France

Nicola Williams, Steve Fallon, Miles Roddis, Daniel Robinson,
Jonathan Knight, Oliver Berry, Andrew Stone, Annabel Hart

Contents

Highlights	6	Massif Central	546
Getting Started	13	Limousin, the Dordogne & Quercy	570
Itineraries	16		
The Authors	23	Atlantic Coast	609
Snapshot	26	French Basque Country	646
History	27	The Pyrenees	667
The Culture	41	Toulouse Area	693
Environment	56	Languedoc-Roussillon	717
Food & Drink	63	Provence	760
Paris	85	Côte d'Azur & Monaco	815
Around Paris	177	Corsica	860
Far Northern France	200	Directory	893
Normandy	235	Transport	914
Brittany	277	Health	929
Champagne	323	World Time Zones	931
Alsace & Lorraine	341	Language	932
The Loire	387	Glossary	938
Burgundy	425	Behind the Scenes	940
Lyon & the Rhône Valley	466	Index	947
French Alps & the Jura	489	Legend	964

FAR NORTHERN
FRANCE
p200

PARIS
p85

NORMANDY
p235

CHAMPAGNE
p323

ALSACE-
LORRAINE
p341

BRITTANY
p277

AROUND PARIS
p177

THE LOIRE
p387

BURGUNDY
p425

FRENCH
ALPS &
JURA
p489

ATLANTIC
COAST
p609

LIMOUSIN,
THE
DORDOGNE
& QUERCY
p570

MASSIF
CENTRAL
p546

LYON &
THE RHÔNE
VALLEY
p466

FRENCH
BASQUE
COUNTRY
p646

THE
PYRENEES
p667

TOULOUSE
AREA
p693

LANGUEDOC-
ROUSSILLON
p717

PROVENCE
p760

CÔTE D'AZUR
& MONACO
p815

CORSICA
p860

Destination France

France is maddening and beautiful, infuriating and inspiring. It is Europe's land of good food and good wine, of royal chateaux and renovated farmhouses, of landmarks known the world over and hidden landscapes few really know. Matisse, Renoir and Picasso painted it. Hemingway wrote about it. Descartes and Sartre defined modern thought in it. And Sinatra sang about it.

People here have *joie de vivre* and savoir-faire. They know how to look good and live well. They eat like there is no tomorrow and drink red wine by the barrelful – with grace and panache. They perfect the art of living. They madden and they inspire.

Their cultural heritage is gargantuan and inexhaustible: savour the multitude of museums, striking architecture and precious works of art packed into the shining capital on the timeless River Seine. See glorious pasts blaze forth at Versailles and in the royal chateaux of the Loire Valley. Travel south for Roman civilisation and the sparkling blue sea. Sense the subtle infusion of language, music and mythology in Brittany brought by 5th-century Celtic invaders. Smell ignominy on the beaches of Normandy and battlefields of Verdun and the Somme. And know that this is but the icing on the cake. How very infuriating.

France's dizzying landscape ensnares mountain peaks and giddy glaciers, jagged ridges and rivers, lakes, white-water canyons, canals and orchards, vineyards and forests and endless coastline. Biking, boating, ballooning and boarding are four of the zillion and one ways to see it, taste it, feel it, love it, hate it. A love-hate relationship it might be, but that is all part of 'old' Europe's French charm.

RICHARD I'ANSON

PARIS (p85)
Wine, dine, view art or just chill out at a café in France's most exciting city

LORRAINE (p370)
Take in Nancy's gilded wrought ironwork and curvaceous Art Nouveau masterpieces

ALSACE (p343)
Gaze in awe at the rose-coloured spires and stained glass of Strasbourg cathedral

AROUND PARIS (p177)
Marvel at the glory of Chartres cathedral, a crowning architectural achievement of Western civilisation

NORMANDY (p235)
Stroll in Monet's garden, visit D-Day beaches and relive William's conquest on the Bayeux Tapestry

BRITTANY (p277)
Play the sailor on wooden boats in Douarnenez's vast Musée du Bateau

THE LOIRE VALLEY (p387)
Discover this fabled region's chateaux and live like royalty

100 km
60 miles

THE NETHERLANDS

GERMANY

BELGIUM

LUXEMBOURG

SWITZERLAND

ENGLAND

WALES

BRITAIN

NORTH SEA

ENGLISH CHANNEL (LA MANCHE)

ATLANTIC OCEAN

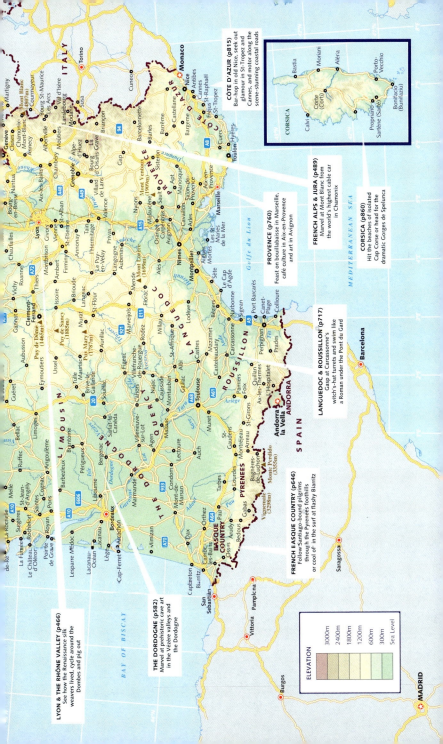

CÔTE D'AZUR (p815)
Bar-hop in old Nice, seek out glamour in St-Tropez and Cannes, and motor along the scene-stunning coastal roads

PROVENCE (p760)
Feast on bouillabaisse in Marseille, café culture in Aix-en-Provence and art in Avignon

FRENCH ALPS & JURA (p489)
Marvel at Mont Blanc from the world's highest cable car in Chamonix

CORSICA (p860)
Hit the beaches of isolated Cap Corse or head for the dramatic Gorges de Spelunca

LANGUEDOC & ROUSSILLON (p717)
Gasp at Carcassonne's witch's-hat turrets and swim like a Roman under the Pont du Gard

FRENCH BASQUE COUNTRY (p646)
Follow Santiago-bound pilgrims through the Pyrenees foothills or cool off in the surf at flashy Biarritz

THE DORDOGNE (p582)
Marvel at prehistoric cave art in the Vézère valleys and the Dordogne

LYON & THE RHÔNE VALLEY (p466)
See how the Renaissance silk weavers lived, cycle around the Dombes and pig out

ELEVATION

	3000m
	2400m
	1800m
	1200m
	600m
	300m
	Sea Level

Whichever chunk of the country you choose, there's no escaping the France of the past. Paris is only the start of a history tour. Prehistory takes the shape of cave art in the **Dordogne** (p591); and there are no better places for Roman relics than the **Rhône Valley** (p486), **Provence** (p792) and **Languedoc** (p733). Medieval and Renaissance old towns abound, **Lyon** (p472), **Lille** (p203), **Strasbourg** (p348) and **Dijon** (p445) among them; while the **Loire Valley chateaux** (p395, p409) make a glorious blast to France's royal past. The **Bayeux Tapestry** (p262), northern France's **WWI battlefields** (p223) and **D-Day landing beaches** (p266) evoke grisly war images.

RICHARD NEBESKY

Revel in *belle époque* Montmartre (p130), the Paris of song and story

Reflect on the ravages of war at the Omaha Beach Memorial (p267)

MICHELLE

Envisage royal courts of the past as you explore the glorious Chateau de Chambord (p401)

CHRIS M

DIANA MAYFIELD

Take a pictorial journey through history as you view favourite masterpieces in the Louvre (p113), Paris, the world's richest art depository

JEAN-BERNARD CARILLET

Contemplate the meaning of the mysterious megaliths at Carnac (p310)

Imagine 17th-century life passing by in the narrow streets of Annecy (p508), on the River Thiou

GLENN VAN DER KNIJFF

There's no end to art and architecture must-sees, Paris alone promising something fabulous around every corner with its architecture and art from all eras. Other treasures – invariably with a generous dose of romance thrown in – include chateaux at **Versailles** (p187), **Chambord** (p401), **Chenonceau** (p410) and **Cheverny** (p402); **Strasbourg** (p348) and **Chartres** (p196) cathedrals; **Vichy's** *belle époque* spa buildings (p556); Avignon's medieval **Palais des Papes** (p786); and Matisse's minimalist chapel in **Vence** (p834). **Provence** (p803) and the **Côte d'Azur's** (p822) modern art portfolio is unsurpassable.

Join pilgrims in Ronchamp at La Chapelle de Notre Dame du Haut (p542), by Le Corbusier

PAUL DAVID HELLANDER

FRANCES LINZEE GORDON

Admire Rouen's French Gothic Cathédrale Notre Dame (p240)

Crane your neck to take in the ultramodern skyscape of La Défense, Paris (p179)

IZZET

IZZET KERIBAR

Be drawn like the tides that surround the sea-splashed Abbaye du Mont St-Michel (p272) and explore the medley of its architectural styles

BETHUNE CARMICHAEL

Journey from impressionism to Art Nouveau at the Musée d'Orsay (p124)

Wander the witch's-capped streets of the medieval La Cité (p730) at Carcassonne

PASCALE BEROUJON

France's natural beauty – and the opportunities it presents – is a big drawcard. Skiing and snowboarding and hiking are invigorating ways to view vistas of the French Alps and the Pyrenees: the breath-taking **Chamonix Valley** (p497) and a heart-stopping **Aiguille du Midi** (p499) cable-car ride are highlights. At lower altitudes, the **Grande Corniche** (p852), with panoramas of the Côte d'Azur and Corsica's **Gorges de Spelunca** (p877) are spectacular. The cliffs and rock formations at **Étretat** (p279) in Normandy, **Brittany's sea-swept islands** (p298, p313) and the **Côte d'Opale** (p215) in far northern France are stunning chunks of coastline.

Hike close to the summer spectacle of Mont Blanc (p497) and stunning mountain tarns

GARETH McC

CHRISTER FREDRIKSSON
Flock to the Camargue delta (p800) to join throngs of pink flamingos

Embrace the inspiration of Monet's garden (p243), Giverny

JOHN HAY

DAVID WALL

Enjoy a bird's-eye view of the French Riviera from the dramatic clifftop vantage point of Èze (p852)

Slow down and relish the leisurely pace of the port of Annecy (p508) on the shores of Lac d'Annecy

GLENN VAN DER KNIJFF

JOHN S KING

Soar above the Pyrenees at Accous (p682)

For many the magnet to France is its food and wine, arguably the Western world's most important and seminal cuisine. Whether it's staples – one of almost 500 types of **cheese** (p63); or the sausages, blood puddings, cured and salted meats called **charcuterie** (p65) – or regional specialities, you'll be tempted and well-fed. For dairy products, nowhere beats **Normandy** (p65). **Périgord** (p68) is famed for its duck and goose liver; produce is at its freshest in sunny **Provence** (p69). Everyone knows the wines from **Bordeaux** (p71) and **Champagne** (p72) but don't overlook those from **Alsace** (p70), the **Loire** (p71) and the **Rhône** (p72).

CHRIS MELLOR

Taste a cloudy, young wine (p71)
in Burgundy

Sample oysters and other shellfish gathered
in waters around Cancale (p67)

OLIVIER CIRENDINI

Salivate to the aroma of freshly baked bread (p63) and baguettes – 'the staff of life'

BETHUNE CAF

Getting Started

Be it a cheap spur-of-the-moment weekend break or a carefully thought-out trip of a lifetime, travel in France requires as little – or as much – money, planning and time as you do or don't have.

WHEN TO GO

French pleasures can be savoured any time, although many Francophiles swear spring is best. Sun-worshippers bake in the hot south between June and early September and winter-sports enthusiasts soar down snow-covered mountains mid-December to late March. Festivals (p903) and gastronomic temptations (p63) around which to plan a trip abound year-round.

School holidays – Christmas and New Year, mid-February to mid-March, Easter, July and August – see millions of French families descend on the coasts, mountains and other touristy areas. Traffic-clogged roads, sky-high accommodation prices and sardine-packed beaches and ski slopes are downside factors of these high-season periods. Many shops take their *congé annuel* (annual closure) in August; Sundays and public holidays (p905) are dead everywhere.

The French climate is temperate, although it gets nippy in mountainous areas and in Alsace and Lorraine. The northwest suffers from high humidity, rain and biting westerly winds, while the Mediterranean south enjoys hot summers and mild winters.

COSTS & MONEY

Accommodation will be your biggest expense: count on a bill of at least €50 a night for a mid-range hotel double. Backpackers staying in hostels and living on bread and cheese can survive on €40 a day; those opting for mid-range hotels, restaurants and museums will spend upwards of €70. For cent savers, see p902.

TRAVEL LITERATURE

France has inspired reams of writing over the centuries. For books on French history and society see the History and Culture (p47) chapters.
An Orderly Man and **A Short Walk from Harrods** (Dirk Bogarde) British film icon renovates his farmhouse in Provence.
A Moveable Feast (Ernest Hemingway) Bohemian literary life in Paris between the wars.
Down and Out in Paris and London (George Orwell) Famous account of the time Orwell spent living with tramps in Paris and London in the late 1920s.
Tender is the Night and **Bits of Paradise** (F Scott Fitzgerald) Vivid accounts of life during the decadent 1920s Jazz Age on the Côte d'Azur.

LONELY PLANET INDEX

Litre of petrol €1.10

Litre bottle of Evian/ Perrier mineral water €0.35/0.75

Cheap/expensive bottle of wine €4/as much as you want to pay

Souvenir T-shirt €15

Croissant & café au lait €2.50

HOW MUCH?

Local/foreign newspaper €1/3

Filled baguette €4

Mid-range hotel double (outside Paris) €60 to €100

Ten-minute taxi ride €15

Metro, tram or city bus ticket €1.20-1.40

DON'T LEAVE HOME WITHOUT...

- Valid travel insurance (p905)
- ID card or passport and visa if required (p911)
- Driving licence, car documents and car insurance (p923)
- Sunglasses, hat, mosquito repellent and a few clothes pegs for the hot south
- A brolly for wet 'n soggy Brittany, neighbouring northern climes and Paris
- An adventurous appetite, a pleasure-seeking palate and a thirst for good wine

TOP TENS
FESTIVALS & EVENTS

France's festival calendar dishes up something for everybody. For a comprehensive listing of events and dates, see p903.

- Carnaval de Nice (Nice) February (p825)
- Pélerinage des Gitans (Stes-Maries de la Mer) May & October (p808)
- Fête des Gardians (Arles) May (p804)
- Grand Prix Automobile de Monaco (Monaco) May (p857)
- Fête de la Musique (countrywide) 21 June (p904)
- Paris Plage (Paris) July-August (p136)
- Festival d'Avignon & Festival Off (Avignon) July (p787)
- Journées du Patrimoine (countrywide) September
- Fête des Lumières (Lyon) December (p476)
- Tour de France (countrywide) July (p45)

BUILDINGS

Ignoring the obvious (the Louvre, Eiffel Tower and so on), here are our Top 10. For a comprehensive look at famous and fascinating buildings in France, see p52.

- Vesunna Musée Gallo-Romain de Périgueux (p585)
- Le Corbusier's Chapelle de Notre-Dame du Haut, Ronchamp (p542)
- Maison Carrée & Carré d'Art, Nîmes (p733)
- Matisse's Chapelle du Rosaire, Vence (p834)
- La Piscine Musée d'Art et d'Industrie, Lille (p205)
- Chartres (p196), Reims (p327) & Strasbourg (p349) cathedrals
- Châteaux de Chambord (p401) and Chenonceau (p410) in the Loire Valley
- Château de Versailles, Versailles (p187)
- Mont St-Michel (p273)
- Fontenay (p459) and Fontevraud (p424) abbeys

OUT OF THE ORDINARY

Keen to travel France on the quirky side (see p20)? Been there, done that; we bet that you have never...

- Scaled Europe's highest sand dune (p644)
- Sailed along subterranean waters (p608)
- Scuttled like a rat through Paris' sewers (p126) and catacombs (p123)
- Celebrated Sunday mass in Breton (p302)
- Found the spring of eternal youth (p318)
- Watched 90 dogs wolf down 90kg of stinking offal in 10 seconds flat (p403)
- Been a space tourist (p700)
- Eaten silk weavers' brains or pig-intestine sausage (p478)
- Seen tender, tragic, fickle and passionate love growing in a garden (p410)
- Gone volcanic (p553)

Flaubert's Parrot (Julian Barnes) A witty homage to one of France's greatest writers.
Home and Dry in France: Or a Year in Purgatory (George East) A nightclub bouncer moves into a water mill in Normandy – and survives to tell the hilarious tale.
Tropic of Cancer and **Tropic of Capricorn** (Henry Miller) Steamy novels set in Paris, published in France in the 1930s, banned in the UK and USA until the 1960s.
A Year in Provence (Peter Mayle) Witty look at the French through English eyes.

See Climate Charts (p899) for more information

INTERNET RESOURCES
French Government Tourist Office (www.francetourism.com) Official tourist site.
Lonely Planet (www.lonelyplanet.com)
Maison de la France (www.franceguide.com) Main tourist office website.
Motorist Information (www.bison-fute.equipement.gouv.fr in French) Road conditions, closures and school holiday schedule.
Meteo France (www.meteo.fr in French) For details of nationwide weather conditions.
SNCF (www.sncf.com) France's national railways website.

Itineraries
CLASSIC ROUTES

THE TIMELESS CLASSICS
Two weeks / Paris to Nice

There's no better place to kick off a whistle-stop tour of classic French sights than Paris where the **Eiffel Tower** (p125), **Arc de Triomphe** (p127), **Notre Dame** (p119) and the **Louvre** (p113) beckon romance seekers. Stroll the banks of the Seine and gardens of **Versailles** (p185), then flee the capital for Renaissance royalty at **Châteaux de Chambord** (p401) and **Chenonceau** (p410). If castles are not your thing, skip the Loire and spend a couple of days in Normandy, not missing Rouen's **Cathédrale Notre Dame** (p240), the **Bayeux Tapestry** (p262), **Mont St-Michel** (p272) and the **D-Day landing beaches** (p266).

Then venture south, visiting the **Bordeaux wine region** (p637) en route. Surfers will find waves in **Biarritz** (p657), while the faithful or faithfully curious might enjoy world-famous **Lourdes** (p675). Otherwise, it's straight to **Carcassonne**'s (p727) turreted city walls; Roman **Nîmes** (p733) with a trip to the **Pont du Gard** (p738); and the papal city of **Avignon** (p783) with its **nursery-rhyme bridge** (p786). Finish on the Côte d'Azur, not missing Grace Kelly's **Monaco** (p854), a flutter in **Monte Carlo** (p857), a portside aperitif in **St-Tropez** (p844), a strut in **Cannes** (p834) and a stroll in **Nice** (p818).

From Paris to Nice, with a few short detours along the way, is a breathtaking 2000km that can be done in a whirlwind fortnight, but definitely merits as much time as you can give it.

COAST TO COAST

Step off the boat in **Calais** (p209) and there's 40km of stunning cliffs, sand dunes and windy beaches – not to mention great views of those white cliffs of Dover across the Channel – on the spectacular **Côte d'Opale** (p215). Speed southwest next, taking in a fish lunch in **Dieppe** (p247), a cathedral-stop in **Rouen** (p240) or a picturesque cliff-side picnic in **Étretat** (p249) on the **Côte d'Albatre** (p248) on your way to your overnight stop: one of Normandy's prettiest seaside resorts – **Honfleur** (p251), **Deauville** (p254) or **Trouville** (p254).

Devote day two to the **D-Day landing beaches** (p266) and abbey-clad **Mont St-Michel** (p272). If island life is more your cup of tea, push on to **Brest** (p296) or **Camaret** (p300) instead, from where you can sail to Brittany's hauntingly beautiful **Île d'Ouessant** (p298). Equally tempting to Robinson Crusoes is **Belle Île** (p313), with its fantastic rock formations, caves and beaches.

A long drive south along the Atlantic Coast rewards you with chic **La Rochelle** (p620) and its lavish portside feasts of seafood and oysters. In **Royan** (p627), catch a ferry across the water to **Soulac-sur-Mer** (p637), a happening seaside resort from where it is simply a matter of wining your way through the **Médoc** (p637) to bustling **Bordeaux** (p628) – city of fine food, wine, museums and nightlife. Next morning, continue south through **Toulouse** (p695) and **Carcassonne** (p727) to the Med. The flamingo- and horse-studded **Camargue** (p806), immediately west of **Marseille** (p763), is a unique patch of coast to explore – and a far cry from the glitz and glamour of the **Riviera** (p816) further east.

The Atlantic to the Mediterranean in a week – 2500km in all – is no mean feat, but one that rewards with stunning vistas, some superb coastal motoring and sensational seafood. For those with more time to play with, activities abound in, on and out of the sea – and there's always Corsica for the truly coast crazy.

TOUR DE FRANCE   One month / Strasbourg to Paris

Get set for your race around the country in Strasbourg: stroll canal-clad **Petite France** (p349), marvel at its **cathedral** (p349) and dine in a **winstub** (p353). Moving on to greener climes, pick up the **Route du Vin d'Alsace** (p357) and tipple your way around the **Vosges** (p367) foothills. But keep a clear head for that splendid Art Nouveau architecture in **Nancy** (p372) where you should spend at least one night to enjoy romantic **place Stanislas** (p372) illuminated. From Lorraine it is guns a-ho to champagne cellars around **Épernay** (p332), then north to the sobering **Battle of Somme memorials** (p223) in far northern France.

Devour Normandy and Brittany's best sights in week two: base yourself in **Bayeux** (p260) to see the **tapestry** (p262), **D-Day landing beaches** (p266) and **WWII memorials** (p267). **Mont St-Michel** (p272) is an astounding pit stop en route to France's Celtic **land of legends** (p279); **St-Malo** (p281) and **Dinard** (p286) are charming places to overnight. Meander around megaliths in **Carnac** (p310), then zoom south for even more prehistory in the **Vézère Valley** (p591).

The pace hots up the third week: from the **Dordogne** (p582), wiggle through the **Upper Languedoc** (p720) – through the spectacular **Gorges du Tarn** (p745) – to **Avignon** (p783). Take a break with local café culture then slog like a Tour de France cyclist up **Mont Ventoux** (p795). Explore Provence's **hilltop villages** (p798) then speed north to the majestic city of **Lyon** (p468), from where an **Alpine mountain adventure** (opposite) is doable.

The last leg takes in wine-rich Burgundy: **Beaune** (p453), **Dijon** (p444) and **Vézelay** (p440) are the obvious places to stop en route to Paris.

Tour de France cyclists take three weeks to bike 3000km around the country. This 3000km tour of France can be done in one month, but warrants much more time than that. As with the world's greatest cycling race, it labours through the Pyrenees and Alps, and finishes on Paris' Champs-Élysées.

ROADS LESS TRAVELLED

A MOUNTAIN ADVENTURE   Two weeks / Chamonix to Cauterets

Start an Alpine adventure in chic **Chamonix** (p497), at the foot of Europe's highest peak (p497): take a cable car to the **Aiguille du Midi** (p499) and **Le Brévent** (p499) or a train to the **Mer de Glace** (p500). Skiing the legendary **Vallée Blanche** (p501), **snowshoeing** (p500) and warmer-weather **paragliding** (p502) are top thrills. For the truly Alpine-dedicated there are always the **Vanoise** (p519) and **Écrins** (p529) national parks to explore.

Hopping across Lake Geneva by boat, the unexplored **Jura** (p535) looms large. Gentle land of cross-country skiing, dog-mushing and cheese dining in **Métabief Mont d'Or** (p543) – not to mention Le Corbusier's **Ronchamp** (p542) chapel – this tranquil region is perfect for peace-seekers.

Alternatively, head southwest for week two, breaking the journey in the **Parc Naturel Régional de Chartreuse** (p516) of potent pea-green liqueur fame or in the cave-riddled **Parc Naturel Régional du Vercors** (p528). Passing through the wild **Cévennes** (p741), walking a stage of Robert Louis Stevenson's **donkey trek** (p743) is a possibility before hitting the Pyrenees.

Once in the **Parc National des Pyrénées** (p680), revitalise weary bones with spa waters in **Bagnères de Luchon** (p690) before hitting the **Vallée d'Ossau** (p684) and **Vallée d'Aspe** (p681) for a heady cocktail of **mountain biking** (p691), wild **walking** (p691) and **vulture spotting** (p685). Use **Cauterets** (p686) – from where you can ski (p688) in season – as your base.

This highly energetic 1500km tour from the French Alps to the Pyrenees will leave you breathless, especially if you take a few days out to indulge in an adrenalin rush of outdoor activity up, down or on the mountain slopes.

QUIRKY FRANCE   One month / A Paris sewer to a Burgundy building site

Forget the Eiffel Tower, St-Tropez and the sweet-smelling lavender fields of Provence. This tour zooms in on France's quirky sights, sounds – and smells in the case of the **Paris sewer** (p126) where its starts. Gawp at more skulls than you can imagine in the capital's **catacombs** (p123), then venture north to the spot near **Compiègne** (p233) where WWI officially ended. Top off your day with a subterranean dose of V2 rocket technology in a **bunker** (p214) near St-Omer.

A few drops of Christ's blood in **Fécamp** (p248) on the Normandy coast inspired monks to concoct Bénédictine: visit the **Palais Bénédictine** (p248) and get a free shot – then tell yourself you're not drunk as you tour the 'laboratory of emotions' in Honfleur's wacky **Les Maisons Satie** (p252). In Brittany find the **forest** (p318) where King Arthur met Viviane.

Steering south along the Atlantic Coast, cartwheel down Europe's highest sand dune near **Arcachon** (p641). Afterwards, head east to Quercy and set sail on an underground river in **Gouffre de Padirac** (p608); then nip to Toulouse to tour **Space City** (p700) and see **Airbus planes** (p700) being built.

Seeing where silk weavers toiled in the 19th century and the tunnels they walked puts **Lyon** (p474) in a different light. Returning north, watch a son et lumière with 60 knights on horseback and 600 actors at a **Burgundy chateau** (p436) and see brickies in costume at the **Chantier Médiéval de Guédelon** (p433), near La Puisaye, build a castle using 13th-century tools.

It might well follow a predictable route – enabling it to be mixed-and-matched with other itineraries in this chapter – but that is about it. Covering 2400km in all, one month scarcely does quirky France justice. Take longer if you can.

TAILORED TRIPS

TASTEBUDS ON TOUR

Eating your way around France is a fulfilling way of seeing it, although the fiercest of appetites will have trouble tasting all that's cooking. When our 'Author's Choice' tastebuds went on tour, they plumped for porky-pig *bouchon* cuisine in **Lyon** (p478), considered the gastronomic capital. Then they hit Burgundy to discover what quintessential French dishes like *escargots* (snails) and **bœuf Bourguignon** (p68) really taste like. The region's gooey, stinky, mouth-melting **époisses cheese** (p64) was a particular hit.

Next stop was Alsace with its **Strasbourg** (p351) brewery tours and wine route through the **Vosges** (p367). Lunch was a **cowherd feast** (p367), **smelly Munster** (p368) included. Then it was north to Champagne for some bubbly and *biscuits roses* in **Reims** (p328).

In Normandy authors ate *tripes à la mode de Caen* (a tripe and trotter dish) in **Caen** (p258); **St-Brieuc** (p67) in Brittany cooked sea urchins; and the Atlantic Coast proffered **oysters** (p645). Zooming south, foie gras tickled tastebuds in **Périgord** (p590); several hours was spent over *bouillabaisse* (a Provençal fish stew) in **Marseille** (p770); then it was all aboard the ferry for *charcuterie* (cold meats), *civet de sanglier* (wild boar stew) and chestnuts in **Corsica** (p69).

THE ARTSY WAY

Provence and the Côte d'Azur have always been an artist's paradise: Matisse lapped up the extraordinary sunlight and Mediterranean vivacity in **Nice** (p823), designing an extraordinary chapel in **Vence** (p834). Picasso set up studio in **Antibes** (p832); **Signac** and other Fauvists found inspiration in **St-Tropez** (p844); while Cézanne spent his artistic career in **Aix-en-Provence** (p779). Looking west along the coast, Dutch-born Van Gogh painted some of his most famous canvases in **Arles** (p803) and **St-Rémy de Provence** (p791).

The Fauvist-favoured port of **Collioure** (p758) on the Côte Vermeille in Roussillon is an essential stop on any art lover's itinerary; as is Henri de Toulouse-Lautrec's hometown in **Albi** (p705), near Toulouse. Moulin Rouge cancan girls and prostitutes the bohemian artist painted in Paris hang in the town's **Musée Toulouse-Lautrec** (p706).

A day trip to Monet's spectacular garden-clad home and studio (now a museum) in **Giverny** (p243) is irresistible for anyone doing France the artsy way from Paris – where, incidentally, Monet's famous painting of **Rouen cathedral** (p240) in the **Musée d'Orsay** (p124) is a must. Renoir hung out with his impressionist buddies in and around **Le Havre** (p249, p252, p244) on the serene Normandy coast, and is buried in **Essoyes** (p340) in Champagne.

KIDDING AROUND

Kidding around France need not be an endurance test: amusements aimed at the biggest and smallest of budgets and ages abound.

Paris offers the **Jardin du Luxembourg** (p123) with play areas and the activity-driven **Cité des Sciences et de l'Industrie** (p131), not to mention **Disneyland Resort Paris** (p184). Heading north, there are fish to be felt in **Boulogne** (p217); ships models in **Dunkirk** (p220); horses in **Compiègne** (p233); and **Nigloland** theme park (p339) in Champagne. Older children might enjoy Alsace's trio of kid-orientated museums: science in **Strasbourg** (p351), cars in **Mulhouse** (p369) and toys in **Colmar** (p364).

Beaches, boats and islands in Brittany and along the Atlantic Coast are the stuff that idyllic childhood holidays are made from. And for rainy days, there are aquariums in **Cherbourg** (p269), **St-Malo** (p284) and **Brest** (p297), and **Futuroscope** theme park (p619) near Poitiers.

Hot-air ballooning (p401, p428), **cycling** (p390, p428) and **canal-cruising** (p428) are big in the Loire Valley and Burgundy. **Lyon** (p473), with its green city parks and puppet theatres, suits kids of all ages; as do the **Alpine mountain resorts** (p495) where supervised *jardins de neige* (snow gardens) take kids from the age of three. At lower altitudes, children can visit farms and ride dog sledges in the **Jura** (p544), and on the island of Corsica **horse-riding** (p864), **snorkelling** (p875) and **sea cruises** (p867) entertain.

WORLD HERITAGE SITES

France is home to 28 World Heritage Sites (http://whc.unesco.org). So put on your historical hat for a tour of the country's most precious treasures.

In Paris revel in the most romantic city on earth from the banks of the **River Seine** (p113) and in royal palaces at **Versailles** (p187) and **Fontainebleau** (p189). In **Chambord** (p401), take your hat off to François I for the 440-room hunting lodge he had built. Cathedrals in **Bourges** (p396) and **Chartres** (p196) make other fine forays from the capital.

Those needing a break from Paris life could consider Burgundy with its medieval abbey in **Fontenay** (p459) and Romanesque basilica in **Vézelay** (p440). The latter – a fortified village – has been the starting point for French pilgrims heading to **Santiago de Compostela** (p440) in Spain for centuries. Their well-trodden paths in France are protected as World Heritage Sites.

Northern gems include Strasbourg's **Grande Île** (p348); a trio of fine squares in **Nancy** (p372); the cathedral, palace-museum and basilica in **Reims** (p327); and **Amiens** (p227) cathedral. Seasplashed **Mont St-Michel** (p272) and its bay is yet another priceless world treasure.

In the south, taste **St-Émilion** (p640), a Bordeaux red produced from listed vineyards. Other jewels include **Carcassonne** (p727); the Roman **Pont du Gard** (p738), **Arles** (p800) and **Orange** (p791); and the historical centres of **Avignon** (p783) and **Lyon** (p468). Several capes and natural beauty spots in **Corsica** (p860) are also protected.

The Authors

NICOLA WILLIAMS   Coordinating Author; Lyon & Rhône Valley

Living in Lyon – crossroads to the Alps and the Mediterranean, not to mention the fabulous 19th-century silk-weaving *canut* she lives in – Nicola considers herself well and truly spoilt. A journalist by training, she worked in the Baltic region as a newspaper features editor and later city-guide series editor for several years before trading in Lithuanian *cepelinai* for Lyonnaise *andouillette* in 1997. Nicola has authored many Lonely Planet titles, including *The Loire* and *Provence & the Côte d'Azur*.

My Favourite Trip

It has to be *Le Train Bleu* (p34): Paris to Marseille at TGV-lightning speed (p918), then along the coast to Nice by snail-slow seaside train. Lingering on steps and squares – at the Sacré Cœur (p130), in front of the Pompidou (p116), beneath the Grande Arche de la Défense (p180) and so on – is the *only* way to see Paris. At Gare de Lyon (p171), lavish frescoes inside the restaurant named after the 1920s train tell a thousand tales of *belle époque* train travel. Then it's southbound for a port-side aperitif and *bouillabaisse* in Marseille (p770), and sunset over the stunning red rocks and coves of Massif de l'Estérel (p841) en route to Nice (p818).

OLIVER BERRY   Burgundy; French Alps & the Jura; Corsica

Oliver graduated from University College London with a degree in English and now works as a writer and journalist in Cornwall and London. His first trip to France was at the tender age of two, and subsequent travels have carried him from the streets of Paris to the Alpine mountains and from the wine regions of southern France to the chestnut forests of Corsica. He is a regular contributor to various film and travel publications and in 2001 he was named *The Guardian* Young Travel Writer of the Year.

STEVE FALLON   Food & Drink; Paris; Around Paris

A native of Boston, Steve graduated from Georgetown University with a Bachelor of Science in modern languages and then taught English at the University of Silesia near Katowice in Poland. After working for several years for a daily newspaper in the USA and earning a master's degree in journalism, his fascination with the 'new' Asia led him to Hong Kong, where he lived for more than a dozen years, working for a variety of media and running a travel bookshop. Steve lived in Budapest for several years before moving in 1994 to London, from where he travels to Paris as often as he can. He has contributed to or written more than two dozen Lonely Planet titles, including *Paris* and *World Food France*.

ANNABEL HART Normandy; Directory; Transport

Tired of university, Annabel left her home town of Melbourne and set off for a four-month trip to Paris to study French. Four years on she's still there, addicted to the ups and downs of life in Paris – where she has spent most of her time working as a freelance writer and practising her Parisian slang. Annabel has contributed to Lonely Planet's Web content and various guidebooks including *Paris Condensed* and *Bretagne*, and has now embarked on a master's degree in world politics. Her travels have taken her throughout France and Europe, Southeast Asia, New Zealand and Australia.

JONATHAN KNIGHT The Loire; Limousin, the Dordogne & Quercy; Atlantic Coast; French Basque Country

Jonathan's interest in France began at 15 after meeting a sassy French girl in Cornwall. She smoked, swore and spoke wiz a Franch accent. Despite her glamour and sophistication, the distance and language proved problematic, and the relationship ended. But an intrigue with all things French had taken hold and holidays to the Alps, Cannes and Paris were followed by a year studying in Nice. Studies complete, he took a job at a radio station in Monte Carlo, enjoying a morning commute along the shores of the Mediterranean. Jonathan now lives in London where he works as a freelance advertising copywriter and travel writer.

DANIEL ROBINSON Far Northern France; Champagne; Alsace & Lorraine

Over the past 15 years, Daniel's articles and books – published in six languages – have covered every French region, but he has a particular fondness for those bits of the *Hexagone* in which Romance and Germanic cultures have mingled for over a thousand years. Seeking out enchanting corners of rust belt France is a long-time hobby, and he takes particular interest in the creativity and panache of dynamic northern cities such as Lille, Nancy and Strasbourg.

Daniel grew up in the United States and Israel and holds a BA in Near Eastern Studies from Princeton University. He is based in Tel Aviv.

MILES RODDIS Brittany; Massif Central; The Pyrenees; Langedoc-Roussillon

Miles' involvement with France began when, 15 and spotty, he noisily threw up the night's red wine in a Paris café. Undeterred by the subsequent monumental hangover, he mainlined in French at university, becoming seriously hooked and spending an idyllic sandwich year in Neuville-sur-Saône, a place quite rightly overlooked by the best guidebooks, including the one in your hand.

Living over the Pyrenees in Valencia, Spain, he and his wife, Ingrid, make a point of visiting France, for work or for sheer fun, at least once a year.

Miles has written or contributed to more than 25 Lonely Planet titles including *France*, *Brittany & Normandy* and *Walking in France*.

ANDREW STONE   Toulouse Area; Provence; Côte d'Azur & Monaco

Andrew's first experience of southern France was as a schoolboy barely out of short trousers and he has never forgotten it. Having arrived late and woken early at his aunt's house, he threw back the shutters on a dazzling Côte d'Azur dawn of cobalt sky and pungent, dark-green pine forest. A large French family (10 cousins) has given Andrew ample opportunities to come back regularly and stay all over the south since then. Trips to France today are divided evenly between recapturing the wonder of that first moment and snuffling out new regional food and wine treats.

Snapshot

Presidential elections aren't until 2007 but contenders are already jockeying for position in a political race riddled with back-stabbing drama and intrigue. Jacques Chirac (1932–) has never recovered from the fact that his old mate Nicolas Sarkozy (1955–) didn't back him in his 1995 run for the Élysée Palace (p127). Since then it has been all-out *guerre froide* (cold war) between the two politicians who – despite being on the same right-wing side of the political fence – make no bones about their dislike for each another.

Unfortunately for French president *Le Grand Jacques*, he is already in his 70s, has two terms under his presidential belt and is too old and too old-hat say critics. And then there is Sarko (as the French press nickname him). A man of the masses and the man of the moment, finance minister Nicolas Sarkozy is dynamic, high-profile, highly ambitious – and short. As interior minister (until April 2004), he put more police on French streets, cracked down on crime and drugs and spoke a lot (but didn't do anything) about helping the country's substantial immigrant population (p45) get on in French life (Sarkozy himself is the son of a Hungarian immigrant).

Enter Alain Juppé (1945–), a Chirac loyalist set to take over the presidential helm until February 2004 when he landed an 18-month suspended jail sentence for his role as Paris deputy mayor in a party funding scam. The scandal – all the more shady given Chirac's job as mayor of Paris (p39) at the time – saw Chirac's centre-right Union pour un Movement Populaire (UMP) party sent to the slaughterhouse by the socialists in countrywide regional elections the following month. European elections in June 2004 were equally disastrous for the UMP. Juppé is expected to be replaced by Sarko as UMP chairman in November 2004.

François Hollande (1954–) might chair France's left-wing Parti Socialiste, but it is Paris mayor Bertrand Delanoë (1948–) who is the Socialist Party's brightest political spark – and its hottest contender for the 2007 race. The dynamo politician – openly gay and survivor of an assassination attempt a couple of years back – brought to an end 130 years of right-wing rule in the capital by landing the Paris mayorship in 2001. Creating a summertime sandy beach (p136) on the banks of the Seine is but one of the fabulously innovative touches he has brought to the French capital.

France's outright opposition to the US-led war in Iraq in 2003 stirred up widespread anti-French sentiment among Americans: many restaurants in the US changed 'French fries' on their menus, to 'freedom fries to avoid having to mention the unspeakable, while US defence secretary Donald Rumsfeld publicly dismissed France (along with Germany) as 'old Europe'.

The government's greatest challenge is to put some wind back in the sails of a sluggish economy. A strong engine for EU growth, rivalled only by Germany, the French economy nonetheless only grew by 0.5% in 2003 – its lowest growth rate since 1993. Despite widespread privatisation in the 1990s, public spending and the public deficit (4.1% of GDP in 2003) are still high. More privatisation, trimming down the state sector (employer of one in four French workers) and slashing costs in France's much-revered healthcare system are among the heavyweight tasks faced by the government.

And all eyes are on it (not least the nation's smokers who watched a packet of their favourite cigarettes hiked up in price by 40% in 2003–04) for what promises to be a thrilling ride.

FAST FACTS

Population: 60.2 million

Area: 551,000 sq km

GDP: €1557.2 billion

GDP growth: 0.5%

Inflation: 2.1%

Unemployment: 9.8%

Highest point: Mt Blanc (4807m)

Internet domain: fr

Mobile phone users: 65% of the population, the lowest percentage of the original 15 countries in the EU at the start of 2004

Annual alcohol consumption (average per person over 15 years): wine 78.9L, beer 41L, cider 6.9L and spirits 9.1L

History

PREHISTORIC PEOPLE

Neanderthals were the first to live in France. Out and about during the Middle Palaeolithic period (about 90,000 to 40,000 BC), these early *Homo sapiens* hunted animals, made crude flake-stone tools and lived in caves. In the late 19th century Neanderthal skeletons were found in caves at Le Moustier (p591) and Le Bugue in the Vézère Valley (p591) in Dordogne.

Cro-Magnons, a taller *Homo sapien* variety who notched up 1.70m on the height chart, followed 35,000 years ago. These people had larger brains than their ancestors, long and narrow skulls, and short, wide faces. Their hands were nimble and with the aid of improved tools they hunted reindeer, bison, horses and mammoths to eat. They played music, danced, performed assorted ceremonies and had fairly complex social patterns. View archaeological finds (decorated tools, primitive musical instruments and so on) from this period in museums in Strasbourg (p350) and Dijon (p448).

Significantly, Cro-Magnons also drew, painted and sculpted, marking the birth of prehistoric. A tour of Grotte de Lascaux II (p591) – a replica of the Lascaux cave where one of the world's best examples of Cro-Magnon drawings were found in 1940 – demonstrates how initial simplistic drawings and engravings of animals gradually became more detailed and realistic. Dubbed 'Périgord's Sistine Chapel', the Lascaux cave is one of 25 known decorated caves in Dordogne's Vézère Valley, the prehistory of which is covered in Les Eyzies de Tayac's Musée National de Prehistoire (p591).

The Neolithic period (about 7500 to 4000 years ago), also called the New Stone Age, created France's incredible collection of menhirs and dolmens: the Morbihan Coast in Brittany (p310) is an ode to megalithic monuments. During this era, warmer weather caused great changes in flora and fauna, and ushered in farming and stock rearing. Cereals, peas, beans and lentils were grown; communities became more settled and villages were established. Decorated pottery, woven fabrics and polished stone tools became commonplace household items.

GAULS & ROMANS

The Celtic Gauls moved into the region between 1500 and 500 BC, establishing trading links by about 600 BC with the Greeks whose colonies included Massilia (Marseille) on the Mediterranean coast. About 300 years later the Celtic Parisii tribe built a few wattle and daub huts on what is now Paris' Île de la Cité (p119).

It was from Wissant (p215) on the Côte d'Opale in far northern France that Julius Caesar launched his invasion of Britain in 55 BC. Centuries of conflict between the Gauls and Romans ended in 52 BC when Julius Caesar's legions crushed a revolt led by Gallic chief Vercingétorix (p551) in Gergovia near present-day Clermont-Ferrand. See Vercingétorix on Clermont-Ferrand's place de la Jaude (p549) and

DID YOU KNOW?

France's oldest prehistoric cave paintings (drawn 31,000 years ago) adorn the Grotte Chauvet-Pont d'Arc (Ardèche, Rhône Valley) and the underwater Grotte Cosquer (near Marseille). Neither can be visited.

Shut to everyone bar a privileged handful of scientists, the Grotte Chauvet-Pont d'Arc makes for a fascinating electronic visit at www .culture.gouv.fr/culture /arcnat/chauvet/en.

It took several years for TV producer and historian Mario Ruspli to come up with the images and texts for *Cave of Lascaux: The Final Photographs*, a rare pictorial insight into what the real Lascaux cave looks like.

TIMELINE

c90,000–30,000 BC	1500–500 BC
Around 30,000 BC, Cro-Magnons start decorating the caves in the Vézère Valley (Dordogne) with a riot of bestial scenes	The Celtic Parisii tribe set up camp on the Île de Cité in Paris

Caesar in action on the façade of the Roman triumphal arch (p792) in Orange.

The subsequent period gave rise to magnificent public baths, temples, aqueducts like the Pont du Gard (p738), arenas and amphitheatres and other splendid public buildings: stand like a plebeian or sit like a Roman patrician in awe-inspiring theatres and amphitheatres at Autun (p461), Lyon (p473), Vienne (p486), Arles (802) and Orange (p792). Lyon also has an excellent Gallo-Roman civilisation museum (p473). In the Dordogne Périgueux's 1st-century Roman amphitheatre (p585) was dismantled in the 3rd century and its stones used to build the city walls. The town's stunningly contemporary Vesunna Musée Gallo-Romain (p586) is a feast to behold.

France remained under Roman rule until the 5th century, when the Franks (thus the name 'France') and the Alemanii overran the country from the east. These peoples adopted important elements of Gallo-Roman civilisation (including Christianity) and their eventual assimilation resulted in a fusion of Germanic culture with that of the Celts and the Romans.

DYNASTY

The Frankish Merovingian and Carolingian dynasties ruled from the 5th to the 10th centuries, the Carolingians wielding power from Laon (p233) in northern France. The Frankish tradition by which the king was succeeded by all of his sons led to power struggles and the eventual disintegration of the kingdom into a collection of small feudal states. In Poitiers (p671) in 732 Charles Martel defeated the Moors, thus preventing France from falling under Muslim rule as Spain had done.

Martel's grandson, Charlemagne (742–814), extended the power and boundaries of the kingdom and was crowned Holy Roman Emperor (Emperor of the West) in 800. But during the 9th century, Scandinavian Vikings (also called Norsemen, thus Normans) raided France's western coast, settling in the lower Seine Valley and forming the duchy of Normandy a century later.

With the crowning of Hugh Capet by the nobles as king in 987, the Capetian dynasty was born. The king's then-modest domain – a paltry parcel of land around Paris and Orléans – was hardly indicative of a dynasty that would rule one of Europe's most powerful countries for the next 800 years.

The tale of how William the Conqueror and his Norman forces occupied England in 1066 (making Normandy and, later, Plantagenet-ruled England, a formidable rival of the kingdom of France) is told on the Bayeux Tapestry, showcased inside Bayeux's Musée de la Tapisserie de Bayeux (p262). In 1152 Eleanor of Aquitaine wed Henry of Anjou (see ornate polychrome effigies of the royal couple in Abbaye de Fontevraud, p424), bringing a further third of France under the control of the English crown. The subsequent rivalry between France and England for control of Aquitaine and the vast English territories in France lasted three centuries.

In Clermont-Ferrand in 1095 Pope Urban II preached the First Crusade, prompting France to play a leading role in the Crusades and giving rise to

55–52 BC
Julius Caesar launches his invasion of Britain from the Côte d'Opale in northern France; the Gauls defeat the Romans at Gergovia

c AD 455–70
The Franks invade and kick out the Romans; Alsace is overrun by the Alemanii

some splendid cathedrals – Reims (p327), Strasbourg (p349), Metz (p377) and Chartres (p196) among them – between the 12th and 14th centuries. In 1309 French-born Pope Clement V moved the papal headquarters from Rome to Avignon, Avignon's third pope Benoît XII (1334–42) starting work on the resplendent Palais des Papes (p786). The Holy See remained in the Provençal city until 1377.

Two Lives of Charlemagne, edited by Betty Radice, is a striking Charlemagne biography, beautifully composed by a monk who spent 23 years in Charlemagne's court.

THE HUNDRED YEARS' WAR

Incessant struggles between the Capetians and England's King Edward III (a Plantagenet) over the powerful French throne degenerated into the Hundred Years' War (1337–1453). The French suffered particularly nasty defeats at Crécy and Agincourt (home to a great multimedia battle museum; p214). Abbey-studded Mont St-Michel (p272) was the only place in northern and western France not to fall into English hands.

Five years later, the dukes of Burgundy (allied with the English) occupied Paris and in 1422 John Plantagenet, duke of Bedford, was made regent of France for England's King Henry VI, then an infant. Less than a decade later he was crowned king of France at Paris' Notre Dame (p119).

Luckily for the French, a 17-year-old virginal warrior in the shape of Jeanne d'Arc (Joan of Arc) came along, the tale of whom is told at Orléans' Maison de Jeanne d'Arc (p391). At Château de Chinon (p416) in 1429, she persuaded French legitimist Charles VII that she had a divine mission from God to expel the English from France and bring about Charles' coronation in Reims. Convicted of witchcraft and heresy by a tribunal of French ecclesiastics following her capture by the Burgundians and subsequent sale to the English in 1430, Joan was burned at the stake in Rouen in 1431: one tower of the castle (p240) where the teenager was imprisoned and the square (p240) where she was burned as a witch remain.

Charles VII returned to Paris in 1437, but it wasn't until 1453 that the English were entirely driven from French territory (with the exception of Calais). At Château de Langeais (p411) in 1491, Charles VIII wed Anne de Bretagne, marking the unification of independent Brittany with France.

Jeanne d'Arc (Joan of Arc, 1999) by Paris-born film director Luc Besson is the seventh film to immortalise the 15th-century virginal warrior on the silver screen. The only scene to be shot in France (at Château de Blois in the Loire Valley) was part of Joan's trial.

RENAISSANCE TO REFORMATION

With the arrival of Italian Renaissance culture during the reign of François I (r 1515–47), the focus shifted to the Loire Valley. Italian artists were recruited in droves to decorate royal castles in Amboise (p412), Blois (p397), Chambord (p401) and Chaumont (403), Leonardo da Vinci making Le Clos Lucé (which can be visited; p413) in Amboise his home from 1516 until his death. Artist and architect disciples of Michelangelo and Raphael were influential, as were writers like Rabelais, Marot and Ronsard. Renaissance ideas of scientific and geographic scholarship and discovery assumed a new importance, as did the value of secular over religious life.

The Reformation swept through Europe in the 1530s, the ideas of Jean (John) Calvin (1509–64) – a Frenchman born in Noyon (Picardie) but exiled to Geneva – strengthening it in France. Following the Edict

Letters, testimonies and trial notes from the 15th century document the meteoric rise and fall of Joan of Arc in *Joan of Arc: By Herself and her Witnesses* by Régine Pernoud (English translation by Edward Hyams).

987
Five centuries of Merovingian and Carolingian rule ends with the crowning of Hugh Capet as king; the Capetian dynasty is born

1066
Duke of Normandy William the Conqueror and his Norman forces occupy England

Listen to the French national anthem (p349), what de Gaulle said when Paris was liberated in 1944 and Chirac's defence of nuclear testing in 1995 on the BBC News website (follow the Europe/Coun try Profile/France/Time line link) at http://news .bbc.co.uk.

of Jan (1562), which afforded the Protestants certain rights, the Wars of Religion (1562–98) broke out between the Huguenots (French Protestants who received help from the English), the Catholic League (led by the House of Guise) and the Catholic monarchy. In 1588 the Catholic League forced Henri III (r 1574–89) to flee the royal court at the Louvre (p113) and the next year the monarch was assassinated.

Henri IV (r 1589–1610) kicked off the Bourbon dynasty, issuing the controversial Edict of Nantes (1598) to guarantee the Huguenots many civil and political rights, notably the freedom of conscience. Ultra-Catholic Paris refused to allow the new Protestant king entry to the city, and a siege of the capital continued for almost five years. Only when Henri IV embraced Catholicism at the cathedral in St-Denis (p182) did the capital submit to him.

Throughout most of his undistinguished reign, Fontainebleau-born Louis XIII (r 1610–43) remained firmly under the thumb of his ruthless chief minister, Cardinal Richelieu, best known for his untiring efforts to establish an all-powerful monarchy in France and French supremacy in Europe.

THE SUN KING

For the classic work on Louis XIV and the country he ruled from Versailles, look no further than *The Sun King* by Nancy Mitford.

At the tender age of five, *le Roi Soleil* (the Sun King) ascended the throne as Louis XIV (r 1643–1715). Bolstered by claims of divine right, he involved France in a rash of wars that gained it territory but terrified its neighbours and nearly bankrupted the treasury. At home, he quashed the ambitious, feuding aristocracy and created the first centralised French state. In Versailles, 23km southwest of Paris, Louis XIV built an extravagant palace and made his courtiers compete with each other for royal favour, reducing them to ineffectual sycophants. In 1685 he revoked the Edict of Nantes.

Sun-king grandson Louis XV (r 1715–74) was an oafish buffoon whose regent, the duke of Orléans, shifted the royal court back to Paris. As the 18th century progressed, the *ancien régime* (old order) became increasingly out of step with the needs of the country. Enlightened anti-establishment and anticlerical ideas expressed by Voltaire, Rousseau and Montesquieu further threatened the royal regime.

The Seven Years' War (1756–63), fought by France and Austria against Britain and Prussia, was one of a series of ruinous wars pursued by Louis

---

VAUBAN'S CITADELS

From the mid-17th century to the mid-19th century, the design of defensive fortifications around the world was dominated by the work of one man: Sébastien le Prestre de Vauban (1633–1707).

Born to a relatively poor family of the petty nobility, Vauban worked as a military engineer during almost the entire reign of Louis XIV, revolutionising both the design of fortresses and siege techniques. To defend France's frontiers, he built 33 immense citadels, many of them star-shaped and surrounded by moats, and he rebuilt or refined over 100 more. Vauban's most famous citadel is situated at Lille, but his work can also be seen at Antibes, Belfort, Belle Île, Bensançon, Concarneau, Perpignan, St-Jean Pied de Port, St-Malo and Verdun.

1309	1431
The Holy See moves from Rome to Avignon in southern France, the Popes staying in southern France until 1377	Jeanne d'Arc (Joan of Arc) is burnt at the stake for heresy in Rouen; the English are not driven out of France until 1453

OFF WITH HIS HEAD

In a bid to make public executions more humane (hanging and quartering – roping the victim's limbs to four oxen which then ran in four different directions – was the favoured method of the day for commoners), French physician Joseph Ignace Guillotin (1738–1814) came up with the guillotine.

Several tests on dead bodies down the line, highwayman Nicolas Jacques Pelletie was the first in France to have his head sliced off by the 2m-odd long falling blade on 25 April 1792 on place de Grève on Paris' Right Bank. His head rolled into a strategically placed wicker basket. During the Reign of Terror, at least 17,000 met their death by guillotine.

By the time the last person in France (murderer Hamida Djandoubi in Marseille) to be guillotined had the chop in 1977 (behind closed doors – the last public execution was in 1939), the lethal contraption had been sufficiently refined to slice off a head in 2/100 of a second. France abolished capital punishment in 1981.

XV, leading to the loss of France's flourishing colonies in Canada, the West Indies and India to the British. The war cost a fortune and, even more ruinous for the monarchy, it helped to disseminate in France the radical democratic ideas that the American Revolution thrust onto the world stage.

REVOLUTION TO REPUBLIC

Social and economic crisis marked the 18th century. With the aim of warding off popular discontent, Louis XVI called a meeting of the *États Généraux* (Estates General) in 1789 made up of representatives of the nobility (First Estate), clergy (Second Estate) and the remaining 90% of the population (Third Estate). When the Third Estate's call for a system of proportional voting failed, it proclaimed itself a National Assembly and demanded a constitution. On the streets, a Parisian mob took the matter into their own hands by raiding the Invalides (p124) for weapons and storming the prison at Bastille (now a very busy roundabout; p119).

France was declared a constitutional monarchy and various reforms enacted. But as the new government armed itself against the threat posed by Austria, Prussia and the many exiled French nobles, patriotism and nationalism mixed with revolutionary fervour. Before long, the moderate republican Girondins lost power to the radical Jacobins led by Robespierre, Danton and Marat, and in September 1792 France's First Republic was declared. Louis XVI was publicly guillotined in January 1793 on Paris' place de la Concorde (p127) and the head of his queen, the vilified Marie Antoinette, rolled several months later.

The terrifying Reign of Terror between September 1793 and July 1794 saw religious freedoms revoked, churches closed, cathedrals turned into 'Temples of Reason' and thousands incarcerated in dungeons in Paris' Conciergerie (p120) before being beheaded (see above).

Afterwards, a five-man delegation of moderate republicans led by Paul Barras set itself up as a *Directoire* (Directory) to rule the Republic – until a dashing young Corsican general named Napoleon Bonaparte (1769–1821) came along.

DID YOU KNOW?

Portrayed as something of a clueless idiot, Louis XVI is reckoned to have written *'rien'* (nothing happened) in his diary the day the Bastille was stormed.

From Joan of Arc to the Eurostar, *Cross Channel* by Julian Barnes is a witty collection of key moments in shared Anglo-French history.

1515	1562–98
With the reign of François I, the royal court moves to the Loire Valley where a rash of regal chateaux and hunting lodges are built	Henry IV gives French Protestants freedom of conscience with the Edict of Nantes

NAPOLEON BONAPARTE

Napoleon Bonaparte's skills and military tactics quickly turned him into an independent political force and in 1799 he overthrew the Directory and assumed power as consul of the First Empire. A referendum in 1802 declared him consul for life, his birthday became a national holiday and in 1804 he was crowned emperor of the French by Pope Pius VII at Paris' Notre Dame (p119). Two years on he commissioned the world's largest triumphal arch (p127) to be built.

To consolidate and legitimise his authority, Napoleon waged several wars in which France gained control of most of Europe. In 1812 his troops captured Moscow, only to be killed off by the brutal Russian winter. Two years later, Allied armies entered Paris, exiled Napoleon to Elba and restored the House of Bourbon to the French throne at the Congress of Vienna (1814–15).

But in 1815 Napoleon escaped from the Mediterranean island-kingdom, landed at Golfe Juan in southern France and proceeded north, triumphantly entering Paris on 20 May. His glorious 'Hundred Days' back in power ended with the Battle of Waterloo and his return to exile (to the South Atlantic island of St-Helena, where he died in 1821). In 1840 his remains were moved to a very grand tomb in the Église du Dôme (p125) on Paris' Esplanade des Invalides.

SECOND REPUBLIC TO SECOND EMPIRE

A struggle between extreme monarchists who sought a return to the *ancien régime*, people who saw the changes wrought by the Revolution as irreversible, and the radicals of the poor working-class neighbourhoods of Paris dominated the reign of Louis XVIII (r 1815–24). Charles X (r 1824–30) responded to the conflict with ineptitude and was overthrown in the so-called July Revolution of 1830. Those who were killed in the Paris street battles that accompanied the Revolution are buried in vaults under the Colonne de Juillet in the centre of place de la Bastille (p119).

DID YOU KNOW?

The *Code Napoléon* (or Civil Code), instituted by French hero Napoleon Bonaparte, forms the basis of the French legal system and many others in Europe.

A History of Modern France by Alfred Cobban is a very readable, three-volume history covering the period from Louis XIV to 1962.

REPUBLICAN CALENDAR

During the Revolution, the Convention adopted a calendar from which all 'superstitious' associations (such as saints' days) were removed. Year 1 began on 22 September 1792, the day the Republic was proclaimed. The 12 months – renamed Vendémiaire, Brumaire, Frimaire, Nivôse, Pluviôse, Ventôse, Germinal, Floréal, Prairial, Messidor, Thermidor and Fructidor – were divided into three 10-day weeks called *décades*.

The poetic names of the months were seasonally inspired: the autumn months, for instance, were Vendémiaire (derived from *vendange*, grape harvest or vintage), Brumaire (from *brume*, mist or fog) and Frimaire (from *frimas*, frost). The last day of each *décade* was a rest day, and the five or six remaining days of the year were used to celebrate Virtue, Genius, Labour, Opinion and Rewards. These festivals were initially called *sans-culottides* in honour of the *sans-culottes*, the extreme revolutionaries who wore pantaloons rather than the short breeches favoured by the upper classes.

While the Republican calendar worked well in theory, it caused no end of confusion and on 1 January 1806 Napoleon switched back to the Gregorian calendar.

1643–1715	1789–94
The Sun King assumes the French throne and shifts the royal court from Paris to a fabulous palace 23km west of the city in Versailles	Revolutionaries storm the Bastille, leading to the public beheading of Louis XVI and Marie Antoinette and the Reign of Terror

FRENCH INVENTIONS

▪ The first digital calculator (Blaise Pascal, 1642)

▪ The hot-air balloon (Jospeh and Étienne Montgolfier, 1783)

▪ A printed language that blind people could read (Louis Braille, 1829)

▪ Margarine (Mège Mouriés, 1869)

▪ Etch-a-Sketch children's toy (Arthur Granjean, 1958)

▪ The installation of a silicon chip computer memory on credit cards (Roland Moreno, 1974)

▪ Minitel, the first public interactive computer network (1980)

Louis-Philippe (r 1830–48), a constitutional monarch of bourgeois sympathies and tastes, was subsequently chosen by parliament, only to be ousted by the 1848 Revolution. The Second Republic was established and elections brought in Napoleon's almost useless nephew, Louis Napoleon Bonaparte, as president. But in 1851 Louis Napoleon led a coup d'état and proclaimed himself Emperor Napoleon III of the Second Empire (1852–70).

France enjoyed significant economic growth at this time. Paris was transformed under urban planner Baron Haussmann (1809–91) who, among other things, created the 12 huge boulevards radiating from the Arc de Triomphe (p127). Napoleon III threw glittering parties at the royal palace (p232) in Compiègne, and breathed in the sea air at fashionable Biarritz (p654) and Deauville (p254).

As his uncle had done before him, Napoleon III embroiled France in various catastrophic conflicts, including the Crimean War (1853–56) and the humiliating Franco-Prussian War (1870–71), which ended with Prussia taking the emperor prisoner. Upon hearing the news, defiant Parisian masses took to the streets demanding a republic; the so-called Wall of the Federalists in Paris' Cimetière du Père Lachaise (p129) serves as a deathly reminder of the subsequent bloodshed.

A Social History of the French Revolution by Christopher Hibbert is the book to buy for those seeking an easy-to-digest social account of the period.

A BEAUTIFUL AGE

There was nothing beautiful about the start of the Third Republic. Born as a provisional government of national defence in September 1870, it was quickly besieged by the Prussians who laid siege to Paris and demanded National Assembly elections be held. Unfortunately, the first move made by the resultant monarchist-controlled assembly was to ratify the Treaty of Frankfurt (1871), the harsh terms of which – a five-billion-franc war indemnity and surrender of the provinces of Alsace and Lorraine – prompted immediate revolt. During *La Semaine Sanglante* (Bloody Week), several thousand rebel Communards (supporters of the hard-core insurgent Paris Commune) were killed and a further 20,000 or so executed.

Despite this bloody start, the Third Republic ushered in the glittering *belle époque* (beautiful age), with Art Nouveau architecture, a whole field of artistic 'isms' from impressionism onwards, and advances in science and engineering, including the construction of the first metro line in

DID YOU KNOW?

Starving citizens baked bread laced with sawdust and ate most of the animals in the city zoo during Prussia's siege of Paris (1870–71).

1799–1815	1858
The rise and fall of dashing Corsican soldier Napoleon Bonaparte	A 14-year-old peasant girl in Lourdes sees the Virgin Mary in a series of 18 visions; the town becomes a world pilgrimage site

Paris. World exhibitions were held in the capital in 1889 (showcased by the Eiffel Tower, p125) and again in 1901 in the purpose-built Petit Palais (p127). Bohemia Paris, with its nightclubs and artistic cafés, was conceived around this time.

Colonial rivalry between France and Britain in Africa ended in 1904 with the *Entente Cordiale* (literally 'Cordial Understanding'), marking the start of a cooperation that has continued, more or less, to this day.

Discover the type of life Alfred Dreyfus would have led on Devil's Island with *Dry Guillotine: 15 Years among the Living Dead*, a gripping account of the South American French penal colony by René Belbenoît, first published in 1938.

THE GREAT WAR

A trip to the Somme (p223) or Verdun (p384) battlefields – places synonymous with wartime slaughter – goes some way to revealing the unimaginable human cost of WWI. Of the eight million French men called to arms, 1.3 million were killed and almost one million crippled. Much of the war took place in northeastern France, trench warfare using thousands of soldiers as cannon fodder to gain a few metres of territory: trenches at the battle ground of Le Linge in Alsace form part of a memorial museum (p368).

Central to France's entry into war against Austria-Hungary and Germany had been its desire to regain Alsace and Lorraine, lost to Germany in 1871. The Great War officially ended in November 1918 with Germany and the Allies signing an armistice in a clearing (p233) near Compiègne. But the details were not finalised until 1919 when the so-called 'big four' – French Prime Minister Georges Clemenceau, British Prime Minister Lloyd George, Italian Premier Vittorio Orlando and US President Woodrow Wilson – gathered in the Palace of Versailles (p187) to sign the Treaty of Versailles. Its harsh terms included the return of Alsace-Lorraine to France and a reparations bill of US$33 billion for Germany.

Battles, battleground tours, a who's who, propaganda posters, diaries and war timeline are among the impressive range of features to be found on this comprehensive site examining the Great War at www.firstworldwar.com.

WWI saw industrial production drop by 40% and France thrown into financial crisis. Yet somehow Paris still sparkled as the centre of the avant-garde in the 1920s and 1930s, with artists pushing into the new fields of cubism and surrealism, Le Corbusier (p53) rewriting the architectural textbook, foreign writers like Ernest Hemingway and F Scott Fitzgerald attracted by the liberal atmosphere of Paris, and nightlife establishing a cutting-edge reputation for everything from jazz to striptease. In 1922 the luxurious *Train Bleu* (Blue Train) made its first run from Calais, via

1870	1914–18
The Third Republic ushers in the *belle époque*	Eight million French men are called to arms during WWI; of these, 1.3 million are killed and almost one million are crippled

Paris, to the Côte d'Azur. The train only had 1st-class carriages and was quickly dubbed the 'train to paradise'.

WWII

The naming of Adolf Hitler as Germany's chancellor in 1933 signalled the end of a decade of accommodation and compromise between France and Germany. Initially the French tried to appease Hitler, but two days after Germany invaded Poland in 1939, France joined Britain in declaring war on Germany.

By June 1940 France had capitulated. The British expeditionary force sent to help the French barely managed to avoid capture by retreating to Dunkirk and crossing the English Channel in small boats. The Maginot Line (p344) had proved useless, German armoured divisions outflanking it by going through Belgium.

Germany divided France into a zone under direct German occupation (in the north and along the western coast) and a puppet state led by ageing WWI hero General Pétain in the spa town of Vichy; the demarcation line between the two ran through Château de Chenonceau (p410) in the Loire Valley. Life in the Nazi-occupied north is examined at La Coupole (p214), a WWII museum inside a subterranean Nazi-built rocket launch site.

The Vichy regime was viciously anti-Semitic, local police invariably proving very helpful to the Nazis in rounding up French Jews and others for deportation to Auschwitz and other death camps. Museums in Grenoble (p524) and Lyon (p475), among others, examine these deportations. The only Nazi concentration camp on French soil was Natzweiler-Struthof (p357); it can be visited.

An 80km-long stretch of beach (p226, p264) and Bayeux's Musée Mémorial 1944 Bataille de Normandie (p262) tell the tale of the D-Day landings on 6 June 1944 when 100,000-plus Allied troops stormed the coastline to liberate most of Normandy and Brittany. Paris was liberated on 25 August by a force spearheaded by Free French units, sent in ahead of the Americans, so the French would have the honour of liberating their own capital.

The US general's war room in Reims (p327) where Nazi Germany officially capitulated in May 1945 is open to the public.

POST-WAR DEVASTATION

France was ruined by the time it was liberated. Over one-third of industrial production fed the German war machine during WWII, the

A detailed history of WWII with Nazi leader biographies and a Holocaust timeline with over 150 images make this website stand out www.historyplace.com

WWI: Trenches on the Web (www.worldwar1.com) provides dozens of hot links to other Great War-related websites.

'A simple story of the nightmare of Flanders mud' is how one critic reviewed *Birdsong* by Sebastian Faulks, a gripping novel about trench warfare in northern France during WWI. The novel spans 1910 to the Armistice.

THE FRENCH RESISTANCE

Despite the myth of '*la France résistante*' (the French Resistance), the underground movement never actually included more than 5% of the population. The other 95% either collaborated or did nothing. Resistance members engaged in railway sabotage, collected intelligence for the Allies, helped Allied airmen who had been shot down and published anti-German leaflets, among other activities. The impact of their pursuits might have been modest but the Resistance served as an enormous boost to French morale – not to mention fresh fodder for numerous literary and cinematic endeavours.

1939	1944
Nazi Germany occupies France and establishes a Vichy regime	Normandy and Brittany are the first to be liberated by Allied troops following the June 1944 D-Day landings

occupiers requisitioning practically everything that wasn't (and was) nailed down: ferrous and nonferrous metals, statues, iron grills, zinc bar tops, coal, leather, textiles and chemicals. Agriculture, strangled by the lack of raw materials, fell by 25%.

In their retreat, the Germans burned bridges (2600 destroyed) and the Allied bombardments tore up railroad tracks (40,000km). The roadways hadn't been maintained since 1939, ports were damaged, and nearly half a million buildings and 60,000 factories destroyed. The French had to pay for the needs of the occupying soldiers to the tune of 400 million francs a day, prompting an inflation riptide.

France's humiliation at the hands of the Germans was not lost on its restive colonies. As the war economy tightened its grip, the native-born people, poorer to begin with, noticed that they were taking the brunt of the pain. In North Africa, the Algerians coalesced around a movement for greater autonomy that blossomed into a full-scale independence movement by the end of the war. The Japanese moved into strategically important Indochina in 1940. A Vietnamese resistance movement that developed quickly took on an anti-French, nationalistic tone setting the stage for Vietnam's eventual independence.

Wine & War by Don & Petie Kladstrup is the cliffhanger story of how France's wine-makers saved their country's greatest treasure – its vineyards – from destruction during WWII.

THE FOURTH REPUBLIC & POST-WAR PROSPERITY

DID YOU KNOW?

Women in France gained the right to vote in 1944.

After the liberation, General Charles de Gaulle (1890–1970) – France's undersecretary of war who had fled Paris for London in 1940 after France capitulated – faced the delicate task of setting up a viable government. Vichy officials were disqualified but what to do about the resistance fighters who had already installed themselves in many municipal offices? Using his personal prestige, de Gaulle kept reprisals to a minimum, convincing resistance fighters to disarm and join a temporary government of national unity.

Elections on 21 October 1945 created a national assembly composed largely of pro-resistant communists. De Gaulle was appointed head of the government, but quickly sensed that the tide was turning against his idea of a strong presidency and in January 1946 he resigned.

The magnitude of France's post-war economic devastation required a strong central government with broad powers to rebuild its industrial and commercial base. Soon after the liberation, most banks, insurance companies, car manufacturers and energy-producing companies passed into the hands of the government. Other businesses remained in private hands, the objective being to combine the efficiency of state planning with the dynamism of private initiative. But progress was slow. By 1947 rationing remained and France was forced to turn to the USA for loans as part of the Marshall Plan to rebuild Europe.

One of the aims of the Marshall Plan was to stabilise post-war Europe financially and politically, thus thwarting the expansion of Soviet power. As the Iron Curtain dropped over Eastern Europe, the pro-Stalinist bent of the Communist Party put it in a politically untenable position. Seeking at once to exercise power within the government and at the same time oppose its measures as insufficiently Marxist, the communists found themselves on the losing end of disputes involving the colonies, workers' demands and American aid. In 1947 they were booted out of government.

DID YOU KNOW?

Charles de Gaulle was a record breaker: he is included in the *Guinness Book of Records* as surviving more assassination attempts – 32 to be precise – than anyone else in the world.

1949	1954–62
France signs the Atlantic Pact uniting North America and Western Europe in a mutual defence alliance (NATO)	The Algerian War of Independence marks the end of French colonialism

While the Communist Party fulminated against the 'imperialism' of American power, de Gaulle founded a new party, the Rassemblement du Peuple Français (RPF), which argued for the containment of Soviet power. In 1949 France signed the Atlantic Pact uniting North America and Western Europe in a mutual defence alliance (NATO). The fear of both communism and a resurgent Germany also led to the first steps towards European integration with the birth of the Council of Europe in 1949, the European Coal and Steel Community in 1951 and military accords in 1954.

For a vivid, in-depth and provocative portrait of de Gaulle go to www .charles-de-gaulle.org.

The economy gathered steam in the 1950s, helped in part by a world-wide economic expansion. The French government invested in hydroelectric plants, nuclear power plants, oil and gas exploration, petrochemical refineries, steel production, naval construction, auto factories, building construction to accommodate a baby boom and consumer goods.

WAR IN THE COLONIES

The 1950s spelled the end of French colonialism. When Japan surrendered to the Allies in 1945, the nationalist Ho Chi Minh launched a drive for an autonomous Vietnam that became a drive for independence. Under the brilliant General Giap, the Vietnamese perfected a form of guerrilla warfare that proved highly effective against the French army (and later the Americans). After their defeat at Dien Bien Phu in 1954, the French threw in the towel and withdrew from Indochina.

The struggle for Algerian independence was nastier. Technically a French *département* (p906), Algeria was in effect ruled by a million or so French settlers who wished to protect their privileges at all costs. Heads stuck firmly in the Saharan sands (especially in the south where the oil was), the colonial community and their supporters in the army and the right wing refused all Algerian demands for political and economic equality.

Past Imperfect: French Intellectuals, 1944–1956 by Tony Judt studies the lively intellectual life of post-war France with flair and authority.

The Algerian War (1954–62) was brutal. Nationalist rebel attacks were met with summary executions, inquisitions, torture and massacres that only made Algerians more determined to gain their independence. The government responded with half-hearted reform and reorganisation programmes that failed to address the fact that most people no longer wished to be a part of France.

International pressure on France to pull out of Algeria came from the UN, the USSR and the USA, while *pieds noirs* (literally 'black feet' –

THE BIRTH OF THE BIKINI

Almost called *atome* (French for atom) rather than bikini after its pinprick size, the scanty little two-piece bathing suit was the 1946 creation of Cannes fashion designer Jacques Heim and automotive engineer Louis Réard.

Top and bottom swimsuits had existed for centuries, but it was the French duo who plumped for the name, bikini – after Bikini, an atoll in the Marshall Islands chosen by the USA in 1946 as the testing ground for atomic bombs.

Once wrapped around the curvaceous buttocks of 1950s sex-bomb Brigitte Bardot on St-Tropez' Plage de Pampelonne, there was no looking back. The bikini was born.

1968	1981
Anti-authoritarian student protests at de Gaulle's style of government by decree escalate into countrywide strike	The super-speedy TGV makes its first commercial journey (Paris to Lyon)

as Algerian-born French people are known in France), elements of the military and extreme right-wingers became increasingly enraged at what they saw as defeatism in dealing with the problem. A plot to overthrow the government and replace it with a military-style regime, raising the serious risk of a civil war in France, was narrowly avoided when de Gaulle agreed to assume the presidency in 1958.

THE FIFTH REPUBLIC & YESTERDAY'S MAN

While it could claim to have successfully reconstructed and expanded the economy and created a certain political stability, the Fourth Republic was ultimately hampered by a weak presidential branch and the debilitating situation in Algeria. De Gaulle remedied the first problem by drafting a new constitution – the Fifth Republic – which gave considerable powers to the president at the expense of the National Assembly.

Algeria was a greater problem, de Gaulle's initial attempts at reform – according the Algerians political equality and recognising their right in principle to self-determination – only serving to further infuriate right-wingers without quenching the Algerian thirst for independence. Following a failed coup attempt by a bunch of military officers in 1961, the Organisation de l'Armée Secrète (OAS; a group of French settlers and sympathisers opposed to Algerian independence) resorted to terrorism. It tried to assassinate de Gaulle several times and in 1961 violence broke out on the streets of Paris. Police violently attacked Algerian demonstrators, murdering more than 100. In 1962 de Gaulle negotiated an end to war in Algeria with the lakeside signing of the *Accord d'Évian* (Evian Accord) in Évian-les-Bains.

By the late 1960s de Gaulle was appearing more and more like yesterday's man. The loss of the colonies, the surge in immigration (p45) and rise in unemployment had weakened his government, while de Gaulle's government by decree was starting to gall the anti-authoritarian baby-boomer generation, which was now at university and gagging for social change. Students reading Herbert Marcuse and Wilhelm Reich found much to admire in Fidel Castro, Che Guevara and the black struggle for civil rights in America and vociferously denounced the American war in Vietnam.

Student protests of 1968 climaxed with a brutal overreaction by police to a protest meeting at Paris' most renowned university(p121). Overnight, public opinion turned in favour of the students, while the students themselves occupied the Sorbonne and erected barricades in the Latin Quarter. Within days, a general strike by 10 million workers countrywide paralysed France.

But such comradeship between worker and student did not last long. While the former wanted a greater share of the consumer market, the latter wanted to destroy it. After much hesitancy, de Gaulle took advantage of this division by appealing to people's fear of anarchy. Just as the country seemed on the brink of revolution and an overthrow of the Fifth Republic, stability returned. The government immediately decentralised the higher education system and followed through in the 1970s with a wave of other reforms (lowering the voting age to 18, an abortion law and so on). De Gaulle meanwhile resigned from office in 1969 after losing

DID YOU KNOW?

L'Imagination au Pouvoir (Power to the Imagination) and *Sous les Pavés, la Plage* (Under the Cobblestones, the Beach) – a reference to Parisians' favoured material for building barricades and what they could expect to find beneath – were slogans drummed up in 1968.

DID YOU KNOW?

France has had 11 constitutions since 1789. The present one, instituted by de Gaulle in 1958, is known as the Fifth Republic.

1994	1995
The 50km-long Channel Tunnel linking mainland France with Britain opens after seven years of hard graft by 10,000 workers	After twice serving as prime minister, Jacques Chirac becomes president of France

an important referendum on regionalisation and suffered a fatal heart attack the following year.

POMPIDOU TO LE PEN

Georges Pompidou (1911–74), prime minister under de Gaulle, stepped onto the podium as president. Despite embarking on an ambitious modernisation programme, investing in aerospace, telecommunications and nuclear power, he failed to stave off inflation and social unrest following the global oil crisis of 1973.

Valéry Giscard d'Estaing (1926–) inherited a deteriorating economic climate and sharp divisions between the left and right upon assuming presidential power in 1974. Hampered by a lack of media nous and an arrogant demeanour that left him ill-equipped to marshal a consensus, d'Estaing proved unpopular. His friendship with emperor and accused child-eater Jean Bédel Bokassa of the Central African Republic did little to win him friends and in 1981 he was ousted by long-time head of the Parti Socialiste (PS; Socialist Party), François Mitterrand (1916–96). As the only surviving French president to remain in politics, the French media nicknamed d'Estaing *l'Ex* (the Ex).

Despite France's first socialist president instantly alienating the business community (the Paris stock market index fell by 30% on news of his victory) by setting out to nationalise 36 privately owned banks, industrial groups and other parts of the economy, Mitterrand did give France a new sparkle. The Minitel – a potent symbol of France's advanced technological savvy – was launched in 1980 and a clutch of *grands projets* (great works; p52) were embarked upon in the French capital. The death penalty was abolished, homosexuality was legalised, a 39-hour work week was instituted, annual holiday time was upped from four to five weeks and the right to retire at 60 was guaranteed.

Yet by 1986 the economy was weakening and in parliamentary elections that year the right-wing opposition, led by Jacques Chirac (Paris mayor since 1977), won a majority in the National Assembly. For the next two years Mitterrand worked with a prime minister and cabinet from the opposition, an unprecedented arrangement known as *cohabitation*. The extreme-right Front National (FN; National Front) meanwhile quietly gained ground by loudly blaming France's economic woes on immigration.

Presidential elections in 1995 ushered Jacques Chirac (an ailing Mitterrand did not run) into the Élysée Palace, the former mayor winning immediate popular acclaim for his direct words and actions in matters relating to the EU and the war raging in Bosnia. Whizz-kid foreign minister Alain Juppé was appointed prime minister and several women were placed in top cabinet positions. Unfortunately, Chirac's attempts to reform France's colossal public sector in order to meet the criteria of European Monetary Union (EMU) were met with the largest protests since 1968, and his decision to resume nuclear testing on the Polynesian island of Moruroa and a nearby atoll was the focus of worldwide outrage.

Always the maverick, Chirac called early parliamentary elections in 1997 – only for his party, the Rassemblement pour la République (RPR;

View pics of all the French presidents, take a virtual tour of the presidential pad and see the Arman-studded room where visiting heads of state are received in the online office of the French president at www .elysee.fr.

In *The Extreme Right in France*, JG Shields digs deep into France's political past to trace the rise of the far right and find out just how Le Pen managed to make such an impact in the 2002 presidential race (p40).

Follow the moves and motions of the National Assembly at www .assemblee-nat.fr.

1999	2002
A fire in the Alpine Mont Blanc tunnel kills 41 people	The French franc, first minted in 1360, is dumped as France adopts the euro (€) as its official currency

Rally for the Republic), to lose out to a coalition of socialists, communists and greens. Another period of *cohabitation* ensued, this time with Chirac on the other side.

Presidential elections in 2002 were a shocker. Not only did the first round of voting see left-wing Socialist Party leader Lionel Jospin eliminated. It also saw racist demagogue Jean-Marie Le Pen (1928–) of the FN scoop 17% of the national vote. In the fortnight preceding the subsequent run-off ballot, demonstrators took to the streets with cries of 'Vote for the crook, not the fascist' ('crook' referring to the various party financing scandals floating around Chirac). On the big day itself, left-wing voters – without a candidate of their own – hedged their bets with the 'lesser-of-two-evils' Chirac to give him 82% of votes. Chirac's landslide victory was echoed in parliamentary elections a month later when the president-backed coalition UMP (Union pour un Mouvement Populaire) won 354 of the 577 parliamentary seats, ending years of *cohabitation* and leaving a seatless Le Pen-led FN feeling very sorry for its xenophobic self. Subsequent claims of nepotism in response to Le Pen trying to pass the party leadership automatically to his daughter weakened the party further.

France is one of the five permanent members of the UN Security Council. It withdrew from NATO's joint military command in 1966 and has maintained an independent arsenal of nuclear weapons since 1960. Despite ritual denunciations of globalisation by politicians and pundits, its economy is heavily dependent on the global marketplace – its export market is Europe's fourth largest and its agricultural sector, the largest in the EU, thanks to generous subsidies awarded to the high-voting, sympathy-inducing agricultural sector.

Keep abreast with the policies, speeches and actions of the *premier ministre* (prime minister) at www.premier-ministre.gouv.fr.

2003	2004
A heatwave across Europe brings sizzling temperatures of 40°C to Paris in August, killing an estimated 14,800 (mainly elderly) people	The National Assembly says yes to a controversial bill banning overtly religious symbols such as the Islamic headscarf in state schools

The Culture

THE NATIONAL PSYCHE

There is nothing more maddening than the shop assistant who unabashedly chats to her mate while you wait, or the post-office clerk who greets you with complete lack of recognition. Dumb insolence some say.

France is a country whose people have attracted more stubborn myths and stereotypes than any other in Europe. Arrogant, rude, bolshy, unbelievably bureaucratic (which, incidentally, is true: you try getting a *carte grise* or car-ownership papers), sexist, chauvinistic, super chic and stylish are among the dozens of tags – true or otherwise – donned on the garlic-eating, beret-wearing French over the centuries. The French, by the way, don't wear berets these days.

Most people are extremely proud to be French and staunchly nationalistic to boot, a result of the country's republican stance that places nationality – rather than religion, for example – at the top of the self-identity list. This has created an overwhelmingly self-confident nation, both culturally and intellectually – a French superiority complex that manifests itself in a pompous refusal to speak any language other than French, according to many Anglophones.

Contrary to popular belief, a surprisingly large number of French speak English or another foreign language very well, are open to travel and are perfectly happy to use their language skills should the need arise. Of course, if monolingual English-speakers don't even attempt '*bonjour*', then there is no way proud French linguists will let on they speak great English with a great sexy accent. French men, by the way, deem an English gal's heavily accented French as downright sexy as many women deem a Frenchman speaking English.

On the subject of sex, not all French men ooze romance or light Gitanes all day. Nor are they as civilised about adultery as French cinema would have you believe. Despite the insouciance with which film-makers treat infidelity, surveys reveal that only 7% of those in a couple strayed in the previous 12 months. *Adieu 'French Lover'* bemoaned *Le Monde* in reporting this unsettling news when it first came out. Adultery, illegal in France until 1975, was actually grounds for automatic divorce until as late as mid-2004.

Suckers for tradition, the French are slow to embrace new ideas and technologies: it took the country an age to embrace the Internet, clinging on to their own Minitel system for dear life. Yet the French are also incredibly innovative (p33) – a dichotomy reflected in practically every facet of French life. they drink and smoke more than anyone else, yet live longer. They eat like kings, but are not fat, and so on…

LIFESTYLE

Peek into the 5th-floor bourgeois apartment of Monsieur et Madame Tout le Monde and you'll see them dunking croissants in bowls of *café au lait* for

By looking at history, Jean-Benoit Nadeau and Julie Barlow find solutions to puzzling dichotomies such as how the French can be so horribly bureaucratic, archaic and inventive all at the same time in *Sixty Million Frenchmen can't be Wrong: What Makes the French so French*.

Gals seeking French chic could try donning Debra Ollivier's *Entre Nous: A Woman's Guide to Finding Her Inner French Girl*, an imaginative little number that delves into the secret of inner (and outer) French beauty.

SACRE BLEU!

'Ooooo la la' they do say, but *'sacre bleu'* they don't. A favourite of writers seeking to add colour to a 'French' scene, this chestnut hasn't been heard in France since the Franco-Prussian War. *'Mon Dieu!'* is one of the gentler expressions of surprise. More popular expletives can't be printed but just sit in a café some afternoon and watch Parisians slip on dog-droppings.

breakfast, buying a baguette every day from the bakery (Monsieur nibbles the top off on his way home) and not recycling bar a few glass bottles. They go to the flicks once a month, work not a second more than 35 hours a week and have a 20-year-old daughter who is 'oh so BCBG, darling'.

Madame buys a clutch of hot-gossip weekly mags, Monsieur enjoys *boules* and August is the *only* month a summer holiday is considered. Dodging dog poo on pavements is a sport practised from birth, Minitel remains the best way to find telephone numbers and in shops everything goes on the *carte bleue*: this *is* the society after all that microchipped credit cards long before anyone else even dreamt of scrapping the swipe-and-sign system.

The couple have a landlord: with a longstanding tradition of renting rather than buying (38% of households rent the property they live in), home ownership is low. Rented accommodation in cities and towns tends to be high-rise apartment blocks.

Jospin's slashing of the standard French working week from 39 to 35 hours in 2000 (applicable to employers of more than 20 from 2002) created jobs, boosted domestic tourism and redefined peak hours as pleasure-thirsty workers headed out to the country on Thursday night (instead of Friday) and returned to urban life on Monday evening. While most French workers, given the choice, would plump for less income and more leisure time, a sizeable chunk of the population still toils 39 hours or more a week. (Since 2003 employers can enforce a 39-hour work week for a negotiable extra cost.)

Rich in play time (a 35-hour work week, five weeks annual holiday and every religious holiday in the book) they might be, but one out of three French can't afford to travel on holiday. Of those that do, only 10% holiday abroad. Women overall earn 12% less than men.

The family plays a vital role, 85% of French defining themselves in terms of their family (rather than profession or friends). Nonetheless, couples are marrying later (men at the age of 30, women at 28) and waiting longer to have children. More children are born out of wedlock (44% in 2002 compared to 11% in 1980) and divorce is on the rise (37% of marriages end in divorce). The traditional sense of duty towards the elderly is also diminishing claim critics who cite the shocking number of elderly Parisians who died during the 2003 heatwave without any relative coming forward to bury them.

Abortion is legal during the first 12 weeks of pregnancy, girls under 16 not needing parental consent providing they are accompanied by an adult of their choice: 30 abortions take place in France for every 100 live births.

Civil unions between two members of the same (or different) sex have been legal since 2000, although this falls short of legal marriages say gay lobbyists who want homosexual couples to be granted the same fiscal advantages and adoptive rights in marriage as heterosexuals. A petition calling for the legal recognition of same-sex marriages in early 2004 was topped off in June that year by the civil wedding of two gay men in Bègles town hall in

DID YOU KNOW?

One out of two French practise a sport regularly, walking being the vastly preferred activity. Five million smooth-movers cruise around on in-line skates.

Find out everything you need to know about buying or selling a home in France, setting up a business, marriage, inheritance and so on, under French law with Notaires de France (French Notaries) at www.notaires.fr (click on the minuscule Union Jack for English).

In *Le Divorce*, Diane Johnson explores expatriate society and French manners through the eyes of a young American woman in 1990s Paris, embroiled in her sister's divorce.

WHAT KIDS DO

French kids start *école maternelle* (nursery) at the age of three; move to *école primaire* (primary school) when they are six; and go to *lycée* (secondary school) from 11 to 16 or 18. The grand finale for academically minded pupils is the *baccalauréat*.

Anyone who's passed the *bac* bags a free place at one of France's 77 overcrowded universities – where 30% of students flunk the compulsory end-of-first-year exams and leave. One-third of French students plump for the University of Paris (p121), of which the historic Sorbonne is part; while the country's top 5% study at one of 140 elite *grandes écoles*.

> **FRENCH KISSING**
>
> Kissing is an integral part of French life. (The expression 'French kissing', as in tongues, doesn't exist in French incidentally.) That said, put a Parisian in Provence and there's no saying they will know when to stop.
>
> Countrywide, people who know each other reasonably well, really well, a tad, barely at all, greet each other with a glancing peck on each cheek. Southern France aside (where everyone kisses everyone), two men rarely kiss (unless they are related or artists) but always shake hands. Boys and girls start kissing as soon as they're out of nappies, or so it seems.
>
> Kissing French-style is not completely straightforward, 'how many' and 'which side first' potentially being problematic. In Paris it is definitely two: unless parties are related, *very* close friends or haven't seen each other in an age, anything more is deemed affected. That said, in certain trendy 20-something circles friends swap three or four cheek-skimming kisses, as do many young teenagers at school *parce qu'ils ont que ça à faire...*
>
> Travel south and the *bisous* (kisses) multiply, three or four being the norm in Provence. The bits of France neighbouring Switzerland around Lake Geneva tend to be three-kiss country (in keeping with Swiss habits); and in the Loire Valley it is four. Corsicans, bizarrely, stick to two but kiss left cheek first – which can lead to locked lips given everyone else in France starts with the right cheek.

Bordeaux. The ground-breaking ceremony, conducted by local mayor and former Green party presidential candidate, Noël Mamère, was the first in France. The gay scene thrives in Paris, Marseille and Lyon (see p904).

POPULATION

France is not that densely populated – 107 people inhabit every square kilometre (compared to 235 in Germany, 240 in the UK and 116 in the EU), although a fat 20% wedge of the national population is packed into the greater metropolitan area of Paris.

The last 10 years have seen rural and suburban areas steadily gaining population; and Paris and the northeast (except Alsace) losing inhabitants to southern France, an increasingly buoyant part of the country where populations are predicted to rise by 30% over the next 30 years.

In keeping with European trends, France's overall population is ageing: by 2050 one in three will be 60 or more (compared to one in five in 2000) – a demographic phenomenon that will be less marked in urban areas like Paris, Lyon and the Rhône Alpes and on the Mediterranean coast where increasing work opportunities ensures a younger, more active population.

For much of the last two centuries, France has had a considerably lower rate of population growth than its neighbours. In the last decade, that trend has changed and the birth rate now equals 2.1 children per woman. By 2050 the population of mainland France is expected to notch up 64 million – five million more than in 2000.

See p45 for a snapshot of France's foreign population.

SPORT

Most French wouldn't be seen dead walking down the street in trainers and tracksuit bottoms. Contrary to appearances though, they do love sport. Shaved-leg cyclists toil up Mont Ventoux (p795) in good weather; anyone who is anyone flits off for the weekend to ski; and football fans fill stadiums during home matches.

France has achieved a strikingly high level in international judo, four-time world champion David Douillet being the star. Les 24 Heures du

A New Yorker transplanted to Paris with a wife and small child takes a wry look at French politics, habits and society in Adam Gopnick's recommended *Paris to the Moon.*

DID YOU KNOW?

French life expectancy is among the world's highest – 82.9 for women and 75.8 for men

Mans and the F1 Grand Prix in Monte Carlo are the world's raciest dates in motor sports.

With the exception of mogul champion, *le boss des bosses* Edgar Gospiron, skiing bizarrely hasn't produced any stars since the 1968 Alpine sweep of Jean-Claude Killy. Chamonix snowboarder Karine Ruby (1978–) won the discipline's first Olympic gold medal in 1998 and holds more World Cup titles than any other boarder. On ice, Marina Anissina and Gwendal Peizerat scooped ice-dancing gold at Salt Lake City in 2002, and Brian Joubert finished second in the 2004 world figure-skating championships.

Paris will know in 2005 if its bid to host the 2012 Summer Olympics is successful. The French capital last hosted the gargantuan event in 1924.

Football

France's greatest sporting moment came at the 1998 World Cup, which the country hosted and won.

At club level, Marseille was the first French side in 1991 to win the European Champions League. In 1994 Paris–St-Germain won the European Cup Winners' Cup. Since the 1995 Bosman decision allowing European clubs to field as many European players as they wish, French football greats (including Zidane and Petit) have been lured to richer clubs in Italy, Britain, Spain and Germany. Other hotshots out of France include Arsenal's French manager Arsène Wenger and striker Thierry Henry.

France's home matches (friendlies and qualifiers for major championships) kick off at St-Denis' magnificent 80,000-capacity Stade de France (p183), built for the World Cup. Other noteworthy stadiums (there are 250-odd in all in France) include the Stade de Gerland (p482) in Lyon, home to national champions Olympique Lyonnais.

Rugby

Rugby league has a strong following in the south and southwest of France, favourite teams being Toulouse, Montauban and St-Godens. Rugby union is more popular still, as the enduring success of the powerful Paris–St-Germain club testifies.

DID YOU KNOW?

Marseille-born Zinedane Zidane transferred from Juventus to Real Madrid in 2001 for US$64.45 million, making him the most expensive player in football history.

Read all about French rugby and keep tabs with the scores on the board at www.francerugby.fr (in French)

DOS & DON'TS

Many visitors to France conclude it would be a great place if it weren't for the French. Adopt some simple dos and don'ts of French etiquette yourself and you could well find your relations with the French so vastly improved you actually start liking them.

■ Say *'Bonjour, monsieur/madame/mademoiselle'* when you walk into a shop or café, and *'Merci, monsieur…au revoir'* when leaving. Use *'Monsieur'* for any male person who isn't a child; *'Madame'* for those you'd call 'Mrs' in English; and *'mademoiselle'* for unmarried women.

■ Touching, fondling or picking up fruit, vegetables, flowers or a piece of clothing in shops attracts immediate killer stares from shop assistants. Ask if you want to look at something.

■ Take a gift – flowers (not chrysanthemums, which are only brought to cemeteries) or wine for more informal gatherings – when invited to someone's home.

■ Going 'Dutch' (splitting the bill) in restaurants is an uncivilised custom for many French. The person who invites generally pays, although close friends often share the cost.

■ Never discuss money, particularly income, over dinner.

■ Knock what your French textbook at school taught you on the head. These days *'s'il vous plaît'* – never *'garçon'* (meaning 'boy') – is the *only* way to summon a waiter in restaurants.

FRENCH BALLS

France's most traditional ball games are *pétanque* and the similar, though more formal, *boules*, which has a 70-page rule book. Both are played by village men in work clothes on a rough gravel or sandy pitch known as a *boulodrome*, scratched out wherever a bit of flat and shady ground can be found. World championships are held for both sports. In the Basque Country, the racquet game of *pelote* (p653) is the thing to do.

France's home games in the Tournoi des Six Nations (Six Nations Tournament) are held in March and April. The finals of the Championnat de France de Rugby take place in late May and early June.

Cycling

In July the world's most prestigious bicycle race, the **Tour de France**, brings together 189 of the world's top male cyclists (21 teams of nine) and 15 million spectators for a spectacular 3000-plus kilometre cycle around the country. The three-week route changes each year, but always labours through the Alps and Pyrenees and finishes on the Champs-Élysées in Paris. The publicity caravan preceding the cyclists showers roadside spectators with coffee samples, logo-emblazoned balloons, pens and other free junk-advertising gifts. Annual tour dates and routes are listed at www.letour.fr.

Drug scandals reduced the 1998 Tour de France to a 'tour of shame', less than 100 riders crossing the finishing line after several teams were disqualified for doping. Since then the race has cleaned up its act, although 2004 started badly with the withdrawal of the French team and banning of the Spanish, both on doping grounds. Brittany-born biking legend Bernard Hinault (1954–), nicknamed *le blaireau* (the badger), won the Tour de France five times before retiring in 1986.

France is the world's top track cycling nation and has a formidable reputation in mountain biking: Christian Taillefer holds the world speed record on a mountain bike, 212.39km/h, which he hit by flying down a snow-covered ski slope.

Tennis

The French Open, held in Paris's Roland Garros Stadium in late May and early June, is the second of the year's four Grand Slam tennis tournaments. Marseille-born Sébastien Grosjean (1978–) has been the highest-ranking French player on the men's circuit for the last few years, and WTA No 1 (September 2004) player Amélie Mauresmo is the French star on the women's circuit.

MULTICULTURALISM

Multicultural France has always drawn immigrants: 4.3 million from other parts of Europe arrived between 1850 and WWI and another three million came between the world wars. During the post-WWII economic-boom years, several million unskilled workers followed from North Africa and French-speaking sub-Saharan Africa. Large-scale immigration peaked in the early 1960s when, as the French colonial empire collapsed, French settlers returned to metropolitan France from Algeria, other parts of Africa and Indochina.

Immigrants today form 7.4% (4.3 million) of the population – a constant since 1975 when France implemented its first immigration law. The largest communities are Algerians (13%), Portuguese (13%), Moroccans (12%) and Italians (9%). Of this ethnic community, only one-third (36%)

Belt up with Les 24 Heures du Mans at www .lemans.org and Monte Carlo's F1 Grand Prix at www.acm.mc.

DID YOU KNOW?

French journalist and cyclist, Henri Desgrange, came up with the Tour de France in 1903 as a means of promoting his sports newspaper *L'Auto* (*L'Équipe* today). With the exception of two world war–induced intervals, it has been held every year since.

Make the Fédération Française de Tennis (French Tennis Federation) your first stop in court for everything to do with tennis in France, including the French Open website www.fft.fr in French).

has French citizenship, which is not conferred at birth but subject to various administrative requirements.

Racial tensions are fuelled by the extreme-right Front National (FN; National Front), whose leader Jean-Marie Le Pen makes no bones about his party's anti-foreigner stance. The politician outraged millions with his dismissal of the Holocaust as a 'mere detail of history' in the 1980s and his 'inequality of races' jargon in the late 1990s. Yet he got through to the second round of elections in the 2002 presidential race (p40), making a right-wing takeover of France a possibility. Though Paris may at times appear to be multiracial heaven, racism does exist here, and what may appear to be exotic to the outsider (an elderly Maghreb man selling salted nuts in the metro) is simply a tough struggle for survival for those who can't find employment. Racist acts of violence have not been uncommon in recent years, particularly in Paris' crowded suburbs. In the workplace, young people of non-French origin face widespread discrimination. How many black waiters do you see in central Paris cafés and restaurants?

The French republican code, while inclusive and nondiscriminatory on the one hand, does little to accommodate a multicultural society. This dichotomy exploded in a riot of demonstrations in 2004 when the Islamic headscarf (along with Jewish skullcaps, crucifixes and other religious symbols) was banned in French schools. The law, intended to place all schoolchildren on an equal footing in the classroom, was slammed by Muslims as intolerant and yet more proof that the French state is not prepared to integrate Muslims into French society.

Some 90% of France's Muslim community are noncitizens; many are illegal immigrants; and most live in depressing poverty-stricken *bidonvilles* (tinpot towns) surrounding major metropolitan centres.

DID YOU KNOW?

Both parents of 10% of children born in France are foreign; another 10% of French children have one foreign parent.

MEDIA

Public licence fees subsidise public broadcaster France Télévisions, which controls 40% of the market with its three TV channels – France 2, 3 and 5 (Arte after 7pm), see p893. Yet in the face of increasingly stiff competition from private broadcasters such as TF1 and M6, its future looks bleak.

Until 2003 cable TV operators could not transmit to more than eight million households each. With this restriction lifted, cable and satellite TV services are expected to grow 127% by 2007 to reach 15.9 million households. TV via broadband ADSL is the other big sell: France Télécom's video-driven MaLigne tv was launched in Lyon in 2003 and Paris the year after.

As in Britain, there is a strong distinction between broadcasting and print media. The press, like TV and radio broadcasters, are independent and free of censorship.

Find out about the public broadcaster behind France 2, 3 and 5 (Arte) with www.francetelevi sions.fr (in French) and its biggest private competitor at www.tf1.fr (in French).

RELIGION

Secular France maintains a rigid distinction between the church and state – to the horror of certain religious groups for whom the state ban on the wearing of religious symbols (above) in schools in 2004 was offensive and discriminative.

Some 55% of French identify themselves as Catholic, although no more than 10% attend church regularly. Another one million people are Protestant, concentrated in Alsace, the Jura, the Massif Central and along the Atlantic Coast.

Coexisting uneasily with this nominally Christian majority is France's five million-strong Muslim community. Most Muslims adhere to a moderate Islam, although the deportation (and subsequent return) in 2004 from Lyon of an Algerian iman in favour of stoning unfaithful wives – one

Listen to the voice of French Jews online at www.col.fr (in French).

of 27 radical Muslim prayer leaders to be deported since 2001 – renewed fears that Islamic fundamentalists are gaining ground. It also prompted calls from more moderate Muslims for the state to help train imans in a French-style Islam and build more mosques. Most of the 1500 or so imans in France are self-taught or have been educated in more radical climes. Almost 90% are employees of Algeria, Saudi Arabia or another Islamic country and work in mosques funded by these countries.

Over half of France's 600,000-strong Jewish population (Europe's largest) lives in and around Paris. Marseille has the next-largest Jewish community. French Jews, the first in Europe to achieve emancipation, have been represented by the Paris-based umbrella organisation the Consistoire since 1808. The number of anti-Semitic incidents is rising.

DID YOU KNOW?

French Muslims were only given a national voice in 2003 with the election of the French Muslim Council (FCMC), an umbrella organisation of 18 representatives from Muslim associations and mosques in France.

WOMEN IN FRANCE

Women were given the right to vote in 1945 by de Gaulle's short-lived post-war government, but until 1964 a woman needed her husband's permission to open a bank account or get a passport. Younger French women especially are quite outspoken and emancipated, but self-confidence has yet to translate into equality in the workplace, where women are often kept out of senior and management positions. The problem of sexual harassment *(harcélement sexuel)* in the workplace is finally beginning to be addressed with a new law imposing financial penalties on the offender.

Feminism in France from 1968 to the mid-1980s is charted by Claire Duchen in *Feminism in France*.

A great achievement in the last decade has been *Parité*, the law requiring political parties to fill 50% of their slates in all elections with female candidates.

ARTS
Literature
COURTLY LOVE TO SYMBOLISM

Lyric poems of courtly love composed by troubadours dominated medieval French literature, while the *roman* (literally 'the romance') drew on old Celtic tales like King Arthur, the search for the Holy Grail and so on. With the *Roman de la Rose*, a 22,000-line poem by Guillaume de Lorris and Jean de Meung, the allegorical figures of Pleasure and Riches, Shame and Fear popped on the scene.

La Pléiade, Rabelais and Montaigne made French Renaissance literature great: La Pléiade was a group of lyrical poets active in the 1550s and 1560s, of whom the best known is Pierre de Ronsard. The highly exuberant narrative of Loire Valley-born François Rabelais (1494–1553) blends coarse humour with encyclopaedic erudition in a vast panorama that includes every kind of person, occupation and jargon existing in mid-16th-century France. Michel de Montaigne (1533–92) meanwhile wrote essays on everything from cannibals, war horses and drunkenness to the uncanny resemblance of children to their fathers.

'*Le grand siècle*' ushered in the great French classical writers with their lofty odes to tragedy. François de Malherbe (1555–1628) brought a new rigour to the treatment of rhythm in poetry; and Parisian Marie de La Fayette (1634–93) penned the first major French novel, *La Princesse de Clèves* (1678).

DID YOU KNOW?

On Victor Hugo's 80th birthday, the street on which he lived in Paris was renamed avenue Victor Hugo. After he died his coffin was laid overnight beneath the Arc de Triomphe for an all-night vigil.

The chateau on the French–Swiss border in the Jura where Voltaire (1694–1778) lived from 1759 can be visited (p545). His philosophical work, together with that of Swiss-born philosopher Jean-Jacques Rousseau, dominated the 18th century. A century on, Besançon (p536) gave birth to Victor Hugo – the key figure of French Romanticism. The breadth of interest and technical innovations exhibited in his poems

PRIZES FOR THE LITERARY

Slammed as conservative (greats like Flaubert, Molière and Balzac weren't allowed in) and chauvinistic (just three of its current 38 members are women) it might be, but there's no disputing one fact: the Paris-based Académie Française (French Academy), founded in 1635 by Cardinal Richelieu to discuss rhetoric and literary criticism, is one of the country's grandest and oldest institutions. Each year it awards 70 or so different literary prizes to the brightest and best writers in French.

Literary prizes awarded outside the academy include the Prix Fémina for works by women writers; the Prix Goncourt for imaginative prose; the Prix Médicis for writers 'whose fame does not match their talent'; and the Prix Interallié, won in 2003 by Frederic Beigbeder's *Windows on the World*, a September 11-inspired novel set in New York in 2002 and named after the World Trade Centre's 107th-floor restaurant.

France honours its literary talent with almost 200 different prizes and awards in all. For a complete list of prizes and authors – present and past – see www.prix-litteraires.net.

A Penguin Classic worth devoting several days of reading time is *Gargantua and Pantagruel* by François Rabelais (translated by JM Cohen), a farcical epic about the adventures of the giant Gargantua and his son Pantagruel.

and novels – *Les Misérables* and *Notre Dame de Paris* (The Hunchback of Notre Dame) among them – was phenomenal.

In 1857 two literary landmarks were published: *Madame Bovary* by Gustave Flaubert (1821–80) and Charles Baudelaire's (1821–67) collection of poems, *Les Fleurs du Mal* (The Flowers of Evil). Émile Zola (1840–1902) meanwhile strove to convert novel-writing from an art to a science in his powerful series, *Les Rougon-Macquart*.

The expression of mind states rather than the detailing of day-to-day reality was the aim of the symbolists, Paul Verlaine (1844–96) and Stéphane Mallarmé (1842–98). Verlaine's poems – alongside those of Arthur Rimbaud (1854–91), with whom Verlaine shared a tempestuous homosexual relationship – are seen as French literature's first modern poems.

MODERN LITERATURE

Les Poètes du 19ème Siècle (Poets of the 19th Century) is an excellent online resource (in French) for anyone interested in reading in-depth about Verlaine, Baudelaire, Rimbaud et al. Go to www.poetes .com.

The world's longest novel – a seven-volume 9,609,000-character giant by Marcel Proust (1871–1922) – dominated the early 20th century: *À la Recherche du Temps Perdu* (Remembrance of Things Past) explores in evocative detail the true meaning of past experience recovered from the unconscious by 'involuntary memory'.

Surrealism proved a vital force until WWII, André Breton (1896–1966) capturing its spirit – a fascination with dreams, divination and all manifestations of 'the marvellous' – in his autobiographical narratives. In Paris the bohemian Colette (1873–1954) captivated and shocked with her titillating novels detailing the amorous exploits of heroines such as schoolgirl Claudine. Of her many Parisian addresses, it is the apartment where she died in the Palais Royal (p115) that is the most illustrious. Otherwise, there's a small museum (p433) in the Burgundian village where she was born.

After WWII, existentialism developed around the lively debates of Jean-Paul Sartre (1905–80), Simone de Beauvoir (1908–86) and Albert Camus (1913–60) in Paris' Left-Bank cafés of St-Germain des Prés. View the graves of Sartre and Beauvoir in the Cimetière du Montparnasse (p123).

The 1950s' *nouveau roman* saw experimental young writers seek new ways of organising narratives, Nathalie Sarraute slashing identifiable characters and plot in *Les Fruits d'Or* (The Golden Fruits). *Histoire d'O* (Story of O), an erotic sadomasochistic novel written by Dominique Aury under a pseudonym in 1954, meanwhile sold more copies than any other contemporary French novel outside France. In the 1960s it was the forbiddingly experimental novels of Philippe Sollers (1936–) that raised eyebrows.

Contemporary authors include Françoise Sagan, Pascal Quignard, Jean Auel, Emmanuel Carrère and Stéphane Bourguignon. Also popular are Frédéric Dard (alias San Antonio), Léo Malet and Daniel Pennac, widely read for his witty crime fiction such as *Au Bonheur des Ogres* (The Scapegoat) and *La Fée Carabine* (The Fairy Gunmother).

Cinema & TV
CINEMA

Watching French classics in the Lyonnaise factory (p475) where those cinematographic pioneers, the Lumière brothers, shot the world's first-ever motion picture in March 1895, is a must for cinema buffs.

French film flourished in the 1920s, Abel Gance (1889–1981) being king of the decade with his powerful antiwar blockbuster *J'Accuse* (I Accuse; 1918) – all the more impressive for its location filming on actual WWI battlefields (p223). The switch to sound ushered in René Clair (1898–1981) and his world of fantasy and satirical surrealism: his exuberant *À Nous La Liberté* (For Us, Liberty; 1931) clearly influenced Charlie Chaplin's famous assembly-line scene in *Modern Times*.

WWI was inspired the 1930s classic, *La Grande Illusion* (The Great Illusion; 1937), a devastating portrayal of the folly of WWI based on the trench warfare experience of director Jean Renoir (1894–1979). Indeed, portraits of ordinary people and their lives dominated film until the 1950s when realism was eschewed by surrealist Jean Cocteau (1889–1963) in two masterpieces of cinematic fantasy: *La Belle et la Bête* (Beauty and the Beast; 1945) and *Orphée* (Orpheus; 1950) are unravelled in Menton's Musée Jean Cocteau (p853) on the Côte d'Azur.

Sapped of talent and money after WWII, France's film industry begged new energy by the 1950s. And so the *nouvelle vague* (new wave) burst forth. With small budgets and no extravagant sets or big-name stars, film-makers produced uniquely personal films using real-life subject matter: Claude Chabrol (1930–) explored poverty and alcoholism in a French village in *Le Beau Serge* (Bitter Reunion; 1958); Alain Resnais (1922–) portrayed the problems of time and memory in his *Hiroshima, Mon Amour* (1959); and François Truffaut (1932–84) dealt with love in its many permutations.

By the 1970s the new wave had lost its experimental edge, handing over the limelight to lesser known directors like Eric Rohmer (1920–), who made beautiful but uneventful films in which the characters endlessly analyse their feelings. Two 1960s movies ensured France's invincibility as land of romance: Claude Lelouch's *Un Homme et une Femme* (A Man and a Woman; 1966), a beautifully photographed love story set in Deauville (p254) and

The vast labour-intensive series of novels, known under the general title of *La Comédie Humaine*, by Tours-born Honoré de Balzac is nothing short of a social history of France.

André Gide found his voice in the celebration of homosexual sensuality and left-wing politics, exposing the hypocrisy and self-deception with which people try to avoid sincerity in his novel *Les Faux-Monnayeurs* (The Counterfeiters).

CÉSARS

The little golden statues handed to actors at the Césars – the French Oscars – are named after the man who made them.

One of the most influential sculptors to emerge after WWII, Marseille-born César Baldaccini (1921–98) used scrap metal and iron to sculpt larger-than-life insects and animals. Proof of the pudding stands on his grave in Paris' Cimetière du Montparnasse (p123).

César was the first to use motorised vehicles as an artistic medium, crushing no less than 23 cars in the name of art between 1960 and 1989; a couple are in Nice's Musée d'Art Moderne et d'Art Contemporain (p822).

Jacques Demy's *Les Parapluies de Cherbourg* (The Umbrellas of Cherbourg; 1964), a wise and bittersweet love story likewise filmed in Normandy.

Big-name stars, slick production values and a strong sense of nostalgia were the dominant motifs in the 1980s as generous state subsidies to film-makers switched to costume dramas, comedies and 'heritage movies' in the face of growing competition from American thrillers and action flicks. Claude Berri's depiction of prewar Provence in *Jean de Florette* (1986), Jean-Paul Rappeneau's *Cyrano de Bergerac* (1990) and *Bon Voyage* (2003) set in 1940s Paris, and *Astérix et Obélix: Mission Cléopâtre* (2001) – all starring France's best known (and biggest-nosed) actor Gérard Depardieu – found huge audiences in France and abroad.

In 2001 the delightfully uncontroversial *Le Fabuleux Destin de Amélie Poulain* (Amélie; 2001), a feel-good story of a winsome Parisian do-gooder directed by Jean-Pierre Jeunet of *Delicatessen* (1991) fame, proved an instant hit – everywhere. French film has enjoyed a massive renaissance ever since, French-film cinema-goers outside of France rising from 17 million in 2000 to a current 37.5 million a year.

Subjects broached by box-office smash hits are wide and varied, among them Jacques Perrin's beautifully photographed animal film *Le Peuple Migrateur* (Winged Migration; 2001) about bird migration; the big-name (Omar Sharif and Isabelle Adjani) *Monsieur Ibrahim et les Fleurs du Coran* (Mr Ibrahim and the Flowers of Coran; 2003) about an Arab grocer living on rue Bleue; and the giggle-guaranteed, Marseille comedy *Taxi 3* (2003).

Existentialist Camus stresses the importance of the writer's political engagement in his work *L'Étranger* (The Outsider), which scooped him the Nobel Prize for Literature in 1957.

DID YOU KNOW?

Colette was the first woman in France to be honoured with a state funeral.

A HISTORY OF FRENCH CINEMA IN 10 FILMS

Grab a bottle of Burgundy, glue yourself to the screen and take a whirlwind tour through French cinematic history (all available on video or DVD) with:

■ *La Règle du Jeu* (The Rules of the Game; 1939) Shunned by the public and censored, Jean Renoir's story of a 1930s bourgeoisie hunting party in the Loire Valley's soggy Sologne (p396) is a dark satirical masterpiece.

■ *Les Enfants du Paradis* (Children of Paradise; 1945) Made during the Nazi occupation of France, Marcel Carné celebrates the vitality and theatricality of a Paris without Nazis.

■ *Et Dieu Créa la Femme* (And God Created Woman; 1956) Roger Vadim's tale of the amorality of modern youth set in St-Tropez made a star out of Brigitte Bardot.

■ *Les Quatre Cents Coups* (The 400 Blows; 1959) Partly based on the rebellious adolescence of the best loved of new-wave directors François Truffaut.

■ *Les Vacances de M Hulôt* (Mr Hulôt's Holiday; 1953) and *Mon Oncle* (My Uncle; 1958) Two films starring the charming, bumbling figure of Monsieur Hulot and his struggles to adapt to the modern age by non-new-wave 1950s director Jacques Tati.

■ *Diva* (1981) & *37°2 le Matin* (Betty Blue; 1986) Two visually compelling films by Jean-Jacques Beineix. *Diva* stars French icon Richard Bohringer.

■ *Shoah* (1985) Claude Lanzmann's 9½-hour-long B&W documentary – interviews with Holocaust survivors worldwide – is disturbing. It took 11 years to make.

■ *Indochine* (Indochina; 1993) An epic love story set in 1930s French Indochina with Catherine Deneuve – timeless beauty et al – as a French plantation owner.

■ *Subway* (1985), *Le Grand Bleu* (The Big Blue; 1988), *Nikita* (1990) and *Jeanne d'Arc* (Joan of Arc; 1999) Take your pick from these box-office hits directed by Luc Besson.

■ *Code Inconnu* (Code Unknown; 2001) Intellectual art-house film starring Oscar-winning French actress Juliette Binoche as an actress in Paris.

An increasing number of French film directors are turning to Hollywood to make big commercial productions and also forsaking their mother tongue to reach wider audiences. French films made in English include Louis Leterrier's *The Transporter* (2002) with a script written by Parisian film director Luc Besson; Michel Gondry's *Eternal Sunshine of the Spotless Mind* (2004) starring Kate Winslet and Jim Carrey; and Jean-Jacques Annaud's *Two Brothers* (2004), about two tiger cubs separated at birth.

The Palme d'Or, awarded each year at Cannes (p836), is the world's most coveted film prize. The French film industry honours its film-makers, actors and so on with Césars (p49).

The unofficial André Bazin website features reams of colourful insight into the *nouvelle vague* www.unofficialbazini antrib.com.

TV

Most French know you don't phone your friends at 8pm, so sacred is *Le Journal*, the evening news slots on TF1 and France 2. Many turn on the box at 7.55pm to enjoy a five-minute satirical summary of world events with the witty Spitting Image-style *Les Guignols de l'Info*. So revered are the sharp-tongued puppets that Canal Plus repeats the entire week's episodes on Sunday around 1pm.

La télé-réalité (reality TV) sees TF1 and M6 vying for prime-time viewers. Not without controversy, reality TV is barred from the public channels, while *Loft Story* – the first such show – outraged viewers when it was aired in 2001. Such was the furore that the Conseil Supérieur de l'Audiovisuel (CSA; www.csa.fr) limited the time cameras in the loft could film. Contestants needed time and a space away from the public eye, the French broadcasting authority ruled.

Jumel Debouzze (1976–; www.jamel.fr) is French TV's funniest man, a feat all the more impressive given the mischievous comic's upbringing as one of five children in an immigrant Moroccan family in a Parisian suburb.

TV news, views, the latest in reality TV, what's on and loads more about French TV is online (in French) at www .toutelatele.com.

Music

There's more to it than accordions and Edith Piaf.

French baroque music influenced European musical output enormously in the 17th and 18th centuries, while French musical luminaries – Charles Gounod (1818–93), César Franck (1822–90) and Carmen-creator Georges Bizet (1838–75), among them – were a dime a dozen in the 19th century. Modern orchestration was founded by Hector Berlioz (1803–69), the greatest figure in the French Romantic movement, born near Grenoble (p521), who demanded gargantuan forces: his ideal orchestra included 240 stringed instruments, 30 grand pianos and 30 harps.

Claude Debussy (1862–1918) revolutionised classical music with his *Prélude à l'Après-Midi d'un Faune* (Prelude to the Afternoon of a Fawn), creating a light, almost Asian musical impressionism; while impressionist comrade Maurice Ravel (1875–1937) peppered his work, including *Boléro*, with sensuousness and tonal colour. Contemporary composer Olivier Messiaen (1908–92) combined modern, almost mystical music with natural sounds such as birdsong. His student Pierre Boulez (1925–) works with computer-generated sound.

Jazz hit 1920s Paris in the banana-clad form of Josephine Baker, a cabaret dancer from the USA (the 15th-century chateau in the Dordogne where the African-American lived after the war can be visited; p597). Post-WWII ushered in a much-appreciated bunch of musicians – Sidney Bechet, Kenny Clarke, Bud Powell and Dexter Gordon, among them. In 1934 a chance meeting between Parisian jazz guitarist Stéphane Grappelli and three-fingered Roma guitarist Django Reinhardt in a Montparnasse

DID YOU KNOW?

By law the lyrics of two out of five songs played on French radio must be French. One in five has to be that of a newcomer.

nightclub led to the formation of the Hot Club of France quintet. Claude Luter and his Dixieland Band was the hot sound of the 1950s.

The *chanson française,* a tradition dating from the troubadours of the Middle Ages, was eclipsed by the music halls and burlesque of the early 20th century, but revived in the 1930s by Piaf and Charles Trenet. In the 1950s the Left Bank cabarets nurtured *chansonniers* (cabaret singers) such as Léo Ferré, Georges Brassens, Claude Nougaro, Jacques Brel and Serge Gainsbourg.

French pop music has evolved massively since the 1960s *yéyé* (imitative rock) days of Johnny Halliday. Particularly strong is world music, from Algerian raï and other North African music (artists include Cheb Khaled, Natacha Atlas, Jamel, Cheb Mami, Racid Taha) to Senegalese *mbalax* (Youssou N'Dour), West Indian *zouk* (Kassav, Zouk Machine). One musician who combines many of these elements to stunning effect is Manu Chao (www.manuchao.net), the Paris-born son of Spanish parents whose albums are bestsellers worldwide.

Another hot musical export is Parisian electro-dance duo, Daft Punk, whose debut album *Homework* (1997) fused disco, house, funk and techno. *Discovery* (2001) adopts a more eclectic approach. Electronica duo, Air, around since the mid-1990s, remains sensational with its third album *Talkie Walkie* (2004). French rap was spearheaded in the 1990s by Senegal-born Paris-reared rapper MC Solaar.

Immigrant life in the French *banlieue* (suburbs) finds expression in the hip-hop lyrics of countless French artists, among them Marseille's hugely successful IAM; Brittany's Manau trio that fuses hip-hop with traditional Celtic sounds; and the Paris-based Triptik trio from Nantes who released its third album *TR-303* in 2003. Hard-core rappers include five-piece rap band KDD from Toulouse and Paris' Suprême NTM (NTM being an abbreviation for a French expression far too offensive to include here).

Architecture
PREHISTORIC TO ART NOUVEAU
From the prehistoric megaliths around Carnac (p311) to Vauban's 33 star-shaped citadels (p30, p205, p382 and p537) built to defend France's 17th-century frontiers, French architecture has always been of *grand-projet* proportions.

Southern France is the place to find France's Gallo-Roman legacy: the Pont du Gard (p738), amphitheatres in Nîmes (p733) and Arles (p802), the theatre at Orange (p792) and Nîmes' Maison Carrée (p733).

Several centuries later, architects adopted architectural elements from Gallo-Roman buildings to create *roman* (Romanesque) masterpieces such as Toulouse's Basilica St-Sernin (p697), Poitier's Église Notre Dame la Grande (p618) and Caen's two famous Romanesque abbeys (p258). Eleventh- and 12th-century Romanesque buildings have round arches, heavy walls whose few windows let in very little light, and a lack of ornamentation bordering on the austere.

Northern France's extraordinary wealth in the 12th century lured the finest architects, engineers and artisans who created impressive Gothic structures with ribbed vaults carved with great precision, pointed arches, slender verticals, chapels along the nave and chancel, refined decoration and stained-glass windows. Avignon's pontifical palace (p786) is Gothic architecture on a gargantuan scale. With the discovery of flying buttresses around 1230, Gothic masterpieces such as the seminal cathedral at Chartres (p196) and its successors at Reims (p327), Amiens (p227) and Strasbourg (p349) appeared.

The worldly-wide travels of Will – misogynist American journalist, woman seducer and high-profile intellectual in Paris – form the basis of Philippe Sollers' novel *Women* (Femmes). Wrapped around the storyline are philosophical reflections on a variety of subjects, including the art of the modern novel and women.

For anyone who reads French, aVoir-aLire.com: l'œil culturel (www.avoir-alire.com) is an essential tool for keeping tabs of the latest literature, music, comic strips and films to be released.

By the 15th century architects had shelved size for ornamentation, conceiving the beautifully lacy Flamboyant Gothic. For an example of such decorative overkill, look at the spire of Strasbourg cathedral. To trace the shift from late Gothic to Renaissance, travel along the Loire Valley: Château de Chambord (p401) illustrates the mix of classical components and decorative motifs typical to early Renaissance architecture. In the mid-16th century, François I had Italian architects design Fontainebleau (p189).

In 1635 early-baroque architect François Mansart (1598–1666) designed the classical wing of Château de Blois (p397), while his younger rival, Louis Le Vau (1612–70), started work on Louis XIV's palace at Versailles (p187).

A quest for order, reason and serenity through the adoption of the forms and conventions of Graeco-Roman antiquity defined neoclassical architecture from 1740 until well into the 19th century. Nancy's place Stanislas (p372) is France's loveliest neoclassical square.

Under Napoleon, many of Paris's best-known sights – the Arc de Triomphe (p127), La Madeleine (p128), the Arc du Carrousel at the Louvre (p113) and the Assemblée Nationale building – were designed.

Art Nouveau (1850–1910) combined iron, brick, glass and ceramics in ways never before seen. See for yourself in Paris with Hector Guimard's noodle-like metro entrances; the fine Art Nouveau interiors in the Musée d'Orsay (p124); and the glass roof over the Grand Palais (p127).

The French Civil Service website contains thousands of invaluable hot links, covering everything from child benefit and family allowance in France to pension information, museum listings, art and architectural sites, cultural services, NGOs and so on at www .service-public.fr

CONTEMPORARY

Chapelle de Notre-Dame du Haut in the Jura (p542) and Couvent Ste-Marie de la Tourette near Lyon (p485) are architectural icons of the 20th century. Designed in the 1950s by France's most celebrated architect, Le Corbusier (1887–1965), the structures rewrote the architectural stylebook with their sweeping lines and functionalised forms perfectly adapted to fit the human form.

French political leaders have long sought to immortalise themselves through the erection of big huge public edifices, otherwise called *grands projects*. Georges Pompidou commissioned the now much-revered Centre Beaubourg (Centre Pompidou; p116) in Paris in 1977; Giscard d'Estaing

---

LOOK TO THE FUTURE

A hat trick of magnificent architectural projects are in the making in the capital – with treasures inside as fabulous as the design outside. Target date for all three is 2006.

The Musée du Quai Branly, named after the riverside quay on which it stands, will showcase 300,000 objects dedicated to arts and civilisations of Africa, Asia, Oceania and the Americas. Designed by French architect Jean Nouvel (www.jeannouvel.fr) in his Paris *atelier* (workshop), the state-of-the-art museum embraces 700,000 sq metres of exhibition space and resembles a huge wooden bridge. Glass walls and display cases place objects against a natural backdrop of foliage. Web cams (www.qualbranly.fr) are rigged up on-site.

West along the Seine in Boulogne-Billancourt, what was a Renault car factory is being transformed by Japanese architect Tadao Ando into an art gallery of proportions sufficiently gigantic to house the contemporary art collection of French multibillionaire François Pinault of Gucci, Yves Saint Laurent, Samsonite and Christie's auction-house fame (he owns the lot). The futuristic building, trapezoid in shape, will appear as a 'spaceship suspended over the Seine'. It is anticipated to be the next big thing after London's Tate Modern.

The 120m-tall metallic tower planned for Le Havre's rejuvenated 19th-century docks on the Frissard peninsula will be impossible to miss. Another Jean Nouvel creation, the striking tower – complete with sky-high exhibition and conference rooms – tops a 12,000-sq-metre aquatic centre with a design inspired by Roman baths.

was instrumental in transforming a derelict train station into the glorious Musée d'Orsay (p124); while François Mitterrand commissioned the capital's best-known contemporary architectural landmarks, including IM Pei's glass pyramid (p114) at the Louvre; the Opéra-Bastille (p119); the Grande Arche (p180) in the skyscraper district of La Défense; Jean Nouvel's Institut du Monde Arabe; and the controversial home of the Bibliothèque Nationale (p129). Paris' 80,000-capacity Stade de France (p183), built for the 1998 football World Cup, has rarely been more than half-full since.

In the provinces, notable buildings include Strasbourg's European Parliament (p350), Dutch architect Rem Koolhaas' Euralille and Jean Nouvel's glass-and-steel Vesunna Musée Gallo-Romain in Perigueux (p586). Otherwise, there's a 1920s Art Deco swimming pool-turned-art museum to see in Lille (p205); an 11th-century abbey-turned-monumental sculpture gallery in Angers (p420); and – come 2007 – a contemporary art museum in Metz (p379) that will blow your mind away.

Painting

French painting began with Nicolas Poussin (1594–1665) according to Voltaire, who clearly rated the classical mythological and biblical scenes bathed in golden light that the baroque painter created. Forward-wind a couple of centuries and modern still life pops onto the scene with the work of Jean-Baptiste Chardin (1699–1779), the first to see still life as an essay in composition rather than a show of skill in reproduction. A century later, neoclassical artist Jacques Louis David (1748–1825) wooed the public (not to mention Napoleon) with his vast portraits; several are in the Louvre.

While Romantics like Eugène Delacroix (buried in Paris' Cimetière du Père Lachaise; p129) revamped the subject picture, the Barbizon School effected a parallel transformation of landscape painting. Barbizons included landscape artist Camille Corot (1796–1875) and Jean-François Millet (1814–75). The son of a peasant farmer from Normandy, Millet took many of his subjects from peasant life and reproductions of his *L'Angélus* (The Angelus; 1857) – the best-known French painting after the *Mona Lisa* – are strung above mantelpieces all over rural France. The original hangs in Paris' Musée d'Orsay (p124).

The latter is also the place to see the Realists, among them Édouard Manet (1832–83) who zoomed in on Parisian middle-class life and Gustave Courbet (1819–77) who depicted the drudgery of manual labour and difficult lives of the working class. The artist himself came from a privileged family; see where he lived at the Musée Courbet (p540), his family home in the Jura.

It was in a flower-filled garden in a Normandy village (p243) that Claude Monet (1840–1926) expounded impressionism, a term of derision taken from the title of his experimental painting *Impression: Soleil Levant* (Impression: Sunrise; 1874). A trip to the Musée d'Orsay unveils a rash of other members of the school – Boudin, Sisley, Pissarro, Renoir, Degas and so on.

BMPT

The anti-Establishment BMPT took its acronymic name from its members (Daniel **B**uren, Swiss-born Olivier **M**osset, Parisian Michel **P**armentier and Italian artist Niele **T**oroni). Founded in France in the mid-1960s, the four-man band painted commune-style, rendering any work they produced the property of the group rather than the individual – a political statement on art ownership that, ironically, backfired given issues of ownership lingered long after the rebels split.

An arthritis-crippled Renoir painted out his last impressionist days in a villa (p833) on the Côte d'Azur. With a warmth and astonishing intensity of light hard to equal, the French Riviera inspired dozens of artists post-Renoir: Paul Cézanne (1839–1906) is particularly celebrated for his postimpressionist still lifes and landscapes done in Aix-en-Provence where he was born and worked (visit his studio; p779); Paul Gauguin (1848–1903) worked in Arles; while Dutch artist Vincent van Gogh (1853–90) painted Arles and St-Rémy de Provence (p803). In St-Tropez pointillism took off: Georges Seurat (1859–91) was the first to apply paint in small dots or uniform brush strokes of unmixed colour, producing fine mosaics of warm and cool tones, but it was his pupil Paul Signac (1863–1935) who is best known for his pointillist works; see them in St-Tropez's Musée de l'Annonciade (p844).

Twentieth-century French painting is characterised by a bewildering diversity of styles, including Fauvism and cubism. Henri Matisse (1869–1954) was the man behind the former (a Fauvist trail around Collioure takes you past scenes he captured on canvas in Roussillon; p758) and Spanish prodigy Pablo Picasso (1881–1973), the latter. Both chose southern France to set up studio, Matisse living in Nice (visit the Musée Matisse; p823) and Picasso opting for a 12th-century chateau (now the Musée Picasso; p832) in Antibes. Cubism, as developed by Picasso and Georges Braque (1882–1963) deconstructed the subject into a system of intersecting planes and presented various aspects of it simultaneously.

No piece of French art better captures Dada's rebellious spirit than Marcel Duchamp's *Mona Lisa* complete with moustache and goatee. In 1922 German Dadaist Max Ernst moved to Paris and worked on surrealism, a Dada offshoot that drew on the theories of Freud to reunite the conscious and unconscious realms and permeate daily life with fantasies and dreams.

With the close of WWII, Paris' role as artistic world capital ended, leaving critics wondering ever since where all the artists have gone. The focus shifted back to southern France in the 1960s with new realists like Arman (1928–) and Yves Klein (1928–62), both from Nice and well represented in contemporary art museums in Paris (p116), Lyon (p475), St-Étienne (p485), Nice (p822), Lille (p203) and Strasbourg (p350).

In 1960 Klein famously produced *Anthropométrie de l'Époque Bleue*, a series of blue imprints made by naked women (covered from head to toe in blue paint) rolling around on a white canvas – in front of an orchestra of violins and an audience in evening dress. A decade on the supports-surfaces movement deconstructed the concept of a painting, transforming one of its structural components (such as the frame or canvas) into a work of art instead.

Artists in the 1990s threw in the towel as far as the grandeur of early French art was concerned, looking to the minutiae of everyday urban life to express social and political angst and turning to mediums other than paint to let rip. Conceptual artist Daniel Buren (1938–) reduced his painting to a signature series of vertical 8.7cm-wide stripes that he applies to every surface imaginable – white marble columns in the courtyard of Paris's Palais Royal (p115) included. The painter (who in 1967, as part of the Radical *groupe BMPT*, signed a manifesto declaring he was not a painter) was the *enfant terrible* of French art in the 1980s. Partner-in-crime Michel Parmentier (1938–2000) insisted on monochrome painting for a while – blue in 1966, grey in 1967 and red in 1968.

Current trends are best expressed by the Palais de Tokyo, a contemporary art space in Paris that opens noon to midnight or thereabouts; encourages art visitors to feel, touch, talk and interact; and bends over backwards to turn every expectation of painting and art on its head.

DID YOU KNOW?

Fauvism took its name from the slur of a critic who compared the exhibitors at the 1906 autumn salon in Paris with *fauves* (wildcats) because of their radical use of intensely bright colours.

Gem-up with what's happening tomorrow in the contemporary art scene in Paris with www.paris-art.com (in French).

Environment

THE LAND

Hexagon-shaped France, the largest country in Europe after Russia and Ukraine, is hugged by water or mountains along every side except its northeastern boundary – a relatively flat frontier abutting Germany, Luxembourg and Belgium.

Its 3200km-long coastline embraces everything from white chalk cliffs (Normandy) and treacherous promontories (Brittany) to fine-sand (Atlantic Coast) and pebble (Mediterranean Coast) beaches. Five major river systems criss-cross the country: the Garonne (which includes the Tarn, Lot and Dordogne) empties into the Atlantic; the Rhône links Lake Geneva and the Alps with the Mediterranean; Paris is licked by the Seine, which snakes through the city en route from Burgundy to the English Channel; while tributaries of the North Sea-bound Rhine drain much of the area north and east of the capital. Then there's France's longest river, the chateau-studded Loire, which meanders from the Massif Central to the Atlantic.

Mountains run riot. Europe's highest peak, Mont Blanc (4807m), spectacularly tops the French Alps that stagger along France's eastern border from Lake Geneva to the Côte d'Azur. North of Lake Geneva the gentle limestone Jura Range runs along the Swiss frontier to reach heights of around 1700m, while the rugged Pyrenees lace France's entire 450km-long border with Spain and peak at 3404m.

Stunning as they are, the Alps, Jura and Pyrenees are mere babies compared to France's ancient massifs, formed 225 to 345 million years ago. The Massif Central covers one-sixth (91,000 sq km) of the country and is renowned for its chain of extinct volcanoes: Puy de Dôme (1465m) last erupted in 5760 BC, the volcanic history and geology of which is explained in the Vulcania centre near Clermont-Ferrand (p553). Other golden oldies, worn down by time, include the forested upland of the Vosges in northeast France; the Ardennes on Champagne's northern edge; and Brittany and Normandy's backbone, the Massif Armoricain.

WILDLIFE

France is blessed with a rich variety of flora and fauna, although few habitats have escaped human impact: urbanisation, pollution, intensive agriculture, wetland draining, hunting, the encroachment of industry and tourism infrastructure developments menace dozens of species.

DID YOU KNOW?

The flow of the Loire is eight times greater in December and January than at the end of summer.

Mont Blanc: Discovery and Conquest of the Giant of the Alps by Stefano Ardito portrays France's most magnificent mountain in all its soaring splendour. Its glossy 200-odd pages are packed with stunning photographs.

RESPONSIBLE TOURISM

Follow the local code of ethics and common decency in nature reserves and national parks:

■ Pack up your litter.

■ Minimise waste by taking minimal packaging and no more food than you need.

■ Don't use detergents or toothpaste, even if they are biodegradable, in or near watercourses.

■ Stick to designated paths in protected areas, particularly in sensitive biospheres, Alpine areas and coastal dunes where flora and fauna may be seriously damaged if you stray.

■ When camping in the wild (check first with the landowners or a park ranger to see if it's allowed), bury human waste in catholes at least 15cm deep and at least 100m from any watercourse.

■ Obey the 'no dogs, tents and motorised vehicles' rule in national parks.

WHERE TO WATCH WILDLIFE

The national parks and their smaller siblings encourage green-eyed visitors to hook up with a naturalistic guide to watch wildlife; details are in the regional chapters. Otherwise, the following observation posts are worth a gander:

- Bisons in Languedoc at the Reserve de Bisons d'Europe near Mende (p745).

- Vultures in the Pyrenees at La Falaise aux Vautours in the Vallée d'Ossau (p685) and in Languedoc at the Belvédère des Vautours in the Parc Naturel Régional des Grands Causses (p747).

- Storks in Alsace at the Centre de Réintroduction des Cigognes in Hunawihr (p361) and the Enclos Cigognes in Munster (p368); on the Atlantic Coast at the Parc Ornithologique in Le Tech (p645) and at the Parc des Oiseaux outside Villars-les-Dombes near Lyon (p645).

- Wolves in Languedoc at the wolf reserve in the Parc du Gévaudan near Mende (p745) and in the Alps with a wolf-watching expedition organised by the Parc National du Mercantour (p822).

Animals

France has more mammals to see (around 110) than other country in Europe. Couple this with its 363 bird species, 30 amphibian types, 36 varieties of reptiles and 72 kinds of fish and wildlife watchers are in paradise.

High-altitude plains in the Alps and Pyrenees shelter the marmot (it hibernates October to April) with its shrill and distinctive whistle; the nimble *chamois* (mountain antelope) with its dark-striped head; and the *bouquetin* (Alpine ibex) that can be seen in large numbers in the Parc National de la Vanoise (p519). The mouflon, introduced in the 1950s, clamber over stony sun-lit scree slopes in the mountains; and the red and roe deer and wild boar are common in lower-altitude forested areas. Winter welcomes the Alpine hare with its white coat, while 19 of Europe's 29 bat species hang out in the dark in the Alpine national parks.

The wolf, which disappeared from France in the 1930s, was spotted in the Parc National du Mercantour in 1992 – much to the horror of the mouflon (on which its preys) and local sheep farmers. Dogs, corrals and sound machines to frighten the 60-odd wolves believed to freely roam in the mountains today are effective alternatives to more murderous means of getting rid of the unwanted predator.

The brown bear also disappeared from the Alps in the mid-1930s. The 300 or so that lived in the Pyrenees at that time have dwindled to no more than five today; see p683 for more details.

A rare but wonderful treat is the sighting of a golden eagle: 40 pairs nest in the Parc National du Mercantour, 20 pairs nest in the Vanoise, 37 in the Écrins and a good handful in the Pyrenees. Other birds of prey include the peregrine falcon, kestrel, buzzard and bearded vulture with its unsavoury bone-breaking habits. The latter – the largest bird of prey with an awe-inspiring wingspan of 2.8m – was extinct in the Alps from the 19th century until the 1980s when it was reintroduced. More recently, the small pale-coloured Egyptian vulture (worshipped by the Egyptians, hence its name) has been spotted; 50 pairs inhabit the Pyrenees.

Even the eagle-eyed will have difficulty spotting the ptarmigan, a chicken-like species around since the Ice Age that moults three times a year to ensure a fool-proof camouflage for every season (brown in summer, white in winter). It lives on rocky slopes and in Alpine meadows above 2000m. The nutcracker with its loud and buoyant singsong

DID YOU KNOW?

Of the 39,000 insect species identified in France, 10,000 creep and crawl around the Parc National du Mercantour in the French Alps.

The Ligue de Protection des Oiseaux (LPO; League for the Protection of Birds) advises birders on what to see where and when. Visit its website (in French) at www.lpo.fr.

Those interested in birds of prey will also enjoy http://percnoptere.lpo.fr and http://balbuzard .lpo.fr.

and larch-forest habitat, the black grouse, rock partridge, eagle owl and three-toed woodpecker are among the other 120-odd species to keep bird-watchers on their toes in mountainous realms.

Elsewhere on the French watch-the-birdie front, there are storks (p361) to see in Alsace; 10% of the world's flamingo population to see in the Camargue (p806); giant black cormorants – some with a wing-span of 170cm – on an island (p289) off the north coast of Brittany; and unique seagull and fishing eagle populations in the Réserve Naturelle de Scandola (p876) on Corsica. The osprey – a once-widespread migratory bird that winters in Africa and returns to France in February or March – only inhabits Corsica and the Loire Valley today.

Identify birds in France by their songs and calls or listen to the sounds of the Jura forests, and so on, with CDs produced by French 'voices of nature' publisher Sitelle www .sittelle.com.

Plants

About 14 million hectares of forest – beech, oak and pine in the main – cover 20% of France, while 4200 different species of plants and flowers are known to grow countrywide (2250 alone grow in the Parc National des Cévennes). In forests near Reims in the Champagne region, beech trees grow in a bizarrely stunted, malformed shape (p331).

The Alpine and Pyrenean regions nurture fir, spruce and beech forests on north-facing slopes between 800m and 1500m. Larch trees, mountain and arolla pines, rhododendrons and junipers stud shrubby subalpine zones between 1500m and 2000m; and a brilliant riot of spring- and summer-time wildflowers carpets grassy meadows above the tree line in the Alpine zone (up to 3000m).

Alpine blooms include the single golden-yellow flower of arnica, still used in herbal and homeopathic bruise-relieving remedies; the flame-coloured fire lily that flowers from December to May; and the hardy Alpine columbine with its delicate blue petals. The rare twinflower only grows in the Parc National de la Vanoise. Of France's 150 orchids, the black vanilla orchid is one to look out for – its small red-brown flowers exude a sweet vanilla fragrance. At Les Fermes de Marie in Megève (p506), dozens of Alpine plants and seeds – gentian, St John's wort, melissa, pulsatilla, pimpernel, cyclamen, hazel seeds and so on – go into beauty care products.

Corsica and the Massif des Maures, west of St-Tropez on the Côte d'Azur, are closely related botanically: both have chestnut and cork oak trees (the bark of which gets stuffed in bottles) and are thickly carpeted with *maquis* – a heavily scented scrubland where dozens of orchids, herbs (the secret behind Provençal cooking) and heathers find shelter: particularly enchanting are the rock rose (a shrub with white flowers with yellow centres or pinkish-mauve flowers), the white-flowering myrtle that blossoms in June and is treasured for its blue-black berries (used to make some excellent liqueurs) and the blue-violet flowering Corsican mint with its heady summertime aroma.

Trip through France's forests with the Office National des Forêts (National Forestry Commission), online (in French) at www.onf.fr.

DID YOU KNOW?

The protected 'queen of the Alps' (alias the Alpine eryngo) might well bear an uncanny resemblance to a purple thistle. It is in fact a member of the Parsley family (to which the carrot also belongs). Find it on grassy ledges.

NATIONAL PARKS

The proportion of land protected in France is low relative to the country's size: six small national parks *(parcs nationaux)* fully protect just 0.8% of the country. Another 7% is protected to a substantially lesser degree by 42 *parcs naturels régionaux* (regional nature parks) and a further 0.4% by 136 smaller *réserves naturelles* (nature reserves), some of which are under the eagle eye of the Conservatoire du Littoral (p60).

While the central zones of national parks are uninhabited and fully protected by legislation (dogs, vehicles and hunting are banned and camping is restricted), the ecosystems they protect spill into populated periph-

Park	Features	Activities	Best Time to Visit	Page
Parc National des Cévennes	wild peat bogs, causses, granite peaks, ravines and ridges bordering the Massif Central and Languedoc (910 sq km); red deer, beavers, vultures, wolves, bison	walking, trekking with donkeys, mountain-biking, horse-riding, cross-country skiing, caving, canoeing, botany (2250 plant species)	spring & winter	p741
Parc National des Écrins	glaciers, glacial lakes and mountain tops soaring up to 4102m in the French Alps (1770 sq km); marmots, lynx, ibex, chamois, bearded vultures	walking, climbing, hang-gliding	spring & summer	p529
Parc National du Mercantour	Provence at its most majestic with 3000m-plus peaks and dead-end valleys along the Italian border; marmots, mouflons, chamois, ibex, wolves, golden and short-toed eagles, bearded vultures	skiing (alpine), white-water sports, mountain-biking, walking, donkey trekking	spring, summer & winter	p822
Parc National de Port Cros	Island marine park off the Côte d'Azur forming France's smallest national park and Europe's first marine park (700 hectares and 1288 hectares of water); puffins, shearwaters, migratory birds	snorkelling, bird-watching, swimming, gentle strolling & sunbathing	summer (water activities) & autumn (bird-watching)	p848
Parc National des Pyrénées	100km of mountains along the Spanish border (457 sq km); marmots, izards, brown bears, golden eagles, vultures, buzzards	skiing (alpine & cross-country), walking, mountaineering, rock-climbing, white-water rafting, canoeing, kayaking mountain-biking	spring, summer & winter (skiing)	p680
Parc National de la Vanoise	post-glacial mountain landscape of Alpine peaks, 80 sq km of glaciers and beech-fir forests, forming France's first national park (530 sq km): chamois, ibex, marmots, golden eagles	skiing (alpine & cross-country), walking, mountaineering, mountain-biking	spring, summer & winter (skiing)	p519

eral zones in which tourism and other (often environmentally unfriendly) economic activities run riot.

Most regional nature parks and reserves were established, not only to improve (or at least maintain) local ecosystems, but to encourage economic development and tourism in areas (such as the Massif Central and Corsica) suffering from diminishing populations and increasing economic problems.

Select pockets of nature – the Pyrenees, Mont St-Michel and its bay, part of the Loire Valley and a clutch of capes on Corsica – are Unesco World Heritage Sites (p22).

ENVIRONMENTAL ISSUES

Summer forest fires are an annual hazard. Great tracts of land sizzle each year, often because of careless day-trippers but occasionally, as is sometimes the case in the Maures and Estérel ranges on the Côte d'Azur, because they are intentionally set alight by people wanting to get licences to build on the damaged lands. Since the mid-1970s, between 67 sq km and 883 sq km of land a year has been reduced to a burnt black stubble by

Get the green low-down (in French) on France's 42 regional nature parks with the Fédération des Parcs Naturels Régionaux de France (Fédération of French Regional Natural Parks) at www.parcs-na turels-regionaux.tm.fr.

an average of 540 fires annually – although the number of fires is falling according to the Office National des Forêts (ONF), the national forestry commission responsible for public forests in France. In the Vosges forests in northern France, acid rain is the bigger menace.

Wetlands – incredibly productive ecosystems that are essential for the survival of a number of bird species, reptiles, fish and amphibians – are shrinking. More than two million hectares – 3% of French territory – are considered important wetlands, but only 4% of this land is protected. The vulnerability of these areas was highlighted in 2003 when lumps of oil landed on beaches in southwestern France following the sinking of the *Prestige* oil tanker off Spain's northwestern coast in late 2002. The slick wrecked beaches, crippled local fishing and seafood industries, and killed hundreds of birds and marine life – to the horror of French environmentalists who were still seething with anger over the 1999 *Erika* oil tanker disaster that fouled more than 400km of shoreline in Brittany and cost US$860 million to clean up.

Men with dogs and guns pose an equally big threat to French animal life. While the number of hunters in France has fallen by 20% in the last decade, there are still way more hunters in France (almost 1.5 million) than in other Western European countries (around 1 million in Spain and Italy, 625,000 in Britain). Despite the Brussels Directive being introduced in 1979 to protect wild birds, their eggs, nests and habitats in the EU, the French government didn't bother to make its provisions part of French law – meaning birds that can safely fly over other countries can still be shot as they cross France. A good handful of those not shot – at least 1000 birds of prey a year – are electrocuted to death by high-voltage power lines instead.

Many traditional animal habitats have been destroyed by huge recreational lakes, created by the state-owned electricity company, Electricité de France (EDF), which dams rivers to produce electricity. Since the 1980s however, almost 80% of the country's electricity has been produced by 19 nuclear power plants. (The French nuclear-power station programme is the most ambitious in the world.) Most are on main rivers or near the coast – the environmental cost of which is high. Radioactive emissions spewed out by the four nuclear plants on the banks of the River Loire alone represent more than 25% of rare gas emissions in France. Blistering hot temperatures in summer 2003 prompted calls for a new round of nuclear plants to be built in a bid to cope with ever-increasing energy demands.

Nuclear waste from France and elsewhere is treated at a plant on the Cotentin Peninsula in Normandy and then pumped into the Channel.

HIGH-FACTOR PROTECTION BY THE SEA

Some 10% of the coastline of mainland France and Corsica is managed by the **Conservatoire du Littoral** (Coastal Protection Agency; ☎ 05 46 84 72 50; www.conservatoire-du-littoral.fr in French; Corderie Royale, BP 13 7, F-1 7306 Rochefort Cedex), an association that acquires threatened natural areas by the sea to restore, rejuvenate and protect.

Rare orchid-studded sand dunes east of Dunkirk (p220), a Corsican desert (p875), the Baie de la Somme with its ornithological park (p217) and several wet and watery pockets of the horse-studded Camargue (p806) rank among the conservatoire's rich pageant of *espaces naturels protégés* (protected natural areas).

Books, guides and maps on the 300 sites and 70,100 hectares managed by the Conservatoire du Littoral sites are sold in its online boutique.

TOP FIVE NATURAL CURIOSITIES

Several up hill and down dales later, here's what tickled us most in France's 42 regional parks:

- Dwarf-mutant beech trees that have grown in all their stunted glory around Reims and Champagne, since the 6th century and are protected today by the Parc Naturel Régional de la Montagne de Reims (p331) in Champagne.

- Europe's highest sand dune (which also happens to move, swallow trees and so on), the Dune de Pyla near Arcachon on the Atlantic Coast (p644).

- Europe's largest extinct volcano (by area), Monts du Cantal, the balding slopes of which can be hiked up in summer and skied down in winter. It falls within the Parc Naturel Régional des Volcans d'Auvergne (p554) in the Massif Central.

- Lunar landscape of underground sink-hills, caves and streams beneath the *causses* (limestone plateaus) of the Parc Naturel Régional des Grands Causses (p746) in Languedoc.

- Prehistoric bird footprints and marine-reptile fossil skeletons in the Réserve Naturelle Géologique de Haute-Provence in the Alps (p811).

Throughout the 1980s and 1990s France's nuclear activity was a particularly hot potato: French agents blew up the Greenpeace ship *Rainbow Warrior* in New Zealand's Auckland harbour in 1985 in an attempt to derail the organisation's campaign against nuclear testing on the Polynesian island of Mururoa and a nearby atoll. France did not sign a worldwide test-ban treaty until 1998.

Cadarache in southeast France is the favoured European contender for the construction of a thermonuclear experimental reactor – a US$5 billion engineering project between the EU, the USA, China and Japan among others that will revolutionise the production of world power should it succeed. Unlike conventional nuclear power plants, fusion reactors produce energy through the fusion of light atom nuclei and produce dramatically less radioactive waste. The cleaner, new-generation reactor will only start churning out energy in 2014.

Environmentalists in Languedoc are none too happy to have one of the world's tallest bridges (p747) slicing across one of their quiet valleys. A motorway will race along it from 2005.

Find out more about France's role in the world quest to develop fusion power at www.iter.org.

Conservation Organisation

A growing network of environmental organisations in France watchdog trouble spots:

- **Les Amis de la Nature** (☎ 01 46 27 53 56; www.amisnature-colombes.org in French; 197 rue Championnet, 75018 Paris) Cycle or walk instead of taking the car. For further tips on how to reduce your impact on the environment, contact nature's friends.

- **Association Nationale de Protection des Eaux de Rivières** (TOS; ☎ 01 43 75 84 04; www.anpertos.org in French; 67 rue de Seine, 94140 Alfortville) Help clean up French rivers with the National Association for the Protection of River Waters.

- **Espaces Naturels de France** (ENF; ☎ 02 38 24 55 00; www.enf.asso.fr in French; 6 rue Jeanne d'Arc, 45000 Orléans) Safeguards 40,000 hectares split across 1350 sites.

- **Fondation Ligue Française des Droits de l'Animal** (LFDA; www.league-animal-rights.org; 39 rue Claude Bernard, 75005 Paris) No to force feeding and foie gras is one of the animal-friendly calls made by the French League for Animal Rights.

- **France Nature Environnement** (☎ 02 38 62 44 48; www.fne.asso.fr in French; 6 rue Dupanloup, 45000 Orléans) Umbrella organisation for 3000-odd nature-protection and environmental groups countrywide.

DID YOU KNOW?

France's last working coal mine (near Creutzwald on the French-German border) closed in April 2004, marking the end of a traditional 300-year-old industry that employed 300,000 until the 1960s when nuclear power took over.

A DEGRADING PROCESS

Make sure that whatever you bring to the mountains leaves with you. Decomposition, always slow, is even more protracted in the high mountains. Typical times:

- paper handkerchief: three months
- apple core: up to six months
- cigarette butt: three to five years
- wad of chewing gum: five years
- lighter: 100 years

- plastic bag: 450 years
- aluminium can: up to 500 years
- plastic bottle: up to 1000 years
- glass bottle: up to 4000 years

- **Greenpeace** (☎ 01 44 64 02 17; www.greenpeace.org; 22 rue des Rasselins, 75020 Paris) For all the environmental hotspots in France.
- **Ligue pour la Préservation de la Faune Sauvage** (ROC; www.roc.asso.fr; 26 rue Pascal, 75005 Paris) The French League for the Protection of Wild Animals also fights for the rights of non-hunters in France (98% of the population).

Food & Drink

'The French think mainly about two things – their two main meals,' a well-fed *bon-vivant* French friend once told us. 'Everything else is in parentheses.' And it's true. While not every French man, woman and child is a walking *Larousse Gastronomique*, the gastronomic Bible of French cuisine, eating and drinking well is still of prime importance to most people in this country and they continue to spend an inordinate amount of time thinking about, talking about and consuming food and wine.

But don't suppose for a moment that this obsession with things culinary means dining out in France has to be a ceremonious occasion or one full of pitfalls for the uninitiated. Approach food and wine here with even half the enthusiasm the French themselves do, and you will be warmly received, encouraged and very well fed.

For a full culinary tour of France, including tips on how to prepare your own French banquet, pick up a copy of Lonely Planet's *World Food France*.

STAPLES & SPECIALITIES

Every nation or culture has its own staples, dictated by climate, geography and tradition. French cuisine has long stood apart for its great use of a variety of foods – beef, lamb, pork, poultry, fish and shellfish, cereals, vegetables and legumes – but its staple 'trinity' is bread, cheese and *charcuterie* (cured, smoked or processed meat products). And as for national and regional specialities, well, *tout est possible* (the sky's the limit).

Staples
BREAD
Nothing is more French than *pain* (bread). More than 80% of all French people eat it at every meal, and it comes in an infinite variety.

All bakeries have *baguettes* (and the similar but fatter *flûtes*), which are long and thin and weigh 250g, and wider loaves of what are simply called *pains*. A *pain*, which weighs 400g, is softer on the inside and has a less crispy crust than a baguette. Both types are at their best if eaten within four hours of baking; if you're not very hungry, ask for a half-loaf: a *demi baguette* or a *demi pain*. A *ficelle* is a thinner, crustier 200g version of a baguette – not unlike a very thick breadstick, really.

Bread has experienced a renaissance in France in recent years and most bakeries also carry heavier, more expensive breads made with all sorts of grains and cereals; you will also find loaves studded with nuts, raisins or herbs. These heavier breads keep much longer than baguettes and standard white-flour breads.

Bread is baked at various times during the day, so it's available fresh as early as 6am and also in the afternoon. Most bakeries close for one day a week, but the days are staggered so that a town or neighbourhood is never left without a place to buy a loaf (except, perhaps, on Sunday afternoon).

CHEESE
France has nearly 500 varieties of *fromage* (cheese) produced at farms, dairies, mountain huts, monasteries and factories. They're made from either cow's, goat's or ewe's milk, which can be raw, pasteurised or *petit-lait* ('little milk', the whey left over after the milk fats and solids have been curdled with rennet, an enzyme derived from the stomach of a calf or young goat).

DID YOU KNOW?

In the Middle Ages soups were closer to what we would call porridge today and the word *soupe* referred to a piece of bread (or sop) boiled in with the *bouillon* (broth or stock).

The choice on offer at a *fromagerie* (cheese shop) can be overwhelming, but *fromagers* (cheese merchants) always allow you to sample before you buy and are usually very generous with their advice and guidance. The following list divides French cheeses into five main groups as they are usually presented in a *fromagerie* and recommends several types to try.

Fromage de chèvre

'Goat's milk cheese' is usually creamy and both sweet and a little salty when fresh, but hardens and gets much saltier as it matures. Among the best are: Ste-Maure de Touraine, a creamy, mild cheese from the Loire region; Crottin de Chavignol, a classic though saltier variety from Burgundy; Cabécou de Rocamadour from Midi-Pyrénées, often served warm with salad or marinated in oil and rosemary; and St-Marcellin, a soft white cheese from Lyon.

DID YOU KNOW?

President Charles de Gaulle, commenting on the near impossibility of uniting the French on a single issue after WWII, famously grumbled: 'You cannot easily bring together a country that has 265 kinds of cheese'. And did you know that the number has now almost doubled to 500?

Fromage à pâté persillée

'Veined' or 'blue cheese' is so called because the veins often resemble *persille* (parsley). Roquefort is a ewe's-milk veined cheese that is to many the king of French cheeses. Fourme d'Ambert is a very mild cow's-milk cheese from the Rhône Valley. Bleu du Haut Jura (also called Bleu de Gex) is a mild blue-veined mountain cheese.

Fromage à pâté molle

'Soft cheese' is moulded or rind-washed. Camembert de Normandie, a classic moulded cheese that for many is synonymous with French cheese, and the refined Brie de Meaux are both made from raw cow's milk; Munster from Alsace and the strong Époisses de Bourgogne are rind-washed, fine-textured cheeses.

Fromage à pâté demi-dure

'Semi-hard cheese' denotes uncooked, pressed cheese. Among the finest are Tomme de Savoie, made from either raw or pasteurised cow's milk; Cantal, a cow's-milk cheese from Auvergne that tastes something like Cheddar; St-Nectaire, a strong-smelling pressed cheese that has a strong and complex taste; and Ossau-Iraty, a ewe's milk cheese made in the Basque Country.

Fromage à pâté dure

'Hard cheese' in France is always cooked and pressed. Among the most popular are: Beaufort, a grainy cow's milk cheese with a slightly fruity taste from Rhône-Alpes; Comté, a cheese made with raw cow's milk cheese in Franche-Comté; Emmental, a cow's-milk cheese made all over

SERVING CHEESE

When cutting cheese at the table, remember that a small circular cheese like a Camembert is cut in slices like a pie. If a larger such cheese (eg Brie) has been bought pre-sliced, cut from the tip to the rind; cutting off the top is considered rude. Slice cheeses whose middle is the best part (eg the blue or veined cheeses) in such a way as to take your fair share of the rind. A flat piece of semi-hard cheese like Emmental is usually just cut horizontally in chunks.

Wine and cheese is a match made in heaven. It's a matter of taste but in general, strong, pungent cheeses require a young, full-bodied red or a sweet wine, while soft cheeses with a refined flavour call for more quality and age in the wine. Some classic pairings include: Alsatian Gewürztraminer and Munster; Côtes du Rhône red and Roquefort; Côte d'Or (Burgundy) red with Brie or Camembert; and mature Bordeaux with Emmental or Gruyère.

France; and Mimolette, an Edam-like bright-orange cheese from Lille that can be aged for up to 36 months.

CHARCUTERIE

Traditionally *charcuterie* is made only from pork, though a number of other meats – from beef and veal to chicken and goose – are used in making sausages, blood puddings, hams and other cured and salted meats. Pâtés, terrines and *rillettes* are essentially *charcuterie* and are prepared in many different ways.

The difference between a pâté and a terrine is academic: a pâté is removed from its container and sliced before it is served or sold while a terrine is sliced from the container itself. *Rillettes*, on the other hand, is potted meat (pork, goose, duck or rabbit) or even fish that is not ground, chopped or sliced but shredded with two forks, seasoned, mixed with fat and spread cold like pâté over bread or toast.

While every region in France produces standard *charcuterie* favourites as well as its own specialities, Alsace, Lyon and the Auvergne produce the best sausages and Périgord and the north of France some of the most acclaimed pâtés and terrines. Among the basic types of *charcuterie* you'll encounter at a *charcuterie* or *charcuterie-traiteur* (see p77):

andouille – large smoked tripe (chitterling) sausage cooked and ready to eat (usually cold) when bought

andouillette – soft raw sausage made from the pig's small intestines that is grilled and sometimes eaten with onions and potatoes

boudin blanc – smooth white sausage made from poultry, veal, pork or even rabbit, which is cooked and can be served with, say, haricot beans or apples

boudin noir – blood sausage or pudding made with pig's blood, onions and spices and usually eaten hot with stewed apples and potatoes

fromage de tête – brawn or head cheese

jambon – ham; smoked or salt-cured pork made from a pig's hindquarters

saucisse – usually a small fresh sausage that is boiled or grilled before eating

saucisson – a large salami usually eaten cold

saucisson sec – air-dried salami

Regional Specialities

There are all sorts of reasons for the amazing variety of France's regional cuisine. Climatic and geographical factors have been particularly important: the hot south tends to favour olive oil, garlic and tomatoes, while the cooler, pastoral northern regions prefer cream and butter. Coastal areas specialise in mussels, oysters and saltwater fish, while those near lakes and rivers make full use of the freshwater fish available.

Diverse though it is, French cuisine is typified by certain regions, most notably Normandy, Burgundy, Périgord, Lyon and, to a lesser extent, the Loire region, Provence and Alsace. Still others such as Brittany, the Auvergne, the Basque Country, Languedoc and Corsica have made incalculable contributions to what can generically be called French food.

NORMANDY

The large fertile region that stretches along the English Channel from northeastern Brittany in the west to Picardy in the east, Normandy is famous for the incredible richness and superior quality of its local produce, but three staples are all-important in the Norman kitchen: milk and other dairy products, apples and seafood.

Each Norman cow produces an average 5000L of milk annually, supplying France with half its milk, cream, butter and cheese. Among the

The Food of France by Waverley Root is *the seminal work* on *la cuisine française* in English, with much focus on historical development, by a long-time American correspondent based in France.

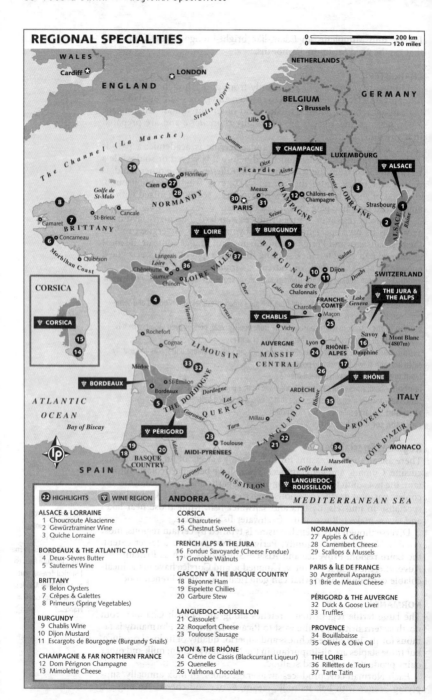

REGIONAL SPECIALITIES

0 — 200 km
0 — 120 miles

WALES
Cardiff ✪
✪ LONDON
ENGLAND
NETHERLANDS
GERMANY
BELGIUM
✪ Brussels
LUXEMBOURG
The Channel (La Manche)
Straits of Dover
Lille ● 13
Somme
Oise
Picardie
Aisne
♥ CHAMPAGNE
♥ ALSACE
Meuse
Lorraine
Rhine
Trouville ● Honfleur
29
Caen ● 27
28
NORMANDY
Meaux ●
30
PARIS 31
♥ CHAMPAGNE ● 12 Châlons-en-Champagne
Strasbourg ● 1
♥ ALSACE 2
3
Golfe de St-Malo
8
Camaret
7 St-Brieuc Cancale
6 Concarneau
BRITTANY
Morbihan Coast
Quibéron
Seine
♥ LOIRE
Langeais
Loire
36
Chênehutte
Saumur
Chinon
LOIRE VALLEY
4
Cher
Vienne
Creuse
♥ BURGUNDY
9
37
BURGUNDY
Côte d'Or
Chalonnais
10 ● Dijon
11
Doubs
Saône
SWITZERLAND
♥ THE JURA & THE ALPS
Lake Geneva
♥ CHABLIS
Charolles
● Mâcon
25
FRANCHE-COMTÉ
Savoy
16 Mont Blanc (4807m)
AUVERGNE
Vichy ●
Lyon ● RHÔNE-ALPES
24
Dauphiné
CORSICA
♥ CORSICA
15
14
Rochefort ●
Cognac ●
LIMOUSIN
MASSIF CENTRAL
26
17 ♥ RHÔNE
Médoc
33 32
♥ BORDEAUX
St-Émilion
Bordeaux
5
THE DORDOGNE
Dordogne
Lot
QUERCY
Garonne
ARDÈCHE
35
ITALY
Rhône
PROVENCE
CÔTE D'AZUR
ATLANTIC OCEAN
Bay of Biscay
♥ PÉRIGORD
23 ● Toulouse
Tarn
Millau ●
LANGUEDOC
21 22
34
MONACO
Marseille ●
19
20
18
BASQUE COUNTRY
MIDI-PYRÉNÉES
Adour
SPAIN
Garonne
ROUSSILLON
ANDORRA
Golfe du Lion
♥ LANGUEDOC-ROUSSILLON
MEDITERRANEAN SEA

22 HIGHLIGHTS   ♥ WINE REGION

ALSACE & LORRAINE
1 Choucroute Alsacienne
2 Gewürztraminer Wine
3 Quiche Lorraine

BORDEAUX & THE ATLANTIC COAST
4 Deux-Sèvres Butter
5 Sauternes Wine

BRITTANY
6 Belon Oysters
7 Crêpes & Galettes
8 Primeurs (Spring Vegetables)

BURGUNDY
9 Chablis Wine
10 Dijon Mustard
11 Escargots de Bourgogne (Burgundy Snails)

CHAMPAGNE & FAR NORTHERN FRANCE
12 Dom Pérignon Champagne
13 Mimolette Cheese

CORSICA
14 Charcuterie
15 Chestnut Sweets

FRENCH ALPS & THE JURA
16 Fondue Savoyarde (Cheese Fondue)
17 Grenoble Walnuts

GASCONY & THE BASQUE COUNTRY
18 Bayonne Ham
19 Espelette Chillies
20 Garbure Stew

LANGUEDOC-ROUSSILLON
21 Cassoulet
22 Roquefort Cheese
23 Toulouse Sausage

LYON & THE RHÔNE
24 Crème de Cassis (Blackcurrant Liqueur)
25 Quenelles
26 Valrhona Chocolate

NORMANDY
27 Apples & Cider
28 Camembert Cheese
29 Scallops & Mussels

PARIS & ÎLE DE FRANCE
30 Argenteuil Asparagus
31 Brie de Meaux Cheese

PÉRIGORD & THE AUVERGNE
32 Duck & Goose Liver
33 Truffles

PROVENCE
34 Bouillabaisse
35 Olives & Olive Oil

THE LOIRE
36 Rillettes de Tours
37 Tarte Tatin

cheeses, Camembert (produced in Normandy since the time of William the Conqueror) reigns supreme, but there are a great many others, including the heart-shaped Neufchâtel, salty Pont l'Évêque and smelly Livarot. Cream and butter go into the creation of the many rich, thick sauces that accompany fish, meat and vegetable dishes in the region.

Trouville and Honfleur are the places to go for fish and seafood; market barrows there are laden with lobsters, crayfish, langoustines, prawns, scallops, oysters, mussels and an endless variety of fish. Specialities include *matelote*, a kind of fish stew made with white wine and cream, and *sole à la normande* served with tiny shrimps.

Apples are the third essential of Norman cuisine, and light, refreshing, slightly alcoholic *cidre* (cider) – be it *doux* (sweet) or *brut* (dry) – is popular. It is also used extensively in cooking, particularly in meat and poultry dishes, including a dish not to everyone's taste: *tripes à la mode de Caen,* tripe combined with ox or calf's trotters, cider or Calvados, carrots, leeks, onions and herbs and slow-cooked in a sealed clay pot.

Calvados is to the apple what Cognac is to the grape. The most celebrated variety of this strong apple brandy comes from the Vallée d'Auge and is widely used in the preparation of sauces and in desserts.

BRITTANY

At the westernmost tip of France and surrounded by open sea on three sides, Brittany is a paradise for lovers of seafood, especially shellfish: oysters from Cancale and the Morbihan Gulf coast; scallops and sea urchins from St-Brieuc; crabs from St-Malo; and lobsters from Camaret, Concarneau and Quiberon. The region enjoys a very mild (though wet) Atlantic climate, which helps to produce some of the finest *primeurs* (spring or early vegetables) in France.

Without a doubt the *crêpe* and the *galette* are the royalty of Breton cuisine. A crepe is made from wheat flour and almost always sweet; the *crêpe beurre-sucre,* made with butter and sugar, is the classic variety but anything ranging from fruit and jam to liqueurs can be added. The flour used in a *galette* is made from buckwheat, a traditional staple of the region, and the fillings are always savoury. A *galette complète,* for example, comes with ham, egg and cheese.

ALSACE

In a traditional Alsatian restaurant you're likely to find *baeckeoffe* (baker's oven), a stew made of several kinds of meat (often pork, mutton and beef) and vegetables that have been marinated for several days. *Choucroute alsacienne* (or *garnie*) is sauerkraut served hot with sausage, bacon, pork loin and/or ham knuckle and accompanied by cold beer or chilled Pinot Noir.

Alsatians love savoury pies and tarts. The most popular is the *flammeküche* (or *tarte flambée*), a thin layer of pastry topped with cream, onion, bacon and sometimes cheese or mushrooms and cooked in a wood-fired oven. *Zwiebelküche* (or *tarte à l'oignon*) is an onion tart, while a *tourte* is a raised pie with ham, bacon or ground pork, eggs and leeks and often flavoured with Riesling. Alsace produces some excellent *charcuterie,* prepared from what is known in these parts as *le seigneur cochon* (the noble pig).

Due to the abundance of fruits and nuts in the region, Alsace's patisseries (pastry shops) are particularly well stocked with scrumptious cakes, tarts and pies, including *kugelhopf,* a mildly sweet, domed sultana-and-almond cake. *Tarte alsacienne* is a custard tart made with local fruits, which also includes the distinctive purple plums called *quetsches.*

DID YOU KNOW?

In Normandy Calvados is sometimes drunk in the middle of a meal as a *trou norman,* a 'Norman hole', to allow room for more courses.

LOIRE REGION

The cuisine of this region should be familiar to most since it was the cooking of the Loire, refined in the kitchens of the region's chateaux from the 16th century onward, that became the cuisine of France as a whole: *rillettes, coq au vin*, basic *beurre blanc* sauce and *tarte Tatin*.

Don't miss the opportunity to try *rillons*, chunks of fatty pork or duck cooked until crisp and crunchy and sometimes mixed with *rillettes* or foie gras. Also try *jambon d'Amboise*, an especially fine ham; *boudin blanc*, a smooth white sausage stuffed with chicken; and some of the freshwater fish (pike, shad, gudgeon, perch and smelt) that abound in the Loire and its many tributaries.

The Loire region has been called the 'garden of France' and quality produce of all types is grown here. But it is especially known for its mushrooms and prunes. The misnamed *champignons de Paris* are raised in 'caves' (actually quarries from where stones for the chateaux were mined) at Langeais and Chênehutte; the *pruneaux de Tours*, prunes dried from luscious Damson plums, are often cooked in poultry, pork or veal dishes or end up stuffed.

BURGUNDY

The cuisine of Burgundy, based on beef, wine and mustard, is solid, substantial and served in generous portions. The region's signature dish, *bœuf bourguignon*, is beef marinated and cooked in red wine with mushrooms, onions, carrots and bits of bacon. Any dish described as *à la bourguignonne* will be prepared with a similar sauce. Quite a few other Burgundian dishes are prepared with cream-based sauces, although *andouillette de Mâcon* (a small pork sausage) is served with a sauce made with the region's most famous condiment, Dijon mustard. The large, black and very tasty *escargots de Bourgogne* are raised on grape leaves.

Other traditional Burgundian products include *pain d'épices*, a gingerbread that traditionally takes up to eight weeks to prepare, and blackcurrants, which are used to make both jams and *crème de cassis*, a sweet blackcurrant liqueur that is combined with white wine (traditionally Aligoté) to make the aperitif known as a *kir*.

LYON

The city of Lyon, at the crossroads of some of France's richest agricultural regions (Burgundy and its wines, Charolles and its beef cattle, Dauphiné and its dairy products), enjoys a supply of quality foodstuffs unequalled in France. Indeed, it is considered by many to be France's *temple de gastronomie*; some of France's most talented chefs work here.

Some typical Lyonnaise dishes include *saucisson de Lyon* pan-fried with apples and *quenelles*, light poached dumplings made of pike (or less frequently chicken) and often served in a *sauce Nantua*, a creamy crayfish sauce. The *marrons glacés*, candied chestnuts from nearby Ardèche, are superb and with Valrhona chocolate (p486) being made at Tain l'Hermitage just downriver, it's no surprise that Lyon's proudest boast is its chocolates, particularly those made by the firm Bernachon (p481).

PÉRIGORD

Better known to many English speakers as the Dordogne (the name of the most important of the region's rivers and of its chief *département*), Périgord is celebrated for its truffles and poultry. Most prized among the latter are the ducks and geese whose fattened livers are turned into *pâté de foie gras* (duck or goose liver pâté) or cooked and stored in their own fat as *confit de canard* and *confit d'oie*. Goose fat is very important in the region's traditional cuisine, and walnut oil is used as a seasoning and in salads.

La cuisine périgourdine is very diverse and also includes freshwater fish (which can be stuffed with foie gras or cooked with truffles, grilled, marinated or cooked in ashes), crayfish, rabbit and beef. One of the best desserts is *gâteau aux châtaignes* (chestnut cake), but also look out for flans and tarts made with plums, quinces, grapes, cherries or pears.

THE AUVERGNE

The terrain, the climate and even the people of the Auvergne (the Massif Central area) are often described in French as *rude* – 'rugged', 'harsh' or 'tough'. In a word this, too, is its cuisine, including *potée auvergnate*, a hearty soup-stew of cabbage, bacon, pork sausages and potatoes, and lots of *charcuterie*, with the celebrated *salaisons d'Auvergne* (salt-cured meats) sold and consumed throughout France.

Specialities of the Auvergne include *lentilles vertes du Puy aux saucisses fumées*, smoked pork sausages with green Puy lentils, and *truffade*, a sticky blend of potatoes, cheese (usually Cantal) and garlic not unlike the *aligot* enjoyed in Languedoc and eaten with sausages.

PROVENCE

The Roman legacy of olives, wheat and wine remain the triumvirate of *la cuisine provençale*, and many dishes are prepared with olive oil and generous amounts of garlic. Provence's most famous dish is *bouillabaisse*, a chowder made with at least three kinds of fresh fish, cooked for 10 minutes or so in broth with onions, tomatoes, saffron and various herbs, and eaten as a main course with toasted bread and *rouille*, a spicy mayonnaise of olive oil, garlic and chilli peppers. Tomatoes, aubergine and squash, stewed together with green peppers, garlic and various aromatic herbs, produce that perennial Provençal favourite, *ratatouille*.

BASQUE COUNTRY

Among the essential ingredients of Basque cooking are the deep-red chillies you'll see hanging out to dry in summer, brightening up houses and adding that extra bite to many of the region's dishes, including the area's signature *jambon de Bayonne*, the locally prepared Bayonne ham. Fish dishes abound on the coast, especially those made with hake; the 'Basque bouillabaisse' called *ttoro* may include hake, eel and monkfish as well as tomatoes, white wine and chillies. Basques love cakes and pastries but the most popular of all is *gâteau basque*, a relatively simple layer cake filled with cream or cherry jam.

Le Grand Atlas des Cuisines de Nos Terroirs from Éditions Atlas is a beautifully illustrated atlas of regional cooking in France with emphasis on cuisine campagnarde (country cooking).

LANGUEDOC

No dish is more evocative of Languedoc than *cassoulet*, a casserole or stew with beans and meat. There are at least three major varieties but a favourite is the cassoulet from Toulouse, which adds *saucisse de Toulouse*, a fat, mild-tasting pork sausage. *Saucisse de Toulouse* often comes *à la languedocienne*, sautéed in goose fat and served with tomato, parsley and capers. But 'in the Languedoc style' is not an immutable recipe; it can also mean a garlicky garnish of tomatoes, aubergines and *cèpes* (boletus mushrooms). France's most famous blue cheese is made at Roquefort, south of Millau.

CORSICA

The hills and mountains of the island of Corsica have always been ideal for raising goats, sheep, cows and pigs; kitchen gardens produce a bounty of courgettes, small, purplish artichokes, asparagus and aubergines. The *maquis*, the dense Corsican underbrush made up of shrubs mixed with wild rosemary, laurel, lavender and thyme, flavours many dishes, along with olive oil, wild mint, fennel, tomatoes, honey, oranges and *cédrat*, a sweeter variety of lemon.

These raw materials have all come together to create such trademark Corsican foods as *stufatu*, a fragrant mutton stew, *premonata*, beef braised with juniper berries, and *lonzo aux haricots blancs*, a Corsican sausage cooked with white beans, white wine and herbs.

The island's most popular cheese is *brocciu*, which can be eaten fresh, when it is almost like ricotta, or as a rather mild and creamy, crumbly cheese when drained, salted and aged. Many sweets are prepared with chestnut flour (once a staple of the island), including *falculelli*, pressed and frittered Corsican *brocciu* cheese served on a chestnut leaf, and *castagnacci*, chestnut-flour pudding.

DRINKS
Alcoholic Drinks
Although alcohol consumption has dropped by a third in less than two decades, France still ranks sixth in the world in the boozing stakes behind Luxembourg, Romania, Portugal, Ireland and the Czech Republic.

WINE
Grapes and the art of wine-making were introduced to Gaul by the Romans. In the Middle Ages, important vineyards developed around monasteries as the monks needed wine to celebrate Mass. Large-scale wine production later moved closer to the ports (eg Bordeaux) from it could be exported.

In the middle of the 19th century, phylloxera aphids were accidentally brought to Europe from the USA. The pests ate through the roots of Europe's grapevines, destroying some 10,000 sq km of vineyards in France alone. European wine production appeared to be doomed until root stocks resistant to phylloxera were brought from California and original cuttings grafted onto them.

Wine-making is a complicated chemical process, but ultimately the taste and quality of the wine depend on four key factors: the type(s) or blend of grape, the climate, the soil and the art of the *vigneron* (wine-maker).

Some viticulturists have honed their skills and techniques to such a degree that their wine is known as a *grand cru* (literally, 'great growth'). If this wine has been produced in a year of optimum climatic conditions it becomes a *millésime* (vintage) wine. *Grands crus* are aged first in small oak barrels and then in bottles, sometimes for 20 years or more, before they develop their full taste and aroma. These are the memorable (and pricey) bottles that wine experts talk about with such passion.

There are dozens of wine-producing regions throughout France, but the seven principal regions are Alsace, Bordeaux, Burgundy, Champagne, Languedoc-Roussillon, the Loire region and the Rhône. Areas such as Burgundy comprise many well-known districts, including Chablis, Beaujolais and Mâcon, while Bordeaux encompasses Médoc, St-Émilion and Sauternes – to name just a few of its many subregions.

With the exception of Alsatian ones, wines in France are named after the location of the vineyard rather than the grape varietal.

Alsace
Alsace has been producing wine since about AD 300. These days, the region produces almost exclusively white wines – mostly varieties produced

nowhere else in France – that are known for their clean, fresh taste and compatibility with the often heavy local cuisine. The vineyards closest to Strasbourg produce light red wines from Pinot Noir that are similar to rosé. This wine is best served chilled.

Alsace's four most important varietal wines are Riesling, known for its subtlety; the more pungent and highly regarded Gewürztraminer; the robust, high-alcohol Pinot Gris; and Muscat d'Alsace, which is not as sweet as that made with Muscat grapes grown further south.

Bordeaux

Bordeaux has been synonymous with full-bodied red wine since the time of the Romans. Britons, who call Bordeaux reds clarets, have had a taste for the wines of this region since the mid-12th century when King Henry II, who controlled the region through marriage, tried to gain the favour of the locals by granting them tax-free trade status with England. Thus began a roaring business in wine exporting that continues to this day.

The reds of Bordeaux, which produces more fine wine than any other region in the world, are often described as well balanced, a quality achieved by blending several grape varieties. The grapes predominantly used are Merlot, Cabernet Sauvignon and Cabernet Franc. Bordeaux's foremost wine-growing areas are Médoc, Pomerol, St-Émilion and Graves; the sweet whites of the Sauternes area are the world's finest dessert wines.

'Bordeaux has been synonymous with full-bodied red wine since the time of the Romans.'

Burgundy

Burgundy has produced wines since the time of the Celts but developed its reputation during the reign of Charlemagne, when monks first began to produce wine here.

Burgundy's red wines are produced with Pinot Noir grapes; the best vintages need 10 to 20 years to age. White wine is made from the Chardonnay grape. The five main wine-growing areas of Burgundy are Chablis, Côte d'Or, Côte Chalonnais, Mâcon and Beaujolais, which alone produces 13 different types of light Gamay-based red wine.

Languedoc

This region is the country's most important wine-growing area, with up to 40% of France's wine – mainly cheap red *vin de table* (table wine) produced here. About 300,000 hectares of the region is 'under vine', which represents one-third of France's total.

In addition to the well-known Fitou label, the area's other quality wines are Coteaux du Languedoc, Faugères, Corbières and Minervois. The region also produces about 70% of France's *vin de pays,* 'country wine' from a particular named village or region, most of which is labelled Vin de Pays d'Oc.

Loire Region

The vineyards of the fertile Loire Valley are small and wine-makers are used to selling directly to day-trippers who make their way here to buy their favourite wines. The Loire's 75,000 hectares of vineyards rank the region as the third-largest area in France for the production of quality wines. Although sunny, the climate is moist and not all grape varieties thrive here.

The most common grapes are the Muscadet, Cabernet Franc and Chenin Blanc varieties. Wines tend to be light and delicate. The most celebrated areas are Pouilly-Fumé, Vouvray, Sancerre, Bourgueil, Chinon and Saumur.

Rhône Region

The Rhône region is divided into northern and southern areas. The different soil, climate, topography and grapes used means there is a dramatic difference in the wines produced by each.

On steep hills by the river, the northern vineyards make red wines from the ruby-red Syrah grape; the aromatic Viognier grape is the most popular for white wines. The south is better known for the quantity rather than quality of the wine it produces. The Grenache grape, which ages well when blended, is used in the reds, while the whites use the Ugni Blanc grape.

CHAMPAGNE

Champagne is made from the red Pinot Noir, the black Pinot Meunier or the white Chardonnay grape. Each vine is vigorously pruned and trained to produce a small quantity of high-quality grapes. Indeed, to maintain exclusivity (and price), the amount of champagne that can be produced each year is limited to between 160 and 220 million bottles, most of which is consumed in France and the UK.

The process of making champagne – carried out by innumerable *maisons* (houses) – is a long and complex one. There are two fermentation processes, the first in casks and the second after the wine has been bottled and had sugar and yeast added.

In the two months that the bottles are aged in cellars kept at 12°C, the wine turns effervescent. The sediment that forms in the bottle is removed by *remuage*, a painstakingly slow process in which each bottle – stored horizontally – is rotated slightly every day for weeks until the sludge works its way to the cork. Next comes *dégorgement:* the neck of the bottle is frozen, creating a blob of solidified Champagne and sediment, which is then removed.

At this stage, the champagne's sweetness is determined by adding varying amounts of syrup dissolved in old champagne. Then the bottles of young champagne are laid in a cellar and aged for between two and five years (sometimes longer), depending on the *cuvée* (vintage).

If the final product is labelled *brut,* it is extra dry, with only 1.5% sugar content. *Extra-sec* means it's very dry (but not as dry as brut), *sec* is dry and *demi-sec* is slightly sweet. The sweetest Champagne is labelled *doux*.

Some of the most famous champagne houses are Dom Pérignon, Möet et Chandon, Veuve Cliquot, Mercier, Mumm, Krugg, Laurent-Perrier, Piper-Heidsieck and Taittinger.

APERITIFS & DIGESTIFS

Meals in France are often preceded by an appetite-stirring *apéritif* such as *kir* (white wine sweetened with cassis or blackcurrant syrup), *kir royale* (champagne with cassis) or *pineau* (cognac and grape juice). *Pastis,* a 90-proof, anise-flavoured alcoholic drink that turns cloudy when you add water, is especially popular at cafés and with your author.

After-dinner drinks are often ordered with coffee. France's most famous brandies are Cognac and Armagnac, both of which are made from grapes in the regions of those names. *Eaux de vie,* literally 'waters of life', can be made with grape skins and the pulp left over after being pressed for wine (Marc de Champagne, Marc de Bourgogne), apples (Calvados), pears (Poire William) as well as such fruits as plums *(eau de vie de prune)* and raspberries *(eau de vie de framboise)*.

BEER & CIDER

The *bière à la pression* (draft beer) served by the *demi* (about 33cL) in bars and cafés across the land is usually one of the national brands such as

Kronenbourg, 33 or Pelforth and totally forgettable. Alsace, with its close cultural ties to Germany, produces some excellent local beers (eg Bière de Scharrach, Schutz Jubilator and Fischer, a hoppy brew from Scilligheim). Northern France, close to Belgium and the Netherlands, has its own great beers as well, including St-Sylvestre Trois Monts, Colvert, Terken Brune and Brasserie Jeanne d'Arc's Grain d'Orge made from barley.

Cidre (apple cider) is made in many parts of France, including Savoy, Picardy and the Basque Country, but its real home is Normandy and Brittany. You'll find *poiré* (perry, or pear cider) in Picardy and Normandy.

Nonalcoholic Drinks

The most popular nonalcoholic beverages consumed in France are coffee and mineral water.

WATER & MINERAL WATER

All tap water in France is safe to drink, so there is no need to buy bottled water. People in cities don't agree, however; less than 1% of the water consumed by a typical Parisian household each day, for example, is actually drunk. Tap water that is not drinkable (eg at most public fountains and on trains) will usually have a sign reading *'eau non potable'*.

If you prefer tap water rather than pricey bottled water, make sure you ask for *de l'eau* (some water), *une carafe d'eau* (a jug of water) or *de l'eau du robinet* (tap water). Otherwise you'll most likely get bottled *eau de source* (spring water) or *eau minérale* (mineral water), which comes *plate* (flat or still) or *gazeuse* (fizzy or sparkling). Popular mineral waters in France:

Badoit – France's oldest bottled mineral water with the tiniest of bubbles and medium taste, from the Loire Valley

Évian – A light, still Alpine mineral water from the spa town Évian-les-Bains, the 'pearl of Lake Geneva' (p508)

Perrier – Well-known, very carbonated mineral water in a distinctive green bottle from Languedoc (p737)

Vittel – Popular still mineral water from Lorraine sold in vending machines everywhere

Volvic – A very neutral still water from the Auvergne (p554)

COFFEE

The most ubiquitous form of coffee here is espresso, made by forcing steam through ground coffee beans. A small espresso, served without milk, is called *un café noir, un express* or simply *un café*. You can also ask for a *grand* (large) version.

Café crème is espresso with steamed milk or cream. *Café au lait* is lots of hot milk with a little coffee served in a large cup or, sometimes, a bowl. A small *café crème* is a *petit crème*. A *noisette* (literally, 'hazelnut') is an espresso with just a dash of milk. Decaffeinated coffee is *café décaféiné*.

CELEBRATIONS

At the risk of sounding facile, food in itself makes French people celebrate, and they'll accept any excuse for a party. There are birthdays and engagements and weddings and christenings and, like everywhere, there are special holidays.

> 'Food in itself makes French people celebrate, and they'll accept any excuse for a party.'

One tradition that is very much alive is called the *jour des rois,* which falls on 6 January and marks the feast of the *Épiphanie* (Epiphany), when the Three Wise Men paid homage to the Infant Jesus. A *galette des rois* (kings' cake), a puff pastry with frangipane cream, a little dried *fève* bean (or plastic or silver figurine) and topped with a gold paper crown that goes on sale in patisseries throughout France after the new year, is placed on the table. The youngest person in the room ducks under the table and calls out which member of the party should get each slice. The person who gets the bean is named king or queen, dons the crown and chooses his or her consort. This tradition is popular not just at home among families but also at offices and dinner parties.

At *Chandeleur* (Candlemas, marking the Feast of the Purification of the Virgin Mary) on 2 February, family and friends gather together in their kitchens to make *crêpes de la Chandeleur* (sweet pancakes).

Pâques (Easter) is marked here as elsewhere with *œufs au chocolat* (chocolate eggs) filled with candy fish and chickens and there is always an egg hunt for the kids. The traditional meal at Easter lunch is *agneau* (lamb) or *jambon de Pâques*, which – like hot-cross buns in Britain – seems to be available throughout the year nowadays.

After the *dinde aux marrons* (turkey stuffed with chestnuts) eaten at lunch on *Noël* (Christmas), a *bûche de Noël*, a 'log' of chocolate and cream or ice cream, is served.

WHERE TO EAT & DRINK

There's a vast number of eateries in France where you can get breakfast or brunch, a full lunch or dinner, and a snack between meals. Most have defined roles, though some definitions are becoming a bit blurred.

Auberge

An *auberge* (inn), which may also appear as an *auberge de campagne* and *auberge du terroir* (country inn), is usually attached to a rural inn or small hotel and serves traditional country fare.

'Unlike the vast majority of restaurants in France, brasseries serve full meals, drinks and coffee from morning till late at night.'

Bar

A *bar* or *bar américain* (cocktail bar) is an establishment dedicated to elbow-bending and rarely serves food beyond pre-made sandwiches or snacks. A *bar à vins* is a 'wine bar', which may or may not (usually the former) serve full meals at lunch and dinner. A *bar à huîtres* is an 'oyster bar'.

Bistro

A *bistro* (often spelled *bistrot*) is not clearly defined in France. It can be simply a pub or bar with snacks and light meals or a fully fledged restaurant.

Brasserie

Unlike the vast majority of restaurants in France, *brasseries* – which can look very much like cafés – serve full meals, drinks and coffee from morning till late at night. The dishes served almost always include *choucroute* and sausages because the brasserie, which actually means 'brewery' in French, originated in Alsace.

Buffet

A *buffet* (or *buvette*) is a kiosk usually found at train stations and airports selling drinks, filled baguettes and snacks.

Café

The main focus of a café is, of course, *café* (coffee) and only basic food is available at most. Common options include a baguette filled with Camembert or pâté and *cornichons* (gherkins), a *croque-monsieur* (grilled ham and toasted cheese sandwich) or a *croque-madame* (a toasted cheese sandwich topped with a fried egg).

Cafétéria

Many cities in France have *cafétérias* (cafeteria restaurants), including Flunch, that offer a decent selection of dishes you can see before ordering – a factor that can make life easier if you're travelling with kids.

Creperie

Creperies (sometimes seen as *galetteries*) specialise in sweet crepes and savoury *galettes* (see p67).

Ferme-Auberge

A *ferme-auberge* (literally 'farm inn') is usually a working farm that serves diners traditional regional dishes made from ingredients produced on the farm itself. The food is usually served *table d'hôte* (literally 'host's table'), meaning in set courses with little or no choice.

Relais Routier

A *relais routier* is a transport café or truck stop, usually found on the outskirts of towns and along major roads, which caters to truck drivers and can provide a quick, hearty break from cross-country driving.

Restaurant

The *restaurant* comes in many guises and price ranges in France. Generally they specialise in a particular variety of food (eg regional, traditional, North African, Vietnamese). There are lots of restaurants where you can get an excellent French meal for under €30 – Michelin's *Guide Rouge* is filled with them – and they usually offer what the French call a *bon rapport qualité-prix* (good value for money). Some of the best French restaurants in the country are attached to hotels, and are usually open to nonguests. Chain restaurants with standard *menus* are a definite step up from fast-food places and usually offer good-value (though uninspired) *menus*. Among the most common are Hippopotamus, Bistrot Romain and Léon de Bruxelles.

Almost all restaurants close for at least 1½ days (ie a full day and either one lunch or one dinner period) each week and this schedule will be posted on the front door. Chain restaurants are usually open throughout the day, seven days a week.

Restaurants almost always have a *carte* (menu) posted outside so you can decide before going in whether the selection and prices are to your liking. Most offer at least one fixed-price, multicourse meal known in French as a *menu*, *menu à prix fixe* or *menu du jour* (daily menu). A *menu* (not to be confused with a *carte*) almost always costs much less than ordering à la carte.

When you order a *menu*, you usually get to choose an entree, such as salad, paté or soup; a main dish (several meat, poultry or fish dishes, including the *plat du jour*, or 'the daily special', are generally on offer); and one or more final courses (usually cheese or dessert). In some places, you may also be able to order a *formule*, which usually has fewer choices but allows you to pick two of three courses – a starter and a main course, say, or a main course and a dessert.

Boissons (drinks), including wine, cost extra unless the *menu* says *boisson comprise* (drink included), in which case you may get a beer or a glass of mineral water. If the *menu* has *vin compris* (wine included), you'll probably be served a 25cL *pichet* (jug) of wine. The waiter will always ask if you would like coffee to end the meal, but this will almost always cost extra.

DID YOU KNOW?

The restaurant as we know it today was born in Paris in 1765 when a certain Monsieur A Boulanger opened a small business in rue Bailleul in the 1er, selling soups, broths and other restoratives.

Restaurant meals here are almost always served with bread, which is rarely accompanied by butter. If you run out of bread in your basket, don't be afraid to ask the waiter for more *('Pourrais-je avoir encore du pain, s'il vous plaît')*.

Restaurant Libre-Service

A *restaurant libre-service* is a 'self-service restaurant' similar to a *cafétéria* (see p75).

Restaurant Rapide

A *restaurant rapide* is a fast-food restaurant be it imported (McDonald's, Pizza Hut and KFC) or home-grown such as Quick.

Restaurant Universitaire

All French universities have several *restaurants universitaires* (refectories or canteens) subsidised by the Ministry of Education and operated by the Centre Régional des Œuvres Universitaires et Scolaires, better known as 'Crous'. They serve very cheap meals (typically under €5) and are usually open to nonstudents.

Salon de Thé

A *salon de thé* (tearoom) is a trendy and somewhat pricey establishment that usually offers quiches, salads, cakes, tarts, pies and pastries in addition to black and herbal teas.

VEGETARIANS & VEGANS

DID YOU KNOW?

France has long been a nation of dyed-in-the-wool carnivores and until modern times the word *viande* (meat) simply meant 'food'.

Vegetarians and vegans make up a small minority in a society where *viande* (meat) once also meant 'food', and they are not particularly well catered for; specialist vegetarian restaurants are few and far between. In fact, the vegetarian establishments that do exist in France often look more like laid-back, 'alternative lifestyle' cafés than restaurants. On the bright side, more and more restaurants are offering vegetarian choices on their set *menus*, and *produits biologiques* (organic products) are all the rage nowadays, even among carnivores. Other options include *saladeries*, casual restaurants that serve a long list of *salades composées* (mixed salads).

DINING WITH CHILDREN

It is sometimes said here that France treats its children as adults until they reach puberty – at which time they revert to being children again. You'll see a few *petits hommes* (little men) and *petites dames* (little ladies) dining decorously on the town with their parents, but most restaurants here do not have highchairs, children's menus or children's portions. In fact, children are rarely seen in most Parisian restaurants, which may explain the popularity of American-style fast-food restaurants and French chain restaurants such as Hippopotamus and Buffalo Grill (see p151), which cater to parents with kids in tow.

HABITS & CUSTOMS

French people do not eat in the clatter-clutter style of the Chinese or with the exuberance and sheer gusto of, say, the Italians. A meal is an artistic and sensual delight to most people here, something to be savoured and enjoyed with a certain amount of style and *savoir-vivre*.

When shopping for provisions, follow the example of the French and shop at speciality stores, whose managers can always offer advice.

When the French Eat

BREAKFAST

What the French call *petit déjeuner* is not every Anglo-Saxon's cup of tea. Masters of the kitchen throughout the rest of the day, French chefs don't seem up to it in the morning. Perhaps the idea is not to fill up – *petit déjeuner* means 'little lunch' and the real *déjeuner* (lunch) is just around the corner!

In the Continental style, people here traditionally start the day with a bread roll or a bit of baguette left over from the night before eaten with butter and jam and followed by a *café au lait* (coffee with lots of hot milk), a small black coffee or even a hot chocolate. Some people also eat cereal, toast, fruit and even yogurt in the morning – something they never did before.

Contrary to what many foreigners think, the French do not eat croissants every day but usually reserve these for a treat at the weekend when they may also choose *brioches, pains au chocolat* or other *viennoiserie* (baked goods).

'Contrary to what many foreigners think, the French do not eat croissants every day'

LUNCH & DINNER

Many French people still consider *déjeuner* (lunch) to be the main meal of the day. But as the pace of life is as hectic here as it is elsewhere in the industrialised world nowadays, the two-hour midday meal has become increasingly rare, at least on weekdays. Dinners, however, are still turned into elaborate affairs whenever time and finances permit. A fully fledged, traditional French meal at home is an awesome event, often comprising six distinct *plats* (courses). They are always served with wine – red, white or rosé (or a combination of two or all three), depending on what you're eating. A meal in a restaurant almost never consists of more than three or four courses: the *entrée* (starter or first course), the *plat principal* (main course), *dessert* and perhaps *fromage* (cheese).

Where the French Shop

Most French people buy a good part of their food from a series of small neighbourhood shops, each with its own speciality (though like everywhere more and more people are relying on supermarkets). At first, having to go to four shops and stand in four queues to fill the fridge (or assemble a picnic) may seem a waste of time, but the ritual is an important part of the way many French people live their daily lives. Note that many food shops are closed Sunday afternoon and all day Monday.

It's perfectly acceptable to purchase only meal-size amounts: a few *tranches* (slices) of meat to make a sandwich, perhaps, or a *petit bout*

FRITES

To make perfectly fried French fries or chips *(frites)* you'll need a *friteuse*, a deep-fryer (either stove-top or electric). Slice the potatoes uniformly, relatively thin (2cm) and about 8cm long. Put them in a bowl of cold salted water and let them soak for an hour, changing the water once or twice to remove some of the excess starch. Then dry them thoroughly on kitchen towels or on a tea towel/dish cloth.

Begin to heat the oil and put the potatoes in a *grille* (deep-frying basket). When the oil reaches 180°C plunge the *grille* into the *friteuse,* which will cause the temperature to drop. After about 10 minutes, when the potatoes start to take on a slightly waxy look and glisten, remove the basket from the oil and let it rest for about five minutes and allow the oil to heat back up. Put the basket back in the deep-fryer and cook till the chips are golden brown (about 10 minutes).

(small hunk) of sausage. You can also request just enough *pour une/deux personne(s)* (for one/two person/s).

BOUCHERIE
A *boucherie* is a general butcher's shop selling fresh beef, lamb, pork, chicken etc, but for specialised poultry you have to go to a *marchand de volaille* (also called a *volailler*), where *poulet fermier* (free-range chicken) and *poulet de grain* (corn-fed chicken) are also sold. A *boucherie chevaline*, easily identifiable by the gilded horse's head above the entrance, sells horsemeat, which some people prefer to beef or mutton, in part because it is less likely to have been produced using artificial hormones and has less fat. A *triperie* has tripe, either fresh or in various sauces.

BOULANGERIE
Fresh bread is baked and sold at France's 36,000 *boulangeries*, which supply three-quarters of the country's bread. Along with bread, bakeries usually sell croissants, *brioches, pains au chocolat* etc – baked goods that are lumped together under the term *viennoiserie*.

CHARCUTERIE
A *charcuterie* is a delicatessen offering sliced meats, pâtés, terrines, *rillettes* etc, though they sometimes do other things like seafood salads and even casseroles like *traiteurs* (opposite) do. Most supermarkets have a *charcuterie* counter.

CHOCOLATERIE
This is a shop selling only chocolate; most specialise in their own bonbons made on the premises.

'Most chocolateries specialise in their own bonbons on the premises'

CONFISERIE
Sweets including chocolate made with the finest ingredients can be found at *confiseries*, which are sometimes combined with *boulangeries* and patisseries.

ÉPICERIE
Literally 'spice shop', this is a small grocery store with a little bit of everything, including fruit and vegetables, and also known as an *alimentation générale*. Some *épiceries* are open on days when other food shops are closed, and many family-run operations close late at night.

FROMAGERIE
If you buy your cheese in a supermarket, you're likely to end up with unripe and relatively tasteless products unless you know how to select each variety. Here's where a *fromagerie*, also known as a *crémerie*, comes in. The owner, a true expert on matters dairy, can supply you with cheese that is *fait* (ripe) to the exact degree that you request and will almost always let you taste before you decide what to buy.

MARCHAND DE LÉGUMES ET DE FRUITS
Fruits and vegetables are sold by a *marchand de légumes et de fruits* (greengrocer) and at food markets and supermarkets. Most *épiceries* have only a limited selection. You can buy whatever quantity of produce suits you, even if it's just three carrots and a peach. *Biologique* (or *bio*) means grown organically (ie without chemicals).

MARCHAND DE VIN

Wine is sold by a *marchand de vin* (or *caviste*), such as the shops of the Nicolas chain. Wine shops in close proximity to the vineyards of Burgundy, Bordeaux, the Loire region and other wine-growing areas are often called *vinothèques* and offer tastings.

MARCHÉ

In most towns and cities, many of the aforementioned products are available one or more days a week at a *marché en plein air* (open-air market), also known as a *marché découvert,* and up to six days a week at a *marché couvert* (covered marketplace), often known as *les halles.* Markets are cheaper than food shops and supermarkets and the merchandise, especially fruit and vegetables, is much more fresh and of better quality.

PATISSERIE

Mouth-watering pastries are available at patisseries. Some of the most common pastries include *tarte aux fruits* (fruit tarts), *pain aux raisins* (a flat, spiral pastry made with custard and sultanas) and *religieuses* (eclairs that – vaguely – resemble a nun's habit).

POISSONERIE

Fresh fish and seafood are available from a *poissonnerie* (fishmonger). People have such a taste for fish in France that fish shops in big cities and towns inland often have as big a selection of fresh fish and crustaceans as the ones closer to the coast do.

SUPERMARCHÉ

Both town and city centres usually have at least one department store with a large *supermarché* (supermarket) section in the basement or on the 1st floor. Most larger supermarkets have *charcuterie* and cheese counters, and many also have in-house *boulangeries.*

TRAITEUR

A *traiteur* (caterer) sells ready-to-eat dishes to take home: casseroles, salads of all shades and hues and many more elaborate dishes. *Traiteurs* are a picnicker's delight and a godsend to people at home who want something better than takeaway but can't be bothered to cook.

COOKING COURSES

What better place to discover the secrets of *la cuisine française* than in front of a stove? Cooking courses are available at different levels and lengths of time and the cost of tuition varies widely. In Paris one of the most popular – and affordable – is **Cours de Cuisine Françoise Meunier** (Map pp96-8; ☎ 01 40 26 14 00; www.fmeunier.com; 7 rue Paul Lelong, 2e; metro Bourse), which offers three-hour courses at 2.30pm on Tuesday and at 10.30am from Wednesday to Saturday for adult/child aged 12 to 14 €90/60. 'Carnets' of five/20 courses cost €400/1500. Other major cooking schools in Paris:

École de Gastronomie Française Ritz Escoffier (Map pp93-5; ☎ 01 43 16 30 50; www .ritzparis.com; 38 rue Cambon, 1er; metro Concorde)

École Le Cordon Bleu (Map pp99-101; ☎ 01 53 68 22 50; www.cordonbleu.edu; 8 rue Léon Delhomme, 15e; metro Vaugirard or Convention)

École Lenôtre (Map pp93-5; ☎ 01 45 02 21 19; www.lenotre.fr; Pavillon Élysée, 10 av des Champs-Élysées, 8e; metro Champs-Élysées Clemenceau)

DID YOU KNOW?

French homemakers have never been averse to letting the experts take care of the more complicated dishes and have used the services of *traiteurs* and *pâtissiers* for centuries.

SOUPE À L'OIGNON GRATINÉE

Nothing is more Parisian than onion soup with a crust of oven-browned grated cheese.

225g onions, thinly sliced	salt and pepper
60g butter	thin rounds of bread
1 tablespoon flour	thin slices of Gruyère cheese
1.5L water	

Cook the sliced onions in butter. When they are golden, sprinkle with flour. Mix well with a wooden spoon and gradually blend in the water. Season with salt and pepper and simmer for 15 minutes. Slice the bread thinly and brown in butter. Ladle the soup into individual earthenware bowls, top with a crouton and cheese and heat in the oven until the cheese begins to brown. Serves 6.

There are a number of regional cooking schools around France:

Domaine de la Tortinière (☎ 02 47 34 35 00; www.tortiniere.com; route de Ballan Miré, Les Gués de Veigné, 37250 Montbazon) Traditional Touraine cuisine courses in a chateau setting.

La Cuisine du Soleil (☎ 04 93 75 78 24; www.moulin-mougins.com; Notre Dame de Vie, 06250 Mougins) Mediterranean cuisine taught by a top chef.

La Manoir d L'Aufragère (☎ 02 32 56 91 92; www.laufragere.com; L'Aufragère, La Croisée, 27500 Fourmetot) Courses are held in a Norman manor house.

Mas de Cornud (☎ 04 90 92 39 32; www.mascornud.com; Petite Route de Mas Blanc, 13210 St-Rémy de Provence) Provençal home cooking.

EAT & DRINK YOUR WORDS

For pronunciation guidelines see p932.

Useful Phrases

I'm hungry/thirsty.
J'ai faim/soif. — zhay fum/swaf

A table for two, please.
Une table pour deux, s'il vous plaît. — ewn ta·bler poor der seel voo play

Do you have a menu in English?
Est-ce que vous avez la carte en anglais? — es·ker voo za·vay la kart on ong·lay

What's the speciality of this region?
Quelle est la spécialité de la région? — kel ay la spay·sya·lee·tay de la ray·zhon

What is today's special?
Quel est le plat du jour? — kel ay ler pla doo zhoor

I'd like the set menu, please.
Je prends le menu, s'il vous plaît. — zher pron ler mer·new seel·voo·play

I'd like some…
Je voudrais du/de la… — zher voo·dray doo/de la…

May I have another…please?
Puis-je avoir encore un/une… *s'il vous plaît?* — pwee zher a·vwa ong·kor un/oon… seel voo play

I'm a vegetarian.
Je suis végétarien/végétarienne. (m/f) — zher swee vay·zhay·ta·ryun/ vay·zhay·ta·ryen

I don't eat (meat).
Je ne mange pas de viande. — zher ne monzh pa de vyond

Is service included?
Le service est compris? — ler sair·vees ay kom·pree

The bill, please.
L'addition, s'il vous plaît. — la·dee·syon seel voo play

Menu Decoder
STARTERS (APPETISERS)

assiette anglaise	plate of cold mixed meats and sausages
assiette de crudités	plate of raw vegetables with dressings
soufflé	a light, fluffy dish of egg yolks, stiffly beaten egg whites, flour and cheese and other ingredients

SOUP

bouillabaisse	Mediterranean-style fish soup, originally from Marseille, made with several kinds of fish, including *rascasse* (spiny scorpion fish); often eaten as a main course
bouillon	broth or stock
bourride	fish stew; often eaten as a main course
potage	thick soup made with puréed vegetables
soupe au pistou	vegetable soup made with a basil and garlic paste
soupe de poisson	fish soup
soupe du jour	soup of the day

MEAT & POULTRY

aiguillette	thin slice of duck fillet
andouille or **andouillette**	sausage made from pork or veal tripe
bifteck	steak
bleu	nearly raw
saignant	very rare (literally: 'bleeding')
à point	medium rare but still pink
bien cuit	literally: 'well cooked', but usually like medium rare
blanquette de veau	veal stew with white sauce
bœuf bourguignon	beef and vegetable stew cooked in red wine
bœuf haché	minced beef
boudin noir	blood sausage (black pudding)
brochette	kebab
canard	duck
caneton	duckling
cassoulet	Languedoc stew made with goose, duck, pork or lamb fillets and haricot beans
charcuterie	cooked or prepared meats (usually pork)
chevreuil	venison
choucroute	sauerkraut with sausage and other prepared meats
civet	game stew
confit de canard (d'oie)	duck (goose) preserved and cooked in its own fat
coq au vin	chicken cooked in wine
côte	chop of pork, lamb or mutton
côtelette	cutlet
cuisses de grenouille	frogs' legs
entrecôte	rib steak
escargot	snail
faisan	pheasant
faux-filet	sirloin steak
filet	tenderloin
foie	liver
foie gras de canard	duck liver pâté
fricassée	stew with meat that has first been fried
gibier	game
gigot d'agneau	leg of lamb
grillade	grilled meats

jambon	ham
langue	tongue
lapin	rabbit
lard	bacon
lardon	pieces of chopped bacon
lièvre	hare
mouton	mutton
oie	goose
pieds de cochon/porc	pigs' trotters
pintade	guinea fowl
quenelles	dumplings made of a finely sieved mixture of cooked fish or (rarely) meat
rognons	kidneys
sanglier	wild boar
saucisson	large sausage
saucisson fumé	smoked sausage
steak	steak
steak tartare	raw ground meat mixed with onion, raw egg yolk and herbs
tournedos	thick slices of fillet
volaille	poultry

FISH & SEAFOOD

anchois	anchovy
anguille	eel
brochet	pike
cabillaud	cod
calmar	squid
chaudrée	fish stew
coquille St-Jacques	scallop
crabe	crab
crevette grise	shrimp
crevette rose	prawn
écrevisse	freshwater crayfish
fruits de mer	seafood
hareng	herring
homard	lobster
huître	oyster
langouste	crayfish
langoustine	very small saltwater 'lobster' (Dublin Bay prawn)
maquereau	mackerel
merlan	whiting
morue	cod
moules	mussels
palourde	clam
rouget	mullet
sardine	sardine
saumon	salmon
thon	tuna
truite	trout

COOKING METHODS, SAUCES & CONDIMENTS

à la vapeur	steamed
aïoli	garlic mayonnaise
au feu de bois	cooked over a wood-burning stove
au four	baked

béchamel	basic white sauce
en croûte	in pastry
farci	stuffed
fumé	smoked
gratiné	browned on top with cheese
grillé	grilled
huile d'olive	olive oil
moutarde	mustard
pané	coated in breadcrumbs
pistou	pesto (pounded mix of basil, hard cheese, olive oil and garlic
provençal(e)	tomato, garlic, herb and olive oil dressing or sauce
rôti	roasted
sauté	sautéed (shallow fried)
tartare	mayonnaise with herbs
vinaigrette	salad dressing made with oil, vinegar, mustard and garlic

DESSERTS & SWEETS

crêpes suzettes	orange-flavoured pancakes flambéed in liqueur
dragées	sugared almonds
éclair	pastry filled with cream
flan	egg-custard dessert
frangipane	pastry filled with cream and flavoured with almonds
gâteau	cake
gaufre	waffle
glace	ice cream
île flottante	literally: 'floating island'; beaten egg white lightly cooked, floating on a creamy sauce
macaron	macaroon (sweet biscuit of ground almonds, sugar and egg whites)
sablé	shortbread biscuit
tarte (aux pommes)	apple tart or pie
yaourt	yogurt

SNACKS

croque-monsieur	grilled ham and cheese sandwich
croque-madame	croque-monsieur with a fried egg
frites	chips (French fries)
quiche	quiche

Food Glossary

BASICS

breakfast	*petit déjeuner*	**lunch**	*déjeuner*
dinner	*dîner*	**food**	*nourriture*
menu	*carte*	**set menu**	*menu/formule*
starter/appetiser	*entrée*	**main course**	*plat principal*
wine list	*carte des vins*	**market**	*marche*
grocery store/		**waiter/**	
delicatessen	*épicerie/traiteur*	**waitress**	*serveur/serveuse*
knife	*couteau*	**fork**	*fourchette*
spoon	*cuillère*	**bottle**	*bouteille*
glass	*verre*	**plate/dish**	*plat/assiette*
hot/cold	*chaud/froid*	**with/without**	*avec/sans*

MEAT & FISH

beef	*boeuf*	**meat**	*viande*
chicken	*poulet*	**pork**	*porc*

fish	poisson	turkey	dinde
lamb	agneau	veal	veau

FRUIT & VEGETABLES

apple	pomme	lemon	citron
apricot	abricot	lentils	lentilles
artichoke	artichaut	lettuce	laitue
asparagus	asperge	mushroom	champignon
banana	banane	onion	oignon
beans	haricots	peach	pêche
beetroot	betterave	peas	petit pois
bilberry		pepper	
(blueberry)	myrtille	(red/green)	poivron (rouge/vert)
blackcurrant	cassis	pineapple	ananas
cabbage	chou	plum	prune
carrot	carotte	potato	pomme de terre
celery	céleri	prune	pruneau
cepe (boletus		pumpkin	citrouille
mushroom)	cèpe	raspberry	framboise
cherry	ceris	rice	riz
cucumber	concombre	shallot	échalotte
French (string)		spinach	épinards
beans	haricots verts	strawberry	fraise
gherkin (pickle)	cornichon	sweet corn	maïs
grape	raisin	tomato	tomate
grapefruit	pamplemousse	turnip	navet
leek	poireau	vegetable	légume

OTHER

bread	pain	jam	confiture
butter	beurre	oil	huile
cheese	fromage	pepper	poivre
cream	crème	salt	set
egg	œuf	sugar	sucre
honey	miel	vinegar	vinaigre

DRINKS

beer	bière	milk	lait
coffee	café	mineral water	eau minérale
with milk	au lait	tea	thé
with sugar	avec sucre	water	eau
juice (apple)	jus (de pomme)	wine (red)	vin (rouge)
juice (orange)	jus (d'orange)	wine (white)	vin (blanc)

Paris

CONTENTS

History	87
Orientation	88
Information	89
Dangers & Annoyances	112
Sights	113
Activities	131
Walking Tour	132
Paris for Children	134
Tours	134
Festivals & Events	135
Sleeping	136
Eating	147
Drinking	158
Entertainment	160
Shopping	167
Getting There & Away	170
Getting Around	171

Paris is to many people the most beautiful and romantic city in the world. The architecture, the parks and squares, the timeless Seine, the café life and the people's *joie de vivre* – and dress sense – all combine to make the 'City of Light' a monumental, handsome and fascinating place in which to live and to visit. But the uninitiated may find it all a bit daunting at first.

Paris has more landmarks familiar to people who have never visited than any other city. First-time visitors often arrive in the French capital with all sorts of expectations and trepidations: of grand vistas, of intellectuals discussing weighty matters in cafés, of romance along the Seine, of sexy cabaret revues and of rude people who don't (or won't) speak English but will happily rip you off. If you look, you'll find all those things – there's no doubt about that. But set aside your preconceptions and explore the city's avenues and backstreets as if the Eiffel Tower and Notre Dame weren't about to pop into view at any moment.

Parisians believe they have savoir-faire – the inherent knowledge of how to live well – and you'll find that Paris is a feast for the senses. It's a city to view: wide boulevards, monuments, works of art and magical lights. It's a city to taste: cheese, wine, *charcuterie*. It's a city to hear: opera, jazz or world music, or just the sound of metro cars whooshing by. It's a city to smell: perfume boutiques, cafés with fresh coffee and croissants, chestnuts roasting in winter. It's a city to feel: the wind in your face as you cycle by the Seine, the *frisson* of fear and pleasure as you peer from the top of the Eiffel Tower. Above all, it's a city to discover. This chapter is designed to whet your appetite and guide you when you arrive. But remember: it's just a guidebook Leave it behind from time to time and wander to find your very own personal Paris.

HIGHLIGHTS

- Take in the contents and rooftop view at the art and cultural complex of **Centre Pompidou** (p116)
- Play 'spot the departed' at **Cimetière du Père Lachaise** (p129), the world's most visited necropolis
- Ascend the **Eiffel Tower** (p125) the image that has become more Parisian than Paris itself
- Visit the **Louvre** (p113) to view old favourites such as the *Mona Lisa* and *Venus de Milo*
- Check out the **Marais** (p117) for stately *hôtels particuliers* (private mansions) by day and the pulsating nightlife after dark
- Say ooooh-la-la to **Montmartre** (p130), the Paris of story, song and myth
- Marvel at the incomparable collection of impressionist art and the architectural beauty of the **Musée d'Orsay** (p124)
- Come to **Notre Dame** (p119) for both the sacred (rose windows, medieval statuary) and the profane (gargoyles, tourist hordes)
- Admire the sublime stained glass of Christ's Passion on a sunny day at **Ste-Chapelle** (p120)

■ POPULATION: 2.1 MILLION	■ AREA: 105 SQ KM

HISTORY

What is now the Île de la Cité was settled in the 3rd century BC by a tribe of Celtic Gauls known as the Parisii. Centuries of conflict between the Gauls and Romans ended in 52 BC, when Julius Caesar's legions crushed a Celtic revolt led by Vercingétorix. Christianity was introduced in the 2nd century AD, and Roman rule ended in the 5th century with the arrival of the Germanic Franks. In 508 Frankish king Clovis I united Gaul as a kingdom and made Paris his seat.

The Middle Ages brought prosperity to Paris. Construction began on the cathedral of Notre Dame in the 12th century, and the marshy Marais area north of the Seine – what would become known as the Right Bank – was drained and settled. The Louvre began as a riverside fortress around 1200, the beautiful Ste-Chapelle was consecrated in 1248 and the Sorbonne opened its doors in 1253.

Scandinavian Vikings (also known as Norsemen or Normans) had begun raids on France's west coast in the 9th century; after three centuries of conflict, they started to push towards Paris. These conflicts heralded the Hundred Years' War between Norman England and Paris' Capetian dynasty, eventually bringing the French defeat at Agincourt in 1415 and English control of the capital in 1420. In 1429 the 17-year-old Jeanne d'Arc (Joan of Arc) rallied the French troops to defeat the English at Orléans. With the exception of Calais, the English were finally expelled from France in 1453.

At the end of the 15th century the Renaissance helped Paris get back on its feet, and many of the city's most famous buildings and monuments were erected at this time. But in less than a century Paris was again in turmoil, this time in the name of religion. Clashes between the Huguenot Protestants and Catholic groups became increasingly commonplace, culminating with the 1572 St Bartholomew's Day massacre of 3000 Huguenots who had gathered in Paris to celebrate the wedding of Henri of Navarre (later King Henri IV).

Louis XIV (le Roi Soleil, or the Sun King) ascended the throne in 1643 at the age of five and held the crown until 1715. During his long reign, he nearly emptied the national coffers with his ambitious building and battling. His most tangible legacy is the palace at Versailles, 21km southwest of Paris. The excesses of Louis XVI and his queen Marie-Antoinette, led to an uprising of Parisians on 14 July 1789 and the storming of the Bastille prison – kick-starting the French Revolution.

After a few short years the populist visions of the Revolution gave way to a Reign of Terror, during which even a few of the original patriots were executed. The unstable post-Revolution government was consolidated in 1799 under a young Corsican general named Napoleon Bonaparte, who declared himself First Consul. In 1804 he had the Pope crown him Emperor of the French and then swept most of Europe under his wing. Napoleon's hunger for more victories and glory led to his defeat, first in Russia in 1812 and later at Waterloo in Belgium in 1815.

After the defeated Napoleon was exiled, France struggled under a string of mostly inept rulers until a coup d'état in 1851 brought emperor Napoleon III to power. He oversaw the construction of a more modern Paris, with wide boulevards, sculptured parks and – not insignificantly – a modern sewer system. Like his uncle, however, this Napoleon and his penchant for pugnacity led to a costly and eventually unsuccessful war, this time with the Prussians in 1870. When the masses in Paris heard of their emperor's capture by the enemy, they took to the streets, demanding that the republic be restored. Despite its bloody beginnings, the Third Republic ushered in the glittering and very creative period known as the *belle époque* (beautiful era).

The *belle époque* was famed for its Art Nouveau architecture and advances in the arts and sciences. By the 1930s Paris had become a centre for the artistic avant-garde and had established its reputation among freethinking intellectuals. This was all cut short by the Nazi occupation of 1940; Paris would remain under direct German rule until 25 August 1944. After the war Paris regained its position as a creative centre and nurtured a revitalised liberalism that reached a climax in the student-led uprisings of 1968. The Sorbonne was occupied, barricades were set up in the Latin Quarter and some nine million people nationwide were inspired to join in a general strike that paralysed the country.

During the 1980s President François Mitterrand initiated several costly *grands projets*, a series of building projects that garnered widespread approval even when the results were popular failures. Responses to the flashier examples, such as the glass pyramids in the courtyard of the Louvre and the Bibliothèque Nationale, have ranged from shock horror to doting rapture; if nothing else, the *projets* provoked dialogue about the Parisian aesthetic.

In May 2001 Bertrand Delanoë, a Socialist with support from the Green Party, became Paris' – and a European capital's – first openly gay mayor. He continues to enjoy widespread popularity, particularly for his efforts to make Paris more liveable by promoting bicycles and buses and to create a more approachable and responsible city administration.

ORIENTATION

Central Paris is relatively small: approximately 9.5km (north to south) by 11km (east to west). Within the 'oval' of central Paris, which Parisians call *intra-muros* (Latin for 'within the walls'), the Rive Droite (Right Bank) is north of the Seine, while the Rive Gauche (Left Bank) is south of it since the river flows from east to west.

Paris is quite an easy city to negotiate, but this chapter offers you three ways to find the addresses listed: by district, map reference and metro station.

Arrondissements

Paris is divided into 20 arrondissements (districts), which spiral out clockwise from the centre like a conch shell. City addresses always include the number of the arrondissement, as streets with the same name exist in different districts.

In this chapter, arrondissement numbers are given after a street address using the usual French notation: 1er for *premier* (1st), 2e for *deuxième* (2nd), 3e for *troisième* (3rd) and so on. On some signs or commercial maps, you will see the variation 2ème, 3ème etc.

Maps

The most useful map of Paris is the 1:10,000-scale *Paris Plan* published by Michelin. It

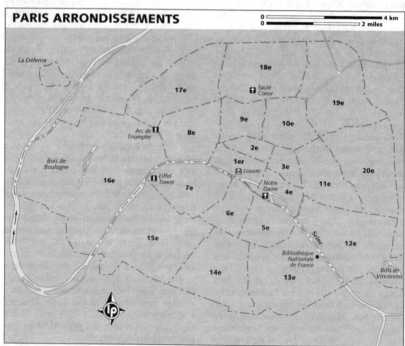

PARIS IN...

Two days

If you've got just a couple of days in Paris you should definitely join a morning tour and then concentrate on the most Parisian of sights and attractions: Notre Dame (p119), the Louvre (p113), the Eiffel Tower (p125) and the Arc de Triomphe (p127). In the late afternoon have a coffee or a pastis on the av des Champs-Élysées (p154) and then make your way to Montmartre (p130) for dinner. The following day take in such sights as the Musée d'Orsay (p124), Ste-Chapelle (p120), Conciergerie (p120), Musée National du Moyen Âge (p121) and/or the Musée Rodin (p125). Have brunch on the place des Vosges (p148) and enjoy a night of mirth and gaiety in the Marais (p158).

Four days

With another day to look around the city, you should consider a cruise (p134) along the Seine or the Canal St-Martin and visit some place further afield – the Cimetière du Père Lachaise (p129), say, or the Parc de la Villette (p130). Take in a concert, opera or ballet (p162) at the Palais Garnier or Opéra Bastille or a play at the Comédie Française (p166). Why not head to a destination in the Île de France on the following day such as Versailles (p185) or Chartres (p196)? Be back in time for a farewell pub and club crawl through Ménilmontant (p160), though.

A week

If you have a full week here you can see a majority of the sights listed in this chapter, visit places 'outside the walls' such as La Défense (p179) and St-Denis (p182), and leave Paris for a couple of days' excursion. Vaux-le-Vicomte (p192) can be easily combined with Fontainebleau (p189), Senlis (p195) with Chantilly (p193) and, if you travel hard and fast, Chartres (p189) with Versailles (p185).

---

comes in booklet form (No 11 or 14; €5.25) or as a fold-out sheet (No 10 or 12; €4.25 to €6) or, under the name *Atlas Paris 15*, in large format (€9). The Lonely Planet *Paris City Map* is available from bookshops in the UK and France.

For a more user-friendly street atlas than the venerable old *Paris par Arrondissement* (€13.50), choose L'Indispensable's *Paris Pratique par Arrondissement* (€5.50), which is a slim, pocket-sized atlas. The larger *Le Petit Parisien* (€7) has three maps for each arrondissement, showing streets, metro lines and bus routes

The best place to find a full selection of maps is the Espace IGN (p906).

Metro Stations

Paris counts some 372 metro stations and there is always one station within a maximum of 500m of wherever you need to go in Paris (see the Metro map, opposite p108). Thus all the offices, museums, hotels and restaurants mentioned here have the nearest metro stop written immediately after the contact details. Metro stations usually have a useful *plan du quartier* (map of the neighbourhood) on the wall near the exits.

INFORMATION
Bookshops

Abbey Bookshop (Map pp105-7; ☎ 01 46 33 16 24; 29 rue de la Parcheminerie, 5e; metro Cluny-La Sorbonne; ☺ 10am-7pm Mon-Sat) Mellow Canadian-owned bookshop not far from place St-Michel celebrated for its free tea and coffee and good selection of new and used books.

Les Mots à la Bouche (Map pp105-7; ☎ 01 42 78 88 30; www.motsbouche.com in French; 6 rue Ste-Croix de la Bretonnerie, 4e; metro Hôtel de Ville; ☺ 11am-11pm Mon-Sat, 2-8pm Sun) 'On the Tip of the Tongue' is Paris' premier gay bookshop. If you're feeling naughty, go down – stairs, that is.

Red Wheelbarrow Bookstore (Map pp105-7; ☎ 01 48 04 75 08; 22 rue St-Paul, 4e; metro St-Paul; ☺ 10am-7pm Mon-Sat, 2-6pm Sun) This relatively new English-language bookshop has arguably the best selection of literature and 'serious reading' in Paris.

Shakespeare & Company (Map pp105-7; ☎ 01 43 26 96 50; 37 rue de la Bûcherie, 5e; metro St-Michel; ☺ noon-midnight) Paris' most famous English-language bookshop has a varied collection of new and used books in English, including paperback novels for as little as €1.

(Continued on page 109)

St Ouen Ⓜ

Mairie
de Clichy Ⓜ

Cimetière
Parisien des
Batignolles

Cimetière de
Levallois

Ⓜ Blvd Bessières

Stade de
Courbevoie

Cimetière
Sud

Pont de
Levallois
Bécon Ⓜ

Pablo
Neruda

21 🛇 Ⓜ
Porte de
Clichy

Louison
Bobet

**See La Défense
Map (p181)**

Île de la
Grande Jatte

Anatole
France

Av de Wagram

Av de Clichy

A14

La
Défense

Av Bineau

See Central Paris - NW Map (pp94-5)

La Défense
Grande Arche Ⓜ

Esplanade de
la Défense Ⓜ

R. de Villiers

Blvd Victor Hugo

Blvd Péripherique

Blvd Malesherbes

17e

Blvd Circulaire

Pont de
Neuilly Ⓜ

Av Charles de Gaulle Ⓜ

Av du Roule

Blvd Pereire

R. de Courcelles

Ga
La
Blvd Hauss

R. de la République

Les Sablons Ⓜ

Av de Friedland

Seine

Blvd Maurice Barrès

Blvd Maillot

Arc de
Triomphe

8e

Mare St
James

Av Foch

Av des Champs Elysées

Île de
Puteaux

Lac Pour
le Patinage

Av Victor Hugo

Av Kléber

Av Marceau

Triangle
d'Or

Avenue
Foch

Parc de
Bagatelle

Lac Inférieur

Cimetière
de Passy

Q d'Orsay   Q Anatole F

15

Racing
Club de
France

Ave Henri
Martin

Av Paul Doumer

7e

Faubourg
St Germain

Hippodrome
de Longchamp

Garde
Républicaine
Cheval

Av Henri Martin

16e

Q. Branly

Eiffel
Tower

Av de la Bourdonnais

Blvd St-Ge

**Bois de
Boulogne**

La
Muette Ⓜ

Q. de Grenelle

Blvd des Invalides

Étang de
Boulogne

Lac
Supérieur

BoulainVilliers 🚉

Ranelagh Ⓜ

Blvd Suchet

Blvd Grenelle

R. de Sèvres

Le
Bar

A13

9

Hippodrome
d'Auteuil

Jasmin Ⓜ

Blvd Grenelle

Blvd Garibald

R. de Sèvres

Porte
d'Auteuil Ⓜ

Michel
Ange
Auteuil Ⓜ

Église
d'Auteuil Ⓜ

R. la Fontaine

Javel Ⓜ

Necker

Stade
Roland
Garros

13

Michel Ange
Molitor Ⓜ

Q. de Grenelle

R. de la Croix Nivert

Gare
Montparnasse

30

15e

R. Lecourbe

Stade
Jean Bouin

Chardon
Lagache Ⓜ

R. de Lourmel

Av de Maur

Parc
des
Princes

Exelmans Ⓜ

R. de la Convention

Ancien
Cimetière Ⓜ

Ⓜ Ⓜ Porte de
St Cloud

Boulevard
Victor

Blvd Victor

Cimetière
de
Vaugirard

See Central Paris - SW Map (pp100-1)

Billancourt Ⓜ

Marcel
Sembat Ⓜ

Nouveau
Cimetière

Issy-
Val-de-
Seine Ⓜ

Blvd Péripherique

Porte de
Versailles Ⓜ

2

Pernety Ⓜ

N10

Pont de
Sèvres Ⓜ

Centre Sportif
Suzanne
Lenglen

Blvd Lefebvre

Plaisance Ⓜ

14e

Stade de
la Porte de
la Plaine

Porte
de Vanves Ⓜ

Île
Seguin

Île St
Germain

Stade
Jean
Bouin

Stade
G. Voisin

Corentin
Celton Ⓜ

Stade Charles
Rigoulot
(Centre Sportif) 25

Stade
Didot

Stade
Jules
Noël

Île de
Billancourt

Seine

Q. de Stalingrad

Jacques
Henri
Lartigue

Mairie d'Issy Ⓜ

Malakoff
Plateau
de Vanves Ⓜ

Por
d'Orlea
Cimetière
de
Montrouge

🚉 Issy Ville

André
Roche

Cimetière
des Longs
Réages

Malakoff
Rue E Dolet Ⓜ

Chatillon Montrouge Ⓜ

INFORMATION
American Hospital in Paris.........................1 B1
Bureau des Objets Trouvés........................2 C5
Hertford British Hospital...........................3 C1
SOS Dentaire..4 E5

SIGHTS & ACTIVITIES   (pp113-32)
Bibliothèque Nationale de France -
  François Mitterrand...............................5 F5
Catacombes..6 E5
Cité de la Musique...................................7 G1
Cité des Sciences et de l'Industrie............8 G1
Hippodrome d'Auteuil..............................9 B4
Manufacture des Gobelins......................10 E5
Musée de la Musique..........................(see 7)
Parc de Bercy..11 G5

Porte de Choisy.....................................12 F6
Stade Roland Garros..............................13 B4

SLEEPING   ⬆ (pp136-47)
Auberge de Jeunesse Le D'Artagnan......14 H3
Camping du Bois de Boulogne...............15 A3
Hôtel de Blois.......................................16 D5
Petit Palace Hôtel..................................17 D5

EATING   🍽 (pp147-58)
L'Avant-Goût...18 F5
La Fleuve de Chine.................................19 F6
Sinorama..20 F5

ENTERTAINMENT   🙂 (pp160-7)
Ateliers Berthier....................................21 D1

Cité de la Musique Box Office................22 G2
Le Batofar..23 G5
Le Zénith..24 G1

SHOPPING   🛍 (pp167-70)
Marché aux Puces de la Porte de
  Vanves...25 D5
Marché aux Puces de Montreuil.............26 H4
Marché aux Puces de St Ouen...............27 E1
Musée & Compagnie.............................28 G5

TRANSPORT   (pp170-6)
Gare Routière Internationale de Paris
  Galliéni...29 H3
Rent a Car Système...............................30 B4

INFORMATION
American Express....................................(see 14)
Art Nouveau Toilets................................ 1 G5
Belgian Embassy..................................... 2 C4
British Consulate..................................... 3 G5
British Embassy....................................... 4 F5
Bureau de Change................................... 5 E5
Canadian Embassy................................... 6 E5
École de Gastronomie Française Ritz
  Escoffier... 7 G5
École Lenôtre.. 8 F5
Espace IGN... 9 E5
German Embassy.................................... 10 E5
Irish Embassy.. 11 C4
Japanese Embassy................................. 12 D3
New Zealand Embassy........................... 13 B5
Paris Convention & Visitors Bureau...... 14 H4
Paris Convention & Visitors Bureau
  (Main Branch)...................................... 15 H6
Pharmacie des Champs.......................... 16 D4
Spanish Embassy................................... 17 D5
Thomas Cook Exchange Office............... 18 D4
US Consulate... 19 G5
US Embassy... 20 G5

SIGHTS & ACTIVITIES   (pp113-32)
Arc de Triomphe.................................... 21 C5
Bateaux Mouches................................... 22 E6
Colonne Vendôme.................................. 23 H5
Église de la Madeleine........................... 24 G5
Flame of Liberty Memorial..................... 25 D6
Galerie Nationale du Jeu de Paume...... 26 G6
Galeries du Panthéon Bouddhique du
  Japon et de la Chine........................... 27 C5
Galeries Nationales du Grand Palais..... 28 F6
Grand Palais..................................(see 28)
Hôtel de la Marine................................ 29 G5

L'Open Tour.. 30 H4
Musée de l'Opéra.................................. 31 H4
Musée de l'Orangerie............................ 32 G6
Musée des Beaux-Arts de la Ville
  de Paris.. 33 F6
Musée Guimet des Arts Asiatiques........ 34 C6
Obélisk... 35 G6
Palais de l'Élysée.................................. 36 F5
Palais Garnier.................................(see 31)
Palais de la Découverte......................... 37 E5
Petit Palais.....................................(see 33)

SLEEPING   (pp136-47)
Hôtel Langlois....................................... 38 H3
Hôtel Britannia..................................... 39 G3
Hôtel Costes... 40 H5
Hôtel de Crillon.................................... 41 G5
Hôtel Eldorado...................................... 42 G2
Hôtel Ritz Paris..................................... 43 H5

EATING   (pp147-58)
Champs-Élysées Bistro Romain.............. 44 D4
L'Ardoise.. 45 G5
Le Roi du Pot au Feu............................ 46 G4
Lina's... 47 G5
Monoprix Supermarket.......................... 48 H5
Monoprix Supermarket.......................... 49 E5
P'tit Bouchon Gourmand....................... 50 C4

DRINKING   (pp158-60)
Bushwacker's.. 51 H5
Harry's New York Bar............................ 52 H5

ENTERTAINMENT   (pp160-7)
Crazy Horse.. 53 D6
Fnac Champs-Élysées............................. 54 E5
Kiosque Théâtre.................................... 55 G5

Le Lido de Paris.................................... 56 D4
Palais Garnier Box Office.................(see 31)
Salle Pleyel.. 57 D3
Théâtre Mogador.................................. 58 H4
Virgin Megastore Champs-Élysées......... 59 E5

SHOPPING   (pp167-70)
Boutique Maille..................................... 60 G5
Boutique PSG.. 61 E5
Colette... 62 H6
Fauchon... 63 G5
Fauchon... 64 G5
Fromagerie Alléosse.............................. 65 C3
Galeries Lafayette................................. 66 H4
Galeries Lafayette................................. 67 H4
Le Printemps de l'Homme...................... 68 H4
Le Printemps de la Beauté
  et Maison.. 69 H4
Le Printemps de la Mode....................... 70 H4
Les Caves Augé..................................... 71 F4
Réciproque... 72 A6
Réciproque... 73 A6

TRANSPORT   (pp170-6)
ADA.. 74 G3
Air France Buses................................... 75 C4
Batobus Stop.. 76 E6
Buses from Beauvais Airport.................. 77 B3
Buses to Beauvais Airport...................... 78 B3
easyCar.. 79 H5
Roissybus... 80 H4

OTHER
Charles de Gaulle Statue....................... 81 F5
Église St Roch....................................... 82 H6
Ministère de la Justice........................... 83 H5
Palais des Congrès de Paris................... 84 B3

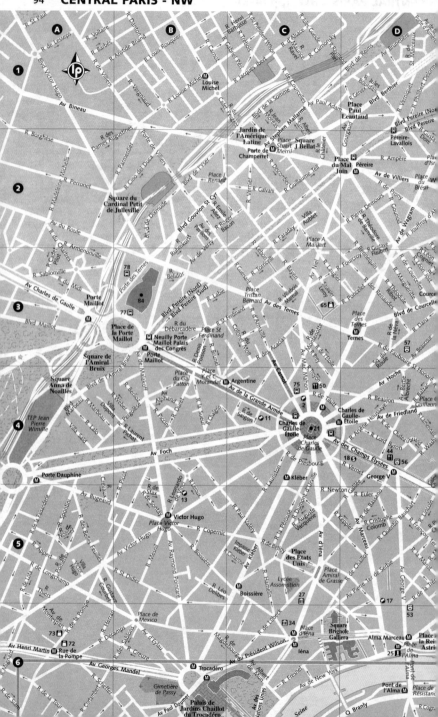

0 — 400 m
0 — 0.2 miles

E **F** **G** **H**

Square Carpeaux

See Montmartre Map (pp108)

Brochant **M**

Cimetière de Montmartre

1

Square des Batignolles

La Fourche **M**

Place de Clichy

Blanche **M**

Blvd de Clichy

Place Blanche

2

Rome **M**

Blvd des Batignolles

Villiers **M**

Place P. Goubaux

Square Berlioz

Place de la République Dominicaine

Monceau **M**

Europe **M**

Place de l'Europe

Liège **M**

Place de Budapest

Trinité **M**

Square d'Estienne d'Orves

Place d'Estienne d'Orves

38

3

Parc de Monceau

R Murillo

Gare St Lazare

St Lazare **M**

R St Lazare

39

R de la Victoire

Square M Pagnol

58

Blvd Haussmann

Place St Augustin **M** St Augustin

71

Square Louis XVI

Blvd Haussmann

R Joubert

68

R de Provence

66 **67**

Place Chassaigne-Goyon

Miromesnil **M**

Havre Caumartin **M**

69 **70**

Auber **R** Place Diaghilev

Chaussée d'Antin **M**

4

St Philippe du Roule **M**

Place Beauvau

14 Auber

30

Place Edouard VIII

Place Ch Garnier

Opéra **M**

Place J Rouché

31

59

49

9

61

Franklin D Roosevelt **M**

Rond Point Champs-Elysée Marcel Dassault

36

4

Place de la Madeleine

Madeleine **M** de la Madeleine blvd

55

24

63

3

51

Blvd des Capucines

Place de l'Opéra

See pp96-7

J

5

Triangle d'Or

Champs-Elysées Clemenceau

Av des Champs Elysées

81

Av Gabriel

60

1

29

41

Place de la Concorde

Concorde **M**

19

47

45

R du Mont Thabor

40

Place Vendôme

Right Bank

43

83 **23**

52

48

Pyramides **M**

15

62 **82**

J

10

37

Grand Palais

28

133

8

Av Edward Tuck

26

R de Rivoli

Tuileries **M**

Place François 1er

35

32

Jardin des Tuileries

Place des Pyramides

6

Port de la Conférence

76

See pp100-1

Seine

Q des Tuileries

Q d'Orsay

Place de Finlande

Invalides

Assemblée Nationale

Q Anatole France

INFORMATION
C'Clean Laverie..................................... 1 E6
Club Alpin Française............................. 2 G2
Cours de Cuisine Françoise Meunier.... 3 B5
FFRP Information Centre & Bookshop....4 F1
Forum Voyages..................................... 5 A6
Laverie Libre Service............................ 6 D6
Laverie Libre Service Primus................ 7 F5
Laverie SBS.. 8 C4
Main Post Office................................... 9 B6
Nouvelles Frontières........................... 10 A6
Paris Convention & Visitors Bureau..... 11 D3
Voyageurs du Monde........................... 12 A5

SIGHTS & ACTIVITIES   (pp113-32)
Louis XIV Memorial.............................. 13 B6
Maison de l'Air.................................... 14 G4
Musée des Arts et Métiers................... 15 C6
Musée Grévin...................................... 16 B4
Oldest House in Paris (3 Rue Volta)..... 17 D6
Paris Canal Croisières.......................... 18 F2
Passage des Panoramas....................... 19 B5
Passage Jouffroy.................................. 20 B4
Passage Verdeau.................................. 21 B4

SLEEPING   (pp136-47)
Auberge de Jeunesse Jules Ferry......... 22 E5
Grand Hôtel de Paris........................... 23 D4
Hôtel Chopin....................................... 24 B4
Hôtel des Arts..................................... 25 B4
Hôtel Favart.. 26 A5
Hôtel Français..................................... 27 D4
Hôtel La Vieille France........................ 28 D3
Hôtel les Trois Poussins....................... 29 A3
Hôtel Peletier-Haussmann Opéra........ 30 A4
Nord Hôtel.. 31 C3
Nord-Est Hôtel.................................... 32 C3
Peace & Love Hostel............................ 33 E2

Sibour Hôtel.. 34 D4
Woodstock Hostel................................ 35 B3

EATING   (pp147-58)
404... 36 C6
Baan Boran... 37 A5
Chez Papa/Espace Sud-Ouest............. 38 E2
Chinese Noodle Shops & Restaurants.. 39 D6
Food Shops.. 40 A3
Food Shops.. 41 C5
Franprix Faubourg St Denis Branch...... 42 C5
Franprix Jean Pierre Timbaud Branch...43 E6
Franprix Jules Ferry Branch.................. 44 E5
Franprix Magenta Branch..................... 45 D4
Fromagerie.. 46 C4
Gare du Nord Buffalo Grill................... 47 C3
Jewish & North African Kosher
    Restaurants..................................... 48 B4
Juan et Juanita.................................... 49 F5
Julien.. 50 C5
Krung Thep.. 51 G4
Kunitoraya... 52 A5
L'Arbre à Cannelle............................... 53 B4
L'Ave Maria... 54 F6
Le Chansonnier................................... 55 E3
Le Villaret... 56 F6
Les Ailes... 57 B4
Lina's.. 58 A6
New Nioullaville................................. 59 F5
Opéra Hippopotamus.......................... 60 A5
Pooja.. 61 C4
Roi du Kashmir.................................... 62 C4
Shalimar.. 63 C5
Terminus Nord..................................... 64 C3
Wally le Saharien................................ 65 B3

DRINKING   (pp158-60)
Cannibale Café.................................... 66 G5

Chez Prune.. 67 E4
Chez Wolf Motown Bar........................ 68 D4
L'Autre Café... 69 F5

ENTERTAINMENT   (pp160-7)
Chez Adel.. 70 E4
Cinémathèque Française....................... 71 C5
Gibus.. 72 E5
La Champmeslé.................................... 73 A5
La Favela Chic..................................... 74 E5
La Java.. 75 F5
Le Cithéa... 76 G6
Le Limonaire....................................... 77 B4
Le Nouveau Casino.............................. 78 F6
Le Pulp.. 79 B5
Le Scorp.......................................(see 79)
New Morning.. 80 C4
Opus... 81 E3
Rex Club.. 82 B5

SHOPPING   (pp167-70)
Anna Joliet.. 83 A6
Kiliwatch... 84 B6
Marché Belleville................................. 85 G5
Marché St-Quentin............................... 86 C3
Rue Montorgueil Market....................... 87 B6

TRANSPORT   (pp170-6)
ADA... 88 F6
RATP Bus No 350 to Charles de Gaulle
    Airport.. 89 D3
RATP Bus No 350 to Charles de Gaulle
    Airport.. 90 D4
Rent A Car Système............................. 91 C3

OTHER
Porte St-Denis..................................... 92 C5
Porte St-Martin.................................... 93 C5

INFORMATION
Alliance Française... 1 H4
American Church in Paris............................2 E1
Australian Embassy...................................... 3 C2
Centre des Étudiants....................................4 E4
Centre Régional Information Jeunesse....5 C2
Dutch Embassy..6 F4
École Le Cordon Bleu..................................7 D6
Italian Embassy...8 G3
Paris Convention & Visitors Bureau........9 C2
South African Embassy..............................10 E1
Swiss Embassy..11 F2
Tea & Tattered Pages.................................12 F4

SIGHTS & ACTIVITIES (pp113-32)
Bike 'n' Roller..13 E2
Cimetière du Montparnasse....................14 G5
Cimetière du Montparnasse Conservation
  Office..(see 14)
Église du Dôme..15 F2
Église St-Louis des Invalides.....................16 F2
Eiffel Tower...17 C2
Fat Tire Bike Tours......................................18 C3
Fat Tire Bike Tours Starting Point...........19 C2
Hôtel Matignon...20 G2
Ministère des Affaires Étrangères...........21 F1

Musée d'Orsay...22 G1
Musée de l'Armée..23 F2
Musée de l'Homme................................(see 24)
Musée de la Marine......................................24 B1
Musée des Égouts de Paris.................25 D1
Musée Rodin..26 F2
Palais de Chaillot...27 B1
Paris Canal Croisières...................................28 G1
Rucher du Luxembourg (Apiary).............29 H4
Tombeau de Napoléon 1er..................(see 15)
Tour Montparnasse.................................... 30 G5

SLEEPING (pp136-47)
Accueil Familial des Jeunes Étrangers.... 31 H3
Celtic Hôtel..32 G5
Hôtel de Danemark.....................................33 H5
Hôtel de Paris...34 G5
Hôtel Delambre..35 G5
Hôtel Lenox St Germain............................ 36 H2

EATING (pp147-58)
Blvd Edgar Quinet Food Market...........37 G5
Brasserie Lipp...38 H3
Creperies..39 G5
Dix Vins...40 F5
Franprix Delambre......................................41 H5

Franprix Supermarket................................42 G5
Inno Supermarket.......................................43 G5
La Coupole..44 H5
Le Dôme..45 H5
Mustang Café...46 G5

DRINKING (p159)
Cubana Café...47 H5

ENTERTAINMENT (pp160-7)
Cinémathèque Française............................48 C1
Kiosque Théâtre..49 G5
Red Light...50 G5
Théâtre du Vieux Colombier...................51 H3

SHOPPING (pp167-70)
Le Bon Marché...52 G3
Rue Cler Market...53 E2

TRANSPORT (pp170-6)
Air France Buses..54 G5
Air France Buses..55 F1
Aérogare des Invalides...............................56 F1
Batobus Stop..57 C1
Batobus Stop.......................................(see 28)
easyCar...58 F6

Rue de la Pompe
R. Greuze
R. Decamps
Av. Georges Mandel
Trocadéro
Av. du Président Wilson
Iéna
Place de l'Alma
Pont de l'Alma
A
B
Place du Trocadéro et du 11 Novembre
Cimetière de Passy
C
Av. d'Iéna
Av. Albert de Mun
R. Fresnel
Av. de New York
D
27
Jardins du Trocadéro
48
Place de la Résistance
R. Cognacq
Pont de l'Alma
25

1
Villa Guibert
R. de la Tour
R. Louis David
Place de Varsovie
24
R. Scheffer
R. Vineuse
R. Benjamin Franklin
Jardins du Trocadéro
Av. des Nations Unies
See pp94-5
R. Cognac
Cité de l'Alma
Av. Franco Russe

R. Nicolo
Av. Paul Doumer
R. Eugène Manuel
Place de Costa Rica
Blvd Delessert
Pont d'Iéna
57
Allée Paul Deschanel
Av. de Montessuy
R. St Valentin
R. Dupont

2
Boulain Villiers
R. Bois le Vent
R. de Passy
Square Charles Dickens
Passy
R. Raynouard
9
12
Eiffel Tower
Eiffel Tower
Av. Gustave Eiffel
R. Edgar Faure
19
Place Jacques Rueff
Parc du Champ de Mars

R. Singer
R. Alfred Bruneau
R. Vignes
R. des Marronniers
R. de l'Annonciation
R. René Boylesve
Champ de Mars-Tour Eiffel
Stade Émile Anthoine
5
R. Jean Rey
3
R. Charles Floquet
Allée Thomy Thierry
Av. Pierre Loti
Av. Anatole France

3
Maison de Radio France
R. Gros
R. Félicien David
Av. de Versailles
Kennedy Radio-France
Q. de Grenelle
R. du Docteur Finlay
Blvd de Grenelle
Place A Sauvy
18
Place Dupleix
Dupleix
Av. de Suffren
Av. de la Motte Picquet

Place de Brazzaville
R. Nélaton
R. Sextius Michel
R. St Charles
R. Viala
R. Juge
R. Fondary
R. Tiphaine
La Motte Picquet Grenelle
Square Cambronne
Place Cambronne
Cambronne

4
Javel
Rond Point du Pont Mirabeau
Q. André Citroën
R. de Lourmel
Square Pablo Casals
Place St Charles
R. Ginoux
Av. Émile Zola
Charles Michels
Av. Émile Zola
R. du Théâtre
Avenue Émile Zola
R. Frémicourt
R. Letellier

5
Square des Cévennes
Parc André Citroën
Cimetière de Grenelle
Rond Point St Charles
R. de la Convention
Jardin Duranton
Boucicaut
Place du Commerce
Commerce
Place Violet
Square Violet
Félix Faure
Square St Lambert
Square Gerbert
Place et Square Adolphe Chérioux
Vaugirard

6
Balard
Av. Félix Faure
Place Balard
Balard
Blvd du Général Martial Valin
Lourmel
Cimetière de Vaugirard
R. de la Croix Nivert
Convention
R. Lecourbe
R. Dombasle
7

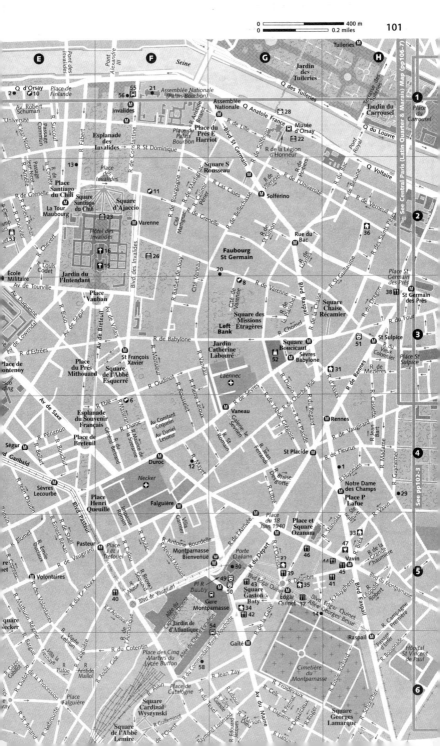

0 — 400 m
0 — 0.2 miles

See Central Paris (Latin Quarter & Marais) Map (pp106-7)

Tuileries M

Jardin des Tuileries

Q des Tuileries

Jardin du Carrousel

Place du Carrousel

Pont des Invalides

Pont Alexandre III

Seine

E · F · G · H

Q d'Orsay   Place de Finlande
2 ● · 10 ●

56 ● · 55 · 21 ●   Assemblée Nationale (Palais Bourbon)

Invalides M

Av. Robert Schuman

Assemblée Nationale   Q Anatole France   28

R Aristide Briand

Musée d'Orsay   22

Q du Louvre

Pont Royal

Jardin du Carrousel

1

Place du Carrousel

'Université   Q Surcouf   R Fabert   R de Constantine
R Jean Nico   Passage Commun

13 ●   Place des Invalides

R St Dominique   Place du Palais Bourbon   Place du Prés E Harriot   R de Lille   Blvd St Germain   R de Solférino   R de la Légion d'Honneur

Q du Bac   Q Voltaire

Place de Grenelle   R de Bourgogne   Square S Rousseau   R de Villersexel   R de Poitiers   R du Bac   R de Beaune   R des Saints Pères

Esplanade des Invalides

Place de Finlande

Q 11   Square d'Ajaccio   R Las Cases   R Casimir Perier   Solférino M   R de l'Université   R de Verneuil

2

Place du Chili   Square Santiago du Chili   23

La Tour Maubourg M   Varenne M   Clé de Martignac   R de Bellechasse   R de Lille   R de Grenelle

Hôtel des Invalides   16   15   26

R de Cléry   Louis Codet   Jardin de l'Intendant

R de Constantine   R de Talleyrand   R de Bourgogne

Rue du Bac M   36

R St Guillaume   R de Beaune

Place St Germain des Prés   38   St Germain des Prés M

Varenne M   20   8   R de Varenne   Blvd Raspail   R de Chaise

R de Grenelle   Cité de Varenne   Faubourg St Germain

R du Dragon   R du Four

3

École Militaire   Place Vauban

Av de Tourville   Av Duquesne   Blvd des Invalides

Square des Missions Étrangères   Square Chaise Récamier

St Sulpice M   51   R du Vieux Colombier   R de Mézières   Place St Sulpice

'lace de ontenoy   Place du Prés Mithouard   St François Xavier M   Square de l'Abbé Esquerré   R de Babylone   Jardin Catherine Labouré   R de Chomel

Square Boucicaut   Sèvres Babylone M   52   31   R de Rennes   R d'Assas

R de Sèvres

R Oudinot

Laennec +

Av de Saxe   R Eblé   6   R Duroc   Au Constant Coquelin   R Pierre Leroux   R Rousselet   Vaneau M   R de l'Abbé Grégoire   R du Cherche Midi   R du Regard   Rennes M   R de Vaugirard

Esplanade du Souvenir Français

Place de Breteuil

Av de Breteuil   R Duroc   R Mizon   Au Daniel Lesueur   Galerie la Sévres   R St Romain   St Placide M   R de Fleurus

Duroc M   12 ●

4

Ségur M   'd Garibaldi   Blvd Garibaldi   R Bargue

Place Henri Queuille

Necker +

Falguière M

1 ●   R Huysmans   Notre Dame des Champs M   Place P Lafue   29 ●

Sèvres Lecourbe M   Blvd Pasteur

Place du 18 Juin 1940   Place et Square Ozanam   33   47   R de la Grande Chaumière

5

M Volontaires   Pasteur M   Place J et I Trefouel   R Antoine Bourdelle   Montparnasse Bienvenüe M   Porte Océane   Place du Départ   37   46   Vavin M   45   41

R de Vaugirard   30 ●   39   43   35   Blvd Edgar Quinet   Blvd du Montparnasse

40   49   Square Gaston Baty   Edgar Quinet M   37   Allée Georges Besse   14 ●

50   Gare Montparnasse   34   42   Blvd Edgar Quinet   Raspail M

Jardin de l'Atlantique   54

quare ecker   Gaîté M

Hôpital St Vincent de Paul

6

Place des Cinq Martyrs du Lycée Buffon   58   R Jean Zay   Cimetière du Montparnasse

Square Cardinal Wyszynski   Place de Catalogne

Square de l'Abbé Lemire   Square Georges Lamarque

See Central Paris (Latin Quarter & Marais) Map (pp106-7)

See pp100-1

See pp100-1

INFORMATION
Centre Gai et Lesbien...................... 1 F3
Forum Voyages............................... 2 C4
Hôpital de la Salpêtrie Emergency
   Entrance.................................... 3 D6
Hôpital de la Salpêtrière................. 4 E6
Laverie Libre Service...................... 5 B4
Laverie Libre Service...................... 6 C4
Laverie Miele Libre Service............. 7 F3
Le Bateau Lavoir (Laundrette)........ 8 C4
Maison des Femmes....................... 9 G4
OTU Voyages Branch..................... 10 A5
Paris Convention & Visitor Bureau...... 11 F4
XS Arena Luxembourg.................... 12 B4

SIGHTS & ACTIVITIES   (pp113-32)
Chapelle de la Sorbonne............... 13 B4
Cimetière du Père Lachaise
   Conservation Office................... 14 H2
Colonne de Juillet......................... 15 E3
École de Botanique....................... 16 D5
Galerie d'Anatomie Comparée et de
   Paléontologie............................ 17 D5
Galerie de Botanique.................... 18 D5
Galerie de Minéralogie, de Géologie
   et de Paléobotanie.................... 19 D5
Gepetto & Vélos (Bicycle Hire)...... 20 C4
Grand Bassin (Bassin du Luxembourg).. 21 A4
Grande Galerie de l'Évolution........ 22 D5
Institut du Monde Arabe............... 23 D4
Jardin Alpin................................. 24 D5
Jardin d'Hiver (Serres Tropicales).... 25 D5
Maison de Victor Hugo.................. 26 E2
Ménagerie du Jardin des Plantes.... 27 D4
Ménagerie Entrance...................... 28 D4
Mosquée de Paris......................... 29 C5
Musée du Luxembourg.................. 30 A4
Nomades..................................... 31 E3
Palais du Luxembourg (Sénat)........ 32 A4
Panthéon..................................... 33 B4
Paris à Vélo, C'est Sympa!............. 34 C3
Sorbonne.................................... 35 B3

SLEEPING   🏠 (pp136-47)
Blue Planet Hostel........................ 36 F4

Centre International BVJ Paris-
   Quartier Latin............................ 37 C4
Comfort Inn Mouffetard................ 38 C5
Familia Hôtel................................ 39 C4
Grand Hôtel du Progrès................ 40 B5
Grand Hôtel St Michel................... 41 B4
Hôtel Baudelaire Bastille................ 42 F3
Hôtel Beaumarchais....................... 43 E1
Hôtel Castex................................. 44 E3
Hôtel Cluny Sorbonne................... 45 B4
Hôtel de l'Espérance..................... 46 C6
Hôtel de la Herse d'Or................... 47 E3
Hôtel de la Place des Vosges......... 48 E2
Hôtel des Grand Écoles................. 49 C4
Hôtel du Panthéon....................... 50 B4
Hôtel Gay Lussac.......................... 51 B5
Hôtel La Demeure......................... 52 D6
Hôtel Lyon Mulhouse.................... 53 E2
Hôtel Minerve.............................. 54 C4
Hôtel Royal Bastille....................... 55 F3
Hôtel St Christophe....................... 56 C5
Hôtel St Jacques........................... 57 B4
Maison Internationale des Jeunes
   pour la Culture et la Paix............ 58 H3
Young & Happy Hostel.................. 59 C5

EATING   🍴 (pp147-58)
Bofinger...................................... 60 E3
Caves St-Gilles............................. 61 E2
Champion Supermarket.................. 62 C4
Chez Léna et Mimille..................... 63 C5
Coffee India................................. 64 F3
Crêpes Show................................ 65 F3
Ed l'Épicier Supermarket................ 66 C5
Fauchon...................................... 67 E3
Founti Agadir............................... 68 C5
Franprix Supermarket.................... 69 C5
Grand Appétit.............................. 70 E3
Indonesia.................................... 71 A4
La Petit Légume........................... 72 C4
La Piragua................................... 73 G1
Le Bistrot du Dôme Bastille............ 74 E3
Le C'Amelot................................. 75 E2
Le Clown Bar............................... 76 E1
Le Foyer du Vietnam..................... 77 C5

Le Square Trousseau...................... 78 F3
Le Vigneron................................. 79 C5
Les Galopins................................ 80 F2
Les Quatre et Une Saveurs............. 81 C4
Monoprix Bastille.......................... 82 F3
Mosquée de Paris Restaurant &
   Tearoom Entrance...................... 83 D5
Perraudin.................................... 84 B4
Place Monge Food Market............. 85 C5
Rue Mouffetard Food Market......... 86 C5
Tao... 87 B5
Tashi Delek.................................. 88 B4
Waly Fay...................................... 89 G2

DRINKING   🍷 (pp158-60)
Barrio Latino................................ 90 F3
Café des Phares............................ 91 E3
Le Salon Egyptien......................... 92 C4
Le Vieux Chêne............................ 93 C5
Piano Vache................................. 94 C4

ENTERTAINMENT   🎭 (pp160-7)
Café de la Danse.......................... 95 F3
Église Royale du Val-de-Grâce........ 96 B5
Fnac Musique Bastille.................... 97 E3
Le Balajo..................................... 98 F3
Le Bataclan.................................. 99 F1
Opéra Bastille.............................. 100 E3
Opéra Bastille Box Office............... 101 E3

SHOPPING   🛍 (pp167-70)
Marché Bastille............................ 102 E2
Rue Mouffetard Market................(see 86)

TRANSPORT   (pp170-6)
Batobus Stop............................... 103 D4
Rent A Car Système....................... 104 G6

OTHER
Arènes de Lutèce.......................... 105 C4
Cirque d'Hiver.............................. 106 E1
Église St Étienne du Mont.............. 107 C4
Fontaine de l'Observatoire............. 108 A5

INFORMATION
Abbey Bookshop................................. 1 C5
Access Academy.................................. 2 B5
Akyrion Net Center............................. 3 G4
Best Change.. 4 C2
Cyberbe@ubourg Internet C@fé........ 5 E2
Espace du Tourisme d'Île de France....(see 31)
Hôtel Dieu (Hospital).......................... 6 E4
Hôtel Dieu Emergency Entrance........ 7 D4
Julice Laverie...................................... 8 B5
Julice Laverie...................................... 9 B5
Laverie Libre Service........................ 10 B2
Laverie Libre Service........................ 11 G3
Laverie Libre Service........................ 12 F3
Laverie Libre Service Primus............ 13 G4
Le Change du Louvre........................ 14 B2
Les Mots à la Bouche........................ 15 F3
Nouvelles Frontières......................... 16 C5
OTU Voyages...................................... 17 E2
Pharmacie Bader................................ 18 C5
Pharmacie des Halles......................... 19 D3
Red Wheelbarrow Bookstore............ 20 H5
Salon d'Accueil (Hôtel de Ville)........ 21 E4
Shakespeare & Company.................. 22 D5
Société Touristique de Services (STS)
    Exchange Office............................. 23 C5
Village Voice...................................... 24 A5
Web 46... 25 G4
XS Arena Les Halles........................... 26 E2

SIGHTS & ACTIVITIES   (pp113-32)
16th-Century Half-Timbered Houses.... 27 F4
Arc de Triomphe du Carrousel.......... 28 A2
Atelier Brancusi................................. 29 E2
Bibliothèque Publique d'Information
    Entrance....................................... 30 E2
Carrousel du Louvre Entrance........... 31 A2
Conseil d'État.................................... 32 B1
Défenseur du Temps Mechanical Clock. 33 E2
Église St Paul-St Louis....................... 34 G4
Église St-Eustache............................. 35 D1
Église St-Germain des Prés............... 36 A5
Église St-Louis-en-l'Île...................... 37 G6
Église St-Sulpice................................ 38 A6
Fontaine des Innocents...................... 39 D2
Forêt de la Licorne............................ 40 C6
Grande Pyramide................................ 41 A2
Hôtel de Ville Exhibition Entrance.....42 E3
Institut de France.............................. 43 B3
Inverted Glass Pyramid...................... 44 A2
Maison Européenne de la
    Photographie................................ 45 G4
Maison Roue Libre (Bicycle Rental).....46 D2
Mechanical Fountains........................ 47 E3
Medieval House (51 Rue de
    Montmorency)............................... 48 F1
Monoprix Supermarket...................... 49 A5
Musée Carnavalet............................... 50 H3
Musée d'Art et d'Histoire du Judaïsme..51 F2
Musée de la Mode et du Textile....... 52 A1
Musée de la Publicité........................(see 52)
Musée des Arts Décoratifs................(see 52)
Musée du Louvre................................ 53 B2
Musée National du Moyen Âge......... 54 C6
Musée Nationale d'Art Moderne....... 55 E2
Musée Picasso.................................... 56 H2
Notre Dame Cathedral....................... 57 E5
Notre Dame North Tower Entrance.... 58 E5
Point Zéro des Routes de France....... 59 E5
Ste Chapelle...................................... 60 D4

Tour de l'Horloge.............................. 61 D4
Tour St Jacques................................. 62 D3

SLEEPING   (pp136-47)
Centre International BVJ Paris-Louvre...63 C1
Grand Hôtel Malher........................... 64 G4
Hôtel Axial Beaubourg...................... 65 E3
Hôtel Caron de Beaumarchais............ 66 F4
Hôtel Central Marais......................... 67 F3
Hôtel d'Angleterre............................ 68 A4
Hôtel de la Bretonnerie.................... 69 F3
Hôtel de Lille Pélican....................... 70 B1
Hôtel de Lutèce................................. 71 F5
Hôtel de Nesle................................... 72 B4
Hôtel de Nice.................................... 73 F4
Hôtel des Deux Continents................ 74 A4
Hôtel des Deux Îles.......................... 75 F5
Hôtel des Marronniers...................... 76 A4
Hôtel du Globe.................................. 77 B5
Hôtel du Septième Art...................... 78 H5
Hôtel du Vieux Saule........................ 79 H1
Hôtel Esmeralda................................ 80 D5
Hôtel Henri IV.................................... 81 D5
Hôtel Henri IV.................................... 82 C4
Hôtel Jeanne d'Arc............................ 83 H4
Hôtel Le Compostelle....................... 84 F4
Hôtel Pratic....................................... 85 H4
Hôtel Relais Christine....................... 86 B4
Hôtel Rivoli....................................... 87 F4
Hôtel Saintonge Marais.................... 88 H2
Hôtel St Honoré................................ 89 C2
Hôtel St Merry.................................. 90 E3
Hôtel St-Louis Marais....................... 91 H5
L'Hôtel.. 92 A4
La Villa St-Germain des Prés............. 93 A4
MIJE Le Fauconnier........................... 94 G5
MIJE Le Fourcy.................................. 95 G4
MIJE Maubuisson............................... 96 F4
Mélia Colbert Boutique Hotel........... 97 D5

EATING   (pp147-58)
Amorino.. 98 B5
Berthillon.. 99 F5
Bouillon Racine............................... 100 C6
Brasserie de l'Isle St-Louis.............. 101 F5
Café Marly....................................... 102 A2
Champion Supermarket.................... 103 B5
Chez Albert...................................... 104 B4
Chez Marianne................................. 105 G3
Chez Nénesse................................... 106 G3
Crèmerie des Carmes (Fromagerie)...(see 133)
Ed l'Epicier Supermarket................. 107 G3
Food Shops.......................................(see 133)
Franprix Châtelet............................. 108 D3
Franprix Marais................................ 109 G3
Franprix Supermarket....................... 110 G5
Franprix Supermarket....................... 111 G4
Franprix Supermarket....................... 112 C2
Fromagerie G Millet......................... 113 H4
Guen Maï.. 114 A5
Joe Allen... 115 E1
L'Alivi... 116 F4
L'Ambassade d'Auvergne................. 117 F1
L'Arbuci.. 118 B5
L'As de Felafel................................. 119 G3
L'Enoteca... 120 G5
L'Épi d'Or.. 121 C1
La Charlotte en l'Île......................... 122 G5
La Perla.. 123 F4
La Soummam.................................... 124 B5

Le Golfe de Naples.......................... 125 A5
Le Mâchon d'Henri.......................... 126 A5
Le Petit Mâchon.............................. 127 B2
Le Petit Picard................................. 128 F3
Le Réconfort.................................... 129 G2
Les Halles Léon de Bruxelles........... 130 D1
Monoprix Supermarket.................... 131 H4
Piccolo Teatro.................................. 132 G4
Place Maubert Market...................... 133 D6
Polidor... 134 B6
Supermarché G20............................ 135 G4
Tea Caddy... 136 D5

DRINKING   (pp158-60)
Au Petit Fer à Cheval...................... 137 G3
Café de Flore.................................... 138 A5
Jokko Bar... 139 G3
L'Apparement Café.......................... 140 H2
Le 10.. 141 B6
Le Fumoir... 142 C2
Les Deux Magots............................. 143 A5
Papou Lounge.................................. 144 B2
Quiet Man.. 145 G2
Stolly's Stone Bar............................ 146 F4

ENTERTAINMENT   (pp160-7)
Bliss Kfé... 147 G4
Châtelet-Théâtre Musical de Paris... 148 D3
Comédie Française........................... 149 A1
Comédie Française Discount Ticket
    Window....................................... 150 A1
Comédie Française Studio Théâtre....(see 31)
Fnac Forum des Halles..................... 151 D2
Le Baiser Salé.................................. 152 D2
Le Caveau de la Huchette................ 153 D5
Le Dépôt.. 154 E1
Le Wagg... 155 B4
Les Bains.. 156 E1
Odéon Théâtre de l'Europe.............. 157 B6
Open Café... 158 F3
Point Virgule.................................... 159 F3
Virgin Megastore Carrousel du
    Louvre...(see 31)

SHOPPING   (pp167-70)
Aboud'Abi Bazar............................. 160 H4
Cacao et Chocolat............................ 161 B5
CSAO Boutique................................ 162 G3
E Dehillerin...................................... 163 C1
Forum des Halles............................. 164 D2
La Petite Scierie.............................. 165 F5
La Samaritaine (Men & Sport)......... 166 C2
La Samaritaine Main Building........... 167 C3
Les Ruchers du Roy.......................... 168 F4
Marché aux Enfants Rouges............. 169 H1
Mélodies Graphiques...................... 170 F4

TRANSPORT   (pp170-6)
Batobus Stop.................................... 171 B3
Batobus Stop.................................... 172 E5
Batobus Stop.................................... 173 F4
Batobus Stop.................................... 174 A3
Eurolines Ticket Office..................... 175 D6
Noctambus (Night Bus) Stops.......... 176 D3
Noctambus (Night Bus) Stops.......... 177 F3

OTHER
Église St Julien le Pauvre................ 178 D5
Guimard Synagogue......................... 179 G4

Rue Montorgueil Market

A B C D

1

R des Pyramides
R d'Argenteuil
Av de l'Opéra
R Ste-Anne
R Molière
R St-Honoré
R de Montpensier
R de Valois
R Coquillière
R Hérold
R Coq Héron
R du Bouloi
R Jean Jacques Rousseau
R Étienne Marcel
R Montorgueil
R Française

Jardin du Palais Royal
Banque de France
Hôtel des Postes
Right Bank

150, 149
Place Colette
32 Palais Royal
R du Colonel Driant
R des Petits Enfants
163
R du Jour
35
130
46

52
31
Place du Palais Royal
Palais Royal Musée du Louvre
Galerie Vero Dodat
121, 70
63
Bourse de Commerce
Place René Cassin
Les Halles
R Rambuteau

2

Jardin du Carrousel
28
Place du Carrousel
44
102
41
53
Cour Carrée
Jardin de l'Oratoire
10, 144
14
127
R de Marengo
R de l'Oratoire
R Berger
R du Louvre
R de Viarmes
R St-Honoré
112
Place M Quentin
89
4
Place M de Navarre
164 Forum des Halles, 151
Châtelet les Halles
Place Jean du Bellay, 3
152

Louvre Rivoli
142
R Perrault
R de Rivoli
Place du Louvre
166
167
R de l'Arbre Sec
R de la Monnaie
R Bailleul
R Boucher
R du Pont Neuf
R des Déchargeurs
R des Lavandières
Châtelet
Châtelet
Châtelet
108
de la Ferronnerie

Pont Neuf
Jardin de l'Infante
Q du Louvre
171
Q de Conti
R Bertin Poirée
Q de la Mégisserie
Av Victoria
Squa de la T St Jacc
148
Place du Châtelet
Châtelet

3

Seine
174
Q Malaquais
Place de l'Institut
43
Square du Vert Galant
Place du Pont Neuf
Pont Neuf
Square Dauphine
82
Place Dauphine
Palais de Justice
Île de la Cité
Conciergerie
61
Q de l'Horloge
Q de la Corse
Pont au Change
Q des G

4

École des Beaux Arts
R des Beaux Arts
92
68
R Visconti
93
74, 76
R Jacob
R Jacques Callot
72
155
R de Nevers
R de Nesle
R du Pont de Lodi
R Christine
R Dauphine
R Guénégaud
R Mazarine
R de Seine
R de Savoie
104
86
60
St Michel Notre Dame
Cité
Cité

5

R Bonaparte
R de Bucí
R St-Benoît
138, 143
49
36
9
118, 161
103
98
2
8, 124
23
R St André des Arts
Place St André des Arts
St Michel
Q St Michel
153
22, 80
136, 178
Square R Viviani
81
St Michel- Notre Dame
R de la Huchette
R St Séverin
Place St Michel
R de la Harpe
R Galande

St Germain des Prés
Place St Germain des Prés
Square F Desruelles
114
Mabillon
24
125
126
Marché St Germain
R du Four
R Clément
R Princesse
R Guisarde
R des Canettes
R Mabillon
R Grégoire de Tours
Cour du Commerce St André
R de l'Éperon
R Suger
R Danton
R Serpente
18
16
Danton Memorial
Odéon
Carrefour de l'Odéon
Place H Mondor
Blvd St Germain
Cluny la Sorbonne

6

Fontaine des Quatre Évêques
St Sulpice
38
Place St Sulpice
R Palatine
R St Sulpice
141
77
R des Quatre Vents
R de Condé
R de Tournon
R Crébillon
Place de l'Odéon
157
Place Paul Claudel
Jardin du Luxembourg
134
100
40, 54
R Racine
R Monsieur le Prince
R Casimir Delavigne
Blvd St Michel
R Pierre Sarrain
R de l'École de Médecine
Square et Place P Painlevé
175
Latin Quarter
Square F.A. Mariette
R des Écoles
R Thénard
R de Latran
R du Sommerard
Maubert Mutualité
R Férou
R Servandoni
R Vaugirard

0 _____ 200 m
0 _____ 0.1 miles

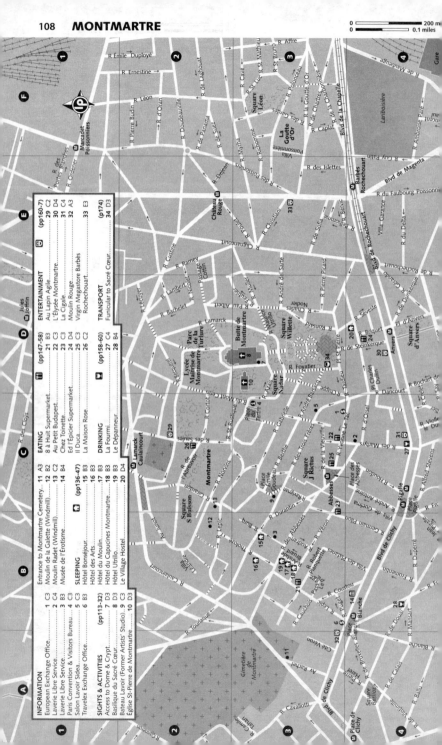

INFORMATION
European Exchange Office............1 C3
Laverie Libre Service..................2 C4
Laverie Libre Service..................3 B3
Paris Convention & Visitors Bureau..4 C3
Salon Lavoir Sidea......................5 C3
Travelex Exchange Office............6 B3

SIGHTS & ACTIVITIES   (pp113-32)
Access to Dome & Crypt................7 D3
Basilique du Sacré Coeur.............8 D3
Bateau Lavoir (Former Artists' Studio)...9 C3
Église St-Pierre de Montmartre.....10 D3

Entrance to Montmartre Cemetery...11 A3
Moulin de la Galette (Windmill).....12 B2
Moulin Radet (Windmill)..............13 C2
Musée de l'Érotisme....................14 B4

SLEEPING   (pp136-47)
Hôtel Bonséjour........................15 B3
Hôtel des Arts..........................16 B3
Hôtel du Moulin........................17 B3
Hôtel du Capucines Montmartre...18 B3
Hôtel Utrillo............................19 B3
Le Village Hostel.......................20 D4

EATING   (pp147-58)
8 à Huit Supermarket.................21 B3
Au Petit Budapest......................22 B3
Chez Toinette..........................23 C3
Ed l'Épicier Supermarket............24 D4
Il Duca...................................25 C3
La Maison Rose.........................26 C2

DRINKING   (pp158-60)
La Fourmi................................27 D3
Le Dépanneur..........................28 B4

ENTERTAINMENT   (pp160-7)
Au Lapin Agile...........................29 C2
L'Élysée Montmartre...................30 D4
La Cigale................................31 C4
Moulin Rouge...........................32 A3
Virgin Megastore Barbès
Rochechouart.........................33 E3

TRANSPORT   (p174)
Funicular to Sacré Coeur.............34 D3

PARIS METRO MAP

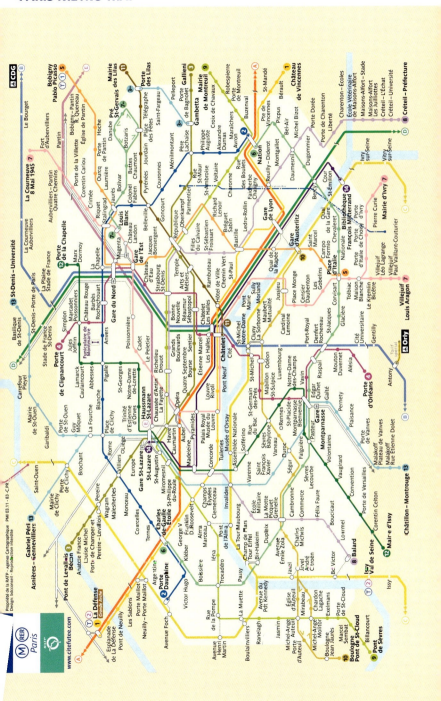

CHRISTOPHER GR

Aerial view of Paris (p85) and the Seine

Ste-Chapelle (p120), Paris

MARTIN MOOS

JONATHAN SMITH

Eiffel Tower (p125)

Centre Pompidou (p116), Paris

MARTIN MOOS

(Continued from page 89)

Tea & Tattered Pages (Map pp99-101; ☎ 01 40 65 94 35; 24 rue Mayet, 6e; metro Duroc; ☺ 11am-7pm Mon-Sat, noon-6pm Sun) T&TP is by far the best and most comprehensive shop selling used English-language books in Paris, with some 15,000 volumes squeezed into two floors.

Village Voice (Map pp105-7; ☎ 01 46 33 36 47; www.villagevoicebookshop.com; 6 rue Princesse, 6e; metro Mabillon; ☺ 2-8pm Mon, 10am-8pm Tue-Sat, 2-6pm Sun) The Voice has an excellent selection of contemporary North American fiction and European literature in translation, lots of readings and helpful knowledgeable staff.

Emergency

The numbers below are to be dialled in an emergency. See p110 for hospitals with 24-hour accident and emergency departments. For nationwide emergency numbers, see inside the front cover.

Ambulance (SAMU Paris; ☎ 01 45 67 50 50)

SOS Médecins (☎ 01 47 07 77 77) 24hr house calls.

SOS Helpline (☎ 01 47 23 80 80) In English.

Urgences Médicales de Paris (Paris Medical Emergencies; ☎ 01 53 94 94 94, 01 48 28 40 40) 24hr house calls.

Internet Access

Some metro and RER stations (eg St-Michel, Miromesnil) offer free Internet access but there's always a queue a mile long. At the same time, some 50 post offices in Paris – up to five in a few arrondissements – have Internet centres called Cyberposte (p905). The centres generally are open from 8am or 9am to 7pm weekdays and till noon Saturday.

The best and most central commercial Internet cafés in Paris:

Access Academy (Map pp105-7; ☎ 01 43 25 23 80; www.accessacademy.com in French; 60-61 rue St-André des Arts, 6e; metro Odéon; per hr approx €3.50, per day/week/month €6.80/14.90/35.70; ☺ 8am-2am) This is France's largest Internet café, with some 400 screens in the heart of St-Germain. Hourly rates depend on what time you log on.

Akyrion Net Center (Map pp105-7; ☎ 01 40 27 92 07; www.akyrion.com in French; 19 rue Charlemagne, 4e; metro St-Paul; adult per 15/30/60min €2.50/4.10/7.30 student €2/3.30/5.90; ☺ 11am-midnight Mon-Sat, 2pm-midnight Sun) This centre in the Marais is popular with students at the nearby university.

Cyberbe@ubourg Internet C@fé (Map pp105-7; ☎ /fax 01 42 71 49 80; 38 rue Quincampoix, 4e; metro Châtelet-Les Halles; per 15/30/45/60min €1.50/3/4.60/6, per 10/20/40hr €29/44/75; ☺ 9am to 11pm)

Web 46 (Map pp105-7; ☎ 01 40 27 02 89; fax 01 40 27 03 89; 46 rue du Roi de Sicile, 4e; metro St-Paul; per 15/30/60min €2.50/4/7, 5hr €29; ☺ 9.30am-midnight) This is a very pleasant, well-run café in the heart of the Marais with 15 modules.

XS Arena Luxembourg (Map pp105-7; ☎ 01 43 44 55 55; 17 rue Soufflot, 5e; metro Luxembourg; per 1/2/3/4/5hr €3/6/8/10/12; ☺ 24hr) This minichain of Internet cafés is bright, buzzy and open round the clock. The **XS Arena Les Halles** (Map pp105-7; ☎ 01 40 13 02 60; 43 rue Sébastopol, 1er; metro Les Halles) branch is just down from the Forum des Halles.

Internet Resources

Mairie de Paris (www.paris.fr) Statistics plus city and tourist information direct from the Hôtel de Ville.

Metropole Paris (www.metropoleparis.com) Excellent online magazine in English.

Paris Pages (www.paris.org) Good links to museums and cultural events.

Paris Tourist Office (www.paris-touristoffice.com) Super site with more links than you'll ever need.

Laundry

There's a *laverie libre-service* (self-service laundrette) around just about every corner in Paris; your hotel or hostel can point you to one in the neighbourhood. Machines usually cost €2.80 to €3.70 for a small load (5kg to 7kg) and €5 to €5.50 for a larger (10kg to 13kg) one. Drying costs €1 for 10 to 12 minutes.

LOUVRE & LES HALLES

Laverie Libre Service (Map pp105-7; 7 rue Jean-Jacques Rousseau, 1er; metro Louvre-Rivoli; ☺ 7.30am-10pm) Near the Centre International BVJ Paris-Louvre hostel.

MARAIS & BASTILLE

Laverie Libre Service (Map pp105-7; 35 rue Ste-Croix de la Bretonnerie, 4e; metro Hôtel de Ville; ☺ 7am-10pm)

Laverie Libre Service (Map pp105-7; 25 rue des Rosiers, 4e; metro St-Paul; ☺ 7.30am-10pm)

Laverie Libre Service Primus (Map pp105-7; 40 rue du Roi de Sicile, 4e; metro St-Paul; ☺ 7.30am-8.30pm)

Laverie Miele Libre Service (Map pp102-4; 2 rue de Lappe, 11e; metro Bastille; ☺ 7am-10pm)

LATIN QUARTER & JARDIN DES PLATES

Laverie Libre Service (Map pp102-4; 216 rue St-Jacques, 5e; metro Luxembourg; ☺ 7am-10pm) Three blocks southwest of the Panthéon.

Le Bateau Lavoir (Map pp102-4; 1 rue Thouin, 5e; metro Cardinal Lemoine; ☺ 7am-10pm) Near place de la Contrescarpe.

ST-GERMAIN, ODÉON & LUXEMBOURG
Julice Laverie (Map pp105-7; 56 rue de Seine, 6e; metro Mabillon; ☯ 7am-11pm)
Julice Laverie (Map pp105-7; 22 rue des Grands Augustins, 6e; metro St-André des Arts; ☯ 7am-9pm)

GARE DU NORD, GARE DE L'EST & RÉPUBLIQUE
Laverie Libre Service (Map pp96-8; 14 rue de la Corderie, 3e; metro République or Temple; ☯ 8am-9pm)
Laverie SBS (Map pp96-8; 6 rue des Petites Écuries, 10e; metro Château d'Eau; ☯ 7am-10pm)

MÉNILMONTANT & BELLEVILLE
C'Clean Laverie (Map pp96-8; 18 rue Jean-Pierre Timbaud,11e; metro Oberkampf; ☯ 8am-10pm)
Laverie Libre Service Primus (Map pp96-8; 83 rue Jean-Pierre Timbaud, 11e; metro Couronnes; ☯ 7.30am-8pm)

MONTMARTRE & PIGALLE
Laverie Libre Service (Map p108; 92 rue des Martyrs, 18e; metro Abbesses; ☯ 7.30am-10pm)
Laverie Libre Service (Map p108; 4 rue Burq, 18e; metro Blanche; ☯ 7.30am-10pm) West of the Butte de Montmartre.
Salon Lavoir Sidea (Map p108; 28 rue des Trois Frères, 18e; metro Abbesses; ☯ 7am-8.50pm)

Left Luggage
All the train stations (see p171) have left-luggage offices or lockers. They charge €3.40/5/7.50 for 48 hours for a medium/large/extra-large bag. After that the fee is a flat €4.50 per day. Be warned that most of these left-luggage offices and lockers are closed to the public from about 11.15pm to between 6.15am and 6.45am.

Media
There are no local English-language newspapers in Paris although freebies such as *Paris Voice, Paris Where* and *The Irish Eyes* proliferate and are available at English-language bookshops, pubs and so on. The Paris-based *FUSAC* (short for *France USA Contacts*), a freebie issued every fortnight, consists of hundreds of ads placed by both companies and individuals. It is distributed free at the same places as well as at the **American Church in Paris** (Map pp99-101; ☎ 01 40 62 05 00; www.acparis.org; 65 quai d'Orsay, 7e; metro Pont de l'Alma or Invalides; reception ☯ 9am-noon & 1-10.30pm Mon-Sat, 9am-noon & 1-7pm Sun), which functions as a community centre for English speakers and is an excellent source of information on au pair work, short-term accommodation etc.

Paris Live Radio (www.parislive.net), the city's first all-English station, can be heard via the Internet, cable, satellite and DAB digital radio (1463.232MHz LG) throughout the day.

Medical Services
DENTAL SURGERIES
For emergency dental care contact either of the following:
Hôpital de la Salpêtrière (Map pp102-4; ☎ 01 42 16 00 00; rue Bruant, 13e; metro Chevaleret) This is the only dental hospital with extended hours. After hours use the **emergency entrance** (Map pp102-4; 83 blvd de l'Hôpital, 13e; metro St-Michel; ☯ 5.30pm-8.30am).
SOS Dentaire (Map pp90-2; ☎ 01 4 3 36 36 00; 87 blvd de Port Royal, 14e; metro Port Royal) This is a private dental office that also offers services when most dentists are off duty – from 8.30pm to 11pm weekdays and from 9.30am to 11pm at the weekend.

HOSPITALS
There are some 50 *assistance publique* (public health service) hospitals in Paris. Major hospitals in the city:
American Hospital in Paris (Map pp90-2; ☎ 01 46 41 25 25; www.american-hospital.org; 63 blvd Victor Hugo, 92200 Neuilly-sur-Seine; metro Pont de Levallois Bécon) Offers emergency 24-hour medical and dental care.
Hertford British Hospital (Map pp90-2; ☎ 01 46 39 22 22; www.british-hospital.org; 3 rue Barbès, 92300 Levallois-Perret; metro Anatole France) This is a less expensive, English-speaking option than the American Hospital.
Hôtel Dieu (Map pp105-7; ☎ 01 42 34 81 31; place du Parvis Notre Dame, 4e; metro Cité) After 8pm use the **emergency entrance** (rue de la Cité).

PHARMACIES
Some pharmacies with extended hours:
Pharmacie Bader (Map pp105-7; ☎ 01 43 26 92 66; 12 blvd St-Michel, 5e; metro St-Michel; ☯ 9am-9pm)
Pharmacie des Champs (Map pp93-5; ☎ 01 45 62 02 41; Galerie des Champs, 84 av des Champs-Élysées, 8e; metro George V; ☯ 24hr)
Pharmacie des Halles (Map pp105-7; ☎ 01 42 72 03 23; 10 blvd de Sébastopol, 4e; metro Châtelet; ☯ 9am-midnight Mon-Sat, 9am-10pm Sun)

Money
Post offices generally offer the best exchange rate and accept both cash and travellers cheques. *Bureaux de change* are faster and easier, open longer hours and give better

rates than most banks. For general advice on exchanging money, see p908.

Among some of the better *bureaux de change* in Paris are the following:

LOUVRE & LES HALLES
Best Change (Map pp105-7; ☎ 01 42 21 46 05; 21 rue du Roule, 1er; metro Louvre Rivoli; ☺ 10am-1pm & 2-7pm Mon-Sat) This *bureau de change* is three blocks southwest of Forum des Halles.
Le Change du Louvre (Map pp105-7; ☎ 01 42 97 27 28; 151 rue St-Honoré, 1er; metro Palais Royal-Musée du Louvre; ☺ 10am-6pm Mon-Sat) This moneychanger is just north of the Louvre.

LATIN QUARTER & JARDIN DES PLANTES
Société Touristique de Services (STS; Map pp105-7; ☎ 01 43 54 76 55; 2 place St-Michel, 6e; metro St-Michel; ☺ 9am-8pm Mon-Sat, 10am-8pm Sun)

ÉTOILE & CHAMPS-ÉLYSÉES
Bureau de Change (Map pp93-5; ☎ 01 42 25 38 14; 25 av des Champs-Élysées, 8e; metro Franklin D Roosevelt; ☺ 9am-8pm)
Thomas Cook (Map pp93-5; ☎ 01 47 20 25 14; 125 av des Champs-Élysées, 8e; metro Charles de Gaulle-Étoile; ☺ 9.15am-8.30pm)

MONTMARTRE & PIGALLE
European Exchange Office (Map p108; ☎ 01 42 52 67 19; 6 rue Yvonne Le Tac, 18e; metro Abbesses; ☺ 10am-6.30pm Mon-Fri, 10.30am-6pm Sat)
Travelex (Map p108; ☎ 01 42 57 05 10; 82-86 blvd de Clichy, 18e; metro Blanche; ☺ 10am-8.30pm Mon-Sat, 9.45am-8.30pm Sun)

Post
The **main post office** (Map pp96-8; ☎ 01 40 28 76 00; 52 rue du Louvre, 1er; metro Sentier or Les Halles; ☺ 24hr), five blocks north of the eastern end of the Louvre, is open round the clock, but only for basic services such as sending letters and picking up poste restante mail (window Nos 5 to 7; €0.46 per letter). Other services, including currency exchange, are available only during regular opening hours. Be prepared for long queues after 7pm. Poste restante mail not specifically addressed to a particular branch post office will be delivered here. There is a one-hour closure from 6.20am to 7.20am Monday to Saturday and from 6am to 7am on Sunday.

Each arrondissement has its own five-digit postcode, formed by prefixing the arrondissement number with '750' or '7500' (eg 75001 for the 1er arrondissement, 75019 for the 19e etc). The only exception is the 16e, which has two postcodes: 75016 and 75116.

You can also buy stamps from *tabacs* (tobacconists).

Telephone
For information on how to use phones in France, see p910. All public telephones in Paris require a *télécarte* (phonecard), which can be purchased at post offices, *tabacs*, supermarket check-out counters, SNCF ticket windows, metro stations and anywhere you see a blue sticker reading '*télécarte en vente ici*'.

Toilets
The public toilets in Paris are signposted as *toilettes* or *WC*. The tan-coloured, self-cleaning cylindrical toilets you see on Paris' pavements are open 24 hours and cost €0.40.

Café owners do not appreciate use of their facilities if you are not a paying customer. If you are desperate, try ducking into a fast-food place, a major department store, Forum des Halles (Map pp105-7) or even a big hotel. There are public toilets (€0.40) underground in front of Notre Dame cathedral (Map pp105-7), near the Arc de Triomphe (Map pp93-5), east down the steps at Sacré Cœur (Map p108) and in a few metro stations. Check out the wonderful Art Nouveau public toilets below place de la Madeleine, 8e (Map pp93-5). They were built in 1905.

In older cafés and bars, the amenities may consist of a *toilette à la turque* (Turkish-style toilet), which is what the French call a squat toilet.

Tourist Information
The main branch of the **Office de Tourisme et de Congrès de Paris** (Paris Convention & Visitors Bureau; Map pp93-5; ☎ 0 892 683 000; www.paris-touristoffice.com; 25-27 rue des Pyramides, 1er; metro Pyramides; ☺ 9am-8pm Apr-Oct, 9am-8pm Mon-Sat & 11am-7pm Sun Nov-Mar) is about 500m northwest of the Louvre. It closes on 1 May only.

In addition the bureau maintains five centres (telephone numbers and website are the same as the main office) elsewhere in Paris.
Eiffel Tower (Map pp99-101; Pilier Nord, Parc du Champ de Mars, 7e; metro Champ de Mars-Tour Eiffel; ☺ 11am-6.45pm 2 May-Sep) In the base of the Eiffel Tower's North Pillar.

Gare de Lyon (Map pp102-4; Hall d'Arrivée, 20 blvd Diderot, 12; metro Gare de Lyon; 8am-6pm Mon-Sat, closed Sun & holidays) In the mainline trains arrivals hall.
Gare du Nord (Map pp96-8; 18 rue de Dunkerque, 10; metro Fare du Nord; 12.30-8pm, closed Christmas Day & 1 May) Under the glass roof of the Île de France departure and arrival area at the eastern end of the station.
Montmartre (Map p108; 21 place du Tertre, 18e; metro Abbesses; 10am-7pm, closed Christmas Day & 1 May)
Opéra/Grands Magasins (Map pp93-5; 11 rue Scribe, 9e; metro Gare de Lyon; 9am-6.30pm Mon-Sat, closed Sun, Christmas Day, 1 Jan & 1 May) In the same building as Opéra's landmark American Express office.

Espace du Tourisme d'Île de France (p179) is responsible for the areas around Paris.

Travel Agencies

You'll find travel agencies everywhere in Paris, but the following are among the largest and offer the best service and (usually) deals.
Forum Voyages (www.forum-voyages.fr in French); Latin Quarter branch (Map pp102-4; ☎ 01 53 10 50 50; 28 rue Monge, 5e; metro Cardinal Lemoine); Opéra branch (Map pp96-8; ☎ 01 42 61 20 20; 11 av de l'Opéra, 1er; metro Pyramides) Forum has nine outlets in Paris that are usually open 9.30am to 7pm Monday to Saturday.
Nouvelles Frontières (☎ 0 825 000 825; www .nouvelles-frontieres.fr in French); Odéon branch (Map pp105-7; ☎ 01 43 25 71 35; 116 blvd St-Germain, 6e; metro Odéon); Opéra branch (Map pp96-8; ☎ 01 42 61 02 62; 13 av de l'Opéra, 1er; metro Pyramides) There are 22 outlets around the city open 9am to 7pm Monday to Saturday.
OTU Voyages (☎ 0 820 817 817; www.otu.fr in French); Luxembourg branch (Map pp102-4; ☎ 0 825 004 027; 39 av Georges Bernanos, 5e; metro Port Royal; 9am-6.30pm Mon-Fri, 10am-noon & 1.15-5pm Sat) There is also a branch opposite the Centre Pompidou (p137).
Voyageurs du Monde (Map pp96-8; ☎ 01 42 86 16 00; www.vdm.com in French; 55 rue Ste-Anne, 2e; metro Pyramides or Quatre-Septembre; 9.30am-7pm Mon-Sat) 'World Travellers' is an enormous agency with more than 10 departments dealing with different destinations.

DANGERS & ANNOYANCES
Crime

In general Paris is a safe city and random street assaults are rare; in fact, criminal acts fell by 7% between 2002 and 2003, with thefts involving violence dropping by almost 10%. The so-called Ville Lumière (City of Light) is generally well lit, and there's no

reason not to use the metro before it stops running at some time between 12.30am and just past 1am. As you'll notice, women *do* travel alone on the metro late at night in most areas, though not all who do so report feeling 100% comfortable.

Metro stations that are probably best avoided late at night include: Châtelet-Les Halles and its seemingly endless corridors; Château Rouge in Montmartre; Gare du Nord; Strasbourg St-Denis; Réaumur Sébastopol; and Montparnasse Bienvenüe. *Bornes d'alarme* (alarm boxes) are located in the centre of each metro/RER platform and in some station corridors.

Nonviolent crime such as pickpocketing and thefts from handbags and packs is a problem wherever there are crowds, especially tourists. Places to be particularly careful include Montmartre (especially around Sacré Cœur); Pigalle; the areas around Forum des Halles and Centre Pompidou; the Latin Quarter (especially the rectangle bounded by rue St-Jacques, blvd St-Germain, blvd St-Michel and quai St-Michel); below the Eiffel Tower; and on the metro during rush hour.

Lost Property

All objects found anywhere across Paris – except those picked up on the trains or in train stations – are eventually brought in to the city's **Bureau des Objets Trouvés** (Lost Property Office; Map pp90-2; ☎ 01 55 76 20 20; fax 01 40 02 40 45; 36 rue des Morillons, 15e; metro Convention; 8.30am-7pm Mon-Fri Jul & Aug, 8.30am-5pm Mon & Wed, 8.30am-8pm Tue & Thu, 8.30am-5.30pm Fri Sep-Jun), which is run by the Préfecture de Police. Since telephone enquiries are impossible, the only way to find out if a lost item has been located is to go there and fill in the forms.

Items lost on the **metro** (☎ 01 44 68 20 20) are held by station agents for three days before being sent to the Bureau des Objets Trouvés.

Anything found on trains or in train stations is taken to the lost-property office – usually attached to the left-luggage office – of the relevant station. Telephone enquiries (in French) are possible:
Gare d'Austerlitz (☎ 01 53 60 71 98)
Gare de l'Est (☎ 01 40 18 88 73)
Gare de Lyon (☎ 01 53 33 67 22)
Gare du Nord (☎ 01 55 31 58 40)

Gare Montparnasse (☎ 01 40 48 14 24)
Gare St-Lazare (☎ 01 53 42 05 57)

Litter & Dog Dirt

In theory Parisians can be fined over €150 for littering but we've never seen (or heard of) anyone ever having to pay up. Don't be nonplussed if you see locals drop paper wrappings or other detritus along the side of the pavement, however; the gutters in every quarter of Paris are washed and swept out daily and Parisians are encouraged to use them where litter bins are not available.

A much greater annoyance are all those dog droppings on the pavements. The Paris municipality spends €11 million each year to keep them relatively free of dog dirt, but it seems that repeated campaigns – including threats of heavy fines (up to €450) and free plastic bags distributed in parks and along the quays – to get people to clean up after their pooches, owned by 160,000 households in Paris, have been less than a howling success, with only an estimated 60% of dog owners doing so.

SIGHTS

Paris' major sights are distributed more or less equally on the Right and Left Banks of the Seine. We start in the heart of the Right Bank in the area around the Louvre and Les Halles, which largely takes in the 1er and follows, more or less, the order of the arrondissements (see p88), ending in the Parc de la Villette in the 19e.

Louvre & Les Halles

The area around the Louvre in the 1er contains some of the most important sights for visitors in Paris. To the northeast, the mostly pedestrian zone between the Centre Pompidou and the Forum des Halles, with rue Étienne Marcel to the north and rue de Rivoli to the south, is filled with people by day and by night, just as it was for the 850-odd years when part of it served as Paris' main marketplace known as *les halles*.

MUSÉE DU LOUVRE

The vast Palais du Louvre was constructed as a fortress by Philippe-Auguste in the early 13th century and rebuilt in the mid-16th century for use as a royal residence. In 1793 the Convention turned it into the **Musée du Louvre** (Louvre Museum; Map pp105-7; ☎ 01 40 20 53

> ### AH, LA CARTE!
>
> The **Carte Musées-Monuments** (Museums-Monuments Card; ☎ 01 44 61 96 60; for 1/3/5 days €18/36/54) is valid for entry to some three dozen sights in Paris – including the Louvre, the Centre Pompidou and the Musée d'Orsay – and another two dozen 22 in the Île de France, including parts of the chateaux at Versailles, Fontaine and Chantilly. The pass is available from the participating venues as well as tourist offices, Fnac outlets, RATP information desks and major metro stations.

17, 01 40 20 51 51; www.louvre.fr; metro Palais Royal-Musée du Louvre; admission to permanent collections/permanent collections & temporary exhibits €7.50/11.50, after 3pm & all day Sun €5/9.50, under 18 free, 1st Sun of month free; 🕑 9am-6pm Thu-Sun, 9am-9.45pm Mon & Wed).

The paintings, sculptures and artefacts on display in the Louvre Museum have been assembled by French governments over the past five centuries. Among them are works of art and artisanship from all over Europe and important collections of Assyrian, Etruscan, Greek, Coptic and Islamic art and antiquities. Traditionally the Louvre's *raison d'être* is to present Western art from the Middle Ages to about the year 1848 (at which point the Musée d'Orsay takes over) as well as the works of ancient civilisations that formed the starting point for Western art. However, in recent years it has acquired or begun to exhibit other important collections as well.

The Louvre may be the most actively avoided museum in the world. Daunted by the richness and sheer size of the place (the side facing the Seine is some 700m long and it is said that it would take nine months just to glance at every piece of art here), both local people and visitors often find the prospect of an afternoon at a smaller museum far more inviting. Eventually, most people do their duty and come, but many leave overwhelmed, unfulfilled, exhausted and frustrated at having got lost on their way to da Vinci's *La Joconde*, better known as *Mona Lisa* (Denon Wing, 1st floor, Rm 13). Since it takes several serious visits to get anything more than a brief glimpse of the works on offer, your best bet – after checking out a few you really want to see – is to choose a particular period or section of the Louvre and pretend that the rest is in another museum somewhere across town.

The most famous works from antiquity include the *Seated Scribe* (Sully Wing, 1st floor), the *Code of Hammurabi* (Richelieu Wing, ground floor) and that armless duo, the *Venus de Milo* (Sully Wing, ground floor) and the *Winged Victory of Samothrace* (Denon Wing, 1st floor). From the Renaissance, don't miss Michelangelo's *The Dying Slave* (Denon Wing, ground floor) and works by Raphael, Botticelli and Titian (Denon Wing, 1st floor). French masterpieces of the 19th century (Sully Wing, 2nd floor) include Ingres' *The Turkish Bath*, Géricault's *The Raft of the Medusa* and works by Corot, Delacroix and Fragonard.

When the museum opened in the late 18th century it contained 2500 paintings; today there are around 30,000 on display. The 'Grand Louvre' project, inaugurated by the late President Mitterrand in 1989, doubled the museum's exhibition space. In recent years new and renovated galleries have opened devoted to *objets d'art* such as Sèvres porcelain and the crown jewels of Louis XV (Sully Wing, 1st floor).

The main entrance and ticket windows in the Cour Napoléon are covered by a 21m-high **Grande Pyramide**, a glass pyramid designed by the Chinese-born American architect IM Pei. You can avoid the queues outside the pyramid or at the Porte des Lions entrance by entering the Louvre complex via the Carrousel du Louvre shopping area or by following the 'Louvre' exit from the Palais Royal-Musée du Louvre metro station. Those in the know buy their tickets in advance by ringing ☎ 0 892 697 073, from the *billeteries* (ticket offices) of Fnac or Virgin Megastores (p161) or from any of the major department stores (see p168), and walk straight in without queuing. Tickets are valid for the whole day, so you can come and go as you please. If planning to visit during one of the two weekly *nocturnes*, remember that on Wednesday virtually the entire museum remains open after 6pm but on Monday evening there's only a *circuit court* (short tour) of selected galleries.

The Musée du Louvre is divided into four sections: the Sully, Denon and Richelieu Wings and the Hall Napoléon. **Sully** creates the four sides of the Cour Carrée (literally 'square courtyard') at the eastern end of the complex. **Denon** stretches along the Seine to the south; **Richelieu** is the northern wing along rue de Rivoli.

The split-level public area under the glass pyramid is known as the **Hall Napoléon** (☺ 9am-10pm Thu-Mon). It has an exhibit on the history of the Louvre, a bookshop, a restaurant, a café, auditoriums for concerts, lectures and films and **CyberLouvre** (☺ 10am-6.45 Wed-Mon), an Internet salon with monitors that allow virtual-reality access to some 20,000 works of art. The centrepiece of the **Carrousel du Louvre shopping centre** (Map pp105-7; ☎ 01 40 20 67 30; 99 rue de Rivoli; ☺ 8.30am-11pm), which runs underground from the pyramid to the Arc de Triomphe du Carrousel in the Jardin du Carrousel, is an **inverted glass pyramid** *(pyramide inversée),* also created by Pei.

Free maps in English of the complex called *Louvre Plan/Information* are available at the information desk in the centre of the Hall Napoléon. Excellent publications to guide you if you are doing the Louvre on your own are *Destination Louvre: A Guided Tour* (€7.50), *Louvre: The Visit* (€7.90) and *The Louvre: Key Art Works* (€15). All are available from the museum bookshop.

English-language guided tours (☎ 01 40 20 52 63) lasting 1½ hours depart from the area marked 'Acceuil des Groupes' (Group Welcome) under the glass pyramid at 11am, 2pm and 3pm Monday to Saturday. Tickets cost €6 (€3.50 for those aged 13 to 18, free for under 12s) in addition to the cost of admission. Groups are limited to 30 people, so it's a good idea to sign up at least 30 minutes before departure time. Audioguide tours in six languages and lasting 1½ hours can be rented for €5 under the pyramid at the entrance to each wing until 4.30pm.

OTHER PALAIS DU LOUVRE MUSEUMS

The Palais du Louvre contains three other museums run by the **Union Centrale des Arts Décoratifs** (UCAD; ☎ 01 44 55 57 50; www.ucad.fr; 107 rue de Rivoli, 1er; metro Palais Royal-Musée du Louvre; adult/18-25 yrs/under 18 €6/4.50/free; ☺ 11am-6pm Tue-Fri, 10am-6pm Sat & Sun) in the Rohan Wing of the Louvre complex. These were revamped or created under the Grand Louvre project. Admission includes entry to all three museums (Map pp105-7).

Musée des Arts Décoratifs The Applied Arts Museum on the 3rd floor displays furniture, jewellery and such *objets d'art* as ceramics and glassware from the Middle

Ages and the Renaissance through the Art Nouveau and Art Deco periods to modern and contemporary. Some departments may be closed over the next several years as the museum undergoes extensive renovations.

Musée de la Publicité The Advertising Museum, which shares the 3rd floor, contains some 100,000 posters dating as far back as the 13th century and innumerable promotional materials touting everything from 19th-century elixirs and early radio advertisements to Air France and electronic publicity. Only certain items are on exhibit at any one time.

Musée de la Mode et du Textile The Museum of Fashion and Textiles on the 1st and 2nd floors warehouses some 16,000 costumes dating from the 16th century till today, but only displays them in unusual themed exhibitions.

JARDIN DES TUILERIES

The formal, 28-hectare **Jardin des Tuileries** (Tuileries Garden; Map pp93-5; metro Tuileries or Concorde; 7am-9pm late Mar-late Sep, 7am-7.30pm late Sep-late Mar), which begins just west of the Jardin du Carrousel, was laid out in its present form – more or less – in the mid-17th century by André Le Nôtre, who also created the gardens at Vaux-le-Vicomte (p192) and Versailles (p185). The Tuileries soon became the most fashionable spot in Paris for parading about in one's finery; today it is a favourite of joggers.

The **Voie Triomphale** (Triumphal Way), also called the Axe Historique (Historic Axis), the western continuation of the Tuileries' east–west axis, follows the av des Champs-Élysées to the Arc de Triomphe and, ultimately, to the Grande Arche in the skyscraper district of **La Défense** (p179).

JEU DE PAUME & ORANGERIE

The **Galerie Nationale du Jeu de Paume** (Jeu de Paume National Gallery; Map pp93-5; ☎ 01 47 03 12 52; www.rmn.fr; 1 place de la Concorde, 1er; metro Concorde; adult/senior, student, senior & 13-18 yrs/under 13 €6/4.50/ free; noon-9.30pm Tue, noon-7pm Wed-Fri, 10am-7pm Sat & Sun) is housed in an erstwhile *jeu de paume* (real, or royal, tennis) court built in 1861 during the reign of Napoleon III in the northwestern corner of the Jardin des Tuileries. Once the home of a good part of France's national collection of impressionist art, now housed across the Seine in the Musée d'Orsay (p124), the two-storey Jeu de Paume stages innovative exhibitions of contemporary art.

The **Musée de l'Orangerie** (Orangery Museum; Map pp93-5; ☎ 01 42 97 48 16; www.rmn.fr; place de la Concorde, 1er; metro Concorde) in the southwestern corner of the Jardin des Tuileries is, with the Jeu de Paume, all that remains of the once palatial Palais des Tuileries, which was razed during the Paris Commune in 1871 (see p33). It exhibits important impressionist works, including a series of Monet's exquisite *Décorations des Nymphéas* (Water Lilies) and paintings by Cézanne, Matisse, Picasso, Renoir, Sisley, Soutine and Utrillo, but was undergoing extensive renovations at the time of research is due to reopen at the beginning of 2005.

PLACE VENDÔME

The octagonal **place Vendôme** (Map pp93-5; metro Tuileries or Opéra) and the arcaded and colonnaded buildings around it were constructed between 1687 and 1721. In March 1796 Napoleon married Josephine, Viscountess Beauharnais, in the building at No 3. Today, the buildings surrounding the square house the posh Hôtel Ritz Paris (p137) and some of the city's most fashionable boutiques. The 43.5m-tall **Colonne Vendôme** (Vendôme Column), that stands in the centre of the square, consists of a stone core wrapped in a 160m-long bronze spiral made from 1250 Austrian and Russian cannons captured by Napoleon at the Battle of Austerlitz in 1805. The statue on top depicts Napoleon as a Roman emperor.

PALAIS ROYAL

The **Palais Royal** (Royal Palace; Map pp105-7; Place du Palais Royal, 1er; metro Palais Royal-Musée du Louvre), which briefly housed a young Louis XIV in the 1640s, lies to the north of place du Palais Royal and the Louvre. Construction was begun in the 17th century by Cardinal Richelieu, though most of the present neoclassical complex dates from the latter part of the 18th century. It now contains the governmental **Conseil d'État** (State Council) and is closed to the public.

The colonnaded building that is opposite place André Malraux is the **Comédie Française** (p166), which was founded in 1680 and is the world's oldest national theatre.

Just north of the palace is the **Jardin du Palais Royal** (Map pp105-7; 7.30am-11pm Jun-Aug, 7.30am-9.30pm Sep, 7.30am-8.30pm Oct-Mar, 7.30am-10.15pm Apr & May), a lovely park surrounded by 19th-century shopping arcades, including **Galerie de Valois** on the eastern side and **Galerie de**

Montpensier to the west. Don't miss the zany Palais Royal-Musée du Louvre **metro entrance** on the place du Palais Royal.

CENTRE POMPIDOU
The **Centre National d'Art et de Culture Georges Pompidou** (Georges Pompidou National Centre of Art & Culture; Map pp105-7; ☎ 01 44 78 12 33; www .centrepompidou.fr; place Georges Pompidou, 4e; metro Rambuteau) is the most successful art and cultural centre in the world. An extensive €85-million renovation was completed at the start of the new millennium, with expanded exhibition space, a new cinema, CD and video centre, and dance and theatre venues, making it even more popular.

The Centre Pompidou, also known as the Centre Beaubourg, has amazed and delighted visitors since it was inaugurated in 1977, not just for its outstanding collection of modern art, but also for its radical architectural statement; it was among the first buildings to have its 'insides' turned outside. But it all began to look somewhat *démodé* by the late 1990s, hence the refit.

The **Forum du Centre Pompidou** (admission free; ⏰ 11am-10pm Wed-Mon), the open space at ground level, has temporary exhibits and information desks.

The 4th and 5th floors of the centre exhibit about a third of the 50,000-plus works of the **Musée National d'Art Moderne** (MNAM, National Museum of Modern Art; adult/senior & 18-25 yrs/under 18 €7/5/free, 1st Sun of month free; day pass incl MNAM & temporary exhibits adult/senior & 18-25 yrs €10/8; permanent collection ⏰ 11am-9pm Wed-Mon), France's national collection of art dating from 1905 onwards and including the work of the Surrealists and Cubists, as well as pop art and contemporary works. The huge (and free) **Bibliothèque Publique d'Information** (BPI; ☎ 01 44 78 12 33; www.bpi.fr in French; ⏰ noon-10pm Mon & Wed-Fri, 11am-10pm Sat & Sun) takes up the 3rd, 2nd and part of the 1st floors, while the 6th floor has three galleries for **temporary exhibitions** (admission usually €7/5).

The **Atelier Brancusi** (Map pp105-7; place Georges Pompidou; ⏰ 2-6pm Wed-Mon), west of the main building, contains some 140 examples of the work of Romanian-born sculptor Constantin Brancusi (1876–1957) as well as drawings, paintings and glass photographic plates. An MNAM ticket includes entry.

Place Georges Pompidou, west of the centre, and the nearby pedestrian streets attract buskers, street artists, musicians, jugglers and mime artists, and can be as much fun as the centre itself. The fanciful **mechanical fountains** (Map pp105-7; place Igor Stravinsky) of skeletons, dragons, G clefs and a big pair of ruby-red lips, just south of the centre and created by Jean Tinguely and Niki de St-Phalle, are a positive delight.

Le Défenseur du Temps (Map pp105-7; Defender of Time; 8 rue Bernard de Clairvaux; ⏰ 9am-10pm), a mechanical clock (1979) whose protagonist does battle on the hour with the elements (air, water and earth in the form of a phoenix, crab and dragon), is a block north of the Centre Pompidou, just off Rue Brantôme (3e) in a development known as Quartier de l'Horloge.

FORUM DES HALLES
Les Halles, the city's main wholesale food market, occupied the area just south of the Église St-Eustache from the early 12th century until 1969, when it was moved to the southern suburb of Rungis. In its place, the unspeakable **Forum des Halles** (Map pp105-7; ☎ 01 44 76 96 56; 1 rue Pierre Lescaut, 1er; metro Les Halles or Châtelet Les Halles), a huge underground shopping centre, was constructed in the glass-and-chrome style of the early 1970s.

Atop the Forum des Halles is a popular **park**. During the warmer months, street musicians, fire-eaters and other performers display their talents throughout the area, especially at **place du Jean du Bellay**, whose centre is adorned by a multitiered Renaissance fountain, the **Fontaine des Innocents**, erected in 1549. It is named after the Cimetière des Innocents, a cemetery on this site from which two million skeletons were disinterred and transferred to the Catacombes (p123) in the 14e after the Revolution.

ÉGLISE ST-EUSTACHE
The majestic **Église St-Eustache** (Map pp105-7; ☎ 01 42 36 31 05; www.st-eustache.org in French; 2 impasse St-Eustache, 1er; metro Les Halles; ⏰ 9am-7.30pm), one of the most beautiful churches in Paris and consecrated to an early Roman martyr who is the patron saint of hunters, is just north of the gardens above the Forum des Halles. Constructed between 1532 and 1640, St-Eustache is primarily Gothic, though a neoclassical façade was added on the western side in the mid-18th century. Inside, there are some exceptional

Flamboyant Gothic arches holding up the ceiling of the chancel, although most of the interior ornamentation is Renaissance and classical. The gargantuan organ above the west entrance, with 101 stops and 8000 pipes, is used for concerts (long a tradition here) and during High Mass on Sunday (11am and 6pm).

TOUR ST-JACQUES

The Flamboyant Gothic, 52m-high **Tour St-Jacques** (St James' Tower; Map pp105-7; place du Châtelet, 4e; metro Châtelet) is all that remains of the Église St-Jacques la Boucherie, built by the powerful butchers guild in 1523 and demolished by the Directory in 1797. The tower is topped by a weather station. It is closed to the public.

LA SAMARITAINE ROOFTOP TERRACE

For an amazing 360-degree, panoramic view of central Paris, head for the roof of this department store's **main building** (Map pp105-7; ☎ 01 40 41 20 20; www.lasamaritaine.com; 19 rue de la Monnaie, 1er; metro Pont Neuf; Ⓨ 9.30am-7pm Mon-Wed & Fri, 9.30am-10pm Thu, 9.30am-8pm Sat). A lift will take you to the 9th floor; you then walk two flights up to the 11th floor. At the time of research the terrace was closed for security reasons.

Marais & Bastille

The Marais, the area of the Right Bank north of Île St-Louis in the 3e and 4e, was exactly what its name implies – 'marsh' or 'swamp' – until the 13th century, when it was put to agricultural use. In the early 17th century, Henri IV built the place Royale (today's place des Vosges), turning the area into Paris' most fashionable residential district and attracting wealthy aristocrats who then erected their own luxurious *hôtels particuliers* (private mansions) and less expensive *pavillons* (smaller residences). Today many of them house museums and government institutions.

When the aristocracy moved out of Paris to Versailles and Faubourg St-Germain during the late 17th and the 18th centuries, the Marais and its townhouses passed into the hands of ordinary Parisians. The 110-hectare area was given a major face-lift in the late 1960s and early 1970s. The Marais has become a much desired address in recent years; it also remains home to a long-established Jewish community and is the centre of Paris' gay life.

Today, the Marais is one of the few neighbourhoods of Paris that still has most of its pre-Revolution architecture. Examples include the **oldest house in Paris** at 3 rue Volta (Map pp96–8) in the 3e, parts of which date back to 1292; the medieval one at 51 rue de Montmorency (Map pp105–7) in the 3e dating back to 1407 and the 16th-century half-timbered buildings at 11 and 13 rue François Miron (Map pp105–7) in the 4e.

After years as a run-down immigrant neighbourhood notorious for its high crime rate, the contiguous Bastille district (11e and 12e) has undergone a fair degree of gentrification, largely due to the opening of the Opéra Bastille back in 1989. Though the area is not the hip nightlife centre it was throughout most of the 1990s, it still has quite a bit to offer after dark, with numerous pubs, bars and clubs lining rue de Lappe and rue de la Roquette.

HÔTEL DE VILLE

After having been gutted during the Paris Commune of 1871, Paris' **Hôtel de Ville** (city hall; Map pp105-7; ☎ 0 820 007 575; www.paris.fr; place de l'Hôtel de Ville, 4e; metro Hôtel de Ville) was rebuilt in the neo-Renaissance style (1874–82). The ornate façade is decorated with 108 statues of noteworthy Parisians. There's a **Salon d'Accueil** (reception hall; 29 rue de Rivoli, 4e; Ⓨ 9.30am–6-7pm Mon-Sat), which dispenses copious amounts of information and brochures and is used for temporary exhibitions.

The Hôtel de Ville faces the majestic **place de l'Hôtel de Ville**, used from the Middle Ages to the 19th century to stage many of Paris' celebrations, rebellions, book burnings and public executions. Known as place de Grève (Strand Square) until 1830, it was in centuries past a favourite gathering place of the unemployed, which is why a strike is called *une grève* in French to this day.

PLACE DES VOSGES

Place des Vosges (Map pp102-7; metro St-Paul or Bastille), inaugurated in 1612 as place Royale, is an ensemble of 36 symmetrical houses with ground-floor arcades, steep slate roofs and large dormer windows arranged around a large square. Only the earliest houses were built of brick; to save time and money, the rest were given timber frames and faced with plaster, which was then painted to resemble brick.

The author Victor Hugo lived at the square's Hôtel de Rohan-Guéménée from 1832 to 1848, moving here a year after the publication of *Notre Dame de Paris* (The Hunchback of Notre Dame). The **Maison de Victor Hugo** (Victor Hugo House; Map pp102-4; ☎ 01 42 72 10 16; www.paris.fr/musees/maison_de _victor_hugo in French; permanent collections admission free, temporary exhibitions adult/senior & student/14-25 yrs/under 14 €5.50/4/2.50/free; ☟ 10am-6pm Tue-Sun) is now a municipal museum devoted to the life and times of the celebrated novelist and poet, with an impressive collection of his drawings and portraits.

MUSÉE CARNAVALET

This museum, also called **Musée de l'Histoire de Paris** (Paris History Museum; Map pp105-7; ☎ 01 44 59 58 58; www.paris.fr/musees/musee_carnavalet in French; 23 rue de Sévigné, 3e; metro St-Paul or Chemin Vert; permanent collections admission free, temporary exhibits adult/senior & student/14-25 yrs/under 14 €5.50/4/2.50/free; ☟ 10am-6pm Tue-Sun), is in two *hôtels particuliers*. It charts the history of Paris from the Gallo-Roman period to the 20th century. Some of the nation's most important documents, paintings and other objects from the French Revolution are here (Rooms 101 to 113), as is Fouquet's magnificent Art Nouveau jewellery shop from the rue Royale (Room 142) and Marcel Proust's cork-lined bedroom from his apartment on blvd Haussmann (Room 147), in which he wrote most of the 7350-page *À la Recherche du Temps Perdu*.

MUSÉE PICASSO

The **Picasso Museum** (Map pp105-7; ☎ 01 42 71 25 21; 5 rue de Thorigny, 3e; metro St-Paul or Chemin Vert; adult/18-25 yrs/under 18 €6.70/5.20/free, 1st Sun of month free; ☟ 9.30am-6pm Wed-Mon Apr-Sep, 9.30am-5.30pm Wed-Mon Oct-Mar), housed in the mid-17th-century Hôtel Salé, is one of Paris' best-loved art museums and includes more than 3500 of the *grand maître*'s engravings, paintings, ceramic works, drawings and sculptures. You can also see part of Picasso's personal art collection, which includes works by Braque, Cézanne, Matisse, Modigliani and Degas.

MUSÉE D'ART ET D'HISTOIRE DU JUDAÏSME

The **Musée d'Art et d'Histoire du Judaïsme** (Art & History of Judaism Museum; Map pp105-7; ☎ 01 53 01 86

60; www.mahj.org; 71 rue du Temple, 3e; metro Rambuteau; adult/student & 18-25 yrs/under 18 €6.10/3.80/free; ☟ 11am-6pm Mon-Fri, 10am-6pm Sun) is housed in the sumptuous, 17th-century Hôtel de St-Aignan. It was formed by combining the crafts, paintings and ritual objects from Eastern Europe and North Africa of the Musée d'Art Juif (Jewish Art Museum) in Montmartre with medieval Jewish artefacts from the Musée National du Moyen Âge (p121). It traces the evolution of Jewish communities from the Middle Ages to the present, with particular emphasis on the history of the Jews in France. Highlights include documents relating to the Dreyfus Affair (1894–1900) and works by Paris-based Jewish artists Chagall, Modigliani and Soutine. Expect a very high level of security at the entrance.

MAISON EUROPÉENNE DE LA PHOTOGRAPHIE

The **Maison Européenne de la Photographie** (European House of Photography; Map pp105-7; ☎ 01 44 78 75 00; www.mep-fr.org in French; 5-7 rue de Fourcy, 4e; metro St-Paul or Pont Marie; adult/senior & 9-25 yrs/under 9 €5/2.50/free, plus 5-8pm Wed free; ☟ 11am-8pm Wed-Sun), housed in the rather overwrought Hôtel Hénault de Cantorbe dating from the early 18th century, has cutting-edge temporary exhibits (usually retrospectives on single photographers) and a huge permanent collection on the history of photography, with particular reference to France.

MUSÉE DES ARTS ET MÉTIERS

The **Musée des Arts et Métiers** (Arts & Crafts Museum; Map pp96-8; ☎ 01 53 01 82 00; 60 rue de Réaumur, 3e; metro

Arts et Métiers; adult/5-18 yrs/family €5.50/3.80/15.25; 10am-6pm Tue, Wed & Fri-Sun, 10am-9.30pm Thu) is a must for anyone with a scientific (or mechanical) bent. Instruments, machines and working models from the 18th to 20th centuries are displayed across three floors, with Foucault's original pendulum (1855) taking pride of place.

PLACE DE LA BASTILLE
The Bastille, built during the 14th century as a fortified royal residence, is the most famous monument in Paris that no longer exists; the notorious prison – the quintessential symbol of monarchical despotism – was demolished by a Revolutionary mob on 14 July 1789 and all seven prisoners were freed. **Place de la Bastille** (Map pp102-4; metro Bastille) in the 12e, where the prison once stood, is now a very busy traffic roundabout.

In the centre of the *place* is the 52m-high **Colonne de Juillet** (July Column), whose shaft of greenish bronze is topped by a gilded and winged figure of Liberty. It was erected in 1833 as a memorial to those killed in the street battles that accompanied the July Revolution of 1830; they are buried in vaults under the column. It was later consecrated as a memorial to the victims of the February Revolution of 1848 (see p32).

OPÉRA BASTILLE
Paris' giant 'second' **opera house** (Map pp102-4; ☎ 0 892 899 090, 01 44 61 59 65; www.opera-de-paris .fr in French; 2-6 place de la Bastille, 12e; metro Bastille), designed by the Canadian architect Carlos Ott, was inaugurated on 14 July 1989, the 200th anniversary of the storming of the Bastille. There are **guided tours** (☎ 01 40 01 19 70; adult/senior & student/under 19 €10/8/5; 1½hr), which usually depart at 1pm and 5pm Monday to Saturday. Tickets go on sale 15 minutes before departure at window No 4 of the **box office** (120 rue de Lyon, 11e; 11am-6.30pm Mon-Sat)

Île de la Cité
The site of the first settlement in Paris around the 3rd century BC and later the Roman town of Lutèce (Lutetia), the Île de la Cité remained the centre of royal and ecclesiastical power even after the city spread to both banks of the Seine during the Middle Ages. The buildings on the middle part of the island were demolished and rebuilt during Baron

Haussmann's great urban renewal scheme of the late 19th century.

NOTRE DAME CATHEDRAL
The **Cathédrale de Notre Dame de Paris** (Cathedral of Our Lady of Paris; Map pp105-7; ☎ 01 42 34 56 10; place du Parvis Notre Dame, 4e; metro Cité; 8am-6.45pm Mon-Fri, 8am-7.45pm Sat & Sun) is the true heart of Paris; in fact, distances from Paris to all parts of metropolitan France are measured from **place du Parvis Notre Dame**, the square in front of Notre Dame. A bronze star, set in the pavement across from the main entrance, marks the exact location of **point zéro des routes de France** (point zero of French roads).

Notre Dame is not only a masterpiece of French Gothic architecture but has also been the focus of Catholic Paris for seven centuries. In recent years its western façade has had a thorough cleaning, which makes it even more attractive and inspiring.

Constructed on a site occupied by earlier churches – and, a millennium before that, a Gallo-Roman temple – it was begun in 1163 and largely completed by the mid-14th century. Architect Eugène Emmanuel Viollet-le-Duc carried out extensive renovations in the 19th century. The interior is 130m long, 48m wide and 35m high and can accommodate more than 6000 worshippers.

Notre Dame is known for its sublime balance, though if you look closely you'll see all sorts of minor asymmetrical elements introduced to avoid monotony, in accordance with standard Gothic practice. These include the slightly different shapes of each of the three main portals, whose statues were once brightly coloured to make them more effective as a *Biblia pauperum* – a 'Bible of the poor' to help the illiterate understand the Old Testament stories, the Passion of the Christ and the lives of the saints. One of the best views of Notre Dame is from **Square Jean XXIII**, the lovely little park behind the cathedral, where you can see the mass of ornate **flying buttresses** that encircle the chancel and support its walls and roof.

Inside, exceptional features include three spectacular **rose windows**, the most renowned of which is the 10m-wide one over the western façade above the 7800-pipe organ, and the window on the northern side of the transept, which has remained virtually unchanged since the 13th century. The central choir with its carved wooden stalls and statues representing the Passion of the Christ is also noteworthy. There are free guided tours (in English) of the cathedral at noon on Wednesday and Thursday and at 2.30pm on Saturday.

The **trésor** (treasury; adult/student/3-12 yrs €2.50/2/1; 9.30am-6pm Mon-Sat, 1.30-5.30pm Sun) in the southeastern transept contains artwork, liturgical objects, church plate and relics, some of them of questionable origin. Among these is the Ste-Couronne, the 'Holy Crown', which is purportedly the wreath of thorns placed on Jesus' head before he was crucified and was brought here in the mid-13th century. It is exhibited at 4.45pm on each Friday of Lent and on the first Friday of each month during the rest of the year.

The entrance to the **tours de Notre Dame** (Notre Dame towers; ☎ 01 53 10 07 00; www.monum.fr; rue du Cloître Notre Dame; adult/student & 18-25 yrs/under 18 €6.10/4.10/free, 1st Sun Oct-Mar free; 9.30am-7.30pm Mon-Fri, 9am-9pm Sat & Sun Jul & Aug, 10am-5.30pm Oct-Mar, 9.30am-7.30pm Apr-Jun & Sep), which can be climbed, is from the **North Tower**, to the right and around the corner as you walk out of the cathedral's main doorway. The 387 spiralling steps bring you to the top of the west façade, where you'll find yourself face-to-face with many of the cathedral's most frightening gargoyles, the 13-tonne bell Emmanuel (all the cathedral's bells are named) in the **South Tower** and a spectacular view of Paris.

STE-CHAPELLE
Ste-Chapelle (Holy Chapel; Map pp105-7; ☎ 01 53 40 60 97; www.monum.fr; 4 blvd du Palais, 1er; metro Cité; adult/18-25 yrs/under 18 €6.10/4.10/free, 1st Sun Oct-Mar free, joint ticket with Conciergerie €10.40/7.40/free; 9.30am-6pm Mar-Oct, 9am-5pm Nov-Feb), the most exquisite of Paris' Gothic monuments, is tucked away within the walls of the **Palais de Justice** (Law Courts). The 'walls' of the **upper chapel** are sheer curtains of richly coloured and finely detailed **stained glass**, which bathe the chapel in an extraordinary light.

Built in just under three years (compared with nearly 200 years for Notre Dame), Ste-Chapelle was consecrated in 1248. The chapel was conceived by Louis IX to house his personal collection of sacred relics (now kept in the treasury of Notre Dame).

CONCIERGERIE
The **Conciergerie** (Map pp105-7; ☎ 01 53 40 60 97; www.monum.fr; 2 blvd du Palais, 1er; metro Cité; adult/18-25 yrs/under 18 €7.50/5.50/free, 1st Sun Oct-Mar free, joint ticket with Conciergerie €10.40/7.40/free; 9.30am-6pm Mar-Oct, 9am-5pm Nov-Feb), built in the 14th century for the concierge of the Palais de la Cité, was the main prison during the Reign of Terror (p31) and used to incarcerate alleged enemies of the Revolution before they were brought before the Revolutionary Tribunal in the Palais de Justice next door. Among the 2700 prisoners held in the **cachots** (dungeons) here before being sent in tumbrels to the guillotine were Queen Marie-Antoinette and, as the Revolution began to turn on its own, the Revolutionary radicals Danton and Robespierre.

The Gothic **Salle des Gens d'Armes** (Cavalrymen's Hall) dates from the 14th century and is a fine example of the Rayonnant Gothic style. It is the largest surviving medieval hall in Europe. The **Tour de l'Horloge** (clock tower; cnr blvd du Palais & quai de l'Horloge), built in 1353, has held a public clock aloft since 1370.

PONT NEUF
The sparkling-white stone spans of Paris' oldest bridge, **Pont Neuf** (Map pp105-7; metro Pont Neuf) – literally 'New Bridge' – have linked the western end of the Île de la Cité with both banks of the Seine since 1607, when King Henri IV inaugurated it by crossing the bridge on a white stallion. The seven arches, best seen from the river, are decorated with humorous and grotesque figures of barbers, dentists, pickpockets, loiterers etc.

Île St-Louis
The smaller of the Seine's two islands, Île St-Louis is just downstream from the Île de la Cité. In the early 17th century, when it was actually two uninhabited islets (Île Notre Dame and Île aux Vaches), a building contractor and two financiers worked out a deal with Louis XIII to create one island out of the two and build two stone bridges to the mainland. In exchange they would receive the right to subdivide and sell the newly created real estate. This they did with great success, and by 1664 the entire island was covered with fine new houses.

Today, the island's 17th-century, greystone houses and the shops that line the streets and quays impart a village-like, provincial calm. The central thoroughfare, **rue St-Louis en l'Île**, is home to a number of upmarket art galleries, boutiques and the

French baroque **Église St-Louis en l'Île** (Map pp105-7; ☎ 01 46 34 11 60; 19bis rue St-Louis en l'Île, 4; metro Pont Marie; ☒ 9am-noon & 3-7pm Tue-Sun), built between 1656 and 1725. The area around **Pont St-Louis**, the bridge linking the island with the Île de la Cité, and **Pont Louis Philippe**, the bridge to the Marais, is one of the most romantic spots in all of Paris.

Latin Quarter & Jardin des Plantes

Known as the Quartier Latin because all communication between students and professors here took place in Latin until the Revolution, this area of the 5e has been the centre of Parisian higher education since the Middle Ages. It still has a large population of students and academics affiliated with the Sorbonne (now part of the University of Paris system), the Collège de France, the École Normale Supérieure and other institutions of higher learning. To the southeast, the Jardin des Plantes, with its tropical greenhouses and Muséum National d'Histoire Naturelle, offers a bucolic alternative to cobbles and chalkboards.

MUSÉE NATIONAL DU MOYEN ÂGE

Sometimes called the Musée de Cluny, the **Musée National du Moyen Âge** (National Museum of the Middle Ages; Map pp105-7; ☎ 01 53 73 78 16, 01 53 73 78 00; www.musee-moyenage.fr in French; Thermes de Cluny, 6 place Paul Painlevé, 5e; metro Cluny-La Sorbonne or St-Michel; adult/senior, student & 18-25 yrs/under 18 €5.50/4/free, 1st Sun of month free; ☒ 9.15am-5.45pm Wed-Mon) is housed in two structures: the **frigidarium** (cooling room) and other remains of Gallo-Roman baths dating from around AD 200, and the late-15th-century Hôtel de Cluny, considered the finest example of medieval civil architecture in Paris.

The spectacular displays at the museum include statuary, illuminated manuscripts, armaments, furnishings and objects made of gold, ivory and enamel. A sublime series of late-15th-century tapestries from the southern Netherlands known as La Dame à la Licorne (The Lady with the Unicorn) is hung in Room 13 on the 1st floor. The **Forêt de la Licorne**, a medieval-style garden, is north of the museum.

SORBONNE

Paris' most renowned university, the **Sorbonne** (Map pp102-4; 12 rue de la Sorbonne, 5; metro Luxembourg or Cluny-La Sorbonne) was founded in 1253 by Robert de Sorbon, confessor to Louis IX, as a college for 16 impoverished theology students. Today, the Sorbonne's main complex (bounded by rue de la Sorbonne, rue des Écoles, rue St-Jacques and rue Cujas, 5e) and other buildings in the vicinity house most of the 13 autonomous universities that were created when the University of Paris was reorganised after violent student protests in 1968.

Place de la Sorbonne links blvd St-Michel and the **Chapelle de la Sorbonne**, the university's gold-domed church constructed between 1635 and 1642. The chapel holds the remains of Cardinal Richelieu (1585–1642).

PANTHÉON

The domed landmark now known simply as the **Panthéon** (Map pp102-4; ☎ 01 44 32 18 00; www.monum.fr; place du Panthéon, 5e; metro Luxembourg; adult/18-25 yrs/under 18 €7/4.50/free, 1st Sun Oct-Mar free; ☒ 9.30am-6.30pm Apr-Sep, 10am-6.15pm Oct-Mar) was commissioned around 1750 as an abbey church dedicated to Ste Geneviève, but because of financial and structural problems it wasn't completed until 1789 – not a good year for churches to open in France. Two years later, the Constituent Assembly converted it into a secular mausoleum for the grands hommes de l'époque de la liberté française (great men of the era of French liberty).

The Panthéon is a superb example of 18th-century neoclassicism but its ornate marble interior is gloomy in the extreme. The 80-odd permanent residents of the crypt include Voltaire, Jean-Jacques Rousseau, Victor Hugo, Émile Zola, Jean Moulin and Nobel Prize winner Marie Curie.

JARDIN DES PLANTES

Paris' 24-hectare **Jardin des Plantes** (Botanical Gardens; Map pp102-4; ☎ 01 40 79 30 00; 57 rue Cuvier, 5e; metro Gare d'Austerlitz, Censier Daubenton or Jussieu; ☒ 7.30am-5.30 to 8pm according to the season) was founded in 1626 as a medicinal herb garden for Louis XIII. Here you'll find the Eden-like **Jardin d'Hiver** (Winter Garden; adult/senior & 16-25 yrs €2.30/1.50; ☒ 1-5pm Mon & Wed-Fri, 1-6pm Sat & Sun Apr-Sep, 1-5pm Wed-Sun Oct-Mar), which is also called the **Serres Tropicales** (Tropical Greenhouses); the **Jardin Alpin** (Alpine Garden; admission free; ☒ 8-11am & 1.30-5pm Mon-Fri Apr-Sep), with 2000 mountain plants; and the gardens of the **École de Botanique** (admission free; ☉ 8-11am & 1.30-5pm Mon-Fri), which is where students of the School of Botany 'practice'.

The **Ménagerie du Jardin des Plantes** (Botanical Garden Zoo; ☎ 01 40 79 37 94; 57 rue Cuvier & 3 quai St-Bernard, 5e; metro Jussieu or Gare d'Austerlitz; adult/senior, student & 4-15 yrs €6/3.50; ☉ 9am-6pm Mon-Sat, 9am-6.30pm Sun Apr-Sep, 9am-5pm Mon-Sat, 9am-5.30pm Sun Oct-Mar), a medium-sized (5.5-hectare) zoo in the northern section of the garden, was founded in 1794. During the Prussian siege of Paris in 1870, most of the animals were eaten by starving Parisians. The **Microzoo** (☉ 10am-noon & 2-5.15pm Apr-Sep, 10am-noon & 1.30-4.45pm Oct-Mar), entry to which is included in the admission fee, features microscopic animals and is open to those over 11.

MUSÉE NATIONAL D'HISTOIRE NATURELLE

The **Musée National d'Histoire Naturelle** (National Museum of Natural History; ☎ 01 40 79 30 00; www.mnhn .fr in French; 57 rue Cuvier, 5e; metro Censier Daubenton or Gare d'Austerlitz), created by a decree of the Revolutionary Convention in 1793, was the site of important scientific research during the 19th century. It is housed in four different buildings (all on Map pp102–4) along the southern edge of the Jardin des Plantes.

The **Grande Galerie de l'Évolution** (Great Gallery of Evolution; 36 rue Geoffroy St-Hilaire, 5e; adult/senior & 16-25 yrs €7/5; ☉ 10am-6pm Wed-Mon) has some imaginative exhibits on evolution and mankind's effect on the global ecosystem spread over four floors and 6000 sq metres of space. The **Salle des Espèces Menacées et des Espèces Disparues** on level 2 displays extremely rare specimens of endangered and extinct species while the **Salle de Découverte** (Room of Discovery) on level 1 houses interactive exhibits for kids. There's a guided tour in English (€5) at 3pm on Saturday but it depends on demand.

The **Galerie de Minéralogie, de Géologie et de Paléobotanie** (36 rue Geoffroy St-Hilaire; adult/senior & 16-25 yrs €5/3; ☉ 10am-5pm Mon-Fri, 10am-6pm Sat & Sun Apr-Oct, 10am-5pm Wed-Mon Oct-Mar), which covers mineralogy, geology and palaeobotany (fossilised plants), has an amazing exhibit of giant natural crystals and a basement display of jewellery and other objects made from minerals. The **Galerie de Botanique** (10-18 rue Buffon, 5e), the Botany Gallery to the east, is used for temporary exhibits. The **Galerie d'Anatomie Comparée et de Paléontologie** (2 rue Buffon; adult/senior & 16-25 yrs €5/3; ☉ 10am-5pm Mon-Fri, 10am-6pm Sat & Sun Apr-Sep, 10am-5pm Wed-Mon Oct-Mar) has displays on comparative anatomy and palaeontology (the study of fossils).

MOSQUÉE DE PARIS

The central **Mosquée de Paris** (Paris Mosque; Map pp102-4; ☎ 01 45 35 97 33; www.mosquee-de-paris .org; 39 rue Geoffroy St-Hilaire, 5e; metro Censier Daubenton or Place Monge; adult/senior & 7-25 yrs €2.30/1.50; ☉ 9am-noon & 2-6pm Sat-Thu), with its striking 26m-high minaret, was built in 1926 in the ornate Moorish style so popular at the time. Visitors must be modestly dressed and remove their shoes at the entrance to the prayer hall. The complex includes a North African-style **salon de thé** (tearoom) and **restaurant** (p152) and a **hammam** (☎ 01 43 31 18 14, 01 43 31 38 20; admission €15; ☉ men 2-9pm Tue & 10am-9pm Sun, women 10am-9pm Mon, Wed, Thu & Sat, 2-9pm Fri), a traditional Turkish-style bathhouse where a massage costs €10/20/30 for 10/20/30 minutes.

St-Germain, Odéon & Luxembourg

Centuries ago the Église St-Germain des Prés and its affiliated abbey owned most of today's 6e and 7e. The neighbourhood around the church began to develop in the late 17th century, and these days it is celebrated for its heterogeneity. Cafés such as Les Deux Magots and Café de Flore (p159) were favourite hangouts of postwar, Left Bank intellectuals and the places where existentialism was born.

ÉGLISE ST-GERMAIN DES PRÉS

Romanesque **Église St-Germain des Prés** (Church of St Germanus of the Fields; Map pp105-7; ☎ 01 43 25 41 71, 01 55 42 81 33; 3 place St-Germain des Prés, 6e; metro St-Germain des Prés; ☉ 8am-7pm Mon-Sat, 9am-8pm Sun), which is the oldest church in Paris, was built in the 11th century on the site of a 6th-century abbey and was the dominant church in Paris until the advent of Notre Dame. It has since been altered many times, but **Chapelle de St-Symphorien**, to the right as you enter, was part of the original abbey and is the final resting place of St Germanus (AD 496–576), the first bishop of Paris. Columns in the chancel were taken from the Merovingian abbey. The bell tower over the western entrance has changed little since 990, although the spire dates only from the 19th century.

INSTITUT DE FRANCE

Bringing together five of France's academies of arts and sciences, the august **Institut de**

France (French Institute; Map pp105-7; ☎ 01 44 41 44 41; www.institut-de-france.fr in French; 23 quai de Conti, 6e; metro Mabillon or Pont Neuf) was created in 1795. The most famous of these is the **Académie Française**, founded by Cardinal Richelieu in 1635. Its 40 members, known as the Immortels (Immortals), are charged with the Herculean (some might say impossible) task of safeguarding the purity of the French language.

The domed building housing the Institut de France, across the Seine from the eastern end of the Louvre, is a masterpiece of 17th-century French neoclassical architecture. There are usually **guided tours** (adult/under 25 €9/6) at 10.30am and 3pm on the first Saturday of the month and occasionally on Sunday. Check *Pariscope* or *L'Officiel des Spectacles* (see p160) under 'Conférences' or ring the institute for details.

JARDIN DU LUXEMBOURG
When the weather is fine Parisians of all ages flock to the formal terraces and chestnut groves of the 23-hectare **Jardin du Luxembourg** (Luxembourg Garden; Map pp102-4; metro Luxembourg; ⏰ 7am-9.30pm Apr-Oct, 8am-sunset Mar-Nov) to read, relax and sunbathe. There are a number of activities for children here, and in the southern part of the garden you'll find urban **orchards** as well as the honey-producing **Rucher du Luxembourg** (Luxembourg Apiary).

Palais du Luxembourg (Luxembourg Palace; rue de Vaugirard, 6e), at the northern end of the garden, was built for Marie de Médicis, Henri IV's consort; it has been the **Sénat** (Senate), the upper house of the French parliament, since 1958. There are **guided tours** (reservations ☎ 01 44 61 20 89; adult/under 25 €9/6) of the interior at 10am on the first Sunday of each month, but you must book by the preceding Wednesday.

The **Musée du Luxembourg** (Luxembourg Museum; ☎ 01 42 34 25 95; 19 rue de Vaugirard, 6e; metro Luxembourg or St-Sulpice; adult/student & 13-26 yrs from €9/6/4; ⏰ 11am-7pm Tue-Thu, 11am-10.30pm Fri-Mon), which opened at the end of the 19th century in the orangery of the Palais du Luxembourg as an exhibition space for living artists, now hosts prestigious temporary art exhibitions. Admission price depends on the exhibit.

Montparnasse
After WWI, writers, poets and artists of the avant-garde abandoned Montmartre and crossed the Seine, shifting the centre of artistic ferment to the area around blvd du Montparnasse. Chagall, Modigliani, Léger, Soutine, Miró, Kandinsky, Picasso, Stravinsky, Hemingway, Ezra Pound and Cocteau, as well as such political exiles as Lenin and Trotsky, all used to hang out in the cafés and brasseries for which the quarter became famous. Montparnasse remained a creative centre until the mid-1930s; the boulevard's many restaurants, cafés and cinemas still attract large numbers in the evening.

TOUR MONTPARNASSE
A steel-and-smoked-glass eyesore built in 1974, the 210m-high **Tour Montparnasse** (Montparnasse Tower; Map pp99-101; ☎ 01 45 38 52 56; www .tourmontparnasse56.com; rue de l'Arrivée, 15e; metro Montparnasse Bienvenüe; to 56th fl adult/senior & student/under 14 €7/6/4.50, to 59th fl €8/6.80/5.50; ⏰ 9.30am-11.30pm Apr-Sep; 9.30am-10.30pm Sun-Thu, 9.30am-11pm Fri & Sat Oct-Mar) affords spectacular views over the city – a view, we might add, that does not take in this ghastly oversized lipstick tube. A lift takes you up to the 56th-floor enclosed **observatory**, with an exhibition centre and a video about Paris. You can combine the lift trip with a hike up the stairs to the **open-air terrace** on the 59th floor.

CIMETIÈRE DU MONTPARNASSE
Cimetière du Montparnasse (Montparnasse Cemetery; Map pp99-101; blvd Edgar Quinet & rue Froidevaux, 14e; metro Edgar Quinet or Raspail; ⏰ 8am-6pm Mon-Fri, 8.30am-6pm Sat, 9am-6pm Sun mid-Mar–early Nov; 8am-5.30pm Mon-Fri, 8.30am-5.30pm Sat, 9am-5.30pm Sun early Nov–mid-Mar) received its first 'resident' in 1824. It contains the tombs of such illustrious personages as Charles Baudelaire, Guy de Maupassant, Samuel Beckett, Constantin Brancusi, Chaim Soutine, Man Ray, André Citroën, Alfred Dreyfus, Jean Seberg, Simone de Beauvoir, Jean-Paul Sartre and the crooner Serge Gainsbourg. Maps showing the location of the tombs are available free from the **conservation office** ☎ 01 44 10 86 50; 3 blvd Edgar Quinet, 14e).

CATACOMBES
In 1785 it was decided to solve the hygiene and aesthetic problems posed by Paris' overflowing cemeteries by exhuming the bones and storing them in the tunnels of three disused quarries. One ossuary created

in 1810 is now known as the **Catacombes** (☎ 01 43 22 47 63; Map pp90-2; www.paris.fr/musees /musee_carnavalet in French; 1 place Denfert Rochereau, 14e; metro Denfert Rochereau; adult/senior & student/ 14-25 yrs/under 14 €5/3.30/2.60/free; ⊙ 10am-5pm Tue-Sun), which can be visited. After descending 20m (130 steps) from street level, visitors follow 1.6km of underground corridors in which the bones and skulls of millions of Parisians are neatly stacked along the walls. During WWII these tunnels were used as a headquarters by the Resistance.

The route through the Catacombes begins at a small, dark-green *belle époque*-style building in the centre of place Denfert Rochereau. The exit is on rue Remy Dumoncel (metro Mouton Duvernet), 700m southwest of place Denfert Rochereau.

Faubourg St-Germain & Invalides

Faubourg St-Germain in the 7e, the area between the Musée d'Orsay and, a kilometre to the south, rue de Babylone, was Paris' most fashionable neighbourhood during the 18th century. Some of the most interesting mansions, many of which now serve as embassies, cultural centres and government ministries, are along three streets running east to west: rue de Lille, rue de Grenelle and rue de Varenne. The **Hôtel Matignon** (Map pp99-101; 57 rue de Varenne, 7e) has been the official residence of the French prime minister since the start of the Fifth Republic in 1958.

MUSÉE D'ORSAY

The **Musée d'Orsay** (Orsay Museum; Map pp99-101; ☎ 01 40 49 48 84; www.musee-orsay.fr; 1 rue de la Légion d'Honneur, 7e; metro Musée d'Orsay or Solférino; adult Mon-Sat/Sun €5/3 senior & 18-25 yrs €3, under 18 free, 1st Sun of month free; ⊙ 9am-6pm Tue, Wed, Fri & Sat, 9am-9.45pm Thu, 9am-6pm Sun late Jun-Sep, 10am-6pm Tue, Wed, Fri & Sat, 10am-9.45pm Thu, 9am-6pm Sun Oct-late Jun) is housed in a former train station (1900) facing the Seine from quai Anatole France. It displays France's national collection of paintings, sculptures, *objets d'art* and other works produced between the 1840s and 1914, including the fruits of the impressionist, postimpressionist and Art Nouveau movements. The Musée National d'Art Moderne (p116) at the Centre Pompidou then picks up the torch.

Many visitors to the museum go straight to the upper level (lit by a skylight) to see the famous **impressionist paintings** by Monet, Pissarro, Renoir, Sisley, Degas and Manet and the **postimpressionist works** by Gauguin, Cézanne, Van Gogh, Seurat and Matisse, but there's also lots to see on the ground floor, including some early works by Manet,

Monet, Renoir and Pissarro. The middle level has some superb **Art Nouveau rooms**.

English-language tours (information ☎ 01 40 49 48 48; admission fee plus €6/4.50; 1½hr) include the 'Masterpieces of the Musée d'Orsay' tour, departing at 11.30am Tuesday to Saturday, with an additional one at 4pm on Thursday from February to August. There's an in-depth tour focusing on the impressionists at 2.30pm on Tuesday and 4pm on Thursday at least once a month. The 1½-hour **audioguide tour** (€5), available in six languages, points out around 80 major works. Be aware that tickets are valid all day so you can leave and re-enter the museum as you please.

MUSÉE RODIN

The **Musée Rodin** (Rodin Museum; Map pp99-101; ☎ 01 44 18 61 10; www.musee-rodin.fr; 77 rue de Varenne, 7e; metro Varenne; adult Mon-Sat/Sun €5/3 senior & 18-25 yrs €3, under 18 free, 1st Sun of month free, garden only €1; 🕙 9.30am-5.45pm Apr-Sep, 9.30am-4.45pm Oct-Mar) is both a sublime museum and one of the most relaxing spots in the city, with a lovely **garden** full of sculptures and shade trees in which to rest and contemplate *The Thinker*. Rooms on two floors of this 18th-century residence display extraordinarily vital bronze and marble sculptures by Rodin, including casts of some of his most celebrated works: *The Hand of God*, *The Burghers of Calais*, *Cathedral*, that perennial crowd-pleaser *The Thinker* and the incomparable *The Kiss*.

HÔTEL DES INVALIDES

The **Hôtel des Invalides** (Map pp99-101; metro Varenne or La Tour Maubourg) was built in the 1670s by Louis XIV to provide housing for 4000 *invalides* (disabled war veterans). On 14 July 1789 a mob forced its way into the building and, after fierce fighting, seized 28,000 rifles before heading on to the prison at Bastille and revolution.

North of the Hôtel des Invalides' main courtyard, the so-called **Cour d'Honneur**, the **Musée de l'Armée** (Army Museum; ☎ 01 44 42 37 72; www.invalides.org; 129 rue de Grenelle, 7e; adult/senior, student & 18-25 yrs/under 18 €7/5.50/free; 🕙 10am-6pm Apr-Sep, 10am-5pm Oct-Mar, closed 1st Mon of month), which holds the nation's largest collection on the history of the French military. To the south are the **Église St-Louis des Invalides**, once used by soldiers, and the **Église du Dôme**, with its sparkling dome (1677–1735) visible throughout the city, which received

the remains of Napoleon in 1840. The very extravagant **Tombeau de Napoléon 1er** (Napoleon's Tomb; 🕙 10am-6pm Apr-Sep, 10am-5pm Oct-Mar, closed 1st Mon of month), in the centre of the church, consists of six coffins that fit into one another like a Russian *matryoshka* doll. Admission to the Army Museum allows entry to all the other sights in the Hôtel des Invalides.

A 500m-long expanse of lawn called the **Esplanade des Invalides** (metro Invalides, Varenne or La Tour Maubourg) separates Faubourg St-Germain from the Eiffel Tower area.

Eiffel Tower Area & 16e Arrondissement

Paris' very symbol, the Eiffel Tower, is surrounded by open areas on both banks of the Seine, which take in both the 7e and 16e, which is perhaps the most chichi and snobby part of Paris. It's not everyone's *tasse de thé* but there are several outstanding museums and sights in this part of the Right Bank.

EIFFEL TOWER

The **Tour Eiffel** (Map pp99-101; ☎ 01 44 11 23 23; www.tour-eiffel.fr; metro Champ de Mars-Tour Eiffel or Bir Hakeim; 🕙 lifts 9am-midnight mid-Jun–Aug, 9.30am-11pm Sep–mid-Jun; stairs 9am-midnight mid-Jun–Aug, 9.30am-6.30pm Sep–mid-Jun) faced massive opposition from Paris' artistic and literary elite when it was built for the 1889 Exposition Universelle (World Fair), marking the centenary of the Revolution. The 'metal asparagus', as some Parisians snidely called it, was almost torn down in 1909 but was spared because it proved an ideal platform for the transmitting antennas needed for the new science of radiotelegraphy. It welcomed two million visitors the year it opened and three times as many climb to the top each year today.

The Eiffel Tower, named after its designer, Gustave Eiffel, is 324m high, including the TV antenna at the tip. This figure can vary by as much as 15cm, however, as the tower's 10,000 tonnes of iron, held together by 2.5 million rivets, expand in warm weather and contract when it's cold.

Three levels are open to the public. The lifts (west and north pillars), which follow a curved trajectory, cost €4 to the 1st platform (57m above the ground), €7.30 to the 2nd (115m) and €10.40 to the 3rd (276m). Children aged three to 11 pay €2.20/4/5.70, respectively; there are no youth or student discounts and children under three are free.

You can avoid the lift queues by taking the stairs (€3.50) in the south pillar to the 1st and 2nd platforms.

CHAMP DE MARS

Running southeast from the Eiffel Tower, the grassy **Champ de Mars** (Field of Mars; Map pp99-101; metro Champ de Mars-Tour Eiffel or École Militaire) is named after the Roman god of war. It was originally a parade ground for the cadets of the 18th-century **École Militaire** (Military Academy), the vast, French-classical building (1772) at the southeastern end of the park, which counted Napoleon among its graduates.

PALAIS DE CHAILLOT

The two curved, colonnaded wings of the **Palais de Chaillot** (Chaillot Palace; Map pp99-101; metro Trocadéro), built for the 1937 World Exhibition held here, and the terrace in between them afford an exceptional panorama of the Jardins du Trocadéro, the Seine and the Eiffel Tower.

At the far eastern tip of the Palais de Chaillot is the main branch of the **Cinémathèque Française** (p161). In its western wing there are two interesting museums. The **Musée de l'Homme** (Museum of Mankind; ☎ 01 44 05 72 72; www.mnhn.fr in French; 17 place du Trocadéro, 16e; adult/senior & student/4-16 yrs €7/5/3; 9.45am-5.15pm Wed-Mon) contains an excellent display on population growth linked with UN databases, as well as anthropological and ethnographical exhibits from Africa and Europe (1st floor) and the Americas, the Pacific and the Arctic (2nd floor). The **Musée de la Marine** (Maritime Museum; ☎ 01 53 65 69 53; www.musee-marine.fr; 17 place du Trocadéro; adult/senior or student/under 18 €7/5.40/free; 10am-6pm Wed-Mon) focuses on France's naval adventures from the 17th century until today and boasts one of the world finest collections of carved model ships.

JARDINS DU TROCADÉRO

The **Trocadero Gardens** (Map pp99-101; metro Trocadéro), whose fountains and statue garden are grandly illuminated at night, are across Pont d'Iéna from the Eiffel Tower. They are named after a Spanish stronghold near Cádiz that was captured by the French in 1823.

MUSÉE GUIMET DES ARTS ASIATIQUES

The **Musée Guimet des Arts Asiatiques** (Guimet Museum of Asian Art; Map pp93-5; ☎ 01 56 52 53 00; www.museeguimet.fr; 6 place d'Iéna; metro Iéna; permanent collections adult Mon-Sat/Sun €5.50/4 student, senior & 18-25 yrs €4, under 18 free, 1st Sun of month free; 10am-6pm Wed-Mon) is France's foremost repository for sculptures, paintings, *objets d'art* and religious articles from Afghanistan, India, Nepal, Pakistan, Tibet, Cambodia, China, Japan and Korea. The core of the collection – Buddhist paintings and sculptures brought to Paris in 1876 by collector Émile Guimet – is housed in the annexe called the **Galleries du Panthéon Bouddhique du Japon et de la Chine** (Buddhist Pantheon Galleries of Japan & China; ☎ 01 47 23 61 65; 19 av d'Iéna; metro Iéna), in the scrumptious Hôtel Heidelbach a short distance to the north. Don't miss the wonderful Japanese garden here.

FLAME OF LIBERTY MEMORIAL

Southeast of the Musée Guimet and over the border to the 8e is **place de l'Alma** (Map pp93-5; metro Alma-Marceau). This is where on 31 August 1997 in the underpass running parallel to the Seine Diana, Princess of Wales, was killed in an automobile accident along with her companion, Dodi Fayed, and their chauffeur, Henri Paul. The bronze **Flame of Liberty** is a replica of the one topping the torch of the Statue of Liberty and was placed here by Paris-based US firms in 1987 on the centenary of the *International Herald Tribune* newspaper as a symbol of friendship between France and the USA. It became something of a memorial to Diana and was decorated with flowers, photographs, graffiti and personal notes for almost five years. In 2002 it was renovated and cleaned and, this being an age of short memories, there are now very few reminders of the tragedy that happened so close by.

MUSÉE DES ÉGOUTS DE PARIS

The **Musée des Égouts de Paris** (Paris Sewers Museum; Map pp99-101; ☎ 01 53 68 27 81; place de la Résistance, 7e; metro Pont de l'Alma; adult/student & 5-16 yrs/under 5 €3.80/3.05/free; 11am-6pm Sat-Wed May-Sep, 11am-5pm Sat-Wed Oct-Apr) is a working museum whose entrance – a rectangular maintenance hole topped with a kiosk – is across the street from 93 quai d'Orsay, 7e. Raw sewage flows beneath your feet as you walk through 480m of odoriferous tunnels, passing artefacts illustrating the development of Paris' waste-water disposal system. It'll take your breath away, it will.

Étoile & Champs-Élysées

A dozen avenues radiate out from place de l'Étoile – officially place Charles de Gaulle – and first among them is the av des Champs-Elysées. This broad boulevard, whose name refers to the 'Elysian Fields' where happy souls dwelt after death, according to Greek mythology, links place de la Concorde with the Arc de Triomphe. Symbolising the style and *joie de vivre* of Paris since the mid-19th century, the avenue remains a popular tourist destination.

Some 400m north of av des Champs-Élysées is rue du Faubourg St-Honoré (8e), the western extension of rue St-Honoré. It is home to some of Paris' most renowned couture houses, jewellers, antique shops and the 18th-century **Palais de l'Élysée** (Map pp93-5; cnr rue du Faubourg St-Honoré & av de Marigny, 8e; metro Champs Élysées Clemenceau), the official residence of the French president.

ARC DE TRIOMPHE

The **Arc de Triomphe** (Triumphal Arch; Map pp93-5; ☎ 01 55 37 73 77, 01 44 95 02 10; www.monum.fr; metro Charles de Gaulle-Étoile; viewing platform adult/ 18-25 yrs/under18 €7/4.50/free, 1st Sun of month free; ☼ 9.30am-11pm Apr-Sep, 10am-10.30pm Oct-Mar) is 2.2km northwest of place de la Concorde in the middle of place Charles de Gaulle or place de l'Étoile), the world's largest traffic roundabout. It was commissioned in 1806 by Napoleon to commemorate his imperial victories but remained unfinished when he started losing battles and then entire wars. It was not completed until 1836. Since 1920, the body of an **Unknown Soldier** from WWI, taken from Verdun in Lorraine, has lain beneath the arch; his fate and that of countless others is commemorated by a **memorial flame** that is rekindled each evening around 6.30pm.

From the **viewing platform** on top of the arch (up 284 steps and well worth the climb) you can see the 12 avenues – many of them named after Napoleonic victories and illustrious generals (including ultra-exclusive av Foch, which is Paris' widest boulevard) – radiating towards every part of the city. Tickets are sold in the underground passageway beneath place de l'Étoile that surfaces on the even-numbered side of av des Champs-Élysées.

GRAND & PETIT PALAIS

Erected for the 1900 World Exposition, the **Grand Palais** (Great Palace; ☎ 01 44 13 17 17; Map pp93-5; www.rmn.fr; 3 av du Général Eisenhower, 8e; metro Champs-Élysées Clemenceau; without/with booking adult Thu-Mon €9/10 Sun €7/8, student & senior €7/8 Thu-Sun, under 18 free, 1st Sun of month free; ☼ without booking 1-8pm Thu-Mon, 1-10pm Wed, with booking 10am-8pm Thu-Mon, 10am-10pm Wed) was houses the **Galeries Nationales du Grand Palais** beneath its huge, Art Nouveau glass roof. Special exhibitions, among the biggest the city stages, last three or four months here.

The **Petit Palais** (Little Palace; ☼ 01 42 65 12 73, 01 44 51 19 31; www.paris.fr/musees in French; av Winston Churchill, 8e; metro Champs-Élysées Clemenceau), which was also built for the 1900 fair, is home to the **Musée des Beaux-Arts de la Ville de Paris**, the Paris municipality's Museum of Fine Arts, with medieval and Renaissance *objets d'art*, tapestries, drawings and 19th-century French painting and sculpture. It was closed at the time of research and is expected to reopen in 2005.

PALAIS DE LA DÉCOUVERTE

The **Palais de la Découverte** (Palace of Discovery; Map pp93-5; ☎ 01 56 43 20 21; www.palais-decouverte.fr in French; av Franklin D Roosevelt, 8e; metro Champs-Élysées Clemenceau; adult/senior, student & 5-18 yrs/under 5 €6/ 3.90/free; ☼ 9.30am-6pm Tue-Sat, 10am-7pm Sun) is a fascinating science museum with interactive exhibits on astronomy, biology, medicine, chemistry, mathematics, computer science, physics and earth sciences. The **planetarium** (admission €3.50 extra) usually has four shows a day in French; ring or consult the website for current schedules.

Concorde & Madeleine

The cobblestone expanses of 18th-century place de la Concorde are sandwiched between the Jardin des Tuileries and the parks at the eastern end of av des Champs-Élysées. Delightful place de la Madeleine is to the north. Both are in the 8e arrondissement.

PLACE DE LA CONCORDE

This square (Map pp93-5; metro Concorde) was laid out between 1755 and 1775. The 3300-year-old pink granite **obelisk** with the gilded top in the middle of the square once stood in the Temple of Ramses at Thebes (today's Luxor) and was given to France in 1831 by Muhammad Ali, viceroy and pasha of Egypt. The **female statues** adorning the four corners of the square represent France's eight largest cities.

In 1793 Louis XVI's head was lopped off by a guillotine set up in the northwest corner of the square, near the statue representing Brest. During the next two years, a guillotine built near the entrance to the Jardin des Tuileries was used to behead some 1343 more people, including Marie-Antoinette and, six months later, the Revolutionary leaders Danton and Robespierre. The square was given its present name after the Reign of Terror (p31), in the hope that it would be a place of peace and harmony.

The two imposing buildings on the north side of the square are the **Hôtel de la Marine**, headquarters of the French navy, and the **Hôtel de Crillon** (p144), one of Paris' swankiest hotels.

ÉGLISE DE LA MADELEINE

The neoclassical **Église de la Madeleine** (Church of St Mary Magdalene; Map pp93–5; ☎ 01 44 51 69 00; rue Royale, 8e; metro Madeleine; ☽ 7.30am-7pm Mon-Sat, 7.30am-1.30pm & 3.30-7pm Sun) is 350m northeast of place de la Concorde. Built in the style of a Greek temple, what is simply called La Madeleine was consecrated in the year 1845 after almost a century of design changes and construction delays. It is surrounded by 52 Corinthian columns, and the marble and gilt interior is topped by three sky-lit cupolas.

Opéra & Grands Boulevards

Place de l'Opéra (Map pp93–5) is the site of Paris' world-famous (and original) opera house. It abuts the Grands Boulevards, the eight contiguous 'Great Boulevards' – Madeleine, Capucines, Montmartre, Poissonnière, Italiens, Bonne Nouvelle, St-Denis and St-Martin – that stretch from elegant place de la Madeleine in the 8e eastwards to the less-than-desirable place de la République in the 3e, a distance of just under 3km.

The Grands Boulevards were laid out in the 17th century on the site of obsolete city walls and served as a centre of café and theatre life in the 18th and 19th centuries, reaching the height of fashion during the *belle époque*. North of the western end of the Grands Boulevards is blvd Haussmann (8e and 9e), the heart of the commercial and banking district and known for some of Paris' most famous department stores, including **Galeries Lafayette** and **Le Printemps** (p168).

PALAIS GARNIER

Palais Garnier (Garnier Palace; Map pp93–5; place de l'Opéra, 9e; metro Opéra), one of the most impressive monuments erected in Paris during the 19th century, stages operas, ballets and classical-music concerts (p162). In summer it can be visited on English-language **guided tours** (☎ 01 40 01 22 63; admission €10; ☽ 10.30am & noon late Jul-early Sep).

Palais Garnier houses the **Musée de l'Opéra** ☎ 01 47 42 07 02, 01 40 01 22 63; www.opera-de-paris .fr in French; adult/senior, student & 10-26 yrs €6/3, under 10 free; ☽ 10am-6pm Jul & Aug, 10am-5pm Sep-Jun), which contains a lot of documentation (it also functions as an important research library) and some memorabilia. More interestingly admission to the museum includes a visit to the opera house itself as long as there's not a daytime rehearsal or performance.

COVERED ARCADES

There are several **passages couverts** (covered shopping arcades; Map pp96–8) off blvd Montmartre (9e) and walking through them is like stepping back into early-19th-century Paris. The **passage des Panoramas** (11 blvd Montmartre, 2e; metro Grands Boulevards), which was opened in 1800 and received Paris' first gas lighting in 1817, was expanded in 1834 with the addition of four other interconnecting passages: Feydeau, Montmartre, St-Marc and Variétés. The arcades are open till about midnight daily.

On the northern side of blvd Montmartre, between Nos 10 and 12, is **passage Jouffroy** (metro Grands Boulevards), which leads across rue de la Grange Batelière to **passage Verdeau**. Both contain shops selling antiques, old postcards, used and antiquarian books, gifts, pet toys, imports from Asia and the like. The arcades are open until 10pm.

MUSÉE GRÉVIN

Inside passage Jouffroy, the **Musée Grévin** (Grévin Museum; Map pp96-8; ☎ 01 47 70 85 05; www .grevin.com in French; 10 blvd Montmartre, 9e; metro Grands Boulevards; adult/student/6-14 yrs €16/13.80/9; ☽ 10am-6.30pm Mon-Fri, 10am-7pm Sat & Sun) boasts some 250 wax figures that look more like caricatures than characters, but where else do you get to see Marilyn Monroe and Charles de Gaulle face to face or the real death masks of French Revolutionary leaders? The admission charge is positively outrageous and just keeps growing.

Ménilmontant & Belleville

A solidly working-class *quartier* with little to recommend it until just a few years ago, Ménilmontant in the 11e now boasts a surfeit of restaurants, bars and clubs. On the other hand, Belleville (20e), home to large numbers of immigrants, especially Muslims and Jews from North Africa and Vietnamese and ethnic Chinese from Indochina), remains for the most part unpretentious and working-class. **Parc de Belleville** (Map pp96-8; metro Couronnes), which opened in 1992 a few blocks east of blvd de Belleville, occupies a hill almost 200m above sea level amid 4.5 hectares of greenery and offers superb views of the city, especially from the **Maison de l'Air** (☎ 01 43 28 47 63; 27 rue Piat, 20e; metro Pyrénées; adult/senior & student €2/1; ☯ 1.30-5.30pm Tue-Sat, 1.30-6.30pm Sun Apr-Sep, 1.30-5pm Tue-Sun Oct-Mar), which stages temporary exhibitions related to ecology and the environment. Paris' most famous necropolis lies just to the south of the park.

CIMETIÈRE DU PÈRE LACHAISE

The world's most visited graveyard, **Cimetière du Père Lachaise** (Père Lachaise Cemetery; Map pp102-4; ☎ 01 55 25 82 10; metro Philippe Auguste, Gambetta or Père Lachaise; ☯ 8am-6pm Mon-Fri, 8.30am-6pm Sat, 9am-6pm Sun mid-Mar–early Nov; 8am-5.30pm Mon-Fri, 8.30am-5.30pm Sat, 9am-5.30pm Sun early Nov–mid-Mar) opened its one-way doors in 1804. Its 70,000 ornate, even ostentatious tombs form a verdant, open-air sculpture garden.

Among the mortal remains of the one million people buried in the cemetery are Chopin, Molière, Apollinaire, Oscar Wilde, Balzac, Proust, Gertrude Stein, Colette, Simone Signoret, Pissarro, Seurat, Modigliani, Sarah Bernhardt, Yves Montand, Delacroix, Edith Piaf, Isadora Duncan and even the immortal 12th-century lovers, Abélard and Héloïse. One particularly frequented grave is that of 1960s rock star **Jim Morrison** (1943–71), who is buried in division No 6.

Père Lachaise has four entrances, two of which are on blvd de Ménilmontant. Maps indicating the location of noteworthy graves are posted around the cemetery including one by the **conservation office** (Map pp102-4; 16 rue du Repos, 20e) on the western side of the cemetery. Better yet, newsstands and flower kiosks in the area, especially those by the metro stations, sell the primitive but useful

Plan Illustré du Père Lachaise (Illustrated Map of Père Lachaise; €2).

13e Arrondissement & Chinatown

The 13e begins a few blocks south of the Jardin des Plantes in the 5e and is undergoing a true renaissance following the opening of the Bibliothèque Nationale de France François Mitterrand, the arrival of the high-speed Météor metro line (No 14) and the start of the ZAC Paris Rive Gauche project, the massive redevelopment of the old industrial quarter along the Seine. The stylishness of the neighbouring 5e extends to the av des Gobelins, while further south, between av d'Italie and av de Choisy, the succession of Asian restaurants, stalls and shops in the capital's version of Chinatown gives passers-by the illusion of having imperceptibly changed continents.

BIBLIOTHÈQUE NATIONALE DE FRANCE FRANÇOIS MITTERRAND

Rising up from the banks of the Seine are the four glass towers of the controversial, €2 billion **Bibliothèque Nationale de France** (National Library of France; Map pp90-2; ☎ 01 53 79 53 79; www .bnf.fr; 11 quai François Mauriac, 13e; metro Bibliothèque Fr Mitterrand; admission per 2 days/1 yr €4.50/46; ☯ 10am-8pm Tue-Sat, noon-7pm Sun), which was conceived by the late President François Mitterrand as a 'wonder of the modern world' and opened in 1988.

No expense was spared to carry out a plan that many said defied logic. While many of the books and historical documents were shelved in the sun-drenched, 23-storey towers – shaped like half-open books – readers sat in artificially lit basement halls built around a 'forest courtyard' of 140 50-year-old pines, trucked in from the countryside. The towers have since been fitted with a complex (and expensive) shutter system, but the basement is prone to flooding from the Seine. The national library contains around 12 million tomes stored on some 420km of shelves and can accommodate 2000 readers and 2000 researchers.

MANUFACTURE DES GOBELINS

The **Manufacture des Gobelins** (Gobelins Factory; Map pp90-2; ☎ 01 44 08 52 00; 42 av des Gobelins, 13e; metro Les Gobelins; adult/8-25 yrs/under 7 €8/6/free; ☯ guided tour 2pm & 2.45pm Tue-Thu) has been weaving *haute lisse* (high-relief) tapestries on specialised looms since the 18th century, along with Beauvais-style *basse lisse* (low-relief) ones and Savonnerie rugs. The factory can be visited by guided tour only three days a week.

Montmartre & Pigalle

During the late 19th and early 20th centuries the bohemian lifestyle of Montmartre in the 18e attracted a number of important writers and artists, including Picasso, who lived at the studio called **Bateau Lavoir** (Map p108; 11bis Émile Goudeau) from 1908 to 1912 during his so-called Blue Period. Although the activity shifted to Montparnasse after WWI, Montmartre retains an upbeat ambience that all the tourists in the world couldn't spoil.

Only a few blocks southwest of the tranquil, residential streets of Montmartre is lively, neon-lit Pigalle (9e and 18e), one of Paris' two main sex districts (the other, which is *much* more low-rent, is along rue St-Denis and its side streets north of Forum des Halles in the 1er). But Pigalle is more than just a sleazy red-light district; there are plenty of trendy nightspots, including clubs and cabarets, here as well.

The easiest way to reach Montmartre is via the RATP's sleek funicular (p173). Montmartrobus, a bus run by the RATP. It makes a circuitous route from place Pigalle through Montmartre to the 18e Mairie on place Jules Joffrin. Detailed maps are posted at bus stops.

BASILIQUE DU SACRÉ CŒUR

The **Basilique du Sacré Cœur** (Basilica of the Sacred Heart; Map p108; ☎ 01 53 41 89 00; www.sacre-coeur -montmartre.com; place du Parvis du Sacré Cœur, 18e; metro Anvers; ⏱ 6am-11pm), perched at the very top of the Butte de Montmartre (Montmartre Hill), was built from contributions pledged by Parisian Catholics as an act of contrition after the humiliating Franco-Prussian War of 1870–71. Construction began in 1873, but the basilica was not consecrated until 1919.

Some 234 spiralling steps lead you to the basilica's **dome** (admission €5; ⏱ 9am-7pm Apr-Sep, 9am-6pm Oct-Mar), which affords one of Paris' most spectacular panoramas; they say you can see for 30km on a clear day.

PLACE DU TERTRE

Half a block west of the **Église St-Pierre de Montmartre**, which once formed part of a 12th-century Benedictine abbey, is **place du Tertre** (Map p108; metro Abbesses), once the main square of the village of Montmartre. These days it's filled with cafés, restaurants, portrait artists and tourists and is always animated. Look for the **Moulin de la Galette** and **Moulin Radet**, two old-style windmills to the west of the square on rue Lepic.

CIMETIÈRE DE MONTMARTRE

Established in 1798, **Cimetière de Montmartre** (Montmartre Cemetery; Map p108; ☎ 01 43 87 64 24; metro Place de Clichy; ⏱ 8am-6pm Mon-Fri, 8.30am-6pm Sat, 9am-6pm Sun mid-Mar–early Nov, 8am-5.30pm Mon-Fri, 8.30am-5.30pm Sat, 9am-5.30pm Sun early Nov–mid-Mar) is perhaps the most famous cemetery in Paris after Père Lachaise. It contains the graves of Zola, Alexandre Dumas the younger, Stendhal, Heinrich Heine, Jacques Offenbach, Hector Berlioz, Degas, François Truffaut and Vaslav Nijinsky – among many others. The entrance closest to Butte de Montmartre is at the end of av Rachel, just off blvd de Clichy or down the stairs from 10 rue Caulaincourt.

MUSÉE DE L'ÉROTISME

The **Musée de l'Érotisme** (Museum of Erotic Art; Map p108; ☎ 01 42 58 28 73; 72 blvd de Clichy, 18e; metro Blanche; adult/student €7/5; ⏱ 10am-2am) tries to put some 2000 titillating statuary and stimulating sexual aids and fetishist items from days gone by on a loftier plane, with erotic art – both antique and modern – from four continents spread over seven floors. But most of the punters know why they are here.

La Villette

The Buttes Chaumont, the Canal de l'Ourcq and especially the Parc de la Villette, with its wonderful museums and other attractions, create the winning trifecta of the 19th arrondissement.

PARC DE LA VILLETTE

The whimsical, 35-hectare **Parc de la Villette** (La Villette Park; Map pp90–2; ☎ 01 04 03 75 75, 01 40 03 75 03; www.villette.com; metro Porte de la Villette or Porte de Pantin) in the city's far northeastern corner, which opened in 1993, stretches from the Cité des Sciences et de l'Industrie (metro Porte de la Villette) south to the Cité de la Musique (metro Porte de Pantin). Split into two sections by the Canal de l'Ourcq (p135), the park is enlivened by shaded walkways, imaginative street furniture, a series of themed gardens for kids and fanciful, bright-red pavilions known as *folies*.

CITÉ DES SCIENCES ET DE L'INDUSTRIE

The huge **Cité des Sciences et de l'Industrie** (City of Science & Industry; Map pp90-2; ☎ 01 40 05 80 00, ☎ reservations 0 892 697 072; www.cite-sciences.fr; 30 av Corentin Cariou, 19e; metro Porte de la Villette; ☑ 10am-6pm Tue-Sat, 10am-7pm Sun), at the northern end of Parc de la Villette, has all sorts of high-tech exhibits. Free attractions:

Aquarium (level -2; ☑ 10am-6pm Tue-Sat, 10am-7pm Sun)

Cité des Métiers (level -1; ☑ 10am-6pm Tue-Fri, noon-6pm Sat) Information about trades, professions and employment.

Cyber-base (level 1; ☑ noon-7.30pm Tue, noon-6.30pm Wed-Sun) Internet centre.

Médiathèque (levels 0 & -1; ☑ noon-7.45pm Tue, noon-6.45pm Wed-Sun) With multimedia exhibits dealing with childhood, the history of science and health.

A free (and very useful) map/brochure in English called *The Keys to the Cité* is available from the information counter at the main entrance to the complex. If you really want to know what's what and what's where, buy a copy of the detailed, 80-page *Guide to the Permanent Exhibitions* (€3) at reception. An audioguide costs €4.

The huge – and rather confusingly laid-out – **Explora** (adult/7-25 yrs/under 7 €7.50/5.50/free) exhibitions are on levels 1 and 2 and cover everything from train technology and space to biology and sound. Tickets are valid for a full day and allow you to enter and exit up to four times.

The **Planétarium** (level 1; admission €3, 3-7 yrs free, under 3 not admitted; ☑ 11am-5pm Tue-Sun) has six shows a day on the hour (except at 1pm) on a screen measuring 1000 sq metres.

The highlight of the Cité des Sciences et de l'Industrie is the brilliant **Cité des Enfants** (Children's Village; level 0; whose colourful and imaginative hands-on demonstrations of basic scientific principles are divided into three sections: one for three- to five-year-olds, and two for five- to 12-year-olds. In the first, kids can explore, among other things, the behaviour of water (waterproof lab ponchos provided). The second allows children to build toy houses with industrial robots and stage news broadcasts in a TV studio equipped with video cameras. The

third, **Électricité**, is a special electricity exhibition devoted to the five-to-12 age group.

Visits to Cité des Enfants lasting 1½ hours begin four times a day: at 9.45am, 11.30am, 1.30pm and 3.30pm on Tuesday, Thursday and Friday and at 10.30am, 12.30pm, 2.30pm and 4.30pm on Wednesday, Saturday and Sunday. Each child is charged €5 and must be accompanied by an adult (maximum two per family). During school holidays it's a good idea to make reservations two or three days in advance by telephone or via the Internet.

CITÉ DE LA MUSIQUE

The **Cité de la Musique** (Music Village; Map pp90-2; ☎ 01 44 84 44 84; www.cite-musique.fr; 221 av Jean Jaurès, 19e; metro Porte de Pantin), on the southern edge of Parc de la Villette, is a striking triangular-shaped concert hall whose brief is to bring non-elitist music from around the world to Paris' multiethnic masses. In the same complex, the **Musée de la Musique** (Music Museum; ☎ 01 44 84 44 84; adult/senior, student & 18-25 yrs/under 18 €6.10/4.80/free; ☑ noon-6pm Tue-Sat, 10am-6pm Sun) displays some 900 rare musical instruments out of a collection of 4500 warehoused, and you can hear many of them being played through the earphones included in the admission cost.

ACTIVITIES

The best single source of information on sports in Paris (but in French only) is the 500-page *Parisports: Le Guide du Sport à Paris* (www.sport.paris.fr) available free from the **Mairie de Paris** information centre in the **Hôtel de Ville** (Map pp105-7; ☎ 0 820 007 575; www.paris.fr; 29 rue de Rivoli, 4e; metro Hôtel de Ville).

Cycling

Paris has some 220km of bicycle lanes running throughout the city as well as a dedicated lane paralleling some two-thirds of the blvd Périphérique. On Sundays and holidays throughout most of the year, large sections of road are reserved for pedestrians, cyclists and skaters under a scheme called 'Paris Respire' (Paris Breathes).

Maison Roue Libre (Map pp105-7; ☎ 0 810 441 534; www.rouelibre.fr; Forum des Halles, 1 passage Mondétour, 1er; metro Les Halles; ☑ 9am-7pm mid-Jan–mid-Dec), sponsored by RATP, the city's public transport system, is the best place to rent a bicycle in Paris. Bicycles cost €3/8/12/14/20 per hour/half-day/10-hour day/24-hour day/ weekend and include insurance, helmet and baby seat.

Other outfits that rent bicycles:

Bike 'n' Roller (Map pp99-101; ☎ 01 45 50 38 27; 38 rue Fabert, 7e; metro Invalides; per 3 hr/day €9/12; ☺ 10am-8pm Mon-Sat, 10am-6.30pm Sun)

Fat Tire Bike Tours (see p134)

Gepetto & Vélos (Map pp102-4; ☎ 01 43 54 19 95; www.gepetto-et-velos.com in French; 59 rue du Cardinal Lemoine, 5e; metro Cardinal Lemoine; per ½ day/day/ weekend/week €7.50/15/23/50; ☺ 9am-1pm & 2-7.30pm Tue-Sat, 9am-1pm & 2-7pm Sun)

Paris à Vélo, C'est Sympa! (Map pp102-4; ☎ 01 48 87 60 01; www.parisvelosympa.com in French; 37 blvd Bourdon, 4e; metro Bastille; per ½ day/day/weekend/week €9.50/12.50/24/59; ☺ 9.30am-1pm & 2-6pm Mon-Fri, 9am-6pm Sat & Sun Nov-Mar, 9.30am-1pm & 2-6.30pm Mon-Fri, 9am-7pm Sat & Sun Apr-Oct)

Skating

Those into in-line skating might want to join in one of the two so-called Skating Rambles *(Randonnées en Roller)* organised each week throughout the year that attract up to 10,000 participants. The **Pari Roller ramble** (information ☎ 01 43 36 89 81; www.pari -roller.com in French) leaves **place Raoul Dautry** (Map pp99-101; metro Montparnasse Bienvenuë), the plaza between gare Montparnasse and Tour Montparnasse in the 14e, at 10pm Friday, returning at 1am. The **Rollers & Coquillages ramble** (☎ 01 44 54 07 44; www.rollers-coquillages.org) departs from **blvd Bourdon** (Map pp102-4; metro Bastille) in the 4e every Sunday at 2.30pm, returning at between 5.30pm and 6pm.

Nomades (Map pp102-4; ☎ 01 44 5 54 07 44; www .nomadeshop.com in French; 37 blvd Bourdon, 4e; metro Bastille; ☺ 11am-1pm & 2-7pm Mon-Fri, 10am-7pm Sat, 10am-6pm Sun) is the Harrods of shops for roller heads and, in addition to renting out skates, it sells equipment and accessories and gives courses at five different levels. Skates rent for €5/8 per half-day/day during the week and €6/9 at the weekend. A weekend/ week (Monday to Friday)/full week costs €16/23/30. Elbow and knee guards/helmets cost €1/2.

Swimming

Paris has 35 swimming pools that are open to the public; check with the **Mairie de Paris** (☎ 0 820 007 575; www.paris.fr) for the one that's nearest you. Most are short-length pools and

finding a free lane for lengths can be nigh on impossible. Opening times vary widely, but avoid Wednesday afternoon and Saturday when kids off from school take the plunge. Unless noted otherwise the entry cost for municipal pools in Paris is €2.40/1.35 for adults/under 21. A carnet of 10 tickets costs €19.80/11.40.

WALKING TOUR

And you thought it was all berets, baguettes and bistros…To be sure Paris is and will always be *français* – the *couturiers* will continue to spin their glad rags, the *boulangeries* will churn out those long, crispy loaves and the terrace cafés will remain the places from which to watch the world go by. But it's a much more international world nowadays, and *Paris Mondial* (literally 'World Paris'), a diverse, dynamic, multicultural city, vibrates to its rhythms.

France ruled a considerable part of the world until as recently as the middle of the 20th century, and today its population includes a large number of immigrants and their descendants from its former colonies and protectorates in Africa, Indochina, the Middle East, India, the Caribbean and the South Pacific. At the same time, France has continued to accept significant numbers of exiles and refugees. Most of these immigrants have settled in specific areas of the capital, especially Belleville in the 19e and 20e, rue du Faubourg St-Denis in the 10e and La Goutte d'Or and Château Rouge in the 18e. A stroll through these quarters will have you touring the globe without even boarding an aeroplane.

Begin the walk at the Pyrénées metro stop in Belleville, a district where Jewish kosher and Muslim halal butchers share the same streets with cavernous Chinese eating establishments, their windows festooned with dripping *cha siu* (roast pork). Walk west on rue de Belleville past the **birthplace of Edith Piaf** (**1**; see p51) at No 72 and turn left (south) onto rue Piat, though you will be forgiven for thinking says 'Piaf'. Rue Piat will bring you to the **Parc de Belleville** (p129) which, at 200m above sea level, offers wonderful views of what is a very flat city. Descend the steps at the end of rue du Transvaal that lead to the **Maison de l'Air** (**2**; p129) nature centre exhibition space and follow the path to rue de Pali Kao and blvd de Belleville.

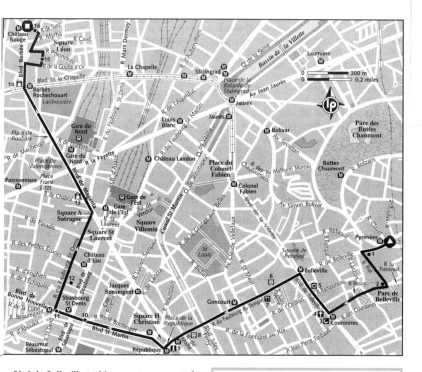

Blvd de Belleville is like a microcosm of Paris Mondial and on market mornings (p169), you might think you've been transported to the Mediterranean, Africa or even Asia. Watch the elegant, turbaned African women in Technicolor *boubous* (West African dress) brush past frenzied, young Asians with mobile phones glued to their ears, and more relaxed Orthodox Jews wearing yarmulkes alongside North Africans in *jellabas* (hooded cloak) on their way to the mosque. At No 39 is the **Mosquée Abou-Bakr (3)** just a few doors down from the modern **Église Notre Dame Réconciliatrice (4)** at the corner of rue de la Fontaine du Roi. About 100m up on the right-hand – or Tunisian – side of blvd de Belleville is the **Synagogue Michkan-Taachov (5)** at No 110. In nearby **rue Ramponeau** you'll encounter a Jewish shop called La Maison du Taleth at No 10 with religious tomes and articles and a kosher butcher Boucherie Zlassi at No 7.

The walk down rue du Faubourg du Temple (11e), left (west) at the top of blvd de Belleville, to place de la République is a long one and you can take the metro for a couple of stops. But in doing so you'd miss the vibrancy and assorted sights: **La Java (6;** p163) at No 105, where Piaf once warbled, and the **Épicerie Asie, Antilles, Afrique (7)** at No 88 that sells edibles from three continents.

Once you've crossed the placid **Canal St-Martin** and walked past the decrepit entrance to the popular clubs **La Favela Chic** and **Gibus (8;** p164), enormous **place de la République** and its ever-present **statue of the Republic (9),** erected in 1883, pop into view. This is where many political rallies and demonstrations in Paris start, end or are taking place. Make your way to the square's northwestern corner and follow blvd St-Martin past **Porte St-Martin (10)** and **Porte St-Denis (11),** two triumphal arches dating from the late 17th century. Turn right (north) and follow **rue du Faubourg St-Denis**, the main artery linking Tamil Nadu with Turkey. **Passage Brady (12**; p156) at No 46, built in 1828 and once housing 100 tiny boutiques, is a warren of Indian, Pakistani and Bangladeshi cafés and restaurants and the perfect spot for a break and refuelling.

Continue northward and when the **Gare de l'Est** comes into view turn left onto blvd Magenta and carry on north past 19th-century **Marché St-Quentin (13**; p169) and the **Gare du Nord**. The landmark pink sign announcing the **Tati department store (14)** marks the start of La Goutte d'Or, the North African quarter called 'The Golden Drop' after a white wine produced here in the 19th century. The district is contiguous with African Château Rouge and outside the metro station you'll most likely be presented with the calling cards of various mediums *(médiums)* or fortune tellers *(voyants)* promising to effect the return of your estranged spouse, unrequited lover or misplaced fortune.

From the metro stop walk northwards up blvd Barbès past numerous goldsmiths and fast-food shops and then turn east into rue de la Goutte d'Or, a great *souk* of a street selling everything from gaudy tea glasses and pointy-toed leather *babouches* (slippers) to colourful belly dancers' costumes. From every direction the sounds of *rä* (a fusion of Algerian folk music and rock) fill the air.

Cut up **villa Poissonnière (15)**, a cobbled street that looks straight out of the 19th-century daguerreotype, and turn left and then right onto **rue des Poissoniers**, the 'Street of Fishermen' that is anything but: here you're more likely to find halal butchers offering special deals on sheep heads and 5kg packets of chicken.

Rue Myrha is the frontier between Central and West Africa and the Maghreb; raï music quickly gives way to Cameroonian *bikutsi* (a fusion of ancestral rhythms and speedy electric guitars) and Senegalese *mbalax*. After crossing over rue Myrha, turn left (west) into **rue Dejean (16)**, where an open-air market is held from 8am to 1pm and 3.30pm to 7.30pm Tuesday to Saturday and 8am to 1pm on Sunday. Here you *will* find fish and lots of it, especially fresh *capitaine* and *thiof* from Senegal, alongside stalls selling fiery Caribbean Scotch Bonnet chillies, plantains and the ever-popular *dasheen* (taro). It's everything you'd need, in fact, to succeed in the art of Afro-Caribbean cuisine.

The Château Rouge metro station is a few steps to the southwest.

PARIS FOR CHILDREN

Paris abounds in places that will delight children, and there is always a special child's entry rate to attractions (though ages of eligibility may vary). Family visits to many areas of the city can be designed around a rest stop (or picnic) at the city's may parks. For details about Disneyland Resort Paris, see p184.

Lonely Planet's *Travel with Children* by Cathy Lanigan includes all sorts of useful advice for those travelling with little ones. If you read French, the daily newspaper *Libération* produces a supplement every other month entitled *Paris Mômes* (Paris Kids), with listings and other information aimed at kids to age 12. An excellent website for information is www.babygoes2.com. *L'Officiel des Spectacles* (p160), the weekly entertainment magazine that appears every Wednesday, lists some *gardes d'enfants* (babysitters) available in Paris.

TOURS
Bicycle

An English-speaking company that consistently gets rave reviews from readers is **Fat Tire Bike Tours** (Map pp99–101; ☎ 01 56 58 10 54; www.fattirebiketoursparis.com; 24 rue Edgar Faure, 15e; metro La Motte-Piquet Grenelle; office ☺ 9am-7pm), formerly Mike's Bike Tours. Fat Tire offers day tours of the city (adult/student €24/22) lasting about four hours at 11am in March and April and September to November, and at 11am and 3.30pm from May to August. Night bicycle tours (adult/student €28/26) depart at 7pm on Sunday, Tuesday and Thursday in March and November and at 7pm daily from April to October. Tours depart from av Gustave Eiffel, 7e (Map pp99–101), just opposite the Eiffel Tower's South Pillar at the start of the Champ de Mars. Costs include bicycle hire and, if necessary, raingear. Three-speeds are also available to rent for €2/15/25/50/65 per hour/day/weekend/week/month.

Boat

Based on the Right Bank just east of the Pont de l'Alma **Bateaux Mouches** (Map pp93-5;

☎ 01 42 25 96 10; www.bateaux-mouches.com; Port de la
Conférence, 8e; metro Alma Marceau; adult/senior & 4-12
yrs/under 4 €7/4/free), the most famous riverboat company in Paris, runs 1000-seat tour
boats, the biggest on the Seine. The tours
leave every half-hour from 10am to 8pm
and every 20 minutes from 8pm to 11pm
between mid-March and mid-November.
For the rest of the year, there are five
daily at 11am, 2.30pm, 4pm, 6pm and
9pm. There may be additional cruises in
winter, depending on demand. The cruise
lasts an hour and commentary is in several
prerecorded languages.

If you prefer to see Paris from one of
its reconditioned canals, **Paris Canal Croisières**
(Map pp96-8; ☎ 01 42 40 96 97; www.pariscanal.com in
French; Bassin de la Villette, 19-21 quai de la Loire, 19e;
adult/senior & 12-25 yrs/4-11 yrs €16/12/9 Mon-Sun
morning, adult, senior & 12-25 yrs/4-11 yrs €16/9 Sun
afternoon) has daily three-hour cruises from
quai Anatole France (7e), just northwest
of the Musée d'Orsay (Map pp99–101) to
Parc de la Villette, 19e (Map pp90–2) via
the charming Canal St-Martin and Canal de
l'Ourcq. Departures are 9.30am from quai
Anatole France and at 2.30pm from Bassin
de la Villette.

Bus
Balabus (in French ☎ 0 892 687 714, in English 6am-
9pm ☎ 0 892 684 114; www.ratp.fr in French; €1.30 or
1 metro/bus ticket; ⏰ 12.30-8pm Sun Apr-Sep) run by
RATP follows a 50-minute route from Gare
de Lyon to La Défense that passes by many
of central Paris' most famous sights. Buses
depart about every 20 minutes.

L'Open Tour (Map pp93-5; ☎ 01 42 66 56 56;
www.paris-opentour.com; 13 rue Auber, 9e; metro Havre
Caumartin or Opéra; 1 day adult/4-11 yrs €25/12, 2 consecutive days €28/12) operates open-deck buses
along four circuits (central Paris, 2¼ hours;
Montmartre-Grands Boulevards, 1¼ hours;
Bastille-Bercy, one hour; and Montparnasse-
St-Germain one hour) daily year-round.
You can jump on and off at more than
50 stops. Schedules vary but buses depart
roughly every 10 to 15 minutes from 9.30am
to 6pm April to October and every 25 to 30
minutes from 9.30am to 4.30pm November
to March.

Walking
Paris Walking Tours (☎ 01 48 09 21 40; www.paris
-walks.com; adult/students under 25/10-18 yrs €10/7/5) has

English-language tours of several different
districts and along different themes, including
Montmartre at 10.30am on Sunday and
Wednesday (leaving from metro Abbesses;
Map p108) and the Marais at 10.30am on
Tuesday and Saturday and 2.30pm on Sunday (departing from metro St-Paul, north
of Île St-Louis; Map pp105–7). There are
other tours focusing on Hemingway, impressionism, Thomas Jefferson, the French Revolution and so on.

FESTIVALS & EVENTS
Innumerable cultural and sporting events
take place in Paris throughout the year;
weekly details appear in *Pariscope* and
L'Officiel des Spectacles (p160). You can
also find them listed month by month
under the heading 'Évènements' (Events)
on the tourist office's website (www.paris
-touristoffice.com).

The following abbreviated list gives you
a taste of what to expect throughout the
year.

January & February
La Grande Parade de Paris (www.parisparade.com)
The city's New Year's Day parade originated in Montmartre
but takes place in different venues (eg along the Grands
Boulevards) depending on the year. Check the website for
details.
Chinese New Year (www.paris.fr) Dragon parades and
other festivities are held in late January or early February
in Chinatown, the area of the 13e between av d'Ivry and
av de Choisy (metro Porte de Choisy or Tolbiac), with
an abridged version along rue Au Maire (metro Arts et
Métiers) in the 3e.
Salon International de l'Agriculture (www.salon
-agriculture.com) A 10-day international agricultural fair
with lots to eat and drink, including dishes and wine from
all over France. Held at the Parc des Expositions at Porte de
Versailles in the 15e (metro Porte de Versailles) from late
February to early March.

March & April
Jumping International de Paris (www.bercy.fr in
French) Annual showjumping tournament, held in early
March, featuring the world's most celebrated jumpers at
the Palais Omnisports de Paris-Bercy in the 12e (metro
Bercy).
Banlieues Bleues (www.banlieuesbleues.org) 'Suburban
Blues' jazz and blues festival (with world, soul, funk and
R&B thrown in for good measure) held in March and April
in St-Denis and other Paris suburbs and attracting big-
name talent.

Marathon International de Paris (www.paris marathon.com) The Paris International Marathon in early April starts on place de la Concorde, 1er, and finishes on av Foch, 16e. The **Semi-Marathon de Paris** is a half-marathon held in March (see the marathon website for details).

Foire du Trône (www.foiredutrone.com in French) Huge fun fair (350 attractions) held on the pelouse de Reuilly of the Bois de Vincennes (metro Porte Dorée) for eight weeks during April and May.

May & June

Foire de Paris (www.comexpo-paris.com) Huge modern living fair, including crafts, gadgets, food and wine, held in early May at the Parc des Expositions at Porte de Versailles in the 15e (metro Porte de Versailles).

Internationaux de France de Tennis (www.french open.org) The glitzy French Open tennis tournament takes place from late May to early June at Stade Roland Garros (metro Porte d'Auteuil) at the southern edge of the Bois de Boulogne in the 16e.

Fête de la Musique (www.fetedelamusique.culture.fr) A national music festival welcoming in summer on 21 June. Caters to a great diversity of tastes (jazz, reggae, classical etc) and features staged and impromptu live performances all over the city.

Gay Pride March (www.gaypride.fr in French) A colourful, Saturday afternoon parade held in late June through the Marais to Bastille celebrates Gay Pride Day, with various bars and clubs sponsoring floats and participants in some pretty outrageous costumes.

Paris Jazz Festival (www.parcfloraldeparis.com) Free jazz concerts every Saturday and Sunday afternoon in June and July in Parc Floral (metro Château de Vincennes).

La Goutte d'Or en Fête (www.gouttedorenfete.org in French) World-music festival (raï, reggae, rap and so on) running from late June to early July at square Léon, 18e (metro Barbès Rochechouart or Château Rouge).

July & August

Bastille Day Paris is *the* place to be on France's national day. Late on the night of the 13th, *bals des sapeurs-pompiers* (dances sponsored by Paris' fire brigades, who are considered sex symbols in France) are held at fire stations around the city. At 10am on the 14th, there's a military and fire-brigade parade along av des Champs-Élysées, accompanied by a fly-over of fighter aircraft and helicopters. In the evening a huge display of *feux d'artifice* (fireworks) is held at around 11pm on the Champ de Mars, 7e.

Tour de France (www.letour.fr) The last stage of the world's most prestigious cycling event ends with a race up av des Champs-Élysées on the 3rd or 4th Sunday of July.

Paris Plage (www.paris.fr) 'Paris Beach', one of the most unique and successful, city recreational events in the world sees 3km of embankment from the quai Henri IV (metro Sully Morland) in the 4e to the quai des Tuileries (metro Tuileries) in the 1er transformed into three sand and pebble beaches, with sun beds, umbrellas, atomisers and plastic palm trees from mid-July to mid-August.

September & October

Jazz à la Villette (www.cite-musique.fr) Super 10-day jazz festival with sessions in Parc de la Villette, at the Cité de la Musique and in surrounding bars in early September.

Festival d'Automne (www.festival-automne.com in French) 'Autumn Festival' of arts – including painting, music, dance and theatre – held in venues throughout the city from mid-September for three months.

November & December

Christmas Eve Mass Celebrated at midnight on Christmas Eve at many Paris churches, including Notre Dame, but get there by 11pm to find a place.

New Year's Eve Blvd St-Michel (5e), place de la Bastille (11e), the Eiffel Tower (7e) and especially av des Champs-Élysées (8e) are the places to be.

SLEEPING

There is a wide choice of accommodation for all budgets throughout much of Paris. When calculating accommodation costs in Paris, assume you'll spend €15 to €25 per person per night in a hostel and at least €30 for a wash-basin-equipped double in a budget hotel (count on closer to €50 if you want your own shower). Bear in mind that you may be charged €2 to €5 to use communal showers in budget hotels. If you can't go without your daily ablutions, it is often a false economy staying at such places.

Mid-range hotels in Paris offer some of the best value for money of any European capital. Hotels at this level always have en suite facilities. All rooms have showers or baths unless noted otherwise. These hotels charge between €65 and €150 for a double and are generally excellent value, especially at the higher end.

Top-end places run the full gamut from tasteful and discreet boutique hotels that will usually cost two people up to €250 a night to deluxe-style palaces with rack rates equivalent to the GNP of a medium-sized Latin American republic.

Breakfast (usually a simple continental affair of bread, croissants, butter, jam and coffee or tea) is served at most hotels with two or more stars and costs from about €6.

Like most cities and towns elsewhere in France, Paris levies a *taxe de séjour* (tourist tax) of between €0.20 (camp site, unclassified hotels) to €1.20 (four-star hotels) per person per night on all forms of accommodation.

Accommodation Services

The Paris tourist office, notably the Gare du Nord branch (p112), can find you a place to stay for the night of the day you stop by. The price for booking a hostel is €1.20, a one-star hotel costing between €40 and €70 for a double is €3 and a two-star (€60 to €100) costs €4. For a three-star hotel costing €100 to €150, you'll pay €6 to book, it's €7.60 for a four-star (€150 to €450) and for a four-star deluxe hotel costing from €260 to €730 it's €8.

Some travel agencies (see p112) can book you reasonably priced accommodation. The student travel agency **OTU Voyages** (Map pp105-7; ☎ 01 40 29 12 22, 0 825 004 024; www.otu.fr in French; 119 rue St-Martin, 4e; metro Rambuteau; ⏰ 9.30am-6.30pm Mon-Fri, 10am-5pm Sat), directly across the *parvis* (square) from Centre Pompidou, can *always* find you accommodation, even in the summer. You pay for the accommodation plus a finder's fee of €12, and the staff give you a voucher to take to the hotel. Prices for singles are around €35, doubles start at about €40. Be prepared for long queues in the high season.

An agency that can arrange bed-and-breakfast accommodation in Paris and gets good reviews from readers is **Alcôve & Agapes** (☎ 01 44 85 06 05; fax 01 44 85 06 14; info@paris -bedandbreakfast.com). Expect to pay between €45 and €100 for a double. **Frendy** (www.frendy .com) is an accommodation booking service (mostly apartments and B&Bs) for gays and lesbians.

Louvre & Les Halles

The very central area encompassing the Musée du Louvre and the Forum des Halles, effectively the 1er and a small slice of the 2e, is more disposed to welcoming top-end travellers, but there are some decent mid-range places to choose from as well. Both airports are linked to nearby metro Châtelet-Les Halles by the RER.

BUDGET

Centre International BVJ Paris-Louvre (Map pp105-7; ☎ 01 53 00 90 90; bvj@wanadoo.fr; 20 rue Jean-Jacques Rousseau, 1er; metro Louvre-Rivoli; dm €25, d per person €28; ✗) This modern hostel run by the

Bureau des Voyages de la Jeunesse (Youth Travel Bureau), has bunks in a single-sex room for two to eight people; rates include breakfast. Guests should be aged under 35. Rooms are accessible from 2.30pm on the day you arrive and all day after that. There are no kitchen facilities and showers are in the hallway. There is usually space in the morning, even in the summer, so stop by as early as you can.

Hôtel de Lille Pélican (Map pp105-7; ☎ 01 42 33 33 42; 8 rue du Pélican, 1er; metro Palais-Musée du Louvre; s/d/tr with washbasin €35/43/65, d with shower €50; ✗) This old-fashioned but clean 13-room hotel down a quiet side street has recently been given a face-lift. Some of its rooms have just a washbasin and bidet, with communal showers in the hallway (€4.50), but most now have their own shower. The friendly and helpful manager speaks good English.

MID-RANGE

Hôtel St-Honoré (Map pp105-7; ☎ 01 42 36 20 38; paris@hotelsthonore.com; 85 rue St-Honoré, 1er; metro Châtelet; s/d/tw/q €59/74/83/92) This upgraded, 29-room hotel is between the Palais Royal and the Seine at the eastern end of a very upmarket shopping street. It offers some fairly cramped rooms and a few more spacious ones for three and four people.

TOP END

Hôtel Ritz Paris (Map pp93-5; ☎ 01 43 16 35 29; www.ritzparis.com; 15 place Vendôme, 1er; metro Opéra; s & d Jul, Aug & Nov-Apr €580-680, May, Jun, Sep & Oct €630-730, junior ste €800-1030, 1-bedroom ste €1050-1500; P ✗ ✗ 🖳 🖾) One of the world's most celebrated hotels, the Ritz Paris – is there any other? – has sparkling rooms and suites. Its **L'Espadon** restaurant has two Michelin stars and the **Hemingway Bar** is where the American author imbibed once he'd made a name for himself – and could afford it.

Marais & Bastille

There are quite a few top-end hotels in the heart of the lively Marais as well as in the vicinity of the elegant place des Vosges, and the choice of lower-priced one- and two-star hotels is excellent. Two-star comfort is less expensive closer to the Bastille in the neighbouring 11e, however. Despite massive gentrification in recent years, there are some fine hostels and some less expensive hotels in the Marais as well. East of Bastille, the relatively untouristed 11e is generally made up of unpretentious, working-class areas and is a good way to see the 'real' Paris up close.

BUDGET

Maison Internationale de la Jeunesse et des Étudiants (☎ 01 42 74 23 45; www.mije.com; ☒ ☐) The MIJE runs three hostels in attractively renovated 17th- and 18th-century *hôtels particuliers* (private mansions) in the heart of the Marais, and it's difficult to think of a better budget deal in Paris. Costs are the same for all three. A bed in a shower-equipped, single-sex dorm sleeping four to eight people is €27 and €42/32/28 per person in a single/double/triple. Rooms are closed from noon to 3pm, and the curfew is 1am to 7am. The maximum stay is seven nights. Individuals can make reservations at any of the three MIJE hostels listed below (all Map pp105–7) by calling the central switchboard or emailing; they'll hold you a bed till noon. During the summer and other busy periods, there may not be space after about mid-morning. There's an annual membership fee of €2.50.

MIJE Le Fourcy (6 rue de Fourcy, 4e; metro St-Paul) The largest of the three branches. There's a cheap eatery here called **Le Restaurant** with a three-course *menu* including a drink for €10.50 and a two-course *formule* plus drink for €8.50.

MIJE Le Fauconnier (11 rue du Fauconnier, 4e; metro St-Paul or Pont Marie) This hostel is two blocks south of MIJE Le Fourcy.

MIJE Maubuisson (12 rue des Barres, 4e; metro Hôtel de Ville or Pont Marie) The pick of the three in our opinion is half a block south of the *mairie* (town hall) of the 4e.

Maison Internationale des Jeunes pour la Culture et la Paix (Map pp102–4; ☎ 01 43 71 99 21; mij.cp@wanadoo.fr; 4 rue Titon, 11e; metro Faidherbe Chaligny; dm €20; ☒ ☐) About 1.3km east of place de la Bastille, this hostel offers accommodation in comfortable but rather institutional rooms for up to eight people, and there's a curfew between 2am and 6am. The upper age limit of 30 is not strictly enforced. Telephone reservations are accepted, but your chance of finding a bed is greatest if you call or stop by between 8am and 10am. The maximum stay is theoretically three days but you can usually stay for a week if there is room.

Hôtel de la Herse d'Or (Map pp102–4; ☎ 01 48 87 84 09; hotel.herse.dor@wanadoo.fr; 20 rue St-Antoine, 4e;

metro Bastille; s/d with washbasin €38/45, d with shower/bath & toilet €58/60) This friendly, 35-room place on busy rue St-Antoine has unsurprising, serviceable rooms down a long stone corridor that have been partially renovated. Hall showers cost €2. And, BTW, *herse* is not 'hearse' in French but 'portcullis'. So let's just call it the 'Golden Gate Hotel'.

Hôtel Rivoli (Map pp105–7; ☎ 01 42 72 08 41; 44 rue de Rivoli or 2 rue des Mauvais Garçons, 4e; metro Hôtel de Ville; s/d with washbasin €27/35, s/d with shower €35/39, d with bath & toilet €49) Long an LP favourite, the Rivoli is forever cheery but not as dirt cheap as it once was, with 20 basic, somewhat noisy rooms. Showers are free. The front door is locked from 2am to 7am.

MID-RANGE

Hôtel du Septième Art (Map pp105–7; ☎ 01 44 54 85 00; hotel7art@wanadoo.fr; 20 rue St-Paul, 4e; metro St-Paul; s with washbasin €59, s & d with shower or bath & toilet €75-130, tw €85-130; ☐) This heavily themed 23-room hotel on the south side of rue St-Antoine is a fun place for film buffs (*le septième art*, or 'the seventh art', is what the French call cinema), with a black-and-white-movie theme throughout, right down to the tiled floors and bathrooms. Oddly, almost all the posters and memorabilia relate to old Hollywood films, with not a reference to a *film français* in sight.

Hôtel Baudelaire Bastille (Map pp102–4; ☎ 01 47 00 40 98; www.tonichotel.com; 12 rue de Charonne, 11e; metro Bastille or Ledru Rollin; s with shower €62-65, d with shower & toilet €65-72, tr €72-82, q €90-100; ☐) Formerly the Pax and now part of the small chain called Tonic Hotels, with three properties elsewhere in France, the one-star Baudelaire Bastille offers large and spotless rooms but does not have a lift.

Hôtel de la Bretonnerie (Map pp105–7; ☎ 01 48 87 77 63; www.bretonnerie.com; 22 rue St-Croix de la Bretonnerie, 4e; metro Hôtel de Ville; s & d €110-145, tr & q €170, ste €180-205) A very charming three-star in the heart of the Marais nightlife area dating from the 17th century. Decorations in each of the 22 rooms and seven suites are unique and some rooms have four-poster and canopy beds.

Hôtel Caron de Beaumarchais (Map pp105–7; ☎ 01 42 72 34 12; www.carondebeaumarchais.com; 12 rue Vieille du Temple, 4e; metro St-Paul; d €120-152; ☒) You have to see this award-winning, themed hotel to believe it. Done up like a private house in the Marais contemporary with the eponymous dramatist – who happens to have written his *chef d'œuvre Le Mariage de Figaro* (The Marriage of Figaro) at No 47 of the same street – the hotel has a prized 18th-century pianoforte, gilded mirrors and candelabras in its front room and stylish (though somewhat small) guest rooms.

Hôtel Castex (Map pp102-4; ☎ 01 42 72 31 52; www .castexhotel.com; 5 rue Castex, 4e; metro Bastille; s €95-115, d €120-140, ste €190-220; 🔡) Once a budget hotel, equidistant from Bastille and the Marais, the Castex has had a major face-lift, but retained some of its 17th-century elements, including a vaulted stone cellar used as a breakfast room, terracotta floor tiles and Toile de Jouy wallpaper. Unusual for a small hotel in Paris, the Castex is fully air-conditioned.

Hôtel Central Marais (Map pp105-7; ☎ 01 48 87 56 08; www.hotelcentralmarais.com; 2 rue Ste-Croix de la Bretonnerie, 4e; metro Hôtel de Ville; r €87, ste €110) This small, seven-room hotel in the centre of gayland caters essentially for gay men, though lesbians are also welcome. Be aware that there is only one bathroom for every two rooms, and the suite for up to four people demands a minimum stay of three nights.

Hôtel Le Compostelle (Map pp105-7; ☎ 01 42 78 59 99; fax 01 40 29 05 18; 31 rue du Roi de Sicile, 4e; metro Hôtel de Ville; s/d with shower & toilet €60/89, d with bath €96) A tasteful 25-room place at the more tranquil end of the Marais not far from place des Vosges and surrounded by excellent restaurants, but the welcome could be a titch warmer.

Hôtel Jeanne d'Arc (Map pp105-7; ☎ 01 48 87 62 11; www.hoteljeannedarc.com; 3 rue de Jarente, 4e; metro St-Paul; small/large s €57/70, d €80, tw/tr/q €95/112/140) This charming hotel near lovely place du Marché Ste-Catherine is a great little *pied-à-terre* for your peregrinations among the museums, bars and restaurants of the Marais, Village St-Paul and Bastille. But everyone knows about it so book early. Do not confuse this two-star place with the two-star Grand Hôtel Jeanne d'Arc in the unlovely 13e.

Grand Hôtel Malher (Map pp105-7; ☎ 01 42 72 60 92; www.grandhotelmalher.com; 5 rue Malher, 4e; metro St-Paul; s low season €86-95, high season €103-115, d €103-112 & €118-132, ste €155-175) With a pretty courtyard in the back, this is a friendly, family-run establishment with nicely appointed rooms. Some of the public areas have been recently renovated, including the lobby.

Hôtel Lyon Mulhouse (Map pp102-4; ☎ 01 47 00 91 50; www.1-hotel-paris.com; 8 blvd Beaumarchais, 11e;

metro Bastille; s €60-85, d €68-75, tw €80-85, tr €90-95, q €100-115) As a former post house, from where carriages would set out for Lyon and Mulhouse in Alsace, this place has been a hotel since the 1920s and has quiet and comfortable rooms. Place de la Bastille and the delightful market on blvd Richard Lenoir (p169) are just around the corner.

Hôtel de Nice (Map pp105-7; ☎ 01 42 78 55 29; fax 01 42 78 36 07; 42bis rue de Rivoli, 4e; metro Hôtel de Ville; s/d/tr €65/100/120) Reception is on the first floor of this especially warm, family-run hotel with 23 comfortable rooms. Some rooms have balconies high above busy rue de Rivoli.

Hôtel de la Place des Vosges (Map pp102-4; ☎ 01 42 72 60 46; hotel.place.des.vosges@gofornet.fr; 12 rue de Birague, 4e; metro Bastille; s €101, d with shower €101-120, tw with bath €106-120, ste 140) This superbly situated two-star hotel due south of sublime place des Vosges has rather average rooms though the public areas are quite impressive. There's a tiny lift from the 1st to 4th floors. Rates include breakfast.

Hôtel Pratic (Map pp105-7; ☎ 01 48 87 80 47; www.hotelpratic.com; 9 rue d'Ormesson, 4e; metro St-Paul; s/d with washbasin & toilet €59/77, with shower €87/98, with bath & toilet €102/117, tr with bath & toilet €135) Opposite the delightful place du Marché Ste-Catherine, this hotel has been thoroughly renovated and the *vieux Marais* theme – exposed beams, gilt frames, striped wallpaper – is almost too much. Rather pricey for what you get, frankly.

Hôtel Royal Bastille (Map pp102-4; ☎ 01 48 05 62 47; hroyalbastille@hotmail.com; 14 rue de la Roquette, 11e; metro Bastille; s/d/tr/q from €78/87/104/123) More upmarket than most of the other lower-priced hotels along lively rue de la Roquette in Bastille, the Royal Bastille is a pleasant 29-room place with good-value rooms.

Hôtel St-Louis Marais (Map pp105 7; ☎ 01 48 87 87 04; www.saintlouismarais.com; 1 rue Charles V, 4e; metro Sully Morland; small/large s €59/91, d/tw/tr €107/125/140) This especially charming hotel in an 17th-century convent is more Bastille than Marais but still within easy walking distance of the latter. Wooden beams, terracotta tiles and heavy drapes tend to darken the 16 rooms but certainly add to the atmosphere.

Hôtel Saintonge Marais (Map pp105-.; ☎ 01 42 77 91 13; www.hotelmarais.com; 16 rue Saintonge, 3e; metro Filles du Calvaire; s €90-105, d €110-115, ste €170) Exposed beams, vaulted cellar and period furniture, makes the 23-room Saintonge

Marais really more Oberkampf/République than the Marais. But with the Musée Picasso practically next door, let's not quibble. You'll get much more bang for your buck here than in the more central parts of Marais, including at the Saintonge's sister property, **Hôtel St-Merry** (below).

TOP END

Hôtel Axial Beaubourg (Map pp105-7; ☎ 01 42 72 72 22; www.axialbeaubourg.com; 11 rue du Temple, 4e; metro Hôtel de Ville; s €110-125, d €155, tw €165; ☒ 및) With newly refurbished 'new look' rooms in the heart of the Marais, the Axial Beaubourg has a name that says it all: modern mixed with historic. It's a very upbeat place to stay and convenient to almost everything.

Hôtel St-Merry (Map pp105-7; ☎ 01 42 78 14 15; www .hotelmarais.com; 78 rue de la Verrerie, 4e; metro Châtelet; d & tw €160-230, tr €205-275, ste €335-407) The inside of this 11-room hostelry with beamed ceilings, church pews and confessionals and wrought-iron candelabra is a Gothic historian's wet dream; you have to see the architectural elements of room No 9 and the furnishings of No 20 to believe them. In reality, it's all a bit of fee-fie *faux* fun.

Île de la Cité & Île St-Louis

Believe it or not, the only hotel on the Île de la Cité is a budget one. However, Île St-Louis, the smaller of the two islands in the Seine, is by far the more romantic and has a string of excellent top-end hotels. It's an easy walk from central Paris.

BUDGET

Hôtel Henri IV (Map pp105-7; ☎ 01 43 54 44 53; 25 place Dauphine, 1er; metro Pont Neuf or Cité; s €24-31, d €31-36, tr €42 with washbasin, d with shower €44, d with shower/bath & toilet €55/68) This decrepit place, with 20 tattered and worn rooms, is popular for its location, location and location right on the tip of the Île de la Cité. It would be impossible to find something this romantic at such a price elsewhere; just don't stay in bed too long. Hall showers cost €2.50 but breakfast is included. Be sure to book well in advance.

TOP END

Hôtel des Deux Îles (Map pp105-7; ☎ 01 43 26 13 35; www.hotel-ile-saintlouis.com; 59 rue St-Louis en l'Île, 4e; metro Pont Marie; s/d & tw €140/158; ☒) While this atmospheric 17-room hotel has rustic

furnishings and an open fire in the lobby, some of the guest rooms are disappointingly small.

Hôtel de Lutèce (Map pp105-7; ☎ 01 43 26 23 52; www.hotel-ile-saintlouis.com; 65 rue St-Louis en l'Île, 4e; metro Pont Marie; s/d/tr €133/158/172; ☒) An exquisite 23-room hotel and more country than city, the Lutèce is under the same friendly and helpful management as the **Hôtel des Deux Îles** (left). The comfortable rooms are tastefully decorated and the location is among the most desirable in the city.

Latin Quarter & Jardin des Plantes

The northern section of the 5e close to the Seine has been popular with students and young people since the Middle Ages.

There are dozens of attractive two- and three-star hotels in the Latin Quarter, including a cluster near the Sorbonne and another group along the lively rue des Écoles. Mid-range hotels in the area are very popular with visiting academics so rooms are hardest to find when conferences and seminars are scheduled (usually from March to July and October). In general this part of the city offers better value among top-end hotels than the neighbouring 6e does. The Luxembourg and Port Royal RER stations are linked to both airports by RER and Orlyval.

BUDGET

Centre International de Séjour BVJ Paris-Quartier Latin (Map pp102-4; ☎ 01 43 29 34 80; bvj@wanadoo .fr; 44 rue des Bernardins, 5e; metro Maubert Mutualité; 1/2/6-bed r per person €35/28/26; ☒) This Left Bank hostel is a branch of the **Centre International BVJ Paris-Louvre** (p137) and has the same rules. All of the rooms here have en suite showers and telephones.

Grand Hôtel du Progrès (Map pp102-4; ☎ 01 43 54 53 18; fax 01 56 24 87 80; 50 rue Gay Lussac, 5e; metro Luxembourg; basic s/d/tr €35/42/55, s/d with shower & toilet €46/54) A budget, 26-room hotel that's been a favourite of students for generations. There are washbasin-equipped singles and large, old-fashioned doubles with a view and a lot of morning sun. Rates include breakfast and the hall showers are free.

Young & Happy Hostel (Map pp102-4; ☎ 01 47 07 47 07; www.youngandhappy.fr; 80 rue Mouffetard, 5e; metro Place Monge; dm €20-22, d per person €23-25; ☒ 및) Although slightly tatty, this is a friendly spot

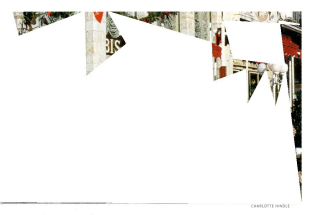

CHARLOTTE HINDLE

Street café scene, Lille (p202)

NEIL SETCHFIELD

ndow details of the Grand' Place
21), Arras

STEPHEN SAKS

Grandes Écuries, Chateau de
Chantilly (p193)

teau de Versailles (p187)

BRENT WINEBRENNER

ROCCO FASANO

River Rance, Dinan (p289)

The white cliffs of Étretat
(p249)

BETHUNE CARMICHAEL

Plage de Bon Secours (p284), St-Malo

ROCCO FASANO

in the centre of the most happening area of the Latin Quarter. It's popular with a slightly older crowd nowadays. The rooms are closed from 11am to 4pm, but the reception remains open; the 2am curfew is strictly enforced. Beds are in smallish rooms for two to four people with washbasins. Rates differ according to the season. In summer the best way to get a bed is to stop by at about 9am.

MID-RANGE

Hôtel Cluny Sorbonne (Map pp102-4; ☎ 01 43 54 66 66; www.hotel-cluny.fr; 8 rue Victor Cousin, 5e; metro Luxembourg; s €69-74, d/tr/q €78/122/130) This hotel, where Rimbaud and Verlaine dallied – and how – in 1872, has 23 pleasant, well-kept rooms; room No 63 has fabulous views of the college and the Panthéon. The lift may only be the size of a telephone box but it will accommodate most travellers and their hat boxes. Service could be better, though.

Comfort Inn Mouffetard (Map pp102-4; ☎ 01 43 36 17 00; www.mouffetard.paris.comfort-inn.fr; 56 rue Mouffetard, 5e; metro Place Monge; s/d €89/119) A chain-like hotel may not be what you had in mind when you decided on Paris, but this one is not entirely without charm on a lovely pedestrians-only street – and it's a hop, skip and a jump from delightful place de la Contrescarpe and one of the best food markets in Paris.

Hôtel La Demeure (Map pp102-4; ☎ 01 43 37 81 25; www.hotel-paris-lademeure.com; 51 blvd St-Marcel, 13e; metro Gobelins; s/d €119-141, ste €198; P ⚄ 🖳) This self-proclaimed *'hotel de caractère'*, owned and operated by a charming father-son team, is just a bit away from the action at the bottom of the 5e. But the refined elegance of its 43 rooms, the almost 'clubby' public areas and the wraparound balconies of the corner rooms make it worth going that extra distance.

Hôtel Esmeralda (Map pp105-7; ☎ 01 43 54 19 20; fax 01 40 51 00 68; 4 rue St-Julien le Pauvre, 5e; metro St-Michel; s with washbasin/shower/bath €35/65/80, d with shower & toilet €80, with bath & toilet €85-95, tr/q from €110/180) The renovated, 19-room Esmeralda is tucked away in a quiet street with full views of Notre Dame. It has been everyone's secret 'find' for years now so book well in advance. This is about as central Latin Quarter as you're ever going to get.

Hôtel de l'Espérance (Map pp102-4; ☎ 01 47 07 10 99; hotel.esperance@wanadoo.fr; 15 rue Pascal, 5e; metro Censier Daubenton; s with shower/bath & toilet €68/76, d with shower/bath & toilet €73/84, tw €84, tr €99) The 'Hotel of Hope', just a couple of minutes' walk south of lively rue Mouffetard, is a quiet and immaculately kept place with *faux* antique furnishings and a warm welcome. Larger rooms have two double beds.

Familia Hôtel (Map pp102-4; ☎ 01 43 54 55 27; www.hotel-paris-familia.com; 11 rue des Écoles, 5e; metro Cardinal Lemoine; s/d with shower & toilet €73.50/90, d/tw/tr/q with bath & toilet €100/102/143.50/180) This very welcoming and well-situated hotel has attractive sepia murals of Paris' landmarks in its rooms. Eight rooms have little balconies, from which you can glimpse Notre Dame. The flower-bedecked windows make the front of the hotel one of the most attractive in the quarter. Rates include breakfast.

Hôtel Gay-Lussac (Map pp102-4; ☎ 01 43 54 23 96; fax 01 40 51 79 49; 29 rue Gay Lussac, 5e; metro Luxembourg; s/d €33/49, with shower €55/64, with shower & toilet €59/68.50, tr/q with shower & toilet €90/95) The Gay-Lussac is a family-run hotel with a lot of character in the southern part of the Latin Quarter. Though the single rooms are small, the others are large and have high ceilings. Rates include breakfast.

Hôtel des Grandes Écoles (Map pp102-4; ☎ 01 43 26 79 23; www.hotel-grandes-ecoles.com; 75 rue du Cardinal Lemoine, 5e; metro Cardinal Lemoine or Place Monge; s & d €105-130, tr €125-150; P) This wonderful hotel, just north of place de la Contrescarpe, has one of the loveliest situations in the Latin Quarter, tucked away in a courtyard off a medieval street with its own garden; if the weather isn't suitable to have breakfast there, you'll enjoy the old-fashioned breakfast just as much. The Irish writer James Joyce lived in one of the courtyard flats in 1921. The owners are especially welcoming and will make you feel at home.

Hôtel Henri IV (Map pp105-7; ☎ 01 46 33 20 20; www.henri-paris-hotel.com; 9-11 rue St-Jacques, 5e; metro St-Michel Notre Dame or Cluny La Sorbonne; s/d/tr €120/140/165) A three-star place awash in antiques, old prints and fresh flowers, the Henri IV is a Latin Quarter oasis mere steps from Notre Dame and the Seine. It's part of the same group as the **Hôtel de Lutèce** and the **Hôtel des Deux Îles** (opposite) on the Île de St-Louis but do *not* confuse this hotel with the bare-bones budget hotel of the same name on the Île de la Cité (see opposite).

Hôtel St-Christophe (Map pp102-4; ☎ 01 43 31 81 54; www.charm-hotel-paris.com; 17 rue Lacépède, 5e;

metro Place Monge; s €104-113, d €115-125) With well-equipped rooms this classy small hotel is on a quiet street between rue Monge in the Latin and the Jardin des Plantes. It's part of the Logis de France umbrella association, always a sign of quality.

Hôtel St-Jacques (Map pp102-4; ☎ 01 44 07 45 45; www.hotel-saintjacques.com in French; 35 rue des Écoles, 5e; metro Maubert Mutualité; s €50-75, d €85-112, tr €105-135; ☐) An adorable place whose balconies overlook the Panthéon. Audrey Hepburn and Cary Grant, who filmed some scenes of *Charade* here a half-century ago, would commend the mod cons that now complement the original 19th-century details (ornamented ceilings, iron staircase and so on), but sadly the service seems to have slipped a notch or two since our last visit. The singles are relatively spacious but not all rooms have toilets.

TOP END

Grand Hôtel St-Michel (Map pp102-4; ☎ 01 46 33 33 02; www.grand-hotel-st-michel.com; 19 rue Cujas, 5e; metro Luxembourg; s/d €120/170, ste €220) Far away from the din of blvd St-Michel, the location of this hotel feels almost remote. Some of the rooms have a balcony and the attached *salon de thé* (tearoom) is quite pleasant.

Mélia Colbert Boutique Hotel (Map pp105-7; ☎ 01 56 81 19 00; melia.colbert@solmelia.com; 7 rue l'Hôtel Colbert, 5e; metro Maubert Mutualité; s & d €260-390, tr & q €442-549, ste €494-602; ✕ ☒ ☐) Unabashedly calling itself a 'boutique hotel', the Colbert has a glorious front courtyard and a namesake address. Well-heeled friends swear by this discreet property.

Hôtel du Panthéon (Map pp102-4; ☎ 01 43 54 32 95; www.hoteldupantheon.com; 19 place du Panthéon, 5e; metro Luxembourg; s €99-213, d €99-223, tr €184-244, f €198-426; ☒ ☐) In the shadow of the capital's largest secular mausoleum and just up the hill from the Jardin du Luxembourg, the Panthéon is a attractive property that feels almost more 'deluxe' than 'top end'. Rates vary so widely according to the season that staff are wary of giving them out. In any case, booking on the web will save you at least 15% on the cost.

Hôtel Relais Christine (Map pp105-7; ☎ 01 40 51 60 80; www.relais-christine.com; 3 rue Christine, 6e; metro Mabillon or St-Michel; s & d €325-425, ste from €475; ✕ ☐) Part of the prestigious Chateaux et Hôtels de France chain, the Relais Christine has an unforgettable courtyard entrance

off a quiet street, a back garden and a spa and fitness centre built in and around an original 13th-century cellar.

St-Germain, Odéon & Luxembourg

The well-heeled St-Germain des Prés is a delightful area to stay but has very little in the way of budget offerings. On the other hand there are some excellent mid-range three-star hotels here.

MID-RANGE

Hôtel des Deux Continents (Map pp105-7; ☎ 01 43 26 72 46; www.2continents-hotel.com; 25 rue Jacob, 6e; metro St-Germain des Prés; s €135, d €145-155, tw €155, tr €190; ☒) The 'Two Continents Hotel' (surely the name is to lure all the Yanks over) is a very pleasant establishment with spacious rooms in a quiet street. The mural in the breakfast room is an early morning eye-opener.

Hôtel de Danemark (Map pp99-101; ☎ 01 43 26 93 78; www.hoteldanemark.com; 21 rue Vavin, 6e; metro Vavin; s €112-145, d €125-145; ✕) This positively scrumptious boutique hotel southwest of the Jardin du Luxembourg has 15 very tastefully furnished rooms – there's original artwork in each, some gaze onto Henri Sauvage's Carreaux Métro, an Art Nouveau tiled apartment building designed in 1912, and the higher priced rooms have Jacuzzis. Montparnasse and all its bars and brasseries are a short walk away.

Hôtel du Globe (Map pp105-7; ☎ 01 43 26 35 50; fax 01 46 33 62 69; 15 rue des Quatre Vents, 6e; metro Odéon;

r with toilet €55, with shower & toilet €70-90, with bath & toilet €105) The Globe is an eclectic, if somewhat dusty, caravansarie with 15 rooms, each with its own theme. We especially like room No 12 and its canopy bed.

Hôtel de Nesle (Map pp105-7; ☎ 01 43 54 62 41; fax 01 43 54 31 88; 7 rue de Nesle, 6e; metro Odéon or Mabillon; s with shower €50-60, d with shower €75, d with bath €100) The Nestle is a relaxed, colourfully decorated hotel with 20 rooms and different themes – from Molière and Africa to 1001 Nights theme – in a quiet street west of place St-Michel. There's also a lovely garden in the back. Reservations are only accepted by telephone and usually only up to a few days in advance.

TOP END

Hôtel d'Angleterre (Map pp105-7; ☎ 01 42 60 34 72; www.hotel-dangleterre.com; 44 rue Jacob, 6e; metro St-Germain des Prés; s €130-220, d €140-230, ste €270-300; 🖳) The 'England Hotel' is a beautiful 27-room property in a quiet street close to busy blvd St-Germain and the Musée d'Orsay. The loyal clientele breakfast or brunch in the courtyard garden patio of this former British Embassy where the Treaty of Paris that ended the American Revolution was signed on 3 September 1783 and where Hemingway spent his first night in Paris (in room No 14 on 20 December 1921, to be precise). Duplex suite No 51 (€300) at the top has beamed ceilings and is the finest in the house.

L'Hôtel (Map pp105-7; ☎ 01 44 41 99 00; www .l-hotel.com; 13 rue des Beaux Arts, 6e; metro St-Germain des Prés; s & d low season €248-529, high season €272-625, ste from €529/625; 🗶 🎇 🖳 🛒) With 20 rooms and tucked away in a quiet quay-side street, the place with the most minimal of names is the stuff of romantic Paris legends. Rock and film star patrons alike fight to sleep in room No 16 where Oscar Wilde died a century ago or in the mirrored Art Deco room (No 36) of legendary dancer Mistinguett. This was also a home away from home for the Argentine writer Jorge Luis Borges (1899–1986), who stayed here many times in the late 1970s and early '80s.

Hôtel des Marronniers (Map pp105-7; ☎ 01 43 25 30 60; fax 01 40 46 83 56; 21 rue Jacob, 6e; metro St-Germain des Prés; s €110, d €150-165, tw €155-170, tr €185-205, q €245; 🎇) At the end of a small courtyard, the 'Chestnut Trees Hotel' has less-than-huge rooms and a magical garden

around the back with a veranda. It's a real oasis in the heart of St-Germain.

La Villa St-Germain des Prés (Map pp105-7; ☎ 01 43 26 60 00; www.villa-saintgermain.com; 29 rue Jacob, 6e; metro St-Germain des Prés; s & d from €240-335, ste from €440; 🗶 🎇) This hotel helped set what has become almost a standard of the Parisian accommodation scene: small, minimalist, discreet. Fabrics, lighting, soft furnishings – all are of the utmost quality and taste.

Montparnasse

Just east of Gare Montparnasse, there are a number of two- and three-star places on rue Vandamme and rue de la Gaîté – though the latter street is rife with sex shops and peep shows. Gare Montparnasse is served by Air France buses from both airports. Place Denfert Rochereau is also linked to both airports by Orlybus, Orlyval and RER. The budget places here don't usually see many foreign tourists.

BUDGET

Hôtel de Blois (Map pp90-2; ☎ 01 45 40 99 48; fax 01 45 40 45 62; 5 rue des Plantes, 14e; metro Mouton Duvernet; s/d with washbasin €40/42, with shower €43/45, with shower & toilet €46/49, tr €61; 🅿) This very friendly, 25-room establishment just off av du Maine offers smallish singles and doubles with both washbasin and bidet and with shower. Triples are fully equipped and have bathtubs.

Celtic Hôtel (Map pp99-101; ☎ 01 43 20 93 53; hotelceltic@wanadoo.fr; 15 rue d'Odessa, 14e; metro Edgar Quinet; s with washbasin/shower €43/54, d with shower & toilet €57-63, tr with shower & toilet €72) An old-fashioned, 29-room place that has undergone only partial modernisation. The Celtic has pretty bare singles and doubles but the Gare Montparnasse is only a convenient 200m away from the hotel.

MID-RANGE

Hôtel Delambre (Map pp99-101; ☎ 01 43 20 66 31; www.hoteldelambre.com; 35 rue Delambre, 14e; metro Montparnasse; s €65-85, d €80-95, tr & q €140) This attractive 30-room hotel just east of the Gare Montparnasse takes wrought-iron as a theme and uses it both in functional pieces and decorative items throughout.

Hôtel de Paris (Map pp99-101; ☎ 01 43 22 10 13; fax 01 40 47 07 58; 51 av du Maine, 14e; metro Montparnasse Bienvenüe; s €68-80, d €75-90, tr €83-90) A simple hotel with the equally simple name; the rooms have little balconies overlooking the Gare Montparnasse.

Petit Palace Hôtel (Map pp90-2; ☎ 01 43 22 05 25; petitpalace@hotelsparisonline.com; 131 av du Maine, 14e; metro Gaîté; s €54-62, d €61-69, tr €69; P ✕) Run by the same family for half a century, this friendly (though rather ambitiously named) two-star hotel has 44 smallish but spotless rooms. All the rooms have showers and toilets.

Faubourg St-Denis & Invalides

The 7e is a lovely arrondissement in which to stay, but apart from the northeastern section – the area east of Invalides and opposite the Louvre – it's fairly quiet here.

Hôtel Lenox St-Germain (Map pp99-101; ☎ 01 42 96 10 95; hotel@lenoxsaintgermain.com; 9 rue de l'Université, 7e; metro Rue du Bac; s €115-120, d €140-150, tw €142-160, ste €255-270; ☼) This mid-range hotel in the posh 7e has simple, uncluttered and comfortable rooms upstairs and a late-opening 1930s-style bar downstairs, which attracts a chic clientele. The Art Deco décor is a treat and the leather armchairs more than comfortable.

Concorde & Madeleine

This area boasts two of Paris' finest hotels – one relatively new and one vintage.

Hôtel Costes (Map pp93-5; ☎ 01 42 44 50 00; fax 01 42 44 50 01; www.hotelcostes.com; 239 rue St-Honoré, 1er; metro Concorde; s & d €350-800, ste from €1200; ✕ ☼ 💻 🛁) The eponymous hotel of Jean-Louis Costes offers a 'luxurious and immoderate home away from home' to the style Mafia. Outfitted in over-the-top camp Second Empire cast-offs, it's the darling of the rich and famous and their hangers-on.

Hôtel de Crillon (Map pp93-5; ☎ 01 44 71 15 00; www.crillon.com; 10 place de la Concorde, 8e; metro Concorde; s €480-575, d €575-855, ste from €945, larger ste from €1400; ✕ ☼ 💻) This colonnaded, 200-year-old palace is the epitome of French luxury. Its sparkling public areas (including **Les Ambassadeurs** restaurant, with its two Michelin stars) are sumptuously decorated with chandeliers, original sculptures, gilt mouldings, tapestries and inlaid furniture. The rooms are spacious and most of them have floor-to-ceiling marble bathrooms to luxuriate in.

Clichy & Gare St-Lazare

These areas offer some excellent mid-range hotels. The better deals are away from Gare St-Lazare but there are several places along rue d'Amsterdam beside the station worth checking out. There's also an unusual place to stay in the budget category.

Hôtel Eldorado (Map pp93-5; ☎ 01 45 22 35 21; eldoradohotel@wanadoo.fr; 18 rue des Dames, 17e; metro Place de Clichy; s/d/tr with shower €45/60/80) This boho place is one of Paris' grooviest finds: a welcoming, well-run place with 40 colourfully decorated rooms in a main building on a quiet street and in an annexe with a private garden at the back. Is this really Paris?

Hôtel Britannia (Map pp93-5; ☎ 01 42 85 36 36; fax 01 42 85 16 93; 24 rue d'Amsterdam, 9e; metro St-Lazare; s & d with shower/bath €78/85, tr with shower or bath €94) The Britannia has narrow hallways but pleasant, clean rooms. It's just opposite Gare St-Lazare and an easy walk to the *grands magasins* on blvd Haussmann. The triples are a bit on the small side though.

Hôtel Favart (Map pp96-8; ☎ 01 42 97 59 83; www .hotel-paris-favart.com; 5 rue Marivaux, 2e; metro Richelieu Drouot; s/d/tr €85/108/130) With rooms facing the Opéra Comique, the Favart is a stylish Art Nouveau hotel that feels like it never let go of the *belle époque*. If you're interested in shopping at the big department stores on blvd Haussmann, this is an excellent choice.

Opéra & Grands Boulevards

The avenues around blvd Montmartre are a popular nightlife area and a lively district in which to stay.

Hôtel des Arts (Map pp96-8; ☎ 01 42 46 73 30; hdag@ free.fr; 7 Cité Bergère, 9e; metro Grands Boulevards; s with shower/bath €68/74, d €74/82, tr €92/98; P) The new management of this hotel has transformed what was once a funky place to stay with loads of character (and resident parrot) into just any other old two-star hotel in the area. But some things never change. The 'Arts Hotel' still has 25 rooms and it remains in a quiet little alley off rue du Faubourg Montmartre. There are some seven other hotels on this street alone.

Hôtel Chopin (Map pp96-8; ☎ 01 47 70 58 10; fax 01 42 47 00 70; 46 passage Jouffroy, entrance at 10 blvd Montmartre, 9e; metro Grands Boulevards; s €57, s with shower & toilet €64-72, d with shower & toilet €73-84, tr with shower & toilet €97) The Chopin, dating back to 1846, is down one of Paris' most delightful 19th-century *passages couverts* (covered shopping arcades; see p128). It may be a little faded around the edges, but it's still enormously evocative of the *belle époque* and the welcome is always warm. After the arcade closes at 10pm, ring the *sonnette de nuit* (night doorbell).

Hôtel Langlois (Map pp93-5; ☎ 01 48 74 78 24; www.hotel-langlois.com; 63 rue St-Lazare, 9e; metro Trinité; s €79-89, d €89-99, tw €99, ste €132) Built in 1870, the hotel formerly known as the Hôtel des Croisés has retained its charming *belle époque* look and feel despite a massive make-over in 1997. The 27 rooms and suites are unusually large for a small-ish hotel in Paris and its very convenient to the department stores on blvd Haussmann.

Hôtel Peletier-Haussmann-Opéra (Map pp96-8; ☎ 01 42 46 79 53; www.peletieropera.com; 15 rue Le Peletier, 9e; metro Richelieu Drouot; s €70-75, d €78-86, tr €86-100; ✕) This is a pleasant, 26-room hotel just off blvd Haussmann and close to the big department stores. There are attractive packages available at weekends, depending on the season.

Gare du Nord, Gare de l'Est & République

The areas east and northeast of the Gare du Nord and Gare de l'Est have always had a more than ample selection of hotels and now you'll also find a hostel within striking distance. At the same time, there are quite a few two- and three-star places around the train stations in the 10e that are convenient if you are catching an early-morning train to London or want to crash immediately upon arrival. Place de la République is convenient for the nightlife areas of Ménilmontant.

Gare du Nord is linked to Charles de Gaulle airport by RER and RATP bus No 350 and to Orly airport by Orlyval. Bus No 350 to/from Charles de Gaulle airport also stops right in front of the Gare de l'Est.

BUDGET

Auberge de Jeunesse Jules Ferry (Map pp96-8; ☎ 01 43 57 55 60; www.fuaj.fr; 8 blvd Jules Ferry, 11e; metro République or Goncourt; dm €19.50, d per person €20; ✕ ▣) This official hostel, three blocks east of place de la République, is somewhat institutional and rooms could be cleaner, but the atmosphere is fairly relaxed. Beds are in two- to six-person rooms, which are locked between 10.30am and 2pm for housekeeping, and there is no curfew. You'll have pay an extra €3 per night if you don't have a Hostelling International card or equivalent. The only other official hostel in central Paris is the **Auberge de Jeunesse Le D'Artagnan** (Map pp90-2; ☎ 01 40 32 34 56; www .fuaj.fr; 80 rue Vitruve, 20e; metro Porte de Bagnolet; dm €20.60; ✕ ▣), which is far from the centre of the action but just one metro stop from the Gare Routière Internationale de Paris-Gallieni (international bus terminal). The largest hostel in France, with 439 beds on seven floors, the D'Artagnan has rooms with two to eight beds, big lockers, laundry facilities, a bar, a cinema and the same rules and regulations as the Jules Ferry hostel.

Peace & Love Hostel (Map pp96-8; ☎ 01 46 07 65 11; www.paris-hostels.com; 245 rue La Fayette, 10e; metro Jaurès or Louis Blanc; dm €17-21, d per person €21-26; ▣) This modern-day hippy hang-out (not an oxymoron, it would appear) is a groovy though chaotically run hostel with beds in smallish, shower-equipped rooms for two to four people. There's a great kitchen and eating area but most of the action seems to revolve around the ground-floor bar (open till 2am) that boasts more than 10 types of beer, including the cheapest *blonde* (that's lager) in Paris.

Sibour Hôtel (Map pp96-8; ☎ 01 46 07 20 74; sibour .hotel@wanadoo.fr; 4 rue Sibour, 10e; metro Gare de l'Est; s & d with washbasin €35, s & d with toilet €40, s/d/tr/q with shower & toilet €50/58/63/80; ℗) A homely and friendly place with well-kept rooms, including some old-fashioned ones. Hall showers cost €3

Hôtel La Vieille France (Map pp96-8; ☎ 01 45 26 42 37; la.vieille.france@wanadoo.fr; 151 rue La Fayette, 10e; metro Gare du Nord; d with washbasin €12, d with shower/ bath & toilet €58/64, tr €78-90) 'The Old France' has relatively spacious and pleasant rooms. At least one reader has written to complain about the noise, however. Hall showers are free.

MID-RANGE

Hôtel Français (Map pp96-8; ☎ 01 40 35 94 14; www .hotelfrancais.com; 13 rue du 8 Mai 1945, 10e; metro Gare de l'Est; s €77-81, d €84-91, tr €109-116; ℗ ✕ ▣) This two-star hotel facing the Gare de l'Est has attractive, almost luxurious rooms (some with balconies). Parking – always difficult around the train stations – in the hotel garage costs a steep €8.

Grand Hôtel de Paris (Map pp96-8; ☎ 01 46 07 40 56; grand.hotel.de.paris@gofornet.com; 72 blvd de Strasbourg, 10e; metro Gare de l'Est; s/d/tr/q €74/79/96/112) A well-run establishment just south of the Gare de l'Est, the Grand has pleasant, soundproofed rooms and a tiny lift.

Nord Hôtel (Map pp96-8; ☎ 01 45 26 43 40; www .nordhotel.com; 37 rue de St-Quentin, 10e; metro Gare du Nord; s €60-79, d €89, tr €109) Just opposite the Gare du Nord, the 'North Hotel' has 46 clean and quiet rooms with shower or bath.

Nord-Est Hôtel (Map pp96-8; ☎ 01 47 70 07 18; hotel .nord.est@wanadoo.fr; 12 rue des Petits Hôtels, 10e; metro Poissonnière; s/d/tr/q €62/72/92/115) This unusual 30-room hotel, charmingly located on the 'Street of Little Hotels', is set away from the street and fronted by a small terrace. It is convenient to both the Gare du Nord and the Gare de l'Est.

Ménilmontant & Belleville

The Ménilmontant nightlife district is an excellent area in which to spend the evening, but the selection of accommodation in all price categories is surprisingly limited.

MID-RANGE

Hôtel Beaumarchais (Map pp102-4; ☎ 01 53 36 86 86; www.hotelbeaumarchais.com; 3 rue Oberkampf, 11e; metro Filles du Calvaire; s €69-85, d €99, ste 140) This brighter-than-bright boutique hotel with its emphasis on sunbursts and bold colours, particularly orange and yellows, is just this side of kitsch. But it makes for a different Paris experience and fits in with its surroundings very well indeed. Some rooms look onto a small leafy courtyard.

Hôtel du Vieux Saule (Map pp105-7; ☎ 01 42 72 01 14; www.hotelvieuxsaule.com; 6 rue Picardie, 3e; metro Filles du Calvaire; s low season €76-91, high season €91-106, d €106-136 & €121-151, VIP r €121-151 & €136-166; P ⊠ ⊠) The flower-bedecked 'Old Willow Tree' is a hostelry in the northern Marais and something of a 'find' because of its slightly unusual location. There's a tranquil little garden and the original 16th-century vaulted cellar (now breakfast room) has antique copper utensils on display. The five rooms on the VIP (4th) floor have been renovated.

Gare de Lyon, Nation & Bercy

The neighbourhood around the Gare de Lyon has a few budget hotels as well as a popular independent hostel.

BUDGET

Blue Planet Hostel (Map pp102-4; ☎ 01 43 42 06 18; www.hostelblueplanet.com; 5 rue Hector Malot, 12e; metro Gare de Lyon; dm €18.30-21; ⊡) This hostel is very close to Gare de Lyon – convenient if you're heading south or west at the crack of dawn. Dorm beds are in rooms for three or four people; the place is closed between 11am and 3pm but there there's no curfew.

Montmartre & Pigalle

Montmartre, encompassing the 18e and the northern part of the 9e, is one of the most charming neighbourhoods in Paris. There is a bunch of top-end hotels in the area and the attractive two-star places on rue Aristide Bruant are generally less full in July and August than in spring and autumn.

The flat area around the base of the Butte Montmartre has some surprisingly good budget deals. The lively, ethnically mixed area east of Sacré Cœur can be a bit rough;

some say it's prudent to avoid Château Rouge metro station at night. Both the 9e and the 18e have fine and recommended hostels.

BUDGET

Hôtel Bonséjour (Map p108; ☎ 01 42 54 22 53; fax 01 42 54 25 92; 11 rue Burq, 18e; metro Abbesses; s with washbasin €22-25, d with washbasin €30-32, d with shower €38-40, tr €53) The 'Good Stay' is at the end of a quiet street in Montmartre. Some rooms (eg Nos 14, 23, 33, 43 and 53) have little balconies and at least one of the rooms (No 55) offers a fleeting glimpse of Sacré Cœur. It's a simple place to stay – no lift, linoleum floors etc – but comfortable and very friendly. Hall showers cost €2.

Le Village Hostel (Map p108; ☎ 01 42 64 22 02; www.villagehostel.fr; 20 rue d'Orsel, 18e; metro Anvers; dm mid-Mar–Oct/Nov–mid-Mar €21.50/20, d per person €25/23, tr €23/21.50; 🖳) 'The Village' is a fine 25-room hostel with beamed ceilings and views of Sacré Cœur. Dorm beds are in rooms for four to six people and all rooms have showers and toilets. Kitchen facilities are available, and there is a lovely outside terrace. Rooms are closed between 11am and 4pm and curfew is 2am.

Woodstock Hostel (Map pp96-8; ☎ 01 48 78 87 76; www.woodstock.fr; 48 rue Rodier, 9e; metro Anvers; dm Oct-Mar/Apr-Sep €15/20, d per person €17/23; 🖳) Woodstock is just down the hill from raucous Pigalle in a quiet, residential quarter. Dorm beds are in rooms for four to six people and there's a kitchen. The rooms are shut from 11am to 3pm; the curfew is 2am. It's a pleasant place with a spoiled feline in residence. The high-season rates also apply over Christmas and the New Year holidays.

MID-RANGE

Hôtel des Arts (Map p100; ☎ 01 46 06 30 52; www .arts-hotel-paris.com; 5 rue Tholozé, 18e; metro Abbesses or Blanche; s/d & tw/tr €64/78/94; 🅿) Part of the Logis de France group, the 'Arts Hotel' is a friendly and attractive place convenient for both Pigalle and Montmartre. Towering over it is the old-style Moulin de la Galette windmill.

Hôtel des Capucines Montmartre (Map p108; ☎ 01 42 52 89 80; fax 01 42 52 29 57; 5 rue Aristide Bruant, 18e; metro Abbesses or Blanche; s €45-50, d €54-60, tr €60-70) This is a decent, family-run hotel with 30 rooms on a small street awash with places to stay.

Hôtel du Moulin (Map p108; ☎ 01 42 64 33 33; www.hotelmoulin.com; 3 rue Aristide Bruant, 18e; metro Abbesses or Blanche; s €54-66, d €59-76, tw €73-79) There are 27 good-sized rooms with toilet and bath or shower at this quiet little hotel. The Korean family who owns the place is very kind. Check out the excellent (and crazy) website.

Hôtel Utrillo (Map p108; ☎ 01 42 58 13 44; adel .utrillo@wanadoo.fr; 7 rue Aristide Bruant, 18e; metro Abbesses or Blanche; s €61, d with shower/bath €73/79, tr €91; 🖳) This friendly 30-room hotel is very nicely decorated and can even boast a small sauna.

TOP END

Hôtel les Trois Poussins (Map pp96-8; ☎ 01 53 32 81 81; www.les3poussins.com; 15 rue Clauzel, 9e; metro St-Georges; s €130-175, d & tw €145-175, tr & q €210, studio for 1 €140-190, for 2 €155-190, for 3 & 4 €225; 🗙 🖳) The 'Hotel of the Three Chicks' (as in little chickens) is a lovely property due south of place Pigalle. Half of the rooms are small studios with their own cooking facilities.

EATING

When it comes to food, Paris has everything – and nothing. As the culinary centre of the most aggressively gastronomic country in the whole world, the city has more 'generic French', regional and ethnic restaurants than any other place in France. But *la cuisine parisienne* (Parisian cuisine) is a poor relation of that extended family known as *la cuisine des provinces* (provincial cuisine). That's because those greedy country cousins have consumed most of what was once on Paris' own plate, claiming it as their own. Today very few French dishes except maybe *vol-au-vent* (light pastry shell filled with chicken or fish in a creamy sauce), *potage St-Germain* (thick green pea soup), onion soup and the humble pig's trotters are associated with the capital.

That said, like the Indian curry and Turkish kebabs of London, over the years ethnic food has become as Parisian as that ubiquitous onion soup; the *nems* and *pâtés impérials* (spring or egg rolls) and *pho* (soup noodles with beef) of Vietnam, the couscous and tajines of North Africa, the *boudin antillais* (West Indian blood pudding) from the Caribbean and the *yassa* (meat or fish grilled in onion and lemon sauce) of Senegal are all eaten with relish throughout the capital. Ethnic food is what

Paris does better than any other city in the country.

Louvre & Les Halles

The area between Forum des Halles (1er) and the Centre Pompidou (4e) is filled with scores of trendy restaurants, but few of them are particularly good and mostly cater to tourists, both foreign and French. Streets lined with places to eat include rue des Lombards, the narrow streets north and east of Forum des Halles and pedestrians-only rue Montorgueil, a market street and probably your best bet for something quick.

If you're in search of Asian food, Japanese businesspeople flock to rue Ste-Anne just west of the Jardin du Palais Royal for the freshest sushi and soba (noodles). There are also some good-value restaurants serving other Asian cuisine in the area.

FRENCH

Café Marly (Map pp105-7; ☎ 01 46 26 06 60; cour Napoléon du Louvre, 93 rue de Rivoli, 1er; metro Palais Royal-Musée du Louvre; starters €8-21, pasta €13-23, sandwiches & snacks €10-14, mains €16-30; ⏲ lunch & dinner to 1am) A classic venue that serves contemporary French fare under the colonnades of the Louvre and overlooks the glass pyramid.

L'Épi d'Or (Map pp105-7; ☎ 01 42 36 38 12; 25 rue Jean-Jacques Rousseau, 1er; metro Louvre-Rivoli; starters €5-15, mains €14-20, menu €18; ⏲ lunch & dinner Mon-Fri, Sat evening till 10pm) This oh-so-Parisian bistro serves well-prepared, classic dishes – such as *gigot d'agneau* (leg of lamb) cooked for seven hours – to a surprisingly well-heeled crowd.

Le Petit Mâchon (Map pp105-7; ☎ 01 42 60 08 06; 158 rue St-Honoré, 1er; metro Palais Royal-Musée du Louvre; starters €6.50-12.50, mains €14-21, lunch menu €16.50; ⏲ lunch & dinner to 11pm Tue-Sun) An upbeat bistro with Lyon-inspired specialities; it's convenient to the Louvre.

AMERICAN

Joe Allen (Map pp105-7; ☎ 01 42 36 70 13; 30 rue Pierre Lescot, 1er; metro Étienne Marcel; brunch €11.90-15, lunch menu €12.90, dinner menus €18 & €22.50; ⏲ noon-midnight) An institution in Paris for some three decades, Joe Allen is little bit of New York in Paris. There's an excellent brunch from noon to 4pm on weekends.

ASIAN

Baan Boran (Map pp96-8; ☎ 01 40 15 90 45; 43 rue de Montpensier, 1er; metro Palais Royal-Musée du Louvre; lunch menu €12.50, meals from €30; ⏲ lunch Mon-Fri, dinner to 11.30pm Mon-Sat) This informal eatery just opposite the Théâtre du Palais Royal is run by two Thai women.

Kunitoraya (Map pp96-8; ☎ 01 47 03 33 65; 39 rue Ste-Anne, 1er; metro Pyramides; soups €8.50-15, noodles €9-16, lunch menu €12.50; ⏲ 11.30am-10pm) With seating on two floors, this simple place has a wide and excellent range of Japanese noodle dishes and set lunches and dinners.

QUICK EATS

L'Arbre à Cannelle (Map pp96-8; ☎ 01 45 08 55 87; 57 passage des Panoramas, 2e; metro Grands Boulevards; dishes €6.50-9.50; ⏲ noon-6.30pm Mon-Sat) A lovely tearoom with original 19th-century décor, *tartes salées* (savoury pies; €6.50 to €7) and excellent salads (€6.25 to €9.30).

SELF-CATERING

There are a number of supermarkets along av de l'Opéra and rue de Richelieu, as well as around Forum des Halles, including a large one in the basement of **Monoprix** (Map pp93-5; 21 av de l'Opéra, 2e; ⏲ 9am-9.50pm Mon-Fri, 9am-8.50pm Sat). Other supermarkets include the following:

Ed l'Épicier (Map pp105-7; 80 rue de Rivoli, 4e; ⏲ 9am-8pm Mon-Sat)

Franprix (Map pp105-7; 35 rue Berger, 1er; ⏲ 8.30am-7.50pm Mon-Sat); Franprix Châtelet branch (Map pp105-7; 16 rue Bertin Poirée, 1er; metro Châtelet; ⏲ 9am-8pm Mon-Sat)

Marais & Bastille

The Marais, filled with small restaurants of every imaginable type, is one of Paris' premier neighbourhoods for eating out. In the direction of place de la République there's a decent selection of ethnic places. If you're looking for authentic Chinese food but can't be bothered going all the way to Chinatown in the 13e or Belleville in the 20e, check out any of the small noodle shops and restaurants along rue Au Maire, 3e (Map pp96-8, metro Arts et Métiers), which is southeast of the Musée des Arts et Métiers. The kosher and kosher-style restaurants along rue des Rosiers, 4e (Map pp105-7), the so-called Pletzel, serve specialities from North Africa, Central Europe and Israel. Many are closed on Friday evening, Saturday and Jewish holidays. Takeaway falafel and *shwarma* (kebabs) are available at several places along the street.

Bastille is another area chock-a-block with restaurants, some of which have added a star or two to their epaulets in recent years. Narrow rue de Lappe and rue de la Roquette, 11e (Map pp102–4), just east of place de la Bastille, may not be as hip as they were a dozen years ago, but they remain popular streets for nightlife and attract a young, alternative crowd.

FRENCH

L'Alivi (Map pp105-7; ☎ 01 48 87 90 20; 27 rue du Roi de Sicile, 4e; metro St-Paul; starters €8-15, mains €14-19.50, lunch menu €15, dinner menu €20; ⓨ lunch & dinner to 11.30pm) This is a rather fashionable Corsican restaurant serving such delectables as *starzapreti* (brocciu cheese and spinach quenelles) and *cabri rôti* (roast kid).

L'Ambassade d'Auvergne (Map pp105-7; ☎ 01 42 72 31 22; 22 rue du Grenier St-Lazare, 3e; metro Rambuteau; starters €9-18, mains €14-19, menu €27; ⓨ lunch & dinner to 10.30pm) The 'Auvergne Embassy', is the place to go if you're really hungry; the sausages and hams of this region are among the best in France, as are the lentils from Puy and the sublime *clafoutis*, a custard and cherry tart baked upside down like a *tarte Tatin* (caramelised apple pie).

Le Bistrot du Dôme Bastille (Map pp102-4; ☎ 01 48 04 88 44; 2 rue de la Bastille, 4e; metro Bastille; starters €8.70-12, mains €18.70-23; ⓨ lunch & dinner till 11pm) This lovely restaurant, little sister to the more established Dôme in Montparnasse (p154), specialises in superbly prepared fish and seafood dishes.

Bofinger (Map pp102-4; ☎ 01 42 72 87 82; 5-7 rue de la Bastille, 4e; metro Bastille; lunch menu €21.50, dinner menu €31.50; ⓨ noon-1am, closed 3-6.30pm Mon-Fri) Founded in 1864, Bofinger is reputedly the oldest brasserie in Paris. Ask for a seat downstairs, under the *coupole* (stained-glass dome); it's the prettiest part of the restaurant.

Chez Nénesse (Map pp105-7; ☎ 01 42 78 46 49; 17 rue Saintonge, 3e; metro Filles du Calvaire; starters €3.50-14.50, mains €12-15, plat du jour €9.50, ⓨ lunch & dinner to 10.30pm Mon-Fri) The atmosphere at Chez Nénesse, an oasis of simplicity and good taste, is 'old Parisian café' and the dishes are prepared with fresh, high-quality ingredients.

Les Galopins (Map pp102-4; ☎ 01 47 00 45 35; 24 rue des Taillandiers, 11e; metro Bastille or Voltaire; starters €6-10.50, mains €11.50-18, lunch menus €11.50 & €15; ⓨ lunch Mon-Fri, dinner to 11pm Mon-Thu, to 11.30pm Fri & Sat) This cute little neighbourhood bistro serves dishes in the best tradition of French

cuisine: *poêlée de pétoncles* (pan-fried queen scallops), *magret de canard* (fillet of duck breast) and *cœur de rumsteck* (tenderloin rump steak).

Le Petit Picard (Map pp105-7; ☎ 01 42 78 54 03; 42 rue Ste-Croix de la Bretonnerie, 4e; metro Hôtel de Ville; lunch menu €12, dinner menus €14.50 & €21.50; ⓨ lunch Tue-Fri, dinner till 11pm Tue-Sun) This popular little restaurant in the centre of the Marais serves traditional French cuisine. If you're very hungry, try the generous *menu traditionel* (€21.50).

Le Réconfort (Map pp105-7; ☎ 01 49 96 09 60; 37 rue de Poitou, 3e; metro St-Sébastien Froissart; starters €6-10, mains €14-20, lunch menus €13 & €17, plat du jour €10, brunch €19; ⓨ lunch & dinner to 11pm Mon-Sat, brunch noon-4pm Sun) 'The Comfort' has generous space between tables, is quiet enough to chat without shouting and the kitchen turns out some very tasty and inventive dishes.

Le Square Trousseau (Map pp102-4; ☎ 01 43 43 06 00; 1 rue Antoine Vollon, 12e; metro Ledru Rollin; starters €6-10, mains €19-16, lunch menu €20, dinner menu €25; ⓨ lunch & dinner to 11.30pm Tue-Sat) This vintage bistro with etched glass, zinc bar and polished wood panelling is comfortable rather than trendy, and attracts a jolly and mixed clientele. Most people come to enjoy the lovely terrace overlooking a small park.

NORTH AFRICAN & MIDDLE EASTERN

404 (Map pp96-8; ☎ 01 42 74 57 81; 69 rue des Gravilliers, 3e; metro Arts et Métiers; couscous & tajines €13-23, lunch menu €17, brunch menu €21; ⓨ lunch Mon-Fri, dinner to midnight daily, brunch to 4pm Sat & Sun) As comfortable a Maghrebi (North African) caravanserai as you'll find in Paris, the 404 not only has excellent couscous and tajines but superb grills (€10 to €21). You'll just love the *One Thousand and One Nights* décor.

La Soummam (Map pp105-7; ☎ 01 43 54 12 43; 25 rue des Grands Augustins, 6e; metro Odéon or St Michael; starters €3.70-7.30, mains €11.50-19, lunch menu €10.50, dinner menus €14.30-24.50; ⓨ lunch & dinner to 11.30pm Mon-Sat) In this restaurant decorated with carpets, pottery and artworks, you can taste the unusual *tammekfoult*, a Berber-style couscous of steamed vegetables accompanied by milk curds, as well as a superb veal tajine with olives, artichokes, prunes and other vegetables.

VEGETARIAN

Grand Apétit (Map pp102-4; ☎ 01 40 27 04 95; 9 rue de la Cerisaie, 4e; metro Bastille or Sully Morland; meals from €15, menus €10-15; lunch Mon-Fri, dinner to 9pm Mon-Wed) 'The Big Appetite', a simple place near Bastille, offers light fare such as miso soup and cereals, as well as strength-building dishes for big eaters only. There's an excellent organic and macrobiotic shop attached.

Piccolo Teatro (Map pp105-7; 01 42 72 17 79; 6 rue des Écouffes, 4e; metro St-Paul; lunch menus €8.20-15.10, dinner menu €21.50; lunch & dinner till 11.30pm) This is an intimate place with exposed stone walls, a beamed ceiling and cosy little tables. Try the *assiette végétarienne* (vegetarian plate; €12.10) or the gratin, the speciality of the house, which combines vegetables, cream and cheese.

OTHER CUISINES

Caves St-Gilles (Map pp102-4; 01 48 87 22 62; 4 rue St-Gilles, 3e; metro Chemin Vert; tapas €5.50-15.70, platters €8-13; lunch & dinner till 11.30pm) This Spanish wine bar a short distance northeast of place des Vosges is the most authentic place on the Right Bank for tapas, paella (at the weekend only; €18) and sangria (€27 for 1L).

Chez Marianne (Map pp105-7; 01 42 72 18 86; 2 rue des Hospitalières St-Gervais, 4e; metro St-Paul; sandwiches €5.50-8, dishes €3.50-20; noon-midnight) Chez Marianne serves Sephardic-style kosher platters with four/five/six different meze (eg falafel, humus) and purées of eggplant, chickpeas and so on cost (€12/14/16). The window of the adjoining deli dispenses killer takeaway falafel sandwiches for €4 and there's an excellent bakery attached.

Coffee India (Map pp102-4; 01 48 06 18 57; 33-35 rue de Lappe, 11e; metro Bastille; starters €5.40-8.40, mains €12-22, lunch menu €9; lunch & dinner to 2am) Despite its confusing name, this restaurant (and cocktail bar/lounge/tearoom/café) serves surprisingly authentic southern Indian fare.

L'Enoteca (Map pp105-7; 01 42 78 91 44; 25 rue Charles V, 4e; metro Sully Morland or Pont Marie; starters €8-13, pasta €10-13, mains €17-20; lunch & dinner to 11.30pm) This trattoria in the historic Village St-Paul quarter, serves *haute cuisine à l'italienne*, and there's an excellent list of Italian wines by the glass (€3 to €9).

La Perla (Map pp105-7; 01 42 77 59 40; 26 rue François Miron, 4e; metro St-Paul or Hôtel de Ville; starters 6.30-8.50, mains €11-15, lunch platters €6-9; lunch & dinner to midnight) A favourite with younger Parisians, 'The Pearl' is a Californian-style Mexican bar-restaurant serving guacamole (€6.30), nachos (€5.50 to €8.50) and burritos

(€7.90 to €8.40). The margaritas (€8.50 to €9.30) are excellent.

Waly Fay (Map pp102-4; 01 40 24 17 79; 6 rue Godefroy Cavaignac, 11e; metro Charonne; starters €5.50-6.50, meze & platters €4.50-10, mains €11.50-15; dinner to 11pm Mon-Sat) For African food with a West Indian twist to the sounds of soul and jazz, try this easygoing 'loungin' restaurant'.

QUICK EATS

L'As de Felafel (Map pp105-7; 01 48 87 63 60; 34 rue des Rosiers, 4e; metro St-Paul; dishes €3.50-7; 11am-midnight Sun-Thu, noon-sunset Fri) This has always been our favourite place for deep-fried balls of chickpeas and herbs (€3.50 to €4).

Crêpes Show (Map pp102-4; 01 47 00 36 46; 51 rue de Lappe, 11e; metro Ledru Rollin; lunch menu €7, dinner menu €11; lunch Mon-Fri, dinner to 1am) An unpretentious little restaurant specialising in sweet crepes and savoury buckwheat *galettes* priced between €3 and €7. There are lots of vegetarian choices, including great salads from €7.

SELF-CATERING

In the Marais, there are a number of food shops and Asian delicatessens on the odd-numbered side of rue St-Antoine, 4e (Map pp105-7) as well as several supermarkets. For cheese, try the excellent **Fromagerie G Millet** (Map pp105-7; 01 42 78 48 78; 77 rue St-Antoine, 4e; 7.30am-1pm & 3.30-8pm Mon-Fri, 7.30am-1pm Sat) and there's a branch of the famous **Fauchon** (Map pp102-4; 01 53 01 91 91; 10 rue St-Antoine, 4e; metro Bastille; 8am-11pm) nearby.

Closer to Bastille, there are lots of food shops along **rue de la Roquette** (Map pp102-4; metro Voltaire or Bastille) up towards place Léon Blum.

Supermarkets include the following:

Franprix (Map pp105-7; 135 rue St-Antoine, 4e; 9am-8.30pm Mon-Sat); Franprix Marais branch (Map pp105-7; 87 rue de la Verrerie, 4e; 9am-8.15pm Mon-Fri, 9am-8.30pm Sat)

Monoprix (Map pp105-7; 71 rue St-Antoine, 4e; 9am-9pm Mon-Sat); Monoprix Bastille branch (Map pp102-4; 97 rue du Faubourg St-Antoine, 11e; metro Ledru Rollin; 9am-10pm Mon-Sat)

Supermarché G20 (Map pp105-7; 115 rue St-Antoine, 4e; 9am-8.30pm Mon-Sat)

Île St-Louis

Famed for its ice cream as much as anything else, the Île St-Louis is generally a pricey place to eat and restaurants are few and far between. It's best suited to those looking for a light snack at one of the lovely tearooms along rue St-Louis en l'Île such as **La Charlotte en Île** (Map pp105-7; ☎ 01 43 54 25 83; rue St-Louis en l'Île 24, 4e; metro Pont Marie; ☺ noon-8pm Thu-Sun) or for ingredients for a picnic along the Seine.

FRENCH

Brasserie de l'Isle St-Louis (Map pp105-7; ☎ 01 43 54 02 59; 55 quai de Bourbon, 4e; metro Pont Marie; ☺ 5pm-1am Thu, noon-1am Fri-Tue) Established in 1870, this brasserie enjoys a spectacular location on the Seine and serves standard brasserie favourites such as *choucroute garnie, jarret* (veal shank) (€16.50 each) and *onglet de boeuf* (prime rib of beef).

QUICK EATS

Berthillon (Map pp105-7; ☎ 01 43 54 31 61; 31 rue St-Louis en l'Île, 4e; metro Pont Marie; 1/2/3/4 scoops €2/3.50/4.50/5.50; takeaway & shop ☺ 10am-8pm Wed-Sun, café ☺ 1-8pm Wed-Fri, 2-8pm Sat & Sun) While the fruit flavours (eg cassis) produced by this celebrated *glacier* (ice-cream maker) are justifiably renowned, the chocolate, coffee, *marrons glacés* (candied chestnuts), *Agenaise* (Armagnac and prunes), *noisette* (hazelnut) and *nougat au miel* (honey nougat) are much richer. Make your choice from among 70 flavours.

SELF-CATERING

On rue St-Louis en l'Île there are **fromageries** and **groceries** (usually closed on Sunday afternoon and all day Monday). There are more **food shops** on rue des Deux Ponts.

Latin Quarter & Jardin Des Plantes

Rue Mouffetard, 5e (Map pp102-4; metro Place Monge or Censier Daubenton), and its side streets are filled with places to eat. It's especially popular with students because of the number of stands and small shops selling baguettes, Italian *panini* and crepes.

Avoid rue de la Huchette and the labyrinth of narrow streets in the 5e across the Seine from Notre Dame (Map pp105-7). The restaurants between rue St-Jacques, blvd St-Germain and blvd St-Michel attract mainly foreign tourists, who appear to be unaware that some people refer to the area as 'Bacteria Alley' because of the meat and seafood ripening in the windows. To add insult to injury, many of the poor souls who eat here are under the impression that this little maze is the celebrated Latin Quarter.

FRENCH

Bouillon Racine (Map pp105-7; ☎ 01 44 32 15 60; 3 rue Racine, 6e; metro Cluny La Sorbonne; starters €7-11.50,

---

FAST-FOOD & CHAIN RESTAURANTS

American fast-food chains have busy branches all over Paris as does the local hamburger chain **Quick**. In addition, a number of restaurants have outlets around Paris with standard menus. They are definitely a cut above fast-food outlets and can be good value in areas such as along the av des Champs-Élysées, where restaurants tend to be over-priced or bad value (or both).

Bistro Romain (starters €4.70-9.50, pasta €9.90-13.40, mains €8.90-17.50, lunch €10.95, dinner menus €14.90 & €22.70; ☺ usually 11.30am-1am) This ever popular bistro-restaurant chain, with some 16 branches in Paris proper, is surprisingly upmarket for its price category. The **Champs-Élysées Bistro Romain** (Map pp93-5; ☎ 01 43 59 93 31; 122 av des Champs-Élysées, 8e; metro George V), one of three along the city's most famous thoroughfare, is a stone's throw from place Charles de Gaulle.

Buffalo Grill (www.buffalo-grill.fr in French; mains €8-15, menus from €8; ☺ usually 11am-11pm Sun-Thu, 11am-midnight Fri & Sat) Buffalo Grill counts some 10 branches in Paris, including the **Gare du Nord Buffalo Grill** (Map pp96-8; ☎ 01 40 16 47 81; 9 blvd de Denain, 10e; metro Gare du Nord). The emphasis here is on grills and steak – from T-bone (€16) to ostrich (€13.50).

Hippopotamus (www.hippopotamus.fr in French; starters €3.90-8.50, mains €9.80-17.50, menus €9.90-22.90; ☺ usually 11.45am-12.30am Sun-Thu, 11.45am-1am Fri & Sat) This chain, which has 10 branches in Paris proper, specialises in solid, steak-based meals. Four of the outlets stay open to 5am daily, including the **Opéra Hippopotamus** (Map pp96-8; ☎ 01 47 42 75 70; 1 blvd des Capucines, 2e; metro Opéra).

Léon de Bruxelles (www.leon-de-bruxelles.com in French; starters €3.80-6, mains €9.50-15, menus €9.90-13.60; ☺ usually 11.45am-11pm) Léon de Bruxelles focuses on one thing: *moules* (mussels). Meal-size bowls of the bivalves, served with chips and bread, start at under €10. There are a 13 Léons in Paris, including the **Les Halles Léon de Bruxelles** (Map pp105-7; ☎ 01 42 36 18 50; 120 rue Rambuteau, 1er; metro Châtelet-Les Halles).

mains €12-17, lunch menu €15, dinner menu €25; ⓨ lunch & dinner to 11pm) This 'soup kitchen' built in 1906 to feed city workers is an Art Nouveau palace though the classic French dishes like *caille confite* (preserved quail) and *cochon de lait* (milk-fed pork) can't hold a candle to the surrounds.

Chez Léna et Mimille (Map pp102-4; ☎ 01 47 07 72 47; 32 rue Tournefort, 5e; metro Censier Daubenton; lunch starters/mains/desserts €7/14/7, dinner menu with wine €35; ⓨ lunch Tue-Fri, dinner till 11pm Mon-Sat) Here is a cosy but elegant French restaurant with excellent food and one of the most fabulous terraces in Paris, overlooking a little park with a fountain.

Perraudin (Map pp102-4; ☎ 01 46 33 15 75; 157 rue St-Jacques, 5e; metro Luxembourg; starters €6-15, mains €14-23, lunch menu €18, dinner menu €26; ⓨ lunch & dinner to 10.30pm Mon-Fri) Perraudin is a traditional French restaurant that hasn't changed much since the late 19th century. If you fancy classics such as *bœuf bourguignon* (€14), *gigot d'agneau* (€15) or *confit de canard* (€15), try this reasonably priced place.

Le Vigneron (Map pp102-4; ☎ 01 47 07 29 99; 18-20 rue du Pot de Fer, 5e; metro Place Monge; starters €6-18, mains €11-24, lunch menus €10.50 & €13.50, dinner menus €16.50 & €25; ⓨ lunch & dinner till midnight) 'The Wine Grower' is one of the better French restaurants in the Mouffetard quarter, specialises in the cuisine of the southwest.

ASIAN

Tao (Map pp102-4; ☎ 01 43 26 75 92; 248 rue St-Jacques, 5e; metro Luxembourg; soups & salads €7-8, mains €8.50-13; ⓨ lunch & dinner to 10.30pm Mon-Sat) A decidedly upmarket Asian restaurant with Zen-ish – Taoist? – décor, this place serves some of the best Vietnamese cuisine in the Latin Quarter.

Tashi Delek (Map pp102-4; ☎ 01 43 26 55 55; 4 rue des Fossés St-Jacques, 5e; metro Luxembourg; soups €3-4, Tibetan bowls €5.35-6.25, lunch menu €12, dinner menu €18; ⓨ lunch & dinner to 11pm Mon-Sat) An intimate little place whose name approximates *tashi dele*, or 'bonjour' in Tibetan, Tashi Delek offers Himalayan dishes that may not be gourmet but are certainly tasty and inexpensive. There are also four vegetarian choices (€6.40 to €8.40).

NORTH AFRICAN & MIDDLE EASTERN

Founti Agadir (Map pp102-4; ☎ 01 43 37 85 10; 117 rue Monge, 5e; metro Censier Daubenton; lunch menus €15 & €18; ⓨ lunch & dinner to 10.30pm Tue-Sun) This popular Moroccan restaurant serves some of the best couscous and tajines (€12.90 to €17) and *pastillas* (chicken pie; €7 to €8) on the Left Bank.

Mosquée de Paris (Map pp102-4; ☎ 01 43 31 38 20; 39 rue Geoffroy St-Hilaire, 5e; metro Censier Daubenton or Place Monge; starters & small dishes €4-12, mains €11-25; ⓨ lunch & dinner to 10.30pm) The central Mosque of Paris (p122) has an authentic restaurant serving couscous (€11 to €25) and tajines (€12 to €16). There's also a North African-style **tearoom** (ⓨ 9am-midnight) where you can enjoy a cup of peppermint tea (€2.50).

VEGETARIAN

La Petit Légume (Map pp102-4; ☎ 01 40 46 06 85; 36 rue des Boulangers, 5e; metro Cardinal Lemoine; salads €10.70-12.90, dishes €6.90-9, menus €8.55-14; ⓨ lunch & dinner to 10pm Mon-Sat) 'The Little Vegetable', a tiny place on a narrow road, is a great choice for house-made vegetarian fare.

Les Quatre et Une Saveurs (Map pp102-4; ☎ 01 43 26 88 80; 72 rue du Cardinal Lemoine, 5e; metro Cardinal Lemoine; lunch menu €13, dinner menus €22 & €25; ⓨ lunch Sun-Fri, dinner to 10.30pm Sun-Thu & Sat) Set back from place de la Contrescarpe, this bright macrobiotic restaurant is extremely popular among health-food lovers. All ingredients are guaranteed 100% organic.

Quick Eats

Le Foyer du Vietnam (Map pp102-4; ☎ 01 45 35 32 54; 80 rue Monge, 5e; metro Place Monge; dishes €3.10-6.50, menu €8.40; ⓨ lunch & dinner to 10pm Mon-Sat) This little place is a favourite meeting spot among the capital's Vietnamese community and serves simple one-dish meals in medium and large portions.

Tea Caddy (Map pp105-7; ☎ 01 43 54 15 56; 14 rue St-Julien le Pauvre, 5e; metro St-Michel; salads €9.50-11, sandwiches €7.50-9, light meals €8.50-11.80; ⓨ noon-7pm Wed-Mon) The most English of 'English' tearooms in Paris, this institution founded in 1928 is a fine place to break for tea (€5.50 to €7.50) and pastries (about €7) after a tour of nearby Notre Dame, Ste-Chapelle or the Conciergerie.

SELF-CATERING

Place Maubert, 5e (Map pp105-7), becomes a lively **food market** four mornings a week. There are also some great provisions shops here, including a cheese shop called **Crémerie des Carmes** (Map pp105-7; ☎ 01 43 54 50 93; 47ter blvd

St-Germain, 5e; metro Maubert Mutualité; 7.30am-1pm & 3.30-8pm Mon-Fri, 7.30am-1pm Sat).

There's a particularly lively **food market** along rue Mouffetard (see p169). On place Monge there's a much smaller **market** (Map pp102-4; place Monge, 5e; metro Place Monge; 8am-2pm Wed, Fri & Sun).

Supermarkets in the area:

Champion (Map pp102-4; 34 rue Monge, 5e; metro Place Monge; 8.30am-9pm Mon-Sat)

Ed l'Épicier (Map pp102-4; 37 rue Lacépède, 5e; 9am-1pm & 3-7.30pm Mon-Fri, 9am-7.30pm Sat)

Franprix (Map pp102-4; 82 rue Mouffetard, 5e; metro Censier Daubenton or Place Monge; 9am-8pm Mon-Sat)

St-Germain, Odéon & Luxembourg

Rue St-André des Arts (Map pp105-7; metro St-Michel or Odéon) is lined with restaurants, including a few down the covered passage de Rohan. There are lots of eateries between Église St-Sulpice and Église St-Germain des Prés as well, especially along rue des Canettes, rue Princesse and rue Guisarde. Carrefour de l'Odéon (metro Odéon) has a cluster of lively bars, cafés and restaurants. Place St-Germain des Prés itself is home to celebrated cafés such as **Les Deux Magots** and **Café de Flore** (p159) as well as the equally celebrated Brasserie Lip.

FRENCH

L'Arbuci (Map pp105-7; 01 44 32 16 00; 25 rue de Buci, 6e; metro Mabillon; meals from €35, lunch menus €15.50 & €20; noon-1am) Though this retro-style brasserie recently got an all-marble, all-glass makeover (boo!), the specialities remain: seafood (especially oysters) and spit-roasted beef, chicken, pork and salmon and – for dessert – pineapple.

Brasserie Lipp (Map pp99-101; 01 45 48 53 91; 151 blvd St Germain, 6e; metro St Germain des Prés; starters €7.70-17.70, mains €15.50-18; noon-1am) The Lipp is a wood-panelled café-brasserie (1880) where politicians rub shoulders with intellectuals, editors and media moguls, and waiters in black waistcoats, bowties and long white aprons serve such brasserie favourites as *choucroute garnie* (€16.60), *tête de veau* and *bœuf gros sel*.

Le Mâchon d'Henri (Map pp105-7; 01 43 29 08 70; 8 rue Guisarde, 6e; metro St-Sulpice or Mabillon; starters €6-8, mains €12-13; lunch & dinner until 11.15pm) A very Parisian bistro in an area awash with bars, this *mâchon* (Lyon-style restaurant)

serves up Lyon-inspired dishes with – go figure – a Mediterranean twist.

Polidor (Map pp105-7; 01 43 26 95 34; 41 rue Monsieur le Prince, 6e; metro Odéon; starters €4-12, mains €7-12, lunch menu €9, dinner menus €18 & €26; lunch & dinner till 12.30am Mon-Sat, to 11pm Sun) A meal at this quintessentially Parisian *crémerie-restaurant* is like a quick trip back to Victor Hugo's Paris – the restaurant and its décor date from 1845 – but everyone knows about it and it's pretty touristy. Specialities include *bœuf bourguignon* (€10), *blanquette de veau* (veal in white sauce; €11) and the most famous *tarte Tatin* (€5) in Paris.

OTHER CUISINES

Chez Albert (Map pp105-7; 01 46 33 22 57; 43 rue Mazarine, 6e; metro Odéon; starters €6-24, mains €17-22, lunch menu €17, dinner menu €28; lunch & dinner to 10.30pm Tue-Sat) This place offers authentic Portuguese food. Try *porc Alentejana aux palourdes* (pork cooked with clams in a casserole), any of the numerous *bacalhau* (salt-dried cod) dishes such as *brandade de morue* (creamed salt cod) or prawns sautéed in lots of garlic.

Le Golfe de Naples (Map pp105-7; 01 43 26 98 11; 5 rue de Montfaucon, 6e; metro Mabillon; starters €8-13, pizza & pasta dishes €9.50-14, mains €11-18.50; lunch & dinner to 11pm) The 'Gulf of Naples' has some of the best pizza and fresh, shop-made pasta in Paris – though more elaborate main courses are something of a disappointment. Don't forget to try the *assiette napolitaine*, a plate of grilled fresh vegetables (€13.50).

Indonesia (Map pp102-4; 01 43 25 70 22; 12 rue de Vaugirard, 6e; metro Luxembourg; lunch menus €9-12.50, dinner menus €13-19; lunch Sun-Fri, dinner to 10.30pm) One of only a couple of Indonesian restaurants in town, this unimaginatively named eatery has all the old favourites – from an elaborate, nine-dish *rijstafel* (€23) to *lumpia* (€4.50), *rendang* (€8.50) and *gado-gado* (€5).

QUICK EATS

Amorino (Map pp105-7; 01 43 26 57 46; 4 rue Buci, 6e; metro St-Germain des Prés; ice creams €3.40-5; noon-midnight Sun-Thu, 1pm-midnight Fri & Sat) We're told that Berthillon (p151) has some serious competition and that Amorino's home-made ice cream (yogurt, forest fruits, caramel, kiwi, strawberry etc) is, in fact – egad! – better. Expect a long wait in the queue.

Guen Maï (Map pp105-7; 01 43 26 03 24; cnr rue Cardinale & rue de l'Abbaye, 6e; metro St-Germain des Prés or Mabillon; soups €4.50, mains €7-10.50; ☺ lunch Mon-Sat) Guen Maï is a health-food shop that also serves macrobiotic and organic *plats du jour* and soups.

SELF-CATERING

With the Jardin du Luxembourg nearby, this is the perfect area for putting together a picnic lunch. There is a large cluster of **food shops** on rue de Seine and rue de Buci, 6e (Map pp105-7; metro Mabillon). The renovated and covered **Marché St-Germain** (Map pp105-7; rue Lobineau, 6e; metro Mabillon), just north of the eastern end of Église St-Sulpice, has a huge array of produce and prepared food. Nearby supermarkets:

Champion (Map pp105-7; 79 rue de Seine, 6e; metro Mabillon; ☺ 1-9pm Mon, 8.40am-9pm Tue-Sat, 9am-1pm Sun)

Monoprix (Map pp105-7; 52 rue de Rennes, 6e; metro St-Germain des Prés; ☺ 9am-10pm Mon-Sat)

Montparnasse

Since the 1920s the area around blvd du Montparnasse has been one of the city's premier avenues for enjoying that most Parisian of pastimes: sitting in a café and checking out the scenery on two legs. Many younger Parisians, however, now consider the area somewhat *démodé* and touristy, which it is to a certain extent, and avoid it.

Montparnasse offers all types of eateries but especially traditional creperies. As Gare Montparnasse is where Bretons arriving in Paris to look for work would disembark (and apparently venture no further), there is no shortage of creperies in the area. There are three at 20 rue d'Odessa (Map pp99–101) alone and at least half a dozen more round the corner on rue du Montparnasse.

FRENCH

La Coupole (Map pp99-101; ☎ 01 43 20 14 20; 102 blvd du Montparnasse, 14e; metro Vavin; starters €7.50-12.50, mains €13.50-18.50, lunch menu €17.50, dinner menus €22.90 & €32.90; ☺ 8am-1am Sun-Thu, to 1.30am Fri & Sat) This 450-seat brasserie, which opened in 1927, has mural-covered columns painted by such artists as Brancusi and Chagall. Its dark-wood panelling and indirect lighting have hardly changed since the days of Sartre, Soutine, Man Ray and the dancer Josephine Baker.

Dix Vins (Map pp99-101; ☎ 01 43 20 91 77; 57 rue Falguière, 15e; metro Pasteur; menu €18.50; ☺ lunch Tue-Sat,

dinner to 11pm Mon-Sat) This tiny little restaurant, which offers a set menu only, is so popular you will probably have to wait at the bar even if you've booked. Be sure to sample one of the carefully chosen wines that the owner will decant into a carafe.

Le Dôme (Map pp99-101; ☎ 01 43 35 25 81; 108 blvd du Montparnasse, 14e; metro Vavin; starters €12.50-23, mains €30.50-56; ☺ lunch & dinner to 12.30am) An Art Deco extravaganza dating from the 1930s, The Dôme is a monumental place for a meal, with the emphasis on the freshest of oysters, shellfish and fish dishes such as *sole meunière*.

QUICK EATS

Mustang Café (Map pp99-101; ☎ 01 43 35 36 12; 84 blvd du Montparnasse, 14e; metro Montparnasse Bienvenüe; starters €6-13.50, salads €6.70-9, mains €7.50-13.30; ☺ 8am-5am) A café that almost never sleeps, the Mustang has passable Tex-Mex combination platters and nachos from €7.50 to €13.30, fajitas for €12.50 and burgers €8.90 to €10.60.

SELF-CATERING

Opposite the Tour Montparnasse there's a outdoor **food market** (Map pp99-101; blvd Edgar Quinet; ☺ 7am-1.30pm Wed & Sat) open two days a week. Supermarkets convenient to the area:

Franprix (Map pp99-101; 55 av du Maine, 14e; metro Gaité; ☺ 8.30am-8pm Mon-Sat); Franprix Delambre branch (Map pp99-101; 11 rue Delambre; metro Vavin; ☺ 8.30am-7.50pm Mon-Sat)

Inno (Map pp99-101; 29-31 rue du Départ, 14e; metro Montparnasse Bienvenüe; ☺ 9am-9.50pm Mon-Fri, 9am-8.50pm Sat)

Étoile & Champs-Élysées

With very few exceptions, eateries lining the touristy 'Avenue of the Elysian Fields' offer little value for money. Restaurants in the surrounding areas can be excellent, however.

FRENCH

L'Ardoise (Map pp93-5; ☎ 01 42 96 28 18; 28 rue du Mont Thabor, 1er; metro Concorde or Tuileries; menu €30; ☺ lunch & dinner to 11pm Wed-Sun) This is a little bistro with no menu as such (*ardoise* means 'blackboard', which is all there is) and the food – rabbit stuffed with plums and beef fillet with morels – is superb.

P'tit Bouchon Gourmand (Map pp93-5; ☎ 01 40 55 03 26; 5 rue Troyon, 17e; metro Charles de Gaulle-Étoile; mains €16-28, menu €25; ☺ lunch Mon-Fri, dinner to 11pm

Mon-Sat) An institution on the Breton coast for almost a quarter, 'Greedy's Little Wine Bar' has at last arrived in *la capitale*. Try the voluptuous *camembert rôti sur son lit de salade* (roasted camembert with salad) and the *millefeuille de boudin noir aux pommes* (black pudding in layered pastry with apples).

QUICK EATS

Lina's (Map pp93-5; ☎ 01 40 15 94 95; 4 rue Cambon, 1er; metro Concorde; salads €4.50-6.10, sandwiches €3.50-7; ⏰ 9.30am-4.30pm Mon-Fri, 10am-5.30pm Sat) This branch of a popular chain of sandwich and soup bars across Paris (some 19 outlets at last count) has upmarket sandwiches, salads and soups. There's also an **Opéra branch** (Map pp96-8; ☎ 01 47 03 30 29; 7 av de l'Opéra, 1er; metro Pyramides).

SELF-CATERING

The huge **Monoprix** (Map pp93-5; 62 av des Champs-Élysées, 8e; metro Franklin D Roosevelt; ⏰ 9am-midnight Mon-Sat) at the corner of rue La Boétie has a big supermarket section in the basement. Nearby **place de la Madeleine** (metro Madeleine) is the luxury food centre of one of the world's food capitals (see p168).

Opéra & Grands Boulevards

The neon-lit blvd Montmartre (metro Grands Boulevards or Richelieu Drouot) and nearby sections of rue du Faubourg Montmartre (neither of which are anywhere near the neighbourhood of Montmartre) form one of the Right Bank's most animated café and dining districts. A short distance to the north there's a large selection of kosher Jewish and North African restaurants on rue Richer, rue Cadet and rue Geoffroy Marie, 9e, south of metro Cadet.

FRENCH

Julien (Map pp96-8; ☎ 01 47 70 12 06; 16 rue du Faubourg St-Denis, 10e; metro Strasbourg St-Denis; starters €6-16, mains €13.50-28, menus with wine €22.90 & €32.90; ⏰ lunch & dinner to 1am) In the less-than-salubrious neighbourhood of St-Denis, Julien offers brasserie food that you wouldn't cross town for, but – mon Dieu! – the décor and the atmosphere: it's an Art Nouveau extravaganza perpetually in motion and a real step back in time.

Le Roi du Pot au Feu (Map pp93-5; ☎ 01 47 42 37 10; 34 rue Vignon, 9e; metro Havre Caumartin; starters €4-6,

mains €15-17, 2-/3-course menus €21 & €25; ⏰ noon-10.30pm Mon-Sat) The typical Parisian bistro atmosphere adds immensely to the charm of 'The King of Hotpots', but why you really want to come here is for a genuine *pot au feu*, a stockpot of beef, aromatic root vegetables and herbs stewed together.

JEWISH & NORTH AFRICAN

Les Ailes (Map pp96-8; ☎ 01 47 70 62 53; 34 rue Richer, 9e; metro Cadet; starters €6-17, mains €18-23; ⏰ lunch & dinner till 11.30pm) Just next door to the celebrated Folies-Bergère, 'The Wings' is a kosher North African (Sephardic) place that offers superb couscous with meat or fish (€18 to €23) and grills. Don't even consider a starter; you'll be inundated with little plates of salad, olives etc before you can say 'L'chaim'.

Wally le Saharien (Map pp96-8; ☎ 01 42 85 51 90; 36 rue Rodier, 9e; metro St-Georges or Cadet; lunch menu €23.50, dinner menu €40.40; ⏰ lunch & dinner to 10.30pm Tue-Sat) This place is several notches above most Maghrebi restaurants in Paris, offering couscous in its pure Saharan form – without any stock or vegetables, just a finely cooked grain served with a delicious sauce, as well as excellent tajines.

Gare du Nord, Gare de l'Est & République

These areas offer all types of food but most notably Indian and Pakistani, which can be elusive elsewhere in Paris. There's a cluster of traditional brasseries and bistros around the Gare du Nord.

FRENCH

Chez Papa/Espace Sud-Ouest (Map pp96-8; ☎ 01 42 09 53 87; 206 rue La Fayette, 10e; metro Charles Dupont; starters €9.15-10.20, salads €7.05-12.30, mains €13.05-16.15; ⏰ 11.30am-1am) Although this place serves southwestern specialities like *cassoulet* and *garbure* (€15.80), most people are here for the famous *salade Boyarde*, an enormous bowl filled with lettuce, tomato, sautéed potatoes, two types of cheese and ham (€7.05; €7.80 if you want two fried eggs thrown in).

Terminus Nord (Map pp96-8; ☎ 01 42 85 05 15; 23 rue de Dunkerque, 10e; metro Gare du Nord; starters €6.50-15.50, mains €13.50-28, menus with wine €22.90 & €32.90; ⏰ 8am-1am) The 'North Terminus' has a copper bar, waiters in white uniforms, brass fixtures and mirrored walls that look as they did when it opened directly opposite the

Gare du Nord in 1925. Breakfast (from €8) is served from 8am to 11am daily, and full meals continuously from 11am to 12.30am.

QUICK EATS
Passage Brady (Map pp96-8; 46 rue du Faubourg St-Denis & 33 blvd de Strasbourg, 10e; metro Château d'Eau; usually lunch & dinner to 11pm) This derelict covered arcade, which could easily be in Calcutta, has dozens of incredibly cheap Indian, Pakistani and Bangladeshi cafés offering excellent value lunches (meat curry, rice and a tiny salad from €5, chicken or lamb biryani for €5 to €8, thalis for €12) and dinners (from €7.60). The pick of the crop:
Pooja (01 48 24 00 83; 91 passage Brady)
Roi du Kashmir (01 48 00 08 85; 76 passage Brady)
Shalimar (01 45 23 31 61; 59 passage Brady)

SELF-CATERING
Rue du Faubourg St-Denis, 10e (metro Strasbourg St-Denis or Château d'Eau), which links blvd St-Denis and blvd de Magenta, is one of the cheapest places in Paris to buy food, especially fruit and vegetables (shop Nos 23, 27-29 and 41-43). It has a distinctively Middle Eastern air, and quite a few of the groceries offer Turkish, North African and subcontinental specialities. Many of the food shops, including the **fromagerie** at No 54, are open Tuesday to noon on Sunday. Further north, you'll find **Marché St-Quentin** (Map pp96-8; metro Gare de l'Est); for details see p169.

There are three Franprix supermarkets convenient to this area:
Franprix (Map pp96-8; 25 rue du Faubourg St-Denis, 10e; metro Strasbourg St-Denis; 9am-7.50pm Mon-Sat)
Franprix (Map pp96-8; 57 blvd de Magenta, 10e; metro Gare de l'Est; 9am-8pm Mon-Sat)
Franprix (Map pp105-7; 49 rue de Bretagne, 3e; metro Arts et Métiers; 9am-8.30pm Tue-Sat, 9am-1.20pm Sun)

Ménilmontant & Belleville
In the northern section of the 11e and into the 19e and 20e arrondissements, rue Oberkampf and its extension, rue de Ménilmontant (Map pp96-8), are popular with diners and denizens of the night though rue Jean-Pierre Timbaud, running parallel to the north, is stealing some of their glory these days. Rue de Belleville and the streets running off it are dotted with Chinese, Southeast Asian and a few Middle Eastern places; blvd de Belleville has some kosher couscous restaurants, most of which are closed on Saturday.

FRENCH
Le C'Amelot (Map pp102-4; 01 43 55 54 04; 50 rue Amelot, 11e; metro St-Sébastien Froissart; lunch menus €16 & €23, dinner menu €32; lunch Tue-Fri, dinner to midnight Mon-Sat) 'The Street Peddler' is the perfect little neighbourhood bistro but on everyone's list so book well in advance.

Le Clown Bar (Map pp102-4; 01 43 55 87 35; 114 rue Amelot, 11e; metro Filles du Calvaire; starters €10, mains €13-15, lunch menu €13.50, dinner menu €18; lunch Mon-Sat, dinner to midnight) A wonderful wine bar-cum-bistro next to the Cirque d'Hiver, the Clown Bar is like a museum with its painted ceilings, mosaics on the wall, lovely zinc bar and circus memorabilia that touches on one of our favourite themes: the evil clown. The food is simple and unpretentious traditional French.

Juan et Juanita (Map pp96-8; 01 43 57 60 15; 82 rue Jean-Pierre Timbaud, 11e; metro Parmentier or Couronnes; starters €5.50, mains €13-15, menu €15; dinner to 2am Tue-Sat) Run by two young women, this place stands out for its over-the-top, slightly camp décor and the exceedingly high standards of its kitchen. Expect innovative dishes and unusual tastes.

Le Villaret (Map pp96-8; 01 43 57 89 76; 13 rue Ternaux, 11e; metro Parmentier; starters €7-15, mains €18-25, lunch menus €20 & €25, dinner sampling menu €46; lunch

---

AUTHOR'S CHOICE
Le Chansonnier (Map pp96-8; 01 42 09 40 58; 14 rue Eugène Varlin, 10e; metro Château Landon or Pierre Dupont; starters €6-12, mains € 13.50-15, lunch menu €10.50, dinner menu €23.50; lunch Mon-Fri, dinner to 11pm Mon-Sat) It may not be the best restaurant in Paris, but if ever there was the perfect example of a *restaurant du quartier*, 'The Singer', named after Lyonnais socialist singer/songwriter Pierre Dupont (1821–70), is it. With its curved zinc bar and Art Nouveau mouldings and windows, it could be a film set. The food is authentic, very good and very substantial; the dinner menu includes *terrine maison à valonté* – essentially all you can eat of four types of terrine. The *saucisson de Lyon* (Lyon sausage) studded with pistachios is an excellent starter while the *daube de joue de bœuf* (beef cheek stewed in a Dutch oven in a rich, wine-laden broth with herbs and vegetables) is the main course of choice. Expect a lot of repeat custom.

Mon-Fri, dinner to 11.30pm Mon & Tue, to 1am Wed-Sat) An excellent neighbourhood bistro serving very rich food, this place has diners coming from across Paris till late to sample such specialities as *velouté de cèpes à la mousse de foie gras* (cepe mushroom soup with foie gras mousse) and *gigot d'agneau de Lozère rôti et son gratin de topinambours* (roast lamb with Jerusalem artichoke gratin).

ASIAN
New Nioullaville (Map pp96-8; ☎ 01 40 21 96 18; 32 rue de l'Orillon, 11e; metro Belleville or Goncourt; starters €5.30-6, rice & noodles €6.90-9, mains €7-14, menus €7.30-12; ☯ lunch & dinner to 12.45am) This cavernous, 500-seat place resembles the Hong Kong Stock Exchange on a busy day. The food is a bit of a mishmash – *dim sum* sits next to beef satay, as do scallops with black bean alongside Singapore noodles. Order carefully and you should be able to approach authenticity.

Krung Thep (Map pp96-8; ☎ 01 43 66 83 74; 93 rue Julien Lacroix, 20e; metro Pyrénées; starters €7-8.50, veg dishes €5.50-7, mains €8.50-18; ☯ dinner till 11pm) The 'Bangkok' (in Thai, anyway) is a small Asio-kitsch place with all our favourites (and then some – there are 130 dishes on the menu): green curries, *tom yam gung* and fish or chicken steamed in banana leaves.

OTHER
L'Ave Maria (Map pp96-8; ☎ 01 47 00 61 73; 1 rue Jacquard, 11e; metro Parmentier; dishes €11-14; ☯ lunch Mon-Fri & dinner to midnight) This fusion place is just like a Brazilian or African canteen, a chic, imaginary and colourful greasy spoon combining flavours of the Southern Hemisphere and creating hearty, hybrid and harmonious dishes. Music livens up towards midnight and dancing carries on to 2am.

La Piragua (Map pp102-4; ☎ 01 40 21 35 98, 6 rue Rochebrune, 11e; metro St-Ambroise; starters €4-6.50, mains €10-13, menus €16 & €18; ☯ dinner to 11.30pm Mon-Thu, to midnight Fri & Sat) La Piragua is a small, brightly coloured eatery with Colombian favourites like *ceviche* (fish marinated in lemon juice) and *badeja paisa*, a concoction of chopped meat, kidney beans, rice and the kitchen sink. The list of Chilean wines is excellent.

SELF-CATERING
Supermarkets in the area include **Franprix** (Map pp96-8; 28 blvd Jules Ferry, 11e; metro République

or Goncourt; ☯ 8am-8pm Mon-Sat) and a **Franprix branch** (Map pp96-8; 23 rue Jean-Pierre Timbaud, 11e; metro Oberkampf; ☯ 8am-8pm Mon-Sat).

13e Arrondissement & Chinatown
Dozens of Asian restaurants – not just Chinese ones – line the main streets of Paris' Chinatown (Map pp90-2), including av de Choisy, av d'Ivry and rue Baudricourt. Another wonderful district for an evening out is the Butte aux Cailles area, just southwest of place d'Italie. It's chock-a-block with interesting addresses.

FRENCH
L'Avant-Goût (Map pp90-2; ☎ 01 53 80 24 00; 26 rue Bobillot, 13e; metro Place d'Italie; starters €8, mains €15, lunch menu €12, dinner menu €26; ☯ lunch & dinner to 11pm Tue-Fri) This prototype of the Parisian 'neo-bistro' (classical yet modern) in the Butte aux Cailles serves some of the most inventive modern cuisine around. It can get noisy at times and there are occasional lapses in the service, but the food is well worth it.

ASIAN
La Fleuve de Chine (Map pp90-2; ☎ 01 45 82 06 88; 15 av de Choisy, 13e; metro Porte de Choisy; dishes €7.60-16.50; ☯ lunch & dinner to 11pm Fri-Wed) 'The River of China', which can also be reached through the Tour Bergame housing estate at 130 blvd Masséna, has some of the most authentic Cantonese and Hakka food to be found in Paris and, as is typical, both the surroundings and service – but definitely not the food – are forgettable.

Sinorama (Map pp90-2; ☎ 01 53 82 09 51; 118 av de Choisy & 23 rue du Docteur Magnan, 13e; metro Tolbiac or Place d'Italie; starters €4-15, mains €8.50-17, rice & noodles €4.50-8, lunch menu €9; ☯ lunch & dinner to 2am) This airport hangar of a Chinese restaurant with two entrances and a camp name serves good Shanghainese dishes, with a smattering of Cantonese choices.

Montmartre & Pigalle
The 18th arrondissement, where you will find Montmartre and the northern half of place Pigalle, thrives on crowds and little else. When you've got Sacré Coeur, place du Tertre and its portrait artists and Paris literally at your feet, who needs decent restaurants? But that's not to say everything is a write-off in this well-trodden tourist

area. You just have to pick and choose a bit more carefully.

FRENCH

Chez Toinette (Map p108; ☎ 01 42 54 44 36; 20 rue Germain Pilon, 18e; metro Abbesses; meals from €23; ⏰ dinner to 11pm Tue-Sat) The atmosphere of this convivial restaurant, which has somehow managed to keep alive the tradition of old Montmartre in one of the capital's most touristy neighbourhoods, is rivalled only by its fine cuisine.

La Maison Rose (Map p108; ☎ 01 42 57 66 75; 2 rue de l'Abreuvoir, 18e; metro Lamarck Caulaincourt; starters €7.80-13, mains €14.50-16.50, menu €14.50; ⏰ lunch & dinner to 10.30pm daily Mar-Oct, lunch Thu-Mon & dinner to 9pm Mon, Thu-Sat Nov-Feb) If you are looking for the quintessential intimate Montmartre bistro, head for the tiny 'Pink House' just north of place du Tertre.

OTHER CUISINES

Au Petit Budapest (Map p108; ☎ 01 46 06 10 34; 96 rue des Martyrs, 18e; metro Abbesses; starters €7.50-15, mains €10.50-16, lunch menu €13.50, dinner menu €17.50; ⏰ lunch Thu-Sun, dinner to midnight Tue-Sun) The old etchings and the requisite Gypsy music here re-create something of the atmosphere of a Hungarian csárda of the late 19th century but the food – from the *paprikash au bœuf épicé* (beef paprika) to the *gâteau au fromage blanc* (cream cheese cake) – is a refined version of popular Hungarian dishes.

Il Duca (Map p108; ☎ 01 46 06 71 98; 26 rue Yvonne le Tac, 18e; metro Abbesses; starters €7-12, pasta €10-13, mains €15-17, menu €14; ⏰ lunch & dinner to 11pm Mon-Fri, to midnight Sat & Sun) 'The Duke' is an intimate little Italian restaurant with good, straightforward food, including shop-made pasta. The selection of Italian wine and cheese is exceptional.

SELF-CATERING

Towards place Pigalle there are lots of grocery stores, many of them open until late at night; try the side streets leading off blvd de Clichy (eg rue Lepic). Heading south from blvd de Clichy, rue des Martyrs, 9e (Map p108), is lined with food shops almost all the way to metro Notre Dame de Lorette. Supermarkets in the area:

8 à Huit (Map p108; 24 rue Lepic, 18e; metro Abbesses; ⏰ 8.30am-9pm Mon-Sat)

Ed l'Épicier (Map p108; 31 rue d'Orsel, 18e; metro Anvers; ⏰ 9am-8pm Mon-Sat)

DRINKING

Traditionally drinking in Paris revolved around a café, where a *demi* looked more like an eyewash than 330mL of beer. But all that has changed and the number of drinking establishments has mushroomed in recent years, especially in the Marais and along the Grands Boulevards. Happy hour – sometimes extending to as late as 9pm – has brought the price of a pint of beer, a glass of wine or a cocktail down to pricey, rather than extortionate, levels.

Louvre & Les Halles

Le Fumoir (Map p105-7; ☎ 01 42 92 00 24; 6 rue de l'Amiral Coligny, 1er; metro Louvre-Rivoli; ⏰ 11am-2am) 'The Smoking Room' is a huge bar/café just opposite the Louvre with a gentleman's club/library theme. It's a friendly, lively place and quite good fun. Happy hour is 6pm to 8pm daily.

Papou Lounge (Map pp105-7; ☎ 01 44 76 00 03; 74 rue Jean-Jacques Rousseau, 1er; metro Louvre-Rivoli; ⏰ 10am-2am Mon-Fri, 11am-2am Sat, 5pm-midnight Sun) The brothers who own this place share a fascination for les Papous (Papuans) and Papua New Guinea, and the tribal masks, carvings and photos on the wall may give you itchy feet.

Marais & Bastille

L'Apparement Café (Map pp105-7; ☎ 01 48 87 12 22; 18 rue des Coutures St-Gervais, 3e; metro St-Sébastien Froissart; ⏰ noon-2am Mon-Fri, 4pm-2am Sat, 12.30pm-midnight Sun) Tucked not so 'Apparently' behind the Musée Picasso, this oasis of peace looks like a private living room.

Barrio Latino (Map pp102-4; ☎ 01 55 78 84 75; 46-48 rue du Faubourg St-Antoine, 11e; metro Bastille; ⏰ 11.30am-2am) Squeezing the salsa craze for everything it's worth, the 'Latin Quarter' is an enormous bar and restaurant spread over three floors that attracts Latinos, Latino wannabes and Latino wanna-haves.

Café des Phares (Map pp102-4; ☎ 01 42 72 04 70; 7 place Bastille, 4e; metro Bastille; ⏰ 7am-3am Sun-Thu, 7am-4am Fri & Sat) The 'Beacons Café' is best known as the city's original philocafé (philosophers' café), established by the late philosopher and Sorbonne professor Marc Sautet (1947–98). If you feel like debating such topics as 'What is a fact?' and 'Can people communicate?', head for the Phares at 11am on Sunday.

Jokko Bar (Map pp105-7; ☎ 01 42 74 35 96; 5 rue Elzévir, 3e; metro St-Paul or Chemin Vert; ⏰ 5pm-12.30am

Wed-Sun) Part of the CSAO group (p170), the Jokko is a delightful spot with colourful African décor, great world music and rum-based cocktails from €8. There are concerts most nights at 7.30pm.

Au Petit Fer à Cheval (Map pp105-7; ☎ 01 42 72 47 47; 30 rue Vieille du Temple, 4e; metro Hôtel de Ville or St-Paul; ✆ 9am-2am) A slightly offbeat bar-restaurant named after its horseshoe-shaped zinc (counter), this tiny place is often filled to overflowing with friendly regulars and boasts one of the best people-watching vantage points in the Marais.

Quiet Man (Map pp105-7; ☎ 01 48 04 02 77; 5 rue des Haudriettes, 3e; metro Rambuteau; ✆ 5pm-2am Sun-Thu, 4pm-2am Fri & Sat) This is about the most authentic Irish pub Paris has to offer, with a real live Irish owner and musicians playing Irish music. There are trad sets every night from 8pm to 1am and happy hour is from 5pm to 8pm daily.

Stolly's Stone Bar (Map pp105-7; ☎ 01 42 76 06 76; 16 rue de la Cloche Percée, 4e; metro Hôtel de Ville; ✆ 4.30pm-2am) This Anglophone bar on a tiny street just above rue de Rivoli is always crowded, particularly during the 4.30pm to 8pm happy hour, when a 1.6L pitcher of cheap *blonde* (house lager) costs €11 and cocktails are €4.60.

Latin Quarter & Jardin des Plantes

Piano Vache (Map pp102-4; ☎ 01 46 33 75 03; 8 rue Laplace, 5e; metro Maubert Mutualité; ✆ noon-2am Mon-Fri, 9pm-2am Sat & Sun) Just down the hill from the Panthéon, 'The Mean Piano' is 'underground' as the films would have us understand the term. Great music (guest DJs) and a good crowd of very mixed ages. Happy hour is from opening to 9pm Monday to Friday.

Le Salon Égyptien (Map pp102-4; ☎ 01 43 25 58 99; 77 rue du Cardinal Lemoine, 5e; metro Cardinal Lemoine; ✆ 11.30am-2am) People come here mainly to smoke hookahs (€4.60), and you'll smell the intoxicating aromas of apricot, honey, apple or strawberry as soon as you walk through the door. Settle into a large pouf and sip tea or the unusual *karkadet* (a hibiscus-derived beverage).

Le Vieux Chêne (Map pp102-4; ☎ 01 43 37 71 51; 69 rue Mouffetard, 5e; metro Place Monge; ✆ 4pm-2am Sun-Thu, 4pm-5am Fri & Sat) 'The Old Oak', popular with students and long a Mouffetard institution (some people believe it is the oldest bar in the city) has jazz at the weekend. Happy hour is from opening until 9pm daily.

St-Germain, Odéon & Luxembourg

Le 10 (Map pp105-7; ☎ 01 43 26 66 83; 10 rue de l'Odéon, 6e; metro Odéon; ✆ 5.30pm-2am) This is a popular cellar pub with smoke-darkened posters on the walls, an eclectic jukebox with everything from jazz and the Doors to Yves Montand, and sangria, the house speciality, always at the ready. Happy hour is from 6pm to 9pm daily.

Café de Flore (Map pp105-7; ☎ 01 45 48 55 26; 172 blvd St-Germain, 6e; metro St-Germain des Prés; ✆ 7.30am-1.30am) The Flore is an Art Deco café where the red, upholstered benches, mirrors and marble walls haven't changed since the days when Sartre, de Beauvoir, Camus and Picasso bent their elbows here. The terrace is a much sought-after place to sip beer (€7.50 for 400mL), the house Pouilly Fumé (€7.50 a glass or €29 a bottle) or coffee (€4).

Les Deux Magots (Map pp105-7; ☎ 01 45 48 55 25; 170 blvd St-Germain, 6e; metro St-Germain des Prés; ✆ 7am-1am) This erstwhile literary haunt, whose name derives not from a couple of disgusting white worms but from the two *magots* (grotesque figurines) of Chinese dignitaries at the entrance, dates from 1914 although it is best known as the favoured hang-out of Sartre, Hemingway, Picasso and André Breton. Everyone has to sit on the terrace here at least once and have a coffee (€4), beer (€5.50) or the famous hot chocolate served in porcelain jugs (€6).

Montparnasse

The most popular places to while away the hours over a drink or coffee in Montparnasse are large café-restaurants like **La Coupole** and **Le Dôme** (p154) on blvd du Montparnasse.

Cubana Café (Map pp99-101; ☎ 01 40 46 80 81; 47 rue Vavin, 6e; metro Vavin; ✆ 11am-3am Sun-Wed, 11am-5am Thu-Sat) The 'Cuban Café' is the perfect bar-restaurant for a couple of 'starter' drinks before carrying on to the nearby Coupole, with Cuban cocktails (€7.30) reduced to €5.30 at happy hour (5pm to 7.30pm daily).

Opéra & Grands Boulevards

Bushwacker's (Map pp93-5; ☎ 01 44 94 95 64; 10 rue de Caumartin, 9e; metro Havre-Caumartin or Opéra; ✆ noon-2am) The name notwithstanding, this very upmarket, Australian-themed bar in the financial district is no den of thieves. Stuffed wallabies, didgeridoos and flat computer screen TVs predominate, and the circular bar encourages interaction.

Harry's New York Bar (Map pp93-5; ☎ 01 42 61 71 14; 5 rue Daunou, 2e; metro Opéra; 🕑 10.30am-4am) One of the most popular American-style bars in the prewar years, Harry's once welcomed such habitués as writers F Scott Fitzgerald and Hemingway, who no doubt sampled the bar's unique cocktail and creation: the Bloody Mary (€9.60). The Cuban mahogany interior dates from the mid-19th century and was brought over from a Manhattan bar in 1911. There's light jazz in the basement piano bar from 10pm to 2am Monday to Saturday.

Gare du Nord, Gare de l'Est & République

Chez Prune (Map pp96-8; ☎ 01 42 41 30 47; 71 quai de Valmy, 10e; metro République; 🕑 8am-2am Mon-Sat, 10am-2am Sun) This Soho-boho café is the venue that put the Canal St-Martin on the map. Most people come here for the vibe and the mojito cocktails.

Chez Wolf Motown Bar (Map pp96-8; ☎ 01 46 07 09 79; 81-83 blvd de Strasbourg, 10e; metro Gare de l'Est; 🕑 24hr except 6am-7pm Sat) This is the place to come in the lonely wee hours when you've got a thirst and a few bob but, alas, no friends; the Motown can sometimes feel like a club.

Ménilmontant & Belleville

L'Autre Café (Map pp96-8; ☎ 01 40 21 03 07; 62 rue Jean-Pierre Timbaud, 11e; metro Parmentier; 🕑 8am-1.30am Mon-Fri, 11.30am-1.30am Sat & Sun) 'The Other Café', which helped move some of the after-dark action north of rue Oberkampf to rue Jean-Pierre Timbaud, attracts a mixed young crowd of locals, artists and party-goers with its long bar, huge open space, relaxed environment and reasonable prices.

Cannibale Café (Map pp96-8; ☎ 01 49 29 95 59; 93 rue Jean-Pierre Timbaud, 11e; metro Couronnes; 🕑 8.30am-2am) The name of this place isn't suggesting that you bring condiments. In fact 'Cannibal Café' couldn't be more welcoming, with its grand rococo-style bar topped with worn zinc, decrepit mirrors, peeling mouldings, wood panelling, Formica tables and red leatherette bench seats. It is a laid-back, almost frayed alternative to the groovy pubs and bars of rue Oberkampf and the perfect place to linger over a coffee (€2) or beer at the bar (€2 a demi or €6.50 a pint).

Montmartre & Pigalle

Le Dépanneur (Map p108; ☎ 01 40 16 40 20; 27 rue Fontaine, 9e; metro Blanche; 🕑 24hr) 'The Repairman', an American diner with postmodern frills open round the clock, has plenty of tequila and fancy cocktails (from €6) and there are DJs after 11pm from Thursday to Saturday.

La Fourmi (Map p108; ☎ 01 42 64 70 35; 74 rue des Martyrs, 18e; metro Pigalle; 🕑 8am-2am Mon-Thu, 10am-4am Fri-Sun) A trendy Pigalle hang-out, the trendy 'Ant' buzzes (marches?) all day and night and is a convenient place to meet before heading off to the clubs.

ENTERTAINMENT
Listings

It's virtually impossible to sample the richness of Paris' entertainment scene without first studying *Pariscope* (€0.40) or *Officiel des Spectacles* (€0.35), both of which come out on Wednesday and are available at newsstands everywhere in the city. *Pariscope* includes a six-page insert in English at the back, courtesy of London's *Time Out* magazine. The weekly magazine *Zurban* (www.zurban.com in French; €0.80), which also appears on Wednesday, offers a fresher look at entertainment in the capital. *Les Inrockuptibles* (www.lesinrocks. com in French; €2.90) is a national culture and entertainment weekly but, predictably, the lion's share of the information concerns Paris.

For up-to-date information on clubs and the music scene, pick up a copy of *LYLO* (an acronym for *Les Yeux, Les Oreilles*, literally 'Ears and Eyes'), a free magazine booklet with excellent listings of rock concerts and other live music. It is available at many cafés, bars and clubs across town. The monthly magazine *Nova* (www.novaplanet .com in French; €2) is an excellent source for information on clubs and the music scene; its *Hot Guide* listings insert is particularly useful. Visit any of the Fnac outlets (see opposite) for free flyers, schedules and programmes.

Other excellent sources for finding out what's on include Radio FG on 98.2MHz FM (www.radiofg.com in French) and Radio Nova on 101.5MHz FM. You can also try www.france-techno.fr (French only) or www .flyersweb.com (French only) for up-to-date information on clubbing.

Tickets & Bookings

You can buy your tickets for cultural events at numerous ticket outlets, including Fnac (rhymes with 'snack') and Virgin Megastore branches, for a small commission. Both accept reservations, ticketing by phone and the Internet and most credit cards. Tickets generally cannot be returned or exchanged unless a performance is cancelled.

Fnac (☎ 0 892 68 36 22; www.fnac.com in French) has 10 outlets in Paris with *billeteries* (ticket offices) including the following:

Fnac Musique Bastille (Map pp102-4; ☎ 01 43 42 04 04; 4 place de la Bastille, 12e; metro Bastille; ✆ 10am-8pm Mon-Sat)

Fnac Champs-Élysées (Map pp93-5; ☎ 01 53 53 64 64; 74 av des Champs-Élysées, 8e; metro Franklin D Roosevelt; ✆ 10am-midnight Mon-Sat, 11am-midnight Sun)

Fnac Forum des Halles (Map pp105-7; ☎ 01 40 41 40 00; Forum des Halles shopping centre, Level 3, 1-7 rue Pierre Lescot, 1er; metro Châtelet-Les Halles; ✆ 10am-7.30pm Mon-Sat)

Virgin (www.virginmega.fr in French) has a half-dozen 'megastores' in the capital; central locations:

Virgin Megastore Champs-Élysées (Map pp93-5; ☎ 01 49 53 50 00; 52-60 av des Champs-Élysées, 8e; metro Franklin D Roosevelt; ✆ 10am-midnight Mon-Sat, noon-midnight Sun)

Virgin Megastore Carrousel du Louvre (Map pp105-7; ☎ 01 44 50 03 10; 99 rue de Rivoli, 1er; metro Palais Royal-Musée du Louvre; ✆ 10am-8.30pm Mon & Tue, 10am-9.30pm Wed-Sun)

Virgin Megastore Barbès (Map p108; ☎ 01 56 55 53 70; 15 blvd Barbès, 18e; metro Barbès Rochechouart; ✆ 10am-10pm Mon-Sat)

DISCOUNT TICKETS

On the day of any play or musical performance, **Kiosque Théâtre** (Map pp93-5; opp 15 place de la Madeleine, 8e; metro Madeleine; ✆ 12.30-7.45pm Tue-Sat, 12.30-3.45pm Sun) sells tickets to plays and other events (concerts, operas, ballets etc) at half-price plus commission of about €2.50. Seats are almost always the most expensive ones in the stalls or 1st balcony. There's also a **Kiosque Théâtre Montparnasse branch** (Map pp99-101; parvis Montparnasse, 15e; metro Montparnasse Bienvenüe) between Gare Montparnasse and Tour Montparnasse, open the same hours. There are no telephone bookings.

Cinemas

Pariscope and *L'Officiel des Spectacles* (see opposite) list Paris' cinematic offerings alphabetically by their French title followed by the English (or other foreign) one.

Visiting to the cinema in Paris is not cheap: expect to pay between €6 and €8 for a first-run film. Students and those aged under 18 or over 60 usually get discounts of about 25% except on Friday, Saturday and Sunday nights. On Wednesday (and some Mondays) most cinemas give discounts of 20% to 30% to everyone.

Cinémathèque Française (☎ 01 56 26 01 01; www.cinemathequefrancaise.com in French; adult/student & child €4.70/3, 10-ticket carnet €44/27) This national cultural institution almost always leaves its foreign offerings – often rarely screened classics – in their original versions. There are two *salles*, the main one at the **Palais de Chaillot** (Map pp99-101; 7 av Albert de Mun, 16e; metro Trocadéro or Iéna; ✆ screenings Wed-Sun), which you enter from the Jardins du Trocadéro, and the more convenient but less dramatic **Grands Boulevards branch** (Map pp96-8; 42 blvd Bonne Nouvelle, 10e; metro Bonne Nouvelle; ✆ screenings).

Gay & Lesbian Venues

The Marais, especially those areas around the intersection of rue Ste-Croix de la Bretonnerie and rue des Archives and eastwards to rue Vieille du Temple, has been Paris' main centre of gay and lesbian nightlife for two decades. There are a few other addresses scattered elsewhere on the Right Bank.

Bliss Kfé (Map pp105-7; ☎ 01 55 34 98 81; 30 rue du Roi de Sicile, 4e; metro St-Paul; ✆ 5.30pm-2am) This dike café-cum-lounge bar is a stylish newcomer to the Marais, with a New York vibe and a somewhat mixed – guys are welcome – crowd.

La Champmeslé (Map pp96-8; ☎ 01 42 96 85 20; 4 rue Chabanais, 2e; metro Pyramides; ✆ 2pm-2am Mon-Thu, 2pm-dawn Fri & Sat) The oldest (established in 1979) lesbian bar in the city that plays mellow music and has regular theme nights, including a cabaret of French chansons commencing at 10pm on Thursday and sometimes Saturday.

Le Dépôt (Map pp105-7; ☎ 01 44 54 96 96; 10 rue aux Ours, 3e; metro Rambuteau or Étienne Marcel; admission €6 12; ✆ 2pm 8am) A huge place with both conversation bars and obscure cruising space. DJ theme nights are scheduled throughout the week.

Open Café (Map pp105-7; ☎ 01 42 72 26 18; 17 rue des Archives, 4e; metro Hôtel de Ville; ✆ 11am-2am) This is where most boyz of most ages head after work before moving on to bigger (maybe) and better (doubtful) things. It's packed but more social than cruisy. Happy hour is 6pm to 9pm daily.

Red Light (Map pp99-101; ☎ 01 42 79 94 94; 34 rue du Départ, 14e; metro Montparnasse Bienvenüe; admission €20; ☺ 11pm-6am Thu-Sun) This underground (literally) venue at the foot of the Tour Montparnasse has become the destination of choice for the young gay crowd, especially on Saturday house nights.

Le Scorp (Map pp96-8; ☎ 01 40 26 28 30; 25 blvd Poissonnière, 2e; metro Grands Boulevards; admission free-€15; ☺ 11.45pm-6.30am Wed & Thu, midnight-7.30am Fri & Sat) The Scorp – short for 'Scorpion' – is one of the more relaxed, mixed gay dance clubs in Paris. On the ground floor is **Le Pulp** (☎ 01 40 26 01 93; admission €9-10; ☺ midnight-6am Thu-Sun), the city's pre-eminent girls-only club (mixed on Thursday).

Live Music
OPERA & CLASSICAL

The **Opéra National de Paris** (ONP; ☎ 0 892 899 090; www.opera-de-paris.fr in French) splits its performance schedule between the Palais Garnier, its original home built in 1875, and the modern Opéra Bastille, which opened in 1989. Both opera houses also stage ballets and classical-music concerts performed by the ONP's affiliated orchestra and ballet companies. The season runs from September to July.

Opéra Bastille (Map pp102-4; 2-6 place de la Bastille, 12e; metro Bastille) Tickets are available from the adjacent **box office** (130 rue de Lyon, 12e; ☺ 11am-6.30pm Mon-Sat) 14 days before the date of the performance, but the only way to ensure a seat is by **post** (120 rue de Lyon, 75576 Paris CEDEX 12) some two months in advance. Operas cost €6 to €114. Ballets cost €13 to €70; seats with limited or no visibility available at the box office only are €6 to €9. Chamber-music concerts, which are also held here throughout the season, cost €6 to €16. If there are unsold tickets, people aged under 26 or over 65 and students can get excellent seats for €20 only 15 minutes before the curtain goes up.

Palais Garnier (Map pp93-5; place de l'Opéra, 9e; metro Opéra) Ticket prices and conditions (including last-minute discounts) at the **box office** (place de l'Opéra, 9e; ☺ 11am-6.30pm Mon-Sat) of the city's original opera house are almost exactly the same as those at the Opéra Bastille.

Along with opera, Paris plays host to dozens of orchestral, organ and chamber-music concerts each week. From October to June the excellent Orchestre de Paris performs at the Châtelet-Théâtre Musical

de Paris and the **Théâtre Mogador** (Map pp93-5; ☎ 01 53 32 32 00; 25 rue de Mogador, 9e; metro St-Lazare) while renovation of the Salle Pleyel is completed.

Châtelet-Théâtre Musical de Paris (Map pp105-7; ☎ 01 40 28 28 40; www.chatelet-theatre.com in French; 2 rue Édouard Colonne, 1er; metro Châtelet; concert tickets €9-60; box office ☺ 11am-7pm) This central venue hosts concerts (including ones by the Orchestre de Paris) as well as operas (€20 to €106; €11 for seats with no visibility), ballets (€21 to €62 or €9 for the cheapest seat), and theatre performances. Classical music is also performed at 11am on Sunday (€20) and at 12.45pm on Monday, Wednesday and Friday (€9). Tickets go on sale 14 days before the performance date; subject to availability, anyone aged under 26 or over 65 can get reduced-price tickets (eg €10 for the Sunday morning concert) from 15 minutes before curtain time. There are no performances in July and August.

Salle Pleyel (Map pp93-5; ☎ 01 45 61 53 00; 252 rue du Faubourg St-Honoré, 8e; metro Ternes) Dating from the 1920s, this highly regarded hall hosts many of Paris' finest classical music concerts and recitals. It was closed in July 2002 for a three-year renovation.

CHURCH CONCERT VENUES

The churches of Paris are popular venues for classical music concerts and organ recitals. The concerts held at **Notre Dame Cathedral** (Map pp105-7; ☎ 01 42 34 56 10; tickets €10-€40) don't keep to any fixed schedule but are advertised on posters around town. There's usually a free organ concert some time between 4.30pm and 5.15pm on Sunday, especially in winter. From April to October classical concerts are also held in **Ste-Chapelle** (Map pp105-7; ☎ 01 53 73 78 51; Île de la Cité, 1er); the cheapest seats cost around €17 (€12 for students aged under 26). From November to June concerts are also held at the exquisite **Église Royale du Val-de-Grâce** (Map pp102-4; ☎ 01 42 01 47 67; 277bis rue St-Jacques, 5e; metro Port Royal; adult/child €18.30/12.20).

ROCK, POP & INDIE

There's rock, pop and indie at bars, cafés and clubs around Paris, and a number of venues regularly host acts by international performers. It's often easier to see big-name Anglophone acts in Paris than in their home countries. The most popular stadiums or other big venues for international acts are the **Palais Omnisports de Paris-Bercy** (Map pp102-4; ☎ 0 825 030 031, 01 46 91 57 57; www.bercy.fr in French; 8 blvd de Bercy, 12e; metro Bercy) in Bercy; the **Stade de France** (Map p182; ☎ 0 892 700 900, 01 55 93 00 00; www.stadedefrance.fr; rue Francis de Pressensé, ZAC du Cornillon Nord, 93216 St-Denis La Plaine; metro St-Denis-Porte de Paris) in St-Denis; and **Le Zénith** (Map pp90-2; ☎ 01 42 08 60 00; www.le-zenith.com in French; 211 av Jean Jaurès, 19e; metro Porte de Pantin) at the Cité de la Musique in the Parc de la Villette, 19e.

Le Bataclan (Map pp102-4; ☎ 01 43 14 35 35; 50 blvd Voltaire, 11e; metro Oberkampf or St-Ambroise; admission €15-50; box office ⏰ 11am-7pm Mon-Sat) Built in 1864 and Maurice Chevalier's debut venue in 1910, this small concert hall draws some French and international acts. It also masquerades as a theatre and dance hall. Le Bataclan usually opens from 8pm for concerts.

Café de la Danse (Map pp102-4; ☎ 01 47 00 57 59; www.cafédeladanse.com in French; 5 Passage Louis-Philippe, 11e; metro Bastille; admission €10-20; box office ⏰ noon-6pm Mon-Fri) Just a few metres down a small passage from 23 rue de Lappe, 'The Dance Café' is a large auditorium with 300 to 500 seats. Almost every day from sometime between 7.30pm and 9pm, it plays host to rock and world music concerts, dance performances, musical theatre and poetry readings.

La Cigale (Map p108; ☎ 01 49 25 89 99; 120 blvd de Rochechouart, 18e; metro Anvers or Pigalle; admission €22-45; box office ⏰ noon-7pm Mon-Fri) 'The Cicada' is an enormous old music hall seating up to 2000 people and hosting international rock acts, jazz and folk groups and full-on dance and variety performances. There's seating in the balcony and dancing up front.

L'Élysée Montmartre (Map p108; ☎ 01 44 92 45 36, 01 55 07 16 00; www.elyseemontmartre.com; 72 blvd de Rochechouart, 18e; metro Anvers; admission €10-34) A huge old music hall with a great sound system, this is one of the better venues in Paris for one-off rock and indie concerts. It opens at 7.30pm for concerts and becomes a popular club on Friday and Saturday from midnight to 6am.

La Java (Map pp96-8; ☎ 01 42 02 20 52; 105 rue du Faubourg du Temple, 10e; metro Goncourt; admission €8-16; ⏰ 11pm-5am Thu-Sat, 2-7pm Sun) The dance hall (1922) where Édith Piaf got her first break now reverberates to the sound of live salsa and other Latino music. There's a *thé dansant* (tea dance) here on Sunday.

JAZZ & BLUES

After WWII Paris was Europe's most important jazz centre and it is again very much à la mode; the city's better clubs attract top international stars.

Le Baiser Salé (Map pp105-7; ☎ 01 42 33 37 71; 58 rue des Lombards, 1er; metro Châtelet; admission free-€22) 'The Salty Kiss' is one of several jazz clubs on the same street. The *salle de jazz* on the 1st floor has concerts of pop rock and *chansons* at 7pm and Afro-jazz and jazz fusion at 10pm. The cover charge depends on the act; it's free during the *soirée bœuf* (jam session) on Monday night. Try to catch the incomparable Pierre Chabrèle on trombone.

Le Caveau de la Huchette (Map pp105-7; ☎ 01 43 26 65 05; 5 rue de la Huchette, 5e; metro St-Michel; adult Sun-Thu €10.50, Fri & Sun €13, student €9; ⏰ 9pm-2.30am Sun-Thu, 9pm-3.30am Fri, 9pm-4am Sat) Housed in a medieval *caveau* (cellar) that was used as a courtroom and torture chamber during the Revolution, this club is where virtually all the jazz greats have played since the end of WWII. It's touristy but the atmosphere can often be more electric than at the more serious jazz clubs. Sessions start at 9.30pm.

New Morning (Map pp96-8; ☎ 01 45 23 51 41; www .newmorning.com in French; 7-9 rue des Petites Écuries, 10e; metro Château d'Eau; admission €14.50-21; ⏰ 8pm-2am) This informal auditorium hosts jazz concerts as well as blues, rock, funk, salsa, Afro-Cuban and Brazilian music three to seven nights a week at 9pm, with the second set ending at about 1am. Tickets (€18.30 to €22.80) are available at the box office (open 4.30pm to 7.30pm) and at the door.

Opus (Map pp96-8; ☎ 01 40 34 70 00; 167 quai de Valmy, 10e; metro Louis Blanc; admission free-€15; ⏰ 8pm-2am Sun & Tue-Thu, 8pm-4am Fri & Sat) Located within a former officers' mess by the Canal St-Martin, this place has moved on from hip-hop to jazz, soul, blues, gospel and *zouk* (a blend of African and Latin American dance rhythms). It's a club-cum-concert venue and there are menus for €33 and €40 (obligatory Thursday to Saturday).

FRENCH CHANSONS

When French music comes to mind, most people hear accordions and *chansonniers* (cabaret singers) such as Edith Piaf, Jacques Brel, Georges Brassens and Léo Ferré. But although you may stumble upon buskers performing *chansons françaises* or playing *musette* (accordion music) in the market, it can sometimes be difficult to catch traditional French music in a more formal setting in Paris. We list a handful of venues where you're sure to hear it – both the traditional and the modern forms.

Au Lapin Agile (Map p108; ☎ 01 46 06 85 87; www .au-lapin-agile.com; 22 rue des Saules, 18e; metro Lamarck Caulaincourt; adult €24, students Sun & Tue-Fri only €17; ✆ 9pm-2am Tue-Sun) This rustic cabaret venue in Montmartre was favoured by artists and intellectuals in the early 20th century and *chansons* are still performed here and poetry read six nights a week starting at 9.30pm. Admission includes one drink.

Chez Adel (Map pp96-8; ☎ 01 42 08 24 61; 10 rue de la Grange aux Belles, 10e; metro Jacques Bonsergent; admission free; ✆ lunch & dinner to 2am Tue-Fri, noon-2am Sat & Sun) Chez Adel is a truly Parisian concept: Syrian hosts with guest *chansonniers* (as well as Gypsy, folk and world) performing most nights to a mixed and enthusiastic crowd.

Le Limonaire (Map pp96-8; ☎ 01 45 23 33 33; 18 cité Bergère, 9e; metro Grands Boulevards; admission free; ✆ 6pm-midnight Tue-Sun) This little wine bar is one of the best places to listen to traditional French bistro music, but come here only if you're serious about the genre; the crowd is almost reverential. Singers (who change regularly) perform at 10pm Tuesday to Saturday and at 7pm on Sunday.

Clubs

The clubs and other dancing venues that are favoured by the Parisian party people change frequently and many are officially private. Single men may not be admitted – even if their clothes are subculturally appropriate – simply because they're men on their own. Women, on the other hand, get in for free on some nights. It's always easier to get into the club of your choice during the week, when things may be hopping even more than they are at the weekend. Remember that Parisians tend to go out in groups and don't mingle as much as Anglo-Saxons do. The truly trendy crowd considers showing up before 1am a serious breach of good taste. Admission fees almost always include one alcoholic drink.

Paris is great for music (techno remains very popular) and there are some mighty fine DJs based here. Latino and Cuban salsa music is also huge. Theme nights at clubs are as common here as they are in, say, London so it's best to consult the sources mentioned earlier (see p160) before making plans

Les Bains (Map pp105-7; ☎ 01 48 87 01 80; www .lesbains-club.com in French; 7 rue du Bourg l'Abbé, 3e; metro Étienne Marcel; admission €16-20; ✆ 11pm-5am Mon-Sat) Housed in a refitted old Turkish hamman, 'The Baths' is still renowned for its surly, selective bouncers on the outside though celebrities and star-struck revellers are thinner on the ground inside. What happened to all the BMWs, Porsches and Rollers waiting at the kerb?

Le Balajo (Map pp102-4; ☎ 01 47 00 07 87; 9 rue de Lappe, 11e; metro Bastille; admission €8-17; ✆ 9-4.30pm Tue-Thu, 11pm-5.30am Fri & Sat, 3-7.30pm Sun) A mainstay of Parisian nightlife since 1936, this ancient ballroom is a bit lower shelf these days but still hosts a number of popular theme nights. Tuesday to Thursday is salsa and Latino music, on Friday and Saturday DJs play rock, disco, R 'n' B and house and from 3pm to 7.30pm on Sunday, DJs play old-fashioned musette (accordion music).

Le Batofar (Map pp90-2; ☎ 01 56 29 10 33; www .batofar.net in French; opposite 11 quai François Mauriac, 13e; metro Quai de la Gare or Bibliothèque; admission free-€12; ✆ 9pm-midnight Mon & Tue, 9 or 10pm-4, 5 or 6am Wed-Sun) What looks like an unassuming tug boat moored near the imposing Bibliothèque Nationale de France is a rollicking dancing spot that attracts some top international techno and funk DJ talent. Jazz concerts usually take place on Monday and Tuesday evening.

Le Cithéa (Map pp96-8; ☎ 01 40 21 70 95; 114 rue Oberkampf, 11e; metro Parmentier or Ménilmontant; admission free-€4; ✆ 5pm-5.30am Tue-Thu, 10pm-6.30am Fri & Sat) This popular and ever-hopping concert venue has bands playing soul, Latin and funk but especially world music and jazz, usually from 10.30pm, with DJs from 1am.

La Favela Chic (Map pp96-8; ☎ 01 40 21 38 14; www .favelachic.com in French; 18 rue du Faubourg du Temple, 10e; metro République; admission free; ✆ 7.30pm-2am Tue-Fri, 9.30pm-4am Sat) The ambience is more *favela* (shantytown) than chic in this restobar-cum-dancehall next to Gibus (following) where Brazilians and French alike get down to the frenetic mix of samba, *baile* funk and classic Brazilian pop.

Gibus (Map pp96-8; ☎ 01 47 00 78 88; www.gibus .fr in French; 18 rue du Faubourg du Temple, 11e; metro République; admission free-€18; ✆ 11pm-dawn Tue-Sat) Gibus, an enormously popular cave-like venue that is halfway between the Canal St-Martin and place de la République, has hard techno on Tuesday with Thermo Tek, acid and trance on Wednesday with Virtual Moon, and techno on Thursday with Parisjuana Night.

Le Nouveau Casino (Map pp96-8; ☎ 01 43 57 57 40; www.nouveaucasino.net in French; 109 rue Oberkampf, 11e; metro Parmentier; admission free-€18; ☺ 9pm or 11pm–btwn 2am & 6am) 'The New Casino' has made quite a splash since opening in 2000, with its electronic live music concerts and DJs. It has a huge dance floor and some pretty impressive acoustic and video systems.

Rex Club (Map pp96-8; ☎ 01 42 36 10 96; 5 blvd Poissonnière, 2e; metro Bonne Nouvelle; admission €8-13; ☺ 11.30pm-6am Wed-Sat) This huge club remains the hottest spot in town for house (Thursday and Saturday) and techno (Friday) and attracts Paris' top DJ talent.

Studio 287 (off Map pp90-2; ☎ 01 48 34 00 00; 33 av de la Porte d'Aubervilliers, 18e; metro Porte de la Chapelle; admission €10-16; ☺ 11pm-5am Tue-Thu, 11pm-noon Fri & Sat) The city's biggest dance club, with a capacity for 2000 gyrating and sweating bods, Studio 287 in the northern reaches of Paris may be a bit too commercial for some but Thursday's Studio 54 disco packs them in and Kit-Kat afters at the weekend often last till midday.

Le Wagg (Map pp105-7; ☎ 01 55 42 22 00; 62 rue Mazarine, 6e; metro Odéon; admission €10-12; ☺ 11pm-5am Wed-Sun) Clerkenwell meets St-Germain in the former Whisky a Go-go and now a UK-style Conran club. Dress light; the temperature rises considerably as the night wears on. Friday is house and electro.

Cabaret

Paris' risqué cabaret revues – those dazzling, pseudo-bohemian productions where the women all wear two beads and a feather (or was it two feathers and a bead?) – are about as representative of the Paris of the 21st century as crocodile-wrestling is of Australia or bronco-busting of the USA. But they continue to draw in the crowds as they did in the days of Toulouse-Lautrec and Aristide Bruant.

Crazy Horse (Map pp93-5; ☎ 01 47 23 32 32; www.lecrazyhorseparis.com; 12 av George V, 8e; metro Alma Marceau) This popular cabaret, whose dressing (or, rather, undressing) rooms were featured in Woody Allen's film *What's New Pussycat?* (1965), has been promoting what it calls *l'art du nu* (nudity) for over half a century. Shows (1¾ hours) are at 8.30pm and 11pm Sunday to Friday and at 7.30pm, 9.45pm and 11.50pm Saturday. Admission

(including two drinks) is €49/69/90 in the bar/mezzanine/orchestra and €110 in the orchestra with a half-bottle of champagne. Students are €29 with one drink.

Le Lido de Paris (Map pp93-5; ☎ 01 40 76 56 10; www.lido.fr; 116bis av des Champs-Élysées, 8e; metro George V) Founded at the close of WWII, the Lido gets top marks for its ambitious sets and the lavish costumes of its 70 artistes. Nightly shows cost €80 at 9.30pm and €60 (€80 on Friday and Saturday) at 11.30pm; €69 to watch from the bar (with two drinks). With dinner, entry to the 9.30pm show costs €140, €170 and €200, depending on the menu chosen, and includes a half-bottle of champagne per person.

Moulin Rouge (Map p108; ☎ 01 53 09 82 82; www.moulinrouge.fr; 82 blvd de Clichy, 18e; metro Blanche) This legendary cabaret founded in 1889, whose dancers appeared in Toulouse-Lautrec's celebrated posters, sits under its trademark red windmill (actually a 1925 copy of the 19th-century original). Champagne dinner shows (at 7pm) cost €130, €145 or €160. The show at 9pm with half a bottle of champers costs €92; at 11pm it drops to €82.

Sport

Parisians are mad about sport. For details of upcoming sporting events, consult the sports daily *L'Équipe* (€0.80; www.lequipe.fr in French) or *Figaroscope* (www.figaroscope.fr in French), an entertainment and activities supplement published with *Le Figaro* daily newspaper each Wednesday.

Most big international sporting events are held are held at the magnificent **Stade de France** (Map p182; ☎ 0 892 700 900; www.stadefrance.com; rue Francis de Pressensé, ZAC du Cornillon Nord, 93216 St-Denis La Plaine) at St-Denis, which was built for the 1998 World Cup.

FOOTBALL

France's home matches (friendlies and qualifiers for major championships) are held at the **Stade de France** (tickets €12 to C70).

The city's only top-division football team, **Paris-St-Germain** (☎ 01 47 43 71 71; www.psg.fr in French) plays its home games at the 45,500-seat **Parc des Princes** (Map pp90-2; ☎ 0 825 075 078; 24 rue du Commandant Guilbaud, 16e; metro Porte de St-Cloud; tickets €12-80; box office ☺ 9am-9pm Mon-Sat), near Stade Roland Garros. Tickets are also available at the more central **Boutique PSG** (Map pp93-5; ☎ 01 56 69 22 22; www.psg.fr in French; 27 av Champs Elysées, 8e; metro Franklin D Roosevelt;

10am-7.45pm Mon-Thu, 10am-9.45pm Fri & Sat, noon-7.45pm Sun).

TENNIS
In late May/early June the tennis world focuses on the clay surface of the 16,500-seat **Stade Roland Garros** (Map pp90-2; ☎ 01 47 43 48 00, 01 47 43 52 52; www.frenchopen.org, www.rolandgarros.com; av Gordon Bennett, 16e; metro Porte d'Auteuil) in the Bois de Boulogne for Les Internationaux de France de Tennis (The French Open), the second of the four Grand Slam tournaments. Tickets are expensive and hard to come by; bookings must usually be made by the previous March at the latest.

The top indoor tournament is the Open de Tennis de la Ville de Paris (Paris Tennis Open), which usually takes place sometime in late October or early November at the **Palais Omnisports de Paris-Bercy** (Map pp102-4; ☎ 01 40 02 60 60; www.bercy.fr in French; 8 blvd de Bercy, 12e; metro Bercy). Tickets are available from the **box office** (☎ 0 892 390 490, from abroad ☎ 33-1 46 91 57 57; 11am-6pm Mon-Sat).

CYCLING
Since 1974 the final stage of the **Tour de France** (www.letour.fr), the world's most prestigious cycling event, has ended on the av des Champs-Élysées. The final day varies from year to year but is usually the 3rd or 4th Sunday in July, with the race finishing sometime in the afternoon. If you want to see this exciting event, find a spot at the barricades before noon.

Track cycling events, a sport at which France excels, are usually held in the *vélodrome* of the Palais Omnisports de Paris-Bercy.

HORSE RACING
One of the cheapest ways to spend a relaxing afternoon in the company of Parisians of all ages and backgrounds is to go to the races. The most accessible of the Paris areas' seven racecourses is **Hippodrome d'Auteuil** (Map pp90-2; ☎ 01 40 71 47 47; www.france-galop.com in French; Champ de Courses d'Auteuil, Bois de Boulogne, 16e; metro Porte d'Auteuil), in the southeastern corner of the Bois de Boulogne. It hosts steeplechases from February to late June/early July and early September to early December.

Races are held about six times a month (check the *France Galop* website for the exact days), with half a dozen or so heats

scheduled from 2pm to 5.30pm. There's no charge to stand on the *pelouse* (lawn) in the middle of the track but a seat in the *tribune* (stands) costs around €3/1.50 for adults/students and seniors on weekdays and €4/2 on Sunday; those under age 18 get in free. Race schedules are published in almost all national newspapers. If you read French, pick up a copy of *Paris Turf* (€1.15), the horse-racing daily.

Theatre
Almost all of Paris' theatre productions, including those written in other languages, are performed in French. There are a few English-speaking troupes around, though; look for ads on metro poster boards and in English-language periodicals such as *FUSAC* (p110), *Paris Voice* and *The Irish Eyes*, which are free at English-language bookshops, pubs, and so on, as well as the website www.parisfranceguide.com.

Comédie Française (Map pp105-7; ☎ 0 825 101 680; www.comedie-francaise.fr; place Colette, 1er; metro Palais Royal-Musée du Louvre; tickets €5-32; box office 11am-6pm Tue-Sat, 1-6pm Sun & Mon) Founded in 1680 during the reign of Louis XIV, the 'French Comedy' theatre bases its repertoire around works of the classic French playwrights such as Molière, Racine and Corneille, though in recent years contemporary and even non-French works have been staged. There are three venues: the main **Salle Richelieu** on place Colette just west of the Palais Royal; the **Comédie Française Studio Théâtre** (Map pp105-7; ☎ 01 44 58 98 58; Galerie du Carrousel du Louvre, 99 rue de Rivoli, 1; metro Palais Royal-Musée du Louvre; box office 1-5pm Wed-Mon); and the **Théâtre du Vieux Colombier** (Map pp99-101; ☎ 01 44 39 87 00; 21 rue du Vieux Colombier, 6e; metro St-Sulpice; box office 11am-6pm Tue-Sat, 1-6pm Sun & Mon). Discount tickets for 95 places near the ceiling (€5) go on sale one hour before curtain time (usually 8.30pm), which is when those aged under 27 years can purchase any of the better seats remaining for €7.50 to €10. The discount tickets are available from the window around the corner from the main entrance and facing place André Malraux.

Odéon-Théâtre de l'Europe (Map pp105-7; ☎ 01 44 41 36 36; www.theatre-odeon.fr; place de l'Odéon, 6e; metro Odéon) This huge, ornate theatre built in the early 1780s, often puts on foreign plays in their original languages (subtitled in French) and hosts theatre troupes from abroad. It was undergoing complete renovation until 2005 during which time plays were being staged at the **Ateliers Berthier** (Map pp90-2; ☎ 01 44 85 40 40; 8 blvd Berthier, 17e; metro Porte de Clichy; tickets €13-26; box office 🕓 11am-6.30pm Mon-Sat).

Point Virgule (Map pp105-7; ☎ 01 42 78 67 03; 7 rue Ste-Croix de la Bretonnerie, 4e; metro Hôtel de Ville; 1/2/3 shows €15/24/27, student Sun-Fri €12) The tiny 'Semicolon' is a popular comedy spot in the Marais offering café-theatre at its best – stand-up comics, performance artists and sometimes musical acts. The quality is variable but it's great fun nevertheless and the place has a reputation of discovering new talent. There are three shows daily at 8pm, 9.15pm and 10.30pm.

SHOPPING
Paris is a wonderful place to shop, whether you're someone who can afford an original Cartier diamond bracelet or you're an impoverished *lèche-vitrine* (literal meaning: 'window-licker') who just enjoys what you see from the outside looking in. From the ultrachic couture houses of av Montaigne and the cubby-hole boutiques of the Marais to the vast underground shopping centre at Les Halles and the flea-market bargains at St-Ouen, Paris is a city that knows how to make it, how to display it and how to charge for it.

Opening Hours
Opening times in Paris are notoriously anarchic, with each store setting its own hours. Most shops will be open at least from 10am to 6pm five days a week (including Saturday) but they may open earlier, close later, close for lunch (usually 1pm to 2 or 2.30pm) or for a full or half-day on Monday or Tuesday. In general, only shops in tourist areas (eg the Champs-Élysées and the Marais) open on Sunday. Many larger shops and department stores also have a *nocturne* – one late shopping night (usually to 10pm and on Thursday) a week.

Clothing & Fashion
HAUTE COUTURE & DESIGNER WEAR
Most of the major French couturiers and ready-to-wear designers have their own boutiques in the capital, but it's also possible to see labelled, ready-to-wear collections at major department stores such as Le Printemps, Galeries Lafayette and Le Bon

Marché. The Right Bank, especially the so-called **Triangle d'Or** (Map pp93-5; metro Franklin D Roosevelt or Alma Marceau, 1er & 8e), **rue du Faubourg St-Honoré** (Map pp93-5; metro Madeleine or Concorde, 8e) and its eastern extension, **rue St-Honoré** (metro Tuileries), **place des Victoires** (Map pp96-8; metro Bourse or Sentier, 1er & 2e) and the Marais' **rue des Rosiers** (Map pp105-7; metro St-Paul, 4e), is traditionally the epicentre of Parisian fashion though **St-Germain** (Map pp105-7; metro St-Sulpice or S-Germain des Prés) on the Left Bank also boasts its fair share of boutiques.

FASHION EMPORIA
There are fashion shops offering creations and accessories from a variety of cutting-edge designers.

Abou Dhabi Bazar (Map pp105-7; ☎ 01 42 77 96 98; 10 rue des Francs Bourgeois, 3e; metro St-Paul; 🕓 2-7pm Sun & Mon, 10.30am-7.15pm Tue-Sat) This fashionable boutique with the odd name is a treasure-trove of smart and affordable ready-to-wear pieces from young designers including Paul & Joe, Isabel Marant and Vanessa Bruno.

Colette (Map pp93-5; ☎ 01 55 35 33 90; 213 rue St-Honoré, 1er; metro Tuileries; 🕓 10.30am-7.30pm Mon-Sat) This highly successful concept store is Japanese-inspired and has an exquisite selection of clothes, accessories and odds and ends. Featured designers include Alexander McQueen, Marko Matysik and Lulu Guinness but it doesn't stop there. Check out the limited edition Nike sneakers, Prada handbags, designer hairpins and cutting-edge clocks.

Kiliwatch (Map pp96-8; ☎ 01 42 21 17 37; 64 rue Tiquetonne, 2e; metro Étienne Marcel; 🕓 2-7pm Mon, 11am-7pm Tue-Sat) This enormous barn of a shop is filled with rack after rack of colourful, original street and club wear, plus a startling range of second hand clothes and accessories in reasonable condition.

Réciproque (Map pp93-5; ☎ 01 47 04 30 28, 01 47 04 82 24; 88 & 95 rue de la Pompe, 16e; metro Rue de la Pompe; 🕓 11am-7pm Tue-Fri, 10.30am-7pm Sat) The biggest *dépôt-vente* (resale stores that sell used or barely used clothes and accessories from one-quarter to one-half off the original price) has rack after rack of Chanel suits as well as bits and pieces from Christian Lacroix, Hermès, Prada, Thierry Mugler, Issey Miyake, Christian Dior, John Galliano, Gucci and Dolce & Gabbana. It's an excellent place to pick up bags and shoes.

Department Stores

Paris boasts a number of *grands magasins* (department stores) including those listed here. *Soldes* (sales) are generally held in January and June/July.

Le Bon Marché (Map pp99-101; ☎ 01 44 39 80 00; www.bonmarche.fr; 24 rue de Sèvres, 7e; metro Sèvres Babylone; ⏰ 9.30am-7pm Mon-Wed & Fri, 10am-9pm Thu, 9.30am-8pm Sat) Opened by Gustave Eiffel as Paris' first department store in 1852, 'The Good Market' (which also means 'bargain') is less frenetic than its rivals across the river, but no less chic. Men's as well as women's fashions are sold.

Galeries Lafayette (Map pp93-5; ☎ 01 42 82 34 56; www.galerieslafayette.com; 40 blvd Haussmann, 9e; metro Auber or Chaussée d'Antin; ⏰ 9.30am-7.30pm Mon-Wed, Fri & Sat; 9.30am-9pm Thu) A vast *grand magasin* in two adjacent buildings, Galeries Lafayette features a wide selection of fashion and accessories. A fashion show (☎ 01 42 82 30 25 to book a seat) takes place at 11am every Tuesday year-round with another show at 2.30pm on Friday April to October.

Le Printemps (Map pp93-5; ☎ 01 42 82 50 00; www.printemps.com; 64 blvd Haussmann, 9e; metro Havre Caumartin; ⏰ 9.35am-7pm Mon-Wed, Fri & Sat, 9.35am-10pm Thu) 'The Spring' (as in the season) is actually three separate stores – one each for women's fashion (De la Mode), one for men (De l'Homme) and one for beauty and household goods (De la Beauté et Maison) – offering a staggering display of perfume, cosmetics and accessories, as well as established and up-and-coming designer wear. There's a fashion show under the 7th-floor cupola at 10am on Tuesday.

La Samaritaine (Map pp105-7; ☎ 01 40 41 20 20; www.lasamaritaine.com; 19 rue de la Monnaie, 1er; metro Pont Neuf; ⏰ 9.30am-7pm Mon-Wed & Fri, 9.30am-10pm Thu, 9.30am-8pm Sat) 'The Samaritan' is in two buildings between Pont Neuf and 142 rue de Rivoli, 1er. The main store's biggest draw is the outstanding view from the rooftop restaurant and café (p117); the building devoted to men's fashion has a large sports department in the basement.

Flea Markets

Paris' *marchés aux puces* (flea markets) can be great fun if you're in the mood to browse for unexpected diamonds in the rough through all the *brocante* (second-hand goods) and bric-a-brac on display. Some new items are also available, and a bit of bargaining is expected. Closing times depend on the season.

Marché aux Puces de Montreuil (Map pp90-2; av du Professeur André Lemière, 20e; metro Porte de Montreuil; ⏰ 7.30 or 8am-6 or 7pm Sat-Mon) This flea market is renowned for its good-quality second-hand clothes and designer seconds. The 500 stalls also sell engravings, jewellery, linen, crockery, old furniture and appliances.

Marché aux Puces de la Porte de Vanves (Map pp90-2; av Georges Lafenestre & av Marc Sangnier, 14e; metro Porte de Vanves; ⏰ 7am-6 or 7pm Sat & Sun) The Porte de Vanves flea market is the smallest and, some say, friendliest of the big three. Av Georges Lafenestre looks like a giant car-boot sale, with lots of 'curios' that aren't quite old (or curious) enough to qualify as antiques. Av Marc Sangnier is lined with stalls with new clothes, shoes, handbags and household items for sale.

Marché aux Puces de St-Ouen (Map pp90-2; www.les-puces.com; rue des Rosiers, av Michelet, rue Voltaire, rue Paul Bert & rue Jean-Henri Fabre, 18e; metro Porte de Clignancourt; ⏰ 9am or 10am-7pm Sat-Mon) This vast flea market founded in the late 19th century and said to be Europe's largest has some 2500 stalls grouped into 10 *marchés* (market areas), each with its own speciality (eg Marché Serpette and Marché Biron for antiques, Marché Malik for second-hand clothing). Check the websites www.libertys.com and www.vernaison.net for further information.

Food & Wine

The food and wine shops of Paris are legendary and well worth seeking out. Many places will vacuum pack or shrink wrap certain food items to guard against spoilage.

Boutique Maille (Map pp93-5; ☎ 01 40 15 06 00; 6 place de la Madeleine, 8e; metro Madeleine; ⏰ 10am-7pm Mon-Sat) This shop specialises in mustards, of which it stocks and/or can make up for you some two dozen different varieties.

Cacao et Chocolat (Map pp105-7; ☎ 01 46 33 77 63; 29 rue du Buci, 6e; metro Mabillon; ⏰ 10.30am-7.30pm Mon-Sat, 11am-1.30pm & 2.30-7pm Sun) You have not tasted chocolate (a veritable religion in France) till you've tasted this stuff. 'Cocoa and Chocolate' is an exotic and contemporary take on chocolate, showcasing the cocoa bean in all its guises, both solid and liquid. The added citrus flavours, spices and even chilli are guaranteed to tease you back for more.

TO MARKET, TO MARKET...

Paris counts some five dozen *marchés découverts* (open-air markets) that pop up in public squares around the city two or three times a week and there are another 19 *marchés couverts* (covered markets) that keep more regular hours: 8am to 1pm and 3.30pm or 4pm to 7pm or 7.30pm from Tuesday to Saturday and till lunchtime on Sunday. Completing the picture are numerous independent *rues commerçantes*, pedestrian streets where the shops set up outdoor stalls. To find out when there's a market near your hotel or hostel, ask the staff or anyone who lives in the neighbourhood.

The following are favourite Paris markets rated according to the variety of their produce, their ethnicity and the neighbourhood. They are *la crème de la crème*.

Marché Bastille (Map pp102-4; blvd Richard Lenoir, 11e; metro Bastille; ⏱ 7am or 8am-1pm Tue & Sun) Stretching as far north as Richard Lenoir metro station, this is arguably the best roving street market in Paris.

Marché Belleville (Map pp96-8; blvd de Belleville btwn rue Jean-Pierre Timbaud & rue du Faubourg du Temple, 11e & 20e; metro Belleville or Couronne; ⏱ 7am or 8am-1pm Tue & Fri) This market offers a fascinating (and easy) entry into the large, vibrant ethnic communities of the *quartiers de l'est* (eastern neighbourhoods), home to African, Middle Eastern and Asian immigrants as well as artists and students.

Rue Cler (Map pp99-101; metro École Militaire; ⏱ 7am or 8am-7pm or 7.30pm Tue-Sat, 8am-noon Sun) This street in the 7e is a breath of fresh air in a sometimes stuffy *quartier* and can almost feel like a party at the weekend when the whole neighbourhood turns out en masse to squeeze, pay and cart away.

Marché aux Enfants Rouges (Map pp105-7; 39 rue de Bretagne, 3e; metro Temple or Arts et Métiers; ⏱ 8am-1pm & 4-7.30pm Tue-Sat, 8am-1pm Sun) This recently reopened covered market south of place de la République has both ethnic (Italian, North African etc) stalls as well as French ones.

Rue Montorgueil (Map pp96-8; rue Montorgueil btwn rue de Turbigo & rue Réaumur, 2e; metro Les Halles or Sentier; ⏱ 7am or 8am-7pm or 7.30pm Tue-Sat, 8am-noon Sun) This is the closest market to Paris' 700-year-old wholesale market, Les Halles, which was moved from this area to the southern suburb of Rungis in 1969.

Rue Mouffetard (Map pp102-4; rue Mouffetard around rue de l'Arbalète; metro Censier Daubenton or Place Monge; ⏱ 7am or 8am-7pm or 7.30pm Tue-Sat, 8am-noon Sun) Rue Mouffetard is the city's most photogenic market street – the place where Parisians send tourists.

Marché St-Quentin (Map pp96-8; 85 blvd de Magenta, 10e; metro Gare de l'Est; ⏱ 8am-1pm & 3.30-7.30pm Tue-Sat, 8am-1pm Sun) This iron-and-glass covered market built in 1866 is a maze of corridors lined mostly with gourmet food stalls.

Les Caves Augé (Map pp93-5; ☎ 01 45 22 16 97; 116 blvd Haussmann, 8e; metro St-Augustin; ⏱ 1-7.30pm Mon, 9am-7.30pm Tue-Sat) 'The Augé Cellars' should be the *marchand de vin* (wine shop) for you if you're following the advice of Marcel Proust. It's now under the stewardship of a passionate and knowledgeable *sommelier*.

Fauchon (Map pp93-5; ☎ 01 47 62 60 11; 26-30 place de la Madeleine, 8e; metro Madeleine; ⏱ 8.30am-7pm Mon-Sat) Paris' most famous caterer has six departments in two buildings selling the most incredibly mouth-watering delicacies from pâté de foie gras to designer *confiture* (jam). Fruit – the most perfect you've ever seen – includes exotic items from Southeast Asia (mangosteens, rambutans etc).

Fromagerie Alléosse (Map pp93-5; ☎ 01 46 22 50 45; 13 rue Poncelet, 17e; metro Termes; ⏱ 9am-1pm & 4-7pm Tue-Sat, 9am-1pm Sun) This is without a doubt the best cheese shop in Paris and well worth a trip across town.

La Petite Scierie (Map pp105-7; ☎ 01 55 42 14 88; 60 rue St-Louis en l'Île, 4e; metro Pont Marie; ⏱ 11am-8pm) This little hole-in-the-wall sells every edible produced by and made from ducks, with the emphasis on foie gras (€30 for 180g).

Les Ruchers du Roy (Map pp105-7; ☎ 01 42 72 02 96; 37 rue du Roi de Sicile, 4e; metro St-Paul; ⏱ 11am-1pm & 3-8pm Tue-Sun) 'The Apiaries of the King' sells dozens of types of honey and apiarian products fit for a king.

Gifts & Souvenirs

Paris has a huge number of speciality shops offering gift items.

Anna Joliet (Map pp96-8; ☎ 01 42 96 55 13; passage du Perron, 9 rue de Beaujolais, 1er; metro Pyramides; ⏱ 10am-7pm Mon-Sat) This wonderful (and tiny) shop at the northern end of the Jardin du Palais Royal specialises in music boxes, both new and old. Just open the door and see if you aren't tempted in.

CSAO Boutique (Map pp105-7; ☎ 01 44 54 55 88; 1-3 rue Elzévir, 3e; metro St-Paul or Chemin Vert; ☻ 11am-7pm Tue-Fri, 11am-7.30pm Sat, 2-7pm Sun) This wonderful gallery and shop distributes the work of African artists and craftspeople. Many of the colourful fabrics and weavings are exquisite and the handmade recycled items – small watering cans from old tuna tins, handbags and caps from soft-drink cans, lamp shades from tomato paste tins – are both amusing and heartbreaking.

E Dehillerin (Map pp105-7; ☎ 01 42 36 53 13; 18-20 rue Coquillière, 1er; metro Les Halles; ☻ 8am-12.30pm & 2-6pm Mon, 8am-6pm Tue-Sat) Spread over two floors and dating back to 1820, E Dehillerin carries the most incredible selection of professional-quality *matériel de cuisine* (kitchenware) in the world. You're sure to find something even the most well-equipped kitchen is lacking.

Mélodies Graphiques (Map pp105-7; ☎ 01 42 74 57 68; 10 rue du Pont Louis-Philippe, 4e; metro Pont Marie; ☻ 2-7pm Mon, 11am-7pm Tue-Sat) 'Graphic Melodies' carries all sorts of items made from exquisite Florentine *papier à cuve* (paper hand-decorated with marbled designs). There are several other fine stationery shops along the same street.

Musée & Compagnie (Map pp90-2; ☎ 01 40 02 98 72; 40-42 Cour St-Émilion, 12e; metro Cour St-Émilion; ☻ 11am-9pm) This large shop sells top-end copies of all those knickknacks and dust-collectors you admired in the museum but couldn't have: Mona Lisa, Venus de Milo, Celtic jewellery and so on. All fakes, of course – but good ones.

GETTING THERE & AWAY

For information on the transport options between the city and Paris' airports, see opposite. For information on international air links to Paris, see p914.

Air

AÉROPORT D'ORLY

Orly (ORY; Map p179; ☎ 01 49 75 15 15, flight info ☎ 0 892 681 515; www.adp.fr), the older and smaller of Paris' two major international airports, is 18km south of the city. Air France and some other international carriers (eg Iberia and TAP Air Portugal) use Orly-Ouest (the west terminal). A driverless overhead train linking Orly-Ouest with Orly-Sud, which is part of the Orlyval system, functions as a free shuttle between the terminals.

AÉROPORT PARIS-BEAUVAIS

The international airport at **Beauvais** (BVA; off Map p179; ☎ 03 44 11 46 86; www.aeroportbeauvais.com), 80km north of Paris, is used by charter companies and discount airline Ryanair for its European flights, including those between Paris and Dublin, Shannon and Glasgow.

AÉROPORT ROISSY CHARLES DE GAULLE

Roissy Charles de Gaulle (CDG; Map p179; ☎ 01 48 62 22 80, 0 892 681 515; www.adp.fr), 30km northeast of Paris in the suburb of Roissy, consists of three terminal complexes, appropriately named Aérogare 1, 2 and 3. Aérogares 1 and 2 are used by international and domestic carriers. Aérogare 3 is used mainly by charter companies.

AIRLINE OFFICES

Contacts for airline offices in Paris can be found in the *Yellow Pages* under 'Transports aériens', among them:

Aer Lingus (☎ 01 70 20 00 72; www.aerlingus.com)
Air Canada (☎ 0 825 880 881; www.aircanada.com)
Air France (☎ arrivals 0 820 820 820, departures ☎ 0 892 681 048; www.airfrance.com)
Air New Zealand (☎ 01 40 53 82 83; www.airnz.com)
British Airways (☎ 0 825 825 400; www.british airways.com)
British Midland (☎ 01 41 91 87 04; www.flybmi.com)
Continental Airlines (☎ 01 42 99 09 09; www .continental.com)
Delta Air Lines (☎ 0 800 354 080; www.delta.com)
easyJet (☎ 0 825 082 508; www.easyjet.com)
Northwest Airlines (☎ 0 890 710 710; www.klm.com)
Qantas Airways (☎ 0 820 820 500; www.qantas.com)
Ryanair (☎ 0 892 682 073; www.ryanair.com)
United Airlines (☎ 0 810 727 272; www.ual.com)
US Airways (☎ 0 810 632 222; www.usairways.com)
Virgin Atlantic (☎ 0 800 528 528; www.virgin-atlantic .com)

Bus

DOMESTIC

Because French transport policy is biased in favour of the excellent state-owned rail system, **Société Nationale des Chemins de Fer Français** (SNCF), the country has extremely limited inter-regional bus services and there are no internal intercity bus services to or from Paris.

INTERNATIONAL

Eurolines (p917) links Paris with destinations in all parts of Western and Central Europe,

Scandinavia and Morocco. The main **Eurolines office** (Map pp105-7; ☎ 01 43 54 11 99, 0 892 899 091; www.eurolines.fr; 55 rue St-Jacques, 5e; metro Cluny-La Sorbonne; ◷ 9.30am-6.30pm Mon-Fri, 10am-1pm & 2-6pm Sat) books seats and sells tickets. The **Gare Routière Internationale de Paris-Gallieni** (Map pp90-2; ☎ 0 892 899 091; 28 av du Général de Gaulle; metro Gallieni), the city's international bus terminal, is in the inner suburb of Bagnolet.

Train

SNCF (www.sncf.fr; ☎ 0 892 353 535) mainline train information is available round the clock.

Paris has six major train stations, each of which handles passenger traffic to different parts of France and Europe and also has a metro station bearing its name. For more information on the breakdown of regional responsibility of trains from each station, see the ferries and train map (p918).

Gare d'Austerlitz (Map pp102-4; blvd de l'Hôpital, 13e; metro Gare d'Austerlitz) Spain and Portugal; Loire Valley and non-TGV trains to southwestern France (eg Bordeaux and Basque Country).

Gare de l'Est (Map pp96-8; blvd de Strasbourg, 10e; metro Gare de l'Est) Luxembourg, parts of Switzerland (Basel, Lucerne, Zurich), southern Germany (Frankfurt, Munich) and points further east; areas of France east of Paris (Champagne, Alsace and Lorraine).

Gare de Lyon (Map pp102-4; blvd Diderot, 12e; metro Gare de Lyon) Parts of Switzerland (eg Bern, Geneva, Lausanne), Italy and points beyond; regular and TGV Sud-Est trains to areas southeast of Paris, including Dijon, Lyon, Provence, the Côte d'Azur and the Alps.

Gare Montparnasse (Map pp99-101; av du Maine & blvd de Vaugirard, 15e; metro Montparnasse Bienvenüe) Brittany and places en route from Paris (eg Chartres, Angers, Nantes), TGV Atlantique trains to Tours, Nantes, Bordeaux and other destinations in southwestern France.

Gare du Nord (Map pp96-8; rue de Dunkerque, 10e; metro Gare du Nord) UK, Belgium, northern Germany, Scandinavia, Moscow etc (terminus of the high-speed Thalys trains to/from Amsterdam, Brussels, Cologne and Geneva and Eurostar to London); trains to the northern suburbs of Paris and northern France, including TGV Nord trains to Lille and Calais.

Gare St-Lazare (Map pp93-5; rue St-Lazare & rue d'Amsterdam, 8e; metro St-Lazare) Normandy (eg Dieppe, Le Havre, Cherbourg).

GETTING AROUND
To/From the Airports
AÉROPORT D'ORLY

There a half-dozen public-transport options to get to and from Orly airport. Apart from

RATP bus No 183, all services call at both terminals. Tickets for the bus services are sold on board. With certain exceptions, children between the ages of two and 11 pay half price. You can also choose to go by shuttle van and taxi.

Air France Bus No 1 (☎ 0 892 350 820; www.cars-airfrance.com in French; one way/return €7.50/12.75; every 15min 6am-11.30pm to Paris, 5.45am-11pm to Orly; journey time 30-45min) This *navette* (shuttle bus) runs to/from the eastern side of Gare Montparnasse (Map pp99-101; rue du Commandant René Mouchotte, 15e; metro Montparnasse Bienvenüe) as well as Aérogare des Invalides (Map pp99-101; metro Invalides) in the 7e. On your way into the city, you can ask to get off at metro Porte d'Orléans or metro Duroc.

Jetbus (☎ 01 69 01 00 09; €5.15; every 15-20min 6.43am-10.49pm to Paris, 6.15am-10.15pm to Orly; journey time 55min) With the exception of RATP bus No 183, Jetbus is the cheapest way to get to/from Orly. It runs to/from metro Villejuif Louis Aragon, which is a bit south of the 13e on the city's southern fringe. From there a regular metro/bus ticket will get you into the centre of Paris.

Orlybus (☎ 0 892 687 714; €5.70; every 15-20min 6am-11.30pm to Paris, 5.35am-11pm to Orly; journey time 30min) This RATP bus runs to/from metro Denfert Rochereau (Map pp90-2) in the 14e and makes several stops in the eastern 14e in each direction.

Orlyval (☎ 0 892 687 714; €8.80 to/from Paris, €10.65 to/from La Défense; every 4-12min 6am-11pm each direction; journey time 33min to Paris, 50min to La Défense) This RATP service links Orly with the city centre via a shuttle train and the RER (p173). A driverless shuttle train runs between the airport and Antony RER station (eight minutes) on RER line B, from where it's an easy journey into the city; to get to Antony from the city (26 minutes), take line B4 towards St-Rémy-lès-Chevreuse. Orlyval tickets are valid for travel on the RER and for metro travel within the city.

RATP Bus No 183 (☎ 0 892 687 714; €1.30 or 1 metro/bus ticket; every 35min 5.35am-8.35pm each direction; journey time 1hr) This is a is a slow public bus that links Orly-Sud (only) with metro Porte de Choisy (Map pp90-2), at the southern edge of the 13e.

RER C (☎ 0 890 361 010; €5.35; every 12-20min 5.45am-11pm each direction; journey time 50min) An Aéroports de Paris (ADP) shuttle bus links the airport with RER line C at Pont de Rungis-Aéroport d'Orly RER station. From the city, take a C2 train towards Pont de Rungis or Massy-Palaiseau. Tickets are valid for onward travel on the metro.

Along with public transport the following private options are available:
Allô Shuttle (☎ 01 34 29 00 80; www.alloshuttle.com)
Paris Airports Service (☎ 01 46 80 14 67; www.paris airportservice.com)

Shuttle Van PariShuttle (☎ 0 800 699 699; www
.parishuttle.com)
World Shuttle (☎ 01 46 80 14 67; www.world
-shuttles.com)

These companies all provide door-to-door
service for about €25 for a single person (from
about €15 to €18 per person for two or more).
Book in advance and allow for numerous
pick-ups and drop-offs. Some readers have
written to say that some shuttle-van services
are less than reliable.

A taxi between central Paris and Orly will
cost about €40 and take 20 to 30 minutes

AÉROPORT ROISSY CHARLES DE GAULLE

Roissy Charles de Gaulle has two train stations: Aéroport Charles de Gaulle 1 (CDG1)
and the sleek Aéroport Charles de Gaulle 2
(CDG2). Both are served by commuter trains
on RER line B3. A free shuttle bus links all of
the terminals with the train stations.

There are various public-transport options
for travel between Aéroport Roissy Charles de
Gaulle and Paris. Tickets for the bus services
are sold on board. With certain exceptions,
children between age two and 11 pay half-
price. As for Orly, shuttle vans and taxis are
also available.

Air France bus No 2 (☎ 0 892 350 820; www.cars
-airfrance.com in French; one way/return €10/17; every
15min 5.45am-11pm each direction; journey time 35-
50min) Air France bus No 2 links the airport with
locations on the Right Bank: near the Arc de Triomphe just
outside 2 av Carnot, 17e (Map pp93-5; metro Charles de
Gaulle-Étoile) and the Palais des Congrès de Paris (Map
pp93-5; blvd Gouvion St-Cyr, 17e; metro Porte Maillot).
Air France bus No 4 (☎ 0 892 350 820; www.cars-air
france.com in French; one way/return €11.50/19.55; every
30min to Paris 7am-9pm, to Roissy Charles de Gaulle
7am-9.30pm; journey time 45-55min) Air France bus No 4
links the airport with Gare de Lyon (Map pp102-4; 20bis
blvd Diderot, 12e; metro Gare de Lyon) and with the Gare
Montparnasse (Map pp99-101; rue du Commandant René
Mouchotte, 15e; metro Montparnasse Bienvenüe).
RATP Bus No 350 (☎ 0 892 687 714; €3.90 or 3 metro/
bus tickets; every 30min 5.45am-7pm each direction;
journey time 1¼hr) This public bus links Aérogares 1 & 2
with Gare de l'Est (Map pp96-8; rue du 8 Mai 1945, 10e;
metro Gare de l'Est) and with Gare du Nord (Map pp96-8;
184 rue du Faubourg St-Denis, 10e; metro Gare du Nord).
RATP Bus No 351 (☎ 0 892 687 714; €3.90 or 3
metro/bus tickets; every 30min 6am-9.30pm to Paris, 6am-
8.20pm to Roissy Charles de Gaulle; journey time 55min)
This public bus links the eastern side of place de la Nation

(Map pp90-2; av du Trône, 11e; metro Nation) with the
Roissy Charles de Gaulle.
RER B (☎ 0 890 361 010; €7.75; every 4-15min 4.56am-
11.40pm in each direction; journey time 30min) RER line
B3 links CDG1 and CDG2 with the city. To get to the airport
take any RER line B train whose four-letter destination
code begins with E (eg EIRE) and a shuttle bus (every
five to eight minutes) will ferry you to the appropriate
terminal. Regular metro ticket windows can't always sell
RER tickets as far as the airport so you may have to buy
one at the RER station where you board.
Roissybus (☎ 0 892 687 714; €8.20; every 15-20min
5.45am-11pm in each direction; journey time 60min) This
public bus links both terminals with rue Scribe (Map pp93-
5; metro Opéra) behind the Palais Garnier in the 9e.

The four shuttle-van companies listed in
the Orly section (p171) will take you from
Roissy Charles de Gaulle to your hotel for
€25 for a single person or €15 to €18 for two
or more people. Book in advance.

Taxis to/from the city centre cost from
€40 to €55, depending on the traffic and
time of day.

BETWEEN ORLY & ROISSY

Air France bus No 3 (☎ 0 892 350 820; www.cars
-airfrance.com in French; €15.50; every 30min 6am-10.30pm;
journey time 50-60min) runs between Orly and
Roissy Charles de Gaulle and is free for
connecting Air France passengers.

The taxi fare from one airport to the
other should cost around €56. Count on
one hour's travel time.

AÉROPORT PARIS-BEAUVAIS

An **express bus** (☎ 0 892 682 064; ⏱ 8.40am-10.10pm
to Paris, 5.45am-7.15pm to Beauvais; journey time 1-1¼hr)
leaves Parking Pershing (Map pp93-5; 1 blvd
Pershing, 17e; metro Porte Maillot) just west of Palais
des Congrès de Paris three hours before
Ryanair departures (you can board up to 15
minutes before) and leaves the airport 20 to
30 minutes after each arrival, dropping off
just south of Palais des Congrès on Place de
la Porte Maillot. Tickets can be bought from
the **Ryanair** (☎ 03 44 11 41 41) counter at the
airport or from a kiosk in the parking lot.

A taxi between central Paris and Beauvais
will cost Paris €110 during the day and €150
at night and all day Sunday.

Boat

From late March to October, a river shuttle
called **Batobus** (☎ 01 44 11 33 99; www.batobus.com

1-day pass adult/2-6 yrs, €11/6, 2-day pass €13/7; every 25min 10am-7pm late Mar-May & Oct, 10am-9pm Jun-Sep) docks at the following eight locations. As you can jump on and off at will, Batobus can be used as a form of transport.

Champs-Élysées (Map pp93-5; port des Champs-Élysées, 8e; metro Champs-Élysées Clemenceau)

Eiffel Tower (Map pp99-101; port de la Bourdonnais, 7e; metro Champ de Mars-Tour Eiffel)

Hôtel de Ville (Map pp105-7; quai de l'Hôtel de Ville, 4e; metro Hôtel de Ville)

Jardin des Plantes (Map pp102-4; quai St-Bernard, 5e; metro Jussieu)

Musée d'Orsay (Map pp99-101; quai de Solférino, 7e; metro Musée d'Orsay)

Musée du Louvre (Map pp105-7; quai du Louvre, 1er; metro Palais Royal-Musée du Louvre)

Notre Dame (Map pp105-7; quai Montebello, 5e; metro St-Michel)

St-Germain des Prés (Map pp105-7; quai Malaquais, 6e; metro St-Germain des Prés)

Car & Motorcycle

While driving in Paris is nerve-racking, it is not impossible, except for the faint-hearted or indecisive. The fastest way to get across the city by car is usually via blvd Périphérique (Map pp90-2), the ring road that encircles the city.

In many parts of Paris you pay €1.50 to €2 an hour to park your car on the street. Large municipal parking garages usually charge €2.60 an hour and between €20 and €23 for 24 hours.

Parking fines are €11 to €33, depending on the offence and its gravity, and parking attendants dispense them with great abandon. You pay them by purchasing a *timbre amende* (fine stamp) for the amount written on the ticket from any *tabac* (tobacconist), affixing the stamp to the pre-addressed coupon and dropping it in a letter box.

RENTAL

You can get a small car (eg a Renault Twingo) for one day, without insurance and 250km mileage, from around €71 with Budget. Most of the larger companies listed below have offices at the airports and several are also represented at **Aérogare des Invalides** (Map pp99-101; metro Invalides) in the 7e.

Avis (☎ 0 802 050 505; www.avis.fr)
Budget (☎ 0 825 003 564; www.budget.fr in French)
Europcar (☎ 0 825 358 358; www.europcar.fr in French)
Hertz (☎ 0 825 861 861; www.hertz.fr)

Smaller agencies can offer much more attractive deals. For example, Rent A Car Système has an economical-class car for from €30 per day and €0.30 per kilometre, €45/69 a day with 100/300km, €90 for a weekend with 500km and €199 for seven days with 800km. The companies below offer reasonable rates; for a wider selection check the *Yellow Pages* under 'Location d'Automobiles: Tourisme et Utilitaires'. It's a good idea to reserve at least three days ahead, especially for holiday weekends and during the summer.

ADA (☎ 0 825 169 169; www.ada-location.com in French); 8e arrondissement branch (**Map pp93-5**; ☎ 01 42 93 65 13; 72 rue de Rome, 8e; metro Rome); 11e arrondissement branch (**Map pp96-8**; ☎ 01 48 06 58 13; 34 av de la République, 11e; metro Parmentier) ADA has a dozen bureaus in Paris.

easyCar (www.easycar.com); Montparnasse branch (**Map pp99-101**; Parking Gaîté, 33 rue du Commandant René Mouchotte, 15e; metro Gaîté); place Vendôme branch (**Map pp93-5**; ☎ /fax 01 40 15 60 17; metro Tuileries or Opéra) Britain's budget car-rental agency hires mini Mercedes from €13 a day plus extras and Smart cars (from €8). Both branches are in underground car parks and are fully automated systems; you must book in advance and fill in all the forms online on location.

Rent A Car Système (☎ 0 891 700 200; www.rentacar .fr); Gare du Nord branch (**Map pp96-8**; ☎ 01 42 80 31 31; 2 rue de Compiègne, 10e; metro Gare du Nord); Bercy branch (**Map pp102-4**; ☎ 01 43 45 98 99; 79 rue de Bercy, 12e; metro Bercy); 16e arrondissement branch (**Map pp90-2**; ☎ 01 42 88 40 04; 84 av de Versailles, 16e; metro Mirabeau) Rent A Car has 16 outlets in Paris.

Public Transport

Paris' public transit system, most of which is operated by the **RATP** (Régie Autonome des Transports Parisians; in French ☎ 0 892 687 714, in English ☎ 0 892 684 114; www.ratp.fr in French; ☑ 6am-9pm), is one of the cheapest and most efficient in the Western world.

Transport maps of various sizes and degrees of detail are available for free at metro ticket windows. RATP's *Paris 1* provides plans of metro, RER, bus and tram routes in central Paris; *Paris 2* superimposes the same plans over street maps; and *Île-de-France 3* covers the area surrounding Paris. For itineraries, traffic and so on, log onto www.citefutee.com (French only).

BUS

Paris' bus system, also operated by the RATP, runs between 5.45am and 12.30am Monday to Saturday. Services are drastically reduced on Sunday and public holidays (when buses run from 7am to 8.30pm) and from 8.30pm to 12.30am daily when a *service en soirée* (evening service) of 20 buses – distinct from the Noctambus overnight services described below – goes into operation.

Fares

Short bus rides (ie rides in one or two bus zones) cost one metro/bus ticket; longer rides require two tickets. Transfer to other buses or the metro is not allowed on the same ticket. Travel to the suburbs costs up to three tickets, depending on the zone. Special tickets valid only on the bus can be purchased from the driver.

Whatever kind of single-journey ticket you have, you must cancel *(oblitérer)* it in the *composteur* (cancelling machine) next to the driver. If you have a Carte Orange, Mobilis or Paris Visite pass, just flash it at the driver when you board. Do not cancel your magnetic coupon accompanying your pass.

A single ride on a Noctambus costs €2.60 and allows one immediate transfer onto another night bus. Noctambus services are free if you have a Carte Orange, Mobilis or Paris Visite pass for the zones in which you are travelling.

Night Buses

After the metro lines have finished their last runs at about 1am, the Noctambus network of night buses lines links the place du Châtelet (1er) and av Victoria just west of the Hôtel de Ville (Map pp105-7) in the 4e with most parts of the city and the suburbs. Look for the symbol of a little black owl silhouetted against a yellow quarter moon. All 18 Noctambus lines depart every hour weekdays and every half-hour at the weekend from 1am to 5.30am daily.

METRO & RER

Paris' underground network consists of two separate but interlinked systems: the **Métropolitain**, known as the *métro*, with 14 lines and 372 stations; and the **RER** (Réseau Express Régional), a network of suburban lines designated A to E and then numbered that pass through the city centre. In this book, the term 'metro' is used to cover both the Métropolitain and the RER system within Paris proper.

Fares

The same RATP tickets are valid on the metro, the RER (for travel within the city limits), buses, the Montmartre funicular and Paris' two tram lines. They cost €1.30 if bought individually and €10 (€5 for children aged four to 11) for a carnet of 10. Tickets are sold at all metro stations, though not always at every entrance. Ticket windows and vending machines accept most credit cards.

One metro/bus ticket lets you travel between any two metro stations for a period of two hours, no matter how many transfers are required. You can also use it on the RER for travel within zone 1. However, a single ticket cannot be used to transfer from the metro to a bus, from a bus to the metro or between buses.

Always keep your ticket until you exit from your station; you may be stopped by a *contrôleur* (ticket inspector) and will have to pay a fine (€20 to €40 on the spot) if you are found to be without a ticket or are holding an invalid one.

Metro Network

Each metro train is known by the name of its terminus. On maps and plans each line has a different colour and number (from 1 to 14).

Blue-on-white directional signs in metro and RER stations indicate the way to the correct platform for your line. On lines that split into several branches (eg line Nos 3, 7 and 13), the terminus served by each train is indicated on the cars with back-lit panels.

Older black-on-orange *correspondance* (transfer) signs and newer ones listing the lines in their individual colours show how to reach connecting trains. In general, the more lines that stop at a station, the longer the transfer will take – and some (eg those at Châtelet and Montparnasse Bienvenüe) are very long indeed.

White-on-blue *sortie* signs indicate the station exits from which you have to choose. You can get your bearings by checking the *plan du quartier* (neighbourhood map) posted at each exit.

The last metro train on each line begins its run sometime between 12.35am and 1.04am. The metro starts up again around 5.30am.

RER Network

The RER is faster than the metro, but the stops are much further apart. Some of Paris'

UNDERGROUND ART

Few underground railway systems are as convenient, as reasonably priced or, at the better stations, more elegant than the Paris one. The following list is just a sample of the most interesting stations from an artistic perspective. The specific platform is mentioned for those stations served by more than one line.

Abbesses (Map p108; line No 12) The noodle-like pale-green metalwork and glass canopy of the station entrance is one of the finest examples of the work of Hector Guimard (1867–1942), the best-known French Art Nouveau architect, whose signature style once graced most metro stations.

Arts et Métiers (Map pp96-8; line No 11 platform) The copper panelling, portholes and mechanisms of this station recall Jules Verne, Captain Nemo and the nearby Musée des Arts et Métiers.

Bastille (Map pp102-4; line No 5 platform) A large ceramic fresco features scenes taken from newspaper engravings published during the Revolution.

Bibliothèque François Mitterrand (Map pp90-2; line No 14) This enormous station – all screens, steel and glass, and the terminus of the high-speed Météor line that opened in 1998 – resembles a high-tech cathedral.

Carrefour Pleyel (Map p182; line No 13) This station just south of St-Denis, and named in hour of composer and piano-maker Ignace Joseph Pleyel (1757–1831), has been reconfigured as a 'contemporary musical instrument', with the rumble of the trains the 'music' and no doubt commuters the 'picks'.

Cluny-La Sorbonne (Map pp105-7; line No 10 platform) A large ceramic mosaic replicates the signatures of intellectuals, artists and scientists from the Latin Quarter through history.

Concorde (Map pp93-5; line No 12 platform) On the walls of the station, what look like children's building blocks in white and blue ceramic are 45,000 tiles spelling out the text of the *Déclaration des Droits de l'Homme et du Citoyen* (Declaration of the Rights of Man and of the Citizen), the document setting forth the principles of the French Revolution.

Louvre-Rivoli (Map pp105-7; line No 1 platform & corridor) Statues, bas-reliefs and photographs offer a small taste of what to expect at the Musée du Louvre above ground.

Palais Royal-Musée du Louvre (Map pp105-7) The unusual modern entrance on the place du Palais Royal, a kind of back-to-the-future look at the Guimard works and designed by young artist Jean-Michel Othoniel, is made up of 800 red, blue, amber and violet glass balls and resembles a crown.

Parmentier (Map pp96-8; line No 3) The theme in this station is agricultural crops, particularly the potato since it was the station's namesake, Antoine-Auguste Parmentier (1737–1817), who brought the potato into fashion in France.

Pont Neuf (Map pp105-7; line No 7) With the old mint and the Musée de la Monnaie de Paris just above, the focus here is on coins: obsolete francs and all-too-current euros.

attractions, particularly those on the Left Bank (eg the Musée d'Orsay, Eiffel Tower and Panthéon), can be reached far more conveniently by the RER than by metro.

RER lines are known by an alphanumeric combination – the letter (A to E) refers to the line, the number to the spur it will follow somewhere out in the suburbs. As a rule of thumb, even-numbered RER lines head for Paris' southern or eastern suburbs while odd-numbered ones go north or west. All trains whose four-letter codes (indicated both on the train and on the light board) begin with the same letter share the same terminus. Stations served are usually indicated on electronic destination boards above the platform.

Suburban Services

The RER and **SNCF commuter lines** (☎ 0 891 362 020, 0 891 676 869; www.sncf.fr) serve suburban destinations outside the city limits (ie zones 2 to 8). Buy your ticket *before* you board the train or you won't be able to get out of the station when you arrive. You are not allowed to pay the additional fare when you get there.

If you are issued with a full-sized SNCF ticket for travel to the suburbs, validate it in one of the time-stamp pillars *before* you board the train. You may also be given a *contremarque magnétique* (magnetic ticket) to get through any metro/RER-type turnstiles on the way to/from the platform. If you are travelling on a multizone Carte Orange, Paris Visite or Mobilis pass, do *not* punch the magnetic coupon in one of SNCF's time-stamp machines. Most – but not all – RER/SNCF tickets purchased in the suburbs for travel to the city allow you to continue your journey by metro.

For some destinations, a ticket can be purchased at any metro ticket window; for others you'll have to go to an RER station on the line you need in order to buy a ticket.

TOURIST PASSES

The rather pricey Mobilis and Paris Visite passes are valid on the metro, the RER, the SNCF's suburban lines, buses, night buses, trams and the Montmartre funicular railway. They do not require a photo but you should write your card number on the ticket. They can be purchased at larger metro and RER stations, at SNCF offices in Paris and at the airports.

The Mobilis card and its coupon allows unlimited travel for one day in two to eight zones (€5.20 to €18.30). It is available at all metro and RER ticket windows as well as SNCF stations in the Paris region but you would have to make at least six metro trips in a day (based on the carnet price) in zones 1 and 2 to break even on this pass.

Paris Visite passes, which allow the holder discounted entry to certain museums and activities as well as discounts on transport fares, are valid for one, two, three or five consecutive days of travel in either three, five or eight zones. The version covering one to three zones costs €8.35/13.70/18.25/26.65 for one/two/three/five days. Children aged four to 11 pay €4.55/6.85/9.15/13.70.

TRAVEL PASSES

The cheapest and easiest way to use public transport in Paris is to get a Carte Orange, a combined metro, RER and bus pass whose accompanying magnetic coupon comes in weekly and monthly versions. You can get tickets for travel in two to eight urban and suburban zones but, unless you'll be using the suburban commuter lines extensively, the basic ticket valid for zones 1 and 2 should be sufficient.

A weekly Carte Orange *(coupon hebdo-madaire)* costs €14.50 for zones 1 and 2 and is valid from Monday to Sunday and can be purchased from the previous Thursday until Wednesday; from Thursday weekly tickets are available for the following week only. Even if you'll be in Paris for only three or four days, it may work out cheaper than

buying carnets and it will certainly cost less than buying a daily Mobilis or Paris Visite pass (opposite). The Carte Orange monthly ticket *(coupon mensuel;* €48.60 for zones 1 and 2) begins on the first day of each calendar month; you can buy one from the 20th of the preceding month. Both are sold in metro and RER stations from 6.30am to 10pm and at some bus terminals. You can also buy a Carte Orange coupon from vending machines.

To buy your first Carte Orange, take a passport-size photograph (four photos are available from photo booths in train and many metro stations for €4) of yourself to any metro or RER ticket window. Request a Carte Orange (which is free) and the kind of coupon (weekly or monthly) you'd like. To prevent tickets from being used by more than one person, you must write your family name *(nom)* and first name *(prénom)* on the Carte Orange, and the number of your Carte Orange on the weekly or monthly coupon you've bought.

Taxi

The *prise en charge* (flag-fall) in a Parisian taxi is €2. Within the city limits, it costs €0.62 per kilometre for travel between 7am and 7pm Monday to Saturday (Tarif A; white light on meter), and €1.06 per kilometre from 7pm to 7am at night, all day Sunday and on public holidays (Tarif B; orange light on meter). Travel in the suburbs (Tariff C) costs €1.24 per kilometre.

There's an extra €2.60 charge for taking a fourth passenger, but most drivers refuse to accept more than three people anyway for insurance reasons. Each piece of baggage over 5kg costs €0.90 extra, an animal costs €0.60 and for pick-ups from SNCF mainline stations there's supplement of €0.70.

Radio-dispatched taxi companies, on call 24 hours:

Alpha Taxis (☎ 01 45 85 85 85)
Artaxi (☎ 01 42 41 50 50)
Taxis Bleus (☎ 01 49 36 10 10)
Taxis G7 (☎ 01 47 39 47 39)
Taxis Radio 7000 (☎ 01 42 70 00 42)
Taxis-Radio Étoile (☎ 01 42 70 41 41)

Around Paris

CONTENTS

La Défense   179
St-Denis   182
Disneyland Resort Paris   184
Versailles   185
Fontainebleau   189
Vaux-le-Vicomte   192
Chantilly   193
Senlis   195
Chartres   196

Paris is encircled by the Île de France (Island of France), the seed from which France the kingdom grew, beginning about AD 1100. Today, the excellent rail and road links between the French capital and the exceptional sights of this region and neighbouring *départements* make it especially popular with day-trippers from Paris.

The Île de France can boast some of the nation's most beautiful and ambitious cathedrals. Closest to Paris, a mere 4km from Porte de la Chapelle, is St-Denis, the last resting place for France's kings until the Revolution. Senlis, just east of Chantilly, has a magnificent Gothic cathedral said to have inspired elements of the (holy) mother of all basilicas: the cathedral at Chartres. The latter, with its breathtaking stained glass and intricately carved stone portals, is arguably the most beautiful in all of Christendom.

While not exactly the Loire Valley, the Île de France counts some of the nation's most extravagant chateaux. Foremost is the palace at Versailles, whose opulence and extravagances were partly what spurred the revolutionary mob to storm the Bastille in July 1789. The chateau at Fontainebleau is one of the most important Renaissance palaces in France while the one at Chantilly is celebrated for its gardens and the artwork it contains. The woodlands and forests surrounding Fontainebleau and Chantilly offer unlimited outdoor activities.

But the Île de France is not stuck in the past. The modern cityscape of La Défense, just over the border from the 17th arrondissement, stands in stark contrast to the Paris of the imagination and reminds visitors that the capital has at least one of its feet firmly in the 21st century. And then there's every kid's favourite, Disneyland Resort Paris, which has added more attractions to its stable and is even easier to reach from central Paris by train.

Other destinations within easy striking distance of Paris include Beauvais (p230) and Compiègne (p231) in Far Northern France and Giverny (p243) in Normandy.

HIGHLIGHTS

- Relive the glory, the over-the-top excess exemplified in the 18th-century **Château de Versailles** (p187)

- Contemplate the awesome stained glass and inspirational west portal of **Cathédrale Notre Dame de Chartres** (p196)

- Get behind the scenes at a new film being shot at Walt Disney Studios, **Disneyland Resort Paris** (p184)

- Wonder at the richness of the 15th-century *Très Riches Heures du Duc de Berry* illuminated manuscript at **Château de Chantilly** (p193)

- Get physical in the **Forêt de Fontainebleau** (p191), the Île de France region's most beautiful and diverse forest

---

- POPULATION: 10.9 MILLION (ÎLE DE FRANCE)   - AREA: 12,000 SQ KM

Orientation & Information

The Île de France is shaped by five rivers: the Epte in the northwest, the Aisne in the northeast, the Eure in the southwest, the Yonne in the southeast and the Marne in the east.

Espace du Tourisme d'Île de France (Map pp105–7; ☎ 0 826 166 666 or from abroad ☎ 33-1 44 50 19 98; www.pidf.com; Galerie du Carrousel du Louvre; 99 rue de Rivoli, 1er; metro Palais Royal-Musée du Louvre; ☺ 10am–7pm) is the central tourist office for the Île de France. It is located in the lower level of the Carrousel du Louvre shopping centre next to IM Pei's famous inverted glass pyramid. This tourist office provides a wealth of information about Île de France and its attractions.

MAPS

If you're visiting the area under your own steam, pick up a copy of IGN's 1:250,000 scale map *Île de France* (€4.90) or the more compact 1:100,000-scale *Paris et Ses Environs* (€3.70), both available from the Espace IGN outlet (see p906) just off the av des Champs-Élysées.

LA DÉFENSE

pop 40,800 (including Park District)

The ultramodern architecture of La Défense, Paris' skyscraper district on the Seine and 3km west of the 17th arrondissement, is so strikingly different from the rest of centuries-old Paris that it's worth a brief visit to put it all in perspective. When

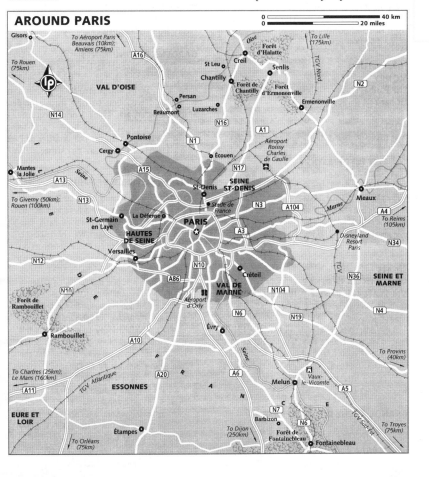

development of the 750-hectare site began in the late 1950s, it was one of the world's most ambitious civil-engineering projects. Its first major structure was the vaulted, largely triangular-shaped **Centre des Nouvelles Industries et Technologies** (CNIT; Centre for New Industries and Technologies), a giant 'pregnant oyster' inaugurated in 1958 and extensively rebuilt 30 years later. But after the economic crisis of the mid-1970s office space in La Défense became hard to sell or lease. Buildings stood empty and further development of the area all but ceased.

Things picked up in the following decades, and today La Défense counts more than 100 buildings, the tallest of which is the 187m **Total Fina Elf Coupole** (1985). Fourteen of France's 20 largest corporations maintain their headquarters here, and a total of 1500 companies of all sizes employ some 150,000 people.

Information

MONEY
BNP Paribas (4 place de la Défense)
CIC bank (11 place de la Défense)

POST
Post Office (Passage du Levant; ground fl, CNIT Bldg)

TOURIST INFORMATION
Espace Info-Défense (☎ 01 47 74 84 24; www.la defense.fr in French; 15 place de la Défense; ☉ 9.30am-5.30pm Mon-Fri Oct-Mar, 10am-6pm Apr-Sep) La Défense's tourist office has reams of free information, details on cultural activities and sells guides to the area's monumental art (€2.30), architecture (€5.40) and history (€6.10).

Sights

MUSÉE DE LA DÉFENSE
The **Musée de la Défense** (La Défense Museum; ☎ 01 47 74 84 24; www.ladefense.fr in French; 15 place de la Défense; admission free; ☉ 10am-6pm Mon-Fri Apr-Sep, 9.30am-5.30pm Mon-Fri Oct-Mar), below the Espace Info-Défense traces the development of La Défense through the decades with drawings, architectural plans and scale models. Especially interesting are the projects that were never built.

GRANDE ARCHE DE LA DÉFENSE
La Défense's most important sight and its biggest draw is the remarkable, cube-like **Grande Arche** (Great Arch; ☎ 01 49 07 27 27; 1 parvis

de le Défense; adult/child & student/family €7.50/6/€16-22; ☉ 10am-6.30pm). Designed by Danish architect Johan-Otto von Spreckelsen and housing government and business offices, it is made of white Carrara marble, grey granite and glass, and measures 110m exactly along each side. Inaugurated on 14 July 1989, the arch marks the western end of the 8km-long **Axe Historique** (Historic Axis), begun in 1640 by André Le Nôtre of Versailles fame and stretching from the Louvre's glass pyramid. The structure, which symbolises a window open to the world, is slightly out of alignment with the Axe Historique – on purpose. Lifts will whisk you up to the 35th floor of the arch, but (frankly) neither the views from the rooftop nor the temporary exhibitions housed in the top storey justify the relatively high ticket price.

GARDENS & MONUMENTS
The Parvis, place de la Défense and Esplanade du Général de Gaulle, which together form a pleasant, kilometre-long pedestrian walkway, have been turned into a **garden of contemporary art**. The 60-odd monumental sculptures and murals here – and west of the Grande Arche in the **Quartier du Parc** (Park District) and **Jardins de l'Arche**, a 2km-

---

IN THE DEFENCE OF PARIS

La Défense is named after *La Défense de Paris*, a sculpture erected here in 1883 to commemorate the defence of Paris during the Franco-Prussian War of 1870–71. Removed in 1971 to facilitate construction work, it was placed on a round pedestal just west of the Agam fountain in 1983.

Many do not like the name La Défense because of its militaristic connotation, and it has caused some strange misunderstandings over the years. A high-ranking official of EPAD, the authority that manages the district, was once denied entry into Egypt because his passport indicated he was the 'managing director of La Défense', which Egyptian officials assumed was part of France's military-industrial complex. And there's an apocryphal story that tells of a visiting Soviet general who once expressed admiration at how well the area's military installations had been camouflaged.

long westward extension of the Axe Historique – include colourful and imaginative works by Calder, Miró, Agam, Torricini and others.

In the southeastern corner of place de la Défense and opposite the Info-Défense office is a much older **La Défense de Paris monument** honouring the defence of Paris during the Franco-Prussian War of 1870–71 (see opposite). Behind is the **Bassin Agam**, a pool with colourful mosaics and computer-controlled fountains; *ballets muets* take place between noon and 2pm and 5pm and 6pm weekdays, and from 3pm to 6pm at the weekend. Water displays accompanied by music are at 1pm on Wednesday and 4pm at the weekend.

Eating

For the most part La Défense is fast-food territory, including the ever-popular **Bistro Romain** (☎ 01 40 81 08 08; 37 Le Parvis; lunch menu €10.95, dinner menus €15.90 & €22.70; ☑ 11.30am-10pm) overlooking the Parvis, but there are a number of independent outlets from which to choose.

Brasserie du Toit de la Grande Arche (☎ 01 49 07 27 27; lunch menu €15; ☑ lunch noon-3.30pm, bar with snacks 10am-7pm) Sitting at the top the Grande Arche, this brasserie offers acceptable French standards at lunch and some of the best views in Paris from 110m up.

Le Petit Bofinger (☎ 01 46 92 46 46; 1 place du Dôme; menus €19.50 & €24; ☑ lunch & dinner until 11pm) Formerly Le Petit Dôme (as it sits

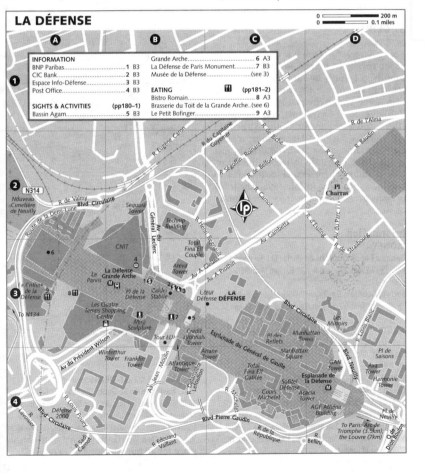

under what was once the IMAX Dôme), this glassed-in dining room with its out-of-the-way feel is a perennial favourite of La Défense *gens d'affaires* (businesspeople).

Getting There & Away

La Défense Grande Arche metro station is the western terminus of metro line No 1; the ride from the Louvre takes about 15 minutes. If you take the faster RER line A, remember that La Défense is in zone 3 and you must pay a supplement (€1.95) if you are carrying a travel pass for zones 1 and 2 only.

Bus 73 from Musée d'Orsay, place de la Concorde and place Charles de Gaulle links central Paris with La Défense Grande Arche (terminus).

ST-DENIS

pop 85,800

For 1200 years St-Denis was the burial place of the royalty of France; today it is a quiet suburb just north of Paris' 18th arrondissement. The ornate royal tombs, adorned with some truly remarkable statuary, and Basilique de St-Denis that contains them (the world's first major Gothic structure) are worth a visit. St-Denis' more recent claim to fame is the Stade de France, just south of the Canal de St-Denis, the futuristic stadium where France beat Brazil to win the World Cup in July 1998. The town is easily accessible by metro in 20 minutes or so.

Information

MONEY

Banque Populaire Nord de Paris (121 rue Gabriel Péri; 9.25am-12.25pm & 1.35-6.05pm Mon-Fri, 8.50am-12.35pm Sat)

Société Générale Basilique (11 place Jean Jaurès; 8.45am-1pm & 2-5.15pm Tue-Fri, 8.45am-12.40pm Sat)

POST

Post Office (59 rue de la République) Just 200m west of the tourist office.

TOURIST INFORMATION

Office de Tourisme de St-Denis La Plaine (☎ 01 55 87 08 70; www.saint-denis-tourisme.com in French; 1 rue de la République; 9.30am-1pm & 2-6pm Mon-Sat, 10am-1pm & 2-4pm Sun Apr-Oct, 9.30am-1pm & 2-6pm Mon-Sat, 10am-2pm Sun Nov-Mar) The tourist office is 100m west of the basilica.

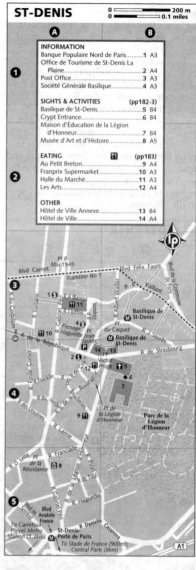

ST-DENIS

0 — 200 m
0 — 0.1 miles

INFORMATION
Banque Populaire Nord de Paris.........1 A3
Office de Tourisme de St-Denis La
Plaine..2 A4
Post Office...3 A3
Société Générale Basilique................4 A3

SIGHTS & ACTIVITIES (pp182-3)
Basilique de St-Denis........................5 B4
Crypt Entrance...................................6 B4
Maison d'Éducation de la Légion
d'Honneur...7 B4
Musée d'Art et d'Histoire..................8 A5

EATING (pp183)
Au Petit Breton...................................9 A4
Franprix Supermarket......................10 A3
Halle du Marché...............................11 A3
Les Arts...12 A4

OTHER
Hôtel de Ville Annexe......................13 B4
Hôtel de Ville...................................14 A4

Sights

BASILIQUE DE ST-DENIS

The **Basilique de St-Denis** (Basilica of St Denis; ☎ 01 48 09 83 54; www.monum.fr; 1 rue de la Légion d'Honneur; basilica free, tombs adult/senior, student & 18-25 yrs/under 18 €6.10/4.10/free; 10am-6.15pm Mon-Sat, noon-6.15pm Sun Apr-Sep, to 5.15pm Oct-Mar) served as the burial place for all but a handful of France's kings and queens from Dagobert I (r 629–39) to Louis XVIII (r 1814–24). Their tombs and mausoleums constitute one of Europe's most important collections of funerary sculpture.

The single-towered basilica, begun around 1135, changed the face of Western architecture. It was the first major structure to be built in the Gothic style and served as a model for many other 12th-century French cathedrals, including the one at Chartres (p196). Features illustrating the transition from Romanesque to Gothic can be seen in the **choir** and **ambulatory**, which are adorned with a number of 12th-century **stained-glass windows**.

During the Revolution and the Reign of Terror, the basilica was devastated; human remains were removed from the royal tombs and dumped into two pits outside the church. The mausoleums were put into storage in Paris, however, and survived. They were brought back in 1816, and the royal bones were reburied in the crypt a year later. Restoration of the structure was begun under Napoleon, but most of the work was carried out by the Gothic Revivalist architect Eugène Viollet-le-Duc from 1858 until his death in 1879.

The **tombs** are decorated with life-size figures of the deceased. Those built before the Renaissance are adorned with *gisants* (recumbent figures). Those made after 1285 were carved from death masks and are thus fairly, well, lifelike; the 14 figures commissioned under Louis IX (St Louis; r 1214–70) are depictions of how earlier rulers might have looked. The oldest tombs (dating from around 1230) are those of **Clovis I** (d 511) and his son **Childebert I** (d 558). Self-paced 1¼-hour tours using CD-ROM headsets (€4; €5.50 for two people sharing) are available at the crypt ticket kiosk.

Just south of the basilica is the former royal abbey and now the **Maison d'Éducation de la Légion d'Honneur**, a school for 500 pupils.

MUSÉE D'ART ET D'HISTOIRE
The excellent **Musée d'Art et d'Histoire** (Museum of Art & History; ☎ 01 42 43 05 10; 22bis rue Gabriel Péri; adult/student & senior/under 16 €4/2/free; 🕙 10am-5.30pm Mon, Wed & Fri, 10am-8pm Thu, 2-6.30pm Sat & Sun) occupies a restored Carmelite convent southwest of the basilica that was founded in 1625 and later presided over by Louise de France, the youngest daughter of Louis XV. Displays include reconstructions of the Carmelites' cells, an 18th-century apothecary and fascinating items found during excavations around St-Denis. There's a section on modern art and politically charged posters, cartoons, lithographs and paintings from the 1871 Paris Commune.

STADE DE FRANCE
The 80,000-seat, cunningly named **Stadium of France** (☎ 0 892 700 900; www.stadefrance.com; rue Francis de Pressensé, ZAC du Cornillon Nord, 93216 St-Denis La Plaine; adult/student/6-11 yrs €10/8.50/7; 🕙 tours on the hour in French 10am-5pm year-round, in English 10.20am & 2.30pm Jun-Aug), just south of central St-Denis and in full view from rue Gabriel Péri, was built for the 1998 World Cup, which the French football team won by miraculously defeating Brazil 3-0. The futuristic and quite beautiful structure, with a roof the size of place de la Concorde, is now used for football and rugby matches, major gymnastic events and big-ticket music concerts. It can be visited on a guided tour from Porte H (Gate H), but they are conducted in English only in summer.

Eating
Les Arts (☎ 01 42 43 22 40; 6 rue de la Boulangerie; starters €4.90-9.50, couscous €7.90-19.20, tajines €9.50-12.50; 🕙 lunch Tue-Sun, dinner to 10.30pm Mon-Sat) This is a central restaurant with French and Maghrebi cuisine that comes recommended locally.

Au Petit Breton (☎ 01 48 20 11 58; 18 rue de la Légion d'Honneur; plat du jour €8, menus €10 & €12; 🕙 8.30am-3.30pm Mon-Sat) 'At the Little Breton' is a decent choice for a light lunch of *galettes* (a savoury version of crepes) and dry cider or a snack of sweet crepes.

The large, multiethnic **food market** (place Jean Jaurès; 🕙 8am-2pm Tue, Fri & Sun) across the street from the tourist office and in the **Halle du Marché**, the large covered market a short stroll away to the northwest, is known in particular for its selection of spices.

There's a **Franprix supermarket** (34 rue de la République; 🕙 9am-1pm & 3-7.15pm Tue-Sat, 8.30am-1pm Sun) in the centre of town near the post office.

Getting There & Away
Take metro line No 13 to the penultimate station, Basilique de St-Denis, for the basilica

and tourist office, or to St-Denis-Porte de Paris for the Musée d'Art et d'Histoire and the Stade de France; the latter can also be reached via RER line B (station: La Plaine-Stade de France). When taking metro line No 13, make sure you board a train heading for St-Denis Université and *not* for Gabriel Péri/Asnières-Gennevilliers, as the line splits at La Fourche station.

DISNEYLAND RESORT PARIS

It took almost €4.6 billion and five years of work to turn the beet fields east of the capital into Europe's first Disney theme park, which opened in 1992 amid much fanfare and controversy. Although Disney stockholders were less than thrilled with the park's performance for the first few years, what was originally known as Euro-Disney is now very much in the black, and the many visitors – mostly families with young children – can't seem to get enough.

Orientation

Disneyland Resort Paris consists of three main areas: commercial Disney Village, with its five hotels, shops, restaurants and clubs; Disneyland Park, with its five theme parks; and Walt Disney Studios Park, which brings film, animation and TV production to life. The first two are separated by the RER and TGV train stations; Walt Disney Studios Park is next to Disneyland Park.

Information

MONEY
Bureaux de change are everywhere, including a **branch** (10am-7pm) at the main entrance to Disneyland Park.

TOURIST INFORMATION
Espace du Tourisme d'Île de France et de Seine et Marne (01 60 43 33 33; www.pidf.com; place des Passagers du Vent, Disneyland Resort Paris, 77705 Marne-la-Vallée; 10am-7pm) The Île de France tourist office branch in the heart of the resort shares space with an office dispensing information on the *département* of Seine et Marne.

Sights

One-day admission fees at **Disneyland Resort Paris** (01 60 30 60 30, UK 0 870 503 0305, USA 407-WDISNEY, 407-934 7639; www.disneylandparis .com, www.needmagic.com) include unlimited access to all rides and activities in either Dis-

neyland Park or Walt Disney Studios Park. Those who opt for the latter, however, can enter Disneyland Park three hours before it closes. Multiple-day passes are also available: a **Passe-Partout** (adult/child €49/39) allows entry to both parks for one day while a **Hopper Ticket** (adult/child high season €109/84, low season €105/78) allows you to enter and leave both parks as you like over three days, which need not be consecutive but must be used within three years.

Disneyland Park (adult/3-11 yrs €40/30 Apr-Oct, €39/29 Nov-Mar; 9am-11pm daily early Jul-Aug, 10am-8pm Mon-Fri, 9am-8pm Sat & Sun Sep-Mar, 9am-8pm daily Apr-early May, 10am-8pm Mon-Fri, 9am-8pm Sat & Sun early May–mid-Jun, 9am-8pm daily mid-Jun–early Jul) is divided into five *pays* (lands). **Main Street, USA**, just inside the main entrance and behind Disneyland Hotel, is a spotless avenue reminiscent of Norman Rockwell's idealised small-town America c1900, complete with Disney characters let loose among the crowds. Adjoining **Frontierland** is a re-creation of the 'rugged, untamed American West'. **Adventureland**, meant to evoke the Arabian Nights and the wilds of Africa (among other exotic lands portrayed in Disney films), is home to that old favourite, Pirates of the Caribbean, as well as Indiana Jones and the Temple of Peril: a roller coaster that spirals through 360° – in reverse! **Fantasyland** brings fairy-tale characters such as Sleeping Beauty, Pinocchio, Peter Pan and Snow White to life; you will also find 'It's a Small World' here. **Discoveryland** features a dozen high-tech attractions and rides (including Space Mountain and Orbitron) and futuristic films at Videopolis that pay homage to Leonardo da Vinci, George Lucas and – for a bit of local colour – Jules Verne.

Walt Disney Studios Park (adult/3-11 yrs €40/30 Apr-Oct, €39/29 Nov-Mar; 9am-6pm daily late Jun-early Sep, 10am-6pm Mon-Fri, 9am-6pm Sat & Sun early Sep-late Jun), which opened in March 2002, has a sound stage, a production backlot and animation studios that help illustrate up close how films, TV programmes and cartoons are produced.

Sleeping & Eating

There are 50 restaurants at Disneyland Resort Paris, including such memorable venues as the **Silver Spur Steakhouse** in Frontierland, the **Blue Lagoon Restaurant** in Fantasyland and **Annette's Diner** in Disney Village. Most have adult menus for between €20 and €28 and a children's one for €10. Restaurants in Disneyland Park open for lunch and dinner according to the season; those in Disney Village open from 11am or 11.30am to about midnight daily. You are not allowed to picnic on resort grounds.

Each of the resort's half-dozen **hotels** (☎ 01 60 30 60 30; www.disneylandparis.com; P X X 🖵 🖼) has its own all-American theme, reflected in the architecture, landscaping, décor, restaurants and entertainment. All of the rooms have two double beds (or, in the case of the Hôtel Cheyenne, one double bed and two bunk beds) and can sleep up to four people. Free shuttle buses link the hotels with the parks.

Rates vary. The vast majority of guests stay on some sort of package. Prices are highest during July and August and around Christmas; on Friday and Saturday nights and during holiday periods from April to October; and on Saturday nights from mid-February to March. The least expensive rates are available on most weeknights (ie Sunday to Thursday or, sometimes, Friday) from January to mid-February, from mid-May to June, for most of September, and from November to mid-December.

THE TENNIS COURT OATH

At Versailles in May 1789, in an effort to deal with the huge national debt and to moderate dissent by reforming the tax system, Louis XVI convened the États-Généraux (States General), a body made up of over 1000 deputies representing the three 'estates': the nobility, the clergy and the so-called Third Estate, representing the middle classes.

When the Third Estate's representatives, who formed the majority of the delegates, were denied entry to the usual meeting place of the États-Généraux, they met in the Salle de Jeu de Paume (Royal Tennis Court), where they constituted themselves as the National Assembly on 17 June. Three days later they took the famous *Serment du Jeu de Paume* (Tennis Court Oath), swearing not to dissolve the assembly until Louis XVI had accepted a new constitution. This act of defiance sparked demonstrations of support and, less than a month later, a mob in Paris stormed the prison at Bastille.

Disneyland Hôtel (d per person €258-599) This property at the entrances to the two parks bills itself as a 'lavish Victorian fantasy' and is the pinnacle of Disney Resort Paris accommodation.

Hôtel Cheyenne (d per person €105-184) The 14 timber-framed buildings of this hotel – each with its own hokey name – are arranged to resemble a Wild West frontier town.

Hôtel Santa Fe (d per person €69-139) Offering the most affordable accommodation in the resort itself, the Santa Fe has an American Southwest style.

Getting There & Away

Marne-la-Vallée/Chessy (Disneyland's RER station) is served by RER line A4; trains run every 15 minutes or so from central Paris (€6, 35 to 40 minutes). The last train back to Paris leaves at about 12.20am.

VERSAILLES

pop 85,300

The prosperous, leafy and very bourgeois suburb of Versailles, 21km southwest of Paris, is the site of the grandest and most famous chateau in France. It served as the kingdom's political capital and the seat of the royal court for more than a century, from 1682 to 1789 – the year Revolutionary mobs massacred the palace guard and dragged Louis XVI and Marie-Antoinette back to Paris where they eventually had their heads lopped off.

Because so many people consider Versailles a must-see destination, the chateau attracts upwards of three million visitors a year. The best way to avoid the queues is to arrive first thing in the morning; if you're interested in just the Grands Appartements, another good time to get here is about 3.30pm or 4pm. The queues are longest on Tuesday, when many of Paris' museums are closed, and on Sunday.

Information

CCF bank (17-19 rue du Maréchal Foch)

Office de Tourisme de Versailles (☎ 01 39 24 88 88; www.versailles-tourisme.com; 2bis av de Paris; 🕑 9am-7pm daily Apr-Oct, 9am-6pm Tue-Sat, 9am-5pm Sun & Mon Nov-Mar) The tourist office has themed guided tours (adult/child €8/4) of the city and chateau throughout the week year-round.

Post Office (av de Paris) On the opposite side of av de Paris from the tourist office.

VERSAILLES

0	600 m
0	0.4 miles

INFORMATION
CCF Bank...1 D5
Office de Tourisme de Versailles.....2 C5
Post Office..3 C5

SIGHTS & ACTIVITIES (pp187-8)
Bassin d'Appollon..............................4 A4
Bassin de Neptune.............................5 C4
Entrée A (Ticket Office)......................6 C5
Entrée C...7 C5
Entrée D...8 C5
Entrée F..9 C5
Grand Trianon..................................10 A3
Hameau de la Reine..........................11 A2
Orangerie......................................(see 12)
Parterre du Midi...............................12 B5

Petit Trianon....................................13 A3
Salle de Jeu de Paume......................14 C5

SLEEPING ⬆ (p188)
Hôtel d'Angleterre............................15 C5
Hôtel du Palais.................................16 C5
Royal Hôtel......................................17 C6

EATING 🍽 (p188)
À la Ferme..18 C6
Crêperie St-Louis..............................19 C5
Le Falher..20 C5
Marché Notre Dame &
    Food Halls....................................21 D4
Monoprix Supermarket.....................22 D5
Pizzeria Via Veneto...........................23 C5

TRANSPORT (pp188-9)
Bicycle Hire......................................24 A4
Bicycle Hire.................................(see 32)
Bus No 171 To/From Paris................25 C5
Local Bus Station..............................26 C5
Phébus Bicycle Rental.......................27 D6

OTHER
Cathédrale St-Louis..........................28 C6
Cour des Ministres............................29 C5
Cour Royale......................................30 C5
Église Notre Dame............................31 C4
Grille de la Reine..............................32 B4
Grille de Neptune.............................33 C4
Grille du Dragon...............................34 C4
Hôtel de Ville...................................35 D5
Les Manèges Versailles Shopping
    Centre...36 C5
Préfecture..37 D5

Sights

CHÂTEAU DE VERSAILLES

The splendid and enormous **Château de Versailles** (Palace of Versailles; ☎ 01 30 83 78 00, 01 30 83 77 77; www.chateauversailles.fr; Passport adult/10-17 yrs €20/6 Apr-Oct, €14.50/4 Nov-Mar; ☼ 9am-6.30pm Tue-Sun Apr-Oct, 9am-5.30pm Tue-Sun Nov-Mar) was built in the mid-17th century during the reign of Louis XIV – the Roi Soleil (Sun King) – to project the absolute power of the French monarchy, which was then at the height of its glory. Its scale and décor also reflect Louis XIV's taste for profligate luxury and his boundless appetite for self-glorification. Some 30,000 workers and soldiers toiled on the structure, the bills for which all but emptied the kingdom's coffers. The chateau has undergone relatively few alterations since its construction, though almost all the interior furnishings disappeared during the Revolution and many of the rooms were rebuilt by Louis-Philippe (r 1830–48).

About two decades into his long reign (1643–1715), Louis XIV decided to enlarge the hunting lodge his father had built at Versailles and turn it into a palace big enough for the entire court, which numbered about 6000 people at the time. To accomplish this he hired three supremely talented men: the architect Louis Le Vau (Jules Hardouin-Mansart took over from Le Vau in the mid-1670s); the painter and interior designer Charles Le Brun; and the landscape artist André Le Nôtre, whose workers flattened hills, drained marshes and relocated forests as they laid out the seemingly endless gardens, ponds and fountains.

Le Brun and his hundreds of artisans decorated every moulding, cornice, ceiling and door of the interior with the most luxurious and ostentatious of appointments: frescoes, marble, gilt and woodcarvings, many with themes and symbols drawn from Greek and Roman mythology. The **Grand Appartement du Roi** (King's Suite), for example, includes rooms dedicated to Hercules, Venus, Diana, Mars and Mercury. The opulence reaches its peak in the **Galerie des Glaces** (Hall of Mirrors), a 75m-long ballroom with 17 huge mirrors on one side and, on the other, an equal number of windows looking out on the gardens and the setting sun.

The chateau complex comprises four main sections: the palace building, a 580m-long structure with multiple wings, grand halls and sumptuous bedchambers (only parts of which are open to the public); the vast gardens, canals and pools to the west of the palace; and two outbuildings, the **Grand Trianon** and, a few hundred metres to the east, the **Petit Trianon**.

The so-called 'Passport' allows entry (via Entrée B2) to the State Apartments, King's Chamber, the Trianons, the gardens, Coach Museum and fountain displays or you can visit sections and sights on a guided tour or individually. The **Grands Appartements** (State Apartments; admission before/after 3.30pm €7.50/5.30, under 18 free; ☼ 9am-6.30pm Tue-Sun Apr-Oct, 9am-5.30pm Tue-Sun Nov-Mar), the main section of the palace that can be visited without a guided tour, include the Galerie des Glaces, the Appartement de la Reine (Queen's Suite) and several other sights. Tickets are on sale at Entrée A (Entrance A), which is off to the right from the equestrian statue of Louis XIV as you approach the palace. If you have a Carte Musées-Monuments (see p113) you don't have to wait in the queue – go straight to Entrée B2.

The section of the vast **chateau gardens** (adult/under 18 €3/free, after 6pm free Apr-Oct, free Nov-Mar; ☼ 9am-sunset Apr-Oct, 8am-5.30pm or 6.30pm Nov-Mar) nearest the palace, laid out between 1661 and 1700 in the formal French style, is famed for its geometrically aligned terraces, flowerbeds, tree-lined paths, ponds and fountains. The many statues of marble, bronze and lead were made by the most talented sculptors of the era. The English-style **Jardins du Petit Trianon** are more pastoral and have meandering, sheltered paths.

The **Grand Canal**, 1.6km long and 62m wide, is oriented to reflect the setting sun. It is traversed by the 1km-long **Petit Canal**, creating a cross-shaped body of water with a perimeter of more than 5.5km. Louis XIV used to hold boating parties here. In season, you too can paddle around the Grand Canal in four-person **rowing boats** (☎ 01 39 66 97 66; per ½hr/hr €8/11; ☼ Mar-Nov); board them at the canal's eastern end. The **Orangerie**, built under the Parterre du Midi (flowerbed) on the southwestern side of the palace, is used to store tropical plants in winter.

The gardens' largest fountains are the 17th-century **Bassin de Neptune** (Neptune's Fountain), 300m north of the palace, whose straight side abuts a small pond graced by a winged dragon, and the **Bassin d'Apollon**, at the eastern end of the Grand Canal, in the centre of which Apollo's chariot, pulled by rearing horses, emerges from the water.

Try to time your visit for the **Grande Perspective** and **Grandes Eaux Musicales** (adult/student & over 11 €6/4.50, after 4.50pm free; ☑ 11am-noon & 3.30-5pm Sat early May-late Sep, Sun early Apr-early Oct) fountain displays.

In the middle of the park, approximately 1.5km northwest of the main building, are Versailles' two smaller palaces, each of which is surrounded by neatly tended flowerbeds. The pink-colonnaded **Grand Trianon** (adult/concession/under 18 €5/3/free; ☑ noon-6.30pm Apr-Oct, noon-5.30pm Nov-Mar) was built in 1687 for Louis XIV and his family as a place of escape from the rigid etiquette of the court. Napoleon I had it redone in the Empire style. The much smaller, ochre-coloured **Petit Trianon** (entry incl with Grand Trianon; ☑ noon-6.30pm Mar-Oct, noon-5.30pm Nov-Feb), built in the 1760s, was redecorated in 1867 by Empress Eugénie, the consort of Napoleon III, who added Louis XVI-style furnishings similar to the uninspiring pieces that now fill its 1st-floor rooms.

Further north is the **Hameau de la Reine** (Queen's Hamlet), a mock village of thatched cottages constructed from 1775 to 1784 for the amusement of Marie-Antoinette, who liked to play milkmaid here.

The **Appartement de Louis XIV** and **Appartements du Dauphin et de la Dauphine** – also called the King's Chamber – can be toured with a one-hour **audioguide** (adult/under 10 €4/free) available at Entrée C. You can begin your visit between 9am and 5pm (4pm from November to March). This is also a good way to avoid the queues at Entrée A.

Several different **guided tours** (☎ 01 30 83 77 88; 1/1½/2hr adult €4/6/8, 10-17 yrs €2.70/4.20/5.50; ☑ 9am-4pm Tue-Sun Apr-Oct, 9am-3.45pm Tue-Sun Nov-Mar) are available in English. Tickets are sold at Entrée D; tours begin across the courtyard at Entrée F and must be booked ahead. All tours require you to purchase a ticket to the Grands Appartements. If you buy a tour ticket at Entrée C or Entrée D you can later avoid the Grands Appartements queue at Entrée A by going straight to Entrée B.

Sleeping

Hôtel d'Angleterre (☎ 01 39 51 43 50; hotel-angleterre@voila.fr; 2bis rue de Fontenay; s & d with washbasin & toilet €35, with shower & toilet €65-71, tr & q €86; Ⓟ)

Less than 300m from the chateau entrance, the 'England' has 18 charming and up-to-date rooms.

Royal Hôtel (☎ 01 39 50 67 31; www.royalhotelversailles.com; 23 rue Royale; s/d with shower & toilet €49-58, d/tr with bath & toilet €61/70) With basic but adequate rooms, the Royal is a central choice, with friendly staff.

Hôtel du Palais (☎ 01 39 50 39 29; hotelpalais@ifrance.com; 6 place Lyautay; d with washbasin €38, with shower €50-55) This well-kept 24-room hotel is an inexpensive option opposite Versailles-Rive Gauche train station.

Eating

Le Falher (☎ 01 39 50 57 43; 22 rue Satory; starters €14-20, mains €23-25, lunch menu €22, dinner menus €29 & €46; ☑ lunch Mon-Fri & dinner to 10.30pm Tue-Sat) This quiet and elegant place not far from the palace has French gastronomic menus.

À la Ferme (☎ 01 39 53 10 81; 3 rue du Maréchal Joffre; starters €6-10, mains €10.50-15, 2-/3-course menus €15.50/19; ☑ lunch & dinner to 11pm Wed-Sun) 'At the Farm' specialises in grilled meats and the cuisine of southwestern France.

Crêperie St-Louis (☎ 01 39 53 40 12; 33 rue du Vieux Versailles; menus €9-14; ☑ lunch & dinner to 11pm) This is a cosy place with Breton specialities including sweet and savoury crêpes and galettes (€3 to €7.50).

Pizzeria Via Veneto (☎ 01 39 51 03 89; 20 rue Satory; pizzas & pasta dishes €7-11; ☑ lunch & dinner to 11pm) A good choice for the specialities.

Marché Notre Dame (place du Marché Notre Dame; ☑ 7.30am-1.30pm Tue, Fri & Sun) This outdoor market north of the tourist office is worth a visit. There are also **food halls** (☑ 7am-1pm & 3.30-7.30pm Tue-Sat, 7am-2pm Sun) surrounding the market place.

Monoprix (9 rue Georges Clemenceau; ☑ 8.30am-8.55pm Mon-Sat) This department store north of av de Paris has a large supermarket section.

Getting There & Away

RATP Bus No 171 (€1.30 or one metro/bus ticket, 35 minutes) links Pont de Sèvres (15e) in Paris with the place d'Armes every eight to 15 minutes daily, with the last bus leaving Versailles just before 1am. Be aware that it's faster to go by RER and you'll have to get to/from Pont de Sèvres metro station on line No 9 if you take the bus.

RER line C5 (€2.35) takes you from Paris' Left Bank RER stations to Versailles-Rive Gauche station, which is only 700m southeast of the chateau and close to the tourist office. The last train to Paris leaves shortly before midnight. RER line C8 links Paris' Left Bank with Versailles-Chantiers station, a 1.3km walk from the chateau.

SNCF operates 70 trains a day from Paris' Gare St-Lazare (€3.20) to Versailles-Rive Droite, which is 1.2km from the chateau. The last train to Paris leaves just after midnight. Versailles-Chantiers station is also served by some 30 SNCF trains a day (20 on Sunday) from Gare Montparnasse; all trains on this line continue to Chartres (€9.90; 45 to 60 minutes).

Getting Around

From February to November, bicycles can be hired from **kiosks** (☎ 01 39 66 97 66; per ½hr/hr/½ day/day €2.50/5/10.50/12; ☼ 10am-close Mon-Fri, 1pm-close Sat & Sun Jun-mid–Sep, 10am-close Sat & Sun Feb-May & mid-Sep–Nov) at Petite Venise at the eastern end of the Grand Canal and next to Grille de la Reine. You can also rent bikes from **Phébus** (☎ 01 39 20 16 60; www.phebus.tm.fr in French; place Raymond Poincaré; per 1hr/2hr/day/week/month €5/10/12/16/25; ☼ 7.15am-7.45pm Mon-Fri, 11am-5pm Sat & Sun) in front of the Versailles-Chantiers metro station.

FONTAINEBLEAU
pop 15,800
The town of Fontainebleau, 67km southeast of Paris, is renowned for its elegant Renaissance chateau – one of France's largest royal residences – whose splendid furnishings make it particularly worth visiting. It's much less crowded and pressured than Versailles. The town itself has a number of fine restaurants and nightspots and is surrounded by the beautiful Forêt de Fontainebleau, a favourite hunting ground of many French kings and today an important recreational centre in the Île de France.

Information

Office de Tourisme de Pays de Fontainebleau (☎ 01 60 74 99 99; www.fontainebleau-tourisme.com; 4 rue Royale; ☼ 10am-6pm Mon-Sat, 10am-12.30pm & 3-5pm Sun Apr-Oct, 10am-1pm Sun Nov-Mar) The tourist office, in a converted petrol station a couple of hundred metres west of the chateau, hires out **bicycles** (per ½ day/day €15/19), as well as self-paced English-language **audioguide tours** (€4.60; 1½hr) of both the palace and the Forêt de Fontainebleau.

Post Office (2 rue de la Chancellerie)

Société Générale (102 rue Grande; ☼ 8.35am-12.30pm & 1.30-5.25pm Mon-Fri, 8.35am-12.30pm & 1.30-4.25pm Sat)

Sights
CHÂTEAU DE FONTAINEBLEAU
The enormous, 1900-room **Château de Fontainebleau** (Palace of Fontainebleau; ☎ 01 60 71 50 70; www.chateaudefontainebleau.net; adult/18-25 yrs/under 18 €5.50/4/free, 1st Sun of month free; ☼ 9.30am-6pm Wed-Mon Jun-Sep, 9.30am-5pm Wed-Mon Oct-May), whose list of former tenants or visitors reads like a who's who of French royalty, is one of the most beautifully decorated and furnished chateaux in France. Every centimetre of wall and ceiling space is richly adorned with wood panelling, gilded carvings, frescoes, tapestries and paintings. The parquet floors are of the finest woods, the fireplaces ornamented with exceptional carvings, and many of the pieces of furniture are originals dating back to the Renaissance era.

The first chateau on this site was built sometime in the early 12th century and enlarged by Louis IX a century later. Only a single medieval tower survived the energetic Renaissance-style reconstruction undertaken by François I (r 1515–47), whose superb artisans, many of them brought from Italy, blended Italian and French styles to create what is known as the First School of Fontainebleau. The *Mona Lisa* once hung here amid other fine works of art of the royal collection.

During the latter half of the 16th century, the chateau was further expanded by Henri II (r 1547–59), Catherine de Médicis and Henri IV (r 1589–1610), whose Flemish and French artists created the Second School of Fontainebleau. Even Louis XIV got in on the act: it was he who hired Le Nôtre to redesign the gardens.

Fontainebleau, which was not damaged during the Revolution (though its furniture was stolen or destroyed), was beloved by Napoleon, who had a fair bit of restoration work carried out. Napoleon III was another frequent visitor.

During WWII the chateau was turned into a German headquarters. After it was liberated by Allied forces under US General George Patton in 1944, part of the complex served as the Allied and then NATO's headquarters from 1945 to 1965.

The **Grands Appartements** (State Apartments) include a number of outstanding rooms. The spectacular **Chapelle de la Trinité** (Trinity Chapel), whose ornamentation dates from the first half of the 17th century, is where Louis XV married Marie Leczinska in 1725 and where the future Napoleon III was christened in 1810. **Galerie François 1er**, a jewellery box of Renaissance architecture, was decorated from 1533 to 1540 by Il Rosso, a Florentine follower of Michelangelo. In the wood panelling, François I's monogram appears repeatedly along with his emblem, a dragonlike salamander.

The **Salle de Bal**, a 30m-long ballroom dating from the mid-16th century that was also used for receptions and banquets, is renowned for its mythological frescoes, marquetry floor and Italian-inspired coffered ceiling. Large windows afford views of the Cour Ovale and the gardens. The gilded bed found in the 17th- and 18th-century **Chambre de l'Impératrice** (Empress' Bedroom) was never actually used by Marie-Antoinette, for whom it was built. The gilding in the **Salle du Trône** (Throne Room), the royal bedroom before the Napoleonic period, is in three shades: gold, green and yellow. Conducted tours of the Grands Appartements in English usually depart at 2.30pm from July to September from the staircase near the ticket windows, but check with staff.

The **Petits Appartements** (Small Apartments) were the private rooms of the emperor and

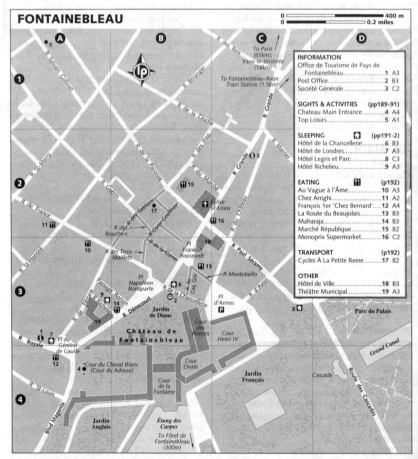

FONTAINEBLEAU

0 ――― 400 m
0 ――― 0.2 miles

INFORMATION
Office de Tourisme de Pays de
Fontainebleau.......................1 A3
Post Office....................................2 B3
Société Générale..........................3 C2

SIGHTS & ACTIVITIES   (pp189–91)
Chateau Main Entrance............4 A4
Top Loisirs...................................5 A1

SLEEPING   (pp191–2)
Hôtel de la Chancellerie...........6 B3
Hôtel de Londres.......................7 A3
Hôtel Legris et Parc...................8 C3
Hôtel Richelieu...........................9 A3

EATING   (p192)
Au Vague à l'Âme.....................10 A3
Chez Arrighi..............................11 A2
François 1er 'Chez Bernard'.....12 A4
La Route du Beaujolais.............13 B3
Maharaja...................................14 B3
Marché République..................15 B2
Monoprix Supermarket............16 C2

TRANSPORT   (p192)
Cycles À La Petite Reine..........17 B2

OTHER
Hôtel de Ville............................18 B3
Théâtre Municipal....................19 A3

empress, and the **Musée Napoléon 1er** (Napoleon I Museum) contains personal effects – such as uniforms, hats, coats, ornamental swords – and knick-knacks that belonged to Napoleon and his relatives. Neither has fixed opening hours and entry is an additional €3/2.30 for adults/ 18 to 25 years (free for those under 18).

As successive monarchs added their own wings to the chateau, five irregularly shaped courtyards were created. The oldest and most interesting is the **Cour Ovale** (Oval Courtyard), no longer oval but U-shaped due to Henri IV's construction work. It incorporates the keep, the sole remnant of the medieval chateau. The largest courtyard is the **Cour du Cheval Blanc** (Courtyard of the White Horse), from where you enter the chateau. Napoleon, about to be exiled to Elba in 1814, bade farewell to his guards from the magnificent 17th-century **double-horseshoe staircase** here. For that reason the courtyard is also called the Cour des Adieux (Farewell Courtyard).

The **chateau gardens** (admission free; ☺ 9am-7pm May-Sep, 9am-6pm Mar, Apr & Oct, 9am-5pm Nov-Feb) are quite extraordinary. On the northern side of the chateau is the **Jardin de Diane**, a formal garden created by Catherine de Médicis. Le Nôtre's formal, 17th-century **Jardin Français** (French Garden), or Grand Parterre, is east of the **Cour de la Fontaine** (Fountain Courtyard) and the **Étang des Carpes** (Carp Pond). The **Grand Canal** was excavated in 1609 and predates the canals at Versailles by more than half a century. The informal **Jardin Anglais** (English Garden), laid out in 1812, is west of the pond.

FORÊT DE FONTAINEBLEAU

This 20,000-hectare **Forêt de Fontainebleau** (Fontainebleau Forest) forest, which begins 500m south of the chateau and surrounds the town, is one of the prettiest woods in the region. The many trails – including parts of the **GR1** and **GR11** (see p897 for general information about walking trails) – are excellent for jogging, walking, cycling, horse riding and climbing. The area is covered by IGN's 1:25,000-scale *Forêt de Fontainebleau* map (No 2417OT; €9). The tourist office sells the *Guide des Sentiers de Promenades dans le Massif Forestier de Fontainebleau* (€7.60), whose maps and text (in French) cover almost 20 walks in the forest, as well as the

comprehensive *La Forêt de Fontainebleau* (€12.50), published by the Office National des Forêts, with almost three dozen walks.

Rock-climbing enthusiasts have long come to the forest's sandstone ridges, rich in cliffs and overhangs, to hone their skills before setting off for the Alps. If you want to give it a go, contact **Top Loisirs** (☎ 01 60 74 08 50; www.toploisirs.fr; 16 rue Sylvain Collinet) about equipment hire and instruction. The tourist office sells the comprehensive *Fontainebleau Climbs* (€25) in English.

Sleeping

Hôtel de Londres (☎ 01 64 22 20 21; www.hotel delondres.com; 1 place du Général de Gaulle; s & d €90-105, ste €125-150; **P**) This fine 12-room hotel opposite the chateau's main entrance dates back to at least the Second Empire and is a very comfortable place to stay. Some rooms (including Nos 2 and 10) have balconies with stunning views of the chateau.

Hôtel Richelieu (☎ 01 64 22 26 46; fax 01 64 23 40 17; 4 rue Richelieu; s €41-57, d €46-62; **P**) The 18-room Richelieu, just north of the chateau, is part of the Logis de France group – always a sign of quality – and has an excellent wine bar and bistro attached.

Hôtel de la Chancellerie (☎ 01 64 22 21 70; hotel .chancellerie@gofornet.com; 1 rue de la Chancellerie; s/d/tr €35/40/58) This hotel opposite the post office

---

AUTHOR'S CHOICE

Hôtel Legris et Parc (☎ 01 64 22 24 24; legris.et.parc@wanadoo.fr; 36 rue Paul Séramy & 6 rue d'Avon; s €46-50, d €61-95, tr €102-145; **P** 💻 🐾) This lovely 32-room hotel, situated in a 17th-century residence where Racine apparently once laid his head, abuts the palace park and boasts its own verdant garden. The hotel has a lovely open-air swimming pool and an excellent restaurant called **L'Éden** (starters €9.50-19, mains €14-35, menu €29). History is all around you at Legris et Parc. Just next door is a synagogue built in 1861 and razed by the Nazis in 1941 and, on the hotel grounds, is a Pavillon de Chasse, a 'Hunting Pavilion' done up in what the French call *style gentleman farmer* where Field Marshal Bernard Montgomery, Commander-in-Chief of all Allied Forces in Europe, held Scottish reels while based here after the war.

has 25 old-fashioned but comfortable and spotless rooms. Rates are about €10 more from April to October.

Eating

Chez Arrighi (☎ 01 64 22 29 43; 53 rue de France; starters €9-20, mains €13.50-23.50, menus €18.80, €23.50 & €31.80; 🕑 lunch & dinner to 11pm Tue-Sun) An elegant place – arguably the best restaurant in Fontainebleau – with traditional gastronomic cuisine.

François 1er 'Chez Bernard' (🕑 01 64 22 24 68; 3 rue Royale; starters €6.90-18.90, mains €14.50-18.60, lunch menu €15, dinner menu €28; 🕑 lunch & dinner to 11pm) This double-barrelled eatery has excellent specialities from Normandy, with an emphasis on seafood.

Maharaja (☎ 01 64 22 14 64; 15 rue Dénecourt; starters €3.50-7.50, mains €5.50-17.50, lunch menus €9 & €14, dinner menu €15; 🕑 lunch & dinner to midnight Mon-Sat) The Maharajah has curries (€7.50 to €9) and tandoori dishes (€5.50 to €17.50) as well as standard starters such as pakoras and samosas.

La Route du Beaujolais (☎ 01 64 22 27 98; 3 rue Montebello; starters €7-14, mains €12-20, lunch menu €12, dinner menus €17 & €24; 🕑 lunch & dinner to 11pm) 'The Beaujolais Way' is no great shakes, but it's central and serves reliable Lyonnaise-style dishes.

Au Vague à l'Âme (☎ 01 60 72 10 32; 39 rue de France; galettes & crêpes €2.50-7.50, menus €25 & €35; 🕑 lunch Tue-Sun, dinner to 1am Tue-Sat) This café-restaurant is the place to come for Breton specialities including fresh oysters and an oyster terrine to die for.

Marché République (rue des Pins; 🕑 8am-1pm Tue, Fri & Sun) Fontainebleau's covered food market is just north of the central pedestrian area.

Monoprix (58 rue Grande; 🕑 8.45am-7.45pm Mon-Sat, 9am-1pm Sun) This department store has a supermarket section on the 1st floor.

Getting There & Around

Up to 30 daily commuter trains link Paris' Gare de Lyon every hour with Fontainebleau-Avon station (€7.30, 40 to 60 minutes); the last train returning to Paris leaves Fontainebleau a bit after 9.45pm weekdays, just after 10pm on Saturday and sometime after 10.30pm on Sunday. SNCF has a package €20/16/8 for adults/ 10 to 17 years/four to nine years that includes return transport from Paris, bus transfers and admission to the chateau.

Local buses (€1.30) link the train station with central Fontainebleau, 2km to the southwest, every 10 minutes from about 6am until about 9.30pm (11.30pm on Sunday). The tourist office hires out normal bicycles (see p189). For mountain bike hire try **Cycles À La Petite Reine** (☎ 01 60 74 57 57; 32 rue des Sablons; per hr/½ day/day/week €5/10/13/54 Mon-Fri, €13/16 Sat & Sun; 🕑 9am-7.30pm Mon-Sat, 9am-6pm Sun).

VAUX-LE-VICOMTE

Privately owned **Château de Vaux-le-Vicomte** (☎ 01 64 14 41 90; www.vaux-le-vicomte.com; adult/senior, student & 6-16 yrs €12/9.50, candlelight visit €15/13, exhibit, garden & museum only €7; 🕑 10am-1pm & 2-6pm Mon-Fri, 10am-6pm Sat & Sun late Mar–mid-Nov, candlelight visit 8pm-midnight Fri Jul & Aug, Sat May–mid-Oct) and its magnificent **formal gardens** (🕑 10am-6pm late Mar–mid-Nov), 20km north of Fontainebleau and 61km southeast of Paris, were designed and built by Le Brun, Le Vau and Le Nôtre between 1656 and 1661 as a precursor to their more ambitious work at Versailles.

Unfortunately the beauty of Vaux-le-Vicomte's turned out to be the undoing of its owner, Nicolas Fouquet, Louis XIV's minister of finance. It seems that Louis, seething with jealousy that he had been upstaged at the chateau's official opening, had Fouquet thrown into prison, where the unfortunate *ministre* died in 1680. Today visitors can view the interior of the chateau, and wander through the gardens and the **Musée des Équipages** (Carriage Museum; 🕑 10am-1pm & 2-6pm Mon-Fri, 10am-6pm Sat & Sun late Mar–mid-Nov).

On the second and the last Saturday of every month from late March to October, there are elaborate *jeux d'eau* (fountain displays) in the gardens from 3pm to 6pm.

Getting There & Away

Unfortunately, Vaux-le-Vicomte is not an easy place to get to by public transport. The chateau is 6km northeast of Melun, which is served by RER line D2 from Paris (€7, 45 minutes). You will have to take a taxi to the chateau from Melun, which will cost between €15 and €20. If you are travelling by car, take the N6 from Paris and the A5a (in the direction of Melun) and exit at Voisenon. From Fontainebleau, follow the N6 and the N36.

CHANTILLY

pop 10,900

The elegant town of Chantilly, 48km north of Paris, has a heavily restored but imposing chateau, surrounded by parkland, gardens, lakes and a vast forest. There's more than ample opportunity here for walking, cycling and horse riding.

Information

Office de Tourisme de Chantilly (☎ 03 44 67 37 37; www.chantilly-tourisme.com; 60 av du Maréchal Joffre; 🕑 9.30am-12.30pm & 1.30-5.30pm Mon-Sat, 10.30am-1.30pm Sun May-Sep, 9.30am-12.30pm & 1.30-5.30pm Mon-Sat Oct-Apr) Ask the staff for a copy of *Circuit Touristique en Ville*, a pamphlet with a 23-stop walk around town starting at the tourist office.

Post Office (26 av du Maréchal Joffre)

Société Générale (1 av du Maréchal Joffre; 🕑 8.30am-12.15pm & 1.45-5.30pm Mon-Thu, 8.30am-12.15pm & 1.45-6.30pm Fri, 9.30am-3.25pm Sat)

Sights

CHÂTEAU DE CHANTILLY

The **Château de Chantilly** (☎ 03 44 62 62 62; www.chateaudechantilly.com; adult/12-17yrs/4-11 yrs €7/6/2.80;

🕑 10am-6pm daily Jul-Aug, 10am-6pm Wed-Mon Mar-Jun, Sep & Oct, 10.30am-12.45pm & 2-5pm Wed-Mon Nov-Feb), left in a shambles after the Revolution, is of interest mainly because of its gardens and a number of superb paintings. It consists of two attached buildings, which are entered through the same vestibule. The **Petit Château** was built around 1560 for Anne de Montmorency (1492–1567), who served six French kings as *connétable* (high constable), diplomat and warrior and died fighting Protestants in the Counter-Reformation. The attached Renaissance-style **Grand Château** was rebuilt 100 years after the Revolution by the Duke of Aumale, son of King Louis-Philippe. It served as a French military headquarters during WWI.

The Grand Château, to the right as you enter the vestibule, contains the **Musée Condé**. Its unremarkable 19th-century rooms are adorned with furnishings, paintings and sculptures haphazardly arranged according to the whims of the duke, who donated the chateau to the Institut de France at the end of the 19th century on the condition that the exhibits not be reorganised and

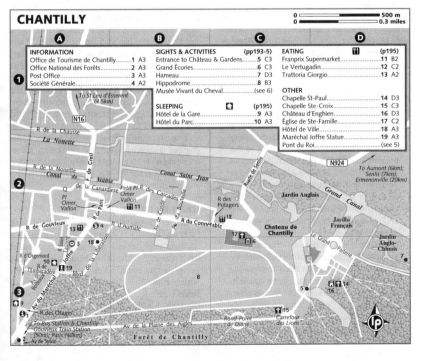

CHANTILLY				0 ⸻ 500 m / 0 ⸻ 0.3 miles
INFORMATION		**SIGHTS & ACTIVITIES**	(pp193-5)	**EATING** 🍴 (p195)
Office de Tourisme de Chantilly........1 A3		Entrance to Château & Gardens........5 C3		Franprix Supermarket................11 B2
Office National des Forêts...............2 A3		Grand Écuries.................................6 C3		Le Vertugadin...........................12 C2
Post Office....................................3 A3		Hameau..7 D3		Trattoria Giorgio........................13 A2
Société Générale............................4 A2		Hippodrome...................................8 B3		
		Musée Vivant du Cheval..............(see 6)		**OTHER**
				Chapelle St-Paul.......................14 D3
		SLEEPING 🛏	(p195)	Chapelle Ste-Croix.....................15 C3
		Hôtel de la Gare............................9 A3		Château d'Enghien.....................16 D3
		Hôtel du Parc...............................10 A3		Église de Ste-Famille..................17 C2
				Hôtel de Ville...........................18 A3
				Maréchal Joffre Statue................19 A3
				Pont du Roi...........................(see 5)

that they remain open to the public. The most remarkable works are hidden away in a small room called the **Sanctuaire**, including paintings by Raphael, Filippino Lippi and Jean Fouquet.

The Petit Château contains the **Appartements des Princes** (Princes' Suites), which are straight ahead from the entrance. The highlight here is the **Cabinet des Livres**, a repository of 700 manuscripts and more than 30,000 volumes, including a Gutenberg Bible and a facsimile of the *Très Riches Heures du Duc de Berry*, an illuminated manuscript dating from the 15th century that illustrates the calendar year for both the peasantry and the nobility. The **chapel**, to the left as you walk into the vestibule, has woodwork and stained-glass windows dating from the mid-16th century and was assembled by the duke in 1882.

The chateau's excellent gardens were once among the most spectacular in France. The formal **Jardin Français**, with flowerbeds, lakes and **Grand Canal** laid out by Le Nôtre in the mid-17th century, is northeast of the main building. To the west, the 'wilder' **Jardin Anglais** was begun in 1817. East of the Jardin Français is the rustic **Jardin Anglo-Chinois**, created in the 1770s. Its foliage and silted-up waterways surround the **Hameau**, a mock village dating from 1774 whose mill and half-timbered buildings inspired the

---

CHÂTEAU DE WHIPPED CREAM

Like every self-respecting 18th-century French chateau, the palace at Chantilly had its own *hameau* (hamlet) complete with *laitier* (dairy), where the lady of the household and her guests could play at being milkmaids, as Marie-Antoinette did at Versailles. But the cows at Chantilly's dairy took their job rather more seriously than their fellow bovines at other faux dairies, and news of the *crème chantilly* (sweetened whipped cream) served at the hamlet's teas became the talk (and envy) of aristocratic Europe. The future Habsburg emperor Joseph II clandestinely visited this '*temple de marbre*' (marble temple), as he called it, to try out the white stuff in 1777, and when the Baroness of Oberkirch tasted the goods she cried, 'Never have I eaten such good cream, so appetising, so well prepared'.

Hameau de la Reine at Versailles. Crème Chantilly – cream beaten with icing and vanilla sugar and dolloped on everything sweet that doesn't move in France – was born here (see left).

A normal ticket allows entry to the chateau, Musée Condé and park, though you can visit just the **park** and **gardens** (adult/4-11 yrs €3/2; 10am-6pm Mar-Oct, 10am-12.45pm & 2-6pm Nov-Feb) separately. Combination tickets include the park and canal boat ride (adult/four to 11 years €8/5); the chateau, museum, park and boat adult/12 to 17 years/four to 11 years €13/11/7); and the chateau, museum, park, boat and minitrain ride through the park (adult/12 to 17 years/four to 11 years €15/13/9).

The **Grandes Écuries** (Grand Stables) of the chateau, built between 1719 and 1740 to house 240 horses and more than 400 hunting hounds, stand apart from the chateau to the west and close to Chantilly's famous **Hippodrome** (racecourse), inaugurated in 1834. They house the **Musée Vivant du Cheval** (Living Horse Museum; 03 44 57 13 13; www.musee -vivant-du-cheval.fr; adult/12-17 yrs/4-11 yrs €8/6.50/5.50; 10.30am-6.30pm Mon & Wed-Fri, 2-6.30pm Tue, 10.30am-7pm Sat & Sun Jul & Aug; 10.30am-6.30pm Mon-Fri, 10.30am-7pm Sat & Sun May & Jun; 10.30am-6.30pm Wed-Mon, 10.30am-7pm Sat & Sun Apr, Sep & Oct; 2-6pm Mon & Wed-Fri, 10.30am-6.30pm Sat & Sun Nov-Mar), whose 30 equines live in luxurious **wooden stalls** built by Louis-Henri de Bourbon, the seventh Prince de Condé. Displays include everything from riding equipment to rocking horses and portraits, drawings and sculptures of famous nags from the past.

The 30-minute **Présentation Équestre Pédagogique** (Introduction to Dressage; 11.30am, 3.30pm & 5.30pm daily Apr-Oct, 3.30pm Mon-Fri, 11.30am, 3.30pm & 5.15pm Sat & Sun Nov-Mar) is included in the entry price.

FORÊT DE CHANTILLY
South of the chateau is the 6300-hectare **Forêt de Chantilly** (Chantilly Forest), once a royal hunting estate and now crisscrossed by a variety of walking and riding trails. Long-distance trails here include the **GR11**, which links the chateau with the town of **Senlis** (see opposite) and its wonderful cathedral; the **GR1**, which goes from **Luzarches** (famed for its cathedral, parts of which date from the 12th century) to **Ermenonville**; and the **GR12**, which goes northeast from four

lakes known as the **Étangs de Commelles** to the **Forêt d'Halatte**.

The area is covered by IGN's 1:25,000-scale *Forêts de Chantilly, d'Halatte and d'Ermenonville* map (No 2412OT; €9). The 1:100,000-scale *Carte de Découverte des Milieux Naturels et du Patrimoine Bâti* (€6.50), available at the tourist office, indicates sites of interest (eg churches, chateaux, museums and ruins). The **Office National des Forêts** (☎ 03 44 57 03 88; www.onf.fr in French; 1 av de Sylvie; 8.30am-noon & 2-5pm Mon-Fri), just southeast of the tourist office, publishes a good walking guide for families called *Promenons-Nous dans les Forêts de Picardie: Chantilly, Halatte & Ermenonville* (€7.50). Mountain bikers might want to pick up a copy of the detailed *Les Cahiers de la Randonnée VTT: Forêts de Chantilly et d'Ermenonville* (€13) at the tourist office.

Sleeping & Eating

Hôtel du Parc (☎ 03 44 58 20 00; www.bestwestern.fr; 36 av du Maréchal Joffre; s €78-88, d €86-96, tr €98-108, ste €112; P) This architecturally bankrupt place is no great shakes, but it's part of the Best Western chain so you can expect a reasonable standard of service. Cheaper rooms face the street.

Hôtel de la Gare (☎ 03 44 62 56 90; fax 03 44 62 56 99; place de la Gare; s & d €49) Opposite the train station, this rambling hotel with a dozen rooms is a surprisingly pleasant place with renovated shower-equipped doubles.

Le Vertugadin (☎ 03 44 57 03 19; 44 rue du Connétable; starters €8-15, mains €15-25, lunch menu €15, dinner menu €23; lunch daily, dinner to 11pm Mon-Sat) This very friendly and highly recommended restaurant has excellent menus and a walled-in garden that is a delight in summer.

Trattoria Giorgio (☎ 03 44 57 00 48; av du Maréchal Joffre; starters €6.90-11.50, pasta €7.90-11, mains €11.50-1810, lunch menu €9.90; lunch & dinner to 11.30pm) Giorgio's is a very central Italian bistro – just the ticket for a pizza or more ambitious meal en route to/from the train station.

Franprix (132 rue du Connétable; 8.30am-12.30pm & 2.30-7.30pm Tue-Thu, 8.30am-7.30pm Fri & Sat, 8.30am-1pm Sun) The supermarket is midway between the train station and the chateau.

Getting There & Away

Château de Chantilly is just over 2km east of the train station (next to the bus station); the most direct route from there is to walk along av de la Plaine des Aigles through a section of the Forêt de Chantilly. You'll get a better sense of the town, however, by taking av du Maréchal Joffre and rue de Paris to connect with rue du Connétable, Chantilly's principal thoroughfare.

Paris' Gare du Nord links with Chantilly-Gouvieux train station (€7.45, 30 to 45 minutes) by a mixture of RER and SNCF commuter trains (almost 40 a day; 20 on Sunday). The last train back to Paris departs daily just before midnight.

SENLIS

pop 16,250

Senlis, just 10km northeast of Chantilly, is an attractive medieval town of winding cobblestone streets, Gallo-Roman ramparts and towers. It was a royal seat from the time of Clovis to Henri IV and contains four small but fine **museums**, devoted to such diverse subjects as art, archaeology, hunting and the French cavalry in North Africa, and an important 12th-century cathedral.

The Gothic **Cathédrale de Notre Dame** (place Notre Dame; 8am-6pm), which is entered through the south portal, was built between 1150 and 1191. The cathedral is unusually bright, but the stained glass, though original, is generally unexceptional. The magnificent carved stone **Grand Portal** (1170), on the western side facing place du Parvis Notre Dame, has statues and a central relief relating to the life of the Virgin Mary. It is believed to have been the inspiration for the portal at the cathedral in Chartres.

The **Office de Tourisme de Senlis** (☎ 03 44 53 06 40; off.tourisme-senlis@wanadoo.fr; place du Parvis Notre Dame; 10am-12.30pm & 2-5pm Mon-Sat, 11.15am-1pm & 2.30-5pm Sun Nov-Feb, 10am-12.30pm & 2-6.15pm Mon-Sat, 10.30am-1pm & 2.30-6.15pm Sun Mar-Oct) is just opposite (and west of) the cathedral.

Sleeping & Eating

Hostellerie de la Porte Bellon (☎ 03 44 53 03 05; www.portebellon.com; 51 rue Bellon; s with shower €52-65, with bath €65-70, d with shower €55-68, with bath €68-73; P) This wonderful 18-room hotel is housed in an 18th-century manor a couple of hundred metres east of the cathedral.

Le Scaramouche (☎ 03 44 53 01 26; 4 place Notre Dame; starters €10-22, mains €14-35, menus €24, €35 & €58; lunch & dinner to 10.30pm Thu-Mon) The up-market Scaramouche is the best and most central place for a meal while visiting the cathedral or museums.

Surrounding the open-air **market** (rue St-Hilaire; 8am-1pm Tue & Fri) southwest of the cathedral are a number of relatively cheap places to eat including pizzerias, creperies and cafés.

Getting There & Away
Buses (€3.10, 25 minutes) link Senlis with Chantilly's bus station just next to its train station about every half-hour on weekdays and hourly on Saturday with about a half-dozen departures on Sunday. The last bus returns to Chantilly at 8pm on weekdays (just after 7pm at the weekend).

CHARTRES
pop 40,250
The magnificent 13th-century cathedral of Chartres, crowned by two very different spires – one Gothic, the other Romanesque – rises from rich farmland 88km southwest of Paris and dominates the medieval town around its base. The cathedral's varied collection of relics, particularly the Ste-Voile (the 'Holy Veil' said to have been worn by the Virgin Mary when she gave birth to Jesus), attracted many pilgrims during the Middle Ages, who contributed to the building and extensions of the cathedral. With its astonishing blue stained glass and other treasures, the cathedral at Chartres is a must-see for any visitor to Paris.

Information
MONEY
Crédit Agricole (1 Cloître Notre Dame; 8.45am-12.30pm & 1.50-5.30pm Tue-Fri, 8.45am-12.30pm & 1.50-4pm Sat)
BNP Paribas (7-9 place des Épars; 8.30am-noon & 1.30-5.35pm Tue, 8.50am-noon & 1.45-5.35pm Wed-Fri, 8.30am-noon & 1.30-4.45pm Sat)

POST
Post Office (place des Épars) Housed in an impressive neogothic building with *fin-de-siècle* mosaics adorning the front.

TOURIST INFORMATION
Office de Tourisme de Chartres (02 37 18 26 26; info@otchartres.fr; place de la Cathédrale; 9am-7pm Mon-Sat, 9.30am-5.30pm Sun Apr-Sep; 10am-6pm Mon-Sat, 10am-1pm & 2.30-4.30pm Sun Oct-Mar) The tourist office, across the square from the cathedral's main

entrance, rents self-paced English-language **audioguide tours** (for 1/2 people €5.50/8.50; 1½hr) of the medieval city.

Sights
CATHÉDRALE NOTRE DAME DE CHARTRES
The 130m-long cathedral **Cathédrale Notre Dame de Chartres** (Cathedral of Our Lady of Chartres; 02 37 21 22 07; www.cathedrale-chartres.com in French; place de la Cathédrale; 8.30am-7.30pm), one of the crowning architectural achievements of Western civilisation, was built in the Gothic style during the first quarter of the 13th century to replace a Romanesque cathedral that had been devastated – along with much of the town – by fire on the night of 10 June 1194. Because of effective fundraising among the aristocracy and donated labour from the common folk, construction took only 30 years, resulting in a high degree of architectural unity.

Excellent English-language **guided tours** (adult/senior/student €6/4/3; noon & 2.45pm Mon-Sat Apr-early Nov; 1½hr) are conducted by Chartres expert Malcolm Miller (02 37 28 15 58; fax 02 37 28 33 03). English-language **audioguide tours** (25/45/70min €2.90/3.80/5.65) with three different themes can be hired from the cathedral bookshop. French-language **guided tours** (adult/senior/student & over 10 €6/4/3; 10.30am Tue-Sat, 3pm daily Apr-Oct, 2.30pm daily Nov-Mar) also depart from here.

The cathedral's west, north and south entrances have superbly ornamented triple **portals**, but the west entrance, known as the **Portail Royal**, is the only one that predates the 1194 fire. Carved from 1145 to 1155, its superb statues, whose features are elongated in the Romanesque style, represent the glory of Christ in the centre, and the Nativity and Ascension to the right and left, respectively. The structure's other main Romanesque feature is the 103m-high **Clocher Vieux** (Old Bell Tower; also called the Tour Sud, or 'South Tower'), which was begun in the 1140s. It is the tallest Romanesque steeple still standing anywhere.

A visit to the 112m-high **Clocher Neuf** (New Bell Tower; adult/18-25 yrs/under 18 €4.60/3.10/free, 1st Sun of certain months free; 9.30am-noon & 2-5.30pm Mon-Sat, 2pm-5.30pm Sun May-Aug, to 4.30pm Sep-Apr), which is also known as the Tour Nord (North Tower), is well worth the ticket price and the climb up the long spiral stairway. Access is just behind the cathedral

CHARTRES

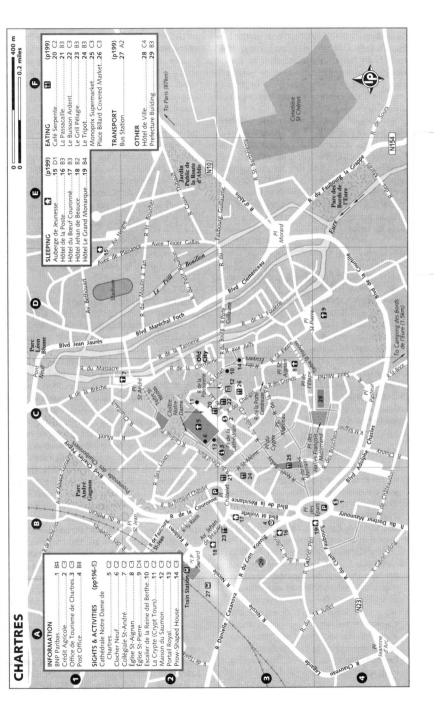

INFORMATION

BNP Paribas...............................1	B4
Crédit Agricole.........................2	C3
Office de Tourisme de Chartres....3	C3
Post Office................................4	B3

SIGHTS & ACTIVITIES (pp196–5)

Cathédrale Notre Dame de	
Chartres................................5	C3
Clocher Neuf............................6	C3
Collégiale St-André..................7	D1
Église St-Aignan......................8	C3
Église St-Pierre.......................9	D4
Escalier de la Reine del Berthe...10	C3
La Crypte (Crypt Tours)............11	C3
Maison du Saumon..................12	C3
Portail Royal...........................13	C3
Prow-Shaped House................14	C3

SLEEPING (p199)

Auberge de Jeunesse..............15	D1
Hôtel de la Poste....................16	B3
Hôtel du Bœuf Couronné.........17	B3
Hôtel Jehan de Beauce.............18	B2
Hôtel Le Grand Monarque.........19	B4

EATING (p199)

Café Serpente........................20	C2
La Passacaille.........................21	B3
Le Buisson Ardent...................22	C3
Le Grill Pélagie.......................23	B3
Le Tripot...............................24	B3
Monoprix Supermarket............25	C3
Place Billard Covered Market....26	C3

TRANSPORT

Bus Station...........................27	A2

OTHER

Hôtel de Ville........................28	C4
Prefecture Building.................29	B3

bookshop. A 70m-high platform on the lacy Flamboyant Gothic spire, built from 1507 to 1513 by Jehan de Beauce after an earlier wooden spire burnt down, affords superb views of the three-tiered flying buttresses and the 19th-century copper roof, turned green by verdigris.

The cathedral's 172 extraordinary **stained-glass windows**, almost all of which date back to the 13th century, form one of the most important ensembles of medieval stained glass in the world. The three most exquisite windows dating from the mid-12th century are in the wall above the west entrance and below the rose window. Survivors of the fire of 1194 (they were made some four decades before), the windows are renowned for the depth and intensity of their blue tones, which have become known as 'Chartres blue'.

The cathedral's 110m-long **crypt** (adult/senior, student & 7-18 yrs €2.60/2; 11am Mon-Sat, 2.15pm, 3.30pm, 4.30pm & 5.15pm daily late Jun-late Sep, 11am Mon-Sat, 2.15pm, 3.30pm & 4.30pm daily Apr-late Jun & late Sep-Oct, 11am Mon-Sat & 4.15pm daily Nov-Mar), a tombless Romanesque structure built in 1024 around a 9th-century predecessor, is the largest in France. Tours in French (with a written English translation) lasting 30 minutes start at **La Crypte** (☎ 02 37 21 56 33; 18 Cloître Notre Dame), the cathedral-run shop selling religious items and souvenirs, from April to October. At other times they begin

at the shop below the North Tower in the cathedral.

The most venerated object in the cathedral's possession is the **Ste-Voile** (Holy Veil) relic, which originally formed part of the imperial treasury of Constantinople but was offered to Charlemagne by the Empress Irene when the Holy Roman Emperor proposed marriage to her in AD 802. It has been in Chartres since 876 when Charles the Bald presented it to the town. The cathedral was built because the veil survived the 1194 fire. It is contained in a cathedral-shaped reliquary and displayed at the moment in a small side chapel off the eastern aisle. It doesn't look like much – a yellowish bolt of silk draped over a support – but as the focus of veneration among millions of the faithful for two millennia it is priceless. We only wonder how they keep it clean.

OLD CITY

Chartres' meticulously preserved old city is northeast and east of the cathedral along the narrow western channel of the River Eure, which is spanned by a number of footbridges. From rue Cardinal Pie, the stairway called **Tertre St-Nicolas** and **rue Chantault** – the latter lined with medieval houses – lead down to the empty shell of the 12th-century **Collégiale St-André**, a Romanesque collegiate church closed in 1791 and severely damaged in the early 19th century and again in 1944.

Rue de la Tannerie and its extension **rue de la Foulerie** along the river's east bank are lined with flower gardens, mill races and the restored remnants of riverside trades: wash houses, tanneries and the like. **Rue aux Juifs** (Street of the Jews) on the west bank has been extensively renovated. Half a block down the hill there's a riverside promenade and up the hill **rue des Écuyers** has many structures dating from around the 16th century, including a half-timbered, **prow-shaped house** at No 26, with its upper section supported by beams. At No 35 is the **Escalier de la Reine Berthe** (Queen Bertha's Staircase), a tower-like covered stairwell clinging to a half-timbered house that dates back to the early 16th century.

Rue du Bourg and **rue de la Poissonnerie** also have some old half-timbered houses; on the latter, look for the magnificent **Maison du Saumon** (Salmon House), also known as the Maison de la Truie qui File (House of the

---

SAVED BY RED TAPE

The magnificent cathedral at Chartres and its priceless stained glass managed to survive the ravages of the Revolution and the Reign of Terror for the same reason that everyday life in France can often seem so complicated: the French bureaucratic approach to almost everything.

As antireligious sentiment was reaching fever pitch in 1791, the Revolutionary government decided the cathedral deserved something more radical than mere desecration: demolition. The question was how to accomplish that. To find an answer, the government appointed a committee, whose admirably thorough members deliberated for four or five years. By then the Revolution's fury had been spent, and – to history's great fortune – the plan was shelved.

Spinning Sow), at No 10-12 with its carved consoles of the Angel Gabriel and Mary, Michael the Archangel slaying the dragon and, of course, the eponymous salmon. It is now a restaurant.

From **place St-Pierre**, you get a good view of the flying buttresses holding up the 12th- and 13th-century **Église St-Pierre** (place St-Pierre; 9am-noon & 2-6pm). Once part of a Benedictine monastery founded in the 7th century, it was outside the city walls and thus vulnerable to attack; the fortress-like, pre-Romanesque **bell tower** attached to it was used as a refuge by monks and dates from around 1000. The fine, brightly coloured **clerestory windows** in the nave, choir and apse date from the early 14th century.

Église St-Aignan (place St-Aignan; 9am-noon & 2-6pm), first built in the early 16th century, is interesting for its wooden barrel-vault roof (1625), arcaded nave and painted interior of faded blue and gold floral motifs (c 1870). The stained glass and the Renaissance **Chapelle de St-Michel** date from the 16th century.

Sleeping

Hôtel Le Grand Monarque (02 37 18 15 15; www .bw-grand-monarque.com; 22 place des Épars; s €85-107, d €105-120, tr €145-155; P ☒ ☐) This three-star hotel is supposedly Chartres' finest but some of the public areas and the guest rooms have a frayed feel and look to them.

Hôtel de la Poste (02 37 21 04 27; fax 02 37 36 42 17; 3 rue du Général Koenig; s with shower/bath €57/62, d €71.50/77.50, tr €94/117; P ☐) A two-star property just off the place des Épars, this place offers superb service and a central location.

Hôtel du Bœuf Couronné (02 37 18 06 06; fax 02 37 21 72 13; 15 place Châtelet; s/d with washbasin & toilet €27/30, with shower €40/50, with bath €43/57) This cosy, Logis de France–affiliated guesthouse in the centre of everything offers excellent value and has a memorable **restaurant** (menus €22 & €26; lunch & dinner to 11pm) with generous menus.

Hôtel Jehan de Beauce (02 37 21 01 41; www .contact-hotel-chartres.com; 19 av Jehan de Beauce; s with washbasin & toilet €29/36, s with shower €43-48, d with shower €50-55, s with bath €48-52, d with bath €55-59, tr €55-61; ☐) If you're looking for budget accommodation, this hotel has relatively clean, but very spartan singles, doubles and triples.

Auberge de Jeunesse (02 37 34 27 64; fax 02 37 35 78 85; 23 av Neigre; dm €11; ☒ ☐) Reception at the hostel, which is about 1.5km east of

the train station via blvd Charles Péguy and blvd Jean Jaurès, opens from 2pm to 10pm daily and curfew is 10.30pm in winter and 11.30pm in summer. To get there from the train station, take bus No 5 (direction: Mare aux Moines) to the Rouliers stop.

Eating

Le Tripot (02 37 36 60 11; 11 place Jean Moulin; starters €11-19, mains €13.50-24, lunch menu €15, dinner menus €22.50, €28.50 & €37.50; lunch Tue-Sun, dinner till 9.30pm Tue-Sat) This wonderful little place just down from the cathedral is one of the best bistros in Chartres.

Le Buisson Ardent (02 37 34 04 66; 10 rue au Lait; starters €9.50-16, mains €13-22, lunch menu €18, dinner menu €22; lunch Thu-Tue, dinner to 10.30pm Mon, Tue, Thu-Sat) 'The Burning Bush' is a charming, old-style place with good-value menus.

La Passacaille (02 37 21 52 10; 30 rue Ste-Même; starters €3.70-8.10, mains €9.90-12.40; lunch & dinner until 10.30pm) This welcoming Italian place has particularly good pizzas (€7.10 to €10.10) and fresh pasta (€8.10 to €9.50).

Le Grill Pélagie (02 37 36 07 49; 1 av Jehan de Beauce; starters €3.70-7.90, mains €9.90-14.80, menus €11.50-18.50; lunch & dinner till 11pm Mon-Sat) This is a popular place specialising in grills and Tex-Mex dishes such as guacamole and quesadillas (€6.50) and fajitas (€13.80 to €15.60).

Café Serpente (02 37 21 68 81; 2 Cloître Notre Dame; salads & omelettes €5.20-1150, dishes €13.50-15; 10am-1pm) The atmospheric Serpente brasserie and *salon de thé* (tearoom) is conveniently located opposite the cathedral.

There are a lot of food shops surrounding the **covered market** (place Billard; 7am-1pm Sat), just off rue des Changes south of the cathedral. The market itself dates from the early 20th century.

The **Monoprix** (21 rue Noël Ballay & 10 rue du Bois Merrain; 9am-7.30pm Mon-Sat) department store with two entrances has a supermarket on the ground floor.

Getting There & Away

Some 30 SNCF trains a day (20 on Sunday) link Paris' Gare Montparnasse (€11.80, 55 to 70 minutes) with Chartres, all of which pass through Versailles-Chantiers (€9.90, 45 to 60 minutes). The last train back to Paris leaves Chartres a bit after 9pm weekdays, just before 9pm on Saturday and sometime after 10pm on Sunday.

200

Far Northern France

CONTENTS

Lille	202
Calais	209
Inland Attractions	213
Côte d'Opale	215
Boulogne-sur-Mer	216
Dunkirk	219
Arras	221
Battle of the Somme Memorials	223
Amiens	227
Beauvais	230
Compiègne	231
Laon	233

The first bit of France seen by visitors coming from the UK is often Le Nord de France, densely populated and laden with declining rust-belt industries. One of the country's more fabled corners it isn't, but the area – made up of three historical regions, Flanders (Flandre or Flandres), Artois and Picardy (Picardie) – has lots to offer those willing to do a bit of exploring.

In the Middle Ages, France's far northern tip, together with much of Belgium and part of the Netherlands, made up a feudal principality known as Flanders. Many people in the area still speak Flemish – essentially Dutch with some variances in pronunciation and vocabulary – and, unlike anywhere else in France, the locals drink more beer than wine. This is especially true during the region's many annual festivals and *braderies* (carnivals; see p29 and p32).

It takes only two hours on the Eurostar to get from London to Lille, the region's surprisingly friendly commercial, cultural and culinary capital. Some 50km to the south, the 17th- and 18th-century Flemish-style buildings in picturesque Arras have no equal anywhere in France. Amiens, not far from a number of moving WWI memorials, is graced by one of France's most magnificent Gothic cathedrals.

Calais' prosperity as the premier trans-Channel port has come partly at the expense of Boulogne-sur-Mer, endowed with a picturesque old city, and Dunkirk (Dunkerque). The spectacular Côte d'Opale stretches from Calais to Boulogne along the Strait of Dover (Pas de Calais), the narrowest bit of the English Channel (La Manche). Inland, you'll find WWII sites, St-Omer, known for its basilica, and hilltop Cassel.

Just outside Greater Paris, Napoleon III's Compiègne is a popular destination for day trippers from Paris, Beauvais is known for its huge, unfinished cathedral, and Laon offers panoramic views from the walls of its hilltop old town.

HIGHLIGHTS

- Visit Lille's superb **museums** (p203), explore the city's **old town** (p203) and partake of its **restaurants** and **nightlife** (p206, p207)

- Ramble along the spectacular windswept **Côte d'Opale coastline** (p215) and gaze across the Channel to the white cliffs of Dover

- Explore Arras' Flemish-style **Grand' Place** and **place des Héros** (p221)

- Admire Amiens' breathtaking **Gothic cathedral** (p227) both inside and out

- Ponder the horrors and sacrifices of WWI at the evocative **Battle of the Somme memorials** (p223)

- Amble around Laon's hilltop fortifications and picturesque **old city** (p234)

Côte d'Opale ★
Lille ★
Arras ★
Battle of the Somme Memorials ★
Amiens ★
Laon ★

| ■ POPULATION: 5,900,000 | ■ AREA: 31,969 SQ KM |

FAR NORTHERN FRANCE

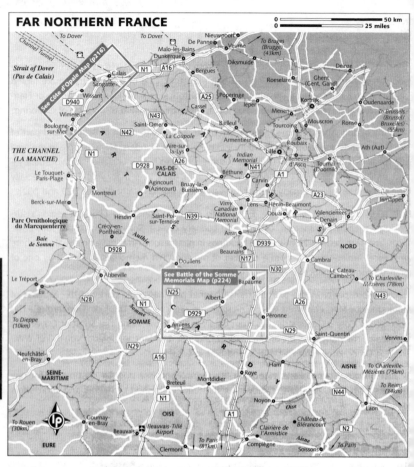

See Côte d'Opale Map (p216)

See Battle of the Somme
Memorials Map (p224)

0 — 50 km
0 — 25 miles

LILLE

pop 1 million

Lively, forward-looking Lille (Rijsel in Flemish) may be France's most underrated major city. Long an industrial centre, Lille's recent history shows how a grimy metropolis, its economy based on declining technologies, can transform itself – with the help of generous government investment – into a glittering and self-confident cultural hub. Highlights for the visitor include an attractive old town with a strong Flemish flavour, two renowned art museums, stylish shopping, some fine dining options and a happening, student-driven nightlife scene. In 2004 Lille (along with Genoa) was the EU's Cultural Capital of Europe.

Orientation

At the heart of Lille are three public squares: place du Général de Gaulle (also called the Grand' Place), place du Théâtre and place Rihour. The area of narrow streets north of place du Général de Gaulle is known as Vieux Lille (Old Lille).

Gare Lille-Flandres is about 400m southeast of place du Général de Gaulle; ultramodern Gare Lille-Europe is 500m east of the square.

Information
BOOKSHOPS

Le Furet du Nord (☎ 03 20 78 43 43; 15 place du Général de Gaulle) The largest bookstore in Europe. Has a wide selection of English-language works.

INTERNET ACCESS
Cybercafé Le Smiley (☎ 03 20 21 12 19; 2 rue Royale; per hr €6.10; ☯ noon-3am Mon-Sat, 4pm-midnight Sun) A lively, gay-friendly and very popular bar with a DJ on Friday nights. Lots of fun, though probably a bit too noisy for writing your thesis.

LAUNDRY
Zombified by too much art and culture? You can stare at the machines going round and round… There are laundrettes at 57 rue du Molinel, 4 rue Ovigneur and 13 rue de la Collégiale. They are open 7am to 7pm or 8pm.

MEDICAL SERVICES
Hôpital Roger Salengro (☎ 03 20 44 61 40/41; rue du Professeur Émile Laine; metro CHR B Calmette; ☯ 24hr) The *accueil urgences* (emergency room/casualty ward) of Lille's vast, 15-hospital Cité Hospitalière is 4km southwest of the city centre.
SOS Médecins (☎ 03 20 29 91 91; day/weekend/night/late-night €30/42.56/58.50/63.50) Doctors make house calls 24 hours a day.

MONEY
There are lots of commercial banks along rue Nationale. The tourist office changes money but the exchange rate is poor.

Exchange bureaus at the train stations:
Lille-Europe (ICE Bureau de Change; ☯ 7.30am-8pm Mon-Sat, 10am-8pm Sun) Near Accès (track access) C.
Lille-Flandres (Travelex bureau; ☯ 8am-8pm Mon-Fri, 10am-6pm Sat & Sun) Next to counter No 14.

POST
Branch Post Office (1 blvd Carnot) In the Chambre de Commerce building; changes money and has a Cyberposte.
Main Post Office (8 place de la République) Changes money and has a Cyberposte.

TOURIST INFORMATION
Tourist Office (☎ 03 59 57 94 00; www.lilletourism com; place Rihour; ☯ 9.30am-6.30pm Mon-Sat, 10am-noon & 2-5pm Sun & holidays) Occupies a remnant of the 15th-century Palais Rihour, a former résidence of the dukes of Burgundy; a war memorial forms the structure's eastern side. A brochure (€1) outlines four walking tours.

Sights
CITY CENTRE
North of place du Général de Gaulle, **Vieux Lille** gleams with restored 17th- and 18th-century houses. The old, brick residences along **rue de la Monnaie** now house chic shops (see also Musée de l'Hospice Comtesse, p205). Other

equally atmospheric streets include **rue de la Grande Chaussée** and **rue Esquermoise**.

The ornate, Flemish-Renaissance **Vieille Bourse** (Old Stock Exchange; place du Général de Gaulle), built in 1652, actually consists of 24 separate buildings. The courtyard in the middle hosts a **book market** (☯ 2-7pm Tue-Sun).

On the southern side of place du Général de Gaulle, the Art Deco home of **La Voix du Nord** (1932), the leading regional daily, has a gilded sculpture of the Three Graces on top. The goddess-topped **column** (1845) in the square's fountain commemorates the Austrian siege of Lille in 1792.

Nearby, place du Théâtre is dominated by the neoclassical **Opéra** and the tower-topped, neo-Flemish **Chambre de Commerce**, both of which date from the early 20th century.

PALAIS DES BEAUX-ARTS
The world-renowned **Fine Arts Museum** (☎ 03 20 06 78 00; place de la République; metro République Beaux Arts; adult/12-25 yrs/under 12 €4.60/3/free; ☯ 2-6pm Mon, 10am-6pm Wed, Thu, Sat & Sun, 10am-7pm Fri) possesses a superb collection of 15th- to 20th-century paintings, including works by Rubens and Van Dyck and a recently acquired Manet. On the ground floor, there's exquisite porcelain and faïence, much of it of local provenance; the basement houses classical archaeological finds, medieval statuary and intricate 18th-century models of the fortified cities of northern France and Belgium. Tickets are valid for the whole day. An audioguide costs €4.60; information sheets are available in each hall.

MUSÉE D'ART MODERNE
The highly regarded **Museum of Modern Art** (☎ 03 20 19 68 68; www.nordnet.fr/mam in French; 1 allée du Musée, Villeneuve-d'Ascq; adult/12-25 yrs €6.50/1.50,

---

LILLE MÉTROPOLE ALL INCLUSIVE
This pass, which comes in one-/two-/three-day versions (€20/30/45), gets you access to most of the museums in greater Lille, discounts on tickets to cultural events and unlimited use of public transport. The three-day version includes various sites in the Nord-Pas-de-Calais region and the use of regional TER trains. It is on sale at the Lille, Roubaix, Tourcoing and Watrelos tourist offices.

LILLE

0	400 m
0	0.2 miles

INFORMATION
Branch Post Office............................1 C4
Cybercafé Le Smiley...........................2 B4
Laundrette.......................................3 C5
Laundrette.......................................4 C5
Laundrette.......................................5 B3
Le Furet du Nord.............................6 C4
Main Post Office..............................7 B5
Tourist Office..................................8 B5

SIGHTS & ACTIVITIES   (pp203-5)
Chambre de Commerce.................(see 1)
Charles de Gaulle's Birthplace.........9 B3
Children's Amusement Park............10 A4
Citadelle..11 A3
Euralille..12 D4
La Voix du Nord............................13 C4
Musée de l'Hospice Comtesse.......14 B3
Opéra..15 C4
Palais des Beaux-Arts....................16 B5
Porte Royale.................................17 A4
Vieille Bourse...............................18 C4

SLEEPING   (pp205-6)
Auberge de Jeunesse.....................19 C5

Central Hôtel.................................20 B5
Grand Hôtel Bellevue....................21 B4
Hôtel Brueghel.............................22 C4
Hôtel de France............................23 C5
Hôtel Faidherbe............................24 C4
Hôtel Flandre-Angleterre................25 C4
Hôtel Le Floréal...........................26 C5
Hôtel Le Globe.............................27 A4
Hôtel Moulin d'Or.........................28 C5

EATING   (pp206-7)
À l'Huîtrière.................................29 C4
Aux Moules..................................30 C5
Boulangerie Notre Dame de la Treille.31 B4
Brasserie La Chicorée....................32 C4
Carrefour Hypermarket..................33 D4
El-Koutoubia................................34 B4
Fromagerie Philippe Olivier...........35 B4
La Pâte Brisée..............................36 B3
La Source....................................37 C5
La Voûte......................................38 C4
Le Hochepot................................39 B4
Match Supermarket.......................40 A5
Monoprix Supermarket..................41 C4
Outdoor Market............................42 B6

Outdoor Market.........................(see 43)
Wazemmes Food Market...............43 A6

DRINKING   ▢   (p207)
Café Oz.......................................44 C3
La Clave......................................45 B5
Le Balatum...................................46 B4
L'Illustration Café.........................47 B4
Vice Versa....................................48 B4

ENTERTAINMENT   ▢ (p207-8)
Cinéma Majestic............................49 B5
Cinéma Metropole.........................50 C4
FNAC Billetterie...........................51 C4
La Scala.......................................52 C3
Le 30..53 C4
Nouveau Siècle Concert Hall..........54 B4

SHOPPING   (p208)
Euralille Shopping Centre.............(see 12)

TRANSPORT   (pp208-9)
ADA...55 C5
Ch'ti Vélo....................................56 C4
DLM..57 C4
Eurolines Bus Stop.......................58 D4
Eurolines Office...........................59 C4
France Cars..................................60 C5
Rent-A-Car Système......................61 C5

10am-2pm 1st Sun of the month admission free; ☺ 10am-6pm Wed-Mon), situated in a sculpture park 8km east of central Lille, displays colourful, playful and just plain weird works by artists including Braque, Calder, Léger, Miró, Modigliani and Picasso. To get there, take metro line No 1 to Pont de Bois and then bus No 41 to Parc Urbain-Musée.

LA PISCINE MUSÉE D'ART ET D'INDUSTRIE
If Paris can turn a disused train station into a world-class museum, why not take an Art Deco municipal swimming pool (built 1927–32) – an architectural masterpiece inspired by civic pride and hygienic high-mindedness – and transform it into a temple of the arts? This innovative **museum** (☎ 03 20 69 23 60; http://museeroubaix.free.fr in French; 23 rue de l'Espérance, Roubaix; metro Gare Jean Lebas; adult €3, incl temporary exhibit €5; ☺ 11am-6pm Tue-Thu, 11am-8pm Fri, 1-6pm Sat & Sun), 11km northeast of central Lille, showcases fine arts, applied arts and sculpture in a delightful watery environment. The amusing website is worth a surf, even if you don't understand French.

MUSÉE DE L'HOSPICE COMTESSE
Housed in an attractive 17th-century poorhouse, the **Hospice Comtesse Museum** (☎ 03 28 36 84 00; 32 rue de la Monnaie; adult/12-25 yrs €2.30/1.50; ☺ 2-6pm Mon, 10am-12.30pm & 2-6pm Wed-Sun) features ceramics, faïence wall tiles and 17th- and 18th-century paintings, furniture and religious art. The **Salle des Malades** (Hospital Hall) is decorated with Lille tapestries.

CHARLES DE GAULLE'S BIRTHPLACE
The upper-middle-class house in which Charles André Marie Joseph de Gaulle (WWII Resistance leader, architect of the Fifth Republic and ferocious defender of French interests) was born in 1890 is being made into an interactive **museum** (☎ 03 28 38 12 05; www.maison-natale-degaulle.org in French; 9 rue Princesse; adult/child/under 9 €9/5/3) intended to present the French leader in the context of his times. Displays (supposed to be open from June 2005) include a dainty baptismal robe and the Citroën in which de Gaulle narrowly escaped an assassination attempt in 1961.

CITADELLE
The world's greatest 17th-century military architect, Sébastien le Prestre de Vauban (see p30), constructed this massive five-pointed, star-shaped **fortress** after the capture of Lille by French forces in 1667. It still functions as a military base but the outer ramparts (2.2km) are open to the public. On the southeastern side, the tree-shaded park has a **children's amusement park**.

Tours
The tourist office (p203) runs English-language **tours of Vieux Lille** (adult/under 16 €7/6; ☺ 2.30pm Sat). There are also **French-language tours** (☺ 3pm Sun May-Aug) of the Citadelle; the meeting point is Porte Royale, the citadel's main gate.

Bike tours (adult/under 16 €7/6) get rolling at 3pm on two Wednesdays a month from May to August.

Festivals & Events
The giants (p208) come out to cavort at the **Fêtes de Lille** street festival, which takes place on the third weekend of June. A flea market extraordinaire, the **Braderie** (below), is held on the first weekend of September. Christmas decorations and other goodies are sold at the **Marché de Noël** (Christmas market; place Rihour; ☺ late Nov-late Dec).

Sleeping
Thanks to the business market, many of the hotels are at their fullest from Monday

---

BRADERIE DE LILLE
During the first weekend in September, Lille's entire city centre is transformed into an enormous flea market – with stands selling antiques, local delicacies, handicrafts and more – called the Braderie de Lille. The extravaganza is believed to date from the Middle Ages, when the Lillois were permitted to hawk old garments from sundown to sunup for some extra cash.

Lille's biggest event of the year, the Braderie runs from 3pm on Saturday to midnight on Sunday, when street sweepers emerge to tackle the mounds of mussel shells and old *frites* (French fries) left behind by the merrymakers. Before the festivities, you can make room for all those extra calories by joining in the half-marathon held at 9am on Saturday. A free map of the market, *Braderie de Lille – Le Plan*, is available from the tourist office (p203).

to Thursday. There are lots of hotels facing Gare Lille-Flandres.

BUDGET

Auberge de Jeunesse (☎ 03 20 57 08 94; lille@fuaj.org; 12 rue Malpart; metro Mairie de Lille; dm with breakfast 1st night/subsequent nights €16.25/13.45; ✆ reception closed 11am-3pm, hostel closed late Dec–late Jan) The spartan rooms of a former maternity hospital, which are locked from 10am to 4.30pm, now house 165 beds (up to six beds per room). Toilets and showers are down the hall.

Hôtel de France (☎ 03 20 57 14 78; fax 03 20 57 06 01; 10 rue de Béthune; s/d from €30/35, with shower & toilet €39/46) You can't get more central than this two-star place; its 32 airy, functional rooms are one of the best deals in town. To get there by car, drive via place Rihour.

Central Hôtel (☎ 03 20 54 64 63; centralhotel@club-internet.fr; 91 rue Boucher de Perthes; s/d €32/40; ✆ reception closed noon-7pm Sun) With one star and 12 spacious rooms, this place – a short walk from the city centre – is a great option if you're looking for peace, quiet and the ambience of days gone by.

Hôtel Faidherbe (☎ 03 20 06 27 93; fax 03 20 55 95 38; 42 place de la Gare; d from €30, with shower & toilet €45) The one-star rooms are cheerful, compact and well-designed – but very simply furnished.

AUTHOR'S CHOICE

À l'Huîtrière (☎ 03 20 55 43 41; www.huitriere .fr; 3 rue des Chats Bossus; lunch menus €43, mains €30-48; ✆ noon-2pm & 7-9.30pm, closed Sun evening & 21 Jul-22 Aug) In 1928, the grandfather of the present owners turned to the nascent Art Deco movement – first exhibited (and named) in Paris just three years earlier – to find suitably elegant decoration for his fish shop, situated in the heart of Vieux Lille on the 'Street of the Hunchback Cats'. The sea-themed mosaics, stained glass and ceramics haven't changed since then, nor has the family's commitment to culinary excellence: the oak-panelled restaurant has held one or two Michelin stars continuously since 1930. Worth a look-in, even if you're not in the mood to dine on super-fresh seafood, accompanied by a wine or two from the 40,000-bottle cellar. Booking ahead is recommended on Friday night, Saturday and holidays.

Hôtel Le Globe (☎ 03 20 57 29 58; 1 blvd Vauban; d/q €35/50.50) The large rooms have French windows that look out on the Citadelle and (in most cases) chimneys that add a dollop of old-fashioned charm.

MID-RANGE

Hôtel Brueghel (☎ 03 20 06 06 69; www.hotel-brueghel .com in French; 5 parvis St-Maurice; d with shower from €44, s/d with shower & toilet €65/71) The two-star rooms are a mix of modern and antique, though they don't have as much Flemish charm as the lobby. The tiny wood-and-wrought-iron lift dates from the 1920s.

Hôtel Flandre-Angleterre (☎ 03 20 06 04 12; www .hotel-flandre-angleterre.fr in French; 13 place de la Gare; s/d €53/63) England certainly isn't bland and neither is Flanders, but the two-star rooms at this place, though comfortable, clean and pastel-hued, are rather lacking in character. Convenient for rail travellers.

Small two-star options near Gare Lille-Flandres include:

Hôtel Le Floréal (☎ 03 20 06 36 21; hotel-le-floreal@ wanadoo.fr; 21 rue Ste-Anne; s/d €50/65; ✆) A friendly nine-room place with linoleum floors.

Hôtel Moulin d'Or (☎ 03 20 06 12 67; francine.boidin@ wanadoo.fr; 15 rue du Molinel; s/d/tr €48/60/68) The 13 rooms are space efficient and unsurprising.

TOP END

Grand Hôtel Bellevue (☎ 03 20 57 45 64; grand.hotel .bellevue@wanadoo.fr; 5 rue Jean Roisin; d from €110) This three-star Best Western–affiliated establishment was grandly built in the early 20th century. A charmingly creaky *belle époque* lift trundles guests to the spacious rooms, which have high ceilings and antique-style French furnishings.

Eating

Lille – and especially Vieux Lille – has an excellent and varied selection of restaurants, many serving Flemish specialities such as *carbonnade* (braised beef stewed with beer and brown sugar); note that not many are open on Sunday.

VIEUX LILLE

Amid this brick-built area's cornucopia of eateries, rue Royale is *the* place for ethnic cuisine.

La Voûte (☎ 03 20 42 12 16; 4 rue des Débris St-Étienne; weekday lunch menus €9, other menus €12-16; ✆ closed Sun & Mon evening) The specialities of

Flanders, including *carbonnade* (€11), are served in a classic bistro ambience

Le Hochepot (☎ 03 20 54 17 59; 6 rue du Nouveau Siècle; menus €18-25; ☉ closed Sun & lunch Sat) This rustic but elegant restaurant specialises in Flemish dishes such as *coq à la bière* (chicken cooked in beer) and *carbonnade*.

La Pâte Brisée (☎ 03 20 74 29 00; 63-65 rue de la Monnaie) This relaxed and ever-popular eatery serves savoury and sweet tarts, salads, meat dishes and gratin in one-/two-/three-course *menus* (€7.90/11.30/14.70), including a glass of wine, *cidre* or beer.

El-Koutoubia (☎ 03 20 55 58 97; 16 rue Royale; mains €9-15; ☉ closed lunch Sun) Moroccan treats such as couscous and tajines are brought steaming to your table amid rich decoration.

SOUTH OF PLACE DE GAULLE

South of place du Général de Gaulle, the rue d'Amiens area is full of restaurants and pizzerias. West of the main post office, there are lots of cheap eats on lively, studenty rue d'Inkermann, rue Solférino and rue Masséna.

Brasserie La Chicorée (☎ 03 20 54 81 52; 15 place Rihour; menus €9.50-25.50; ☉ meals served 10-4.30am Sun-Thu, 10-6.30am Fri & Sat) Dine on regional treats such as *carbonnade* and *waterzoë* (three kinds of fish prepared with beer) at practically any time of the day or night.

Aux Moules (☎ 03 20 57 12 46; 34 rue de Béthune; ☉ meals served noon-midnight) An informal, brasserie-style place specialising in Flemish dishes such as rabbit in Kriek beer sauce with *frites* (€9), and, of course, mussels (€10 to €11.50). Kriek beer, a Flanders speciality, is made with sour cherries.

La Source (☎ 03 20 57 53 07; 13 rue du Plat; 2-course menus €7.50-11; ☉ meals served 11.30am-2pm Mon-Sat, 7-9pm Fri) This organic food shop serves vegetarian and fish *plats du jour* (daily specials).

SELF-CATERING

The old-time *flûtes* (thin baguette) and *pain à l'ancienne* (traditionally baked bread) at **Boulangerie Notre Dame de la Treille** (26 rue Basse; ☉ 7.30am-7.30pm, closed Sun & holidays) are especially scrumptious.

Wazemmes food market (place Nouvelle Aventure; metro Gambetta; ☉ 7am-6pm Tue-Thu, to 8pm Fri & Sat, to 2pm Sun) is a lively covered market 1.2km southwest of the centre. The city's largest **outdoor market** (☉ until 1.30pm or 2pm Tue, Thu & Sun) is outside, and there's another **outdoor market**

(place Sébastopol; ☉ Wed & Sat mornings) a bit nearer the centre than Wazemmes. Other shopping options:

Carrefour hypermarket (upper level, Euralille shopping centre; ☉ 9am-10pm Mon-Sat)

Fromagerie Philippe Olivier (3 rue du Curé St-Étienne; ☉ Tue-Sat)

Match supermarket (97 rue Solférino; ☉ 9am-9pm Mon-Sat)

Monoprix supermarket (31 rue du Molinel; ☉ 8.30am-8.30pm Mon-Sat)

Drinking

Lille has two main nightlife zones: Vieux Lille, where bars – including a number of gay places – tend to be small and oriented towards a fairly chic clientele; and, 750m southwest of the tourist office, rue Masséna and rue Solférino, where inexpensive high-decibel bars draw mainly students.

Café Oz (☎ 03 20 55 15 15; 33 place Louise de Bettignies; ☉ 2pm-3am Apr-Oct, 5pm-3am Nov-Mar, happy hour 6-9pm Mon-Sat) A branch of Paris' famous Australian bar, the Oz attracts lots of international students. Footy on the wide screen, Australiana on the walls, Fosters on tap (€2.60) – what more could you ask for?

L'Illustration Café (☎ 03 20 12 00 90; 18 rue Royale; ☉ 12.30pm-3am) This mellow but smoky bar, decorated with Art Nouveau woodwork and paintings by local artists, attracts *artistes* and *intellectuels* in the mood to exchange weighty ideas – or just shoot the breeze.

Le Balatum (☎ 03 20 57 41 81; 13 rue de la Barre; ☉ 4pm-2am, to 3am Fri & Sat) This laid-back, funky, dimly lit place is ideal for a tête-à-tête. The paintings and lamps were made by the very creative owner; theme nights occur frequently. Gay friendly.

La Clave (☎ 03 20 30 09 61; 31 rue Masséna; ☉ 6pm-3am Mon-Sat) The tone at this unpretentious bar is set by Caribbean-style murals, salsa, rumba and rum (€4). Draws a mixed-age crowd. Occasionally hosts live concerts.

Entertainment

Lille's free French-language entertainment guide, *Sortir*, is issued each Wednesday and available at the tourist office, cinemas and event venues.

Tickets for Lille's rich cultural offerings can be purchased at the **Fnac billetterie** (ticket agency; ☎ 03 20 15 58 59; www.fnac.com in French; ☉ 10am-7.30pm Mon-Sat), opposite 15 rue du Sec-Arembault.

CINEMAS

For nondubbed films:

Cinéma Majestic (☎ 08 92 08 00 73; 54 rue de Béthune) Has six projection spaces.

Cinéma Metropole (☎ 03 20 15 92 20, 08 36 68 00 73; 26 rue des Ponts des Comines) An art cinema.

GAY & LESBIAN

Lille has an open and active gay scene.

Vice Versa (☎ 03 20 54 93 46; 3 rue de la Barre; ☺ 11am-3am Mon-Fri, 2pm-3am Sat, 4pm-midnight Sun) This mellow and very popular place is a mainly gay *café alternatif* that takes eclectic décor – created by the staff and changed regularly – in bold new directions.

LIVE MUSIC

The **Orchestre National de Lille** (☎ 03 20 12 82 40; www.onlille.com in French) plays in the **Nouveau Siècle** concert hall (place Pierre Mendès-France; concert tickets adult €10-34, over 60 €16-29, under 26 from €8).

Le 30 (☎ 03 20 30 15 54; www.le30club-concert.fr.st in French; 30 rue de Paris; admission free; ☺ 9.30pm-4am Mon-Sat) With its soft modular couches, this bar looks like a 1960s airport VIP lounge. There's live jazz, blues and Latin American music nightly from 10.30pm to 1.30am (to 2.30am on Friday and Saturday).

NIGHTCLUBS

Thanks to a change in local bylaws, you no longer have to cross the Belgian frontier (eg to Gand) to dance past 4am, though some locals still do because, they say, the techno is edgier, the prices lower, substances more available and the closing time even later (1pm!).

La Scala (☎ 03 20 42 10 60; 32 place Louise de Bettignies; admission free; ☺ 11pm-8am Mon-Sat) Pulsating music and gyrating bodies under the arches of a brick cellar. Music and ages are varied.

Shopping

Lille's snazziest clothing and house-wares shops are in the old city and are especially thick along rue de la Monnaie and rue de la Grande Chausée.

The cavernous Euralille shopping centre, a project of the 90s designed by Dutch architect Rem Koolhaas, lies between the two train stations.

Getting There & Away

BUS

Eurolines (☎ 03 20 78 18 88; 23 parvis St-Maurice; ☺ 9.30am-12.30pm & 1.30-6pm, in summer to 7pm Mon-Fri, 1-6pm Sat) destinations include Brussels (€10, 1½ to two hours), Amsterdam (€34, six hours) and London (€39, six hours). Buses depart from the unsignposted bus parking lane on rue de Turin, on the northeast side of Gare Lille-Europe.

CAR

Driving into and out of Greater Lille is incredibly confusing, even with a good map.

THE GIANTS

In far northern France, *géants* (giants) – wickerwork body masks up to 8.5m tall animated by someone (or several someones) inside – emerge for local carnivals and on feast days to dance and add to the general merriment. Each has a name and a personality, usually based on the Bible, legends or local history. Giants are born, grow up, marry and have children (though never really die), creating, over the years, complicated family relationships. They serve as important symbols of town, neighbourhood and village identity.

Medieval in origin and also found in places as far afield as the Iberian Peninsula (eg in Catalonia, www.gegants.org), the Austrian Tyrol, Mexico, Brazil and India, giants have been a tradition in this region since the 16th century. Over 300 of the creatures, also known as *reuze* (in Flemish) and *gayants* (in Picard), now 'live' in French towns, including Arras, Boulogne, Calais, Cassel, Douai, Dunkirk and Lille; local associations look after their every need. Giants make appearances year-round, but your best chance to see them is at pre-Lenten carnivals, during Easter and at summer festivals: dates and places – as well as the latest marriages and births – appear in the annual French-language brochure *Le Calendrier des Géants* (www.geants-carnaval.org), available at tourist offices.

At the **Maison des Géants** (☎ 32-68 26 51 70; www.ath.be/maisondesgeants in French; 18 rue de Pintamont, Ath, Belgium; adult/student €4/3; ☺ 10am-noon & 1-5pm or 6pm Tue-Fri, 2-6pm Sat, Sun & holidays), 60km due west of Lille, you can see how the popular creatures are brought to life.

Parking at the Champ de Mars (the huge car park just east of the Citadelle) costs €2, including travel to the city centre on the Citadine bus line. Parking is free along the streets southwest of rue Solférino and up around the house where Charles de Gaulle was born (p205).

Car hire for less than the biggies charge is available at:

ADA (☎ 03 20 57 03 25; 2 rue Gustave Delory)
DLM (☎ 03 20 06 18 80; 32 place de la Gare)
France Cars (☎ 03 20 57 58 99; 114 rue du Molinel)
Rent-A-Car Système (☎ 03 20 40 20 20; 113 rue du Molinel)

TRAIN

Lille's two train stations are one stop apart on metro line No 2.

Gare Lille-Flandres is used by almost all regional services and most TGVs to Paris' Gare du Nord (€33.70 or €45.80 depending on service, 62 minutes, one to two hourly).

Gare Lille-Europe – topped by what looks like a 20-storey ski boot – handles pretty much everything else, including Eurostar trains to London, TGVs/Eurostars to Brussels (weekday/weekend €22.40/14.40, 38 minutes, 12 to 14 daily) and TGVs to Nice (€104.90 or €123.70, 7¼ hours, two direct daily). Fares are higher in peak periods.

For details on getting to/from Amiens, Arras, Boulogne, Calais, Dunkirk and St-Omer, see those sections.

Getting Around

There are plans to pedestrianise virtually the whole city centre by 2006 or 2007.

BICYCLE

Not-for-profit **Ch'ti Vélo** (☎ 03 28 53 07 49; 10 av Willy Brandt; ☑ 7.30am-7.30pm Mon-Fri, 9am-7.30pm Sat, Sun & holidays), on the northern side of Gare Lille-Flandres, rents city bikes for €5 per day.

BUS, TRAM & METRO

Lille's two speedy metro lines, two tramways and bus lines – several of which cross into Belgium – are run by **Transpole** (☎ 08 20 42 40 40), which has an **information window** (☑ closed Sun) in the Gare Lille-Flandres metro station.

Tickets (single/10 €1.15/10) are sold on buses but must be purchased (and validated in the orange posts) *before* boarding

a metro or tram. A Pass' Journée day pass costs €3.35. To buy a weekly pass (€11), valid from Monday to Sunday, you'll need a Carte Blanche photo ID (€1.50), available at the Transpole office.

CALAIS

pop 75,000

Never in the history of tourism have so many travellers passed through a place, and so few stopped to visit. Except for some better-than-expected restaurants, two small museums and Rodin's *The Burghers of Calais* (below), there's not very much to encourage the 22 million people who travel by way of Calais each year to stop and explore. However, the town – a mere 34km from the English town of Dover (Douvres in French) – does make a convenient base for visiting French Flanders and the Channel coast.

In the 14th century the English were so covetous of Calais – in part to control its audacious pirates – that King Edward III took over the town in 1347, thus beginning over two centuries of English rule.

THE BURGHERS OF CALAIS

Rodin sculpted *Les Bourgeois de Calais* in 1895 to honour six local citizens who, in 1347, after eight months of holding off the besieging English forces, surrendered themselves and the keys to the starving city to Edward III of England. Their hope: that by sacrificing themselves they might save the town and its people. Moved by the entreaties of his consort, Philippa, Edward eventually spared both the Calaisiens and their six brave leaders.

Actually, you don't have to visit Calais' Flemish Renaissance-style town hall (1911–25) to see Rodin's masterpiece. Other casts of the six emaciated but proud figures, with varying degrees of copper-green patina (many were made posthumously), can be seen in London (next to the Houses of Parliament), the USA (New York, Washington, Philadelphia, Omaha, Pasadena, Stanford University) and even Japan (Shizuoka Prefecture). So moved by the work that you want one at home? You can buy a 66cm-high copy from www.bronzedirect.com – a bargain at US$2500!

CALAIS

0 ————— 400 m
0 ————— 0.2 miles

The Channel (La Manche)

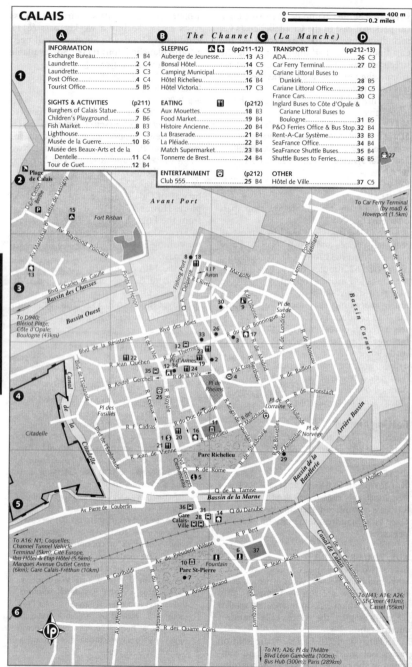

INFORMATION
Exchange Bureau.....................1 B4
Laundrette...............................2 C4
Laundrette...............................3 C3
Post Office...............................4 C4
Tourist Office...........................5 B5

SIGHTS & ACTIVITIES (p211)
Burghers of Calais Statue..........6 C5
Children's Playground................7 B6
Fish Market...............................8 B3
Lighthouse...............................9 C3
Musée de la Guerre.................10 B6
Musée des Beaux-Arts et de la
  Dentelle..............................11 C4
Tour de Guet..........................12 B4

SLEEPING (pp211-12)
Auberge de Jeunesse.............13 A3
Bonsaï Hôtel...........................14 C5
Camping Municipal.................15 A2
Hôtel Richelieu.......................16 B4
Hôtel Victoria.........................17 C3

EATING (p212)
Aux Mouettes.........................18 B3
Food Market............................19 B4
Histoire Ancienne....................20 B4
La Braserade...........................21 B4
La Pléiade...............................22 B4
Match Supermarket.................23 B4
Tonnerre de Brest....................24 B4

ENTERTAINMENT (p212)
Club 555.................................25 B4

TRANSPORT (pp212-13)
ADA..26 C3
Car Ferry Terminal...................27 D2
Cariane Littoral Buses to
  Dunkirk................................28 B5
Cariane Littoral Office.............29 C5
France Cars.............................30 C3
Ingland Buses to Côte d'Opale &
  Cariane Littoral Buses to
  Boulogne..............................31 B5
P&O Ferries Office & Bus Stop.32 B4
Rent-A-Car Système.................33 B3
SeaFrance Office.....................34 B4
SeaFrance Shuttle Buses..........35 B4
Shuttle Buses to Ferries...........36 B5

OTHER
Hôtel de Ville.........................37 C5

Avant Port

Fort Risban

To Car Ferry Terminal
(by road) &
Hoverport (1.5km)

Av. Maréchal & Lattre de Lassigny

Av. Raymond Poincaré

Blvd Charles de Gaulle

Bassin des Chasses

To D940;
Blériot Plage;
Côte d'Opale;
Boulogne (43km)

Bassin Ouest

Ports H Hénon

Fishing Port

R. de Dépelière

R E Rivet

R. Margollé

R. Avron

R.I.P

Plage
de Calais

Dig. de Carron Béthune

Bassin Carnot

R du Q. de la Loire

Q. de la Loire

Pont
Vetillard

R. Lamy

R. de la Tamise

R. de Londres

R. de Moscou

Pl de
Suède

Blvd des Alliés

Blvd de la Resistance

R. de la Mer

R. du Cdt Bonningue

R. de Madrid

R. Berthois

R. de Croix

R. de Thermes

Pl d'Armes

R. Jean Quéhen

R. André Gerchell

R. de la Paix

Pl de
Rheims

R. Royale

R. Leveux

R. du Duc de Guise

R. F Cadras

R. Richelieu

R. Seig. du Maréchau

Pl de
Lorraine

R. de Ballon

R. de Cronstadt

R. de Hollande

Pl de
Norvège

R. Amsterdam

Pl des
Fusillés

Citadelle

Blvd de l'Esplanade

Canal de la Citadelle

Parc Richelieu

R. de Rome

Bassin de la
Batellerie

Arrière Bassin

Q. de la Tamise

R. Mollien

R. Descartes

Bassin de la Marne

Av. Pierre de Coubertin

R Georges Clemenceau

Gare
Calais-
Ville

Q. du Danube

R P Bert

R. Jean Jaurès

Blvd Léon Gambetta

Q. de la Gendarmerie

Q. du Commerce

Canal de Calais

To A16; N1; Coquelles;
Channel Tunnel Vehicle
Terminal (5km); Cité Europe;
Ibs Hôtel & Etap Hôtel (5.5km);
Marques Avenue Outlet Centre
(6km); Gare Calais-Fréthun (10km)

Av. du Président Wilson

R. Garibaldi

R. du Onze

Av. Alfred Delcluze

R. des Quarre Coins

Parc St-Pierre

Fountain

R. Aristide Briand

Blvd Jacquard

To N43; A16; A26;
St-Omer (41km);
Cassel (55km)

To N1; A26; Pl du Théâtre;
Blvd Léon Gambetta (100m);
Bus Hub (300m); Paris (289km)

Orientation

Gare Calais-Ville (the train station) is 650m south of the main square, place d'Armes, and 700m north of Calais' relatively untouristed commercial district (around blvd Léon Gambetta and the place du Théâtre bus hub).

The car ferry terminal is 1.5km northeast of place d'Armes; the Hoverport (for SeaCats) is another 1.5km further out. The Channel Tunnel's vehicle loading area is about 6km southwest of the town centre.

Information

LAUNDRY

Be fully prepared for British border formalities – cross the Channel with clean undies. There are laundrettes on the eastern side of place d'Armes (open 7am to 9pm) and at 36 rue de Thermes (open 7am to 7pm and longer in summer).

MONEY

Currency exchange is possible aboard car ferries and SeaCats. In town, banks (open Tuesday to Friday and Saturday morning) are clustered along rue Royale.
Exchange Bureau (5 rue Royale; ⊙ 9.30am-6pm Mon-Sat)

POST

Post Office (place de Rheims) Has a Cyberposte terminal.

TOURIST INFORMATION

Tourist Office (☎ 03 21 96 62 40; www.calais-cotedopale.com; 12 blvd Georges Clemenceau; ⊙ 9am-7pm Mon-Sat, 10am-1pm Sun & holidays Easter-Aug, 10am-1pm & 2-6.30pm Mon-Sat Sep- Easter)

Sights & Activities

You can watch huge car ferries sailing majestically towards Dover from Calais' sandy cabin-lined **beach**, which begins 1km northwest of place d'Armes and is linked to town by a **bike path**. The sand continues westward along 8km-long, dune-lined **Blériot Plage**, named after pioneer aviator Louis Blériot, who began the first ever trans-Channel flight from here in 1909. Both beaches are served by bus No 3.

If you're willing to burn calories for a superb panorama, you can climb the 271 stairs to the top of the **lighthouse** (☎ 03 21 34 33 34; blvd des Alliés; adult/5-15 yrs €2.50/1.50; ⊙ 10amnoon & 2-5.30pm or 6.30pm Sat, Sun & holidays year-round,

2-5.30pm or 6.30pm Mon-Fri Jun-Sep, Wed Oct-May & during school holidays), built in 1848.

You won't be exhausted by a visit to the **Musée des Beaux-Arts et de la Dentelle** (Museum of Fine Arts & Lace; ☎ 03 21 46 48 40; 25 rue Richelieu; adult/student €3/1.50, admission free Wed; ⊙ 10am-noon & 2-5.30pm Mon & Wed-Fri, 10am-noon & 2-6.30pm Sat, 2-6.30pm Sun), with exhibits that focus on mechanised lace-making (the first machines were smuggled to Calais from England in 1816), 15th- to 20th-century painting and modern sculptures, including pieces by Rodin.

World War II artefacts (uniforms, weapons, proclamations) fill the display cases of the **Musée de la Guerre** (☎ 03 21 34 21 57; adult/student/family of 4 incl audioguide €6/5/14; ⊙ 10am-6pm May-Aug, 11am-5.30pm Apr & Sep, 11am-5pm Wed-Mon mid-Feb–Mar, noon-5pm Wed-Mon Oct–mid-Nov), housed in a concrete bunker that used to be German naval headquarters. It sits incongruously in **Parc St-Pierre**, next to a *boules* ground and a **children's playground**.

The 13th-century **Tour de Guet** (watchtower; place d'Armes) is a rare remnant of pre–20th-century Calais – the rest of the town was virtually demolished during WWII.

Sleeping

A number of two-star hotels can be found along rue Royale.

Auberge de Jeunesse (☎ 03 21 34 70 20; www.auberge-jeunesse-calais.com in French; av Maréchal de Lattre de Tassigny; dm with breakfast €15.20; ⊙ 24hr; **P**) Modern and well equipped, and just 200m from the beach, its a good source of information on local events. Bikes can be rented in the warm season. It is served by bus No 3.

Hôtel Richelieu (☎ 03 21 34 61 60; www.hotel-richelieu-calais.com; 17 rue Richelieu; d/2-room q from €46/92) At this quiet two-star place, the 15 cheery rooms, each one unique, are outfitted with antique furniture redeemed by the owner from local markets.

Bonsai Hotel (☎ 03 21 96 10 10; www.bonsai-hotel.tm.fr; 2 quai du Danube; d/tr €27/31) This prefab place is the ultimate in charmless ticky-tacky cheapness. Sneezing within 20cm of the pressboard walls could possibly result in structural damage to the building. In triple rooms, the third bed is a bunk above the double bed.

In Coquelles next to the Cité Europe shopping mall (and near the Channel Tunnel vehicle loading area) are **Ibis Hôtel** (☎ 03 21 46 37

AUTHOR'S CHOICE

Hôtel Victoria (☎ 03 21 34 38 32; hotelvic toria@wanadoo.fr; 8 rue du Commandant Bon- ningue; d from €26, with shower & toilet €37) The 14 well-lit and comfortable two-star rooms have walls thin enough to let you get a good sense of how your fellow guests are getting on with each other. One theory has it that the mere act of crossing the Chan- nel does wonders for the ardour of many Brits, though it's not clear whether the hotel's namesake would approve of this, or even understand what you were talking about if you tried to explain it to her. The joyous sounds of schoolchildren carousing in the school playground across the street greet you bright and early, a reminder of the many happy children on both sides of the Channel who owe their very existence to the seductive romance of this seemingly average hotel.

00; place de Cantorbéry; d €49) and **Etap Hôtel** (☎ 08 92 68 30 59; place de Cantorbéry; s/d €29/35).

CAMPING

Camping Municipal (☎ 03 21 97 89 79; av Raymond Poincaré; per adult/site €3.24/2.27; ☺ year-round) Oc- cupies a grassy but soulless site inside Fort Risban. Served by bus No 3.

Eating

Calais is a good place for a first or last meal on the Continent. Rue Royal and place d'Armes are lined with eateries.

La Pléiade (☎ 03 21 34 03 70; 32 rue Jean Quéhen; 3-/4-/6-course menus €22/35/50; ☺ closed Sun & Mon) Some loyal customers come over from Eng- land just to dine here on *filet de bar rôti* (sea bass with almond sauce and a dollop of *pistou*) and other fish dishes.

Aux Mouettes (☎ 03 21 34 67 59; 10 rue Jean Pierre Avron; menus €15-32; ☺ closed Mon & dinner Sun) Fish- erfolk sell their daily catch across the street at the quay – easy to see why this unassum- ing place is known for serving only the very freshest fish.

Histoire Ancienne (☎ 03 21 34 11 20; 20 rue Royale; 2-/3-/5-course menus €11/17.50/30; ☺ closed Sun & din- ner Mon) Specialising in meat and fish dishes grilled over a wood fire, this Paris-style bis- tro also has *pieds de cochon* (pigs' trotters) and *escargots à l'ail* (snails with garlic).

La Braserade (☎ 03 21 97 02 59; 8 rue Jean de Vienne; menus from €14.94; ☺ closed lunch Mon & Sat) Gussied up like an Alpine chalet, this restaurant serves reasonably priced Savoyarde dishes such as *raclette* (melted cheese with cold cuts and pickles) and *braserade* (meat dishes you barbecue yourself at the table). The pricier *menus* (€17.53 to €29.73) include access to an all-you-can-eat seafood buffet and a bottom- less glass of red wine, beer or soft drink.

Tonnerre de Brest (☎ 03 21 96 95 35; 16 place d'Armes; crepes €2.50-6.80; ☺ closed Mon except Jul & Aug) At this rustic informal eatery, run by two sisters, you can wash down with *cidre* 19 kinds of savoury *galettes* and 27 sorts of sweet crepes.

SELF-CATERING

Feed yourself by shopping at the **food mar- ket** (place d'Armes; ☺ Wed & Sat morning) or **Match supermarket** (place d'Armes; ☺ 9am-7.30pm Mon-Sat year-round, 9am-noon Sun Jul & Aug)

Entertainment

Club 555 (☎ 03 21 34 74 60; www.le555.com in French; 63 rue Royale; admission incl one drink €10; ☺ 11pm- 5am Tue-Sun) This spot, one of the nightspots and bars along rue Royale, is a '70s-style discotheque with flashing lights, space for 700 revellers and plenty of banquettes for hanging out. The music is mixed; there's a theme party every Friday.

Getting There & Around

For details on getting across the Channel, see p917 and p920.

BOAT

Every day, 45 to 54 car ferries from Dover dock at the busy car ferry terminal, about 1.5km northeast of place d'Armes. Com- pany bureaus:

P&O Ferries car ferry terminal (☎ 03 21 46 10 10; ☺ 24hr); place d'Armes (☎ 01 55 69 82 28; 41 place d'Armes)

SeaFrance car ferry terminal (☎ 03 21 46 80 05; ☺ 6am-10.45pm); place d'Armes (☎ 03 21 19 42 42; 2 place d'Armes)

Shuttle buses (€1.50 for P&O) coordinated with departure times link Gare Calais-Ville and each company's office at place d'Armes with the car ferry terminal.

Hoverspeed's car-carrying SeaCats to Dover (operational from mid-March to 22

December) use the **Hoverport** (high-speed ferry terminal; ☎ 03 21 46 14 00, 008 00 12 11 12 11), which is 3km northeast of the town centre. Alas, hovercraft – the pride of British maritime engineering in the 1960s – no longer lumber up the beach here. *Some* SeaCat arrivals and departures are met by shuttle buses to/from Gare Calais-Ville (€1.50).

BUS
Inglard (☎ 03 21 96 49 54; car ferry terminal) links Calais' train station with the beautiful Côte d'Opale (p215) and Boulogne (€4.70, 1¼ hours; three daily except Sunday and holidays), stopping at 75 blvd Daunou in Boulogne.

    Cariane Littoral (☎ 03 21 34 74 40; office 10 rue d'Amsterdam) operates express services from Calais' train station to Boulogne (€6.40, 40 minutes, five daily Monday to Friday, two on Saturday), where bus stops are at the train station and place Dalton, and Dunkirk (€7, 40 minutes, 12 daily Monday to Friday, three on Saturday).

CAR & MOTORCYCLE
To reach the Channel Tunnel's vehicle loading area at Coquelles, follow the road signs on the A16 to the Tunnel Sous La Manche (Tunnel under the Channel) at exit No 13.

    The following companies generally have cheaper walk-in rates than the car ferry terminal offices of Avis, Budget, Europcar, Hertz and National-Citer, which – like their Hoverport outlets – are not always staffed.

ADA (☎ 03 21 36 50 12; 15 rue de Thermes)
France Cars (☎ 03 21 96 08 00; 47 blvd des Alliés)

Rent-A-Car Système (☎ 03 21 34 41 99; 1 rue de Thermes)

TAXI
To order a cab, call **Taxis Radio Calais** (TRC; ☎ 03 21 97 13 14).

TRAIN
Calais has two train stations: Gare Calais-Ville in the city centre; and Gare Calais-Fréthun, a TGV station 10km southwest of town near the Channel Tunnel entrance. They are linked by the free Navette TER, which is a bus service operated by Cariane Littoral.

    From Gare Calais-Ville you can travel to Amiens (€19.70, two to 2½ hours, two or three direct Monday to Saturday), Arras (€16.90, two hours, 10 daily Monday to Friday, six or seven daily Saturday and Sunday), Boulogne (€6.60, 27 to 48 minutes, 15 to 19 daily Monday to Saturday, nine daily Sunday), Dunkirk (€7, 50 minutes, four daily Monday to Friday, two on Saturday) and Lille-Flandres (€14, 1¼ hours, 18 daily Monday to Friday, 11 on Saturday, seven on Sunday).

    Calais-Fréthun is served by TGVs to Paris' Gare du Nord (€35.50 or €47.90, 1½ hours, five daily Monday to Saturday, two on Sunday) as well as the Eurostar to London.

INLAND ATTRACTIONS
You don't have to stray far from the Channel to find beautiful countryside, typical French towns and WWII relics.

SHOP TILL YOU DROP IN CALAIS

Calais' shops and hypermarkets supply day-tripping *rosbifs* (Britons) with everything except, perhaps, roast beef. Items eagerly sought 'on the Continent' include delicious edibles (terrines, cheeses, gourmet-prepared dishes) and drinks (wine, champagne, beer and spirits) that are hard to find – or much more expensive – in the land of the pound sterling.

    The enormous steel-and-glass shopping centre **Cité Europe** (☎ 03 21 46 47 48; www.cite europe .com; boulevard du Kent; ⏲ 10am-8pm Mon-Thu, 10am-9pm Fri, 9am-8pm Sat) is in Coquelles, next to the vehicle-loading area for the Channel Tunnel. Its 130 shops include a vast **Carrefour hypermarket** (⏲ 9am-10pm Mon-Sat) and wine shops where buying alcohol in bulk to carry home in the boot is made easy.

    Right nearby is the new **Marques Avenue** (☎ 03 21 17 07 70; www.marquesavenue.com; ⏲ 10am-8pm Mon-Thu, 10am-9pm Fri, 9am-8pm Sat) outlet centre, which boasts discount clothing and accessories by 80 designer brands.

    To get to Cité Europe by car, take the A16 to exit Nos 12 or 14; for Marques Avenue, use exit No 12.

St-Omer
pop 14,400

St-Omer, said to be the first truly French town you come to after landing at Calais – its river, the Aa, is the certainly first one you'll come across in any alphabetised list of the world's waterways – is justly renowned for its richly furnished 13th- to 15th-century **basilica** (until at least 5pm), formerly a cathedral. The only major Gothic church in the region, it's a real gem: much of the woodwork, including the main altar and breathtaking baroque organ, dates from the 1700s. The mechanism of the mechanical clock, in the north transept, was put together back in 1558.

The **tourist office** (03 21 98 08 51; www.tour isme.fr/saint-omer; 4 rue du Lion d'Or; 9am-6pm Mon-Sat, 10am-1pm Sun & holidays Easter-Sep, 9am-12.30pm & 2-6pm Mon-Sat except holidays Oct-Easter) is one block north of place Foch, the vast square in front of the **town hall** (1830).

The **Musée Sandelin** (03 21 38 00 94; http://m3.dnsalias.com/sandelin in French; 14 rue Carnot; adult/15-25 yrs €4.50/3; 10am-noon & 2-6pm Wed-Sun, to 8pm Thu), with its recently renovated displays that include ceramics, *objets d'art* and paintings, is housed in a harmonious townhouse built in 1776; a number of rooms are furnished in the style that suited the refined lifestyle of the Enlightenment elite. To get there from place Foch, walk a block south and then a long block east.

The **Musée Henri Dupuis** (03 21 38 24 13; 9 rue Henri Dupuis; adult/15-25 yrs €2.50/1.50; 10am-noon & 2-6pm Wed-Sun), midway between place Foch and the basilica, displays bric-a-brac (ceramics, minerals) assembled during the late 19th century by a wealthy local.

A bit northeast of town, the market gardens of the swampy **Marais Audemarois**, rich in wildlife (including 250 kinds of bird, 19 species of dragonfly and 11 types of bat), can be visited on foot or by rowboat.

There are many good-value restaurants (lunch *menus* €10 to €13), frequented by repeat visitors from the UK, around the perimeter of place Foch and adjacent place P Bonhomme, and along rue Louis Martel.

Le Vivier (03 21 95 76 00; levivier@wanadoo.fr; 22 rue Louis Martel; d €52), a block south of the town hall, has seven comfortable but standard two-star rooms and a fine fish and seafood **restaurant** (menus €16-35; closed Sun evening). A lively **food market** (place Foch) is held every Saturday morning.

St-Omer's train station, 1.5km northeast of the town hall, is on the rail line (15 daily Monday to Friday, seven daily Saturday and Sunday) linking Calais (€6.40, 30 minutes) with Lille-Flandres (€9.50, 50 minutes).

La Coupole

A subterranean V2 launch site just five minutes' flying time from London – almost (but not quite) put into operation in 1944 – now houses **La Coupole** (03 21 12 27 27; www.lacoupole .com; adult/5-16 yrs €9/6; 9am-6pm, to 7pm Jul & Aug, closed 25 Dec-2 Jan), an exhibition centre that uses the latest museological techniques and lots of moving images to present:

- Life in northern France during the Nazi occupation
- The German's secret programmes to build V1 and V2 rockets (which could fly at 650km/h and an astounding 5780km/h respectively).
- The post-war conquest of space with the help of V2 rocket technology – and V2 engineers.

Built by POWs (mainly Soviets), the complex is buried deep in a hillside and is topped by a 72m-wide concrete dome (thus the name). English commentary is provided by a headset; a full tour of the site takes about 2½ hours.

La Coupole is 5km south of St-Omer (the circuitous route is signposted but confusing) just outside the town of Wizernes, near the intersection of the D928 and the D210. From the A26, take exit No 3 or 4.

Cassel
pop 2200

The compact and very Flemish village of Cassel, on a hilltop 57km east of Calais, affords panoramic views of the verdant Flanders plain. It served as Maréchal Ferdinand Foch's headquarters at the beginning of WWI and, in 1940, was the site of intensive rearguard resistance by British troops defending Dunkirk during the evacuation.

The **tourist office** (03 28 40 52 55; www.ot-cassel.fr in French; 23 Grand' Place; 8.30am-noon & 1.30-5.30pm Mon-Fri year round, plus 9am-noon & 2-5.30pm Sat May-Sep & 2.30pm–5.30pm Sun Jun-Sep) is on the main square.

Eight or 10 generations ago, wheat flour was milled and linseed oil pressed just as it is today at the wooden **moulin** (windmill; adult/

child €2.80/2.40; 🕙 10am-noon & 2-5.30pm Apr-Sep & during school holidays, open Sat noon & Sun Oct–mid-Dec & mid-Jan–Mar), perched on the highest point in town to catch the wind. The 30-minute, hands-on tour is noisy but interesting.

Le Foch (☎ 03 28 42 47 73; www.hotel-foch.net; 41 Grand' Place; d €72, if you also take dinner €62) has six charming rooms with an antique feel. The elegant **restaurant** (menus €16-32; 🕙 closed dinner Sun & perhaps Tue) specialises in traditional French cuisine.

Taverne Flamande (☎ 03 28 42 42 59; 34 Grand' Place; menus €14-22; 🕙 closed Wed & dinner Tue) serves tasty Flemish dishes in a dining room that dates from 1933.

CÔTE D'OPALE

The 40km of cliffs, sand dunes and beaches between Calais and Boulogne, known as the Opal Coast because of the ever-changing interplay of greys and blues in the sea and sky, are a dramatic and beautiful introduction to France. The coastal peaks (frequently buffeted by gale-force winds), wide beaches and rolling farmland are dotted with the remains of Nazi Germany's Atlantic Wall, a chain of fortifications and gun emplacements built to prevent the Allied invasion that in the end took place in Normandy. The seashore has been attracting British beach lovers for over a century.

Part of the **Parc Naturel Régional Nord-Pas-de-Calais**, the Côte d'Opale area is criss-crossed by hiking paths, including the GR Littoral trail that hugs the coast. Some routes are also suitable for mountain biking and horse riding. Each village along the Côte d'Opale has at least one camping ground.

By car, the D940 offers some spectacular vistas. Inglard buses link all the sights and villages mentioned below with Calais and Boulogne (see p213).

Sights

The Channel Tunnel slips under the Strait of Dover 8km west of Calais at the village of **Sangatte**, known for its wide beach. Southwest of there, the coastal dunes give way to cliffs that culminate in windswept, 134m-high **Cap Blanc-Nez**, which affords spectacular views of the Bay of Wissant, the port of Calais, the Flemish countryside (pockmarked by Allied bomb craters) and the cliffs of Kent. The grey **obelisk** honours the WWI Dover Patrol.

The well-off and very French seaside resort of **Wissant** (☎ tourist office 03 21 82 48 00), a good base for walks in the rolling countryside, boasts a vast fine-sand beach – in 55 BC Julius Caesar launched his invasion of Britain from here. **Hôtel Le Vivier** (☎ 03 21 35 93 61; www.levivier.com; place de l'Église; d with breakfast from €54), across the street from the church, has mid-sized pastel rooms and a nautically themed **restaurant** (menus €25-35; 🕙 closed Tue & Wed) specialising in fish and seafood.

Topped by a lighthouse and a radar station serving the 600 ships that pass by each day, the 45m-high cliffs of **Cap Gris-Nez** are only 28km from the English coast. The name 'Grey Nose' is a corruption of the archaic English 'craig ness', meaning 'rocky promontory'. The area is a stopping-off point for millions of migrating birds.

The village of **Ambleteuse**, on the northern side of the mouth of Slack River, is blessed by a lovely beach once defended from attack by 17th-century **Fort Mahon**. Just south of town is a protected area of grass-covered dunes known as **Dunes de la Slack**.

THE BATTLE OF AGINCOURT

Agincourt (Azincourt) entered the history books on 25 October 1415 when English archers and men-at-arms – led by King Henry V – inflicted an overwhelming defeat on superior French forces in one of the bloodiest engagements of the Hundred Years' War. Against minimal losses of their own, the axe- and sword-wielding English killed 6000 of their opponents, whose cavalry and foot soldiers were weighed down by heavy armour made all the more cumbersome by the soggy terrain.

The **Centre Historique Médiéval Azincourt** (☎ 03 21 04 41 12; www.azincourt-medieval .com; adult/under 16 €6.50/5; 🕙 9am-7pm Jul & Aug, 10am-5pm or 6pm Sep-Jun) uses the latest audiovisual technology (English available) and copies of 15th-century armaments to bring alive both the battle and its context. Is the steep admission fee needed (if partial) revenge for France's battlefield debacle?

The **Champ de Bataille** (battlefield), 2.5km southeast of the museum, along the D71 (at the intersection of the D107-E2 and the D104), is marked by a granite column and a viewpoint indicator showing the battle's progression.

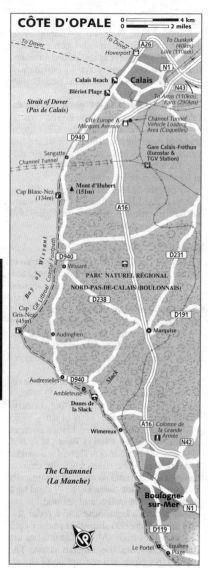

CÔTE D'OPALE

The well-organised **Musée 39-45** (☎ 03 21 87 33 01; http://musee3945.com; adult/7-14 yrs €6/4.30; ☀ 9.30am or 10am-6pm Apr–mid-Oct, Sat & Sun only Mar & mid-Oct–Nov), devoted to the wartime period, has a 30-minute English-language film and oodles of authentic paraphernalia. Make sure you see the displays of field rations – yum!

BOULOGNE-SUR-MER
pop 44,000

Boulogne, by far the most interesting of France's Channel ports, makes a decent first stop in France, especially if combined with a swing through the Côte d'Opale. Most of the city is an uninspiring mass of postwar reconstruction, but the attractive Ville Haute (Upper City), perched high above the rest of town, is girded by a 13th-century wall. The city is also home to one of France's premier aquariums.

Orientation

Central Boulogne consists of the hilltop Ville Haute and, on the flats below, the Basse Ville (Lower City). The main train station, Gare Boulogne-Ville, is 1.2km southeast of the centre.

Information

There are laundrettes at 235 rue Nationale and 62 rue de Lille. Both are open 7am to 8pm. Several commercial banks can be found on or near rue Victor Hugo.

Main Post Office (place Frédéric Sauvage) Changes money and has a Cyberposte.

Tourist Office (☎ 03 21 10 88 10; www.tourisme -boulognesurmer.com in French; 24 quai Gambetta; ☀ 9am-7pm Mon-Sat, 10am-1pm & 3-6pm Sun Jul & Aug, 9.15am-12.30pm & 1.45-6pm Mon-Sat Sep-Jun, 10.15am-1pm Sun Apr, May & Jun, 3-5.30pm Sun Sep-Nov)

Sights
VILLE HAUTE

You can walk all the way round the Upper City – an island of centuries-old buildings and cobblestone streets – on top of the rectangular, tree-shaded **ramparts**, a distance of just under 1.5km. Among the impressive buildings around place Godefroy de Bouillon are the neoclassical **Hôtel Desandrouin**, built in the 1780s and later used by Napoleon, and the **town hall** (1735), with its square medieval belfry.

Basilique Notre Dame (☀ 9am-noon & 2-6pm Apr-Aug, to 5pm Sep-Mar), with a towering, Italianate dome visible from all over town, was built from 1827 to 1866 with little input from trained architects. The partly Romanesque **crypt** and **treasury** (☀ 2-5pm Tue-Sun; admission €2) are eminently skippable.

Everything from Egyptian mummies to 19th-century Inuit masks to Oceanic art, with an *in situ*, 4th-century Roman wall thrown in for good measure, is on view at **Château-Musée** (☎ 03 21 10 02 20; adult €3.50, student & senior €2.50; ⏰ 10am-5pm Mon & Wed-Sat, 10am-5.30pm Sun), which is being renovated but should reopen in early 2005. The whole eclectic collection is housed in a 13th-century fortified castle built by the counts of Boulogne.

And now for something completely unexpected: the house where José de San Martín, the exiled hero of Argentine, Chilean and Peruvian independence, died in 1850 has been turned into the **Musée Libertador San Martín** (☎ 03 21 31 54 65; 113 Grande Rue; admission free; ⏰ 10am-noon & 2-6pm Fri-Tue), owned by the Argentine government. Ring the bell for a free English tour of this piece of South America, complete with memorabilia related to San Martín's life and lots of fancy military uniforms.

VILLE BASSE

The most interesting thing to do in the Lower City is to stroll along the **fishing port** (Quai Gambetta), where you'll find fish vendors – and hungry seagulls diving and squawking overhead. The **shopping precinct** is centred around rue Victor Hugo and rue Adolphe Thiers.

NAUSICAÄ

This first-class **marine aquarium** (☎ 03 21 30 99 99; www.nausicaa.fr; blvd Ste-Beuve; adult/3-12 yrs Apr-Sep €12.50/9, Oct-Mar €11/8, audioguide €3; ⏰ 9.30am-8pm Jul & Aug, 9.30am-6.30pm Sep-Jun, closed 3 weeks in mid-Jan) focuses on the sustainable use of marine resources, comes with lots of kid-friendly activities (fish petting, a sea-lion tank, feeding sessions) and has signs in English. Educational in the best sense of the word, you

---

BIRD-WATCHERS' PARADISE

South of Boulogne on the Baie de la Somme, **Parc Ornithologique du Marquenterre** (☎ 03 22 25 68 99; www.baiedesomme.org/marquenterre; St-Quentin-en-Tourmont; adult/6-16 yrs €9.60/7.10; ⏰ 10am-7.30pm Apr-Sep, to 5.30pm Oct-Mar) is a stopover for hundreds of species of migrating birds on their way from northern and central Europe to warmer climes around the Mediterranean and Africa. The Somme estuary, which is 5km wide, is the largest in northern France. Several walking routes are available for bird-watchers and guided visits are also available.

---

can see everything from sharks to speckled caimans (in a tropical forest) to see-through jellyfish up close; the new **Maison Planetaire** focuses on energy efficiency in the home. From April 2005 through the end of 2006, a special exhibit will cover South Africa and its two oceans, the Pacific and the Atlantic.

At the cafés you can buy tuna sandwiches – kind of like a zoo that sells lionburgers, some might say, but don't forget that Boulogne is Europe's most important fish-processing centre. If the prices look like they'll do to your pocket what drag nets do to the oceans, remember that you'd pay about the same to see two Hollywood movies.

BEACHES

Boulogne's beach begins just north of Nausicaä, across the mouth of the Liane from the vaguely menacing steelworks, now closed and set for demolition and decontamination. There are other fine beaches 4km north of town at **Wimereux** (bus 1 and 2, two to four times per hour), a partly *belle époque*–style resort founded by Napoleon in 1806; 2.5km southwest at **Le Portel** (bus 23); and 5km south at **Equihen Plage** (bus 11).

A bit further afield, the beach resort of **Le Touquet** (Paris Plage; ☎ tourist office 03 21 06 72 00; www.letouquet.com), 30km south of Boulogne, was hugely fashionable in the interwar period, when the English upper crust found it positively smashing (in 1940 a politically oblivious PG Wodehouse was arrested here by the Germans). These days it offers a wide selection of year-round outdoor activities for the whole family.

Sleeping

Auberge de Jeunesse (☎ 03 21 99 15 30; boulogne-sur-mer@fuaj.org; place Rouget de Lisle; dm with breakfast & sheets €15.50; ⏰ closed Jan; 🖳) This modern outfit has spacious rooms with shower, toilet and three or four beds – fairly luxurious as far as hostels go. Kitchen facilities are available; there's a billiard table near the bar.

Hôtel Faidherbe (☎ 03 21 31 60 93; fax 03 21 87 01 14; 12 rue Faidherbe; d €45-60, Oct-Mar €5 less) The doors of the 34 modern, smallish rooms are upholstered so, at least upstairs, you won't hear Victor, the talking (or squawking) mynah bird who greets guests in the lobby. The new owners of this two-star place are wine connoisseurs and invite their guests to sample selected vintages at reasonable prices.

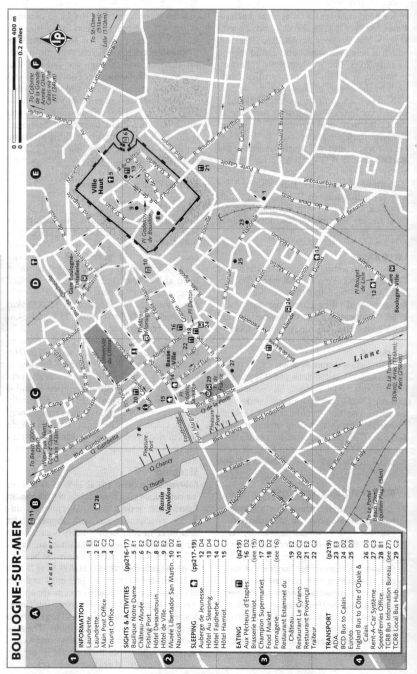

Hôtel Hamiot (☎ 03 21 31 44 20; hotelrestaurant hamiot@wanadoo.fr; 1 rue Faidherbe; d from €55) This three-star place has 12 very comfortable wood-panelled rooms with gleaming tile bathrooms.

Hôtel Au Sleeping (☎ 03 21 80 62 79; fax 03 21 10 63 97; 18 blvd Daunou; s/d €30/34; ☼ reception closed after 1pm Sun except Jul & Aug) It may have only one star and the furnishings may be simple, but the welcome is warm and the 12 rooms are well lit and clean.

Eating
VILLE HAUTE
There are quite a few intimate restaurants – most of them moderately priced – along rue de Lille.

Restaurant Estaminet du Château (☎ 03 21 91 49 66; 2 rue du Château; menus €10-30; ☼ closed Thu & Wed evening; ☒) Meat dishes are an option but this place – a veteran French-style restaurant with an informal rustic feel – is especially strong on fish and seafood.

Restaurant Provençal (☎ 03 21 80 49 03; 107 rue Porte Gayole; ☼ Wed-Mon) Serves tasty Moroccan couscous with raisins (vegetarian €7.60, meat €11 to €19.80) and tajines (€15) amid over-the-top Oriental décor.

VILLE BASSE
Thanks to its ready supply, Boulogne is an excellent place for fresh fish. The area between rue Coquelin and place Dalton has a good choice of eateries.

Aux Pêcheurs d'Étaples (☎ 03 21 30 29 29; 31 Grande Rue; menus €13-24; ☼ closed Sun evening) Walk in past the fresh fish on ice and you arrive at a fine seafood restaurant with a modern nautical ambience. Cabillaud (cod), caught nearby, is a speciality.

Brasserie Hamiot (☎ 03 21 31 44 20; plat du jour €7.50, 3-course menus €16-28, kids' menus €6.50; ☼ noon-midnight) This bustling and hugely popular wood-panelled brasserie has a terrace in summer. See also Hôtel Hamiot (above).

Restaurant Le Cyrano (☎ 03 21 31 66 57; 9 rue Coquelin; 3-course menus from €8.25; ☼ 11.30am-10pm Mon-Sat) At this unpretentious but welcoming place, a full meal – for example, mussels, steak and dessert – comes at a good price.

SELF-CATERING
Food shops are sprinkled around rue de la Lampe and rue Adolphe Thiers and, in the Ville Haute, along rue de Lille.

Food market (place Dalton; ☼ Wed & Sat mornings) Held the day before if Wednesday or Saturday is a holiday.

Fromagerie (23 Grande Rue; ☼ closed Sun & Mon morning) This place is next door to Aux Pêcheurs d'Étaples.

Traiteur (1 Grande Rue; ☼ closed Mon & Sun afternoon) Ready-to-eat delicacies.

There's also a **Champion supermarket** (53 blvd Daunou).

Getting There & Around
BOAT
SpeedFerries (UK ☎ 01304-20 3000, France ☎ 03 21 10 50 00; www.speedferries.com) offers an ultramodern, ultrafast catamaran service between Boulogne and Dover (50 minutes, five daily). Foot passengers without cars cannot be accommodated.

BUS
For details on bus service to the beautiful Côte d'Opale and Calais, see p212.

Most local bus lines, run by **TCRB** (☎ 03 21 83 51 51), stop at place de France.

CAR
Discount rental agencies include:
ADA (☎ 03 21 80 80 82; 211 rue Nationale)
Euroto (☎ 03 21 30 32 23; 96 rue Nationale)
Rent-A-Car Système (☎ 03 21 80 97 34; 26 rue de la Lampe)

TAXI
To order a cab, ring ☎ 03 21 91 25 00.

TRAIN
Gare Boulogne-Ville has services to Amiens (€15.70, 1½ hours, five to eight daily), Calais-Ville (€6.60, 27 to 48 minutes, 15 to 19 daily Monday to Saturday, nine daily Sunday), Étaples-Le Touquet (€4.70, 20 minutes, 10 to 21 daily), Lille-Flandres or Lille-Europe (€17.80, one to two hours, 10 to 13 daily) and Paris' Gare du Nord (€27.50, 2¾ hours, six to nine daily).

DUNKIRK
pop 209,000
Dunkirk (Dunkerque), flattened during WWII, was rebuilt during one of the most uninspired periods in Western architecture, so unless you're the world's only fan of 1950s brick low-rise, want to hang out on

the Malo-les-Bains beach or plan to join in a colourful pre-Lent carnival, there's little reason to spend much time here.

Under Louis XIV, Dunkirk – whose name means 'church of the dunes' in Flemish – served as a base for French privateers, including the infamous Jean Bart (1650–1702), whose daring attacks on English and Dutch ships have ensured his status as a local hero: the city centre's main square, suitably adorned with a dashing statue, bears his name.

Orientation & Information

The train station is 600m southwest of Dunkirk's main square, place Jean Bart. The beach and its waterfront esplanade, Digue de Mer, are 2km northeast of the centre – via av des Bains – in the faded, turn-of-the-20th-century seaside resort of Malo-les-Bains.

The **tourist office** (☎ 03 28 66 79 21; www.ot -dunkerque.fr; rue de l'Amiral Ronarc'h; ☼ 9am-12.30pm & 1.30-6.30pm Mon-Fri, 9am-6.30pm Sat, 10am-noon & 2-4pm Sun & holidays, no midday closure Jul & Aug) is in the base of a medieval belfry.

THE EVACUATION OF DUNKIRK

In May and June 1940, Dunkirk earned a place in the history books when the British Expeditionary Force and French and Belgian units found themselves almost completely surrounded by Hitler's armies, which had advanced into far northern France.

In an effort to salvage what it could, Churchill's government ordered British units to make their way to Dunkirk, where naval vessels and hundreds of fishing boats and pleasure craft – many manned by civilian volunteers – braved intense German artillery and air attacks to ferry 340,000 men to the safety of England. Conducted in the difficult first year of WWII, this unplanned and chaotic evacuation – dubbed Operation Dynamo – failed to save any of the units' heavy equipment but was, nevertheless, seen as a key demonstration of Britain's resourcefulness and determination.

Dunkirk's wide, promenade-lined beach, Plage des Alliés, named in honour of the Allied troops evacuated to England from here in 1940, is in the seaside Dunkirk suburb of Malo-les-Bains.

Sights & Activities

The **Musée Portuaire** (Harbour Museum; ☎ 03 28 63 33 39; 9 quai de la Citadelle; adult/under 18 €4/3; ☼ 10am-12.45pm & 1.30-6pm, probably closed Tue, no midday closure Jul & Aug), housed in a one-time tobacco warehouse, will delight ship-model lovers of all ages. Forty-five minute guided **tours** (adult/under 18 €4/3.50) take visitors aboard a barge, a lighthouse ship (to open 2005) and the *Duchesse Anne*, a three-masted merchant marine training ship built in Germany in 1901 and acquired by France as WWII reparations.

Stretching east of Dunkirk to the Belgian border, *les dunes flamandes* (Flemish dunes) represent a unique ecosystem harbouring hundreds of plant species, including rare orchids. The area – including the **Dewulf and Marchand dunes** – is served by bus No 2B (3B on Sunday and holidays), which continues on to Adinkerke in Belgium (€1.30, an extra €0.80 to cross the border).

Tours

The tourist office has details on **boat tours** (adult €7.50; ☼ Tue-Sun Jul & Aug) of Dunkirk's huge port (France's third largest) and some of the country's most important (and odoriferous) steel and iron works; departures are from place du Minck.

Festivals & Events

Dunkirk's **carnival**, held at the beginning of Lent, originated as a final fling for the town's cod fishermen before they set out for months on the waters off Iceland. The biggest celebration is on the Sunday right before Mardi Gras, when costumed citizens march around town behind fife-and-drum bands, and general merriment reigns. At the climax of the festivities, the mayor and other dignitaries stand on the town hall balcony and pelt the assembled locals with dried salted herrings.

Getting There & Away

For details on links to Calais, see p212. Almost all trains to Lille stop at Lille-Flandres (€11.60, 1¼ hours, nine to 21 daily).

Ferries run by **Norfolk Line** (☎ 03 28 59 01 01; www.norfolkline.com) link Loon Plage, about 25km west of the town centre, with Dover (from €155 one way for car and five passengers, two hours, 10 daily).

ARRAS

pop 40,000

Arras (the final 's' is pronounced), former capital of Artois, is worth seeing mainly for its harmonious ensemble of Flemish-style arcaded buildings; the rest of the city, seriously damaged during both world wars, is a mixture of 19th-century and postwar architecture. The city is a good base for visits to the Battle of the Somme memorials, especially if you have a car.

Orientation

The centre of Arras is the historic Grand' Place and the almost-adjoining place des Héros (the Petite Place), where you'll find the town hall. The train station is 600m to the southeast. The pedestrianised area southeast of place des Héros, including rue Ronville, is the commercial centre.

Information

Banks can be found along rue Gambetta and its continuation, rue Ernestale.

Laundrette (17 place d'Ipswich; ⏰ 7am-8pm)

Post Office (rue Gambetta) Has a Cyberposte and changes money.

Tourist Office (☎ 03 21 51 26 95; www.ot-arras .fr; place des Héros; ⏰ 9am or 10am-noon & 2-6pm or 6.30pm Mon-Sat, no midday closure May-Sep, 10am-12.30pm or 1pm & 2.30pm or 3-6pm or 6.30pm Sun & holidays) Inside the town hall.

Sights & Activities

Arras' two market squares, **place des Héros** and the **Grand' Place**, with a history stretching back to the 11th century, are surrounded by Flemish-Baroque houses build in the 1600s and 1700s. These vary in all sorts of decorative details but their 345 sandstone columns form a common arcade unique in France. The tourist office offers a **self-guided tour** (adult/student €5.35/3.05) of the city centre.

The Flemish-Gothic **Hôtel de Ville** (town hall, place des Héros) dates from the 16th century but was completely rebuilt after WWI. Three giants (see p208) – Colas, Jacqueline and their son Dédé – make their home in the lobby.

The basement of the town hall is a veritable hub of activity. If you're in the mood for a panoramic view, this is the place to hop on the lift to the top of the 75m **belfry** (adult/student €2.30/1.60; ⏰ 9am or 10am-noon & 2-6pm or 6.30pm Mon-Sat, no midday closure May-Sep, 10am-12.30pm or 1pm & 2.30pm or 3-6pm or 6.30pm Sun & holidays). The **Histo-**

rama (adult €2.30, student & child €1.55) presents the city's history in a 20-minute slide show (in English). But for a truly unique perspective on Arras, head into the slimy **souterrains** (tunnels; adult €4.40, student & child €2.40). Also known as *boves* (cellars), they run under place des Héros and were turned into British command posts, hospitals and barracks during WWI. Each spring, in a brilliant juxtaposition of underground gloom and horticultural exuberance, plants and flowers turn the tunnels into the life-affirming **Jardin des Boves** (⏰ 20 Mar-20 Jun). Tours of the *souterrains* (40 to 50 minutes, English translation available) *generally* begin at 10am, 11am, 2.30pm, 3.30pm and 4.30pm from Monday to Friday, and every 30 minutes or so on Saturday and Sunday. All three attractions can be visited with the **combined ticket** (forfait; adult €6.80, student & child €4).

Highlights at the **Musée des Beaux-Arts** (Fine Arts Museum; ☎ 03 21 71 26 43; 22 rue Paul Doumer; adult €4, student, over 65 & teacher €2; ⏰ 9.30am-noon & 2-5.30pm Wed-Mon, no midday closure Thu), housed in a neoclassical former Benedictine abbey, include the original copper lion from the town hall belfry, medieval sculpture (including a 15th-century skeletal figure whose stomach is being devoured by worms) and 17th-century religious paintings. **Le City Pass** (adult €9.80, student & child €6) gets you into the museum, belfry, Historama and *souterrains*.

The 18th-century house where Arras-born lawyer and Jacobin radical Maximilien Robespierre lived just before the Revolution, the **Maison Robespierre** (9 rue Maximilien Robespierre; admission free; ⏰ 2-5.30pm Tue & Thu, 3.30-6.30pm Sat & Sun), houses a small exhibit on traditional construction crafts prepared by an association of master craftsmen.

Sleeping

BUDGET

Auberge de Jeunesse (☎ 03 21 22 70 02; arras@fuaj.org; 59 Grand' Place; bed 1st night/subsequent nights €11.70/8.90; ⏰ reception open 7.30am-noon & 5-11pm, hostel closed Jan & perhaps Dec) Modern and superbly situated in the town centre, this has cheerful rooms for two to 10; almost all beds are bunks. Full kitchen facilities are available.

Hôtel du Beffroi (☎ 03 21 23 13 78; fax 03 21 23 03 08; 28 place de la Vacquerie; s/d from €30/34, with shower & toilet €40/45; ⏰ reception closed after noon Sun) Only one star hangs by the door but the 15 rooms are tasteful and squeaky clean. Room No 16, a veritable suite, comes with a romantic view.

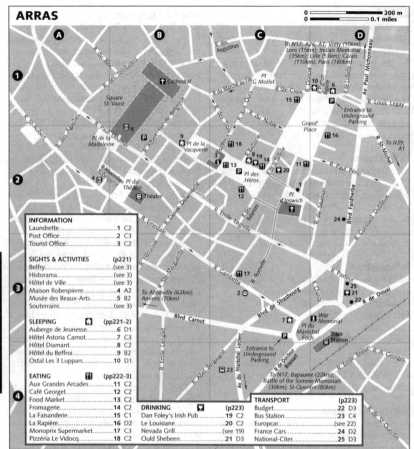

ARRAS

INFORMATION	
Laundrette	1 C2
Post Office	2 C3
Tourist Office	3 C2

SIGHTS & ACTIVITIES	(p221)
Belfry	(see 3)
Historama	(see 3)
Hôtel de Ville	(see 3)
Maison Robespierre	4 A2
Musée des Beaux-Arts	5 B2
Souterrains	(see 3)

SLEEPING	(pp221-2)
Auberge de Jeunesse	6 D1
Hôtel Astoria Carnot	7 C3
Hôtel Diamant	8 C2
Hôtel du Beffroi	9 B2
Ostal Les 3 Luppars	10 D1

EATING	(pp222-3)
Aux Grandes Arcades	11 C2
Café Georget	12 C2
Food Market	13 C2
Fromagerie	14 C2
La Faisanderie	15 C1
La Rapière	16 D2
Monoprix Supermarket	17 C2
Pizzéria Le Vidocq	18 C2

DRINKING	(p223)
Dan Foley's Irish Pub	19 C2
Le Louisiane	20 C2
Nevada Grill	(see 19)
Ould Shebeen	21 D3

TRANSPORT	(p223)
Budget	22 D3
Bus Station	23 C4
Europcar	(see 22)
France Cars	24 D2
National-Citer	25 D3

MID-RANGE

A number of city-centre hostelries offer good value for money.

Ostel Les 3 Luppars (☎ 03 21 60 02 03; www.ostel-les-3luppars.com in French; 47 Grand' Place; s/d/q from €44/60/75) Homy and centred on a courtyard, this 'ho(s)tel' occupies the Grand' Place's only non-Flemish-style building (it is Gothic and dates from 1370). The rooms are comfortable, if a tad too standard. Ostel Les 3 Luppars has a sauna, which costs €5 per person.

Hôtel Astoria Carnot (☎ 03 21 71 08 14; www.hotelcarnot.com; 10 place du Maréchal Foch; s/d/q €47/51/66) The well-lit, two-star rooms are spiffy and quite modern and come with spacious tile bathrooms.

Hôtel Diamant (☎ 03 21 71 23 23; www.arras-hotel-diamant.com; 5 place des Héros; s/d from €50/56 □) The 12 two-star rooms are compact but pleasant; the buffet breakfast costs €7.50.

Eating

Lots of eateries are hidden away under the arches of the Grand' Place.

La Faisanderie (☎ 03 21 48 20 76; 45 Grand' Place; menus €25-65; ⏱ 12.15-2pm & 7.30-9.15pm, closed Mon, lunch Tue & Sun evening) An exceptionally elegant French restaurant under vaulted brick ceilings. The menu changes with the seasons so the ingredients are always fresh.

La Rapière (☎ 03 21 55 09 92; 44 Grand' Place; menus €17-27; ⏱ closed Sun evening) Regional cuisine, including *flan de maroilles* (flan made with a local cows' milk cheese), is elegantly served in a contemporary ambience.

Aux Grandes Arcades (☎ 03 21 23 30 89; 10 Grand' Place; menus €15-35, plat du jour €11; ☺ daily) This brasserie-style place focuses on regional dishes such as *potje vleesch* (Flemish terrine made with veal, rabbit and fowl, €15).

Café Georget (☎ 03 21 71 13 07; 42 place des Héros; plat du jour €7.50; ☺ noon-2pm Mon-Sat) An unpretentious eatery serving hearty, homemade French dishes.

Pizzéria Le Vidocq (☎ 03 21 23 79 50; 24 rue des Trois Visages; pizzas €6.35-9.90; ☺ closed Sun, dinner Wed & lunch Sat) The pizzas arrive steaming from a wood-fired oven. Also on offer are pasta, 12 kinds of veal and 12 varieties of salad (about €8).

SELF-CATERING
There's a **food market** (☺ Wed & Sat mornings) in the square around the Hôtel de Ville, and a **Monoprix supermarket** (30 rue Gambetta).

Fromagerie (37 place des Héros; ☺ 9.30am-12.30pm & 2.30-7.15pm Tue-Thu, 8.30am-7.15pm Fri & Sat) Several other food shops are right nearby.

Drinking
Cafés and pubs line the northern side of place des Héros and adjacent rue de la Taillerie. **Dan Foley's Irish Pub** (7 place des Héros) doesn't have much that's authentically Irish except Guinness; a quintessentially French eatery, the Nevada Grill, is next door.

Ould Shebeen (☎ 03 21 71 87 97; 6 blvd Faidherbe; ☺ 11am-1am Mon-Thu, until 2am Fri & Sat) This down-to-earth Irish pub, with its rough-hewn décor, attracts native English speakers as well as Francophone locals. Thursday is trivia night (at about 10.30pm); questions are in English and French.

Le Louisiane (☎ 03 21 23 18 00; 12 rue de la Taillerie; ☺ noon-1am or 2am, from 3pm on Sun) This yuppy-ish café-bar comes with mellow background music and two billiard tables.

Getting There & Away
BUS
For details on buses from Arras' **bus station** (☎ 03 21 51 34 64; rue Abel Bergaigne; ☺ office 7am-6.30pm Mon-Fri, to 12.30pm Sat) to the Vimy Canadian National Memorial and Albert, see p225 and p227.

TRAIN
Arras is on the main line linking Lille-Flandres (€8.60, 40 minutes to one hour,

11 to 17 daily) with Paris' Gare du Nord (€27.20 or €36.90 by TGV, 52 minutes, 12 to 15 daily). Other destinations include Amiens (€9.60, 50 minutes, seven to 11 daily) and Calais-Ville (€16.90, two hours, 10 daily Monday to Friday, six or seven daily Saturday and Sunday).

CAR
Budget (☎ 03 21 60 76 76; 5 rue de Douai)
Europcar (☎ 03 21 07 29 54; 5 rue de Douai)
France Cars (☎ 03 21 50 22 22; 31 blvd Faidherbe) Less expensive than the majors.
National-Citer (☎ 03 21 71 49 14; 14 blvd Faidherbe)

TAXI
Companies available pretty much 24 hours include **Taxis GT** (☎ 03 21 71 64 32) and **Alliance Taxi** (☎ 03 21 23 69 69). Both can take you to Somme battlefield sites.

BATTLE OF THE SOMME MEMORIALS
The First Battle of the Somme, a WWI Allied offensive waged in the villages and woodlands northeast of Amiens, was designed to relieve pressure on the beleaguered French troops at Verdun (see p382). On 1 July 1916, British, Commonwealth and French troops 'went over the top' in a massive assault along a 34km front. But German positions proved virtually unbreachable, and on the first day of the battle an astounding 21,392 British troops were killed and another 35,492 were wounded. Most casualties were infantrymen mown down by German machine guns.

By the time the offensive was called off in mid-November, 1.2 million lives had been lost on both sides. The British had advanced 12km, the French 8km. The Battle of the Somme has become a metaphor for the meaningless slaughter of war and its killing fields have since become a site of pilgrimage.

INFORMATION
A variety of brochures, including *A Guide to Australian Memorials on the Western Front*, can be picked up at area tourist offices. For information on the Commonwealth War Grave Commission see p225.

TOURS
Touring the area is easiest by car, but quite a few sites can be visited by train or bus from

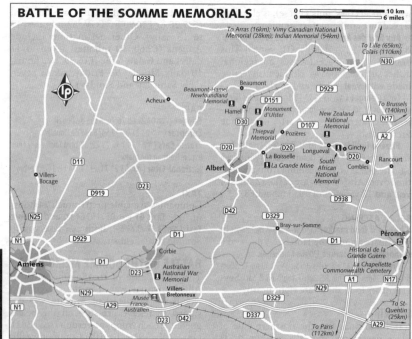

BATTLE OF THE SOMME MEMORIALS

Amiens and/or Arras – details on public transport options appear after each listing. Cycling is also an option.

Experienced companies offering minibus tours from Albert include:

Battlefield Tours (☎/fax 03 21 50 18 87, 06 87 43 10 49; www.somme-normandy-tours.com; half-/full day per person from €22/52; ☼ tours begin 10am & 3pm year-round) Pick-up in Arras or Amiens is an option.

Salient Tours (☎ France 06 86 05 61 30, ☎ UK 01225-812299; www.salienttours.com; half-day per person from €22; ☼ tours begin 10am & 3pm Tue-Sun Easter-late Oct)

North of Arras

The area north of Arras has a couple of noteworthy memorials and numerous military cemeteries.

VIMY CANADIAN NATIONAL MEMORIAL & PARK

Whereas the French, right after the war, attempted to erase all signs of battle and return the Somme region to agriculture and normalcy, the Canadians decided that the most evocative way to remember their fallen was to preserve pieces of the crater-pocked battlefields. As a result, the best place to get some sense of the unimaginable hell known as the Western Front is at the chilling, eerie moonscape of **Vimy Ridge**. Visitors can also see **tunnels** (☼ May-Nov) and reconstructed **trenches**.

Of the 66,655 Canadians who died in WWI, 3589 lost their lives in April 1917 taking this ridge, a German defensive line, the highest point of which was later chosen as the site of Canada's **WWI memorial** (inaccessible due to repairs until mid-2006). The allegorical figures, carved from huge blocks of limestone, include a cloaked, downcast female figure representing a young Canada mourning her fallen. The base is inscribed with the names of 11,285 Canadians who went missing in action. The 1-sq-km park also includes two **Canadian cemeteries** and, at the vehicle entrance to the main memorial, a **monument to the Moroccan Division** (in French and Arabic).

The **Historical Interpretive Centre** (☎ 03 21 58 19 34; www.vac-acc.gc.ca; ☼ 10am-6pm May-Dec, 9am-5pm Jan-Apr), staffed by Canadian students, will at some point be replaced by a new museum near the trenches. The **Canadian Virtual War Memorial** (www.virtualmemorial.gc.ca) has details on over 116,000 Canadian war dead.

Getting There & Away

From Arras, you can take bus No 91 (about €2, 20 minutes, six or seven daily Monday to Saturday) towards Lens; ask the bus driver to stop at Vimy Ridge, 3.2km from the memorial.

Trains link Arras with the town of Vimy (€2.50, 12 minutes, six daily Monday to Friday, two on Saturday), 6km east of the memorial.

A taxi from Arras costs about €20 return, plus €19 for each hour the driver spends waiting.

INDIAN MEMORIAL

The fascinating and seldom-visited **Mémorial Indien**, vaguely Moghul in architecture, records the names of Commonwealth soldiers from the Indian subcontinent who 'have no known grave'. The units (31st Punjabis, 11th Rajputs, 2nd King Edward's Own Gurkha Rifles) and the ranks of the fallen (sepoy, havildar, *naik, sowar*, labourer, follower) engraved on the walls evoke the pride, pomp and exploitation on which the British Empire was built.

To get there from La Bassée, take the northbound D947 to its intersection with the D171.

South of Arras

Some of the bloodiest fighting of WWI took place around the town of Albert (p227). The farmland north and east of the town is dotted with dozens of Commonwealth cemeteries.

PÉRONNE

The best place to start a visit to the Somme battlefields is in the river port of Péronne, at the well-designed and informative **Historial de la Grande Guerre** (☎ 03 22 83 14 18; www .historial.org; Château de Péronne; adult/senior €7/6, student, teacher & ex-serviceman €3.50; ۞ 10am-6pm Apr-Sep, 10am-6pm Tue-Sun Oct–mid-Dec & mid-Jan–Mar). This innovative museum tells the story of the war chronologically, with equal space given to the German, French and British perspectives on what happened, how and why. A great deal of visually engaging material, including period films and the bone-chilling engravings of Otto Dix, capture the aesthetic sensibilities, enthusiasm, naive patriotism and unimaginable violence of the time. The proud uniforms of various units and armies are shown laid out on the ground, as if on freshly – though bloodless – dead soldiers. Not much glory here.

On the N17 at the southern edge of town, **La Chapellette Commonwealth Cemetery** has separate British and Indian sections.

One bus line links Péronne with Albert (€3.50, 50 minutes, three or four a day Monday to Saturday); another goes to both Villers-Bretonneux (€4.50, 50 minutes, one

---

COMMONWEALTH CEMETERIES & MEMORIALS

Over 750,000 soldiers from Australia, Canada, the Indian subcontinent, New Zealand, South Africa, the UK, the West Indies and other parts of the British Empire died on the Western Front, two-thirds of them in France. By Commonwealth tradition, they were buried where they fell, in over 1000 military cemeteries and 2000 civilian cemeteries. Today, hundreds of neatly tended Commonwealth plots – marked by white-on-dark-green signs – dot the landscape along a wide swathe of territory running roughly from Albert and Cambrai north via Arras and Béthune to Armentières and Ypres (Ieper) in Belgium. Many of the headstones bear inscriptions composed by family members. Twenty six memorials (20 of them in France) bear the names of over 300,000 Commonwealth soldiers whose bodies were never recovered or identified. French, American and German war dead were reburied in large cemeteries after the war.

Except where noted, all the monuments listed in this section are always open. Many Commonwealth cemeteries have a plaque with historical information. The bronze Cemetery Register boxes contain a booklet with details of the site; you can record your impressions in the visitors' book.

The website of the **Commonwealth War Graves Commission** (www.cwgc.org) has a search function that can find details on individual war dead.

or two daily Monday to Saturday) and Amiens' bus station (€4.50, 1¼ hours).

THIEPVAL MEMORIAL
Dedicated to 'the Missing of the Somme', this **memorial** – the region's most visited place of pilgrimage – was built in the early 1930s on the site of a German stronghold that was stormed on 1 July 1916 with unimaginable casualties. The columns of the arches are inscribed with the names of 73,367 British and South African soldiers whose remains were never found. The modern but discreet **Thiepval Visitors Centre** (www.thiepval.org.uk), built almost entirely below ground level, opened its doors in mid-2004, on the 90th anniversary of the start of WWI.

AUSTRALIAN NATIONAL WAR MEMORIAL
During WWI, 313,000 Australians (out of a total population of 4.5 million) volunteered for military service; 46,000 met their deaths on the Western Front (14,000 others perished elsewhere). The **Australian National War Memorial**, a 32m tower engraved with the names of 10,982 soldiers who went missing in action, stands on a hill where Australian and British troops repulsed a German assault on 24 April 1918. It was dedicated in 1938; two years later its stone walls were scarred by the guns of Hitler's invading armies.

The nearest town is **Villers-Bretonneux**, an ugly bourg that still hasn't completely recovered from the war. For Aussies, though, it's a heart-warming place that bills itself as *l'Australie en Picardie*, and Anzac Day is religiously commemorated. In 1993, the unidentified remains of an Australian soldier were transferred from Adelaide Cemetery, on the N29 at the western edge of town, to the Tomb of the Unknown Soldier in Canberra.

The **Musée Franco-Australien** (☎ 03 22 96 80 79; www.villers-bretonneux.com/Australian.htm; École Victoria, 9 rue Victoria, Villers-Bretonneux; adult/student €3.05/1.55; ☒ 10am-12.30pm & 2-6pm Wed-Sun & Tue afternoon, plus 2-6pm on 1st & 3rd Sun of month) has intimate, evocative displays of WWI Australiana, including letters, photographs of life on the Western Front, and a small Anzac library. The front steps are a favoured trysting spot for local teens.

The Villers-Bretonneux train station, linked to Amiens (€3, 12 minutes, five to eight daily), is 700m south of the museum (along rue de Melbourne) and an easily walkable 3km south of the Australian National War Memorial. Bus No 13 links Villers-Bretonneux with Amiens (€3.40, 25 minutes, three daily Monday to Saturday) and Péronne (€4.50, 50 minutes, one or two daily Monday to Saturday).

A **taxi** (☎ 03 22 48 49 49) to the memorial from Villers-Bretonneux costs €12 return, plus €3 for every 10 minutes spent waiting at the site.

BEAUMONT-HAMEL NEWFOUNDLAND MEMORIAL
Like Vimy (p224), the evocative **Mémorial Terre-Neuvien** preserves part of the Western Front in the state it was in at fighting's end. The zigzag trench system, which still fills with mud in winter, is clearly visible, as are countless shell craters and the remains of barbed-wire barriers.

On 1 July 1916, the volunteer Royal Newfoundland Regiment stormed entrenched German positions and was nearly wiped out; a sign explains blandly that 'strategic and tactical miscalculations led to a great slaughter'. You can survey the whole battlefield from the **caribou statue**, surrounded by plants native to Newfoundland. Canadian students based at the **visitors centre** (☎ 03 22 76 70 87; ☒ 10am-6pm May–mid-Nov, to 5pm mid-Nov–Apr, closed late Dec-early Jan), designed to look like a typical Newfoundland fisher's house, give free guided tours from May to mid-November (and on some days the rest of the year).

MONUMENT DE L'ULSTER
Built on a German frontline position assaulted by the overwhelmingly Protestant 36th (Ulster) Division on 1 July 1916, the **Tour d'Ulster** (Ulster Tower) is a replica of Helen's Tower near Bangor, County Down, where the unit did its training. Dedicated in 1921, it has long been a Unionist pilgrimage site. An obelisk known as the **Orange Memorial to Fallen Brethren** stands near the entrance.

SOUTH AFRICAN & NEW ZEALAND NATIONAL MEMORIALS
The **South African National Memorial** (Mémorial Sud-Africain) stands in the middle of shell-pocked **Delville Wood**, which was almost captured by a South African brigade

in the third week of July in 1916. The avenues through the trees are named after streets in London and Edinburgh. The star-shaped **museum** (☎ 03 22 85 02 17; ☉ 10am-5.45pm Apr–mid-Oct, to 3.45pm in winter, closed Mon, holidays & 11 Nov-early Feb) was dedicated amid much apartheid-related controversy in 1986.

The **New Zealand National Memorial** is 1.5km due north of Longueval.

LA GRANDE MINE

This enormous **crater** – one of many made by tunnelling under enemy (in this case German) trenches and planting vast quantities of explosives – looks like the site of a meteor impact. Some 100m across and 30m deep and officially known as the Lochnagar Crater Memorial, it was created at 7.30am on 1 July 1916, and is a testament to the boundless ingenuity human beings show when determined to kill their fellow creatures.

ALBERT

The most noteworthy landmark in this rather unfetching town (population 10,000), virtually flattened during WWI, is neo-Byzantine-style **Basilique Notre-Dame de Brebières**, topped by a gilded statue of the Virgin Mary, famously left dangling by a German shell. For great views, you can climb the 70m-high belfry from April to September.

Right next to the basilica, the **Musée des Abris Somme 1916** (☎ 03 22 75 16 17; www.somme-1916.org; rue Anicet Godin; adult/under 18 €4/2.50; ☉ 9am-noon & 2-6pm Feb–mid-Dec, no midday closure Jun-Sep), housed in dank underground galleries, does a good job of evoking the grim lives of soldiers and local civilians at the front line.

The **tourist office** (☎ 03 22 75 16 42; www.tourismc albert.net in French; 9 rue Gambetta; ☉ 9am-noon or 12.30pm & 1.30pm or 2pm 6.30pm Mon-Sat, 10am-12 30pm Sun & holidays Apr-Sep, to 5pm Mon-Sat Oct-Mar) is 50m towards the train station from the basilica. Year-round, it arranges tours of the WWI memorials (phone ahead for reservations) and rents out bicycles (per day €12).

Trains (six to 12 daily) link Albert's train station – the monoplane hanging in the waiting hall is a Potez 36 from 1933 – with Amiens (€5.40, 25 minutes) and Arras (€6.30, 25 minutes).

AMIENS
pop 132,000

Amiens, the comfy if reserved former capital of Picardy, boasts one of France's most magnificent Gothic cathedrals. Local people out for a quick bit of shopping, a bite or just a stroll animate the post-war city centre, a mostly pedestrianised precinct with clean-lined, modernist buildings that have aged remarkably well. The city is a good base for visits to the Battle of the Somme memorials – and its 26,000 students give the place a young, lively feel.

Orientation

Commercial life is based around place Gambetta, two blocks west of the cathedral. The train station is about 1km southeast of place Gambetta; you can find it from most anywhere in town by looking for the 26-storey Tour Perret.

Information

Banks can be found around place René Goblet and along pedestrianised rue des Trois Cailloux.

Laundrette (10 rue André; ☉ 8am-7pm)

Main Post Office (7 rue des Vergeaux) Has currency exchange and a Cyberposte.

Neurogame Cybercafé (☎ 03 22 72 68 79; 16 rue des Chaudronniers; per hr €3.50; ☉ 10am-midnight Mon-Sat, 2-8pm Sun) Internet access.

Tourist Office (☎ 03 22 71 60 50; www.amiens.com /tourisme; 6bis rue Dusevel; ☉ 9.30am-6pm or 7pm Mon-Sat, 10am-noon & 2-5pm Sun) Can supply details on visiting the Somme war monuments, including minibus tours, and on summer boat tours of St-Leu.

Sights & Activities
CATHÉDRALE NOTRE DAME

This spectacular **Gothic cathedral** (place Notre Dame; ☉ 8.30am-6.15pm Apr-Sep, 8.30am-noon & 2pm-5.15pm Oct-Mar), the largest in France and a Unesco World Heritage site, was begun in 1220 to house the (purported) head of St John the Baptist, now enclosed in gold in the northern outer wall of the ambulatory. Connoisseurs rave about the soaring Gothic arches, unity of style and immense interior but for locals, the 17th-century statue known as the **Ange Pleureur** (Crying Angel), in the ambulatory opposite the axial chapel, remains a favourite.

The nave is lined with beautifully decorated chapels and graced by 13th-century **bronze figures** of the bishops who built the

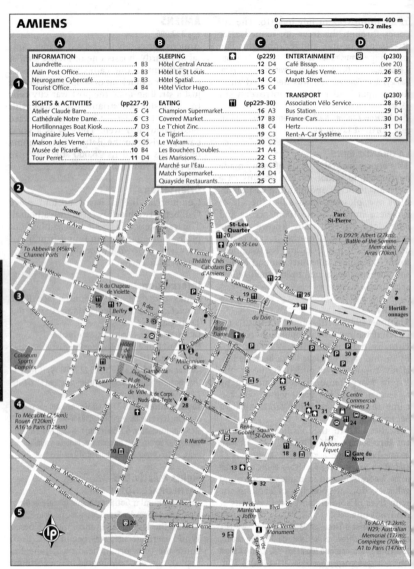

AMIENS

0 — 400 m
0 — 0.2 miles

INFORMATION
Laundrette.................................1 B3
Main Post Office.......................2 B3
Neurogame Cybercafé...............3 B3
Tourist Office............................4 B4

SIGHTS & ACTIVITIES (pp227-9)
Atelier Claude Barre..................5 C4
Cathédrale Notre Dame.............6 C3
Hortillonnages Boat Kiosk.........7 D3
Imaginaire Jules Verne..............8 C4
Maison Jules Verne...................9 C5
Musée de Picardie...................10 B4
Tour Perret............................11 D4

SLEEPING (p229)
Hôtel Central Anzac................12 D4
Hôtel Le St Louis....................13 C5
Hôtel Spatial..........................14 C4
Hôtel Victor Hugo...................15 C4

EATING (pp229-30)
Champion Supermarket............16 A3
Covered Market.......................17 B3
Le T'chiot Zinc........................18 C4
Le Tigzirt...............................19 C3
Le Wakam..............................20 C2
Les Bouchées Doubles..............21 A4
Les Marissons........................22 C3
Marché sur l'Eau....................23 C3
Match Supermarket.................24 D4
Quayside Restaurants..............25 C3

ENTERTAINMENT (p230)
Café Bissap.......................(see 20)
Cirque Jules Verne..................26 B5
Marott Street.........................27 C4

TRANSPORT (p230)
Association Vélo Service............28 B4
Bus Station............................29 D4
France Cars...........................30 D4
Hertz....................................31 D4
Rent-A-Car Système................32 C5

cathedral. The choir, with its 110 sumptuously carved oak **choir stalls** (1508–22), is separated from the ambulatory by gilded wrought-iron grates and choir screens with painted, haut-relief stone figures that illustrate the lives of St John the Baptist (1531) and the first bishop of Amiens and patron saint of Picardy, St Firmin (1495). The black-and-white 234m-long **maze** embedded in the floor of the nave is easy to miss as the soaring vaults draw the eye ever upward. Plaques in the south transept arm commemorate Australian, British, Canadian, New Zealand and US troops who died in WWI.

A free 45-minute light show bathes the cathedral façade in vivid medieval colours nightly from 15 June to 30 September and 15 December to 6 January; the photons start flying at 8pm in winter and sometime between 9.45pm (September) and 10.45pm (June) in summer.

OTHER SIGHTS & ACTIVITIES

The medieval **St-Leu Quarter**, north of the cathedral along the Somme, is the best place in town for a riverside stroll. Postwar renovations have left parts of the area too cute by half, but the many neon-lit quayside restaurants and pubs make it especially lively at night. Another product of postwar exuberance, the concrete **Tour Perret** (built 1948–54), at one time the tallest building in Europe, faces the train station.

The lawns, lakes, waterways and bridges of **Parc St-Pierre** stretch eastwards from St-Leu all the way to the **Hortillonnages** – also known as the Jardins Flottants (Floating Gardens) – a 330-hectare area of market gardens that have supplied the city with vegetables and flowers since the Middle Ages. From April to October, one-hour **cruises** (adult/11-16 yrs/4-10 yrs €5/4.20/2.50) of the peaceful canals – in 12-person gondola-like boats – depart from a riverside **kiosk** (☎ 03 22 92 12 18; 54 blvd de Beauvillé) daily from 2pm until between 5pm and nightfall; get there before 4pm to buy tickets.

The **Musée de Picardie** (☎ 03 22 97 14 00; 48 rue de la République; adult/6-18 yrs €4/2.50; ☑ 10am-12.30pm & 2-6pm Tue-Sun), housed in a dashing Second Empire structure (1855–67), is surprisingly well-endowed with archaeological exhibits, medieval art, 18th-century French paintings (including royal commissions) and Revolution-era ceramics. Some 80 works from here spent part of 2004 hanging out in California – at the Santa Barbara Museum of Art.

Ever wonder how stained glass is actually designed and put together? You can see firsthand at **Atelier Claude Barre** (☎ 03 22 91 81 18; 40 rue Victor Hugo; adult €4, child & student €2; ☑ 3pm Mon-Sat). Visitors get to see the workshop – the eight artisans fill commissions from both churches and private collectors – and a collection of 11th- to 20th-century stained glass.

Jules Verne (1828–1905) wrote many of his best-known works of brain-tingling – and eerily prescient – science fiction during the two decades he lived in Amiens. His grand turreted house is now the **Maison Jules Verne** (☎ 03 22 45 37 84; www.jules-verne.net in French; 2 rue Charles Dubois; adult/student €3/1.50; ☑ 10am-noon & 2-6pm Tue-Fri, 2-6pm Sat, Sun & holidays), the furnished rooms of which have been left just as they were back when going round the world in 80 days sounded utterly fantastic. Verne fans may also want to check out the changing exhibitions at the new **Imaginaire Jules Verne** (☎ 03 22 45 37 84; 36 rue de Noyon; adult/student €2/1; ☑ 11am-7pm mid-Jun–Sep, 3-7pm Tue-Sun Oct–mid-Jun), the bookshop of which carries Verne classics in English. The centenary of his death will be celebrated across France in 2005.

Sleeping

Amiens' hotels often fill up with businesspeople from Monday through Thursday.

Hôtel Victor Hugo (☎ 03 22 91 57 91; fax 03 22 92 74 02; 2 rue de l'Oratoire; d/tw €38/44) Just a block from the cathedral, this charming family-run hostelry has two stars and 10 modern stylish rooms that retain touches of days gone by.

Hôtel Le St Louis (☎ 03 22 91 76 03; www.le-saint louis.com in French; 24 rue des Otages; d/q from €47/76) All the mod cons with more than a dash of 19th-century French class. The 16 two-star rooms are spacious and tasteful.

Hôtel Spatial (☎ 03 22 91 53 23; www.hotelspatial .com; 15 rue Alexandre Fatton; s/d from €28/33, with shower & toilet €38/43; **P**) Staying here is hardly a scintillating aesthetic experience, but this two-star place is practical, welcoming and spotless.

Hôtel Central Anzac (☎ 03 22 91 34 08; hotel -central2@wanadoo.fr; 17 rue Alexandre Fatton; s/d from €26/30, with shower & toilet €36/40; **P**) Founded decades ago by an Australian ex-serviceman, this bland two-star place is now run by a friendly French family. The rooms are clean and comfortable, although small. Hall showers cost €2.50.

Eating

The area right around place du Don and the quays across the river in St-Leu (quai Bélu) are bursting with dozens of restaurants and cafés.

Les Marissons (☎ 03 22 92 96 66; pont de la Dodane; menus €18.50-49; ☑ closed Sun & lunch Sat) Occupying a 14th-century boatwright's workshop, this may well be the finest eatery in town; it's certainly the most elegant. Traditional French dishes and *cuisine du marché*, tailor-made to take advantage of fresh seasonal ingredients available in the market, are the specialities; the chef's personal favourite – it's his own invention – is *lotte rotie aux abricots* (monk-fish roasted with apricots, €25).

Le T'chiot Zinc (☎ 03 22 91 43 79; 18 rue de Noyon; menus €11.40-27.70; ☽ closed Sun & lunch Mon) Inviting, bistro-style décor – banquettes, light fixtures and mirrored walls reminiscent of the *belle époque* – provides a perfect backdrop for the tasty French and Picard cuisine, including lots of fish and seafood.

Les Bouchées Doubles (☎ 03 22 91 00 85; 11bis rue Gresset; dishes €9.20-18.20; ☽ noon-2.30pm & 7.30-11.30pm) A contemporary brasserie that specialises in succulent beef dishes.

Le Wakam (☎ 03 22 72 51 50; 48 rue St-Leu; lunch menus €10-16; ☽ 12.30-2pm Mon-Fri, 7.30pm-midnight) At this chic and very mellow place, mouth-watering 'Afrotropical' (mainly West African) dishes can be washed down with fine South African wines and rums shipped in from Guyana and Jamaica.

Le Tigzirt (☎ 03 22 91 42 55; courtyard, 7 place du Don; dishes €9.50-20; ☽ closed Mon, dinner Sun & lunch Sat) The Algerian Berber-style couscous and tajines are steamed, boiled, grilled and baked to perfection. Often crowded. To get in, press intercom button No 6.

SELF-CATERING
Fruit and vegetables grown in the Hortillonnages are sold at the **marché sur l'eau** (floating market; place Parmentier; ☽ until 12.30pm Sat, to 1pm in summer), now held on dry land.

Other places to stock up for a picnic include **Champion supermarket** (22bis rue du Général Leclerc; ☽ 9am-7.30pm Mon-Sat), the **covered market** (Halles du Beffroi; rue de Metz; ☽ 9am-1pm & 3-7pm Tue-Thu, 9am-7pm Fri & Sat, 8.30am-12.30pm Sun) and **Match supermarket** (Centre Commercial Amiens 2; ☽ 9am-8pm Mon-Sat).

Entertainment
Café Bissap (☎ 03 22 92 36 41; 50 rue St-Leu; ☽ noon-3am Tue-Sat, to 1am Sun & Mon) A mixed and very laid-back crowd, including lots of students, sips West African beers amid décor from the Senegalese proprietor's native land. There's live jazz every Sunday from 9pm to midnight; the rest of the time, the beat is Afrosalsa.

Marott Street (☎ 03 22 91 14 93; 1 rue Marotte; ☽ 11am-1am) This building started out as an insurance office, designed by Gustave Eiffel's architectural firm in 1892. It has since been turned into a chic bar where the trendy sip champagne, suspended – on clear glass tiles – over the wine cellar.

Concerts are often held at **Cirque Jules Verne** (place Longueville), a 16-sided circus venue built in 1889 for the centennial of the French Revolution, and **Mégacité** (www.megacite.com; av Hippodrome), about 2km west of the centre.

Getting There & Away
For details on visiting the Battle of the Somme memorials by public transport, see p225.

BUS
The **bus station** (☎ 03 22 92 27 03; ☽ office 6am-7pm Mon-Fri, 7am-6.45pm Sat), in the basement of the Centre Commercial Amiens 2, is accessible only from rue de la Vallée.

TRAIN
From the train station in the town centre, Amiens is linked to Arras (€9.60, 50 minutes, seven to 11 daily), Boulogne (€15.70, 1½ hours, five to eight daily), Calais-Ville (€19.70, two to 2½ hours, two or three direct Monday to Saturday), Lille-Flandres (€16.20, 1½ hours, six to nine daily) and Paris' Gare du Nord (€16.50, 1¼ to two hours, 25 daily Monday to Friday, 15 daily Saturday and Sunday). SNCF buses (45 minutes) go to the Haute Picardie TGV station, 42km east of the city.

CAR
ADA (☎ 03 22 46 49 49; 387 chaussée Jules Ferry) Situated 2.4km southeast of the train station and served by bus No 1.

France Cars (☎ 03 22 72 52 52; 75 blvd d'Alsace-Lorraine)

Hertz (☎ 03 22 91 26 24; 3 blvd d'Alsace-Lorraine)

Rent-A-Car Système (☎ 03 22 82 44 55; 19 rue des Otages)

Getting Around
There's free parking one or two blocks northeast of the Victor Hugo, Spatial and Central Anzac Hotels, on rue Lameth, rue Cardon, rue Jean XXIII and rue de la Barette.

Association Vélo Service (☎ 03 22 72 55 13; 3 rue des Corps Nuds-sans-Teste; per hr/day €1/5, tandems €2/8; ☽ 9am-12.30pm & 1.30-7pm) is a nonprofit group that rents bikes. A €100 deposit is required; helmets are free.

BEAUVAIS
pop 547,000
For the French, the name 'Beauvais' conjures up images of medieval Picardy at its most extravagant. Famed for the titanic hubris

of its cathedral, doomed to remain forever unfinished, it has been a tapestry-making centre since the time of Louis XIV and is often mentioned in the same breath as Gobelins (p129) and Aubusson (p578). Alas, the modern-day town, rebuilt after being bombed in 1940, is far from enchanting.

Information

The **tourist office** (☎ 03 44 15 30 30; ot.beauvaisis@ wanadoo.fr; 1 rue Beauregard; ❧ 9.30am or 10am-6pm or 6.30pm Mon-Sat, 10am-5pm Sun & holidays May-Sep, to 1.30pm Sun & holidays Oct-Apr) is about 200m southeast of the cathedral.

Sights

The history of the unfinished (but nevertheless stunning) **Cathédrale St-Pierre** (❧ 9am-12.15pm & 2-6.15pm Apr-Sep, 9am-12.15pm & 2-5.30pm Oct-Mar, no midday closure Jul & Aug) has been one of insatiable ambition and colossal failure. When Beauvais' Carolingian cathedral (parts of which can still be seen) was partly destroyed by fire in 1225, the bishop and local nobles decided that its replacement should surpass anything ever built. Unfortunately, their richly adorned creation also surpassed the limits of technology, and in 1284 the 48m-high vaults – the highest ever built – collapsed. There was further damage in 1573 when the 153m spire, the tallest of its era, came a-tumblin' down. Today, the flamboyant Gothic choir and transept stand nave-less, seemingly held up by huge wood beams (in fact, these have helped stabilise the building – so did pouring tonnes of concrete under the floor – and are to be removed as soon as funding comes through). One of the **astronomical clocks** (adult/17-25 yrs/6-16 yrs €4/2.50/1) dates from the 14th century; the other, finished in 1868, does its thing at 10.40am, 11.40am, 2.40pm, 3.40pm and 4.40pm, with additional demonstrations at 12.40pm and 5.40pm in July and August.

Just west of the cathedral, head through the two round bastions – a relic of the early 1300s – to the excellent **Musée Départemental de l'Oise** (☎ 03 44 11 11 30; 1 rue du Musée; adult €2, 18-25 yrs & senior €1, under 18 free; ❧ 10am-noon & 2-6pm Wed-Mon, no midday closure in summer). Highlights in this former bishops' palace include the *Dieu Guerrier Gaulois*, a slender and aristocratic Celtic warrior made of hammered sheet brass in the 1st century AD; a sinuous Art Nouveau dining room; a rich selection

of 19th-century French painting; and medieval wood carvings (in the reception area).

Tapestries made in the workshops of Beauvais and Gobelins are presented in themed temporary exhibitions at France's national tapestry museum, **Galerie Nationale de la Tapisserie** (☎ 03 44 15 39 10; rue St-Pierre; adult €4.60, 18-25 yrs & senior €3.10, under 18 free; ❧ 9.30am or 10am-12.30pm & 2-6pm Tue-Sun Apr-Sep, to 5pm Oct-Mar, closed btwn exhibitions), just east of the cathedral.

You can see strikingly modern tapestries actually being made, using techniques perfected over centuries, at the state-owned **Manufacture Nationale de la Tapisserie** (☎ 03 44 14 41 90; 24 rue Henri Brispot; tours adult/7-17 yrs €3.20/1; ❧ tours approximately 2pm & 3pm Tue-Thu), 1km south of the cathedral. All the projects underway have been commissioned by the French government to add panache to embassies and other official buildings.

Sleeping & Eating

JP Pub Hôtel (☎ 03 44 45 07 51; fax 03 44 45 71 25; 15 place Jeanne Hachette; d €38) Burned out in a fire started by someone's mobile-phone charger, this place, 250m south of the tourist office, should be back in action (and fireproofed) by the time you read this. Reception (at the bar) is closed until 2pm on Sunday.

Nouvelles Galeries supermarket (2 rue Carnot) Two short blocks east of the tourist office; the food section is in the basement.

Getting There & Away

Beauvais-Tillé Airport (☎ 08 92 68 20 66; www.aero portbeauvais.com), a few kilometres northeast of the centre, is thriving thanks to cheap Ryanair flights; destinations include Dublin, Glasgow and Shannon.

Rail destinations include Paris' Gare du Nord (€10.70, 1¼ hours, 11 to 16 daily).

COMPIÈGNE

pop 45,000

Favoured by French rulers as a country retreat since Merovingian times, Compiègne reached its glittering zenith under Napoleon III (ruled 1852–70). These days the city, 80km northeast of Paris, is a favourite day trip for Parisians, particularly on Sunday.

On 23 May 1430, Joan of Arc (Jeanne d'Arc) – honoured by two statues in the city centre – was captured at Compiègne by the Burgundians, who later sold her to their allies, the English.

During WWII, 49,860 people – *résistants,* political prisoners and Jews – were held in a transit camp in the Compiègne suburb of Royallieu before being shipped by train to Buchenwald, Mauthausen, Dachau and other Nazi concentration camps. A memorial-museum is planned to open in late 2006.

Information

The **tourist office** (☎ 03 44 40 01 00; compiegne .tourisme.infos@wanadoo.fr; place de l'Hôtel de Ville; ⏰ 9.15am-12.15pm & 1.45-6.15pm Mon-Sat, 10am-1pm & 2.30-5pm Sun Apr-Sep, to 5.15pm & closed Mon morning Oct-Mar) is next to the ornate, 15th-century Gothic town hall, and opposite a statue of Jeanne d'Arc.

Sights

CHÂTEAU DE COMPIÈGNE

Napoleon III's glittering hunting parties drew well-connected participants from all around the continent to the vast **royal palace** (☎ 03 44 38 47 00; www.musee-chateau-comp iegne.fr in French; place du Général de Gaulle; adult/18-25 yrs/under 18 €4.50/3/free, adult Sun €3; ⏰ tours 10am-5.15pm Wed-Mon, to 3.45pm Nov-Feb). The chateau's sumptuously decorated **Grands Appartements** (Imperial Apartments), including the empress' bedroom and a ballroom lit by 15 chandeliers, can be seen on a one-hour tour (in French, English brochure are available; departures every 15 or 20 minutes). The **Musée du Second Empire** (open by request only – ask if a staff member is available to accompany you) illustrates the life of Napoleon III and that of his family (mid-1800s) amid a lot of gaudy gilding.

Vehicles that predate the internal combustion engine and early motorcars are the main attraction at the **Musée de la Voiture** (Vehicle Museum; adult/under 18 €2.60/free, incl the Grands Appartements adult/18-25 yrs/under 18 €5.50/4/free). Tours are in French only and last one hour.

To the east of the chateau, the English-style **Petit Parc** gardens link up with the **Grand Parc** and the **Forêt de Compiègne**, which surrounds Compiègne from the east and southeast, and is a favourite venue for hiking, cycling and horse riding.

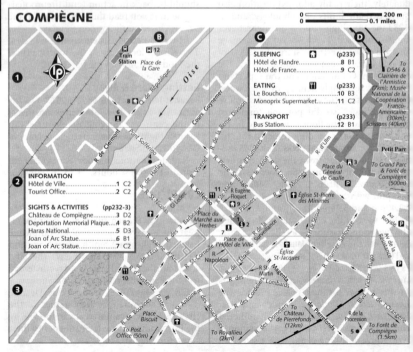

COMPIÈGNE

0 ————— 200 m
0 ————— 0.1 miles

SLEEPING	🏠	(p233)
Hôtel de Flandre		.8 B1
Hôtel de France		.9 C2

EATING	🍽	(p233)
Le Bouchon		.10 B3
Monoprix Supermarket		.11 C2

| TRANSPORT | | (p233) |
| Bus Station | | .12 B1 |

INFORMATION	
Hôtel de Ville	.1 C2
Tourist Office	.2 C2

SIGHTS & ACTIVITIES	(pp232-3)
Château de Compiègne	.3 D2
Deportation Memorial Plaque	.4 B2
Haras National	.5 D3
Joan of Arc Statue	.6 B1
Joan of Arc Statue	.7 C2

To D546 & Clairière de l'Armistice (7km); Musée National de la Coopération Franco-Américaine (30km); Soissons (40km)

Petit Parc

To Grand Parc & Forêt de Compiègne (500m)

To Château de Pierrefonds (12km)

To Post Office (50m)

To Royallieu (2km)

To Forêt de Compiègne (1.5km)

HARAS NATIONAL
You can wander among stalls housing magnificent thoroughbreds, trotters, saddle horses, ponies and draught horses at the **National Stud Farm** (☎ 03 44 38 54 50; 6 rue de la Procession; admission free; ⏰ 2-4.30pm Mon-Fri except holidays, closed Mar–mid-Jul). It was established in 1876 in the chateau's former stables, built for Louis XV in 1738, and is now run by the Ministry of Agriculture.

CLAIRIÈRE DE L'ARMISTICE
The armistice that came into force on 'the 11th hour of the 11th day of the 11th month' – the year was 1918 – and finally put an end to WWI was signed 7km northeast of Compiègne (towards Soissons) in the railway carriage of the Allied supreme commander, Maréchal Ferdinand Foch.

On 22 June 1940, in the same railway car, the French – with Hitler looking on smugly – were forced to sign the armistice that recognised the German conquest of France. Taken for exhibition to Berlin, the carriage was destroyed in April 1945 on the Führer's personal orders lest it be used for a third surrender – his own.

In the middle of a thick forest, the **Armistice Clearing** (☎ 03 44 85 14 18; adult/7-13 yrs €3/1.50; ⏰ 9am-12.15pm & 2-6pm Wed-Mon Apr-Sep, 10am-noon & 2-5pm Wed-Mon Oct-Mar), staffed by volunteers (mainly French army veterans), commemorates these events with monuments and a museum with 700 stereoscopic (3D) photos that give you an eerie feeling of being right there in the mud, muck and misery of WWI. The wooden rail wagon now on display is of the same type as the original; the furnishings, hidden away during WWII, were the ones actually used in 1918. Since 1927, only visiting heads of state and government, along with a few very lucky ministers or ambassadors, have been allowed to go inside the wagon. By tradition, the president of France pays an official visit to the site every year ending in eight (1998, 2008 etc).

Festivals & Events
One of the world's most gruelling one-day cycling races, **Paris-Roubaix** (www.letour.com/indexus.html), starts at place du Général de Gaulle on the first Sunday after Easter. The 261km competition is famous for its 50km of bone-jarring sections over *pavé*

(cobblestone) roads, including an especially tough 2.4km bit through the Forêt d'Arenberg.

Sleeping
Most of the hotels are situated between the train station and the chateau.

Hôtel de France (☎ 03 44 40 02 74; contact@restauranthoteldefrance.fr; 17 rue Eugène Floquet; s/d from €50/60) A lovingly looked-after two-star place with chintz and antiques everywhere.

Hôtel de Flandre (☎ 03 44 83 24 40; fax 03 44 90 02 75; 16 quai de la République; s/d from €27/30, with shower & toilet €42/52) This straightforward two-star hotel offers more convenience than charm. Some of the rooms have river views.

Eating
The streets southwest of Église St-Jacques, including rue Magenta and rue des Lombards, are home to lots of restaurants.

Le Bouchon (☎ 03 44 20 02 03; 4 rue d'Austerlitz; menus €10.50-25) An old-style bistro and wine bar, this place has a sunny terrace and stick-to-the-ribs main courses such as duck *cassoulet* (casserole, €12).

Picnic supplies are sold at the **Monoprix supermarket** (37 rue Solférino).

Getting There & Around
Trains link Compiègne to Amiens (€10.50, 1½ hours, five to eight daily) and Paris' Gare du Nord (€11.40, 40 minutes to one hour 20 minutes, 15 to 26 daily).

Local buses are free except on Sunday, when service is limited. Lines No 1 and 2 link the train station with the chateau.

There's nonmetered parking in front of the chateau (place du Général de Gaulle) and along av Royale and av de la Résistance southeast of there.

LAON
pop 26,300
Laon (the name has one syllable and rhymes with *enfant*) served as the capital of the Carolingian Empire until it was brought to an end in 987 by Hugh Capet, who was rather partial to Paris. The walled, hilltop Ville Haute (Upper Town) commands fantastic views of the surrounding plains and has a fine Gothic cathedral. About 100m below sits the Ville Basse (Lower Town), completely rebuilt after being flattened in WWII.

WHEN BENNY MET LOUIE

In these days of 'freedom fries' and diplomatic hauteur, it's something of a relief to glance back at times gone by when relations between France and the USA were warmer, if not always free of rivalry. From the American Revolution (when French generals led American patriots, and Benjamin Franklin lobbied Louis XVI) through WWI (when American volunteers carried out humanitarian work long before the Doughboys arrived) and WWII (when the Parisians didn't exactly liberate themselves, whatever de Gaulle might have proclaimed), the USA and France have had a prickly but ardent love affair. All this and more is presented through art and artefacts at the **Musée National de la Coopération Franco-Américaine** (☎ 03 23 39 60 16; adult/18-25 yrs/under 18 €3/2.30/free; ☺ 10am-12.30pm & 2-5.30pm Wed-Mon), 30km northeast of Compiègne in the 17th-century Château de Blérancourt. The **Jardins du Nouveau Monde** (☺ 8am-7pm) showcase 'exotic' flowers, shrubs and trees (eg the sequoia) that are native to the Americas.

Information

In the Ville Haute, the **tourist office** (☎ 03 23 20 28 62; tourisme.info.laon@wanadoo.fr; place de la Cathédrale; ☺ 9.30 or 10am-12.30pm & 2-6pm Mon-Sat, 1-5pm or 6pm Sun & holidays, no midday closure & open Sun morning Jul & Aug) is next to the cathedral in a 12th-century hospital. It holds a 1/600-scale model of Laon as it looked in 1854 and has excellent English brochures.

Sights & Activities

A model for a number of its more famous Gothic sisters – Chartres, Reims and Dijon among them – **Cathédrale Notre Dame** (☺ 9am-6pm or 6.30pm) was built (1150–1230) in the transitional Gothic style on Romanesque foundations. The 110m-long interior has a gilded wrought-iron choir screen and is remarkably well lit; some of the stained glass dates from the 12th century. A memorial plaque for Commonwealth WWI dead hangs inside the west façade. Underneath the cathedral (and much of the town) there are three levels of **caves and quarries** (☺ tours daily Jul & Aug, Sat & Sun Jun, Sep & Oct).

The Ville Haute's narrow streets are rich in historic buildings, making Laon a particularly rewarding place for keen-eyed wandering. The octagonal 12th-century **Chapelle des Templiers** is in the garden of the archaeologically orientated **Musée de Laon** (☎ 03 23 20 19 87; 32 rue Georges Ermant; admission €3.20; ☺ 11am-6pm Tue-Sun Jun-Sep, 2-6pm Tue-Sun Oct-May).

The 7km-long **ramparts**, with their three fortified gates, are lovely for a stroll; paths known as *grimpettes* take you along the steep forested slopes. For panoramic views, head to the 13th-century **Porte d'Ardon**, circular **Batterie Morlot** and **rue du Rempart St-Rémi**. Local Jesuit missionary Jacques Marquette (1637–75), a pioneer explorer of the Mississippi River and the first European to live in what later became Chicago, is commemorated by a **statue** on rue de la Libération.

Sleeping & Eating

Rue Chatelaine, which links the cathedral with place du Général Leclerc, is home to several food shops.

Hôtel Les Chevaliers (☎ 03 23 27 17 50; hotel chevaliers@aol.com; 3-5 rue Sérurier; s from €28, d with shower & toilet €58; ☺ mid-Jan–mid-Nov) Parts of this two-star 14-room hostelry, around the corner from the Haute Ville's town hall, date from the Middle Ages. Rooms are simple, with a touch of rusticity and rates include breakfast.

Hôtel du Commerce (☎ 03 23 79 57 16; hotel.commerce.laon@wanadoo.fr; 11 place de la Gare; d from €26, with shower & toilet €37) Facing the train station, this welcoming two-star hotel has rooms that are modestly furnished but offer good value.

Getting There & Around

There are direct rail services to Amiens (€14, 1½ hours, four or five daily), Paris' Gare du Nord (€17.40, 1¾ hours, 13 daily Monday to Friday, seven on Saturday, four on Sunday) and Reims (€7.70, 40 minutes, eight daily Monday to Friday, three or four daily Saturday and Sunday).

The Ville Haute is a steep 20-minute walk from the train station – the stairs begin at the upper end of av Carnot. More fun is the overhead **Poma funicular railway** (return €1; ☺ every 3min 7am-8pm Mon-Sat except holidays year-round, 2.30-7pm Sun Jul & Aug), which links the train station with the Ville Haute.

Normandy

CONTENTS

Rouen	**238**
Around Rouen	243
Dieppe	245
Côte d'Albâtre	248
Le Havre	249
Calvados	**251**
Honfleur	251
Trouville & Deauville	254
Caen	256
Bayeux	260
D-Day Beaches	266
Manche	**268**
Cherbourg	269
Coutances	271
Mont St-Michel	272
Alençon	275

236

Normandy is a land of tradition, of quintessential grey farmhouses rising out of rolling green pastures, of blackberried hedgerows lining patchwork fields of artichokes, cauliflower and corn. It's a land of apples and crustaceans, of generous meals, half-timbered houses and honest fishing villages where deep rural countryside meets the bracing sea.

Normandy is a land steeped in history, the subject of successive invasions and decisive battles. A place where monasteries rise up from the sea and where tapestries recount historical watersheds, home to the thighbone of William the Conqueror, the garden of Claude Monet and over six million cows.

And while you can feel the proximity to English history and geography, the region retains its own distinctive culture and identity. With its swish seaside resorts, postwar reconstructions and busy universities, it is not at odds with modernity but is a place that has had to re-create itself constantly, all the while maintaining its strong link with the past.

For the visitor the charm is twofold: the peaceful country and coastal landscape, and the fascinating cities and towns. The city of Rouen is well endowed with medieval architecture, including a spectacular cathedral; Caen boasts some fine Norman Romanesque abbeys; Bayeux, home to the 11th-century Bayeux Tapestry, is only a dozen kilometres from the D-Day landing beaches. The Battle of Normandy (1944) left its mark on the region, reducing many towns to rubble. In cities such as Le Havre and Caen, postwar architecture predominates.

The coastline stretches 600km from the dramatic chalk cliffs of the Côte d'Albâtre to the celebrated island abbey of Mont St-Michel. Impressionist artists were drawn to Normandy's shores, lined with picturesque seaside resorts such as Fécamp, Honfleur and the fashionable twin towns of Deauville-Trouville. Inland lie fertile farmland and wooded valleys.

HIGHLIGHTS

- Soak everything, from your coffee to your Camembert, in local **Norman Calvados** (p251), an apple liqueur
- Fresh, fine seafood at the picturesque port of **Honfleur** (p251), where explorers set sail for the New World
- Stroll around **Giverny** (p243), the luxuriant garden planted and painted by Monet
- **D-Day landing beaches** (p266) – pay homage to those who fell during Operation Overlord in WWII
- Watch the waters rise around the bay of the soaring Gothic abbey on **Mont St-Michel** (p272)
- Relive William's conquest of England along the 70m **Bayeux Tapestry** (p255)
- Swing with the movers and shakers when Hollywood descends on seaside **Deauville** (p249)
- View the stunning Manneporte rock arch from the top of the white cliffs at Étretat (p249)

▪ POPULATION: 3,202,400	▪ AREA: 29,900 SQ KM

NORMANDY

NORMANDY

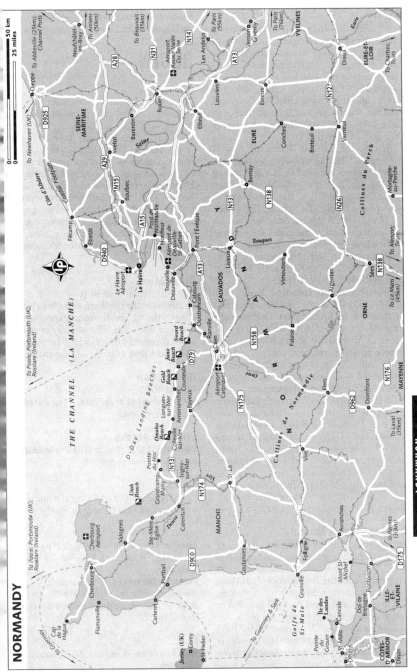

History

The Vikings invaded what is now Normandy in the 9th century. Originally made up of bands of plundering pirates, many of these raiding groups from Scandinavia established settlements in the area and adopted Christianity. In 911 the French king Charles the Simple and the Viking chief Hrölfr agreed that the Rouen region become home to these Norsemen (or Normans), who gave their name to the region.

In 1066 the duke of Normandy crossed the English Channel with 6000 soldiers. His forces crushed the English in the Battle of Hastings, and the duke – who became known in history as William the Conqueror – was crowned king of England. The Channel Islands (Îles Anglo-Normandes), just off the Norman coast, came under English rule in the same year and remain so to this day. During the 11th and 12th centuries, many churches were built in Normandy and England in the Romanesque style.

Throughout the Hundred Years' War (1337–1453) the duchy switched back and forth between French and English rule. England dominated Normandy (except for Mont St-Michel) for about 30 years until France gained permanent control in 1450. In the 16th century, Normandy, a Protestant stronghold, was the scene of much fighting between Catholics and Huguenots.

In 1942 a force of 6000, mostly Canadian, troops participated in a disastrous landing near Dieppe. On 6 June 1944 – better known as D-Day – 45,000 Allied troops landed on beaches near Bayeux. The Battle of Normandy (p264) followed, with more than 425,000 Allied and German casualties and more than 15,000 civilian deaths. Eventually, the German resistance was broken. Paris was liberated on 25 August.

Getting There & Around

Ferries to and from England and Ireland dock at Cherbourg, Ouistreham, Le Havre and Dieppe. The Channel Islands are most accessible from the Breton port of St-Malo, but in the warm season from Cherbourg, Carteret, Granville and Portbail as well. For more information on ferries, see p919.

Normandy is easily accessible by train from Paris. All major towns in Normandy are well connected by rail, but the buses between smaller towns and villages are infrequent.

Visitors who want to explore Normandy's rural areas should consider renting a car.

ROUEN

pop 108,750

The city of Rouen is known for the lofty spires and craggy church towers that make up its delightful medieval centre, where you'll find over 2000 half-timbered houses. Rouen also has a renowned Gothic cathedral and a number of excellent museums. The city was occupied by the English during the Hundred Years' War when the young French heroine Joan of Arc (Jeanne d'Arc) was tried for heresy and burned at the stake.

Today, Rouen boasts a thriving cultural scene and excellent restaurants. It's an excellent base for visiting Monet's home in Giverny.

Orientation

The main train station (Gare Rouen-Rive Droite) is at the northern end of rue Jeanne d'Arc, the main thoroughfare running south to the Seine. The old city is centred around rue du Gros Horloge between the place du Vieux Marché and the cathedral.

Information

BOOKSHOPS

ABC Bookshop (☎ 02 35 71 08 67; 11 rue des Faulx) English-language books.

INTERNET ACCESS

PlaceNet (☎ 02 32 76 02 22; 37 rue de la République; per 15min €1; ☼ 10am-midnight)

LAUNDRY

Laundrettes at 47 and 55 rue d'Amiens, are open 7am or 8am to 8pm or 9pm.

MONEY

American Express (☎ 02 35 89 48 60; 25 place de la Cathédrale; ☼ 9am-1pm & 2-6pm Mon-Sat) In the tourist office.

Bureau de Change (7-9 rue des Bonnetiers; ☼ 7am-10pm) Decent exchange rates. Banks with ATMs line rue Jeanne d'Arc between the Théâtre des Arts and place Maréchal Foch.

POST

Main Post Office (45 rue Jeanne d'Arc) It has a Cyberposte terminal.

ROUEN

0 ━━━━━━━━━━ 400 m
0 ━━━━━━━━━━ 0.2 miles

INFORMATION
ABC Bookshop..**1** D4
American Express.........................(see 7)
Bureau de Change....................................**2** C5
Laundrette...**3** D4
Laundrette...**4** D4
Main Post Office.......................................**5** B3
PlaceNet...**6** C4
Tourist Office...**7** B4
Voyages Wasteels Travel Agency........**8** C2

SIGHTS & ACTIVITIES   (pp240–1)
Aître St-Maclou..**9** D5
Cathédrale Notre Dame........................**10** C4
Église Jeanne d'Arc...............................**11** A4
Église St-Éloi..**12** A4
Église St-Maclou.....................................**13** C5
Église St-Ouen..**14** D4
Gros Horloge...**15** B4
La Tour Jeanne d'Arc.............................**16** C3
Monument Juif..**17** B4
Musée de la Céramique........................**18** B3
Musée des Beaux-Arts...........................**19** C3
Musée Jeanne d'Arc...............................**20** A4
Musée Le Secq des Tournelles.............**21** C3

Palais de Justice Courtyard............(see 17)
Palais de Justice....................................**22** B4
Town Hall..**23** D4

SLEEPING   (p241)
Hôtel Andersen......................................**24** B2
Hôtel Dandy..**25** A3
Hôtel de la Cathédrale..........................**26** C4
Hôtel des Carmes...................................**27** C4
Hôtel Dieppe..**28** C2
Hôtel Le Palais.......................................**29** B4
Le Vieux Carré..**30** C3

EATING   (pp241–2)
Alimentation Générale..........................**31** C4
Au Temps des Cerises...........................**32** B3
Covered Food Market............................**33** A4
Food & Clothing Market........................**34** D5
Gill...**35** B5
Gourmand'grain.....................................**36** B4
Le P'tit Bec...**37** D4
Les Maraîchers.......................................**38** A4
Les Nymphéas..**39** A3
Monoprix Supermarket.........................**40** B4
Pascaline...**41** B4
Thé Majuscule..**42** C5

DRINKING   (p242)
L'Euro...**43** A4
L'Insolite...**44** D5
Le Saxo...**45** D5

ENTERTAINMENT   (p242)
Cinéma Le Melville................................**46** B5
Théâtre des Arts.....................................**47** A5

TRANSPORT   (pp242–3)
Bus Station...**48** A5
Espace Métrobus/CNA Bus....................**49** A5
Rouen Cycles..**50** A4

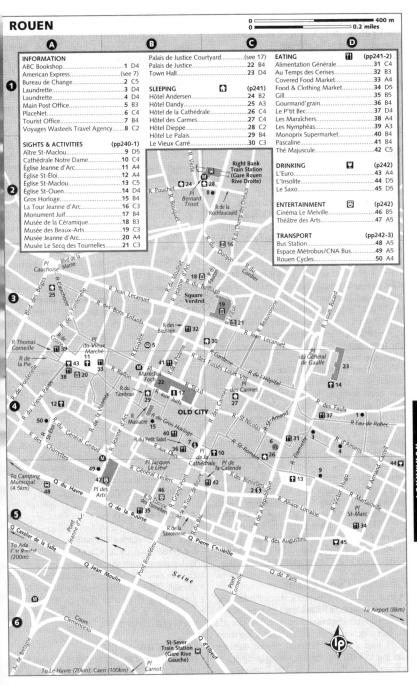

NORMANDY

TOURIST INFORMATION

Tourist Office (☎ 02 32 08 32 40; www.rouentour isme.com; 25 place de la Cathédrale; ⏰ 9am-7pm Mon-Sat, 9.30am-12.30pm & 2-6pm Sun May-Sep, 9am-6pm Mon-Sat, 10am-1pm Sun Oct-Apr)Staff make hotel reservations in the area for €1.50.

TRAVEL AGENCIES

Voyages Wasteels (☎ 0 825 887 057; 111bis rue Jeanne d'Arc) Discount travel agent.

Sights

OLD CITY

Rouen suffered enormous damage during WWII but has been painstakingly restored. The main street, rue du Gros Horloge, runs from the cathedral to **place du Vieux Marché**, where 19-year-old Joan of Arc was executed for heresy in 1431. The striking **Église Jeanne d'Arc** (⏰ 10am-12.15pm & 2-6pm Mon-Sat), marking the site contains marvellous 16th-century stained-glass windows. Tacky **Musée Jeanne d'Arc** (33 place du Vieux Marché; admission €4; ⏰ 9.30am-7pm May-Sep, 10am-noon & 2-6.30pm Oct-Apr) across the square might interest the kids.

Rue du Gros Horloge is spanned by an early-16th-century gatehouse holding aloft the **Gros Horloge**, a large medieval clock with only one hand.

The ornate **Palais de Justice** (Law Courts), which was left a shell at the end of WWII, has been restored to its early-16th-century Gothic glory, though the 19th-century western façade still shows extensive damage. During construction of the city's underground (subway) system, archaeologists discovered a 3rd-century Gallo-Roman settlement.

The **courtyard** of the Palais de Justice, which you can enter through a gate on rue aux Juifs, is worth a look for its spires, gargoyles and statuary. The two-storey building under the courtyard is the **Monument Juif**, the oldest such monument in France and the only reminder of Rouen's ancient Jewish community, expelled by Philippe le Bel in 1306. It is closed to the public indefinitely.

CATHÉDRALE NOTRE DAME

A masterpiece of French Gothic architecture, Rouen's **Cathédrale Notre Dame** (⏰ 8am-6pm) was a subject of impressionist painter Claude Monet's exploration of light. Built between 1201 and 1514, it suffered severe damage during WWII; the decades-long restoration process is nearly complete. The Romanesque

crypt was part of a cathedral completed in 1062 and destroyed by fire in 1200. Note also the Flamboyant Gothic **Tour de Beurre**, with its apt yellow stonework, paid for out of the alms donated by various members of the congregation who wanted to eat butter during Lent. There are several guided visits to the crypt, ambulatory and **Chapel of the Virgin** on weekends, and daily in July and August.

MUSEUMS

In a desanctified 16th-century church, the fascinating **Musée Le Secq des Tournelles** (☎ 02 35 71 28 40; 2 rue Jacques Villon; adult/concession €2.30/1.55; ⏰ 10am-1pm & 2-6pm Wed-Mon) is devoted to the blacksmith's craft. It displays some 12,000 locks, keys and other wrought-iron utensils made between the 3rd and 19th centuries.

The **Musée des Beaux-Arts** (Fine Arts Museum; ☎ 02 35 71 28 40; 26bis rue Jean Lecanuet; adult/student €3/2; ⏰ 10am-6pm Wed-Mon) features paintings from the 15th to the 20th centuries.

Housed in a 17th-century building with a fine courtyard, the **Musée de la Céramique** (☎ 02 35 07 31 74; 1 rue du Faucon; admission €3; ⏰ 10am-1.30pm & 2-6pm Wed-Sat) is known for its 16th- to 19th-century faïence (decorated earthenware).

CHURCHES

The **Église St-Maclou** (⏰ 10am-noon & 2-6pm Mon-Sat, 3-5.30pm Sun) is a Flamboyant Gothic church built between 1437 and 1521, but much of the decoration dates from the Renaissance. The entrance is next to 56 rue de la République.

The **Église St-Ouen** (⏰ 10am-noon & 2-6pm Wed-Mon mid-Mar–Oct, 10am-12.30pm & 2-4.30pm Wed, Sat & Sun Nov–mid-Mar), a 14th-century abbey, is a marvellous example of Rayonnant Gothic style. The entrance is through a lovely garden along rue des Faulx.

AÎTRE ST-MACLOU

A curious ensemble of half-timbered buildings, **Aître St-Maclou** (186 rue Martainville; admission free; ⏰ 8am-8pm), built between 1526 and 1533, is decorated with macabre carvings of skulls, crossbones, gravediggers' tools and hourglasses. The courtyard was used as a burial ground for victims of the plague as late as 1781 and is now the municipal **École des Beaux-Arts**. Enter behind Église St-Maclou.

LA TOUR JEANNE D'ARC

La Tour Jeanne d'Arc (☎ 02 35 98 16 21; rue du Donjon; adult €1.50; ⏰ 10am-12.30pm & 2-6pm Wed-Sat & Mon,

2-6.30pm Sun Apr–Sep; 10am-12.30pm & 2-5pm Wed-Sat & Mon, 2-5.30pm Sun Oct-Mar) is the sole survivor of eight towers that once ringed a huge 13th century chateau built by Philippe Auge. Joan of Arc was imprisoned here before her execution. The tower has two exhibition rooms.

Tours
The tourist office runs **guided tours** (French only; adult/student €6/4; 2hr) of the city at 2.30pm at least twice a week from March to November, and daily in July and August.

Festivals & Events
The next **Rouen Armada** (www.armada.org), a big week-long festival with concerts, fireworks and a parade of sailing boats and warships, will be in 2007. Accommodation is booked up about a year in advance.

Sleeping
If you're staying over a weekend, ask the tourist office about its 'Bon Week-end' offer of two nights for the price of one in some hotels.

BUDGET
Hôtel Le Palais (☎ 02 35 71 41 40; 12 rue du Tambour; r €28-40) This hotel is in a highly advantageous location right near the Palais de Justice and the Gros Horloge. The rooms, all of which have showers, are good value. For an extra €2 you can have an en suite toilet.

Camping Municipal (☎ 02 35 74 07 59; rue Jules Ferry, Déville-lès-Rouen; camping €9.70) Modern facilities just 5km northwest of the city. From the Théâtre des Arts or the bus station, take bus No 2 and get off at the *mairie* (town hall) of Déville-lès-Rouen.

MID-RANGE
Hôtel de la Cathédrale (☎ 02 35 71 57 95; www.hotel -de-la-cathedrale.fr; 12 rue St-Romain; s/d from €49/59) Behind the beautiful 17th-century timber-panelled façade and the plant-filled inner courtyard you'll find small but comfortable, prettily decorated rooms. All in all a wonderful and atmospheric hotel.

Hôtel des Carmes (☎ 02 35 71 92 31; www.hotel descarmes.fr.st in French; 33 place des Carmes; r €42-58; P) In a 19th-century building, this romantic place is the sweetest little hotel in town. The rooms of varying sizes are decorated with colour and flair. Some are equipped with a huge and gleaming bath.

Hôtel Andersen (☎ 02 35 71 88 51; www.hoteland ersen.com; 4 rue Pouchet; d from €40) A welcoming, family-run establishment housed in an elegant 19th-century mansion. The bright, airy rooms are surprisingly large and comfortable, decorated in the Directory style of post-Revolutionary France.

Le Vieux Carré (☎ 02 35 71 67 70; www.vieux-carre .fr; 34 rue Ganterie; d €58) This gorgeous, half-timbered hotel is a true gem. The elegant rooms manage to simultaneously embrace tradition and avoid tackiness, and many give onto the tranquil inner courtyard.

TOP END
Hôtel Dieppe (☎ 02 35 71 96 00; place Bernard Tissot; d €77-90; P X 🖳) This attractive hotel has been lovingly restored and is well worth its three stars. The rooms are smallish but plush and very well equipped, and the service is top notch. Special weekend rates are available.

Hôtel Dandy (☎ 02 35 07 32 00; www.hotels-rouen .net; 93 rue Cauchoise; r €72-95; P) A delightful option in a quiet location, decorated in Old Normandy style with much polished wood, gleaming mirrors and plush furnishings. The rooms are exceedingly comfortable and have their own coffee maker.

Eating
BUDGET
Gourmand'grain (☎ 02 35 98 15 74; 3 rue du Petit Salut; menus from €8.10; 🕑 lunch only, closed Mon) This lunch-time vegetarian café with good salads and health-food *menus* is about the only place in town with vegan options.

Le P'tit Bec (☎ 02 35 07 63 33; 182 rue Eau de Robec; lunch menus €11-13.50, mains €7-9; 🕑 lunch Mon-Sat, dinner Fri & Sat) Good news for the weight-conscious traveller: here you can fill up on things fresh and light, such as tarts, poached fish and steamed vegetables.

MID-RANGE
Les Maraîchers (☎ 02 35 71 57 73; 37 place du Vieux Marché; menu €18) While the food here is great, it is clearly outdone by the magnificent décor. Gleaming with mirrors, polished wood, pewter and tiles, the restaurant has been classified a *café historique d'Europe*.

Pascaline (☎ 02 35 89 67 44; 5 rue de la Poterne; menus €12.95-21.90) This atmospheric bistro has a Pianola. It has wonderful duck dishes – the chef is a master *canardier* who prepares the famous *caneton à la Rouennaise*.

Au Temps des Cerises (☎ 02 35 89 98 00; 4-6 rue des Basnage; lunch menu €10.50, dinner menus from €15; ☺ closed Sun, Mon & lunch Sat) Cheese, cheese and more cheese: turkey breast with Camembert, *oeufs cocotte* (eggs cooked in ramekins and topped with a cheese sauce) and, of course, fondue. There's a vegetarian menu.

Thé Majuscule (☎ 02 35 71 15 66; 8 place de la Calende; tartes €6.95; ☺ noon-6.30pm Mon-Sat) A tearoom and second-hand bookshop that serves up home-made tarts, desserts and exotic teas in a smoke-free environment.

TOP END

Gill (☎ 02 35 71 16 14; 8 quai de la Bourse; weekday menu €38, weekend menus €54-74; ☺ Tue-Sat) This is the finest restaurant in these parts. The food is of exceptional quality, as witnessed by the scallops served with finely sliced truffles or ravioli with fennel and crayfish in a sauce of divine inspiration.

Les Nymphéas (☎ 02 35 89 26 69; 7 rue de la Pie; weekday menu €27, weekend menus €34-44; ☺ Tue-Sat) Patrice Kukrudz, the chef of this superb establishment, is one of the stars of Norman cuisine. He succeeds in using cider and Calvados to amplify the refined flavours of foie gras and soufflés.

SELF-CATERING

Rue Rollon has several good fruit stalls, cake shops and bakeries. The **covered food market** (place du Vieux Marché; ☺ 6am-1.30pm Tue-Sun) offers dairy products, fish and fresh produce. But there's a more lively daily **food and clothing market** (place St-Marc).

There's an **Alimentation Générale** (78 rue de la République) and a **Monoprix supermarket** (65 rue du Gros Horloge).

Drinking

L'Euro (☎ 02 35 07 55 66; 41 place du Vieux Marché; ☺ around 4pm-2am) You can nibble and sip the evening away on the terrace sampling tapas and tropical cocktails. When the sun goes down a DJ spins house for the upstairs lounge and dance floor.

Le Saxo (☎ 02 35 98 24 92; 11 place St-Marc; ☺ 9am-2am) This place moves to the tune of jazz and blues – it's a must on the nightcrawler's itinerary, especially on weekends when there are sometimes live concerts.

L'Insolite (☎ 02 35 88 62 53; 58 rue d'Amiens) This is the newest bar on the gay and lesbian scene in Rouen but heteros are also welcome.

Check out the 'vivarium' that includes reptiles and a parrot.

Entertainment

Cinéma Le Melville (☎ 02 32 76 73 21; 12 rue St-Étienne des Tonneliers) occasionally runs non-dubbed English-language films.

Théâtre des Arts (☎ 02 35 71 41 36; place des Arts; tickets from €20) Rouen's premier music venue and home to the Opéra de Normandie, the theatre also runs concerts and ballets.

Getting There & Away

The **Aéroport Rouen Vallée du Seine** (☎ 02 35 79 41 00) is 8km southeast of town at Boos. There are weekday direct flights to Lyon that connect with other cities in France as well as to international destinations.

CNA (☎ 0 825 076 027; 9 rue Jeanne d'Arc) runs services throughout Seine-Maritime, including Dieppe (€10.65, two hours, three daily), and towns along the coast west of Dieppe, including Fécamp (€14.45, 3¼ hours, one daily) and Le Havre (€12.65, three hours, five daily). Buses to Dieppe and Le Havre are slower and pricier than the train. Buses leave from quai du Havre and quai de la Bourse.

From Gare Rouen-Rive Droite, an Art-Nouveau edifice built in 1912–28, there's a frequent express train to/from Paris' Gare St-Lazare (€17.40, 70 minutes). Other services include Amiens (€15.50, 1¼ hours), Caen (€19.40, two hours), Dieppe (€9, 45 minutes) and Le Havre (€11.80, one hour). Gare Rouen-Rive Gauche has regional services.

Getting Around

There is no public transport into town from the airport; a taxi costs about €20.

Both Rouen's extensive local bus network and its metro line are operated by **TCAR** (Espace Métrobus). The metro runs from 5am (6am Sunday) to 11.30pm and is most useful for getting from the train station to the centre of town. A ticket valid for an hour of unlimited travel costs €1.30, a 10-ticket magnetic card costs €10. A Carte Découverte (one/two/three days €3.50/5/6.50) public transport pass is available at the tourist office.

For taxis, **Radio Taxi** (☎ 02 35 88 50 50) operates 24 hours.

Rouen Cycles (☎ 02 35 71 34 30; 45 rue St-Éloi) rents mountain bikes for €12 per day.

For car rental, try **ADA** (☎ 02 35 72 25 88; 34 av Jean Rondeaux). **Avis** (☎ 02 35 88 60 94) and **Hertz**

(☎ 02 35 70 70 71) are both in the Gare Rouen-Rive Droite train station.

AROUND ROUEN

Lovely day trips can be made from Rouen, particularly in the landlocked Eure *département*. The beautiful gardens of Claude Monet are at Giverny. From the 12th-century Château Gaillard in Les Andelys, a breathtaking panorama takes in the bend of river banks that rise to forested hills and white bluffs.

Les Andelys

pop 8500

Some 39km to the southeast of Rouen lies Les Andelys, a small, elongated town at the confluence of the mighty Seine and the tiny Gambon. The main reason for coming to the town is to visit the ruins of Château Gaillard, a 12th-century stronghold of English king Richard the Lion-Heart.

ORIENTATION & INFORMATION

The town is split into two parts: Grand Andely, whose main square is place Poussin, and to the west the older Petit Andely, which lies on the banks of the mighty Seine.

The tiny **tourist office** (☎ 02 32 54 41 93; 24 rue Philippe-Auge; ☼ 9.30am-noon & 2-6pm Mon-Sat, to 5.30pm Sun Jun-Sep; 2-5.30pm Mon-Fri Oct-May) is in Petit Andely at the foot of the cliffs, which form the base of the chateau.

CHÂTEAU GAILLARD

Built in 1196–97, **Château Gaillard** (☎ 02 32 54 04 16; admission €3; ☼ 10am-1pm & 2-6pm Wed-Mon) secured the western border of English territory along the Seine until Henry IV ordered its destruction in 1603. More impressive than the ruins is the fantastic view over the Seine, whose white cliffs are best seen from the platform north of the castle. The chateau is a 20-minute climb via a path that begins about 100m north of the tourist office. By car, take the turn-off opposite Église Notre Dame in Grand Andely and follow the signs.

SLEEPING & EATING

The tourist office has a list of *chambres d'hôtes* (B&Bs).

Hôtel Normandie (☎ 02 32 54 10 52; 1 rue Grande; d €54) Watch the boats and ducks go by along the Seine from the flowery terrace of this pleasant establishment. The hotel offers comfortable, nicely fitted rooms.

Hôtel and Restaurant de la Chaine d'Or (☎ 02 32 54 00 31; www.lachainedor.com; 27 rue Grande; r €72-122; P 🖳) This romantic hideaway in Petit Andely has peaceful, comfortable rooms, many of which look out on the Seine. The hotel has a **restaurant** (menus €27-55.50; ☼ closed Mon & dinner Sun) that offers fine regional specialties. A buffet breakfast on the terrace is an extra €12 but is well worth it.

Camping Château Gaillard (☎ 02 32 54 18 20; route de la Mare; adult/tent €5/4.20; ☼ Feb-Dec) A good choice for camping, 800m southeast of the chateau and 200m from the Seine.

Villa du Vieux Château (☎ 02 32 54 30 10; 78 rue G Nicolle; menus €25 & €31; ☼ closed Sun dinner, Mon & Tue) In Petit Andely, this restaurant does excellent fish *menus*. There are restaurants around place Poussin in Grand Andely.

GETTING THERE & AWAY

There's no train station in Les Andelys. **CNA buses** (☎ 0 825 076 027) link Grand Andely (place Poussin) and Rouen at least twice daily (€7.49, 1¼ hours).

Giverny

pop 550

Between Paris and Rouen and an ideal day trip from either, this small village contains the Musée Claude Monet. First opened to the public in 1980, the garden museum is immensely popular with visitors, many of whom also come to view the fine impressionist collection of the Musée d'Art Américain.

MUSÉE CLAUDE MONET

Musée Claude Monet (☎ 02 32 51 28 21; adult/student/child €5.50/4/3; ☼ 9.30am-6pm Tue-Sun Apr-Oct, Mon if public holiday) was Monet's home and studio. The hectare of land that Monet owned has become two distinct areas cut by the Chemin du Roy, a train line that was unfortunately changed into what is now the D5 road.

The northern part is the **Clos Normand** where Monet's famous pastel pink and green house and Water Lily studio stand. His studio is now the entrance hall, adorned with reproductions of his works and ringing with cash register bells from busy souvenir stands. Outside are the symmetrically laid-out gardens.

From the Clos Normand's far corner, a tunnel leads under the D5 to the **Jardin d'Eau** (Water Garden). Having bought this piece of land in 1895 after his reputation had been established, Monet dug a pool (fed by the Epte, a tributary of the nearby Seine), planted water lilies and constructed the Japanese bridge, which has since been rebuilt. Draped with purple wisteria, the bridge blends into the asymmetrical foreground and background, creating the intimate atmosphere for which the 'Painter of Light' was famous.

Seasons have an enormous effect on the gardens at Giverny. From early to late spring, daffodils, tulips, rhododendrons, wisteria and irises appear, followed by poppies and lilies. By June, nasturtiums, roses and sweet peas are in flower. Around September, there are dahlias, sunflowers and hollyhocks.

MUSÉE D'ART AMÉRICAIN

The **Musée d'Art Américain** (American Impressionist Museum; ☎ 02 32 51 94 65; www.maag.org; 99 rue Claude Monet; adult/student/child €5.50/4/3; ⏰ 10am-6pm Tue-Sun Apr-Oct) contains works of American impressionist painters who flocked to France in the late 19th and early 20th centuries. It's housed in a garish building 100m down the road from Musée Claude Monet.

GETTING THERE & AWAY

Giverny is 76km northwest of Paris and 66km southeast of Rouen. The nearest town is Vernon, nearly 7km to the west on the Paris–Rouen train line.

From Paris' Gare St-Lazare (€10.80, 50 minutes) there are two early trains to Vernon. For the return trip there's about one direct train an hour between 5pm and 9pm. From Rouen (€8.60, 40 minutes), four trains leave before noon; to get back, there's about one train every hour between 5pm and 10pm.

Once in Vernon it's still a hike to Giverny. **Shuttle buses** (☎ 02 35 71 32 99) meet most trains and cost €2 each way. You can rent a bike from the **Café de Chemin de Fer** (☎ 02 32 21 16 01) for €12 a day.

CLAUDE MONET

Everyone discusses my art and pretends to understand, as if it were necessary to understand, when it is simply necessary to love.

Claude Monet

The undisputed leader of the impressionists, Claude Monet was born in Paris in 1840 and grew up in Le Havre, where he found an early affinity with the outdoors. Monet disliked school and would spend his time drawing and caricaturing his professors in the margins of his exercise books. By 15 his skills as a caricaturist were known throughout Le Havre, where he sold his portraits. Eugène Boudin, his first mentor, convinced him to turn his attention to the landscapes, light, shadows and nature that later defined Monet's work.

In 1860 military service interrupted Monet's studies at the Académie Suisse in Paris and took him to Algiers, where the intense light and colours further fuelled his imagination. The young painter became fascinated with capturing a specific moment in time, the immediate impression of the scene before him, rather than the precise detail.

From 1867 Monet's distinctive style began to emerge, focusing on the effects of light and colour and using the quick, undisguised broken brushstrokes that would characterise the impressionist period. His contemporaries were Pissarro, Renoir, Sisley, Cézanne and Dégas. The young painters left the studio to work outdoors, experimenting with the shades and hues of nature, arguing and sharing ideas. Their work was far from welcomed by critics; one of whom condemned it as 'impressionism', in reference to Monet's *Impression: Sunrise* (1874), which became the name of their movement.

From the late 1870s Monet concentrated on painting in series, seeking to re-create a landscape by showing its transformation under different conditions of light and atmosphere. *Haystacks* (1890–91) and *Rouen Cathedral* (1891–95) are some of the best-known works of this time. In 1883 he moved to Giverny, planting his property with a variety of flowers around an artificial pond, in order to paint the subtle effects that varying tones of sunlight had on nature. Here he painted the *Nymphéas* (Water Lilies) series. The huge dimensions of some of these works, together with the fact that the pond's surface takes up the entire canvas, meant the abandonment of composition in the traditional sense and the virtual disintegration of form. Despite his failing eyesight, Monet completed the series just before his death in 1926.

DIEPPE
pop 35,700

Dieppe is an ancient seaside town and a favourite among British weekenders. It's not the prettiest place in Normandy, but its location – set between two limestone cliffs – and its medieval castle are dramatic. Dieppe also has the attractive, gritty appeal of an old-fashioned port.

Privateers based in Dieppe pillaged Southampton in 1338 and blockaded Lisbon two centuries later. The first European settlers in Canada included many Dieppois. The town was one of France's most important ports during the 16th century, when ships regularly sailed from Dieppe to West Africa and Brazil.

Orientation

The town centre is largely surrounded by water. Boulevard de Verdun runs along the lawns – a favourite spot for kite flyers – that border the beach. Most of the Grande Rue and rue de la Barre has been turned into a pedestrianised area. Quai Duquesne and its continuation quai Henri IV follow the western and northern sides of the port area. Ferries dock at the terminal on the north-eastern side of the port, just under 2km on foot from the tourist office.

Information

INTERNET ACCESS
La Au Bar (☎ 02 35 40 48 35; 19 rue de Sygogne; ♡ 10am-2am Mon-Sat, 2-7pm Sun; per 15min/hr €1/4)

LAUNDRY
Laundrette (44 rue de l'Épée; ♡ 7am-9pm)

MONEY
Banque Populaire (15 place Nationale) One of several on place Nationale.
Crédit Maritime Mutuel (3 rue Guillaume Terrien) One of the few banks open Monday.

POST
Main Post Office (2 blvd Maréchal Joffre) It has Cyberposte.

TOURIST INFORMATION
Tourist Office (☎ 02 32 14 40 60; www.dieppetour isme.com; Pont Jehan Ango; ♡ 9am-1pm & 2-8pm Mon-Sat, 10am-1pm & 3-6pm Sun Jul & Aug, 9am-1pm & 2-7pm Mon-Sat, 10am-1pm & 3-6pm Sun May-Jun & Sep, 9am-noon & 2-6pm Mon-Sat Oct-Apr) On the western side of the port area. Hotel reservations in the area cost €3.50.

Château Musée

High over the city to the west, **Château Musée** (☎ 02 35 84 19 76; adult/student €3/1.50; ♡ 10am-noon 2-6pm Jun-Sep, 10am-noon & 2-5pm Wed-Mon Oct-May) is Dieppe's most impressive landmark. Dating from the 15th century it offers sweeping views over the sea. The museum is devoted to Dieppe's maritime and artistic history, a large portion of which involved the dubious practice of separating African elephants from their tusks and shipping the ivory back to Dieppe. The craft of ivory-carving reached extraordinary heights in Dieppe during the 17th century and the results are on display.

Cité de la Mer

Exhibits at the **Cité de la Mer** (☎ 02 35 06 93 20; 37 rue de l'Asile Thomas; adult/under-16s €5/3; ♡ 10am-12.30pm & 2-6.30pm Jun-Aug, 10am-noon & 2-6pm Sep-May) are devoted to fishing techniques, shipbuilding, cliffs and even pebbles. The visit ends with five large aquariums filled with happy living examples of sea creatures that are usually found on French plates: octopus, lobsters, turbot and cod.

Other Sights

Although the white cliffs on either side of Dieppe have been compared to those at Dover, the **beach** is gravelly and at times very windy.

The vast **lawns** between blvd de Verdun and the beach were laid out in the 1860s by that seashore-loving imperial duo, Napoleon III and his wife, Eugénie. **Église St-Jacques**, a Norman Gothic church at place St-Jacques, has been reconstructed several times since the early 13th century.

The **Canadian Military Cemetery** is 4km towards Rouen. Take av des Canadiens (the continuation of av Gambetta) south and follow the signs.

The **GR21 hiking trail** follows the Côte d'Albâtre southwest from Dieppe all the way to Le Havre. Maps and topoguides for hikes and easy walks in the surrounding area are available from the tourist office.

Water in the Olympic-sized **swimming pool** (☎ 02 35 06 05 66; promenade Plage; ♡ 10am-7.30pm) is heated to 25°C and there are diving boards.

Sleeping
BUDGET
Auberge de Jeunesse (☎ 02 35 84 85 73; 48 rue Louis Fromager; dm €8.90; ♡ mid-May–mid-Sep; P)

NORMANDY

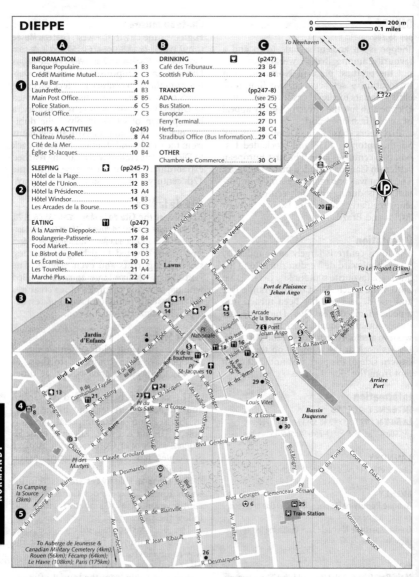

DIEPPE

INFORMATION		
Banque Populaire	1	B3
Crédit Maritime Mutuel	2	C3
La Au Bar	3	A4
Laundrette	4	B3
Main Post Office	5	B5
Police Station	6	C5
Tourist Office	7	C3

SIGHTS & ACTIVITIES		(p245)
Château Musée	8	A4
Cité de la Mer	9	D2
Église St-Jacques	10	B4

SLEEPING		(pp245-7)
Hôtel de la Plage	11	B3
Hôtel de l'Union	12	B3
Hôtel la Présidence	13	A4
Hôtel Windsor	14	B3
Les Arcades de la Bourse	15	C3

EATING		(p247)
Á la Marmite Dieppoise	16	C3
Boulangerie-Patisserie	17	B4
Food Market	18	C3
Le Bistrot du Pollet	19	D3
Les Écamias	20	D2
Les Tourelles	21	A4
Marché Plus	22	C4

DRINKING		(p247)
Café des Tribunaux	23	B4
Scottish Pub	24	B4

TRANSPORT		(pp247-8)
ADA	(see 25)	
Bus Station	25	C5
Europcar	26	B5
Ferry Terminal	27	D1
Hertz	28	C4
Stradibus Office (Bus Information)	29	C4

OTHER		
Chambre de Commerce	30	C4

About 4km southwest of the train station, this hostel provides a kitchen and laundry. From the train station, walk straight up blvd Bérigny to the Chambre de Commerce from where you take bus No 2 Val Druel to the Château Michel stop.

Hôtel de l'Union (☎ 02 35 84 35 52; 47-49 rue du Haut Pas; s/d from €22.90/24.50) This family-run

establishment has somewhat faded rooms of varying sizes. It also hosts a good little restaurant.

Camping

Camping La Source (☎ 02 35 84 27 04; adult/site €4/6; ☼ mid-Mar–mid-Oct) This camping ground is 3km southwest of Dieppe in a lovely creekside location, just off the D925 (well signposted). Take bus No 4 to the Petit-Appeville train station (10 minutes), walk beneath the railway bridge and up the marked gravel drive.

MID-RANGE & TOP END
Les Arcades de la Bourse (☎ 02 35 84 14 12; fax 02 35 40 22 29; 1-3 Arcade de la Bourse; r from €49; **P**) This is an elegant, old-style hotel in the centre of town, by the port. All rooms have a private bathroom, TV and telephone, and the more expensive ones have views over the port.

Hôtel Windsor (☎ 02 35 84 15 23; 18 blvd de Verdun; r from €58; **P**) This hotel *is* on the seafront, though you'll have to walk across all those lawns to get to the water. The décor is a little garish but the rooms are comfortable and many offer sea views and balconies.

Hôtel de la Plage (☎ 02 35 84 18 28; 20 blvd de Verdun; r €48-73; **P** **🖳**) These well-equipped rooms either give onto the seafront, or onto the interior garden and courtyard. Some are more attractively decorated than others; those with sea views are larger (and more expensive).

Hôtel La Présidence (☎ 02 35 84 31 31; www .hotel-la-presidence.com in French; blvd de Verdun; r €78-93; **P** **✕** **🖳**) This large, sleek, modern hotel has all the comforts you would expect. The huge restaurant has sea views, as do many of the rooms. Some apartments with kitchenettes are available.

Eating
Les Tourelles (☎ 02 35 84 15 88; 43 rue du Commandant Fayolle; menus €9.50-19; 🕑 closed Mon & dinner Sun) This is an old-fashioned restaurant with an everchanging array of simple, generous dishes and a decent selection of wines. Its fresh seafood and convivial atmosphere attract tourists, families and local office workers alike.

Le Bistrot du Pollet (☎ 02 35 84 68 57; 23 rue Tête de Boeuf; weekday lunch menu €11.50; 🕑 closed Sun & Mon) A gem for fish lovers, hidden away from the tourist crowds in the old fishermen's quarter. The à la carte offerings might include *lotte* (monkfish) marinated in wine and *daurade* (sea bream) with herbs. The restaurant is small so it's best to reserve.

Les Écamias (☎ 02 35 84 67 67; 129 quai Henri IV; menus €13.50-20; 🕑 closed Mon, dinner Sun & Tue) This is a simple, family-style place serving fresh, tasty seafood at reasonable prices. You can't go wrong with a delicious pile of mussels or the *raie* (ray) with butter sauce.

À la Marmite Dieppoise (☎ 02 35 84 24 26; 8 rue St-Jean; menus €26-39; 🕑 closed Mon & dinner Sun) If you really want to taste Dieppe's *fruits de la mer* at their best, head for this intimate establishment in the old city. Their speciality is *marmite Dieppoise*, a delicious fish stew.

SELF-CATERING
There's a **food market** (🕑 6am-1pm Tue & Thu, 7am-5pm Sat) between place St-Jacques and place Nationale and two wonderful **boulangeries** (15 quai Henri IV; 🕑 Tue-Sun; 14 rue de la Boucherie; 🕑 Thu-Tue). The **Marché Plus supermarket** (22 quai Duquesne) is open long hours.

Drinking
Dieppe has loads of pubs and bars full of interesting characters, but don't be surprised if you have to buzz to be let in.

Scottish Pub (☎ 02 35 84 13 16; 12 rue St-Jacques) This is a good place to kick off a pub crawl, and the friendly bar staff will point you in the right direction.

Café des Tribunaux (☎ 02 32 14 44 65; place du Puits Salé) This sprawling 18th-century building was a preferred hang-out for impressionist painters in the late 19th century. It remains an impressive venue to this day.

Getting There & Away
The bus station is in the same cavernous building as the train station. CNA runs services to Fécamp (€11.40, 2¼ hours, at least two daily) and Rouen (€10.65, two hours, three daily). No buses run on Saturday or Sunday afternoons.

The first ferry service from Dieppe to the UK began in 1790. These days **Hoverspeed** (☎ 08 20 00 35 55) runs car and pedestrian ferries between Dieppe and Newhaven. Boats depart from the ferry terminal on the northeastern side of the port area at the end of quai de la Marne. For further ferry information, see p919.

From Dieppe's **train station** (🕑 02 35 06 69 33), the paucity of direct trains to Paris' Gare St-Lazare (€22.80, 2¼ hours, four daily) is offset by frequent services to Rouen (€9, 50 minutes, 10 daily), where there is a connecting service to Le Havre (€16, two hours from Dieppe).

Getting Around
Stradibus (☎ 02 32 14 03 03) operates 13 local lines that run until 6pm or 8pm. All buses

stop at either the train station or the nearby Chambre de Commerce, on quai Duquesne. It has an information office on this road. A single ticket costs €1.05, a 10-ticket carnet €7. Buses shuttle foot passengers between the ferry terminal and the tourist office (€2).

ADA (☎ 02 35 84 32 28; train station)

Europcar (☎ 02 35 04 97 10; 33 rue Thiers)

Hertz (☎ 02 32 14 01 70; 5 rue d'Écosse)

Taxis (☎ 02 35 84 20 05) Fare from the ferry pier to the city centre is about €7.50.

CÔTE D'ALBÂTRE

Stretching 100km southwest from Dieppe to Étretat are the tall white cliffs and pebbled beaches of the Côte d'Albâtre (Alabaster Coast). Small villages and resorts nestle in the dry valleys leading down from the Pays de Caux, a chalky inland plateau. Towards the southwest are the Côte d'Albâtre's two main centres: Fécamp and Étretat.

Without a car, the Côte d'Albâtre is rather inaccessible. However, walkers can follow the coastal GR21 footpath from Dieppe to Le Havre. If you are driving, take the coastal road, which starts at the D75 west of Dieppe, and not the inland D925.

Fécamp
pop 21,500

Fécamp was a fishing village until the 6th century, when a few drops of Christ's blood miraculously found their way here and attracted hordes of pilgrims. Benedictine monks soon established a monastery and the 'medicinal elixir' they concocted in the early 16th century helped keep Fécamp on the map. The recipe, lost during the Revolution, was rediscovered in the 19th century and the after-dinner liqueur was produced commercially. Today, Bénédictine is one of the most widely marketed *digestifs* in the world.

INFORMATION

Tourist Office (☎ 02 35 28 51 01; www.fecamp.com in French; 113 rue Alexandre Le Grand; ⏰ 9am-12.30pm & 2.30-6pm Apr-Sep, 9am-noon & 2.30-6pm Oct-Mar) In the town centre, this is the main source of information.

Tourist Office (☎ 02 35 29 16 94; quai de la Vicomté; ⏰ 11am-2pm & 3-7.30pm Jul & Aug) Another, smaller office at the port that opens over the summer months.

PALAIS BÉNÉDICTINE

In an ornate 1900 building, mixing Flamboyant Gothic and other eclectic styles, is

the **Palais Bénédictine** (☎ 02 35 10 26 10; 110 rue Alexandre Le Grand; adult/student €5/3.70; ⏰ 10am-6pm Jul & Aug, 10am-noon & 2-5pm Apr-Jun & Sep, 10.30-11.45am & 2-5pm Feb, Mar & Oct-Dec, closed Jan). It was inspired by the 15th-century Hôtel de Cluny in Paris. It's geared up to tell you everything about the history and making of its aromatic liqueur – except the exact recipe.

Tours start in the art museum, which houses the private collection of founder Alexandre Le Grand, and continues through a hall where hundreds of bottles of bootlegged Bénédictine are proudly displayed. In the fragrant Plant & Spice Room, you can smell a handful of some of the ingredients used to make the potent drink. The tour ends in the attractive modern art gallery, which has changing exhibits.

The admission price includes a free shot of Bénédictine.

ABBATIALE DE LA STE-TRINITÉ

Built from 1175 to 1220 under the instigation of Richard the Lion-Heart, the **Abbatiale de la Ste-Trinité** (☎ 02 35 28 84 39; place des Ducs Richard; ⏰ 9am-6pm) was the most important pilgrimage site in Normandy until the construction of Mont St-Michel, thanks to the drop of holy blood that miraculously floated to Fécamp in the trunk of a fig tree. Among the many treasures inside is the late-15th-century *Dormition de la Vierge*.

Across from the abbey are the remains of the **fortified chateau** built by the earliest dukes of Normandy in the 10th and 11th centuries.

SLEEPING & EATING

Hôtel de la Mer (☎ 02 35 28 24 64; 89 blvd Albert 1er; r €35-53) A cool, modern establishment, this place is the pick of the bunch of the various beachfront hotels. The rooms are very comfortably outfitted, and many have balconies with sea views.

Camping Renéville (☎ 02 35 28 20 97; Côte de Renéville; site €9.50) Dramatically situated on the western cliffs overlooking the beach, this is a prime position for camping.

Marée (☎ 02 35 29 39 15; 75 quai Bérigny; menus €17.60-34; ⏰ closed Sun, Mon & dinner Thu) An extension of a fish shop, this place offers the freshest, tastiest fish in town. The *choucroute de la mer* (seafood with sauerkraut) has just the right touch of tang but all the fish and seafood is prepared with a minimum of fuss. Finish off with *crème brûlée à la Bénédictine*.

GETTING THERE & AWAY
Fécamp is accessible by bus from Dieppe, Le Havre and Rouen, and by train from Le Havre. The **train station** (☎ 02 35 28 24 82) is conveniently located. **Autocars Gris** (☎ 02 35 22 34 00) has 10 buses daily to Le Havre (€7.30, 1½ hours) via Étretat and five on Sunday.

Étretat
pop 1650
The small village of Étretat, which is 20km southwest of Fécamp, is renowned for its two cliffs: the Falaise d'Amont and the Falaise d'Aval. Featuring the most unusual rock formations in the area, you'll see them long before you arrive. They appear somewhat deceivingly to be one rock.

Beyond the Falaise d'Aval, southwest of the village, is the stunning Manneporte rock arch and the 70m-high Aiguille (Needle), which pierces the surface of the water behind the arch. From the western end of Étretat's stony beach, a steep path leads to the top of the cliff, which affords fine views. On the Falaise d'Amont opposite, a memorial marks the spot where two aviators were last seen before their attempt to cross the Atlantic in 1927. Do *not* explore the base of the cliffs outside low tide.

The **tourist office** (☎ 02 35 27 05 21; www.etretat .net; place Maurice Guillard; ⏲ 10am-7pm mid-Jun–mid-Sep, 10am-noon & 2-6pm mid-Mar–mid-Jun & mid-Sep–mid-Nov, 10am-noon & 2-6pm Fri & Sat mid-Nov–mid-Mar) posts accommodation lists for the area on the door outside opening hours. It also has a map of the cliff trails and rents bicycles.

The only way to reach Étretat is on the bus line that runs from Fécamp to Le Havre, stopping at Yport. See p250.

LE HAVRE
pop 193,250
Le Havre is France's second-most important port and a bustling gateway for ferries to Britain, but it wouldn't win any prizes in a beauty contest.

All but obliterated by WWII bombing raids, Le Havre was rebuilt by Auguste Perret, who also designed the city's 100m-high 'Stalinist Baroque' church. While the regimented boulevards and concrete buildings make this urban landscape uninviting, the very newness of the city can be intriguing. The sophisticated André Malraux fine-arts museum is one of the best in Normandy. You can also enjoy the wide, rocky beach, good seafood restaurants, lots of parking and a number of good-value hotels.

Orientation
The main square is the enormous place de l'Hôtel de Ville. Avenue Foch runs westwards to the sea and the Port de Plaisance recreational area. Boulevard de Strasbourg goes eastwards to the train and bus stations. Rue de Paris cuts south past Espace Oscar Niemeyer, a square named after the Brazilian who designed two cultural centre buildings (which have been compared to a truncated cooling tower and a toilet bowl).

Rue de Paris ends at the quai de Southampton and the Bassin de la Manche, from where ferries to Britain set sail out of the Terminal de la Citadelle, southeast of the central square. Within easy walking distance of the terminal is the Quartier St-François, Le Havre's 'old city'.

Information
INTERNET ACCESS
Microminute (☎ 02 35 22 10 15; 7 rue Casimir Perier; per hr €3.60; ⏲ 2-7pm Mon, 10am-7pm Tue-Sat)

LAUNDRY
Laundrette (5 rue Georges Braque)

MONEY
Exchange Bureau (41 Chaussée Kennedy) Opposite the old Irish Ferries terminal.
Société Générale (2 place Léon Meyer) Plus other banks along blvd de Strasbourg.

POST
Main Post Office (62 rue Jules Siegfried) It has Cyber poste.

TOURIST INFORMATION
Tourist Office (☎ 02 32 74 04 04; www.lehavretour isme.com in French; 186 blvd Clemenceau; ⏲ 9am-7pm Mon-Sat, 10am-12.30pm & 2.30-6pm Sun Jun-Sep, 9am-6.30pm Mon-Fri, 9am-12.30pm & 2-6.30pm Sat, 10am-1pm Sun Oct-May) On the waterfront about 650m southwest of city hall. Staff reserve local accommodation for free.

Sights
The main highlight of Le Havre is the hypermodern **Musée des Beaux-Arts André-Malraux**

NORMANDY

(☎ 02 35 19 62 62; 2 blvd Clemenceau; adult/student €3.80/2.20; ⏰ 11am-6pm Mon-Wed, 11am-7pm Sat & Sun), about 800m south of the tourist office. There is an excellent collection of impressionist art, including paintings from Monet, Sisley, Renoir and Le Havre native Eugène Boudin. Another large section is devoted to Fauvist Raoul Dufy who was also born in Le Havre.

Sleeping

Hôtel Celtic (☎ 02 35 42 39 77; www.hotel-celtic.com in French; 106 rue Voltaire; r €31-48) Rooms in varying in size are brightly painted and furnished in a traditional style. The more expensive have views over the Bassin du Commerce but all are equipped with private facilities and satellite TV.

Le Petit Vatel (☎ 02 35 41 72 07; www.multimania .com/lepetitvatel; 86 rue Louis Brindeau; s/d €35/43) A modern, efficient and comfortable choice, this hotel lacks character but offers small, bright rooms that are good value for money. All rooms have satellite TV and windows are double glazed to assure a sound night's sleep. More expensive rooms are available with bathtubs and views.

Hôtel Vent d'Ouest (☎ 02 35 42 50 69; www .ventdouest.fr; 4 rue de Caligny; r €75-105; **P**) This carpeted and comfortable three-star hotel is very big on décor. Each of the rooms has its own personalised style based upon the themes of mountain, countryside or sea.

CAMPING
Camping de la Forêt de Montgeon (☎ 02 35 46 52 39; chlorophile1@wanadoo.fr; camping €12.20; ⏰ year-round) Nearly 3km north of town in a 250-hectare forest, this is a lovely shaded site. From the station, take bus No 11 and alight after the 700m-long Jenner Tunnel. Then walk north 1.5km through the park.

Eating

La Marine Marchande (☎ 02 35 25 11 77; 27 blvd Amiral Mouchez; lunch menu €10; ⏰ lunch only Mon-Sat) Here you can chow down with hungry sailors at a full buffet table of hors d'oeuvres, plus a main course, cheese, dessert and wine. They might open for dinner if you call ahead. To get there take rue Charles Laffitte from the train station, follow it to the right as it becomes rue Marceau, and onto blvd Amiral Mouchez.

L'Odyssée (☎ 02 35 21 32 42; 41 rue du Général Faidherbe; menus €21-34; ⏰ closed Mon, lunch Sat & din-

ner Sun) This refined dining room is one of the best spots in Le Havre for superb fish dishes. The cheaper *menus* are only available during the week.

Les Trois Pics (☎ 02 35 48 20 60; Promenade des Régates, Sente Alphonse Karr, Ste-Adresse; weekday lunch menus €13-17, dinner menus €23 & €35; ⏰ closed Mon & dinner Sun) When the locals of Le Havre are looking for the very best in seafood, they head out to Ste-Adresse for a whiff of salt air, excellent service and piles of shells.

La Villa (☎ 02 35 54 70 80; 66 blvd Albert 1er; weekday lunch menu €29.50, dinner menus €46-125; ⏰ closed Mon & dinner Sun & Wed) People come from miles around for the astonishing cuisine of master chef Jean-Luc Tartarin. The marvellous *menus* changes according to the market and the chef's inspiration.

For self-caterers, there's a **Champion** supermarket (cnr rue de la République & rue Turenne).

Drinking & Entertainment

Le Camp Gourou (☎ 02 35 22 00 92; 163 rue Victor Hugo) As its play-on-words name suggests, this raucous and highly popular student bar attracts lots of Australians.

Le Havana Café (☎ 02 35 42 35 77; 173 rue Victor Hugo) The Havana will brighten your day with its tropical ambience and reasonably priced drinks. The musical programme is varied, although there is a Latin night once a month.

L'Agora (☎ 02 32 74 09 70; Espace Oscar Niemeyer) Not only do you get to see the inside of Le Havre's most striking building but there's a bar and concert hall that hosts an eclectic selection of musical acts from hip-hop to something called celtic-rock-latino.

Getting There & Away
AIR
The **airport** (☎ 02 35 54 65 00), 6km north of town in Octeville-sur-Mer, mainly serves Lyon.

BOAT
P&O European Ferries (☎ 0 803 013 013; ⏰ information desk 9am-7pm), which links Le Havre with Portsmouth, uses the new Terminal de la Citadelle on av Lucien Corbeaux, just over 1km southwest of the train station.

BUS
Caen-based **Bus Verts du Calvados** (☎ 08 10 21 42 14) and Rouen's **CNA** (☎ 0825 07 60 27) run frequent services from the bus station (be-

hind the train station) to Honfleur (€6.80, 30 minutes), Rouen (€12.65, 2½ hours), Deauville-Trouville (€9.35, 1¾ hours) and Caen (€20, two to three hours). **Autocars Gris** (☎ 02 35 22 34 00) has 10 buses daily to Le Havre (€7.30, 1½ hours) via Étretat (one hour) and five on Sunday.

TRAIN
Le Havre's **train station** (cours de la République) is east of the city centre. Chief destinations are Rouen (€11.80, one hour, 15 daily) and Paris' Gare St-Lazare (€25.20, 2¼ hours, 10 daily). A secondary line goes north to Fécamp (€6.70, 1¼ hours, five daily) with a change at Bréauté-Beuzeville.

Getting Around
There's no public transport to town from the airport. A taxi will cost about €12.

Bus Océane (☎ 02 35 22 35 00; place de l'Hôtel de Ville) runs 14 lines in Le Havre. Single tickets cost €1.40 and a carnet of 10 is €9.20; a day ticket costs €3.20 and gives unlimited bus travel for that day.

To order a **taxi**, call (☎ 02 35 25 81 81) or (☎ 02 35 25 81 00).

CALVADOS

The *département* of Calvados stretches from Honfleur in the east to Isigny-sur-Mer in the west. It's famed for its rich pastures and farm products: butter, cheese, cider and an apple-flavoured brandy called Calvados. The D-Day beaches extend along almost the entire coast of Calvados.

HONFLEUR
pop 8350
The gateway to the sea, the picturesque harbour town of Honfleur recalls a time when fishermen, pirates and explorers set sail to seek their fortunes over the seas. It has long been popular with Parisian weekenders, who flock to the pretty town and its sandy beaches.

The stone dwellings constructed at the height of Honfleur's glory in the 17th and 18th centuries survive largely intact in a warren of streets around its old harbour. Because of extensive siltation, centuries-old wooden houses that once lined the seafront quay now lie several hundred metres inland.

In the 19th century Honfleur attracted a steady stream of artists, among them many impressionists.

The graceful 2km-long Pont de Normandie over the Seine, linking Honfleur with Le Havre for the first time, opened in 1995. Just 15km southwest are the coastal resorts of Deauville and Trouville.

History
Honfleur's seafaring tradition dates back over a millennium. After the Norman invasion of England in 1066, goods bound for the conquered territory were shipped across the Channel from Honfleur.

In 1608 Samuel de Champlain left from here on his way to found Quebec City. In 1681 Cavelier de la Salle started out from Honfleur to explore what is now the USA. He reached the mouth of the Mississippi and named the area Louisiana in honour of King Louis XIV, ruler of France at the time. During the 17th and 18th centuries, Honfleur achieved a degree of prosperity through trade with the West Indies, the Azores and the colonies on the western coast of Africa.

Orientation
Honfleur is centred around the Vieux Bassin (old harbour). To the east is the heart of the old city, known as the Enclos because it was once enclosed by fortifications. To the north is the Avant Port (outer harbour) where the fishing fleet is based. Quai Ste-Catherine fronts the Vieux Bassin on the west, and rue de la République runs southwards from it. The Plateau de Grâce, with Chapelle Notre Dame de Grâce on top, is west of town.

Information
Lavomatic (4 rue Notre Dame; ☼ 8am-9pm) Laundry.
Léviathan (☎ 02 31 87 92 95, 11 blvd Charles V, per 30min €1.50; ☼ 2.30pm-1am Mon-Sat) Internet access.
Main Post Office (rue de la République) Southwest of the centre, just past place Albert Sorel. It has a Cyberposte terminal.

> ### PASSE MUSÉE
> The **Passe Musée** (adult/student €9/6) is on sale in museums and allows one visit to each of the town's four museums, except the Clocher. Bought at any museum, you can use it over a one-year period.

NORMANDY

Tourist Office (☎ 02 31 89 23 30; www.ot-honfleur.fr; quai Lepaulmier; ☷ 10am-7pm Mon-Sat, 10am-5pm Sun Jul & Aug, 10am-12.30pm & 2-6.30pm Mon-Sat 10am-5pm Sun Apr-Jul & Sep, 10am-12.30pm & 2-6pm Mon-Sat 10am-5pm Sun Oct-Mar) Helps visitors find accommodation.

Sights

ÉGLISE STE-CATHERINE

Wooden **Église Ste-Catherine** (place Ste-Catherine; ☷ 10am-noon & 2-6pm, except during services), whose stone predecessor was destroyed during the Hundred Years' War, was built by the people of Honfleur during the late 15th and the early 16th centuries. It is thought that they chose wood, which could be worked by local shipwrights, in an effort to save stone for strengthening the fortifications of the Enclos. The structure that the town's carpenters created, which was intended to be temporary, has a vaulted roof that looks like an overturned ship's hull. The church is also remarkable for its twin naves, each topped by vaulted arches supported by oak pillars.

CLOCHER STE-CATHERINE

The church's free-standing wooden bell tower, **Clocher Ste-Catherine** (☎ 02 31 89 54 00; adult/ student incl admission to Musée Eugène Boudin €4.40/2.70; ☷ 10am-noon & 2-6pm Wed-Mon mid-Mar-Sep, 2.30-5pm Mon-Fri, 10am-noon & 2.30-5pm Sat & Sun Oct-mid-Mar), dates from the second half of the 15th century. It was built apart from the church for both structural reasons (so the church roof would not be subject to the bells' weight and vibrations) and for safety (a high tower was more likely to be hit by lightning). The former bell-ringer's residence at the base of the tower houses a small museum of liturgical objects, but the huge, rough-hewn beams are of more interest.

MUSÉE EUGÈNE BOUDIN

Named in honour of the early impressionist painter born here in 1824, **Musée Eugène Boudin** (☎ 02 31 89 54 00; rue de l'Homme de Bois; adult/ student incl admission to Clocher Ste-Catherine €4.40/2.70, Jun-Nov €5.10/3.60; ☷ 10am-noon & 2-6pm Wed-Mon mid-Mar-Sep, 2.30-5pm Mon-Fri, 10am-noon & 2.30-5pm Sat & Sun Oct-mid-Mar) has a good collection of impressionist paintings from Normandy, including works by Dubourg, Dufy and Monet. An entire room is devoted to the works of Eugène Boudin, whom Baudelaire called the 'king of skies' for his luscious skyscapes.

LES MAISONS SATIE

The delightful **Les Maisons Satie** (☎ 02 31 89 11 11; 67 blvd Charles V; adult/student €5.10/3.60; ☷ 10am-7pm Wed-Mon Jun-Sep, 11am-6pm Wed-Mon Oct-May) imaginatively captures the spirit of composer Erik Satie (1866–1925) who lived and worked in Honfleur. 'Esoteric' Satie was known for his surrealistic wit as much as for his starkly beautiful piano compositions. Located in Satie's birthplace, visitors wander through the museum with a headset playing Satie's music and excerpts from his writings (in French or English). Each room is a surprise. One features a winged pear. Another, the Laboratory of Emotions, has a whimsical contraption that is pedalled.

HARBOURS

The **Vieux Bassin**, from where ships bound for the New World once sailed, now shelters mainly pleasure boats. The nearby quays and streets, especially **quai Ste-Catherine**, are lined with tall, narrow houses dating from the 16th to 18th centuries. The **Lieutenance**, once the residence of the town's royal governor, is at the mouth of the old harbour.

The **Avant Port**, on the other side of the Lieutenance, is home to Honfleur's 50 or so fishing vessels. Further north, dikes line both sides of the entrance to the port.

Either harbour makes a pleasant route for a walk to the seashore. Honfleur is a good launching pad for boat tours of the region.

MUSÉE DE LA MARINE

Honfleur's small **Musée de la Marine** (☎ 02 31 89 14 12; adult/student €3/1.80, incl admission to Musée d'Ethnographie et d'Art Populaire Normand €4.20/2.60; ☷ 10am-noon & 2-6pm Tue-Sun Apr-Sep, 2-6pm Mon-Fri, 10am-noon & 2-6pm Sat & Sun Oct-mid-Nov & mid-Feb-Mar, closed mid-Nov-mid-Feb) is on the eastern side of the Vieux Bassin in the deconsecrated Église St-Étienne, which was begun in 1369 and enlarged during the English occupation of Honfleur (1415–50). Displays include assorted model ships, ships' carpenters' tools and engravings.

MUSÉE D'ETHNOGRAPHIE ET D'ART POPULAIRE NORMAND

Next to the Musée de la Marine on rue de la Prison (an alley off quai St-Étienne), the **Musée d'Ethnographie et d'Art Populaire Normand** (☎ 02 31 89 14 12; adult/student €3/1.80, incl admission to Musée de la Marine €4.20/2.60; ☷ 10am-noon & 2-6pm

NORMANDY

Tue–Sun Apr–Sep, 2–6pm Mon–Fri, 10am–noon & 2–6pm Sat & Sun Oct–mid–Nov & mid–Feb–Mar, closed mid–Nov–mid–Feb) occupies a couple of houses and a former prison dating from the 16th and 17th centuries. Its rooms re-create the homes and furnishings of Honfleur in the 16th to 19th centuries.

GRENIERS À SEL

The two huge **Greniers à Sel** (salt stores; ☎ 02 31 89 02 30; rue de la Ville), along from the tourist office, were built in the late 17th century to store the salt needed by the fishing fleet to cure its catch of herring and cod. During July and August the stores host art exhibitions and concerts.

CHAPELLE NOTRE DAME DE GRÂCE

Built between 1600 and 1613, the **Chapelle Notre Dame de Grâce** is at the top of the Plateau de Grâce, a wooded, 100m-high hill about 2km west of the Vieux Bassin. There's a great view of the town and port.

Tours

Within Honfleur, the tourist office runs two-hour **guided tours** (adult/student €6/4; ◷ 3pm Mon) of the town in English and a variety of themed tours in French.

Fifty-minute **boat tours** of the Vieux Bassin and the port area with Vedettes Stéphanie, Alphée and Evasion cost €6.50. Vedette la Jolie France goes to the Pont de Normandie (€8). Tours run from March to mid-October. Boarding is from the quai des Passagers or the quai de la Quarantaine. The schedule depends upon the tides.

Sleeping

BUDGET & MID-RANGE

Auberge de la Claire (☎ 02 31 89 05 95; 77 cours Albert Manuel; apt from €70) Those keen to do their own cooking – with fresh local produce – will be pleased to find these tidy apartments with kitchenettes about 900m southwest of the Vieux Bassin.

Hôtel Belvédère (☎ 02 31 89 08 13; 36 rue Emile Renouf; s/d €51/62; **P**) Less than 1km east of the town centre, this tranquil retreat has a relaxing garden and terrace. Ask for room 11 to secure a view of the Pont de Normandie.

Hôtel des Loges (☎ 02 31 89 38 26; www.hoteldesloges.com; 18 rue Brûlée; r from €90; **P**) A romantic choice with soft lighting and elegant design. Rooms are minimalist but comfortable and

the ambience is friendly and fuss-free. Families will like the baby-sitting service (per hour €8).

Camping

Camping du Phare (☎ 02 31 89 10 26; blvd Charles V; site €10.65; ◷ Apr–Sep) This camping ground is the closest to town. From the town centre, follow rue Haute about 500m northwest of the Vieux Bassin.

TOP END

Hôtel du Dauphin (☎ 02 31 89 15 53; www.hotel-du-dauphin.com; 10 place Pierre-Berthelot; r €66-151; **P** ✖ ▣) Behind a 17th-century, half-timbered façade lies this modern and charming hotel. The colourful rooms are bound to cheer you up on a grey Norman day, and the more expensive rooms even have spa baths.

Hôtel Le Cheval Blanc (☎ 02 31 81 65 00; www.hotel-honfleur.com; 2 quai des Passagers; r €70-230; **P** ✖) This luxurious establishment is in a 15th-century mansion overlooking the port. The rooms, which have views over the Vieux Bassin, are modern with plush furniture and exposed beams.

Eating

Places to dine in Honfleur are abundant, especially along quai Ste-Catherine.

La Cidrerie (☎ 02 31 89 59 85; 26 place Hamelin; menu €9; ◷ closed Tue-Wed Oct-Jun) The crepes and *galettes* are sure to please, but the main attraction is the wide selection of beverages that are based almost exclusively on apples and pears. *Cidre* (cider), *pommeau*, *poiré* (perry or pear cider) and Calvados are served in surprising ways.

La Tortue (☎ 02 31 89 04 93; 36 rue de l'Homme de Bois; menus €16-30; ◷ closed Tue & dinner Mon) Mmmm… fried fois gras in truffle juice! Here you can enjoy fine cuisine in a refreshingly relaxed and informal setting. Vegetarians will be relieved to discover a decent meat-free *menu*.

L'Absinthe (☎ 02 31 89 39 00; 10 quai de la Quarantaine; menus €29/€48/€63) Located in a ravishing 18th-century mansion, this is one of the finest restaurants in Normandy. The cuisine is sumptuous and sophisticated, even on its cheapest *menu*. Do reserve in advance.

SELF-CATERING

The **market** (place Ste-Catherine; ◷ 9am-1pm Sat) has an excellent selection of local products and

NORMANDY

an organic food market. There's a Champion supermarket just west of rue de la République, near place Albert Sorel.

Drinking

Café L'Albatros (☎ 02 31 89 25 30; 32 quai Ste-Catherine) Sailors, students, philosophers and layabouts are all at home at this café-bar, from breakfast through beer and sandwiches and on to nightcaps.

Le Perroquet Vert (☎ 02 31 89 14 19; 52 quai Ste-Catherine) The 'green parrot' has an excellent selection of beer and a good terrace for people-watching.

Getting There & Around

The **bus station** (☎ 02 31 89 28 41) is southeast of the Vieux Bassin on rue des Vases. **Bus Verts** (☎ 0 810 214 214 Caen) No 20 runs via Deauville-Trouville (€3.40, 30 minutes, five per day) to Caen (€11.05, €13.70 by express bus, one hour). The same line goes northwards to Le Havre (€6.80, 30 minutes, five per day) via the Pont de Normandie.

Honfleur is very small and can be visited on foot. A small tourist train does take people up the hill as part of a guided tour.

TROUVILLE & DEAUVILLE

pop 5600 (Trouville) / pop 4300 (Deauville)
Roughly 15km southwest of Honfleur lie Trouville and Deauville, two seemingly similar seaside resorts that maintain distinctly different personalities. Chic Deauville has been a playground of the wealthy ever since it was founded by Napoleon III's cousin, the duke of Morny, in 1861. Often called the '21st *arrondissement*' for its masses of Parisian weekenders, Deauville cultivates this 'lifestyles of' reputation with its designer boutiques, casino, racetrack and annual Festival of American Film.

Trouville is more down to earth, offers better-value accommodation and some decent restaurants. The town attracted a series of painters and writers during the 19th-century, such as Mozin and Flaubert. One thing both towns have in common are wide, sandy beaches lined with bathhouses.

Orientation

The towns are separated only by the River Touques, with Trouville on the eastern bank and Deauville on the western bank, respectively, and linked by the Pont des Belges. The combined train and bus station is situated just west of the bridge. Beaches line the coast to the north of both towns on either side of the port.

Information
INTERNET ACCESS
Gestimedia (☎ 02 31 14 04 61; 6 rue Thiers, Deauville; per hr €6; ☿ 9am-1pm & 2-6pm Mon-Fri)

MONEY
Crédit du Nord (84 rue Eugène Colas, Deauville) Has an ATM.
Société Générale (9 place Morny, Trouville) Has an ATM.

POST
Deauville Post Office (rue Robert Fossorier) Has Cyberposte and exchanges currency.
Trouville Post Office (16 rue Amiral de Maigret)

TOURIST INFORMATION
Deauville Tourist Office (☎ 02 31 14 40 00; www .deauville.org; place de la Mairie; ☿ 9am-7pm Jul-Sep, 9am-6.30pm May & Jun, 9am-12.30pm & 2-6.30pm Mon-Sat, 10am-1pm & 2-5pm Sun mid-Sep–Apr) Pick up a copy of the free, outlandishly glossy magazine *Deauville Passions* for an overview of annual events.
Trouville Tourist Office (☎ 02 31 14 60 70; www .trouvillesurmer.org; 32 blvd Fernand Moureaux; ☿ 9.30am-7pm Mon-Sat, 10am-4pm Sun Jul & Aug, 9.30am-noon & 2-6.30pm Mon-Sat Apr-Jun & Sep-Oct, 9.30am-noon & 1.30-6pm Mon-Sat Nov-Mar)

Sights & Activities
In Deauville, the rich, famous and assorted wannabes strut along the beachside **Promenade des Planches**, a 500m-long boardwalk lined with private swimming huts, before losing a wad at the **Casino de Deauville** 200m to the south.

About 1km to the northeast of the Trouville tourist office is the **Musée de Trouville** (☎ 02 31 88 16 26; 64 rue du Général Leclerc; adult/student €2/1.50; ☿ 2-6.30pm Wed-Mon Apr-Sep), in the magnificent Villa Montebello. The villa has a panoramic view over the beaches, and the museum recounts the history of Trouville and features work from Charles Mozin and Eugène Boudin. There are temporary exhibitions by local artists.

On Trouville's beachside promenade, you'll see several illustrious **19th-century villas**. The beach is also home to the remarkably varied **Aquarium Vivarium de Trouville** (☎ 02 31 88 46 04; adult/student €6.50/4.50; ☿ 10am-noon &

2-6.30pm Easter-Jun & Sep-Oct, 10am-7pm Jul & Aug, 2-6pm Nov-Easter), which aside from wild and wonderfully colourful fish also houses some fearsome reptiles (snakes, crocodiles and iguanas among them) and weird insects.

Festivals & Events

Deauville's answer to Cannes is the **American Film Festival** (www.festival-deauville.com), which is open to all and attracts a procession of Hollywood stars in the first week of September.

Trouville's **Festival Folklorique** fills the streets with colourfully clad musicians and dancers in the third week of June.

Deauville is renowned for its equestrian tradition. The **horse-racing season**, which runs from early July to mid-October, is held at two local racetracks: Hippodrome La Touques for gallop races and jumping events and Hippodrome Clairfontaine with galloping, trotting and steeplechase.

Sleeping

The best-value hotels are all in Trouville, and the town participates in the 'Bon Week-end' two-nights-for-the-price-of-one programme from November to March.

Hôtel de la Paix (☎ 02 31 88 35 15; hoteldela paix@hotmail.com; 4 place Fernand Moureaux, Trouville; d €50-61) Quite recently – and tastefully – renovated, this hotel has retained its traditional features while brushing up its amenities. The more expensive rooms overlook the port.

La Maison Normande (☎ 02 31 88 12 25; www .maisonnormande.com in French; 4 place de Lattre de Tassigny, Trouville; r with shower €44, with bathroom €52-64) A real Norman house in quintessential Norman style, with crisscrossing beams, flowery furnishings and traditional touches. You'll feel like you're visiting your new Norman grandma.

The most luxurious establishments in Deauville are the **Hôtel Normandy** (☎ 02 31 98 66 22; www.lucienbarriere.com; 38 rue Jean Mermoz; r from €238; **P** **X**) and the **Hôtel Royal Barrière** (☎ 02 31 98 66 33; www.lucienbarriere.com; 14 blvd Cornuché; r €229-1165; **P** **X** **Q** **Q**), which are as much tourist attractions as hotels.

CAMPING
Le Chant des Oiseaux (☎ 02 31 88 06 42; fax 02 31 98 16 09; 11 route d'Honfleur; adult/site €2.50/5; ⏲ Apr-Oct) About 1km east of Trouville, this camping ground has a sweeping view of the coast.

Eating

Deauville has a somewhat overpriced dining scene. For better value, head to Trouville.

Bistrot Sur Le Quai (☎ 02 31 81 28 85; 68 blvd Fernand Moureaux, Trouville; lunch menu €12, dinner menus €15-25; ⏲ closed Wed) One of the better choices of the waterfront eateries in Trouville, Bistro Sur Le Quai serves great seafood and has a very agreeable terrace.

Brasserie Le Central (☎ 02 31 88 13 68; 158 blvd Fernand Moureaux, Trouville; menus from €16.20) Parisians will feel right at home in this large dining room reminiscent of some of the capital's most celebrated brasseries. Portions are quite copious; one main course is usually sufficient.

La Petite Auberge (☎ 02 31 88 11 07; 7 rue Carnot, Trouville; menus €25-42; ⏲ closed Tue & Wed) It doesn't get much more Norman than this, from the traditional décor to the well-chosen *menu*. Prices are reasonable considering the quality of the cuisine.

SELF-CATERING
Mamy Crêpe (☎ 02 31 14 96 44; 16 rue Désiré-le-Hoc, Deauville) sells excellent crepes and sandwiches. There is also a **Monoprix** (blvd Fernand Moureaux; ⏲ closed Sun) and a **food market** (place du Maréchal Foch; ⏲ Wed & Sat mornings).

Drinking & Entertainment

Zoo Bar (☎ 02 31 81 02 61; 53 rue Désiré-le-Hoc, Deauville) Dim lighting, deep house and designer-clad clients make this postmodern-style bar popular with the fashionable fauna of Deauville.

La Maison (☎ 02 31 81 43 10; 66 rue des Bains, Trouville) A welcome exception to the snooty seaside vibe is this casual, atmospheric wine bar where you can drink vintage wine by the glass and enjoy cheese and *charcuterie* platters. Concerts and art exhibitions are held regularly.

Casino de Deauville (☎ 02 31 14 31 14; av Lucien Barrière, Deauville; ⏲ 11am-2am Mon-Fri, 10am-4am Sat, 10am-3am Sun) Dress is formal, but men can borrow a jacket and tie from reception.

Louisiane Follies (☎ 02 31 87 75 00; place du Maréchal Foch, Trouville; ⏲ 10am-2am) This beachfront casino is a more relaxed affair with an adjoining cinema and nightclub.

Getting There & Around

Aéroport de Deauville-St-Gatien (☎ 02 31 65 65 65) is 10km northeast of Deauville-Trouville. There is no public transport into town.

Bus Verts (☎ 0 810 214 214) has very frequent services to Caen (€8.50, 1¼ hours), Honfleur (€3.40, 30 minutes) and Le Havre (via Honfleur; €9.35, one hour).

Train services from Deauville-Trouville require changes at Lisieux (€5.10, 20 minutes, 10 daily). Trains go to Caen (€12.40, one to 1½ hours, 13 daily), Rouen (€19.90, 3¼ hours, four daily) and Dieppe (via Rouen; €28.90, 3½ hours, four daily).

CAEN

pop 117,000

Today, Caen is a bustling university city with some fine museums and historical sites and a massive 11th-century chateau. Unfortunately, it has little else of great interest to visitors, having been decimated during WWII and rebuilt in a utilitarian, though not entirely unpleasing, style.

The capital of Basse Normandie, Caen was bombed on D-Day and burned for over a week before being liberated by the Canadians – only to be then shelled by the Germans. The only vestiges of the past to have survived are the ramparts around the chateau and the two abbeys, all built by William the Conqueror when he founded the city in the 11th century. Much of the medieval city was built from 'Caen stone', a creamy local limestone exported for centuries to England.

Caen makes a good base for exploring the D-Day beaches. Linked to the sea by a canal running parallel to the River Orne, Caen is gateway for Ouistreham, a minor passenger port for ferries to England.

Orientation

Caen's modern heart is made up of a few pedestrianised shopping streets and some busy boulevards. The largest, av du 6 Juin, links the centre, which is based around the southern end of the chateau, with the canal and train station to the southeast. What's left of the old city is centred around rue du Vaugueux, a short distance east of the chateau.

Information

BOOKSHOPS

Hemisphères (☎ 02 31 86 67 26; 15 rue des Croisières) Guidebooks in English, including Lonely Planet titles.

INTERNET ACCESS

M.I.G. (☎ 02 31 93 09 09; 74-76 av de la Libération; per hr €3; ☒ 2.30-7pm Mon, 10am-noon & 2.30-7pm Tue-Sat)

LAUNDRY

Laundrette (127 rue St-Jean)

MONEY

Crédit Agricole (1 blvd Maréchal Leclerc) There's an exchange bureau here.

POST

Main Post Office (place Gambetta) It has Cyberposte.

TOURIST INFORMATION

SNCF Boutique (8 rue St-Pierre) For train information and reservations.

Tourist Office (☎ 02 31 27 14 14; www.caen.fr/tourisme; place St-Pierre; ☒ 9am-7pm Mon-Sat, 10am-1pm & 2-5pm Sun Jul & Aug, 9.30am-6.30pm Mon-Sat & 10am-1pm Sun Jun & Sep) Information on sites and entertainment.

Mémorial – Un Musée pour la Paix

Caen's best-known museum, **Mémorial – Un Musée pour la Paix** (Memorial – A Museum for Peace; ☎ 02 31 06 06 44; www.memorial-caen.fr in French; adult /student €18/16, WWII veterans free; ☒ 9am-8pm Jun-Sep, 9am-7pm Oct-May, closed 1st 2-3 weeks of Jan), provides an outstanding and vivid account of the Battle of Normandy and the challenges to world peace from WWII to today.

The visit begins with a history of Europe's descent into total war, tracing events from the end of WWI through the rise of Fascism to the Battle of Normandy in 1944. Telling the story through artefacts, sound, lighting, film footage, documents and animation, the exhibits graphically evoke the horrors of war, the occupation and the battle for liberation. A recently installed section of the museum focuses on the Cold War, decolonisation and the emergence of the European Union. The exhibition is poignant and stirring; the hordes of noisy school children certainly aren't. All signs are in French, English and German.

The memorial is about 3km northwest of the tourist office on Esplanade Dwight Eisenhower. To reach it, take bus No 17 from opposite the tourist office at place St-Pierre; the last bus back departs at 8.45pm (earlier on Sunday). By car, follow the multitude of signs with the word 'Mémorial'.

Château de Caen

An enormous fortress surrounded by a dry moat, **Château de Caen** (www.chateau.caen.fr; ☒ 6am-10pm May-Sep, 6am-7.30pm Oct-Apr) was begun by

CAEN

NORMANDY

0 400 m
0 0.2 miles

INFORMATION
Crédit Agricole	1 E2
Hemisphères	2 C2
Laundrette	3 E3
Main Post Office	4 C3
MJG	5 D1
Police Kiosk	6 D2
SNCF Boutique	7 D2
Tourist Office	8 D2

SIGHTS & ACTIVITIES (pp256–8)
Abbaye aux Dames	9 E1
Abbaye aux Hommes	10 B2
Château de Caen	11 D1
Musée de Normandie	12 D1
Musée des Beaux-Arts	13 D1

SLEEPING (pp258)
Hôtel Bernières	14 D2
Hôtel des Cordeliers	15 C1
Hôtel des Quatrans	16 D1
Hôtel du Château	17 D2
Hôtel Le Dauphin	18 C2

EATING (pp258–60)
Dolly's Café & Tea Rooms	19 D2
Épicerie de Nuit	20 D1
L'Alcide	21 E2
La Petite Auberge	22 E2
Le Costa	23 E2
Le Météor	24 F4
Monoprix Supermarket	25 D3

DRINKING (pp260)
6X	26 C2
El Ché Guevara	27 C2
Le Carré	28 E2
Le Vertigo	29 C2
Le Zinc	30 D1
Théâtre de Caen	31 D3

ENTERTAINMENT (pp260)
Le Farniente	32 C2

TRANSPORT (pp260)
F/DA	33 F4
Bus Station	34 F4
Bus Verts Information Kiosk	35 E2
Car Rental Agencies	36 F4
CTAC	37 F4

William the Conqueror in 1060 and extended by his son Henry I. It has been used over the centuries by royals, revolutionaries, townsfolk and the military.

Take a walk around the **ramparts** and visit the 12th-century **Chapelle de St-Georges** and the **Échiquier** (Exchequer), which dates from about AD 1100 and is one of the oldest civic buildings in Normandy. Of special interest is the **Jardin des Simples**, a garden of medicinal and aromatic herbs cultivated during the Middle Ages – some of which are poisonous. A book (written in French) on the garden is on sale inside the **Musée de Normandie** (☎ 02 31 30 47 50; adult/student €1.50/0.80; ⏰ 9.30am-6pm Wed-Mon), which contains historical artefacts illustrating life in Normandy. There are explanatory signs in English.

The **Musée des Beaux-Arts** (☎ 02 31 30 47 70; admission €3.80, Wed free; ⏰ 9.30am-6pm Wed-Mon) is based in a modern building nearby. It houses an extensive collection of paintings dating from the 15th to 20th centuries (including the wonderful *Marriage of the Virgin* painted by Pietro Vannucci in 1504), ceramics and a noteworthy collection of engravings.

Abbeys

Caen's two Romanesque abbeys were built by William the Conqueror and his wife, Matilda of Flanders, after the distant cousins had been absolved by the Roman Catholic church for marrying. The **Abbaye aux Hommes** (☎ 02 31 30 42 81; adult/student €2/1, free Sun, guided visit €4; ⏰ 8.50am-noon & 2-7.30pm, guided visits 9.30am, 11am, 2.30pm & 4pm), with its multiturreted Église St-Étienne, is at the end of rue Écuyère and was William's resting place. The tomb was destroyed in turn by a 16th-century Calvinist mob and by 18th-century revolutionaries – a solitary thighbone is all that's left of Will's mortal remains. The convent buildings are today home to the town hall.

The starker **Abbaye aux Dames** (☎ 02 31 06 98 98; admission free; guided tours 2.30pm & 4pm), at the eastern end of rue des Chanoines, incorporates the Église de la Trinité. Access to the abbey, which houses regional government offices, is by guided tour only. Look for Matilda's tomb behind the main altar.

Sleeping
BUDGET
Cité de Lébisey (☎ 02 31 46 74 74; fax 02 31 46 74 76; Cité de Lébisey, 114-116 rue de Lébisey, BP 5153, 14070 Caen Cedex 5; student/nonstudent per day €7.50/11, per 2 weeks €60.25/78.85, per month €120.45/153; 🖥) These university dormitories offer a good deal for clean doubles with showers in the hall. Reservations must be made by mail or fax. The dormitories are just north of the chateau.

Hôtel Bernières (☎ 02 31 86 01 26; www.hotelberni eres.com; 50 rue de Bernières; s/d €35/45) This friendly place is a particularly good find for the price with cosy, comfortable rooms. Bear in mind that in some rooms there's only a curtain separating the shower from the sleeping area.

MID-RANGE & TOP END
Hôtel des Cordeliers (☎ 02 31 86 37 15; fax 02 31 39 56 51; 4 rue des Cordeliers; d from €45) One of the rare Caen hotels in an 18th-century building, this hotel has more character than most. The rooms are attractive with white walls and plain pine furniture, and open directly onto a relaxing interior garden.

Hôtel du Château (☎ 02 31 86 15 37; www.hotel -chateau-caen.com; 5 av du 6 Juin; s/d €45/55; 🅿) This is an excellent location just a stone's throw from the chateau. The rooms are simple but quite generous in size, each painted a different colour of the rainbow. Front windows are double glazed and there's an elevator.

Hôtel des Quatrans (☎ 02 31 86 25 57; www .hotel-des-quatrans.com; 17 rue Gémare; s/d €48/58; 🅿) Taking care not to break that unspoken agreement among hotel owners to match the bedspreads with the curtains, this hotel offers calm, fairly plush rooms and modern comforts such as satellite TV.

Hôtel Le Dauphin (☎ 02 31 86 22 26; www.le-dau phin-normandie.com; 29 rue Gémare; r €70-150; 🅿 ✂) With warm, calming colours and discerning details such as antiques, polished wood doors and exposed beams, this former priory offers a touch of class (Rm 310 is particularly romantic). There's also a fancy restaurant.

Eating
In one of Caen's few remaining old quarters, the area around rue du Vaugueux is a popular dining spot offering a wide range of prices and cuisines.

La Petite Auberge (☎ 02 31 86 43 30; 17 rue des Équipes d'Urgence; menus €12 & €19; ⏰ closed Sun & Mon) This is a cosy little place for a home-style meal. The dishes are simple and delicious, including, of course, the ubiquitous tripe, a local Caen speciality. The €11 *menu* is available on weekdays only.

L'Alcide (☎ 02 31 44 18 06; 1 place Courtonne; menus €14.50-22.50; ☺ closed Sat) This is an excellent address for sampling Caen cuisine, especially the infamous *tripes à la mode de Caen*. Connoisseurs say that the tripe here are served in a sauce so flavoursome you can almost forget you're eating intestines.

Le Météor (☎ 02 31 82 31 35; 55 rue d'Auge; menu €10; ☺ lunch only Mon-Sat) A good three-course *menu* for €10 is already a great find. At this little restaurant by the train station, they'll also throw in a glass of wine. We're not complaining.

Dolly's Café & Tea Rooms (☎ 02 31 94 03 29; 16-18 av de la Libération; breakfast €6-12, dishes around €8.50; ☺ 10am-7.30pm Tue-Sat, 9.30am-6pm Sun) Just what you've been craving after all those croissants: a full, hearty, savoury English breakfast that is served all day. Daily specials can include fish and chips. Cross-Channel products such as tea, jam and newspapers are available next door at The English Shop.

Le Costa (☎ 02 31 86 28 28; 13 rue Guilbert; menus from €21; ☺ closed Sun) Slide through the revolving door into the sleek, Art-Deco interior of this chic restaurant, where you will dine on modern French classics. The *saumon sauvage* (wild salmon) is a particularly fine choice.

WILLIAM CONQUERS ENGLAND

The son of Robert I of Normandy and his concubine Arlette, William 'the Conqueror' (commonly referred to as 'William the Bastard') ascended the throne of Normandy at the tender age of five. Thwarting several attempts by rivals – including members of his own family – to kill him and his advisers, William took over the reign of Normandy aged 15. He soon set about regaining his lost territory and feudal rights, quashing several rebellions along the way.

William had twice been promised the throne of England: once from the king himself, Edward the Confessor (William's relative), and once from the most powerful Saxon lord in England, Harold Godwinson of Wessex, who had the misfortune of being shipwrecked on the Norman coast.

In January 1066 Edward died without an heir. Harold was immediately crowned king, with the support of the great nobles of England (and very likely the majority of the Saxon people).

One of several pretenders to the throne, William was preparing to send an invasion fleet across the Channel, when a rival army (consisting of an alliance between Harold's estranged brother Tostig and Harold Hardrada of Norway) landed in the north of England. In a September battle at Stamford Bridge, near York, Harold defeated and killed both Hardrada and Tostig.

Meanwhile, William had crossed the Channel unopposed with an army of about 6000 men, including a large cavalry force. They landed at Pevensey before marching to Hastings on 13 October, where Harold faced William with about 7000 men from a strong defensive position. The battle began the next day.

Although William's archers scored many hits among the densely packed and ill-trained Saxon peasants, the latter's ferocious defence ended a charge by the Norman cavalry and drove them back in disarray. William faced the real possibility of losing the battle. Summoning the knowledge and tactical ability he had gained in numerous campaigns against rivals in Normandy, he used the cavalry's rout to draw the Saxon infantry out from their defensive positions, whereupon the Norman infantry turned and caused heavy casualties on the undisciplined Saxon troops. The battle started to turn against Harold, who was slain (by an arrow through the eye, according to the Bayeux Tapestry) late in the afternoon. The embattled Saxons fought on until sunset and then fled. William immediately marched to London, ruthlessly quelled the opposition, and was crowned king of England on Christmas Day.

William thus became the ruler of two kingdoms, bringing England's feudal system of government under the control of Norman nobles. Ongoing unrest among the Saxon peasantry soured William's opinion of the country and he spent the rest of his life after 1072 in Normandy, only going to England when compelled to do so. William left most of the governance of the country to the bishops.

In Normandy William continued to expand his influence through military campaigns, strategic marriages and the ruthless elimination of all opposition. In 1087 he was injured during an attack on Mantes. He died at Rouen a few weeks later and was buried at Caen.

SELF-CATERING

There's a downstairs supermarket at **Mono-prix** (45 blvd Maréchal Leclerc; ☽ 8.30am-8.30pm Mon-Sat). Late-night purchases can be made at **Épicerie de Nuit** (23 rue Porte au Berger; ☽ 8pm-2am Tue-Sun).

For food markets check out place St-Sauveur on Friday, blvd Leroy (behind the train station) on Saturday and place Courtonne on Sunday.

Drinking & Entertainment

We're not sure where this Caen–Havana connection originated, but Cuban-style bars are all the rage here. The general idea is cool, rum-laced cocktails, hot Latin music and the odd cigar. Some of the better places include **El Che Guevara** (☎ 02 31 85 10 75; 53 rue de Geôle), popular with young beer drinkers early in the evening and smart 30-somethings later on, and **Le Farniente** (☎ 02 31 86 30 00; 13 rue Paul Doumer) where a cool crowd dances it up.

Students always know where to find good vibes and cheap drinks: in Caen they flock to **6X** (☎ 02 31 86 36 98; 7 rue St-Sauveur; ☽ noon-1am Mon-Sat, 4pm-1am Sun) and **Le Vertigo** (☎ 02 31 85 43 12; 14 rue Écuyère).

Le Carré (☎ 02 31 38 90 90; 32 quai Vendeuvre) This is one of the region's the slickest discos, with theme nights and a strict, selective door policy. The décor is kind of disco-baroque and the music mainly '70s and '80s. You must be over 27 and dressed smartly.

Le Zinc (☎ 02 31 93 20 30; 12 rue du Vaugueux) This is one of the better gay bars in town. It can get quite packed with a young, sometimes mixed, crowd. The DJ spins house and techno and there's a terrace in summer.

Théâtre de Caen (☎ 02 31 30 48 00; 135 blvd Maréchal Leclerc) In the centre of town, this hall offers a season of opera, dance, jazz and classical concerts that runs from October to May.

Getting There & Away

AIR

Caen's **airport** (☎ 02 31 71 20 10) is 5km west of town in Carpiquet.

BOAT

Brittany Ferries (☎ 02 31 36 36 36) sail from Ouistreham, 14km northeast of Caen, to Portsmouth in England. For more information see p919.

BUS

Bus Verts (☎ 0 810 214 214; information kiosk place Courtonne) serves the entire Calvados *département*, including Bayeux (€5.80, 50 minutes), Courseulles-sur-Mer (€4.80, 30 minutes) as well as Deauville-Trouville (€8.50, 1¼ hours), Honfleur (€10.20 via Cabourg and Deauville, or €13.70 by express bus) and the ferry port at Ouistreham (€3.40, 25 minutes). It also runs two buses a day to Le Havre (€20, 1½ hours).

See p268 for details on getting to the D-Day beaches.

Most buses stop at the bus station and in the centre of town at place Courtonne. When leaving or arriving at Caen by bus, your ticket will be valid for public transport to/from the bus station.

CAR

Rental places include **Hertz** (☎ 02 31 84 64 50; 34 place de la Gare), **Europcar** (☎ 02 31 84 61 61; 36 place de la Gare), **Avis** (☎ 02 31 84 73 80; 44 place de la Gare) and **ADA** (☎ 02 31 34 88 89; 26 rue d'Auge).

TRAIN

Caen is on the Paris–Cherbourg line. There are regular connections to Paris' Gare St-Lazare (€26.20, 2½ hours, 13 daily), as well as Bayeux (€5.10, 20 minutes, 15 per day), Cherbourg (€16.60, 3¼ hours, four daily), Pontorson (€20.40, 2½ hours, daily), Rennes (€27.30, three hours, two daily), Rouen (€19.40, two hours, 10 daily) and Tours (via Le Mans; €28.40, 3¾ hours, five daily).

Getting Around

A bus links the airport with Caen's train station. A taxi costs about €15.

CTAC (☎ 02 31 15 55 55) runs city bus No 7 and the more direct No 15 between the train station and the tourist office (stop: St-Pierre). There's also a tram line connecting the train station with the university, stopping at quai de Juillet, rue de Bernières, place St-Pierre and the chateau. A single ride on either costs €1.05 and a carnet of 10 tickets costs €9. Services end between 6pm and 8pm.

There are a couple of options for **taxis** (☎ 02 31 26 62 00, 02 31 52 17 89).

BAYEUX

pop 15,400

Stately Bayeux proudly possesses the only pictorial record of William the Conqueror's trans-Channel invasion in 1066 – the Bayeux Tapestry. This invaluable stretch of embroidered cloth is the magnet for several million tourists each year and, with a majestic cathedral, the British War Cemetery and some excellent museums, a visitor can easily pass an absorbing few days here. Bayeux was the first town liberated after the D-Day landings and is one of the few in Calvados to have survived WWII unscathed.

Orientation

The Cathédrale Notre Dame, the major landmark in the centre of Bayeux and visible throughout the town, is 1km northwest of the train station. The River Aure, with

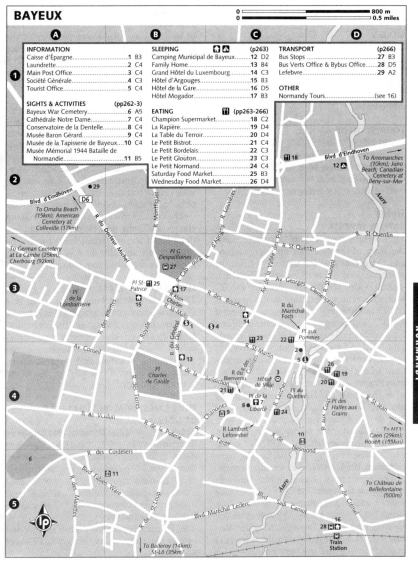

BAYEUX

0 _____ 800 m
0 _____ 0.5 miles

INFORMATION	
Caisse d'Épargne	1 B3
Laundrette	2 C4
Main Post Office	3 C4
Société Générale	4 C3
Tourist Office	5 C4

SIGHTS & ACTIVITIES	(pp262-3)
Bayeux War Cemetery	6 A5
Cathédrale Notre Dame	7 C4
Conservatoire de la Dentelle	8 C4
Musée Baron Gérard	9 C4
Musée de la Tapisserie de Bayeux	10 C4
Musée Mémorial 1944 Bataille de Normandie	11 B5

SLEEPING	(p263)
Camping Municipal de Bayeux	12 D2
Family Home	13 B4
Grand Hôtel du Luxembourg	14 C3
Hôtel d'Argouges	15 B3
Hôtel de la Gare	16 D5
Hôtel Mogador	17 B3

EATING	(pp263-266)
Champion Supermarket	18 C2
La Rapière	19 D4
La Table du Terroir	20 D4
Le Petit Bistrot	21 C4
Le Petit Bordelais	22 C3
Le Petit Glouton	23 C3
Le Petit Normand	24 C4
Saturday Food Market	25 B3
Wednesday Food Market	26 D4

TRANSPORT	(p266)
Bus Stops	27 B3
Bus Verts Office & Bybus Office	28 D5
Lefebvre	29 A2

OTHER	
Normandy Tours	(see 16)

several attractive little mills along its banks, flows northwards on the eastern side of the centre.

Information
INTERNET ACCESS
You can log on at the tourist office for €10 per 1½ hours.
LAUNDRY
Laundrette (13 rue du Maréchal Foch)

MONEY
Caisse d'Épargne (59 rue St-Malo) ATM.
Société Générale (26 rue St-Malo) ATM.

POST
Main Post Office (14 rue Larcher) Has Cyberposte and changes money.

TOURIST INFORMATION
Tourist Office (☎ 02 31 51 28 28; www.bayeux-tour ism.com; pont St-Jean; ☒ 9am-noon & 2-6pm Mon-Sat, 9.30am-noon & 2.30-6pm Sun Jul & Aug) Just off the northern end of rue Larcher. Will change money when the banks are closed and can book accommodation (€2 fee).

Sights
BAYEUX TAPESTRY
The world-famous **Bayeux Tapestry** recounts the story of the Norman invasion of 1066 and the events that led up to it – from the Norman perspective. Scholars believe that Bishop Odo of Bayeux, William's half-brother, commissioned the 70m-long tapestry for the opening of the Bayeux cathedral in 1077. The story of the Norman conquest is presented in 58 remarkable scenes, briefly captioned in Latin. The main narrative fills up the centre of the canvas, while depictions of the daily life of 11th-century Norman France – men's labours, dress, animals, weapons, feasts and battles – unfolds in the top and bottom edges, rendered in startling detail. The Saxons are depicted with moustaches and the backs of the Norman soldiers' heads are shaved. Halley's Comet, which passed through our part of the solar system in 1066, also makes an appearance.

The tapestry is housed in the **Musée de la Tapisserie de Bayeux** (☎ 02 31 51 25 50; rue de Nesmond; adult/student incl admission to Musée Baron Gérard €7.40/3; ☒ 9am-6.30pm mid-Mar–Apr & Sep-Nov, 9.30am-12.30pm & 2-6pm Nov–mid-Mar, 9am-7pm May-Aug). The excellent taped commentary (€1) makes viewing the upstairs exhibits a bit unnecessary. A 14-minute film on the 2nd floor is screened eight to 13 times a day in English (last showing 5.15pm, or 5.45pm May to August).

CATHÉDRALE NOTRE DAME
Most of Bayeux's spectacular **Cathédrale Notre Dame** (place de la Liberté; ☒ 8.30am-6pm Oct-Jun, 8.30am-7pm Jul-Sep), a fine example of Norman Gothic architecture, dates from the 13th century, though the crypt, the arches of the nave and the lower portions of the towers on either side of the main entrance are 11th-century Romanesque. The central tower was added in the 15th century; the copper dome dates from the 1860s.

CONSERVATOIRE DE LA DENTELLE
The fascinating **Conservatoire de la Dentelle** (Lace Conservatory; ☎ 02 31 92 73 80; 6 rue du Bienvenu; admission free; ☒ 10am-12.30pm & 2-6pm Mon-Sat) is dedicated to the preservation of traditional Norman lace-making. You can watch some of France's most celebrated lace-makers, who create intricate designs using dozens of bobbins and hundreds of pins.

The conservatory also offers lace-making classes and sells materials (pins, bobbins, thread and so on). Small lace objects, the product of something like 50 hours' work, are on sale from €30 to €300.

MUSÉE BARON GÉRARD
The pleasant **Musée Baron Gérard** (☎ 02 31 92 14 21; 6 rue Lambert Leforestier; adult/student €2.60/1.60; ☒ 10am-12.30pm & 2-6pm), in the mansion, Hôtel du Doyen, specialises in local porcelain, lace and 15th- to 19th-century paintings (Italian, Flemish and impressionist). Admission is free if you buy a ticket to the tapestry museum.

MUSÉE MÉMORIAL 1944 BATAILLE DE NORMANDIE
Bayeux's huge **Musée Mémorial 1944 Bataille de Normandie** (☎ 02 31 92 93 41; blvd Fabien Ware; adult/student €5.50/2.60; ☒ 9.30am-6.30pm May–mid-Sep, 10am-12.30pm & 2-6pm mid-Sep–Apr) rather haphazardly displays thousands of photos, uniforms, weapons, newspaper clippings and lifelike scenes associated with D-Day and the Battle of Normandy.

A 30-minute film in English is screened two to five times a day (always at 10.45am and 5pm).

BAYEUX WAR CEMETERY

This peaceful cemetery, on blvd Fabien Ware a few hundred metres west of the war museum, is the largest of the 18 Commonwealth military cemeteries in Normandy. It contains 4868 graves of soldiers from the UK and 10 other countries. Many of the 466 Germans buried here were never identified, and the headstones are simply marked *'Ein Deutscher Soldat'* (A German Soldier). There is an explanatory plaque in the small chapel to the right as you enter the grounds. The large structure across blvd Fabien Ware commemorates the 1807 Commonwealth soldiers missing in action.

Festivals & Events

The first weekend in July, **Fêtes Médiévales de Bayeux** holds parades and medieval song and dance for the anniversary of the Battle of Formigny, which put an end to the Hundred Years' War.

Sleeping

BUDGET

Family Home (☎ 02 31 92 15 22; fax 02 31 92 55 72; 39 rue du Général de Dais; dm incl breakfast €18-20) This is an excellent, friendly old hostel and a great place to meet other travellers. Multicourse French dinners with wine (€11) are often served. Vegetarian dishes are available on request or you can cook for yourself.

Hôtel de la Gare (☎ 02 31 92 10 70; fax 02 31 51 95 99; 26 place de la Gare; r €24.50-48; **P**) This is a fair compromise: it's old but well maintained; the rooms are slightly cramped but well-equipped; and it's by the station but still quiet at night (as there are few late trains). Normandy Tours (see p268) operates from the hotel.

Camping

Camping Municipal de Bayeux (☎ 02 31 92 08 43; blvd d'Findhoven; adult/site €2.90/3.60, mid Mar mid-Nov) This camping ground is about 2km north of the town centre. Bus No 3 stops three times daily at nearby Les Cerisiers.

MID-RANGE

The tourist office has a list of *chambres d'hôtes* in the Bayeux area. The cheapest cost is about €34 for two people, with breakfast.

Hôtel Mogador (☎ 02 31 92 24 58; hotel.mogador@wanadoo.fr; 20 rue Alain Chartier; d €45-50; **P**) Exposed ceiling beams and old-fashioned décor

add a touch of warmth and character to this two-star establishment. The rooms are restful and comfortable and many face a pleasant interior courtyard.

Hôtel d'Argouges (☎ 02 31 92 88 86; dargouges@aol .com; 21 rue St-Patrice; r €80-100; **P**) The former 18th-century mansion of the d'Argouges family, this stately residence is now a graceful hotel. The rooms are elegant, while the inner garden allows for some peaceful time out.

Grand Hôtel du Luxembourg (☎ 02 31 92 00 04; hotel.luxembourg@wanadoo.fr; 25 rue des Bouchers; r €99-115; **P** ✕) This hotel combines businesslike comfort with a warm and friendly welcome. It manages to connect with tradition without appearing old-fashioned, and contains an excellent restaurant.

Château de Bellefontaine (☎ 02 31 22 00 10; hotel.bellefontaine@wanadoo.fr; 49 rue de Bellefontaine; s/d €108/120; **P** ✕) Surrounded by five acres of groomed parkland, this majestic 18th-century castle makes for some very luxurious accommodation. Rooms Nos 4, 5 and 6 have their own chimney and boast a fine view over the park.

Eating

Le Petit Normand (☎ 02 31 22 88 66; 35 rue Larcher; menus €9.50-23; ✕ closed Thu Oct-Apr) That ever-present regional staple, apple cider, makes it into most of the traditional Norman recipes at this popular little restaurant, which has a view over the cathedral.

La Table du Terroir (☎ 02 31 92 05 53; 42 rue St-Jean; menus lunch €11, dinner €14-26; ✕ closed Sun & Mon) The extension of a butcher shop, this is a no-go for vegetarians but the cuts are of high quality. The big wooden tables fill up with a carnivorous crowd who come for the excellent *menus*.

La Rapière (☎ 02 31 21 05 45; 53 rue St-Jean; lunch menu €15, dinner menus €24 & €30, ✕ closed Wed & Thu) A real highlight here is the quite extraordinary salad Rapière, with foie gras, *gesiers* (gizzards – sounds better in French!) and langoustines. And why not conclude with a Camembert in Calvados?

Le Petit Bistrot (☎ 02 31 51 85 40; 2 rue du Bienvenu; menus €16 & €28; ✕ closed Sun & Mon Sep-Jun) This is a charming little eatery whose strong suit is the intelligent use of fresh local ingredients. The fish and duck *menus* are an excellent choice.

Le Petit Bordelais (☎ 02 31 92 06 44; 15 rue du Maréchal Foch; dishes €7.20-16; ✕ lunch to 2.30pm, drinks

NORMANDY

THE BATTLE OF NORMANDY

In early 1944 an Allied invasion of Continental Europe seemed inevitable. Hitler's folly on the Russian front and the Luftwaffe's inability to control the skies had left Germany vulnerable.

Normandy was to be the spearhead into Europe. Codenamed 'Operation Overlord', the invasion entailed an assault by three paratroop divisions and five seaborne divisions, along with 13,000 aeroplanes and 6000 vessels. The total initial invasion force was 45,000, and 15 divisions were to follow once successful beachheads had been established.

The Straits of Dover seemed the most likely invasion spot to the Germans who set about heavily reinforcing the area around Calais and the large Channel ports. Allied intelligence went to extraordinary lengths to encourage the German belief that the invasion would be north of Normandy, even creating phoney airfields and military bases across from the Pas de Calais.

Because of the tides and unpredictable weather patterns, Allied planners had only a few days available each month in which to launch the invasion. On 5 June, the date chosen, very bad weather set in, delaying the operation. The weather had only improved slightly the next day, but General Dwight D Eisenhower, Allied commander-in-chief, gave the go-ahead: 6 June would be D-Day.

In the very early hours of 6 June the first troops were on the ground. British commandos captured key bridges and destroyed German communications, while the paratroops weren't far behind them. Although the paratroops' tactical victories were few, they caused enormous confusion in German ranks. More importantly, because of their relatively small numbers, at first, the German high command didn't believe that the real invasion had begun.

Sword, Juno & Gold Beaches

These beaches, stretching for about 35km from Ouistreham to Arromanches, were attacked by the British 2nd Army, which included sizable detachments of Canadians and smaller groups of Commonwealth, Free French and Polish forces.

At Sword Beach, initial German resistance was quickly overcome by the Allies and the beach was secured after approximately two hours. Infantry pushed inland from Ouistreham to link up with paratroops around Ranville, but it wasn't long before they suffered heavy casualties as their supporting armour fell behind, trapped in a massive traffic jam on the narrow coastal roads. Nevertheless, they were within 5km of Caen by 4pm, but a heavy German armoured counterattack forced them to dig in. Thus, in spite of the Allies' successes, Caen was not taken on the first day as planned.

At Juno Beach, Canadian battalions landed quickly but had to clear the Germans trench by trench before moving inland. Mines took a heavy toll on the infantry, but by noon they were south and east of Creuilly. Late in the afternoon the German armoured divisions that had halted the British coming from Sword Beach were deflected towards the coast and held Douvres, thus threatening to drive a wedge between the Sword and Juno forces. But the threat of encirclement made them withdraw by the next day.

At Gold Beach, the attack by the British forces was at first chaotic as unexpectedly high waters obscured German underwater obstacles. By 9am, though, Allied armoured divisions were on the beach and several brigades pushed inland. By afternoon they'd joined up with the Juno forces and were only 3km from Bayeux. On all three of these beaches, odd-looking 'Funnies' – specially designed armoured amphibious vehicles made to clear minefields, breach walls and wire entanglements, and provide support and protection for the infantry – proved their worth. Their construction and successful deployment was due to the ingenuity and foresight of British Major-General Hobart.

Omaha & Utah Beaches

The struggle on Omaha Beach (Vierville, St-Laurent and Colleville beaches) was by far the bloodiest of the day. Omaha Beach stretched 10km from Port-en-Bessin to the mouth of the River Vire and was backed by 30m-high cliffs. The beach was heavily defended by three battalions of heavily armed, highly trained Germans supported by an extensive trench system, mines and underwater obstacles. Men disembarked their landing craft in choppy seas and under heavy German fire; the naval bombardment had done little damage to German positions at the top of the cliffs and only two of the 29 Sherman tanks expected to support the troops made it to shore. Man by man, metre by metre, the GIs gained a precarious toehold on the beach and scaled the cliffs. A naval destroyer finally opened fire and the Germans, lacking reserves, had to fall back a short distance. Nevertheless, 1000 soldiers were killed at Omaha on D-Day, out of a total of 2500American casualties.

At Utah, US forces faced little resistance, and got off the beach after two hours. By noon, the beach had been cleared with the loss of only 12 men. Pockets of troops held large tracts of territory to the west of the landing site, and the town of Ste-Mère-Église was captured.

The Beginning of the End
Four days later, the Allies held a coastal strip about 100km long and 10km deep. British Field Marshal Montgomery's plan successfully drew the weight of German armour towards Caen, where fierce fighting continued for more than a month and reduced the city to rubble. This enabled the US army who were stationed further west to consolidate and push northwards up the Cotentin Peninsula.

The prized port of Cherbourg fell to the Allies on 27 June, after a series of fierce battles. However, its valuable facilities were blown up by the Germans so it remained out of service until autumn. To overcome such logistical problems, the Allies had devised the remarkable 'Mulberry Harbours'. These were enormous floating harbours that were towed from England, and set up off the Norman coast. They were indispensable in allowing large amounts of supplies to be quickly taken off ships and onto the roads leading to the front. A big storm from 19 to 22 June, however, destroyed the harbour stationed at Omaha Beach and damaged the Gold Beach installation.

The fierce Battle of the Hedgerows was fought mainly by the Americans up and down the Cotentin Peninsula. The *bocage* (farmland crisscrossed by walled roads and hedgerows) made ideal territory for defending and the Germans made good use of it. Nevertheless, once the Allies finally broke out from the beachheads, their superior numbers prevailed.

By the end of July, US army units had smashed through to the border of Brittany. By mid-August, two German armies had been surrounded and destroyed near Falaise and Argentan, and on 20 August, US forces crossed the Seine at several points about 40km north and south of Paris.

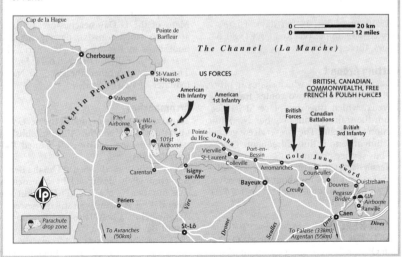

to 7pm Tue-Sat) This little wine cellar makes a brilliant lunch destination. You can enjoy the plat du jour or sample an assortment of cheeses, all complemented with excellent – and inexpensive – vintages.

SELF-CATERING
Takeaway shops are near rue St-Martin and rue St-Jean, including **Le Petit Glouton** (☎ 02 31 92 86 43; 42 rue St-Martin). There's also a **Champion supermarket** (blvd d'Eindhoven).

Rue St-Jean has an open-air food market on Wednesday morning, as does place St-Patrice on Saturday morning. Don't miss *tergoule,* a sweet, cinnamon-flavoured rice pudding typical of the Bayeux region.

Entertainment
Bayeux is not known for its hot nightlife, but there are frequent concerts and theatrical events staged in venues around town. Check the free booklet *Sorties Plurielles* for listings.

Getting There & Away
Bus Verts (☎ 0 810 214 214; opposite the train station in Bayeux) offers rather infrequent services from the train station and place St-Patrice to Caen, the D-Day beaches (see p268), Vire and elsewhere in the Calvados *département.* The schedules are arranged for school children coming into Bayeux in the morning and going home in the afternoon.

Train services from Bayeux include Paris' Gare St-Lazare (€28.80) via Caen (€5.10, 20 minutes, 15 per day), as well as Cherbourg (€13.30, one hour, 10 per day). There's a service to Quimper (via Rennes; €45.80, 5¾ hours, three per day).

Getting Around
Bybus (☎ 02 31 92 02 92), which shares an office with Bus Verts, has two routes traversing Bayeux, which finish at place St-Patrice. From the train station, take bus No 3 (direction J Cocteau). The bus service is geared to students and is thus infrequent. There's no bus service on Sunday.

Family Home (☎ 02 31 92 15 22; 39 rue du Général de Dais) rents out bikes for about €12 per day.

Call for a **taxi** (☎ 02 31 92 92 40, 02 31 92 04 10) round the clock.

D-DAY BEACHES
The D-Day landings, codenamed 'Operation Overlord', were the largest military op-

eration in history. Early on the morning of 6 June 1944, swarms of landing craft – part of a flotilla of over 6000 boats – hit the beaches, and tens of thousands of soldiers from the USA, UK, Canada and elsewhere began pouring onto French soil.

The majority of the 135,000 Allied troops stormed ashore along 80km of beaches north of Bayeux codenamed (from west to east) Utah, Omaha (in the US sector), Gold, Juno and Sword (in the British and Canadian sectors). The landings on D-Day – called Jour J in French – were followed by the Battle of Normandy, which would lead to the liberation of Europe from Nazi occupation. In the 76 days of fighting, the Allies suffered 210,000 casualties, including 37,000 troops killed. German casualties are believed to be around 200,000; and another 200,000 German soldiers were taken prisoner. Caen's memorial museum provides the best introduction to the history of what took place here and also attempts to explain the rationale behind each event. Once on the coast, travellers can take a well-marked circuit that links the battle sites, close to where holiday-makers sunbathe.

Fat Norman cows use the bombed-out bunkers to shield themselves from the wind. Many of the villages near the D-Day beaches have small museums with war memorabilia on display collected by local people after the fighting.

Information
Maps of the D-Day beaches are available at *tabacs* (tobacconists), newsagents and bookshops in Bayeux and elsewhere. The best one is called *D-Day 6.6.44 Jour J.* The area is also called the Côte du Nacre (Mother-of-Pearl Coast).

Arromanches
To make it possible to unload the necessary quantities of cargo, the Allies established two prefabricated ports code-named **Mulberry Harbours**.

The harbour established at Omaha Beach was completely destroyed by a ferocious gale just two weeks after D-Day, but the second, Port Winston, can still be viewed at Arromanches, a seaside town 10km northeast of Bayeux.

The harbour consists of 146 massive cement caissons towed from England and sunk to form a semicircular breakwater in which floating bridge spans were moored. In the three months after D-Day, 2.5 million men, four million tonnes of equipment and 500,000 vehicles were unloaded there. At low tide you can walk out to many of the caissons. The best view of Port Winston is from the hill, east of town, topped with a statue of the Virgin Mary.

The well-regarded **Musée du Débarquement** (Invasion Museum; ☎ 02 31 22 34 31; place de 6 Juin; adult /child €6/4; ☺ 9am-7pm Jul & Aug, 9.30am-12.30pm & 1.30-5.30pm Sep-Jun), right in the centre of Arromanches, explains the logistics and importance of Port Winston and makes a good first stop before visiting the beaches. The last guided tour (in French, with text in English) leaves 45 minutes before closing time.

Longues-sur-Mer

The massive casemates and 152mm German guns on the coast near Longues-sur-Mer, 6km west of Arromanches, were designed to hit targets some 20km away, which in June 1944 included both Gold Beach (to the east) and Omaha Beach (to the west). Half a century later, the mammoth artillery pieces are still sitting there in their colossal concrete emplacements. (In wartime they were covered with camouflage nets and tufts of grass.)

Parts of an American film about D-Day, *The Longest Day* (1962), were filmed both here and at Pointe du Hoc. On clear days, Bayeux's cathedral, 8km away, is visible to the south.

Omaha & Juno Beaches

The most brutal fighting on D-Day took place 15km northwest of Bayeux along 7km of coastline known as Omaha Beach.

A memorial marks the site of the first US military cemetery on French soil, which contained the bodies of soldiers killed on the beach as they ran inland towards German positions on the nearby ridge. Their remains were later reinterred at the American Military Cemetery at Colleville-sur-Mer or in the USA.

These days, Omaha Beach is lined with holiday cottages and is popular with swimmers and sunbathers. Little evidence of the war remains apart from a single concrete boat used to carry tanks ashore and, 1km further west, the bunkers and munitions

sites of a German fortified point (look for the tall obelisk on the hill).

Dune-lined Juno Beach, 12km east of Arromanches, was stormed by Canadian troops on D-Day. A Cross of Lorraine marks the spot where General Charles de Gaulle came ashore shortly after the landings.

Military Cemeteries

The bodies of the American soldiers who lost their lives during the pivotal Battle of Normandy were either sent back to the USA (if their families so requested) or buried in the **American Military Cemetery** (☎ 02 31 51 62 00; ☺ 9am-6pm mid-Apr–Sep, 9am-5pm Oct–mid-Apr) at Colleville-sur-Mer, 17km northwest of Bayeux. The cemetery contains the graves of 9386American soldiers and a memorial to 1557 others whose remains were never found.

The huge, immaculately tended expanse of lawn, with white crosses and Stars of David set on a hill overlooking Omaha Beach, testifies to the extent of the killings that took place around here in 1944. There's a large colonnaded memorial, a reflecting pond and a chapel for silent meditation. The staff at the welcome centre are highly efficient at finding specific graves.

By tradition, soldiers from the Commonwealth killed in the war were buried near where they fell. As a result, the 18 **Commonwealth Military Cemeteries** in Normandy follow the line of advance of British and Canadian troops.

Many of the gravestones bear epitaphs written by the families of the dead. The Commonwealth cemeteries are always open. There is a **Canadian Military Cemetery** at Bény-sur-Mer, a few kilometres south of Juno Beach and 18km east of Bayeux. See p263 for information on the mostly British Bayeux War Cemetery.

Some 21,000 German soldiers are buried in the **German Military Cemetery** near the village of La Cambe, 25km west of Bayeux. Hundreds of other German dead were buried in the Commonwealth cemeteries, including the one in Bayeux.

Pointe du Hoc Ranger Memorial

At 7.10am on 6 June 1944, 225 US Army Rangers scaled the 30m cliffs at Pointe du Hoc, where the Germans had a battery of huge artillery guns. However, the guns had been transferred elsewhere, but the Americans captured the gun emplacements (two huge circular cement structures) and the German command post (next to the two flag poles), and then fought off German counterattacks for two days. By the time they were relieved on 8 June, 81 of the rangers had been killed and 58 more had been wounded.

Today the site, which France turned over to the US government in 1979, looks much as it did half a century ago. The ground is still pockmarked with 3m bomb craters. Visitors can walk among and inside the German fortifications, but they are warned not to dig: mines and explosive materials may remain below the surface. In the German command post, you can see where the wooden ceilings were charred by American flame-throwers. As you face the sea, Utah Beach, which runs roughly perpendicular to the cliffs, is 14km to the left. Pointe du Hoc, which is 12km west of the American Military Cemetery, is always open. The command post is open the same hours as the cemetery.

Tours

A bus tour is an excellent way to see the D-Day beaches. **Normandy Tours** (☎ 02 31 92 10 70; Hôtel de la Gare, Bayeux; per person €35 incl museum admission) has four-hour tours stopping at Longues-sur-Mer, Arromanches, Omaha Beach, the American Military Cemetery and Pointe du Hoc for €35.

D-Day Tours (☎ 02 31 22 00 08; fax 02 31 51 74 74; www.d-daybeaches.com; BP 48525, 14400 Bayeux; per adult/student €45/40 incl museum admission) are best booked through the Family Home hostel (see p266). They'll collect you from place du Quebec in Bayeux.

The Mémorial museum tours include a combined ticket that includes a visit to the Mémorial – Un Musée pour la Paix (p256) and a half-day tour of the landing beaches for €67.50 (€55.50 for veterans, those under 18 and morning departures). The visit and tour can be done separately or on the same day but must be booked in advance. Tours leave at 1pm daily from mid-January to March and October to December; and at 9am and 2pm daily from April to September.

Getting There & Away
BUS
From Bayeux, bus No 70, run by **Bus Verts** (☎ 0 810 214 214), goes west to the American

Military Cemetery at Colleville-sur-Mer and Omaha Beach, and on to Pointe du Hoc and the town of Grandcamp-Maisy. Bus No 74 (No 75 during summer) serves Arromanches, Gold and Juno Beaches, and Courseulles. Bus No 30 will get you from Caen to Bayeux.

During July and August, the Côte de Nacre line goes to Caen via Arromanches, Gold, Juno and Sword Beaches, and Ouistreham; Circuit 44 links Bayeux and Caen via Pointe du Hoc, the American Military Cemetery, Arromanches and Mémorial – Un Musée pour la Paix. You can start the journey in Caen (€17 return), Courseulles (€15 return), Arromanches (€12 return) or Bayeux (€13 return). Prices are for all bus lines.

D-Day Lines (☎ 0 810 214 214; www.busverts14.fr /dday60) runs summer services along the coast from Bayeux, past all the major beaches to Grand Caen.

Local transport company Bus Verts runs a summer service from Caen, Bayeux and Deauville. The day circuits visit one of the major landing beaches, stopping at points of interest, major cemeteries and museums along the way (discounts are offered for museum entry). Cost is €14 for all of them.

Caen – to Arromanches and Omaha Beach. Leaves from place Courtonne at 9.35am.

Bayeux – two circuits leave from place St-Patrice at 9.42am: one to Arromanches and Omaha Beach, and the other to Utah Beach via St-Mère-Église.

Deauville – to Sword Beach and Ouistreham. Leaves from the station at 9.20am.

CAR
For three or more people, renting a car can be cheaper than a tour. **Lefebvre Car Rental** (☎ 02 31 92 05 96; blvd d'Eindhoven), at the Esso petrol station in Bayeux, charges €78 per day with 200km free (more than enough for a circuit to the beaches along coastal route D514), or €135 for two days with 400km free.

MANCHE

The Manche *département* includes the entire Cotentin Peninsula from Utah Beach to the magnificent Mont St-Michel. The peninsula's northwest corner is especially captivating, with unspoiled stretches of rocky coastline sheltering tranquil bays and villages. Due west lie the Channel Islands of Jersey and Guernsey. The fertile inland areas, crisscrossed with hedgerows, produce an abundance of cattle, dairy products and apples.

Sadly, over the past two decades, the Manche region has become known as Europe's nuclear dump due to its uranium waste treatment plant (Cap de la Hague), its sprawling power plant (Flamanville) and its nuclear submarines construction (at the Cherbourg shipyards).

CHERBOURG

pop 26,750

At the very tip of the Cotentin Peninsula sits Cherbourg, the largest but hardly the most appealing town in this part of Normandy. Transatlantic cargo ships, passenger ferries from Britain, yachts and warships pass in and out of Cherbourg's monumental port. The port took on an enormous strategic importance during the D-Day landings, as it was indispensable in resupplying the invasion forces.

Don't expect to find any of the romance portrayed in Jacques Demy's 1964 classic film *Les Parapluies de Cherbourg* (The Umbrellas of Cherbourg) here.

Orientation

The Bassin du Commerce, a wide central waterway, separates the 'living' half of Cherbourg to the west from the deserted streets to the east. The attractive Avant Port (Outer Harbour) lies to the north.

Information

INTERNET

Forum Espace Culture (☎ 02 33 78 19 30; place Centrale; per 10/30min €1.50/2.35; ☺ 2-7pm Mon, 10am-7pm Tue-Sat) The Internet café is on the upper floor of this cultural centre.

LAUNDRY

Laundrette (67 rue au Blé)

MONEY

Crédit Lyonnais (16 rue Maréchal Foch) ATM.

POST

Main Post Office (1 rue de l'Ancien Quai) It has a Cyberposte and exchanges currency.

TOURIST INFORMATION

Tourist Office (☎ 02 33 93 52 02; www.ot-cherbourg -cotentin.fr in French; 2 quai Alexandre III; ☺ 9am-

6.30pm Mon-Sat, 10am-12.30pm Sun Jul & Aug, 9am-12.30pm & 2-6.30pm Mon-Sat Sep-Jun)

Tourist Office Annexe (☎ 02 33 44 39 92; ferry terminal) Open for ferry arrivals.

Sights & Activities

Upstairs in a cultural centre, **Musée Thomas Henry** (☎ 02 33 23 02 23; 4 rue Vastel; adult/child €2.3/1.10; ☺ 10am-noon & 2-6pm Tue-Sat, 2-6pm Sun & Mon May-Sep, 2-6pm Wed-Sun Oct-Apr) has 200 works by French, Flemish, Italian and other artists. Highlights include *Atalante et Maleagre* by Van Dyck, *Conversion de St-Augustin* by Fra Angelico and 30 paintings by Jean-François Millet.

The new **Cité de la Mer** (☎ 02 33 20 26 26; www .citedelamer.com; Gare Maritime Transatlantique adult/ child €13/9.50; ☺ 9.30am-7pm Jun–mid-Sep, 10am-6pm mid-Sep–May), north of the city centre, contains half a million litres of water and is the largest aquarium in Europe. There is also a former nuclear submarine – children under six cannot visit it.

Cherbourg is a big sailing centre. At the entrance to the Port de Plaisance Chantereyne, **Station-Voile Cherbourg-Hague** (☎ 02 33 78 19 29; www.cherbourg-hague-nautisme.com in French) runs half-day beginners sailing courses (€92) and a range of other activities such as kayaking, rowing and paragliding.

Sleeping

Auberge de Jeunesse (☎ 02 33 78 15 15; cherbourg@ fuaj.org; 55 rue de l'Abbaye; dm €16.05) This comfortable, ultramodern hostel opened in 1998 and is still going strong. Take bus No 3 or 5 to the Hôtel de Ville stop.

Quai de Caligny has plenty of mid-range options. There are cheaper places in the backstreets north of the tourist office.

Hôtel Moderna (☎ 02 33 43 05 30; www.moderna -hotel.com; 28 rue de la Marine; r €39-48; P ✗) The comfortable, well-equipped rooms (ask for a port view) are decorated in soft pastels and come with satellite TVs and telephones. A good spot for a stopover before catching the ferry.

Hôtel Renaissance (☎ 02 33 43 23 90; fax 02 33 43 96 10; 4 rue de l'Église; r €49-58) This large hotel has modern facilities and a prime location: smack in the centre of town and right near the ferry terminals. Recently renovated, the rooms have views of the port.

Hôtel La Croix de Malte (☎ 02 33 43 19 16; hotel .croix.malte@wanadoo.fr; 5 rue des Halles; r €35-48) Near

NORMANDY

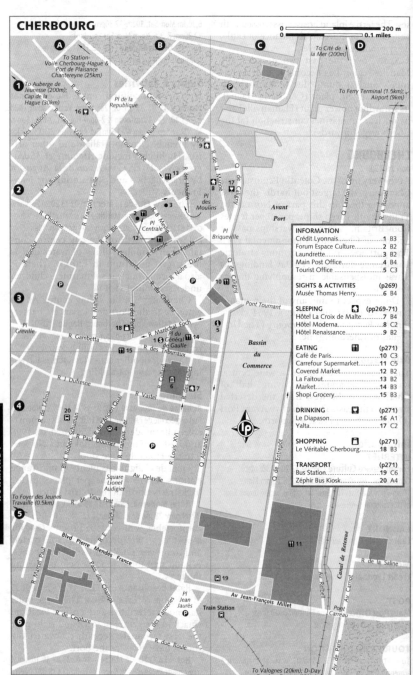

CHERBOURG

To Station-
Voile Cherbourg-Hague &
Port de Plaisance
Chantereyne (25km)

To Auberge de
Jeunesse (200m);
Cap de la
Hague (30km)

To Cité de
la Mer (200m)

To Ferry Terminal (1.5km);
Airport (9km)

Pl de la
République

Av Cessart

R de la Paix

R Grande Vallée

R des Bastions

R de l'Église

R Tour Carrée

R de la Marine

R Talluau

R François Lavieille

R Christine

R au Blé

Pl
Centrale

R Gde Mesnil

PB Mesnil

R Grande

R des Moulins

Pl
des
Moulins

Avant
Port

Q de Caligny

Q Lawton Collins

Q A Rossel

R Bondor

R du Commerce

R des Fossés

R Notre Dame

Pl
Briqueville

R de Chaleur

R de Châteaur

Q de Caligny

Pont Tournant

Pl
Greville

R Mahieu

R des Portes

R Maréchal Foch

Pl du
Général
de Gaulle

R des Tribunaux

Bassin
du
Commerce

R Gambetta

R J Dufresne

R Choiseul

R aux Halles

R Vastel

R de l'Alma

R Paul Doumer

Blvd Robert Schuman

R de l'Ancien Quai

R François Ier

Q Alexandre III

Square
Lionel
Audigier

Av Delaville

Q de l'Entrepôt

To Foyer des Jeunes
Travaille (0.5km)

Vieux Pont

R de l'E

Pass des Champs

Blvd Pierre Mendes France

Q Louis XVI

R Martel Paul

Canal de Retenue

R de la Saline

Av Rebull

Av Carnot

Pont
Carreau

R de Ceinture

R des Tanneries

Pl
Jean
Jaurès

Av Jean-François Millet

Train Station

R due Roule

Av de Paris

To Valognes (20km); D-Day

0   200 m
0   0.1 miles

INFORMATION
Crédit Lyonnais...............................1 B3
Forum Espace Culture.....................2 B2
Laundrette......................................3 B2
Main Post Office............................4 B4
Tourist Office 5 C3

SIGHTS & ACTIVITIES   (p269)
Musée Thomas Henry.....................6 B4

SLEEPING   (pp269-71)
Hôtel La Croix de Malte.................7 B4
Hôtel Moderna...............................8 C2
Hôtel Renaissance..........................9 B2

EATING   (p271)
Café de Paris................................10 C3
Carrefour Supermarket..................11 C5
Covered Market............................12 B2
La Faitout.....................................13 B2
Market...14 B3
Shopi Grocery..............................15 B3

DRINKING   (p271)
Le Diapason.................................16 A1
Yalta...17 C2

SHOPPING   (p271)
Le Véritable Cherbourg................18 B3

TRANSPORT   (p271)
Bus Station..................................19 C6
Zéphir Bus Kiosk.........................20 A4

NORMANDY

the Théâtre de Cherbourg (built in 1882), this hotel has well-equipped doubles.

Eating

Rue Tour Carrée, rue de la Paix and around place Centrale offer a wide choice in both cuisine and price.

Café de Paris (☎ 02 33 43 12 36; 40 quai de Caligny; menus €17-21; ✆ closed Mon & dinner Sun Oct-May) It's not the place for a romantic tête-à-tête with the constant crowds and bustle, but the seafood is the freshest in town.

La Faitout (☎ 02 33 04 25 04; 25 rue Tour Carrée; menu €19; ✆ closed Sun & Mon) Of course the other dishes are great, but at this popular and atmospheric restaurant it's all about the show-stopping crusty duck. On weekends it's best to reserve a table.

SELF-CATERING

Cherbourg's market days are Tuesday and Thursday until 5pm at place de Gaulle and the covered place Centrale. The latter operates on Saturday morning. There's **Carrefour supermarket** (Centre Continent quai de l'Entrepôt) and the **Shopi grocery store** (57 rue Gambetta).

Entertainment

Yalta (☎ 02 33 43 02 81; 46 quai de Caligny) This is the sizzling centre of Cherbourg nightlife, attracting sailors, students and sophisticates alike. There are usually two or three jazz, rock or blues concerts a month and occasionally French singers.

Le Diapson (☎ 02 33 01 21 43; 21 rue de la Paix) This place has a little bit of everything – a philosophy night, art exhibits and the occasional concert. There's a good selection of beer and a varied musical programme.

Shopping

The umbrellas of Cherbourg are beautifully made and the best place to buy them is at **Le Véritable Cherbourg** (☎ 02 33 93 66 60; 30 rue des Portes), which has a stunning selection starting at €85.

Getting There & Away

AIR

Cherbourg's airport is 9km east of town at Maupertus-sur-Mer.

BOAT

The three companies with services to either England or Ireland have bureaus in the ferry terminal *(gare maritime)*. Their desks are open two hours before departure and for 30 minutes after the arrival of each ferry.

Brittany Ferries (☎ 02 33 88 44 44) covers the route to Poole in England; **Irish Ferries** (☎ 02 33 23 44 44) sails to Rosslare, Ireland; and **P&O** (☎ 02 33 88 65 70) handles the link to Portsmouth. For further details and schedules see p919.

BUS

The main regional bus line (which stops at the station on av Jean-François Millet) is **STN** (☎ 02 33 44 32 22). It has services to Valognes (€3.90, 30 minutes, six daily) and Barfleur (€4.30, 40 minutes, two daily).

TRAIN

Services from the **train station** (☎ 02 33 57 50 50; ✆ 6am-10pm) include one direct to Paris' Gare St-Lazare (€36.60, 3½ hours, seven daily) and another via Caen (€60, 1½ hours, eight daily). There are also trains to Rennes and Pontorson. Most destinations require a change at either Caen or Lisons.

Getting Around

There's no public transport from the airport into town. A taxi will cost about €20.

City buses are run by **Zéphir** (☎ 08 10 81 00 50; 40 blvd Robert Schuman). Buses leave from either outside the kiosk or at various points around place Jean Jaurès, in front of the train station. Single tickets cost €1 and a carnet of 10 is €8. There's a shuttle-bus service linking the ferry terminal, the town centre and the train station.

Taxis can be called on ☎ 02 33 53 36 38. The trip between the train station and ferry terminal costs about €8. **Station-Voile** (see p269) rents mountain bikes.

COUTANCES

pop 9700

The medieval hilltop town of Coutances, 77km south of Cherbourg, has two major sights: a remarkable cathedral and a stunning landscape garden. Together they justify a day trip from Bayeux, or a pleasant stopover on the road to Mont St-Michel further south.

Orientation & Information

The town centre is compact and confined by blvd Alsace-Lorraine in the northwest and blvd Jeanne Paynel to the east. At the centre of town is the cathedral and town hall. The train and bus stations are about 1km southeast of the town centre.

Post Office (10 rue St-Dominique) Exchanges money and has a Cyberposte terminal.

Société Générale (8 rue Daniel) Bank opposite the tourist office.

Tourist Office (☎ 02 33 19 08 10; tourisme-coutan ces@wanadoo.fr; place Georges Leclerc; ⏰ 10am-12.30pm & 2-5.30pm Mon, 10am-12.30pm & 2-6pm Tue, Wed & Fri, 10am-6pm Thu, 10am-12.30pm & 2-5pm Sat)

Sights & Activities

The lofty 13th-century Gothic **Cathédrale de Coutances** (admission free; ⏰ 9am-7pm) is one of France's finest, prompting Victor Hugo to call it the prettiest he'd seen after the one at Chartres. Its airy Norman-Romanesque design is enhanced by the use of light-hued limestone. There are several frescoes worth a look, including a 13th-century St George slaying the beast. There are **tours** (adult/student €5/3; ⏰ 3.30pm Mon-Fri summer) in English available, which also afford sweeping views from the galleries in the lantern tower.

Opposite place Leclerc lies the splendid **Jardin des Plantes** (⏰ 9am-8pm mid-Sep–Oct & Apr-Jun, 9am-11.30pm Jul–mid-Sep, 9am-5pm Oct-Mar), a grand 19th-century landscape garden that blends symmetrical French lines with Italianate terraces, English-style copses, a maze and fountains. Its varied stock of ornamental trees includes giant redwood, cedar of Lebanon, New Zealand beech and Canadian nut. Like the cathedral, the grounds are illuminated on summer nights. During the day it's ideal for picnics.

Sleeping & Eating

Hôtel des Trois Piliers (☎ 02 33 45 01 31; 11 rue des Halles; r €25) Rooms are small but well equipped. The bar downstairs draws a young, noisy crowd and the hotel is often booked out by students during holiday periods.

Hôtel le Parvis (☎ 02 33 45 13 55; fax 02 33 45 68 00; place de la Cathédrale; r €42-67) This is an unremarkable but resolutely comfortable hotel, where all the rooms have en suites and English TV. If you're a die-hard fan of *choucroute,* you might like to try their restaurant, which specialises in the Alsacian dish commonly known as sauerkraut.

Restaurant le Vieux Coutances (☎ 02 33 47 94 78; 55 rue Geoffroy de Montbray; menus €10.70-32;

⏰ closed Mon) This former post office is a small, intimate Norman eatery with excellent fish or meat *menus.* We think this is the best address in town.

The market is held on Thursday morning. Look for the delicious local Coutances cheese with its creamy centre.

Getting There & Away

The SNCF runs buses to Granville (€7.40, 30 minutes, up to five daily). In July and August there are buses to the beaches (20 minutes, three daily). Regular train services include Cherbourg (€15.30, two hours, six daily), Caen (€13.50, 1½ hours, six daily) and Paris' Gare du Nord (€34.70, four hours, twice daily).

MONT ST-MICHEL

pop 42

It's difficult not to be impressed with your first sighting of Mont St-Michel. Covering the summit is the massive abbey, a soaring ensemble of buildings in a hotchpotch of architectural styles. The abbey (80m above the sea) is topped by a slender spire with a gilded copper statue of Michael the Archangel slaying a dragon. Around the base are the ancient ramparts and a jumble of buildings that house the handful of true residents. At night the whole structure is brilliantly illuminated.

Mont St-Michel's fame derives equally from the bay's extraordinary tides. Depending on the gravitational pull of the moon and, to a lesser extent, the sun, the difference between low and high tides can reach 15m. The Mont either looks out onto bare sand stretching many kilometres into the distance or, at high tide (only about six hours later), the same expanse under water. However, the Mont and its causeway are completely surrounded by the sea only at the highest of tides, which occur at seasonal equinoxes.

Most people will stay at Pontorson, the town opposite.

History

According to Celtic mythology, Mont St-Michel was one of the sea tombs to which the souls of the dead were sent. In 708 the saint appeared to Bishop Aubert of Avranches and told him to build a devotional chapel at the summit. In 966, Richard I, duke of Normandy, gave Mont St-Michel to the Benedictines, who turned it into an important centre of learning and, in the 11th century, into something of an ecclesiastical fortress, with a military garrison at the disposal of the abbot and the king.

In the 15th century, during the Hundred Years' War, the English blockaded and besieged Mont St-Michel three times. The fortified abbey withstood these assaults; it was the only place in western and northern France not to fall into English hands. After the Revolution, Mont St-Michel was turned into a prison. In 1966 the abbey was symbolically returned to the Benedictines as part of the celebrations marking its millennium. Mont St-Michel and the surrounding bay became a Unesco World Heritage Site in 1979.

Orientation

There is only one opening in the ramparts, Porte de l'Avancée, immediately to the left as you walk down the causeway. The Mont's single street – Grande Rue – is lined with restaurants, a few hotels, souvenir shops and entrances to some rather tacky exhibits in the crypts below. There are several large car parks (€4 per day) close to the Mont.

Pontorson (population 4200), the nearest town to Mont St-Michel, is 9km south and the base for most travellers. Route D976 from Mont St-Michel runs right into Pontorson's main thoroughfare, rue du Couësnon.

Information

MONEY
There is an ATM next to the tourist office in Mont St-Michel.

CIN bank (98 rue du Couësnon, Pontorson; Tue-Sat) Better exchange rates than the Mont.

Société Générale ATM just inside the Porte de l'Avancée.

POST
Pontorson Post Office (place de l'Hôtel de Ville)

Mont St-Michel Post Office (Grande Rue)

TOURIST INFORMATION
Mont St-Michel Tourist Office (02 33 60 14 30; www.ot-montsaintmichel.com; 9am-7pm Jul & Aug, 9am-noon & 2-5.30pm Sep-Jun) Up the stairs to the left as you enter Porte de l'Avancée. If you're interested in what the tides will be doing, look for the table of tides (horaire des marées) posted outside. A detailed map of the Mont is available at the tourist office for €3.50.

Pontorson Tourist Office (02 33 60 20 65; fax 02 33 60 85 67; mont.st.michel.pontorson@wanadoo.fr; place

de l'Église; 9am-noon & 2-7pm Mon-Fri, 10am-noon & 3-6pm Sat, 10am-noon Sun Apr-Sep, 9am-noon & 2-6pm Mon-Fri, 10am-noon & 3-6pm Sat Oct-Mar) Friendly staff and heaps of information about local walks, tours and events.

Walking Tour

When the tide is out, you can walk all the way around Mont St-Michel, a distance of about 1km. Straying too far from the Mont could be risky: you might get stuck in wet sand – from which Norman soldiers are depicted being rescued in one scene of the Bayeux Tapestry.

Abbaye du Mont St-Michel

The Mont's major attraction is the renowned **abbey** (02 33 89 80 00; adult/18-25/under 18 incl 1hr guided tour €7/4.50/free; 9am-7pm May-Sep, 9.30am-6pm Oct-Apr). To reach it, walk to the top of the Grande Rue and then climb the stairway. From Monday to Saturday between mid-May and September, there are self-paced illuminated night-time visits of Mont St-Michel complete with music from 9pm to midnight.

Most rooms can be visited without a guide, but it's worthwhile taking the tour included in the ticket price. One-hour tours in English depart three to eight times daily (the last leaves about 1½ hours before closing). It is also possible to rent an audioguide with recorded commentary (€4) if you miss the tour.

The **Église Abbatiale** (Abbey Church) was built at the rocky tip of the mountain cone. The transept rests on solid rock while the nave, choir and transept arms are supported by the massive rooms below. The church is famous for its mixture of architectural styles: the nave and south transept (11th and 12th centuries) are Norman Romanesque, while the choir (late 15th century) is Flamboyant Gothic. Mass is at 12.15pm from Tuesday to Sunday.

The buildings on the northern side of the Mont are known as **La Merveille** (literally 'the marvel'). The famous **cloître** (cloister) is surrounded by a double row of delicately carved arches resting on granite pillars. The early-13th-century **réfectoire** (dining hall) is illuminated by a wall of recessed windows – remarkable, given that the sheer drop precluded the use of flying buttresses – which diffuses the light beautifully. The Gothic

Salle des Hôtes (Guest Hall), dating from 1213, has two giant fireplaces. Watch out for the **promenoire** (ambulatory), with one of the oldest ribbed vaulted ceilings in Europe, and **La Chapelle de Notre Dame sous Terre** (Underground Chapel of Our Lady), one of the earliest rooms built in the abbey and rediscovered in 1903.

The masonry used to build the abbey was brought to the Mont by boat and pulled up the hillside using ropes. What looks like a treadmill for gargantuan gerbils was in fact powered in the 19th century by half a dozen prisoners who, by turning the wheel, hoisted the supply sledge up the side of the abbey.

Église Notre Dame de Pontorson
Though no match for its dramatic sister to the north, the 12th-century Church of Our Lady in Pontorson is a good example of the Norman Romanesque style of architecture. To the left of the altar is a 15th-century relief of Christ's Passion, which was mutilated during the Religious Wars and again during the Revolution.

Grande Rue
Of the several so-called **museums** (adult/child per museum €4/2) along the street, two might merit a visit. Children may find the **Archéoscope**, a smart 20-minute multimedia history of the Mont with lights, video and even smoke, as exciting as the actual bricks and mortar. The **Musée de la Mer et de l'Écologie** is informative about Mont St-Michel's complex tidal patterns and merits a visit if model ships excite you.

Sleeping
There are eight hotels within the walls of Mont St-Michel and several more at the end of the causeway. All tend to be fully booked in summer, often by large coach parties. We recommend that you beat a retreat further afield. The following hotels are in Pontorson:

Centre Duguesclin (☎ /fax 02 33 60 18 65; aj@ville -pontorson.fr; blvd du Général Patton; r per person €7.30; year-round) About 1km west of the train station, this modern, newly renovated hostel offers four- to six-bed rooms and kitchen facilities. The hostel closes from 10am to 6pm, but there's no curfew. It is in an old three-storey stone building opposite No 26.

Hôtel de Bretagne (☎ 02 33 60 10 55; www.le bretagnepontorson.com; 59 rue du Couësnon; s €35-48, d €39-64) Rooms in this attractive mid-range option are brighter than its rather dreary reception area. Its quite formal **restaurant** offers excellent service and food, from the two-course *formule* (€11) to a gourmet *menu* (€38).

Hôtel Montgomery (☎ 02 33 60 00 09; www.hotel -montgomery.com; 13 rue du Couësnon; r €77-225; P) A lovely 16th-century mansion with a vine-covered Renaissance façade. Each room is different and has been decorated with period furnishings and equipped with modern amenities. The restaurant is excellent.

CAMPING
Camping Haliotis (☎ 02 33 68 11 59; www.camp ing-haliotis-mont-saint-michel.com in French; adult/site €4.20/3.50; Apr-Oct;) Just off blvd Général Patton, this complex has a heated pool.

Eating
MONT ST-MICHEL
Tourist restaurants around the base of the Mont have lovely views, but although *menus* start at about €12 the quality can be mediocre. Cosy **Crêperie La Sirène** (☎ 02 33 60 08 60; galettes €6.40-8.20) offers reasonable value.

La Mère Poulard (☎ 02 33 89 68 68; Grande Rue; lunch menus €29-39, dinner menus €45-55; 11am-10pm) Established in 1888, this tourist institution turns out its famous *omelettes à la Mère Poulard* (soufflé omelettes cooked in a wood-fired oven) at astronomical prices. Autographed photos of visiting film stars and politicians adorn the walls. The choices also include seafood, free-range chicken and *agneau pré-salé* (lamb from animals that have grazed the salt meadows in the surrounding area).

PONTORSON
You'll find a few cheap, unexceptional eateries along main rue du Couësnon but if you're looking for anything special, choose a hotel restaurant.

In addition to the eateries listed above, the **Hôtel La Tour Brette** (☎ 02 33 60 10 69; latourbrette@wanadoo.fr; 8 rue du Couësnon) and **Hôtel La Cave** (☎ 02 33 60 11 35; www.hotel-la-cave .com; 37 rue Libération) both have lovely restaurants with traditional French *menus* for €12 to €20.

SELF-CATERING

The nearest supermarket is across from the Hôtel Mercure on the causeway, 2km from the Mont. In Pontorson, there's the **8 à Huit** (5 rue du Couësnon).

Getting There & Away

BUS

Courriers Bretons (☎ 02 33 60 11 43) runs between Pontorson and Mont St-Michel (€1.70, 15 minutes, seven to 10 daily) and also to/from St-Malo (€7.80, one hour).

TRAIN

Services from Pontorson include Caen (via Folligny; €19.20, 2¼ hours, two daily), Rennes (via Dol; €10.50, 50 minutes, two daily) and Cherbourg (€20.70, 2½ hours, two daily). To get to Pontorson, from Paris, take the train to Caen (from Gare St-Lazare), to Rennes (from Gare Montparnasse), or travel directly to Pontorson via Folligny (from Gare Montparnasse; €35.60).

Getting Around

You can rent bicycles from **Camping Haliotis** (☎ 02 33 68 11 59; off blvd Général Patton) and **VMPS** (☎ 02 33 60 28 76, 06 86 90 95 01). VMPS delivers to your hotel or camp site. For a taxi, call ☎ 02 33 60 33 23.

ALENÇON

pop 30,400

In the far south of Normandy, on the edge of the Normandie-Maine nature reserve, lies the former lace-making hub of Alençon. The town exudes an aura of genteel wealth – harking back to its days as a Norman tax-collecting centre in the 17th century – and makes a nice breather en route to/from Paris, 193km to the south.

Orientation

The old town and its sights are about 1.5km southwest of the train station, via av du Président Wilson and rue St-Blaise. The River Sarthe snakes past the old quarter to the south.

Information

Crédit Mutuel (89bis rue aux Sieurs) ATM.
Espace Internet (☎ 02 33 32 40 33; 6-8 rue des Filles Notre Dame; ☼ 8.30am-7pm Mon-Sat) Internet access.
Laundrette (5 rue du Collège)

Post Office (16 rue du Jeudi) It has Cyberposte and exchanges currency.
Tourist Office (☎ 02 33 80 66 33; alencon.tourisme@wanadoo.fr; place La Magdelaine; ☼ 9.30am-6pm Mon-Sat, 10am-12.30pm & 3-5.30pm Sun Jul & Aug, 9.30am-noon & 2-6.30pm Mon-Sat Sep-Jun) In the turreted Maison d'Ozé, this tourist office will book accommodation for free. Ask for the walking tour brochure *Alençon Foot*.

Sights

The old town, especially along the **Grande Rue**, is full of atmospheric Second Empire houses and wrought-iron balconies dating from the 18th century. To the southeast looms the crowned turret of the **Château des Ducs**, which was used by the Nazis as a prison during WWII (closed to the public).

Occupying an old Jesuit schoolhouse, the **Musée des Beaux-Arts et de la Dentelle** (☎ 02 33 32 40 07; 12 rue Charles Aveline; adult/child €2.90/2.40; ☼ 10am-noon & 2-6pm Jul & Aug, Tue-Sun Sep-Jun) has a so-so collection of Flemish, Dutch and French artworks from the 17th to 19th centuries and an exhaustive (some might say exhausting) exhibit on the history of lace-making. There's also an unexpected section of Cambodian artefacts – including buddhas, spears and tiger skulls – donated by a former (French) governor of Cambodia.

The **Église Notre Dame** (Grande Rue; ☼ 8.30am-noon & 2-5.30pm) has a stunning Flamboyant Gothic portal from the 16th century and some superb stained glass in the chapel where St Theresa was baptised. The house in which St Theresa was born is next door.

The **Musée Leclerc** (☎ 02 33 26 27 26; 33 rue du Pont Neuf; adult/child €2.25/1.20; ☼ 10am-noon & 2-6pm Apr-Sep, 10.30am-noon & 2-5.30pm Oct-Mar) details the history of Alençon during WWII, including some fascinating wartime photos. The town was liberated in August 1944 by General Leclerc, whose statue stands guard out front.

Sleeping & Eating

Hôtel Le Grand St-Michel (☎ 02 33 26 04 77; fax 02 33 26 71 82; 7 rue du Temple; r with washbasin/bathroom €32/43; P) In the centre of old Alençon and on a quiet street, this place has the air of a traditional country house. The rooms are comfortable in a casual, thrown-together way.

Hôtel-Restaurant Le Grand Cerf (☎ 02 33 26 00 51; 21 rue St-Blaise; s/d €51/59; P ✗ ▣) This stately old building on the edge of the old

NORMANDY

town offers more luxury, with plush rooms and a delightfully traditional décor. It has a garden patio and a good **restaurant** (menus from €13.50; ☯ closed Sat & Sun).

Camping Municipal (☎ 02 33 26 34 95; 69 rue de Guéramé; adult/site €2.10/2.45) Southwest of town on the Sarthe, this well-outfitted location has only 87 sites.

Restaurant Au Petit Vatel (☎ 02 33 26 23 78; 72 place du Commandant-Desmeulles; menus €18.50-69; ☯ closed Wed & dinner Sun) Recently taken over by new owners, this well-known restaurant serves refined cuisine in an equally refined dining room. Go on, try the *beignet de Camembert* (Camembert fritters).

Getting There & Around
STAO (☎ 02 33 26 06 35) buses connects Alençon with Sées (€4.60, 20 minutes, once daily) and Mortagne-au-Perche (€6.10, one hour, four daily).

From Alençon there are frequent train services to Gare Montparnasse in Paris (€47.20, 1¾ hours), Caen (€14.50, 1¾ hours), Pontorson (€30.40, four hours) and Le Mans (€8.10, 45 minutes), among other destinations.

Altobus (☎ 08 00 50 02 29) has three routes that serve the city including one, Line A, which runs from the train station to the town centre.

Brittany

CONTENTS

North Coast	**281**
St-Malo	281
Dinard	286
Cancale	289
Pointe du Grouin	289
Dinan	289
Paimpol	292
Perros-Guirec	293
Finistère	**294**
Roscoff	294
Around Roscoff	296
Brest	296
Le Conquet	298
Île d'Ouessant	298
Presqu'île de Crozon	300
Huelgoat	301
Douarnenez & Locronan	302
Quimper	302
Concarneau	305
Around Concarneau	308
Morbihan Coast	**308**
Lorient	308
Carnac	310
Quiberon	312
Belle Île	313
Vannes	314
Around Vannes	317
Eastern & Central Brittany	**318**
Josselin	318
Forêt de Paimpont	318
Rennes	319

Brittany stands slightly aloof from the rest of France, set apart by its Celtic roots and a stubborn independent streak. Even on the map it seems to want to break away – a granite prow yearning westwards into the Atlantic, reaching towards Canada, the Caribbean and Cape Horn.

Much of the region's charm lies in its Celtic culture and intimate relationship with the sea. Brittany's intricately fretted shoreline – mirrored in the Gothic tracery of its cathedrals and the patterns of its traditional lace headdresses – has some of France's finest coastal scenery, while its music and cultural festivals are among the liveliest and most colourful in Europe.

Although for centuries the ocean has been a hard taskmaster for Breton sailors, for today's visitor it is both playground and larder. Brittany boasts dozens of classic seaside resorts, such as Dinard, Perros-Guirec and Bénodet, and offers some of the best yachting, windsurfing, sea-kayaking and coastal hiking in France. When it's time to eat, the harvest of the sea – from mussels and oysters to lobster and sea bass – is on the menu. Washed down, of course, with a glass of Breton cider or a crisp Muscadet wine from the vineyards of Nantes, to the south.

The Celtic culture planted in Brittany 1500 years ago put down strong roots, which neither union with France nor Revolution was able to rip out. Bretons care for and cherish their past. You'll sense it in the serried megaliths of Carnac, the stone calvaries of Finistère and the upholding of the ancient traditions of *pardons* (religious pilgrimages). You see it in the old wooden sailing boats, redolent of tar and turpentine, straining at their moorings in Breton harbours, and hear it in the strident wail of traditional musical instruments, the *biniou* and *bombarde*.

It's a past leavened with the spice of myth and legend. The region abounds with tales of lost, sunken cities; and of Ankou (Death) prowling darkened villages in his creaking, wooden cart.

Brittany may show a French face to the world but it possesses a Celtic soul all its own.

HIGHLIGHTS

- Walk the rugged coastline of the **Île d'Ouessant** (p298) or another of Brittany's seaswept islands
- Ponder the meaning of Carnac's **megaliths** (p311)
- Cycle forest trails in the **Forêt de Paimpont** (p318)
- Wander the streets of St-Malo's old **walled city** (p281)
- Cruise up the River Rance to the medieval city of **Dinan** (p289)
- Play the sailor on the traditional wooden boats in Douarnenez's vast **Musée du Bateau** (p302)
- Sprawl on Dinard's swanky **beach** (p286)
- Dance till you drop at Lorient's **Festival Interceltique** (p309)

★ Île d'Ouessant ★★ Dinard ★ St-Malo
★ Dinan
★ Douarnenez
Lorient ★   ★ Forêt de Paimpont
Carnac ★

■ POPULATION: 2,905,000	■ AREA: 27,210 SQ KM

BRITTANY

History

Brittany's earliest known inhabitants were Neolithic tribes whose menhirs and dolmens still poke skywards (see p311). In the 6th century BC, the first wave of Celts swept in and named their new homeland 'Armor', the land beside the sea. In 56 BC Julius Caesar conquered the region, which remained in Roman hands until the 5th century AD.

After the Romans withdrew, a second wave of Celts – driven from what is now Britain and Ireland by the Anglo-Saxon invasions – crossed the Channel and settled in Brittany. They brought with them Christianity, spread by Celtic missionaries, after whom many Breton towns, such as St-Malo and St-Brieuc, were named.

In the 9th century, Brittany's national hero, Nominoë, revolted against French rule. But, sandwiched geographically between two more powerful kingdoms, the duchy of Brittany was contested by both France and England throughout the Middle Ages until, after a series of strategic royal weddings, the region became part of France in 1532.

Over the centuries, Brittany has retained a separate regional identity. To this day, some Bretons retain the hope that their region might one day regain its independence.

KING ARTHUR

Breton culture abounds in mysterious legends and the most famous of all is that of King Arthur, which spread to England in the Middle Ages via Celtic Cornwall. In Brittany many sites still recall Arthur, Lancelot his favourite knight, Merlin the magician and the fairies Vivian and Morgan le Fay.

Île Grande and Île d'Aval, close to Perros-Guirec, both lay claim to be the island of Avalon where, legend says, Arthur is buried. Deep in the Forêt d'Huelgoat, one of the last vestiges of the old, vast inland forest, is where Arthur searched in vain for the Holy Grail. Merlin's mistress, Vivian (the mysterious Lady of the Lake), prowled the Forêt de Paimpont (or Brocéliande), southwest of Rennes; deep within it, the wizard's spring of eternal youth still trickles. Vannes, for its part, was the capital of the kingdom ruled by Ban, Lancelot's father, while Nantes, in many versions of the myth, is where King Arthur held court.

The latest violent manifestation of Breton nationalism was in April 2000, when a bomb attack on a McDonald's fast-food restaurant in Quévert, near Dinan, left one person dead. Despite this isolated, tragic event, the overwhelming body of nationalist sentiment in Brittany is entirely peaceful.

Most Bretons retain a strong bond with their native culture without feeling the need to belong to any separatist movement. Nowadays, there's a drive for cultural and linguistic renewal – and a consciousness of Brittany's place within a wider Celtic culture that embraces Ireland, Wales, Scotland, Cornwall and Galicia in Spain, with all of whom stronger ties have been established.

Climate

Brittany's coast is washed by the Gulf Stream, a warm ocean current flowing from the Gulf of Mexico towards northwest Europe. As a result, the region enjoys a gentle climate with warm, but never too warm, summers and mild winters. Even though Brittany records France's highest annual rainfall, it rarely pours for many consecutive days, even during the wettest months (January to May).

The Culture

Breton customs and language are more evident in Basse Bretagne (lower Brittany), the western half of the peninsula, and particularly in Cornouaille, its southwestern tip. Haute Bretagne (upper Brittany), the eastern half (which includes St-Malo), has retained little of its traditional way of life.

You might be lucky enough to see traditional costumes, including the tall lace headdresses of the women, at a *fest-noz* (night-time dance and music fiesta) or *pardon*. Brittany's two major cultural festivals are Quimper's Festival de Cornouaille in late July and Lorient's Festival Interceltique in early August.

Language

Breton (Breiz) is a Celtic language related to Cornish and Welsh and, more distantly, to Irish and Scottish Gaelic. You might well hear Breton in western Brittany (especially in Cornouaille), where as many as 600,000 people have some degree of fluency. However, as with so many minority languages, the number of Breton-speaking households is diminishing.

BRITTANY

50 km
25 miles

To Caen (32km)

ORNE

CALVADOS

MANCHE

To Domfront (32km)

To Le Mans (100km)

Laval

MAYENNE

Château-Gontier

MAINE-ET-LOIRE

Vire

Avranches

Mont St-Michel

Fougères

Vitré

ILLE-ET-VILAINE

N157

Ancenis

LOIRE-ATLANTIQUE

Loire

Granville

Îles Chausey

Îles des Landes

Cancale

Pontorson

Rennes

N137

N137

Châteaubriant

N824

Nantes

To The Channel Islands; Plymouth; Poole (UK)

Pointe du Grouin

St-Malo

Dol-de-Bretagne

Côte d'Émeraude

Dinard

St-Briac

St-Cast

Dinan

N24

Forêt de Paimpont

St-Nazaire

Cap Fréhel

Le Val-André

Lamballe

N12

Plémet

Brest Canal

Redon

La Baule

Golfe de Saint Malo

Binic

St-Brieuc

Étang au Duc

Josselin

Nantes-Brest Canal

N165

Le Croisic

Île de Bréhat

Paimpol

Guingamp

Loudéac

Pontivy

MORBIHAN

Vannes

Bird Sanctuary

Île d'Houat

Côte de Granit Rose

Ploumanac'h

Perros-Guirec

Trégastel-Plage

Trébeurden

Lannion

Plouha

Lac de Guerlédan

N164

Locmariaquer

Port Navalo

Île de Hoëdic

CÔTES D'ARMOR

B R I T T A N Y

Carnac

Gulf of Morbihan

Morlaix

Roscoff

St-Pol-de-Léon

Callac-Plouguer

Châteauneuf

Auray

Plouharnel

Quiberon

Belle Île

To Plymouth; Rosslare (UK); Cork (Ireland)

N12

St-Thégonnec

Huelgoat

FINISTÈRE

Quimperlé

Lorient

Le Palais

Île de Batz

Sizun

Guimiliau

Lampaul-Guimiliau

Landivisiau

Lesneven

Landerneau

Monts d'Arrée

Parc d'Armorique

Montagnes Noires

N165

Concarneau

Île de Groix

Île d'Ouessant

Île Molène

Plougastel

Brest

Ménez Hom

Châteaulin

Locronan

Quimper

CORNOUAILLE

Pont-Aven

Port-Manec'h

Île de Gléan

Le Conquet

Camaret-sur-Mer

Crozon

Presqu'île de Crozon

Douarnenez

Audierne

Bénodet

Pont-l'Abbé

St-Guénolé

Pointe du Raz

Île de Sein

ATLANTIC OCEAN

LP

THE GWENN HA DU: BRITTANY'S FLAG

Wherever you go in Brittany, you'll see the distinctive monochrome Breton flag, the *Gwenn ha Du* (White and Black). Invented in 1923, it took its inspiration from the USA's stars and stripes. The nine horizontal stripes – five black and four white – represent the five ancient bishoprics of Haute Bretagne (Upper Brittany) and the four of Basse Bretagne (Lower Brittany). In the upper left corner is a field of stylised ermines, the device on the coat of arms of the former duchy of Brittany.

Legend has it that Anne de Bretagne adopted the ermine as a symbol of Brittany. The duchess was watching an ermine (a stoat in its white winter coat) being chased by hunters, when the tiny animal stopped and accepted death rather than cross a patch of muddy ground and stain its pure white fur. The motto of the duchy of Brittany was *'Plutôt la mort que la souillure'* – 'Rather death than the stain (of dishonour)'.

After the Revolution, the new government made a concerted effort to suppress the Breton language and replace it with French. Indeed, no more than 25 years ago, if school children spoke Breton in class they might have been punished. Things have changed, however, and nowadays some 20 privately subsidised schools – including several at the secondary level – teach in Breton.

Activities

On the coast, even quite small resorts offer the opportunity for sailing, windsurfing, canoeing and kayaking – and scuba diving around the rocky archipelagos is among the best in France.

A leisurely way to tour the region is by canal boat along the waterways from Brest or Dinan to Nantes. For information on boats, moorings and locks contact the **Service de la Navigation** (in Rennes ☎ 02 99 59 20 60, in Lorient ☎ 02 97 64 85 20).

Getting There & Around

Ferries link St-Malo with the Channel Islands and the English ports of Portsmouth, Poole and Weymouth. From Roscoff, there are ferries to Plymouth (UK) and Cork (Ireland).

Brittany's major towns and cities are linked by rail but routes leave the interior poorly served. The bus network is extensive, but services are often infrequent.

It's well worth renting a car or motorbike or bringing your own, especially if you're keen on exploring out-of-the-way destinations. Brittany – especially Cornouaille and the interior – is an excellent area for cycling, and bike-rental places are never hard to find.

NORTH COAST

The central swathe of Brittany's north coast is shared between the *départements* of Ille-et-Vilaine and Côtes d'Armor. It's as wild or tame, as family-friendly or look-at-me cool as you care to make it.

All along the Côte d'Émeraude (Emerald Coast), which transcends both *départements*, are promontories with spectacular sea views, emerald-green shallows and aquamarine deeps. The long, broad, safe strands of golden sand are backed by small, well-resourced resorts, each ideal for a family holiday. Smarter and more substantial are exclusive Perros-Guirec and its rival, Dinard, chic as they come with its casino and distinctive striped bathing tents.

Eastwards, across the Rance Estuary (do take the scenic passenger ferry across its mouth if you're travelling light) is St-Malo, with the ramparts and narrow streets of Intra-Muros, its old quarter, faithfully reconstructed after the devastation of WWII. Nearby, Cancale, famous for its oyster beds, is a must for all serious seafood scoffers.

Allow a full day too to venture inland and visit the charming walled medieval city of Dinan, left behind a bit by the tide of coastal development but still hugely – excessively in high summer – popular with day visitors.

ST-MALO

pop 52,700

The port of St-Malo is one of Brittany's most popular tourist destinations. Squatting at the mouth of the River Rance, it's famed for its walled city, nearby beaches – and one of the world's highest tidal ranges.

BRITTANY

ST-MALO & ST-SERVAN

INFORMATION
Cyberl@n............................1 E1
Laundrette..........................2 F1
Main Post Office..................3 D1
Tourist Office......................4 C2

SIGHTS & ACTIVITIES (pp283-4)
Cathédrale St-Vincent...........5 B2
Château de St-Malo..............6 C1
Fort de la Cité.....................7 C4
Fort National.......................8 D1
Mémorial 39-45....................9 C4
Musée du Château..............10 B1
Musée International du Long
  Cours Cap-Hornier...........11 D4
Tour Solidor....................(see 11)

SLEEPING (pp284-5)
Camping Aleth.....................12 C4
Hôtel Aux Vieilles Pierres.....13 A3
Hôtel Brocéliande................14 F1
Hôtel de la Mer...................15 D3
Hôtel de la Rance...............16 D4
Hôtel de l'Univers...............17 B1
Hôtel France et
  Chateaubriand.................18 B1

EATING (p285)
Borgnefesse.......................22 B2
Crêperie Chez Gaby.............23 B3
Glacier Sanchez..................24 B2
Hall au Blé (Covered
  Market)...........................25 B2
La Chasse-Marée.................26 A2
La Coquille d'Oeuf...............27 B1
Le Maclow.........................28 B1
Le Petit Crêpier..................29 B2
Rue de l'Orme Food Shops..30 B2

Hôtel Le Neptune................19 E1
Hôtel San Pedro..................20 A2
Quic-en-Grogne..................21 A3

DRINKING (p285)
L'Aviso..............................31 A2

TRANSPORT (pp285-6)
Boat Trips to Dinan.........(see 33)
Bus Offices....................(see 4)
Bus Station........................32 C1
Corsaire Ferry to Dinard......33 B4
Europcar...........................34 E2
Gare Maritime de la
  Bourse...........................35 D3
Gare Maritime du Naye........36 D3

St-Malo was a key port during the 17th and 18th centuries, serving as a base for both merchant ships and government-sanctioned pirates, known euphemistically as privateers. Although fortification began in the 12th century, the most imposing military architecture dates from the 17th and 18th centuries, when the English, the favourite targets of Malouin privateers, posed a constant threat.

Orientation

The St-Malo conurbation consists of the harbour towns of St-Malo and St-Servan plus the modern suburbs of Paramé and Rothéneuf to the east. The old walled city of St-Malo is known as Intra-Muros ('within the walls') or Ville Close. From the train station, it's a 15-minute walk westwards along av Louis Martin.

Information

Cyberl@n (☎ 02 99 56 07 78; 68 chaussée de Sillon; per hr €4; ⏰ noon-1am Mon-Sat, 3pm-1am Sun) Internet access.

Laundrette (25 blvd de la Tour d'Auvergne; ⏰ 7.30am-9pm)

Main Post Office (1 blvd de la Tour d'Auvergne)

Tourist Office (☎ 02 99 56 64 48; www.saint-malo -tourisme.com; esplanade St-Vincent; ⏰ 9am-7.30pm Mon-Sat, 10am-6pm Sun Jul & Aug, 9am-12.30pm & 1.30-6pm or 6.30pm Mon-Sat Sep-Jun, 10am-12.30pm & 2.30-6pm Sun Easter-Jun & Sep)

Sights & Activities

OLD CITY

The old walled city was originally an island, which became linked to the mainland by the sandy isthmus of Le Sillon in the 13th century.

During August 1944, the battle to drive German forces out of St-Malo destroyed around 80% of it. The main historical monuments were faithfully reconstructed, while the rest of the area was rebuilt in the style of the 17th and 18th centuries.

Constructed between the 12th and 18th centuries, the town's centrepiece, **Cathédrale St-Vincent** (place Jean de Châtillon; ⏰ 9.30am-6pm), was severely damaged by the 1944 bombing. Highlights are the striking modern bronze altar and the glowing, harlequin colours of the modern stained glass in the traceried windows of the east wall.

If the narrow streets become claustrophobic, escape to the **ramparts**, constructed at the end of the 17th century under the great military architect Vauban. You can make a complete circuit (around 2km); there's free access at several places, including all the main city gates.

From their northern stretch, you can look across to the remains of **Fort National** (admission free; ⏰ Jun-Sep). Accessible only at low tide, this fort, also Vauban-designed, was long used as a prison.Within **Château de St-Malo**, built by the dukes of Brittany in the 15th and 16th centuries, is the **Musée du Château** (☎ 02 99 40 71 57; adult/child €4.80/2.40; ⏰ 10am-noon & 2-6pm Apr-Sep, Tue-Sun Oct-Mar). Covering the history of the city and the St-Malo region, the museum's most interesting exhibits are in the Tour Générale – the history of cod fishing on the Grand Banks on the ground floor and the photos of St-Malo after WWII.

COMBINED TICKET

A combined ticket (adult/child €11.75/5.90) gives access to St-Malo's three major monuments: the Musée du Château de St-Malo, Musée International du Long Cours Cap-Hornier and Mémorial 39-45. It can be purchased at any of the three participating museums and is valid for the duration of your stay in St-Malo.

ÎLE DU GRAND BÉ

You can walk to the rocky islet of Île du Grand Bé, where the great 18th-century writer Chateaubriand is buried, via the Porte des Bés. Once the tide rushes in, the causeway remains impassable for about six hours so check tide times with the tourist office.

ST-SERVAN

Fort de la Cité was constructed in the mid-18th century and used as a German base during WWII. One of the bunkers now houses **Mémorial 39-45** (☎ 02 99 82 41 74; adult/child €4.8/2.40; guided visits 2pm, 3.15pm & 4.30pm Tue-Sun Apr-Jun & Sep-Mar, 6 times daily Jul & Aug), which depicts St-Malo's violent WWII history and liberation and includes a 45-minute film in French.

Musée International du Long Cours Cap-Hornier (Museum of the Cape Horn Route; ☎ 02 99 40 71 58; adult/ child €4.8/2.40; ⏰ 10am-noon & 2-6pm Apr-Sep, Tue-Sun Oct-Mar) is in the 14th-century Tour Solidor. Presenting the life of the hardy sailors who

BRIT

followed the Cape Horn route, it offers superb views from the top of the tower.

AQUARIUM

The **Grand Aquarium** (☎ 02 99 21 19 00; av Général Patton; adult/child €13/9.50; ☎ at least 10am-6pm Feb-Dec), about 4km south of the city centre, is an excellent wet-weather alternative for kids with its mini-submarine descent and *bassin tactile* (touch pool), where you can fondle rays, turbot – even a baby shark (don't fear for their fingers; it's small and not noticeably carnivorous!). Bus No 5, direction Grassinais, passes by every half-hour.

BEACHES

West of the city walls is **Plage de Bon Secours** with a protected tidal pool for bathing. St-Servan's **Plage des Bas Sablons** has a cement wall to keep the sea from receding completely at low tide. The **Grande Plage**, much larger, stretches northeast along the isthmus of Le Sillon. **Plage de Rochebonne** is another 1km to the northeast. The stretch from Grande Plage to Plage des Bas Sablons via the ramparts of the old city makes a wonderful sunset stroll.

BOAT TRIPS

Corsaire (☎ 02 23 18 15 15) runs ferries from just outside the Porte de Dinan to Îles Chausey (adult/child €26/15.60 return, 1½ hours, July to August), the Île Cézembre (€12/7 return, 20 minutes, April to September) and Dinan (adult/child one way €18/11, return €24/14.50, 2½ hours, May to September). For ferries to Dinard see p288.

Sleeping

Auberge de Jeunesse (☎ 02 99 40 29 80; info@centre varangot.com; 37 av du Père Umbricht; dm €13.20, s €20.70-22, d €29.40-32, all with breakfast) Choose the more expensive option for a considerably more luxurious stay than the usual hostel fare. Take bus No 5 from the train station or No 1 (July and August only) from the bus station and tourist office.

BEYOND THE WALLS

There are plenty of hotels for all budgets near the train station and around the beaches of Sillon and Grande Plage.

Hôtel Le Neptune (☎ 02 99 56 82 15; 21 rue de l'Industrie; d €20-27.50, with bathroom €27-42) Close to the Grande Plage, this comfortable, family-run place is above a small, cheerful bar.

Hôtel Brocéliande (☎ 02 99 20 62 62; 43 chaussée du Sillon; d €84-125) The Brocéliande is a delightful, cosy place. Most rooms – including the breakfast room with its picture window – directly overlook the Grande Plage and bedrooms are individually and tastefully decorated.

HOTELS – INTRA-MUROS

Hôtel Aux Vieilles Pierres (☎ 02 99 56 46 80; 4 rue des Lauriers; d €29, with bathroom €45) This friendly, intimate, family-run hotel, the cheapest in the old city, has only six rooms so it's wise to reserve in advance. For dinner, step no further than its equally cosy downstairs restaurant.

Hôtel San Pedro (☎ 02 99 40 88 57; www.san pedro-hotel.com; 1 rue Ste-Anne; s/d €50/55; ☒ Feb-Nov) Tucked at the back of the old city, the San Pedro, extensively renovated in 2003, offers impeccable rooms, the warmest of welcomes and sea views.

Hôtel France et Chateaubriand (☎ 02 99 56 66 52; www.hotel-fr-chateaubriand.com; place Chateaubriand; s €64-73, d €74.50-95.50) This smart, two-star establishment faces the entrance to the chateau. Its 80 rooms – the more expensive ones overlook the sea – are plush, speaking of the baroque, and several have wheelchair access.

Hôtel de l'Univers (☎ 02 99 40 89 52; www.hotel -univers-saintmalo.com in French; place Chateaubriand; s €44-71.50, d €58-81) Also attractive, in the same square and more modestly priced, it may lack the France et Chateaubriand's sea views but oh, what a bar (see opposite)!

Quic-en-Groigne (☎ 02 99 20 22 20; www.quic-en -groigne.com; 8 rue d'Estrées; s €48, d €53-62; [P]) This tranquil, mid-range choice occupies two floors (there's no lift so be prepared to flex your muscles and drag your bags) in a quiet street off main rue de Dinan.

HOTELS – ST-SERVAN

Hôtel de la Rance (☎ 02 99 81 78 63; www.larance hotel.com; 15 quai Sébastopol; d €55-81) This small, welcoming 11-room hotel overlooking Port Solidor has spacious and stylish rooms – try to get one at the front with a balcony and sea view.

Hôtel de la Mer (☎ 02 99 81 61 05; 3 rue Dauphine; d €31) This hotel, with a couple of public car parks nearby, is an excellent deal and particularly convenient if you've been decanted from an evening ferry from the UK. It's small – so best to book ahead.

CAMPING
Camping Aleth (☎ 02 99 81 60 91; camping@ville
-saint-malo.fr; allée Gaston Buy, St-Servan; camping €11.10;
🕑 Apr-Sep) Camping Aleth (also spelt Alet),
next to Fort de la Cité, enjoys an exceptional view in all directions. Take bus No 1
in July and August or No 6 year-round.

Eating
The old city has lots of tourist restaurants,
creperies and pizzerias in the area bounded
by Porte St-Vincent, the cathedral and the
Grande Porte.

Le Maclow (☎ 02 99 56 50 41; 22 rue Ste-Barbe;
sandwiches €2.50-4) Although it looks like a
burger chain clone, this little sandwich bar
is fine for cheap, no-nonsense takeaway
grub.

Le Petit Crêpier (☎ 02 99 40 93 19; 6 rue Ste-
Barbe; dishes €5.50-8; 🕑 closed Tue-Wed except Jul &
Aug) This famous creperie is known for its
gourmet specialities such as a *galette* with
plaice in a seaweed and Muscadet sauce or
a crepe with a mousse of dates and spices.

Other worthwhile places for a snack
include the tiny, hole-in-the-wall **Crêperie
Chez Gaby** (2 rue de Dinan), which has excellent
galettes and crepes costing from €1.75 to
€5.50, and **Glacier Sanchez** (☎ 02 99 56 67 17;
9 rue de la Vieille Boucherie), serving up great ice
cream (€4 for three scoops).

La Chasse-Marée (☎ 02 99 40 85 10; 4 rue du
Grout-St-Georges; mains €12-23, menus €14-23) Here
you can enjoy excellent seafood, beef and
lamb in a dining room with exposed timber
beams. The dinner *menu* includes half a
dozen oysters, a main course and cheese.

La Coquille d'Oeuf (☎ 02 99 40 92 62; 20 rue de
la Corne de Cerf; menus €12-23.50) Neat, trim and
with a nautical theme, this small restaurant
with its tables for two makes for intimate,
good value dining.

Borgnefesse (☎ 02 99 40 05 05; 10 rue du Puits-
aux Braies; mains €11.50, full meal €21; 🕑 closed lunch
Sat-Mon) Fish and seafood are the main ele-
ments on the short but impressive menu.
Ask the owner, an exuberant Captain
Haddock figure, to explain just why his
restaurant is called Borgnefesse (But One
Buttock)…

SELF-CATERING
Among the food shops along rue de l'Orme
is a truly excellent **cheese shop** (🕑 Tue-Sat) at
No 9. Just down the street is **Hall au Blé**,
once the town's grain store and now its
covered market.

Drinking
Hôtel de l'Univers (see opposite) has a magnificent, snug bar, all in wood and clad with
maritime photos and prints.

L'Aviso (☎ 02 99 40 99 08; 12 rue Point du Jour;
🕑 5pm-2am) With 300 beers on offer, over
10 of them on draught, this cheerful place
is for serious hopheads. It sometimes has
live music.

Entertainment
In summer, classical music concerts are
held in Cathédrale St-Vincent and elsewhere in the city.

Getting There & Away
AIR
See Dinard Getting There & Away (p288)
for flight details.

BOAT
Brittany Ferries (☎ reservations France 08 25 82 88
28, ☎ UK 0870 556 1600; www.brittany-ferries.com)
sail between St-Malo and Portsmouth and
Condor Ferries (☎ France 08 25 16 03 00, ☎ UK 0845
345 2000; www.condorferries.co.uk) run to/from
both Poole and Weymouth via Jersey or
Guernsey.

Hydrofoils and catamarans depart from
the Gare Maritime de la Bourse; car ferries
leave from the Gare Maritime du Naye.

From April to September, **Corsaire** (☎ 02
23 18 15 15) runs the Bus de Mer (Sea Bus;
adult/child €5.90/3.60 return, 10 minutes,
hourly) shuttle service between St-Malo
and Dinard.

BUS
All intercity buses stop by both train and
bus stations.

Courriers Bretons (☎ 02 99 19 70 80) has
services to Cancale (€3.80, 30 minutes),
Fougères (€13.90, 1¾ hours, one to three
daily), Pontorson (€8.30, one hour) and
Mont St-Michel (€9.20, 1½ hours, three
to four daily). It also offers all-day tours to
Mont St-Michel (return €25, Tuesday and
Saturday June to September).

TIV (☎ 02 99 82 26 26) has buses to Dinard
(€3.40, 30 minutes, hourly) and Rennes
(€9.90, one to 1½ hours, three to six
daily).

BRITTANY

CAT (☎ 02 99 82 26 26) bus No 10 goes to Dinan (€5.70, 50 minutes, three to eight daily) via the Barrage de la Rance.

CAR & MOTORCYCLE

Avis (☎ 02 99 40 18 54) has a desk at both the main train station and Gare Maritime du Naye. **ADA** (☎ 02 99 56 06 15) has a booth in the train station, while **Europcar** (☎ 02 99 56 75 17; 16 blvd des Talards) is across the street.

TRAIN

Trains or SNCF buses run between St-Malo and Rennes (€11.40, one hour, frequent), Dinan (€7.60, one hour, five daily) and Lannion (€21.60, four hours, seven daily). Change at Rennes for Paris' Gare Montparnasse (€53, 4¼ hours, eight to 10 daily).

Getting Around

St-Malo city buses (single journey €1.10, 10-trip carnet €7.80, 24hr pass €3.20) operate until about 8pm with some lines extending until around midnight in summer. Between esplanade St-Vincent and the train station, take bus Nos 1 (July to August only), 2, 3 or 4.

Call ☎ 02 99 81 30 30 for a taxi.

DINARD

pop 10,100

Dinard has attracted a well-heeled clientele, especially from the UK, since the mid-19th century. Indeed, it retains something of the feel of a late-19th-century beach resort with its striped bathing tents, beachside carnival and pinnacled *belle époque* mansions perched above the water. And there's an annual festival of British cinema, held in early October.

Orientation

Dinard's focal point is Plage de l'Écluse (also called Grande Plage), flanked by Pointe du Moulinet and Pointe de la Malouine. To get to this beach from the Embarcadère (where boats from St-Malo dock), climb the stairs and walk 200m northwest along rue Georges Clemenceau.

Information

Cyberk@w@ (☎ 02 99 46 79 01; 32 rue de la Gare; per hr €4; 🕑 11am-1am Tue-Sat, 2-11pm Sun-Mon)
Lavomatic de la Poste (10 rue des Saules; 🕑 8am-7pm Jun-Sep, Mon-Sat Oct-May)
Main Post Office (place Rochaid)

Tourist Office (☎ 02 99 46 94 12; www.ville-dinard .fr; 2 blvd Féart; 🕑 9.30am-7.30pm Jul & Aug, core hours 9am-12.15pm & 2-6pm Mon-Sat Sep-Jun) Staff will book accommodation for free.

Sights

As befits a classic seaside resort, Dinard's main attractions are its beaches, cafés and waterfront walks. Take a stroll along **promenade du Clair de Lune** (Moonlight promenade). With a free sound-and-light spectacle in summer, it runs from just north of place Général de Gaulle to the Embarcadère, offering views of St-Malo's old city across the River Rance estuary.

Guided walks (🕑 2.30pm & 4.30pm, Mon & Wed-Sat) covering the town's history, art and architecture, depart from the tourist office.

BARRAGE DE LA RANCE

This 750m bridge over the Rance estuary carries the D168 between St-Malo and Dinard, lopping a good 30km off the journey. The **Usine Marémotrice de la Rance**, jutting below it, generates over 3% of Brittany's electricity. Its 24 turbines churn out over 600 million kWh annually by exploiting the lower estuary's extraordinary high tidal range – a difference of 13.5m between high and low tide.

If you're even slightly mechanically minded, visit **Espace Découverte** (admission free; 🕑 1-7pm Tue-Sun) on the Dinard bank. Illustrating the power station's construction and environmental impact, it runs an interesting film in English.

Activities

SWIMMING

Wide, sandy **Plage de l'Écluse** is fringed with Dinard's trademark blue-and-white striped bathing tents and overlooked by fashionable hotels, a casino and some attractive neo-Gothic villas. Picasso used the beach as the setting for several canvases in the 1920s and you may see reproductions of them planted in the sand. A **statue** of film director Alfred Hitchcock, with a seagull perched on each shoulder, stands near the beach's entrance in honour of the annual festival of British film.

The **Piscine Olympique** (☎ 02 99 46 22 77; promenade des Alliés; adult/student €4/2.55), an indoor Olympic-sized swimming pool right beside the beach, is filled with heated sea water.

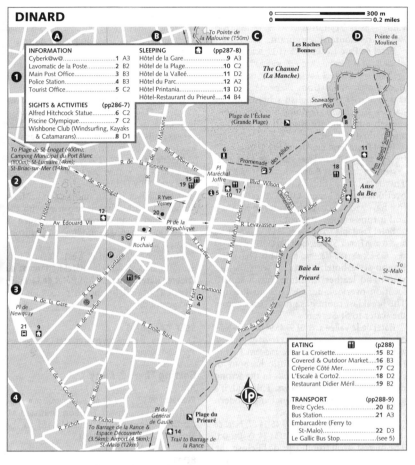

DINARD

INFORMATION	
Cyberk@w@	1 A3
Lavomatic de la Poste	2 B2
Main Post Office	3 B3
Police Station	4 B3
Tourist Office	5 C2

SIGHTS & ACTIVITIES	(pp286-7)
Alfred Hitchcock Statue	6 C2
Piscine Olympique	7 C2
Wishbone Club (Windsurfing, Kayaks & Catamarans)	8 D1

SLEEPING	(pp287-8)
Hôtel de la Gare	9 A3
Hôtel de la Plage	10 C2
Hôtel de la Vallée	11 D2
Hôtel du Parc	12 A2
Hôtel Printania	13 D2
Hôtel-Restaurant du Prieuré	14 B4

EATING	(p288)
Bar La Croisette	15 B2
Covered & Outdoor Market	16 B3
Crêperie Côté Mer	17 C2
L'Escale à Corto2	18 D2
Restaurant Didier Méril	19 B2

TRANSPORT	(pp288-9)
Breiz Cycles	20 B2
Bus Station	21 A3
Embarcadère (Ferry to St-Malo)	22 D3
Le Gallic Bus Stop	(see 5)

Plage du Prieuré, 1km to the south, may not be as chic as Plage de l'Écluse but you'll find it less crowded. **Plage de St-Énogat** is 1km west of Plage de l'Écluse, on the far side of Pointe de la Malouine.

WALKING & CYCLING

Beautiful seaside trails extend along the coast in both directions. Particularly spectacular is a traverse of the splendid shoreline from Plage du Prieuré to Plage de St-Énogat via Pointe du Moulinet. For other hiking opportunities throughout the *département*, pack the Institut National Géographique (IGN) 1:50,000 map *Ille-et-Vilaine: Randonnées en Haute Bretagne,* which highlights walking trails.

WINDSURFING & KAYAKING

At Plage de l'Écluse, **Wishbone Club** (☎ 02 99 88 15 20; ⏰ 9am-9pm Jun-Sep, 10am-noon & 2-6pm Oct-May), next to the open-air swimming pool, offers windsurfing lessons (€30 per hour) and also hires out boards (€14 to €19 per hour, €30 to €40 per half-day) and catamarans/kayaks (€30/10 per hour).

Sleeping

Dinard can be an expensive place to stay; you might want to base yourself in St-Malo and hop over on the ferry.

Hôtel de la Gare (☎ 02 99 46 10 84; 28 rue de la Corbinais; d €20-26) Station Hotel, still so called even though trains no longer pass and the station is long demolished, is a fair hike from the beach but the rooms are undeniably good value – as is **L'Épicurien** (menu €9, ☺ lunch only Mon-Fri), its Routard restaurant.

Hôtel du Parc (☎ 02 99 46 11 39; hotel.du.parc@ infonie.fr; 20 av Édouard VII; d €28, with bathroom €47; ☺ Easter-Sep & school holidays) This medium-sized hotel, 500m from Plage de l'Écluse, is a favourite with English school journey parties. Corridors are dingy but the rooms, though smallish, are more than adequate and bathed in light.

Hôtel-Restaurant du Prieuré (☎ 02 99 46 13 74; fax 02 99 46 81 90; 1 place Général de Gaulle; d €38.50-46; ☺ Feb-Dec, closed Mon & dinner Sun except Jul & Aug) This is a lovely, old-fashioned little place overlooking the beach. Of its seven rooms, five have views across the water to St-Malo and it runs a fine **restaurant**.

Hôtel Printania (☎ 02 99 46 13 07; www.printania hotel.com in French; 5 av George V; s/d €50/55, d with sea view €75-85; ☺ mid-Mar–mid-Nov) This charming Breton-style hotel, complete with mature wood and leather furniture, has a superb location overlooking the Baie du Prieuré. The breakfast room has grand views across the water to St-Servan.

Hôtel de la Vallée (☎ 02 99 46 94 00; www.hotel delavallee.com; 6 av George V; d incl breakfast from €60, with sea view from €70; ☺ mid-Dec–mid-Nov) Facing the Printania across the little harbour of Anse du Bec, the Vallée looks in the wrong direction for expansive views. This said, it's a pleasant blend of traditional and modern with bright, cheerful rooms.

Hôtel de la Plage (☎ 02 99 46 14 87; hotel-de -la-plage@wanadoo.fr; 3 blvd Féart; d €51-84; ☺ Dec-Oct) The merest stroll from Plage de l'Écluse, the 'Beach Hotel' is a fine, stone-built structure with 18 well-appointed rooms. The dearer ones have a balcony with sea views.

CAMPING
Camping Municipal du Port Blanc (☎ 02 99 46 10 74; camping.dinard@free.fr; rue Sergeant Boulanger; camping €18.70; ☺ Apr-Sep) It's close to the beach, about 2km west of Plage de l'Écluse.

Eating
Bar La Croisette (☎ 02 99 46 43 32; 4 rue Yves Verney; menus €11 & 17; ☺ mid-Dec–mid-Nov, closed Tue Oct-Mar) La Croisette, easily recognised by the blonde, bikini-clad mannequin on the roof, is a cheerful eatery and bar where portions are ample. It carries a wide selection of wines by the glass.

Restaurant Didier Méril (☎ 02 99 46 95 74; 6 rue Yves Verney; menus €27-37; ☺ closed 5-20 Jan & Wed except school holidays) This altogether more sophisticated place takes its food *very* seriously. With a young, talented, creative chef, it has rapidly gained a reputation for itself that extends way beyond Brittany.

Crêperie Côte Mer (☎ 02 99 16 80 30; 29 blvd Wilson; galettes €2.60-7.20, other dishes €4.60-7.80) A crisp little creperie with pine tables, the Côte Mer serves grills, salads and *moules-frites* as well as crepes, galettes and ice cream.

L'Escale à Corto (☎ 02 99 46 78 57; 12 av George V; mains €10.20-22; ☺ dinner only school holidays, Tue-Sun rest of year) This fashionable, intimate restaurant specialises in fish and seafood. Meals are all à la carte; the menu varies with the seasons and features creative dishes such as sea bream with ginger and lime and saffron-scented scallops.

Some of Dinard's best restaurants are attached to hotels. **Hôtel-Restaurant du Prieuré**, **Hôtel Printania** and **Hôtel de la Vallée** (see left) are all top-notch places for fish and seafood.

SELF-CATERING
Dinard has a large **covered market** (place Rochaid; ☺ 7am-1.30pm).

Getting There & Away
AIR
Ryanair (☎ 02 99 16 00 66; www.ryanair.com) has daily flights to/from London Stansted. A daytime/evening taxi from Dinard to the airport costs around €10/15.

BOAT
From April to September, **Corsaire** (☎ 02 23 18 15 15) runs the Bus de Mer (Sea Bus; adult/child €5.90/3.60 return, 10 minutes, hourly) shuttle service between Dinard and St-Malo.

BUS
TIV (☎ 02 99 82 26 26) buses (€3.40, 30 minutes, hourly) connect Dinard and the train station in St-Malo via the Barrage de la Rance. Dinard's bus station is southwest of the town centre at place de Newquay; Le Gallic bus stop, outside the tourist office, is more convenient.

TAE (☎ 02 99 26 16 00) runs five buses daily between Dinard and Rennes (€11.80, two hours) via Dinan (€3.80, 25 minutes).

Getting Around

You can hire bicycles (€5.50/8 per half-/full day) and motor scooters (€11/38 per hour/day) to get around at **Breiz Cycles** (☎ 02 99 46 27 25; 8 Rue St-Énogat).

For a taxi, telephone ☎ 02 99 46 88 80 or ☎ 02 99 88 15 15.

CANCALE
pop 5200

Cancale, a relaxed fishing port 14km east of St-Malo, is famed for its offshore *parcs à huîtres* (oyster beds), which each year yield around 4000 tonnes of prize mollusc. The town even has a small museum dedicated to oyster farming and shellfish, the **Ferme Marine** (Marine Farm; ☎ 02 99 89 69 99; Corniche de l'Aurore; adult/child €6.10/3.10; mid-Feb–Oct, tours in English 2pm mid-Jun–mid-Sep), southwest of the port, where you can take a guided tour.

The *marché aux huîtres* (oyster market) is just a cluster of little stalls in the shadow of the Pointe des Crolles lighthouse. Numbered according to size and quality, oysters cost from €2.50 per dozen for the smallest *huîtres creuses* (No 5) to as much as €20 for saucer-sized *plates de Cancale*.

The **tourist office** (☎ 02 99 89 63 72; www.ville -cancale.fr; 9.30am-12.30pm & 2-6pm or 7pm Mon-Sat, 9.30am-12.30pm Sun) is at the top of rue du Port. Startlingly uninformed – even about its own opening hours – it does, however, rent bicycles (per half-day/day from €8/11).

There's a seasonal tourist office **annexe** on quai Gambetta in the wooden house where the fish auction takes place.

Sleeping

Auberge de Jeunesse (☎ 02 99 89 62 62; cancale@fuaj .org; Port Pican; dm €9.30; Feb–mid-Dec). Cancale's HI-affiliated youth hostel overlooks the beach at Port Pican, 3km north of the town, to where the St-Malo–Cancale bus continues.

Hôtel La Mère Champlain (☎ 02 99 89 60 04; 1 quai Thomas; interior d €30-45, with sea view €50-65) Rooms at this recently renovated hotel have great sea views. There's a nice **restaurant** deck, complete with crisp linen, heavy cutlery and smart waiters with black bow ties.

CAMPING

Camping Municipal Le Grouin (☎ 02 99 89 63 79; fax 02 99 89 96 31; Pointe du Grouin; camping €12.70; Mar-Oct) This area, 6km north of Cancale

near Pointe du Grouin, overlooks a fine beach and is one of several in the area.

Eating

Cancale boasts over 50 restaurants, most of which specialise in – you've guessed it – oysters, starting at around €6.50 per dozen.

Le Surcouf (☎ 02 99 89 61 75; 7 quai Gambetta; menus €18-50, mains €19-24; closed Wed-Thu except Jul & Aug) Le Surcouf is among the best of the many quality seafood restaurants that line the waterfront.

Au Pied d'Cheval (☎ 02 99 89 76 95; 10 quai Gambetta; 9am-9pm) At this rustic little place, the *assiette du capitaine* (captain's plate; €5.60) gives you half a dozen oysters, direct from their farm, washed down with a glass of Muscadet while their *super plateau* (a mega seafood platter) for two costs a bargain €30.50.

Getting There & Away

Buses stop behind the church on place Lucidas and at Port de la Houle, next to the pungent fish market. **Courriers Bretons** (☎ 02 99 19 70 70) and **TIV** (☎ 02 99 82 26 26) have year-round services to/from St-Malo (€3.80, 30 minutes). At least three Courriers Bretons buses daily continue to Port Pican and Port Mer, near Pointe du Grouin.

POINTE DU GROUIN

This nature reserve lies on a headland at the tip of the wild, beautiful coast between Cancale and St-Malo. Cancale tourist office's free map covers the coastline well. **Île des Landes**, just offshore, is home to a colony of giant black cormorants, whose wingspan can reach 170cm.

Via the GR34 coastal hiking trail, Pointe du Grouin is a stunning 7km hike from Cancale and 18km from St-Malo. By the D201 road, it's 4km from Cancale.

DINAN
pop 11,000

Perched above the River Rance 22km south of Dinard, this walled, medieval city has some beautiful 15th-century half-timbered houses. During Fête des Remparts, held every second year in late July, Dinannais decked out in medieval garb are joined by some 40,000 visitors for a rollicking two-day festival in the tiny old city.

BRITTANY

Orientation

Nearly everything of interest – except the picturesque port area on the River Rance – is within the tight confines of the old city, at its heart place des Cordeliers and adjacent place des Merciers.

Information

@rospace (☎ 02 96 87 04 87; 9 rue de la Chaux; per 15 min €1.50; ☺ 10am-12.30pm & 1.30-7pm Tue-Sat) Internet access.
Main Post Office (7 place Duclos)
Tourist Office (☎ 02 96 87 69 76; www.dinan-tour isme.com; 9 rue du Château; ☺ 9am-7pm Mon-Sat, 10am-12.30pm & 2.30-6pm Sun mid-Jun–mid-Sep, 9am-12.30pm & 2-6pm Mon-Sat mid-Sep–mid-Jun)

Sights

OLD TOWN

Within the cobbled streets of the old town, attractive half-timbered houses overhang place des Cordeliers and place des Merciers. A few paces south, the **Tour de l'Horloge** (adult/under 18 €2.60/1.65; ☺ 10am-6.30pm Jun-Sep, 2-6.30pm Apr-May), a 15th-century clock tower whose tinny chimes ping every quarter-hour, rises from rue de l'Horloge. It's well worth the climb up to its tiny balcony.

In the north transept of **Basilique St-Sauveur** (place St-Sauveur; ☺ 9am-6pm), with soaring Gothic chancel, is a 14th-century grave slab, reputed to contain the heart of Bertrand du Guesclin, a 14th-century knight noted for his hatred of the English and his fierce battles to expel them from France.

Just east of the church, beyond the tiny **Jardin Anglais** (English Garden), a former cemetery and nowadays a pleasant little park, is the 13th-century **Tour Ste-Cathérine**, with great views down over the viaduct and port.

Rue du Jerzual and its continuation, steep **rue du Petit Fort**, both lined with art galleries, antiques shops and restaurants, lead down to the **Vieux Pont** (Old Bridge), from where the little **port** extends northwards while the 19th-century **Viaduc de Dinan** soars high above to the south.

CHÂTEAU & MUSÉE DE DINAN

Dinan's **museum** (☎ 02 96 39 45 20; rue du Château; adult/child €4/1.55; ☺ 9am-noon & 2-7pm mid-Jun–Aug, 1.30-5.30pm Sep-Dec & Feb–mid-Jun) is in the keep of the ruined 14th-century castle. It presents the town's history, especially its textile industry, together with a collec-tion of 16th-century polychrome wooden statues and a fine collection of *coiffes* (traditional lace headdresses).

Activities

BOAT TRIPS

Between May and September, **Corsaire** (☎ 02 96 39 18 04) runs boats along the River Rance to Dinard and St-Malo (one way/return €17.30/23, 2½ hours). There's usually one sailing a day, the morning departure time linked to the tide and the return trip (by boat) occurring the following day. From Dinard or St-Malo, you can easily return to Dinan by bus (and, from St-Malo, by train too).

WALKING

Ask at the tourist office for its leaflet *Discovery Tours*, in English, which plots three walking itineraries around town.

Sleeping

Auberge de Jeunesse Moulin de Méen (☎ 02 96 39 10 83; dinan@fuaj.org; Vallée de la Fontaine des Eaux; dm €9.30) Dinan's HI-affiliated youth hostel is in a lovely old water mill about 750m north of the port. It has limited camping space and five much-coveted double rooms.

Hôtel Duchesse Anne (☎ 02 96 39 09 43; fax 02 96 87 57 26; 10 place Duguesclin; d €28, with bathroom €36-40) This inexpensive, central place has cramped yet acceptable accommodation. It runs a reasonable restaurant and there's public parking right opposite.

Hôtel Les Grandes Tours (☎ 02 96 85 16 20; carregi@wanadoo.fr; 6 rue du Château; d €35, with bathroom €45-50; ☺ Feb–mid-Dec; **P**) Venerable, altogether larger and once upon a time called Hôtel des Messageries; it was here that Victor Hugo slept with his very good friend Juliette Drouet in 1836. It has smallish but attractively renovated rooms.

Hôtel Tour de l'Horloge (☎ 02 96 39 96 92; hil iohotel@wanadoo.fr; 5 rue de la Chaux; d €48-54) The 12-room Horloge occupies a charming 18th-century house on a cobbled, car-free lane. Top-floor rooms have exposed wooden beams and a splendid view of the clock tower.

Hôtel Le d'Avaugour (☎ 02 96 39 07 49; www .avaugourhotel.com; 1 place du Champ; d with breakfast €119-176; ☺ mid-Feb–mid-Nov) In an elegant 18th-century town house just inside the city walls, the Avaugour is a peaceful luxury hotel with tastefully decorated rooms and

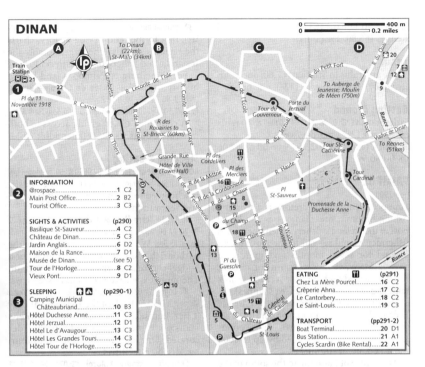

DINAN

0 — 400 m
0 — 0.2 miles

INFORMATION		
@rospace	1	C2
Main Post Office	2	B2
Tourist Office	3	C3

SIGHTS & ACTIVITIES	(p290)	
Basilique St-Sauveur	4	C2
Château de Dinan	5	C3
Jardin Anglais	6	D2
Maison de la Rance	7	D1
Musée de Dinan	(see 5)	
Tour de l'Horloge	8	C2
Vieux Pont	9	D1

SLEEPING	(pp290-1)	
Camping Municipal		
Châteaubriand	10	B3
Hôtel Duchesse Anne	11	C3
Hôtel Jerzual	12	D1
Hôtel Le d'Avaugour	13	C3
Hôtel Les Grandes Tours	14	C3
Hôtel Tour de l'Horloge	15	C2

EATING		(p291)
Chez La Mère Pourcel	16	C2
Crêperie Ahna	17	C2
Le Cantorbery	18	C2
Le Saint-Louis	19	C3

TRANSPORT	(pp291-2)	
Boat Terminal	20	D1
Bus Station	21	A1
Cycles Scardin (Bike Rental)	22	A1

a pretty rear garden. There's ample public parking right opposite.

Hôtel Jerzual (☎ 02 96 87 02 02; www.bestwestern
.com/fr/jerzual; 26 quai des Talards; s €75-108, d €80-148;
ℙ 🏊) Outside the city walls, the Jerzual overlooks the port. Modern and sensitively constructed in stone and slate, its 52 rooms have every last comfort while the restaurant merits a visit for its own sake. They rent bikes – ideal for a towpath spin – to guests.

CAMPING
Camping Municipal Châteaubriand (☎ 02 96 39 11
96; fax 02 96 85 06 97; 103 rue Chateaubriand; camping €7;
⏰ Easter-Sep) The nearest camping ground is this small, unexceptional two-star place, at the foot of the ramparts.

Eating
Le Cantorbery (☎ 02 96 39 02 52; 6 rue Ste-Claire;
menus €22-32; ⏰ closed Wed & dinner Sun Oct-Apr) Occupying a magnificent 17th-century house, this elegant, intimate restaurant changes its menu regularly, according to the rhythm of the seasons, and does an excellent-value lunch *formule* (€15).

Chez La Mère Pourcel (☎ 02 96 39 03 80; 3 place
des Merciers; menus €28-62.50, mains €18-33; ⏰ Tue-Sat
& lunch Sun) La Mère Pourcel is a Dinan institution: a wonderful beamed dining room, mostly 15th-century, that serves specialities of the region such as salt-marsh lamb.

Le Saint-Louis (☎ 02 96 39 89 50; 9-11 rue de Léhon;
lunch menus Mon-Fri €11.50, dinner menus €16.50 & €20;
⏰ closed Wed & lunch Mon) This popular place is famous for its good-value, all-you-can-eat buffets. In season, walk through to the charming floral patio at the rear.

Crêperie Ahna (☎ 02 96 39 09 13; 7 rue de la Poisson-
nerie; galettes €6-7.85; ⏰ Mon-Sat) This excellent place, in the family for three generations, tosses up gourmet, inventive crepes and galettes; the speciality of the house is a galette filled with duck breast and cooked with garlic-and-herb butter.

Getting There & Away
BUS
Buses leave from place Duclos and the bus station. **CAT** (☎ 02 96 39 21 05) bus No 10 goes to St-Malo (€5.70, 50 minutes, three to eight daily). **TAE** (☎ 02 99 26 16 00) runs five daily

292 NORTH COAST •• Paimpol

services to Dinard (€3.80, 25 minutes) and Rennes (€8.80, 1½ hours).

TRAIN
There are trains to St-Malo (€7.60, one hour, five daily) and Rennes (€11.90, one hour).

Getting Around
Cycles Scardin (☎ 02 96 39 21 94; 30 rue Carnot) rents bikes for €12/72 per day/week.

Call a taxi on ☎ 02 96 39 06 00 or ☎ 06 08 00 80 90.

PAIMPOL
pop 7900
Paimpol (Pempoull in Breton) is a working fishing harbour, once famous as the home port of the Icelandic fishery. Then, the town's fishermen would set sail to the seas around Iceland for seven months and more at a stretch. Many, victims of storms or disease, never returned and are now recalled in folk tales and *chants de marins* (sea shanties).

Paimpol is the closest port to Île de Bréhat (Enez Vriad in Breton), a tiny, car-free island 8km north of town, whose population of 350 is overwhelmed by up to 4000 tourists daily in summer.

The centre of Paimpol, to the south of the two harbours, is around the market square of place du Martray. Bus and train stations are both 100m south of this square.

The **tourist office** (☎ 02 96 20 83 16; www.paimpol-goelo.com; ☉ 9.30am-7.30pm Mon-Sat & 10am-6pm Sun Jun-Sep, 9.30am-12.30pm & 1.30-6.30pm Mon-Sat Oct-May) is on place de la République.

Sights
The splendid **Musée de la Mer** (☎ 02 96 22 02 19; rue Labenne; adult/child €4.25/2.10; ☉ 10.30am-noon &

2.30-6pm mid-Jun–Aug, 2.30-6pm mid-Apr–mid-Jun & early Sep), in a former cod-drying factory, charts the region's maritime heritage, notably the Icelandic cod fishery of the 19th century.

For something of Paimpol's land-bound history, visit the **Musée du Costume Breton** (☎ 02 96 22 02 19; rue Raymond Pellier; adult/child €2.50/1.30; ☉ 10.30am-12.30pm & 2.30-6pm Jul & Aug).

A combined ticket, giving access to both museums, costs €5.40/2.60 per adult/child.

Sleeping & Eating
Auberge de Jeunesse (☎ 02 96 20 83 60; paimpol@fuaj .org; Château de Kerraoul) This HI-affiliated hostel is scheduled to re-open in 2005 after extensive renovations.

Hôtel Le Terre-Neuvas (☎ 02 96 55 14 14; fax 02 96 20 47 66; 16 quai Duguay Trouin; d €31-37; ☉ mid-Jan–mid-Dec) With a good location beside the harbour, the Terre-Neuvas is Paimpol's best budget choice and runs a decent restaurant. The more expensive rooms have sea views.

K" Loys (☎ 02 96 20 40 01; www.k-loys.com; 21 quai Morand; d €65-120) Each of the 15 rooms at cosy 'Chez Louise', in its time a ship-owner's mansion, is individually and tastefully decorated. One, accommodating up to four, has disabled facilities.

Crêperie-Restaurant Morel (☎ 02 96 20 86 34; 11 place du Martray; galettes €4.20-6.90) On Paimpol's main square, the Morel is much favoured by locals during the low season. Help your galette down with a glass of their refreshing draught cider.

L'Islandais (☎ 02 96 20 93 80; 19 quai Morand; menus €16.50 & €24.50) This attractive, bustling harbourside restaurant serves, predominantly and appropriately, fish and seafood. For something lighter, try their salads (€7.70) or a galette (€3.40 to €6.10).

LA GRANDE PÊCHE

It was the fishermen of Brittany who, way back in the 16th century, pioneered *La Grande Pêche à la Morue* (The Great Cod Fishery), long-lining for cod on the Grand Banks of Newfoundland. Braving the stormy waters of the north Atlantic, the *morutiers* (cod-fishing boats) would be away from their home ports for up to six months at a time, their crews suffering lives of unimaginable hardship – a tradition that continued until the 1930s.

During the peak of *La Grande Pêche* in the late 19th and early 20th centuries, boats from St-Malo favoured the Newfoundland (Terre-Neuve) fishing grounds, while the fishermen of Paimpol and nearby Binic frequented the Icelandic fishery. Their *goélettes* (schooners), with a crew of only a dozen or so men, were small and fast but often exposed to dangerous conditions. In the 19th and early 20th centuries, the Paimpol region lost a total of 100 ships and more than 2000 men to the sea in only 80 years.

Paimpol's Tuesday **market** spreads over place Gambetta and place du Martray. At the weekend, vendors sell freshly-shucked oysters at quai Duguay Trouin.

CAMPING
Camping Municipal de Cruckin (☎ 02 96 20 78 47; rue de Cruckin; camping €12.40; ⊗ Easter-Sep) This quiet, two-star camping ground is on the beautiful Baie de Kérity, 2km southeast of town off the road to Plouha.

Getting There & Around
BICYCLE
Cycles du Vieux Clocher (☎ 02 96 20 83 58; place Verdun) rents bikes (per day €11). It's south of the tourist office near the Vieux Clocher (Old Bell Tower).

BOAT
Vedettes de Bréhat (☎ 02 96 55 79 50; www.vedettesdebrehat.com) operates ferries (adult/child €7.50/6.50 return, 15 minutes, hourly sailings 8.30am to 7pm April to September, at least eight daily October to March) goes to Île de Bréhat from Pointe L'Arcouest, 6km north of Paimpol.

BUS & TRAIN
CAT (☎ 02 96 68 31 20) runs buses to/from St-Brieuc (€7.60, 1½ hours). In summer most continue to Pointe L'Arcouest.

There are several trains or SNCF buses daily between Paimpol and Guingamp (€5.80, 45 minutes), where you can pick up connections to Brest, St-Brieuc and Rennes.

PERROS-GUIREC
pop 7900
The chic resort of Perros-Guirec sits on a rocky peninsula at the eastern end of the Côte de Granit Rose (Pink Granite Coast). It's an exclusive town, flanked by a new marina to the southeast and the old fishing port of Ploumanac'h, about 3km to the northwest; in between lie granite cliffs and coves where sea otters still feel at home.

Orientation
Perros has two distinct parts: the upper town on the hill and the marina area at its base, to the south. They're about 1km apart if you make your way up through the back streets, or double that distance if you follow the main coastal road (blvd de la Mer and

blvd Clemenceau) around Pointe du Château, at the eastern end of town.

Information
Laverie du Port (7 rue Anatole le Braz; ⊗ 9.15am-7.15pm) For your laundry needs.
Main Post Office (rue de la Poste)
Tourist Office (☎ 02 96 23 21 15; www.perros-guirec .com; 21 place de l'Hôtel de Ville; ⊗ 9am-7.30pm Mon-Sat, 10am-12.30pm & 4-7pm Sun Jul & Aug, 9am-12.30pm & 2-6.30pm Mon-Sat Jun-Sep)

Activities
SWIMMING & WALKING
Of several beaches close to Perros, the main one is **Plage de Trestraou**, to the north about 1km from the tourist office. The others, attractive **Plage de Trestrignel** and **Plage du Château**, on either side of Pointe du Château, are smaller, prettier but often more crowded.

The **sentier des douaniers** (custom officer's trail) follows the spectacular 5km coastline from Plage de Trestraou to Ploumanac'h through a wilderness of massive, pink granite boulders and outcrops.

Sleeping
Hôtel du Port (☎ 02 96 23 21 79; www.caféduport.fr; 85 rue Ernest Renan; d €38-47) This hotel has a dozen modern, double-glazed rooms, with bathroom, TV and telephone. The pricier ones have balconies overlooking the marina.

Hôtel Le Gulf Stream (☎ 02 96 23 21 86; www .gulf-stream-hotel-bretagne.com; 26 rue des Sept-Îles; d €40-48, with bathroom €55-68) The Gulf Stream is a lovely villa perched above the eastern end of Plage de Trestraou. Its 12 modest – and very pleasant – rooms (eight with sea views) contrast with its grand and decidedly up-market **restaurant**.

Hostellerie les Feux des Îles (☎ 02 96 23 22 94; www.feux-des-iles.com; 53 blvd Clemenceau, s €61-90, d €92-112; ⊗ closed 1-15 Oct) Surrounded by a large, flower-filled, clifftop garden looking out towards the Sept-Îles, 'Island Lights' is a magnificent stone villa with a modern wing attached. Its **restaurant** specialises in gourmet seafood.

CAMPING
Camping de Trestraou (☎ 02 96 23 08 11; fax 02 96 23 26 06; 89 av du Casino; camping €20; ⊗ May–mid-Sep) Ideally positioned, this camping area is close to the centre of Perros-Guirec and only a few minutes' walk from Plage de Trestraou.

BRITTANY

Eating

Crêperie du Trestraou (☎ 02 96 23 04 34; blvd Thalassa; galettes €3-9.40; ☺ closed Mon & Thu except Jul & Aug) Although this creperie looks more like a standard pizza joint from the outside, it has an excellent selection of crepes and galettes, as well as salads, seafood and grills.

Crêperie Les Vieux Gréements (☎ 02 96 91 14 99; 19 rue Anatole Le Braz; galettes €5.50-9; ☺ Tue-Sun, closed 2 weeks in Oct, 1-15 Dec) In an old shipowner's house overlooking the marina, this creperie has a pleasant outdoor terrace. On the 1st floor is a *moulerie*, serving mussels, mussels and more mussels.

Digor Kalon (☎ 02 96 49 03 63; 89 rue du Maréchal Joffre; menus €12-17.50; ☺ dinner only, closed Mon & Tue except Jul & Aug) This Celtic-themed pub-cum-restaurant is an Aladdin's cave of bric-a-brac. The food – snacky stuff such as mixed tapas (€6.50), mussels (€8.50 to €9.50) and Breton cakes – is good and they do a great line in local beers.

SELF-CATERING

At the **Marché des Pêcheurs** (Marina; ☺ 8.30am-12.30pm Jul & Aug, 2-3 times weekly Sep-Jun), the fisherfolk sell their catch directly. Nearby, **Biocoop** (67 rue Anatole le Braz) is a neat little cooperative that sells only organic produce.

Getting There & Around

CAT (☎ 02 96 68 31 20) bus No 15 (€3, 30 minutes, five to eight daily) links Perros-Guirec with Lannion's train station, calling at Ploumanac'h, Trégastel and Trébeurden. From Lannion, there are rail links via Plouaret Trégor eastwards to Guingamp (€7, 40 minutes) and on to St-Brieuc (€10.30, one hour); and westwards via Morlaix (€7, one hour) to Roscoff (€22.10, three hours) and Brest (€13.90, 1¾ hours).

Perros-Cycles (☎ 02 96 23 13 08; 129 rue Maréchal Joffre) rents out city/mountain bikes for €12/23 per day.

FINISTÈRE

To really delve into Breton culture and tradition, push west to Finistère (Land's End), its heartland. On the northern knuckle of this fist thrust into the Atlantic, you stand the greatest chance of hearing native Breton spoken. Here is the greatest concentration of *enclos paroissiaux* (parish closes), intricately sculpted groups decorating village churchyards and peculiar to Brittany.

The islands off the coast are buffeted by wild seas and strong tidal currents while some 350 lighthouses, beacons, buoys and radar installations stand watch over the busy, treacherous sea lanes leading into the Channel.

Cornouaille (meaning Cornwall) differs in mood from the wilder, more sparsely populated north of Finistère. Holiday resorts are livelier, fishing ports bigger and more bustling and the coastline is more dramatic.

Build in time to visit Quimper, capital of the *département*, with its cobbled streets, half-timbered houses and waterways, and Brest, host to the world's largest boat festival. You'll find the tang of salt strong too in the still active fishing ports and seaside resorts of Concarneau and Douarnenez (give yourself a good half-day to explore its huge maritime museum).

ROSCOFF
pop 3600

Protected from the furious seas by the little island of Batz, Roscoff (Rosko in Breton), whose 16th-century granite houses cluster around a bay, is the southernmost – and arguably the most attractive – French channel ferry port.

Beneath the waters around Roscoff grow a wide variety of algae, some of which are used in *thalassothérapie*, a health and beauty treatment based on sea water.

Roscoff's fertile hinterland is known for its *primeurs* (early fruits and vegetables), such as cauliflower, onions, tomatoes, new potatoes and artichokes. Before the advent of large roll-on roll-off ferries, Roscoff farmers, known as 'Johnnies', would load up boats with the small pink onions grown locally, cross the Channel, then peddle – and pedal; they strung their onions from the handlebars of their bikes – them around the towns of the UK.

Orientation

Roscoff ranges around a north-facing bay, with its fishing port and pleasure harbour on the western side. Quai d'Auxerre leads northwest – becoming quai Charles de Gaulle, then rue Amiral Réveillère – to the main place Lacaze-Duthiers.

THE SEAWEED HARVESTERS

All along much of the north coast of Brittany, the receding tide exposes vast areas of sea bed covered in a thick growth of seaweed (*goémon*). For centuries, a small band of seaweed harvesters (*goémoniers*) have collected the weed washed up along the shore or set out in boats to dredge it fresh from its rocky bed. Long used as an agricultural fertiliser, the seaweed is today dried and used for various purposes in the food and cosmetics industries.

Roscoff's **Centre de Découverte des Algues** (☎ 02 98 69 77 05; 5 rue Victor Hugo; admission free; ☼ 9am-noon & 2-7pm Mon-Sat) has a small permanent display (in French) about the history, harvesting and multiple uses of seaweed and also organises guided walks.

The car ferry terminal is at Port de Bloscon, 2km east of the town centre.

Information
LAUNDRY
Ferry Laverie (23 rue Jules Ferry; ☼ 9am-8pm)

MONEY
The **ferry terminal** has a 24hr banknote exchange and ATM.

POST
Post Office (19 rue Gambetta)

TOURIST INFORMATION
Tourist Office (☎ 02 98 61 12 13; www.roscoff-tourisme.com; 46 rue Gambetta; ☼ 9am-12.30pm & 1.30-7pm Mon-Sat, 10am-12.30pm Sun Jul & Aug, 9am-noon & 2-6pm Mon-Sat Sep-Jun) Occupies a fine old stone building just north of place de la République.

Sights & Activities
The 16th-century flamboyant Gothic **Eglise Notre Dame de Kroaz-Batz** (place Lacaze-Duthiers) with its Renaissance belfry is one of Brittany's most spectacular churches.

Aquarium de Roscoff (☎ 02 98 29 23 25; place Georges Teissier), just northwest of the church, was closed for extensive renovations at the time of writing.

Maison des Johnnies (☎ 02 98 61 25 48; 48 rue Brizeux; admission €4; ☼ afternoons Jun–mid-Sep, Sat & Sun mid-Feb–May & late Sep) is a museum devoted

to the itinerant onion vendors of times past who enjoy near-hero status hereabouts.

Thalasso Roscoff (☎ 08 25 00 20 99; www.thalasso.com in French; rue Victor Hugo) offers a huge range of health-inducing activities including a heated seawater pool, hammam and Jacuzzi (each €9 or all three for €16).

Sleeping
Hôtel Les Arcades (☎ 02 98 69 70 45; lesarcadesroscoff@wanadoo.fr; 15 rue Amiral Réveillère; d with toilet €32-36, with bathroom €48-60; ☼ Mar–mid-Nov) This two-star hotel, run by the same family for nearly a century, overlooks the bay. It has simple but modern rooms and – who knows – you may find yourself in the same bed that Jane Fonda and Roger Vadim once shared.

Hôtel Les Chardons Bleus (☎ 02 98 69 72 03; www.chardonsbleus.fr.st in French; 4 rue Amiral Réveillère; d 48-55; ☼ Mar-Jan, closed Sat & Sun except Jul & Aug) The 'Thistles', a Logis de France, is also good value, with quiet rooms and a pleasant restaurant.

Hôtel Talabardon (☎ 02 98 61 24 95; www.talabardon.fr in French; place de l'Église; s €84-127, d €112-174; ☼ Mar-Oct) Roscoff's oldest hotel, established in 1890, offers spacious, comfy rooms, many with balconies looking over the sea. You may find the welcome rather frostier than the weather.

CAMPING
Camping de Perharidy (☎ 02 98 69 70 86; www.aquacamp.fr in French; Le Ruguel; per person/tent/car €2.70/2.45/1.15; ☼ Easter-Sep) This spot is close to a sandy beach in the grounds of a lovely 19th-century mansion. It's approximately 3km southwest of Roscoff.

Eating
In Roscoff, France's premier crabbing port, seafood reigns supreme.

La Moule au Pot (☎ 02 98 19 33 60; 13 rue Édouard Corbière; ☼ May-Oct, closed Wed except Jul & Aug) With fresh flowers, wooden beams, a huge fireplace and a leafy rear terrace, the 'Mussel in the Pot' is a wonderful place for a substantial snack, such as a platter of mussels or one of their giant salads (€8).

L'Écume des Jours (☎ 02 98 61 22 83; quai d'Auxerre; menus €18-43; ☼ closed Wed Jul & Aug, Tue-Wed Sep-Jun) In a beautiful 16th-century house overlooking the harbour, this is one of Roscoff's top seafood restaurants with a warm, friendly atmosphere. Highly recommended.

BRITTANY

Le Surcouf (☎ 02 98 69 71 89; 14 rue Amiral Réveil-lère; ⊙ Feb-Dec, closed Wed Jul & Aug, Tue-Wed Sep-Dec & Feb-Jun) This pleasant, brasserie-style restaurant specialises in seafood, drawing strongly upon local produce and culinary tradition.

Hôtel Les Arcades (see p295) has a quality restaurant, strong on seafood, does a particularly good value lunch *menu* and has superb views of the harbour. The gourmet restaurant (*menus* €19 to €44) of **Hôtel Talabardon** (see p295) also has stunning views over the bay.

Getting There & Away
BOAT
Brittany Ferries (☎ reservations 08 25 82 88 28; www .brittany-ferries.com) links Roscoff to Plymouth in England (five to nine hours, one to three daily, year-round) and Cork in Ireland (14 hours, once weekly, June to September). Boats leave from Port de Bloscon, about 2km east of the town centre.

BUS & TRAIN
The combined bus and train station is on rue Ropartz Morvan.

Cars Bihan (☎ 02 98 83 45 80) operates buses from Roscoff to Brest (€9.70, 1½ to two hours; up to four daily) departing from the ferry terminal (Port de Bloscon) and passing by the town centre.

There are regular trains and SNCF buses to Morlaix (€8.60, 45 minutes), where you can make connections to Brest, Quimper and St-Brieuc.

AROUND ROSCOFF
Île de Batz
pop 600
A 20-minute ferry trip north of Roscoff, Île de Batz (pronounced ba; Enez Vaz in Breton) is a charming little island with some good beaches. Just 4 sq km, it's one big, fertile vegetable garden with soil fertilised by seaweed.

Jardins Georges Delaselle (☎ 02 98 61 75 65; adult/child €4/2; ⊙ 1-6pm Jul & Aug, 2-6pm Wed-Mon Apr-Jun & Sep-Oct), founded in the 19th century, has a luxuriant display of over 1500 plants from all five continents.

GETTING THERE & AROUND
The ferry (adult/child €6.50/3.50 return, bike €6 return) between Roscoff and Île de Batz runs every 30 minutes between 8am and 8pm from late-June to mid-September;

there are about eight sailings daily during the rest of the year.

On the island, **Vélos et Nature** (☎ 02 98 61 75 75), **Le Saout** (☎ 02 98 61 77 65) and **Prigent** (☎ 02 98 61 77 65) all rent bicycles.

BREST
pop 149,600
Rainy Brest, sheltered by its magnificent natural harbour, is one of France's most important naval and commercial ports. Flattened by air attacks during WWII, it was rebuilt as a modern – and not particularly attractive – city. Even though the medieval port area and its narrow streets are long gone, you'll still see the crisp, white uniforms of French sailors everywhere.

History
Brest grew up around its castle, built to defend the harbour on the River Penfeld. Following the 1532 union of Brittany and France, both the castle and its harbour became a royal fortress.

During the reign of Louis XIV, Brest and its naval dockyards became one of France's four naval main military ports. In WWII, this strategically important city, occupied by German forces, was bombarded intensively and virtually razed by allied aircraft. These days, Brest is still a major port and naval base. And, although its shipbuilding and heavy industries have waned, it is reinventing itself as a centre for high-tech, tourism and service industries.

Orientation
Brest sprawls along the northern shore of the deep natural harbour known as the Rade de Brest. Its castle, the naval base (Arsenal Maritime) and Port de Commerce are on the waterfront. From the castle, rue de Siam runs northeast to place de la Liberté, the city's main square, then it intersects with av Georges Clemenceau, the main northwest to southeast traffic artery.

Information
Laverie du Père Denis (8 place de la Liberté; ⊙ 7am-8.30pm) Laundry.
Main Post Office (place Général Leclerc)
Net@rena (☎ 02 98 33 61 11; 30 rue Yves Collet; per hr €3.50; ⊙ 11am-1am Mon-Thu, 11-4am Fri & Sat, 1-11pm Sun) Internet access.

Tourist Office (☎ 02 98 44 24 96; office.de.tourisme .brest@wanadoo.fr; place de la Liberté; 9.30am-7pm Mon-Sat & 10am-noon Sun mid-Jun–mid-Sep, 9.30am-12.30pm & 2-6pm Mon-Sat mid-Sep–mid-Jun)

Sights & Activities
OCÉANOPOLIS
Within the huge aquariums of Brest's ultra-modern **Océanopolis** (☎ 02 98 34 40 40; www .oceanopolis.com in French; port de Plaisance; adult/child €14.50/10; 9am-6pm Apr-Aug, 10am-5pm Tue-Sun Sep-Mar), about 3km east of the city centre, are kelp forests, seals, crabs, anemones, penguins, sharks and so much more that swims or crawls. Take bus No 7 from place de la Liberté.

MUSÉE DE LA MARINE
The **Naval Museum** (☎ 02 98 22 12 39; adult/child €4.60/free; 10am-6.30pm Apr–mid-Sep, 10am-noon & 2-6pm Wed-Mon mid-Sep–Mar) is within the fortified, 13th-century **Château de Brest** (one of the few buildings to survive WWII bombing), from whose ramparts there are striking views of the harbour and naval base.

TOUR TANGUY
The paintings, photographs and dioramas in this 14th-century **tower** (☎ 02 98 00 88 60; place Pierre Péron; admission free; 10am-noon & 2-7pm Jun-Sep, 2-5pm Wed-Thu & 2-6pm Sat & Sun Oct-May) trace the history of Brest – in particular how it was on the eve of WWII. Don't miss the documented visit of three Siamese ambassadors in 1686 who presented gifts to the court of Louis XIV; rue de Siam was renamed to commemorate the occasion.

Tours
Between April and September, **La Société Maritime Azenor** (☎ 02 98 41 46 23) offers cruises (adult/child €14/10, 1½ hours, two or three times daily) around the harbour and naval base, departing from both the Port de Commerce (near the castle) and the Port de Plaisance (opposite Océanopolis). **Vedettes Armoricaines** (☎ 02 98 44 44 04) operates similar cruises, sailing from the Port de Commerce. The tourist office sells tickets for both.

Festivals & Events
The big summer attraction is **Les Jeudis du Port** (Harbour Thursdays; admission free; 7.30pm-midnight Thu mid-Jul–late Aug) with live bands, concerts, street theatre and children's events.

Brest 2008 is the title of the next mega-moot of around 2000 traditional sailing craft from around the world that the city hosts in an intensive week of July every four years.

Sleeping
Auberge de Jeunesse (☎ 02 98 41 90 41; brest.aj.cis@ wanadoo.fr; rue de Kerbriant; dm B&B €12.10) Brest's modern youth hostel is near Océanopolis and a stone's throw from the artificial beach at Moulin Blanc. Take bus 7 from the train station to the terminus (Port de Plaisance).

Hôtel Le Régent (☎ 02 98 44 29 77; www.brestle -regent.fr.st in French; 22 rue d'Algésiras; s/d from €30/33) With its lovely Art-Nouveau café-bar, this place speaks attitude and offers excellent value. All 18 rooms have private bathrooms and at weekends rates fall as low as €24.

Hôtel Continental (☎ 02 98 80 50 40; continental -brest@hotel-sofibra.com; rue Émile Zola; s €101-133, d 109-141) The Continental is the smartest spot in Brest city centre. The exterior is just plain dull but the Art-Deco interior will suck your breath away.

CAMPING
Camping du Goulet (☎ 02 98 45 86 84; camping dugoulet@wanadoo.fr; Ste-Anne du Portzic; per person/ tent/car €3.50/4/1.30) This huge, hilly camping ground is in Ste-Anne du Portzic, 6km southwest of Brest and 400m from the sea. Take bus No 14 from the train station to Le Cosquer stop.

Eating
Amour de Pomme de Terre (☎ 02 98 43 48 51; 23 rue Halles St-Louis; menus €9-26) 'Potato Love' serves up all manner of dishes – just as long as they have potatoes. You also get a delightful mini-salad of the freshest fruit and veg from the covered market opposite – and a dip into a basket of rich dried sausages, from which you hack off a hunk.

Fleur de Sel (☎ 02 98 44 38 65; 15bis rue de Lyon; mains €16-23.50; closed Sun & lunch Sat) This stylish Art-Deco restaurant, its minimalist décor contrasting with the warm atmosphere, serves creative French cuisine, with dishes such as veal kidneys sizzled in truffle vinegar.

Ma Petite Folie (☎ 02 98 42 44 42; Port de Plaisance; menus €18-25; Mon-Sat) This superb seafood restaurant is in an old lobster-fishing boat, forever beached at Moulin Blanc, near the *auberge de jeunesse*.

Le Ruffé (☎ 02 98 46 07 70; 1bis rue Yves Collet; menus €25-30, mains €13.50-18; ☼ closed dinner Sun) With its unostentatious maritime décor, Le Ruffé, airy, friendly and highly regarded, is among the best places in town for seafood and quality, creative fish dishes.

Les Halles Ste-Marie, Brest's covered market, is a rich resource for self-caterers.

Getting There & Away

AIR
Ryanair has a daily flight to/from London (Stansted).

BOAT
Ferries to Île d'Ouessant (see p300) leave from the Port de Commerce.

BUS
Brest's bus station (☎ 02 98 44 46 73) is beside the train station. Routes include Le Conquet (€4.45, 45 minutes, six daily) and Roscoff (€9.70, 1½ to two hours, four daily).

CAR & MOTORCYCLE
Hire companies include **ADA** (☎ 02 98 44 44 88; 9 av Georges Clemenceau) and **Europcar** (☎ 02 98 44 66 88; rue Voltaire).

TRAIN
There are frequent trains or SNCF buses to Quimper (€13.80, 1¼ hours) and Morlaix (€8.80, 45 minutes), which has connections to Roscoff (€12, 1½ hours). There are also around 15 TGV trains daily to Rennes (€29.40, two hours) and Paris (Gare Montparnasse; €66.30, 4½ hours).

Getting Around
The local bus network **Bibus** (☎ 02 98 80 30 30) sells tickets for €1, carnets of 10 for €8.30 and day passes for €3. It also has an information kiosk on place de la Liberté.

Torch'VTT (☎ 02 98 46 06 07; 93 blvd Montaigne) rents bicycles.

To order a taxi call ☎ 02 98 80 43 43 or ☎ 02 98 42 11 11.

LE CONQUET
pop 2150
Perched on the westernmost tip of Brittany, the pretty fishing village of Le Conquet (called, engagingly, Konk Leon in Breton) lies close to some pristine beaches and lovely coastal paths. It's largely ignored by

tourists, who generally leave their cars here, then pile onto the Île d'Ouessant ferry.

Information
The **tourist office** (☎ 02 98 89 11 31; www.leconquet .fr in French; ☼ 9am-1pm & 3-7pm Mon-Sat, 9am-1pm Sun Jul & Aug, 9am-noon Tue-Sat Sep-Jun) is in the town hall in the Parc de Beauséjour.

Activities
The tourist office's free town plan details a couple of good **walks** in and around Le Conquet. A clifftop stride leads to **Phare de Kermorvan**, a 37m-high lighthouse perched on the Kermorvan Peninsula, which guards the harbour entrance. To its north lies **Plage des Blancs Sablons**, a lovely, wide beach.

A 5km hike along the coastal path south of Le Conquet leads to **Pointe St-Mathieu**. At the foot of its conspicuous lighthouse are the spectacular ruins of the 16th-century Benedictine **Abbaye St-Mathieu**.

Sleeping & Eating
Le Relais du Vieux Port (☎ 02 98 89 15 91; 1 quai du Drellac'h; d €37-55) Le Relais, with seven comfortable rooms (three with four-poster beds), enjoys an appealing setting beside the waterfront at the old (inner) harbour and represents excellent value. Staff are friendly and there's a cosy creperie and restaurant on the ground floor.

Hostellerie de la Pointe St-Mathieu (☎ 02 98 89 00 19; www.pointe-saint-mathieu.com; Pointe St-Mathieu; s €58-66, d €63-80; dinner menus €25-64) Five kilometres south of Le Conquet, this lovely hotel has a swimming pool, stylish bar and gourmet restaurant with a Gothic fireplace and stone vaulting.

Getting There & Away
Buses operated by **Les Cars St-Mathieu** (☎ 02 98 89 12 02) link Brest with Le Conquet (€4.65, 45 minutes, six daily).

Ferries to Île d'Ouessant depart from the *embarcadère* (ferry terminal) in the outer harbour.

ÎLE D'OUESSANT
pop 950
Île d'Ouessant (Enez Eusa in Breton, meaning 'Island of Terror'; Ushant in English) is rugged and hauntingly beautiful. About 20km from the mainland and some 7km by 4km, it serves as a beacon for over 50,000 ships entering the English Channel each year.

Traditionally, the sea provided the islanders with both a livelihood and resources. The menfolk, mostly sailors, would be away for as much as two years at a time and it was the women who tilled the fields and pulled in the seaweed. The interior of the houses, partitioned by little more than wooden panels, could almost be the inside of a boat, the furniture often fashioned from driftwood. To mask its imperfections, it was usually painted in bright colours – green for hope or blue and white symbolising the Virgin Mary.

Although the island is no longer isolated (day visitors by the thousand pour from the ferries in high summer), a few local traditions persist. Old women still make delicate lace crosses in memory of husbands who never returned from the sea, little black sheep are free to roam as they please and the delicious local dish, *ragoût de mouton* (lamb roasted in an extempore peat oven), is prepared on special days.

The entire island is ideal for windy walks. A 45km path follows the craggy, rocky coastline amid some very grand scenery.

Orientation & Information

The ferry landing is at Port du Stiff on the east coast. The island's only village is Lampaul, 4km away. On the west coast, there's a handful of hotels, restaurants and shops.

The tiny **tourist office** (☎ 02 98 48 85 83; www ot-ouessant.fr in French; ⏰ 10am-noon & 1.30-6pm Mon-Sat, 10am-noon Sun) is on place de l'Église in Lampaul. It sells an English-language version of its brochure *Circuits de Randonnée Pédestre* (€2.30) with stylised maps and descriptions of four coastal walks varying between 10km and 16km.

Sights & Activities

MUSEUMS

Black-and-white striped Phare de Créac'h is the world's most powerful lighthouse, its beam (two white flashes every 10 seconds) visible for over 50km. Beneath is the island's main museum, the **Musée des Phares et des Balises** (Lighthouse & Beacon Museum; ☎ 02 98 48 80 70; adult/child €4/2.50; ⏰ 10.30am-6.30pm Apr-Sep, 1.30-5pm or 5.30pm Oct-Mar). In the old lighthouse generator rooms, it tells the story of these vital navigation aids. Unless you're of a technical bent, you'll probably find the section on shipwrecks and underwater archaeology more interesting.

The small **Écomusée d'Ouessant** (☎ 02 98 48 86 37; Maison du Niou; adult/child €3.20/2; ⏰ as Musée des Phares et des Balises) occupies two typical local houses, one recreating a traditional homestead, the other exploring the island's history and customs.

A combined ticket giving entry to both museums costs €6.30/2.

CYCLING

The most practical and enjoyable way to get around the island is by bike (for details of bicycle hire, see p300).

BEACHES

Plage de Corz, 600m south of Lampaul, is the island's best beach. Other good spots to stretch out are **Plage du Prat**, **Plage de Yuzin** and **Plage Ar Lan**. All are easily accessible by bike from Lampaul or Port du Stiff.

Sleeping & Eating

Auberge de Jeunesse (☎ 02 98 48 84 53; fax 02 98 48 87 42; La Croix-Rouge, Lampaul; dm B&B €13.70; ⏰ closed last 3 weeks Jan) This friendly hostel, on the hill above Lampaul, has two- to six-person bedrooms. Reservations are essential since it's very popular with school and walking groups.

Hôtel Roc'h Ar Mor (☎ 02 98 48 80 19; www .rocharmor.com in French; d €59-82.50; ⏰ mid-Feb–Dec) This modern 15-room hotel has bright, cheerful rooms, enjoys a superb location next to the Baie de Lampaul and runs a good **restaurant** with a terrace overlooking the sea.

Camping Municipal (☎ 02 98 48 84 65; fax 02 98 48 83 99; Stang Ar Glan, Lampaul; per person/site €2.65/2.70; ⏰ Apr-Sep) About 500m east of Lampaul, it looks more like a football field than a camping ground.

Crêperie Ti A Dreuz (☎ 02 98 48 83 01; Lampaul; galettes €3-9; ⏰ Easter–mid-Sep) This pretty little blue-and-white creperie (named 'the slanting house' because of its somewhat wonky walls) serves delicious galettes. Try the *ouessantine*, with its creamy potato, cheese and sausage topping.

Ty Karn (☎ 02 98 48 87 33; Lampaul; lunch menu €12-15, dinner €20-28) The ground floor of this hyperfriendly place is a bar, offering tasty midday snacks in summer, while upstairs there's an agreeable restaurant.

If you forgot the sandwich filling, you'll find three minimarkets in Lampaul.

BRITTANY

Getting There & Away

AIR

Finist'air (☎ 02 98 84 64 87; www.finistair.fr) flies from Brest's small airport to Ouessant in a mere 15 minutes. There are two flights daily (adult/child €61/35).

BOAT

Two companies operate ferries to Ouessant year-round. Fares quoted are all return.

Penn Ar Bed (☎ 02 98 80 80 80; www.pennarbed.fr) sails from the Port de Commerce in Brest (adult/child €30/18, 2½ hours) and from Le Conquet (€25.90/15.50, 1½ hours). Boats run between each port and the island two to five times daily from May to September and once daily between October and April.

In season, Penn Ar Bed also operates from Camaret (€26.80/16.10, two hours, once daily mid-April to mid-September).

Finist'mer (☎ 02 98 89 16 61; www.finist-mer.fr in French) runs faster boats to the island up to six times daily from Le Conquet (€25.50/14, 40 minutes, mid-April to September) and from Camaret (adult/child €26.50/15, one hour, daily mid-July to mid-August, Wednesday only Easter to mid-July).

Buy ferry tickets at the ports or at the Brest or Le Conquet tourist offices. In high summer, it's prudent to reserve at least one day in advance and check in 30 minutes before departure.

Getting Around

BICYCLE

Several bike hire operators have kiosks at the Port du Stiff ferry terminal and compounds just up the hill. They also have outlets in Lampaul. The going rate for town/mountain bikes is €10/14.

Cycling on the coastal footpath is forbidden – the fragile turf is strictly for walkers.

MINIBUS

Several islanders – including **Lucien Malgorn** (☎ 06 84 42 12 70) and **Dominique Etienne** (☎ 06 07 90 07 43) – run minibus services. They meet the ferry at Port du Stiff and will shuttle you to Lampaul or your accommodation for a flat fare of €1.50 (in July and August, book ahead to guarantee a seat). For the return journey, the pick-up point is the car park beside Lampaul's church.

Minibus owners also offer two-hour guided tours (€12 per person) of the island.

PRESQU'ÎLE DE CROZON

The tempting Crozon Peninsula, part of the Parc Naturel Régional d'Armorique, offers wild and spectacular sea cliffs at Pointe de Dinan and Pointe de Pen-Hir and, in Morgat and Camaret, a pair of sheltered resort towns with beaches.

Ménez-Hom

The rounded, 330m-high, heather- and grass-clad hump of Ménez-Hom guards the eastern end of the peninsula. The summit – a surfaced road leads right to the top – offers a superb panorama over the Baie de Douarnenez and is also a popular hang-gliding and paragliding site. The **Club Celtic de Vol Libre** (☎ 02 98 81 50 27; www.vol-libre-menez -hom.com in French) offers half-day hang-gliding and *parapente* sessions for €70.

Landévennec

To the north of Ménez-Hom, the River Aulne flows into the Rade de Brest beside the pretty little village of Landévennec, famous for its ruined Benedictine **Abbaye St-Guénolé**. The abbey **museum** (☎ 02 98 27 35 90; admission €4; ⏰ 10am-7pm Jul–mid-Sep, 2-6pm Sun-Fri May-Jun & late Sep) records the history of the settlement founded by St Guénolé in AD 485 and the oldest Christian site in Brittany. Nearby, a new abbey is home to a contemporary community of monks, who run a little shop selling, among the usual tourist paraphernalia, delicious, home-made fruit jellies.

Camaret-sur-Mer

Until early last century, Camaret was France's biggest crayfish port, its boats roaming as far as the Indian Ocean in search of this expensive crustacean. Today, the carcasses of abandoned fishing boats line the harbour, sad testimony to this once-thriving local industry. But it's a lively place in summer and a popular yachting harbour that depends on the annual flood of summer visitors for a living.

The **Chapelle Notre-Dame-de-Rocamadour**, its timber roof like an inverted ship's hull, is dedicated to the sailors of Camaret, who have adorned it with votive offerings of oars, lifebuoys and model ships.

The **tourist office** (☎ 02 98 27 93 60; www.camaret-sur-mer.com in French; 15 quai Kléber; ⏰ 9am-7pm Mon-Sat & 10am-1pm Sun Jul & Aug, 10am-noon & 2-5pm Mon-Sat Sep-Jun) is on the waterfront.

Pointe de Pen-Hir

Pointe de Pen-Hir, 3km south of Camaret, is a spectacular headland bounded by steep sea cliffs. It bears two WWII memorials; one commemorates the Bretons who died, the other, a bunker, is to soldiers and sailors who perished during the Battle of the Atlantic. The line of sea stacks off the point is known as the Tas de Pois – rather more euphonic in French than its translation, 'Pile of Peas'.

Crozon & Morgat

pop 7800

Crozon, the largest town on the peninsula, provides shops and services for the more alluring resort of Morgat, 2km south, which makes a good base for exploring this outstandingly beautiful peninsula.

INFORMATION

The **Crozon tourist office** (☎ 02 98 27 07 92; croz on.maison.du.tourisme@wanadoo.fr; blvd Pralognan; 🕑 9.15am-12.30pm & 2-7pm Mon-Sat, 10am-noon Sun Jul & Aug, 9.15am-noon & 2-5.30pm or 6pm Mon-Sat Sep-Jun) is on the main road to Camaret 500m west of the church.

The seasonal **Morgat tourist office** (☎ 02 98 27 29 49; 🕑 Jul & Aug) overlooks the promenade at the corner of blvd de la Plage.

ACTIVITIES

Beyond the marina at the southern end of Morgat's fine sandy **beach**, the coastal path offers an excellent 8km hike along the sea cliffs to **Cap de la Chèvre**.

A couple of Morgat-based companies, **Vedettes Rosmeur** (☎ 02 98 27 10 71) and **Vedettes Sirènes** (☎ 02 98 26 20 10) operate 45-minute boat trips to the colourful **sea caves** along the coast. Tours (adult/child €9/6) depart from Morgat harbour several times daily from April to September.

SLEEPING & EATING

Hôtel de la Baie (☎ 02 98 27 07 51; hotel.delabaie@ presquile-crozon.com; 46 blvd de la Plage, Morgat; d with shower €33, with bathroom €37-45.50; Ⓟ) This jolly, family-run place on Morgat's promenade is one of the best deals in town; parking's free and it's also one of the very few hotels to remain open year-round.

Camping Les Pieds Dans l'Eau (☎ 02 98 27 62 43; St-Fiacre; per person/tent/car €3.75/3.75/2; 🕑 mid-Jun–mid-Sep) 'Camping feet in the water' (almost literally so at high tide since the beach is only a well-cast pebble away) is one of nine camping grounds along the peninsula.

La Grange de Toul-Boss (☎ 02 98 27 17 95; 1 place d'Ys; galettes €3-7.50, menus €13, mains €10-18.50) Near the Morgat tourist office, this restaurant, creperie and tearoom occupies an old traditional Breton barn. The *menu* is exceptionally good value; starters include half a crab or six oysters and the mains are principally large portions of fish.

Les Échoppes (☎ 02 98 26 12 63; 24 quai du Kador, Morgat; menus €15-30; 🕑 lunch & dinner Jul & Aug, dinner only May, Jun & Sep) This unassuming stone cottage at the southern end of the waterfront specialises in seafood – the catch of the day is advertised on a sign outside. It's so small that we advise reserving, whatever the day.

GETTING THERE & AROUND

There are five buses daily from Quimper to Crozon (€9.30, 1¼ hours), continuing to Camaret (€9.50) and up to four from Camaret and Crozon to Brest (€9, 1¼ hours, daily). Buses also run between Morgat, Crozon and Camaret several times daily (€1.70, 10 minutes).

To rent a bike, contact **Presqu'îles Loisirs** (☎ 02 98 27 00 09; 13 rue de la Gare, Crozon), opposite Crozon's tourist office, **Point Bleu** (☎ 02 98 27 09 04; Quai Kador, Morgat) or, in summer, the open-air stall in front of Morgat's tourist office. The going rate is about €10 per day.

HUELGOAT

pop 1750

Huelgoat (An Uhelgoat in Breton), 30km south of Morlaix, makes an excellent base for exploring what's left of the forested Argoat. The village borders the unspoiled Forêt d'Huelgoat – where King Arthur's treasure is said to be buried – with its unusual rock formations, caves, menhirs and abandoned silver and lead mines. To the east and northeast are the Forêt de St-Ambroise and the Forêt de Fréau. All have a good network of walking trails.

Orientation & Information

Huelgoat sits beside a small Y-shaped lake that empties into the Argent, a mere trickle of a river. Between June and September, the **tourist office** (☎ 02 98 99 72 32; fax 02 98 99 75 72; 🕑 10am-12.30pm & 2-5.30pm Mon-Sat Jul & Aug, 10am-noon & 2-4.30pm Mon-Fri Sep-Jun) is in the Moulin du Chaos, an old mill beside the

BRITTANY

bridge at the eastern end of the lake. During the rest of the year it operates within the town hall (place Alphonse Penven).

Activities
WALKING
Huelgoat gets busy in summer and the network of forest tracks is best appreciated in the relative calm of spring and autumn. An undemanding walking trail (45 minutes round trip) heads downstream from the bridge, initially on the opposite bank to the tourist office. Here, the river disappears into a picturesque, wooded valley where giant granite boulders lie pell mell, each upholstered with shaggy green moss.

Longer hikes (1½ to two hours) lead along the Promenade du Canal to some old silver mines and to the unremarkable Grotte d'Artus (Arthur's Cave).

Sleeping & Eating
Hôtel-Restaurant du Lac (☎ 02 98 99 71 14; fax 02 98 99 70 91; 9 rue Général de Gaulle; d €45-58; ☼ mid-Feb–mid-Dec) Huelgoat's only hotel, a Logis de France that's a mere 200m from the tourist office, is fine, if not as charming as its name and lakeside location might suggest. Its popular **restaurant** serves steaks, pizzas and salads.

Camping Municipal du Lac (☎ 02 98 99 78 80; rue Général de Gaulle; per person/site €2.90/3.40; ☼ mid-Jun–mid-Sep) This camping ground is on the lakeside around 500m west of the town centre.

Crêperie des Myrtilles (☎ 02 98 99 72 66; 26 place Aristide-Briand; crepes €2-6, menus from €8; ☼ Jan-Oct, closed Mon except Jul & Aug) This pretty little creperie on the town's main square has a pleasant summer terrace. Try their juicy, signature *crêpe aux myrtilles* (crepes with bilberry, picked locally).

Getting There & Away
EFFIA (☎ 02 98 93 06 98) runs at least two services daily to Morlaix (€8.70, one hour) to the north and Carhaix to the southeast. Buses stop in front of the Chapelle de Notre-Dame in place Aristide-Briand.

DOUARNENEZ & LOCRONAN
In Breton, the good folk of Douarnenez are called *penn sardin* (sardine head), a nickname derived from former days when it was home port to more than 1000 sardine boats, whose catch was processed by over 30 canneries. Today it's still an important fishing

port, but it has also re-invented itself as a guardian of Brittany's – and France's – maritime traditions.

The action part of Douarnenez sits on a stubby peninsula. From it, streets fall steeply west to the narrow, river-mouth harbour of Port Rhu. Eastwards, the narrow alleys of the old town lead more gently down to the old port of Rosmeur.

The **tourist office** (☎ 02 98 92 13 35; www.douarnenez-tourisme.com in French; 2 rue Docteur Mével; ☼ 10am-noon & 2-7pm Mon-Sat, 10am-1pm Sun Jul & Aug, 10am-noon & 2-5pm or 6pm Mon-Sat Sep-Jun) is beside place Édouard Vaillant.

On Port Rhu's lively waterfront are **Port-Musée** and the **Musée du Bateau** (☎ 02 98 92 65 20; quai du Port Rhu; combined ticket adult/child €6.20/3.85; ☼ 10am-7pm mid-Jun–mid-Sep, 10am-12.30pm & 2-6pm Tue-Sun Apr–mid-Jun & mid-Sep–Oct). Moored at open-air Port-Musée are around 20 traditional vessels, ranging from a Breton *langoustier* (cray-fishing boat) to a Norwegian masted sailing ship. Within the vast Musée du Bateau, occupying a former sardine cannery, are around 40 smaller traditional boats such as an Inuit kayak and a Welsh coracle as well as local craft.

On the other side of town is the old port area of **Rosmeur**, an attractive waterfront lined with fishermen's bars and touristy restaurants.

CAT (☎ 02 98 90 68 40) runs buses to/from Quimper (€6, 35 minutes, six to 10 daily).

To the east of Douarnenez, Locronan has changed little outwardly since the 18th century – and so has been much in demand as a film location, most famously in 1979 for Roman Polanski's *Tess*.

It may have evaded the passage of time, but Locronan certainly doesn't escape the passage of thousands of tourists every year. To savour the atmosphere of *les temps perdus*, it's best to visit very early in the morning or outside the summer season.

Locronan's **tourist office** (☎ 02 98 91 70 14; www.locronan.org in French; place de la Mairie; ☼ Apr-Sep) is on the main square.

Between two and seven buses daily run to Locronan from both Quimper and Camaret.

QUIMPER
pop 59,400
Quimper (kam-pair), lying where the small Rivers Odet and Steïr meet, takes its name

from the Breton word *kemper,* meaning 'confluence'. Strongly Breton in character and administrative capital of the *département* of Finistère, it's very much the cultural and artistic capital too, with its cobbled streets, half-timbered houses, waterways and magnolias, imparting a pleasing village feel.

Orientation
The old city, much of it pedestrianised, clusters around the cathedral on the north bank of the Odet, overlooked by Mont Frugy on the south bank.

Information
Eixxos (☎ 02 98 64 40 56; 12 blvd Dupleix; per hr €3.50; ⏱ 11am-10pm Mon-Thu, 11am-1am Fri & Sat, 2-10pm Sun) Internet access.
Laverie de la Gare (4 av de la Gare; ⏱ 8am-8pm) Laundry.
Main Post Office (blvd Amiral de Kerguélen)
Tourist Office (☎ 02 98 53 04 05; www.quimper-tourisme.com in French; place de la Résistance; ⏱ 9am-7pm Mon-Sat, 10am-1pm & 3-5.45pm Sun Jul & Aug, 9.30am-12.30pm & 1.30-6pm or 6.30pm Mon-Sat Sep-Jun, 10am-12.45pm Sun Jun & 1-15 Sep) Can reserve accommodation. Arranges weekly guided city tours in English, July-August.

Sights & Activities
CATHÉDRALE ST-CORENTIN
The twin spires and soaring vertical lines of Quimper's **cathedral** dominate the city centre. Begun in 1239, it wasn't fully completed until the 1850s, when those spires that meld so harmoniously into the original structure were added. The inside, recently scrubbed, renovated and repainted, gives an extraordinary feeling of light and space. High up on the west façade, between the spires, is an equestrian statue of King Gradlon, the city's mythical 5th century founder.

MUSEUMS
Musée Départemental Breton (☎ 02 98 95 21 60; 1 rue du Roi Gradlon; adult/child €3.80/2.50; ⏱ 9am-6pm Jun-Sep, 9am-noon & 2-5pm Tue-Sat & 2-5pm Sun Oct-May) is in what used to be the bishop's palace, beside the cathedral. It has superb exhibits on the history, furniture, costumes, crafts and archaeology of the area. Adjoining the museum is the **Jardin de l'Évêché** (Bishop's Palace Garden; admission free; ⏱ 9am-5pm/6pm).
Musée de la Faïence (☎ 02 98 90 12 72; 14 rue Jean-Baptiste Bousquet; adult/child €4/2.30; ⏱ 10am-6pm Mon-Sat mid-Apr–mid-Oct) occupies a one-

time ceramics factory and displays over 2000 pieces of choice china.
Musée des Beaux-Arts (☎ 02 98 95 45 20; 40 place St-Corentin; adult/child €4/2.50; ⏱ 10am-7pm Jul & Aug, 10am-noon & 2-6pm Wed-Mon Apr-Jun & Sep-Oct, 10am-noon & 2-6pm Wed-Sat & Mon, 2-6pm Sun Nov-Mar) in the town hall displays European paintings from the 16th to early 20th centuries.

WALKING
A nice way to get the feel of Quimper is to simply stroll along the banks of River Odet, where flowers cascade from its numerous foot bridges, or around place Médard, rue Kéréon, rue des Gentilhommes and its continuation, rue du Sallé, to place au Beurre. Most of old Quimper's **half-timbered houses** are concentrated in this tight triangle.
If you're feeling a little more energetic, climb 72m-high **Mont Frugy**, which offers great views of the city. Follow the switchback path that starts just east of the tourist office.

Tours
From May to September **Vedettes de l'Odet** (☎ 02 98 57 00 58) runs boat trips (adult/child €21.50/13, 1¼ hours) from Quimper along the wonderfully scenic Odet estuary to Bénodet, departing from quai Neuf.

Festivals & Events
The **Festival de Cornouaille** (www.festival-cornouaille.com in French), a showcase for traditional Celtic music, costumes and culture, takes place between the third and fourth Sundays of July. After the traditional festival, classical music concerts are held at different venues around town. Ask the tourist office for times and venues of a local *fest-noz* (night festival).

Sleeping
Auberge de Jeunesse (☎ 02 98 64 97 97; quimper@fuaj.org; 6 av des Oiseaux; dm €8.90) Quimper's youth hostel, with self-catering facilities, is beside Camping Municipal (see below), on the edge of a wooded park.
Hôtel TGV (☎ 02 98 90 54 00; www.hoteltgv.com in French; 4 rue de Concarneau; d €36-42) One among several hotels around the train station, the TGV, recently under new ownership, has small but well-appointed rooms. A reader reports that noise from the bar beneath can be intrusive so aim high, for one of the top-floor rooms.
Hôtel Gradlon (☎ 02 98 95 04 39; www.hotel-gradlon.com in French; 30 rue de Brest; d €82-99; ⏱ closed

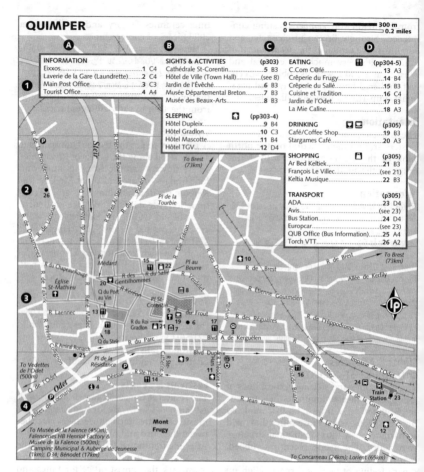

QUIMPER

INFORMATION	
Eixxos	1 C4
Laverie de la Gare (Laundrette)	2 C4
Main Post Office	3 C3
Tourist Office	4 A4

SIGHTS & ACTIVITIES	(p303)
Cathédrale St-Corentin	5 B3
Hôtel de Ville (Town Hall)	(see 8)
Jardin de l'Évêché	6 B3
Musée Départemental Breton	7 B3
Musée des Beaux-Arts	8 B3

SLEEPING	(pp303-4)
Hôtel Dupleix	9 B4
Hôtel Gradlon	10 C3
Hôtel Mascotte	11 B4
Hôtel TGV	12 D4

EATING	(pp304-5)
C.Com C@fé	13 A3
Crêperie du Frugy	14 B4
Crêperie du Sallé	15 B3
Cuisine et Tradition	16 C4
Jardin de l'Odet	17 B3
La Mie Câline	18 A3

DRINKING	(p305)
Café/Coffee Shop	19 B3
Stargames Café	20 A3

SHOPPING	(p305)
Ar Bed Keltiek	21 B3
François Le Villec	(see 21)
Keltia Musique	22 B3

TRANSPORT	(p305)
ADA	23 D4
Avis	(see 23)
Bus Station	24 D4
Europcar	(see 23)
QUB Office (Bus Information)	25 A4
Torch VTT	26 A2

20 Dec-20 Jan) This comfortable place, full of character, is almost a home from home. Rooms are set around a pretty courtyard with a rose garden at its heart and there's a convivial bar with an open fire for winter evenings.

Hôtel Dupleix (☎ 02 98 90 53 35; www.hotel-dup leix .com in French; 34 blvd Dupleix; d €82-105; **P**) The Dupleix, reliable if bland, is part of a business complex overlooking the River Odet opposite the town hall. All rooms are modern and well equipped and some have a balcony and view of the cathedral.

Hôtel Mascotte (☎ 02 98 53 37 37; www.hotel-sofi bra.com; 6 rue Théodore Le Hars; s €55-77, d €64-77) The Mascotte is spruce and reliable, if short on character. Rooms are double glazed and sizeable and there's adjacent public parking. Just don't expect anything out of the ordinary.

CAMPING

Camping Municipal (☎ /fax 02 98 55 61 09; av des Oiseaux; per person/tent/car €3.26/0.75/1.55) This park is 1km west of the old city. From quai de l'Odet follow rue Pont l'Abbé northwestwards and continue straight ahead where it veers left. Alternatively, take bus No 1 from the train station to the Chaptal stop.

Eating

Crêperie du Frugy (☎ 02 98 90 32 49; 9 rue Ste-Thérèse; galettes €3.70-6.55; ⏰ closed Sun & lunch Mon) This tiny place, in the shadow of Mont Frugy, dishes up excellent inexpensive crepes and galettes.

Crêperie du Sallé (☎ 02 98 95 95 80; 6 rue du Sallé; galettes €3-9; ⊗ Tue-Sat) Locals crowd into this bright and breezy creperie at lunchtime so arrive early to guarantee a table. Sample some real Breton specialities, tucked away inside your galette, such as *saucisse fumée* (smoked sausage; €6.60) and coquilles St-Jacques (scallops; €8.60).

Jardin de l'Odet (☎ 02 98 95 76 76; 39 blvd Amiral de Kerguélen; menus €19-35; ⊗ Mon-Sat) This stylish Art-Deco restaurant overlooks part of the Jardin de l'Évêché. Specialising in Breton and French cuisine, it takes familiar dishes, then twists and modifies them creatively.

SELF-CATERING
La Mie Câline (14 quai du Steir) is a hugely popular bakery where you can get a whopping filled baguette, pastry and soft drink for only €5.20. If the midday line is too long – or if you want something a bit more subtle – just cross the stream to **C.Com C@fé** (9 quai du Port au Vin). Here, they do great sandwiches and garnished salads – so the midday queues are likely to be just as long.

Cuisine et Tradition (45 av de la Gare) is a delicatessen with a huge choice of cured meats, tarts, pies and ready-prepared dishes.

Drinking
Rue du Frout near the cathedral has a couple of small pubs that attract a Breton-speaking clientele.

Stoke up a hookah at **Stargames Café**. Primarily an Internet café, Stargames has a lovely little oriental café, all cushions and low seating, on the ground floor.

Café/Coffee Shop (20 Rue du Frout; ⊗ 6pm-1am) is a popular gay venue.

Entertainment
From late June to the first week in September, there's traditional Breton music and dance (admission €4) every Thursday evening at 9pm in the Jardin de l'Évêché.

Shopping
Ar Bed Keltiek (Celtic World; ☎ 02 98 95 42 82; 2 rue du Roi Gradlon) has a wide selection of Celtic books, music, pottery and jewellery.

Keltia Musique (☎ 02 98 95 45 82; 1 place au Beurre) carries an excellent range of CDs and books on Breton and Celtic music and art.

François Le Villec (☎ 02 98 95 31 54, 4 rue du Roi Gradlon) is an excellent place to shop for

faïence and creative textiles based upon traditional Breton designs.

Getting There & Away
BUS
CAT (☎ 02 98 90 68 40) bus destinations include Brest (€13.30, 1¼ hours) and Douarnenez (€6, 35 minutes, six to 10 daily).

Caoudal (☎ 02 98 56 96 72) runs buses to Concarneau (€4.60, 45 minutes, seven to 10 daily); three daily continue to Quimperlé (€8.90, 1½ hours).

CAR
ADA (☎ 02 98 52 25 25), **Europcar** (☎ 02 98 65 10 05) and **Avis** (☎ 02 98 90 31 34) all have offices right outside the train station.

TRAIN
There are frequent trains to Brest (€13.80, 1¼ hours, up to 10 daily), Lorient (€9.70, 40 minutes, six to eight daily), Vannes (€15.90, 1½ hours, seven daily), Rennes (€27.60, 2½ hours, five daily) and Paris (Gare Montparnasse; €63.30, 4¾ hours, eight daily).

Getting Around
BICYCLE
Torch VTT (☎ 02 98 53 84 41; 58 rue de la Providence; ⊗ Tue-Sat) rents mountain bikes for €15 per day. The friendly owner is a fount of information about local cycle routes.

CAR & MOTORCYCLE
Leave your car in the vast Parking de la Providence, which can accommodate over 1000 vehicles.

PUBLIC TRANSPORT
The information office of **QUB** (☎ 02 98 95 26 27; 2 quai de l'Odet), the local bus company, is opposite the tourist office.

TAXI
For a taxi, call ☎ 02 98 90 21 21.

CONCARNEAU
pop 18,600
Concarneau (Konk-Kerne in Breton), 24km southeast of Quimper, is France's third-most important trawler port after Boulogne and Lorient. Much of the tuna brought in here is caught in the Indian Ocean or off the coast of Africa; look out for handbills announcing the size of the incoming fleet's catch.

BRITTANY

The city has the refreshingly unpretentious air of a working fishing port, its charms supplemented by Ville Close, the walled old town perched on a rocky islet, and several good nearby beaches.

Orientation

Concarneau hugs the western side of the harbour at the mouth of the River Moros. Ville Close and its ramparts separate the Port de Plaisance, to the south, from the busy fisheries area of the Port de Pêche. Quai d'Aiguillon, becoming quai Peneroff, runs from north to south beside the harbour.

Information

Laundrette (21 av Alain Le Lay; ☉ 7am-8pm)
Post Office (14 quai Carnot)
Tourist Office (☎ 02 98 97 01 44; www.ville-concarneau.fr in French; quai d'Aiguillon; ☉ 9am-7pm Jul & Aug, 9am-12.30pm & 1.45-6.30pm Mon-Sat, 9.30am-12.30pm Sun April-Jun & 1-15 Sep, 9am-noon & 2-6pm Mon-Sat mid-Sep–March) Our sole candidate for the least friendly tourist office in Brittany award.

Sights

VILLE CLOSE

The **walled town**, fortified between the 14th and 17th centuries, is on a small island linked to place Jean Jaurès by a footbridge. Heed that timely warning on a sundial by the entrance: 'Time passes like a shadow'.

Savour rue Vauban and place St-Guénolé, their old stone houses converted into shops, restaurants and galleries, then return via the **ramparts** on the southern side of the island for views over the town, port and bay.

MUSEUMS & VISITS

The excellent **Musée de la Pêche** (Fisheries Museum; ☎ 02 98 97 10 20; 3 rue Vauban; adult/child €6/4; ☉ 9.30am-8pm Jul & Aug, 10am-noon & 2-6pm Sep-Jun, closed 3 weeks in Jan) has offshore fishing boats, a retired trawler, model ships and exhibits on everything you might want to know about the fishing industry.

The **Marinarium** (☎ 02 98 50 81 64; place de la Croix; adult/child €5/3; ☉ 10am-7pm Jul & Aug, 10am-noon & 2-6pm Apr-Jun & Sep, 2-6pm Oct-Dec & Feb), founded in 1859, is the world's oldest institute of marine biology. It has 10 aquariums and exhibits on oceanography and marine flora and fauna.

Maison Courtin (☎ 02 98 97 01 80; 3 quai du Moros; adult/child €2/free; ☉ tours 9.30am, 10.30am, 11.30am & 2.30pm Tue-Sun Jun-Sep, 10.30am & 11.30am Tue-Fri Sep-

Jun), one of Concarneau's last functioning canning factories, does cannery tours that include a film of the cannery in peak production and free sampling.

BEACHES

Plage des Sables Blancs is on Baie de la Forêt, 1.5km northwest of the town centre; take bus No 2, northbound, from the tourist office. For Plage du Cabellou, 5km south of town, take bus No 2, southbound.

Activities

WALKING

The tourist office sells a walking guide, *Balades au Pays des Portes de Cornouaille* (€4; in French), that describes half-a-dozen walks around Concarneau. One good walk, the *Boucle de Moros* (5km), is a loop trail following the banks of the River Moros upstream.

SEA ANGLING

If you fancy catching your own fish, the **Santa Maria** (☎ 02 98 50 69 01; adult/child €31/16 incl equipment hire; sailing 8am Mon, 8am & 1.30pm or 2pm Tue-Fri) does four-hour sea-angling trips daily in July and August. It's moored alongside quai d'Aiguillon near the tourist office.

Tours

In July and August, **Vedettes Glenn** (☎ 02 98 97 10 31) does four-hour river trips (adult/child €24/12, sailing 2.15pm Tuesday to Friday and Sunday) from Concarneau along the gorgeously scenic estuary of the River Odet.

Sleeping

Auberge de Jeunesse (☎ 02 98 97 03 47; concarneau.aj.cis@wanadoo.fr; quai de la Croix; dm €10) This friendly hostel is right on the waterfront, next to the Marinarium.

Hôtel des Halles (☎ 02 98 97 11 41; www.hoteldeshalles.com; place de l'Hôtel de Ville; s €42, d €47-56) A quiet, older-style hotel with comfortable, renovated rooms, the Halles is only a few minutes' stroll from Ville Close.

Hôtel de France et d'Europe (☎ 02 98 97 00 64; hotel.france-europe@wanadoo.fr; 9 av de la Gare; d €48-59; (P)) The 26 rooms at this conveniently central place, a member of the Citôtel group, are all bright and modern.

Hôtel Modern (☎ 02 98 97 03 36; fax 02 98 97 89 06; 5 rue du Lin; d €40, with bathroom €55-60; (P)) With its friendly landlady, this is a cosy, 1950s, put-your-feet-up kind of place.

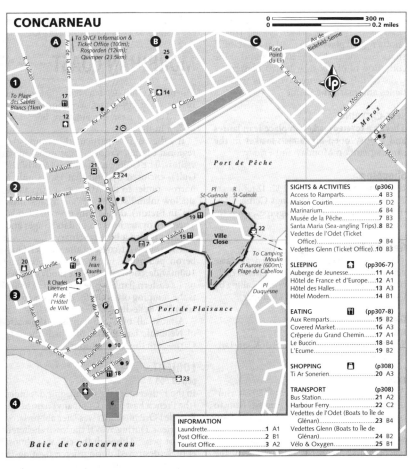

CONCARNEAU

SIGHTS & ACTIVITIES	(p306)
Access to Ramparts	4 B3
Maison Courtin	5 D2
Marinarium	6 B4
Musée de la Pêche	7 B3
Santa Maria (Sea-angling Trips)	8 B2
Vedettes de l'Odet (Ticket Office)	9 B4
Vedettes Glenn (Ticket Office)	10 B3

SLEEPING	(pp306-7)
Auberge de Jeunesse	11 A4
Hôtel de France et d'Europe	12 A1
Hôtel des Halles	13 A3
Hôtel Modern	14 B1

EATING	(pp307-8)
Aux Remparts	15 B2
Covered Market	16 A3
Crêperie du Grand Chemin	17 A1
Le Buccin	18 B4
L'Ecume	19 B2

SHOPPING	(p308)
Ti Ar Sonerien	20 A3

TRANSPORT	(p308)
Bus Station	21 A2
Harbour Ferry	22 C2
Vedettes de l'Odet (Boats to Île de Glénan)	23 B4
Vedettes Glenn (Boats to Île de Glénan)	24 B2
Vélo & Oxygen	25 B1

INFORMATION	
Laundrette	1 A1
Post Office	2 B1
Tourist Office	3 A2

CAMPING

Camping Moulin d'Aurore (☎ 02 98 50 53 08; www .moulinaurore.com in French; 49 rue de Trégunc; per person/site €4/4; ☼ Apr-Sep) This area is only 600m southeast of the harbour and a mere 50m from the sea. Take bus No 1 or 2 to Le Rouz stop from the tourist office or the ferry from Ville Close, then walk southeast along rue Mauduit Duplessis.

Eating

Crêperie du Grand Chemin (☎ 02 98 97 36 57; 17 av de la Gare; crepes €1.30-3.80; ☼ closed Mon except Jul & Aug) For excellent Breton crepes, try this unpretentious little place. Your basic *crêpe au beurre* (buttered crepe) costs only €1.30 or you can make a meal of it with crepes

from starter to finish (three-course *menus* €8 to €12.30).

Le Buccin (☎ 02 98 50 54 22; 1 rue Dougay Trouin; menus €16-34; ☼ closed Thu, lunch Sat & dinner Sun except Jul & Aug) Elegant Le Buccin (The Whelk) is the place where Concarneau's gourmets gather to enjoy whatever harvest of the sea has been landed at the Port de Pêche that morning.

You can eat well in La Ville Close – and prices aren't necessarily top-tourist.

Aux Remparts (☎ 02 98 50 65 66; 31 rue Théophile Louarn; ☼ Easter-Oct) Enjoy their very Breton lunchtime *menu* (€11) of fish soup, *moules frites* and *far breton*. Or, for something lighter, choose from their inventive range of galettes (€6 to €8.45).

L'Écume (☎ 02 98 97 15 98; 3 place St-Guénolé; menus €10-13; ☺ Thu-Tue mid-Mar–mid-Sep) This is another good place for a meal or substantial snack. As you tuck in, glance around at the collection of old postcards that plaster the walls of this cosy retreat with its wooden tables and maritime theme.

SELF-CATERING
There's a **covered market** on place Jean Jaurès and a busy open-air **farmers market** in the same square on Monday and Friday.

Shopping
Ti Ar Sonerien (☎ 02 98 50 82 82; 12 rue Dumont d'Urville) specialises in all things Celtic: CDs, music, books, *bodhrans*, bagpipes, even tin whistles.

Getting There & Away
There's no train station in Concarneau. **Caoudal** (☎ 02 98 56 96 72) runs up to 10 buses daily between Quimper and Quimperlé, calling by Concarneau (€4.60 to/from Quimper).

Getting Around
BICYCLE
Vélo & Oxygen (☎ 02 98 97 09 77; 65 av Alain Le Lay) Rents bikes for €10 per day.

BOAT
A stubby little passenger ferry (€0.80; running 8am to 11pm July to August, 8am to 6.30 or 8.30pm Monday to Saturday, 9am to 12.30pm and 2pm to 6.30pm Sunday September to June) links Ville Close with place Duquesne on the eastern side of the harbour.

TAXI
Call ☎ 02 98 97 10 93 or ☎ 02 98 50 70 50.

AROUND CONCARNEAU
The **Îles de Glénan** are a cluster of nine little islands about 20km south of Concarneau. Several are nature reserves; **Île de St-Nicolas**, a mere 900m by 300m, is the only one accessible to visitors.

Vedettes de l'Odet (☎ 02 98 57 00 58; adult/child return €25/13; sailings 1-4 daily May-Sep, Wed-Thu Apr & Oct) sails from Bénodet. It also does a guided cruise (adult/child €38.50/20) around the islands with English commentary.

Vedettes de l'Odet (sailings twice daily mid-Jul–Aug, Thu Jun–mid-Jul) also sails from Concarneau, as

do **Vedettes Glenn** (☎ 02 98 97 10 31; adult/child return €24/12; sailings twice daily 10am & 2.15pm Jul & Aug).

MORBIHAN COAST

Morbihan, the *département* that covers Brittany's south-central section, stretches from Lorient near the Finistère border to Redon in the east.

It's the coast – particularly around the regional capital, Vannes – that draws most visitors. The Golfe du Morbihan (Morbihan Gulf), enclosed by land that leaves only a narrow outlet to the Atlantic, is virtually a shallow inland sea (*mor bihan* means 'little sea' in Breton), dotted with over 40 islands. There are oyster beds around its fringes and the area is also a bird sanctuary.

The wild west coast of the slender Quiberon peninsula, in places no more than 100m wide, contrasts with the sandy beaches on its eastern flank, while the town at its tip is the jumping off point for day visits to the island of Belle-Île-en-Mer.

Almost all of Morbihan is a showcase of Neolithic landmarks, of which those at Carnac are the most famous.

LORIENT
pop 62,000
In the 17th century the Compagnie des Indes (the French East India Company) named the Port de l'Orient, which was later abbreviated to Lorient. During WWII the town sheltered U-boat pens. Although the city was almost entirely destroyed during fierce fighting in 1945, it remains an important port.

Lorient (An Oriant in Breton) is not a particularly pretty city – like Brest, it was almost completely rebuilt after its hammering in WWII – and it has few specific attractions. All the same, its tidy streets, upbeat atmosphere and large student community make it worth a visit. Fans of Celtic music and culture will enjoy the Festival Interceltique, which takes place every summer.

Orientation
Lorient creeps along the western side of a large natural harbour, the Rade de Lorient, at the mouth of the River Scorff. The centre of town is near the canal-like Port de Plaisance, about 1km south of the train and bus stations. From these terminals, you can

reach it by walking down cours de Chazelles and its continuation, rue Maréchal Foch, or by taking bus No D, direction Carnel.

Information

INTERNET ACCESS
No Work Tech (☎ 02 97 84 72 09; 5 place de la Libération; per hr €4; ⏰ 2pm-1am Mon, 10am-1am Tue-Sat, 3-11pm Sun)

LAUNDRY
There are two laundrettes on blvd Cosmao Dumanoir beside the bus station.

POST
Main Post Office (9 quai des Indes)

TOURIST INFORMATION
Tourist Office (☎ 02 97 21 07 84; www.lorient-tourisme.com; quai de Rohan; ⏰ 9am-7pm Mon-Sat, 10am-1pm Sun Jul & Aug, 9am or 10am-12.30pm & 1.30-5pm or 6pm Mon-Fri Sep-Jun, 9am-noon & 2-6pm Sat Apr-Jun & Sep, 10am-12.30pm Sat Oct-Mar)

Sights
The oceanographic research vessel **Thalassa** (☎ 02 97 35 13 00; quai de Rohan; adult/child €6.30/4.90; ⏰ 9am-7pm Jul & Aug, 9am-12.30pm & 2-6pm Tue-Fri, 2-6pm Sat-Mon Sep-Jun), permanently moored at the Port de Plaisance, enjoys life as an oceanography museum and hands-on exhibition.

In Port Louis, 5km south of Lorient, the magnificent 16th-century **citadel** (adult/student/child €4.60/3/free; ⏰ 10am-6.30pm Wed-Mon Apr–mid-Sep, 2-6pm Wed-Mon mid-Sep–mid-Dec & Feb-Mar) has two worthwhile museums. **Musée de la Compagnie des Indes** (☎ 02 97 82 19 13) traces the history of the French East India Company and its lucrative trade with India, China, Africa and the New World from 1660 to the end of the 18th century through its fascinating display of documents, maps and artefacts. **Musée National de la Marine** (☎ 02 97 82 56 72) illustrates the themes of safety at sea and underwater archaeology, with a rich treasure trove from the world's oceans.

To reach Port Louis and the museum, take the **Batobus** (☎ 02 97 21 28 29; one way €1.15) ferry, which runs between Lorient and Port Louis, leaving every half-hour between 6.45am and 8pm. It departs from Lorient's Port de Pêche from Monday to Saturday and from the Embarcadère de la Rade on Sunday.

Île de Groix, 8km long by 3km wide and about 14km offshore, was once a major tuna fishing port. With its excellent beaches and a 25km coastal footpath, it makes a great day trip (for ferries, see p310).

Festivals & Events
For 10 days in early August, Lorient throbs to the **Festival Interceltique** (☎ 02 97 21 24 29; www.festival-interceltique.com). At this celebration of Celtic music, literature and dance, which attracts around 500,000 visitors, folk from the Celtic countries and regions – Ireland, Scotland, Wales, Cornwall, Isle of Man and Galicia (in northwest Spain) – join the Bretons in celebrating their common heritage.

Sleeping
Auberge de Jeunesse (☎ 02 97 37 11 65; lorient@fuaj.org; 41 rue Victor Schoelcher; dm €9.30) Lorient's HI-affiliated hostel is 4km from town in a beautiful waterside setting on the banks of the River Ter. From the bus stop on cours de Chazelles, outside the bus station, take bus No B2.

Bar-Hôtel Les Pêcheurs (☎ 02 97 21 19 24; fax 02 97 21 13 19; 7 rue Jean Lagarde; d €18-21, with shower or toilet €23-29, with bathroom €34; ⏰ Mon-Sat; P) The cheery 'Fishermen', with rooms above a cosy neighbourhood bar, is excellent value. Ask for a room at the bar, which usually closes well before bedtime.

Hôtel Victor Hugo (☎ 02 97 21 16 24; hotelvictorhugo.lorient@wanadoo.fr; 36 rue Lazare Carnot; d €27, with bathroom €42-48; P) The 30-room Victor Hugo is warm and welcoming. Rooms overlooking the street are soundproofed, public areas are bright and rooms are tasteful and spotless.

Rex Hôtel (☎ 02 97 64 25 60; www.rex-hotel-lorient.com; 28 cours de Chazelles; s €43, d €46-54; P) Rooms positively gleam at this tautly run ship – almost literally so; the reception desk has the shape of a boat's prow, there's woodwork everywhere and a tape of waves breaking and seagulls mewing plays in the small lounge.

Eating
Bistro Le Clos des Vignes (☎ 02 97 64 15 72; 7 cours de la Bôve; menus €11, weekdays €15.75) All polished wood, brass rails and crisp white tablecloths, this lively bistro dishes up seafood and Lyonnais specialities. Finish off with a selection from their splendid cheeseboard.

Restaurant Les Papilles (☎ 02 97 21 08 44; 63 rue Maréchal Foch; mains €9.50-11, menus €20-25; ⏰ closed Mon, Sat & dinner Sun) Les Papilles serves classic French cuisine at reasonable prices; the lunch *menu* at €11.50 is particularly good value.

Le Jardin Gourmand (☎ 02 97 64 17 24; 46 rue Jules-Simon; meals €18-48; ☺ Tue-Sat) The minimalist décor at this highly regarded restaurant, a couple of blocks north of the train station, contrasts with the rich, subtle cuisine. The menu, based upon what's best in the market that morning, changes regularly.

SELF-CATERING
Stock up at the **Halles de Merville**, one of Lorient's two covered markets.

Getting There & Away
BOAT
The **Société Morbihannaise de Navigation** (SMN; ☎ 08 20 05 60 00; www.smn-navigation.fr in French) operates car ferries between the Gare Maritime and Île de Groix (adult/child €24.15/15.30 return, 45 minutes, seven to eight daily). From mid-July to the end of August, SMN runs a passenger-only ferry to Sauzon on Belle Île (adult/child €29.25/15.55 return, one hour, once daily).

BUS
The **bus station** (☎ 02 97 21 28 29) is linked to the train station by a footbridge. Destinations include Josselin (€11) and Pontivy (€9.20).

TRAIN
There are several trains a day from Lorient to Quimper (€9.70, 40 minutes), Vannes (€8.10, 40 minutes) and Rennes (€22.70), plus TGVs to Paris (Gare Montparnasse; €59.10 to €69.70, four hours).

Getting Around
City **buses** (☎ 02 97 21 28 29; ticket €1.15, 10-trip carnet €10, 24hr pass €3.50) run until around 8pm.
    For a taxi, call ☎ 02 97 21 29 29.

CARNAC
pop 4600
Carnac (Garnag in Breton) has the world's greatest concentration of megalithic sites, erected between 5000 BC and 3500 BC. About 32km west of Vannes, it consists of an attractive old village, Carnac-Ville, and a modern seaside resort, Carnac-Plage, with its 2km-long sandy beach.

Orientation
Carnac-Ville is 1.5km north of Carnac-Plage. The megalithic sites of Le Ménec and Kermario are 1km north of Carnac-Ville.

Information
INTERNET ACCESS
Le Bao-Bab (3 allée du Parc, Carnac-Plage; per hr €4) A friendly bar with four terminals.

POST
Main Post Office (av de la Poste, Carnac-Ville)

TOURIST INFORMATION
Main Tourist Office (☎ 02 97 52 13 52; www.carnac .fr; 74 av des Druides, Carnac-Plage; ☺ 9am-7pm Mon-Sat & 3-7pm Sun Jul & Aug, 9am-noon or 12.30pm & 2-6pm Mon-Sat Sep-Jun)
Tourist Office Annexe (☎ 02 97 52 13 52; place de l'Église, Carnac-Ville; ☺ Apr-Sep & school holidays)

Sights
MUSÉE DE PRÉHISTOIRE
To set the scene, pass by the **Museum of Prehistory** (☎ 02 97 52 22 04; 10 place de la Chapelle, Carnac-Ville; adult/child €5/2.50; ☺ 10am-12.30pm & 1.30-6pm or 7pm Thu-Tue & Wed morning Oct-May) A block northeast of place de l'Église, it chronicles life in and around Carnac from the Palaeolithic and Neolithic eras to the Middle Ages. There's a free English-language booklet to guide you through the exhibits.

MAISON DES MÉGALITHES
Opposite the Alignements du Ménec is the **Maison des Mégalithes** (☎ 02 97 52 89 99; route des Alignements; admission free; ☺ 9am-8pm Jul & Aug, to 5.15pm Sep-Apr, to 7pm May-Jun), where you sign on for guided visits to the alignments. This recently opened information centre has rolling video, topographic models and a good selection of books about the sites (including the official *The Carnac Alignments* in English; €6). Its rooftop terrace gives a good view of the menhirs.

THE MEGALITHS
The best way to get a feel for the alignments is to walk or bike between the Le Ménec and Kerlescan groups, with menhirs almost constantly in view. Between June and September, seven buses a day run between the two sites and both Carnac-Ville and Carnac-Plage.
    Because of severe erosion, the sites are fenced off to allow the vegetation to regenerate. However, between 10am and 5pm from October to May, you can wander freely through parts (exactly where changes so check the frequent site billboards or ask at the Maison des Mégalithes). For the rest of the

MORBIHAN'S MIGHTY MEGALITHS

The whole Morbihan region is a showcase of Neolithic landmarks – menhirs, dolmens, cromlechs, tumuli and cairns; the very vocabulary is mostly Breton in origin. The most famous of these are the megaliths (the word means simply 'big stone' in Greek) around Carnac – the densest concentration in the world – erected between 5000 BC and 3500 BC.

Carnac's megalithic sites stretch 13km north from Carnac-Ville and east as far as the village of Locmariaquer. Don't expect Britain's Stonehenge, though; most menhirs are no more than 1m high and scarcely reach your thigh – yet they predate Stonehenge by at least 1000 years. What *will* impress you is the sheer weight of their numbers – over 3000 of them. And their cumulative weight too; just how *did* the original constructors hew, then haul these blocks (the heaviest weighs 300 tonnes), millennia before the wheel and the mechanical engine reached Brittany?

And why? The question continues to bewilder historians. Theories and hypotheses, from the inspired to the barking mad, are multiple. A fertility cult (those thousands of erect, phallic menhirs are a stiff argument in favour of such an interpretation)? Manifestations of sun-worship? The stylised representation of some divinity, long forgotten by the corporate consciousness? For the moment, the cumulative best offer of all this pondering is the vague yet commonly agreed notion that they served some kind of sacred, religious purpose – the same spiritual impulsion that has led to so many of the world's greatest monuments built by humankind.

year, there are **guided visits** (€4; regularly in French, at least once daily in English, Jul & Aug, Sat & Sun Apr-Jun).

Tumulus St-Michel, at the end of rue du Tumulus and 400m northeast of the Carnac-Ville tourist office, dates back to at least 5000 BC. From the top, capped by a much weathered 16th-century cross, there's a fine view of the estuary and inland plain.

The largest menhir field – with no less than 1099 stones – is the **Alignements du Ménec**, 1km north of Carnac-Ville, its rows of stones easily seen from the road. From here, the D196 heads northeast for about 1.5km to the equally impressive **Alignements de Kermario**. Climb the stone observation tower midway along the site to see the alignment from above, threading like rows of pulled teeth. Another 500m further on are the **Alignements de Kerlescan**, a smaller grouping.

Between Kermario and Kerlescan and 500m to the south of the D196 is the small, well-preserved **Tumulus de Kercado** (admission €1), dating from 3800 BC and the burial site of a Neolithic chieftain. During the French Revolution it was used as a hiding place for Breton royalists.

From the parking area 300m further along the D196, a 15-minute walk brings you to the **Géant du Manio**, highest menhir in the whole complex, and the **Quadrilatère**, a group of mini-menhirs, close-set in a rectangle.

Near Locmariaquer, 13km southeast of Carnac-Ville, the major monuments are the **Table des Marchands**, a 30m-long dolmen,

and the **Grand Menhir Brisé** (adult/student/child €4.70/3/free; 9am-8pm Jul & Aug, 9am-7pm May-Jun, 9.30am-12.30pm & 2-5.15pm Sep-Apr), the region's largest menhir, which once stood 20m high but now lies broken on its side. Both are off the D781, just before the village.

Just south of Locmariaquer and by the sea is the **Dolmen des Pierres Plates**, a 24m-long chamber whose rocky walls are decorated with still visible engravings.

Sleeping

Auberge Le Ratelier (☎ 02 97 52 05 04; www.le-ratelier .com; 4 Chemin du Douet, Carnac-Ville; d with shower €38-46, with bathroom €43-55; Feb-Dec) This delightfully rustic eight-room hotel – a former farmhouse that's all low ceilings with traditional timber furnishings – is in a quiet street one block southwest of place de l'Église.

Hôtel Ho-Ty (☎ 02 97 52 11 12; fax 02 97 52 89 52; 15 av de Kermario, Carnac-Plage d €37-59, Easter–mid-Nov) A mere minute's walk from the beach, the Ho-Ty is a traditional family seaside hotel in a lovely blue and white 1930s building. Given its location, its eight rooms, recently renovated, represent great value.

Hôtel Le Bateau Ivre (☎ 02 97 52 19 55; fax 02 97 52 84 94; 71 blvd de la Plage, Carnac-Plage; d with breakfast €83-113.50;) Set in landscaped gardens with a small heated swimming pool, the Bateau Ivre is one of Carnac's more luxurious hotels. All rooms have a balcony and overlook the beach. Avoid August, when it's significantly overpriced at €160.

BRITTANY

CAMPING

There are over 15 camping grounds around Carnac.

Camping des Menhirs (☎ 02 97 52 94 67; www .lesmenhirs.com; 7 allée St-Michel, Carnac-Plage; per peson/site €7.20/27; ☑ May–late-Sep; ☒) This luxury complex – complete with pool, sauna, massage and cocktail bar – is just 300m north of the beach.

Eating

Le Jardin de Valentin (☎ 02 97 52 19 12; 2 rue St-Cornély, Carnac-Ville; menus €8.50-12, salads €9; ☑ Jan–mid-Nov) You can eat in the stylishly decorated restaurant or in the courtyard of this delightful little place, tucked away down a short alley. Save room for one of their desserts.

Auberge Le Ratelier (see Sleeping; menus €17-40; ☑ May-Sep, Thu-Mon Oct-Apr) This hotel restaurant serves gourmet *menus* in a pleasant low-beamed dining room with whitewashed walls. The English version of the menu, with its 'banana greediness to rhum' and other verbal tidbits, is also to be savoured.

Crêperie St-George (☎ 02 97 52 18 34; 8 allée du Parc, Carnac-Plage; galettes, buckwheat pancakes €3.20-6.70, menu €9; ☑ Apr-Sep & school holidays) Set in the Galeries St-George shopping centre, this chic, modern creperie is one of the best-value eating places in town.

Getting There & Away

BUS

The main bus stops are in Carnac-Ville outside the police station on rue St-Cornély and in Carnac-Plage beside the tourist office. Buses go to Auray (€4), Vannes (€6.90) and Quiberon (€3.80).

TRAIN

The nearest year-round train station is in Auray, 12km to the northeast. SNCF has an office above the Carnac-Plage tourist office.

Getting Around

You can hire bikes from **Lorcy** (☎ 02 97 52 09 73; 6 rue de Courdiec, Carnac-Ville) and **Le Randonneur** (☎ 02 97 52 02 55; 20 av des Druides, Carnac-Plage).

For a taxi, call ☎ 02 97 52 75 75.

QUIBERON

pop 4600

At the tip of a slim, 14km-long peninsula, Quiberon (Kiberen in Breton) is a popular seaside town fringed by sandy beaches and a wild sea-swept coastline. It's the major port for ferries to Belle Île.

Orientation & Information

The D768, leads along the peninsula and into Quiberon, ending at the train station. From here rue de Verdun winds down to the sheltered bay of Port-Maria, pincered by the town's main beach, La Grande Plage, to its east and the ferry harbour to the west.

The **tourist office** (☎ 02 97 50 07 84; www .quiberon.com; 14 rue de Verdun; ☑ 9am-1.30pm & 2-7pm Mon-Fri, to 5pm Sat, 10am-1pm & 2-5pm Sun Jul & Aug, 9am-12.30pm & 2-6pm Mon-Sat Sep-Jun) is between the train station and Grande Plage.

Sights & Activities

Conserverie La Belle-Iloise (☎ 02 97 50 08 77; rue de Kerné; ☑ 9-11.30am & 2-6pm Jul & Aug, 10-11am & 3-4pm Mon-Fri Sep-Jun), north of the train station and one of only two remaining sardine canning factories, offers guided visits around its former cannery.

Grande Plage attracts families; bathing spots towards the peninsula's tip are larger and less crowded. The peninsula's rocky western flank is known as the **Côte Sauvage** (Wild Coast). It's great for a windy walk though usually too rough for swimming.

Sleeping

Many hotels close between November and March or April.

Auberge de Jeunesse – Les Filets Bleus (☎ 02 97 50 15 54; 45 rue du Roch Priol; dm €7.70; ☑ Apr-Sep) Quiberon's HI-affiliated hostel is in a quiet part of town 800m east of the train station. There's limited camping in the grounds.

Hôtel Le Roc'h Priol (☎ 02 97 50 04 86; www .hotelrochpriol.fr; 1-5 rue des Sirènes; d €54-89; ☑ mid-Feb–mid-Nov; ℗) The bright, modern Roc'h Priol is in a quiet corner of town, 800m east of the centre.

Hôtel L'Océan (☎ 02 97 50 07 58; hotel-de-locean .com in French; 7 quai de l'Océan; d €34-60; ☑ Easter-Sep) You can't miss this pleasant family hotel, overlooking the harbour. Look for the big white house with multicoloured shutters. The top rate gets you a harbour view.

Hôtel Albatros (☎ 02 97 50 15 05; fax 02 97 50 27 61; 24 quai de Belle-Île; d €54-82) The modern, 35-room Albatros looks over the waterfront between the harbour and Grande Plage. Paying top whack will secure a comfy room with a big balcony and a view of Belle-Île.

CAMPING

Camping du Conguel (☎ 02 97 50 19 11; www
.campingduconguel.com; blvd de la Teignouse; camping
€15-33; ⏰ Apr-Oct; 🏊) This luxury four-star
option, with aquapark, is one of the peninsula's 15 camping grounds. Just 2km
east of the town centre, it's beside Plage du
Conguel. Rates rocket in July and August.

Eating

Creperies, pizzerias and snack bars line
quai de Belle-Île, promenade de la Plage
and rue de Port Maria.

La Closerie de St-Clément (☎ 02 97 50 40 00; 36
rue de St-Clément; galettes €4-8.20; ⏰ closed Wed & dinner Sun except Jul & Aug) This rustic creperie, with
gnarled timber beams and chunky wooden
furniture, has a garden terrace for summer
and a cosy fireplace for winter.

Restaurant-Crêperie du Vieux Port (☎ 02 97
50 01 56; 42-44 rue Surcouf; menu €11, mains around €12,
galettes €4-7; ⏰ mid-Feb–Oct) Overlooking Port-
Haliguen, 1km northeast of Grande Plage,
this eatery occupies an old stone house
with a beautiful, flower-filled garden.

La Criée (☎ 02 97 30 53 09; 11 quai de l'Océan; mains
€15-18; ⏰ Tue-Sun Feb-Dec) On the seafront and an
easy walk from the ferry terminal, this splendid restaurant offers quite the finest seafood
(laid out enticingly on a table for you to take
your pick) and freshest fish in town.

Getting There & Away
BOAT

For ferries between Quiberon and Belle-Île,
see p314.

BUS

Quiberon is connected by **Cariane Atlantique**
(☎ 02 97 47 29 64) buses with Carnac (€3.80),
Auray (€6.30) and Vannes (€9.10, 1¾ hours).
Buses stop at the train station and place
Hoche near the tourist office and beach.

CAR & MOTORCYCLE

Drive your car into Quiberon town centre
during July and August and you'll spend
the day stuck in a traffic jam. During high
summer, we strongly recommend leaving
your vehicle at the 1200-place Sémaphore
car park (up to four hours €3.40, 24 hours
€9), 1.5km north of the beach, then walking or taking the free shuttle bus into town.
Even better: leave the car at Auray station
and hop on the Tire-Bouchon train.

TRAIN

A shuttle train called the 'Tire-Bouchon'
(corkscrew) runs several times a day between Auray and Quiberon in July and
August only (€2.60, 40 minutes). From September to June a SNCF bus service links
Quiberon and Auray train stations (€6.20,
50 minutes) four times a day.

Getting Around

Cycles Loisirs (☎ 02 97 50 31 73; 3 rue Victor Golvan),
200m north of the tourist office, charges
€8/13 a day to rent a touring/mountain bike.
Cyclomar (☎ 02 97 50 26 00; 47 place Hoche) rents
both bikes and scooters. The shop, which
is around 200m south of the tourist office,
also runs an operation from the train station
during July and August.

To order a taxi ring ☎ 02 97 50 11 11.

BELLE ÎLE
pop 5200

Belle-Île-en-Mer, about 15km south of Quiberon, is just what its name suggests: a beautiful island. About 20km by 9km and the
biggest of Brittany's islands, it's exposed to
the full force of Atlantic storms to the west.
Its eastern waters are relatively sheltered.

Although the summer daytime population can swell to over 35,000, the island
rarely feels crowded.

Information

Turn left as you leave the ferry in Le Palais
for the main **tourist office** (☎ 02 97 31 81 93;
www.belle-ile.com; quai Bonnelle; ⏰ 8.45am-7.30pm
Mon-Sat & 8.45am-1pm Sun Jul & Aug, 9am-12.30pm &
2-6pm Mon-Sat, 10-12.30pm Sun Sep-Jun).

There's a summer-only **information kiosk**
(☎ 02 97 31 69 49; ⏰ Easter-Sep) on the quay in
Sauzon.

Sights & Activities

Le Palais is a cosy port dominated by the
citadel, which Vauban strengthened in 1682
after centuries of Anglo-French dispute over
control of the area. The citadel now houses
the **Musée Historique** (☎ 02 97 31 84 17; adult/child
€6.10/3.05; ⏰ 9.30am-6pm May-Oct, 9.30am-noon & 2-
5pm Nov-Apr), which examines Belle Île's past.

Belle-Île's wild, deeply eroded southwestern coast, known with reason as the **Côte Sauvage**, has spectacular rock formations and a
number of caves. The most famous, **Grotte
de l'Apothicairerie** (Cave of the Apothecary's

BRITTANY

Shop), is an awesome cavern where the waves roll in from two sides.

Port de Donnant has a beautiful beach, popular with surfers, though swimming here is dangerous. **Port Kérel** is the best one for children is **Plage des Grands Sables**, 2km long, is the island's biggest and busiest strand.

The large-scale maps in *Guide des Randonnées Pédestres et Cyclistes* (Walking and Cycling Trail Guide; €8), on sale at the tourist office, are excellent for navigation. The ultimate hike is a circuit of the 95km **coastal footpath** that follows the island's coastline.

Sleeping

Auberge de Jeunesse Haute Boulogne (☎ 02 97 31 81 33; belle-ile@fuaj.org; Le Palais; dm €9.30; ♥ closed Oct) This modern HI-affiliated hostel is to the north of the citadel.

Hôtel La Frégate (☎ 02 97 31 54 16; fax 02 97 31 33 13; quai de l'Acadie, Le Palais; d €29, with bathroom €39; ♥ Apr–mid-Nov) Facing the ferry dock, the Frégate is a good economical choice though the interior décor doesn't live up to the appeal of the colourful exterior. There's a lively bar beneath and a spacious guest living room overlooking the harbour.

Hôtel Vauban (☎ 02 97 31 45 42; www.hotelvauban .com in French; 1 rue des Ramparts, Le Palais; s €39, d €1-70; ♥ mid-Feb–Oct) The Vauban has 16 comfortable, spacious rooms and a grand location, perched beside the coastal path high above the ferry landing. By car, it's signed from place de la République. On foot, turn second left up a steep, narrow alley that becomes rue des Remparts.

CAMPING

There are 10 camping areas around Belle-Île; most open from April or May to September or October.

Camping Municipal Les Glacis (☎ 02 97 31 41 76; Le Palais; per person/tent/car €4/4.50/2, site €2; ♥ Apr-Sep) This camping area is at the base of the citadel in Le Palais.

Eating

Le Goéland (☎ 02 97 31 81 26; 3 quai Vauban, Le Palais; mains €10-16; ♥ Thu-Mon Mar–mid-Nov) The Goéland (seagull) in Le Palais is an excellent restaurant, whether you choose the lively bar-brasserie on the ground floor or the more formal restaurant upstairs. The menu concentrates on seafood, augmented by local lamb, fattened on the island, and salads.

Getting There & Away
FROM QUIBERON

The shortest crossing to Belle-Île is from Quiberon. **SMN** (☎ 08 20 05 60 00; www.smn-navi gation.fr in French) operates car ferries (45 minutes, year-round) and fast passenger ferries (20 minutes, July to August) to Le Palais, and fast passenger ferries to Sauzon (April to mid-September). An adult/child return fare is €25.50/16.10 for boats and €28/17.65 for the fast ferry. There are five crossings a day – more than double that in July and August.

FROM VANNES

Navix operates a ferry at least daily between May and mid-September from Vannes.

FROM LORIENT

From mid-July to the end of August, **SMN** runs a fast passenger-only ferry (adult/child €29.25/15.55 return, one hour, once daily) from Lorient to Sauzon.

Getting Around

There are lots of places in Le Palais where you can hire bicycles/motor scooters for around €12/35 a day.

VANNES
pop 55,000

Gateway to the islands of the Golfe du Morbihan, Vannes (Gwened in Breton) is a lovely town – small enough to feel intimate, close enough to the sea to taste the salt air and old enough to have an interesting history. Its medieval heart, lively with students from the Vannes branch of the Université de Rennes, must be as vital as it was centuries ago.

History

In pre-Roman times Vannes was the capital of the Veneti, a Gaulish tribe of sailors who fortified their town with a sturdy wall (some of which remains) and built a formidable fleet of sailing ships. The Veneti were conquered by Julius Caesar in the 1st century BC. Under the 9th-century Breton hero Nominoë, the town became the centre of Breton unity, while in 1532 the union of the duchy of Brittany with France was proclaimed here in Vannes.

Orientation

Vannes' small marina sits at the end of a canal-like waterway about 1.5km from the gulf's entrance. Roughly 3.5km south of town, the Île de Conleau, also known as the Presqu'île de Conleau (Conleau Peninsula) is linked to the mainland by a causeway.

Information

Futur i Média (☎ 02 97 01 84 09; 14 rue de la Boucherie; €4 per hr; ☽ noon-1am Mon-Fri, 2pm-1am Sat & Sun) Internet access.

Laverie Automatique (5 av Victor Hugo; ☽ 7am-9pm) For washing those clothes.

Main Post Office (2 place de la République)

Tourist Office (☎ 02 97 47 24 34; www.tourisme-vannes .com in French; 1 rue Thiers; ☽ 9am-7pm Jul & Aug, 9.30am-12.30pm & 2-6pm Mon-Sat Sep-Jun) Occupies a lovely 17th-century half-timbered house.

Sights

Vannes' **old town** is a maze of narrow alleys ranged around the Gothic splendour of **Cathédrale St-Pierre**, built in the 13th century and remodelled several times since.

Part of the **ramparts**, which afford views over the manicured gardens, is accessible for wandering (the stairs are tucked away behind rue des Vierges). You can see the black-roofed **Vieux Lavoirs** (Old Laundry Houses), though you'll get a better view from the **Tour du Connétable** or **Porte Poterne** to the south.

Musée de la Cohue (☎ 02 97 47 35 86; 9-15 place St-Pierre; adult/child €4/2.50; ☽ 10am-6pm Jul-Sep, 1.30-6pm Oct-Jun), named after the venerable 14th-century building that houses it, has been, over the centuries, a produce market, a law

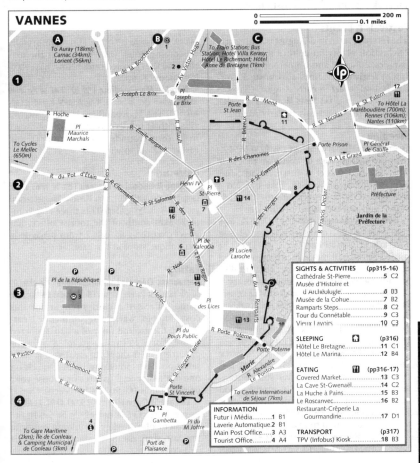

VANNES

SIGHTS & ACTIVITIES   (pp315-16)
Cathédrale St-Pierre..................5 C2
Musée d'Histoire et
    d'Archéologie.......................6 D3
Musée de la Cohue....................7 B2
Ramparts Steps..........................8 C2
Tour du Connétable....................9 C3
Vieux Lavoirs...........................10 C3

SLEEPING   (p316)
Hôtel Le Bretagne.....................11 C1
Hôtel Le Marina.........................12 B4

EATING   (pp316-17)
Covered Market..........................13 C3
La Cave St-Gwenaël....................14 C2
La Huche à Pains........................15 B3
Le Roscanvec.............................16 B2
Restaurant-Crêperie La
    Gourmandine.........................17 D1

INFORMATION
Futur i Média............1 B1
Laverie Automatique..2 B1
Main Post Office.........3 A3
Tourist Office............4 A4

TRANSPORT   (p317)
TPV (Infobus) Kiosk..................18 B3

BRITTANY

court and the seat of the Breton parliament. Today it's a museum of fine arts, displaying mostly 19th-century paintings, sculptures, engravings and temporary exhibits.

Musée d'Histoire et d'Archéologie (☎ 02 97 47 35 86; 2 rue Noë; adult/child €3/1.50; ☉ 10am-6pm mid-Jun–mid-Sep), in the 15th-century Château Gaillard, exhibits primarily artefacts from the megalithic sites at Carnac and Locmariaquer plus Roman and Greek finds. Outside the summer season, it's closed for extensive renovation works.

Tours

From April to September **Navix** (☎ 02 97 46 60 00) offers a range of cruises on the Golfe du Morbihan, departing from the Gare Maritime, 2km south of the tourist office.

Festivals & Events

The **Fêtes d'Arvor** in mid-August is a three-day celebration of Breton culture that includes parades, concerts and numerous *festoú noz* (night festivals). Vannes also hosts a four-day **Festival de Jazz** in early August. Classical music concerts, **Les Nuits Musicales du Golfe**, take place from mid-July to early August.

Sleeping

Centre International de Séjour (☎ 02 97 66 94 25; cis.sene@wanadoo.fr; route de Moustérian; dm €10.60) This 100-bed hostel is just beyond Séné, 7km southeast of Vannes. Take bus No 4 from place de la République to Le Stade stop – and reserve ahead in summer.

Hôtel Le Richemont (☎ 02 97 47 17 24; www .hotel-richemont-vannes.com in French; 26 place de la Gare; d with toilet €33, with bathroom €47-52; P) Don't be misled by the naff mock-medieval breakfast room; the 28 bedrooms are comfortable, soundproofed and strictly contemporary.

Hôtel Anne de Bretagne (☎ 02 97 54 22 19; www .anne-bretagne.com; 42 rue Olivier de Clisson; d €32, with bathroom s €42-45, d €48-61; P) This is another friendly port of call with well-kept, slightly dated rooms that offer good value for money.

Hôtel Le Bretagne (☎ 02 97 47 20 21; hotel.le .bretagne@wanadoo.fr; 34-36 rue du Mené; d €35-40) Just outside the old city walls yet still conveniently central, Le Bretagne is another good economical choice with decent doubles above its poky staircase. Others realise this too so you'd do well to reserve in advance.

Hôtel Le Marina (☎ 02 97 47 22 81; lemarina hotel@aol.com; 4 place Gambetta; s/d €35/38, with shower

€46/49, with bathroom €49/54) This comfortable, welcoming hotel, with views over the marina and the crowded cafés below, has relaxing, modern rooms.

Hôtel La Marébaudière (☎ 02 97 47 34 29; www .marebaudiere.com in French; 4 rue Aristide-Briand; d €62-107; P) The Marébaudière is a large Breton villa with 41 modern, refurbished rooms set in its own grounds just 10 minutes' walk east of the old town.

CAMPING

Camping Municipal de Conleau (☎ 02 97 63 13 88; camping.conleau@tiscali.fr; av du Maréchal Juin; per person/site €4.10/8.80; ☉ Apr-Sep) This three-star complex, 3km south of the tourist office, has views over the gulf. Bus 2 from place de la République stops at the gate.

Eating

Restaurant-Crêperie La Gourmandine (☎ 02 97 01 00 20; 18 rue St-Patern; menus €8-15, mains €9-15) The name reflects the twin strengths of this cosy, affable, warmly recommended eatery, on the ground floor of a half-timbered house. For a full meal, go for a *menu* or pick from their short but creative à la carte selection. For something lighter, snack on one of their special galettes or choose your own toppings (€0.90 to €1.90 each).

La Cave St-Gwenaël (☎ 02 97 47 47 94; 23 rue St-Gwenaël; galettes €3-6.50; menu €9; ☉ Tue-Sat) In the basement of a medieval building opposite the cathedral, the St-Gwenaël is an excellent creperie.

Le Roscanvec (☎ 02 97 47 15 96; 17 rue des Halles; menus €17-74; ❤ Mon-Sat Jul & Aug, Tue-Sat Sep-Jun) The Roscanvec is the best of several tempting eateries along rue des Halles. Set in a lovely 16th-century timbered house, it has a superb menu of seafood and game. The cheapest menu is available for weekday lunches only while the most expensive offers lobster in just about every way it can be prepared.

SELF-CATERING
On Wednesday and Saturday mornings, a **produce market** takes over place du Poids Public and the surrounding area. Vannes' **covered market** is just around the corner.

La Huche à Pains (23 place des Lices) is a popular patisserie that sells *kouign amann* (butter cake) and other enticing Breton pastries.

Getting There & Away
BUS
TIM (☎ 02 97 01 22 10) buses serve Pontivy (€8.50, 50 minutes, three daily) while **Cariane Atlantique** (☎ 02 97 47 29 64) runs via Auray to Carnac (€6.90 1¼ hours) and on to Quiberon (€9.10, 1¾ hours). A SNCF express bus goes to/from St-Brieuc (€15.30, two hours, four daily) via Pontivy (€8.85, 55 minutes).

The small bus station is opposite the train station.

CAR & MOTORCYCLE
Europcar (☎ 02 97 42 43 43) and **ADA** (☎ 02 97 42 59 10) are in the train station. **Budget** (☎ 02 97 54 25 22) is opposite, in the bus station.

TRAIN
There are frequent trains westwards to Auray (€3.40, 12 minutes), Lorient (€8.10, 40 minutes) and Quimper (€15.90, 1½ hours). Eastbound trains serve Rennes (€16.50, 1½ hours) and Nantes (€17.40, 1½ hours). For Quiberon (€9.50 to €11), take the train to Auray and continue by SNCF bus or, in July and August, train.

Getting Around
TPV (☎ 02 97 01 22 23; ticket €1.10, 10-trip carnet €8.50) runs eight city bus lines till 8.15pm. Its Infobus kiosk is on place de la République. Bus Nos 3 and 4 link the train station with place de la République.

You can hire bikes from **Cycles Le Mellec** (☎ 02 97 63 00 24; 51ter rue Jean Gougaud) for €12 a day.

To order a taxi, ring ☎ 02 97 54 34 34.

AROUND VANNES
Golfe du Morbihan Islands
Of the 40 inhabited islands in the Golfe du Morbihan, **Île d'Arz** and **Île aux Moines**, the two largest, are popular day-trip destinations from Vannes.

From the Vannes' Gare Maritime, **Navix** (☎ 02 97 46 60 00; www.navix.fr in French) offers a range of cruises on the Golfe du Morbihan between April and September. Its 'Grand Tour du Golfe' (adult/child €21.50/14, 3¼ hours) includes optional visits to Île aux Moines and Île d'Arz (supplementary €5/4).

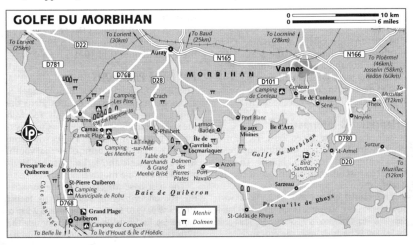

GOLFE DU MORBIHAN

BRITTANY

Le Passeur de l'Île d'Arz (☎ 02 97 50 83 83) runs ferries from Île de Conleau, 3.5km south of Vannes, to Île d'Arz (adult/child return €6/3.50, 15 minutes, hourly year-round).

Izenah (☎ 02 97 26 31 45) boats make the short crossing from Port Blanc, 13km southwest of Vannes, to Île aux Moines (adult/child return €3.5/2, five minutes, half-hourly year-round).

EASTERN & CENTRAL BRITTANY

Eastern Brittany encompases the inland portion of the *département* of Ille-et-Vilaine. A region of fertile farmland and gently rolling countryside, it marks the one-time frontier between Brittany and France. Rennes, capital of Ille-et-Vilaine and of Brittany as a whole, may not feel all that Breton but it's a bustling university city in its own right and has an attractive old quarter.

Central Brittany is split between the *départements* of Côtes d'Armor and Morbihan. The Forêt de Paimpont (or Brocéliande), where King Arthur and his court once held sway and Merlin wove his magic, is wonderful for cycling and walking. Throughout, small villages with character are tucked away, far from any tourist track – though today charming Josselin with its stunning 14th-century chateau has been very much 'discovered'.

JOSSELIN
pop 2400

The picturesque village of Josselin, 43km northeast of Vannes, was the seat of the counts of Rohan for several centuries. Overlooking the River Oust, their imposing castle hosted many of the dukes of Brittany during their progressions through the duchy.

Orientation & Information

Josselin lies on the River Oust. Its centre, place Notre Dame, is a beautiful square of 16th-century half-timbered houses. The castle and tourist office are south, below rue des Trente, the main through street.

The **tourist office** (☎ 02 97 22 36 43; www .paysdejosselin.com; place de la Congrégation; ☽ 10am-6pm Jul & Aug, 10am-noon & 2-6pm Mon-Fri, 10am-noon Sat Sep-Jun) is beside the castle entrance.

Sights & Activities

The three huge round towers of the 14th-century **Château de Josselin** (☎ 02 97 22 36 45; adult/child €6.60/4.50; ☽ 10am-6pm mid-Jul–Aug, 2-6pm Jun–mid-Jul & Sep, Sat & Sun Apr-May & Oct) dominate the riverbanks. Behind them, the elegant Gothic-Renaissance building dates from the late 15th and early 16th centuries.

The **Basilique Notre Dame du Roncier** (place Notre Dame), parts of which date from the 12th century, has some superb 15th- and 16th-century stained glass in the south aisle. In the chapel northeast of the choir is the finely carved marble tomb of Olivier de Clisson, who fortified the chateau during the Hundred Years' War, together with his wife.

Sleeping & Eating

Hôtel-Restaurant du Château (☎ 02 97 22 20 11; www.hotel-chateau.com in French; 1 rue Général de Gaulle; d €31, with shower €43, with bathroom €55.50-60; ☽ closed Sun-Mon Nov-Mar; Ⓟ) Pay top whack to enjoy a room with the most magnificent view of the chateau, looming above this delightfully cosy hotel. Its **restaurant** (menus €14-40) also has a gorgeous picture window.

Camping du Bas de la Lande (☎ 02 97 22 22 20; campingbasdelalande@wanadoo.fr; Guégon; per person/tent/ car €3/3/2; ☽ Apr-Oct) This spot is about 2km west of Josselin, on the south bank of the Oust.

There are several popular creperies on and around place Notre-Dame. Down the hill, **Crêperie-Grill Sarrazine** (☎ 02 97 22 37 80; 51 rue Glatinier; menus from €9, galettes & salads from €6) packs in the locals.

Getting There & Away

Josselin is on the main **CTM** (☎ 02 97 01 22 01) bus route between Pontivy (€6.20, 30 minutes) and Rennes (€11.10, 1½ hours).

FORÊT DE PAIMPONT

The Paimpont Forest (or Brocéliande) is about 40km southwest of Rennes. Here, the young King Arthur traditionally received the sword Excalibur from Viviane, the mysterious Lady of the Lake. Visitors still come here in search of the spring of eternal youth, where the magician Merlin first met Viviane, who became his lover.

The best base for exploring the forest is the lakeside village of **Paimpont**. Its **tourist office** (☎ 02 99 07 84 23; ☽ 10am-noon & 2-5pm or 6pm Jun-Sep, Tue-Sun Oct-Dec & Feb-May) is beside the 12th-century **Église Abbatiale** (Abbey Church).

It has a free walking/cycling map detailing over 50km of trails, or you can buy the more complete *Brocéliande à Pied* walking guide, which describes over 30 forest paths. In July and August the tourist office leads guided tours (half/full day €8/10) of the forest.

Sleeping & Eating

Auberge de Jeunesse (☎ 02 97 22 76 75; dm €7.70; ☺ Jun–mid-Sep) This hostel occupies a lovely stone farmhouse at Choucan-en-Brocéliande, 5km north of Paimpont.

Hôtel Le Relais de Brocéliande (☎ 02 99 07 84 94; www.le-relais-de-broceliande.fr; 7 rue du Forges, Paimpont; d €34, with shower €42, with bathroom €48, menus €16-68.60) This 24-room hotel has pleasantly rustic rooms with all mod cons, as well as an excellent restaurant.

Camping Municipal de Paimpont (☎ 02 99 07 89 16; rue du Chevalier Lancelot du Lac; per person/tent/car €2.50/2.20/1; ☺ May-Sep) This small camping ground is near the lake.

For a cheaper bite, try the **Crêperie au Temps des Moines** (☎ 02 99 07 89 63; 16 av Chevalier Ponthus) in a pleasing granite house overlooking the lake.

Getting There & Around

TIV (☎ 02 99 30 87 80) runs buses to/from Rennes (€2.85, one hour).

You can rent mountain bikes (per half/full day €9/14) from **Bar Le Brécilien** (☎ 02 99 07 81 13; rue Général de Gaulle), beside Paimpont's tourist office.

RENNES
pop 203,500

The attractive university town of Rennes has been an important crossroads from Roman times onwards. Capital of Brittany since its incorporation into France in the 16th century, it developed at the junction of the highways linking the northern and western ports of St-Malo and Brest with the former capital, Nantes (see p612), and the inland city of Le Mans.

Orientation

The city centre is divided by La Vilaine, a river channelled into a cement-lined canal that disappears underground just before the central square, place de la République. The northern area includes the pretty, pedestrianised old city, while the south is garishly modern.

Information

France Telecom (place de la République, beside the post office; per 20 min €1; ☺ noon-7pm Mon-Sat) Internet access.

Laundrette (23 rue de Penhoët; ☺ 7am- 8pm)

Main Post Office (place de la République)

Tourist Office (☎ 02 99 67 11 11; www.ville-rennes.fr; 11 rue St-Yves; ☺ 9am-6pm/7pm Mon-Sat, 11am-6pm Sun) Staff will book local accommodation for a fee of €1.

Sights & Activities

OLD CITY

Much of medieval Rennes was gutted by the great fire of 1720, started by a drunken carpenter who accidentally set alight a pile of shavings. The half-timbered houses that survived now make up the old city, Rennes' most picturesque quarter.

Among the prettiest streets are **rue St-Michel** and **rue St-Georges**. The latter bisects the enormous place de la Mairie and place du Palais, site of the 17th-century **Palais du Parlement de Bretagne**, the former seat of the rebellious Breton parliament and more recently, the Palais de Justice. In 1994 this building too was destroyed by fire, started by demonstrating fishermen. Now restored, it houses the Court of Appeal.

One of the most stylish half-timbered houses is **Maison du Guesclin** (3 rue St-Guillaume), named after the 14th-century Breton warrior. Nearby is 17th-century **Cathédrale St-Pierre** (☺ 9.30am-noon & 3-6pm) with its pure neoclassical interior.

MUSEUMS

The city's former university building now houses the **Musée des Beaux-Arts** (☎ 02 99 28 55 85; 20 quai Émile Zola; adult/child €4/2; ☺ 10am-noon & 2-6pm Wed-Mon), unexceptional except for rooms devoted to the Pont-Aven school.

Temporarily sharing premises are the most important elements of the **Musée de Bretagne** (☎ 02 99 28 55 84), with displays on Breton history and culture. It's scheduled to move to a new cultural complex – the futuristic **Champs Libres** (cours des Alliés), due to open in 2005, which will also house **Espace des Sciences**, an interactive science museum.

ACTIVITIES

To see Rennes from a special perspective, hire an electric boat from **urbaVag** (☎ 02 99 33 16 88; rue Canal St Martin; per hr €15-25) and cruise its waterways. Boats take up to seven

BRITTANY

RENNES

| 0 | 300 m |
| 0 | 0.2 miles |

INFORMATION
France Telecom..........................1 B4
Laundrette................................2 B2
Main Post Office.......................3 B4
Tourist Office...........................4 A3

SIGHTS & ACTIVITIES (pp319-21)
Cathédrale St-Pierre..................5 A3
Champs Libres (Opens 2005)....6 C5
Maison du Guesclin...................7 A3
Musée de Bretagne...................(see 8)
Musée des Beaux Arts...............8 C4
Palais du Parlement de Bretagne.9 C2

SLEEPING (p321)
Hôtel d'Angleterre....................10 C4
Hôtel de la Tour d'Auvergne....11 A5
Hôtel des Lices.........................12 A2
Hôtel-Restaurant Au Rocher de
Cancale..................................13 B2

EATING (p321)
Bistrot des Alibantes................14 C2
Hôtel-Restaurant Au Rocher de
Cancale e...............................(see 13)
L'Ouvrée..................................15 A2
Léon le Cochon.......................16 C4
Les Halles Centrales (Covered
Market)..................................17 B4
St-Germain-des-Champs..........18 C3

To Auberge de
Jeunesse (600m);
urbaVag boat
hire (1.5km);
Hédé (25km);
Bécherel (33km);
St-Malo (60km)

To Camping des
Gayeulles (3km);
Mont St-Michel
(50km)

R d'Échange
R St-Malo
Pl Ste-Anne
Ste-Anne
R d'Antrain
R de la Visitation
R St-Louis
R St-Michel
Pl St-Michel
Penhoët
Pl des Lices
R de
Pl du Champ-Jacquet
R le Bastard
Monnaie
R Victor Hugo
R de la
R St-Guillaume
R St-Georges
R du Chapitre
R de Rohan R de l'Horloge
Pl de la Mairie
Pl du Maréchal Foch
R St-Yves
R F Buisson
Pont de Nemours
Pl St-Germain
Q Duguay Trouin
Pl de la République
Q Chateaubriand
Q Lamennais
République
La Vilaine
Q Émile Zola
Pl de Bretagne
R Chalotais
R du Pré Botté
R Toullier
R Dupont des Loges
Blvd de la Tour d'Auvergne
R Poullain Duparc
Pl Honoré Commeurec
R Jules Simon
R Vasselot
R Maréchal Joffre
Blvd de la Liberté
R Chicotte
Blvd de la Liberté
R Thiers
Pl du Parlement de Bretagne
La Vilaine
R St-Hélier
R de Plélo
Charles de Gaulle
Pl Charles de Gaulle
R du Puits Mauger
R d'Isly
Shopping Centre
Cours des Allées
Pl du Colombier
Blvd Magenta
Av Jean Janvier
R J M Duhamel
R Gurvand
R de l'Alma
Blvd du Colombier
Blvd de Beaumont
Blvd Solférino
Pl de la Gare
Gares
Train Station
To Airport (6km);
Forêt de Paimpont
(40km); Vannes
(111km)
To Nantes (107km)

ENTERTAINMENT (p322)
Ciné TNB................................19 D4
Cinéma Arvor.........................20 C1
Théâtre National de Bretagne..(see 19)

TRANSPORT (p322)
Allo Stop Bretagne..................21 B5
Bus Station.............................22 D6
Car Hire.................................23 D6
City Bus Station......................24 C3
STAR Office...........................25 C3
STAR Office...........................26 B4

BRITTANY

passengers and the price drops significantly by each extra hour of rental.

Festivals & Events

Rennes is at its most lively during the **Tombées de la Nuit** festival in the first week of July when the old city is lively with music, theatre and locals togged out in medieval costume.

Yaouank (☎ 02 99 30 06 87) is a huge *fest-noz* (night festival), held on the third Saturday in November.

Sleeping

Auberge de Jeunesse (☎ 02 99 33 22 33; rennes@fuaj .org; 10-12 Canal St-Martin; dm with breakfast €13.25) Rennes' youth hostel has a canal-side setting. Take bus No 18 from place de la Mairie.

Hôtel de la Tour d'Auvergne (☎ 02 99 30 84 16; fax 02 23 42 10 01; 20 blvd de la Tour d'Auvergne; d €25, with bathroom €38) The spick-and-span rooms at this warm, inviting place, only a 10-minute walk from the old town, are a real bargain.

Hôtel d'Angleterre (☎ 02 99 79 38 61; fax 02 99 79 43 85; 19 rue Maréchal Joffre; s €23, d with shower €32, with bathroom €38-47) The Angleterre occupies a grand old town house with monumental staircases, echoing corridors and spacious, if somewhat tired, rooms.

Hôtel-Restaurant Au Rocher de Cancale (☎ 02 99 79 20 83; 10 rue St-Michel; d €37-46) Set in a half-timbered house and one of the few options in the old town, this fine restaurant (see right) has four pretty, renovated rooms upstairs.

Hôtel des Lices (☎ 02 99 79 14 81; www.hotel-des -lices.com in French; 7 place des Lices; s/d €54/57) Bright and breezy Hôtel des Lices offers comfortable, attractive, soundproofed rooms in a superb location; the ones on the upper floors have good views over the old town.

CAMPING

Camping des Gayeulles (☎ 02 99 36 91 22; fax 02 23 20 06 34; rue Professeur Audin; per person/tent/car €3.35/5/40/1.50) Rennes' only camping ground is in Parc des Bois, about 4.5km northeast of the train station. Take bus No 3 from place de la République to the Gayeulles stop.

Eating

Rue St-Georges and rue St-Malo are lined with creperies and ethnic eateries – from Indian to Brazilian.

AUTHOR'S CHOICE

Léon le Cochon (☎ 02 99 79 37 54; 1 rue Maréchal Joffre; mains €10.50-12.50; ☼ closed Sun Jul & Aug only) Bustling and justifiably basking in the plaudits of almost every French gastronomic guidebook, 'Leo the Pig' is agreeably informal and laid-back for all that and offers great value. As you'd anticipate, pork (indeed porcine products in all their rich manifestations) features prominently on the menu. Leave your tip in the piggy bank on the bar.

L'Ouvrée (☎ 02 99 30 16 38; 18 place des Lices; menus €15-32; ☼ Tue-Fri, lunch Sun & dinner Sat) You'll relish highly-reputed L'Ouvrée for the subtle blends of its main dishes, so attractively presented that it's almost a shame to tuck into them.

St-Germain-des-Champs (☎ 02 99 79 25 52; 12 rue Vau St-Germain; mains €9, menu €15, ☼ lunch Tue-Fri, dinner Fri & Sat) Even ardent carnivores will enjoy this organic-food-only vegetarian restaurant with its tranquil rear terrace. It also does sandwiches and dishes to take away (€4.50 to €6).

Bistrot des Alibantes (☎ 02 99 84 02 02; 36 rue de la Visitation; lunch menu €10, dinner menu €17; ☼ closed Sun, dinner Mon & Tue) This attractive bistro, all antique furniture and wooden floors, serves great classic French and Breton dishes. The lunch *menu* is particularly good value.

Hôtel-Restaurant Au Rocher de Cancale (see Sleeping; mains €9-13, menus €14-25; ☼ Mon-Fri) This delightful restaurant serves mainly fish. Settle into their *plateau du rocher* (€20), a seafood platter that includes oysters, winkles, whelks and *amandes de mer*, a kind of giant clam.

SELF-CATERING

Les Halles Centrales (place Honoré Commeurec) is the larger of Rennes' two covered markets. On Saturday morning there's a huge fresh produce market on place des Lices.

Drinking

Students usually head to Rue St-Michel – renamed 'Rue de la Soif' (Street of Thirst) – for bars, pubs and cafés. Rue St-Malo also has lots of music bars and cafés, of a slightly scruffier, more eclectic nature.

BRITTANY

Entertainment

Nondubbed films are screened at both **Cinéma Arvor** (☎ 02 99 38 72 40; 29 rue d'Antrain) and **Ciné TNB** (☎ 02 99 30 88 88; 1 rue St-Hélier) at the Théâtre National de Bretagne. *Ciné Spectacles* is the free weekly guide.

Getting There & Away

Cariane Atlantique (☎ 02 40 18 42 00) offers services to Nantes (€14.50, two hours). **CTM** (☎ 02 97 01 22 01) runs an express bus service to/from Pontivy (€15, two hours, eight daily). **TAE** (☎ 02 99 26 16 00) runs five times daily to Dinard (€11.80, two hours) via Dinan (€8.80, 1½ hours); **TIV** (☎ 02 99 26 11 26) serves St-Malo (€9.90, one to 1½ hours, three to six daily), Fougères (€8.50, one hour) and Paimpont (€2.85, one hour).

CAR & MOTORCYCLE

ADA (☎ 02 99 67 43 79), **Europcar** (☎ 02 23 44 02 72), **National Citer** (☎ 02 23 44 02 78) and **Hertz** (☎ 02 23 42 17 01) all have offices at the train station.

TRAIN

Destinations with frequent services include St-Malo (€11.40, one hour), Dinan (€11.90, one hour), Vannes (€16.50, 1½ hours), Nantes (€18.90, 1¼ hours), Brest (€29.40, two hours), Quimper (€27.60, 2½ hours) and Paris' Gare Montparnasse by TGV (€59.80, 2¼ hours).

HITCHING

Allo Stop Bretagne (☎ 02 99 67 34 67; www.allosto prennes.com in French; 20 rue d'Isly; ☺ 9.30am-12.30pm & 2-6pm Mon-Sat), in the Trois Soleils shopping centre, matches up hitchers with drivers for a fee of €6.10.

Getting Around

Rennes has an efficient local bus network and a very smart, 22nd-century single-line metro, both run by **STAR** (☎ 08 20 03 20 02; www.star.fr in French). Bus and metro tickets (single journey €1, 10-trip carnet €9.20, 24hr pass €3) are interchangeable.

To get to the town centre from the train or bus station, take bus No 17 to place de la République.

The metro line runs northwest to southeast. Main stations of interest to visitors are Gares (train stations), République (place de la République) and Ste-Anne (old town).

Ring ☎ 02 99 30 79 79 for a taxi.

Champagne

CONTENTS

Reims	325
Around Reims	331
Épernay	331
Troyes	334
Côte des Bar	340

Champagne, known in Roman times as Campania (literally 'Land of Plains'), is a largely agricultural region famed around the world for the sparkling wines that have been made here since the days of Dom Pérignon. According to French law, only bubbly from the region – grown in designated areas, then aged and bottled according to the strictest standards – can be labelled as champagne. Nothing will drive the locals into fits of righteous indignation faster – or will elicit more searing expressions of contempt mixed with pity – than a mention of that absurd liquid marketed as 'California champagne'!

The production of the celebrated wine takes place mainly in two *départements:* Marne, whose metropolis is the 'Coronation City' of Reims, famed for its medieval churches; and the less prestigious Aube, whose *préfecture* is the ancient and picturesque city of Troyes, one of the best places in France to stroll among half-timbered houses.

The town of Épernay, a bit south of Reims, is the de facto capital of champagne (the drink) and is the best place to head for *dégustation* (tasting). The Route Touristique du Champagne (Champagne Tourist Route) wends its way through the region's diverse vineyards, taking visitors from one picturesque – and prosperous – village to the next. A number of big *maisons* (champagne houses) have achieved international renown, but much of the region's liquid gold is made by 5000 small-scale *vignerons* (wine producers), many of whose family-run facilities welcome visitors. The regional tourism committee's website is www.tourisme-champagne-ardenne.com.

HIGHLIGHTS

- Inhale the heady odours of maturing champagne on a cellar tour in **Épernay** (p332) or **Reims** (p328)
- Explore the rolling vineyards along Champagne's scenic **wine route** (p331, p340)
- Stroll among half-timbered houses and duck into Gothic churches in Troyes' medieval **old city** (p336)
- Admire modern and medieval paintings and ancient hand tools in Troyes' fine **museums** (p337)

★ Reims
★ Épernay

★ Troyes

- POPULATION: 1.3 MILLION
- AREA: 25,720 SQ KM

REIMS
pop 206,000

Meticulously reconstructed after WWI and WWII, Reims (pronounced something like 'rance') is a neat and orderly city with wide avenues and well-tended parks. Together with Épernay, it's the most important centre of champagne production.

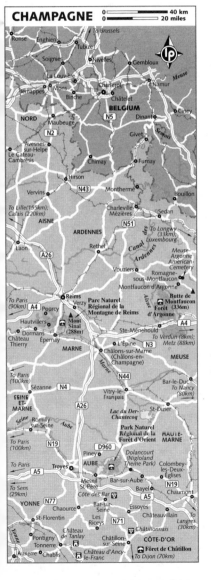

After Clovis I, founder of the Frankish kingdom, was baptised here in AD 496, Reims (often anglicised as Rheims) became the traditional site of French coronations. From 816 to 1825, 34 sovereigns – among them 25 kings – began their reigns as Christian rulers in the city's famed cathedral.

Orientation

In the commercial centre (northwest of the cathedral), the main streets are rue Carnot, rue de Vesle, rue Condorcet and, for shopping, rue de Talleyrand. The train station is about 1km northwest of the cathedral, across square Colbert from place Drouet d'Erlon, the city's major nightlife centre. Virtually every street in the city centre is one way.

Information

INTERNET ACCESS

Clique et Croque Cybercafé (☎ 03 26 86 93 92; 27 rue de Vesle; per hr €4.20; ⏱ 10am-12.30am Mon-Sat, 2-9pm Sun) In the courtyard of the shopping arcade.

LAUNDRY

Laundrette (59 rue Chanzy; ⏱ 7am-9.30pm)

MONEY

There's a cluster of commercial banks on rue Carnot; several more can be found at the southern end of place Drouet d'Erlon. The tourist office changes money on Sunday and holidays.

POST

Branch Post Office (2 rue Cérès) Through the arches on the eastern side of place Royale. Has currency exchange and a Cyberposte.
Main Post Office (2 rue Olivier Métra; ⏱ 8am-7pm Mon-Fri, 8am-noon Sat) Has a Cyberposte.

TOURIST INFORMATION

Tourist Office (☎ 03 26 77 45 00; www.reims-tourisme .com; 2 rue Guillaume de Machault; ⏱ 9am-7pm Mon-Sat, 10am-6pm Sun & holidays early Apr–mid-Oct, 10am-5pm

---

MUSEUM PASS

All four museums run by the municipality – St-Rémi, Reddition, Beaux-Arts and the Ancienne Collège des Jésuites – as well as the Chapelle Foujita are covered by a single entry fee of €3 (free for students; valid one month).

CHAMPAGNE

REIMS

0 — 400 m
0 — 0.2 miles

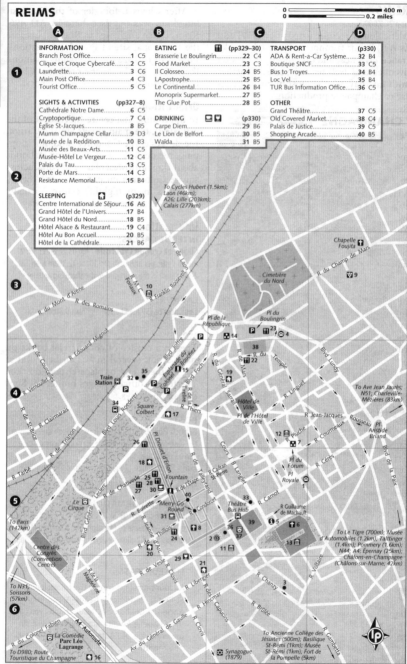

INFORMATION
Branch Post Office....................1 C5
Clique et Croque Cybercafé.......2 C5
Laundrette.............................3 C6
Main Post Office.....................4 C3
Tourist Office.........................5 C5

SIGHTS & ACTIVITIES (pp327–8)
Cathédrale Notre Dame............6 C5
Cryptoportique.......................7 C4
Église St-Jacques....................8 B5
Mumm Champagne Cellar........9 D3
Musée de la Reddition............10 B3
Musée des Beaux-Arts.............11 C5
Musée-Hôtel Le Vergeur..........12 C4
Palais du Tau........................13 C5
Porte de Mars.......................14 C3
Resistance Memorial...............15 B4

SLEEPING (p329)
Centre International de Séjour...16 A6
Grand Hôtel de l'Univers..........17 B4
Grand Hôtel du Nord..............18 B5
Hôtel Alsace & Restaurant.......19 C4
Hôtel Au Bon Accueil.............20 B5
Hôtel de la Cathédrale............21 B6

EATING (pp329–30)
Brasserie Le Boulingrin............22 C4
Food Market.........................23 C3
Il Colosseo............................24 B5
L'Apostrophe.........................25 B5
Le Continental.......................26 B4
Monoprix Supermarket............27 B5
The Glue Pot.........................28 B5

DRINKING (p330)
Carpe Diem..........................29 B6
Le Lion de Belfort..................30 B5
Waïda.................................31 B5

TRANSPORT (p330)
ADA & Rent-a-Car Système.....32 B4
Boutique SNCF......................33 C5
Bus to Troyes........................34 B4
Loc Vel...............................35 B4
TUR Bus Information Office......36 C5

OTHER
Grand Théâtre.......................37 C5
Old Covered Market...............38 C4
Palais de Justice.....................39 C5
Shopping Arcade...................40 B5

To Cycles Hubert (1.5km);
Laon (46km);
A26; Lille (203km);
Calais (277km)

Chapelle
Foujita

Cimetière
du Nord

R. du Champ de Mars

R. du Mont d'Arène

R. des Romains

R. du Mont d'Arène

R. Franklin Roosevelt

R.M.C
Feraux

R des Romains

R. Edouard Mignot

Pl de la
République

Pl du
Boulingrin

Blvd Lundy

To Ave Jean Jaurès;
N51; Charleville-
Mézières (83km)

R. de Courcelles

Blvd Joffre

Esplandade du
Colonel Boulmez

Blvd Foch

R. du
Temple

R. du Mars

R. Linguet

Train
Station

R. de Vernouillet

R. Clairmarais

R. de St-Brice

Blvd Louis Roederer

Square
Colbert

R. de
Trelon

R. de la
Trentelle

R. de
Sarrail

R. Thiers

Hôtel de
Ville

Pl de l'Hôtel
de Ville

R. Jean-Jacques

R. Courmeaux

Rousseau Pl
Aristide
Briand

R. de Trianon

R. Tarbé

R. du
Colonel

Blvd Général Leclerc

R. de Charlevoie

R. Drouet d'Erlon

R. de l'Etape

R. de Talleyrand

Cours J.B
Langlet

R. Cadan
St-Pierre

Pl du
Forum

Pl
Royale

R. Céres

Blvd de la Paix

To Paris
(142km)

Le
Cirque

Merry Go
Round

Fountain

R. Buirette

R. de Condorcet

Théâtre
Bus Hub

R. Carnot

R Guillaume
de Machault

R de Vesle

R. Jeanne d'Arc

R. du Thillois

R. de Chanzy

Centre des
Congrès
(Convention
Centre)

To N31;
Soissons
(57km)

R. de la
Magdelaine

R. de Vesle

R. de Clovis

R. Libergier

R. Hincmar

R. Chanzy

R. Brûlée

To Le Tigre (700m); Musée
d'Automobiles (1.2km); Taittinger
(1.4km); Pommery (1.6km);
N44; A4; Épernay (25km);
Châlons-en-Champagne
(Châlons-sur-Marne; 42km)

R. du Colonel Fabien

La Comédie
Parc Léo
Lagrange

A4 Autoroute

Av. du Général de Gaulle

R. de Clovis

Synagogue
(1879)

To Ancienne Collège des
Jésuites (500m); Basilique
St-Rémi (1km); Musée
St-Rémi (1km); Fort de
la Pompelle (5km)

To D980; Route
Touristique du Champagne

R. de Vesle

R. Capucins

R. Voltaire

Blvd Gambetta

LP

Mon-Sat, 11am-4pm Sun & holidays mid-Oct–early Apr) Has an Internet post that runs on a France Télécom *télécarte*.

Churches & Museums

Imagine the pomp, the extravagance, the over-the-top costumes and the egos writ large of a French royal coronation. For centuries, the focal point of such affairs was Reims' **Cathédrale Notre Dame** (☿ approx 7.30am–7.30pm, closed during Sun morning Mass), a Gothic edifice begun in 1211 – on a site occupied by churches since the 5th century – and mostly completed a century later.

The most famous event in the cathedral's history was the coronation of Charles VII – with Joan of Arc at his side – on 17 July 1429. Very badly damaged (like the whole city) by artillery and fire during WWI, it was restored with funds donated largely by John D Rockefeller; reconsecration took place in 1938, just in time for the next world war.

The 138m-long cathedral is more interesting for its dramatic history than for its heavily restored architectural features. The finest stained-glass windows are the western façade's 12-petalled **great rose window**, its smaller downstairs neighbour, and the rose window in the north transept arm, above the Flamboyant Gothic organ case (15th and 18th centuries). Nearby is a 15th-century **astronomical clock**. There's a window by Chagall in the axial chapel (behind the high altar) and, two chapels to the left, a statue of Joan of Arc.

The hearty might want to climb to the **cathedral roof** (adult €4.60, incl Musée du Tau €7.50; ☿ Tue-Sat & Sun afternoon early May-early Sep, Sat & Sun afternoon mid-Mar–early May & early Sep-Oct) on a one hour tour – the Palais du Tau has details.

Palais du Tau (☎ 03 26 47 81 79; adult/18-25 yrs/under 18 €6.10/4.10/free; ☿ 9.30am-6.30pm Tue-Sun early May-early Sep, 9.30am-12.30pm & 2-5.30pm Tue-Sun early Sep-early May), a former archbishop's residence constructed in 1690, was where French princes stayed right before their coronations – and where they played host to a sumptuous banquet right afterwards. Now a museum, it displays truly exceptional statues, ritual objects and tapestries from the cathedral, some in the impressive Salle du Tau.

Way back in the AD 400s, Bishop Remigius baptised Clovis and 3000 Frank-

ish warriors; 121m-long **Basilique St-Rémi** (place St-Rémi) is named in his honour. Once a Benedictine abbey church and now a Unesco World Heritage Site (along with the cathedral and the Palais du Tau), its Romanesque nave and transept – worn but stunning – date mainly from the mid-11th century. The choir (constructed between 1162 and 1190) is in the early Gothic style, with a large triforium gallery and, way up top, tiny clerestory windows. The 12th-century-style chandelier has 96 candles, one for each year of the life of St-Rémi, whose tomb (in the choir) is marked by a mausoleum from the mid-1600s.

An **evocation lumière** (a sort of sound & light show; admission free) takes place inside at 9.30pm on Saturday from July to September. The basilica is about 1.5km southeast of the tourist office; to get there by bus take the Citadine 1 or 2 lines to St-Rémi.

Just 100m from the western façade of Basilique St-Rémi, **Musée St-Rémi** (☎ 03 26 85 23 36; 53 rue Simon; ☿ 2-6.30pm Mon-Fri, 2-7pm Sat & Sun) displays archaeological items, tapestries and 16th- to 19th-century weapons.

Musée-Hôtel Le Vergeur (☎ 03 26 47 20 75; 36 place du Forum; adult/student/10-18 yrs €3.90/2.80/1; ☿ tours begin 2-5pm or 5.30pm Tue-Sun, also at 10am Tue-Fri Jun-Aug), in a 13th- to 16th-century town house, displays some lovely furniture and art objects.

About 1.5km southeast of the cathedral, the **Musée d'Automobiles** (☎ 03 26 82 83 84; 84 av Georges Clemenceau; adult/student/6-10 yrs/family of 4 €5/4/2.50/15; ☿ 10am-noon & 2-6pm Wed-Mon) displays 140 motor vehicles from the 1920s to the 1970s. To get there by public transport, take bus D to the Boussinesq stop.

WWII IN EUROPE ENDED IN REIMS

Nazi Germany capitulated on 7 May 1945 in US General Dwight D Eisenhower's war room (another surrender document was signed two days later near Berlin), now a museum known as the **Musée de la Reddition** (Surrender Museum; ☎ 03 26 47 84 19; 12 rue Franklin Roosevelt; ☿ 10am-noon & 2-6pm Wed-Mon).

The original Allied battle maps are still affixed to the walls of the one-time technical college, now known as Lycée Franklin Roosevelt. Signs are in French.

CHAMPAGNE

Other Sights

Reims' main nightlife can be found at **place Drouet d'Erlon**, a huge pedestrianised square with runway lights, almost as much neon as Times Square and dozens of places to eat and drink. Southeast of the **fountain** – crowned by a gilded statue of Winged Victory – is a covered **shopping arcade**. At rue Condorcet, the 12th- to 14th-century **Église St-Jacques** has some pretty awful post-war stained glass.

The handsome **place Royale**, surrounded by neoclassical arcades, reflects the magnificence of Louis XV's France (that's him on the pedestal).

Relics of the Roman period include **Porte de Mars** (place de la République), a Roman triumphal arch from the 3rd century AD and the **Cryptoportique** (place du Forum; admission free; ♥ 2–5pm Tue–Sun mid-Jun–mid-Sep), a 3rd-century Roman gallery that was apparently used for grain storage.

Champagne Cellars

The musty *caves* (cellars) and dusty bottles of about a dozen Reims-area champagne houses can be visited on guided tours. The following places all have fancy websites, cellar temperatures of 8°C to 10°C and offer frequent English-language tours that end with a tasting session. For details of the champagne production process see p72.

The headquarters of the **Taittinger** (☎ 03 26 85 84 33; www.taittinger.com; 9 place St-Nicaise; tours adult/under 12 €7/free) empire is 1.5km southeast of the cathedral. It is an excellent place to come for a clear, straightforward presentation on how champagne is actually made – no clap-trap about 'the champagne mystique' here! On the one-hour tours visitors are shown everything from *remuage* (bottle turning) to *dégorgement* (sediment removal at -25°C) to the corking machines. Parts of the cellars occupy 4th-century Roman stone quarries; other bits were made by 13th-century Benedic-

tine monks. For €270 you can purchase a 6L Mathusalem, though for a really big bash you'll surely want a Nabuchodonosor (15L) – and a Bible to figure out why oversized champagne bottles have such bizarre names! Tours begin from 9.30am to 11.45am and 2pm to 4.20pm (closed on weekends from December to mid-March).

Mumm (pronounced moom; ☎ 03 26 49 59 70; www .mumm.com; 34 rue du Champ de Mars; tours adult/under 16 €7/free) was founded in 1827 and is now the world's third-largest producer (eight million bottles a year). Mumm offers edifying, one-hour cellar tours – completely revamped in 2004 – that end with a *flûte* of Cordon Rouge. They run from 9am to 11am and 2pm to 5pm from March to October, and also take place on weekend and holiday afternoons – and (if you reserve in advance) from Monday to Friday – from November to February. A tasting session with oenological commentary is available for €13/18 for two/three champagnes.

Pommery (☎ 03 26 61 62 55; www.pommery.com; 5 place du Général Gouraud; tours adult/student/under 12 €7.50/6/free) is located in an Elizabethanstyle hilltop campus (built 1868–78) 1.8km southeast of the cathedral, Pommery has cellar tours that take you 30m underground to Gallo-Roman quarries and 25 million bottles of bubbly; they operate from 10am to 5pm (to 4pm or 4.30pm from mid-November to March). Weekends can get crowded so phoning ahead is a good idea. The complex often hosts contemporary art exhibitions.

Tours

Mumm (see above) arranges **vineyard visits** (per person €25; ♥ Mar–Oct) by six-person minibus; reserve in advance.

The tourist office offers a self-guided tour of the cathedral and the city centre (about €8 for one or two people) and English-language guided tours of the cathedral (in summer, around 2.30pm).

Festivals & Events
In June, the six-day **Les Sacres du Folklore**, one of northern France's most colourful folk festivals, takes place concurrently with **Les Fêtes Johanniques**, an over-the-weekend medieval celebration that re-enacts Joan of Arc's arrival in Reims.

From July to early August, **Les Flâneries Musicales d'Été** brings over 100 concerts (most of them free) to historic venues all over town.

Sleeping
The city centre offers a wide range of good-value accommodation options.

BUDGET
Centre International de Séjour (CIS; ☎ 03 26 40 52 60; www.cis-reims.com; chaussée Bocquaine; dm in a 2- or 3–5-bed room €12/11, with shower & toilet €16/13, s €28; ☺ 24hr; ▫) The 189 rooms are institutional, brightly painted and have not a drop of charm – but the friendly atmosphere more than makes up for it. A great place to meet people! To get there take bus B, K, M or N to the Comédie stop or bus H to the Pont de Gaulle stop.

Hôtel Alsace (☎ 03 26 47 44 08; fax 03 26 47 44 52; 6 rue du Général Sarrail; s/d/tr with shower from €26/29/34, with shower & toilet €29/32/37) Run by the friendly son of a Yorkshireman who married a Frenchwoman during the war, this 24-room place has large rooms that are being redecorated as we go to press. In winter reception is closed on Sunday afternoon – call ahead if you'll be arriving then.

Hôtel Au Bon Accueil (☎ 03 26 88 55 74; fax 03 26 05 12 38; 31 rue de Thillois; s from €22, d with shower & toilet €35) This place almost (but not quite) lives up to its name, but it does offer clean, eminently serviceable rooms. Hall showers cost €1.50.

MID-RANGE
There are a number of two- and three-star hotels at place Drouet d'Erlon and along adjacent rue Buirette.

Hôtel de la Cathédrale (☎ 03 26 47 28 46; fax 03 26 88 65 81; 20 rue Libergier; d/q from €56/77) Charm, graciousness – and some very shiny brass, lovingly polished – greet guests at this family-run two-star place, whose tasteful rooms have high ceilings.

Grand Hôtel du Nord (☎ 03 26 47 39 03; www.hotel-reims.com; 75 place Drouet d'Erlon; d from €55) Has a sunny breakfast room and cheerful, upbeat rooms, some with views of the square.

Grand Hôtel de l'Univers (☎ 03 26 88 68 08; hotel-univers@ebc.net; 41 blvd Foch; d from €68, Nov–mid-Mar from €62.50) This venerable three-star place has large rooms, tastefully appointed, with high ceilings, bathrooms with space to move around and odd plastic keys.

Eating
Place Drouet d'Erlon is lined with pizzerias, brasseries, cafés, pubs and sandwich places.

FRENCH
The restaurant attached to the **Hôtel Alsace** (see left; 3-course menu €9.90; ☺ lunch Mon-Sat) has one of the best midday deals in town.

Le Continental (☎ 03 26 47 01 47; 95 place Drouet d'Erlon; menus, some with wine €18.50-36; ☺ noon-2.30pm & 7-11pm or later) Built in the early 20th century, this marble-floored place serves up panoramic views and classic French dishes such as *magret de canard* (fillet of duck breast); seafood is the speciality from September to May. The tablecloths are very pink.

Brasserie Le Boulingrin (☎ 03 26 40 96 22; 48 rue de Mars; menus €16-23; ☺ Mon-Sat) Offers a mini-trip back in time with original 1920s décor, including an old-time zinc bar. The culinary focus is on meat and fish.

OTHER
Il Colosseo (☎ 03 26 47 68 50; 9 rue de Thillois; ☺ 11.30am-2.30pm & 6.30-11.30pm Tue-Sat) Reached through a dilapidated – one could even say decadent – Art Nouveau theatre façade, this place serves pizzas and pastas (€7.70 to €11.50) as well as salads (€8 to €10.50).

The Glue Pot (☎ 03 26 47 36 46; 49 place Drouet d'Erlon; ☺ 10am-3am, meals served noon-2.30pm & 7-11pm, until 1.30am Fri & Sat nights) An eatery that

---

AUTHOR'S CHOICE

L'Apostrophe (☎ 03 26 79 19 89; 59 place Drouet d'Erlon; 2-course weekday menu €13, salads €11-14, mains €12.50-23) This bustling café-brasserie serves generous portions of very French intellectual pretension (the walls are lined with books!) – and some mean cocktails – along with its very international cuisine. Don't feel you have to discuss metaphysics, though: the arty types and local literary figures who flock here are more interested in the chic atmosphere, summertime terrace and good value.

only the French genius for eclecticism could have created: this Irish pub doubles as a Tex-Mex restaurant (*fajitas* are €13.60, *quesadillas au chèvre* €13.15) that serves burgers (the Big Boy has an egg on top) and pizzas (€6.60 to €9.90) to patrons seated on bright red banquettes. Believe it or not, the food is pretty good!

SELF-CATERING
Facing the cathedral's western front, a bunch of **shops** sell champagne. Fresh food choices include the **food market** (place du Boulingrin; ⏰ until 1.30pm Wed) and **Monoprix Supermarket** (21 rue de Chativesle; ⏰ 9am-8pm Mon-Sat).

Drinking
Terraced brasseries and cafés line brightly lit place Drouet d'Erlon, the focal point of Reims' nightlife; some places stay open till 3am. *Les Rendez-Vous,* a free guide published each Wednesday, lists concerts and other cultural events.

Waïda (☎ 03 26 47 44 49; 5 place Drouet d'Erlon; ⏰ 7.30am-7.30pm Tue-Sat, 7.30am-1pm & 3.30-7pm Sun) An old-fashioned patisserie with mirrors, mosaics and marble from 1960.

Le Lion de Belfort (☎ 03 26 47 48 17; 37 place Drouet d'Erlon; ⏰ 7am-3am) This quintessentially French café-bar is, oddly, outfitted with tea-related British colonial memorabilia.

Carpe Diem (☎ 03 26 02 00 41; http://lecarpediem .free.fr in French; 6 rue des Capucins; ⏰ from 9pm) This gay, bi and transsexual bar, situated above a kebab place, flies its rainbow flags proudly and has frequent theme nights.

Le Tigre (☎ 03 26 82 64 00; 2bis av Georges Clemenceau; ⏰ 5pm-4am Mon-Thu, 5pm-5am Fri & Sat, weekends only Aug) Funky, sprawling and student-oriented, this bar-disco is about 1km east of the cathedral, has live rock and reggae bands (€5) on Friday and Saturday starting at 9pm (but not in July and August). At 11pm from Thursday to Saturday, Le Tigre becomes a disco (Thursday free, Friday and Saturday €6).

Getting There & Away
BUS
The best way to get to Troyes (€19.70, 1¾ to 2¼ hours, three or four daily weekdays, two on Saturday, one on Sunday except during university breaks, none on holidays) is to take a bus operated by **TransChampagne** (STDM; ☎ 03 26 65 17 07). The stop is next to the train station; hours are posted.

CAR
Rental companies with offices facing the train station car park:
ADA (☎ 03 26 50 08 40)
Loc Vel (☎ 03 26 40 43 38)
Rent-a-Car Système (☎ 03 26 77 87 77)

TRAIN
Reims' train station is on the secondary Paris–Longwy line. Destinations with direct services include Épernay (€5.20, 21 to 45 minutes, 23 daily weekdays, 14 daily weekends), Laon (€7.70, 40 minutes, eight daily Monday to Friday, three or four daily Saturday and Sunday) and Paris' Gare de l'Est (€20.30, 1¾ hours, 12 to 16 daily).

In the city centre, information and tickets are available at the **Boutique SNCF** (1 cours JB Langlet; ⏰ 10am-7pm Mon-Sat).

Getting Around
BICYCLE
The **Centre International de Séjour** (see p329) rents city bikes to the public for €10/15 for a half/whole day.

BUS
The local bus company is **TUR** (☎ 03 26 88 25 38; office at 6 rue Chanzy; ⏰ closed Sun & holidays). Two circular lines, Citadine 1 and Citadine 2 (single ticket €0.80), serve most of the sights mentioned in this section. Most lines begin their last runs at about 8.50pm.

PARKING
Just east of the train station, the car park at esplanade du Colonel Bouchez is unmetered (at least it was at the time of writing). There's plenty of free parking north and northwest of the train tracks.

TAXI
For a taxi, call ☎ 03 26 47 05 05.

FLIGHT OF THE HUMBLED KING

Louis XVI's attempt to escape from Paris in 1791 ended at **Ste-Ménehould** (pronounced Saint Menoo), 79km east of Reims, when the soon-to-be-beheaded monarch and Marie-Antoinette were recognised by the postmaster thanks to the king's portrait printed on a banknote.

AROUND REIMS

The **Route Touristique du Champagne** (Champagne Route) weaves its way among neatly tended vines covering the slopes between small villages, some with notable churches or speciality museums, some quite ordinary. All along the route, beautiful panoramas abound and small-scale *producteurs* (champagne producers) welcome travellers in search of bubbly; many are closed during the *vendange* (grape harvest), ie September and into October. Tourist offices can supply you with an excellent colour-coded booklet, *The Sparkling Vineyards*, which lists up-to-date addresses, emails and websites. In this region you must phone before stopping by.

The signposted tertiary roads that make up the Champagne Route – 600km in all, divided into six circuits – meander through the Marne's three most important wine-growing areas:

- **Montagne de Reims** – between Reims and Épernay
- **Côte des Blancs** – south of Épernay towards Sézanne
- **Vallée de la Marne** – west of Épernay towards Dormans and Château Thierry

For details on the Côte des Bar region, see p340.

Hautvillers

Three centuries ago it was in this tidy and conspicuously prosperous village (population 860), 7km north of Épernay, that Dom Pérignon created champagne as we know it. His tomb is next the altar of the **Église Abbatiale** (abbey church), which has lots of 17th-century woodwork; the abbey itself was burnt down by the English during the Hundred Years' War. Great vineyard views await a few hundred metres north of the centre along route de Fismes (D386); and south along route de Cumières (a road leading to the D1). Hautvillers is twinned with Eguisheim in Alsace, which may help explain why two **storks** live in a cage 800m towards Épernay along the D386.

Details on the village and region are available at the **tourist office** (☎ 03 26 57 06 35; www.ccgvm.com in French; place de la République; ⏰ 9.30am-1pm & 1.30-6pm Mon-Sat, 10am-5pm Sun mid-Apr–Oct, 10am-noon & 2-5pm Mon-Sat Nov–mid-Apr, 11am-4pm Sun Nov & mid-Mar–mid-Apr).

Parc Naturel Régional de la Montagne de Reims

The section of the Route Touristique nearest Reims skirts the Montagne de Reims Regional Park, endowed with lush forests and a botanical curiosity, the mutant beech trees known as **faux de Verzy** (see above). To get to the faux from the village of Verzy, follow the signs up the D34; the first trees can be seen about 1km from 'Les Faux' car park.

Across the D34, a short trail leads through the forest to the *point de vue* (panoramic viewpoint) atop 288m-high **Mont Sinaï**. Visitors are asked to refrain from worshipping golden calves, roasting marshmallows over the burning bush and doing impious impressions of Charlton Heston.

ÉPERNAY
pop 26,000

Épernay, a well-to-do provincial town 25km south of Reims, is home to some of the world's most famous champagne houses. Beneath the streets in some 100km of subterranean cellars, 200 million of bottles of champagne, just waiting to be popped open for some sparkling celebration, are being aged. In 1950, one such cellar – owned by

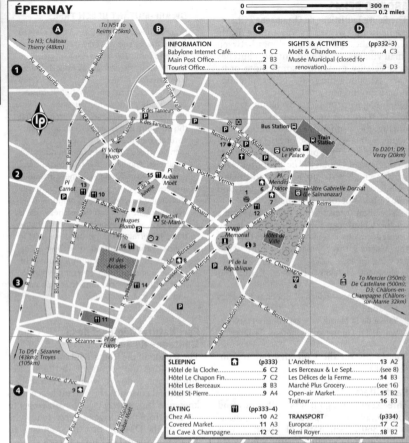

ÉPERNAY

0 — 300 m
0 — 0.2 miles

INFORMATION
Babylone Internet Café...................1 C2
Main Post Office............................2 B3
Tourist Office................................3 C3

SIGHTS & ACTIVITIES (pp332–3)
Moët & Chandon...........................4 C3
Musée Municipal (closed for
   renovation)................................5 D3

To N51 to Reims (25km)
To N3; Château Thierry (48km)
Av Jean Jaurès
R de Bréban
R des Tanneurs
R des Tanneurs
Bus Station
Train Station
To D201; D9; Verzy (20km)
R Pasteur
Av Jean Jaurès
PI Victor Hugo
Rempart
17
Blvd de la Motte
Cinéma Le Palace
R du Docteur Verron
PI Auban Moët
15
PI Mendès-France
6
Théâtre Gabrielle Dorziat (le Salmanazar)
R de Reims
PI Carnot
13
10
R du Paulmier
18
R Flodoard
7
12
R Gambetta
R de la Juvence
R de la Fauvette
PI Hugues Plomb
Portail St-Martin
2
R Professeur Langevin
16
R Jean Moët
WWII Memorial
3
Hôtel de Ville
R Pupin
PI des Arcades
8
R Cuisine
R Eugène Mercier
PI de la République
Av de Champagne
R de Berceaux
14
5
To Mercier (350m); De Castellane (500m); D3; Châlons-en-Champagne (Châlons-sur-Marne 32km)
Blvd du Cubry
Blvd Léger Bertin
11
R Jean Chandon-Moët
R de Bernon
R de Sézanne
PI de l'Europe
To D51; Sézanne (43km); Troyes (105km)
R Jeanne d'Arc
9
Av Paul Chandon
R des Hôtels Auban Moët

SLEEPING (p333)
Hôtel de la Cloche..........................6 C2
Hôtel Le Chapon Fin.......................7 C2
Hôtel Les Berceaux.........................8 B3
Hôtel St-Pierre...............................9 A4

EATING (pp333–4)
Chez Ali......................................10 A2
Covered Market...........................11 A3
La Cave à Champagne..................12 C2

L'Ancêtre....................................13 A2
Les Berceaux & Le Sept...........(see 8)
Les Délices de la Ferme................14 B3
Marché Plus Grocery................(see 16)
Open-air Market.........................15 B2
Traiteur......................................16 B3

TRANSPORT (p334)
Europcar....................................17 C2
Rémi Royer.................................18 B2

the irrepressible Mercier – hosted a car rally without the loss of a single bottle!

The town, set amid the gentle, vineyard-covered slopes of the Marne Valley, is the best place in Champagne to tour cellars and sample fizzy wine. It can easily be visited as a day trip from Reims – or even Paris.

Orientation

Mansion-lined av de Champagne, where many of Épernay's champagne houses are based, stretches east from the town's commercial heart (around place des Arcades), whose liveliest streets are rue Général Leclerc and rue St-Thibault. The area south of place de la République is given over to car parks.

Information

Babylone Internet Café (☎ 03 26 55 96 44; 25 rue Gambetta; per hr €4; ⏰ noon-10pm Tue-Thu, noon-1am Fri & Sat, 3-10pm Sun)

Main Post Office (place Hugues Plomb; ⏰ 8am-7pm Mon-Fri, 8am-noon Sat) Has currency exchange and a Cyberposte.

Tourist Office (☎ 03 26 53 33 00; www.ot-epernay.fr; 7 av de Champagne; ⏰ 9.30am-12.30pm & 1.30-7pm Mon-Sat, 11am-4pm Sun & holidays mid-Apr–mid-Oct, 9.30am-12.30pm & 1.30-5.30pm Mon-Sat mid-Oct–mid-Apr) Has details on activities in the region, including cellar visits and options for walking and cycling.

Champagne Houses

Épernay's champagne houses cannot be accused of cowering behind excessive modesty or aristocratic understatement. When it comes to PR for brand-name bubbly, dignified razzle-dazzle is the name of the game. Many of the well-touristed *maisons* on or near av de Champagne offer interesting, informative tours, followed by tasting and a visit to the factory-outlet bubbly shop. For details on the champagne production process, see p72).

The prestigious **Moët & Chandon** (☎ 03 26 51 20 20; www.moet.com; adult/12-16 yrs €7.50/4.50; 18 av de Champagne) produces more champagne (25 to 30 million bottles a year) than anyone else and offers one-hour tours that are among the region's most impressive. They depart every 10 or 20 minutes from 9.30am to 11.30am and 2pm to 4.30pm (closed weekends from mid-November to mid-March). Super-premium Dom Perignon will set you back at least €94 a bottle; a 1962 vintage is a bargain at €650.

The 45-minute tours at **De Castellane** (☎ 03 26 51 19 19; www.castellane.com in French; 64 av de Champagne; adult/10-18 yrs €6/4.50) take in the *maison's* informative bubbly **museum**, dedicated to elucidating the *méthode champenoise* and its diverse technologies. The reward for climbing the 237 steps up the 60m tower: a panoramic view. Tours run from 10.30am to 11.15am and 2.30pm to 5.15pm, April to November.

Mercier (☎ 03 26 51 22 22; www.champagnemercier.com; 68-70 av de Champagne; adult/12-15 yrs €6.50/3; ☯ mid-Jan–about 20 Dec, closed Tue & Wed except mid-Mar–mid-Nov), the most popular brand in France (and No 2 in overall production), has thrived on unabashed self-promotion since it was founded in 1847 by Eugène Mercier, a trailblazer in the field of eye-catching publicity stunts and the virtual creator of the cellar tour. Everything here is flashy, including the 160,000L barrel that took two decades to build (for the Universal Exposition of 1889) and the lift that transports you 30m underground to a laser-guided train that gets confused by forward-facing camera flashes and has been known to veer into the bottles that line its route. There are entertaining 45-minute tours from 9.30am to 11.30am and 2pm to 4.30pm.

Vineyard Tour
Champagne Domi Moreau (☎ 06 30 35 51 07 or after 6.30pm 03 26 59 45 85; www.champagne-domimoreau.com; adult €20; departures 9.30am &/or 2.30pm except

Wed & during the 2nd half of Aug, the Christmas period & Feb school holidays) runs three-hour minibus tours to nearby vineyards. Pick-up is across the street from the tourist office. Call ahead for reservations.

Sleeping
Épernay's hotels are especially full on weekends from Easter to September and on weekdays in May, June and September.

Hôtel St-Pierre (☎ 03 26 54 40 80; fax 03 26 57 88 68; 1 rue Jeanne d'Arc; s/d from €21/24, d with shower & toilet from €34; P) Occupying an early-20th-century mansion that has hardly changed in half a century, this place has simple rooms that retain the charm and atmosphere of yesteryear. Reception *may* be closed on Sunday from 2pm to 6pm.

Hôtel Les Berceaux (☎ 03 26 55 28 84; les.berceaux@wanadoo.fr; 13 rue des Berceaux; d €66-75) The rooms of this three-star institution, founded in 1889, are endowed with a certain Champenoise ambience.

Hôtel de la Cloche (☎ 03 26 55 15 15; hotel-de-la-cloche.c.prin@wanadoo.fr; 5 place Mendès-France; d from €39) Has two stars and 19 cheerful, pastel rooms.

Hôtel Le Chapon Fin (☎ 03 26 55 40 03; fax 03 26 54 94 17; 2 place Mendès-France, d €34) The rooms are plain but perfectly serviceable; the floors are not linoleum, we're told, but imitation wood.

Eating
Rue Gambetta is home to four pizzerias.

L'Ancêtre (☎ 03 26 55 57 56; 20 rue de la Fauvette; menus €15.50-29; ☯ closed Tue, Wed lunch & in Jul) An intimate, country-style eatery with traditional French cuisine and just six tables.

La Cave à Champagne (☎ 03 26 55 50 70; 16 rue Gambetta; menus €14.50-28; ☑ Thu-Tue) Designed to look like a wine cellar, this place specialises in Champenoise cuisine.

Chez Ali (☎ 03 26 51 80 82; 27 rue de la Fauvette; menus €12-18.50; ☑ closed Mon & dinner Sun) Serves up steaming Algerian couscous.

The venerable **Hôtel Les Berceaux** (see p333) has two in-house eateries. **Les Berceaux** (weekday menu with/without wine €38/28, other menus €46 & €61; ☑ Wed-Sun) is a sparklingly elegant *gastronomique* restaurant. As we went to press the staff was in mourning over having lost their Michelin star (one of the authors made the unpardonable faux pas of asking about it) but we're betting that the shock and humiliation will inspire them to try even harder. **Le Sept** (menus €16-22) is a more popularly priced place with traditional French cuisine.

SELF-CATERING
Fresh food is abundant at the **covered market** (Halle St-Thibault; rue Gallice; ☑ 8am-noon Wed & Sat) and the modest **open-air Market** (place Auban Moët; ☑ Sun morning).

Traiteur (9 place Hugues Plomb; ☑ 8am-12.45pm & 3-7.30pm except Sun & Wed) sells scrumptious prepared dishes and **Les Délices de la Ferme** (19 rue St-Thibault; ☑ approximately 9am-noon & 3-7pm Tue-Sat) has wonderful cheeses.

Another option is **Marché Plus Grocery** (13 place Hugues Plomb; ☑ 7am-9pm Mon-Sat, 9am-1pm Sun).

Getting There & Around
The **train station** (place Mendès-France) has direct services to Nancy (€23.80, two hours, four or five daily), Reims (€5.20, 21 to 45 minutes, 23 daily weekdays, 14 daily weekends) and Paris' Gare de l'Est (€17.50, 1¼ hours, 10 to 16 daily).

Cars can be hired from **Europcar** (☎ 03 26 54 90 61; 20 rempart Perrier).

Parking in the lots south of place de la République is free for the first hour and costs about €1.50 per hour after that.

Mountain bikes can be rented from **Rémi Royer** (☎ 03 26 55 29 61; 10 place Hugues Plomb; half-/whole day €10/17; ☑ 9am-noon & 2-7pm Tue-Sat). The tourist office sells cycling maps.

TROYES
pop 123,000
Troyes – like Reims, one of the historic capitals of Champagne – has a lively old city that is graced with one of France's fin-

est ensembles of medieval and Renaissance half-timbered houses. It is thus one of the best places in France to get a sense of what Europe looked like back when William Shakespeare was alive. Several unique and very worthwhile museums and a number of ancient churches provide further reasons to spend some time here.

Troyes does not have any champagne cellars. However, you can shop till you drop in its scores of outlet stores specialising in brand-name clothing and accessories.

Orientation
Although Troyes hardly benefits from the champagne trade, the medieval city centre– bounded by blvd Gambetta, blvd Victor Hugo, blvd du 14 Juillet and the Seine – is, ironically, shaped like a champagne cork *(bouchon)*. The main commercial street is rue Émile Zola. Most of the city's sights and activities are in the old city, centred on the 17th-century town hall and Église St-Jean.

Information
INTERNET ACCESS
Open Games Cybercafé (☎ 03 25 41 58 71; 24 rue Claude Huez; per hr €2.80; ☑ 2-10pm Mon, 11am-10pm Tue-Thu, 11am-midnight Fri & Sat, 2-8pm Sun) You can order a *really* tacky tombstone down the block at No 14.

LAUNDRY
Laundrette (9 rue Georges Clemenceau; ☑ 7am-8pm) Duds meet suds in a gripping contest of wills.

MONEY
The tourist office annexe changes money when the banks are closed but the rate is poor.
BNP Bank (53 rue Général de Gaulle, ☑ 8.30am-12.15pm & 1.30-6pm)

PASS' TROYES

This new discount pass (€12), on sale at the tourist office and (oddly) packaged differently for men and women, is a great deal. Among its benefits: free entry to all five of the old city's museums; a champagne tasting session; a guided or audioguided tour of the old city; a horse-drawn carriage ride (in summer); and discounts at various factory outlet shops.

TROYES

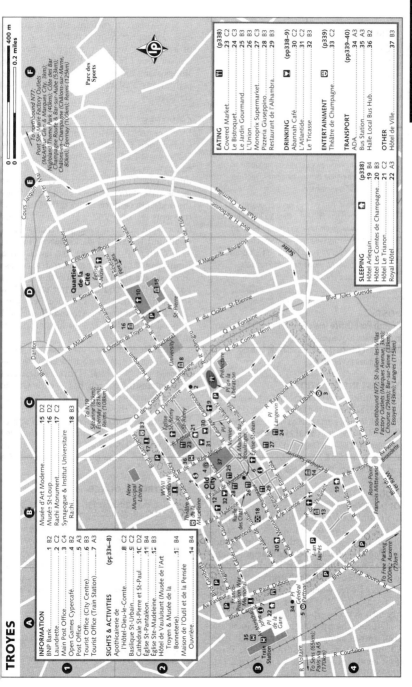

INFORMATION
BNP Bank.................................1 B2
Laundrette................................2 C2
Main Post Office.........................3 C4
Open Games Cypercafé...............4 B2
Post Office.................................5 A3
Tourist Office (City Centre)..........6 B3
Tourist Office (Train Station)........7 A3

Musée d'Art Moderne................15 D2
Musée St-Loup..........................16 D2
Rachi Monument........................17 C2
Synagogue & Institut Universitaire
Rachi...................................18 B3

SIGHTS & ACTIVITIES   (pp334–8)
Apothicairerie de
l'Hôtel-Dieu-le-Comte................8 C2
Basilique St-Urbain....................9 C2
Cathédrale St-Pierre et St-Paul....10 D2
Église St-Pantaléon..................11 B4
Église Ste-Madeleine.................12 B3
Hôtel de Vauluisant (Musée de l'Art
Troyen & Musée de la
Bonneterie)..........................13 B4
Maison de l'Outil et de la Pensée
Ouvrière...............................14 B4

EATING   (p338)
Covered Market.........................23 C2
Le Bistroquet.............................24 C3
Le Jardin Gourmand....................25 B3
L'Union....................................26 B3
Monoprix Supermarket................27 C3
Pizzeria Giuseppino....................28 B3
Restaurant de l'Alhambra.............29 B3

DRINKING   (pp338–9)
Abannah Café...........................30 C2
L'Atlantide................................31 C2
Le Tricasse...............................32 B3

ENTERTAINMENT   (p339)
Théâtre de Champagne...............33 C2

TRANSPORT   (pp339–40)
ADA...34 A3
Bus Station................................35 A3
Halle Local Bus Hub....................36 B2

OTHER
Hôtel de Ville.............................37 B3

SLEEPING   (p338)
Hôtel Arlequin...........................19 B4
Hôtel Les Comtes de Champagne...20 B3
Hôtel Le Trianon.........................21 C2
Royal Hôtel...............................22 A3

0   400 m
0   0.2 miles

TROYES AND YOU

Chances are Troyes has already played a role in your life:

■ If you've ever enjoyed a story about Lancelot or King Arthur's search for the Holy Grail you owe a debt to the 12th-century poet Chrétien (Chrestien) de Troyes (http://camelot.celtic-twilight .com/chretien).

■ Every time you've purchased gold bullion (or gold jewellery) you've done so using the troy ounce or some fraction thereof (see right).

■ Whenever you've put on a Lacoste shirt (www.lacoste.fr), Petit Bateau kids clothing (www.petit-bateau.com in French) or Dim underwear (www.dim.fr in French) you've paid homage to a brand name created right here in France's knitwear capital.

POST

Branch Post Office (place Général Patton) Has currency exchange and a Cyberposte.

Main Post Office (38 rue Louis Ulbach) Exchanges currency and has a Cyberposte.

TOURIST INFORMATION

Tourist Office (www.tourisme-troyes.com) Train Station (☎ 03 25 82 62 70; 16 blvd Carnot; ☻ 9am-12.30pm & 2-6.30pm Mon-Sat except holidays year-round, 10am-1pm Sun Nov-Mar) City Centre (☎ 03 25 73 36 88; rue Mignard; ☻ 10am-7pm Jul–mid-Sep, 9am-12.30pm & 2-6.30pm Mon-Sat, 10am-noon & 2-5pm Sun & holidays May, Jun & mid-Sep–Oct) Faces the west façade of Église St-Jean.

Sights

OLD CITY

Half-timbered houses line the streets of Troyes' old city, rebuilt after a devastating fire in 1524 – streets worth exploring include **rue Paillot de Montabert**, **rue Champeaux** and **rue de Vauluisant**. An effort is being made to uncover many of the half-timbered façades plastered over when buildings were 'modernised' after WWII (for example, along recently spruced-up rue Émile Zola).

Off rue Champeaux (between No 30 and 32), a stroll along tiny **ruelle des Chats** (Alley of the Cats), as dark and narrow as it was four centuries ago, is like stepping back into the Middle Ages. You half expect a group of Shakespearean ruffians, singing drunkenly, to appear from around the corner, or a sneering wench to empty a chamber pot on your head from the top floor. The stones along the sides were installed to give pedestrians a place to stand when horses clattered by.

CHURCHES

Incorporating elements from every period of Champenois Gothic architecture, **Cathédrale St-Pierre et St-Paul** (☻ 10am-1pm & 2-6pm except Mon morning, longer hours Jul–mid-Sep) is an architectural mishmash. The Flamboyant Gothic **west façade**, part of it recently cleaned, dates from the mid-16th century, whereas the choir and transepts are over 250 years older. The interior is illuminated by a spectacular series of around 180 **stained-glass windows** (13th to 17th centuries) that shine like jewels on a sunny day. Also of some interest: a fantastical baroque **organ** (1730s) sporting musical *putti* (cherubs) and a tiny **treasury** (☻ Jul & Aug). A dramatic scene unfolded here during 1429, when Joan of Arc and Charles VII stopped by on their way to his coronation in Reims.

Église Ste-Madeleine (rue Général de Gaulle; ☻ 10am-noon & 2-5pm except Sun morning & Mon morning, longer hours Jul–mid-Sep), Troyes' oldest and most interesting church, has an early Gothic nave and transept that date from the mid-12th century; the choir and tower weren't built until the Renaissance. The main attraction is the splendid Flamboyant Gothic **rood screen**, which dates from the early 1500s. In the nave, the statue of a deadly serious **Ste**

THE TROYES OUNCE

During the 12th and 13th centuries, Troyes grew exceptionally prosperous thanks to its three-month trade fairs, which attracted artisans and merchants from as far afield as Scotland and Constantinople. The fairs' *bureaux de change* were kept very busy exchanging ducats for dinars and crowns for pounds, and the standards of measurement that were established eventually spread throughout Europe and the entire world. That's why, to this day, precious metals such as gold and silver are measured in units known as troy weight (one pound equals 12 troy ounces, one troy ounce equals 31.1g).

CHAMPAGNE

Marthe (St Martha), around the pillar from the wooden pulpit, is considered a masterpiece of the 15th-century Troyes School.

Other churches worth a visit include **Église St-Pantaléon** (rue de Turenne; ⊙ same as Église Ste-Madeleine). Built from 1508 to 1672 in the Renaissance-style on the former site of a synagogue. The interior is decorated with dozens of 16th-century statues, most of them carved locally.

Basilique St-Urbain (place Vernier; ⊙ same as Église Ste-Madeleine) is a Gothic structure begun in 1262 by Pope Urban IV, who was born in Troyes and whose father's shoemaker shop once stood on this spot. It has some fine 13th-century stained-glass windows. In the choir is *La Vierge au Raisin*, a graceful early-15th-century stone statue of the Virgin.

MUSEUMS
Centuries-old hand tools, worn to a sensuous lustre by generations of skilled hands, bring to life a world of manual skills largely destroyed by the Industrial Revolution at the **Maison de l'Outil et de la Pensée Ouvrière** (Museum of Tools & Crafts; ☎ 03 25 73 28 26; www.maison -de-l-outil.com; 7 rue de la Trinité; adult/student €6.50/5; ⊙ 10am-6pm). A new exhibit features locksmithing. Videos show artisans at work. Run by a national crafts guild, this unique and – if you'll excuse the expression – riveting museum is housed in the magnificent Renaissance-style Hôtel de Mauroy (mid-1500s).

Musée d'Art Moderne (☎ 03 25 76 26 80; place St-Pierre; adult/student under 25 €5/free; ⊙ 11am-6pm except Mon & holidays) owes its existence to all those alligator shirts, whose global success

allowed the museum's benefactors, Lacoste entrepreneurs Pierre and Denise Lévy, to amass this outstanding collection. Housed in a one-time bishop's palace (16th to 18th centuries), the museum focuses on glass, ceramics and French painting (including lots of Fauvist works) created between 1850 and 1950. Featured artists include Derain, Dufy, Matisse, Modigliani, Picasso, Soutine and local favourite Maurice Marinot.

Musée St-Loup (☎ 03 25 76 21 68; 1 rue Chrestien de Troyes; adult/student under 25 €4/free; ⊙ 10am-noon & 2-6pm except Tue & holidays), across the street from the cathedral, has a varied and sometimes surprising collection of medieval sculpture, enamel, archaeology and natural history. The stuffed mammals and birds at the entrance give the completely wrong impression!

If you come down with an old-fashioned malady – scurvy, perhaps, or unbalanced humours – the place to go is the **Apothicairerie de l'Hôtel-Dieu-le-Comte** (☎ 03 25 80 98 97; quai des Comtes de Champagne; ⊙ irregular hours), a fully outfitted, wood-panelled pharmacy from the early 1700s.

Hôtel de Vauluisant (☎ 03 25 73 05 85; 4 rue de Vauluisant; adult/student under 25 €3/free; ⊙ 10am-noon or 1pm & 2-6pm except Tue & holidays, also closed Mon Oct-May), a haunted-looking Renaissance-style mansion-turned-museum, has two sections:
- **Musée de l'Art Troyen** (Museum of Troyes Art) Features the evocative paintings, stained glass and statuary (stone and wood) of the Troyes School, which flourished here during the economic prosperity and artistic ferment of the 1500s.

RASHI

During the 11th and 12th centuries, a small Jewish community was established in Troyes under the protection of the counts of Champagne. Its most illustrious member was Rabbi Shlomo Yitzhaki (Solomon son of Isaac; 1040–1105), better known as Rashi (Rachi in French).

Rashi's commentaries on the Bible and the Talmud, which combine literal and non-literal methods of interpretation and make extensive use of allegories and parables as well as symbolic meanings, are still vastly important to Jews; they have also had an impact on Christian Bible interpretation. Rashi's habit of explaining difficult words and passages in the local French vernacular – transliterated into Hebrew characters – has made his writings an important resource for scholars of Old French. In 1475 (a mere 30 years after Gutenberg) Rashi's Bible commentary became the first book to be printed in Hebrew.

In Troyes (pronounced 'Troysh' in Rashi's transliteration), the striking **Rachi monument** (next to the Théâtre de Champagne) stands on the site of a medieval Jewish cemetery. A local institute of Jewish studies, the **Institut Universitaire Rachi** (www.institut-rachi-troyes.com), is named in his honour. The 900th anniversary of his death will be marked with a big bash in June 2005.

CHAMPAGNE

■ **Musée de la Bonneterie** (Hosiery & Knitwear Museum) Showcases the sock-strewn story of Troyes' 19th-century knitting industry. Some of the machines on display look like enormous Swiss watches.

Festivals & Events

A celebrity musical performer helps select the theme and artists featured at the weeklong **Nuits de Champagne** (www.nuitsdechampagne.com in French), held in late October or early November.

La Ville en Musique brings music of all sorts (classical, jazz, rock, organ etc) to Troyes from late June to late August.

Sleeping

Hôtel Les Comtes de Champagne (☎ 03 25 73 11 70; www.comtesdechampagne.com; 56 rue de la Monnaie; d from €28, with shower & toilet €37; **P**) This superwelcoming place has been held up for centuries by the same massive wooden ceiling beams. A huge and very romantic double with balcony costs €60 – an excellent deal!

Royal Hôtel (☎ 03 25 73 19 99; www.royal-hotel -troyes.fr; 22 blvd Carnot; d from €70; ☒ closed for 3 weeks around New Year) This family-run hostelry has restrained rooms with bright, shiny bathrooms and the usual three-star comforts.

Hôtel Le Trianon (☎ 03 25 73 18 52; 2 rue Pithou; d from €25, with shower €34; ☒ reception 11am-8pm Mon, 6.30am-8pm Tue-Sat, 9am-1pm Sun) At this gay-friendly place the French tricolour flies proudly from the balcony, a rainbow flag next to it. The eight rooms, above a jaunty yellow bar, are spacious but ordinary.

Eating

Rue Champeaux is lined with eateries. Ethnic restaurants, cafés and student-oriented takeaways can be found just west of the cathedral along rue de la Cité.

FRENCH

Le Bistroquet (☎ 03 25 73 65 65; place Langevin; menus €16.90-26.90; ☒ closed dinner Sun, also lunch Sun mid-Jun–mid-Sep) This Parisian-style brasserie, hugely popular with locals, offers excellent French dining value. Among the specialities: *andouillette de Troyes* (chitterling sausages), not for the fainthearted but nevertheless the city's culinary pride and joy.

Le Jardin Gourmand (☎ 03 25 73 36 13; 31 rue Paillot de Montabert; menu €16.50; ☒ closed Sun & lunch Mon) Elegant without being overly formal,

this intimate eatery uses only the freshest ingredients for its French and Champenoise dishes (meat and fish). The estimable wine list includes 25 vintages available by the glass. There's a terrace in summer.

L'Union (☎ 03 25 40 35 76; 34 rue Champeaux; 2-/3-course menus €12.50/18.50; ☒ Mon-Sat) Suffused with the atmosphere of 1950s Paris – with just a touch of the classic American diner – this place serves solid brasserie-style food.

OTHER

Pizzeria Giuseppino (☎ 03 25 73 92 44; 26 rue Paillot de Montabert; pasta & pizzas €6.50-9; ☒ Tue-Sat) Troyes' best pizza – ultrathin and crispy – is on offer at this chummy student hang-out.

Restaurant de l'Alhambra (☎ 03 25 73 18 41; 31 rue Champeaux) Amid Moorish-style décor (brought over from Morocco), you can sip Algerian wines and dine on couscous (€12 to €16) and tajines.

SELF-CATERING

There is a **covered market** (☒ 8am-12.45pm & 3.30-7pm Mon-Thu, 7am-7pm Fri & Sat, 9am-12.30pm Sun) for self-caters.

The **Monoprix Supermarket** (71 rue Émile Zola; ☒ 8.30am-8pm Mon-Sat) may be the most beautiful supermarket in France – the upper floors recently got their half-timbers buffed and shined.

Drinking

Abannah Café (☎ 03 25 73 99 02; 12 rue Pithou; ☒ 2pm-3am Mon-Sat) When live bands drop by to play jazz, rock and Cuban music (two Fridays a month from about 9.30pm), patrons – a mix of students and factory workers – dance on the chairs of this vaguely Cuban-style bar, which also doubles as a Tex-Mex restaurant.

It is shirts-optional for the bar guys. There's a theme night each Thursday at 8pm. The people caricatured in the murals – drawn by one of the *serveurs* – are Abannah *habitués*. This place regularly produces champion darts teams.

Le Tricasse (☎ 03 25 73 14 80; 16 rue Paillot de Montabert; 3pm-3am Mon-Sat) For decades, revellers with bourgeois tendencies – including students, both foreign and domestic – have headed to this bar, named after a local Gallic tribe. DJs spin CDs on Friday and Saturday from 10pm (and often on Thursday, too). You can try your skill in a genteel game of pool.

L'Atlantide (☎ 03 25 73 85 83; 2 place Claude Huez; admission free Thu, €5-10 Fri-Sun; 11pm-4am or 5am Thu-Sun) Enter the rounded plate-metal entrance, walk down the stairs to the cellar and you could almost be in Berlin or Zurich. The 18-to-25 crowd – their white T-shirts fluorescing in the black light – boogie to house, techno and R&B in one vast space, while the over-25s congregate in the quieter **Privilege** enjoying the sweet sounds of the '80s and '90s. The stats: three bars, two DJs and lots of locals out to party.

Shopping

Troyes is famous across France for its **magasins d'usine** (factory outlets; generally 10am-7pm, closed most Sun, some also closed Mon until 2pm), a legacy of the local knitwear industry. Brand-name sportswear, underwear, baby clothes, shoes and so on – discontinued styles, unsold stock, returns, prototypes – attract bargain-hunters by the coachload.

Most stores are situated in two main zones:

- **St-Julien-les-Villas** – About 3km south of the city centre on blvd de Dijon (the N71

to Dijon). **Marques Avenue** (☎ 08 25 85 86 87; www.marquesavenue.com; av de la Maille) boasts 240 name brands.

- **Pont Ste Marie** – About 3km northeast of Troyes' city centre along rue Marc Verdier, which links av Jean Jaurès (the N77 to Châlons-en-Champagne) with av Jules Guesde (the D960 to Nancy). **McArthur Glen** (☎ 03 25 70 47 10; www.mcarthurglen.fr in French) is a huge strip mall with some 84 shops. Close to McArthur Glen **Marques City** (☎ 03 25 46 37 48; 35 rue Danton; www.marquescity.com in French) houses 30 more stores.

Getting There & Away

BUS

Coach services fill some of the gaping holes left by Troyes' rather pathetic rail services. The **bus station office** (☎ 03 25 71 28 42; 8.30am-12.30pm & 2-6.30pm Mon-Fri), run by Courriers de l'Aube, is in a corner of the train station building. Schedules are posted on the uprights next to each bus berth. For details on getting to Reims, see p330.

CAR

Vehicles can be rented from **ADA** (☎ 03 25 73 41 68; 2 rue Voltaire).

TRAIN

Troyes is on the rather isolated line linking Basel (Bâle) with Paris' Gare de l'Est (€19.90, 1½ hours, 13 to 15 daily). A change of trains gets you to Dijon (€24.40, 2½ to four hours, three to five daily).

Getting Around

Old-city street improvements will continue through to 2006 so there may be changes to the one-way street grid.

NIGLOLAND THEME PARK

The third most popular amusement park in France (Disneyland Resort Paris, p184, is No 1), **Nigloland** (☎ 03 25 27 94 52; www.nigloland.fr; adult/under 12 & over 60 €15.50/14; 10am-6pm or 7pm mid-Jun–Aug & during Apr school holidays, to 5.30pm or 6pm on most weekends & some weekdays May, Jun, Sep & Oct) may be even cheesier than its competitors, but the place is still a huge hit with kids, especially those aged three to 12. Homesick Americans can drop by 1950s-style **Hollywood Boulevard** and take a road trip (without autoroute tolls!) along **Route Nationale 66**, both in the **Village Rock'n'Roll**. It's not clear why there's a Caribbean pirate galleon (a giant swing), a California gold rush-style roller coaster and a paddlewheel river steamer named the *King of Mississippi* in the **Village Canadien** (Canadian Village), but you might want to mention this arrangement the next time you hear a snooty European making condescending noises about North Americans' ignorance of world geography. The park is on the N19 40km east of Troyes in Dolancourt. If you're on the A5 take exit No 22 or 23.

All city-centre parking is metered except for one free segment at the western end of blvd Gambetta. There's a large free car park a block south of blvd du 1er RAM.

TCAT (☎ 03 25 70 49 00; www.tcat.fr in French) has its main bus hub, known as Halle, next to the covered market.

To order a taxi, call ☎ 03 25 78 30 30 or ☎ 03 25 76 06 60.

CÔTE DES BAR

Although the Aube *département,* of which Troyes is the capital, is a major producer of champagne (it has 65 sq km of vineyards), it gets little of the recognition accorded the Marne *département* and the big *maisons* around Reims and Épernay. Much of the acrimony dates from 1909, when the Aube growers were excluded from the growing area for Champagne's Appellation d'Origine Contrôlée (AOC). Two years later, they were also forbidden to sell their grapes to producers up north, resulting in months of strikes and chaos; eventually the army was called in. It was another 16 years before the Aube wine growers could again display the prestigious (and lucrative) AOC tag on their labels, but by then the producers in the region's north had come to dominate the champagne market.

Today, champagne production in the southeastern corner of the Aube – about 35km southeast of Troyes and just north of Burgundy's Châtillonnais vineyards (see p459) – is relatively modest in scale, though the reputation of the area's wines has been on an upward trajectory in recent years.

The Côte des Bar section of the **Route Touristique du Champagne** (see p331) passes through **Bar-sur-Aube** (☎ tourist office 03 25 27 24 25), graced by a medieval quarter and two churches, and **Colombey-les-Deux-Églises**, Charles de Gaulle's burial place. **La Boisserie** (☎ 03 25 01 52 52; adult/under 12 €4/free, incl memorial adult/student €7/6; ☒ 10am-12.30pm & 2-6.15pm mid-Apr–mid-Oct, 10am-12.30pm & 2-4.45pm mid-Oct–Nov, 20 Dec-4 Jan & Feb–mid-Apr), the general's family home from 1934 to 1970, is now a museum and place of Gaullist pilgrimage. The 43.5m-high Lorraine cross (1972), symbol of the Resistance, was paid for by public subscription.

Also along the route is **Essoyes**, Renoir's burial place. **Maison de la Vigne** (☎ 03 25 29 64 64; ☒ 2.30-6.30pm Easter-1 Nov) has exhibits on wine-growing in Champagne. **Bayel** (☎ tourist office 03 25 92 42 68; www.bayel-cristal.com) is a village known for its long tradition of crystal-making. Tours of the **Cristalleries Royales de Champagne** (Champagne Royal Glassworks) generally begin at 9.30am and 11am Monday to Friday.

Les Riceys (☎ tourist office 03 25 29 15 38; www .les-riceys-champagne.com) is a *commune* noted for its three churches, three different AOCs and exceptional rosé wines.

Langres
pop 10,000 / elevation 466m

Langres, 75km southeast of Bar-sur-Aube and about the same distance north of Dijon, is both an elongated hilltop bastion, with six towers and seven fortified gates, and a cheese with an orangey-yellow crust. The town's most famous son is Denis Diderot (1713–84), the great encyclopaedist; his statue graces place Diderot, the main square in the centuries-old, stone town centre.

Two blocks north of place Diderot is **Cathédrale St-Mammès**, whose classical façade (1758), with its mammoth columns, hides a late-Romanesque and early-Gothic interior. The modern **Musée d'Art et d'Histoire** (☎ 03 25 87 08 05; place du Centenaire; admission free; ☒ 10am-noon & 2-5pm or 6pm Wed-Mon), two short blocks west of the cathedral, has a collection that ranges from archaeology to the local faïence, cutlery and tinware industries. Circumambulating the **ramparts** – on the inside or the outside – is a 3.5km affair.

The **tourist office** (☎ 03 25 87 67 67; office .tourisme.pays.de.langres@wanadoo.fr; square Olivier Lahalle; ☒ Mon-Sat year-round, Sun & holidays May-Sep) is next to one of the town gates, **Porte des Moulins** (1647).

The two-star, Logis de France-affiliated **Grand Hôtel de l'Europe** (☎ 03 25 87 10 88; hotel -europe.langres@wanadoo.fr; 23 rue Diderot; s/d from €45/55), in a one-time post house two blocks north of place Diderot, has rooms that boast 'bourgeois comfort'. The rustic **restaurant** (menus €14.50-46) specialises in game (in season) and dishes made with local cheese.

Langres' train station, on the flats about 3km west of the old town centre, has services to Dijon (€12.10, one hour, two to four daily), Reims (€25.70, 2½ hours, two to four daily) and Troyes (€16.90, 1¼ hours, five to seven daily). It's linked to the city centre by bus (every 60 to 90 minutes from 6.22am to 6.44pm Monday to Saturday).

Alsace & Lorraine

CONTENTS

Alsace   **343**
Strasbourg   345
Route du Vin d'Alsace   357
Colmar   362
Massif des Vosges   367
Mulhouse   369
Écomusée d'Alsace   370
Lorraine   **370**
Nancy   370
Baccarat   376
Metz   377
Fort du Hackenberg   382
Verdun   382
Verdun Battlefields   384
American Memorials   386
Fort de Fermont   386

ALSACE & LORRAINE

Though often spoken of as if they were one, Alsace and Lorraine, neighbouring regions in France's northeastern corner, are linked by little more than a common border through the Vosges Mountains and the imperial ambitions of late-19th-century Germany. In 1871, after the Franco-Prussian War, the newly created German Reich annexed Alsace and part of Lorraine, making the regions' return to rule from Paris a rallying cry of French nationalism.

The charming and beautiful region of Alsace, long a meeting place of Europe's Latin and Germanic cultures, is nestled between the Vosges Mountains and the River Rhine – along which the long-disputed Franco-German border has found a final resting place. Popularly known as a land of storks' nests and colourful half-timbered houses sprouting geraniums, Alsace also offers a wide variety of outdoor activities – including hiking, mountain biking and skiing – in and around its gentle, forested mountains. Throughout France, the people of Alsace have a reputation for being hard-working, well organised and tax-paying.

Lorraine, a region of prairies and forests popularly associated with quiche and de Gaulle's double-barred cross *(croix de Lorraine)*, has little of the picturesque quaintness of Alsace. However, it is home to two particularly handsome cities, both former capitals. Nancy, one of France's most refined and attractive cities, is famed for its Art Nouveau architecture, while Metz, 54km to the north, is a dynamic place known for its Germanic architecture and the stunning stained glass in its marvellous cathedral. The town of Verdun bears silent testimony to the destruction and insanity of WWI.

HIGHLIGHTS

- Crane your neck to see the rose-coloured spires and stained glass of Strasbourg's splendiferous **cathedral** (p349)

- Take in Nancy's supremely refined **wrought iron grillwork** (p372) and **Art-Nouveau masterpieces** (p372)

- Watch storks glide majestically above their rooftop nests in **Hunawihr** (p361), **Munster** (p368) and along the **Route du Vin d'Alsace** (p357)

- Marvel at Colmar's medieval **Issenheim Altarpiece** (p364)

- Be dazzled by the curtains of stained glass in the **Gothic cathedral** (p377) at Metz

- Gaze out on the Vosges, the Rhine, the Black Forest and the Alps from the **Grand Ballon** or the **Ballon d'Alsace** (p368)

REGIONS: ALSACE 　　　　　LORRAINE	POPULATION: 1.7 MILLION POPULATION: 2.3 MILLION	AREA: 8332 SQ KM AREA: 23,669 SQ KM

ALSACE

Alsace occupies an area 190km long and no more than 50km wide and is made up of two rival *départements:* Bas-Rhin (Lower Rhine; www.tourisme67.com in French), the area around the dynamic regional (and European) capital, Strasbourg; and Haut-Rhin (Upper Rhine; www.tourisme68.com), which covers the region's more southerly reaches, including the picturesque *département* capital, Colmar, and the industrial city of Mulhouse. Germany is just across the busy, barge-laden Rhine, whose left bank is Alsatian as far south as the Swiss city of Basel.

History

French influence in Alsace began in the 1500s during the Wars of Religion (1562–98) and increased during the Thirty Years' War (1618–48) when Alsatian cities, caught between opposing Catholic and Protestant factions, turned to France for assistance. Most of the region was attached to France in 1648 under the Treaty of Westphalia. Today one-fifth of Alsatians are Protestants.

By the time of the French Revolution, the Alsatians felt far more connected to France than to Germany, but the passage of time did little to dampen Germany's appetite for the region known in German as Elsass (Elsaß). The Franco-Prussian War of 1870–71, a supremely humiliating episode

ALSACE & LORRAINE

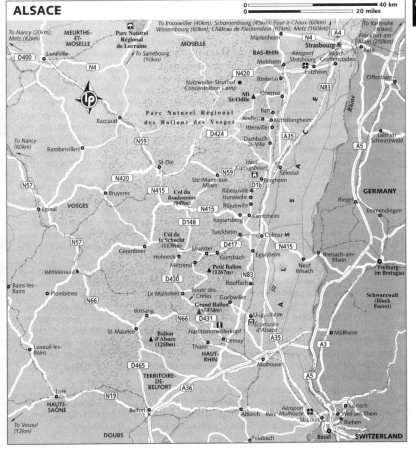

ALSACE

in French history, ended with the Treaty of Frankfurt (1871), by which an embittered France was forced to cede Alsace and the northern part of Lorraine (Lothringen) to the Second Reich.

Following Germany's defeat in WWI, Alsace and Lorraine were returned to France, but the French government's programme to reassimilate the area (eg by banning German-language newspapers) gave rise to a strong home-rule movement. These days, similar sentiments fuel support for the far-right Front National party, at 22% (in the first round of the 2004 regional elections) the highest in the country.

Germany's second annexation of Alsace and Lorraine in 1940 (and indeed the occu-pation of all of France) was supposed to have been made impossible by the state-of-the-art Maginot Line (see below). Immediately after Nazi Germany took over the area, about half a million Alsatians fled to occupied France. This time, the Germanisation campaign was particularly harsh: anyone caught speaking French was imprisoned, and even the Alsatian language was banned.

After the war, Alsace was once again returned to France. Intra-Alsatian tensions ran high, however, as those who had left came back and confronted neighbours whom they suspected of having collaborated with the Germans: 140,000 Alsatians, as annexed citizens of the Third Reich, had been conscripted into Hitler's armies. Known as the 'Malgré-Nous' because the vast majority

THE MAGINOT LINE

The famed **Ligne Maginot** (www.maginot.org), named after France's minister of war from 1929 to 1932, was one of the most spectacular blunders of WWII. This elaborate, mostly subterranean defence network, built between 1930 and 1940 (and, in the history of military architecture, second only to the Great Wall of China in sheer size), was the pride of prewar France. It included everything France's finest military architects thought would be needed to defend the nation in a 'modern war' of poison gas, tanks and aeroplanes: reinforced concrete bunkers, subterranean lines of supply and communication, minefields, antitank canals, floodable basins and even artillery emplacements that popped out of the ground to fire and then disappeared. The only things visible above ground were firing posts and lookout towers. The line stretched along the Franco–German frontier from the Swiss border all the way to Belgium where, for political and budgetary reasons, it stopped. The Maginot Line even had a slogan: 'Ils ne passeront pas' (They won't get through).

'They' – the Germans – never did. Rather than attack the Maginot Line straight on, Hitler's armoured divisions simply circled around through Belgium and invaded France across its unprotected northern frontier. They then attacked the Maginot Line from the rear. Against all the odds – and with most of northern France already in German hands – some of the fortifications held out for a few weeks. When resistance became hopeless, thousands of French troops managed to escape to Switzerland, where the Swiss promptly interned them (they were freed the following year).

Parts of the Maginot Line – remarkably preserved – are open to visitors, but without your own wheels they're a bit hard to get to. In Lorraine, visitors can tour over a dozen sites, including Fort du Hackenberg (p382) and Fort de Fermont (p386). Major Maginot sites in Alsace:

Four-à-Chaux (☎ 03 88 94 48 62, at the Lembach tourist office ☎ 03 88 94 43 16; www.ot-lembach.com) Captured by the Germans after a week of fighting in June 1940, this fort is 60km north of Strasbourg on the tiny D65 (a few kilometres east of Lembach). **Guided tours** (in French and German with English text; adult/student/under 12 €4.50/3.50/2) last 1½ to two hours, involve 1.7km of walking and begin at 10am, 2pm and 3pm daily from late March to early November. There are additional tours at 11am from July to September, 4pm from May to September and 5pm in July and August. From early November to late March, tours start at 10.30am and 2.30pm on Saturday and Sunday.

Schœnenbourg (Hunspach tourist office ☎ 03 88 80 59 39; www.lignemaginot.com; adult/6-18 yrs €5/3) The largest visitable Maginot fortress, this concrete behemoth is about 45km north of Strasbourg. You can begin a self-guided tour of the two-hour, 2.5km route (signs in English) from 2pm to 4pm Monday to Saturday from Easter to September and from 9.30am to 11am and 2pm to 4pm on Sunday from April to October.

had gone off to war against their will, over half never returned from the Russian front and post-war Soviet prison camps. To make Alsace a symbol of hope for future Franco-German (and pan-European) cooperation, Strasbourg was chosen as the seat of the Council of Europe (in 1949) and, later, of the European Parliament.

Language

Alsatian (Elsässisch; www.heimetsproch.org), the language of Alsace, is an Alemannic dialect of German not unlike the dialects spoken in nearby parts of Germany and Switzerland. It has no official written form (spelling – including on menus – is something of a free-for-all), and pronunciation varies considerably from one area to another (especially between the north and south). Despite a series of heavy-handed attempts by both the French and the Germans to impose their languages on the region, in part by restricting (or even banning) the use of Alsatian, it is – miraculously – still used in everyday life by people of all ages, in the villages as well as the cities. You're likely to hear its sing-songy cadences whenever you happen upon locals who are just being themselves – for instance, in a *boulangerie*.

STRASBOURG

pop 427,000

Prosperous, cosmopolitan Strasbourg (City of the Roads) is France's great northeastern metropolis and the intellectual and cultural capital of Alsace. Situated only a few kilometres west of the Rhine, the city is aptly named, for it is on the vital transport arteries that have linked northern Europe with the Mediterranean since Celtic times. Strasbourg continues to serve as an important European crossroads thanks to the presence of the European Parliament, the Council of Europe, the European Court of Human Rights, the Eurocorps (www.eurocorps.org), the Franco-German TV network Arte (www.arte-tv.com in French) and a student population of some 48,000, 20% from outside France.

Towering above the restaurants, *winstubs* (traditional Alsatian eateries) and pubs of the lively old city – a wonderful area to explore on foot – is the cathedral, a medieval marvel in pink sandstone. Nearby you'll find one of the finest ensembles of museums anywhere in France.

Accommodation is extremely difficult to find during European Parliament sessions (p352).

History

Before it was attached to France in 1681, Strasbourg was effectively ruled for several centuries by a guild of citizens whose tenure accorded the city a certain democratic character. A university was founded in 1566 and several leaders of the Reformation took up residence here. Johannes Gutenberg worked in Strasbourg from about 1434 to 1444, perfecting his printing press and the moveable metal type that made it so revolutionary. Three centuries later, the German poet, playwright, novelist and philosopher Johann Wolfgang von Goethe (1749–1832) studied law here.

Orientation

Strasbourg's train station is 400m west of the Grande Île (Big Island), the core of ancient and modern Strasbourg, whose main squares are place Kléber, place Broglie (pronounced **broag**-lee), place Gutenberg and place du Château. The quaint Petite France area in the Grande Île's southwestern corner is subdivided by canals. Much of the city centre is for pedestrians only.

The European Parliament building and Palais de l'Europe are about 2km northeast of the cathedral.

The city centre is about 3.5km west of Pont de l'Europe, the bridge that links the French bank of the Rhine with the German city of Kehl.

Information

BOOKSHOPS

Géorama (☎ 03 88 75 01 95; 20-22 rue du Fossé des Tanneurs; ☷ closed Sun & Mon morning) Has a huge selection of hiking maps and topoguides.

The Bookworm (☎ 03 88 32 26 99; 3 rue de Pâques; tram stop Ancienne Synagogue) Carries new and used English-language books, including Lonely Planet guides.

INTERNET ACCESS

L'Utopie (☎ 03 88 23 89 21; 21-23 rue du Fossé des Tanneurs; per hr €3; ☷ 7am-11.30pm Mon-Sat, 8am-10pm Sun) The computers are in the basement. A Wireless Internet connection for your laptop costs €3 per hour.

NeT SuR CouR (☎ 03 88 35 66 76; 18 quai des Pêcheurs; tram stop Gallia; per hr €2; ☷ 9.30am-9.30pm Mon-Fri, 2-8pm Sat & Sun) At the end of a narrow courtyard.

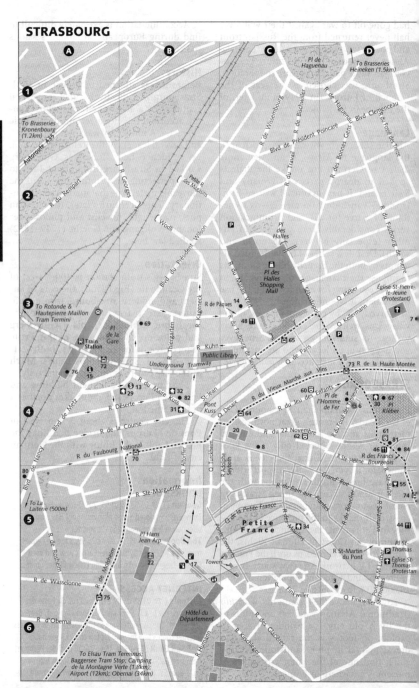

STRASBOURG

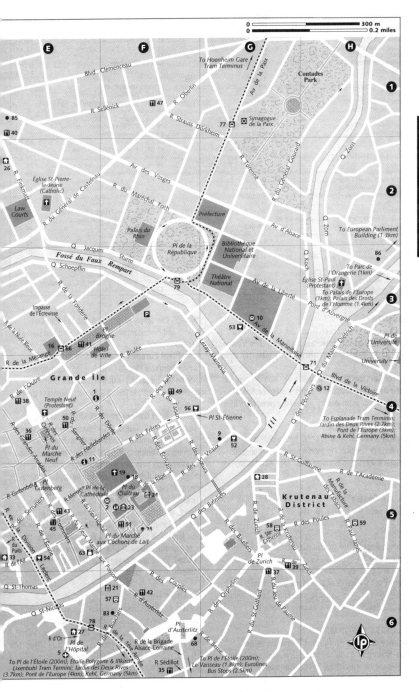

ALSACE & LORRAINE

0 ——— 300 m
0 ——— 0.2 miles

E **F** **G** **H**

Blvd Clemenceau

To Hoenheim Gare
Tram Terminus

Av de la Paix

Contades Park

1

R Sellénick   R Oberlin

🏛 47

● 85

R Strauss Dürkheim   77 🔲

🏛 40

✠ Synagogue
de la Paix

Q Zorn

🏠 26

R du Général Gouraud

R Totlenne

2

Av des Vosges

R du Maréchal Foch

Église St-Pierre-le-Jeune (Catholic)
✠

R du Général de Castelnau

Q Zorn

Q Koch

To European Parliament
Building (1.3km)

Law Courts

R du Général de Castelnau

Préfecture

● 86

Palais du Rhin

Pl de la République

Bibliothèque National et Universitaire

Av d'Alsace

To Parc de
l'Orangerie (1km)

Q Jacques   Sturm

Église St-Paul
(Protestant) ✠

Fossé du Faux Rempart

Q Schoepflin

Théâtre National

Av de la Liberté

To Palais de l'Europe
(1km); Palais des Droits
de l'Homme (1.4km)

🔲 79

Pont d'Auvergne

3

Impasse de l'Écrevisse

R de la Fonderie

Pl de l'Université

R de la Nuée Bleue

🅿

Pl Broglie

⏰ 10

R du Maire Dietrich

University

16 🔲 66 🏛 41
Hôtel de Ville

R Brûlée

53 🔲

Av de la Marseillaise

71 🔲

Blvd de la Victoire

Grande Île

Q Lezay-Marnésia

R des Pêcheurs @ 12

4

R de l'Outre

🏛 38

Temple Neuf
(Protestant)

R des Juifs

🏛 49

R du Faisan

56 🔲

Pl St-Étienne

To Esplanade Tram Terminus;
Jardin des Deux Rives (2.7km);
Pont de l'Europe (3km);
Rhine & Kehl, Germany (5km)

50 🏛   1 ℹ

R des Frères

🏛 36

R des Hallebardes

9 ℹ

R des Veaux

52 🔲

R St-Guillaume

R de l'Académie

Pl du Marché Neuf

ℹ 11

R des Écrivains

R des Sœurs

🏛 19   18 ●

Pl du Château

🏛 28

R de la Manufacture des Tabacs

Krutenau District

5

R Gutenberg   Pl Gutenberg

2 ℹ 🏛 23

🏛 21

R Mercière

R du Vieil Hôpital

R des Bateliers

R de l'Académie

R des Serruriers

🏛 43

R des Cordonniers

45

R du Vieux Marché aux Poissons

🏛 91   95

Pl du Marché aux Cochons de Lait

R de Zurich

58 🔲

R Ste-Catherine

R des Poules

🔲 59

R du Jeu de Paume

Q du Puits

🏠 33

54 🔲

R de l'Ail

63 🔲

Pl de Zurich

Pl de Zurich

R de Zurich   39 🏛

Q St-Thomas

🏛 21

57 🔲

R d'Austerlitz

🏛 42

37 🔲

R du Jeu de Paume

6

Q St-Nicolas

83 ●

78

Pl d'Austerlitz

R des Orphelins

🏠 27

R d'Or

Pl de l'Hôpital

5

R des Bouchers

R de la Brigade Alsace-Lorraine

68

R de Berne

To Pl de l'Étoile (200m);
Étoile Polygone & Illkirch-
Lixenbuhl Tram Termini; Jardin des Deux Rives
(3.7km); Pont de l'Europe (4km); Kehl, Germany (5km)

R Sédillot

35 🏛

To Pl de l'Étoile (200m);
Le Vaisseau (1.8km); Eurolines
Bus Stops (2.5km)

LP

INFORMATION	
Agence de Développement Touristique en	
Bas-Rhin..1 E4	
Branch Post Office....................................2 F5	
Espace Services (Laundrette)....................3 D6	
Géorama...4 D4	
Hôpital Civil (Hospital)............................5 E6	
L'Utopie...6 D4	
Laundrette..7 D3	
Laundrette..8 C4	
Laundrette..9 G4	
Main Post Office.....................................10 G3	
Main Tourist Office.................................11 E4	
NeT SuR CouR..12 H4	
Société Générale Bank............................13 B4	
The Bookworm..14 C3	
Tourist Office Annexe.............................15 A4	

SIGHTS & ACTIVITIES	(pp348–52)
Banque de France....................................16 E3	
Barrage Vauban & Terrasse Panoramique.17 B5	
Cathedral's South Entrance......................18 F5	
Cathédrale Notre Dame............................19 F5	
Église St-Pierre-le-Vieux (Protestant &	
Catholic)..20 C4	
Musée Alsacien..21 F6	
Musée d'Art Moderne et Contemporain..22 B5	
Musée de l'Œuvre Notre Dame.................23 F5	
Palais Rohan (Musée Archéologique, Musée des	
Arts Décoratifs & Musée des	
Beaux-Arts)..24 F5	
Strasbourg Fluvial Boat Excursions...........25 F5	

SLEEPING	(pp352–3)
CIARUS Hostel...26 E2	
Hôtel Au Cerf d'Or..................................27 E6	

Hôtel Aux Trois Roses.............................28 G5	
Hôtel du Rhin...29 B4	
Hôtel Kléber...30 D4	
Hôtel Le Colmar......................................31 B4	
Hôtel Le Grillon......................................32 B4	
Hôtel Patricia..33 E5	
Hôtel Régent Petite France......................34 C5	

EATING	(pp353–4)
Adan..35 F6	
Atac Supermarket....................................36 E4	
Au Cèdre...37 G6	
Au Crocodile...38 E4	
Au Renard Prêchant.................................39 G5	
Cash' Center Supermarket........................40 E1	
Food Market..41 E3	
Food Shops..42 F6	
Fromagerie des Tonneliers.......................43 E5	
L'Assiette du Vin.....................................44 D5	
La Cloche à Fromage...............................45 E5	
Lafayette Gourmet Supermarket..............46 D4	
Le King...47 F1	
Le Sahara..48 C3	
Tiger Wok...49 F4	
Winstub le Clou.......................................50 E4	
Winstubs s'Muensterstuewel....................51 F5	

DRINKING	(pp354–5)
Au Brasseur...52 C4	
La Taverne Française...............................53 C3	
Route 66...54 E5	
The Irish Times..55 D5	
Zanzibar..56 F4	

ENTERTAINMENT	(pp355–6)
Bar Le Zoo..57 F6	

Café des Anges.......................................58 G5	
La Salamandre..59 H5	
Le Star Cinema.......................................60 C4	
Odyssée Cinema.....................................61 D4	
Star St Exupéry Cinema..........................62 C4	

SHOPPING	(p356)
Marché de Brocante................................63 D5	

TRANSPORT	(pp356–7)
Alt Winmärik Tram Stop..........................64 C4	
Ancienne Synagogue-Les Halles Tram	
Stop...65 C3	
Broglie Tram Stop...................................66 E3	
CTS Bus Information Bureau....................67 D4	
Eurolines Office.......................................68 F6	
Europcar...69 B3	
Faubourg National Tram Stop.................70 B4	
Gallia Tram Stop.....................................71 H4	
Gare Centrale Tram Stop.........................72 A4	
Homme de Fer Tram Hub........................73 D4	
Langstross Grand' Rue............................74 D5	
Musée d'Art Moderne Tram Stop............75 A6	
National-Citer & Avis..............................76 A4	
Parc du Contades Tram Stop....................77 G1	
Porte de l'Hôpital Tram Stop...................78 E6	
République Tram Stop.............................79 F3	
Sixt...80 A5	
SNCF Boutique.......................................81 D4	
Vélocation Bicycle Rental........................82 B4	
Vélocation Bicycle Rental........................83 F6	

OTHER	
German Consulate...................................84 D4	
Strasbourg Section of Club Vosgien.........85 E1	
US Consulate...86 H3	

LAUNDRY

There are laundrettes at 29 Grand' Rue, 8 rue de la Nuée Bleue and 15 rue des Veaux. Opening hours are about 7.30am to 8pm or 9pm.

Espace Services (2 quai Finkwiller; ☼ 8am-7.45pm) Has better views than any other laundrette in France. Special facilities let you wash and dry your *petit* or *grand chien* (dog).

MEDICAL SERVICES

Hôpital Civil (☎ 03 88 11 67 68; 1 place de l'Hôpital; tram stop Porte de l'Hôpital; ☼ 24hr) A new 15-block hospital complex is set to open just west of the Hôpital Civil in 2006.

MONEY

Société Générale (8 place de la Gare; ☼ 2-6pm Mon, 8.30am-noon & 1.30-6pm Tue-Fri)

POST

Branch Post Office (place de la Cathédrale; ☼ 8am-6.30pm Mon-Fri, 8am-5pm Sat) Has extended Saturday hours and currency exchange.

Main Post Office (5 av de la Marseillaise; tram stop République) In a neo-Gothic structure built by the Germans in 1899. Has exchange services and a Cyberposte.

TOURIST INFORMATION

Agence de Développement Touristique en Bas-Rhin (☎ 03 88 15 45 80; www.tourisme67.com in French; 9 rue du Dôme; ☼ 9.30am-noon & 1.30-6pm

Mon-Fri) Can supply excellent English brochures on Jewish and Protestant sites, cycling, hiking and skiing in northern Alsace.

Info-Point Europe (☎ 03 88 15 70 80; 26a av de la Paix; tram stop Parc du Contades; ☼ 10am-noon & 2-5pm) Can supply you with a vast number of official brochures – mostly in French – on every aspect of the EU project.

Main Tourist Office (☎ 03 88 52 28 28; www.ot -strasbourg.fr; 17 place de la Cathédrale; ☼ 9am-7pm) Next door to the ornate, 16th-century Maison Kammerzell. Walking-tour brochure (€1) and free bus/tram and cycling maps available here. The Strasbourg Pass (€10.60), a coupon book valid for three consecutive days, may save you a fair bit of cash.

Tourist Office Annexe (☎ 03 88 32 51 49; tram stop Gare Centrale; ☼ 9am-7pm Jun-Sep & Dec, 9am-12.30pm & 1.45-6pm Apr, May, Oct & Nov, closed Sun Jan-Mar & Nov) In front of the train station in the subterranean Galerie de l'En-Verre (underneath place de la Gare). There are plans to move it into the train station building at some point.

Grande Île

With its bustling public squares, busy pedestrianised areas and upmarket shopping streets, the Grande Île, declared a World Heritage Site by Unesco, is a paradise for the aimless ambler. The narrow streets of the **old city**, particularly right around the cathedral, are especially enchanting at night. There are watery views from the paths along the **River Ill** and its canalised branch, the **Fossé du Faux Rempart**; the grassy quays, frequented by swans, are a great venue for a picnic or a romantic stroll.

Crisscrossed by narrow lanes, canals and locks, **Petite France** is the stuff of fairy tales. The half-timbered houses, meticulously maintained and sprouting veritable thickets of geraniums, and the riverside parks attract multitudes of tourists. However, the area still manages to retain its Alsatian atmosphere and charm, especially in the early morning and late evening.

The romantic Terrasse Panoramique on top of **Barrage Vauban** (admission free; 9am-7.30pm), a dam built to prevent river-borne attacks on the city, affords panoramas of the River Ill.

Cathédrale Notre Dame

Strasbourg's lacy, almost fragile-looking Gothic **Cathédrale Notre Dame** (7am-7pm) is one of the marvels of European architecture. The west façade, most impressive if approached from rue Mercière, was com-

pleted in 1284, but the 142m spire – the tallest of its time – was not in place until 1439; its southern companion was never built. The cathedral served as a Protestant church from 1521 to 1681.

On a sunny day, the 12th- to 14th-century **stained-glass windows** – especially the rose window over the western portal – shine like jewels. The colourful **organ case** on the northern side dates from the 14th century, while the 30m-high Gothic and Renaissance contraption just inside the southern entrance is the **horloge astronomique** (astronomical clock), a late-16th-century clock (the mechanism dates from 1842) that strikes solar noon every day at 12.30pm. There's a €1 charge to see the carved wooden figures whirl through their paces, which is why only the cathedral's **south entrance** is open from a bit after 11.40am until the end of the show.

The 66m-high **platform** (03 88 43 60 40; adult/student & under 18 €3/1.50; 9am-5pm Mon-Fri, 10am-5pm Sat & Sun Apr-Oct, 9am-4.30pm Mon-Fri, 10am-4.30pm Sat & Sun Nov-Mar) above the façade – from which the **tower** and its Gothic openwork **spire** soar another 76m – affords a spectacular stork's-eye view of Strasbourg. The entrance to the 330 spiral steps is at the base of the bell tower that was never built.

Musée de l'Œuvre Notre-Dame

Occupying a group of magnificent 14th- and 16th-century buildings, the renowned **Musée de l'Œuvre Notre-Dame** (03 88 32 88 17; 3 place du Château; adult/student under 26 & senior/under 18 & disabled incl audioguide €4/2/free; 10am-6pm Tue-Sun) houses one of Europe's premier collections of Romanesque, Gothic and Renaissance sculptures (including many originals from the cathedral), 15th-century paintings and stained glass. *Christ de Wissembourg* (c1060; Room 2) is the oldest work of stained glass in France. The celebrated figures of a downcast and blindfolded *Synagogue* (representing Judaism) and a serenely victorious *Église* (the Church), which date from approximately 1230 and once flanked the southern entrance to the cathedral (the statues that stand there now are copies), are on the right and left walls, respectively, of Room 7.

Hollywood gore seems pretty milquetoasty compared to what they came up with back when Hell really was hell. *Les Amants Trépassés* (the Deceased Lovers; Room 23),

---

LA MARSEILLAISE

Though you'd never know it from the name, France's stirring national anthem, 'La Marseillaise', was written in Strasbourg. In April 1792, at the beginning of the war with Austria, the mayor of Strasbourg – in whose city a garrison was preparing for battle – suggested that the revolutionary army could use a catchy and patriotic tune to sing while marching off to spread the blessings of liberty throughout Europe. He approached Claude Rouget de Lisle, a young army engineer with a minor reputation as a composer, who after a furious all-night effort came up with a marching song entitled 'Chant de Guerre de l'Armée du Rhin' (War Song of the Rhine Army). The mayor himself first performed it in his home, which stood at the western end of place Broglie (on the site of the present Banque de France building). The soul-stirring tune and its bloody lyrics became popular immediately, and by August were on the lips of volunteer troops from Marseille as they marched northwards to defend the Revolution.

painted in 1470, shows a remarkably ugly couple being punished for their illicit lust: both of their entrails are being devoured by dragon-headed snakes while a toad feasts on her pudenda. If this work isn't enough to scare you into a life of chastity nothing will!

Musée d'Art Moderne et Contemporain

The outstanding **Musée d'Art Moderne et Contemporain** (Museum of Modern & Contemporary Art; ☎ 03 88 23 31 31; place Hans Jean Arp; tram stop Musée d'Art Moderne; adult/student/over 60 & under 18 €5/2.50/free; ☑ 11am-7pm Tue, Wed, Fri & Sat, noon-10pm Thu, 10am-6pm Sun) has an exceptionally diverse collection of works representing every major art movement of the past century or so, including impressionism, symbolism, Fauvism, cubism, Dadaism and surrealism. Laminated cards provide background in English (except for temporary exhibits).

Palais Rohan

Palais Rohan (☎ 03 88 52 50 00; 2 place du Château; for the whole complex adult/student under 26 & senior/under 18 & disabled €6/3/free, for each museum €4/2/free; ☑ 10am-6pm Wed-Mon) was built between 1732 and 1742 as a residence for the city's princely bishops. In the basement the **Musée Archéologique** (audioguide included in ticket price) takes you from the Palaeolithic period to AD 800. On the ground floor is the **Musée des Arts Décoratifs**, which has a series of lavish rooms featuring the lifestyle of the rich and powerful during the 18th century. Louis XV and Marie-Antoinette once slept here – in 1744 and 1770, respectively. On the 1st floor the **Musée des Beaux-Arts** has a rather staid collection of French, Spanish, Italian, Dutch and Flemish masters from the 14th to the 19th centuries.

MUSEUMS

The **Pass Musées** (one-day/three-day/annual €6/8/20, one-day version for students under 26 & seniors €3) gets you into all of Strasbourg's museums, including temporary exhibitions.

All of Strasbourg's **museums** (www.musees-strasbourg.org) are free on the first Sunday of the month. On other days tickets are valid all day long so you can enter and re-enter as you please.

Musée Alsacien

Housed in three typical houses from the 1500s and 1600s, the **Musée Alsacien** (☎ 03 88 52 50 01; 23 quai St-Nicolas; tram stop Porte de l'Hôpital; adult/student under 26 & senior/under 18 & disabled €4/2/free; ☑ 10am-6pm Mon & Wed-Sun Jan-Mar, Jul & Aug, noon-6pm Mon & Wed-Sat, 10-6pm Sun rest of year), affords a fascinating glimpse of Alsatian life over the centuries. Displays in the museum's two dozen rooms include kitchen equipment (stoves, ceramics, biscuit cutters), children's toys, colourful furniture and even a tiny 18th-century synagogue.

European Institutions

The home of the relatively toothless 785-member **European Parliament** (Parlement Européen; ☎ 03 88 17 20 07; www.europarl.eu.int; rue Lucien Fèbvre; tram stop Wacken), used just 12 times a year for four-day 'part-sessions' (plenary sessions), is 2km northeast of the cathedral. When it's in session (dates are available from the tourist office or on the EU website under 'Plenary Sessions' in the Activities section), you can sit in on debates for up to one hour; it's first-come first-served and no reservations are possible. The best times to come (with ID) are from 5pm to 6pm on Monday (the session often continues until late at night) and from 9am (10am on Thursday) to noon and 3pm to 6pm Tuesday to Thursday. The rest of the time the building is inaccessible because of strict post-9/11 security measures.

Across the Ill, the Council of Europe's **Palais de l'Europe** (☎ 03 88 41 20 29; www.coe.int), once used by the European Parliament, can be visited on free one-hour weekday tours; ring a day ahead for reservations. During the four annual sessions of the council's 45-country *assemblée parlementaire* you can sit in on debates (no reservations required). To get there by bus, take No 6, 30 or 72.

Just across the Canal de la Marne, the striking **Palais des Droits de l'Homme** (☎ 03 88 41 34 95; www.echr.coe.int), home of the European Court of Human Rights since 1995, completes the city's ensemble of major European institutions. Sitting in on one of the two to five monthly court sessions, which begin at 9am or 9.30am Tuesday to Thursday and last about 90 minutes, is possible if there's space – check the website under 'pending cases' for dates and get there with ID a half-hour ahead. The *palais* is served by bus Nos 6, 30 and 72.

ALSACE & LORRAINE

JEWISH ALSACE

Interest in Alsace's rich Jewish heritage (www.sdv.fr/judaisme in French), spanning a thousand years, has grown tremendously in recent times. Indeed, the European Day of Jewish Culture (www.jewishheritage.org), marked in early September in 23 countries, grew out of a local initiative in northern Alsace. Famous people of Alsatian-Jewish origin include the Marx Brothers and the actress Julia Louis-Dreyfus, who played Elaine Benes on *Seinfeld*.

Towns all over the region, including many along the Route du Vin d'Alsace (p357), have historic **synagogues**. Museums with exhibits related to Alsatian Judaism include Strasbourg's Musée de l'Œuvre Notre Dame (p349) and Musée Alsacien (p350); Colmar's Musée Bartholdi (p364); and the **Musée Judéo-Alsacien** (☎ 03 88 70 97 17; 62 Grand' Rue; ☺ 9am-noon & 2-5pm Tue-Fri mid-Mar–mid-Sep) in Bouxwiller, 40km northeast of Strasbourg. Several tourist offices (eg Strasbourg and Colmar) offer walking tours of Jewish sites, though these are usually in French.

The Agence de Développement Touristique en Bas-Rhin (p348) has published an excellent brochure *Discovering Alsatian Judaism*.

East & South of the Grande Île

Many of Strasbourg's most impressive (and German-built) public buildings are just northeast of the Grande Île around **place de la République** (tram stop République). The neighbourhood that stretches from there eastwards to Parc de l'Orangerie is dominated by solid, stone buildings inspired by late-19th-century Prussian tastes. Most are some sort of 'neo' – Romantic, Gothic or Renaissance – and you can see that some had the initials RF (République Française) hastily added after 1918 to replace the original German insignia.

Across av de l'Europe from Palais de l'Europe, the flowerbeds, playgrounds, shaded paths and swan-dotted lake of **Parc de l'Orangerie** are hugely popular with local families, especially on sunny Sunday afternoons. In the warm months you can rent **rowing boats** on Lac de l'Orangerie. To get there by bus, take No 6, 30 or 72.

Le Vaisseau (the Vessel; pont d'Ankara; http://levaisseau.cg67.fr), an interactive, hands-on science and technology museum inspired by Paris' La Villette, is due to open in late 2004/early 2005. Situated 2.5km southeast of the cathedral, its exhibits – all of them trilingual (English, French and German) – are aimed at kids aged three to 15.

As a concrete (but very green) expression of Franco-German friendship, Strasbourg and its German neighbour Kehl have turned areas once used by customs posts and military installations into the 60-hectare **Jardin des Deux Rives** (Two-Shores Garden; opened April 2004), whose play areas, promenades and gardens stretch along both banks of the Rhine just south of Pont de l'Europe. The centrepiece is a sleek (and hugely expensive) **suspension bridge** for pedestrians and cyclists, designed by the French architect Marc Mimram (www.mimram.com in French); one of the walkways is 275m long, the other 387m long.

Tours

CITY TOURS

Boat excursions (70 minutes in length) that take in Petite France and the European institutions are run by **Strasbourg Fluvial** (☎ 03 88 84 13 13, 03 88 32 75 25; behind the Palais Rohan; adult/student €6.80/3.40, at night €7.20/3.60; at least 4 times daily).

The tourist office offers 1½-hour Walkman tours of the cathedral and the old city (adult/student €6/3).

BREWERIES

Brasseries Kronenbourg (☎ 03 88 27 41 59; siege.visites@kronenbourg-fr.com; 68 route d'Oberhausbergen; tram stop Ducs d'Alsace), which sells one billion litres of beer in France every year (that is enough beer to fill over 300 Olympic swimming pools!), has a brewery 2.5km northwest of the Grande Île in the suburb of Cronenbourg. Interesting and thirst-quenching tours (adult/12 to 18 years €3/2) take place on weekdays and, from May to September and in December, on Saturday; call ahead for times and reservations.

Brasseries Heineken (☎ 03 88 19 57 55; 4 rue St-Charles) is 2.5km north of the Grande Île in Schiltigheim, near the intersection of rue St-Charles and route de Bischwiller. Free, two-hour tours in French, German or English (depending on group bookings) are held on weekdays; phone ahead for times and reservations. Take the No 4 bus (northbound) to the Schiltigheim Mairie stop.

HIKING, CYCLING & SNOW-SHOEING
The Strasbourg section of the **Club Vosgien** (☎ 03 88 35 30 76; www.club-vosgien-strasbourg.net in French; 71 av des Vosges; ☻ staffed 4-6.30pm Mon-Fri, 10am-noon Sat), a regional walking organisation founded in 1872, runs walks, cycling excursions and snow-shoe trips for its members (guests welcome) in the Vosges and other parts of Alsace; there are departures at around 8am each Sunday and sometimes on other days too. No reservations are needed for trips by private car (passengers pay €0.06 per kilometre) or train; reserve a few days ahead for bus trips (€12). Insurance costs €4.

Festivals & Events
The **Festival International de Musique** (International Music Festival; ☎ 03 88 15 44 66) is held in mid-June and **Musica** (☎ 03 88 23 46 46), a feast of contemporary music runs from mid-September to early October.

Marché de Noël (Christkindelsmärik in Alsatian, ie Christmas Market; place Kléber, place de la Cathédrale, place Broglie & place de la Gare) is a huge and justifiably renowned outdoor market selling Christmas decorations and seasonal treats such as mulled wine. It's held from the last weekend in November until 31 December (until 24 December at place Broglie).

Sleeping
It is *extremely* difficult to find last-minute accommodation from Monday to Thursday when the European Parliament is in plenary session (generally for one week each month; see p350). Because of the Christmas Market, weekends in December are also a problem. If you're stuck, the tourist office can provide details of same-night room availability and may be able to reserve a room. Hotel reservations can also be made via www.strasbourg.com/hotels.

BUDGET
Centre International d'Accueil et de Rencontre Unioniste de Strasbourg (CIARUS; ☎ 03 88 15 27 88; www.ciarus.com; 7 rue Finkmatt; dm in 8-/4-/2-bed rooms incl breakfast €16.50/20/22.50; P ▣) This welcoming Protestant-run hostel, outfitted

with 295 beds, is so stylish it even counts a few European Parliament members among its regular clients. The 700 groups it puts up (with) every year are equally international. There are frequent social events in the evening. No HI card is necessary. Dorm rooms have industrial-strength furniture, toilets and showers; facilities for the disabled are available. By bus, take No 2, 4 or 10 to the Place de Pierre stop

Hôtel Patricia (☎ 03 88 32 14 60; www.hotelpatricia.fr.st; 1a rue du Puits; d from €30, with shower & toilet €40; ☻ reception 8am-8pm Mon-Sat, 8am-2pm Sun) The dark, rustic interior and Vosges sandstone floors – the 16th-century structure was once a convent – fit in well with the local ambience. Rooms are simply furnished but spacious and soundproofed; some also have great views. Hall showers cost €2. The best budget bet on the island.

Hôtel Le Colmar (☎ 03 88 32 16 89; hotel.le.colmar@wanadoo.fr; 1 rue du Maire Kuss; tram stop Alt Winmärik; s/d from €24.50/27.50, with shower & toilet €37/40; ☻ reception closed 1.30-5.30pm Sun) This cheapie offers a unique combination of light, linoleum and loquaciousness – it ain't stylish but it's convenient and good value. Showers are €2.50.

Camping
Camping de la Montagne Verte (☎ 03 88 30 25 46; 2 rue Robert Forrer; per adult/site €3.35/4.50; ☻ mid-Mar–Oct & late Nov-early Jan) A grassy municipal camping ground a short walk from the Nid de Cigognes stop on bus line No 2.

MID-RANGE
Two- and three-star hotels line place de la Gare.

Hôtel du Rhin (☎ 03 88 32 35 00; www.hotel-du-rhin.com; 7-8 place de la Gare; tram stop Gare Centrale; d from €34, with shower & toilet €60) This two-star establishment, run by the same family since 1941, makes at least token efforts at being stylish (tatami mats line the hallways). The rooms are comfortable and soundproofed; thanks to the timeless décor, some of them would make a good set for a French film about a tawdry love affair, c 1972.

Hôtel Le Grillon (☎ 03 88 32 71 88; www.grillon.com; 2 rue Thiergarten; tram stop Gare Centrale; s/d from €30/37, old room with shower & toilet €40/47, new room €55/62; ▣) This informal two-star place has old-style rooms that are bland and have prefab bathroom modules, and new-style rooms that come with wooden floors, proper tiled bathrooms and sleeker furnishings. Internet access is free for the first 15 minutes.

Hôtel Au Cerf d'Or (☎ 03 88 36 20 05; fax 03 88 36 68 67; 6 place de l'Hôpital; tram stop Porte de l'Hôpital; s/d from €50.30/61; 🖳) A Jacuzzi, small swimming pool and sauna (half-hour €8) are the cherry on the icing of this Logis de France-affiliated hotel, a golden *cerf* (stag) hanging proudly out front. On the ground floor there's a traditional French restaurant and a homey sitting area with two pianos; upstairs, the spacious and very comfortable rooms have solid all-tile bathrooms.

Hôtel Aux Trois Roses (☎ 03 88 36 56 95; www .hotel3roses-strasbourg.com; 7 rue de Zurich; s/d from €47/63; P) Housed in a handsome building classified as a historic monument, this two-star hotel has cheery rooms with lots of pine; the cheaper ones are on the small side. A sauna costs €5. Two rooms are outfitted for disabled guests.

Hôtel Kléber (☎ 03 88 32 09 53; hotel.kleber@goffornet .com; 29 place Kléber; s/d with shower €32/37, with shower & toilet €40.50/47.50) You're likely to be disappointed by this superbly situated two-star unless you've got a thing for loveably bad taste. The public areas retain echoes of the 1970s, while the rooms – cramped unless you pay €69 – have laughably cheap wood-panel ceilings and plastic faux-plaster walls.

TOP END

Hôtel Régent Petite France (☎ 03 88 76 43 43; 5 rue des Moulins; www.regent-hotels.com; s/d from €223/243, ste for 2 €366-455; P 🖳) Guests of this luxurious four-star hotel enjoy romantic watery views, a sauna and marble bathrooms worthy of a Roman emperor. If you're in one of the rooms over the lock your stay will be accompanied by the rush of water, which can be either calming (no need to bring along a relaxation CD) or nerve-wracking (New Yorkers might try pre-recording the sound of honking cars and ambulance sirens). The breakfast room is decorated with giant paintings inspired by angry underclass graffiti, so paying €18.50 is both an act of self-indulgence and a safe and sophisticated way of slumming it. Bringing along Fido or Mitzi will set you back €18.50. Facilities for the disabled are available.

Eating

Strasbourg is a gastronomer's dream. Just south of place Gutenberg, pedestrianised rue des Tonneliers is lined with mid-range restaurants of all sorts, both ethnic and French. Inexpensive student eateries can be found northeast of the cathedral along rue des Frères, especially towards place St-Étienne.

WINSTUBS & FRENCH

Winstub Le Clou (☎ 03 88 32 11 67; 3 rue du Chaudron; 🕙 meals served 11.45am-2pm & 5.30pm-midnight except Sun, holidays & lunch Wed) Diners sit together at long tables with paisley tablecloths, so come here for an evening in the company of fellow diners, not an intimate tête-à-tête. Specialities include *baeckeoffe* (€16.50) and *wädele braisé au pinot noir* (€14.50). The selection of Alsatian and French wines is quite good.

L'Assiette du Vin (☎ 03 88 32 00 92; 5 rue de la Chaîne; lunch menu €19.90, 2-/3-course menus €21/26, 4-course menu with 4 wines €45; 🕙 closed Sun, lunch Mon & Sat) At this mellow and elegant French restaurant, the décor changes with the seasons (the summer flowers come from the chef's mother's garden) as does the cuisine, inspired by what's available fresh in the marketplace. The wine list is extensive, with over 180 options; 12 to 15 vintages can be sampled by the glass (€3 to €7).

La Cloche à Fromage (☎ 03 88 23 13 19; 27 rue des Tonneliers; 🕙 closed lunch Tue) The world's largest cheese platter – with some 90 different cheeses – greets you at the door of this haven for the lactose addicted, a perennial favourite of local *fromage* connoisseurs. A plate of 15 cheeses matured and selected by a master *fromager* costs €21.50; *fondue Savoyarde* (cheese fondue) will warm your insides for €20.50.

> ### WINSTUBS
>
> A *winstub* (literally 'wine room') is a traditional Alsatian restaurant renowned for its warm, homey atmosphere. Most dishes are based on pork and veal; specialities include *baeckeoffe* (meat stew), *jambonneau* (knuckle of ham), *wädele braisé au pinot noir* (ham knuckles in wine) and *jambon en croûte* (ham wrapped in a crust). Vegetarians can usually order *Bibeleskas* (*fromage blanc*; soft white cheese mixed with fresh cream) and *pommes sautées* (sautéed potatoes). Few *winstubs* offer fixed-price *menus*; many have nonstandard opening hours.

ALSACE & LORRAINE

Au Renard Prêchant (☎ 03 88 35 62 87; 33 place
de Zurich; mains €9-16; ❧ closed lunch both Sat & Sun)
Occupying a 16th-century chapel, this convivial and often crowded restaurant offers
excellent, reasonably priced French and
regional cuisine. The atmosphere is warm,
woody and very Alsatian; décor includes
stained glass, a stuffed *renard* (fox) and a
mural of historic Strasbourg. *Gibier* (game)
is a seasonal speciality.

Winstub s'Muensterstuewel (☎ 03 88 32 17 63;
8 place du Marché aux Cochons de Lait; lunch menu €23;
❧ Tue-Sat) Though in the middle of a touristy area, this *winstub* has an excellent reputation – for mains and desserts – thanks to
its English-speaking, Paul Bocuse-trained
owner, who's happy to whip up vegetarian
options on demand.

ASIAN & NORTH AFRICAN

Tiger Wok (☎ 03 88 36 44 87; 8 rue du Faisan; lunch incl a
drink €13, dinner €14, all-you-can-eat €22; ❧ noon-2.15pm
& 7-10.30pm, to 11.30pm Fri & Sat) Locals chic-sters
tired of pigs' knuckles and fois gras flock
to this wokkery, where you choose your ingredients (vegies, fish, meat) and then tell
your personal *wokeur* (wok guy) – muscular
and short-sleeved – how to prepare them
and with which sauces. The result: a quick
crunchy meal eaten with giant wooden
tweezers (is someone afraid of chop sticks?)
Chic and modern in a Zen sort of way.

Au Cèdre (☎ 03 88 25 14 69; 1 rue St-Gothard; meat
mains €12.20-16; ❧ closed lunch both Sat & Sun) Au-

thentic Lebanese cuisine and a good selection of vegetarian dishes have made this
somewhat formal restaurant hugely popular. The multidish *mezza menu* costs €19
(minimum two people).

Le Sahara (☎ 03 88 22 64 50; 3 rue du Marais Vert;
tram stop Ancienne Synagogue; lunch menu €9; ❧ closed
Sun) A favourite of people who work in the
neighbourhood, this unpretentious Berber
restaurant serves copious portions of steaming couscous (€6.20 to €14.50).

VEGETARIAN & KOSHER

Adan (☎ 03 88 35 70 84; 6 rue Sédillot; menu €11;
❧ 11.30am-2pm Mon-Sat) Adan is an informal
vegetarian-organic restaurant serves tasty
soups, salads and four kinds of quiches,
including two without milk products.

Le King (☎ 03 88 52 17 71; 28 rue Sellénick; tram
stop Parc du Contades; 2-course menu €10; ❧ closed
Sat & dinner Fri) In the heart of Strasbourg's
Jewish neighbourhood, this kosher place
specialises in Moroccan-style grilled meats
and fish.

SELF-CATERING

A few blocks south of the cathedral, pedestrianised rue d'Austerlitz is home to quite
a few **food shops**.

The **food market** (place Broglie; ❧ until at least
4pm, often until 6pm Wed & Fri) moves to place
Kléber during the Christmas market.

Stock up on cheese at **Fromagerie des Tonneliers** (32 rue des Tonneliers; ❧ 9.15am-12.15pm &
2.30-7pm Mon-Fri, 8.15am-6.30pm Sat).

Supermarkets in Strasbourg:
Atac supermarket (47 rue des Grandes Arcades;
❧ 8.30am-8pm Mon-Sat)
Cash' Center (22 rue Finkmatt; ❧ 9am-7.30pm Mon-
Thu, 8.30am-3pm or 4pm Fri, 9am-1pm & 3-7pm Sun) An
all-*cacher* (kosher) supermarket that serves Strasbourg's
large Jewish community.
Lafayette Gourmet supermarket (34 rue du 22
Novembre; ❧ 9am-8pm Mon-Sat) On the ground floor of
the Galeries Lafayette department store.

Drinking

La Taverne Française (☎ 03 88 24 57 89; 12 av de la
Marseillaise; tram stop République or Gallia; ❧ 8.30am-
2am Mon-Thu, 8.30am-3am Fri, 2pm-3am Sat) At this
mellow café – favoured by actors from the
nearby theatre, musicians and students – a
mixture of the old-fashioned and the endearingly tacky creates the ideal atmosphere for
stimulating conversation. Bring along some

fresh salmon and by the end of the evening you'll have lox.

Zanzibar (☎ 03 88 36 66 18; 1 place St-Étienne; ⏰ 5pm-4am) A friendly laid-back bar in the heart of the Grande Île's student quarter. Local groups (plus a few from abroad) play rock, reggae, pop, jazz etc in the funky cellar starting at 10pm on Thursday, Friday and Saturday (except from mid-July to August). Admission is usually free.

The Irish Times (☎ 03 88 32 04 02; 19 rue St-Barbe; ⏰ 4pm-1.30am Mon-Fri, 2pm-1.30am Sat & Sun) A congenial and genuinely Irish pub with a very international clientele. There's live music (mainly Irish) from about 9.30pm to 12.30am on Friday and Saturday; Thursday is open-mike night (9pm), Wednesday features a trivia quiz with prizes (9.30pm). Major sports events – shown on the two wide screens – often push back Sunday opening to kick-off time.

Au Brasseur (☎ 03 88 36 12 13; 22 rue des Veaux; ⏰ 11am-1am) Four beers – *brune, ambrée, blonde* and *blanche* – are brewed on the premises of this warm, dimly lit microbrewery, which also has some of the best deals in town on Alsatian treats: *baeckhoffe* is €13.50, while all-you-can-eat *Flammekueche* (served at all hours) with 0.9L of beer will set you back just €12.50. Local groups play rock and blues from 9.30pm to 1am on Friday and Saturday.

Route 66 (☎ 03 88 32 89 79; 15 rue de la Division Leclerc; ⏰ 3pm-4am Tue-Sun) Mercifully short on ersatz Americana (despite the name), the student crowd at this friendly downto-earth bar is sprinkled with American year-abroaders and players from Étoile Noire (the local 1st-division ice-hockey team). As for the background music, almost anything that sounds good loud – except techno and rap – goes, especially if it is rock.

Entertainment

The Strasbourgeois may head to bed earlier than their counterparts in other major French cities but the city's entertainment options are legion – despite a new ordinance that killed the late-late scene by forcing nightspots to close between 4am and 6am. Details on cultural events appear in the free monthly *Spectacles* (www.spectacles-publications.com in French), available at the tourist office.

CINEMAS
Nondubbed film venues:

Le Star (☎ 03 88 32 44 97; www.cinema-star.com in French; 27 rue du Jeu des Enfants)

Odyssée (☎ 03 88 75 10 47; www.cinemaodyssee .com in French; 3 rue des Francs Bourgeois) An art-house cinema.

Star St-Exupéry (☎ 03 88 22 28 79; www.cinema-star .com in French; 18 rue du 22 Novembre)

GAY & LESBIAN VENUES
Bar Le Zoo (☎ 03 88 24 55 33; www.lezoobar.com in French; 6 rue des Bouchers; tram stop Porte de l'Hôpital; ⏰ 6pm-2am) This friendly mostly gay bar has a mellow cellar lounge with sofas and frequent theme nights. On Wednesday from 9pm there's a *soirée poste*, during which patrons post letters to each other. *Kfé Kuchen*, a coffee and cake combo, is served up on Sunday (6pm to 9pm). In summer you can sit out on the terrace.

LIVE MUSIC
A number of the places listed under Drinking (above) host live concerts.

Strasbourg's most vibrant venue for live music of every sort is **La Laiterie** (☎ 03 88 23 72 37; www.artefact.org in French; 11-13 rue du Hohwald; tram stop Laiterie; ⏰ closed Jul, Aug & around Christmas), about 1km southwest of the train station. It puts on about 20 concerts a month. Tickets (€5 to €25) are available either at the door (telephone bookings aren't accepted) or for a slight surcharge at an Fnac or Virgin ticket outlet in the city. On Friday nights from midnight to 6am, La Laiterie turns into a techno disco (€5).

NIGHTCLUBS
La Salamandre (☎ 03 88 25 79 42; www.lasalamandre -strasbourg.fr in French; 3 rue Paul Janet; adult/student incl a drink €10/6; ⏰ 10pm-4am Wed-Sun) Billed as a *barclub spectacles*, this discotheque – warmly lit, friendly and with a marble fountain in the middle – has theme nights each Friday (salsa, disco, 1980s etc). Wednesday and Thursday are student nights (open to all). From October and April there's a *bal musette* (dancing to live French accordion music, salsa, tango and 1950s rock and roll; adult/student €12/8) on Sunday from 5pm to 10pm.

Café des Anges (☎ 03 88 37 12 67; 5 rue Ste Catherine; admission generally free; ⏰ 9pm-4am Mon-Sat, 7pm-4am Sun) On the ground floor – that is, *au paradis* (in paradise) – the DJ spins disks (everything from gypsy to *bal musette*) from inside a psychodelic Austin Mini amid décor inspired by Austin Powers: welcome (back) to the early 1970s. In the cellar – *en enfer* (in hell) – the darker world of *A Clockwork Orange* sets the tone: stage lights sweep the dance floor and drinks can be ordered at the bright red bar. Things don't start until midnight or 1am. There salsa every Sunday starting at 7pm.

Shopping

The city's fanciest shopping can be found on and around **rue des Hallebards**; the super-elegant window displays are real eye candy.

Second-hand goods and antiques are on sale at the small **Marché de Brocante** (southern end of rue du Vieux Marché aux Poissons; 9am-6pm Wed & Sat).

Getting There & Away

AIR

Strasbourg's **airport** (03 88 64 67 67; www.strasbourg.aeroport.fr) is 12km southwest of the city centre (towards Molsheim) near the village of Entzheim.

Ryanair (www.ryanair.com) no longer has cheap flights to Strasbourg (they were deemed a violation EU rules against state subsidies) but the company does link London Stansted with Karlsruhe–Baden Baden airport (www.badenairpark.de), about 50km to the northeast; both cities are linked to Strasbourg by train (about €15; 35 minutes).

BUS

As part of the French government's relentless campaign to restrict private-sector competition with the state-owned SNCF and 44.7% state-owned Air France, Eurolines buses must now stop 2.5km south of the **Eurolines office** (03 90 22 14 60; 6D place d'Austerlitz; 10am-6.30pm Mon-Fri, 10am-noon & 2-5pm Sat) near Stade de la Meinau (the city's main football stadium), on rue du Maréchal Lefèbvre about 200m west of av de Colmar and the Lycée Couffignal tram stop.

Strasbourg city bus No 21 (€1.20) links place Gutenberg with the Stadthalle in Kehl, the German town just across the Rhine.

CAR

Rental options:
Avis (03 88 32 30 44) In the train station's arrival hall.
Europcar (03 88 15 55 66; 16 place de la Gare)

National-Citer (03 88 23 60 76) In the train station's arrival hall.
Sixt (03 88 23 72 72; 31 blvd de Nancy)

TRAIN

Train information and tickets are available on the Grande Île at the **SNCF Boutique** (5 rue des France-Bourgeois; 10am-7pm Mon-Fri, to 5pm Sat).

The train station, built in 1883 and now being given a pre-TGV upgrade, is linked to Metz (€19.10, 1¼ hours, five to nine daily), Nancy (€18.40, 1¼ hours, nine to 12 daily), Lyon (€42.30, five hours, four or five direct daily) and Paris' Gare de l'Est (€40.90, four to 4½ hours, eight to 12 daily); and, internationally, to Basel (Bâle; €17.40, 1¼ hours, 15 direct each weekday, 11 daily on weekends), Frankfurt (€35.60, 2½ hours, six to eight nondirect daily) and Budapest (€147.80, 14 hours, nightly).

Route du Vin destinations include Colmar (€9.30, 31 to 60 minutes, 36 each weekday, 20 daily weekends), Dambach-la-Ville (€6.80, 45 to 70 minutes, 16 daily on weekdays, nine on Saturday, three on Sunday), Obernai (€4.70, 27 to 50 minutes, 20 daily weekdays, 10 on Saturday, three on Sunday) and Sélestat (€6.70, 20 to 40 minutes, 43 each weekday, 21 daily weekends).

In 2007, when the long-planned TGV-Est line (at 320km/h the fastest TGV yet) is supposed to go into operation, the trip from Strasbourg to Paris will take a mere two hours 20 minutes.

Getting Around

TO/FROM THE AIRPORT

CTS's **Navette Aéroport** (03 88 77 70 70) links the Baggersee tram stop with the airport (€4.80, 12 minutes). It runs every 20 minutes (every 20 or 30 minutes on weekends) until at least 9.50pm.

BICYCLE

Strasbourg, a European leader in bicycle-friendly planning, has an extensive and ever-expanding *réseau cyclable* (network of cycling paths and lanes; www.strasbourg.fr/Strasbourgfr/GB/SeDeplacer/Avelo). Free maps are available at the tourist office.

The city government's **Vélocation system** can supply you with a well-maintained one-speed bike for €4/7 per half-/whole day (plus a €100 deposit) – and just €18 a month for students! Outlets:

City Centre (☎ 03 88 24 05 61; 10 rue des Bouchers; tram stop Porte de l'Hôpital; 🕑 9.30am-noon & 2-6.30pm Mon-Fri, to 7pm Sat, Sun & holidays Apr-late Oct, 10am-5pm Mon-Fri late Oct-Mar)

Train Station (☎ 03 88 23 56 75; 4 rue du Maire Kuss; tram stop Alt Winmärik; 🕑 6am-7.30pm Mon-Fri, 9.30am-noon & 2-7pm Sat year-round, 9.30am-noon & 2-7pm Sun & holidays Apr-late Oct)

BUS & TRAM

Four highly civilised tram lines – to which a fifth line, 13.5km of track and 22 stations are to be added by 2007 – form the centrepiece of Strasbourg's excellent public transport network, run by **CTS** (☎ 03 88 77 70 70; information bureau 31 place Kléber). The main hub is at place de l'Homme de Fer. Buses – few of which pass through the Grande Île – run until about 11.30pm; trams generally operate until about 12.30am. This being earnest, hard-working Strasbourg there are no night buses.

Single bus/tram tickets, sold by bus drivers and the ticket machines at tram stops, cost €1.20. The Tourpass (€3), valid for 24 hours from the moment you time-stamp it, is sold at tourist offices and ticket machines. The weekly Hebdopass (€11, free CTS photo ID required) is good from Monday to Sunday.

In this chapter, tram stops are mentioned for places outside of the Grande Île, where relevant.

PARKING

Virtually the whole city centre is either pedestrianised or a hopeless maze of one-ways, so don't even think of getting around the Grande Île by car – or parking there for more than a couple of hours. For details on parking options check out www .parcus.com.

At Strasbourg's eight Park-and-Ride (Parking-Relais) lots, all on tram lines, the €2.40 all-day fee gets the driver and each passenger a free round-trip tram ride into the city centre. If you'd like to visit the city without car hassles this is the way to do it. To get to a Park-and-Ride lot from the autoroute, follow the signs marked 'P+R Tram'.

TAXI

Round-the-clock companies:

Alsace France Taxi (☎ 03 88 22 19 19)
Taxi Treize (☎ 03 88 36 13 13)

ROUTE DU VIN D'ALSACE

Meandering for some 120km along the eastern foothills of the Vosges, the Alsace Wine

---

NATZWEILER-STRUTHOF CONCENTRATION CAMP

A mere 50km southwest of Strasbourg stands the only Nazi concentration camp on French soil, Natzweiler-Struthof. The site was chosen by Hitler's personal architect, Albert Speer, because of the nearby deposits of valuable pink granite, in whose extraction – in the **Grande Carrière** (Large Quarry) – many inmates were worked to death as slave labourers. In all, some 10,000 to 12,000 of the camp's prisoners died; many were shot or hung and some were gassed. In early September 1944, as the Allies were approaching, the 5517 surviving inmates were sent to Dachau.

The camp provided the Reichsuniversität (Reich University) in Strasbourg with inmates for use in often lethal pseudo-medical experiments involving chemical warfare agents (mustard gas, phosgene) and infectious diseases such as hepatitis and typhus. In April 1943 86 Jews (including 30 women) specially brought from Auschwitz were gassed here to supply the university's anatomical institute with skulls and full skeletons for its anthropological and racial skeleton collection. After liberation, their bodies, preserved in alcohol, were found by Allied troops in Strasbourg.

Today, visitors can see the remains of the **camp** (☎ 03 88 97 04 49; adult/under 16 €1.52/free; 🕑 10am-6pm Jul & Aug, 10am-noon & 2-5.30pm Mar-Jun, 10am-noon & 2-5pm Sep-24 Dec), whose barracks – one housing a **museum** – are still surrounded by guard towers and two rows of barbed wire. The **chambre à gaz** (gas chamber), an ordinary-looking building 1.7km down the D130 from the camp gate, the **four crématoire** (crematorium oven) and the **salle d'autopsie** (autopsy room) bear grim witness to the unspeakable atrocities committed here.

To get to Natzweiler-Struthof from Obernai, take the D426, D214 and D130; follow the signs to 'Le Struthof' or 'Camp du Struthof'.

Route passes through villages guarded by ruined hilltop castles, surrounded by vine-clad slopes and coloured by half-timbered houses. Combine such charms with numerous roadside *caves* (wine cellars), where you can sample Alsace's crisp white varietal wines (in particular Riesling and Gewürztraminer – the accent is on the 'tra'), and you have one of France's busiest tourist tracks. Local tourist offices can supply you with an English-language map-brochure, *The Alsace Wine Route*.

The Route du Vin, at places twee and commercial, stretches from Marlenheim, about 20km west of Strasbourg, southwards to Thann, about 35km southwest of Colmar. En route are some of Alsace's most picturesque villages (and some very ordinary ones, too), many extensively rebuilt after being flattened in WWII. Ramblers can take advantage of the area's *sentiers viticoles* (signposted vineyard trails) and the paths leading up the eastern slopes of the Vosges to the remains of medieval bastions.

The villages mentioned below – listed from north to south – all have plenty of hotels, camping areas and restaurants. *Chambres d'hôtes* (B&Bs) can cost as little as €25 (plus breakfast) for a double – tourist offices can provide details on local options.

Tours
For minibus tours of the Route du Vin:

LCA Top Tour (☎ 03 89 41 90 88, after hours ☎ 06 88 40 21 02; www.alsace-travel.com; 6 place de la Gare, Colmar; half-day €47.50) Reservations can be made via the Colmar tourist office.

Regioscope (☎ 06 88 21 27 15; www.regioscope.com; morning/afternoon tour €39/48) Based in Mulhouse. Also offers visits to the Vosges.

Getting There & Around
The Route du Vin, which is not just one road but also a composite of several (the D422, D35, D1bis and so on), can be followed by car or bicycle. It is well signposted but you might want to pick up a copy of Blay's colour-coded map, *Alsace Touristique* (€5.65). Cyclists will find IGN maps such as *Le Haut-Rhin à Vélo* (€5.40) invaluable.

Parking can be a nightmare in the high season, especially in Ribeauvillé and Riquewihr. Your best bet is to park outside town centres and walk.

It's possible to get around the Route du Vin by public transport since most of the towns and villages mentioned below are served by train and/or bus from Strasbourg (see p356) and Colmar (see p367). On many trains you can take along a bicycle.

Obernai
pop 9600

This walled town, 35km south of Strasbourg, is centred on the picturesque place du Marché, an ancient market square that's still put to use each Thursday morning. Around the square you'll find the mainly 16th-century **hôtel de ville** (town hall), decorated with baroque trompe l'œil; the Renaissance **Puits aux Six Seaux** (Well of the Six Buckets), across rue du Général Gouraud (the main street); and the partly stone **Halle aux Blés** (Corn Exchange; 1554), from whose flanks pedestrianised rue du Marché and tiny parallel ruelle du Canal de l'Ehn – just a hand's breadth wide – lead to the Vosges-sandstone **synagogue** (1876). The cool and flower-bedecked courtyards and alleyways (such as little ruelle des Juifs, next to the tourist office) are fun to explore, as are the 1.75km-long, 13th-century **ramparts**.

A number of wine cellars are just a short walk from town. From the hilltop cross north of town, the 1.5km **Sentier Viticole du Schenkenberg** takes you through vineyards.

The **tourist office** (☎ 03 88 95 64 13; www.obernai.fr; place du Beffroi; ⏱ 9.30am-12.30pm & 2-7pm daily Jul & Aug, 9am-noon & 2-6pm daily Apr-Jun, Sep & Oct, 9am-noon & 2-5pm Mon-Sat Nov-Mar) is behind the *hôtel de ville*, opposite the 59m **Kapellturm** (Belfry), completed in 1280.

La Cloche (☎ 03 88 95 52 89; 90 rue du Général Gouraud; s/d from €30/37.50, with shower & toilet €39/47), a two-star Logis de France-affiliated hotel facing the *hôtel de ville*, has 20 spacious, wood-furnished rooms, some with classic views of the ancient town centre. Charming and atmospheric, its rustic **restaurant** (menus €13-26; ⏱ closed dinner Sun Dec-Feb) serves delicious bourgeois Alsatian cuisine.

The train station is about 300m east of the old town.

Mont Ste-Odile
Occupied by a convent originally founded in the 8th century (it's been destroyed and rebuilt several times since), the 763m-high summit of Mont Ste-Odile is a place of great

spiritual meaning for many Alsatians, in part because it affords spectacular views of the wine country and, nearer the Rhine, the fields of white cabbage (for sauerkraut) around Krautergersheim. Vestiges of the 10km **Mur Païen** (Pagan Wall), built by the Celts around 1000 BC and fixed up by the Romans, are nearby. The summit, surrounded by conifer forests, can be reached on foot via a network of trails that come from every direction, including Obernai, 12km to the northeast.

Mittelbergheim
pop 620

A solid hillside village with no real centre, Mittelbergheim is awash with Sylvaner grape vines, its tiny streets lined with ancient houses in subdued tones of tan, mauve and terra cotta. From **Parking de Zotzenberg** (northern edge of the village on the D362), named after the local *grand cru* (a wine grown in a vineyard bearing the region's most prestigious AOC classification), a paved *sentier viticole* heads across the slopes toward the two towers of the Château du Haut Andlau and the Vosges. A stroll along rue Principale (the main street) will take you past the red sandstone **Catholic Église St-Martin** (next to No 17) built in 1893 and, a block down, the Protestant **Église St-Étienne** (next to No 30) dating from the 12th to the 17th centuries.

The two-star **Hôtel Gilg** (☎ 03 88 08 91 37; www.reperes.com/gilg; 1 route du Vin - the D362; d €47-68; ♥ reception closed Tue & Wed), built in 1614 (the trompe l'oeil dates from 2001), has woodpanelled rooms – reached via a spiral stone staircase – that are as almost as romantic as the village. Reserve well in advance for May, September and October. The rustically elegant **restaurant** (menus €18-66; ♥ closed Tue & Wed) serves classic French and Alsatian cuisine.

Private accommodation is easy to come by – you'll see *'chambres/zimmer'* signs in windows all over town; a list of about two dozen options is posted outside the Renaissance **hôtel de ville** (☎ tourist office 03 88 08 01 66; 2 rue Principale).

Dambach-la-Ville
pop 2000

Surrounded by vines, this village has plenty of wine cellars but manages to avoid touristic overload. The best-preserved sections of the 14th-century, pink-granite **ramparts** are along the southwestern side of the old

town; three of the four original watchtowers still stand. Some of the superb half-timbered houses date from before 1500.

The neo-Romanesque **Église St-Étienne** (place de l'Église) and the **synagogue** (rue de la Paix), unused since WWII, both date from the 1860s.

The **tourist office** (☎ 03 88 92 61 00; www.pays-de -barr.com; place du Marché; ♥ 9am-noon & 2-6pm Mon-Sat, 10am-12.30pm Sun Jul & Aug, 10am-noon & 2-6pm Mon-Fri, 2-6pm Sat rest of year), in the mid-16th-century Renaissance-style **hôtel de ville**, can supply you with a walking-tour brochure.

The renowned Frankstein *grand cru* vineyards cover the southern and southeastern slopes of four granitic hills west and southwest of Dambach. The two-hour **Sentier Viticole du Frankstein** meanders among the hallowed vines, passing by the hillside **Chapelle St-Sebastien** (♥ 9am-7pm May-Oct, 9am-4pm or 5pm Sat, Sun & holidays Nov-Apr), known for its Romanesque tower, Gothic choir, Renaissance windows and baroque high altar. The granite 12th-century **Château du Bernstein**, with its pentagonal tower, is about an hour's walk westwards up the hill.

The train station is about 1km east of the old town.

Sélestat
pop 17,500

Sélestat is the largest town between Strasbourg, 50km to the north, and Colmar, 23km to the south. Its claim to cultural fame is the 15th- and 16th-century **Bibliothèque Humaniste** (Humanist Library; ☎ 03 88 58 07 20; 1 rue de la Bibliothèque; adult/student €3.60/2; ♥ 9am-noon & 2-6pm Mon & Wed-Fri, Sat morning year-round, also open 2-5pm Sat & Sun Jul & Aug), whose displays include a 7th-century book of Merovingian liturgy, a 10th century treatise on Roman architecture and a copy of *Cosmographiae Introductio*, printed in 1507 in the Vosges town of St-Dié, in which the New World was referred to as 'America' for the very first time. An audioguide costs €1.55; explanatory sheets are available in six languages.

Maison du Pain (☎ 03 88 58 45 90; rue du Sel; admission €4.60; ♥ 10am-noon & 2-6pm Tue-Fri, 2-6pm Sat, 10am-1pm & 2-5pm Sun year-round, also 10am-1pm Sat Jul & Aug), 50m from the Bibliothèque Humaniste, showcases not S&M but rather the art of bread-making. It is run by local *boulangers*.

The 13th- to 15th-century **Église St-Georges**, one of Alsace's loveliest Gothic churches, has curtains of stained glass – some from the 1300s and 1400s – in the choir. Nearby, the 12th-century Romanesque **Église St-Foy** was heavily restored in the 19th century.

Vieux Sélestat, the old town area south and southwest of the churches, is a mainly post-war commercial precinct dotted with half-timbered and *trompe-l'œil* shop buildings. An **outdoor market**, held since 1435, takes over the streets around Église St-Foy from 8am to noon every Tuesday.

The turn-off to the **cimetière israélite** (Jewish cemetery; ☉ 8am-6pm Apr-Sep except Sat & Jewish holidays, to 4pm Oct-Mar) is 1.8km north of Sélestat's water tower along the N83. The key is kept by the people in the house facing the entrance.

The usual information is available at the **tourist office** (☎ 03 88 58 87 20; www.selestat-tourisme.com in French; blvd du Général Leclerc; ☉ 9am-noon & 2-5.45pm, to 5pm Sat, closed Sun & holidays year-round, longer hours & open 11am-3pm Sun & holidays Jul & Aug).

The train station is 1km west of the Bibliothèque Humaniste.

Bergheim
pop 1830

The delightful walled town of Bergheim – overflowing with geraniums, dotted with flowerbeds and enlivened by half-timbered houses in shocking pastels – is more spacious than its neighbours. But things have not always been so cheerful: over the centuries, the town has passed from one overlord to another – having been sold, ceded or captured – some 20 times; and between 1582 and 1630, 35 women and one man were burnt at the stake here for witchcraft. **Maison des Sorcières** (House of the Witches; ☎ 03 89 73 85 20; rue de l'Église; adult €3; ☉ 2-6pm Wed-Sun Jul & Aug, 2.30-6.30pm Sun & holidays May, Jun, Sep & Oct) takes a hard look at the local witch hunts.

The centre, spared the ravages of WWII, is dominated by the 14th-century, early-Gothic **church**, significantly modified in the early 1700s. The wall-mounted **sundial** at 44 Grand' Rue has its origins in 1711. The tile-roofed, 14th-century, Gothic **Porte Haute** is the only one of the village's original three main gates still extant; across the car park, the **Herrengarten lime tree**, planted around 1300, is hanging in there but looks like it could use a hug. Bergheim's *grands crus* are Kanzlerberg and Altenberg de Bergheim.

The tiny **tourist office** (☎ 03 89 73 31 98; ☉ most days Jun-Sep), staffed by volunteers, is between the well-proportioned **hôtel de ville**, constructed of red sandstone in 1767, and the **synagogue**, built in 1863 on the site of an early-14th-century synagogue.

Just inside the Porte Haute, **La Cour du Bailli** (☎ 03 89 73 73 46; www.cour-bailli.com; 57 Grand' Rue; 2–8-person studio mid-Jun–early Oct & Dec €65-110, rest of year €56-99; ☉ reception 10am-6pm) is a three-star apartment hotel built around a flowery, 16th-century courtyard. Its 24 spacious and very comfortable studios come with kitchenettes. There are several reasonable **restaurants** between here and the *hôtel de ville*.

Haut Kœnigsbourg
Perched on a lushly forested promontory and offering superb vistas, the imposing red-sandstone **Château du Haut Kœnigsbourg** (☎ 03 88 82 50 60; adult/student under 26/under 18 €7/4.50/free, adult €5.50 if you buy your ticket at the Riquewihr or Ribeauvillé tourist offices; ☉ 9.30am-6.30pm Jun-Aug, 9.30am-5.30pm Apr, May & Sep, 9.45am-5pm Mar & Oct, 9.45am-noon & 1-5pm Nov-Feb) makes a very medieval impression despite having been reconstructed in the early 1900s – with German imperial pomposity – by Kaiser Wilhelm II (r 1888–1918).

Ribeauvillé
pop 4750

Ribeauvillé, some 19km northwest of Colmar, is arguably the most heavily touristed of all the villages on the Route du Vin. It's easy to see why: this little village, nestled in a valley and brimming with 18th-century overhanging houses and narrow alleys, is picture-perfect.

Don't miss the 17th-century **Pfifferhüs** (Fifers' House; 14 Grand' Rue), which once housed the town's fife-playing minstrels and is now home to a friendly *winstub*; the **hôtel de ville** (town hall; across from 64 Grand' Rue) and its Renaissance fountain; or the nearby clock-equipped **Tour des Bouchers** (Butchers' Bell-tower; 13th and 16th centuries).

Just across the traffic roundabout from the tourist office, the **Cave Vinicole** (☎ 03 89 73 61 80; www.cave-ribeauville.com; 2 route de Colmar; admission & tasting free; ☉ 9am-noon & 2-6pm), a winegrowers' cooperative founded way back in 1895, has a small museum and very informative brochures in English.

West and northwest of Ribeauvillé, the remains of three 12th- and 13th-century hilltop castles – **St-Ulrich** (530m), **Giersberg** (530m) and **Haut Ribeaupierre** (642m) – can be reached on a three-hour hike. The local *grands crus* are Kirchberg de Ribeauvillé, Osterberg and Geisberg.

The **tourist office** (☎ 0 820 360 922, from abroad ☎ 03 89 49 08 40; www.ribeauville-riquewihr.com; 1 Grand' Rue; ⏰ 9.30am-noon & 2-6pm Mon-Sat Apr-Oct & Dec, 10am-1pm Sun May-Oct & Dec, 10am-noon & 2-5pm Mon-Fri & alternate Sat rest of year), the area's best equipped, is at the southern end of the main street, the one-way (south-to-north) Grand' Rue.

Hunawihr
pop 515
About 1km on foot south of Ribeauvillé, this quiet hamlet, surrounded by a 14th-century wall and vineyards, feels more solid and serious than its neighbours do. On a hillside just outside the centre, the 16th-century fortified **church**, surrounded by a hexagonal wall, has been a *simultaneum* – that is, it has served both the Catholic and Protestant communities – since 1687.

About 500m east of Hunawihr, the **Centre de Réintroduction des Cigognes** (Stork Reintroduction Centre; ☎ 03 89 73 28 48; adult/5-14 yrs €7.50/5; ⏰ 10am-noon & 2pm-btwn 5pm & 7pm, no midday closure weekends & Jun-Aug, closed mid-Nov–late Mar) is *the* place in Alsace to see storks up close (see below). Home base for about 150 free-flying storks (who gobble up 45 tonnes of chopped meat each year), the centre is also working to reintroduce otters to the area. Cormorants, penguins, otters and a sea lion show off their fishing prowess several times each afternoon.

At the nearby **Jardins des Papillons** (Butterfly Gardens; ☎ 03 89 73 33 33; ⏰ Apr-1 Nov) you can stroll among exotic free-flying butterflies.

Riquewihr
pop 1080
This largely pedestrianised village is every bit as popular with visitors as Ribeauvillé, 5km to the north, but feels much more medieval. The 16th-century **ramparts** are great for exploring, as are the alleys and courtyards. The *grands crus* here are Schoenenbourg (north of town) and Sporen (southeast of town).

The late-13th-century **Dolder** (admission €2; ⏰ daily Jul & Aug, Sat, Sun & holidays Easter-Jun & Sep-2 Nov) is a stone and half-timbered gate – topped by a bell tower – with a small local-history museum inside. From there, rue des Juifs leads to the **Tour des Voleurs** (Thieves' Tower; admission incl

STORKS

White storks *(cigognes)*, long a feature of Alsatian folklore, are one of the region's most beloved symbols. Believed to bring luck (as well as babies), they winter in Africa and then spend the warmer months in Europe, feeding in the marshes (their favourite delicacies include worms, insects, small rodents and even frogs) and building their nests of twigs and sticks on church steeples, rooftops and tall trees.

When mid-August arrives, instinct tells young storks – at the age of just a few months – to fly south for a two- or three-year, 12,000km trek to sub-Saharan Africa (Alsatian storks are particularly fond of Mali and Mauritania), from where they return to Alsace ready to breed – if they return at all. Research has shown that over 90% die en route because of electrocution, hunting, exhaustion and dehydration. In subsequent years, the adult storks – 1m long, with a 2m wingspan and weighing 3.5kg – make only a short trek south for the winter, returning to Alsace to breed after a few months in Africa.

Since about 1960, however, the draining of the marshes along the Rhine, hunting and droughts in Africa, chemical poisons and – most lethal of all – high-tension lines have reduced stork numbers catastrophically. By the early 1980s there were only two pairs left in the wild in all of Alsace.

In the 1970s and 1980s, research and breeding centres were set up with the goal of establishing a permanent, year-round Alsatian stork population. The young birds spend the first three years of their lives in captivity, which causes them to lose their migratory instinct and thus avoid the rigours and dangers of migration. The programme has been a huge success, and today Alsace – the western extremity of the storks' range – is home to 250 pairs.

See above and p368 for details of stork-breeding centres.

the Dolder €3; (✓) Easter-2 Nov), a former dungeon containing some extremely efficient-looking implements of torture. The **Château des Princes de Wurtemberg-Montbéliard**, (1540), now houses the **Musée de la Communication** (☎ 03 89 47 93 80; (✓) Wed-Mon early Apr-1 Nov), which traces the development of written and voice communications, especially in Alsace, from the Roman period to the present. A must for fans of mail coaches!

The **tourist office** (2 rue de la Première Armée) has the same contact details and opening hours as its Ribeauvillé colleague.

Le Sarment d'Or (☎ 03 89 86 02 86; www.riquewihr -sarment-dor.com; 4 rue du Cerf; d €57-77), a two-star hotel with 10 rooms, has a very local atmosphere and charming touches in every corner. The attached **restaurant** (menus €18-52; (✓) closed Mon, lunch Tue & dinner Sun) is resolutely French. To get there walk down the narrow medieval street across from 60 rue du Général de Gaulle.

Kaysersberg
pop 3000
In the middle of the picture-perfect centre of Kaysersberg, 10km northwest of Colmar, stands the red-sandstone Catholic **church** (12th to 15th centuries), which has the ornate Renaissance **hôtel de ville** (1605) on one side and a Renaissance **fountain** on the other. Up the main street, av du Général de Gaulle (one way going west to east, ie downhill), there are lots of colourful old houses, many half-timbered, others showing baroque influences; further along is the squat, **fortified bridge** (next to No 84), built to span the River Weiss in 1514.

You can see master glass-blowers practising their magic at **Verrerie d'Art** (☎ 03 89 47 14 97; 30 rue du Général de Gaulle; (✓) 10am-12.15pm & 2-5.45pm Tue-Sat year-round, 2-5.45pm Sun mid-Apr–late Dec).

The house where the musicologist, medical doctor and 1952 Nobel Peace Prize winner **Albert Schweitzer** (1875–1965) was born is now a **museum** (☎ 03 89 47 36 55; 126 rue du Général de Gaulle; adult/child €2/1; (✓) 9am-noon & 2-6pm Apr-11 Nov & weekends late Nov-late Dec) with exhibits on the good doctor's life in Alsace and Gabon.

On the hill above town, the remains of a massive, crenellated **chateau** stand surrounded by vines. Footpaths lead in all directions from Kaysersberg through glen and vineyard; possible destinations include

Riquewihr (1½ hours), Labaroche (2½ hours) and Ribeauvillé (three hours).

The **tourist office** (☎ 03 89 78 22 78; www.kayser sberg.com; 37 rue du Général de Gaulle; (✓) 9am-12.30pm & 1.30-6.30pm Mon-Sat, 10am-2pm Sun Jul & Aug, 8.30am-noon & 1-5.30pm Mon-Sat Sep-Jun) is inside the *hôtel de ville*.

Painted yellow-orange and very Alsatian in ambience, the **Hôtel Arbre Vert** (☎ 03 89 47 11 51; http://perso.wanadoo.fr/arbrevertbellepromenade; 1 rue Haute du Rempart; d from €61; (✓) reception closed 11am-2pm or 3pm Mon, Tue & Thu-Sat, closed after 7pm Mon, hotel closed Jan), with two stars and 22 rooms, is at the western edge of the town centre next to 135 rue du Général de Gaulle.

COLMAR
pop 67,000
The centre of the harmonious town of Colmar, capital of the Haut-Rhin *département*, is a maze of cobbled pedestrian malls and Alsatian-style buildings from the late Middle Ages or the Renaissance. Many of the half-timbered houses are painted in tones of blue, orange, red or green. The Musée d'Unterlinden is renowned worldwide for the profoundly moving *Issenheim Altarpiece*.

The Route du Vin (p357) can be explored by bike, car and even bus using Colmar as a base. And for something a bit different, it's easy to take day trips to the German university city of Freiburg and the Swiss city of Basel, each about an hour away.

Orientation
Avenue de la République links the train station and the intercity bus terminal with the Musée d'Unterlinden and the nearby tourist office, a distance of about 1km. The old city, much of it pedestrianised, is southeast of the Musée d'Unterlinden. The Petite Venise quarter runs along the River Lauch, at the southern edge of the old city.

Information
Cyber Didim (☎ 03 89 23 20 44; 9 rue du Rempart; per hr €2.70; (✓) theoretically 10am-midnight Mon-Sat, 2-11pm Sun) Upstairs at the döner kebab place.
Hôpital Pasteur; ☎ 03 89 12 40 94; 39 av de la Liberté; (✓) 24hr) Situated 700m west of the train station and served by bus lines 1, 3, 10, A, C and S.
Laundrette (1b rue Ruest; (✓) 7am-9pm)
Le Poussin Vert cybercafé (☎ 03 89 41 18 58; 37 route de Neuf-Brisach; per hr €2; (✓) 1pm-1.30am Mon-Sat, 3pm-1.30am Sun)

COLMAR

INFORMATION
Cyber Didim...................................1 C1
Laundrette......................................2 E1
Le Poussin Vert Cybercafé...........3 E1
Main Post Office...........................4 B3
Tourist Office................................5 C1

SIGHTS & ACTIVITIES   (pp364–5)
Ancienne Douane..........................6 D3
Collégiale St Martin......................7 D2
Église des Dominicains.................8 C2
Entrance to Église des
  Dominicains................................9 C2
Maison des Têtes................(see 18)
Maison Pfister.............................10 D2
Musée Bartholdi..........................11 D2
Musée du Jouet...........................12 E1
Musée d'Unterlinden...................13 C1
Rue de Turenne Bridge................14 D3
Synagogue...................................15 E2
Temple St-Mathieu......................16 D2

SLEEPING   (pp365–6)
Grand Hôtel Bristol......................17 A4
Hôtel des Têtes...........................18 C2
Hôtel Kempf................................19 C2

EATING   (p366)
Aux Trois Poissons......................20 D3
Covered Market...........................21 D3
Djerba La Douce..........................22 D2
Fromagerie St-Nicolas..................23 D2
La Maison des Têtes...........(see 18)
La Maison Rouge..........................24 D3
Le Temps des Délices...................25 E2
Les Gourmets d'Asie....................26 E2
Monoprix Supermarket................27 D1

DRINKING   (p366)
Bar Le Seven & Club VIP..............28 B2
Blue Cat's Club............................29 C1

ENTERTAINMENT   (pp366–7)
Théâtre Municipal........................30 C1

TRANSPORT   (p367)
ADA..31 B2
Bus Terminal.................................32 A4
Colmarvélo...................................33 C2
Cycles Geiswiller..........................34 C2
Unterlinden/Point Central Bus
  Hub..35 C1
Water Tower.................................36 C4

ALSACE & LORRAINE

To Statue of Liberty (3km);
Riquewihr (15km);
Kaysersberg (11km);
Strasbourg (67km)

To N415;
Freiburg-im-Breisgau
(Germany 50km)

N442

To Hôtel Beau
Séjour (500m)

Route de Neuf-Brisach

Av d'Alsace

R. de l'Est

R. de la Grenouillère
R. de la Cigogne

Quartier
des
Tanneurs

Pl. de la
Montagne
Verte

Police
Nationale

Lunch

R. Schwendi

R. des Fleurs

Old City

Petite
Venise

R. de la Poissonnerie

R. de Turenne

Blvd St-Pierre

R. des Américains

R. Barthold i

Route de Bâle

R. des Écoles

R. St-Jean

R. des Augustins

Pl.
du Marché
aux Fruits

R. des Marchands

R. Berthe Molly

R. des Boulangers

R. St-Éloi

R. Vauban

R. Ruest

R. d'Alspach

R. des Clefs

R. du
Mouton

R. Jeanne
d'Arc

Pl. du
2 Février

Pl. de
l'Ancienne
Douane

R. des Tanneurs

R. Mercière

Pl. de la
Cathédrale

R. des Serruriers

R. St-Nicolas

R. des Prêtres

R. du Rapp

R. Étoile

Hôtel
de Ville

Pl. de
la Mairie

Ste-
Anne

Cours
Ste-
Anne

R. du Rempart

R. du Nord

Route de Neuf-Brisach

R. des Ancêtres

R. des
Dominicains

Pl. des
Dominicains

R. Kléber

R. des Têtes

R. des Boulangers

R. Chasseur

R. de Turenne

Blvd du Général Leclerc

Blvd du Champ de Mars

Champ
de
Mars

Pl. Rapp

Merry-Go-Round
& Children's
Playground

R. Hérlich

Av Jean de Lattre de Tassigny

Pl. Jean
de Lattre R Stanislas
de Tassigny

R. Stanislas

R. Édouard Richard

R. Jacques Preiss

R. des Îles

R. des Îlandais

R. de la Marne

Av de la République

R. Buat

R. Camille Schlumberger

R. Gambetta

R. Me-Jmv

Courthouse

R. de Reims

Av de la Gare

Pl. de
la Gare Train
Station

Pedestrian
Tunnel

R. des Trois
Épis

R. Bruat

Av de la Liberté

R. du Tir

R. du Schauenberg

To Hôpital
Pasteur
(300m)

To D417; Vallée de
de Munster

Av de Munster

R. du Canal

To Rouffach (12km);
Guebwiller (26km);
Thann (35km); Route
de Rouffach; N83; Cernay
(35km); Route des Crêtes

To A35; Mulhouse
(45km); Basel (67km)

Route d'Ingersheim

To La Manufacture (200m);
Auberge de Jeunesse
Mittelhart (1km); N415

Pl. de
la Sinn

Av Raymond Poincaré

300 m
0.2 miles

0
0

Main Post Office (36 av de la République; ☒ 8am-6.30pm Mon-Fri, 8.30am-noon Sat) Has exchange services and a Cyberposte.

Tourist Office (☎ 03 89 20 68 92; www.ot-colmar.fr; 4 rue des Unterlinden; ☒ 9am-noon & 2-6pm Mon-Sat, 10am-1pm Sun & holidays, longer hours in some seasons) Can supply you with information on cultural events, hiking, cycling and bus travel along the Route du Vin and in the Massif des Vosges.

Sights

OLD CITY

The medieval streets of the old city, including **rue des Clefs**, the **Grand' Rue** and **rue des Marchands**, are lined with dozens of restored, half-timbered houses. **Maison Pfister** (1537), opposite 36 rue des Marchands, is remarkable for its exterior decoration, including delicately painted panels, an elaborate oriel window and a carved wooden balcony. The house next door at 9 rue des Marchands, which dates from 1419, has a wooden sculpture of an uptight-looking *marchand* (merchant) – has his tulip portfolio just tanked? – on the corner. **Maison des Têtes** (House of the Heads; 19 rue des Têtes), built in 1609, has a fantastic façade crowded with 106 grimacing stone faces and animal heads.

LADY LIBERTY IN COLMAR

On 4 July 2004 Colmar celebrated the centenary of the death of Frédéric Auguste Bartholdi (1834–1904) by inaugurating a 12m-high replica of the Statue of Liberty at the town's northern entrance. Made of stratified resin supported by an Eiffelesque internal metal frame, Lady Liberty II bears her torch 3km north of the old city on route de Strasbourg (the N83), in the middle of a traffic roundabout near Colmar-Houssen airfield. Around her base congregate the huddled masses, yearning for another glassful of Gewürztraminer... By the way, the copper-skinned New York original (www.nps.gov/stli), which was dedicated in 1886, is four times as tall (eight times as tall including the pedestal).

A €0.90 French **postage stamp** featuring the *Statue de la Liberté* and honouring Bartholdi was issued in Colmar and Paris on 21-22 February 2004. In 1986 France and the USA issued identical stamps in honour of the statue's 100th anniversary.

Colmar has a number of small *quartiers* (quarters) – often not much more than a single street – which preserve the ambience that reigned back when each was home to a specific guild. **Rue des Tanneurs**, with its tall houses and rooftop verandas for drying hides, intersects **quai de la Poissonnerie**, the former fishers' quarter, which runs along the Lauch. The river provides the delightful **Petite Venise** (Little Venice) area – also known as Quartier de la Krutenau – with its rather fanciful appellation. It is best appreciated from the **rue de Turenne bridge**.

At the southeastern end of rue des Marchands, near **Quartier des Tanneurs** (Tanners' District), is the **Ancienne Douane** (Koïfhus in Alsatian; Old Customs House), built in 1480 and topped with a variegated tiled roof. Now used for temporary exhibitions and concerts, it is the town's best example of late-medieval civil architecture.

Colmar's historic buildings are lit up after nightfall by computer-controlled spotlights every Friday and Saturday (daily during festival periods and from late November to December).

MUSEUMS

The **Issenheim Altarpiece** (Rétable d'Issenheim), acclaimed as one of the most dramatic and moving works of art ever created, is the pride and joy of the **Musée d'Unterlinden** (☎ 03 89 20 15 50; www.musee-unterlinden.com; 1 rue d'Unterlinden; adult/student under 26 incl an audioguide €7/5; ☒ 9am-6pm daily May-Oct, 9am-noon & 2-5pm Wed-Mon Nov-Apr). Other exhibits range from an Alsatian wine cellar to medieval armour and from Strasbourg faïence to Revolutionary memorabilia.

Dedicated to the Colmar native who created New York's Statue of Liberty, the **Musée Bartholdi** (☎ 03 89 41 90 60; 30 rue des Marchands; adult/student/under 12 €4.10/2.50/free; ☒ 10am-noon & 2-6pm Wed-Mon Mar-Dec) displays the works (including models) and memorabilia of Frédéric Auguste Bartholdi in the house where he was born. Highlights include a full-size plaster model of the Lady Liberty's left ear (the lobe is watermelon-sized!) and the Bartholdi family's sparklingly bourgeois apartment. A ground-floor room is dedicated to 18th- and 19th-century Jewish ritual objects.

At the **Musée du Jouet** (Toy Museum; ☎ 03 89 41 93 10; 40 rue Vauban; adult/6-17 yrs €4/3, for groups of 4 or more €3/1.50; ☒ 9am-6pm daily Jul-Sep, 10am-noon &

2-6pm Wed-Mon Oct-Jun), kids of every age will be delighted to see toys, dolls and trains from generations past.

HOUSES OF WORSHIP

The 13th- and 14th-century Gothic **Collégiale St-Martin** (place de la Cathédrale; 8am-6.30pm except during services) has a sombre ambulatory and a peculiar, Mongol-style copper spire (1572).

The celebrated triptych *La Vierge au Buisson de Roses* (The Virgin in the Rose Bush), painted by Martin Schongauer in 1473, can be seen inside the desanctified Gothic **Église des Dominicains** (adult/student €1.30/1; 10am-1pm & 3-6pm Apr-Dec). In 1972 the work made world headlines when it was stolen, not to be recovered until 18 months later. The stained glass is from the 14th and 15th centuries.

Temple St-Mathieu (Grande' Rue; 10am-noon & 3-5pm around Easter, 20 May-about 7 Jun & end Jul-about 7 Oct), typically Protestant in its austerity, has something of a split personality. From 1715 to 1987, a wall cut off the soaring 14th-century Gothic choir – a Catholic hospital chapel until 1937 – from the nave, long a Protestant church. Thanks to this odd architectural arrangement, the 14th-century *jubé* (rood screen) – such structures were removed from most Catholic churches during the counter-Reformation – survived. The elaborate Silbermann organ is used for concerts.

God only knows why Colmar's classical-style 1843 **synagogue** (3 rue de la Cigogne) has its very own belfry (Jews have no tradition of ringing bells), but if 19th-century neo-Moorish synagogues (eg the Great Synagogue of Budapest) can have minarets, why not?

Festivals & Events

From mid-May to mid-September, **Soirées Folkloriques** (free performances of Alsatian music and dancing) are held at 8.30pm on Tuesday at place de l'Ancienne Douane.

Vintners display their creations at the **Foire Régionale des Vins d'Alsace** (Regional Wine Fair of Alsace), which attracts large numbers of visitors from the weekend before 15 August until the following weekend. Local food specialities are also on offer. During the summer, villages all over Alsace hold **Fêtes du Vin** (Wine Festivals) featuring wine and song; the tourist office supplies details.

During the first two weeks of July, Colmar plays host to a number of music festivals, including the Western-classical **Festival International de Colmar** (www.festival-colmar.com). The **Festival de Jazz** takes place in early or mid-September.

Colmar's magical **Marché de Noël** (Christmas Market; www.noel-colmar.com) runs from the last Saturday in November to 31 December.

Sleeping

In December (during the Christmas market), around Easter and from mid-July to mid-August (especially during the wine fairs) most hotels are booked up well in advance.

BUDGET

Auberge de Jeunesse Mittelhart (☎ 03 89 80 57 39; fax 03 89 80 76 16; 2 rue Pasteur; dm/d with 2 bunks incl breakfast €11.65/28.30; reception 8-10am & 5-11pm, to midnight during daylight savings time, closed mid-Dec–mid-Jan) This one-time orphanage isn't cheery (it's not hard to imagine lonely children crying themselves to sleep) but the management does its best. An old-style place with 110 beds, hall showers and kitchen facilities, it's situated 1.2km northwest of the tourist office, just around the corner from 76 route d'Ingersheim. Curfew is 11pm (midnight during daylight savings time). By bus take No 4, 5, 6, 12 or 15 to the Pont Rouge stop.

Hôtel Kempf (☎ 03 89 41 21 72; www.chez.com/mawo/kempf.html; 1 av de la République; d from €28, with shower & toilet €40) The phone system may date from before Sputnik and the rooms may be plain Jane, but the mattresses at this family-run two-star place are especially comfortable and the showers squirt torrents of hot water. To get there by car, follow the signs to the Rapp car park.

MID-RANGE & TOP END

Hôtel Beau Séjour (☎ 03 89 20 66 66; www.beausejour.fr; 25 rue du Ladhof; d depending on size & season €49-85, apt-style d per week €180-330; P) This venerable and very classy three-star hostelry, built in 1913, has been run by the Keller family for five generations. Everything about it oozes charm, from the rooms, some with Provençal or Louis XV décor, to the elegant restaurant. Situated about 1km northeast of the centre.

Grand Hôtel Bristol (☎ 03 89 23 59 59; www .grand-hotel-bristol.com; 7 place de la Gare; d from €75; **P**) A marble stairway leads from the plush lobby of this Best Western-affiliated three-star place (built in 1925) to grand hallways and rooms in which you're unlikely to bump your head: not only are the ceilings sky-high and the floor padded with leafy carpeting, but hanging pillows protect guests who collapse onto the bed after one too many varietals. Handicapped facilities available.

Hôtel des Têtes (☎ 03 89 24 43 43; www.la-maison -des-tetes.com; 19 rue des Têtes; d €131-269, low season €91-209; **P** ✗ ✗) This impeccable four-star hostelry, luxurious but never flashy, is definitely honeymoon material. Situated in and around the magnificent Maison des Têtes (p364), each of its 21 rooms offers rich wood panelling, an elegant sitting area, a mostly marble bathroom and romantic views.

Eating

Restaurants are sprinkled all over Colmar's old city, especially around place de l'Ancienne Douane.

ALSATIAN & FRENCH

La Maison des Têtes (☎ 03 89 24 43 43; 19 rue des Têtes; menus €28-60; ✓ closed Mon, lunch Tue & dinner Sun) Behind the leaded windows of the spectacular Maison des Têtes (p364) awaits a truly grand dining room, built in 1898 and decorated with grape bunches in wood, wrought iron and stained glass. The chef's *cuisine française actuelle* includes *foie gras au Riesling* and, in season, fish and game. Known for its superb wine list.

La Maison Rouge (☎ 03 89 23 53 22; 9 rue des Écoles; menus €16.90-34.30; ✓ Mon-Sat; ✗) A good variety of hearty Alsatian specialities, including mouthwatering *jambon braisé* (spit-roasted ham; €10.90), are on offer at this rustic city restaurant.

Aux Trois Poissons (☎ 03 89 41 25 21; 15 quai de la Poissonnerie; menus €21-45; ✓ closed Wed, dinner both Sun & Tue) Oil paintings on the walls and Persian carpets on the floor give this mainly fish restaurant an atmosphere of hushed and very civilised elegance. The chef's speciality is *sandre à la choucroute* (pike-perch with sauerkraut; €20). Provençal frogs' legs will hop onto your plate for €15.

Le Temps des Délices (☎ 03 89 23 45 57; 23 rue d'Alspach; lunch menu €18, other menus €23-50;

✓ noon-1.30pm & 7-9pm, closed Mon, dinner both Sun & Thu; ✗) A classy Franco-Italian restaurant with space for just 15 to 20 diners. All ingredients are fresh, and there's a terrace in summer.

OTHER

Les Gourmets d'Asie (☎ 03 89 41 75 10; 20b rue d'Alspach; menus €11.75-21.20; ✓ closed Mon & lunch Tue) Authentic Vietnamese cuisine is served with exceptional elegance.

Djerba La Douce (☎ 03 89 24 17 12; 10 rue du Mouton; ✓ Mon-Sat) You'll be given a welcome as warm and gentle as the beaches of Jerba. Steaming Tunisian couscous costs €9.50 to €17.50.

SELF-CATERING

Buy fresh ingredients at **food markets** (place de l'Ancienne Douane & in the covered market on rue des Écoles; ✓ 8am-noon or to 12.30pm Thu). Market gardeners once unloaded their produce directly from boats at the handsome sandstone *marché couvert* (1865).

Prepare yourself to be overcome by the heady odours of unpasteurised cheese at **Fromagerie St-Nicolas** (18 rue St-Nicolas; ✓ 9am-12.30pm & 2-7pm Mon afternoon & Tue-Fri, 9am-7pm Sat), and there is a **Monoprix supermarket** (✓ 8am-8pm Mon-Sat) across the square from Musée d'Unterlinden.

Drinking

Blue Cat's Club (☎ 03 89 23 31 57; 17 rue du Rempart ✓ 5pm-1.30am) Colmar may be pretty conservative but this relaxed bar, where Cuban and American themes mix promiscuously, is pretty hip. The mint juleps are highly recommended.

Bar Le Seven (☎ 03 89 23 32 72; www.seven-vip .com in French; 6 rue des Trois Épis; admission free; ✓ 6pm-2.30am) Rock concerts play on huge TVs while under-30s play darts or down pints at high, round tables. Wednesday is karaoke night (from 8.30pm). *Soirées à thème* (theme nights) often begin at 10pm on Friday or Saturday; there are live concerts about once a month. The adjacent **Club VIP** is a cosy, dimly lit lounge that attracts a mainly over-30 crowd.

Entertainment

Colmar's main concert and theatre venues are **La Manufacture** (☎ 03 89 24 31 78; www.atelier durhin.com in French; 6 route d'Ingersheim), housed in a former factory 400m northwest of the tourist office, and the **Théâtre Municipal** (☎ 03 89 20 29 02), next to the Musée d'Unterlinden.

Getting There & Away
BUS
Public bus may not be the quickest way to explore Alsace's Route du Vin but it *is* a viable option; destinations served include Riquewihr, Hunawihr, Ribeauvillé, Kaysersberg and Eguisheim. In the Vosges you can bus it to Munster, Col de la Schlucht and Col du Bonhomme.

Buses and bus-train combos (via Bresach) also serve the German city of Freiburg (€6.15, 1¼ hours, seven daily weekdays, four daily weekends and holidays). From Monday to Friday the last bus back leaves Freiburg at 10.10pm.

The bus terminal – little more than a car park – is to the right as you exit the train station. Timetables are posted and available at the tourist office or online (www.l-k.fr in French). Services are severely reduced on Sunday and holidays.

CAR
Cars can be hired from **ADA** (☎ 03 89 23 90 30; 22bis rue Stanislas).

TRAIN
Colmar has train connections to Basel (Bâle; €10.20, 50 minutes, 11 to 17 daily), Mulhouse (€6.60, 20 to 40 minutes, 32 each weekday, 20 daily weekends), Paris' Gare de l'Est (€46.20, five to six hours via Strasbourg) and Strasbourg (€9.30, 31 to 60 minutes, 36 each weekday, 20 daily weekends).

Route du Vin destinations accessible by train include Dambach-la-Ville (€4.90) and Obernai (€6.70), both of which require a change of trains at Sélestat (€3.80, 11 to 20 minutes, 33 daily weekdays, 21 daily weekends). About 16 daily autorails or buses (10 daily on weekends) link Colmar with the Vallée de Munster towns of Munster (€3.10, 35 minutes) and Metzeral (€3.90, 45 minutes); the last run back begins at 7.24pm.

Getting Around
BICYCLE
Colmarvélo (☎ 03 89 41 37 90; place Rapp; per half-/whole day €3/4.50; ⊙ 8.30am-noon & 2-8pm Jun-Sep, 9am-noon & 2-7pm Apr, May & Oct), run by the municipality, rents city bikes (deposit €50).

Hybrid bikes for Route du Vin touring can be rented from **Cycles Geiswiller** (☎ 03 89 41 30 59; 4-6 blvd du Champ de Mars; per half-/whole day €5/9.50; ⊙ Tue-Sat).

BUS
Colmar's 16 local bus lines, which run until sometime between 6pm and 8.30pm Monday to Saturday, are operated by **TRACE** (☎ 03 89 20 80 80). The main hub is Unterlinden-Point Central.

PARKING
Unmetered parking can be found a few blocks east of the train station (around the water tower) and in *part* of the lot at place de la Montagne Verte.

TAXI
For a cab call **Taxi Gare** (☎ 03 89 41 40 19) or **Radios Taxis** (☎ 03 89 80 71 71).

MASSIF DES VOSGES
The delightful and sublime **Parc Naturel Régional des Ballons des Vosges** covers about 3000 sq km in the southern part of the Vosges range. In the warm months, the gentle, rounded mountains, deep forests, glacial lakes and rolling pastureland are a walker's paradise, with an astounding 10,000km of marked trails, including GRs (GR5, GR7, GR53 etc) and their variants. Cyclists also have hundreds of kilometres of idyllic trails. In winter 36 inexpensive skiing areas offer modest downhill pistes and cross-country options.

For details of outings sponsored by the Strasbourg section of the Club Vosgien, see p352.

For information on bus and train connections to access towns in the Vosges region, see left.

MOUNTAIN DINING

On weekends, many Alsatians head to a *ferme-auberge* (farm restaurant) in the Vosges for a *repas marcaire* (cowherd's meal), which usually includes *tourte* (pork pie), *Roïgabrageldi* (potatoes with bacon and onion), *Schiffala* (smoked pork), *Siesskass* (soft white cheese with cream and Kirsch brandy) and, of course, a cheese such as Munster – made right on the farm!

ALSACE & LORRAINE

Vallée de Munster

This lush, verdant river valley – its pastureland dotted with tiny villages, its upper slopes thickly forested – is one of the loveliest in the Vosges range. Walking and cycling trails abound.

MUNSTER

The quiet streamside town of Munster (population 5000; the name means 'monastery'), famed for its eponymous cheese, is a good base for exploring the valley. It grew up around Abbaye St-Grégoire, a Benedictine abbey founded by monks from Ireland in AD 660.

At **place du Marché** (food market on Tuesday and Saturday mornings), the roof and chimneys of the **Maison du Prélat** (former prelate's quarters) are the year-round home of about a dozen pairs of storks. About 250m behind the Renaissance **hôtel de ville** (across the square from the Maison du Prélat) is the **Enclos Cigognes** (Stork Enclosure; see p361), where a half-a-dozen frisky young birds dine on chopped meat, fish and day-old male chicks (sorry cuddly chick lovers, but storks are avid carnivores).

Information

Maison du Parc (☎ 03 89 77 90 34; www.parc-ballons -vosges.fr in French; 1 rue du Couvent; ☯ 10am-noon & 2-6pm Tue-Sun May–mid-Sep, 2-6pm Mon-Fri mid-Sep–Apr, also open 10am-noon Mon-Fri during school holidays) The regional park's visitor centre has ample

---

THE CONTINENTAL DIVIDE

The Massif des Vosges serves as a *ligne de partage des eaux* (continental divide): a raindrop that falls on the range's eastern slopes will flow to the Rhine and eventually make its way to the icy waters of the North Sea, but a drop of rain that lands on the southern slopes of the Ballon d'Alsace – perhaps only a few metres from its Rhinebound counterpart – will eventually end up in the Rhône before merging with the warm waters of the Mediterranean. The Vosges' western slopes feed the Moselle, which joins the Rhine at Koblenz.

The Danube (Donau), which meanders through Vienna and Budapest on its way to the Black Sea, rises 100km east of the Vosges in the mountains of the Black Forest.

---

information in English. To get there walk through the arch of the Maison du Prélat.

Tourist Office (☎ 03 89 77 31 80; www.la-vallee-de -munster.com; 1 rue du Couvent; ☯ 9.30am-12.30pm & 1.30-6pm or 6.30pm Mon-Sat, 10am-12.30pm Sun Jul & Aug, 9.30am-12.30pm & 2-6pm Mon-Fri, 10am-noon & 2-4pm Sat Sep-Jun) Has information – some in English – on the whole Munster Valley, including visits to cheese-makers. In the same building as the Maison du Parc but around the other side.

Sleeping & Eating

Hôtel des Vosges (☎ 03 89 77 31 41; hotelbardesvosges@ wanadoo.fr; 58 Grand' Rue; d with toilet & with/without shower €47/34; ☯ reception closes at 1pm Sun except Jul & Aug) This family-run two-star place, on the main commercial street, has rather bland soundproofed rooms with huge bathrooms. There are several **restaurants** in the immediate vicinity.

Super U supermarket (☯ 8am-7pm Mon-Sat, to 8pm Fri, to 6.30pm Sat) Situated on the southern outskirts of Munster (towards Colmar) on the D417.

LE LINGE

Carved into the sandstone hilltop, the German fortifications at Le Linge (986m) were the object of a French offensive launched in July 1915. Some 10,000 French troops and 7000 Germans died in the assaults and subsequent hand-to-hand warfare between trenches only metres apart. The battle site, which has one of the best-preserved WWI trench networks in France, is still surrounded by rusted tangles of the original barbed wire. Some areas have yet to be cleared of live munitions and still contain human remains.

The forested memorial site, on the D11-VI, affords gorgeous views of tree-covered hills and pastoral hamlets – making for a jarring contrast with the trenches and rifle slits. WWI relics are displayed in the small **memorial museum** (adult/under 16 €2/free; ☯ 9am-12.30pm & 2-6pm 15 Apr-1 Nov).

Route des Crêtes

The Route of the Crests, part of it built during WWI to supply French frontline troops, takes you to (or near) the Vosges' highest *ballons* (bald, rounded mountain peaks) as well as to several WWI sites. Mountaintop lookouts afford spectacular views of the Alsace plain, the Schwartzwald (Black Forest) across the Rhine in Germany, the Jura and, on clear days, the Alps.

Starting in Cernay, the Route des Crêtes continues northeast and then north along the D431, D430, D61 and D148 to the **Col du Bonhomme** (949m), often impassable due to snow in the winter months and early spring.

The site of the bloodiest WWI fighting in Alsace, **Hartmannswillerkopf** – known as **Vieil Armand** to the French troops – saw the deaths of some 30,000 French and German soldiers as the strategic hilltop fortress changed hands several times. The remains of trenches and fortifications, most of them German, can be seen near the hilltop fortress (956m), marked by a 22m-high white cross.

At the dramatic, windblown summit of the **Grand Ballon** (1424m), the highest point in the Vosges, a trail takes you to a radar ball and a weather station. If the unsurpassed panorama doesn't blow you away, the howling wind just might.

From **Col de la Schlucht** (1139m), home to a small ski station, trails lead in various directions; walking north along the GR5 will take you to three lakes, **Lac Vert**, **Lac Noir** and **Lac Blanc** (Green, Black and White Lakes).

The **Ballon d'Alsace** (1250m), 20km southwest of the Grand Ballon as the crow flies (by road, take the D465 from St-Maurice), is the meeting point of four *départements* (Haut-Rhin, Territoire de Belfort, Haute-Saône and Vosges) and of three regions (Alsace, Franche-Comté and Lorraine). Between 1871 and WWI, the border between France and Germany passed by here, attracting French tourists eager to catch a glimpse of France's 'lost province' of Alsace from the heroic equestrian **statue of Joan of Arc** (1909) and the cast-iron **orientation table** (1888). During WWI the mountaintop was heavily fortified, but the trenches, whose shallow remains can still be seen, were never used in battle.

The Ballon d'Alsace is a good base for day walks. The GR5 passes by here, as do other trails; possible destinations include **Lac des Perches** (four hours).

MULHOUSE
pop 234,000

The industrial city of Mulhouse (pronounced 'moo-**looze**'), 43km south of Colmar, was al-

lied with the cantons of nearby Switzerland before voting to join revolutionary France in 1798. Largely rebuilt after the ravages of WWII, it has none of the quaint Alsatian charm that you find further north – but the city's world-class industrial museums are well worth a stop.

Information

The **tourist office** (☎ 03 89 35 48 48; www.tourism-mulhouse.com; 9 av du Maréchal Foch; 9am-noon & 2-6pm Mon-Fri) is 250m due north of the train station. In the heart of the old city, the **tourist office annexe** (place de la Réunion; 10am-6pm Mon-Sat, 10am-noon & 2-6pm Sun & holidays year-round, to 7pm Jul, Aug & Dec) is in the 16th-century former **hôtel de ville** (town hall). English-language brochures detail walking tours of medieval **Vieux Mulhouse** and the 19th-century **Nouveau Quartier**.

Museums

The wonderful **Musée National de l'Automobile** (☎ 03 89 33 23 23; www.collection-schlumpf.com; 192 av de Colmar; tram stop Musée de l'Auto; adult/7-17 yrs/student/family incl an English audioguide €10/5/7.50/27.50; 10am-6pm Apr-Oct, to 5pm Nov-May, from 1pm Mon-Fri early Jan-early Feb) displays 400 rare and beautiful European motorcars produced since 1878 by over 100 different companies, including Bugatti, whose factory was in nearby Molsheim. The collection was secretly assembled by Fritz Schlumpf, a self-made textile magnate whose passion – indeed, obsession – for fast cars only grew as his worsted-wool empire nosedived. In 1977, after he had gone bust and fled to Switzerland, outraged former workers occupied the one-time factory that housed the glittering collection, which they saw as a symbol of capitalist greed. By car, exit the A36 at the Mulhouse Centre exit.

A gricer's dream, the **Musée Français du Chemin de Fer** (☎ 03 89 42 83 33; 2 rue Alfred de Glehn) displays the SNCF's superb collection of locomotives and carriages, perhaps the finest in Europe. It should have reopened by the time you read this.

One long block northeast of the station, **Musée de l'Impression sur Étoffes** (Museum of Textile Printing; ☎ 03 89 46 83 00; www.musee-impression.com; 14 rue Jean-Jacques Henner; adult/student €6/3; ⏰ 10am-noon & 2-6pm Tue-Sun) covers the history of the industry that made Mulhouse – the 'French Manchester' – incredibly wealthy. Its unique collection of over six million printed fabric samples, assembled since 1833 and now the most extensive in the world, is a mecca for fabric designers. There are printing demonstrations at 3pm on Wednesday, Friday and Sunday.

Has wallpaper always been something of a wallflower in your life? The delightful **Musée du Papier Peint** (Wallpaper Museum; ☎ 03 89 64 24 56; www.museepapierpeint.org; 28 rue Zuber, Rixheim; adult/student over 12 €6/4.50; ⏰ 9am or 10am-noon & 2-6pm daily Jun-Sep, closed Tue Oct-May), home to an unparalleled collection of wallpaper and the machines used to make it since the 18th century, will change all that. Situated a couple of kilometres southeast of central Mulhouse on the D66, it's easy to get to: by car take the A36 and get off at Rixheim; by bus take line No 10 from place de l'Europe to the Commanderie stop.

Getting There & Around

France's second train line, linking Mulhouse with Thann, opened in 1839. Today, the **train station** (10 av du Général Leclerc), just south of the city centre, has direct services to Colmar (€6.60, 20 to 40 minutes, 32 each weekday, 20 daily weekends) and Strasbourg (€14.10, one hour, 19 to 25 daily).

Mulhouse is getting a two-line, 20km tram system; until construction of the first phase is finished sometime in 2005, the city centre will remain in a state of traffic chaos.

ÉCOMUSÉE D'ALSACE

In Ungersheim about 17km northwest of Mulhouse (off the A35 to Colmar), **Écomusée d'Alsace** (☎ 03 89 74 44 74; www.ecomusee-alsace.com

in French; adult/4-14 yrs/student €14.50/9.50/13, slightly less in winter; ⏰ tickets sold & artisans at work 9.30am-7pm Jul & Aug, 10am-6pm late Feb-Jun, Sep & Oct, to 5pm Nov-early Jan, closed early Jan-late Feb, restaurant & park open until 11pm) is a 'living museum' in which some 20 smiths, cartwrights, coopers and other craftspeople do their thing in and among 70 centuries-old Alsatian buildings – a veritable village – brought here for preservation (and so storks can build nests on them) from seven different Alsatian subregions. The whole thing is much less hokey than it sounds and in fact inspires real enthusiasm from Alsatians proud of their heritage. Traditional agriculture and its implements are showcased on Sundays. By the time you read this there should be signs in English.

That industrial relic next door is the **Rodolphe Potassium Mine**, shut down in 1976. Now affiliated with the Écomusée, parts can be visited with a retired miner (additional fee).

LORRAINE

Lorraine is fed by the Rivers Meurthe, Moselle and Meuse – hence the names of three of its four *départements* (the fourth is Vosges).

NANCY
pop 331,000

Delightful Nancy has an air of refinement found nowhere else in Lorraine. With a magnificent central square, several fine museums and sparkling shop windows, the former capital of the dukes of Lorraine seems as opulent today as it did in the 16th to 18th centuries, when much of the city centre was built.

Nancy has long thrived on a combination of innovation and sophistication. The Musée de l'École de Nancy features the dream-like sinuous works of the Art Nouveau movement, which flourished here (as the Nancy School) thanks to the rebellious spirit of local artists – including Émile Gallé (1846–1904) – who set out to prove that everyday objects could be drop-dead gorgeous. Further examples of their work can be found at the Musée des Beaux-Arts and throughout the city: keep an eye out for the stained-glass windows and elaborate

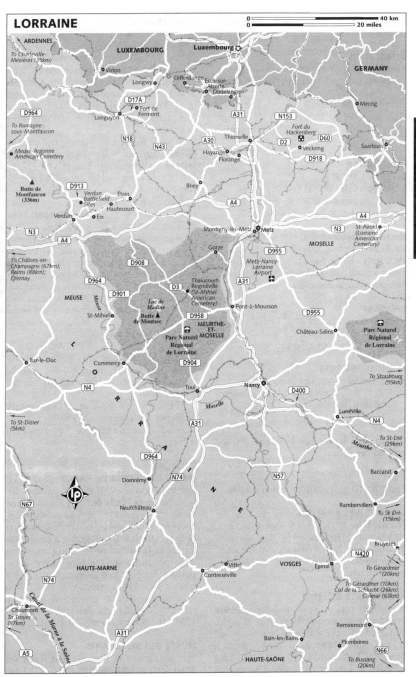

grillwork that grace the entrances to many offices, shops and private homes.

Orientation

Place Stanislas – now off limits to motor vehicles – connects the narrow, twisting streets of the medieval Vieille Ville (Old Town), centred on the Grande Rue, with the rigid right angles of the 16th-century Ville Neuve (New Town) to the south. The train station is 800m southwest of place Stanislas.

Information

INTERNET ACCESS

E-café Cyber Café (☎ 03 83 35 47 34; 11 rue des Quatre Églises; per min/hr €0.09/5.40; ☉ 11am-9pm Mon, 9am-9pm Tue-Sat, 2-8pm Sun) Has UK and US keyboards on hand.

Musée du Téléphone (☎ 03 83 86 50 00; 11 rue Maurice Barrès; per hr adult/student & senior €4/3; ☉ 10am-7pm Tue-Sat, 2-6pm 1st Sun of month) This telecommunications museum has saved itself from obsolescence by adding an Internet café.

LAUNDRY

There are laundrettes at 124 rue St-Dizier (open 7.45am to 9.30pm) and 1 rue de l'Armée Patton (open 7am to 9pm).

MEDICAL SERVICES

Hôpital Central (casualty ward/emergency room ☎ 03 83 85 14 61; 29 av Maréchal de Lattre de Tassigny; ☉ 24hr) About 1km southeast of place Stanislas.

MONEY

Commercial banks can be found on and around rue St-Jean.

POST

Post Office (10 rue St-Dizier) Does currency exchange.

TOURIST INFORMATION

Tourist Office (☎ 03 83 35 22 41; www.ot-nancy.fr; place Stanislas; ☉ 9am-7pm Mon-Sat, 10am-5pm Sun & holidays Apr-Oct, 9am-6pm Mon-Sat, 10am-1pm Sun & holidays Nov-Mar) Inside the *hôtel de ville*. Has free walking tour brochures.

Architecture & Sights

Beautifully proportioned, neoclassical **place Stanislas**, impressively illuminated at night, is named after the man who commissioned it (and whose **statue** stands in the middle), Stanislaw Leszczynski. The dethroned king of Poland, Leszczynski ruled Lorraine as

duke in the middle decades of the 17th century, thanks to his son-in-law Louis XV. The opulent buildings that surround the square (including the **hôtel de ville**), the dazzling gilded **wrought-iron gateways** by Jean Lamour, and the rococo fountains **Fontaines de Neptune** and **d'Amphitrite** by Guibal form one of the finest ensembles of 18th-century architecture and decorative arts anywhere in France.

A block to the east, 90m-square **place de l'Alliance** is graced by lime trees and a **baroque fountain** by Bruges-born Louis Cyfflé (1724–1806); it was inspired by Bernini's *Four Rivers* fountain in Rome's Piazza Navona.

Adjoining place Stanislas – on the other side of Nancy's own **Arc de Triomphe**, built in honour of Louis XV in the mid-1750s – is larger and quieter **place de la Carrière**, once a riding and jousting arena. A Unesco World Heritage Site (as are place Stanislas and place de l'Alliance), it is graced by four rows of linden trees and stately rococo gates in gilded wrought iron. A block to the east you'll find **Parc de la Pépinière**, a delightful formal garden that boasts cafés, a rose garden and a small zoo.

North of the Vieille Ville, Art Nouveau townhouses include the **Maison Weissenburger** (1 blvd Charles V), built in 1904, and the **Maison Huot** (92 quai Claude de Lorrain), constructed a year earlier.

The interior of the domed, 18th-century **cathédrale** (rue St-Georges) is a sombre mixture of neoclassical and baroque. The organ loft is from 1757.

Museums

MUSÉE DE L'ÉCOLE DE NANCY

The highlight of a visit to Nancy is the brilliant **Musée de l'École de Nancy** (School of Nancy Museum; ☎ 03 83 40 14 86; 36-38 rue du Sergent Blandan; adult/student & senior €4.575/2.29; ☉ 10.30am-6pm Wed-Sun), which brings together a heady collection of furnished rooms and curvaceous glass produced by the turn-of-the-20th-century Art Nouveau movement (p53). It's housed in a 19th-century villa about 2km southwest of the city centre – to get there take bus No 122 to the Painlevé stop or No 123 to the Nancy Thermal stop.

MUSÉE DES BEAUX-ARTS

Star attractions at the excellent **Musée des Beaux-Arts** (Fine Arts Museum; ☎ 03 83 85 30 72; 3 place

Stanislas; adult/student & senior €5.34/3.05; 10am-6pm Wed-Mon) include a superb collection of Daum-made Art Nouveau glass and a rich and varied selection of paintings from the 14th to 18th centuries. Laminated information sheets in English are available.

MUSÉE HISTORIQUE LORRAIN

The mostly 16th-century Palais Ducal, splendid former residence of the dukes of Lorraine, now houses the **Musée Historique Lorrain** (Lorraine Historical Museum; 03 83 32 18 74; 64 & 66 Grande Rue; adult/student for both sections €4.60/3.10, for 1 section €3.10/2.30; 10am-12.30pm & 2-6pm Wed-Mon). The part dedicated to **fine arts and history** (at No 64) has rich collections of medieval statuary, engravings and faïence, as well as Judaica from before and after the Revolution; the section dedicated to **regional art and folklore** (at No 66) is housed in the 15th-century **Couvent des Cordeliers**, a former Franciscan monastery. Inside, the late-15th-century Gothic **Église des Cordeliers** and the adjacent **Chapelle Ducale** (Ducal Chapel; 1607) modelled on the Medici Chapel in Florence, served as the burial place of the dukes of Lorraine.

Tours

The tourist office offers MP3 tours (€5) of the historic centre (two hours) and the Art-Nouveau quarters (three hours).

Sleeping

BUDGET

Auberge de Jeunesse Château de Remicourt (03 83 27 73 67; aubergeremicourt@mairie-nancy.fr; 149 rue de Vandœuvre in Villers-lès-Nancy; dm in 3-10-bunk room €13.50, in double with shower €15.50, rates incl sheets & breakfast) Surrounded by a peaceful park, this fantastic old chateau, with 60 beds, is 4km south of the centre. Check-in is between 2pm (5.30pm on Sunday) and 9pm. By bus, take No 126 to the St-Fiacre stop or Nos 134 and 135 to Villers Lycée Stanislas.

Hôtel de l'Académie (03 83 35 52 31; fax 03 83 32 55 78; 7bis rue des Michottes; s/d with shower from €23.50/26.50, r with shower & toilet from €29.50) This offbeat place has a tacky fountain that sounds like a broken urinal and cheaply furnished rooms with acoustic tile ceilings. Gallé would have been appalled but you can't beat the price.

MID-RANGE

Hôtel de Guise (03 83 32 24 68; www.hoteldeguise.com; 18 rue de Guise; s/d/q €46/56/73;) A grand

stone staircase leads to extra-wide hallways and bright, spacious rooms. The bathrooms are as modern as the 18th-century hardwood floors are charmingly creaky. The building, in the heart of the old city, dates from 1680.

Hôtel des Portes d'Or (03 83 35 42 34; www.hotel-lesportesdor.com; 21 rue Stanislas; d from €51) This welcoming and very cosy two-star hostelry, superbly situated just metres from place Stanislas, has charming rooms of almost three-star quality. Often full so call ahead.

Hôtel des Prélats (03 83 32 11 52; fax 03 83 37 58 74; 56 place Monseigneur Ruch; tram stop Cathédrale; r €51-88) In a grand historic building that has served as a hotel since 1906, this place is being completely restored and renovated.

Eating

No less than 20 reasonably priced eateries of all sorts line rue des Maréchaux, just west of the Arc de Triomphe; lunch *menus* start at just €9. North of there, intimate eateries can be found all along the Grande Rue. There are lots of cheapies in the vicinity of the covered market.

Brasserie Excelsior (03 83 35 24 57; 50 rue Henri Poincaré; tram stop Nancy Gare; lunch & after-10pm menu €20.50, other menu €29.90; 8am-12.30am Mon-Sat, 8am-11pm Sun; meals served noon-3pm & 7pm-closing time) Built in 1910, this sparkling brasserie's sumptuous Art Nouveau décor makes every meal memorable. Six kinds of pork are on offer; the sauerkraut options include one *choucroute à trois poissons* with salmon, haddock and scallops.

Restaurant Le Gastrolâtre (03 83 35 51 94; 1 place Vaudémont; lunch menu €18, other menus €30-40; closed Sun, lunch Mon & dinner Thu) Warm and lived-in, this restaurant has been serving Lorraine cuisine – with some Provençal touches – since 1970. Specialities with deep regional roots include *boekoffe à foie gras*

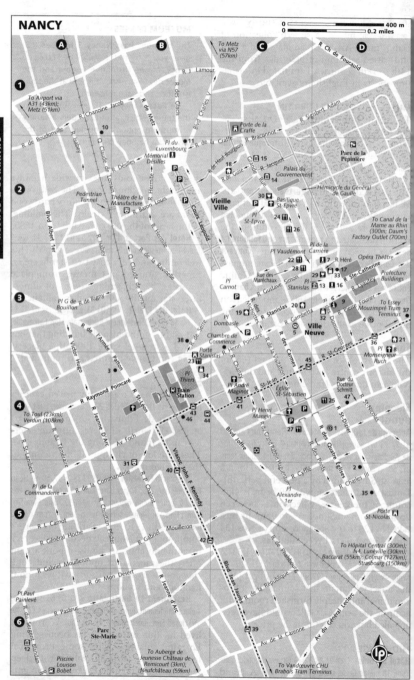

NANCY

0 |========| 400 m
0 |========| 0.2 miles

To Metz
via N57
(57km)

R Ch de Foucauld

To Airport via
A31 (43km);
Metz (51km)

R J Lamour

R Chanoine Jacob

R des Glacis

R de Metz

R de Boudonville

R Isabey

Q Claude de Lorrain

R Désilles

R Hermite

10

Porte de la
Craffe

R Bracannot

R Sigisbert Adam

Parc de la
Pépinière

Pl du
Luxembourg

11

R de la Craffe

R de Haut-Bourgeois

R de Guise

18

Mémorial
Désilles

R Jacquot

Grande Rue

15

Palais du
Gouvernement

14

Pedestrian
Tunnel

Théâtre de la
Manufacture

R Baron Louis

Cours Léopold

Vieille
Ville

30

Basilique
St-Epvre

Hémicycle du Général
de Gaulle

R Charles V

Blvd Charles V

Blvd Albert 1er

R de la Ravinelle

R Claude de Lorrain

Pl
St-Epvre

24

26

To Canal de la
Marne au Rhin
(300m; Daum's
Factory Outlet (700m

Pl de la
Carrière

Pl Vaudémont

22

7

R Héré

Opéra Théâtre

Pl G de
Bouillon

R de Rigny

R Victor Hugo

R de l'Armée Patton

R de Serre

28

Rue des
Maréchaux

R Gustave Simon

29

17

33

R Ste-Catherine

Préfecture
Buildings

13

16

R Lyautey

Pl
Carnot

Pl
Stanislas

Pl
Dombasle

R Stanislas

19

R des Ponts-Mouja

20

R Stanislas

R Gambetta

6

9

R Pierre Fourier

32

Ville
Neuve

4 @

To Essey
Mouzimpré Tram
Terminus

37

38

Chambre de
Commerce

Porte
Stanislas

Henri Poincaré

R de la Visitation

5

R St-Dizier

R St-Georges

R St-Georges

36

21

Pl
Monseigneur
Ruch

8

23

34

Pl
Thiers

3

Train
Station

Pl André
Maginot

41

Chang

45

Rue du
Docteur
Schmitt

47

25

R Raymond Poincaré

R St-Léon

R Jeanne d'Arc

R du Tènedize

R St-Lambert

To Toul (23km);
Verdun (108km)

Av Foch

43

46

44

Église
St-Sébastien

Pl Henri
Mangin

27

R des Quatre Églises

@ 1

R St-Nicolas

31

Viaduc John F Kennedy

R P Chalnot

Blvd Joffre

R du Grand Rabbi Haguenau

R Cyffle

R des Ponts

2

Pl de la
Commanderie

R de la Commanderie

R Christian Pfister

R Gabriel

40

Pl
Alexandre
1er

R Charles III

35

R L Carnot

R Général Hoche

Mouilleron

42

Av de la Carrière

Porte
St-Nicolas

To Hôpital Central (300m);
N4; Lunéville (30km);
Baccarat (55km); Colmar (127km);
Strasbourg (150km)

R Gabriel Mouilleron

R de Mon Désert

R Jeanne d'Arc

Blvd Jean Jaurès

R de la République

Pl Paul
Painlevé

R Pasteur

Parc
Ste-Marie

12

R du Sergent Blandan

Piscine
Louison
Bobet

39

Av du Général Leclerc

To Auberge de
Jeunesse Château de
Remicourt (3km);
Neufchâteau (59km)

To Vandœuvre CHU
Brabois Tram Terminus

INFORMATION			SLEEPING		(p373)	SHOPPING		(p376)
E-café Cyber Café	1	D4	Hôtel de Guise	18	C2	Baccarat Shops	32	D3
Laundrette	2	D5	Hôtel de l'Académie	19	C3	Daum	33	D3
Laundrette	3	B4	Hôtel des Portes d'Or	20	C3	Lefèvre-Lemoine	34	B4
Musée du Téléphone	4	D3	Hôtel des Prélats	21	D3	St Sébastien Shopping Centre		
Post Office	5	C3				Centre	(see 27)	
Tourist Office	6	D3	EATING		(pp373–5)			
			Aux Croustillants	22	C3	TRANSPORT		(p376)
SIGHTS & ACTIVITIES		(pp372–3)	Brasserie Excelsior	23	B4	ADA	35	D5
Arc de Triomphe	7	D3	Chez Bagot-Le Chardon Bleu	24	C2	Cathédrale Tram Stop	36	D3
Cathédrale	8	D3	Covered Market	25	D4	Cyclotop Bike Rental	37	D3
Couvent des Cordeliers	(see 15)		La Basse Cour	26	C2	Europcar	38	B3
Hôtel de Ville	9	D3	Monoprix Supermarket	27	C4	Garenne Tram Stop	39	C6
Maison Huot	10	A1	Restaurant Le Gastrolâtre	28	C3	Kennedy Tram Stop	40	B5
Maison Weissenburger	11	B2				Maginot Tram Stop	41	C4
Musée de l'École de Nancy	12	A6	DRINKING		(p375)	Mon Désert Tram Stop	42	B5
Musée des Beaux-Arts	13	D3	L'Arquebuse	29	D3	Nancy Gare Tram Stop	43	B4
Musée Historique Lorrain (Fine Arts &			Le Ch'timi	30	C2	Nancy République Bus Hub	44	B4
History Section)	14	C2				Point Central Tram Stop	45	C4
Musée Historique Lorrain (Regional			ENTERTAINMENT		(p375)	STAN Tram & Bus Information		
Arts & Folklore Section)	15	C2	Blue Note III Club	(see 19)		Office	46	B4
Statue of Stanislaw Leszczynski	16	D3	Caméo Cinema	31	B5	STAN Tram & Bus Information		
Wrought-Iron Gateway	17	D3	Le Varadero	(see 26)		Office	47	D4

ALSACE & LORRAINE

de canard (meat stew with duck *foie gras*). Black truffles take centre stage from December to March.

La Basse Cour (☎ 03 83 36 67 29; 23 Grande Rue; menu €16; ⏱ 6.30-11pm or later Mon-Sat) A bourgeois apartment in a 16th- and 17th-century townhouse has been transformed into a homey, intimate eatery specialising in mouth-watering Lorraine-style *cuisine de campagne* (farm-fresh country cuisine). One of the chef's favourites is vol-au-vent filled with lamb sweetbread, ham and morilles mushrooms, but it's poultry that rules the roost, on the menu as well the walls.

Chez Bagot-Le Chardon Bleu (☎ 03 83 37 42 43; 45 Grande Rue; lunch menu €14.50, other menus €21.50-31; ⏱ 12.15-1.45pm & 7.15-10pm, closed Mon, lunch Tue & dinner Sun) This very popular restaurant, elegant yet convivial, is known for its creative French cuisine. Specialities include fish.

SELF-CATERING

Aux Croustillants (10 rue des Maréchaux; ⏱ 24hr except from 9pm Sun to 5.30am Tue) is an almost-24/7 *boulangerie*. Other options are the **covered market** (place Henri Mangin; tram stop Point Central; ⏱ 7am-6pm Tue-Thu, 7am-6.30pm Fri & Sat) and the **Monoprix supermarket** (⏱ 8.30am-8.30pm Mon-Sat), inside the St-Sébastien shopping mall.

Drinking

Le Ch'timi (☎ 03 83 32 82 76; 17 place St-Epvre; ⏱ 9am-2am Mon-Sat, 9am-8pm Sun) At this unpretentious mellow bar, spread out over three brick-and-stone storeys, you can choose from 200 different beers, 16 of them on tap.

L'Arquebuse (☎ 03 83 32 11 99; 13 rue Héré; ⏱ 6.30pm-4am Tue-Sat) This very stylish candle-lit bar has superb views of place Stanislas and, from about 11pm, dancing to salsa, zouk etc; the clientele comes mainly from the over-35 demographic. Sushi (about €1 per piece) is served until 10pm.

Entertainment

Details on cultural events appear in the free monthly *Spectacles* (www.spectacles-publications.com in French).

CINEMA

There's a good selection of nondubbed films at the **Caméo** (☎ 03 83 28 41 00; www.cine-cameo.com in French; 16 rue de la Commanderie; tram stop Kennedy), a four-screen art cinema.

LIVE MUSIC

Blue Note III Club (☎ 03 83 30 31 18; 3 rue des Michottes; ⏱ 10pm-4am Wed, Thu & Sun, 11pm-5am Fri & Sat) This vaulted subterranean discotheque, at the far end of the courtyard, has concerts (€3 to €5) and student nights (€2) – and after 2am a disco – on Wednesday and Thursday; live jazz and blues (until 1am) and two dance floors (one Latino, the other disco; €10) on Friday and Saturday; and karaoke (and after 2am a disco) on Sunday. Twenty-somethings predominate.

Le Varadero (☎ 03 83 36 61 98; 27 Grande Rue; admission free; ⏱ 6pm-2am Mon-Sat Apr-Sep, 8pm-2am Tue-Sat Oct-Mar) Named after a beach in Cuba, this laid-back radical-chic student hangout has live Joan Baez-style folk music from 8.30pm to 10pm every Friday and Saturday; after that a Latino-oriented DJ takes over. There are often student nights on Wednesdays.

Shopping

The main commercial thoroughfares in the city are rue St-Dizier, rue St-Jean and rue St-Georges.

Exquisite crystal and jewellery is on display at the **Baccarat shops** (☎ 03 83 30 55 11; 2 rue des Dominicains & next door at 3 rue Gambetta; ☑ closed Mon morning & Sun), where the cheapest wine glass – impossibly delicate – costs €54. At **Daum** (☎ 03 83 32 21 65; 14 place Stanislas; ☑ closed Mon morning & Sun), you can watch a video showing crystal artisans at work and visit a small **museum** of early-20th-century pieces.

Daum's factory outlet (☎ 03 83 32 14 55; 17 rue des Cristalleries; tram stop Cristalleries; ☑ 9.30am-12.30pm & 2.30-6.30pm Mon-Sat), about 1km northeast of place Stanislas, sells discontinued designs and unsigned seconds.

Bergamotes de Nancy, the local confectionery speciality, are hard candies made with bergamot, a citrus fruit – also used to flavour Earl Grey tea – that grows on the slopes of Mt Etna. The only confectioner allowed to sell *bergamottes* (with two Ts) is **Lefèvre-Lemoine** (Au Duché de Lorraine; ☎ 03 83 30 13 83; 47 rue Henri Poincaré; tram stop Nancy Gare; ☑ 8.30am-7pm Mon-Sat, 9.30am-12.30pm Sun), founded in 1840 and last redecorated – with Gilded Age panache – way back in 1928. One of its old-fashioned sweets tins made a cameo appearance in the film *Amélie.*

Getting There & Away

CAR

Rental options:
ADA (☎ 03 83 36 53 09; 138 rue St-Dizier)
Europcar (☎ 03 83 37 57 24; 18 rue de Serre)
National-Citer (☎ 03 83 37 38 59; in the train station departure hall; tram stop Nancy Gare)

TRAIN

The **train station** (place Thiers; tram stop Nancy Gare) is on the line linking Paris' Gare de l'Est (€35.30, three hours, 12 to 14 daily) with Strasbourg (€18.40, 1¼ hours, nine to 12 daily). Other destinations include Baccarat (€8.50, 40 to 70 minutes, six to nine daily) and Metz (€8.30, 40 to 70 minutes, 34 daily Monday to Friday, 22 on Saturday, 14 on Sunday).

Getting Around

BICYCLE

Cyclotop (☎ 03 83 40 31 31; 89 rue St-Georges; tram stop Cathédrale; per half-/full day €5/7; ☑ 9am-noon & 2-6pm except Sat afternoon, Mon morning & Sun), run by the municipality, rents distinctive yellow-and-red city bikes.

BUS & TRAM

The local public transport company, **STAN** (☎ 03 83 30 08 08; www.reseau-stan.com in French; offices at 3 rue du Docteur Schmitt & place de la République; ☑ 7am-7.25pm Mon-Sat), has its main hubs at Nancy République and Point Central. The tram line – the first of three planned – uses innovative new technology that's based on rubber-tyred street cars guided by a single rail. One/10 tickets cost €1.15/8.20.

PARKING

There's free parking 600m northeast of place Stanislas on the other side of Canal de la Marne au Rhin, and in the working-class neighbourhoods west of the train tracks.

TAXI

A **taxi** (☎ 03 83 37 65 37) is just a telephone call away.

BACCARAT

pop 5000

For centuries Nancy and southern Lorraine have produced some of the world's finest crystal and glassware. The most famous *cristallerie* (crystal glassworks) of all, founded in 1764, is at Baccarat, 55km southeast of Nancy. At the **Musée du Cristal** (☎ 03 83 76 61 37; www.baccarat.fr; adult/under 10 €2.50/free; ☑ 9.30am-12.30pm & 2-6.30pm Apr-Oct, 10am-noon & 2-6pm Nov-Mar), on the grounds of the Baccarat glassworks, you can admire 1100 exquisite pieces.

Across the River Meurthe, the concrete **Église St-Rémy**, built in the mid-1950s to replace an earlier church destroyed by Allied bombing in 1944, is decorated with over 4000 panels of coloured Baccarat crystal.

The **tourist office** (☎ 03 83 75 13 37; www.ville-baccarat.fr/accotgb.htm; ☑ 9am-noon & 2-5.30pm Mon-Sat year-round, 10am-noon Sun & holidays Jul & Aug) is in the car park behind the church.

Hôtel La Renaissance (☎ 03 83 75 11 31; www.hotel-la-renaissance.com; 31 rue des Cristalleries; s/d €43/47), just down the block from the museum, is a two-star Logis de France–affiliated hotel with attractive rooms and an excellent French restaurant.

Baccarat's train station is a few hundred metres north of the Musée du Cristal, with trains to Nancy (€8.50, 40 to 70 minutes, six to nine daily).

METZ

pop 322,000

Present-day capital of the Lorraine region and an important high-tech centre, Metz is a dignified city with stately public squares, shaded riverside parks, a large university and a historic commercial centre. The Gothic cathedral, with its stunning stained glass, is the most outstanding attraction.

Metz became part of France in 1648. When Germany annexed the city in 1871, a quarter of the population fled to French territory; many went to nearby Nancy, which remained French. Quite a few of the most impressive buildings date from the 48-year period when Metz was part of the German empire.

Orientation

The cathedral, on a hill above the River Moselle, is a bit over 1km north of the train station. The city centre's main public squares are place d'Armes, next to the cathedral; place St-Jacques, in the heart of the pedestrianised commercial precinct; place St-Louis; and, 400m to the west, place de la République.

Information

EMERGENCY

Police (Hôtel de Police; ☎ 03 87 16 17 17; 6 rue Belle Isle; 🕒 24hr)

INTERNET ACCESS

Diacom Internet Café (☎ 03 87 63 08 85; 20 rue Gambetta; per hr €3; 🕒 10am-9pm Mon-Sat, 11am-9pm Sun)

LAUNDRY

There are laundrettes at 11 rue de la Fontaine, 4 rue des Allemands, 22 rue du Pont des Morts and 23 rue Taison. All are open 7am to 8pm.

MEDICAL SERVICES

Notre Dame de Bonsecours CHR (Bldg F emergency room/casualty ward ☎ 03 87 55 34 91/2; 1 place Philippe de Vigneulles; 🕒 24hr)

MONEY

There are commercial banks at place St-Louis and on the southeastern side of place de la République. The tourist office charges a 5.5% commission to change money.

POST

Main Post Office (9 rue Gambetta) Has currency exchange and a Cyberposte.

TOURIST INFORMATION

Tourist Office (☎ 03 87 55 53 76; http://tourisme.mairie -metz.fr; place d'Armes; 🕒 9am-8.30pm Mon-Sat Jul & Aug, to 7pm Mar-Jun & Sep-Nov, to 6.30pm Dec-Feb, plus 10am-3pm Sun & holidays year-round) In a one-time guardroom built in the mid-1700s. The free monthly *Ce Mois-Ci à Metz* lists cultural events. Has a free walking and cycling map and an Internet terminal that works with a *télécarte*.

Cathédrale St-Étienne

Metz' spectacular Gothic **Cathédrale St-Étienne** (🕒 8am-7pm May-Sep, to 6pm Oct-Apr), built between 1220 and 1522, is famed for its veritable curtains of 13th- to 20th-century stained glass, among the finest in France. The superb **Flamboyant Gothic windows** (1504), on the main wall of the north transept arm, provide a remarkable stylistic contrast with the glorious **Renaissance windows** on the main wall of the south transept arm, created a mere two decades later. There are distinctive windows by **Chagall** on the western wall of the north transept arm and in the nearby section of the ambulatory (over the entrance to the Grande Sacristie), where you'll also find the **treasury** (adult/student €1.50/1). In the 15th-century **crypt** (below the altar; adult/student €1.50/1) you can see a 15th-century sculpture of the Graoully ('**grau**lee' or '**grau**-yee'), a dragon that is said to have terrified pre-Christian Metz. Try to visit on a bright day. Like the city centre's other major monuments, the cathedral is beautifully illuminated at night (until 1am).

Musée La Cour d'Or

The truly excellent **Musée La Cour d'Or** (☎ 03 87 68 25 00; 2 rue du Haut Poirier; adult/senior & student under 26/under 12 €4.60/2.30/free, 1st Sun of month free; 🕒 9am-5pm Mon & Wed-Fri, 10am-5pm Sat & Sun) has an outstanding collection of Gallo-Roman antiquities, paintings, and early-medieval religious art and stonework. It is housed in a maze of 60 rooms that were originally part of a 15th-century granary and a 17th-century convent.

City Centre

On the eastern edge of the city centre, triangular **place St-Louis** is surrounded by medieval arcades and merchants' houses dating from the 14th to 16th centuries.

Neoclassical **place de la Comédie**, bounded by one of the channels of the Moselle, is home to the city's **théâtre** (1738–53), the oldest theatre building in France that's still in

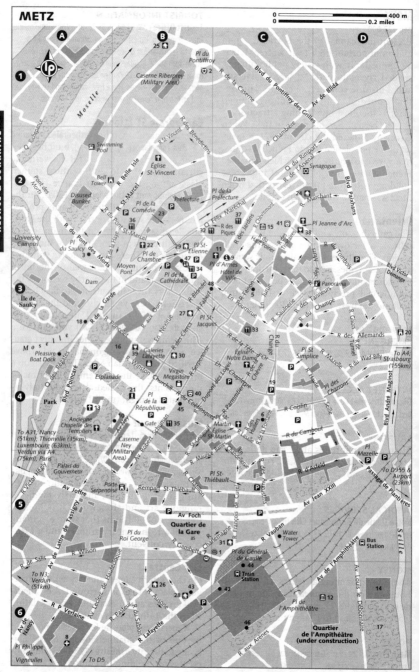

METZ

0 ————— 400 m
0 ————— 0.2 miles

INFORMATION		
Diacom Internet Café	1	C5
Hôtel de Police	2	B1
Laundrette	3	A3
Laundrette	4	C3
Laundrette	5	C3
Laundrette	6	C4
Main Post Office	7	B5
Notre Dame de Bonsecours CHR		
(Hospital)	8	A6
Tourist Office	9	C3

SIGHTS & ACTIVITIES	(pp377–80)	
Arsenal Cultural Centre	10	B4
Cathédrale St-Étienne	11	C3
Centre Pompidou-Metz		
(2007)	12	D6
Église St Pierre-aux-Nonains	13	A4
Les Arènes	14	D6
Musée La Cour d'Or	15	C2
Palais de Justice	16	B4
Parc de la Seille	17	D6
Pedal Boats Hire	18	A3
Place St-Louis	19	C4

Porte des Allemands	20	D3
Statue of Marshall Ney	21	B4
Temple Neuf	22	B3
Théâtre	23	B2

SLEEPING	(p380)	
Auberge de Jeunesse		
Carrefour	24	C2
Auberge de Jeunesse		
Metz-Plage	25	B1
Cécil Hôtel	26	B6
Grand Hôtel de Metz	27	B3
Hôtel Bristol	28	B6
Hôtel de la Cathédrale	29	B3
Hôtel Lafayette	30	B4
Hôtel Métropole	31	C5

EATING	(pp380–1)	
À La Ville de Lyon	32	B2
Atac Supermarket	33	C3
Covered Market	34	B3
L'Étude	35	B4
Restaurant du Pont St Marcel	36	B2
Taj Mahal	37	C2

DRINKING		(p381)
Café Jehanne d'Arc	38	C2
L'Appart	39	B4

ENTERTAINMENT		(p381)
Arsenal Cultural Centre	(see 10)	
Le Tiffany	40	B4
Les Arènes	(see 14)	
Salle des Trinitaires	41	C2

TRANSPORT	(pp381–2)	
Arrival Hall	42	C6
Budget	43	B6
Departure Hall	44	C6
TCRM Bus Information		
Office	45	B4
Train Station Back Entrance	46	C6
Vélocation	47	B3
Vélocation	(see 42)	

OTHER		
'Appel' Upright	48	B3
Centre St Jacques Shopping		
Mall	(see 33)	

ALSACE & LORRAINE

use. During the Revolution, place de l'Égalité (as it was then known) was the site of a guillotine that lopped the heads off 63 'enemies of the people'. The neo-Romanesque **Temple Neuf** (Protestant Church), sombre and looming, was constructed under the Germans in 1903.

The formal flowerbeds of the **Esplanade** – and its **statue** of a gallant-looking Marshall Ney, sword dangling at his side (1859) – are flanked by imposing public buildings, including the **Arsenal Cultural Centre** (1863) and the sober, neoclassical **Palais de Justice** (late 18th century). **Église St-Pierre-aux-Nonains** (admission free; 1-6pm Tue-Sat & 2-6pm Sun mid-Jun–21 Sep, 1-6pm Sat & 2-6pm Sun late Sep-early May) was originally built around AD 400 as part of a Gallo-Roman spa complex (the wall sections that have horizontal red-brick stripes are Roman originals). For a thousand years – from the 6th to the 16th centuries – the structure served as the abbey church of a women's monastery.

West and northwest of the Esplanade, on both sides of blvd Poincaré, is a lovely **riverside park** graced with statues, ponds, swans and a fountain. **Pedal boats** can be rented on quai des Régates in the warm months.

The crenellated **Porte des Allemands** (Gate of the Germans; interior closed) was first erected around 1230 when a wall to surround this part of the city was constructed. It owes its name, not (heaven forbid!) because of a fondness for the Germans, but to the friars of Notre-Dame-des-Allemands, who ran a hospital near here in the Middle Ages. The gate, overlooking the River Seille, was severely damaged during the liberation of the city by Allied forces in November 1944.

Quartier de la Gare

The solid and bourgeois buildings and broad avenues of Quartier de la Gare, including rue Gambetta and av Foch, were constructed in the decades leading up to WWI. Built with the intention of Germanising the city by emphasising Metz' post-1871 status as an integral part of the Second Reich, its neo-Romanesque and neo-Renaissance buildings are made of dark-hued sandstone, granite and basalt, rather than the yellow-tan Jaumont limestone characteristic of French-built neoclassical structures.

The massive, grey-sandstone **train station**, completed in 1908 and decorated with Teutonic sculptures whose common theme was German imperial might, was designed with military needs clearly in mind. With a length of 300m, it could handle the loading or unloading of 20,000 troops and their equipment in just 24 hours. The massive **main post office**, built in 1911 of red Vosges sandstone, is as solid and heavy as the cathedral is light and lacy.

Quartier de l'Amphithéâtre

'The wrong side of the tracks', until recently a wasteland of abandoned hangars and depots, is undergoing a complete transformation thanks to Metz' seemingly boundless cultural ambitions (and development budget). The Amphitheatre Quarter already boasts **Les Arènes** (Palais Omnisports), a vast steel-and-glass venue for sports events and concerts, and the green riverside lawns of **Parc de la Seille**. But you ain't seen nothin' yet: come 2007, the **Centre Pompidou-Metz** – a branch of the inside-out original in Paris –

is supposed to open its doors. The winning design, by Shigeru Ban (Tokyo), Jean de Gastines (Paris) and Philip Gumuchdjian (London), is like nothing else ever conceived by the human mind. Suffice it to say that the whole thing will be covered by an undulating, translucent 'membrane' of Teflon-coated fibreglass. The project may just do for Metz what the Guggenheim did for Bilbao.

Tours
The tourist office's 1½-hour *visites audio-oguidées* (Walkman tours; €7) of the city centre are available in six languages.

Sleeping
In general, Metz' hotels offer excellent value. Except in summer, they are at their fullest from Monday to Thursday.

BUDGET
Auberge de Jeunesse Carrefour (☎ 03 87 75 07 26; ascarrefour@wanadoo.fr; 6 rue Marchant; dm in 3–4-bedroom €12.35, s/d €14.10/28.20, rates incl breakfast) This hostel for young working people has plain rooms, accessible all day long, in which showers and toilets are being installed. There's no curfew. From the train station, take bus Nos 3 or 11 to the St-Georges stop.

Auberge de Jeunesse Metz-Plage (☎ 03 87 30 44 02; aubjeumetz@aol.com; dm €12.30, s €15.30, rates incl breakfast ; ☺ check-in 8am-10am & 5-10pm) This old-time hostel, with 62 beds, has decades-old facilities but offers room access (with a code) all day long; there's no curfew. Kitchen facilities are available. By bus, take the No 3 or 11 to the Pontiffroy stop.

Hôtel Lafayette (☎ 03 87 75 21 09; fax 03 87 75 66 87; 24 rue des Clercs; d with toilet or shower €28, d/tr with shower & toilet €33/41) The spotless rooms, many with old-fashioned touches (eg chimneys), are a bit ragged around the edges but the staff is welcoming and you can't beat the location.

MID-RANGE
Hôtel Métropole (☎ 03 87 66 26 22; www.hotel metropole-metz.com; 5 place du Général de Gaulle; s/d from €38/45/57; ☒) Built as a hotel at the tail end of the German period (1912), this two-star place has rooms that are so bright and cheery they're almost spiritually uplifting. Excellent value for money.

Cécil Hôtel (☎ 03 87 66 66 13; www.cecilhotel-metz .com; 14 rue Pasteur; d €54) Built in 1920, right after Metz was returned to France, this charming two-star hotel has modern, pastel rooms with spacious tile bathrooms. From Thursday to Sunday nights, the buffet breakfast (€6) is free if you stay at least two days.

Hôtel Bristol (☎ 03 87 66 74 22; www.hotel-bristol -57.com; 7 rue Lafayette; s/d from €28/32, larger d €45) Bring your bell-bottoms and nose plug – at the Bristol it's still the 1970s, the period authenticity certified by the fusty odour of furnishings undisturbed since Elvis didn't die. The two-star rooms can charitably be termed compact (in the cheaper ones the word 'cramped' also comes to mind).

Grand Hôtel de Metz (☎ 03 87 36 16 33; www .grandhotelmetz.com in French; 3 rue des Clercs; d from €59) At this two-star place, you can luxuriate in a two-person bathtub in one of the romantic minisuites (€90), big enough for ball-room dancing (our advice to management: lose the plastic plants), and make your own eggs at the buffet breakfast (€6.50). By car, take rue Fabert from the cathedral, push the button on the 'appel' upright and explain you're going to the hotel.

Eating
Place St-Jacques is taken over by cafés in the warmer months. Cheap student eats are available near the university on grungy rue du Pont des Morts.

À la Ville de Lyon (☎ 03 87 36 07 01; next to 13 rue des Piques; menus €19-45.80, children's menu €6.90; ☺ closed Mon & dinner Sun) This elegant and very formal restaurant features traditional French dishes as well as the cuisine of Lorraine. Specialities include quiche Lorraine and *soufflé glacé à la mirabelle* (chilled soufflé with mirabelle plums).

Restaurant du Pont St-Marcel (☎ 03 87 30 12 29; 1 rue du Pont St-Marcel; menus €18-29) Everything

---

AUTHOR'S CHOICE

Hôtel de la Cathédrale (☎ 03 87 75 00 02; www.hotelcathedrale-metz.fr in French; 25 place de Chambre; d €55-80, ste €90). Ensconced in a gorgeous 17th-century townhouse, this three-star place positively oozes romance! The 20 large rooms are tastefully furnished with antiques and silks that perfectly complement the ancient wooden beams overhead. The wrought ironwork is by Jean Lamour (1698–1771), creator of the gilded masterpieces that adorn Nancy's place Stanislas.

AUTHOR'S CHOICE

L'Étude (☎ 03 87 36 35 32; www.l-etude.com in French; 11 av Robert Schuman; 2-/3-course menus €19.80/23.80, when there's live music €22.60/26.30; ☺ Mon-Sat) Hugely popular with local cognoscenti, this eatery is a real quintessential French mixture of the intellectual (with book-lined walls) and the gastronomic (French, of course). There's live music (jazz, blues, Roma, Cuban – the website has the schedule) commencing at 8.30pm on Friday and Saturday (reservations recommended).

---

here is typical of Lorraine, from the succulent dishes to the white cotton hats, billowy shirts, black vests and long skirts worn by the waitresses.

Taj Mahal (☎ 03 87 74 33 23; 16 rue des Jardins) This place has a weekday, all-you-can-eat Indian lunch buffet for just €8.50 and vegetarian mains for €7.

SELF-CATERING

For food supplies there is the **covered market** (place de la Cathédrale; ☺ approx 7am-6pm Tue-Sat) or the **Atac supermarket** (place St-Jacques; ☺ 8.30am-7.30pm Mon-Sat), on the lower level of the Centre St-Jacques shopping mall.

Drinking

Café Jehanne d'Arc (☎ 03 87 37 39 94; place Jeanne d'Arc; ☺ noon-2.30am Mon-Fri, 3pm-3.30am Sat) This establishment bears its long history – the roof beams are from the 1500s, the frescoes two or three centuries older – with good humour and mellowness. The sound track is pure jazz. There's a refreshing terrace in the warm months.

L'Appart (☎ 03 87 18 59 26; 2 rue Haute Pierre; ☺ 5pm-3am Sun Thu, 7pm-7am or 8am Fri & Sat) The house in which the poet Paul Verlaine Arthur Rimbaud's lover and almost his assassin – was born in 1844 is now a laid-back mainly gay bar with campy chandeliers, a retro 1950s ceiling, a bright orange floor and centuries-old carved wood panelling (protected by law). It is a disco on Sunday.

Entertainment

The city's main concert venues are the **Arsenal cultural centre** (☎ 03 87 39 92 00; av Ney), **Les Arènes** (☎ 03 87 62 82 93 60; www.arenes-de-metz.com in French), and the smaller **Salle des Trinitaires**

(place Jeanne d'Arc). Details on cultural events appear in the free monthly *Spectacles* (www .spectacles-publications.com in French).

The gyrating bodies and ultramodern décor of **Le Tiffany** (☎ 03 87 75 23 32; 24 rue du Coët-losquet; admission free except Fri/Sat €10/12; ☺ 11pm-5am Wed-Sat) would have knocked the socks off the medieval people who built the vaulted cellar it has occupied since 1972. Each of the three dance halls features a different type of music (soul, R&B, house, retro etc).

Getting There & Away

CAR
Rental options:

Budget (☎ 03 87 66 36 31; 5 rue Lafayette)
Europcar (☎ 03 87 62 26 11; in the train station's arrival hall)
National-Citer (☎ 03 87 38 09 99; in the train station's arrival hall)

TRAIN

Metz' train station is on the line linking Paris' Gare de l'Est (€35.30, three hours, seven to nine daily) with Luxembourg (€11.20, 50 minutes, 11 to 19 daily). Direct trains also go to Nancy (€8.30, 40 to 70 minutes, 27 to 37 daily Monday to Saturday, 15 on Sunday), Strasbourg (€19.10, 1¼ to 1¾ hours, five to nine daily) and Verdun (€11.40, 1¼ hours, three each weekday, one daily weekends).

Getting Around

BICYCLE
Three-speed city bikes can be rented from non-profit **Vélocation** (per half-/whole day €3/5) outlets:

Train station (☎ 03 87 62 61 79; in the arrival hall; ☺ 9am-8pm, to 6pm Sat & Sun, closed Sat & Sun Christmas-Feb)
Under the covered market (☎ 03 87 74 50 43; rue d'Estrées ☺ 8am-7pm, to 6pm Sat & Sun)

BUS

The local bus system, run by **TCRM** (☎ 03 87 76 31 11; office at 1 av Robert Schuman; ☺ Mon-Sat) operates from 6am to about 8pm daily (bus No 11 also has runs at about 10pm, 11pm and midnight). One/six rides cost €0.90/4.10 and the all-day Visipass is €3.

PARKING

Near the train station, there's free parking under the trees on av Foch and, to the northeast, at place Mazelle.

TAXI
You can order a **taxi** (☎ 03 87 56 91 92) day or night.

FORT DU HACKENBERG
The largest single Maginot Line bastion (p344) in the Metz area was the 1000-man **Fort du Hackenberg** (☎ 03 82 82 30 08), which is 30km northeast of Metz near the village of Veckring, whose 10km of galleries were designed to be self-sufficient for three months and, in battle, to fire four tonnes of shells a minute. Two-hour tours (adult/child under 16 €5/2.50) begin every 15 minutes between 2pm and 3.30pm on Saturday and Sunday from April to October. An electric trolley takes visitors along 4km of the fortress' underground tunnels – always at 12°C – past a variety of subterranean installations (kitchen, hospital, electric plant etc).

VERDUN
pop 21,000
The horrific events that took place in and around Verdun between February 1916 and August 1917 – *l'enfer de Verdun* (the hell of Verdun) – have turned the town's name into a byword for wartime slaughter. During the last two years of WWI, over 800,000 soldiers – some 400,000 French and almost as many Germans, along with thousands of the Americans who arrived in 1918 – lost their lives here.

After the annexation of Alsace and part of Lorraine by Germany in 1871, Verdun became a frontline outpost. Over the next four decades, it was turned into the most important – and most heavily fortified – element in France's eastern defensive line. During WWI Verdun itself was never taken by the Germans, but the evacuated town was almost totally destroyed by artillery bombardments. In the hills to the north and east of Verdun, where most of the fighting took place, the brutal combat (carried out with artillery, flame-throwers and poison gas) completely wiped out nine villages.

These days, Verdun is an economically depressed and profoundly provincial backwater, though the dispatch of French troops based near Verdun to peacekeeping missions abroad has made world politics a very local – and for some, personal – affair.

Orientation
Central Verdun straddles the River Meuse and its two canals, but the livelier Ville Haute (Upper Town) is on the river's western bank, which rises to the cathedral. The train station is 700m northwest of the cathedral. The main drag is known as rue St-Paul and rue Mazel.

Information
Commercial banks can be found around the intersection of rue Mazel and rue Beaurepaire. The tourist office exchanges US dollars and pounds sterling on weekends and holidays.
Laundrette (2 place Chevert; ☼ 6.30am-8pm, to 9pm Jun-Sep)
Main Post Office (av de la Victoire) Has currency exchange and a Cyberposte.
Tourist Office (☎ 03 29 86 14 18; www.verdun-tourisme.com; place de la Nation; ☼ 8.30am-6.30pm Mon-Sat May-Sep, 9am-noon & 2-5pm or 6pm Mon-Sat Oct-Apr, 9.30am-5pm Sun & holidays Apr-Sep, 10am-1pm Sun & holidays Oct-Mar)

Citadelle Souterrraine
In 1916 Verdun's huge **Citadelle Souterrraine** (Underground Citadel; ☎ 03 29 86 62 02; tourist entrance on av du 5e RAP; adult/5-15 yrs €5.40/2.30), with its 7km of underground galleries, was turned into an impregnable command centre in which 10,000 *poilus* (French WWI soldiers) lived, many while waiting to be dispatched to the front. About 10% of the galleries have been converted into an imaginative audiovisual re-enactment of the war, making this an excellent introduction to the WWI history of Verdun. The citadel was designed by Vauban (p30) in the 17th century and completed in 1838.

Half-hour tours, in battery-powered cars and available in six languages, depart every five minutes from 9am (10am from December to March) to 11.30am or noon and 2pm to 4.30pm (5pm in October and November, 6pm or 6.30pm from April to September, when there's no midday closure). The citadel is closed during the second and third weeks of January.

Centre Mondial de la Paix
The **Centre Mondial de la Paix** (World Centre for Peace; ☎ 03 29 86 55 00; place Monseigneur Ginisty; adult/student €5.50/3; ☼ 9.30am-7pm Jun–mid-Sep, 9.30am-noon & 2-6pm mid-Sep–May, closed Jan) has

imaginative and moving exhibits – accompanied by English commentary (via headsets) and video images – on the themes of peace and human rights in light of the horrific carnage of WWI. The exhibits are different from what many people expect as the focus here is on human beings rather than political or military developments – or army hardware. The centre is housed in Verdun's handsomely classical (and classically handsome) former bishop's palace built in 1724.

Other Sights

Inside **Cathédrale Notre Dame** (place Monseigneur Ginisty; ⏰ 8am-6pm or 7pm), a gilded baroque **baldachin** and 18th-century furnishings add some character to the heavily restored Romanesque and Gothic structure. Much of the most-colourful stained glass is from the interwar period.

The colossal **Monument à la Victoire** (Victory Monument), built from 1920 to 1929 and overlooking rue Mazel, portrays a warrior and is flanked by two cannons. Its almost Fascist-looking countenance is softened somewhat by the new cascading fountain.

Two one-time city gates are the **Porte Chaussée** (rue Chaussée), built in the 14th century and later used as a prison, and **Porte St-Paul** (rue St-Paul), built in 1877 and rebuilt between 1919 and 1929. The Rodin bronze was given to the city by the Netherlands.

ALSACE & LORRAINE

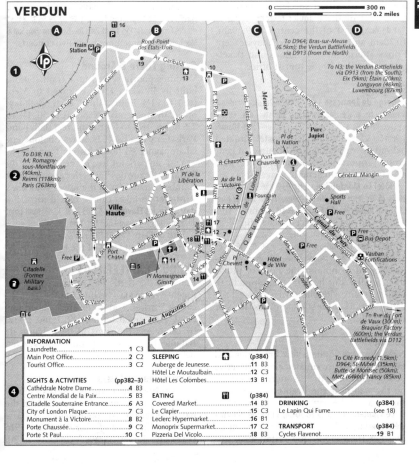

VERDUN

0 — 300 m
0 — 0.2 miles

INFORMATION	
Laundrette	1 C3
Main Post Office	2 C2
Tourist Office	3 C2

SIGHTS & ACTIVITIES	(pp382–3)
Cathédrale Notre Dame	4 B3
Centre Mondial de la Paix	5 B3
Citadelle Souterraine Entrance	6 A3
City of London Plaque	7 C3
Monument à la Victoire	8 B2
Porte Chaussée	9 C2
Porte St Paul	10 C1

SLEEPING	⌂ (p384)
Auberge de Jeunesse	11 B3
Hôtel Le Moutaulbain	12 C3
Hôtel Les Colombes	13 B1

EATING	⊞ (p384)
Covered Market	14 B3
Le Clapier	15 C3
Leclerc Hypermarket	16 B1
Monoprix Supermarket	17 C2
Pizzeria Del Vicolo	18 B3

DRINKING	(p384)
Le Lapin Qui Fume	(see 18)

TRANSPORT	(p384)
Cycles Flavenot	19 B1

LA PETITE AMERIQUE

Verdun had a significant American military presence until Charles de Gaulle pulled France out of NATO's integrated military command in 1966. In **Cité Kennedy**, a neighbourhood that once housed American military families, the streets still bear names such as av d'Atlanta, av de Floride, av de Géorgie and impasse de Louisiane.

Tours

For details on tours of the Verdun Battlefields, see p384.

Dragées (pronounced 'dra-**zhay**'; sugared almonds) – not to be confused with *draguer* (dra-**gay**), which means to chat up – have long been a Verdun speciality. There are tours (€2) of the **Braquier factory** (50 rue du Fort de Vaux), east of the centre, at 9.30am, 10.30am and 2.30pm on weekdays except Friday afternoon; reservations and ticketing are handled by the tourist office.

Sleeping

Auberge de Jeunesse (☎ 03 29 86 28 28; ajverdun@wanadoo.fr; place Monseigneur Ginisty; dm €9.30; ☺ reception 8am-12.30pm & 5-11pm Mon-Fri, 8-10am & 5-9pm Sat & Sun) This modern hostel, situated behind the cathedral, has 70 bunks of generous proportions. Rooms are accessible all day long; a kitchenette is available.

Hôtel Le Montaulbain (☎ 03 29 86 00 47; fax 03 29 84 75 70; 4 rue de la Vieille Prison; d with shower from €32, with shower & toilet €38) The 10 rooms at this family-run two-star place are cheerful, well-tended and fairly spacious.

Hôtel Les Colombes (☎ 03 29 86 05 46; 9 av Garibaldi; d €34; ☺ reception closed Sun afternoon Nov-Feb) Named to honour the dove of peace, this family-run hostelry has practical, well-lit rooms with cheap rugs but real tile bathrooms. Has one star but offers two-star comfort.

Eating

Near the river, quite a few brasseries and fast-food joints are situated along attractive pedestrianised quai de Londres (a plaque on the wall near rue Beaurepaire explains the origin of the name).

Le Clapier (☎ 03 29 86 20 14; 34 rue des Gros Degrés; menu €13; ☺ Mon-Sat) A real *restaurant du quartier* (neighbourhood restaurant), this

intimate place serves up traditional home cooking in a homey atmosphere.

Pizzeria Del Vicolo (☎ 03 29 83 93 93; 33 rue des Gros Degrés; ☺ closed Sun & lunch Mon) Tasty pizzas from the wood-fired oven (€6.30 to €9.70), pasta dishes (€6.50 to €7.90) and meat mains (€8.20 to €11.90) are the specialities.

SELF-CATERING

The **food market** (rue Victor Hugo; ☺ 7am-12.30pm Fri & perhaps other days), renovated in 2004, is under the arches of the old covered market. The **Leclerc hypermarket** (☺ 9am-8pm Mon-Sat) is cross the car park from the train station and there is a **Monoprix supermarket** (rue Mazel; ☺ 9am-noon & 2-7pm Mon-Sat, to 8.30pm Fri).

Drinking

Up for a pint in a friendly neighbourhood bar? Try **Le Lapin Qui Fume** (☎ 03 29 86 15 84; 31 rue des Gros Degrés; ☺ 11am-2am Tue-Sat, 6pm-2am Sun & Mon), which sometimes hosts live concerts.

Getting There & Around

Verdun's poorly served little train station, built by Eiffel in 1868, is linked to Metz (€11.40, 1¼ hours, three each weekday, one daily weekends), Nancy (€14.50, 1½ to 2½ hours, two to four nondirect daily) and Paris' Gare de l'Est (€29.50 via Châlons-en-Champagne, 3½ hours, two to four daily).

You can park for free in the lots on av du 8 Mai 1945, rue des Tanneries and rue Léon Gambetta and next to the upper Citadelle.

Mountain bikes can be rented for €15 a day at **Cycles Flavenot** (☎ 03 29 86 12 43; rond-point des États-Unis; ☺ 9am-noon & 2-7pm Tue-Sat).

Taxis de Place (☎ 03 29 86 05 22 or 03 29 84 53 59) is based right in front of the tourist office.

VERDUN BATTLEFIELDS

Much of the Battle of Verdun (p385) was fought 5km to 8km (as the crow flies) northeast of Verdun. Today, the area – again forested – is served by the D913 and D112; by car follow the signs to the 'Champ de Bataille 14-18'. The opening hours given below may be modified in 2005.

Information & Tours

The Verdun tourist office (p382) can supply practical and historical information on the battlefields; books on offer include Alistaire Horne's *The Price of Glory: Verdun 1916* (€13) and Robert Graves' *Goodbye to All*

That (€9). The tourist office's four-hour minibus tours (€25.50 including entrance fees; English text available) of the five main battle sites begin at 2pm from May to mid-September.

Mémorial de Verdun

The village of Fleury, wiped off the face of the earth in the course of being captured and recaptured 16 times, is now the site of the **Mémorial de Verdun** (Musée Mémorial de Fleury; ☎ 03 29 84 35 34; adult/11-16 yrs €7/3.50; ⊙ 9am-6pm Apr-early Sep, 9am-noon & 2-6pm early Sep-late Dec, Feb & Mar). The story of the battle is told using evocative (and in some cases gruesome) photos, documents, weapons and other objects; downstairs is a re-creation of the battlefield as it looked on the day the guns finally fell silent. Admission includes a film, available in English.

In the grassy crater-pocked centre of **Fleury**, a few hundred metres down the road from the memorial, signs among the low ruins indicate the village's former layout.

Ossuaire de Douaumont

The sombre, 137m-long **Douaumont Ossuary** (☎ 03 29 84 54 81), inaugurated in 1932, is one of France's most important WWI memorials. It contains the remains of about 130,000 unidentified French and German soldiers collected from the battlefields after the war. An excellent, 20-minute **audiovisual presentation** (adult/8-12 yrs €4/3; ⊙ no screenings in Jan or mornings in Dec & Feb) on the battle and its participants begins every 30 minutes from 9am to 11.30am and 2pm to sometime between 4.30pm (in November) and 6pm (May to August); there's no midday break from April to September. With the same ticket you can climb the 46m-high **bell tower**, which houses a small museum.

Fort de Douaumont

About 2km northeast of the Douaumont Ossuary on the highest of the area's hills stands **Fort de Douaumont** (☎ 03 29 84 41 91; adult/8-15 yrs €3/1.50; ⊙ 9am-6.30pm Apr-Aug, 10am-noon & 2-6pm Sep-Mar, to 5pm Dec, closed Jan), the strongest of the 39 fortresses and bastions built along a 45km front to protect Verdun. Because the French high command disregarded warnings of an impending German offensive, Douaumont – whose 3km network of cold, dripping galleries was built between 1885 and 1912 – had only a skeleton crew when the Battle of Verdun began. By the fourth day it had been captured easily; four months later it was retaken by colonial troops from Morocco.

Tranchée des Baïonnettes

On 12 June 1916 two companies of the 137th Infantry Regiment of the French army were

---

THE BATTLE OF VERDUN

The outbreak of WWI in August 1914 was followed on the Western Front by a long period of trench warfare in which neither side made any significant gains. To break the stalemate, the Germans decided to change tactics, attacking a target so vital for both military and symbolic reasons that the French would throw every man they had into its defence. These troops would then be slaughtered, 'bleeding France white' and causing the French people to lose their will to resist. The target selected for this bloody plan by the German general staff was the heavily fortified city of Verdun.

The Battle of Verdun began on the morning of 21 February 1916. After the heaviest shelling of the war to that date (something like two million shells were fired in 10 hours), German forces went on the attack and advanced with little opposition for four days, capturing, among other unprepared French positions, Fort de Douaumont. Thus began a 300-day battle fought by hundreds of thousands of cold, wet, miserable and ill-fed men, sheltering in their muddy trenches and foxholes amid a moonscape of craters.

French forces were regrouped and rallied by General Philippe Pétain (later the leader of the collaborationist Vichy government during WWII), who slowed the German advance by launching several French counterattacks. He also oversaw the resupply of Verdun via the **Voie Sacrée** (Sacred Way), the 75km road from Bar-le-Duc, maintained by territorial troops from Senegal. The Germans weren't pushed back beyond their positions of February 1916 until American troops and French forces launched a coordinated offensive in September 1918.

sheltering in their *tranchées* (trenches), *baïonnettes* (bayonets) fixed, waiting for a ferocious artillery bombardment to end. It never did – the incoming shells covered their positions with mud and debris, burying them alive. They weren't found until three years later, when someone spotted several hundred bayonet tips sticking out of the ground. The victims were left where they died, their bayonets still poking through the soil. The site is always open. The tree-filled valley across the D913 is known as the **Ravin de la Mort** (Ravine of Death).

Fort de Vaux

On 1 June 1916 German troops managed to enter the tunnel system of the **Fort de Vaux** (☎ 03 29 88 32 88; adult/8-15 yrs €3/1.50; ☺ 9am-6.30pm Apr-Sep, 10am-5pm Oct-Mar, closed Jan), attacking the French defenders from inside their own ramparts. After six days and seven nights of brutal, metre-by-metre combat along the narrow passageways (the most effective weapons were grenades, flame throwers and poison gas) the steadfast French defenders, dying of thirst (drops of moisture off the walls had become their only water source), were forced to surrender. The fort was re-captured by the French five months later.

The interior of Vaux, built between 1881 and 1912 and encased in 2.5m of concrete, is smaller, more reconstructed and less dreary – and thus less interesting – than Douaumont.

Fort de Souville

This unrestored fort (built 1875–77), some of whose underground galleries have col-lapsed, sits in the **Forêt Domaniale de Verdun** (Verdun Forest) on a gravel track linked to the D112 and D913. All around, post-war trees and undergrowth sprout from shell craters and traces of the trench lines. Na-ture heals all – but very slowly.

AMERICAN MEMORIALS

The largest US military cemetery in Europe, the WWI **Meuse-Argonne American Cemetery**, is at Romagne-sous-Montfaucon, 41km north-west of Verdun along the D38 and D123. Just east of Montfaucon d'Argonne (about 10km southeast of the cemetery), a 58m-high col-umn atop the 336m-high **Butte de Montfaucon** commemorates the US 1st Army's Meuse-Argonne offensive of 1918.

About 40km southeast of Verdun, the WWI **St-Mihiel American Cemetery** is on the outskirts of Thiaucourt-Regniéville. From there, a 15km drive to the southwest takes you to the 375m-high **Butte de Montsec**, site of a US monument with a bronze relief map surrounded by a round, neoclassical colonnade.

The WWII **Lorraine American Cemetery** is about 45km east of Metz just outside of St-Avold.

These sites are managed by the **American Battle Monuments Commission** (www.abmc.gov).

FORT DE FERMONT

One of the larger underground fortresses on the Maginot Line (p344), **Fermont** (☎ 03 82 39 35 34; www.ligne-maginot-fort-de-fermont.asso.fr) is approximately 56km north of Verdun. Around 30m deep, it withstood three days of heavy bombardment when the Germans attacked on 21 June 1940 but surrendered a few days later. During the 2½-hour tour (adult/seven to 12 years €5/3), in English for Anglophone groups (the rest of the time a written translation is available), a small electric trolley transports you from one subterranean army block to another. Tours begin between 2pm and 4.30pm daily from July to 19 September, at 3pm Monday to Friday in May and June and at 2pm and 3.30pm on Saturday, Sunday and holidays from April to June and 20 September to October.

The Loire

CONTENTS

Orléanais	**390**
Orléans	390
Orléans to Sully-sur-Loire	394
Gien to Sancerre	396
Bourges	396
La Sologne	396
Blésois	**397**
Blois	397
Around Blois	401
Touraine	**404**
Tours	404
Around Tours	409
Tours Area Chateaux	409
Amboise	412
Pagode de Chanteloup	415
Loches	415
Chinon	416
Anjou	**418**
Angers	418
Around Angers	422
Saumur & Troglodyte Valley	423

THE LOIRE

388

Some French words are understood the world over. 'Chateau' is one of them. Its very mention inspires images of grand towers rising to the heavens, of extravagant dining rooms for hundreds of guests, of exquisite gardens and shimmering moats. It says banquets, balls and decadence; crystal chandeliers and candelabras. It encapsulates both the intrigue of French history and our vision of romantic France. It's a word that belongs to the Loire Valley.

From the 15th to the 18th centuries, this area served as the playground of kings, princes, dukes and nobles, who expended family fortunes and the wealth of the nation to turn it into a vast neighbourhood of lavish (and not-so-lavish) chateaux. The result is a rich and concentrated collection of architectural treasures – indeed, its historical importance was recognised in 2000 when Unesco named the entire region a World Heritage Site. The Renaissance architecture to be found at Chambord, Chaumont, Chenonceau and Azay-le-Rideau is truly stunning; earlier defensive fortresses, simpler in design but no less significant, can be glimpsed at Angers, Chinon and Loches. Numerous other chateaux, big and small, dot the landscape.

The Loire is France's longest, most regal river. From its source in the Massif Central, it follows a 1020km course through Bourgogne, Orléanais, Blésois, Touraine and Anjou, into the Atlantic. It cuts a wide, flat valley through stunning countryside, making cycling a popular way to get around, although amateur cyclists should be aware that up to 50km can be clocked up for a return trip to just one chateau.

There are other attractions here too – religious architecture, curious caves and regional gastronomy in particular – but make no mistake, the real stars of the Loire are, in a word, the chateaux.

HIGHLIGHTS

- Explore the lifestyle of early royalty at the huge, gracious **Château de Chambord** (p401)
- Enjoy the quiet grandeur of **Chenonceau** (p410), a beautiful château built on the River Cher
- Splash out on a luxurious stay at **Château de Brissac** (p395)
- Take in the views of the Loire Valley from on high with a **hot-air balloon ride** (p401)
- Sniff out the vineyards and of **Sancerre** (p395) & **Vouvray** (p409)
- Try out the numerous restaurants in **Tours** (p407) and drinking at bustling **place Plumereau** (p408)
- Experience history through the sound-and-light show at eclectic **Château de Blois** (p397)
- Marvel at the control of the dog trainers at La Soupe des Chiens at **Château de Cheverny** (p402)

- POPULATION: 2,220,039
- AREA: 26,411 SQ KM

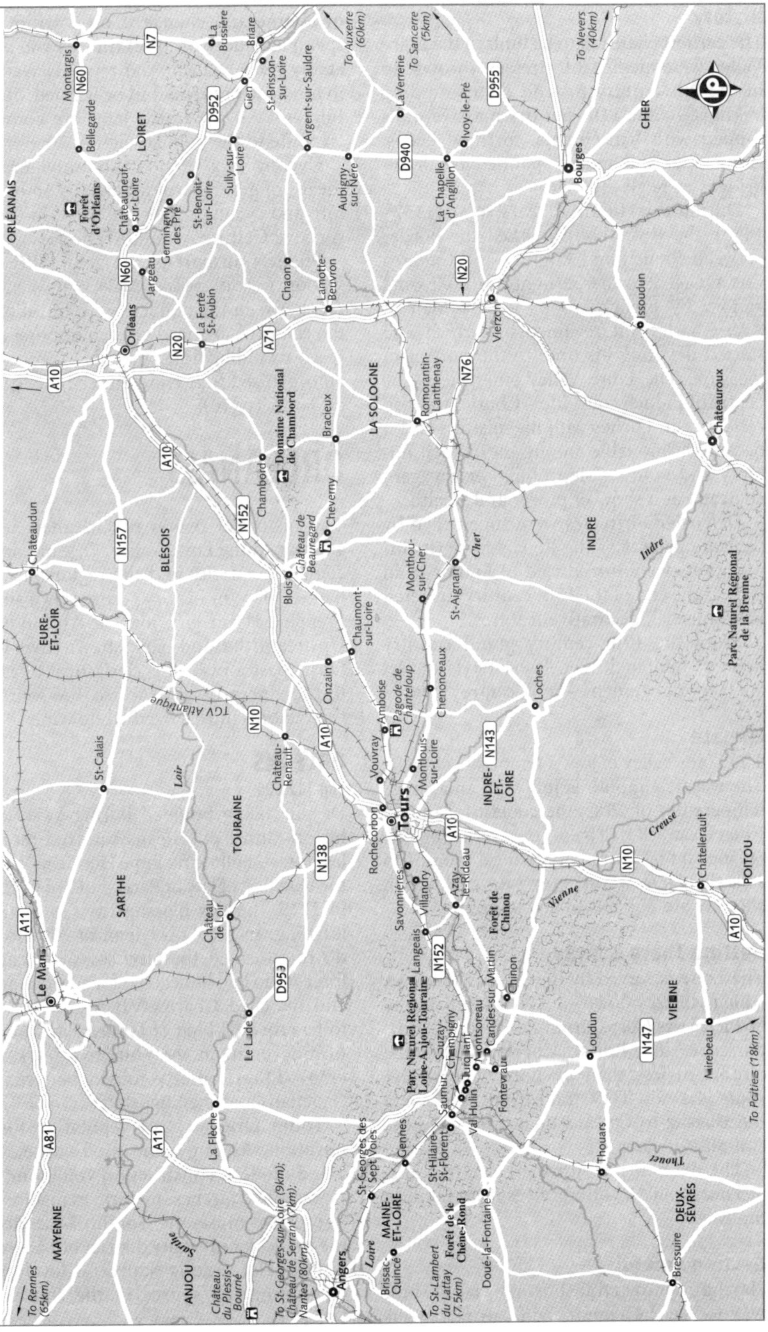
LOIRE VALLEY
0 50 km
0 25 miles
ORLÉANAIS
LOIRET
Montargis
Bellegarde
La Bussière
Briare
Gien
St-Brisson-sur-Loire
Argent-sur-Sauldre
Sully-sur-Loire
St-Benoît-sur-Loire
Germigny-des-Prés
Châteauneuf-sur-Loire
Forêt d'Orléans
Jargeau
Orléans
La Ferté St-Aubin
Chaon
Lamotte-Beuvron
Aubigny-sur-Nère
La Verrerie
To Auxerre (60km)
To Sancerre (5km)
To Nevers (40km)
Ivoy-le-Pré
La Chapelle d'Angillon
Bourges
CHER
Vierzon
Issoudun
Châteauroux
Romorantin-Lanthenay
LA SOLOGNE
Bracieux
Domaine National de Chambord
Chambord
Cheverny
Château de Beauregard
Blois
BLÉSOIS
Châteaudun
EURE-ET-LOIR
TGV Atlantique
Chaumont-sur-Loire
Onzain
Monthou-sur-Cher
St-Aignan
Cher
INDRE
Indre
Parc Naturel Régional de la Brenne
Loches
Chenonceaux
Amboise
Pagode de Chanteloup
Vouvray
Montlouis-sur-Loire
Château-Renault
St-Calais
Loir
TOURAINE
SARTHE
Rochecorbon
Tours
INDRE-ET-LOIRE
Creuse
Châtellerault
POITOU
Vienne
Savonnières
Villandry
Azay-le-Rideau
Forêt de Chinon
Langeais
Château de Loir
Le Mans
Le Lude
Chinon
Candes-sur-Martin
Montsoreau
Fontevraud
Loudun
VIENNE
Mirebeau
To Poitiers (18km)
Saumur
Champigny
Souzay
Parc Naturel Régional Loire-Anjou-Touraine
Val Hulin
St-Hilaire-St-Florent
Gennes
St-Georges des Sept Voies
La Flèche
Thouars
Thouet
DEUX-SÈVRES
Bressuire
Doué-la-Fontaine
Forêt de le Chêne-Rond
To St-Lambert du Lattay (7.5km)
Brissac-Quincé
MAINE-ET-LOIRE
Loire
Angers
To St-Georges-sur-Loire (9km); Château de Serrant (7km); Nantes (80km)
Château du Plessis-Bourré
ANJOU
Sarthe
MAYENNE
To Rennes (65km)
A81
A11
A10
N10
N138
N152
N143
N147
D953
N157
N152
A10
N20
A71
N60
N7
D952
D940
D955
N76
N20

THE LOIRE

History

The earliest chateaux to be built in the Loire Valley were medieval fortresses, thrown up in the 9th century to fend off marauding Vikings. By the 11th century massive walls topped with battlements, fortified keeps, arrow slits and moats spanned by drawbridges were all the rage.

During the Hundred Years' War (1337–1453), the River Loire marked the border between French and English, and the area was ravaged by fierce fighting. Following victory by French troops led by Joan of Arc, Charles VII regained his crown and started devoting his time to the pursuit of pleasure. The Loire Valley emerged as the centre of French court life – Charles took up residence in Loches with his mistress and it became fashionable among the French nobility and bourgeoisie to build extravagant chateaux as a show of power and wealth.

Defensive fortresses were superseded by pleasure palaces as the Renaissance (its innovations were introduced to France from Italy at the end of the 15th century) ushered in whimsical, decorative features.

From the 17th century grand country houses – built in the neoclassical style and set amid formal gardens – took centre stage.

Climate

The Loire Valley enjoys a temperate climate. The warmest month is July with an average temperature of 25°C, the coolest is January when it can fall well below the average of 5°C. Spring and late summer are ideal months to visit thanks to warm, sunny days, although showers are possible in any season.

Getting There & Away

The Loire is served by the TGV Atlantique, which whizzes down to Tours (and nearby St-Pierre des Corps) from Paris' Gare Montparnasse and Roissy Charles de Gaulle airport in less than an hour. The slower route is a non-TGV train from Paris' Gare d'Austerlitz to Orléans or nearby Gare des Aubrais-Orléans.

The main airport for the Loire region is at Tours (p408), with services from London Stansted.

Getting Around

Having your own transport is by far the best way to see the region. You can plan your own itinerary, change it on a whim and spend as much (or little) time as you'd like at any given chateau. Car rental is available in most major towns, but be warned, during July and August traffic jams are common en route to the popular sights.

Cycling is a popular and invigorating means of getting around; details on bicycle hire and cycling routes are listed in the respective Getting Around sections.

Public transport is not great. **SNCF train services** (national enquiries ☎ 36 35; www.sncf.com) run between the major towns, but most of the chateaux are hard or even impossible to reach by public transport. It's easier to join an organised tour from either Blois (p399) or Tours (p410).

ORLÉANAIS

The historical region of Orléanais is the gateway to the Loire Valley. Orléans, an ancient Roman city and the region's capital, had its place in history secured by a simple French peasant girl, Joan of Arc, in 1429. Upstream, the sand-bank-strewn River Loire twists past a rash of ecclesiastical treasures to the vineyards of Sancerre, the source of the region's most prized white wine.

ORLÉANS

pop 112,600

Despite being bombed during WWII, the historic heart of Orléans survived more or less intact. Following Pope Honorius' ban on the teaching of law in Paris (but not Orléans) in 1219, the city blossomed as a centre of learning. In May 1429 Joan of Arc (Jeanne d'Arc) stormed the city, smashed English forces who had besieged it for seven months, and marched Charles VII north to Reims to be crowned king of France. This was the turning point in the Hundred Years' War (1337–1453), bitterly fought between the Capetians and the English.

Today Orléans has a reputation for innovation. Among some tired corners and bland modern construction you'll find Romanesque churches, historic mansions and impressive museums. South of the city, in the modern university district of La Source, is Parc Floral de la Source, a lovely park containing the source of the short river Loiret.

Orientation

The River Loire snakes along the southern fringe of the city centre. Rue de la République links place du Martroi, the main square, with the central train station (Gare d'Orléans) and the adjoining Centre Commercial place d'Arc, a shopping complex that lies 400m to the north. The station for trains to and from Paris (Gare des Aubrais-Orléans) is 2km further north from Gare d'Orléans. The historic quarter of the city is east of place du Martroi, along rue Jeanne d'Arc.

Information

INTERNET ACCESS
BSP Info (☎ 02 38 77 02 82; 125 rue Bannier; per hr €4; ☼ 10am-8pm Tue-Sat, 2-8pm Sun & Mon)

Médiatheque (☎ 02 38 65 45 37; per hr €3.60; 1 place Gambetta; ☼ 10am-6pm Tue, Wed, Fri & Sat, 1-8pm Thu)

Odysseus Cyber Café (☎ 02 38 77 98 48; 32 rue du Colombier; per hr €4.50; ☼ 9am-9pm Mon-Wed, 9am-1am Thu & Fri, 11am-1am Sat)

MONEY
There are several commercial banks on place du Martroi. The post office at place du Général de Gaulle deals with currency exchange.

POST
Post Office (place du Général de Gaulle)

TOURIST INFORMATION
Espace d'Accueil Touristique (☎ 02 38 53 33 44; 6 rue Jeanne d'Arc; ☼ 2-5pm Tue-Sat, 10am-noon Sun)

Tourist Office (☎ 02 38 24 05 05; www.ville-orleans fr; 6 rue Albert 1er; ☼ 10am-1pm & 2-6.30pm Mon, 9am-1pm & 2-6.30pm Tue-Sat)

Sights

HÔTEL GROSLOT
A flamboyant, Renaissance style *hôtel particulier* (private mansion), **Hôtel Groslot** (☎ 02 38 79 22 30; place de l'Étape; admission free; ☼ 10am-noon & 2-6pm Sun-Fri, 4.30-6pm Sat Oct-Jun, 5-8pm Sat Jul-Aug) was built between 1550 and 1552 for Jacques Groslot, a city bailiff whose family lived here until 1790 when the French Revolution turned it into the town hall. Its lavish interior dates from 1850–54. The bedroom in which the 17-year-old king of France François II died in 1560 is today used as a marriage hall. Guided tours are possible on request.

MUSÉE DES BEAUX ARTS
The **Musée des Beaux Arts** (Museum of Fine Arts; ☎ 02 38 79 21 55; 1 rue Fernand Rabier; adult/student €3/1.60; ☼ 9.30am-12.15pm & 1.30-5.45pm Tue-Sat, 2-6pm Sun) houses an impressive collection of European art from the 15th to 20th centuries. Numerous religious works of art and treasures from surrounding chateaux that were seized during the French Revolution are among the displays.

CATHÉDRALE STE-CROIX
Orléans' Flamboyant Gothic **Cathédrale Ste-Croix** (☎ 02 38 77 87 50; place Ste-Croix; admission free; ☼ 9.15am-noon & 2.15-6pm), was built under Henri IV from 1601. Louis XIII (1610–43) had the choir and nave restored, Louis XIV (1638–1715) built the transept, and the next two Louis (1715–74) rebuilt the western façade and its towers. The spire (1858) completed the project. **Stained-glass windows** (1895) in the lower nave depict the life of Joan of Arc, France's patron saint who was canonised in 1920.

MAISON DE JEANNE D'ARC
The timber-framed **Maison de Jeanne d'Arc** (☎ 02 38 52 99 89; 3 place du Général de Gaulle; adult/student €2/1; ☼ 10am-12.15pm & 1.30-6pm Tue-Sun May-Oct, 1.30-6pm Tue-Sun Nov-Apr) is a reconstruction of the 15th-century house where Joan of Arc stayed for 11 days in April and May 1429. The original building was destroyed during WWII. Timber beams from a house dating from the same era were used to build the current edifice in 1965. The building houses an exhibition dedicated to the 17-year-old virgin warrior.

Festivals & Events
Since 1430 the Orléanais have celebrated the annual **Fête Johanniques**, which falls around 8 May and commemorates Joan of Arc's liberation of the city. A week of street parties, medieval costume parades and concerts climaxes with a solemn Mass at the cathedral.

Sleeping
Decent budget accommodation is scarce in Orléans, although a few cheaper hotels can be found on rue du Faubourg Bannier just north of place Gambetta. Better to spend a bit more on the good-value mid-range options. Most hotel reception desks close on Sunday afternoons.

THE LOIRE

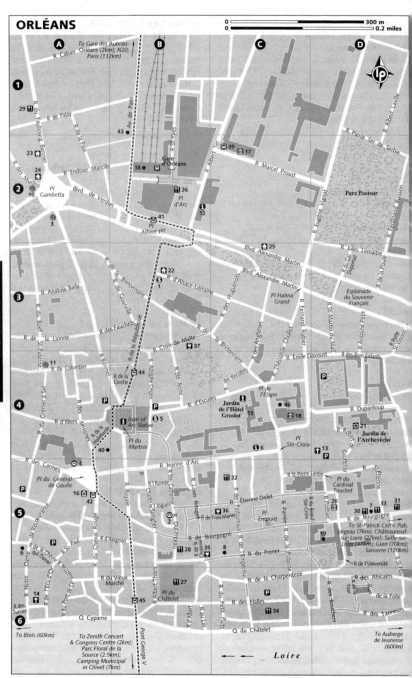

THE LOIRE

INFORMATION			Musée des Beaux Arts	18	C4	L'Estaminet	33	D5
Banque de France	1	B3	Préfecture	19	D5	Marché de la Charpenterie	34	C6
Branch Post Office	2	B5	Salle des Thèses	20	D5			
BSP Info	3	A2	Synagogue	21	D4	DRINKING		(p394)
Central Post Office	4	A5				Bel Air	35	B5
Crédit Lyonnais	5	B4	SLEEPING		(pp391–3)	Cats des Trois Maries	36	C5
Espace d'Acceuil Touristique	6	C4	Hôtel de l'Abeille	22	B3	Le Saint-Andrews	37	D5
Laundrette	7	D5	Hôtel Le Bannier	23	A2			
Laundrette	8	C5	Hôtel St Aignan	24	A2	TRANSPORT		(p394)
Laundrette	9	A5	Hôtel St-Martin	25	C3	Avis	38	B2
Médiathèque	10	A2				Bus Station	39	C2
Odysseus Cyber Café	11	A4	EATING		(pp393–4)	Espace Transport	40	A4
Tourist Office	12	B2	Carrefour Supermarket	(see 26)		Gare d'Orléans Tram Stop	41	B2
			Centre Commercial Place d'Arc	26	B2	Général de Gaulle Tram Stop	42	A5
SIGHTS & ACTIVITIES		(p391)	Covered Market	27	B6	Rent-Van & Car Ecoto	43	B1
Cathédrale Ste-Croix	13	D4	Espace Canal	28	B5	République Tram Stop	44	B4
Église Notre Dame de Recouvrance	14	A6	Intermarché Supermarket	29	A1	Royale Châtelet Tram Stop	45	B6
Hôtel Groslot	15	C4	La Petite Marmite	30	D5			
Maison de Jeanne d'Arc	16	A5	Le Gargantua	31	D5	OTHER		
Musée d'Orléans	17	C2	Le KT	32	C5	Hôtel de Ville	46	C4

BUDGET
Auberge de Jeunesse (☎ 02 38 53 60 06; asse.crjs@ libertysurf.fr; 1 blvd de la Motte-Sanguin; dm €7, sheets €2.50; reception 8am-9.30pm) Occupying an imposing neoclassical building in a park east of the town centre, this hostel has mainly small dorms with two beds and a shower. Take bus SY to the 'Pont Bourgogne' stop.

Hôtel Le Bannier (☎ 02 38 53 25 86; 13 rue du Faubourg Bannier; r with shower €25, with bath & toilet €28) This zero-star hotel above a bar is a cheerful place for budget travellers, once you get past the moody cigar-smoking patron. The simple rooms hold the record for world's thinnest walls.

Camping
Camping Municipal (☎ 02 38 63 53 94; fax 02 38 63 58 96; rue du Pont Bouchet; camping €14.20; Apr–mid-Oct) This camping ground is 7km south of Orléans in Olivet.

MID-RANGE
Hôtel St Aignan (☎ 02 38 53 15 35; www.contact -hôtel.com; 3 place Gambetta; s/d from €45/51; P) This high-rise two-star hotel is modern, comfortable and spacious – the bathrooms are as big as some bedrooms in town. Popular with business travellers.

Hôtel de l'Abeille (☎ 02 38 53 54 87; www.ho teldelabeille.com in French; 64 rue Alsace-Lorraine; r with toilet/shower from €37/42) On the edge of the pedestrian zone, this lovingly restored, century-old hotel is furnished with beautiful antiques and Jeanne d'Arc memorabilia. The creaky floorboards can definitely be excused; this is good value for such a charming place.

Hôtel St-Martin (☎ 02 38 62 47 47; www.hotel -orleans-st-martin.com; 52 blvd Alexandre Martin; d with/

without shower & toilet €43/35) This friendly, tidy hotel near the station has well-furnished rooms and showers of the small, plastic capsule variety. It's on a main road; rooms at the back are quieter.

Eating
The stretch of rue du Bourgogne between the *préfecture* and rue St-Etienne is loaded with places to eat. Take your pick from Moroccan, Indian, Chinese and plenty of French eateries.

Le Gargantua (☎ 02 38 54 30 80; 136 rue Bourgogne; menus €13-25) Among an appropriate setting of wooden beams and red-checked tablecloths you can sample the cuisine of times gone by such as veal's head, tongue and *andouille* (tripe sausage). Not for the faint-hearted – or vegetarian.

L'Estaminet (☎ 02 38 54 27 57; 148 rue Bourgogne; mains €8-14) A small, atmospheric place serving French fare with an international twist. The delicious foie gras tagliatelle is a popular speciality. With only seven tables, it's wise to book ahead in busy periods.

La Petite Marmite (☎ 02 38 54 23 83; 178 rue de Bourgogne; mains €14-22, menus €20 & €32;) Warm, cosy and always busy, this nonsmoking restaurant in a beautiful old timber-framed house serves up tasty regional fare.

Espace Canal (☎ 02 38 62 04 30; 6 rue Ducerceau; dishes €11-13; lunch Mon-Fri, dinner Thu-Sat) A unique cellar restaurant where you can swirl, sip and swallow or spit local wines while feasting on fine French food. A prestigious place, let down only by the uncomfortable chrome chairs.

Le KT (☎ 02 38 52 90 69; 13 rue des Pastoureaux; menu €5.30, plat du jour €5; 11.30am-2pm Mon-Fri) A canteen run by catering students.

THE LOIRE

THE LOIRE

SELF-CATERING

Snack food and cafés abound along Rue de Bourgogne. **Marché de la Charpenterie** (rue des Halles; ⏰ 4-10.30am Tue, Thu & Sat) is an outdoor market. The **covered market** (place du Châtelet; ⏰ 7.30am-7pm Tue-Sun) also has a good selection of fresh produce.

There is an **Intermarché supermarket** (49 rue du Faubourg Bannier), as well as a massive **Carrefour supermarket** inside the Centre Commercial place d'Arc.

Drinking

Bel Air (☎ 02 38 77 08 06; 44 rue du Poirier; ⏰ 6pm-1am Tue-Sat) The bar of the moment is the sophisticated Bel Air. All atmospheric red lights, soft furnishings, mellow house tunes and €10 cocktails.

Cats des Trois Maries (☎ 02 38 54 68 68; 2 rue des Trois Maries; ⏰ 6pm-3am Wed-Sat) The spot for jazz, blues and funk, with live bands from 9.30pm Friday and Saturday.

Other busy drinking holes include the Irish **St-Patrick Celtic Pub** (☎ 02 38 54 53 50; 1 rue de Bourgogne; ⏰ noon-1am) and **Le St-Andrews** (☎ 02 38 54 44 00; 15 rue Croix-de-Malte; ⏰ 1pm-1am Tue-Sat), a very British pub.

Entertainment

What's-on listings fill **Orléans Poche** (www.orleanspoche.com in French), a free monthly events magazine available at the tourist office.

The tourist office **billetterie** (☎ 02 38 24 05 05) sells tickets for choral concerts at Cathédrale Ste-Croix and classical (and occasionally rock) concerts at **Zénith** (☎ 02 38 25 05 05; 1 rue President Schuman), the city's concert and congress centre.

Getting There & Away

BUS

From the **bus station** (☎ 02 38 53 94 75; 1 rue Marcel Proust), **Les Rapides du Val de Loire** (☎ 02 38 61 90 00; www.rvl-info.com in French) operates buses to/from Châteauneuf-sur-Loire (€5.40, 35 minutes, four to six daily), Gien (€11.40, 1¾ hours, one daily) and Jargeau (€4.30, 45 minutes, three daily).

CAR

There is an office of **Avis** (☎ 02 38 62 27 04; ⏰ 8am-noon) inside the central train station. **Rent-Van & Car Ecoto** (☎ 02 38 77 92 92; 19 av de Paris), which is behind the Ibis hotel, offers competitive rates.

TRAIN

Shuttle trains (every eight minutes) link the **central train station** (Gare d'Orléans; ☎ 02 38 79 91 00; 1 rue St-Yves) with Gare des Aubrais-Orléans, 2km north.

From Orléans, most westbound trains along the Loire Valley stop at both train stations, including trains to/from Blois (€8.60, 30 minutes, about 20 trains daily), St-Pierre des Corps (€14.70, one to two hours, six daily), Nantes (€32.10, 2½ hours, three daily) and Tours (€14.80, 1¼ to 1¾ hours, four daily).

Most trains to/from Paris' Gare d'Austerlitz use Gare des Aubrais-Orléans (€15.50, one hour, 10 to 15 daily) but some continue on to central Gare d'Orléans.

Getting Around

Tickets and timetables for Semtao city buses and trams are available at **Espace Transport** (☎ 02 38 71 98 38; rue de la Hallebarde; ⏰ 9am-6.30pm Mon-Sat). It sells Liberté tickets (€3) allowing unlimited travel on buses and trams. Otherwise one-way tram/bus tickets purchased from the driver cost €1.20.

Orléans' 18km north–south tramline links Gare des Aubrais-Orléans with the central train station, rue de la République and place du Général de Gaulle in the centre of town, and the Parc Floral de la Source on the Loire's southern banks.

ORLÉANS TO SULLY-SUR-LOIRE

Medieval chateaux are overshadowed by ecclesiastical treasures along the eastern stretch of the River Loire between Orléans and Sully-sur-Loire. Its northern bank is flanked by the elk-rich **Forêt d'Orléans**, 38,234 hectares and the only place in France to shelter nesting osprey.

The riverside town of **Jargeau** (population 3561), which is 20km east of Orléans, is home to the Confrèrie des Chevaliers du Goûte Andouille (Tripe Sausage Brotherhood), dedicated to *andouille* – a fat tripe sausage, typical to the region, and sold at Monsieur Guibet's *charcuterie* at 14 place du Matroi.

The history of trade along the mighty River Loire comes alive in the **Musée de la Marine** (☎ 02 38 46 84 46; 1 place Aristide Briand; adult/child €5/2.50; ⏰ 10am-6pm Wed-Mon Apr-Oct, 2-6pm Wed-Mon Nov-Mar), a marine museum that is housed in an 11th- to 17th-century chateau in **Châteauneuf-sur-Loire**, 7km further east. The **tourist office** (☎ 02 38 58 44 79; 3 place Aristide Briand; 9.30am-12.30am & 2-7pm Mon-Sat Jun-Sep, to 6pm Oct-Mar) has information on cycling routes in the area.

In **Germigny des Prés**, 6km further east, the historically significant **Église de Germigny des Prés** is a rare example of Carolingian architecture. Dating to AD 806, this is one of France's oldest churches. The Greek-cross-shaped floor plan and 9th-century mosaic in its eastern apse are unique.

The 11th-century Romanesque **Basilique de St-Benoît** in **St-Benoît-sur-Loire**, 12km further east, shelters the relics of St Benedict (480–547). The heavily ornamented capitals supporting the monumental porch tower illustrate scenes from the Bible's Book of Revelations.

Château de Sully-sur-Loire (☎ 02 38 36 36 86; adult/child €5/3.50; 10am-6pm Apr-Sep, 10am-noon & 2-5pm Feb-Mar & Oct-Dec), with its fairy-tale moats and its thick-set towers, is a quintessential medieval fortress. It was built at the end of the 14th century to defend one of the River Loire's few crossings.

Sleeping & Eating

The **tourist office** (☎ 02 38 36 23 70; ot.sully.sur .loire@wanadoo.fr; place du Général de Gaulle; 9.30am-12.30pm & 2-7pm Mon-Sat May-Sep, 9.30am-noon & 2.30-6.30pm Tue-Sat Oct-Apr) in Sully-sur-Loire has accommodation details.

Hôtel de la Poste (☎ 02 38 36 26 22; fax 02 38 36 39 35; 11 rue Faubourg St-Germain; d from €46; P) in the village has comfortable rooms. The lovely courtyard **restaurant** (menu €15) dishes up memorable cuisine.

La Ferme des Châtaigniers (☎ 02 38 36 51 98; chemin des Châtaigniers; lunch menu €18, dinner menus €19-34) restaurant is run by a young couple who enthusiastically welcome guests to their rustic old chestnut farm, 2.5km west of Sully-sur-Loire off the D951.

LIVE LIKE A KING

Living in a château may be beyond the reach of most of us, but it is possible to experience the romantic magic of château life by staying in one of these *châteaux chambres d'hôtes*. You can't send the staff to the gallows on a whim but in most cases you'll get a queen-size bed, and breakfast fit for a king. These are our top five choices; a useful website for others is www .chateaux-france.com.

Château de Brissac (☎ 02 41 91 22 21; www.chateau-brissac.fr; r incl breakfast €390, dinner €77; P) The huge, extravagantly furnished rooms have to be seen to be believed: antique four-poster beds, wood panelling, hidden doors and historically significant tapestries are unique extras you won't get anywhere else. The chateau itself is grand, tall and set in well-tended gardens. All round, an exceptional experience and worth the royal price tag for the finest rooms, and setting, in the Loire.

Château de Verrieres (☎ 02 41 38 05 15; http://chateau-verrieres.com; 53 rue d'Alsace, Saumur; r €120-240, dinner €38; P) An elegant town chateau in the southwest of Saumur (p423) set in four acres of a tree-filled English park. It was built in 1890 and inside, the furnishings and décor remain pretty much as they were then – graceful, refined and ornate.

Château des Réaux (☎ 02 47 95 14 40; www.allchateaux.com/chateau-reaux.html; d incl breakfast €120-250; P) With its moat, brick and stone cheeseboard-effect towers and flower-filled garden this little chateau is undeniably beautiful. The rooms are not as grand as at some of the other chateau on offer, but it is a family home rather than a royal residence. Also open to day visitors between March and November. It's 12km north of Chinon (p416); take the D749 towards Bourgueil, and turn off onto the D238.

Château de la Verrerie (☎ 02 48 81 51 60; www.chateaux-france.com/verrerie; d €140-395; P) This 16th-century chateau was built as a summer house for the Scottish Stuart clan. It's in an idyllic spot, edging a tranquil lake and surrounded by forest. There are 12 luxury rooms, a 1.6km lake-side walking trail and a handy heliport on site. It's 8km north of Château d'Ivoy in Aubigny-sur-Nère.

Château d'Ivoy (☎ 02 48 58 85 01; chateau.divoy@wanadoo.fr; d incl breakfast €170; P) A modestly sized 16th to 17th-century chateau set in 10 hectares of prime hunting land. The six spacious rooms are exquisitely decorated with period furnishings. Dogs can be accommodated in the kennels. It's 30km west of Sancerre (p396) on the D12 in Ivoy-le-Pré.

THE LOIRE

GIEN TO SANCERRE

Corn and asparagus fields line the southern banks of the Loire from Sully-sur-Loire to picture-postcard **Gien** (population 16,477), 23km east. The town is known for its distinctive *bleu de Gien* earthenware, and bridle paths, ideal for cycling, skirt the river.

From Gien, the GR3 shadows the river on its course to Briare. Privately owned 17th-century **Château de la Bussière** (☎ 02 38 35 93 35; adult/child €7/4; ✆ Apr-Sep), which showcases fishing memorabilia and a 13th-century vegetable garden, and **Château de St-Brisson** (☎ 02 38 36 71 29; €7/4; ✆ Apr-Sep), known for its display of medieval stone-fed war machines, can be visited en route.

The industrial town of **Briare**, 15km east of Gien, is of little interest beyond its magnificent Art Nouveau canal bridge that spans the Loire. Built from iron between 1604 and 1642, the 662m canal bridge is Europe's longest. **Cruises** (adult/child €6/1; ✆ Apr-Nov) depart from **Port de Commerce** (☎ 02 38 37 12 75), in Briare and take 1½ hours.

The vineyards around **Sancerre** produce the region's best-known white wine. The **tourist office** (☎ 02 48 54 08 21; www.sancerre.net; Nouvelle Place; ✆ 10am-12.30pm & 2.30-5.30pm daily Apr–mid-Nov, closed Sun rest of year), in the village, has a list of places where you can taste and buy the local vintage.

Château d'Ivoy (p395) and Château de la Verrerie (p395), both west of Sancerre, are two remarkable places to stay and eat.

BOURGES

pop 76,000

The bustling city of Bourges is in the Berry region, southwest of Sancerre on the D955. Not part of the Loire Valley castle circuit, Bourges is known for its maze of cobbled streets, its culinary specialities and – above all – its magnificent cathedral. First settled by the Gauls, Bourges was the home of the future king Charles VII and later the centre of arms production under Napoleon III. Evening illuminations between May and August show the town in its best light.

The **tourist office** (☎ 02 48 23 02 60; www.ville -bourges.fr; 21 rue Victor Hugo; ✆ 9am-7pm Apr-Sep, 9am-6pm Mon-Fri & 2-5pm Sun Oct-Mar) is opposite the cathedral. Bourges is south of Gien along the D940, and on direct train lines from Orléans, Nantes and Tours; from Paris, change at Vierzon.

Cathédrale St-Étienne (☎ 02 48 65 49 44; place Étienne Dolet), a gothic masterpiece begun by Henri de Sully in 1195, has impressive medieval stained-glass windows and an incredible astronomical clock, designed in 1424 as a wedding present to Charles VII and Marie d'Anjou.

Hotel Le Berry (☎ 02 48 65 99 30; www.le-berry .com in French; 3 place Général Leclerc; r €55-62; P ✖), opposite the station, is a large hotel with modern rooms.

There are a few lively places to eat on rue Porte Jaune, just north of the cathedral, including **Le Latino** (☎ 02 48 65 26 37; 17 rue Porte Jaune; menus €10-15) with Latin American specialities and English *menus*.

LA SOLOGNE

The French associate the soggy wetland of La Sologne with one thing: hunting. A vast 490,000 hectares of ponds and woodland between the Rivers Loire and Cher, it has forests rich in deer, while eels, carp and pike fill its lakes and rivers.

La Sologne's 'capital' is Romorantin-Lanthenay, 41km southeast of Blois on the D765, a pretty little town straddling the River Sauldre. The **tourist office** (☎ 02 54 76 43 89; www.tourisme-romorantin.com in French; ✆ 10am-12.15pm & 2-6.30pm Mon, 8.45am-12.15pm & 1.30-6.30pm Tue-Fri, 8.45am-12.15pm & 2-6pm Sat year-round, plus 1am-noon Sun & holidays) has free brochures on driving and walking tours in the area.

La Sologne became a royal hunting playground under François I (r 1515–47). Years of war, disease and floods turned the area into waterlogged, malaria-infested swamp until the mid-19th century, when the plateau was drained by Napoleon III and regained its hunting prestige. Today the private hunting lifestyles of the rich and famous are unapologetically revealed in the **Maison du Braconnage** (House of Poaching; ☎ 02 54 88 68 68; adult/7-18 yrs €3/2.30; ✆ 2-6pm Wed-Mon Jul-Sep, 2-6pm Wed, Sat, Sun & holidays Apr-Jun & Oct–mid-Nov), which is in Chaon (about 11km east of Lamotte-Beuvron).

Aside from hunting, La Sologne is known for *tarte Tatin*, the famous and delicious upside-down apple tart accidentally created in 1888 by the Tatin sisters from Lamotte-Beuvron a small town south of Orléans on the N20.

There's an unexpectedly stylish hotel in town, the four-star **Grand Hotel du Lion d'Or**

MICHAEL GEBICKI

Vineyards along the scenic Route Touristique du Champagne (p331) near Reims

Cathédrale Notre Dame (p348), Strasbourg

CHRIS MELLOR

ELLIOT GERARD DANIEL

Half-timbered houses in the old city of Troyes (p336)

CHRIS MELLOR

Street cafés and wrought ironworks, place Stanislas, (p372) Nancy

Château de Chenonceau (p410), Loire Valley

Ornate keyboard, Château de Blois (p397), Loire Valley

Cloisters of Abbaye de Fontenay (p459), near Dijon

Hôtel-Dieu des Hospices de Beaune (p454) on the Côte d'Or

(☎ 02 54 94 15 15; www.hotel-liondor.fr; 69 rue Georges Clemenceau; r from €122; ⊗ closed mid-Feb–mid-Mar; P 😼 🖳), which occupies a 16th-century *hôtel particulier*. Rooms have been individually refurbished to an exceptionally high standard in keeping with the buildings origins. The hotel's acclaimed **restaurant** (menus €79-115; ⊗ lunch closed Tue) has two Michelin stars.

There are daily trains to Romorantin-Lanthenay from Tours (€12.40, 1¼ to 1½ hours, three daily) and Orléans (€12, 1½ to 1¾ hours, three daily).

BLÉSOIS

Blésois is graced with some of the Loire's finest chateaux, including stunning Chambord, magnificently furnished Cheverny, romantic Chaumont and modest Beauregard. Blois' tourist office has information on son et lumières (sound-and-light shows) hosted by these and other chateaux.

BLOIS
pop 49,300

Medieval Blois (pronounced blwah) was once the seat of the powerful counts of Blois, from whom France's Capetian kings were descended. From the 15th to the 17th century, Blois was a hub of court intrigue, and in the 16th century it served as a second capital of France. Several dramatic events – involving some of the most important personages in French history such as kings Louis XII, François I and Henri III – took place inside the city's outstanding attraction, Château de Blois.

The old city, seriously damaged by German attacks in 1940, retains its steep, twisting medieval streets.

Orientation

Blois, on the northern bank of the Loire, is a compact town – almost everything is within 10 minutes' walk of the train station. The old city is the area south and east of Château de Blois, which towers over place Victor Hugo. Blois' modern commercial centre is focused around pedestrianised rue du Commerce, rue Porte Chartraine and rue Denis Papin, which is connected to rue du Palais by a monumental staircase built in the 19th century.

Information

Several commercial banks face the river along quai de la Saussaye near place de la Résistance.

3'me Monde (☎ 02 54 74 38 22; 39 av Jean Laigret; per hr €4; ⊗ 11am-9pm) Internet access.

Centre Hospitalier de Blois (☎ 02 54 55 66 33; mail Pierre Charlot) Two kilometres northeast of the town centre.

Post Office (rue Gallois) Has a Cyberposte.

Tourist Office (☎ 02 54 90 41 41; www.ville-blois .fr in French & www.loiredeschateaux.com; 23 place du Château; ⊗ 9am-7pm Mon-Sat, 10am-7pm Sun Apr-Sep, 9am-12.30pm & 2-6pm Mon-Sat, 9.30am-12.30pm Sun Oct-Mar) Charges €2.30 to make hotel or B&B reservations.

Sights
CHÂTEAU DE BLOIS

The ornate and serendipitous **Château de Blois** (☎ 02 54 90 33 32; adult/student/child €6.50/4.50/2; ⊗ 9am-7pm Jul & Aug; 9am-6pm Apr-Jun, Sep & Oct; 9am-12.30pm & 2-5.30pm Nov-Mar) is a useful crash course in château architecture of the Loire. It's formed of four distinct wings constructed around a central courtyard, each reflecting the favoured style of the period in which it was built: medieval (13th century); Flamboyant Gothic (1498–1503), from the reign of Louis XII; early Renaissance (1515–24), from the reign of François I; and classical (17th century).

During the Middle Ages, the counts of Blois meted out justice in the huge **Salle des États Généraux** (Estates General Hall), a part of the feudal castle that survived wars, rebuilding and, most dangerous of all, changes in style and taste. It was used as a film set by the French film director Luc Besson for the trial scene in his box-office hit *Jeanne d'Arc* (1999).

A few steps away, but worlds apart in terms of design, the distinctive brick-and-stone **Louis XII section**, which includes the hall where entrance tickets are sold, is ornamented with porcupines – Louis XII's heraldic symbol. The king himself is also featured among the intricate decoration on the façade, cutting a dashing figure on horseback. The royal apartments on the first floor house the **Musée des Beaux-Arts**.

Started just 15 years later, the **François I wing** illustrates the speed at which Italian-influenced Renaissance design gained popularity in France. The famous projecting **spiral staircase**, a magnificent structure decorated

THE LOIRE

BLOIS

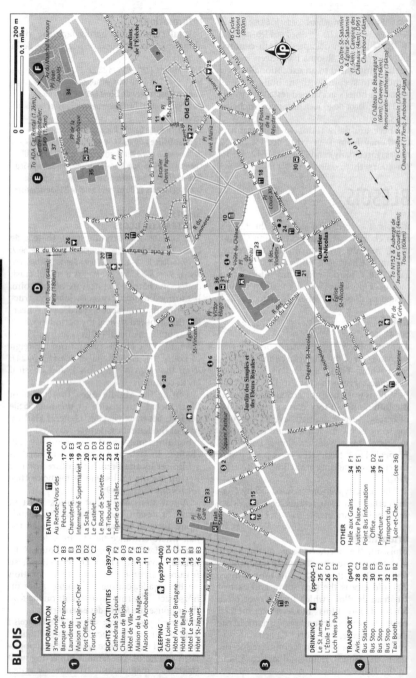

INFORMATION		
3'me Monde	1	C2
Banque de France	2	B3
Laundrette	3	E3
Maison du Loir-et-Cher	4	D3
Post Office	5	D2
Tourist Office	6	C2

SIGHTS & ACTIVITIES	(pp397-9)	
Cathédrale St-Louis	7	F2
Château de Blois	8	D3
Hôtel de Ville	9	F2
Maison de la Magie	10	E3
Maison des Acrobates	11	F2

SLEEPING	(pp399-400)	
Côté Loire	12	D4
Hôtel Anne de Bretagne	13	C2
Hôtel du Bellay	14	D1
Hôtel Le Savoie	15	B3
Hôtel St-Jacques	16	B3

EATING		(pp400)
Au Rendez-Vous des Pêcheurs	17	C4
Charcuterie	18	E3
Intermarché Supermarket	19	A3
La Scala	20	D1
Le Castelet	21	D3
Le Rond de Serviette	22	D2
Le Triboulet	23	D3
Triperie des Halles	24	E3

DRINKING		(pp400-1)
Le St James	25	F2
L'Étoile Tex	26	D1
Loch Ness Pub	27	E2

TRANSPORT		(p401)
Avis	28	C2
Bus Station	29	B2
Bus Stop	30	E3
Bus Stop	31	D3
Bus Stop	32	E1
Taxi Booth	33	B2

OTHER		
Halle aux Grains	34	F1
Justice Palace	35	E1
Point Bus Information Office	36	D2
Préfecture	37	E1
Transports du Loir-et-Cher	(see 36)	

with François I's insignia, a capital 'F' and a salamander, dominates the exterior.

The fourth wing to be built, the **Gaston d'Orléans wing**, is an impressive example of French classical architecture. Again, the monumental staircase is the most notable aspect of the construction, a double-vaulted design adorned with allegorical sculpture.

The most infamous episode in the history of the chateau occurred during the chaotic 16th century. King Henri III summoned his great rival, the ultra-powerful duke of Guise – a leader of the Catholic League (which threatened the authority of the king, himself a Catholic) – to his Counsel Chamber. There, he was set upon by 20 royal bodyguards armed with daggers and swords. When the violence was over, the joyous king, who had been hiding behind a tapestry, stepped into the room to inspect the duke's perforated body. Henri III was himself assassinated eight months later.

There's a **son et lumière** (☎ 02 54 78 72 76; adult/student/child €9.50/6/4.50; 🕐 9.30pm, 10pm, 10.15pm & 10.30pm early May–mid-Sep) and a show in English on Wednesday in May, June, August and September. Tickets are sold 30 minutes before the show starts. Combined same-day tickets (€12/8.50/5.50) are available for the show and chateau.

MAISON DE LA MAGIE
The **Maison de la Magie** (House of Magic; ☎ 02 54 55 26 26; 1 place du Château; adult/12-17 yrs/6-11 yrs €7.50/6.50/5; 🕐 10am-12.30pm & 2-6.30pm Jul & Aug, 10am-12.30pm & 2-6pm Tue-Sun Apr-Jun, 10am-noon & 2-6pm Wed, Thu, Sat & Sun Sep-Mar) faces Château de Blois and has magic shows, interactive exhibits and displays of clocks invented by the Blois-born magician Jean-Eugène Robert-Houdin (1805–71), after whom the great Houdini named himself. Tickets combining magic and *son et lumière* shows are available.

OLD CITY
Around the old city, large brown explanatory signs indicate tourist sights. **Cathédrale St-Louis** (🕐 7.30am-6pm) was rebuilt in a late Gothic style following the devastating hurricane of 1678.

Immediately behind is the **Hôtel de Ville**. Note the unusual double-aspect **sundial**, across the courtyard in a corner of the

Ecclesiastical Tribunal building. There's a great view of Blois and the Loire from the lovely **Jardins de l'Évêché** (Gardens of the Bishop's Palace), behind the cathedral.

Across the square from the cathedral, 15th-century **Maison des Acrobates** (House of the Acrobats; 3bis rue Pierre de Blois), is so-named because its timbers are decorated with characters taken from medieval farces. It was one of the few medieval houses to survive the bombings of WWII.

Tours
Transports du Loir-et-Cher (TLC; ☎ 02 54 58 55 55; adults/student & child €10/8; 🕐 mid-May–early-Sep) operates chateau excursions from Blois to Chambord and Cheverny. Tours depart twice daily from Blois train station at 9.10am and 1.20pm, arriving back in Blois at 1.10pm and 6pm respectively. Admission fees to the two chateaux are not included but tour participants are eligible for reduced tariffs. Tickets are sold on the bus, or in advance from the tourist office and the TLC's **Point Bus information office** (☎ 02 54 78 15 66; 2 place Victor Hugo) in Blois.

Sleeping
Reservations for Gîtes de France *chambres d'hôtes* (B&Bs) can be made at the **Maison du Loir-et-Cher** (☎ 02 54 58 81 64; www.gites-de -france-blois.com in French; 5 rue de la Voûte du Château; 🕐 9am-5pm Mon-Fri).

BUDGET
The **Auberge de Jeunesse Les Grouëts** (☎ 02 54 78 27 21; blois@fuaj.org; 18 rue de l'Hôtel Pasquier; dm €7, sheets €2.70, breakfast €3.20; 🕐 Mar–mid-Nov) is in Les Grouëts, 4.5km southwest of Blois train station. Be sure to call before arriving as it's often full. Beds are in two 24-bed, single-sex dorms and kitchen facilities are available. To get there, take local TUB bus No 4 (runs until 7pm) from place de la République (linked to the train station by TUB bus No 1).

Hôtel du Bellay (☎ 02 54 78 23 62; http://hotel dubellay.free.fr; 12 rue des Minimes; d with washbasin €23-25, d/tr/q with shower & toilet €35/45/55) It's easy to miss the tiny entrance to this ancient stone house, the original doorway obviously having been built in times when people were much smaller. Some of the rooms are tiny too, but all have charm, lovingly adorned with older-style, mumsy wallpaper.

THE LOIRE

Hôtel St-Jacques (☎ 02 54 78 04 15; www.hotel saintjacquesblois.com; 7 rue Ducoux; s/d with washbasin €25/27, with shower & toilet €35/37) A functional one-star hotel next to the station where friendly, helpful staff will show you to amply sized but uninspiring rooms. There are bicycles to rent for €12.50 per day.

Camping

Camping des Châteaux (☎ 02 54 78 82 05; camping with/without electricity €10/8; ☉ Jul-Sep) This two-star camping ground is in Vineuil, about 4km south of Blois. There is no bus service from town except in July and August (phone the camping ground or the tourist office for details).

MID-RANGE

Côté Loire (☎ 02 54 78 07 86; www.coteloire.com; 2 place de la Grève; r from €39, Apr-Oct €46) Full of wooden-beamed character, this small, higgledy-piggledy hotel has had a recent spruce-up with new beds, carpets and a colour scheme. A good choice, if you can get one of the seven rooms.

Hôtel Anne de Bretagne (☎ 02 54 78 05 38; fax 02 54 74 37 79; 31 av Jean Laigret; s/d with shower or bath & toilet from €33/48) A pretty, two-star hotel with bright, comfortable rooms overlooking a leafy crescent. The location is handy for the chateau and there's a small terrace for breakfast.

Hôtel Le Savoie (☎ 02 54 74 32 21; hotel.le.sa voie@wanadoo.fr; 6 rue Ducoux; s/d with shower & toilet from €37/41) A quiet, family-run hotel, conveniently located for the station. The two-star rooms are well equipped with extras like English TV channels.

Eating

In addition to those mentioned below, popular restaurants line rue Foulerie and several café-brasseries dot place de la Résistance.

Au Rendez-Vous des Pêcheurs (☎ 02 54 74 67 48; 27 rue du Foix; mains €21-28; ☉ Tue-Sat) Perhaps the finest seafood restaurant in town, this pretty cottage-style place specialises in fish from the River Loire and the Atlantic Ocean. The setting may be relaxed, but the food is of the highest quality.

La Scala (☎ 02 54 74 88 19; 8 rue des Minimes; pizza & pasta €6-10; ☉ noon-11pm) Prompt service and decent, good value Italian food are what makes this pizzeria popular and lively. If the *quatrro fromaggio* pizza isn't cheesy

enough for you, the huge Venice mural and life-size gondola will be!

Le Triboulet (☎ 02 54 74 11 23; Place du Château; menus €16.50-23.50; ☉ closed Sun & Mon) A busy restaurant right by the château offering traditional French dining. The tasty *menu du terroir* (€23.50) showcases seasonal Loire area specialities. After the architectural delights of its neighbour, the simple interior is nothing to get excited about but there's a pleasant garden and terrace nice on hotter days.

Le Castelet (☎ 02 54 74 66 09; 40 rue de Saint Lubin; menus €15.40-24.80; ☉ closed Wed & Sun) A convivial restaurant with the motto '*classic cooking in tune with the seasons*'. This translates to traditional French cuisine with a regional market-fresh twist. It has a vegetarian *menu* (€15.40) on offer. One of the two dining rooms is nonsmoking.

Le Rond de Serviette (☎ 02 54 74 48 04; 18 rue Beauvoir; menus €5.50 & €7.80, mains €5-7; ☉ closed Sun lunch) This cosy little pizzeria markets itself as Blois' cheapest and most humorous restaurant. The €5.50 *menu* is certainly unbeatable, but the Lonely Planet sign out the front has nothing to do with us.

SELF-CATERING

There is an **Intermarché supermarket** (av Gambetta; ☉ 9am-12.30pm & 3-7.15pm Mon-Sat). In the old city, a food market fills rue Anne de Bretagne on Tuesday, Thursday and Saturday until 1pm. There are a number of **charcuteries** in the area around Place Louis XII offering cold meats and prepared dishes. For tasty tripe, try the **Triperie des Halles** (☎ 02 54 78 14 63; 5 rue Anne de Bretagne).

Drinking

The best of the bars can be found in the old town, particularly in the small alleys and squares off rue Foulerie. Several pubs overlook place Av Maria.

Le St James (☎ 02 54 74 44 99; 50 rue Foulerie; ☉ 10pm-5am Thu-Sun) A lively bar with a choice of 162 cocktails and an atmospheric courtyard in which to install yourself while you try them all.

Loch Ness Pub (☎ 02 54 56 08 67; cnr rue des Juifs & rue Pierre de Bois) Another popular watering hole with a younger crowd and Guinness on tap. The two floors get busier and noisier as the night gets longer, especially on karaoke Thursdays.

L'Étoile Tex (☎ 02 54 78 46 93; 9 rue du Bourg Neuf)
For a student vibe, head to this busy bar/
Tex-Mex place at the top of the hill hosting rock concerts every Saturday night at
9.30pm (free entry). Modern, trendy and
sophisticated it's not, but the unpretentious
vibe is refreshing. Good fun.

Getting There & Away
For information on transport to/from Blésois
chateaux, see p399. Further details appear
under each chateau listing.

BUS
The **TLC bus network** (☎ 02 54 58 55 44) has a
very limited service, reduced further during the holidays and on Sunday. TLC buses
to destinations around Blois leave from in
front of the **Point Bus information office** (☎ 02
54 78 15 66; 2 place Victor Hugo; ✆ 1.30-6pm Mon, 8am-
noon & 1.30-6pm Tue-Fri, 1.30-4.30pm Sat) and the bus
station – a patch of car park with schedules
posted – in front of the train station. Verify
departure times before travelling.

Bus No 2 travels between Chambord and
Blois (€3.25, 45 minutes), from Monday to
Saturday. It departs from Blois station at
12.15pm, and leaves Chambord at 6.45pm
for the return trip. On Sunday buses leave
Blois at 1.45pm.

Your other option is the TLC's tourist bus
(p399), or hiring a minibus (see right).

CAR
On the D149, **ADA** (☎ 02 54 74 02 47; 108 av du
Maréchal Maunoury) is 3km northeast of the train
station. Take bus No 1 from the train station
or bus No 4 from place de la République to
the Cornillettes stop. **Avis** (☎ 02 54 74 48 15; 6 rue
Jean Moulin) also has an office in Blois.

TRAIN
The **train station** (av Dr Jean Laigret) is at the western end of the street.

There are frequent trains to/from Amboise (€5.50, 20 minutes, hourly), Tours
(€8.30, 40 minutes, 11 to 17 daily) and the
nearest TGV station, St-Pierre des Corps
(€8, 25 to 35 minutes, half-hourly).

There are four direct non-TGV trains
daily from Blois to Paris' Gare d'Austerlitz
(€20.80, 1½ to two hours), plus several
more if you change trains in Orléans. There
are also direct trains to Nantes (€27.10, two
hours, three daily).

Getting Around
BICYCLE
Hire two wheels from **Cycles Leblond** (☎ 02
54 74 30 13; 44 levée des Tuileries; bike hire per day/week
€12.50/80; ✆ 9am-9pm). Levée des Tuileries is
the continuation of promenade du Mail.

BUS
TUB (☎ 02 54 78 15 66) operates buses around
Blois. Buses run until about 8pm and a one-
way ticket costs €1; bus No 5 links the train
station with the chateau. Point Bus information office (see left) has information and
timetables.

TAXI
The **taxi booth** (Taxi Radio; ☎ 02 54 78 07 65; place
de la Gare) is in front of the train station. For
chateau trips, air-conditioned eight-person
minibuses can be hired. A return trip to
Chambord and Cheverny with an hour
at each costs €74; to Chaumont, Amboise
and Chenonceau €115. Prices go up 50%
on Sundays and holidays. You can choose
which chateau to visit; it's best to book well
in advance.

AROUND BLOIS
Château de Chambord
The pinprick village of Chambord is dominated by the spectacular **Château de Chambord**
(☎ 02 54 50 50 02; www.chambord.org; adult/18-25 yrs/
child €7/4.50/free; ✆ 9am-6.15pm Apr-Sep, 9am-5.15pm

Oct-Mar), which François I had built from 1519 as a base for hunting game in the Sologne forests. Ironically, the king chose the site for its easy two-day ride by horse and carriage from Paris, but he stayed here a total of only 42 days during his reign (1515–47).

The Renaissance chateau has a feudal ground plan. You'll see the king's emblems – the royal monogram (a letter 'F') and salamanders of a particularly fierce disposition – adorning many parts of the building. Though forced by liquidity problems to leave his two sons unransomed in Spain and to help himself to both the wealth of his churches and his subjects' silver, François I kept 1800 workers and artisans busy for 15 years.

The chateau's famed **double-helix staircase**, attributed by some to Leonardo da Vinci who lived in Amboise (34km southwest) at the invitation of François I from 1516 until his death three years later, consists of two spiral staircases that wind around a central axis but never meet. The ornamentation is early French Renaissance.

The double-helix staircase leads up to the Italianate **rooftop terrace**. Standing here, surrounded by towers, cupolas, domes, chimneys, mosaic slate roofs and lightning rods, is rather like standing on an overcrowded chessboard. It was on the terrace that the royal court assembled to watch military exercises, tournaments and the hounds and hunters returning from a day of stalking deer.

Ticket sales end 30 minutes before the chateau closes. As well as free mini-guides in English distributed on arrival, you can rent an audioguide (€4). Free, one-hour guided tours are available daily in French (and often in English) from around 10am.

DOMAINE NATIONAL DE CHAMBORD

The chateau is in the middle of the **Domaine National de Chambord**, a 54-sq-km hunting preserve reserved solely for the use of the president of France (a right that Jacques Chirac has chosen not to exercise). A 32km stone wall built between 1542 and 1645 surrounds the estate. **Walking and mountain bike trails** crisscross 12 sq km on the western side and there's **aires de vision** (observation towers) where you can spot animals.

The **estate** (☎ 02 54 50 50 00) runs fun and informative **4WD forest tours** (up to 8 people €125; ☑ Apr-Sep) and bike tours (see right).

ENTERTAINMENT

Night promenades (adult/child €12/7, combination show & chateau ticket €14/9; ☑ nightfall Mon-Sat Jun-Aug, Fri & Sat Sep) Chambord runs 'metamorphose' night promenades, where the chateau is lit up with a variety of images and scenes, with music playing in the background. Visitors are then free to wander around at their own leisure; the grounds stay open until 10pm or midnight.

GETTING THERE & AWAY

Chambord is 16km east of Blois and 20km northeast of Cheverny. To/from Blois there are TLC buses during the school year (p401) and coach tours to Chambord and Cheverny between mid-May and 31 August (p399).

In Chambord TLC public buses use the stop on the westbound D33.

GETTING AROUND

Bicycles, perfect for exploring Forêt de Chambord and around, can be rented in Chambord from the **Echapée Belle kiosk** (☎ 02 54 33 37 54; bike hire per hr/day/weekend €5.50/13/24) next to Pont St-Michel in the castle grounds. From July to September the estate authorities (p402) organise two-hour **cycling tours** (adult €10), not including bike hire.

Château de Cheverny

The elegant, perfectly symmetrical **Château de Cheverny** (☎ 02 54 79 96 29; www.chateau-cheverny .fr; adult/student/child €6.10/4.10/3; ☑ 9.15am-6.45pm Jul & Aug, 9.15am-6.15pm Apr-Jun & Sep, 9.30am-noon & 2.15-5.30pm Oct & Mar, 9.30am-noon & 2.15-5pm Nov-Feb), built between 1625 and 1634, is the region's most magnificently furnished chateau. Sitting like a sparkling white ship amid a sea of beautifully manicured gardens, the chateau is graced with a finely proportioned neoclassical façade. Inside visitors are treated to room after sumptuous room fitted out with the finest of period appointments. The most richly furnished rooms are the **Chambre du Roi** (in which no king ever slept because no king ever stayed at Cheverny) and the **Grand Salon**. In the 1st-floor dining room, 36 panels illustrate the story of *Don Quixote*.

The grounds shelter the 18th-century **Orangerie**, where Leonardo da Vinci's *Mona Lisa* was hidden during WWII.

The château was also the inspiration for the mythical Marlinspike Hall, home

THE LOIRE

of French fictional favourite *Tintin*. It features in many of Tintin's adventures and in honour of this, a permanent Tintin exhibition, **Les Secrets de Moulinsart** (The Secrets of Marlinspike Hall; adult/student/child combined chateau & exhibition ticket €10.50/8.40/6.20), has been created in the grounds; opening hours are the same as Château de Cheverney. The colourful, interactive display, aimed squarely at kids and Tintin fans, re-creates scenes from some of the character's best-known adventures.

GETTING THERE & AWAY

Cheverny is 16km southeast of Blois and 20km southwest of Chambord. The TLC bus No 4 from Blois to Villefranche-sur-Cher stops at Cheverny (€2.40, 25 to 35 minutes). Buses leave Blois at 12.25pm Monday to Friday. Returning to Blois, the last bus leaves Cheverny at 6.52pm. Departure times can vary and are different on Sundays and holidays; check with TLC or the Blois tourist office (p397). Between mid-May and 31 August, TLC operates coach tours (p399) from Blois.

Château de Chaumont

It's a short, healthy climb up to **Château de Chaumont** (☎ 02 54 51 26 26; adult/18-25 yrs/child €5.50/3.50/free; ⏰ 9.30am–6pm mid-Mar–mid-Oct, 10am-4.30pm mid-Oct–mid-Mar), which is set on a bluff overlooking the Loire. The entrance,

across a wooden drawbridge between two wide towers, opens onto an inner courtyard from where there are stunning views. The building itself, resembling a feudal castle, is modestly sized for a chateau. It's easy to imagine enjoying a family meal in the homely dining room, or popping into the tiny chapel for prayer and solitude. Opposite the main entrance are the luxurious **stables**, built in 1877.

In 1560 Catherine de Médicis (France's powerful queen mother) took revenge on Diane de Poitiers, the mistress of her late husband, Henry II, by forcing her to accept Chaumont in exchange for her much more favoured residence, Château de Chenonceau (p410).

GETTING THERE & AWAY

Chaumont-sur-Loire is 17km southwest of Blois and 20km northeast of Amboise, on the Loire's southern bank. The path leading to the park and chateau starts at the intersection of rue du Village Neuf and rue Maréchal Leclerc (D751).

By public transport, the only way to get to Chaumont-sur-Loire is via local train on the Orléans–Tours line. Get off the train at Onzain (10 minutes), from where it is about a 20-minute, 2km walk across the river to the chateau. Single rail fares to Onzain from Blois/Tours/Orléans cost €2.80/6.60/10.30.

LA SOUPE DES CHIENS

As was the custom among the nobility of centuries past, the Viscount de Sigalas – whose family has owned Cheverny since it was built – hunts with hounds. His 100 dogs – most a cross between English fox terriers and French *poitevins* – are quite beautiful, no matter what you think of the practice of using them to kill stags.

Each dog has a name, posing a fantastic memory feat for the two dog trainers who do, indeed, know every dog and its name. The *soupe des chiens* (feeding of the dogs) is an awe-inspiring demonstration of the exact control they exercise over the pack. A massive 90kg of animal parts is brought by wheelbarrow into the cement enclosure each day and methodically arranged in a 2m-wide mountain while the hounds whimper and sniff from inside the kennel. The tiny kennel door is then opened and 100 dogs bundle and squeeze out as fast as they can – but not until the dog master cracks the whip does the pack dare so much as sniff at their daily 1kg ration. The stinking offal is then ripped to shreds and gobbled up in minutes. Double portions are doled out after the twice-weekly winter hunt.

The *soupe des chiens* takes place in the *chenils* (kennels) at 5pm daily in summer. In January, February and between mid-September and December, the dogs are fed at 3pm on Monday, Wednesday, Thursday and Friday only. The pack hunts every Tuesday and Saturday between September and March, departing from the majestic front entrance of the chateau if hunting in the Forêt de Cheverny.

By bicycle, the sleepy back roads on the southern bank of the river are a tranquil option. The Chaumont-sur-Loire **tourist office** (☎ 02 54 20 91 73; 24 rue du Maréchal Leclerc; ☼ 9.30am-7.30pm mid-Jun–Sep, 9.30am-12.30pm & 1.30-6pm Apr–mid-Jun, Sep & Oct, 9.30am-12.30pm & 1.30-5.30pm Nov-Mar) rents bicycles for €10 per day.

Château de Beauregard

Built in the early 16th century to serve as a hunting lodge for François I, the most famous feature of **Château de Beauregard** (☎ 02 54 70 36 74; adult/student & child €6.50/4.50; ☼ 9.30am-7.30pm Jul & Aug, 9.30am-12.30pm & 2-6.30pm Apr-Jun & Sep, 9.30am-12.30pm & 2-5pm Thu-Tue Oct-Dec & mid-Feb–Mar) is its **Galerie des Portraits**, the walls of which are plastered with 327 portraits of notable faces dating from the 14th to 17th century.

GETTING THERE & AWAY

Beauregard is 6km south of Blois. It can also be reached via a pleasant 15km cycle ride through the forest from Chambord. There is road access to the chateau from the Blois–Cheverny D765 and the D956 (turn left at the village of Cellettes).

The **TLC** (☎ 02 54 58 55 44) bus from Blois to St-Aignan stops at Cellettes (€1.50), 1km southwest of the chateau, Monday to Friday at 7.50am and on Wednesday, Friday and Saturday; the first bus from Blois to Cellettes leaves at 12.25pm.

Unfortunately, there's no afternoon bus back except for the Châteauroux–Blois line operated by **Transports Boutet** (☎ 02 54 34 43 95), which passes through Cellettes around 6.15pm on Monday to Saturday, and – except during August – at roughly 6pm on a Sunday.

TOURAINE

With the exception of the medieval fortresses at Chinon and Loches, the castles of Touraine – Azay-le-Rideau, Chenonceau, Langeais and Villandry – date to the Renaissance. They were designed purely to pamper the soul and pander to the physical pleasures of the queen, king and his multitude of royal mistresses.

Tours is the historical capital of Touraine and an inexpensive base from which to explore the region.

TOURS

pop 270,000

Lively Tours has the cosmopolitan, bourgeois air of a miniature Paris, with wide 18th-century avenues, formal public gardens, café-lined boulevards and a thriving university – home to 30,000 students. The French spoken in Tours is said to be the purest in France. Twice in its history Tours briefly hosted the French government: in 1870 during the Franco-Prussian War and again in 1940, with the onset of WWII. Since then, it has become better known for its crisp white Vouvray and Montlouis wines.

Orientation

Thanks to the spirit of the 18th century, Tours is efficiently laid out. Its focal point is place Jean Jaurès, where the city's major thoroughfares – rue Nationale, blvd Heurteloup, av de Grammont and blvd Béranger – meet. The train station is 300m east of place Jean Jaurès. The old city is centred on place Plumereau, which is about 400m west of rue Nationale. The northern boundary of the city is demarcated by the River Loire, which flows roughly parallel to the River Cher, 3km south.

Information

BOOKSHOPS

Géothèque (☎ 02 47 05 23 56; 6 rue Michelet) Travel bookshop selling maps and guides.
La Boîte à Livres de l'Étranger (☎ 02 47 05 67 29; 2 rue du Commerce) English-language fiction and nonfiction.

EMERGENCY

Police Station (☎ 02 47 33 80 69; 70-72 rue Marceau; ☼ 24hr)

INTERNET ACCESS

Alli@nce Micro (☎ 02 47 05 49 50; calliance-micro@wanadoo.fr; 7ter rue de la Monnaie; per hr €3; ☼ 9.30am-7pm Mon-Sat)
CyberGate (☎ 02 47 05 95 94; 11 rue du Président Merville; per hr €3; ☼ 11am-midnight Tue-Sat, 2-10pm Sun & Mon)

LAUNDRY

Laundrette (22 rue Bernard Palissy; ☼ 7am-8.30pm)

MONEY

The post office has an exchange service. There are commercial banks around place Jean Jaurès.

Credit Agricole (av de Grammont)
Exchange Kiosk (☺ 8.45am-6pm Mon-Sat; closed Jan)
In the train station. Offers good rates.

POST
Post Office (1 blvd Béranger) Has a Cyberposte.

TOURIST INFORMATION
Tourist Office (☎ 02 47 70 37 37; www.ligeris.com;
78-82 rue Bernard Palissy; ☺ 8.30am-7pm Mon-Sat,
10am-12.30pm & 2.30-5pm Sun mid-Apr–mid-Oct;
9am-12.30pm & 1.30-6pm Mon-Sat, 10am-1pm Sun
mid-Oct–mid-Apr)

Sights

MUSÉE DES BEAUX-ARTS
Occupying three floors of an impressive
17th- to 18th-century archbishop's palace,
the **Musée des Beaux-Arts** (☎ 02 47 05 68 73;
18 place François Sicard; adult/student/child €4/2/free;
☺ 9am-12.45pm & 2-6pm Wed-Mon) has an excellent collection of paintings, furniture and
objets d'art from the 14th to the 20th century. Contemporary works include *le Jardin
de la France* by local artist Max Ernst, an
abstract marriage of a Loire Valley landscape and the female form.

CATHÉDRALE ST-GATIEN
Various parts of Tours' Gothic-style **Cathédrale St-Gatien** (☺ 9am-7pm, closed during services)
represent the 13th century (the choir), 14th
century (the transept), 14th and 15th centuries (the nave) and 15th and 16th centuries
(the west façade). The domed tops of the
two 70m-high **towers** (closed to the public)
date from the Renaissance. There's a fine
view of the **flying buttresses** from behind the
cathedral. Spectacular exterior aside, the interior is renowned for its marvellous 13th-
to 15th-century **stained-glass windows**.

You can also visit the Renaissance **Cloître
de la Psallette** (☎ 02 47 47 05 19, adult/child €2.50/
free; ☺ 9.30am-12.30pm & 2-6pm Mon-Sat, 2-6pm Sun
Apr-Sep, 2-5pm daily Oct-Mar).

MUSÉUM D'HISTOIRE NATURELLE
Housed in an 18th-century bailiff's tribunal,
the modern **Muséum d'Histoire Naturelle** (☎ 02
47 64 13 31; 3 rue du Président Merville; adult/student & child
€4/2; ☺ 10am-noon & 2-6pm Tue-Fri, 2-7pm Sat & Sun)
has a colourful collection of permanent and
temporary exhibits. Kids can get up close to
all kinds of (stuffed) creatures; hedgehogs,
badgers, otters and plenty of birds and fish.

There are also life-size lions, crocodiles and
bears to scare any pint-size visitors. Long-
term temporary exhibits include dinosaur-
and volcano- themed displays. There are no
explanations in English, but that doesn't detract from this largely visual experience.

JARDIN BOTANIQUE
About 1km west of the city centre, the **Jardin
Botanique** (blvd Tonnelle; admission free; ☺ 7.45am-
sunset) is a great place for a stroll or a picnic.
Created between 1831 and 1843 on reclaimed
land on the banks of St Anne stream, the
five-hectare landscaped park has a tropical
greenhouse, medicinal herb garden and petting zoo. There are also emus and kangaroos
bouncing around. To get there, it's a short
walk or take Bus No 4 (€1.05, every 10 minutes) along blvd Béranger.

MUSÉE DE L'HÔTEL GOÜIN
This archaeological museum, **Musée de l'Hôtel
Goüin** (☎ 02 47 66 22 32; 25 rue du Commerce; adult/
child €3.50/2.60; ☺ 9.30am-12.30pm & 1.15-6.30pm Apr-
Sep, 9.30am-12.30pm & 2-5.30pm Oct-Mar) is housed in
Hôtel Goüin, a Renaissance residence built
around 1510 for a wealthy merchant. Its
Italian-style façade is worth seeing, even if
the eclectic assemblage of prehistoric, Gallo-
Roman, medieval, Renaissance and 18th-
century artefacts doesn't interest you.

Tours
For details on chateau tours, see p400.

Sleeping
There are lots of good value hotels and
other accommodation options to be found
in Tours.

BUDGET
Auberge de Jeunesse du Vieux Tours (☎ 02 47 37
81 58; tours@fuaj.org; 5 rue Bretonneau; dm HI members/
nonmembers €12.70/15.60; reception ☺ 8am-12.30pm,
6-10pm; 🖳) A new and well-equipped hostel
near the old town. It's a large place with a
friendly feel, and has a decent-size kitchen
for cooking and a lounge for hanging out
and playing foosball.

Hôtel Val de Loire (☎ 02 47 05 37 86; hotel.val
.de.loire@club-Internet.fr; 33 blvd Heurteloup; r €29-40) A
delightful two-star hotel in a century-old
bourgeois home near the station. The cheaper
rooms are quite simple, but the larger rooms
are individually furnished with the occasional

THE LOIRE

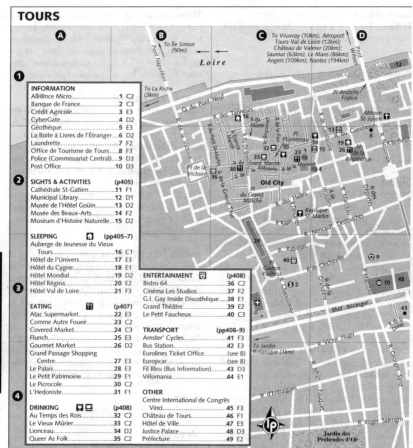

TOURS

INFORMATION	
Alli@nce Micro	1 C2
Banque de France	2 C3
Crédit Agricole	3 E3
CyberGate	4 D2
Géothèque	5 E3
La Boîte à Livres de l'Étranger	6 D2
Laundrette	7 F2
Office de Tourisme de Tours	8 F3
Police (Commissariat Central)	9 D3
Post Office	10 D3

SIGHTS & ACTIVITIES	(p405)
Cathédrale St-Gatien	11 F1
Municipal Library	12 D1
Musée de l'Hôtel Goüin	13 D2
Musée des Beaux-Arts	14 F2
Muséum d'Histoire Naturelle	15 D2

SLEEPING 🏠	(pp405–7)
Auberge de Jeunesse du Vieux Tours	16 C1
Hôtel de l'Univers	17 E3
Hôtel du Cygne	18 E1
Hôtel Mondial	19 D2
Hôtel Régina	20 E2
Hôtel Val de Loire	21 F3

EATING 🍴	(p407)
Atac Supermarket	22 E3
Comme Autre Fouée	23 C2
Covered Market	24 C3
Flunch	25 E3
Gourmet Market	26 D2
Grand Passage Shopping Centre	27 E3
Le Palais	28 E3
Le Petit Patrimoine	29 E1
Le Picrocole	30 C2
L'Hedoniste	31 F1

DRINKING 🍷 🍺	(p408)
Au Temps des Rois	32 C2
Le Vieux Mûrier	33 C2
Lionceau	34 D2
Queer As Folk	35 C2

ENTERTAINMENT 🎭	(p408)
Bistro 64	36 C2
Cinéma Les Studios	37 F2
G.I. Gay Inside Discothèque	38 E1
Grand Théâtre	39 E2
Le Petit Faucheux	40 C3

TRANSPORT	(pp408–9)
Amster' Cycles	41 F3
Bus Station	42 E3
Eurolines Ticket Office	(see 8)
Europcar	(see 8)
Fil Bleu (Bus Information)	43 D3
Vélomania	44 E1

OTHER	
Centre International de Congrès Vinci	45 F3
Château de Tours	46 F1
Hôtel de Ville	47 E3
Justice Palace	48 D3
Préfecture	49 E2

ornate fireplace, antique wardrobe or writing desk. The 1st-floor rooms have high ceilings and full-length windows.

Hôtel Régina (☎ 02 47 05 25 36; fax 02 47 66 08 72; 2 rue Pimbert; s/d with washbasin €21/24, s/d/q with shower from €25/29/38) The best of the lower-priced options, this popular and good value hotel has a range of rooms depending on your budget. It's clean, if a little smoky-smelling and the matronly manageress doesn't stand for any mischief.

Camping
Camping Municipal des Rives du Cher (☎ 02 47 27 27 60; fax 02 47 25 82 89; 61 rue de Rochpinard, St-Avertin; camping €11; ⏰ Apr–mid-Oct) This three-star camping ground is 5km south of Tours.

To get there, take bus No 5 from place Jean Jaurès to the St-Avertin bus terminal, then follow the signs.

MID-RANGE
Hôtel du Cygne (☎ 02 47 66 66 41; hotelcygne .tours@wanadoo.fr; 6 rue du Cygne; r €40-60; 🅿) A pretty hotel on a quiet side street in the old town; wooden-shuttered windows, high ceilings, blooming flowerboxes, chandeliers and period detail. The spacious 1st-floor rooms tick all the boxes, but it loses a couple of marks for the dreary reception/breakfast room and its smaller upper-floor rooms.

Hôtel Mondial (☎ 02 47 05 62 68; www.hotel mondialtours.com; 3 place de la Résistance; s/d from €34/40, breakfast €6) A modern two-star option with

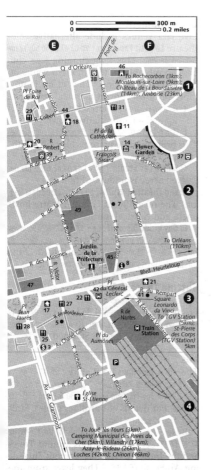

immaculate, carpeted rooms overlooking place de la Résistance. There's a sunny room on the second floor to enjoy the buffet breakfast, which could take all morning with the spread they provide here.

TOP END

Hôtel de l'Univers (☎ 02 47 05 37 12; www.hotel -univers-loirevalley.com; 5 blvd Heurteloup; standard €185, superior €255; ✗ ⊠ ⊑) Tours' swishest town-centre hotel is unapologetically old-fashioned, from the wood-panelled whisky-and-cigar bar to the Chesterfield-scattered reception. The grand old building dates from 1846; upstairs the refined rooms offer spaciousness and a good level of four-star comfort.

Eating

In the old city, place Plumereau and nearby rue du Grand Marché and rue de la Rôtisserie are loaded with restaurants, cafés, creperies and *boulangeries* – many have lovely street terraces. Another cluster of places serving tasty food grace rue Colbert.

L'Hedoniste (☎ 02 47 05 20 40; 16 rue Lavoisier; lunch/dinner menus from €11/16) In this convivial, cave-like place, a regional French menu is enhanced by an exhaustive range of wines and the viticultural knowledge of the proprietor. He can advise on the perfect glass of wine to have with every dish, selecting from row upon row of bottles decorating the stone walls.

Le Picrocole (☎ 02 47 20 68 13; 28-30 rue du Grand Marché; menus €11 & €17) Occupying a series of cosy rooms in an old house, this popular place serves regional and French specialities. It's a good place to try *rillons*; another popular choice is their renowned chocolate *fondant* cake.

Le Palais (☎ 02 47 61 48 54; 15 place Jean Jaurès; lunch/dinner menus €9.90/15.90) Trendy pizzeria/brasserie serving the usual pizzas and salads plus more unusual mains (€8 to €9) including rabbit, and marinated salmon. Cool music, relaxed surroundings and attentive service all add to the vibe and there's a terrace outside for people-watching.

Le Petit Patrimoine (☎ 02 47 66 05 81; 58 rue Colbert; lunch menu €9, dinner menus €12-26) This relaxed eatery is always busy and is excellent value for such tasty, well-presented French food. The restaurant, simple but atmospheric with stone walls and a wood-beamed ceiling, may be small, but the portions are not.

Flunch (☎ 02 47 64 56 70; 14 place Jean Jaurès; menu €6, mains €4-10; ☺ 11am-10pm) A canteen chain with cheap prices and décor.

SELF-CATERING

Sandwich stalls sell filled baguettes and pastries in the **Grand Passage shopping centre** (18 rue de Bordeaux).

Tours has some 30 markets around town on various days of the week; your best bet is the large, permanent **covered market** (place Gaston Pailhou), or the open-air **gourmet market** (place de la Résistance; ☺ 4-10pm 1st & 3rd Fri of month).

There is also an **Atac supermarket** (5 place du Général Leclerc; ☺ 8.30am-8pm Mon-Sat & 9.30am-12.30pm Sun).

THE LOIRE

AUTHOR'S CHOICE

Comme Autre Fouée (☎ 02 47 05 94 78; 11 rue de la Monnaie; lunch/dinner menus from €10/19.50) *Fouée* (or *fouaces*), is an age-old regional speciality, a small disc of dough thrown into a woodfired oven for 45 seconds and served immediately, piping hot. The pitta-like bread is used to scoop up *fouéefuls* of *rillettes, haricots blanc* or farmhouse goat's cheese for a hearty, filling, country-style meal. At Comme Autre Fouée, a pun on Comme Autre Fois (just like the old days), you can install yourself in this old stone building for a good few hours while they constantly replenish your basket with oven-fresh *fouée*.

Drinking

You don't need to look very hard for bars and cafés in Tours – the old town is full of them. A good starting point is place Plumereau, which fills to bursting in the summer with tourists and locals sipping wine or espresso.

There are also a few lively student bars situated along rue de la Longue Echelle and the southern strip of adjoining rue du Dr Bretonneau.

Le Vieux Mûrier (☎ 02 47 61 04 71; 11 place Plumereau; 🕑 11am-midnight) This stylish place is favourite for people-watching in the bustling heart of the old-town, with tables spilling out into place Plumereau.

Au Temps des Rois (☎ 02 47 05 04 51; 3 place Plumereau; 🕑 11am-2am) Also with a great location in place Plumereau, this café attracts a younger, livelier student-type crowd. It is quite a popular place to hang out and look cool.

Le Palais (🕑 11am-2am) The ground floor bar at Le Palais is a trendy place for a drink and there are tables outside so patrons can enjoy a beer in the sunshine. Things liven up after about 11pm with regular DJs and karaoke evenings.

Queer As Folk (☎ 02 47 75 04 27; 108 rue de Commerce; 🕑 6pm-2am) Unashamedly camp bar, with blue neon lights, zebra-print soft furnishings and plenty of trash techno, euro-pop and '80s disco.

Lionceau (55 rue de Commerce; 🕑 7pm-2am) Ole-in-the-wall gay bar favoured by a slightly older crowd than Queer As Folk.

Entertainment

Live jazz venues include alternative café-theatre **Le Petit Faucheux** (☎ 02 47 64 50 50; 12 rue Leonard de Vinci) This long-running jazz club has recently moved to a modern venue on rue Leonard de Vinci. The set-up is now more sit-down concert than laid-back café, but it continues to attract an exceptional line-up and an appreciative crowd.

Bistro 64 (☎ 02 47 38 47 40; 64 rue du Grand Marché) This brilliant place presents blues in a 16th-century setting.

Cinémas Les Studio (☎ 02 47 64 42 61; 2 rue des Ursulines) Screens undubbed films.

Grand Théâtre (☎ 02 47 60 20 20; 34 rue de la Scellerie) The magnificent Grand Théâtre hosts opera and classical music.

GI Gay Inside Discothêque (☎ 02 47 66 29 96; www .gidiscotheque.com in French; 13 rue Lavoisier; admission Fri/Sat €5/8; 🕑 11pm-5am) A gay nightclub of the flashing-lights-and-nude-torsos variety.

Getting There & Away
AIR

From **Aéroport Tours-Val de Loire** (☎ 02 47 49 37 00; www.tours-aeroport.com) Ryanair operates direct flights to London Stansted.

BUS

There's a **Eurolines ticket office** (☎ 02 47 66 45 56; 76 rue Bernard Palissy; 🕑 2-6pm Mon, 9am-noon & 1.30-6.30pm Tue-Fri, 9am-noon & 1.30-5.30pm Sat) in Tours. For details of Eurolines routes, fares and deals, see p917.

Buses operated by **Touraine Fil Vert** (☎ 02 47 47 17 18) serve destinations around Tours and the Indre-et-Loire department, including Amboise (€2.10). They leave from the **bus station** (☎ 02 47 05 30 49; place du Général Leclerc), which has an **information desk** (☎ 02 47 05 30 49; 🕑 7am-7pm Mon-Sat), only drivers sell tickets.

In July and August you can make an all-day circuit by public bus from Tours to Chenonceaux and Amboise by taking the 10am bus to Chenonceaux (€2.10, 1¼ hours), then the 12.40pm bus from Chenonceaux to Amboise (€1.05, 25 minutes). Return buses from Amboise to Tours (€2.10) leave at 4.25pm, 5.25pm and 6.20pm. Double-check times and schedules before departing.

CAR

Car-rental offices:

Avis (☎ 02 47 20 53 27) At the train station.

Europcar (☎ 02 47 64 47 76; 76 blvd Bernard Palissy)

TRAIN

The **train station** (place du Général Leclerc) has an **information office** (8.30am-6.30pm Mon-Sat, closed public holidays). Tours is linked to St-Pierre des Corps (Tours' TGV train station) by shuttle train.

Local trains run between Tours and Orléans at least hourly (€15, 1¼ hours). Stops on this route include St-Pierre des Corps (€1.20, five minutes), Montlouis-sur-Loire (€2.20, 12 minutes), Amboise (€4.40, 20 minutes) and Blois (€8.30, 35 minutes). There are trains southbound to Loches (€7.20, one hour, two daily) and westbound to Saumur (€9.20, 40 minutes, 13 daily).

To get from Paris to Tours by rail take a TGV from Gare Montparnasse (€35 to €45, 1¼ hours, 10 to 15 daily). This trip often requires a change of trains at St-Pierre des Corps; or a direct non-TGV from Gare d'Austerlitz (€25.80, two to three hours, five to eight daily). There are TGV and non-TGV services to Bordeaux (€37, 2½ hours by TGV), Poitiers (€16, one hour) and Nantes (€22.50, two hours). Change trains in Poitiers to get to/from La Rochelle (€29.80, two to three hours).

Getting Around
TO/FROM THE AIRPORT

A **shuttle bus** (one way €5) leaves Tours bus station at 3.45pm daily, stopping at the train station (3.55pm) before continuing to the airport in time for the daily Ryanair departure at 5.20pm. Arriving passengers can catch it back into town at 5.30pm.

BICYCLE

From May to September friendly **Amster' Cycles** (02 47 61 22 23; 5 rue du Rempart; 1-/2-/7-day bike hire €14/21/55), rents out road and mountain bikes. Staff provide cyclists with a puncture-repair kit and map.

Vélomania (02 47 05 10 11; 109 rue Colbert) is another bike-rental outlet charging the same.

BUS

The network serving Tours and its suburbs is run by **Fil Bleu** (02 47 66 70 70), which has an **information office** (5bis rue de la Dolve). Most lines stop around the periphery of place Jean Jaurès. Tickets, which are valid for one hour after being stamped, cost €1.05.

AROUND TOURS

Vineyards carpet **Vouvray** (population 2900) and **Montlouis-sur-Loire** (population 8000), 10km east of Tours on the northern and southern bank respectively of the Loire. For centuries wine growers have stored their wines in *caves* (wine cellars), hewn out of the white tufaceous cliffs that line this stretch. Neither village is overly attractive, but each offers ample opportunity to taste and buy Appellation d'Origine Contrôlée (AOC) Vouvray and Montlouis wines.

The **Vouvray tourist office** (02 47 52 68 73; cnr route du Vignoble on the N152 & av Brulé, the D46; 9am-6pm Mon-Sat, 9am-1pm Sun Apr-Sep, 9am-1pm Tue-Sat rest of year), has information on wine-tasting options and rents bicycles. Opposite, the **Maison du Vouvray** (02 47 52 72 51; 24 av Brulé; 9am-12.30pm & 1.45-7pm) is a good place to kick off a *dégustation* (tasting) spree.

In Montlouis-sur-Loire the **tourist office** (02 47 45 00 16; www.ville-montlouis-loire.fr in French; place de la Mairie; 9am-12.30pm & 2-6.30pm Mon-Sat May-Sep, plus 10am-1pm Sun Jul & Aug, 10am-noon & 2-5pm Mon-Sat Oct-Apr) and the **Maison de la Loire** (02 47 50 97 52; 60 quai Albert Baillet; 2-6pm) can provide information.

A unique spot to stay and eat in the surrounds is **Les Hautes Roches** (02 47 52 88 88; www.leshautesroches.com; 86 quai de la Loire; d €125-255; menus €45-61) in the northern suburb of Rochecorbon. Dug by monks as a haven during the Wars of Religion, the caves now form part of a four-star hotel/restaurant. (For more troglomania see p423.)

GETTING THERE & AWAY

Fil Bleu's bus No 61 links Tours' place Jean Jaurès with Vouvray (€1.05, 20 minutes). Montlouis-sur-Loire is served by bus line C2 (€2.20, 45 minutes) operated by Fil Vert.

TOURS AREA CHATEAUX

A number of the most interesting Loire chateaux make an easy day trip from Tours. Those accessible by train or SNCF bus from Tours include Chenonceau, Villandry, Azay-le-Rideau, Langeais, Amboise (p412), Chaumont (p403), Chinon (p416) and Saumur (p423). Transport details are listed at the end of each chateau listing.

The tourist office in Tours has details of *son et lumières*, medieval re-enactments, and other spectacles performed at the chateaux during summer.

Tours

Touring chateaux by public transport can be horribly slow and expensive, so even veteran backpackers should consider taking an organised bus tour. The interesting English-language tours are surprisingly relaxed and informal. Most allow you between 45 minutes and one hour at each chateau. Tour prices do not include entrance fees, but if you're part of a group you may be entitled to discounts. If you can get five to seven people together, you can design your own minibus itinerary.

There are three companies offering minibus tours from Tours: **Acco-Dispo** (☎ 06 82 00 64 51; www.accodispo-tours.com), **Quart de Tours** (☎ 06 85 72 16 22; www.quartdetours.com) and **St-Eloi Excursions** (☎ 02 47 37 08 04; www.saint-eloi.com). Typical prices are from €18 to €31 for a half-day trip to various chateaux sharing a minibus for up to eight people. Reservations can be made at the Tours tourist office or via its website.

Services Touristiques de Touraine (STT; ☎ 02 47 05 46 09; www.stt-millet.fr) runs full-sized coaches for individuals rather than groups from April to mid-October. Many tours include wine tasting in Vouvray or Montlouis-sur-Loire. Afternoon/day tours taking in three chateaux cost €34, which includes admission fees.

For something a bit different and to get away from peak-season crowds, it's possible to take to the air for a birds-eye view of the chateaux. The Tours tourist office has details of **aerial excursions** by helicopter, plane, microlight and hot-air balloon (p401).

See p399 for information about tours departing from Blois.

Château de Chenonceau

With its stylised moat, turrets, drawbridge and towers from the 16th-century, **Château de Chenonceau** (☎ 08 20 20 90 90; www.chenonceau .com; adult/student & child €8/6.50; 🕑 9am-7pm mid-Mar–mid-Sep, 9am-4.30pm to 6.30pm rest of year) is everything a fairy-tale castle should be, although its interior – crammed with period furniture, tourists, paintings, tourists, tapestries and tourists – is only of moderate interest. If you are visiting during the low season, check on opening hours because they vary.

Chenonceau's vast park, with landscaped gardens and forests, covering 70 hectares either side of the River Cher, affords some stunning vistas of the chateau exterior. Diane de Poitiers, mistress of King Henri II, one of the series of remarkable women who created Chenonceau, planted the garden to the left (east) as you approach the chateau. After Henri's death in 1559 she was forced to give up Chenonceau by Henri II's widow, the vengeful Catherine de Médicis, who applied her own energies to the chateau and laid out the garden to the right (west) as you approach the castle.

In the 18th century, Madame Dupin, the chateau's owner at the time, brought Jean-Jacques Rousseau to Chenonceau as a tutor for her son. During the French Revolution, the affection with which the peasantry regarded Madame Dupin saved the chateau from the violent fate of its neighbours.

GETTING THERE & AWAY

Château de Chenonceau, in the town of Chenonceaux (the village has an 'x' at the end), is 34km east of Tours, 10km southeast of Amboise and 40km southwest of Blois.

Chenonceaux SNCF train station is in front of the chateau. Between Tours and Chenonceaux there are four to six trains daily (€5.20, 30 minutes).

Château de Villandry

Château de Villandry (☎ 02 47 50 02 09; www.cha teauvillandry.com; admission chateau & gardens adult/child €7.50/5, gardens only €5/3.50; 🕑 chateau 9.30am-5pm or 6.30pm mid-Feb–mid-Nov, gardens 9am-dusk year-round) has some of the most spectacular formal gardens in France. **Jardin d'Ornement** (Ornamental Garden) comprises intricate, geometrically pruned hedges and flowerbeds loaded with romantic symbolism so abstract that you can tour the entire garden without comprehending its true meaning (even with the aid of the free English-language brochure available at the entrance). Between the chateau and the village church, the **potager** (kitchen garden) is a cross between the vegetable plots in which medieval monks grew their food and the formal gardens so beloved of 16th-century France.

All told, Villandry's gardens occupy five hectares and include in excess of 1150 lime trees, hundreds of grape trellises and 52km of landscaped plant rows. Villandry is at its most colourful from May to mid-June and August to October, but is worth a visit year-round.

The chateau itself was completed in 1536, making it the last of the major Renaissance chateaux to be built in this area. The interior has undergone extensive refurbishment and although not yet finished, it's worth exploring. Furnished in comfortable 18th-century style, the rooms and hallways are adorned with dark and moody Spanish paintings and large, faded tapestries. An unusual 13th-century **Moorish ceiling** is thought to have been bought here from Toledo, Spain.

The corner **tower** is all that remains of the original medieval structure on which the current chateau was built. From the tower, the intricate gardens can be seen in their entirety, as can the parallel Rivers Loire and Cher.

GETTING THERE & AWAY
Villandry is 17km southwest of Tours, 31km northeast of Chinon and 11km northeast of Azay-le-Rideau. By road the shortest route from Tours is the D7, but cyclists will find less traffic on the D88 (which runs along the southern bank of the Loire) and the D288 (which links the D88 with Savonnières). If heading southwest from Villandry towards Langeais, the best bike route is the D16; it has no verges and only light traffic. Villandry is included on most organised tour circuits (p405).

By public transport the only way of travelling between Tours and Villandry is the largely inconvenient train to Savonnières (€2.60, 13 minutes), about 4km east of Villandry. During the week the first train from Tours is at 12.28pm; heading back, there is a direct train to Tours at 1.42pm (13 minutes) and another at 5.40pm via Langeais (1¼ hours). On Saturday there is an additional direct train from Savonnières to Tours at 5.37pm. On Sunday the only train to Tours is at 1.42pm.

Château d'Azay-le-Rideau
Château d'Azay-le-Rideau (☎ 02 47 45 42 04; adult/18-25 yrs/child €6,10/4 10/free; ✆ 9.30am-6pm Apr-Jun & Sep-Oct, 9.30am-7pm Jul & Aug, 9.30am-12.30pm & 2-5.30pm Nov-Mar), built on an island in the River Indre and surrounded by a quiet pool and park, is harmonious and elegant. It is adorned with stylised fortifications and turrets intended both as decoration and to indicate the rank of the owners. Inside, seven rooms are open to the public, but, beyond a few 16th-century Flemish tapestries, they

are disappointing. Forty-five minute **tours** (adult €4) in several languages take place at regular intervals.

The bloodiest incident in the chateau's history occurred in 1418. During a visit to Azay, then a fortified castle, the crown prince (later King Charles VII) was insulted by the Burgundian guard. Enraged, he had the town burned and executed some 350 soldiers and officers. The present chateau was begun exactly a century later by Giles Berthelot, one of François I's less-than-selfless financiers. When the prospect of being audited and hanged drew near, Berthelot fled abroad. The finishing touches were added in the 19th century.

GETTING THERE & AWAY
Château d'Azay-le-Rideau, 26km southwest of Tours, features on most tour itineraries from Tours (p405). The D84 and D17, either side of the Indre, are a delight to cycle along.

Azay-le-Rideau is on the SNCF Tours–Chinon line (four or five daily Monday to Saturday and one on Sunday). From Tours the 30-minute trip (50 minutes by SNCF bus) costs €4.40; the station is 2.5km from the chateau. The last train/bus to Tours leaves Azay at about 6.35pm (8pm on Sunday).

Château de Langeais
Built in the late 1460s to cut off the most likely invasion route from Brittany, **Château de Langeais** (☎ 02 47 96 72 60; adult/senior/student & child €6.50/5.50/4; ✆ 9.30am-8pm mid-July–mid-Aug, 9.30am-6.30pm Apr–mid-Jul & mid-Aug–mid-Oct, 10am-5.30pm mid-Oct-Mar), in flowery Langeais presents two faces to the world. From the town it appears a 15th-century fortified castle – nearly windowless with machicolated ramparts (ie walls from which missiles and boiling liquids could be dropped on attackers) rising forbiddingly from the drawbridge. The sections facing the courtyard, however, are outfitted with the large windows, dormers and decorative stonework characteristic of later chateaux designed for more refined living. The **ruined dungeon** in its grounds dates from around 944 and is the oldest such structure in France.

Langeais has a truly interesting interior. The unmodernised configuration of the rooms and the **period furnishings** give you a pretty good idea of what the place looked like during the 15th and 16th centuries. The walls are decorated with fine but somewhat faded Flemish and Aubusson **tapestries**, representing the most extensive and significant tapestry collection in France other than at the Louvre.

In one room, wax figures re-enact the marriage of King Charles VIII and Duchess Anne of Brittany, held here on 6 December 1491. The event brought about the final union of France and Brittany.

GETTING THERE & AWAY

Langeais is 14km west of Villandry and about 24km southwest of Tours. Its **train station** (☎ 02 47 96 82 19), 400m from Château de Langeais, is on the Tours–Savonnières–Saumur line. The last train to Tours (€4.30, 15 to 25 minutes, three to six daily) is at 6.37pm (5.30pm on Saturday, 7.15pm or 8.20pm on Sunday and holidays). Tickets from Langeais cost €2.20 to Savonnières (4km from Villandry) and €6.20 to Saumur (25 minutes).

AMBOISE

pop 11,000

The picturesque town of Amboise, nestling under its fortified chateau on the southern bank of the Loire, reached its peak during the decades around 1500, when the luxury-loving King Charles VIII enlarged it and King François I held raucous parties here. These days the town makes the most of its association with Leonardo da Vinci, who lived his last years here under the patronage of François I.

Amboise is protected from the river by a dyke, and its flower-covered heights are a great place for a riverside promenade. Tours, 23km downstream, and Blois, 34km upstream, are easy day trips from here. Amboise makes a good base for visiting the chateaux east of Tours (p410).

Orientation

Amboise train station, across the river from the town centre, is about 800m north of Château d'Amboise. Le Clos Lucé, Leonardo da Vinci's former home, is 500m southeast of the chateau along rue Victor Hugo. The island in the middle of the Loire is called Île d'Or.

Place Michel Debré – effectively an extension of rue Victor Hugo and sometimes called place du Château – stretches westwards from the northern end of rue de la Tour to pedestrian rue Nationale, Amboise's main commercial and touristy street.

Information

Several banks dot rue Nationale.

Playconnect (119 rue Nationale; ☎ 02 47 57 18 04; ⏰ 1-10pm Mon, 10am-10pm Tue-Thu, 10am-midnight Fri & Sat) In addition to Internet and games, Playconnect will transfer your digital photos onto CD.

Post Office (20 Quai du Général de Gaulle)

Tourist Office (☎ 02 47 57 09 28; www.amboise-va ldeloire.com; ⏰ 10am-1pm & 2-6pm Mon-Sat, 10am-1pm & 3-6pm Sun Apr-Jun & Sep, 9am-8pm Mon-Sat & 10am-6pm Sun Jul & Aug, 10am-1pm & 2-6pm Mon-Sat & 10am-1pm Sun Oct-Mar) In a pavilion opposite 7 quai du Général de Gaulle, stocks walking and cycling maps, and supplies a free English-language brochure for walking around Amboise.

Sights & Activities

CHÂTEAU D'AMBOISE

The fortified rocky outcrop topped by **Château d'Amboise** (☎ 02 47 57 00 98; place Michel Debré; adult/student/7-14 yrs €7.50/6.50/4.20; ⏰ 9am-7.30pm Jul & Aug, 9am-6.30pm Apr-Jun, Sep & Oct, 9am-noon & 2-5pm Nov-May). Charles VIII (r 1483–98), who was born and brought up here, enlarged the chateau in 1492 after a visit to Italy, where he was impressed by that country's artistic creativity and luxurious lifestyle. He died six years later after hitting his head on a low lintel while on his way to a *jeu de paume* (the precursor to tennis) game. His widow, the 22-year-old Anne de Bretagne, was obliged by contract to marry the new king of France, Louis XII.

King François I (r 1515–47) also grew up here as did his sister, the reform-minded French Renaissance author Margaret of Angoulême (also known as Margaret of Navarre). François I lived in the chateau during the first few years of his reign, a lively period marked by balls, masquerade parties, tournaments and festivities of all sorts.

Today just a few of the 15th- and 16th-century structures survive. These include the Flamboyant Gothic **Chapelle St-Hubert** and the **Salle des États** (Estates Hall), where a group of Protestant conspirators were tried before being hanged from the balcony in 1560. From 1848 to 1852, Abdelkader, the military and political leader of the

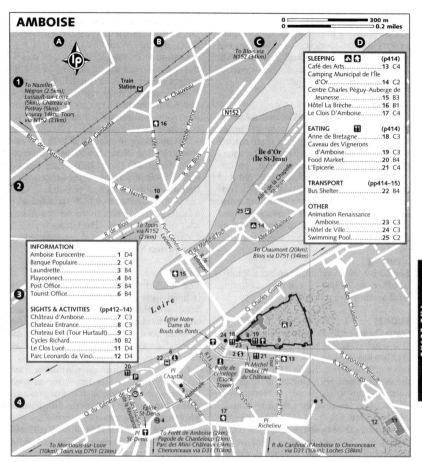

AMBOISE

0 ___ 300 m
0 ___ 0.2 miles

INFORMATION
Amboise Eurocentre...................1 D4
Banque Populaire.......................2 C4
Laundrette.................................3 B4
Playconnect...............................4 B4
Post Office.................................5 B4
Tourist Office.............................6 B4

SIGHTS & ACTIVITIES (pp412–14)
Château d'Amboise.....................7 C3
Chateau Entrance......................8 C3
Chateau Exit (Tour Hurtault).....9 C3
Cycles Richard..........................10 B2
Le Clos Lucé............................11 D4
Parc Leonardo da Vinci.............12 D4

SLEEPING (p414)
Café des Arts............................13 C4
Camping Municipal de l'Île
d'Or.....................................14 C2
Centre Charles Péguy-Auberge de
Jeunesse.............................15 B3
Hôtel La Brèche........................16 B1
Le Clois D'Amboise...................17 C4

EATING (p414)
Anne de Bretagne.....................18 C3
Caveau des Vignerons
d'Amboise............................19 C3
Food Market.............................20 B4
L'Epicerie.................................21 C4

TRANSPORT (pp414–15)
Bus Shelter...............................22 B4

OTHER
Animation Renaissance
Amboise..............................23 C3
Hôtel de Ville...........................24 C3
Swimming Pool........................25 C2

To Blois via N152 (34km)
To Nazelles-Négron (2.5km); Lussault-sur-Loire (5km); Château du Pintray (5km); Vouray 14km; Tours via N152 (23km)
Train Station
Île d'Or (Île St-Jean)
To Tours via N152 (23km)
To Chaumont (20km); Blois via D751 (34km)
Loire
Église Notre Dame du Bouts des Ponts
Pl Chaptal
Porte de l'Horloge (Clock Tower)
Pl Michel Debré (Pl du Château)
Église St-Denis
Pl St-Denis
To Montlouis-sur-Loire (10km); Tours via D751 (23km)
To Forêt de Amboise (2km); Pagode de Chanteloup (2km); Parc des Mini-Châteaux (3km); Chenonceaux via D31 (10km)
Pl Richelieu
R du Cardinal d'Amboise to Chenonceaux via D31 (10km); Loches (38km)

THE LOIRE

Algerian resistance to French colonialism, was imprisoned here. The chapel is said to be the final resting place of Leonardo da Vinci, a modest monument to such a great man.

The **ramparts** afford a panoramic view of the town and the Loire Valley.

The entrance to the chateau is located at the end of rampe du Château. On Wednesday and Saturday evenings between mid-June and the end of August, the chateau stages an evening show – a re-enactment of the life and times of François I – in its courtyard. Tickets can be bought in advance from **Animation Renaissance Amboise** (☎ 02 47 57 14 47; www.renaissance-amboise.com; adult grandstand/stalls €16/13, child €16/7).

LE CLOS LUCÉ

Leonardo da Vinci came to Amboise in 1516 at the invitation of François I. Until his death three years later at the age of 67, Leonardo lived and worked in **Le Clos Lucé** (☎ 02 47 57 62 88; 2 rue du Clos Lucé; adult/student/6-15 yrs €9.50/7.50/5; ⏰ 9am-8pm Jul & Aug, 9am-7pm Apr, Jun, Sep & Oct, 9am-6pm Nov, Dec, Feb & Mar, 9am-5pm Jan), a brick manor house, which contains restored rooms and scale models of Leonardo's inventions, including a proto-automobile, armoured tank, parachute and hydraulic turbine. It's a fascinating place offering a unique insight into the mind of the genius.

The house is set in the lovely **Parc Leonardo da Vinci** (⏰ Apr-Nov; adult/student/6-15 yrs combined ticket for Le Clos Lucé & Parc Leonardo da Vinci €11/9/6.50);

it has the same opening hours as Le Clos Lucé. Following the circuit around the park reveals life-size models (some working) of some of the prototypes and a presentation hall with a short video and a 6m model of his famous flying machine.

WINE TASTING

The innovative **Caveau des Vignerons d'Amboise** (☎ /fax 02 47 57 23 69; 🕑 10am-7pm Mar-Nov), inside the chateau walls opposite 42 place Michel Debré, is a *cave* (wine cellar) run by enterprising local wine growers. Here you can taste – for free – six white, three red and two rosé wines, as well as two types of Touraine Crémant de Loire (a sparkling drink likened to champagne). To ensure the most untickled of tastebuds are titillated, the wine growers offer different local foods to taste.

Sleeping

For B&B accommodation contact the tourist office, which has a list of homes offering B&B around Amboise.

BUDGET

Centre Charles Péguy-Auberge de Jeunesse (☎ 02 47 30 60 90; fax 02 47 30 60 91; Île d'Or; dm €8.60; reception 🕑 2-8pm Mon-Fri, 6-8pm Sat & Sun) An efficiently run youth hostel on the Île d'Or in the middle of the Loire, with singles, doubles and dorms for up to six people. If reception is closed, try screeching into the intercom.

Café des Arts (☎ /fax 02 47 57 25 04; 32 rue Victor Hugo; s/d/q with washbasin €15/29/52, This funky little place, a centuries-old town house turned hip place to stay, is situated above a happening café. It's the best budget deal in town by a margin.

Camping

Camping Municipal de l'Île d'Or (☎ 02 47 57 23 37; Île d'Or; camping €9.25; 🕑 Apr-Sep) There is minigolf, a mountain bike circuit and on-site tennis courts at this camping ground. Admission to the neighbouring swimming pool costs €2/1.20 for adults/children.

MID-RANGE

Hôtel La Brèche (☎ 02 47 57 00 79; www.labreche -amboise.com; 26 rue Jules Ferry; d with shower & toilet €50-64; 🕑 Feb-Nov) Across the river from the town centre this hotel, with red sun-shades and colourful flower boxes, is comfortable and full of charm. The friendly owner is

very knowledgeable about the local area. On warm days guests breakfast outside on a tree-shaded terrace.

Château de Pintray (☎ 02 47 23 22 84; www.cha teau-de-pintray.com; d with breakfast €95) Five kilometres west in Lussault-sur-Loire, is a small 16th-century chateau with five traditionally furnished rooms. You can taste and buy AOC Montlouis wines produced on the estate here.

Le Clois D'Amboise (☎ 02 47 30 10 20; www.leclos amboise.com; 27 rue Rabelais; r high season €75-150, low season €65-129; P ⌘) This place is a gem; a grand old 17th-century bishops' residence with a tranquil walled garden. The building itself has been renovated to a high standard with a fantastic selection of individually and lavishly furnished rooms. The terrace is perfect for a pre-chateau-tour breakfast, the outdoor pool perfect for an after-tour splash.

Eating

The southern side of place Michel Debré is lined with light, lunchtime snack spots. Sandwich shops, *boulangeries*, creperies, and fast-food outlets line rue Nationale. An open-air food market spills across quai du Général de Gaulle on Friday and Sunday morning.

Caveau des Vignerons d'Amboise (see left) serves lunchtime platters – *assiettes* filled with regional produce, such as foie gras and goat's cheese (€6 to €7) – perfect for foodies who are seeking a taste of Touraine.

L'epicerie (☎ 02 47 57 08 94; 46 place Michel Debré; menus €10.50-35) A quaint and friendly little restaurant, this place serves regional French cuisine. Fish is a speciality; you'll often find *sandre* from the River Loire on the *menu*.

Anne de Bretagne (☎ 02 47 57 05 46; 1 rampe du Château; mains €7-10) Big salads, pasta and *galettes*, as well as a vegetarian *menu* and a host of tempting, alcohol-soaked crepes. It's also a good spot to grab coffee and an outside table, and watch the world go by.

Getting There & Around

BICYCLE

Hire mountain bikes at **Cycles Richard** (☎ 02 47 57 01 79; 2 rue de Nazelles; bike hire per day €11; 🕑 9am-noon & 2.30-7pm Mon-Sat).

BUS

Buses to/from Amboise stop at the bus shelter across the car park from the tourist office.

CAT's line No 10 links the town with Tours' bus terminal (one way €2.10, 30 to 50 minutes, eight daily Monday to Saturday, six daily during summer holidays). There are likewise round trips, from Monday to Saturday, between Amboise and Château de Chenonceau). Buses depart from outside the central post office at 10.52am (one way €1.05, 25 minutes) and return from Chenonceaux at 5pm.

TRAIN
The **train station** (☎ 02 47 23 18 23; blvd Gambetta), across the river from the centre of town, is served by trains from Paris' Gare d'Austerlitz (€24.20, 2¼ to three hours, 11 daily).

About three-quarters of the trains on the Blois–Tours line (11 to 17 daily) stop at Amboise. Fares are €5.50 to Blois (20 minutes) and €4.40 to Tours (20 minutes).

PAGODE DE CHANTELOUP
The 44m-high, Chinese-style **Pagode de Chanteloup** (☎ 02 47 57 20 97; adult/student/7-15 yrs €6/5/4; ❧ 10am-6.30pm May, Jun & Sep, 9.30am-7.30pm Jul & Aug, 10am-noon & 2-5.30pm Mar, Apr & Oct, 2-5pm Mon-Fri, 10am-noon & 2-5pm Sat & Sun Feb & Nov) is one of the 18th century's more pleasing follies. Built between 1775 and 1778, it combines contemporary French architectural fashions with elements from China, a subject of great fascination at the time. From the top of the pagoda, visitors are rewarded with an impressive view of the Loire Valley.

This eccentric pagoda is a delightful picnic venue. **Hampers** (€10) bursting with regional treats are sold at the May-to-October entrance. You can hire a **boat** (per hour €6) to row your sweetheart around the lake and there is a fun collection of old-fashioned games to play for free.

The pagoda is about 2km south of Amboise. Take rue Bretonneau and follow the plentiful signs to 'La Pagode'. Public buses between Amboise (see p414) and Tours (see p408) stop at the 'Pagode' stop.

LOCHES
pop 6550
Medieval Loches, with its cobbled streets and imposing keep perched on a rocky spur, could be a film set. The 11th-century keep was built by Foulques Nerra (Falcon the Black; r 987–1040), while its feudal chateau witnessed Joan of Arc persuade Charles VII

to march north in June 1429 to be crowned. The royal court he consequently established here was notorious for its wild banquets, thrown primarily to woo the scandalously wicked yet stunningly beautiful Agnès Sorel, a royal mistress who died aged 28. Her tomb lies in Loches. The town's golden age ended in 1461 with the ascension of Louis XI to the throne. The new king turned the keep into a state prison.

Orientation & Information
Loches is about 40km southeast of Tours. The citadel sits south of the old town, on the western bank of the Indre. The train and bus stations are across Pont Pierre Senard on the eastern bank of the river.
Post Office (rue Descartes) Has a Cyberposte.
Tourist Office (☎ 02 47 91 82 82; www.lochesentouraine.com; place de la Marne; ❧ 9.30am-7pm Mon-Sat mid-Jun–mid-Sep, 9.30am-12.30pm & 2-6.30pm Mon-Sat mid-Sep–mid-Jun) The tourist office is wedged between Pont Pierre Senard and rue de la République, the main commercial street.

Sights
CITADEL
The 11th-century **Porte Royale** (Royal Gate), up the hill on rue de la Porte, is flanked by two 13th-century towers and remains the only opening in the sturdy 2km wall that encircles the citadel.

Inside, the **Donjon** (Castle Keep; adult/7-18 yrs €5/3.50; ❧ 9am-7pm Apr-Sep, 9am-12.30pm & 2-5pm Oct-Mar) at the southernmost point of the rocky promontory is the oldest structure within the citadel (built 1010–35). The notorious **Round Tower** and **Martelet** were built under Louis XI as prisons. Inmates were tortured in a cage weighing 2.5 tons, a replica of which is on display.

The northern end of the citadel contains the **Logis Royal** (Royal Residence; adult/7-18 yrs €3.80/2; ❧ 9am-7pm Apr-Sep, 9am-12.30pm & 2-5pm Oct-Mar). The 15th-century funerary urn of Agnès Sorel is in the northern wing of the residence, built for Charles VIII and Anne de Bretagne in the 16th century. A **combined ticket** (adult/7-14 yrs €7/4.50) to Donjon and Royal Lodge is available.

In summer **son et lumières** (☎ 02 47 59 01 76) are held in the citadel at 10pm Friday and Saturday. The terrace offers a fine panorama of Loches village tumbling down the hillside towards the Indre Valley.

THE LOIRE

Sleeping & Eating
The tourist office has plenty of information on camping grounds and *chambre d'hôtes* in the area.

Hôtel de France (☎ 02 47 59 00 32; hotelde france@aol.com; 6 rue Piçois; r €42-64; P) In the centre of the medieval district, this imposing two-star hotel has an impressive entranceway and a pleasant courtyard **restaurant** (menus €15-43). The rooms, by comparison, are cheaply decked-out, although perfectly comfortable.

La Crêpicoise (☎ 02 47 59 25 59; 3 rue Piçois; mains €8-15; ⊗ lunch Fri-Wed, dinner Fri-Tue) Decent, simple food such as crepes, salads and grills in unfussy surroundings.

CAK'T (☎ 02 47 59 39 35; 6 Grande Rue; set lunch €8, cakes from €1.50; ⊗ lunch noon-7pm daily, dinner Jul & Aug) Quirky little tearoom with art hanging on the walls and tempting cakes displayed on the trolley. The lunch *menus* are good value.

A **food market** fills place du Marché and rue St-Antoine on Wednesday morning.

Getting There & Around
Loches is on the Tours–Châteauroux train line. The train and bus stations are across Pont Pierre Senard on place des Cordeliers. There are trains to and from Tours (€7.20, 45 minutes, two daily) and SNCF buses (€10.70, 50 minutes, three or four daily).

Peugeot Cycles-JM Jourdain (☎ 02 47 59 02 15; 7 rue des Moulins; road/mountain bike hire per day €8/12, per week €40/65) rents out road and mountain bikes.

CHINON
pop 8627
Chinon's massive fortress – 400m long – looms above the town's medieval quarter. The uneven, cobblestone streets are lined with ancient houses, some built of decaying tufa stone, others half-timbered and brick. The contrast between the triangular, black slate roofs and the whitish-tan tufa gives the town its distinctive appearance.

Villandry, Azay-le-Rideau and Langeais all can easily be visited from Chinon if you are using your own transport. The Forêt de Chinon (Chinon Forest), which is a wooded area ideal for walking and cycling, begins a couple of kilometres northeast of town and stretches along the D751 all the way to Azay-le-Rideau.

Chinon's vineyards stretch north, south and east of the town, on both banks of the Vienne.

Orientation & Information
Rue Haute St-Maurice, the main street in the medieval quarter, becomes rue Voltaire as you move east. The train station is 1km east of the town's commercial hub, place du Général de Gaulle (also called place de l'Hôtel de Ville).

Internet access is available at Hôtel le Menestrel (see p417) for €0.40 per minute and there are several banks near the post office.

Post Office (quai Jeanne d'Arc)

Tourist Office (☎ 02 47 93 17 85; www.chinon.com; place Hofheïm; ⊗ 10am-7pm May-Sep, 10am-noon & 2-6pm Mon-Sat Oct-Apr)

Sights
CHÂTEAU DE CHINON
Perched atop a rocky spur high above the River Vienne, this huge, mostly ruined medieval fortress, **Château de Chinon** (☎ 02 47 93 13 45; adult/student or child €6/4.50; ⊗ 9am-7pm Apr-Sep, 9.30am-5pm Oct-Mar), consists of three parts separated by waterless moats: the 12th-century **Fort St-Georges** (of which little remains), which protected the chateau's vulnerable eastern flank; the **Château du Milieu** (the Middle Castle); and, at the western tip, the **Château du Coudray**. From the ramparts there are great views in all directions.

After crossing the moat (once spanned by a drawbridge) and entering Château du Milieu, you pass under the **Tour de l'Horloge** (Clock Tower). The four rooms inside are dedicated to the career of Joan of Arc, who picked out Charles VII from among a crowd of courtiers in 1429 in the castle's **Salle du Trône** (Throne Room). Other parts of the almost undecorated **Grand Logis Royal** (Royal Apartments), built during the 12th, 14th and 15th centuries, are in slightly better condition.

To get to the chateau, walk up the hill to rue du Puits des Bancs and turn left. By car, route de Tours (the continuation of the D751 from Tours) will take you to the rear of the chateau.

MUSÉE ANIMÉ DU VIN
The kitsch **Musée Animé du Vin** (Animated Wine Museum; ☎ 02 47 93 25 63; 12 rue Voltaire; adult/child €3.80/3.20; ⊗ 10.30am-12.30pm & 2-7pm Apr-Sep) has

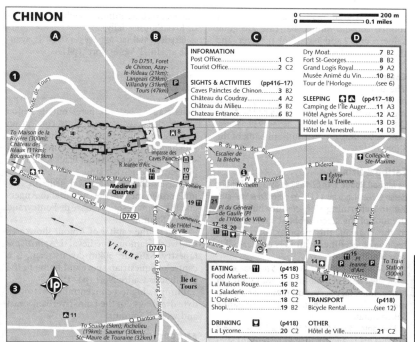

CHINON

INFORMATION	
Post Office.........................1 C3	
Tourist Office.....................2 C2	

SIGHTS & ACTIVITIES	(pp416–17)
Caves Painctes de Chinon.........3 B2	
Château du Coudray...............4 A2	
Château du Milieu................5 B2	
Chateau Entrance.................6 B2	

Dry Moat..........................7 B2
Fort St-Georges...................8 B2
Grand Logis Royal.................9 A2
Musée Animé du Vin...............10 B2
Tour de l'Horloge............(see 6)

SLEEPING	(pp417–18)
Camping de l'Île Auger..........11 A3	
Hôtel Agnès Sorel...............12 A2	
Hôtel de la Treille.............13 D3	
Hôtel le Menestrel..............14 D3	

To D751, Foret de Chinon, Azay-le-Rideau (21km); Langeais (29km); Villandry (31km); Tours (47km)

To Maison de la Rivière (300m); Château des Réaux (11km); Bourgueil (19km)

Route de Tours

R. Voltaire

Q. Pasteur

Q. Charles VII

Medieval Quarter

(D749)

Vienne

(D749)

Île de Tours

R. du Faubourg St-Jacques

To Seuilly (5km); Richelieu (19km); Saumur (30km); Ste-Maure de Touraine (32km)

Q. Danton

Impasse des Caves Painctes

R. Jeanne d'Arc

(R Haute St-Maurice)

R. Voltaire

Escalier de la Brèche

R. du Puits des Bancs

Pl R J-J Rousseau Hofheim

R. Carnot

R. du Commerce

R. de l'Hôtel de Ville

Pl du Général de Gaulle (Pl de l'Hôtel de Ville)

R. Rabelais

Q. Jeanne d'Arc

R. Diderot

Église St-Étienne

R. Marceau

R. Hoche

R. Buffon

Collégiale Ste-Maxime

Pl Jeanne d'Arc

R. de 11 Novembre

To Train Station (300m)

EATING	(p418)
Food Market......................15 D3	
La Maison Rouge.................16 B2	
La Saladerie....................17 C2	
L'Océanic.......................18 C2	
Shopi...........................19 B2	

DRINKING	(p418)
La Lycorne......................20 C2	

TRANSPORT	(p418)
Bicycle Rental..............(see 12)	

OTHER	
Hôtel de Ville..................21 C2	

0 ———— 200 m
0 ———— 0.1 miles

THE LOIRE

life-size mechanical figures that demonstrate how wine and wine barrels are made, accompanied by a piped commentary in English. The admission price includes a sample of local wine and *confiture de vin* (sweet wine jam or jelly).

CAVES PAINCTES DE CHINON

Underneath the ruins of the chateau are the **Caves Painctes de Chinon** (☎ 02 47 93 30 44; impasse des Caves Painctes; admission €3; ♥ guided tours 11am, 3pm, 4.30pm & 6pm, Tue-Sun Jul–mid-Sep), former quarries converted into wine cellars during the 15th century and hardly touched since. The extensive network of caves is filled with row upon row of bottles; guided tours conclude with a free glass of the local produce. This is also a good source of information on regional wines, local growers and possible *dégustations*.

Festivals & Events

On the third weekend in August, musicians, dancers and locals dress up in period costume for the **Marché à l'Ancienne**, a re-creation of a 19th-century farmers' market,

where wines and traditional food products from the Loire region are sold.

Sleeping

The tourist office has a list of *chambres d'hôtes* in the area including Château des Réaux (p395) 11km north of town.

Hôtel Agnès Sorel (☎ 02 47 93 04 37; www.agnes -sorel.com; 4 quai Pasteur; d €46-56, with private terrace €72) A lovely riverside spot run by a friendly family; choose from older-style rooms, immaculately furnished with sturdy wooden beds in the original building, or comfortable, modern rooms with terrace in the annexe. Access for disabled guests.

Hôtel de la Treille (☎ 02 47 93 07 71; fax 02 47 93 94 10; 4 place Jeanne d'Arc; d with washbasin €28, with shower & toilet €36-40; P) Simple, but rustic with a 14th-century stone staircase leading to five cosy rooms. The bustling downstairs **restaurant** (menus €11-18) is a great value place to eat.

Hôtel le Menestrel (☎ 02 47 93 07 20; fax 02 47 93 48 75; place Jeanne d'Arc; d with shower from €28; 🖳) Wooden beams, fussy bedspreads and flowery wallpaper all contribute to the feel of a stay at grandma's house. The homely rooms, above a simple bar-café are good value; rooms 2 and 3 overlook the river (and the main road).

Camping
The tourist office can reserve a site at one of five camping grounds nearby, including the well-equipped **Camping de l'Île Auger** (☎ 02 47 93 08 35; quai Danton; camping €9.50; ☺ mid-Mar–mid-Oct; ☒), on the southern bank of the Vienne.

Eating & Drinking
La Maison Rouge (☎ 02 47 98 43 65; 38 rue Voltaire; menus €17-23, lunch from €12; ☺ closed Fri & Nov–mid-Mar) In a charming 13th-century building at the foot of the steep cobbled street leading to the chateau, this popular place serves regional specialities with jugs of local Chinon wine.

La Saladerie (☎ 02 47 93 99 93; 5 rue Rabelais; salads & mains €8-10) A hole-in-the-wall gourmet bistro, this place serves up main-size salads, meat dishes and *chaud' patats* (gigantic baked potatoes).

L'Océanic (☎ 02 47 93 44 55; 13 rue Rabelais; menus €21-50) This is a fairly formal restaurant specialising in fresh and tasty seafood. There's a small terrace outside; reserve a table if you're planning to visit for a summertime lunch.

Rue Rabelais is the most likely spot for an evening tipple or two.

La Lycorne (☎ 02 47 93 94 94; 15 rue Rabelais; ☺ noon-midnight, closed Mon) A large, lively pub-brasserie with occasional live music.

SELF-CATERING
A handy supermarket is **Shopi** (22 place du Général de Gaulle). At the northern end of place du Général de Gaulle, there's an **outdoor market** (☺ 8am-6pm Thu, to 1pm Sat & Sun). Place Jeanne d'Arc plays host to a **food market** on Thursday morning.

Getting There & Around
Chinon is 47km southwest of Tours, 21km southwest of Azay-le-Rideau and 80km north of Poitiers.

The **train station** (☎ 02 47 93 11 04), 300m east of place Jeanne d'Arc, is linked with Tours (€7.40, 50 minutes, 11 trains or SNCF buses on weekdays, five on Saturday and two on Sunday and holidays) and Azay-le-Rideau

(€3.90, 20 to 30 minutes, eight to 12 trains or SNCF buses daily).

Bicycle rental (per half-/full-day €8/14) is available at Hôtel Agnès Sorel (p417).

ANJOU

Renaissance chateaux peter out in Anjou where chalky-white tufa cliffs conceal an astonishing underworld of wine cellars, mushroom farms and monumental art sculptures. Above ground, black slate roofs pepper the vine-rich land.

Outstanding architectural gems in Anjou's crown include the cathedral in Angers and the Romanesque Abbaye de Fontevraud east of Saumur.

Angers, the capital of Anjou, showcases the world-famous medieval *L'Apocalypse* tapestry. Saumur, 50km downstream, is a centre of equestrian sport and home to the prestigious Cadre Noir (p424).

Europe's highest concentration of troglodyte dwellings dot the Loire riverbanks east and west of Saumur.

ANGERS
pop 141,500
Angers, 70km west of Chinon, straddles the River Maine. The city was settled by the Andes Celtic tribe and became an administrative capital under the Romans. In the 9th century it served as the seat of the powerful counts of Anjou who controlled a vast territory embracing most of southwestern France by the 12th century.

Much of the city was bombed during WWII; the city housed an exiled Polish government in 1940 and the regional headquarters of the Gestapo in 1942.

Angers is pleasantly walkable. Its richest treasure, displayed inside its mighty chateau, is a medieval tapestry depicting scenes from the Apocalypse.

The city hosted the royal court until the 12th century when Henri II shifted it east to Chinon.

Orientation
Angers' historic quarter lies on the eastern bank of the Maine, bordered by blvd Ayrault and its continuation, blvd Carnot, to the north; blvd du Maréchal Foch to the east; and blvd du Roi René to the south.

ANGERS

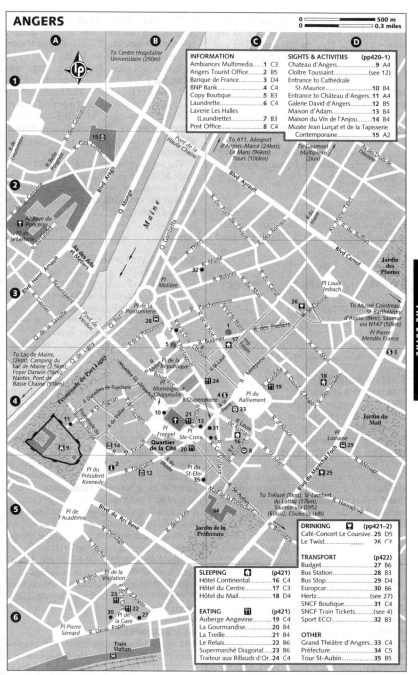

0 — 500 m
0 — 0.3 miles

INFORMATION

Ambiances Multimedia......**1** C3
Angers Tourist Office........**2** B5
Banque de France.............**3** D4
BNP Bank........................**4** C4
Copy Boutique.................**5** B3
Laundrette......................**6** C4
Laverie Les Halles
(Laundrette)...............**7** B3
Post Office......................**8** C4

SIGHTS & ACTIVITIES (pp420–1)

Chateau d'Angers.............**9** A4
Cloître Toussaint..............(see 12)
Entrance to Cathédrale
St-Maurice..................**10** B4
Entrance to Château d'Angers..**11** A4
Galerie David d'Angers......**12** B5
Maison d'Adam................**13** B4
Maison du Vin de l'Anjou....**14** B4
Musée Jean Lurçat et de la Tapisserie
Contemporaine...............**15** A2

SLEEPING (p421)

Hôtel Continental............**16** C4
Hôtel du Centre...............**17** C3
Hôtel du Mail.................**18** D4

EATING (p421)

Auberge Angevine............**19** C4
La Gourmandise..............**20** B4
La Treille.......................**21** B4
Le Relais.......................**22** B6
Supermarché Diagonal......**23** B4
Traiteur aux Rillauds d'Or..**24** C4

DRINKING (pp421–2)

Café-Concert Le Coursive..**25** D5
Le Twist.........................**26** C3

TRANSPORT (p422)

Budget..........................**27** B6
Bus Station.....................**28** B3
Bus Stop........................**29** D4
Europcar.........................**30** B6
Hertz.............................(see 27)
SNCF Boutique................**31** C4
SNCF Train Tickets...........(see 4)
Sport ECO......................**32** B3

OTHER

Grand Théâtre d'Angers....**33** C4
Préfecture......................**34** C5
Tour St-Aubin.................**35** B5

THE LOIRE

The train station is 800m south of place du Président Kennedy, the square at the western end of blvd du Roi René. The bus station overlooks the river on place de la Poissonnerie.

Information

INTERNET ACCESS
Ambiances Multimedia (☎ 02 41 18 26 24; 10 rue Bodinier; per hr €3; ⏲ 9am-9pm Mon-Fri, 9am-midnight Sat, 3-7pm Sun)
Copy Boutique (☎ 02 41 88 96 26; 48 rue Plantagenêt; per hr €4; ⏲ 9am-7.30pm Mon-Fri, 9am-12.30pm & 2-7pm Sat)

MONEY
Both the post office and the tourist office have exchange services. There are commercial banks on blvd Maréchal Foch and place Molière.

POST
Post Office (1 rue Franklin Roosevelt) Has a Cyberposte.

TOURIST INFORMATION
Tourist Office (☎ 02 41 23 50 00; www.angers-tour isme.com; 7 place du Président Kennedy; ⏲ 9am-7pm Mon-Sat, 10am-1pm & 2-6pm Sun May-Sep; 9am-1pm Mon, 9am-6pm Tue-Sat, 10am-1pm Sun Oct-Apr)

Sights & Activities

CHÂTEAU D'ANGERS
This 13th-century fortress **Château d'Angers** (☎ 02 41 86 48 77; 2 promenade du Bout du Monde; adult/student & child €6.10/4.10; ⏲ 9.30am-6.30pm May-Sep, 10am-5.30pm Oct-Apr) is one of the finest examples of feudal architecture in the Loire Valley. Its 17 dark-grey, black schist towers stand 30m tall, on a rocky promontory on the eastern bank of the Maine. The **royal residence**, **chapel** and **landscaped gardens** inside the walls were built in the 14th and 15th centuries to host the court of the Anjou dukes.

Most people visit Château d'Angers to see the magnificent **L'Apocalypse** (the Apocalypse), a series of 68 medieval scenes that form the oldest tapestry of its size in the world. It was commissioned by Louis I in 1375 and illustrates the last book of the Bible according to St John. The 103m tapestry has been showcased in a purpose-built bunker inside the fortress since 1996. Free brochures are available in English, and there are also guided tours. Last admission is 6.15pm.

CATHÉDRALE ST-MAURICE
Angers' magnificent 12th- to 13th-century **Cathédrale St-Maurice** (☎ 02 41 87 58 45; place Freppel; admission free; ⏲ 8.30am-7pm Apr-Nov, 8.30am-5.30pm Dec-Mar), in the centre of the historic **quartier de la Cité**, has a striking Norman porch (c 1170) and nave (c 1150–1250). The latter features three convex vaults forming a perfect square, outstanding examples of mid-12th-century Angevin vaulting. The collection of **stained-glass windows** date from the 12th to the 16th centuries.

The square in front of the cathedral, Place Monseigneur Chappoulie, is linked to the River Maine by a **monumental staircase**. Behind the cathedral on place Ste-Croix is **Maison d'Adam** (c 1500), a half-timbered town house with an ornate façade studded with wooden sculptures.

GALERIE DAVID D'ANGERS
Monumental sculptures by Angers-born sculptor David d'Angers (1788–1856) are displayed in **Galerie David d'Angers** (☎ 02 41 87 21 03; 33bis rue Toussaint; adult/child €2/1; ⏲ 9.30am-6.30pm mid-Jun–mid-Sep, 10am-noon & 2-6pm Tue-Sun mid-Sep–mid-Jun). The gallery is housed in an 11th-century abbey (Cloître Toussaint), transformed into a masterpiece of contemporary architecture by French architect Pierre Prunet in 1980–94. Natural light floods in through a glass roof supported by steel beams and the resultant play of sun and shadow on the sculptures is stunning.

MUSÉE JEAN LURÇAT ET DE LA TAPISSERIE CONTEMPORAINE
Housed in the Gothic-vaulted sick wards of a former hospital (1180–1865), **Musée Jean Lurçat et de la Tapisserie Contemporaine** (☎ 02 41 87 41 06; 6 blvd Arago; adult/under 18 yrs €3.50/1.75; ⏲ 9.30am-6.30pm mid-Jun–mid-Sep, 10am-noon & 2-6pm Tue-Sun mid-Sep–mid-Jun) showcases a series of 10 monumental tapestries woven in the 1960s by French-born artist Jean Lurçat (1892–1966). Entitled *Le Chant du Monde* (The Song of the World), the hangings illustrate the horror story of human destruction. A disturbing green skeleton depicts 'Hiroshima Man'.

MUSÉE COINTREAU
The rich, intoxicating aroma emanating from the copper stills at the **Musée Cointreau** (☎ 02 41 31 50 50; www.cointreau.com; blvd des Breton-

nières; adult/12-18 yrs €5.50/2.60; tours ⓨ 10.30am, 2.30pm, 3.30pm & 4.30pm Jul & Aug, 10.30am & 3pm Mon-Sat plus additional tour 4.30pm Sun May, Jun, Sep & Oct, 3pm Mon-Sat plus additional tour 4.30pm Sun Nov-Apr) is enough to send anyone running for the gift shop to stock up. The exact ingredients required for the famous orange liquor are top secret, known to just a select few. As such, every bottle of Cointreau sold anywhere in the world is produced right here; 30 million bottles a year. The displays and thorough guided tour are interesting and professional, but it's that sublime aroma – of orange peel and summertime – that lingers.

The museum is off the ring road to the east of Angers. Take bus No 7 from Angers bus station to the 'Cointreau' stop.

WINE TASTING

The **Maison du Vin de l'Anjou** (☎ 02 41 88 81 13; www.vins-valdeloire.com in French; 5bis place du Président Kennedy; admission free; ⓨ 9.30am-1pm & 3-6.30pm Tue-Sun Apr-Sep, 9am-1pm & 3-6.30pm Tue-Sat Oct-Mar), across from the chateau, is the perfect spot to sample Anjou and Saumur wines.

Sleeping
BUDGET

Foyer Darwin (☎ 02 41 22 61 20; contact@foyerdarwin .com; 3 rue Darwin; dm €10.50) Five kilometres west of Angers and not far from the lake, Foyer Darwin is a large, 300-bed hostel on the Bellebeille Cité Université campus. Facilities here are good; there's a decent lounge with billiards and foosball, plus a self-service canteen and mountain bikes for hire. To get there, take bus No 6 or No 8 from Angers train station.

Hôtel du Centre (☎ 02 41 87 45 07; 12 rue St-Laud; d with shower & toilet €28) In a pretty pedestrian street, it has ordinary rooms above a popular, comfy-leather-sofa-filled bar of the same name.

Camping

Camping du Lac de Maine (☎ 02 41 73 05 03; fax 02 41 73 02 20; av du Lac de Maine; camping €9.70-13; ⓨ mid-Mar–mid-Oct) overlooking a lake, is approximately 2.5km southwest of Angers. To get to this 162-site area from town, take bus No 6 from the stop at the train station.

MID-RANGE

Hôtel du Mail (☎ 02 41 25 05 25; hoteldumailangers@ yahoo.fr; 8-10 rue des Ursules; s/d from €37/49; Ⓟ) This

fantastic not-quite-boutique hotel fills a lovely townhouse set around a quiet courtyard. The beautiful, well-furnished interior is immaculate and the overall experience is better than its two-star rating would imply.

Hôtel Continental (☎ 02 41 86 94 94; www .hotellecontinental.com; 12-14 rue Louis de Romain; s/d €42/56) Right in the centre of town, this reliable two-star has a stylised 1920s logo and, modern, if unspectacular rooms. The buffet breakfast (€6) is good value. It is accessible to disabled travellers.

Eating

Auberge Angevine (9 rue Cordelle; ⓨ noon-2pm, 6-11pm Tue-Sat) Wenches in medieval costume serve up platters of wild boar and goblets of red wine in this themed restaurant that doesn't take itself too seriously. The venue is a cavernous old chapel, with wooden benches and candelabras. Good fun and great value; Tuesday evening sees kids entertainment.

La Treille (☎ 02 41 88 45 51; 12 rue Montault; lunch menu €10, dinner menus €14-19; ⓨ Tue-Sat) A traditional, homely little restaurant at the back of the cathedral, boasting a terrace opposite Maison d'Adam and a good value lunch *menu*. Known locally for top-notch food and service.

Le Relais (☎ 02 41 88 42 51; 9 rue de la Gare; lunch menu €14.50, dinner menus €18.80-30; ⓨ Tue-Sat) A refined, turn-of-the-century ambience is to be found at this classy restaurant, but it's in an odd choice of area, down by the station. Traditional gourmet *plats* (specials), excellent fresh market cuisine and an extensive wine list.

SELF-CATERING

For top-rate sandwiches, filled baguettes and other satisfying lunchtime bites, head to **La Gourmandise** (cnr place Ste-Croix & rue St-Aubin; ⓨ 7am-7.30pm Mon-Sat). Count on a long queue at peak meal times.

Near the train station, **Supermarché Diagonal** (4 rue de la Gare; ⓨ 8am-8pm Mon-Sat) is a small grocery store.

Traiteur aux Rillauds d'Or (☎ 02 41 88 03 13; 59 rue St-Laud) sells prize-winning *rillons* (fat-fried pork cubes) and other meaty treats.

Drinking

Pubs and bars bespeckle the southern end of rue St-Laud. Irish bars dot the pedestrian section of nearby rue des Poeliers.

THE LOIRE

Le Twist (☎ 02 41 88 72 00; 8 rue St-Étienne; 🕙 11.30am-2am Tue-Sat) Slick back your hair and head down to this fun – if a little kitsch – 50's style American bar. Traditional cocktails and tequila shots get this place buzzing until the early hours.

Café-Concert Le Coursive (☎ 02 41 25 13 87; 7bis blvd du Maréchal Foch; 🕙 5pm-2am Mon-Sat) Live concerts are held regularly at this laid-back venue. The music is predominately on a jazz tip, but it's worth checking the listings for other genres.

Entertainment
For the latest information on cinema, music, and theatre, pick up a copy of *Angers Poche*, a free weekly gig guide available at the tourist office.

Getting There & Away
AIR
Aéroport d'Angers-Marcé (☎ 02 41 33 50 00) is 24km northeast of the centre in Marcé, off the A11.

BUS
Eurolines buses depart from quai H at Angers **bus station** (place de la Poissonnerie).

Regional services from the bus station are operated by **Anjou Bus** (☎ 02 41 88 59 25). Destinations include Brissac-Quincé (€1.40, 25 minutes, six daily); St-Georges-sur-Loire (€1.40, 40 minutes, about five daily), take bus No 7; and Saumur (€6.50, 1½ hours, about 10 daily), take bus No 11.

TRAIN
Angers' sparkling new glass and steel **SNCF train station** (Angers St-Laud; place de la Gare) is well served, and there is an **SNCF Boutique** (5 rue Chaperonnière). There is at least one train hourly to/from Tours (€14/16.90 for a non-TGV/TGV, 50 minutes to 1½ hours), Saumur (€6.80, 20 minutes) and St-Pierre des Corps (€16.90, one hour). Change trains in Tours or St-Pierre des Corps to get to/from Blois (€19.40, 1½ hours), Orléans (€24.60, two hours), and various other eastern Loire destinations. Trains run daily to/from Nantes (€13.50, 30 minutes, at least half-hourly), from where there are connecting southbound rail services to La Rochelle, Bordeaux and Toulouse.

There are TGV services between Angers and Paris' Gare Montparnasse (€41.40 to €52.50, 1½ hours, 10 to 15 daily).

Getting Around
BICYCLE
Sport ECO (☎ 02 41 87 07 77; 45 rue Maillé; per day/weekend/week €11/20/45; 🕙 10am-noon & 2-7pm Tue-Sat) rents bicycles or rollerblades.

CAR
Car-rental companies:
Budget (☎ 02 41 88 23 16; 16 rue Denis Papin) Opposite the station.
Europcar (☎ 02 41 87 87 10; place de la Gare)
Hertz (☎ 02 41 88 15 16; rue Denis Papin) Also opposite the station.

AROUND ANGERS
South of Angers, the River Maine joins the Loire for the final leg of its journey to the Atlantic. The river banks immediately west of this confluence remain the source of some of the valley's most noble wines – Savennières, Coteaux du Layon and so on.

The **Musée de la Vigne et du Vin d'Anjou** (Museum of Anjou Wine and Vines) 17km south of Angers in St-Lambert du Lattay, is the best place to learn more about these wines.

The 13th-century **Prieuré de l'Epinay** (☎ 02 41 39 14 44; bernard.gaultier3@wanadoo.fr; d with breakfast €70; 🕙 Easter-Sep; 🅿) in St-Georges-sur-Loire, 1km southwest of Serrant, is a delightful place to stay (and eat) for wine lovers. The *chambre d'hôte* is run by a wine connoisseur who takes guests on tours of surrounding wine cellars. The priory rents bicycles.

Château de Serrant
Château de Serrant (☎ 02 41 39 13 01; adult/child €8.40/4.60; 🕙 Apr–mid-Nov), 15km west of Angers, is a perfect example of Renaissance architecture, with an unusually well-furnished interior. Its library has over 12,000 books. The 17th-century ebony cabinet in the drawing room conceals 33 secret drawers and is one of four known to exist in the world (the others are in Windsor Castle, Château de Fontainebleau and Amsterdam's Rijksmuseum). Guided tours depart at 20 minutes past the hour from 10.20am to 5.20pm, with extra tours at 10 minutes to the hour in July and August (no tours 11.20am to 2.20pm).

GETTING THERE & AWAY
Château de Serrant is 15km west of Angers on the N23. It's an easy cycle from Angers. Bus Nos 18 and 18B to St-Georges-sur-Loire (40 minutes, five daily) stop nearby.

Château de Brissac

This highly ornate chocolate-box folly **Château de Brissac** (☎ 02 41 91 22 21; adult/student & child €7/5.50; 🕑 10am-6pm Jul–mid-Sep, 10am-noon & 2.15-5.15pm Apr-Jun & Sep-Oct) is 15km south of Angers in Brissac-Quincé. Home to the dukes of Brissac since 1502, it is the tallest castle in the Loire at seven storeys and sits regally amid grounds studded with cedar trees and stretching across 800 hectares.

Inside, flamboyant furnishings and ornamentation coat its 203 rooms. The theatre, lit with chandeliers, was the whimsical creation of the Vicomtesse de Trèdene, a soprano with a passion for the arts. Château de Brissac can be visited with an hourly guided tour.

You can stay at the château (p395).

GETTING THERE & AWAY

Travelling from Angers, Brissac-Quincé can be reached via the D748 and its continuation, the D761. Bus Nos 9 and 9B link Angers bus station with Brissac-Quincé (€3, 25 minutes, six daily); the village bus stop is on place de la République, in front of the chateau.

SAUMUR & TROGLODYTE VALLEY

pop (Saumur) 30,100

The notability of small-town Saumur, 70km southeast of Angers, rides on the renowned National Equestrian School, stabled in St-Hilaire-St-Florent on its western outskirts. In the town centre, military personnel from the calvary school – stationed here since 1599 – buzz around town on bicycles, creating a pleasant old-fashioned atmosphere.

In the Revolution, *troglodytes* – Swiss-cheese-like caves hollowed in the chalky buffs that dominate the river banks around Saumur – provided a refuge for 75% of the populations of Angers and Saumur. Today the caves are used to store wine, grow mushrooms and bake *fouaces,* a kind of pitta bread that is typical of this valley.

Information

Doué-la-Fontaine Tourist Office (☎ 02 41 59 20 49; tourisme@ville-douelafontaine.fr; 30 place des Fontaines) On the central square.

Saumur Tourist Office (☎ 02 41 40 20 60; www.saumur-tourisme.com; place de la Bilange; 🕑 9.15am-7pm Mon-Sat, 10.30am-12.30pm & 2.30-5.30pm Sun mid-May–mid-Oct; 9.15am-12.30pm & 2-6pm Mon-Sat mid-Oct-Apr) Near the bridge (Pont Cessart), inside the old theatre.

Saumur

The historic heart of Saumur, on the south bank of the Loire, is dominated by **Château de Saumur** (☎ 02 41 40 24 40; adult/child €6/4; 🕑 9.30am-6pm Jul & Aug, 10am-1pm & 2-5.30pm Sep-Jun, closed Tue Nov-Mar & Mon Jan), a stunning, fairy-tale castle cornered by pointed towers. It was built under Louis XI from 1246 and has been used as a dungeon, a fortress and a country residence. Today it houses two museums, one dedicated to horses and the other to decorative arts.

The **École Nationale d'Équitation** (National Equestrian School; ☎ 02 41 53 50 60; www.cadrenoir.fr), 3km west of the town centre in St-Hilaire–St-Florent, trains instructors and riders at competition level, prepares teams for the Olympic Games and is home to the elite Cadre Noir (p424). The school sports Europe's largest indoor riding arena. Guided **tours** (morning/afternoon €7/5; 🕑 9.30am Tue-Sat, btwn 2-4pm Sat & Sun Apr-Sep) include watching a Cadre Noir training session. Advance reservations are essential; tours are held in English when there are enough Anglophones.

Surrounding **mushroom farms** recycle the 10 tonnes of droppings dumped daily by the school's 400 horses. The **Musée du Champignon** (☎ 02 41 50 31 55; adult/student/children €6.50/5/4; 🕑 10am-7pm), tucked in a cave in St-Hilaire-St-Florent, is a living example of the area's thriving button-mushroom industry that occupies 800km of Saumurois caves and accounts for 65% of national production.

West of Saumur

Caves riddle this stretch, dubbed 'Troglodyte Valley'. **St-George des Sept Voies**, 23km west of Saumur, is home to the **Hélice Terrestre de l'Orbière** (☎ 02 41 57 95 92; Espace d'Art Plastique Contemporain; admission €4; 🕑 11am-8pm May-Sep, 2-6pm Oct-Apr), a startling piece of monumental art, sculpted underground by local artist Jacques Warminski (1946–96). The screw-shaped subterranean gallery, duplicated in reverse above ground, can be explored on foot.

In **Gennes**, 8km southeast, there's a **Gallo-Roman amphitheatre** (☎ 02 41 51 55 04), built around AD 150, which in summer hosts lively (bloodless) re-enactments of the bloody spectacles once staged by the Romans. From here, the scenic D69 cuts south through the green **Forêt de le Chêne-Rond** to **Doué-la-Fontaine** (population 7200), an ideal base for exploring Troglodyte Valley. In the town **zoo** (☎ 02 41 59

CADRE NOIR

Three moves set the Cadre Noir apart from its equestrian counterparts in Vienna: the *croupade*, which requires the horse to stretch its hind legs 45° into the air while its front legs stay on the ground; the *courbette*, which sees its front legs raised and tucked firmly into its body; and the demanding *cabriole*, which elevates the horse into the air in a powerful four-legged leap. These acrobatic feats, far from being crude or cruel, are considered the height of grace, elegance and Classicism. They are achieved after 5½ years of training, which starts when a horse is three years old. Daily training sessions last 1½ hours, following which the horse is untacked, washed down, dried and boxed for the remaining 22hrs of the day.

A black cap and jacket, gold spurs and three golden wings on the rider's whip are the distinctive trademarks of the elite Cadre Noir rider.

18 58; adult/child €12/6; 🕙 9am-7pm Apr-Sep, 10am-6pm Oct-Mar), off route de Cholet (D960), giraffes hang out in former falun pits and crocodiles bathe in pools inside clammy caves. Other troglodytic sites here include **Les Perrières** (☎ 02 41 59 71 29; 545 rue des Perrières), where falun rock was quarried in the 18th century; and the **Cave aux Sarcophages** (☎ 02 41 59 24 95; 1 rue Croix Mordret), an ancient Merovingian cave where 35,000-odd Monolithic sarcophagi were manufactured from the 6th to the 9th centuries.

The abandoned troglodytic village of **Rochemenier,** about 6km north of Doué via the D761, is also open to visitors from April to October.

East of Saumur

Saumur's eastern Troglodyte Valley is dominated by underground wine cellars. Fruity Saumur-Champigny red wine, the most respected Saumurois appellation, can be sampled at various cave cellars in **Souzay-Champigny**, 6km east of Saumur.

Subterranean **Musée de la Pomme Tapée** (Museum of Tapped Apples; ☎ 02 41 51 48 30; adult/child €4.80/2.80; 🕙 2.30-6pm Tue-Fri, 10am-noon & 2.30-6pm Sat & Sun Jul & Aug, Sat & Sun only Apr-Jun & Sep-Nov) in Val Hulin, 3km further east along the riverside D947, demonstrates how apples

were dried, squashed and rehydrated into spiced mulled wine in the 19th century.

Button mushrooms are the gastronomic speciality of the **Cave à Champignons** in Le Saut aux Loups, a few kilometres east of Musée de la Pomme Tapée.

The neighbouring medieval villages of **Montsoreau** (population 560) and **Candes-sur-Martin** (240) are a blend of mellow-hued rooftops, snug on the confluence of the Loire and the Vienne.

The breathtaking, 12th-century Romanesque **Abbaye de Fontevraud** (☎ 02 41 51 71 41), 4km south of Montsoreau, forms the largest monastic ensemble in France. Until it closed in 1793, it was unique in that its nuns and monks were governed by a woman: the abbess. It was also one of France's harshest prisons between 1804 and 1963 – now people pay to stay in luxury at this Unesco World Heritage Site.

Sleeping & Eating

See p395 for information on staying at the grand Château de Verrieres in Saumur.

Prieuré St-Lazare (☎ 02 41 51 73 16; www.hotelfp-fontevraud.com; d €60-85), a converted priory in the grounds of Abbaye de Fontevraud, is a prestigious choice. Despite its 12th-century origins, the rooms are modern and comfortable. The cloister restaurant is renowned for its gastronomic menu and wine list.

Auberge de la Route d'Or (☎ 02 41 95 81 10; 2 place de l'Église, Candes-sur-Martin; lunch menu €12.90, dinner menus €19.90-31; 🕙 daily Jul & Aug, Thu-Mon Sep-May), just under the church in Candes-sur-Martin, is well worth a gastronomical detour: it has a roaring fire in winter, a terrace in summer and delicious *menus*.

Other options in town include **Camping Caravaning l'Île d'Offard** (☎ 02 41 40 30 00; fax 02 41 67 37 81; rue de Verden, Saumer; camping €13.50-18.50; 🕙 Mar-Nov) on the island at Saumur and **Centre International de Séjour l'Île d'Offard** (dm incl breakfast €10.50, d with shower €31) next door.

Getting There & Away

From Angers, **Anjou Bus** (☎ 02 41 88 59 25) operates regular daily buses to/from Saumur (1½ hours) and Doué-la-Fontaine (€5, 55 minutes, about six daily).

Saumur is on the train line between Tours (€9.20, 30 to 50 minutes) and Angers (€6.80, 30 minutes) with regular trains – at least hourly – in both directions.

Burgundy

CONTENTS

Yonne	**429**
Auxerre	429
Around Auxerre	433
Avallon	437
Vézelay	440
Around Vézelay	442
Parc Naturel Régional	
du Morvan (Nièvre)	**442**
Saulieu	443
Chateau Chinon	444
Maquis Bernard Résistance	
Cemetery	444
Côte d'Or	**444**
Dijon	444
Côte d'Or Vineyards	452
Beaune	453
Northwest of Dijon	457
Saône-et-Loire	**459**
Autun	459
Le Creusot	462
Cluny	463
North of Cluny	465
Mâcon	465

Bordered to the south and east by the snow-crowned Alps, and to the north and west by the hills and flat plains of Champagne and the Massif Central, Burgundy is in many ways the real heartland of France. It's also at the epicentre of two of the country's greatest passions: food and wine. Some of the most prestigious vintages are produced in northern Burgundy around Chablis, and along the sun-baked Côte d'Or south of Beaune. It's certainly a place where you can eat and drink to your heart's content, but there's more to Burgundy than gastronomic greatness.

Until the 15th century Burgundy was an independent kingdom from the rest of France, with a vast territory that extended far beyond its own borders. The remnants of its rich heritage are scattered across the region, from the glorious medieval and Renaissance architecture of Dijon and Beaune to the grand chateaux of Tanlay, St-Fargeau and Ancy-le-Franc. In the Middle Ages Burgundy was also one of the most important religious centres in France. Nearly every town boasts an impressive church, and the magnificent abbeys of Auxerre, Vézelay, Pontigny and Fontenay are some of the best preserved in the country.

Burgundy is also a great place to experience the French countryside. Whether exploring the wild reaches of the Parc Naturel Régional du Morvan, floating down the waterways of the Yonne or sailing across the Côte d'Or vineyards in a hot-air balloon, you'll find Burgundy is one of France's most varied *départements* – an enticing blend of hilltop villages and bustling market towns, grand chateaux and tiny churches, patchwork fields and abandoned abbeys.

Burgundy is divided into four *départements:* Yonne (capital: Auxerre) in the northwest, Côte d'Or (capital: Dijon) in the northeast, Saône-et-Loire (capital: Mâcon) in the south, and the southwestern Nièvre *département,* which is mostly taken up by the Parc Naturel Régional du Morvan.

HIGHLIGHTS

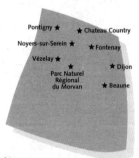

- Wander through the lavish mansions of **Ancy-le-Franc** (p436), **Tanlay** (p436) and **St-Fargeau** (p436)
- Sample the local wines in the cellars of **Beaune** (p454) and the **Côte d'Or** (p453)
- Explore the walled village of **Noyers-sur-Serein** (p435)
- The hilltop town of **Vézelay** (p440)
- Imagine the life of Cistercian monks at the abbeys of **Fontenay** (p459) and **Pontigny** (p434)
- Hike and bike in the **Parc Naturel Régional du Morvan** (p442)
- Delve into Dijon's medieval and Renaissance past captured in the city's **museums** and **architecture** (p445)

▪ POPULATION: 1.6 million	▪ AREA: 31,582 SQ KM

History

At its height in the 14th and 15th centuries, the dukedom of Burgundy (Bourgogne in French) was one of the richest and most powerful states in Europe, second only to Venice in terms of wealth. The Valois Dukes commanded a vast swathe of territory encompassing Holland, Flanders, Luxembourg, Belgium, Picardy, Alsace and Lorraine, and their rivalry with their French neighbours was bitter (during the Hundred Years War, it was the Burgundians who sold Joan of Arc to the English). At the time, it seemed more likely that the kingdom of France would become part of Burgundy, rather than the other way around. But in the

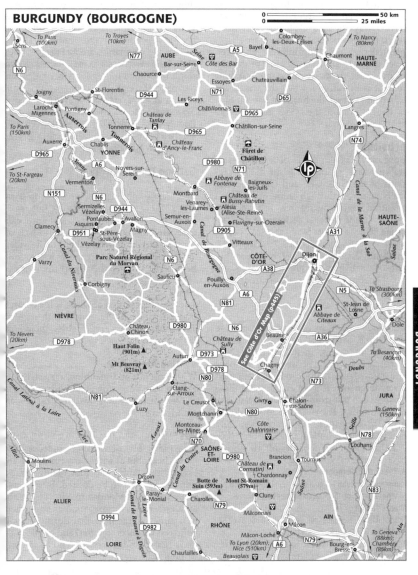

BURGUNDY (BOURGOGNE)

end, when Duke Charles the Bold was killed during the siege of Nancy, it was Burgundy that became part of France, in 1477.

Climate
Burgundy shares a similar climate to much of the rest of the country. The mixture of sunshine and showers in spring and the long, hot summers make for perfect wine-growing weather. Burgundy's cold winters have always been a challenge to *viticulteurs;* the region's best vineyards are always planted high up along hillsides and sheltered slopes to afford them some protection from winter frosts. Perhaps the best time to visit is in autumn, when the weather is warm and settled, the bustle of harvest time is dying down and the woods and fields are ablaze with colour.

Activities
Burgundy has hundreds of kilometres of walking and cycling trails, including sections of the GR2, GR7 and GR76. Several trails take you through some of the most beautiful wine-growing areas in France.

The **Comité Régional de Tourisme de Bourgogne** (Regional Tourism Board; ☎ 03 80 28 02 80; www.burgundy-tourism.com; BP 1602, 21035 Dijon CEDEX) publishes English-language brochures on outdoor activities (including walking and canal boating) that are available from tourist offices.

BOATING
Burgundy's 1200km of waterways include the Yonne, Saône and Seille Rivers and a network of canals, including the 242km Canal de Bourgogne. Between mid-October and mid-March many canals are emptied for maintenance. Known as *chômages,* these closures can last from several weeks to one or two months. The rivers are almost always open for navigation. Locks are open daily except on major holidays.

Reliable rental companies offering boats from March to November:

Bateaux de Bourgogne (☎ 03 86 72 92 10; sla@ tourisme-yonne.com; 1-2 quai de la République, 89000 Auxerre) A group of 15 rental companies based above Auxerre's tourist office.

France Afloat (Burgundy Cruisers; ☎ /fax 03 86 81 67 87, UK ☎ /fax 08700 110 538; www.franceafloat.com; 1 quai du Port, 89270 Vermenton) Based 23km southeast of Auxerre, this agency represents 10 rental companies.

Locaboat Plaisance (☎ 03 86 91 72 72; www.locaboat.com; Port au Bois, BP 150, 89303 Joigny CEDEX) Offers boats from many locations in France, including Joigny (27km northwest of Auxerre) and Venarey-les-Laumes (67km northwest of Dijon).

HOT-AIR BALLOONING
From April to October you can take a stunning *montgolfière* (hot-air balloon) ride over Burgundy from €230 per person (under 12 years €115). Note that balloon rides are heavily dependent on the weather.

Two big companies are **Air Escargot** (☎ 03 85 87 12 30; www.air-escargot.com), based 16km south of Beaune in Remigny (bookings can be made through the Beaune tourist office); and **Air Adventures** (☎ 03 80 90 74 2; www.airadventures.fr), based 50km west of Dijon near Pouilly-en-Auxois. Flights last between one and two hours and usually leave during early morning or late afternoon.

Getting There & Away
AIR
Burgundy's only regional airport is in **Dijon** (☎ 03 80 67 67 67; www.dijon.aeroport.fr), but regular chartered flights to French and European cities are currently on hold, due to lack of demand and the unpredictability of the wider airline industry. Plans are under way to find new carriers to keep the airport running.

TRAIN
The mainline station at Dijon is the central transport hub for Burgundy, with regular TGV links to most French cities, including Lyon and Paris.

Getting Around
With patience and planning, it's relatively easy to tour Burgundy by public transport. Details on trains and buses appear under each listing.

BUS
Burgundy's bus network is extensive and fairly cheap, but as with many rural areas in France, timetables and punctuality sometimes leave a lot to be desired. Buses generally run from Monday to Saturday, with Sunday services during summer and other peak times. Remember that during school holidays *(vacances scolaires)* and public holidays *(jours feriés),* services tend to change without warning.

GARETH McCORMACK

Parc National de la Vanoise (p519),
Rhône-Alpes

NICOLA WILLIAMS

Pont d'Arc p488),
Rhône Valley

GLENN VAN DER KNIJFF

Cathédrale St-Jean (p472), Vieux Lyon

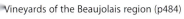

Vineyards of the Beaujolais region (p484)

PASCALE BEROUJON

JEAN-BERNARD CARILLET

Musée d'Histoire Naturelle
(p612), Nantes

JULIA WILKINSON

Le Thot – Espace Cro-Magnon
(p594), Vézère Valley

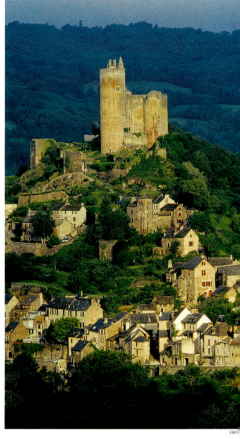

EMI

The *bastide* village of Najac (p606), Quercy

MARTIN MOOS

Seafood harvest at La Rochelle (p620) on the Atlantic Coast

CAR

As always, the most convenient way to get around is by car, which will allow you to get off the beaten track and explore some of the lesser known areas of Burgundy. Major car-hire firms are found in most large towns.

CYCLING

Since most of Burgundy is (fairly) flat, cycling is also a great way of getting around. Tourist offices stock a selection of guidebooks and leaflets detailing possible routes – the most popular criss-cross through the Morvan National Park and the wine territory of the Côte d'Or. Bikes are widely available for hire.

TRAIN

The train is probably the best way of getting around if you're planning on taking public transport. Services connect Auxerre, Avallon, Beaune and Montbard, from where you can catch regional trains to most areas around Burgundy.

YONNE

The Yonne *département,* roughly midway between Dijon and Paris, has long been the gateway to Burgundy. The region is home to the riverside city Auxerre; the white-wine centre, Chablis; medieval towns Pontigny, Noyers-sur-Serein and Tonnerre; the chateaux of Tanlay and Ancy-le-Franc; Avallon's hilltop city; and the medieval village of Vézelay.

AUXERRE

pop 37,800

Auxerre (pronounced oh-*sair*) is one of the oldest and most alluring towns in the Yonne. The city's varied architecture reflects its age; wandering through the maze of cobbled streets in the old city, you'll pass Roman remains, Gothic churches, and timber-framed medieval houses, and gaze across a jumble of belfries, spires and steep tiled rooftops all the way to the wide River Yonne.

Auxerre makes a good base for visiting northern Burgundy, and the city's pleasure-boat port makes it an excellent place to rent a canal boat (p428).

History

The area around Auxerre has been inhabited since long before the birth of Christ, but the first significant settlement grew up under the auspices of the Romans, and the city still retains some of its Gallo-Roman architecture. Auxerre became an important religious centre from the 4th century, especially following the construction of the town's impressive abbey, built to house the tomb of St-Germain. The town found much of its wealth in the Middle Ages as a river-port and centre for the wine-growing industry, but after the coming of the railways, most of the heavy industry moved elsewhere and the town slipped into economic decline.

These days Auxerre has reinvented itself as a pleasure port and a bustling provincial town, and also boasts one of the country's top football teams.

Orientation

The old city climbs from the left bank of the River Yonne, while the train station is 700m east of the river in the industrial zone. The commercial centre stretches uphill from Cathédrale St-Étienne to the post office, with shops lining rue de Paris and rue du Temple. The liveliest areas are around pedestrianised rue de l'Horloge and place Charles Surugue.

Information

INTERNET ACCESS

Maison de la Jeunesse (pl de l'Arquebuse; Internet access free; Mon-Fri 10am-12pm & 2-6pm) Youth centre (inside the France Telecom building) offering free Internet access.

LAUNDRY

Laundrette (138 rue de Paris; 8am-9pm)

MONEY

Banks can be found between place Charles Surugue and place Charles Lepère. The tourist office changes small amounts of money on Sunday and holidays.

POST

Post Office (pl Charles Surugue)

TOURIST INFORMATION

Tourist Office (03 86 52 06 19; www.ot-auxerre.fr; 1-2 quai de la République; 9am-1pm & 2-7pm Mon-Sat,

AUXERRE

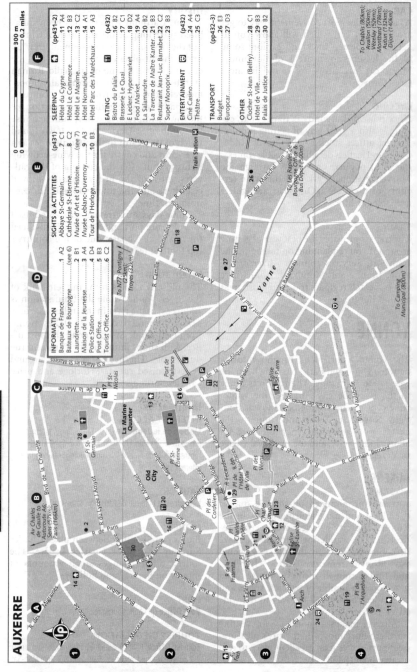

INFORMATION
Banque de France..................1 A2
Bateaux de Bourgogne............(see 6)
Laundrette...........................2 B1
Maison de la Jeunesse...........3 A4
Police Station......................4 D4
Post Office..........................5 B3
Tourist Office......................6 C2

SIGHTS & ACTIVITIES (p431)
Abbaye St-Germain...............7 C1
Cathédrale St-Étienne............8 C2
Musée d'Art et d'Histoire.......(see 7)
Musée Leblanc-Duvernoy.......9 A3
Tour de l'Horloge.................10 B3

SLEEPING (pp431-2)
Hôtel du Cygne....................11 A4
Hôtel le Commerce................12 B3
Hôtel Le Maxime..................13 C2
Hôtel Normandie..................14 A1
Hôtel Parc des Maréchaux......15 A3

EATING (p432)
Bistrot du Palais...................16 B2
Brasserie Le Quai.................17 C1
E Leclerc Hypermarket...........18 D2
Food Market.......................19 A4
La Salamandre.....................20 B2
La Taverne de Maître Kanter....21 B3
Restaurant Jean-Luc Barnabet...22 C2
Super Monoprix....................23 B3

ENTERTAINMENT (p432)
Ciné Casino.........................24 A4
Théâtre..............................25 C3

TRANSPORT (pp432-3)
Budget...............................26 E3
Europcar.............................27 D3

OTHER
Clocher St-Jean (Belfry).........28 C1
Hôtel de Ville......................29 B3
Palais de Justice...................30 B2

9.30am-1pm & 3-6.30pm Sun mid-Jun–mid-Sep; 9.30am-12.30pm & 2-6pm Mon-Fri, 9.30-12.30pm & 2-6.30pm Sat, 10am-1pm Sun mid-Sep–mid-Jun)

Sights & Activities

Wonderful views of the city are available from **Pont Paul Bert** (1857) and the arched footbridge opposite the tourist office. Both bridges are ideal places for starting a walk around the city. Auxerre's oldest architecture is found along the streets leading from the river towards the abbey and the cathedral.

ABBAYE ST-GERMAIN

The ancient **Abbaye St-Germain** (☎ 03 86 18 05 50; pl St-Germain; adult €4.20; ⏰ 10am-6.30pm Wed-Mon Jun-Sep, 10am-noon & 2-6pm Wed-Mon Oct-May) began as a basilica above the tomb of St Germain, founder of the first monastery in Auxerre. Over the centuries, as the site's importance grew, so did the abbey. During the Middle Ages, it attracted pilgrims from all over Europe.

The atmospheric **crypts** (last tour at 5pm or 5.30pm) contain some of the only surviving examples of Carolingian architecture in France. Supported by 1000-year-old oak beams, the walls and vaulted ceiling are decorated with 9th-century frescoes, and the far end of the crypt houses the tomb of St Germain himself. Guided tours (in French) are provided several times daily. Excavation has uncovered sarcophagi from as early as the 6th century, as well as the foundations of previous buildings. Left in situ, they now form a fascinating exhibit.

MUSÉE D'ART ET D'HISTOIRE

Housed in the eastern section of Abbaye St-Germain, and included in the abbey's admission price, this intriguing museum displays prehistoric artefacts, Gallo-Roman remains and sculpture and pottery discovered in and around Auxerre.

The same ticket includes entry to **Musée Leblanc-Duvernoy** (☎ 03 86 52 44 63; 9bis rue d'Églény; separate admission €2.10; ⏰ 2-6pm Wed-Mon), which has a fine collection of china and *faïence* (decorated pottery).

CATHÉDRALE ST-ÉTIENNE

The vast Gothic **Cathédrale St-Étienne** (place St-Germain; ⏰ 7.30am-7pm summer, 7.30am-5.30pm winter) and its stately 68m-high bell tower dominate Auxerre's skyline (and most of the postcards, too). The building was mainly constructed between the 13th and 16th centuries, though the choir, ambulatory and vivid **stained-glass windows** date from the 1200s. The Gothic western front was badly damaged by the hammer-happy Huguenots, who decapitated most of the statues during the Wars of Religion.

The **crypt** (admission €2.30; ⏰ 9am-noon & 2-6pm, closed Sun morning in summer) contains frescoes dating from the 11th to 13th centuries, including a scene of Christ on horseback unknown anywhere else in Christendom. Sitting in the underground chapel, with light filtering through the little windows and faint echoes of voices in the cathedral above, it's easy to imagine the power such places held for medieval pilgrims.

Upstairs, the modest **treasury** (admission €1.50) displays what was left of the cathedral's riches after the revolutionary mobs came calling.

From June to September a 75-minute sound-and-light show is held nightly in the cathedral, and from June to August hour-long organ concerts are held every Sunday.

TOUR DE L'HORLOGE

The spire-topped **Tour de l'Horloge** (clock tower; rue de l'Horloge) was built in 1483 as part of the city's fortifications. On the 17th-century clock faces (there's one on each side), the sun-hand indicates the time of day; the moon-hand shows what day of the lunar month it is, making a complete rotation every 29½ days. Look out for the fibreglass statue of Marie Noël, Auxerre's best known poet, near the clock tower.

Sleeping
BUDGET

Hôtel Le Commerce (☎ 03 86 52 03 16; hotel_du _commerce@ipoint.fr; 5 rue René Schaeffer; s/d/f €41/45/55) A cheap, welcoming place in the centre of town. The rooms are hardly luxurious, but the old building is full of character with original beams and a timber-framed frontage. The **restaurant** (mains €8-12) serves up Italian and French cuisines.

Camping Municipal (☎ 03 86 52 11 15; 8 route de Vaux; camping from €2.30; ⏰ Apr-Sep) A shaded, grassy place 1.5km south of the train station (and across the street from the football stadium). From place de l'Arquebuse, take bus A (two to three per hour until 7pm) to the Stades Arbre Sec stop.

MID-RANGE

Hôtel Parc des Maréchaux (☎ 03 86 51 43 77; www
.hotel-parcmarechaux.com; 6 av Foch; s €70, d €75-90;
P) One of Auxerre's best hotels, housed
in a former private mansion near the old
city. The 25 rooms are all named after
French marshals, and the best have balconies overlooking the peaceful garden,
where you can enjoy a luxurious summertime breakfast.

Hôtel Le Maxime (☎ 03 86 52 14 19; www.lemax
ime.net; 2 quai de la Marine; s/d €65/75, ste €100-120;
P 🔀) In a wonderful spot with views over
the River Yonne, this upmarket place offers
impeccable rooms and first-class service.
The attached restaurant is also very good,
if a little pricey.

Hôtel Normandie (☎ 03 86 52 57 80; normandie@
acom.fr; 41 blvd Vauban; s €49-55, d €55-75; 🕑 closed early
Feb; **P**) On the tree-lined square of blvd
Vauban, this is a great value hotel just outside the old city. The ivy-covered frontage,
friendly staff and understated rooms make
it feel like a much more expensive country
hotel.

Hotel du Cygne (☎ 03 86 52 26 51; fax 03 86 51
68 33; 14 rue du 24 Août; s/d €47/52; **P**) A cheaper
place outside the city centre, in a modern
building near place Arquebuse. The 30
plain rooms have all the mod-cons including satellite TV and minibars.

Eating

Bistrot du Palais (☎ 03 86 51 47 02; 69 rue de Paris;
mains €10; 🕑 lunch & dinner Tue-Sat) A classic
French bistro with tiny tables, checked
tablecloths and the essential sound of clat-
tering saucepans. It offer homely country
cooking, Lyonnaise sausages and Burgundian stews are specialities.

La Salamandre (☎ 03 86 52 87 87; 84 rue de Paris;
lunch menu €22, dinner menus €30-51; 🕑 closed Sun, dinner Wed, lunch Sat) A refined seafood restaurant,
with dishes ranging from pan-fried scallops
and *fruits de mer* (seafood) to wild turbot
and skate wing.

La Taverne de Maître Kanter (☎ 03 86 52 16 21;
11 pl Charles Lepère; mains €12-16; 🕑 lunch & dinner)
A reliable restaurant that serves enormous
plates of *sauerkraut* and more kinds of sausages than you knew existed.

Brasserie Le Quai (☎ 03 86 51 66 67; 4 pl St-Nicolas;
pizzas €8-10.50, menus €16-23; 🕑 lunch & dinner) Situated in a gorgeous fountainside setting
within a stone's throw of the river, this chic,

contemporary brasserie serves a good selection of salads, pizzas and pasta classics.

Restaurant Jean-Luc Barnabet (☎ 03 86 51 68
88; 14 quai de la République; menus €34-66, children's menu
€16; 🕑 lunch Wed-Sun, dinner Wed-Sat) Auxerre's
finest food is along the quay at Restaurant
Jean-Luc Barnabet. The owner's innovative versions of traditional French dishes
have earned many accolades, including a
Michelin star.

SELF-CATERING

A large **food market** (pl de l'Arquebuse) springs to
life on Tuesday and Friday mornings. There
are plenty of food shops along rue de Paris.

Supermarkets include a **Super Monoprix** (pl
Charles Surugue; 🕑 8.30am-8pm Mon-Sat) and a vast
E Leclerc hypermarket (14 av Jean Jaurès; 🕑 9am-8pm
Mon-Fri).

Entertainment

CINEMAS

Ciné Casino (☎ 03 86 52 36 80; 1 blvd du 11 Novembre)
This cinema has eight screens and shows
mainstream releases and art-house films
(often nondubbed).

THEATRE & MUSIC

Théâtre (☎ 03 86 72 24 24; 54 rue Joubert) The city's
Art Deco style theatre produces dance,
drama and theatre, and hosts Le Studio, a
regular event that brings top jazz talent to
the town from mid-October to early June.

Getting There & Away

BUS

Buses run by **Les Rapides de Bourgogne** (☎ 03
86 94 95 00; 3 rue des Fontenottes; 🕑 9am-noon Mon-Fri,
9am-noon Sat afternoon) link the train station and
place de l'Arquebuse with Chablis (€4.20,
35 minutes, two daily Monday to Friday
and usually one on Saturday) and Pontigny
(€3, 35 minutes, one or two daily except
Sunday). The tourist office has timetables.

CAR

Car-rental companies:
Budget (☎ 03 80 18 00 88; 32 av Gambetta)
Europcar (☎ 03 86 46 99 08; 9 av Gambetta)

TRAIN

Trains run from the Auxerre–St-Gervais **station** (rue Paul Doumer) to the mainline Laroche-
Migennes station (€3.30, 20 minutes, 12 to 15
daily), where you can change for Paris' Gare

de Lyon (€20.60, two to three hours, eight to 10 daily); Dijon (€20.80, two hours, three direct and 10 nondirect daily); and Montbard (€13.70 from Auxerre, 1½ hours, six to 10 daily), which is near Abbaye de Fontenay. Trains also go to Sermizelles-Vézelay (€6.40, 45 minutes, three to five daily) and Avallon (€8.10, one hour, three to five daily).

Getting Around
Free parking is available on quai de la Marine and quai de la République, and on the *boulevards périphériques* around the old city: de la Chainettes, Vauban, du 11 Novembre and Vaulabelle. The city's one-way system can be very confusing – bring a good map if you're driving.

For a taxi call ☎ 03 86 94 02 02 or ☎ 03 86 46 95 67.

AROUND AUXERRE
Between the River Yonne and the Canal de Bourgogne lie the Auxerrois and the Tonnerrois, rural areas covered with forests, fields, pastures and vineyards. The quiet back roads, such as the D124, and many of the walking trails make for excellent cycling.

La Puisaye
The countryside west of Auxerre is known as **La Puisaye**, a sparsely-populated landscape of woods, winding creeks and dark hills. The area is best-known as the birthplace of Colette (1873–1954), author of *La Maison de Claudine* and *Gigi*, and still one of France's most popular women writers. Colette was born in the tiny town of St-Sauveur-en-Puisaye, southwest of Auxerre, and much of her work explores her rural childhood in Burgundy. The **Musée Colette** (Colette Museum; ☎ 03 86 45 61 95; admission €4.30; ☻ 10am–6pm Wed-Mon Apr-Oct, weekends & public holidays only Nov-Mar), on the outskirts of St-Sauveur-en-Puisaye, houses a collection of her manuscripts, letters and belongings.

Other sights include the chateaux of **St-Fargeau** and **Ratilly** (see p436), and the **Chantier Médiéval de Guédelon** (☎ 03 86 45 66 66; www .guedelon.org; adult/child €8/6; ☻ 10am-6pm Thu-Tue & 10am-7pm Sun Mar-Jun, 10am-7pm Jul & Aug, 10am-5.30pm Thu-Tue Sep-Nov), near St-Fargeau, where for the last six years, a huge team of builders, stonemasons and carpenters (in period costume) have been constructing a medieval

castle with only 13th-century tools and materials. No-one seems to have any idea when the project is likely to be finished.

The **Musée de la Reproduction du Son** (☎ 03 86 74 13 06; musee.son@wanadoo.fr; St-Fargeau; admission €5.50; ☻ 10am-noon & 2-6pm Apr-Nov, to 7pm Jul & Aug, also open 2-6pm school holidays year-round), in St-Fargeau itself, is also well worth investigating. This extraordinary little museum houses one of the country's finest collections of early sound-recording equipment, from pump-operated barrel organs to self-playing pianos – the noise when they're all going at once is unforgettable (and quite deafening).

Chablis
pop 2600
The well-to-do but sleepy town of Chablis, 19km east of Auxerre, has made its fortune growing, ageing and marketing the white wines that bear its name. True Chablis derives its character from the area's unique clay and limestone soil, which contains millions of fossilised oyster shells.

Most of Chablis' shops are closed on Monday and from noon to 3pm on other days. In winter many cellars and *domaines* close down, but in summer, especially around harvest-time, it's a great place to come to watch the wine industry in full swing.

HISTORY
The village of Chablis originally grew up around a small monastery in the 9th century. The original building was replaced by the present-day Église St-Martin, (modelled on the Gothic cathedral in Sens) during the 12th century. Monks from Chablis and the nearby Abbatiale at Pontigny were among the first to perfect the process of making white wine, and the town's vintages were highly prized as far back as the Middle Ages. The town grew rich on the proceeds of the wine industry, and its reputation for making some of France's best white wines continues to this day.

ORIENTATION & INFORMATION
Chablis' main street is known as rue Auxerroise (west of the main square, place Charles de Gaulle) and rue du Maréchal de Lattre de Tassigny (east of place Charles de Gaulle).

BURGUNDY

CHABLIS CLASS

Chablis is one of the largest wine-producing areas in Burgundy. The dry, light white wine is made exclusively from Chardonnay grapes, and is divided into four Appellations d'Origine Contrôlées (AOC): Petit Chablis, Chablis, Chablis Premier Cru and, most prestigious of all, Chablis Grand Cru. The seven *grands crus,* lovingly grown on just 1 sq km of land on the hillsides north of town, are Blanchot, Bougros, Les Clos, Grenouilles, Preuses, Valmur and Vaudésir.

Wine can be sampled and bought at dozens of places – the tourist office has a comprehensive list. One of the largest is **La Chablisienne** (☎ 03 86 42 89 89; blvd Pasteur; ☽ 9am-12.30pm & 2-7pm), a cooperative cellar 1km south of town on the D91 towards Noyers-sur-Serein. Free *dégustation* is possible year-round. Another good house is the family-run **Cave du Connaisseur** (☎ 03 86 42 87 15; www.chablis.net/caveduconnaisseur in French; rue des Moulins; ☽ 9am-noon & 2-6pm).

The **tourist office** (☎ 03 86 42 80 80; www.chablis .net; 1 quai du Biez; ☽ 10am-12.30pm & 1.30-6pm Mon-Sat, 10am-12.30pm Sun Dec-Mar) is just east of place Charles de Gaulle.

SIGHTS & ACTIVITIES
The 12th- and 13th-century early Gothic **Église St Martin** (☽ Jul & Aug), founded in the 9th century by monks fleeing the Norman attacks on Tours, is north of place Charles de Gaulle. South along rue Porte Noël are the twin bastions of **Porte Noël** (1778), which hosts art exhibitions from mid-June to mid-September. Nearby is the shell of a 16th-century building known (inaccurately) as the **synagogue** (12 rue des Juifs). **Petit Pontigny** (rue de Chichée) was once used by the Cistercian monks of Pontigny as a fermentation cellar.

Vineyard walks from Chablis include the **Sentier des Grands Crus** (8km) and the **Sentier des Clos** (13km to 24km, depending on your route). The tourist office sells a French-language topoguide (€5.50).

Cycling is a popular way to tour the surrounding countryside, and the tourist office helpfully hires **bikes** (2hr/full-day €3.80/12) from Easter to early October.

Nearby villages worth exploring include **Courgis**, which offers great views; **Chichée** and **Chemilly**, both on the River Serein; and **Chitry-le-Fort**, famous for its fortified church.

SLEEPING & EATING
Hôtel Bergerand's (☎ 03 86 18 96 08; www.bergerand -chablis-france.com; 4 rue des Moulins; d €55-75) A pleasant, rustic hotel within stumbling distance of the centre of Chablis – a bonus if you've gone a little wild on the wine-tasting.

Hostellerie des Clos (☎ 03 86 42 10 63; www.hos tellerie-des-clos.fr; rue Jules-Rathier; s €50-71, d €58-84; ☽ mid-Jan–mid-Dec; P ⌘) A luxurious, three-star hotel housed in the town's former hospices, with lavish rooms and enclosed gardens. A separate building offers suites and apartments (€100 to €183). The **restaurant** (menus €33-70) bears one Michelin star, and as you'd expect, the wine-list is rather impressive.

Many restaurants around place Charles de Gaulle have outside terraces. **Le Syracuse** (☎ 03 86 42 19 45; 19 rue du Maréchal de Lattre de Tassigny; menus €12-23.50; ☽ closed Sun night & Mon) This place serves regional specialities and pizzas (from €7.50) in a vaulted, 13th-century dining room.

Except for the **Petit Casino grocery** (rue du Maréchal Leclerc; ☽ Mon-Sat), all the food shops along rue Auxerroise are closed on Sunday afternoon and Monday.

Chablis has an **outdoor food market** (place Charles de Gaulle; ☽ until 1pm Sun).

GETTING THERE & AWAY
Place Charles de Gaulle is linked to Auxerre by **Les Rapides de Bourgogne** (☎ 03 86 94 95 00) bus (€4.20, 35 minutes, two daily on weekdays, usually one on Saturday).

Pontigny
pop 825
Rising from flat fields 25km north of Auxerre, Pontigny's **Abbatiale** (abbey church; ☎ 03 86 47 54 99; ☽ 9am-6pm), is one of the last surviving examples of Cistercian architecture in Burgundy. The simplicity and purity of its construction reflects the austerity of the Cistercian order. On summer days sunshine filtering through the high windows bathes the abbey in light, creating an amazing sense of peace and tranquillity.

The Gothic sanctuary, 108m long and lined with 23 chapels, was built in the mid-

12th century, but the wooden choir screen, stalls and organ loft were added in the 17th and 18th centuries. Monks from the abbey were the first to perfect the production of Chablis wine.

The **tourist office** (☎ 03 86 47 47 03; pontigny@ wanadoo.fr; 22 rue Paul Desjardins; ☟ 10am-12.30pm & 2-6pm Mon-Fri Apr-Oct, to 4.30pm Tue-Fri Nov-Mar), across the road from the Abbatiale, has information on accommodation and walking trips.

The only hotel in Pontigny is **Le Relais de Pontigny** (☎ 03 86 47 96 74; d from €30), a roadside bar 400m along the N77 from the tourist office. The 10 upstairs rooms are bland but cheap, and you can find food at the attached truckers' **restaurant** (menus €13-16). Or try the nearby **Moulin de Pontigny** (☎ 03 86 47 44 98; menus €20, €27 & €33; ☟ lunch Mon-Sat, dinner Fri & Sat) offers fine rural cooking in the town's old mill – frog's legs, braised ham and *andouillette* (tripe sausage) are on the menu.

Supplies are available at the **Proximarché grocery** (43 rue Paul Desjardins; ☟ 8.30am-1pm & 3-7.30pm, closed Sun afternoon).

Les Rapides de Bourgogne (☎ 03 86 94 95 00) runs daily buses to Pontigny from Auxerre (€3, 35 minutes).

Noyers-sur-Serein
pop 810

Surrounded by rolling pastureland and wooded hills, the tiny medieval village of Noyers (pronounced nwa-*yer*) is 30km southeast of Auxerre. Stone ramparts and fortified battlements hem the village in on every side, and from the imposing stone gateway, cobbled streets lead past 15th- and 16th-century gabled houses and half-timbered buildings. Many of the streets still bear their medieval names – look out for rue du Grenier-à-Sel (Salt Store) and place du Marché-au-Blé (Flour Market).

A KNIGHT IN SHINING PETTICOATS

Speculation about the cross-dressing habits of the French secret agent Charles Chevalier d'Éon de Beaumont (1728–1810), born in Tonnerre, has been rife for centuries, especially in sex-obsessed England, where he spent much of his life wearing the latest women's fashion and spying for Louis XV. The locals, at least, have no doubt about the brave chevalier's suitability as a role model for today's youth: they've named the local secondary school after him.

Lines carved into the façade of the 18th-century **village hall**, next to the library, mark the level of historic floods. Across the street you'll find the **tourist office** (☎ 03 86 82 66 06; 22 pl de l'Hôtel de Ville; ☟ 9am-noon & 2.30-6.30pm, closed Sat & Sun Oct-Easter).

Musée de Noyers (☎ 03 86 82 89 09; rue de l'Église; admission €3.05; ☟ 11am-6.30pm Wed-Mon Jun-Sep, 2.30-6.30pm Sat & Sun Oct-May), along a back-street near the 15th-century church, displays a collection of **naive art** assembled by a local art historian.

Just outside the clock-topped southern gate, Chemin des Fossés leads eastwards towards the River Serein and a **riverside walk** around Noyers' 13th-century **fortifications.**

The only place to stay in the village is **Hôtel de la Vieille Tour** (☎ 03 86 82 87 69; fax 03 86 82 66 04; 59 place du Grenier-à-Sel; d €40-55; ☟ Apr-Sep), a charming, ivy-covered hotel along one of the cobbled streets. The nicest rooms look onto the river behind the village, and there's a sweet garden where you can relax in summer.

There's a **camping ground** outside the city walls, on the left as you approach the southern gates, near the post office. The two grocery stores inside the gates are closed on Sunday afternoon.

Les Rapides de Bourgogne (☎ 03 86 94 95 00) runs buses from Avallon (€6, one or two daily and none on Sunday or during school holidays).

Tonnerre
pop 6000

The town of Tonnerre is best known for **Hôtel-Dieu** (rue de l'Hôpital; adult/concession €3.50/2.50; ☟ 9am-11.30 & 2-5.30pm Mon-Sat), a charity hospital founded in 1293 by Marguerite de

Bourgogne, sister-in-law of St Louis. At the eastern end of the barrel-vaulted patients' hall, near the chapel and Marguerite's tomb, is an extraordinary 15th-century Entombment of Christ, carved from a single stone. The **tourist office** (☎ 03 86 55 14 48; 🕒 9am-12.30pm & 2-6.30pm Mon-Sat, 10am-noon & 2-5pm Sun) is housed inside.

About 400m west, some 100L of water per second gush from **Fosse Dionne**, a natural spring – its weird blue-green tint hints at its great depth. The pool is surrounded by an 18th-century washing house and a semicircle of ancient houses. Legend has it that a serpent lurks at the bottom of the spring.

The nicest place to stay in town overlooks the Fosse Dionne. **La Ferme de Fosse Dionne** (☎ 03 86 54 82 62; www.fermefossedionne.com; 11 rue de la Fosse Dionne; d from €48) has six tasteful rooms of varying sizes. Downstairs, the owner runs a café and antique shop; ask nicely and he might play one of his old gramophones.

Budget accommodation can be found at the dingy **Hotel du Centre** (☎ 03 86 55 10 56; 65 rue de l'Hôpital; s €21.50-32, d €22-40, tr €35.10) on the main road through town.

Tonnerre, 19km to the northeast of Chablis, is on the train line linking Dijon (€30.60, one hour, eight to 10 daily) with Laroche–Migennes.

Les Rapides de Bourgogne (☎ 03 86 94 95 00) has buses (one or two daily except Sunday and Saturday during school holidays) to Auxerre (€6, 80 minutes) and to Chablis (€2.40, 35 minutes).

Château de Tanlay

The French Renaissance–style **Château de Tanlay** (☎ 03 86 75 70 61; adult/child €7/3; 🕒 Wed-Mon Apr–mid-Nov), an elegant product of the 17th century, is surrounded by a wide moat and elaborately carved outbuildings. Interior highlights include the Grande Galerie, whose walls and ceiling are completely covered with trompe l'œil. One-hour tours are offered from 9.30am to 11.30am and 2.15pm to 5.15pm. The chateau is 10km east of Tonnerre in the village of Tanlay.

Château d'Ancy-le-Franc

The Italian Renaissance makes an appearance at the square **Château d'Ancy-le-Franc**

MOATS & MANSIONS

The following are five chateaux off Burgundy's beaten track.

St-Fargeau (☎ 03 86 74 05 67; www.chateau-de-st-fargeau.com in French; 40km southwest of Auxerre on the D965; admission €7; 🕒 10-noon & 2-6pm Apr-Sep) This fabulous pentagonal red-brick chateau, set around a vast central courtyard, dates mainly from the 15th century. From mid-July to mid-August a huge outdoor spectacle involving 60 mounted knights and 600 actors takes place every Friday and Saturday at 10pm in the chateau's grounds.

Ratilly (☎ 03 86 74 79 54; 12km southeast of St Fargeau; admission €3.50; 🕒 10am-noon & 2-5pm Mon-Fri Sep-Jun, 10am-6pm Jun-Sep) A 13th-century stone castle surrounded by dense forests and a dry moat. The chateau is privately owned and displays sculptures, stonework and pottery exhibitions in its grounds.

Bussy-Rabutin (☎ 03 80 96 00 03; 15km northeast of Semur-en-Auxois, just off D954; admission €6.10; 🕒 9am-noon & 2-6pm Tue-Sun mid-May–mid-Sep, 9am-noon & 2-5pm Tue-Sat mid-Sep–mid-May) A 16th- to 17th-century chateau with twin turrets bordered by formal gardens. Inside you'll find over 200 17th-century paintings collected by Roger Bussy-Rabutin, a scurrilous member of Louis XIV's court. Entry includes a guided tour.

La Rochepot (☎ 03 80 21 71 37; www.larochepot.com; 22km southeast of Beaune, off the N6; admission €5.50; 🕒 10am-6pm Wed-Mon Jul-Aug, 10-11.30am & 2-5.30pm Wed-Mon Sep-Apr) The conical towers of this 15th-century chateau rise from thick woods above the ancient village of Rocheport. Inside you can view the chateau's beautifully-preserved architecture, including the dining room, former guard's room and chapel.

Sully (☎ 03 85 82 10 27; www.chateaudesully.com; 15km northeast of Autun along the D973; admission €6, gardens €2.50; 🕒 10am-6pm Apr-Nov) On the outskirts of the village of Sully, this chateau was the birthplace of Marshall Mac-Mahon, duke of Magenta and president of France from 1873 to 1879; today it is still occupied by his descendants. The four wings are decorated with elaborate towers and spiky turrets. Hourly guided tours are available.

(☎ 03 86 75 00 25; www.chateau-ancy.com; adult/ student/under 15 €6/5/3; ⊙ Apr-early Nov), built in the 1540s by the celebrated Italian architect Serlio. The richly painted interior was mostly completed by Italian artists brought to Fontainebleau by François I. One-hour tours begin at 10.30am, 11.30am, 2pm, 3pm and 4pm (and at 5pm from June to August). Overlooking huge stables, a large park and the Canal de Bourgogne, the chateau is 19km southeast of Tonnerre. In summer there are outdoor classical concerts followed by tours of the chateau.

AVALLON

pop 9500

The walled town of Avallon, set on a picturesque hilltop overlooking the River Cousin and the far reaches of the Parc Naturel Régional du Morvan, has been an important strategic site since Roman times. Over the centuries the town has witnessed many bloody conflicts but the majority of its 15th- and 16th-century fortifications are still standing, and are best appreciated from the lush river valley below the city. Avallon is at its most animated during the Saturday morning market. The city makes a good base for exploring Parc Naturel Régional du Morvan and Vézelay.

Orientation

The old city is built on a triangular granite hilltop, with steep ravines to the east and west. The train station is 900m northeast of place Vauban. The main commercial thoroughfare is Grande Rue Aristide Briand, which runs through town to the old city gates, passing the tourist office en route.

Information

INTERNET ACCESS

Tourist Office (per 15min €3) See Tourist Information.

MONEY

Banks are dotted along Grande Rue Aristide Briand.

POST

Post Office (9 place des Odebert)

TOURIST INFORMATION

Tourist Office (☎ 03 86 34 14 19; www.avallonnais -tourisme.com in French; 6 rue Bocquillot; ⊙ 10am-7.30pm Jul & Aug, 10am-noon & 2-6pm Mon afternoon-Sat morning Sep-Jun) In a 15th-century house near the old city gates.

Sights

WALLED CITY

Construction of Avallon's fortifications, which tower over the green terraced slopes of the Cousin Valley, was begun in the 9th century. The city was contested by the first French kings, the dukes of Burgundy and English armies during the Hundred Years' War, and was pillaged during the Wars of Religion for good measure. A stroll around the walls, past the 15th- to 18th-century towers, ramparts and bastions, is an excellent way to appreciate the town's battle-scarred past.

Église St-Lazare (rue Bocquillot; ⊙ Easter-Sep) was built in the 12th century. Soon after the huge numbers of pilgrims drawn here by a piece of the skull of St Lazarus (believed to provide protection from leprosy) rendered the structure inadequate. As a result, the façade was moved 20m west. The church once had three **portals**, but one was crushed when the northern belfry collapsed in 1633. The two remaining portals are grandly decorated in the Burgundian Romanesque style, though much of the exterior carving has been damaged. Nearby, the 15th-century **Tour de l'Horloge** (clock tower) spans the southern end of Grande Rue Aristide Briand.

South of the church is the city's ancient gateway, the **Bastion de la Petite Porte**. A pathway meanders from the gateway and gives fine views over the Cousin Valley. On clear days you can see all the way to the hilltops of the Parc Naturel Régional du Morvan.

OTHER SIGHTS

Regular art exhibitions are held in the **Église St-Pierre**, next door to Église St-Lazare, and across the street in the 18th-century **Grenier à Sel** (Salt Store).

Musée de l'Avallonnais (☎ 03 86 34 03 19; pl de la Collégiale; adult/student/under 18 €3/1.50/free; ⊙ 2-6pm Wed-Mon May-Oct), founded in 1862, displays religious art, fossils and expressionist sketches by Georges Rouault (1871–1958).

About 100 costumes from the 18th to 20th centuries are displayed at the **Musée du Costume** (☎ 03 86 34 19 95; 6 rue Belgrand; adult/ student €4/2.50; ⊙ 10.30am-12.30pm & 1.30-5.30pm Easter-Oct).

AVALLON

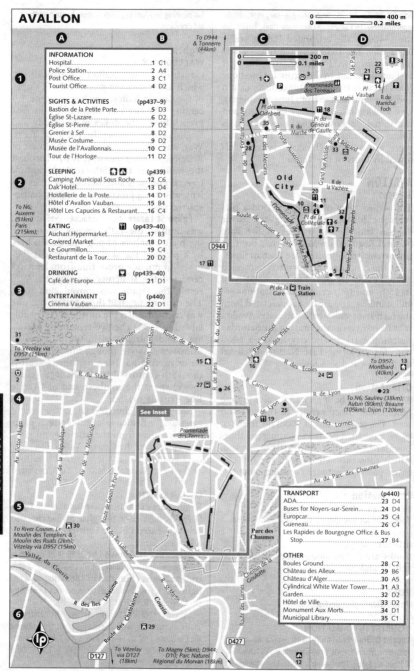

INFORMATION	
Hospital	1 C1
Police Station	2 A4
Post Office	3 C1
Tourist Office	4 D2

SIGHTS & ACTIVITIES	(pp437–9)
Bastion de la Petite Porte	5 D3
Église St-Lazare	6 D2
Église St-Pierre	7 D2
Grenier à Sel	8 D2
Musée Costume	9 D2
Musée de l'Avallonnais	10 C2
Tour de l'Horloge	11 D2

SLEEPING	(p439)
Camping Municipal Sous Roche	12 C6
Dak'Hotel	13 D4
Hostellerie de la Poste	14 D1
Hôtel d'Avallon Vauban	15 B4
Hôtel Les Capucins & Restaurant	16 C4

EATING	(pp439–40)
Auchan Hypermarket	17 B3
Covered Market	18 D1
Le Gourmillon	19 C4
Restaurant de la Tour	20 D2

DRINKING	(pp439–40)
Café de l'Europe	21 D1

ENTERTAINMENT	(p440)
Cinéma Vauban	22 D1

TRANSPORT	(p440)
ADA	23 D4
Buses for Noyers-sur-Serein	24 D4
Europcar	25 C4
Gueneau	26 C4
Les Rapides de Bourgogne Office & Bus Stop	27 B4

OTHER	
Boules Ground	28 C2
Château des Alleux	29 B6
Château d'Alger	30 A5
Cylindrical White Water Tower	31 A3
Garden	32 D2
Hôtel de Ville	33 D2
Monument Aux Morts	34 D1
Municipal Library	35 C1

BURGUNDY

Activities

An excellent route for a walk or bike ride in the Vallée du Cousin is the shaded, one-lane D427, which follows the River Cousin through dense forests and open meadows. You can head west towards Pontaubert and Vézelay, or east towards Magny.

The tourist office provides maps for walking tours, as well as information on Parc Naturel Régional du Morvan. You can also pick up the *Passeport Cœur en Bourgogne* (€5) booklet, which offers discounts on sights and activities, including museums and chateaux.

Sleeping
BUDGET

Dak'Hotel (☎ 03 86 31 63 20; www.dak-hotel.com in French; route de Saulieu; s/d €46/51; P ⚓) This functional chain hotel is a little way out of town towards Saulieu. The concrete exterior is far from beautiful, and the modern bedrooms might be a little boxy and bland, but there's an onsite swimming pool and it's a handy option for those with their own car.

Hôtel Le St Vincent (☎ 03 86 34 04 53; 3 rue de Paris; d €28-60; reception ⏰ usually closed Sun) Above a busy restaurant on a main roundabout, this is an acceptable alternative if everywhere else is full.

Camping

Camping Municipal sous Roche (☎ /fax 03 86 34 10 39; per adult/tent/car €2/2/2; ⏰ mid-Mar–mid-Oct) Two kilometres southeast of the old city on the banks of the Cousin.

MID-RANGE

Hotel d'Avallon Vauban (☎ 03 86 34 36 99; www .avallonvaubanhotel.com; 53 rue de Paris; s/d €45/51, tr €61-88; P) The best deal near the city centre, housed inside an old coaching inn on the road towards Tonnerre. The 26 rooms all have private phones and satellite TV, and there are four self-contained apartments in the attached garden.

Hôtel les Capucins (☎ 03 86 34 06 52; hotelles capucins@aol.com; 6 av Paul Doumer; d/tr €50/60; P) Eight simple rooms are offered above its stylish restaurant (see right), which is quite handy if you've sipped a little too much *vin rouge* over supper.

Le Moulin des Templiers (☎ 03 86 34 10 80; www .hotel-moulin-des-templiers.com; 10 route de Cousin; s €42-52, d €52-60; P) This beautifully converted mill is tucked away in a shady location in the Cousin Valley, about 5km south of town. The cosy bedrooms, rustic dining room and country furnishings are brimming with charm, and there's a delightful outside terrace next to the rushing river, which makes an ideal place for sipping an early evening aperitif.

TOP-END

Hostellerie de la Poste (☎ 03 86 34 14 19; www.hos telleriedelaposte.com; 13 pl Vauban; s/d €98/114, ste €167; P) Set around a quaint cobbled courtyard where horse-drawn carriages once clattered, this has been Avallon's top hotel for 200 years. The rooms are lavishly furnished, and the only downside is its position on busy place Vauban.

Le Moulin des Ruats (☎ 03 86 34 97 00; www .moulin-des-ruats.com; Vallée du Cousin; d €70-140) This former flour mill is a little closer to town than Moulin des Templiers, and a lot more expensive, but the fantastic wooded location, luxurious rooms and riverside terraces justify the price.

Eating & Drinking

Hôtel des Capucins restaurant (☎ 03 86 34 06 52; 6 av Paul Doumer; menus €23-52; ⏰ closed Wed year-round & Tue Sep-Jun) This elegant hotel serves French cuisine with a modern twist – roast rabbit and rump steak in red butter are some of the items you might find on its *carte*.

Restaurant de la Tour (☎ 03 86 34 24 84; 84 Grande Rue Aristide Briand; pizza & pasta €5.50-8, plats du jour €7-8; ⏰ lunch & dinner Mon-Sat) A lively bistro that serves good antipasti, pizza and pasta, and has a tempting selection of *plats du jour*.

Le Gourmillon (☎ 03 86 31 62 01; 8 rue de Lyon; menus €13-27; ⏰ closed dinner Sun) French and Burgundian dishes are served in the bright dining room of this down-to-earth restaurant: try the country paté and delicious *crème brûlée*.

Café de l'Europe (☎ 03 86 34 04 45; 7 place Vauban; ⏰ 8am-2am) The often-crowded Café de l'Europe is a lively café-bar-brasserie with billiards, lottery tickets and meals available at all hours.

SELF-CATERING

The **covered market** (marché couvert; ⏰ until 1pm Sat) and place du Général de Gaulle fill with food stalls on Saturday morning. There are several food shops nearby.

BURGUNDY

The vast **Auchan hypermarket** (rue du Général Leclerc; ✆ 8.30am-9pm Mon-Sat) is north of the town centre.

Entertainment

Cinéma Le Vauban (☎ /fax 03 86 34 22 87; 1 rue du Maréchal Foch) Shows new release films (usually in French) in an endearingly run-down old building near the town centre.

Getting There & Away

BUS
Service No 49 run by **Transco** (☎ 03 80 42 11 00) goes to Dijon (€15.77, two hours, two or three daily). **Les Rapides de Bourgogne** (☎ 03 86 34 00 00; 39 rue de Paris; ✆ 8am-noon & 3-5pm Mon-Fri, 9.30am-11.30am Sat) buses travel to Noyers (€6, one hour, one or two daily except Sunday and school holidays). Timetables are available from the tourist office.

CAR
Car-rental companies include **ADA** (☎ 03 86 34 20 38; 64 rue de Lyon) and **Europcar** (☎ 03 86 34 39 36; 28 rue de Lyon).

TRAIN
Trains link Avallon with Auxerre (€8.10, one hour, three to five daily) and the mainline Laroche–Migennes station (€10.10, two hours, three to five daily). Change at Laroche–Migennes for Paris' Gare de Lyon (€25.40, three to four hours, three or four daily) and Dijon (€14.90, two hours, two or more daily).

SNCF buses go to Montbard (€7.30, 50 minutes, two or three daily), also on the Paris–Dijon line (near the Abbaye de Fontenay). Trains/buses serve Saulieu (€6.60, one hour, two or three daily) and Autun (€11.70, 1¾ hours, one daily).

Getting Around
Parking marked by blue lines require a timer *disque* (disk) available at tobacconists; spaces with white lines are unrestricted.

VÉZELAY
pop 570
Despite the hordes of tourists who descend on Vézelay in summer, this tiny, hilltop village is one of France's architectural gems. Perched on a rocky spur crowned by slender buildings and the ancient abbey church of Basilique Ste-Madeleine, surrounded by a patchwork of vineyards, sunflower fields, and grazing sheep, Vézelay seems to have been lifted from another age.

History
Thanks to the relics of St Mary Magdalene, Vézelay's Benedictine monastery became an important pilgrimage site in the 11th and 12th centuries, and served as the starting point for one of the four pilgrimage routes to Santiago de Compostela in Spain. The town reached the height of its renown in the 12th century, when St Bernard, leader of the Cistercian order, preached the Second Crusade in Vézelay, and King Philip Augustus of France and King Richard the Lion-Heart of England met up here before setting out on the Third Crusade.

Information

MONEY
There are no banks in Vézelay, but there is an ATM by the post office.

POST
Post Office (pl Charles Surugue)

TOURIST INFORMATION
Tourist Office (☎ 03 86 33 23 69; www.vezelaytourisme.com in French; rue St-Pierre; ✆ 10am-1pm & 2-6pm Jun-Oct, closed Thu Nov-Apr) A new location on place du Champ-de-Foire is under construction.

Sights & Activities

BASILIQUE STE-MADELEINE
Originally established in the 880s, Vézelay's abbey, **Basilique Ste-Madeleine**, has had a very turbulent history. The original basilica was rebuilt between the 11th and 13th centuries, trashed by the Huguenots in 1569, desecrated during the Revolution and, to top off the human ravages, repeatedly struck by lightning.

By the mid-1800s it was on the point of collapse. In 1840 the architect Viollet-le-Duc undertook the daunting task of rescuing the structure. His work, which included reconstructing the western façade and its doorways, helped Vézelay – previously a ghost town – spring back to life.

On the 12th-century **tympanum** inside the church, Romanesque carvings show Jesus radiating his holy spirit to the Apostles. The **nave**, rebuilt following the great fire of 1120, has round arches and tiny windows, typical

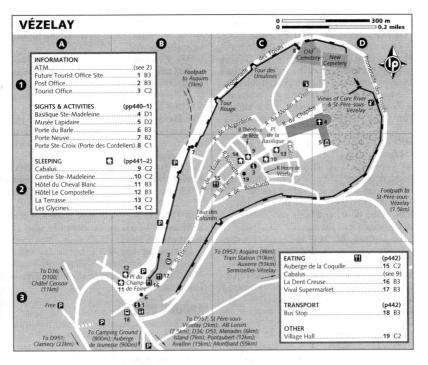

VÉZELAY

INFORMATION	
ATM	(see 2)
Future Tourist Office Site	1 B3
Post Office	2 B3
Tourist Office	3 C2

SIGHTS & ACTIVITIES	(pp440–1)
Basilique Ste-Madeleine	4 D1
Musée Lapidaire	5 D2
Porte du Barle	6 B3
Porte Neuve	7 B2
Porte Ste-Croix (Porte des Cordeliers)	8 C1

SLEEPING	(pp441–2)
Cabalus	9 C2
Centre Ste-Madeleine	10 C2
Hôtel du Cheval Blanc	11 B3
Hôtel Le Compostelle	12 B3
La Terrasse	13 C2
Les Glycines	14 C2

EATING	🍴	(p442)
Auberge de la Coquille	15 C2	
Cabalus	(see 9)	
La Dent Creuse	16 B3	
Vival Supermarket	17 B3	

TRANSPORT	(p442)
Bus Stop	18 B3

OTHER	
Village Hall	19 C2

features of the Romanesque style; the transept and choir (1185) have ogival arches and larger windows, hallmarks of Gothic architecture. Under the transept there is a mid-12th-century **crypt** with a reliquary dedicated to Mary Magdalene.

The abbey can be visited all day except during prayers (sometimes held in the cloister chapel), which visitors are welcome to attend. Services are sung in haunting four-voice harmonies by the monks and nuns of the Fraternité Monastique de Jérusalem several times daily. Prayers last 30 to 40 minutes (1¼ hours for the 6pm Mass and, on Sunday and holidays, the 11am Mass). From April to September concerts are held in the main nave.

The **park** behind Ste-Madeleine affords wonderful views of the Cure Valley and nearby villages, including St-Père-sous-Vézelay. From the northern side, a dirt road leads down to the **old cemetery**. The **Promenade des Fossés** circumnavigates Vézelay's medieval ramparts.

While you're wandering around Vézelay, look out for the brass shells on the cobbled street – they mark the original pilgrims' trail to the abbey.

CANOEING & CYCLING
Bicycles can be rented and kayak trips can be arranged at **AB Loisirs** (☎ 03 86 33 38 38; www .abloisirs.com in French; route du Camping, St-Père-sous-Vézelay; 🕙 9.30am-6.30pm), 400m southeast of the D957 along the D36.

Sleeping
BUDGET
Hôtel du Cheval Blanc (☎ 03 86 33 22 12; fax 03 86 33 34 29; pl du Champ-de-Foire; d €32-38; 🕙 Feb-Nov, reception closed Mon & after 5.30pm Sun) Good basic hotel at the bottom of the hill from town, with eight rooms and a homely restaurant.

La Terrasse (☎ 03 86 33 25 50; pl de la Basilique; d €25-35; 🕙 Easter–mid-Nov) This handy option for those on a tight budget has seven rooms, some with toilets across the garden.

Auberge de Jeunesse (☎/fax 03 86 33 24 18; route de l'Étang; dm €8-10; 🕙 Apr-Oct) Nine hundred metres southwest of place de Champ-de-Foire towards Étang-sur-Arroux. Kitchen facilities are available, but sheets aren't.

BURGUNDY

There's a **camping ground** nearby (☎ 03 86 33 24 18; route de l'Étang; camping €7; ☺ Apr-Sep).

Centre Ste Madeleine (☎ 03 86 33 22 14; rue St-Pierre; dm €8.50, s/d €13.50/19; ☺ year-round) This friendly hostel is housed in a spick-and-span medieval building, once inhabited solely by the town's religious fraternity. Today, it's a pleasant (if rather starchy) place run by surprisingly with-it Franciscan nuns.

MID-RANGE & TOP-END

Cabalus (☎ 03 86 33 20 66; www.cabalus.com in French; rue St-Pierre; d €38-54) This charming B&B, housed in the abbey's former hostelry, offers four highly individual rooms with exposed stonework, wrought-iron balconies, stone floors and huge windows, right in the shadow of the basilica.

Les Glycines (☎/fax 03 86 32 35 30; lesglycines .bourgogne@club-Internet.fr; rue St-Pierre; s €35, d €50-80; ☺ Feb-Dec) An extraordinary little hotel with brick floors, wooden beams and offbeat character a few steps from the basilica. The rooms are all named after famous artists (*Paul Claudet* is the one to get). No TV or telephones – the emphasis is on quiet contemplation.

Hôtel Le Compostelle (☎ 03 86 33 28 63; le.compostelle@wanadoo.fr; 1 pl du Champ-de-Foire; d €46-56, f €66-78; ☺ mid-Feb–Dec) The 18 spotless rooms overlook the valley or the garden, but the ones facing uphill towards the basilica are the ones to choose.

Eating

There are lots of lively restaurants, cafés and delicatessens along rue St-Pierre. **Cabalus** runs an excellent tearoom with an open fire in the hostelry's old kitchens. Delicious *croques-monsieurs*, crepes, bruschetta and cakes are all under €8, and the coffee, tea and hot chocolate come in little earthenware cups. It's highly recommended.

Auberge de la Coquille (☎ 03 86 33 35 57; 81 rue St-Pierre; crepes €3-8, menus €13-23; ☺ lunch & dinner Feb-Nov, Sat & Sun & some lunch Nov-Jan) A traditional country creperie that also serves hearty French cuisine in its small low-ceilinged dining room. Budget diners can go for the standard selection of sweet and savoury crepes; those with deeper pockets could try *coq au vin* and *jambon persillé*.

La Dent Creuse (☎ 03 86 33 36 33; pl du Champ-de-Foire; menus €13-30; ☺ lunch & dinner) A large and rather formal restaurant that specialises in Burgundian roasts, fish and chicken dishes,

and also boasts the town's best terrace overlooking the fields and distant forests below the town.

The **Vival supermarket** (rue St-Étienne; ☺ 9am-12.30pm daily, 4-7pm Tue, Thu & Sat & most afternoons Jul & Aug) sells groceries.

Getting There & Away

Vézelay is 15km from Avallon (19km via the gorgeous D427 via Pontaubert). For cars, there's a free car park 250m from place du Champ-de-Foire.

Three to five trains a day link **Sermizelles-Vézelay train station** (☎ 03 86 33 41 78), about 10km north of Vézelay, with Avallon (€2.60, 15 minutes) and Auxerre (€6.40, one hour). **Taxis** (☎ 03 86 32 31 88, 03 86 88 19 06) to/from Sermizelles-Vézelay cost about €16 (€20 at night and on Sunday).

In summer one SNCF bus a day links Vézelay with Avallon (€3, 20 minutes) and Montbard (€3, 70 minutes) on the Paris–Dijon line.

AROUND VÉZELAY

Parc Naturel Régional du Morvan is within easy reach of Vézelay. A footpath links Promenade des Fossés with the village of **Asquins**, from where trails lead to the River Cure.

Southeast of Vézelay at the base of the hill, **St Père-sous-Vézelay** contains a Flamboyant Gothic church and several upmarket restaurants. Three kilometres south along the D958 are the **Fontaines Salées** (☺ Thu-Tue Easter-Oct), saltwater hot springs where excavations have uncovered a Celtic sanctuary (2nd century BC) and Roman baths (1st century). A few kilometres south is **Pierre-Perthuis**, named after a natural stone arch; nearby, a graceful stone bridge (1770) spans the forested River Cure Gorge.

PARC NATUREL RÉGIONAL DU MORVAN (NIÈVRE)

In the Nièvre *département*, the 2304-sq-km **Parc Naturel Régional du Morvan** is a granite plateau bounded by Vézelay, Avallon, Saulieu, Autun and Chateau Chinon. It includes 700 sq km of dense woodland, 13 sq km of lakes, and rolling farmland broken by hedgerows, stone walls and stands of beech, hornbeam and oak. The majority of the area's 34,000 residents earn their living from farming, ranching, logging and even growing Christmas trees. The time when the impoverished Morvan (a Celtic name meaning 'Black Mountain') supplied wet nurses to rich Parisians has passed long ago.

Visitors to the park can now enjoy walking, mountain biking, horse riding, rock climbing, fishing and water sports. Rafting, canoeing and kayaking are possible on the Rivers Chalaux, Cousin, Cure and Yonne.

EDIBLE ESCARGOT

In France *helix pomatia* (otherwise known as the edible snail) is known as *escargot de Bourgogne* – the Burgundy snail. The humble crawler was once a regular – and unwelcome – visitor to the vineyards of Burgundy (hence the name) and was all but killed off after the introduction of industrial-strength pesticides in the 19th and 20th centuries. Ironically, the vast majority of the snails eaten in France are now imported from Eastern Europe.

St-Brisson Visitors Centre

Surrounded by hills, forests and lakes, the **Maison du Parc** (03 86 78 79 00; http://parcdumorvan.org in French) is 14km west of Saulieu in St-Brisson. General information, including hiking and cycling guides, is available either in the **Accueil building** (9.30am-5pm Mon-Sat & 10am-1pm & 2.30-6pm Sun Easter-Oct, longer hours Jul & Aug) or in the **Administration building** (8.30am-noon & 1.30-5pm Mon-Fri Nov-Easter), both in the Maison du Parc complex. Guided walks of the park are arranged in July and August.

The **Écomusée du Morvan** (03 86 78 79 06; admission free; 10.15am-6pm Easter-Nov), which explores traditional Morvan life and customs, has five sites around the park with two more planned.

Morvan was a major stronghold for the Resistance in WWII; the **Musée de la Résistance en Morvan** (03 86 78 72 99; adult/student €4/2.50; 10.15am-6pm Easter–mid-Nov) chronicles key events and characters.

The **Verger Conservatoire**, established in 1995, is an orchard that cultivates 200 varieties of rare fruit trees. Half a dozen **trails** pass by St-Brisson.

SAULIEU
pop 2900

Once an overnight stop on the Paris–Lyon coach road, the village of Saulieu – approximately 40km from Avallon and Autun – has been renowned for its cooking for a long time, and today remains a gastronomic centre.

The **tourist office** (03 80 64 00 21; saulieu.tourisme@wanadoo.fr; 24 rue d'Argentine; 9am-12.30pm & 2-7pm daily mid-Jun–mid-Sep, 9am-noon &

2-5pm Tue-Sat mid-Sep–Feb, 9am-noon & 2-6pm Tue-Sat Mar–mid-Jun), on the N6, covers the Parc Naturel Régional du Morvan including cycling and hiking.

Musée François Pompon (03 80 64 19 51; 3 rue du Docteur Roclore; adult/student €4/2.50; 10am-noon & 2-6pm Mon & Wed-Sat, 10.30am-noon & 2-5.30pm Sun & holidays, closed Jan & Feb) displays medieval statuary and work by the local animal sculptor François Pompon (1855–1933). Next to the museum, the **Basilique St Andoche** is known for its carved capitals depicting flora, fauna and Biblical stories.

Sleeping & Eating

La Vieille Auberge (03 80 64 13 74; 15 rue Grillot; menus €12-29; closed Jan & Feb) This is a traditional inn serving Burgundy cooking at a fair price. Rustic rooms are available upstairs.

La Côte d'Or (03 80 90 53 53; www.bernard-loiseau.com; 2 rue d'Argentine; menus €122-185) The main restaurant of one of France's renowned chefs, Bernard Loiseau. The sophisticated country cuisine has earned three Michelin stars: despite the price, you won't get a table without a reservation.

Atac supermarket (rue Jean Bertin; 8.45am-12.15pm & 2.45-7pm Mon-Sat) is 300m downhill from the Restaurant Bernard Loiseau, on the D26.

Getting There & Away

SNCF trains and/or buses go to Autun (€6.90, 50 minutes, four or five daily and two on Sunday and holidays) and Avallon (€11.70, 50 to 60 minutes, three daily). **Transco** (03 80 42 11 00) runs bus No 48 to Dijon (€12, 1½ hours, once daily except on Sunday and holidays).

BURGUNDY

CHATEAU CHINON
pop 2720

Château Chinon is best known for having had François Mitterrand as its mayor from 1959 to 1981, and it was once a key strategic point for defending upper Burgundy. It now makes a convenient base for exploring the Morvan, but the modern town hasn't got much to offer.

The **tourist office** (☎ 03 86 85 06 58; otsi.chateau -chinon@wanadoo.fr; pl Notre Dame; ☒ 9am-12.30pm & 2-6pm Mon-Thu, 9am-12.30pm & 2-5pm Fri year-round) supplies brochures, maps and topoguides.

Jean Tinguely and Niki de St-Phalle's **fountain** in front of the town hall resembles the one at the Centre Pompidou in Paris.

The **Musée du Septennat** (☎ 03 86 85 19 23; 6 rue du Château; adult/concession €4/2; ☒ 10am-noon & 2-6pm Wed-Mon mid-Feb–Jun & Sep-Dec, 10am-1pm & 2-7pm Jul & Aug) displays official trinkets presented to Mitterrand during his two *septennats* (seven-year presidential terms, now reduced to five). Next door the **Musée du Costume** (☎ 03 86 85 18 55; 4 rue du Château; adult/student €4/2; ☒ 10am-noon & 2-6pm Wed-Mon Apr-Jun & Sep, 10am-1pm & 2-7pm Jul & Aug) explores French fashion since the 18th century.

Hôtel Le Vieux Morvan (☎ 03 86 85 05 01; fax 03 86 85 02 78; 8 place Gudin; d from €45; ☒ closed mid-Dec– mid-Jan, reception closed Sun night & Mon approx Nov-Apr) long served as Mitterrand's official local residence. The attached **restaurant** (menus €15-39) serves French and regional cuisine.

Hôtel Lion d'Or (☎ 03 86 85 13 56; fax 03 86 79 42 22; 10 rue des Fossés; d from €25-40; reception ☒ closed Fri evening & often Sun evening approx Nov-Mar), through the arch from place Notre Dame, is an older place with seven plain, one-star rooms.

For buses see Autun (p462).

MAQUIS BERNARD RÉSISTANCE CEMETERY

Seven RAF airmen – the crew of a bomber shot down near here in 1944 – and 21 *résistants* are buried in the neatly tended **Maquis Bernard Résistance Cemetery**, surrounded by the dense forests in which British French paratroops operated with Free French forces. The nearby **drop zone** is marked with signs.

The cemetery is about 8km southwest of Montsauche-les-Settons (along the D977) and 5.6km east of Oroux-en-Morvan (along the D12), near the tiny hamlet of Savelot. From the D977, go 2.8km along the narrow dirt road to Savelot.

CÔTE D'OR

The Côte d'Or *département* is named after one of the world's foremost wine-growing regions, which stretches from Dijon south to the wine town of Beaune and beyond. In the far northwest, Châtillon-sur-Seine displays spectacular Celtic treasures, while in the west you can visit Abbaye de Fontenay and the walled town of Semur-en-Auxois. South of Dijon is Abbaye de Cîteaux, once hugely influential.

DIJON
pop 230,000

Dijon, mustard capital of the universe, is one of France's most appealing provincial cities, with an inviting centre graced by elegant medieval and Renaissance buildings. Despite its long history, modern Dijon is a lively, dynamic city with 24,000 university students and a thriving cultural scene.

History

Dijon served as the capital of the dukes of Burgundy from the 11th to 15th centuries, reaching its golden age during the 14th and 15th centuries under Philippe-le-Hardi (Philip the Bold), Jean-sans-Peur (John the Fearless) and Philippe-le-Bon (Philip the Good). During their reigns Dijon was turned into one of the great centres of European art, but the chasm between rich and poor was always vast, and the city endured a turbulent time during the Revolution.

Orientation

Dijon's commercial centre stretches from the tourist office eastwards to Église St Michel; the main shopping streets are rue de la Liberté and rue du Bourg. Place Grangier, with its many bus stops, is north of rue de la Liberté, while the train station is at the western end of av Maréchal Foch. The old city is around place François Rude and the surrounding streets.

Information
EMERGENCY
Police Station (☎ 03 80 44 55 00; 2 place Suquet; ☒ 24hr) Access between 6pm and 7.30am is on rue du Petit Cîteaux.

INTERNET ACCESS

Multi-Rezo (☎ 03 80 66 33 21; 74 rue Vannerie; per 12min/hr €1/5; ☺ 9am-midnight Mon-Sat, 2-10pm Sun)

Netwave (☎ 03 80 30 55 16; 10 rue de la Liberté; per hour €4; h10am-10pm Mon-Sat, 4-8pm Sun)

LAUNDRY

There are laundrettes at 41 rue Auguste Comte, 28 and 55 rue Berbisey and 8 place de la Banque They are generally open 7.30am to 9pm.

MEDICAL SERVICES

The duty pharmacy and doctors are listed outside the tourist office.

Hôpital Général (☎ 03 80 29 30 31; 3 rue du Faubourg Raines; ☺ 24hr)

MONEY

Banque de France (2 place de la Banque) Usually changes money on weekday mornings.

POST

Main Post Office (pl Grangier)

TOURIST INFORMATION

Tourist Office (☎ 03 80 44 11 44; www.dijon-tourism .com; place Darcy; ☺ 9am-7pm May–mid-Oct, 10am-6pm mid-Oct–Apr) There's a branch at the airport open for incoming flights.

Tourist Office Annexe (☎ 03 80 44 11 44; 34 rue des Forges; ☺ 9am-noon & 2-6pm Mon-Sat)

UNIVERSITIES

The main **Dijon University** campus is 2km east of the centre.

Sights
MEDIEVAL & RENAISSANCE ARCHITECTURE

Once home to the region's rulers, the **Palais des Ducs et des États de Bourgogne** (Palace of the Dukes & States of Burgundy) is an elaborate complex in the heart of old Dijon. The building received its neoclassical façade in the 17th and 18th centuries when it was the seat of Burgundy's parliament. The palace overlooks **place de la Libération**, a public arcade designed by Jules Hardouin-Mansart (an architect of Versailles) in 1686.

The west wing is occupied by Dijon's **city hall**. The eastern wing houses the Musée des Beaux-Arts (see later); its entrance is next to the **Tour de Bar**, a squat 14th-century tower that once served as a prison.

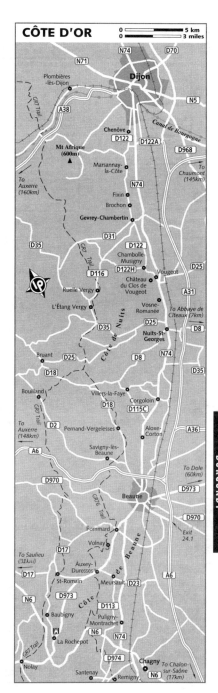

BURGUNDY

DIJON

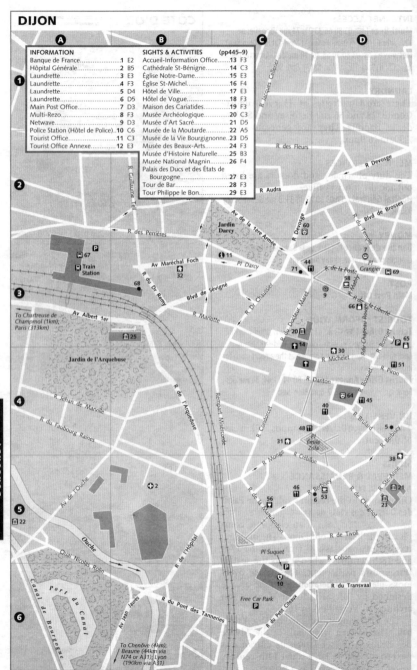

INFORMATION
Banque de France	**1** E2
Hôpital Générale	**2** B5
Laundrette	**3** E3
Laundrette	**4** F3
Laundrette	**5** D4
Laundrette	**6** D5
Main Post Office	**7** D3
Multi-Rezo	**8** F3
Netwave	**9** D3
Police Station (Hôtel de Police)	**10** C6
Tourist Office	**11** C3
Tourist Office Annexe	**12** E3

SIGHTS & ACTIVITIES (pp445–9)
Accueil-Information Office	**13** F3
Cathédrale St-Bénigne	**14** C3
Église Notre-Dame	**15** E3
Église St-Michel	**16** F4
Hôtel de Ville	**17** E3
Hôtel de Vogüe	**18** F3
Maison des Cariatides	**19** F3
Musée Archéologique	**20** C3
Musée d'Art Sacré	**21** D5
Musée de la Moutarde	**22** A5
Musée de la Vie Bourguignonne	**23** D5
Musée des Beaux-Arts	**24** F3
Musée d'Histoire Naturelle	**25** B3
Musée National Magnin	**26** F4
Palais des Ducs et des États de Bourgogne	**27** E3
Tour de Bar	**28** F3
Tour Philippe le Bon	**29** F3

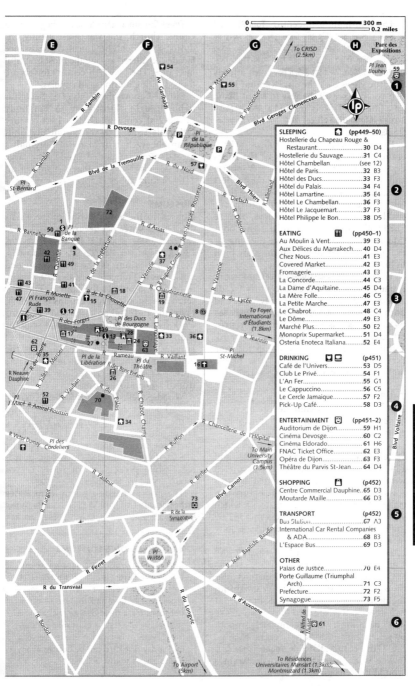

0 ────── 300 m
0 ────── 0.2 miles

E F G H

To CRISD
(2.5km)

Parc des
Expositions

Pl Jean
Bouhey 59

🚌 54

🚌 55

Av Garibaldi

R Marceau

R Parmentier

Blvd Geroges Clemenceau

R Sambin

R Devosge

Pl
de la
République

R du Nord

Blvd de la Tremouille

R Lallemand

Blvd Thiers

R Dietsch

R Diderot

Pl
St-Bernard

R Samblin

57 🚌

72

R d'Assas

R Jean-Jacques Rousseau

R Vannerie

R du Lycée

50 1 🏧 Pl
de la
Banque

R Bannelier

R Chabot

R de la Préfecture

42 🏛

3

49

4 ◆ 🏛
37

Auguste Comte

R Verrerie

R Chaudronnerie

43

47

41

Pl François
Rude

39 12

R Musette

R de la Chouette

15

R des Forges

18 🏛

19 🏛

8 @

R Jeannin

To Foyer
International
d'Étudiants
(1.8km)

62

35

R du Bourg

R Mercier

17 🏛

29

13

28

R Jeannin

24

33

36

Pl
St-Michel

63

R Neauve
Dauphine

R Jules Mercier

Pl de la
Libération

Pl du
Théâtre

Rameau

R Vaillant

16

R Vauban

52

J Macé

R Amiral Roussin

R du
Palais

70

R des Bons Enfants

26

34

R Victor Dumay

Pl des
Cordeliers

R Chabot Charny

R Chancellerie de l'Hôpital

To Main
University
Campus
(1.5km)

R Pasteur

R Berbier

Blvd Carnot

73

R de la
Synagogue

R Turgot

R Ferret

Pl
Wilson

2 Jedi Baptiste Baudin

R du Longvic

R d'Auxonne

R du Transvaal

R Bossut

R Alfred de
Musset

61

To Airport
(5km)

To Résidences
Universitaires Mansart (1.3km);
Montmuzard (1.3km)

Blvd Voltaire

BURGUNDY

SLEEPING 🏠 (pp449–50)
Hostellerie du Chapeau Rouge &
  Restaurant.........................**30** D4
Hostellerie du Sauvage..........**31** C4
Hôtel Chambellan..............(see 12)
Hôtel de Paris......................**32** B3
Hôtel des Ducs.....................**33** F3
Hôtel du Palais....................**34** F4
Hôtel Lamartine...................**35** E4
Hôtel Le Chambellan............**36** F3
Hôtel Le Jacquemart.............**37** F3
Hôtel Philippe le Bon............**38** D5

EATING 🍽 (pp450–1)
Au Moulin à Vent.................**39** E3
Aux Délices du Marrakech.....**40** D4
Chez Nous..........................**41** E3
Covered Market....................**42** E3
Fromagerie..........................**43** E3
La Concorde........................**44** C3
La Dame d'Aquitaine.............**45** D4
La Mère Folle......................**46** C5
La Petite Marche..................**47** E3
Le Chabrot..........................**48** C4
Le Dôme.............................**49** E3
Marché Plus.........................**50** E2
Monoprix Supermarket..........**51** D4
Osteria Enoteca Italiana.........**52** E4

DRINKING 🍷🍺 (p451)
Café de l'Univers.................**53** D5
Club Le Privé.......................**54** F1
L'An Fer.............................**55** G1
Le Cappuccino.....................**56** C5
Le Cercle Jamaïque...............**57** F2
Pick-Up Café.......................**58** D3

ENTERTAINMENT 🎭 (pp451–2)
Auditorium de Dijon.............**59** H1
Cinéma Devosge...................**60** C2
Cinéma Eldorado..................**61** H6
FNAC Ticket Office...............**62** E3
Opéra de Dijon....................**63** F3
Théâtre du Parvis St-Jean.......**64** D4

SHOPPING 🛍 (p452)
Centre Commercial Dauphine..**65** D3
Moutarde Maille..................**66** D3

TRANSPORT (p452)
Bus Station.........................**67** A3
International Car Rental Companies
  & ADA............................**68** B3
L'Espace Bus.......................**69** D3

OTHER
Palais de Justice...................**70** E4
Porte Guillaume (Triumphal
  Arch)..............................**71** C3
Prefecture...........................**72** F2
Synagogue..........................**73** F5

The 46m-high, 15th-century **Tour Philippe le Bon** (Tower of Philip the Good; place des Ducs de Bourgogne; adult/concession €2.30/1.20; 9am-noon & 1.45-5.30pm Thu-Tue Easter-end Nov, 9am-11pm Thu-Tue & 1.30-3.30pm Wed Sat & Sun Nov-Easter) affords fantastic views over the city. Rumour has it that you can see all the way to Mont Blanc on a fine day. Tickets are sold at the nearby **Accueil-Information office** (03 80 74 52 71; until 5.30pm or 6pm).

Dijon's finest **hôtels particuliers** (aristocratic townhouses) are north of the Palais des Ducs around rues Verrerie, Vannerie and des Forges. The street names reflect the industries that once thrived along them (glassmakers, basket-weavers and metalsmiths respectively); these days, they're lined with antique shops and designer boutiques. Some houses still have their medieval timbered frontages, but most are built in luxurious Renaissance stone.

The **Maison des Cariatides** (28 rue Chaudronnerie) is particularly fine; its 17th-century façade is decorated with stone caryatids, vines and horns. Nearby, the splendid **Hôtel Chambellan** (34 rue des Forges) is occupied by the tourist office annexe. From the interior courtyard, a spiral stone staircase leads up to some carved vaulting and a great view of the building's 17th-century architecture.

CHURCHES
All of Dijon's major churches are open until sunset (approximately 8pm in summer) every day.

A little way north of the Palais des Ducs, **Église Notre Dame** was built between 1220 and 1240. The façade's three tiers are decorated with leering gargoyles separated by two rows of columns and the 14th-century **Horloge à Jacquemart** (Jacquemart Clock), which was transported from Flanders in 1382 by Philip the Bold, who claimed it as a trophy of war. It chimes every quarter-hour. The interior has a vast transept crossing and 13th-century stained glass.

Outside, **rue de la Chouette** is named after the small stone *chouette* (owl) carved into the north wall of the church. Said to grant happiness and wisdom to those who stroke it, it's been worn almost completely smooth by generations of fortune-seekers. Nearby, the 17th-century **Hôtel de Vogüé** (8 rue de la Chouette) is renowned for the ornate carvings around its Renaissance courtyard.

Église St-Michel (place St-Michel) began as a Gothic church, but was subsequently endowed with a richly ornamented Renaissance façade considered among the most beautiful in France. The two 17th-century towers are topped with glittering gold cupolas.

Situated above the tomb of St Benignus (who brought Christianity to Burgundy in the 2nd century), Dijon's 13th-century **Cathédrale St-Bénigne** was originally built as an abbey church. Many of Burgundy's great figures are buried inside. The large **crypt** (admission €1) is all that remains of an 11th-century abbey chapel.

MUSEUMS
Housed in the eastern wing of the Palais des Ducs, **Musée des Beaux-Arts** (03 80 74 52 70; adult/senior/student €3.40/1.60/free, Sun free; 9.30am-6pm Wed-Mon May-Oct, 10am-5pm Wed-Mon Nov-Apr) is one of the most renowned museums in France – considered by many to be second only to the Louvre. The museum has important collections of French, Flemish and Italian art, and contains work by local figures such as the sculptor Francis Rude and the designer/architect Hugues Sambin. You can also visit the huge **ducal kitchens**. The kitchens and the museum's modern art section are closed from 11.45am to 1.45pm.

Wood-panelled **Salle des Gardes** (Guards' Room) houses the carved sepulchres of two of the Valois dukes of Burgundy, Philippe le Hardi, and Jean sans Peur and his wife Marguerite de Bavière. Both tombs are topped by life-size figures attended by angelic guardians, while processions of finely carved mourners adorn the sides.

The city's archaeological museum, **Musée Archéologique** (03 80 30 88 54; 5 rue du Docteur Maret; adult/senior/student €2.20/1.10/free, Sun free;

VISITING DIJON'S MUSEUMS

Dijon has several outstanding museums. The **Dijon Card** (1-/2-/3-day pass €8/11/14) gets you into the main ones, and includes a guided city tour and the use of public transport. It's a great deal unless you're a student, in which case most museums are free. Several museums are free to everyone on Sunday. The card can be bought at any of the town's tourist offices.

9.30am-12.30pm & 1.30-6pm Wed-Sun Oct-May, 9.30am-6pm Jun-Sep), displays Celtic artefacts and a particularly fine 1st-century bronze of the goddess Sequana standing on a boat. The 11th-century chamber on the lowest level was once part of a Benedictine abbey.

Housed in a 17th-century *hôtel particulier*, **Musée National Magnin** (☎ 03 80 67 11 10; 4 rue des Bons Enfants; adult/student €3/2.30, Sun €2.30, first Sun of month free; ☺ 10am-noon & 2-6pm Tue-Sun) displays works of art donated to the city in 1938 by the brother and sister team of Jeanne and Maurice Magnin.

In the copper-domed chapels of a neoclassical church (1709), the ecclesiastical **Musée d'Art Sacré** (☎ 03 80 44 12 69; 15 rue Ste Anne; adult/senior/student €2.80/1.60/free, Sun free; ☺ 9am-noon & 2-6pm Wed-Mon) displays objects from the 12th to 19th centuries. Almost next door and included in the ticket price, **Musée de la Vie Bourguignonne** (☎ 03 80 44 12 69; 17 rue Ste Anne; ☺ 9am-noon & 2-6pm Wed-Mon) occupies a 17th-century Cistercian convent and explores rural life in Burgundy in past centuries.

Finally, you can't leave Dijon without paying homage to the city's most famous export, **Musée de la Moutarde** (Musée Amora; 48 quai Nicolas Rolin; adult/under 12 incl tour €3/free; tours ☺ 3pm Mon-Sat Jun-Sep, Wed & Sat Oct). Visits to the mustard museum at the factory of Amora, Dijon's main mustard company, must be arranged at the tourist office on place Darcy.

In Dijon's botanical park, **Jardin de l'Arquebuse**, you'll find a stream, pond and formal gardens. The city's **Musée d'Histoire Naturelle** (Natural History Museum; ☎ 03 80 76 82 76; adult/student €2/free, Sun free; ☺ 9am-noon & 2-6pm except Tue, Sat & Sun morning) is near the entrance.

OTHER SIGHTS

Dijon has plenty of green spaces. Try **Jardin Darcy** (next to the tourist office), **Jardin de l'Arquebuse**, **place des Ducs de Bourgogne** (just north of the Palais des Ducs) and **place St-Michel** (next to Église St Michel).

Founded in 1383 **Chartreuse de Champmol** (Carthusian monastery; 1 blvd Chanione Kir; ☺ 8am-6pm) was almost completely destroyed during the Revolution. The famous **Puits de Moïse** (Well of Moses), a grouping of six Old Testament figures by Claus Sluter between 1395 and 1405, is undergoing restoration. Another Sluter work, the **Portail de la Chapelle** (Chapel Doorway) is nearby. The site, 1.2km west of the train station, is now occupied (bizarrely) by a psychiatric hospital.

Tours

The tourist office (p445) publishes the *Owl's Trail* (€2), a brochure detailing a self-guided walking tour of the city centre; the route is marked on the pavement by red arrows. The tourist office also runs English-language walking tours of the city, including *nocturnes* at 10pm in July and August. They cost €6/9/3 for adults/couples/concessions. The two-hour Visite Audioguidée (Walkman tour) costs €6.

Circuits des Châteaux bus tours to the region's chateaux, churches and abbeys run most Sundays from late June to September. They cost €40/50 per half-/full day. Commentary is in French. Tickets are arranged through the tourist office. You can also reserve places for Couleurs Bourgogne, two- or three-day trips around Burgundy with a gastronomic theme.

Wine & Voyages (☎ 03 80 61 15 15; www.wineandvoyages.com; 2/3hr tours €45/50, full day €95; ☺ early Mar–mid-Dec) runs minibus tours in French and English, including circuits of the Côte de Nuits vineyards. It's essential to reserve ahead.

Festivals & Events

The **Folkloriades Internationales et Fêtes de la Vigne** is week-long dance festival held in August or September. **Foire Internationale et Gastronomique**, in late-October to November and held at the Parc des Expositions, gives visitors the chance to sample cuisines from Burgundy and around the world. **L'Estivade** brings theatre, ballet and concerts to town in late June to July.

Sleeping

The best hotels in Dijon are around the old city or near the restaurants and bars southwest of the centre. Considering the city's size and prosperity, hotels in Dijon are surprisingly affordable.

BUDGET

Centre de Rencontres Internationales et de Séjour de Dijon (CRISD; ☎ 03 80 72 95 20; reservation@auberge -cri-dijon.com; 1 blvd Champollion; s/d/q per person €26/16/14) An institutional, 260-bed place 2.5km northeast of the centre. By bus, take

BURGUNDY

No 5 (towards Épirey) from place Grangier; at night take line A to Épirey.

Hôtel le Chambellan (☎ 03 80 67 12 67; hotel chambellan@aol.com; 92 rue Vannerie; s €34-48, d €42-52) A great deal on one of the city's oldest streets. The pretty building is typical of the area, with flower boxes and shuttered windows, and there is a small 17th-century courtyard where breakfast is served in summer.

Hôtel Lamartine (☎ 03 80 30 37 47; www.ot-dijon .fr; 12 rue Jules Mercier; s/d €31/47; reception ⏰ closed noon-3pm) On a shabby backstreet just off rue du Bourg. The 14 rooms are plain and the street views are uninspiring, but the location is unbeatable – the Palais des Ducs is a few steps from the front door.

Hôtel de Paris (☎ 03 80 43 41 88; hoteldeparis dijon@minitel.net; 9-11 av du Maréchal Foch) This hotel is on the traffic-thronged road to the train station, so it can get noisy, but it's a useful option if you're got an early connection. Pastel shades and boxy rooms make for a cosy night's sleep.

MID-RANGE

Hôtel du Palais (☎ 03 80 67 16 26; fax 03 80 65 12 16; 23 rue du Palais; s with shower €30-37, d with shower €34-43, s with bath €40-45, d with bath €48-65, tr with bath €52-70) One of Dijon's best-kept secrets, a smart hotel housed in a former *hôtel particulier* near the Quartier d'Antiquaires. The rooms are spacious and welcoming (the best are on the first floor), and the place oozes old-fashioned charm from every corner.

Hostellerie du Sauvage (☎ 03 80 41 31 21; hotel dusauvage@free.fr; 64 rue Monge; d from €41) On a charming cobbled courtyard in a 15th-century *relais de poste* (relay posthouse), this great value hotel is off buzzy rue Monge. Parking is available in the old carriage-houses for €4 per day.

Hôtel Le Jacquemart (☎ 03 80 60 09 60; www .hotel-lejacquemart.fr; 32 rue Verrerie; d €28-54, ste €60) Right in the heart of old Dijon in a 17th-century building, this hotel offers 31 quaint and comfortable rooms. The window boxes make it a pretty place to arrive in summer.

Hôtel des Ducs (☎ 03 80 67 31 31; fax 03 80 67 19 51; 5 rue Lamonnaye; d €54-74, tw €79-87, ste €106; Ⓟ 🔀) A modern hotel, opposite the Opéra de Dijon and around the corner from Église St-Michel. Most rooms have small balconies onto the street. If you're looking for a city-style hotel, this is a good choice.

TOP END

Hôtel Philippe le Bon (☎ 03 80 30 73 52; www.hotel philippelebon.com in French; 18 rue Ste-Anne; d €79-103; Ⓟ 🔀) Thirty-six stylish, contemporary rooms in a buzzy setting near the cafés and restaurants of rue Berbisey. There is a small garden, a decent restaurant and parking is included.

Hostellerie du Chapeau Rouge (☎ 03 80 50 88 88, www.chapeau-rouge.fr; 5 rue Michelet; d €130-197; 🔀) A Dijon institution since 1847, and one of the city's most luxurious places to stay, with four stars, 30 Jacuzzi-equipped rooms and an inevitably stuffy atmosphere. The attached restaurant is one of the city's best.

Eating

As Burgundy's foremost city, Dijon has no shortage of excellent places to eat, ranging from cheap creperies to the highest *haute cuisine*. The best restaurants are around rue Berbisey and place Émile Zola, and along rue Bannelier and rue Quentin, next to the covered market.

RESTAURANTS

Hostellerie du Chapeau Rouge (see above; menus with/without wine €42/35) Features bold, creative French cuisine based on traditional ingredients and top-quality local produce. For gastrophiles, the restaurant offers two gourmet menus; €75 buys seven sumptuous courses, while €100 gets a belt-busting 11.

La Dame d'Aquitaine (☎ 03 80 30 45 65; 23 pl Bossuet; menus €18-36; ⏰ closed Sun & lunch Mon) Excellent Burgundian and southwestern French cuisine and the atmospheric location in a vaulted 13th-century cellar make this one of Dijon's most renowned restaurants.

Le Chabrot (☎ 03 80 30 69 01; 36 rue Monge; menus €11-27; ⏰ lunch & dinner Mon-Sat) An attractive wine bar serving traditional French cooking. The relaxed atmosphere, candle-lit tables and rustic décor make it popular with gourmets and wine-lovers alike.

Aux Délices du Marrakech (☎ 03 80 30 82 69; 20 rue Monge; dishes €10-25; ⏰ closed lunch Mon), On the same street as Le Chabrot, this excellent Moroccan restaurant boasts an ornately decorated dining room with an unmistakably North-African ambiance, and the huge portions of tajine and couscous are just as authentic.

La Mère Folle (☎ 03 80 50 19 76; 102 rue Berbisey; menus €12-22; ⏰ closed lunch Sat) A relaxed and

BURGUNDY

rather camp French restaurant serving unusual variations on traditional dishes, such as *bœuf bourguignon* with tagliatelle. The restaurant itself is crammed with character, from the baroque mirrors on the walls to the pineapple-shaped lights on the tables – even the drinking water is different (appropriately enough, it's served in watering cans).

La Petite Marche (☎ 03 80 30 15 10; 27-29 rue Musette; menus €10-15; ☺ lunch Mon-Sat) Vegetarians tired of Burgundy's meat-heavy menus should head for this popular organic restaurant, renowned as one of the best in France.

Osteria Enoteca Italiana (☎ 03 80 50 07 36; 32 rue Amiral Roussin; lunch menu €14; ☺ Tue-Sun) A small Italian diner with delicious pasta and fish dishes.

CAFÉS & QUICK EATS
Au Moulin à Vent (☎ 03 80 30 81 43; 8 pl François Rude; ☺ closed Mon & dinner Sun) A quintessentially French street-side café opposite the fountain on place François Rude. There's a large terrace outside and a snug restaurant upstairs serving local specialities.

La Concorde (☎ 03 80 30 69 43; 2 pl Darcy) This classic Art Deco styled café and brasserie occupies a great position overlooking busy Darcy. The pavement conservatory is the place for morning coffee and late-night drinking, and inside there's a fine restaurant serving excellent bistro food.

Le Dôme (☎ 03 80 30 58 92; 16bis, rue Quentin; menus from €12, formule midi €12; ☺ closed dinner Sun) In the dynamic area around the covered market, this smart café has lots of outside tables where you can sit and watch the city go by. The *formule midi* includes entrée, plat du jour and coffee.

SELF-CATERING
For picnic treats head for the 19th-century **covered market** (Halles du Marché; rue Quentin; ☺ until 1pm Tue & Thu-Sat) and the nearby **fromagerie** (28 rue Musette; ☺ closed Sun & Mon morning). Supermarkets include **Monoprix supermarket** (11-13 rue Piron; ☺ 9am-9pm Mon-Sat) and **Marché Plus** (rue Bannelier; ☺ 7am-9pm Mon-Sat, 9am-noon Sun).

Drinking
Pick-Up Café (☎ 03 80 30 61 44; 9 rue Mably; ☺ 8am-2am) A typically French idea of an American bar-diner, complete with jukeboxes and pinball machines.

Le Cercle Jamaïque (Rhumerie; ☎ 03 80 73 52 19; 14 place de la République; ☺ 2pm-4am Tue-Sat) A large bar that specialises in rum cocktails and is decked out with tacky Chinese-baroque décor. There's often live music (ranging from Cuban to jazz) from about 11pm to 3.30am. Downstairs, there's a **club** (☺ 11pm-4am Thu-Sat) that plays everything but techno (cover charge from €6).

Café de l'Univers (☎ 03 80 30 98 29; 47 rue Berbisey; ☺ 9am-2am) One of many convivial café-bars along rue Berbisey. Downstairs there's a cellar with a small **dance floor** (☺ 10pm-2am Thu-Sun, to noon weekends).

Le Cappuccino (☎ 03 80 41 06 35; 132 rue Berbisey; ☺ 3pm-2am) Despite the name, this is one of Dijon's most popular beer bars, with a varied selection of bottled and draught beers from all over Europe. The dimly lit interior regularly hosts bands and live music events, and it's always jammed with a lively crowd on weekends.

Entertainment
For the latest on Dijon's cultural scene, pick up *Spectacles*, available free from the tourist office. Events tickets are sold at the **Fnac ticket office** (☎ 08 92 68 36 22; www.fnac.com in French; 24 rue du Bourg; ☺ 10am-7pm Tue-Fri, 9.30-7pm Sat, 1-7pm Mon).

NIGHTCLUBS
Dijon's club scene is centred around place de la République.

L'An-Fer (☎ 03 80 70 03 69; 8 rue Marceau; admission with/without drink Wed & Thu €7/5, Fri €9.50, Sat & Sun €8; ☺ 11pm-5am Wed-Sun, closed Wed mid-Jul–mid-Sep) L'An-Fer achieved fame for pioneering techno music (Laurent Garnier worked here for four years); house takes centre stage on Saturday.

Club Le Privé (☎ 03 80 73 39 57; 20 av Garibaldi; admission Sun-Thu €5, Fri & Sat €8; ☺ 10pm-5am) The bright lights and leopard-skin banquettes say it all – this is a cheesy club popular with Dijon's students and bright young things.

CINEMAS
Cinéma Eldorado (☎ 03 80 66 51 89; 21 rue Alfred de Musset; ☺ closed mid-Jul–mid-Aug) A three-screen arts cinema where nondubbed films flicker nightly.

Cinéma Devosge (☎ 03 80 30 74 79; 6 rue Devosge) Usually has a nondubbed film playing next to the new releases.

THEATRE

Théâtre du Parvis St-Jean (☎ 03 80 30 12 12; www.tdb-cdn.com in French; rue Monge) In the converted Église St-Jean on rue Monge, presents dance, music and theatre, including classics and new work.

CLASSICAL MUSIC & DANCE

Auditorium de Dijon (☎ 03 80 60 44 44; www.leduodijon.com in French; 11 blvd de Verdun) Presents concerts, opera and dance from September through to June.

Shopping

Moutarde Maille (☎ 03 80 30 41 02; 32 rue de la Liberté; 9am-7pm Mon-Sat) Buy gourmet mustard at this factory shop of the company that makes Grey-Poupon. You can even have it dispensed from the pump.

Mulot & Petitjean (☎ 03 80 30 07 10; mulot.petitjean@wanadoo.fr; 13 place Bossuet; 9am-noon & 2-7pm, closed Sun morning) Dijon has lots of sumptuous patisseries; one of the best-known is Mulot & Petitjean, which sells the finest *pains d'épices* in town.

Getting There & Away

AIR

Aéroport Dijon-Bourgogne airport (☎ 03 80 67 67 67; www.dijon.aeroport.fr) is 5km southeast of the city centre, but lack of demand has meant regular scheduled flights are currently suspended.

BUS

The bus station is in the train station complex. Details on services are available at the **Transco information counter** (☎ 03 80 42 11 00; 5.30am-8.30pm Mon-Fri, 6.45am-12.30pm & 4-8.30pm Sat, 10am-1pm & 4pm-8.30pm Sun). Timetables are posted on the platforms; tickets are sold on board.

Lines to the Côte d'Or include No 44 to Beaune and No 60, which serves Gevrey-Chambertin (€1.70, 30 minutes, 15 to 18 Monday to Saturday, fewer on Sundays) via Fixin and Marsannay-la-Côte. See the following sections for details about Transco transport to/from Autun (p462), Avallon (p440), Châtillon-sur-Seine (p459), Saulieu (p443) and Semur-en-Auxois (p458).

CAR

Major rental companies and **ADA** (☎ 03 80 53 15 56) have *bureaux* in the train station.

TRAIN

The **train station** (rue du Docteur Remy) is in the western part of Dijon. Paris' Gare de Lyon is just 1¾ hours away by TGV (€46.20, nine to 16). Most trains to Lyon (€22.50, two hours, at least 12 daily) go to Gare de la Part-Dieu. Other long-haul destinations include Nice (€76.20, six hours, two daily) and Strasbourg (€34.60, four hours, three or four non-direct daily).

Getting Around

BUS

Details on Dijon's bus network, operated by STRD, are available from **L'Espace Bus** (☎ 03 80 30 60 90; pl Grangier; 7.15am-7.15pm Mon-Fri, 7.15am-12.15pm & 2.15-7.15pm Sat). Single tickets, sold by drivers, cost €0.80 and last for an hour; a Forfait Journée ticket is valid all day and costs €2.70 (available from the tourist office or L'Espace Bus).

Bus lines are known by their number and destination. In the city centre, seven lines stop along rue de la Liberté, and five more have stops around place Grangier. Most lines operate until 8.30pm; after that, the six lines of the Réseau du Soir (A, B, C, D, E and F) run every 30 minutes or so until 12.15am. The train station is linked with the city centre (rue de la Liberté) by bus Nos 1, 9 and 12.

CAR & MOTORCYCLE

All city centre parking is metered. Free spots are available (clockwise from the train station): northwest of rue Devosge, northeast of blvd Thiers, southeast of blvd Carnot and south of rue du Transvaal. There's a big free car park at place Suquet, just south of the police station. As in many French cities, the one-way system is hellish – a detailed city map (such as Michelin) is a very good idea.

TAXI

A taxi is just a phone call away on ☎ 03 80 41 41 12, available 24 hours a day.

CÔTE D'OR VINEYARDS

Burgundy's finest vintages come from the vine-covered Côte d'Or (Golden Hillside; p445), the narrow, eastern slopes of a limestone, flint and clay ridge that run south from Dijon for about 60km. The northern section, the **Côte de Nuits**, stretches from the village of Fixin south to Corgoloin and produces reds known for their full-bodied, robust character. The southern section, the **Côte de Beaune**, lies between Aloxe-Corton and Santenay and produces great reds and great whites.

The wonderful wine-making villages of the Côted'Or include (from north to south): Marsannay-la-Côte, Fixin, Brochon, Gevrey-Chambertin, Vougeot, Vosne-Romanée, Nuits-St-Georges, Pernand-Vergelesses, Aloxe-Corton and Savigny-lès-Beaune, all north of Beaune; and Pommard, Volnay, St-Romain, Auxey-Duresses, Meursault, Puligny-Montrachet, Rochepot and Sante-nay, all south of Beaune. Just hearing these names makes wine-buffs go weak at the knees.

Wine Tasting

Look for signs reading *dégustation* (tasting), *domaine* (wine-making estate), *chateau*, or *cave* (wine cellar) around the villages of Côte d'Or. Another key term is *gratuit* (free); visitors are still expected to be serious about making a purchase. Places offering more than a few wines to try usually charge a fee.

Walking & Cycling

The GR7 and GR76 run along sections of the Côte d'Or. Much of the route follows tertiary roads west of the N74. The Beaune tourist office sells cycling guides covering Côte d'Or villages.

To get from Dijon to Beaune by bike, follow the quiet D122 through the vineyards until Nuits-St-Georges, and then take the D8 and the D115C. The ride takes three or four hours and covers about 40km. To avoid cycling both ways, you can take your bike on the train for the return trip, but this is possible only on certain runs – contact the SNCF for details.

Getting Around

Apart from hiring a hot-air balloon or cycling, the best way to see the Côte d'Or is by car. Getting around by bus and train is possible but can be taxing.

The best trail for wine-lovers to follow is the 'Route des Grands Crus', a signposted route that winds through the region's most famous villages – though if you're tasting wine at every stop, you might not get very far in a day.

BURGUNDY WINE: TOP FIVE FACTS

- Red wines in Burgundy are made only with the Pinot Noir grape; whites are made with the Chardonnay grape.

- Burgundy has 37,500 hectares of vineyards, which produce around 40m gallons of wine every year.

- Cistercian monks were the first to plant vines on the Côte d'Or in the 12th century.

- The outbreak of the phylloxera bug in 1878 decimated the majority of Burgundy's vineyards.

- The best wines come from the higher slopes of the Côte d'Or.

BEAUNE
pop 22,000

Beaune (pronounced similarly to bone) is the unofficial capital of the Côte d'Or. The thriving town's *raison d'être* is wine – making it, tasting it, selling it, but most of all, drinking it. Consequently Beaune is one of the best places in France for wine-tasting. The old city also contains the magnificent Hôtel-Dieu, France's most beautiful medieval charity hospital.

History

Like many other towns in Burgundy, Beaune was founded on the site of a Roman fort (named Belen after a Gaulish sun god). For a short time during the reign of the dukes of Burgundy, Beaune became the region's capital, but declined in political importance following the death of the last Valois dukes. Beaune later became a centre for the cloth and wine industries, and remains a hugely prosperous commercial centre, but the town's fortified walls and martial architecture (as well as its vast medieval hospices) are reminders of more unsettled times.

Orientation

The old city is partly enclosed by ramparts and encircled by a one-way boulevard. The train station is 1km east of the tourist office, and most of the town's sights. The main commercial area centres on place Carnot. Rue Monge and rue Carnot are pedestrianised.

BURGUNDY

Information
BOOKSHOPS
Athenaeum de la Vigne et du Vin (☎ 03 80 25
08 30; 7 rue de l'Hôtel-Dieu; ⏰ 10am-7pm) Specialist
bookseller with thousands of oenological titles (the art and
science of wine-making).

LAUNDRY
Laundrette (19 rue du Faubourg St-Jean; ⏰ 7.00am-9pm)

MONEY
The tourist office changes money on Saturday, Sunday and holidays in summer.
Banque de France (26 pl Monge) May change money
from 8.45am to noon Monday to Friday.

POST
Post Office (7 blvd St Jacques)

TOURIST INFORMATION
Tourist Office (☎ 03 80 26 21 30; www.beaune
-burgundy.com; 1 rue de l'Hôtel-Dieu; ⏰ 9.30am-8pm
Mon-Sat 21 Jun-21 Sep, 9.30am-7pm Mon-Sat Apr-20 Jun
& 22 Sep–mid-Nov, 10am-6pm Mon-Sat mid-Nov–Mar,
10am-12.30pm & 2-5pm or 6pm Sun year-round)

Sights
Hôtel-Dieu des Hospices de Beaune (☎ 03 80 24
45 00; rue de l'Hôtel-Dieu; adult/student/under 18 €5.40/
4.50/2.60; ⏰ 9am-6.30pm Easter–mid-Nov, 9am-11.30am
& 2pm-5.30pm mid-Nov–Easter), Beaune's celeb
rated charity hospital, was founded in 1443
by Nicolas Rolin (chancellor to Philip the
Good). Behind the Gothic frontage, the
hospice opens into a stone courtyard, surrounded by ornate turrets and pitched
rooftops covered in multicoloured tiles.

PASS BEAUNE

This pick-and-mix pass, offered by the
Beaune tourist office, offers discounts on
local attractions. Sample itineraries include
Pass Beaune Maxi (€21.20), which gives
admission to Hôtel-Dieu, Beaune's museums, a wine cellar visit and a tourist train-
ride; and **Pass Chateau Trio** (€14.85), which
gives admission to the chateaux of Sully,
Rochepot and Demigny. Alternatively, you
can devise your own itinerary (possible
items include hot-air balloon flights, abbey
visits and cellar tours). In general the passes
offer 5%, 10% or 15% off for two, three or
four attractions.

You can also visit the Grande'Salle, the
hospice's main sick room (look out for
dragon-motifs on the roof-beams) and the
18th-century pharmacy, lined with pottery flasks once filled with newt's eyes and
vomit-nut powder. Another highlight is
the graphic **Polyptych of the Last Judgement**
(1443), an ornate altar-piece by the Flemish painter Roger van der Weyden.

Basilique Collégiale Notre Dame (admission tapestries €2.30; ⏰ 9am-7pm, tapestries 9.30am-12.30pm &
2-5pm Mon-Sat mid-Apr–mid-Nov), a 11th- to 15th-
century church affiliated with the Cluny
Monastery, it displays medieval tapestries
commissioned by the Rolin clan.

Musée du Vin de Bourgogne (Museum of Burgundy
Wines; ☎ 03 80 22 08 19; rue d'Enfer; admission €5.40;
⏰ 9.30am-5pm Wed-Mon Jan-Mar, 9.30am-6pm Wed-Mon
Apr-Dec) has exhibits on wine production.

Musée des Beaux-Arts (☎ 03 80 24 98 70; 6 blvd
Perpreuil; admission €5.40; ⏰ 2-6pm Apr-Sep) features
Gallo-Roman carvings and assorted paint-
ings, including works by Beaune-born Félix
Ziem (1821–1911).

Musée Marey (☎ 03 80 24 56 92; rue de l'Hôtel de
Ville; admission €5.40; ⏰ 2-6pm Apr-Oct), in the southern wing of the Hôtel de Ville (town hall), is
dedicated to early cinematography.

Beaune's stone **ramparts**, which shelter
private wine cellars and wild, overgrown
gardens, are ringed by a pathway that
makes a lovely afternoon stroll.

Activities
WINE TASTING
Underneath Beaune, millions of dusty bottles of wine are being aged to perfection in
cool, dark, cobweb-lined cellars. Everyone
in town seems to be cultivating their own
personal *cave* – to get you started, there are
many places in town where you can sample
fine wines.

Marché aux Vins (☎ 03 80 25 08 20; www
.marcheauxvins.com in French; 2 rue Nicolas Rolin; tastings
⏰ 10-11am & 2-5pm mid-Sep–mid-Jun, 9.30am-5.45pm
mid-Jun–mid-Sep) During this tour, using a
tastevin (a flat metal cup with shiny surfaces, which help you admire the wine's colour) you'll sample 18 wines in the candle-lit
former Église des Cordeliers and its cellars.
Tastings last an hour.

Reine Pédauque (☎ 03 80 22 23 11; www.reine
-pedauque.com in French; rue de Lorraine; tastings
⏰ 10-11.30am & 2-4pm mid-Nov-Mar, 9.30-11.30am
& 2-5.30pm Apr–mid-Nov) During a 45-minute

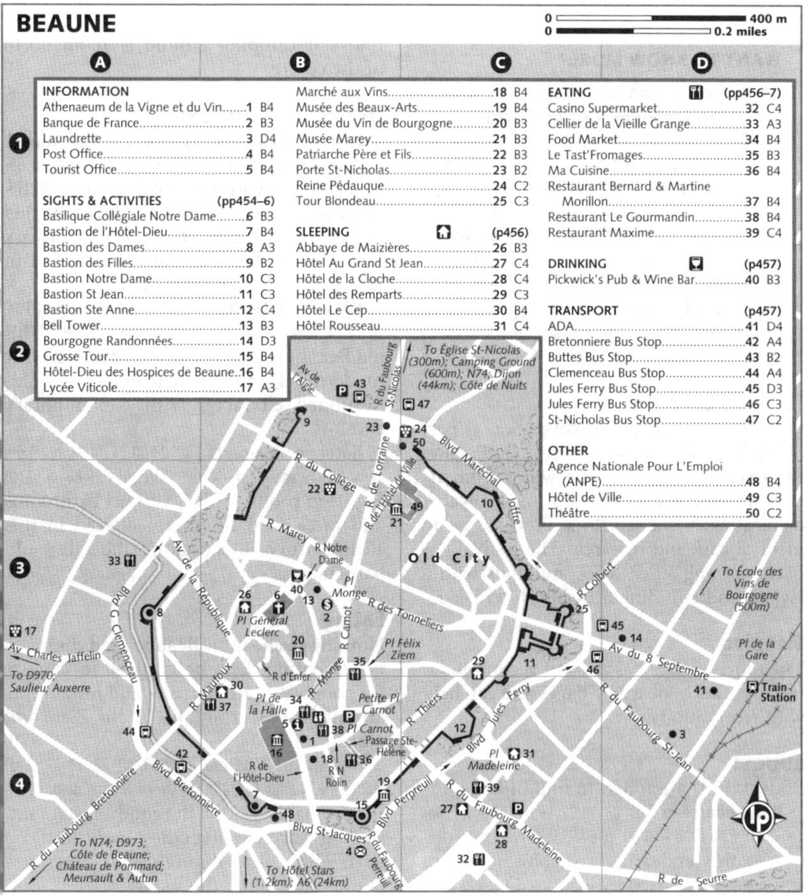
BEAUNE
0 400 m
0 0.2 miles
A B C D
1 2 3 4
INFORMATION
Athenaeum de la Vigne et du Vin 1 B4
Banque de France 2 B3
Laundrette 3 D4
Post Office 4 B4
Tourist Office 5 B4
SIGHTS & ACTIVITIES (pp454–6)
Basilique Collégiale Notre Dame 6 B3
Bastion de l'Hôtel-Dieu 7 B4
Bastion des Dames 8 A3
Bastion des Filles 9 B2
Bastion Notre Dame 10 C3
Bastion St Jean 11 C3
Bastion Ste Anne 12 C4
Bell Tower 13 B3
Bourgogne Randonnées 14 D3
Grosse Tour 15 B4
Hôtel-Dieu des Hospices de Beaune 16 B4
Lycée Viticole 17 A3
Marché aux Vins 18 B4
Musée des Beaux-Arts 19 B4
Musée du Vin de Bourgogne 20 B3
Musée Marey 21 B3
Patriarche Père et Fils 22 B3
Porte St-Nicholas 23 B2
Reine Pédauque 24 C2
Tour Blondeau 25 C3
SLEEPING (p456)
Abbaye de Maizières 26 B3
Hôtel Au Grand St Jean 27 C4
Hôtel de la Cloche 28 C4
Hôtel des Remparts 29 C3
Hôtel Le Cep 30 B4
Hôtel Rousseau 31 C4
EATING (pp456–7)
Casino Supermarket 32 C4
Cellier de la Vieille Grange 33 A3
Food Market 34 B4
Le Tast'Fromages 35 B3
Ma Cuisine 36 B4
Restaurant Bernard & Martine Morillon 37 B4
Restaurant Le Gourmandin 38 B4
Restaurant Maxime 39 C4
DRINKING (p457)
Pickwick's Pub & Wine Bar 40 B3
TRANSPORT (p457)
ADA 41 D4
Bretonniere Bus Stop 42 A4
Buttes Bus Stop 43 B2
Clemenceau Bus Stop 44 A4
Jules Ferry Bus Stop 45 D3
Jules Ferry Bus Stop 46 C3
St-Nicholas Bus Stop 47 C2
OTHER
Agence Nationale Pour L'Emploi (ANPE) 48 B4
Hôtel de Ville 49 C3
Théâtre 50 C2
To Église St-Nicolas (300m); Camping Ground (600m); N74; Dijon (44km); Côte de Nuits
Old City
To École des Vins de Bourgogne (500m)
Pl de la Gare
Train Station
To D970; Saulieu; Auxerre
To N74; D973; Côte de Beaune; Château de Pommard; Meursault & Autun
To Hôtel Stars (1.2km); A6 (24km)
Av de l'Aigle
R du Faubourg St-Nicolas
R du Collège
R de Lorraine
R de l'Hôtel de Ville
Blvd Maréchal Joffre
R Marey
R Notre Dame
Pl Monge
R des Tonneliers
Av de la République
Blvd G Clemenceau
Av Charles Jaffelin
Pl Général Leclerc
R Carnot
R d'Enfer
R Monge
Pl Félix Ziem
R Maufoux
Pl de la Halle
Petite Pl Carnot
Pl Carnot
Passage Ste-Hélène
R de l'Hôtel-Dieu
R N Rolin
R Thiers
Blvd Jules Ferry
Pl Madeleine
R Colbert
Av du 8 Septembre
R du Faubourg St-Jean
R du Faubourg Madeleine
Blvd Perpreuil
R du Faubourg Perpreuil
Blvd St-Jacques
Blvd Bretonnière
R du Faubourg Bretonnière
R de Seurre

guided tour (in English upon request) of the 18th-century cellar you'll be able to sample one white, three reds and Belen, an aperitif. Given the thick cobwebs on the ceiling, you wouldn't want to be in here if gravity reversed itself.

Patriarche Père et Fils (☎ 03 80 24 53 78; www.patriarche.com; 5 rue du Collège; guided audio tour & tastings €9, tastings ⏲ 9.30-11.30am & 2-5.30pm) The largest cellars in Beaune are rather like Paris' Catacombs except that the corridors are lined with dusty wine bottles instead of human bones. You have the opportunity to compare 13 wines during the audio tour; circuits take 40 minutes.

Lycée Viticole (☎ 03 80 26 35 81; 16 av Charles Jaffelin; ⏲ 8am-noon & 2-5.30pm Mon-Fri, 8am-noon Sat) One of 14 French secondary schools that train young people to grow vines and ferment, age and bottle wine. You can visit the cellars and taste the excellent wines made by the students as part of their studies.

Tours

The tourist office (p454) hosts English-language **walking tours** (per person/couple €6.50/11) from July to mid-September. It also arranges **minibus tours** (tours €40-66) of the vineyards and hot-air balloon rides (p428).

CYCLING

Bourgogne Randonnées (☎ 03 80 22 06 03; 7 av du 8 Septembre; ⏲ 9am-noon & 1.30-7pm Mon-Sat, 10am-noon & 2-7pm Sun Apr-Oct) arranges tailor-made bike tours around the Côte d'Or. Bikes cost €15/69/170 per day/week/month.

WANT TO KNOW MORE?

For more information about Côte d'Or wines, the **École des Vins de Bourgogne** (☎ 03 80 26 35 10; www.vins-bourgogne.fr; 6 rue du 16eme Chasseurs, Beaune) runs tailor-made wine courses to educate your palate. A good reference guide is Sylvain Pitiot & Jean-Charles Servant's *The Wines of Burgundy* (€13.95, 10th edition), or you could consult www.frenchwines.com, where you'll find maps of the Côte d'Or villages and lists of growers, *climats* and vintage years.

Festivals & Events

On the third Sunday in November, as part of the 'Trois Glorieuses' Festival, the **Hospices de Beaune** auctions off the wines from its endowment, 58 hectares of prime vineyards bequeathed by benefactors. Proceeds go to medical care and research. The festival has been running since 1859, and ends with a lavish candle-lit dinner inside Hôtel Dieu.

Sleeping

The tourist office has a list of accommodation options in nearby villages and can help with reservations.

BUDGET

Budget deals are tough to find in Beaune.

Hôtel Rousseau (☎ 03 80 22 13 59; 11 place Madeleine; s €24-40, d €30-50, tr €47-55) The best option is this endearingly shabby hotel run since 1959 by a friendly woman *d'un certain âge*. Some of the old-fashioned rooms have showers or toilets. Reception occasionally shuts for a while without warning.

Hôtel Au Grand St Jean (☎ 03 80 24 12 22; hotel-au-grand-st-jean@wanadoo.fr; 18 rue du Faubourg Madeleine; d/q from €41/51; ☼ Jan–mid-Nov) This big, institutional hotel has lots of plain rooms and it's cheap – at least for Beaune.

Hôtel de France (☎ 03 80 24 10 34; fax 03 80 24 96 78; 35 av du 8 Septembre; s €38-65, d €51-75, tr €61-75; **P**) Perhaps not the period hotel you were dreaming of in Beaune, but it's comfortable enough and affordable. The sparse modern rooms are clean and it's near the train station.

Camping

Camping ground (☎ 03 80 22 03 91; 10 rue Auguste Dubois; per adult/tent €3/4; ☼ mid-Mar–Oct) This four-star camping ground is 700m north of the centre.

MID-RANGE & TOP END

Abbaye de Maizières (☎ 03 80 24 74 64; www.abbayedemaizieres.com in French; 19 rue Maizières; d 65-87, tr €104-120) A quirky hotel inside a 12th-century chapel, with lovingly converted rooms making use of the old brickwork and wooden beams. The restaurant is in the abbey's Romanesque cellar.

Hôtel de la Cloche (☎ 03 80 24 66 33; fax 03 80 24 04 24; 40/42 place Madeleine; d from €69; **P**) This old Beaune establishment has been recently modernised, and now manages to mix old-fashioned character with contemporary comfort.

Hôtel des Remparts (☎ 03 80 24 94 94; hotel.des.remparts@wanadoo.fr; 48 rue Thiers; d €51-80, q €110) Eighteen rooms with luxurious bathrooms and brick-tiled floors are offered in this 17th-century house along the city's old battlements.

Eating

Nothing is cheap in Beaune, and dining is no exception. The best places to explore for good value are the cafés and restaurants around place Carnot, place Félix Ziem and place Madeleine.

Restaurant Maxime (☎ 03 80 22 17 82; 3 pl Madeleine; menus €16-28; ☼ closed Mon & dinner Sun) A reasonably priced Burgundy restaurant, serving delicacies including traditional *coq au vin* in a small dining room. Other restaurants surround the square.

Ma Cuisine (☎ 03 80 22 30 22; passage Ste Hélène; menu €16; ☼ lunch & dinner Mon-Fri, closed lunch Wed, Sat & Sun) Excellent French and Burgundian dishes offer good value at this busy bistro, and there's a nice outdoor terrace.

Restaurant Bernard & Martine Morillon (☎ 03 80 24 12 06; 31 rue Maufoux; menus €35-77; ☼ closed lunch Mon, Tue & Fri & Jan) This restaurant provides sophisticated French dining with a substantial price-tag. Gastrophiles might try the lobster, oysters, or pigeon with fresh figs, and in season, could even order truffles (€84).

Restaurant Le Gourmandin (☎ 03 80 24 07 88; 8 pl Carnot; lunch menu €14, other menus €20-54) An intimate place that offers regional specialities, including *bœuf bourguignon* and *jambon persillé*, cooked with loving care and attention.

SELF-CATERING

The covered market in place de la Halle hosts a **food market** (🕑 until 1pm Sat) and a much smaller **marché gourmand** (gourmet market; 🕑 Wed morning). The nearest *fromagerie* is **Le Tast' Fromages** (23 rue Carnot; 🕑 closed Sun & Mon mid-Nov–mid-Apr).

Casino supermarket (28 rue du Faubourg Madeleine; 🕑 8.30am-7.30pm Mon-Sat) is through an archway on rue Faubourg Madeleine.

Wine can be purchased *en vrac* (in bulk) for as little as €1.10 per litre (from €3.40 per litre for AOC vintages), not including the container, at **Cellier de la Vieille Grange** (27 blvd Georges Clemenceau; 🕑 closed Sun afternoon).

Drinking

Pickwick's Pub & Wine Bar (🕿 03 80 24 72 59; 2 rue Notre Dame; 🕑 11am-3pm & 5pm-2am Mon-Sat, 12.30-2.30pm & 5-9pm Sun) A convincingly English-style pub, with leather armchairs, an open fireplace and lots of beers and whiskies behind the counter. There's live music most Saturdays.

Getting There & Away

BUS

Service No 44 run by **Transco** (🕿 03 80 42 11 00) links Beaune with Dijon (€5.80, one hour, six to nine daily, two on Sunday and holidays), stopping at wine-growing villages such as Vougeot, Aloxe-Corton and Nuits-St-Georges. Buses serve villages south of Beaune (eg Pommard, Volnay, Meursault and Rochepot). In Beaune, buses stop along the boulevards around the old city. The tourist office has timetables.

CAR

You can rent cars from **ADA** (🕿 03 80 22 72 90; 26 av du 8 Septembre).

TRAIN

Beaune's **train station** (pl de la Gare) is outside the city walls, about 500m east of the town centre.

There are frequent trains to Dijon (€6, 20 minutes, 15 to 20 daily) and the Côte d'Or village of Nuits-St-Georges (€3, 10 minutes, 15 to 20 daily). The last train from Beaune to Dijon leaves at about 11.20pm.

Other destinations include Paris' Gare de Lyon (from €35.30, two direct TGVs daily), Autun (€11.90 via Étang, 1¾ hours, two daily), Mâcon (€11.60, one hour, 11 to 15

AUTHOR'S CHOICE

Hôtel le Cep (🕿 03 80 22 35 48; www.hotel-cep beaune.com; 27 rue Maufoux; s €125, d €160-190, ste €240-320) Quite simply, this is one of France's very finest hotels. Housed in an absolutely stunning 16th-century mansion in the old quarter of Beaune, Le Cep offers the kind of old-fashioned luxury and effortless grandeur you don't find very often these days. The hotel is furnished in lavish Renaissance style, with grand salons, four-poster beds, marble statues, enormous open fireplaces, original wooden beams and a colonnaded courtyard, and the bedrooms are all named after famous wines of the Côte d'Or. If all that is not enough to convince you, rumour has it that Louis XIV preferred staying here, rather than at the Hôtel-Dieu. Now that is some recommendation!

daily) and one or both of Lyon's train stations (€19.20, 1½ to 2¼ hours, seven to nine daily).

Getting Around

Parking is free outside the town walls. When your legs get tired you can take a **taxi** (🕿 06 09 42 36 80, 🕿 06 09 43 12 08).

From April to October, Bourgogne Randonnées (p455) hires bikes.

NORTHWEST OF DIJON

The area northwest of Dijon is a mainly rural landscape of broad fields, sharp hills and wooded escarpments dotted with fortified towns perched on the hilltops, notably at Flavigny and Semur-en-Auxois. This region was once one of the main Celtic strongholds in Burgundy, and one of the country's most important pre-Roman treasure troves (the Trésor de Vix) was discovered near Châtillon-sur-Seine. Its strategic position also made it an important military site – Gaulish resistance against Roman rule was crushed once and for all on the plains below the village of Alice-Ste-Reine.

Semur-en-Auxois
pop 4500

Surrounded by a hairpin curve in the River Armançon, this beautiful fortified town is criss-crossed by cobbled lanes and arched

BURGUNDY

ABBAYE DE CÎTEAUX

It was largely due to St Bernard (1090–1153) that the **Abbey of Cîteaux** (☎ 03 80 61 32 58; www .citeaux-abbaye.com in French), south of Dijon, became the headquarters of a vast monastic order, the Cistercians, which once had 600 abbeys stretching from Sweden to the Near East.

In contrast with the showy Benedictines of Cluny, the Cistercian order was known for its discipline and humility. Monks were required to engage in manual labour, and as a result became expert wine-growers, farmers, builders and metal-workers. Founded in 1098 Cîteaux was mostly destroyed during the Revolution, so there are few historic buildings left. Monks didn't return to the abbey until 1898.

From early May to mid-October, you can visit the monastery on a 1¾-hour guided **tour** (adult/ student €7/3.50; tours ☺ 10.30am, 11.30am, 2.30pm, 3.15pm, 4pm & 4.45pm Tue-Sat, except Fri from mid-Jun–mid-Sep; 12.15pm, 1pm, 2pm, 3pm, 4pm & 5pm Sun). It's in French (English text supplied) and is described as 'more spiritual than architectural'; a 30-minute audiovisual presentation offers wordless insights into the life of the abbey's 30 modern-day monks. Phone ahead for reservations.

arcades, guarded by four massive, 13th- and 14th-century pink-granite bastions. Dotted with artists' galleries, timber-framed houses and antique shops, it is a lovely place to while away a summer afternoon.

The **tourist office** (☎ 03 80 97 05 96; www.ville -semur-en-auxois.fr; 2 pl Gaveau; ☺ 9am-7pm Mon-Sat mid-Jun–Sep, 2-6pm Mon, 9am-noon & 2-6pm Tue-Sat Oct–mid-Jun, 10am-noon & 3-6pm Sun Apr-Sep) has a free brochuredetailing walking tours.

The handsome buildings in the **old city** were built when Semur was an important religious centre, boasting no less than six monasteries. The **Promenade du Rempart** affords panoramic views from the medieval battlements.

Inside the twin-towered **Église Notre-Dame** (☺ 9am-noon & 2-6.30pm, until 5.45pm in winter), restored in the mid-19th century, are a stained-glass window (1927) and a plaque commemorating American soldiers who fell in WWI.

The exhibits of the **Musée Municipal** (☎ 03 80 97 24 25; rue Jean-Jacques Collenot; adult/concession €3.15/1.35; ☺ 2-6pm Wed-Mon May–mid-Jun, 10am-noon & 2-6pm Wed-Mon mid-Jun–mid-Sep, 2-5pm except Tue & Sat & Sun mid-Sep–Apr), which range from fossils and stuffed fauna to archaeology, sculpture and oil paintings, are still arranged much as they were in the 19th century.

SLEEPING & EATING
Hôtel Cymaises (☎ 03 80 97 21 44; www.proveis .com/lescymaises in French; rue du Renandot; d from €35) A good, uncomplicated hotel housed in an 18th-century *maison bourgeoise*, set around a quiet courtyard. The rooms are simple and there's a bright conservatory for breakfast.

Hôtel de la Côte d'Or (☎ 03 80 97 28 28; 3 pl Gaveau; low/high season €45/58; P) This attractive hotel, housed in a pretty white building with blue shuttered windows opposite the tourist office, offers carefully-kept rooms with a hint of bygone days.

Le Calibressan (☎ 03 80 97 32 40; 16 rue Févret; menus €13-28; ☺ closed Mon, lunch Sat & dinner Sun) A rustic eatery that mixes old Burgundian favourites with modern Californian cuisine, run by a Franco-American husband and wife team.

Hôtel Les Gourmets (☎ 03 80 97 09 41; 4 rue Varenne; ☺ closed Tue & dinner Mon) In a 16th-century house in the old city, this family-run restaurant serves home-style cooking made to traditional Burgundy recipes. Plain bedrooms are available upstairs.

Pub Le Lion (☎ 03 80 97 26 68; 4 rue de l'Ancienne Comédie; ☺ 9am-2am Mon-Sat) The centre of local nightlife, with five billiard tables and a good wine and beer selection.

GETTING THERE & AWAY
Two or three SNCF buses a day go to Saulieu (€4.80, 34 minutes) and Montbard (on the Paris–Dijon line; €3.10, 21 minutes). **Transco** (☎ 03 80 42 11 00) runs bus No 49 to/ from Dijon (€9.60, one hour 20 minutes, two or three daily).

Flavigny-sur-Ozerain & Alésia
Flavigny, 16km east of Semur, is a delightful hilltop village surrounded by ramparts and rolling pastureland. Neither over-restored nor touristy, it's straight out of the Middle Ages, which is why movies such as *Chocolat* have been filmed here. The local sweet,

anis de Flavigny, consists of an anise seed wrapped in rock-hard candy.

Flavigny's only hotel, the seven-room **Le Relais de Flavigny** (☎ 03 80 96 27 77; www.le-relais .fr; rue des Anciennes Halles; d from €31; ✛ closed Jan), is above a local bar and restaurant in the middle of the old city. Rooms are very simple, but have a certain rustic charm.

Local farmers cook up their produce at **La Grange** (☎ 03 80 96 20 62; mains €8-10; ✛ Sun & holidays Mar-Nov, 12.30-5pm Tue-Fri, 12.30-6pm Sat, 12.30-8pm Sun Jul-Sep), next to the church. In recent years this place has started drawing diners from far and wide, and it's a fantastic way to try traditional Burgundy cooking.

Diehard fans of Roman military history should drop by **Alésia** (Alice-Ste-Reine), a few kilometres northwest of Flavigny, where the Celtic chief Vercingétorix was defeated by Julius Caesar in 52 BC. In addition to the **archaeological excavations** (✛ closed winter) a few hundred metres from the village, there's a small **museum** and a hilltop **statue of Vercingétorix** erected on the orders of Napoleon III. The nearby viewpoint indicator shows the presumed battle lines.

Abbaye de Fontenay

Fontenay Abbey (☎ 03 80 92 15 00; adult/concession €7.50/3.75), founded in 1118 and restored to its medieval glory over the past century, offers a fascinating glimpse of how the Cistercian monks once lived. Set in a wooded riverside valley, the abbey grounds include a beautifully simple chapel, the barrel-vaulted monks' dormitory, landscaped gardens, and even the old forge, bakery and trout farm. Guided **tours** (✛ hourly 10am-noon & 2-5pm Mar-Nov) are in French (printed information in English is available); unguided visits are possible year-round.

A **taxi** (☎ 06 08 82 20 61) from Montbard's train station – served from Dijon (€9.90, 10 minutes) and Paris' Gare de Lyon (non-TGV/TGV train €25.70/30.60, two to 2½ hours) – costs €8 to €10.

Châtillon-sur-Seine
pop 6800

Châtillon's main claim to fame is the **Trésor de Vix**, a treasure trove of Celtic, Etruscan and Greek objects found in the tomb of a Celtic princess believed to have controlled the trade in British tin and Baltic amber. The collection is displayed at the **Musée du Châtil-**lonnais (☎ 03 80 91 24 67; rue du Bourg; adult/under 15 €4.30/2.30; ✛ 9.30am-noon & 2-5pm Wed-Mon Sep-Jun, 10am-6pm Jul & Aug) and includes the princess' gold tiara and a 1.64m-high, bronze Greek vase (krater) that held a bladder-bursting 1100L of wine.

Châtillon's **tourist office** (☎ 03 80 91 13 19; tourism-chatillon-sur-seine@wanadoo.fr; pl Marmont; ✛ 2-5pm Mon, 9am-noon & 2-5pm Tue-Sat) is at the fountain roundabout. The town was heavily bombed during WWII; the postwar commercial centre is bordered by two branches of the Seine, here hardly more than a stream.

Near the **Source de la Douix**, you can climb up to the 16th-century **Tour de Gissey**, where there's a fine view of the whole town; access is via the cemetery. Overlooking the village is the 10th-century **Église St-Vorles**. The **Châtillonnais vineyards**, northwest of town, produce wines including Burgundy's own bubbly, *crémant de Bourgogne*.

Accommodation is limited: there's **Hotel de la Côte d'Or** (☎ 03 80 97 28 28; 2 rue Charles-Ronot; s/d €45/58; **P**), a pleasant hotel with shuttered windows off the main street, and the ultra-budget rooms above the run-down bar-restaurant of **Hotel Le Cheval Rouge** (☎ 03 80 81 53 70; pl du 8 Mai; d from €28).

Transco (☎ 03 80 42 11 00) has buses to Dijon (line No 50; €13.28, 1½ hours, two or three daily).

SAÔNE-ET-LOIRE

The Saône-et-Loire *département*, in Burgundy's south, has important Gallo-Roman ruins in Autun, glorious Romanesque churches (or what's left of them) in Cluny and Paray-le-Monial, a fascinating industrial heritage in Le Creusot, and vineyards around Mâcon and between Tournus and Cluny. Several rivers and the Canal du Centre meander among its green hills.

AUTUN
pop 18,000

Eighty-five kilometres southwest of Dijon, Autun is a quiet provincial town but two millennia ago – under the name Augustodunum – it was one of the most important cities in Roman Gaul, boasting 6km of ramparts, two theatres, an amphitheatre and a system of aqueducts. From AD 269

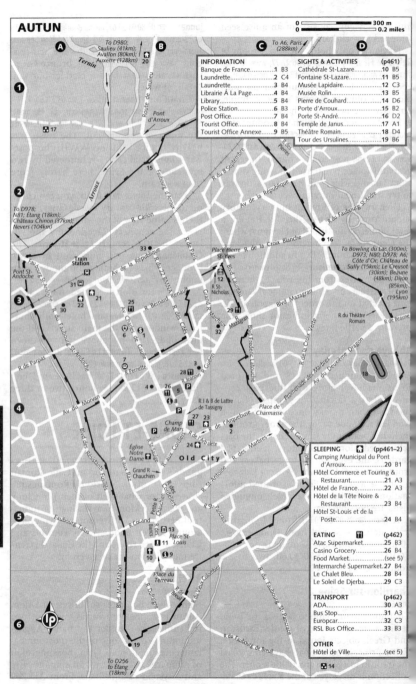

AUTUN

| 0 | 300 m |
| 0 | 0.2 miles |

To D980;
Saulieu (41km);
Avallon (80km);
Auxerre (128km)

To A6; Paris
(288km)

INFORMATION
Banque de France	1	B3
Laundrette	2	C4
Laundrette	3	B4
Librairie À La Page	4	B4
Library	5	B4
Police Station	6	B3
Post Office	7	B4
Tourist Office	8	B4
Tourist Office Annexe	9	B5

SIGHTS & ACTIVITIES (p461)
Cathédrale St-Lazare	10	B5
Fontaine St-Lazare	11	B5
Musée Lapidaire	12	C3
Musée Rolin	13	B5
Pierre de Couhard	14	D6
Porte d'Arroux	15	B2
Porte St-André	16	D2
Temple de Janus	17	A1
Théâtre Romain	18	D4
Tour des Ursulines	19	B6

To D978;
N81; Étang (18km);
Château Chinon (37km);
Nevers (104km)

To Bowling du Lac (300m);
D973; N80; D978; A6;
Côte d'Or; Château de
Sully (15km); Le Creusot
(30km); Beaune
(48km); Dijon
(85km);
Lyon
(195km)

Old City

SLEEPING 🏠 (pp461–2)
Camping Municipal du Pont		
d'Arroux	20	B1
Hôtel Commerce et Touring &		
Restaurant	21	A3
Hôtel de France	22	A3
Hôtel de la Tête Noire &		
Restaurant	23	B4
Hôtel St-Louis et de la		
Poste	24	B4

EATING 🍴 (p462)
Atac Supermarket	25	B3
Casino Grocery	26	B4
Food Market	(see 5)	
Intermarché Supermarket	27	B4
Le Chalet Bleu	28	B4
Le Soleil de Djerba	29	C3

TRANSPORT (p462)
ADA	30	A3
Bus Stop	31	A3
Europcar	32	C3
RSL Bus Office	33	B3

OTHER
| Hôtel de Ville | (see 5) | |

To D256
to Étang
(18km)

BURGUNDY

onwards the city was repeatedly sacked by Barbarian tribes, but its fortunes turned in the Middle Ages, when an impressive cathedral was built. Many of the town's buildings date from the 17th and 18th centuries.

Autun is an excellent base for exploring the southern Parc Naturel Régional du Morvan.

Orientation

The train station is linked to Autun's common-turned-car park, the Champ de Mars, by the town's main thoroughfare, av Charles de Gaulle. The hilly area around Cathédrale St-Lazare, reached via narrow cobblestone streets, is known as the old city. The main shopping area is around rue St-Saulge.

Information

BOOKSHOPS
Librairie À La Page (☎ 03 85 52 24 72; 17bis av Charles de Gaulle; ☒ closed Mon morning & Sun)

EMERGENCY
Police Station (☎ 03 85 86 01 80; 29ter av Charles de Gaulle; ☒ 24hr)

LAUNDRY
There are laundrettes at 18 rue de l'Arquebuse (open 7am to 9pm) and 1 rue Guérin (7am to 8pm).

POST & MONEY
The Post Office is opposite 8 rue Pernette.

TOURIST INFORMATION
Tourist Office (☎ 03 85 86 80 38; www.autun.com; 2 av Charles de Gaulle; ☒ 9am-7pm Jun-Sep, 9am-noon & 2-6pm Mon-Fri, 9am-12.30pm & 2.30-6pm Sat Oct-May) Offers a self-guided walking-tour brochure and pamphlets on Parc Naturel Régional du Morvan.
Tourist Office Annexe (☎ 03 85 52 56 03; 5 pl du Terreau; ☒ 10am noon & 2-6pm Jun-mid-Oct)

Sights

Built during the reign of Constantine, **Porte d'Arroux** was one of Augustodunum's four gates. Constructed entirely without mortar, it has four arches: two for vehicles and two for pedestrians. **Porte St-André** is similar in design.

The **Théâtre Romain** (Roman Theatre), designed to hold 16,000 people, was damaged in the Middle Ages (much of its stone was plundered for new buildings). Thanks to

19th-century restorations it's now possible to imagine the place filled with cheering (or jeering) spectators. From the top of the theatre, you can see southwest to **Pierre de Couhard** (Rock of Couhard), the 27m-high remains of a Gallo-Roman pyramid that was probably a tomb.

Long associated (wrongly) with the Roman god Janus, the 24m-high **Temple de Janus** – in the middle of farmland 800m north of the train station – is thought to have been a site for Celtic worship. Only two of its massive walls are still standing.

Cathédrale St-Lazare (place du Terreau; ☒ 8am-8pm) was built in the 12th century to house the sacred relics of St Lazarus. Later additions include the 15th to 16th bell tower, upper choir and chapels, and the 19th-century square towers over the entrance. The Romanesque **tympanum** – inhabited by tiny chirping bats – over the main doorway shows the Last Judgement, and was carved in the 1130s by Gislebertus, whose name is written below Jesus' right foot. Across the bottom, the saved are on the left while the damned – including a woman whose breasts are being bitten by snakes (symbolising lust) – are on the right. The Renaissance-style fountain next to the cathedral, **Fontaine St-Lazare**, dates from the 16th century.

Musée Rolin (☎ 03 85 52 09 76; 5 rue des Bancs; adult/student €3.05/1.50; ☒ 9.30am-noon & 1.30-6pm Wed-Mon Apr-Sep, 10am-noon & 2-5pm Wed-Mon Oct-Mar) displays Gallo-Roman artefacts, Romanesque sculptures and 15th- and 16th-century French and Flemish paintings.

For a **stroll** along the city walls (part-Roman but mostly medieval), walk from av du Morvan south to the 12th-century **Tour des Ursulines** and follow the walls to the northeast. You can also walk to the Pierre de Couhard, where you can pick up the Circuit des Gorges, three marked forest trails ranging from 4.7km to 11.5km – ask for a brochure at the tourist office.

Tours

From July to mid-September, there are daily **walking tours** (€5.50), sometimes in English, of the old city and the cathedral. They are run by the tourist office.

Sleeping

Hôtel Commerce et Touring (☎ 03 85 52 17 90; fax 03 85 52 37 63; 20 av de la République; d €32-42) A tidy, simple 21-room hotel at the bottom of town, near the train station, with neat and unremarkable rooms.

Hôtel de France (☎ 03 85 52 14 00; fax 03 85 86 14 52; 18 av de la République; d €22-39) Near the Hotel Commerce, this 26-room, family-run hostelry is another basic option for tight purse strings.

Hôtel de la Tête Noire (☎ 03 85 86 59 99; www .hoteltetenoire.fr; 3 rue de l'Arquebuse; d €44-65) This great value hotel is in an excellent position between old and new cities. The newly renovated rooms are spacious and comfortable, and the buffet breakfast is huge. There's a lift to the upper floors.

Hôtel St-Louis et de la Poste (☎ 03 85 52 01 01; louisposte@aol.com; 6 rue de l'Arbalète; d €70-100, deluxe ste from €200) A luxurious four-star establishment, justly proud of its lavish lobby – and the fact that Napoleon once slept here. The Suite Napoléon costs a mere €230.

Camping
Camping Municipal du Pont d'Arroux (☎ 03 85 52 10 82; route de Saulieu; per adult/tent/car €2.50/2.15/1.30; ☀ 1 week before Easter-Oct) In a beautiful (if cramped) spot on the River Ternin.

Eating
Le Chalet Bleu (☎ 03 85 86 27 30; 3 rue Jeannin; menus €14-43; ☀ closed Tue, dinner Mon) Creative French cuisine served in a light, modern dining room decorated with potted plants. Regional produce forms the heart of the varied menu.

Le Soleil de Djerba (☎ 03 85 86 17 77; 17 rue Mazagran; menus €10-19; ☀ Mon-Sat) Very popular with the Autunois, this small Tunisian restaurant serves generous portions of excellent couscous as well as good French menus.

SELF-CATERING
The square outside the town hall hosts a **food market** (☀ until noon or 12.30pm Wed & Fri).

Other grocery options include an **Atac supermarket** (av Charles de Gaulle; ☀ 8.30am-7pm Mon-Sat); a **Casino grocery** (6 av Charles de Gaulle; ☀ 7.30am-12.30pm & 3-7.30pm Tue-Sat, 8.30am-noon & 4-6pm Sun); and an **Intermarché supermarket** (21 rue J&B de Lattre de Tassigny; ☀ 8am-7.30pm Mon-Sat).

Getting There & Away
BUS
From the bus stop next to the train station, RSL buses travel to Château Chinon

(€5.35, one hour, one daily Monday to Friday, Saturday during school terms) and other towns in the Parc Naturel Régional du Morvan. There's an **RSL Bus Office** (☎ 03 85 86 92 55; 13 av de la République; ☀ 8.15am-noon & 2-6pm Mon-Thu, to 5pm Fri). Timetables are available at the tourist office or the bus station.

Transco (☎ 03 80 42 11 00) has daily buses to Dijon (€12.84, 2¼ hours) via Beaune and the Côte d'Or wine-making villages.

CAR
You can rent cars from **ADA** (☎ 03 85 52 64 03; 8 av de la République) and **Europcar** (☎ 03 85 52 13 31; 3 Grande rue Marchaux).

TRAIN
Autun's **train station** (av de la République; ☀ until 6.30pm most days) is on a very slow line that requires a change of train (or bus) to get anywhere except Saulieu (€6.90, 50 minutes, four or five daily, two on Sunday) and Avallon (€11.70, 1¾ hours, two or three daily, one on Sunday).

Except on Sunday and holidays, one or two trains a day go to Auxerre (€17.60, 2¾ hours).

LE CREUSOT
pop 28,900

Le Creusot is, frankly, an ugly industrial town, but the story of how it got that way is fascinating (at least if you like industrial history). After all, this is where the power hammer was invented in 1841 – the towering gadget at the southern entrance to town was the mightiest power hammer in the world when it was built in 1876.

Thanks to abundant coal deposits and cheap transport via the Canal de Charolais (1793), Le Creusot became a major steel-making centre during the 19th century. The story of the smoke-belching Schneider steelworks is told at **Château de la Verrerie** (☎ 03 85 73 92 00; adult/student/f €5.95/3.80/15.25; ☀ 10am-7pm Mon-Fri, 2-7pm Sat & Sun Jun-Sep, 9am-noon & 2-6pm Mon-Fri, 2-6pm Sat & Sun Sep-May), an 18th-century glassworks turned into a private mansion by the Schneiders, undisputed masters of the town.

The chateau's **Musée de l'Homme et de l'Industrie** (☀ 10am-noon & 2-6pm Mon-Fri, 2-6pm Sat & Sun) tells the story of the Schneider dynasty and exhibits some marvellous 1:14-scale steam locomotives. Across the courtyard, the **Académie François Bourdon** (🕑 11am-12.30pm & 3-6pm Mon-Fri, 3-6pm Sat & Sun, longer hours in summer) has models of various flagship Schneider products (including railway locomotives, bridges, naval vessels and nuclear power plants).

The **tourist office** (☎ 03 85 55 02 46; lecreusot.net; 🕑 9am-noon & 2-6pm Mon-Fri, 2-5pm Sat & Sun) can be found in the chateau's gatehouse.

The town is linked to the Le Creusot TGV station by **TGV Bus** (☎ 03 85 73 01 10) (€1, 20 minutes, two to four daily) and to Autun by the **SNCF** (€6, 45 minutes, six to eight daily, two on Sunday).

CLUNY
pop 4400

The remains of Cluny's great abbey – which was Christendom's largest church until the construction of St Peter's Basilica in the Vatican – are fragmentary and scattered, barely discernible among the houses and green spaces of the modern-day town. But with some imagination, it's possible to picture how things looked in the 12th century, when Cluny's Benedictine abbey, answerable only to the Pope, held sway over 1100 priories and monasteries stretching from Poland to Portugal. A smaller version of Cluny's lost abbey can be seen 30km west in the little town of **Paray-le-Monial**.

Orientation & Information

Cluny's main street is known (from southeast to northwest) as place du Commerce, rue Filaterie, rue Lamartine and rue Mercière.

Post Office (rue de la Levée)

Tourist Office (☎ 03 85 59 05 34; cluny@wanadoo.fr; 6 rue Mercière; 🕑 10am-12.30pm & 2.30-7pm Apr-Sep, 10am-7pm Jul & Aug, 10am-12.30pm & 2.30-5pm Mon-Sat Nov-Mar) Has good English-language brochures.

Sights

The vast **Église Abbatiale** (☎ 03 85 59 89 99; adult/18-25 yrs/under 18 €6.10/4.10/free; 🕑 9.30am-6.30pm May-Aug, 9.30am-noon & 1.30-5pm Sep-Apr, closed major holidays), built between 1088 and 1130, once stretched from the **map table** in front of Musée Ochier to the trees near the **Clocher de l'Eau Bénite** (Tower of the Holy Water) and its neighbour, **Tour de l'Horloge** – a distance of 187m. The original building boasted two towers, several belfries and some 300 windows, but as the influence of the Cluny order waned, so did the abbey's importance, and

the building fell into disrepair and was finally closed in 1790. During the Revolution, angry mobs set out to sack the building but lost interest (it took them a week just to burn the archives), and the abbey was instead sold to a local property developer, who carved it up piece by piece and auctioned off the stone for building material.

Cluny has two other churches: the **Église St Marcel** (rue Prud'hon; 🕑 closed to public), topped by an octagonal, three-storey belfry; and the 13th-century **Église Notre Dame**, across the street from the tourist office.

Tickets and guide leaflets are purchased at **Musée Ochier** near the abbey ruins, and open at the same times. Much of the remaining site (including the southern transept and 18th-century chapel) is occupied by the **École Nationale Supérieure d'Arts et Métiers** (ENSAM; place du 11 Août), an institute for training engineers. You can wander around the grounds at noon and for around an hour after closing time. Free guided tours in English take place in July and August.

The best place to appreciate the abbey's scale is from the top of the **Tour des Fromages** (Tower of Cheeses; adult/student €1.25/0.80), once used to ripen cheeses. Access to the tower's 120 steps is through the tourist office.

The **Haras National** (National Stud Farm; 2 rue Porte des Prés; 🕑 9am-7pm), founded by Napoleon in 1806, houses some of France's finest thoroughbreds, ponies and draught horses. Visitors are welcome to wander the grounds.

Sleeping

Hôtel Bourgogne (☎ 03 85 59 00 58; www.hotel-cluny .com; pl de l'Abbaye; d €78-150; P) Tucked away beside the remains of the abbey, this smart brick-fronted hotel is the most comfortable place to stay in Cluny, with modern rooms and a flowery outside terrace.

Hôtel de l'Abbaye (☎ 03 85 59 11 14; hotel@abbaye -cluny.fr; av Charles de Gaulle; s €30-48, d €48-52; P) Hard to miss thanks to its vicious peach exterior, this is a more affordable option on the outskirts of town. The rural atmosphere and cosy rooms are pleasant, and the regional restaurant is good too.

Hôtel du Commerce (☎ 03 85 59 03 09; fax 03 85 59 00 87; 8 pl du Commerce; s/d €24-39) A very central, one-star, 17-room hotel that has little to recommend it apart from the price. Reception closes from noon to 4.30pm.

BURGUNDY

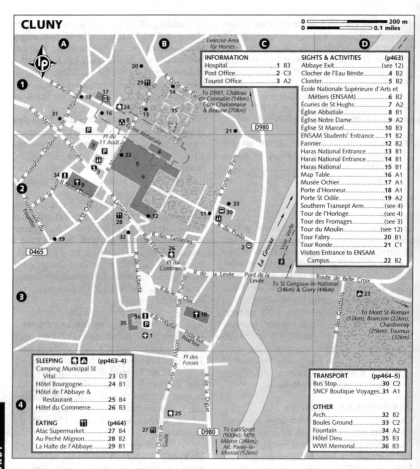

CAMPING

Camping Municipal St Vital (☎ 03 85 59 08 34; rue des Griottons; camping €10.20; ☼ May-Sep) A grassy camping area slightly east of town.

Eating

La Halte de l'Abbaye (☎ 03 85 59 28 49; 3 rue Porte des Prés; 4-course lunch menu €10; ☼ 9am-6pm Thu-Tue, lunch 11.30am-2.30pm) A classic little French bistro that specialises in Charolais beef dishes. The dining room is packed with wooden tables and overhead beams, and there are regional beers on tap.

Au Pêché Mignon (☎ 03 85 59 11 21; 25 rue Lamartine; ☼ 7.30am-8pm) Cluny's gourmet patisserie offers all kinds of sweet and sticky delights – home-made nougat, jams, choc-

olate, sumptuous cakes and a house speciality – 'monk's truffles'. There's also an attached teashop.

There are several other cafés and restaurants around place de l'Abbaye and rue Lamartine. Cluny's food shops – virtually all closed on Monday – are along place du Commerce, rue Lamartine and rue Mercière. There's also an **Atac supermarket** (av Charles de Gaulle; ☼ 8.45am-7.15pm Tue-Sat, 9am-noon Sun).

Getting There & Away

The bus stop on rue Porte de Paris is served by the SNCF coach line between Chalon-sur-Saône's train station (€7.50, 1-1½ hours, four daily), Mâcon's train station (€3.90, 45 minutes, six daily) and the Mâcon-Loché

TGV station. Tickets are available at the **SNCF's Boutique Voyages** (☎ 03 85 59 07 72; 9 rue de la République; ⏰ 9am-noon & 1.30-5.30pm Tue-Fri & Sat morning).

NORTH OF CLUNY

An old railway line stretching 44km from Cluny to Givry and a former canal towpath form the flat **Voie Verte** (Green Road), which is perfect for walking, cycling and in-line skating.

Tournus, known for its 9th- to 12th-century church, is 33km northeast of Cluny. The medieval village of **Brancion** sits at the base of its chateau, while **Chardonnay** is surrounded by vineyards. There's a panoramic view from 579m **Mont St-Romain.**

The **Côte Chalonnaise** wine-growing area runs from St-Gengoux-le-National northwards to **Chagny** (south of the vineyards of the Côte de Beaune); tourist offices have wine route maps.

Fourteen kilometres north of Cluny, the Renaissance-style **Château de Cormatin** (☎ 03 85 50 16 55; adult/student/under 17 €6.50/5/4; ⏰ 10am-noon & 2-5.30pm Apr-May & Oct–mid-Nov, 10am-noon & 2-6.30pm Jun-Sep; 10am-6.30pm mid-Jul–mid-Aug) is renowned for its opulent 17th-century, Louis XIII-style interiors. Cormatin is linked to Cluny by seven SNCF buses daily (€2.80, 25 minutes).

MÂCON

pop 37,200

The town of Mâcon, on the right bank of the Saône, is a good base for exploring the **Mâconnais,** Burgundy's southernmost wine-growing area. The area's best vintage is Pouilly Fuissé, a renowned white produced southwest of Mâcon.

The **tourist office** (☎ 03 85 21 07 07; www.macon -tourism.com; 1 place St-Pierre; ⏰ 10am-7pm Mon-Sat, 3-7pm Sun & holidays Jun-Sep, 10am-12.30pm & 2-6pm Mon-Sat Oct-May) has information on the Mâconnais and Beaujolais vineyards. It's across the street from the **town hall**, part of which was built around 1750 as the most splendid mansion in town. You can visit some of the interior.

The shops in Mâcon's pedestrianised centre reflect the town's prosperity. The 16th-century **Maison de Bois** (☎ 03 85 38 37 70; rue Dombey) is decorated with carved wooden figures, some of them on the cheeky side – these days it's an upmarket pub. The early-19th-century **Cathédrale St Vincent** (pl Lamartine) was briefly known as Église St-Napoléon.

Musée Lamartine (☎ 03 85 38 96 19; 41 rue Sigorgne; adult/student €2.30/free; ⏰ 10am-noon & 2-6pm Mon-Sat, 2-6pm Sun & holidays) explores the life and times of the Mâcon-born Romantic poet and left-wing politician Alphonse de Lamartine (1790–1869). **Musée des Ursulines** (☎ 03 85 39 90 38; adult/student €2.30/free; ⏰ 10am-noon & 2-6pm, closed Sun morning & Mon), housed in a 17th-century Ursuline convent, features Gallo-Roman archaeology and 16th- to 20th-century paintings.

You'll find restaurants and bars near the tourist office on rue Joseph Dufour, and along the river south of Pont St Laurent.

Mâcon's elegant riverfront and proximity to the Alps made it a popular destination with 19th-century tourists – when Queen Victoria visited, she took up an entire floor of the **Hôtel d'Europe et d'Angleterre** (☎ 03 85 38 27 94; fax 03 85 39 22 54; 92-109 quai Jean Jaurès; d €50-70). The hotel's old-world grandeur may have faded a little since then, but it's still an atmospheric place to stay, with a lovely 19th-century lobby, extravagant spiral staircase and quaint rooms.

The Mâcon-Ville train station is linked to Dijon (€15.90, 1½ hours, 15 to 20 daily) and Lyon's two stations (€11.70, 30 to 45 minutes, 14 to 23 daily). SNCF buses travel daily to Cluny from the train station (€3.90, 45 minutes).

The Mâcon-Loché TGV station is 5km southwest of town.

BURGUNDY

Lyon & the Rhône Valley

CONTENTS

Lyon	468
North & West of Lyon	484
St-Étienne	485
Downstream along the Rhône	486

Plumb at the crossroads to central Europe and the Atlantic, the Rhineland and the Mediterranean, the Rhône Valley has been the envy of many a soul for centuries. Roman Lyon – the region's cultural highlight – is majestic and elegant with artistic and culinary riches exceeded only by those of Paris; gastronomy-wise, it is on a par – if not better. The city is, after all, France's gastronomic capital, say gourmets. Nearby, you can visit the Gallo-Roman ruins at Vienne (of jazz festival fame), the industrial museums of St-Étienne, and medieval Pérouges.

The Rhône wiggles through Lyon on its 813km-long journey from Lake Geneva to the Mediterranean. Around 2000 BC during the Bronze Age, its waters were a prime trade route for amber and tin. Under the Romans, wine-making flourished in the region, and it continues to do so – highly regarded Côtes du Rhône appellations grow between Vienne and the unassuming town of Valence, as well as in vineyards south of sweet Montélimar.

The Gorges de l'Ardèche (Ardèche Gorges) bring the River Ardèche tumbling to the gates of Provence and Languedoc. For Rhône Valley sights further south (eg, Orange, Avignon), see the Provence chapter.

HIGHLIGHTS

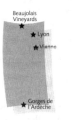

- Explore the diverse neighbourhoods of **Vieux Lyon** (p472) or the **Croix Rousse** *canuts* (p474)
- Ride the funicular railway up **Fourvière hill** (p473)
- Step back in time with a visit to the Roman archaeological museums in **Lyon** (p473) and **Vienne** (p486)
- Salivate over some mouth-watering **Valrhona chocolate** (p486) and **Montélimar nougat** (p487)
- Enjoy some porky piggy-part cuisine in Lyon's traditional **bouchons** (p478)
- Exercise legs and wine palates visiting **Beaujolais vineyards** (p484) by pedal-power
- Rush headlong into white-water sports in **Gorges de l'Ardèche** (p488)

- POPULATION: 5,645,407
- AREA: 43,698 SQ KM

LYON & THE RHÔNE VALLEY

LYON

pop 415,000

Grand old Lyon (Lyons in English) – the focal point of a prosperous urban area of almost two million people, France's second-largest conurbation – has spent the last 500 years as a commercial, industrial and banking powerhouse. At the forefront of scientific research, it produced physicist André-Marie Ampère (1775–1836), after whom the basic unit of electrical current was named, and the Lumière brothers, creators of the world's first motion picture in 1895.

Outstanding museums, a dynamic cultural life, a hotter-than-hot clubbing and bar scene, a thriving university and fantastic shopping endow this thriving metropolis – making it no mean surprise for anyone who ventures its way. Green parks, riverside paths and a historical centre sufficiently precious to be protected as a Unesco World Heritage Site is there to be explored on foot or by bicycle, while gourmets can indulge their wildest gastronomic fantasies with a dining scene that is both sharp and savvy.

History

Founded in 43 BC as a Roman military colony called Lugdunum, Lyon served as the capital of the Roman territories known as the Three Gauls under Augustus. The city's extraordinary prosperity took root in the 15th century when, with the arrival of moveable type in 1473, Lyon became one of Europe's foremost publishing centres, with several hundred resident printers. By the mid-18th century, the city's silk weavers emerged as a force to be reckoned with, making what had been a textiles centre since the 15th century the silk-weaving capital of Europe.

The international police agency Interpol has been headquartered here since 1989.

Orientation

The city centre is on the Presqu'île, a 500m-to 800m-wide peninsula bounded by the Rhône and the Saône. Public squares running down the peninsula from north to south include place de la Croix Rousse, in the hilltop neighbourhood of Croix Rousse; place Louis Pradel, just north of the opera house; place des Terreaux; place de la République, attached to pedestrianised rue de la République; vast place Bellecour; and place

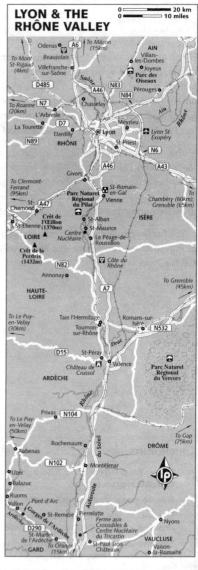

LYON & THE RHÔNE VALLEY

Carnot, just north of Gare de Perrache, one of Lyon's two mainline train stations.

On the western bank of the Saône, Vieux Lyon (Old Lyon) is sandwiched between the river and the hilltop area of Fourvière.

The districts east of the Rhône are known as Lyon-Rive Gauche (Lyon-Left Bank). Gare de la Part-Dieu, the city's other mainline

THE BUTCHER OF LYON

Klaus Barbie (1913–91) – 'the butcher of Lyon' – was Lyon's Gestapo commander from 1942 to 1944. Under him, some 4000 people (including Resistance leader Jean Moulin) were killed and 7500 others – including many *résistants* and Jews – were deported to Nazi death camps. The bloody years of Nazi rule ended in September 1944, when the retreating Germans blew up all but two of Lyon's 28 bridges.

After the war, Barbie worked for US counter-intelligence (1947–51) then settled in Bolivia with his family under the name Klaus Altmann. In 1952 and again in 1954, he was sentenced to death in absentia by a Lyonnais court but it was not until 1987, following his extradition from Bolivia, that he was tried in person for crimes against humanity. Barbie was sentenced to life imprisonment and died of leukaemia in prison three years later.

The life and times of Klaus Barbie are the subject of the epic 4½-hour film *Hôtel Terminus*.

train station, is 1.5km east of the Rhône in La Part-Dieu, a modern commercial centre dominated by *le crayon* – the pencil-shaped Crédit Lyonnais tower.

Lyon is divided up into nine arrondissements (districts); the arrondissement number appears after each street address in this chapter.

Information
BOOKSHOPS
Decitre (Map pp470-2; ☎ 04 26 68 00 30; 6 place Bellecour, 2e; metro Bellecour; ⏰ 9.30am-7pm Mon-Sat) English-language fiction, travel guides and maps.
Raconte-Moi La Terre (Map pp470-2; ☎ 04 78 92 60 20; www.raconte-moi.com; 38 rue Thomassin, 2e; metro Cordeliers; ⏰ 10am-7.30pm Mon-Sat) Travel bookshop, predominantly French titles.

EMERGENCY
Police Station (Map pp470-2; Commissariat de Police; ☎ 04 78 42 26 56; 47 rue de la Charité, 2e; metro Perrache or Ampère)

INTERNET ACCESS
The Albion (Map pp470-2; ☎ 04 78 28 33 00; 12 rue Ste-Catherine, 1er; metro Hôtel de Ville; ⏰ 7pm-2am Sun-Thu, 7pm-3am Fri & Sat) English pub with free WiFi zone and free Internet access on two terminals.
Connectik Café (Map pp470-2; ☎ 04 72 77 98 85; 19 quai St-Antoine, 2e; metro Cordeliers; per 15min/hr/10hr €3/6/45; ⏰ 10am-7pm Mon-Sat)
Raconte-Moi La Terre (Map pp470-2; see Bookshops above; per hr/3hr €4/10) First-floor Internet café.

INTERNET RESOURCES
www.lyon.fr Official city of Lyon website.
www.lyonclubbing.com The very latest (in French) on Lyon's nightlife scene; bars, clubs, live music, celebrities, hot gossip and so on.

www.lyonresto.com Restaurant listings with reviews, menu prices and ratings for food, atmosphere, service, quality and quantity (in French).
www.petitpaume.com Search electronically through the best city guide (in French) on Lyon, compiled by university students and distributed for free just one day a year in October.
www.rhonealpes-tourisme.com Regional tourist information site.

LAUNDRY
Laundrette (Map pp470-2; 10 rue Ste-Catherine, 1er; metro Hôtel de Ville; ⏰ 6.30am-8.30pm)
Lav'+ (Map pp470-2; rue Terme, 1er; metro Hôtel de Ville; ⏰ 6am-9pm)

MEDICAL SERVICES
Duquesne Pharmacy (off Map pp470-2; ☎ 04 78 93 70 96; 30 rue Duquesne, 6e; metro Foch; ⏰ 24hr)

CENT SAVER

The **Lyon City Card** (€15/25/30 for 1/2/3 days) gains you admission into every museum in Lyon, onto the roof of Basilique Notre Dame de Fourvière, and up Fourvière's Tour de l'Observatoire. It also includes the cost of one of the tourist office's guided or audioguided city tours, and – between April and October you can also set sail on a river excursion. Last but not least, the Lyon City Card – sold by the tourist office and also available at certain hotels – gets you unlimited travel on buses, trams, the funicular and the metro.

Cent savers note that the Musée de la Civilisation Gallo-Romaine in Fourvière and the Musée de la Poupée are free on Thursday.

LYON & THE RHÔNE VALLEY

LYON

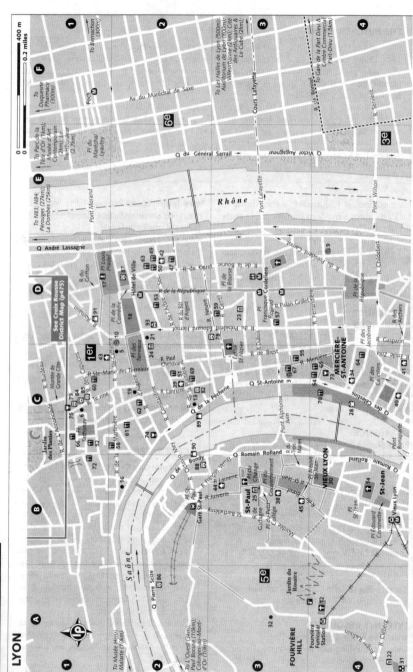

To Musée Henri
Malaire (1km)

To L'Ouest (3km);
Paul Bocuse (10km);
Collonges-au-Mont-
d'Or (10km)

To N83, N84:
Pérouges (27km);
La Dombes (25km)

To Parc de la
Tête d'Or (1km);
Musée d'Art
Contemporain
(2km); Le
TransBordeur (2.2km)

To Bernachon
(800m)

To Les Halles de Lyon (500m);
Auditorium de Lyon (800m);
Cité Villeurbanne (2km); Cité
des Antiquaires &
Le Cube (2km)

To Le Sofitel;
To Gare de la Part Dieu &
Centre Commercial
Part-Dieu (1.5km)

To Duquesne
Pharmacy (500m)

See Croix Rousse
District Map (p475)

Jardin
des Plantes

Saône

Rhône

FOURVIÈRE
HILL

Fourvière Funicular
Station

Jardin du
Rosaire

VIEUX LYON

MERCIÈRE-
ST-ANTOINE

400 m
0.2 miles

⑤

⑥

⑦

⑧

Cours de la Liberté

Ⓜ Guillotière

To Hôtel de Noailles
(150m); Le Fridge
(500m); Musée Lumière,
Hangar du Premier Film &
Mur du Cinéma Mural (2.5km);
Hôpital Edouard Herriot (3km);
Grande Mosquée de Lyon (4km)

LYON-
RIVE
GAUCHE

🏠

7e

R. Pasteur

R. de Marseille

Cours Gambetta

Victor Augagneur Ⓠ

83 🏛

80 🏦

Quai Claude Bernard

R. de l'Université

University

R. Pasteur

R. Chevreul

Rhône

R. de la Barre

68 🏠

R. des Marronniers

Pl. Antonin
Poncet

🏠 26 ●

81 🏨

PRESQU'ÎLE

Bellecour Ⓜ

1 ①

11 🏠

36 🏠

Quai du Docteur Gailleton

Pont de l'Université

Pont Gallieni

To Au Bureau (500m);
Tony Garnier (2.5km);
Maison de la
Danse (3km); A43
to Lyon St-Exupéry
Aéroport (25km);
Grenoble (110km)

To Le Bureau (500m);
Fresque de Gerland
Mural (3km); Parc &
Stade de Gerland (3km)

27 🏦

🏛 15

Quai Claude Bernard

71 🏠

4 ●

56 🏠 🏠
76

Pl. Bellecour

20 🏠

Bellecour Ⓜ

R. de la Charité

R. Sala

R. des Remparts d'Ainay

7 🏛

**Quartier
Auguste Comte**

R. Auguste Comte

R. Ste-Hélène

2e

R. Victor Hugo

Pl. Ampère
Ampère Ⓜ

37 🏠

R. Franklin

R. de Condé

8 ●

46 🏠

R. Dubuamel

To Vienne
(32km); Valence
(106km); Montélimar
(152km); Marseille
(315km via the A7)

Quai Tilsit

R. du Plat

R. Jarente

77 🏠

R. Henri IV

Pl.
Carnot

ramp

Av. Berthelot

Quai Fulchiron

R. de Doyenné

R. d'Enghien

R. de Condé

R. Général Plessier

R. Vaubecour

Cours de Verdun

R. du Bélier

48 🏠

🏠

5 🏠

92 🏠

Ⓜ
Perrache

R. St-Georges

Église
St-Georges

St-Georges

Quai St-Georges

Monte du Chemin Neuf

33 🏛

⑤ 🚠 29

Minimes
Funicular Stop 🚠

To St-Just
Funicular Station

🚉 Gare de
Perrache

Saône

A6

Quai Rambaud

To Musée de la Poupée
(5km); Camping
International (5km);
Beaujolais (40km);
A6 to Paris (460km)

N7

To Aquarium du
Grand Lyon (3km)

⑥

⑦

⑧

To Musée des
Confluences (200m)

INFORMATION	
AOC Exchange.................................1 C5
Central Post Office..........................2 D6
Connectik Café...............................3 C3
Decitre...4 C5
Laundrette....................................5 C2
Lav' +...6 C1
Musée des Tissus............................7 C7
Police Station.................................8 C7
Raconte-Moi La Terre.......................9 D4
The Albion...................................10 D2
Tourist Office...............................11 D5

SIGHTS & ACTIVITIES	(pp472–6)
Basilique Notre Dame de Fourvière......12 A4
Bibliothèque de la Cité Mural.............13 C2
Cathédrale St-Jean.........................14 B4
Centre d'Histoire de la Résistance et de la	
Déportation.............................15 D8
Fresque des Lyonnais......................16 B2
Homme de la Liberté Statue..............17 D1
Hôtel de Ville...............................18 D2
Le Cri du Kangaroo.........................19 C2
Louis XIV Statue............................20 C5
Lyon Parc Auto.............................21 D2
Musée de la Civilisation Gallo-Romaine..22 A4
Musée de l'Imprimerie.....................23 D3
Musée des Arts Décoratifs...............(see 7)
Musée des Beaux-Arts.....................24 C2
Musée Gadagne............................25 B3
Nature & Découvertes.....................26 D5
Navig-Inter (cruises)......................27 D8
Navig-Inter (river excursions)...........28 C4
Odéon..29 A5
Palais de Justice............................30 B4
Théâtre Romain............................31 A4
Tour Métallique.............................32 A3

SLEEPING	(pp476–8)
Auberge de Jeunesse du Vieux Lyon...33 B5
Comfort Hôtel St-Antoine................34 C4
Gîtes de France.............................35 B7
Hilton Lyon..................................36 D5
Hôtel Alexandra............................37 C7
Hôtel Cour des Loges.....................38 B3
Hôtel de Paris...............................39 C2
Hôtel des Artistes..........................40 C4
Hôtel des Celestins.........................41 C4
Hôtel Iris.....................................42 D2
Hôtel Ste-Catherine.......................43 C1
Hôtel St-Paul................................44 B3
La Tour Rose................................45 B3
Sofitel Royal Lyon..........................46 C8

EATING	(pp478–81)
Alyssaar......................................47 D2
Brasserie Georges..........................48 C8
Café 100 Tabac.............................49 D2
Café 203......................................50 D2
Café des Fédérations......................51 C2
Café-Restaurant des Deux Places......52 C1
Chez Hugon.................................53 D2
Commanderie des Antonins.............54 C4
Gaston Restaurant Agricole..............55 C3
Giraudet.....................................56 C5
Grand Café des Négociants..............57 D3
La Halle de la Martinière..................58 C2
La Meunière.................................59 D3
La Soup'ente................................60 C1
La Table d'Hippolyte.......................61 C2
La Vieille Réserve...........................62 C2
Le Garet......................................63 D2
Le Pâtisson..................................64 C4
L'Épicérie.....................................65 C4
Les Enfants Gâtés..........................66 C1

Lolo Quoi....................................67 C3
Maison Perroudon........................68 D5
Moinon.......................................69 C2
Outdoor Food	
Market....................................70 C4
Pagès Védrenne............................71 C5
Restaurant Albert..........................72 B1

DRINKING	(pp481–2)
Elle..73 C4
Le Voxx.......................................74 C2
Palais de la Bière...........................75 C1
Richart.......................................76 C5
Thé Cha Yuan...............................77 C6

ENTERTAINMENT	(pp482–3)
CNP-Terreaux Cinema....................78 D3
Edy'ns Club..................................79 C1
Fish...80 E5
Fnac Billetterie..............................81 D5
Hot Club de Lyon..........................82 C2
La Marquise.................................83 E5
Le Madras....................................84 C1
L'Opéra Rock................................85 C1
Nightclubs...................................86 A2
Opera House................................87 D2
Théâtre Le Guignol........................88 B2

SHOPPING	(p483)
Book Market.................................89 C2
Crafts Market................................90 C2
Lyon-créateur.com.........................91 D1

TRANSPORT	(pp483–4)
Bus Station...................................92 B8
SNCF Boutique...........................(see 4)
Taxi Rank.....................................93 D2

Hôpital Édouard Herriot (off Map pp470-2; ☎ 08 20 08 20 69; 5 place d'Arsonval, 3e; metro Grange Blanche) 24hr emergency room; 4km southeast of place Bellecour.
Maisons Médicales de Garde (☎ 04 72 33 00 33; ☽ 7pm-midnight Mon-Fri, noon-midnight Sat, Sun & holidays) After-hours medical care.

MONEY

Commercial banks abound on rue Victor Hugo, 2e; rue du Bât d'Argent, 1er; and rue de la République, 1er.
AOC Exchange (Map pp470-2; 20 rue Gasparin, 2e; metro Bellecour; ☽ 9.30am-6.30pm Mon-Sat)

POST

Central Post Office (Map pp470-2; 10 place Antonin Poncet, 2e; metro Bellecour)

TOURIST INFORMATION

Tourist Office (Map pp470-2; ☎ 04 72 77 69 69; www .lyon-france.com; place Bellecour, 2e; metro Bellecour; ☽ 9am-7pm Mon-Sat, 10am-6pm Sun mid-Apr–mid-Oct, 10am-6pm Mon-Sat, 10am-5.30pm Sun mid-Oct–mid-Apr)

Sights

VIEUX LYON

Old Lyon (Map pp470–2), with its cobblestone streets and **medieval and Renaissance houses** below Fourvière hill, is divided into three quarters: St-Paul at the northern end, St-Jean in the middle and St-Georges in the south. Facing the river is the **Palais de Justice** (Law Courts; quai Romain Rolland).

Lovely old buildings languish on **rue du Bœuf, rue St-Jean** and **rue des Trois Maries**. Look up to see the gargoyles and other cheeky stone characters that sit on the window ledges along **rue Juiverie**, home to Lyon's Jewish community in the Middle Ages.

The partly Romanesque **Cathédrale St-Jean** (place St-Jean, 5e; metro Vieux Lyon; ☽ 8am-noon & 2-7.30pm Mon-Fri, 8am-noon & 2-5pm Sat & Sun), seat of Lyon's 133rd bishop, was built from the late 11th to the early 16th centuries. The portals of its Flamboyant Gothic façade (completed in 1480) are decorated with 280 square stone medallions (early 14th century). The **astronomical clock** in the north transept arm chimes at noon, 2pm, 3pm and 4pm. Organ concerts (free) are held at 6pm on the third Sunday of each month.

The **Musée Gadagne** (☎ 04 78 42 03 61; www .museegadagne.com in French; place du Petit Collège, 5e; metro Vieux Lyon; adult/under-18 €3.80/free; ☽ 10.45am-6pm Wed-Mon), housed in a 16th-century mansion once owned by two rich Florentine bankers, houses a local history museum and a puppet museum.

FOURVIÈRE

Over two millennia ago, the Romans built the city of Lugdunum on the slopes of Fourvière (Map pp470–2). Today, Lyon's 'hill of prayer' – topped by a basilica and the **Tour Métallique**, a grey, Eiffel Tower–like structure built in 1893 and used as a TV transmitter – affords spectacular views of Lyon and its two rivers. Several footpaths wind uphill but the funicular departing from place Édouard Commette in Vieux Lyon is the easiest way up; use a metro ticket or buy a funicular return ticket (€2.20).

Crowning the hill is the ornate **Basilique Notre Dame de Fourvière** (www.lyon-fourviere.com in French; ◷ 8am-7pm), a superb example of the exaggerated enthusiasm for embellishment that dominated French ecclesiastical architecture during the late 19th century. **Guided tours** (☎ 04 78 25 86 19; adult/child €4/2.50; ◷ 2.30pm & 4pm Mon-Sun Jun-Sep, 2.30pm Oct & Nov, 2.30pm & 4pm Apr & May) last 1¼ hours and take in the roof and various bits inside, and end up at the top of the **Tour de l'Observatoire** (Observatory Tower). There's an equally stunning city view from the less-giddying terrace below.

Extraordinary artefacts found in the Rhône Valley, including the remains of a four-wheeled vehicle from around 700 BC, several sumptuous mosaics and lots of Latin inscriptions are displayed in the **Musée de la Civilisation Gallo-Romaine** (Museum of Gallo-Roman Civilisation; ☎ 04 72 38 81 90; 17 rue Cléberg, 5e; Fourvière funicular station; adult/under 18 €3.80/free, free for everyone Thu; ◷ 10am-6pm Tue-Sun Mar-Oct, 10am-5pm Tue-Sun Nov-Feb). Next door is the **Théâtre Romain**, built around 15 BC and enlarged in AD 120 to seat an audience of 10,000, and the smaller **odéon** where Romans held poetry readings and musical recitals.

PRESQU'ÎLE

The centrepiece of Presqu'île's (Map pp470–2) beautiful **place des Terreaux** (metro Hôtel de Ville), 1er, is a 19th-century fountain made of 21 tonnes of lead and sculpted by Frédéric-Auguste Bartholdi, creator of New York's Statue of Liberty. The four horses pulling the chariot symbolise rivers galloping seawards. The contemporary fountains dotting the square were designed by Burden. The **Hôtel de Ville** (City Hall) fronting the square was built in 1655 but given its present ornate façade in 1702.

Next door, the **Musée des Beaux-Arts** (Museum of Fine Arts; ☎ 04 72 10 17 40; 20 place des Terreaux, 1er; metro Hôtel de Ville; adult/under 18 €6/free; ◷ 10am-6pm Wed-Mon, from 10.30pm Fri) showcases France's finest collection of sculptures and paintings from every period of European art outside Paris. The free **cloister garden** is a great picnic venue.

Lyon's neoclassical, glass-topped **opera house** (place de la Comédie, 1er; metro Hôtel de Ville) was

---

TOP FIVE: LYON FOR KIDS

There's no end to kidding around Lyon, proof of the pudding being in the city's quarterly what's-on-for-kids listings magazine *Bulles de Gones* (www.bullesdegones.com in French). Parks, biking and boats aside, how about …

Aquarium du Grand Lyon (off Map pp470-2; ☎ 04 72 66 65 66; www.aquariumlyon.fr in French; 6 place du Général Leclerc, La Mulatière; adult/child €11/7; ◷ 10am-5pm Mon-Fri, 10am-6pm Sat & Sun school holidays, 10am-6pm Sat & Sun rest of year) Watch sharks and feel fish at this well thought-out aquarium, 4km south of the city centre in La Mulatière. Bus No 15 from place Bellecour.

A Puppet Show in Parc de la Tête d'Or (off Map pp470-2; ☎ 04 78 71 75); at Vieux Lyon's Théâtre Le Guignol (Map pp470-2; ☎ 04 78 28 92 57; 2 rue Louis Carrand, 5e; metro Vieux Lyon; adult/child €8/6); or at the Théâtre de la Croix Rousse (off Map p475; ☎ 04 72 32 11 55; 65 blvd des Canuts, 4e; metro Hénon).

A Nature Workshop Making a barometer, mini-vegetable garden, star spotting and the like – organised by Nature & Découvertes (Map pp470-2; ☎ 04 78 38 38 74; 58 rue de la République, 2e; metro Bellecour).

Musée de l'Automobile Henri Malartre (Car Museum; off Map pp470-2; ☎ 04 78 22 18 80; Château de Rochetaillée; adult/under 18 €5.30/free; ◷ 9am-6pm Tue-Sun) Ogle at 120 vintage cars and 50-odd motorbikes at this 15th-century chateau-museum, 10km north in Rochetaillée-sur-Saône. Bus No 40 or 70.

Musée de la Poupée (Doll Museum; off Map pp470-2; ☎ 04 78 87 87 00; www.lacroix-laval.com in French; Parc de Lacroix-Laval, route de St-Bel, Marcy l'Étoile; adult/under 18 €3.80/free, everyone free on Thu; ◷ 10am-5pm Tue-Sun) Little girls will love this fairy-tale castle, surrounded by a dreamy 115-hectare park, where dolls from all eras and countries live.

erected in 1832. Skateboarders and roller-bladers buzz around the fountains of riverside **place Louis Pradel**, surveyed by the figure of **Homme de la Liberté** (Man of Freedom) on roller-skates, sculpted from scrap metal by Marseille-born César (1921–98).

The **Musée de l'Imprimerie** (Printing Museum; ☎ 04 78 37 65 98; 37 rue de la Poulaillerie, 2e; metro Cordeliers; adult/under 18 €3.80/free; ☼ 9.30am-noon & 2-6pm Wed-Sun) focuses on a technology established in Lyon by the 1480s.

Extraordinary Lyonnais silks, French and Asian textiles, and carpets are included in the collection of the **Musée des Tissus** (Textile Museum; ☎ 04 78 38 42 00; www.musee-des-tissus.com; 34 rue de la Charité, 2e; metro Ampère; adult/under 18 €4.60/free; ☼ 10am-5.30pm Tue-Sun). Next door, the **Musée des Arts Décoratifs** (Decorative Arts Museum; free with Textile Museum ticket; ☼ 10am-noon & 2-5.30pm Tue-Sun) showcases 18th-century furniture, tapestries, wallpaper, ceramics and silver.

Laid out in the 17th century, **place Bellecour** (metro Bellecour) – one of Europe's largest public squares – is pierced by an equestrian **statue of Louis XIV**. From here, pedestrianised **rue Victor Hugo** runs southwards to place Carnot and Gare de Perrache.

South of the train station lies the **Confluent de Lyon** (off Map pp470-2; www.lyon-confluence.fr), one of the city's most exciting urban areas where the Rhône and the Saône meet.

Watch this space for the spacey science-orientated **Musée des Confluences** to open in 2007. As much a stunning piece of contemporary architecture as museum, it will be housed in a gigantic glass riverside crystal. The exhibition space inside will be shaped like a cloud.

CROIX ROUSSE

The hilltop neighbourhood of Croix Rousse (Map opposite), to the north up the steep *pentes* (slopes) from central Lyon, is known for its village air, bohemian inhabitants and outdoor market. Following the introduction of the mechanical Jacquard loom in 1805, Lyonnais *canuts* (silk weavers) built workshops here with beamed ceilings high enough to accommodate the new machines. During the bitter 1830–31 *canut* uprisings, triggered by low pay and dire working conditions, hundreds of weavers were killed.

The labour-intensive life of 19th-century silk weavers comes to life at the riveting **Atelier de Passementerie** (off Map pp475; ☎ 04 78 27 17 13; www.soierie-vivante.asso.fr; 21 rue Richan, 4e; metro Croix Rousse; adult/child €1.90/1.40; ☼ 2-6.30pm Tue, 9am-noon & 2-6.30pm Wed-Sat), an authentic workshop where *canuts* (weavers) weaved until as late as 1979. The Passementerie workshop is one of three that can be visited by guided tour only. In the **Atelier de Tissage**

TROMPE-L'ŒIL MURALS

Famous Lyonnais, past and present, beckon from a series of huge wall murals painted by Cité de la Création (www.cite-creation.fr), a local artists' group set up in the early 1980s.

Some 25 local personalities stare out from the seven-storey **Fresque des Lyonnais** (Map pp470-2; cnr rue de la Martinière & quai de la Pêcherie, 1er; metro Hôtel de Ville). More-familiar faces include loom inventor Joseph-Marie Jacquard (1752–1834), Renaissance poet Maurice Scève (c 1499–c 1560), superstar chef Paul Bocuse (see p479) and explorer Giovanni da Verrazzano, a Florentine shipmaster and navigator who discovered what is now New York in 1524 (he left it untouched, enabling the Dutch to settle it a century later, though he did earn a narrows and a bridge for his efforts). The yellow-haired Little Prince is a tribute to his creator, author Antoine de St-Exupéry, born in Lyon in 1900. Up the hill in Croix Rousse, the **Mur des Canuts** (Map opposite; cnr blvd des Canuts & rue Denfert-Rochereau, 4e; metro Hénon) celebrates the quarter's silk-weaving tradition.

At the **Musée Urbain Tony Garnier** (off Map pp470-2; ☎ 04 78 75 16 75; www.museeurbaintonygarnier .com; 4 rue des Serpollières, 8e; admission free; ☼ 2-6pm Tue-Fri & Sun, 10am-noon & 2-7pm Sat), 25 murals painted on apartment blocks illustrate different aspects of 'the ideal city' as perceived by Tony Garnier (1869–1948), the Lyonnais architect who designed the 1930s housing estate in which the urban museum is housed. Bus No 53 from Gare de Perrache stops outside the museum.

Other monumental murals include **Bibliothèque de la Cité** (Map pp470-2; cnr quai de la Pêcherie & rue de la Platière, 1er; metro Hôtel de Ville) featuring five storeys of shelved books; and **Mur du Cinéma** (off Map pp470-2; cnr cours Gambetta & Grand Rue de la Guillotière, 7e; metro Guillotière), which illustrates the city's marvellous cinematic history.

Mécanique (Mechanical Weaving Workshop) an entire family of weavers lived and worked in just 65 sq metres for decades.

RIVE GAUCHE

Lyon's 117-hectare **Parc de la Tête d'Or** (off Map right; ☎ 04 72 69 47 60; blvd des Belges, 6e; metro Masséna; 🕐 6am-11pm mid-Apr–mid-Oct, to 9pm mid-Oct–mid-Apr), landscaped in the 1860s, is graced by a lake, a botanical garden with greenhouses, an Alpine garden, rose garden and zoo. When it's warm you can rent boats, ride ponies and play miniature golf. The park is served by bus No 41 or 47 from metro Part-Dieu.

The park's northern realms snug up to the brick-and-glass **Cité Internationale**, designed by Italian architect Renzo Piano to host the G7 summit in 1996. Inside, the **Musée d'Art Contemporain** (off Map right; Museum of Contemporary Art; ☎ 04 72 69 17 17; www.moca-lyon.org; 81 quai Charles de Gaulle, 6e; adult/under 18 €3.80/free; 🕐 noon-7pm Wed-Sun) displays works created after 1960.

The WWII headquarters of Gestapo chief Klaus Barbie (see p469) houses the evocative **Centre d'Histoire de la Résistance et de la Déportation** (Map pp470-2; ☎ 04 78 72 23 11; 14 av Berthelot, 7e; metro Perrache or Jean Macé; adult/under 18 €3.80/free; 🕐 9am-5.30pm Wed-Sun). Multimedia exhibits present the history of Nazi atrocities and the heroism of French Resistance fighters.

Cinema's glorious beginnings are featured at the **Musée Lumière** (off Map pp470-2; ☎ 04 78 78 18 95; www.institut-lumiere.org; 25 rue du Premier Film, 8e; metro Monplaisir-Lumière; adult/student €6/5; 🕐 11am-6.30pm Tue-Sun), 3km southeast of place Belle-cour on cours Gambetta. It's in the home of Antoine Lumière who, with his sons Auguste and Louis, shot the first reels of the world's first motion picture, *La Sortie des Usines Lumières* (Exit of the Lumières Factories) on 19 March 1895. Classic films are screened at the **Hangar du Premier Film** (p482).

The **Grande Mosquée de Lyon** (off Map pp470-2; ☎ 04 78 76 00 23; 146 blvd Pinel, 8e; metro Laënnec; 🕐 9am-noon Sat-Thu), 5km east of Presqu'île, fuses traditional North African architecture and calligraphy with contemporary Western styles.

Activities
BLADING

Rollerbladers (www.generationsroller.asso.fr) meet on Fridays at 9pm on place Bellecour for a mass swirl around the city. Otherwise, they

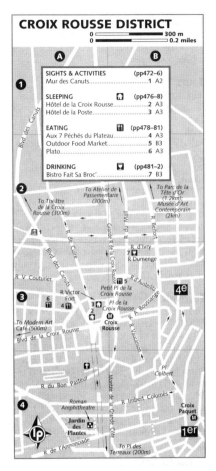

CROIX ROUSSE DISTRICT

0 ———— 300 m
0 ———— 0.2 miles

SIGHTS & ACTIVITIES	(pp472–6)
Mur des Canuts	1 A2

SLEEPING	🏠 (pp476–8)
Hôtel de la Croix Rousse	2 A3
Hôtel de la Poste	3 A3

EATING	🍴 (pp478–81)
Aux 7 Péchés du Plateau	4 A3
Outdoor Food Market	5 B3
Plato	6 A3

DRINKING	🍷 (pp481–2)
Bistro Fait Sa Broc'	7 B3

blade by the rivers; in Parc de la Tête d'Or (off Map pp475); and in the **skate park** (off Map pp470-2; ☎ 04 78 69 17 86; 24 rue Pierre de Coubertin, 7e; metro Gerland) in Parc de Gerland, south of the city at the confluence of the Rhône and the Saône.

Le Cri du Kangourou (Map pp470-2; ☎ 04 78 39 59 26; 21 rue d'Algérie, 1er; metro Hôtel de Ville) rents blades.

CYCLING

Cycle paths run beside both rivers; the tourist office has details. Bicycles can be rented from **Lyon Parc Auto** (Map pp470-2; ☎ 04 78 30 11 10; 23 place des Terreaux, 1er; metro Hôtel de Ville; €7/12 per half-/full day; 🕐 9am-7pm), the subterranean car park underneath place des Terreaux.

LYON & THE RHÔNE VALLEY

Motorists who park in the **car park** (☎ 04 78 42 50 09; www.vincipark.com; parking per hr/24hr €1.50/20.50; ☼ 24hr) beneath place Bellecour can borrow a bike for free.

Tours
The tourist office runs thematic English-language **walking tours** (adult €9 or €12) of Vieux Lyon and Croix Rousse. Alternatively, DIY with a set of headphones (€8/12 per half-/full day) or a copy (€1.50) of *Lyon Balades: Decouvrez Lyon à pied* (Lyon Walks: Discover Lyon on foot) or *à vélo* (by bike) in hand. The tourist office stocks both.

Navig-Inter (☎ 04 78 42 96 81; www.naviginter.fr in French) runs 1¼-hour afternoon **river excursions** (Map pp470–2; from the dock at 3 quai des Célestins, 2e; metro Bellecour or Vieux Lyon; adult/child €7/5) from April to October. Advance bookings are vital for its **lunch** and **dinner cruises** (adult/child from €24/37), departing from 23 quai Claude Bernard, 7e (Map pp470–2).

Festivals & Events
In June and July, **Les Nuits de Fourvière** (☎ 04 72 32 00 00; www.nuitsdefourviere.fr in French) brings a multitude of open-air concerts to Fourvière's Théâtre Romain (Map pp470–2).

For several days around 8 December, Lyon is lit up by the **Fête des Lumières** (Festival of Lights), marking the Feast of the Immaculate Conception. Sound-and-light shows are projected onto the city's most important buildings (place des Terreaux is always a key festival venue; Map p475) and everyone puts candles in the windows of their homes.

Even-numbered years host the month-long **Biennale de la Danse** (Dance Biennial) in September and odd-numbered years hail the **Biennale d'Art Contemporain** (Contemporary Art Biennial) between July and September.

Sleeping
BUDGET
Auberge de Jeunesse du Vieux Lyon (Map pp470-2; ☎ 04 78 15 05 50; lyon@fuaj.org; 41-45 montée du Chemin Neuf; metro Vieux Lyon, 5e; dm €12.70; reception ☼ 7am-1pm & 9m or 10pm-1am) Rates include breakfast at this superbly located hostel above Vieux Lyon. Its 180 beds are split between rooms for two to seven people.

Hôtel Iris (Map pp470-2; ☎ 04 78 39 93 80; hoteliris@ freesurf.fr; 36 rue de l'Arbre Sec, 1er; metro Hôtel de Ville; s/d with hand basin €29/32, with shower & toilet from €36/39). The location of this two-star hotel inside a wonderful, four-centuries-old convent could not be better – so get in quick to snag one of its 11 simple rooms overlooking a quiet courtyard.

Hôtel de la Poste (Map p475; ☎ /fax 04 78 28 62 67; 1 rue Victor Fort, 4e; metro Croix Rousse; s/d/q with shared shower from €17/17/33, d/tr with shower €33/46; reception ☼ 6.30am-8.30pm) Rooms share toilets on the corridor (some showers too) at this back-to-basics hotel where price – not prettiness – pulls in the punters. Fourth-floor rooms command a bird's-eye view of Croix Rousse's central square.

TRABOULES

There's more to Lyon than meets the eye. Beneath and between the city's chic shops and cafés, dark and dingy (and invariably smelly) *traboules* (secret passages) wind their way through apartment blocks, under streets and into courtyards. In all, 315 passages link 230 streets and have a combined length of 50km.

Although a couple of Vieux Lyon's *traboules* date from Roman times, most were constructed by *canuts* (silk weavers) in the 19th century to facilitate the transport of silk in inclement weather. Resistance fighters found them equally handy during WWII.

Genuine *traboules* (derived from the Latin *trans ambulare* meaning 'to pass through') cut from one street to another, often wending their way up fabulous spiral staircases en route. Passages that fan out into a courtyard or lead into a cul de sac are not *traboules*, but rather *miraboules*.

Vieux Lyon's most celebrated *traboules* include those linking 54 rue St-Jean with 27 rue du Bœuf (push the intercom button to buzz open the door), 24 rue St-Jean with 1 rue du Bœuf and 10 quai Romain Rolland with 2 place du Gouvernement. In Croix Rousse, step into the city's underworld at 9 place Colbert, crossing cours des Voraces – renowned for its monumental staircase that zigzags up seven floors – and emerging at 29 rue Imbert Colomès.

The tourist office runs *traboules* guided tours (above).

Camping

Wanting to pitch up on a farm around Lyon? Contact Gîtes de France (see below).

Camping Municipal International (off Map pp470-2; ☎ 04 78 35 64 55; camping-lyon@marie-lyon.fr; allée du Camping, Portes de Lyon; camping €13.70; reception ⏰ 8am-8pm Mon-Fri, 12.30-8pm Sat & Sun 🚇) About 10km northwest of central Lyon in Dardilly, this 215-site area can be reached by bus No 3 from metro Hôtel de Ville or bus No 89 from metro Gare de Vaise.

MID-RANGE

From a room above a village *épicerie* to a suite in a Second Empire mansion in Beaujolais, **Gîtes de France** (Map pp470-2; ☎ 04 72 77 17 50; www.gites-de-france-rhone.com; 1 rue Général Plessier, 2e; metro Perrache; B&B for 2 people €40-100; ⏰ 9am-noon & 1-6pm Mon-Fri, 10am-1pm Sat) organises B&B around Lyon to suit all budgets and tastes. Many places cook dinner (€10 to €25 per person).

Hôtel St-Paul (Map pp470-2; ☎ 04 78 28 13 29; www .hotelstpaul.fr; 6 rue Lainerie, 5e; metro Vieux Lyon; d with shower €38, d/q with shower & toilet €45/68) Two stars stud this 20-room inn in Vieux Lyon where medieval stonework mixes with modern blandness. Rooms facing the shabby but interior courtyard promise a quieter night's sleep than those facing the street.

Hôtel Alexandra (Map pp470-2; ☎ 04 78 37 75 79; 49 rue Victor Hugo, 2e; metro Ampère; d with shower/shower & toilet €43.50/49.50) Another one-star establishment with a smidgen of old-fashioned charm thrown.

Hotel des Artistes (Map pp470-2; ☎ 04 78 42 04 88; www.hoteldesartistes.fr; 8 rue Gaspard André, 2e; metro Bellecour or Hôtel de Ville; s €70-102, d €79-108) Theatrically furnished rooms are the trademark of this very red, very charming, three-star pad in the heart of Presqu'île shopping land. Rates reflect what's in the bathroom (shower or bath) and the view.

Hôtel de Paris (Map pp470-2; ☎ 04 78 28 00 95; www .hoteldeparis-lyon.com; 16 rue de la Platière, 1er; metro Hôtel de Ville; small s/d €42/49, lux d €53-68). Middle-of-the-road sums up this mid-range hotel bang slap in central Lyon's commercial heart. The priciest doubles have a minibar and a big bath to wallow in as well as a shower.

Hôtel de la Croix Rousse (Map p475; ☎ 04 78 28 29 85; 157 blvd de la Croix Rousse, 4e; metro Croix Rousse; d €46; Ⓟ) Croix Rousse's simple, village-style hotel touts 18 rooms – furnished several decades ago but spick, span and spotlessly

HAVE A GOOD WEEKEND

City-breakers arriving in Lyon on Friday or Saturday can take advantage of the city's 'Bon Week-end à Lyon' deal, whereby selected hotels offer the second night free to guests staying in a single or double room for two consecutive nights. *Bon* weekenders also get a free Lyon City Card (see p469). Book at least 24 hours in advance directly through the hotel, mentioning 'Bon Week-end à Lyon'.

clean. Reception shuts for the night around midnight; ask for the code to get back in if you intend staying out late.

Hôtel de Noailles (off Map pp470-2; ☎ 04 78 72 40 72; hotel-de-noailles-lyon@wanadoo.fr; 30 cours Gambetta, 7e; metro Saxe-Gambetta; s/d from €54/62; Ⓟ) This charming 24-room place is a comfortable choice for those seeking a bed on the *rive gauche* (left bank). Part of the Logis de France association (always a safe bet), everything about this place is reassuringly unsurprising.

Hôtel des Celestins (Map pp470-2; ☎ 04 72 56 08 98; www.hotelcelestins.com; 4 rue des Archers, 2e; metro Bellecour; courtyard s/d €56/60, theatre d €63) Families with kids – cot or camp-bed size (both provided for free) – are welcome at this friendly, theatre-side hotel; it goes out of its way to ensure guests get the most out of their stay in Lyon.

Comfort Hôtel St-Antoine (Map pp470-2; ☎ 04 78 92 91 91; www.hotel-saintantoine.fr; 1 rue du Port du Temple, 2e; metro Cordeliers; s/d from €63/66; Ⓟ Ⓓ) A stylish mix of old and new – a WiFi Internet zone and period furnishings – greet guests at this thoroughly modern hotel that occupies an 18th-century townhouse.

Hôtel Ste-Catherine (Map pp470-2; ☎ 04 78 37 44 91, fax 04 78 42 90 17; 28 rue Ste-Catherine, 1er; metro Hôtel de Ville; street-facing s/d €50/55, garden-facing €58/63) This charming old 29-room pile in the heart of kebab land is slowly getting a contemporary face-lift, meaning things get shabbier the higher you ascend. Pricier but quieter 'garden'-facing rooms peep out onto a pocket-sized interior courtyard with a couple of flowerbeds.

TOP END

Hôtel Cour des Loges (Map pp470-2; ☎ 04 72 77 44 44; www.courdesloges.com; 2-8 rue du Bœuf, 5e; metro Vieux

BOUCHONS

A *bouchon* might be a 'bottle stopper' or 'traffic jam' elsewhere in France, but in Lyon it's a small, friendly, more local-than-local bistro that cooks up the city's traditional cuisine.

Kick-start what will definitely be a memorable gastronomic experience with a *communard,* an aperitif of red Beaujolais wine and *crème de cassis* (blackcurrant liqueur), named after the supporters of the Paris Commune killed in 1871. Blood-red in colour, the mix would be considered criminal elsewhere in France. When ordering wine, don't bother asking for a wine list. Simply order a *pot* – a thick glass bottle adorned with an elastic band to prevent wine drips – of red Côtes du Rhône or Beaujolais.

Next comes the entrée of *tablier de sapeur* (literally 'fireman's apron', but actually meaning breaded, fried stomach) or *salade de cervelas* (salad of boiled pork sausage, sometimes studded with pistachio nuts or specks of black truffle) perhaps. Hearty main dishes to sink meat-frantic gnashers into include *boudin blanc* (veal sausage), *boudin noir aux pommes* (blood sausage with apples), *quenelle* (a lighter-than-light flour, egg and cream dumpling), *quenelle de brochet* (pike quenelle, usually served in a creamy crayfish sauce) and *andouillette* (sausages made from pigs' intestines). If none of those appeal, try wrapping your lips around some *pieds de mouton/veau/couchon* (sheep/calf/piggie trotters).

The cheese course usually comprises a choice of three things: a bowl of *fromage blanc* (a cross between cream cheese and natural yogurt) with or without cream; *cervelle de canut* (literally 'brains of the silk weaver'), *fromage blanc* mixed with chives and garlic that originated in Croix Rousse and accompanied every meal for 19th-century weavers; or a round of local St-Marcellin ripened to perfection by the legendary Mère Richard for three generations. Desserts are unadventurous and rarely that inspiring. Think *tarte aux pommes* (apple tart) or *fromage blanc* (again) with a fruit coulis dribbled on top.

Little etiquette is required to eat in *bouchons*. Seldom do you get clean cutlery for each course, mopping your plate with a chunk of bread is fine; and, if the tablecloth is of the paper variety, that's probably where your bill will be added up.

In keeping with tradition, many *bouchons* are closed weekends and in August.

Lyon; ste from €230/440; (P ⊠ 🞬 💻) This haven of peace and tranquillity languishes in four beautiful Renaissance mansions wrapped around a *traboule*. Some suites have a fireplace and *plafond à la française* (a hefty wooden-beamed ceiling typical to Lyon), and there's a sauna to sweat it out. Kenzo, Kissinger and Phil Collins star in the *livre d'or* (guest book).

La Tour Rose (Map pp470-2; ☎ 04 78 92 69 10; 22 rue du Bœuf, 5e; metro Vieux Lyon; d €230-540; (P ⊠ 🞬 💻) The 12 lavishly appointed suites in this four-star beauty built from three 13th- to 18th-century buildings honour Lyon's silky traditions. Prices reflect room size. One restaurant spectacularly reclines in an old chapel with cobbled floor and glass roof.

Sofitel Royal Lyon (Map pp470-2; ☎ 04 78 37 57 31; H2952@accor-hotels.com; 20 place Bellecour, 2e; metro Bellecour; s/d from €136/150, lux from €215/241, ste €492; (P ⊠ 🞬 💻) The most prestigious address on place Bellecour has lavished tender loving luxurious care upon its guests ever since

1895 when it first opened (at that time under the name Hôtel Royal). Service is four star and royal here, and 24-hour hotel parking costs €16.

Hilton Lyon (Map pp470-2; ☎ 04 78 17 50 50; www.hilton-lyon.com; 70 quai Charles de Gaulle, 6e; s/d from €136/150, lux s/d from €215/241, ste €492; (P ⊠ 🞬 💻) The city's other big-name hotel is a shimmering, state-of-the-art, sun-lit glass palace with 201 rooms wedged between the River Rhône and Parc de la Tête d'Or. Suites on the top floor command a stunning city panorama.

Eating
BOUCHONS
Reservations are recommended at these quintessentially Lyonnais establishments (see above).

Café des Fédérations (Map pp470-2; ☎ 04 78 28 26 00; www.lesfedeslyon.com in French; 8 rue Major Martin, 1er; metro Hôtel de Ville; dinner menu €23; 🕒 Mon-Fri) For proof of the pudding that some things never change, plop yourself down at this splendid *bouchon* and feast on *caviar de la Croix Rousse* (lentils dressed in a creamy sauce) and other age-old dishes.

Chez Hugon (Map pp470-2; ☎ 04 78 28 10 94; 12 rue Pizay, 1er; metro Hôtel de Ville; menu €22; ⏺ Mon-Fri) Madame Hugon serves typical meaty treats on red-and-white checked tablecloths in an interior that can only be described as a blast from the past – 1937 to be precise.

Café-Restaurant des Deux Places (Map pp470-2; ☎ 04 78 28 95 10; 5 place Fernand Rey, 1er; metro Hôtel de Ville; menu €22; ⏺ Mon-Fri) Checked curtains and an interior crammed with antiques and old photographs contribute to the overwhelmingly traditional feel of this well-placed *bouchon*. Its pavement-terrace beneath trees on a quiet village-like square is a major drawcard.

Le Garet (Map pp470-2; ☎ 04 78 28 16 94; 7 rue du Garet, 1er; metro Hôtel de Ville; lunch menu €17, dinner menu €21; ⏺ Mon-Fri) Yet another in the great cluster of typical *bouchons*, Le Garet – named after the small street on which it stands no less – is within spitting distance of the opera house, making it a particularly tasty choice for the city's cultural set.

La Meunière (Map pp470-2; ☎ 04 78 28 62 91; 11 rue Neuve, 1er; metro Hôtel de Ville; lunch menu €17, dinner menus €22 & €27; ⏺ Tue-Sat) Excellent trotter selection, snails and ox muzzle.

FRENCH

Plato (Map p475; ☎ 04 72 00 01 30; 1 rue Villeneuve, 4e; metro Croix Rousse; lunch menus €15 & €19.50; ⏺ Mon-Sat) Sweep through thick pink curtains into this stylish plateau restaurant, decked out in with contemporary flair and oozing theatre. Creative dishes – think mussel carpaccio, a whole roasted Bourg en Bresse chicken and the like – are just divine, darling.

Aux 7 Péchés du Plateau (Map p475; ☎ 04 78 28 48 82; place Tapis 3, 4e; metro Croix Rousse; menus €18 & €30; ⏺ Mon-Sat) Make no bones about it – diners come here for the meat, not the décor which is strictly bare-bones. This butcher's restaurant serves *salade de rognons blancs et ris d'agneau* (white kidney salad with sweet breads), *tête de veau* (calf's head) and several beef cuts.

Commanderie des Antonins (Map pp470-2; ☎ 04 78 37 19 21; www.commanderie-antonons.fr in French; 30 quai St-Antoine, 2e; metro Bellecour; lunch menu €15, dinner menu €19.90) Another meaty choice, albeit it a highly refined one, this ode to the carnivorous cooks meat the old-fashioned way – slowly over a low heat in a wood-burning oven – and serves it with a flourish in a medieval banquet hall. Once a month it hosts thematic meal-accompanied, gastronomy lectures.

La Soup'ente (Map pp470-2; ☎ 04 78 39 32 64; 6 place des Capucins, 1er; metro Hôtel de Ville; plat du jour €8; ⏺ Tue-Sun) A charming traffic-free courtyard terrace is the main draw of this unpretentious art, sound and food concept restaurant where a cultured crowd munches simple food platters (€9).

La Table d'Hippolyte (Map pp470-2; ☎ 04 78 27 75 59; 22 rue Hippolyte Flandrin, 1er; lunch menu €17, full dinner around €45; ⏺ closed Sun, Mon & lunch Sat) Traditional French cuisine is concocted with the freshest seasonal ingredients at this pocket-sized place with a pocket-sized pavement terrace in summer. What's at the market dictates what is chalked up on the board.

Restaurant Albert (Map pp470-2; ☎ 04 78 27 95 56; 10 place Fernand Rey, 1er; metro Hôtel de Ville; menu €27; ⏺ Tue-Sat) Albert fuses the eclectic with the traditional to create an intimate,

AUTHOR'S CHOICE

L'Ouest (off Map pp470-2; ☎ 04 37 64 64 64; www.bocuse.com; 1 quai du Commerce, 9e; metro Gare de Vaise; starters/mains around €14/20; ⏺ lunch & dinner) No other chef has done more to secure Lyon's reputation as French gastronomic capital than Paul Bocuse, one of the oldest and most respected names in the business who has revolutionised fine dining in the city with his four-card pack of contemporary dining spaces. (He still runs his self-named, 'old-school' haute cuisine restaurant in Collonges-au-Mont d'Or, 10km north, too.) With the focus at Ouest (meaning 'west') being on island cuisine – any island that is – Bocuse-trained chefs cook up everything from crab 'n' saffron soup to Indonesian-inspired cod and straight-forward lamb chops – all in front of diners' eyes in a state-of-the-art stainless-steel open kitchen. Décor is minimalist and avant garde (think glass and wood), fashion TV flashes (rather annoyingly so) across flat wall TV screens, and a vast decking space outside overlooks the murky grey waters of the Saône.

bistro where delicious fare rules. Service veers on the bohemian and Albert's *raviolis d'escargots maison* (snail-stuffed pasta cushions) followed by *rognons de veau au vinaigre de zérès* (veal kidneys in sherry vinegar) are memorable musts.

Cobbled rue Mercière (2e) is crammed with eating options, terraces overflowing in summer.

Gaston Restaurant Agricole (Map pp470-2; ☎ 04 72 41 87 86; 41 rue Mercière, 2e; metro Cordeliers; lunch buffet €12; ☜ Mon-Sat) Pack a hearty thirst and giant-sized appetite before venturing into this feisty agricultural restaurant complete with rusty old tractor parked up front and a liberal scattering of vegie-filled wheelbarrows. Dining is around shared wooden tables and the feast-until-you're-full lunchtime buffet of cold meat and vegies is a steal.

Lolo Quoi (Map pp470-2; ☎ 04 72 77 60 90; 40-42 rue Mercière, 2e; metro Cordeliers; pasta €12, starters €5, mains €15; ☜ noon-2pm & 7pm-midnight) Sleekly kitted

---

out in wood and slate, Italianate Lolo Quoi is hugely trendy and very chic. Pastas with innovative sauces are the speciality.

Brasserie Georges (Map pp470-2; ☎ 04 72 56 54 54; 30 cours de Verdun, 2e; metro Perrache; menus €19 & €21.50; ☜ 11.30am-11.15pm Sun-Thu, 11.30am-12.15am Fri & Sat) Going strong since 1836, this brasserie seats over 500 people amid ornate 1920s Art Deco ceiling murals, floor tiles and upholstered red banquettes. Food is of the onion soup, mussels and sauerkraut variety.

ETHNIC & VEGETARIAN

Alyssaar (Map pp470-2; ☎ 04 78 29 57 66; 29 rue du Bât d'Argent, 1er; metro Hôtel de Ville; menus €12, €15 & €19; ☜ dinner Tue-Sat) Aleppo is undoubtedly 'the gastronomic capital of the Middle East' as far as the Syrian-born owner of this cheap, cheerful and tasty joint is concerned.

Le Pâtisson (Map pp470-2; ☎ 04 72 41 81 71; www .lepatisson.com in French; 17 rue du Port du Temple, 2e; metro Bellecour; menus €15.50 & €18.50; ☜ closed Sun, lunch Sat & dinner Fri) A *médaillon de tofu* and *escalope d'aubergine* are among the refreshingly imaginative dishes cooked up with flair at this well established vegetarian restaurant.

Rue Ste-Marie-des-Terreaux and rue Ste-Catherine, 1er (metro Hôtel de Ville), are lined with Chinese, Turkish and Indian places offering cheap eats.

CAFÉS

Outdoor cafés spill across place des Terreaux (metro Hôtel de Ville) and seemingly every square and street in Vieux Lyon (metro Vieux Lyon) in summer. Our perennial favourites follow.

Maison Perroudon (Map pp470-2; ☎ 04 78 37 37 56; 6 rue de la Barre, 2e; metro Bellecour; ☜ 7am-7.30pm Tue-Sun; ☒) Smoking is no go in this cake shop's contemporary-styled café where a predominantly female crowd lunches on light salads. Its cakes are to die for.

Giraudet (Map pp470-2; ☎ 04 72 77 98 58; www .giraudet.fr; 2 rue Colonel Chambonnet, 2e; metro Bellecour; ☜ lunch 11.30am-2.30pm Mon-Sat) Essentially a small sleek boutique selling *quenelles* (flour, egg and cream dumplings), Giraudet also has tables and a bar where you can taste the Lyonnais speciality and unusual soups (watercress, curry, broad bean and cumin etc).

Café 203 (Map pp470-2; ☎ 04 78 28 66 65; 9 rue du Garet, 1er; metro Hôtel de Ville; 1-/2-/3-course menu €7/9.50/12; ☜ 7am-2am) One of the most popular addresses in city-slick circles, 203 oozes

---

BREAKFAST & BRUNCH

A clutch of inspired breakfast and brunch joints guarantees to drag the laziest of bones out of bed. **Café 203** (see right) cooks up a simple croissant or waffle, juice and coffee breakfast (€5); and the **Modern Art Café** (see opposite) does weekend brunch. Otherwise try:

- **Les Enfants Gâtés** (Map pp470-2; ☎ 04 78 30 91 14; 3 place Sathonay, 1er; metro Hôtel de Ville; breakfast from €6, lunch menu €8.50; ☜ Tue-Sun) The Spoilt Children leaves breakfast and brunch lovers feeling thoroughly spoilt. Pick from a French breakfast, English breakfast or giant-sized mix of both at this unpretentious café with a pavement terrace on one of the city's prettiest squares.

- **L'Épicérie** (Map pp470-2; ☎ 04 78 37 70 85; 2 rue de la Monnaie, 2e; metro Cordeliers; breakfasts €4.90 & €6.90; ☜ 8am-1am) Enjoy breakfast *comme à la maison* (like at home) – bread with jam, honey and nutella, plus coffee, tea or chicory – or indulge in *brioche* (sweet bread) too *comme chez mémé* (like at grandma's) at this family-run bistro, decked out like a 1950s grocery store.

TASTEBUD TICKLERS

Titillate your tastebuds or those of Granny's back home with...

■ *Boudins, andouillettes* and other porky piggy Lyonnais sausages from **Moinon** (Map pp470-2; 18 rue de la Plaitière, 1er; metro Hôtel de Ville; ⊙ Tue-Sat & Sun morning), the best sausage maker in town.

■ The best Côte du Rhône money can buy from **La Vieille Réserve** (Map pp470-2; 1 place Tobbie Robatel, 1er; metro Hôtel de Ville; ⊙ Tue-Sat), an exclusive wine shop.

■ Hand-painted spice chocolates from **Richart** (Map pp470-2; 1 rue du Plat, 2e; metro Bellecour; ⊙ Mon-Sat).

■ A strawberry, peach, blueberry or other fruity liqueur from **Pagès Védrenne** (Map pp470-2; 5 place Bellecour, 2e; metro Bellecour; ⊙ Tue-Sat).

■ Lyon's finest cakes and pastries from **Bernachon** (off Map pp470-2; www.bernachon.com in French; 42 cours Franklin Roosevelt, 6e; metro Foch; ⊙ Tue-Sun).

---

atmosphere and is simply a great place to breakfast (see opposite), lunch, dine in the evening or just drink. It also runs **Café 100 Tabac** (Map pp470-2; 23 rue de l'Arbre Sec; ⊠) around the corner – same hours, prices, genre but no smoking.

Grand Café des Négociants (Map pp470-2; ☎ 04 78 42 50 05; 2 place Francisque Regaud, 2e; metro Cordeliers; ⊙ 7am-1am) Mirror-lined walls and impeccable service characterise this refined café-cum-brasserie where Lyonnais have met for coffee or to lunch since 1864. Its buzzing pavement terrace makes it a popular choice.

SELF-CATERING

Central Lyon has two fantastic **outdoor food markets** (Riverfront Map pp470-2; quai St-Antoine, 2e; metro Bellecour or Cordeliers; ⊙ Tue-Sun morning; Croix Rousse Map p475; blvd de la Croix Rousse, 4e; metro Croix Rousse; ⊙ Tue-Sun morning), stuffed with fruits, vegetables, meats, cheese, bread and so on.

Les Halles de Lyon (off Map pp470-2; 102 cours Lafayette, 3e; metro Part-Dieu; ⊙ 7am-noon & 3-7pm Tue-Thu, 7am-7pm Fri & Sat, 7am-noon Sun) and **La Halle de la Martinière** (Map pp470-2; 24 rue de la Martinière, 1er; metro Hôtel de Ville; ⊙ 8am-12.30pm & 4-7.30pm Tue-Sun) are the main indoor food markets. Mère Richard (see Bouchons, p478) has a stall at Les Halles.

Drinking

The bounty of café-terraces on place des Terreaux, 1er, buzz with drinkers day and night. English-style pubs are clustered on rue Ste-Cathérine, 1er (metro Hôtel de Ville) and in Vieux Lyon.

Modern Art Café (off Map p475; ☎ 04 72 87 06 82; www.modernartcafé.net; 65 blvd de la Croix Rousse, 4e; metro Croix Rousse; ⊙ 5am-1am Mon-Fri, 11am-1am Sat & Sun) Retro furnishings, changing art on the walls, a *plage* (beach) with deckchairs, weekend brunch and a clutch of music- and video-driven happenings make this art bar one cool place to lounge.

Bistro Fait Sa Broc' (Map p475; ☎ 04 72 07 93 97; 1-3 rue Dumenge, 4e; metro Croix Rousse; ⊙ 5.30pm-1am Mon-Sat) A rainbow greets punters at this colourful wine bar, known for its retro furnishings (you try spotting two chairs that match), changing wall art and occasional live bands. Regional cheeses, cold meats and light snacks are served all hours.

Elle (Map pp470-2; ☎ 04 78 42 92 83; 2 rue de la Monnaie, 2e; metro Cordeliers; ⊙ 10.30am-12.30am Tue-Sat) A Moroccan-inspired interior means floor poufs, comfy sofas with an abundance of cushions, and low tables bedecked with pots of complimentary almonds and raisins for this oh-so-chic bar.

Le Voxx (Map pp470-2; ☎ 04 78 28 33 87; 1 rue d'Algérie, 1er; metro Hôtel de Ville; ⊙ 8am-2am Mon-Sat, 10am-2am Sun) What adds up to one of the Presqu'île's most hip and trendy bars boasts a minimalist interior – only really visible by day when there's less of a crowd – and a Saône-side pavement terrace where you can watch impatient motorists wait for the lights to turn green.

Palais de la Bière (Map pp470-2; ☎ 04 78 27 94 00; 1 rue Terme, 1er; metro Hôtel de Ville; ⊙ 6pm-2am Tue-Thu, 6pm-3am Fri & Sat) With 15 beers on tap (€3.40/4.20 for a 25cL glass before/after 9pm) and 300 different types of bottled beers, pint lovers won't go thirsty. An Ardèche-brewed *bière aux marrons* (chestnut beer) is about the only beer produced in the wine-loving

Rhône Valley. The truly thirsty can embark on a 15-beer *tour du monde* (world tour).

Thé Cha Yuan (Map pp470-2; ☎ 04 72 41 04 60; 7-9 rue des Remparts d'Ainay, 2e; metro Ampère; 🕑 9am-7pm Tue-Sat) Some 300 kinds of tea are brewed at this tea room that also serves dim sum – a sublime combination of French elegance and traditional Chinese serenity.

Entertainment

The tourist office has loads of information on Lyon's rich and varied entertainment scene. Locally published listings guides include the weekly *Lyon Poche* (www.lyonpoche.com in French; €1 at newsagents); the quarterly *Progrescope* (www.progrescope.com) distributed every three months with the local daily newspaper *Le Progrès* (www.leprogres. fr; €0.80 at newsagents); and the free weekly *Le Petit Bulletin* (www.petit-bulletin.fr) available at the tourist office. See p469 for online entertainment information.

Tickets for most events are sold at the **Fnac Billetterie** (ticket office; Map pp470-2; ☎ 04 72 40 49 49; 85 rue de la République, 2e; metro Bellecour; 🕑 10am-7.30pm Mon-Sat).

CINEMAS

Nondubbed films are the staple diet at **CNP-Terreaux** (Map pp470-2; ☎ 08 92 68 69 33; 40 rue du Président Édouard Herriot, 1er; metro Hôtel de Ville).

Hangar du Premier Film (off Map pp470-2; ☎ 04 78 78 18 95; www.institut-lumiere.org; 25 rue du Premier Film, 8e; metro Monplaisir Lumière) screens films of every sort and from every era, moving onto the square outside the theatre on Tuesday evenings from June to September.

In summer films (usually with a musical or pop slant) are shown on a big screen outside at Ninkasi (see below).

LIVE MUSIC

Hot Club de Lyon (Map pp470-2; ☎ 04 78 39 54 74; www .hotclubjazz.com in French; 26 rue Lanterne, 1er; metro Hôtel de Ville; adult €9-12, student €7-9; 🕑 9pm-1am Tue-Thu, 9.30pm-1am Fri, 4-7pm & 9.30pm-1am Sat) This non-profit musical landmark since 1948 stages five weekly concerts of live jazz (big band, swing, bebop, contemporary etc), plus a free Saturday afternoon jamming session.

Ninkasi (off Map pp470-2; ☎ 04 72 76 89 00; www .ninkasi.fr in French; 267 rue Marcel Mérieux, 7e; tram stop Stade de Gerland; 🕑 10am-1am Mon-Wed, 10am-3am Thu-Sat & 4-11pm Sun) This micro-brewery near the stadium lures a frenetic crowd who steam

in to drink beer, listen to DJ beats and jive to bands. In summer everything (including films on Tuesday and Wednesday) spills onto the vast bamboo terrace outside. Ninkasi runs three other joints in town

Le Transbordeur (off Map pp470-2; ☎ 04 72 43 09 99; www.transbordeur.fr; 3 blvd de Stalingrad, Villeurbanne) Lyon's prime concert venue in an old industrial building is on the big-time European concert-tour circuit and draws international stars. Take bus No 59 or 70 from metro Part-Dieu or No 4 from metro Foch.

NIGHTCLUBS

Fish (Map pp470-2; ☎ 04 72 84 98 98; 21 quai Victor Augagneur, 3e; metro Guillotière; admission €10; 🕑 8pm-5am Wed & Thu, 8pm-6am Fri & Sat). Hugely popular with the trendy set, this huge *discothèque* (capacity over 1000) occupies a boat moored on the Rhône's left bank. DJs spin varied sounds.

Le Fridge (off Map pp470-2; ☎ 04 72 61 13 61; 67 rue des Rancy, 3e; metro Guillotière; admission €10, free for women Wed & Fri; 🕑 10.30pm-5am Wed-Sat) Hip hop, house, groove and techno are the order of the day at this DJ-driven club.

La Marquise (Map pp470-2; ☎ 04 37 40 13 93; www .marquise.net; 20 quai Victor Augagneur, 3e; metro Guillotière; admission free; 🕑 10pm-5am Wed-Sat) A 'good vibes generator' is how this moored barge sells itself. Come here for electronic music of all sorts – drum and bass, soul, rap etc.

Le Cube (off Map pp470-2; ☎ 04 78 17 29 84; 115 blvd Stalingrad, Villeurbanne; admission free; 🕑 8pm-5.30am Wed-Sat) The Cube is just that – a glass box where the Lyonnais jet set flock to jive the night away. House reigns at this trend temple.

Edy'ns Club (☎ 04 78 30 02 01; 3 rue Terme, 1er; free: 🕑 10pm-12.30am Thu-Sat), **Le Madras** (☎ 04 78 30 62 30; 3 rue Terme, 1er; 🕑 10pm-late Fri & Sat) and karaoke club **L'Opéra Rock** (☎ 04 78 39 99 88; 7 rue Terme, 1er; admission €11; 🕑 10.30pm-late Tue-Sat) are a trio of dancing venues near the opera (Map pp470-2). Otherwise, nightclubs dot the length of quai Pierre Scize, 5e, along the Saône north of Vieux Lyon.

SPORT

When at home, the national football champions **Olympique Lyonnais** (http://olweb.fr) kick off at the **Stade de Gerland** (off Map pp470-2; ☎ 04 72 76 01 70; 353 av Jean Jaurès, 7e), the city stadium built in 1926 and overhauled for the 1998 World Cup. Match tickets (☎ 08 92 46 12 30) are sold online.

THEATRE, DANCE & CLASSICAL MUSIC

Opera House (Map pp470–2; ☎ 04 72 00 45 45; www.opera
-lyon.com in French; place de la Comédie, 1er; metro Hôtel de
Ville; box office ⏰ 11am-7pm Mon-Sat) Opera, ballet
and classical concerts are presented mid-
September to early July.

Maison de la Danse (off Map pp470–2; ☎ 04 72
78 18 00; www.maisondeladanse.com in French; 8 av Jean
Mermoz, 8e; tram stop Bachut-Mairie du 8e; box office
⏰ 11.45am-6.45pm Mon-Fri, 2-6.45pm Sat) Stunning performances of contemporary dance,
tango, flamenco etc.

Auditorium de Lyon (off Map pp470–2; ☎ 04 78 95
95 95; www.auditoriumlyon.com in French; 82 rue de Bonnel,
3e; metro Part-Dieu; box office ⏰ 11am-6pm Mon-Fri, 2pm
Sat) Home to the Orchestre National de Lyon;
also hosts workshops and jazz and world
music concerts September to late June.

Shopping

The **Presqu'île** (Map pp470–2) is the place
to shop: Mainstream shops line rue de la
République and rue Victor Hugo, its continuation south of place Bellecour. Upmarket
boutiques and big-name design houses stud
parallel rue du Président Édouard Herriot,
rue de Brest and the trio of streets fanning
from place des Jacobins to place Bellecour.
Lyon-créateur.com (33 rue Romarin, 1er; metro Hôtel de
Ville) sells clothes by Lyon designers.

More big-name fashion designers are
clustered alongside art galleries and antique
shops in **Quartier Auguste Comte** (Map pp470–
2), an exclusive quarter around rue Auguste
Comte, 2e, south of place Bellecour. At least a
hundred antique dealers operate from **La Cité
des Antiquaires** (off Map pp470–2; www.cite-antiquaires
.fr; 117 blvd Stalingrad, Villeurbanne; metro Charpennes;
⏰ 9.30am-12.30pm & 2.30-7pm Thu, Sat & Sun).

Centre Commercial La Part-Dieu (off Map pp470–2;
metro Part-Dieu; ⏰ 9.30am-7.30pm Mon-Sat) is Lyon's
vast indoor shopping centre, with a large
supermarket, cafés and dozens of shops.

Markets for browsing away sunny days:
Book Market (Map pp470–2; quai de la Pêcherie, 1er;
metro Hôtel de Ville; ⏰ 7am-6pm Sat & Sun)
Crafts Market (Map pp470–2; quai de Bondy, 5e; metro
Vieux Lyon; ⏰ 9am-noon Sun)

Getting There & Away

AIR

Flights from cities around Europe land at
Aéroport Lyon–St-Exupéry (formerly Lyon-Satolas; off
Map pp470–2; ☎ 0 800 826 826; www.lyon.aeroport.fr),
25km east of the city.

BUS

In the Perrache complex (Map pp470–2),
Eurolines (☎ 04 72 56 95 30), **Intercars** (☎ 04 78
37 20 80) and Spain-oriented **Linebús** (☎ 04 72
41 72 27) have offices on the bus-station level
of the Centre d'Échange (follow the 'Lignes
Internationales' signs).

CAR & MOTORCYCLE

Major car-rental companies have offices at
Gare de la Part-Dieu, east of the centre, and
Gare de Perrache.

TRAIN

Lyon has two mainline train stations: **Gare
de la Part-Dieu** (off Map pp470–2; metro Part-Dieu),
1.5km east of the Rhône, which handles all
long-haul trains; and **Gare de Perrache** (Map
pp470–2; metro Perrache), on the Presqu'île, which
is becoming just a regional station. Many
long-distance trains stop at both. Just a few
local trains stop at **Gare St-Paul** (Map pp470–2;
metro Vieux Lyon) in Vieux Lyon. Tickets are sold
at all three stations and in town at the **SNCF
Boutique** (Map pp470–2; 2 place Bellecour, 2e; metro Bellecour; ⏰ 9am-6.45pm Mon-Fri, 10am-6.30pm Sat).

Destinations by direct TGV include Paris'
Gare de Lyon (€55.60, two hours, every 30
to 60 minutes), Lille-Europe (€85.80, three
hours, nine daily), Nantes (€102.20, 4¾
hours, six daily), Beaune (€19.20, 1½ hours
to 2¼ hours, seven to nine daily), Dijon
(€24.20, 1¾ hours to two hours, at least 12
daily) and Strasbourg (€42.30, five hours,
four or five direct daily).

Getting Around

TO/FROM THE AIRPORT

Lyon–St-Exupéry airport is linked to the city
by **Satobus** (☎ 04 72 68 72 17; www.satobus.com; adult
one way/return €8.40/14.90; every 20min 5am-9pm from the
centre, 6am 11.20pm from the airport). The trip takes
45 minutes from Gare de Perrache (from
the international bus station in the Centre
d'Échange) and 35 minutes from Gare de
la Part-Dieu. A one-way/return Rhône Pass
(€9.30/18.60) covers a one-hour ride on the
metro as well as the trip to/from the airport.

By taxi, the 30-minute trip from the airport to the city centre costs upwards of €45
depending on the time of day.

PUBLIC TRANSPORT

Public transport – buses, trams, a four-line
metro and two funiculars linking Vieux

Lyon to Fourvière and St-Just – is run by **TCL** (☎ 08 20 42 70 00; www.tcl.fr in French; office at 17bis blvd Vivier Merle, 3e; metro Part-Dieu; ☒ 8.30am-5pm Mon-Fri). It operates from around 5am to midnight.

Tickets cost €1.40/11.50 for one/10 and are available from bus and tram drivers and from machines at metro entrances. Tickets allowing unlimited travel for two hours/one day €2/4.20 are also available, as are a couple of *tickets jumelés* which combine a return public-transport ticket with admission to the Musée Lumière (adult/child €7/6) or aquarium (€11/7). On all forms of public transport tickets must be time-stamped; a regular single ticket is valid for one hour after being stamped and allows up to three transfers (but no return journey).

TAXI

Taxis hover at stands in front of both train stations; on the place Bellecour end of rue de la Barre, 2e; and at the northern end of rue Chenavard, 1er. Otherwise call:

Allo Taxi (☎ 04 78 28 23 23; www.allotaxi.fr in French)
Taxis Lyonnais (☎ 04 78 26 81 81)
Taxi-Radio (☎ 04 78 28 13 14)

NORTH & WEST OF LYON

Hills, lakes and vineyards are but a short ride away from cosmopolitan Lyon.

Beaujolais

Hilly Beaujolais is a land of streams (all tributaries of the Saône), granite peaks (the highest is 1012m Mont St-Rigaud), pastures

---

AUTHOR'S CHOICE

There's no better spot to lunch à la Dombes than at **La Bicyclette Bleue** (☎ 04 74 98 21 48; www.labicyclettebleue.fr in French; lunch menu from €10, dinner menu €18; ☒ closed Wed & dinner Tue), an intimate family-run place 7.5km southeast of Villars-les-Dombes in Joyeux. As well as serving delicious local fare – including must-try *grenouilles fraîches en persillade* (frogs legs cooked up in butter and parsley) – it rents kids, adults and tandem bicycles (bikes/tandems per hr €4.50/8, per half-day €12.50/20) to explore the many surrounding *étangs*. Cyclists can pick from 11 different mapped circuits, 12km (one hour) to 59km (four hours) long.

---

and forests northwest of Lyon. The region is famed for its fruity red wines, especially its 10 premium *crus*, and the Beaujolais *nouveau*, drunk at the tender age of just six weeks. Vineyards stretch south from Mâcon (see p465) along the right bank of the Saône for some 50km.

At the stroke of midnight on the third Thursday in November (late Wednesday night) – as soon as French law permits – the *libération* or *mise en perce* (tapping; the opening) of the first bottles of cherry-bright Beaujolais *nouveau* is celebrated with much hype and circumstance around France and the world. In the town of **Beaujeu**, 64km northwest of Lyon, there's free Beaujolais *nouveau* for all at a grand street party known as the Sarmentelles de Beaujeu.

For details on B&Bs and chateaux where you can taste and buy wine, contact Beaujeu's **tourist office** (☎ 04 74 69 22 88; www.beaujeu.com in French; place de l'Église; ☒ 10am-noon & 2-6pm) next to the church. Down the block, the giant statue – with arms outstretched – honours **Gnafron**, a puppet character known for his exceptional fondness for Beaujolais wine.

The region's other gastronomic highlights include fine oils – such as pecan, almond and pine kernel – available at the **Huilerie Beaujolaise** (☎ 04 74 69 28 06; 29 rue des Echarmeaux), on Beaujeu's northern edge; and the prize-winning honey sold at the **Miellerie du Fût** (☎ 04 74 69 92 03) in **Avenas**, a village surrounded by pastures and forests and endowed with a 12th-century Romanesque church.

Exploring Beaujolais by **mountain bike** is uplifting, its gentle hills suitable for the least experienced of cyclists. Fifteen routes (230km) for two-wheelers are detailed in the topoguide *Le Beaujolais à VTT*. **Évasion Beaujolaise** (☎ 04 74 02 06 84) in Marchampt, 10km south of Beaujeu, rents bicycles and maps showing thematic circuits for cyclists. **Walking** the area's many footpaths is another delightful option.

Rewarding spots to sleep, wine and dine include the two-star, seven-room **Anne de Beaujeu** (☎ 04 74 04 87 58; 28 rue de la République; d from €57; ☒ closed Mon, lunch Tue & dinner Sun), a charming hotel-restaurant in Beaujeu; and **Restaurant Christian Mabeau** (☎ 04 74 03 41 79; menus €34-54.50; ☒ closed Mon, dinner Sun & most of Jan & Sep) in Odenas, 10km south of Beaujeu via the D37. Its French *gastronomique* cuisine, including lots of fish dishes, can be enjoyed on the extraordinary rear terrace overlooking a vineyard.

Your own wheels or a sturdy set of walking boots is really the only way to explore Beaujolais.

Pérouges & La Dombes

The medieval village of **Pérouges** (population 850), a bit too perfectly restored, has starred in a number of films. In the warm months, day-trippers flock here to stroll its cobbled alleys, admire its half-timbered and stone houses, and devour *galettes de Pérouges* (sweet tarts, served warm and crusted with sugar) with cider. The old **liberty tree** at place de la Halle, planted in 1792, has seen better days but is still hanging in there. Bus Nos 126 and 130 link the village, perched on a hill 27km northeast of Lyon, with Gare de Perrache.

Northwest is **La Dombes**, a marshy area whose hundreds of *étangs* (shallow lakes), created from malarial swamps over the past six centuries by local farmers, are used as fish ponds and then drained so crops can be grown on the fertile lake bed. The area, famed for its production of frogs' legs, attracts lots of wildlife, particularly waterfowl. Local and exotic birds, including dozens of pairs of storks, can be observed at the more kid-friendly **Parc des Oiseaux** (☎ 04 74 98 05 54; www.parc-des-oiseaux.com in French; admission depending on season €7.50-11; ⏰ 10am-nightfall), an extremely well-run and beautifully landscaped bird park and ornithological research centre just outside Villars-les-Dombes on the N83.

Couvent Ste-Marie de la Tourette

This modernistic **convent** (☎ 04 74 26 79 70; www.couventlatourette.com; guided tour adult/child €5/free), 30km west of Lyon in La Tourette, is a mecca for dedicated fans of the architect Le Corbusier (p53), renowned for his stark, concrete buildings and innovative furniture design. The convent is currently under renovation meaning no overnight accommodation or guided tours by the white-robed Dominican monks living here. Until work is complete only parts of the building will be open to visitors; check its website for the latest update.

From Lyon's Gare de Perrache (10 daily) and Gare St-Paul (20 daily), trains go to L'Arbresle (€3.90, 40 minutes), 2km north of La Tourette; call ☎ 04 74 26 90 19 for a taxi or walk (around 25 minutes). By car

> ### NUCLEAR TOURISM
>
> Nuclear tourism enjoys a twist at the **Ferme aux Crocodiles** (☎ 04 75 04 33 73; www.lafermeauxcrocodiles.com; adult/child €8.30/6; ⏰ 9.30am-7pm Mar-Sep, 9.30am-5pm Oct-Feb), a crocodile farm, which is 20km south of Montélimar in Pierrelatte, where 350-odd grouchy Nile crocodiles slumber in tropical pools heated by a neighbouring nuclear power plant.
>
> The **Centre Nucléaire du Tricastin** plant has four 915-megawatt reactors, sufficiently productive to heat 42 hectares of greenhouses and 2400 local homes. Nearby, the **Centre Nucléaire de St-Alban–St-Maurice**, 20km south of Vienne on the Rhône's left bank, has two pressurised water reactors rated at a mighty 1300 megawatts, enough to supply the needs of Lyon 10 times over.

follow the westbound N7 out of Lyon or the more scenic D7.

ST-ÉTIENNE
pop 200,000

The best bits of St-Étienne – an unpretentious, down-to-business industrial city 62km southwest of Lyon – look like the dullest bits of Paris, but don't let the greyness scare you off: the city has three excellent museums that merit a visit.

The city's industrial heritage, including the local bicycle industry founded in 1886, feature at the **Musée d'Art et d'Industrie** (☎ 04 77 33 04 85; 2 place Louis Comte; adult/child €4.40/free; ⏰ 10am-6pm Wed-Mon) and the **Musée de la Mine** (☎ 04 77 43 83 26; 3 blvd Franchet d'Espérey; adult/child €5.60/free; ⏰ Wed-Mon) has a mine active from 1910 to 1973 where you can see coal-extraction technology in situ and get a sense of what it was like to work as a collier. Underground tours departing several times daily are by train.

On a considerably brighter note, the internationally renowned **Musée d'Art Moderne** (☎ 04 77 79 52 52; adult/child €4.40/free; ⏰ 10am-6pm Wed-Mon) has a flamboyant collection of paintings, sculptures and photographs including classics from the early 20th century as well as contemporary works. It is in La Terrasse, a neighbourhood on the northern edge of the city. To get there, take tram No 4.

Should you need to spend the night in St-Étienne, the **tourist office** (☎ 08 92 70 05 42;

www.tourisme-st-etienne.com; 16 av de la Libération; 9am-7pm Mon-Sat, 9am-noon Sun Apr-Sep, 9am-6pm Mon-Sat, 9am-noon Sun Oct-Mar), 1km southwest of the main train station, St-Étienne Châteaucreux, has accommodation lists.

Getting There & Around

Ryanair flies from London Stansted to/from tiny **Aéroport de St-Étienne-Bouthéon** (☎ 04 77 55 71 71; www.saint-etienne.aeroport.fr), 15km northwest of the city. Local bus No 100 (€2.80, 14 to 17 daily Monday to Saturday, five on Sunday) links the roundabout outside the airport with place Chavanelle, near the St-Étienne tourist office. Ryanair buses to Lyon are coordinated with the flight times (adult one way/return €20/30).

France's very first train line, which was built between 1824 and 1833, connected St-Étienne with Lyon. Today, trains linking St-Étienne Châteaucreux with Lyon (€8.60, 50 minutes) go to either Gare de la Part-Dieu or Gare de Perrache (both at least hourly).

DOWNSTREAM ALONG THE RHÔNE

South of Lyon, vineyards meet nuclear power plants – not the most auspicious juxtaposition perhaps, but worth a stop for Lyon-based day-trippers or those bound south.

TAIN'S CHOCOLATE FACTORY

There's more to Tain l'Hermitage than just revered red wine. Its other *grand cru* is **Valrhona chocolate**, produced in the village in all its guises – be it bitter dark, milky caramel, with orange slices or hazelnut slivers – since 1924. Indulge your wildest chocolate fantasy at its **shop** (14 av du Président Roosevelt; 9am-7pm Mon-Fri, 9am-6pm Sat) in Tain.

As well as running workshops for professional pastry chefs and chocolate-makers, the prestigious chocolate-maker of world renown runs sweet courses for individuals in its **École du Grand Chocolate** (☎ 04 75 07 90 90; www.valrhona.com; quai du Général de Gaulle). A sweet tooth for chocolate is about the only qualification you need to sign up for Valrhona's four-day 'Chocolate Experience' course (€822) devoted to the use of chocolate in pastries, or its three-day 'Basic Chocolate Candies' course (€632).

Vienne

pop 29,900

This one-time Gallo-Roman city, now a disappointingly average town 30km south of Lyon, is only worth a stop if you're an aficionado of the Romans, or you're around during its famous two-week **jazz festival** (☎ 08 92 70 20 07; www.jazzavienne.com) at the end of June.

The Corinthian columns of the superb **Temple d'Auguste et de Livie** (place Charles de Gaulle), built about 10 BC to honour the Emperor Augustus and the lovely Livia (his wife), in the small old town are a fine sight. Across the river in St-Romain-en-Gal, the excavated remains of the Gallo-Roman city form the archaeological **Musée Gall-Romain** (☎ 04 74 53 74 01; 2 chemin de la Plaine Gal; adult/under 18 €3.80/free, free 1st Sun of month; 10am-6pm Tue-Sun Mar-Oct, 10am-5pm Tue-Sun Nov-Feb). There are great town views from the **Belvédère de Pipet**, a viewing balcony with a 6m-tall statue of the Virgin Mary, immediately above Vienne's fabulous **Théâtre Romain** (☎ 04 74 85 39 23; rue du Cirque; admission €2, free 1st Sun of month; 9.30am-1pm & 2-6pm Apr-Aug, 9.30am-1pm & 2-6pm Tue-Sun Sep & Oct, 9.30am-12.30pm & 2-5pm Tue-Sat, 1.30-5.30pm Sun Jan-Mar, Nov & Dec). The vast Roman amphitheatre, built around AD 40–50, tumbles majestically down the hillside and is a key jazz-festival venue.

The **tourist office** (☎ 04 74 53 80 30; www.vienne-tourisme.fr; 3 cours Brillier; 9am-noon & 1.30-6pm Mon-Sat, 10am-noon & 2-5pm Sun) has information on guided walking tours of the city, festivals, markets and other sights and activities in and around town.

SLEEPING & EATING

Auberge de Jeunesse (☎ 04 74 53 21 97; 11 quai Riondet; dm €10; reception 5-8pm Mon-Thu, 2-5pm Fri) Vienne's 54-room riverside hostel is a two-minute strut south of the tourist office. At weekends and in winter, call ahead to make sure someone is in when you arrive.

Grand Hôtel de la Poste (☎ 04 74 85 02 04; 47 cours Romestang; d/tr/q €45/55/65; P) This old-time, two-star hotel with 36 spacious rooms sits plumb on the main, tree-lined avenue. Night owls beware; the front door closes at midnight (11pm weekends).

Hôtel de la Pyramide (☎ 04 74 53 01 96; www.lapyramide.com in French; 14 blvd Fernand-Point; s/d/ste from €160/175/240; menus €49, €85 & €130; restaurant Thu-Mon; P) So called because of its location overlooking La Pyramide de la Cirque (a 15.5m-tall obelisk that in Roman

AS NUTTY AS NOUGAT

There is just one sweet reason to stop in Montélimar – to eat its nutty chewy nougat.

Produced in the otherwise ordinary town, 46km south of Valence, since the 17th century, *nougat de Montélimar* took off after WWII when holidaying motorists on their way to Provence and the Côte d'Azur stopped off in the Rhône-side town to buy the sweeter-than-sweet treat.

Traditional Montélimar nougat consists of at least 28% almonds, 25% lavender honey, 2% pistachio nuts, sugar, egg white and vanilla. Nougat varies in texture (more or less tender), honey taste (more or less strong) and crispness of the nuts. Some nougats are coated in chocolate and others have fruit (try the one with figs), but traditional Montélimar nougat is quite simply off-white.

A dozen nougat producers in Montélimar offer free tours of their sweet factories; pick a small (rather than an industrial) confectioner and arrange your visit to coincide with the morning cooking session. Most producers spend the afternoon cutting and packing their morning's production.

- **Le Gavial** (☎ 04 75 01 67 19; 6 chemin de Géry; ⏰ 8-11.30am & 2-5pm) Four-person workshop producing the best nougat according to a taste test by the French *Gault & Millau* food guide.

- **Le Chaudron d'Or** (☎ 04 75 01 03 95; www.chaudron-dor.com; 7 av du 52e Regiment d'Infanterie; ⏰ 8am-7pm) The Golden Cauldron warrants a peek for the 'show' by the loveable confectioner.

- **Diane de Poytiers** (☎ 04 75 01 67 02; www.diane-de-poytiers.fr; 99 av Jean Jaurès; ⏰ 8.30-11.45am & 2-5.15pm) Slightly south of town but the trip through this refurbished factory is worth it.

- **Musée du Nougat Arnaud Soubeyran** (☎ 04 75 51 01 35; www.nougatsoubeyran.com; Quartier des Blaches, RN7; shop ⏰ 9am-7pm Mon-Sat, 10am-noon & 2.30-6.30pm Sun, guided tours 9.30am, 10.30am & 11.30am, 2pm, 3pm, 4pm & 5pm) Large factory-cum-museum and shop with a café where you can sample fruit-flavoured nougats.

The **tourist office** (☎ 04 75 01 00 20; www.montelimar-tourisme.com; allées Provençales; ⏰ 9am-12.15pm & 2-6.30pm Mon-Sat), across the park from the train station, has more detailed information on visiting nougat producers. In town, souvenir and nougat shops on allées Provençales sell 200g bags of *papillotes* (bite-sized nougat chunks wrapped in shiny paper) for €4 to €5.50.

Montélimar is on the train line linking Valence-Ville (€6.90, 23 minutes, five daily) with Avignon-Centre (€10.90, 45 minutes, hourly).

times pierced the centre of a hippodrome), this apricot villa with powder-blue shutters is a four-star haven of peace and tranquillity. French chef Patrick Henriroux works wonders in the kitchen with lobsters, foie gras, fresh black truffles (in season), *coquilles St-Jacques* (mussels) and other gourmet treats.

Less-grand eating options abound along cours Romestang and cours Brillier near the tourist office.

GETTING THERE & AWAY

Trains and buses link Vienne with Lyon's Gare de Perrache (€5.40, 20 to 32 minutes, at least hourly) and Valence (€10.20, 45 minutes, at least hourly).

Towards Valence

The **Parc Naturel Régional du Pilat** spills across 650 sq km southwest of Vienne and offers some breathtaking panoramas of the Rhône Valley from its highest peaks, Crêt de l'Œillon (1370m) and Crêt de la Perdrix (1432m). The Montgolfier brothers, inventors of the hot-air balloon in 1783, were born – and held their first public *montgolfière* demonstration – in **Annonay**, 50km northwest of Valence on the park's southeastern boundary.

The north section of the Côtes du Rhône wine-growing area, known for vintages offering particularly good value, stretches from Vienne south to Valence. Two of the area's most respected *appellations*, St-Joseph and Hermitage, grow around **Tain l'Hermitage**, an ordinary bourg on the Rhône's left bank. Its **tourist office** (☎ 04 75 08 06 81; place de l'Église; ⏰ 9am-noon & 2-6pm Mon-Sat) has a list of cellars where you can taste and buy wine.

One or two trains every hour link Tain l'Hermitage with Valence (€3.10, 12 minutes) and Lyon (most trains use Gare de Perrache; €11.70, one hour).

Valence

pop 63,400

Several Rhône Valley towns claim to be the gateway to Provence, but Valence has a better claim than most. Alas, the threshold is rather less interesting than what slumbers inside...

In Vieux Valence, the city's old town, the main landmark is **Cathédrale St-Apollinaire**, a late-11th-century pilgrimage church (thus the ambulatory), largely destroyed in the Wars of Religion and rebuilt in the 17th century. Nearby, allegorical sculpted heads adorn **Maison des Têtes** (57 Grande Rue), a blend of Flamboyant Gothic and Renaissance built in 1530. The main commercial streets are rue Émile Augier and Grande Rue.

Grand panoramas of the Rhône Valley can be enjoyed from the clifftop ruins of 12th-century **Château de Crussol** (admission free; 24hr), accessible from **St-Péray**, a village 5km northwest along the N532.

The local shortbread speciality, *le Suisse*, is a crunchy, orange-rind-flavoured biscuit shaped like one of the Vatican's Swiss guards. Said to commemorate Pope Pius VI's imprisonment and death in Valence in 1799, it's available at patisseries.

The Valence **tourist office** (04 75 44 90 40; www.tourisme-valence.com; 9am-6.30pm Mon-Fri, 9am-5pm Sat, also 9am-noon Sun Jul & Aug) is in the train-station building. There is a complete list of accommodation options available online at www.hotels-valence.com.

SLEEPING & EATING

Hôtel des Senteurs (04 75 44 15 32; www.pic-valence.com; 285 av Victor Hugo; d low/high season from €145/165;) Run with loving tender care by the Pic family since the late 19th century, this Provençal-style Relais & Châteaux hotel stuns. Relax in the reading room or billiard room, or over a gastronomic feast in the gourmet **Restaurant Pic** (04 75 44 15 32; 285 av Victor Hugo; lunch menu €50, dinner menus €75-135; closed Mon, dinner Sun year-round plus Tue Nov-Mar) or on the terrace of the less-formal **Auberge du Pin** (04 75 44 53 86; 285bis av Victor Hugo; menus €26 & €30; lunch & dinner year-round). Anne-Sophie Pic, the gourmet force behind Pic, is the only female chef in France with two Michelin stars.

GETTING THERE & AWAY

Train destinations include Montélimar (€6.90, 23 minutes, five daily), Lyon (€13.70, 1¼ hours, 12 daily), Avignon-Centre (€15.90, 1¼ hours, four to six direct daily) and Grenoble (€12.80, 1¼ hours, nine daily).

Frequent trains and buses (€2) link the city centre train station (Valence-Ville) with the Valence TGV Rhône-Alpes Sud station, 10km east.

Gorges de l'Ardèche

The serpentine River Ardèche slithers and churns past towering cliffs of mauve, yellow and grey limestone – dotted with vegetation typical of the Midi – as it makes its way from near **Vallon Pont d'Arc** to **St-Martin de l'Ardèche**, a few kilometres west of the Rhône. Eagles nest in the cliffs and there are numerous *grottes* (caves) – some inhabited as far back as 40,000 years ago – to explore. One of the area's most famous features is the **Pont d'Arc**, a natural stone bridge created by the river's torrents.

About 300m above the canoeable waters of the gorge (half- and full-day river expeditions can be arranged in Vallon Pont d'Arc and St-Martin de l'Ardèche) is the **Haute Corniche** (D290), which affords a magnificent series of *belvédères* (panoramic views). It turns into a huge and chaotic traffic jam in summer. On the plateaus above the gorges, typically Midi villages (eg St-Remèze) are surrounded by garrigue, lavender fields and vineyards.

From Vallon Pont d'Arc, the scenic D579 takes cyclists and motorists northwest to **Ruoms**; across the river, the D4 (signposted 'Largentière') snakes wildly along the **Défilé de Ruoms** (a narrow tunnel of rock) and the **Gorges de la Ligne** for 8km. From Bellevue, bear north on the D104 for 2km to Uzer, then east on the D294 to **Balazuc**, one of France's prettiest villages.

From Balazuc the D579 leads northwards to **Aubenas**, from which point a multitude of scenic roads fans out into the surrounding Cévenol countryside. This is a land of chestnuts where the dark brown fruit is turned into everything from *crème de châtaigne* (a sweet purée served with ice cream, crepes or cake) to *bière aux marrons* (chestnut beer). Unique to the region is *liqueur de châtaigne*, a 21% alcohol-by-volume liqueur which makes a sweet aperitif when mixed with white wine. Buy a bottle at the **Palais du Marron** (04 75 64 35 16; 10 cours de l'Esplanade) in **Privas**.

French Alps & the Jura

CONTENTS

Savoy	**497**
Chamonix	497
Megève & St-Gervais	506
Les Portes du Soleil	507
Thonon-les-Bains	507
Annecy	508
Around Annecy	512
Chambéry	512
Around Chambéry	516
Méribel	516
Val d'Isère	517
Parc National de la Vanoise	519
Dauphiné	**521**
Grenoble	521
Around Grenoble	528
Les deux Alpes	530
Alpe d'Huez	531
Briançon	532
Around Briançon	535
The Jura	**535**
Besançon	536
Around Besançon	540
Belfort & Around	542
Métabief Mont d'Or	543
Around Métabief Mont d'Or	544
Parc Naturel Régional du Haut-Jura	544

'Lances des glaciers fiers, rois blancs' (Lances of proud glaciers, white kings)
from Voyelles, Arthur Rimbaud (1854–91)

The French Alps, where green valleys meet soaring peaks topped with craggy, snowbound summits, form one of the most awesome mountain ranges in the world. Created by the impact of two huge continental plates over 200 million years ago, the icy spikes, needles and snowy peaks of the Alpine mountains have inspired Roman generals, Romantic poets and madcap mountaineers alike. These days, the region may no longer be an isolated wilderness, but the Alps continue to excite and inspire their visitors all the same.

Blanketed by snow and ice in winter, and bathed with warm sunshine and blue skies in summer, the mountains and valleys of the French Alps contain some of the country's top tourist destinations. The Alps are the spiritual home of winter sports, and skiing and snowboarding are the region's main attractions, especially around the high-octane resorts of Chamonix, Megève and Val d'Isère. But the mountains are also a hugely popular destination in summer, when the snow melts away to reveal lush valleys, green meadows and fields of wildflowers, as well as hundreds of kilometres of walking trails.

While thrill-seekers indulge in warm-weather sports ranging from paragliding to white-water rafting, hikers can head out into one of the region's many national parks in search of golden eagles, mountain goats and the elusive ibex. History buffs should head for the medieval towns of Annecy and Chambéry, and big city thrills can be found in the dynamic capital of the Alps, Grenoble. North of Lake Geneva (Lac Léman), in the Jura region, the old city of Besançon and the villages of Arbois and Baume-les-Messieurs make ideal bases for exploring the little-visited Franche-Comté region and the wild reaches of Parc Naturel Régional du Haut-Jura.

HIGHLIGHTS

- Riding the world's highest, scariest **cable car** (p500) in Chamonix
- Stroll the lantern-lit lanes of **Annecy** (p508)
- Absorb the big-city ambience of **Grenoble** (p521), capital of the Alps
- Explore the high mountain trails of the **Parc National de la Vanoise** (p519)
- Pass some time exploring the clocks and citadel of **Besançon** (p536)
- Get back to nature in the mountains, forests and waterfalls of the **Jura** (p544)
- Sample freshly made cheese in **Poligny** (p541)
- Join the architects' pilgrimage to Le Corbusier's futuristic chapel at **Ronchamp** (p542)

★ Ronchamp
★ Besançon
★ Poligny
Parc Naturel Régional du Haut-Jura
★ Annecy ★ Chamonix
★ Parc National de la Vanoise
★ Grenoble

- POPULATION: 5,600,000
- AREA: 210,000 SQ KM

History

For much of their history, the French Alps have been a place of transition, a bridge between the warmer climes of the Mediterranean and the cooler regions of northern Europe. Little is known of the earliest settlers of the Alps (mainly thought to be Neolithic tribes, who arrived around 3000 BC, and later Bronze Age settlers). Migrant tribes of Celtic, Gaulish and Teutonic origin also made their home in various places around the Alps, and by the time of Christ permanent communities were well established, especially around the lakes of Geneva, Bourget and Annecy, and the Tarentaise and Maurienne valleys.

The Alps became an important strategic stronghold during the years of Roman conquest and, after years of struggle, were finally placed under Roman control during the reign of Augustus. Over the following centuries, the Frankish kings of the Merovingian and Carolingian empires laid the foundations for the modern Alps and its distinctive dialects, traditions and cultures.

During the 13th and 14th centuries, the Alps were fiercely contested by the feudal houses of Savoy, the Dauphiné and Provence, but by the end of the 14th century only the house of Savoy remained as serious opposition to the kingdom of France and its Italian rivals. The ensuing centuries were marked by successive wars and occupations, with each side swapping and reoccupying towns and territories – a cycle which was only finally ended with the union of Savoy with France in 1860. Savoy was divided into two *départements* (Savoie and Haute-Savoie), and the Alps were finally integrated into the wider French Republic.

During the Industrial Revolution, the abundant natural resources of the Alps led to the growth of heavy industry, especially hydroelectric power, mining, metalworking and agriculture. Tourism had also been a growing industry since the first holiday-makers made their way to the area around Chamonix and Mont Blanc in the late 19th century, a trend which continued in the early 20th century with the foundation of the first spa towns and holiday resorts.

During WWII, the Alps were occupied by German and Italian forces, but much of the population despised the Vichy French regime and the mountains became one of the main strongholds for the French resistance. Liberation finally came in 1944, but the region had been badly scarred by the years of occupation, and it took many years for the region to recover its economic strength. Modern industry, huge urban development and large-scale tourism all contributed to the regeneration of the Alps in the post-war years. Though its rural traditions and heritage may have largely disappeared today, the Alps remain one of the most popular and economically successful areas in France.

Geography

The Alps have served as a barrier between Europe's peoples since ancient times. Formed some 44 million years ago, the peaks and valleys of the Alpine ranges have been sculpted by erosion and massive glaciers. Both have endowed the river valleys with mild climates and rich soils, making them very suitable for human settlement. The Alps stretch for 370km from Lake Geneva (Lac Léman) in the north, almost to Provence in the south. France's border with Italy follows the Alps' highest ridges and peaks.

The two major historic regions are Savoy and Dauphiné. Savoy covers the northern area and culminates in Europe's highest mountain, Mont Blanc (4807m), with the town of Chamonix at its base. To the west, Annecy is the gateway to Savoy, while further south sits the region's historic capital, Chambéry. Dauphiné, which is south of Savoy and stretches eastwards all the way to Briançon and the Italian border, is home to Grenoble, the main city of the Alps.

North of Lake Geneva, the Jura Mountains form an arc that extends northwards along the River Doubs towards Alsace.

The Alps are characterised by extreme climatic diversity. There's enough snow most years from December to April for skiing even at lower-altitude stations. In spring (and late spring and summer at higher elevations), carpets of flowers bloom beside the magnificent forests. Throughout the year, weather conditions can change rapidly.

For weather information, call the **météo** (weather bureau; regional report ☎ 08 36 68 00 00, snow & mountain report ☎ 08 36 68 04 04; www.meteo.fr in French). For the departmental report, dial ☎ 08 36 68 02 followed by the two-digit

FRENCH ALPS & THE JURA

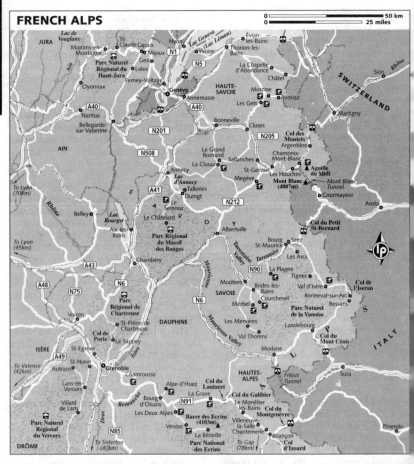

FRENCH ALPS

departmental number (p907). Year-round, daily weather bulletins are pinned outside the tourist office in ski resorts.

National & Regional Parks

Unlike other similar-size mountain ranges around the world, the Alps are not a pristine wilderness. In fact, the habitable parts of the French Alps support a dense population, and the region's villages, towns and ski resorts are linked by an extensive network of roads (and motorways). Fortunately, parts of the Alps are within the boundaries of three national and four regional parks, in which wildlife is carefully protected (p58).

The national parks – Vanoise (in Savoy), Écrins (in Dauphiné) and Mercantour (in

Provence, along the Italian border) – are surrounded by larger zones where industry and human habitation are permitted. Including the regional parks of Queyras (on the Italian border south of Briançon), the Vercors (southwest of Grenoble), Chartreuse (north of the Vercors) and Massif des Bauges (north of Chartreuse), the Alps are endowed with the greatest concentration of parks in France.

The Jura region is home to the Parc Naturel Régional du Haut-Jura.

Dangers & Annoyances

Despite precautions such as anti-avalanche fences and tunnels, avalanches pose a very real danger in snowbound areas. Every year

RESCUE SERVICES

The **PGHM** (Peloton de Gendarmerie de Haute Montagne; in Chamonix ☎ 04 50 53 16 89) is the main mountain rescue service in the Alps. Each resort has its own branch.

people are killed as a result of these disasters, and whole valleys can be cut off for days.

The daily avalanche risk is announced through signs and coloured flags outside all ticket kiosks, at the base of most ski lifts and dotted around resorts and slopes:

- yellow=low risk,
- black/yellow=heightened risk
- black=severe risk.

All avalanche warning signs should be heeded, whether they are along roads or on ski slopes. They are there for a reason.

On glaciers, be careful of crevasses. An accident in an isolated area can be fatal, so never ski, hike or climb alone. At high altitudes, where the sun's ultraviolet radiation is much stronger than at sea level (and is intensified by reflection off the snow), wear sunglasses and put sunscreen on exposed skin.

The air is often dry in the Alps – carry water when hiking, and drink more than you would at lower altitudes. Also, be aware of the possibility of hypothermia after a long climb or a sudden storm, as you'll cool off quickly while enjoying the cold, windy panorama.

Skiing & Snowboarding

Snow sports, once reserved for the truly wealthy, are now accessible to most people. Each winter millions of holiday-makers head to the 200-plus resorts in the French Alps for Alpine (downhill) skiing, cross-country treks, ski touring, and snowboarding – not to mention the après-ski.

The ski season starts just before Christmas and finishes at the end of April. In years of heavy snowfall, it's possible to ski from November until mid-May in higher-altitude resorts. At the beginning and end of the season, and in January, accommodation and lift tickets are discounted, and many resorts offer deals. Give the slopes a wide berth over Christmas and New Year, and during school holidays in late February and early March, when prices are sky-high and accommodation is scarce.

Summer skiing on high-altitude glaciers is usually possible in July and August in some areas. Most resorts have a combination of cross-country areas, Alpine runs and snowboard parks.

Off-piste skiing, known in French as *hors piste* (skiing outside groomed trails on fresh or powder snow), is popular, but off-piste skiers should exercise extreme caution as these areas usually do not have any warning signs. Take a guide with you.

Experienced off-piste skiers can ski tour – skiing and climbing the less accessible peaks, ridges and glaciers outside resort areas. Most tours last from three to seven days with accommodation in mountain *refuges*. Depending on the exact itinerary, three-day tours start at around €400. Experienced guides can be contacted in most resorts at the Bureau des Guides (p494) and ESF (p495).

Known in French as *ski de fond,* cross-country skiing is most popular in the Jura. Cross-country stations are more relaxed and casual than the higher ski resorts, with prices reflecting the lower altitudes, smaller snowfalls and shorter ski season.

Snowboarding is a fast-growing Alpine sport. Chamonix, Chamrousse, Les Arcs, Espace Killy, Les Deux Alpes, La Plagne and Méribel all have large snowparks equipped with half-pipes, quarter-pipes, gaps, rails and ramps.

INFORMATION

Every ski station has a tourist office that provides information on skiing, indoor

WEB WORLD

- **www.natives.co.uk** Excellent website aimed at seasonal ski workers.

- **www.planetmountain.com** Comprehensive website with advice on classic Alpine ski routes.

- **www.planetsubzero.com** Book seasonal and long-term ski accommodation online.

- **www.skifrance.fr** Official website for the main Alpine ski resorts.

- **www.thealps.com** Useful resort guide with some great photo galleries.

SKIING & SNOWBOARDING IN THE ALPS

Resort	Trademarks	Alpine runs	Cross-country trails	Difficulty level	Ski lifts	Ski pass (6 days)
Chamonix-Mont Blanc	High in altitude & attitude; young, trendy & full of fun	155km	45km	Intermediate, advanced, off-piste	47	€176
Portes du Soleil	Exclusive resort attracting a more sedate crowd	650km	130km	All abilities, off-piste	209	€176
St-Gervais & Megève	Pricey, chic & full of Alpine charm	300km	76km	Beginners, intermediate	79	€154
La Clusaz	A cheaper spot, popular locally	132km	70km	Beginners, intermediate	55	€137.50
Trois Vallées	Méribel: heavy traffic & bars packed with Brits	600km	130km	All abilities	200	€198
La Plagne	The family choice; Olympic bobsleigh run	225km	85km	Beginners, intermediate	111	€176
Les Arcs	Top skiing & snowboarding; car-free but little charm	200km	30km	All abilities, off-piste	54	€181
Val d'Isère	Unrivalled Alpine skiing; buzzy nightlife	300km	44km	Intermediate, advanced, off-piste	97	€181
Les Deux Alpes	Snowboarders' delight; summer skiing; lively bar scene	220km	20km	Intermediate, advanced	54	€158
Alpe d'Huez	Snowboarding park; longest black run; summer skiing	236km	50km	All abilities	87	€178.50
Le Grand Serre Chevalier	Door-to-door skiing from several resorts	250km	35km	All abilities, off-piste	74	€160
Métabief Mont d'Or	Low altitude; snow not guaranteed	40km	250km	Predominantly cross-country	23	€97.20
Les Rousses	Popular with French & Swiss day-trippers	42km	260km	Predominantly cross-country	38	€94

and outdoor activities, and public transport. The local accommodation service, ski school and **Bureau des Guides**, an association of professional, independent guides, are often conveniently located in the same building (usually known as the Maison de la Montagne). Nearly all resorts have post offices, banks, bakeries and supermarkets.

SkiFrance (☎ 01 47 42 23 32; skifrance.fr; 61 blvd Haussmann, F-75008 Paris) and the **Fédération Française de Ski** (☎ 04 50 51 40 34; www.ffs.fr; 50 rue des Marguisats, BP 2451, F-74011 Annecy) provide information on all French ski resorts.

Downhill runs range in length from a few hundred metres to 20km and are colour-coded to indicate the level of difficulty of the runs: green (beginners), blue (intermediate), red (advanced) and black (very advanced). Summer skiing on glaciers tends to be on short green or blue runs.

Cross-country ski trails are designated as easy or difficult. The resorts charge fees for the upkeep of the trails. Single resort ski passes for cross-country skiing only are usually around €6/27 per day/week (Métabief Mont D'Or; website: www.montdor-2lacs .com/actihiver.htm).

EQUIPMENT

Skis, snowboards, boots and poles can be hired in every resort. Alpine equipment starts at €18/50 per day/week. Cross-country equipment ranges per day from €6.50 to €33 and per week from €14 to €65, and snowboards and boots per day from around €17 to €25 and per week from €140 to €190. You can hire monoskis and telemark skis in most resorts, too.

Take a note of the serial number marked on your skis. If you lose them, you have to pay for a replacement pair (take out insurance to cover this cost). Most ski shops have a locker room where you can leave your skis free of charge overnight. Always equip yourself with UV-protective sunglasses, gloves, a piste map (free from tourist offices), warm and water-resistant clothing, and sunscreen.

If you're looking to purchase your gear, one of the best ideas is to head for the resorts towards the end of the winter season, when many shops clear out last year's stock at rock-bottom prices. Look out for shop windows announcing *liquidation* or *fin de serie*.

LIFT PASSES

A daunting range of contraptions *(remon-tées mécaniques)* cover the slopes to whisk skiers uphill. Lifts include *téléskis* (drag lifts), *télésièges* (chair lifts), *télécabines* (gondolas), *téléphériques* (cable cars) and *funiculaires* (funicular railways).

Daily, weekly, monthly or seasonal ski passes – *forfaits* – offer the best value. Passes give access to one or more ski sectors and sometimes include neighbouring resorts. Passes are cheaper for children and seniors, and many resorts offer package deals covering a six-day ski pass and six half-day group lessons. Others offer packages incorporating a six-day ski pass with accommodation or ski school.

For prices see opposite.

SCHOOLS

France's leading ski school, the **École de Ski Français** (ESF; www.esf.net) has branches in most stations and generally offers tuition at better rates than the smaller, independent ski schools. ESF also offers group or private snowboarding lessons.

Prices vary greatly between resorts: in general, the more expensive the resort, the pricier the lessons are likely to be. If you're looking to learn from scratch, the smaller ski resorts will offer much better value. A six-day course (three hours of group tuition daily) costs between €80 and €300; private one- or two-hour lessons cost between €30 and €80. All resorts offer lessons for children; some have snow gardens for toddlers aged from three to five to play in.

PACKAGE DEALS

Package deals are by far the cheapest way to ski. Most resorts offer excellent-value discount packages that usually include a week's accommodation, ski pass, and sometimes equipment hire and ski lessons.

The FUAJ (p894) has 17 hostels in the French Alps and offers some good-value package deals in winter, starting from about €300/420 in the low/high season for six days' hostel accommodation, meals, ski pass and equipment hire.

INSURANCE

Insurance is a necessity if you're planning a trip to the snow. If you're hurt on the slopes, all the services that come to your aid from the ambulance that ferries you down the mountainside to the doctor who treats you – will charge. If you require evacuation by helicopter, the bill you receive on your hospital bed might do you more lasting damage than your injuries.

Most package deals include insurance, but *Carte Neige* is a flexible policy (available for a few days to a full season) offered by nearly all resorts. It often entitles the holder to extra deals, such as discounted ski lessons and lift passes. Full cover includes mountain rescue costs and medical treatment. It costs between €40 and €60 per year (€20 to €30 for cross-country skiers), depending on the level of cover you choose and where you buy the insurance.

All resorts also offer *Carré Neige*, a daily insurance scheme that offers similar cover to the *Carte Neige*. It can be purchased from ticket kiosks at the same time as your lift pass, and costs €2.50 to €3 per day. Insurance is also available from most equipment hire shops to cover the cost of any damage to your equipment – it's usually a wise purchase.

Warm-Weather Activities

The Alps come alive in spring and summer, when the snow cover melts and carpets of wildflowers reclaim the mountainsides. Fantastic hiking trails criss-cross national parks; the GR5 traverses the entire Alps. Rafting, canoeing and mountain biking are also popular, as are the more sedate pastimes of horse riding and ice-skating. Warm-weather activities can be enjoyed at most larger ski resorts.

A popular Alpine activity is *parapente* (paragliding), the sport of floating down from somewhere high suspended from a wing-shaped, steerable parachute. The ESF in most resorts offers courses: an initiation flight costs from €60 to €90. A five-day beginner course costs from €360 to €550. A second five-day course, which prepares you to pursue the sport on your own, costs the same.

Skydiving costs a lot more: €200 to €220 for a day of instruction and a first jump from 1200m.

Sleeping & Eating

Most resorts have a central reservation service that books accommodation in hotels, studios, apartments and chalets. Prices vary drastically between the low and high seasons, and hotels generally offer full or half-board. Most apartments and studios have kitchenettes – the cheapest option for budget travellers. Gîtes de France publishes the annual *Gîtes de Neige* guide (p894).

The **Club Alpin Français** (Map p333-33; ☎ 01 53 72 87 00; www.clubalpin.com; 24 av de Laumière, 19e, Paris;

metro Laumière) has numerous mountain *refuges* in the Alps, for which advance reservations are usually required. Contact the relevant office in the place you are visiting.

Restaurants in ski resorts tend to offer poor-quality cuisine at heightened prices. On the slopes, you'll ski past plenty of restaurants with prices that reflect the high altitude.

Getting There & Around

The Alps' closest international airport is Aéroport International de Genève (Geneva international airport), near Geneva, and Lyon St-Exupéry, just outside Lyon. Allow ample time to check in as the airport can become almost impassable with the hordes of skiers, snowboarders and their oversized luggage.

Geneva airport is split into Swiss and French sectors and you may have to travel between both sides (to pick up or drop a hire car, for example), which means negotiating customs, police and baggage reclaim – often with lengthy queues – all over again.

On a clear day and with the right flight path, the view through the plane window is the best introduction to the Alps you can possibly have. In winter there are direct bus connections from both airports to numerous ski resorts with **Geneva's Aeroski bus** (☎ 022-798 20 00; www.gva.ch/en/inst/aeroskibus.htm) and **Lyon's Satobus-Alpes** (☎ 04 37 25 52 55; www.satobus-alps .com).

The Eurostar speeds its way through the Channel Tunnel from London (Waterloo station) to Moûtiers (8¾ hours) and Bourg St-Maurice (9½ hours) on Saturday during the ski season. Train services within France to many parts of the Alps are excellent. Full details are published in the SNCF's *La Neige en Direct* brochure, which you can pick up at most stations.

To reach some ski resorts by car you may need snow chains after heavy snowfalls, and in the high season, traffic on the high mountain passes leading to the resorts can be hellish. The Fréjus road tunnel connects the French Alps with Italy, as do a number of major passes: Col du Petit St-Bernard (2188m) near Bourg St-Maurice, Col du Mont Cénis (2083m) in the Haute Maurienne Valley, and Col du Montgenèvre (1850m) near Briançon. Certain high-altitude passes, such as the Col du Galibier

(2558m) and the Col de l'Iseran (2770m), are usually closed between November and June, although this depends on snowfall. Road signs indicate well in advance if passes are blocked.

SAVOY

Bordered by Switzerland and Italy, Savoy (Savoie; pronounced sav-*wa*) rises from the southern shores of Lake Geneva (Lac Léman) and keeps rising until it reaches the massive Mont Blanc, which dominates the town of Chamonix. To the southwest, long U-shaped valleys are obvious relics of ancient glaciers that created lakes such as Lac d'Annecy, as well as France's largest natural lake, Lac Bourget, near Aix-les-Bains.

Savoy is divided into two *départements,* Haute-Savoie and Savoie, and the people of the region are known as Savoyards. Despite centuries of French cultural influence, they have managed to keep their identity and often speak their own dialect, which reveals Provençal influences. In the remote valleys, such as in the Haute Maurienne, rural life goes on as it has for centuries, and the people continue to struggle with the harsh climate and the ever-present threat of avalanches.

History

Savoy was long ruled by the House of Savoy, founded by Humbert I (the Whitehanded) in the mid-11th century. During the Middle Ages, the dukes of Savoy extended their territory eastwards to other areas of the western Alps, including the Piedmont region of what is now Italy.

In the 16th century the dukes of Savoy turned towards their Italian territories; in 1563 they moved their capital from Chambéry to Turin. However, they continued to rule Savoy and resisted repeated French attempts to take over the region. Savoy was annexed by France in 1792 but was returned 23 years later.

In 1720 Victor Amadeus II, duke of Savoy, became king of Sardinia and over the next century important territories in northern Italy, including Genoa, came under Savoyard control. In the mid-19th century the House of Savoy worked to unify Italy under Piedmontese leadership, a goal they achieved in 1861 with the formation of the Kingdom

of Italy under King Victor Emmanuel II of the House of Savoy. However, in exchange for Napoleon III's acceptance of this new arrangement and the international agreements that led up to it, Savoy – along with the area around Nice – was ceded to France.

CHAMONIX
pop 10,000 / elevation 1037m
The town of Chamonix is surrounded by the most spectacular scenery in the French Alps. The area, a leading mountaineering centre, is almost Himalayan: deeply crevassed glaciers point towards the valley from the icy crown of Mont Blanc, which soars 4.8km above sea level. Chamonix has been a summer resort since the 18th century and a winter one from 1903. It's also gained a reputation as one of the top spots in the Alps for heli-skiing (p501). Since 1965, when the 11.6km Mont Blanc tunnel – the world's highest rock-covered tunnel (2480m) – was opened, Chamonix has been linked by road to Courmayeur in Italy.

The tunnel was closed in March 1999 following a devastating fire, which started when a goods lorry carrying flour and margarine burst into flames and quickly spread to nearby vehicles. The blaze burned for over two days and killed 39 people. A massive investigation was launched after the fire had been extinguished. The tunnel's safety systems and emergency procedures were completely overhauled, and after three years of exhaustive repairs, it finally reopened to cars and other vehicles in 2002.

Orientation
Chamonix runs along the banks of the River Arve for about 2km. The Mont Blanc massif looms over the east side of the valley, while the Aiguilles Rouges range lines the western edge. The two main streets, rue du Docteur Paccard and rue Joseph Vallot, contain most of the town's shops and restaurants. The bus and train stations are across the river, 500m east of the town centre at the end of av Michel Croz.

Information
BOOKSHOPS
Librairie VO (☎ 04 50 53 24 41; 20 av Ravanel -le-Rouge; ☻ 9am-noon & 2-7.30pm Mon-Sat) Sells English books, including many (as you might expect) with a mountaineering theme.

Photo Alpine Tairraz (☎ 04 50 53 14 23; 162 av Michel Croz) A photographic shop that also sells mountaineering books and prints.

EMERGENCY

PGHM (Peloton Gendarmerie Haute Montagne; ☎ 04 50 53 16 19; 69 rue de la Mollard) The main mountain rescue service for the Mont Blanc area.

Police Station (☎ 04 50 53 00 55; 111 rue de la Mollard)

INTERNET ACCESS

As well as the following internet cafés, there are a number of bars and restraurants in Chamonix that offer Internet access at around 15 to 20 cents a minute.

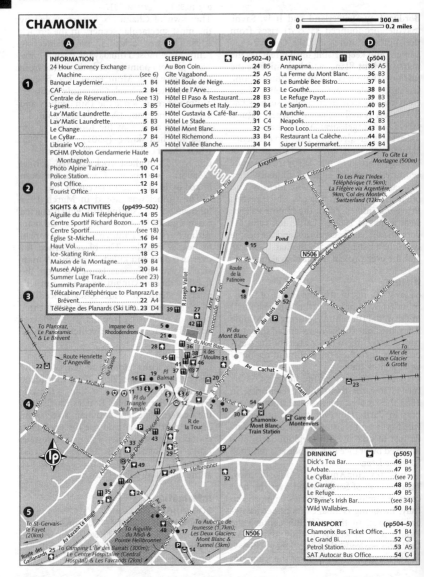

CHAMONIX

0 ___ 300 m
0 ___ 0.2 miles

INFORMATION
24 Hour Currency Exchange
Machine...................................(see 6)
Banque Laydernier.........................**1** B4
CAF...**2** B4
Centrale de Réservation..........(see 13)
i-guest...**3** B5
Lav'Matic Laundrette.....................**4** B5
Lav'Matic Laundrette.....................**5** B3
Le Change.....................................**6** B4
Le CyBar.......................................**7** B5
Librairie VO...................................**8** A5
PGHM (Peloton Gendarmerie Haute
Montagne)..................................**9** A4
Photo Alpine Tairraz....................**10** C4
Police Station...............................**11** B4
Post Office....................................**12** B4
Tourist Office................................**13** B4

SIGHTS & ACTIVITIES   (pp499–502)
Aiguille du Midi Téléphérique.....**14** B5
Centre Sportif Richard Bozon......**15** C3
Centre Sportif............................(see 18)
Église St-Michel............................**16** B4
Haut Vol......................................**17** B5
Ice-Skating Rink...........................**18** C3
Maison de la Montagne................**19** B4
Museé Alpin.................................**20** B4
Summer Luge Track....................(see 23)
Summits Parapente.......................**21** B3
Télécabine/Téléphérique to Planpraz/Le
Brévent......................................**22** A4
Télésiège des Planards (Ski Lift)...**23** D4

SLEEPING 🏠 (pp502–4)
Au Bon Coin.................................**24** B5
Gîte Vagabond.............................**25** A5
Hôtel Boule de Neige...................**26** B3
Hôtel de l'Arve.............................**27** B3
Hôtel El Paso & Restaurant...........**28** B3
Hôtel Gourmets et Italy................**29** B4
Hôtel Gustavia & Café-Bar...........**30** C4
Hôtel Le Stade..............................**31** C4
Hôtel Mont Blanc.........................**32** C5
Hôtel Richemond..........................**33** B4
Hôtel Vallée Blanche....................**34** B4

EATING 🍴 (p504)
Annapurna....................................**35** A5
La Ferme du Mont Blanc...............**36** B3
Le Bumble Bee Bistro....................**37** B4
Le Gouthé.....................................**38** B4
Le Refuge Payot............................**39** B3
Le Sanjon.....................................**40** B5
Munchie.......................................**41** B4
Neapolis.......................................**42** B3
Poco Loco.....................................**43** B4
Restaurant La Calèche...................**44** B4
Super U Supermarket.....................**45** B4

DRINKING 🍷 (p505)
Dick's Tea Bar...............................**46** B4
L'Arbate.......................................**47** B5
Le CyBar....................................(see 7)
Le Garage.....................................**48** B5
Le Refuge.....................................**49** B5
O'Byrne's Irish Bar.....................(see 34)
Wild Wallabies.............................**50** B4

TRANSPORT (pp504–5)
Chamonix Bus Ticket Office..........**51** B4
Le Grand Bi..................................**52** C3
Petrol Station................................**53** A5
SAT Autocar Bus Office................**54** C4

i-guest (☎ 04 50 55 98 58; iguestchx@yahoo.fr;
22 Galerie Blanc Neige; per min around €0.10-0.15, per hr
around €7.50; 2-8pm) In a small shopping arcade just
off rue Docteur Paccard.
Le CyBar (☎ 04 50 53 69 70; www.cybarchamonix
.com; 80 rue des Moulins; per min from €0.10; 10am-
1.30am) Has computers spread over two floors. You can
also bring your own laptop to connect.

INTERNET RESOURCES
www.chamonix.com Official website for the Chamonix
valley, with comprehensive information on staying and
playing in the Mont Blanc massif.
www.chamonix.net Companion site, which offers more
advice on accommodation, entertainment and nightlife in
Chamonix.
www.compagniedumontblanc.com The company
that handles most tourist activities in Chamonix.

LAUNDRY
Lav'Matic Laundrette (40 impasse des Primevères;
 9am-8pm)
Lav'Matic Laundrette (174 av de l'Aiguille du Midi;
 9am-8pm)

MEDICAL SERVICES
Duty Chemist (☎ 04 50 53 36 79)
Duty Dentist (☎ 04 50 66 17 19)
Duty Doctor (☎ 04 50 53 48 48)
Le Centre Hospitalier (Central Hospital; ☎ 04 50 53
84 00; 509 route des Pélerins) In Les Favrands about 2km
south of Chamonix centre. A list of medical practitioners
can be obtained from the tourist office.

MONEY
There are several seasonal exchange places
between the tourist and post offices. Most
banks in town have an ATM.
Le Change (21 place Balmat; 9am-1pm & 3-7pm
May, Jun & early Sep–Nov, 8am-8pm Jul–early Sep &
Dec-Apr) Generally offers the best rate in town. Outside, a
24-hour ATM accepts banknotes in 15 currencies.

POST
Post Office (place Balmat; 8am-noon & 2-6pm Mon-
Fri, 8am noon Sat Sep Jun, 8am 7pm Mon Fri, until noon
Sat Jul & Aug) Right in the centre of town.

TOURIST INFORMATION
Centrale de Réservation (☎ 04 50 53 23 33;
reservation@chamonix.com; Tourist Office; 24hr)
Usually takes accommodation bookings for stays of three
nights minimum.
Club Alpin Français (CAF; ☎ 04 50 53 16 03; fax 04 50
53 27 52; 136 av Michel Croz; 3.30-7.30pm Mon, Tue &

Fri, 3-6.15pm Thu, 9am-noon Sat) Looks after most Mont
Blanc *refuges*, and runs climbing excursions and tours.
Seasonal hours vary.
Tourist Office (☎ 04 50 53 00 24; www.chamonix.com;
85 place du Triangle de l'Amitié; 8.30am-12.30pm &
2-7pm Jun-Sep & Dec-Apr, 9am-12.30pm & 2-6.30pm Oct,
Nov & May) Offers hundreds of brochures on accommoda-
tion and activities, and also sells ski passes.

Sights
AIGUILLE DU MIDI
A jagged pinnacle of rock rising above
glaciers, snowfields and rocky crags, 8km
from the domed summit of Mont Blanc, the
Aiguille du Midi is one of Chamonix's most
famous landmarks. If you can handle the
height, the panoramic views from the summit are absolutely breathtaking and should
not be missed.

Cable-car tickets (advance reservations 24hr ☎ 08 92
68 00 67; adult/child return €34/24, one way/return to Plan
de l'Aiguille €12.30/14.40; 7am-5.30pm summer, 8am-
3.30pm winter) from Chamonix to Aiguille du
Midi are available; a ride to the *téléphérique's*
halfway point, Plan de l'Aiguille (2317m) is
an excellent place to start hikes in summer.

The *téléphérique* leaves from the end of av
de l'Aiguille du Midi and runs year-round.
Be prepared for long queues. Note that making advance reservations on the 24-hour
number incurs a booking fee of €2.

From the Aiguille du Midi, between May
and September, you can make the 5km ride
in the panoramic Mont Blanc cable car to
Pointe Helbronner (3466m) on the Italian
border, crossing a vista of glaciers, snow
plains and shimmering ice-fields en route.
Another *téléphérique* from Pointe Helbronner descends to the Italian ski resort
of Courmayeur, but the views alone are
worth the trip.

LE BRÉVENT
The highest peak on the western side of the
valley, **Le Brévent** (2525m) has fabulous views
of the Mont Blanc massif. It can be reached
by **télécabine** (larger than a *téléphérique*) and
téléphérique (☎ 04 50 53 13 18; adult/child return
€15.50/11; 8am-5.45pm summer, 9am-5pm winter),
from the end of rue de la Mollard.

Several hiking trails can be picked up at
Le Brévent or at the *télécabine's* midway
station, **Planpraz** (one way/return €8.50/10.50), at
2000m. There is a great restaurant at the
summit of Le Brévent (p504).

MER DE GLACE

The **Mer de Glace** (Sea of Ice), the second-largest glacier in the Alps, is 14km long, 1800m wide and up to 400m deep. During a visit to Chamonix in 1741, Englishman William Windham was the first foreigner to set eyes on the glacier, which he described as 'a sort of agitated sea that seemed suddenly to have become frozen' (hence the name). The glacier moves 45m a year at the edges, and up to 90m a year in the centre, and has become a popular tourist attraction thanks to the rack-and-pinion railway line built between 1897 and 1908.

Since 1946, the **Grotte de la Mer de Glace** (ice cave; ☼ late May-late Sep) has been carved every spring – work begins in February and takes three months. The interior temperature is between -2°C and -5°C. Look down the slope for last year's cave to see how far the glacier has moved.

With avalanche proofing over parts of the tracks, the train – which leaves from **Gare du Montenvers** (☎ 04 50 53 12 54; 35 place de la Mer de Glace; adult return €14; ☼ 10am-4pm winter, 8.30am-5.30pm May-Jun & Sep, 6.30am-6pm Jun & Jul, 6am-7.30pm Aug) in Chamonix and creeps up to Montenvers (1913m) – runs year-round and takes 20 minutes. From Montenvers, a *téléphérique* takes tourists to the cave. A **combined ticket** (adult/child €21/15) is valid for the train, *téléphérique* and admission to the cave.

The Mer de Glace can be reached on foot via the Grand Balcon Nord trail from Plan de l'Aiguille. The uphill trail from Chamonix (two hours) begins near the summer luge track. Traversing the glacier and its crevasses requires proper equipment and an experienced guide.

MUSÉE ALPIN

The **Musée Alpin** (☎ 04 50 53 25 93; 89 av Michel Croz; adult/child €4/1.50; ☼ 2-7pm summer, 10am-noon school holidays, closed rest of year), just off av Michel Croz, occupies a grand building that once housed one of Chamonix's most luxurious hotels. Exhibits include artefacts, lithographs and photos illustrating the history of mountain climbing and other Alpine sports.

Activities

WINTER ACTIVITIES

Maison de la Montagne

The **Maison de la Montagne** (190 place de l'Église) is across the square from the tourist office, and should be your first port of call for finding out about the Mont Blanc area.

On the ground floor, the **Compagnie des Guides** (☎ 04 50 53 00 88; www.chamonix-guides.com; ☼ 8am-noon & 3.30-7.30pm Jul & Aug, closed Sun Sep-Jun) is the central base for Chamonix' professional mountain guides. Guides for skiing, mountaineering, hiking, mountain-biking and just about every other alpine pastime can be hired year-round (starting from €250 per day for four people).

École Ski Français (ESF; ☎ 04 50 53 22 57; www.esf-chamonix.com; per hr from €20; ☼ 8.15am-7pm Mon-Sat in winter) is on the 1st floor and offers tailor-made programmes for all levels, from complete novices to seasoned skiers looking to improve their technique. Discounts are available for longer courses.

On the 2nd floor, the **Office de Haute Montagne** (☎ 04 50 53 22 08; www.ohm-chamonix.com

---

CHAMONIX'S CABLE-CAR

The **téléphérique** (☎ 04 50 53 30 80) from Chamonix to the Aiguille du Midi (3842m) has deservedly earned its reputation as the highest (and scariest) cable car in Europe. The idea of a floor-to-peak cable-car was first conceived in 1909, but the technical challenges proved enormous, and engineers initially had to settle for a lower-altitude version, completed in 1924. After WWII, the original dream was revived and the spectacular full-altitude cable car finally swung into action in 1955.

It's an amazing feat of engineering, climbing from the valley floor to a terrace beneath the Aiguille at 3777m in just 20 minutes. From far below, the Aiguille looks like a single peak; in fact, it has twin spires connected by a gravity-defying footbridge. There is even a restaurant where you can savour the afternoon tea of a lifetime: the **3842** (☎ 04 50 55 82 23; mains from €6; ☼ late morning-télepherique closing).

The last few metres to the summit itself are by elevator. From the viewing platform at the top, there are stunning 360° views of the surrounding mountains. Often you can watch mountain climbers on nearby ridges or brave skiers setting out for the daunting Vallée Blanche descent.

COMPAGNIE DES GUIDES

Founded between 1821 and 1823, the Compagnie des Guides is the oldest organisation of its kind in the world. Its members are all highly skilled mountain experts with unparalleled experience in the Alpine ranges. The selection process is famously gruelling – until recently, only young men born in the Chamonix valley were even considered for selection. The present membership is more diverse, and includes a number of female guides – a major shift pioneered by women mountaineers like climber and guide Sylviane Tavernier.

The guides take their work (and reputation) very seriously – the annual **Fête des Guides,** when new members are welcomed and lost colleagues remembered, is one of the highlights of the Chamonix year. The son-et-lumière show usually takes place in mid-August, with fireworks, concerts and mountaineering displays, and culminates in a solemn ceremony at the Église St-Michel in Chamonix.

in French; 🕑 9am-12.30pm & 2.30-6.30pm Mon-Sat), which serves walkers, hikers and mountain climbers, provides information on trails, hiking conditions and *refuges* (staff can help make reservations).

Skiing & snowboarding

Chamonix is most famous for its world-class skiing and snowboarding. Of the nine main areas, the best for beginners are Le Tour, Les Planards, Le Brévent and La Flégère (the latter two are connected by *téléphérique*). Les Chosalets and Les Grands Montets, accessible from Argentière 9km north of Chamonix, offer accomplished skiers the most challenging skiing. There are also more advanced runs in most areas.

Les Grands Montets has a snowpark equipped with a half-pipe, kicker ramps and other obstacles for snowboarders, and most of Chamonix's runs are open to boarders and skiers. The valley has produced several champion snowboarders in recent years.

The region also has a large number of marked but ungroomed trails suitable for skiers looking for off-piste thrills. The famous 20km **Vallée Blanche descent** is one of the world's most celebrated runs, and remains a life-long dream for most serious skiers. The route leads from the Aiguille du Midi over the Mer de Glace and through the forests back to Chamonix, covering a drop in altitude of just under 2760m (9200ft). It should *only* be tackled with a guide – the route crosses the crevasse-riddled glacier and passes through avalanche-prone areas. It takes four to five hours and a guide costs €235 for up to four people, but this is one skiing experience you will never forget. Contact the ESF or Compagnie des Guides for details.

Lift Passes

The tourist office and the kiosks next to ski-lifts sell several ski-passes for the Chamonix area. The most popular is the **Cham' Ski pass** (per day/week/season €40/176/650), valid for all the valley lifts and free bus transport. Family, seniors' and beginners' passes are available too. You can also buy passes for a single ski area. The more expensive Ski-Pass Mont Blanc covers Megève–St-Gervais as well as the Chamonix Valley.

Ski Touring & Heli-skiing

One of Chamonix's great attractions is the possibility for *ski de randonnée* (ski touring). The range of tours is almost endless. It's possible to travel for a week or longer, skiing all the way to Switzerland or Italy, staying in mountain *refuges* (or if you're really unhinged, tents) along the way. A three-day *stage* package starts at around €400 per person. During winter, it's illegal to make overnight trips in the Chamonix–Mont Blanc area without the permission of the Compagnie des Guides, due to the danger of avalanches.

The king of ski tours is the classic six-day **Haute Route** (per person incl guide 730; 🕑 Mar & Apr) between Chamonix and Zermatt in Switzerland, opened by guides in 1927. Skiers should be experienced in off-piste skiing and will need to be very fit.

Other classic routes include the **Oberland** to Switzerland (six days, from €830), which traverses steep mountain descents and glacial areas including the famous Konkordiaplatz, and the **Tour des Jorasses** from Argentière to the Géant glacier through the rocky spires of the Grandes Jorasses range (five days, starting from €640).

Heli-skiing is also possible: contact **Chamonix Mont-Blanc Helicopters** (☎ 04 50 54 13 82; info@helico.fr), **SAF Chamonix Helicopters** (☎ 04 50 54 07 86; www.saf-helico.com) or the Compagnie des Guides for details. Prices range from €230 to €370. A 10-minute panoramic **helicopter flight** (per person from €65) is available with a minimum of four people.

SUMMER ACTIVITIES
Walking
In late spring and summer (about mid-June to October), 310km of spectacular walking trails open up around Chamonix. The most rewarding are the high-altitude trails reached by cable car. The *téléphériques* shut down in the late afternoon, but in June and July there is enough light to walk until 9pm or later.

Combined map and guide *Carte des Sentiers du Mont Blanc* (Mountain Trail Map; €4) is ideal for straightforward day walks. The most useful map is the 1:25,000 IGN map entitled *Chamonix-Massif du Mont Blanc* (No 3630OT; €9). Both are sold at Photo Alpine Tairraz (p498).

The **Grand Balcon Sud** trail along the western side of the valley stays at around 2000m and affords great views of Mont Blanc. On foot, it can be reached from behind Le Brévent's *télécabine* station. For less uphill walking, take either the Planpraz or La Flégère lifts.

A number of routes start from Plan de l'Aiguille, including the **Grand Balcon Nord**, which takes you to the Mer de Glace, from where you can walk or take the train down to Chamonix.

There are also trails to **Lac Blanc** (White Lake) at 2350m, a turquoise lake (despite its name) surrounded by mountains, from either the top of Les Praz-l'Index cable car (€12) or La Flégère (€1), the line's midway point.

Canyoning
Chamonix Guide (☎ 04 50 53 05 16; www.chamonixguide.com; 44 chemin de l'Ordon) offers summer canyoning expeditions in the mountains around Mont Blanc and other destinations in the Alps.

Summer Luge
The **summer luge track** (☎ 04 50 53 08 97; per ride €5.50; 🕒 1.30-6.30pm Sat & Sun Jun, 10am-7.30pm Jul & Aug) is near the *télésiège des Planards*. If there is no snow the luge also opens in May.

Cycling
Many lower-altitude trails (like the Petit Balcon Sud) are perfect for mountain biking. See p505 for information on bike rental. The Compagnie des Guides can organise one-day mountain-bike tours for €50 per person per day, and also offers three-, four- or five-day tours of Mont Blanc.

Paragliding
The sky above Chamonix is often dotted with colourful paragliders wheeling down from the snowy heights. Starter flights from Planpraz (2000m) cost €90 (€220 from the Aiguille du Midi). A five-day course starts at €420. Contact **Haut Vol** (☎ 04 50 53 98 01; haut.vol@tiscali.fr; 14 place de Chamonix Sud) or **Summits Parapente** (☎ 04 50 53 50 14; www.summits.fr; 28 impasse des Primevères).

Ice-Skating & Other Sports
An indoor **ice-skating rink** (patinoire; adult/child €4.10/3.30, skate rental €3; 🕒 10am-noon & 3-6pm Mon-Tue & Thu-Sun, 2-6pm & 9-11pm Wed) is located near the **Centre Sportif Richard Bozon** (☎ 04 50 53 09 07; 214 av de la Plage), where you'll also find a huge outdoor swimming pool and squash and tennis courts. *Location patins* is French for skate rental.

Sleeping
The cheapest way to visit Chamonix is through a package deal. If you decide to go it alone, Chamonix has no shortage of hotels – though finding one with an available bed might be the greatest challenge of your season.

During July, August and the ski season, hotels are heavily booked, so reserve ahead. Many prefer guests who take full or half-board. Accommodation can be booked in advance through Centrale de Réservation (p499).

Les Carnets de l'Hébergement, available free from the tourist office, lists most of the region's camping grounds, *refuges, gîtes d'étape, chambres d'hôtes*, apartments and hotels. In the low/high season expect to pay from €160/245 per week for a two-person studio.

Most mountain *refuges* (€14 to €20 a night) are accessible to hikers, though some can be reached only by mountain climbers. Breakfast and dinner, prepared by the warden, are often available for an extra fee.

It's essential to reserve a place – you don't want to hike halfway across Mont Blanc to find the refuge full. For information, contact the CAF (p499). When the office is closed, pick up a list detailing CAF *refuges* from outside the office. Many are minor architectural miracles, built at crazy angles or teetering precariously over stomach-churning drops.

BUDGET
Budget accommodation is always scarce in Chamonix, and in high season you'll have to book several months in advance. Gîte accommodation can be a good way to cut costs, though space to dry your gear after a day's skiing can be hard to find.

There are some 14 camping grounds in the Chamonix region, but you'd be a brave soul (or have an industrial-strength sleeping bag) to make use of them in winter. Because of the altitude, it's nearly always chilly at night.

Auberge de Jeunesse (☎ 04 50 53 14 52; chamonix@fuaj.org; 127 montée Jacques Balmat; dm incl breakfast summer €13.25-17; check-in ☽ 8am-noon & 5-10pm, closed early May & Oct–mid-Dec) About 2km southwest of Chamonix in Les Pélerins, this hostel can be reached by bus. Take the Chamonix–Les Houches line and get off at the Pélerins École stop. In winter, only weekly packages are available, including bed, food, ski pass and ski hire for six days. There's no kitchen.

Gîte La Montagne (☎ 04 50 53 11 60; 789 promenade des Crémeries; dm €12; ☽ closed 11 Nov–20 Dec) An attractive *gîte* in a traditional alpine-style building on a forested site, about 1.5km north of the train station (near La Frasse bus-stop).

Gîte Vagabond (☎ 04 50 53 15 43; www.levaga bond.co.uk; 365 av Ravanel-le-Rouge; dm €12.50, half-board €28; ☐) A neat hostelry with a kitchen, bar-restaurant with Internet access, BBQ area, climbing wall and parking. Beds are in four- or six-person dorms.

Au Bon Coin (☎ 04 50 53 15 67; hotelauboncoin@ wanadoo.fr; 80 av de l'Aiguille du Midi; d with bath & view €55-62; P) One of the best year-round deals in Chamonix. Perched above busy shops, it looks drab from the front, but the rear rooms are south-facing, and most have small balconies offering views of Mont Blanc. There are no TVs – but with views like this, who needs light entertainment?

Hôtel Le Stade (☎ 04 50 53 05 44; 79 rue Whymper; s/d from €34/46) Dull but pleasant rooms, though its position above shops on a busy roundabout can be a headache in high season. The entrance is around the back, up steps to the 1st floor.

Hôtel Boule de Neige (☎ 04 50 53 04 48; 362 rue Joseph Vallot; s/d from €36/56) A chalet-style hotel halfway up the lively rue Joseph Vallot. The rooms are as basic as they come, but there's an attractive mountain-town feel helped by the little local bar downstairs.

Hôtel El Paso (☎ 04 50 53 64 20; fax 04 50 53 64 22; 37 impasse des Rhododendrons; d with shared bath low/ high season €42/50) Looks like a cheap hotel in a Mexican border-town, but the rowdy atmosphere and Tex-Mex *menu* in the downstairs bar are just the trick for young boarders abroad – and it comes at a price that's hard to beat.

Camping
L'Île des Barrats (☎ 04 50 53 51 44; 185 chemin d'Île des Barrats; ☽ May-Oct) A three-star camping ground in a quiet clearing, near the base of the Aiguille du Midi *téléphérique*.

Les Deux Glaciers (☎ 04 50 53 15 84; glaciers@ clubInternet.fr; 80 route des Tissières; ☽ closed mid-Nov–mid-Dec) Another three-star camping ground in Les Bossons, 3km south of Chamonix. To get there, take the train to Les Bossons or the Chamonix bus to the Tremplin-le-Mont stop.

MID-RANGE
Most of Chamonix's hotels fall into this bracket, and what you get for your money can vary wildly.

Hôtel de l'Arve (☎ 04 50 53 02 31; www.hotelarve -chamonix.com; 60 impasse des Anémones; d high season €78-104; P) Built to resemble a traditional mountain chalet, this hotel is tucked away in a quiet courtyard off rue Joseph Vallot. All the rooms have lots of Alpine atmosphere and the best have a stunning view down the valley to Mont Blanc.

Hôtel Vallée Blanche (☎ 04 50 53 04 50; www .val lee-blanche.com; 36 rue du Lyret; d low/high season €67/130; P) This place is hard to miss, thanks to its shocking pink exterior and the bright-red telephone box outside, but inside, the hotel has a sophisticated feel that wouldn't be out of place in the smarter ski resorts. The nicest rooms look onto the river or the Mont Blanc range.

Hôtel Gourmets et Italy (☎ 04 50 53 01 38; www
.hotelgourmets-chamonix.com; 96 rue du Lyret; d low/high
season €75/157) Just along the street from Hôtel
Vallée Blanche, this smart hotel sometimes
offers good deals in the shoulder months.
The rooms are decorated in plain, warm
tones and all have minibars, bathrobes and
satellite TV, and there's a lovely flower-
filled garden to enjoy in summer.

Hôtel Gustavia (☎ 04 50 53 00 31; fax 04 50 55 86
39; www.hotel-gustavia.com; 272 av Michel Croz; d low/high
season from €71/144) A large, three-star hotel with
attractive double rooms, the best of which
have mountain views. It's popular with
young skiers and snowboarders, with a busy
après ski bar, and is near the train station.

Hôtel Richemond (☎ 04 50 53 08 85; www.riche
mond.fr; 228 rue du Docteur Paccard; s low season €53-
60, high season €83-96; P) A vast, austere hotel
where the prices stay low even in high season, which means it's nearly always full.
The best rooms have mountain views; the
worst have views of the car park.

TOP END
Hôtel Mont Blanc (☎ 04 50 53 05 64; www.bestmont
blanc.com; 62 allée du Majestic; d with half-board per person
low/high season €103/183; P ⊠ ⊞ ⊡) South of
the tourist office, this is one of Chamonix's
top hotels, boasting four stars and all the
luxury you could possibly wish for.

Eating
RESTAURANTS
In season, most of Chamonix's restaurants
are open daily for lunch and dinner.

Neapolis (☎ 04 50 53 98 41; 79 Gallerie Alpina; pizza
& pasta €6.40-9.90; ⊙ Mon-Sat) This simple Italian restaurant overlooks the river and has
cheap, wholesome cooking – which makes
it very popular.

Restaurant La Calèche (☎ 04 50 55 94 68; 18
rue du Docteur Paccard; evening menus from €17) One
of many restaurants around place Balmat
aimed squarely at undiscriminating holiday
makers. Still, the fondue is very good, which
is more than can be said for the décor.

Annapurna (☎ 04 50 55 81 39; 62 av Ravanel-Le
Rouge; mains €6-15) If you're feeling chilly after
the snow, how about a volcanic curry? This
snazzy Indian place has a good vegetarian
selection – try the chickpea curry or the
vegetarian platter.

Le Sanjon (☎ 04 50 53 56 44; 5 av Ravanel Le
Rouge; menus €15-25, fondue €11-21) A picturesque

wooden chalet restaurant serving *raclette* –
a block of melted cheese, usually eaten with
potatoes and cold meats and fondue.

Munchie (☎ 04 50 53 45 41; 87 rue des Moulins; mains
€10-25; ⊙ closed lunch) A trendy hang-out with
great pan-Asian food. Mains include black-
ened salmon *sashimi*, authentic sushi and
Thai Chicken with pimento and ginger.

Le Panoramic (☎ /fax 04 50 53 44 11; Le Brévent;
menus from €15) At Le Brévent cable station, this
is the place to choose for a lofty lunch with
an incredible view of Mont Blanc. The selection of *menus* include local cheese, cured
meat, potatoes and salad, and a warming
glass of *vin chaud* will perk you up on a
snowy winter's day.

CAFÉS & QUICK EATS
Le Gouthé (☎ 04 50 53 58 95; 95 rue des Moulins; cakes
& pastries €1-4; hot drinks €1.50-3) Head here for
the best cakes, pastries and hot chocolate
in town.

Le Bumble Bee Bistro (☎ 04 50 53 50 03; 65 rue
des Moulins; mains €5-10) A tiny, welcoming café
that serves hot, hearty meals throughout the
day. Cod fritters, chargrilled chicken, steak
and ale pie, and potato wedges are ideal after
a hard day on the slopes, but vegetarians
should try the Red Dragon Pie, stuffed full
of vegetables, lentils and spicy beans.

Poco Loco (☎ 04 50 53 43 03; 47 rue du Docteur
Paccard; crepes from €1.50, pizza €5-7, menus from €7)
One of several sandwich shops near place
Balmat, with hot paninis, sweet crepes and
huge burgers.

SELF-CATERING
There's a **Super U Supermarket** (117 rue Joseph Vallot; ⊙ 8.15am-7.30pm Mon-Sat, 8.15am-12.45pm Sun winter). **Le Refuge Payot** (☎ 04 50 53 18 71; 166 rue Joseph
Vallot) and **La Ferme du Mont Blanc** (☎ 04 50 53 37
13; 202 rue Joseph Vallot) stock an excellent range
of cheeses, meats and other local products.

Getting There & Away
BUS
The bus station is in the train station building. The office of **SAT Autocar** (☎ 04 50 53 01 15;
www.satobus-alps.com in French; ⊙ 6.45am-10.30am &
1.25-4.45pm Mon-Fri, 6.45am-11.00am & 1.25-4.45pm Sat &
Sun winter) is near the train station entrance;
seasonal hours vary. Buses operate to Geneva
bus station (€33, 1½ to two hours), Annecy
(€15.30, three hours) and Geneva airport
(€33, 2¼ hours). Services to Italy, through

APRÈS-SKI IN CHAMONIX

Chamonix's humming nightlife is one of its main attractions, and there are enough bars and clubs to keep you going for a whole season.

Popular places include the café-bar of **Hôtel Gustavia** (see p504), which has a happy hour most evenings, and a lively terrace outside, and **O'Byrne's Irish Bar** at Hôtel Vallée Blanche (see p503), which does a decent Murphy's and attracts an older crowd.

Le Cybar (p499) regularly hosts après-ski bands and comedy nights and usually has a happy hour from 6pm to 7pm. You can grab a warming snack (tortillas, jacket potatoes, burgers and paninis for €4 to €8) or watch a DVD in the upstairs lounge.

Dick's Tea Bar (☎ 04 50 53 19 10; www.dicksteabar.com; rue des Moulins), is Chamonix's outpost of the Alpine nightclub chain. Club classics and weird cocktails are the order of the day.

Wild Wallabies (☎ 04 50 53 01 31; 1 rue de la Tour) is a grungy Australian-themed joint that offers pool, table football and bar snacks. As you might imagine it's a popular place with the snow-crowd from Down Under.

Le Refuge (☎ 04 50 53 00 94; 275 rue du Docteur Paccard) and **L'Arbate** (☎ 04 50 53 80 23; www.arbate .com; 80 chemin du Sapi) are buzzy late-night destinations. Chamonix's biggest, cheesiest disco is **Le Garage** (☎ 04 50 53 64 49; 200 av de l'Aiguille du Midi), down an alleyway off av Michael Croz.

---

the Mont Blanc tunnel, include Courmayeur (€18 return) and Aoste (€22 return).

CAR

If you're coming to Chamonix from Italy, you'll arrive via the **Mont Blanc Tunnel** (cars single/return €29/36), which enters town in the southern suburb of Les Pélerins. From France, the N205 travels to Les Houches and Les Bossons before arriving in Chamonix.

Parking in town can be tricky. Car parks (some free) are scattered along Route du Bouchet, around Rue des Allobroges and in Chamonix Sud, but in season they're likely to be full. Another option is to park outside town and connect by bus or train: contact **Chamonix Parc-Auto** (☎ 04 50 53 65 71; weekly rates from €31).

TRAIN

Chamonix–Mont Blanc **train station** (☎ 04 50 53 12 98; ticket counter 6am 8pm) is at the end of av Michel Croz. It has a **left-luggage counter** (1st/additonal piece luggage €3/1.50; 6am-8pm).

Major destinations include Paris' Gare de Lyon (€87, six to seven hours, five daily), Lyon (€32, 4½ hours via Annecy), Annecy (€18, 2½ hours), Geneva (€17, four hours via Annecy or Chambéry), and Grenoble (€28, five hours via Annecy). There's an overnight train to Paris (€99, 10 hours) year-round.

The narrow-gauge train line from St-Gervais–le Fayet (23km west of Chamonix) to Martigny, Switzerland (42km north of Chamonix), stops at 11 towns in the valley

including Argentière. There are nine to 12 return trips a day. From St-Gervais–le Fayet, there are trains to all parts of France.

Getting Around

BICYCLE

Between June and September, **Le Grand Bi** (☎ 04 50 53 14 16; 240 av du Bois du Bouchet; 3-/10-speed mountain bike hire per day €15/22; 9am-12.30pm & 2.30-7pm Tue-Sat) rents bikes.

BUS

Bus transport is handled by **Chamonix Bus** (☎ 04 50 53 05 55; place du Triangle de l'Amitié; 7am-7pm winter, 8am-noon & 2-7pm Jun-Aug).

Bus stops are marked by black-on-yellow roadside signs. From mid-December to mid-May, there are numerous lines to the ski lifts. During the rest of the year there are only two lines, both leaving from place de l'Église and passing by the Chamonix Sud stop. One line goes south to Les Houches; the other goes north via Argentière to Col des Montets. Buses stop running between 6pm and 7pm, depending on the season. In winter, buses are free for holders of ski passes; others pay €1.50 for one sector during the day, €2 at night.

TAXI

There's a **taxi stand** (☎ 04 50 53 13 94) outside the train station. Tariffs are posted inside the station. Minibuses for two to eight people are available from **Chamonix Transfer** (☎ 06 07 67 88 85; www.chamonix-transfer.com in French).

MEGÈVE & ST-GERVAIS

Megève (population 4700, elevation 1113m), 36km southwest of Chamonix, and neighbouring St-Gervais (population 5400, elevation 810m) sit below Mont Blanc and are connected by a common network of ski lifts. These tiny ski villages are among the oldest in the Alps.

Megève was developed as a resort in the 1920s for a French baroness following her disillusionment with Switzerland's crowded St-Moritz. Today it remains an expensive, trendy resort with an old square accessed by old narrow medieval-style streets and lanes. On the eastern outskirts of the village are some chapels and oratories that trace the Stations of the Cross in baroque, rococo, and Tuscan-style woodcarvings.

Summer hiking trails in the Bettex, Mont d'Arbois and Mont Joly areas are accessible from both villages. Mountain biking is equally popular; some of the best terrain is found along marked trails between Val d'Arly, Mont Blanc and Beaufortain.

Information

Megève has a **tourist office** (☎ 04 50 21 27 28; www.megeve.com; rue de Monseigneur Conseil; ☼ 9am-12.30pm & 2-7pm Mon-Sat, 9am-12.30pm & 4-7pm Sun winter). The **accommodation service** (☎ 04 50 21 29 52; reservation@megeve.com) is based here too.

Megève's **ESF** (☎ 04 50 21 00 97; www.megeve-ski.com; 76 rue Ambroise Martin) and the **Bureau des Guides** (☎ 04 50 21 55 11; www.bureaudesguides.com; 76 rue Ambroise Martin) are inside Maison de la Montagne. Megève's **International Ski School** (ESI; ☎ 04 50 58 78 88; www.esimegeve.com) is at the bottom of the Mont d'Arbois cable car.

In St-Gervais the **tourist office** (☎ 04 50 47 76 08; fax 04 50 47 75 69; 115 av Mont Paccard; ☼ 9am-noon & 2.30-7.30pm high season, 9am-noon & 2-6pm low season) also has an **accommodation service** (☎ 04 50 93 53 63). There are also **ESF** (☎ 04 50 47 7621; promenade du Mont Blanc) and **Bureau des Guides** (☎ 04 50 47 76 55; place du Mont Blanc) offices here.

Sleeping

Both tourist offices stock lists of accommodation, but Megève isn't cheap. Studios for two people per week in the low/high season start at €230/310.

Bookings for CAF *refuges* in St-Gervais and Megève can be made through the CAF office in Chamonix (p499) or through the

Refuge du Val-Monjoie (☎ 04 50 47 76 70; 73 av de Miage, St-Gervais).

Alp Hôtel (☎ 04 50 21 07 58; www.alp-hotel.fr; 434 route de Rochebrune; half-board d €53-62) A friendly chalet-style place in Megève with comfortable, rustic two-star rooms.

Hôtel Au Coeur de Megève (☎ 04 50 21 25 30; www.hotel-megeve.com; rue Charles Feige; r €104-163) Near the centre of Megève, this three-star hotel has pleasant rooms and balconies looking onto the street.

Au Vieux Moulin (☎ 04 50 21 22 29; www.vieux moulin.com; 188 rue Ambroise-Martin; d €146-250; P ☼) One of Megève's oldest hotels, housed in a beautiful refurbished alpine chalet with lots of luxurious touches.

Eating

Les Fermes de Marie (☎ 04 50 93 03 10; www.fermes demarie.com; chemin de Riante Colline; mains €12-20, menus from €35; ☼ lunch & dinner) A renowned Alpine spa-resort boasting not one but three of the top restaurants in Megève – a formal dining room, a traditional Alpine rotisserie, and a cheese restaurant serving fondue and *raclette*.

La Ferme de mon Père (☎ 04 50 21 01 01; www .marc-veyrat.com; 367 route du Crêt; mains €75-105, menus €270/360; ☼ lunch & dinner Dec-Apr) This celebrated gastronomic restaurant is owned by one of France's top chefs, Marc Veyrat. In keeping with the rest of Megève, the prices are sky-high, but with dishes such as *sirène de macaron meringuée* (mermaid macarooned meringue) and *coquillages en folie* (joyous shellfish) on the menu, you're guaranteed a truly unique dining experience

Getting There & Away

There's a **SAT bus** and **SNCF office** (☎ 04 50 47 73 88) opposite the tourist office in St-Gervais. In Megève, contact the **bus station** (☎ 04 50 21 25 18) and **train station** (☎ 08 92 35 35 39) for further information on transfers to and from Megève.

Many trains to/from Paris via Annecy stop at Sallanches (13km from Megève) and St-Gervais–le Fayet (16km from Megève and 2km from St-Gervais). All trains terminate in St-Gervais–le Fayet.

There are four buses daily between St-Gervais, Megève and Chamonix (€8.50, 55 minutes). Seven buses daily link Megève and St-Gervais with St-Gervais–le Fayet and Sallanches train stations. There are also five buses daily in winter to/from Geneva airport (€33, 1½ hours).

From St-Gervais–le Fayet and St-Gervais, the **Mont Blanc tramway** (☎ 04 50 47 51 83) rattles its way up to Bellevue (1800m), offering staggering mountain views en route. A return ticket costs €15.

LES PORTES DU SOLEIL

The dozen villages linked by lifts along the French–Swiss border in the northern Chablais – dubbed the Portes du Soleil (Gates of the Sun) – comprise the largest ski area in France. Some 650km of slopes and trails criss-cross the region. You can buy a ski pass covering some or all of them.

The largest village is **Morzine** (population 3000, elevation 1000m) in Haute Savoie, retaining some (but not much) of its traditional Alpine village atmosphere. Accommodation can be booked through the **accommodation service** (☎ 04 50 79 11 57; reservation@morzine-avoriaz .com) inside the **tourist office** (☎ 04 50 74 72 72; www.morzine-avoriaz.com in French; place de la Crusaz; ☼ 8.30am-7.30pm Sun-Fri, plus 8am-8pm Sat during winter & summer seasons). There's also an **Auberge de Jeunesse** (☎ 04 50 79 14 86; morzine@fuaj.org; dm €12; ☼ Christmas-Apr & Jun-Sep).

Avoriaz (1800m), a few kilometres up the valley from Morzine, is among the most expensive of the French ski resorts. Built in the 1960s, Morzine's high-rise apartment blocks manage to blend into their surroundings because each one is covered with wooden shingles. Apart from two four-star hotels and a **Club Méditerranée** (☎ 04 50 74 28 70; fax 04 50 74 03 61; all-inclusive package per week from €805), all accommodation is in studios or apartments, which can be booked through the **tourist office** (☎ 04 50 74 02 11; www.avoriaz .com; ☼ 8.30am-7pm). Avoriaz is a car-free resort but there are outdoor and covered car parks. Transport is by horse-and-sleigh in winter. There's a special course for mountain bikes with jumps and other obstacles. It's free, but only open in summer.

If you're arriving by road via Cluses, **Les Gets** (population 1300, elevation 1172m) is the first village of the Portes du Soleil. Quieter than Morzine and cheaper than Avoriaz, it has plenty of accommodation; contact the **tourist office** (☎ 04 50 75 80 80; www .lesgets.com; place de la Mairie; ☼ 8.30am-7pm in winter, 8.30am-12.30pm & 2-7pm Mon-Fri, 8.30am-7pm Sat & Sun in summer) or the **accommodation booking office** (☎ 04 50 75 80 51; reservations@lesgets.com) housed in the same building.

Getting There & Away

Free shuttle buses serve the lifts of Télécabine Super Morzine, Télécabine du Pléney and Téléphérique Avoriaz.

During the ski season, Morzine is linked by bus to Geneva airport (€29), 50km north. From Morzine there are regular **SAT buses** (☎ 04 50 79 15 69) to Les Gets and Avoriaz. There are also buses from Morzine to its closest train stations: Thonon-les-Bains (34km to the north) and Cluses (31km to the south).

THONON-LES-BAINS

pop 30,000 / elevation 430m

Thonon-les-Bains is the largest town on the French side of Lake Geneva (Lac Léman), and the capital of the Chablais area. Just across the water from the Swiss city of Lausanne, the modern town sits on a bluff above the lake and is linked to the marina (port des Rives) by a 230m-long **funiculaire** (☎ 04 50 71 21 54; one way/return €1/1.80; ☼ 8am-12.30pm & 1.30-6.30pm, 8am-11pm summer). Thonon makes for a peaceful overnight stop in summer, with serene lake cruises and pleasant lakefront walks – but the town itself hasn't got much to offer. From the port, quai de Ripaille follows the lake 1km east to **Château de Ripaille** (☎ 04 50 26 64 44; admission incl tour €6; tours 3pm).

The **tourist office** (☎ 04 50 71 55 55; www.thonon lesbains.com; place du Marché; ☼ 9am-noon & 2-6pm Mon-Sat Sep-Jun, 8.30am-12.30pm & 1.30-7pm Mon-Sat, 10am-noon Sun Jul & Aug) operates a lakeside **annexe** (☎ 04 50 26 19 94; port des Rives; ☼ 10.30am-12.30pm & 2-7pm Jul & Aug) during summer. The annexe sells tickets for Lake Geneva cruises, run mainly by the Swiss **CGN company** (☎ 04 50 71 14 71) and **Navirives** (☎ /fax 04 50 71 52 42).

Accommodation can be found at the old **Hôtel à l'Ombre des Marronniers** (☎ 04 50 71 26 18; fax 04 50 26 27 47; 17 place de Crète; d €44-46), beside the train station, or the modern **Hôtel Ibis** (☎ 04 50 71 24 24; fax 04 50 71 87 76; 2ter av d'Évian; d €55-75) near the town centre.

SAT (☎ 04 50 71 00 88; 11 av Jules Ferry) has regular buses to/from Thonon to Évian (€1.50, 15 minutes) and into the Chablais Mountains, including to Morzine. The **train station** (☎ 08 36 35 35 35; place de la Gare) is southwest of place des Arts, the main square. Trains go to Geneva (€6.30, 40 minutes) and Bellegarde (€9.60, 1¼ hours) via Thonon-les-Bains.

HEALTH FARMS & HOT WATER

Nine kilometres east of Thonon is **Évian-les-Bains**, famous for its mineral water. Known as the 'Pearl of Lake Geneva', Évian was a favourite country retreat of the dukes of Savoy, but was razed during the Wars of Religion. It reinvented itself as a luxury tourist resort in the 18th century when the fashion for spa baths reached its height. Though the health benefits of sitting in tubs of mineral water were never quite established, drinking the stuff caught on in a big way: bottled mineral water now accounts for most of Évian's economy. The water takes 15 years to trickle down through the Chablais mountains, gathering minerals en route, before emerging at a constant temperature of 11.4°C (52.8°F).

If you're interested, it's possible to visit the Évian factory; ask at the **tourist office** (☎ 04 50 75 04 26; www.eviantourism.com; place d'Allinges; 🕑 8.30am-12.30pm & 2-7pm Mon-Fri, 9am-noon & 3-7pm Sat, 10am-noon & 3-6pm Sun Jul & Aug, to 6pm mid-May–mid-Sep, 8.30am-noon & 2-6pm Mon-Fri Oct-Apr) for details or head straight for the factory's **Public Relations Office** (☎ 04 50 26 80 80; 22 av des Sources). Tours are free but must be booked in advance. You might even get a free sample.

ANNECY

pop 50,000 / elevation 448m

Annecy, the chic capital of Haute-Savoie, is a pretty lakeside town, criss-crossed with ancient canals and lined with medieval houses and arched alleyways. Visitors can stroll along the lakefront or mosey around the old city, admiring the Alpine peaks and the geranium-covered bridges or take to the waters of Lac d'Annecy in *pedalos*, canoes and cruise-boats. Annecy makes the perfect place to kick back and relax after the adrenaline-fuelled Alpine resorts – except in summer, when the bumper-to-bumper traffic can be a little taxing.

Orientation

The train and bus stations are 500m northwest of the Vieille Ville (old town), which is huddled around the River Thiou (split into Canal du Thiou to the south and Canal du Vassé to the north). The town centre is between the post office and the purpose-built Centre Bonlieu, which houses the city's theatre and the tourist office, near the shores of Lac d'Annecy.

Information

INTERNET ACCESS

Syndrome Cybercafé (☎ 04 50 45 39 75; infos@syndrome.com; per 15min/hr €2/6; 3bis av de Chevêne; 🕑 noon-midnight)

LAUNDRY

Lav' Confort Express (4 rue de la Gare; 🕑 7am-9pm)

MONEY

Convenient branches include Crédit Lyonnais in the Bonlieu Centre and Banque Populaire (Faubourg Ste-Claire), with an ATM and currency-exchange machine.

Banque de France (9bis av de Chambéry; 🕑 8.45am-noon & 1.45-3.45pm Mon-Fri)

POST

Post Office (4bis rue des Glières)

TOURIST INFORMATION

Annecy Sport Information (☎ 04 50 33 88 31; 🕑 3-7pm Mon, 2.30-7pm Tue-Fri, 10am-noon Sat) Also in Centre Bonlieu.

Tourist Office (☎ 04 50 45 00 33; www.lac-annecy .com; 1 rue Jean Jaurès; 🕑 9am-12.30pm & 1.45-6pm Mon-Sat mid-Sep–mid-May, 9am-6.30pm Mon-Sat mid-May–mid-Sep, Sun summer) In Centre Bonlieu.

Sights & Activities

Wandering around the old town and the lakefront are the essence of a visit to Annecy. Just east of the Vieille Ville, behind the town hall, are the flowery **Jardins de l'Europe**, shaded by Californian giant redwoods. **Champ de Mars** is a popular park across the Canal du Vassé from the redwoods. Both are linked by the elegant arch of the Pont des Amours.

VIEILLE VILLE

The Vieille Ville, a warren of narrow streets and colonnaded passageways, retains much of its 17th-century appearance. On the central island, the imposing **Palais de l'Isle** (☎ 04 50 33 87 31; adult/student €3.05/0.75; 🕑 10am-6pm Jun-Sep, 10am-noon & 2-6pm Wed-Mon Oct-May) was once a prison, but is now home to local-history displays. Between mid-June and September there are guided tours in English around Vieille Ville – contact the tourist office for details.

CHÂTEAU D'ANNECY
In the 13th- to 16th-century castle above town, the **Musée Château** (☎ 04 50 33 87 30; adult/student €4.70/1.60; ⏰ 10am-noon & 2-6pm Wed-Mon Oct-May, 10.30am-6pm Jun-Sep) is a fine museum that explores traditional Savoyard art and crafts, and has a display on Alpine natural history. It also holds frequent special exhibitions. The

climb to the chateau is worth it just for the view over the old town's crowded rooftops.

SUNBATHING & SWIMMING
The lakefront is lined with parks and grassy areas where you can picnic, sunbathe and swim in the warm months. **Plage d'Annecy-le-Vieux** (admission free) is 1km east of the

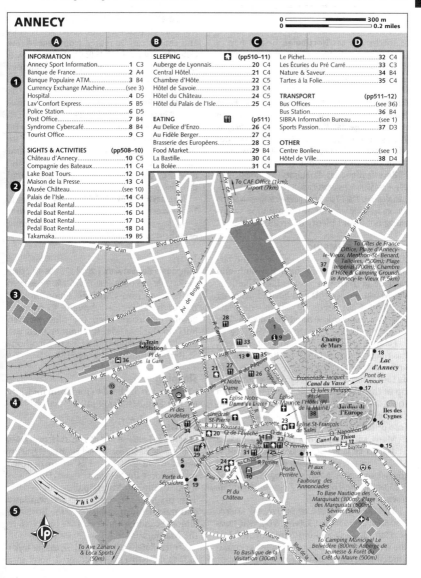

ANNECY

INFORMATION	
Annecy Sport Information	1 C3
Banque de France	2 A4
Banque Populaire ATM	3 B4
Currency Exchange Machine	(see 3)
Hospital	4 D5
Lav'Confort Express	5 B5
Police Station	6 D5
Post Office	7 B4
Syndrome Cybercafé	8 B4
Tourist Office	9 C3

SIGHTS & ACTIVITIES	(pp508–10)
Château d'Annecy	10 C5
Compagnie des Bateaux	11 D4
Lake Boat Tours	12 D4
Maison de la Presse	13 C4
Musée Château	(see 10)
Palais de l'Isle	14 C4
Pedal Boat Rental	15 D4
Pedal Boat Rental	16 D4
Pedal Boat Rental	17 D4
Pedal Boat Rental	18 D4
Takamaka	19 B5

SLEEPING	(pp510–11)
Auberge de Lyonnais	20 C4
Central Hôtel	21 C4
Chambre d'Hôte	22 C5
Hôtel de Savoie	23 C4
Hôtel du Château	24 C5
Hôtel du Palais de l'Isle	25 C4

EATING	(p511)
Au Delice d'Enzo	26 C4
Au Fidèle Berger	27 C4
Brasserie des Européens	28 C3
Food Market	29 B4
La Bastille	30 B4
La Bolée	31 C4

Le Pichet	32 C4
Les Écuries du Pré Carré	33 C3
Nature & Saveur	34 B4
Tartes à la Folie	35 C4

TRANSPORT	(pp511–12)
Bus Offices	(see 36)
Bus Station	36 B4
SIBRA Information Bureau	(see 1)
Sports Passion	37 D3

OTHER	
Centre Bonlieu	(see 1)
Hôtel de Ville	38 D4

OUT & ABOUT IN ANNECY

Annecy hosts many events and exhibitions throughout the year. Highlights include a **Venetian carnival** in March, Spanish and Italian **film festivals** in March and October, a major **animation festival** in June, a **fireworks display** over the lake in August (Fête du Lac), and **Le Retour des Alpages**, a street festival celebrating Savoyard traditions and folklore in October. Another exciting annual spectacle is **Les Noctibules**, held in July, when the night-time streets of Annecy are taken over by street performers.

Champ de Mars. Closer to town is **Plage Impérial** (admission €3), which has changing rooms. **Plage des Marquisats** (admission free) is 1km south of the Vieille Ville along rue des Marquisats. The beaches are officially open from June to September.

Base Nautique des Marquisats (☎ 04 50 45 39 18; 29 rue des Marquisats; adult/under 18 €3.50/2.50; ☼ 9am-7pm Mon-Sat, 10am-7pm Sun & holidays May–early Sep, to 7.30pm Jul–early Sep) has three outdoor swimming pools and plenty of green spaces.

WALKING & CLIMBING

A fine stroll can be followed from the Jardins de l'Europe along quai Bayreuth and quai de la Tournette to the Base Nautique des Marquisats (right) and beyond. Another excellent walk begins at Champ de Mars and goes eastwards around the lake towards Annecy-le-Vieux.

Forêt du Crêt du Maure, south of Annecy, has many walking trails, but there are better areas in two nearby nature reserves: **Bout du Lac** (20km from Annecy on the southern tip of the lake) and **Roc de Chère** (10km from town on the eastern shore of the lake). Both can be reached by Voyages Crolard buses (see p512).

Maps and topoguides can be purchased at **Maison de la Presse** (13 rue Vaugelas; ☎ 04 50 51 73 51; ☼ 9am-noon & 2-6pm Mon-Sat) and the tourist office. A good walking map is the 1:25,000-scale Top 25 IGN map entitled *Lac d'Annecy* (No 3431OT).

The **CAF** (☎ 04 50 09 82 09, 04 50 27 29 45; 77 rue du Mont Blanc; ☼ 3-7pm Wed, 5.30-7pm & 8-9pm Fri, 10am-noon Sat) office is about 1.5km northeast of the train station. Takamaka (right) arranges guided hikes and climbs.

CYCLING & IN-LINE SKATING

There's a cycling path (also popular with in-line skaters) along the western shore of the lake. It starts 1.5km south of Annecy (on rue des Marquisats) and travels to Duingt, 12km further south. See p512 for information on bicycle and in-line skate rental.

WATER SPORTS

The **Base Nautique des Marquisats** (31 rue des Marquisats) is a centre for aquatic activities. Kayaks and canoes can be rented from **Canoë-Kayak Club d'Annecy** (☎ 04 50 45 03 98; ☼ 9am-noon & 1-5pm Jun-Sep), which is at Base Nautique des Marquisats.

Between June and mid-September, the **Société des Régates à Voile d'Annecy** (SRVA; ☎ 04 50 45 48 39; fax 04 50 45 64 64; 31 rue des Marquisats; sailing boat hire per 2hr €40; ☼ 9am-noon & 2-5pm Mon-Fri) rents all sorts of sailing boats. Between late March and late October, pedal boats and small motor-boats can be hired along the quays of the Canal du Thiou and Canal du Vassé.

Takamaka (☎ 04 50 45 60 61; www.takamaka.fr; 17 rue Faubourg Ste-Claire) arranges rafting (from €49), kayaking (from €39) and canyoning expeditions (€47 to €95).

Tours

Compagnie des Bateaux (☎ 04 50 51 08 40; 2 place aux Bois; 1hr lake cruise adult/child €10/8; ☼ summer) boats leave from Canal du Thiou on quai Bayreuth. Tickets are bought 15 minutes before departure from the blue wooden huts on the lakeside. In summer there are also boat trips across the lake to Menthon-St-Bernard and Talloires (p512).

Sleeping

Cheap hotels are hard to find from mid-July to mid-August – book in advance.

BUDGET

Auberge de Jeunesse (☎ 04 50 45 33 19; annecy@fuaj .com; 4 route du Semnoz; dm incl breakfast €12) This smart wood-clad hostel is south of town in the Forêt du Semnoz, about 1km away from Camping Municipal Le Belvédère. The plain décor, large picture windows and modern furnishings give the hostel an almost Scandinavian feel. Take bus No 6 to the Marquisats stop.

Central Hôtel (☎ 04 50 45 05 37; 6bis rue Royale; s €37-42, d €44-49) This ivy-covered hotel in a quiet, shabby courtyard is one of the cheapest places close to the Vieille Ville – but the rooms are a little basic. **Auberge du Lyonnais** (☎ 04 50 51 26 10; fax 04 50 51 05 04; 14 quai de l'Évêché; r €29-45) In the heart of the old city, this hotel-restaurant occupies an idyllic setting next to the canal – but there are only nine rooms, so be quick.

Camping
There are several camping grounds near the lake in Annecy-le-Vieux.
Camping Municipal Le Belvédère (☎ 04 50 45 48 30; fax 04 50 45 55 56; camping €13) In the Forêt du Crêt du Maure, is 2.5km south of the train station.

MID-RANGE & TOP END
One **chambre d'hôte** (☎ 04 50 23 34 43; 2 av de la Mavéria; d €35-50) overlooks the lake next to the Impérial Palace. Alternatively, there's a **chambre d'hôte** (☎ 04 50 45 72 28; rampe du Château; d €60-80) in a big period house next to Hôtel du Château.
Hôtel du Château (☎ 04 50 45 27 66; fax 04 50 52 75 26; 16 rampe du Château; r €45-60; P) Just below one of the towers of the chateau, this small, hilltop hotel is hard to beat for a serene view over Annecy's lantern-lit lanes. The rooms are cosy and there's a great terrace overlooking the city's rooftops.
Hôtel du Palais de L'Isle (☎ 04 50 45 86 87; fax 04 50 51 87 15; 13 rue Perrière; d €69-88) Next to Le Pichet restaurant, this is an upmarket hotel with 26 well-kept modern rooms, many of which look over the canal.
Hôtel de Savoie (☎ 04 50 45 15 45; fax 04 50 45 11 99; 1 place de St-François; s/d €45/70) Once a convent, this characterful little hotel has its entrance on the left side of Église St-François de Sales. It's a small, friendly place with simple rooms and in a great location.

Eating
RESTAURANTS
In the Vieille Ville, the quays along both sides of Canal du Thiou are lined with cafés and restaurants. There are lots of cheap places along rue du Pâquier.
Au Delice d'Enzo (☎ 04 50 45 35 36; 17 rue du Pâquier; pizza or pasta €6.50-10; ☼ lunch & dinner) One of several restaurants under the arched colonnades of rue du Pâquier, this tiny little Italian joint has a streetside terrace and serves good, simple pizza and pasta.

Brasserie des Européens (☎ 04 50 51 30 70; 23 rue Sommeiller; mains €8-20; ☼ lunch & dinner) A popular brasserie with a 1920s ambience, specialising in mussels; try the *Moules Spéciales Brasserie* cooked in beer. It also has a fresh seafood takeaway counter.
Les Écuries du Pré Carré (☎ 04 50 45 59 14; 10 rue Vaugelas; menus €15-25; ☼ Mon-Sat) South of Brasserie des Européens in a small courtyard off rue Vaugelas, this is a pricey, classy place which usually has lake fish on its varied menu.
La Bolée (☎ 04 50 45 26 62; 14 rue de l'Isle; crepes €7-9.15; ☼ Thu-Tue May-Sep) A simple Breton creperie with regional variations on the theme. Try the *Savoyard*, with bacon and local *reblochon* cheese.
Le Pichet (☎ 04 50 45 32 41; 13 rue Perrière; menus €18-29; ☼ Thu-Mon) Next door to the Hôtel du Palais de L'Isle, this restaurant has a big terrace and a range of Savoyard dishes, including delicious, diet-busting *tartiflette* (sliced potatoes and *reblochon* cheese baked in the oven).
La Bastille (☎ 04 50 45 09 37; 3 quai des Vieilles Prisons; menus €11-20; ☼ lunch & dinner) A great little canalside restaurant with a sheltered terrace, opposite the old city prison. *Tartiflette*, steaks and Savoyard fondues are all delicious.

CAFÉS
Rue Perrière and rue de l'Isle have several cheap sandwich shops.
Tartes à la Folie (7-9 rue Vaugelas) Sweet and savoury tarts are on offer at this little café – don't miss out on the scrumptious rhubarb and nut tarts.
Au Fidèle Berger (cnr rue Royale & rue Carnot; ☼ 9.15am-7pm Tue-Fri, 9am-7.30pm Sat) A traditional tearoom and patisserie with a fantastic old-world feel.
Nature & Saveur (place des Cordeliers; ☼ 8.30am-7pm Tue-Sat) A cosy organic café with a terrace on the quayside, offering smoothies, fresh juices and organic salads and snacks.

SELF-CATERING
In the Vieille Ville, there is a popular **food market** (rue Faubourg Ste-Claire; ☼ 8am-noon Sun, Tue & Fri).

Getting There & Away
AIR
Annecy's small **airport** (☎ 04 50 27 30 06; www.annecy.aeroport.fr; 8 route Côte Merle) is north of the

city in Meythet, just west of the autoroute to Geneva. The airport has daily flights to Paris' Orly Sud (from €250, one hour 20 minutes).

BUS
The bus station, **Gare Routière Sud** (rue de l'Industrie), is next to the train station. Exits from the train station platforms lead directly to the bus station. Tickets can be purchased from the bus offices at the bus station.

Voyages Crolard (☎ 04 50 45 08 12; ☼ 7.15am-12.30pm & 1.45-7.30pm Mon-Sat, also Sun in peak seasons), based at the bus station, serves various points around Lac d'Annecy, including Menthon, Talloires and Roc de Chère on the eastern shore; Sévrier on the western shore; and Bout du Lac on the southern tip. Other destinations include La Clusaz (€9.20, 50 minutes), Albertville (€7.70, 1¼ hours) and Chamonix (€16, two hours).

Autocars Frossard (☎ 04 50 45 73 90; ☼ 7.45-11am & 2-7.15pm Mon-Fri, 7.45am-1pm Sat), at the bus station, sells tickets to Annemasse, Chambéry, Évian, Geneva, Grenoble, Nice and Thonon.

TRAIN
There are information counters at the **train station** (☎ 08 36 35 35 35; place de la Gare; information counters ☼ 9am-noon & 2-7pm, ticket windows ☼ 5am-10.30pm Mon-Fri, 9am-7.30pm Sat & Sun).

There are frequent trains to Paris' Gare de Lyon (€77 by TGV, 3¾ hours), Nice (€66, 7½ hours), Lyon (€19, three hours), Chamonix (€18, 2½ to three hours), Aix-les-Bains (€6.20, 30 minutes) and Chambéry (€9.60, one hour).

The night train to Paris (€70, eight hours), often full on weekends, leaves between 9pm and 10pm. Couchettes cost extra.

Getting Around
BICYCLE & IN-LINE SKATING
Bikes can be hired from **Loca Sports** (☎ 04 50 45 44 33; 2 av de Zanaroli), southwest of the Vieille Ville. **Sports Passion** (☎ 04 50 51 46 28; 3 av du Parmelan) rents out tandems, mountain bikes and in-line skates.

BUS
The municipal bus company is **SIBRA** (☎ 04 50 51 72 72). The **SIBRA information bureau** (☎ 04 50 10 04 04; Centre Bonlieu; ☼ 8.30am-7pm Mon-Sat) is at Centre Bonlieu.

Buses run from 6am to 8pm Monday to Saturday. On Sunday, 20-seat minibuses (identified by letters rather than numbers) provide a limited service. Tickets cost €1, an eight-ride carnet costs €6.50 and weekly coupons cost €10.

TAXI
Taxis (☎ 04 50 45 05 67) are based at the bus station; otherwise call **Taxi Plus** (☎ 04 50 68 93 33).

AROUND ANNECY
When the sun shines, the villages of **Sévrier**, 5km south on Lake Annecy's western shore, and **Menthon-St-Bernard**, 7km south on the lake's eastern shore, make good day trips. **Talloires**, just south of Menthon, is Annecy's most exclusive lakeside spot.

Skiing is the Annéciens' main weekend activity in winter. Eighteen km south is the cross-country resort of **Le Semnoz** (1700m). Further afield are **La Clusaz** (1100m), 32km east of Annecy, and **Le Grand Bornand** (1000m), 34km northeast. Accommodation in La Clusaz is handled by the **tourist office** (☎ 04 50 32 65 00; www.laclusaz.com).

CHAMBÉRY
pop 58,000
Chambéry, which lies in a wide valley between Annecy and Grenoble, has long served as one of the principal gateways between France and Italy. Occupying the entrance to the valleys that lead to the main Alpine passes, the town was the capital of Savoy from the 13th century until 1563. Its charming old quarter, crammed with courtyards and cobbled streets, grew up around the castle, which once served as the seat of power for the dukes of Savoy.

Orientation
Busy dual carriageways along a narrow canal separate the town's compact old section from the northern sprawl, which starts near the train station at the northern end of rue Sommeiller. Place des Éléphants – the old city's focal point – is at the northeastern end of rue de Boigne.

Information
LAUNDRY
Laverie Automatique (1 rue Doppet; ☼ 7.30am-8pm).
Lavomatique (37 place Monge; ☼ 7am-10pm)

CHAMBÉRY

0 ————— 200 m
0 ————— 0.1 miles

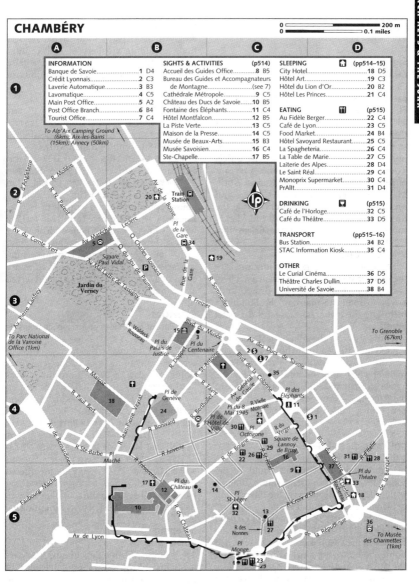

INFORMATION		
Banque de Savoie	1	D4
Crédit Lyonnais	2	C3
Laverie Automatique	3	B3
Lavomatique	4	C5
Main Post Office	5	A2
Post Office Branch	6	B4
Tourist Office	7	C4

SIGHTS & ACTIVITIES	(p514)	
Accueil des Guides Office	8	B5
Bureau des Guides et Accompagnateurs		
de Montagne	(see 7)	
Cathédrale Métropole	9	C5
Château des Ducs de Savoie	10	B5
Fontaine des Éléphants	11	C4
Hôtel Montfalcon	12	B5
La Piste Verte	13	C5
Maison de la Presse	14	C5
Musée de Beaux-Arts	15	B3
Musée Savoisien	16	C4
Ste-Chapelle	17	B5

SLEEPING	(pp514–15)	
City Hotel	18	D5
Hôtel Art	19	C3
Hôtel du Lion d'Or	20	B2
Hôtel Les Princes	21	C4

EATING	(p515)	
Au Fidèle Berger	22	C4
Café de Lyon	23	C5
Food Market	24	B4
Hôtel Savoyard Restaurant	25	C5
La Spagheteria	26	C5
La Table de Marie	27	C5
Laiterie des Alpes	28	D4
Le Saint Réal	29	D4
Monoprix Supermarket	30	C4
PrAllt	31	C5

DRINKING	(p515)	
Café de l'Horloge	32	C5
Café du Théâtre	33	D5

TRANSPORT	(pp515–16)	
Bus Station	34	B2
STAC Information Kiosk	35	C4

OTHER		
Le Curial Cinéma	36	D5
Théâtre Charles Dullin	37	D5
Université de Savoie	38	B4

MONEY

Most branches in the city have ATMs.
Banque de Savoie (6 blvd du Théâtre)
Crédit Lyonnais (26 blvd de la Colonne)

POST

Post Office (sq Paul Vidal)
Post Office Branch (place de l'Hôtel de Ville)

TOURIST INFORMATION

Parc National de la Vanoise Office (☎ 04 79 62 30 54; fax 04 79 96 37 18; 135 rue du Docteur Julliand; ☺ 8am-noon & 2-6pm Mon-Fri) Parc National de la Vanoise's main headquarters.

Tourist Office (☎ 04 79 33 42 47; www.chambery-tourisme.com in French; 24 blvd de la Colonne; ☺ 9am-noon & 1.30-6pm Mon-Sat mid-Sep–mid-Jun, 9am-

12.30pm & 1.30-6.30pm Mon-Sat, 10am-12.30pm Sun mid-Jun–mid-Sep)

Sights

CHÂTEAU DES DUCS DE SAVOIE

Chambéry's forbidding 14th-century **Château des Ducs de Savoie** (place du Château; tours adult/student €4/3; ✆ 7.30am-7pm, tours 10.30am, 2.30pm, 3.30pm, 4.30pm & 5.30pm Jul-Aug) now houses the region's Conseil Général (County Council).

The château can be visited only on guided one-hour tours run by the tourist office. Tours take place daily but times vary out of season. There is one daily tour in April, May, June, September and October, and on low-season weekends. Tours start at the tourist office. Between January and March, tours start outside the **Accueil des Guides office** (☎ 04 79 85 93 73; place du Château; ✆ 1.30-5.30pm Mon, Tue, Thu & Fri).

Some of the city's finest architecture is in the quarter surrounding the chateau. There is currently a huge restoration project underway to renovate many of the buildings, including the elaborate façade of the **Hôtel Montfalcon**.

Tours also visit the adjoining **Ste-Chapelle**, built in the 15th century to house the Shroud of Turin. Chambéry lost the relic to Turin in 1860 when Savoy became part of France. You can visit the 70-bell **Grand Carillon** in Ste-Chapelle – Europe's largest bell chamber – on a guided **tour** (adult €4; ✆ 10.30am & 5.30pm Sat).

FONTAINE DES ÉLÉPHANTS

With its four huge carved elephants, this bizarre **Fontaine des Éléphants** could be the model for an Indian postage stamp. It dominates place des Éléphants at the intersection of blvd de la Colonne and rue de Boigne, and was sculpted in 1838 in honour of Général de Boigne (1751–1830), a local who made his fortune in the East Indies. When he returned home, he bestowed some of his wealth on the town and was honoured posthumously with this monument. The arcaded street that leads from the fountain to Château des Ducs and bears his name was one of his most important local projects.

MUSEUMS

South of the fountain, near the 15th- and 16th-century **Cathédrale Métropole**, is **Musée Savoisien** (☎ 04 79 33 44 48; sq de Lannoy de Bissy;

adult/student €3/1.50; ✆ 10am-noon & 2-6pm Wed-Mon), which displays local archaeological finds, including a gallery of 13th-century wall paintings discovered behind a false roof inside a local mansion. Exhibits of traditional Savoyard mountain life are displayed on the 2nd floor.

Musée des Beaux-Arts (☎ 04 79 33 75 03; place du Palais de Justice; adult/student €3/1.50; ✆ 10am-noon & 2-6pm Wed-Mon) houses a rich collection of 14th- to 18th-century Italian works.

Musée des Charmettes (☎ 04 79 33 39 44; chemin des Charmettes; adult/student €3/1.50; ✆ 10am-noon & 2-6pm Wed-Mon Apr-Sep, to 4.30pm Oct-Mar), 1km southeast of the town, occupies the country house of philosopher and writer Jean-Jacques Rousseau, who lived here from 1736 to 1742 with his lover, Baronne Louise Éléonore de Warens. From mid-July to the end of August, night-time shows in period costume *(visite-spectacle costumée)* take place on Wednesday and Friday evenings. Tickets can be reserved at the tourist office.

Activities

The **Bureau des Guides et Accompagnateurs de Montagne** (☎ 04 79 33 81 62) has an **information desk** (✆ 2-6pm) inside the tourist office. It arranges canyoning, rock and ice climbing, skiing and caving expeditions, as well as local walks.

The tourist office sells walking maps and cycling guides covering the Chartreuse and Vanoise parks, as does **La Piste Verte** (☎ 04 79 33 57 31; 172 rue Croix d'Or; ✆ 9am-noon & 2-6pm Mon-Sat) and **Maison de la Presse** (☎ 04 79 33 41 62; 139 place St-Léger; ✆ 9am-6pm Mon-Sat). Various **walking tours** (tours €4-5; ✆ Jul & Aug) are offered by the tourist office, taking in everything from Chambéry's network of alleyways to its colourful trompe-l'oeil wall paintings.

Sleeping

BUDGET

The nearest Auberge de Jeunesse is in Aix-les-Bains (p516). Chambéry's selection of hotels leaves a lot to be desired. The best places are nearer the town centre.

City Hotel (☎ 04 79 85 76 79; fax 04 79 85 86 11; 9 rue Denfert Rochereau; d €35-50) Southeast of the centre, this is a functional, modern place near the theatre. The best rooms overlook place du Théâtre.

Hôtel du Lion d'Or (☎ 04 79 69 04 96; fax 04 79 96 93 20; 13 av de la Boisse; s €22-32, d €33-42) One of several hotels opposite the train station, with large, drab rooms and a busy brasserie adjoining the hotel.

Camping
There are several camping grounds outside Chambéry.

Alp'Aix (☎ 04 79 88 97 65; 20 blvd du Port-aux-Filles, Le Bourget du Lac; camping €11-15; ☼ Apr-Sep) A good choice just north of Chambéry. Take bus H from the place des Éléphants stop or the train station to the terminus, from where it's a 400m walk.

MID-RANGE
Hôtel Art (☎ 04 79 62 37 26; fax 04 79 62 49 98; 154 rue Sommeiller; d €44-51; P) Though the concrete façade looks uninspiring, this modern hotel has nicely furnished rooms with bath and TV, and is one of the city's better options.

Hôtel Les Princes (☎ 04 79 33 45 36; fax 04 79 70 31 47; 4 rue de Boigne; s/d €60/70; P ☼) Housed in one of the arcaded buildings close to the centre, this is by far the nicest hotel in Chambéry. Rooms are tastefully furnished and very comfortable.

Eating
RESTAURANTS
La Spagheteria (☎ 04 79 33 27 62; 43 rue St-Réal; pizza & pasta €5.95-10.35, menus €12 & €16; ☼ lunch & dinner Mon-Sat) Lively little Italian restaurant tucked away down a narrow alleyway, with flowers on the tables, plenty of Mediterranean atmosphere and a great range of pizzas and pastas.

Hôtel Savoyard (☎ 04 79 33 36 55; 35 place Monge; menus €12-21; ☼ lunch & dinner) The place to come in Chambéry for Savoyard specialities; its *tartiflette* (oven-cooked potatoes and *reblochon* cheese) and *gratin de crozets* (Savoyard pasta with cheese) are out of this world. It also has a children's *menu*. Try Mondeuse, Savoy's almost berry-like red wine.

La Table de Marie (☎ 04 79 85 99 76; 193 rue Croix d'Or; menus €13-18; ☼ dinner) An excellent little home-style restaurant at the end of busy place St-Léger, with Savoyard mains and an intimate, candle-lit atmosphere.

Le St-Réal (☎ 04 79 70 09 33; 10 rue St-Réal; mains €25-90; ☼ Mon-Sat) The best restaurant in Chambéry, with several menus exploring a varied range of Alpine and French cuisine. It's a little starchy, and expensive too, but the food is wonderful. The €90 *menu* includes seven courses.

CAFÉS
Au Fidèle Berger (☎ 04 79 33 06 37; rue de Boigne; ☼ Mon-Sat) This traditional *salon de thé* has exquisite chocolates and cakes.

Café de Lyon (place Monge; lunch menu €8.50-11; ☼ 7am-midnight Mon-Sat) This is a busy brasserie that overlooks a main thoroughfare of Chambéry.

SELF-CATERING
On Saturday morning a **food market** (place de Genève) is held. There's a **Monoprix supermarket** (place du 8 Mai 1945; ☼ 8.15am-7.30pm Mon-Sat). **Laiterie des Alpes** (88 rue d'Italie) stocks a wide variety of local cheeses and dairy products. Italian products are sold at **Pr.Al.It** (67 rue d'Italie).

Drinking
The huge open square of place St-Leger is the heart of Chambéry's night-time scene.

Café de l'Horloge (☎ 04 79 33 39 26; 107 place St-Léger) This great old-world café offers 200 brands of bottled beer, 30 brands of whisky and nine draught beers, as well as a fine selection of ice-cream sundaes.

Café du Théâtre (☎ 04 79 33 16 53; place du Théâtre) A lively café-bar with a large outside terrace in front of the Théâtre Charles Dullin, great for people-spotting and soaking up the Alpine sunshine.

Entertainment
Le Curial Cinéma (☎ 04 79 85 55 43; commalraux@wanadoo.fr; place François Mitterrand; tickets adult/concession €7/5) Part of the Éspace Malraux arts and exhibition complex located just south of rue de la République.

Getting There & Away
BUS
There's a **ticket office** (☼ 6.15am to 7pm) at **Chambéry bus station** (☎ 04 79 69 11 88; place de la Gare), south of the train station. From the station, there are buses to Aix-les-Bains (€2.80, 35 minutes, five daily), Annecy (€8.20, 50 minutes, seven daily), and Grenoble (€8.90, 1½ hours, 10 daily). There's one bus to Geneva and Nice every day, and five buses to Lyon St-Exupéry airport (€20, one hour).

TRAIN
The Chambéry **train station** (☎ 08 36 35 35 35; place de la Gare; ticket office ☼ 5.45am-8.30pm Mon-Sat, 6.45am-9.30pm Sun) is located at the end of rue Sommeiller.

There are major rail connections to Paris' Gare de Lyon (€76 by TGV via Lyon or Aix-les-Bains, 3¾ hours, 11 daily), Lyon (€14, 1¼ hours, 12 daily), Annecy (€7.90, one hour, 25 daily) and Grenoble (€9, one hour, 10 to 13 daily).

There are also trains up the Maurienne Valley to Modane (€13, one hour, nine daily), which continue to Turin, Rome and Naples in Italy.

Getting Around

BUS

The main hub for local buses is run by **STAC** (☎ 04 79 68 67 00; blvd de la Colonne), near Fontaine des Éléphants; there's also a **STAC information kiosk** (☎ 04 79 70 26 27; blvd de la Colonne; ☺ 7.15am-7.15pm Mon-Fri, 8.30am-12.15pm & 2.30-6.30pm Sat). Many buses also stop at the train station. In general, they run Monday to Saturday until about 8pm. Single tickets cost €1 and a carnet of 10 costs €6.20.

AROUND CHAMBÉRY

Chambéry town is wedged in between two regional nature parks – **Parc Naturel Régional de Chartreuse** in the southwest and **Parc Naturel Régional du Massif des Bauges** to the northeast. Covering an area of 800 sq km, the Massif des Bauges offers some excellent hiking opportunities. The nature reserve in the north of the park is home to more than 600 chamois and mouflon.

The **main tourist office** (☎ 04 79 54 84 28; www.lesbauges.com; ☺ 9am-noon & 2-6pm Mon-Sat) for the Massif des Bauges is in Le Châtelard. The **Chartreuse national park headquarters** (☎ 04 76 88 75 20; www.parc-chartreuse.net) is located in St-Pierre-de-Chartreuse.

From the thermal spa of **Aix-les-Bains**, 11km northwest of Chambéry, you can tour **Lac Bourget** – France's largest natural lake – by boat. Contact **Bateaux d'Aix-les-Bains** (☎ 04 79 88 92 09) at the Grand Port or **Aix-les-Bains tourist office** (☎ 04 79 88 68 00; www.aixlesbains.com; place Maurice Mollard; ☺ 9am-6pm or 6.30pm daily Apr-Sep, Mon-Sat Oct, Nov & Mar, to 5.30pm Mon-Sat Dec-Feb), next to the port.

Albertville, 39km from Chambéry on the eastern park boundary, played host to the 1992 Winter Olympics. The Olympic highs and lows are colourfully told at the **Maison des Jeux Olympiques** (☎ 04 79 37 75 71; 11 rue Pargoud; ☺ 9am-7pm Mon-Sat, 2-7pm Sun Jul & Aug, 9am-noon & 2-6pm Mon-Sat Sep-May).

MÉRIBEL

elevation 1450m

Méribel lies at the heart of one of the largest skiable areas in the world – the Trois Vallées (Three Valleys), which also includes the resorts of Courchevel and Belleville. The wealthy, purpose-built ski station, 42km southeast of Albertville and 88km from Annecy and Chambéry, was established in 1938 by Scotsman Colonel Peter Lindsay, and today remains one of the most 'British' resorts in France.

Despite the circus of pubs and shops that have cropped up to appease its predominantly British clientele, Méribel has just about managed to retain an Alpine village atmosphere, thanks to a decision made in the mid-1940s to use only traditional Savoyard building styles.

Information

Méribel's central **Maison du Tourisme** (www.meribel.net; ☺ 9am-7pm winter, closed noon-3pm summer) houses the **tourist office** (☎ 04 79 08 60 01; info@meribel.net), the **accommodation service** (☎ 04 79 00 50 00; reservation@meribel.net) and the **ESF** (☎ 04 79 08 60 31; www.esf-meribel.com; ☺ 9am-noon Mon-Fri), as well as a transport information counter.

The glossy French-English booklet *Méribel – Very Belle!* is available free from the tourist office and has a full listing of all the resort's facilities. Alternatively, consult www.meribel.net for the latest prices.

Activities

SKIING & SNOWBOARDING

One of the best skiing resorts in France, the vast area around Méribel can satisfy skiers of all levels. Above Val Thorens, there is summer skiing on the Glacier de Péclet.

Méribel Valley alone has 73 Alpine ski runs (150km), 47 ski lifts, two snowboarding parks, a slalom stadium, and two Olympic downhill runs built for the 1992 Winter Olympics. Many of these runs pass through Mottaret, a transit point 300m above the town, from where the valley's highest lift (2910m) climbs Mont Vallon.

The Trois Vallées pass (one/six days €41/198) allows use of all the area's lifts. Passes valid for more than six days also allow one day of skiing at Espace Killy, La Plagne, Les Arcs, Peisey Vallandry, Pralognan la

Vanoise or Les Saisies. Cheaper ski passes that only cover Méribel Valley are available (€34/161).

SUMMER ACTIVITIES

The *Guide des Sentiers* (available at the tourist office) details 20 marked walking trails in Méribel Valley. Particularly enticing is the botanical trail around Lake Tueda in the Réserve Naturelle de Tueda (Tueda Nature Reserve).

The **Bureau des Guides** (☎ 04 79 00 30 38; guides .meribel@laposte.net; ☒ 9.30am-noon & 4-7pm Sun-Fri) inside the tourist office organises rock climbing, walking and mountain-biking expeditions. Contact **AN Rafting** (☎ 04 79 09 72 79; www.an-rafting.com in French; per day €95) about courses on white-water rafting.

Sleeping

Of the seven hotels built for the 1992 Olympics, all but two have three or four stars – one-star hotels became almost extinct in Méribel long ago. Accommodation prices are high, but studio and apartment prices are around €330 to €450 per week for two people. Contact the reservation service for more details.

The cheapest options are **Hôtel du Moulin** (☎ 04 79 00 52 23; fax 04 79 00 58 84; d €73) and **Hôtel Le Doron** (☎ 04 79 08 60 02; hotel-doron@wanadoo.fr; d from €92), both no-star hotels within reach of the town centre. At the other end of the scale is **Hôtel Mont Vallon** (☎ 04 79 00 44 00; montvallon - meribel@laposte.fr; r with half-board €150-700), one of Méribel's oldest and best hotels.

Getting There & Away

The four-lane A43, built for the 1992 Olympics, links Chambéry (88km northwest) with the nearest town, Moûtiers, 18km north of Méribel.

There are shuttle buses from Méribel to Geneva airport (€64, four hours) and Lyon St-Exupéry airport (€57, three to four hours). There's a **SNCF information bureau** (☎ 04 79 00 53 28) at the tourist office. The closest **train station** (☎ 08 36 35 35 35) is in Moûtiers from where there are connections to Paris (€59.30, 4½ hours) and Chambéry (€10.40, 1¼ hours).

Regional buses are operated by **Transavoie** (☎ 04 79 24 21 58) and run between Méribel and Moûtiers (€10.30, four to six Monday to Friday, 10 to 12 Saturday and Sunday).

VAL D'ISÈRE

pop 1738 / elevation 1850m

It's hip to be seen in Val d'Isère, a trendy resort in the upper Tarentaise Valley, 31km southeast of Bourg St-Maurice. Until the 1930s, Val d'Isère – a former hunting ground for the dukes of Savoy – was a remote village in the upper reaches of the eastern Alps. Today, Val d'Isère offers everything the discerning snow-junky could wish for – vast areas of groomed snow, plenty of off-piste thrills, modern lift systems allowing easy access to the slopes, a thriving commercial centre, and an animated après-ski scene.

On the other hand, if you're looking for a traditional Alpine atmosphere, then Val d'Isère is hardly ideal – the town's oldest building is the 11th-century church, with the rest of the village made up of Savoyard stone houses, chalet-style hotels and apartment blocks. But serious snow-goers rate Val d'Isère as one of the Alps' best all-round resorts, which accounts for the thousands of British, German and Scandinavian tourists who flock here every year, while French skiers head for quieter slopes.

Along with the high-altitude, purpose-built resort of **Tignes** (2100m), Val d'Isère and four other villages combine to form **Espace Killy** – named after local skiing legend Jean-Claude Killy, a triple gold medallist at the 1968 Winter Olympics.

The resort's most famous run is **La Face de Bellevarde**, a 63% black ski slope peaking at 2809m, used for the men's downhill skiing events in the 1992 Winter Olympics. Anyone daring or reckless enough to do it can. The Olympic gold medallist, Austrian Patrick Ortlieb, completed the enormous run in one minute 50.37 seconds.

Orientation

The majority of Val d'Isère is concentrated along the main central street, which runs directly on from the D902 into town. The bus station is at the bottom of the village, while most of the bars, restaurants and hotels are in the centre. The nearby resorts of Tignes and Val Claret are reached by the twisting D87, which branches off the main road just before the Lac du Chevril.

Information

The **tourist office** (☎ 04 79 06 06 60; www.valdisere .com; place Jacques Mouflier; ☒ 8.30am-7.30pm Sun-Fri,

8.30am-8pm Sat) is in the village centre and the Bureau des Guides has a desk inside during summer. The **Val Hôtel Accommodation Service** (☎ 04 79 06 18 90; valhotel@valdisere.com) makes bookings for four days and over.

There are ATMs in the village and a couple of seasonal exchange offices.

Activities
WINTER ACTIVITIES

Espace Killy offers some of the best skiing in the country between 1550m and 3450m. Ski touring is also excellent, especially in the Parc National de la Vanoise. The snowboarders' Snowspace Park in La Deille has a half-pipe, tables, gaps, quarter-pipes, and kicker ramps, while the runs around Tignes are popular with both snowboarders and skiers. In July and August you can ski on the glacier.

Val d'Isère has no less than 11 ski schools and many more independent instructors. The **ESF** (☎ 04 79 06 02 34; esf.valdisere@wanadoo .fr; ✆ 8.30am-7pm) is housed in a large building off place Jacques Mouflier. Nearby **Misty Fly Snowboard School** (☎ 04 79 40 08 74; lionel .surf@infonie.fr; place Jacques Mouflier) specialises in snowboarding while **Alpine Experience** (☎ 04 79 06 28 81; www.alpineexperience.com) runs courses in off-piste skiing.

During special periods, Espace Killy ski passes (one/six days €39/187) include one day's skiing in La Plagne, Les Arcs, Les Trois Vallées or Valmorel.

Heli-skiing, ice diving, ice climbing, snowshoeing, snowmobiling and husky-drawn sledge rides are some of the more unusual activities on offer in Val d'Isère. The tourist office has full details.

SUMMER ACTIVITIES

One of the best walks from Val d'Isère is to the village of Tignes along the Gorges de la Daille or the high road along Vallon de la Tovière. Other walks include the classic route across the high mountain pass of Col de l'Iseran, or the trek to the Glacier des Sources d'Isère, but there are many more trails in the nearby Parc National de la Vanoise.

The valleys and trails from Val d'Isère into the Vanoise National Park offer many possibilities for mountain biking and fishing. The Bureau des Guides organises, among other things, visits to a local cheese farm and Alpine bird-watching treks. **Safaris Vanoise** (☎ 04 79 06 00 03; www.valgliss.com in French)

organises animal photography and filming expeditions. The ESF runs *parapente* (paragliding) lessons in summer.

Sleeping

Accommodation in Val d'Isère is geared towards package skiers, which makes independent travelling expensive. Advance bookings are essential and can be made through Val Hôtel Accommodation Service (left).

Apartments, ranging from private shortterm lets to purpose-built apartment blocks, are more accommodating to a range of budgets. Val Hôtel Accommodation Service is the best place to find out what's available. Two-person apartments in the low/ high season start at €190/330 per week, but prices vary widely so shop around.

There are really no budget hotels in Val d'Isère, so unless you plan well ahead, accommodation is likely to take a major bite out of your budget.

MID-RANGE

Hôtel l'Avancher (☎ 04 79 06 02 00; route Fornet; d with half-board €77-100, ✆ usually closed summer; **P**) One of several hotels on the more affordable east side of town. The alpine chalet-style building looks just the ticket, especially when it's covered in snow and icicles are hanging from the eaves.

Hôtel Les Chardons (☎ 04 79 06 00 15; www .hotel-les-chardons.com; d €91-124, with half-board €98-142; **P**) Twenty-seven unfussy rooms in an attractive timber-clad building a short walk from the town centre.

Relais du Ski (☎ 04 79 06 02 06; fax 04 79 41 10 64; d winter €57-65, summer €50-58) An affordable hotel with more basic double rooms. The inhouse restaurant is also good, with an *Assiette Montagnarde* for €13, which includes local cheeses and cold meats.

TOP END

If you feel like doing Val d'Isère in style, there are plenty of top-end hotels to choose from. Try the refurbished **Hôtel Christiania** (☎ 04 79 06 08 25; www.hotel-christiania.com; d €169-277; **P** 🍴 🛢) with its roaring fireplace, or the lavish **Hôtel Tsanteleina** (☎ 04 79 06 12 13; www.hoteltsanteleina.com; d €103-243; **P** 🍴).

Eating

Eating in Val d'Isère is a hit-and-miss affair. With 70 restaurants in the village catering

---

THE DISAPPEARING LAKE

Look out for Lac du Chevril on your right as you approach Val d'Isère. The lake and dam were created amid much controversy between 1947 and 1955 by the French Electricity company EDF to generate hydroelectric power. The village of Tignes-le-Lac, once home to 500 people, was abandoned as a result of the project and now lies at the bottom of the lake. You can hardly miss Lac du Chevril – that is, if it's there…

Every 10 years the EDF drain the lake to carry out dam maintenance, leaving a huge hole where the lake used to be. In the mud you can still spot the remains of the doomed Tignes-le-Lac – houses, tree trunks and even an old car, and on the southern side the remains of a couple of bridges. Sightseers flock to the muddy floor of Lac du Chevril to wander among the debris of this bizarre spectacle and a solemn commemorative Mass is held on the lake bed before it is refilled, a process that takes two months. The lake was last emptied in March 2000 and won't be emptied again until 2010.

---

to a largely English clientele, the quality of cuisine is varied and unpredictable. Better deals are to be had opting for half- or full-board in your hotel.

Nonetheless, try the central **Samovar** (☎ 04 79 06 13 51; mains €12-20) for French and Savoyard cuisine, or **Bananas** (☎ 04 79 06 04 23; mains €8-15), near the bottom of the Olympic run, for a selection of Tex-Mex food.

SELF-CATERING

At the eastern end of the village is a **Spar supermarket** (☒ 8am-noon & 2-7pm) with a well-stocked wine cellar, cheese and meat counter and plenty of DIY meal items.

Drinking

Val d'Isère has gained a reputation as one of the biggest party towns in the Alps, and there are loads of bars in the village.

Dick's Tea Bar (☎ 04 79 06 14 87; www.dicksteabar.com; admission €12, free before 11.30pm; ☒ 3pm-4am) The Val d'Isère outpost of the Alpine nightclub chain. If you've been to any of the others – or to a student night in a British nightclub – you'll know what to expect.

Café Face (☎ 04 79 06 29 80) Opposite Dick's, this chic après-ski bar is something of an institution in Val d'Isère, boasting moody lighting, stylish retro furniture and enough cocktails to keep you going all season.

Warm'Up Cafés (☎ 04 79 06 27 00; ☒ from 10am) A big, pub-style drinking hole on the main street, with live music, lots of tables and a large central bar.

Getting There & Away

Autocars Martin (☎ 04 79 06 00 42; ☒ 9.15am-12.30pm & 1.15-7pm) runs four buses daily to Val

d'Isère and Tignes (€10.50, 20 to 30 minutes) from Bourg St-Maurice, the nearest train station. There is a **SNCF counter** (☒ 9am-noon & 3-7pm) here too.

Satobus-Alpes (☎ 04 37 25 52 55) operates four buses every day (three on Sunday) from Val d'Isère to Lyon St-Exupéry airport via Bourg St-Maurice (€50, three to four hours). The service runs only from mid-December to April and on Saturday in July and August.

Getting Around

Val d'Isère is served by free buses operating around the resort. The *train rouge* (red train), a network of 23 shuttle buses, connects Val d'Isère with Tignes and other villages, including Les Boisses and the Grand Motte funicular. Timetables are posted at bus stops.

PARC NATIONAL DE LA VANOISE

A wild mix of high mountains, steep valleys and vast glaciers, the Parc National de la Vanoise was declared the country's first national park in 1963. It covers 530 sq km between the Tarentaise Valley to the north and the Maurienne Valley to the south. The park is a hiker's heaven, with 500km of waymarked trails (including the GR5 and GR55) and 42 remote *refuges* for overnight shelter. The scenery is spectacular – snowcapped peaks mirrored in icy lakes are only just the start of what you can expect to see here. Marmots and chamois, as well as France's largest colony of Alpine ibex, graze free and undisturbed among the larch trees, and above them all reigns the mighty eagle.

A SHAGGY GOAT STORY

The animal most synonymous with the French Alps is without a doubt the Alpine ibex, a hardy mountain goat identifiable by its huge, curly horns and fondness for sickeningly high mountain ledges. In the 16th century, the Alps were full of ibex (*bouquetin* in French), but unfortunately their extravagant horns – which can measure one metre in length and weigh over five kilograms – became the must-have item for every self-respecting gentleman's trophy cabinet in the 19th century, and within a few years the animals had been hunted to the brink of extinction. Following lengthy conservation campaigns and the foundation of national reserves such as the Parc National de la Vanoise, populations have steadily recovered. But don't be surprised if you don't see one – thankfully, the ibex seems to have learned that humans can be bad for its health.

Orientation

The park is divided into two main areas: the *zone central* (central zone), which is highly protected and is bordered by five designated nature reserves, and the *zone périphérique* (peripheral zone), where the nearest villages and tourist centres to the park are located. The most convenient bases are along the southern edge of the park in Bonneval-sur-Arc and Lanslebourg, and to the southwest around Modane and Saint-André.

Information

The Parc National de la Vanoise Office (p513) in Chambéry has information on the park and a list of *refuges*. To book *refuges* in June, July or August call ☎ 04 79 08 71 49. The park newspaper, *Estive*, contains a full listing of all *refuges* complete with direct contact numbers, and is available free from tourist offices.

Park information is available at the **Tourist Office** (☎ 04 79 05 95 95; www.bonneval-sur-arc .com; ☽ 9am-noon & 2-6.30pm Mon-Sat in season, to 6pm rest of year) in Bonneval-sur-Arc and **Maison du Val Cénis** (☎ 04 79 05 23 66; www.valcenis.com; ☽ 9am-noon & 3-7pm) in Lanslebourg. A good regional map is the 1:50,000-scale IGN map *Parc de la Vanoise* (No 11).

Activities

SKIING

Lanslebourg and Bonneval-sur-Arc are popular cross-country skiing resorts. Both offer limited Alpine skiing as well. The **ESF** (☎ 04 79 05 95 70) is inside the Bonneval-sur-Arc tourist office.

In summer it's possible to ski on the Grand Pissaillas glacier at Col de l'Iseran, 23km northeast of Lanslebourg. The best skiing is between March and early May.

WALKING

Walkers have a network of small trails to choose from – the Maison du Val Cénis (see Information) has a trails booklet. The **Bureau des Guides** (☎ 04 79 05 95 70) inside Bonneval-sur-Arc tourist office and **Guide de Haute-Montagne** (☎ 04 79 05 94 74) run guided walks and climbs.

The trail from Lanslebourg up to the Turra Fort (2500m), from where there are great views over the Lac du Mont Cénis, generally takes about three hours. To really take in the region, you can follow all or part of Le Grand Tour de Haute Maurienne – a hike of five days or more around the upper reaches of the valley. There are 15 *refuges* or *gîtes d'étape* en route.

The GR5 and GR55 pass through the park and there are also trails linked to the Écrins National Park to the south and Grand Paradiso National Park in Italy. Tracks are usually passable from June to October.

Sleeping

Auberge de Jeunesse Hameau des Champs (☎ 04 79 05 90 96; fax 04 79 05 82 52; dm €7.30, breakfast €2.90; ☽ mid-Dec–mid-Sep), which is located in the hamlet of Les Champs, is on the eastern side of Lanslevillard.

There are five hotels in Lanslebourg, including **Hôtel La Vieille Poste** (☎ 04 79 05 93 47; fax 04 79 05 86 85; d €40-44; ☽ closed mid-Apr–Jun & Nov-Jan). This warm and welcoming two-star place is on the main road through town.

Hôtel La Bergerie (☎ 04 79 05 94 97; fax 04 79 05 93 24; d €48; ☽ closed May–mid-Jun & Oct–mid-Dec) is in pretty Bonneval-sur-Arc.

Camping Les Balmasses (☎ 04 79 05 82 83; ☽ Jun-Sep) is in Lanslebourg.

Getting There & Away

The trains serving the valley leave from Chambéry and run as far as the **Modane train** station (☎ 08 36 35 35 35), 23km southwest of Lanslebourg.

From Modane, **Transavoie buses** (☎ 04 79 05 01 32) go to Lanslebourg (€9.30, one hour). Once daily (in the evening) they continue to Bessans and Bonneval-sur-Arc. In winter a shuttle bus runs several times daily between Lanslebourg and Bonneval-sur-Arc.

DAUPHINÉ

Dauphiné, which encompasses the territories south and southwest of Savoy, stretches from the River Rhône in the west to the Italian border in the east. It includes the city of Grenoble and, a little further east, the mountainous Parc National des Écrins. The gentler terrain of the western part of Dauphiné is typified by the Parc Naturel Régional du Vercors, much loved by cross-country skiers. In the east, the town of Briançon stands guard on the Italian frontier.

History
The area now known as Dauphiné was first inhabited by the Celts and the Romans. By the 11th century it was under the rule of Guigues I, the count of Albon, whose great-grandson Guigues IV (ruled 1133–42) was the first count to bear the name of 'dauphin'. By the end of the 13th century, the name 'dauphin' had become a title and the fiefs held by the region's ruling house, La Tour du Pin, were known collectively as Dauphiné. The rulers of Dauphiné continued to expand their territories, which gave them control of all the passes through the southern Alps.

In 1339 Humbert II established a university at Grenoble. A decade later, lacking money and a successor, he sold Dauphiné to the French king, Charles V, who started the tradition whereby the eldest son of the king of France (the crown prince) ruled Dauphiné and bore the title 'dauphin'. The region was annexed to France by Charles VII in 1457.

GRENOBLE
pop 156,000
The elegant, modern city of Grenoble is the intellectual and economic capital of the Alps. Spectacularly sited in a broad valley surrounded by snow-capped mountains – the Chartreuse to the north, the Vercors to the southwest and the Italian Alps to the

east – the city is also the centre of the Dauphiné region. The modern shops, broad boulevards and varied architecture make it a great place to spend a few days soaking up the big-city atmosphere.

Grenoble gained a reputation for progress in the 1960s, when the Socialist Hubert Dubedout served as mayor. People from all over France were attracted by the city's social, artistic and technological innovations. The large university serves a student body of 50,000 and has a thriving foreign student exchange programme. Grenoble also has important facilities for nuclear and microelectronic research.

The city hosts a jazz festival in March, a rock festival in April, and a theatre festival in June and July. Given Grenoble is the capital of Dauphiné, this is *the* place to sample the popular French dish *gratin dauphinois* (finely-sliced potatoes cooked with milk and Gruyère cheese). *Noix de Grenoble* (a sweet walnut candy) and *gâteau aux noix* (walnut cake) are the local specialities for those with a sweet tooth.

Orientation
Grenoble can be a difficult city to negotiate, especially from behind the wheel, thanks to the bewildering one-way system. The old city is centred around place Grenette and place Notre Dame, both about 1km east of the train and bus stations. The main university campus is a couple of kilometres east of the old centre on the southern side of the River Isère.

Information
BOOKSHOPS
Arthaud (☎ 04 76 42 49 81; 23 Grande Rue; ⏱ 10.30am-7pm Mon, 9.30am-7pm Tue-Sat) The best bookshop in Grenoble for new titles, although mostly French.
Librairie le Sphinx (☎ 04 76 44 55 08; genevieve journault@wanadoo.fr; 6 place Notre Dame; ⏱ noon-8.30pm Mon-Fri, Sat noon-7pm) A wonderful, chaotic place above the Tonneau de Diogène café that specialises in French philosophy books.

EMERGENCY
Duty Pharmacy (☎ 04 76 63 42 55)
Grenoble University Hospital (☎ 04 76 76 75 75; www.chu-grenoble.fr in French) There are two main sites: Hôpital Nord La Tronche and Hôpital Sud.
Police Station (☎ 04 76 69 48 00; 21 av Léon Blum)

GRENOBLE

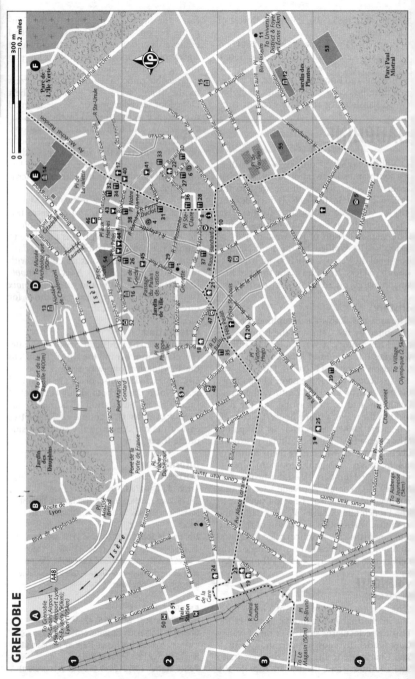

INFORMATION		SLEEPING	🏠	(pp525–6)	DRINKING	🍸🍷	(p527)
Arthaud...**1** D2		Hôtel Acacia..**18** C2			Bar 1900...**40** E2		
Banque de France...........................**2** C2		Hôtel Alizé...**19** A3			Barberousse.......................................**41** E2		
Lavomatique......................................**3** C4		Hôtel Angleterre...............................**20** D3			Café Tamara..**42** D1		
Le New Age Cyber Café....................**4** E2		Hôtel de l'Europe..............................**21** D2			Chorus Café...**43** E1		
Librairie Le Sphinx.....................(see 34)		Hôtel le Moucherotte......................**22** E2			Le Couche Tard..................................**44** D1		
Main Post Office...............................**5** E4		Hôtel Lux..**23** A3			Le Saxo Pub...**45** D2		
Neptune Internet Services.............**6** E2		Hôtel Suisse et Bordeaux................**24** A2			Le Twenty..**46** E1		
Post Office Branch............................**7** E2		Hôtel Victoria.....................................**25** C4					
TAG Information Desk..................(see 8)					ENTERTAINMENT	🎭	(p527)
Tourist Office.....................................**8** E2		EATING	🍴	(pp526–7)	Fnac...**47** D2		
		Café de la Table Ronde.....................**26** D2			La Nef Cinema....................................**48** C2		
SIGHTS & ACTIVITIES		(pp523–5)	Ciao a Te...**27** E2			Les 6 Rex...**49** D3		
Bishop's Palace.............................(see 17)		Food Market...................................(see 36)					
CAF...**9** B2		La Fôret Noire.....................................**28** E2			TRANSPORT		(pp527–8)
Maison de la Montagne..................**10** E3		La Mère Ticket....................................**29** D2			Bus Station...**50** A2		
Maison de la Nature et de		La Panse..**30** E2			Car Rental		
l'Environment............................**11** F3		La Voile Blanche.................................**31** E2			Companies....................................**51** A2		
Mountain Wilderness...................(see 11)		L'Amphitryon......................................**32** E1			Métro-Vélo.....................................(see 51)		
Musée d'Histoire Naturelle............**12** F3		Le Mal Assis...**33** E2			Téléphérique to		
Musée Dauphinois..........................**13** D1		Le Tonneau de Diogène....................**34** E1			Fort de la Bastille.........................**52** D2		
Musée de Grenoble.........................**14** E1		Les Archers..**35** C3					
Musée de la Résistance et de la Déportation		Les Halles Ste-Claire.........................**36** E2			OTHER		
de L'Isère.....................................**15** F2		Monoprix Supermarket....................**37** D2			Hôtel de Ville......................................**53** F4		
Musée Stendhal.................................**16** D2		Restaurant des Montagnes..............**38** E2			Palais de Justice.................................**54** D1		
Notre-Dame & St-Hugues Cathedral...**17** E1		Subway...**39** C4			Préfecture..**55** E3		

INTERNET ACCESS
Le New Age Cyber Café (☎ 04 76 51 94 43; 1 rue Bernave; per 15min/hr €2/3.50; ⏱ 8am-10pm Mon-Sat, 10am-9pm Sun) Cheap access noon-2pm.

Neptune Internet Services (☎ 04 76 63 94 18; salle -Internet@neptune.fr; 2 rue de la Paix; per 15min/hr €2/3.50, discounts noon-2pm & 7-9pm; ⏱ 9am-9pm Mon-Fri, 9am-8pm Sat, 1-8pm Sun) WiFi and laptop connection points.

INTERNET RESOURCES
www.grenoble-isere.info Official site for the Grenoble tourist office.

LAUNDRY
Lavomatique (14 rue Thiers; ⏱ 7am-10pm) Opposite Hôtel Victoria.

MEDIA
Le Petit Bulletin Published every Wednesday. Free listings guide to the week's events.

MONEY
ATMs are found at most main banks.
Banque de France (cnr blvd Édouard Rey & av Félix Vialet; ⏱ 8.45am-12.15pm & 1.30-3.30pm Mon-Fri) Usually changes money at a good rate.

POST
Post Office (7 blvd Maréchal Lyautey; ⏱ 8am-6.45pm Mon-Fri, until noon Sat).

Post Office Branch (rue de la République; ⏱ 8am-5.30pm Tue-Sat) Next to the tourist office.

TOURIST INFORMATION
Cargo Kiosk (⏱ 1-6.30pm Tue-Sat) For events tickets.
SNCF Counter (⏱ 8.30am-6.30pm Mon-Fri, 9am-6pm Sat) For train information.

TAG Office (⏱ 8.30am-6.30pm Mon-Fri, 9am-6pm Sat) For local bus information.

Tourist Office (☎ 04 76 42 41 41; www.grenoble-isere .info; 14 rue de la République; ⏱ 9am-6.30pm Mon-Sat, 10am-1pm Sun, longer hours in summer) Inside the large purpose-built Maison du Tourisme on rue de la République.

Sights
FORT DE LA BASTILLE
Looming above the old city on the northern side of the River Isère, the **Fort de la Bastille** is Grenoble's best known landmark. Constructed during the 16th century (and expanded in the 19th) to control the approaches to the city, the stronghold has long been a focus of military and political action.

These days, its strategic importance may have waned, but the views are as spectacular as ever, with vast mountains on every side, the bridges and grey waters of the Isère river below, and the wide streets of modern Grenoble stretching out into the south. On clear days, you can even catch a glimpse of Mont Blanc, northeast along the jagged Grésivaudan valley. Three viewpoint indicators – one west of the *téléphérique* station, the other two on the roof of the building just to the east – explain the surrounding vistas, and a sign near the disused Mont Jalla chairlift indicates nearby hiking trails.

To get to the fort, a **téléphérique** (☎ 04 76 44 33 65; adult/student one way €3.80/3, return €5.50/4.40; ⏱ 10.45am-6.30pm Nov-Feb, 9.30am-11.45pm Mar-May, 9.15-12.15am Jun-Aug) leaves from quai Stéphane Jay between the Marius Gontard and St-Laurent bridges. The rapid ascent in egg-shaped pods, which climb 264m from the quay over the swift waters of the river, is almost more fun than the fort itself. Unsurprisingly, it gets crowded in summer – leave early to avoid the worst queues.

The *téléphérique* hours vary on Sundays and in high season – check the time for the last return car before you leave, as it's a long walk back to town if you miss it. A number of trails and a road lead up the hillside to the fort.

MUSEUMS
Dauphiné's foremost city has no shortage of excellent museums, ranging from world-renowned arts collections to exhibits on local culture and history.

Several of Grenoble's museums offer free entry. The **MultiPass Grenoble** (per day €10) is also a good deal. It's available from the tourist office and includes admission to one of the city's (paying) museums or Le Magasin arts centre (below), a return ticket on the Grenoble–Bastille *télépherique*, guided city tour, day pass for Grenoble's public transport, and a parking ticket worth €2 for the Museum or Verdun car parks.

Musée de Grenoble
The sleek glass and steel exterior of Grenoble's boldest museum stands at the southern end of place Notre Dame. Also known as the Musée des Beaux-Arts, **Musée de Grenoble** (☎ 04 76 63 44 44; 5 place de Lavalette; www.museede grenoble.fr; adult/student €5/2; ☺ 10am-6.30pm, closed Tue) is renowned for its distinguished modern collection, including various works by

---

LE MAGASIN

Grenoble has lots of art galleries and exhibition places, but the most impressive (and not just in terms of size) is **Le Magasin** (the Shop; ☎ 04 76 21 95 84; www.magasin-cnac .org in French; 155 cours Berriat; adult/concession €3.50/2), one of Europe's leading centres of contemporary art, created in 1986 in a vast warehouse built by employees of Gustave Eiffel. There are two exhibition areas – 'The Rue', a permanent 1000 sq m space with a huge glass roof, and 'The Galleries', a flexible space of about 900 sq m. Exhibitions change almost daily – call to find out the latest news and opening hours. Charles Saatchi would be green with envy.

---

famous artists Chagall, Matisse, Modigliani, Monet, Picasso, Pissaro, Gauguin among others. There are 1½-hour guided **tours** (adult €3; ☺ Sat & Sun 3pm) available.

Musée d'Histoire Naturelle
Alpine flora and fauna, a 'carnival of insects' and an aquarium are housed in the **Musée d'Histoire Naturelle** (Museum of Natural History; ☎ 04 76 44 05 35; 1 rue Dolomieu; adult/student €2.20/1.50; ☺ 9.30am-noon & 1.30-5.30pm Mon-Fri, 2-6pm Sat & Sun), overlooking the Jardin des Plantes. The grounds also include a botanical garden.

Musée Dauphinois
The **Musée Dauphinois** (☎ 04 76 85 19 01; www .musee-dauphinois.fr in French; 30 rue Maurice Gignoux; ☺ 10am-7pm Wed-Mon May-Oct, until 6pm Nov-Apr) documents the cultures, crafts and traditions of Alpine life. The museum occupies a beautiful 17th-century convent, nestled at the foot of the hill below Fort de la Bastille. From the city centre, it is most easily reached by the Pont St-Laurent footbridge.

East of the museum, also in the historic St-Laurent quarter, is **Musée Archéologique** (☎ 04 76 44 78 68; www.musee-archeologique-grenoble .com in French; ☺ 9am-6pm Wed-Mon), housed in a 12th-century church.

Musée de l'Ancien Évêché
The **Notre Dame and St-Hugues Cathedral** (place Notre Dame) and the adjoining 14th-century **Bishop's Palace** (☎ 04 76 03 15 25; www.ancien -eveche-isere.com in French; 2 rue Très Cloîtres; admission free; ☺ 9am-6pm Mon-Sat except Tue, 10am-7pm Sun) have had complete facelifts and now contain three museums: the **crypte archéologique**, with Roman walls and a baptistery dating from the 4th to 10th centuries; the **Musée d'Art Sacré**, which contains liturgical and religious objects; and the **Centre Jean Achard**, with exhibits of art from the Dauphiné region.

Musée de la Résistance et de la Déportation de l'Isère
This moving **Musée de la Résistance et de la Déportation de l'Isère** (☎ 04 76 42 38 53; 14 rue Hébert; admission free; ☺ 9am-7pm Wed-Mon Jun-Aug, 9am-noon & 2-6pm Wed-Mon, from 10am Sun Sep-May) examines the deportation of Jews and other 'undesirables' from Grenoble to Nazi camps during WWII, and explores the role of the Vercors region in the French Resistance. Captions are in French, English and German.

Musée Stendhal

Stendhal, author of *Le Rouge et le Noir* (The Red and the Black), was born in Grenoble in 1783. The tourist office distributes a free brochure called *Route Historique – Stendhal*, which traces the life and works of the author from his birthplace to the outlying villages where he found inspiration. **Musée Stendhal** (☎ 04 76 54 44 14; 1 rue Hector Berlioz; ☺ 9am-noon & 2-6pm Tue-Sat), overlooks the formal Jardin de Ville, only opens in the afternoon in winter.

Activities

SKIING

The tourist office has comprehensive information, including accommodation lists, for Grenoble and all of its surrounding ski resorts.

WALKING

For information on outdoor activities, head for the **Maison de la Montagne** (☎ 08 25 82 55 88; www.grenoble-montagne.com in French; 3 rue Raoul Blanchard). All the main organisations are housed under one roof. The **Bureau Info-Montagne** (☎ 04 76 42 45 90; fax 04 76 42 87 08; ☺ 9am-noon & 2-6pm Mon-Fri, 10am-1pm & 2-6pm Sat) can give advice on just about every imaginable mountain activity except skiing. It sells hiking maps and has information on *gîtes d'étape* and *refuges*. The **Bureau des Guides de Grenoble** (☎ 04 38 37 01 71; www .guide-grenoble.com in French; ☺ 9am-noon & 1-6pm; Mon afternoon-Sat) and the **Accompagnateurs en Montagne Alpes-Dauphiné** both provide guiding services in the Dauphiné region and further afield.

The **Club Alpin Français** (CAF; ☎ 04 76 87 03 73; 32 av Félix Viallet; www.clubalpin-grenoble.com in French; ☺ 2-6pm Tue-Wed, 2-8pm Thu-Fri) manages *refuges* and organises walking, mountain-biking and skiing trips. Other walking clubs include **Mountain Wilderness** (☎ 04 76 84 54 42; fax 04 76 84 54 44; 5 place Bir-Hakeim) in the Maison de la Nature et de l'Environment.

Festivals & Events

Grenoble Jazz Festival (☎ 04 76 51 65 32; www .jazzgrenoble.com in French; 3-/5-night pass €42/75) has been bringing a wide selection of jazz greats and outdoor concerts to Grenoble for the last 30 years. The festival is held annually in March; full details are available from the tourist office or the festival website.

Sleeping

Grenoble's hotels are expensive, but compared to the sky-high prices of nearby ski resorts, many offer good value. Special deals are available at certain hotels through the **'Bon Weekend en Ville' scheme** (www.bon-week-end -en-villes.com). In general, if you reserve your room at a participating hotel in advance, and stay for two nights, arriving on a Friday or Saturday, the second night is free. Make sure you receive confirmation before arrival.

Parking in Grenoble can often be a problem. Few hotels have private garages, which means you'll have to factor in the cost of a city car park (usually between €6 to €10 for 24 hours). Some hotels have special arrangements with local car parks – ask when you book your room.

BUDGET

Auberge de Jeunesse (☎ 04 76 09 33 52; grenoble@fuaj .org; 10 av du Grésivaudan; B&B €12; reception ☺ 7.30am-11pm) Five kilometres south of the train station in the Echirolles district. From Cours Jean Jaurès, take bus No 1 to the Quinzaine stop (look for the Casino supermarket).

Hôtel de l'Europe (☎ 04 76 46 16 94; www.hotel europe.fr; 22 place Grenette; s €26-53, d €28-59) One of the city's oldest establishments, housed in a classic Grenoblois building above place Grenette. It's a great value hotel, with big rooms and a fabulous spiral staircase to the top floor. The front rooms have balconies offering views of Fort Bastille and the mountains beyond.

Hôtel du Moucherotte (☎ 04 76 54 61 40; fax 04 76 44 62 52; 1 rue Auguste Gaché; s/d from €28/30) The murky Moucherotte is one of the cheapest options near the city centre. Despite its dingy exterior, the rooms are clean but basic in the extreme.

Hôtel Alizé (☎ 04 76 43 12 91; fax 04 76 47 62 79; 1 rue Amiral Courbet; s/d €31/36, tr €44-48) In the area near the train station, this hotel is small, simple and very cheap, which makes it popular – book in advance if you can.

Hôtel Victoria (☎ 04 76 46 06 36; 17 rue Thiers; r with shower from €32-36; ☺ Sep-Jul; Ⓟ) Located in the place Condorcet area, this is the best of the bunch – tucked away in a quiet courtyard, with old-fashioned floral décor and friendly owners. The lively place Condorcet area has lots of low-rent restaurants and scruffy bars.

MID-RANGE

The following hotels are in the city centre.

Hôtel Angleterre (☎ 04 76 87 37 21; www.hotel
-angleterre.fr; 5 place Victor Hugo; d €91-155) The pick
of several three-star hotels in the area,
thanks to its luxurious rooms and a great
location opposite the fountain-adorned
place Victor Hugo. It accepts reservations
for 'Bon-Weekend' packages.

Hôtel Acacia (☎ 04 76 87 00 71; fax 04 76 47 21 25;
13 rue de Belgrade; s/d/tw €36/49/56) As boxy and
boring as they come, but the city-centre position is ideal. If you've ever stayed in a city
motel you'll know what to expect. Accepts
'Bon-Weekend' reservations.

The following hotels are in the area
around the train station.

Hôtel Lux (☎ 04 76 46 41 89; www.hotel-lux.com in
French; 6 rue Crépu; s/d/tw €41/44/47) A tidy, friendly
two-star place on a quiet back street near
the station. It looks utilitarian from the outside, but the rooms are pleasant and there's
a car park close by.

Hôtel Suisse et Bordeaux (☎ 04 76 47 55 87; www
.hotel-sb-grenoble.com; 6 place de la Gare; s/d/tr €41/48/58)
One of three huge hotels facing the sta-
tion. In its heyday it must have been a fine
establishment, with big balconies and lavish
décor; these days it's a little run-down, but
still nicer than some hotels nearby.

Eating

Eating out in style is easy in Grenoble. The
main food thoroughfares are around place
Grenette, place Notre Dame, place St-André
and rue Brocherie, but there are interesting
places scattered all over the city.

RESTAURANTS

Le Mal Assis (☎ 04 76 54 75 93; 9 rue Bayard; evening
menu €21; ⏰ lunch & dinner Tue-Sat) A cosy, upmarket restaurant serving delicious *cuisine bourgeoise*. The surrounding streets are packed
with antique shops and art galleries, so expect a smart, cultured crowd. Reservations
are recommended.

La Panse (☎ 04 76 54 09 54; 7 rue de la Paix; lunch
menu €11, all-day menu €13; ⏰ lunch & dinner Mon-Sat)
A relaxed option, popular with the architects and media types who have offices in
this quarter of the city. The lunchtime and
all-day menus offer traditional dishes with
a contemporary twist.

La Voile Blanche (☎ 04 76 44 22 62; 4 rue Pierre
Duclot; menus €15-35; ⏰ closed Mon & dinner Sun) Rec-

ommended by readers and locals alike. The
restaurant has been refurbished (and has
changed its name) but still offers the same
seasonal cuisine, with seafood and local
dishes a speciality. The €15 menu includes
two courses, wine and coffee.

La Mère Ticket (☎ 04 76 44 45 40; 13 rue Jean-
Jacques Rousseau; lunch menu €11; ⏰ lunch & 8-11pm
Mon-Sat) A tiny, traditional French restaurant
tucked away on a busy shopping street. The
homely country cooking is fantastic value,
especially at lunchtime. The delicious *poulet aux écrevisses* (chicken with crayfish)
and *gratin dauphinois* come highly recommended.

Restaurant des Montagnes (☎ 04 76 15 20 72; 5
rue Brocherie; salads from €5.90, fondue per person €12.50-
21; ⏰ 7pm-midnight Sep-Jun) Grenoble's premier
place for fondue and *tartiflette*. This is a restaurant where waistline worries should be
left at the door. Loosen your belt and order
one of the 13 kinds of sumptuous fondue
instead. You need a minimum of two people
for the fondue.

Les Archers (☎ 04 76 46 27 76; 2 rue Docteur Bailly;
mains €8-15; ⏰ 11am-1am) A brasserie with great
outside seating in summer. Fish and seafood
are especially good, with delicacies including pan-fried trout and grilled sea bass.

Ciao a Te (☎ 04 76 42 54 41; 2 rue de la Paix; salads
from €10; ⏰ Tue-Sat) A vibrant Italian restaurant that serves great pasta. If you're feeling
hungry, try the filling, delicious cannelloni.

L'Amphitryon (☎ 04 76 51 38 07; 9 rue Chenoise; couscous €9-13; ⏰ Mon-Sat) With its stark, minimalist décor, this is one of Grenoble's funkiest
restaurants, serving great, generous couscous and North African cuisine.

CAFÉS

Le Tonneau de Diogène (☎ 04 76 42 38 40; 6 place
Notre Dame; menu from €6, plat du jour €10; ⏰ 8.30am-
1am) Grenoble's best known philo-café, a
cramped, wonderfully atmospheric place,
decked out with polished wood, leather
booths, and lots of tightly packed tables.
If you feel like strutting your philosophical stuff, discussions are usually held on
Thursday evenings.

Café de la Table Ronde (☎ 04 76 44 51 41; 7 place
St-André; lunch menu €10, dinner €10-28; ⏰ 7am-midnight
Mon-Sat) Another of Grenoble's most famous
cafés. The establishment, which dates from
1739, was a favoured haunt of Stendhal and
Rousseau, and the old-world atmosphere

and period furnishings don't seem to have changed much since they were around. In summer, place St-André is one of the city's liveliest squares, especially after dark.

Subway (☎ 04 76 87 31 67; cnr rue Lakanal & blvd Gambetta; salads €3.50-7.60; ⏰ 10am-1am Mon-Sat, from 5pm Sat & Sun) The best breakfast option in town for late risers. The sandwiches are cheap and generous, the beer is cold, and there's usually reggae, dub or rock on the stereo – which makes this a popular student hangout by night.

La Forêt Noire (☎ 04 76 44 54 98; 5 rue Alphand; cakes €2-6, mains €6-12) A Grenoble institution for afternoon tea. The café serves a lavish range of cakes, tarts and *viennoiseries*, as well as light meals. Look no further for something sweet and sticky.

SELF-CATERING

Les Halles Ste-Claire (place Ste-Claire; ⏰ 6am-1pm Tue-Sun) is Grenoble's lovely old covered market. Even if you're not going there to shop, the market atmosphere is worth investigating. There's also a busy **food market** (place Ste-Claire; ⏰ Wed-Mon).

The **Monoprix supermarket** (cnr rue de la République & rue Lafayette; ⏰ 8.30am-7.30pm Mon-Sat) has a basement grocery section and a *boulangerie*. For cake fiends, patisseries can be found around place Notre Dame.

Drinking

Barberousse (☎ 04 76 57 14 53; 8 rue Hache; ⏰ 5pm-1am) There are 33 sorts of aromatic rum fermenting in giant glass flasks behind the counter at Barberousse. Try downing a shot of cherry, apple, papaya or other fruit-flavoured liqueurs.

Bar 1900 (place Notre Dame; ⏰ 5pm-1am) Right next door to the chiming clock-tower of the Notre Dame cathedral, this is an atmospheric little bar with a great outdoor terrace onto the square.

La Twenty (☎ 04 76 51 13 74; 20 rue Chenoise; ⏰ 11am-1am Mon-Sat) A funky bar in the heart of the old city with kitsch, colourful décor and an equally colourful management. The huge lunchtime platters have a national theme (Italian, Savoyard, Chinese etc) and are great value. By night, you can sample house-special Chartreuse cocktails in the company of a relaxed, friendly crowd.

Le Couche Tard (☎ 04 76 44 18 79; 1 rue du Palais; ⏰ 4pm-1am) and **Le Saxo Pub** (☎ 04 76 51 06 01;

5 rue d'Agier; ⏰ 6pm-2am) are two of Grenoble's popular late-night drinking spots, but there are loads more to discover – Rue Brocherie, place St-André, and the streets around rue Thiers are all good places for night-owls to explore.

Also worth a look are **Café Tamara** (☎ 04 76 63 85 88; 3 rue du Palais; ⏰ 1pm-2am Mon-Sat, 2pm-1am Sun), a chic piano-bar with great coffee and cocktails, and **Chorus Café** (☎ 04 76 15 22 89; 8 rue Brocherie; ⏰ 6pm-1am Tue-Sun), a fun place where the walls are covered with graffiti.

Entertainment

Grenoble's best art cinema is the seven-screen **La Nef** (☎ 04 76 46 53 25; 18 blvd Edouard Rey; ⏰ from 7pm), which shows a great selection of art-house and independent films. For new releases, **Les 6 Rex** (☎ 08 92 68 00 31; 13 rue St-Jacques; ⏰ from 7pm) is the most central.

As a thriving student city, Grenoble has lots of music venues. The best place to find out what's on is the huge **Fnac** (☎ 04 76 85 85 85; www.fnac.com in French; 4 rue Félix Poulet), just off place Grenette, which has an in-store ticket booking agency.

Getting There & Away

AIR

Domestic flights are handled by **Grenoble -St-Geoirs airport** (☎ 04 76 65 48 48), 45km northwest of Grenoble. International flights operate to/from **Lyon St-Exupéry airport** (☎ 08 26 80 08 26), 90km from the city off the A43 to Lyon.

BUS

The **bus station** (☎ 04 76 87 90 31; rue Émile Gueymard; ⏰ 6.30am-7pm Mon-Sat, 7.15am-7pm Sun) is next to the train station, and is the main terminus for several bus companies. **VFD** (☎ 08 20 83 38 33; www.vfd.fr in French; ⏰ 8am-6pm Tue-Fri, 8am noon & 1.30-4.30pm Sat & Mon) serves most Alpine destinations; tariffs are worked out on a zone system according to how far you travel. Destinations include Chambéry (€4.90, 1¾ hours), Chamrousse (€6, 1¼ hours), Bourg d'Oisans (€4.90, 50 minutes), Les Deux Alpes (€4.90, 1¾ hours) and the Vercors ski stations.

Intercars (☎ 04 76 46 19 77; www.intercars.fr in French; station office ⏰ 9am-noon & 2-6pm Mon-Fri, 9am-noon & 2-5pm Sat) handles long-haul destinations including Berlin (€87, 21 hours), Munich (€72, 10 hours), Rome (€48, 10 hours), Milan

(€23, 5½ hours), Zurich (€31, eight hours) and Geneva (€12, four hours). It operates buses departing from Annecy, Chambéry, Chamonix and Lyon too.

TRAIN

The huge, modern **train station** (☎ 08 36 35 35 35; rue Émile Gueymard; ⊙ 4.30am-2am) is next to the Gare Europole tram stop, which is served by both tramlines (see Getting Around).

Destinations served include Paris' Gare de Lyon (from €64, 3½ hours by TGV), Chambéry (€9, one hour, 14 daily) and Lyon (€16, 1½ hours, five daily), from where you can catch trains to Nice and Monaco. There are also daily trains to Turin (€44, 3½hours), Milan (€54, five hours, change at Chambéry), and Geneva (€20, two hours).

Getting Around
TO/FROM THE AIRPORT

The bus to **Lyon St-Exupéry airport** (☎ 04 76 87 90 31) stops at the bus station (one way/return €20/30, 65 minutes). Buses to the Grenoble-St-Geoirs domestic airport depart from the bus station (one way/return €13/20, 45 minutes).

BICYCLE

If you can't face another tram-ride into town, **Métro-Vélo** (☎ 08 20 22 38 38; bike hire per day €5; ⊙ 7am-8pm Mon-Fri, 9am-noon & 2-7pm Sat & Sun), opposite the car-hire offices underneath the station, rent out bikes.

BUS & TRAM

The pride of Grenoble's public transport system are its two pollution-free tram lines – sensibly called A and B (plans are underway for a third). Both stop at the tourist office and the train station, and run through the heart of town. They're fast, reliable and almost silent, which makes you wonder why all big cities don't have them – until you've almost been run over for the nineteenth time.

Bus and tram tickets cost €1.20 and are available from ticket machines at tram stops or from drivers. They must be time-stamped in the blue machines located at each stop before boarding. Tickets are valid for transfers – but not return trips – within one hour.

A carnet of 10 tickets costs €9.50. Daily/five-day passes (Visitag) are available for

€3.20/11 from the **TAG information desk** (☎ 04 76 20 66 66) at the tourist office, or from the TAG office outside the train station. Family passes are also available.

The majority of the buses on the 20 different lines stop running quite early, usually between 6pm and 9pm. Trams run daily from 5am (6.15am on Sunday) until just after midnight.

CAR

Having a car in the city is of little benefit, since the roads are confusing and parking is expensive. If you're looking for four wheels to explore the surrounding countryside, all the main agencies are underneath the station, including **ADA** (☎ 04 67 43 00 36; ⊙ 8am-noon &1-6.30pm Mon-Fri, 8am-noon & 2-5pm Sat).

TAXI

Taxis can be ordered by calling the central reservation line on ☎ 04 76 54 42 54.

AROUND GRENOBLE

The low-altitude regions surrounding Grenoble attract a relaxed crowd in search of cheap winter skiing or summer walking. Stations known for their cross-country skiing include Lans-en-Vercors and Villard de Lans, southwest of Grenoble in the Vercors range; and Col de Porte and Le Sappey, north of Grenoble in the Chartreuse. Summer skiing can be found further east in **Les Deux Alpes** and **Alpe d'Huez**.

Chamrousse, the nearest ski resort to Grenoble, was built for the 1968 Winter Olympics. The family resort, popular for its wide and gentle slopes, hosts the snowboarding World Cup and the French freestyle ski championships every March. Chamrousse's **tourist office** (☎ 04 76 89 92 65; www.chamrousse .com; 42 place de Belledonne; ⊙ 9am-6pm ski season, 9am-noon & 1.30-5pm rest of year) can help with accommodation. There are several VFD buses daily from Grenoble to Chamrousse (€6, 1¼ hours).

Parc Naturel Régional du Vercors

Immediately southwest of Grenoble the Parc Naturel Régional du Vercors (1750 sq km) is a large cross-country skiing, caving and hiking area. During WWII it became a stronghold of the Resistance movement and was given the name the 'Fortresse de la Résistance'.

Lans-en-Vercors (population 1450, elevation 1020m), 25km southwest of Grenoble, is the leading ski village on the Vercors plateau. There's none of the adrenaline of the high-Alpine descents here, nor is there a bustling nightlife. From Lans-en-Vercors, hourly shuttle buses travel to the Stade de Neige (Snow Stadium), an area of wooded slopes crowned by Le Grand Cheval (1807m), about 4km east.

The equally sedate village of **Villard de Lans** (population 3350, elevation 1050m), 9km up the valley from Lans-en-Vercors, is linked by ski lifts and roads to neighbouring resort **Corrençon-en-Vercors** (1111m).

INFORMATION

The **park headquarters** (☎ 04 76 94 38 26; www.pnr -vercors.fr; 255 chemin des Fusillés; ⏲ 8.30am-12.30pm & 2-5pm Mon-Fri) is inside the Maison du Parc in Lans-en-Vercors. The **tourist office** (☎ 04 76 95 42 62; www.ot-lans-en-vercors.fr; place de la Mairie; ⏲ 9am-12.30pm & 1.30-6pm daily high seasons, 9am-noon & 2-6pm Mon-Fri, 10am-noon & 2-5pm Sat & Sun rest of year) in Lans-en-Vercors and the **tourist office** (☎ 04 76 95 10 38; www.villarddelans.com; place Mure Ravaud; ⏲ 9am-12.30pm & 2-7pm summer, 9am-7pm winter; 9am-noon & 2-6pm Mon-Sat rest of year) in Villard de Lans provide extensive information on activities in the park.

The free brochure *Welcome to Vercors* lists walks as well as driving and caving tours; *Site National Historique de la Résistance en Vercors* traces the footsteps of the Resistance movement.

GETTING THERE & AWAY

From Lans-en-Vercors, **VFD** (☎ 04 76 95 11 24) runs six buses daily (five at the weekend) to and from Grenoble (€6, 50 minutes), Villard de Lans (€1.80, 10 minutes) and Corrençon (€1.40, 15 minutes).

Parc National des Écrins

The spectacular Parc National des Écrins (930 sq km) was created in 1973. Stretching between the towns of Bourg d'Oisans, Briançon and Gap, it is France's second-largest national park. The area is enclosed by steep, narrow valleys, sculpted by the Romanche, Durance and Drac rivers and their erstwhile glaciers.

The **main park headquarters** (☎ 04 92 40 20 10; ecrins-parcnational@espaces-naturels.fr; ⏲ 8am-noon & 1-5pm Mon-Fri) is at the Domaine de la Cha-

rance, F-05000 Gap. There's a large **park office** (☎ 04 92 21 08 49; ecrins.briançonnais@espaces-naturels .fr; place Médecin Général Blanchard; ⏲ 9.30am-7pm Jul & Aug; 9.30am-noon & 2-7pm Sep-Jun) in Briançon.

Bourg d'Oisans (population 3000, elevation 720m), 50km southeast of Grenoble, and Briançon, another 67km in the same direction, make good bases for exploring the park. The **Maison du Parc** (☎ 04 76 80 00 51; ecrins .oisans@espaces-naturels.fr; rue Gambetta; ⏲ 8am-noon & 1.30-7pm summer, 8am-noon & 1.30-5.30pm Mon-Fri rest of year) sells maps and guides including the invaluable IGN 1:25,000 *Les Deux Alpes–Le Parc National des Écrins* (No 3336ET) and *Bourg d'Oisans-Alpe d'Huez* (No 3335ET). The town's **tourist office** (☎ 04 76 80 03 25; www .bourgdoisans.com; ⏲ 8.30am-noon & 2-5.30pm Mon-Sat, 8.30am-noon Sun winter; 9am-7pm Mon-Sat, 10am-noon & 3-6pm Sun summer) is well stocked too. You'll find it on the main road just before the River Romanche at quai Girard.

ACTIVITIES
Walking

There are plenty of zigzagging paths used for centuries by shepherds and smugglers from points all along the Romanche Valley.

From Bourg d'Oisans there is a path up to Villard Notre Dame (1525m, two hours). From Venosc, a tiny mountain village in the Vénéon Valley, about 12km southeast of Bourg d'Oisans, there is a trail to the popular skiing resort of Les Deux Alpes (1660m, 1½ hours).

Dix Itinéraires (a publication in French) is a good companion for 10 different treks and climbs of up to seven hours. *Venosc/Vallée de Vénéon* is another good publication.

The Bourg d'Oisans tourist office sells six different walking maps (in English and French) entitled *Oisans au Bout des Pieds* (Oisans Under Your Feet).

Other Activities

Air Écrins Club de Parapente de l'Oisans (☎ /fax 04 76 11 00 35; 23 rue Général de Gaulle, Bourg d'Oisans) runs canoeing, kayaking and *parapente* schools.

At St-Christophe, near Venosc, **Vénéon Eaux Vives** (☎ 04 76 80 23 99) organises similar activities and hires out mountain bikes.

SLEEPING & EATING

Most of the park's 32 **refuges** (dm €10-12) are run by the CAF. Several **gîtes d'étape** (dm €12-15) on the outskirts of the park are open year-round. For a full listing, ask at the Bourg d'Oisans tourist office for the free *Guide des Hébergements*.

Maison des Jeunes Le Paradis (☎ 04 76 80 01 76; 50 rue Thiers; dm €10; ☺ closed May & Oct), in Bourg d'Oisans, has dorm beds in rooms for 12 people and can also arrange mountain biking, kayaking, canoeing etc.

Bourg d'Oisans also has about 10 hotels, the cheaper ones being around the bus station on rue de la Gare. You can find simple doubles at **Le Moulin des Fruites Bleues** (☎ 04 76 80 00 26; d €30-50), **Hôtel Le Rocher** (☎ 04 76 80 01 53; fax 04 76 79 11 94; d from €35) and **Hôtel de l'Oberland Français** (☎ 04 76 80 24 24; d from €35).

Hôtel Le Florentin (☎ 04 76 80 01 61; fax 04 76 80 05 49; rue Thiers; s €43-52, d €55-59; ☺ closed mid-Dec–Sep) is a family-run hotel with a friendly welcome.

There are plenty of camping grounds in Bourg d'Oisans – the best is **La Cascade** (☎ 04 76 80 02 42; fax 04 76 80 22 63; camping €18; ☺ mid-Dec–Sep), near the tourist office. Most of the cheaper camping grounds are only open from June to September.

There are plenty of small supermarkets and grocery stores in Bourg d'Oisans to stock up on supplies.

GETTING THERE & AWAY
VFD buses (☎ 04 76 80 00 90; Bourg d'Oisans) serve the Romanche Valley and Briançon. They operate from the **bus station** (av de la Gare), on the main road into Bourg d'Oisans. From Grenoble, VFD bus No 3000 goes to Bourg d'Oisans (€2.70, 80 minutes) up to eight times a day, while the No 3030 and the No 3020 from Grenoble stop in Bourg d'Oisans on their way to Les Deux Alpes and Alpe d'Huez.

LES DEUX ALPES
elevation 1600m
Les Deux Alpes, 28km southeast of Bourg d'Oisans, has the largest summer skiing area in Europe. From mid-June to early September, you can ski on the Glacier du Mont de Lans (3200m to 3425m), which offers panoramic views of Mont Blanc, Massif Central and Mont Ventoux.

Les Deux Alpes is a popular winter skiing resort too, as well as one of France's top snowboarding spots. The never-ending stream of traffic clogging up the main street belies its lowly beginnings as a mountain pasture for local sheep flocks.

Orientation
Les Deux Alpes is mostly centred around the long main street (av de la Muzelle), which cuts north-south through town from the road from Grenoble. The central square of place des Deux Alpes is about 700m into the resort. The Maison de la Montagne is a short way north, while the main car parks and bus stops are further south towards the end of the street.

Information
Everything in town revolves around the **Maison des Deux Alpes** (place des Deux Alpes). It houses the **tourist office** (☎ 04 76 79 22 00; www.les2alpes .com; ☺ 8am-7pm high season, 9am-noon & 2-6pm Mon-Fri rest of year) and **accommodation service** (☎ 04 76 79 24 38; res2alp@les2alpes.com), as well as the **ESF** (see opposite).

The main **Bureau des Guides** (☎ 06 11 32 71 88) inside the **Maison de la Montagne** (av de la Muzelle), north of the main tourist office, arranges ice climbing, rock climbing, walking, rafting and mountain-bike expeditions with experienced guides.

The *les2alpes Magazine* and the annual *Winter Guide*, both available free from the tourist office, have stacks of useful information in English about the resort.

Sights
A 6m-tall dinosaur, Alpine flowers and shepherds are just some of the ice-sculptures you'll find in the **grotte de glace** (ice cave; cable-car & cave entry adult/child €20/15; ☺ 9.30am-4.30pm) carved into the Glacier du Mont de Lans at Dôme de Puy Salié (3425m). Take the Jandri Express *télécabine* to 3200m (change of *télécabine* at 2600m), from where you can take the underground Dôme Express funicular to 3400m.

For a glimpse of traditional Alpine life as it once was, visit the **Maison de la Montagne** (☎ 04 76 79 53 15; av de la Muzelle; admission €2; ☺ 10am-noon & 3-7pm summer, 2-6pm winter).

Activities
SKIING & SNOWBOARDING
The main skiing domain lies below La Meije (3983m), one of the highest peaks in the Parc National des Écrins. There are 200km of marked pistes, 20km of cross-country trails, and in the snowpark (2600m), a 600m-long axe pipe, 110m-long half-pipe and numerous jumps.

ESF (☎ 04 76 79 21 21; esf.les2alpes@wanadoo.fr) and the **École de Ski International St-Christophe** (☎ 04 76 79 04 21; ecole.ski.internationale@wanadoo.fr; av de la Muzelle), close to place des Deux Alpes, run skiing and snowboarding schools for all levels.

WARM-WEATHER ACTIVITIES
Numerous walks are listed in the free brochure *Le Guide des Randonnées Pédestres au Départ des Deux Alpes* available at the tourist office.

Parapente ESF (☎ 06 07 72 26 60; ☽ 6-7.30pm; parapente@2alpes.com; 1-day course €60), inside the Maison des Deux Alpes, offers paragliding courses.

Sleeping
The accommodation service (see Information opposite) inside the Maison des Deux Alpes arranges accommodation within the resort. Two-person apartments cost around €190/250 a week in the low/high season – bookings, as usual, should be made well in advance.

Off-piste skiers wishing to tackle the challenge of the fearsome La Grave descent should consider basing themselves in the village of La Grave, 21km to the east of Les Deux Alpes.

The **Auberge de Jeunesse** (☎ 04 76 79 22 80; les-deux-alpes@fuaj.org; Les Brûleurs de Loups; dm €11) is in the heart of town. It only offers weekly packages in winter, including seven days' accommodation, food and a ski-lift pass. Prices start at €290/400 in the low/high season.

Auberge Edelweiss (☎ 04 76 79 90 93; edelweiss@waw.com; s/d high season €40/52) is a homely little hotel that caters to individual and small groups. Rooms here are cosy. There is also a restaurant and a Jacuzzi to thaw out tired skiers.

Getting There & Away
VFD operates buses running to Les Deux Alpes from Grenoble (€2.70, 1¾ hours, eight daily), 77km northwest.

In Les Deux Alpes, reserve tickets in advance from the **VFD office** (☎ 04 76 80 51 22; 112 av de la Muzelle) or from the tourist office. Buses stop at Bourg d'Oisans (40 minutes) en route to Grenoble. There are also services to Lyon St-Exupéry, Alpe d'Huez, Briançon and Geneva airports.

ALPE D'HUEZ
elevation 1860m
The ski resort of Alpe d'Huez sits 13km above Bourg d'Oisans, and is reached by a steep road (La Montée de l'Alpe d'Huez) which is best known as one of the 'classic' ascents often included in the Tour de France cycle race.

Alpe d'Huez has winter runs for skiers and snowboarders of all abilities. At 16km, La Sarenne is the longest black run in the French Alps. Experienced skiers can also ski in July and August on glaciers (ranging from 2530m to 3330m). The panoramic view from Pic du Lac Blanc (3330m), the highest point accessible year-round from the village by the Tronçon *télécabines*, is particularly impressive.

Information
The **tourist office** (☎ 04 76 11 44 44; info@alpedhuez .com; ☽ 9am-12.30pm & 2.30-6pm), **accommodation centre** (☎ 04 76 11 44 44; resa@alpedhuez.com; ☽ 9am-12.30pm & 2.30-6pm) and **ESF** (☎ 04 76 80 31 69; ☽ 9am-12.30pm & 2.30-6pm) are inside the **Maison de l'Alpe** (place Joseph Paganon).

The **Bureau des Guides** (☎ 04 76 80 42 55) and the **Taburle École du Snowboard Français** (☎ 04 76 80 95 82) are both off place du Cognet at the Rond Point des Pistes, the northernmost point of the village. The annual *Le Guide de l'Alpe* booklet, free from the tourist office, has a full listing of all facilities in the resort.

Sleeping
The accommodation centre (see Information above) takes accommodation bookings. Expect to pay €215/350 in the low/high season for a small, two-person studio. With some 28 hotels and another 27 rental places, accommodation is plentiful but demand is high in season.

One of the least expensive hotels in Alpe d'Huez, **Gai Vallon** (☎ 04 76 80 98 37; rue de l'Église; r from €37, half-board from €41) is one-star and offers simple, neat rooms.

Hôtel Alp'Azur (☎ 04 76 80 34 02; place Jean Molin; d €67-82; ☽ closed Apr-Jun) is a friendly, helpful, two-star place. Its rates include breakfast.

Getting There & Away
VFD buses (☎ 04 76 80 31 61) run from Grenoble to Alpe d'Huez (€15.50, 1¾ hours, eight daily) via Bourg d'Oisans.

BRIANÇON
pop 11,300 / elevation 1026m

Jutting out from a rocky outcrop at the meeting of five valleys, the hilltop city of Briançon stands like a sentinel between the French Alps and Italy, which is 20km to the northeast.

Long a frontier post, the fortified old city of Briançon overlooks the road to the Col de Montgenèvre (1850m), an ancient Roman mountain pass that was made into a reliable road by Napoleon. Briançon's lofty ramparts and sheer walls are more reminiscent of the towns of northern Burgundy than its Alpine neighbours, but the town's main claim to fame is its altitude – at 1320m, it is the highest town in Europe and boasts approximately 300 days of sunshine a year.

During the late 17th century, the military architect Vauban was called in to make the town impregnable to attack after it had been razed during a regional war. Since then, the town has crept down the slopes to encompass the Durance Valley. The lower town has a lift station to the ski resort of Le Grand Serre Chevalier. Sadly, it's inherited none of the charm of the old town, and generally looks its best covered with a blanket of snow.

Briançon is sandwiched between Parc National des Écrins to the west and Parc Naturel Régional du Queyras to the south, making it an excellent base for outdoor pursuits.

Orientation
The town is divided into two sections: the Vieille Ville (old city), with its pedestrianised streets and battlements, and the modern Ville Basse (lower town), which sprawls out beneath the old city at the junction of two rivers. The upper and lower towns are connected by the steep hill of av de la République.

Entry to the Vieille Ville is from place du Champ de Mars (on the old city's northern side) or, if you're walking up the hill from the lower town, through the Porte d'Embrun. The train station is in the suburb of Ste-Catherine.

Information
LAUNDRY
LavPlus (Central Parc; ☺ 7am-7pm)

MONEY
Banque Populaire (20 av Maurice Petsche) Exchanges currency.
Crédit Agricole (10 Grande Rue; ☺ 8am-noon & 1.55-5pm Mon-Fri, until 4.30pm Sat) The branch in the old city.
Crédit Agricole (Le Moulin shopping mall)

POST
Post Office (place du Champ de Mars) Opposite the entrance to the old town.
Post Office Branch (Parc Chancel) In the lower town just off av du 159 RIA.

TOURIST INFORMATION
Maison du Parc (☎ 04 92 21 42 15; ecrins.briançonnais@espaces-naturels.fr; Place Médecin Général Blanchard; ☺ 9.30am-7pm Jul & Aug, 9.30am-noon & 2-7pm Sep-Jun) At the southern end of Grande Rue in the Vieille Ville, provides information on the Parc National des Écrins.
Tourist Office (☎ 04 92 21 08 50; office-tourisme-briancon@wanadoo.fr; 1 place du Temple; ☺ 9am-noon & 2-6pm Mon-Sat, 10am-12.30pm & 3-5pm Sun Sep-Jun, 9am-7pm Jul & Aug) In Vieille Ville.

Sights
VIEILLE VILLE
The old city is a fine place to spend an afternoon drinking in the mountain air and admiring the views from the city's battlements. In high summer the throngs of tourists can be troublesome, but off-season the town is quiet and the atmosphere is tranquil. If you've spent a week in the sardine-can ski resorts of the central Alps, it makes an ideal place to rest those weary bones before the journey home.

At the top of the old city is the **Porte de Pignerol**, a daunting gateway hewn from dark stone. The steep main street, Grande Rue, is known as the Grande Gargouille (Great Gargoyle) because of the drain that gushes down its middle, and there are several fountains in the old part of town, spouting water from underground springs. The brightly coloured buildings, all earthy reds, rich pinks and ochre yellows, lend the town an almost Tuscan air – a reminder that the Italian border lies just a few miles east. There are also a couple of tiny, tumbledown chapels along Briançon's back streets.

The coral-pink **Collégiale** (Church of Our Lady & St Nicholas) is a more permanent relic. Built by Vauban in the early 18th century, the twin-towered church is characteristically heavy and fortified. The baroque

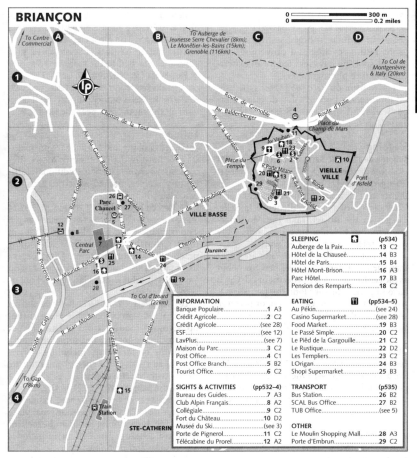

BRIANÇON

0 ____ 300 m
0 ____ 0.2 miles

To Centre **A**
Commercial

To Auberge de **B**
Jeunesse Serre Chevalier (8km);
Le Monêtier-les-Bains (15km);
Grenoble (116km)

C

D
To Col de
Montgenèvre
& Italy (20km)

1

Route de Grenoble

Av Baldenberger

Route d'Italie

Chemin de la Tour

Av du Caul Barbot

Av de la Libération

Place du
Champ de Mars

Av Vauban

Place du
Temple

R Porte Méane

**VIEILLE
VILLE**

Pont
d'Asfeld

2

Av René Froger

R René Frager

R Pasteur Collaud

Av de la République

VILLE BASSE

Parc
Chancel

Durance

Chemin Vieux

Av de Provence

Central
Parc

R Centrale

Av Maurice Petsche

To Col d'Izoard
(22km)

3

Route de Gap

R Jean Moulin

Av du Général de Gaulle

To Gap
(78km)

4

Train
Station

STE-CATHERIN

INFORMATION	
Banque Populaire	1 A3
Crédit Agricole	2 C2
Crédit Agricole	(see 28)
ESF	(see 7)
LavPlus	(see 7)
Maison du Parc	3 C2
Post Office	4 C1
Post Office Branch	5 B2
Tourist Office	6 C2

SIGHTS & ACTIVITIES	(pp532–4)
Bureau des Guides	7 A3
Club Alpin Français	8 A3
Collégiale	9 C2
Fort du Château	10 D2
Musée du Ski	(see 3)
Porte de Pignerol	11 C2
Télécabine du Prorel	12 A2

SLEEPING	(p534)
Auberge de la Paix	13 C2
Hôtel de la Chauseé	14 B3
Hôtel de Paris	15 B4
Hôtel Mont-Brison	16 A3
Parc Hôtel	17 B3
Pension des Remparts	18 C2

EATING	(pp534–5)
Au Pékin	(see 24)
Casino Supermarket	(see 25)
Food Market	19 B3
Le Passé Simple	20 C2
Le Pièd de la Gargouille	21 C2
Le Rustique	22 D2
Les Templiers	23 C2
L'Origan	24 B3
Shopi Supermarket	25 B3

TRANSPORT	(p535)
Bus Station	26 B2
SCAL Bus Office	27 B2
TUB Office	(see 5)

OTHER	
Le Moulin Shopping Mall	28 A3
Porte d'Embrun	29 C2

paintings and gilt chapels inside are worth a closer look.

The 18th-century **Fort du Château** sits above the old city and offers magnificent views of the surrounding mountains. Guided **tours** (adult/concessions €4.50/3; Jul-Aug) are organised by the tourist office, but if you don't think you're up to the uphill climb, av Vauban, which runs along the town's ramparts, affords fine views of the snowy peaks of the Écrins national park.

TÉLÉCABINE DU PROREL

The **télécabine du Prorel** (av René Froger; return ticket/day pass €5.30/9; 8.45am-4.15pm Mon-Fri, 7am-5.15pm Sat & Sun ski season & summer mid-Jun–mid-Sep), which leaves from the Briançon-Serre-

Chevalier 1200 station in the lower town, climbs to Le Prorel (2566m), one of the highest points of Le Grand Serre Chevalier mountain range.

Activities

In winter there is skiing at Le Grand Serre Chevalier (p535), the range that stretches from Briançon to Le Monêtier-les-Bains, 15km northwest. The **ESF** (☎ 04 92 20 30 57; www.esf-serrechevalier.com; 7 av René Froger) and various ski-hire shops are inside the *télécabine* du Prorel station. **CAF** (☎ 04 92 20 16 52; 6 av René Froger; 5-7pm Tue-Sat) is near the ski-lift station.

During winter, ice climbing and ski tours can be organised by the **Bureau des Guides**

(☎ 04 92 20 15 73; fax 04 92 20 46 49; Central Parc; day trip per person around €25; ⏰ 9.30am-noon & 1.30-7pm Jul-Sep). In summer it organises treks, *parapente*, rafting, cycling and canyoning, and animal-spotting day treks led by an experienced nature photographer.

The Maison du Parc (p532) sells the useful *Promenades* booklets that detail numerous walks and hikes in the Briançon, Oisans and Vanoise region.

Sleeping

Auberge de Jeunesse Serre Chevalier (☎ 04 92 24 74 54; serre-chevalier@fuaj.org; BP 2, 05240 Serre-Chevalier Cedex; dm summer €12; ⏰ Dec-Apr & Jun-Nov) This is the nearest hostel, 8km northwest at Serre Chevalier-le-Bez near Villeneuve-la-Salle. To get to the hostel, take the Monêtier-les-Bains bus to Villeneuve-Pre-Long. Only weekly rates are available in winter.

The hotels in the Vieille Ville are nicer than their counterparts in the new town, but as the central streets are pedestrianised, you'll have to park your car along the ramparts. If you need to catch an early train, or if you're skiing, the Basse Ville is a more practical base. Prices rise during the skiing season.

OLD TOWN

Pension des Remparts (☎ 04 92 21 08 73; 14 av Vauban; d with shower €35-44) One of the cheapest places in the old city. The front rooms face the mountains and the bar downstairs is a popular haunt with Briançon's flat-cap crowd.

Auberge de la Paix (☎ 04 92 21 37 43; fax 04 92 20 44 45; 3 rue Porte Méane; d €39-55; P) Twenty comfortable rooms in an old inn near the Grande Rue, though some of the rooms are quite dark because of the minuscule windows. The attached restaurant is one of the best in town.

NEW TOWN

Hôtel de la Chaussée (☎ 04 92 21 10 37; fax 04 92 20 03 94; 4 rue Centrale; d €37-42, tw/tr €51/58; P) An alpine-style hotel in the lower town that has better than two-star rooms and is usually very quiet.

Hôtel Mont-Brison (☎ 04 92 21 14 55; 3 av du Général de Gaulle; d €30-49; ⏰ Jan-Oct) Another two-star place at the bottom of the hill from the old city. The rooms are showing their age and it's on a busy roundabout, but it's clean and central.

Hôtel de Paris (☎ 04 92 20 15 30; fax 04 92 20 30 82; 41 av du Général de Gaulle; s/d/tr 39/43/42; ⏰ closed early Oct & end Apr) The most convenient option for the station has lots of space and a nice sunroom attached to the side.

Parc Hôtel (☎ 04 92 20 37 47; fax 04 92 20 53 74; cnr av Maurice Petsche & av du 159 RIA, Central Parc; s/d/tr €63/71/79; P ✗) A blocky purpose-built hotel with all the mod-cons, near the ski-lift.

Eating

Savoyard cooking and fondues are the mainstays of most of the restaurants. Many offer a *menu Vauban* featuring traditional 18th-century recipes, named after the architect who shaped the town.

Le Pied de la Gargouille (☎ 04 92 20 12 95; 64 Grande Rue; menus €16-18, fondues & tartiflettes from €13) The friendliest and homeliest restaurant in town is run by a local couple who know practically everyone in town. Don't expect too many frills, but for grilled meats and Savoyard fondues, the Gargoyle's Foot is recommended.

Les Templiers (☎ 04 92 20 29 04; 20 place du Temple; ⏰ 6.30-11pm Dec-Oct) This place rustles up Savoyard fondues from €12 to €15 per person, simple pizzas, and some intriguing variations of *tartiflette*, including *chèvriflette* (made with goats' cheese) and *ratiflette* (made with *raclette* cheese).

Le Passé Simple (☎ 04 92 21 37 43; 3 rue Porte Méane; menus €15-22; ⏰ lunch & dinner) Inside the Auberge de la Paix, this is a traditional place with a big, busy dining room and excellent Savoyard cooking. The €19 menu includes onion soup and *filet de boeuf*.

Le Rustique (☎ 04 92 21 00 10; 36 rue du Pont d'Asfeld; ⏰ until 11pm) For local dishes and traditional fondue, try this cavernous place. It has a non-smoking room, and house specialities include locally caught trout. Gourmands should try its apple tart with *foie gras* or quail roasted in honey.

L'Origan (☎ 04 92 20 10 09; 25 rue Centrale; pizza from €5.80) is a pizzeria with lots of varieties. **Au Pékin** (☎ 04 92 21 24 22; menus from €10; ⏰ 11am-2pm & 6-11pm) is in the same building as L'Origan, and offers the usual Chinese favourites.

SELF-CATERING

There's a **food market** (⏰ Wed) in the car park next to the fire station, just off rue Centrale. Numerous food shops line Grande Rue in the Vieille Ville.

Briançon has a **Shopi supermarket** (av Maurice Petsche; ☎ 8.30am-12.30pm & 2.30-7.30pm Mon-Sat, 8.45am-noon Sun) and a huge **Casino supermarket** (Le Moulin shopping mall).

Getting There & Away
BUS
The **bus station** (cnr av du 159 RIA & rue Général Colaud) is simply a bus stop marked Autocar Arrêt. **SCAL** (☎ 04 92 21 12 00; 14 av du 159 RIA; ☎ 8am-noon & 2-6pm Mon-Fri) has an office next door. It runs a daily bus to Gap (€9.25, two hours), Digne (€17, 3¼ hours, no bus on Sunday), Marseille (€26, 5¾ hours), and Aix-en-Provence (€23, five hours).

VFD buses (p527) in Grenoble travel from Briançon via Bourg d'Oisans (€12, 1¾ hours) to Grenoble (€25, 2¼ hours) twice daily.

TRAIN
Briançon's **train station** (☎ 04 92 51 50 50; av du Général de Gaulle) is at the southern end of the street, about 1.5km from the Vieille Ville. There are **ticket windows** (☺ 5.30am-12.20am Mon-Fri, until 10pm Sat & Sun). Left luggage costs €2 per piece.

To Paris' Gare d'Austerlitz, a direct overnight train leaves at 8.30pm (€90, 10 hours). Faster daytime services go via Grenoble or Valence (€69.50, 6½-seven hours). Other destinations include Gap (€11, 1¼ hours), Grenoble (€25, 4½ hours) and Marseille (€33, four hours).

Getting Around
BUS
Local buses run by TUB – Nos 1, 2 and 3 – connect the train station to place du Champ de Mars, from about 7am to 6pm Monday to Saturday. Line 1 runs slightly later. On Sunday, Line D runs from around 9am to 5pm. A single ticket costs €1 and a carnet of 10, €7 (available from the TUB office, *tabacs* and the tourist office). The **TUB office** (☎ 04 92 20 47 10; tub@wanadoo.fr; place de Suse, ☎ 9am-noon & 1.30-5.30pm Tue-Fri) is in Parc Chancel.

TAXI
You can also call a **taxi** (☎ 04 92 21 14 42).

AROUND BRIANÇON
Le Grand Serre Chevalier
Le Grand Serre Chevalier is a ski area above the Serre Chevalier Valley in the Hautes-Alpes. There are 13 villages along the valley floor, but the lift system only reaches Briançon and the villages of Chantemerle, Villeneuve-la-Salle and Le Monêtier-les-Bains. Chantemerle (Serre Chevalier 1350) and Villeneuve-la-Salle (Serre Chevalier 1400) are the central resorts. Le Monêtier-les-Bains (Serre Chevalier 1500) is quieter, while Briançon has the cheapest accommodation.

The main tourist office is in Briançon, but there is a small **tourist office** (☎ 04 92 24 98 97) in Chantemerle, a **tourist office** (☎ 04 92 24 98 98) in Villeneuve-la-Salle and a **tourist office** (☎ 04 92 24 98 99) in Le Monêtier-les-Bains. All are open 9am to noon and 2pm to 7pm daily in high season, but close an hour earlier and on Sunday the rest of the year. Accommodation can be booked through the **central reservation office** (☎ 04 92 24 98 90; resa@ot-serrechevalier .fr) at Briançon tourist office.

There are lots of passes available covering the different ski areas – ask at any of the ski-lift stations or pick up the free guidebook *(Guide d'Accueil)*, which lists tariffs. A pass for Serre Chevalier costs €32/160 per day/six days.

The Bureau des Guides in Briançon (p535) and the **Maison de la Montagne** (☎ 04 92 24 75 90) in Villeneuve-la-Salle offer winter ski tours and summer mountaineering trips.

GETTING AROUND
There are buses from Briançon (€4.15, 20 minutes, 10 daily) to Villeneuve-la-Salle. In winter, lifts operate and free shuttle buses ply the route between Le Monêtier-les-Bains and Briançon.

THE JURA

The dark wooded hills and granite plateaus of the Jura Mountains stretch for 360km along the Franco-Swiss border from the Rhine to the Rhône. Part of the historic Franche-Comté region, the Jura is one of the least explored regions in France, which makes it a fine place to escape the Alpine crowds. If you're looking for a taste of traditional mountain life, the Jura makes a far better destination than the ruthlessly modernised and tourist-orientated resorts elsewhere in the Alps.

The Jura – from a Gaulish word meaning 'forest' – is an important agricultural area, best known for its unique wines and cheeses. It is

FRENCH ALPS & THE JURA

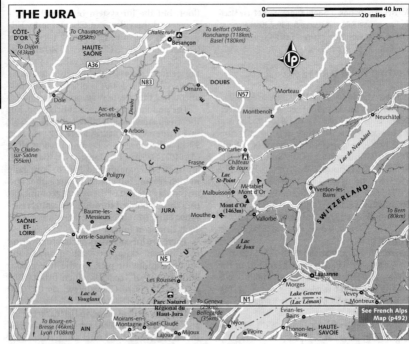

THE JURA

also France's premier cross-country skiing area. The range is dotted with ski stations from Pontarlier south to Bellegarde; Métabief Mont d'Or, north of the Parc Naturel Régional du Haut-Jura, is the main station, as popular for its superb hiking and nature trails as for its gentle slopes. Every year the region hosts the Transjurassienne, one of the world's toughest cross-country skiing events.

BESANÇON

pop 125,000

Besançon, capital of the Franche-Comté region, is surrounded by hills on the northern reaches of the Jura range. First settled in Gallo-Roman times, it became an important stop on the early trade routes between Italy, the Alps and the Rhine.

Since the 18th century, it has been a noted clock-making centre. Victor Hugo, author of *Les Misérables*, and the film-pioneering Lumière brothers, were all born on the square now known as place Victor Hugo in Besançon's old town.

Noted for its vast parks, clean streets and few tourists, Besançon is considered one of the most liveable cities in France. It has one of the country's largest foreign student populations and the old town's cobbled streets hum with bars and bistros. The Battant quarter, originally settled by wine-makers, is the most historic area of town.

Orientation

Besançon's old city is neatly encased by the curve of the River Doubs called the Boucle du Doubs. The tourist office and train station are both just outside this loop to the north and northwest. The Battant quarter straddles the northwest bank of the river around rue Battant. Grande Rue, the pedestrianised main street, slices through the old city from the river to the gates of the citadel.

Information

INTERNET ACCESS

Optimum (☎ 03 81 82 13 07; www.optimum.fr; 31 rue d'Arènes; per 10min/1hr €1/3.50; 10am-10.30pm Mon-Sat, 2-10pm Sun)

LAUNDRY

Blanc-Matic (14 rue de la Madeleine; 7am-8pm)

MONEY

Foreign currency can be changed at the tourist office, post office and the train-station information office. Most banks have ATMs. **Banque de France** (19 rue de la Préfecture) Usually changes money.

POST

Post Office (23 rue Proudhon; ⏰ 9am-noon & 2-6pm) In the old city.
Post Office Branch (rue Battant)

TOURIST INFORMATION

Tourist Office (☎ 03 81 80 92 55; www.besancon -tourisme.com; 2 place de la 1ère Armée Française; ⏰ 10am-7pm Mon, 9am-7pm Tue-Sat, 10am-noon & 3-5pm Sun Apr-Sep, 10am-6pm Mon, 9am-6pm Tue-Sat Oct-Mar, 10am-noon Sun mid-Sep–mid-Jun)

Sights & Activities

MUSÉE DES BEAUX-ARTS ET D'ARCHÉOLOGIE

Thought to be France's oldest museum, the **Musée des Beaux-Arts** (☎ 03 81 87 80 49; 1 place de la Révolution; adult/student €3/free; ⏰ 9.30am-noon & 2-6pm Wed-Mon) houses an impressive collection of paintings, including primitive and Renaissance works. Franche-Comté's long history of clock-making is also displayed here.

CITADEL

Built by Vauban for Louis XIV between 1688 and 1711, Besançon's **citadel** (☎ 03 81 87 83 33; rue des Fusillés de la Résistance; adult/concession/child €7/6/4; ⏰ 9am-7pm Jul & Aug, 9am-6pm Apr-Jun, Sep & Oct, 10am-5pm Nov-Mar) sits at the top of rue des Fusillés de la Résistance. It's a steep 15-minute walk from the **Porte Noire** (Black Gate; rue de la Convention), a triumphal arch left over from Besançon's Roman days, dating from the 2nd century AD.

Inside the walls of the citadel, and open at the same times, are three museums focusing on local culture: the **Musée Comtois**, the **Musée d'Histoire Naturelle** (Natural History Museum) and the **Musée de la Résistance et de la Déportation**, which examines the rise of Nazism and fascism and the French Resistance movement.

Less sobering are the colourful collections of insects, fish and nocturnal rodents exhibited in the **insectarium**, **aquarium** and **noctarium**. Siberian tigers prowl the **parc zoologique**. Admission to the citadel includes entry to all the museums.

HORLOGE ASTRONOMIQUE

Housed in the 18th-century **Cathédrale St-Jean** (rue de la Convention; admission €2.50; ⏰ closed Tue Apr-Sep, Tue & Wed Oct-Mar, closed Jan), this incredible astronomical clock has 30,000 moving parts, 62 dials and, among other things, tells the time in 16 places, the tides in eight different ports, and the time of sunrise and sunset. It really has to be seen to be believed. There are guided **tours** (⏰ 9.50-11.50am & 2.50-5.50pm).

Activities

Club Alpin Français (CAF; ☎ 03 81 81 02 77; 14 rue Luc Breton; ⏰ 5-7pm Tue-Fri) provides information on walking, skiing and mountain biking, and sells useful topoguides and maps.

Tours

Two boat companies based in Villers-le-Lac with vessels docked beneath the Pont de la République in Besançon – **CNFS** (☎ 03 81 68 05 34; fax 03 81 68 01 00; adult/child €8/7; ⏰ Jul & Aug) and **Les Vedettes Bisontines** (☎ 03 81 68 13 25; fax 03 81 68 09 85; adult/child €8/7; ⏰ Apr-Oct depending on weather conditions) – offer 1¼-hour river trips along the Boucle du Doubs. In summer there are usually three trips a day.

Sleeping

Auberge de Jeunesse Les Oiseaux (☎ 03 81 40 32 00; 48 rue des Cras; dm incl breakfast €20) Two kilometres east of the train station is this hostel. Rates include breakfast and bedding; subsequent nights cost €2 less. Take bus No 7 from the tourist office in the direction of Orchamps and get off at Les Oiseaux.

Hôtel du Nord (☎ 03 81 81 34 56; 8 rue Moncey; d €30-52; 🅿) Excellent city hotel along a smart street in the old quarter. The more expensive rooms are huge and have great, spacious bathrooms. Parking is off-site in an underground garage.

Hôtel de Paris (☎ 03 81 81 36 56; hoteldeparis@ hotmail.com; 33 rue des Granges; d €15-60; 🅿) One of the best deals in Besançon, this efficient and comfortable hotel has 60 rooms that vary in quality – ask to see a couple before you choose. The ample car park is a real bonus – entry to the car park is from rue de la République

Hôtel Regina (☎ 03 81 81 18 30; 91 Grande Rue; d €35-50; 🅿) Down a quiet alley in the heart of the old city, this two-star hotel offers cosy, floral rooms with shower, toilet and TV. There's

BESANÇON

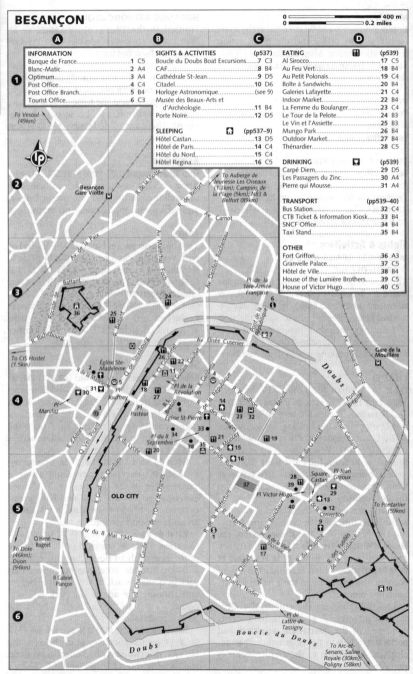

0 ————— 400 m
0 ————— 0.2 miles

INFORMATION	
Banque de France	1 C5
Blanc-Matic	2 A4
Optimum	3 A4
Post Office	4 C4
Post Office Branch	5 B4
Tourist Office	6 C3

SIGHTS & ACTIVITIES	(p537)
Boucle du Doubs Boat Excursions	7 C3
CAF	8 B4
Cathédrale St-Jean	9 D5
Citadel	10 D6
Horloge Astronomique	(see 9)
Musée des Beaux-Arts et	
d'Archéologie	11 B4
Porte Noire	12 D5

SLEEPING	(pp537–9)
Hôtel Castan	13 D5
Hôtel de Paris	14 C4
Hôtel du Nord	15 C4
Hôtel Regina	16 C5

EATING	(p539)
Al Sirocco	17 C5
Au Feu Vert	18 B4
Au Petit Polonais	19 C4
Boîte à Sandwichs	20 B4
Galeries Lafayette	21 C4
Indoor Market	22 B4
La Femme du Boulanger	23 C4
Le Tour de la Pelote	24 B3
Le Vin et l'Assiette	25 B3
Mungo Park	26 B4
Outdoor Market	27 B4
Thénardier	28 C5

DRINKING	(p539)
Carpé Diem	29 D5
Les Passagers du Zinc	30 A4
Pierre qui Mousse	31 A4

TRANSPORT	(pp539–40)
Bus Station	32 C4
CTB Ticket & Information Kiosk	33 B4
SNCF Office	34 B4
Taxi Stand	35 B4

OTHER	
Fort Griffon	36 A3
Granvelle Palace	37 C5
Hôtel de Ville	38 B4
House of the Lumière Brothers	39 C5
House of Victor Hugo	40 C5

enough parking space for just three cars in the lane.

Hôtel Castan (☎ 03 81 65 02 00; fax 03 81 83 01 02; 6 square Castan; d €65-95) Housed in an ivy-covered 18th-century townhouse on a little shaded square in the old city, this is one of the nicest places to stay in town. Book well ahead for one of the 10 tastefully furnished rooms.

CAMPING
Camping de la Plage (☎ 03 81 88 04 26; route de Belfort; camping €11; May-Sep) The closest camping ground is at Chalezeule, 5km northeast of Besançon on the N83.

Eating
RESTAURANTS
Au Petit Polonais (☎ 03 81 81 23 67; 81 rue Granges; mains €8-15; closed Sun & dinner Sat) One of Besançon's oldest restaurants, founded in 1870 by Polish émigrés and still pulling in the punters with delicious offerings of cooked meats, fondues and sausages.

Au Feu Vert (☎ 03 81 82 17 20; 11 place de la Révolution; menus from €9; noon-10.30pm) A simple restaurant with a colourful dining room and a cheap and generous *menu*, offering regional specialities such as *gratin de saucisse de Morteau* (a cheesy potato and sausage bake).

Thénardier (☎ 03 81 82 06 18; 11 place Victor Hugo; menus from €8) A good option for lunch, with cheap, filling salads, light meals, good coffee and speedy service.

Al Sirocco (☎ 03 81 82 24 05; 1 rue Chifflet; closed Sun & lunch Mon) Great, traditional Italian diner with little tables and fishing nets hanging from the ceiling. Locals come here for the best pizza and pasta in Besançon.

La Tour de la Pelote (☎ 03 81 82 14 58; 41 quai de Strasbourg; menus from €22; Tue-Sun) Popular with tourists and housed in a 16th-century stone tower. Offers the usual selection of French cuisine mixed with local specialities.

Le Vin et l'Assiette (☎ 03 81 81 48 18; 97 rue Battant; menu €18; Tue-Sat) An intimate bistro and wine bar, above the Caves Marcellin (Marcellin wine cellars). Sample local Jura wine accompanied by meats and cheeses.

Mungo Park (☎ 03 81 81 28 01; 11 rue Jean Petit; menus from €39-89; noon-3.30pm & 5.30-9.30pm Tue-Sat) Named after a Scottish explorer, this is one of the town's most renowned restaurants. Braised fish in peppered artichokes and Charollais beef fillet are just some of the items you might try.

QUICK EATS
La Femme du Boulanger (☎ 03 81 82 86 93; 6 rue Morand; cakes €2-5, breakfast €4-8) Scrumptious bakery and coffee bar, offering home-made breads, sweet and savoury tarts, healthy breakfasts and not-so-healthy cakes. There is no obvious sign outside, so look for the blackboard and the bread displays.

Boîte à Sandwichs (☎ 03 81 81 63 23; 21 rue du Lycée; sandwiches €2.80-4.50) Offers cheap, filling sandwiches.

SELF-CATERING
Fresh fish, meat, vegetables and cheeses are sold at the large **indoor market** (cnr rue Paris & rue Claude Goudimel). The nearby **outdoor market** (place de la Révolution) sells mainly fresh fruit and vegetables.

Galeries Lafayette (9am-7pm Mon-Sat) Enter from 69 Grande Rue or opposite the Hôtel de Paris on rue des Granges. There's a grocery section in the basement.

Drinking
Besançon is an old town with a young heart. The nightlife is mostly concentrated around the river and in the old Battant quarter.

Carpé Diem (☎ 03 81 83 11 18; 2 place Jean Gigoux; salads from €2.60 & plats du jour €8) A small, rough-and-ready café-bar. The wooden bar, smoky atmosphere and tattered posters covering the wall make it an ideal hangout for lost bohemians.

Pierre qui Mousse (☎ 03 81 81 15 25; 1 place Jouffrey; 9am-1am) A popular bar-brasserie right on the riverfront, where you can sup Belgian beer (€3.50) under low wooden beams. Happy hour is usually from 6pm to 7pm.

Les Passagers du Zinc (☎ 03 81 81 54 70; 5 rue de Vignier; 5pm-1am Tue-Fri, 5pm-2am Sat & Sun) A grungy bar and club that hosts tapas nights, live bands and music nights; it's where Besançon's hip brigade can be found by night. Step through the bonnet of an old Citroën DS to reach the cellar.

Getting There & Away
BUS
Buses operated by **Monts Jura** (☎ 08 25 00 22 44) depart from the **bus station** (9 rue Proudhon; 8-10am & 4-6.30pm Mon-Fri, 8am-1pm & 2.30-5.30pm Sat). There are daily services to Ornans and Pontarlier.

TRAIN
Around 800m uphill from the city centre is **Besançon Gare Viotte** (☎ 08 36 35 35 35; ticket office 5am-10.30pm). Train tickets can be bought in advance at the **SNCF office** (44 Grande Rue).

Major connections include Paris' Gare de Lyon (from €45 non-TGV, three hours, three daily), Dijon (€14, 50 minutes, 20 daily), Lyon (€32, three hours, eight daily), Belfort (€13, 1¼ hours, six daily), Arbois (€7.40, six to eight daily) and Arc-et-Senans (€5.60, 35 minutes, four daily). To get to Frasne (near Métabief), change trains in Mouchard (€12.90, 2½ hours).

Getting Around
BUS
Local buses are run by **CTB** (☎ 03 81 48 12 12), which has a **ticket & information kiosk** (place du 8 Septembre; 9am-12.30pm & 1-7pm Mon-Sat). A single ticket/day ticket/carnet of 10 costs €1/3.20/8.50. Bus Nos 8 and 24 link the train station with the centre.

TAXI
You can phone for a **taxi** (☎ 03 81 88 80 80) or pick one up next to the town hall.

AROUND BESANÇON
Saline Royal
Envisaged by its designer, Claude-Nicolas Ledoux, as the 'ideal city', the 18th-century **Saline Royale** (Royal Salt Works; ☎ 03 81 54 45 45; fax 03 81 54 45 46; adult/student/child €7/4.50/2.80; 9am-7pm Jul-Aug, 9am-6pm Jun & Sep, 9am-noon & 2-6pm Apr, May & Oct, 10am-noon & 2-5pm Nov-Dec, Jan-Mar) at **Arc-et-Senans**, 30km southwest of Besançon, is a showpiece of early Industrial Age town planning. Although his urban dream was never realised, Ledoux's semicircular saltworks is now listed as a Unesco World Heritage site.

The **tourist office** (☎ 03 81 57 43 21; www.ot-arcetsenans.fr; Saline Royale; 2-5pm Mon-Wed, 10am-noon & 2-5pm Fri & Sat, closed Thus & Sun) is housed inside the gateway of the Salt Works, and can help with finding local homestays and B&Bs. One option nearby is **Hotel Relais** (☎ 03 81 57 40 60; fax 03 81 57 46 17; d €32-35), a family-run place in the centre of the village, with 10 cosy double rooms in a traditional red-roofed house.

Camping des Bords de Loue (☎ 03 81 57 42 20, 03 81 57 43 21; camping €12-18; May-Oct) is a 1.5km-hike signposted off the main road.

There are regular trains running from Besançon (€5.60, 35 minutes, eight to 10 daily) to Arc-et-Senans.

Ornans
pop 4015
Ornans, 25km southeast of Besançon, is known as Franche-Comté's 'Little Venice'. The River Loue cuts through the heart of the pretty old town, above which towers the **Château d'Ornans**.

Realist painter Gustave Courbet (1819–77) was born in Ornans, and his house is now occupied by the **Musée Courbet** (☎ 03 81 62 23 30; summer/winter €6.70/3.40; 10am-noon & 2-6pm, closed Tue Nov-Mar), which displays some of the famous works of Courbet, including a self-portrait painted while he was in prison.

Chocoholics should aim to hit Ornans in March for the annual **Chocolate Festival** (☎ 03 81 40 21 01; www.rec-production.com).

The best hotel in Ornans is the smart **Hôtel de France** (☎ 03 81 62 24 44; hoteldefrance@europost.org; 51-53 rue Pierre-Vernier; P), opposite the bridge across the river Loue.

Close to Ornans, the **Vallée de la Loue** (Loue Valley) is a popular destination for mountain biking, canoeing and kayaking enthusiasts. Contact the **Syratu sports club** (☎ 03 81 57 10 82; fax 03 81 57 18 49; 2 route de Montgesoye) for information. Ornans' **tourist office** (☎ /fax 03 81 61 21 50; 7 rue Pierre Vernier; 9.30am-noon & 3-5.30pm Mon-Fri, 9.30am-noon & 2-6pm Sat) has plenty of walking and cycling information.

There are nine buses daily (€3.30, 45 minutes) from Besançon to Ornans.

Route Pasteur & Route du Vin
Nearly every town in the Jura seems to have a street, square or garden (sometimes all three) named after Louis Pasteur, the great 19th-century chemist who invented pasteurisation and developed the first rabies vaccine (he also made great leaps in the treatment of ailing silkworms). And rightly so – though much of his working life was spent in Paris, Pasteur was born and raised in the Jura, and he returned for holidays until his death in 1895.

Pasteur was born in **Dole**, 20km west of Arc-et-Senans along the D472. His childhood home, **La Maison Natale de Pasteur** (☎ 03 84 72 20 61; www.musee-pasteur.com; 43 rue Pasteur; adult/child €4.50/2; 10am-6pm Mon-Sat, 2-6pm Sun Jul & Aug, 10am-noon & 2-6pm Mon-Sat, 2-6pm Sun Apr-Jun, Sep & Oct,

10am-noon & 2-6pm Sat & Sun Nov-Mar), overlooking the Canal des Tanneurs in the old town, is now an atmospheric museum housing letters, artefacts and exhibits including his university cap and gown.

In 1827, the Pasteur family settled in the rural community of **Arbois**, about 35km east of Dole. His laboratory and workshops in Arbois are on display at **La Maison de Louis Pasteur** (☎ 03 84 66 11 72; 83 rue de Courcelles; adult/child €5.50/2.80). Visits are only by **tour** (⏰ hourly 9.45-11.45am & half-hourly 2.15-6.15pm Jun-Sep, hourly 2.15-5.15pm Apr, May & 1-15 Oct). The house is still decorated with its original 19th-century fixtures and fittings.

Despite his international reputation, Pasteur was an active member of village life, and often found himself called upon to dispense neighbourly advice on subjects ranging from sickly vines to sickly children (despite the fact that he was a chemist by profession). He also regularly took part in the **Fête de Bou**, a traditional harvest festival that still takes place every year in Arbois.

No visit to Arbois, the wine capital of the Jura, would be complete without sampling a glass of *vin jaune*. The history of this nutty 'yellow wine', which is matured for six years in oak casks, is recounted in the **Musée de la Vigne et du Vin** (☎ 03 84 66 26 14; percee@jura.vins .com; ⏰ 10am-noon & 2-6pm Wed-Mon Feb-Jun & Sep, 10am-6pm Wed-Mon Jul & Aug) inside the restored **Château Pécaud**, a turreted mansion that once formed part of the city's fortifications.

High above Arbois, along the twisting Route du Vin, is **Pupillin**, a quaint, yellow-brick village (population 220) famous for its wine production. Some 10 different *caves* are open to visitors, but there is no public transport to Pupillin and it's a long 2.5km walk uphill from Arbois.

The **tourist office** (☎ 03 84 37 47 37; www.arbois .com; rue de l'Hôtel de Ville; ⏰ 9.30am-noon & 2-6pm Sep-Easter, 9am-12.30pm & 2-6.30pm Easter-Sep) offers advice on cycling routes in the Arbois area. The SNCF office is housed in the same building. There are regular trains to Arbois from Besançon via Mouchard (€14.80, 40 minutes, eight to 10 daily).

Poligny & Baume-les-Messieurs

Whereas much of nearby Burgundy relies on the fruits of the vine for its livelihood, the Jura is best known for its cheese. Poligny is the capital of the Comté cheese-making industry, and you can find out all about this venerable cheese at the **Maison du Comté** (☎ 03 84 37 23 51; av de la Résistance; admission free; ⏰ 9.30am-noon & 2.30-5pm Tue-Sun summer).

Some 40 million tonnes of Comté are produced each year, mostly by *fruitières* (cheese dairies) located in the Franche-Comté area. The **tourist office** (☎ 03 84 37 24 21; tourisme.poligny@ wanadoo.fr; rue Victor Hugo; ⏰ 9am-noon & 2-6pm Mon-Fri,

---

THE CHEESE ROUTE

One of the best ways to taste the Jura's cheeses is to head to a traditional *fruitière* (cheese dairy). Not only will you be able to see cheeses being made in the traditional way, you'll also get to sample regional varieties including Comté, Morbier, Bleu de Gex and Mont d'Or.

Le Hameau du Fromage (☎ 03 81 62 41 51; Cleron, 7km west of Ornans; www.hameaudufromage.com; ⏰ 9am-7pm year-round) This is a good place to start your tour, with two films on cheese-making (in English on request), a cheese museum, cheese restaurant and huge cheese shop.

Fructeries Vagne de Château-Chalon (☎ 03 84 44 92 25; vagne-fromageries@wanadoo.fr; Château-Chalon, 10km southwest of Poligny; ⏰ 11am-12.30pm & 2-7pm mid-Jun–mid-Sep, 11am-12.30pm & 2-6pm Fri-Sun rest of year) Traditional village *fruitière* offering guided tours and tastings of most of the region's main cheeses.

Musées des Maisons Comtoises (☎ 03 81 55 29 77; maisons-comtoises.org; Nancray, 20km east of Besançon; ⏰ 10am-7pm Apr-Oct, 2-5pm mid-Mar–Apr & Oct–mid-Nov) Reconstructed cheese farm dating from the 19th century, now turned into an intriguing museum.

La Fruitière du Massif Jurassien (☎ 03 84 51 24 00; juraterroir.com; Pont-du-Navoy, 10km southeast of Poligny; ⏰ 8am-noon & 2-6pm) One of the largest Comté producers in the Jura. Tasting and tours available.

Fruitière bio de la Chaux de Gilley (☎ 03 81 43 30 35; La Chaux, 20km northeast of Pontarlier; ⏰ 9am-noon & 6-7pm) One of the only entirely organic cheese farms in the region. English, German and Spanish tours available.

For further info, check out **www.lesroutesducomte.com**, where you'll find other theme tours around the Jura, including suggested routes through the region's lakes, forests, and clock-making centres.

9am-noon & 2-5.30pm Sat) in Poligny has a list of local cheese shops that visitors can tour.

Baume-les-Messieurs (population 200) is an extraordinarily pretty village of cob houses and red-tiled rooftops, nestled between three glacial valleys, 20km south of Poligny. The town is best known for its abandoned **Benedictine abbey** (☎ 03 84 44 99 28; admission €3; ☼ 10am-6pm mid-Jun–mid-Sep). Nearby, the **Grottes de Baume** (Baume Caves; ☎ 03 84 44 61 58), are accessible by road from the foot of the 10m-tall **Cascade de Baume** (Baume Waterfall). Guided **tours** (☼ 10am-5.30pm Apr-Sep) of the 30 million-year-old caves are available.

Immediately to the east of Baume-les-Messieurs is the Jura's **Région des Lacs** (Lakes District).

SLEEPING & EATING

Opposite Baume-les-Messieurs' abbey is **Le Grand Jardin** (☎ 03 84 44 68 37; d €45-60), a traditional village house offering quaint double rooms. Book well ahead in summer.

Café de l'Abbaye (☎ 03 84 44 63 44; ☼ lunch & dinner Mon-Sat summer) is a lovely little café in one of the abbey's old buildings which offers salads, cheese tarts, *tartiflette* and a delicious *cassolette franc-comtoise* (a casserole of potatoes, onions, cheese and local sausage).

Le Comptois (☎ /fax 03 84 25 71 21; d €35-55) is some 5km east in Doucier. Don't miss out on its Jurassien fondue. Le Comptois also organises gastronomic tours of the region.

BELFORT & AROUND

Belfort (population 50,125), just across the border from Germany and Switzerland, is as Alsatian as it is Jurassien. Historically part of Alsace, it became part of the Franche-Comté region in 1921. Today the city is best known as the manufacturer of the TGV train.

Belfort's **tourist office** (☎ 03 84 55 90 90; www .ot-belfort.fr; 2 rue Clemenceau; ☎ 9am-noon & 2-6pm Mon-Fri) can provide city maps and accommodation lists.

The **Musée d'Art et d'Histoire** (☎ 03 84 54 25 51; ☎ 10am-6pm, Wed-Mon Apr-Sep, 10am-noon & 2-6pm Wed-Mon Oct-Apr) is inside the **Vauban citadel**. Open-air concerts are held on Wednesday in summer. At the foot of the citadel stands **Le Lion de Belfort**, created by Frédéric-Auguste Bartholdi, who also designed the Statue of Liberty in New York. The 11m-tall lion commemorates Belfort's resistance to the Prussians in 1870–71 – while the rest of Alsace was annexed as part of the greater German Empire, Belfort stubbornly remained a part of France.

In July, Belfort hosts **Les Eurockéennes** (☎ 03 84 57 01 92; fax 03 84 28 15 12), a three-day open-air rock festival. In **Sochaux**, 12km south of Belfort near Montbéliard , car enthusiasts can visit the **Musée Peugeot** (☎ 03 81 99 42 03; adult/child €7/3.50; ☎ 10am-6pm). The modernist **Sacré-Coeur church** at Audincourt, 4km southeast, is a must for architecture buffs.

The **Massif du Ballon d'Alsace** (1247m), 20km north of Belfort in the southern Vosges Mountains, offers winter skiing, summer walking, mountain biking, kayaking and hot-air ballooning.

Ronchamp

Ronchamp has a **tourist office** (☎ 03 84 63 50 82; 14 place du 14 Juillet; ☎ 9am-noon & 2-6pm Mon & Fri, 9am-noon & 2-5pm Sat Jun-Oct).

La Chapelle de Notre Dame du Haut (Chapel of our Lady of the Height; ☎ 03 84 20 65 13; admission €2; ☎ 9.30am-6.30pm Apr-Sep, to 4pm Oct-Mar), Ronchamp's striking modernist chapel, sits on a hill overlooking the old mining town, 20km west of Belfort. Designed by the Swiss architect Le Corbusier between 1950 and 1955 to replace a church destroyed in WWII, the chapel is considered one of the 20th century's architectural masterpieces – making it a pilgrimage site for thousands of architects every year. The chapel's surreal design and sweeping concrete roof are said to have been inspired by a hermit crab shell.

In summer, Sunday service is at 11am. Over 3000 pilgrims gather here each year on 8 September. A 15-minute walking trail leads uphill from the centre of Ronchamp to the chapel.

Sleeping & Eating

In Ronchamp, **Hôtel à la Pomme d'Or** (☎ 03 84 20 62 12; fax 03 84 63 59 45; d €38-45) is at the foot of the hill leading up to the chapel, while the rustic **Hôtel Carrer** (☎ 03 84 20 62 32; fax 03 84 63 57 08; d €35-40) is 2km north of Ronchamp in Le Rhien.

Don't leave Belfort without biting into a Belfore, a scrumptious almond-flavoured pastry filled with raspberries and topped with hazelnuts.

HOT BOX, CHRISTMAS ICE & JESUS

It's hot, it's soft and it's packed in a box. *Vacherin Mont d'Or* is the only French cheese to be eaten with a spoon – hot (or cold for that matter). Made between 15 August and 15 March with *lait cru* (unpasteurised milk), it derives its unique nutty taste from the spruce bark in which it's wrapped.

Louis XV adored it. In the 18th century it was called fat cheese, wood cheese or box cheese. Today, *vacherin Mont d'Or* is named after the mountain village from which it originates. Connoisseurs top the soft-crusted cheese with chopped onions, garlic and white wine, wrap it in aluminium foil and bake it for 45 minutes to create a *boîte chaude* (hot box).

Only 11 factories in the Jura are licensed to produce *vacherin Mont d'Or* which, ironically, has sold like hot cakes since 1987, when 10 people in Switzerland died from listeriosis after consuming the Swiss version of Mont d'Or. Old-fashioned cheese buffs in Mont d'Or believe the bacterial tragedy, which claimed 34 lives between 1983 and 1987, only happened because the Swiss copycats pasteurised their milk.

Mouthe, 15km south of Métabief Mont d'Or, is the mother of *liqueur de sapin* (fir-tree liqueur). *Glace de sapin* (fir-tree ice cream) also comes from Mont d'Or, known as the North Pole of France due to its seasonal sub-zero temperatures (record low –38°C). Sampling either is rather like ingesting a Christmas tree. Then there's Jesus. *Jésus* – a small, fat version of *saucisse de Morteau* (Morteau sausage) – is the gastronomic delight of the village of Morteau. *Jésus* is easily identified by the wooden peg on its end, attached after the sausage is smoked with pine-wood sawdust in a traditional *tuyé* (mountain hut). Morteau residents claim their sausage is bigger and better than any other French sausage. They host a **sausage festival** (☎ 03 81 50 69 43) every August.

Getting There & Away

Major connections from Belfort's train station include Paris' Gare de Lyon via Besançon (from €53, 4½ hours, three daily), Montbéliard (€3.10, 15 minutes, 20 daily) and Besançon (€13, 1¼ hours, six daily).

From Belfort there are one or two trains a day to/from Ronchamp (€3.80, 20 minutes). On weekdays there are also two buses a day to/from Ronchamp (€3.60, 35 minutes).

MÉTABIEF MONT D'OR

pop 700 / elevation 1000m

Métabief Mont d'Or, 18km south of Pontarlier on the main road to Lausanne, is the region's leading cross-country ski resort. All year, lifts take you almost to the top of Mont d'Or (1463m), the area's highest peak, from where a fantastic 180° panorama stretches over the foggy Swiss plain to Lake Geneva (Lac Léman) and from the Matterhorn all the way to Mont Blanc. Métabief is famed for its unique *vacherin Mont d'Or* cheese.

Orientation & Information

The main lift station for downhill skiers is in Métabief. There are smaller lifts in Les Hôpitaux Neufs, 2km northeast.

In Métabief, the local **tourist office** (☎ 03 81 49 16 79; ot@metabief-montdor.com; ☻ 9am-noon & 2-5pm, closed Sun Sep–mid-Dec) and **École du Ski Français** (ESF; ☎ 03 81 49 04 21; ☻ 9am-noon & 2-5pm) are housed in the **Centre d'Accueil** (6 place Xavier Authier).

There is another **tourist office** (☎ 03 81 49 13 81; fax 03 81 49 09 27; 1 place de la Mairie) in Les Hôpitaux Neufs, open until 6pm daily in season.

Fromagerie du Mont d'Or

Comté, *morbier* and *vacherin Mont d'Or* cheese have been produced by the Sancey-Richard family in Métabief since 1953. The **Fromagerie du Mont d'Or** (☎ 03 81 49 02 36; www.fromageriedumontdor.fr; rue Moulin; admission free; cheese shop ☻ 9am-12.15pm & 3-7pm Mon-Sat, 9am-noon Sun), which produces over 200 tonnes of cheese a year, is open to visitors. Guided **tours** (☻ 9.30am) include a visit to the dairy's salting rooms, where the *vacherin Mont d'Or* cheeses are washed with salt water, and the maturing cellars where the 45kg rounds of Comté cheese are turned by hand twice weekly for up to 12 months. If you want to see cheese being made, arrive with the milk lorry before 10.30am.

Sleeping & Eating

Both tourist offices have comprehensive lists of hotels and apartments to rent in Métabief.

FRENCH ALPS & THE JURA

GRANDE TRAVERSÉE DU JURA

The Grande Traversée du Jura (GTJ) – the Grand Jura Crossing – is a 210km cross-country skiing track from Villers-le-Lac (north of Pontarlier) to Hauteville-Lompnes (southwest of Bellegarde). The path peaks at 1500m near the town of Mouthe (south of Métabief) and follows one of the coldest valleys in France. After the first 20km the route briefly crosses into Switzerland, but mostly runs along the border on the French side. Well maintained and very popular, the track takes 10 full days of skiing to cover – a feat even for the ultrafit.

Part of the GTJ – the 76km from Lamoura to Mouthe – is traversed each year during the world's second-largest cross-country skiing competition, the Transjurassienne. Held in late February, the challenge is taken up by more than 4000 skiers, who charge off in a blaze of colour.

For information on the GTJ and accommodation along the route, contact **Relais de Randonnée Étapes Jura** (☎ 03 84 41 20 34; F-39310 Lajoux); or **GTJ-Espace Nordique Jurassien** (☎ 03 84 52 58 10; rue Baronne-Delort, F-39300 Champagnole). The best map of the area is the IGN 1:50,000-scale map entitled *Ski de Fond – Massif du Jura*.

Hôtel Étoile des Neiges (☎ 03 81 49 11 21; fax 03 81 49 26 91; rue du Village; s/d/tr low season €49/59/72; menus €10-28), in Métabief, is a family-run chalet with good, cosy rooms. Local dishes such as *raclette*, fondue Comtoise, *Mont d'Or chaud* and *la saucisse Jésus de Morteau* are served in its excellent restaurant, which is also open to nonguests. Tickle your tastebuds first with a hearty shot of *anis de Pontarlier* (a liquorice-flavoured aperitif), the Jura's answer to Provençal pastis.

Getting There & Away

The closest **train station** (☎ 08 36 35 35 35) is at Frasne, 25km northwest on the rail line between Dijon, Arc-et-Senans and Vallorbe (9km east in Switzerland). From Frasne, there are daily buses that pass through Métabief and Les Hôpitaux Neufs.

AROUND MÉTABIEF MONT D'OR

Winter skiers keen for a break from the slopes should head a few kilometres south to **L'Odyssée Blanche – Parc du Chien Polaire** (White Odyssey Polar Dog Park; ☎ 03 81 69 20 20; fax 03 81 69 13 02; adult/child €6.50/4.90; ☺ 10am-noon & 2-6pm Tue-Sun) in Chaux Neuve. Try your hand at 'mushing' on a dog-drawn sledge, or simply tour the kennels and coo over the huskies and malamutes instead. A 90-minute dog sleigh expedition costs €45 to €50.

The **Château de Joux** (☎ 03 81 69 47 95; adult/student/child €5/4.25/2.55; ☺ 9am-6pm Jul-Aug, 10-11.30am & 2-4.30pm Apr-Jun, tours 10am, 11.30am, 2pm, 3.15pm & 4.15pm Oct-May), 10km north of Métabief, guards the entrance from Switzerland into northern and central France. It sits atop Mont Larmont (922m), overlooking a dramatic **cluse**

(transverse valley). Part of *Les Misérables* (1995) was filmed here, and during the First Empire, the castle was a state prison. Today it houses France's most impressive arms museum. The music and theatre festival, **Festival des Nuits de Joux**, takes place here in mid-July.

Montbenoît (population 230), 20km further north, is the capital of the tiny **Saugeais Republic**. The folkloric republic, declared in 1947, has its own flag, national anthem, postage stamp and a 94-year-old president, Gabrielle Pourchet, who is featured on the Saugeais banknote. During summer a customs officer greets tourists as they enter the town.

PARC NATUREL RÉGIONAL DU HAUT-JURA

The Haut-Jura Regional Park covers an area of 757 sq km, stretching from Chapelle-des-Bois in the north almost to the western tip of Lake Geneva. Each year in February its abundant lakes, mountains and low-lying valleys play host to the Transjurassienne, the world's second longest cross-country skiing race (above). Exploring this region is difficult without private transport.

The largest town in the park, **Ste-Claude** (population 12,704), is best known for its illustrious wooden pipe-making and diamond-cutting traditions, the history of which unfolds in the local pipe and diamond museum. The **CAF** (☎ 03 84 45 58 62; fax 03 84 60 36 88; 8 blvd de la République) provides information on its *refuges* in the Jura. Dubbed the French capital of wooden toys, **Moirans-en-Montagne**, 14km west, is an apt home for the playful **Musée du Jouet** (Toy Museum).

Les Rousses (population 2850, elevation 1100m) on the northeastern edge of the park, is the main centre for winter sports, walking and mountain biking. Three of its four small, gently sloped downhill ski areas – Les Jouvencelles, Le Noirmont and La Serra – are in France; the fourth – La Dole – is in Switzerland. Extensive cross-country trails take skiers as far north as Métabief Mont d'Or as well as eastwards across the Swiss border.

The **tourist office** (☎ 03 84 60 02 55; www.les rousses.com; rue Pasteur), **SNCF bureau** (☎ 03 84 60 01 90) and the **Club des Sports** (☎ 03 84 60 35 14) are inside the **Maison du Tourisme** (route Blanche), next to the bus station.

The Jura's most staggering view can be savoured from the **Col de la Faucille**, 20km south of Les Rousses. As the N5 twists and turns its way down the Jura Mountains past the small ski resort of **Mijoux**, the panoramic view of Lake Geneva embraced by the French Alps and Mont Blanc beyond is startling. For the best vantage point, take a *télécabine* from Mijoux or head for the terrace restaurant of La Mainaz (right).

Continuing a further 25km southeast you arrive at the French–Swiss border, passing through **Ferney-Voltaire**, 5km north of Geneva en route. Following his banishment from Switzerland in 1759, Voltaire lived in Ferney until his return to Paris and death in 1778. There are guided **tours** (admission €4; ☺ 10am-6pm Oct-Apr, closed Mon May-Sep) of his estate, which includes a chateau, chapel and seven-hectare park. Past visitors include Auden, Blake and Flaubert, all of whom wrote about the philosopher's home in exile.

AUTHOR'S CHOICE

La Mainaz (☎ 04 50 41 31 10; mainaz@club -Internet.fr; 5 route du Col de la Faucille; d €57-89) What better way to round off your journey in the Jura than at this beautiful, classy hotel, at the edge of the Haut-Jura National Park? There are lots of luxury hotels in the Alps, but you'll need a second mortgage to pay for most of them – the Mainaz manages to combine old-fashioned Alpine charm, modern-day comfort and fantastic value. The rooms are spacious and beautifully presented, but the real draw is the absolutely unbelievable view of the Alps, which you can savour either from your room or the panoramic restaurant terrace. By sunset it's a sight never forgotten.

Massif Central

CONTENTS

Clermont-Ferrand	548
Around Clermont-Ferrand	553
Parc Naturel Régional	
des Volcans d'Auvergne	**554**
Vichy	554
Orcival	558
Col de Guéry	558
Le Mont-Dore	558
Around le Mont-Dore	561
Puy Mary	562
Murat	562
Parc Naturel Régional	
Livradois-Forez	**563**
Thiers	563
Ambert	564
La Chaise Dieu	564
Le Puy-en-Velay	564
Around Le Puy-en-Velay	568

The Massif Central is France's spine, its vertebrae the spiky plugs and rounded grassy cones of extinct volcanoes called *puys*, (pronounced 'pwee'). Down in the relatively rich volcanic soil of its plains and valleys, maize, tobacco and vines all thrive. Its rumpled slopes are clad in either dense forest or pasture, offering sweet grazing for the cattle and sheep that are the source of Auvergnat cheeses, some of France's finest.

At valley level too you'll find spa towns that these days pull in both the hale and those seeking health. Vichy is for those who treasure a touch of faded elegance while St-Nectaire, home to the smooth, eponymous cheese, and Le Mont-Dore, ski resort in winter and summertime trekking base, both still speak of *la belle époque*.

Clermont-Ferrand is the only city of consequence. It's home to the Michelin tyre giant – though you'd never guess it as you roam the narrow streets of the old quarter. It's a great base for exploring the northern *puys* – and for visiting Vulcania, a breathtaking multimedia exhibition about all things volcanic.

But the Massif Central, with its superb walking and mountain biking, is above all for those who love the great outdoors. Two large regional parks, the dramatic Parc Naturel Régional des Volcans d'Auvergne and its tamer eastern neighbour, the Parc Naturel Régional du Livradois-Forez, together make up France's largest environmentally protected area. And from the Massif Central, which is roughly coextensive with the Auvergne, trickle the myriad streams that band together to form some of France's mightiest rivers such as the Dordogne, Allier and Loire.

MASSIF CENTRAL

HIGHLIGHTS

- Drink in views of all southeastern France from **Mont Mézenc's summit** (p569)
- Live a little of the *belle époque* life in the spa town of **Vichy** (p554)
- Puff your way to the tiptop of spectacular **Puy Mary** (p562)
- Survive a virtual volcanic eruption at state-of-the-art **Vulcania** (p553)
- Crunch across **volcanic cinders** (p554), tiny and light as Rice Krispies
- Tuck into windy picnics up high, sampling each day a different **Auvergnat cheese** (p562)

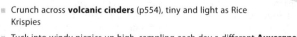

- POPULATION: 1,310,000
- AREA: 26,015 SQ KM

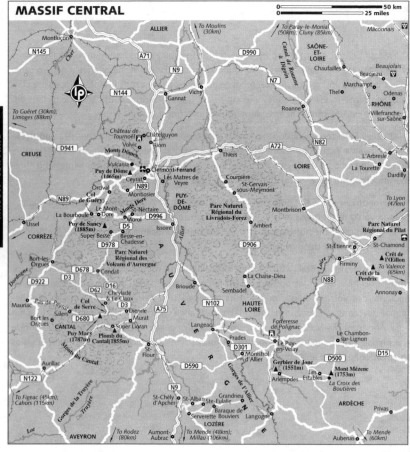

MASSIF CENTRAL

Activities

Walking rivals skiing as the most popular activity in the Massif Central, which is crisscrossed by 13 GR tracks (including the spectacular GR4, which cuts through the range from north to south) and hundreds of other footpaths. Some of these trails are also suitable for mountain biking and the publisher Chamina puts out a series of excellent topoguides for the region.

Several ski resorts, particularly Le Mont-Dore, Super Besse and Super Lioran (near Murat), provide full Alpine skiing facilities and the Massif Central's undulating terrain is great for cross-country skiing.

The region's topography and thermal currents also mean it's ideal for hang-gliding

and *parapente* (paragliding), for which the *puys* are used as take-off platforms (p553).

CLERMONT-FERRAND

pop 137,000 / elevation 400m

The lively city of Clermont-Ferrand, the Massif Central's principal urban centre, makes a good base for exploring the north of the region. A student population of some 30,000 gives vitality to the town centre, built on top of a long-extinct volcano.

Clermont-Ferrand is the centre of France's rubber industry, better known to the world as the Michelin tyre empire. The company got into the sideline of guidebook publishing in 1898 to promote motor-car tourism – and thus the use of its pneumatic tyres.

Orientation

The old city is bounded by av des États-Unis, rue André Moinier and blvd Trudaine. The partly pedestrianised commercial centre stretches westwards from the cathedral to av des États-Unis and place de Jaude, then along rue Blatin.

Information

BOOKSHOP
Book'in (☎ 04 73 36 40 06; 38 av des États-Unis) Has a small selection of used English-language books.

INTERNET ACCESS
Lepton (16 av des Paulines; per hr €2.50; ☺ 11am-midnight Mon-Sat, 2pm-midnight Sun; from 2pm school holidays)
Visio2 Paulines (14 av des Paulines; per hr €2.50; ☺ 10am-midnight Mon-Sat, 1-8pm Sun) Carnot (11 av Carnot; per hr €2.50; ☺ 10am-midnight Mon-Sat)

LAUNDRY
Laundrette (6 place Hippolyte Renoux; ☺ 7am-8.30pm)

POST
Main Post Office (rue Maurice Busset)

TOURIST INFORMATION
Espace Massif Central (☎ 04 73 42 60 00; ☺ Mon-Sat) In the same building as the tourist office and observing similar hours. Provides information on the region's outdoor activities. Partly run by Chamina, the excellent Massif Central topoguide publisher, it carries a full range of walking guides.
Tourist Office (☎ 04 73 98 65 00; www.clermont-fd .com; place de la Victoire; ☺ 9am-7pm Mon-Fri, 10am-6pm Sat & Sun May-Sep; 9am-6pm Mon-Fri, 10am-1pm & 2-7pm Sat, 9.30am-12.30pm & 2-6pm Sun Oct-Apr) *Espace Art Roman* downstairs is an excellent free exhibition highlighting the region's outstanding Romanesque churches. There's a 30-minute film with optional English audio.

Sights

The soaring, Gothic **Cathédrale Notre Dame** (☺ 8am-6pm Jun–mid-Sep, 8am-noon & 2-6pm mid-Sep–May) looks smog-blackened and grim. But the structure's volcanic stones, dug from the quarries of nearby Volvic, were the same blackish-grey hue the day the finishing touches were put to the choir seven centuries ago.

The twin towers are from the 19th century, when the west façade too was restored by the Gothic revivalist Viollet-le-Duc. The architects took full advantage of the strength yet lightness of Volvic stone to create a vast, double-aisled nave, held aloft by particularly slender pillars and vaults. Stand before the altar steps and marvel at the glowing 14th-century rose windows at each end of the transept. Several stained glass windows in the choir and side-chapels are also from the 13th and 14th centuries.

From place de la Poterne and its early-16th-century **Fontaine d'Amboise**, two blocks north of the cathedral, there's a fine view of the Puy de Dôme and nearby peaks.

Flanking the narrow streets east of the cathedral are some of Clermont-Ferrand's finest 17th- and 18th-century townhouses, including **Hôtel Reboul-Sadourny** (9 rue Savaron), fronting a small courtyard, and **Hôtel de Chazerat** (4 rue Blaise Pascal).

Rue Blaise Pascal, with several antique shops that merit a browse, leads, via rue du Port, to the 12th-century **Basilique Notre Dame du Port** (☺ 8am-8pm May-Sep, 8am-6pm Oct-Apr), a Unesco World Heritage Site. The highlight of this truly magnificent example of Auvergnat-Romanesque is its choir, into which the light streams on a summer's day. Notice too the delightfully naive carving on the capitals of the four easternmost pillars.

The **Musée Bargoin** (☎ 04 73 91 37 31; 45 rue Ballainvilliers; adult/student/child €4/2.50/free; ☺ 10am-noon & 1-6pm Tue-Sat, 2-5pm Sun) has excellent prehistory and Gallo-Roman sections on the ground floor. Between November and March it mounts temporary exhibitions upstairs.

Just down the street, **Musée Lecoq** (☎ 04 73 91 93 78; 15 rue Bardoux; adult/student/under 18 €4/2/free; ☺ 10am-noon & 2-6pm Mon-Sat May-Sep, to 5pm Oct-Apr; 2-6pm Sun year-round) is a natural history museum with an impressive collection of rocks, fossils, stuffed fauna and pickled things that creep.

The most striking feature of **Place de Jaude**, the city's main square, is the equestrian statue of Vercingétorix, the Celtic chief who almost foiled Julius Caesar's conquest of Gaul (p551).

The quiet, none-too-prosperous suburb of **Montferrand**, 2.5km northeast of the cathedral, beyond the vast Michelin works, is worth a visit for its many **Gothic and Renaissance houses**, especially around where rue de la Rodade meets rue des Cordeliers. Many have stone-built ground floors and overhanging, half-timbered upper floors.

MASSIF CENTRAL

CLERMONT-FERRAND

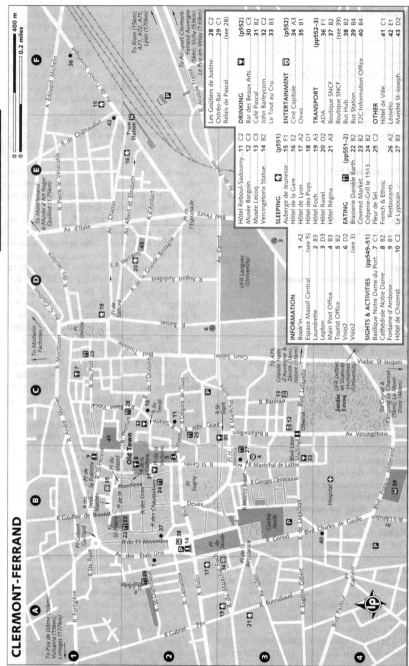

0 — 0 — **400 m**
0 — 0 — **0.2 miles**

To Riom (15km);
A71, A72, A75;
Lyon (170km)

To Aéroport Clermont-
Ferrand Auvergne
(5km); Vichy (53km);
Le Puy-en-Velay (130km)

To Montferrand
& Musée d'Art Roger
Quilliot (1.75km)

To Michelin
Factories

To Puy de Dôme (10km);
Volcania (15km);
Limoges (177km)

To A75;
Grande Halle
d'Auvergne (3km);
Issoire (38km)

To Ceyrat &
Camping Le Chanset
(5km); Le Mont-
Dore (46km)

INFORMATION	
Book'in......................................	1 A2
Espace Massif Central................	(see 5)
Laundrette................................	2 B3
Lepton......................................	3 D3
Main Post Office.......................	4 B3
Tourist Office............................	5 D2
Visio2.......................................	6 D2
Visio2.......................................	(see 3)

SIGHTS & ACTIVITIES	(pp549–51)
Basilique Notre Dame du Port....	7 C1
Cathédrale Notre Dame..............	8 B2
Fontaine d'Amboise...................	9 B1
Hôtel de Chazerat......................	10 C2

Hôtel Reboul-Sadourny..............	11 C2
Musée Bargoin...........................	12 C3
Musée Lecoq.............................	13 C3
Vercingétorix Statue..................	14 B2

SLEEPING	(p551)
Auberge de Jeunesse..................	15 F1
Hôtel de la Gare........................	16 E2
Hôtel de Lyon...........................	17 A2
Hôtel des Puys...........................	18 D1
Hôtel Foch................................	19 A3
Hôtel Ravel................................	20 D2
Hôtel Regina.............................	21 A3

EATING	(pp551–2)
Brasserie Danièle Barth..............	22 B2
Covered Market.........................	23 B2
Crêperie-Grille 1513..................	24 B2
Fleur de Sel...............................	25 C2
French & Ethnic	
Restaurants............................	26 A2
Le Lypocan................................	27 B3

DRINKING	(p552)
Les Goûtiers de Justine..............	28 C2
Ostréo-Bar................................	29 C1
Relais de Pascal.........................	(see 28)
Bar des Beaux Arts.....................	30 C3
Café Pascal................................	31 B2
John Barleycorn.........................	32 C2
Le Tout au Cru...........................	33 B3

ENTERTAINMENT	(p552)
Ciné Capitole.............................	34 A3
Oxxo...	35 B1

TRANSPORT	(pp552–3)
ADA..	36 F1
Boutique SNCF..........................	37 B2
Boutique SNCF..........................	(see 39)
Bus Hub....................................	38 B4
Bus Station...............................	39 B4
T2C Information Office...............	40 B4

OTHER	
Hôtel de Ville............................	41 C1
Léovelo.....................................	42 E1
Marché St-Joseph......................	43 D2

Viaduc St-Jacques

Old Town

Train Station

CELTIC HERO

Vercingétorix, chief of the Celtic Arverni tribe, almost foiled Julius Caesar's conquest of Gaul. With most of Gaul overrun and Caesar slyly playing one tribe off against the other, Vercingétorix pulled together the tribes between the Loire and Garonne rivers and forged a force that could match the Roman legions in discipline.

In the summer of 52 BC, it thrashed Caesar's troops at Gergovia near Clermont-Ferrand, in the tribe's heartland. Glimpsing hope, all but five of the Gallic tribes rose against Rome and joined forces, led by Vercingétorix.

For a couple of years, the Gauls hounded the Romans with guerrilla warfare and stood up to them in several match-drawn pitched battles. But gradually Gallic resistance collapsed and Roman rule in Gaul reigned supreme.

Vercingétorix was captured and taken to Rome, where he was paraded in chains in Caesar's triumphal procession. As a final insult, he was left languishing in prison for six years before being put to death by strangulation.

The **Musée d'Art Roger Quilliot** (☎ 04 73 16 11 30; place Louis Deteix; adult/child €4/free; �' 10am-6pm Tue-Sun) is an excellent fine arts museum in an architecturally superb complex in Montferrand. It has a fascinating, chronologically arranged collection of sculpture, painting and art objects from the late Middle Ages to the 20th century. To get to Montferrand, take bus No 16 from place de Jaude or Nos 1 and 9 from the bus station.

Sleeping
Auberge de Jeunesse (☎ 04 73 92 26 39; fax 04 73 92 99 96; 55 av de l'Union Soviétique; dm €8.90; ☑ May-Oct) The Auberge du Cheval Blanc (White Horse Inn), Clermont's HI-affiliated hostel, is only 100m from the bus and train stations.

Hôtel Ravel (☎ 04 73 91 51 33; hotelravel63@ wanadoo.fr; 8 rue de Maringues; s/d €35/42) With its eccentric mosaic façade and pleasant old-fashioned rooms, the Ravel is a good bet if you like your accommodation with character – something the landlady too has, in spades! It's in a quiet part of town, where the only bustle comes from the St-Joseph morning market, around which there's free parking, once evening falls.

Hôtel de la Gare (☎ 04 73 92 07 82; garehotel63@aol .com; 76 av Charras; s/d €35/40) One of several hotels in a quiet street near the train station, the 19-room Hôtel de la Gare, fully renovated in 2003, is a good two-star choice.

Hôtel Régina (☎ 04 73 93 44 76; regina.foch@ wanadoo.fr; 14 rue Bonnabaud; d €36, s/d with bathroom €46/52; P) On a quiet street, just off place de Jaude in the heart of town, Hôtel Régina has trim, comfortable rooms and private parking (€6) right opposite.

Hôtel Foch (☎ 04 73 93 48 40; regina.foch@wanadoo .fr; 22 rue Maréchal Foch; d €32, s with bathroom €37-46, d €42-50; P) Owned by the same family as the Régina, Hôtel Foch is an equally central, marginally more economical choice with smaller rooms, some of which have air-con.

Hôtel de Lyon (☎ 04 73 17 60 80; hotelde.lyon@ wanadoo.fr; 16 place de Jaude; s €53.50-60.50, d €67-75; P) This 33-room hotel on place de Jaude couldn't possibly be more central – and it has private parking so your car needn't be an encumbrance. Most rooms overlook the square and are double glazed throughout so you needn't be apprehensive about noise from the square-side pub.

Hôtel des Puys (☎ 04 73 91 92 06; www.hoteldespuys .fr; 16 place Delille; s €67-75, d €83-90; P) In most rooms, toilet and bathroom are separate and the majority share a balcony overlooking busy place Delille. All have been recently and comprehensively renovated and – rare for France – one floor is reserved for nonsmokers. Equally recently renamed, this three-star hotel still features in many information sources as Hôtel des Puys d'Arverne.

CAMPING
Camping Le Chanset (☎ 04 73 61 30 73; camping .lechanset@wanadoo.fr; av Jean Baptiste, Ceyrat; per person/tent/car €2.60/4/1.50; ☑ year-round) The nearest camping ground is in Ceyrat, virtually a suburb of Clermont-Ferrand. Bus No 4 stops right outside.

Eating
RESTAURANTS
Two blocks north of place de Jaude, rue St-Dominique and nearby rue St-Adjutor

sprawl with reasonably priced **French and eth-nic restaurants**, including Tunisian, Indian, Vietnamese, Italian, Tex-Mex, Portuguese and Cuban.

Brasserie Danièle Bath (☎ 04 73 31 23 22; place St-Pierre; menu €21, mains €15-25; ☺ Tue-Sat, closed mid-end Feb & 18-31 Aug) This classy little place serves top-quality dishes based on fresh local ingredients from the central market opposite. Dining is a delight on its summer terrace.

Fleur de Sel (☎ 04 73 90 30 59; 8 rue Abbé Girard; menus €25 & €40, mains €25-30; ☺ Tue-Sat Sep-Jul) Fleur de Sel specialises in fine fish and seafood, which feature in every dish except the desserts. It's small, stylishly furnished and popular so you'll need to reserve.

Relais de Pascal (☎ 04 73 92 21 04; 15 rue Blaise Pascal; weekday lunch menus €8-10.50, dinner €19.50; ☺ Tue-Sat) This seething *bar-restaurant du quartier* serves pork-based Auvergnat dishes on marble tables. Ample platters of pig-based *charcuterie* (€5.60 to €9.20) are dished up any old time.

Crêperie-Grill le 1513 (☎ 04 73 92 37 46; 3 rue des Chaussetiers; menus €13.50-23, crepes €2.50-5.50) This cavernous restaurant occupies the ground floor of a sumptuous mansion built in 1513 – hence the name. For a hefty snack, go for a *galette* (savoury buckwheat pancake). For the ravenous, the French fries that accompany the mains must have depleted half a potato field. Go downstairs to the lovely internal terrace for summer dining.

Ostréo Bar (☎ 04 73 91 58 28; 63bis rue du Port; ☺ 7.30am-8pm Mon-Sat) This tiny hole in the wall offers oysters (€13 per dozen, €8.50 to take away) whenever there's an 'r' in the month.

Le Lypocan (☎ 04 73 92 67 24; 16 place Hippolyte Renoux; ☺ lunch & dinner Sat, dinner Tue-Fri, lunch Mon) This is an informal, immensely popular pizza and pasta joint that also does meaty mains with an Italian touch.

CAFÉS
Les Goûters de Justine (☎ 04 73 92 26 53; 11bis rue Blaise Pascal; ☺ noon-7pm Tue-Sat) This charming tearoom – it's rather like stepping into your great aunt's parlour – is a haven of calm and mellowness in the heart of the city that also does a range of snacks.

SELF-CATERING
The city's **covered market** (☺ 6am-7pm Mon-Sat) is a jumble of blue, yellow and grey cubes splaying across place St-Pierre.

Drinking
Café Pascal (4 place de la Victoire) This favourite exchange-student hang-out is most times packed to the gunnels inside and you'll be lucky to find a chair on its popular summertime terrace.

Bar des Beaux Arts (4 rue Ballainvilliers) This bar too pulls in the student crowd, here to enjoy its recently renovated interior or to sit and sip at the tables that take over most of the adjacent square.

Le Tout au Cru (9 blvd Léon Malfreyt; dishes €8) This pleasant, intimate wine bar with its wooden counter and tables serves a variety of wines by the glass and snacks. You'll enjoy its plate of cold cuts and salad.

John Barleycorn (9 rue du Terrail; ☺ 2pm-2am Mon-Sat May-Aug, 5pm-2am Mon-Sat Sep-Apr) This long-established Celtic pub serves liquids brewed from both barley and corn.

Entertainment
Oxxo (☎ 04 73 14 11 11; 14-16 rue des Deux Marchés; admission €5; ☺ 10pm-4am Wed-Sat) The downstairs dance floor at this rough-hewn discotheque-bar, popular with students, only begins to fill up after 11pm.

There are nondubbed films at the five-screen **Ciné Capitole** (☎ 08 92 68 73 33; 32 place de Jaude).

The city's main venue for concerts and spectacles is the striking, ultramodern **Zénith** (☎ 04 73 77 24 24), which can accommodate up to 8500 spectators. Inaugurated in late 2003 and part of the Grande Halle d'Auvergne complex, it's southeast of the city centre.

Getting There & Away
AIR
The **Clermont-Ferrand Auvergne airport** (☎ 04 73 62 71 00), a major Air France hub for domestic and European flights, is 7km east of the city centre.

BUS
The **bus station** (69 blvd François Mitterrand) has an efficient **information office** (☎ 04 73 93 13 61).

Bus No 73 runs to Riom (€3.60, 15-30 minutes, nine daily) and No 1 serves Thiers (€7.90, 1¼ hours, up to 10 daily). For Vichy, you're better off by train.

Intercars (☎ 04 73 29 70 05) handles Eurolines ticketing. **Linebus** (☎ 04 73 34 81 16; ☺ 10am-7pm Mon-Sat) has buses to a wide number of destinations in Spain.

CAR & MOTORCYCLE

Try **ADA car rental** (☎ 04 73 91 66 07; 79 av de l'Union Soviétique).

TRAIN

Clermont-Ferrand is the Massif Central's most important rail junction. It has two **boutiques SNCF** (ticketing offices; ☎ 08 92 35 35 35; 43 rue du 11 Novembre & bus station).

Destinations include Paris' Gare de Lyon (€39, 3½ hours, six to nine daily) and Lyon (€23.20 via St-Étienne, three hours, up to 12 daily). The route through the Gorges de l'Allier to Nîmes (€31.80, five hours, two or three daily) via Langeac (€13.40) and Monistrol d'Allier (€16.10), known as Le Cévenol, is one of the most scenic in France.

Short-haul trains run to/from Le Mont-Dore (€10.70, 1¼ hours, four or five daily), Le Puy-en-Velay (€18.10, 2¼ hours, four daily), Murat (€14.50, 1½ hours, six to 10 daily), Riom (€2.60, 10 minutes, frequent), Vichy (€8.10, 40 minutes, frequent) and Thiers (€7.30, 40 to 55 minutes, eight to 10 daily).

Getting Around

Léovélo (☎ 04 73 14 12 36; av de l'Union Soviétique; 7am-7pm Mon-Sat), a splendid public sector initiative, rents bikes for a bargain €3/5 per half-/full-day. You need to drop a refundable deposit of €150.

The local bus company, **T2C** (☎ 04 73 28 56 56), has an information office on place de Jaude.

Call **Allo Taxi** (☎ 04 73 19 53 53).

AROUND CLERMONT-FERRAND
Puy de Dôme

Covered in outdoor adventurers in summer and snow in winter, the balding Puy de Dôme (1465m) gives a panoramic view of Clermont-Ferrand and scores of volcanoes. The Celts, then Romans, worshipped their gods from the summit. Nowadays, dominated by a TV transmission tower resembling a giant rectal thermometer, it's a popular launching platform for *parapente* and hang-gliding enthusiasts.

You can reach the summit either by the 'mule track' – a steepish hour's climb starting at the Col de Ceyssat, 4km off the D941A – or by the 4km **toll road** (per vehicle €4.50; 8am-dusk Mar-Nov, weekends only Dec). This road is closed to private cars from 10am to 6pm daily in July and August and between 12.30pm and 6pm on weekends in May, June and September – then, you take a shuttle bus (per adult/child €3.50/1.40 return).

Vulcania

Vulcania (☎ 08 20 82 78 28; www.vulcania.com; adult/child €19/12; 9am-6pm or 7pm Apr-Aug, Wed-Sun mid-Feb–Mar & Sep–mid-Nov) is 15km to the west of Clermont-Ferrand on the D941B. A hugely spectacular multimedia visitors centre in an architecturally innovative site, it illustrates the workings of volcanoes and their role in the development of our planet.

Riom
pop 18,800

Riom, 15km north of Clermont-Ferrand on the train line to Vichy, makes a convenient day or half-day trip from Clermont-Ferrand. The streets of the austere old city, in the Middle Ages the capital of the Auvergne region, are lined with magistrates' mansions built of dark Volvic stone.

ORIENTATION & INFORMATION

The main arteries of the old city are the north–south rue du Commerce, plus its northern extension, rue de l'Horloge, and the east–west rue de l'Hôtel de Ville. The train station is 400m southeast of the old city at the end of av Virlogeux.

The **tourist office** (☎ 04 73 38 59 45; www.riom-auvergne.com in French; 16 rue du Commerce; 9.30am-noon & 2-5.30pm Tue, Wed, Fri & Sat, 2-5.30pm Mon & Thu Sep-Jun, 9.30am-12.30pm & 2-6.30pm Mon-Sat, 10am-1pm Sun Jul & Aug), 100m south of rue de l'Hôtel de Ville, supplies an English-language walking-tour brochure.

SIGHTS

The 15th-century **Église Notre Dame du Marthuret** (rue du Commerce), about 200m from the tourist office, has a fine pair of 14th-century statues of the Virgin: the *Vierge à l'Oiseau* (Virgin with Bird; the figure over the entrance is a copy – the original is inside, in the first chapel to the right) – and the squat *Vierge Noire* (Black Virgin), in the next chapel eastwards.

Transitional **Église St-Amable** (rue St-Amable) has a Gothic choir and a Romanesque nave, its pillars topped by wonderful painted capitals.

MASSIF CENTRAL

Riom has two **museums** (combined ticket adult/child €5.60/2.60; ☑ 10am-noon & 2.30-6pm Tue-Sun Jun-Sep, 10am-noon & 2-5.30pm Tue-Sun Oct-May), both of which merit a visit. The **Musée Francisque Mandet** (☎ 04 73 38 18 53; 14 rue de l'Hôtel de Ville) has a collection of classical antiquities, medieval sculptures and 17th- to 19th-century paintings while the excellent **Musée d'Auvergne** (☎ 04 73 38 17 31; 10bis rue Delille) has displays documenting rural life in Auvergne.

Volvic

About 7km southwest of Riom is the town of **Volvic**, famous for its spring water and quarries which provided the lightweight but strong volcanic stone used in so many local buildings, including Clermont-Ferrand's cathedral.

Even if you don't go inside, it is well worth the walk up to the ruins of the nearby **Château de Tournoël** (adult/child €5/3; ☑ Apr-Sep) to enjoy the splendid panoramic view from its base.

PARC NATUREL RÉGIONAL DES VOLCANS D'AUVERGNE

An ideal area for great walking is the 3950-sq-km, 120km- long **Parc Naturel Régional des Volcans d'Auvergne** (information office ☎ 04 73 65 64 00). Volcanic activity started about 20 million years ago, with the last eruptions petering out about 5000 years ago.

The northernmost range, the **Monts Dômes**, are a chain of some 80 'recent' cinder cones, the best known being the Puy de Dôme (see p553). Three million years older, the **Monts Dore** culminate in the Puy de Sancy (1885m), the Massif Central's highest point and a popular downhill ski station in winter. At its foot lies the spa town of Le Mont-Dore, an ideal base from which to explore the area.

The wilder, rugged **Monts du Cantal**, all that remains of a super-volcano worn down over the millennia, dominate the south of the park. The highest point is the Plomb du Cantal (1855m), a desolate peak often shrouded in heavy, swirling clouds, even in summer.

VICHY
pop 27,000

The spa resort of Vichy exudes faded *belle époque* charm. The town became enormously fashionable after visits by Napoleon III in the 1860s. These days, however, the average age of *curistes* (patients taking the waters) must equal that of any old folk's home. Most come seeking relief from rheumatism, arthritis and digestive ailments under France's generous social security system.

Since July 1940, Vichy has enjoyed dubious fame as the wartime capital of Marshal Philippe Pétain's collaborationist 'Vichy French' government, attracted to the town by the availability of hotel rooms and phone lines.

Orientation

Vichy is centred around triangular Parc des Sources, 800m west of the train station along rue de Paris. Rue Georges Clemenceau, the main shopping thoroughfare, crosses the partly pedestrianised city centre.

Information

Échap (☎ 04 70 32 28 57; 12 rue Source de l'Hôpital; per hr €4; ☑ noon-midnight Tue-Sat, 2pm-midnight Sun) Internet access.
Main Post Office (place Charles de Gaulle)
Multi-Nett (12 rue Source de l'Hôpital; ☑ 7am-9pm) Laundrette.
Tourist Office (☎ 04 70 98 71 94; www.vichytourisme .com; 19 rue du Parc; ☑ 9am-7.30pm Mon-Sat, 9.30am-12.30pm & 3-7pm Sun Jul & Aug, 9am-12.30pm & 1.30-7pm Mon-Sat, 9.30am-12.30pm & 3-7pm Sun Apr-Jun & Sep, 9am-noon & 1.30-6pm Mon-Fri, 9am-noon & 2-6pm Sat, 2.30- 5.30pm Sun Oct-Mar)

Sights & Activities

To savour the full richness of Vichy's Second Empire and *belle époque* heritage, pick up a couple of flimsy pamphlets (in French but very visual) from the tourist office. *Vichy Pas à Pas* describes a couple of walking routes while *Quartier Thermal Vichy: Exercices de Styles* explores the spa area in more depth.

The bench-lined walkways of **Parc des Sources**, created in 1812, are enclosed by a covered promenade. At the park's northern end is the glass-enclosed **Hall des Sources** (☑ 6.15am-6/7/8.30pm), whose taps deliver six types of mineral water, three of them warm (up to 43.3°C). There's no charge to sit in

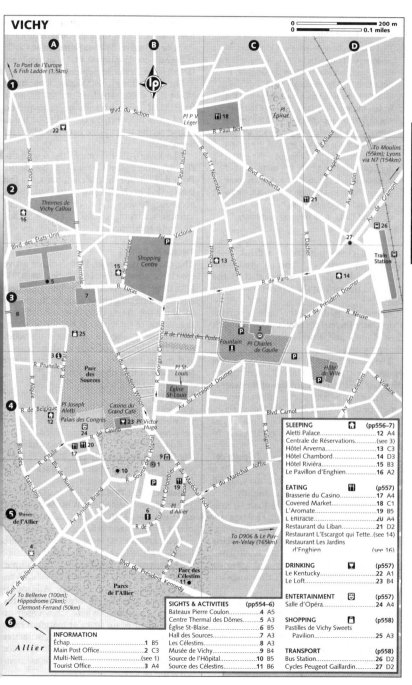

VICHY

0 ———————— 200 m
0 ———————— 0.1 miles

To Pont de l'Europe
& Fish Ladder (1.5km)

Blvd du Sichon

Pl P V Léger

R Paul Bert

Pl d'Epinat

22

R Louis Blanc

Thermes de
Vichy Callou

16

R Jean Jaurès

R du 11 Novembre

Blvd Gambetta

R d'Alsace

R Capelet

Av de Lyon

To Moulins
(55km); Lyons
via N7 (154km)

Av de Cramont

Blvd des États-Unis

Av Victoria

21

Av Thermale

R Dacher

27

Train Station

Shopping Centre

15

R Thibaudière

R Lucas

R Desbrest

13

R Beaupradat

R de Paris

14

26

5

7

8

25

R Prunelle

R de Paris

R du Président Wilson

R Georges Clémenceau

R de l'Hôtel des Postes

Fountain

Pl Charles de Gaulle

2

R Neuve

R du Président Doumer

3

Pl St-Louis

Église St-Louis

Hôtel de Ville

R Alquié

R de Belgique

Parc des Sources

Pl Joseph Aletti

Casino du Grand Café

Av du Président Doumer

Blvd Carnot

R des Célestins

R Voltaire

Palais des Congrès

12

24

23

Pl Victor Hugo

R du Casino

R Saligny

SLEEPING (pp556–7)
Aletti Palace..........................12 A4
Centrale de Réservations.....(see 3)
Hôtel Arverna.......................13 C3
Hôtel Chambord...................14 D3
Hôtel Riviéra........................15 B3
Le Pavillon d'Enghien...........16 A2

R d'Italie

17

20

Blvd des États-Unis

Blvd de Russie

Source de l'Hôpital

9

1

19

R H Colomber

R Besse

R du Maréchal Foch

10

Av Arisède Briand

Pl d'Allier

6

R de la Tour

EATING (p557)
Brasserie du Casino..............17 A4
Covered Market....................18 C1
L'Aromate...........................19 B5
L'Entracte...........................20 A4
Restaurant du Liban.............21 D2
Restaurant L'Escargot qui Tette..(see 14)
Restaurant Les Jardins
  d'Enghien (see 16)

Parc de l'Allier

R de la Gare

To D906 & Le Puy-
en-Velay (165km)

DRINKING (p557)
Le Kentucky........................22 A1
Le Loft...............................23 B4

4

Blvd du Président Kennedy

Parc des Célestins

11

ENTERTAINMENT (p557)
Salle d'Opéra......................24 A4

Pont de Bellerive

To Bellerive (100m);
Hippodrome (2km);
Clermont-Ferrand (50km)

Parcs de l'Allier

Allier

SHOPPING (p558)
Pastilles de Vichy Sweets
  Pavilion............................25 A3

SIGHTS & ACTIVITIES (pp554–6)
Bateaux Pierre Coulon...........4 A5
Centre Thermal des Dômes.....5 A3
Église St-Blaise.....................6 B5
Hall des Sources...................7 A3
Les Célestins........................8 A3
Musée de Vichy....................9 B4
Source de l'Hôpital..............10 B5
Source des Célestins.............11 B6

INFORMATION
Échap.................................1 B5
Main Post Office...................2 C3
Multi-Nett........................(see 1)
Tourist Office.......................3 A4

TRANSPORT (p558)
Bus Station.........................26 D2
Cycles Peugeot Gaillardin.....27 D2

MASSIF CENTRAL

LADY OF LETTERS

That *grande dame* of letter writing, Mme de Sévigné, visiting Vichy in 1676, wrote to her friend and confidante Mme de Grignon in her usual breezy epistolary style:

'So, my dearest, I took the plunge and the waters this morning. Lord, how foul they are! About six in the morning you go to the spring, where just everyone who matters is already there. You all sip and sup and pull the ugliest of faces because – just imagine – the waters are boiling hot and have the quite vilest of sulphury tastes. You stroll up and down, come and go, listen to Mass, go walkabout, throw up, confide discreetly just how you threw up – and that's it, all the way to midday...'

the metal chairs but taking a drink costs €1.65 from April to October. A graduated, urine-sample-style cup is included in the price and the taste of the hotter brews is not dissimilar.

Across the path sits the Indo-Moorish-style **Centre Thermal des Dômes**, adorned with tiled domes and towers and nowadays a shopping arcade.

The taps of **Source de l'Hôpital** (🕙 8am-8.30pm Apr-Dec), first used in Gallo-Roman times, dispense unlimited quantities of the warm-ish, odoriferous and rather bitter mineral waters of the Hôpital and Célestins springs. If you're sick the former might make you well, but if you're well it's just as likely to make you sick.

In the ornate, oval pavilion of **Source des Célestins** (blvd du Président Kennedy; 🕙 8am-8.30pm Apr-Sep, to 6pm Oct-Mar), you can drink your fill of the famous slightly saline, slightly fizzy mineral water, of which more than 60 million bottles are sold annually. The taps are shut in winter to prevent the pipes freezing.

The wonderful Art-Deco **Église St-Blaise** (rue de la Tour), built in the 1930s, is enriched by neo-Byzantine mosaics and glowing stained-glass windows depicting angular, muscle-bound figures.

The small **Musée de Vichy** (🕿 04 70 32 12 97; 15 rue du Maréchal Foch; admission free; 🕙 2-6pm Tue-Fri, 2-5pm Sat) occupies three small rooms in an Art-Deco theatre. Surprisingly slight for a city with such a history, it displays paintings, sculpture, a few archaeological finds and a few telegrams from Marshal Pétain.

The flowery **Parcs de l'Allier** border the River Allier. Below these gardens, alongside Pont de Bellerive, **Bateaux Pierre Coulon** (🕿 04 73 26 62 00) do 45-minute **boat trips** (adult/child €6/4.50) from Easter to September.

For a little flutter, visit Vichy's **Hippodrome** (🕿 04 70 32 47 00), which is one of France's finest and most prestigious racecourses, just across the river on the Bellerive bank. Horse racing takes place between May and September.

The River Allier is one of the few in the country where salmon still swim. Beside the Pont de l'Europe on the right bank is a **fish ladder** (🕙 3-7pm Tue-Thu, Sat & Sun Mar-Aug) where, according to season, you can see migratory salmon, sea trout, eels and lampreys, in addition to local species.

THERMAL BATHS

The most luxurious of Vichy's three active spas is the ultramodern **Les Célestins** (🕿 04 70 30 82 00; 111 blvd des États-Unis) with its beauty, fitness and slimming programs. Walk-in treatments include a *douche de Vichy* (a four-hand massage as you're sprayed with hot spring water; €41), *hydromassage* (a massage with water jets; €28), *illutation* (a body mud mask; €41) and the *jet tonifiant* (a high-powered water jet – the sort that disperses riots; €28).

Sleeping

Vichy's many hotels offer some of the country's best deals. Those we include are open year-round unless otherwise noted.

Rooms can be booked without charge at the **Centrale de Réservations** (🕿 04 70 98 23 83), sharing office space with the tourist office (p554).

Hôtel Riviéra (🕿 04 70 98 22 32; fax 04 70 96 14 09; 5 rue de l'Intendance; s/d €30/33) With large rooms and bathroom, Hôtel Riviéra is one of several places on this street offering good value.

Hôtel Arverna (🕿 04 70 31 31 19; www.hotels -vichy.com in French; 12 rue Desbrest; s/d from €39/45; ⊠) A dynamic, engaging young couple, fleeing Paris for quieter quarters, have recently taken over this hotel. All rooms are double glazed and most overlook the small internal patio, where vines creep up the walls. For more space at marginal extra cost, ask for one of the four large, attractive rooms with a small salon (€51). Rare for such a relatively small place, there are non-smoking rooms.

Pavillon d'Enghien (☎ 04 70 98 33 30; www.pavil londenghien.com; 32 rue Callou; s €45-70, d €57-76; closed 20 Dec–1 Feb; P ⚏) Rooms in this converted mansion are trim and attractive. Each is individually furnished without one square centimetre of plastic in sight, except for the minibar. Nearly all rooms have a bathtub and most overlook the internal garden and small pool. Next door is its fantastic restaurant, **Les Jardins d'Enghien**, whose *menu terroir et découverte* (€18), an ample selection of local specialities, is quite outstanding value.

Hôtel Chambord (☎ 04 70 30 16 30; le.chambord@ wannadoo.fr; 82-84 rue de Paris; s €35-42, d €38-51) This hotel, handy for the station, has been run by the same family for three generations. Welcoming and relaxed, it runs a decent restaurant, **L'Escargot qui Tette** (The Suckling Snail; menus €26 & 33).

Aletti Palace (☎ 04 70 30 20 20; www.aletti.fr; 3 place Joseph Aletti; s €92-138, d €107-153; ✗ ⚏) This is *the* place to stay to get a sense of what a visit during the *belle époque* must have been like for the affluent. Nothing could be more of the era and more French – except that, as a sign of more modern times, it has now become part of a multinational chain. But no chain-smoking here – an impressive 40% of the rooms are tobacco-free.

Eating

For two excellent hotel restaurants, see Les Jardins d'Enghien, at Le Pavillon d'Enghien, and L'Escargot qui Tette, at Hôtel Chambord (above).

Brasserie du Casino (☎ 04 70 98 23 06; 4 rue du Casino; lunch menu €14, fish menu €24; ✆ Thu-Mon, closed mid-Oct–mid-Nov & mid-end-Feb) This is a wonderful pre-WWII brasserie, its walls plastered with signed photos of the once-famous artistes who dropped in from the Opéra, just across the road. Count on around €35 for an à la carte meal with wine.

Restaurant du Liban (☎ 04 70 31 14 79; 51 blvd Gambetta; mezze €3-4.30; closed lunch Mon) This unpretentious place serves tasty Lebanese food, offering more than 50 different kinds of mezze. For a variety of taste sensations, go for the *mini mezze* (€22 for two people), a selection of 10 of the best.

L'Entracte (☎ 04 70 59 85 68; 10 rue du Casino; ✆ Tue-Sat) Essentially a wine bar clad in attractive antique wood panelling, this is a great place for an open toasted sandwich (€7.50) or a platter of Auvergnat cheese (€6), sluiced down with fine wine from the select wine list, available by the glass.

SELF-CATERING

The cavernous **covered market**, built in the mid-1930s in a heavy, unadorned Stalinist style, is on place PV Léger.

Drinking

There's little after dark in Vichy to make young blood tingle.

Le Kentucky (14 blvd du Sichon; ✆ 5pm-2am Mon-Sat) pulls in a young crowd and has a decent range of draught beers. Thursday night is student night.

Le Loft (☎ 04 70 97 16 46; 7 rue du Casino; admission €8; ✆ from 11pm Thu-Sun), below the Casino du Grand Café, is a popular discotheque.

Entertainment

Grab *Vichy Mensuel*, a free monthly what's-on guide, at the tourist office or around town.

Vichy was once known as the 'French Bayreuth', and even today operas, operettas, dance performances and concerts are regularly staged in the ornate 1902 **Salle d'Opéra** (☎ 04 70 30 50 50; rue du Casino) in the Palais des Congrès (formerly Vichy's Grand Casino).

AUTHOR'S CHOICE

L'Aromate (☎ 04 70 32 13 22; 9 rue Besse; menus €13.50-31, mains €16-18; ✆ mid-Aug–mid-Jul, closed Wed, dinner Tue & Sun) With its pillars topped by ornate capitals holding up the high ceiling – which, it must be said, bears a crack or two – its softly piped classical music and tall, gilded mirrors, L'Aromate speaks of a lost elegance. But the food is imaginative, stylishly presented and strictly contemporary. It's a fairly formal place, reservations are all but essential and even if you strike lucky with a lunchtime walk-in, you won't be all that well regarded. And don't expect lightning service; good food, as the menu points out, takes time. So set aside a good two hours of your life. By the end, you won't regret it and, as a souvenir of a special meal, you can take away a pot of one of their exotic home-made jams.

MASSIF CENTRAL

Shopping

You can sample and purchase the octagonal mint, aniseed and lemon lozenges known as *pastilles de Vichy*, pride of the city since 1825, at the **sweets pavilion** of the **Parc des Sources** (Apr-Oct).

Getting There & Around

Major train destinations include Paris' Gare de Lyon (€36.20, three hours, six to eight daily), Clermont-Ferrand (€8.10, 40 minutes, frequent), Riom (€6.20, 25 minutes, frequent) and Lyon (€20.50, 2½ hours, six to eight daily).

Cycles Peugeot Gaillardin (04 70 31 52 86; 48 blvd Gambetta) hires both town and mountain bikes year-round (half-/full-day €5/8) and requires a refundable deposit of €80.

ORCIVAL
pop 290 / elevation 860m

The delightful, slate-roofed village of Orcival lies midway between the Puy de Dôme and Le Mont-Dore. Beside the gurgling River Sioulet, it's a perfect base for day hikes and, despite the coachloads of quick-fix tourists, a lovely spot to spend a few soothing days.

Hanging over the entrance of the superb 12th-century Auvergnat-Romanesque **basilica** are balls and chains left in gratitude by released prisoners. Perched on a pillar behind the altar is a squat 12th-century statue of the Virgin, fashioned from gilded silver over wood.

Turreted 15th-century **Château de Cordès** (04 73 65 81 34; adult/student/child €4/3/2.30; 10am-noon & 2-6pm Easter-Oct) is about 2.5km to the north. It's well worth the short detour to enjoy the rich 18th-century furnishings and the formal gardens, laid out by Le Nôtre, designer of the gardens of Versailles and of London's Greenwich and St James's parks.

The **tourist office** (04 73 65 89 77; terresdomes .sancy@wanadoo.fr; 10am-noon & 2-7pm Mon-Sat, 10am-noon Sun Jul & Aug, 10am-noon & 2-6pm Tue-Sat Jun & Aug, 2-6pm Tue-Sat other school holidays) is opposite the church.

Sleeping & Eating

Les Bourelles (04 73 65 82 28; d €25; Easter-Sep) Set back from the road, Les Bourelles has a lovely, flowery terrace and seven simple rooms giving beautiful views.

Hôtel Notre Dame (/fax 04 73 65 82 02; d €32-36; Feb-Dec) This hotel belongs to the same friendly couple who run Les Bourelles and is excellent value. All seven rooms have views of the basilica and have been recently renovated. Ask for No 26, which has its own large terrace. The **restaurant** has filling *menus* (€10.50 to €19.50).

COL DE GUÉRY

The D27 from Orcival to the Col de Guéry (1268m), 8.5km to its south, passes through spectacular scenery.

In summer, the **Maison des Fleurs d'Auvergne** (04 73 65 20 09; 10am-7pm mid-Jun–mid-Sep, Sat & Sun only May–mid-Jun) presents the area's flora. Although in French, the display is highly visual and in the *jardin écologique* grow many of the plants and trees you'll encounter on walks in the area. From the first snowfall, the centre becomes the **Foyer Ski de Fond Orcival Guéry** (9am-7pm), a cross-country skiing centre from which radiate nearly 30km of groomed pistes. Hire of cross-country equipment costs €9.20 per day and snowshoes are €5.50.

Auberge du Lac de Guéry (04 73 65 02 76; www .auberge-lac-guery.fr in French; d €50; mid-Jan–mid-Oct) Rooms are relatively plain but the site, on the southern shore of **Lac de Guéry**, is unbeatable. You'll eat well in its **restaurant** (menus from €10.50), where the fish, selected from the nearby fish farm, couldn't come fresher.

LE MONT-DORE
pop 1800 / elevation 1050m

This lovely little spa town, 44km southwest of Clermont-Ferrand, is ideal for exploring the Puy de Sancy area on foot, by bicycle or by car. It stretches along a narrow, wooded valley beside the Dordogne, not far from the river's source. Built from locally quarried dark stone, the town bustles with skiers in winter, then hikers and *curistes*, attracted by the hot springs and spa, in summer.

Information

Laundrette (place de la République; 9am-7pm)
Post Office (place Charles de Gaulle)
Tourist Office (04 73 65 20 21; www.mont-dore .com; av de la Libération; 9am-12.30pm & 2-6.30pm Mon-Sat, 9am-noon Sun, also 2-5pm Sun school holidays) Has a France Telecom Internet post.

Sights & Activities

The waters (37°C to 40°C) of the huge **Établissement Thermal** (hot springs complex; ☎ 04 73 65 05 10; place du Panthéon; ☼ May–mid-Oct) soothe respiratory ailments and rheumatism. The spa also offers fitness programmes for the hale and hearty (from €91, minimum three days), or you can test the waters with its one-day introductory programme (€43). There are 45-minute **guided tours** (adult/child €3/2; hourly 2-5pm Mon-Sat May–mid-Oct; 3pm Mon-Fri mid-Oct–Apr), of the sumptuous 19th-century neo-Byzantine interior, which retains vestiges from Gallo-Roman times.

The **Funiculaire du Capucin** (☎ 04 73 65 01 25; av René Cassin; single/return €3.30/4.20; ☼ May–mid-Oct) runs to Les Capucins, a 1270m-high wooded plateau above town. France's oldest funicular railway, built in 1898, it creeps up at precisely one metre per second. From the upper station, multiple signed walking possibilities open up such as linking with the GR30, which wends its way southwards towards the Puy de Sancy, continuing to the Pic du Capucin (1450m; about 45 minutes one way) or dropping steeply back to town.

A cable-car lift, the **Téléphérique du Sancy** (☎ 04 73 65 02 73; single/return €5.20/6.50; ☼ 9am-6pm Jul & Aug, 9.30am-12.30pm & 1.30-5pm May, Jun & Sep, ski-season hours vary with daylight & operation of other lifts), about 3.5km south of town, swings to the summit of the Puy de Sancy (also known as the Pic de Sancy). Here, you can take in the stunning panorama of the northern puys and the southern Monts du Cantal before starting a hike or, in winter, slip-sliding down the slopes.

A session at the town's **ice-skating rink** (☎ 04 73 65 06 55; allée Georges Lagaye; ☼ Dec-Aug) costs €6.15, including skate hire.

Mont-Dore Aventures (☎ 04 73 65 00 00; www .montdoreaventures.com in French; le Salon du Capucin; adult/under 14/under 10 €19/14/10; ☼ 9am or 10am-7pm Jun-Aug; 1-7pm Sat & Sun Apr-May & Sep-Nov) is great for playing Tarzan for an hour or two, as you clamber and swing your way around the circuits up in the trees. It's 150m from the Funiculaire du Capucin's upper station. Alternatively, take the winding 4km road via the D465.

SKIING

The northern side of the spectacular Puy de Sancy has 42km of runs. Another 45km splay over the hill down to **Super Besse**, on the

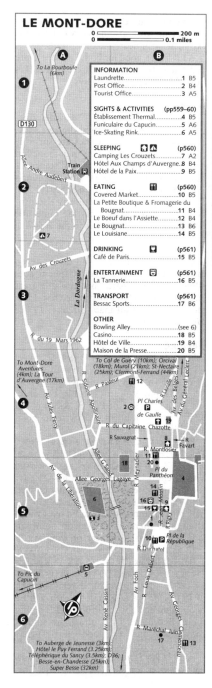

mountain's southeastern slopes. The cross-country network around Le Mont-Dore is excellent, with nearly 40km of trails.

A lift ticket, good for both Le Mont-Dore and Super Besse, costs €20/52 (under 12s €14/37.50) for one/three days.

WALKING
Lonely Planet's *Walking in France* describes two of the best trails around the area's forests, lakes and peaks. Routes are superbly indicated; a signpost at every major junction bristles with arrows showing distance or time to the next landmark. Buy Chamina's 1:30,000-scale map *Massif du Sancy* (€5.35). This sterling Auvergnat company also produces a walking guide with the same title (€6.70), describing 30 hikes in the area.

CYCLING
You can't avoid the ups and downs (even though the Funiculaire du Capucin *does* allow bikes on board) but it's still great biking terrain. The tourist office has a free mountain bike trail map, *Circuit VTT: Le Mont-Dore Sancy*.

Sleeping
Auberge de Jeunesse (☎ 04 73 65 03 53; le-mont-dore@fuaj.org; route du Sancy; dm with breakfast €11.70; ❤ Dec–mid-Nov) This HI-affiliated youth hostel, Le Grand Volcan (The Big Volcano), sits in the shadow of Puy de Sancy about 3.5km south of town. It's wise to book ahead in summer.

Hôtel Aux Champs d'Auvergne (☎ 04 73 65 00 37; fax 04 73 65 00 30; 18 rue Favart; s/d €18/25, with bathroom €29/36, half-board €30/39; ❤ late Dec–mid-Oct) This friendly, laid-back place has 23 cosy rooms and does plentiful meals, cooked with flair and strictly for guests. Go for half-board; dinner is a splendid five-course affair and there's home-made pumpkin jam at breakfast to smear on your warm croissant.

Hôtel de la Paix (☎ 04 73 65 00 17; www.hotel-de-la-paix.info; 8 rue Rigny; s/d €37/47; menu €19; ❤ mid-Dec–mid-Oct) Built in 1880, it retains much of its *fin de siècle* grandeur with a little bijou salon and a wonderfully lavish dining room. Bedrooms, by contrast, are simple, comfortable and very good value. There's also a highly regarded restaurant.

Hôtel le Puy Ferrand (☎ 04 73 65 18 99; www.hotel-puy-ferrand.com; d €45-78; ❤ Dec-Sep) This

cosy mid-range hotel, 150m below the Puy de Sancy cable car, has an excellent restaurant, sauna and year-round covered pool.

CAMPING
Camping Les Crouzets (☎ & fax 04 73 65 21 60; per person/site €2.60/2.35; ❤ mid-Dec–mid-Oct) It's municipal and conveniently opposite the train station.

Camping L'Esquiladou (☎ 04 73 65 23 74; camping.esquiladou@wanadoo.fr; per person/site €3/2.45; ❤ May–mid-Oct) About 1.5km north of town and signposted from the train station, L'Esquiladou, also municipal, is altogether more tranquil and roomy.

Eating
Several hotels (including the three we recommend) offer good *menus*.

Le Bougnat (☎ 04 73 65 28 19; 23 rue Georges Clemenceau; menus €15-23; closed Nov–early Dec) With its low-beamed wooden interior hung with appealing farmhouse clutter and an attractive, flowery terrace, this splendid place offers rich Auvergnat dishes confected from local produce. A recent change of ownership does not seem to have affected quality.

Le Louisiane (☎ 04 73 65 03 14; 2 rue Jean Moulin; menus €12-25; closed Wed mid-Oct–Apr) Spacious and airy, Le Louisiane is an odd yet pleasing marriage with its décor, which owes much to the deep south of the US, grafted onto the vast dining room of what was once the largest luxury hotel in the region. Go for a *brochette* (skewer) of succulent meat (€16) or fish (€17). Also surprising for a restaurant that couldn't possibly be farther from the sea, the quality of its fish dishes is superb.

Le Bœuf dans l'Assiette (Beef on the Plate; ☎ 04 73 65 01 23; 9 av Michel Bertrand; mains €7-11.50, menus €10.40-14.50; ❤ Tue-Sun) As its name suggests, this place is for serious carnivores as photographs of cows gaze down on you from the walls like film stars' portraits.

SELF-CATERING
There's a small **covered market** (place de la République, ❤ 8am-1pm Tue-Sun).

La Petite Boutique du Bougnat (1 rue Montlosier), sister to the restaurant of the same name, positively bursts with the best local cured and canned meats, hams, sausages and over 30 varieties of Auvergnat wine. Right opposite, its *fromagerie* is just as enticing.

Drinking

Café de Paris (8 rue Jean Moulin) is a convivial, crowded old-time café where clients, mainly from the town, play cards, flirt and chat until the cows come home.

Entertainment

La Tannerie (☎ 04 73 65 02 67; rue du Docteur Perpère) is the town's sole discotheque.

Getting There & Around

From the sleepy Le Mont-Dore **train station** to Paris' Gare de Lyon (€42.80, 5½ hours), change at Clermont-Ferrand (€10.70, 1¼ hours, up to four or five daily).

In winter, a free skiers **shuttle bus** *(navette)* regularly plies between Le Mont-Dore and the cable car. From mid-May to September, the service operates four or five times daily (single/return €2/3), continuing to La Bourboule (single/return €3/5.50).

Bessac Sports (☎ 04 73 65 02 25; 3 rue Maréchal Juin) hires out mountain bikes from €10/15 per half-/full-day and can also put you wise about the most attractive routes.

The Téléphérique du Sancy and Funiculaire du Capucin are other means of transport (p559).

AROUND LE MONT-DORE

Only 7km downriver westwards, **La Bourboule**, Le Mont-Dore's slightly larger sister spa, has some lovely *belle époque* buildings. The **tourist office** (☎ 04 73 65 57 71; www.bourboule .com in French; place de la République) is in the town hall. The train trip to/from Le Mont-Dore (€1.30, seven daily) takes eight minutes.

About 10km east of Le Mont-Dore, the 12th-century **Château de Murol** (☎ 04 73 88 67 11; www.chateaudemurol.com in French; adult/child €4/3; ☼ daily Apr–mid-Nov & school holidays, Sat & Sun mid-Nov Mar) sits squat atop a knoll overlooking the village of the same name. In July and August, actors in period costume recreate medieval castle life.

Lac Chambon

This pleasant little beach resort, beside the natural lake of the same name, is 1.5km west of Murol. Among its string of hotels, a couple at the northern end that are just that little bit higher offer the best views of the lake. Try **Hôtel La Mouteroun** (☎ 04 73 88 63 18; fax 04 73 88 61 07; d with shower €35, with bathroom €45; ☼ year-round) and its equally impressive

neighbour, **Hôtel Restaurant Beau Site** (☎ 04 73 88 61 29; fax 04 73 88 66 73; d €40-48; menus €16-24; ☼ Feb-Oct), which also runs a fine, highly recommended restaurant.

Also at the northern end are **Sancy Loisirs** (☎ 04 73 88 67 07), which rents canoes, dinghies and windsurfs.

Besse-en-Chandesse

Picturesque Besse-en-Chandesse is 25km southeast of Le Mont-Dore. There's a small **tourist office** (☎ 04 73 79 52 84; place du Docteur Pipet; ☼ 9am-noon & 2-6pm Dec-Sep, Mon-Sat Oct-Nov).

With cobbled streets and houses of solid rectangular basalt block, it's known for its cheese production (in fact processing much more St-Nectaire cheese than the town of St-Nectaire itself). Several of the 15th- to 18th-century houses along rue de la Boucherie were built of basalt quarried right beside each home – and the quarry became the cheese cellar.

The 15th-century **Maison de la Reine Margot** is home to a small **ski museum** (☎ 04 73 79 57 30; admission €2.50; ☼ 9am-noon & 2-7pm school holidays). Pierre-André, who's collected more than 300 pairs of vintage skis and other mountain gear, will himself guide you around with his charmingly eccentric English.

The mostly Romanesque **Église St-André** has a 12th-century nave with finely carved capitals.

The ski station of **Super Besse** (p559), established in the 1960s as a purpose-built resort, is 7km west. On the way, pause after 4km at **Lac Pavin**, an attractive near-circular lake, Auvergne's deepest, in the hollow of an extinct volcano. A gentle walk around its perimeter takes about 45 minutes.

St-Nectaire

Famed for its 50 natural springs and eponymous soft and flavoursome cheese, St-Nectaire merits a visit. Straggling for more than 2km from St-Nectaire-le-Haut (the upper) to St-Nectaire-le-Bas (the lower), it's a lively place with still a whiff of faded charm from its days as a spa town.

The efficient **tourist office** (☎ 04 73 88 50 86; ☼ 9-11.45am & 2-4.45pm Jul & Aug, Mon-Sat Sep-Jun) is in St-Nectaire-le-Bas.

The Romans were the first to steep themselves in the waters, both hot and cold, of the **Grottes du Cornadore** (☎ 04 73 88 57 97; adult/child

AUVERGNAT CHEESES

From as early as the 1st century AD, the lush grasses of Auvergne's volcanic soils have fed the cows that gave the milk that farmers ferment into its range of excellent cheeses. The region has no less than five classified as Appellation d'Origine Contrôlée (AOC; the highest category of French cheese, with an officially controlled declaration of origin): Cantal, white and full flavoured; Salers, similar, from the same area but made only from the milk of cows that graze on high summer pastures; St-Nectaire, rich-scented, flat and round like a discus; Fourme d'Ambert, a mild, smooth blue cheese; and Bleu d'Auvergne, also blue and stronger, with a creamier texture than its much-touted cousin, Rocquefort.

Take your pick; each in its distinct way makes a delightful sandwich filling.

€5.80/4.30; ☉ mid-Feb–Oct). Perfect natural baths, these caves today make an impressive underground spectacle.

At the **Grottes de Jonas** (☎ 04 73 88 57 98; adult/child €5.80/4.30; ☉ mid-Feb–Oct), 6km south of town, are more than 60 interconnecting troglodyte caves hewn into the cliff, several retaining traces of medieval frescoes.

Maison du St-Nectaire (☎ 04 73 88 57 96; adult/child €4.40/3.40; ☉ mid-Dec–mid-Nov) is a small exhibition that takes you through the cheese-making process and includes a guided tasting and introductory film.

At the top of the town, highlights of the delightful Romanesque **church** (☉ 9am-7pm Apr-Oct, 10am-12.30pm & 2-6pm Nov-Mar) are its 103 carved polychrome capitals and a fine 12th-century statue of the virgin.

PUY MARY

Majestic Puy Mary (1787m) is an easy, 30-minute ascent from **Pas de Peyrol**, a 1582m pass on the D680 that's blocked by snow-drifts between late October and May.

North of Puy Mary is **Col de Serre** (1364m), a notch 3km northeast of the Pas de Peyrol. From here the D62 drops tortuously to the green River Cheylade valley, passing through rich pasture and deciduous forests.

Alternatively, take the D680 from Col de Serre to follow the gentle Santoire Valley eastwards to the tidy little village of **Dienne**, and continue to the town of Murat.

MURAT

pop 2400 / elevation 930m

Murat sits at the foot of a basaltic crag topped by a giant white statue of the Virgin Mary. It makes a good base for exploring the Monts du Cantal, including **Puy Mary** and the 1855m **Plomb du Cantal**. Walks bagging each peak, starting from the ski station of **Super Lioran**, are described in Lonely Planet's *Walking in France*.

The friendly **tourist office** (☎ 04 71 20 09 47; www.ville-de-murat.com in French; 2 rue du Faubourg Notre-Dame; ☉ 9am-12.30pm & 1.30-7pm Mon-Sat, 9.30am-1pm & 2.30-6.30pm Sun Jul & Aug, 9am-noon & 2-6pm Mon-Sat Sep-Jun) is beside the town hall.

Armed with its free pamphlet, *The Picturesque Visit in the Old Murat* (sic; the text flows better than the title), you can happily spend a pleasant hour or so browsing Murat's steep, narrow streets.

Maison de la Faune (☎ 04 71 20 00 52; just off place de l'Hôtel de Ville; adult/child €4/2.40; ☉ 10am-12.30pm & 2-7pm Mon-Sat, 10am-noon & 3-7pm Sun Jul & Aug, 10am-noon & 2-6pm Mon-Sat, 2-6pm Sun other school holidays) occupies an elegant 16th-century house. On the ground floor are more than 10,000 mounted insects, starring some truly dazzling tropical butterflies. Upper levels display local stuffed and mounted wildlife in a natural, well documented – in French – setting. This said, there's a chilling irony – the frequent green spots on individual labels denote endangered species; lift your eyes and there's the hapless creature, staring back at you in death.

AUTHOR'S CHOICE

Auberge du Maître Paul (☎ 04 71 20 14 66; fax 04 71 20 22 20; 14 place du Planol; s/d €30/36) Upstairs, this jolly, family-friendly *gîte* with attitude has winding corridors and spruce, charmingly decorated rooms that put many a pension to shame. Popular with walkers in summer and skiing families when the snow's on the heights, its restaurant is worth dropping into even if you're lodged elsewhere. Pick up a pizza (€6.90; to eat in or take away) the size of a flying saucer or indulge in the excellent *menu* (€17) that's rich in local specialities. If you're overnighting, find space in the small, free public parking lot just behind the *auberge*. If you're just visiting, leave your car in the square beside the town hall.

A steepish ascent (45 minutes round trip from the tourist office) takes you up to Rocher de Bonne Vie with its statue of the Virgin. Follow the red-and-white GR flashes northwestwards out of town, then signs for the Rocher, to enjoy a magnificent view of the town and the higher peaks to the west.

Sleeping & Eating

Hostellerie Les Breuils (☎ 04 71 20 01 25; fax 04 71 20 33 20; 34 av du Docteur Mallet; d €62-76; ��� mid-May–mid-Oct; **P** ��) Converted from a private 19th-century mansion and still in the hands of the original family, Les Breuils' more modern features include a heated pool. Ivy-clad and welcoming with a lovely garden, it makes a excellent mid-range choice. The pricier rooms are very large and those on the 1st floor still have the original furniture.

Hôtel Les Messageries (☎ 04 71 20 04 04; www .hotel-les-messageries.com in French; 18 av Docteur Mallet; s/d €35/41; menus €12-25; closed Nov-Christmas; ��) Overlooking the train station, this Logis de France is more characterful than its bland exterior suggests. Its restaurant is strong on Auvergnat dishes and there's a sauna (€3.80), pool and mini-gym, should you still have energy to expend after a day's hiking.

CAMPING

Camping Municipal Stalapos (☎ 04 71 20 01 83; rue du Stade; person/pitch €2/1.60; ��� May-Sep) Beside the River Alagnon, this attractive camping area is 750m south of the train station.

Getting There & Away

Trains running between Clermont-Ferrand (€14.50, 1½ hours) and Aurillac (€7.50, 45 minutes) call by Murat six to 10 times daily. One or two continue beyond Aurillac to Toulouse (€28.50, 4½ hours).

PARC NATUREL RÉGIONAL LIVRADOIS-FOREZ

One of France's largest protected areas, this nature park slopes away gently to the west to the plains of Limagne while the Monts du Forez, dropping abruptly to the upper Loire valley, form a natural eastern limit.

The **park information office** (☎ 04 73 95 57 57; www.parc-livradois-forez.org in French; ��� 9am-12.30pm & 1.30-4.40pm or 5.30pm Mon-Fri year-round, 3-7pm Sat & Sun May–mid-Sep) is just off the D906 in St-Gervais-sous-Meymont. It produces an excellent brochure, *La Route des Métiers* (The Cottage Industry Trail). This describes and pinpoints on the map 40 small museums and cottage industries, all open to the public, which produce items as diverse as lace, honey, medicinal plants and perfumes. Its *Guide de la Randonnée et des Loisirs de Plein Air* gives a host of suggestions for treks and mountain bike routes, cross-referring to the relevant topoguides. Both are in French and free.

Getting Around

The observation car of the **Discovery Train** (Train de la Découverte; ☎ 04 73 82 43 88) is a superb way to see the heart of the park. In July and August, it runs for 85km between Courpière (15km south of Thiers) via Ambert (adult/child €11/7) to Sembadel (6km south of La Chaise-Dieu; adult/child €18/13). From Ambert to Sembadel is €12/9. Check the variable timetable with the park office, or Ambert and La Chaise Dieu tourist offices.

THIERS

pop 14,800 / elevation 420m

Down below, beside the Gorges de la Durolle, you could convince yourself that Thiers is a town seriously on the skids. The thundering river that once drove the mills that ground the knives roars on but the abandoned factories along its banks are a sad testament to an outmoded way of production.

Nevertheless, Thiers remains Steel City with more than 60 workshops and factories producing some 70% of knives sold in France. To understand its unique industrial history, you need to visit the Musée de la Coutellerie and the Vallée des Rouets.

The **Musée de la Coutellerie** (Cutlery Museum; ☎ 04 73 00 50 06; 23 & 58 rue de la Coutellerie; adult/child €4.75/2.30; ��� year-round, tours & demonstrations 10am-6.30pm Jul & Aug, 10am-noon & 2-6pm Tue-Sun Sep-Oct & Mar-Jun, Wed-Sun Nov-Dec & Feb) presents cottage-industry cutlery manufacturing with demonstrations by skilled craftspeople.

The **Vallée des Rouets** (Valley of the Waterwheels; ��� noon-6.30pm Jul & Aug, noon-6pm Tue-Sun Jun & Sep), about 10km upstream from Thiers, is an open-air museum to the self-employed knife grinders who spent their working days stretched along a wooden plank above their grindstone. You can follow either an easy 1km signed walking trail or another, scarcely more arduous, of 2.5km. In July and August a shuttle bus runs hourly from opposite the town hall. Otherwise, take the N89 towards Lyon.

A combined ticket (adult/child €5.80/2.50) covers the shuttle bus and admission to both the museum and Vallée des Rouets.

The friendly **tourist office** (☎ 04 73 80 65 65; www.ville-thiers.fr in French; 1 place du Pirou; ☼ 9am–1pm & 1.30-7pm Mon-Sat, 10am–noon & 2-6pm Sun mid-Jun–mid-Sep, 9.30am–noon & 2-6pm Mon-Sat mid-Sep–Jun) is in the Château du Pirou. Nearby is the **Maison de l'Homme de Bois** (21 rue de la Coutellerie), named after the bizarre figure in skins carved in wood on the left of the façade. It's one of several fine wood and half-timbered 15th-century mansions in the old quarter.

AMBERT

Back in the 16th century, Ambert, 30km north of La Chaise-Dieu, had more than 300 small water-powered mills. The little town fed the printing presses of Lyon and was France's most important paper producer until the Industrial Revolution. Today it's renowned for the fine Fourme d'Ambert cheese and is a centre for the surrounding agricultural area.

The **tourist office** (☎ 04 73 82 61 90; 4 place de l'Hôtel de Ville; ☼ 9am-6pm Mon-Sat, 10am–noon Sun Jul & Aug, 9am–noon & 2-6pm Mon-Fri, 10am–noon Sat Sep-Jun) is opposite the town hall. At 3pm on Thursdays during July and August, it organises **guided walks** (adult/child €4/2) in English around old Ambert.

Maison de la Fourme d'Ambert (☎ 04 73 82 49 23; rue des Chazeaux; adult/child €4.20/3.40; ☼ 9am-7pm Jul & Aug, 9am-noon & 2-7pm Tue & Thu-Sat Oct-Jun) explains via a short video in French the production process of rich, mellow blue Fourme d'Ambert cheese. It has a display of traditional cheese-making implements – and also graciously displays Auvergne's other fine cheeses.

Musée Agrivap (☎ 04 73 82 60 42; rue de l'Industrie; adult/child €4.80/3; ☼ 10am-1pm & 2-7pm Jul & Aug; 2-6pm Easter-Jun & Sep–mid-Oct) is a collection of vintage agricultural machinery and traction engines.

Moulin Richard de Bas (☎ 04 73 82 03 11; adult/child €5.50/3.60; ☼ 9am-8pm Jul & Aug, 9am-noon & 2-6pm Sep-Jun) occupies a 14th-century mill and produces handmade paper using traditional techniques. It's 4km out of town on the D57 towards Valeyre.

Ambert's round **town hall** was originally the town's grain store. Notice the grotesque gargoyles sprouting like warts all along the exterior southern wall of Gothic **Église St-Jean**. There are some lovely half-timbered, mainly 15th-century houses along rue du Château, rue de la République and place Minimes.

LA CHAISE DIEU

Early in the 14th century, an 11-year-old novice monk, Pierre Roger de Beaufort, joined the **Église Abbatiale de St-Robert** (adult/student/child €3/2/1; ☼ 9am-noon & 2-7pm Jun-Sep, 10am-noon & 2-5pm Mon-Sat, 10am–noon Sun Oct-May). Later, as Pope Clement VI, he bequeathed funds for a fundamental reconstruction of this abbey church, originally built in 1044 – and for the placing of his tomb at its heart.

Although sacked by Huguenots in 1562, ravaged by fire in 1695 and despoiled by revolutionary mobs in the late 18th century, it's still deeply impressive.

At the west end is an elaborately carved 18th-century wooden organ gallery. Plumb in the centre of the choir sits the black-and-white marble tomb of the good pope, surrounded by 144 14th-century choir stalls in pale oak. Lift your eyes to take in the magnificent 17th-century Flemish tapestries above them.

By the northern aisle is an unfinished 15th-century fresco of the **Dance of Death** where sinuous skeletons mock human figures representing the various classes of society.

Outside, the **Salle de l'Écho** has led to all sorts of speculation. Whisper, facing the wall, in one corner and someone listening in the opposite corner will hear you perfectly. Was it, as some maintain, for hearing the confession of lepers? Or of indiscreet fellow monks? Or is it no more than an unanticipated architectural and acoustic fluke?

The abbey and village of La Chaise Dieu are internationally renowned for their annual festival of sacred music, held during the last 10 days of August.

LE PUY-EN-VELAY
pop 20,500 / elevation 630m
From Le Puy-en-Velay protrude a trio of striking volcanic plugs. Surrounded by a fertile valley, the city, capital of the Haute- Loire

département, is proud of its lace-making tradition – and its pedigree green lentils, which have earned Appellation d'Origine Contrôlée status, just like a fine wine, thanks to the area's uniquely rich volcanic soil.

In medieval times, the cathedral of Le Puy was one of four French departure points for pilgrim routes to Santiago de Compostella in Spain. Known as the Via Podiensis, it's today called, more prosaically, the GR65, a 1600km long-distance walking trail.

From nearby Le Monastier-sur-Gazeille begins an equally famous and much less arduous trail, the GR70, following in the donkey tracks of Robert Louis Stevenson (p743).

Orientation
North of the main square, place du Breuil, lies the pedestrianised old city, its narrow streets leading uphill to the cathedral. Le Puy-en-Velay's commercial centre is around the town hall and between blvd Maréchal Fayolle and rue Chaussade.

Information
INTERNET ACCESS
Cyb'Aire (17 rue Général Lafayette; per hr €3.50; 10am-midnight Mon-Sat, 2pm-midnight Sun)

LAUNDRY
There are laundrettes at 24 rue Portail d'Avignon (open daily) and 12 rue Chèvrerie (open Monday to Saturday).

POST
Main Post Office (8 av de la Dentelle)

TOURIST INFORMATION
Main Tourist Office (☎ 04 71 09 38 41; www.ot-lepuyenvelay.fr; place du Breuil; 8.30am-7.30pm Jul & Aug, 8.30am-noon & 1.30-6.15pm Sep-Jun, closed Sun pm Oct Easter) Has good walking tour leaflet in English, *Historical Visits*, describing three walks around town.
Tourist Office Annexe (23 rue des Tables; late Jun—early-Sep)

Sights & Activities
Medieval, Gothic and Renaissance houses of dark volcanic stone border rue Chaussade, rue du Collège, rue Porte Aiguière and rue Pannessac.

God beams down from each of Le Puy's three lava pinnacles: the largest, around whose skirts the old city fans, has the cathedral; the highest bears a giant statue of the Virgin; and on the steepest, a few hundred metres further north, perches a 10th-century gravity-defying chapel.

Cathédrale Notre Dame is a heavily restored Romanesque cathedral. The most impressive way to enter it is through the massive arches at the top of cobbled rue des Tables. Byzantine and Moorish elements include the six domes over the nave and the ornately patterned stonework. A 17th-century **Black Virgin** takes pride of place on the high altar.

The beautiful 12th-century **cloister** (adult/18-25 yrs/under 18 €4.60/3.10/free; 9am-6.30pm Jul & Aug, 9am-noon & 2-6.30pm mid-May–Jun & Sep, to 5pm Oct–mid-May) with its multicoloured building blocks would look perfectly at home in Moorish Spain.

The massive **Rocher Corneille** (adult/child €3/1.50; 9am-6/7/7.30pm mid-Mar–Sep; 10am-5pm Oct–mid-Nov & Feb–mid-Mar) is just north of the cathedral and accessible via rue du Cloître. It was crowned in 1860 by a jarringly red, 16m-high statue of Notre Dame de France made from melted-down cannons captured in the Crimean War. She looks for all the world like something in raspberry from the top of a wedding cake but the view from her feet is superb.

Chapelle St-Michel d'Aiguilhe (adult/child €2.50/1; 9.30am-6.30pm May-Sep, 9.30am-noon & 2-5.30pm mid-Mar–Apr & Oct–mid-Nov, 2-5pm Feb–mid-Mar) perches at the summit of an 85m-high volcanic plug. The 10th-century choir is pre-Romanesque and you can still see traces of the 12th-century murals. It's an easy walk – as far as the base, that is! Or take bus No 6 to the base.

You can admire antique and modern lace and take lace-making classes (€8 per hour) at the **Centre d'Enseignement de la Dentelle au Fuseau** (☎ 04 71 02 01 68; 38-42 rue Raphaël; admission €2; 9am-noon & 1.30-5.30pm Mon-Fri, 9.30am-4.30pm Sat mid-Jun–mid-Sep, 10am-noon & 2-5pm Mon-Fri mid-Sep–mid-Jun), a nonprofit museum and educational centre that seeks to preserve what

---

DISCOUNT ADMISSION

Between February and October you can visit Le Puy's four major sights – the cathedral cloister, Rocher Corneille, Chapelle St-Michel d'Aiguilhe and the Musée Crozatier – with an open-dated discount combination ticket (€7.50), available at the tourist office and each location.

MASSIF CENTRAL

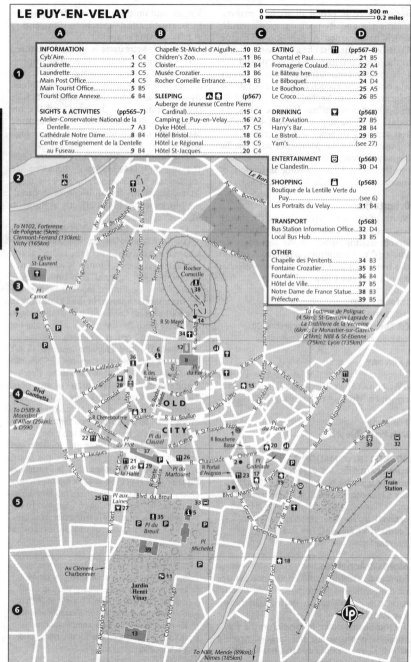

LE PUY-EN-VELAY

0		300 m
0		0.2 miles

INFORMATION
Cyb'Aire.................................1 C4
Laundrette.............................2 C5
Laundrette.............................3 C5
Main Post Office...................4 C5
Main Tourist Office..............5 B5
Tourist Office Annexe..........6 B4

SIGHTS & ACTIVITIES   (pp565–7)
Atelier-Conservatoire National de la
   Dentelle...........................7 A3
Cathédrale Notre Dame......8 B4
Centre d'Enseignement de la Dentelle
   au Fuseau.........................9 B4

Chapelle St-Michel d'Aiguilhe....10 B2
Children's Zoo.....................11 B6
Cloister.................................12 B4
Musée Crozatier..................13 B6
Rocher Corneille Entrance....14 B3

SLEEPING   (p567)
Auberge de Jeunesse (Centre Pierre
   Cardinal).........................15 C4
Camping Le Puy-en-Velay...16 A2
Dyke Hôtel..........................17 C5
Hôtel Bristol........................18 C5
Hôtel Le Régional................19 C5
Hôtel St-Jacques.................20 C4

EATING   (pp567–8)
Chantal et Paul....................21 B5
Fromagerie Coulaud............22 A4
Le Bâteau Ivre.....................23 C5
Le Bilboquet.........................24 D4
Le Bouchon..........................25 A5
Le Croco..............................26 B5

DRINKING   (p568)
Bar l'Aviation.......................27 B5
Harry's Bar...........................28 B4
Le Bistrot.............................29 B5
Yam's...............................(see 27)

ENTERTAINMENT   (p568)
Le Clandestin......................30 D4

SHOPPING   (p568)
Boutique de la Lentille Verte du
   Puy................................(see 6)
Les Portraits du Velay.........31 B4

TRANSPORT   (p568)
Bus Station Information Office..32 D4
Local Bus Hub.....................33 B5

OTHER
Chapelle des Pénitents.........34 B3
Fontaine Crozatier...............35 B5
Fountain.............................36 B4
Hôtel de Ville......................37 B5
Notre Dame de France Statue..38 B3
Préfecture...........................39 B5

Le Bor

Av de Bonneville

16
10

Av de Bonneville

To N102, Forteresse
de Polignac (5km);
Clermont-Ferrand (130km);
Vichy (165km)

Église
St-Laurent

Chemin du Cimetière

Pl
Carnot

Rocher
Corneille

38

R St-Mayol

14

34

Henri Pourrat

To Fortresse de Polignac
(4.5km); St-Germain Laprade &
La Distillerie de la Verveine
(6km); Le Monastier-sur-Gazeille
(21km); N88 & St-Etienne
(75km); Lyon (135km)

Av de la Cathédrale

36
6
8

12

15

R de Vienne

Blvd
Gambetta

9
28

31

OLD

R Jules Vallès

To D589 &
Monistrol
d'Allier (25km);
& D590

22

CITY

1

Pl
du Planet

R de la Gazelle

30

32

Pl
du Plot

20

Train
Station

21
29

26

23

19

24

Av Charles Dupuy

25

27

33

5

35

Blvd du Breuil

Pl aux
Laines

Pl du
Breuil

39

Pl
Michelet

18

Av Clément
Charbonnier

11

Jardin
Henri
Vinay

13

Cours Victor Hugo

To N88, Mende (89km);
Nîmes (185km)

LP

was once an important local industry (in 1900 the Haute-Loire *département* had 5000 lace workshops).

You might also want to take a look at the state-owned **Atelier-Conservatoire National de la Dentelle** (☎ 04 71 09 74 41; 2 rue Duguesclin), just west of place Carnot. Here, the French government orders some of the prestigious gifts it gives to visiting heads of state. Free hour-long visits start at 10am and 2pm on Monday, Tuesday, Thursday and Friday.

Jardin Henri Vinay, in the heart of town, is a pleasant park with a swan lake and small children's zoo. At its southern end is **Musée Crozatier** (☎ 04 71 09 38 90; adult/18-25 yrs/under 18 €3/1.20/free; ⏱ 10am-noon & 2-6pm mid-Jun–mid-Sep, Wed-Mon mid-Sep–mid-Jun, to 4pm Oct-Apr). Exhibits include some impressive Romanesque capitals, local folk costumes and lace, a sad collection of stuffed birds and animals and some ingenious late-19th-century mechanical devices, among them the first patented sewing machine.

La Distillerie de la Verveine du Velay (☎ 04 71 03 04 11; 45min tour adult/student/child €5.30/4/2; ⏱ 10am-noon & 1.30-6.30pm Jul & Aug, Tue-Sat Mar-Jun & Sep-Dec) is famous for its bright green firewater, first brewed in 1859. It's 6km east of town in St-Germain Laprade; take the N88 then the C150.

Festivals & Events

The **Fêtes Renaissance du Roi de l'Oiseau** are four days of street fun in mid-September. The tradition dates to 1524 when the title of King *(Roi)* was first accorded to the archer who brought down a straw bird, the *oiseau*. Among other concessions, the winner was exempt from all local taxes for the following year. Today's prize, alas, is markedly less generous but there's still heaps of fun for all.

Interfolk, Le Puy's annual week-long folk festival, in the second half of July, is nearly 40 years old but remains as fresh as ever.

Sleeping

Auberge de Jeunesse (☎ 04 71 05 52 40; auberge@maire-le-puy-en-velay.fr; 9 rue Jules Vallès; dm €7.70; ⏱ Apr-Sep, Mon-Fri Oct-Mar) The youth hostel, which occupies part of Centre Pierre Cardinal, has a members kitchen.

Hôtel Le Régional (☎ 04 71 09 37 74; 36 blvd Maréchal Fayolle; d €21.50, with bathroom €26-34) This is a good budget option whose 12 rooms

are altogether cosier than the hotel's stark exterior might suggest.

Hôtel St-Jacques (☎ 04 71 07 20 40; www.hotel-saint-jacques.com; 7 place Cadelade; s €43, d €43-50; P) Hôtel St-Jacques, intimate, friendly and well maintained, has 12 tidy rooms, one with disabled access, on four floors overlooking a pedestrian square.

Hôtel Bristol (☎ 04 71 09 13 38; www.hotelbristol-lepuy.com; 7-9 av Maréchal Foch; s €38, d €42-49; ⏱ closed 1-15 Jan & 2 weeks in Mar; P) This Logis de France, its 40 rooms recently and comprehensively refurbished, is a good two-star option with a garden, attractively retro restaurant and small, cosy bar.

Dyke Hôtel (☎ 04 71 09 05 30; fax 04 71 02 58 66; 37 blvd Maréchal Fayolle; d €40-48; P) This warm, welcoming place has 15 attractive, modern rooms, some with balconies. That name may be something of a *faux ami* – or *fausse amie; dyke* (pronounced 'deek') here means a volcanic spire.

CAMPING

Camping Le Puy-en-Velay (☎ 04 71 09 55 09; chemin de Bouthezard; camping €9.10; ⏱ Easter-Sep) Le Puy's camping ground is attractively situated beside the River Borne. Bus No 6 delivers you outside.

Eating

Chantal et Paul (☎ 04 71 09 09 16; 8 place de la Halle; menus €9 & €12.20; ⏱ closed Sun, dinner Sat) Popular with downtown workers, this unpretentious husband-and-wife restaurant offers unbeatable value for the few euros you drop.

Le Bateau Ivre (☎ 04 71 09 67 20; 5 rue Portail d'Avignon; menus €18-29; ⏱ Tue-Sat) This long, thin place exudes elegance with polished wooden tables and stylish cutlery – each fork a miniature Neptune's trident. Portions are generous and the cuisine is imaginative; the *fricassée de cailles*, sautéed quail nestling in a green salad sprinkled with a variety of nuts, makes a superb starter. For dessert indulge yourself with the *assiette gourmande*, a selection of exotic fruits, mousses and other soft, calorie-rich temptations.

Le Croco (☎ 04 71 02 40 13; 5 rue Chaussade; lunch menus €11-13; ⏱ Tue-Sat) While not eschewing red meat, Le Croco (The Crocodile; tuck into your cheek the pair of croc jelly babies/jellybeans that come with your bill) is particularly strong on bushy salads and equally

MASSIF CENTRAL

enormous, mainly vegetarian *plats compo-sés* (mixed platters).

Le Bouchon (☎ 04 71 05 41 42; 3 blvd St-Louis; menus €13-22; closed dinner Tue & Wed) Le Bouchon is another highly popular venue, rich in local fare. The *menu du terroir* (€16) is a stimulating four-course exploration of local specialities.

Le Bilboquet (☎ 04 71 09 74 24; 52 rue du Faubourg St-Jean; menus €15-45; closed Sun dinner Sep-Apr) It pulls in the diners by the sheer quality of its regional cuisine and the friendliness of the family owners. Australian readers are assured of a special welcome; just ask the *patronne* about her brother in Brisbane.

SELF-CATERING

Just west of the town hall, there's a good Saturday morning **food market** sprawling over place du Plot, place de la Halle and rue St-Jacques. **Fromagerie Coulaud** (24 rue Grenouil-lit; ☺ Tue-Sat) is one of France's disastrously declining number of specialist cheese shops and merits your patronage.

Drinking

Harry's Bar (37 rue Raphaël), a congenial place for a drink, these days pounds to a Latin beat. **Bar l'Aviation** (place aux Laines) and its neighbour **Yam's** pack in a youthful crowd. **Le Bistrot** (7 place de la Halle) is a great watering hole if you've a taste and thirst for good beer.

Entertainment

Le Clandestin (☎ 04 71 05 77 53; 20 rue de la Gazelle; ☺ Fri & Sat plus Wed & Thu school holidays) is Le Puy-en-Velay's only discotheque.

Shopping

Several shops sell handmade lace. Pieces marked *dentelle du Puy* were made in Le Puy-en-Velay many years ago (there's no longer any commercial lace production here); lace marked *fait main* (handmade) has probably been imported from China.

Les Portraits du Velay (☎ 04 71 06 00 94; www .dentelledupuy.com in French; 10 rue Raphaël; ☺ Easter-Sep, afternoons only Mon-Sat Oct-Easter), a lace shop, has lace-making demonstrations between Easter and August.

Le Puy's other Big L is the humble lentil. But not just any old pulse. To be sure of the real AOC thing – and to learn more than you ever thought you wanted to know about lentils – visit **Boutique de la Lentille**

Verte du Puy (☎ 04 71 02 60 44; 23 rue des Tables; ☺ Jun-Sep), sharing an address with the tourist office's summer annexe (p565).

Getting There & Away

The bus station and its **information office** (☎ 04 71 09 25 60) is just north of the train station. Three buses run to/from Mende on weekdays, and two travel to/from St-Étienne, which has good onwards bus and rail connections.

Le Puy-en-Velay's sleepy **train station** (av Charles Dupuy) has limited rail services. Destinations include Lyon (€18.10, 2½ hours, three daily), Clermont-Ferrand (€18.10, 2¼ hours, four daily) and St-Étienne (€11.10, 1½ hours, five to seven daily), which connects with the TGV network.

Getting Around

All six lines of the local **TUDIP** bus network (single ticket/10-trip carnet €1/7) pass by place Michelet.

For a taxi call ☎ 04 71 05 42 43.

AROUND LE PUY-EN-VELAY
Forteresse de Polignac

Perched atop yet another volcanic plug, about 5km northwest of Le Puy centre, are the crumbling remains of this 11th-century fortress whose 32m-high **Donjon** remains nearly intact, if much restored over the years. Once home to the powerful Polignac family, who virtually ruled Velay from the 11th to the 14th centuries, it's scheduled to re-open to the public in 2005.

Gorges de l'Allier

About 30km west of Le Puy-en-Velay, the salmon-filled River Allier – paralleled by the scenic Langeac-Langogne stretch of the Clermont-Ferrand–Nîmes rail line (two to three trains daily) – weaves between rocky, scrub-covered hills and steep cliffs. Above the river's right (eastern) bank, the narrow D301 gives fine views as it passes through wild countryside and a number of remote, mud-puddle hamlets. Several villages in the area have Romanesque churches. The one in **Prades** – where you can laze on the village's small sand beach – has an expressive 15th-century polychrome wood entombment of Christ, and a rich baroque altarpiece.

AN Rafting (☎ 04 71 57 23 90; www.an-rafting.com in French), in scenic **Monistrol d'Allier**, does river

---

QUIET HEROISM IN LE CHAMBON-SUR-LIGNON

The village of Le Chambon-sur-Lignon is in the Montagne Protestante, a remote highland area with a long-standing Protestant majority. Its tradition of sheltering the persecuted began in the 17th century, when Huguenots fled here. Throughout WWII, Chambon and nearby hamlets 'hid, protected and saved' around 3000 refugees, including hundreds of Jewish children, being hunted by French police and the Gestapo. A crucial role in this resistance to the Nazis was played by the local religious leadership, led by Pastor André Trocmé.

Today Chambon continues its venerable tradition of welcoming the disadvantaged by taking in orphans and children from troubled families, both in institutions (such as the Collège-Lycée International Cévenol) and in local homes.

---

descents to Prades by raft and inflatable canoe (€40) between April and September and also organises canyon descents and rock climbing.

Hôtel des Gorges (☎ 04 71 57 24 50; fax 04 71 57 25 36; d with shower/bathroom €35/38; ☻ Apr-Sep) does a special deal for pilgrims and hikers: €20 for dinner and a bunk bed in a double room – it'll want to see your backpack to confirm that you're more than a motorist on the scrounge, though. The hotel does a plentiful *menu* for all comers at €12.

In tidy **Langeac** (population 4500), at the northern extremity of the Allier's most interesting stretch, drop into the **Collégiale St-Gal**, a 15th-century Gothic church, and, beside it, **Le Jaquemard**, a small museum of local traditions.

Langeac has a well-equipped **tourist office** (☎ 04 71 77 05 41; place Aristide Briand; ☻ 9am-noon & 2-7pm Mon-Fri, 5pm Sat, 10am-noon Sun May-Sep, 9am-noon & 2-5.30pm Tue-Sat Oct-Apr).

Le Chambon-sur-Lignon

'L'espace ouvert, l'esprit aussi' (open space, open mind) is the motto of this quiet, neat village, 45km east of Le Puy-en-Velay, which played a courageous role in WWII.

Across the street from the Protestant **temple** is a bronze **plaque** erected in Chambon's honour by Jews sheltered here as children. Every July and August there's an exhibition on the town's WWII history. Ask at the **tourist office** (☎ 04 71 59 71 56; www.ot-lechambonsurlignon .fr; rue des Quatre Saisons; ☻ 9am-noon & 2-6.30pm Mon-Sat, 10am-noon Sun Jun-Sep, 9am-noon & 3-6pm Mon-Sat Oct-May) for details.

Mont Mézenc

South of Le Chambon-sur-Lignon, the D500 and D262 take you to the scenic D410, from which the D400 winds its way up to the col of La Croix des Boutières (1508m). Here you can link up with the GR7 and GR73 trails for the half-hour hike to the summit of Mont Mézenc (1753m; pronounced meh-*zang*).

On a clear day, you can see the entire southeastern quarter of France, from Mont Blanc, 200km to the northeast, right around to Mont Ventoux, 140km in the southeast of the region.

MASSIF CENTRAL

Limousin, the Dordogne & Quercy

CONTENTS

Limousin	**573**
Limoges	573
Around Limoges	577
Aubusson	578
Uzerche	579
Brive-la-Gaillarde	579
Northeast of Brive	579
Southeast of Brive	581
The Dordogne	**582**
Périgueux	583
Bertric Burée	587
Sarlat-la-Canéda	587
Prehistoric Sites & the Vézère Valley	591
Dordogne Périgourdine	595
Monpazier	597
Château de Biron	597
Bergerac	597
Quercy	**598**
Cahors	599
East of Cahors	603
West of Cahors	607
Northern Quercy	607

The adjacent regions of Limousin, the Dordogne and Quercy are tucked away in southwestern France between the Massif Central and the vineyard-covered lowlands around Bordeaux. Although they share similar histories and are firmly steeped in rural life, each has its own distinctive landscape, ambience and cuisine.

Limousin is the least densely populated region in France. Its main city, Limoges, known for fine china and enamelware, is a good staging post. But the real draw is the countryside; a verdant landscape of hills, rivers and woodland dotted with tiny hamlets. The beautiful village of Gimel-les-Cascades, surrounded by brooks and pine-clad hills, is idyllic enough to inspire visitors to move here. Indeed, plenty of Britons now have homes or second homes in this region.

The Brits, however, were not the first to discover these parts. Around the Dordogne River (known as Périgord), prehistoric paintings in limestone caves point to the existence of civilisations some 14,000 years ago. Paintings, such as those at Lascaux, are among the most significant examples of prehistoric art in the world. More recent attractions include hilltop chateaux and fortified *bastide* villages, so there's plenty above ground to explore too.

Quercy, the southernmost area, is warmer and drier, being not far from Toulouse and the Pyrenees. It's not as well-known as its neighbours to the north, but this area also harbours magnificent prehistoric art, majestic castles and pretty villages alongside the steep, dramatic limestone canyons cut by the River Lot.

The best way to experience the beauty of this river-rich region is by boat. Whether it's a white-knuckle canoe ride down the Dordogne or a few days relaxing on a houseboat on the River Lot, the glistening waters offer a raft of opportunities for fun and adventure.

LIMOUSIN, THE DORDOGNE & QUERCY

HIGHLIGHTS

- Marvel at incredible prehistoric cave paintings in the **Vézère Valley** (p591)

- Taste the local foie gras and truffles at the medieval town of **Sarlat-la-Canéda** (p587)

- Shop at the open-air market in **Villefranche de Rouergue** (p605)

- Stroll through the pretty villages of **Gimel-les-Cascades** (p580) and **Collongnes-la-Rouge** (p581)

- Explore the *bastides* of **Domme** (p595), **Monpazier** (p597) and **Najac** (p606)

- Relax on a houseboat on the River Lot near **Cahors** (p599)

- Take a cruise on the underground river at **Gouffre de Padirac** (p608)

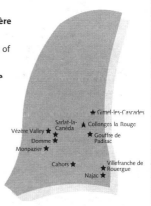

★ Gimel-les-Cascades
Sarlat-la-Canéda ★ ▲ Collongnes la Rouge
Vézère Valley ★ ★
Domme ★ ★ Gouffre de Padirac
Monpazier ★
Cahors ★ Villefranche de Rouergue ★
Najac ★

POPULATION: 1,134,959	AREA: 25,654 SQ KM

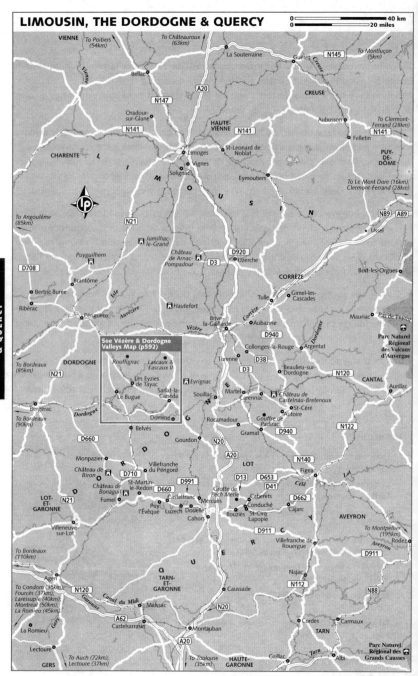

LIMOUSIN, THE DORDOGNE & QUERCY

0 — 40 km
0 — 20 miles

See Vézère & Dordogne Valleys Map (p592)

Getting There & Around

The major transportation hub for the region is Limoges (p577): the A20 motorway heads northwards from here to Paris and continues south through the region to Toulouse, trains serve Paris and neighbouring regions, and planes arrive from around France and across the channel in the UK. Bergerac airport (p598) also has services to and from the UK.

The best way to see the region is by car, although there is a useful rail link that wiggles down to Toulouse from Limoges via Brive, Souillac and Cahors. Train services are supplemented by SNCF buses.

LIMOUSIN

The tranquil, green hills of Limousin, dotted with old churches and castles, present the quintessential image of rural France. Long overlooked by tourists, the region's many rivers, springs and lakes now attract visitors interested in such outdoor pursuits as sailing, canoeing, kayaking and fishing. The local economy is based on agriculture, in particular cattle and sheep farming.

Limousin is made up of three *départements:* Haute-Vienne, in the west, whose *préfecture* is the city of Limoges; the rural Creuse, in the northeast; and, in the southeast, the Corrèze, blessed with many of the region's most beautiful sights.

LIMOGES

pop 200,000

The pleasant, although hardly compelling, city of Limoges has long been acclaimed for its production of enamelware and fine porcelain. Museums and galleries dedicated to these arts are among the city's main attractions. Known around Europe for its top-flight basketball team, Limoges also has a small but animated nightlife scene, thanks largely to the presence of some 17,000 university students.

Orientation

The train station is located 500m northeast of place Jourdan. The Cité Quarter and its cathedral are southeast of place Jourdan and east of the partly pedestrianised commercial centre, the chateau-less Château Quarter.

Information

INTERNET ACCESS

Le Cybar (☎ 05 55 32 31 71; 33 rue Delescluze; per hr €4; 🕒 10am-1am Mon-Wed, 10am-2am Thu-Sat)

LAUNDRY

There are laundrettes at 28 rue Delescluze and 9 rue Monte a Regret; both are open until 9pm.

MONEY

There are several banks on place Jourdan and place Wilson and the post office also changes money.

Banque de France (8 blvd Carnot; money exchange 🕒 8.45am-noon Mon-Fri)

POST

Main Post Office (29 av de la Libération) Offers currency exchange services, a Cyberposte and an ATM.

Post Office (6 blvd de Fleurus) Has Cyberposte and ATM.

TOURIST INFORMATION

Maison du Tourisme (☎ 05 55 79 04 04; 4 place Denis Dussoubs; 🕒 8.30am-noon & 1.30-6.30pm Mon-Sat) Provides information on the Haute-Vienne, including B&B reservations and organised cycling and hiking trips.

Tourist Office (☎ 05 55 34 46 87; otlimoges.haute-vienne@en-france.com; 12 blvd de Fleurus; 🕒 9am-7pm Mon-Sat, 10am-6pm Sun mid-Jun–mid-Sep, 9am-noon & 2-7pm Mon-Sat mid-Sep–mid-Jun) The office also organises guided walks of the town from February to June.

Sights

PORCELAIN & ENAMEL

The **Musée National Adrien Dubouché** (☎ 05 55 33 08 50; 8bis place Winston Churchill; adult/18-25 yrs/under 18 €4/2.60/free; 🕒 10am-12.30pm & 2-5.45pm Wed-Mon, no lunch break Jul & Aug) has one of France's two most outstanding ceramics collections (the other is in Sèvres, southwest of Paris). An English language brochure is available at the entrance.

The **Bernardaud porcelain factory** (☎ 05 55 10 55 91; 27 av Albert Thomas), 1km northwest of the Musée National Adrien Dubouché, can be visited daily June to September; **tours** (adult/under 12 €4/free) are from 9.15am to 11am and 1pm to 4.30pm and include a demonstration. The rest of the year tours take place Monday to Friday (and sometimes on Saturday), but you have to phone ahead.

In Limoges *émail* (eh-*my*) has nothing to do with the Internet, it means 'enamel', which has been produced here since the 12th

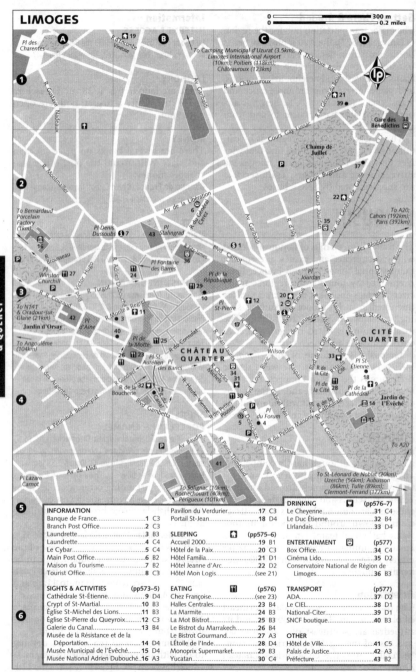

LIMOGES

INFORMATION	
Banque de France	1 C3
Branch Post Office	2 C3
Laundrette	3 B3
Laundrette	4 C4
Le Cybar	5 C4
Main Post Office	6 B2
Maison du Tourisme	7 B2
Tourist Office	8 C3

SIGHTS & ACTIVITIES	(pp573–5)
Cathédrale St-Étienne	9 D4
Crypt of St-Martial	10 B3
Église St-Michel des Lions	11 B3
Église St-Pierre du Queyroix	12 C3
Galerie du Canal	13 B4
Musée de la Résistance et de la Déportation	14 D4
Musée Municipal de l'Évêché	15 D4
Musée National Adrien Dubouché	16 A3
Pavillon du Verdurier	17 C3
Portail St-Jean	18 D4

SLEEPING	(pp575–6)
Accueil 2000	19 B1
Hôtel de la Paix	20 C3
Hôtel Familia	21 D1
Hôtel Jeanne d'Arc	22 D2
Hôtel Mon Logis	(see 21)

EATING	(p576)
Chez Françoise	(see 23)
Halles Centrales	23 B4
La Marmite	24 B3
La Mot Bistrot	25 B3
Le Bistrot du Marrakech	26 B4
Le Bistrot Gourmand	27 A3
L'Étoile de l'Inde	28 D4
Monoprix Supermarket	29 B3
Yucatan	30 C4

DRINKING	(pp576–7)
Le Cheyenne	31 C4
Le Duc Étienne	32 B4
L'Irlandais	33 D4

ENTERTAINMENT	(p577)
Box Office	34 C4
Cinéma Lido	35 D2
Conservatoire National de Région de Limoges	36 B3

TRANSPORT	(p577)
ADA	37 D2
Le CIEL	38 D1
National-Citer	39 D1
SNCF boutique	40 B3

OTHER	
Hôtel de Ville	41 C5
Palais de Justice	42 A3
Préfecture	43 B2

century. The Musée Municipal (below) has a fine collection of *émaux* (plural). Stunning (but pricey) contemporary works can be admired at **Galerie du Canal** (☎ 05 55 33 14 11; 15 rue du Canal; ☑ 10am-noon & 2-7pm Tue-Sat; also Mon in Jul, Aug & Dec), a cooperative gallery run by six master enamellists.

Traditional porcelain and enamel galleries can be found south of the tourist office along blvd Louis Blanc.

CHÂTEAU QUARTER

All that remains of the great pilgrimage abbey of St-Martial, founded in AD 848, is an outline on place de la République. The **Crypt of St-Martial** (☑ mid-Jun–mid-Sep), from the 9th-century, contains the tomb of Limoges' first bishop, who converted the population to Christianity. It can be visited.

Église St-Pierre du Queyroix (place St-Pierre) half a block southeast of place de la République, has an impressive 13th-century tower. Across place St-Pierre is the **Pavillon du Verdurier**, an octagonal, porcelain-faced structure that dates from 1900.

Église St-Michel des Lions (rue Adrien Dubouché), named for the two granite lions standing on either side of the tower door, has a huge copper ball perched atop its 65m-high spire. Built between the 14th and 16th centuries, it contains St-Martial's relics (including his head) and a number of beautiful 15th-century stained-glass windows.

Just off place St-Aurélien, the pedestrianised **rue de la Boucherie** – so named because of the butcher's shops that lined the street in the Middle Ages – and nearby streets are graced with half-timbered houses.

CITÉ QUARTER

The crumbly granite **Cathédrale St-Étienne** – one of the few Gothic churches built south of the Loire – was begun in 1273 and completed in 1888. Facing place St-Étienne, the Flamboyant Gothic **Portail St-Jean** (the carved portal of the northern transept arm) dates from the early 1500s. Inside, the richly decorated Renaissance rood screen, once situated at the entrance to the choir (c 1300), is now in a less conspicuous location at the far end of the nave. Note the cathedral's remarkably slender pillars.

The **Musée Municipal de l'Évêché** (☎ 05 55 45 98 10; place de la Cathédrale; admission free; ☑ 10-11.45am & 2-6pm Wed-Mon, to 5pm Oct-May, also Tue Jul-Sep) spe-

cialises in 12th- to 20th-century enamel but also has a handful of lesser-known works by Pierre-Auguste Renoir, born in Limoges in 1841. Across the courtyard, the **Musée de la Résistance et de la Déportation** (☎ 05 55 45 98 10; admission free; ☑ 10-11.45am & 2-6pm Wed-Mon Jun-mid-Sep, 2-5pm mid-Sep–May, also Tue Jul-Sep) illustrates the exploits of the Resistance and the suffering of the deportees with the help of photos, handbills, maps and military equipment. Both 18th-century buildings are in a peaceful, terraced garden.

The cathedral is surrounded by the **Jardin de l'Évêché**, Limoges' botanical garden, whose formal beds include both medicinal and toxic herbs and lots of flowers. Nearby **rue Haute Cité** is lined with 16th- and 17th-century houses that have granite lower floors and half-timbered upper storeys.

Sleeping
BUDGET
Hôtel Mon Logis (☎ 05 55 77 41 43; www.hotel-limoges-monlogis.com in French; 16 rue du Général du Bessol; s from €24, s/d with shower from €26/29.50; P) Don't be put off by the fierce-looking Alsatian guard dog – this one-star hotel, close to the station, is about the best budget option. The simple, brown-carpeted rooms have toilet cubicles and hairdryers; some have TVs.

Accueil 2000 (☎ 05 55 77 63 97; fjt.accueil-2000@wanadoo.fr; 20 rue d'Encombe Vineuse; s incl breakfast €14; reception ☑ 24hr) A charmless 93-room co-ed hostel for young working people. It accepts travellers year-round, though rooms are most likely to be available in summer.

Camping
Camping Municipal d'Uzurat (☎ 05 55 38 49 43; av d'Uzurat; sites 2 people & tent €9; ☼ Jul-Aug) This is a three-star camping ground on the edge of the Bastide forest about 3.5km north of the train station. By bus, take No 20 to av Louis Armand stop and then walk along the lake for about 400m.

MID-RANGE
Hôtel de la Paix (☎ 05 55 34 36 00; fax 05 55 32 37 06; 25 place Jourdan; d with shower/& toilet from €36/47; (P)) This is the place where time has stood still. Antique gramophones and related memorabilia clutter the corridors, floral print runs wild and the impeccable, courteous service can only be from times gone by. A delightful old hotel with modern, comfortable rooms; the spacious ones on the 2nd floor have balconies. Free parking out the front.

Hôtel Jeanne d'Arc (☎ 05 55 77 67 77; www.hotel jeannedarc-limoges.fr; 17 av du Général de Gaulle; s/d with shower €53/62.50, s/d with bath €68/78; (P)) This old blue-shuttered coaching inn has been transformed into a charming three-star hotel. The elegant, traditionally furnished rooms come with big beds, armchairs and desks.

Hôtel Familia (☎ 05 55 77 51 40; 18 rue du Général du Bessol; d with shower & toilet €40) A very well-maintained, two-star hotel in a quiet spot close to the station. The rooms are spotless and fully equipped although the building itself is nothing special.

Eating
Two areas in particular have a good concentration of restaurants; around Halles Centrales in the Château Quarter, and around rue Haute Cité in the Cité Quarter.

Chez Françoise (☎ 05 55 32 32 79; Halles Centrales; menus €8.50/15; ☼ lunch only, closed Sun & holidays) Fast food, local style. Find a space between the friendly market workers on these long benches and tuck in to a hearty, three-course feed for €8.50. There's a limited choice – usually a couple of meat options plus a fish choice for the main – but it's great value.

Le Bistrot du Marrakech (☎ 05 55 34 49 68; 11 place de la Motte; mains €12-16) Despite tacky Moroccan décor and sloppy presentation, this intimate restaurant serves delicious sizzling tagines.

The melt-in-the-mouth lamb and prune tagine (€12) is an absolute winner.

La Mot Bistrot (☎ 05 55 34 47 19; 22 place de la Motte; mains €7.50-12) In a sunny corner overlooking bustling place de la Motte, this is a good place to people-watch and work on the facial tan while tucking into traditional French café-bistro fare or sipping an espresso.

Yucatan (☎ 05 55 33 67 77; 3 rue Charles Michels; mains €6-9.80; ☼ Tue-Sun) Sombrero lamp shades, fake cacti and colourful ponchos fill this lively Tex-Mex place; fajitas, tacos, burgers and cocktails fill the menu. This is one of a handful of busy eateries at the bottom of rue Charles Michels.

La Marmite (☎ 05 55 33 38 34; 1 place Fontaine des Barres; menus €16.50-37; ☼ Tue-Sat) In a pretty square of lop-sided medieval houses, this intimate place occupying a rustic, 17th-century building, offers traditional Périgord specialities.

Le Bistrot Gourmand (☎ 05 55 10 29 29; 5-7 place Winston Churchill; ☼ noon-3pm & 7-11.30pm Mon-Sat; mains €7.90-16.50) This large and popular bistro-style restaurant serves tasty fish and meat mains. Choose from the cosy inside room or the sunny conservatory.

L'Étoile de l'Inde (☎ 05 55 32 46 95; 7 rue Haute Cité) French waitresses finely dressed in full Indian regalia serve up tasty tandoori and curry dishes (some vegetarian) from €5, though the screeching Goa techno is a bit unnecessary.

SELF-CATERING
Stock up at the **Halles Centrales** (covered market; place de la Motte; ☼ to 1pm), or the **Monoprix supermarket** (42 rue Jean Jaurès; ☼ 8.30am-8pm Mon-Sat).

Drinking
Rue Charles Michels, with its many watering holes, has been nicknamed 'rue de la Soif' (Thirst St) by local students.

Le Cheyenne (☎ 05 55 32 32 62; 4 rue Charles Michels; ☼ 7pm-1am Mon-Sat) A small, lively spot for cowboys and students.

Le Duc Étienne (place St-Aurélien; ☼ 2pm-2am Mon-Sat, 6pm-2am Sun) Also in the Cité Quarter area is this small, mellow bar popular with students.

Le Trompe L'Oeil (☎ 05 55 32 51 03; 26 place de la Motte; ☼ 11am-midnight Tue-Sat) A trendy new café-bar in a charming medieval building, with tables that spill out onto the square.

L'Irlandais (☎ 05 55 32 46 47; 2 rue Haute Cité; Ⓨ 5pm-1am Tue-Fri, 3pm-2am Sat & Sun) In the hip Quartier de la Cathédrale, L'Irlandais is run by a Breton and is a friendly little place. In an atmospheric old building with a wooden interior, it has live music on Friday and Saturday and seats outside in summer.

Entertainment
Tickets for cultural events all over southwestern France are available from **box office** (☎ 05 55 33 28 16; 15 rue Jean Jaurès; Ⓨ Tue-Sat).

Conservatoire National de Région de Limoges (☎ 05 55 45 95 50; 9 rue Fitz-James) holds regular concerts and lessons in traditional musical instruments.

Cinéma Lido (☎ 05 36 68 20 15; 3 av du Général de Gaulle) screens nondubbed films.

Getting There & Away
AIR
Just off the A20, **Limoges International Airport** (☎ 05 55 43 30 30; www.aeroportlimoges.com in French) is 10km west of Limoges. It is served by domestic flights and Ryanair flights from the UK.

BUS
Buses to destinations such as Oradour-sur-Glane (€3), St-Léonard de Noblat (€3 by SNCF bus), Tulle (€16.30 by SNCF bus), Solignac (€2) and Rochechouart (€5) depart from **Le CIEL** (Centre Intermodal d'Échanges de Limoges; ☎ 05 55 45 10 10), the bus terminal that is situated right across the tracks from the train station.

CAR
Hire cars from **ADA** (☎ 05 55 79 61 12; 27 av du Général de Gaulle) or **National-Citer** (☎ 05 55 77 10 10; 8 cours Gay-Lussac).

TRAIN
The green-domed, Art Deco-style **Gare des Bénédictins** (☎ 0 836 353 535), completed in 1929, is one of the most striking train stations in France.

Train destinations include Paris' Gare d'Austerlitz (€39.50, three hours, 12 daily), Aubusson (€12.30, 1¾ hours, three daily, one on Sunday), Cahors (€23.30, 2¼ hours, five daily), Périgueux (€13.30, one hour, 13 daily) and Uzerche (€9, 40 minutes, 11 daily).

Tickets are also available from the **SNCF boutique** (4 rue Othon Péconnet).

AROUND LIMOGES
Oradour-sur-Glane
This village, site of a horrific SS massacre in 1944 (below), has been turned into a moving and evocative memorial.

Seven buses daily link Le CIEL in Limoges with Oradour-sur-Glane (€3, 30 minutes). By car, take the D9 and follow the road signs to the *village martyr* (martyred village).

SILENCE BEARS WITNESS

Oradour-sur-Glane, 21km northwest of Limoges, was an unexceptional Limousin town until the afternoon of 10 June 1944, when German lorries bearing an SS detachment rumbled into town.

The town's entire population was ordered to assemble at the market square. The men were divided into groups and forced into *granges* (barns), where they were gunned down before the structures were set alight. Several hundred women and children were herded into the church, inside which a bomb was detonated; those who tried to escape through the windows were shot before the building was set on fire. The Nazi troops then burned down the entire town: inside the 328 buildings left smouldering that evening were the corpses of dozens of civilians who had hidden to avoid capture. Of the people rounded up that day – among them refugees from Paris and a couple of Jewish families living under assumed names – only one woman and five men survived; 642 people, including 205 children, were killed.

Since these events, the entire **village** (admission free; Ⓨ 9am-5pm, to 7pm mid-May–mid-Sep) has been left untouched to serve as a memorial. The tram tracks and overhead wires, the prewar-style electricity lines and the rusting hulks of 1930s automobiles give a pretty good idea of what the town must have looked like on the morning of the massacre.

Entry to the village is via the **Centre de la Mémoire** (adult/child, student & war veteran €6/4; Ⓨ same as the village) which describes the village before the massacre and shows survivors' testimonies and executioners' confessions.

After the war, a larger Oradour was built a few hundred metres west of the ruins.

Solignac
pop 1350

The pretty medieval village of Solignac, 10km south of Limoges on the River Briance, owes its outsized, 75m-long granite **church** to its popularity as a stopover on the pilgrimage route to Santiago de Compostela (Spain; p604). Built during the second quarter of the 1100s in the Limousin-Romanesque style, the sober, one-time abbey church is – thanks to the domed roof – remarkably wide (14m) and (considering that it's pre-Gothic) pretty well lit. The **stalls** in the nave, made for the Benedictines in the late 1400s, are decorated with carved human heads, bizarre animals and a monk mooning the world. Above the stalls, the **capitals** of the columns – intended to further the moral education of the faithful – are decorated with human figures being devoured by dragons and serpents. There's a 15th-century **fresco** of St-Christophe on the southern (right-hand) wall of the choir. One of the transept arms is crowned with a dome, the other by a barrel arch.

The 12km-long **Sentier de la Briance**, with yellow trail markings, leads you through the surrounding countryside, much of it forested. Shorter trails are also marked; maps are available at the tourist office. The **Parc du Reynou** (☎ 05 55 00 40 00; www.parczooreynou.com in French; exit 37 off the A20; adult/child €9/6.50; ☯ 10am-8pm Apr-Sep; 1-5pm Wed, Sat & Sun Oct-Mar) is a free-range exotic animal park a few kilometres away in Le Vigen, popular with children.

Solignac's **tourist office** (☎ 05 55 00 42 31; tourisme-solignac@wanadoo.fr; ☯ 10am-1pm & 2.30-6.30pm Tue-Sat, 10am-1pm & 3-6pm Sun May-Sep; 9am-noon & 2-6pm Tue-Fri & 9am-noon Sat Oct-Apr) is in the car park across the street from the church. When it's closed, brochures are available from the Secretariat on the 1st floor of the *mairie* (village hall) at 57 av St-Eloi, 150m west of the church.

Hôtel Le St-Eloi (☎ 05 55 00 44 52; fax 05 55 00 55 56; 66 av St-Eloi; r from €43), 150m from the church's western front, has 15 Provençal-style rooms. It has an attached **restaurant** (menus from €14; ☯ closed Sun evening, Mon lunch & Jan).

When school is in session, three buses daily (except Sunday) link Le CIEL in Limoges with Solignac (€3, 25 minutes, two the rest of the year); and the neighbouring hamlet of Le Vigen (€3, 35 minutes, two or three daily year-round). The Solignac–Le Vigen train station is linked to Limoges (€2.50, 10 minutes) and Uzerche (€9, 40 minutes) by one or two trains daily.

AUBUSSON
pop 5000

Aubusson, about 90km from both Limoges and Clermont-Ferrand, has been acclaimed for its exquisite tapestries and carpets for over 500 years.

Sights

These days the town, in something of an economic slump, and nearby Felletin (10km to the south) are home to about 30 tapestry workshops. Their products, both traditional and contemporary, are on display in season at the **L'Exposition Tapisseries d'Aubusson-Felletin** (admission €3; ☯ 9am-12.30pm & 2-6pm Jun-Sep, no lunch break Jul & Aug), held inside the town hall on the Grande Rue (the main drag).

Across the curvaceous River Creuse, on the other side of the hill (on top of which sit the ruins of a chateau), is the modest **Musée Départemental de la Tapisserie** (☎ 05 55 83 08 30; adult/child €4/2.50; ☯ 9.30am-noon & 2-6pm Wed-Mon, no lunch break Jul & Aug). The museum houses changing exhibits of antique and modern tapestries. The town's tapestry workshops include the large **Manufacture St-Jean** (☎ 05 55 66 10 08; av des Lissiers; ☯ 9am-noon & 2-5.30pm Mon-Fri), 200m from the Musée Départemental, which can be toured for €6.50. Call in advance to book a tour.

Aubisson's **tourist office** (☎ 05 55 66 32 12; ☯ 10am-7pm Mon-Sat, 10am-noon & 2.30-5.30pm Sun & holidays mid-Jun–mid-Sep; 9.30am-12.30pm & 2-6pm Mon-Sat mid-Sep–Easter; to 6.30pm Mon-Sat & to 5.30pm Sun Easter–mid-Jun), down the alley from 65 Grande Rue, has details about visiting many of the area's other tapestry *ateliers*, most of which have no admission fee. Next door, the 16th-century **Maison du Tapissier** (admission €3) houses a museum of the history of tapestry-making. Opening hours are the same as those of the tourist office, which handles ticket sales.

Sleeping & Eating

Hôtel du Lissier (☎ 05 55 66 14 18; fax 05 55 66 33 87; 84 Grande Rue; s/d with shower & toilet €34/39; reception ☯ closed Sun, & Mon night in winter) The Hôtel du Lissier has brand-new colour-coordinated rooms that are bright and spacious. The attached restaurant downstairs has a small selection of standard, good-value dishes (€7.50 to 11.50).

Hôtel Le France (☎ 05 55 66 10 22, 05 55 66 88 64; 6 rue des Déportés; r from €46) This is a charming hotel occupying an 18th-century *hôtel particulier* with an imposing white-shuttered façade. The spotlessly clean rooms are comfortable and well-equipped.

Getting There & Away
Aubusson is linked to Limoges by four SNCF buses each day (€12.10, 1¾ hours), except on Sunday.

UZERCHE
pop 3500
Set on a promontory high above the River Vézère, the picturesque town of Uzerche – much quieter now the A20 diverts most traffic around the town – is known for its 15th- and 16th-century **Maisons à Tourelles**, which look like small castles thanks to their turrets. Some fine examples can be seen around **Porte Bécharie**, a 14th-century town gate near place Marie Colein.

At the top of the hill, high above the steep, dark-grey slate rooftops, is **Église St-Pierre**. A barrel-vaulted, Romanesque abbey church, it has a typically Limousin-style belfry and an 11th-century crypt, reached through a squat door in the outside wall of the choir.

Take the D3 under the railway viaduct to get a panoramic view of the town.

Orientation & Information
The old city is perched on a hill almost entirely surrounded by a hairpin curve in the Vézère. The only street into the old city is at shop-lined place Marie Colein, which is about 500m up the D920 (av de Paris) from the D3.

Tourist Office (☎ 05 55 73 15 71; ot.uzerche@wanadoo fr; place de la Libération; ☼ 10am-12.30pm & 2.30-5.30pm Mon-Sat, 10am-12.30pm & 2.30-6pm Sun Jun-Sep, 10am-noon & 2-5.30pm Mon-Fri Apr, May & Oct, 10am-noon Mon-Fri Nov-Mar) Behind the church.

Sleeping & Eating
Hôtel Jean Teyssier (☎ 05 55 73 10 05; http://hotel teyssier.free.fr in French; rue du Pont-Turgot; d from €47; ☼ reception closed Tue & Wed, except from 5pm mid-Jul–mid-Sep) An attractive, two-star place with 14 rooms, at the intersection of the N20 and D3; it has a **restaurant** (menus €18-33; ☼ closed Wed).

Hôtel Ambroise (☎ 05 55 73 28 60; fax 05 55 98 45 73; 34 av de Paris; r with shower €38) A rustic family

hotel with a pretty garden right on the river. The two-star rooms have older-style furnishings and lovely river views.

Getting There & Away
Uzerche is linked to Limoges, 56km to the north, by train (€9, 40 minutes, 11 daily). The train station is 2km north of the old city along the N20.

BRIVE-LA-GAILLARDE
pop 51,590
Brive-La-Gaillarde (Brive), known for its champion rugby team, is sprawling, ugly and of little interest to most travellers. However, nearby areas of the Corrèze *département* include some of Limousin's most attractive towns and villages. A major rail junction, Brive can be used as a transport, provisioning and accommodation base.

The **tourist office** (☎ 05 55 24 08 80; www.brive -tourisme.com in French; place du 14 Juillet; ☼ 9am-7pm Mon-Sat, 10am-1pm Sun Jul & Aug, 9am-noon & 2-6pm Mon-Sat except holidays Sep-Jun) is housed in a 19th-century water tower.

A cluster of cheap hotels near the train station includes the **Hôtel Le France**(☎ 05 55 74 08 13; 60 av de la Gare; r from €32) with tiny rooms into which a shower and toilet have been squeezed. For more comfort, the three-star **Hôtel Le Quercy** (☎ 05 55 74 09 26; fax 05 55 74 06 24; r €49; P ☼) offers spacious rooms with carpeted walls, cable TV and large baths. It's opposite the tourist office.

Brive is the region's major rail and bus hub – see the relevant town and city listings for details. The **bus station** (☎ 05 55 17 91 19; place du 14 Juillet; ☼ 8.15am-noon & 2-6.15pm Mon-Sat) is next to the tourist office. Local and intercity buses do not run on Sunday or holidays.

The train station is linked to the tourist office and bus station, 1.3km to the southwest, by the hourly bus No 5, which runs until a little before 7pm.

NORTHEAST OF BRIVE
Aubazine
The restful, idyllic village of Aubazine sits on a hilltop surrounded by forests, sloping pastures and verdant valleys. The small **tourist office** (☎ 05 55 25 79 93; place de l'Église) is in the village hall on the main square. Opening hours vary.

The 12th-century Romanesque **church** contains an extremely rare oak **armoire liturgique** (liturgical chest) from the late 1100s, as well as the elaborately carved, 13th-century limestone **tomb** of Étienne d'Obazine, founder of the Cistercian abbey to which the church once belonged. About 300m north, along route de Tulle, the small, Greek Melchite (Catholic) monastery has a modern, Byzantine-style **Chapelle Grecque** (Greek Chapel).

One of the area's footpaths heads up the hill to the **Puy de Paulliac** (or Pauliat; 520m), which has a *cromlech* (dolmen) at the top and affords fine views. For part of the way it follows the abbey's one-time aqueduct, the **Canal des Moines**.

Hôtel Le Saint Étienne (☎ 05 55 25 71 01; hotel.saint-etienne@netcourrier.com; place du Bourg; r from €43; ☻ Mar-Nov), a two-star inn, is housed in a 14th-century chateau in the centre of the village. Its 41 rooms are simply designed but comfortable. The adjoining **restaurant** (menus €15-19.50; ☻ closed Mon & dinner Sun) serves traditional French cuisine in a sunny courtyard.

Tulle
pop 15,500

The town of Tulle (pronounced with a long 'Toole'), prefecture of the Corrèze *département* and home of France's last accordion factory, stretches along both banks of the River Corrèze for some 3km. The river itself is hard to spot, as it's choked with lines of traffic along both banks. The train station is 2km southwest of the cathedral.

Opposite the cathedral (and next to the ornate **Maison de Loyac**) is Tulle's **tourist office** (☎ 05 55 26 59 61; office-de-tourisme-de-tulle@wanadoo.fr; ☻ 2-6pm Mon, 9am-noon & 2-6pm Tue-Sat & 10am-noon Sun Jul & Aug).

There's a busy market selling local produce, lace and clothes in front of the cathedral on Wednesday mornings.

Next door to the Romanesque and Gothic **cathedral**, which consists of just a nave (the transept collapsed in 1796), a 13th-century cloister leads to the **Musée du Cloître** (☎ 05 55 26 91 05; adult/student/under 7 yrs €2.35/1.10/free; ☻ closed Wed morning & Sat), which displays an eclectic collection that includes lace, ceramics and religious sculpture. Walking around the tranquil cloistered courtyard is free.

At the other end of town and across the river from the train station, the **Musée des Armes Anciennes** (Armaments Museum; ☎ 05 55 20 28 28; 1 rue du 9 Juin 1944; ☻ 9am-noon & 2-6pm Mon-Fri Jul & Aug, 2-6pm Wed & 9am-noon & 2-6pm Thu & Fri Sep-Jun)

displays firearms collected over the last two centuries by the city's national armaments manufactory.

Hôtel Le Bon Accueil (☎ /fax 05 55 26 70 57; 8-10 rue du Canton; d €30; ☻ reception usually closed Sat night & Sun), right across the river from the cathedral, is a one-star place whose average rooms are brightened up with cheesy photos of cats and fast cars. The attached rustic **restaurant** (menus from €12) has hearty, family-style French meals.

Despite its position overlooking the station, the brightly painted **Hôtel de la Gare** (☎ 05 55 20 04 04; 25 av Winston Churchill; d from €39) is a good mid-range option worth its two stars.

Le Richlieu (☎ 05 55 26 42 18; 8 av Charles de Gaulle) is a friendly, traditional bar where locals hang out. You can buy a sandwich at the adjacent patisserie and eat it at the bar's outdoor tables.

Tulle is linked by train and SNCF bus to Brive (€4.40, 25 minutes, nine to 15 daily) and Clermont-Ferrand (€19.60, three hours, three to seven daily).

Gimel-les-Cascades
pop 650

This tiny, flower-filled village, lying 37km northeast of Brive-la-Gaillarde, is set amid some of the most spectacular scenery in Limousin. It's an ideal spot to come for a picturesque stroll and a picnic.

A few hundred metres down the hill from the late-15th-century **Église St-Pardoux**, known for its late-12th-century enamel reliquary, are the **Cascades**, three waterfalls that drop 143m into a gorge aptly named the Inferno. They're within a privately owned **park** (☎ 05 55 21 26 49; adult/6-14 yrs €4/3; ☻ 10am-6pm Mar-Oct).

Other sights in and around Gimel-les-Cascades include the **Pont de Péage**, a medieval toll bridge rebuilt in the 1700s; the ruins of the **Château de Roche Haute**; the remains of the Romanesque **Église St-Étienne de Braguse**; and the Big Dipper–shaped, 20-hectare **Étang de Ruffaud**, a lake that offers a refreshing dip and a shady retreat for a picnic. Walking options include the trails along the **Gorges de la Vallée de la Montane**. Details are available at the **tourist office** (☎ 05 55 21 44 32; ☻ 10am-6pm Jul & Aug), 50m up the hill from the church.

Hostellerie de la Vallée (☎ 05 55 21 40 60; fax 05 55 21 38 74; d with shower/bath €41/43; ☻ Mar-Dec) is a two-star place between the church and the tourist office. Its nine simple, newly renovated rooms are small but the view and sound of the nearby cascades from the bedroom windows more than make up for the lack of space. The attached **restaurant** (menus €19.50-30; ☺ Thu-Tue), overlooking the gorge, offers delicious home-cooked food using local produce.

SOUTHEAST OF BRIVE

This part of Limousin is very near Carennac (p608), Rocamadour (p607), Château de Castelnau-Bretenoux (p608) and the Gouffre de Padirac (p608).

Turenne

pop 755

The pretty hilltop village of Turenne, 11km west of Collonges-la-Rouge on the D8 road, and 28km south of Brive, enjoyed considerable independence – under a viscount – from about 1000 until 1738. However, it was sold to Louis XV, whose taxation sent the town into precipitous decline as the artisan class fled. Dominating the village is the **chateau** (☎ 05 55 85 90 66; adult/under 18 €3/2; ☺ 10am-7pm Jul & Aug, 10am-noon & 2-6pm Apr-Jun, Sep & Oct, 2-5pm Sun Nov-Mar), on a sheer limestone outcrop that affords superb panoramas of the surrounding countryside. The massive 17th-century **Collégiale** (Collegiate Church) is in the style of the Counter-Reformation. Turenne is on the GR46 footpath.

The **tourist office** (☎ 05 55 85 94 38; ☺ 9am-12.30pm & 3-6.30pm Jul & Aug, 10am-12.30pm & 3-6pm Apr-Jun & Sep) is a few metres from place du Foirail (on the D8). The rest of the time, brochures can be picked up at the village hall, 200m to the west, on weekday and Saturday mornings and in the afternoon on Tuesday, Thursday and Friday.

La Maison des Chanoines (☎ 05 55 85 93 43; d €60-85; ☺ Apr-Oct), surrounded by 15th- to 18th-century slate-roofed houses, is a charming, six-room hotel in the centre of the village. It has stylish accommodation and there is an attached **restaurant** (menus €30-36) with a tree-shaded terrace, serving creative French food.

Turenne Gare, 3km southeast of the village, is served by a daily train from Brive (€2.80, 14 minutes). From Monday to Saturday there are buses from Brive (€2.80, 25 minutes, one or two daily).

Collonges-la-Rouge

pop 50

On a gently angled slope above a tributary of the Dordogne, the narrow alleyways of 'Collonges-the-Red', built entirely of bright red sandstone, squeeze between wisteria-covered houses topped with round turrets. Surrounded by lush greenery, and in the spring flowers of every colour, this tiny hamlet is a delightful place for a stroll.

The part Romanesque **church**, constructed from the 11th to the 15th centuries on the foundations of an 8th-century Benedictine priory, was an important resting place on the pilgrimage to Santiago de Compostela (p604). In the late 16th century local Protestants held prayers in the southern nave and their Catholic neighbours prayed in the northern nave, where there is still a gilded-wood retable erected in the 17th century. Nearby, the ancient wood and slate roof of the **old covered market**, held up by stone columns, shelters an ancient baker's oven.

The **tourist office** (☎ 05 55 25 47 57; ☺ 10am-7pm Jul & Aug, 10am-12.30pm & 2.30-7pm Jun & Sep, 11am-noon & 2-5pm Mon-Fri Oct-Mar) is next to the town hall on the village's 'main' road, a turning from the D38.

Relais de St-Jacques de Compostelle (☎ 05 55 25 41 02; fax 05 55 84 08 51; d with shower & toilet €50-65; ☺ mid-Mar–mid-Nov), the only place to stay, has 11 rooms. It's in a partly medieval building in the centre of the village. The attached **restaurant** (menus from €18-45) has traditional regional fare.

Collonges is linked by bus with Brive, 18km to the northwest along the D38 (€3, 30 minutes, six on weekdays and one only on Saturday).

Beaulieu-sur-Dordogne

pop 1300

The verdant, aptly named town of Beaulieu (literally 'beautiful place'), one of the most attractive medieval villages along the upper Dordogne, is well worth at least an overnight visit.

INFORMATION

Tourist Office (☎ 05 55 91 09 94; www.beaulieu -sur-dordogne.fr in French; place Marbot; ☺ 9am-7pm Jul & Aug, 10am-12.30pm & 2.30-5pm Mon-Sat Sep-Jun, 10am-12.30pm & 2.30-5pm Apr-Sep) On the D940, it has an English-language walking guide (€2) and Internet access (€6 per hour).

LIMOUSIN, THE DORDOGNE & QUERCY

SIGHTS

Beaulieu is famed for the majestic **Abbatiale St-Pierre**, a 12th-century Romanesque abbey church that was a stop on the Santiago de Compostela pilgrimage (p604). The southern portal's brilliant **tympanum** (c 1130), based upon prophecies from the books of Daniel and the Apocalypse, illustrates the Last Judgement with vivid scenes including monsters devouring the condemned. The **treasury**, with its 12th-century gilded Virgin and 13th-century enamel reliquary, is on view inside. The nearby streets have picturesque houses that date from the 14th and 15th centuries.

Lovely areas for a stroll include **Faubourg de la Chapelle**, a neighbourhood of 17th- and 18th-century houses on the banks of the Dordogne, especially up towards **Chapelle des Pénitents**, a Romanesque chapel. The river can be crossed on foot at the dam. The GR480, a spur of the GR46, passes by here.

SLEEPING

Auberge de Jeunesse de la Riviera Limousine (☎ 05 55 91 13 82; www.fuaj.org/aj/beaulieu; place du Monturu; dm €9.20; ☒ Apr-Nov, reception 6-9pm) This is a homey, 28-bed place idyllically situated along the river, occupying a partly 14th-century building. Kitchen facilities are available. Bags can be left during the day.

Auberge Les Charmilles (☎ 05 55 91 29 29; charme@club-Internet.fr; 20 blvd Rodolphe de Turenne; d with large bathroom €52) Housed in a lovely old building overlooking the river, Auberge Les Charmilles has eight delightful rooms and a garden.

Hôtel L'Étape Fleurie (☎ 05 55 91 11 04; 17 place du Champ de Mars; s from €28, d with shower/bath €38/42). A welcoming 18-room, one-star place with bright, modern rooms.

Camping

Camping des Îles (☎ 05 55 91 02 65; per person €5-7, per car €2.50; ☒ Apr-Oct) On the other side of the old city from the tourist office, this lovely, shaded camping ground is on an island sandwiched between two branches of the Dordogne. Its three-star facilities include tennis, children's play area and fishing.

EATING

Hôtel L'Étape Fleurie (☎ 05 55 91 11 04; 17 place du Champ de Mars; lunch/dinner menus from €10/16.50) This rustic restaurant in the hotel serves family-style regional specialities in a central spot overlooking the main square.

Auberge Les Charmilles (☎ 05 55 91 29 29; charme@club-Internet.fr; 20 blvd Rodolphe de Turenne; ☒ closed Tue & Wed Oct-Apr) This place offers delicious, classic French cuisine. Try a dozen oysters or pork in balsamic vinegar.

Au Beau Lieu Breton (☎ 05 55 91 20 46; rue du Presbytère; crepes €4-7; ☒ closed Mon Sep-Mar) On an alley behind (west of) the church, Au Beau Lieu Breton serves sweet and savoury crepes as well as omelettes and salads.

On Wednesday and Saturday mornings, an open-air market is held next to the village church. At least one of the two grocery stores on place Marbot – the Suprette and the Casino – are open daily (closed Sunday afternoon except in July and August); midday closure for both lasts from 12.30pm to 2.30pm or 3pm.

GETTING THERE & AWAY

Beaulieu is situated 70km east of Sarlat-la-Canéda and 47km northeast of the Gouffre de Padirac (p608).

From Monday to Saturday, there are buses linking Beaulieu with Brive (€5.90, one hour, one to three daily, none to two daily during school holidays). Schedules are posted at the bus shelter on place du Champ de Mars (opposite Hôtel L'Étape Fleurie) and outside the tourist office.

THE DORDOGNE

Known to the French as Périgord, the Dordogne *département*, named after the most important of the region's seven rivers, was one of the prehistoric cradles of human civilisation. The remains of Neanderthal and Cro-Magnon people have been discovered throughout the region, and quite a number of local caves, including the world-famous Lascaux, are decorated with extraordinary works of prehistoric art. Périgord's numerous hilltop chateaux (p585) and *bastides* (opposite) bear witness to the bloody battles waged here during the Middle Ages and the Hundred Years' War.

To make the region's attractions more accessible to visitors, Périgord has been divided into four areas, each assigned a colour according to its most prominent feature. The fields and forests to the north and northwest are known as Périgord Vert (green). In the centre, the area of limestone surrounding the capital, Périgueux, and along the River Isle is known as Périgord Blanc (white). The wine-growing area of Périgord Pourpre (purple) lies to the southwest, around Bergerac. Périgord Noir (black), known for its dark forests and many chateaux, encompasses the Vézère Valley and, to the south, part of the Dordogne valley; between the two valleys lies the attractive medieval town of Sarlat-la-Canéda.

Warm-weather sports that are popular within the region include canoeing, kayaking, fishing, rock climbing, horse riding and cycling. Tourist offices have details and can supply you with informative, English-language brochures.

During the warmer months, the Dordogne, famed for its rich cuisine, attracts vast numbers of tourists, including many from the UK. In winter the region goes into deep hibernation, and many hotels, restaurants and tourist sites close.

PÉRIGUEUX

pop 33,294

Périgueux, prefecture of the Dordogne *département,* has a restored medieval and Renaissance quarter, much of it built of dazzling white limestone, and one of France's best museums of prehistory. Founded over 2000 years ago on a hill bounded by a curve in the gentle River Isle, the city is at its liveliest during the Wednesday and Saturday truffle and foie gras markets (p586).

Périgueux is located 45km northwest of the Vézère Valley.

Orientation

The medieval and Renaissance old city, known as Puy St-Front, is on the hillside between the Isle (to the east), blvd Michel Montaigne and place Bugeaud (to the west). On the other side of place Bugeaud is the old city's historic rival, the largely residential Cité, centred around the ruins of a Roman amphitheatre. The train station is about 1km northwest of the old city.

Information

EMERGENCY

Hôtel de Police (police station; ☎ 05 53 06 44 44; place du Président Roosevelt; ⏰ 24hr) Across from 20 rue du 4 Septembre.

> **BASTIDES**
>
> In the early 1200s the population of southwestern France was growing, as was a certain discontent with feudalism. Local suzerains and bishops, seeing in the new demographics an opportunity to enhance their authority and increase their income from rents, tolls and tariffs, turned to ancient Roman models of urban planning. Over the next 150 years they established more than 300 towns and villages known as *bastides*.
>
> Generally surrounded by defensive walls, these 'new towns' had a regular street grid (terrain permitting), numbered building lots of uniform shape and size (to facilitate tax collection) and a charter granting various privileges to the inhabitants; the arcaded market square – which was the centre of the town's commercial life – often had a church in one corner. *Bastides* that are covered in this chapter include Villefranche de Rouergue (p605), Najac (p606), Monpazier (p597) and Domme (p595).

INTERNET ACCESS
Cybertek (☎ 05 53 06 89 65; 14 cours Fénelon; ⏰ Tue-Sat)

LAUNDRY
There are laundrettes at place Hoche (open 8am to 8pm), 18 rue des Mobiles de Coulmiers (open to 9pm) and 61 rue Gambetta (open to 9pm, except Saturday to 8pm).

MONEY
There are several banks on place Bugeaud.
Banque de France (1 place du Président Roosevelt; money exchange ⏰ 8.45am-12.15pm Mon-Fri)

POST
Main Post Office (1 rue du 4 Septembre) Offers money exchange and a Cyberposte.

TOURIST INFORMATION
Espace Tourisme Périgord (☎ 05 53 35 50 24; 25 rue du Président Wilson; ⏰ 9am-noon & 2-5pm Mon-Fri) Provides information on the Dordogne département.
Tourist Information Kiosk (place André Maurios; ⏰ 9am-8pm Jun-Sep)
Tourist Office (☎ 05 53 53 10 63; tourisme .perigueux@perigord.tm.fr; 26 place Francheville; ⏰ 9am-1pm & 2-6pm Mon-Sat year-round & 10am-1pm & 2-6pm Sun mid-Jun–mid-Sep) The main tourist office.

PÉRIGUEUX

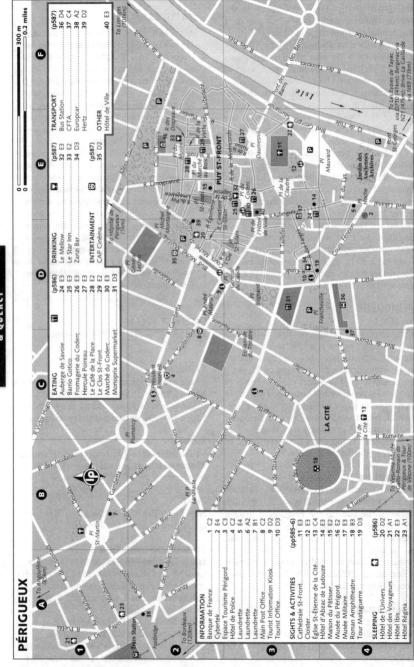

INFORMATION
Banque de France......................1	C2
Cybertek.................................2	E4
Espace Tourisme Périgord............3	C3
Hôtel de Police.........................4	C2
Laundrette..............................5	E4
Laundrette..............................6	A2
Laundrette..............................7	B1
Main Post Office.......................8	C2
Tourist Information Kiosk.............9	D2
Tourist Office..........................10	D3

SIGHTS & ACTIVITIES (pp585–6)
Cathédrale St-Front...................11	E3
Cloister................................12	E3
Église St-Étienne de la Cité.........13	C4
Hôtel d'Abzac de Ladouze............14	E3
Maison du Pâtisser....................15	E2
Musée du Périgord....................16	E3
Musée Militaire........................17	E3
Roman Amphitheatre..................18	B3
Tour Mataguerre.......................19	D3

SLEEPING (p586)
Hôtel de l'Univers.....................20	D2
Hôtel des Voyageurs...................21	A1
Hôtel Ibis..............................22	E3
Hôtel Régina...........................23	A1

EATING (p586)
Auberge de Savoie....................24	E3
Barrio Gotico...........................25	E3
Fromagerie du Coderc.................26	E3
Hercule Poireau.......................27	E3
Le Café de la Place....................28	E3
Le Clos St-Front.......................29	E2
Marché du Coderc....................30	E3
Monoprix Supermarket................31	D3

DRINKING
Le Mellow.............................32	E3
Le Star Inn.............................33	C4
Zanzi Bar..............................34	D3

ENTERTAINMENT (p587)
CAP Cinéma...........................35	D2

TRANSPORT (p587)
Bus Station............................36	D4
CFTA..................................37	C4
Europcar..............................38	A2
Hertz..................................39	D2

OTHER
Hôtel de Ville.........................40	E3

Sights

PUY ST-FRONT

The **Musée du Périgord** (☎ 05 53 06 40 70; 22 cours Tourny; adult/student/under 18 €4/2/free; 11am-6pm Mon, Wed-Fri, 1-6pm Sat & Sun Apr-Sep, 10am-5pm Mon, Wed-Fri, 1-6pm Sat & Sun Oct-Mar, closed holidays) is well known for its rich collection of prehistoric tools and implements; Gallo-Roman and medieval artefacts are also on display. There's free admission from midday to 2pm Monday to Saturday between mid-September and mid-June.

When seen against the evening sky, the **Cathédrale St-Front** (place de la Clautre; admission free; 8am-12.30pm & 2.30-7.30pm), topped with five bump-studded domes and many more equally bumpy domelets, looks like something you might come across in Istanbul. However, by day, the sprawling structure, 'restored' by Abadie (the creator of Paris' Sacré Cœur) in the late 19th century, looks contrived and overwrought in the finest pseudo-Byzantine tradition. The carillon sounds the same hour chime as Big Ben. The best views of the cathedral (and the town) are from **Pont des Barris**.

The ancient cobblestone streets north of the cathedral are lined with centuries-old limestone houses, such as along **rue du Plantier**. A few short blocks to the west, the area's main thoroughfare, **rue Limogeanne**, has graceful Renaissance buildings at Nos 3 and 12. There are more such structures on nearby streets, including **rue Éguillerie** (such as the Renaissance-style **Maison du Pâtisser** at place St-Louis) and **rue de la Miséricorde**. The 15th- and 16th-century houses along **rue Aubergerie** include the **Hôtel d'Abzac de Ladouze** (across from No 19) with its two octagonal towers.

The **Musée Militaire** (☎ 05 53 53 47 36; 32 rue des Farges; admission €3.50; 1-6pm Mon-Sat Apr-Sep, 2-6pm Mon-Sat Oct-Dec, Wed & Sat Jan-Mar, closed holidays), founded right after WWI, has a varied collection of swords, firearms, uniforms and insignia from the Napoleonic wars and the two world wars.

Of the 28 towers that once formed Puy St-Front's medieval fortifications, only **Tour Mataguerre**, a stout, round bastion next to the main tourist office, remains. It was given its present form in the late 15th century.

LA CITÉ

Only a few arches of Périgueux's 1st-century **Roman amphitheatre** are still standing – the rest of the massive structure, designed to hold 30,000 spectators, was disassembled and carried off to construct the city walls in the 3rd century.

The **Église St-Étienne de la Cité** (place de la Cité), constructed in the 11th and 12th centuries, served as Périgueux's cathedral until 1669. Only two cupolas and two bays survived the

CHATEAUX

The Dordogne and Quercy aren't in the same league as the Loire Valley, but they do have quite a few impressive chateaux, many of them massive fortresses built in the Middle Ages. This chapter provides details on visiting the chateaux of Beynac (p596), Biron (p597), Bonaguil (p607), Carennac (p608), Castelnau-Bretenoux (p608), Castelnaud (p596), Milandes (p597) and Najac (p606), as well as Turenne (p581) in southern Limousin.

There are a number of other chateaux in the region:

Jumilhac-le-Grand (☎ 05 53 52 42 97; adult/child €6/4; Jun–Sep, weekends & holidays May, Oct–mid-Nov) A turreted 15th- to 17th-century chateau about 50km northeast of Périgueux along the N21 and D78.

Puyquilhem (☎ 05 53 54 82 18; adult/child €5.20/3.20) A Renaissance-influenced chateau 30km north of Périgueux near Villars.

Hautefort (☎ 05 53 50 51 23; adult/child €8/4; late Mar–Oct, Sun afternoons Nov–mid-Mar, closed mid-Dec–mid-Jan) An imposing neoclassical chateau 40km east of Périgueux. It has an English-style garden and French flower terraces.

Eyrignac (☎ 05 53 28 99 71; adult/child €8/4) Around 13km northeast of Sarlat, this chateau is famed for its exquisite 18th-century French-style gardens.

Puymartin (☎ 05 53 59 29 97; adult/child €6/3; Apr-Nov) A castle-like and partly furnished chateau 8km northwest of Sarlat.

Losse (☎ 05 53 50 80 08; adult/student/child €6/5/3; Easter-Oct) In the Vézère Valley 5km southwest of Montignac, Losse is decorated with 16th- and 17th-century tapestries and furniture.

devastation wrought by the Huguenots during the Wars of Religion (1562–98). Two blocks to the south, the **Vesunna Musée Gallo-Romain de Périgueux** (☎ 05 53 53 00 92; rue Claude Bernard; adult/child €5.50/3.50; ☼ 10am-7pm Jul & Aug, 10am-12.30pm & 2-5.30pm Sep-Jun) is a new museum built to showcase the ruins of a 1st-century Roman villa uncovered in pretty good nick in 1959. The excavations have revealed a treasure-trove of Roman artefacts, jewellery, cooking utensils and some incredible murals. In the grounds stands the **Tour de Vésone**, shaped like a gargantuan anklet, the only remaining section of a Gallo-Roman temple thought to have been dedicated to the goddess Vessuna, protector of the town (and the Roman name for Périgueux).

Tours

There are French-language **guided tours** of the city with guides who speak English two to four times a week (daily in summer). Tickets cost €5 (12 to 18 years and students €3.80); the details are available at the tourist office. Ask also about the less regular **bicycle tours**.

Sleeping

There's a lack of decent accommodation in town in every price range; options are functional rather than memorable. The tourist office can provide details of camping grounds, *chambres d'hôtes* (B&Bs) and youth hostels.

Hôtel de l'Univers (☎ 05 53 53 34 79; fax 05 53 06 70 76; 18 cours Michel Montaigne; s €42.70, d €45-53.35; ☼ Feb-Dec) This welcoming, two-star hotel has a varied selection of generously sized rooms. Most have high ceilings and bathrooms; the two attic rooms are a touch cheaper. There's a decent restaurant (right) downstairs.

Hôtel des Voyageurs (☎ 05 53 53 17 44; 26 rue Denis Papin; s/d from €14/16) This is one of half a dozen inexpensive hotels near the train station, along rue Denis Papin and rue des Mobiles de Coulmiers. The rock-bottom prices here mean tiny rooms and flimsy furniture, but the rooms are perfectly clean, and the creaky staircase helps to drown out the noise from the rowdy bar next door.

Hôtel Régina (☎ 05 53 08 40 44; comfort.perigueux@ wanadoo.fr; 14 rue Denis Papin; d from €42/46; P) This place is one of the better two-star options

in the hotel ghetto around the station, but it may not be to everyone's taste, with pastel walls and brightly coloured soft furnishings. Comfortable, modern and good value. Suitable for disabled guests.

Hôtel Ibis (☎ 05 53 53 64 58; HO636@accor.hotels .com; 8 blvd Georges Saumande; s/d from €41/50; P) The Ibis is a comfortable chain hotel.

Eating

Hercule Poireau (☎ 05 53 08 90 76; 2 rue de la Nation; mains €15-25; ☼ Mon-Fri) An exceptionally stylish eatery in an old stone-arched building opposite the cathedral, serving delicious Périgord specialities. The restaurant has a trendy anteroom for drinks next door.

Le Clos St-Front (☎ 05 53 46 78 58; 12 rue St-Front; menus €16-20; ☼ Tue-Sat) Tucked away in a quiet corner of town, this upmarket place has French *menus* that vary depending on the fresh produce available in the marketplace. The pretty garden is perfect for a long summer lunch.

Auberge de Savoie (☎ 05 53 09 58 32; 19 rue Aubergerie; menus €10-24) Reliable, good-value regional specialities are offered by this mini-chain that prides itself on friendly service as well as tasty food. The sunny terrace, surrounded by medieval buildings, is a winner in season.

Le Café de la Place (☎ 05 53 08 21 11; 7 place du Marché au Bois; mains €11-15) A bohemian, old-style bar where artists and students hang out on the terrace. It serves a large selection of tasty regional dishes, (including the house speciality foie gras) plus salads and local wines by the glass.

Hôtel de l'Univers (☎ 05 53 53 34 79; fax 05 53 06 70 76; 18 cours Michel Montaigne; menus €15-35; ☼ closed Mon & lunch Tue) A refined restaurant popular for its tasty Périgord and Breton specialities (including fish and lobster). Inside, the restaurant lacks atmosphere, but there's a delightful vine-covered terrace.

Barrio Gotico (☎ 05 53 05 07 33; 12 rue de la Sagesse; tapas €1.50-4; ☼ 6.30pm-1am Tue-Sat) A funky little tapas bar, off place St-Louis, serving cheap hot and cold tapas to the strain of Latin beats. There's a lively vibe, with DJs playing later in the evening.

SELF-CATERING

On Wednesday and Saturday mornings from mid-November to mid-March, black truffles, wild mushrooms, foie gras, *confits* duck or goose conserve), cheeses and other local delicacies are sold at the Marché de Gras (on place St-Louis) in Puy St-Front.

On Wednesday and Saturday mornings year-round, there's a food market on place de la Clautre, near the cathedral. Not far from the southern end of rue Limogeanne is the **Marché du Coderc** (covered market; ⌚ to about 1.30pm). Across the square is **Fromagerie du Coderc** (⌚ Tue-Sat & Sun morning).

There's an upstairs **Monoprix supermarket** (⌚ 8.30am-8pm Mon-Sat) between place Bugeaud and place Francheville.

Drinking
Le Mellow (☎ 05 53 08 53 97; 4-6 rue de la Sagesse; ⌚ 5pm-2am Tue-Sat) One of a handful of bars along this stretch in Puy St-Front, this is by far the trendiest, with a good-looking crowd enjoying cool music and cocktails.

Zanzi Bar (☎ 05 53 53 28 99; 2 rue Condé; ⌚ 6.30pm-2am Tue-Sat) A lively place with a tropical ambiance and exotic cocktails. The salsa lessons on Wednesday evenings at 8pm and 9.30pm get easier in direct proportion to the number of cocktails drunk!

Le Star Inn (☎ 05 53 08 56 83; place du Musée; ⌚ 8pm-2am Mon-Sat May-Sep, 8pm-1am Mon-Sat Oct-Apr) A welcoming pub across from 23 rue St-Front, run by a British couple and something of a hang-out for English speakers. English books are available to borrow.

Entertainment
The seven-screen **CAP Cinéma** (☎ 05 53 09 40 09; 19 blvd Michel Montaigne) screens nondubbed films.

Getting There & Away
BUS
The Périgueux **bus station** (place Francheville) is on the southern side of the square; hours are posted at the bus stops. One of the carriers, **CFTA** (☎ 05 53 08 43 13; ⌚ Mon-Fri), has an office on the storey overlooking the waiting room. The tourist office and the train station information office can supply you with schedules.

Except on Sunday and holidays, destinations include Bergerac (€6.80, 70 minutes, three daily), Ribérac (€5.15, one hour, four daily, one on Saturday) and Sarlat-la-Canéda (€8.35, 1½ hours, two daily, fewer in July and August) via the Vézère Valley town of Montignac (€5.85, 55 minutes).

CAR
Hire cars from **Europcar** (☎ 05 53 08 15 72; 7 rue Denis Papin) or **Hertz** (☎ 05 53 53 88 88; 20 cours Michel Montaigne).

TRAIN
The **train station** (rue Denis Papin) is served by local bus Nos 1, 4 and 5. Destinations with direct services include Bordeaux (€16.30, 1¼ hours, nine to 13 daily), Brive-La-Gaillarde (€10.30, one hour, three to five daily), Les Eyzies de Tayac (€6.30, 30 minutes, two to four daily) and Limoges (€10, one hour, seven to 11 daily, three on Saturday).

Train services to Paris' Gare d'Austerlitz (€45.90, three to five hours, 12 to 16 daily) are via Limoges. To get to Sarlat-la-Canéda (€12) you have to change at Brive.

Getting Around
Allo Taxi (☎ 05 53 09 09 09) is available 24 hours a day.

BERTRIC BURÉE
This tiny village (population 399), 35km northwest of Périgueux between Ribérac and Verteillac on the D708, draws thousands of gourmands and onlookers for the annual **snail festival** (☎ 05 53 91 94 96), held on the first Monday in May.

SARLAT-LA-CANÉDA
pop 10,000
The beautiful, well-restored town of Sarlat, administratively twinned with nearby La Canéda, is the capital of Périgord Noir. Its medieval and Renaissance townscape, much of it built of tan sandstone in the 16th and 17th centuries, attracts large numbers of tourists, especially for the year-round Saturday market.

Sarlat is an excellent base for car trips to the prehistoric sites of the Vézère Valley and to the Dordogne Périgourdine.

Orientation
The heart-shaped Cité Médiévale (Medieval Town) is bisected by the ruler-straight rue de la République (La Traverse), which (along with its continuations) stretches 2km north from the viaduct and nearby train station to the Auberge de Jeunesse. The Cité Médiévale is centred on place de la Liberté, rue de la Liberté and place du Peyrou.

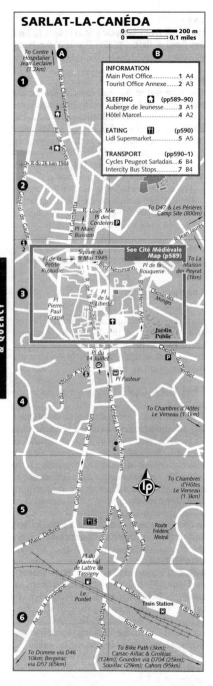

Information

MONEY

There are several banks along rue de la République.

POST

Main Post Office (Map left; place du 14 Juillet) Currency exchange and a Cyberposte.

TOURIST INFORMATION

Main Tourist Office (Map left; ☎ 05 53 31 45 45; www.ot-sarlat-perigord.fr in French; rue Tourny; ⌚ 9am-7pm Mon-Sat, 10am-noon Sun Apr-Oct, 9am-noon & 2-7pm Mon-Sat Nov-Mar) In a building attached to the cathedral. Staff can supply the *Visitors' Map of the Medieval Town*, which takes you on a walking tour of the historic centre, and brochures on hikes and car tours in the area. In summer there is a €2 charge for making hotel and B&B bookings.

Tourist Office Annexe (Map p588; ☎ 05 53 59 18 87; av du Général de Gaulle; ⌚ 9am-noon & 2-6pm Mon-Sat Jul & Aug).

Sights & Activities

Once part of Sarlat's Cluniac abbey, **Cathédrale St-Sacerdos** (Map opposite) is a real hotchpotch of styles. The wide, airy nave and its chapels date from the 17th century, the cruciform chevet (at the far end from the entrance) is from the 14th century; and the western entrance and much of the belfry above it are 12th-century Romanesque. The organ dates from 1752.

Behind the town's cathedral is **Jardin des Enfeus** (Map opposite), Sarlat's first cemetery, and the 12th-century **Lanterne des Morts** (Lantern of the Dead; Map opposite), a short tower that looks like the top of a missile. It may have been built to commemorate St-Bernard, who visited Sarlat in 1147 and whose relics were given to the abbey.

Across the square from the front of the cathedral is the ornate façade of the Renaissance **Maison de la Boétie** (Map opposite), the birthplace of the writer Étienne de la Boétie (1530–63).

The alleyways of the quiet, largely residential area west of rue de la République, many of them lined with centuries-old stone houses, are also worth exploring. **Rue Jean Jacques Rousseau** makes a good starting point.

A **bicycle path** *(piste cyclable)* begins 3km southeast of Sarlat (near the intersection of the D704 and the D704A), and takes you along an old railway grade to Carsac-Aillac (12km from Sarlat) and across the river to

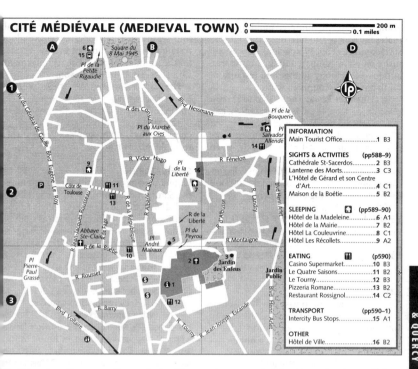

CITÉ MÉDIÉVALE (MEDIEVAL TOWN)

INFORMATION	
Main Tourist Office	1 B3

SIGHTS & ACTIVITIES	(pp588–9)
Cathédrale St-Sacerdos	2 B3
Lanterne des Morts	3 C3
L'Hôtel de Gérard et son Centre	
d'Art	4 C1
Maison de la Boétie	5 B2

SLEEPING	(pp589–90)
Hôtel de la Madeleine	6 A1
Hôtel de la Mairie	7 B2
Hôtel La Couleuvrine	8 C1
Hôtel Les Récollets	9 A2

EATING	(p590)
Casino Supermarket	10 B3
Le Quatre Saisons	11 B2
Le Tourny	12 B3
Pizzeria Romane	13 B2
Restaurant Rossignol	14 C2

TRANSPORT	(pp590–1)
Intercity Bus Stops	15 A1

OTHER	
Hôtel de Ville	16 B2

Groléjac. It will eventually reach Souillac (about 30km from Sarlat).

L'Hôtel de Gérard et son Centre d'Art (Map above; ☎ 05 53 59 57 97; 1 passage de Gérard du Barry) is an arts centre housed in a beautiful medieval building off rue Fénelon, which offers week-long painting courses in the first week of July and September.

Sleeping

Sarlat has no really cheap hotels. On holiday weekends during spring and in July and August, virtually everything is booked up way in advance. The tourist office has a full list of the area's many *chambres d'hôtes*.

BUDGET

Auberge de Jeunesse (Map opposite; ☎ 05 53 59 47 59, 05 53 30 21 27; 77 av de Selves; dm €10) is a modest but friendly 15-bed hostel with cooking facilities; call ahead for a reservation.

Chambres d'Hôtes Le Verseau (☎ 05 53 31 02 63; 49 route des Pechs; d incl breakfast €24-44) Just four rooms are available in this friendly place, with a leafy garden ideal for breakfast, picnics and barbecues. It's 2.2km north of the train station

along route Frédéric Mistral – if you call from the station the owner will pick you up.

Hôtel Les Récollets (Map above; ☎ 05 53 31 36 00; www.hotel-recollets-sarlat.com; 4 rue Jean-Jacques Rousseau; d from €39) Lost in narrow alleys of the Medieval Town, this delightful old building has been renovated inside with 18 fully equipped two-star rooms. While some of the charm of the building has been lost, the larger rooms (and breakfast room) retain some stone-walled character. The nearest parking is a block up the hill on blvd Eugène Le Roy.

MID-RANGE

Hôtel La Couleuvrine (Map above; ☎ 05 53 59 27 80; www.la-couleuvrine.com; 1 place de la Bouquerie; d from €55; P) A beautiful, chateau-like, three-star place, parts of which date from the 13th to 15th centuries. The accommodation, beautifully furnished with old, dark wood furniture, combines rustic comfort and medieval minimalism. Try room No 19, an atmospheric family room in the turret.

Hôtel de la Madeleine (Map above; ☎ 05 53 59 10 41; www.hoteldelamadeleine-sarlat.com; 1 place de la Petite Rigaudie; s/d from €62/71; Feb-Dec; P) This grand old wooden-shuttered building dominates the square and offering refined three-star comfort. The 39 spacious rooms are just a bit plain compared to the impressive, antique-filled lobby, lounge and restaurant. Look out for discounts in winter.

La Maison des Peyrat (☎ 05 53 59 00 32; www .maisondespeyrat.com; Le Lac de la Plane; r €47-95; half-board per person €51-75) This tastefully renovated 17th-century house with tranquil gardens is set on a hill about 1.5km from the town centre, with great views over the surrounding countryside. It's one of the most charming hotels in the area, renowned for its good food and welcoming atmosphere.

Other possibilities:

Hôtel de la Mairie (Map p589; ☎ 05 53 59 05 71; fax 05 53 59 59 95; 13 place de la Liberté; d €43-45) This hotel is slap-bang central with loads of character.

Hôtel Marcel (Map p588; ☎ 05 53 59 21 98; fax 05 53 30 27 77; 50 av de Selves; d €45-55) Cheerful two-star rooms.

Eating

There are quite a few tourist-oriented restaurants along the streets north, northwest and south of the cathedral. Périgord's famous gastronomy can be sampled at a number of establishments.

Hôtel La Couleuvrine (Map p589; see Sleeping; menus €18-32; ☺ mid-Feb–mid-Jan) The popular restaurant here is a bit special. A huge medieval fireplace, glowing chandeliers and a scattering of French antiques help to create a traditional country atmosphere. The gastronomic and regional *menus* are superb, and there's a great value lunch *menu* on Tuesday, Wednesday and Friday with two courses and a glass of wine for €14.

Restaurant Rossignol (Map p589; ☎ 05 53 31 02 30; 15 rue Fénelon; menus €19-60; ☺ Fri-Wed) A spacious, refined restaurant with starched white tablecloths and sparkling wine glasses. The service is exemplary, but the real attraction is the delicious €60 menu, full of Périgord specialities including foie gras and truffles.

Le Tourny (Map p589; ☎ 05 53 29 17 80; 1 rue Tourny; menus €16-22.50; ☺ Tue-Sun) A few doors down from the tourist office, this friendly little restaurant, popular with the locals, is renowned for Basque specialities as well as traditional Périgord cuisine. The dish to try is the succulent duck-based *confit de canard en croûte* (€13.50).

Le Quatre Saisons (Map p589; ☎ 05 53 29 48 59; 2 Côte de Toulouse; menus €18-29; ☺ closed Wed Sep-Jun)

This family-run place is indeed good for all four seasons with a modern, stylish indoor restaurant and a couple of breezy terraces for the summer months. The regional menu varies according to the season.

Pizzeria Romane (Map p589; ☎ 05 53 59 23 88; 3 Côte de Toulouse; mains from €6) A small, pack-em-in, no-frills pizzeria in the back alleys of the Medieval Town, serving good value, good quality Italian staples. Pasta dishes from €6, pizzas from €7.

SELF-CATERING

Long a driving force in the local economy, the Saturday market on place de la Liberté and along rue de la République offers edibles in the morning and durables such as clothing all day. Depending on the season, Périgord delicacies on offer include truffles, foie gras, mushrooms and goose-based products. A smaller fruit and vegetable market on place de la Liberté is held on Wednesday morning. Quite a few shops around town sell foie gras and other pricey regional specialities.

The **Casino supermarket** (Map p589; 32 rue de la République; ☺ 8am-12.15pm & 2.30-7.15pm Tue-Sat, 8.30am-12.15pm Sun) keeps longer hours in July and August. The **Lidl supermarket** (Map p588; av Aristide Briand; ☺ 9am-12.30pm & 2.30-7.30pm Mon-Fri, 9am-7pm Sat) is at the southern end of the avenue.

Getting There & Away
BUS

Services are very limited; schedules are available at the tourist office. There's no bus station – departures are from the train station, place Pasteur or place de la Petite Rigaudie, depending on where you're going. There are one or two buses daily (fewer in July and August) to Périgueux (€6.80, 1½ hours) via the Vézère Valley town of Montignac.

TRAIN

The **train station** (☎ 05 53 59 00 21), 1.3km south of the old city at the southern end of av de la Gare, is poorly linked with the rest of the region. The ticket windows are staffed until 7pm.

Destinations include Bordeaux (€19.90, 2½ hours, two to four direct daily) which is on the same line as Bergerac, Périgueux (change at Le Buisson; €12.00, 1½ hours, two daily), and Les Eyzies de Tayac (train at Le Buisson; €7.10, 50 minutes to 2¼ hours depending on connections, two daily). The SNCF bus to Souillac (€4.90, 40 minutes, two to four daily) passes through Carsac-Aillac (on the scenic D703) and links up with trains on the Paris (Gare d'Austerlitz)–Limoges–Toulouse line.

Getting Around

BICYCLE
The Sarlat area has nine bike-rental outlets including **Cycles Peugeot Sarladais** (Map p588; ☎ 05 53 28 51 87; 36 av Thiers).

CAR & MOTORCYCLE
Free parking is available around the perimeter of the Medieval Town along blvd Nessmann, blvd Voltaire and blvd Henri Arlet. Cars are banned from the Medieval Town from June to September, and rue de la République is pedestrianised in July and August.

PREHISTORIC SITES & THE VÉZÈRE VALLEY
Of the Vézère Valley's 175 known prehistoric sites, the most famous ones, including the world-renowned cave paintings in Lascaux, are situated between **Le Bugue** (near the confluence of the Vézère and Dordogne) and Montignac, 25km to the northeast. The sites mentioned here are just the highlights and are listed roughly from southwest to northeast.

Many of the villages that are situated in the area, including Les Eyzies de Tayac and Montignac, have one or more hotels. You can also use Périgueux (p583) and Sarlat-la-Canéda (p587) as bases to explore the area. Most of the valley's sites are closed in winter; the best time to visit is in spring or autumn, when the sites are open but the crowds are not overwhelming.

Getting Around
The Vézère Valley is well signed; arrows at every crossroads direct you to both major and minor sights. Public transport in the area is limited, see p587, opposite and p592.

Les Eyzies de Tayac
pop 850
The two museums in the one-street touristy village of Les Eyzies de Tayac provide an excellent introduction to the valley's prehistoric legacy.

INFORMATION
Tourist Office (☎ 05 53 06 97 05; www.leseyzies.com; 🕑 9am-7pm Mon-Sat, 10am-noon & 2-6pm Sun Jul & Aug, 9am-noon & 2-6pm Mon-Sat, 10am-noon & 2-5pm Sun Sep-Jun, closed Sun Oct-Apr) On Les Eyzies' main street, the D47, right below the most prominent part of the cliff.
Librairie de la Préhistoire (🕑 8.30am-12.30pm & 3-7pm Mar-Nov, no lunch break Jun-Aug, 8.30am-noon Dec-Feb) Sells IGN maps and topoguides; across from the tourist office.

SIGHTS
The very interesting **Musée National de Préhistoire** (National Museum of Prehistory; ☎ 05 53 06 45 45; adult/18-25 yrs/under 18 yrs €4.50/3/free, on Sun adults €3; 🕑 9.30am-6.30pm Jul & Aug, 9.30am-noon & 2-5.30pm Wed-Mon Sep-Jun) is built into the cliff above the tourist office (with an expanded exhibition space that opened in mid-2004). Its well-presented collection of artefacts provides a great introduction to the area's prehistoric human habitation.

About 250m north of Musée National de Préhistoire along the cliff face is the **Abri Pataud** (☎ 05 53 06 92 46; adult/6-12 yrs €5.20/3.20; 🕑 10am-7pm Jul & Aug, 10am-7pm Tue-Thu & Sun Sep-Jun), a Cro-Magnon shelter *(abri)* inhabited over a period of 15,000 years starting some 37,000 years ago; bones and other artefacts discovered during the excavations are on display. The ibex carved into the ceiling dates from about 19,000 BC. The admission price includes a one-hour guided tour (the guides generally know some English).

SLEEPING & EATING
Hostellerie du Passeur (☎ 05 53 06 97 13; www .hostellerie-du-passeur.com; place de la Mairie; d €62-85; 🕑 Feb-Oct; P) In a great spot overlooking the Vézère, this superb two-star hotel, in an old bourgeois mansion house, has pretty country-style rooms. The **restaurant** (menus from €22; 🕑 closed Mon & Tue lunch), with a shady terrace, serves traditional Périgord and French fare. It's next door to the tourist office.

Hôtel des Roches (☎ 05 53 06 96 59; hotel@roches -les-eyzies.com; 15 av de la Forge; d €75-85; 🕑 Apr-Nov; P 🕿) On the edge of town, this comfortable 41-room, three-star place is set in pretty gardens. It also has a swimming pool.

Camping & Caravanning Le Vézère Périgord (☎ 05 53 06 96 31; fax & off season 05 53 06 79 66; route de Montignac, Tursac; camping for 2 people €16, extra person €5; 🕑 Apr-Oct; P 🕿) This excellent three-star place is in the middle of a forest 6km

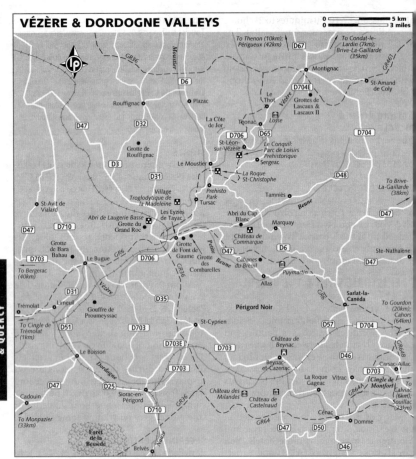

VÉZÈRE & DORDOGNE VALLEYS

north of Les Eyzies (on the D706). It's quiet, well maintained and in a beautiful setting with swimming pool, tennis courts and children's playground.

GETTING THERE & AWAY
The **train station** (☎ 05 53 06 97 22) is 700m north of the tourist office (and 200m off the D47). The ticket windows are staffed until at least 6pm (but closed until noon at the weekend).

Destinations include Bordeaux (change trains at Le Buisson; €28.40, two to three hours, eight or nine daily), Sarlat-la-Canéda (change at Le Buisson; €7.50, 50 minutes to two hours depending on connections, three daily), Périgueux (€6.30, 30 minutes, four

or five daily) and Paris' Gare d'Austerlitz (€48.70, five hours, three daily).

GETTING AROUND
Bicycles can be rented at the tourist office for €8 per half-day or €12 per day.

Limeuil
This charming walled village, perched high above the confluence of the Rivers Vézère and Dordogne, is known for its municipal gardens. **Hôtel Au Bon Accueil** (☎ 05 53 63 30 97; d with/without shower €35/27; ✆ Easter-Oct), with 10 rooms, is just down the one-way street from place des Fosses. The attached **restaurant** (menus €15-23; ✆ closed Mon Sep & Oct) serves traditional Périgord-style *menus*.

THE DORDOGNE •• Prehistoric Sites & the Vézère Valley **593**

Grotte de Font de Gaume

Just over 1km northeast of Les Eyzies on the D47, this **cave** (☎ 05 53 06 86 00; www.leseyzies .com/grottes-ornees; adult/18-25 yrs/under 18 €6.10/4.10/free; 9am-12.30pm & 2-5.30pm Sun-Fri, no lunch break Jun-Sep) has one of the most astounding collections of prehistoric paintings still open to the public. About two dozen of its 230 remarkably sophisticated polychrome figures of mammoths, bison, horses, reindeer, bears and other creatures, created by Cro-Magnon people 14,000 years ago, can be visited. A number of the animals, engraved and/or painted in red and black, are depicted in movement or in three dimensions.

To protect the cave, discovered in 1901, the number of visitors is limited to 200 per day, and the 45-minute group tours (explanatory sheets in English available) are limited to 20 participants and must be reserved a few days ahead (a week or two ahead from July to September) by phone or via the website.

Grotte des Combarelles

The long and very narrow Combarelles Cave, 3km northeast of Les Eyzies and 1.6km east of Grotte de Font de Gaume, averages only 80cm in width. Discovered in 1894 it is renowned for its 600 often-superimposed engravings of animals, especially reindeer, bison and horses; there are also some human or half-human figures. The works date from 12,000 to 14,000 years

ago. To reserve a place in a six-person group (tours last 45 to 60 minutes), call the Grotte de Font de Gaume – opening hours, admission costs and reservation guidelines are the same for both sites.

Abri du Cap Blanc

High-relief and low-relief figures of horses, reindeer and bison, created 14,000 years ago, decorate this natural shelter, formed by an overhanging rocky outcrop. Situated on a pristine, forested hillside, the privately owned **shelter** (☎ 05 53 59 21 74; adult/7-15 yrs €5.90/3.50; Apr-Nov) can be visited on guided tours lasting an hour (English explanatory sheets available), between 10am and noon and between 2pm and 6pm (7pm in July and August, when there's no midday closure).

The Abri, 8km east of Les Eyzies along the beautiful D48, is a fine place to begin a day hike.

Grotte du Grand Roc

The **Grand Roc Cave** (☎ 05 53 06 92 70; www.grand roc.com; adult/child €7/3.50; 10am-6pm Jul & Aug, 10am-5pm Sep-Jun), known for its masses of delicate, translucent stalactites and stalagmites, is a few kilometres northwest of Les Eyzies along the D47. Nearby is the prehistoric site of **Abris de Laugerie Basse** (adult/child €6/3; same as Grand Roc) and a still-inhabited troglodytic hamlet.

Grotte de Rouffignac

About 15km north of Les Eyzies, the cave at **Rouffignac** (☎ 05 53 05 41 71; adult/child €6/3.50; tours in French 9am-11.30am & 2-6pm Jul & Aug, from 10am Sep-Nov & Apr-Jun), the largest in the area (it has some 10km of galleries), is known for its 250 engravings and paintings of mammoths and other animals.

Village Troglodytique de la Madeleine

This cave-dwelling **village** (☎ 05 53 06 92 49; adult/family/5-12 yrs €5/16/3; 9.30am-7pm Jul & Aug, 10am-6pm Sep-Jun, to 5pm Dec & Jan), 8km north of Les Eyzies along the D706, is in the middle of a delightfully lush forest overlooking a hairpin curve in the River Vézère. The site has two levels: 10,000 to 14,000 years ago, prehistoric people lived on the bank of the river in an area now closed to the public; and 500 to 700 years ago, medieval French people built a fortified village – which is now lies in ruins – halfway up the cliff face. Their chapel, dedicated to Ste-Madeleine, gave its name to the site, and to the entire Magdelenian era. On the plateau above the cliff are the ruins of a 14th-century castle (closed to the public). Many of the artefacts discovered here are at the prehistory museum in Les Eyzies. Several walking trails pass by the site.

Guided tours (in French; 50 minutes) begin every half-hour or so; a free English-language brochure is available.

La Roque St-Christophe

This 900m-long series of terraces and **caves** (☎ 05 53 50 70 45; www.roque-st-christophe.com; adult/student/5-11 yrs €6/5/3; ☯ 10am-6pm Apr-Oct, to 7pm Jul & Aug, 11am-5pm Nov-Mar) sits on a sheer cliff face 30m above the Vézère. It has had an extraordinary history as a natural bastion, serving Mousterian (Neanderthal) people some 50,000 years ago, enemies of the Normans in the 10th century, the English from 1401 to 1416, as well as Protestants in the late 16th century.

La Roque St-Christophe is on the D706, 9km northeast of Les Eyzies. At the ticket kiosk, you can borrow an informative brochure that makes a valiant effort to make the now-empty caverns come alive.

Le Moustier

Across the River Vézère from La Roque St-Christophe is Le Moustier – the findings here gave the Mousterian era its name.

Dhagpo Kagyu-Ling (☎ 05 53 50 70 75; www .dhagpo-kagyu.org; s/d from €10.70/12.20; meals from €2.30), a centre for Tibetan Buddhist studies and meditation that was founded in 1975, is 1km up the hill from the church – you will know you have found it when you see the gold-topped stupa, the small, Tibetan-style temple, a row of prayer wheels and lots of fluttering prayer flags. The centre offers day, weekend and longer courses (from €9 per day) on Buddhist philosophy and meditation, many in English, and also hosts inter-religious dialogue. Accommodation is available for varying prices; advance reservations are essential.

St-Léon-sur-Vézère

pop 427

This quiet, one-time river port, on a picturesque loop of the River Vézère 10km southwest of Montignac, is a good base for day hikes. It has two small castles (both closed to the public): the 14th-century **Manoir de la Salle**, with its squat, square donjon; and the more refined, 16th-century **Château de Clérens**, adorned with Renaissance turrets. The interior of the 11th- and 12th-century Romanesque **church** has a wooden ceiling; the half-dome above the choir shows remnants of medieval frescoes.

The **Auberge du Pont Restaurant** (☎ 05 53 50 73 07; menu €21-35; ☯ closed Wed) serves Périgord and Provençal specialities.

Le Thot

The museum and animal park known as **Le Thot – Espace Cro-Magnon** (☎ 05 53 50 70 44; adult/6-12 yrs €5/3; ☯ 9am-7pm Jul & Aug, 10am-noon & 2-5.30pm Tue-Sun Sep-Jun, closed Jan), intended as an introduction to the world of prehistoric people, has models of animals that appear in prehistoric art, live specimens of similar animals, and exhibits on the creation of Lascaux II. See Lascaux II (opposite) for details of combined tickets.

Montignac

pop 3101

The relaxing and picturesque town of Montignac, on the Vézère 25km northeast of Les Eyzies, achieved sudden fame after the discovery of the nearby Grotte de Lascaux. The attractive old city and commercial centre is on the river's right bank, but of more use for touristic logistics is the left-bank area around place Tourny. Rue du 4 Septembre links the D65 with the D704 and the D704E to Lascaux.

ORIENTATION & INFORMATION

There are three banks right around the tourist office.

Maison de la Presse (☯ closed Sun afternoon except Jul & Aug) Across the street from the tourist office, it sells IGN maps and topoguides.

Post Office (place Tourny) Offers currency exchange.

Tourist Office (☎ 05 53 51 82 60; www.bienvenue -montignac.com in French; place Bertrand de Born; ☯ 9am-7pm Jul-Sep, 9am-noon & 2-6pm Mon-Sat Oct-Jun) Around 200m west of place Tourny and next to the 14th-century Église St-Georges le Prieuré.

SLEEPING & EATING

Hôtel de la Grotte (☎ 05 53 51 80 48; fax 05 53 51 05 96; place Tourny; d with shower/bath €42/47) With a very pleasant garden on the banks of the river, this charming place, 200m east of the tourist office, offers 10 very comfortable rooms. Its restaurant has traditional and creative Périgord-style *menus* from €18 (€11.50 at lunch) to €38.

Le Relais du Soleil d'Or (☎ 05 53 51 80 22; www.le-soleil-dor.com in French; 16 rue du 4 Septembre; d €81-110; ⌚ closed mid-Jan–mid-Feb; P ⌘) An old post house that is now home to a swish three-star hotel and restaurant. There's a large shaded garden with a swimming pool, and a charming, antique-filled lounge for relaxing. The rooms are not quite as exciting, but are well-equipped with minibars and satellite TVs. Its fine dining restaurant has regional *menus* from €19.

Bar des Arcades (☎ 05 53 51 95 73; 37 rue du 4 Septembre; ⌚ 8am-8pm in winter, to 2am in summer) A cosy, traditional café, popular with locals, serving good snacks and regional specialities such as *cassoulet de canard* (duck casserole; €8.50).

Le Tourny (☎ 05 53 51 59 95; place Tourny) This is both a brasserie and a bar with DJs, sports on the TV and regular concerts. It usually opens 7.30am to 1am in winter (2.30am in summer), but stays open to 4am or 5am when there's a live concert, which is generally on Saturday night and, from April to September, on Friday night from 10pm to 2am.

Casino supermarket (place Tourny; ⌚ Tue-Sat & Sun morning, closed 12.30-3pm) Next to the post office.

ENTERTAINMENT
Nondubbed films are screened at **Cinéma Vox** (☎ 05 53 51 87 24), across the car park from the tourist office.

GETTING THERE & AWAY
For information on buses to/from Montignac, see p587 and p590. There's a bus stop (hours posted) at place Tourny.

Grottes de Lascaux & Lascaux II
Lascaux Cave, 2km southeast of Montignac at the end of the D704E, is adorned with some of the most extraordinary prehistoric paintings ever found. Discovered in 1940 by four teenage boys who, it is said, were out searching for their dog, the cave's main room and a number of steep galleries are decorated with figures of wild oxen, deer, horses, reindeer and other creatures depicted in vivid reds, blacks, yellows and browns. The drawings and paintings, shown

by carbon dating to be between 15,000 and 17,000 years old, are thought to have been done by members of a hunting cult.

The cave, in pristine condition when found, was opened to the public in 1948 but was closed 15 years later when it became clear that human breath and the resulting carbon dioxide and condensation were causing the colours to fade and a green fungus – and even tiny stalactites – to grow over the paintings.

In response to massive public curiosity about prehistoric art, a precise replica of the most famous section of the original cave was meticulously re-created a few hundred metres away. **Lascaux II** (☎ 05 53 51 95 03; adult/6-12 yrs €8/4.50; ⌚ 9am-7pm Jul & Aug, 10am-noon & 2-5.30pm Tue-Sun Sep-Jun, closed Jan) opened in 1983, and although the idea sounds kitschy, the reproductions are surprisingly evocative and well worth a look.

The 40m-long Lascaux II can handle 2000 visitors daily (in guided groups of 40). The last tours (40 minutes) begin about an hour before the morning and afternoon closing times. From April to October, tickets are sold *only* in Montignac (next to the tourist office). Reservations are not necessary except for groups. Combined tickets (€9/5) are available for Lascaux II and Le Thot (opposite).

DORDOGNE PÉRIGOURDINE
The term Dordogne Périgourdine is used to describe the part of Périgord that stretches along the River Dordogne.

Domme
pop 1030
Set on a steep promontory high above the Dordogne, the trapezoid-shaped walled village of Domme is one of the few *bastides* to have retained most of its 13th-century ramparts, including three fortified gates. A bit too perfectly restored, it attracts more than its share of coach tours, but they in no way spoil the stunning panorama from the cliff-side **Esplanade du Belvédère** and the adjacent **Promenade de la Barre**, which stretches west along the forested slope to the Jardin Public (a public park).

Across from the **tourist office** (☎ 05 53 31 71 00; place de la Halle; ⌚ 10am-7pm Jul & Aug, 10am-noon & 2-6pm Feb-Jun & Sep–mid-Nov, 2-5pm Mon-Fri mid-Nov–Dec, closed Jan) is the 19th-century reconstruction of a 16th-century *halle* (covered market).

This houses the entrance to the **grottes** (adult/student/child €6/5/3.50; ✆ guided tours every 20-30min 10.30am-6.40pm), 450m of stalactite-filled galleries below the village; a lift whisks you back up at the end of the 30-minute tour. Except in January, tours take place whenever the tourist office, which sells tickets, is open; the last tour leaves 30 minutes before closing time in the morning and the afternoon.

On the far side of the square from the tourist office, the **Musée d'Arts et Traditions Populaires** (adult/student/child €3/2.50/2; ✆ Apr-Sep) has nine rooms of artefacts (clothing, toys and tools), mainly from the 19th century.

ACTIVITIES
From March to September or mid-October (unless the river is too high), **canoe and kayak trips** can be arranged through **Randonnée Dordogne** (☎ 05 53 28 22 01; randodordogne@wanadoo.fr), a highly professional, English-speaking outfit whose base is in Cénac, 300m to the right as you approach the D46 bridge over the River Dordogne from the south (ie from Domme). Day trips cost €22 per person or €38 for a double kayak, including transport. Half-day trips are available from €14 per person.

SLEEPING
Hôtel Les Quatre Vents (☎ 05 53 31 57 57; fax 05 53 31 57 59; d with shower & toilet €40-48; 🏊) A two-star place with 26 comfortable rooms, two swimming pools and gardens.

Château de Castelnaud
The 12th- to 16th-century **Château de Castelnaud** (☎ 05 53 31 30 00; adult/10-17 yrs €6.60/3.30; ✆ 9am-8pm Jul & Aug, 10am-7pm May, Jun & Sep, 10am-6pm Mar, Apr & Oct–mid-Nov, 2-5pm Sun-Fri mid-Nov–Feb), 11km west of Domme along the D50 and D57, has everything you'd expect from a cliff-top castle: walls up to 2m thick (as you can see from the loopholes, some designed for crossbows, others for small cannons); a superb panorama of the meandering Dordogne; and fine views of the fortified chateaux (including arch rival Château de Beynac) that dot the nearby hilltops. The interior rooms are occupied by a **museum of medieval warfare**, whose displays range from daggers and spiked halberds to huge catapults. The houses of the medieval village of Castelnaud cling to the steep slopes below the fortress. An English-language guidebook can be borrowed at the ticket counter.

La Roque Gageac
This hamlet of tan stone houses is built halfway up the cliff face on the right bank of one of the *cingles* (hairpin curves) in the River Dordogne. When the tiny **tourist office** (☎ 05 53 29 17 01; ✆ 9am-12.30pm & 2-6pm Easter-Oct) shed in the car park is closed, brochures can be picked up at the post office.

The **Fort Troglodyte** (☎ 05 53 31 61 94; adult/child €4/2; ✆ 10am-7pm Mon-Fri, Apr–mid-Nov & usually in off season, also Sat Jul & Aug) consists of a number of medieval military positions built into the cliff. There's some tropical foliage in the small, free **Jardin Exotique** (Exotic Garden), next to the tiny **church**. Down below, the quay serves as a launch point for short **river cruises** – contact **Gabares Norbert** (☎ 05 53 29 40 44).

Canoes can be rented from **Canoë Dordogne** (☎ 05 53 29 58 50; 1-person canoe travelling 7/14/21km €12/18/24, 2-person canoe €20/25/32), next to the car park, which also offers rock climbing and spelunking daily from April to October (often booked out in July and August).

East of La Roque Gageac, the beautiful D703 follows the northern bank of the serpentine Dordogne, passing by the **Cingle de Montfort** (a particularly sharp hairpin curve). Unfortunately, it's too narrow and busy for cycling – bikers are much better off taking the old railroad tracks, sections of which have been turned into a bike path (look for signs to the *piste cyclable*).

The place with the sign that reads **Bar-Hôtel** (☎ 05 53 29 51 63; d with shower €29; ✆ Easter-Oct) offers basic accommodation.

Hôtel La Belle Étoile (☎ 05 53 29 51 44; fax 05 53 29 45 63; d €46-70; ✆ Apr-Oct) has 16 two-star rooms.

Château de Beynac
This dramatic **fortress** (☎ 05 53 29 50 40; adult/5-11 yrs €7/3; ✆ 10am-6pm) is perched on a sheer cliff, dominating a strategic bend in the Dordogne. A steep trail links it to the centre of the village of **Beynac-et-Cazenac**, 150m below on the river bank (and the D703). Opening times may vary slightly according to the owners' discretion.

Loyal to the king of France, the fort, built from the 12th to 14th centuries (and later modified), was long a rival of Castelnaud, just across the river, which owed its allegiance to the king of England. The interior is architecturally interesting – you get a good idea of the layout of a medieval fortress – but is only partly furnished. From mid-March to mid-November, one-hour guided tours (in French) take place every half-hour.

In a stunning spot, with the château high above and the river just below, is the stylish **Hôtel-Restaurant du Château** (☎ 05 53 29 19 20; www.hotelduchateau-dordogne.com; d from €50; Feb-Dec), with spacious rooms. The rooms at the front have been redecorated with minimalist chic; four rooms have castle views. The **restaurant** (menus €17.50-22) specialises in traditional Périgord cuisine. It's on the main road through Beynac.

Château des Milandes

The claim to fame of the smallish, late-15th-century **Château des Milandes** (☎ 05 53 59 31 21; adult/4-15 yrs €7.50/5.50; 9am-7pm Jul & Aug, 10am-6pm Apr-Jun, Sep & Oct) is its post-war role as the home of the African-American dancer and music-hall star Josephine Baker (1906–75), who helped bring black American culture to Paris in the 1920s with her *Revue Nègre* and created a sensation by appearing on stage wearing nothing but a skirt of bananas.

Baker was awarded the Croix de Guerre and the Legion of Honour for her work with the French Resistance during WWII and was later active in the US civil rights movement. She established her Rainbow Tribe here in 1949, adopting 12 children from around the world as 'an experiment in brotherhood'.

The last obligatory, bilingual guided tour (lasting about 60 minutes) begins about an hour before closing time. The fierce-looking birds of prey in the courtyard are the stars of falconry displays several times a day (only in the afternoon in April, September and October).

MONPAZIER

pop 560

Of all the *bastides* in southwestern France, Monpazier (about 45km from both Sarlat-la-Canéda and Bergerac), founded by a representative of the king of England in 1284, is one of the most attractive, and popular with warm-season tourists.

The arcaded market square, **place des Cornières** (place Centrale), is surrounded by a motley assemblage of well-preserved stone houses that reflect centuries of building and rebuilding. The rectangular street grid is no longer enclosed by ramparts, but

three of the town **gates** still stand. Thursday is market day, as it has been since the Middle Ages.

The **tourist office** (☎ 05 53 22 68 59; www.pays-des-bastides.com in French; place des Cornières; 10am-7pm Jul & Aug, 10am-12.30pm & 2-6.30pm Apr-Jun & Sep, to 6pm Mon-Sat, 2.30-6pm Sun Oct-Mar), in the southeastern corner of the square, has an informative historical brochure in English.

Two-star **Hôtel de Londres** (☎ 05 53 22 60 64; fax 05 53 22 61 98; Foirail Nord; d with shower & toilet €35-45), on the way into Monpazier (on the D53), has 10 spacious rooms that are in need of a lick of paint. Even a good clean would help. The attached **restaurant** (menus from €17), with shaded terrace, serves traditional French and Périgord dishes and also has a vegetarian *menu* (€14.50).

The **Casino grocery** (place des Cornières; 8am-12.30pm & 2.30-7pm Tue-Sat & Sun morning, also Mon in Jul & Aug) is on the northern side of the square.

CHÂTEAU DE BIRON

Over the course of eight centuries, the Gontaud (or Gontaut) Biron family built, expanded and rebuilt this **castle** (☎ 05 53 63 13 39; adult/student & child €4.60/2.60; 10am-12.30pm & 2-6pm end Apr–mid-Oct, closed Mon, Fri & Sat end Oct–mid-Apr & Jan). In the early 1900s the castle was sold off, along with its contents, to pay for the extravagant lifestyle of a particularly irresponsible heir.

The castle's gloriously eclectic mixture of architectural styles, the oldest from the 12th century, is a bit hard to fathom if you don't take one of the free, French-language tours (a sheet in English is available). The realistic re-creations of medieval life that fill some of the rooms were once movie sets (the chateau itself is frequently used as a backdrop for films).

The GR36 links Biron with Monpazier, 8km to the north.

BERGERAC

pop 27,000

The less-than-thrilling town of Bergerac, the capital of the Périgord Pourpre wine-growing area, is surrounded by 125 sq km of vineyards. A Protestant stronghold in the 16th century, it sustained heavy damage during the Wars of Religion, but the old city and the old harbour quarter have retained some of their old-time ambience and are worth a stroll. Bergerac makes a convenient stopover on the way from Périgueux (47km to the northeast) to Bordeaux (93km to the west).

The dramatist and satirist Savinien Cyrano de Bergerac (1619–55) may have put the town on the map, but his connection with his namesake is extremely tenuous: it is believed that during his entire life he stayed here a few nights at most.

Information

The **tourist office** (☎ 05 53 57 03 11; www.bergerac -tourisme.com; 97 rue Neuve d'Argenson; ☘ 9.30am-7.30pm Mon-Sat, 10.30am-1pm & 2-7pm Sun Jul & Aug, 9.30am-1pm & 2-7pm Mon-Sat Sep-Jun) supplies useful brochures in English, including information on cycling and wine-tasting in the region.

Sights

Bergerac has long been an important centre for tobacco-growing, which is why it has the **Musée du Tabac** (Tobacco Museum; ☎ 05 53 63 04 13; 10 rue de l'Ancien Port; adult/child €3/1.50; ☘ 10am-noon & 2-6pm Tue-Fri Jan-Dec, 2-6pm Sat & Sun Mar-Nov & Mon Jul & Aug), housed in the early-17th-century, elegant Maison Peyrarède.

The **Musée du Vin et de la Batellerie** (☎ 05 53 57 80 92; place de la Mirpe; adult/child €0.60; ☘ 10am-noon & 2-5.30pm Tue-Fri, 10am-noon Sat) showcases local wine-making and the historic role of the river as a vital transport artery.

Cloître des Récollets (☎ 05 53 63 57 55; admission free; ☘ 10am-12.30pm & 2-6pm Mon-Sat May-Sep, Tue-Sat Oct-Apr), a 16th-century cloister along the river, is occupied by the local Maison des Vins, which offers free wine-tasting.

Sleeping & Eating

The tourist office can provide a full list of *chambres d'hôtes* in the area.

Le Colombier de Cyrano & Roxane (☎ 05 53 57 96 70; bluemoon2@club-Internet.fr; 17 place de la Mirpe; d incl breakfast from €45) About the only *chambre d'hôte* in town, and the most attractive place to stay, this quirky 16th-century building with sloping floors and rickety stairs is the oldest house still standing in Bergerac. The rooms are true to the period theme, though the bathrooms are modern.

Le Moderne (☎ 05 53 57 19 62; 19 av du 108e RI; d from €26, with shower & toilet €36) One of a few small hotels near the station offering good value, this two-star option has 11 rooms above a fairly quiet bar.

Restaurant La Treille (☎ 05 53 57 60 11; 12 quai Salvette; mains €12-18) This restaurant occupies a scenic spot near the riverbank at the edge of the old town. It serves tasty traditional French food on an outside terrace.

Getting There & Away

Bergerac is on the tertiary train line that links Bordeaux and St-Émilion with Sarlat. The airport, 4km southeast of town, is served by flights from Paris (Air France) and the UK (Ryanair).

QUERCY

Southeast of the Dordogne *département* lies the warm, unmistakably southern region of Quercy, many of whose residents still speak Occitan (Provençal). The dry limestone plateau that is found in the northeast is covered with oak trees and cut by dramatic canyons created by the serpentine River Lot and its tributaries. The main city of Cahors is not far away from some of the region's finest vineyards.

Boating

One of the most relaxing ways to see the cliffs and villages along the 64km, navigable stretch of the Lot between St-Cirq Lapopie and Luzech – Cahors is about midway between the two – is to rent a houseboat. Over the next few years, there are plans to open up more of the River Lot to navigation, making it possible to travel downstream to Fumel and upstream to Cajarc.

For detailed information, contact the Centrale de Réservation Loisirs Accueil (p601); or **Les Bateaux Safaraid** (☎ 05 65 30 22 84; fax 05 65 35 98 89) in Bouziès; **Baboumarine** (☎ 05 65 30 08 99; fax 05 65 23 92 59) in Cahors; **Crown Blue Line** (☎ 05 65 20 08 79; fax 05 65 30 97 96) in Douelle; or **Locaboat Plaisance** (head office ☎ 03 86 91 72 72; fax 03 86 62 42 41) in Luzech.

For general information on boating in France, see p922.

Walking & Cycling

In addition to the GR36 and the GR65, both of which pass through Cahors, Quercy has numerous marked trails for day walks. Other Grande Randonnée trails that cross the Lot *département* include the GR6, GR46 and GR652. A variety of topoguides for walkers and cyclists are available from tourist offices.

CAHORS

pop 21,432

Cahors, former capital of the Quercy region, is a quiet town with a relaxed Midi atmosphere. Surrounded on three sides by a bend in the River Lot and ringed by hills, it is endowed with a famous medieval bridge, a large (if unspectacular) medieval quarter and a couple of minor Roman sites. The weather is mild in winter, hot and dry in summer and generally delightful in the spring and autumn. Cahors makes an excellent base for exploring Quercy.

Orientation

The town's main commercial thoroughfare, the north–south oriented blvd Léon Gambetta, is named in honour of Cahors-born Léon Gambetta (1838–82), one of the founders of the Third Republic and briefly premier of France (1881–82). It divides Vieux Cahors (Old Cahors) to the east from the new quarters to the west. At its northern end is place Général de Gaulle, essentially a giant car park; about 500m to the south is place François Mitterrand, home of the tourist office. An even-numbered street address is often blocks away from a similar odd-numbered one.

Information

INTERNET ACCESS

INIT (☎ 05 65 22 00 81; 100 rue Jean Vidal; per hr €2; ⊙ 8.30am-noon & 1.30-5pm Mon-Fri)

Les Docks (see Entertainment; per hr €3; ⊙ 2-8pm Mon & Tue, 2-10pm Wed-Fri, 2-6pm Sat & Sun)

LAUNDRY

There are laundrettes at place de la Libération and 208 rue Georges Clemenceau; both are open 7am to 9pm.

MEDICAL SERVICES

Centre Hospitalier Jean Rougier (☎ 05 65 20 50 50) The ramp to the 24 hour Urgences (casualty ward) is just across from 428 rue Président Wilson.

MONEY

There are banks offering money exchange along blvd Léon Gambetta, open either Tuesday to Saturday or Monday to Friday.

POST

Main Post Office (257 rue Président Wilson) Has a Cyberposte.

TOURIST INFORMATION

Tourist Office (☎ 05 65 53 20 65; cahors@wanadoo.fr; place François Mitterrand; ⊙ 9am-12.30pm & 1.30-6pm Mon-Sat, 10am-noon Sun & holidays Jul & Aug) Efficient, with several excellent brochures in English on offer.

Comité Départemental du Tourisme (☎ 05 65 35 07 09; www.tourisme-lot.com; 1st fl, 107 quai Eugène Cavaignac; ⊙ 8am-12.30pm & 1.30-6pm Mon-Thu, to 5.30pm Fri) Provides information on the Lot *département*.

Sights & Activities

It is possible to walk around three sides of Cahors by following the **quays** along the town's riverside perimeter. Sights below are listed more or less anticlockwise from the bridge. **Pont Valentré**, one of France's finest fortified medieval bridges, consists of six arches and three tall towers, two of them outfitted with machicolations (projecting parapets equipped with openings that allow defenders to drop missiles on attackers below). Built in the 14th century (the towers were added later), it was designed as part of the town's defences, not as a traffic bridge.

Two millennia ago, the **Fontaine des Chartreux** was used in the worship of Divona, the namesake of Gallo-Roman Cahors. A large number of coins, minted between 27 BC and AD 54 and apparently thrown into the water as offerings, were discovered by archaeologists a few years back. The flooded cavern under the pool has been explored by divers to a depth of 137m.

In the Middle Ages Cahors was a prosperous commercial and financial centre. To this day **Vieux Cahors**, the medieval quarter east of blvd Léon Gambetta, is densely packed with old (though not necessarily picturesque) four-storey houses linked by streets and alleyways that are so narrow you can almost touch both walls. At place St Urcisse, there's a fascinating **mechanical clock** (1997) that drops metal balls through a series of improbable contraptions.

The cavernous nave of the Romanesque-style **Cathédrale St-Étienne** (admission free), which was consecrated in 1119, is crowned with two 18m-wide cupolas (the largest in France) that were inspired by the architecture of the Near East. The chapels along the nave (repainted in the 19th century) are Gothic, as are the choir and the massive western façade. The wall paintings between the organ and the interior of the western façade are early 14th-century originals.

LIMOUSIN, THE DORDOGNE & QUERCY

CAHORS

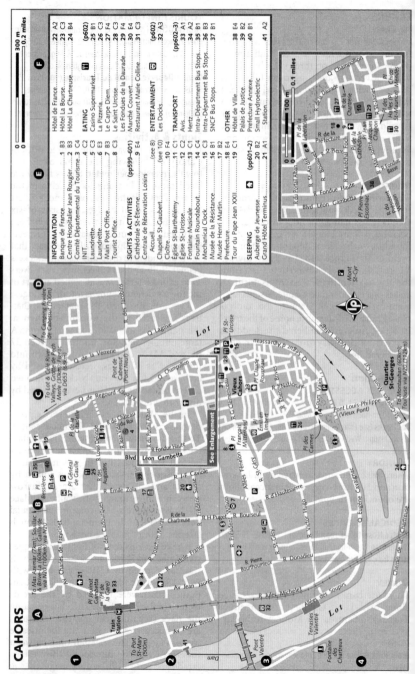

LIMOUSIN, THE DORDOGNE & QUERCY

INFORMATION
Banque de France.................1	B3
Centre Hospitalier Jean Rougier....2	B3
Comité Départemental du Tourisme..3	C4
INIT.............................4	C3
Laundrette......................5	C2
Laundrette......................6	B3
Main Post Office................7	B3
Tourist Office..................8	C3

SIGHTS & ACTIVITIES (pp599–601)
Cathédrale St-Étienne............9	E4
Centrale de Réservation Loisirs Accueil...(see 8)
Chapelle St-Gaubert............10	F4
Cloître........................11	C1
Église St-Barthélémy...........12	C1
Église St-Urcisse..............13	C1
Fontaine Musicale..............14	C4
Fountain Roundabout...........15	C3
Mechanical Clock...............16	B1
Musée de la Résistance.........17	B2
Musée Henri Martin.............18	E4
Prefecture....................19	C1
Tour du Pape Jean XXII.........	

SLEEPING (pp601–2)
Auberge de Jeunesse...........20	B2
Grand Hôtel Terminus..........21	A1
Hôtel de France...............22	A2
Hôtel La Bourse...............23	C3
Hôtel La Chartreuse...........24	B4

EATING (p602)
Casino Supermarket............25	B1
La Pizzeria...................26	C3
Le Carpe Diem................27	F4
Le Saint Urcisse..............28	C3
Les Fondues de la Daurade.....29	F4
Marché Couvert...............30	E4
Restaurant Marie Colline......31	C3

ENTERTAINMENT (p602)
Les Docks....................32	A3

TRANSPORT (pp602–3)
Avis..........................33	A1
Hertz.........................34	A2
Intra-Department Bus Stops....35	B1
Intra-Department Bus Stops....36	B3
SNCF Bus Stops................37	B1

OTHER
Hôtel de Ville................38	E4
Palais de Justice.............39	B2
Prefecture Annexe............40	B1
Small Hydroelectric Station....41	A2

Accessible from the cathedral's choir or through the arched entrance opposite 59 rue de la Daurade de la Chantrerie, the heavily mutilated **cloître** (cloister; ⓨ Jun-Sep), is in the Flamboyant Gothic style of the early 16th century. Off the cloister, **Chapelle St-Gausbert** (admission €3), named after a late-9th-century bishop of Cahors, houses a small collection of liturgical objects. The frescoes of the Final Judgement date from around 1500.

The **Musée Henri Martin** (Musée Municipal; ☎ 05 65 30 15 13; 792 rue Émile Zola; ⓨ Wed-Mon) has some archaeological artefacts and a collection of works by the Cahors-born pointillist painter Henri Martin (1893–1972). It opens only when there are temporary exhibitions, usually from June to September.

To get to the 1989 **Fontaine Musicale** (Musical Fountain), go down the alley next to 70 rue Louis Deloncle.

The **Tour du Pape Jean XXII** (1-3 blvd Léon Gambetta), a square, crenellated tower – at 34m the tallest structure in town – was built in the 14th century as part of the home of Jacques Duèse, later Pope John XXII from 1316 to 1334. The second of the Avignon popes, he established a university in Cahors in 1331. The interior is closed to the public. Across the street is the 14th-century **Église St-Barthélémy**, with its massive brick and stone belfry.

The small **Musée de la Résistance** (☎ 05 65 22 14 25; place Général de Gaulle; admission free; ⓨ 2-6pm), on the northern side of the square, presents illustrated exhibits on the Resistance, the concentration camps and the liberation of France.

WALKING

The 264m-high antenna-topped hill of **Mont St-Cyr**, across the river from Vieux Cahors, affords excellent views of the town and the surrounding countryside. It can easily be climbed on foot with some sturdy shoes, the trail begins near the southern end of Pont Louis-Philippe (1838).

Tours

The **Centrale de Réservation Loisirs Accueil** (☎ 05 65 53 20 90; loisirs.accueil.lot@wanadoo.fr; place François Mitterrand; ⓨ 8am-noon & 1.30-6.30pm Mon-Fri, also Sat Jun-Sep), in the tourist office building, arranges canoe, bicycle and horse-riding excursions, cookery courses and houseboat rental. If you want a hassle-free walk, it can provide

an itinerary and arrange for accommodation, meals and even the transport of your bags. Activities can often be booked at short notice.

Festivals & Events

Around Bastille Day (14 July), the week-long **Festival de Blues** brings big-name jazz stars to town.

Sleeping

Rooms are hardest to come by in July and August. Many cheapies do not register new guests on Sunday unless you make advance arrangements by phone.

The staff at Centrale de Réservation Loisirs Accueil (left) can organise accommodation in the area's many *chambres d'hôtes* and *gîtes*.

BUDGET

Auberge de Jeunesse (☎ 05 65 35 64 71; fax 05 65 35 95 92; 20 rue Frédéric Suisse; dm €9.30; check-in ⓨ 24hr; 🖳) The 40-bed youth hostel is located in the same building as the Foyer des Jeunes Travailleurs. The hostel's staff are helpful and efficient and there's a cheap canteen. Smaller rooms for one or two people are often full, so accommodation is usually in dorms of four to 10 beds; telephone reservations advisable.

Hôtel La Bourse (☎ /fax 05 65 35 17 78; 7 place Claude Rousseau; d from €28) Despite the entrance being down a dark, dingy alleyway around the corner from the bar/reception, the 10 rooms here are all spacious and clean. It's also the only decent budget option in the medieval quarter.

Camping

Camping Rivière de Cassebut (☎ 05 65 30 06 30; www.cabessut.com; sites €8 & per person €3, ⓨ Apr-Oct, 🖳) This three-star camping ground is situated on the left bank of the River Lot about 1km north of Pont de Cabessut (the bridge just east of Vieux Cahors).

MID-RANGE

Grand Hôtel Terminus (☎ 05 65 53 32 00; terminus .balandre@wanadoo.fr; 5 av Charles de Freycinet; d €60-160; 🅿 ⊠) Not your run-of-the-mill station hotel, this exceptional place is both luxurious and full of character. Built around 1920, the hotel has recently been refurbished to a high standard with period detail including ornamental radiators, stained-glass windows and roll-top baths. The rooms are beautifully furnished and the huge beds are perfect for holiday lie-ins.

Hôtel La Chartreuse (☎ 05 65 35 17 37, www.hotel -la-chartreuse.com; chemin de la Chartreuse; d with shower/ bath from €49/62; P ☒ ☒ ☒) This comfortable three-star hotel, although in an ugly, modern building, occupies a great spot on the southern bank of the River Lot. The rooms (some with balconies) have the usual three-star comforts and views across the river and to the town on the far side.

Hôtel de France (☎ 05 65 35 16 76; www.hotel defrance-cahors.fr in French; 252 av Jean Jaurès; d from €42; P ☒ ☒) Near the train station and the Pont Valentré is this modern, reliable three-star hotel with good-sized rooms. Facilities include minibars and international TV channels. Good value.

Eating

Les Fondues de la Daurade (☎ 05 65 35 27 27; place Jean Jacques Chapon; lunch menus from €8.60, dinner menus from 14.50) For something quick and hearty, this snackery gets the thumbs up. Fondues (€14) are its speciality, but it's also good for *tartines*, crepes, omelettes and other snacks and there's a sunny terrace overlooking the square.

Le Carpe Diem (☎ 05 65 35 68 28; 219 rue Maréchal Foch; mains €10-15; ☒ Wed-Sat) A quirky little place whose speciality is cooking with tea. Tea is used as a spice to liven up mainly traditional French dishes and to create unusual combinations such as river perch infused with Egyptian tea (€13.80) – it's tastier than it sounds!

Le Saint Urcisse (☎ 05 65 35 06 06; place St-Urcisse; mains €15-22; ☒ Tue-Sat) With a delightful walled

---

AUTHOR'S CHOICE

Restaurant Marie Colline (☎ 05 65 35 59 96; 173 rue Clemenceau; ☒ noon-2pm Tue-Fri) This is a rarity in France – a fantastic vegetarian restaurant! Choose from a changing menu of just two or three delicious dishes such as *Aubergine Lasagne* or *Dauphinois of Pumpkin*. Mains are €7; entrées and desserts are €3.50 each. The white wooden floors and garden chairs create a rustic ambiance, and there are three tables outside in the sunshine. Advance bookings essential.

---

garden and birds chattering away, this place is hard to beat for summer lunch, especially with the weekday lunch time *menu du jour* at just €11.80. There's a good choice of traditional French cuisine, including some very moorish desserts! Just don't plan too much for the afternoon...

La Pizzeria (☎ 05 65 35 12 18; 58 blvd Léon Gambetta; pizza from €7; ☒ Mon-Sat, also Sun lunch May-Oct) An extremely popular and good value pizzeria where the pizzas are created and fired in full view – always a good sign. Pastas and large salads also on offer.

SELF-CATERING

Marché Couvert (place des Halles; ☒ 7.30am-12.30pm & 3-7pm Tue-Sat, 9am-noon Sun & most holidays) A covered market also known as Les Halles. There's an open-air market on Wednesday and Saturday mornings around the covered market and on place Jean-Jacques Chapou. Nearby, food shops can be found around place des Halles and along rue de la Préfecture.

There's a **Casino supermarket** (☒ closed Wed) on place Général de Gaulle.

Entertainment

Les Docks (☎ 05 65 22 36 38; 430 allées des Soupirs) This one-time warehouse is now a municipal cultural centre, with a concert hall, a venue for small-scale theatre productions, music lessons (€2 per hour) and practice rooms for young musicians (€1 per hour per musician), a free skate park (for fans of in-line skates and skateboards) and an Internet café (p599).

Getting There & Away

BUS

The bus services linking Cahors with destinations around Lot *département*, designed primarily to transport school children, are a mess. To check your limited options, ask at the tourist office.

There are daily SNCF bus services from Cahors' train station and place Charles de Gaulle to Bouziès (see opposite), Tour de Faure (St-Cirq Lapopie, see opposite), Figeac (see p604) and Mercuès, Castelfranc, Luzech and Puy l'Évêque (see p607).

CAR

Choose from **Avis** (☎ 05 65 30 13 10; place de la Gare) or **Hertz** (☎ 05 65 35 34 69; 385 rue Anatole France) opposite the train station.

Free parking is available all along the river and in the westernmost sections of the car parks along allées Fénelon (behind the tourist office) and also at place Charles de Gaulle.

TRAIN

Cahors' **train station** (place Jouinot Gambetta, aka place de la Gare) is on the main SNCF line (four to nine daily) linking Paris' Gare d'Austerlitz (€59.60, five hours). Trains stop at Limoges (€23.30, two hours), Souillac (€9.20, 45 minutes), Brive-La-Gaillarde (€13.20, one hour) and Toulouse (€14.70, 1½ hours). To get to Sarlat-la-Canéda, take a train to Souillac and an SNCF bus from there (€13.80, three hours, three daily).

EAST OF CAHORS

The limestone hills between Cahors and Figeac are cut by the dramatic, cliff-flanked Rivers Lot and Célé. The narrow, winding and supremely scenic D662 (signposted 'Vallée du Lot') follows the River Lot, while the even narrower and more spectacular D41 (signposted 'Vallée du Célé') follows the tortuous route of the River Célé.

Bouziès

pop 70

The quiet hamlet of Bouziès, on the left bank of the Lot between the cliffs and the river bank, is home to the welcoming, two-star **Hôtel Les Falaises** (☎ 05 65 31 26 83; www.mona lisahotels.com; r €42-58; ☼ Apr-Oct; 🅿 🐾). Prices depend on the season Mountain bikes, canoes and kayaks are rented out to guests and visitors alike. The attached **restaurant** (menus from €13) serves regional meals.

Les Bateaux Safaraid (p598) rents *gabarres* (flat-bottomed river boats) and six-person houseboats.

The SNCF bus (four to six daily) that links Cahors (€4.40, 25 minutes) with Figeac (€7.50, 70 minutes) stops on the D662 just across the narrow suspension bridge from Bouziès. If you make advance reservations, the hotel will send its minivan to pick you up at Cahors' train station or drop you off at the starting point of a hike.

Grotte de Pech Merle

The spectacular, 1200m-long **Pech Merle Cave** (☎ 05 65 31 27 05; www.pechmerle.com; adult/5-18 yrs mid-Jun–mid-Sep €7/4.50, mid-Sep–mid-Jun €6/3.80),

30km northeast of Cahors, is first and foremost a natural wonder, with thousands of stalactites and stalagmites of all varieties and shapes. It also has dozens of paintings of mammoths, horses and 'negative' human handprints, drawn by Cro-Magnon people 16,000 to 20,000 years ago in red, black, blue and dark grey. Prehistoric artefacts that have been found in the area are on display in the museum.

From April to October one-hour guided tours (English text available) take place every 45 minutes (every 15 minutes in summer) from 9.30am to noon and 1.30pm to 5pm daily. It's well worth the admission price. During the months when there are lots of tourists around (especially July and August), get there early as only 700 people daily are allowed to visit. Telephone reservations are accepted.

The cave is 8km from the Bouziès bridge and 3km from Cabrerets along the D41, D13 and D198. On foot the cave is about 3km from Bouziès via the GR651.

Conduché

Le Bureau des Sports Nature (☎ 05 65 24 21 01; perso.wanadoo.fr/bureau-sports-nature; ☼ Mon-Fri year round, Sat & Sun in Jul & Aug), based in the village of Conduché (near the confluence of the Rivers Lot and Célé), offers guided **rock climbing** and **spelunking**, guided **walks**, **canoe trips** and off-road **mountain biking**, weather permitting. Prices vary depending on numbers and activities; guided canoe trips start at €19 for a half day.

St-Cirq Lapopie

pop 50

St-Cirq Lapopie, 25km east of Cahors and 44km southwest of Figeac, is perched on a cliff top 100m above the River Lot. The spectacular views and the area's natural beauty more than make up for the village's self-conscious charm.

The fortified, early-16th-century **Gothic church** is of no special interest except for its stunning location. The ruins of the 13th-century **chateau**, at the top of the hill, also afford a fine panorama. Below, along the narrow alleyways, the restored stone and half-timbered houses, topped with steep, red-tiled roofs, shelter **artisans' studios** offering leather goods, pottery, jewellery and various wooden items. The **Musée Rignault**

SANTIAGO DE COMPOSTELA

The prospect of a few less years in purgatory through the granting of a soul-cleansing plenary indulgence may have motivated the early pilgrims to Santiago de Compostela in northwest Spain. However, for the thousands of contemporary spiritualists and atheists who undertake the long and rocky road to this important medieval site each summer, the incentive may be a little more palpable.

In the early 9th century a hermit, Pelayo, led by a vision, stumbled across the 800-year-old tomb of the apostle James, brother of John the Evangelist. Soon after his remains were authenticated, a shrine was established and by the 12th century Santiago de Compostela had become as significant a site of pilgrimage as Jerusalem and Rome. Four traditional routes through France now exist, the most popular of which passes through Figeac (below) and Cahors (p599). Though you can pick up the trail from any number of points, it's possible to follow a road from Paris for an arduous 2000km hike. Numerous points of worship or *refuges* were established en route, encouraging the welcome patronage of passing pilgrims. Walkers or those on horseback who complete the final 100km to Santiago (cyclists the final 200km) qualify for a Compostela Certificate issued on arrival at the cathedral.

(admission €2; ☉ 10am-12.30pm & 2.30-6pm Apr-Oct, to 7pm Jul & Aug) has a delightful garden and an eclectic collection of French furniture and art from Africa and China.

The **tourist office** (☎ 05 65 31 29 06; saint-cirq .lapopie@wanadoo.fr; ☉ 10am-1pm & 2-7.30pm Jun-Sep, to 6pm Apr, May & Oct, to 5pm Sun & closed Mon Nov-Mar) in the village hall can supply you with an English-language brochure.

The riverside **Camping de la Plage** (☎ 05 65 30 29 51; site for 2 people with/without electricity €17.80/14.80; ☉ Apr-Nov) is on the left bank of the Lot at the bridge linking the D662 (Tour de Faure) with the road up to St-Cirq Lapopie.

The **Hôtel de La Pelissaria** (☎ 05 65 31 25 14; http://perso.wanadoo.fr/hoteldelapelissaria; r €71-130; ☉ Apr-Oct; ☒), a short way down the hill from the tourist office, has rooms in a lovely 16th-century house, perched dramatically on the edge of the cliff. There are panoramic views of the town and the river from the terrace.

St-Cirq Lapopie is 2km across the river and up the hill from Tour de Faure (on the D662), from where SNCF buses go to Cahors (€4.80, 35 minutes, four to six daily) and Figeac (€7.90, one hour, five daily).

Figeac

pop 9500

The harmonious riverside town of Figeac, on the River Célé 70km northeast of Cahors, has a picturesque **old city**, with many houses dating from the 12th to 18th centuries. Founded in the 9th century by Benedictine monks, it became a prosperous medieval market town, an important stopping place for pilgrims travelling to Santiago de Compostela (above) and, later, a Protestant stronghold (1576–1623).

ORIENTATION & INFORMATION

The main commercial thoroughfare is the north–south blvd Docteur G Juskiewenski, which runs perpendicular to the Célé and its right-bank quays. Pedestrianised rue Gambetta, four short blocks east, is also perpendicular to the river. The train station, about 600m to the southeast, is across the river from the centre of town, at the end of av Georges Clemenceau.

The **tourist office** (☎ 05 65 34 06 25; http://figeac .quercy-tourisme.com; place Vival; ☉ 10am-7.30pm Jul & Aug, 10am-12.30pm & 2.30-6pm Mon-Sat & 10am-12.30pm Sun May, Jun & Sep, 10am-noon & 2.30-6pm Mon-Sat Oct-Apr) is one block north of the river and two blocks east of blvd Docteur G Juskiewenski.

The **post office** (8 av Fernand Pezet), a block west of blvd Docteur G Juskiewenski, offers currency exchange. There are a couple of banks along the same street.

The **Allo Laverie laundrette** (☉ 6am-10pm) is next to the tourist office.

SIGHTS

The tourist office is housed in a handsome, 13th-century building. Upstairs is the **Musée du Vieux Figeac** (adult/child €2/1; ☉ same as tourist office), with a varied collection of antique clocks, coins, minerals and a propeller blade made by a local aerospace firm.

Figeac's most illustrious son is the brilliant linguist and founder of the science of Egyptology, Jean-François Champollion

(1790–1832), who managed to decipher the written language of the pharaohs by studying the Rosetta Stone, an edict issued in 196 BC in Greek and two Egyptian scripts, demotic and hieroglyphic. Discovered by Napoleon's forces in 1799 during their abortive invasion of Egypt, the stone was captured by the English in 1801 and taken to the British Museum, where it remains; an enlarged copy fills the ancient courtyard next to Champollion's childhood home, now the **Musée Champollion** (☎ 05 65 50 31 08; rue des Frères Champollion; adult/student & child €3.10/1.85; ⏰ 10am-noon & 2.30-6.30pm Tue-Sun Mar-Oct, also Mon in Jul & Aug, 2.30-6.30pm Tue-Sun Nov-Feb) on a tiny street four blocks north of the tourist office (along pedestrianised rue de la République). There is a small collection of Egyptian antiquities. Some of the explanatory signs are in English.

North of the Musée Champollion and place Champollion, **rue de Colomb**, favoured by the local aristocracy in the 18th century, is lined with centuries-old mansions in sandstone, half-timbers and brick. Near the river on rue du Chapitre, the musty **Église St-Sauveur**, a Benedictine abbey church built from the 12th to 14th centuries, features stained glass installed during the last half of the 19th century.

SLEEPING

Hôtel-Café Champollion (☎ 05 65 34 04 37; fax 05 65 34 61 69; 3 place Champollion; d with bath €47) This is a funky, modern hotel with 10 nicely designed rooms, right in the heart of the old city. Good breakfasts with real coffee and fresh juice are available at its adjoining café.

Hôtel Le Terminus (☎ 05 65 34 00 43; www.hotel-terminus.fr; 27 av Georges Clemenceau; d with shower & toilet €46; **P**) This reasonable two-star hotel opposite the train station has 12 bright, cheery rooms and a decent **restaurant** (menus €23-50) with tender Quercy lamb a particular speciality.

Grand Hôtel Le Pont D'Or (☎ 05 65 50 95 00; hotel.pont.or@free.fr; 2 av Jean Jaurès; d €60-76; **P** ✗ ❄ 💻 🌐) Overlooking the river Célé, this 13th-century building has been completely renovated inside to create a characterless but comfortable three-star hotel. Top-notch facilities include pool, sauna and fitness room. Riverside rooms are larger (and more expensive).

EATING

Cuisine du Marché (☎ 05 65 50 18 55; 15 rue Clermont; menus €18-35; ⏰ Mon-Sat) Regional gastronomy can be sampled in the old city at this airy and refined establishment. *Menus* feature contemporary variations on Quercy cuisine and there's an extensive wine list.

Le Crepuscule (☎ 05 65 34 28 53; rue de la République) A plain but friendly diner-style place, popular with locals, serving tasty pizzas, savoury crepes and grills.

Le Marrakech (☎ 05 65 34 69 25; 7 rue des Maquisards; mains €10-15) A harem-like, dark and cosy place beside the steps of the old city, offering authentic Moroccan tagines (stews) and couscous.

There is a **Centre L Gambetta (Leclerc) supermarket** (32 rue Gambetta; ⏰ 8.30am-12.30pm & 2pm-7.30pm Mon-Sat), and place Carnot hosts a food market on Saturday morning.

GETTING THERE & AWAY

Four SNCF buses daily travel to Cahors (€10.20, 1¾ hours) via Bouziès and Tour de Faure (St-Cirq Lapopie). Stops are at Figeac's train station and on av Maréchal Joffre (which runs along the river) behind Lycée Champollion.

The **train station** (☎ 05 65 04 94 79) is on two major lines: the one that links Clermont-Ferrand (€25.70, four hours) with Villefranche de Rouergue (€5.70, 40 minutes), Najac (€7.70, 50 minutes) and Toulouse (€18.60, 2½ hours); and the route from Paris' Gare d'Austerlitz (€50.10, about 4½ hours) to Limoges (€22.10, 2¼ hours), Brive (€11.80, 1¼ hours), Rocamadour-Padirac (€6.70, 35 minutes) and Rodez (€10.20, 2¼ hours). There are four or five trains daily to each destination.

Villefranche de Rouergue
pop 12,300

Villefranche, 61km east of Cahors, is – like most *bastides* – centred around an arcaded central square, **place Notre Dame**. In one corner is the Languedoc Gothic **Collégiale Notre Dame**, a flying buttress-less structure built in the 14th and 15th centuries, whose never-completed belfry is held aloft by massive supports. The 15th-century **choir stalls** are ornamented with humorous figures.

A few blocks to the southwest along streets lined with stone and half-timbered houses, the **Musée Urbain Cabrol** (☎ 05 65 45 44 37;

rue de la Fontaine; ⓨ Mon-Sat Jun–mid-Sep, Mon-Fri mid-Sep–May) has an eclectic but fascinating collection of prehistory, religious art, local folk art and 19th-century medical equipment. The **fountain** at the front, decorated with stone carvings from 1336, gushes naturally.

Approximately 500m towards Najac from the train station, the **Chartreuse St-Sauveur**, a 15th-century monastery once affiliated with the austere Carthusian order, now houses a hospital. Of interest are the vaulted Gothic **cloister** (ⓨ 24hr) and the **chapel** (ⓨ 2-5pm Mon-Fri, 9-11am Sun), topped by a square belfry.

The large Thursday morning market on place Notre Dame is a real draw for tourists and locals alike, where everything from Chinese herbal medicine to organic produce and handmade kites is sold.

Next to the town hall, the **tourist office** (☎ 05 65 45 13 18; www.villefranche.com in French; promenade du Guiraudet; ⓨ 9am-noon & 2-6pm Mon-Sat May-Oct, also 10am-noon Sun Jul & Aug, 9am-noon & 2-6pm Mon-Fri Nov-Apr) has a walking tour brochure in English.

Hôtel Bellevue (☎ 05 65 45 23 17; 3 av de Segala; d from €30), at the intersection of the D922 and the D911, across the tracks and half a block up the hill from the train station, is a small, family-run place with simple rooms.

Le Relais de Farrou (☎ 05 65 45 18 11; fax 05 65 45 32 59; route de Figeac; s/d from €43/48.50; P ⓡ), 4km from town, offers three-star comfort in an old *relais de poste* (postal station) at very reasonable rates.

L'Assiette Gourmande (☎ 05 65 45 25 95; place Andrée Lescur; menus €12.50-28; ⓨ closed Sun, Tue & Wed evening), just off place Notre Dame, is a snazzy restaurant with an outside terrace, offering fine regional and French cuisine. The tasty four-course *menu de saison* is good value at €17.50.

La Mestiça (☎ 05 65 45 68 20; 12 rue Prestat; mains from €4.50) is a cosy little creperie selling good value snacks and salads as well as crepes. The lunch-time menu is a bargain €4 including wine. It's half a block west of place Notre Dame.

Villefranche's train station (across the river from the tourist office) is linked with regular trains to Figeac (€5.70, 40 minutes) and Capdenac (€4.90, 30 minutes) from where there are SNCF buses to Cahors (€13.90) and Brive (€15.30).

Najac

pop 250

The beautifully preserved, fairytale-like *bastide* village of Najac grew in the 13th century around the **Fortresse Royal** (☎ 05 65 29 71 65; ⓨ Apr-Sep), also known as the Château Fort, built on a rocky, easily defensible hill high above a hairpin curve in the River Aveyron. A bit to the west is the massive, Midi-Gothic **Église St-Jean l'Évangéliste**, which the locals were forced to construct by the Inquisition in 1258 as punishment for their Catharist tendencies.

The medieval parts are spread out along one, east–west-oriented street that runs 1.2km along the crest of the hill; it links the church with the sloping **place du Faubourg**, a charming, *bastide*-style central square surrounded by houses – each unique – from as early as the 13th century.

The **tourist office** (☎ 05 65 29 72 05; otsi .najac@wanadoo.fr; place du Faubourg; ⓨ 9am-noon & 2-5.45pm Mon-Sat Apr-Sep, also 10am-noon Sun Jul & Aug, 9am-noon & 2-5.45pm Mon-Fri & Sat morning Oct-Mar) is on the southern side of the square.

Najac makes a good base for kayaking, rafting, cycling and hiking (a topoguide is available at the tourist office). **Najac de la Vallée**, along the river, is 3km (by road) down the hill near the train station (see p605 for train information).

Oustal del Barry (☎ 05 65 29 74 32; www.oustaldel barry.com; place du Faubourg; d €66.50-89, ⓨ late Mar–mid-Nov), just up the hill from the tourist office, is a two-star place in an old wooden-beamed building with stunning views of the valley and the fortress. The attached **restaurant** (menus from €22.30; ⓨ closed Tue lunch & Mon Oct-Jun) has *menus* made with fresh local products.

Le Belle Rive (☎ 05 65 29 73 90; fax 05 65 29 76 88; Le Roc du Pont; d with shower or bath €50-53; P ⓡ) is a two-star, family-run hotel 1.5km from the village, past the train station. It has 30 comfortable rooms, a swimming pool, tennis court and billiard room.

La Salamandre (☎ 05 65 29 74 09; rue du Barriou; menus €16-20; ⓨ closed Wed dinner Dec & Jan), just downhill from the tourist office, is a stylish, contemporary restaurant serving inventive variations on traditional cuisine. The wonderful panoramic terrace has giddying views of the roller-coaster valley below.

Il Capello (☎ 05 65 29 70 26; route de la Gare; menu €10, pizza €5.80-7.30; ⓨ closed Wed dinner) is a busy, rustic restaurant packed with locals, serving pizzas, grills and hearty homemade local dishes.

The most scenic way to get to Villefranche de Rouergue, 23km to the north, is via the twisting, one-lane D638, which intersects the D339 about 5km northeast of Najac.

WEST OF CAHORS

Downstream from Cahors, the lower River Lot follows an impossibly serpentine route through the rich vineyards of the Cahors Appellation d'Origine Contrôlée (AOC) region, passing the dams at **Luzech**, whose medieval section sits at the base of a donjon, and **Castelfranc**, with a suspension bridge.

Along (and above) the river's right bank, the D9 – too narrow and heavily trafficked for cycling – affords superb views of the vines and the river's many hairpin curves. Château de Biron and Monpazier (p597) are nearby.

Four to seven SNCF buses each day link Cahors with Luzech (€3, 20 minutes) and Puy l'Évêque (€5.50, 45 minutes).

Puy l'Évêque
pop 2200

The once-important riverside port of Puy l'Évêque, on a rocky hillside above the right bank of the Lot, has an intimate, stone centre with numerous, centuries-old stone houses. It is a good base for exploring the lower Lot area, including the Cahors AOC wineries. The town is 31km from Cahors.

The Puy l'Évêque **tourist office** (☎ /fax 05 65 21 37 63; ☺ 8.30am-12.30pm & 2-6.30pm Mon-Fri, to 6pm Sat, Sep-Jun, 9.30am-12.30pm & 2.30-6.30pm Mon-Sat, 10am-12.30pm Sun Jul & Aug), in the golden-hued village hall building – at the base of a square, 13th-century donjon – can supply you with an English-language brochure on day hikes.

About 4km north up the hill and through the forest, the austere **Église de Martignac** (☺ 10am-7pm), topped by a peculiar half-timbered belfry, is decorated with 15th-century frescoes, protected for centuries by layers of whitewash. The surrounding area is perfect for quiet walks.

Hôtel Henry (☎ 05 65 21 32 24; www.hotel-henry .com; 23 rue du Docteur Roumat; d €32-38, with garden view €43-47; ☒) is a very well appointed two-star hotel near the old town with a leafy terrace and small garden. The attached **restaurant** (menus €15-28; ☺ closed Sun night & some Sat in winter) has French and Quercy-style *menus*.

Château de Bonaguil

This imposing feudal **fortress** (☎ 05 53 71 90 33; adult/7-16 yrs €4.50/3; ☺ 10am-6pm Jun-Aug, 10.30am-1pm & 2.30-5pm Sep, 11am-1pm & 2.30-5pm Oct, 11am-1pm & 2.30-5.30pm Feb & Mar, 11am-1pm & 2.30-5.30pm Apr & May; 2.30-4.30pm Sun & holidays Nov-Jan) is a fine example of late-15th-century military architecture, featuring the artful integration of cliffs, outcrops, towers, bastions, loop-holes, machicolations and crenellations. It's situated about 15km west of Puy l'Évêque (and on the GR36 footpath). Optional guided tours (1½ hours), in English three times daily in July and August, generally take place on the hour, with the last one about an hour before closing time.

About 5km to the southeast is the attractive village of **St-Martin-le-Redon**, in a quiet little valley along the River Thèze (and just off the D673).

NORTHERN QUERCY

The northern edge of Quercy is not far from Collonges-la-Rouge, Beaulieu-sur-Dordogne and Turenne (p581).

Rocamadour
pop 630

Except in winter, when it's nearly dead, the spectacularly situated pilgrimage centre of Rocamadour, 59km north of Cahors and 51km east of Sarlat, is a touristic nightmare, overrun with coaches and crammed with tacky souvenir shops.

Perched on a 150m-high cliff face above the River Alzou, the old city – known as the **Cité** – was, from the 12th to 14th centuries, an important stop on one of the pilgrimage routes to Santiago de Compostela (p604). These days, coach tourists with glazed eyes obediently plod through a number of over-restored Gothic chapels, including **Chapelle Notre Dame**, home to a 12th-century Black Madonna said to have miraculous powers.

The Cité's only street is connected to the chapels and the plateau above, known as **L'Hospitalet**, by the **Grand Escalier** (Great Staircase). The pious once climbed this on their knees, and there's a path whose switchbacks are marked with graphic Stations of the Cross. At the top of the stairs is the 14th-century **chateau** (charging €2.50 for a view from the ramparts).

Sights in L'Hospitalet include the **Grotte des Merveilles** (☎ 05 65 33 67 92; ☺ Apr–mid-Nov), a one-room cave with some mediocre stalactites and prehistoric cave paintings.

The Cité **tourist offices** (☎ 05 65 33 62 59) is on the main street, and there's another **branch** (☎ 05 65 33 22 00) at L'Hospitalet, next to the Grotte des Merveilles.

Gouffre de Padirac

The truly spectacular **Padirac Cave** (☎ 05 65 33 64 56; adult/6-9 yrs €8/5.20; ☉ 9am-6pm Jul, 8.30am-6.30pm Aug 9am-noon & 2-6pm Apr-Jun & Sep-early Oct), 15km northeast of Rocamadour and 10km southeast of Carennac, offers the closest thing – at least in *this* world – to a cruise to Hades across the River Styx. Discovered in 1889, the cave's navigable river, 103m below ground level, is reached through a 75m-deep, 33m-wide chasm.

Boat pilots, who speak only Occitan and Midi-accented French, ferry visitors along a 500m stretch of the subterranean waterway, guiding them up and down a series of stairways to otherworldly pools and vast, floodlit caverns.

The whole cave operation is unashamedly mass-market, but it retains an innocence and style reminiscent of the 1930s, when the first lifts were installed. The temperature inside the cave is a constant 13°C. The 1¼-hour visits take place from April to early October.

Château de Castelnau-Bretenoux

A stunning hilltop silhouette greets you as you approach this feudal **fortress** (☎ 05 65 10 98 00; adult/18-25 yrs/under 18 €6.10/4.10/free; ☉ 9.30am-7pm Jul & Aug, 9.30am-12.30pm & 2-6.30pm May & Jun, 10am-12.30pm & 2-5.30pm Wed-Mon Sep-Apr). One of France's most impressive, it is 9km east of Carennac. It dominates the valleys of the Rivers Dordogne, Cère and Bave, with its sandy limestone hues ranging from golden yellow to deep red. Most of the complex – which, mercifully, has not been over-restored – dates from the 12th to the 15th centuries. The site has signs in English.

Ticket sales stop 45 minutes before the morning and afternoon closing times. The seven eclectically furnished rooms must be visited with a guide (English information sheet available).

Carennac
pop 370

The narrow alleyways of this delightful medieval village, on the left bank of the Dordogne, meander among tile-roofed houses made of golden-hued stone, some built as early as the 10th century (and most occupied only in the summer).

An arched stone gate leads to the 16th-century **Château du Doyen**, which houses a heritage centre, **L'Espace Patrimoine** (☎ 05 65 33 81 36; patrimoine-vallee-dordogne@wanadoo.fr; admission free; ☉ 10am-noon & 2-6pm Tue-Fri Apr-Jun, Tue-Sun Jul-Sep), showcasing the art and history of the region. Above is the square **Tour de Télémaque**, named after the hero of Fénelon's *Les Aventures de Télémaque,* written here in 1699.

Next to the chateau is the **priory**, reached via the same stone gate. Over the entrance to the Romanesque **Église St-Pierre** is an exceptional **tympanum** depicting Jesus in majesty, carved in the Languedoc Romanesque style in the mid-12th century. Just off the **cloître** (cloister; adult/child €2.50/0.80), heavily damaged in the Revolution, is a remarkable, late-15th-century **Mise au Tombeau** (Statue of the Entombment), once brightly painted. Its opening hours are the same as the **tourist office** (☎ 05 65 10 97 01; ot.intercom.carennac@wanadoo .fr; ☉ 10am-7pm mid-Jun–Sep, 10am-noon & 2-6pm Mon-Sat, 2-6pm Sun Oct–mid-Jun) next door.

Walking options include the GR652, which links the village of Mézels (on the river to the northwest) with the Gouffre de Padirac (to the southeast). For a lovely drive, follow the D30 southeast along the Dordogne.

Hôtel des Touristes (☎ 05 65 10 94 31; www .hotel-touristes.com; d from €40; ☉ closed Christmas) is a cosy, renovated nine-room place run by the same family for four generations and open pretty much year-round. The lovely double rooms have wooden floorboards, cool blue tones and river views. Half-board (from €47 per person, including the room) may be required in July and August. The **restaurant** (menus €14.50-24; ☉ closed dinner Fri & Sat Oct–mid-Apr) features traditional regional cuisine.

The only place to buy food is the small **grocery** (☉ closed 12.30-3pm, also Sun & Mon afternoons) next to the post office.

Atlantic Coast

CONTENTS

Nantes	612
Poitiers	617
Around Poitiers	619
La Rochelle	620
Île de Ré	625
St-Martin de Ré	625
South of La Rochelle	626
Cognac	627
Bordeaux	628
Bordeaux Wine-Growing Region	637
The Médoc	637
St-Émilion	639
Arcachon	641
Around Arcachon	644

It may not have the glitz and glamour associated with its counterpart on the Mediterranean, but France's Atlantic coast is just as appealing. Of course, there's the scorching sunshine and miles of sandy beaches, but there's so much more to this region than bucket-and-spade summer days.

Lively Bordeaux is emerging from an ambitious makeover to become one of France's hot destinations. Rich in museums, restaurants and nightlife, the city centre has been scrubbed, polished and pedestrianised to great effect, showcasing its grand neoclassical architecture. Then there's the wine. The city is surrounded by one of the most renowned wine-growing regions, from the pompous chateaux of the Médoc to the distinguished wineries of St-Émilion.

On the coast itself, the relaxed seaside resorts of Soulac-sur-Mer and Arcachon sit at either end of the Côte d'Argent, a long stretch of virtually deserted sand beaches and dunes best explored on bicycle. If you prefer riding the waves rather than two-wheelers, you're also in luck. The surf here is about the best in Europe.

The charming, picturesque ports of La Rochelle and on nearby Île de Ré are the nearest you'll find to the yacht-glamour of the Med, but these unpretentious places are known more for *poisson* than posing, with succulent, fresh seafood on the menu. Inland diversions include the famed brandy town of Cognac, the historic and commodious city of Nantes and the superb Romanesque churches at Poitiers.

The area in this chapter straddles three regions; Pays de la Loire in the north around Nantes; Poitou-Charentes from Poitiers to the coast; and Aquitaine, south of the Gironde Estuary. That may help to explain the sheer diversity of attractions on offer here.

HIGHLIGHTS

- Surf's up! Catching the waves (or a lesson) at **Arcachon** (p641) or **Soulac-sur-Mer** (p638)
- Wine tasting, chateaux visits and long lunches at **St-Émilion** (p639) and the **Médoc** (p637)
- Gorging on magnificent seafood in **La Rochelle** (p623)
- Run, jump or cartwheel down **Dune de Pyla** (p644)
- Laugh, cry and applaud at the Opera House, **Nantes** (p616)
- Explore the restaurants, bars and clubs of **Bordeaux** (p634)
- Laze around on the beaches at **Île de Ré** (p626)

- POPULATION: 4,529,642
- AREA: 51,597 SQ KM

ATLANTIC COAST

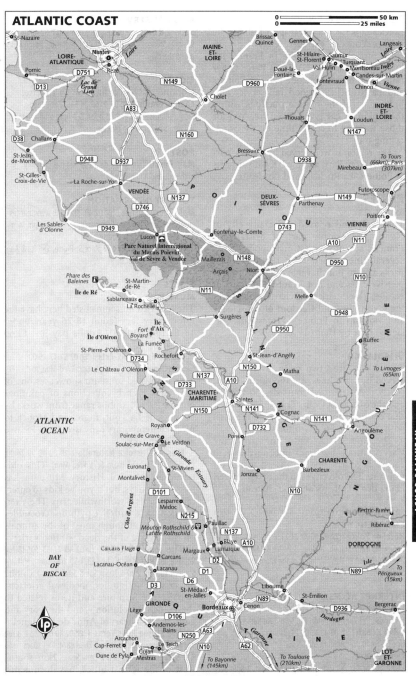

ATLANTIC COAST

0 _____ 50 km
0 _____ 25 miles

St-Nazaire

LOIRE-ATLANTIQUE

Nantes

Loire

Rezé

Pornic

D751

D13

Lac de Grand Lieu

N149

Cholet

A83

MAINE-ET-LOIRE

Brissac-Quincé

Gennes

Langeais

St-Hilaire-St-Florent

Saumur

Turquant

Val Hulin

Montsoreau

Candes-sur-Martin

Doué-la-Fontaine

Fontevraud

Chinon

Vienne

INDRE-ET-LOIRE

D960

Thouars

Loudun

N147

D38

Challans

N160

Bressuire

D938

Mirebeau

To Tours (66km); Paris (307km)

St-Jean-de-Monts

D948

D937

Futuroscope

St-Gilles-Croix-de-Vie

La Roche-sur-Yon

VENDÉE

N137

DEUX-SÈVRES

Parthenay

N149

Poitiers

VIENNE

D746

Les Sables-d'Olonne

D949

Luçon

Fontenay-le-Comte

D743

A10

N11

Parc Naturel Interrégional du Marais Poitevin, Val de Sèvre & Vendée

Maillezais

N148

Arçais

Niort

D950

N10

Phare des Baleines

St-Martin-de-Ré

Île de Ré

Sablanceaux

La Rochelle

N11

Melle

D948

Île d'Aix

Fort Boyard

Île d'Oléron

La Fumée

St-Pierre-d'Oléron

Rochefort

D734

Le Château d'Oléron

N137

A10

D733

CHARENTE-MARITIME

Surgères

St-Jean-d'Angély

N150

Matha

Ruffec

To Limoges (65km)

Saintes

N141

Cognac

N141

Angoulême

ATLANTIC OCEAN

N150

Royan

Pointe de Grave

Le Verdon

Soulac-sur-Mer

D732

Pons

Jonzac

Barbezieux

CHARENTE

Euronat

St-Vivien

Gironde Estuary

N10

Bectric-Rurée

Montalivet

Ribérac

D101

DORDOGNE

Lesparre-Médoc

N215

Mouton Rothschild & Lafitte Rothschild

Pauillac

N137

A10

Isle

To Périgueux (15km)

N89

Carcans Plage

Margaux

Blaye

BAY OF BISCAY

Carcans

Lamarque

D2

Libourne

Lacanau-Océan

Lacanau

D1

St-Émilion

Bergerac

D3

D6

St-Médard-en-Jalles

N89

D936

Dordogne

Lège

GIRONDE

Bordeaux

Cenon

D106

Andernos-les-Bains

A63

Garonne

LOT-ET-GARONNE

Arcachon

N250

Cap-Ferret

Le Teich

N10

A62

Dune de Pyla

Gujan-Mestras

To Bayonne (145km)

To Toulouse (210km)

Getting There & Away
Bordeaux is the main transport hub for the region. You can get there easily by train from just about anywhere in France; it's just three hours by TGV from Paris. Other rail arrival options include Nantes, Poitiers and La Rochelle. A good rail service also links most of the main attractions within the region. A car gives added freedom for those wanting to spend time on the wine-tasting trail.

The region is well-served by flights, particularly from Paris and the UK with airports at Poitiers, La Rochelle and Bordeaux.

NANTES
pop 277,728
The lively and relaxed university city of Nantes, historically part of Brittany, is France's seventh-largest metropolis. It has several fine museums, carefully tended parks and an unbelievable number of inexpensive cafés and restaurants. The Edict of Nantes, a landmark royal charter guaranteeing civil rights and freedom of conscience and worship to France's Protestants, was signed here by Henri IV in 1598.

Orientation
The city centre's two main arteries, both served by tram lines, are the north–south, partly pedestrianised cours des 50 Otages, and the east–west Cours Franklin Roosevelt that connects the train station (to the east) with quai de la Fosse (to the west).

The commercial centre runs from the Gare Centrale bus/tram hub northeast to rue de la Marne and northwest to rue du Calvaire. The old city is to the east, between cours des 50 Otages and the chateau.

Information
EMERGENCY
Hôtel de Police (☎ 02 40 37 21 21; 6 place Waldeck Rousseau; tram stop Motte Rouge) Police Nationale's 24-hour station is 1km northeast of the Monument des 50 Otages.

INTERNET ACCESS
Cyber House (☎ 02 40 12 11 84; 8 quai de Versailles; per hr €3; 2pm-2am Mon-Fri, 3pm-2am Sat)
Cyber Kebab (☎ 02 40 47 09 21; 30 rue de Verdun; per hr €3; 10am-midnight Mon-Sun)
Cyber Planet (☎ 02 51 82 47 97; 18 rue de l'Arche Sèche; per hr €3; 10am-midnight Mon-Sat, 2-8pm Sat)

MEDICAL SERVICES
Service d'Urgence (emergency room; ☎ 02 40 08 38 95; quai Moncousu) Of the vast CHR de Nantes hospital is along the river.

MONEY
Commercial banks line rue La Fayette.
Change Graslin (☎ 02 40 69 24 64; 17 rue Jean-Jacques Rousseau; 9am-noon & 2-6pm Mon-Fri, to 4.45pm Sat) Exchange bureau.

POST
Main Post Office (place de Bretagne) Has currency exchange and a Cyberposte.

TOURIST INFORMATION
Main Tourist Office (☎ 02 40 20 60 00; www.nantes-tourisme.com; place du Commerce; 10am-7pm Mon-Sat) In the Palais de la Bourse.
Tourist Office Annexe (2 place St-Pierre; Jul & Aug) Next to the cathedral.

Sights
MUSEUMS
The first two museums listed here have the same entry fees (adult/18-26 years/under 18 €3.10/1.60/free). Adults pay just €1.60 after 4.30pm.

Musée des Beaux-Arts (☎ 02 51 17 45 00; 10 rue Georges Clemenceau; 10am-6pm Wed-Mon, to 8pm Fri) This renowned museum showcases one of the finest French collections of paintings outside Paris. Exhibits range from works by Georges de La Tour, Ingres and Monet, to more contemporary canvasses from Picasso and Kandinsky.

Musée d'Histoire Naturelle (☎ 02 40 99 26 20; 12 rue Voltaire; 10am-6pm Wed-Mon) This old-fashioned Natural History Museum has seen better days, but if you've kids to entertain it makes a worthwhile trip. The **vivarium** is stocked with live pythons, crocodiles and iguanas although most of the animals on display are of the dead, stuffed variety.

The **Musée Dobrée** (☎ 02 40 71 03 50; 18 rue Voltaire; adult/student & child €3/1.50, free Sun; 1.30-5.30pm Tue-Fri, 2.30-5.30pm Sat & Sun) has exhibits of classical antiquities, medieval artefacts, Renaissance furniture and items related to the French Revolution – and the ivory and gold-encased heart of Anne de Bretagne!

The **Musée Jules Verne** (☎ 02 40 69 72 52; 3 rue de l'Hermitage; adult/student & child €8/4; 10am-noon & 2-6pm Mon & Wed-Sat, 2-6pm Sun), 2km southwest of the tourist office, has documents, posters, first-editions and other items connected with Jules Verne, the visionary sci-fi writer, who was born in Nantes in 1828.

OTHER ATTRACTIONS

From the outside, the **Château des Ducs de Bretagne** (Chateau of the Dukes of Brittany; ☎ 02 40 41 56 56; admission to grounds free; 🕙 10am-6pm) looks like your standard medieval castle. Inside, the parts facing the courtyard are in the style of a Renaissance pleasure palace. Walking along part of the ramparts is free.

Inside the Flamboyant Gothic **Cathédrale St-Pierre et St-Paul** (place St-Pierre), the **tomb of François II** (r 1458–88), duke of Brittany, and his second wife, Marguerite de Foix, is considered a masterpiece of Renaissance art. The statue facing the nave represents **Prudence**.

The **Jardin des Plantes**, across blvd de Stalingrad from the train station, is one of the most exquisite botanical gardens in France. Founded in the early 19th century, it has beautiful flowerbeds, duck ponds, fountains and even a few California redwoods (sequoias). There are **hothouses** and a **children's playground** at the northern end.

The channels of the Loire that once surrounded **Île Feydeau** (the neighbourhood south of the Gare Centrale) were filled in after WWII, but you can still see the area's 18th-century mansions, built by rich merchants. Some are adorned with stone carvings of the heads of African slaves.

Two blocks northwest of Île Feydeau is **Passage Pommeray**, a delightful shopping arcade that opened in 1843. Nearby are **place Royale**, laid out in 1790, and **place Graslin**, on the northern side of which stands the imposing, neoclassical **Théâtre Graslin**, built in 1788 and beautifully renovated in 2003 (see p616).

Sleeping

In addition, to the hotels reviewed, the tourist office has a list of camping grounds and hostels in town. Most places close reception on Sunday afternoons.

BUDGET

Hôtel St-Daniel (☎ 02 40 47 41 25; hotel.st.daniel@ wanadoo.fr; 4 rue du Bouffay; d from €29) In the heart of the old town, this great value budget place offers rooms with un-budget extras

like spaciousness, TV, hairdryer and double-glazing. Some rooms have been renovated and boast flashy wooden floors. There are a few family rooms for €39.

Hôtel de la Bourse (☎ 02 40 69 51 55; fax 02 40 71 73 89; 19 quai de la Fosse; d from €19, with shower & toilet €24) The emphasis here is on low prices rather than style and location, unless you like cheap pine furniture, feline art and car park views. As a place to sleep though, the clean, tidy rooms here are a steal. Hall showers cost €2.20.

Hôtel Fourcroy (☎ 02 40 44 68 00; 11 rue Fourcroy; s/d with shower & toilet €30/32; P) In a nondescript building tucked away down a side-street, this great value hotel has 19 exceptionally well-kept rooms, with modern bathrooms and upholstered doors.

MID-RANGE & TOP END

Hôtel de France (☎ 02 40 73 57 91; www.hotels-exclusive .com/hotels/france; 24 rue Crébillon; s €60-99, d €63-102; P) A three-star place in an 18th-century mansion, with Louis XVI-style furnishings. It's showing its age a bit now; some of the high-ceilinged rooms don't quite match up to the grandeur of the opulent entrance hall. Rooms with disabled access available.

Hôtel Graslin (☎ 02 40 69 72 91; fax 02 40 69 04 44; 1 rue Piron; d €57-70; 🖳) Modern three-star hotel with all the in-room facilities you could wish for including bathrobes, minibar and matching yellow curtains, bedspreads and chairs. Good location off Place Graslin.

Grand Hôtel Nantes Central (☎ 02 51 82 10 00; H1985@accor-hotels.com; 4 rue du Couedic; s/d €130/140, ste €160; P 🗙 😭 🖳) Part of the Mercure chain, this well-appointed hotel offers very

ATLANTIC COAST

AUTHOR'S CHOICE

Hôtel Pommeraye (☎ 02 40 48 78 79; www .hotel-pommeraye.com; 2 rue Boileau; s/d from €35/43 weekends, €49/59 weekdays; P 🖳) A new, stylish boutique hotel within an older building, mixing the classic and the contemporary with great success. Relax to the gentle sounds of the water feature while using the free lobby Internet, or walk straight out into the heart of Nantes' shopping district. Comfortable, well-equipped rooms are presented in warm, modern colours. Cheaper rooms are a bit small, but you can pay extra to 'Go Large'.

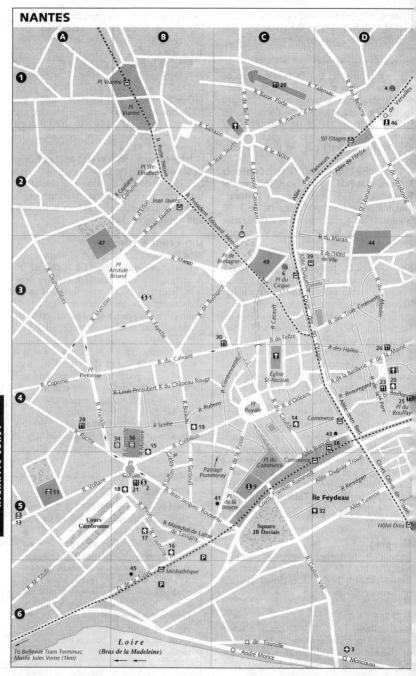

NANTES

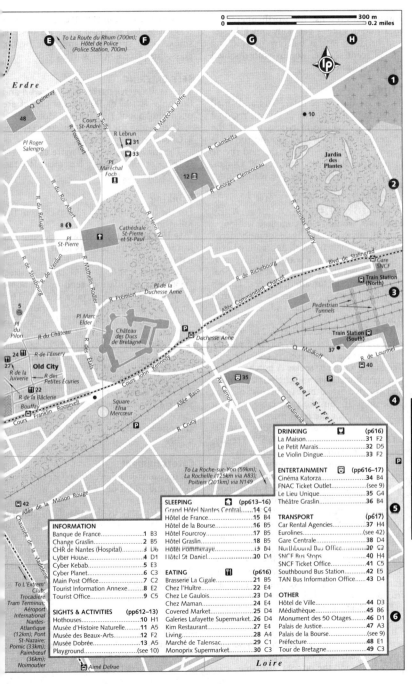

INFORMATION

Banque de France	1	B3
Change Graslin	2	B5
CHR de Nantes (Hospital)	3	D6
Cyber House	4	D1
Cyber Kebab	5	E3
Cyber Planet	6	C3
Main Post Office	7	C2
Tourist Information Annexe	8	E2
Tourist Office	9	C5

SIGHTS & ACTIVITIES (pp612–13)

Hothouses	10	H1
Musée d'Histoire Naturelle	11	A5
Musée des Beaux-Arts	12	F2
Musée Dobrée	13	A5
Playground	(see 10)	

SLEEPING (pp613–16)

Grand Hôtel Nantes Central	14	C4
Hôtel de France	15	B4
Hôtel de la Bourse	16	B5
Hôtel Fourcroy	17	B5
Hôtel Graslin	18	B5
Hôtel Pommeraye	19	B4
Hôtel St Daniel	20	D4

EATING (p616)

Brasserie La Cigale	21	B5
Chez l'Huître	22	E4
Chez Le Gaulois	23	D4
Chez Maman	24	E4
Covered Market	25	D4
Galeries Lafayette Supermarket	26	D4
Kim Restaurant	27	E4
Living	28	A5
Marché de Talensac	29	C1
Monoprix Supermarket	30	C3

DRINKING (p616)

La Maison	31	F2
Le Petit Marais	32	D5
Le Violin Dingue	33	F2

ENTERTAINMENT (pp616–17)

Cinéma Katorza	34	B4
FNAC Ticket Outlet	(see 9)	
Le Lieu Unique	35	G4
Théâtre Graslin	36	B4

TRANSPORT (p617)

Car Rental Agencies	37	H4
Eurolines	(see 42)	
Gare Centrale	38	D4
Northbound Bus Office	39	G3
SNCF Bus Stops	40	H4
SNCF Ticket Office	41	C5
Southbound Bus Station	42	E5
TAN Bus Information Office	43	D4

OTHER

Hôtel de Ville	44	D3
Médiathèque	45	B6
Monument des 50 Otages	46	D1
Palais de Justice	47	A3
Palais de la Bourse	(see 9)	
Préfecture	48	E1
Tour de Bretagne	49	C3

Map labels:
- Erdre
- To La Route du Rhum (700m); Hôtel de Police (Police Station, 700m)
- Q Ceineray
- R Tournefort
- Pl Roger Salengro
- Cours St-André
- R St-André
- R Lebrun
- R Maréchal Joffre
- R Gambetta
- Jardin des Plantes
- Pl Maréchal Foch
- R du Roi-Albert
- R Georges Clemenceau
- R du Refuge
- R de Verdun
- R de Strasbourg
- Pl St-Pierre
- Cathédrale St-Pierre et St-Paul
- R Henri IV
- R Mathelin Rodier
- R Stanislas Baudry
- Blvd de Stalingrad
- Gare SNCF
- R de Richebourg
- Train Station (North)
- Pl de la Duchesse Anne
- R Prémion
- Pl Marc Elder
- Pl du Pilori
- R du Château
- Château des Ducs de Bretagne
- R des États
- Allée Commandant Charcot
- Pedestrian Tunnels
- Train Station (South)
- Duchesse Anne
- Cours John Kennedy
- Q Malakoff
- R de Lourmel
- R de l'Emery
- Old City
- R de la Juiverie
- R des Petites Écuries
- R de la Bâclerie
- Bouffay
- Square Élisa Mercœur
- Allée Baco
- Av Carnot
- Canal St-Félix
- Cours Franklin Roosevelt
- R Crucy
- Q Ferdinand
- Q de la Madeleine
- Allée de la Maison Rouge
- Chaussée de la Madeleine
- To L'Extrem' Club; Trocadière Tram Terminus; Aéroport International Nantes-Atlantique (12km); Pont St-Nazaire; Pornic (33km); Paimbœuf (36km); Noirmoutier
- To La Roche-sur-Yon (59km); La Rochelle (125km via A83); Poitiers (201km) via N149
- Aimé Delrue
- Loire

Scale: 0 — 300 m / 0 — 0.2 miles

comfortable rooms. It's worth upgrading to a junior suite – generally much bigger and brighter with a balcony overlooking the adjacent square. Rooms with disabled access available.

Eating

There are dozens of cafés, bars and small restaurants, many of them French-regional or ethnic, a couple of blocks west of the chateau in the lively area around rue de la Juiverie, rue des Petites Écuries and rue de la Bâclerie. West of cours des 50 Otages, you'll find eateries along rue Jean-Jacques Rousseau and rue Santeuil.

Brasserie La Cigale (☎ 02 51 84 94 94; 4 place Graslin; menus €15.20 & €24.80; ⏰ 7.30-12.30am) A trip to Nantes wouldn't be complete without a stop at the exquisite Cigale, grandly decorated with 1890s tilework and painted ceilings that mix baroque with Art Nouveau. If you can't get there for a meal (traditional French) drop in for afternoon tea. There's no better place – you can choose from a wide range of fusion teas and select a cake from the trolley.

Chez Maman (☎ 02 51 72 20 63; 2 rue de la Juiverie; mains from €10; ⏰ lunch & dinner Tue-Sun) Traditional home-made French cooking, just like Maman used to make! A hotchpotch of mis-matching tables and chairs, chandeliers and assorted bric-a-brac in this bistro-cum-junk-shop. If you like your table, you can take it home for the right price!

Living (☎ 02 40 69 67 22; 32 rue Scribe; menus €17 & €28.50; ⏰ lunch Tue-Fri, dinner Tue-Sat) Trendy, cavernous restaurant-bar buzzing with fashionable 30-something Nantoise. Surprisingly, the food is not so cutting-edge with standard, but well-presented French fare. Open til 2am Friday and Saturday.

Chez Le Gaulois (☎ 02 40 08 22 98; 8 rue de la Paix; mains €9.50-17; ⏰ Mon-Sat) You can't get any more 'French carnivore' than this place with giant legs of ham hanging from the rafters and piles of *saucisson* just waiting to be scoffed. Specialities include *raclette*, fondue and *tartiflette*. Leave your vegetarian friends behind and bring a big appetite!

Kim Restaurant (☎ 02 40 35 18 40; 4 rue de la Juiverie; menus €10 & €15.50; ⏰ Mon-Sat) Tasty Thai, Chinese and Vietnamese specialities are served at this popular place. Speedy service and pack-'em-in tables keeps the atmosphere lively and the prices reasonable.

Chez l'Huître (☎ 02 51 82 02 02; 5 rue des Petites Écuries; dishes €6-7.5; ⏰ Mon-Sat) With oysters, smoked fish specialities and wine by the glass, this place is well worth a visit.

SELF-CATERING
The small **covered market** (place du Bouffay) and the huge **Marché de Talensac** (rue Talensac) are open until about 1pm (closed Monday).

There's also the **Monoprix supermarket** (2 rue du Calvaire; ⏰ 9am-9pm Mon-Sat).

The massive **Galeries Lafayette department store** (rue de la Marne) has a basement **food section** (⏰ 9am-7.30pm Mon-Sat).

Drinking

For the hard stuff, take your pick from the following bars.

Le Lieu Unique (see below) Super-hip bar in the arts centre. It hosts local and international DJs.

La Maison (☎ 02 40 37 04 12; 4 rue Lebrun; ⏰ 3pm-2am) An hilarious send-up of a home furnished in very bad taste c 1970. This convivial bar plays mainly house music and is a perfect place for a chat (and is thus popular with loquacious students).

Le Violin Dingue (☎ 02 40 74 09 29; 1 rue Lebrun; ⏰ 7.30pm-2am Tue-Sun) A mellow bar that often has live music from 8.30pm (diverse concerts cost around €5).

Le Petit Marais (☎ 02 40 20 15 25; 15 rue Kervégan; ⏰ 6.30pm-4am Mon-Sat, 6pm-2am Sun) Friendly place with a mainly gay crowd. There are often concerts Thursday and Friday nights.

Entertainment

Listings of cultural events appear in *Nantes Poche* and *Pil'* (both €0.50). *Le Mois Nantais*, available at the tourist office and tobacconists, has day-by-day details of cultural events. What's-on websites include www .vivanantes.com in French. Tickets are available across the hall from the tourist office at the **Fnac billeterie** (ticket outlet; ☎ 02 51 72 47 23; ⏰ 10am-8pm Mon-Sat).

The beautiful **Théâtre Graslin** (☎ 02 40 69 77 18; Place Graslin) is the home of the Nantes Opera. Recently refurbished and reopened, the venue hosts lavish productions in its stunning blue-seated auditorium.

Le Lieu Unique (☎ 02 40 12 14 34; www.lelieuunique .com in French; 2 rue de la Biscuiterie) is the city's wonderful industrial-chic-style concert venue, occupying the one-time Lu biscuit factory. This former artists squat offers dance and theatre performances, eclectic and electronic music, philosophical sessions and contemporary art. It also has a bar and restaurant.

NIGHTCLUBS

La Route du Rhum (☎ 02 40 74 48 57; quai Henri Barbusse; tram stop Motte Rouge; ⏰ 8pm-4am Tue-Sun) This two-storey houseboat sitting around 1km northeast of the Monument des 50 Otages has jam sessions and concerts of blues, rock and reggae music.

L'Extrem' Club (☎ 02 28 00 11 46; 44 Bouaye, Les Landes Bigots; ⏰ midnight-5am Fri-Sun) South of the Loire in Les Landes Bigots (about 10 minutes south by car from the chateau, in the direction of Pornic-Noirmoutier), is currently the area's hottest gay disco.

CINEMAS

The six-screen **Cinéma Katorza** (☎ 02 51 84 90 60; 3 rue Corneille) offers nondubbed films.

Getting There & Away
AIR
Aéroport Nantes-Atlantique International (☎ 02 40 84 80 00; www.nantes.aeroport.fr) is 12km southeast of town.

BUS
The southbound **bus station** (☎ 0 825 087 156), across from 13 allée de la Maison Rouge, is used by CTA buses serving areas of the Loire-Atlantique *département* south of the Loire River.

The northbound **bus office** (☎ 0 825 087 156; 1 allée Duquesne, on cours des 50 Otages), run by Cariane Atlantique, handles buses to destinations north of the Loire.

There's also a **Eurolines office** (☎ 02 51 72 02 03, allée de la Maison Rouge; ⏰ 8am 6pm Mon Fri, 8am-12.30pm Sat).

CAR
Budget, Europcar and Hertz have offices right outside the train station's southern entrance.

TRAIN
The **train station** (☎ 36 35; 27 blvd de Stalingrad) is well connected to most of France. Destinations include Paris' Gare Montparnasse (€49.10 to €61.40, 2¼ hours by TGV, 15 to 20 daily), Bordeaux (€37, four hours, three

or four daily) and La Rochelle (€21, 1¾ hours, three or four daily).

Tickets and information are also available at the **SNCF ticket office** (La Bourse, 12 place de la Bourse; ⏰ 10am-7pm Mon, 9am-7pm Tue-Sat) in the city centre.

Getting Around
TO/FROM THE AIRPORT
A public bus known as TAN-Air links the airport with the Gare Centrale bus/tram hub and the train station's southern entrance (€6, 20 minutes) from about 5.30am (2pm Sunday) until 9pm. For information call **Allotan** (☎ 0 810 444 444).

BUS & TRAM
The **TAN network** (☎ 0 801 444 444; www.tan.fr in French), which has an **information office** (2 allée Brancas, place du Commerce; ⏰ Mon-Sat), includes three modern tram lines that intersect at the Gare Centrale (Commerce), the main bus/tram transfer point. Buses run from 7.15am to 9pm. Night services continue until 12.30am.

Bus/tram tickets can be purchased individually (€1.20) from bus (but not tram) drivers and at tram stop ticket machines, and are valid for one hour after being time-stamped. A *ticket journalier,* good for 24 hours, costs €3.30; time-stamp it only the first time you use it.

CAR & MOTORCYCLE
There's free parking in the car park 200m east of the southbound bus station; in the car park across the street from the Médiathèque tram stop (except for the first few rows, marked *payant*); and south of the train station along the southern section of quai Malakoff.

TAXI
To order a taxi, call ☎ 02 40 69 22 22.

POITIERS
pop 120,000
Poitiers, the former capital of Poitou, is home to some of France's most remarkable Romanesque churches. It is not a particularly fetching city – it fits very tightly into its hilltop site – but the pedestrian-only shopping precinct has its charms.

In the year AD 732 somewhere near Poitiers (the exact site is not known), the cavalry of Charles Martel defeated the Muslim forces of Abd ar-Rahman, governor of Córdoba, thereby ending Muslim attempts to conquer France.

Orientation

The train station is about 600m west and down the slope from the old city and commercial centre, which begins just north of Poitiers' main square, place du Maréchal Leclerc, and stretches northeast to Église Notre Dame la Grande. Rue Carnot heads south from place du Maréchal Leclerc.

Information

Commercial **banks** can be found around place du Maréchal Leclerc.

Cybercafé Poitiers (☎ 05 49 39 51 87; www.cyber café-poitiers.fr in French; 171 Grand'Rue; per hr €5.50; ☼ 10am-8pm Mon-Sat, 4-8pm Sun, to 10pm Jul & Aug) East of Église Notre Dame.

Post Office (21 rue des Écossais) Has a Cyberposte and changes money.

Tourist Office (☎ 05 49 41 21 24; accueil@ot-poitiers .fr; 45 place Charles de Gaulle; ☼ 9.30am-7pm Mon-Sat, 10am-6pm Sun Jun-Sep; 10am-6pm Mon-Sat Oct-May) Near Église Notre Dame.

Sights

The Romanesque **Église Notre Dame la Grande** (place Charles de Gaulle; ☼ 8.30am-7pm Mon-Sat, 2-5pm Sun) is in the pedestrianised old city. It dates from the 11th and 12th centuries, except for three of the five choir chapels (added in the 15th century) and all six chapels along the northern wall of the nave (added in the 16th century). The atrociously painted decoration in the nave is from the mid-19th century; the only original **frescoes** are the faint 12th- or 13th-century works that adorn the U-shaped dome above the choir. The celebrated **west façade** is beautifully decorated with three layers of stone carvings based on the Old and New Testaments. On summer evenings between late June and late September, the characters adorning the façade are colourfully illuminated.

At the northeastern end of rue Gambetta, the Palais de Justice (law courts) occupies a one-time palace of the counts of Poitou and the dukes of Aquitaine. Inside, you can visit the **Salle des Pas-Perdus** (☼ 9am-6pm Jul & Aug, 8.45am-5.30pm Mon-Fri Sep-Jun), a vast, partly 14th-century hall with three huge fireplaces.

At the bottom of the street (500m east of Église Notre Dame la Grande), the vast, Angevin (or Plantagenet) Gothic-style **Cathédrale St-Pierre** (rue de la Cathédrale; ☼ 8am-6pm) – so unlike its Gothic cousins to the north – was built from 1162 to 1271; the west façade and the towers date from the 14th and 15th centuries. At the far end of the choir, the stained-glass window of the Crucifixion and the Ascension is among the oldest in France.

Constructed in the 4th and 6th centuries on Roman foundations, **Baptistère St-Jean** (rue Jean Jaurès; admission €0.60; ☼ 10.30am-12.30pm & 3-6pm Wed-Mon Apr-Oct, 2.30-4.30pm Wed-Mon Nov-Mar), a block south of the cathedral, was rebuilt in the 10th century and used as a parish church. The octagonal hole under the frescoes was used for total-immersion baptisms, practised until the 7th century. It now houses a museum of Merovingian sarcophagi (from the 5th to 7th centuries).

The worthwhile **Musée Ste-Croix** (☎ 05 49 41 07 53; www.musees-poitiers.org in French; 3 rue Jean Jaurès; adult/child €3.50/free; ☼ 1.15-6pm Mon, 10am-noon & 1.15-6pm Tue-Fri, 10am-noon & 2-6pm Sat & Sun Jun-Sep; only to 5pm Mon-Fri & afternoons Sat & Sun Oct-May) is across the lawn from Baptistère St-Jean, and was built atop Gallo-Roman walls that were excavated and left *in situ*. It has exhibits on the history of Poitou from prehistoric times to the 19th century. Admission here also affords access to the **Musée Rupert de Chièvre** (☎ 05 49 41 07 53; 9 rue Victor Hugo; ☼ same hours as Musée Ste-Croix), which displays furniture, paintings and art from the 19th century.

Sleeping

Other than a couple of unappealing places opposite the station, Poitiers is short on budget accommodation. A better option is to spend a bit extra on one of the decent mid-range options.

MID-RANGE

Hôtel de l'Europe (☎ 05 49 88 12 00; www.hotelde leuropepoitiers.com; 39 rue Carnot; s/d from €47.50/53; **P**) This charming hotel is worth more than its official two stars. The main building, dating from 1710, has a sweeping staircase, oversized rooms and pleasing older-style décor. The annex has modern rooms for the same price. Breakfast is served in the lovely garden room.

Hôtel du Plat d'Étain (☎ 05 49 41 04 80; hotelduplat detain@wanadoo.fr; 7-9 rue du Plat d'Étain; d with shower or bath & toilet €45-50; P) In a pedestrian street half a block north of place du Maréchal Leclerc (through the arch next to the theatre), is this cosy two-star hotel, next to a late-opening bar. Up three flights of narrow stairs, the tranquil third floor attic rooms look on to the adjacent church and across the town.

Le Grand Hôtel (☎ 05 49 60 90 60; www.grand hotelpoitiers.fr; 28 rue Carnot; s/d €65.50/80.50; P 🕱) Faux Art Deco furnishings and fittings give this three-star hotel character. The rooms, popular with business travellers, are spacious and well-equipped.

Eating & Drinking

The most promising area for dining is south of place du Maréchal Leclerc, especially rue Carnot. The Grand'Rue also has some good eateries.

La Serrurerie (☎ 05 49 41 05 14; 28 rue des Grandes Écoles; mains €10-14) This atmospheric, lively and hugely popular café *bistrot* does great meals and huge weekend brunches (€14). Temporary exhibitions showcase local art and sculpture.

La Joyeuse Marmite (☎ 05 49 88 14 59; 66 Grand' Rue; menu €10; 🕒 lunch only Mon-Fri) A merry local bistro serving hearty lunch meals including wine. Just north of Place de la Cathédrale.

The **Marché Notre Dame** (🕒 7am-1pm Tue-Sat) is right next to Église Notre Dame la Grande. About 200m to the south, the **Monoprix supermarket** (🕒 9am-7.30pm Mon-Sat) is across from 29 rue du Marché Notre Dame (behind the Palais de Justice).

Bars and pubs can be found along rue Carnot and one block north of place du Maréchal Leclerc along rue du Chaudron d'Or.

Getting There & Away

The modern **train station** (☎ 0 836 353 535; blvd du Grand Cerf) has direct links to Bordeaux (€28.70, 1¾ hours), La Rochelle (€19.80, one hour 20 minutes), Tours (€16, one hour) and many other cities. TGV tickets from Paris' Gare Montparnasse (1½ hours, 12 daily) cost from €43. SNCF buses go to Nantes (€23, 3¼ hours).

AROUND POITIERS
Futuroscope

With striking domes, pods and towers rising from the French countryside like a James Bond movie set, **Futuroscope** (☎ 05 49 49 30 80;

www.futuroscope.com; Jaunay-Clan; adult/5-12 yrs Apr-Sep & weekends €30/22, Mon-Fri Oct-Mar €21/16; 🕒 10am-at least 10.15pm Apr-Sep, to 6pm Sun-Fri & to 10pm Sat Feb, Mar, Oct & Nov, closed mid-Nov–mid-Feb) is a unique cinema theme park whose 22 attractions make for a hugely entertaining day. There are evening lakeside **laser and firework shows** (Apr-Aug, Sat & Sun Mar-Nov) – as a result, closing times range from 6pm to 11pm. On show days, a ticket costs €15/9 if you arrive after 6pm. Allow a minimum of five hours to see all the major attractions or two days to see everything.

Attractions include **Cyberworld**, an action-packed 3D trip inside a computer with a Lara Croft-style cyber-guide. The journey features a dizzying array of spectacular 3D effects, plus a cameo appearance by the Pet Shop Boys. At **Cosmos**, board a spaceship for a journey through the solar system and beyond; back on planet earth, take a trip to the Rio Carnivale at **Couleurs Bresil**, where a 360° screen puts you in the heart of the action.

The films, which last four to 40 minutes, showcase the park's cinematic technological wizardry, so don't come expecting convincing acting or intelligent plots. A free infrared headset lets you pick up soundtracks in English, German and Spanish.

Futuroscope is 10km north of Poitiers in Jaunay-Clan (take exit No 28 off the A10). TGV trains link the park's TGV station with Paris (€43.20, 1½ hours, three daily), Tours (€14.90, 30 minutes, three daily) and Bordeaux (€29.60, 1¾ hours, two to three daily).

Local **STP buses** (☎ 05 49 44 66 88) Nos 9, 16 and 17 (€1.30, 30 minutes) link Futuroscope (Parc de Loisirs stop) with Poitiers' train station (the stop in front of Avis car rental); there are one to two buses an hour from 6.15am until 7.30pm or 9pm.

Marais Poitevin

Known as Venise Verte (Green Venice) for its green waterways, the Marais Poitevin (*marais* means marsh) is a marvellous wetland, with a rich and varied birdlife. Part of the protected Parc Naturel Interrégional du Marais Poitevin, it covers a sprawling 80,000 hectares of wet marsh and drained marsh, interspersed with villages and woods.

The main modes of transport around the area are **canoeing** and **boating**. To rent a boat or bicycle, or to organise gîtes and *chambres* *d'hôtes* accommodation, contact **Venise Verte Loisirs** (☎ 05 49 35 43 34; www.veni severteloisirs.fr in French; 10 chemin du Charret, Arçais).

The main stepping stone to the Marais is Niort, 76km southwest of Poitiers, where there's a **tourist office** (☎ 05 49 24 18 79; 16 rue du Petit St-Jean). Niort station connects with Poitiers (€12.60, 50 minutes), and there are some bus services to villages – after that you need to explore by foot, boat or bike.

LA ROCHELLE
pop 120,000

The lively and increasingly chic port city of La Rochelle, midway down France's Atlantic coast, gets lots of tourists, especially in July and August, but most of them are of the domestic, middle-class variety: unpretentious families or young people out to have fun.

La Rochelle's focal point is the picturesque café- and restaurant-lined old port, which basks in the bright Atlantic sunlight by day and is grandly illuminated by night.

Despite a progressively more sophisticated feel, La Rochelle remains a great destination for families, with decent kid-friendly attractions and kilometres of fine-sand beaches on nearby Île de Ré.

History

La Rochelle was one of France's foremost seaports from the 14th to 17th centuries, and local shipowners were among the first to establish trade links with the New World. Many of the early French settlers in Canada, including the founders of Montreal, set sail from here in the 17th century.

During the 16th century, La Rochelle, whose spirit of mercantile independence made it fertile ground for Protestant ideas, incurred the wrath of Catholic loyalists, especially during the Wars of Religion. After the notorious St Bartholomew's Day Massacre of 1572, many of the Huguenots who survived took refuge here.

In 1627 La Rochelle – by that time an established Huguenot stronghold – was besieged by Louis XIII's forces under the personal command of his principal minister, Cardinal Richelieu. By the time they surrendered after 15 months of resistance, all but 1500 of the city's 20,000 residents had died of starvation. The city recovered slowly, but was dealt further blows by the revocation of the Edict of Nantes in 1685

and the loss of French Canada – and the right to trade with North America – to the English in 1763.

Orientation

La Rochelle is centred around the Vieux Port (Old Port), to the north of which lies the old city. The tourist office is on the southern side of the Vieux Port in an area of brightly-painted wooden buildings known as Le Gabut. The train station is linked to the Vieux Port by the 500m-long av du Général de Gaulle. Place du Marché and place de Verdun are at the northern edge of the old city.

The university campus is midway between the Vieux Port and the seaside neighbourhood of Les Minimes, 3km southwest of the city centre.

Information
BOOKSHOPS
Planète Bleue (☎ 05 46 34 23 23; 41 rue des Merciers)

EMERGENCY
Hôtel de Police (police station; ☎ 05 46 51 36 36; 2 place de Verdun; ☒ 24hr)
Médecins d'Urgence (emergency doctors; ☎ 05 46 67 33 33)

INTERNET ACCESS
Cyber Club (☎ 05 49 76 76 76; 20 rue Cordouan; per hr €6; ☒ noon-8pm Mon-Tue, noon-2am Wed-Sat, 2-8pm Sun)

MONEY
In the old city, there are a number of banks on rue du Palais. The post office also has exchange services.

POST
Post Office (6 rue de l'Hôtel de Ville) Has exchange services and a Cyberposte.

TOURIST INFORMATION
Tourist Office (☎ 05 46 41 14 68; http://larochelle -tourisme.com or www.ville-larochelle.fr; Le Gabut; ☒ 9am-8pm Mon-Sat, 11am-5.30pm Sun Jul & Aug; 9am-7pm Mon-Sat, 11am-5pm Sun Jun & Sep; 9am-6pm Mon-Sat, 10am-1pm Sun Oct-May)

Sights & Activities
To protect the harbour at night and defend the city in times of war, an enormous chain used to be stretched between the two

LA ROCHELLE

0 — 300 m
0 — 0.2 miles

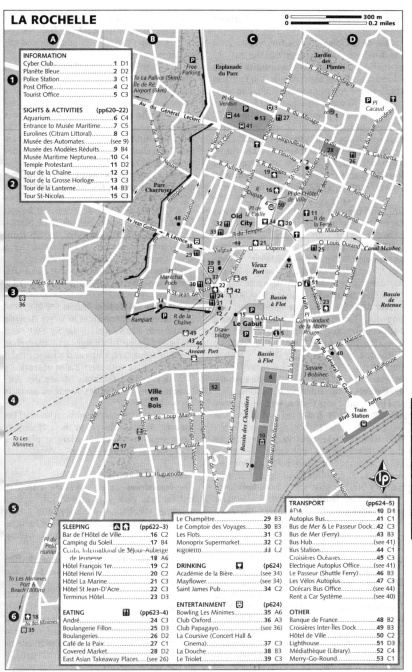

INFORMATION
Cyber Club..............................1 D1
Planète Bleue..........................2 D2
Police Station..........................3 C1
Post Office..............................4 C2
Tourist Office..........................5 C3

SIGHTS & ACTIVITIES   (pp620–22)
Aquarium................................6 C4
Entrance to Musée Maritime......7 C5
Eurolines (Citram Littoral)..........8 C3
Musée des Automates............(see 9)
Musée des Modèles Réduits........9 B4
Musée Maritime Neptunea........10 C4
Temple Protestant...................11 D2
Tour de la Chaîne....................12 C3
Tour de la Grosse Horloge........13 C3
Tour de la Lanterne..................14 B3
Tour St-Nicolas.......................15 C3

SLEEPING   (pp622–3)
Bar de l'Hôtel de Ville..............16 C3
Camping du Soleil...................17 B4
Centre International de Séjour-Auberge
  de Jeunesse..........................18 A6
Hôtel François 1er....................19 C2
Hôtel Henri IV.........................20 C2
Hôtel La Marine......................21 C3
Hôtel St Jean-D'Acre................22 C3
Terminus Hôtel.......................23 D3

EATING   (pp623–4)
André....................................24 C3
Boulangerie Fillon...................25 D3
Boulangeries...........................26 D2
Café de la Paix........................27 C1
Covered Market.......................28 D2
East Asian Takeaway Places....(see 26)
Le Champêtre..........................29 B3
Le Comptoir des Voyages..........30 B3
Les Flots................................31 C3
Monoprix Supermarket.............32 C2
Rigoletto................................33 C2

DRINKING   (p624)
Académie de la Bière.............(see 34)
Mayflower.............................(see 34)
Saint James Pub......................34 C2

ENTERTAINMENT   (p624)
Bowling Les Minimes................35 A6
Club Oxford...........................36 A3
Club Papagayo.....................(see 36)
La Coursive (Concert Hall &
  Cinema)...............................37 C3
La Douche..............................38 B3
Le Triolet...............................39 C3

TRANSPORT   (pp624–5)
......................................40 D4
Autoplus Bus..........................41 C1
Bus de Mer & Le Passeur Dock..42 C3
Bus de Mer (Ferry)...................43 B3
Bus Hub..............................(see 41)
Bus Station.............................44 C1
Croisières Océanes...................45 C3
Electrique Autoplus Office......(see 41)
Le Passeur (Shuttle Ferry).........46 B3
Les Vélos Autoplus...................47 C3
Océarc Bus Office................(see 44)
Rent a Car Système...............(see 40)

OTHER
Banque de France....................48 B2
Croisières Inter-Îles Dock..........49 B3
Hôtel de Ville.........................50 C2
Lighthouse.............................51 D3
Médiathèque (Library)..............52 C4
Merry-Go-Round.....................53 C1

ATLANTIC COAST

14th-century stone towers at the harbour entrance.

Tour de la Chaîne affords fine views from the top and has displays on the history of the local Protestant community in the basement. Across the harbour you can also climb to the top of the 36m-high, pentagonal **Tour St-Nicolas** if you don't get lost in the maze of stairs and corridors.

West of Tour de la Chaîne, the medieval wall leads to the steeple-topped, 15th-century **Tour de la Lanterne**, also known as Tour des Quatre Sergents in memory of four sergeants from the local garrison who were executed in 1822 for plotting to overthrow the newly reinstated monarchy. The English-language graffiti on the walls was carved by English privateers who were held here during the 18th century.

The three **towers** (☎ 05 46 34 11 81; admission per tower adult/18-25 yrs/child €4.60/3.10/free; ☉ 10am-7pm Apr-Sep, 10am-12.30pm & 2-5.30pm Tue-Sun Oct-May, closed during holidays) can be visited on a combined ticket which costs €10/6.50.

Tour de la Grosse Horloge (Quai Duperré), the imposing Gothic-style clock tower, has a 14th-century base and an 18th-century top. The arch leads to arcaded **rue du Palais**, La Rochelle's main shopping street, which is lined with 17th- and 18th-century shipowners' homes. Two blocks to the east, **rue des Merciers** is also lined with arcades.

The Flamboyant Gothic wall of the **town hall** (☎ 05 46 41 14 68; place de l'Hôtel de Ville) was built in the late 15th century, while the Renaissance-style courtyard dates from the 16th century. There are guided tours (€3/1.50 for adults/under 12) at 3pm on weekends and holidays; at 3pm and 4pm daily in July, August and school holidays.

The austere **Temple Protestant** (2 rue St-Michel) was built in the late 17th century, though it became a Protestant church only after the Revolution; the interior took on its present form during the last 75 years of the 19th century.

Just south of Le Gabut is the impressive **Aquarium** (☎ 05 46 34 00 00; adult/student & child €10/7; ☉ 9am-11pm Jul & Aug, to 8pm Apr-Jun & Sep, 10am-8pm Oct-Mar) a relatively new attraction, thoughtfully laid-out and well-stocked with over 10,000 specimens of sea-based flora and fauna. Kids can scurry off to explore little underwater rooms and get up close to the fish; even the shark tank has an indented

glass capsule that creates the sensation of being in there with the 2.7m Bull Sharks. For €3.50 you can hire an amusing and entertaining audio-tour.

The innovative **Musée Maritime Neptunea** (Maritime Museum; ☎ 05 46 28 03 00; adult/student & child €7.60/5.30; ☉ 10am-7.30pm Jul & Aug, til 6.30pm Apr-Jun & Sep, 2-6.30pm Oct-Mar) at Bassin des Chalutiers is the permanent home of Jacques Cousteau's research ship, *Calypso*, presently awaiting repairs. Admission includes tours of a *chalutier* (fishing boat) and a meteorological research vessel.

About midway between the Vieux Port and Les Minimes is the **Musée des Automates** (☎ 05 46 41 68 08; 14 rue La Désirée; adult/child 3-10 yrs €6.50/4; ☉ 9.30am-7pm Jun-Aug; 10am-noon & 2-6pm Feb-May, Sep & Oct; 2-6pm Nov-Jan), which displays – in action – some 300 automated dolls from the last two centuries. It's laid out like a small theme park, including a near-life-size recreation of bygone Montmartre in Paris, complete with Moulin Rouge and funicular railway.

At **Musée des Modèles Réduits** (☎ 05 46 41 64 51; rue La Désirée; adult/under 10 €6.50/4; ☉ 9.30am-7pm Jun-Aug; 10am-noon & 2-6pm Feb-May, Sep & Oct; 2-6pm Nov-Jan), children of all ages can marvel at the miniature cars, ships and a huge model railway display with over 200m of track.

A ticket good for both Musée des Automates and Musée des Modèles Réduits costs €10/5.50.

The modern resort neighbourhood of **Les Minimes**, 3km southwest of the city centre, has a small **beach** and the largest pleasure craft port on Europe's Atlantic coast.

Festivals & Events
The **Francofolies** (☎ 05 46 28 28 28), a six-day festival held each year in mid-July, brings together vocalists and performing artists from all over La Francophonie (the French-speaking world) and attracts lots of young people.

The 10-day **Festival International du Film** (☎ 01 48 06 16 66 or 05 46 51 54 00) runs from the end of June to early July.

Sleeping
La Rochelle has a shortage of cheap hotels. Most places charge high-season rates from sometime in the spring until September or October. During July and August, virtually all the hotels are full.

BUDGET

Centre International de Séjour-Auberge de Jeunesse (☎ 05 46 44 43 11; fax 05 46 45 41 48; av des Minimes; bus No 10; dm/d with breakfast €13/32) This place is 2km southwest of the train station in Les Minimes. Check-in is possible from 8am to midnight.

Bar de l'Hôtel de Ville (☎ 05 46 41 30 25; 5 rue St-Yon; d from €32, with shower & toilet €39; 1-3-person studio per night/week €54/305) This busy nine-room hotel attached to the Bar de l'Hôtel de Ville represents the only budget accommodation in town. The simple rooms are popular with students on long-stays, so it's often difficult to bag a bed. The studio apartments are available only in July and August.

Camping

During the warmer months, dozens of camping areas open up around La Rochelle and on the Île de Ré, but most are full during July and August. The tourist office has a list of those outside the town.

Camping du Soleil (☎ 05 46 44 42 53; av Marillac; bus No 10; camping €16.65; ⌣ mid-May–mid-Sep) Nearest camping area to the city centre but it is often completely full.

MID-RANGE

Hôtel La Marine (☎ 05 46 50 51 63; www.hotel-marine.com in French; 30 quai Duperré; r May-Sep €70-95, Oct-May €59-75) This two-star hotel is in a fantastic location overlooking the port. Most rooms have recently been refurbished with neutral tones and designer furniture – rooms 1, 6, 9 and 13 stand out, with first class views.

Hôtel François 1er (☎ 05 46 41 28 46; www.hotelfrancois1er.fr; 15 rue Bazoges; d €50-85; P) Charming, quiet hotel with a cobbled courtyard entrance and traditionally furnished rooms. In the 15th and 16th centuries a number of French kings stayed in this building. It certainly has some king-size rooms, but you pay more for the extra space.

Terminus Hôtel (☎ 05 46 50 69 69; hotel.terminus@tourisme-francais.com; 7 rue de la Fabrique; s/d from low season €39/47, high season €53/53) Near to the tourist office, this welcoming hotel has 32 comfortable rooms that vary in price depending on the season. Each room is named after one of the offshore islands; the bright, sunny ones at the front are the best. Access for disabled guests.

Hôtel St Jean-D'Acre (☎ 05 46 41 73 33; www.hotel-la-rochelle.com; 4 place de la Chaîne; r high/low season from €65/60; ▢) Situated near a cluster of good seafood restaurants, this modern three-star hotel has views of the port and the Tour de la Chaîne. Part of the Inter Hotel chain.

Hôtel Henri IV (☎ 05 46 41 25 79; henriIV@wanadoo.fr; 31 rue des Gentilshommes; d low/high season from €40/54, with shower & toilet €50/77) In a late-16th-century building in the middle of the pedestrianised old city.

Eating

According to locals, La Rochelle has so many restaurants, you could dine out every day of the year and never eat at the same place twice. Dozens of eateries can be found along the northern side of the Vieux Port, especially on quai Duperré, cours des Dames, rue de la Chaîne and rue St-Jean du Pérot. The place du Marché area has several inexpensive restaurants and pizzerias.

Café de la Paix (☎ 05 46 41 39 79; 54 rue Chaudrier; menus €14 & €19, children €8, mains €15-20; ⌣ 7am-9.30pm) This century-old place is a grand, atmospheric brasserie-bar with high, painted ceilings, gold-edged mirrors and all the traditional choices: beef, duck, foie gras and salads. Also a good spot for breakfast (€6.50) or afternoon tea.

Le Comptoir des Voyages (☎ 05 46 50 62 60; 22 rue St-Jean du Perot; menu €22, mains €11) A chic and ambient new place. The emphasis is on 'world food', meaning international flavours

AUTHOR'S CHOICE

André (☎ 05 46 41 28 24; 5 rue St-Jean du Perot; mains €12-22) Something of an institution, this restaurant has been serving up fresh seafood for more than 50 years. It started life as a small bar serving seafood; as its popularity grew, André began buying adjacent shops. There are now eight interconnecting rooms, each with its own individual ambience from traditional bistro to contemporary café to port-holed cabin. Each one is packed with fish-hungry punters, and in each the menu is the same – not just traditional dishes, but innovative creations like monkfish infused with mango and Indian spices (delicious) or the knock-out *cassate Charentaise* (regional fruit flan) both on the €35 menu. An exceptional dining experience.

(Madrid, Madras, Madagascar) but regional produce. The colourful food contrasts fittingly with the cool, understated design.

Le Champêtre (☎ 05 46 41 12 17; 22 rue Verdière; menu €22, mains around €12; ⊙ dinner only from 7.30pm Tue-Sat) An unfussy and intimate little place away from the main restaurant strips, but worth seeking out. You'll find classic (mainly meat-based) French dishes and an enthusiastic patron.

Les Flots (☎ 05 46 41 32 51; 1 rue de la Chaîne; mains €12-22; ⊙ closed dinner Sun) Serves up stylish seafood. Overlooks the port.

Rigoletto (☎ 05 46 41 05 00; 12-14 rue Chef de Ville; pizzas & pasta €6-9; ⊙ closed dinner Sun) What more can we say – it's a busy pizzeria.

SELF-CATERING
The best place to pick up your own edibles is the lively, 19th-century **covered market** (place du Marché; ⊙ 7am-1pm).

Food shops in the vicinity include two cheap East Asian **takeaway places** (4 & 10 rue Gambetta) and **boulangeries** (8 & 29 rue Gambetta).

In the old city, there's **Monoprix supermarket** (30-36 rue du Palais; ⊙ 8.30am-8pm Mon-Sat) and **Boulangerie Fillon** (18 quai Louis Durand; ⊙ 6am-10.30pm Mon & Thu, to 8pm Tue, to 1pm Sun, 6am-2am Fri & Sat).

Drinking
For *salon de thé* ambience, make for the beautifully traditional **Café de la Paix** (p623) where smart waiters will bring you any number of speciality teas.

During the day, the best place for a drink is around the port. For an evening tipple, there are three trusty drinking holes side by side in tiny cour Temple: the **Saint James Pub** (☎ 05 46 41 72 11), the **Mayflower** (☎ 05 46 50 51 39) and the cosy **Académie de la Bière** (☎ 05 46 41 03 44).

Entertainment
The discos **Club Oxford** and **Club Papagayo** (☎ 05 46 41 51 81 for both; admission with one drink €10; ⊙ 11pm-5am Tue-Sun, plus Mon in Jul & Aug) are on the waterfront about 500m west of Tour de la Lanterne, dishing out a standard, eclectic French soundtrack. A newer, more trendy option in the area is **La Douche** (☎ 05 46 41 24 79; 14 rue Léonce; admission €10, free on Thu & Sun; ⊙ 11pm-5am Thu-Sun) spinning house tunes to a mixed gay and straight crowd.

In the port area, **Le Triolet** (☎ 05 46 41 03 58; 8 rue des Carmes; ⊙ 7pm-3am) is known as *le*

cool club for over 25s. There's a laid-back jazzy vibe earlier in the evening but the music gets livelier after 11pm when the disco kicks off.

In Les Minimes, **Bowling Les Minimes** (☎ 05 46 45 40 40; rue Trinquette; ⊙ 10am-2am daily) is situated in an alley next to the youth hostel.

The two auditoriums of **La Coursive** (☎ 05 46 51 54 00; 4 rue St-Jean du Pérot; ⊙ early Sep-late Jul) host concerts and nondubbed art films.

Getting There & Away
AIR
From **La Rochelle Airport** (☎ 05 46 42 30 26; www .larochelle.aeroport.fr in French; north of city centre off the N237) there are flights throughout France and to London Stansted (with Ryanair) and Southampton (with Flybe) in the UK.

BUS
The **bus station** and bus information offices are at place de Verdun. **Océcars** (☎ 05 46 00 95 15) runs services to regional destinations like Royan. See p626 for details on bus services to the island.

Eurolines ticketing is handled by **Citram Littoral** (☎ 05 46 50 53 57; 30 cours des Dames; ⊙ closed Sat afternoon, Mon morning & Sun).

CAR
For rental, there's **ADA** (☎ 05 46 41 02 17; 19 av du Général de Gaulle) and **Rent A Car Système** (☎ 05 46 27 27 27; 27 av du Général de Gaulle).

TRAIN
The **train station** (☎ 0 836 353 535) is linked by TGV to Paris' Gare Montparnasse (€53.60, three hours, five or six direct daily). Other destinations served by direct trains include Nantes (€22, two hours, five or six daily), Poitiers (€19.80, 1½ hours, nine to 10 daily), Rochefort (€6.20, 20 minutes, five to seven daily) and Bordeaux (€22.60, two hours, five to seven daily).

Getting Around
BICYCLE
At **Les Vélos Autoplus** (☎ 05 46 34 02 22) you can hire a bike for free for the first two hours; after that the charge is €1 per hour. Child seats, but not bike helmets, are available for no extra charge. Bikes are available at the **Electrique Autoplus office** (☎ 05 46 34 84 58; place de Verdun; ⊙ 7.30am-7pm Mon-Sat, 1-7pm Sun). From May to September, they can also be picked

up at the **Vieux Port** (across the street from 11 quai Valin).

BOAT
Autoplus' **Le Passeur** (€0.60; ⏰ 7.45am-8pm, to 10pm Apr & May, to midnight Jul & Aug) is a ferry service that links Tour de la Chaîne with the Avant Port. It runs when there are passengers – just press the red button on the board at the top of the gangplank.

The ferry **Bus de Mer** (€1.50; €1.70 Jul & Aug), also run by Autoplus, links Tour de la Chaîne with Les Minimes (20 minutes). It runs daily April to September; at weekends and holidays only from October to March. Boats from the Vieux Port depart every hour on the hour (except at 1pm) from 10am to 7pm (every half-hour and until 11.30pm in July and August).

BUS
The innovative local transport system, **Autoplus** (☎ 05 46 34 02 22), has a main bus hub and **information office** (place de Verdun; ⏰ 7am-7.30pm Mon-Sat). Most lines run until sometime between 7.15pm and 8pm. Tickets cost €1.20.

Bus No 21 runs from place Verdun to the train station, returning via the Vieux Port. No 10 links place de Verdun with the youth hostel and Les Minimes.

CAR & MOTORCYCLE
The **Electrique Autoplus office** (place de Verdun; see opposite) rents electric-powered motorcars €10/16 with a range of 50km for €10/16 per half-day/day. The deposit is €500.

There is free parking on the side streets north of place de Verdun; at esplanade des Parcs, which is a few hundred metres northwest of place de Verdun; and around Neptunea. There's an underground garage at place de Verdun.

Avoid the city centre, especially on market mornings (Wednesday and Saturday).

TAXI
Taxis can be ordered 24 hours a day on ☎ 05 46 41 55 55 or ☎ 05 46 34 02 22.

ÎLE DE RÉ
pop 16,000
This flat island, whose eastern tip is 9km west of the centre of La Rochelle, gets more hours of sunshine than any part of France

away from the Mediterranean coast. In summer its many beaches and seasonal camping grounds are a favourite destination for families with young children; the water is shallow and safe and the sun is bright and warming, but less harsh than along the Mediterranean. Île de Ré can easily be visited as a day trip from La Rochelle.

Île de Ré's main town is the fishing port of St-Martin de Ré, on the northern coast about 12km from the toll bridge. In most of the island's villages, the houses are traditional in design: one- or two-storey whitewashed buildings with green shutters and red Spanish-tile roofs.

The Île de Ré boasts 70km of coastline, including 20km to 30km of fine-sand beaches. Most of the northern coast is taken up by mudflats and oyster farms. The island's western half curves around a bay known as the Fier d'Ars, which is lined with *marais salants* (salt evaporation pools), saltwater marshes and a nature reserve for birds, **Lilleau des Niges**.

There are virtually no budget hotels on the island. Every hotel and camping ground on the island is *totally* full from 14 July to 25 August.

ST-MARTIN DE RÉ
pop 2500
This picturesque little fishing village, which is entirely surrounded by 17th-century fortifications, is especially attractive when the white houses and sailboats are bathed in the bright coastal sun. You can stroll along most of the ramparts but the **citadel** (1681), which has been a prison for over two centuries is closed to the law-abiding public.

Information
In St-Martin, the **tourist office** (☎ 05 46 09 20 06; www.iledere.com; av Victor Bouthillier; ⏰ 10am-1pm & 2-7pm, closes noon Sun Sep-Jun) is a block east of the port (across the street from the Rébus bus stop).

Sleeping
Hôtel de Sully (☎ 05 46 09 26 94; rue Jean Jaurès; r €32-45, Jul-Sep €39-48) Located 150m south of the port in a pretty pedestrian street, this reasonable one-star place is a cheap option with wood panelling and trippy '60s bathroom tiles. It's in an old, converted house so some of the rooms are very small.

Hôtel du Port (☎ 05 46 09 21 21; iledere-hot
.port@wanadoo.fr; quai de la Poithevinière; d/q from €50/65,
Jul-Sep €60/90) A modern two-star hotel right
on the port with bright, spacious rooms.
The wonderful views from the north-facing
rooms are worth the extra outlay.

Hôtel la Jetée (☎ 05 46 09 36 36; info@hotel-lajetee
.com; 23 quai Georges Clemenceau; r €49-76, Jul-Sep €78-
99; P) A contemporary villa-style building
designed around a quiet courtyard. The
three-star hotel, at the eastern edge of the
port, has decent-sized doubles as well as
family rooms with a mezzanine level.

CAMPING
Camping Municipal (☎ 05 46 09 21 96; camping €14;
Mar-mid-Oct) A grassy and shaded site situated a few hundred metres to the south of
the church. Pitching your tent anywhere
but in an official camping area is strictly
forbidden.

Eating
You can find touristy restaurants in the port
area. The friendly **Bistrot du Marin** (☎ 05 46 68
74 66; 10 quai Nicolas Baudin; mains €10-15) is a quaint,
bustling bar-*bistrot*.

In St-Martin, the **covered market** (rue Jean
Jaurès; 8.30am-1pm) is on the southern side
of the port with a cluster of **food shops** nearby, although it's much cheaper to buy food
in La Rochelle.

Beaches
The best beaches on the Île de Ré are
along the southern edge of the island (east
and west of La Couarde) and around the
western tip of the island (northeast and
southeast of Phare des Baleines). Near
Sablanceaux, there are sandy beaches along
the south coast towards Ste-Marie. Many
of the beaches are bordered by dunes that
have been fenced off to protect the vegetation. There's an unofficial **naturist beach** near
the outskirts of Les Portes; access is via the
Forêt du Lizay.

Getting There & Away
For automobiles, the bridge toll (paid on
your way *to* the island; nothing to leave) is
€9 (a whopping €16.50 from mid-June to
mid-September).

Year-round, excruciatingly slow buses
run by **Rébus** (☎ 05 46 09 20 15) link La Rochelle (the train station car park, Tour de

la Grosse Horloge and place de Verdun)
with all the major towns on the island. The
company also covers intra-island routes.

Getting Around
Cycling is an extremely popular way to get
around the island, which is flat and has an
extensive network of paved bicycle paths. A
biking map is available at tourist offices. In
summer practically every hamlet has somewhere to hire bikes.

At Sablanceaux, from mid-June to mid-
September, bikes can be hired at Cycland,
in a **kiosk** (☎ 05 46 09 97 54) in one of the little
buildings to the left as you come off the
bridge. It's best to call one to two days in
advance. The rest of the year, call **Cycland's
office** (☎ 05 46 09 65 27; www.cycland.fr in French) in
La Flotte and it'll deliver a bike to the bridge
in about 15 minutes. Bicycles/mountain
bikes/tandems cost €7/11.50/18 per day.

SOUTH OF LA ROCHELLE
The crescent-shaped **Île d'Aix** (pronounced
'eel day') is a 1.33-sq-km, car-free island
16km due south of La Rochelle, was fortified by Vauban and later used as a prison. It
has some very nice beaches and is served by
regular ferries from La Fumée (see opposite
for information on getting to La Fumée by
bus). **Fort Boyard**, built during the first half of
the 19th century, is an oval-shaped island/
fortress between the Île d'Aix and the **Île
d'Oléron** – the latter is a larger and less picturesque version of the Île de Ré. You can
travel to the Île d'Oléron from Rochefort
by bus.

Companies offering cruises include **Croisières Océanes** (☎ 05 46 50 68 44; cours des Dames, La
Rochelle), which has daily sailings from Easter
to early November.

About 30km southeast of La Rochelle,
Rochefort (population 25,500), founded as a
fortified town in the late 1600s has several
interesting museums and a good market
every Wednesday and Saturday. A guided
tour of the town leaves from the **tourist office** (☎ 05 46 99 08 60; av Sadi Carnot; 9am-8pm Jul
& Aug, 9am-12.30pm & 2-6pm Mon-Sat Oct-Mar) every
Thursday morning at 10am between May
and September.

In a central location, opposite the tourist
office, **Hôtel de France** (☎ 05 46 99 34 00; 55 rue du
Dr Peltier; s/d from €36/38) has standard chain-
hotel rooms at a good price.

Keolis Littoral buses (☎ 05 46 82 31 31) operates services to the Île d'Oléron and to La Fumée, from where there are ferries to the Île d'Aix. Rochefort is on the La Rochelle/Bordeaux train line.

About 40km south of Rochefort is **Royan** (population 16,800), flattened by Allied bombing in early 1945 and rebuilt after the war in the modernist style of the early 1950s. It's a good place to start a visit to the Médoc thanks to the ferry to Pointe de Grave (p638). Trains go to Cognac and, via Saintes, to Nantes and Bordeaux.

COGNAC
pop 19,500
Cognac, surrounded by rolling vineyards and quiet villages, is famed around the world for the double-distilled spirit that bears the town's name, and on which the local economy is based.

Orientation
The train station is on the southern edge of the town centre, while the four cognac distilleries mentioned below are on the other side of town, about 1.5km to the north, near the River Charente. Place François 1er, 200m northeast of the tourist office (follow rue du 14 Juillet), is linked to the river by blvd Denfert Rochereau.

Information
Cyber Espace (☎ 05 45 36 85 60; 68 blvd Denfert Rochereau; per hr €0.75; ⏲ 2-6pm Mon-Fri) Internet access.
Post Office (2 place Bayard) ATM and currency exchange facilities.
Société Générale (33 rue Angoulême) With exchange facilities.
Tourist Office (☎ 05 45 82 10 71; www.tourism-cognac.com; 16 rue du 14 Juillet; ⏲ 9am-7pm Mon-Sat, 10am-6pm Sun Jul & Aug; 9.30am-5.30pm Mon-Sat May, Jun & Sep; 10am 5pm Mon-Sat Oct-Apr) Can supply a town map.

Sights & Activities
The narrow streets of the **Vieille Ville** (Old City), between the partly Romanesque **Église St-Léger** (rue Aristide Briand) and the river, are lined with half-timbered 15th- to 17th-century buildings.

The **Musée de Cognac** (☎ 05 45 32 07 25; 48 blvd Denfert Rochereau; adult/student €2.20/1.20; ⏲ 10am-6pm Jun-Sep, 2.30-5.30pm Wed-Mon Oct-May) has a varied collection that covers fine arts, local

folk traditions and, in the basement, Cognac production.

The Musée de Cognac is in the southern corner of the **Jardin Public** (Public Park). The small zoo is home to a few deer.

COGNAC HOUSES
The most famous cognac distilleries offer tours of their *chais* (cellars; pronounced 'shay') and production facilities, that end with a tasting session. Reservations are only necessary for groups.

Camus (☎ 05 45 32 28 28; www.camus.fr; 29 rue Marguerite de Navarre) is 250m northeast of the Jardin Public. From June to September, 1¾-hour tours (adult/child €5/free) begin at 9.45am, 10.45am, 1.45pm, 2.30pm, 3.15pm and 4pm daily. In May and October, tours begin at 10.45am, 2.30pm and 4pm on weekdays.

The informative tours (adult/student/child €4/2/free) of the sprawling **Martell complex** (☎ 05 45 36 33 33; place Édouard Martell), 250m northwest of the tourist office, last one hour and are sometimes in English. June to September, tours run from 9.30am to 6pm daily, last tour at 5pm; October to May, tours run on weekdays (except Friday afternoon) at 9.30am, 11am, 2.30pm, 3.45pm and 5pm. Call to check times for foreign-language tours.

The **Château de Cognac** (127 blvd Denfert Rochereau), 650m north of place François 1er, was the birthplace in 1494 of King François I and has been home to **Otard** (☎ 05 45 36 88 86; www.otard.com) since 1795. From April to October, the well-conducted, one-hour tours (adult/12 to 18 years, €5/2.50) with commentary available in seven languages begin at 10am, 11am, 2pm, 3pm, 4pm and 5pm daily. Phone in advance to find out when English tours are scheduled, and for all tours between December and March.

The 1¼-hour tours (adult/student and child €6/free) of the **Hennessey facility** (☎ 05 45 35 72 68; 8 rue Richonne), 100m up the hill from quai des Flamands, which runs along the river, include a film (in English) and a boat trip across the Charente to visit the cellars. June to September they run every half-hour daily from 10am to 6pm; March to December, they begin every 45 minutes from 10am to 5pm. Private tours with fancier tastings cost €17 to €30.

The tourist office can supply you with a list of smaller cognac houses near town; most are closed from October to mid-March. **Rémy Martin** (☎ 05 45 35 76 66; www .remy.com) is a few kilometres southwest of town towards Pons. One-hour mini-train tours (adult/12 to 18 years €6/3) run from April to October (except Sunday in April and October). English tours usually leave at 3.30pm, but it is strongly advised to ring in advance to reserve tours.

Sleeping

Hôtel d'Orléans (☎ 05 45 82 01 26; fax 05 45 82 20 33; 25 rue d'Angoulême; d €42; **P**) A wonderful, rambling 17-century house in the heart of the pedestrianised district which, despite a splash of paint and a few recent improvements, hasn't lost any of its charm. Even the staircase is listed as a historic monument.

Hôtel Le Cheval Blanc (☎ 05 45 82 09 55; www .hotel-chevalblanc.fr; 6 place Bayard; s/d/tr €41/46/53; **P**) You'll get a friendly welcome at this efficiently-run two-star place, 100m west of the tourist office. Although the rooms here aren't huge, they are spotlessly clean and well-equipped. There's also a vending machine stocked with miniature bottles of cognac, for those midnight cravings! Access for disabled guests.

Hôtel François 1er (☎ 05 45 32 07 18; www.hotel -francois1er.com; 3 place François 1er; d/tw with shower €44/51; **P**) Occupying a lovely mid-19th century building in central Cognac, this three-star hotel has spacious, renovated rooms with high ceilings and wooden floors.

Eating

There are a number of restaurants and bars to be found in the immediate vicinity of place François 1er and the tourist office.

La Belle Époque (see Hôtel d'Orléans, p628; mains €12-15; lunch Mon-Sat, dinner Tue-Sat) Like Hôtel d'Orléans to which this restaurant belongs,

there's a fading, atmospheric grandeur here, enhanced by the slow ceiling fans, sweeping wooden bar and background jazz. The traditional French food on the menu is also served in the shady courtyard.

La Boune Goule (☎ 05 45 82 06 37; 42 allée de la Corderie; mains €5-11; May-Sep, Mon-Sat Oct-Apr), across the square from the Martell complex, offers local Charentaise dishes at reasonable prices.

SELF-CATERING

There is an **Ecofrais supermarket** (32 place Bayard; 9am-12.30pm & 3-7.30pm Mon-Fri, 8am-noon Sun) opposite the post office. About 300m to the north of place François 1er, the **covered market** (57 blvd Denfert Rochereau; open until 1pm) is just across from the Musée de Cognac.

The friendly and informative **Cognathèque** (☎ 05 45 82 43 31; 10 place Jean Monnet; 9am-7pm) sits 100m from the tourist office. Over 250 different cognacs costing up to €1500 a bottle are available.

Getting There & Away

Cognac's **train station**, at the southern end of av du Maréchal Leclerc, is on the line that links Angoulême with Royan (40 minutes). There are daily trains to/from La Rochelle (€13.80, 1¼ hours).

BORDEAUX

pop 735,000

Bordeaux is buzzing. Long known as *La Belle Au Bois Dormant* (Sleeping Beauty), the city developed a reputation as a dull place with neglected buildings and a chronic lack of urban planning or infrastructure. The then controversial ex-Prime Minister Alain Juppé became mayor. With his blunt, no-nonsense approach he pushed through massive investment in the city; buildings were cleaned, traffic-choked roads pedestrianised, squares re-paved and trees planted. A state-of-the-art tram system was built and plans were drawn up for the redevelopment of the run-down riverside areas. Such sweeping changes have been causing major disruption for several years but at last, the work is nearly finished, and a new, reinvigorated Bordeaux is emerging as one of the country's finest cities. Against a backdrop of neoclassical architecture, wide avenues and pretty parks, the city boasts excellent museums, a vibrant nightlife, an ethnically diverse population and a lively university community.

History
About 100km from the Atlantic at the lowest bridging point on the Garonne River, Bordeaux was founded by the Romans in the 3rd century BC. From 1154 to 1453, the city prospered under the rule of the English, whose fondness for the Bordeaux region's red wine – known across the Channel as claret – provided the impetus for the eventual creation of Bordeaux's international reputation for quality wines.

Orientation
The city centre lies between place Gambetta and the 350m- to 500m-wide Garonne, which is usually a muddy brown as it flows either towards the sea or inland, depending on the tides. From place Gambetta, place de Tourny is 500m northeast, and the tourist office is 400m to the east.

The train station, Gare St-Jean, is in a seedy area about 3km southeast of the city centre. Cours de la Marne stretches from the train station to place de la Victoire, which is linked to place de la Comédie by the long and straight pedestrianised shopping street, rue Ste-Catherine.

Information
BOOKSHOPS
Bradley's Bookshop (☎ 05 56 52 10 57; 8 cours d'Albret; ☼ 9.30am-12.30pm & 2-7pm Tue-Sat, 2-7pm Mon)
Librarie Mollat (☎ 05 56 56 40 40; 15 rue Vital Carles; ☼ 9.15am-7pm Mon-Sat)

INTERNET ACCESS
Cyberstation (☎ 05 56 01 15 15; 23 cours Pasteur; ☼ 9.30am-2am Mon-Sat, 2pm-2am Sun; per hr €3)
NetZone (☎ 05 57 59 01 25; 209 rue Ste-Catherine; ☼ 9.30am-midnight; per hr €3)
Tribal (☎ 05 56 92 99 22; 71 cours Pasteur; ☼ 8.30am-7.30pm Mon-Thu, 8.30am 7pm Fri, 9.30am-6pm Sat; per hr €4.60)

LAUNDRY
There is a full-service laundrette at 31 rue du Palais Gallien, which is open 8am to 9pm, while self-service options are at 32 rue des Augustins, 5 rue de Fondaudège and 8 rue Lafaurie de Monbadon. These are open 7am to 9pm.

MEDICAL SERVICES & EMERGENCY
Hôpital St-André (☎ 05 56 79 56 79; 1 rue Jean Burguet) 24-hour casualty ward.
Police Station (☎ 05 56 99 77 77; 29 rue Castéja; ☼ 24hr)

MONEY
Banks offering currency exchange can be found near the tourist office on cours de l'Intendance, rue de l'Esprit des Lois and cours du Chapeau Rouge.
American Express (☎ 05 56 00 63 36; 11 cours de l'Intendance; ☼ 9am-noon & 1.30-5.30pm Mon-Fri Apr-Sep, to 5pm Mon-Fri Oct-Mar, plus 9.30am-12.30pm Sat Jun-Sep)

POST
Main Post Office (37 rue du Château d'Eau) Currency exchange and Cyberposte.
Post Office (43 place Gambetta; ☼ 10am-7pm Mon & Thu, 9am-7pm Tue, Wed, Fri, 9am-5pm Sat) Extended hours here.
Post Office (place St-Projet)

TOURIST INFORMATION
Maison du Tourisme de la Gironde (☎ 05 56 52 61 40; www.tourisme-gironde.cg33.fr in French; 21 cours de l'Intendance; ☼ 9am-6pm Mon-Fri, to 7pm Apr-Oct, 10am-1pm & 2-6.30pm Sat) For brochures on Gironde *département*.

MUSEUM PRICES & PASSES
The municipal museums in Bordeaux, which include Musée d'Art Contemporain (CAPC), Musée d'Histoire Naturelle, Musée des Arts Décoratifs, Musée des Beaux-Arts and Musée d'Aquitaine, are free to those under 18 and students holding a valid student card. They're also free for everyone on the first Sunday of each month.

The admission for adult/concession is €4/2.50 for each museum's permanent collections and €5.50/3 for temporary exhibits. Concession prices refer to people over the age of 60 or under 25 (though sometimes under 25s can enter free, even without a student card).

The municipal **Carte Pass** is €15.25 and is valid for 10 admissions into the eight municipal museums – those mentioned above, plus the Centre Jean Moulin, the Musée Goupil and the Jardin Botanique – great value for museum buffs.

ATLANTIC COAST

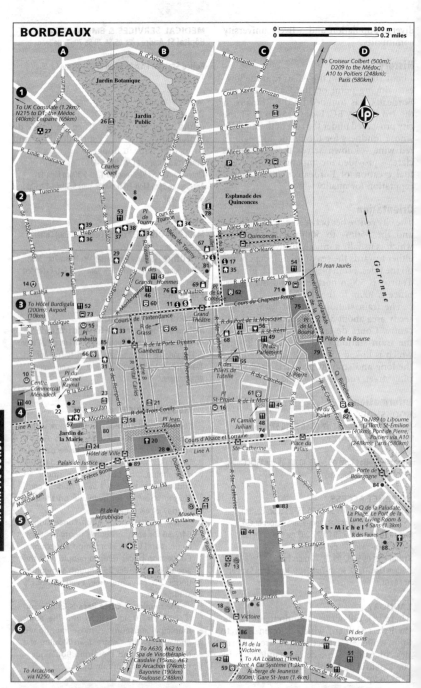

BORDEAUX

0 ——— 300 m
0 ——— 0.2 miles

To Croiseur Colbert (500m);
D209 to the Médoc;
A10 to Poitiers (248km);
Paris (580km)

Jardin Botanique

Jardin Public

To UK Consulate (1.2km);
N215 to D1; the Médoc
(40km); Lesparre (65km)

Esplanade des Quinc;onces

Pl Charles Gruet

Pl de Tourny

Pl des Grands Hommes

Pl Gambetta

To Hôtel Burdigala
(200m); Airport
(10km)

Grand Théâtre

Pl du Colonel Raynal

Centre Commercial Ménadeck

G a r o n n e

Place de la Bourse

Pl du Parlement

Pl St-Pierre

Pl du Palais

To N89 to Libourne
(31km); St-Emilion
(40km); Pont de Pierre;
Poitiers via A10
(248km); Paris (580km)

Jardin de la Mairie

Hôtel de Ville

Pl Jean Moulin

Pl St-Projet

Pl Camille Jullian

Place du Palais

Palais de Justice

Porte de Bourgogne

Pl de la République

Musée d'Aquitaine

To Q de la Paludate,
La Plage, Le Port de la
Lune, Living Room &
Sans (1.3km)

St-Michel

To Arcachon
via N250

Pl de la Victoire

To A630, A62 to
Spa de Vinothérapie
Caudalie (15km); A63
to Arcachon (74km);
Bayonne (190km);
Toulouse (248km)

To AA Location (1km);
Rent A Car Système (1.2km);
Auberge de Jeunesse
(800m); Gare St-Jean (1.4km)

Pl des Capucins

ATLANTIC COAST

INFORMATION		
American Express	.1	B3
Bradley's Bookshop	.2	A4
Cyberstation	.3	B5
Hôpital St-André	.4	B5
Laundrette	(see 29)	
Laundrette	.5	C6
Laundrette	.6	C6
Laundrette	.7	A3
Laundrette	.8	B2
Librarie Mollat	.9	B3
Main Post Office	.10	A4
Maison du Tourisme de la Gironde	.11	B3
Maison du Vin de Bordeaux	.12	B3
Net Zone	.13	C5
Police Station	.14	A3
Post Office (extended hours)	.15	A3
Post Office	.16	C4
Tourist Office	.17	C3
Tribal	.18	C6

SIGHTS & ACTIVITIES	(pp631–2)	
CAPC Musée d'Art Contemporain	.19	C1
Cathédrale St-André	.20	B4
Centre National Jean Moulin	.21	B4
École du Vin	(see 12)	
Galerie des Beaux-Arts	.22	A4
Musée des Arts Décoratifs	.23	A4
Musée des Beaux-Arts	.24	A4
Musée d'Aquitaine	.25	B5
Musée d'Histoire Naturelle	.26	A1
Palais Gallien	.27	A1
Tour Pey-Berland	.28	B4

SLEEPING	(pp632–4)	
Hôtel Balzac	.29	B3
Hôtel Boulan	.30	A4
Hôtel Bristol	.31	A4
Hôtel de Famille	.32	B2
Hôtel de la Tour Intendance	.33	B3
Hôtel de Sèze	.34	B2
Hôtel des 4 Soeurs	.35	C3
Hôtel Excelsior	.36	A2
Hôtel Studio	.37	B2
Hôtel Touring	.38	B2
La Maison du Lierre	.39	A2

EATING	(p634)	
Auchan Supermarket	.40	A4
Bodega Bodega	.41	C3
Cassolette Café	.42	C6
Champion Supermarket	.43	B3
Champion Supermarket	.44	C5
Claret's	.45	C4
Fromagerie	.46	B3
Fruit & Vegie Stalls	.47	D6
La Petite Brasserie	.48	C4
Le Bistrot d'Édouard	.49	C3
Le Fournil des Capucins	.50	D6
Marché des Capucins	.51	D6
Restaurant Agadir	.52	A3
Restaurant Baud et Millet	.53	B2
Restaurant Jean Ramet	.54	C3
Taj Mahal	.55	C4

DRINKING	(pp634–5)	
Bodega Bodega	(see 41)	
Café Brun	.56	C3
Connemara	.57	A4

ENTERTAINMENT	(p635)	
Bar de l'Hôtel de Ville	.58	B4
Box Office	(see 68)	
Café des Sports	.59	C6

Centre Jean Vigo	.60	B3
Cinéma Utopia	.61	C4
Grand Théâtre	.62	C3
La Reine Carotte	.63	D4
Le Plana	.64	C6
Théâtre Femina	.65	B3
Virgin Megastore Billeterie	.66	A3

SHOPPING	(p636)	
Bordeaux Magnum	.67	B2
Galerie Bordelaise	.68	C3
L'Intendant	.69	B3

TRANSPORT	(pp636–7)	
Bus Hub	.70	C3
CGFTE Bus Information Office	.71	C3
Halte Routière (Bus Station)	.72	C2
Jet'Bus (Airport Bus)	.73	A3
Le 63	.74	C4

OTHER		
Bourse du Commerce	.75	C3
Église Notre Dame	.76	B3
Église St-Michel	.77	D5
Girondins Fountain-Monument	.78	B2
Hôtel de la Douane	.79	D3
Hôtel de Ville	.80	A4
Merry-Go-Round	.81	B3
Porte Cailhau	.82	D4
Porte de la Grosse Cloche	.83	C5
Porte des Salinières	.84	D5
Porte Dijeaux	.85	A3
Porte d'Aquitaine	.86	C6
Synagogue	.87	C5
Tour St-Michel	.88	D5
Tribunal de Grande Instance	.89	B4

Tourist Office (☎ 05 56 00 66 00; www.bordeaux -tourisme.com; 12 cours du 30 Juillet; ⏰ 9am-7.30pm Mon-Sat Jul & Aug, to 7pm May & Jun, to 7pm Sep & Oct, 9.30am-6.30pm Sun May-Oct; 9am-6.30pm Mon-Sat, 9.45am-4.30pm Sun Nov-Apr) Right next to the tram stop Comédie. Ask here about the *Passport Gourmand* (€50), which offers reductions on restaurants, activities and some museums and is worth considering if you're staying a while in Bordeaux. The *Plan Guide du Patrimoine* (€1), has information on the city's architectural heritage and suggests two walking itineraries.

Tourist Office Annexe (⏰ 9am-noon & 1-6pm Mon-Sat, 10am-noon & 1-3pm Sun May-Oct; 9.30am-12.30pm & 2-7pm Mon-Fri Nov-Apr) At the train station.

Sights

The sights mentioned appear pretty much from north to south.

The **Croiseur Colbert** (☎ 05 56 44 96 11; adult/ student & child €7.30/5.80; ⏰ 10am-7pm Jun-Aug; 10am-6pm Mon-Fri, 10am-6pm Sat & Sun Apr, May & Sep, 10am-6pm Wed, Sat, Sun & school holidays Oct-Mar), a 180m-long French navy missile cruiser, was in service from 1957 to 1991. It is now docked at quai des Chartrons, (500m north of the Musée d'Art Contemporain) and offers a glimpse of life aboard a battleship.

Entrepôts Lainé was built in 1824 as a warehouse for the rare and exotic products of France's colonies (such as coffee, cocoa, peanuts and vanilla). Its capacious spaces now house the **CAPC Musée d'Art Contemporain** (Museum of Contemporary Art; ☎ 05 56 00 81 50; Entrepôt 7, rue Ferrére; ⏰ 11am-6pm Tue, Thu-Sun, to 8pm Wed, closed Mon). Most of the exhibits and installations that the museum hosts are temporary, presenting major artistic movements over the last 30 years.

The beautifully landscaped **Jardin Public** (cours de Verdun), established in 1755 and laid out in the English style a century later, includes the meticulously catalogued **Jardin Botanique** (☎ 05 56 52 18 77; admission free; ⏰ 8.30am-6pm), founded in 1629 and at this site since 1855; and the **Musée d'Histoire Naturelle** (Natural History Museum; ☎ 05 56 48 29 86; ⏰ 11am-6pm Mon & Wed-Fri, 2-6pm Sat & Sun). There's a **children's playground** on the island.

Nearby, off rue de Fondaudège, is the city's most impressive Roman site, **Palais Gallien** (rue du Dr Albert Barraud; adult/under 12 €1.50/free; ⏰ 3-7pm Jun-Sep), the ruins of a 3rd-century amphitheatre.

The most prominent feature of **esplanade des Quinconces**, a vast square laid out in 1820, is the fountain monument to the Girondins, a group of moderate, bourgeois National Assembly deputies during the French Revolution, 22 of whom were executed in 1793 after being convicted of Counter-Revolutionary

ATLANTIC COAST

activities. The entire 50m-high ensemble, completed in 1902, was dismantled in 1943 by the Germans so the statues could be melted down for their 52 tonnes of bronze. Restoration took years and was not completed until 1983.

The 4km-long **riverfront esplanade** is gradually being redeveloped as part of the town's facelift. The section just north of esplanade des Quinconces is the first to benefit, featuring a park with trees, playgrounds and bicycle paths. However, the six lanes of traffic that clog up adjacent Quai Louis XVIII mean that this spot isn't as peaceful as it might be.

Nowadays, **place Gambetta** is an island of greenery in the midst of the city centre's hustle and bustle, but during the Reign of Terror that followed the Revolution, a guillotine placed here severed the heads of 300 alleged counter-revolutionaries.

A few blocks south of place Gambetta, the **Musée des Arts Décoratifs** (Museum of Decorative Arts; ☎ 05 56 00 72 50; 39 rue Bouffard; museum ⏱ 2-6pm Wed-Mon, temporary exhibits from 11am Mon-Fri) specialises in faïence, porcelain, silverwork, glasswork, furniture and the like.

The **Musée des Beaux-Arts** (☎ 05 56 10 20 56; 20 cours d'Albret; ⏱ Wed-Mon 11am-6pm) occupies two wings of the Hôtel de Ville (city hall) complex (built in the 1770s); between them is a verdant public park, the **Jardin de la Mairie**. Founded in 1801 the museum has a large collection of paintings, including Flemish, Dutch and Italian works from the 17th century and a particularly important work by Delacroix. At nearby place du Colonel Raynal, the museum's annexe, the **Galerie des Beaux-Arts**, hosts short-term exhibitions.

In 1137 the future King Louis VII married Eleanor of Aquitaine in **Cathédrale St-André** (☎ 05 56 81 26 25; admission free; ⏱ 10-11.30am & 2-6.30pm Mon, 7.30-11.30am & 2-6pm Tue-Fri, 9-11.30am & 2-7pm Sat, 8am-12.30pm Sun, but 2.30-5.30pm 1st Sun of month), now a Unesco World Heritage Site. The exterior wall of the cathedral's nave dates from 1096; most of the rest of the structure was built in the 13th and 14th centuries. Renovation of the north portal has uncovered fantastic carvings under centuries of grime. Behind the choir, the 50m-high belfry, 15th-century **Tour Pey-Berland** (adult/student/child €4.60/3.10/free; ⏱ 10am-midday & 2-6pm) has a panoramic view at the top of 232 narrow steps.

The outstanding **Musée d'Aquitaine** (Museum of Aquitaine; ☎ 05 56 01 51 00; 20 cours Pasteur; ⏱ 11am-6pm Tue-Sun) presents 25,000 years of Bordeaux's history and ethnography. Exceptional artefacts include several stone carvings of women and a collection of Gallo-Roman steles, statues and ceramics. The English-language catalogue is worth borrowing at the ticket counter (€1.50 deposit).

Activities

WINE-TASTING & -BATHING

For many visitors, Bordeaux is all about wine; tasting it, drinking it, and of course buying it. To get the most out of your visit, consider enrolling at the **Ecole du Vin** (☎ 05 56 00 22 88; http://ecole.vins-bordeaux.fr; 3 cours du 30 Juillet) at the Maison du Vin de Bordeaux. Introductory two-hour courses are available in English between June and September (€20), but to really develop your nose and impress dinner-party guests with your knowledge of vinification, sign up for a more extensive three- to four-day course (from €375). The courses offer an entertaining introduction to the techniques and vocabulary of tasting and wine-making. Chateaux visits are included to test your new skills.

If you've over-indulged in the local produce, try bathing in it! At the **Spa de Vinothérapie Caudalie** (☎ 05 57 83 83 83; www.sources-caudalie.com; Chemin de Smith Haut Lafitte, Martillac) you can benefit from the blood-strengthening, anti-ageing effects of vine and grape extracts. Take a red-wine bath, enjoy a Merlot wrap or order a Cabernet body scrub. It's 20 minutes south of Bordeaux next to Chateau Smith Haut Lafitte. Leave the A62 at junction 1.

Tours

The tourist office runs a range of guided tours, including a two-hour bilingual **walking tour** of the city (adult/senior or student €6.50/6) at 10am daily. From mid-April to mid-November the tours on Wednesday and Saturday are only by bus.

The tourist office also offers two-hour, bilingual 'Introduction to Wine Tasting' courses (adult/senior or student €20/17) every Thursday at 4.30pm (and on Saturday from mid-July to mid-August).

Sleeping

Budget and mid-range options are plentiful and competitive, but there's a dearth of good top-end accommodation in town. The quality of rooms (particularly in the budget category) can vary enormously, sometimes even within the same hotel, so have a look before you sign up.

BUDGET
Most of the decent budget accommodation is in the area just west of place de Tournay. If possible, don't stay in the seedy area around the train station.

Auberge de Jeunesse (☎ 05 56 33 00 70; fax 05 56 33 00 71; 22 cours Barbey, annexe at 208 cours de l'Argonne; dm €16/17.50 HI member/nonmember incl breakfast; 🖳) Unexpectedly flash for a youth hostel, this place is ultra-modern, well-equipped and open 24 hours. There's a café-bar, kitchen, laundry and facilities for the disabled. All the rooms are dorms, but most are for just four people or less, so you won't have to share your digs with hundreds of smelly-footed students. Take bus No 7/8 to the Meunier stop.

Hôtel Boulan (☎ 05 56 52 23 62; fax 05 56 44 91 65; 28 rue Boulan; s/d €20.25/23.50, with shower €28.25/28.50) Tucked away in a quiet side-street, but still handy for many of the sights (and the Connemara bar!) this friendly place has rooms of a good standard for this price.

Hôtel Excelsior (reception at Hôtel Studio; see below) A better option than its sister hotel up the road. The simple, functional rooms here have all had a lick of paint and are larger and brighter than those at Hôtel Studio, although facilities and prices are identical.

Hôtel de Famille (☎ 05 56 52 11 28; fax 05 56 51 94 43; 76 cours Georges Clemenceau; s & d €18-22, with shower, toilet & TV €29-36) A variety of ordinary but homey rooms. There's no lift, so the higher your room, the cheaper (and smaller) it is. Light sleepers beware – there's no double-glazing.

Hôtel Studio (☎ 05 56 48 00 14; www.hotel-bordeaux.com; 26 rue Huguerie; d/tw/tr €22.80/24.40/27.50; 🅿 🖳) This is the headquarters of Bordeaux's cheap hotel empire – the same family owns at least seven other hotels in town. This particular establishment is a bit dark and stuffy with decrepit rooms. On the upside, a shower, telephone and TV (with a couple of English channels) are all included in the cheap price. A better option from the same owners is the Excelsior, a few doors up the road. The hotel's Internet café charges guests €1.50 per hour.

Hôtel Balzac (☎ 05 56 81 85 12; 14 rue Lafaurie de Monbadon; s/d with shower & toilet €28/31) This is another budget priced option worth trying.

Hôtel Touring (☎ 05 56 81 56 73; le-touring@wanadoo.fr; 16 rue Huguerie; s/d with shower & toilet €36.90/40.30) Don't be put off by the dodgy '70s wallpaper – this place is an excellent deal. The 12 older-style rooms have comfortable beds and sturdy dark-wood furniture; those on the first floor are especially spacious.

MID-RANGE
La Maison du Lierre (☎ 05 56 51 92 71; www.maisondulierre.com; 57 rue Huguerie; s/d €63/73; 🅿) Occupying a sympathetically restored townhouse with a beautiful Bordeaux stone staircase and a pretty courtyard for breakfast in summer, this delightful hotel has a relaxed and friendly *chambre d'hôte* feel. The 12 mid-sized rooms are nicely decorated with warm colours and parquet floors; four rooms have balconies.

Hôtel des 4 Soeurs (☎ 05 57 81 19 20; http://4soeurs.free.fr; 6 cours du 30 Juillet; s/d from €60/70; 🗷 🞨 🖳) An appealing three-star hotel in a great location with the tourist office, Maison du Vin and Grand Theatre all right on the doorstep. The very comfortable rooms boast extras such as hairdryers and English-language TV channels and some overlook place de la Comédie.

Hôtel Bristol (☎ 05 56 81 85 01; www.hotel-bordeaux.com; 14ter place Gambetta; r €32-46) An attractive two-star option from the Hôtel Studio group in a central location overlooking place Gambetta. The 27 cheerful and well-equipped rooms are priced according to size. All have showers, toilets, TVs, mini-bars and all-important double-glazing.

Hôtel de Sèze (☎ 05 56 52 65 54; hotelsezmedoc@aol.com; 7 rue de Sèze; s/d from €46/53; 🅿) A charming three-star hotel occupying an elegant 18th-century building with 69 individually styled rooms. Some rooms are worn, but it serves to enhance the character of this place.

Hôtel de la Tour Intendance (☎ 05 56 44 56 56; fax 05 56 44 54 54; 14-16 rue de la Vieille Tour; s/d with shower & toilet €68/78; 🅿). This place is usually a very good two-star option.\

TOP END
Hôtel Burdigala (☎ 05 56 90 16 16; www.burdigala.com; 6 cours du 30 Juillet; traditional/superior/ste from €170/200/370; 🅿 🗷 🞨 🖳) A modern, four-star hotel, this is Bordeaux's best bet for top-end comfort, although there's nothing

particularly special about it. The standard rooms, although comfortable, are a bit pokey. The larger suites are of questionable design, with red leather sofas a big feature. Wheelchair friendly.

Eating

Bordeaux has some excellent restaurants, many of which offer reasonably priced lunch *menus*. There's a good choice of places along rue St-Remi and in the streets to the south including place du Parlement and rue du Pas St Georges. There are also many inexpensive cafés and restaurants around place de la Victoire, an area that's hugely popular with students.

There's a cluster of sandwich joints around the top end of rue Ste-Catherine and along rue du Palais Gallien.

Claret's (☎ 05 56 01 21 21; 46 rue du Pas St Georges; lunch menu €10, dinner menus €16-20; 🕑 closed Sat lunch & Sun) A chic little venue on place Camille-Jullian offering an interesting selection of southwestern French and Japanese specialities. Despite the sleek wood-toned décor and smooth service, the prices here are very reasonable. In the immediate vicinity there are a number of other intimate restaurants and trendy terrace cafés.

Cassolette Café (☎ 05 56 92 94 96; www.cassolette café.com in French; 20 place de la Victoire; cassolette - 5 choices - €10.50, lunch menu €8.50, dinner menu €10.50; 🕑 noon-midnight) Extremely popular and great value, this is the place to come for hearty French family-style cooking. You order your menu or the ingredients of your *casso-lette* (casserole cooked on a terracotta plate) using a check-off form and your choices appear promptly. Weekend nights have been known to get a bit rowdy with song-singing students, but it's all good fun.

Le Bistrot d'Édouard (☎ 05 56 81 48 87; 16 place du Parlement; menus €11-20; 🕑 lunch & dinner) The great-value three-course menu at €11 keeps this *bistrot* packed. Outside tables are in a calming spot by the fountain in place du Parlement. If you can't get a table here, try next door at L'Ombrière. It's run by the same owners and has an identical menu.

La Petite Brasserie (☎ 05 56 52 19 79; 43 rue du Pas St Georges; menus €25/35; 🕑 Wed-Sun) An unpretentious place offering fine brasserie-style dining in a relaxed and cosy atmosphere. The traditional bordelaise cuisine, extensive wine list and attentive service all get top marks.

Taj Mahal (☎ 05 56 51 92 05; 24 rue du Parlement Ste Catherine; lunch menu from €9.50, dinner menu from €16) Sitting on exquisite carved teak chairs, being served by waiters wearing traditional *shal-war kameez*, feasting on authentic dishes from India and Pakistan; you'll think you've been transported to the subcontinent.

Restaurant Baud et Millet (☎ 05 56 79 05 77; 19 rue Huguerie; menus €22.10-26.70; 🕑 11am-midnight Mon-Sat) For something a bit different, try this unusual, well-respected eatery with over 250 different cheeses on offer and almost as many international wines lining the walls. The mostly vegetarian cuisine includes an all-you-can-eat cheese buffet *(raclette)* for €18.50. The same street is home to a number of other reasonably priced eateries.

Restaurant Jean Ramet (☎ 05 56 44 12 51; jean. ramet@free.fr; 7 place Jean Jaurès; lunch menu €28, dinner menus €45 & €56; 🕑 Tue-Sat) This very formal establishment is a classy choice serving traditional *gastronomique* French and Bordelais cuisine amid mirrors, white tablecloths and sparkling tableware.

Other places you might like to try:

Restaurant Agadir (☎ 05 56 52 28 04; 14 rue du Palais Gallien; couscous €12-17)

Bodega Bodega (☎ 05 56 01 24 24; 4 rue des Piliers de Tutelle; 🕑 noon-3.15pm & 7pm-2am Mon-Sat, 7pm-2am Sun). Tapas bar, see opposite.

SELF-CATERING

A few blocks east of place de la Victoire is **Marché des Capucins** (🕑 6am-1pm Tue-Sun), a one-time wholesale market. Nearby rue Élie Gintrec has super-cheap **fruit and vegie stalls** on weekdays and Saturday until 1pm or 1.30pm.

Champion supermarket (place des Grands Hommes; 🕑 8.30am-7.30pm Mon-Sat) is in the basement of the Marché des Grands Hommes. Nearby, you'll find a fine **fromagerie** (2 rue Montesquieu; 🕑 closed Mon morning & Sun), while there's another **Champion supermarket** (190 rue Ste-Catherine; 🕑 8.30am-8pm Mon-Sat).

Auchan supermarket (opposite 58 rue du Château d'Eau; 🕑 8.30am-10pm Mon-Sat) is a vast, cheap place in the Centre Commercial Mériadeck.

Le Fournil des Capucins (62-64 cours de la Marne), near place de la Victoire, is a bakery that never closes.

Drinking

Connemara (☎ 05 56 52 82 57; 18 cours d'Albret; 🕑 noon-2am) Popular with both locals and expats, this lively Irish bar gets absolutely packed on major sporting occasions. Get there early to bag a seat in front of the big screen. There's also darts, pool and regular live music as well as pub food.

Bodega Bodega (☎ 05 56 01 24 24; 4 rue des Piliers de Tutelle; ☾ noon-3.15pm & 7pm-2am Mon-Sat, 7pm-2am Sun) Two floors of tapas, tunes and trendy types; this is the biggest and best Spanish bar in town. Mind your head on the giant hams hanging up above the bar when you order a drink.

Café Brun (☎ 05 56 52 20 49; 45 rue St-Rémi; ☾ 10am-2am) This bar-bistro with a warm atmosphere and cool jazz is great for an evening aperitif.

Entertainment

Bordeaux has a really vibrant nightlife scene; details of events appear in *Bordeaux Plus* and *Clubs & Concerts* (www.clubsetconcerts.com in French), both free and available at the tourist office. The fortnightly *Spectaculaire*, €0.50 at newsstands, lists music, cinema, theatre and dance events.

Student nightlife is centred around place de la Victoire, which can be somewhat seedy at night.

Tickets for events such as concerts and bullfights can be purchased from the **Virgin Megastore billeterie** (☎ 05 56 56 05 55; 17place Gambetta; ☾ 10am-7.30pm Mon-Thu, 10am-9.30pm Fri & Sat, 3-6.30pm Sun) or the **Box Office** (☎ 05 56 48 26 26; Galerie Bordelaise).

NIGHTCLUBS & LIVE MUSIC

For zoning reasons, many of the city's late-late dance venues are a few blocks northeast of Gare St-Jean along the river, on quai de la Paludate (just south of the railway bridge) and perpendicular rue du Commerce. Most places are not huge clubs but bars with DJs and dancing. Bouncers can be selective but there's normally no cover charge.

Le Port de la Lune (☎ 05 56 49 15 55; portdelalune@wanadoo.fr; 58 quai de la Paludate; ☾ 7pm-2am) Jazz club and bistrot. A dark, smoky and atmospheric place in the best jazz tradition. The large venue hosts live jazz virtually every night while the restaurant with tables either in the main room or in the quieter room next door offers seasonal menus (€18 to €20).

La Plage (☎ 05 56 49 02 46; 40 quai de la Paludate; ☾ 11pm-5am Wed-Sat) Popular local DJs serve up a mix of banging house and techno tunes

to a happy crowd of 20- to 30-somethings. The tropical beach theme adds to the fun. Don't forget your sun-tan lotion.

Café des Sports (5 cours de l'Argonne) If you've had a big feed at the Cassolette Café next door, it's just a short stagger to get the drinks in at this lively student hang-out. Beer on tap, football on the telly.

4 Sans (☎ 05 56 49 40 05; 40 rue Armagnac; international/local acts €5-10/free; ☾ from midnight Thu-Sat) Trendy night club featuring top-notch local and international house, techno and drum 'n' bass DJs.

Living Room (☎ 05 56 85 71 85; 14 rue du Commerce; ☾ midnight-5am) If staying in is the new going out, this is a comfortable home from home. The cosy oriental-lounge décor (lots of rugs and couches) and techno/house sound attracts a slightly older crowd.

Le Plana (☎ 05 56 91 73 23; 22 place de la Victoire; ☾ 7am-2am Mon-Sat, 2pm-2am Sun) A lively, animated student hang-out. Except in July and August, it has live jazz every Sunday at about 10.30pm, and concerts (ranging from rock to funk and soul, some of them jam sessions) at 10.30pm Monday to Wednesday.

GAY & LESBIAN VENUES

Bar de l'Hôtel de Ville (☎ 05 56 44 05 08; 4 rue de l'Hôtel de Ville; ☾ 6pm-2am) It's often very busy and there's a spirited 95% gay crowd at this bar. Shows are held on some Sundays.

La Reine Carotte (☎ 05 56 01 26 68; 32 rue du Chai des Farines; ☾ 7pm-2am Tue & Sat) This is a mellow place attracting a clientele that's about 50% lesbian.

CLASSICAL MUSIC

Except in August and September, the 18th-century **Grand Théâtre** (☎ 05 56 00 85 95; place de la Comédie) stages operas, ballets and concerts of orchestral and chamber music; there's a **ticket office** (☾ 11am-6pm Tue-Sat). For the operettas, plays, dance performances and variety shows held at **Théâtre Femina** (10 rue de Grassi), there is a ticket office in the nearby **Galerie Bordelaise** (☎ 05 56 48 26 26; ☾ 10am-7pm Tue-Sat, 2-7pm Mon).

CINEMAS

Nondubbed films are screened at two art-house cinemas, **Centre Jean Vigo** (☎ 05 56 44 35 17; 6 rue Franklin), and the popular, five-screen **Cinéma Utopia** (☎ 05 56 52 00 03; 3 place Camille Jullian).

Shopping

The main shopping artery is the 1.2km **rue Ste-Catherine**, reputed to be the longest pedestrianised shopping street in Europe.

Galerie Bordelaise, a 19th-century shopping arcade, is at the intersection of rue de la Porte Dijeaux and rue Ste-Catherine.

The city's luxury shopping district, formed by the Allée de Tourny, Cours Georges Clemenceau and Cours de l'Intendance, is called **le triangle d'or** (the golden triangle).

Bordeaux wine in all price ranges is on sale at several speciality shops near the tourist office, including **Bordeaux Magnum** (☎ 05 56 48 00 06; 3 rue Gobineau; ✆ 10am-7.30pm Mon-Sat) and **L'Intendant** (☎ 05 56 48 01 29; 2 Allée de Tourny; ✆ 10am-7.30pm).

There are antique shops along rue Bouffard, near the Musée des Arts Décoratifs.

Getting There & Away

AIR

Bordeaux airport (☎ 05 56 34 50 50; www.bordeaux .aeroport.fr) is in Mérignac, 10km west of the city centre. In addition to domestic services operated by Air France, Ryanair (www .ryanair.com) has regular flights from the UK and low-cost Dutch airline Basiq Air (www.basiqair.com) fly from Amsterdam. A taxi from the airport into town costs €15 to €20.

BUS

Buses to places all over the Gironde (and parts of nearby *départements*) leave from the **Halte Routière** (bus terminal; allées de Chartres), in the northeast corner of esplanade des Quinconces; schedules are posted. For details on buses to the Médoc see p638 and St-Émilion see p641. **Citram Aquitaine** runs most buses to destinations in the Gironde and has an **information kiosk** (☎ 05 56 43 68 43; ✆ 1-8pm Mon-Fri, 9am-1.30pm & 5-8pm Sat) at the Halte Routière.

Eurolines (☎ 05 56 92 50 42; 32 rue Charles Domercq; ✆ Mon-Sat) faces the train station.

CAR

The big boys have offices in the train station building, all the way to the left as you exit. Inexpensive rental companies close to the train station:

AA Location (☎ 05 56 92 84 78; 185 cours de la Marne; ✆ Mon-Sat) About 400m from the station.

Rent A Car Système (☎ 05 56 33 60 75; 204 cours de la Marne; ✆ Mon-Sat)

TRAIN

Bordeaux is one of France's most important rail transit points. The station, **Gare St-Jean**, is about 3km from the city centre at the southern terminus of cours de la Marne. Be extra-careful with your bags here.

Destinations from Bordeaux include Paris' Gare Montparnasse (€58.90, three hours, at least 16 daily), Bayonne (€24.40, 1¾ hours, eight daily), Nantes (€37, four hours, five or six daily), Poitiers (€28.70, 1¾ hours, nine daily), La Rochelle (€22.50, two hours, five to seven daily) and Toulouse (€27.70, two to three hours, nine to 14 daily).

Getting Around

TO/FROM THE AIRPORT

The train station and place Gambetta are connected to the airport (single/return €6.50/11, 35 minutes, every 45 minutes at the weekend) by **Jet'Bus** (☎ 05 56 34 50 50) from 5.30am until 9.30pm (last departure from the airport 10.45pm). The trip takes approximately 45 minutes; much more if there are traffic jams.

BICYCLE

Le 63 (☎ 05 56 51 39 41, 06 74 82 27 62; 63 cours d'Alsace et Lorraine; ✆ 24hr) rents out bicycles (€3/14/18 for one/eight/24 hours) and *go-ped* motorised scooters (€15/45 per hour/day).

BUS

Bordeaux's urban buses are run by **CGFTE** (Allo Bus; ☎ 05 57 57 88 88). The company has Espace Bus information/ticket offices at the train station, place Gambetta (4 rue Georges Bonnac).

The train station is linked with the city centre by bus Nos 7 and 8; line No 1 runs along the waterfront from the train station north to Le Croiseur Colbert and beyond. Single tickets (€1.15), sold on board, are *not* valid for transfers. The Bordeaux Découverte card, available at the tourist office, allows unlimited travel for one/three/six days (€3.60/8.30/11.80). Time-stamp it only the first time you use it.

There are night bus services on nights when big shows and sporting events take place at the Grand Théâtre, Palais des Sports and Théâtre Femina. On weekends, night buses run on line S11, between place de la Victoire and the night-club zone on quai de la Paludate.

CAR
Parking in the city centre is hard to find and pricey. Places to look for free spaces include the side streets north of the Musée d'Art Contemporain and west of the Jardin Public. Many hotels provide parking for around €6 to per night. There are large parking lots to the north of esplanade des Quinconces and opposite place de la Bourse.

TAXI
To order a taxi call ☎ 05 56 99 28 41.

TRAM
The first section of the new tramway system, Line A, opened in December 2003. It starts at the Mériadeck shopping centre to the west of the city centre, and continues east along cours d'Alsace et Lorraine before crossing the river and continuing 10km eastwards to the suburb of Cenon. Another two lines were due to open as this book went to press. Line B will start at esplanade des Quinconces, heading south to place de la Victoire and on to the university. Line C will link esplanade des Quinconces with the train station via the riverside.

When the service is fully operational, trams will run every 10 minutes between 5am and 1am. Purchase a ticket (€1.15) from the machine at your tram stop and stamp it on board. Découverte cards are also valid on the trams.

BORDEAUX WINE-GROWING REGION
The 1000-sq-km wine-growing area around the city of Bordeaux is, along with Burgundy, France's most important producer of top-quality wines. The region is divided into 57 appellations (production areas whose soil and microclimate impart distinctive characteristics on the wine produced there) that are grouped into seven *familles* and subdivided into a hierarchy of designations (eg *premier grand cru classé*, the most prestigious) that often vary from appellation to appellation.

The majority of the region's many wines – reds, rosés, sweet and dry whites and sparkling wines – have all earned the right to include the abbreviation AOC (Appellation d'Origine Contrôlée) on their labels, indicating that the contents have been grown, fermented and aged according to strict regulations governing such matters as the number of vines permitted per hectare and acceptable pruning methods.

Bordeaux has over 5000 chateaux (also known as *domaines, crus* or *clos*), a term that in this context refers not to palatial residences but rather to the properties where grapes are raised, picked, fermented and then matured as wine. The smaller chateaux sometimes accept walk-in visitors, but at many places, especially the better-known ones, you have to make advance reservations by phone. Many chateaux are closed during the *vendange* (grape harvest) in October.

Information
In Bordeaux, the **Maison du Vin de Bordeaux** (☎ 05 56 00 22 88; 3 cours du 30 Juillet; ◷ 8.30am-4.30pm Mon-Fri), across the street from the tourist office, can supply you with a free, colour-coded map of production areas, details on chateau visits, and the addresses of local *maisons du vin* (tourist offices that deal mainly with winery visits).

Tours
On Wednesday and Saturday (daily from May to October) at about 1.30pm, the Bordeaux tourist office runs five-hour bus tours in French and English to wine chateaux in the area (adult/student/child under 12 €26/23/11.50). From May to October all-day trips (adult/student/child €47/40/23.50) to wine chateaux, starting with a tour and lunch in Bordeaux, begin at 9.15am on Wednesday and Saturday.

More information on winery tours appears on p640.

THE MÉDOC
Northwest of Bordeaux, along the western shore of the Gironde Estuary – formed by the confluence of the Garonne and Dordogne Rivers – lie some of Bordeaux's most celebrated vineyards. To the west, fine-sand beaches, bordered by dunes and *étangs* (lagoons), stretch for some 200km from Pointe de Grave south along the **Côte d'Argent** (Silver Coast) to the Bassin d'Arcachon and beyond; seaside resorts include **Soulac-sur-Mer** (see later), **Carcans Plage, Lacanau-Océan** and **Cap Ferret**. The coastal dunes abut a vast pine forest planted in the 19th century to stabilise the drifting sands and prevent them from encroaching on areas further inland.

ATLANTIC COAST

Getting There & Away

The northern tip of the Médoc, Pointe de Grave, is linked to Royan by **car ferries** (☎ 05 46 38 35 15; one-way person/bicycle/motorcycle/car €3/1.50/9.40/20; 25min) that run six times daily in winter and every 45 minutes in summer. The service runs until sometime between 6.30pm and 8.30pm (7.15pm and 9.30pm from Royan), depending on the season.

There is another **car ferry** (☎ 05 57 42 04 49; one-way person/bicycle/car/motorcycle €3/1.50/12/7) linking Lamarque (between Pauillac and Margaux on the D2) with Blaye, running five to 10 times daily (every 1½ hours June to September). This service starts around 7.30am and ends between 6.30pm and 8pm (until 9pm Saturday and Sunday June to September).

Citram Aquitaine buses (☎ 05 56 43 68 43) link Bordeaux with Margaux (€5.70, 50 minutes), Pauillac (€8.60, 1½ hours), Lesparre Médoc (€11.40, 1½ hours), Soulac-sur-Mer (€13.30, two hours) and Point de Grave (€13.30, 2¼ hours).

Soulac is also linked to Bordeaux by train (€13.60, two hours, change at Lesparre, four daily) and SNCF buses (€13.80, two hours, two to five daily).

To reach the Médoc by car from Bordeaux, take exit *(sortie)* 7 to get off the Bordeaux Rocade (ring road).

Pauillac & Médoc Wine Information Centre

While Pauillac is a fairly unremarkable port town by the banks of the muddy Gironde, it is at the heart of the wine country, surrounded by the distinguished Haut-Médoc, Margaux and St-Julien appellations. The Pauillac wine appellation encompasses 18 *crus classés* including the world-renowned Mouton Rothschild, Latour and Lafite Rothschild.

The Pauillac tourist office houses the **Maison du Tourisme et du Vin** (☎ 05 56 59 03 08; www .pauillac-medoc.com; ☽ 9am-7pm Jul–mid-Sep; 9.30am-12.30pm & 2-6.30pm Jun & mid-Sep–Nov; 9.30am-12.30pm & 2-6pm Mon-Sat, 10.30am-12.30pm & 3-6pm Sun Dec-May), an excellent centre for information about the Médoc region. They can also make appointments (for €3.90) to visit specific wine cellars, and have information on the many *chambres d'hôtes* (B&Bs) in the area. A good resource available here is the Médoc *Guide Découverte* brochure, which lists chateaux and how to visit them.

Vineyards & Chateaux

The gravelly soil of the Médoc's gently rolling hills supports orderly rows of meticulously tended grape vines (mainly Cabernet Sauvignon) that produce some of the world's most sought-after red wines. The most beautiful part of this renowned wine-growing area is north of Pauillac, along the D2 and the D204 (towards Lesparre). To the north, the vines give way to evergreen forests.

Chateaux in the Pauillac appellation that welcome visitors by appointment include the beautifully landscaped **Château Lafite Rothschild** (☎ 05 56 73 18 18; www.lafite.com; admission free; ☽ Mon-Fri Nov-Jul), famed for its premier *grand cru classé*, and whose free, bilingual, one-hour tours (including a tasting session) take place on weekdays; and the equally illustrious **Château Mouton Rothschild** (☎ 05 56 73 21 29; fax 05 56 73 21 28; ☽ daily Apr-Nov, Mon-Fri Jan-Dec), whose tours, frequently in English, cost €5 (more including a tasting session). Both places require you to make advance reservations.

About 20km to the south in Margaux, you can visit the celebrated **Château Margaux** (☎ 05 57 88 83 83; www.chateau-margaux.com; ☽ 10am-noon & 2-4pm Mon-Fri Sep-Jul). It is closed during the grape harvest.

Château Palmer (☎ 05 57 88 72 72; www.chateau -palmer.com), on the D2, 3km south of Margaux in Issan, has one-hour tours (€5) including tastings on weekdays (daily from April to September). Again, both chateaux require advance reservations.

Soulac-sur-Mer

pop 2800

Soulac, which is 9km south of Pointe de Grave and 90km north of Bordeaux, is a lively seaside resort in summer and an almost dead seaside town the rest of the year. The beach, fronted by a promenade, is wide and safe. The mellow waves here are ideal for learning to surf; a variety of courses are offered by **Soulac Surf School** (reservations through the tourist office) between April and October.

ORIENTATION & INFORMATION

The commercial centre is along pedestrianised rue de la Plage, which runs perpendicular to the beach. The train station is 700m south of the town's Romanesque church, buried by drifting dunes in 1757 and dug out a century later.

The **tourist office** (☎ 05 56 09 86 61; www.sou lac.com; 68 rue de la Plage; ⏱ 9am-7pm Jul & Aug; 9am-12.30pm & 2-5.30pm Mon-Fri, 10am-12.30pm & 3-5.30pm Sat Sep-Jun; plus 10am-12.30pm & 3-5.30pm Sun during Apr-Jun & school holidays), is across from the **marché municipal** (a covered food market that opens every morning).

The **post office** (rue du Maréchal d'Ornano), which does currency exchange, is one block northeast of the tourist office.

SLEEPING & EATING

Ask at the tourist office about furnished villa rental. Rooms and camping grounds are always full in July and August.

Hôtel L'Hacienda (☎ 05 56 09 81 34; www.logis -gironde.com in French; rue des Lacs; r in winter/summer €42/58) The amiable, multilingual couple that run this two-star hotel have individually decorated the rooms to a high standard. It's in a quiet spot, 150m south of the church, with a shady garden. The **restaurant** (closed Sunday night in winter) serves good seafood and generous *menus* (€10/18/25). The interior is a bit dull, but meals are also served in the garden in season.

Hôtel La Dame de Cœur (☎ 05 56 09 80 80; www.hotel-damedecoeur.com; 103 rue de la Plage; s/d/tr €31/40/46, Jul & Aug €36.50/52/62.50) A two-star hotel notable more for its giant Queen of Hearts playing card sign than for its ordinary rooms. Reception opens at 6pm in the low season. During July and August, the price includes compulsory breakfast.

There are **pizzerias**, **Tex-Mex** and **seafood** eateries along rue de la Plage.

ST-ÉMILION

pop 2500

The medieval village of St-Émilion, 39km east of Bordeaux, is surrounded by vineyards renowned for their full-bodied, deeply coloured red wines. It is named after Émilion, a miracle-working Benedictine monk who came here from Brittany and lived in a cave between 750 and 767. The monastery founded on this site later became a stop on medieval pilgrimage routes.

Today, St-Émilion and seven surrounding districts have been recognised as a Unesco World Heritage Site. Situated on two limestone hills that look out over the Dordogne River valley, its ramparts (dating to the 13th century) and the rest of the town take on a luscious golden hue as the sun

sets. Not even the vast numbers of tourists who flock here can spoil the charm.

Information

The **tourist office** (☎ 05 57 55 28 28; www.saint -emilion-tourisme.com; place des Créneaux; ⏱ 9.30am-7pm mid-Jun–mid-Sep, 9.30am-12.30pm & 1.45-6pm mid-Sep–mid-Jun) has brochures in English and details on visiting almost 100 nearby chateaux. During the summer the tourist office opens an **information kiosk** (place de l'Église Monolithe), selling tickets to places of interest. Opening times vary (usually 10am to noon and 2pm to 6pm Monday to Friday and some weekends).

The post office, which can exchange currency, the pharmacy, and banks are along rue Guadet.

Sights

The town's most interesting historical sites can only be visited with one of the tourist office's 45-minute guided tours. The worthwhile tours (adult/student/child €5.50/3.60/2.90, plus entry to the sites) depart regularly throughout the day. Most are in French, although an English translation is available – call ahead to check English tour times (usually at 1pm).

The tour is the only way to see the astounding **Église Monolithe**, carved out of limestone from the 9th to the 12th centuries; and the **Grotte de l'Ermitage**, the hermit saint's famous cave where his uncomfortable-looking stone bed can be seen.

You can climb the **clocher** (bell tower; ☎ 05 57 55 28 28; entrance on place des Créneaux; admission €1; ⏱ 9.30am-7pm mid-Jun–mid-Sep, 9.30am-12.30pm & 1.45-6pm mid-Sep–mid-Jun) above the church for a splendid view of the village. If it's closed, they'll give you a key at the tourist office.

The impressive former **Collégiale** (Collegiate Church) has a narrow, domed, Romanesque nave that dates from the 12th century, and a spacious vaulted choir (14th to 16th century) that's almost square. Free concerts are held here during summer (every Thursday, 6pm). **Cloître de l'Église Collégiale**, the church's tranquil 14th-century cloister, is accessible through the tourist office building.

Several of the city's medieval gates survive, including **Porte de la Cadène** (Gate of the Chain), off rue Guadet. Next door is **Maison de la Cadène**, a half-timbered house from the early 16th century.

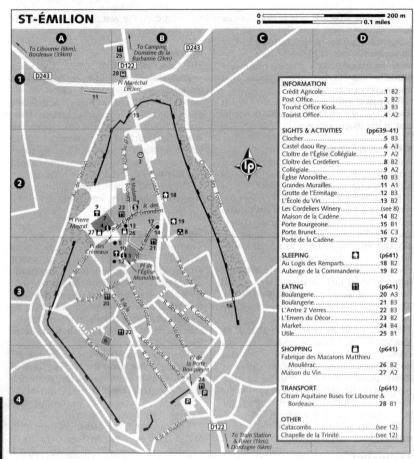

ST-ÉMILION

0   200 m
0   0.1 miles

To Libourne (8km);
Bordeaux (39km)

To Camping
Domaine de la
Barbanne (2km)

INFORMATION
Crédit Agricole...1 B2
Post Office..2 B2
Tourist Office Kiosk................................3 B3
Tourist Office...4 A2

SIGHTS & ACTIVITIES   (pp639–41)
Clocher..5 B3
Castel daou Rey......................................6 A3
Cloître de l'Église Collégiale....................7 A2
Cloître des Cordeliers............................8 B2
Collégiale...9 A2
Église Monolithe...................................10 B3
Grandes Murailles..................................11 A1
Grotte de l'Ermitage...............................12 B3
L'École du Vin......................................13 B2
Les Cordeliers Winery.........................(see 8)
Maison de la Cadène.............................14 B2
Porte Bourgeoise...................................15 B1
Porte Brunet..16 C3
Porte de la Cadène................................17 B2

SLEEPING   (p641)
Au Logis des Remparts...........................18 B3
Auberge de la Commanderie....................19 B2

EATING   (p641)
Boulangerie...20 A3
Boulangerie...21 B3
L'Antre 2 Verres....................................22 B3
L'Envers du Décor.................................23 B2
Market..24 B4
Utile..25 B1

SHOPPING   (p641)
Fabrique des Macarons Matthieu
    Mouliérac.......................................26 B2
Maison du Vin......................................27 A2

TRANSPORT   (p641)
Citram Aquitaine Buses for Libourne &
    Bordeaux...28 B1

OTHER
Catacombs...(see 12)
Chapelle de la Trinité..........................(see 12)

To Train Station
& River (1km);
Dordogne (6km)

Cloître des Cordeliers (rue des Cordeliers; admission free; ☺ year-round) is a ruined monastery. **Les Cordeliers** (☎ 05 57 24 72 07), the winery that has occupied part of the site for over a century, makes sparkling wine. It runs interesting **guided cellar tours** (admission €3.80; ☺ 11am, 3pm, 5pm & 6.30pm Jun–mid-Jul, Sep & Oct; 11am, 3pm, 4.30pm, 5.30pm, 6.30pm & 7.30pm mid-Jul–Aug; 3pm & 5.15pm Apr, Nov & Dec, 4.30pm Jan-Mar) that include a wine and macaroon tasting.

The 13th-century donjon known as the **Castel daou Rey** (Tour du Roi, King's Tower; admission €1; ☺ 9.30am-8.30pm Jun-Sep; variable opening hours out of season), the only remains of what is believed to have been a royal fortress, affords exceptional views of the town and the Dordogne Valley.

Activities
Introductory wine-tasting classes are available in English every day at **L'École du Vin** (☎ 05 57 74 44 29; www.vignobleschateaux.fr; Vignobles & Châteaux, 4 rue du Clocher). The courses (3pm; 1½ hours; €20) are great fun, with games to identify aromas and tastes plus a blind tasting session. Between November and March they're by appointment only. From mid-July to mid-September, the **Maison du Vin** (opposite) also offers bilingual, 1½-hour classes daily (€17).

Tours
The tourist office organises two-hour afternoon **chateau visits** (adult/12-17 yrs €9/6; ☺ Mon-Sat May-Sep) in French and English. It also has

details of concerts and wine-tasting events taking place in local chateaux.

Sleeping

Accommodation in St-Émilion can get very pricey in summer. The tourist office has a list of nearby **chambres d'hôtes**, which generally charge €40 to €70 for a double.

Auberge de la Commanderie (☎ 05 57 24 70 19; www.aubergedelacommanderie.com; rue des Cordeliers; d €60-100, q duplex apartments €120; ⚑ mid-Feb–mid-Jan) Despite the building being of medieval origin, the rooms are modern and very comfortable. The relative appeal of the giant, gaudy in-room murals is a matter of personal taste. A few of the rooms have vineyard-views.

Au Logis des Remparts (☎ 05 57 24 70 43; logis-des-remparts@saint-emilion.org; 18 rue Guadet; d €68-130; ⚑ mid-Jan–mid-Dec; P ⚑) This appealing Gothic house has been completely renovated for three-star comfort, although occasional stained-glass windows and exposed stone keep it true to its origins. Facilities include 17 pleasant rooms, an air-conditioned bar and a large sunny terrace.

CAMPING

Camping Domaine de la Barbanne (☎ 05 57 24 75 80; www.camping-saint-emilion.com; route de Montagne; camping €12.50-18; ⚑ Apr-Sep; ⚑) With three stars and two swimming pools, this place is about 2km north of St-Émilion on the D122.

Eating

L'Envers du Décor (☎ 05 57 74 48 31; rue du Clocher; menus €15 & €25, mains €9-14; ⚑ closed dinner Sun) Inside is an attractive, ambient restaurant/wine bar; outside is a tranquil terrace backing on the Collégiale. Take a seat in either for tasty bistro-style cuisine and fine wine by the glass or the bottle.

L'Antre 2 Verres (☎ 05 57 24 09 73; escalette de la Tour du Roi; menus €14.50-25; ⚑ lunch daily, dinner Sat & Sun) An atmospheric, cave-like eatery occupying limestone hollows at the foot of the Castel daou Rey. Traditional and creative French dishes with, unsurprisingly, a big choice of local wines.

SELF-CATERING

The grocery **Utile** (⚑ 8am-7pm Mon-Sat, 8am-1pm Sun Jun–mid-Sep; 8am-12.30pm & 2-7pm Mon-Fri, 8am-1pm Sun mid-Sep–May) is on the D122, 150m north of town.

There are two **boulangeries** at rue Guadet and rue de la Grande Fontaine; both open to 6pm or 7pm.

There is a **market** every Sunday on place de la Porte Bouqueyre.

Shopping

St-Émilion's quaint streets and squares are lined with wine shops – about 50 of them, one for every eight of the old city's residents!

Maison du Vin (☎ 05 57 55 50 55; place Pierre Meyrat; ⚑ 9.30am-12.30pm & 2-6pm Sep-Jul, 9.30am-7pm Aug), owned by the 250 chateaux whose wines it sells, has exhibitions and publications on local wines.

The recipe for *macarons* (macaroons) was brought to St-Émilion in the 17th century by Ursuline nuns. To this day, the local biscuits are renowned for their soft, fluffy texture and subtle almond flavour. **Fabrique des Macarons Matthieu Mouliérac** (Tertre de la Tente; ⚑ closed mornings Jan-Mar) charges €5 per two dozen. There's another macaroon bakery next to the post office.

Getting There & Away

St-Émilion can be visited as a day trip from Bordeaux by bus and/or train. **Citram Aquitaine** (☎ 05 56 43 68 43) buses to/from Bordeaux's Halte Routière run at least once daily (except on Sunday and holidays from October to April) to Libourne (€5.70, 45 minutes); from there you take a **Marchesseau** (☎ 05 57 40 60 79) bus to St-Émilion (€2, 10 minutes). There's talk of operating a direct service during July and August; contact Citram Aquitaine for the latest.

The SNCF has three autorails daily (two on Sunday and holidays) from Bordeaux (€6.80, 40 minutes); the last train back usually departs at 6.26pm.

By car from Bordeaux, follow the signs for Libourne and take the D243.

Year-round, the tourist office rents out bicycles for €9.15/13.75 per half-day/day.

ARCACHON

pop 11,800

The coastal resort of Arcachon became popular with bourgeois residents of Bordeaux at the end of the 19th century. It's not hard to see why – beach lovers can frolic away sunny days on the long, sandy seashore and nearby Dune de Pyla (p644),

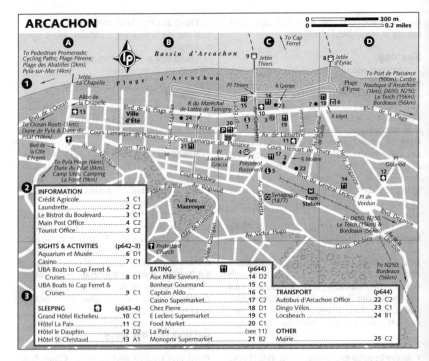

ARCACHON

0 ▬▬▬▬ 300 m
0 ▬▬▬▬ 0.2 miles

Bassin d'Arcachon

INFORMATION	
Crédit Agricole	1 C1
Laundrette	2 C2
Le Bistrot du Boulevard	3 C1
Main Post Office	4 C2
Tourist Office	5 C2

SIGHTS & ACTIVITIES	(p642–3)
Aquarium et Musée	6 D1
Casino	7 C1
UBA Boats to Cap Ferret &	
Cruises	8 D1
UBA Boats to Cap Ferret &	
Cruises	9 C1

SLEEPING	(p643–4)
Grand Hôtel Richelieu	10 C1
Hôtel La Paix	11 C2
Hôtel le Dauphin	12 D2
Hôtel St-Christaud	13 A1

EATING	(p644)
Aux Mille Saveurs	14 D2
Bonheur Gourmand	15 C1
Captain Aldo	16 C2
Casino Supermarket	17 C2
Chez Pierre	18 D1
E Leclerc Supermarket	19 C1
Food Market	20 C1
La Paix	(see 11)
Monoprix Supermarket	21 B2

TRANSPORT	(p644)
Autobus d'Arcachon Office	22 C2
Dingo Vélos	23 C1
Locabeach	24 B1

| **OTHER** | |
| Mairie | 25 C2 |

Europe's highest sand dune. The town itself is not overly attractive but it does have a certain laid-back charm and a pretty inner-suburb of heyday villas harks back to its golden era.

Arcachon makes an easy day trip from Bordeaux, meaning it's often crowded in summer. To escape the hordes, grab a bike and explore the practically deserted out-of-town beaches.

Orientation

Arcachon is on the southern side of the triangular Bassin d'Arcachon (Arcachon Bay), which is linked to the Atlantic by a 3km-wide channel just west of town. The narrow peninsula of Cap Ferret is on the other side of the outlet. The Dune de Pyla begins 8km to the south of Arcachon along the D218.

Arcachon's main commercial streets run parallel to the beach: blvd de la Plage, cours Lamarque de Plaisance and cours Héricart de Thury. Perpendicular to the beach, busy streets include av Gambetta and rue du Maréchal de Lattre de Tassigny.

Information

Credit Agricole (252 Blvd de la Plage) Only bank that will change money.

Le Bistrot du Boulevard (☎ 05 56 83 45 67; 230 blvd de la Plage; per hr €7.50; ☺ 11am-11pm)

Post Office (place Président Roosevelt) Offers currency exchange services, has Cyberposte.

Tourist Office (☎ 05 57 52 97 97; www.arcachon.com; place Président Roosevelt; ☺ 9am-7pm Jul & Aug; 9am-6.30pm Mon-Fri, 9am-5pm Sat, 10am-noon & 1-5pm Sun Apr-Jun & Sep; 9am-6pm Mon-Fri, 9am-5pm Sat Oct-Mar)

Sights

The flat area that abuts the **Plage d'Arcachon** (the town's beach) is known as the **Ville d'Été** (Summer Quarter). The liveliest section is around **Jetée Thiers**, one of the two piers.

In front of the eastern pier, **Jetée D'Eyrac**, stands the town's appealing **casino** building, resembling a Renaissance château transplanted from the Loire. The intricate lines of the façade are juxtaposed against brash neon signs after dark.

The **Aquarium et Musée** (☎ 05 56 83 33 32; 2 rue du Professeur Jolyet; adult/student/under 10 €4.40/3/2.80; ☺ 9.45am-12.15pm & 1.45-7pm Jun-Aug, to 6.30pm Mar-

May & Sep-Nov; closed Dec-Feb) in a wooden shack opposite the casino, is uninspiring with a collection of fish in small tanks and other basic displays.

The elegant **Ville d'Hiver** (Winter Quarter), on the tree-covered hillside south of the Ville d'Été, dates back 100 years. Over 300 villas, many decorated with delicate wood tracery, range in style from neo-Gothic through to colonial. The easy stroll up to the higher ground is aided by the unusual deco-style **public lift** (€0.15; ☾ 9am-12.45pm, 2.30-7pm). The lift is in Parc Mauresque at the southern end of rue du Maréchal de Lattre de Tassigny.

A lovely **pedestrian promenade** lined with trees and playgrounds runs west and then south from the Plage d'Arcachon to **Plage Péreire**, **Plage des Abatilles** and **Pyla-sur-Mer**.

Activities

High-quality **cycle paths** link Arcachon with the Dune de Pyla and Biscarosse (30km to the south), and go all the way around the Bassin d'Arcachon to Cap Ferret. From here, a cyclable path parallels the near-deserted beaches all the way to Pointe de Grave. You can take cycles aboard the boat to Cap Ferret.

The exposed ocean beaches to the south of town generally offer good conditions for surfing. Lessons and equipment hire are offered by **Ocean Roots** (☎ 06 62 26 04 11; 27 av Saint Francois Xavier; oceanrclub@hotmail.com).

Centre Nautique d'Arcachon (☎ 05 56 22 36 83; quai Goslar; ☾ Apr-Sep), 1.5km east of the Jetée d'Eyrac at the Port de Plaisance (Pleasure Boat Port), rents sea kayaks, windsurfing and diving equipment, and offers courses.

Tours

Les Bateliers Arcachonnais (UBA; ☎ 05 57 72 28 28; www.bateliers-arcachon.asso.fr in French) runs ferries from Jetée Thiers to the pine-shaded town of **Cap Ferret** (return ticket adult/child €10/6), across the mouth of the Bassin d'Arcachon. From April to October, boats run four to 20 times daily, depending on the season; the rest of the year there are two sailings on Monday, Wednesday and Friday and four sailings on Saturday and Sunday.

The company also runs daily, year-round cruises around the **Île aux Oiseaux** (adult/child €13/9), the uninhabited island in the middle of the bay. It's a haven for tern,

curlew and redshank, so take your binoculars. There's also an informative running commentary. In July and August there are all-day excursions to the **Banc d'Arguin**, the sand bank off the Dune de Pyla (€15/10, leaving Arcachon 11am).

Sleeping

During July and August, prices go up dramatically and it is extremely difficult to find accommodation. Some hotels require that you take half-board. The tourist office can provide information on furnished rental houses and apartments.

Hôtel La Paix (☎ 05 56 83 05 65; fax 05 56 83 05 65; 8 av de Lamartine; s/d from €25.80/28.90, with shower & toilet €33.30/36.10, half-board d €54-62, studio apartments for 2 per week from €152.40-290, in summer from €320-487; ☾ late Apr-Nov) A charming, friendly and down-to-earth place in a quaint old house, 200m from the beach. Prices vary greatly according to season; from June to September, half-board is obligatory.

Hôtel St-Christaud (☎ /fax 05 56 83 38 53; 8 allée de la Chapelle; d with washbasin €21-35, with shower & toilet €31-47; ☾ year-round) A rambling old house with a maze of simple rooms in varying states of renovation. Facilities are basic, but prices are reasonable.

Hôtel le Dauphin (☎ 05 56 83 02 89; www.dauphin-arcachon.com; 7 av Gounod; d €55-84, q €60-105; P ☒ ☒) This attractive patterned-brick mansion house dates from 1818, although the décor, all tiling and cork panelling, is unmistakably 1970s. Back-lit mirrors and brown-toned bathrooms continue the theme. As well as spotless doubles, there are some family rooms available, all of which have satellite TV.

Grand Hôtel Richelieu (☎ 05 56 83 16 50; www .grand-hotel-richelieu.com; 185 blvd de la Plage; standard d €60-98, deluxe d €120-160; P ☒) With a hint of the grand bourgeois Arcachon of 100 years ago, this refined hotel, just a few steps from the beach, is the best located in town. The only drawback is the smallish size of some of the rooms. Deluxe rooms are larger, with bath and fantastic bay views.

Camping

The steep, inland side of the Dune de Pyla, 10km south of town, is gradually burying five large and rather pricey camping grounds, most of them half-hidden in a forest of pine trees.

La Forêt (☎ 05 56 22 73 28; www.campinglaforet.fr; route de Biscarosse; camping €12.25-26.50; 🏕 Apr–mid-Oct; 🏊) A well-run, three-star place with plenty of shade and good amenities. Prices vary depending on the season.

Eating

The beachfront promenade between Jetée Thiers and Jetée d'Eyrac is lined with **tourist restaurants** and places offering pizza and crepes. Locals tend to avoid this slightly tacky strip, but it has a lively atmosphere and competition keeps prices reasonable.

For a quick lunch-time bite or something to take to the beach, head for **Bonheur Gourmand** (🏕 10.30am-6pm), a tiny kiosk near Jetée Thiers making delicious sandwiches to order.

Chez Pierre (☎ 05 56 22 52 94; 1 blvd Veyrier Montagnères; menus from €19) One of the better (and more upmarket) restaurants on the seaside strip. As you enjoy the seafood specialities on offer, you can gaze out from the terrace to the rippling waters.

La Paix (see Sleeping; menus from €10; 🏕 Jun–mid-Sep) One of the more unusual and appealing places to eat in town, this conservatory-like wood and glass enclosure is dripping with assorted greenery. Traditional French food is on the menu.

Captain Aldo (☎ 05 56 83 78 81; 22 blvd Veyrier Montagnères; menus from €19) Another popular eatery on the beach, with a relaxed and family-friendly terrace. Choose from the lobsters in the tank or from the large selection of fresh fish on display. If you're over-fished, there are Italian options too.

Aux Mille Saveurs (☎ 05 56 83 40 28; 25 blvd du Général Leclerc; menus €13.50-39; 🏕 closed Sun dinner, Mon) Fine, traditional dining in genteel surroundings.

SELF-CATERING

The lively **food market** (rue Roger Expert; 🏕 8am-1pm) is just north of the Mairie on the ground floor of a parking garage.

There's a **Casino supermarket** (57 blvd du Général Leclerc; 🏕 9am-12.30pm & 3-7pm Mon-Sat, 9am-noon Sun). Other supermarkets include **E Leclerc** (224 blvd de la Plage; 🏕 9am-7.30pm Mon-Sat & 9.30am-12.30pm Sun) and **Monoprix** (46 cours Lamarque de Plaisance; 🏕 8.30am-12.30pm & 2-7.30pm Mon-Sat).

Getting There & Away

Some of the trains from Bordeaux to Arcachon (€8.60, 50 minutes, 11 to 18 daily) are coordinated with TGVs from Paris' Gare Montparnasse. The last train back to Bordeaux usually leaves Arcachon at 8.15pm (9.51pm on Sundays and holidays).

Getting Around

There is unmetered parking south of the casino along av de Général de Gaulle.

Locabeach (☎ 05 56 83 39 64; www.locabeach.com; 326 blvd de la Plage; 🏕 9am-12.30pm & 2.30-7pm) rents out scooters and motorcycles starting at €39/215 per day/week.

To order a cab, call ☎ 05 56 83 88 88.

BICYCLE

At **Dingo Vélos** (☎ 05 56 83 44 09; www.dingovelos.com; rue Grenier; 🏕 9.30am-6.30pm daily Apr-Sep, until midnight July & Aug) you can rent tandems, *triplos*, *quatros* and *quintuplos* (bikes with places for two to five riders, half/full day €16/23) and pushme-pullyous (tandems whose riders face in opposite directions; 30 minutes for €4). Five-speeds/mountain bikes start at €10/13 per day.

AROUND ARCACHON
Dune de Pyla

This remarkable sand dune, also known as the Dune du Pilat, stretches from the mouth of the Bassin d'Arcachon southwards for almost 3km. Studies have shown it to be creeping eastwards at about 4.5m a year – it has already swallowed trees, a road junction and even an entire hotel, and at this rate the camping area at the base of the dune's steep eastern side appears to have a limited lifespan.

The view from the top – approximately 114m above sea level – is magnificent. To the west you can see the sandy shoals at the mouth of the Bassin d'Arcachon, including the **Banc d'Arguin bird reserve** and **Cap Ferret**. In the other direction, dense pine forests stretch from the base of the dune eastwards almost as far as the eye can see.

Caution is advised while swimming in this area: powerful currents swirl out to sea from the deceptively tranquil *baïnes* (baylets) that jut into the beach.

GETTING THERE & AWAY

There's a car park at the northern end of the dune.

The local bus company, **Autobus d'Arcachon** (☎ 05 57 72 45 00; 47 blvd du Général Leclerc), has daily

buses from the SNCF station in Arcachon to the Pyla Plage (Haïtza), 1km north of the dune (€2.70).

From mid-June to mid-September, buses continue south to the dune's car park, the camping grounds and Biscarosse.

Gujan Mestras

A bit east of Arcachon, the town of Gujan Mestras sprawls along 9km of coastline. This stretch of the bay is home to seven picturesque and lively oyster ports.

The **tourist office** (☎ 05 56 66 12 65; www.ville -gujanmestras.fr; 16 av De Lattre de Tassigny) is at the western edge of town in La Hume.

About 4km to the east, **Port de Larros**, the largest of the town's seven oyster ports, is lined with weathered wood shacks, with flat-bottom oystering boats moored out the front. The small **Maison de l'Huître** (☎ 05 56 66 23 71; adult/child €2.80/2; 10am-12.30pm & 2.30-6pm Mon-Sat) has a display on oyster farming including a short film in English.

Just 100m away you'll find the little shop **Cap Noroit** (☎ /fax 05 56 66 04 15; 112 allée du Haurat), where you can buy super-fresh Banc d'Arguin oysters (the area's finest) direct from the growers. A dozen medium oysters costs just €3. Seafood restaurants nearby include **Les Viviers** (☎ 05 56 66 01 04), at the port, and **Les Pavois** (☎ 05 56 66 38 71; closed Mon), next to the Maison de l'Huitre. Both charge from around €12 for a dozen oys-

ters which they serve on their waterside terraces.

The Gujan Mestras **train station**, not far from Port de Larros, is on the train line linking Bordeaux with Arcachon. The tiny train station in La Hume is 50 metres west of the tourist office.

Le Teich Parc Ornithologique

Only 29% of the shallow Bassin d'Arcachon, a 155-sq-km tidal bay, is underwater at low tide, making it an ideal habitat for birds. Indeed, some 260 species, both migratory and nonmigratory, visit each year.

The idyllic **Parc Ornithologique** (Bird Reserve; ☎ 05 56 22 80 93; www.parc-ornithologique-du-teich .com; adult/child 5-14 yrs €6.40/4.60; 10am-8pm Jul & Aug, to 7pm mid-Apr–Jun & early Sep–mid-Sep, to 6pm mid-Sep–mid-Apr) at Le Teich, in the southeastern corner of the bay at the mouth of the multi-channelled River Leyre (l'Eyre), is an important centre for the preservation of endangered species. It's an outstanding place to see some of Europe's rarest and most beautiful birds.

It's easiest to observe the birds at high tide. Tidal schedules, available at local tourist offices, appear on the back page of the regional daily *Sud Ouest*.

The Parc Ornithologique is in Le Teich, 15km east of Arcachon on the D650. Le Teich's train station, 1.2km south of the park, is linked with Bordeaux and Arcachon.

French Basque Country

CONTENTS

Bayonne	649
Biarritz	654
St-Jean de Luz & Ciboure	658
Around St-Jean de Luz	662
St-Jean Pied de Port	663
Around St-Jean Pied de Port	666

The Basque Country ('Euskal Herria' in the Basque language) – the area around the western foothills of the Pyrenees (Pyrénées in French) as it slopes down to the Bay of Biscay – has been home to the Basque people for many centuries. The area straddles modern-day France and Spain (with roughly 20% on the French side) but it's still a land apart, stubbornly independent and profoundly different from either of the nation-states that have adopted it.

The French side (called 'Iparralde' in Basque or 'Le Pays Basque' in French), less populous and industrialised than the Spanish Basque region, is perhaps best known for its glitzy beach resort, Biarritz. But the medium-rise town, with bronzed surfers hooning around on mopeds and swarms of peak-season sun-seekers, is the least Basque of the area's towns.

More authentic is the cultural and administrative capital, Bayonne, where French and Basque influences successfully combine to create a unique atmosphere. Traditional Basque music, sports and festivals are a big part of the summer's entertainment and it's not just for the benefit of tourists. Bayonne is also an excellent base from which to explore the region as it has good transport links, restaurants and sleeping options.

To the southwest is St-Jean de Luz, a relaxed family beach resort. There's also a bustling fishing port there, so bring along an appetite and tuck into some tasty Basque seafood specialities.

You'll find the 'Iparralde' of old away from the coast and into the hills, with little one-street villages to discover and green valleys to explore. St-Jean Pied de Port offers a likely base for such excursions, as an age-old pit stop for pilgrims heading over the border to Santiago de Compostela.

HIGHLIGHTS

- Taste the delicious chocolates in **Bayonne** (p653)
- Surf the world-class waves at **Anglet Beach** (p654) near Biarritz
- Catch a frantic game of high-speed *pelote basque* (p653)
- Creep up the mountainside railway on **Le Petit Train de la Rhune** (p662)
- Follow the centuries-old footsteps of pilgrims near **St-Jean Pied de Port** (p665)

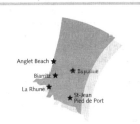

- POPULATION: 574,000
- AREA: 13,383 SQ KM

FRENCH BASQUE COUNTRY

History

The origins and early history of the Basque people are a mystery. Roman sources mention a tribe called the Vascones living in the area and it's attested that the Basques took over what is now southwestern France in the 6th century. Converting to Christianity in the 10th century, they are still known for their strong devotion to Catholicism.

After resisting invasions by Visigoths, Franks, Normans and Moors, the Basques on both sides of the Pyrenees emerged from the turbulent Middle Ages with a fair degree of local autonomy, which they retained in France until the Revolution. The French Basque Country, then part of the duchy of Aquitaine, was under Anglo-Norman rule from the mid-12th century until the mid-15th century.

Basque nationalism flourished before and during the Spanish Civil War (1936–39). Until the death of Franco, the Spanish dictator, in 1975, many Basque nationalists and anti-Franco guerrillas from the other side of the Pyrenees sheltered in France.

Some Basques still dream of carving an Euskadi state out of the Basque areas of Spain and France, and a few support the terrorist organisation Euskadi ta Azkatasuna (ETA), whose name means 'Basque Nation and Liberty'. While France remains peaceful, bombings and other barbarities are not uncommon in the Spanish Basque Country, and Spanish ETA terrorists often seek sanctuary in France.

Language

Basque (Euskara), the only language in southwestern Europe to have withstood the onslaught of Latin and its derivatives, is probably unrelated to any other tongue on earth. No one knows its origins. Theories relating it to languages of the Caucasus, east of the Black Sea, are nowadays discredited and many linguists think that similarities with the long-dead Iberian language come simply from contact between the Iberians and Basques rather than from a common source.

The first book in Basque, marking the beginning of Basque literature, was printed in 1545. Basque is now spoken by approximately a million people throughout Spain and France, nearly all of whom are bilingual. In the French Basque Country, the

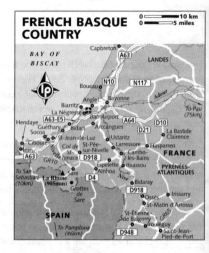

FRENCH BASQUE COUNTRY

language, widely spoken in Bayonne, is even more common in the hilly hinterland. Two TV stations in Spain and one in France broadcast in Basque, and you'll occasionally see on shop doors 'Hemen Euskara emaiten dugu' (Basque spoken here).

Basque Symbols

The Basque flag resembles the UK's but with a red field, a white vertical cross and a green diagonal one. Another common Basque symbol – the *lauburu* – resembles a curly swastika and is a sign of good luck or protection.

Sleeping

In coastal resorts, many holiday-makers return to the same hotel year after year. It can be extremely difficult to find a room in July and August, when room prices rise substantially and some hotels will insist on half board.

Sport

For a canter through the various kinds of *pelote basque,* see p653. To find out where to see them played, turn to the Sport sections in most towns.

Corrida, Spanish-style bullfighting in which the bull is killed, has devotees all over the Basque Country. Corridas take place intermittently during summer and advance reservations are usually necessary; enquire at either the Bayonne or Biarritz tourist offices.

Getting There & Away

All roads and train lines lead to Bayonne, which is easily accessible from the rest of France.

For rail travel to Spain, switch trains at the frontier since the Spanish track gauge is narrower. Take an SNCF train to Hendaye, where you can pick up the EuskoTren, familiarly known as 'El Topo' (The Mole), a shuttle train that runs via Irún to San Sebastián every half-hour until 9pm.

Year-round, the Spanish company Sema runs twice-daily buses between Bayonne and San Sebastián via St-Jean de Luz, while ATCRB operates a summer-only service.

The airport (p653) serving Bayonne and Biarritz has domestic flights as well as services to Switzerland and the UK.

Getting Around

A good rail service links the major towns and plentiful buses connect Bayonne, Biarritz and the surrounding beaches.

BAYONNE

pop 42,000

Founded as Lapurdum by the Romans, Bayonne ('Baiona' in Basque, meaning 'the good river') is the cultural and economic capital of the French Basque Country. Together with sprawling Anglet (the final 't' is pronounced) and Biarritz, 8km to the west, Bayonne forms an urban area (population around 100,000) sometimes known as BAB.

In contrast to the more upmarket seaside resort of Biarritz, Bayonne retains much of its Basqueness: the riverside buildings with their red and green shutters are typical of the region and you'll hear almost as much Euskara as French in certain quarters. Most of the graffiti around town are the work of nationalist groups seeking an independent Basque state.

The town is known for its smoked ham, chocolate and marzipan. According to tradition, the *baïonnette* (bayonet) was developed here in the early 17th century.

Orientation

The Rivers Adour and Nive split Bayonne into three: St-Esprit, the area north of the Adour; Grand Bayonne, the oldest part of the city, on the western bank of the Nive; and the very Basque Petit Bayonne quarter to its east.

MAPS

Local bus company STAB's free local bus map gives a stylised overview of the BAB conurbation. For something more detailed, buy Blay Foldex's *Bayonne Biarritz Anglet* or the Michelin equivalent.

Information

BOOKSHOPS

Mattin Megadenda (☎ 05 59 59 35 14; place de l'Arsenal) Texts on Basque history and culture, walking in the Basque Country, maps and CDs of Basque music.

INTERNET ACCESS

Cyber Net Café (☎ 05 59 50 85 10; place de la République; per hr €4.50; ⏰ 7am-11pm Mon-Sat, noon-11pm Sun)

LAUNDRY

Laverie St-Esprit (16 blvd Alsace-Lorraine; ⏰ 8am-8pm)
Hallwash (6 rue d'Espagne; ⏰ 8am-8pm)

POST

Main Post Office (rue de la Nouvelle Poste) About 1km northwest of the city centre.
Post Office (11 rue Jules Labat)
Post Office (21 blvd Alsace-Lorraine)

TOURIST INFORMATION

Tourist Office (☎ 05 59 46 01 46; www.bayonne-tourisme.com; place des Basques; ⏰ 9am-7pm Mon-Sat, 10am-1pm Sun Jul & Aug, 9am-6.30pm Mon-Fri, 10am-6pm Sat Sep-Jun) Has useful free brochures including *Fêtes*, listing French Basque Country cultural and sporting events, and *Tout à Loisir*, for hiking, biking and other activities. From July to mid-September, the office organises guided tours of the city (€5) at 10am from Monday to Saturday (in French except for Thursday's English-language tour).

Sights & Activities

RAMPARTS

Thanks to Vauban's 17th-century fortifications (see 'Vauban's Citadels', p30), now grass-covered and dotted with trees, a slim, green belt surrounds the city centre. You can walk the stretches of the old ramparts that rise above blvd Rempart Lachepaillet and rue Tour de Sault.

CATHÉDRALE STE-MARIE

Construction of Bayonne's Gothic **cathedral** (⏰ 7.30-11.45am & 3-5.45pm Mon-Sat, 3.30-5.45pm Sun) began in the 13th century, when Bayonne was ruled by the Anglo-Normans, and was completed well after France assumed control

FRENCH BASQUE COUNTRY

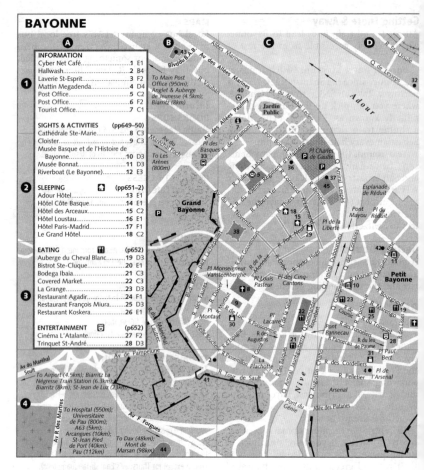

BAYONNE

INFORMATION	
Cyber Net Café	1 E1
Hallwash	2 B4
Laverie St-Esprit	3 F2
Mattin Megadenda	4 D4
Post Office	5 C2
Post Office	6 F2
Tourist Office	7 C1

SIGHTS & ACTIVITIES	(pp649–50)
Cathédrale Ste-Marie	8 C3
Cloister	9 C3
Musée Basque et de l'Histoire de Bayonne	10 D3
Musée Bonnat	11 D3
Riverboat (Le Bayonne)	12 E3

SLEEPING	(pp651–2)
Adour Hôtel	13 E1
Hôtel Côte Basque	14 E1
Hôtel des Arceaux	15 C2
Hôtel Loustau	16 E1
Hôtel Paris-Madrid	17 F1
Le Grand Hôtel	18 D3

EATING	(p652)
Auberge du Cheval Blanc	19 D3
Bistrot Ste-Cluque	20 E1
Bodega Ibaia	21 C3
Covered Market	22 C3
La Grange	23 D3
Restaurant Agadir	24 F1
Restaurant François Miura	25 D3
Restaurant Koskera	26 E1

ENTERTAINMENT	(p652)
Cinéma L'Atalante	27 F2
Trinquet St-André	28 D3

in 1451. These political changes are reflected in the ornamentation on the nave's vaulted ceiling, which includes both the English coat of arms (three lions) and that most French of emblems, the fleur-de-lys. The entrance to the stately 13th-century **cloister** (9am-12.30pm & 2-6pm Tue-Sun mid-May–mid-Sep, 9am-12.30pm & 2-5pm Tue-Sun mid-Sep–mid-May) is on place Louis Pasteur.

MUSÉE BASQUE ET DE L'HISTOIRE DE BAYONNE

This **museum** (05 59 46 61 90; 37 quai des Corsaires; adult/student/under 18 €5.50/3/free; 10am-6.30pm Tue-Sun May-Oct, 10am-12.30pm & 2-6pm Tue-Sun Nov-Apr) presents the history and culture of this unique people and also of Bayonne, their

prime fishing port and maritime window on the wider world.

There is a **combined ticket** (adult/student €9/4.50) to both the Musée Basque and **Musée Bonnat** (05 59 59 08 52; 5 rue Jacques Lafitte; adult/student/child €5.50/3/free; 10am-6.30pm Wed-Mon May-Oct, 10am-12.30pm & 2-6pm Wed-Mon Nov-Apr), which is an art gallery featuring canvases by El Greco, Goya and Degas, and a roomful of works by Rubens.

RIVER TRIPS

From mid-June to mid-September, the riverboat **Le Bayonne** (06 80 74 21 51) runs two-hour cruises on the River Adour from 10am until noon and 2.45pm until 7pm, if enough passengers turn up.

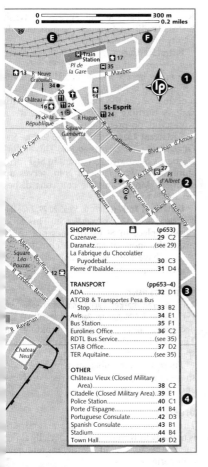

0 ___ 300 m
0 ___ 0.2 miles

SHOPPING	🛍	(p653)
Cazenave		29 C2
Daranatz		(see 29)
La Fabrique du Chocolatier		
Puyodebat		30 C3
Pierre d'Ibaïalde		31 D4

TRANSPORT		(pp653-4)
ADA		32 D1
ATCRB & Transportes Pesa Bus		
Stop		33 B2
Avis		34 E1
Bus Station		35 F1
Eurolines Office		36 C2
RDTL Bus Service		(see 35)
STAB Office		37 D2
TER Aquitaine		(see 35)

OTHER		
Château Vieux (Closed Military		
Area)		38 C2
Citadelle (Closed Military Area)		39 E1
Police Station		40 C1
Porte d'Espagne		41 B4
Portuguese Consulate		42 D3
Spanish Consulate		43 B1
Stadium		44 B4
Town Hall		45 D2

Festivals & Events

The town's premier fiesta is the five-day **Fêtes de Bayonne**, beginning on the first Wednesday in August. It includes a 'running of the bulls', like in Pamplona, Spain, only more benign. Here, they use cows not bulls – and most of the time, participants chase the frisky beasts rather than vice versa. The festival also includes Basque music, bullfights, fireworks, a float parade and rugby.

During Easter week, the town hosts a **Ham Fair**, honouring the *jambon de bayonne*, the acclaimed local ham. The **Journées du Chocolat**, on a variable weekend in May, are a celebration of chocolate, Bayonne's other claim to gastronomic fame.

Sleeping

Accommodation is extremely difficult to find from mid-July to mid-August – and it's near impossible to find during the Fêtes de Bayonne.

BUDGET

Hôtel Paris-Madrid (☎ 05 59 55 13 98; sorbois@wanadoo.fr; place de la Gare; s/d from €16/22, r with shower from €25; P) This friendly place is highly recommended, especially for those arriving at the station just across the road. The owners speak English and the rooms are good value – murals and large papier-mâché animals add some colour and artistic flair.

Hôtel des Arceaux (☎ 05 59 59 15 53; hotel.arceaux@wanadoo.fr; 26 rue Port Neuf; r with washbasin/shower €28/38) The rooms are well priced, if not particularly welcoming, but the new owners are embarking on a complete overhaul so by the time you read this, they should be offering sparkling new rooms for the same price. Rooms at the front have large windows overlooking the bustling pedestrian street below.

The **Auberge de Jeunesse** (☎ 05 59 58 70 00; anglet@fuaj.org; 19 route des Vignes, Anglet; B&B €17 first night, €14.20 subsequent nights; ⊙ mid-Feb–mid-Nov) in Anglet, complete with a Scottish pub, is lively and popular. Reservations are essential in summer. See p655 for details of the outdoor sports courses Anglet offers. The hostel also has some **camping** sites (per adult incl breakfast €10).

From Bayonne station, take STAB bus No 2 (direction Anglet). At the Cinq Cantons stop, change to No 72 (direction Les Plages), which stops at the hostel. Alternatively – and in high season when bus No 72 doesn't operate – take No 2 to the Moulin Barbot stop, from where the hostel is a 10-minute signed walk. On Sunday take line C from the town hall. From Biarritz station or place Clemenceau, take bus No 9 to the Moulin Barbot stop.

See p656 for details of BAB's camping grounds.

MID-RANGE

Hôtel Loustau (☎ 05 59 55 08 08; hotel.loustau@wanadoo.fr; 1 place de la République; s/d/tr/q from €72/76/82/88; ⊠ ⊠) A tall and attractive 18th-century building on the St-Esprit side of the town, with comfortable three-star rooms. On the southern side of the building, the full-length windows open out onto views of the River Adour.

FRENCH BASQUE COUNTRY

Adour Hôtel (☎ 05 59 55 11 31; www.adourhotel .net; 13 place Ste-Ursule; d/tr/q from €47/50/64) Just north of the River Adour and conveniently near the station, this friendly and helpful establishment has bright, airy rooms decorated along regional themes including bullfighting, rugby and gastronomy.

Hôtel Côte Basque (☎ 05 59 55 10 21; fax 05 59 55 39 85; 2 rue Maubec; d €40-46, tr €46-55) This place, also near the station, has taken a leap forward under its new owners. The rooms are pleasant and, for the most part, freshly decorated.

TOP END

Le Grand Hôtel (☎ 05 59 59 62 00, www.bw-legrand hotel.com; 21 rue Thiers; s €59-112, d €65-122; 🅿 🗙) This tastefully refurbished hotel, part of the Best Western chain, offers spacious creamtoned rooms with three-star facilities, including cable TV and room service. The old building was once a convent; you'd never guess from the slick, modern interior, but the grand façade has a certain amount of character.

Eating

You'll find a good selection of medium-priced restaurants around the covered market and all along quai Amiral Jauréguiberry.

Restaurant François Miura (☎ 05 59 59 49 89; 24 rue Marengo; menus €18.30 & €29; 🏵 closed Sun dinner & Wed) This ultrastylish place contrasts original postmodern décor with the raw timelessness of a 19th-century cloister. It's the place to be seen in Petit Bayonne, where the food, such as tender pigeon stuffed with foie gras, is just as fashionable as the clientele.

Bodega Ibaia (☎ 05 59 59 86 66; 45 quai Amiral Jauréguiberry; mains €8-12; 🏵 closed Sun & Mon lunch) This atmospheric Basque restaurant/tapas bar with wooden benches, sawdust on the floor and traditional Spanish tiling is less formal than most of the terrace restaurants on this popular stretch.

Auberge du Cheval Blanc (☎ 05 59 59 01 33; 68 rue Bourgneuf; menus €22, €32 & €68; closed Sun dinner & Mon Sep-Jun) Renowned as one of the town's most exclusive restaurants, this refined eatery fully deserves its Michelin star for its mouth-watering creative French cuisine. A must with the business set at lunch times.

La Grange (☎ 05 59 46 17 84; 26 quai Galuperie; mains €12-38; 🏵 closed Sun) With a shady outside terrace, this popular place overlooking the

River Nive has the ambience of a stylish bistro. Traditional French flavours include plenty of seafood options.

Bistrot Ste-Cluque (☎ 05 59 55 82 43; 9 rue Hugues; menu €16; open lunch & dinner to 10pm) There's only one *menu* here – a large blackboard that's propped up before you. Noisy (the music's a decibel or two too loud), smoky and with waiters bustling about everywhere, it's a wonderful, no-pretensions place.

Restaurant Agadir (☎ 05 59 55 66 56; 3 rue Ste-Catherine; menu €15.50; closed lunch Mon) This enthusiastically decorated restaurant in St-Esprit, shimmering with red and gold, serves up southern Moroccan-style couscous dishes priced €9 to €13.

Restaurant Koskera (☎ 05 59 55 20 79; 2 rue Hugues; menus around €10; 🏵 lunch Mon-Sat) This dark, cavelike place in St-Esprit does not really make the most of the local climate, but it does have inexpensive daily specials of hearty Basque fare.

SELF-CATERING

The **covered market** (quai Commandant Roquebert; 🏵 7am-1pm & 3.30-7pm Fri, 8am-1pm Mon-Thu & Sat) occupies an imposing riverside building. On Tuesday, Thursday and Saturday the market spills out onto the surrounding streets.

There are a number of tempting food shops and delicatessens along rue Port Neuf and rue d'Espagne.

Drinking

The greatest concentration of pubs and bars is in the Petit Bayonne area, especially along rue Pannecau, rue des Cordeliers and quai Galuperie.

Entertainment

Every Thursday in July and August, there's traditional **Basque music** (admission free) at 9.30pm in place Charles de Gaulle.

Between October and June **Trinquet St-André** (☎ 05 59 59 18 69; rue du Jeu de Paume; tickets around €9) stages *main nue* matches (see Pelota, p653) every Thursday at 4.30pm.

In summer, corridas are held from time to time at **Les Arènes** (av du Maréchal Foch), 1km west of the city centre. The tourist office has details of upcoming corridas and also sells tickets.

A filmgoers' cooperative, **Cinéma L'Atalante** (☎ 05 59 55 76 63; 7 rue Denis Etcheverry; adult/student €5.65/3.80) screens nondubbed films.

Cirque de Gavarnie (p690), Pyrenees

Sanctuaires Notre Dame
de Lourdes (p677)

Traditional houses along the River Nive in the Basque resort of St-Jean Pied de Port (p663)

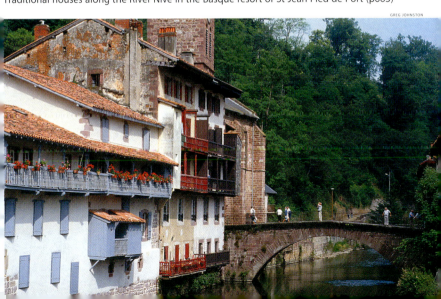

CHRISTOPHER WOOD

Cathédrale St-Étienne (p688),
Toulouse

Quai de la Daurade, River Garonne,
Toulouse (p695)

CHRISTOPHER WOOD

Unesco World Heritage–protected Pont du Gard (p738), north of Nîmes

PELOTA

Pelota (*pelote basque* in French) is the generic name for a group of games native to the Basque Country, all played using a hard ball with a rubber core (the *pelote*) which is struck with bare hands (*mains nues*), a wooden paddle *(pala or paleta)*, or a scoop-like racquet made of wicker, leather or wood and strapped to the wrist *(chistera)*.

Cesta punta, also known as jai alai, the world's fastest ball game and the most popular variety of pelota, became faster and faster after the introduction of rubber made it possible to produce balls with more bounce. The game is played with a *chistera*, with which players catch and hurl the ball with great force. Matches take place in a jai alai, or *cancha*, a three-walled court, usually a precise 53m long.

The walls and floor are made of materials that can withstand the repeated impact of the ball, which can reach speeds of up to 300km/h. A cancha and its tiers of balconies for spectators constitute a fronton. Other types of pelota (such as *joko-garbi, main nue, pala, paleta, pasaka, rebot* and *xare*) are played in outdoor, one-wall courts, also known as frontons, and in enclosed structures called *trinquets*.

Shopping

Bayonne is famous throughout France for its ham. For the lowest prices, visit the covered market (p652). For the best quality, visit a specialist shop such as **Pierre d'Ibaïlde** (☎ 05 59 25 65 30; 42 rue des Cordeliers) where you can taste before you buy.

The town's other claim to gastronomic fame is its chocolate. Two traditional *chocolateries* are **Daranatz** (☎ 05 59 59 03 05; 15 rue Port Neuf) and **Cazenave** (☎ 05 59 59 03 16; 19 rue Port Neuf) where you'll find chocolate pralines the size of apples to challenge even the most devout chocoholics. You can also see chocolate-making in progress at **La Fabrique du Chocolatier Puyodebat** (☎ 05 59 59 20 86; 5/7 rue de Luc; ⏰ 10.30am-noon & 4.30-6pm Tue-Sat).

Getting There & Away

AIR

Biarritz-Anglet-Bayonne airport (☎ 05 59 43 83 83; www.biarritz.aeroport.fr in French) is 5km southwest of central Bayonne and 3km southeast of the centre of Biarritz. Air France flies to/from Paris Orly about eight times daily and less frequently to Lyon and Geneva. Ryanair has a daily flight to/from London Stansted.

Bus No 6 links both Bayonne and Biarritz with the airport (buses depart roughly hourly). A taxi from the town centre costs around €14.

BUS

From place des Basques, **ATCRB buses** (☎ 05 59 26 06 99) follow the coast to the Spanish border. There are 10 services daily to St-Jean de Luz (€3.60, 40 minutes) with connections for Hendaye (€5.60, one hour). Summer beach traffic can double journey times. Transportes Pesa buses leave twice a day for Irún and San Sebastián in Spain (€6.20, 1¾ hours).

From the car park at the train station, **RDTL** (☎ 05 59 55 17 59) runs services northwards into Landes. For beaches north of Bayonne, such as Mimizan Plage and Moliets Plage, get off at Vieux Boucau (1¼ hours, six or seven daily). **TER Aquitaine** (☎ 05 59 27 45 98) has two buses daily to Pau (€14.50, 2¼ hours).

Bayonne is one of three centres in southwest France for **Eurolines** (☎ 05 59 59 19 33; 3 place Charles de Gaulle). Its buses stop in the square, opposite the company office.

CAR & MOTORCYCLE

Among several rental agencies near the train station are **ADA** (☎ 05 59 50 37 10; 11 quai de Lesseps) and **Avis** (☎ 05 59 55 06 56; 1 rue Ste-Ursule). Both open Monday to Saturday.

TRAIN

TGVs run between Bayonne and Paris' Gare Montparnasse (€71.60, five hours, five daily). Within the Basque Country, there are fairly frequent trains to Biarritz (€2.10, 10 minutes), St-Jean de Luz (€3.90, 25 minutes) and St Jean Pied de Port (€7.50, one hour), plus the Franco-Spanish border towns of Hendaye (€5.80, 40 minutes) and Irún (€6.10, 45 minutes).

There are also train services to Dax (€7.60, 40 minutes, up to 10 daily), Lourdes (€17.80, 1¾ hours, six daily), Bordeaux (€24.40, 2¼ hours, at least 10 daily), Pau (€13.70, 1¼ hours, eight daily) and Toulouse (€33.10, 3¾ hours, at least four daily).

Getting Around
BICYCLE
Near the train station, Adour Hôtel (p652) rents bikes, for €9/12.50/30 per half-day/full day/three days.

BUS
STAB buses link Bayonne, Biarritz and Anglet. A single ticket costs €1.15 while carnets of five/10 are €4.75/9.50. STAB has an **information office** (☎ 05 59 52 59 52) in the northeastern corner of the town hall. Bus Nos 1, 2 and 6 run between Bayonne and Biarritz and stop at the town halls of both towns.

CAR & MOTORCYCLE
There's free parking along av des Allées Paulmy, which is within easy walking distance of the tourist office. From here there's a bright-orange shuttle bus that travels the short distance to the town centre.

TAXI
Call **Taxi Bayonne** (☎ 05 59 59 48 48) or **Taxi Gare** (☎ 05 59 55 13 15).

BIARRITZ
pop 30,000
The stylish coastal town of Biarritz, 8km west of Bayonne, took off as a resort in the mid-19th century when Napoleon III and his Spanish-born wife, Eugénie, visited regularly. These days, Biarritz is known for its beaches and some of Europe's best surfing.

The town can be expensive. If you're travelling on a budget, consider staying in Bayonne and visiting Biarritz from there, as many French holiday-makers do. Many surfers camp or stay at one of the two excellent youth hostels in Biarritz and in Anglet.

Orientation
Place Clemenceau, the heart of town, is south of the main beach (Grande Plage). Pointe St-Martin, topped with a lighthouse, rounds off Plage Miramar, the northern continuation of the Grande Plage, which is bounded on its southern side by Pointe Atalaye.

Both train station and airport are about 3km southeast of the centre.

Information
BOOKSHOPS
The Bookstore (☎ 05 59 24 48 00; place Clemenceau) Has a small selection of English books.

INTERNET ACCESS
Génius Informatique (☎ 05 59 24 39 07; 60 av Édouard VII; per hr €5; ☺ 10am-12.30pm & 2-7.30pm Tue-Sat)
Plat-Net (☎ 05 59 24 54 48; 6 rue Guy Petit; per hr €4.50; ☺ 10am-8pm Mon-Sat)

LAUNDRY
Laundrette (11 av de la Marne; ☺ 7am-9pm)

POST
Main Post Office (rue de la Poste)

TOURIST INFORMATION
Tourist Office (☎ 05 59 22 37 10; www.biarritz.fr; 1 square d'Ixelles; ☺ 8am-8pm Jul & Aug; 9am-6pm Mon-Sat, 10am-5pm Sun Sep-Jun) Publishes *Biarritzcope*, a free monthly what's-on guide.
Tourist Office Annexe At the train station in July and August.

Sights & Activities
BEACHES
Biarritz' fashionable beaches are wall-to-wall on hot summer days. In the high season, the **Grande Plage** and also **Plage Miramar** to its north are lined with striped tents. Beyond Pointe St-Martin, the superb surfing beaches of **Anglet** stretch northwards for more than 4km. To get there, take the eastbound bus No 9 from place Clemenceau.

Beyond long, exposed **Plage de la Côte des Basques**, some 500m south of Port Vieux, are **Plage de Marbella** and **Plage de la Milady**. Both can be reached by westbound bus No 9.

MUSÉE DE LA MER
Biarritz' **Musée de la Mer** (Sea Museum; ☎ 05 59 22 75 40; www.museedelamer.com; Esplanade de la Vierge; adult/child €7.20/4.60; ☺ minimum 9.30am-12.30pm, 2-6pm, closed Mon Nov-Mar) overlooks Rocher de la Vierge. The ground-floor aquarium has 24 tanks seething with underwater life from the Bay of Biscay (Golfe de Gascogne). On the 1st floor are exhibits on commercial fishing and whaling, telling stories of Biarritz' whaling past. On the 3rd floor, it's feeding time for a pair of seals at 10.30am and 5pm. A nearby pool holds a couple of sleek sharks, while the top floor has a rather mournful display of stuffed birds.

Tickets are €0.80 cheaper at the tourist office.

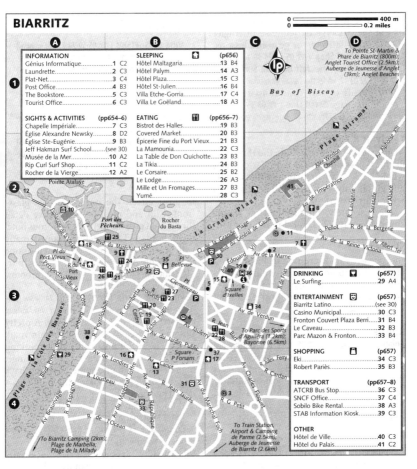

BIARRITZ

INFORMATION	
Génius Informatique	1 C2
Laundrette	2 C3
Plat-Net	3 C4
Post Office	4 B3
The Bookstore	5 C3
Tourist Office	6 C3

SIGHTS & ACTIVITIES	(pp654–6)
Chapelle Impériale	7 C3
Église Alexandre Newsky	8 D2
Église Ste-Eugénie	9 B3
Jeff Hakman Surf School	(see 30)
Musée de la Mer	10 A2
Rip Curl Surf Shop	11 C2
Rocher de la Vierge	12 A2

SLEEPING	(p656)
Hôtel Maïtagaria	13 B4
Hôtel Palym	14 A3
Hôtel Plaza	15 C3
Hôtel St-Julien	16 B4
Villa Etche-Gorria	17 C4
Villa Le Goëland	18 A3

EATING	(pp656–7)
Bistrot des Halles	19 B3
Covered Market	20 B3
Épicerie Fine du Port Vieux	21 B3
La Mamounia	22 C3
La Table de Don Quichotte	23 B3
La Tikia	24 B3
Le Corsaire	25 B2
Le Lodge	26 A3
Mille et Un Fromages	27 B3
Yumé	28 C3

DRINKING	(p657)
Le Surfing	29 A4

ENTERTAINMENT	(p657)
Biarritz Latino	(see 30)
Casino Municipal	30 C3
Fronton Couvert Plaza Berri	31 B4
Le Caveau	32 B3
Parc Mazon & Fronton	33 B4

SHOPPING	(p657)
Eki	34 C3
Robert Pariès	35 B3

TRANSPORT	(pp657–8)
ATCRB Bus Stop	36 C3
SNCF Office	37 C4
Sobilo Bike Rental	38 A3
STAB Information Kiosk	39 C3

OTHER	
Hôtel de Ville	40 C3
Hôtel du Palais	41 C2

OTHER ATTRACTIONS

Stroll over the footbridge at the end of Pointe Atalaye to **Rocher de la Vierge** (Rock of the Virgin), named after the white statue of the Virgin and child. From this impressive outcrop, there are views northwards of the Landes coastline and, far to the south, the mountains of the Spanish Basque Country.

Once a lively fishing port, **Port des Pêcheurs** is nowadays a haven only to pleasure craft. Above it, the Byzantine and Moorish-style **Église Ste-Eugénie** was built in 1864 for – who else? – Empress Eugénie.

Dominating the northern end of the Grande Plage is the stately **Hôtel du Palais**, also built for Empress Eugénie in 1854 and now a luxury hotel. Opposite is **Église**

Alexandre Newsky (8 av de l'Impératrice), a Russian Orthodox church built by and for the Russian aristocrats who frequented Biarritz until the Soviet Revolution. Eugénie was also the inspiration for the nearby doll's-house **Chapelle Impériale** (2-7pm Mon-Sat Jul-Sep, 3-7pm Tue, Thu & Sat Apr-Jun, 3-5pm Thu Oct-Mar), constructed in 1864.

To the north on Pointe St-Martin is the **Phare de Biarritz** (admission €1.50; 10am-noon & 3-7pm Tue-Sun Jul & Aug, 3-7pm Sat & Sun mid-Apr–Jun), the town's lighthouse, which is 73m tall and was erected in 1834.

SURFING

The 4km-long stretch of Anglet beach ranks among Europe's finest surfing venues. The best rental and lesson bargains are to be had at the Auberge de Jeunesse in Anglet (p651). Alternatively, for gear and lessons, try **Rip Curl Surf Shop** (☎ 05 59 24 38 40; 2 av de la Reine Victoria) or the **Jeff Hakman Surf School** (☎ 05 59 22 03 12; under the Casino Municipal).

For details of surf conditions ring the French-language **Swell Line** (☎ 08 36 68 40 64; www.swell-line.com in French) or see its webcam.

Festivals & Events

Major surfing events include the three-day **Biarritz Maider Arosteguy** around Easter and a whole week of surfing competitions, films and gigs in July. For dates and details, go to www.biarritzsurffestival.com (in French).

More sedately, **Fêtes Musicales de Biarritz** covers five days of classical music in April.

Sleeping

Inexpensive hotels are rare in Biarritz and any kind of room is at a premium in July and August. Outside high season, however, you can pick and choose; most prices fall by a good 25%.

BUDGET

Auberge de Jeunesse (☎ 05 59 41 76 00; biarritz@fuaj .org; 8 rue Chiquito de Cambo; dm incl breakfast €14.90; ☷ mid-Jan–mid-Dec) Like Anglet's youth hostel this popular place offers a host of outdoor activities such as surfing, sailing and guided walks. To get here from the train station, follow the railway westwards for 800m.

Camping

Camping de Parme (☎ 05 59 23 03 00; www.camping deparme.com; route de l'Aviation; camping €15.50-23) BAB's only year-round camping ground is in a leafy spot 800m northeast of the train station. It's usually fully booked months in advance for July and August.

Biarritz Camping (☎ 05 59 23 00 12; www.biarritz -camping.fr; 28 rue d'Harcet; camping €13.50-19.50; ☷ mid-May–mid-Sep; ☙) Spacious and shady sites can be found at this summer camping ground, 3km southwest of the centre. Take westbound bus No 9 to the Biarritz Camping stop.

MID-RANGE

Hôtel Plaza (☎ 05 59 24 74 00; hotel.plaza.biarritz@ wanadoo.fr; 20 av Édouard VII; s/d from €81/103; ☒) The Plaza is a three-star Art Deco delight overlooking Grande Plage. Recently refurbished

to great effect, the original 1930s glass-fronted lift and plenty of decorative detail throughout give the feel of a glamorous hotel in its heyday. The spacious rooms (many with beach views) are decked out in the same theme, with Art Deco dressing tables, purple armchairs and marble-effect bathrooms. Highly recommended.

Villa Etche-Gorria (☎ 05 59 24 00 74; www.hotel -etche-gorria.com; 21 av du Maréchal Foch; r with/without bathroom €60/35; ☷ mid-Dec–3rd week Nov) A pretty Basque villa set back from the main road, run by Pierre, the amiable, English-speaking owner. The rooms on the 1st floor are huge, high-ceilinged affairs, some of which have large balconies overlooking the public garden. The small, cheaper attic rooms on the 2nd floor are about the best value in town.

Hôtel Maïtagaria (☎ 05 59 24 26 65; www.hotel -maitagaria.com; 34 av Carnot; d from €56) Spotless, modern rooms and swish bathrooms make this friendly place good value, especially the large, two-roomed family suite (€99). There's an intimate garden at the rear for summer breakfasts (€6).

Hôtel St-Julien (☎ 05 59 24 20 39; www.hotel-saint -julien.com; 20 av Carnot; s/d €59/75; ☷ mid-Jan–mid-Dec) A stylish two-star option in a quiet but central location. Some rooms on the 3rd floor have mountain views.

Hôtel Palym (☎ 05 59 24 16 56; fax 05 59 24 96 12; 7 rue du Port Vieux; r with basin/bathroom from €37/49) A cosy little hotel occupying a brightly painted town house on a busy tourist street. The bedrooms are colourful but the bathrooms are very small.

Eating

Le Corsaire (☎ 05 59 24 63 72; Port des Pêcheurs; mains €9-22; ☷ lunch & dinner Tue-Sat) The service may be excruciatingly slow at peak times, but at least you get an opportunity to enjoy the delightful harbourside setting from the terrace. It's all about seafood down here by the water's edge, with dishes including *dorade à l'espagnole* (€14.50) and *grilled cod with chorizo* (€12.20). This is one of three incredibly popular seafood restaurants here, with neighbouring **Casa Juan Pedro** (☎ 05 59 24 00 86) offering a similar *menu*, and **Chez Albert** (☎ 05 59 24 43 84; mains €17-25) offering a slightly more refined, gastronomic approach.

La Tikia (☎ 05 59 24 46 09; 1 place Ste Eugénie; menus €12.50; lunch & dinner) 'Tikia' is the Basque word for small, but although the restaurant is modestly sized, the same can't be said of the *brochettes,* giant skewers of duck (€12.50), steak (€14.50) or seafood (€13.50). For lighter appetites, there's a good selection of big and small salads. There's also a good choice of local wines, all topped off with friendly service.

Le Lodge (☎ 05 59 24 73 78; 1 rue du Port Vieux; mains €13-17; closed Sun & Mon) A buzzing new restaurant and gallery featuring traditional cuisine and contemporary art. This place dispenses with the minimalist look in favour of a clutter of zebra- and leopard-skin tablecloths and African wall art, but the overall effect works well.

Bistrot des Halles (☎ 05 59 24 21 22; 1 rue du Centre; mains €13-17; lunch & dinner until 10pm) One of a cluster of decent restaurants along rue du Centre that take their produce fresh from the nearby covered market. This bustling place serves three-course meals from the blackboard menu for about €25, including wine.

Yumé (☎ 05 59 22 01 02; 6 rue Jean Bart; menus €28-48; closed Sun) A stylish, gastronomic Japanese restaurant offering authentic, well-presented sushi, sashimi and tempura dishes.

La Mamounia (☎ 05 59 24 76 08; 4 rue Jean Bart) The extravagant North African décor, the centrepiece of which is a ridiculously huge Moroccan teapot, makes this a suitable place to tuck into delicious tagine (€15 to €16) and couscous (€13 to €19.50) dishes.

SELF-CATERING
Biarritz has a **covered market** (7am-1.30pm). Just downhill, **La Table de Don Quichotte** (12 av Victor Hugo) sells all sorts of Spanish hams, sausages and wines, while you'll find a tempting array of cheeses, wines and pâtés at nearby **Mille et Un Fromages** (8 av Victor Hugo). Down at

sea level, **Épicerie Fine du Port Vieux** (41bis rue Mazagran) is another excellent delicatessen.

Drinking
There are good bars along rue du Port Vieux and the streets radiating from it. It's also well worth snooping around place Clemenceau and the central food market area.

Le Surfing (☎ 05 59 24 78 72; 9 blvd Prince des Galles) After a hard day's surfing, this is the place to come and discuss waves and wipe-outs. The bar is full of surfing memorabilia and there's an outside terrace with decent views.

Entertainment
In high summer there are free Friday evening **classical music concerts** in front of Église Ste-Eugénie and at other venues.

If you fancy frittering away your travel money, step into the white slab of Biarritz' **Casino Municipal** (1 av Édouard VII; 10am-3am Mon-Fri, 10am-4am Sat & Sun). Constructed in 1928, gambling (slot) machines whir and chink until the wee hours.

Two discos near the town centre are **Le Caveau** (☎ 05 59 24 16 17; 4 rue Gambetta; 11pm-5am) and **Biarritz Latino** (☎ 05 59 22 77 59; 11pm-5am Tue-Sat). Both venues are within the Casino Municipal.

At the **Fronton Couvert Plaza Berri** (☎ 05 59 22 15 72; 42 av du Maréchal Foch) there's pelota (p653) at 9pm every Tuesday and Friday from June to early September. Other tournaments are held here year-round, often on Sunday afternoons. From July to mid-September, the open-air fronton at **Parc Mazon** has regular *chistera* matches at 9pm on Monday. Admission to each is around €8.

Between mid-June and mid-September, **Euskal-Jaï** (☎ 05 59 23 91 09; av Henri Haget) in the Parc des Sports d'Aguiléra complex, 2km east of central Biarritz, has regular professional *cesta punta* matches at 9pm. Tickets cost between €10 and €20, Bus No 1 stops nearby.

Shopping
For Basque music, crafts and guidebooks, visit **Eki** (☎ 05 59 24 79 64; 21 av de Verdun). For scrumptious chocolates and Basque sweets, drop in on **Robert Pariès** (1 place Bellevue).

Getting There & Away
AIR
Biarritz-Anglet-Bayonne is the nearest airport (p653). Take STAB bus No 6 or, on

Sunday, line C to/from Biarritz' town hall. Each runs once or twice hourly, from 6am until about 7pm.

BUS

Stopping outside the tourist office, there are nine daily **ATCRB buses** (☎ 05 59 26 06 99) that follow the coast southwestwards to St-Jean de Luz (€2.80, 30 to 40 minutes) and Hendaye (€4.90, one hour five minutes). For other destinations, it's better to go from Bayonne – not least in order to ensure a seat in high season.

TRAIN

Biarritz–La Négresse train station is about 3km from the town centre. Bus Nos 2 and 9 connect the two. **SNCF** (13 av du Maréchal Foch; ☺ Mon-Fri) has a town-centre office. Times, fares and destinations are much the same as those detailed on p653.

Getting Around
BUS

Most services stop beside the town hall, from where route Nos 1 and 2 go to Bayonne's town hall and station. **STAB** (☎ 05 59 24 26 53) has an information kiosk just outside the tourist office.

MOTORCYCLE & BICYCLE

You can rent several varieties of wheeled transport from **Sobilo** (☎ 05 59 24 94 47; 24 rue Peyroloubilh): mountain bikes (€12 per day), scooters (from €31) and even in-line skates (€12).

TAXI

Call **Taxis Biarritz** (☎ 05 59 23 05 50).

ST-JEAN DE LUZ & CIBOURE
pop 19,450

St-Jean de Luz ('Donibane Lohizune' in Basque), 24km southwest of Bayonne at the mouth of the River Nivelle, is the most Basque of the region's beach resorts. Hugging one side of a sheltered bay, it has a colourful history of whaling and piracy. Together with its twin town of Ciboure, it makes a pleasant day trip from either Bayonne or Biarritz.

St-Jean de Luz is still an active fishing port, renowned for large catches of sardines (from the waters off Portugal and Morocco), tuna (from the Bay of Biscay and West Africa) and anchovies (from the Bay of Biscay).

Ciboure is St-Jean de Luz' quiet alter ego. Many whitewashed Basque houses, timber-framed and shuttered in green or oxblood-red, survive just south of rue Agorette.

Places mentioned in this section are in St-Jean de Luz unless stated otherwise.

Orientation

St-Jean de Luz and its long beach is on the eastern side of Baie de St-Jean de Luz, with smaller Ciboure on the western curve of the bay. A tiny but active fishing harbour nestles at the mouth of the River Nivelle, dividing the two towns. The axis of St-Jean de Luz is pedestrianised rue Gambetta with bustling place Louis XIV at its southwestern end.

Information

Cyber-Café Azerty (☎ 05 59 51 22 50; 8 blvd Thiers; per hr €5; ☺ 9am-12.30pm & 2-7pm Mon-Fri) Has six terminals for Internet access.

Laverie du Port (place Maréchal Foch; ☺ 7am-9pm) For washing those travelling clothes.

Post Office St-Jean de Luz (cnr blvd Victor Hugo & rue Salagoity) Ciboure (quai Maurice Ravel)

Tourist Office (☎ 05 59 26 03 16; www.saint-jean-de-luz.com; place Maréchal Foch; ☺ 9am-7.30pm Mon-Sat, 10am-1pm & 3-7pm Sun Jul & Aug, 9am-12.30pm & 2.30-6.30pm Mon-Sat, 10am-1pm Sun Sep-Jun)

Sights & Activities

The promontory of **Pointe Ste-Barbe,** at the northern end of the Baie de St-Jean de Luz, is great for panoramas of the town and the wind-tossed sea. It's 1km northeast of the St-Jean de Luz beach, via blvd Thiers and the seaside promenade des Rochers.

The heart of **Socoa** is about 2.5km west of Ciboure along the continuation of quai Maurice Ravel. Its prominent **fort** was built in 1627 and later improved by Vauban. You can walk out to the **Digue de Socoa** breakwater or climb to the **lighthouse** via rue du Phare, then out along rue du Sémaphore for fabulous coastal views.

BEACHES

St-Jean de Luz' family-friendly sandy beach sprouts bathing tents (€6.25 per day) from June to September. Ciboure has its own modest beach.

Plage de Socoa, 2km west of Socoa on the corniche (the D912), is served by ATCRB buses (p662) en route to Hendaye and in high season by boats (p662).

ST-JEAN DE LUZ

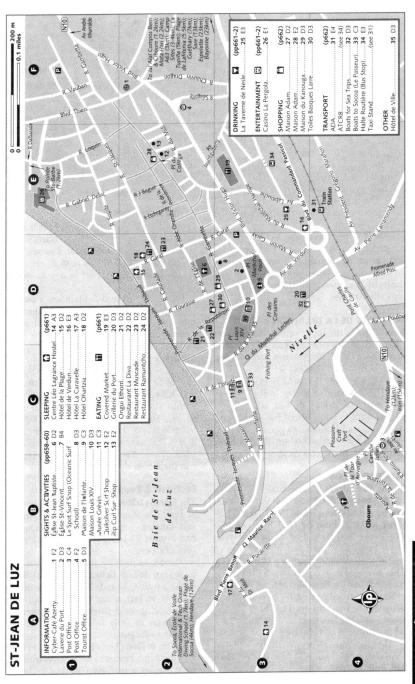

INFORMATION
Cyber-Café Azerty	1 F2
Laverie du Port	2 D3
Post Office	3 C4
Post Office	4 F2
Tourist Office	5 D3

SIGHTS & ACTIVITIES (pp658–60)
Église St-Jean Baptiste	6 D2
Église St-Vincent	7 B4
Le Spot Surf Shop (Oceanic Surf School)	8 D3
Maison de l'Infante	9 C3
Maison Louis XIV	10 D3
Musée Grévin	11 C3
Quiksilver Surf Shop	12 E2
Rip Curl Surf Shop	13 D3

SLEEPING (p661)
Centre Léo Lagrange Hostel	14 A3
Hôtel de la Plage	15 D2
Hôtel de Verdun	16 E3
Hôtel La Caravelle	17 A3
Hôtel Ohartzia	18 D2

EATING (p661)
Covered Market	19 E3
Grillerie du Port	20 D3
Ongui Ethorri	21 D3
Restaurant La Diva	22 D2
Restaurant Muscade	23 D2
Restaurant Ramuntcho	24 D2

DRINKING (pp661–2)
La Taverne de Nesle	25 E3

ENTERTAINMENT (pp661–2)
Casino La Pergola	26 E1

SHOPPING (p662)
Maison Adam	27 D2
Maison Adam	28 E2
Maison du Kanouga	29 D3
Toiles Basques Larre	30 D3

TRANSPORT (p662)
ADA	31 E4
ATCRB	(see 34)
Boats for Sea Trips	32 D3
Boats to Socoa (Le Passeur)	33 C3
Halte Routière (Bus Stop)	34 E3
Taxi Stand	(see 31)

OTHER
Hôtel de Ville	35 D3

CHURCHES

The plain façade of France's largest and finest Basque church, **Église St-Jean Baptiste** (rue Gambetta; ☺ 8.30am-noon & 2-7pm), conceals a splendid interior, where Louis XIV and Maria Teresa (Marie Thérèse) of Spain were married in 1660. After rings were exchanged, the couple walked down the aisle and out of the south door, which was then sealed to commemorate the *rapprochement* between France and Spain. You can still see its outline, opposite No 20 rue Gambetta.

Until as recently as the Second Vatican Council (1962–65), Basque churches such as this had separate areas for men and women. Here, the men occupied the tiers of grand oak galleries and sang as a chorus, while the women's seating was on the ground floor.

Église St-Vincent (rue Pocalette), in Ciboure, was constructed in the 16th and 17th centuries and has an octagonal bell tower topped by an unusual three-tiered wooden roof. Inside, the lavish use of wood and tiered galleries are typically Basque.

ÉCOMUSÉE DE LA TRADITION BASQUE

Beside the N10, this multimedia **museum** (☎ 05 59 51 06 06; www.ecomusee.com in French; adult/student/child €5.50/5/2.30; ☺ 10am-6.30pm Jul & Aug, 9.30am-12.15pm & 2-5.15pm Mon-Sat, 9.30am-12.15pm Sun Apr-Jun & Sep, 10.30-11.30am & 2.45-4.45pm Mon-Sat, 10.30-11.30am Sun & school holidays Jan-Mar & Oct-Dec), 2km north of St-Jean de Luz, will tell you all you want to know about Basque life and traditions – and probably a good deal more; once you have embarked on the 1½-hour guided tour, there's no escape.

PLACE LOUIS XIV

Beside this pleasant pedestrianised square sits **Maison Louis XIV** (☎ 05 59 26 01 56; ☺ 10.30am-noon & 2.30-5.30pm Jun & Sep, 10.30am-12.30pm & 2.30-6.30pm Jul & Aug), built in 1643 by a wealthy shipowner and furnished in period style. Here, Louis XIV lived out his last days of bachelorhood before marrying Maria Teresa. This arranged marriage between the French monarch and the daughter of King Philip IV of Spain signalled peace after 24 years of war between the two nations. Half-hour guided tours (with English text) cost €4.60/2.75 for adults/students and children.

Alongside, and rather dwarfed by its more imposing neighbour, is St-Jean de Luz' **town hall**, built in 1657.

In the days before her marriage, Maria Teresa stayed in another shipowner's mansion, the brick-and-stone Maison Joanoenia, off place Louis XIV and now called **Maison de l'Infante** (☎ 05 59 26 36 82; quai de l'Infante; adult/child €2.30/free; ☺ 2.30-6.30pm Mon, 11am-12.30pm & 2.30-6.30pm Tue-Sat mid-Jun–mid-Oct).

Next door at the **Musée Grévin** (☎ 05 59 51 24 88; 3 rue Mazarin; adult/student/child €5.50/4.40/2.75; ☺ 10am-noon & 2-6pm Apr-Jun, Sep & Oct, 10am-noon & 2-6.30pm Jul & Aug) are some 50 figures from the local nobility plus others more humble, including fishwives and pirates. However, the definition of 'musée' is rather stretched for this nationwide chain of waxworks.

OTHER ACTIVITIES

From Easter to September, **École de Voile International** (☎ 05 59 47 06 32) in Socoa offers windsurfing lessons and catamaran courses.

Tech Ocean (☎ 05 59 47 96 75; 45 av Commandant Passicot) below Socoa Fort is a year-round diving school.

From May to mid-September, a couple of boats leave quai du Maréchal Leclerc for morning deep-sea fishing trips and afternoon cruises.

SURFING

For some prime surfing, head 5.5km northeast of St-Jean de Luz to **Plage de Lafitenia**; ATCRB's Biarritz and Bayonne buses pass within 1km (Martienia or Bubonnet stop, €1.50). Surf schools based in the **Rip Curl** (☎ 05 59 26 81 95; 72 rue Gambetta), **Quiksilver** (☎ 06 86 94 95 27; 68 rue Gambetta) and **Le Spot** (Oceanic Surf School; ☎ 05 59 26 07 93; 16 rue Gambetta) surf shops run their own shuttle buses.

Festivals & Events

The **Fêtes de la St-Jean** – with a choral concert at Église St-Jean Baptiste, bonfires, music and dancing – are celebrated on the weekend nearest 24 June, coinciding with midsummer's eve.

There's something fishy about festivals in St-Jean de Luz. **La Nuit de la Sardine** (Night of the Sardine) sounds like a horror movie but it is, in fact, a night of music, folklore and dancing held twice each summer on a Saturday in early July and the Saturday nearest 14 August.

La Fête du Thon (Tuna Festival), on another July weekend, brings to town street buskers, rock, Basque music, dancing and midnight fireworks, while numerous stands sell all sorts of tuna dishes.

Folk dancers from all across the Spanish and French Basque Country congregate for **Danses des 7 Provinces Basques** in late May or early June, while **Régates de Traînières** is a weekend of whaleboat races on the first weekend in July.

Sleeping

You will need to reserve your accommodation well in advance for visits between July and mid-September. There are very few budget hotels, although off-season prices for mid-range hotels can fall relatively low.

Centre Léo Lagrange (☎ 05 59 47 04 79; 8 rue Simone Menez; dm with breakfast €10) This cheap hostel in Ciboure offers the bare essentials. It's best to phone before arriving in high summer, when it's often full.

Hôtel Ohartzia (☎ 05 59 26 00 06; www.hotel -ohartzia.com in French; 28 rue Garat; r €75-84 high season, €59-65 low-season) This beautifully tranquil Basque house, just a few steps from the beach in St-Jean de Luz, is a world away from the bustle. The immaculate rooms are well furnished and equipped, but the highlight is the rear garden courtyard, an oasis of calm with a gentle twittering of birds: perfect background noise for a siesta.

Hôtel La Caravelle (☎ 05 59 47 18 05; www.hotel lacaravelle.com; blvd Pierre Benoît; r €50-80; P) This nautical themed place in Ciboure comprising two former fishermen's cottages has recently been updated to provide 20 modern rooms, seven of which have fantastic views over the bay.

Hôtel de la Plage (☎ 05 59 51 03 44; www.hotelde laplage.com; 33 rue Garat; r €59-118; mid-Feb–mid-Dec; P) Located right on the main stretch of beach in St-Jean de Luz, this white-painted red-shuttered building is in a fantastic spot. Most rooms have tiny balconies, enough to fit a table and two chairs. The drawback is that it can get noisy in peak season, especially when the bar downstairs is full.

Hôtel de Verdun (☎ 05 59 26 02 55; 13 av de Verdun; r €26-63) Opposite the train station in St-Jean de Luz, this simple place has a complicated pricing structure, which involves taking half board in high season, which is probably not the best option if you want to explore the town's better restaurants. At other times it's good value for relatively spacious, if plain, rooms.

CAMPING

Between St-Jean de Luz and Guéthary, 7km northeast up the coast, are no fewer than 16 camping areas. ATCRB's Biarritz and Bayonne buses stop within 1km of them all. The selection includes the four-star **Camping International Erromardie** (☎ 05 59 26 07 74; www .erromardie.com; camping €15-26; mid-Apr–Sep) in Erromardie.

Eating

There are a number of fancy restaurants along rue de la République and more, interspersed with cafés, around place Louis XIV.

Grillerie du Port (☎ 05 59 51 18 29; quai du Maréchal Leclerc; mid-Jun–mid-Sep) For the freshest seafood in town – guaranteed – join the crowds in this old shack by the port gorging themselves on fresh sardines, salads and slabs of tuna steak fresh off the boat. Informal, economical and enormously popular.

Restaurant La Diva (☎ 05 59 51 14 01; 7 rue de la République; menus €15, €18 & €25; Mar-Oct) Less hearty and more relaxed than Grillerie du Port, this restaurant's cuisine is still firmly fishy, with an emphasis on Basque and Spanish flavours. It's one of many decent options on this restaurant-packed street.

Ongui Ethorri (☎ 05 59 26 85 07; 15 rue de la République; menus €17 & €26; lunch & dinner Mar-Nov) Another popular Basque seafood place on this stretch. If you're feeling a bit peckish, try the house speciality, *parrillada de poissons* (€46 to €54), a huge seafood platter with langoustines, mussels, prawns and five types of fish!

Restaurant Ramuntcho (☎ 05 59 26 03 89; 24 rue Garat; menus €18 & €23; closed Mon low season) This lively place, whose owner hails from Normandy, successfully blends the cuisine of northern and southwestern France. Duck and fish dishes feature prominently, as do tasty jugs of sangria.

Restaurant Muscade (☎ 05 59 26 96 73; 20 rue Garat; Feb-Dec) Mixed salads (€8 to €11) and tasty pies and tarts (€5 to €€8) feature here.

SELF-CATERING

There is a food market that operates every Tuesday and Friday mornings (plus Saturdays in July and August) at the covered market, which spills into blvd Victor Hugo.

Drinking & Entertainment

La Taverne de Nesle (☎ 05 59 26 60 93; www.lataverne .best.cd in French; 5 av Labrouche; 1pm-3am Mon-Sat,

5pm-3am Sun) This cheery neighbourhood pub has a DJ every Friday year-round, and more frequently in summer.

Although swarming with people in high season, St-Jean de Luz has only two discos: **Mata Hari** (☎ 05 59 26 04 28; 48 av André Ithurralde), 2km east of the train station, and **La Tupiña** (☎ 05 59 54 73 23), 5km east on the N10.

Casino La Pergola (☎ 05 59 51 58 58; rue Dalbarade) – with slot machines operating from 11am to 3am daily, and gaming from 9pm to 3am from Tuesday to Sunday – is bang on the beach.

SPORT
In July and August, there's *cesta punta* at the **Jaï Alaï Compos Berri** (☎ 05 59 51 65 30) on route de Bayonne (the N10), 1km northeast of the train station. Matches start at 9pm every Tuesday and Friday, and half-time is spiced up with music or dancing. Tickets are available at the tourist office and are priced between €9 and €20, depending on the crowd-pulling capacity of the players.

Shopping
Agonise over the rich choice of high-calorie Basque pastries and sweets at **La Maison du Kanouga** (9 rue Gambetta). Equally tempting are the two branches of **Maison Adam** (49 rue Gambetta & 6 rue de la République), which has been making sweets since the 17th century.

St-Jean de Luz is also a good place to purchase Basque linen – for example, at **Toiles Basques Larre** (4 rue de la République). In summer, linen woven by the local manufacturer Créations Jean-Vier is on sale at **Maison de l'Infante** (see p660).

Getting There & Away
BUS
Buses run by **ATCRB** (☎ 05 59 26 06 99) pass the Halte Routière bus stop near the train station on their way northeast to Biarritz (€2.80, 30 minutes, over 10 daily Monday to Saturday, six on Sunday) and Bayonne (€3.60, 40 minutes, same frequency as to Biarritz). Southwestwards, there are around 15 services daily to Hendaye (€2.80, 25 minutes), of which four follow the coast and a couple continue to Irún (€3.10) in Spain.

Also passing Halte Routière, Spanish company Transportes Pesa has twice-daily buses to San Sebastián (€3.60, one hour), to which ATCRB runs a summer-only service.

From April to October **Le Basque Bondissant** (The Leaping Basque; ☎ 05 59 26 30 74) runs buses to La Rhune and the Grottes de Sare (p663).

TRAIN
There are frequent trains to Bayonne (€3.90, 25 minutes) via Biarritz (€2.50, 15 minutes) and to Hendaye (€2.50, 15 minutes), with connections to San Sebastián.

Getting Around
BOAT
Between June and September, the good ship **Le Passeur** (☎ 06 81 20 84 98) plies between quai de l'Infante and Socoa (€2 one way) every half-hour.

BUS
Between June and September, the Navette Intercommunale, run by ATCRB, provides a local daily bus service and a skeleton service during the rest of the year. Take Line A for Erromardie and the camping grounds north of town, and Line D for Socoa via Ciboure.

CAR
Car-rental company **ADA** (☎ 05 59 26 26 22) has an office at the train station.

MOTORCYCLE & BICYCLE
Based at the train station, **Fun Bikes** (☎ 05 59 26 75 76) rents cycles (€12 per day) and scooters (€31 per day).

TAXI
The train station has a taxi rank, or call ☎ 05 59 26 10 11 to book a car.

AROUND ST-JEAN DE LUZ
La Rhune
La Rhune ('Larrun' in Basque), a 905m-high, antenna-topped mountain, lies 10km south of St-Jean de Luz. Half in France and half in Spain, it's something of a Basque symbol. Views are spectacular from its peak, which is best approached from **Col de St-Ignace**, which is 3km northwest of Sare on the D4 (the St-Jean de Luz road). From here, you can take a pleasant if fairly strenuous walk or hop onto **Le Petit Train de la Rhune** (☎ 05 59 54 20 26; www.rhune.com; single/return adult €9/11, children €5.50/6.50). This charming little train takes 30 minutes to haul itself up the 4km from col to summit. It runs from Easter to mid-November with departures roughly

every half-hour from 9am (8.30am in July and August), depending on the crowds. Be prepared for a wait of up to an hour in high summer.

Sare

Sare sits in the skirts of La Rhune. At its heart is place du Fronton, where you'll find the **tourist office** (☎ 05 59 54 20 14) sharing premises with the town hall and another sturdy Basque parish church.

Along the D306, 6km south of the village, is the **Grottes de Sare** (☎ 05 59 54 21 88; adult/child €6/3; ⏲ 10am-7pm Jul & Aug, 10am-6pm Easter-Jun & Sep, 10am-5pm Oct–mid-Nov, 2-5pm mid-Nov–Dec & Mar-Easter, 2-4pm Feb), whose gaping entrance leads via narrow passages to a huge central cavern, first inhabited at least 20,000 years ago. To reach it, you need to join one of the obligatory multilingual tours.

Espelette

Whether you like your food sweet or spicy, Espelette should appeal. Above all, the village is famous for its dark red peppers, an essential ingredient of so much Basque cuisine. So prized is *le piment d'Espelette* that it's been accorded *Appellation d'Origine Contrôlée* (AOC) status, much like a fine wine. Arrive in the autumn and you can scarcely see the walls of the houses, which are masked by rows of peppers, threaded with string and hung up to dry. The last weekend in October marks Espelette's **Fête du Piment**, with processions, a formal blessing of the peppers and the ennoblement of a *chevalier du piment* (a knight of the pimento).

Although some like it hot, others may prefer sweeter pleasures. **Chocolats Anton** (☎ 05 59 93 80 58; place du Marché) is a specialist chocolatemaker that offers free tastings of its delightful wares.

The **tourist office** (☎ 05 59 93 95 02) is within a small stone chateau and shares its premises with the town hall. On the 2nd floor of the chateau is a photographic exhibition about – what else? – peppers around the world.

ST-JEAN PIED DE PORT

pop 1400

The walled Pyrenean town of St-Jean Pied de Port (Donibane Garazi in Basque), 53km southeast of Bayonne, was once the last stop in France for pilgrims who converged here from all over the country. Refreshed, they headed south over the Spanish border, a mere 8km away, and on to Santiago de Compostela in western Spain.

Nowadays the town is a popular departure point for hikers and bikers attempting the pilgrim trail.

A pretty little town, St-Jean Pied de Port desperately needs a traffic bypass but it does make for a pleasant day trip from Bayonne. Half the reason for coming here is the scenic journey south of Cambo-les-Bains, as both railway and road (the D918) pass through rocky hills, forests and lush meadows dotted with white farmhouses whose signs announce *ardi* ('cheese' in Basque) for sale.

The town can be hideously crowded in summer. Consider staying the night and exploring before breakfast or visit in low season. Even better, to leave it all behind, rent a bike or pull on your boots and head for the surrounding hills.

Information

Bar Paris (☎ 05 59 37 01 47; 33 av Renaud; per hr €4) For Internet access; a few steps from the station.
Tourist office (☎ 05 59 37 03 57; www.pyrenees -basques.com; place Charles de Gaulle; ⏲ 9am-7pm Mon-Sat, 10am-4pm Sun Jul & Aug; 9am-noon & 2-6pm Mon-Sat Sep-Jun plus 10am-4pm Sun Apr-Jun)

Sights & Activities

OLD TOWN

The church of **Notre Dame du Bout du Pont**, with foundations as old as the town itself, was thoroughly rebuilt in the 17th century. Beyond **Porte de Notre Dame**, which abuts the church, is the photogenic **Vieux Pont** (Old Bridge) from where there's a fine view of whitewashed houses with balconies leaning out above the water. Fishing is forbidden where the River Nive passes through town, and the fat, gulping trout seem to know it. Over the bridge is the commercial artery of rue d'Espagne. A pleasant 500m riverbank stroll upstream brings you to the steeply arched so-called **Pont Romain** (meaning Roman Bridge, but in fact dating from the 17th century).

Rue de la Citadelle is bordered by substantial, pink-granite 16th- to 18th-century residences. Look for the construction date on door lintels (the oldest we found was 1510). A common motif is the scallop shell, symbol

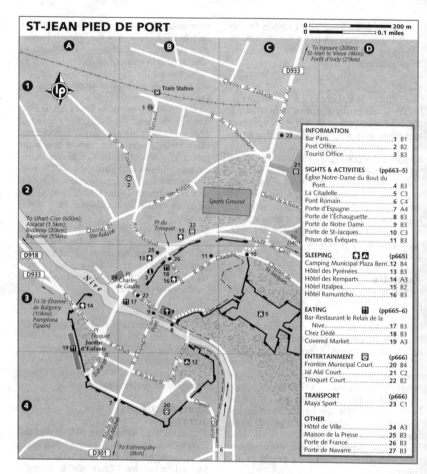

ST-JEAN PIED DE PORT

INFORMATION
Bar Paris...............................**1** B1	
Post Office...........................**2** B2	
Tourist Office.......................**3** B3	

SIGHTS & ACTIVITIES (pp663–5)
Église Notre-Dame du Bout du Pont..................................**4** B3	
La Citadelle..........................**5** C3	
Pont Romain.........................**6** C4	
Porte d'Espagne....................**7** A4	
Porte de l'Échauguette..........**8** B3	
Porte de Notre Dame..............**9** B3	
Porte de St-Jacques..............**10** C3	
Prison des Évêques...............**11** B3	

SLEEPING (p665)
Camping Municipal Plaza Berri..**12** B4	
Hôtel des Pyrénées...............**13** B3	
Hôtel des Remparts...............**14** A3	
Hôtel Itzalpea......................**15** B3	
Hôtel Ramuntcho...................**16** B3	

EATING (pp665–6)
Bar-Restaurant le Relais de la Nive................................**17** B3	
Chez Dédé............................**18** B3	
Covered Market.....................**19** A3	

ENTERTAINMENT (p666)
Fronton Municipal Court.........**20** B4	
Jaï Alaï Court........................**21** C2	
Trinquet Court......................**22** B2	

TRANSPORT (p666)
Maya Sport...........................**23** C1	

OTHER
Hôtel de Ville........................**24** A3	
Maison de la Presse...............**25** B3	
Porte de France....................**26** B3	
Porte de Navarre...................**27** B3	

of St-Jacques (St James or Santiago) and of the Santiago de Compostela pilgrims, and perhaps an early example of come-hither advertising by the boarding housekeepers of the time. Pilgrims would enter the town through the **Porte de St-Jacques** on the northern side of town, then, refreshed and probably a little poorer, head for Spain through the **Porte d'Espagne**, south of the river.

LA CITADELLE

From the top of rue de la Citadelle, a rough cobblestone path ascends to the massive citadel itself, from where there are splendid views of the town, the River Nive and the surrounding hills. Constructed in 1628, the fort was rebuilt around 1680 by military

engineers of the Vauban school. Nowadays it serves as a secondary school and is closed to the public.

If you've a head for heights, descend by the steps signed *escalier poterne* (rear stairway). Steep and slippery after rain, they plunge beside the moss-covered ramparts to **Porte de l'Échauguette** (Watchtower Gate).

PRISON DES ÉVÊQUES

The so-called **Prison des Évêques** (Bishops' Prison; 41 rue de la Citadelle; €3; 11am-12.30pm & 2.30-6pm Easter–mid-Oct), a claustrophobic vaulted cellar, gets its history muddled. It indeed served as the town jail from 1795, as a military lock-up in the 19th century, then as a place of internment during WWII for those caught trying to flee to nominally neutral Spain. The lower section dates from the 13th century when St-Jean Pied de Port was a bishopric of the Avignon papacy, but the building above it dates from the 16th century, by which time the bishops were long gone.

WALKING & CYCLING
St-Jean Pied de Port is a fine place from which to walk or cycle into the Pyrenean foothills, where the loudest sounds you'll hear are cowbells and the wind. Both the GR10 (the trans-Pyrenean long-distance trail running from the Atlantic to the Mediterranean) and the GR65 (the Chemin de St-Jacques pilgrim route) pass through town. **Maison de la Presse** (place Charles de Gaulle) carries a good selection of walking maps.

Pick up a copy of *25 Randonnées en Pays Basque* (€6.10) from the tourist office. Written in French but with explicit maps, it gives enough ideas for walking or mountain-bike routes to keep you active and happy for a good two weeks or more.

To cycle the easy way while enjoying the best of the views of the Nive Valley, load your bicycle onto the train in Bayonne – they're carried free on most services – and roll back down the valley from St-Jean Pied de Port. If you find the ride all the way back to the coast daunting, rejoin the train at Pont-Noblia, for example, or Cambo-les-Bains. For local bike hire, see p666.

Tours
In July and August, the tourist office organises tours of the old town (in French) and Friday morning visits to the citadel.

Festivals & Events
In high summer there is a weekly handicraft and food fair, held most Thursdays, in the covered market.

Sleeping
The tourist office has details of *gîtes* and *chambres d'hôtes* in the area, primarily but not exclusively, for walkers and pilgrims.

Hôtel Itzalpea (☎ 05 59 37 03 66; itzalpea@wanadoo .fr; 5 place du Trinquet; d/tr/q with bathroom €35/46/54) This family-run budget option is sure to please.

Hôtel des Remparts (☎ 05 59 37 13 79; remparts .hotel@wanadoo.fr; 16 place Floquet; d with bathroom €40-50; ⓨ Feb-Sep) A red-shuttered, chalet-style building with functional, good-sized rooms and

sturdy wooden furniture. It's the best of the cheaper options and is popular with walkers swapping tips and comparing blisters.

Hôtel Ramuntcho (☎ 05 59 37 03 91; fax 05 59 37 35 17; 1 rue de France; d with bathroom €45-59; ⓨ closed Wed off-season) A pleasant Logis de France (see p895) within the old walls, this rustic place offers smallish but well-maintained rooms. Some rooms (3, 4, 10 and 11) have balconies that directly overlook the red-brown ramparts and beyond to the mountains. There's also a good restaurant (p665).

Hôtel des Pyrénées (☎ 05 59 37 01 01; hotel .pyrenees@wanadoo.fr; 19 place Charles de Gaulle; r €92-155; ⓨ mid-Jan–mid-Nov; Ⓟ ✕ Ⓡ ▯) The town's classiest hotel offers large, luxurious rooms of contemporary design inside a traditional Basque building. Balconies reveal stunning views of the surrounding mountains, and there's a much-acclaimed restaurant (p665).

CAMPING
Riverside **Camping Municipal Plaza Berri** (☎ 05 59 37 11 19; av du Fronton; per adult/tent/car €2/1.50/1.50; ⓨ Apr-Oct) has ample shade.

Eating
Chez Dédé (☎ 05 59 37 16 40; 3 rue de France; menu €10, full meals €14-15; ⓨ closed Thu & dinner Wed) Nestled in the ramparts of the old town, this busy place, pulling in pilgrims and walkers, is hot on Basque peppers. The flexible, pick-and-mix menu includes entrees (€4), mains (€8 to €9) and desserts (€2). Try the *piquillos farcis à la morue* (sweet peppers stuffed with cod in a rich tomato sauce).

Bar-Restaurant le Relais de la Nive (☎ 05 59 37 04 22; place du Marché; menus €18.50 & €25; ⓨ closed Thu & Dec-Feb) This eatery occupies a wonderful spot beside the river and has views of the Vieux Pont, which is perfectly reflected by day and floodlit at night.

Most the hotels recommended in the Sleeping section also have worthwhile restaurants. Both **Hôtel Itzalpea** (menus €10.70-14.50) and **Hôtel Ramuntcho** (menus €11.20-17.50) offer family-style, regional cuisine at a budget price. In its own league, **Hôtel des Pyrénées** (menus €40-85) is a highly respected gastronomic establishment, with a quiet, refined ambience. The Michelin-starred French and Basque cuisine is reason enough to come to St-Jean; creations such as *raviolis de langoustines au caviar d'aquitaine* (€45) justify all the hype.

SELF-CATERING
Farmers bring in their fresh produce for the town's **Monday market** (place Charles de Gaulle).

Entertainment
In high summer, there are performances of Basque music and dancing in the jai alai court at 9.30pm on Thursdays.

At 5pm every Monday, coinciding with market day, there's a bare-handed pelota tournament at the **trinquet court** (place du Trinquet).

In summer, variants of pelota are played according to the day of the week at the *trinquet, fronton municipal* and jai alai courts. Check schedules at the tourist office. Admission to each costs about €10.

Getting There & Away
Train is the best option; the irregular bus service to/from Bayonne is a huge detour. The train journey to/from Bayonne up the Nive Valley to the end of the line (€7.50, one hour, four daily) is just beautiful.

For a day trip, take the 8.55am from Bayonne. The last train back leaves St-Jean Pied de Port at 4.53pm (check these times, which may vary according to season).

Getting Around
BICYCLE
Maya Sport (☎ 05 59 37 15 98; 18 av du Jaï Alaï) has mountain bikes for hire.

CAR
Parking can be a real pain in summer. The car parks beside the covered market and by the jai alai pelota court, both free, are the largest.

TAXI
To order a taxi, call ☎ 05 59 37 05 00 or ☎ 05 59 37 13 37.

AROUND ST-JEAN PIED DE PORT
The village of **St-Étienne de Baïgorry** along with its outlying hamlets straggle across the Vallée de Baïgorry. Tranquillity itself, after busy St-Jean Pied de Port, and stretched thinly along a branch of the Nive, the village has, like so many Basque settlements, two focal points: the church and the fronton court.

Irouléguy is the French Basque Country's only AOC wine – and most of it comes from the Vallée de Baïgorry. Just north of town, the **wine-growers' cooperative** (☎ 05 59 37 41 33) organises vineyard visits (€3) in July and August. It's open year-round for sales and tasting.

Both St-Étienne de Baïgorry and its near-neighbour **Bidarray**, further down the valley, make excellent bases for walking. The tourist office in St-Jean Pied de Port has a booklet on walks in the area (€6.10) and accommodation details.

The Pyrenees

CONTENTS

Pau	669
Lourdes	675
Around Lourdes	680
Parc National des Pyrénées	680
Vallée d'Aspe	681
Vallée d'Ossau	684
Cauterets	686
Vallée des Gaves & Around	690
Upper Garonne Valley	690
Vallée de l'Ariège	691

As the crow flies, the Pyrenees (Pyrénées) stretch for 430km, sea to sea, forming a natural boundary between France and Spain. Had you sufficient time and energy, you could follow the GR10 walking trail that bucks and twists from Hendaye beside the Bay of Biscay on France's Atlantic coast all the way to Banyuls beside the Mediterranean. But few travellers have such luxuries in abundance so you'll probably have to select from its three distinct zones.

The Pyrénées-Atlantiques rise steadily from the Atlantic, their lush green heads poking through mist and cloud, their skirts of rustling beech forest.

The Hautes Pyrénées, focus of this chapter, are wilder and higher. Their rugged peaks and ridges, deep valleys and high cols are protected territory, falling within the narrow strip of the Parc National des Pyrénées that shadows the frontier for about 100km. Here, you can disappear into the mountains for days and spot only other walkers, marmots, izards (cousin to the chamois) – and, if you're *very* lucky, one of the Pyrenees' last surviving brown bears.

Stunning valleys, such as the Vallée d'Aspe and the Vallée d'Ossau, cut laterally into the central Pyrenees, their lower reaches rich pasture, their narrow, southern necks steeper and more enclosed. Here up high, shimmering lakes and tarns are fed by swift mountain streams punctuated by gushing cascades. Towns, such as the winter ski resorts and summer walking bases of Cauterets and Bagnères de Luchon, are appropriately small, deferring to the sheer grandeur of the mountains.

To the north of their foothills sit the sedate yet dynamic cities of Pau and Lourdes, one of Christianity's most important pilgrim towns.

Eastwards, in the Pyrénées Orientales, the climate becomes warmer and drier, the vegetation pricklier, squatter and more abundant as the mountains taper down into Roussillon, then finally dip into the Mediterranean.

HIGHLIGHTS

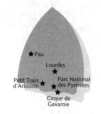

- Catch a first glimpse of **snow-capped mountains** (p669) from Pau's stylish blvd des Pyrénées
- Mingle with the faithful at **Lourdes** (p677), one of the world's most important pilgrimage sites
- Trek in the **Parc National des Pyrénées** (p680), one of western Europe's wildest areas
- Trundle along in the open-topped **Petit Train d'Artouste** (p686) at a constant 2000m
- Gasp at the magnificent wrap-around sweep of the **Cirque de Gavarnie** (p690)

■ POPULATION: 3,017,200	■ AREA: 8400 SQ KM

Information

Information on the Pyrenees is available in Paris, from the **Maison des Pyrénées** (☎ 01 42 86 51 86; pyrenees.paris@cg65.fr; 15 rue St-Augustin, 2e; metro Quatre Septembre).

PAU

pop 81,000

Pau (rhymes with 'so') is famed for its mild climate, flower-filled public parks and magnificent views of the Pyrenees. In the 19th century it was a favourite wintering spot for wealthy English and Americans. In recent years, the city has owed its prosperity to a high-tech industrial base and the huge natural gas field, plus spin-off chemical plants, at nearby Lacq. Nowadays, it's also at the cutting edge of communications technology and has attracted such giants of the trade as Microsoft, Intel, IBM and Toshiba.

Elegant, stylish (the shopping's great, especially if you're of a gourmet bent), it also has a fun-loving undertow, as befits a long-standing university city, and makes a good base for forays into the Pyrenees.

Orientation

The town centre sits on a small hill with the River Pau (Gave de Pau) at its base. Along its crest stretches blvd des Pyrénées, a wide promenade offering Cinemascope views of the mountains. The town's east–west axis is the thoroughfare of cours Bosquet, rue Maréchal Foch and rue Maréchal Joffre, with place Clemenceau at its heart. Small Vieille Ville (old town) surrounds the chateau.

Information

BOOKSHOP

Librairie des Pyrénées (☎ 05 59 27 78 75; 14 rue St-Louis) Carries an excellent selection of walking maps and guidebooks in French.

INTERNET ACCESS

C Cyber Café (☎ 05 59 82 89 40; 20 rue Lamothe, per hr €4.50; 🕑 10am-2am Mon-Fri, 2pm-2am Sat & Sun)
Cyber Coyote (☎ 05 59 27 04 03; 11 rue Duboué; per hr €4.80; 🕑 11.30am-11pm Mon-Thu, 11am-2am Fri & Sat, 2-8pm Sun)

LAUNDRY

Laundrette (66 rue Émile Garet; 🕑 7am-8pm)

POST

Main Post Office (21 cours Bosquet)

TOURIST INFORMATION

Tourist Office (☎ 05 59 27 27 08; www.pau.fr; place Royale; 🕑 9am-6pm Jul & Aug, closed Sun afternoon Sep-Jun) Offers the free booklet *Béarn: Leisure Activities*, a detailed summary of almost everything to do and see in the region.

Sights

CHÂTEAU

Pau's **château** (☎ 05 59 82 38 19; adult/18-25 yrs/under 18 €4.50/3/free; 🕑 9.30am-12.15pm & 1.30-5.45pm mid-Jun–mid-Sep, 9.30-11.45am & 2-4.15pm or 5pm mid-Sep–mid-Jun) was originally the residence of the monarchs of Navarre. It was transformed into a Renaissance chateau, bedecked with gardens, by Marguerite d'Angoulême in the 16th century. Marguerite's grandson, the future Henri IV, was born here – cradled, so the story goes, in an upturned tortoise shell.

Neglected in the 18th century and used as barracks after the Revolution, the chateau was in a sorry state by 1838, when King Louis-Philippe ordered a complete interior renovation, completed by Napoleon III. The whole, especially the façade, has recently been painstakingly re-restored.

The chateau holds one of Europe's richest collections of 16th- to 18th-century Gobelins tapestries and some fine Sèvres porcelain. These items apart, most of the ornamentation and furniture, including an oak dining table that can seat 100, dates from Louis-Philippe's intervention. In the room where Henry IV was born is what's claimed to be that tortoise-shell cradle.

Within the brick-and-stone **Tour de la Monnaie** below the main chateau, a free, modern lift hauls you from place de la Monnaie up to the ramparts.

Admission includes an obligatory and less than arresting guided tour in rapid-fire French or Spanish (though a printed version in English is available).

PYRENEES PANORAMA

From majestic blvd des Pyrénées, there's a breathtaking panorama of the Pyrenean summits on clear days, prevalent in autumn and winter. The **orientation table** opposite No 20 details the names of the peaks.

VIEILLE VILLE

Little is left of Pau's labyrinthine old centre. An area of around 300m in diameter is all that remains, yet it's rich in restored medieval and Renaissance buildings.

PYRENEES (PYRÉNÉES)

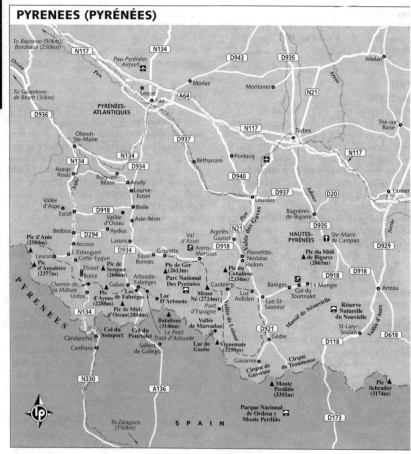

MUSÉE BERNADOTTE

The **Musée Bernadotte** (☎ 05 59 27 48 42; 8 rue Tran; adult/child €2/1; ⏰ 10am-noon & 2-6pm Tue-Sun) has exhibits illustrating the improbable yet true story of how a French general, Jean-Baptiste Bernadotte, born in this very building, became king of Sweden and Norway (see the boxed text, p672). You'll spot the building from a distance by the blue and yellow Swedish flag fluttering outside.

MUSÉE DES BEAUX-ARTS

Pau's **Musée des Beaux-Arts** (Fine Arts Museum; ☎ 05 59 27 33 02; entrance on rue Mathieu Lalanne; adult/child €2/1; ⏰ 10am-noon & 2-6pm Wed-Mon) features 15th- to 20th-century European paintings, including works by Rubens, El Greco and Degas.

Activities

Romano Sport (see p675) rents equipment for a whole range of outdoor activities, including walking (you can hire a pair of mountain boots, even just for the weekend), climbing, skiing, canyon clambering – and also hires bikes.

Festivals & Events

The **Festival de Pau** is an extravaganza of dance, music and theatre, held mid-June to mid-July, with events at the Théâtre St-Louis, Palais Beaumont and several outdoor venues.

L'Été à Pau (Summer in Pau) is a time for free music concerts, often of high quality, at venues throughout the town – notably the amphitheatre in parc Beaumont.

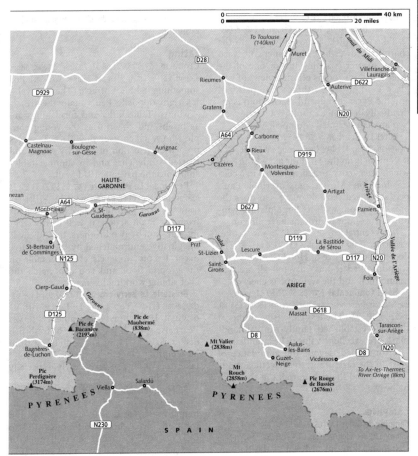

March sees both Carnival week and the month-long **Festival de Dance**, a celebration of contemporary dance.

If cars, whether they are venerable and distinguished or mean and growling, captivate you, plan to spend the week before Whitsuntide in Pau. On the first weekend, there's a parade of vintage vehicles, followed by the **Grand Prix Historique.** On the second weekend, a Formula 3 Grand Prix motor race howls and whines through the city's streets.

Every October, the **Concours Complet International** brings together some of the world's best horse riders in a gruelling competition embracing dressage, cross-country and jumping.

Sleeping

Hôtel de la Pomme d'Or (☎ 05 59 11 23 23; fax 05 59 11 23 24; 11 rue Maréchal Foch; s/d €20/23, with shower €24-28, with bathroom from €25/29) On the 1st floor of a former coaching inn, this is a decent economical choice. Ask for a room facing away from the busy street. Go into the recessed courtyard and you'll find the entrance on the left.

Hôtel Adour (☎ 05 59 27 47 41; www.hotel-adour-pau .com in French; 10 rue Valérie Meunier; s/d with shower €30/32, with bathroom from €40/42; **P** **X**) Even though the street isn't particularly noisy, rooms overlooking this central hotel are *triple* glazed. The other client-sensitive touch is its non-smoking rooms – a welcome feature absent from many hotels with greater pretensions.

Hôtel le Postillon (☎ 05 59 72 83 00; www.hotel -le-postillon.fr in French; 10 cours Camou; s €40, d €43-52) Take your pick; a room giving onto the charming, flower-bedecked inner courtyard of this former coaching inn or one of the three top-floor rooms offering views of vast place Verdun (where there's free parking) and the Pyrenees beyond. Each room is individually decorated in soft pastel tones and two are handicapped equipped.

Hôtel Le Bourbon (☎ 05 59 27 53 12; le-bour bon@wanadoo.fr; 12 place Clemenceau; s/d €47/56; ☒) Reception is on the 1st floor of Le Bourbon, which offers cosy, practical rooms in a central location. Most rooms overlook Pau's pedestrianised central square – as does the breakfast room with its large picture windows. Top-floor bedrooms have air-con.

Hôtel Central (☎ 05 59 27 72 75; www.hotelcen tralpau.com; 15 rue Léon Daran; s €31-45, d €31-58) The decoration and size of Hôtel Central's fully soundproofed rooms vary but all are well maintained and the welcome is cheery.

Hôtel Continental (☎ 05 59 27 69 31; www.best western.com/fr/continental; 2 rue Maréchal Foch; s €55-80, d €62-95; ℗ 🖵) The less expensive rooms at this long-established, family-run Pau landmark are excellent value. The grandeur is far from faded; savour the abundance of glass in the restaurant, the eclectic antique furniture and the rich mosaics in the main hallway.

CAMPING

Camping de Gelos (☎ 05 59 06 57 37; bearn.camping@ wanadoo.fr; per adult/tent/car €3/4.20/1.20; 🕓 Jun-Sep) It's about 3km out of town at the Base de Plein Air recreational area. Take bus No 1 from place Clemenceau to the Mairie de Gelos stop. Pau's **Auberge de Jeunesse** (☎ 05 59 35 09 99; fjt@ldjpau.org; dm €8.50; 🕓 year-round) is beside it.

Eating

L'Entracte (☎ 05 59 27 68 31; 2bis rue St-Louis; dishes around €8; 🕓 lunch Mon-Sat, dinner Wed-Sat) For something light, L'Entracte (The Interval – it's right opposite Pau's main theatre) is a winner. Tablecloths and furnishings are as bright and cheerful as the young couple who've taken over this place. It serves up a wide selection of crunchy salads and toasted sandwiches and in summer tables spill onto the pavement/sidewalk.

Restaurant La Michodière (☎ 05 59 27 53 85; 34 rue Pasteur; menus €14 & €24; mains €11-20; 🕓 Mon-Sat, closed Aug) This gem of a place, a little apart from the main action, is well worth seeking out. Run by two brothers, the cuisine is imaginative and matched by the attractive décor. It's on two levels; choose a table on the ground floor and you can watch the chef sibling working his magic.

Brasserie Le Berry (☎ 05 59 27 42 95; 4 rue Ga-chet; mains €11-14) Top-value Le Berry with its original 1950s brasserie ambience serves Béarnaise specialities and lots of fresh fish dishes. Save a cranny for something from its tempting range of desserts. They don't take reservations so arrive early, especially at lunchtime.

Au Fruit Défondu (☎ 05 59 27 26 05; 3 rue Sully; 🕓 dinner only) This intimate place offers participatory dinners, with cheese, fish and meat and even chocolate fondues (€11 to €15), as well as grill-it-yourself duck or beef *pierrades*, sizzled over a hot stone (€12 to €15).

Chez Pierre (☎ 05 59 27 76 86; 16 rue Louis Barthou; menu €34; 🕓 closed Sun, lunch Sat & Mon) Chez Pierre

---

FRANCE'S SWEDISH KING

Jean-Baptiste Bernadotte, an enthusiastic supporter of the French Revolution, was a distinguished general and diplomat serving both the Revolutionary government and Napoleon and acquiring a reputation as a talented and humane administrator.

Meanwhile, in Stockholm, the Swedish Riksdag (parliament) reckoned that the only way out of the country's dynastic and political crisis was to stick a foreigner on the throne. Admiring French military prowess, they turned to Bernadotte, electing him crown prince in 1810.

Contrary to Napoleon's expectations, Bernadotte didn't follow a pro-French foreign policy. Indeed, in the Battle of Leipzig (1813), Swedish troops under his command helped the allied army give Napoleon his first serious whipping. In 1818, Bernadotte became King Charles XIV. He died in office in 1844 but his line lives on: the present king of Sweden is the seventh ruler in the Bernadotte dynasty.

THE PYRENEES

PAU

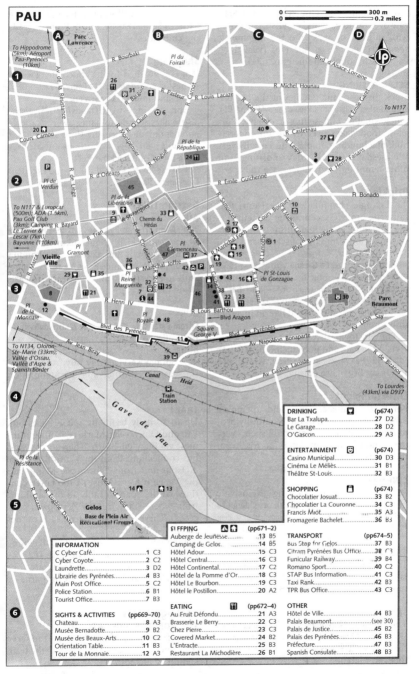

INFORMATION
C Cyber Café	1	C3
Cyber Coyote	2	C2
Laundrette	3	D2
Librairie des Pyrénées	4	B3
Main Post Office	5	C2
Police Station	6	B1
Tourist Office	7	B3

SIGHTS & ACTIVITIES (pp669–70)
Chateau	8	A3
Musée Bernadotte	9	B2
Musée des Beaux-Arts	10	C2
Orientation Table	11	B3
Tour de la Monnaie	12	A3

SLEEPING (pp671–2)
Auberge de Jeunesse	13	B5
Camping de Gelos	14	B5
Hôtel Adour	15	C3
Hôtel Central	16	C3
Hôtel Continental	17	C2
Hôtel de la Pomme d'Or	18	C3
Hôtel Le Bourbon	19	C3
Hôtel le Postillon	20	A2

EATING (pp672–4)
Au Fruit Défondu	21	A3
Brasserie Le Berry	22	C3
Chez Pierre	23	C3
Covered Market	24	B2
L'Entracte	25	B3
Restaurant La Michodière	26	B1

DRINKING (p674)
Bar La Txalupa	27	D2
Le Garage	28	D2
O'Gascon	29	A3

ENTERTAINMENT (p674)
Casino Municipal	30	D3
Cinéma Le Méliès	31	B1
Théâtre St-Louis	32	B3

SHOPPING (p674)
Chocolatier Josuat	33	B2
Chocolatier La Couronne	34	C3
Francis Miot	35	A3
Fromagerie Bachelet	36	B3

TRANSPORT (pp674–5)
Bus Stop for Gelos	37	B3
Citram Pyrénées Bus Office	38	C3
Funicular Railway	39	B4
Romano Sport	40	C2
STAP Bus Information	41	C3
Taxi Rank	42	B3
TPR Bus Office	43	C3

OTHER
Hôtel de Ville	44	B3
Palais Beaumont	(see 30)	
Palais de Justice	45	B2
Palais des Pyrénées	46	B3
Préfecture	47	B3
Spanish Consulate	48	B3

is highly reputed and much garlanded. Salivate over the lobster and crayfish, garnished with saffron, or tuck into the *mignon de veau aux morilles et foie gras* (veal fillet, wild mushrooms and foie gras; €24).

SELF-CATERING
Stock up on picnic goodies at the big **covered market** (place de la République). **Marché Bio**, much smaller and selling exclusively organic food, takes over the gaunt concrete hulk of a building on place du Foirail every Wednesday and Saturday morning. For other tempting food choices, see right.

Drinking
'Le Triangle', bounded by rue Henri Faisans, rue Émile Garet and rue Castetnau is the centre of student nightlife. Most bars stay open until 2am out of season and until 3am in summer.

Good bets are **Le Garage** (☎ 05 59 83 75 17; 49 rue Émile Garet) – look for the giant stucco mechanic sitting on the roof – and **Bar La Txalupa** (34 rue Émile Garet; ☺ Oct-Jun, Tue-Sat Jul-Sep), all in wood and shaped like an inverted ship's hull.

The old town also has its share of convivial little bars and pubs including **O'Gascon** (☎ 05 59 27 64 74; 13 rue du Château), which also serves up Béarnaise cuisine.

Entertainment
For theatre, music, dance and upcoming exhibitions, get hold of the beautifully produced *La Culture à Pau*, published every three months and available for free from the tourist office.

CINEMAS
Pau's only cinema showing exclusively nondubbed films is the excellent **Cinéma Le Méliès** (☎ 05 59 27 60 52; 6 rue Bargoin; adult/student €5.40/4.30).

CASINO
The **Casino Municipal** (☎ 05 59 27 06 92; ☺ 10am-3am Mon-Fri, 10am-4am Sat & Sun) occupies a sumptuous building within Parc Beaumont.

SPORT
The renowned **Hippodrome du Pont Long** (☎ 05 59 13 07 07; 462 blvd du Cami-Salié), 5km north of the town centre, has steeplechases from October to March.

Rugby fans will want to take in a home game of **Section Paloise**, one of France's leading club sides.

Shopping
Pau is renowned for its chocolate. Two of its best *chocolatiers* are **La Couronne** (place Clemenceau) and **Josuat** (23 rue Serviez).

Still on things sweet, **Francis Miot** (48 rue Joffre) also makes wonderful jams, sweets/candies and handmade chocolates (how about a box of *couilles du Pape* – the Pope's testicles – for a loved one back home?).

Cheese lovers should call by the excellent **Fromagerie Bachelet** (24 rue Maréchal Joffre).

Getting There & Away
AIR
The **Aéroport Pau-Pyrénées** (☎ 05 59 33 33 00; www.pau.aeroport.fr) is about 10km northwest of town. Ryanair flies daily to/from London (Stansted). Air France has four to six flights daily to Paris (Orly) and up to three to Paris (Roissy).

BUS
Citram Pyrénées (☎ 05 59 27 22 22) buses roll up the Vallée d'Ossau to Laruns (€7.30, one hour, two to five daily Monday to Saturday; Sunday service only July, August and ski season). Its office and bus stand is on rue Gachet.

TRAIN
Up to 10 daily trains or SNCF buses link Pau and Oloron-Ste-Marie (€5.70, 40 minutes) via Buzy-en-Béarn. There are onward bus connections from Buzy into the Vallée d'Ossau and from Oloron-Ste-Marie into the Vallée d'Aspe. Most of the latter continue to the Spanish railhead of Canfranc, from where trains run to Zaragoza (Saragossa). There are frequent trains to Lourdes (€6.10, 30 minutes).

Frequent direct trains run to Bayonne (€13.40, 1¼ hours) and Toulouse (€23.60, 2¾ hours, up to 10 daily). There are four daily TGVs to Paris' Gare Montparnasse (€74, five hours).

Getting Around
TO/FROM THE AIRPORT
A bus (€5) runs to/from the airport to serve the London Ryanair flight, leaving the train station at 12.15pm.

BICYCLE

At **Romano Sport** (☎ /fax 05 59 98 48 56; 1 rue Jean Réveil; ❤ 9am-noon & 3-7pm Mon-Sat) you can rent town bikes (€10/27/55 per day/three days/week) and mountain bikes (€15/40/85), along with other sporting equipment.

CAR & MOTORCYCLE

There's extensive free parking on place de Verdun. Rental agencies in town include **ADA** (☎ 05 59 72 94 40; 3bis route de Bayonne) and **Europcar** (☎ 05 59 92 09 09; 115 av Jean Mermoz), both in the suburb of Billère.

FUNICULAR RAILWAY

The train station is linked to blvd des Pyrénées by a free funicular railway, a wonderful creaky little contraption. But unless you're heavily laden or a railway nut, it's scarcely worth the wait; the walk itself, even uphill, takes much the same time.

PUBLIC TRANSPORT

The local bus company, **STAP** (☎ 05 59 14 15 16), has a sales and information office on rue Gachet. Single tickets/daily passes/eight-ride *carnets* cost €1/2.50/5.50.

TAXI

For a taxi call ☎ 05 59 02 22 22.

LOURDES

pop 15,000 / elevation 400m

Lourdes, 43km southeast of Pau, was just a sleepy market town until 1858, when Bernadette Soubirous (1844–79), a near-illiterate, 14-year-old peasant girl, saw the Virgin Mary in a series of 18 visions that came to her in a grotto. The Vatican eventually confirmed them as bona fide apparitions and, having lived out her short life as a nun, she was declared Ste Bernadette in 1933.

Nowadays Lourdes is one of the world's most important pilgrimage sites, descended upon annually by some five million visitors from all over the world. Well over half are pilgrims, including many invalids seeking cures. Nowadays, 45% of pilgrims come from beyond France's frontiers – and two-thirds are over 45 years old.

But accompanying the fervent piety of the pilgrims is an astounding display of tacky commercial exuberance – shake-up snow domes, baseball caps, and plastic bottles in the shape of the Virgin (just add holy water

at the shrine) are but a sample. It's easy to mock but remember that some people spend their life savings to come here.

Orientation

Lourdes' two main east–west streets are rue de la Grotte and blvd de la Grotte, both leading to the Sanctuaires Notre Dame de Lourdes. The principal north–south thoroughfare, called av Général Baron Maransin where it passes above blvd de la Grotte, connects the train station with place Peyramale, where you'll find the tourist office.

The huge religious complex that has grown up around the original cave where Bernadette's visions took place is across the River Pau, west of the town centre.

Information
BOOKSHOPS

The Book Shop (☎ 05 62 42 27 94; www.lourdes-bookshop.com; 13 rue du Bourg) Mainly stocks titles relating to the shrine of Lourdes plus a few novels, travel titles and a good range of walking maps.

INTERNET ACCESS

Difintel (5 rue de la Grotte; per hr €3; ❤ 9am-noon & 2-7pm Mon-Sat)
B&W (46 place du Champ Commun; per hr €4; ❤ 2pm-midnight)

LAUNDRY

Laundrette (10 av du Général Baron Maransin; ☎ 8am-7pm)

POST

Main Post Office (1 rue de Langelle)

PASSPORTS & PASSES

If you're intent upon doing Lourdes thoroughly, you save by picking up a *visa passeport touristique* (adults/children €34/17), giving free access to five museums, the little train that circumnavigates the town and a trip on the spectacular Pic du Jer funicular railway, plus an audio-guide to the Grotte de Massabielle.

Alternatively, pick up the free *Lourdes Pass*, pay the normal tariff for five of the seven attractions (Musée de Lourdes, Château Fort/Musée Pyrénéen, Musée de la Nativité, Musée Grévin, Funiculaire du Pic du Jer, Musée du Petit Lourdes, Le Petit Train) and get the last two free.

THE PYRENEES

LOURDES

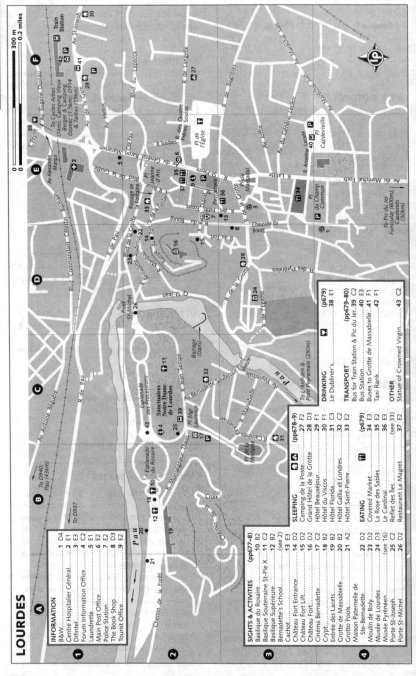

0   300 m
0   0.2 miles

INFORMATION
B&W..............................1 D4
Centre Hospitalier Général......2 E1
Dfintel...........................3 E3
Forum Information Office........4 C2
Laundrette.......................5 E1
Main Post Office.................6 E2
Police Station...................7 E2
The Book Shop...................8 D3
Tourist Office...................9 E2

SIGHTS & ACTIVITIES (pp677–8)
Basilique du Rosaire...........10 B2
Basilique Souterraine St-Pie X...11 C2
Basilique Supérieure...........12 B2
Bernadette's School............(see 2)
Cachot.........................13 E3
Château Fort Entrance..........14 D2
Château Fort Lift..............15 D2
Château Fort...................16 D2
Cinéma Bernadette..............17 C2
Crypt..........................18 B2
Entrée des Lacets..............19 B2
Grotte de Massabielle..........20 B2
Grotto Pools...................21 A2
Maison Paternelle de
  Ste-Bernadette...............22 D2
Moulin de Boly.................23 D2
Musée de Lourdes...............24 D3
Musée Pyrénéen.................(see 16)
Porte St-Joseph................25 C2
Porte St-Michel................26 D2

SLEEPING (pp678–9)
Camping de la Poste............27 F2
Grand Hôtel de la Grotte.......28 D3
Hôtel Beauséjour...............29 F1
Hôtel du Viscos................30 F1
Hôtel Florida..................31 C3
Hôtel Gallia et Londres........32 C2
Hôtel Saint-Pierre.............33 E2

EATING (p679)
Covered Market.................34 E3
La Rose des Sables.............35 E2
Le Cardinal....................36 E3
Reflet des Îles................(see 33)
Restaurant Le Magret...........37 E2

DRINKING (p679)
Le Dubliner's..................38 E1

TRANSPORT (pp679–80)
Bus for Train Station & Pic du Jer..39 C2
Bus Station....................40 E3
Buses to Grotte de Massabielle..41 F1
Taxi Rank......................42 F1

OTHER
Statue of Crowned Virgin.......43 C2

TOURIST INFORMATION

Tourist Office (☎ 05 62 42 77 40; www.lourdes-info tourisme.com; place Peyramale; ⏰ 9am-7pm Mon-Sat, 10am-6pm Sun Jul & Aug, 9am-6.30pm Mon-Sat, 10am-12.30pm Sun Apr-Jun & Sep–mid-Oct, 9am-noon & 2-6pm Mon-Sat Jan-Mar & mid-Oct–Dec)

Forum Information office (☎ 05 62 42 78 78; www .lourdes-france.com; Esplanade des Processions; ⏰ 8.30am-12.15pm & 1.45-6.30pm Apr-Oct, 9am-noon & 1.30-5.30pm or 6pm Nov-Mar) For information on the Sanctuaires Notre Dame de Lourdes.

Sights

SANCTUAIRES NOTRE DAME DE LOURDES

The development of the Sanctuaries of Our Lady of Lourdes began within a decade of the miraculous events of 1858. The most revered site is known variously as the **Grotte de Massabielle** (Massabielle Cave or Grotto), the Grotte Miraculeuse (Miraculous Cave) and the Grotte des Apparitions (Cave of the Apparitions). Open 24 hours, its walls are worn smooth by the touch of millions of hands over the years. Nearby are 19 **pools** in which 400,000 pilgrims seeking cures immerse themselves each year. Miraculous cures are becoming rarer and rarer; the last medically certifiable case took place in 1987 and, after an exhaustive 12-year investigation, was recognised by the church as a miracle.

The main 19th-century section of the sanctuaries has three parts. On the western side of Esplanade du Rosaire, between the two ramps, is the neo-Byzantine **Basilique du Rosaire** (Basilica of the Rosary). One level up is the **crypt**, reserved for silent worship. Above is the spire-topped, neo-Gothic **Basilique Supérieure** (Upper Basilica).

From Palm Sunday (the Sunday before Easter) to at least mid-October, there are solemn **torchlight processions** nightly at 9pm from the Massabielle Grotto, while at 5pm there's the **Procession Eucharistique** (Blessed Sacrament Procession), where pilgrims bearing banners process along the Esplanade des Processions.

When it's wet, the latter ceremony is held inside the vast, bunker-like **Basilique Souterraine St-Pie X** (Underground Basilica of St Pius X) with a capacity for 20,000 worshippers. Built in 1959 in the fallout-shelter style then all the rage, it's redeemed to some extent by vibrantly warm back-lit works of *gemmail*, superimposed pieces of coloured glass embedded in enamel.

Visitors to the sanctuaries should dress modestly. Smoking is forbidden throughout the complex.

All four places of worship open 6am to 10pm in summer and 7am to 7pm in winter. You can enter the grounds around the clock via the Entrée des Lacets on rue Monseigneur Theas. The **Porte St-Michel** and **Porte St-Joseph** entrances are open 5am to midnight year-round.

CHEMIN DE LA CROIX

Also known by the name Chemin du Calvaire (Way of Calvary), the 1.5km **Chemin de la Croix** (Way of the Cross; ⏰ 6am-7pm Easter-Oct, 8am-6pm Oct-Easter), leading up the forested hillside from near the Basilique Supérieure, is punctuated by the 14 Stations of the Cross. Especially devout pilgrims mount to the first station on their knees.

OTHER BERNADETTE SITES

In addition, vistors can see four other places that figured prominently in the life of Ste Bernadette.

On rue Bernadette Soubirous are the **Moulin de Boly** (Boly Mill; No 12; admission free), Bernadette's birthplace, and the **Maison Paternelle de Ste-Bernadette** (No 2; admission €1), the house that the town of Lourdes bought for the Soubirous family after Bernadette saw the apparitions.

The **Cachot** (15 rue des Petits Fossés; admission free), a former prison, is where Bernadette lived during the apparitions.

Bernadette's school (av du Général Baron Maransin; admission free), where she studied and lived from 1860 to 1866 with the Sœurs de Notre Dame de Nevers (Sisters of Our Lady of Nevers), contains some of her personal effects and is now part of the town's Centre Hospitalier Général.

MUSÉE DE LOURDES

The **Musée de Lourdes** (☎ 05 62 94 28 00; adult/child €5.50/2.50; ⏰ 9-11.45am & 1.30-6.45pm Apr-Oct), west of the Cinéma Pax in the Parking de l'Égalité, portrays the life of Ste Bernadette as well as the general history of Lourdes.

CINÉMA BERNADETTE

If you've a yen to learn yet more about Ste Bernadette or simply want to rest your feet, the **Cinéma Bernadette** (☎ 05 62 42 79 19; 6 av Monseigneur Schoepfer; adult/under 18 €6/4.50) shows the same two-hour feature film entitled (you've guessed it) *Bernadette* with optional English dialogue at 2pm, 4.30pm and 8.30pm daily from Easter to October.

CHÂTEAU FORT

There are great bird's eye views of town from the **Château Fort** (Fortified Castle; adult/child €5/2.50; h 9am-noon & 1.30-6.30pm Easter-Oct, 9am-noon & 2-6pm Nov-Easter), up on its rocky pinnacle. Within is the **Musée Pyrénéen**, with displays on folk art and tradition.

Take the free lift (elevator) from rue Baron Duprat or walk up the ramp at the northern end of rue du Bourg.

PIC DU JER

There's a splendid panoramic view of Lourdes and the central Pyrenees from the summit of Pic du Jer (948m). It's but a six-minute ride from valley level by the **funicular railway** (☎ 05 62 94 00 41; blvd d'Espagne; adult/child one way €6/4.50, return €8/6; h 10am-6pm Easter-Oct).

More strenuously and satisfyingly, follow the signed trail to the summit from the lower station (allow 2½ to three hours for the return journey). The ticket booth has a free stylised map.

Take bus No 2 from place Monseigneur Laurence.

Activities

To get away from Bernadette Soubirous, put on your walking shoes or hire a cycle (see p679) and do some or all of the 17km **Voie Verte des Gaves** (Mountain Streams Green route). It follows the old Lourdes–Cauterets train line (parallel to the Cauterets road) up the attractive Vallée des Gaves as far as Soulom, from where walkers can catch a bus back to town.

Festivals & Events

Lourdes' renowned **Festival International de Musique Sacrée** is two weeks of sacred music held around Easter.

Sleeping

Since Lourdes has over 350 hotels – in France, only Paris has more – you shouldn't need our help to find one of the 32,000 available beds. Even so, you may have to scout around during Easter, Whitsuntide, Ascension Day, May and from August to the first week of October. By contrast, the town is so quiet in winter, when most hotels shut down, that it would need a miracle to bring it to life. Given the nature of their clientele, a high proportion have facilities for the handicapped.

BUDGET

Hôtel du Viscos (☎ 05 62 94 08 06; fax 05 62 94 26 74; 6bis av St-Joseph; d €29, with bathroom €34; h Feb–mid-Dec) This friendly, family-run place has a bustling bar for guests, offers great value and couldn't be handier for the station.

Hôtel Saint-Pierre (☎ 05 62 42 30 31; fax 05 62 94 80 32; 4-6 passage de la Fontaine; s/d €25/30; h Apr–Oct) Rooms at this recently renovated hotel are smallish but quite satisfactory. There's a bar for guests, a pleasant street-side patio and a restaurant, Reflet des Îles, serving exotic fare (see p679).

Camping

Camping de la Poste (☎ 05 62 94 40 35; 26 rue de Langelle; 2 people & car €9; h Easter–mid-Oct) Right in the heart of town, it's tiny, friendly – and consequently often full. It also rents eight excellent-value rooms with bathroom (d/tr/q €25/32/40).

Among the nearest of the dozen or so camping grounds ringing town are **Camping Vieux Berger** (☎ 05 62 94 60 57; h mid-Jun–mid-Oct) and **Camping Domec** (☎ /fax 05 62 94 08 79; h Easter-Oct). Both are on route de Julos, just off blvd de Centenaire, the eastern ring road.

MID-RANGE

Hôtel Beauséjour (☎ 05 62 94 38 18; www.hotel-beausejour.com; 16 av de la Gare; s/d €60/70; P X ⌨) At the three-star Beauséjour, with its scrubbed white and ox-blood façade, parking is free and a full third of its 45 rooms are non-smoking. Recently affiliated to the Best Western group, it runs a good **restaurant** (menu €14). Rooms at the rear, though a little smaller, have an incomparable view of town and the Pyrenees beyond.

Grand Hôtel de la Grotte (☎ 05 62 94 58 87; www.hotel-grotte.com; 66 rue de la Grotte; s €66-113, d €74-140; h Apr-Oct; P X) Established in 1872, this charming *fin de siècle* place has belonged to the same family for four generations. With a gorgeous garden, bar and a couple of prestige restaurants, it's an excellent choice for those who like comfort, maturity and old world courtesy.

Hôtel Gallia et Londres (☎ 05 62 94 35 44; www
.hotelgallialondres.com; 26 av Bernadette Soubirous; s
€78-83, d €100-110; ⏰ Apr-Oct; P 🍴 💻) Much
in the same mould, the spacious bedrooms
at this hotel too are each individually and
attractively decorated à la Louis XVI. You'll
gasp at the chandeliers and wooden panelling of the dining room with its side alcoves
for more intimate eating. Equally seductive
is the lovely little garden, a rarity in this
town of stone and concrete.

Hôtel Florida (☎ 05 62 94 51 15; flo_aca_mira
_hotels@hotmail.com; 3 rue Carrières Peyramale; s €46.50,
d €60; ⏰ Apr-Oct; P 🍴) All 117 rooms at this
large mid-range, renovated, family-owned
hotel have air-con and double glazing, while
as many as 20 are equipped for the disabled.
There are fine views of the sanctuaries from
its open air terrace.

Eating

Most hotels offer half- or full-board; some
even require guests to stay on those terms,
especially in high season. Restaurants close
early in this pious town; even the local Mc-
Donald's slams shut at 10.30pm.

Le Cardinal (☎ 05 62 42 05 87; 11 place Peyramale;
salads €5.50-6, menu du jour €8.50; ⏰ Mon-Sat) This
unpretentious bar/brasserie is where the
staff of the tourist office lunch – and they
should know what's best. Tuck into steak,
chips and salad for only €6.50.

La Rose des Sables (☎ 05 62 42 04 82; 8 rue des
Quatre Frères Soulas; ⏰ Tue-Sun) This North African restaurant – a bold Muslim presence in
such a fervently Catholic town – specialises
in couscous (€12 to €14).

Reflet des Îles (⏰ Apr-Oct) This, the restaurant of Hôtel Saint-Pierre (see 678) serves

---

AUTHOR'S CHOICE

Restaurant le Magret (☎ 05 62 94 20 55;
10 rue des Quatre Frères Soulas; menus €24 & 33;
⏰ Tue-Sun Feb-Dec) This pleasant restaurant,
its agreeably rustic décor embellished with
early photos of Lourdes, offers an innovative menu with a pronounced regional
flavour. The friendly, courteous *maître* – a
dead ringer for a portly Lenin – talks you
through the dishes you've ordered and
offers informed rugby chat too, if you've
the inclination. It's prudent to reserve in
advance.

---

spicy dishes from the Indian Ocean island
of La Réunion as well as less exotic French
cuisine. Count on about €15 for a three-
course meal.

L'Ardiden (☎ 05 62 94 30 55; 48 av Peyramale; lunch
menu €10, dinner menus €12 & €16, mains €8-13; ⏰ Wed-
Sun) It's well worth the short walk upstream
to L'Ardiden, pleasantly situated beside Pont
Peyramale and the river and strong on pizza
and pasta.

SELF-CATERING
Lourdes' **covered market** occupies most of
place du Champ Commun.

Drinking

There's not much to rave about after dark;
Lourdes has only one Madonna and she's
far from being a Material Girl.

However, poke your nose into **Le Dublin-
er's** (☎ 05 62 42 16 38; 7 av Alexandre Marqui) and – a
rarity for France – you stand a chance of
actually meeting an Irish drinker in an Irish
pub; every year over 250,000 Hibernians
make the pilgrimage to Lourdes.

Getting There & Away
BUS
The **bus station** (place Capdevieille) has services
northwards to Pau (€7.20, 1¼ hours, four to
six daily) and is a stop for buses running between Tarbes and Argelès-Gazost (at least
eight daily) to the south and gateway to the
Pyrenean communities of Cauterets, Luz-
St-Sauveur and Gavarnie. SNCF buses to
Cauterets (€6.10, one hour, six daily) leave
from the train station.

TRAIN
Many pilgrims arrive by rail and Lourdes
is well connected by train to cities all over
France, including Bayonne (€17.80, 1¾
hours, three to four daily), Pau (€6.20, 30
minutes, over 10 daily) and Toulouse (€20.90,
1¾ hours, seven daily) There are four daily
TGVs to Paris' Gare Montparnasse (€72.40
to €81.40, six hours).

Getting Around
BICYCLE
Opposite Leclerc supermarket, **Cycles Arbes**
(☎ 05 62 94 05 51; 51bis av Alexandre Marqui) hires
out both mountain and town bikes. **Roue
Libre** (☎ 06 87 14 93 48), at the base of the Pic du
Jer cable railway, rents mountain bikes.

THE PYRENEES

CAR & MOTORCYCLE

Lourdes is one big, fuming traffic jam in summer. If you have a vehicle, your best bet is to leave it near the train or bus station, where there's free parking, and walk.

PUBLIC TRANSPORT

The local bus No 1 links the train station with place Monseigneur Laurence and the Sanctuaries.

TAXI

Call ☎ 05 62 94 31 30.

AROUND LOURDES

The **Grottes de Bétharram** (☎ 05 62 41 80 04; adult/child €9/4.50; ⊙ 9am-noon & 1.30-5.30pm Apr-Oct, 2.30-4pm Mon-Fri Jan-Mar), 14km west of town along the D937, are among France's most spectacular limestone caves. Guided visits, by mini-train and barge, last 1½ hours. In summer, it's best to arrive early in the morning to avoid long queues.

To see fauna that you'd be extremely lucky to stumble across higher up the valley in the Parc National des Pyrénées, you might want to visit **Parc Animalier des Pyrénées** (☎ 05 62 97 91 07; www.parc-animalier-pyrenees.com in French; adult/child €9/6; ⊙ 9am-7pm Jun-Aug, 9am-noon & 2-6pm Apr-May & Sep, 1-6pm Oct) at the northern entrance to the village of **Argelès-Gazost**. Residents of this small animal park include marmots, mouflons, otters and a couple of brown bears.

PARC NATIONAL DES PYRÉNÉES

The Parc National des Pyrénées (Pyrenees National Park) extends for about 100km along the Franco-Spanish border, from the Vallée d'Aspe in the west to the Vallée d'Aure in the east. Never broad, its width varies from 1.5km to 15km. Created in 1967, it covers an area of 457 sq km, within which are 230 lakes and Vignemale (3298m), whose summit is the highest in the French Pyrenees. To the south is Spain's 156-sq-km Parque Nacional de Ordesa y Monte Perdido, with which the French park collaborates closely.

Its many streams are fed by both springs and some 2000mm of annual precipitation, much of which falls as snow. The French slopes, especially in the west, are much wetter and greener than the dun-coloured Spanish side.

The vast and varied park is exceptionally rich in both fauna and plant life (over 150 species of flora are endemic). Keep glancing up: its wilder reaches rank among the best places in Europe to see large birds of prey such as golden eagles, griffon and bearded vultures, booted eagles, buzzards and falcons.

The animal population includes 42 of France's 110 species of mammal. Look out for marmots – or rather, listen out for their distinctive whistle. Having become extinct in the Pyrenees, they were successfully reintroduced from the Alps, where they thrive. Another success story is that of the izard, a close relative of the chamois, which was all but blasted out of existence half a century ago, mainly by firearms left over from WWII. Nowadays, thanks to careful control and monitoring, the park is home to about 5000 izards while numbers on both sides of the Pyrenees exceed 20,000. By contrast, brown bears, once numerous, are now extremely scarce; indeed, it's possible that the last survivors may have disappeared by the time you read this.

Each year, the park receives over two million visitors, 80% of whom increase the pressure upon three beleaguered sites: Cirque de Gavarnie, Pont d'Espagne above Cauterets and the Réserve Naturelle de Néouvielle in the eastern sector.

Park boundaries are marked by a red izard head on a rectangular white background, painted on rocks and trees.

MAPS & BOOKS

Each of the six park valleys (Vallée d'Aure, Vallée de Luz, Vallée de Cauterets, Val d'Azun, Vallée d'Ossau and Vallée d'Aspe) is covered by a national park folder or booklet in French, *Randonnées dans le Parc National des Pyrénées*, describing 10 to 15 walking itineraries. Worthwhile for the route maps alone, they're on sale at local park and tourist offices.

The park is covered by IGN's 1:25,000 Top 25 maps 1547OT *Ossau*, 1647OT *Vignemale*, 1748OT *Gavarnie* and 1748ET *Néouvielle*.

The Pyrenees chapter in Lonely Planet's *Walking in France* centres on the Vallée d'Aspe and Vallée de Cauterets. It describes in detail a variety of day walks plus a three-day tour in and around the valleys and suggests extended treks within the park.

Fleurs des Pyrénées Faciles à Reconnaître by Philippe Mayoux, published by Rando Éditions, is a handy, well-illustrated pocket guide in French.

Information

There are **national park offices** with visitors centres at (from west to east) Etsaut, Laruns, Arrens-Marsous, Cauterets, Luz-St-Sauveur, Gavarnie and St-Lary-Soulon. Most – although not the Cauterets or Gavarnie ones – close during the cold half of the year.

For information about the park, its flora and fauna and activities, go to www.parc -pyrenees.com.

Activities
WALKING

The Parc National des Pyrénées is criss-crossed by 350km of waymarked trails (including the Mediterranean to Atlantic GR10), some of which link up with trails in Spain.

The park has about 20 *refuges* (mountain huts or lodges), the majority run by the Club Alpin Français (CAF). Most are staffed only from July to September but retain a small wing year-round.

SKIING

The Pyrenees receive less snow than the much higher Alps and what snow falls is generally wetter and heavier. Despite this, there's reasonable downhill skiing and snowboarding for beginners and intermediates. The potential for cross-country skiing, ski touring and, increasingly, snowshoeing, is also good. The ski season normally lasts from December to early April, depending upon snow conditions.

Ski resorts dot both sides of the Pyrenees. The French side alone has over 20 downhill ski stations, most of them quite modest, and more than 10 cross-country areas

One of the oldest resorts is **Cauterets**, which usually has the longest season and most reliable snow conditions. The largest is the combined resort of **Barèges-La Mongie** (tourist office ☎ 05 62 92 16 00), 39km southeast of Lourdes, with 64 runs and over 50 lifts.

For some of the best cross-country skiing, head for **Val d'Azun** (tourist office in Arrens-Marsous; ☎ 05 62 97 49 49), about 30km southwest of Lourdes. It has 110km of trails between 1350m and 1600m.

WHITE-WATER SPORTS

Rivers racing from the Pyrenean heights offer some of France's finest white water, which, as spring snowmelt is supplemented by modest year-round rain, have a fairly steady annual flow. Organisations offering rafting and canoeing within, or downstream from, the Parc National include **A Boste Sport Loisir** (☎ 05 59 38 57 58; www.aboste.com in French; rue Léon Bérard, 64390 Sauveterre de Béarn) and **Centre Nautique de Soeix** (☎ 05 59 39 61 00; fax 05 59 39 65 16; quartier Soeix, 64400 Oloron-Ste-Marie).

VALLÉE D'ASPE

The River Aspe (Gave d'Aspe) flows for some 50km from the Col du Somport, which marks the frontier with Spain, down to Oloron-Ste-Marie. Fewer than 3000 people live in the 13 villages of the valley, whose upper reaches have always been among the remotest corners of the French Pyrenees and one of the final refuges of their more timid wildlife.

But such seclusion may soon be lost as juggernauts plough through the Pyrenees' newest road tunnel, 8km long and completed in 2003. Despite concessions such as ring roads around the luckier villages of the lower valley, its impact upon the fragile higher reaches of the valley in particular can only be negative.

The Vallée d'Aspe has been a transfrontier passage ever since Julius Caesar's Roman legionaries marched through. A railway line, completed in 1928 and a minor masterpiece of engineering, forged its way up the valley before tunnelling through to meet the Spanish railhead at Canfranc. Services stopped when a bridge collapsed in 1970 and the railway, still visible for most of its length, has been allowed to rust away.

MAPS

The 1:50,000 scale *Béarn: Pyrénées Carte No 3*, published by Rando Éditions, is a practical general trekking map of the area. A more detailed option is IGN's 1:25,000-scale Top 25 map No 1547OT, *Ossau*.

The National Park's *Randonnées dans le Parc National des Pyrénées: Aspe* is a pack of information sheets on 11 walks, varying from 1½ hours to eight hours, in and around the valley.

Information

The valley's friendly **tourist office** (☎ 05 59 34 57 57; www.aspecanfranc.com in French & Spanish; place

Sarraillé; ⏰ 9am-12.30pm & 2-5.30pm or 6.30pm Mon-Sat) is in the main square of **Bedous.** It and **Librairie d'Aspe** (rue de la Caserne) both carry a reasonable selection of walking maps.

The **Maison du Parc National des Pyrénées** (park information centre; ☎ 05 59 34 88 30; ⏰ 10.30am-12.30pm & 2-6.30pm May-Oct) occupies the old train station in **Etsaut** and houses a good display (in French) about the fauna of the Pyrenees.

Getting There & Away

SNCF (☎ 08 92 35 35 35) buses and trains connect Pau and Oloron-Ste-Marie up to 10 times daily (see 674). From Oloron, there are four onward bus connections into the valley via Bedous to Etsaut, the majority continuing to Somport and the Spanish railhead of Canfranc.

Two short cuts over the tops link the Aspe and Ossau valleys. Take the narrow, steeply winding D294 between Escot and Bielle for a spectacular 21km drive over the Col de Marie-Blanque (1035m). The D918, linking Asasp-Arros and Arudy is a more gentle, still attractive yet less spectacular alternative.

Bedous

Bedous, the valley's biggest village – with, despite this superlative, under 600 inhabitants – is 25km south of Oloron-Ste-Marie, where the valley's still wide.

Moulin d'Orcun (☎ 05 59 34 74 91; adult/child €4/3; ⏰ visits 11am & hourly 3-6pm Jul & Aug, by appointment Sep-Jun), 0.5km out of Bedous on the Aydius road, is a working 18th-century watermill.

OUTDOOR ACTIVITIES

The tourist office in Bedous and other outlets in the valley sell the excellent locally produced guide *45 Randonnées dans la Vallée d'Aspe.*

Montagne Nature (☎ 05 59 34 75 77; montagne .nature@wanadoo.fr; ⏰ 10am-12.30pm & 3-7.30pm Jul & Aug, 4-7pm Fri-Sun Sep-Jun), a cooperative of specialists in outdoor-activity, offers just about everything energetic you might want to do in the valley. It rents mountain bikes (€9/15 per half/full day), runs guided cycling outings and does canyon clambering, climbing, skiing, snowshoeing and winter mountaineering trips.

SLEEPING & EATING

Le Mandragot (☎ 05 59 34 59 33; place Sarraillé; beds €10) Accommodation in this welcoming *gîte*

d'étape with its cosy common room is in rooms for two to eight. It has self-catering facilities.

Camping Municipal de Carole (☎ 05 59 34 59 19; per person/tent/car €2.50/2/2; ⏰ Mar-Oct) Around 300m west of the N134, it's well signposted from the main highway.

Chez Michel (☎ 05 59 34 52 47; abr.michel@free.fr; rue Gambetta; d €42 with breakfast; menus €10 & €16.50) On the main street, Chez Michel has a sauna, free for overnighters, and also runs a neat little **restaurant**. Go for the *menu saveur du pays* ('flavours of the region'; €13) of *garbure* (a scrumptious local pork-based gruel, thick with vegetables and pulses), trout with *cèpe* mushrooms and bilberry pie.

Restaurant des Cols (☎ 05 59 34 70 25; ⏰ closed 1-15 Oct) This little place merits a 50km detour for its sumptuous *menus* (€10 to 21.50) Happily it's a mere 6.5km east of Bedous in the hamlet of Aydius. It also has three delightful doubles (€29) with self-catering facilities. The only downsides: the stuffed wildlife in the restaurant and those rabbit skin (or could it be cat?) barstool cushions…

Accous

This little village, 2.5km south of Bedous and 800m east of the highway, sits at the yawning mouth of the Vallée Berthe with a splendid backdrop of 2000m-plus peaks. North of here, the Vallée d'Aspe is broad and fertile. To the south, it closes in dramatically.

The **Fermiers Basco-Béarnais cheese centre** (☎ 05 59 34 76 06; ⏰ 9am-noon & 2-6pm Mon-Fri, 10am-noon & 3-6pm Sat, plus Sun during school holidays), a farmers' cooperative and thriving *fromagerie*, is beside the N134. It has free sampling and offers a 20-minute audiovisual presentation in French, plus the opportunity to buy the best of local ewe, goat and cow's-milk cheeses.

ACTIVITIES

Tiny Accous boasts two *parapente* (paragliding) schools. **Ascendance** (☎ 05 59 34 52 07; www.ascendance.fr in French) offers accompanied 15-minute introductory flights for €65 and five-day induction courses for €366. It also advertises the valley's only Internet point although you'll be turned away if they're busy parapenting. **Air Attitude** (☎ 05 59 34 50 06; www.air-attitude.com in French), newer and offering a wider range of courses and flights, has similar prices.

Starting at Easter through to November, hiring a horse at Auberge Cavalière (see below) will cost you €43/65 per half/full day. Alternatively for an investment of €580 you can enjoy half-board and half a day's riding for the entire week. The hotel also arranges pony treks of four to seven days and walking holidays, supplying detailed maps for circular day walks based from the hotel.

SLEEPING & EATING

Auberge Cavalière (☎ 05 59 34 72 30; www.auberge -cavaliere.com; d €38.50; menus €17 & €20; ☺ year-round) About 3km south of Accous and just off the main road, this well-established place has a strong equine flavour. Dining – and you dine well – in the cosy low-beamed restaurant with sheep and goat pelts around the walls is rather like eating in a particularly cosy barn.

Camping Despourrins (☎ 05 59 34 71 16; per person/site €2.50/2.65; ☺ Mar-Oct) This tiny camping ground is just off the N134, tucked behind the Fermiers Basco-Béarnais cheese centre.

Lescun

The bridge at L'Estanguet that collapsed in 1970 and finished off the valley's train traffic is about 4km south of Bedous. Nearby, a steeply hairpinned, 5.5km detour climbs southwest to the mountain village of Lescun (900m), whose slate roofs once sheltered a leper colony.

It's worth a touch of vertigo on the ascent for the breathtaking, photogenic view westwards of the Cirque de Lescun, an amphitheatre of jagged limestone mountains, backed by the 2504m Pic d'Anie.

WALKING

A number of splendid walks can be started from Lescun. For a day walk with spectacular views back over the Vallée de Lescun and the distinctive Pic du Midi d'Ossau, follow the GR10 northwest via the Refuge de Labérouat and along the base of Les Orgues de Camplong (Camplong Organ Pipes) up to the Cabane du Cap de la Baigt, a *fromagerie* (open only in the summertime), where you can buy fresh cheese directly from the shepherd.

THE BROWN BEAR'S LAST STAND?

The brown bear *(ursos arctos)*, widespread throughout Europe 3000 years ago, was mercilessly hunted and captured for public display. Although rigorously protected for nearly half a century, its very existence is threatened by loss of habitat, tourism and road building – and not helped by its long, precarious two-year breeding cycle. Brown bears disappeared from the French Alps in 1937 while the Pyrenees sustain only a minute population, boosted by a trio from Slovenia, who have successfully bred. However, it's quite possible that, as you read this, the last brown bear will have disappeared from the Hautes-Pyrénées.

As we went to print, there were probably five at the very most roaming the Aspe and Ossau valleys. No one really knows for sure since the evidence comes primarily from footprints, often indistinct and ambiguous and nowadays on occasion supplemented by DNA traces. Best estimates are that there are a couple of youngsters out there, plus the venerable old male Papillon who, experts fear, can't manage it any more, Canelle, the only female, and Néré, imported from Slovenia and released amid great controversy.

In Pyrenean valleys, you'll see slogans daubed on rocks: 'Non aux ours' (No to the bears), 'Pas d'ours' (No bears) and, our favourite, 'Bonne année et longue vie aux ours!' (Happy New Year and long life to the bears!).

Little Borce used to have a couple of Pyrenean bears, Ségoulène and her cub, Myrtille, on display. Criticised by many yet well presented, this brought pleasure to thousands and helped to sensitise visitors to the probable extinction of their cousins in the wild.

Then, in the summer of 2004, Borce established **Espace Animalier** (☎ 05 59 34 89 33; adult/child €7/4.50; ☺ 9.30am-7pm Jul-Sep, 2-6pm Oct-Jun), a large open area above the village where the animals live in semi-captivity.

Here, Ségoulène, her cub, Myrtille, and a young male, a recent arrival (could there be romance in the air?) roam freer, together with izards, roe deer, marmots and mouflons –though higher authority, under pressure from local herders, did veto plans to introduce a small pack of wolves.

Lonely Planet's *Walking in France* describes other tempting walks from Lescun and also from Etsaut, higher up the Vallée d'Aspe.

SLEEPING

Gîte & Camping du Lauzart (☎ & fax 05 59 34 51 77; campinglauzart@wanadoo.fr; per person/tent/car €2.20/ 3.80/1; ⏱ 20 Apr-20 Sep) Spacious, friendly and beautifully situated, this pleasant camping area is 1.5km southwest of the village. A dorm bed in the *gîte* costs €9.35.

Hôtel du Pic d'Anie (☎ 05 59 34 71 54; hotel .picdanie@club-Internet; s/d €32/40; ⏱ May–mid-Sep) In the village itself, the hotel does particularly hearty meals (*menus* €15 – including a vegetarian option – and €23). A couple of doors away is its year-round *gîte* (dorm bed €11) with self-catering facilities.

Maison de la Montagne (☎ 05 59 34 79 14; les cun.dom@clubInternet.fr; dm €11, half-board €26) This cosy, rustic *gîte* has been adapted from an old barn. The owner, a qualified guide, leads mountain walks.

Etsaut & Borce

The twin villages of Etsaut and Borce are set back on either side of the N134, 11km south of Bedous. Both are popular bases for higher-elevation walks. For details of its National Park office, see p681.

Up the hill, Borce is one of the trimmest little hamlets in all the Pyrenees, restored and documented with care – just see how the telephone booth and public toilets blend harmoniously with the village's mellow stone domestic architecture! – yet still a living community, just on the right side of twee.

AUTHOR'S CHOICE

Au Château d'Arance (☎ 05 59 34 75 50; www.auchateaudarance.com in French; d €54-60) From the hamlet of Cette-Eygun, climb eastwards up a narrow, winding lane for 2.25km to reach this delightfully renovated 13th-century castle. For a castle, it's decidedly intimate with only eight rooms, one of which has facilities for the handicapped. Its **restaurant** (menus €15 & €25) is equally stylish and the sweeping view of the valley below from the terrace makes a sundowner taste all the sweeter.

One route for medieval pilgrims heading for Santiago de Compostela (nowadays the GR653 long-distance trail) was via the Vallée d'Aspe, through Borce and over the Col du Somport. **Hospitalet de St-Jacques de Compostelle** (☎ 05 59 34 88 99; admission free; ⏱ 10am-6.30pm) in Borce is a tiny museum, housed in a former pilgrims' lodging and 15th-century chapel. Pop two euros in the slot for 20 minutes of haunting plainsong.

WALKING

For a challenging half-day walk, pick up the GR10 in Borce or Etsaut and follow it south to Fort du Portalet, a 19th-century fortress used as a prison in WWII by the Germans and Vichy government. Here, head east to negotiate the Chemin de la Mâture, a vertiginous path, originally hacked into the vertical cliff face to allow bullock trains to transport timber for ships' masts from the upper slopes.

Prefer hands-in-pockets walking? **Rand'en Âne,** run by the friendly folk at La Garbure (see below) can line you up with a donkey (per hour/half-/full day €11/22/33) to take the strain.

SLEEPING & EATING

La Garbure (☎ 05 59 34 88 98; www.garbure.net; dm €11, half-board €23.50) This popular *gîte d'étape*, down the alleyway beside Etsaut's parish church, has donkeys to rent. The owners have a mountain of information about local walks and there's a kitchen for self-caterers. The same family also runs **La Maison de l'Ours** (☎ 05 59 34 86 38; prices as La Garbure) in the village square. In July and August, you can sit on its terrace and savour their lipsmacking home-made ice cream.

Hôtel des Voyageurs (☎ 05 59 34 88 05; d €31; menus €16.50 & €26; ⏱ mid-Dec–Oct, closed Sun-Mon except school holidays) This unpretentious hotel with its cosy rooms offers just about the best value cuisine in the whole valley. It's in Urdos, 5km south of Etsaut and the last village before the Spanish frontier.

VALLÉE D'OSSAU

The River Ossau makes a 60km journey from the watershed at Col du Pourtalet (1794m) to its confluence with the Aspe at Oloron-Ste-Marie. The Vallée d'Ossau, through which the river cuts a swathe, is one of contrasts. The lower, northern

Harbour at Cassis (p771), Provence

Traditional Provençal costume, Digne-les-Bains (p810)

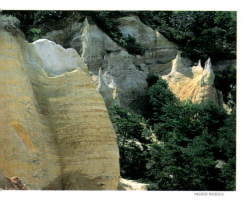

Intriguing rock formations of the Lubéron hills (p799) of Provence

Palais des Papes (p786), Avignon

Limestone outcrops off the Corsican coast near Bonifacio (p886)

Casino de Monte Carlo (p859), Monaco

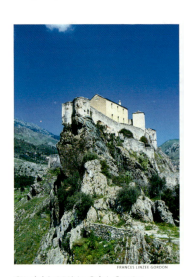

Citadel (p872) in Calvi, Corsica

Rue Grande, St-Paul de Vence (p833), Côte d'Azur

reaches as far as Laruns are broad, green and pastoral. Then, as it cuts more deeply and more steeply into the Pyrenees, it becomes narrow, confined, wooded and looming before broadening out again near the hamlet of Gabas.

MAPS & BOOKS

The most practical general walking map of the area is the 1:50,000-scale *Béarn: Pyrénées Carte No 3,* published by Rando Éditions. For more detail, consult three IGN 1:25,000-scale Top 25 maps – Nos 1547OT *Ossau,* 1647OT *Vignemale* and 1546ET *Laruns.*

The tourist office produces *Randonnées en Vallée d'Ossau* (€7), describing 30 signed walks between 5km and 16km, plus five mountain-bike routes. The quality of the mapping, reproduced from IGN originals, is excellent. The National Park visitor centre stocks *Randonnées dans le Parc National des Pyrénées: Vallée d'Ossau* (€6.40), describing 14 more challenging walks in the area, supported by 1:50,000-scale maps.

Information

INTERNET ACCESS

Refuge-Auberge L'Embaradère (under Laurens, right) Has an Internet point that functions with a France Telecom phonecard.

TOURIST INFORMATION

La Maison de la Vallée d'Ossau (☎ 05 59 05 31 41; ossau.tourisme@wanadoo.fr; place de La Mairie, Laruns; 9.30am-noon & 2-6pm Mon-Sat plus 9am-noon Sun school holidays only) The valley's tourist office, on Laruns' main square.

National Park Visitor Centre (☎ 05 59 05 41 59; pnpossau@espaces-naturels.fr; 9am-12.30pm & 1.30-6pm Jun-Sep, Mon-Fri Oct-May) Beside the Laruns tourist office.

Getting There & Around

Citram Pyrénées (☎ 05 59 27 22 22) runs buses from Pau to Laruns (€7.30, one hour, two to five daily Monday to Saturday – Sunday service only July, August and ski season).

SNCF trains from Pau stop at Buzy-en-Béarn from where there are at least three onward bus connections daily as far as Laruns (40 minutes).

During school holidays, **SARL Canonge** (☎ 05 59 05 30 31) runs a morning and an evening bus between Laruns and Artouste-Fabrèges (€6.10 return, 35 minutes, daily). The summer service continues as far as Col du Pourtalet (€6 one way).

For scenic routes between the Ossau and Aspe valleys, see p682.

Falaise aux Vautours

The gliding flight of the griffon vulture *(Gyps folvus)* is once more a familiar sight over the Pyrenees. It feeds exclusively on carrion, thus acting as a kind of alpine dustman.

This 82-hectare reserve originally protected around 10 griffon vulture pairs nesting in the limestone cliffs above the villages. Now, there are more than 100 nesting pairs, plus various other raptors – notably a couple of migratory Egyptian vultures.

La Falaise aux Vautours (Cliff of the Vultures; ☎ 05 59 82 65 49; www.falaise-aux-vautours.com in French; adult/child €6/4; 10.30am-12.30pm & 2-6.30pm Jun-Aug, 2.30-5.30pm or 6.30pm May-Jun, Sep & other school holidays) in Aste-Béon shows round-the-clock live, big-screen images from nests up on the cliffs. Time it right and you can peek in on nesting, hatching and feeding in real time. There's also an interactive display about vultures with captions in English.

Laruns

pop 1500 / elevation 536m

Laruns, 6km south of Aste-Béon and 37km from Pau, is the valley's principal village.

Refuge-Auberge L'Embaradère (☎ 05 59 05 41 88; www.gite-embaradere.com in French; 13 av de la Gare; dm €10, half-board €25; menus €11 & €16; mid-Jun–mid-Sep, Tue-Sun mid-Sep–mid-Jun) This welcoming walkers' favourite has self-catering facilities – and the valley's only Internet access, open to anyone with a France Telecom phone card. Try its *assiette béarnaise* (€8.50), a rich selection of regional cold cuts.

Hôtel de France (☎ 05 59 05 33 71; fax 05 59 05 43 83; av de la Gare; r €29, with bathroom €39-44) Although no longer young (and all the more characterful for that), this place is spotless and spruce. It serves real jam in real jam pots for breakfast, unlike the usual sealed-plastic goo. The friendly family owners readily dispense information about hiking opportunities.

Camping areas sprawl nearby. At most, however, you're hemmed in by caravans and mobile homes.

Camping du Valentin (☎ 05 59 05 39 33; pelphi@infonie.fr; per person/site €3.15/4.75; May-Oct) By contrast, this highly recommended camping ground, 2.4km south of the village beside the D918, has separate zones for mobile homes, caravans and family tents. Overlooking all, and enjoying the best of the impressive views northwards, is an area for lightweight campers.

Gabas

Tiny Gabas, with less than 50 souls, is now mainly a trekking base, 13km south of Laruns. Its equally small-scale 12th-century **chapel** is the only vestige of what was once a monastery and the last Santiago de Compostela pilgrim hostel before the Spanish frontier at Col du Pourtalet. Pick up a hunk of tangy *fromage d'Ossau*, made in the high mountains from ewe's milk and matured in the hamlet.

The Club Alpin Français **refuge** (CAF; ☎ 05 59 05 33 14; dm €7.60, half-board €23; ☉ Jun–Sep & school holidays, Sat & Sun only other times, closed Nov–mid-Dec), 500m south of Gabas, offers cheery accommodation in rooms for four to 12 and a culinary reputation that extends way beyond the valley; Madame's home-made desserts are to die for.

Hôtel-Restaurant le Biscaü (☎ 05 59 05 31 37; fax 05 59 05 43 23; s/d with shower €17/32.50, with bathroom €27.50/40; menus €9.50-15; ☉ mid-Dec–Oct) Le Biscaü is Gabas' most comfortable option and offers hearty cuisine (save room for the cheese course; the owner himself matures cheeses brought in by the local shepherds).

From the CAF *refuge*, a 3.5km forest track brings you to Lac de Bious-Artigues (1420m) and a superb view southeast to Pic du Midi d'Ossau and southwest to Pic d'Ayous.

Le Petit Train d'Artouste

Winter skiers and summer holiday-makers converge upon charmless, lakeside Artouste-Fabrèges (1250m), 6km by road east of Gabas, to squeeze into the cable car which soars up the flanks of the 2032m Pic de la Sagette. Between June and September, an open-topped **train** (☎ reservations 05 59 05 49 61; adult/child €17/13), built for dam workers in the 1920s, runs for 10km at a constant 2000m from the upper cable car station to Lac d'Artouste (1991m). Views are constantly heart stopping and the 'little train' tucks away over 100,000 passengers annually in its four months of operation. Allow a good

four hours. For walkers, the one-way/return cable-car fare is €3.70/5.70.

There's a seasonal **tourist office** (☎ 05 59 05 34 00; ☉ Jun–Sep & other school holidays) beside the cable car.

CAUTERETS

pop 1300 / elevation 930m

The thermal spa and ski resort of Cauterets, less than 30km south of Lourdes, nestles in a tight valley, crowded in by steep slopes rising to 2800m. In summer, it's a superb base for exploring the forests, meadows, lakes and streams of the Parc National des Pyrénées. In winter, Cauterets is blessed with an abundance of snow; it's usually the first of France's Pyrenean ski stations to open and the last to close.

Information

INTERNET ACCESS

Pizzeria Giovanni (see p689; per hr €4 for nondiners)

LAUNDRY

Laverie Ydéaly (19 rue Richelieu; ☉ 8am-8pm)

TOURIST INFORMATION

Maison de la Presse (8 place Maréchal Foch) For walking maps and international newspapers.

Maison du Parc National des Pyrénées (☎ 05 62 92 52 56; place de la Gare; ☉ 9.30am-noon & 3-7pm Jun–mid-Sep, 9.30am- noon & 3-6pm Mon-Tue & Thu-Sat mid-Sep–Apr) Sells walking maps, has an impressive free exhibition on Pyrenean flora and fauna and shows park-related films. Organises guided walks (per half/full day €9.15/15.25; Jul & Aug).

Pont d'Espagne Information Office (☎ 05 62 92 52 19; ☉ Jun–mid-Oct & mid-Dec–Mar)

Tourist Office (☎ 05 62 92 50 50; www.cauterets.com in French; place Maréchal Foch; ☉ 9am-noon & 2-6pm Mon-Sat, 9am-noon Sun)

Sights & Activities

WALKING

Cauterets makes a particularly good base for day walks since so many start right from town or from Pont d'Espagne at the end of the spectacular D920 road, 8km south, 600m higher and accessible in season by shuttle bus (see p689). For a week or more's stimulating walking in the area, consult Lonely Planet's *Walking in France*.

The area west of Cauterets is covered by IGN's 1:25,000-scale Top 25 map No 1647OT *Vignemale*; land east of town fea-

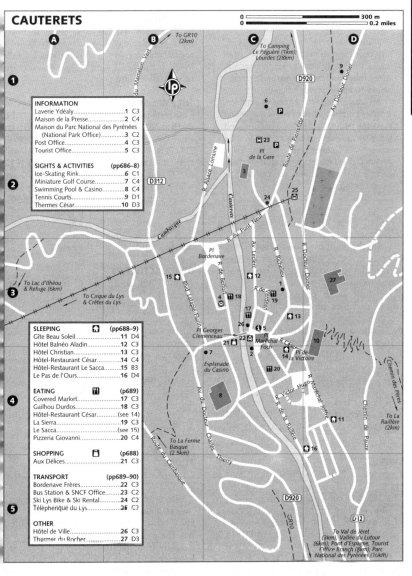

CAUTERETS

0   300 m
0   0.2 miles

To GR10 (2km)

To Camping Le Péguère (1km); Lourdes (28km)

D920

INFORMATION
Laverie Ydéaly...........................1 C3
Maison de la Presse....................2 C4
Maison du Parc National des Pyrénées
(National Park Office)............3 C2
Post Office................................4 C3
Tourist Office............................5 C3

SIGHTS & ACTIVITIES   (pp686–8)
Ice-Skating Rink........................6 C1
Miniature Golf Course................7 C4
Swimming Pool & Casino............8 C4
Tennis Courts............................9 D1
Thermes César.........................10 D3

To Lac d'Ilhéou & Refuge (6km)

To Cirque du Lys & Crêtes du Lys

D312

Pl de la Gare

R. Alsace Lorraine

Cambasque

Cauterets

R. du Pont Neuf

Pl Bordenave

R. de Belfort

R. de Verdun

R. Richelieu

R. Docteur Domer

Av Leclerc

Pl Georges Clemenceau

Pl Maréchal Foch

Av du Docteur Charles Thierry

Esplanade du Casino

R. Maréchal Joffre

Pl de la Victoire

R. César

R. Victor Hugo

R. de la Raillère

Chemin de Pauze

Chemin des Pères

To La Raillère (2km)

SLEEPING   (pp688–9)
Gîte Beau Soleil........................11 D4
Hôtel Balnéo Aladin..................12 C3
Hôtel Christian.........................13 C3
Hôtel-Restaurant César.............14 C4
Hôtel-Restaurant Le Sacca........15 B3
Le Pas de l'Ours.......................16 D4

EATING   (p689)
Covered Market........................17 C3
Gailhou Durdos........................18 C3
Hôtel-Restaurant César........(see 14)
La Sierra..................................19 C3
Le Sacca..............................(see 15)
Pizzeria Giovanni.....................20 C4

SHOPPING   (p688)
Aux Délices.............................21 C3

TRANSPORT   (pp689–90)
Bordenave Frères......................22 C3
Bus Station & SNCF Office.........23 C2
Ski Lys Bike & Ski Rental...........24 C2
Téléphérique du Lys..................25 C2

OTHER
Hôtel de Ville...........................26 C3
Thermes du Rocher...................27 D3

To La Ferme Basque (2.5km)

D920

GR10

D12

To Val de Jéret (3km), Vallée du Lutour (6km); Pont d'Espagne, Tourist Office Branch (8km); Parc National des Pyrénées (10km)

tures on No 1748OT *Gavarnie*. Rando Éditions' *Bigorre Carte No 4* covers the region at 1:50,000.

The Parc National produces *Randonnées dans le Parc National des Pyrénées: Vallée de Cauterets* (€6.40), a loose-leaf pack describing, in French and with a detailed map, 15 walks. The tourist office carries *Sentiers du Lavaudon* (€5), describing seven easy walks in the area.

A painless way to gain height from Cauterets is to take the Téléphérique du Lys cable car (see 689).

For a pleasant day walk from Cauterets (allow around six hours), follow the Vallée de Lutour southwards as far as Lac

---

A LITTLE SWEETENER

Halitosis is never fun. Back in the 19th century, once the *curistes* of Cauterets had swallowed their daily dose of sulphurous spa water, they – and their nearest and dearest – would complain of dog's breath.

An enterprising villager, seeing a chance, set about making a boiled sweet that would mask the odour. Shaped like a humbug and made in a rainbow of colours, *berlingots*, a speciality of Cauterets, are on sale in town. At **Aux Délices** (place Clemenceau), if you happen by at the right time, you can see the sweets being made.

---

d'Estom, where the lakeside *refuge* offers refreshments.

From the giant car park at **Pont d'Espagne**, Chemin des Cascades passes by a series of spectacular waterfalls as it drops northwards towards Cauterets.

Heading south from Pont d'Espagne, you've a choice of two valleys, each different in character. Following the Gave de Gaube upstream through a pine wood brings you to the popular **Lac de Gaube** and, nearby, **Hôtellerie de Gaube** which does drinks, snacks and midday *menus*. Three hours, not counting breaks, is generous for this out-and-back walk.

A longer trek up the gentler, more open **Vallée de Marcadau** leads to **Refuge Wallon** (☎ 05 62 92 64 28; ◉ Mar-Oct) at 1866m. Allow about five hours for the round trip.

SKIING

Cauterets is linked to the 23-run **Cirque du Lys** by the Téléphérique du Lys cable car. The 35km of runs, ranging from 2450m to 1850m, are best for beginner and intermediate **downhill** skiers. Low/high-season lift passes cost €20/23 per day and €102/148.50 per week.

Pont d'Espagne (1450m) is primarily a **cross-country** skiing area. From it, 37km of maintained trails, paralleled in their lower reaches by a piste for walkers and snowshoers, lead up the Vallée du Marcadau. A one-day/week trail pass costs €8/39.

Several shops in Cauterets hire ski equipment. Typical prices per day are downhill €12 to €20, snowboards €19 to €25 and cross-country gear €8 to €12.

SNOWSHOE TREKS

Several mountain guides organise increasingly popular day and half-day treks into spectacular scenery. Typical prices are €20 to €31 per day including transport, and hire of snowshoes and poles.

THERMAL SPAS

Cauterets' hot springs, blooping from the earth at 36°C to 53°C, have attracted *curistes* since the 19th century. **Thermes César** (☎ 05 62 92 14 20; rue Docteur Domer; ◉ Feb-Nov) offers a variety of water-based, tone-up activities (€10 to €33) for weary walkers, skiers and those who just want to indulge. Particularly sensuous is the *pelothérapie* option (€18.50), where you get plastered in mud.

Year-round, **Hôtel Balnéo Aladin** (see p689) does the same though its water is artificially heated, not deep from the earth.

OTHER ACTIVITIES

About 200m southwest of the tourist office are Esplanade du Casino and Esplanade des Oeufs (Egg Esplanade, so named, in an age before public-relations officers and spin doctors held sway, for the stench the sulphurous waters gave off). Here you'll find cafés, an indoor swimming pool, a miniature golf course and the town's large casino. It would be an even more lovely little open space for promenading, if only they'd banish the parked cars.

Cauterets also has an **ice-skating rink** (place de la Gare; adult/child €5.50/3).

Sleeping
BUDGET

Cauterets has two particularly attractive *gîtes*:

Gîte Beau Soleil (☎ 05 62 92 53 52; gite.beau .soleil@wanadoo.fr; 25 rue Maréchal Joffre; per person €16; ◉ closed Nov-first snows) The Beau Soleil has the comfort of a hotel as well as the friendly informality of a *refuge*. Beds are in spick and span doubles or quads with bathrooms and there's also a kitchen for self-caterers.

Le Pas de l'Ours (☎ 05 62 92 58 07; www.lepas delours.com in French; 21 rue de la Raillère; dm €15, with half-board €32, d with bathroom €57-61.50, with half-board per person €42.50; ◉ mid-May–Sep & Dec–mid-Apr) 'The Bear's Footstep' is both hotel and *gîte*. Dorm prices include use of the kitchen and all guests can use the sauna (€8).

Camping

Camping Le Péguère (☎ 05 62 92 52 91; camping peguere@wanadoo.fr; 2 people & car €10.50; 🕙 Apr-Sep) This grassy, shady camping ground, 1.5km north of town on the D920, has some choice sites right beside the Gave de Cauterets.

MID-RANGE

Hôtel Christian (☎ 05 62 92 50 04; www.hotel-chris tian.fr in French; 10 rue Richelieu; s/d €44/56 with breakfast; 🕙 Dec-Sep) Rooms are large and comfortable at this friendly hotel, in the hands of the same Cauterets family for three generations.

Hôtel-Restaurant César (☎ 05 62 92 52 57; www .cesarhotel.com; 3 rue César; d €46-50; 🕙 closed May & Oct) This cosy option, run by an engaging husband and wife team, has attractively furnished rooms and represents excellent value. They also run an impressive restaurant.

Hôtel-Restaurant Le Sacca (☎ 05 62 92 50 02; hotel.le.sacca@wanadoo.fr; 11 blvd Latapie-Flurin; d €40-46; 🕙 closed 10 Oct-20 Dec) Le Sacca is another excellent mid-range choice, run by the same husband and wife team for three decades. It too has a great restaurant and most of the 48 rooms have separate bathroom and toilet.

Hôtel Balnéo Aladin (☎ 05 62 92 60 60; www .hotel-balneo-aladin.com in French; 11 av Général Leclerc; d €110-130 incl breakfast; 🕙 Christmas-Apr & Jun-Sep) Cauterets' only three-star hotel, the Aladin also doubles as a private spa (see p688). Strikingly modern – brash even – in a resort where venerable hotels are closing or converting into apartments, it offers every luxury. A stay of four nights is normally expected, although this is negotiable outside peak periods.

Eating

Le Sacca (see Hôtel-Restaurant Le Sacca, above; menus €12-27) Here is by common consent the finest place to eat in Cauterets with a range of *menus* to suit most pockets. Whether you're down from the mountains or fresh from Lourdes and the plains, make a pilgrimage to savour its subtle cuisine.

Hôtel-Restaurant César (see Sleeping; menus €20-40; 🕙 closed lunch in winter) With its crisp white tablecloths and napkins, the César offers elegant dining. The food is excellent and there's a good range of regional wines at reasonable prices.

La Sierra (☎ 06 61 35 57 15; 8 rue Verdun; lunch menu €10.50, dinner menu €13.50-19) This intimate little place, tucked away down a side street, of-

fers excellent value. Service is cheerful and friendly and the menu is varied.

Pizzeria Giovanni (☎ 05 62 92 57 80; 5 rue de la Raillère; menu €14; 🕙 dinner only except school holidays, closed mid-May–mid-Jun & Nov–mid-Dec) Pizzas (around €9, to eat in or take away) are superior, a generous steak costs €13 and the home-cooked desserts (€4 to €5.50) are a dream. A nice touch: diners can check out their emails for free.

La Ferme Basque (☎ 05 62 92 54 32; route de Cambasque) Around 4km by road west of town, it has a superb plunging view of Cauterets from its terrace and makes a great spot for a daylight drink. But don't bother dining here: the food is indifferent and the service excruciatingly slow.

SELF-CATERING

Stalls are few but Cauterets' **Covered market** (av Leclerc) is a gastronome's delight. Inside, a stall does tasty takeaway regional dishes such as *garbure* while its neighbours sell wonderful mountain cheeses. Just follow your nose…

Gailhou Durdos (rue de Belfort), opposite the post office, has a rich selection of local wines and specialities.

Getting There & Away

The last train steamed out of Cauterets' magnificent, all-wood station in 1947. Like something left over from a cowboy film set, it now serves as the **bus station** (☎ 05 62 92 53 70).

SNCF buses run between Cauterets and Lourdes train station (€6.10, 50 minutes, five to seven daily).

Getting Around

BICYCLE

Rent mountain bikes from **Ski Lys** (☎ 05 62 92 58 30; route de Pierrefitte; per half/full day from €16/25).

CABLE CAR

The two-stage Téléphérique du Lys operates mid June to mid-September and from December to the end of the ski season. It rises over 900m to the Cirque du Lys, where you can catch the Grand Barbat chair-lift up to Crêtes du Lys (2400m). A return trip costs €4.50/6.50 to Cirque du Lys or €5/9 to Crêtes du Lys.

TAXI

Bordenave Frères (☎ 05 62 92 53 68, 06 71 01 46 86; place Clemenceau), who also call itself Allo Taxis, operates a shuttle service between the bus station and Pont d'Espagne (single/return €3.50/5) during the ski season (twice daily) and in summer (six times daily).

Year-round, a taxi between Cauterets and Pont d'Espagne costs €13.

VALLÉE DES GAVES & AROUND

Vallée des Gaves (Valley of the Mountain Streams), gentle and pastoral, extends south from Lourdes to Pierrefitte-Nestalas. Here, the valley forks, narrows, twists and becomes more rugged. The eastern tine pokes into the Pyrenees via Gavarnie while the western prong leads up to Cauterets.

Pic du Midi de Bigorre

Lament the fact or love it, the Pic du Midi (2877m), until recently almost exclusively the preserve of astronomers and scientists, is now accessible to all by **cable car** (☎ 08 25 00 28 77; adult/student/child €23/18/12; ♥ daily Jun-Sep, Thu-Mon Oct & Dec-May). Leaving from the ski resort of La Mongie (1800m), it gives access to one of the Pyrenees' most soul-stirring panoramas, albeit at heart-stopping prices.

Gavarnie

pop 175 / elevation 1360m

In winter, Gavarnie, 52km south of Lourdes at the end of the D921, offers limited downhill and decent cross-country skiing plus snowshoe treks. In summer, it's a popular take-off point for walkers. And take off they do, as quickly as their feet will carry them: by 10am the village and its tawdry souvenir stalls are overrun by trippers.

Consult the IGN Top 25 map No 1748OT *Gavarnie* (€9) or the National Park pack *Randonnées dans le Parc National des Pyrénées: Vallée de Luz* (€6.40) for the rich menu of routes.

The most frequented trail, accessible to all, leads to the **Cirque de Gavarnie**, a breathtaking rock amphitheatre, 1500m high, dominated by ice-capped peaks. The round-trip walk to its foot takes around two hours. Between June and September, you can sit astride a horse or donkey (about €20 round trip). In mid-July, Gavarnie hosts an arts festival in the dramatic setting of the Cirque.

The **tourist office** (☎ 05 62 92 49 10; www.gavarnie.com; ♥ 8.30am-7pm Jul & Aug, 9am-noon & 2-6pm Sep-Jun) occupies new premises at the northern entrance to the village.

The **National Park office** (☎ 05 62 92 42 48; ♥ 9.30am-noon & 1.30-6pm Tue-Sat school holidays, Mon-Fri rest of year) is 200m beyond.

Camping Le Pain de Sucre (☎ 05 62 92 47 55; www.camping-gavarnie.com; per person/site €3.25/3.40; ♥ mid-Dec–mid-Apr & Jun-Sep) enjoys a lovely riverside spot a little north of town.

In summer only, two buses operate daily between Gavarnie and Luz-St-Sauveur, from where there are connections to Lourdes.

Cirque de Troumouse

From Gèdre, 6.5km north of Gavarnie, a toll road (€4 per vehicle) winds southeast up a desolate valley into the Pyrenees to the base of the Cirque de Troumouse, wilder, infinitely less trodden and almost as stunning as the Cirque de Gavarnie. Snows permitting, the road is open between May and October.

UPPER GARONNE VALLEY
St-Bertrand de Comminges

On an isolated hillock, St-Bertrand and its **Cathédrale Ste-Marie** (adult/child €4/1.50; ♥ 9am-7pm Mon-Sat, 2-7pm Sun May-Sep, 10am-noon & 2-5pm or 6pm Mon-Sat, 2-5pm or 6pm Sun Oct-Apr) loom protectively over the Vallée de Garonne and the much-pillaged remains of the Gallo-Roman town of Lugdunum Convenarum, where you can wander at will for free.

The splendid Renaissance oak choir stalls sit below the soaring Gothic east end of the cathedral. Carved in 1535 by local artisans, they blend the serene and spiritual with an earthy realism. The adjacent **tourist office** (☎ 05 61 95 44 44; ♥ 10am-6pm or 7pm Apr-Oct, 10am-5pm Tue-Sun Nov-Dec & Feb-Mar) has a detailed pamphlet in English.

Bagnères de Luchon

pop 3100 / elevation 630m

Bagnères de Luchon (or simply Luchon) is a trim little town of gracious 19th-century buildings, expanded to accommodate the *curistes* who came to take the waters at its splendid spa.

The **tourist office** (☎ 05 61 79 21 21; www.luchon.com; ♥ 9am-7pm Jul & Aug & Dec-Mar, 9am-12.30pm & 1.30-7pm Sep-Nov & Apr-Jun) is at 18 allées d'Étigny.

SIGHTS & ACTIVITIES

Once only for the ailing, the **Thermes** (Health Spa; ☎ 05 61 79 22 97; ♥ Apr-Oct), at the southern end of allées d'Étigny, now also offers relaxation and fitness sessions for weary skiers and walkers, mainstay of the town's tourism-based economy. It's €13 to loll in the scented steam of the 160m-long underground *vaporarium*, then dunk yourself in the caressing 32°C waters of its pool. Follow this with a flutter in the elegant surroundings of the casino and you'll have had a good night out.

The stylish allées d'Étigny, flanked by cafés and restaurants, links place Joffre with the Thermes. Just to the west of this boulevard is the base of the **cabin lift** (single/return €4.90/7.50), which hauls you up to **Superbagnères**, at 1860m the starting point for winter skiing and summer walking. It operates daily in the ski season and during July and August (weekends only during most other months).

Cycling
Although you'll huff and puff, the area is rich in opportunities for mountain biking. Pick up a free copy of *Guide des Circuits VTT*, prepared by the local mountain-bike club, from the tourist office. To rent a bike, see right.

Walking
An amazing 250km of marked trails, ranging from gentle valley-bottom strolls to more demanding high-mountain treks, thread their way from Luchon and Superbagnères. Lonely Planet's *Walking in France* describes five days of walks in the area and the tourist office carries a useful pamphlet, *Sentiers Balisés du Pays de Luchon*. Pick up IGN 1:25,000 map No 1848OT *Bagnères de Luchon*, pull on your boots and you're away.

Other Activities
The skies above Superbagnères are magnificent for **parapenting**. Contact **École Soaring** (☎ /fax 05 61 79 29 23; 14 rue Sylvie). More down-to-earth, **Pyrénées Aventure** (☎ 05 61 79 20 59; 9 rue Docteur Germès) arranges **canyon clambering**, plus **rafting** and **canoeing** on the River Garonne.

SLEEPING
Hôtel des Sports (☎ 05 61 79 97 80; www.hotel-des-sports.net; 12 av Maréchal Foch; s/d €30/38) This hotel is that rare institution in France – an entirely non-smoking hotel, where the friendly owner, himself a hiker, happily dispenses local walking information and advice.

Camping Beauregard (☎ 05 61 79 30 74; fax 05 61 79 04 35; 37; av de Vénasque; per person/site €4/5; ⏲ Apr–mid-Oct) It's the larger and more welcoming of Luchon's two camping grounds.

EATING
Allées d'Étigny is packed with bars and restaurants, some fine delicatessens and the usual pizza-'n'-pasta joints. Two restaurants offer excellent value:

L'Arbesquens (☎ 05 61 79 33 69; 47 allées d'Étigny; menus from €13) Its speciality is *fondue* (€14, minimum two people) in 14 different varieties. Help it down with a jug of their fine Jurançon white wine.

Caprices d' Étigny (☎ 05 61 94 31 05; 30bis allées d'Étigny; menus €14 & €20; ⏲ Fri-Wed) Just across the road and staffed by a young, friendly crew, it does great grilled meats (three-course *menu* €17) on its open fire.

Le Jardin des Cascades (☎ 05 61 79 83 09; menu €24.50, mains €13-20; ⏲ Apr-Sep) In the hamlet of Montauban de Luchon, 1.5km east of Luchon, this restaurant more than merits the steep walk up from its parking lot. Cascading with fresh flowers and tastefully furnished in blue, it's justifiably renowned for its fine cuisine.

Self-caterers should pass by Luchon's daily **market**, established in 1897 and offering fine fresh fare ever since.

GETTING THERE & AROUND
There are SNCF trains and buses between Luchon and Montréjeau (€5.75, 50 minutes, five to seven daily), which has frequent connections to Toulouse (€16.80) and Pau (€17.70).

There's free parking around the Casino and cabin lift station.

For bicycle hire, contact **Liberty Cycles Demiguel** (☎ 05 61 79 12 87; 82 av Foch) – look for the Statue of Liberty sign. Mountain bikes cost €18/51/75 per day/three days/week.

VALLÉE DE L'ARIÈGE
The Vallée de l'Ariège offers some great pre-Pyrenean walking. Tourist offices carry *Guide Randonnée*, a useful free booklet in French that recommends hikes for all levels, including family outings.

Foix
pop 9950
Foix, county seat of the Ariège *département*, merits a small detour from the N20 to visit its castle, 11th-century church and streets lined with medieval, half-timbered houses.

The town sits in the crook of the confluence of the Rivers Ariège and Arget. Its oldest, most attractive quarter is on the west bank of the Ariège.

INFORMATION

The **tourist office** (☎ 05 61 65 12 12; www.ot-foix.fr; ☉ 9am-7pm Mon-Sat, 9.30am-12.30pm & 2-6pm Sun Jul & Aug, 9am-noon & 2-6pm Mon-Sat Sep-Jun) is beside the covered market on cours Gabriel Fauré, the wide main thoroughfare.

SIGHTS

Imposing **Château des Comtes de Foix** (☎ 05 34 09 83 83; adult/child €4/2; ☉ 9.45am-6.30pm Jul & Aug, 9.45am-noon & 2-6pm May-Jun & Sep, 10.30am-noon & 2-5.30pm Wed-Sun & daily in school holidays Oct-Dec & Feb-Apr), with its three crenellated, gravity-defying towers, stands guard over the town. Constructed in the 10th century as a stronghold for the counts of Foix, the castle served as a prison from the 16th century onwards; look for the graffiti scratched into the stones by some hapless prisoner. Today it houses a small **archaeological museum**. In July and August, there are several daily guided visits in French and one in English at 1pm.

ACTIVITIES

Go canyon clambering, mountain biking or hiking with **Pyrénévasion** (☎ 05 61 65 01 10; www.pyrenevasion.com in French) or **Maison de la Montagne** (☎ 05 61 02 68 19; e.mayodon@free.fr).

SLEEPING & EATING

Hôtel Lons (☎ 05 61 65 52 44; www.hotel-lons-foix.com; 6 place Dutilh; d €48-70) Once a coaching inn, it's now a three-star Logis de France with attractive, good-value rooms, nine of which overlook the river. The hotel's **restaurant** (☉ closed Fri dinner & Sat lunch Sep-mid-Jul) offers similar river views through its picture windows.

Camping du Lac (☎ 05 61 65 11 58; www.campingdulac.com in French; 2 people & car €11-17; ☉ year-round; 🏊) Situated on the RN20 2.5km north of Foix, this attractive camp site has a pool and restaurant.

Le Sainte Marthe (☎ 05 61 02 87 87; place Lazéma; menus €24-51; ☉ Jul & Aug, Thu-Mon Sep-Jun) This gourmet restaurant specialises in Ariègeois cuisine, especially *cassoulet* (€16). It can rustle up a vegetarian menu on request and has a non-smoking room.

GETTING THERE & AWAY

Trains and buses (€12, 50 minutes, seven to 15 daily) connect Toulouse and Foix.

Around Foix

Beneath **Labouiche**, 6km northwest of Foix on the D1, flows Europe's longest navigable underground river, along which you can take a spectacular 1500m, 75-minute **boat trip** (☎ 05 61 02 90 77; adult/child €7.50/5.50; ☉ 9.30am-5.15pm Jul & Aug, 10-11.15am & 2-5.15pm Apr-Jun & Sep, 10-11.15am & 2-4.30pm Sat & Sun Oct-mid-Nov).

Ax-les-Thermes

pop 1500 / elevation 720m

Ax-les-Thermes flourishes as a small base for skiing in winter and, with over 60 hot-water springs, as a spa town. Like Foix, it lies at the confluence of two rivers: the Ariège and its near namesake the Oriège. The **tourist office** (☎ 05 61 64 60 60; www.vallees-ax.com; ☉ 9am-noon & 2-7pm Jul & Aug, to 6pm Sep-Jun) is on av Delcassé.

The heart of town is place du Breilh. On one side of the square is the faded elegance of the casino. On the other side is the **Bassin de Ladres**, a pool originally built to soothe the wounds of Knights Templar injured in the Crusades and the ulcers of the town's leper colony. Pull off your socks, follow the example of the knights and steep in its waters.

There are a couple of interesting narrow streets with overhanging buildings between place du Breilh and place Roussel. The **Thermes du Teich** (☎ 05 61 65 86 60; ☉ Apr–mid-Nov), beside the River Oriège, has a pool, sauna, hammam and aquagym (€12 per session), open to all comers.

If you are heading up to or down from Andorra and the Pyrenees, Ax makes a good meal or snack stop.

Le Grand Café (☎ 05 61 64 67 16; 1 av Delcassé) is strong on atmosphere and dishes up good salads and snacks. Its high walls, stucco ceilings and tall etched-glass windows speak of the classic French town café, while the funky music and impressive collection of beer mats and drip towels are decidedly more contemporary.

La Petite Fringale (☎ 06 87 74 03 21; 6 rue Rigal; mains €13-14.50) This popular, friendly place has a small summertime terrace. It does *fondues* (€14 to €17), lots of tempting cheese-based dishes and meaty mains.

La Pizzatière (☎ 05 61 64 33 95; 2 rue Rigal), a couple of doors away, does a huge range of takeaway pizzas, from single slice to giant (55cm across).

Most buses and trains serving Foix (see left) continue as far as Ax.

Toulouse Area

CONTENTS

Toulouse	695
Albi	705
Castres	709
Montauban	709
Moissac	711
Auch	711
Condom	713
Around Condom	715

Not quite the Pyrenees (Pyrénées) and no longer part of Languedoc-Roussillon (after regional boundaries were redrawn in the 1960s), Languedoc's traditional centre, Toulouse, may be in geographical limbo but it's a fascinating region full of historical sights and activities.

Central to the area is Toulouse itself, one of France's fastest-growing cities. Bolstered by its booming hi-tech industries (most notably aerospace – this is the epicentre of the huge Europe-wide EADS aircraft manufacturing consortium) the city is an increasingly self-confident one. It has a vibrant centre with a subtle Spanish flavour and a large student population. To the south of Toulouse lie the Pyrenees, while within easy reach are four towns with strong historical connections: Albi, 75km to the northeast, birthplace of Toulouse-Lautrec; Montauban, 53km north, a Huguenot stronghold in the 16th century; Condom, 110km to the northwest, with a host of 18th-century *hôtels particuliers;* and Auch, 77km west, a key Roman trading route.

West of Toulouse city, the region of Gascony (Gascogne) rolls all the way to the Atlantic. Famous for its lush countryside, sleepy *bastides* (medieval villages), fine wines, foie gras and Armagnac liqueur, slow-paced Gascony is ideal for experiencing some of France's finest examples of medieval and Renaissance architecture.

HIGHLIGHTS

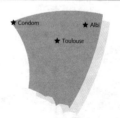

- Sample the delights of **Gascon cuisine** (p702) in Toulouse
- Trace the development of an artistic master at the **Musée Toulouse-Lautrec** (p706), in Albi
- Absorb the ambience of the **bastide villages** (p715) around Condom
- Mix with the revellers enjoying **Toulouse's busy bar scene** (p703)
- Expand your mind and universe at **Cité de l'Espace** (p700)

- POPULATION: 2,551,687
- AREA: 45,349 SQ KM

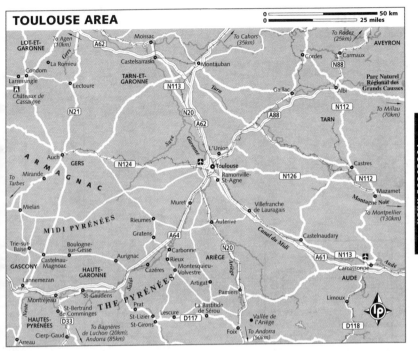

TOULOUSE

pop 398,423

Be warned, even the grannies will want to fight you in Toulouse according to the lyrics of *Oh! Toulouse*, a bittersweet tribute to the city by the late crooner Claude Nougaro, a kind of Sinatra figure in France, who was born and bred here.

Nougaro may have had a hard time growing up on the streets of *la ville rose* (the pink city – so named because of the profusion of rose-red brick buildings), but these days you're more likely to find a good time in Toulouse than you are to bump into any pugilistic pensioners.

Toulouse is a lively, friendly city, with an economy bolstered by its booming aerospace industries and with plenty to offer the visitor.

Anywhere that's home to 100,000 students can't really fail to be a buzzing, busy place with a terrific café and bar scene, a decent club scene and dozens of good affordable places to eat.

Signs of a rich (and tumultuous) history crowd around you in the narrow medieval streets and inside the many churches and cathedrals of the city, which is the capital of the Midi-Pyrénées region and France's fourth-largest city.

History

Toulouse, known to the Romans as Tolosa, was the Visigoth capital from AD 419–507. In the 12th and 13th centuries the counts of Toulouse supported the Cathars (see p756). Three centuries later, during the Wars of Religion, the city sided with the Catholic League. Toulouse merchants grew rich in the 16th and 17th centuries from the woad (blue dye) trade, which collapsed when the Portuguese began importing indigo from India. The Toulouse Parliament ruled Languedoc from 1420 until the 1789 Revolution.

During WWI, Toulouse became a centre for the manufacture of arms and aircraft. In the 1920s, Antoine de St-Exupéry, author of *Le Petit Prince* (The Little Prince), and other daring pilots pioneered mail flights to northwestern Africa and South America, often staying in the city between sorties. After WWII, Toulouse became the nucleus of

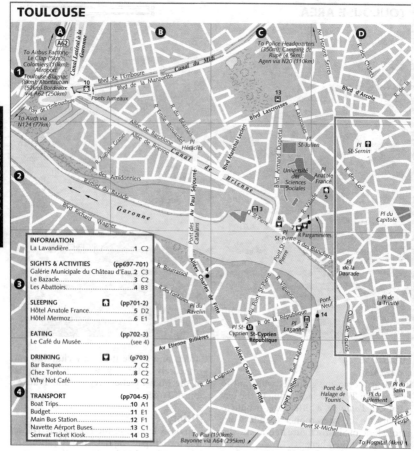

TOULOUSE

INFORMATION	
La Lavandière	1 C2

SIGHTS & ACTIVITIES	(pp697-701)
Galérie Municipale du Château d'Eau	2 C3
Le Bazacle	3 C2
Les Abattoirs	4 B3

SLEEPING	🏠	(pp701-2)
Hôtel Anatole France		5 D2
Hôtel Mermoz		6 E1

EATING	(pp702-3)
Le Café du Musée	(see 4)

DRINKING	🍷	(p703)
Bar Basque		7 C2
Chez Tonton		8 C2
Why Not Café		9 C2

TRANSPORT	(pp704-5)
Boat Trips	10 A1
Budget	11 E1
Main Bus Station	12 F1
Navette Aéroport Buses	13 C1
Semvat Ticket Kiosk	14 D3

the country's aerospace industry. Passenger planes built here have included the Caravelle and the Concorde as well as the latest 555-seat Airbus A380, and local factories also produce the Ariane rocket. These are boom times for Airbus, and especially good ones for Toulouse, as the HQ of the consortium overtook its great US rival Boeing in 2004 in terms of sales of new aircraft. It's a rare success story of Europe outdoing the USA.

Orientation

The heart of Toulouse is bounded to the east by blvd de Strasbourg and its continuation, blvd Lazare Carnot, and, to the west, by the River Garonne. Its two principal squares are place du Capitole and, 200m east, place

Wilson. From the latter, the wide allées Jean Jaurès leads northeast to the main bus station and Gare Matabiau, the train station, both just across the Canal du Midi.

From place du Capitole, rue du Taur runs north to the Basilique St-Sernin, while pedestrianised rue St-Rome and rue des Changes lead south from the square to the transport hub of place Esquirol.

Information
BOOKSHOPS

Bookshop (Map p699; ☎ 05 61 22 99 92; 17 rue Lakanal) Has an excellent range of English-language books and operates an information board.

Ombres Blanches (Map p699; ☎ 05 34 45 53 33; 48-50 rue Gambetta) A friendly and accessible place specialising

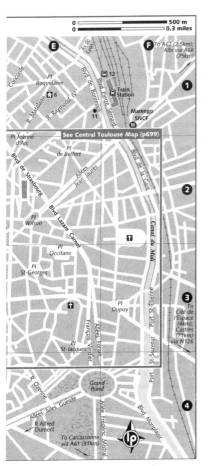

in travel guides, including a good range of Lonely Planet titles and maps.

INTERNET ACCESS
Cyber King (Map p699; 31 rue Gambetta; per hr €4.55; 11am-midnight Mon-Fri, 11.30am-2am Sat, 2-10pm Sun) Centrally located.

Résomania (Map p699; 85 rue Pargaminières; per hr €3-4; 9.30am-midnight Mon-Fri, noon-midnight Sat & Sun)

LAUNDRY
Befitting a city with so many students in digs, Toulouse is well endowed with laundrettes. Two located centrally are:

Hallwash (Map p699; 7 rue Mirepoix)

La Lavandière (Map pp696-7; 29 rue Pargaminières)

POST
Main Post Office (Map p699; 9 rue la Fayette)

TOURIST INFORMATION
Tourist Office (Map p699; ☎ 05 61 11 02 22; www.ot
-toulouse.fr; square Charles de Gaulle; 9am-7pm Mon-Sat, 10am-1pm & 2-6.15pm Sun Jun-Sep, 9am-6pm Mon-Fri, 9am-12.30pm & 2-6pm Sat, 10am-12.30pm & 2-5pm Sun Oct-May) In the base of the Donjon du Capitole, a 16th-century tower. Wine lovers planning to visit *caves* and vineyards in the Toulouse region should pick up the excellent and free *Guide des Vins du Sud-Ouest* plus a free wine map here.

Sights
PLACE DU CAPITOLE
Bustling and pedestrianised **place du Capitole** (Map p699) is the city's main square. On the ceiling of the arcades on its western side are 29 vivid illustrations of the city's history, from the *Venus of Lespugue* (a prehistoric representation of woman) through to the city's role during the crusades and its modern-day status as a hub for the aeronautics industry, by contemporary artist Raymond Moretti.

On the eastern side of the square is the 128m-long façade of Toulouse's city hall, the **Capitole** (9am-5pm Mon-Fri, 9am-1pm Sat mid-Jun–mid-Sep, Mon-Fri mid-Sep–mid-Jun). Built in the early 1750s, it is a focus of civic pride. Within the Capitole is the **Théâtre du Capitole** (☎ 05 61 63 13 13), one of France's most prestigious opera and operetta venues. The interior of the Capitole also includes the over-the-top, late 19th-century **Salle des Illustres** (Hall of the Illustrious).

On the Capitole's eastern side is the green square Charles de Gaulle, or Jardin du Capitole.

VIEUX QUARTIER
The small, 18th-century **Vieux Quartier** (Old Quarter; Map p699) is a web of narrow lanes and plazas south of place du Capitole and place Wilson. Place de la Daurade is the city's 'beach' beside the River Garonne, peaceful by day and romantic by night, overlooking the floodlit Pont Neuf. Well worth the walk.

BASILIQUE ST-SERNIN
Once a Benedictine abbey church, **Basilique St-Sernin** (Map p699; ☎ 05 61 21 80 45; place St-Sernin; 8.30am-5.45pm Mon-Sat, 8.30am-7.30pm Sun Jul-Sep,

8.30-11.45am & 2-5.45pm Mon-Sat Oct-Jun) was once an important stop on the Santiago de Compostela pilgrimage route. The chancel of this vast, 115m-long brick basilica, France's largest and most complete Romanesque structure, was built between 1080 and 1096, and the nave was added in the 12th century. The basilica is topped by a magnificent eight-sided 13th-century **tower** and spire, added in the 15th century.

Directly above the double-level crypt is the 18th-century **tomb of St-Sernin** beneath a sumptuous canopy. In the north transept is a well-preserved **12th-century fresco** of Christ's Resurrection.

Visiting hours for the **ambulatory chapels** and **crypt** (admission €2; 10am-6pm Mon-Sat, 12.30-6pm Sun Jul-Sep, 10-11.30am & 2.30-5pm Mon-Sat, 2.30-5pm Sun Oct-Jun) are shorter than those for the basilica. There are also guided tours of the crypt (10am and 2.30pm Monday to Saturday).

MUSÉE DES AUGUSTINS
The **Musée des Augustins** (Augustins Museum; Map p699; 05 61 22 21 82; www.augustins.org; 21 rue de Metz; adult/child €2.20/1.10; 10am-6pm Thu-Mon, 10am-9pm Wed) houses a superb collection ranging from Roman stone artefacts to paintings by Rubens, Delacroix and Toulouse-Lautrec. The museum occupies a former Augustinian monastery, and the gardens of its two 14th-century **cloisters** are among the prettiest in southern France. A rather striking row of gargoyles lines one side of the cloister.

ÉGLISE DES JACOBINS
This extraordinary Gothic structure, flooded by day in multicoloured light from the huge stained-glass windows, seems to defy gravity. A single row of seven 22m-high columns, running smack down the middle of the nave, looks for all the world like palm trees as they spread their fanned vaulting.

Construction on the **Église des Jacobins** (Map p699; parvis des Jacobins; 9am-7pm), the mother church of the Jacobins, was begun soon after St Dominic founded the order in 1215 to preach Church doctrine to the Cathars. It was completed in 1385.

Interred below the modern, grey-marble altar on the northern side are the remains of St Thomas Aquinas (1225–74), an early head of the Dominican order. From outside, admire the 45m-high, octagonal, 13th-century **belfry**. Admission to the tranquil **cloister** costs €1.50.

The 14th-century refectory, entered via the Église des Jacobins, nowadays hosts temporary art exhibitions.

CATHÉDRALE ST-ÉTIENNE
The **Cathédrale St-Étienne** (Cathedral of St Stephen; Map p699; place St-Étienne; 7.30am-7pm) has a bizarre layout. The vast, 12th-century nave is out of kilter with the huge choir, built in northern French Gothic style as part of an ambitious and unfinished late-13th-century plan to realign the cathedral along a different

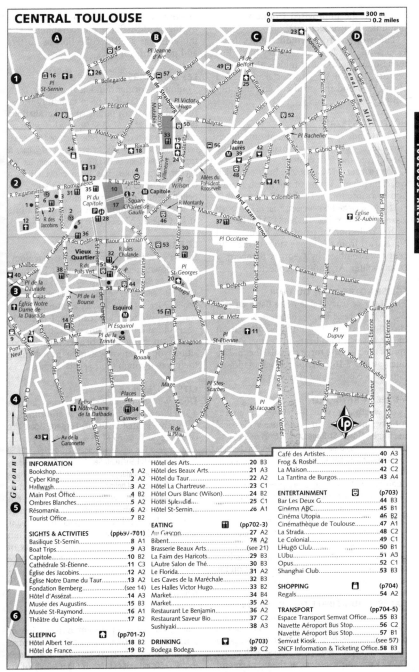

CENTRAL TOULOUSE

0   300 m
0   0.2 miles

INFORMATION	
Bookshop	1 A2
Cyber King	2 A2
Hallwash	3 A2
Main Post Office	4 B2
Ombres Blanches	5 A2
Résomania	6 A2
Tourist Office	7 B2

SIGHTS & ACTIVITIES	(pp697-701)
Basilique St-Sernin	8 A1
Boat Trips	9 A3
Capitole	10 B2
Cathédrale St-Étienne	11 C3
Église des Jacobins	12 A2
Église Notre Dame du Taur	13 A2
Fondation Bemberg	(see 14)
Hôtel d'Assézat	14 A3
Musée des Augustins	15 B3
Musée St-Raymond	16 A1
Théâtre du Capitole	17 B2

SLEEPING	(pp701-2)
Hôtel Albert 1er	18 B2
Hôtel de France	19 B2

EATING	(pp702-3)
Au Gascon	27 A2
Bibent	28 A2
Brasserie Beaux Arts	(see 21)
La Faim des Haricots	29 B3
L'Autre Salon de Thé	30 B3
Le Florida	31 A2
Les Caves de la Maréchale	32 B3
Les Halles Victor Hugo	33 B2
Market	34 B4
Market	35 A2
Restaurant Le Benjamin	36 A2
Restaurant Saveur Bio	37 C2
Sushiyaki	38 A3

DRINKING	(p703)
Bodega Bodega	39 C2

Hôtel des Arts	20 B3
Hôtel des Beaux Arts	21 A3
Hôtel du Taur	22 A2
Hôtel La Chartreuse	23 C1
Hôtel Ours Blanc (Wilson)	24 B2
Hôtel Splendid	25 C1
Hôtel St-Sernin	26 A1

Café des Artistes	40 A3
Frog & Rosbif	41 C2
La Maison	42 C2
La Tantina de Burgos	43 A4

ENTERTAINMENT	(p703)
Bar Les Deux G	44 B3
Cinéma ABC	45 B1
Cinéma Utopia	46 B2
Cinémathèque de Toulouse	47 A1
La Strada	48 C2
Le Colonial	49 C1
L'Hugô Club	50 B1
L'Ubu	51 A3
Opus	52 C1
Shanghai Club	53 B3

SHOPPING	(p704)
Regals	54 A2

TRANSPORT	(pp704-5)
Espace Transport Semvat Office	55 B3
Navette Aéroport Bus Stop	56 C2
Navette Aéroport Bus Stop	57 B1
Semvat Kiosk	(see 57)
SNCF Information & Ticketing Office	58 B3

TOULOUSE AREA

axis (note the improvised Gothic vaulting that links the two sections).

The western rose window dates from 1230, while the layer-cake belfry has a Romanesque base, a Gothic middle and a 16th-century top. The western portal was added about 1450 and the northern entrance not until 1929.

HÔTEL D'ASSÉZAT

Toulouse boasts about 50 handsome *hôtels particuliers* – grand, private mansions mostly dating from the 16th century.

Hôtel d'Assézat (Map p699), built by a rich woad merchant, is one of the finest. It now houses a museum, the **Fondation Bemberg** (☎ 05 61 12 06 89; www.fondation-bemberg.fr; rue de Metz; adult/student €4.60/2.75; 🕙 10am-12.30pm & 1.30-6pm Tue-Sun), with a collection of paintings, bronzes and *objets d'art* from the Renaissance to the 20th century assembled by Georges Bemberg, a cosmopolitan Argentinean collector.

ÉGLISE NOTRE DAME DU TAUR

The 14th-century **Église Notre Dame du Taur** (Map p699; 12 rue du Taur; 🕙 10am-noon & 2-7.15pm) was constructed to honour St-Sernin, patron of the basilica that bears his name. At the end of the nave are three chapels, the middle one housing a 16th-century Black Madonna known as Notre Dame du Rempart.

MUSÉE ST-RAYMOND

Well worth the visit for anyone even remotely interested in Toulouse's classical heritage, **Musée St-Raymond** (☎ 05 61 22 31 44; place St Sernin; adult/child €2.40/1.20, free 1st Sun of month; 🕙 10am-7pm Jun-Aug, to 6pm Sep-May) houses a rich collection of Roman sculpture of exceptional quality, much of it superbly preserved, some of it faintly surreal fragments: a foot or a knee here, a row of decapitated heads there. There's also a collection of early Christian sarcophagi, a treasure house of gold Gaulish torcs and coins, delicate glassware and some good background on the villa where much of the sculpture was found. Ask at reception for the explanatory notes in English.

GALERIE MUNICIPALE DU CHÂTEAU D'EAU

Occupying a 19th-century *château d'eau* (water tower), **Galerie Municipale du Château d'Eau** (Map pp696-7; ☎ 05 61 77 09 40; www.galerie chateaudeau.org in French; place Laganne; adult/student €2.50/1.50; 🕙 1-7pm Tue-Sun), at the western end of Pont Neuf, puts on superb exhibitions by the world's finest photographers. The museum has a great collection of posters and postcards for sale.

LES ABATTOIRS

Toulouse's former municipal abattoir, constructed in 1831, has been tastefully transformed into a vast public space. **Les Abattoirs** (Map pp696-7; ☎ 05 62 48 58 00; www.lesabattoirs.org in French; 76 allées Charles de Fitte; adult/child for permanent exhibitions €3.05/1.55, for permanent exhibitions & temporary exhibitions €6.10/3.05; 🕙 noon-8pm Tue-Sun summer, to 7pm winter) has been recycled as a contemporary art museum, with some excellent temporary exhibitions.

It's worth stopping for a drink or a bite at Le Café du Musée (see p702).

LE BAZACLE

If you've a feel for industrial archaeology, walk downstream from Pont St-Pierre to take in **Le Bazacle** (Map pp696-7; ☎ 05 62 30 16 00; 11 quai St-Pierre; admission free; 🕙 10am-noon & 2-6pm Mon-Fri, 2-7pm Sat & Sun Sep-Jul), a monument to water power with a hydro plant over 100 years old and the remains of a 13th-century mill. Even if you aren't of a technical disposition, you can enjoy watching the fish make their way through their special bypass.

CITÉ DE L'ESPACE

Dock your own space shuttle, try to launch a satellite without crashing it and jump as if weightless inside **Cité de l'Espace** (Space City; off Map pp696-7; ☎ 05 62 71 64 80; www.cite-espace .com; av Jean Gonord; adult/student/child €16/13/11.50 Jul & Aug, €14/11.50/10.50 Sep-Jun; 🕙 9am-7pm daily Jul-Aug & school holidays, 9.30am-5pm Tue-Fri, 9.30am-6pm Sat-Sun & school holidays rest of year), a museum and planetarium with dozens of excellent hands-on exhibits demonstrating basic physical laws and various space-based technologies. Great for adults and a lot of fun for children. On the eastern outskirts of the city, it's marked by a 55m-high space rocket. Take bus No 15 from allées Jean Jaurès to the end of the line, then walk about 600m, aiming for that big rocket.

AIRBUS

The aerospace company **Airbus** (based in Colomiers, about 10km west of the city centre; off Map pp696-7) runs 1½-hour **tours** (adult/child €9/7.50, incl visit to Concorde €13.50/10.50) of its huge Clément Ader aircraft factory, where you can visit the Airbus assembly line and see large chunks of massive airliners being ferried about or unloaded from the huge, bulbous-bodied 'Beluga' transport aircraft that line the runway.

In May 2004, Airbus' A380 factory was opened. This aircraft is the world's largest airliner, with a capacity of 555 passengers. The assembly facility is one of the largest buildings in the world, measuring 490m by 250m, with a height of 46m.

To book a tour, contact **Taxiway** (☎ 05 61 18 06 01; www.taxiway.fr), ideally at least a week in advance for tours in English. Be sure to take a passport or other ID.

Activities

The city's many canalside paths are peaceful places to walk, run or cycle. Port de l'Embouchure (Map pp696-7) is the meeting point of the Canal du Midi (1681; linking Toulouse with the Mediterranean), the Canal Latéral à la Garonne (1856; flowing to the Atlantic) and the Canal de Brienne (1776).

Tours

A number of Toulouse operators run short trips on the canals, including Canal du Midi, or the River Garonne, leaving from Quai de la Daurade or Ponts Jumeaux. Most of the boats operate between 11am and 7pm daily in July and August and at weekends from April to June, September and October. Prices vary with the duration and inclusions for each tour. Try **Toulouse Croisières** (☎ 05 61 25 72 57; www.toulouse-croisieres .com in French) or **Baladines** (☎ 06 07 43 48 28; www .bateaux-toulaisans.com).

Festivals & Events

Major annual events in Toulouse include **Festival Garonne**, a riverside celebration of music, dance and theatre in July; **Piano Jacobins** featuring classical piano recitals in the Église des Jacobins during September; and **Jazz sur Son 31**, an international jazz festival held in October.

Sleeping

Many Toulouse hotels cater for business people so rooms are easiest to find at weekends, when there are great discounts in all price ranges and, surprisingly, during most of the July and August holiday period. Many

mid-range places offer much better value for money than budget alternatives. Strangely for such a major city, Toulouse has no hostel.

BUDGET

Hôtel Splendid (Map p699; ☎ /fax 05 61 62 43 02; 13 rue Caffarelli; r from €17, s/d with shower €23/26, s/d/tr with bathroom €25/29/37) This is a good downtown budget choice though the price of the hall showers (€3.05) may induce temporary hydrophobia.

Hôtel des Arts (Map p699; ☎ 05 61 23 36 21; fax 05 61 12 22 37; 1bis rue Cantegril; s/d with washbasin €24/28, with shower €28/32) Just off place St-Georges and well situated for the evening action. Toilets are in the hall.

Hôtel La Chartreuse (Map p699; ☎ 05 61 62 93 39; la.chartreuse@wanadoo.fr; 4bis blvd Bonrepos; r with bathroom €29) Family-run with an intimate feel, this is a decent budget bet among some fairly scruffy offerings near the station.

Hôtel Anatole France (Map pp696-7; ☎ 05 61 23 19 96; fax 05 61 62 58 17; 46 place Anatole France; d with washbasin €19-22, with shower €22-25, with bathroom €29; **P**) Handy for place du Capitole, it has double glazing and parking spaces.

Camping

Camping de Rupé (off Map pp696-7; ☎ 05 61 70 07 35; 21 chemin du Pont de Rupé; camping €12.50; ☺ for caravans year-round, tents mid-Jun–mid-Sep) This place is often packed. It's 6km northwest of the train station. From place Jeanne d'Arc take bus No 59.

MID-RANGE

The area around place Victor Hugo has plenty of two-star hotels.

Hôtel du Taur (Map p699; ☎ 05 61 21 17 54; www .hotel-du-taur.com; 2 rue du Taur; s €38-52, d €48-56, tw/tr €56/63) Sports the naff-paintings-and-textured-wallpaper look but it's comfortable, friendly enough and rooms overlook a quiet interior courtyard. Its killer attraction is location: roll out of bed and you'll find yourself on place du Capitole.

Hôtel St-Sernin (Map p699; ☎ 05 61 21 73 08; fax 05 61 22 49 61; 2 rue St-Bernard; s/d/tr from €44/48/68; **P**) A peaceful, well-located place with private parking (€8). Ask for a room overlooking the Basilique. The fun-size baths are only for munchkins or very supple contortionists though.

Hôtel Ours Blanc (Wilson) (Map p699; ☎ 05 61 21 62 40; www.hotel-oursblanc.com; 2 rue Victor Hugo; s €43-59, d €53-65; ⊠) The best and most central of the trio of Ours Blanc places in the centre. It has smart, modern rooms and satellite TV.

Hôtel de France (Map p699; ☎ 05 61 21 88 24; www .hotel-france-toulouse.com; 5 rue d'Austerlitz; s €38, d €42-50, q €64-74; ⊠) It has spotless rooms, all with bathroom, some with views of the small, pretty garden. Rooms with air-con cost €4 extra.

Hôtel Albert 1er (Map p699; ☎ 05 61 21 17 91; www .hotel-albert1.com; 8 rue Rivals; r with bathroom & air-con €45-67; ⊠) A pleasant, well-maintained and fairly central family hotel with satellite TV.

TOP END

Hôtel des Beaux Arts (Map p699; ☎ 05 34 45 42 42; www.hoteldesbeauxarts.com; 1 place Pont du Neuf; r with shower €88, river view with bath €110-168, suite €188; ⊠) Surely the most romantic spot in town, with great views over river and bridge by day or night. The rooms are soothingly decorated and there's a smart, modern **brasserie** downstairs (see right).

Hôtel Mermoz (Map pp696-7; ☎ 05 61 63 04 04; www.hotel-mermoz.com; 50 rue Matabiau; d/tr €97/103; P ⊠) Off an ugly street but in a very pretty little nook with a peaceful terrace/garden and bright, welcoming rooms.

Eating

You'll find plenty of places around town offering excellent-value lunch *menus* for under €16 including the great-value places above Les Halles Victor Hugo (see below).

Both blvd de Strasbourg and the perimeter of place du Capitole are lined with restaurants and cafés. The terrace cafés of place St-Georges are lively.

Les Caves de la Maréchale (Map p699; ☎ 05 61 23 89 88; 3 rue Jules Chalande; menus €14-23, mains €18-21; ☽ Tue-Sat & dinner Mon) Dine under the eyeless gaze of classical statues in the magnificently vaulted brick cellar of a pre-Revolution convent. The excellent lunchtime *menu* (€14) of hors d'oeuvre buffet, a *pichet* of wine and main course is an absolute steal. The *menu* at €23 has a wide choice of inventive dishes.

Au Gascon (Map p699; ☎ 05 61 21 67 16; 9 rue des Jacobins; menus €9-20; ☽ lunch & dinner Mon-Sat) Terrific value for hearty, filling and artery-thickening Gascon comfort food comprised almost entirely of duck, foie gras and dauntingly large, oily and utterly delicious servings of *cassoulet au confit* (a haricot bean stew with confit of duck).

Restaurant Saveur Bio (Map p699; ☎ 05 61 12 15 15; 22 rue Maurice Fonvieille; menus €15 & €19.50; ☽ lunch & dinner Mon-Sat) A mainly vegie place given to proselytising about all things organic, it serves tasty, imaginative vegetarian food, including a lunchtime mixed plate (€8) and a great-value evening buffet (€8). It also serves fresh takeaway salads and dishes (€4 to €8).

La Faim des Haricots (Map p699; ☎ 05 61 22 49 25; 3 rue du Puits Vert; menus €8 & €11; ☽ lunch Mon-Sat, dinner Thu-Sat) Offers friendly service and a pick-'n'-mix all-vegetarian menu. There are salad and dessert bars, home-made soups (winter) and a *plat du jour*.

Restaurant Le Benjamin (Map p699; ☎ 05 61 22 92 66; 7 rue des Gestes; lunch menu €14, dinner menu €28) Serves excellent *nouvelle cuisine* rich in duck dishes with a goose variant here and there.

Sushiyaki (☎ 05 61 12 00 60; 9 rue Ste-Ursule; menus €10-20; ☽ lunch & dinner Mon-Sat) Head for this small, intimate, reasonably priced sushi and *teppanyaki* place when you can't face any more duck or *cassoulet*.

Brasserie Beaux Arts (Map p699; ☎ 05 61 21 12 12; 1 quai Daurade; menus €20 & 32; ☽ lunch & dinner) A smart, modern brasserie with a retro '30s feel serving fresh seafood and classic French dishes with style and bustling efficiency.

Le Café du Musée (Map pp696-7; ☎ 05 61 59 33 56; 76 allées Charles de Fitte; plat du jour €7.50, formule du jour €12; ☽ 11am-8pm Tue-Sun) A bright and light space in one of the outbuildings of Les Abattoirs museum (see p700). The *formule du jour* – the daily special, entrée or dessert, drink and coffee – is very good value. This café is also a great spot for an afternoon coffee, some home-made cake, dessert or ice cream.

AUTHOR'S CHOICE

Many of Toulouse's best-value places are the small, spartan, lunchtime-only **restaurants** above the appetite-sharpening food stalls of **Les Halles Victor Hugo** (Map p699), Toulouse's classy covered market. Fast, packed and no-nonsense, catering for market vendors and shoppers alike, they serve up generous, delicious *menus* of hearty fare for €11 to €19, Tuesday to Sunday.

CAFÉS & TEAHOUSES

L'Autre Salon de Thé (Map p699; ☎ 05 61 23 46 67; 16 place St Georges) Very civilised teahouse serving a good range of darjeelings and green teas along with rich, filling desserts inside and (if you're lucky enough to find a free seat) out in the pleasant square.

Two of the best places to linger by day or night over a coffee or something stronger in place du Capitole (Map p699) include **Le Florida** (12 place du Capitole) and **Bibent** (5 place du Capitole), with an ornate plastered, chandeliered and mirrored interior and lots of style.

SELF-CATERING

For fresh produce, visit **Les Halles Victor Hugo** (Map p699; place Victor Hugo), the large covered food market, or the **market** (Map p699; place des Carmes) to the south. Both open until 1pm, Tuesday to Sunday. Another small **market** (Map p699; place du Capitole) spreads across the square selling organically grown food on Tuesday and Saturday mornings.

Drinking

PUBS & BARS

Almost every square in the Vieux Quartier has at least one café, busy day and night. Most cafés are open from early morning until at least midnight, while the bars generally open late morning until the small hours.

Bodega Bodega (Map p699; 1 rue Gabriel Péri) A popular *bodega* (wine bar) with live music and lively crowds at weekends in this small but bustling nightlife enclave close to Jean Jaurès metro stop.

La Tantina de Burgos (Map p699; 27 av de la Garonnette) Another popular *bodega* that is an especially good bet for the strongly Spanish flavour lent by the bullfighting posters, the tapas and the buzzing atmosphere most nights. There is live music here as well at weekends. **Frog & Rosbif** (Map p699; 14 rue de l'Industrie) Very British. A lively expat pub, east of blvd de Strasbourg, with a dartboard and its own microbrewery churning out ales and stouts.

La Maison (Map p699; 9 rue Gabriel Péri) Very French. a cosy place with a log fire in winter where you can smoke while arguing animatedly, or at least watch the youngish local crowd doing so over a glass of excellent red, white or dessert wine.

Rue des Blanchers has several 'alternative' joints. Those clustered around place

St-Pierre beside the Garonne pull in a predominantly young crowd. **Chez Tonton** (Map pp696-7; place St-Pierre) and Spanish-flavoured **Bar Basque** (Map pp696-7; place St-Pierre) are sports bars. Nearby are the **Why Not Café** (Map pp696-7; 5 rue Pargaminières), with its beautiful rear terrace (summer only), and **Café des Artistes** (Map p699; 13 place de la Daurade), an art-student hang-out.

Entertainment

For what's on where, grab yourself a copy of *Toulouse Hebdo*, *Le Flash*, both weekly, or *Intramuros* (which is free from major hotels and cinemas).

NIGHTCLUBS

Toulouse has dance venues aplenty. There are a fair few fully fledged nightclubs, but many bars in town also double up as clubs on certain nights.

Opus (Map p699; 24 rue Bachelier) Offers food until 1.30am, a huge blackboard on which to pen your thoughts and dancing all night (rock upstairs, funk and disco down below).

L'Hugo Club (Map p699; 18 place Victor Hugo) This place is a slightly smarter dance bar attracting an older crowd.

Two hot spots near the centre are **La Strada** (Map p699; 4 rue Gabriel Péri; ☽ midnight-dawn Tue-Sat) and **L'Ubu** (Map p699; ☎ 05 61 23 26 75; 16 rue St-Rome; ☽ Mon-Sat), which has a choosy door policy, so dress smartly.

Out of town, the intrepid may like to risk **Le Clap** (off Map pp696-7; 146 chemin des Étroits); take exit 24 off the A64.

GAY VENUES

Toulouse is a very gay city – it ain't called *la ville rose* just for those pink bricks. Popular **Bar Les Deux G** (Map p699; 5 rue Baronie) attracts a mixed gay and lesbian crowd. **Shanghai Club** (Map p699; 12 rue de la Pomme; ☽ midnight-dawn) is a long-established gay club, also with a mixed clientele. The sauna-like **Le Colonial** (Map p699; 8 place de Belfort; ☽ noon-1am) is much more a male haunt.

CINEMAS

The three-screen **Cinéma Utopia** (Map p699; ☎ 05 61 23 66 20; 24 rue Montardy) and **Cinéma ABC** (Map p699; ☎ 05 61 29 81 00; 13 rue St-Bernard) both show nondubbed foreign films. **Cinémathèque de Toulouse** (Map p699; ☎ 05 62 30 30 10; 69 rue du Taur) also frequently has nondubbed screenings.

THEATRE
Toulouse also has a vibrant theatre scene. The tourist office offers comprehensive information on venues and up-to-the-minute listings.

Shopping

Toulouse's main shopping district, rich in department stores and expensive boutiques, embraces rue du Taur, rue d'Alsace-Lorraine, rue de la Pomme, rue des Arts and nearby streets. Place St-Georges is also surrounded by fashionable shops.

Regals (Map p699; ☎ 05 61 21 64 86; 25 rue du Taur) sells edible specialities such as chocolates, cakes, liqueurs and sweets containing or made of violets or violet flavourings. Place du Capitole (Map p699) hosts a huge **flea market** (including books) each Wednesday and there's another on Saturday and Sunday on place St-Sernin (Map p699). You'll find an antiquarian **book market** (Map p699; place St-Étienne) on Saturday.

Getting There & Away

AIR

Aéroport Toulouse-Blagnac (☎ 05 61 42 44 00; www.toulouse.aeroport.fr) is 8km northwest of the city centre. Air France and easyJet between them have over 30 flights daily to/from Paris (mainly Orly). There are also daily or almost-daily flights to/from many other cities in France and Europe. EasyJet and BA each fly from Gatwick at least twice daily.

Flybe and BMIBaby operate services from various UK regional airports.

BUS

Toulouse's modern **bus station** (Map pp696-7; ☎ 05 61 61 67 67; blvd Pierre Sémard; information office ☺ 8am-7pm) is just north of the train station. Services are listed below.

destination	one-way fare (€)	duration (hr)	frequency
Agen	12.00	3	1 daily
Albi	12.20	1½	1 daily
Andorra	21.00	3½	1–2 Wed, Fri & Sun
Auch	12.10	1¼	2 daily
Castres	9.80	1½	5–7 daily
Foix	9.20	1½	2 daily
Millau	23.80	4	3 daily
Montauban	6.70	1¼	5–7 daily

Semvat's (☎ 05 61 61 67 67) Arc-en-Ciel buses, serving local destinations in Haute-Garonne and nearby *départements,* also use the station, as do **Intercars** (☎ 05 61 58 14 53) and **Eurolines** (☎ 05 61 26 40 04) buses.

CAR

Most car-rental agencies have desks at the train station and airport.
ADA Train Station (☎ 05 61 63 68 63) Airport (☎ 05 61 30 00 33)
Europcar Train Station (☎ 05 62 73 41 64) Airport (☎ 0825 825 514)
Budget (☎ 05 61 63 18 18; 49 rue Bayard)

TRAIN

The **train station** (Gare Matabiau; ☎ 36 35; blvd Pierre Sémard), is about 1km northeast of the city centre. Local destinations served by frequent direct trains are listed below.

destination	one-way fare (€)	duration (hr)	frequency
Albi	11.80	1¼	at least 10 daily
Bayonne	44.80	3¾	at least 5 daily
Bordeaux	27.70	2–3	9–14 daily
Carcassonne	12.10	1hr	10–15 daily
Castres	11.60	1¼	5–9 daily
Foix	11.30	1¼	3–11 daily
Lourdes	20.90	2¼	7 daily
Montauban	7.60	½	at least hourly

The fare from Toulouse to Paris is €80 by Corail (6½ hours, to Gare d'Austerlitz) and €77.10 by TGV (5½ hours, to Gare Montparnasse via Bordeaux).

There is an information and ticketing office for **SNCF** (☎ 08 92 35 35 35; 5 rue Peyras; ☺ 9.30am-6.30pm Mon-Sat) in the town centre.

Getting Around

TO/FROM THE AIRPORT

The **Navette Aéroport bus** (☎ 05 34 60 64 00) links town and airport every 20 minutes and costs €3.90/5.90 single/return. The last run to the airport is at 8.20pm, Sunday to Friday (7.40pm on Saturday). Pick it up at the bus or train station, outside Jean Jaurès metro station or place Jeanne d'Arc. From the airport, the last bus leaves at 11.30pm daily.

An airport taxi costs about €20.

BICYCLE

Semvat (see below) hires bikes for almost nothing. Call by its **Espace Transport base** (Map p699; 05 34 30 03 00; 7 place Esquirol; ☺ 6.45am-6.30pm Mon-Fri, 9am-noon Sat & Sun). Rates are €2.30/2.70 per day/24 hours, although a €260 deposit is required.

BUS & METRO

The local bus network and 15-station metro line are run by **Semvat** (☎ 05 61 41 70 70; www.sem vat.com in French). A ticket for either service costs €1.30 and a 10-ticket carnet costs €10.30.

Most of the bus lines run daily until at least 8pm. The seven 'night' bus lines all start at the train station and run from 10pm to just after midnight.

The metro runs northeast to southwest from Jolimont to Basso-Cambo. Major city stops are Jean Jaurès, Capitole, Esquirol and Marengo SNCF (the train station). These last two are also important metro/bus interchanges. It's fully automated – no driver, no conductor, just lots of short, swift trains speeding under the city. A second line is under construction.

Semvat has ticket and information kiosks across town, including at Marengo and Basso-Cambo metro stations and at 9 place du Capitole. There's also an **Espace Transport Semvat office** (Map p699; 7 place Esquirol; ☺ 8.30am-6.30pm Mon-Fri, 9am-7pm Sat & Sun). All supply route maps, as does the tourist office.

CAR

Parking is tight in the city centre. There are huge car parks under place du Capitole, beneath allées Jean Jaurès, just off place Wilson and above the covered market on place Victor Hugo. At place St-Sernin you can park for free (except Sunday) if you can find a spot. Parking in the municipal multistoreys costs around € 1.80/11.80 per hour/day.

TAXI

There are 24-hour taxi stands at the **train station** (☎ 05 61 21 00 72), **place Wilson** (☎ 05 61 21 55 46) and **place Esquirol** (☎ 05 61 80 36 36).

ALBI

pop 49,106

The massive, fortress-like Gothic cathedral dwarfing the rest of town is an unmissable reminder of Albi's violent religious past.

Albi was the location of the so-called Albigensian heresy of the 12th and 13th centuries and the bloody crusade that crushed it (see The Cathars, p756). Almost all of central Albi, including the cathedral, is built from bricks of reddish clay, dug from the nearby Tarn River.

Two things make a trip here more than worthwhile: that extraordinary cathedral and the excellent museum dedicated to artist Henri de Toulouse-Lautrec, who hailed from Albi. It has the most extensive collection of his work anywhere.

Orientation

Cathédrale Ste-Cécile dominates the heart of the old quarter. From it, a web of narrow, semi-pedestrianised streets stretches southeast to place du Vigan, Albi's commercial hub. The train station is about 1km southwest of the city centre.

Information

INTERNET ACCESS

Ludi.com (64 rue Séré de Rivières; per hr €4.60; ☺ 11am-midnight Mon-Sat, 2pm-midnight Sun)
Mediathèque (av Général de Gaulle; per hr €3.80; ☺ 1-6pm Mon & Tue, 10am-noon & 1-6pm Wed & Sat, 10am-6pm Fri) Albi's splendid, 21st-century public-sector Internet café.

LAUNDRY

Lavomatique (10 rue Émile Grand; ☺ daily)
Lavotop (96 av Général de Gaulle; ☺ daily)

POST

Main Post Office (place du Vigan) With Cyberposte.
Post Office (place de Verdun)

TOURIST INFORMATION

Tourist Office (☎ 05 63 49 48 80; www.tourisme.fr /albi; place Ste-Cécile; ☺ 9am-7pm Mon-Sat, 10am-12.30pm & 2.30-6.30pm Sun Jul-Sep, 9am-12.30pm & 2-6pm Mon-Sat, 10am-12.30pm & 2.30-5pm Sun Oct-Jun) Has a free pamphlet in English, *Three Cultural Heritage Routes*, which describes a trio of signposted walks in the semipedestrianised old quarter.

Cathédrale Ste-Cécile

As much a fortress as a church, the mighty **Cathédrale Ste-Cécile** (place Ste-Cécile; admission free; ☺ 8.30am-6.45pm Jun-Sep, 9am-noon & 2-6.30pm Oct-May) was begun in 1282, not long after the Cathar movement was crushed. Built, to impress and subdue, of red brick in the southern (or

TOULOUSE AREA

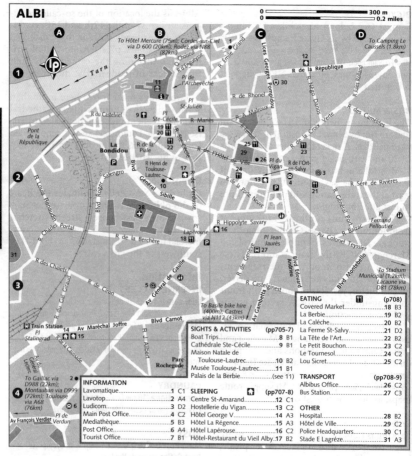

ALBI

0 — 300 m
0 — 0.2 miles

To Hôtel Mercure (75m); Cordes-sur-Ciel via D 600 (20km); Rodez via N88 (82km)

To Camping Le Caussels (1.8km)

To Stadium Municipal (1.2km); Lacaune via D81 (78km)

To Gaillac via D988 (2km); Montauban via D999 (72km); Toulouse via A68 (76km)

To Basile bike hire (400m); Castres via N112 (43km)

INFORMATION
Lavomatique.........................1 C1
Lavotop..............................2 A4
Ludicom.............................3 D2
Main Post Office...................4 C2
Mediathèque........................5 B3
Post Office..........................6 A4
Tourist Office......................7 B1

SIGHTS & ACTIVITIES (pp705-7)
Boat Trips...........................8 B1
Cathédrale Ste-Cécile............9 B1
Maison Natale de
  Toulouse-Lautrec..............10 B2
Musée Toulouse-Lautrec......11 B1
Palais de la Berbie...........(see 11)

SLEEPING (pp707-8)
Centre St-Amarand..............12 C1
Hostellerie du Vigan............13 C2
Hôtel George V..................14 A3
Hôtel La Régence...............15 A3
Hôtel Lapérouse..................16 C2
Hôtel-Restaurant du Vieil Alby..17 B2

EATING (p708)
Covered Market..................18 B3
La Berbie...........................19 B1
La Calèche.........................20 B2
La Ferme St-Salvy...............21 D2
La Tête de l'Art...................22 B2
Le Petit Bouchon.................23 C2
Le Tournesol......................24 C2
Lou Sicret.........................25 C2

TRANSPORT (pp708-9)
Albibus Office.....................26 C2
Bus Station........................27 C3

OTHER
Hospital............................28 B2
Hôtel de Ville.....................29 C2
Police Headquarters............30 C1
Stade E Lagréze..................31 A3

Meridional) Gothic style, it was finished approximately a century later. Attractive isn't the word – indeed, the cathedral's dominant feature is its sheer mass rising over town like some Tolkeinesque dark lord's tower rather than a place of Christian worship. It's a haunting sight when illuminated at night.

When you step inside, however, the contrast with that brutal exterior is total. No surface was left untouched by the Italian artists who, in the early 16th-century, painted their way along its vast nave.

An intricately carved, lacy **rood screen**, many of its statues smashed in the Revolution, spans the sanctuary. The **stained-glass windows** in the apse and choir date from the 14th to 16th centuries.

On no account miss the **grand chœur** (great choir; admission €1) with its frescoes, chapels and 30 fine biblical polychrome figures carved in stone.

At the western end, behind today's main altar, is *Le Jugement Dernier* (The Last Judgement; 1490), a particularly vivid Doomsday horror-show of the damned being boiled in oil, beheaded or imaginatively but casually tortured by demons and monsters.

Musée Toulouse-Lautrec

Beside the tourist office, the **Musée Toulouse-Lautrec** (☎ 05 63 49 48 70; www.musee-toulouse-lautrec .com; place Ste-Cécile; adult/student/child €4.50/2.50/free; ☼ 9am-6pm Jul & Aug, 9am-noon & 2-6pm Sep, 10am-noon & 2-5pm or 5.30pm Oct-Jun, closed Tue Oct-Mar) occupies the **Palais de la Berbie**, the vast, fortress-like 13th- to 15th-century archbishop's palace.

The museum boasts over 500 examples of the artist's work, giving both an excellent idea of his development as an artist and the way individual works evolved – everything from simple pencil sketches and rough pastel drafts to the final works such as his celebrated Parisian brothel scenes, including the *Salon de la rue des Moulins* taking pride of place. On the top floor are works by artists such as Degas, Matisse and Rodin. Audioguides in English cost €3. The attractive ornamental palace gardens and courtyard outside are well worth a wander.

The tourist office runs 45-minute guided **tours** (adult/student/child €7.10/6.50/free) of the museum in French twice daily at Easter and from July to early September.

A short walk away, a plaque on the wall of the privately owned **Maison Natale de Toulouse-Lautrec** (14 rue Henri de Toulouse-Lautrec) marks the house where the artist was born.

Tours

From mid-June to mid-September you can take 35-minute **boat trips** (adult/student or child €5/3) – departures every half-hour daily – from just below the Palais de la Berbie on a *gabarre*, a flat-bottomed sailing barge of the kind that used to haul goods down the Garonne to Bordeaux.

Festivals & Events

There's music for all tastes in Albi's cultural calendar. The **Festival Albi-Jazz** is in late June, while **Musiques en Albigeois**, in the last two weeks of July, offers classical-music concerts in a variety of venues around town. Albi celebrates **Carnaval** at the beginning of Lent with particular gusto.

Sleeping
BUDGET
Centre St-Amarand (☎ 05 63 48 18 29; 16 rue de la République; s/d €16/23; ☺ year-round) A religious centre, about 300m northeast of place du Vigan, offering spotless if spartan budget accommodation to young travellers. Take bus No 1 from the train station to the République stop and look for the courtyard entrance under the 'Tarn Libre' sign.

Hôtel George V (☎ 05 63 54 24 16; www.hotel georgev.com; 29 av Maréchal Joffre; d with shower €33, with bathroom from €41) A recommended family-run place, this hotel has spacious rooms, is handy for the bus and train stations and has a small breakfast terrace.

Camping
Camping Le Caussels (☎ /fax 05 63 60 37 06; camping €12; ☺ Apr–mid-Oct) It's just off route de Millau 2km northeast of place du Vigan. Take bus No 5 from place du Vigan to the terminus. There's running water but few other facilities.

PAINTER, LITHOGRAPHER, POSTER DESIGNER &....COOK?

Henri de Toulouse-Lautrec (1864-1901), Albi's most famous son, was famously short. As a teenager he broke both legs in separate accidents, stunting his growth and leaving him unable to walk without his trademark cane.

He spent his early twenties studying painting in Paris where he mixed with other artists including Van Gogh. In 1890, at the height of the *belle époque*, he abandoned impressionism and took to observing and sketching Paris's colourful nightlife. His favourite subjects included the cabaret singer Aristide Bruant, cancan dancers from the Moulin Rouge and prostitutes from the rue des Moulins, sketched to capture movement and expression in a few simple lines.

With sure, fast strokes he would sketch on whatever was to hand – a scrap of paper or a tablecloth, tracing paper or buff-coloured cardboard. He also became a skilled and sought-after lithographer and poster designer until drinking and general overindulgence in the heady nightlife scene led to his premature death in 1901.

If you want to taste, rather than see, a Toulouse-Lautrec creation, you may find some of Albi's restaurants offering versions of the recipes devised by the keen amateur chef Lautrec (for more information, ask at the tourist office). Alternatively, try to track down the out-of-print *The Art of Cooking* (in French or English), a collection of his amusing, whimsical recipes which include advice on how to cook a squirrel or stew a 'marmot you caught that very same morning sunning himself on a rock'.

MID-RANGE

Hôtel-Restaurant du Vieil Alby (☎ 05 63 54 14 69; fax 05 63 54 96 75; 25 rue Henri de Toulouse-Lautrec; r with bathroom €45-65; closed 2nd half Jan & late Jun/early Jul; P ⊠) Above an excellent restaurant (see below), this is a family-run, good-value place. Parking, difficult hereabouts, costs €7.

Hotel Mercure (☎ 05 63 46 66 66; fax 05 63 46 18 40; 41 rue Porta; s/d €72/80, with river views €80/90; P ⊠ ⊠) Occupying a handsome old brick building hogging a prime riverside spot, the rooms are recently and handsomely refurbished and there's a great terrace from which to gaze back across to town. There's also WiFi access.

Hostellerie du Vigan (☎ 05 63 43 31 31; fax 05 63 47 05 42; 16 place du Vigan; d/tr from €50/65; P ⊠) At the heart of town this place has spacious, modern rooms and a popular brasserie below.

Hôtel La Régence (☎ 05 63 54 01 42; www.hotel laregence.com in French; 27 av Maréchal Joffre; r with shower/ bathroom from €30/42; P) Next door to Hôtel George V, this hotel is warm in its welcome and there's a small garden out the back.

Hôtel Lapérouse (☎ 05 63 54 69 22; fax 05 63 38 03 69; 21 place Lapérouse; r €35-59; P ⊠) This place has cosy rooms with bathrooms and there's a small pool.

Eating & Drinking

Le Petit Bouchon (☎ 05 63 54 11 75; 77 rue de la Croix Verte; menus €8-25; ☽ lunch Mon-Sat, closed early Aug) A small, bustling joint serving simple fare at reasonable prices.

La Tête de l'Art (☎ 05 63 38 44 75; 7 rue de la Piale; menus €14-28; ☽ lunch & dinner daily May-Jul & Sep, Thu-Mon rest of year) Dishes for the adventurous such as jugged hare, tripe and pork foot mix with more traditional local stuff. It also does excellent desserts (pistachio and chocolate tart) and gourmet takeaways.

La Calèche (☎ 05 63 54 15 52; 6 rue de la Piale; menus €14-25; ☽ lunch & dinner) Opposite La Tête de l'Art, you'll also find the classics with the odd quirk among them including frogs' legs, marinated herring and a vegetarian platter (€13).

Lou Sicret (☎ 05 63 38 26 40; 1 rue Timbal; mains €12-17; ☽ lunch & dinner Tue-Sat, dinner only Sun & Mon) Tucked away down an alley at the northwestern corner of place du Vigan, this is friendly and bustling and serves delightful regional cuisine in a secluded courtyard.

Hôtel-Restaurant du Vieil Alby (see above; ☎ 05 63 38 28 23; menus €16-45, lunch €12; ☽ lunch Tue-Sun,

closed late Jul) The very best in local fare is served with the local Gaillac wine. Foie gras with caramelised apples, cassoulet, filet mignon with a cep sauce and mandarin and champagne sorbet are some menu examples. There are also vegetarian options.

Le Tournesol (☎ 05 63 38 38 14; 11 rue de l'Ort-en-Salvy; plat du jour €7.50; ☽ lunch Tue-Sat) A highly popular vegetarian restaurant, airy and full of light. Mixed salad platters start at €8.

Le Grand Pontié (☎ 05 63 54 16 34; place du Vigan; pizzas from €7, menus €10-25; ☽ brasserie lunch, lunch & dinner) A large, grand place with a pizzeria on the mezzanine floor, a brasserie below and a pleasant pavement café spilling onto the square, great for nursing a coffee and watching the action on the square.

Hostellerie du Vigan (see left; menus €16-23, salads €6-8; ☽ lunch & dinner Mon-Sat) A popular bar/ brasserie.

La Berbie (☎ 05 63 54 13 86; 17 place St-Cecile; ☽ 9am-6pm Sun-Thu, 8am-3pm Fri & Sat) A cosy *salon de thé* with great cakes and a fine *tarte tatinand*. There's a great choice of teas served in heavy cast-iron pots (the Darjeeling is especially good).

SELF-CATERING

Fresh fare can be picked up from the temporary (until 2006) **covered market** (place Lapérouse; ☽ morning-early afternoon Tue-Sun) while a car park is built beneath the old and stylish market on place St-Julien. An animated Saturday morning **farmers' market** overflows from place Ste-Cécile into the surrounding streets.

Pick up the very best in cheese from **La Ferme St-Salvy** (53 rue Séré de Rivières), one of France's dwindling number of *fromageries* (specialist cheese shops).

Getting There & Away

BUS

The **bus station** (☎ 05 63 54 58 61), little more than a parking area, is on the southwestern corner of place Jean Jaurès. Ask at the tourist office for a timetable. Services include Cordes (€4.70, 50 minutes, two daily weekdays), Castres (€5.25, 50 minutes, up to 10 daily), Montauban (€11.50, 1¼ hours, two daily) and Toulouse (€11.20, 1½ hours, three daily).

TRAIN

The **train station** (place Stalingrad) is linked by Bus No 1 with the bus station and place du

Vigan. There are multiple trains to/from Rodez (€11.30, 1¼ hours), Millau (€19, 2¾ hours), Toulouse (€10.80, 1¼ hours) and Cordes (€6.50, one hour). For Montauban (€16), change in Toulouse.

Getting Around

You can rent mountain bikes from **Basile** (☎ 05 63 38 43 09; 18 av Maréchale Foch; per day/week €15/73).

Leave your vehicle in the large car park at Le Bondidou, near the cathedral.

Local bus services are run by **Albibus** (☎ 05 63 38 43 43), Monday to Saturday. It has an information office beside the Hôtel de Ville.

Phone for a **taxi** (☎ 05 63 47 99 99, 05 63 54 85 03).

CASTRES

Castres is a worthwhile detour if you are travelling between Albi and Toulouse, Carcassonne or the Mediterranean coast. It was founded by the Romans as a settlement, or *castrum*. At its heart is place Jean Jaurès, which is named in honour of Castres' most famous son and founding father of French socialism.

Castres' **tourist office** (☎ 05 63 62 63 62; 3 rue Milhau Ducommun; ☻ 9.30am-6.30pm Mon-Sat, 3-5pm Sun, closed 12.30-2pm Sep-Jun) is on the eastern bank of the River Agoût, near Pont Vieux.

The **Musée Goya** (☎ 05 63 71 59 30; Hôtel de Ville, rue de l'Hôtel de Ville; admission Apr-mid-Sep €3, mid-Sep–Mar €2.30, under 18 free; ☻ 9am-noon & 2-6pm daily Jul & Aug; 9am-noon & 2-5pm or 6pm Tue-Sun Sep-Jun), well worth a visit, contains France's most important collection of Spanish art, including many paintings and engravings by Goya himself.

Parc de Gourjade (av de Roquecourbe, the D89) is a vast municipal park north of the town centre with camp sites, golf course, about 15km of jogging trails, riding centre, **L'Archipel** (☎ 05 63 62 54 00) water park and an ice-skating rink. You can take bus No 6 or 7 from the Arcades stop on place Jean Jaurès but it's more fun to hop aboard **Le Miredames** (☎ 05 63 62 41 71; adult/child €4/1.60 return), a replica river barge that runs to/from the park from the quay in front of the tourist office three to five times daily from June to September.

MONTAUBAN

pop 54,421

On the right bank of the River Tarn, Montauban was founded in 1144 by Count Al-

phonse Jourdain of Toulouse who, legend has it, was so charmed by its trailing willow trees (*alba* in Occitan) that he named the place Mont Alba.

Montauban, southern France's second-oldest *bastide*, sustained significant damage during the Albigensian crusade. It became a Huguenot stronghold in 1570. The Edict of Nantes (1598) brought royal concessions to the Huguenots but, after its repeal by Louis XIV in 1685, the town's Protestants again suffered persecution.

Montauban's many classical townhouses date from the prosperous decades following the Catholic reconquest.

Orientation

Place Nationale, surrounded by attractive arcaded 17th-century brick buildings and a grid of semipedestrianised streets, sits at the heart of the old city. Place Franklin Roosevelt, overlooked by the cathedral, lies to its south.

The train station is about 1km from place Nationale, across the River Tarn at the western end of av Mayenne.

Information

3D Gamma (103 Faubourg Lacapelle; per hr €4.80; ☻ 11am-midnight Mon-Fri, 2pm-midnight Sat) Internet access.

Laundrette (26 rue de l'Hôtel de Ville; ☻ 7am-7.30pm)

Tourist Office (☎ 05 63 63 60 60; www.montauban-tourisme.com; place Prax-Paris; ☻ 9.30am-6.30pm Mon-Sat Jul & Aug, 9.30am-12.30pm & 2-6.30pm rest of year) Has a free pamphlet in English, *On the Paths to Heritage,* describing an exhaustive walking tour around the old town. It also sells tickets for the town's festivals.

Sights

MUSÉE INGRES

Jean Auguste Dominique Ingres, the sensual neoclassical painter and accomplished violinist, was a native of Montauban. Many of his works, plus canvases by Tintoretto, Van Dyck, Courbet and others, are exhibited in the **Musée Ingres** (☎ 05 63 22 12 91; 19 rue de l'Hôtel de Ville; adult/student & under 18 €4/free; ☻ 10am-6pm daily July & Aug, 10am-noon & 2-6pm Tue-Sat Sep-Jun & Sun Easter–mid-Oct), a former bishop's palace. Reception can provide explanatory notes in English.

For €4.50 you can buy a combined pass that also admits you to the nearby museums of Histoire Naturelle (natural history),

Terroir (local costumes and traditions) and Résistance et Déportation (with mementos of WWII).

CHURCHES
The 18th-century **Cathédrale Notre Dame de l'Assomption** (place Franklin Roosevelt), with its clean, classical lines, contains one of Ingres' masterpieces, *Le Vœu de Louis XIII*, depicting the king pledging France to the Virgin. The fine 13th-century **Église St-Jacques**, also in mellow pink brick, still bears cannonball marks from Louis XIII's 1621 siege of the town.

Festivals & Events
Montauban has summer music fun and historical celebrations.

Alors Chante in May is a festival of traditional French song. **Jazz à Montauban** is a giant jam in the second week of July. The **Fête des Quatre-Cent Coups** (400 Blows) is a weekend street festival in the first half of September. It commemorates the moment when, says local lore, a fortune-teller told Louis XIII, besieging Montauban in 1621, to blast off 400 cannons simultaneously against the town, which still failed to fall.

Sleeping
Hôtel du Commerce (☎ 05 63 66 31 32; 9 place Franklin Roosevelt; r with bathroom €44-70) Central and recently renovated. It does a very generous buffet breakfast (€6).

Hôtel Le Lion d'Or (☎ 05 63 20 04 04; fax 05 63 66 77 39; 22 av Mayenne; s/d from €24/48) A trim two-star option near the train station.

Hôtel d'Orsay (☎ 05 63 66 06 66; www.hotel-restaurant-orsay-com; av Roger Salengro; r with bathroom €47-54; P ☒) Next door to Hôtel Le Lion d'Or and a notch up, this hotel offers comfortable enough, if rather dated, rooms and an upmarket restaurant (see right).

Etap Hôtel (☎ 08 92 68 09 79; www.etaphotel.com; rue Léon Cladel; s/d/tr €32/38/44; P ☒) Just out of the town centre but reasonable value. Inside the ugly concrete bunker exterior are modern, smart (if uniform) rooms. Parking is free, breakfast is €4.

Eating
Bistrot du Faubourg (☎ 05 63 63 49 89; 111 Faubourg Lacapelle; menus €11, €17 & €23; ☺ lunch & dinner Mon-Fri, lunch Sat 15 Aug-Jul) Montauban's best value for money is perhaps found here, as its 'house full' notice regularly attests.

Brasserie des Arts (☎ 05 63 20 20 90; 4 place Nationale; menus €15-19.25, daily special €7.30; ☺ lunch only). One of several brasseries on place Nationale, this popular choice offers a good range of fish dishes.

Agora Café (☎ 05 63 63 05 74; 9 place Nationale; mains €7; ☺ lunch) Local specialities of *piperade* (sweet pepper dish), cassoulet or lentils are served alongside salads (€5.50 to €7) here.

Restaurant Au Fil de l'Eau (☎ 05 63 66 11 85; 14 quai du Dr Lafforgue; menus €24, €38 & €53; ☺ lunch Tue-Sun) Beside the River Tarn, tempting *menus* and a window full of merited recommendations from Gallic gastronomic guides beckon you in. Typical *menu* examples include: frog soufflé, foie gras terrine, pork with confit onions and mustard, *crème brûlée* with star anise.

La Cuisine d'Alain (☎ 05 63 66 06 66; Hôtel d'Orsay, av Roger Salengro; menus €22, €32 & €52; ☺ lunch & dinner Wed-Sun, lunch Mon) Trying to match Restaurant Au Fil de l'Eau in quality, it's especially strong on seafood including oysters, scallops and fish such as *rouget* and offers free wine and coffee with lunch.

Morning **farmers' markets** are on Saturday (place Prax-Paris) and Wednesday (place Lalaque), as well as a smaller, daily one (place Nationale).

Getting There & Away
BUS
Several daily buses for Toulouse (€7) are run by **Autocar Jardel** (☎ 05 63 22 55 00) and to Moissac and Agen by **Autocar Barrière** (☎ 05 63 93 34 34). Since Montauban has no bus station, intercity buses stop at a bewildering – and changing – number of points. Ask at the tourist office for the stop of the week.

From the train station, two SNCF buses run to Albi (€10.20, 1¼ hours, daily except Saturday).

TRAIN
There are Corail trains to Paris' Gare d'Austerlitz (€71, four to six hours) and TGVs to Gare Montparnasse (€71 to €81, five hours, four daily). Regional services include Toulouse (€7.60, 30 minutes, frequent), Bordeaux (€23.30, two hours, frequent) via Agen (€11.50, 45 minutes) and Moissac (€4.80, 20 minutes, up to six daily).

Getting Around
BUS
The train and bus stations are connected with the town centre by bus Nos 3 and 5.

CAR
There may be free parking under Pont Vieux when you read this (although the mayor wants to install meters). Alternatively **Parking Occitan** (place Prax-Paris), where the above-ground section – markedly cheaper than the adjacent underground park – charges €2 for a full day.

TAXI
If you need a taxi, the company to call is **Radio Taxis** (☎ 05 63 66 99 99).

MOISSAC
pop 12,744
Moissac, a day trip from Montauban or Toulouse, was once a stop for Santiago de Compostela pilgrims. **Abbaye St-Pierre** (€5; 9am-noon & 2-7pm Jul & Aug, to 6pm mid-Mar–Jun & Sep–mid-Oct, to 5pm mid-Oct–mid-Mar, but subject to change), resplendent with France's finest Romanesque sculpture, became a model for ecclesiastical buildings in southern France.

Above the **south portal**, completed around 1130, is a superb tympanum depicting St John's Vision of the Apocalypse, with Christ in majesty flanked by the apostles, angels and 24 awestruck elders.

In the **cloister** 116 delicate marble columns support wedge-shaped, deeply carved capitals, each a little masterpiece of foliage, earthy figures or biblical scenes. The Revolution's toll is everywhere – nearly every face is smashed.

You enter the cloister through the **tourist office** (☎ 05 63 04 01 85; www.moissac.fr; place Durand de Bredon; 9am-noon & 2-7pm Jul & Aug, to 6pm mid-Mar–Jun & Sep–mid-Oct, to 5pm mid-Oct–mid-Mar). It shows a free 10-minute video (English version available) and sells a detailed guidebook, also in English. Admission to the cloister also includes a museum of folk art and furnishings, and a library containing replicas of the monastery's beautiful illuminated manuscripts.

There are up to six trains daily to/from Montauban (€4.80, 20 minutes), the majority also serving Toulouse (€7.60). You can park for free in place des Récollets (the market square) and just above (north of) the tourist office.

AUCH
pop 23,501
Auch (pronounced similarly to poche or cloche) has been an important trade cross-roads since the Romans conquered a Celtic tribe called the Auscii and established Augusta Auscorum on the flats east of the River Gers. The town's heyday was in the Middle Ages when the counts of Armagnac (and their archbishops) built the city's cathedral. Its second flowering was in the late 18th century, following the building of new roads to Toulouse and into the Pyrenees. A slide into rural obscurity followed the Revolution in 1789.

Auch is the place to enjoy genuine Gascon cuisine and makes a convenient base for exploring the Gers region's underrated gentle countryside.

Orientation
Hilltop Auch, with place de la Libération, place de la République and the cathedral at its heart, has most of the sights, restaurants, shops and hotels. Pedestrianised rue Dessoles is the principal shopping street. The old town, tumbling away to the south, is a web of lanes, steps and little courtyards. Across the Gers River is the 'new' Auch and the train station.

Information
Bureau Information Jeunesse (16bis rue Rouget de Lisle; per hr €3; 11am-6.30pm Mon-Sat) Cheap Internet access.
Main Post Office (rue Gambetta) With Cyberposte.
Tourist Office (☎ 05 62 05 22 89; www.mairie-auch.fr in French; 1 rue Dessoles; 9.15am-7pm daily Jul & Aug; 9am-noon & 2-6pm Mon-Sat, 9am-noon Sun Easter–mid-Sep) In Maison Fedel, a handsomely restored 15th-century building. Its town map shows a couple of signposted walking tours. Ask for the English version of the exhaustively detailed accompanying leaflet. The office can provide some good recommendations, itineraries and leaflets for exploring the surrounding countryside, villages and public gardens.

Sights
CATHÉDRALE STE MARIE
This magnificent building, now a Unesco World Heritage Site, moved Napoleon II to exclaim 'A cathedral like this should be put in a museum!'. Constructed over two centuries, from 1489 to 1680, **Cathédrale Ste-Marie** (☎ 05 62 05 72 71; 9.30am-noon & 2-5pm) ranges in style from pure Gothic to Italian Renaissance. To appreciate the contrast, take a look at the doorway in the external north wall; the lower part is lacy Gothic

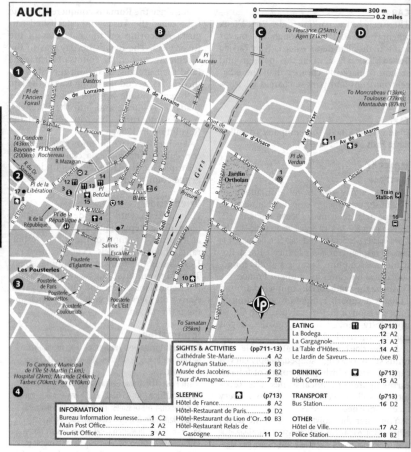

AUCH

0 ————— 300 m
0 ————— 0.2 miles

To Fleurance (25km);
Agen (71km)

To Moncrabeau (13km);
Toulouse (77km);
Montauban (87km)

To Condom
(43km);
Bayonne
(200km)

To Samatan
(35km)

To Camping Municipal
de l'île St-Martin (1km);
Hospital (2km); Mirande (24km);
Tarbes (70km); Pau (110km)

SIGHTS & ACTIVITIES	(pp711–13)
Cathédrale Ste-Marie	4 A2
D'Artagnan Statue	5 B3
Musée des Jacobins	6 B2
Tour d'Armagnac	7 B2

SLEEPING	(p713)
Hôtel de France	8 A2
Hôtel-Restaurant de Paris	9 D2
Hôtel-Restaurant du Lion d'Or	10 B3
Hôtel-Restaurant Relais de	
Gascogne	11 D2

EATING	(p713)
La Bodega	12 A2
La Gargagnole	13 A2
La Table d'Hôtes	14 A2
Le Jardin de Saveurs	(see 8)

DRINKING	(p713)
Irish Corner	15 A2

TRANSPORT	(p713)
Bus Station	16 D2

OTHER	
Hôtel de Ville	17 A2
Police Station	18 A2

INFORMATION	
Bureau Information Jeunesse	1 C2
Main Post Office	2 A2
Tourist Office	3 A2

while the upper, unadorned arch is purest Florentine.

Though the heavy western façade impresses by its sheer bulk – and looks imposingly grand illuminated at night – the real splendour is within: 18 vivid 16th-century Renaissance **stained-glass windows** and the astonishing **choir** (admission €1.50 incl guide sheet in English), featuring over 1500 individual carvings of biblical scenes and mythological creatures in the 113 oak choir stalls.

Behind the cathedral, the 14th-century, 40m-high **Tour d'Armagnac** served Auch's medieval archbishops (and later Revolutionaries) as a prison. It's closed to the public.

MUSÉE DES JACOBINS

The eclectic **Musée des Jacobins** (☎ 05 62 05 74 79; 4 place Louis Blanc; adult/child €3/1.50; ☒ 10am-noon & 2-6pm daily May-Sep, to 5pm Tue-Sun Oct-Apr), sometimes referred to as the Musée d'Auch, was established in 1793, its original collection selected from property seized during the Revolution. Occupying a 15th-century Dominican monastery, it is one of France's oldest and best provincial museums. If you show your entry ticket to the cathedral's choir, you will receive a 50% reduction on the museum admission.

Highlights of this eclectic collection include frescoes and other artefacts from an early Gallo-Roman villa, landscapes by locally born painter Jean-Louis Rouméguère

(1863–1925) and a collection of the ethnography of the Americas, from pre-Colombian pottery to 18th-century religious art.

ESCALIER MONUMENTAL

Auch's 370-step, 19th-century Monumental Stairway drops to the river from place Salinis. Near the bottom swaggers a statue of d'Artagnan, the fictional swashbuckling Gascon hero immortalised by Alexandre Dumas in *Les Trois Mousquetaires* (The Three Musketeers). Nearby, a series of narrow, stepped alleyways, collectively called Les Pousterles, also plunge to the plain.

Sleeping

There's no hostel in town and budget accommodation is scarce.

Hôtel-Restaurant de Paris (☎ 05 62 63 26 22; fax 05 62 60 04 27; 38 av de la Marne; s/d from €24/27, with bathroom from €39/45; ☺ Dec-Oct; ℗) Pleasantly old-fashioned with cosily furnished rooms and a good restaurant that serves copious quantities. Private parking costs €4.

Hôtel-Restaurant du Lion d'Or (☎ 05 62 63 66 00; fax 05 62 63 00 38; 7 rue Pasteur; r with bathroom €30-60) A rambling old place near the river whose cheaper rooms are reasonable value.

Hôtel-Restaurant Relais de Gascogne (☎ 05 62 05 26 81; fax 05 62 63 30 22; 5 av de la Marne; s/d/tr/q with bathroom €45/49/60/72; ☺ mid-Jan–mid-Dec; ℗) A member of the Logis de France chain with comfortable, well-tended rooms.

Hôtel de France (☎ 05 62 61 71 71; auchgarreau@intercom.fr; 2 place de la Libération; s/d from €62/78, with half-board from €88/131; ℗ ☒) A very comfortable three-star establishment up in the old town with a grand, old-fashioned fine dining restaurant attached (see below).

CAMPING

Camping Municipal de l'Île St-Martin (☎ 05 62 05 00 22; ☺ mid-Apr–mid-Nov) A spartan place 1.5km south of town. Take bus No 5 from place de la Libération to the Mouzon stop.

Eating & Drinking

La Table d'Hôtes (☎ 05 62 05 55 62; 7 rue Lamartine; menus €15-30; ☺ lunch & dinner, closed Wed & Sun) Usually full of locals enjoying the great food, much of it local Gascon fare with interesting twists, for example a heavenly pasta with foie gras and morels.

Le Jardin des Saveurs (☎ 05 62 61 71 71; Hôtel de France, 2 place de la Libération; menus from €25; ☺ lunch & dinner Mon-Sat, lunch Sun) Chef Roland Garreau is an acknowledged specialist in Gascon food but it needn't bust your budget: enticing *menus* begin at only €25, rising to the gastronomic revelations of his *menu gourmand du chef* at €48.

La Bodega (☎ 05 62 05 69 17; 7 rue Dessoles; lunch menu €11, mains €13 & €15; ☺ lunch & dinner Mon-Sat, dinner Sun) Serves full meals of Spanish and Basque origin by day and tapas by night and attracts a youngish crowd.

La Gargagnole (☎ 05 62 05 09 64; 10 rue Dessoles; plat du jour €7, salads €6-7, mains €9-11; ☺ lunch & dinner Mon-Sat) Bang opposite La Bodega, this is a bustling, popular place.

Irish Corner (1 place Betclar) French-run, and not an Irish accent in ear shot but convivial and lively all the same, this is a good central spot for a Guinness.

Getting There & Around

Useful bus connections include Condom (€5.80, 50 minutes, three or four daily), Montauban (€11.90, 1¾ hours, up to three daily) and Tarbes (€10.80, 1¾ hours, three daily). These services stop at both the **bus station** (☎ 05 62 05 76 37) and **train station** (☎ 05 62 60 62 12).

SNCF buses operate between Auch and Agen (€9.80, 1½ hours, six to eight services daily), while five to seven trains and two SNCF buses link Auch and Toulouse (€12.10, 1¾ hours).

There's extensive free parking along the length of allées d'Étigny.

CONDOM

pop 7555

Poor Condom, whose name has made it the butt of so many nudge-snigger, English-language jokes (the French don't even use the word, preferring *préservatif* or, more familiarly, *capote anglaise*, meaning 'English hood' – touché!).

Condom is actually a self-confident town beside the River Baïse, and is well worth a visit for its decorative cathedral, some fine restaurants and a clutch of sober neoclassical mansions.

Information

La Lavandière (5 rue Jules Ferry; ☺ 7am-10pm) Open daily to keep your clothes clean.

Tourist Office (☎ 05 62 28 00 80; place Bossuet; ☺ 9am-7pm Mon-Sat, 10am-noon Sun Jul & Aug,

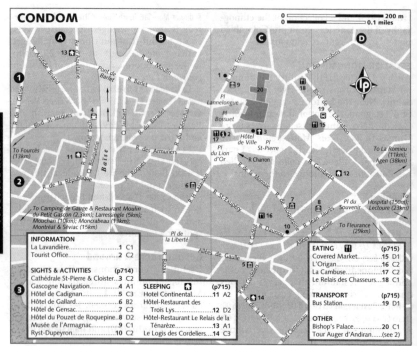

CONDOM

INFORMATION
La Lavandière.........................1 C1
Tourist Office.........................2 C2

SIGHTS & ACTIVITIES (p714)
Cathédrale St-Pierre & Cloister..3 C2
Gascogne Navigation.............4 A1
Hôtel de Cadignan.................5 C3
Hôtel de Gallard....................6 B2
Hôtel de Gensac....................7 C2
Hôtel du Pouzet de Roquepine..8 D2
Musée de l'Armagnac.............9 C1
Ryst-Dupeyron......................10 C2

SLEEPING (p715)
Hotel Continental..................11 A2
Hôtel-Restaurant des
    Trois Lys..........................12 D2
Hôtel-Restaurant Le Relais de la
    Ténarèze.........................13 A1
Le Logis des Cordeliers.........14 C3

EATING (p715)
Covered Market.....................15 D1
L'Origan...............................16 C2
La Cambuse..........................17 C2
Le Relais des Chasseurs.......18 C1

TRANSPORT (p715)
Bus Station..........................19 D1

OTHER
Bishop's Palace....................20 C1
Tour Auger d'Andiran......(see 2)

9am-noon & 2-6pm Mon-Sat Sep-Jun) Located in the 13th-century Tour Auger d'Andiran, just west of the cathedral. Its *Condom: Porte du Bonheur* (Condom: Gateway to Happiness) describes a walking tour of the town.

Sights

Condom's 16th-century **Cathédrale St-Pierre** (place St-Pierre), with its lofty nave and elaborately carved chancel, is a rich example of southern Flamboyant Gothic architecture. Its most richly sculpted entrance – much defaced during the Revolution – gives onto the square. Abutting the cathedral on its northern side is the delicately arched cloister, now occupied in part by the Hôtel de Ville.

Around the corner from the cathedral, **Musée de l'Armagnac** (☎ 05 62 28 47 17; 2 rue Jules Ferry; adult/child €2.20/1.10; ☷ 10am-noon & 3-6pm Wed-Mon Apr-Oct, 2-5pm Wed-Sun Nov, Dec, Feb & Mar, closed Jan) portrays the traditional production of Armagnac, Gascony's fiery rival to Cognac that's distilled to the north in the Bordeaux vineyards.

For a taste of the real stuff, head to **Ryst-Dupeyron** (☎ 05 62 28 08 08; 36 rue Jean Jaurès; ☷ 10am-noon & 2-6.30pm Mon-Fri year-round, 3.30-6.30pm Sat-Sun

Jul & Aug), one of several Armagnac producers offering free tastings. It occupies the 18th-century Hôtel de Cugnac.

Among the town's most elegant 18th-century *hôtels particuliers* mansions are **Hôtel de Gallard** (rue H Cazaubon), **Hôtel de Gensac** (rue de Roquepine), **Hôtel du Pouzet de Roquepine** (rue Jean Jaurès) and **Hôtel de Cadignan** (allées de Gaulle). None is open to the public.

Tours

During July and August, **Gascogne Navigation** (☎ 05 62 28 46 46; quai Bouquerie; adult/child €7/5.50) runs 1½-hour cruises at 3pm and 4.30pm Monday to Saturday from its quayside base, La Capitainerie. It also hires small motor boats by the hour or day (€23/92) and bigger ones by the week.

Festivals & Events

Held on the second weekend in May, **Bandas à Condom** (www.festival-de-bandas.com) brings marching and brass bands from all over Europe for 48 hours of nonstop oompah. In July and August you can listen to operetta in the cloister during **Les Nuits Musicales**.

Sleeping

Hôtel-Restaurant Le Relais de la Ténarèze (☎ 05 62 28 02 54; fax 05 62 28 46 96; 22 av d'Aquitaine; d/tr/q with bathroom €40/49/60) A family-run place with plain but comfortable rooms and an good-value restaurant (see right).

Hôtel Continental (☎ 05 62 68 37 00; www.le continen tal.net; 20 av Maréchal Foch; r with bath/shower €39/47; 🔃) Modern, welcoming and fairly central with a reasonable restaurant attached. Guests benefit from discounted entry to Aquablue, the local pool and sauna. Avoid the road-facing rooms.

Le Logis des Cordeliers (☎ 05 62 28 03 68; www .logisdescordeliers.com; rue de la Paix; r €46-68; 🔆 Feb-Dec; **P** 🔏 🔃) Family-run and tranquil, with an attractive small garden, pool and bar.

Hôtel-Restaurant des Trois Lys (☎ 05 62 28 33 33; www.lestroislys.com; 38 rue Gambetta; r €80-150) Occupying an 18th-century mansion complete with pool and superb restaurant (see right), this is a good place to indulge yourself.

CAMPING

Camping de Gauge (☎ 05 62 28 17 32; fax 05 62 28 48 32; route d'Eauze; 🔆 Apr–mid-Sep) Well equipped and beside the River Baïse, 2.3km southwest of town along the D931. There's a sports centre with pool nearby.

Eating

For a small town, Condom is disproportionately rich in good-value restaurants.

L'Origan (☎ 05 62 68 24 84; 4 rue Cadéot; pizzas €7-8.80, mains €7-10; 🔆 lunch & dinner Tue-Sat year-round,

---

> ### VULGAR VILLAGES
>
> The more puerile English-speaking visitors to France have long been amused by place names such as Condom (not to mention the likes of Pissy or Stains), but the French are in on the act now too. In an attempt to really put themselves on the map, in 2003 a group of French villages with names that mean silly or rude things in French staged their first summit meeting of 'Villages of lyric or burlesque names' in a tiny village outside Toulouse called Mingocebos (or 'eat onions' in the old Occitan tongue). Members include Saligos ('filthy pig'), Beaufou ('beautiful mad') and Cocumont ('cuckold hill'), although Trecon ('very stupid') and Montcuq ('my arse') have yet to join.

---

plus dinner Mon Jul & Aug) Takes over the street in summer and does takeaways. It's good-value, offering a choice of robust Italian dishes.

Le Relais des Chasseurs (☎ 05 62 28 20 14; 3 blvd de la Libération; menus €10-25; 🔆 lunch & dinner Tue-Sat, lunch Mon) An unpretentious place, popular with workers. Its midday *menu* at €10 including wine is particularly good value.

Hotel-Restaurant Le Relais de la Ténarèze (see left; 3-course dinner menus €10.50 & €22; 🔆 daily Jun-Sep, lunch only Mon-Sat Oct-May) Dishes up hearty meals. Often as not, there's no menu and you take what Madame has simmering in the pot.

Hôtel-Restaurant des Trois Lys (see left; menus €20 & €30, à la carte dishes €21-35) The finest Gascon cuisine is found here, with such delights as cod terrine with ceps, crab raviolis in bisque and a *menu terroir* (regional *menu*) at €27.

Restaurant Moulin du Petit Gascon (☎ 05 62 28 28 42; menus €16-32; 🔆 lunch & dinner daily Jul–mid-Sep, closed dinner Sun rest of year) Occupies an unparalleled site on the river close to Camping de Gauge and serves fine food.

La Cambuse (☎ 05 62 68 48 95; place Bossuet; salads €6-9, sandwiches €2.50-3.50, plat du jour €7.90; 🔆 lunch Mon-Sat, dinner Tue, Thu & Fri) A quick-fix place beside the tourist office. Good for eating in or takeaway, the restaurant spills onto place Bossuet in summertime.

SELF-CATERING

The **farmers market**, rich in local produce, is held on Wednesday and Saturday mornings in the covered market. There's a small, Sunday morning market on blvd St-Jacques.

Getting There & Around

Condom, with the nearest train station in Auch, is ill served by public transport. There are three or four daily buses to Auch (€5.80, 50 minutes), including one that continues to Toulouse (€13.90, 2½ hours) and one early-bird run to Bordeaux (€17.70, 2¾ hours Monday to Saturday). There is also one bus a day to Pau (€19.60, 2½ hours) and also to Agen (€7.70, 45 minutes).

Camping de Gauge (see left) rents bikes for €7 per day.

AROUND CONDOM

Condom makes an excellent base for exploring the gentle Armagnac countryside and its attractive villages. Bus services, except to/from Lectoure, are nonexistent but the mild undulation makes it ideal cycling country.

TOULOUSE AREA

Château de Cassaigne

At the 13th-century **Château de Cassaigne** (☎ 05 62 28 04 02; www.chateaudecassaigne.com; ☻ 9am-noon & 2-7pm), the old country house of the bishops of Condom, you can enjoy a free visit, then sample Armagnac from its 18th-century distillery. It's 6.5km southwest of Condom, just off the D931 to Eauze.

Fourcès

Fourcès (pronounce that 's'), 13km north-west of Condom via the D114, is a picturesque *bastide* on the River Auzoue. Uniquely circular, its shady expanse is ringed by well-restored medieval houses. You can sip a drink or have a pleasant but none too copious lunch on the terrace of **L'Auberge** (☎ 05 62 29 40 10; menus €15, €20.50 & €30). Opposite is the tiny, dusty **Musée des Vieux Métiers** (Museum of Ancient Crafts).

The village bursts into colour during the last weekend of April as thousands pour in for its **Marché aux Fleurs**, more a flower festival than market.

The tiny seasonal **tourist office** (☎ 05 62 29 50 96; ☻ Jun-Sep) is in the square (or, more accurately, circle).

Larressingle

Larressingle, 5km west of Condom on the D15, is probably France's cutest fortified village. It is certainly the most besieged, bravely withstanding armies of tourists and Compostela pilgrims.

This textbook bastion bears witness to the troubled times of medieval Gascony. Within the largely intact original walls are the remains of a **castle-keep**, once the principal residence of the bishops of Condom, and the very sturdy Romanesque **Église St-Sigismond**.

Montréal & Séviac

Montréal, established in 1255, was one of Gascony's first *bastides*. Its chunky Gothic church squats beside place Hôtel de Ville, the arcaded main square.

At Séviac, 1.5km southwest of Montréal, are the excavated remains of a 4th-century **Gallo-Roman villa** (admission €3.50; ☻ 10am-7pm Jul & Aug, 10am-noon & 2-6pm Mar-Jun & Sep-Nov). Discovered by the local parish priest in 1868, the site is still being excavated. What archaeologists have revealed are the remains of a luxurious villa, including baths and outbuildings, on the agricultural estate of a 4th-century

Roman aristocrat. Large areas of the villa's spectacular mosaic floors (over 450 mosaics have been uncovered) have survived.

The admission price includes entry to the **museum**, located with Montréal's **tourist office** (☎ 05 62 29 42 85; place Hôtel de Ville; both ☻ 10am-12.30pm & 2.30-6pm Mon-Sat, 11am-5pm Sun Feb-Dec), where artefacts from Séviac are displayed. Ask for its explanatory sheet in English.

La Romieu

La Romieu, 11km northeast of Condom and once an important stopover on the Santiago de Compostela route, takes its name from the Occitan *roumieu*, meaning pilgrim. It's dominated by the magnificent 14th-century collegiate **Église St-Pierre** (admission €3.05). Just opposite the entrance is the **tourist office** (☎ 05 62 28 86 33; ☻ 10am-12.30pm & 2-7.30pm Jul & Aug, to 7pm Jun & Sep, to 6pm Feb-May & Oct-Dec, closed Sun morning year-round), whose staff will let you into the fine Gothic cloister that gives onto the church. Left of the altar is the **sacristy** where original medieval frescoes include arcane biblical characters, black angels and esoteric symbols. Climb the 136 steps of the double-helix stairway to the top of the octagonal tower for a good view over the countryside.

About 500m west of the village is the **Arboretum Coursiana** (☎ 05 62 68 22 80; with/without guided tour €5/4; ☻ 9am-8pm mid-Mar–Nov), an initiative of a local agricultural engineer, where over 650 trees and rare plants flourish.

Lectoure

Lectoure's main claim to fame is its superb **Musée Lapidaire** (☎ 05 62 68 70 22; place Général de Gaulle; adult/child €2.30/1.50; ☻ 10am-noon & 2-6pm daily Mar-Sep, 10am-noon & 2-6pm Wed-Mon Oct-Feb) in the the former Episcopal palace, today the Hôtel de Ville. The museum displays finds from local Gallo-Roman sites, and includes some Roman jewellery and mosaics, as well as an early Christian marble sarcophagus.

Rearing over the museum is the bulk of the 15th-century **Cathédrale St-Gervais et St-Protais** with its curious, ornate tower.

The **tourist office** (☎ 05 62 68 76 98; www.lectoure.fr; ☻ 9am-12.30pm & 2.30-7pm Jul & Aug, 9am-noon & 2-6pm Mon-Sat, 2-5pm Sun Sep-Jun) is next door.

Lectoure is 23km east of Condom and 36km north of Auch. SNCF's Auch–Agen buses stop here eight times daily Monday to Friday, less often at weekends (Auch €5.65, 40 minutes; Agen €5.80, 50 minutes).

Languedoc-Roussillon

CONTENTS

Languedoc	**720**
Montpellier	720
Around Montpellier	725
Sète	725
Agde	726
Béziers	727
Narbonne	727
Carcassonne	727
Nîmes	733
Around Nîmes	737
Alès & Around	739
Parc National des Cévennes	741
Florac	742
Mende	744
Around Mende	745
Gorges du Tarn	745
Parc Naturel Régional des Grands Causses	746
Millau	747
Around Millau	750
Roussillon	**751**
Perpignan	751
Around Perpignan	756
Têt Valley	757
Côte Vermeille	758

Languedoc-Roussillon is something of a three-eyed hybrid, cobbled together in the 1980s by the merging, for administrative purposes, of two historic regions. Bas Languedoc (Lower Languedoc), land of bullfighting, rugby and robust red wines, looks towards the more-sedate Provence. On the plain are all the major towns, such as Montpellier, the vibrant capital, sun-baked Nîmes with its fine Roman amphitheatre – and fairy-tale Carcassonne, with its witches'-hat turrets. On the coast, good beaches abound, old Agde lies somnolent beside the River Hérault and Sète, a thriving port, adds a touch of commercial vigour.

Deeper inland, Haut Languedoc (Upper Languedoc) is quite distinct from the sun-soaked lowlands. A continuation of the Massif Central, this rugged, sparsely populated mountainous terrain shares great trekking, mountain pasture, forests and hearty cuisine with Auvergne. It's a more isolated land for lovers of solitude and the outdoors, where the small towns of Mende, Florac, Alès and Millau are like oases within the greater wilderness. The Parc National des Cévennes is a wild, mountainous area, long the refuge of hermits and exiles and criss-crossed by marked trails. Trekking country too are the bare limestone plateaus of the Grands Causses, sliced through by deep canyons such as the Gorges du Tarn, perfect for a day's canoeing.

Roussillon, abutting the Pyrenees, constantly glances over the frontier to Catalonia, in Spain, with which it shares a common language and culture. Nestling alongside the rocky coastline are attractive little resorts such as Collioure, which drew the likes of Matisse and Picasso, attracted by its special light, while the gentle Têt and Tech Valleys stretch away inland. To their south, the Pic de Canigou, highest summit in the eastern Pyrenees and symbol of Catalan identity, pokes its nose, white in winter, to the clouds while, further east, the foothills are capped by stark, lonely Cathar fortresses.

HIGHLIGHTS

- Gasp at your first glimpse of **La Cité's witches'-hat turrets** (p727) above Carcassonne
- Spot vultures looping and swooping high above **Gorges de la Jonte** (p747)
- Swim under the bridge for an original perspective of the **Pont du Gard** (p738)
- Drift lazily down the **Gorges du Tarn** (p745) in a canoe
- Walk a stage or two of Robert Louis Stevenson's **Cévennes donkey trek** (p743)
- Enjoy spectacular Pyrenean scenery from the trundling **Train Jaune** (Yellow Train; p757)
- Take a slow boat along the **Canal du Midi** (p726)

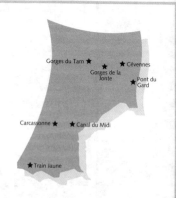

- POPULATION: 2,295,000
- AREA: 27,375 SQ KM

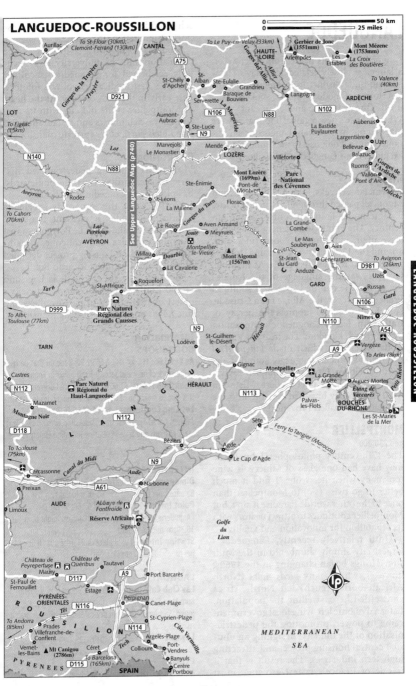

LANGUEDOC-ROUSSILLON

0 ⟨──────⟩ 50 km
0 ⟨──────⟩ 25 miles

LANGUEDOC

Languedoc takes its name from *langue d'oc,* a language closely related to today's Catalan and quite distinct from *langue d'oïl,* the forerunner of modern French, spoken to the north (the words *oc* and *oïl* meant 'yes'). When France's new regional boundaries were mapped out in the 1980s, Languedoc's traditional centre, Toulouse, to the southwest, was excluded from Languedoc-Roussillon.

History
Phoenicians, Greeks, Romans, Visigoths and Moors all passed through Languedoc before it came under Frankish control in the 8th century. The Franks were generally happy to leave affairs in the hands of local rulers and, around the 12th century, Occitania (today's Languedoc) reached its zenith. At the time, Occitan was the language of the troubadours and the cultured speech of southern France. However, the Albigensian Crusade, launched in 1208 to suppress the 'heresy' of Catharism, led to Languedoc's annexation by the French kingdom. The treaty of Villers-Cotterêts (1539), which made *langue d'oïl* the realm's official language, sounded the death knell for Occitan, though a revival spearheaded by the poet Frédéric Mistral in the 19th century breathed new life into the language now called Provençal.

MONTPELLIER
pop 230,000
The 17th-century philosopher John Locke may have had one glass of Minervois wine too many when he wrote: 'I find it much better to go twise (sic) to Montpellier than once to the other world'. Paradise it ain't, but Montpellier continues to attract visitors with its reputation for innovation and vitality.

Until relatively recently, Languedoc's largest city simply slumbered in the Midi sun. Things began changing in the 1960s, however, when many *pieds noirs* (North African–born French) left North Africa and settled here, swelling the population. Later a dynamic left-wing local government came to power, promoting the pedestrianisation of the old city, designing an unusual central housing project and attracting high tech industries. The result is that it is one of France's fastest-growing, most self-confident cities with a public transport system second to none.

Students form nearly a quarter of the population and the university is particularly celebrated for its medical faculties; Europe's first medical school was founded here early in the 12th century. At the heart of Montpellier is the old city with its narrow alleys, rich in bars and restaurants, and fine *hôtels particuliers* (private mansions).

Orientation
Montpellier's mostly pedestrianised historic centre, girdled by wide boulevards, has place de la Comédie at its heart.

Northeast of this square is esplanade Charles de Gaulle, a pleasant tree-lined promenade. To the east is Le Polygone, a vast shopping complex, and Antigone, a mammoth neoclassical housing project designed by the Spanish architect Ricardo Bofill.

Westwards, between rue de la Loge and Grand Rue Jean Moulin, sprawls the city's oldest quarter, a web of narrow alleys and fine *hôtels particuliers* (private mansions).

Information
BOOKSHOPS
As You Like It (☎ 04 67 66 22 90; 8 rue du Bras de Fer) Large stock of new and second-hand books in English.
Bookshop (☎ 04 67 66 09 08; 4 rue de l'Université) Carries a good selection of novels and travel guides in English.
Les Cinq Continents (☎ 04 67 66 46 70; 20 rue Jacques Cœur) Specialist travel bookshop with an excellent stock of maps and travel literature including Lonely Planet guides.

INTERNET ACCESS
Dimension 4 Cybercafé (☎ 04 67 60 57 57; 11 rue des Balances; per hr €3.85; ☽ 10am-midnight)
Point Internet (☎ 04 67 54 57 60; 54 rue de l'Aiguillerie; per hr €1.60; ☽ 9.30am-midnight Mon-Sat, 10.30am-midnight Sun)
St@tion Internet (6-8 place du Marché aux Fleurs; €4 per hr; ☽ 10am-7pm Mon-Sat)

LAUNDRY
Lav'Club Café (6 rue des Écoles Laïques; ☽ 9.30am-8pm Mon-Sat, 2-7pm Sun; closed Wed morning year-round, Sun Jun-Sep) A laundry-café; sip a coffee or grab a snack as your smalls spin.
Lavasud (19 rue de l'Université; ☽ 7am-9pm)

POST
Main Post Office (13 place Rondelet)

TOURIST INFORMATION

Main Tourist Office (☎ 04 67 60 60 60; www.ot-mont pellier.fr; ⊙ 9am-6.30pm or 7.30pm Mon-Fri, 10am-6pm Sat, 10am-1pm & 2-5pm Sun) At southern end of esplanade Charles de Gaulle.

Tourist Office Annexe (train station; ⊙ Jul-Aug)

Sights

HÔTELS PARTICULIERS

During the 17th and 18th centuries, Montpellier's wealthier merchants built grand private mansions with large inner courtyards. Fine examples are **Hôtel de Varennes** (2 place Pétrarque), a harmonious blend of Romanesque and Gothic, and **Hôtel St-Côme** (Grand Rue Jean Moulin), the city's first anatomy theatre for medical students and nowadays its Chambre de Commerce. The 17th-century **Hôtel des Trésoriers de France** (7 rue Jacques Cœur) today houses the Musée Languedocien. Within the old quarter are several other mansions, each marked by a descriptive plaque in French.

MUSEUMS

Musée Fabre (☎ 04 67 14 83 00; 39 blvd Bonne Nouvelle), the city's cultural showpiece, is undergoing fundamental renovation and will remain closed until at least mid-2006. In the interim the **Pavillon du Musée Fabre**, across the esplanade, continues to host temporary displays.

Musée Languedocien (☎ 04 67 52 93 03; 7 rue Jacques Cœur; adult/student €5/3; ⊙ 3-6pm Mon-Sat Jul-Aug, 2-5pm Mon-Sat Sep-Jun) displays the area's rich archaeological finds as well as *objets d'art* from the 16th to 19th centuries.

Musée du Vieux Montpellier (☎ 04 67 66 02 94; 2 place Pétrarque; admission free; ⊙ 9.30am-noon & 1.30-5pm Tue-Sat), a storehouse of the city's memorabilia from the Middle Ages to the Revolution, is upstairs in the Hôtel de Varennes.

Musée Atger (☎ 04 67 66 27 77; 2 rue de l'École de Médecine; admission free; ⊙ 1.30-5.45pm Mon, Wed & Fri) displays a striking collection of French, Italian and Flemish drawings. Housed within the medical faculty, it's closed during university holidays.

AROUND PLACE ROYALE DU PEYROU

This wide, tree-lined esplanade is dominated by the **Arc de Triomphe** (1692) at its eastern end, and the **Château d'Eau** (Water Tower) at the other. Leading from this hexagonal water tower is the 18th-century **Aqueduc de St-Clément**, under which there's an organic food and second-hand books market on

Saturday and *pétanque* (a variant on bowls) most afternoons. To the north, off blvd Henri IV, is the **Jardin des Plantes**, France's oldest botanic garden (1593). Opposite the garden is **Cathédrale St-Pierre**, with its disproportionately large 15th-century porch.

Tours

The main tourist office offers two-hour **walking tours** (€6.50; in English 10.30am Tue & Sat Jul-Aug, 10.30am Sat Sep, 3.30pm Sat Oct-Jun; in French 10am & 5pm daily Jul-Aug, 5pm daily Sep, 3pm Wed, Sat & Sun Oct-Jun) of the old town. Ring at least 48 hours in advance to reserve.

Festivals & Events

Montpellier hosts **Le Printemps des Comédiens**, a popular theatre festival, in June and a two-week international dance festival in June/July. The **Festival de Radio France et Montpellier** in the second half of July brings in top notch classical music and jazz and the majority of events are free.

Sleeping

Auberge de Jeunesse (☎ 04 67 60 32 22; montpellier@ fuaj.org; 2 impasse de la Petite Corraterie; dm €8.90; ⊙ mid-Jan–mid-Dec) Montpellier's HI-affiliated youth hostel is just off rue des Écoles Laïques. The grandiose mosaic entrance contrasts with its basic dorms but who can complain when there's a friendly bar and a cheap bed? Take the tram to the Louis Blanc stop.

Hôtel des Étuves (☎ 04 67 60 78 19; www.hoteldes etuves.fr; 24 rue des Étuves; s €20.50-31, d €32-38) This welcoming, 13-room family hotel creeps around a spiral staircase like a vine. Room

---

AUTHOR'S CHOICE

Hôtel Le Guilhem (☎ 04 67 52 90 90; www .hotel-le-guilhem.com; 18 rue Jean-Jacques Rousseau; s €71-78, d €71-135; ⊠) Occupying a couple of interconnecting 16th-century buildings, the Hôtel Le Guilhem's guest rooms are exquisitely and individually furnished. Nearly all have views of the cathedral and overlook the tranquil garden of nearby Restaurant Le Petit Jardin. Room No 100 (€135) has its own little terrace and garden. All rooms have bathtubs and some have separate toilets. It's wise to reserve at any time of year since Le Guilhem has its faithful clientele who return again and again.

LANGUEDOC-ROUSSILLON

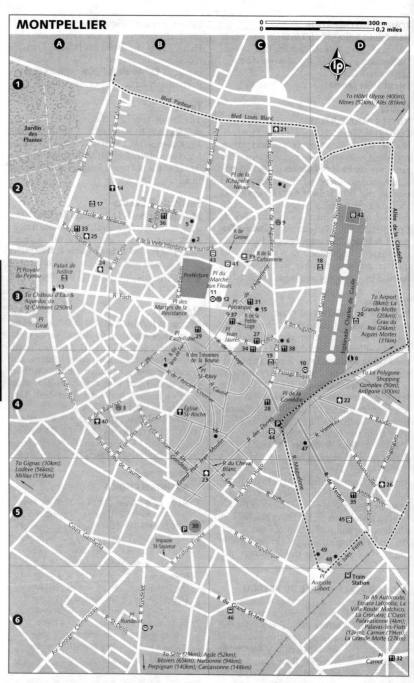

MONTPELLIER

0 _____ 300 m
0 _____ 0.2 miles

Jardin des Plantes

Blvd Pasteur

Blvd Louis Blanc

To Hôtel Ulysse (400m); Nîmes (52km); Alès (81km)

21

Pl de la Chapelle Neuve

4

14

17

R de l'École de Médecine

R Candolle

Pl Candolle

36

5

R de la Vieille Intendance

R Fournarie

2

R de Girone

9

33

25

R St-Croix

39

R de la Carbonnerie

43

41

Palais de Justice

24

Préfécture

Pl du Marché aux Fleurs

11

18

R de l'Aiguillerie

42

Pl Royale du Peyrou

13

To Château d'Eau & Aqueduc de St-Clément (250m)

Pl Giral

R Foch

Pl des Martyrs de la Résistance

12

Pl Pétrarque

37

R de la Petite Loge

31

15

27

R des Augustins

Esplanade Charles de Gaulle

Blvd Bonne Nouvelle

Blvd Sarrail

Allée de la Citadelle

To Airport (8km); La Grande Motte (20km); Grau du Roi (26km); Aigues Mortes (31km)

20

Pl Castellane

29

Pl Jean Jaurès

34

6

38

19

Cours

10

Passage Bruyas

8

22

R des Trésoriers de la Bourse

3

Pl St-Ravy

R Cauzit

R Guilhem

R des Balances

1

40

R de l'Ancien Courrier

Grand Rue Jean-Moulin

R des Étuves

Pl de la Comédie

28

44

47

R Vanneau

R Baudin

Église St-Roch

16

R du Cheval Blanc

23

R Loys

Blvd Victor Hugo

R Joffre

R Marquerose

R Aristide Olivier

R Sérane

26

35

To Gignac (30km); Lodève (56km); Millau (115km)

Blvd du Jeu de Paume

30

Impasse St-Sauveur

R Anatole France

R de la République

45

Cours Gambetta

49

48

R Jules Ferry

Pl Auguste Gibert

Train Station

To A9 Autoroute; Espace Latipolia; La Villa Route; Matchico; La Croisière; L'Oasis Palavasienne (4km); L'Oasis Palavas-les-Flots (12km); Carnon (19km); La Grande Motte (27km)

R Georges Clemenceau

R St-Denis

Pl Rondelet

R Rondelet

7

R du Grand St-Jean

46

To Sète (29km); Agde (52km); Béziers (65km); Narbonne (94km); Perpignan (140km); Carcassonne (148km)

Pl Carnot

32

INFORMATION			Musée Languedocien (Hôtel des Trésoriers de			Restaurant Verdi	**35**	D5
As You Like It	1	B4	France)	19	C4	Roule Ma Poule	**36**	B2
Bookshop	2	B2	Pavillon du Musée Fabre	20	D3	Salmon Shop	**37**	C3
Dimension 4 Cybercafé	3	B4				Tripti Kulai	**38**	C3
Lav'Club Café	4	C2	SLEEPING		(pp721-3)			
Lavasud	5	B2	Auberge de Jeunesse	21	C1	DRINKING		(p724)
Les Cinq Continents	6	C3	Hôtel de la Comédie	22	D4	L'Heure Bleue	**39**	C3
Main Post Office	7	B6	Hôtel des Étuves	23	B5	Mannekin-Pis	**40**	A4
Main Tourist Office	8	D4	Hôtel du Palais	24	A3			
Point Internet	9	C2	Hôtel Le Guilhem	25	A2	ENTERTAINMENT		(p724)
Post Office	10	C3	Hôtel le Mistral	26	D5	Café de la Mer	**41**	C3
Post Office	11	C4				Le Corum	**42**	D2
St@tion Internet	12	C3	EATING		(pp723-4)	Le Heaven	(see 41)	
			Caves Jean Jaurès	27	C3	Le Village	**43**	C3
SIGHTS & ACTIVITIES		(p721)	Chez Fels	28	C4	Opéra-Comédie Box Office	**44**	C4
Arc de Triomphe	13	A3	Halles Castellane Market	29	B3	Rockstore	**45**	D5
Cathédrale St-Pierre	14	B2	Halles Laissac Market	30	B5			
Hôtel de Varennes	15	C3	La Diligence	31	C3	TRANSPORT		(p725)
Hôtel St-Côme	16	C4	Le Ban des Gourmands	32	D6	Bus Station	**46**	C6
Musée Atger	17	A2	Le Petit Jardin	33	A2	Eurolines Ticket Office	**47**	C4
Musée du Vieux Montpellier	(see 15)		Pizzeria Aïda	(see 35)		TaM Office	**48**	D5
Musée Fabre	18	D3	Restaurant Cerdan	34	C3	TaM Vélo	**49**	D5

No 2, one of six overlooking the quiet pedestrian street, has a bath while the rest are equipped with showers.

Hôtel le Mistral (☎ 04 67 58 45 25; www.hotel-le-mistral.com in French; 25 rue Boussairolles; basic s €26, with bathroom s €37-39.50, d €38.50-46; P) This spruce, cosy, friendly 20-room place offers great value and is handy for both the station and heart of town.

Hôtel du Palais (☎ 04 67 60 47 38; fax 04 67 60 40 23; 3 rue du Palais; s €54, d €59-71; P ❄) All 26 rooms of this delightful hotel overlooking a quiet square are decorated by a local artist and tastefully and individually furnished.

Hôtel de la Comédie (☎ 04 67 58 43 64; hotel delacomedie@wanadoo.fr; 1bis rue Baudin; s €44, d €52-69; ❄) This cosy family-run place, just off place de la Comédie, is a favourite with visiting musicians and theatre troupes. All 20 rooms have air-con and heating and are double glazed.

Hôtel Ulysse (☎ 04 67 02 02 30; www.hotel-ulysse .com; 338 av St-Maur; s €49.50-54.50, d €59-66; P) The Ulysse is in a quiet neighbourhood no more than a 10 minute walk from place de la Comédie. It has a small garden and attractive breakfast salon. Each of its 23 rooms, all with bathtubs, is decorated individually and pleasingly furnished in wood and wrought iron.

CAMPING
The closest camping grounds are around the suburb of Lattes, some 4km south of the city centre.

L'Oasis Palavasienne (☎ 04 67 15 11 61; www .oasis-palavasienne.com; route de Palavas; camping according to season €16.70-24.50; ❄ mid-May–Aug) This shady camping ground has a large pool. Take bus No 17 from Montpellier bus station.

Eating
You'll find plenty of cheap and cheerful eateries on rue de l'Université, rue des Écoles Laïques and the streets interlinking them.

Roule Ma Poule (☎ 04 67 60 36 15; 20 place Candolle; plat du jour €7.50) Like most places in the area, it pulls in a mainly student crowd with its decent, uncomplicated fare. Happy-go-lucky and with rapid service, it's a little shrine to the motorbike with posters, pictures, a platoon of crash helmets and models all along the lintel above the bar.

Chez Fels (3 Grand Rue Jean Moulin; ❄ 8am-7.30pm Mon-Sat) Just off place de la Comédie, this hole-in-the-wall sandwich shop does the crunchiest of baby baguettes, stuffed with salad and Alsatian goodies.

Le Ban des Gourmands (☎ 04 67 65 00 85; 5 place Carnot; menu €25, mains €16-18; ❄ Tue-Fri & dinner Sat Sep-Jul) South of the train station and a favourite of locals in the know, this appealing restaurant, run by a young family team, serves delicious local cuisine.

Caves Jean Jaurès (☎ 04 67 60 27 33; 3 rue Collot; menu €17, mains €12-15; ❄ closed Sun, lunch Mon & Wed) Scan this attractive restaurant's range of tasty dishes on the chalkboard that the waiter props against a nearby table. A glass of wine? Select from the bottles of the day on the bar counter. Rather more? Pick from the shelves; every bottle has its price marked and the range is superlative.

Restaurant Verdi (☎ 04 67 58 68 55; 10 rue Aristide Olivier; menus €22-26; ❄ Mon-Sat) This restaurant does delicious Italian fare, especially fish dishes, in an Italian ambience – walls are plastered with posters relating to the eponymous Verdi – and has an outstanding wine list. Two doors away, **Pizzeria Aïda**

LANGUEDOC-ROUSSILLON

serves pasta, pizzas and salads from the same kitchen and in a more informal setting.

Tripti Kulai (☎ 04 67 66 30 51; 20 rue Jacques Cœur; salads €8.50, menus €11 & €15; ☺ noon-9.30pm Mon-Sat) Barrel-vaulted and cosy, this popular vegetarian place stands out for the inventiveness of many of its dishes. To finish, you could drink an infusion of tea a day for more than a month and still not exhaust their selection.

Le Petit Jardin (☎ 04 67 60 78 78; 20 rue Jean-Jacques Rousseau; lunch menu €14, dinner menus €20-28; ☺ Tue-Sun Feb-Dec) 'The Little Garden' is just that: a restaurant offering imaginative cuisine, its big bay windows overlooking a shady, fairytale greenness at the rear, where you could be 100km from Montpellier's bustle.

Restaurant Cerdan (☎ 04 67 60 86 96; 8 rue Collot; menus €12.60-32.50; ☺ closed all Sun, lunch Sat & Mon) This much garlanded family restaurant carries a good list of local wines and offers five different *menus*, each rich in local fare with a leavening of dishes from Normandy, Mme Cerdan's home region.

La Diligence (☎ 04 67 66 12 21; 2 place Pétrarque; lunch menu €17, dinner menus €33-59; ☺ closed all Sun, lunch Sat & Mon) Dine beneath attractive vaults and arches and savour the elegant rear patio beneath a gallery of the Hôtel de Varennes. The lunch *menu* I excellent value.

Salmon Shop (04 67 66 40 70; 5 rue de la Petite Loge; mains €12; ☺ Mon-Sat, closed Sun & lunch Mon) For something fishy, head for the Salmon Shop with its mock log-cabin décor. Most dishes, including the plat du jour, feature salmon, prepared 11 different ways.

SELF-CATERING
The city's **food markets** include **Halles Castellane** (rue de la Loge), the biggest and **Halles Laissac** (rue Anatole France). There's a farmers market every Sunday morning on av Samuel de Champlain in the Antigone complex.

Drinking
All summer long, place de la Comédie is alive with café's where you can drink, grab a quick bite and watch street entertainers strut their stuff. Smaller, more intimate squares include place Jean Jaurès and place St-Ravy.

L'Heure Bleue (1 rue de la Carbonnerie; ☺ Tue-Sun) At this tea salon, you can sip Earl Grey to a background of classical music. It also does light lunches with plenty of choice for vegetarians.

With more than 60,000 students, Montpellier has a profusion of places to drink and dance. You'll find dense concentrations around rue En-Gondeau, off Grand Rue Jean Moulin, around place Jean Jaurès and around the intersection of rue de l'Université and rue Candolle.

If beer is your favourite tipple, call by **Mannekin-Pis** (110 rue des Balances), a neighbourhood bar whose *patron* runs a temple to the amber nectar with eight brands on draught, approximately 100 in bottle and drip mats – a mere sample from his vast collection, built up over 25 years – plastered all over.

Entertainment
Montpellier has a busy cultural calendar. To find out what's on where, pick up the free weekly *Sortir*, available around town and at the tourist office.

Tickets for Montpellier's numerous theatres are sold at the **Opéra-Comédie box office** (☎ 04 67 60 05 45; place de la Comédie). **Le Corum** (☎ 04 67 61 67 61), at the northern end of esplanade Charles de Gaulle, is the city's prime concert venue.

In central Montpellier you'll recognise longstanding discothèque **Rockstore** (☎ 04 67 06 80 00; 20 rue de Verdun) by the rear of a classic American '70s car protruding above the entrance.

There's a critical mass of discos outside town in Espace Latipolia, about 10km out of town on route de Palavas heading towards the coast. These include **La Villa Rouge** (☎ 04 67 06 52 15), **Matchico** (☎ 04 67 64 19 20) and **La Croisière** (☎ 04 67 64 19 52).

L'Amigo, a night bus, does a circuit of these and other dance venues on the periphery of town, leaving Le Corum at midnight, 12.45am and 1.30am, returning at 2.30am, 3.30am and (yawn!) 5am.

GAY VENUES
To tune into the active men-on-men scene (many reckon Montpellier is France's most gay-friendly city), call by **Le Village** (☎ 04 67 60 29 05; 3 rue Fournarié), a shop specialising in queer gear and gay literature, or **Café de la Mer** (☎ 04 67 60 79 65; 5 place du Marché aux Fleurs), just around the corner, where the friendly staff will arm you with a map of gay venues. Right next door, **Le Heaven** (1 rue Delpech) is an exclusively men's bar, which gets busy from 8pm.

Getting There & Away

AIR

Montpellier's **airport** (☎ 04 67 20 85 00; www
.montpellier.aeroport.fr) is 8km southeast of town.
British Airways flies three times per week
(daily in summer) to/from London (Gatwick) and Ryanair operates daily to/from
London (Stansted). Air France has up to 10
daily flights to Paris.

BUS

The **bus station** (☎ 04 67 92 01 43; rue du Grand St-
Jean) is an easy walk from the train station.
Hérault Transport (☎ 08 25 34 01 34) runs hourly
buses to La Grande Motte (No 106; €1.25,
35 minutes) via Carnon from Odysseum at
the end of the tram line. Some continue to
Aigues Mortes (€6, 1½ hours, six daily) and,
in July and August, Stes-Maries de la Mer in
the Camargue (€9.30, two hours).

Eurolines (☎ 04 67 58 57 59; ticketing & information office 8 rue de Verdun) has buses to most European destinations including Barcelona
(€27, five hours), London (€93, 17 hours)
and Amsterdam (€87, 21 hours). **Linebus**
(☎ 04 67 58 95 00) mainly operates services to
destinations in Spain.

TRAIN

Major destinations from Montpellier's two-
storey train station include Paris' Gare de
Lyon by TGV (€70 to €83, 3½ hours, 12
daily), Carcassonne (€19.50, 1½ hours, six
to eight daily), Millau (€21.80, 1½ hours,
two daily) and Perpignan (€19.20, two hours,
frequent).

More than 20 trains daily go northwards
to Nîmes (€7.50, 30 minutes) and southwards
to Narbonne (€12.80, one hour) via Sète
(€4.60), Agde (€7.50) and Béziers (€9.90).

Getting Around

TO/FROM THE AIRPORT

A shuttle bus (€4.80, 15 minutes, 12 daily)
runs between the airport and bus station.

BICYCLE

Montpellier encourages cycling with more
than 100km of bicycle track. **TaM Vélo** (☎ 04
67 92 92 67; 27 rue Maguelone; ☒ 9am-7pm Mon-Sat,
9am-1pm & 4-7pm Sun), an admirable urban initiative, rents town bikes and electric bikes per
hour/half-day/full-day for €1.50/3/6 and
tandems per half-day/full-day for €12/15.
You'll need to leave a deposit (cheque,

credit card or cash) of €150/300 per bike/
electric bike.

PUBLIC TRANSPORT

Take a ride, even just for fun, on Montpellier's high tech, high-speed leave-your-car-
at-home tram. Like city buses, it's run by
TaM (☎ 04 67 22 87 87; 6 rue Jules Ferry) and runs
until midnight. Regular buses run until
about 8.30pm daily.

Single-journey tickets, valid for bus or
tram, cost €1.20. A one-day pass/10-ticket
carnet costs €3/10. Pick them up from
newsagents or any tram station.

TAXI

To call a cab, ring **Taxi Bleu** (☎ 04 67 03 20 00)
or **Taxi 2000** (☎ 04 67 04 00 60).

AROUND MONTPELLIER

The closest beaches are at **Palavas-les-Flots**,
12km south of the city and very much
Montpellier-on-Sea in summer. Take TaM
bus No 17 or 28 (€2.10, 35 minutes, frequent) from the Port Marianne tram stop.
Heading north on the coastal road towards
Carnon, you stand a good chance of seeing
flamingos snuffling the shallows of the lagoons on either side of the coastal D21.

Carnon itself comes out fairly low in the
charm stakes despite its huge marina. Continue hugging the coast along the D59 (Le
Petit Travers), bordered by several kilometres of white sand beach, uncrowded and
without a kiosk or café in sight.

Further northwards and about 20km
southeast of Montpellier is **La Grande Motte**,
sitting on what was once mosquito ridden
salt marsh. Purpose-built on the grand
scale back in the 1960s to plug the tourist
drain southwards into Spain, its architecture, considered revolutionary at the time,
now comes over as fairly heavy and leaden,
contrasting with the more organic growth
of adjacent **Grau du Roi**, deeper rooted and a
still-active fishing port.

Aigues Mortes, situated on the western edge
of the Camargue (p806), is another 11km
to the east.

SÈTE

pop 40,300

Twenty-six kilometres southwest of Montpellier, Sète is France's largest Mediterranean fishing port and its biggest commercial

port after Marseille. Established by Louis XIV in the 17th century, it prospered as the harbours of Aigues Mortes and Narbonne, to north and south, were cut off from the sea by silt deposits.

Huddled east of Mont St-Clair, from where there are great views of town and port, Sète has lots in its favour: waterways and canals, beaches, outdoor cafés and shoals of fish and seafood restaurants.

For the **tourist office** (☎ 04 67 74 71 71; www .ot-sete.fr; 60 Grand'Rue Mario Roustan; ☒ 9.30am-7.30pm Jul-Aug; 9.30am-12.30pm & 2-6pm Mon-Sat, 10am-noon & 2-5pm Sun May-Jun & Sep; 9.30am-12.30pm & 2-5.30pm Mon-Fri, 10am-noon & 2-5pm Sat Oct-Apr), take bus No 2 from the train station.

Sète was the birthplace of the symbolist poet Paul Valéry (1871–1945), whose remains lie in the **Cimetière Marin**, inspiration for and title of his most famous poem. Overlooking this cemetery is the **Musée Paul Valéry** (☎ 04 67 46 20 98; rue François Desnoyer; adult/child €3/1.50; ☒ 10am-noon & 2-6pm daily Jul-Aug, Wed-Mon Sep-Jun), which hosts temporary exhibitions and has one room devoted to the poet.

The town was also the childhood home of singer and infinitely more accessible poet Georges Brassens (1921–81), whose mellow voice still speaks and sings over the headphones at **Espace Georges Brassens** (☎ 04 67 53 32 77; 67 blvd Camille Blanc; adult/child €5/2; ☒ 10am-noon & 2-6pm Tue-Sun), a multimedia centre set up in his memory. Ask for the English synopsis.

Sète Croisières (☎ 04 67 46 00 46; quai Général Durand) does a variety of boat trips, including a one-hour **harbour tour** (adult/child €10/5).

On the first weekend in July, Sète celebrates **La Fête de la St-Pierre**, or Fête des Pêcheurs (Fisherfolks Festival). The **Fête de la St-Louis** fills six frantic days around 25 August with *joutes nautiques*, where participants in competing boats try to knock each other into the water.

Sleeping & Eating
Auberge de Jeunesse (☎ 04 67 53 46 68; fax 04 67 51 34 01; rue Général Revest; dm €9.30; ☒ Jan–mid-Dec) It's 1km northwest of the tourist office in rather glum former administrative buildings, but enjoys a lovely wooded site with great views over the town and harbour.

Hôtel la Conga (☎ 04 67 53 02 57; plage de la Corniche; d €25-40 Sep-Jun, €38-52 Jul-Aug) This pleasant hotel overlooks the beach, 2.25km west of the port area. You'll need to reserve at its

popular restaurant **La Table de Jean** (menus €12-25), justifiably famous for its fish dishes.

Le Chalut (☎ 04 67 74 81 52; 38 quai Maximin Licciardi; menus €14-30, mains €14-20; ☒ closed Wed Oct-Jun) Right on the quayside, this is a local favourite for Sètois delicacies. You can dine in the sober, wood-panelled interior or on the colourful terrace, which teeters just the right side of kitsch.

Les Demoiselles Dupuy (☎ 04 67 74 03 46; 4 quai Maximin Licciardi) This tiny, vital place is only four doors but half a world away from Le Chalut. Crowded, rough and ready, it serves up deliciously fresh seafood at economical prices in unpretentious surroundings.

Getting There & Away
Should you want to head across the Med, both Comanav and Comarit, a pair of Moroccan companies, run ferries to the port of Tangier (Tanger) from quai d'Alger about every four days. For tickets, schedules and information, consult agents **SNCM** (☎ 04 67 46 68 00; fax 04 67 74 93 05; 4 quai d'Alger).

AGDE
pop 22,300
Originally a Phoenician, then a Greek settlement at the mouth of the River Hérault, Agde (from *agathos*, Greek for 'good') is a picturesque fishing port with a small attractive inland old quarter. Make time for a short boat trip along the Canal du Midi, which joins the River Hérault just upstream from the old quarter. The tourist office sells tickets for both **Bateaux du Soleil** (☎ 04 67 94 08 79) and **Bateau Roussillon Languedoc** (☎ 04 67 01 71 93).

The **tourist office** (☎ 04 67 94 29 68; ☒ 9am-7pm Mon-Sat, 10am-1pm Sun Jul-Aug, 9am-noon & 2-6pm Mon-Sat Sep-Jun) is at 1 place Molière.

The dark grey basalt of older buildings, such as the fortress-like, mainly 12th-century **Cathédrale St-Étienne**, motivated Marco Polo to describe the town as the 'black pearl of the Mediterranean'.

Hôtel des Arcades (☎ 04 67 94 21 64; 16 rue Louis Bages; basic rooms €30, with shower €40, with bathroom €45) is an exceptionally friendly place occupying a former convent.

There are some attractive restaurants terraces stretch along the quayside. The fish couldn't be fresher at **Restaurant du Port** (☎ 04 67 94 97 58; 24 rue Chassefière; menu €12; ☒ lunch & dinner May-Sep, lunch only Oct-Apr), which has its own boat. It also does a vegetarian *menu* (€10).

Buses ply the 6km route at least hourly to the modern tourist resort of **Le Cap d'Agde**, named for its long beaches and large nudist colony – a little township in itself with more than 20,000 bare bodies in high season.

BÉZIERS
pop 70,000

Béziers, first settled by the Phoenicians, became an important military post in Roman times. It was almost completely destroyed in 1209 during the Albigensian Crusade, when some 20,000 'heretics', many seeking refuge in the cathedral, were slaughtered. In happier times, the local tax collector Paul Riquet (1604–80) moved heaven and earth to build the Canal du Midi, a 240km-long marvel of engineering with its aqueducts and more than 100 locks, enabling cargo vessels to sail from the Atlantic to the Mediterranean without having to circumnavigate Spain. There's a fine statue to Béziers' most famous son on allées Jean-Jaurès, a wide, leafy esplanade at the heart of the town.

The **tourist office** (☎ 04 67 76 84 00; 29 av St-Saens; ⏰ 9am-7pm Jul-Aug, 9am-noon & 2-6pm Mon-Sat Sep-Jun) is in the Palais des Congrès.

Fortified **Cathédrale St-Nazaire** (⏰ 9am-noon & 2.30-5.30pm), surrounded by narrow alleys, is typical of the area, with massive towers, an imposing façade and a huge 14th-century rose window.

Musée du Biterrois (☎ 04 67 36 71 01; place St Jacques; adult/child €2.35/1.60; ⏰ 10am-6pm Tue-Sun Jul-Aug, 9am-noon & 2-5pm or 6pm Tue-Sun Sep-Jun) is a well displayed and illuminated museum of the town's history, its largest sections devoted to Roman artefacts and wine-making.

As the wine capital of Languedoc, Béziers holds its grape harvest festival in October. Year-round, visit **Terroirs et Cépage** (av Président Wilson) for a little *dégustation* (tasting).

Popular annual events include the week-long **Festa d'Oc**, a celebration of Mediterranean music and dance, in late July, and the **féria** (bullfighting festival) in early August.

NARBONNE
pop 48,000

Once a coastal port but now a whole 13km inland because of silting-up, Narbonne in its time was capital of Gallia Narbonensis and one of the principal Roman cities in Gaul.

The **tourist office** (☎ 04 68 65 15 60; place Roger Salengro; ⏰ 8.30am-7pm Mon-Sat, 9.30am-12.30pm Sun Jun–mid-Sep; 8.30am-noon & 2-6pm Mon-Sat mid-Sep–May) is just northwest of the massive cathedral.

The splendid **Cathédrale St-Just** (entry on rue Armand Gauthier; ⏰ 10am-7pm Jul-Sep, 9am-noon & 2-6pm Oct-Jun) is, in fact, no more than its towers and a soaring choir – at 41m, one of France's highest – construction having stopped in the early 14th century. The Notre Dame de Bethlehem ambulatory chapel has a haunting alabaster Virgin and Child and fine polychrome stone carving, although it is much knocked about. The **treasury** (admission €2.20) has a beautiful Flemish tapestry of the Creation while grotesque gargoyles peer down upon the 16th-century **cloister**.

Adjoining the cathedral to the south and facing place de l'Hôtel de Ville, the fortified **Palais des Archevêques** (Archbishops' Palace) includes the **Donjon Gilles Aycelin** (admission €2.20; ⏰ 11am-6pm Jul-Sep, 9am-noon & 2-6pm Oct-Jun), a large, square 13th-century keep.

The **town hall**, with its mock-Renaissance 19th-century façade by Viollet-le-Duc, is home to Narbonne's **Musée d'Art** and **Musée Archéologique**, the latter with its impressive collection of Roman mosaics and paintings on stucco. Nearby is the **Horreum**, an underground gallery of Gallo-Roman shops. A combined ticket (adult/child €5.20/3.20) gives access to all three.

Take in too Narbonne's imposing Art Nouveau **covered market**, a colourful place to stock up on food and an architectural jewel in it own right.

Just off the A9, 15km south of Narbonne, is the **Réserve Africaine de Sigean** (☎ 04 68 48 20 20; adult/child €20/16; ⏰ 9am-4.30pm up to 8pm according to season), where lions, tigers and other 'safari' specimens live in semi-liberty. If you arrive by bike or on foot, there's free – in a manner of speaking – transport around the reserve. From the A9, take exit 39.

CARCASSONNE
pop 46,250

From afar, Carcassonne looks like some fairy-tale medieval city. Bathed in late-afternoon sunshine and highlighted by dark clouds, La Cité, as the old walled city is known, is truly breathtaking.

Once you're inside the fortified walls, La Cité is far less magical. Luring more than two million visitors each year, it can be a tourist hell in high summer.

CARCASSONNE

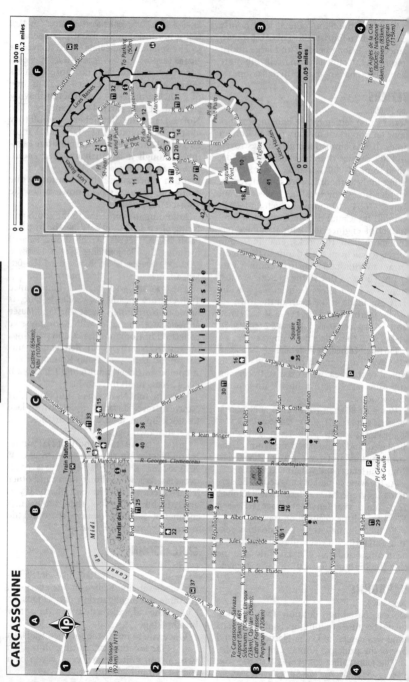

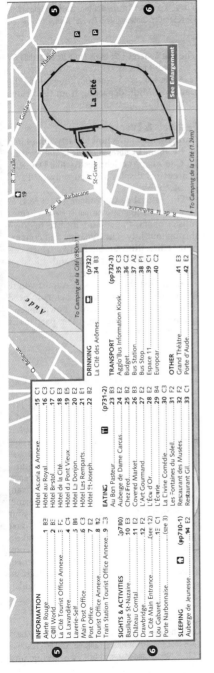

INFORMATION
Alerte Rouge...................................1 B3
C@ll World.......................................2 BE
La Cité Tourist Office Annexe..........3 F.
La Lavandière................................4 B4
Laverie-Self....................................5 B4
Main Post Office............................6 C3
Post Office......................................7 E2
Tourist Office Annexe....................8 B2
Train Station Tourist Office Annexe...9 C3

SIGHTS & ACTIVITIES (pp730)
Basilique St-Nazaire.....................10 E3
Château Comtal............................11 E2
Drawbridge...................................12 F2
La Cité Main Entrance...............(see 12)
Lou Gabaret..................................13 C1
Porte Narbonnaise.....................(see 3)

SLEEPING (pp730-1)
Auberge de Jeunesse....................14 E2

Hôtel Astoria & Annexe...............15 C1
Hôtel au Royal..............................16 C3
Hôtel Bristol..................................17 C1
Hôtel de la Cité............................18 E3
Hôtel du Pont Vieux.....................19 E5
Hôtel Le Donjon...........................20 E2
Hôtel Les Remparts.......................21 E1
Hôtel St-Joseph............................22 B2

EATING (pp731-2)
Au Bon Pasteur.............................23 B3
Auberge de Dame Carcas..............24 E2
Chez Fred......................................25 B2
Covered Market.............................26 B3
L'Art Gourmand............................27 E2
L'Écu d'Or......................................28 E2
L'Écurie...29 B4
La L'ivine Comédie........................30 C1
Les Fontaines du Soleil.................31 F2
Restaurant des Musées..................32 F2
Restaurant Gil..............................33 C1

DRINKING (p732)
La Cité des Arômes........................34 B3

TRANSPORT (pp732-3)
Agglo'Bus Information Kiosk.........35 C3
Budget..36 C2
Bus Station....................................37 A2
Bus Stop..38 F1
Espace 11......................................39 C1
Europcar.......................................40 C2

OTHER
Grand Théatre...............................41 E3
Porte d'Aude................................42 E2

Today's city walls are but the last in a line of fortifications built by Gauls, Romans, Visigoths, Moors and Franks. In the 13th century, they protected one of the major Cathar strongholds (see p756). After 1659, when Roussillon was annexed to France, Carcassonne, no longer a frontier town, began its slow decline. By the 19th century La Cité was 'little more than a slum' and only the elaborate intervention of Viollet-le-Duc, the influential but controversial to this day 19th-century restorer, who, in addition to reworking Carcassonne, also profoundly changed, for example, the cathedrals of Notre Dame in Paris and Vézelay in the Massif Central – prevented the remaining fortifications from just tumbling away.

Carcassonne is not just La Cité, however. The Ville Basse (Lower Town), established in the 13th century and a more modest stepsister to camp Cinderella up the hill, also merits a browse.

Orientation
The River Aude separates the Ville Basse from the Cité, up on a hill 500m southeast. Pedestrianised rue Georges Clemenceau leads from the train station and Canal du Midi southwards through the heart of the lower town.

Information
INTERNET ACCESS
Alerte Rouge (73 rue de Verdun; per hr €4; ☻ 10am-11pm Mon-Sat, 1-8pm Sun)
C@ll World (32 rue de la République; per hr €3.50; ☻ 10am-11pm Mon-Sat, 2-11pm Sun)

LAUNDRY
La Lavandière (31 rue Aimé Ramon; ☻ 8am-7pm Mon-Sat)
Laverie-Self (63 rue Aimé Ramon; ☻ 7am-9pm)

POST
Main Post Office (40 rue Jean Bringer, Ville Basse)
Post Office (rue Porte d'Aude, Là Cité)

TOURIST INFORMATION
La Cité Tourist Office Annexe (Porte Narbonnaise; ☻ 9am-5pm or 7pm according to season)
Main Tourist Office (☎ 04 68 10 24 30; www.carcassonne-tourisme.com; 28 rue de Verdun; ☻ 9am-7pm Jul-Aug, 9am-6pm Sep-Jun)
Train Station Tourist Office Annexe (av du Maréchal Joffre; ☻ Apr-Oct) Kiosk just south of the train station.

LANGUEDOC-ROUSSILLON

Sights

LA CITÉ

Just beside the main entrance to La Cité, a magnificent reconditioned 19th-century merry-go-round (carousel) gyrates to old Julie Andrews numbers. It's emblematic of the blend of tack and charm within.

La Cité, dramatically illuminated at night and enclosed by two rampart walls punctuated by 52 stone towers, is one of Europe's largest city fortifications. But only the lower sections of the walls are original; the rest, including the anachronistic witches'-hat roofs (the originals were altogether flatter and weren't covered with slate), were stuck on by Viollet-le-Duc in the 19th century.

From square Gambetta, it's an attractive walk to La Cité across Pont Vieux, along rue de la Barbacane, then up and in through Porte d'Aude. Catching a bus is also an option (p732).

If you pass over the drawbridge and through the main entrance, you're faced with a massive bastion, the **Porte Narbonnaise** and, just inside, the tourist office annexe. Rue Cros Mayrevieille, suffocating in kitschy souvenir shops, leads up to place du Château, heart of La Cité.

Through another archway and across a second dry moat is the 12th-century **Château Comtal** (adult/student/under 18 €6.10/4.10/free; ⏰ 9.30am-6.30pm Apr-Sep, 9.30am-5pm Oct-Mar). The entrance fee lets you visit the castle itself and also join a 30 to 40-minute guided tour of both castle and ramparts. You may have to wait some time until a critical mass of visitors assembles and the quality of the guiding is variable.

South of place du Château is **Basilique St-Nazaire**. Highlights are the graceful Gothic transept arms with a pair of superb 13th- and 14th-century rose windows at each end.

There's numerous hole-in-the-wall private museums and initiatives, each eager to separate you from your money and including Memories of the Middle Ages, a Schooldays Museum, the Haunted House – and a particularly repellent exhibition of replica medieval torture instruments. All are very resistible.

FALCONRY

Birds of prey dive and swoop at **Les Aigles de la Cité** (☎ 04 68 47 88 99; adult/child €8/5; ⏰ from 2.30pm Apr-Oct), 800m south of the Cité walls.

There's a 45-minute **demonstration** (3pm in Apr-Jun & Sep-Oct, continuously 3-7pm Jul-Aug).

Tours

The **Lou Gabaret** (☎ 04 68 71 61 26; adult/child €7/5.50; sailings 4 times daily mid-Jun–mid-Sep, 2.30pm Tue-Sun Apr–mid-Jun, mid-Sep–mid-Oct) chugs along the Canal du Midi, departing from the bridge just south of the train station.

Festivals & Events

Carcassonne knows how to party. On 14 July at 10.30pm, **L'Embrasement de la Cité** (Setting La Cité Ablaze) celebrates Bastille Day with a fireworks display rivalled only by Paris' pyrotechnics.

The **Festival de Carcassonne** (☎ 04 68 11 59 15; www.festivaldecarcassonne.com in French) brings music, opera, dance and theatre to town throughout July. The dynamic and concurrent **Festival Off** is an alternative fringe celebration with street theatre and a host of events, both free and paying.

In the first three weeks of August you're likely to bump into B-movie actors in need of a crust playing knights, bowmen and troubadours, all playing their part in La Cité's **Fêtes Médiévales**.

Sleeping

BUDGET

Auberge de Jeunesse (☎ 04 68 25 23 16; carcassonne@fuaj.org; rue Vicomte Trencavel; B&B €15.50; ⏰ Feb–mid-Dec) Carcassonne's cheery, welcoming, HI-affiliated youth hostel is in the heart of La Cité. It has a members kitchen, snack bar offering light meals, great outside terrace and one Internet station. Although it has 120 beds, it's smart to reserve year-round.

Sidsmums (☎ 04 68 26 94 49; www.sidsmums.com; 11 chemin de la Croix d'Achille; dm €18) In Preixan, 10km south of Carcassonne, this is a warmly recommended place to relax, recharge your batteries and savour a little of the TLC that lucky Sid enjoys. You can hire a bike, take a guided walk with George the dog and cook for yourself in the self-contained kitchen. There's a twice daily free run into Carcassonne for guests. Otherwise, take the Quillan bus (four daily).

Camping

Camping de la Cité (☎ 04 68 25 11 77; www.campeoles.com; route de St-Hilaire; camping according to season €13.50-19; ⏰ mid-Mar–mid-Oct) A walking and cycling trail leads from the site to both La Cité and the Ville Basse. From mid-June to mid-September, bus No 8 connects the camping ground with La Cité and the train station.

MID-RANGE – VILLE BASSE

Hôtel Astoria (☎ 04 68 25 31 38; hotel-astoria@wanadoo .fr; 18 rue Tourtel; d €20, with shower €29, with bathroom €32-36; (P)) New owners have repainted all rooms and laid fresh tiles or parquet at this hotel and its equally agreeable annexe. Bathrooms are a bit pokey but all in all it's a welcoming place that offers good value. Parking is free.

Hôtel St-Joseph (☎ 04 68 71 96 89; hotel.saint joseph@wanadoo.fr; 81 rue de la Liberté; d €35-42; (P)) A statue of the eponymous saint guards the entrance to this trim hotel, popular with cyclists riding the Canal du Midi towpath and with itinerant railway staff. The most pleasant rooms have been recently renovated in attractive blue and ochre.

Hôtel Bristol (☎ 04 68 25 07 24; hotel.bristol11@ wanadoo.fr; 7 av du Maréchal Foch; s €54-65, d €65-80; (Y) Mar-Nov) A plaster horse's head peers down, indicating that this 19th-century inn was in its time a staging post. Choose between a room overlooking the Canal du Midi or one giving onto the quiet inner courtyard.

Hôtel du Pont Vieux (☎ 04 68 25 24 99; www .hoteldupontvieux.com; 32 rue Trivalle; d mid-Aug–mid-Jul €45-77, mid-Jul–mid-Aug €89-119; (P) (X)) Most bedrooms, with attractively rough-hewn walls, have a bathtub. Those overlooking the large, peaceful garden have air-con while ones overlooking the street are double glazed. On the third floor are rooms 18 and 19, each with unsurpassed views of the Cité, and a small terrace, accessible to all guests. A truly gargantuan buffet breakfast (€7) is laid on.

Hôtel au Royal (☎ 04 68 25 19 12; godar tcl@wanadoo .fr; 22 blvd Jean Jaurès; d €36-65; (Y) Jan-Nov; (P)) At this attractive mid-range option too, you're guaranteed a copious, varied breakfast. Rooms are comfortable, well appointed and equipped with ceiling fans and those facing the busy street all have double glazing.

MID-RANGE – LA CITÉ

Hôtel Le Donjon et Les Remparts (☎ 04 68 11 23 00; www.hotel-donjon.fr; 2 rue du Comte Roger; d €74-145; (P) (X) (X) (💻)) Low-beamed, thick-walled and cosy, Le Donjon makes a most attractive top-end option with rooms overlooking either the ramparts or its shady garden. Les Remparts, effectively its annexe (you check in at Le Donjon), is equally comfortable but shorter on charm – as, it must be said, is the madame at reception.

Hôtel de la Cité (☎ 04 68 71 98 71; www.hotelde lacite.orient-express.com; place Auguste Pont; d €250-550; (Y) mid-Jan–Nov; (P) (X) (🔊)) Hôtel de la Cité has rooms fit for royalty (literally so: 'A favourite hideaway for Europe's crowned heads, film stars, writers and intellectuals,' proclaims its glossy brochure), should you fancy a retreat in such august company.

Eating

Even if it's a boiling summer's day, don't leave town without trying cassoulet, a piping hot dish blending white beans, juicy pork cubes, even bigger cylinders of meaty sausage and, in the most popular local variant, a hunk of duck.

VILLE BASSE

Au Bon Pasteur (☎ 04 68 25 49 63; 29 rue Armagnac; menus €13-22; (Y) closed Sun & Mon Jul-Aug, Sun & Wed Sep-Jun) At this welcoming, intimate family restaurant, where the simple wooden tables and chairs belie the sophistication of the cooking, you can warm yourself in winter with the yummy cassoulet or *choucroute* (sauerkraut), 100% authentic since the chef hails from Alsace. Year-round, their *menu classique* (€13) and *formules de midi* (lunch specials; €9.50 to €11) both represent excellent value.

Chez Fred (☎ 04 68 72 02 23; 31 blvd Omer Sarraut; menus €18-27; (Y) closed lunch Wed & Sat year-round, dinner Tue Sep-Jun) With its all-orange interior and pleated drapes, Chez Fred recalls a bordello while its large protected outdoor terrace makes for pleasant summer dining. The cooking has a marked Andalucian touch and its weekday lunchtime *menu bistro* (€12) is especially worthwhile.

La Divine Comédie (☎ 04 68 72 30 36; 29 blvd Jean Jaurès; pizzas €8-9.50, mains €12.50-14.50; (Y) Mon-Sat) Beside Hôtel Central, this restaurant serves both pizzas and regional dishes on its pleasant outside terrace.

Restaurant Gil (☎ 04 68 47 85 23; 32 route Minervoise; menus €15-33, mains €9-19) Here, you'll enjoy quality, Catalan-influenced cuisine. Its particular strength is the sheer quality of its fresh sea food and fish dishes (€10 to €15), mostly served grilled and unsmothered by superfluous sauces or adornment.

L'Écurie (☎ 04 68 72 04 04; 43 blvd Barbès; menus €22-28; ☺ closed Wed & dinner Sun) Enjoy fine fare either within this attractively renovated 18th-century stable, all polished woodwork, brass and leather, or in the large, shaded garden. Pick from its long, carefully selected list of local wines.

LA CITÉ
Place Marcou is hemmed in on three sides by eateries and every second building in La Cité seems to be a café or restaurant. For those we recommend, it's wise to reserve, particularly for lunch.

Restaurant des Musées (☎ 06 17 05 24 90; 17 rue du Grand Puits) This simple unpretentious place has three rear terraces with views of the ramparts, bakes its own organic bread and offers excellent value meals, including a couple of vegetarian *menus* (€8.50). Although they don't serve alcohol, you can bring in a bottle from the excellent wine shop next door and there's no corkage charge.

Auberge de Dame Carcas (☎ 04 68 71 23 23; 3 place du Château; menus €14 & €24; ☺ Thu-Tue Feb-Dec) This casual place specialises in pork products (model piggies, large and small, displayed all around the restaurant give you a clue) and carries a fine selection of well-priced local wines. Downstairs is cosy and agreeably rustic and you can see the chefs at work while the larger upstairs room offers more light.

Les Fontaines du Soleil (☎ 04 68 47 87 06; 32 rue du Plô; menus €17-45) Seek out this restaurant, just off crowded place Marcou. With its shady terrace, attractive interior and great cooking, it has tempting *menus* to suit every pocket.

L'Écu d'Or (☎ 04 68 25 49 03; 7-9 rue Porte d'Aude; menus €20-32) This stylish place serves, among many other delightful dishes, six varieties of cassoulet and a delicious range of creative desserts.

SELF-CATERING
There's a **covered market** (rue du Verdun; ☺ Mon-Sat) and an **open-air market** (place Carnot; ☺ Tue, Thu & Sat). Chocolate fiends should head straight for the irresistible **L'Art Gourmand** (13 rue St-Louis), which sells a creative range of calorie-laced goodies. The ice cream is pretty great too – all 33 varieties of it.

Drinking
Cafés overlooking place Carnot in the Ville Basse spill onto the square in summer. In the northwestern corner, **La Cité des Arômes** indeed wafts out scents of rich *arabica* and carries a huge selection of coffees.

In La Cité, place Marcou is one big outside café.

Getting There & Away
AIR
Carcassonne-Salvaza airport (☎ 04 68 71 96 46), 5km from town, has precisely two flights daily – **Ryanair** (☎ 04 68 71 96 65) services to/from London (Stansted) and to/from Brussels (Charleroi).

BUS
We can only reiterate the advice of the tourist office: take the train. Eurolines and such intercity buses as there are stop on blvd de Varsovie, 500m southwest of the train station.

TRAIN
Carcassonne is on the main line linking Toulouse (€12.10, 50 minutes, frequent) with Narbonne (€8.60, 30 to 45 minutes), Béziers (€11.50, 50 minutes) and Montpellier (€18.90, 1½ hours). For Perpignan (€15.60), change in Narbonne.

Getting Around
TO THE AIRPORT
Agglo'Bus No 7 runs to/from the airport (€5, 20 minutes), leaving square Gambetta 90 minutes before each Ryanair departure. By car, take the Carcassonne Ouest A61 motorway exit.

BICYCLE
You can rent mountain bikes at **Espace 11** (☎ 04 68 25 28 18; 3 route Minervoise; 1 day/3 days/week €13/35/61; ☺ Tue-Sat).

CAR & MOTORCYCLE
Europcar (☎ 04 68 25 05 09; 7 blvd Omer Sarraut) and **Budget** (☎ 04 68 72 31 31; 5 blvd Omer Sarraut) are both a two-minute walk from the train station.

Cars are forbidden in La Cité during the day. Leave your vehicle in the huge car park (€3.50/5 cars/camper vans) just east of the main entrance.

PUBLIC TRANSPORT
Agglo'Bus, the city bus company, has an **information kiosk** (☎ 04 68 47 82 22; square Gambetta). Buses run until about 7pm from Monday

to Saturday. A single ticket/10-ticket *carnet* costs €0.90/6.90.

Bus No 2 runs about every 40 minutes from the Ville Basse to La Cité's main entrance. From mid-July to mid-August, a free **navette** (shuttle service; every 15 min, 9.30am-7.30pm Mon-Sat) plies between La Cité, square Gambetta and place Carnot.

TAXI
Ring ☎ 04 68 71 50 50.

NÎMES
pop 134,000

Nîmes, encircled by vineyards, *garrigue* (scrub), headily scented rosemary, lavender and thyme, is a little bit Provençal but with a soul as Languedocien as *cassoulet*. It's graced by some of France's best-preserved Roman buildings. Founded by Emperor Augustus, the Roman Colonia Nemausensis reached its zenith in the 2nd century AD, receiving its water from a Roman aqueduct system that included the Pont du Gard, a magnificent arched bridge 23km northeast of town (p738). The sacking of the city by Vandals in the early 5th century began a downwards spiral from which it never quite recovered. Mind you, lazy, laid-back Nîmes does get more than 300 days of sunshine every year.

DENIM DE NÎMES

During the 18th century, Nîmes' sizable Protestant middle class – banned from government posts and various other ways of earning a living – turned its energies to trade and manufacturing. Among the products of Protestant-owned factories was a twilled fabric known as *serge*. Soft yet durable, it became very popular among workers and, stained blue, was the uniform of the fishermen of Genoa.

When a Bavarian-Jewish immigrant to the USA, Levi Strauss (1829–1902), began to make trousers in California during the 1849 gold rush, he soon realised that the miners needed garments that would last. After trying tent canvas, he began importing *serge de Nîmes*, now better known as denim.

Orientation
Almost everything, including traffic, revolves around Les Arènes, the roman am-

phitheatre. North of here, the fan-shaped, largely pedestrianised old city is bounded by blvd Victor Hugo, blvd Amiral Courbet and blvd Gambetta. The main squares are place de la Maison Carrée, place du Marché and place aux Herbes.

Information
INTERNET ACCESS
@dd-on System (11 rue Nationale; per hr €3; ☺ 11am-midnight Mon-Fri, 11am-2am Sat)
PC Gamer (2 rue Nationale; per hr €2.50; ☺ 9.30am-1am)

LAUNDRY
There are laundrettes at 14 rue Nationale (open 7am to 9pm) and 24 rue Porte de France (8am to 8pm).

POST
Post Office (blvd de Bruxelles)

TOURIST INFORMATION
Tourist Office (☎ 04 66 58 38 00; www.ot-nimes.fr; 6 rue Auguste; ☺ 8am-8pm Mon-Fri Jul & Aug, 8.30am-7pm Mon-Fri Sep-Jun, plus 9am-7pm Sat & 10am-5pm Sun year-round)
Maison du Tourisme (☎ 04 66 36 96 30; www.cdt-gard.fr; 3 place des Arènes; ☺ 8am-7pm Jul & Aug Mon-Fri, 8.45am-6pm Mon-Fri Sep-Jun, plus 9.30am-noon Sat year-round). For information about the Gard *département*.

Sights
LES ARÈNES
The superb Roman amphitheatre **Les Arènes** (adult/child €4.65/3.40; ☺ 9am-7pm mid-Mar–mid-Oct, 10am-5pm mid-Oct–mid-Mar), built around AD 100 to seat 24,000 spectators, is wonderfully preserved, even retaining its upper storey, unlike its counterpart in Arles. The interior has a system of exits and passages (called, engagingly, *vomitories*), designed so that patricians attending animal and gladiator combats never had to rub shoulders with the plebs up top.

Covered by a removable roof in winter, Les Arènes lives on as a frequent sporting and cultural venue – an excellent thing in itself though the scaffolding and temporary barriers do detract from its appeal as a historical site. Buy your ticket at the reception point, tucked into its northern walls.

MAISON CARRÉE
The **Maison Carrée** (Square House; admission free; ☺ as Les Arènes) is a remarkably preserved

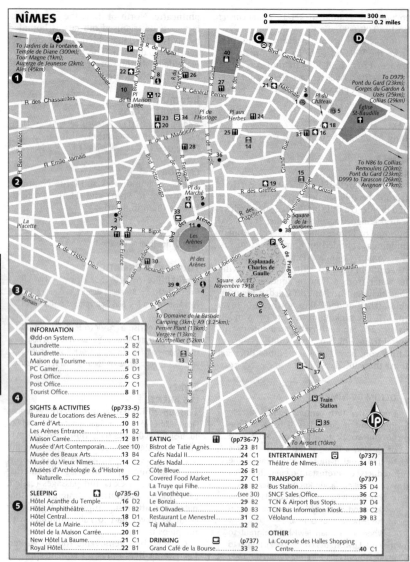

NÎMES

0 _____ 300 m
0 _____ 0.2 miles

To Jardins de la Fontaine &
Temple de Diane (300m);
Tour Magne (1km);
Auberge de Jeunesse (2km);
Alès (45km)

To D979;
Pont du Gard (23km);
Gorges du Gardon &
Uzès (25km);
Collias (29km)

To N86 to Collias,
Remoulins (20km);
Pont du Gard (23km);
D999 to Tarascon (26km);
Avignon (47km)

To Domaine de la Bastide
Camping (3km); A9 (3.25km);
Perrier Plant (13km);
Vergèze (13km);
Montpellier (52km)

To Airport (10km)

INFORMATION	
@dd-on System................................1	C1
Laundrette.....................................2	B2
Laundrette.....................................3	C1
Maison du Tourisme.......................4	B3
PC Gamer......................................5	D1
Post Office....................................6	C3
Post Office....................................7	C1
Tourist Office................................8	B1

SIGHTS & ACTIVITIES	(pp733–5)
Bureau de Locations des Arènes....9	B2
Carré d'Art..................................10	B1
Les Arènes Entrance.....................11	B2
Maison Carrée..............................12	B1
Musée d'Art Contemporain......(see 10)	
Musée des Beaux Arts...................13	B4
Musée du Vieux Nîmes..................14	C2
Musées d'Archéologie & d'Histoire	
Naturelle....................................15	C2

SLEEPING	☆ (pp735–6)
Hôtel Acanthe du Temple..........16	D2
Hôtel Amphithéâtre.....................17	B2
Hôtel Central...............................18	D1
Hôtel de La Mairie.......................19	C2
Hôtel de la Maison Carrée............20	B1
New Hôtel La Baume....................21	C1
Royal Hôtel.................................22	B1

EATING	🍴 (pp736–7)
Bistrot de Tatie Agnès..................23	B1
Cafés Nadal II.............................24	C1
Cafés Nadal.................................25	C2
Côte Bleue...................................26	B1
Covered Food Market...................27	C1
La Truye qui Filhe........................28	B2
La Vinothèque........................(see 30)	
Le Bonzai....................................29	B2
Les Olivades................................30	B3
Restaurant Le Menestrel...............31	C2
Taj Mahal...................................32	B2

DRINKING	🍷 (p737)
Grand Café de la Bourse..............33	B2

ENTERTAINMENT	🎭 (p737)
Théâtre de Nîmes........................34	B1

TRANSPORT	(p737)
Bus Station.................................35	D4
SNCF Sales Office........................36	C2
TCN & Airport Bus Stops..............37	D4
TCN Bus Information Kiosk............38	B2
Véloland......................................39	B3

OTHER	
La Coupole des Halles Shopping	
Centre....................................40	C1

rectangular Roman temple that was constructed around AD 5 to honour Emperor
Augustus' two adopted sons. It has survived
the centuries as a medieval meeting hall,
private residence, stable, church and, after
the Revolution, archive.

The striking glass and steel building
across the square, completed in 1993, is the

Carré d'Art (Square of Art), which houses the
municipal library and Musée d'Art Contemporain (opposite). The work of British architect Sir Norman Foster, it harmonises well
with the Maison Carrée and is everything
modern architecture should be: innovative,
complementary and beautiful – a wonderful, airy building just to float around.

LANGUEDOC-ROUSSILLON

JARDINS DE LA FONTAINE

The elegant Fountain Gardens are enriched by Nîmes' other major Roman monuments. Statue-adorned paths run around inky waterways. The **Source de la Fontaine** was the site of a spring, temple and baths in Roman times. The **Temple de Diane** – 'it is strictly forbidden to escalade this monument,' says the sign in quaint near-English – is left (west) through the main entrance.

A 10- to 15-minute uphill walk brings you to the crumbling shell of the 30m high **Tour Magne** (adult/child €2.50/2; ☼ as for Les Arènes), raised around 15 BC and the largest of a chain of towers that once ran along the city's 7km-long Roman ramparts. From here, there's a magnificent view of Nîmes and the surrounding countryside.

MUSEUMS

Each of Nîmes' **museums** (☼ 10am-6pm Tue-Sun) follows a common timetable. Most are in sore need of a new broom.

Musée du Vieux Nîmes (place aux Herbes; admission free), in the 17th-century episcopal palace, is a small, eccentric museum; one room showcases denim, with smiling pin-ups of Elvis, James Dean and Marilyn Monroe, while two others are devoted entirely to what must be the world's largest – perhaps only? – collection of domestic graters and mincers.

Musée d'Archéologie (13 blvd Amiral Courbet; admission free) brings together some interesting Roman and pre-Roman artefacts unearthed around Nîmes. However, too many exhibits bear nothing more than a peeling paper label with an enigmatic number. The museum also houses a hotchpotch of artefacts from Africa, piled high and tagged with yellowing captions such as 'Abyssinia' and 'Dahomey'. In the same building, **Musée d'Histoire Naturelle** has a musty collection of stuffed animals gazing bleakly out. Only the custodians, protected from importunate visitors inside their own glass case, have life.

Musée des Beaux-Arts (rue de la Cité Foulc; adult/child €4.65/3.40) has a wonderfully preserved Roman mosaic (look down upon it from the first floor). This apart, it houses a fairly pedestrian collection of Flemish, Italian and French works.

The refreshing **Musée d'Art Contemporain** (adult/child €4.65/3.40) in the Carré d'Art makes a welcome contrast. Housing both permanent and rotating exhibitions of modern art, it merits a visit, even if only to prowl the innards of this striking building.

Tours

The tourist office runs two-hour French-language city tours (€5.50) at 10am on Tuesday, Thursday and Saturday in summer, and 2.30pm on Saturday the rest of the year.

Taxi TRAN (☎ 04 66 29 40 11) offers a one-hour tour of the city (€25 to €30 for up to six people) with a cassette commentary in English. Enquire at the tourist office.

Festivals & Events

July and August bring forth an abundance of dance, theatre, rock, pop and jazz events. The tourist office produces *Festivités à Nîmes*, a free annual calendar of events.

FÉRIAS & BULLFIGHTS

Nîmes becomes more Spanish than French during its *férias*. Each – the three-day **Féria Primavera** (Spring Festival) in February, the five-day **Féria de Pentecôte** (Whitsuntide Festival) in June, and the three-day **Féria des Vendanges** coinciding with the grape harvest on the third weekend in September – is marked by daily *corridas* (bullfights). The **Bureau de Locations des Arènes** (☎ 04 66 02 80 90; 2 rue de la Violette) sells tickets.

JEUDIS DE NÎMES

Every Thursday between 6pm and 10.30pm in July and August, artists, artisans and vendors of local food specialities take over the main squares of central Nîmes.

Sleeping

During Nîmes' *férias*, many hotels raise their prices and accommodation can be hard to find.

BUDGET

Auberge de Jeunesse (☎ 04 66 68 03 20; nimes@fuaj .org; 257 chemin de l'Auberge de Jeunesse, la Cigale; dm incl breakfast €13.25) Freshly and comprehensively renovated, it's in a lovely park 3.5km northwest of the train station. Take bus No 2, direction Alès or Villeverte, and get off at the Stade stop.

Hôtel de La Mairie (☎ 04 66 67 65 91; fax 04 66 76 07 92; 11 rue des Greffes; s with washbasin €23, with shower €30, d with bathroom €39-42; ☒ closed 15-31 Oct) Several rooms in this hyperfriendly two-star, 13-room hotel have separate toilets. Ceilings are high and rooms cool, even in high summer. To watch the world go by in the quiet street below, ask for room 3 with its tiny balcony.

Hôtel de la Maison Carrée (☎ 04 66 67 32 89; fax 04 66 76 22 57; 14 rue de la Maison Carrée; s €35, d €45) This hotel has recently changed hands. Long popular as a budget venue, its new owner is slowly pulling it more into the medium-range bracket and upgrading its facilities.

Hôtel Central (☎ 04 66 67 27 75; www.hotel-central .org; 2 place du Château; basic s €30, d with bathroom €45; ☒) With its creaky floorboards and bunches of wild flowers painted on each bedroom door, this hotel is full of character. Garage parking costs €6.50.

Hôtel Acanthe du Temple (☎ 04 66 67 54 61; www .hotel-du-temple.com in French; 1 rue Charles Babut; ☒ ☒) Just opposite the Central, it has spick-and-span rooms, even if some of the wallpaper (different in every room) might induce biliousness. Room and garage prices are – more than coincidentally – within a couple of euros of its neighbours. All rooms have fans, some have separate toilets and a few are non-smoking.

Camping
Camping Domaine de la Bastide (☎ /fax 04 66 38 09 21; camping €11.85; ☒ year-round) is 4km south of town on the D13. Take bus D and get off at La Bastide, the terminus.

MID-RANGE & TOP END
Hôtel Amphithéâtre (☎ 04 66 67 28 51; hotel-amphi theatre@wanadoo.fr; 4 rue des Arènes; s €37-40, d €47-59; ☒ Feb-Dec; ☒ ☒) The welcoming Amphithéâtre, once a pair of 18th-century mansions, has recently been taken over by a young family. Rooms are decorated in warm, woody colours and named after writers or painters; we suggest dipping into Montesquieu or Arrabal (€59), both large and with a balcony overlooking pedestrian place du Marché. Some are non-smoking, most have a bathtub and those on the third floor have air-con.

Royal Hôtel (☎ 04 66 58 28 27; fax 04 66 58 28 28; 3 blvd Alphonse Daudet; s/d with shower €46/62, s with bathroom €51-66, d €67-87) With canvases just about everywhere, the huge dove cage beside reception and the local intelligentsia discoursing over coffee in **La Bodeguita** (☒ 6pm-late Mon-Sat), its very Spanish café, it's evident that *la patronne* is herself an artist. Rooms, all with ceiling fan and most with bathtubs are comfortable and furnished with flair. Some overlook pedestrian place d'Assas; fine for the view though the noise might be intrusive on summer nights.

New Hôtel La Baume (☎ 04 66 76 28 42; www.new -hotel.com; 21 rue Nationale; s/d €95/120; ☒ ☒ ☒) In fact far from new, this 34-room hotel occupies an attractive 17th-century town mansion with a glorious interior courtyard and has every comfort, though you may find it a little short on human warmth.

Eating
Nîmes' gastronomy owes as much to Provence as it does to Languedoc. Spicy southern delights, such as *aïoli, rouille*, are as abundant in this city as cassoulet. Sample the Costières de Nîmes wines from the pebbly vineyards to the south. If you're teetotal, your water couldn't come fresher: Perrier, the famous fizzy French mineral water, comes from nearby Vergèze (opposite).

La Truye qui Filhe (☎ 04 66 21 76 33; 9 rue Fresque; menu €8.70; ☒ noon-2pm Mon-Sat, closed Aug) Within the vaults of a restored 14th-century inn, this, the bargain of Nîmes, blends a self-service format with a homely atmosphere and does a superb-value *menu* that changes daily.

Bistrot de Tatie Agnès (☎ 04 66 21 00 81; 16 rue de la Maison Carrée; ☒ lunch only, Mon-Sat, closed 1-21 Aug) The toasted sandwiches (€7.50) at this recommended lunch spot are as original as its name and you can make a meal out of the giant salads (€7.50 to €8.50).

Côte Bleue (☎ 04 66 67 36 12; rue du Grand Couvent; menus €7.50 & 13, mains €9-11.50; ☒ Mon-Sat Jun-Sep, lunch only Oct-May) Decked in attractive Provençal blues and deep yellows, tiny and bustling, this intimate place is as attractive inside as on its summer terrace. Save a cranny for the *gâteau de marrons et noix*, a dessert that looks like sludge, tastes like ambrosia and comes with a generous squirt of Chantilly cream.

Les Olivades (☎ 04 66 21 71 78; 18 rue Jean Reboul; lunch/dinner menu €11/18.50; ☒ Tue-Sun) There's an intimate dining area to the rear of this excellent wine shop. Just one negative: the uncomfortable chairs will have you sitting ramrod straight to enjoy its excellent fare.

Restaurant Le Menestrel (☎ 04 66 67 54 45; 6 rue École Vieille; menus €15-22; ☺ closed Mon & lunch Tue) This is *the* place for quality local cuisine. Observe yourself in the giant overhead mirror as you tuck away one of its imaginative *menus*.

Rue Porte de France has a scattering of ethnic places: **Taj Mahal** (☎ 04 66 67 37 53; 15 rue Porte de France; mains €8.50-10) is an Indian place; **Le Bonzai** (☎ 04 66 21 84 76; 32 rue Porte de France; ☺ Tue-lunch Sun), opposite, is a touch of Japan.

SELF-CATERING
There are colourful Thursday **markets** in the old city in July and August. The large **covered food market** is in rue Général Perrier.

Quaint **Cafés Nadal**, overlooking place aux Herbes, specialises in local herbs, oils and spices, while its branch on rue St-Castor sells the finest coffees and chocolate. Knowledgeable staff at **La Vinothèque**, which shares premises with Les Olivades, can guide you through their unbeatable choice of local wines.

Drinking
Place aux Herbes is one communal outside café in summer. Equally bustling, beneath the huge palm tree that sprawls in its centre, is place du Marché. On the terrace or inside, **Grand Café de la Bourse**, vast, flamboyant and bang opposite Les Arènes, is great for breakfast or a quick coffee.

Entertainment
Pick up *Nîmescope*, a free fortnightly entertainment listing, available at the tourist office and major hotels. Les Arènes is a major venue for theatre performances and concerts.

Théâtre de Nîmes (☎ 04 66 36 02 04; place de la Calade) has drama, music and opera performances throughout the year.

Getting There & Away
AIR
Nîmes' **airport** (☎ 04 66 70 49 49), 10km southeast of the city on the A54, handles precisely one plane daily – the Ryanair flight to/from London Stansted.

BUS
The **bus station** (☎ 04 66 29 52 00; rue Ste-Félicité) is immediately south of the train station.

Regional destinations include Pont du Gard (€5.40, 45 minutes, up to seven daily), Uzès (€5.70, 45 minutes, eight daily) and Alès (€6.80, 1¼ hours, five daily). There are also buses to/from Avignon (€7.30, 1½ hours, seven daily).

Long-haul operator **Eurolines** (☎ 04 66 29 49 02) covers most European destinations including London (€95) and Amsterdam (€87) and, together with **Line Bus** (☎ 04 66 29 50 62), services to/from Spain.

CAR & MOTORCYCLE
Europcar (☎ 04 66 70 49 22) and **Avis** (☎ 04 66 70 49 26) have kiosks at both the airport and train station.

TRAIN
There's an **SNCF sales office** (11 rue de l'Aspic).

Ten TGVs daily run to/from Paris' Gare de Lyon (€68.90 to €82.80, three hours). There are frequent services to/from Alès (€7.60, 40 minutes), Arles (€6.60, 30 minutes), Avignon (€7.40, 30 minutes), Marseille (€16.20, 1¼ hours), Sète (€10.60, one hour) and Montpellier (€7.50, 30 minutes). Five SNCF buses or trains go to Aigues Mortes in the Camargue (€6.20, 1¼ hours).

Getting Around
TO THE AIRPORT
An airport **bus** (☎ 04 66 29 27 29; €4.50, 30min) meets and greets the daily Ryanair flight, leaving from the train station at 9.15am. To confirm times, ring.

BICYCLE
Véloland (☎ 04 66 36 01 80; 4 rue de la République; ☺ Mon afternoon & Tue-Sat) rents mountain bikes (per half-/full-day €9/15).

PUBLIC TRANSPORT
Local buses are run by **TCN**, which has an information kiosk (☎ 04 66 38 15 40) in the northeast corner of esplanade Charles de Gaulle, the main centre for buses. The cost of a single ticket/five-ticket *carnet* is €1/4.

TAXI
Ring ☎ 04 66 29 40 11.

AROUND NÎMES
Perrier Plant
Ever wondered how they get the bubbles into a bottle of Perrier water? Or why it's

that stubby shape? Take the one-hour tour of **Perrier's spring and bottling plant** (☎ 04 66 87 61 01; admission €5; tours at least every ½hr 9.30-10.30am & 1-3pm Mon-Thu, 2-5pm Sat & Sun Feb-Dec). It's in Vergèze, on the RN113, 13km southwest of Nîmes. We trust their tongue is firmly in their cheek when they advertise *'dégustation gratuité'* (free tasting)!

Pont du Gard

The Pont du Gard, a Unesco World Heritage Site, is an exceptionally well-preserved, three-tiered Roman aqueduct that was once part of a 50km-long system of canals built about 19 BC by the Romans to bring water from near Uzès to Nîmes. The scale is huge: the 35 arches of the 275m-long upper tier, running 50m above the River Gard, contain a watercourse designed to carry 20,000 cubic metres of water per day and the largest construction blocks weigh more than five tonnes.

From car parks either side of the River Gard, you can walk along the road bridge, built in 1743 and running parallel with the lower tier of the aqueduct. The best view of the Pont du Gard is from upstream, beside the river, where you can swim on hot days.

The complex receives many more than a million visitors each year, averaging an horrendous 15,000 or so daily in high summer. There's an **information centre** (☎ 08 20 90 33 30) on each bank.

There's a **museum** (admission €6; captions in English) featuring the bridge, aqueduct and the role of water in Roman society and a 25-minute large-screen **film** (€3; with English version). To retreat from the ever-increasing commercialism, take **Mémoires de Garrigue**, a 1.4km walking trail with interpretive signs that winds through this typical Mediterranean bush and scrubland – though you'll need the explanatory booklet in English (€4) to get the most out of it.

A combined ticket (adult/child €10/8) gives access to all three activities, plus **Ludo**, a children's activity play area.

A spectacular free **light show** (nightly Jul-Aug, Fri & Sat Jun & Sep) should again be beaming out (the installations – and much else on the right bank – were badly damaged by floods in 2002).

If you simply want to enjoy the bridge, head on down. You can ramble round for free around the clock, though the car parks close between 1am and 7am.

GETTING THERE & AWAY

The Pont du Gard is 21km northeast of Nîmes, 26km west of Avignon and 12km southeast of Uzès. Buses to/from each town stop 1km north of the bridge beside the Auberge Blanche. There are five buses daily from Nîmes, two of which continue to Collias, and three from Avignon that continue to Uzès and Alès.

The extensive car parks on each bank of the river cost a whopping €5 (reimbursed if you sign on for the combined ticket).

River Gard

The wild, unpredictable River Gard descends from the Cévennes mountains. Torrential rains can raise the water level by as much as 5m in a flash. During long dry spells, by contrast, it sometimes almost disappears.

The river has sliced itself a meandering 20km gorge (Les Gorges du Gardon) through the hills from **Russan** to the village of **Collias**, about 6km upstream from the Pont du Gard. The GR6 runs beside it most of the way.

In Collias, 4km west of the D981, **Kayak Vert** (☎ 04 66 22 80 76; www.canoefrance.com) and **Canoë Le Tourbillon** (☎ 04 66 22 85 54), both based near the village bridge, rent out kayaks and canoes.

You can paddle 7km down to the Pont du Gard (€17 per person, two hours), or arrange to be dropped 22km upstream at Russan, from where there's a great descent back through Gorges du Gardon (€26, full day), usually possible only between March and mid-June, when the river is high enough.

Uzès

pop 7650

Uzès is a laid-back little hill town 25km northeast of Nîmes. With its faithfully restored Renaissance façades, impressive Duché (Ducal Palace), narrow, semi-pedestrianised streets and ancient towers, it's a charming place for a brief wander.

The **tourist office** (☎ 04 66 22 68 88; www.ville -uzes.fr in French; ☷ 9am-6pm Mon-Fri, 10am-1pm & 2-5pm Sat & Sun Jun-Sep; 9am-noon & 1.30-6pm Mon-Fri, 10am-1pm Sat Oct-May) is on place Albert I, beside the ring road and just outside the old quarter.

SIGHTS & ACTIVITIES

The tourist office carries a useful free pamphlet in English, *Tour of the Historic Town.*

Whether you follow this guided walk or not, let your steps take you through **Place aux Herbes**, Uzès' shady, arcaded central square, its odd angles defying geometrical classification.

The **Duché** (Château Ducal; ☎ 04 66 22 18 96; 10am-1pm & 2-6.30pm Jul–mid-Sep, 10am-noon & 2-6pm mid-Sep–Jun) is a fortified chateau that has belonged to the Dukes of Uzès for more than 1000 years. Altered and expanded almost continuously from the 11th to 18th century, it has some fine period furniture, tapestries and paintings. You can take the **guided tour** (one hour, in French; adult/child €11/8) or wander at will around the **keep** (€6).

Close by, just off rue Port Royal, is the beautifully landscaped **Jardin Médiéval** (Medieval Garden; admission €2; 10.30am-12.30pm & 2-6pm daily Jul-Aug; 2-5pm or 6pm Mon-Fri, 10.30am-12.30pm & 2-5pm or 6pm Sat & Sun Apr-Jun & Sep-Oct).

Musée du Bonbon (☎ 04 66 22 74 39; Pont des Charrettes; adult/child €4.50/2.50; 10am-7pm daily Jul-Sep, 10am-1pm & 2-6pm Tue-Sun Oct-Dec & Feb-Jun) is the place for a little indulgence. As a plaque at the entrance declares, 'This museum is dedicated to all who have devoted their lives to a slightly guilty passion – greed'. Signs at this shrine to sticky sweets are multilingual and you come away with a copious goody bag.

FESTIVALS & EVENTS
Uzès is big on festivals and fairs. The town positively reeks on 24 June, the date of the **Foire à l'Ail** (Garlic Fair). On Saturday mornings between November and March, there's a **truffle market** (place aux Herbes), while the third Sunday in January sees a full-blown **Truffle**

Fair. The town is also renowned for its **Nuits Musicales d'Uzès**, an international festival of baroque music held in the second half of July.

GETTING THERE & AWAY
The *gare routière* – grandly named and in fact a bus stop – is on av de la Libération. Between Avignon (€8.10) and Alès (€6.70) buses run two to four times daily. There are also six to 10 daily to/from Nîmes (€5.70).

ALÈS & AROUND
pop 41,000

Alès, 45km from Nîmes, 70km from Montpellier and snuggled against the River Gard, is the Gard *département*'s second-largest town. Coal was mined here from the 13th century, when monks first dug into the surrounding hills, until the last pit closed in 1986.

The pedestrianised heart of town, having long ago shed its sooty past, is pleasant, if unexciting, to stroll through. Gateway to the Cévennes mountains and bright with flowers in summer, Alès is also a convenient base for visiting a trio of unique exhibitions close by.

The **tourist office** (☎ 04 66 52 32 15; tourisme@ville-ales.net; place Hôtel de Ville; 9am-7pm Mon-Sat, 9am-noon Sun Jul-Aug; 9am-noon & 1.30-5.30pm Mon-Sat Sep-Jun) occupies a modern building set into the shell of a baroque chapel.

Sights
Mine Témoin (☎ 04 66 30 45 15; chemin de la Cité Ste-Marie; adult/child €6.70/3.50; 10am-6pm Jul-Aug, 9am-5pm Jun, 9am-11am & 2-4pm Apr-May & Sep–mid-Nov) in Alès is no museum. Don a safety helmet and

THE CAMISARD REVOLT
Early in the 18th century, a guerrilla war raged through the Cévennes as Protestants took on Louis XIV's army. The revocation of the Edict of Nantes in 1685 removed rights that the Protestant Huguenots had enjoyed since 1598. Many emigrated, while others fled deep into the wild Cévennes, from where a local leader named Roland, only 22 at the time, led the resistance against the French army sent to crush them.

Poorly equipped but knowing the countryside intimately, the outlaws resisted for two years. They fought in their shirts – *camiso* in *langue d'oc*; thus their popular name, Camisards. Once the royal army gained the upper hand, the local population was either massacred or forced to flee. Roland was killed and most villages were methodically destroyed.

Each year, on the first Sunday of September, thousands of French Protestants meet at Roland's birthplace in Le Mas Soubeyran, a sleepy hamlet near the village of Mialet, just off the Corniche des Cévennes. It's now the Musée du Désert, which details the persecution of Protestants in the Cévennes between 1685 and the 1787 Edict of Tolerance, marking the reintroduction of religious freedom.

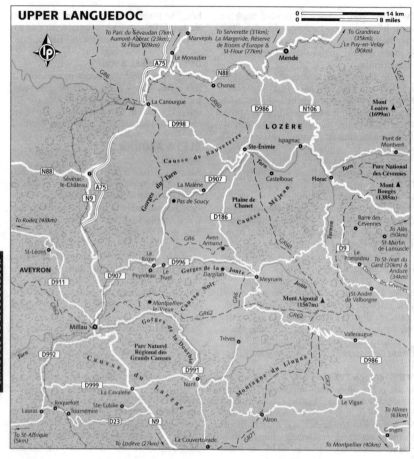

UPPER LANGUEDOC

take the cage down an actual mine. Preceded by a 20-minute video (in French), the one-hour **guided tour** (option in English, July to mid-August, if you ring to reserve; at other times, ask for the free pamphlet in English) leads you along 650m of underground galleries.

The huge **Bambouseraie de Prafrance** (Bamboo Grove; ☎ 04 66 61 70 47; adult/child €6.50/4; ☉ 9.30am-dusk Mar–mid-Nov) was founded in 1855 by a spice merchant. Here in Générargues, 12km southwest of Alès, 150 bamboo species sprout amid aquatic gardens and an Asian village. A fun way to get there is on the Cévennes steam train (opposite).

Musée du Désert (☎ 04 66 85 02 72; adult/child €4/3; ☉ 9.30am-7pm Jul-Aug, 9.30am-noon & 2-6pm Mar-Jun & Sep–mid-Nov) portrays the clandestine way of life of the Camisards. It's in the charming hamlet of Le Mas Soubeyran, 5km north of the Bambouseraie.

Sleeping & Eating

Hôtel Le Riche (☎ 04 66 86 00 33; www.leriche.fr in French; 42 place Pierre Sémard; s €34-40 d €48; ☉ Sep-Jul; P ❄) Opposite the train station, this hotel is highly recommended, as much for its fine restaurant (*menus* €16.50 to €47) as for its pleasant, modern rooms.

Hôtel Durand (☎ 04 66 86 28 94; fax 04 66 30 52 68; 3 blvd Anatole France; s/d €27.50/30.50; P) More modest and about 100m east of Hôtel Le Riche down a side street, it has trim rooms and also represents excellent value.

Camping

Camping la Croix Clémentine (☎ 04 66 86 52 69; www.clementine.fr in French; camping according to season €10.60-19.60; ☟ Apr–mid-Sep) This place is in Cendras, 4km northwest of Alès.

Getting There & Away

BUS

From the **bus station** (place Pierre Sémard), south of the train station, one bus daily heads into the Cévennes to Florac (€12, 1½ hours), and two to four to Uzès (€6.70, 50 minutes), continuing to Avignon (€13.80, 1¾ hours).

TRAIN

There are 10 trains daily to/from Montpellier (€13.30, 1½ hours), some requiring a change in Nîmes (€7.60, 45 minutes). Three trains daily link Alès and Mende (€15, 2¼ hours).

From April to October the little **Train à Vapeur des Cévennes** (Cévennes steam train; ☎ 04 66 60 59 00; adult/child one-way €8/6, return €10.50/7; daily Apr–mid-Sep, Tue-Sun mid-Sep–Oct) takes 40 minutes to chug the 13km between St-Jean du Gard and Anduze via the Bambouseraie, making four return trips each day.

PARC NATIONAL DES CÉVENNES

The heart of the Cévennes was designated a national park in 1970 and is also recognised as a Unesco World Biosphere Reserve. In general drier and hotter than the Auvergne to its north, it has more in common with Mediterranean lands. Sprinkled with isolated hamlets, it harbours a huge diversity of fauna and flora (an astounding 2250 plant species have been recorded). Several of its animals,

including red deer, beavers and vultures, have been successfully reintroduced over the last 25 years. The park covers four main areas: Mont Lozère, much of the Causse Méjean, the Vallées Cévenoles (Cévennes Valleys) and Mont Aigoual. Florac makes a good base for exploration.

The park has three **ecomuseums**: the Écomusées du Mont Lozère, de la Cévenne and du Causse, each of which has several different sites. For more details, ask at the excellent Maison du Parc National des Cévennes (p742).

History

The 910-sq-km park was created to bring ecological stability to an area that, because of religious and later economic upheavals, has long had a destabilising human presence. Population influxes, which saw the destruction of forests for logging and pasture, were followed by mass desertions as people gave up the fight against the inhospitable climate and terrain. Emigration led to the abandonment of hamlets and farms, many of which were snapped up in the 1960s by wealthy Parisians and foreigners.

Maps

The best overall map of the park is the IGN's *Parc National des Cévennes* (€7) at 1:100,000.

Mont Lozère

This 1699m-high lump of granite in the north of the park is shrouded in cloud and ice in winter and covered with heather and blueberries, peat bogs and flowing streams

---

CHESTNUT: THE ALL-PURPOSE TREE

In the Cévennes, the chestnut tree (known as *l'arbre à pain*, or the bread tree) was the staple food of many Auvergnat families. The nuts were eaten raw, roasted and dried, or ground into flour. Blended with milk or wine, chestnuts were the essence of *bajanat*, a nourishing soup. Part of the harvest would feed the pigs while the leaves of pruned twigs and branches provided fodder for sheep and goats.

Harvested at ground level with small forks – of chestnut wood, of course – the prickly husks (called *hérissons*, or hedgehogs) were removed by being trampled upon in spiky boots. Nowadays, they're the favourite food of the Cévennes' wild boars and still feature in a number of local sauces and desserts.

Nothing was wasted. Sections of hollowed-out trunk would serve as beehives, smaller branches would be woven into baskets while larger ones were whittled into stakes for fencing or used to build trellises. The wood, hard and resistant to parasites was used for rafters, rakes and household furniture – everything from, quite literally, the cradle to the coffin.

in summer. **Écomusée du Mont Lozère** (☎ 04 66 45 80 73; adult/child €3.50/2.50; ⏲ 10.30am-12.30pm & 2.30-6.30pm Easter-Sep) has a permanent exhibition at Pont de Montvert, 20km northeast of Florac.

Vallées Cévenoles

First planted back in the Middle Ages, *châtaigniers* (sweet-chestnut trees), carpet the Vallées Cévenoles (Cévennes Valleys), the park's central region of plunging ravines and jagged ridges, along one of which runs the breathtaking Corniche des Cévennes.

Mont Aigoual

Mont Aigoual (1567m) and the neighbouring Montagne du Lingas region are renowned for their searing winds and heavy snowfall. The area is dense with beech trees, thanks to a successful reforestation programme that has counteracted years of uncontrolled logging. The observatory atop the breezy summit has an **exhibition** (admission free; ⏲ May-Sep), portraying the mountain through the seasons and the play of wind and water upon it.

Activities

In winter there's **cross-country skiing** (more than 100km of marked trails) on Mont Aigoual and Mont Lozère, and **donkey treks** are popular in the park in warmer months. There are 600km of donkey- and horse-riding trails and 200km marked out for mountain-bike enthusiasts.

An equally well-developed network of trails makes the park a **walking** paradise year-round. The free French pamphlet *Itinéraires et Sentiers Pédestres* summarises the dozen GR trails that crisscross the park. In addition, there are 22 shorter signposted walks of between two and seven hours' duration and 20 easy, educational trails.

Florac's Maison du Parc has 11 excellent wallets (€5 each) describing circular walks from various starting points within the park. Ask about the Festival Nature, a summertime mix of outdoor activities, lectures and field trips.

Getting There & Away

By car, the most scenic route is the Corniche des Cévennes, a ridge road that winds along the mountain crests of the Cévennes for 56km from St-Jean du Gard to Florac.

FLORAC
pop 2100

Florac, 79km northwest of Alès and 38km southeast of Mende makes a great base for exploring the Parc National des Cévennes and the upper reaches of the Gorges du Tarn. Lively in summer, it's draped along the west bank of River Tarnon, one of the tributaries of the Tarn, with the fortress-like cliffs of the Causse Méjean looming 1000m overhead.

Information

Florac On-Line (1 rue du Pêcher; per hr €6) Internet access.
Laundrette (11 rue du Pêcher; ⏲ 8.30am-7.30pm)
Tourist Office (☎ 04 66 45 01 14; www.mescevennes .com; av Jean Monestier; ⏲ 8.30am-1.30pm & 2.30-7pm daily Jul-Aug, 9am-noon & 2-6pm Mon-Sat Sep-Jun)

Activities

The tourist office has details on a whole summer's worth of outdoor activities. For information on the park's rich walking potential, contact **Maison du Parc National des Cévennes** (☎ 04 66 49 53 01; www.cevennes-parcnational .fr; ⏲ 9.30am-6pm Jul-Aug; 9.30am-12.30pm & 1.30-6.30pm Easter-Jun, Mon-Fri Sep-Easter) It occupies the handsome restored 17th-century Château de Florac, stocks an English version of the guidebook *Parc National des Cévennes* (€15) and has a splendidly informative **interactive exhibition** (admission €3.50), *Passagers du Parc*, with captions and a recorded commentary in English (delivered, alas, by a couple of glum, monotone native speakers) and a 15-minute slide show.

Activities in the Parc National des Cévennes section (left) has more information. Lonely Planet's *Walking in France* describes three varied day walks, each accessible from Florac.

DONKEY TREKS

Why not follow the lead of Robert Louis Stevenson and hire a pack animal? Several companies are in the donkey business. They include **Genti-Âne** (☎ 04 66 41 04 16; anegenti@free .fr) in Castagnols and **Tramontane** (☎ 04 66 45 92 44) in St-Martin de Lansuscle. Typical prices are €35 to €45 per day and €190 to €220 per week and both outfits can reserve accommodation along the route. Though each is outside Florac, they'll transport the dumb creatures to town or a place of your choosing for a fee (around €0.75/km).

TRAVELS WITH A DONKEY

The Cévennes were even wilder and more untamed back in October 1878, when Scottish writer Robert Louis Stevenson crossed them with only a donkey, Modestine, for company.

'I was looked upon with contempt, like a man who should project a journey to the moon, but yet with a respectful interest, like one setting forth for the inclement Pole,' Stevenson wrote in *Travels with a Donkey in the Cévennes*, published in 1879.

Accompanied by the wayward, mouse-coloured Modestine, bought for 65 francs and a glass of brandy, Stevenson took a respectable 12 days to travel the 232km on foot (Modestine carried his gear) from Le Monastier-sur-Gazelle, southeast of Le Puy-en-Velay, to St-Jean du Gard, west of Alès. Afterwards, he sold his ass – and wept.

The Stevenson trail, first retraced and marked with the cross of St Andrew by a Scottish woman in 1978, is nowadays designated the GR70.

Whether you're swaying on a donkey or simply walking, you'll find *The Robert Louis Stevenson Trail* by Alan Castle an excellent, practical, well-informed companion. Consult too www.chemin-stevenson.org and pick up the free pamphlet *Sur Le Chemin de Robert Louis Stevenson* (On The RLS Trail), stocked by tourist offices, which has a comprehensive list of accommodation en route.

OTHER ACTIVITIES

Cévennes Évasion (☎ 04 66 45 18 31; www.cevennes-evasion.com; 5 place Boyer) rents mountain bikes for €12/18 per half-/full-day and furnishes riders with handy colour route maps. In summer it'll take you for free up to the Causse Méjean, from where you can whiz effortlessly back down (minimum five persons). It also arranges caving, rock-climbing and canyon-clambering expeditions (each €42 to €50).

Sleeping

Gîte d'Étape (☎ 04 66 45 24 54; lagrave.alain@wanadoo.fr; 18 rue du Pêcher; dm €11; ☼ Feb–mid-Nov) This welcoming trekkers' favourite with doubles and quads occupies an 18th-century house and has self-catering facilities.

Hôtel Central de La Poste (☎ 04 66 45 00 01; www.archibald-hotel.com in French; 4 av Maurice Tour; d €37-42) A husband-and-wife team has taken over this ex-coaching inn (which needed a feminine touch after some years in the hands of three young men). Lower floors are renovated and they're working their way up. It runs a decent restaurant, the **Archibald**, with a summertime rear terrace overlooking the river.

Hôtel Les Gorges du Tarn (☎ 04 66 45 00 63; gorges-du-tarn.adonis@wanadoo.fr; 48 rue du Pêcher; d €30, with shower €36, with bathroom €42; ☼ Easter-Oct; **P**) Down a quiet side street, rooms in the main building are freshly renovated while those in the annexe are more spacious, if less sparkling. It's restaurant, **L'Adonis** (menus €17-35), merits a visit in its own right.

Grand Hôtel du Parc (☎ 04 66 45 03 05; www.grandhotelduparc.fr; 47 av Jean Monestier; d €41.50-53; ☼ mid-Mar–Nov) This venerable building with its spacious rooms enjoys its own grounds with a pool and delightful gardens. It's a great spot to recharge the batteries and also has a creditable **restaurant** (menus €15-29.50).

Camping

Florac has a pair of municipal riverside camping grounds, each 1.5km from town. **Camping Le Pont du Tarn** (☎ 04 66 45 18 26; pontdutarne@aol.com; camping €8-14; ☼ Apr–mid-Oct; 🐾) is to the north, off the N106, while **Camping La Tière** (☎ 04 66 45 00 53; per person/tent/car €2.50/2.40/1.60; ☼ Jul-Aug) is smaller and to the south. La Tière is right beside the river and may well be less crowded.

Eating

L'Esplanade, a shady, pedestrianised allée, becomes one long dining area in summer. Here, you can eat well and economically at one of the restaurant terraces. The three hotels we recommend on this page all have impressive restaurants.

Le Chapeau Rouge (☎ 04 66 45 23 40; 3bis rue Roussel; menus €15-29) A dynamic young crew have recently taken over The Red Hat, beside the tourist office. It's excellent value and the service is friendly, though they do have trouble coping if the place is full. In summer, the shady terrace, its canopy a thick foliage of vines, is a delight.

La Source du Pêcher (☎ 04 66 45 03 01; 1 rue de Remuret; menus €25-40; ☼ Apr-Oct) With a wonderful open-air terrace, perched above the little River Pêcher, it's very good and oh, they know and show it (a Dutch family walked out the night we dined there) and they still observe the outmoded practice of handing Madame a menu with nothing so vulgar as prices indicated. This said, you'll eat very well indeed, if you can stomach a little ritual humiliation. They don't take reservations, so arrive early.

Maison du Pays Cévenol (3 rue du Pêcher) This gastronomic treasure trove sells local specialities – liqueurs, jams, Pélardon cheese and chestnuts in all their guises.

Getting There & Away
It's a pain without your own transport. One **Autocars Reilhes** (☎ 04 66 45 00 18) minibus runs to/from Alès (€12, 1½ hours), Monday to Saturday, leaving from the old railway station. And that's it for public transport, so keep your hitching thumb supple.

MENDE
pop 13,300
Mende, a quiet little place straddling the River Lot, is the capital of Lozère, France's least populous *département*. Its oval-shaped centre is ringed by a one-way road. This acts as something of a *cordon sanitaire*, leaving the old quarter relatively traffic-free.

Information
Salle Multimédia, (2nd fl, new town hall above the tourist office; place Charles de Gaulle; per hr €1.50; 2-8pm Tue-Fri, 9am-noon Sat) Internet access.
Tourist Office (☎ 04 66 94 00 23; www.ot-mende.fr; place Charles de Gaulle; 9am-12.30pm & 2-7pm Mon-Sat, 9am-noon Sun Jul-Aug; 9am-12.30pm & 2-6pm Mon-Fri, 9am-noon Sat Sep-Jun)

Sights
The English tourist office brochure, *Mende: Heritage Visit of the City,* describes every nook and cranny of historical interest. The dark interior of the 14th-century, twin-towered **Cathédrale Notre Dame** (place Urbain V) makes the magnificent stained-glass windows glow but you'll have to peer hard to make out detail on the eight 17th-century Aubusson tapestries, which are hung high above the nave.

Sleeping & Eating
Hôtel le Commerce (☎ 04 66 65 13 73; www.le commerce-mende.com in French; 2 blvd Henri Bourrillon; s €31, d €37-40; closed 2 weeks in Apr) Opposite place du Foirail on the busy ring road, this pleasantly labyrinthine hotel, run by the same family for three generations, has impeccable, tastefully furnished rooms. The owner – away on a beer tour of Germany when we last called by – is an ale fanatic and its popular **bar** carries an impressive range.

Hôtel de France (☎ 04 66 65 00 04; www.hotelde france-mende.com; 9 blvd Lucien Arnault; d €42-45; menus €21-24; mid-Jan–Dec; P) Most rooms at this Logis de France and one-time coaching inn have sweeping views over the small valley and gardens below. For the smallest of supplements, enjoy the extra space and bright, coordinated colours in room 20 or 21 (€50). The owner speaks excellent English. On the ring road, it's also a first class place to eat.

Restaurant Les Voûtes (☎ 04 66 49 00 05; 13 rue d'Aigues-Passes; menus €17-24; daily Jun-Aug, Tue-Sun Sep-May, closed 1-15 Oct) This restaurant enjoys a splendid setting, deep in the vaults of an ex-convent. Run by a cheerful young team (average age 22), it offers something for everyone: salads big enough to fill a fruit bowl (€7 to €7.50), pizzas (€6.50 to €8.40) – to eat in or takeaway – grills (€10 to €12.50) and a great, recommended lunchtime *menu express* (€12.50).

Le Mazel (☎ 04 66 65 05 33; 25 rue du Collège; menus €13-25; Wed-Mon lunch mid-Mar–mid-Nov) This stylishly decorated restaurant – do not be deterred by the bleakly modern surroundings – offers mainly local cuisine, imaginatively prepared. A recognised gourmet venue, it's true value.

Getting There & Away
Buses leave from the train station and most pass by place du Foirail. On weekdays, there's one daily to Rodez (three hours) and Le Puy-en-Velay (SNCF; two hours). Northbound, two SNCF buses run daily to/from Clermont-Ferrand in the Massif Central (€25.40, three hours).

The train station is 1km north of town across the River Lot. There are three trains daily to Montpellier (€23.80, 3½ hours) via Alès (€14.60, 2¼ hours) and Nîmes (€19.40, three hours).

Getting Around
Rent a mountain bike at **Espace Bike** (☎ 04 66 65 01 81; 1 blvd du Soubeyran; Tue-Sat) for €8/12 per half-/full-day.

AROUND MENDE
Wolf Reserve
Wolves once roamed freely through the Lozère forests but today you'll see them only in the **Parc du Gévaudan** (☎ 04 66 32 09 22; www .loupsdugevaudan.com; adult/child €6/3; ⏰ 10am-7pm Jun-Aug; 10am-5pm or 6pm Apr-May & Sep-Dec) in Ste-Lucie, 7km north of Marvejols. The park sustains more than 100 Mongolian, Canadian, Siberian and Polish wolves living in semi-freedom.

Réserve de Bisons d'Europe
Above the village of Ste-Eulalie en Margeride, the **Réserve de Bisons d'Europe** (☎ 04 66 31 40 40; www.bisoneurope.com in French; ⏰ 10am-5pm or 6pm or 7pm depending on season), above the village of Ste-Eulalie en Margeride, was established with 25 European bison transferred from the Bialowieza forest in Poland.

Within their 200-hectare reserve, the bison roam freely. Visitors, by contrast, must follow a 50-minute **guided tour**, either by horse-drawn carriage (adult/child €10/5.50) or by sledge (€14/8), or take a defined walking path (€5.50/4; from May to August).

GORGES DU TARN
From the village of Ispagnac, 9km northwest of Florac, the spectacular Gorges du Tarn wind southwestwards for about 50km, ending just north of Millau. En route are two villages: medieval Ste-Énimie (a good base for canoeing and walking along the gorges) and, 13km downstream, La Malène, smaller but equally attractive.

The gorge, 400m to 600m deep, marks the boundary between the Causse Méjean to the south and the Causse de Sauveterre to the north. From these plateaus, it looks like a white, limestone abyss, its green waters dotted here and there with bright canoes and kayaks. In summer the riverside road (the D907bis) is often jammed with cars, buses and caravans: every summer's day, more than 3000 cars grind through Ste-Énimie.

Activities
BOATING & CANOEING
Riding the River Tarn is at its best in high summer when the river is usually low and the descent a lazy trip over mostly calm water. You can get as far as the impassable Pas de Soucy, a barrier of boulders about 9km downriver from La Malène.

Various companies organises canoe and kayak descents. Among the longest established are **Canoë Paradan** (☎ 04 66 48 56 90) and **ADN La Cazelle** (☎ 04 66 48 46 05), both in Ste-Énimie, **Locanoë** (☎ 04 66 48 55 57) in Castelbouc and **Au Moulin de la Malène** (☎ 04 66 48 51 14) in La Malène. Prices per person vary little. Typical trips are: Ste-Énimie to La Malène (€17, 13km, 3½ hours) and Ste-Énimie to the Pas de Soucy (€23, 23km, 6½ hours).

The Ste-Énimie tourist office carries information on all companies offering rafting and canoe descents of the River Tarn.

If you'd rather someone else did the hard work, spend a lazy, effortless hour with **Les Bateliers de la Malène** (☎ 04 66 48 51 10; ⏰ Apr-Oct), who, for €18 per person will punt you down an 8km stretch of the gorge, leaving from La Malène, and drive you back.

WALKING & CYCLING
The Sentier de la Vallée du Tarn trail, blazed in yellow and green, runs for around 250km, from Pont de Montvert on Mont Lozère, down the Gorges and all the way to Albi. The GR60 follows an old drovers' route, winding down from the Causse de Sauveterre to Ste-Énimie, crossing the bridge and continuing southwards up to the Causse Méjean in the direction of Mont Aigoual.

Less strenuously, there are 23 circular, signposted walks, each between four and seven hours' duration, in the stretch between Ispagnac and La Malène.

La Cazelle in Ste-Énimie (see the previous Boating & Canoeing section), rents out mountain bikes (per half-/full-day €20/30).

The Ste-Énimie tourist office sells the useful *Vallée et Gorges du Tarn – Balades à Pied et à VTT* (€15), published by Chamina, which details various walking and cycling routes in the area.

HORSE RIDING
Centre Équestre La Périgouse (☎ 04 66 48 53 7; www.perigouse.com in French) in Ste-Énimie hires out horses for €13/32/48 per hour/half-/full-day.

Sleeping & Eating
Château de la Caze (☎ 04 66 48 51 01; www.cha teaudelacaze.com; d €108-162; ⏰ Easter–mid-Nov) This fairy-tale 15th-century castle, next to the Tarn 2km north of La Malène, is a fabulous top-end option. Rooms are the last word

in luxury and it boasts a renowned gourmet restaurant. Accommodation in the annexe is less romantic but much easier on the pocket and guests have access to all the hotel's facilities.

Camping Les Gorges du Tarn (☎ 04 66 48 50 51, fax 04 66 48 59 37; per person/tent/car €2/1/40/1/10; ☼ Easter–mid-Sep) This park is approximately 800m upstream from Ste-Énimie and is the cheapest of the riverside camping sites. It also hires out canoes and kayaks.

Ste-Énimie
pop 200

Ste-Énimie, 27km from Florac and 56km from Millau, tumbles like an avalanche of grey-brown stone, blending into the steep, once-terraced slope behind it. Long isolated, it's now a popular destination for day-visitors from Millau, Mende and Florac and one of the starting points for descending the Tarn by canoe or kayak.

Ste-Énimie's **tourist office** (☎ 04 66 48 53 44; www.gorgesdutarn.net in French; ☼ 9am-7pm daily Jul-Aug, 9am-12.30pm & 1.30-5.30pm Mon-Fri Sep-Jun) is 100m north of the bridge. It stocks maps and walking guides, including IGN Top 25 map No 2640OT *Gorges du Tarn*. There's also a small **annexe** (☼ Jul-Aug) in La Malène.

Highlights are the Romanesque **Église de Ste-Énimie** and, just behind it, the tiny **Écomusée Le Vieux Logis** (combined ticket adult/child €2/1; ☼ visits at least 10am & 4pm Mon-Fri Jul-Aug, Wed-Sun Jun & Sep), its one vaulted room crammed with antique local furniture, lamps, tableware and costumes.

PARC NATUREL RÉGIONAL DES GRANDS CAUSSES

This nature park is mainly harsh limestone plateau. Scorched in summer and windswept in winter, the stony surface holds little moisture as water filters through the limestone to form an underground world ideal for cavers.

The Rivers Tarn, Jonte and Dourbie have sliced deep gorges through the 5000-sq-km plateau, creating four *causses* ('plateaus' in the local patois): Sauveterre, Méjean, Noir and Larzac, each different in its delicate geological forms. One may look like a dark lunar surface, another like a Scottish moor covered with the thinnest layer of grass, while the next is gentler and more fertile. But all are eerie and empty except for the occasional

shepherd and his flock – and all offer magnificent walking and mountain biking.

Millau, at the heart of the park, is a good base for venturing into this wild area. The southern part of the park, home to France's 'king of cheeses' (p750), is known as Le Pays du Roquefort (Land of Roquefort). The Gorges de la Jonte, where birds of prey wheel and swoop, skim the park's eastern boundary and rival the neighbouring, more famous Gorges du Tarn in beauty.

Information
Parc Naturel Régional des Grands Causses office (☎ 05 65 61 35 50; parc.grands.causes@wanadoo.fr; 71 blvd de l'Ayrolle, Millau; ☼ 9am-noon or 12.30pm & 2-5pm or 6pm Mon-Fri)

Causse de Sauveterre

The northernmost of the causses is a gentle, hilly plateau dotted with a few compact and isolated farms resembling fortified villages. Every possible patch of fertile earth is cultivated, creating irregular, intricately patterned wheat fields.

Causse Méjean

Causse Méjean, the highest, is also the most barren and isolated. It's a land of poor pasture enriched by occasional fertile depressions, where streams gurgle down into the limestone through sinkholes, funnels and fissures.

Underground, this combination of water and limestone has created some spectacular scenery. The cavern of **Aven Armand** (☎ 04 66 45 61 31; adult/child €8/5; ☼ 9.30am-7pm Jun-Aug; 9.30am or 10am-noon & 1.30-5pm or 6pm Apr-May & Sep-Oct) on the plateau's southwestern side lies about 75m below the surface. Stretching some 200m, it bristles with a subterranean forest of stalagmites and stalactites. A **combination ticket** (adult/child €10/6) also includes admission to the Chaos de Montpellier-le-Vieux (opposite).

Nearby is the equally spectacular, even larger cavern of **Dargilan** (☎ 04 66 45 60 20; adult/child €8/4; ☼ Jul-Aug 10am-6.30pm, Easter-Jun & Sep-Oct 10am-noon & 2-4.30pm or 5.30pm). A one-hour tour culminates in a sudden exit to a ledge with a dizzying view of the Gorges de la Jonte (opposite) way below.

Causse Noir

Rising immediately east of Millau, the 'Black Causse' is bounded by gorges. It is known best for the **Chaos de Montpellier-le-Vieux** (☎ 05 65 60 66 30; adult/child €5/3; ☼ 9.30am-6pm or 7pm Apr-Oct), an area of jagged rocks 18km northeast of Millau overlooking the Gorges de la Dourbie. Water erosion has created more than 120 hectares of weird limestone formations with fanciful names such as the Sphinx and the Elephant. Three trails, lasting one to three hours, cover the site, as does a tourist train (adult/child €3/2).

If you're here outside official opening times, there's nothing to stop you wandering around freely.

Causse du Larzac

The Causse du Larzac (800m to 1000m) is the largest of the four causses. An endless sweep of distant horizons and rocky steppes broken by medieval villages, it's known as the 'French Desert'.

It's known in particular for old, fortified villages such as **Ste-Eulalie**, long the capital of the Larzac *région*, and **La Couvertoirade**, which were both built by the Knights Templar, a religious military order that distinguished itself during the Crusades.

Gorges de la Jonte

The dramatic Gorges de la Jonte cut east–west from Meyrueis to Le Rozier, below the western slopes of the Aigoual massif. West of Le Truel on the D996 is **Belvédère des Vautours** (Vulture Viewing Point; ☎ 05 65 62 69 69; www.vautours-lozere.com; adult/child €6/3; ☼ 10am-5pm or 6pm mid-Mar–mid-Nov), above which the birds nest high in the cliffs. Reintroduced after having all but disappeared locally, they now freely wheel and plane in the Causses skies.

The viewing point has an impressive multimedia exhibition, including live video transmission from the nesting sites of what must be the world's most heavily researched vultures. It also organises half-day **birding walks** (adult/child €6.50/3; reservation essential) to the surrounding gorges.

MILLAU
pop 22,500

Millau (pronounced mee-yo) sits between the Causse Noir and Causse du Larzac at the confluence of the Rivers Tarn and Dourbie. Falling just over the border into the Midi-Pyrénées *département* of Aveyron, it's tied to Languedoc historically and culturally. Once prosperous and still famous for glove-making, it's fairly run down these days. But as the main centre for the Parc Naturel Régional des Grands Causses, it comes to life at holiday time as a centre for hiking and other outdoor activities – particularly hang-gliding and parapente, exploiting the uplifting thermals.

Information

Laundrette (14 av Gambetta; ☼ 7am-9pm)
Main Post Office (12 av Alfred Merle)
Posanis (5 rue droite; ☼ 10am-10pm Mon-Sat) Internet access.
Tourist Office (☎ 05 65 60 02 42; www.ot-millau.fr; 1 place du Beffroi; ☼ 9am-7pm Mon-Sat Jul-Aug, 9am-12.30pm & 2-6.30pm Mon-Sat Sep-Jun, 10am-12.30pm & 3-6.30pm Sun Easter-Sep)

Sights

The 42m-tall **beffroi** (belfry; rue Droite; adult/under 19 €2.50/free; ☼ 10am-11am & 2.30-6pm Jul-Aug, 3-5pm 15-30 Jun & Sep) has a square base which dates from the 12th century and tapers into a 17th-century octagonal tower, from where there's a great view.

VIADUC DE MILLAU

This brand-new toll bridge, slung across the wide Tarn Valley to link the Causse du Larzac and Causse Rouge, takes the breath away. Designed by the British architect Sir Norman Foster and due for inauguration in January 2005, it's a true work of industrial art and an amazing feat of engineering. Only seven pylons, hollow and seemingly slim as needles, support 2.5km of four-lane motorway. Rising to 340m above the valley bottom, it ranks among the tallest road bridges in the world.

More than three years in construction, it gobbled up 127,000 cu metres of concrete, 19,000 tonnes of reinforcing steel and 5000 tonnes of cables and stays. Yet despite these heavyweight superlatives, it still looks like a gossamer thread. Far from detracting from the charms of the hitherto unspoilt countryside around the town of Millau, this vital link in the A75 motorway is a true icon for the 21st century.

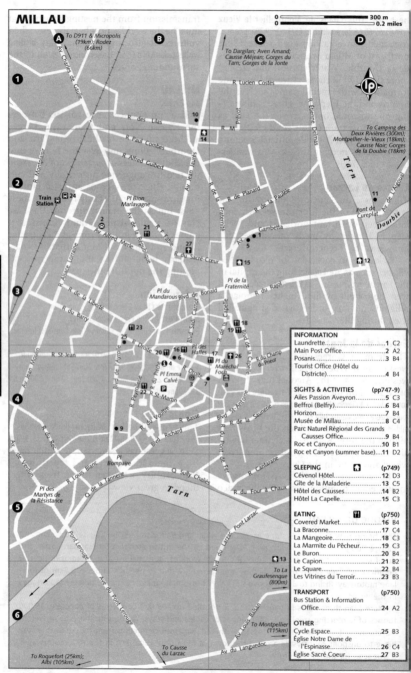

MILLAU

To D911 & Micropolis (19km); Rodez (66km)

To Dargilan; Aven Amand; Causse Méjean; Gorges du Tarn; Gorges de la Jonte

R Lucien Costes

R des Lilas

R Paul Combes

R Alfred Guibert

R M

Train Station

Pl Bion Marlavagné

Av Alfred Merle

Av de la République

Av Jean Jaurès

R de la Fraternité

R de Planard

R de la Pauble

Gambetta

R F Fabre

R du Sacré-Coeur

Pl de la Fraternité

Pl du Mandarous Blvd de Bonald

R du Barry

R Alsace Lorraine

R de la Liberté

Blvd Sadi Carnot

R du Rajol

R de la Capelle

R St-Jean

R Droite

Pl des Halles

Pl du Maréchal Foch

R du Champ du Prieur

R Droite

Pl Emma Calvé

R St-Martin

Blvd de l'Ayrolle

R du Voultre

R Basse

Blvd St-Antoine

R de la Saunerie

Av Jean Moulin

Pl Bompaire

Blvd Richard

R du Pont de Fer

R Capelaure

Av de Verdun

R du Dr Roc

R Louis Blanc

Q de la Tannerie

Tarn

Q Sully Chaliès

R Four à Chaux

Pl des Martyrs de la Résistance

Pont Lerouge

Pont Larzac

Blvd du Larzac

Av du Pont Lerouge

To La Graufesenque (800m)

To Roquefort (25km); Albi (105km)

To Causse du Larzac

Av Louis Balsan

Av du Languedoc

To Montpellier (115km)

To Camping des Deux Rivières (300m); Montpellier-le-Vieux (18km); Causse Noir; Gorges de la Doubie (18km)

Tarn

Doubie

Pont de Cureplat

Av de l'Aigoual

0 — 300 m
0 — 0.2 miles

INFORMATION	
Laundrette............................1	C2
Main Post Office.................2	A2
Posanis..............................3	B4
Tourist Office (Hôtel du Districte)......................4	B4

SIGHTS & ACTIVITIES	(pp747-9)
Ailes Passion Aveyron.........5	C3
Beffroi (Belfry)...................6	B4
Horizon..............................7	B4
Musée de Millau..................8	C4
Parc Naturel Régional des Grands Causses Office.......9	B4
Roc et Canyon...................10	B1
Roc et Canyon (summer base)...11	D2

SLEEPING	(p749)
Cévenol Hôtel....................12	D3
Gîte de la Maladerie...........13	C5
Hôtel des Causses..............14	B2
Hôtel La Capelle.................15	C3

EATING	(p750)
Covered Market..................16	B4
La Braconne......................17	C4
La Mangeoire.....................18	C3
La Marmite du Pêcheur........19	C3
Le Buron...........................20	B4
Le Capion..........................21	B2
Le Square..........................22	B3
Les Vitrines du Terroir.........23	B3

TRANSPORT	(p750)
Bus Station & Information Office............................24	A2

OTHER	
Cycle Espace......................25	B3
Église Notre Dame de l'Espinasse...................26	C4
Église Sacré Coeur.............27	B3

LANGUEDOC-ROUSSILLON

Musée de Millau (☎ 05 65 59 01 08; place du Maréchal Foch; adult/student/under 18 €5/3.50/free; ☺ 10am-6pm daily Jul-Aug, 10am-noon & 2-6pm Apr-Jun & Sep, Mon-Sat Oct-Mar) has a rich collection of fossils, including mammoth molars and a dinosaur skeleton from the Causse du Larzac. In the cellar is a huge array of plates and vases from **La Graufesenque**, in its time the largest pottery workshop in the western Roman Empire. The 1st-floor leather and glove section illustrates Millau's tanneries and their products through the ages.

You can buy a **combined ticket** (€6), which also includes admission to La Graufesenque archaeological site, at the confluence of the Rivers Tarn and Dourbie.

Activities

HANG-GLIDING & PARAPENTE

Companies running introductory courses (average cost €325 to €350 for five or six days) as well as tandem flights (around €65) include:

Ailes Passion Aveyron (☎ 05 65 61 20 96; www.ailes-passion.com in French; 12 av Gambetta)

Horizon (☎ 05 65 59 78 60; www.millau-vol-libre.com; 6 place Lucien Grégoire) Just off place Maréchal Foch. Also offers caving, canyon descents and rock climbing.

Roc et Canyon (☎ 05 65 61 17 77; www.roc-et-canyon.com in French; 55 av Jean Jaurès) In summer you'll find it beside Pont Cureplat. Also on offer is caving, rock climbing, canyon descents, rafting, canoeing – and bungee jumping.

ROCK CLIMBING

The 50m- to 200m-high cliffs of the Gorges de la Jonte are an internationally renowned venue for climbers of all levels – in 2000 Millau hosted the world climbing championships. Both Horizon and Roc et Canyon offer monitored climbs and can put you in touch with local climbers.

WALKING & CYCLING

Pick up a copy of *Les Belles Balades de l'Aveyron* (€8), which is on sale at the tourist office. You can navigate by the explicit maps even if you don't read French. It describes 22 walks around Millau, the Gorges du Tarn and the Grands Causses, all way-marked and varying from 1½ to six hours, and also details 10 mountain-bike and 10 tourer routes.

If you're after more demanding trekking, the GR62 goes over the Causse Noir, passing Montpellier-le-Vieux before winding

down to Millau, while the GR71 and its spurs thread across the Causse du Larzac and through its Templar villages.

Festivals & Events

During mid-August, the four-day *pétanque* world series is held in Millau. Its 16 competitions (including just one for women in this male-dominated sport) attract some 6000 players and even more spectators. Millau hosts a seven-day jazz festival in the third week of July.

Sleeping

Gîte de la Maladerie (☎ 05 65 60 41 84; chemin de la Graufesenque; dm €10) In grounds on the south bank of the Tarn, this friendly gîte is open year-round. On foot, follow the river upstream. If you're driving, turn left (east) after Pont du Larzac.

Hôtel La Capelle (☎ 05 65 60 14 72; fax 05 65 60 22 69; 7 place de la Fraternité; d €26, with bathroom €39-42; ☺ year-round) In the converted wing of a one-time leather factory, La Capelle has new owners, long in the hotel trade and keen to make their mark. The hotel's large terrace with views towards the Causse Noir makes for a perfect breakfast spot.

Hôtel des Causses (☎ 05 65 60 03 19; fax 05 65 60 86 90; 56 av Jean Jaurès; d €40-45; menus €14.50-29) This hotel too has new owners, who have already comprehensively renovated and repainted all 19 rooms. A Logis de France with double glazing throughout, it has a good restaurant with an enticing regional *menu* and several hearty dishes from the Lyon area, the chef/owner's home town.

Cévenol Hôtel (☎ 05 65 60 74 44; www.cevenol-hotel.fr; 115 rue Rajol; d €56-59; ☺ mid-Mar–mid-Nov; P ☺) On the fringe of town, this modern concrete block with its uninspiring exterior is considerably more cosy within. Its 42 rooms – two with disabled access – are spacious (ask for one facing south room, with views over the Causses) and there's a pleasant open-air terrace.

Camping

For visitors in person, the tourist office will make a hotel reservation (€1.50 fee).

Camping des Deux Rivières (☎ 05 65 60 00 27; camping.deux-rivieres@wanadoo.fr; 61 av de l'Aigoual; camping €12; ☺ Apr-Oct) Just east of Pont de Cureplat, this is the closest of several huge riverside camping sites east of town.

Eating

La Braconne (☎ 05 65 60 30 93; 7 place du Maréchal Foch; menus from €15; ☷ closed dinner Sun) This cosy restaurant with an outside terrace overlooking Millau's main square has excellent regional *menus* and is famed for its roast lamb. It has a good selection of Faugères wines.

La Mangeoire (☎ 05 65 60 13 16; 8 blvd de la Capelle; lunch/dinner menu €16/43) This long-established place in the vaults beneath the former city walls serves delightful mainly regional dishes. The lunch *menu* is a midday special but dinner is a mouth-watering gourmet blow-out.

La Marmite du Pêcheur (☎ 05 65 61 20 44; 14-16 blvd de la Capelle; mains €11; ☷ Thu-lunch Tue, closed 22 Jun-1 Jul) A few doors away from la Mangeoire and run by an engaging young couple, it's also attractively vaulted and has hearty regional *menus* within much the same price range. Try the innovative *salade au Roquefort et chataîgnes* (Roquefort and chestnut salad).

Le Square (☎ 05 65 61 26 00; 10 rue St-Martin; menus €16 & €24; ☷ Thu-lunch Tue, closed Wed, dinner Tue & all Mar) It's essential to book at this intimate, highly regarded restaurant with its tempting *menus* and pleasant contemporary décor.

Le Capion (☎ 05 65 60 00 91; 3 rue J-F Alméras; mains 11.50-17, menus €16-35; ☷ closed Wed, dinner Tue & 1-21 Jul) Peer into the kitchen to see the young team at work as you walk past on the way to the main dining room with its warm ochre and salmon colours. Portions are tasty and plentiful – none more so than the rich cheese platter (where, of course, Roquefort stars) and trolley of tempting homemade desserts.

SELF-CATERING

There are **markets** on Wednesday and Friday morning in place du Maréchal Foch, place Emma Calvé and the covered market at place des Halles.

Les Vitrines du Terroir (17 blvd de l'Ayrolle) and **Le Buron** (18 rue Droite) are *fromageries* selling local specialities including Roquefort and Perail du Larzac cheeses.

Getting There & Away

The **bus station and information office** (☎ 05 65 59 89 33) are beside the train station. Buses travel to Toulouse (€24, four hours, one daily), Montpellier (€15.90, 2¼ hours, seven daily), and Rodez (€11, 1½ hours, eight to 10 daily) via Albi (€15.30, 2½ hours).

THE KING OF CHEESES

The mouldy blue-green veins that run through Roquefort are, in fact, the spores of microscopic mushrooms, cultivated on leavened bread.

During the cheese's ripening process – which takes place in natural caves cut in the mountainside – draughts of air called *fleurines* sweep through the cave, encouraging the blue *penicillium roqueforti* to eat its way through the white cheese curds.

Roquefort is one of France's priciest and most noble cheeses. In 1407 Charles VI granted exclusive Roquefort cheese-making rights to the villagers of Roquefort and in the 17th century, the Sovereign Court of the Parliament of Toulouse imposed severe penalties against fraudulent cheese makers trading under the Roquefort name.

Connections from Millau include Béziers (€15.20, 1¾ hours, two to three daily) and Rodez (€10.30, 1½ hours, five to eight daily).

Getting Around

Millau is a compact, walkable town.

'Le Vélo est Mon Métier' ('Bikes are my Business') is the cheery slogan of the young owner of **Cycle Espace** (☎ 05 65 61 14 29; 21 blvd de l'Ayrolle), who supplies chat in plenty for free and cycles at €11/60 per day/week. Roc et Canyon (p749) also rents bikes.

AROUND MILLAU
Roquefort

In the heart of Parc Naturel Régional des Grands Causses and 25km southwest of Millau, the small village of Roquefort-sur-Soulzon turns ewe's milk into France's most famous blue cheese. Its steep, narrow streets, permeated with a cheesy smell, seethe with tourists heading for the cool natural caves, where seven different producers ripen some 22,000 tonnes of Roquefort cheese every year.

La Société (☎ 05 65 59 93 30; www.roquefort-soci ete.com) has 45-minute **guided tours** (adult/under 16 €3/free; ☷ 9.30am-6.30pm Jul-Aug, 9.30am-noon & 1.30-5pm Sep-Jun) that include a rather feeble sound-and-light show and a sample of the three varieties the company makes. Established in 1842, it is the largest Roquefort producer, churning out 70% of the world's supply, 30% of which is exported.

Tours of the equally pungent caves of **Le Papillon** (☎ 05 65 58 50 08; www.roquefort-papillon .com in French; rue de la Fontaine; ✆ 9.30am-6.30pm Jul-Aug, 9.30am-12.30pm & 1.30-4.30pm or 5.30pm Sep-Jun) are free and include a 15-minute film.

Between mid-June and mid-September, you can also visit farms in the area, from which some 130 million litres of ewe's milk are collected annually. For details of tours, contact the **tourist office** (☎ 05 65 58 56 00; www .roquefort.com; ✆ 9am-7pm daily July & Aug; 9am-6pm Mon-Sat Apr-Jun & Sep-Oct; 10am-5pm Mon-Fri Nov-Mar) at the western entry to the village.

Micropolis

'La Cité des Insectes' (Insect City), **Micropolis** (☎ 05 65 58 50 50; www.micropolis.biz; adult/child €9.60/7.10; ✆ 10am-6pm daily Jul-Aug; 10am-5pm Sun-Sun Jun & Sep; 11am-4pm Tue-Fri, 10am-5pm Sat & Sun Mar, May & Oct) is just outside the village of St-Léons, off the D911 19km northwest of Millau.

Ever felt small? This mind-boggling high tech experience happens in a building where grass grows 6m high. The swarms of facts and statistics about insect life, all compellingly presented, seem equally tall but are all true. Admission includes an optional English audiowand and all captions are bilingual. Allow a good 1½ hours, perhaps rounding off with a meal at its pleasant, reasonably priced restaurant.

ROUSSILLON

Roussillon, sometimes known as French Catalonia, sits on Spain's doorstep at the eastern end of the Pyrenees. It's the land of the Tramontane, a violent wind which howls down from the mountains, chilling to the bone in winter and in summer strong enough to overturn a caravan. The main city is Perpignan, capital of the Pyrénées-Orientales *département*.

Long part of Catalonia (which nowadays officially designates only the autonomous region over the border in northeast Spain), Roussillon retains many symbols of Catalan identity. The *sardane* folk dance is still performed and the Catalan language (closely related to Occitan – which is also known as Provençal) is widely spoken.

History

People have lived here since prehistoric times, and one of Europe's oldest skulls was found in a cave near Tautavel (p756).

Roussillon's relatively modern history was for a long time closely bound with events over the Pyrenees in present-day Spain. In 1172 it came under the control of the realm of Catalonia-Aragon. Then, flourishing in its own right as the capital of the kingdom of Mallorca for most of the next two centuries, it again came under alien Aragonese rule for much of the late Middle Ages.

In 1640 the Catalans on both sides of the Pyrenees revolted against the Castilian kings in distant Madrid, who had engulfed Aragon. Perpignan endured a two-year siege, which was only relieved with the help of the French to the north. The subsequent 1659 Treaty of the Pyrenees defined the border between Spain and France once and for all, ceding the northern section of Catalonia, Roussillon, to the French, much to the indignation of the locals.

Geography

Roussillon occupies the southern end of the Lower Languedoc plain. Its highest point is Mont Canigou (2786m), a peak revered by the Catalan people. The flat coastline ends abruptly at the rocky foothills of the Pyrenees, backdrop to the Côte Vermeille (Vermilion Coast), a coastal area of deep-red rocks and soil that inspired Fauvist artists such as Matisse and Derain.

PERPIGNAN
pop 108,000

As much Catalan as French, Perpignan (Perpinyà in Catalan) was, from 1278 to 1344, capital of the kingdom of Mallorca, which stretched northwards as far as Montpellier and included the Balearic Islands. The town later became an important commercial centre and remains the third-largest Catalan city after Barcelona and Lleida in Spain.

It isn't southern France's most attractive city though it's far from a 'villainous ugly town' – the verdict of traveller Henry Swinburne in 1775. At the foothills of the Pyrenees and with the Côte Vermeille to the southeast, it makes a great base for day trips along the coast or to the mountains and Cathar castles of the interior.

LANGUEDOC-ROUSSILLON

PERPIGNAN

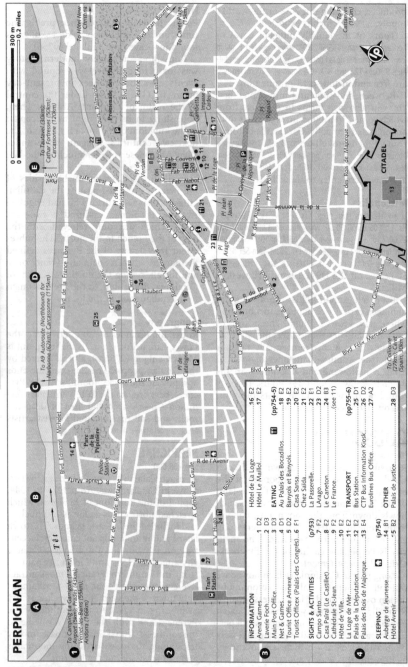

INFORMATION
Arena Games...............................1 D2
Laverie Foch...............................2 D3
Main Post Office...........................3 D3
Net & Games...............................4 D1
Tourist Office Annexe......................5 D2
Tourist Office (Palais des Congrès)........6 F1

SIGHTS & ACTIVITIES (p753)
Campo Santo...............................7 F2
Casa Pairal (Le Castillet).................8 E2
Cathédrale St-Jean.........................9 F2
Hôtel de Ville............................10 E2
La Loge de Mer............................11 E2
Palais de la Députation...................12 E2
Palais des Rois de Majorque...............13 E4

SLEEPING (p754)
Auberge de Jeunesse.......................14 B1
Hôtel Avenir..............................5 B2

Hôtel de La Loge.........................16 E2
Hôtel Le Maillol.........................17 E2

EATING (pp754-5)
Au Palais des Bocadillos.................18 E2
Banyols et Banyols.......................19 E2
Casa Sansa...............................20 E2
Chez Saïda...............................21 E2
La Passerelle............................22 E1
L'Arago..................................23 D2
Le Caneton...............................24 B3
Le France................................(see 11)

TRANSPORT (pp755-6)
Bus Station..............................25 D1
CTP Bus Information Kiosk................26 D2
Eurolines Bus Office.....................27 A2

OTHER
Palais de Justice........................28 D3

It's also commendably well documented – outside every major historical building is a freestanding sign with information in French, Catalan and English.

Orientation
Two rivers flow through the city: the Têt and its tributary, the narrow, crystal-clear Basse, banked with trim gardens. The heart of the partly pedestrianised old town lies around place de la Loge and place de Verdun.

Information

INTERNET ACCESS
Arena Games (9bis rue Docteur Pous; per hr €3; ⏲ 11am-2am Tue-Sat, 3pm-1am Sun & Mon)
Net & Games (45bis av Général Leclerc; per hr €3; ⏲ noon-1am Mon-Sat, 1-8pm Sun)

LAUNDRY
Laverie Foch (23 rue du Maréchal Foch; ⏲ 7am-8.30pm)

POST
Main Post Office (quai de Barcelone)

TOURIST INFORMATION
Tourist Office (☎ 04 68 66 30 30; www.perpignan tourisme.com; ⏲ 9am-7pm Mon-Sat, 10am-4pm Sun mid-Jun–mid-Sep; 9am-6pm Mon-Sat, 9am-noon Sun mid-Sep–mid-Jun) In the Palais des Congrès, off promenade des Platanes.
Tourist Office Annexe (⏲ Oct-May; Espace Palmarium, place Arago)

Sights

PLACE DE LA LOGE
Place de la Loge has three fine stone structures. **La Loge de Mer** was constructed in the 14th century and rebuilt during the Renaissance. At various times Perpignan's stock exchange and maritime tribunal, its ground floor is now occupied by the splendid café-restaurant le France (p754). Sandwiched between it and the **Palais de la Deputation**, once seat of the local parliament, is the **Hôtel de Ville** with its typically Roussillon pebbled façade of river stones. Pass by on Sunday morning and you can watch locals of all ages dancing the graceful *sardane*, folk dance of the Catalans.

LE CASTILLET & CASA PAÏRAL
The museum of Roussillon and Catalan folklore, **Casa Païral** (☎ 04 68 35 42 05; place de Verdun; adult/student €4/2; ⏲ 10am-6.30pm Wed-Mon May-Sep, 11am-5.30pm Wed-Mon Oct-Apr), occupies Le Castillet, a 14th-century red-brick town gate. Once a prison, it's the only vestige of Vauban's fortified town walls, which surrounded the city until the early 1900s. The museum houses bits and pieces of everything Catalan – from traditional bonnets and lace mantillas to a 17th-century kitchen. From the rooftop terrace there are great views of the old city and citadel.

PALAIS DES ROIS DE MAJORQUE
The **Palais des Rois de Majorque** (Palace of the Kings of Mallorca; ☎ 04 68 34 48 29; entrance on rue des Archers; adult/child €4/2; ⏲ 10am-5pm or 6pm) sits on a small hill. Built in 1276 for the ruler of the newly founded kingdom, it was at one time surrounded by extensive fig and olive groves and a hunting reserve, which were lost once Vauban's formidable citadel walls enclosed the palace.

Bizarre but true: the princes of Aragon used to keep lions in the dried-up moat of the castle and the goats that constituted the lions' diet grazed the surrounding meadows, from which commoners' flocks were banned.

CATHÉDRALE ST-JEAN
Topped by a typically Provençal wrought-iron bell cage, **Cathédrale St-Jean** (place Gambetta; ⏲ 9am-noon & 3-6.30pm), begun in 1324 and not completed until 1509, has a flat façade of red brick and smooth river stones in a zigzag pattern. Inside the cavernous single nave, notice particularly the fine carving and relative sobriety of the Catalan altarpiece.

Immediately south of the cathedral (leave by a small door in the south aisle) is the early-14th-century **Campo Santo** (⏲ noon-7pm Tue-Sat Apr-Jun & Sep, 11am-5pm Oct-Mar, closed Jul & Aug), France's only cloister-cemetery, lined with white-marble Gothic niches.

Festivals & Events
As befits a town so close to the Spanish border, Perpignan is strong on fiestas.

For the Good Friday **Procession de la Sanch**, penitents wearing the *caperutxa* (traditional hooded red or black robes) parade silently through the old city. A 'sacred' flame is brought down from Mont Canigou during the week-long **Fête de la St-Jean**, marking midsummer, while in September half the town dons tights and wimples for the **Marché Médiéval** (Medieval Market).

Shutterbugs will be in their element in the first half of September, when, for a full two weeks, the town hosts **Visa Pour l'Image**, the world's major festival of photojournalism, open to the general public.

Perpignan holds a **jazz festival** throughout October and, on the third weekend in October, a **wine festival**, when a barrel of the year's new wine is ceremonially borne to Cathédrale St-Jean to be blessed.

Sleeping

Auberge de Jeunesse (☎ 04 68 34 63 32; fax 04 68 51 16 02; allée Marc Pierre; dm €8.90; ♥ late-Jan–mid-Dec) Perpignan's HI-affiliated youth hostel is just north of Parc de la Pépinière.

Hôtel Avenir (☎ 04 68 34 20 30; www.avenirhotel .com; 11 rue de l'Avenir; s/d €16/21, d with bathroom from €33.60; **P**) Among the string of budget hotels along and around av Général de Gaulle the Avenir is a particularly friendly, highly recommended place. Several rooms have a small terrace and each is uniquely and charmingly decorated by the proprietor. Savour too the delightful first-floor terrace.

Hôtel New Christina (☎ 04 68 35 12 21; www .hotel-newchristina.com; 51 cours Lassus; s/d €62/67; **P** ✕ 🏊) At the excellent, family-run New Christina, rooms are attractively decorated in blue and beige and bathrooms, all with bathtubs, are separate from toilets. Those at the front overlook a public park. The open-air pool, up on the roof, has an even better view. There's also a decent restaurant (*menu* €20).

Hôtel Le Maillol (☎ 04 68 51 10 20; hotel.lemai llol@worldonline.fr; 14 impasse des Cardeurs; d €36-41) Occupying a 17th-century building, Le Maillol, at the end of a cul-de-sac off a pedestrian street, couldn't be more tranquil. Of its smallish but quite adequate rooms on three floors, those overlooking the interior patio have more light.

Hôtel de La Loge (☎ 04 68 34 41 02; www.hotel delaloge.fr; 1 rue des Fabriques Nabot; s €37 d €42-64) Disregard the threadbare stair carpet; the bedrooms themselves are a good deal more pleasant though their furniture varies from attractive and antique to flea market. Of the more expensive rooms, which have air-con and separate toilets, Nos 106 and 206 (each €57) overlook place de la Loge.

Camping

Camping La Garrigole (☎ 04 68 54 66 10; 2 rue Maurice Lévy; camping €13; ♥ year-round) This small camping ground is 1.5km west of the train station. Take bus No 2 and get off at the Garrigole stop.

Eating

Au Palais des Bocadillos (☎ 04 68 35 36 08; place de Verdun; ♥ 7.30am-9.30pm) Planted in one of the old quarter's main squares, the Sandwich Palace serves up a variety of superior sandwiches and baguettes plus a plat du jour, all of which you can eat in or take away.

Chez Saïda (☎ 06 71 82 74 82; 5 rue Lazare Escarguel; mains €10-16) Recently opened, this tiny place specialises in reasonably priced seafood plus, in summer, crunchy salads. You can slurp down a plate of oysters or indulge in a variety of seafood platters, such as their plentiful Étoile.

Le France (☎ 04 68 51 61 71; place de la Loge; mains €13-32; ♥ lunch Mon-Sun) Popular and stylish, Le France manages to blend harmoniously the modern – right down to the all-glass hand basins in the toilets – within a historical setting. Portions are smallish but attractively presented and the wine list is almost as vast as the palatial setting of what was once Perpignan's stock exchange. The lunchtime *formule rapide* (quick *menu*) at €12.50 is great value.

L'Arago (☎ 04 68 51 81 96; 1 place Arago; mains €12.50-18) Here's another restaurant that's much in demand so you may have to hang around a while for a free table. It does pizzas (€7.70 to €9.40) and has a strong and

---

AUTHOR'S CHOICE

Banyols et Banyols (☎ 04 68 34 48 40; 7 rue des Cardeurs; mains €13-18; ♥ Tue-Sat) This recently opened restaurant, stripped back to its brick and girders may be small but it's delightfully light and airy. The chef/owner moves among diners speaking with passion about his cooking before darting back to the kitchen area to stir a sauce, shake a pan and advise his minions, all in full view of the diners. The creative menu changes regularly; do start with the risotto with chestnuts and prawns if it still features. Banyols et Banyols? It's the family name of this talented father and daughter team.

varied à la carte selection. Sample its fine local wines, sold by the glass or bottle.

Casa Sansa (☎ 04 68 34 21 84; entrances 2 rue des Fabriques Nadal & rue des Fabriques Couvertes; mains €12.50-16) This is another highly popular place – or rather two adjacent places. Choose the older, more southerly one, its walls scarcely visible for posters and the photos of the famous and less than famous who have enjoyed its fine Catalan cuisine. It too has a great selection of wines, also available by the glass.

La Passerelle (☎ 04 68 51 30 65; 1 cours Palma-role; mains €16-22; ☾ dinner Mon-Sat) Its attractive marine décor hints at the riches within the kitchen. La Passerelle is *the* restaurant in Perpignan for Mediterranean fish, guaranteed fresh and without a whiff of freezer or fish farm.

Near the train station are plenty of cheap-and-cheerful options, including Arab, Turkish and Alsacien joints. **Le Caneton** (☎ 04 68 34 20 60; 12 rue Victor Hugo; menu €5; ☾ lunch Mon-Fri) must rank as one of France's best-value and tiniest restaurants. It's little more than a room in a private house run by a doughty old couple who do a daily three-course *menu*.

Entertainment

The tourist office publishes *L'Agenda*, a comprehensive free monthly guide to exhibitions and cultural events. *Aware, Le Mag* is one of several competing free, what's-on breakdowns of the club scene and nightlife.

Getting There & Away

AIR

Perpignan's **airport** (☎ 04 68 52 60 70) is 5km northwest of the town centre. Air France flies three to four times daily to/from Paris (Orly) while Ryanair runs a daily flight to/from London Stansted.

BUS

From the **bus station** (☎ 04 68 35 29 02; av Général Leclerc), **Courriers Catalans** services coastal resorts, running two to seven buses daily (€6.60) to/from Collioure and Port-Vendres, most continuing to Banyuls (1¼ hours).

Seven buses daily travel along the Têt Valley to Vernet-les-Bains (€9.60, 1½ hours) via Prades (€8.15) and Villefranche (€9.60) and three of these continue as far as La Tour de Carol (€12.60). Up the Tech Valley, there are up to nine buses daily to Céret (€5.80, 50 minutes).

For long-distance buses, the **Eurolines office** (☎ 04 68 34 11 46; 10 av Général de Gaulle) is just east of the train station.

CAR

Rental companies include **ADA** (airport ☎ 04 68 61 50 95) and **Budget** (airport ☎ 04 68 61 38 85).

TRAIN

Perpignan's small train station – centre of the universe according to Salvador Dalí (below) – is served by bus Nos 2 and 19.

Major destinations include Barcelona (€30 direct, €15 change at Cerbère/Portbou, up to three hours, three daily). There are frequent trains to Montpellier (€19.20, two hours) via Narbonne (€9, 45 minutes) and Béziers (€11.90). For Paris (€68 to €91), change in Montpellier; for Carcassonne (€15.60), in Narbonne.

Closer to home is Cerbère/Portbou on the Spanish border (€6.60, 40 minutes, approximately 15 daily) via Banyuls, Collioure and Port-Vendres.

The nearest you can get to Andorra by train is La Tour de Carol (€20.30, four hours, two to four daily, some changing in Villefranche) via Prades (€6.30, 40 minutes) and Villefranche (€7, at least six daily). From La Tour de Carol, a connecting bus takes you on to Andorra.

Getting Around

The local bus company, CTP, has an **information kiosk** (☎ 04 68 61 01 13; 27 blvd Clemenceau).

DALÍ'S TRAIN OF THOUGHT

You may choose to dissent from Salvador Dalí's no doubt chemically induced claim that Perpignan's train station is the centre of the universe. According to local lore (reinforced by a plaque in front of the building), the Catalan surrealist painter (1904–89) was visiting the capital of French Catalonia in 1965 when he experienced an epiphany 'Suddenly before me, everything appeared with the clarity of lightning,' he wrote. 'I found myself in the centre of the universe.' Dalí went on to describe this nondescript place as *'la source d'illuminations'* and *'la cathédrale d'intuitions'* – no doubt putting a smile on the faces of local tourism authorities and most Perpignanais.

LANGUEDOC-ROUSSILLON

One ticket costs €1.10, a one-day pass *(ticket visite)* is €4.10 and a 10-ticket *carnet*, €7.80.

Bright yellow and red, *Le P'tit Bus* is a free minibus that plies a circular route around the old town. It runs about every five minutes from 8am to 7pm, Monday to Saturday, except – come on now, we're in France! – between 12.30pm and 1.30pm.

For a taxi, call **Accueil Perpignan Taxis** (☎ 04 68 35 15 15).

AROUND PERPIGNAN
Coastal Beaches

The nearest beach – all 5km of it – is at **Canet-Plage**, backed by a sprawl of hotels and apartment blocks. There's a small **tourist office** (☎ 04 68 86 72 00; 9am-7pm daily Jul-Aug; 9am-noon & 2-6pm Mon-Sat, 10am-noon & 3-5pm Sun Sep-Jun). Rent a bicycle (€12.50 per day) from **Sun Bike 66** (☎ 04 68 73 88 65) and cruise the promenade or ride around the Étang de Canet, a small inland lake and nature reserve.

From Argelès-Plage south, wide sandy beaches give way to rocky coastline as the Pyrenees tumble to the sea, their steep flanks terraced with vineyards.

Céret

It's mainly the **Musée d'Art Moderne** (☎ 04 68 87 27 76; 8 blvd Maréchal Joffre; adult/student/child €8/6/free; 10am-6pm or 7pm Wed-Mon) that draws visitors to this town of 8000 souls, settled snugly in the Pyrenee foothills just off the Tech Valley. Superbly endowed for such a small community, its collection owes much to an earlier generation of visitors and residents, including Picasso, Braque, Chagall, Matisse, Miró, Dalí, Juan Gris and Manolo, all of whom donated works (53 from Picasso alone).

Firmly Catalan, Céret is also splendidly disproportionate in the number and vigour of its festivals. Famous for its juicy cherries (the first pickings of the season are packed off to the French president), it kicks off with the **Fête de la Cerise** (Cherry Festival) in late May. Summer sees the **féria** with bullfights and roistering and **La Fête de la Sardane**, celebrating the *sardane*, folk dance par excellence of the Catalans – and, of course, yet more bullfights. More sedately, **Les Méennes** is a festival of primarily classical music. Contact the **tourist office** (☎ 04 68 87 00 53; www.ot-ceret.fr; 1 av Clemenceau) for details.

Tautavel

The Arago Cave, on the slopes above the village of Tautavel, 30km northwest of Perpignan along the D117, has yielded a human skull, estimated to be 450,000 years old, along with many other prehistoric items.

THE CATHARS

The term *le Pays Cathar* (Cathar Land) recalls the cruel Albigensian Crusade – the hounding and extermination of a religious sect called the Cathars.

Cathars (from the Greek word *katharos* meaning 'pure') believed that God's kingdom was locked in battle with Satan's evil world and that humans were evil at heart. But, they reckoned, a pure life followed by several reincarnations would free the spirit from its satanical body. The ascetic *parfaits* ('perfects') followed strict vegetarian diets and abstained from sex.

Catharism spread from the Balkans to Languedoc between the 11th and 13th centuries. Reacting against worldly Rome and preaching in *langue d'oc*, the local tongue, the sect gained many followers.

In 1208 Pope Innocent III preached a crusade against the Cathars, who were closely associated with the Albigenses, a sect based in the city of Albi. The Albigensian Crusade was a chance for northern rulers to expand their territory into Languedoc, supported spiritually by St-Dominic of Toulouse, founder of the Dominican order of monks, and in the field by the cruel Simon de Montfort.

After long sieges, the major Cathar centres at Béziers, Carcassonne, the village of Minerve and the dramatically sited fortresses of Montségur, Quéribus and Peyrepertuse were taken and hundreds of 'perfects' were burned as heretics. In Béziers as many as 20,000 of the faithful were slaughtered. Another cruel massacre took place at Montségur in 1244, when 200 Cathars, refusing to renounce their faith when the castle was captured after a 10-month siege, were burned alive in a mass funerary pyre. In 1321 the burning of the last 'perfect', Guillaume Bélibaste, marked the end of Catharism in Languedoc.

Musée de la Préhistoire (Prehistory Museum; ☎ 04 68 29 07 76; av Jean Jaurès; admission €7; ☼ 10am-8pm Jul-Aug; 10.30am-12.30pm & 1.30-5pm Apr-Jun & Sep; 1.30-5.30pm Feb-Mar, Oct-Nov; Mon only Dec-Jan) has a full-size reproduction of the cave, complete with holograms, dioramas, TVs dispensing knowledge from every corner and lots of fossilised bones and stone tools. The audio-wand (included in the admission fee) has an English channel. There's also a secondary exhibition (ask for the English-language sheet 'The First Inhabitants of Europe'), 300m away on rue Anatole France. Allow a good 1½ hours to take in both elements.

Cathar Fortresses

When the Albigensian Crusade forced the Cathars into the arid mountains that once marked the frontier between France and Aragon, they sought refuge in these inaccessible fortresses. The most famous are **Peyrepertuse** (adult/child €4/2; ☼ 8.30am-8.30pm Jun-Sep, 10am-5pm Feb-Mar & Nov-Dec, 9am-7pm Apr-May & Oct) and **Quéribus** (adult/child €5/2; ☼ 9am-8pm Jul-Aug, 9.30am-6.30pm or 7.30pm Apr-Jun & Sep-Oct, 10am-5pm Jan-Feb & Nov-Dec). Off the D117 about 50km northwest of Perpignan, they can be combined in a day trip that takes in the Musée de la Préhistoire in Tautavel (above) as well. Both, alas, are all but inaccessible without your own wheels.

The larger, Peyrepertuse, approached along the twisting, narrow Gorges de Galamus and occupying one of the most dramatic sites of any castle anywhere, squats high on a ridge with a drop of several hundred metres on all sides. Quéribus, perched precariously at 728m on a rocky spur, marked the Cathars' last stand in 1255.

It's wild country and views from both make the pulse race. They can be hot as hell in summer so be sure to pack extra water.

TÊT VALLEY

Fruit orchards carpet the lower reaches of the Têt Valley. Beyond the strategic fortress town of Villefranche-le-Confluent, the scenery becomes wilder, more open and undulating as the valley climbs towards Spanish Catalonia and Andorra.

Le Train Jaune

Carrying nearly half a million passengers during the three peak months of high summer, **Le Train Jaune** (Yellow Train) runs from Villefranche to La Tour de Carol (return €32) through spectacular Pyrenean scenery. There are five trains daily in July and August, four in June and September and two between October and May. You can't reserve and it's wise to arrive an hour before departure time in high summer.

Prades

pop 6000

Prades, at the heart of the Têt Valley, is internationally famed for its annual music festival. It's an attractive town with houses of river stone and brick, liberally adorned with pink marble from nearby quarries.

The exceptionally friendly **tourist office** (☎ 04 68 05 41 02; www.prades-tourisme.com; ☼ 9am-noon & 2-6pm Mon-Sat, 10am-noon Sun Jul-Aug; 9am-noon & 2-5pm Mon-Fri Sep-Jun, 9am-noon Sat Jun & Sep) is at 4 rue des Marchands.

The belltower of **Église St-Pierre** is all that remains of the original 12th-century Romanesque church. The wonderfully expressive 17th-century *Entombment of Christ* at the western end (the light switch is just to the right) is by the Catalan sculptor Josep Sunyer, who also carved the exuberant main altarpiece, a *chef d'oeuvre* of Catalan Baroque and reputedly the largest in France.

The small **Musée de la Soie** (Silk Museum; ☎ 04 68 96 33 75; av Général Roques; adult/child €6/4; ☼ 10am-7pm daily Jul-Aug; 10am-noon & 2-6pm Tue-Sun Apr-Jun & Sep-Oct) evokes Prades' past as a producer of cocoons for Perpignan's silk industry.

ACTIVITIES

Hiking & Walking Around Prades details in English 20 easy-to-moderate walks lasting from 2½ to four hours. *Six Grandes Randonnées en Conflent* in French describes six more challenging day walks, including the classic ascent of Mont Canigou (2786m). The tourist office sells both guides at €3 each.

VTT en Conflent details nine mountain-bike routes varying from easy to seriously tough. **Cycles Flament** (☎ 04 68 96 07 62; 8 rue Arago) rents out mountain bikes.

The **Festival Pablo Casals** (☎ 04 68 96 33 07; festival.casals@wanadoo.fr), held over two weeks in late July/early August, brings top-flight classical musicians to this small town.

Villefranche-de-Conflent

Villefranche, sitting at the strategic confluence of the valley of the Rivers Têt and Cady

LANGUEDOC-ROUSSILLON

(hence the 'de Conflent' of its name), is encircled by thick fortifications, built by Vauban in the 17th century to strengthen and augment the original 11th-century defences, which have survived intact.

The small **tourist office** (☎ 04 68 96 22 96; www.villefranche-de-conflent.com in French; 32bis rue St-Jacques; ⏰ 10am-1pm & 2-6pm May-Oct; 10.30am-12.30pm & 2-5.30pm Feb-Mar & Nov-Dec, closed Jan) arranges admission to the **ramparts** (adult/student/child €4/3/free; audioguide €3).

The stronghold high above the town, built originally by Vauban (p30) and strengthened under Napoleon III, is the heavily promoted **Château-Fort Liberia** (☎ 04 68 96 34 01; admission €5.50; ⏰ 10am-8pm Apr-Oct, 10am-6pm Nov-Mar), from where there are spectacular views.

Vernet-les-Bains
pop 1500

Busy in summer and almost a ghost town for the rest of the year, this small spa was much frequented by the British aristocracy in the late 19th century (there's still a small Anglican church). Nowadays, it's an alternative to Prades for hiking and, particularly, for attacking **Mont Canigou**, the Pyrenees' easternmost major peak. Three tracks wind up from Vernet. To bag the summit the easy way, bounce up in a 4x4 (about €25 per person return) with **Sport Garage Villaceque** (☎ 04 68 05 51 14; rue du Conflent) or **Jean-Paul Bouzon** (☎ 04 68 05 62 68; 17 blvd des Pyrénées) as far as Les Cortalets (2175m), from where the summit is a three-hour round trip.

Vernet's **tourist office** (☎ 04 68 05 55 35; www .ot-vernet-les-bains.fr) is on place de l'Ancienne Mairie.

CÔTE VERMEILLE

The Côte Vermeille (Vermilion Coast) runs south from Collioure to Cerbère on the Spanish border, where the Pyrenees foothills reach the sea. Against a backdrop of vineyards and pinched between Mediterranean and mountains, it's riddled with small, rocky bays and little ports. These once engaged in sardine and anchovy fishing but now have economies based primarily on tourism.

Resorts are served by regular train and less frequent bus services (p755).

Collioure
pop 2930

In picturesque Collioure, boats bob against a backdrop of houses washed in soft pastel colours. Once Perpignan's port, it found fame early this century when it inspired the Fauvist art of Henri Matisse and André Derain. Later both Picasso and Braque came here to paint (below).

The **tourist office** (☎ 04 68 82 15 47; www.col lioure.com; ⏰ 9am-8pm Mon-Sat, 10am-noon & 3-6pm Sun Jul-Aug; 9am-noon & 2-7pm Mon-Sat May-Jun & Sep; 2-6pm Mon, 9am-noon & 2-6pm Tue-Fri, 9am-noon Sat Oct-Apr) is on place 18 Juin.

Across the creek is the **Château Royal de Collioure** (☎ 04 68 82 06 43; adult/child €4/2; ⏰ 10am-6pm Jun-Sep, 9am-5pm Oct-May). Originally a Templar settlement built upon Roman foundations, the castle enjoyed its greatest splendour as the summer residence of the kings of Mallorca. Vauban added its towering defensive walls in the 17th century.

The medieval church tower of **Notre Dame des Anges** at the northern end of the harbour once doubled up as a lighthouse (the pink dome that gives it the air of a giant penis was

---

THE FAUVISTES & COLLIOURE

'No sky in all France is more blue than that of Collioure. I only have to close the shutters of my room and there before me are all the colours of the Mediterranean.' So effused Henri Matisse (1869–1954), instigator and chief exponent of Fauvism.

The movement briefly embraced many of the principal artists of the day such as Georges Rouault, Raoul Dufy and Georges Braque. Reacting against impressionism, Les Fauves (The Wild Ones) worked with pure colour. Stripping a scene to its most basic elements, they abandoned perspective, filling their canvases with firm lines and stripes, rectangles and splashes of bright colour.

The **Chemin du Fauvisme** (Fauvism Trail) is a walking route around Collioure that passes 20 reproductions of works by Matisse and his younger colleague André Derain. You can pick up a French-language guide booklet (€5.50) from the tourist office or from **Espace Fauve** (quai de l'Amirauté), which does guided tours (€6) of Collioure during school holidays.

added in 1810). Inside is a superb altarpiece, crafted by the Catalan master Josep Sunyer.

The **Musée d'Art Moderne** (☎ 04 68 82 10 19; Villa Pams, route de Port-Vendres; adult/child €2/1.50; ☻ 10am-noon & 2-6pm or 7pm; closed Tue Oct-May) is another stimulating stop for contemporary art lovers.

To sample and pick up some of the best local Collioure wine, visit **La Maison de la Vigne et du Vin** (☎ 04 68 82 49 00; ☻ daily Jul-Sep; weekends May-Jun) in the place de la Mairie.

Collioure's Good Friday procession of hooded penitents is about the richest this side of the Pyrenees. Altogether more joyous are **Fêtes de la St-Vincent** (14-18 August), celebrations in honour of the town's patron saint, their highlight a spectacular firework display on the 16th.

From May to September, leave your car in Parking Relais and take the shuttle bus that runs to the village every 10 minutes. For the rest of the year, there's a large car park behind the castle.

Port-Vendres

Three kilometres south of Collioure, Port-Vendres, Roussillon's only natural harbour and deep-water port, has been exploited ever since Greek mariners roamed the rocky coastline. A significant entrepôt until the independence of France's North African territories in the 1960s, it remains an important coastal fishing and leisure port, though it is the least interesting of the Côte Vermeille resorts. The small **tourist office** (☎ 04 68 82 07 54; 1 quai François Joly; www .port-vendres.com) is in the port's northwestern corner.

Banyuls
pop 5000
Banyuls, 7km south of Port-Vendres, has a small pebble beach, overlooked by the **tourist office** (☎ 04 68 88 31 58; www.banyuls-sur-mer.com; av de la République; ☻ 9am-8pm daily Jul-Aug, 9am-noon & 2.30-6pm Mon-Sat Sep-Jun). The town is the starting point for the GR10, the long distance trail that snakes along the Pyrenees all the way to Hendaye, beside the Atlantic.

At the promenade's southern limit is the **Aquarium du Laboratoire Arago** (☎ 04 68 88 73 39; adult/child €4.20/2.10; ☻ 9am-1pm & 2-9pm Jul-Aug, 9am-noon & 2-6.30pm Sep-Jun). Much more than yet another commercial enterprise with smiling dolphins, it also functions as the oceanographic research station of Paris' Université Pierre et Marie Curie.

More strenuously aquatic but well worth the effort, staff of the **Réserve Naturelle Marine** (Marine Nature Reserve; ☎ 04 68 88 56 87) have mounted a splendid initiative – a 250m **underwater 'trail'** (admission free; ☻ noon-6pm Jul-Aug) that you snorkel around. Just off Plage de Peyrefite, midway between Banyuls and Cerbère, it's punctuated by information points and you can hire fins and masks (€5) up to 5pm (if you have your own gear, you can swim the trail at any time).

LANGUEDOC-ROUSSILLON

Provence

CONTENTS

Marseille Region	**763**
Marseille	763
Aix-en-Provence	776
The Vaucluse	**783**
Avignon	783
Around Avignon	791
Orange	791
Vaison-la-Romaine	793
Mont Ventoux	795
Carpentras	796
Fontaine de Vaucluse	797
Gordes	798
Around Gordes	799
Roussillon	799
Apt & the Lubéron	799
Arles & the Camargue	**800**
Arles	800
The Camargue	806
Northeastern Provence	**810**
Digne-les-Bains	810
Gorges du Verdon	812
Pra-Loup & La Foux d'Allos	814

PROVENCE

First-time visitors may be as captivated by the beauty of this ruggedly lovely chunk of France as the painter Van Gogh was when he arrived from a gloomy Paris in 1888. 'What intensity of colours, what pure air, what vibrant serenity,' he wrote. He wasn't wrong. That colourful intensity in land, sea and sky is brought out by the glorious sun. Along the coast, its rays lend the sea gem-like blues and greens. Inland, the hues are more subtle: roofs in improbably pretty ochres and terracottas and serried rows of lavender.

It's a culturally and historically rich region, too. Van Gogh wasn't the first, or last, painter, writer or thinker to fall for Provence. Its towns and cities are dotted with galleries containing the works of Europe's most celebrated artists.

The Romans were among the first to spot its charms, invading it then sending their favourite legions to retire here. They left many unmissable monuments behind, including theatres and thermal baths (some still in use) in places such as Arles (p802), Aix (p779), Orange (p792) and Vaison-la-Romaine (p794).

Towns boast generous public spaces – just as they did under Augustus. It's an outdoor life, perhaps spent sipping *pastis* (a liquorice-flavoured aperitif) in cafés or playing *pétanque*, a type of bowls using heavy metal balls, under the shade of the region's plane trees.

The area has its own distinct smells and flavours, best experienced in the sensory trance that a visit to a Provençal market induces. The region's abundant fresh produce and seafood are best accompanied with a fresh rosé wine, a delightful and inexpensive local speciality.

HIGHLIGHTS

- Savour **bouillabaisse** (p770), Marseille's fishy speciality
- Smell, taste and buy the best local produce at one of the region's many **superb markets** (p776)
- Walking or cycling in the lovely **Parc Naturel Régional du Lubéron** (p800)
- Get down and boogy in **Aix's lively nightlife** (p782)
- Discover the many gems of Renaissance art at Avignon's **Musée du Petit Palais** (p786)
- Submerge yourself in the thermal baths and spas in **Aix-en-Provence** (p779) or **Digne-les-Bains** (p811)
- Tackle rock climbing, canyoning, canoeing and hiking in the **Gorges du Verdon** (p813)
- Peeking at the **Camargue's abundant bird life** (p806)

| POPULATION: 4,632,600 | AREA: 25,851 SQ KM |

PROVENCE

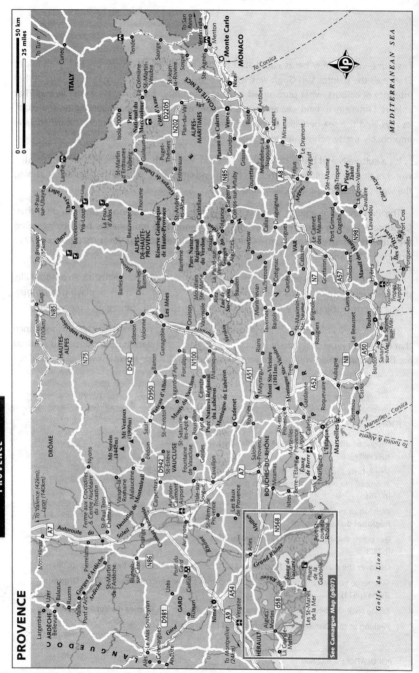

See Camargue Map (p807)

History

Provence was settled over the centuries by the Ligurians, the Celts and the Greeks, but really began to flourish under the Romans after its conquest by Julius Caesar in the mid-1st century BC. The Romans called the area between the Alps, the sea and the River Rhône Provincia Romana, from which the name Provence is derived.

After the collapse of the Roman Empire in the late 5th century, Provence suffered invasions by the Visigoths, Burgundians and the Ostrogoths. The Arabs – who for some time held the Iberian Peninsula and parts of France – were defeated in the 8th century.

During the 14th century, the Catholic Church – under a series of French-born popes – moved its headquarters from feud-riven Rome to Avignon, thus beginning the most resplendent period in that city's history. Provence became part of France in 1481, but Avignon and Comtat Venaissin, with its seat at Carpentras, remained under papal control until the Revolution.

Geography

Provence stretches along both sides of the River Rhône from just north of Orange down to the Mediterranean, and along France's southern coast from the Camargue salt marshes in the west to Marseille in the east. Beyond Marseille is the Côte d'Azur, which, though historically part of Provence, appears in a separate chapter in this book along with Monaco.

South of Arles, the Camargue marshlands – actually the delta of the Rhône – are within a triangle formed by the Grand Rhône to the east and the Petit Rhône to the west.

Most of the region's mountains and hills lie east of the Rhône: the Baronnies; 1909m Mont Ventoux; the Vaucluse plateau; the rugged Lubéron Range and the little Alpilles. Further east is Europe's most spectacular canyon, the Gorges du Verdon.

Climate

Provence's weather is bright, sunny and dry for much of the year, although when the cold, dry winds of the mistral strike southwards down the Rhône Valley – often with surprising fury and little warning – they can turn a fine spring day into a bone-chilling wintry one.

The mistral – formed by the coincidence of high-pressure air over central France and low-pressure air over the Mediterranean – tends to blow continuously for several days. It can reach speeds of more than 100km/h, damaging crops, whipping up forest fires and generally driving everybody around the bend. It is most common in winter and spring.

Language

The various dialects of Provençal – more closely related grammatically to Catalan and Spanish than French – are still spoken every day by thousands of people across southern France, especially by older residents of rural areas.

From around the 12th to the 14th centuries, Provençal was the literary language of France and northern Spain, and was used as far afield as Italy. During that period, it was the principal language of the medieval troubadours – poets, often courtiers and nobles – whose melodies and elegant poems were motivated by the ideal of courtly love.

A movement for the revival of Provençal literature, culture and identity began in the mid-19th century. The movement's most prominent member was the poet Frédéric Mistral (1830–1914), recipient of the Nobel Prize for literature in 1904. In recent years the language has again enjoyed something of a revival, and in many areas signs are written in Provençal and French.

Getting There & Away

For information on ferry services from Marseille to Sardinia and Tunisia see p920. For details on ferries from Marseille to Corsica see p865.

MARSEILLE REGION

MARSEILLE
pop 807,071

In parts very African, in others distinctly Middle Eastern but in its entirety unmistakeably French, the cosmopolitan port of Marseille (spelt Marseilles in English but pronounced the same) is a brusque, bustling place with bags of character. There's the pretty old port, the gritty (and often stinking) backstreets, lively markets with the atmosphere of a Moroccan souk, heavenly

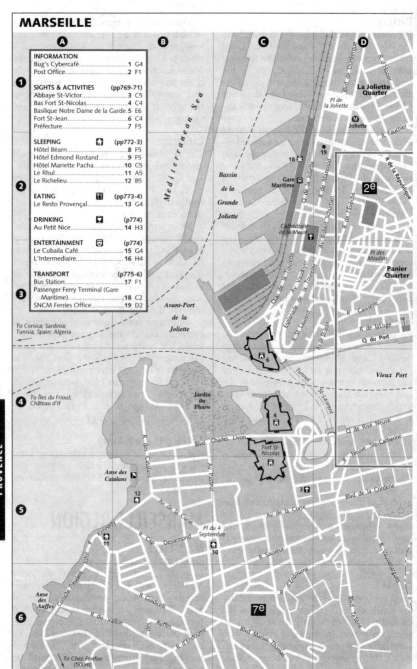

MARSEILLE

INFORMATION
Bug's Cybercafé.....................1 G4
Post Office.............................2 F1

SIGHTS & ACTIVITIES (pp769-71)
Abbaye St-Victor....................3 C5
Bas Fort St-Nicolas................4 C4
Basilique Notre Dame de la Garde.5 E6
Fort St-Jean..........................6 C4
Préfecture.............................7 F5

SLEEPING (pp772-3)
Hôtel Béarn..........................8 F5
Hôtel Edmond Rostand...........9 F5
Hôtel Mariette Pacha............10 C5
Le Rhul..............................11 A5
Le Richelieu.........................12 B5

EATING (pp773-4)
Le Resto Provençal................13 G4

DRINKING (p774)
Au Petit Nice........................14 H3

ENTERTAINMENT (p774)
Le Cubaila Café....................15 G4
L'Intermediaire.....................16 H4

TRANSPORT (p775-6)
Bus Station..........................17 F1
Passenger Ferry Terminal (Gare Maritime)............................18 C2
SNCM Ferries Office..............19 D2

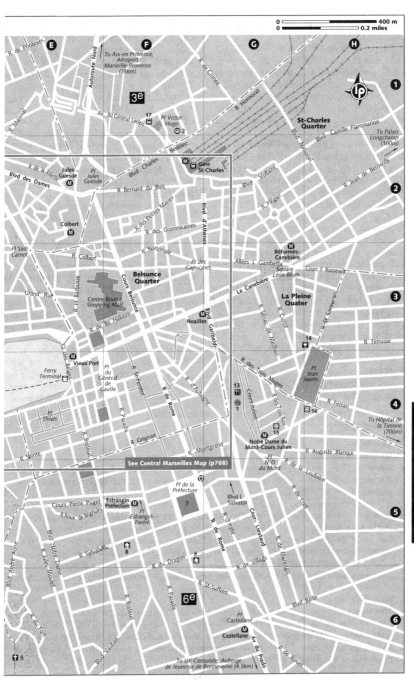

PROVENCE

harbourside restaurants and an increasingly buzzing nightlife.

France's second city with over 800,000 inhabitants, Marseille has not been prettified for the benefit of tourists. Its urban atmosphere – utterly atypical of the rest of Provence – is a function of the diversity of its inhabitants, many of them immigrants from the Mediterranean basin, West Africa and Indochina.

Speak to more provincial French folk and they'll recoil in fear if you mention Marseille. For many it remains a byword for crime and racial tensions but it's an undeserved reputation: an extensive programme of building and development, the high-speed rail link to Paris in particular, is giving the city an increasing dynamism. Parisians are taking weekend breaks here, the arts, music and clubbing scenes are burgeoning and large companies are renting office space; Marseille is becoming *branché* (trendy).

Visitors who enjoy exploring on foot will be rewarded with more sights, sounds and smells than they'll get almost anywhere else in the country. Quaint it ain't but you'll miss a lot if you swerve it. There really is no other city quite like it in France.

History

Greek mariners founded Massilia, a trading post on what is now Marseille's old port, around 600 BC. In the 1st century BC, the city backed Pompey the Great rather than Julius Caesar, whose forces captured Massilia in 49 BC and exacted commercial revenge by confiscating the fleet and directing Roman trade elsewhere.

Massilia retained its status as a free port and was, for a while, the last Western centre of Greek learning, but the city soon declined and became little more than a collection of ruins. It was revived in the early 10th century by the counts of Provence.

The Aragonese pillaged Marseille in 1423, but the greatest calamity in its history took place in 1720, when the plague (carried by a merchant vessel from Syria) killed around 50,000 of the city's 90,000 inhabitants.

Marseille became part of France in the 1480s but soon acquired a reputation for rebelling against the central government. The local population enthusiastically embraced the Revolution, and sent 500 volunteers to defend Paris in 1792. As the troops headed north, they sang a catchy new march composed a few months earlier in Strasbourg and ever after dubbed *La Marseillaise* (now France's national anthem).

Marseille prospered from colonial trade in the 19th century and commerce with North Africa grew rapidly after France occupied Algeria in 1830. Maritime opportunities expanded further when the Suez

MARSEILLE IN...

Two days

Breakfast at **Le Pain Quotidien** (p773), meander around the old port's old forts and its **fish market** (p771), then learn about Marseille's Greek and Roman past in the **Musée d'Histoire de Marseille** (p769). Before lunch on or near the quay, drop in at **La Maison du Pastis** (p774) for tastings of the local firewater.

After lunch, swan along corniche Président John F Kennedy aboard the open-topped **Le Grand Tour** (p771) tourist bus and jump off at **Basilique Notre Dame de la Garde** (p770) for sea breezes and commanding city views. For a late-afternoon coffee or pre-dinner drinks, it's back to the many bars along the quays, then dinner, probably in the streets behind the quai de Rive Neuve. Then it's time to hit the pubs and clubs either along the quays again or up near place Jean Jaurès.

After breakfast the next morning, hit the remaining museums in town or, if the day is right, hone your haggling skills at one of the busy, Moroccan-style **markets** (p771) out of the centre.

Four days

Take a boat from the old port to the romantic fortress/prison **Château d'If** (p770) and the pretty **Îles du Frioul** (p770). On your return, head around the corniche for dinner at one of the **seaside restaurants** (p773) specialising in *bouillabaisse*. On the fourth day, plan a day trip out to the **Calanques** (p771) east of Marseille for sunbathing, a picnic or a seafood lunch and a glass of the delicate local white at the pretty port of Cassis.

Canal opened in 1869. During WWII, Marseille was bombed by the Germans and Italians in 1940, and by the Allies in 1943–44.

Today, Marseille is renowned as Europe's second-largest port and France's most important seaport.

Orientation

The city's main thoroughfare, the wide boulevard called La Canebière, stretches eastwards from the Vieux Port (Old Port). The train station is north of the Canebière at the northern end of blvd d'Athènes. Just a few blocks south of La Canebière is the bohemian cours Julien, a large pedestrianised square dominated by a water garden, fountains and palm trees, and lined with some of Marseille's hippest cafés, restaurants and theatres. The city's commercial heart is around rue Paradis, which gets more fashionable as you move south. The new ferry terminal is west of place de la Joliette, a few minutes walk north of the Cathédrale de la Major.

Marseille is divided into 15 arrondissements; however, most travellers will only be concerned with the central three or four. Places mentioned in the text have the arrondissement (1er, 2e, etc) listed after the street address.

Information
BOOKSHOPS

The northern end of rue Paradis (1er) is lined with bookshops.

Fnac (Map p768; ☎ 04 91 39 94 00; Centre Bourse shopping centre) On the top floor of the centre off cours Belsunce (1er).

Librairie de la Bourse (Map p768; ☎ 04 91 33 63 06; 8 rue Paradis, 1er) Best range of maps, travel books and Lonely Planet guides in Provence.

Librairie Lamy (Map p768; ☎ 04 91 33 57 91; 21 rue Paradis, 1er) A very good selection of English language novels.

EMERGENCY

Préfecture de Police (Map p768; ☎ 04 91 39 80 00; place de la Préfecture, 1er; ☉ 24hr)

INTERNET ACCESS

Bug's Cybercafé (Map pp764–5; ☎ 04 96 12 53 43; 68 cours Julien, 6e; per hr €3.60; ☉ 9.30am-8pm Mon-Wed, 9.30am-10pm Thu-Sat)

Info Cafe (Map p768; ☎ 04 91 33 74 98; 1 quai du Rive Neuve, 1e; per 30 min/hr €2/3.60; ☉ 9am-10pm Mon-Sat, 2.30-7.30pm Sun)

LAUNDRY

Laverie des Allées (Map p768; 15 allées Léon Gambetta; ☉ 8am-8pm) Near place des Capucins.

Laverie Self-Service (Map p768; 5 rue Justice Breteuil, 1er)

MEDICAL SERVICES

Hôpital de la Timone (☎ 04 91 38 60 00; 264 rue St-Pierre, 5e) East of the city centre.

MONEY

There are a number of banks and exchange bureaus on La Canebière near the old port.

Canebière Change (Map p768; 39 La Canebière, 1er).

POST

Branch Post Office (Map pp764–5; 11 rue Honnorat, 3e) Close to the train station but doesn't change money.

Main Post Office (Map p768; 1 place de l'Hôtel des Postes, 1er) Offers currency exchange.

TOURIST INFORMATION

Tourist Office (Map p768; ☎ 04 91 13 89 00; www .marseille-tourisme.com; 4 La Canebière, 1er; ☉ 9am-7pm Mon-Sat, 10am-5pm Sun, to 7.30pm mid-Jun–mid-Sep) Make hotel reservations at this often overwhelmed and understaffed place.

Tourist Office Annexe (Map p768; ☎ 04 91 50 59 18; main train station; ☉ 10am-1pm & 2-6pm Mon-Sat) Go to the central office for hotel reservations.

MARSEILLE CITY PASS

It's worth considering buying a **Marseille City Pass** (1-/2-day pass €16/23), which gives access to the city's museums, guided tours of the town, free access to all metro and bus services, and other discounts, including a reduction for Le Grand Tour tourist bus.

Dangers & Annoyances

Despite its fearsome reputation for crime, Marseille is not significantly more dangerous than other French cities. Avoid street crime by keeping your wits about you and your valuables hidden from view. *Never* leave anything you value in a parked car. Even better, leave it in a garage. It's seldom cheap, though – €14 for anything longer than nine hours and up to 24 hours in one of the central covered car parks is standard, although many hotels have cheaper parking arrangements.

PROVENCE

CENTRAL MARSEILLE

0 — 300 m
0 — 0.2 miles

INFORMATION
Canebière Change.....................1 C3
Info Café...................................2 B3
Laverie des Allées....................3 D2
Laverie Self-Service.................4 C4
Librairie de la Bourse..............5 C3
Librairie Lamy.........................6 C3
Main Post Office......................7 B2
Post Office...............................8 C3
Préfecture de Police................9 D4
Tourist Office.........................10 B3
US Consulate..........................11 C4

SIGHTS & ACTIVITIES   (pp769-71)
Centre de la Vieille Charité.....12 A1
Fish Market.............................13 B3
Jardins des Vestiges...............14 C2
Musée d'Histoire de Marseille...15 C2
Musée de la Mode..................16 C3
Musée des Dock Romains.......17 A2
Musée du Santon....................18 A4
Musée du Vieux Marseille.......19 A2

SLEEPING   (pp772-3)
Etap Hotel..............................20 B4
Grand Hôtel Le Préfecture......21 D4
Hôtel Alizé.............................22 C3
Hôtel d'Athènes.....................23 D1
Hôtel Hermes.........................24 B3
Hôtel Little Palace..............(see 23)

Hôtel Lutetia.........................25 D2
New Hotel Select....................26 D2
New Hôtel Vieux Port.............27 C3

EATING   (pp773-4)
Fruit & Vegetable Market........28 B5
La Boutique du Glacier...........29 C3
Le Bistro à Vin.......................30 C4
Le Mérou Bleu.......................31 B3
Le Pain Quotidien..................32 B4
Lemongrass............................33 B4
Les Arcenaulx........................34 B4
Marché des Capucins.............35 D2
O'Stop...................................36 C3
Pizzeria Chez Mario...............37 B4
Roi du Couscous....................38 B1
Une Table Au Sud..................39 B3

DRINKING   (p774)
Le Bar de la Marine................40 B4
LHeure Verte..........................41 A3
O'Malleys..............................42 B3

ENTERTAINMENT   (p774)
Énigme..................................43 C3
La Caravelle...........................44 B3
Le Trolleybus.........................45 A4
MP Bar...................................46 C3
Virgin Megastore....................47 C4

SHOPPING   (p774-5)
Ducs de Gascogne..................48 B4
La Cie de Provence............(see 50)
La Maison du Pastis...............49 A3
Le Comptoir du Panier............50 A2
Maison Debout.......................51 C4

TRANSPORT   (p775-6)
Algérie Ferries........................52 A1
Boats to Château d'If & Îles du Frioul..53 B3
Espace Infos-RTM...................54 C3
Eurolines/Intercars.................55 D2
GACM Office.......................(see 53)
Navette Buses to Airport.........56 D1
SNCF Boutique.......................57 D4
Thrifty....................................58 D1

OTHER
Opéra.....................................59 C4

At night, avoid walking alone in the Belsunce area, a poor neighbourhood southwest of the train station bounded by La Canebière, cours Belsunce and rue d'Aix, rue Bernard du Bois and blvd d'Athènes.

Sights

Marseille grew up around the old port, where ships have docked for at least 26 centuries. The majority of Marseille's sights cluster close to the port. Head along corniche Président John F Kennedy, though, for some great sea views or up to the commanding heights occupied by the striking Basilique Notre Dame de la Garde, from where you can really get a handle on Marseille's layout. The ever-circling hop-on-hop-off tourist bus service (see p771) is another good way to acquaint yourself with the city and its sights.

MUSEUMS

Unless noted otherwise, the museums listed here are open 10am to 5pm Tuesday to Sunday October to May and 11am to 6pm June to September. Admission to permanent exhibitions costs €2/1 for adults/children and temporary exhibitions usually cost €3/1.50.

Centre de la Vieille Charité

The **Centre de la Vieille Charité** (Old Charity Cultural Centre; Map opposite; ☎ 04 91 14 58 80; 2 rue de la Charité, 2e) is in the mostly North African Panier Quarter. The superb permanent exhibits and imaginative temporary exhibitions are housed in this handsome workhouse and hospice built around a monastery-like cloister between 1671 and 1745, and restored after serving as a barracks (1905), a rest-home for soldiers (WWI) and low-cost housing for people who lost their homes in WWII. It is also home to **Musée d'Archéologie** (☎ 04 91 14 58 80) and **Musée des Arts Africains, Océaniens & Amérindiens** (Museum of African, Oceanic & American Indian Art; ☎ 04 91 14 58 38), which has a diverse and often striking collection, including masks from the Americas, Africa and the Pacific plus some lovingly decorated human skulls.

A combined ticket covering all of the above costs €4; individual tickets are available too at €3 for the Centre de la Vieille Charité and €2 for the others.

Musée d'Histoire de Marseille

The small **Musée d'Histoire de Marseille** (Map opposite; ☎ 04 91 90 42 22; ground fl, Centre Bourse shopping centre, 1er; ⏰ noon-7pm Mon-Sat) is just north of La Canebière. It's packed with artefacts and displays that give a wonderful overview of the cultures that have made their home in Marseille and the crafts they practised over the centuries. Exhibits include the remains of a merchant vessel – discovered by chance in the old port in 1974 – that plied the waters of the Mediterranean in the early 3rd century AD. The 19m-long timbers, which include five different kinds of wood, show evidence of having been repaired repeatedly. To preserve the soaked and decaying wood, the whole thing was freeze-dried right where it now sits – hidden behind glass in a dimly lit room.

Fragments of Roman buildings, uncovered during the construction of the Centre Bourse shopping centre, can be seen outside the museum in the **Jardin des Vestiges** (Garden of Ruins), which fronts rue Henri Barbusse (1er).

Musée de la Mode

Glitz and glamour is the name of the game at the **Musée de la Mode** (Fashion Museum; Map opposite; ☎ 04 91 56 59 57; 11 La Canebière, 1er; adult/child €3/1). Housed in Marseille's superb Espace Mode Méditerranée (Mediterranean Fashion Space), the museum looks at French fashion trends over the past 30 years and displays over 2000 different items of clothing and accessories.

Musée du Santon

The private collection of 18th- and 19th-century *santon* (fingernail-sized nativity figures that are typical of Provence) gathered by *santon*-maker Marcel Carbonnel is displayed at the **Musée du Santon** (Map opposite; ☎ 04 91 54 26 58; 47 rue Neuve Ste-Catherine, 7e; admission free; ⏰ 10am-noon & 2-6.30pm Tue-Sun). Entrance to the adjoining **ateliers** (workshops; ⏰ 8am-1pm & 2-5.40pm Mon-Thu), where you can watch the minuscule 2.5cm- to 15cm-tall figures being crafted, is also free. Guided tours (in French only) are usually conducted on Tuesday and Thursday at 2.30pm.

Continuing 100m up the hill from the museum, you come to the imposing Romanesque **Abbaye St-Victor** (Map pp764-5; ☎ 04 91 05 84 48; ⏰ 8am-7pm), built in the 12th century on the site of a 4th-century martyr's tomb. Marseille's annual sacred-music festival is held here.

Palais de Longchamp

The grand, colonnaded **Palais de Longchamp** (Longchamp Palace; off Map pp764-5; blvd Philippon, 4e), constructed in the 1860s, is at the eastern end of blvd Longchamp. The palace was designed in part to disguise a *château d'eau* (water tower) built at the terminus of an aqueduct from the River Durance. The two wings house Marseille's oldest museum, the **Musée des Beaux-Arts** (☎ 04 91 14 59 30), which specialises in 15th- to 19th-century paintings, including a few by Rubens, Courbet, David and Ingres. There are also sculptures by Marseille-born Pierre Puget. The rather more missable **Musée d'Histoire Naturelle** (☎ 04 91 62 30 78) is also housed here.

BASILIQUE NOTRE DAME DE LA GARDE

Not to be missed for great panoramas and some handsome, if rather overwrought, 19th-century architecture, is a trip up to the **Basilique Notre Dame de la Garde** (Map pp764-5; ☎ 04 91 13 40 80; admission free; ⊙ basilica & crypt 7am-8pm summer, 7am-10pm mid-Jun–mid-Aug, 7am-7pm winter), an enormous Romano-Byzantine basilica 1km south of the old port. It stands on a hilltop (162m) – the highest point in the city – and provides staggering views of sprawling Marseille.

The domed basilica, ornamented with coloured marble, intricate mosaics, murals and gilded objects, was built between 1853 and 1864. The bell tower is topped by a 9.7m-tall gilded statue of the Virgin Mary on a 12m-high pedestal. The great bell inside is 2.5m tall and weighs a hefty 8324kg (the clapper alone is 387kg). Bullet marks and vivid shrapnel scars on the cathedral's northern façade mark the fierce fighting that took place here during Marseille's Battle of Liberation (15–25 August 1944).

Dress conservatively when you visit. Bus No 60 links the old port (from cours Jean Ballard) with the basilica. Count on 30 minutes each way by foot.

CHÂTEAU D'IF

Château d'If (off Map pp764-5; ☎ 04 91 59 02 30; adult/student €4.60/3.10; ⊙ 9.30am-6pm Sep-Mar, 9.30am-6.30pm Jun-Aug), the 16th-century fortress-turned-prison made infamous by Alexandre Dumas' classic work of fiction *Le Comte de Monte Cristo* (The Count of Monte Cristo) is on a 30-sq-km island 3.5km west of the entrance to the old port. Among the people incarcerated here were all sorts of political prisoners, hundreds of Protestants (many of whom perished in the dungeons), the Revolutionary hero Mirabeau, the rebels of 1848 and the Communards of 1871.

Boats run by **GACM** (Map p768; ☎ 04 91 55 50 09; www.answeb.net/gacm in French; 1 quai des Belges, 1er) to the Château d'If leave from outside the GACM office in the old port. There are boats at 9am, 10.30am, noon, 2pm and 3.30pm (€9 return, 20 minutes).

ÎLES DU FRIOUL

The islands of **Ratonneau** and **Pomègues**, each of which is about 2.5km long, are a few hundred metres west of the Château d'If. They were linked by a dyke in the 1820s. From the 17th to 19th century, the islands were used as a place of quarantine for the

---

A SIMMERING ARGUMENT

The French enjoy quarrelling about what makes a good *bouillabaisse* – Provence's seafood stew made with onions, white wine and tomatoes, flavoured with fennel and saffron and served with *rouille* (a delightful, garlicky mayonnaise) and croutons – almost as much as they do actually cooking and eating it.

Everyone agrees the soup must be boiled *(bouillir)* briefly but furiously and the heat lowered *(baisser)* thereafter. At least five or six types of Mediterranean fish plus crab or shrimp are generally held to be essential.

While some add lobster, langoustines or mussels, others regard this as unforgivable sacrilege. Many of Toulon's restaurants add potatoes too; another sinister act according to purists. Then there's the violent schism over how it should be served: in two courses with the broth first, or eaten together with the broth ladled periodically over the fish to keep it warm.

What is indisputable is that however you eat this great local dish (and be warned, some of the better places require you order 24 hours ahead), it's sensational accompanied by a bottle of the delightful local Cassis white wine.

unfortunate people suspected of carrying plague or cholera.

Today, the rather barren islands (total area about 200 hectares) shelter sea birds, rare plants and bathers, and are dotted with fortifications (which were used by German troops during WWII), the ruins of the old quarantine hospital, Hôpital Caroline, and Fort Ratonneau.

Boats to the Château d'If also serve the Îles du Frioul (€14 return; €19 if you want to stop at Château d'If too). In addition to these boats, there are departures at 6.45am, 5pm and 6.30pm for the Îles du Frioul alone.

OLD PORT AREA
Although the main commercial docks were transferred to the Joliette area on the coast north of here in the 1840s, the old port remains an active and charming harbour for fishing craft, pleasure yachts and ferries to the Château d'If. Several stalls sell fresh fish, squid, octopus and spiny *oursins* (sea urchins) during the day here.

The harbour entrance is guarded by **Bas Fort St-Nicolas** (on the southern side) and, across the water, **Fort St-Jean**, founded in the 13th century by the Knights Hospitaller of St John of Jerusalem. In 1943 the neighbourhood on the northern side of the quai du Port – at the time a seedy area with a strong Resistance presence – was systematically dynamited by the Germans. This neighbourhood was rebuilt after the war.

The 17th-century **town hall** has two museums nearby: the **Musée des Docks Romains** and the **Musée du Vieux Marseille**. The **Panier Quarter**, many of whose residents are North African immigrants, is a bit further north. The **Centre de la Vieille Charité** and its museums, well worth a visit, sit at the top of the hill.

On the southern side of the old port, the large and lively **place Thiars** and **cours Honoré d'Estienne d'Orves** pedestrian zone, with its late-night restaurants and cafés, stretches south from quai de Rive Neuve.

The liveliest part of Marseille – always crowded with people of all ages and ethnic groups – is situated around the intersection of La Canebière and cours Belsunce. The area just north of La Canebière and east of cours Belsunce, which is known as **Belsunce**, is a poor immigrant neighbourhood undergoing a slow rehabilitation.

The fashionable **6th arrondissement** is well worth a stroll, especially the area between La Canebière and the **Prefecture building**. **Rue St-Ferréol** is a bustling pedestrian shopping street.

MARKETS
Marseille is home to a colourful array of markets, including the small but absorbing daily fresh **fish market** (Map p768; quai des Belges; 8am-1pm), where you can buy the makings of a *bouillabaisse*.

Cours Julien hosts a Wednesday morning fruit-and-vegetable market. Stalls laden with everything from second-hand clothing to pots and pans fill nearby **place Jean Jaurès** (8am-1pm Sat).

Tours
Le Grand Tour (☎ 04 91 91 05 82; adult/student/child €16/12/8; 10am-at least 4pm); This hop-on-hop-off, open-topped, double-decker tourist bus service, is an excellent way to get acquainted with the city or to travel between the main sights and museums in Marseille. Tours navigate the old port, head around the corniche and up to Notre Dame de la Garde. Headphones provide commentary in five languages.

The tourist office offers various guided tours, including a **walking tour** of the city (€6.50) departing from outside the tourist office at 2pm from Monday to Saturday (2.30pm Sunday).

In summer **GACM** (Map p768; ☎ 04 91 55 50 09) runs boat trips (with French commentary only) from the old port to Cassis and back (€20), which pass by the stunning

---

THE CALANQUES
If you've got wheels, get away from it all just a few miles east of busy, built-up Marseille along the Calanques: small inlets along the rocky, indented coast, sometimes with a small patch of beach on which to soak up the sun. A trip to the pretty nearby fishing village of **Cassis** makes an ideal day out and is a good place to grab lunch and sample the subtle local white wine. The **tourist office** (☎ 04 42 01 71 17; quai des Moulins; 9am-12.30pm & 2-6pm Tue-Sat) supplies a free list and map of the all the *caves* (cellars) you can visit for tastings.

Calanques, dramatic formations of coastal rock that attract unusual wildlife.

Sleeping

Generally speaking, the better hotels cluster around the old port (where budget options are pretty much nonexistent) and as you head east out of the centre along the corniche. The city also has some of France's cheapest hotels, a good percentage of them dodgy dives. Establishments mentioned here are clean and reputable. Prices in Marseille hotels vary little throughout the year.

BUDGET

Auberge de Jeunesse de Bonneveine (☎ 04 91 17 63 30; fax 04 91 73 97 23; impasse du Docteur Bonfils, 8e; dm incl breakfast €14.55; ⊗ Feb-Dec) A good bet for its proximity to the sea and the Calanques, this hostel is about 4.5km south of the centre. Take bus No 44 from the Rond Point du Prado metro stop and get off at the Place Bonnefons stop.

Hôtel Béarn (Map pp764-5; ☎ 04 91 37 75 83; www .hotel-bearn.com; 63 rue Sylvabelle, 6e; s/d with shower €25/35, with shower & toilet €29/40) Although it's a bit shabby, Hôtel Béarn is clean and quiet with colourfully decorated rooms. Reception closes at 11pm or midnight and access after 11pm is via security code.

Grand Hôtel Le Préfecture (Map p768; ☎ 04 91 54 31 60; fax 04 91 54 24 95; 9 blvd Louis Salvator, 6e; r with shower €29, with shower, toilet & TV €32, with bath €37) Far from grand, this place is perfectly acceptable for the price (avoid the run-down 1st-floor rooms).

Le Richelieu (Map pp764-5; ☎ 04 91 31 01 92; hotelmer@club-Internet.fr; 52 corniche Président John F Kennedy, 7e; road-facing r €34-41, sea-facing r €41-53) An idyllic, two-star place with ace views, Le Richelieu is built onto the rocks right next to plage des Catalans. Road-facing rooms can be noisy. Some sea-facing rooms have balconies. Make sure you book ahead.

MID-RANGE

Hôtel Hermes (Map p768; ☎ 04 96 11 63 63; hotel .hermes@wanadoo.fr; 2 rue de la Bonneterie, 1er; s/d from €45/67; P ✗ ✗) Right on the quayside, Hôtel Hermes is bright, cheerful and good value given the location. The roof terrace and the honeymoon-room balcony have terrific views over the harbour and out to Basilique Notre Dame. Nearby secure parking for guests costs €6.

Hôtel Alizé (Map p768; ☎ 04 91 33 66 97; alize -hotel@wanadoo.fr; 35 quai des Belges, 1er; rear-facing s/d €58/63, harbour-facing s/d €75/80; ✗) An elegant, central old pile, Alizé's big draw is its location, right on the old port with great views across it up to the Basilique. The rooms are decent enough (if in need of less-dated decoration). All come with satellite TV and soundproofing.

Etap Hotel (Map p768; ☎ 0 892 680 582; fax 04 91 54 95 67; 46 rue Sainte; s €46, d & tr €50; P ✗ ✗) Set just back from the port (so no maritime views) but it's good value and close to the restaurants and cafés of place Thiers. Try to get one of the large, wood-beamed rooms in the old building (an old sea galley captain's house). Covered parking is €6.

New Hôtel Vieux Port (Map p768; ☎ 04 91 99 23 23; www.new-hotel.com; 3bis rue Reine Elisabeth, 1er; s/d from €86/92, junior ste €145; ✗ ✗) This hotel has been recently and stylishly redesigned throughout, from the lobby's impressive glass lift shaft to the large, plush rooms decked out with classy understatement in several different ethnic styles. It's very central and the pricier rooms have harbour views. Weekend deals may be available.

Hôtel Edmond Rostand (Map pp764-5; ☎ 04 91 37 74 95; www.hoteledmondrostand.com in French; 31 rue du Dragon, 6e; r with 1 or 2 beds €54; ✗) This place may be a little way out of the centre but it's small, efficient and quiet with sleek, modern rooms that come with telephone, TV and minibar.

Hôtel d'Athènes (Map p768; ☎ 04 91 90 12 93; fax 04 91 90 72 03; 37-39 blvd d'Athènes, 1er; s/d with shower €24/34, s/d/tw with shower & toilet €39/46/56) You'll find this place at the foot of the grand staircase leading from the train station into town. It has average but well-kept rooms and an elevator. It also runs the adjoining one-star **Hôtel Little Palace** (r with shower €25-34).

Hôtel Lutetia (Map p768; ☎ 04 91 50 81 78; www .hotellutetia13.com in French; 38 allées Léon Gambetta; s/d/tr from €46/51/70) Close to the New Hotel Select, the Lutetia is homely and spotless. The smallish rooms are equipped with TVs and phones.

New Hotel Select (Map p768; ☎ 04 91 95 09 09; www.new-hotel.com; 4 allées Léon Gambetta, 1er; s/d €65/72; ✗ ✗) This hotel is pleasant, modern and efficiently run. Rooms have TVs, phones and minibars. Rates are about 20% cheaper at the weekend.

Hôtel Mariette Pacha (Map pp764-5; ☎ 04 91 52 30 77; mpacha@hotelselection.com; 5 place du 4 Septembre;

r with shower & TV €56, with shower, toilet & TV €60, with bath, toilet & TV €66) Quiet and tucked away, this hotel is elegant and homely. There are some triples and adjoining rooms for families.

Le Rhul (Map pp764-5; ☎ 04 91 52 01 77, 04 91 52 49 82; 269 corniche Président John F Kennedy; s/d €75/80, bouillabaisse dinner & r for 2 €175) Enchanting sea views from all bedrooms, which are attractive, large and airy (some have balconies). The restaurant (also overlooking the sea) turns out a decent *bouillabaisse*. It's a great option if you want to escape the centre's hustle and bustle.

Eating

Marseille's restaurants offer an incredible variety of cuisines, but no trip here is complete without sampling *bouillabaisse* (see p770). For Vietnamese and Chinese fare, the many restaurants on, or just off, rue de la République are worth a visit.

RESTAURANTS

Fish is predominant and plentiful in Marseille, be it soup, *huîtres* (oysters), *moules* (mussels) or other shellfish. The quai de Rive Neuve (1er) is plastered with outdoor cafés and touristy restaurants touting *bouillabaisse*; those along quai du Port are better but pricier. Expect to pay about €50 for two people. The pedestrian streets around place Thiars are packed with terrace cafés and restaurants in the warmer months.

Chez Fonfon (off Map pp764-5; ☎ 04 91 52 14 38; 140 rue du Vallon des Auffes, 7e; bouillabaisse €40;

AUTHOR'S CHOICE

Une Table au Sud (Map p768; ☎ 04 91 90 63 53; unetableausud@wanadoo.fr; 2 quai du Port; menus €39/49/69; ⏰ closed Sun & Mon) This understatedly elegant restaurant overlooking the old port, turns out inventive, delicately delicious cuisine. There's often a nod to Far Eastern flavours: light foie gras raviolis in a clear chicken broth (basically fancy French won tons) or a very faintly sweet-and-sour tang to vegetables slow roasted with a red wine reduction and served with tender *rouget* fillets. The trademark sweet fennel *tatin* sounds so wrong but tastes so right. Pricey but definitely worth splashing out on.

⏰ closed Mon lunch & Sun) Overlooking a pretty and authentic little harbour, this restaurant has long been, and remains, legendary for serving a very fine *bouillabaisse* indeed. There's a good range of local rosés or the delicious local white Cassis to accompany it. Book ahead.

Lemongrass (Map p768; ☎ 04 91 33 97 65; 8 rue Fort-Notre-Dame, 1e; menus €20; ⏰ closed Sun) A refreshingly different place among the many pizza and *bouillabaisse* places close to the old port, Lemongrass serves inexpensive and interesting menus of fusion Asian/French food using Eastern herbs and spices with restraint.

Le Mérou Bleu (Map p768; ☎ 04 91 54 23 25; 32-36 rue St-Saëns, 1er; dishes €8-19) This is a popular restaurant with a lovely terrace. It has *bouillabaisse* (€30), excellent seafood, meat and pasta.

Les Arcenaulx (Map p768; ☎ 04 91 54 85 38; 27 cours Honoré d'Estienne d'Orves, 1er; mains from €10; ⏰ Mon-Sat) An unusual, beautifully restored complex wrapped around cours des Arcenaulx. It contains a delightful restaurant and *salon de thé*. Book ahead.

Le Bistro à Vin (Map p768; ☎ 04 91 54 02 20; 17 rue Sainte, 6e; dishes €12; ⏰ closed Sun & Sat lunch) This rustic bistro has beamed ceilings and wooden tables. The wine selection is excellent and the accompaniments – *tapenade*, artisanal cheeses and unusual meat parts – are equally enticing.

It may also be worth following your nose to cours Julien, near the Notre Dame du Mont-Cours Julien metro station (Marseille Map) and lined with of French, Indian, Antillean, Pakistani, Thai, Armenian, Lebanese, Tunisian and Italian restaurants.

Le Resto Provençal (Map pp764-5; ☎ 04 91 48 85 12; 64 cours Julien, 1er; regional menu €21, plat du jour €9, lunch menu €12; ⏰ closed Sat lunch & Sun) A winning combination of agreeable outside dining terrace and consistently good Provençal dishes.

At the snackier end of the dining spectrum are **Le Pain Quotidien** (Map p768; ☎ 04 91 33 55 00; 18 place Aux Huiles; breakfast €5-8) for a decent breakfast, **Pizzeria Chez Mario** (Map p768; ☎ 04 91 54 48 54; 8 rue Euthymènes, 1er; mains €8.50-15) for good fish, grilled meats, pizza and pasta, **Roi du Couscous** (Map p768; ☎ 04 91 91 45 46; 63 rue de la République, 2e; couscous €8-12; ⏰ Tue-Sun), serving large and delicious portions of steamed semolina with meats and vegetables, and **O'Stop**

(Map p768; ☎ 04 91 33 85 34; 15 rue St-Saëns, 1er; menu €9; ☼ 24hr) for nonstop sandwiches, pasta and simple, authentic regional specialities.

CAFÉS

Quai de Rive Neuve and cours Honoré d'Estienne d'Orves (1er), a large, long, open square two blocks south of the quay, are crowded with cafés. There is another cluster overlooking place de la Préfecture, at the southern end of rue St-Ferréol (1er). There's also plenty of choice along the quaysides.

La Boutique du Glacier (Map p768; ☎ 04 91 33 76 93; 1 place du Général de Gaulle) Not a good place for people-watching but good for light and lovely daytime pastries and coffee.

SELF-CATERING

Fruit and vegetables are sold at **Marché des Capucins** (Map p768; place des Capucins, 1er; ☼ Mon-Sat), one block north of La Canebière, and at the **fruit-and-vegetable market** (Map p768; cours Pierre Puget, 6e; ☼ Mon-Sat). There are also a couple of supermarkets in the monstrously ugly concrete bunker that is the Centre Bourse shopping centre (Map p768).

Drinking

The Vieux Port is a great place to gravitate towards for a relaxed, scenic coffee by day or night. If you're after clusters of livelier, mainly night-time venues, two especially good areas are the bars and clubs around quai de Rive Neuve and, a fair hike away, the bars and cafés around place Jean Jaurès.

Le Bar de la Marine (Map p768; ☎ 04 91 54 95 42; 15 quai de Rive Neuve, 1er; ☼ 7am-2am) Chic metropolitan espresso sippers mix it with grizzled *pastis*-gulping sailor types at this gregarious bar right on the water.

O'Malleys (Map p768; ☎ 04 91 33 65 50; 9 quai de Rive Neuve, 1er) Overlooking the old port, on the corner of rue de la Paix, this is a friendly place and there are concerts on Wednesday night of Celtic and Irish music.

L'Heure Verte (Map p768; ☎ 04 91 90 12 73; 106 quai du Port; ☼ 11am-11pm high season) This is the place to go to sample many different types of *pastis*, including the house-made ones, steeped for weeks in different herbs and some fierce absinthe. The shop next door (see right) will also sell you bottles of all this stuff to take with you.

Au Petit Nice (Map pp764-5; ☎ 04 91 48 43 04; 28 place Jean Jaurès; ☼ 6am-2am) A favourite with locals for its cosy café feeling. It's more like a local British boozer than anything else.

Entertainment

Cultural event listings can be found in the monthly *Vox Mag* and weekly *Taktik* and *Sortir*, all distributed free of charge at the tourist office, cinemas and the ticket offices mentioned here. Comprehensive listings also appear in the weekly *L'Officiel des Loisirs*. It's worth consulting the website www.marseillebynight.com in French.

Tickets for most cultural events are sold at *billetteries* (ticket counters) in **Fnac** (☎ 04 91 39 94 00) on the top floor of the Centre Bourse shopping centre (Map p768), **Virgin Megastore** (Map p768; ☎ 04 91 55 55 00; 75 rue St-Ferréol, 1er) and **Arcenaulx** (Map p768; ☎ 04 91 59 80 37; 25 cours Honoré d'Estienne d'Orves, 1er).

NIGHTCLUBS

Le Trolleybus (Map p768; ☎ 04 91 54 30 45; 24 quai Rive Neuve; ☼ 11pm-dawn Wed-Sat) Inside the various sections of this tunnel-like club by the harbour there could be techno, funk and indie all playing at the same time. The sound system is great.

La Caravelle (Map p768; ☎ 04 91 90 36 64; 34 quai du Port, 2e; ☼ 7am-2am) This is a trendy place in the Hôtel Bellevue hosting jazz sessions on weekends (November to March). It's in a marvellous location overlooking the port with a small balcony. Great for predinner sundowners served with tasty (and free) bar nibbles.

Le Cubaila Café (Map pp764-5; ☎ 04 91 48 97 48; 40 rue des Trois Rois, 6e; ☼ 10.30pm-2am) This is a great place, even if all you do about Latin dancing is watch it. The food is good, too.

L'Intermediaire (Map pp764-5; ☎ 04 91 47 01 25; 39 cours Julien; ☼ 7pm-2am Mon-Sat) Intimate, vibrant, friendly and often packed, this is one of the happening bars and live-music venues in town, showcasing everything from cover bands to blues and up-and-coming local acts.

Two popular gay bars close to the centre (and attracting a youngish, male gay crowd) are **Énigme** (Map p768; ☎ 04 91 33 79 20; 22 rue Beauvau, 1er) and **MP Bar** (Map p768; ☎ 04 91 33 64 79; 10 rue Beauvau, 1e).

Shopping

La Maison du Pastis (Map p768; ☎ 04 91 90 86 77; 108 quai du Port) Run by the same proprietor as

L'Heure Verte (see opposite), La Maison du Pastis offers informative tastings in English of the southern aperitif of choice, *pastis*, and sells a wide variety of the aniseedy tipple along with it's bad big brother absinthe.

Ducs de Gascogne (Map p768; ☎ 04 91 33 87 28; 20 cours Honoré d'Estienne d'Orves) A truly mouthwatering selection of foie gras (goose liver pâté), Provençal wines and other culinary delights awaits at Ducs de Gascogne.

Maison Debout (Map p768; 46 rue Francis Davso, 1er) This traditional and very quaint shop offers a rich array of coffee, tea and chocolate.

La Cie de Provence (Map p768; ☎ 04 91 56 20 94; 1 rue Caisserie) and **La Comptoir du Panier** (Map p768; ☎ 04 91 56 20 94; 1 rue Caisserie) are both good bets for present buying or for simply treating yourself to Provençal clothes, decorations and household goodies.

Getting There & Away

AIR
Aéroport Marseille-Provence (☎ 04 42 14 14 14), also known as Aéroport Marseille-Marignane, is 28km northwest of town in Marignane.

BOAT
Marseille's **passenger ferry terminal** (gare maritime; Map pp764-5; ☎ 04 91 56 38 63; fax 04 91 56 38 70) is 250m south of place de la Joliette (2e). It's modern and spacious, but facilities for foot passengers are fairly sparse. There is a poorly stocked snack bar, no ATMs and little to keep you amused while waiting for a boat.

The **Société Nationale Maritime Corse Méditerranée** (SNCM; Map pp764-5; ☎ 0 836 679 500; fax 04 91 56 35 86; 61 blvd des Dames, 2e; 🕑 8am-6pm Mon-Fri, 8.30am-noon & 2-5.30pm Sat) links Marseille with Corsica (see p865), Sardinia and Tunisia. It also serves the ports of Algiers, Annaba, Bejaia, Oran and Skikda in Algeria, although services are prone to disruption/cancellation because of the political troubles there.

There is an office for **Algérie Ferries** (Map pp764-5; ☎ 04 91 90 64 70; 29 blvd des Dames, 2e; 🕑 9-11.45am & 1-4.45pm Mon-Fri). Ticketing and reservations for the Tunisian and Moroccan ferry companies, **Compagnie Tunisienne de Navigation** (CTN) and **Compagnie Marocaine de Navigation** (COMANAV; ☎ 04 67 46 68 000), with departures from 4 quai d'Alger in Sète, are handled by SNCM.

For more information on ferry services to/from North Africa and Sardinia see p920.

BUS
The **bus station** (gare des autocars; Map pp764-5; ☎ 04 91 08 16 40; 3 place Victor Hugo, 3e) is 150m to the right as you exit the train station. Tickets are sold at company ticket counters (closed most of the time) or on the bus.

Buses travel to Aix-en-Provence (€4.20, 35 minutes via the autoroute or one hour via the N8, every five to 10 minutes), Avignon (€17, two hours, one daily), Cannes (€21, two hours, four daily), Carpentras (€12, two hours), Cassis (€3.30, 1¼ hours), Cavaillon (€9.50, one hour), Nice (€22, 2¾ hours), Nice airport, Orange, Salon-de-Provence and other destinations. There is a service to Castellane on Saturday morning at 8.30am.

Eurolines (☎ 0 892 289 9091, 04 91 50 57 55; fax 04 91 08 30 01) has buses to Spain, Belgium, the Netherlands, Italy, Morocco, the UK and other countries. Its counter is in the bus station. **Intercars** (☎ 04 91 50 08 66; fax 04 91 08 72 34), with an office next to Eurolines in the bus station, has buses to the UK, Spain, Portugal, Morocco, Poland and Slovakia. There's also a joint **office** (Map p768; ☎ 04 91 50 57 55; 3 allées Léon Gambetta) for these two firms nearer the Vieux Port.

CAR
Rental agencies offering better rates include **Thrifty** (Map p768; ☎ 04 91 95 00 00; 8 blvd Voltaire, 1er), situated near the train station, and **Europcar** (Map p768; ☎ 04 91 99 40 90), inside the train station.

TRAIN
Marseille's passenger train station, served by both metro lines, is called Gare St-Charles. The **information and ticket reservation office** (🕑 9am-8pm Mon-Sat; ticket purchases 4am-1am) is one level below the tracks, next to the metro entrance. Luggage may be kept at the **left-luggage office** (small bag for 72hr €3.40, 🕑 7.15am to 10pm), next to platform A.

In town, tickets can be bought at the **SNCF Boutique** (Map p768; 🕑 9.30am-6.30pm Mon-Fri, 10am-6pm Sat), near place de la Préfecture.

From Marseille there are trains to more or less any destination in France and beyond. Some sample destinations include Paris' Gare de Lyon (€83.90, three hours, 17 daily), Nice (€25, 2½ hours, 21 daily), Avignon (€19.40, 30 minutes, 27 daily), Lyon (€39.40, 3¼ hours, 16 daily), Barcelona (€66.80, 8½ hours) and Geneva (€58, 6½ hours).

Getting Around

TO/FROM THE AIRPORT

Navette (☎ Marseille 04 91 50 59 34, ☎ airport 04 42 14 31 27) shuttle buses link Marseille-Provence airport (€8.50, one hour) with Marseille's train station. Buses heading to the airport leave from outside the station's main entrance every 20 minutes between 5.30am and 9.50pm, and buses to the train station depart the airport between 6.10am and 10.50pm.

BUS & METRO

Marseille is served by two well-maintained, fast metro lines (Métro 1 and Métro 2), a tramline and an extensive bus network.

The metro and most buses run from 5am to 9pm. From 9.25pm to 12.30am, metro and tram routes are covered every 15 minutes by buses M1 and M2 and Tramway 68; stops are marked with fluorescent green signs reading *métro en bus* (metro by bus). Most of the 11 **Fluobus** (☎ information 04 91 91 92 10) night buses leave from in front of the **Espace Infos-RTM** (Map p768; ☎ 04 91 91 92 10; 6 rue des Fabres, 1er; ☯ 8.30am-6pm Mon-Fri, 9.30am-12.30pm & 2-5.30pm Sat). This office distributes route maps and sells tickets.

Bus/metro tickets (€1.50) can be used on any combination of metro and bus for one hour after they've been time-stamped (no return trips). A pass for one/three days costs €4/9.50.

TAXI

There's a taxi stand to the right as you exit the train station through the main entrance.

Marseille Taxi (☎ 04 91 02 20 20) and **Taxis France** (☎ 04 91 49 91 00) run taxis 24 hours a day.

AIX-EN-PROVENCE

pop 137,067

Aix-en-Provence, or just Aix (pronounced like the letter 'x'), is one of France's most graceful and popular cities. Its harmonious fusion of majestic public squares, shaded avenues and mossy fountains, many of which have gurgled since the 18th century, couldn't form a greater contrast to its rowdier, less-polished neighbour, Marseille, only 25km down the road.

There's something for everyone here: the art heritage of Cézanne who lived and painted here, a good choice of fine dining, a lively nightlife and plenty of charm. Cours Mirabeau, a graceful, plane tree–lined boulevard overlooked by the haughty stone lions guarding the large central fountain, is the perfect place to amble, shop and, most importantly, watch the world pass as you nurse a slow espresso in one of the many large cafés lining it.

Some 200 elegant mansions in the city centre date from the 17th and 18th centuries. Many are Italian baroque in style and coloured that distinctive Provençal yellow.

The city – its bars and cafés in particular – is enlivened by the presence of the University of Aix-Marseille, the forerunner of which was established in 1409. The university has 30,000 students, many of them foreigners undertaking intensive French-language courses.

TOP FIVE PROVENÇAL MARKETS

■ **Aix** (p780) Lose track of time among colourful produce on place des Prêcheurs (Tuesday, Thursday and Saturday) and place Richelme (daily). Flowers are on sale at place de l'Hôtel de Ville (Tuesday, Thursday and Saturday morning) and place des Prêcheurs on Sunday morning.

■ **Marseille** (p771) Mooch among the stalls at the tiny but captivating quayside fish market on the old port (daily) or the livelier, Middle Eastern–style bazaars (on weekends) further out of the city.

■ **Apt** (p779) Go crazy at the huge Saturday market packed with scrumptious local fare, including the local speciality, crystallised fruit, then demolish your purchases on a picnic in the lovely Parc Naturel Régional du Lubéron.

■ **Carpentras** (p797) Stock up on nougat, great local cheeses, lavender marmalade and the luscious local melons at the market (Friday) in this untouristy, down-to-earth town.

■ **Arles** (p805) Head here for the large, varied Saturday market stretching the length of the main boulevard and selling great cheese, Camargue salt, olive oil, spices and gifts.

AIX-EN-PROVENCE

0 ___ 200 m
0 ___ 0.1 miles

A · B · C · D

INFORMATION
Book In Bar.................................1 C5
Change L'Agence........................2 B5
Change Nazareth.........................3 B4
Hub Lot Cybercafé......................4 C3
Laundrette..................................5 D5
Laundrette..................................6 A4
Laundrette..................................7 A4
Laundrette..................................8 D3
Paradox Librairie Internationale....9 C5
Post Office...............................10 A5
Tourist Office...........................11 B5

SIGHTS & ACTIVITIES   (pp778-80)
Bouldrome Municipal...................12 C6
Cathédrale St-Sauveur................13 B2
Flea Market...............................14 C4
Galerie d'Art du Conseil Général....15 B5
Musée Granet............................16 D5
Musée Paul Arbaud.....................17 C5
Thermes Sextius.........................18 A3

SLEEPING   (pp780-1)
Grand Hôtel Nègre Coste............19 C4
Hôtel Cardinal...........................20 C5
Hôtel Cardinalx (Annexe).............21 D5
Hôtel des Arts...........................22 D4
Hôtel des Augustins....................23 B4
Hôtel des Quatre Dauphins..........24 C5
Hôtel du Globe..........................25 A3
Hôtel Le Manoir.........................26 A4

EATING   (pp781-2)
Boulangerie...............................27 C4
La Boulangerie du Coin...............28 C3
La Brocherie..............................29 C5
La Fontaine...............................30 B4
LAixquis...................................31 B4
Le Dernier Bistrot......................32 C3
Les Baccanales..........................33 B4
Les Deux Garçons......................34 C4
Les Tournesols..........................35 B3
Market.....................................36 B3
Monoprix Department Store.........37 B4
Petit Casino..............................38 D5
Yôji..39 B5

DRINKING   (p782)
L'unic.....................................40 B3
La Belle Époque........................41 C4
Red Clover..............................42 B4

ENTERTAINMENT   (p782)
Bar Sextius..............................43 A4
Le Scat Club............................44 B3

SHOPPING   (p782)
Cave du Felibrige......................45 B3
Maison Bechard.......................46 B5

TRANSPORT   (pp782-3)
Bus Station..............................47 A6

OTHER
Hôtel de Ville...........................48 B3
Pétanque Course......................49 C6
Théâtre...................................50 D4

PROVENCE

History

Aix was founded as a military camp named Aquae Sextiae (Waters of Sextius) in 123 BC on the site of thermal springs, which are still flowing to this day. Fortunately for stuck-up Aix, the settlement became known as Aix – not Sex.

The town was established after Roman forces under the proconsul Sextius Calvinus had destroyed the Ligurian Celtic stronghold of Entremont, 3km to the north, and enslaved its inhabitants. In the 12th century the counts of Provence made Aix their capital, which it remained until the revolution, when Marseille was declared the new regional capital.

The city reached its zenith as a centre of art and learning under the enlightened King René (1409–80), said to have been a brilliant polyglot who brought painters to his court from around Europe (especially Flanders) and instituted administrative reforms for the benefit of his subjects.

Bypassed by the Marseille-bound railway line in the 19th century, Aix lost out in terms of trade but remains an important legal and academic centre today, as well as a popular commuter town for Marseille's office workers.

Orientation

Cours Mirabeau, Aix's main boulevard, stretches from La Rotonde, a roundabout with a huge fountain and also called place du Général de Gaulle, eastwards to place Forbin. The oldest part of the city, Vieil Aix, is north of cours Mirabeau; most of the streets, alleys and public squares in this part of town are closed to traffic.

South of cours Mirabeau is the Mazarin Quartier, with a regular street grid that was laid out in the 17th century. The entire city centre is ringed by a series of one-way boulevards.

Aix's chicest shops are clustered along pedestrian rue Marius Reinaud, which winds its way behind the Palais de Justice on place de Verdun.

Information

BOOKSHOPS
Book in Bar (☎ 04 42 26 60 07; 1bis rue Cabassol) Bookshop-cum-café selling English-language novels and guidebooks, including Lonely Planet guides. Buys/sells second-hand books.

Paradox Librairie Internationale (☎ 04 42 26 47 99; 15 rue du Quatre Septembre)

INTERNET ACCESS
Hub Lot Cybercafé (☎ 04 42 21 37 31; 15-27 rue Paul Bert; per min €0.06; ✆ 8am-midnight) WiFi access here, helpful service from English owner and there's a sometimes lively bar.

LAUNDRY
There are laundrettes at 3 rue de la Fontaine, 34 cours Sextius, 3 rue de la Fonderie and 60 rue Boulegon. All are open from 7am or 8am to 8pm.

MONEY
Commercial banks mass along cours Mirabeau and cours Sextius, which runs north–south to the west of La Rotonde.
Change L'Agence (15 cours Mirabeau) Local American Express agent.
Change Nazareth (7 rue Nazareth; ✆ 9am-7pm Mon-Sat, 9-5pm Sun Jul & Aug)

POST
Post Office (cnr av des Belges & rue Lapierre)

TOURIST INFORMATION
Tourist Office (☎ 04 42 16 11 61; www.aixenprovenc etourism.com; 2 place du Général de Gaulle; ✆ 8.30am-7pm Mon-Sat, 10am-1pm & 2-6pm Sun Jul & Aug; 8.30am-7pm Mon-Sat, 10am-1pm & 2-7pm Sun Sep-Jun) Highly efficient place but still gets very busy indeed.

Sights

Aix's social scene centres on shaded **cours Mirabeau**, a wide avenue laid out during the latter half of the 1600s and named after the revolutionary hero Comte de Mirabeau. Trendy cafés spill out onto the footpaths on the sunny northern side of the street, which is crowned by a leafy roof of plane trees. The shady southern side shelters a string of elegant Renaissance *hôtels particuliers* (private mansions); **Hôtel d'Espargnet** (1647) at No 38 is among the most impressive (today it houses the university's economics department). The Marquis of Entrecasteaux murdered his wife in their family home, **Hôtel d'Isoard de Vauvenarges** (1710), at No 10.

The large, cast-iron fountain at the western end of cours Mirabeau, **Fontaine de la Rotonde**, dates from 1860. At the avenue's eastern end, the **fountain** at place Forbin is decorated with a 19th-century statue of King

René holding a bunch of Muscat grapes, a varietal he is credited with introducing to the region. Moss-covered **Fontaine d'Eau Thermale** at the intersection of cours Mirabeau and rue du Quatre Septembre spouts water at a temperature of 34°C.

Other streets and squares lined with *hôtels particuliers* include **rue Mazarine**, which is one block south of cours Mirabeau; **place des Quatre Dauphins**, two blocks further south with a fountain that dates from 1667; the eastern continuation of cours Mirabeau, **rue de l'Opéra** (at Nos 18, 24 and 26); and the pretty, fountain-clad **place d'Albertas**, just west of **place St-Honoré**, where live music is sometimes performed on balmy summer evenings.

South of Aix's historic centre is the very pleasant **parc Jourdan**, a spacious green park dominated by Aix's largest fountain and home to the town's **Boulodrome Municipal**. Old men gather here, or on the court on av du Parc, opposite the park entrance, beneath the shade of the trees, to play *pétanque*. Spectators are welcome.

MUSEUMS

The tourist office sells a Visa for Aix-en-Provence for €2 that offers reduced entry for many city and regional museums.

Sadly, Aix's finest museum, **Musée Granet**, housed in a 17th-century priory of the Knights of Malta, will be closed until at least 2006 while it undergoes massive works that will see it triple in size. Exhibits in the reopened museum will include Celtic statues from Entremont as well as Roman artefacts, 16th- to 19th-century Italian, Dutch and French paintings as well as some of Aix-born Cézanne's lesser-known pieces.

Musée Paul Arbaud (☎ 04 42 38 38 95; 2a rue du Quatre Septembre; adult/student €2.50/1.50; ☼ 2-5pm Mon-Sat) displays books, manuscripts and a collection of Provençal faïence – tin-glazed earthenware.

Galérie d'Art du Conseil Général (☎ 04 42 93 03 57; 21bis cours Mirabeau; ☼ 10.15am-12.45pm & 1.30-5.30pm Mon-Sat) also has exhibitions of photography and contemporary art.

CATHÉDRALE ST-SAUVEUR

Cathédrale St-Sauveur (rue J de Laroque; ☼ 8am-noon & 2-6pm) is a interesting ragtag of styles through the ages, incorporating architectural features of every major period from the 5th to 18th centuries stuck onto one another with some modern touches, such as the chunky, golden contemporary altar piece. The main Gothic structure, built between 1285 and 1350, includes the Romanesque nave of a 12th-century church as part of its southern aisle; the chapels were added in the 14th and 15th centuries, and there is a 5th-century sarcophagus in the apse.

Mass is held here at 8am (Saturday at 6.30pm, and Sunday at 9am, 10.30am and 7pm). Gregorian chants are often sung here at 4.30pm on Sunday – an experience not to be missed.

The 15th-century *Triptyque du Buisson Ardent* (Triptych of the Burning Bush) in the nave is by Nicolas Froment; it is usually only opened for groups. Near it is a triptych panel illustrating Christ's passion. The tapestries encircling the choir date from the 18th century and the fabulous gilt organ is baroque. There's a son-et-lumière (sound-and-light) show at 9.30pm most nights in summer.

CÉZANNE TRAIL

Paul Cézanne (1839–1906), Aix's most celebrated son (at least after his death), did much of his painting in and around the city. If you are interested in the minutiae of his day-to-day life – where he ate, drank, played and worked – just follow the **Circuit de Cézanne**, which is marked by round, bronze markers in the footpaths and begins at the tourist office. The markers correspond with an English-language guide called *Cézanne's Footsteps*, which is available free from the tourist office.

Cézanne's last studio, now opened to the public as **Atelier Paul Cézanne** (☎ 04 42 21 06 53; 9 av Paul Cézanne; adult/student €5.50/2; ☼ 10am-noon & 2-5pm), is atop a hill approximately 1.5km north of the tourist office. It has been left exactly as it was when he died and though none of his works hang here, his tools do. Take bus No 1 to the Cézanne stop.

THERMAL SPA

Thermes Sextius (☎ 04 42 23 81 82; 55 cours Sextius) is the place to do as the Romans did on the same spot: chill out and get pampered silly at the thermal spas. By no means cheap, it's the place for luxurious treats such as 'zen spray massage' and a range of beauty treatments. A day's access to the fitness centre or a massage both start at €32.

MARKETS

Aix is the premier market town in Provence. A mass of fruit-and-vegetable stands are set up each morning on place Richelme, just as they have been for centuries. Depending on the season, you can buy olives, *chèvre* (goat's cheese), garlic, lavender, honey, peaches, melons and a whole host of other sun-kissed products.

Another **grocery market** (place des Prêcheurs) is set up on Tuesday, Thursday and Saturday morning.

A **flower market** is set up on place des Prêcheurs (Sunday morning) and on place de l'Hôtel de Ville (Tuesday, Thursday and Saturday mornings). There's also a **flea market** (place de Verdun).

Tours

Between April and October, the tourist office runs a packed schedule of guided bus tours around the region in English and in French. There's also the guided Émile Zola literary walk or a free, self-guided *Literary Walk* brochure. Ask for the free *Guide Map* at the tourist office for details of all tours or study the noticeboard outside. Prices start from around €35.

Festivals & Events

Aix has a sumptuous cultural calendar. The most sought-after tickets are for the month-long **Festival International d'Art Lyrique d'Aix-en-Provence** (International Festival of Lyrical Art; www.festival-aix.com) in July, which brings the most refined classical music, opera and ballet to such city venues as the Théâtre de l'Archevêché, outside the Cathédrale St-Sauveur. Meanwhile, buskers bring the festival spirit to cours Mirabeau.

Other festivals include **Rencontres du 9ème Art** (www.bd-aix.com in French), a brand-new annual comic book, animation and cartoon-art festival in March, the two-day **Festival du Tambourin** (Tambourine Festival) in mid-April and the **Fête Mistralienne**, marking the birthday of Provençal hero Frédéric Mistral on 13 September. For detailed information contact the tourist office.

Sleeping

Despite being a student town, Aix is not cheap. Even so, the centre can fill up fast in summer and during busy conference and law exam times, so booking ahead is always

a good idea. The tourist office has comprehensive details of *chambres d'hôtes* (B&Bs) and *gîtes ruraux* (country cottages) in and around Aix. The tourist office also has a list (which is updated weekly) of all types of accommodation – including farmhouses – to rent on a long-term basis. Hotel bookings are coordinated through one address (resaix@aixenprovencetourism.com).

BUDGET

Auberge de Jeunesse du Jas de Bouffan (☎ 04 42 20 15 99; fax 04 42 59 36 12; 3 av Marcel Pagnol; dm incl breakfast & sheets €15) This is a smart, modern place with great views of a distant Mont Ventoux. It's about 2km west of the centre. Rooms are locked between 9am and 5pm. Take bus No 4 from La Rotonde to the Vasarely stop.

Hôtel des Arts (☎ 04 42 38 11 77; fax 04 42 26 77 31; 69 blvd Carnot; s/d from €29/33) Laid-back and friendly, Hôtel des Arts has decent rooms at least partially soundproofed from street noise by double glazing. Although on the city centre's eastern fringe (second entrance at 5 rue de la Fonderie) it's still only a short stroll from the milling crowds of the centre.

Hôtel Paul (☎ 04 42 23 23 89; hotel.paul@wanadoo.fr; 10 av Pasteur; s/d/tr €35/45/55) Although less central than others, Hôtel Paul has simple but welcoming rooms and a pleasant courtyard garden, making it an appealing budget option. Just north of blvd Jean Jaurès, it's a 10-minute walk from the tourist office or take minibus No 2 from La Rotonde or the bus station.

Camping

Camping Arc-en-Ciel (☎ 04 42 26 14 28; route de Nice; camping €17.10; ☼ Apr-Sep) There are peaceful wooded hills out the back of this place, but a busy motorway in front. It's 2km south east of town, at Pont des Trois Sautets. Take bus No 3 to Les Trois Sautets stop.

MID-RANGE

Hôtel Le Manoir (☎ 04 42 26 27 20; www.hotelmanoir .com; 8 rue d'Entrecasteaux; d/tr with toilet & shower from €54/72, with bath & toilet from €66/82; P) Immaculately kept and occupying a quiet yet central corner of town, Le Manoir has 40 individually decorated rooms with modern comforts and dark-wood period furniture. Enjoy breakfast (€7) under the 14th-century cloister and gaze onto that pleasant garden.

Hôtel Cardinal (☎ 04 42 38 32 30; fax 04 42 26 39 05; 24 rue Cardinale; s/d €47/60, self-catering ste €76) This is a charming place with large (mostly) en suite rooms and a mix of modern and period furniture. The upper rooms offer pretty views across town. The small self-catering suites are in its annexe at 12 rue Cardinale.

Hôtel des Quatre Dauphins (☎ 04 42 38 16 39; fax 04 42 38 60 19; 54 rue Roux Alpheran; s with shower & toilet €45, d with shower & toilet €55-74) Another hotel in a period building near the Cardinal, this place has character, although the rooms lack extensive facilities.

Hôtel du Globe (☎ 04 42 26 03 58; hotel-du-globe@wanadoo.fr; 74 cours Sextius; s with toilet €36, d/tw/tr with shower or bath €59/62/67; P) Just out of the pedestrianised area, Hôtel du Globe is comfortable and reasonable value. Garage parking costs €8 a night and air-con costs €4 extra in July and August.

TOP END

Aix is well endowed with three- and four-star hotels, though many are on the outskirts of town.

Hôtel des Augustins (☎ 04 42 27 28 59; www .hotel-augustins.com; 3 rue de la Masse; standard/superior r low season €95/110, high season €110/125; 🞬) An elegant and atmospheric 15th-century former convent, this place is very comfortable, central and tastefully furnished. All rooms have air-con, cable TV, minibars and telephones. If the weather's good, have breakfast on the roof terrace beneath the bell tower.

Grand Hôtel Nègre Coste (☎ 04 42 27 74 22; www.hotelnegrecoste.com; 33 cours Mirabeau; r €78-100; P 🞬) Right in the heart of the action, this was the hotel of choice for Louis XIV in 1660 and many businesspeople today. The large, comfortable three-star rooms are showing their age somewhat but all are well equipped. Garage parking is available.

Eating

Aix and the surrounding area is a rich hunting ground for fine dining if you've got the budget for it. Ethnic cuisine in town is usually high quality and generally inexpensive and there are enough restaurants to satisfy most mouths. Aix's cheapest dining street is rue Van Loo, lined with restaurants offering Italian and various Asian cuisines.

Aix's sweet speciality is the *calisson*, a soft, lozenge-shaped chew made with almond paste and fruit syrup.

RESTAURANTS

Rue de la Verrerie and rue Félibre Gaut offer a good range of culinary options, including a number of Vietnamese and Chinese restaurants.

Numerous cafés, brasseries and restaurants can be found nearby, in the heart of the city on place des Cardeurs and place de l'Hôtel de Ville.

La Brocherie (☎ 04 42 38 33 21; 5 rue Fernand Dol; menus €15-33; 🕑 closed Sat lunch & Sun) A decent, affordable lunch and dinner option, La Brocherie serves imaginative Provençal mains, good wine and desserts.

Les Tournesols (☎ 04 42 38 30 88; 1 rue Cardinale; menus €16-20; 🕑 closed Sat & Mon dinner, Sun) Painted in sunflower yellow (*tournesols* is French for sunflowers), this tiny place serves up good-value salads and tarts as well as heartier regional dishes.

La Fontaine (☎ 04 42 27 53 35; 40 rue de la Verrerie; menus €17; 🕑 7pm-12.30am Tue-Sat) Named after the pretty little fountain that flows on its outside terrace, La Fontaine offers hearty, generous *menus* of Provençal food.

Le Dernier Bistrot (☎ 04 42 21 13 02; 15-19 rue Constantin; lunch menu €10, dinner menus €16-23; 🕑 Mon-Sat) This bistro boasts a lovely terrace and dishes that mix traditional bistro recipes with Provençal culinary fodder such as beef daubes and *carpaccios, soupe au pistou* and courgette flan with a tomato and basil coulis.

Les Bacchanales (☎ 04 42 27 21 06; 10 rue de la Couronne; lunch menu €18, menu gourmand €63; 🕑 closed Wed & Sat lunch, Tue) An upmarket spot offering a delectable Provençal menu that usually offers several fish choices (such as delicately fennel-scented *rouget*) as well as heavier, traditional meat fare, including a good daube.

Yôji (☎ 04 42 38 84 48; 7 av Victor Hugo; lunch menus from €9.50, dinner menus €16-20) Yôji is often packed even midweek in low season and you'll taste why if you can get in (book ahead) The sushi is first rate and there are some tasty occidental/oriental fusion twists (the sake martini is an unlikely hit, as is the toothsome green-tea *brulée*). For real theatre, choose the sizzling Korean barbeques brought to your table (oh, so that's what those fancy smoke hoods above the tables are for).

L'Aixquis (☎ 04 42 27 76 16; 22 rue Victor Leydet; menus €18 & €60; 🕑 lunch & dinner Tue-Sat) Although small, L'Aixquis is celebrated for its use of fresh produce, tried-and-tested Provençal classics, a good wine list and elaborately presented desserts. The kitchen turns out a good, richly flavoured *pieds et paquets* (slow stewed tripe 'n' trotter) but be warned you'll need to be a fan of that unique glue-and-gristle texture.

CAFÉS

Les Deux Garçons (☎ 04 42 26 00 51; 53 cours Mirabeau) Aix's most renowned café, Les Deux Garçons is on the sunny side of the street. No visit to Aix is complete without a pose here behind your shades. Dating from 1792, this pricey brasserie is a former artist's and intellectual's hang-out – Cézanne and his novelist mate Zola were patrons here.

Not quite so conspicuous are the plentiful open-air cafés that sprawl across the squares, such as place des Cardeurs, forum des Cardeurs, place de Verdun and place de l'Hôtel de Ville.

SELF-CATERING

The next best thing to bread from the market is the fresh and often-warm loaves sold at **La Boulangerie du Coin** (4 rue Boulegon; 🕑 Tue-Sun). It is also one of the few *boulangeries* to bake on Sunday, along with the **boulangerie** (5 rue Tournefort) that never closes, making it ideal for post-pub or club snacks.

Groceries are available in the basement supermarket at **Monoprix Department Store** (cours Mirabeau; 🕑 8.30am-8pm Mon-Sat) and at **Petit Casino** (rue Cardinale; 🕑 9am-7pm Mon-Sat).

Drinking

Several lively pubs and clubs have sprung up on and around rue de la Verrerie.

Red Clover (☎ 04 42 23 44 61; 30 rue de la Verrerie) An Irish pub attracting a studenty crowd and occasionally screening live sport, as does the late-closing bar and Internet café Hub Lot.

La Belle Époque (☎ 04 42 27 65 66; 29 cours Mirabeau; 🕑 6.30am-2.30am) This place buzzes during its two-hour-plus happy 'hour' and boasts large TV screens and DJs playing Latino, house and funk every evening.

L'unic (☎ 04 42 96 38 28; place Richelme) Good for laid-back drinks or brasserie-style fare.

Entertainment

Pick up a free copy of the monthly *In Aix* at the tourist office to find out what's on where and when. Ballet fans may want to check out **Le Ballet Preljocaj** (www.preljocaj.org), a company that made Aix its permanent base in 2005.

NIGHTCLUBS

Le Damier Club (☎ 04 42 27 03 23; 31 av Infirmeries) Providing a good mixture of musical dance styles – rap, pop, nostalgia – Le Damier Club is spread over three floors.

Le Scat Club (☎ 04 42 23 00 23; 11 rue de la Verrerie, 🕑 from 11pm Tue-Sat) An institution in Aix, Le Scat Club presents rock and jazz bands to a young, casual crowd.

Bar Sextius (☎ 04 42 26 07 21; 13 cours Sextius; 🕑 7am-2am Mon-Sat) Another small, intimate venue, Bar Sextius has live music (Thursday) and DJs playing house (Saturday), reggae and raga (Tuesday).

Shopping

Cave du Felibrige (18 rue des Cordeliers) Sells a splendid array of local wines – some *very* expensive.

Maison Bechard (12 cours Mirabeau) A classy patisserie and *confiseur*. What sweeter way to end that sunny summer picnic than with a couple of Aix's traditional almond confections or some great pastries?

Aix's rue Fabrot is also one of the best places in Provence to seek out desirable designer threads, with several boutiques to choose from.

Getting There & Away

AIR

Marseille-Provence airport is 25km from Aix-en-Provence and is served by regular shuttle buses (see opposite).

BUS

Aix's **bus station** (☎ information office 04 42 91 26 80; av de l'Europe) is a 10-minute walk southwest from La Rotonde. It is served by numerous companies.

There are buses to Marseille (€4.20, 35 minutes via the autoroute or one hour via the N8, every five to 10 minutes), Arles (€11.30, 1¾ hours, five daily), Avignon via the autoroute (€13.90, one hour, six daily) or the national road (€11.70, 1½ hours, four daily) and Toulon (€13.40, one hour, four daily Monday to Saturday).

Sumian buses serve Apt (€8, two daily) and Castellane (Monday, Wednesday and Saturday).

CAR

Getting into Aix by car can be a headache: the one-way, three-lane orbital system ringing the old town is busy and street parking can be hard to find, although (pricier) covered parking just around the edges of old town is plentiful.

TRAIN

Aix's tiny **train station** (5am-9.15pm Mon-Fri, 6am-9.15pm Sat & Sun, information office 9am-7pm) is at the southern end of av Victor Hugo. There are frequent services to Briançon (€28.80, 3½ hours), Gap (€22.44, two hours) and, of course, Marseille (€4.10, 35 minutes, at least 18 daily), from where there are connections to just about everywhere.

Aix's new TGV station is 8km from the city centre, accessible by shuttle bus (see below).

Getting Around
TO/FROM THE AIRPORT & TGV STATION

Both the new TGV station and the airport are linked to Aix's bus station (€7.50, from around 5am to 11.30pm) by the half-hourly **Navette** (04 42 93 59 13).

BUS

The city's 14 bus and three minibus lines are operated by **Aix en Bus** (04 42 26 37 28; 8.30am-7pm Mon-Sat). The information desk is inside the tourist office.

La Rotonde is the main bus hub. Most of the services run until 8pm. A single/*carnet* (book) of 10 bus tickets costs €1.10/7.70. A day pass costs €3.50. Minibus No 1 links the bus station with La Rotonde and cours Mirabeau. Minibus 2, starting at the train station, follows much the same route.

TAXI

You can usually find taxis outside the bus station. To order one, call **Taxi Radio Aixois** (04 42 27 71 11) or **Taxi Mirabeau** (04 42 21 61 61).

THE VAUCLUSE

The Vaucluse is Provence at its most picturesque. Many of the towns date from Roman times and boast impressive Gallo-Roman structures. The villages, which spring to life on market days, are surrounded by some of France's most attractive countryside, brightened by the rich hues of wild herbs, lavender and vines. The Vaucluse is

watched over by Mont Ventoux, which, at 1909m, is Provence's highest peak.

The Vaucluse is shaped like a fan, with Avignon, the region's capital, at the hinge. Orange, famed for its Roman theatre, and the smaller Roman town of Vaison-la-Romaine are north of Avignon and west of Mont Ventoux. Carpentras, near the centre of the Vaucluse, also dates from Roman times but is better known for its ancient Jewish community. Just to the south is Fontaine de Vaucluse, to the east of which are Gordes and Roussillon, enticing Provençal villages overlooking a fertile valley. Further east still is Apt, one of the best bases for exploring the pretty Lubéron Range to the south.

Getting Around

If you don't have access to a car, it is possible to get from town to town by local bus, but the frequency and pace of services are very much in keeping with the relaxed tempo of Provençal life.

AVIGNON
pop 88,312

Avignon is synonymous in France with the annual performing arts festival held here each summer. There's also plenty to see during the rest of the year.

Inside the 4km ring of superbly preserved ramparts, towers and crenellations that fence in the old city's narrow streets and ancient tenements you'll find café-filled squares, a number of interesting museums, the famous Pont d'Avignon and the massive fortress and des res of the medieval popes, the Palais des Papes.

History

The city first acquired wealth and power, its mighty ramparts and its reputation as a city of art and culture during the 14th century, when Pope Clement V and his court fled political turmoil in Rome and established themselves near Avignon. From 1309 to 1377, the seven French-born popes based themselves here, and invested huge sums of money in building and decorating the papal palace. Under the popes' tolerant rule, Jews and political dissidents took shelter here.

Opponents of the move to Avignon – many of them Italians, such as the celebrated poet Petrarch, who lived in Fontaine de Vaucluse at the time – called Avignon

AVIGNON

PROVENCE

0 — 500 m
0 — 0.3 miles

Rhône

To Villeneuve-lès
Avignon (500m);
Tour
Philippe-le-Bel (1.2km);
Fort St-André (2.1km)

To Lyons (227km)
To Orange-
Lyons (28km)
Route de Lyon
D225
Porte St-Lazare
Blvd Quai St-Lazare

Blvd Limbert
Montfavet
Route de

Av
Pierre

Aéroport (8km);
Caumont (8km);
Aix-en-Provence (80km);
Marseilles (99km)

To Centre Hospitalier
(2.5km); Arles (36km)

R des Infirmières
Pl des Carmes
R Palaphamerie
R Campane
R Paul Sain
R Louis Pasteur
R Thiers
R St-Christophe
Quartier des Teinturiers
R des Teinturiers
R Guillaume Puy
Philonarde
Sorgue

Blvd St-Michel

R Bertrand
Banasterie
Rocher (les Doms)
(Jardins des Doms)
Blvd de la Ligne
Pont St-Bénézet
Cours Châtelet
Blvd du Rhône
R Petite Fusterie
R des Grottes
R de la Balance
R Campana
R de la République
R Carnot
R Paul Sain
Pl Pie
R Bonneterie
R du Roi René
R Noël Biret
R du Portail Magnanen
R des Corps Saints
R St-Michel
Blvd St-Michel

Pl des Corps Saints
R St-Michel

R Henri Fabre
R des Trois Faucons
Cours Jean Jaurès
Porte de la République
R du Rempart St-Michel

Blvd St-Roch
Gare Avignon Centre (Train Station)
Porte St-Roch

R des Lices
Pl Jérusalem
R de Mons
R Galante
R de la Bancasse
R Viala
R Bouquerie
R Joseph Vernet
R Violette
R Joseph Vernet
R Lanterne
R Victor Hugo
R Annanelle
R St-Charles
Cours Président Kennedy

R Vernet
R Eugène
R Agricol Perdiguier
R Joseph Vernet
Porte de l'Oulle
Blvd de l'Oulle
Allées de l'Oulle
Porte de l'Oulle
Porte St-Dominique
Blvd de St-Dominique
R Velouterie
Av Eisenhower
Av de la Foire (80m)
R Paul Mérindol

Rhône
Pont Édouard Daladier
Chemin des Berges
Île de la Barthelasse

To Nîmes (47km)

Pont de l'Europe

To Gare Avignon
TGV Courtine (4km)

Pl du Palais

INFORMATION		
Bureau du Festival	1	C4
Chez Wam	2	E3
CIC	3	C2
Laverie la Fontaine	4	D3
Lavmatic	5	D3
Main Post Office	6	C4
Shakespeare	7	F1
Tourist Office	8	C3
Webzone	9	D2

SIGHTS & ACTIVITIES		(pp786-7)
Cathédrale Notre Dame des Doms	10	D1
Église St-Pierre	11	D2
Hôtel de Villeneuve-Marrignan & Musée		
Calvet	12	C3
Mireio Embarcadère	13	B2
Musée du Petit Palais	14	C1
Musée Lapidaire	15	C3
Palais des Papes	16	D2
Point d'Argent	17	C4
Synagogue	18	D2

SLEEPING		(pp787-8)
Auberge Bagatelle	(see 19)	
Camping Bagatelle	19	B1
Hôtel Colbert	20	D4
Hôtel de Blauvac	21	C2
Hôtel de la Mirande	22	D2

Hôtel du Palais des Papes	23	C1
Hôtel du Parc	24	D3
Hôtel Innova	25	C3
Hôtel Le Provençal	26	C2
Hôtel L'Europe	27	C2
Hôtel Médiéval	28	D2
Hôtel Mignon	29	C2
Hôtel Monclar	30	D4
Hôtel Splendid	31	D4

EATING		(pp788-9)
Boulangerie Pâtisserie	32	C2
Casino	33	C2
La Compagnie des Comptoirs	34	C3
La Fourchette	35	C2
La Marmiton	(see 22)	
La Tropézienne	(see 33)	
Le Bistrot d'Utopia	(see 58)	
Le Brantes	36	C2
Le Caveau du Théâtre	37	D3
Les Halles & Food Market	38	D3
Maison Nani	39	C3
Restaurant Song Long	40	D2
Tapalocas	41	D2

DRINKING		(p789)
Bleu les Thés	42	C3
Le Café d'Utopia	(see 58)	
L'Electro	43	D2

ENTERTAINMENT		(pp789-90)
Cinéma Utopia	(see 58)	
Fnac	44	C3
Opéra d'Avignon	45	C2
Red Lion	46	D2
Red Zone	47	D2

SHOPPING		(p790)
Comtesse du Barry	48	C2
Instant du Sud	49	D2
Le Lavandin	50	C1
Oliviers & Co	51	C2

TRANSPORT		(pp790-1)
Agence Commerciale TCRA	52	C4
Bus No 10 Stop	(see 6)	
Bus Station	53	D4
La Barthelasse Bus Stop	54	B1
Provence Bike	55	D4
Shuttle boat embarkment point	56	C1
TGV Shuttle Bus Stop	(see 6)	

OTHER		
Hôtel de Ville	57	C2
La Manutention	58	D1
Palais de Justice	59	D2
Pont St-Bénézet Entrance	(see 61)	
Swimming Pool	60	B1
Tour de Châtelet	61	C1

'the second Babylonian captivity' and a den of criminals and brothel-goers, unfit for papal habitation.

Pope Gregory XI left Avignon in 1376, but his death two years later led to the Great Schism (1378–1417), during which rival popes – up to three at one time – resided at Rome and Avignon and spent most of their energies denouncing and excommunicating one another.

Even after the schism was settled and a pope – Martin V – acceptable to all factions established himself in Rome, Avignon remained under papal rule and continued to serve as an important cultural centre. The city and the nearby Comtat Venaissin (now the *département* of Vaucluse) were ruled by papal legates until 1791, when they were annexed to France.

Orientation

The main avenue within the walled city (*intra-muros*) runs northwards from the train station to place de l'Horloge; it's called cours Jean Jaurès south of the tourist office and rue de la République north of it.

Place de l'Horloge is 300m south of place du Palais, which abuts the Palais des Papes. The city gate nearest the train station is Porte de la République, while the city gate next to Pont Édouard Daladier, which leads to Villeneuve-lès-Avignon, is Porte de l'Oulle. The rehabilitated Quartier des Teinturiers (old dyers' quarter), centred around rue des

Teinturiers, southeast of place Pie, is Avignon's bohemian part of town.

Information
BOOKSHOPS

The tourist office has a small boutique that sells maps and regional guides in both French and English.

Shakespeare (☎ 04 90 27 38 50; 155 rue Carreterie; ⏰ 9.30am-12.30pm & 2-6.30pm Tue-Sat) English bookshop and *salon de thé* – enjoy scones with your tomes.

INTERNET ACCESS

Chez Wam (☎ 04 90 86 19 03; 68 rue Guillaume Puy; per 30 min/hr €3/5; ⏰ 7am-1am Mon-Fri, noon-1am Sat & Sun)

Webzone (☎ 04 32 76 29 47; 3 rue St Jean le Vieux; per hr €4.57; ⏰ 11am-10pm Mon-Sat, noon-5pm Sun)

LAUNDRY

Laverie La Fontaine (66 place des Corps Saints; ⏰ 7am-8pm)

Lavmatic (27 rue du Portail Magnanen; ⏰ 7am-7.30pm)

MEDICAL SERVICES

Centre Hospitalier (☎ 04 32 75 33 33; rue Raoul Follereau) 2.5km south of the train station, at the southern terminus of bus line Nos 1 and 3 (marked on bus maps as 'Hôpital Sud').

MONEY

CIC (13 rue de la République) In the train station forecourt with a 24-currency changing machine and ATM.

PROVENCE

POST
Main Post Office (cours Président Kennedy) Currency exchange and Cyberposte.

TOURIST INFORMATION
Tourist Office (☎ 04 32 74 32 74; www.ot-avignon.fr; 41 cours Jean Jaurès; ⌚ 9am-6pm Mon-Sat, 9am-5pm Sun Apr-Jun & Aug-Oct, 9am-6pm Mon-Fri, 9am-5pm Sat, 10am-noon Sun Nov-Mar, 9am-7pm Mon-Sat, 10am-5pm Sun Jul) Around 300m north of the train station. During the Avignon Festival it opens 9am to 7pm (5pm on Sunday). On Tuesday, Thursday and Saturday between 1 April and 31 October, two-hour **city tours** (adult/child €10/7) in English and French depart from the tourist office at 10am.

AVIGNON PASSION

To encourage maximum sightseeing the tourist office has devised the Avignon Passion museum pass. Here's how it works: pay full price at the first monument or museum you enter and you receive a card entitling you to a reduced price in all other museums and discounts on the tourist office walking tours. The pass is good for 15 days in all the museums of Avignon as well as Villeneuve-lès-Avignon and covers a family of five. The discounted price is equal to the admission for students, so it's unnecessary for those with an ISIC card.

Sights & Activities
PONT ST-BÉNÉZET (LE PONT D'AVIGNON)
Pont St-Bénézet (St Bénézet's Bridge; ☎ 04 90 27 51 16; full price/pass €3.50/3; ⌚ 9am-7pm Apr-Jun & Oct & Nov, 9am-8pm Jul-Sep, 9.30am-5.45pm Nov-Mar, to 9pm during theatre festival in Jul) was built between 1177 and 1185 to link Avignon with the settlement across the Rhône that later became Villeneuve-lès-Avignon. By tradition, the construction of the bridge is said to have begun when Bénézet (Benedict the Bridge Builder), a pastor from Ardèche, was told in three visions to get the Rhône spanned at any cost. Yes, this is also the Pont d'Avignon mentioned in the French nursery rhyme. In actual fact, people did not dance *sur le pont d'Avignon* (on the bridge of Avignon) but *sous* (under) it in between the arches.

The 900m-long wooden structure was repaired and rebuilt several times before all but four of its 22 spans were washed away once and for all in the mid-1600s.

Admission to the bridge is via cours Châtelet. Many people find a distant view of the bridge from the Rocher des Doms or Pont Édouard Daladier much more interesting. And it is, of course, free. Another pleasant alternative is to cross the river and take in the view with a stroll on the Île de la Barthelasse, on the promenade des Berges.

WALLED CITY
Avignon's most interesting bits are within the roughly oval walled city, which is surrounded by almost 4.5km of ramparts built between 1359 and 1370. The ramparts were restored during the 19th century, but the original moats were not, leaving the crenellated fortifications looking purposeless and certainly less imposing than they once did. Even in the 14th century this defence system was hardly state-of-the-art: the towers were left open on the side facing the city, and machicolations (openings in the parapets for dropping things such as boiling oil or for shooting arrows at attackers) are lacking in many sections.

Palais des Papes
The huge **Palais des Papes** (Palace of the Popes; ☎ 04 90 27 50 00; place du Palais; full price/pass €9.50/7.50; ⌚ 9am or 9.30am-6.30pm or 7pm Oct-Jun, 9am-8pm Jul-Sep, to 9pm during theatre festival in Jul) was built during the 14th century as a fortified palace for the pontifical court. The cavernous stone halls and extensive grounds testify to the enormous wealth amassed by the papacy during the 'Babylonian Captivity'. The palace is an outstanding example of Gothic architecture but the undecorated rooms are nearly empty except for occasional art exhibits. The view of the palace complex is more impressive than the visit and the best view is from across the river along the chemin des Berges on the Île de la Barthelasse. The fabulous cours d'Honneur – the palace's main courtyard – has played host to the Avignon festival since 1947.

The admission price includes hire of a very user-friendly audioguide in English. Call for the schedule of guided tours in English given in July and August.

Musée du Petit Palais
During the 14th and 15th centuries **Musée du Petit Palais** (☎ 04 90 86 44 58; place du Palais; full price/pass €6/3; ⌚ 10am-1pm & 2-6pm Wed-Mon Jun-Sep, 9.30am-1pm & 2-5.30pm Wed-Mon Oct-May) served

as a bishops' and archbishops' palace. It now houses an outstanding collection of lavishly coloured 13th- to 16th-century Italian religious paintings from artists including Botticelli, Carpaccio and Giovanni di Paolo. There are accompanying information sheets in English in each room.

Rocher des Doms
Just up the hill from the cathedral is **Rocher des Doms**, a delightful bluff-top park that affords great views of the Rhône, Pont St-Bénézet, Villeneuve-lès-Avignon and the Alpilles. A semicircular viewpoint indicator tells you what you're looking at. There's shade, breeze and benches aplenty up here and it's a good spot for a picnic.

Musée Calvet
Housed in the elegant Hôtel de Villeneuve-Martignan (1741–54), **Musée Calvet** (☎ 04 90 86 33 84; 65 rue Joseph Vernet; full price/pass €6/3; 10am-1pm & 2-6pm Wed-Mon) has an impressive collection of artefacts dating from prehistory to the Roman times, as well as paintings from between the 16th and the 20th centuries.

Musée Lapidaire
Not far from the tourist office, **Musée Lapidaire** (☎ 04 90 86 33 84; 27 rue de la République; full price/pass €2/1; 10am-1pm & 2-6pm Wed-Mon) is inexpensive and well worth a quick look for its somewhat random collection of Egyptian, Roman, Etruscan and early Christian bric-a-brac ranging from large sections of marble statuary and hieroglyphics to delicate vases and bronze figurines.

BOATING
Les Grands Bateaux de Provence (☎ 04 90 85 62 25; bateaugbp@aol.com; allées de l'Oulle; based at the Mireio Embarcadère opposite the Porte de l'Oulle, runs excursions from Avignon down the Rhône to Arles, vineyard towns and even the Camargue (€45 including a meal). There are also less-ambitious journeys to Villeneuve-lès-Avignon and Île de la Barthelasse from two to six times daily in July and August.

A free shuttle boat near Pont St-Bénézet connects the walled city with the **Île de la Barthelasse** (10am-12.30pm & 2-6.30pm Apr-Jun, 11am-9pm Jul & Aug, 2-5.30pm Wed, 10am-noon & 2-5.30pm Sat & Sun Oct-Dec).

Tours
Autocars Lieutaud (☎ 04 90 86 36 75; www.cars-lieutaud.fr in French), based at the bus station, offers a variety of thematic whole- and half-day bus tours between April and October, including the Pont du Gard (€15, 4½ hours), Nîmes, Arles and the Camargue (€48, seven hours), Vaison-la-Romaine and Orange (€29, 4½ hours), the Lubéron (€21, 4½ hours) and to the wine cellars at Châteauneuf-du-Pape (€14, three hours).

Festivals & Events
Avignon's streets buzz with life, buskers, street theatre, and leafleters enticing you into the hundreds of shows held during the city's now-world-famous **Festival d'Avignon**, founded in the late 1940s and held every year from early July to early August. It attracts many hundreds of performance artists (actors, dancers and musicians) who put on some 300 *spectacles* of all sorts each day in every imaginable venue. There are, in fact, two simultaneous events: the prestigious, government-subsidised and expensive official festival; and the fringe one, Festival Off.

Tickets for official festival performances in the Palais des Papes' cours d'Honneur cost around €30. A Carte Public Adhérent (€14) gives you a 30% discount on all Festival Off performances and can be obtained at the Conservatoire de Musique. Contact **Avignon Public Off** (☎ 01 48 05 01 19; www.avignon-off.org in French) for the schedule.

Information on the official festival can be obtained from the **Bureau du Festival** (☎ 04 90 27 66 50; www.festival-avignon.com; Espace St-Louis, 20 rue du Portail Boquier). Tickets can be reserved from mid-June.

Sleeping
During the festival, it's practically impossible to find a hotel room unless you've reserved months in advance. Hotel rooms are readily available in August, however, when places in the rest of the Vaucluse *département* are at a premium.

BUDGET
Auberge Bagatelle (☎ 04 90 85 78 45; auberge.bagatelle@wanadoo.fr; Île de la Barthelasse; dm €11-11.50, d with/without shower €34/26.50) Auberge Bagatelle has 210 beds and is part of a large, park-like area that includes Camping Bagatelle.

Rooms are for two, four, six or eight but are rather cramped.

YMCA-UCJG (☎ 04 90 25 46 20; www.ymca-avignon .com; 7bis Chemin de la Justice; s/d/tr/q with washbasin €22/28/33/44, s/d/tr with shower & toilet €33/42/51) This is a good hostel in Villeneuve-lès-Avignon with well-maintained rooms in a variety of sizes. Take bus No 10 to the Pont d'Avignon stop Monteau.

Camping

Camping Bagatelle (☎ 04 90 86 30 39; camping .bagatelle@wanadoo.fr; Île de la Barthelasse; sites s/d with tent & car high season €11/13; ☽ reception 8am-9pm) This attractive, shaded, three-star camping ground is just north of Pont Édouard Daladier, 850m from the walled city. Take bus No 10 from the main post office to the La Barthelasse stop. Follow the river to the camping ground.

MID-RANGE

Hôtel Innova (☎ 04 90 82 54 10; hotel.innova@wanadoo.fr; 100 rue Joseph Vernet; r with shower €32, with shower & TV €40, with shower, toilet & TV €44) This one-star place is always busy so book ahead. It has bright, comfortable and soundproofed rooms.

The following three hotels are close to each other on the same street. **Hôtel du Parc** (☎ 04 90 82 71 55; www.hotelduparc.fr.fm; 18 rue Agricol Perdiguier; s/d with shower €35/43, with shower & toilet €47/47; P) has one-star rooms, **Hôtel Splendid** (☎ 04 90 86 14 46; www.avignon-splendid-hotel.com; 17 rue Agricol Perdiguier; s/d with shower €37/49, with shower & toilet €43/54; P) is friendly with recently renovated rooms, and **Hôtel Colbert** (☎ 04 90 86 20 20; www.lecolbert-hotel.com; 7 rue Agricol Perdiguier; s with shower & toilet €35-55, d with shower & toilet €45-60; ☒), which smells of disinfectant, is good value.

Hôtel Monclar (☎ 04 90 86 20 14; www.hotel -monclar.com; 13 av Monclar; s/d with washbasin €20/30, s/d with shower €26/45; P) Occupying a handsome, peppermint-shuttered 18th-century building by the train station (next to the tracks, in fact, so noise can be a problem). This place has considerable charm. Rooms have washbasins and bidets, a couple have kitchenettes and there's a pretty back garden. Parking costs €4.50.

Hôtel de Blauvac (☎ 04 90 86 34 11; www.hotel -blauvac.com; 11 rue de la Bancasse; s/d/tr €48/51/65) Down a dark, scruffy side street just off the main square you'll find this hidden gem inside the lovely 17th-century former townhouse of the Marqui de Blauvac. The

hotel is friendly, comfortable and central; the rooms convivial and stylish.

Hôtel Médiéval (☎ 04 90 86 11 06; hotel.medieval@ wanadoo.fr; 15 rue Petite Saunerie; s/d €37/58) Hôtel Médiéval is another pretty good central bet. Also in a restored 17th-century house, it's down a quiet street not far from the Palais des Papes. It rents studios on a weekly or monthly basis.

Hôtel du Palais des Papes (☎ 04 90 86 04 13; www.hotel-avignon.com in French; 1 rue Gérard Philippe; s/d/q with shower, toilet & breakfast from €65/75/130) This is a sparsely appointed but nonetheless appealing old-world place with large rooms. The pricier rooms sport a view of the Palais des Papes.

Hôtel Mignon (☎ 04 90 82 17 30; www.hotel-mi gnon.com; 12 rue Joseph Vernet; s with shower €33, d/tw/tr with shower, toilet & breakfast €50/55/61; P) Fairly central and reasonable value, Hôtel Mignon offers spotless, well-kept and soundproofed rooms with multichannel TV. The service is especially helpful and friendly.

Hôtel le Provençal (☎ 04 90 85 25 24; fax 04 90 82 75 81; 13 rue Joseph Vernet; s/d with shower & toilet €46/47) A comparable standard of accommodation to the Mignon opposite. It's popular so book ahead.

TOP END

Hôtel L'Europe (☎ 04 90 14 76 76; www.heurope.com; 12 place Crillon; r €129-410; P ☒ ☒) This is a great four-star place with bags of charm. Napoleon Bonaparte is just one of the historic figures, artists and writers to have enjoyed its lovely plane tree–shaded courtyard and the large, graceful rooms. Garage parking costs €15.

Hôtel de la Mirande (☎ 04 90 14 20 20; www .la-mirande.fr; 4 place de la Mirande; r Nov-Mar from €280, Apr-Oct from €340; P ☒ ☒) Avignon's most exclusive hotel, furnished in lavish but supremely tasteful period style. It occupies a former 14th-century cardinal's palace behind the Palais des Papes and has its own cooking school, Le Marmiton, which also runs an educational evening table d'hôte (see opposite).

Eating

From Easter until mid-November, half of place de l'Horloge is taken over by tourist restaurants and cafés. *Menus* start at about €14. Many restaurants open just for the festival; most have special (and more expensive) festival *menus*.

Tapalocas (☎ 04 90 82 56 84; 15 rue Galante; dishes from €2; 🕑 11.45am-1am) This is a down-to-earth Spanish tapas bar, selling cheap, beer-session ballast.

Le Brantes (☎ 04 90 86 35 14; 2 rue Petite Fusterie; menus €11-23) Serving above-average pizza and pasta that you can enjoy in the flowery courtyard out back.

Maison Nani (☎ 04 90 82 60 90; 29 rue Théodore Aubanel; plat du jour €9; 🕑 closed Sun, Mon-Thu dinner) A cheerful, popular bistro, Maison Nani serves Provençal salads, grilled meat and fresh fish.

Le Bistrot d'Utopia (☎ 04 90 27 04 96; 4 rue des escaliers Ste-Anne; mains from €13) Inside a high-ceilinged, elegantly distressed dining room in the Manutention cultural centre, the Utopia is great for atmosphere and simple, quality food. Peppery-leafed salads, mushroom tarts with buttery pastry, duck breasts done to a turn and ace desserts such as slender lemon curd tart topped with a sliver crystallised orange are typical fare.

La Fourchette (☎ 04 90 85 20 93; 17 rue Racine; menus from €24.40; 🕑 Mon-Fri) A classical French restaurant west of place de l'Horloge, La Fourchette offers a wide choice of dishes on its fixed-price *menu*. The *sauté d'agneau* is a house speciality. Book ahead.

Le Caveau du Théâtre (☎ 04 90 82 60 91; 16 rue des Trois Faucons; lunch/dinner menus €10/18; 🕑 closed Sat lunch & Sun) South of the square, this restaurant turns out rich, traditional French fare with some more adventurous items thrown in, such as butter fried fish in a curry paste with sun-dried tomatoes.

Heading east from place de l'Horloge, you come to rue Carnot, home to a handful of Vietnamese and Chinese places.

Restaurant Song Long (☎ 04 90 86 35 00; 1 rue Carnot; lunch/dinner menus from €5.35/6.90) Offers a wide variety of excellent Vietnamese dishes, including 16 *plats végétariens*.

La Compagnie des Comptoirs (☎ 04 90 85 99 04; 83 rue Joseph Vernet; mains €13-28, lunch formule €15) Opposite the Hôtel Innova, inside Le Cloître des Arts, this is a sophisticated restaurant wrapped around an enchanting 18th-century courtyard. The restaurant has an excellent selection of vegetarian and seafood dishes. Examples from the menu include raviolis of *queue de bœuf* (oxtail) and *daurade* (sea bream) fillets with fennel, *confit* tomatoes and basil. There are also lighter, Asian-flavoured dishes such as sushi.

Le Marmiton (☎ 04 90 85 93 93; 4 place de l'Ami rande; table d'hôte €80; 🕑 dinner Tue-Sat) If you want to watch and learn how typical Provençal food should be prepared as well as eating it, consider the four-course feast cooked before you at a large scrubbed wood table in the intimate kitchen at the Hôtel de la Mirande (budget allowing of course).

SELF-CATERING
Les Halles has a great **food market** (place Pie; 🕑 7am-1pm Tue-Sun).

Boulangerie Pâtisserie (17 rue St-Agricol; 🕑 7.45am-7.30pm Mon-Sat), for breads and sandwiches, is near place de l'Horloge. For groceries there's **Casino** (22 rue St-Agricol; 🕑 8am-12.45pm & 3-7.30pm Mon-Sat). After picking up healthy fruit at Casino, misbehave next door at **La Tropézienne** (☎ 04 90 86 24 72; 22 rue St-Agricol; 🕑 8.30am-7.30pm Mon-Sat), with sinfully delicious pastries, pralines, candied fruit, jams and the creamy *tarte tropézienne*.

Drinking
You can't fail to find a decent café to sit and people watch on the main square around the Opéra.

L'Electro (☎ 06 99 48 97 49; 2 rue du Portail; 🕑 till late) This is a cosy, low-key but hip café-cum-bar that opens until the small hours most nights. At weekends, DJs get busy on the decks.

Le Café d'Utopia (☎ 04 90 27 04 96; 4 rue des escaliers Ste-Anne; 🕑 11.30am-1am) Try this relaxed café/bar inside La Manutention, an entertainment and cultural centre where Avignon's resident artists and intellectuals chew over the cultural scene, including the latest films at the adjacent Cinéma Utopia, on plush banquettes.

Bleu les Thés (☎ 04 32 76 23 69; 26 rue Bouquerie; 🕑 salon de thé 2.30-6.30pm Mon-Fri) A smart, civilised place for an afternoon cuppa or the special house hot chocolate.

Entertainment
For information on the Festival d'Avignon and Festival Off, see p787. Tickets for many cultural events and performances are sold at the tourist office.

Events listings are included in the free *César* weekly magazine and in the tourist office's fortnightly newsletter, *Rendez-vous d'Avignon*. Tickets for most events are sold at **Fnac** (☎ 04 90 14 35 35; 19 rue de la République; 🕑 10am-7pm Mon-Sat).

PROVENCE

Opéra d'Avignon (☎ 04 90 82 23 44; place de l'Horloge; ⏰ box office 11am-6pm Mon-Sat) Housed in an imposing structure built in 1847, Opéra d'Avignon stages operas, operettas, plays, symphonic concerts, chamber music concerts and ballet.

Cinéma Utopia (☎ 04 90 82 65 36; 4 rue des escaliers Ste-Anne; admission €3-5) In the cultural centre tucked behind the Palais des Papes, this cinema screens dubbed and subtitled films.

NIGHTCLUBS

Red Zone (☎ 04 90 27 02 44; 25 rue Carnot) Test drive those new dancing trousers at Red Zone, which rocks most nights. Monday is Afro, Tuesday is salsa, Wednesday there's a live concert and Thursday to Sunday there are DJs playing house, techno etc.

Red Lion (☎ 04 90 86 40 25; 21-23 rue St Jean le Vieux) Part ye-olde-English pub, part nightclub, the Red Lion is a lively spot with a different dance genre each night, including a Thursday disco.

Shopping

Instant du Sud (☎ 04 90 82 24 48; 1 place Nicolas Saboly) You can make your own perfume here.

Le Lavandin (☎ 04 90 85 90 01; 4 rue du puits de la Reille) Offers typically Provençal goods and presents such as elegantly patterned and coloured tablecloths.

Oliviers & Co (☎ 04 92 70 48 20; 19 rue St-Agricol) Sells the very finest olive oil and olive oil–based products such as soap, hand cream and biscuits.

Comtesse du Barry (☎ 04 90 82 62 92; 25 rue St-Agricol) Stock up on gourmet goodies such as fine wine and foie gras.

Getting There & Away

AIR

The **Aéroport Avignon-Caumont** (☎ 04 90 81 51 51) is 8km southeast of Avignon. There is no public transport into town; a taxi costs about €15.

BUS

The **bus station** (halte routière; ☎ 04 90 82 07 35; blvd St-Roch; ⏰ information window 10.15am-1pm & 2-6pm Mon-Fri) is in the basement of the building down the ramp to the right as you exit the train station. Tickets are sold on the buses, which are run by many different companies.

Places you can get to by bus include Aix-en-Provence (via the motorway €13.90, one

hour; on secondary roads €11.70, 1½ hours, four to six daily), Arles (€8.50, 1½ hours, six daily), Carpentras (€3.80, 45 minutes, 27 daily), Marseille (€16.40, 35 minutes direct, one daily), Nice (€27, one daily), Nîmes (€8.10, 1¼ hours, five daily) and Orange (€5.10, 40 minutes, about 20 daily). Most lines operate on Sunday at reduced frequency.

Long-haul bus companies **Linebus** (☎ 04 90 85 30 48) and **Eurolines** (☎ 04 90 85 27 60; www .eurolines.fr) have offices at the far end of the bus platforms.

CAR

Most car-rental agencies are either inside the main train station complex or nearby (follow the signs). They include **Europcar** (Ibis Bldg ☎ 04 90 85 01 40, TGV station ☎ 04 32 74 63 40).

TRAIN

The **main train station** (⏰ information counter 9am-6.15pm Mon-Sat) is across blvd St-Roch from Porte de la République. The left-luggage room, to the left as you exit the station, opens from 6am to 10pm. Luggage left in the automatic lockers (security-controlled) costs €3 to €6.10 depending on size.

The TGV station, specially constructed to receive the super-fast trains from Paris and Lyon, is a few kilometres from town. A shuttle bus (€2) takes you from the TGV station to the bus stop just outside the main post office. It runs every 30 minutes from about 5.30am to 10.50pm.

There are trains to Arles (€5.70, 20 minutes, 14 to 18 daily), Marseille (€15.50, 40 minutes), Nice (€38.80, three hours), Nîmes (€7.40, 30 minutes, 15 daily), Orange (€4.70, 20 minutes, 17 daily) and, by TGV, Paris' Gare de Lyon (€67, 2½ hours) and Lyon (€29.60, one hour).

Getting Around

BIKE

There are several bike-hire places in town, including **Provence Bike** (☎ 04 90 27 92 61; www .provence-bike.com; 52 blvd St Roch), which also rents scooters and motorbikes.

BUS

Local TCRA bus tickets cost €1.05 each if bought from the driver; a *carnet* of 10 tickets costs €8 at TCRA offices. Buses run from 7am to about 7.40pm (8am to 6pm and less frequently on Sunday). The two most important bus transfer points are the Poste stop at the main post office and place Pie.

Carnets and free bus maps *(plan du réseau)* are available at the **Agence Commerciale TCRA** (☎ 04 32 74 18 32; av de Lattre de Tassigny; ⏱ 8.30am-12.30pm & 1.30-6pm Mon-Fri).

Villeneuve-lès-Avignon is linked with Avignon by bus No 10, which stops in front of the main post office and on the western side of the walled city near Porte de l'Oulle.

TAXI

Pick up a taxi outside the train station or call the **place Pie taxi stand** (☎ 04 90 82 20 20; ⏱ 24hr).

AROUND AVIGNON
Villeneuve-lès-Avignon

Villeneuve-lès-Avignon, across the Rhône from Avignon (and in a different *département*), was founded in the late 13th century. It became known as the City of Cardinals because many primates affiliated with the papal court built large residences in the town, despite the fact that it was in territory ruled by the French crown and not the pope.

Avignon's picturesque sister city, Villeneuve also has a few interesting sights, all of which are included in the Avignon Passion pass (p786). From Avignon, Villeneuve can be reached by foot or bus No 10 (from the main post office).

Chartreuse du Val de Bénédiction (☎ 04 90 15 24 24; 60 rue de la République; full price/pass €5.50/3.50; ⏱ 9am-6.30pm May-Aug, 9.30am-5.30pm Sep-Apr) is a well-preserved Carthusian monastery, once the largest and most important in France.

Musée Pierre de Luxembourg (☎ 04 90 27 49 66; rue de la République; full price/pass €3/1.90; ⏱ 10am-12.30pm & 2-6.30pm, closed Mon mid-Sep–mid-Jun) has a mostly middling collection of religious paintings, with one exception. If you're remotely interested in religious art it's well worth the visit for Enguerrand Quarton's lavish and dramatic 1453 painting *The Crowning of the Virgin*. It's worth asking for the accompanying notes, which give an interesting insight into the commissioning of the painting and the religious dogma that underpins its composition.

Tour Philippe-le-Bel (☎ 04 32 70 08 57; full price/pass €1.60/0.90; ⏱ 10am-12.30pm & 2-6.30pm, closed Mon mid-Sep–mid-Jun), a defensive tower built in the 14th century at what was then the northwestern end of Pont St-Bénézet, has great views of Avignon's walled city, the river and the surrounding countryside. The spiral stairs up are narrow and numerous, though. Another Provençal panorama can be enjoyed from 14th-century **Fort St-André** (☎ 04 90 25 45 35; full price/pass €4.60/3.10; ⏱ 10am-1pm & 2-6pm Apr-Sep, 10am-1pm & 2-5pm Oct-Mar).

Les Baux de Provence
pop 468

Twenty five kilometres south of Avignon, past the small town of St-Rémy de Provence (population 9340), is Les Baux de Provence, vividly immortalised on canvas by Van Gogh during his stay in an asylum in 1889–90. This breathtaking fortified village, named after the 245m-high *baou* (rocky spur) on which it is perched, pulls in some 2.5 million tourists a year (putting it on a par with Mont St-Michel in Normandy as one of France's biggest tourist attractions outside of Paris). The castle looms over a beautiful crescent of vineyards and olive groves set beneath dramatic limestone hills on one side and a picturesque valley on the other.

The most pleasant time to visit **Château des Baux** (☎ 04 90 54 55 56; adult/student €7/5.50; ⏱ 9am-7.30pm May & Jun, 9am-8.30pm Jul & Aug, 9am-5pm Sep-Apr), a former feudal home of Monaco's Grimaldi royal family, is early evening after the caterpillar of tourist coaches has evacuated the village. Audioguides in several languages give a thorough explanation of the history of the castle, village and region and there are demonstrations of medieval warfare in summer.

The **tourist office** (☎ 04 90 54 34 39; fax 04 90 54 51 51) has information on Les Baux's few accommodation options. Note, there is no free parking within 800m of the village. Park for free at the car park of the **Cathédrale d'Images** – a rather uninspiring and very overpriced sound and light show (€7) set in a former quarry cave just north of the village. From here, you can easily walk back to Les Baux.

ORANGE
pop 28,889

If it weren't for the Romans, Orange would be a rather workaday town, scarcely worth a visit. Fortunately, the Romans built a splendid theatre and triumphal arch, which have survived largely intact and are the pride of Provence. The town's network of plazas,

PROVENCE

fountains and pedestrian streets are agreeable to stroll along, but not hard to leave.

Through a 16th-century marriage with the German House of Nassau, the House of Orange (the princely dynasty that had ruled Orange since the 12th century) became active in the history of the Netherlands and later, through William III (William of Orange), also in England. Orange (Arenja in Provençal), which had earlier been a stronghold of the Reformation, was ceded to France in 1713 by the Treaty of Utrecht, but to this day many members of the royal house of the Netherlands are known as the princes and princesses of Orange–Nassau.

Orientation

Orange's train station is just over 1km east of place de la République, the city centre, along av Frédéric Mistral and rue de la République. Rue St-Martin links place de la République and nearby place Clemenceau with the tourist office, which is 250m to the west. Théâtre Antique, Orange's magnificent Roman theatre, is two blocks south of place de la République. The tiny River Meyne lies north of the centre. From the train station, bus No 2 from rue Jean Reboul (first left after exiting the station) goes to the Théâtre Antique or République stop.

Information

LAUNDRY
Laundrette (5 rue St-Florent; ☉ 7am-8pm)

MONEY
There are lots of banks along the rue Aristide Briand.
Crédit Lyonnais (7 place de la République)

POST
Post Office (blvd Édouard Daladier) Has a Cyberposte.

TOURIST INFORMATION
Tourist Office (☎ 04 90 34 70 88; www.provence-orange .com; 5 cours Aristide Briand; ☉ 9am-7pm Mon-Sat, 10am-6pm Sun Apr-Sep, 10am-1pm & 2-5pm Mon-Sat Oct-Mar)
Tourist Office Annexe (place des Frères Mounet; ☉ 10am-1pm & 2.15-7pm Mon-Sat, 10am-12.30pm & 2.30-6pm Sun Apr-Sep) In front of the Roman theatre.

Sights
THÉÂTRE ANTIQUE
Orange's magnificent **Roman theatre** (☎ 04 90 51 17 60; adult/student €7.50/5.50; ☉ 9am-6.30pm Apr-

early Oct, 9am-noon & 1.30-5pm early Oct-Mar), designed to seat 10,000 spectators, was probably built during the time of Augustus Caesar (who ruled from 27 BC to AD 14). Its stage wall *(mur de scène)*, the only such Roman structure still standing in its entirety (minus a few mosaics and the roof), is 103m wide and 37m high. Its plain exterior can be viewed from adjacent place des Frères Mounet to the north. Admission price includes an audio tour and entry to the attached museum across the road, worth a quick look for the friezes of Amazons and Centaurs that used to form part of the theatre's scenery.

For a panoramic view of the Roman masterpiece, follow montée Philbert de Chalons or montée Lambert to the top of **Colline St-Eutrope** (St-Eutrope Hill; elevation 97m), where a circular viewing table explains what's what. En route you pass the ruins of a 12th-century **chateau**, the former residence of the princes of Orange.

Those not into walking can always hop aboard the 54-seat **Orangeois tourist train** that departs every 30 minutes or so from outside the Théâtre Antique. The city tour (€5) lasts 30 minutes and takes in all the major sights.

ARC DE TRIOMPHE
Orange's Roman **triumphal arch**, one of the most remarkable of its kind in France, is at the northern end of plane tree–lined av de l'Arc de Triomphe, about 450m from the centre of town. Probably built around 20 BC, it is 19m in height and width, and 8m thick. The exceptional friezes commemorate Julius Caesar's victories over the Gauls in 49 BC, triumphs of which the Romans wished to remind every traveller approaching the city. The arch has been restored several times since 1825.

Festivals & Events
In June and August Théâtre Antique comes alive with all-night concerts, cinema screenings and musical events during **Les Nuits du Théâtre Antique**. During the last fortnight in July, it plays host to **Les Chorégies d'Orange**, a series of weekend operas, classical concerts and choral performances. Seats (€15 to €160) for the festival must be reserved months beforehand, although it is possible to catch a free glimpse of the action from the lookout atop Colline St-Eutrope. Orange also plays host to a week-long **jazz festival** in June.

Tickets for events held in the Théâtre Antique can be reserved at the **Location Théâtre Antique** (☎ 04 90 34 24 24; www.choregies.asso.fr; 14 place Silvain).

Sleeping
BUDGET
Camping Le Jonquier (☎ 04 90 34 49 48; www.avignon -et-provence.com/le-jonquier; 1321 rue Alexis Carrel; camping low/high season €18.50/24.40; ⊙ Apr-Sep) A three-star place near the Arc de Triomphe. Take bus No 1 from the République stop (av Frédéric Mistral, 600m from the train station) to the Arc de Triomphe. From there, walk 100m back, turn right onto rue des Phocéens and right again onto rue des Étudiants. The camping ground, which has a pool, tennis courts and a golf course, is across the football field.

MID-RANGE
Hôtel Arcotel (☎ 04 90 34 09 23; fax 04 90 51 61 12; 8 place aux Herbes; s/d with washbasin €20/27, with shower & toilet €38/38) A friendly, basic establishment, Hôtel Arcotel has well-maintained, if bland rooms near the Théâtre Antique.

Hôtel St-Florent (☎ 04 90 34 18 53; fax 04 90 51 17 25; 4 rue du Mazeau; s/d from €27/55, f €70) Around the corner from Hôtel Arcotel, this place is atmospheric, with great rooms with giant murals painted on the walls and antique wooden beds adorned with crushed and studded velvet.

Le Glacier (☎ 04 90 34 06 26; www.le-glacier.com; 46 cours Aristide-Briand; d & tw €45-61, tr & q €61-79; P 😊) Close to the Théâtre Antique, this is a welcoming place with well-equipped rooms and willing hosts who rent bikes and can recommend good touring itineraries of the nearby countryside and villages.

Eating
East of place Clemenceau, there are a number of moderately priced restaurants.

Le Marrakech (rue A Lacour; couscous €10) Cheap as chips, serving mounds of couscous.

La Sangria (☎ 04 90 34 31 96; 3 place de la République; lunch menu €8.50, dinner menus €11-19.50; ⊙ closed Sun & Tue dinner) Tasty crepes and salads.

Chez Daniel (☎ 04 90 34 63 48; rue Second Weber; menu €24, pizzas €9.50; ⊙ closed Tue dinner, Wed Sep-Jun & Jul & Aug) Near La Sangria, Chez Daniel has delicious Provençal dishes from Estouffade de Lotte Provençale for fish lovers and roast lamb with *chèvre* (goat's cheese) sauce for adventurous meat lovers.

Le Yaca (☎ 04 90 34 70 03; 24 place Silvain; menus €12-22; ⊙ Thu-Tue) Highly recommended for its local fare, served up in a romantic little space marked by beams and stone walls.

Thursday is market day in Orange. Otherwise, self-caterers can pick up supplies at **Petit Casino** (35 rue St-Martin).

Getting There & Away
BUS
The **bus station** (☎ 04 90 34 15 59, 04 90 34 13 39; cours Pourtoules) is southeast of the city centre of the city. Buses from here go to Avignon (€5.10), Carpentras (€4.20), and Vaison-la-Romaine (€4.40), as well as Marseille.

TRAIN
Orange's tiny **train station** (☎ 04 90 11 88 64, 3635; av Frédéric Mistral) is 1.5km east of the tourist office.

Trains travel in two directions: south to Avignon (€4.70, 15 minutes, 17 daily), Marseille (€18.40, 1½ hours, 10 daily) and beyond and north to Lyon (€23, 2¼ hours, 13 daily) and Paris' Gare de Lyon (€75, two hours).

VAISON-LA-ROMAINE
pop 5986
Vaison-la-Romaine, 23km and 47km northeast of Orange and Avignon respectively, is endowed with extensive Roman ruins, a picturesque medieval city and plenty of tourists. However, it's not so overrun that you can't enjoy the sights and relax with a drink in the pretty tree-lined square.

In the 2nd century BC, the Romans conquered an important Celtic city on this site and renamed it Vasio Vocontiorum. The Roman city flourished, in part because it was granted considerable autonomy, but around the 6th century the Great Migrations forced the population to move to the hill across the river, which was easier to defend. The counts of Toulouse built a castle on top of the hill in the 12th century.

The resettlement of the original city site began in the 17th century.

The Roman remains discovered at Vaison include villas decorated with mosaics, colonnaded streets, public baths, a theatre and an aqueduct; the latter brought water down from Mont Ventoux.

The two-week Choralies, a choral festival held each year in August in the Roman

PROVENCE

theatre, is said to be the largest of its kind in Europe.

Vaison, like Malaucène and Carpentras 10km and 27km to the south, is a good base for exploring the Mont Ventoux region.

Orientation

Vaison is bisected by the ever-flooding River Ouvèze. The Roman city centre, on top of which the modern city centre has been built, is on the river's north bank; the medieval Haute Ville is on the south bank.

Pedestrianised Grand' rue heads northwest from the Pont Romain, changing its name near the Roman ruins to av du Général de Gaulle.

To get from the bus station to the tourist office, turn left as you leave the station then left again into rue Colonel Parazols, which leads past the Fouilles de Puymin excavations along rue Burrhus.

Information

Vaison's **tourist office** (☎ 04 90 36 02 11; www .vaison-la-romaine.com; place du Chanoine Sautel; ☑ 9am-noon & 2-5.45pm Mon-Sat, 9am-noon Sun Apr-Jun & Sep-Oct, 9am-noon & 2-6.45pm daily Jul & Aug) is inside the Maison du Tourisme et des Vins, just off av du Général de Gaulle.

The post office, opposite place du 11 Novembre, has an exchange service and Cyberposte.

Sights

GALLO-ROMAN RUINS

The Gallo-Roman ruins that have been unearthed in Vaison can be visited at two sites: **Fouilles de Puymin**, the excavations on the eastern side of av du Général de Gaulle, and (to the west of the same road) **Fouilles de la Villasse** (adult/student/child €7/3.50/3 for both; ☑ 10am-12.30pm & 2-6pm Mar-May, 9.30am-6.15pm Jun & Sep, 9.30am-6.45pm Jul & Aug, 10am-12.30pm & 2-5.30pm Feb & Oct; 10am-noon & 2-4.30pm Nov-Jan).

Fouilles de Puymin, with its entrance opposite Vaison's tourist office, is the more interesting of the pair. This site includes houses, mosaics and a theatre (designed to accommodate 6000 people) built around AD 20 under the reign of Tiberius. **Musée Archéologique** displays some of the artefacts. Its collection of statues includes the silver bust of a 3rd-century patrician and likenesses of Hadrian and his wife Sabina. At Fouilles de la Villasse, you can visit the mosaic-

and fresco-decorated house in which the silver bust was discovered.

From April to September, there are free guided tours in English; check the schedule at the tourist office.

MEDIEVAL QUARTER

Across the much-repaired **Pont Romain**, on the southern bank of the Ouvèze, lies the **Haute Ville**, which dates from the 13th and 14th centuries. Cobblestone alleyways lead up the hill past restored houses. At the summit, which affords a nice view, is an imposing 12th-century **chateau**, modernised in the 15th century only to be later abandoned.

Sleeping

The tourist office has comprehensive accommodation lists, including details on *chambres d'hôtes* and self-catering places in the surrounding region. The hotels are few and far between.

BUDGET

Escapade (☎ 04 90 36 00 78; fax 04 90 36 09 89; av César Geoffray; dm with obligatory half-board €39) Around 500m southeast of town along the river, Escapade is a modern place in large, quiet grounds with views of Mont Ventoux.

Camping du Théâtre Romain (☎ 04 90 28 78 66; info@camping-theatre.com; chemin de Brusquet; camping €18.50; ☑ 15 Mar-15 Nov; ☒) Located opposite Théâtre Antique in the northern section of the Fouilles de Puymin.

MID-RANGE

Hôtel Le Burrhus (☎ 04 90 36 00 11; www.burrhus .com; 1 place de Montfort; d €44-79; ☑ closed 12 Nov-20 Dec & Sun in Jan & Feb) Recently refitted superbly, this hotel is the pick in town. It's right on the square, near all the cafés, and boasts large, light, smart rooms decorated with considerable contemporary flair and modern fittings. Book ahead.

Shopping

Wine such as Gigondas, Châteauneuf-du-Pape and Villages des Côtes du Rhône, honey and honey nougat are all local specialities, but nothing can compare with the delectable black truffles harvested around Vaison-la-Romaine. They don't come cheap (€15 for 12.5g), but just a few shavings of the black fungus will turn the most prosaic plate of pasta into a bite-sized helping of heaven.

Maison des Vins, in the basement of the Maison du Tourisme et des Vins, has local wines and local food products for tasting and purchase.

A vast and varied market snakes through the town centre every Tuesday from 6.30am to 1pm.

Getting There & Away

The bus station, where **Lieutard buses** (Vaison ☎ 04 90 36 05 22, Avignon ☎ 04 90 86 36 75; av des Choralies; ☺ 9am-noon & 2-7pm Mon-Fri, Sat morning) has an office, is east of the modern town. There are limited services geared to the schedules of students from Vaison to Orange (€4.60, 45 minutes), Avignon (€7, 1¼ hours) and Carpentras (€3.90, 45 minutes).

MONT VENTOUX

Standing guard over the surrounding country and visible from as far away as Avignon, Mont Ventoux, is the most prominent geographical feature in northern Provence, thanks to its height (1909m) and its isolation. The radar- and antenna-studded summit, accessible by road, affords spectacular views of Provence, the southern Alps and – when it's especially clear – even the Pyrenees.

Mont Ventoux marks the boundary between the fauna and flora of northern France and that of southern France. Some species, including the snake eagle, numerous spiders and a variety of butterflies, are only found here. The mountain's forests were felled 400 years ago to build ships, but since 1860 some areas have been reforested with a variety of species, including the majestic cedar of Lebanon. The mix of deciduous trees makes the mountain especially colourful in autumn.

Since the summit is considerably cooler than the surrounding plains – there can be a difference of up to 20°C – and receives twice as much precipitation, bring warm clothes and rain gear at any time of the year. Areas above 1300m are usually covered in snow from December to April.

Mont Ventoux's mostly gradual but relentless gradients are regularly included in the route of the Tour de France, and it was here that British cyclist Tommy Simpson collapsed and died during the 1967 event. There is a memorial to him.

Just to the west of Mont Ventoux rise the sharp pinnacles of the limestone **Dentelles de Montmirail**; the surrounding area makes great hiking terrain. Near the eastern end of the Mont Ventoux massif is the village of **Sault** (800m), surrounded in summer by a patchwork of purple lavender.

Malaucène, which is about 10km south of Vaison-la-Romaine and is the former summer residence of the Avignon popes, is where most people begin their forays into the surrounds of Mont Ventoux, about 21km to the east.

Come winter, **Mont Serein** (1445m), about 16km east of Malaucène and 5km from Mont Ventoux's summit on the D974, is transformed into a bustling ski station.

Information

Information Chalet (☎ 04 90 63 42 02; Mont Serein)
Malaucène Tourist Office (☎ 04 90 65 22 59; ot
-malaucene@axit.fr; place de la Mairie; ☺ 10am-noon & 2-4.30pm Apr-Jun, 9.30am-12.30pm & 2.30-6pm Jul & Aug, 10am-noon & 2-4.30pm Mon-Sat Sep-Mar)
Sault Tourist Office (☎ 04 90 64 01 21; ot-sault@axit .fr; av de la Promenade; ☺ 10am-noon & 2-6pm Apr-Jun & Sep, 9am-1pm & 2-7pm Jul & Aug, 10am-noon & 2.30-4.30pm Tue-Sat Oct-Mar)

Walking

The GR4, running from the River Ardèche to the west, crosses the Dentelles de Montmirail before climbing up the northern face of Mont Ventoux. It then joins the GR9, and both trails follow the bare, white ridge before parting ways, with the GR4 winding eastwards to the Gorges du Verdon.

The GR9, which takes you across most of the area's ranges (including the Monts du Vaucluse and Lubéron Range), is arguably the most spectacular walking trail in all of Provence.

MAPS

Didier-Richard's 1:50,000 map No 27, *Massif du Ventoux*, includes Mont Ventoux, the Monts du Vaucluse and the Dentelles de Montmirail. It is available at some of the area's larger tourist offices, and many bookshops and newsagents. More detailed is IGN's Série Bleue 1:25,000 *Mont Ventoux* (No 3140ET).

Getting There & Around

If you've got a car, the summit of Mont Ventoux can be reached from Sault via the D164 or – in summer – from Malaucène

PROVENCE

or St-Estève via the switchback D974, built in the 1930s. This mountain road is often snow-blocked until as late as April. For information on bus services in the area, see opposite.

ACS (☎ 04 90 65 15 42) in Malaucène rents mountain bikes.

CARPENTRAS
pop 27,250

Drowsy Carpentras, equidistant from Avignon (25km) to the southwest and Orange to the northwest, is a small agricultural town, largely untouched by hordes of summer visitors and best known for its bustling Friday markets. The town hosts the eclectic Estivales de Carpentras, a two-week music, dance and theatre festival, in July.

History

Carpentras was an important trading centre in Greek times and later a Gallo-Roman city before becoming the capital of the papal territory of the Comtat Venaissin in 1320. It flourished in the 14th century, when it was visited frequently by Pope Clement V (who preferred it to Avignon) and numerous cardinals. During this time, Jews expelled from territory controlled by the French crown sought refuge in the Comtat Venaissin, where they lived – subject to certain restrictions – under the pope's protection. Today, Carpentras' 14th-century synagogue is the oldest such structure in France still in use.

Orientation

In the 19th century the city's fortifications and walls were replaced by a ring of boulevards: av Jean Jaurès, blvd Alfred Rogier, blvd du Nord, blvd Maréchal Leclerc, blvd Gambetta and blvd Albin Durand. The largely pedestrianised old city lies inside.

If you arrive by bus, walk northeastwards to place Aristide Briand, a major intersection at the southernmost point on the heart-shaped ring of boulevards. Avenue Jean Jaurès leads to the tourist office, while pedestrian-only rue de la République, which heads due north, takes you to the 17th-century Palais de Justice and the cathedral. The town hall is a few blocks northeast of the cathedral.

Information

There are commercial banks on central place Aristide Briand and blvd Albin Durand.

Banque de France (161 blvd Albin Durand; ◐ 9amnoon & 1.30-3.30pm Mon-Fri)
Laundrette (118 rue Porte de Monteux; ◐ 7am-8pm) On the road linking place du Général de Gaulle and blvd Albin Durand.
Post Office (65 rue d'Inguimbert)
Tourist Office (☎ 04 90 63 00 78; www.provenceguide .com; place Aristide Briand; ◐ 9am-7pm Mon-Sat, 9.30am-1pm Sun mid-Jun–mid-Sep, 9.30am-12.30pm & 2-6pm Mon-Sat mid-Sep–mid-Jun) Sells a good range of regional maps and guides, and organises guided **city tours** (adult/child €4/2) from April to September. Ask for the free English-language brochure *Discover Carpentras Tour* if you prefer to do it yourself.

Sights
SYNAGOGUE

Carpentras' wonderful **synagogue** (☎ 04 90 63 39 97; place Juiverie; admission free; ◐ 10am-noon & 3-5pm Mon-Thu, 10am-noon & 3-4pm Fri) was founded on this site in 1367, rebuilt between 1741 and 1743 and restored in 1929 and 1954. For centuries, it served as the focal point of the town's 1000-strong Jewish community. The sanctuary on the 1st floor is decorated with wood panelling and liturgical objects from the 18th century. You'll find the synagogue opposite the town hall (look for the stone plaque inscribed with Hebrew letters). About 100 Jewish families live in Carpentras today.

CATHEDRAL

Carpentras' one-time **cathedral** (◐ 10am-noon & 2-4pm Wed-Mon, to 6pm in summer), now officially known as Église St-Siffrein, was built in the Méridional (southern French) Gothic style between 1405 and 1519. The 17th-century doorway is of classical design and in need of renovation. The bell tower is modern. **Trésor d'Art Sacré** (Treasury of Religious Art) displays various liturgical objects and reliquaries from the 14th to 19th centuries, including the St-Mors, the Holy Bridle bit supposedly made by St Helen for her son Constantine from a nail taken from the True Cross.

MUSEUMS

Carpentras' museums open 10am to noon and 2pm to 4pm (till 6pm April to September) Wednesday to Monday. Admission is €0.50. **Musée Comtadin** (243 blvd Albin Durand), which displays artefacts related to local history and folklore, and **Musée Duplessis** (243 blvd Albin Durand), with paintings from the personal collection of Monseigneur d'Inguimbert, are on the western side of the old city.

Musée Sobirats (112 rue du Collège), one block west of the cathedral, is an 18th-century private residence decorated and crammed with furniture, faïence and *objets d'art* in the Louis XV and Louis XVI styles.

The hospital in the 18th-century **Hôtel Dieu** (place Aristide Briand) has an old-time **pharmacy** and a **chapel**, but you must make arrangements with the tourist office to visit it. There are guided tours every Friday at 3pm year-round and an additional tour on Tuesday in July and August (€4).

MARKETS
Every Friday Carpentras hosts one of the most colourful and mouth-watering markets in Provence, which is saying something. Rue d'Inguimbert and most of av Jean Jaurès are laden with tables covered with nougat, strong local cheeses, orange and lavender marmalade, cauldrons of paella, buckets of olives and fresh fruit (especially the wonderful local melons). From November to the beginning of March, truffles are sold on **place Aristide Briand** (8-10am Fri). Carpentras' biggest fair is held on the Fête de St-Siffrein (Feast of St Siffrein) on 27 November. In July and August, there's a **wine market** in front of the tourist office.

Sleeping & Eating
Hôtel du Théâtre (☎ 04 90 63 02 90; hotel.dutheatre@wanadoo.fr; 7 blvd Albin Durand; d/tr from €56/76) A recently refurbished hotel overlooking place Aristide Briand. Rooms are large and quiet, with double-glazed windows and private bathrooms.

Hôtel La Lavande (☎ 04 90 63 13 49; 282 blvd Alfred Rogier, d with/without shower €38/28) A basic but comfortable eight-room hotel at the northern end of town. From the tourist office, follow blvd Jean Jaurès northeast into blvd Alfred Rogier; the hotel is on the left just past the intersection of rue Porte de Mazan.

Le Fin de Siècle (☎ 04 90 71 12 27; 46 place du Clos; lunch menus €13, lunch menus €20-27, dinner menus €20 & €27) A good, inexpensive lunch bet, Le Fin de Siècle offers things such as *moules frites* among *belle époque* surroundings. The tables spill onto the street in summer.

Le Marijo (☎ 04 90 60 42 65; 73 rue Raspail; menus €20; lunch & dinner Mon-Sat except Wed lunch) Regional fare rules here. Try the goat's cheese

marinated for 15 days in herbs and olive oil and sprinkled with *marc*, a local eau de vie.

Le Vert Galant (☎ 04 90 67 15 50; 12 rue de Clapiès; menus €28-46; closed Mon lunch & Sun May-Sep, Sun dinner & Mon Oct-Apr) Holds a prized Michelin star and serves extremely palatable truffles in season (January to March).

Chocolats Clavel (☎ 04 90 63 07 59; 30 Porte d'Orange; Mon-Sat) This shop appears to be selling cheese and olives but the displays are deceptive. Everything in this cosy place is made of sweets, including sculptured edifices carved from *berlingot*, a hard caramel candy and a local speciality.

Getting There & Away
The train station is served by goods trains only, so buses operated by Cars Comtadins and Cars Arnaud provide Carpentras' only intercity public transport. The **bus station** (place Terradou) is 150m southwest of place Aristide Briand.

Schedules are available from **Cars Comtadins** (☎ 04 90 67 20 25; 38 av Wilson) across the square and from **Cars Arnaud** (☎ 04 90 63 01 82; 8 av Victor Hugo). The tourist office can also help.

There are hourly services to Avignon (€3.80, 45 minutes) and infrequent runs to Vaison-la-Romaine (€3.90, 45 minutes) via Malaucène and Bédoin (€3.50, 40 minutes) at the southwestern foot of Mont Ventoux and Cavaillon (€4.60, 45 minutes), L'Isle-sur-Sorgue (€3.40, 20 minutes), 7km west of Fontaine de Vaucluse.

FONTAINE DE VAUCLUSE
pop 610

The mighty spring for which Fontaine de Vaucluse (Vau-Cluso La Font in Provençal) is named is actually the spot where the River Sorgue ends its subterranean course and gushes to the surface. Pretty Fontaine de Vaucluse lies about 1km downstream from the spring, the crystal waters of which flow animatedly and picturesquely through the village.

Up to 200 cu metres of water per second spill forth magnificently from the base of the cliff in late winter, forming one of the world's most powerful springs. During drier periods, the much reduced flow simply seeps through the rocks at various points downstream from the cliff, and the spring itself becomes little more than a still, very deep pond. Following numerous unsuccessful human and robotic

PROVENCE

attempts to reach the bottom, an unmanned submarine touched base – 315m down – in 1985.

Some 1.5 million visitors descend upon the village each year to stroll about its streets and throw pebbles into its deep, deep pond.

Information

If you come by car, you will have no choice but to fork out €3 for the privilege of parking. There is no free parking to be found *anywhere*.

Tourist office (☎ 04 90 20 32 22; officetourisme .vaucluse@wanadoo.fr; chemin de la Fontaine; ⊗ 9am-7pm Tue-Sat) Southeast of central place de la Colonne on the way to the spring.

Sights
MUSEUMS

For its size, the attractive village has an inordinate number of small museums, dealing with many diverse subjects.

Musée d'Histoire 1939–1945 (☎ 04 90 20 24 00; admission €3.50; ⊗ 10am-noon & 2-6pm Sat & Sun Mar, 10am-noon & 2-6pm Wed-Mon Apr-Jun, 10am-noon & 2-6pm Wed-Mon Jul & Aug, 10am-noon & 2-6pm Wed-Mon Sep & Oct, 10am-noon & 2-5pm Sat & Sun Nov & Dec), adjoining the tourist office, tells the story of the resistance movement during WWII.

Moulin à Papier (⊗ 04 90 20 34 14; chemin de la Fontaine; admission free; ⊗ 9am-12.30pm & 2-5pm Mon-Sat, 10.30am-12.30pm & 2-5pm Sun Sep-Jun, 9am-7pm Jul & Aug) is a reconstructed paper mill, built on the site of Fontaine de Vaucluse's old mill on the river banks opposite the tourist office. Beautiful, flower-encrusted paper, made as it was in the 16th century, is sold in the adjoining boutique and art gallery.

The Italian Renaissance poet Petrarch lived in Fontaine de Vaucluse from 1337 to 1353, immortalising his true love, Laura, wife of Hugues de Sade, in verse. **Musée Pétrarque** (☎ 04 90 20 37 20; admission €3.50; ⊗ 10am-noon & 2-6pm Wed-Mon Apr-Sep, 10am-noon & 2-5pm Oct), on the left bank of the Sorgue, is devoted to his work, sojourn and broken heart.

Sleeping

Auberge de Jeunesse (☎ 04 90 20 31 65; fax 04 90 20 26 20; Chemin de la Vignasse; dm €8) This hostel is south of the Fontaine de Vaucluse in the direction of Lagnes (walk uphill from the bus stop).

The tourist office has a list of *chambres d'hôtes* in the village. Fontaine de Vaucluse

has three hotels. **Font de Lauro** (☎ /fax 04 90 20 31 49; plan de Saumane; d €27-37.50), a small, family-run, 16-room place is the best of the three. The rooms are pretty basic but they are decorated in an attractive Provençal style and there's a small pool.

Hôtel du Poète (☎ 90 20 34 05; www.hoteldupoete .com; r €115; ℗ ⊠ ⊡) The pick of the places in town if the budget allows, this is a charming place surrounded by gurgling crystal waters and tall trees right in the heart of the village. The 23 rooms are comfortable and well equipped.

Camping

Camping Municipal Les Prés (☎ 04 90 20 32 38; route du Cavaillon) West of the village centre, this camping park is near the large public car park and the Sorgue.

Getting There & Away

Fontaine de Vaucluse is 21km southeast of Carpentras and 7km east of L'Isle-sur-Sorgue, the nearest 'real' town. From Avignon, Voyages Arnaud runs a bus (€4.50, one hour, two or three daily) with a stop at Fontaine de Vaucluse, from where it's a short walk to the spring. There are Arnaud buses from Carpentras to L'Isle-sur-Sorgue (20 minutes).

GORDES
pop 2127

On the white, rocky, southern face of the Vaucluse plateau, the tiered village of Gordes forms an amphitheatre that overlooks the Rivers Sorgue and Calavon. The top of the village is crowned by a sturdy chateau built between the 11th and 16th centuries. In summer this once-typical Provençal village is frighteningly overrun with tourists, but it's still worth a wander around if you've got the wheels to get you there.

The **tourist office** (☎ 04 90 72 02 75; www.gordes -village.com; place du Château; ⊗ 9am-12.30pm & 2-6pm Jun-Sep, 9am-noon & 2-5pm Oct-May) is in the chateau's Salle des Gardes (Guards' Hall).

Gordes is about 20km west of Apt and 18km east of Fontaine de Vaucluse. The closest town is Cavaillon, 16km to the southwest, which is served by train and bus from many cities and towns in Provence. Buses run by **Les Express de la Durance** (☎ 04 90 71 03 00) link Gordes with Cavaillon twice a day except on Sunday.

AROUND GORDES

The main reason people come to Gordes is to visit the walled **Village des Bories** (☎ 04 90 72 03 48; adult/under 17 €5.50/3; ☼ 9am-7.30pm), 4km southwest of Gordes, just off the D2 heading for Cavaillon. *Bories* are one- or two-storey beehive-shaped huts constructed without mortar using thin wedges of limestone. They were first built in the area in the Bronze Age and were continuously lived in, renovated and even built anew until as late as the 18th century. It is not known what purpose they first served, but over the centuries they have been used as workshops, wine cellars, shelters and storage sheds. The 'village' contains about 20 such structures, restored to their appearance of about 150 years ago. Some people say the *bories* remind them of Ireland's *clochàn*.

ROUSSILLON

pop 1200

Roussillon lies in the valley between the Vaucluse plateau and the Lubéron Range. Two millennia ago, the Romans used its distinctive ochre earth to produce pottery glazes. These days the whole village – even the cemetery's gravestones – is built of the reddish local stone, making it a popular place for painters eager to try out the range of their palettes. The red and orange hues are especially striking given the yellow-white bareness of the surrounding area and the green conifers sprinkled around town.

Information

The **tourist office** (☎ /fax 04 90 05 60 25; place de la Poste; ☼ 10am-noon & 1.30-6.30pm Mon-Sat Apr-Sep, 9.30am-noon & 1.30-6pm Tue-Fri, 10am-noon & 2-5.30pm Mon & Sat Oct-Mar) is in the centre of Roussillon. A complete list of hotels, *chambres d'hôtes* and restaurants in and around Roussillon is pinned up outside the office.

Sights & Activities

Take a walk in nature's powder paint palette on the 1km **Sentier des Ocres** (Ochre Trail; admission €2; ☼ 9.30am-5.30pm Mar-11 Nov). It begins approximately 100m north of Roussillon's centre and will lead you through fairy-tale groves of chestnuts, maritime pines and scrub to the bizarre and beautiful ochre formations blushing the colours of a sunset and created by erosion and fierce winds over the centuries. Don't wear light colours

or precious shoes; you'll return smudged in rust-coloured dust.

Getting There & Away

Roussillon, 9km east of Gordes in the direction of Apt (11km east again), is inaccessible by public transport. The GR6 walking trail passes through here.

APT & THE LUBÉRON

The beautiful Lubéron hills stretch from Cavaillon in the west to Manosque in the east, and from Apt southwards to the River Durance. The area is named after the main range, a compact massif with a gentle, 1100m-high summit. Its oak-covered northern face is a steep, striking natural rampart while its gentler southern face is drier and more Mediterranean in both climate and flora. Whichever side of the range you're on, the country around you will be enchantingly pretty.

Much of the Lubéron Range is within the boundaries of the Parc Naturel Régional du Lubéron. If you want to explore, the area has some excellent walking trails and is an excellent place for cycling.

The Lubéron area is dotted with *bories* (see left). The town of Apt, an ideal base for exploring the Lubéron, is largely unexceptional except for its grapes, cherries and *fleurions*, candied or crystallised fruits, which are sold everywhere. It celebrates its Cherry Festival each year in May and is renowned for its large and festive Saturday morning market.

Maps

The tourist office sells regional maps such as the Top 25 (3242OT) *Map of Apt and the Parc Naturel Régional du Lubéron*, or the *Cavaillon* map (3142OT). They cost €11.50 and €9 respectively.

Information

Maison du Parc (☎ 04 90 04 42 00; www.parcdu luberon.fr; 60 place Jean Jaurès; ☼ 8.30am-noon & 1.30-7pm Mon-Sat Apr-Sep, to 6pm Mon-Fri Oct-Mar) Has information on the Parc Naturel Régional du Lubéron, including details of the park's two dozen *gîtes d'étape* (hikers' accommodation). The centre has plenty of information on hiking and cycling in the park and sells an excellent range of guides, including the recommended topoguide *Le Parc Naturel Régional du Lubéron à Pied* (€11.90), which details 24 walks including the GR9, GR92 and GR97 trails (in French only).

PROVENCE

Tourist Office (☎ 04 90 74 03 18; www.ot-apt.fr; 20 av Philippe de Girard; ☺ 9am-7pm Mon-Sat & 9.30am-12.30pm Sun Jul & Aug, 9am-noon & 2-6pm Mon-Sat & 9.30am-12.30pm Sun Jun-Sep, 9am-noon & 2-6pm Mon-Sat Oct-May) Over the bridge as you enter Apt from Cavaillon. Ask for the leaflet *Apt –à Découvrir*, which details, in English and French, two one-hour city tours signposted around town with colour-coded markers.

Parc Naturel Régional du Lubéron

The park's 1200 sq km encompass numerous villages, desolate forests, unexpected gorges and abandoned farmhouses well on the way to ruin – or perhaps restoration by fans of Peter Mayle. His purchase and renovation of a house just outside the pretty village of **Ménerbes** in the late 1980s formed the basis of his whimsical, best-selling books *A Year in Provence* and *Toujours Provence*.

Sleeping & Eating

Hôtel L'Aptois (☎ 04 90 74 02 02; fax 04 90 74 64 79; 289 cours Lauze de Perret; d with washbasin from €32, with shower & toilet from €46) A smartly refurbished place on the edge of the old town.

Auberge du Lubéron (☎ 04 90 74 12 50; www.auberge-luberon-peuzin.com; 8 place Faubourg du Ballet; r €52-73) On the opposite side of the river from Hôtel L'Aptois, Auberge du Lubéron is part of the Logis de France chain and offers a fine **restaurant** (menus €29-68). Rooms are cosy and contemporary Provençal in style.

Hostellerie le Paradou (☎ 04 90 08 54 94; www.laparadou-lacascade.com in French; route d'Apt, Lourmarin; r €55, half-board per person €77; P) About 15km out of Apt, this is a charming guesthouse in an idyllic country setting just on the edge of Lourmarin, one of the prettiest Lubéron villages. The rooms are comfortable, basic-farmhouse style and the friendly owners run an accomplished **restaurant** (menus from €22) that's good on the Provençal classics.

Camping

Camping Municipal Les Cèdres (☎ /fax 04 90 74 14 61; route de Rustrel; camping with electricity €12.70; ☺ 25 Feb-14 Nov) This is a basic, no-frills camping ground by the river, just out of town.

Getting There & Away

Buses going to Aix-en-Provence (€12.35, 1½ hours, two daily) leave from the **bus station** (☎ 04 90 74 20 21; 250 av de la Libération) east of the centre. There are services to/from Avignon (€7.20, 1¼ hours, three or four daily),

Digne-les-Bains (€7.30, two hours, one or two daily), Cavaillon (€4.70, 40 minutes, two or three daily) and Marseille (€17.65, 2½ hours, two daily).

ARLES & THE CAMARGUE

ARLES

pop 51,614

Arles' most famous resident was Vincent Van Gogh (1853–90) and it's easy to see why the painter may have found Arles both soothing and visually exciting. Little has changed since Van Gogh immortalised the city's winding streets and shady squares. The baking sun casts a glow over the colourful old houses, keeping the tempo slow. The pace picks up quickly when the matadors come to town, for Arles is *corrida* (bullfighting) crazy and regularly presents bullfights in its Roman amphitheatre.

Arles sits on the northern tip of the Camargue alluvial plain on the Grand Rhône River, just south of where the Petit Rhône splits off from it.

The town began its ascent to prosperity and political importance in 49 BC, when the victorious Julius Caesar – to whom the city had given its support – captured and plundered Marseille, which had backed Caesar's rival, the general and statesman Pompey the Great.

Arles soon replaced Marseille as the region's major port and became the sort of Roman provincial centre that, within a century and a half, needed a 12,000-seat theatre and a 20,000-seat amphitheatre to entertain its citizens. These days, the two structures are still used to stage cultural events and bullfights.

Orientation

Arles is enclosed by the Grand Rhône River to the northwest, blvd Émile Combes to the east and, to the south, blvd des Lices and blvd Georges Clemenceau. It's shaped like a foot, with the train station, place de la Libération and place Lamartine (where Van Gogh once lived) at the ankle, les Arènes at the anklebone and the tourist office under the arch. Covering a relatively small area, it's easily explored on – what else? – foot.

ARLES

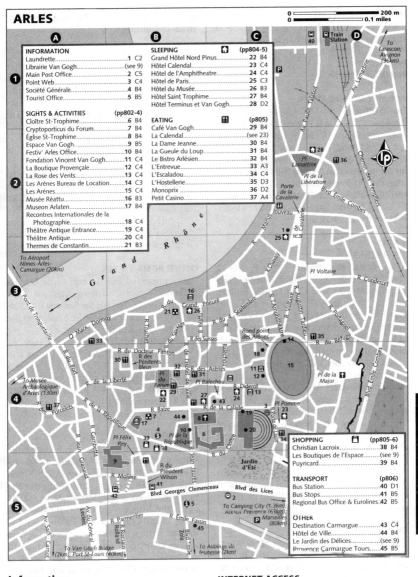

0 — 200 m
0 — 0.1 miles

INFORMATION
Laundrette..............................**1** C2
Librairie Van Gogh...............(see 9)
Main Post Office....................**2** C5
Point Web.............................**3** C4
Société Générale....................**4** B4
Tourist Office.........................**5** B5

SIGHTS & ACTIVITIES (pp802–4)
Cloître St-Trophime................**6** B4
Cryptoporticus du Forum........**7** B4
Église St-Trophime.................**8** B4
Espace Van Gogh...................**9** B5
Festiv' Arles Office................**10** B4
Fondation Vincent Van Gogh...**11** B4
La Boutique Provençale.........**12** C4
La Rose des Vents.................**13** C4
Les Arènes Bureau de Location..**14** C3
Les Arènes..........................**15** C4
Musée Réattu......................**16** B3
Museon Arlaten....................**17** B4
Recontres Internationales de la
   Photographie....................**18** C4
Théâtre Antique Entrance......**19** C4
Théâtre Antique...................**20** C4
Thermes de Constantin.........**21** B3

SLEEPING (pp804–5)
Grand Hôtel Nord Pinus.........**22** B4
Hôtel Calendal.....................**23** C4
Hôtel de l'Amphitheatre........**24** C4
Hôtel de Paris.......................**25** C3
Hôtel du Musée....................**26** B3
Hôtel Saint Trophime............**27** B4
Hôtel Terminus et Van Gogh...**28** D2

EATING (p805)
Café Van Gogh.....................**29** B4
La Calendal.........................(see 23)
La Dame Jeanne...................**30** B4
La Gueule du Loup................**31** B4
Le Bistro Arlésien.................**32** B4
L'Entrevue..........................**33** A3
L'Escaladou.........................**34** C4
L'Hostellerie.......................**35** D3
Monoprix............................**36** D2
Petit Casino.........................**37** A4

SHOPPING (pp805–6)
Christian Lacroix...................**38** B4
Les Boutiques de l'Espace......(see 9)
Puyricard............................**39** B4

TRANSPORT (p806)
Bus Station..........................**40** D1
Bus Stops............................**41** B5
Regional Bus Office & Eurolines.**42** B5

OTHER
Destination Carmargue...........**43** C4
Hôtel de Ville......................**44** B4
Le Jardin des Délices.............(see 9)
Provence Carmargue Tours.....**45** B5

PROVENCE

Information

BOOKSHOPS

Librairie Van Gogh (☎ 04 90 96 86 65; 1 place Félix Rey; ☽ 10am-12.30pm & 2-6.30pm Tue-Sat) Wrapped around the courtyard of Espace Van Gogh, this is a fantastic bookshop with an extensive range of art and history books in French and English, as well as a good variety of regional travel guides.

INTERNET ACCESS

Point Web (☎ 04 90 18 91 54; 10 rue du 4 Septembre; per 10min €1; ☽ 9am-7pm Mon-Sat) This is the best place to get on the Web. It is cheaper and the connection faster than other internet cafes in town.

LAUNDRY

Laundrette (6 rue de la Cavalerie; ☽ 7am-7pm)

MONEY
There are several banks along rue de la République, including Société Générale.

POST
Post Office (5 blvd des Lices)

TOURIST INFORMATION
Tourist Office main office (☎ 04 90 18 41 20, accommodation bookings 04 90 18 41 22; www.tourisme.ville-arles .fr; esplanade Charles de Gaulle; ☺ 9am-6.45pm Apr-Sep, 9am-4.45pm Mon-Sat, 10.30am-2.30pm Sun Oct-Mar); train station (☎ 04 90 49 36 90; ☺ 9am-1pm Jun-Sep) The main office is a short trip along blvd des Lices. The offices also sell a discounted combination ticket to all of Arles' sights for adult/student €13.50/12; museums sell the pass too. From mid-June to mid-September the tourist office runs several thematic city tours.

Sights
LES ARÈNES
Arles' **Roman amphitheatre** (☎ 04 90 96 03 70; adult/student €6/3; ☺ 9am-6.30pm May-Sep, 9am-5.30pm Mar, Apr & Oct, 10am-4.30pm Nov-Feb), built in the late 1st or early 2nd century and marginally larger than its counterpart in Nîmes, originally staged sporting contests, chariot races and bloodier spectacles: wild animals or gladiators (usually slaves or criminals) pitted against each other to the death.

In the early medieval period, during the Arab invasions, les Arènes was transformed into a fortress; three of the four defensive towers can still be seen around the structure. These days, les Arènes has a capacity of more than 12,000 and still draws a full house during the bullfighting season (see p804).

Les Arènes is hidden away in the web of narrow streets in the city centre. Its *bureau de location* (ticket office) is on the northern side of the amphitheatre on Rond point des Arènes.

THÉÂTRE ANTIQUE
The **Théâtre Antique** (Roman theatre; ☎ 04 90 96 93 30; adult/student €3.50/2.60; ☺ 9am-6.30pm May-Sep, 9am-11.30am & 2-5.30pm Mar & Apr, 9-11.30am Oct, 10-11.30am & 2-4.30pm Nov-Feb), which dates from the end of the 1st century BC, was used for many hundreds of years as a convenient source of construction materials, so little of the original structure – measuring 102m in diameter – remains, except for two imposing columns. Entered through the Jardin d'Été (Summer Garden) on blvd des Lices,

it hosts open-air dance, film and music festivals in summer.

ÉGLISE ST-TROPHIME
This austere Provençal Romanesque-style **church** was once a cathedral, as Arles was an archbishopric from the 4th century until 1790. It stands on the site of several earlier churches, and was built in the late 11th and 12th centuries, perhaps using stone cut from the Théâtre Antique. The church is named after St Trophimus, a late-2nd- or early-3rd-century bishop of Arles.

Across the courtyard is serene **Cloître St-Trophime** (☎ 04 90 49 36 36; adult/student €3.50/2.60; ☺ 9am-6.30pm May-Sep, 9am-5.30pm Mar, Apr & Oct, 10am-4.30pm Nov-Feb), surrounded by superbly sculptured columns. The two Romanesque galleries date from the 1100s, while the two Gothic galleries are from the 14th century.

OTHER ROMAN SITES
Partly preserved Roman baths, the **Thermes de Constantin** (rue du Grand Prieuré; adult/student €3/2.20; ☺ 9am-noon & 2-6.30pm May-Sep, 9am-noon & 2-5.30pm Mar, Apr & Oct, 10am-noon & 2-5pm Feb & Nov), near the river, were built in the 4th century.

Cryptoporticus du Forum (adult/student €3.50/2.60; ☺ 9-11.30am & 2-6.30pm May-Sep, 9-11.30am & 2-4.30pm Mar, Apr & Oct, 10-11.30am & 2-4.30pm Feb & Nov) are underground storerooms, most of which were carved out in the 1st century BC. To gain access you need to go through a 17th-century Jesuit chapel on rue Balze.

MUSEUMS
Housed in a strikingly modern building, the **Musée d'Archéologique d'Arles** (Musée de l'Arles Antique; ☎ 04 90 18 88 88/89; adult/student €5.50/4; ☺ 9am-7pm Mar-Oct, 10am-5pm Nov-Feb) brings together the rich collections of the former Musée d'Art Païen and Musée d'Art Chrétien (Museums of Pagan and Christian Art). Exhibits include Roman statues, artefacts, marble sarcophagi and an assortment of 4th-century Christian sarcophagi. The museum is 1.5km southwest of the tourist office at av de la 1ère Division Française Libre on the Presqu'île du Cirque Romain.

Museon Arlaten (☎ 04 90 93 58 11; 29 rue de la République; adult/student €4/3; ☺ 9.30am-1pm & 2-6.30pm Jul & Aug, 9.30am-12.30pm & 2-6pm Tue-Sat Apr-Jun & Sep, 9.30am-12.30pm & 2-5pm Tue-Sat Oct-Mar), occupying a 16th-century townhouse, was founded by the Nobel Prize–winning poet

Frédéric Mistral (see p763). The museum is dedicated to preserving and displaying everyday objects related to traditional Provençal life: furniture, crafts, costumes, ceramics, wigs, a model of the Tarasque (a people-eating amphibious monster of Provençal legend) etc.

Musée Réattu (☎ 04 90 96 37 68; 10 rue du Grand Prieuré; adult/student €4/3; 🕑 10am-noon & 2-5pm Mar, Apr & Oct; 10am-noon & 2-6.30pm May-Sep, 1-5pm Nov-Feb) is housed in a former 15th-century priory. It exhibits works by some of the world's finest photographers, modern and contemporary works of art and paintings by 18th- and 19th-century Provençal artists. The museum also has 57 Picasso drawings, sketched by the artist between December 1970 and November 1971.

VAN GOGH TRAIL
The fact that Arles does not have a single painting from Van Gogh's amazingly productive stay in the area may be a huge disappointment for visitors today, but there's a certain poetic justice to it since the town was hardly kind to Van Gogh during his stay.

Far from treating him sympathetically while he was recovering from his first mental attack (the one that led him to threaten his housemate Paul Gauguin in place Victor Hugo with a cut-throat razor before using it slice off part of his left ear), a petition was raised, his house was sealed and he was locked up for a month on the mayor's orders.

There are fitting tributes to his art, however, at **Fondation Vincent van Gogh** (☎ 04 90 49 94 04; 24bis Rond Point des Arènes; adult/student €7/5; 🕑 10am-7pm Apr-15 Oct, 9.30am-noon & 2-5.30pm Tue-Sun 16 Oct-Mar), inside the Palais de Luppé, from some important modern-day artists, including David Hockney, Francis Bacon and Fernando Botero. It is well worth a visit.

Gallery **La Rose des Vents** (☎ 04 90 93 25 96; 18 rue Diderot; 🕑 10.30am-12.30pm Tue-Sat, 3-7pm Tue-Sun) displays various Van Gogh reproductions, as well as copies of letters written by the artist to his brother Theo.

Various art exhibitions take place at **Espace van Gogh** (☎ 04 90 49 39 39; place Félix Rey), housed in the old Hôtel Dieu and former hospital, where Van Gogh spent some time.

Tours
Jeep tours of the Camargue are organised by many companies, including **Provence Camargue Tours** (☎ 04 90 96 69 20; 1 rue Émile Fassin) and **Destination Camargue** (☎ /fax 04 90 96 94 44; 14bis rue de la Calade). The latter organises half-day trips (adult/child €30/15) departing daily from Arles at 3pm in summer. Reservations can also be made at **La Boutique Provençale** (☎ 04 90 49 84 31; 8 Rond Point des Arènes). For further operators see p808.

Festivals & Events
Arles' biggest event of the year is the **Feria Pascale**, which takes place around Easter and

---

VINCENT VAN GOGH
Vincent Van Gogh (1853–90) revelled in Provence's intense light and colours when he arrived here in 1888. During a highly productive year in Arles he worked with a burning fervour, unfazed even by howling mistrals, during which he would either kneel on his canvases and paint horizontally or lash his easel to iron stakes he had driven deep into the ground.

During his stay he painted, among many other locations, the Pont de Langlois, a little (rebuilt) bridge 3km south of Arles (from town, take bus No 1 to the Pont Van Gogh terminus). Some of Van Gogh's other best-known canvases – *Sunflowers, Van Gogh's Chair* and *Café at Night* – were painted in Arles.

In 1888 Van Gogh's friend and fellow artist Paul Gauguin came to stay with him for several months. But their different temperaments and approaches to art soon led to a quarrel and Van Gogh's first attack of mental illness. In May 1889, because of recurrent attacks, he voluntarily entered an asylum in St-Rémy de Provence (25km northeast of Arles over the Alpilles). During his year here he continued to be amazingly productive. In 1890, while staying in Auvers-sur-Oise (just north of Paris), Van Gogh – lonely, despairing and afraid his madness was incurable – shot and killed himself.

There are few tangible remains of Vincent Van Gogh's stay in Arles. All trace of his rented yellow house on place Lamartine was wiped out during WWII.

marks the beginning of the bullfight season. Bullfighting fans and a trail of pickpockets fill the town, creating traffic chaos and driving up hotel prices, but it is an exciting time.

In addition, Arles has a full calendar of summertime cultural events. In early July, **Les Rencontres Internationales de la Photographie** (International Photography Festival) attracts photographers and aficionados from around the world. The two-week **Fêtes d'Arles**, which usually kicks off at the end of June, brings dance, theatre, music and poetry readings to the city. For more information contact the **Festiv'Arles office** (☎ 04 90 96 47 00, 04 90 96 81 18; fax 04 90 96 81 17; 35 place de la République).

The **Fête des Gardians** in May features a procession of Camargue cowboys through the streets of town, the election of the Queen of Arles and Camargue games in the arena.

Other events include the **Festival Ame Gitane** in mid-August, which celebrates Gypsy (Romany) culture, and the 10-day-long **Fête des Prémices du Riz**, held in September, which marks the start of the rice harvest.

Sleeping

Except during festivals, bullfights and July and August, Arles has plenty of reasonably priced accommodation. There are lots of **gîtes ruraux** (for reservations ☎ 04 90 59 49 40) in the surrounding countryside, especially the Camargue. Ask the tourist office for the list.

BUDGET

Auberge de Jeunesse (☎ 04 90 96 18 25; arles@fuaj .org; 20 av Maréchal Foch; dm incl breakfast 1st night €13.50,

then €13.70; 🕙 5 Feb-20 Dec; **P**) This 100-bed place is 2km from the centre. Take bus No 3 or 8 from blvd Georges Clemenceau (No 8 from place Lamartine) to the Fournier stop. You must have an FUAJ card.

Hôtel Terminus et Van Gogh (☎ /fax 04 90 96 12 32; 5 place Lamartine; s/d with shower & toilet €36.60; **P**) Close to the station, this hotel is welcoming and has good-value rooms with private bathrooms.

Hôtel de Paris (☎ 04 90 96 05 88; 8 rue de la Cavalerie; r from €23) Above a cheap café, Hôtel de Paris provides cheap one-star rooms.

Camping

Camping City (☎ 04 90 93 08 86; www.camping-city .com; 67 route de Crau; camping €16; 🕙 Apr-Sep) The closest camping ground to town, Camping City is 1km southeast of the city centre on the road to Marseille. Take bus No 2 to the Hermite stop.

MID-RANGE

Hôtel de l'Amphitheatre (☎ 04 90 96 10 30; www .hotelamphitheatre.fr; 5-7 rue Diderot; s/d €45/49; 🐾) The wooden-beamed, 17th-century building this hotel occupies has been colourfully and tastefully decorated, as have most of the large, attractive rooms. There's also one room with wheelchair access. The fine breakfast (€6) served here is worth going for. This is one of the best all-round options in town.

Hôtel Calendal (☎ 04 90 96 11 89; www.lecalendal .com; 5 rue Porte de Laure; r €45-99; **P** 🐾 🐾 🖳) This is an attractive place next to the amphitheatre

---

BULLFIGHTING

In *mise à mort* bullfighting (*corrida*) a bull bred to be aggressive is killed in a colourful and bloody ceremony involving picadors, bandilleros, matadors and horses. For bullfighting aficionados in Spain, Latin America and parts of southern France, the *corrida* is not a sport as it does not involve a contest between the matador and the bull. The spectacle is a tragedy in three acts that centre on the inevitable death of the bull. When performed correctly (which is rarely the case) the matador and the bull execute a kind of dance in which each demonstrates heroism under pressure. Aside from the theatrical purpose, the bull must be killed because, after having been in a *corrida*, it is said to be too dangerous to be again placed in a ring with a matador. After the event, the bull is carved up and sold for meat. Because the growing bulls roam free and graze on grass, the meat has a different flavour than that of ordinary steers.

But not all bullfighting ends with a dead animal. In a *course Camarguaise* (Camargue-style bullfight), white-clad *razeteurs* try to remove ribbons tied to the bull's horns with hooks held between their fingers.

In Arles, the bullfighting season begins around Easter with a bullfighting festival known as the Feria (or Féria) Pascale and runs until the September rice harvest festival.

and overlooking the Théâtre Antique. Rooms are bright, airy and well equipped. There's a peaceful garden terrace at the back. Garage parking costs €10.

Hôtel Saint Trophime (☎ 04 90 96 88 38; fax 04 90 96 92 19; 16 rue de la Calade; s €40, d €55-65; P ⊠ ☒) Occupying a fully renovated old building, Hôtel Saint Trophime is replete with antiques, high ceilings, a grand staircase (there's also an elevator) and stylish – if rather bare – rooms, which are of different sizes but all are beautifully maintained and have modern bathrooms.

Hôtel du Musée (☎ 04 90 93 88 88; www.hotel dumusee.com.fr; 11 rue du Grand Prieuré; r with shower €40-51, with bath €56-61) Another period hotel in a fine 12th- to 13th-century building. An appealing 20-room, two-star place with well-furnished rooms, it's spacious and has a rear terrace garden. The road-facing rooms can be noisy though.

TOP END

Grand Hôtel Nord Pinus (☎ 04 90 93 44 44; www.nord -pinus.com; place du Forum; r €137-275; P ☒) Models, circus performers, matadors, show people and artists have flocked here since 1927. The tastefully eccentric décor centres on bullfighting themes but also includes antiques and curios from Provence, Spain and North Africa. If the comfortable rooms are too steep for your budget, at least stop by the bar and check out the ever-changing photo exhibits.

Eating

Blvd Georges Clemenceau and blvd des Lices are lined with plane trees and brasseries with terraces. The latter are fine for a meal if you don't mind dining à la traffic fumes.

RESTAURANTS

Place du Forum, an intimate square shaded by eight large plane trees, turns into one big dining table at lunch and dinner time.

Le Bistrot Arlésien (☎ 04 90 96 07 22; place du Forum; salads €4-8, plats du jour €8) A no-frills place serving basic but decent staples at reasonable prices right in the heart of town.

La Dame Jeanne (☎ 04 90 96 37 09; 4 rue des Pénitents Bleus; menus €13-17) Unpretentious La Dame Jeanne offers three-course (and a four-course) menus.

L'Entrevue (☎ 04 90 93 37 28; 23 quai Max Dormoy; mains €7.70-15, menu €22.90; ☒ 9-12.30am) Occupies a calm, cool spot down by the riverfront, in a cinema and bookshop complex. It doesn't offer a view of the water (it's blocked by high river ramparts) but is a stylish, laid-back place serving modern Asian and Caribbean-inspired cuisine, including a fantastic couscous royal and wonderfully refreshing mint and pine kernel tea.

L'Hostellerie (☎ 04 90 96 13 05; 62 rue du Refuge; menus €14.50-25.50; ☒ Wed-Mon) If you can, dine on the terrace at L'Hostellerie, which has an excellent view towards the amphitheatre. It offers a good selection of salads and a bargain lunch *formule*.

La Gueule du Loup (☎ 04 90 96 96 69; 39 rue des Arènes; meals €12; ☒ noon-4pm) A cosy, family-run place where you can watch your meal being prepared in the open kitchen. The food is typically regional and the standards are high. Try the herb-infused *crème brûlée*.

L'Escaladou (☎ 04 90 96 70 43; 23 rue Porte de Laure; menus €15-20) This place concentrates on fish. Try the *brandade* (€9), *bouillabaisse* (€20) or *aïoli* (€11).

CAFÉS

Café Van Gogh (☎ 04 90 96 44 56; place du Forum; menus €12-16) This very yellow café pays homage to the artist's Arles roots in its attempt to re-create the subject of his canvas *Café de Nuit*. Café Van Gogh is a busy bar by night.

La Calendal (☎ 04 90 96 11 89; 22 place Pomme; meals €12; ☒ noon-4pm) An endearing *salon de thé*–cum-restaurant-cum-hotel. Sip a cuppa between the dining room's cool, stone walls and beamed ceilings or in that quiet, shaded garden. There's also an all-you-can-eat daily buffet for €12.

SELF-CATERING

There is a **Petit Casino** (rue des Porcelets; ☒ 9am-7pm Mon-Sat) and a **Monoprix** (place Lamartine; ☒ 8.30am-7.25pm Mon-Sat).

On Wednesday, market stalls sprawl the length of blvd Émile Combes, along the outside of the city walls. The food section is at the northern end. On Saturday morning, the market moves to blvd des Lices and blvd Georges Clemenceau.

Shopping

Les Boutiques de l'Espace (Espace van Gogh, place Félix Rey) is a good place for gifts, postcards, souvenirs and art books. **Puyricard** (54 rue de la République) offers exquisite Provençal chocolates, while **Christian Lacroix** (52 rue de la République), next door, is the very first boutique of the famous Arlesienne clothes designer.

Getting There & Away

AIR

The **Aéroport Nîmes-Arles-Camargue airport** (Garons airport; ☎ 04 66 70 49 49) is 20km northwest of the city on the A54. There is no public transport into town.

BUS

The **bus station** (☎ information office 0 800 199 413, 0 810 000 816; av Paulin Talabot; ☺ 7.30am-4pm Mon-Sat) is about 1km north of les Arènes. Most intercity buses stop here. Some also stop at 24 blvd Georges Clemenceau. **Telleschi** (☎ 04 42 28 40 22) runs services to Aix-en-Provence (€11.30, 1¾ hours).

Buses also link Arles with various parts of the Camargue, including Les Stes-Maries de la Mer (€6, one hour, two daily in winter and six to nine daily in summer), Port St-Louis (€6.40, one hour five minutes, six daily) and many places en route, such as Mas du Pont de Rousty, Pioch Badet and Pont de Gau.

Eurolines (☎ 04 90 96 94 78), the long-haul bus company, sells tickets at 24 blvd Georges Clemenceau.

TRAIN

Arles' **train station** (☺ information office 9am-12.30pm & 2-6.30pm Mon-Sat) is just across from the bus station. Some major rail destinations include Nîmes (€6.60, 30 minutes), Montpellier (€12.20, one hour), Marseille (€11.60, 40 minutes) and Avignon (€5.70, 20 minutes).

Getting Around

BUS

Local buses are operated by **STAR** (☎ 04 90 96 87 47; information office 24 blvd Georges Clemenceau; ☺ 7.45am-12.45pm & 1.15-6pm Mon-Fri). This office, west of the tourist office, is the main bus hub, although most buses also stop at place Lamartine, a short walk south of the train station. In general, STAR buses run from 7am to 7pm (5pm on Sunday). A single ticket costs €0.80; a 10-ticket *carnet* €7. In addition to its 11 bus lines, STAR runs minibuses called Starlets that circle most of the old city every 30 minutes from 7.15am to 7.40pm Monday to Saturday. Best of all, they're free.

TAXI

If you need a taxi, the number to call is ☎ 04 90 49 69 59.

THE CAMARGUE

Utterly different from the rest of Provence, the haunting, sparsely populated Camargue, a 780-sq-km delta of the River Rhône, is famed for its desolate beauty and for the white horses and black bulls that graze among the rice fields and breeze-blown bull rushes.

The delta's extensive marshes and unique freshwater and saltwater habitats also support incredibly varied bird life: over 500 species of permanent and migratory land and water birds, including storks and bee-eaters. Huge flocks of pink flamingos nest here during spring and summer, many of them near the Étang de Vaccarès and Étang du Fangassier lakes.

The Camargue has been formed over the ages by sediment deposited by the Rhône as it flows into the Mediterranean. There are enormous salt-evaporation pools around Salin de Giraud on the Camargue's southeastern tip.

The northern part of the delta consists of dry land, and in the years following WWII huge tracts were desalinated as part of a drainage and irrigation programme designed to make the area suitable for large-scale agriculture, especially the cultivation of rice.

Most of the Camargue wetlands are within Parc Naturel Régional de Camargue, set up in 1970 to preserve the area's fragile ecosystems by maintaining a balance between its ecosystems and the region's economic mainstays of agriculture, salt production, hunting, grazing and tourism. Shaped like a croissant with the Étang de Vaccarès in the centre, the 850-sq-km park is enclosed by the Petit Rhône and Grand Rhône Rivers. The Étang de Vaccarès and nearby peninsulas and islands form the Réserve Nationale de Camargue, a 135-sq-km nature reserve.

Those black bulls are raised for bullfighting and roam free under the watchful eyes of a mounted *gardian* (or cowboy). But you're much more likely to see bulls grazing in fenced-in fields; and those white horses that are saddled and tethered, waiting in rows under the blazing sun for tourists willing to pay for a ride.

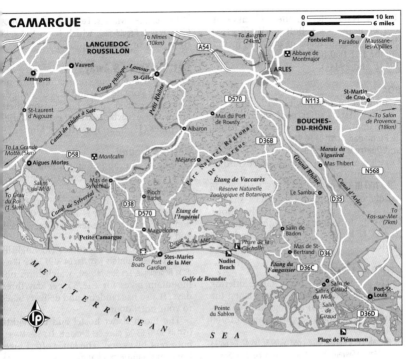

The Camargue is a wonderfully relaxing region to explore by bike, boat and horseback. Just beware of that other traditional Camargue phenomenon: the area's savage mosquitoes, which flourish on the blood of hapless passers-by. Pack *plenty* of insect repellent.

The two most important centres in the Camargue are the seaside resort of Les Stes-Maries de la Mer and the tiny, walled town of Aigues Mortes to the northwest. Both Aigues Mortes and Les Stes-Maries are larded with restaurants, usually offering good-value fare. Look for delicious *gardianne de taureau* (beef stew) and the delicate, thumbnail-sized clams that are called *tellines* on the menu.

Information

Parc Naturel Régional de Camargue information

centre (☎ 04 90 97 86 32; www.parc-camargue .fr in French; Pont de Gau; admission free; ♥ 10am-6pm Apr-Sep, 10am-5pm Sat-Thu Oct-Mar) Four kilometres north of Les Stes-Maries, this centre's exhibits focus on environmental issues. From the glassed-in foyer you can watch birds through powerful binoculars. It also has plenty of information on walking and bird-watching.

Réserve Nationale de Camargue office (☎ 04 90 97 00 97; La Capelière; ♥ 9am-noon & 2-5pm Mon-Sat) Along the D36B, on the eastern side of Étang de Vaccarès. It also has exhibits on the Camargue's ecosystems, flora and fauna, and many trails and paths fan out from the area.

Sights & Activities
MUSÉE CAMARGUAIS

The **Camargue Museum** (Museon Camarguen in Provençal; ☎ 04 90 97 10 82; Mas du Pont de Rousty; adult/student €4.60/2.30; ♥ 9am-6pm Apr-Oct, 10am-5pm Wed-Mon Oct-Mar) is housed in a sheep shed built in 1812. Located 10km southwest of Arles on the D570 to Les Stes-Maries, it's an excellent introduction to the history, ecosystems, flora and fauna of the Camargue river delta. Much attention is given to traditional life in the Camargue (sheep and cattle raising, salt production at Salin de Giraud). A 3.5km nature trail, which ends at an observation tower, begins at the museum.

WALKING

There are numerous walking paths and trails in the Parc Naturel Régional and the

PROVENCE

Réserve Nationale, on the embankments and along the coast. Both park offices sell detailed walking maps of the area, including the 1:25,000 IGN Série Bleue maps Nos 2944E and 2944O.

BOATING

A number of companies with offices in Les Stes-Maries offer boat excursions of the Camargue, including **Camargue Bateau de Promenade** (☎ 04 90 97 84 72; 5 rue des Launes) and **Quatre Maries** (☎ 04 90 97 70 10; 36 av Théodore Aubanel). Both depart from the Port Gardian in the centre of Les Stes-Maries.

Le Tiki III (☎ 04 90 97 81 68) is a beat-up old paddleboat that plies the delta's shallow waters and charges €10 for a 1½-hour tour. Le Tiki is docked at the mouth of the Petit Rhône 1.5km west of Les Stes-Maries de la Mer.

OTHER ACTIVITIES

There are numerous horse farms offering **horse riding** (*promenade à cheval*) along the D570 (Route d'Arles) leading into Les Stes-Maries. Expect to pay approximately €15/60 an hour/day.

Kayak Vert Camargue (☎ 06 09 56 06 47, 04 66 73 57 17; Mas de Sylvéréal), 14km north of Les Stes-Maries off the D38, arranges canoeing and kayaking on the Petit Rhône.

Tours

La Maison du Guide (☎ 06 12 44 73 52; www.maison duguide.camargue.fr in French) at Montcalm, between Aigues Mortes and Les Stes-Maries on the D58, organises a variety of guided tours with a variety of transport modes – on foot, by boat and by bike.

In Les Stes-Maries, **Le Gitan** (☎ 04 66 70 09 65; 17 av de la République), which is on the seafront, also organises jeep safaris.

Getting There & Away

For details about bus connections to/from Arles (via Pont de Gau and Mas du Pont de Rousty) see p806. In the high season, there are two buses each day from Les Stes-Maries to Nîmes (1¼ hours) via Aigues Mortes.

Getting Around

As long as you can put up with the ubiquitous insect pests and the stiff sea breezes, bicycles are a fine way to explore the Camargue, which is, of course, very flat. East of Les Stes-Maries, areas along the seafront and further inland are reserved for walkers and cyclists.

For a list of cycling routes (in English) go to **Le Vélo Saintois** (☎ /fax 04 90 97 74 56; 19 rue de la République, Les Stes-Maries), which hires out mountain bikes for €15/35 per day/three days. It also has tandems and delivers bikes to your hotel door.

The Pioch Badet hostel and **Le Vélociste** (☎ 04 90 97 83 26; place des Remparts, Les Stes-Maries) both rent bikes, too. The latter offers bike, horse and canoe packages.

Les Stes-Maries de la Mer
pop 2478

This coastal resort is known for its nearby beaches and fortified Romanesque church (12th to 15th century), a pilgrimage site for centuries. The neat, treeless rows of low houses are built to endure the three Camargue seasons: sun, wind and mosquitoes. Sandwiched between the sea and the

---

THE GITAN PILGRIMAGE

For two days at the end of each May, Gitans (Romany people, formerly called gypsies) from all over Europe gather at the Camargue fishing village of Les Stes-Maries de la Mer to honour their patron saint, Sarah. According to a Provençal legend, Sarah (along with Mary Magdalene, Mary Jacob, Mary Salome and other Biblical figures) fled the Holy Land in a small boat and landed near the River Rhône.

In 1448 skeletal remains said to belong to Sarah and the Marys were found in a crypt in Les Stes-Maries. Ever since, Gitans have been making the pilgrimage here, dancing and playing music in the streets or carrying a statue of Sarah through town, many of them in traditional dress. The Sunday in October closest to the 22nd is the date for another pilgrimage, dedicated to the Saintes Maries. *Courses Camarguaises* (nonlethal bullfights) are also held. The annual Festival Ame Gitane, a celebration of Gitan culture with theatre, music, film and dance, is held in Arles in mid-August.

marshes, either windswept or sunbaked, this bleached-out town blossoms each summer with pink-faced tourists, Gitans and bullfighters. There's a very Spanish flavour to this town, and not just because of the black bulls. On festival days, proud horse riders sporting traditional costume parade through the town and flamenco is danced in the squares.

INFORMATION
The modern **tourist office** (☎ 04 90 97 82 55; www.saintesmaries.com; 5 av Van Gogh; ⏰ 9am-8pm Jul & Aug, 9am-7pm Apr-Jun & Sep, 9am-6pm Mar & Oct, 9am-5pm Nov-Feb) has an excellent website.

SIGHTS
Les Stes-Maries is most animated during the Gitan pilgrimage (opposite), held annually on 24-25 May.

There is a **Musée des Gitanes** (Panorama du Voyage; ☎ 04 90 97 52 85; Pioch Badet; admission €3; ⏰ 10am-6pm Sep-Jun, 10am-8pm Jul & Aug), next to the Auberge de Jeunesse.

Tickets for bullfights at the **Méjanes arena** (☎ reservations 04 90 97 10 60; av Van Gogh), held in Les Stes-Maries' Arènes, are sold at the ticket office, tucked into its outer walls, between 3pm and 7pm Monday to Saturday.

The coast near Les Stes-Maries is lined with around 30km of uninterrupted finesand **beaches**. The area around **Phare de la Gacholle**, the lighthouse 11km east of town, is frequented by *naturalistes* (nudists).

SLEEPING & EATING
Auberge de Jeunesse (☎ 04 90 97 51 72; fax 04 90 97 54 88; Pioch Badet; ⏰ reception 7.30-10.30am & 5-11pm, to midnight Jul & Aug) This hostel is 8km north of Les Stes-Maries on the D570 to Arles. Les Cars de Camargue buses from Arles drop you at the door (see p806 for details).

A number of old *mas* (farmhouses) surround Les Stes-Maries; many have rooms to let.

Mas de la Grenouillère (☎ 04 90 97 90 22; fax 04 90 97 70 94; d/tr incl breakfast from €60/80; P ⏰ ⏰) Small but comfortable rooms. They have a terrace overlooking open fields full of frogs, which sing guests to sleep each night. La Grenouillère (literally 'The Frog Farm') has stables and organises horse-riding trips. It's 1.5km down a dirt track signposted 1km north of Les Stes-Maries off the D570.

Étrier Camarguais (☎ 04 90 97 81 14; www.letrier .com; d low/high season from €85/105, high season half-board €133/171; P ⏰) This farmhouse-hotel built from 'a dream, flowers and the sun', is idyllic. The hotel is 500m before La Grenouillère along the same dirt track. The reception of the 'Camargue Stirrup' is in a traditional *cabane de gardian* (cowboy cabin). There's a large veranda with parasols to enjoy the food and a large swimming pool to cool off in. Note that half-board is mandatory in July and August.

Heaps of hotels – mostly three or four stars, in the low-rise 'farmhouse style' and generally costing €50 – line the D570, the main road from Arles into Les Stes-Maries. Most hotels in town are equally expensive.

Les Vagues (☎ /fax 04 90 97 84 40; 12 av Théodore Aubanel; d without/with shower from €31/46) On the road that runs along the port west of the tourist office, Les Vagues has decent rooms with bathrooms and some have balconies with sea views.

Hôtel Méditerranée (☎ 04 90 97 82 09; fax 04 90 97 76 31; 4 av Frédéric Mistral; r €39-46) In the centre of town, this place is one of the cheapest options and also offers a homy, familial environment with a flower-decked terrace for breakfast.

Le Tamaris (☎ 04 90 97 93 29; 4 place des Remparts; menu from €11; ⏰ closed Tue Oct-Mar) and **Le Delta** (1 place Mireille; menus €13-24) are both local favourites where you can dine well on little money.

Camping
Camping La Brise (☎ 04 90 97 84 67; fax 04 90 97 72 01; av Marcle Carrière; camping €13; ⏰) Three-star camping northeast of the centre of town.

Aigues Mortes
pop 6084
On the western edge of the Camargue, 28km northwest of Les Stes-Maries, is the curiously named, walled town of Aigues Mortes (which could be translated as 'Dead Waters'). Aigues Mortes was established on marshy flat land in the mid-13th century by Louis IX (St Louis) so the French crown would have a Mediterranean port under its direct control. (At the time, the area's other ports were controlled by various rival powers, including the counts of Provence.) In 1248, Louis IX's ships – all 1500 of them – gathered here before setting sail to the Holy Land for the Sixth Crusade.

Aigues Mortes' sturdy, rectangular ramparts, the tops affording great views over the marshlands, can be scaled from Tour de

PROVENCE

Constance. Inside the walls, there's a fair bit of tourist hype, though the restored Église Notre Dame des Sablons is worth a look.

INFORMATION

Tourist office (☎ 04 66 53 73 00; www.ot-aigues mortes.fr; place St-Louis; ﹠ 9am-noon & 1-6pm Sep-Jun, 9am-8pm Jul & Aug) Inside the walled city at Porte de la Gardette.

SLEEPING & EATING

L'Escale (☎ 04 66 53 71 14; av Tour Constance; s/d/tr €26/29/59) Just outside the walls, L'Escale is a central budget option, although aesthetics are not its strong point: the rooms are rather dark, very simple chalet-style affairs out the back of the old-school bar that fronts the place.

Le Victoria (☎ 04 66 51 14 20; fax 04 66 51 14 21; place Anatole-France; r from €46; menus €14-29) Just opposite the Tour Constance, this place is a cut above, as you'd expect from a Logis de France establishment. It also has a traditional restaurant serving all the local classics such as *soupe de poissons* and *gardienne de taureau.*

Camping Le Clos du Rhône (☎ 04 90 97 85 99; fax 04 90 97 78 85; route d'Aigues Mortes; camping €21.40; 🖳) At this park you can also rent four-person bungalows.

La Salicorne (☎ 04 66 53 62 67; 9 rue Alsace Lorraine; menus €25 & €31) Offers some imaginative culinary flourishes. It's especially strong on fish, for example *carpaccio de lotte* (fresh slivers of raw local fish marinated in lime juice).

NORTHEASTERN PROVENCE

DIGNE-LES-BAINS

pop 17,680 / elevation 608m

Provence hits the Alps, and the land of sun and olive trees meets the land of snow and melted cheese, around Digne-les-Bains, which is about 100km northeast of Aix-en-Provence and 152km northwest of Nice. This laid-back town is named after its thermal springs, visited annually by 11,000 people seeking to pamper themselves or ease rheumatism and respiratory ailments.

The area is also known for lavender production. The harvest is in August and honoured in Digne with a five-day festival, Corso

de la Lavande, starting on the first weekend of the month, and with Les Journées Lavande throughout the region in mid-August. In summer you'll smell the little purple flower everywhere.

Digne itself is unremarkable, although it makes a good base for walking and a wide range of adrenaline sports. The shale around Digne is rich in fossils.

The route Napoléon (now the N85), which Bonaparte followed in 1815 en route to Paris after escaping from Elba, passes through Digne and Castellane, the gateway to the Gorges du Verdon.

Orientation

Digne is built on the eastern bank of the shallow River Bléone. The major roads into town converge at the Point Rond du 11 Novembre 1918, a roundabout 400m northeast of the train station. The main street is blvd Gassendi, which heads northeastwards from the Point Rond and passes the large place du Général de Gaulle, the main square.

Information

INTERNET ACCESS

Cybercafé (☎ 04 92 30 87 17; 48 rue de l'Hubac; per hr €5; ﹠ 10am-7pm Tue-Sat) In the centre of the town.

LAUNDRY

There are laundrettes at 4 place du Marché, in the old city (open 8am to 7pm Monday to Saturday), and 99 blvd Gassendi (open 9am to 7pm).

MONEY

BNP Paribas (5 blvd Gassendi)

POST

Post Office (4 rue André Honnorat) East of the tourist office.

TOURIST INFORMATION

Relais Départemental des Gîtes de France (☎ 04 92 31 30 40; www.gites-de-france.com; ﹠ 9am-noon & 1-5pm Mon-Fri, 9am-noon Sat) Also in the Maison du Tourisme, it books accommodation at *gîtes* in the area. Bookings are only made between 9am and 11am and 1pm to 4pm.

Tourist Office (☎ 04 92 36 62 62; www.ot-dignelesbains .fr; place du Tampinet; ﹠ 8.45am-noon & 2-6pm Mon-Sat, 10am-noon Sun Sep-Jun, 8.45am-12.30pm & 1.30-6.30pm Jul & Aug) Inside the Maison du Tourisme, with information on a variety of guided tours in the region, including lavender tours towards the end of August. The office also supplies some good walking and cycling maps of the area.

Sights & Activities
FONDATION ALEXANDRA DAVID-NÉEL
Paris-born writer and philosopher Alexandra David-Néel, made an incognito voyage in the 1900s to Tibet before settling in Digne. Her memory – and her interest in Tibet – are kept alive by the **Fondation Alexandra David-Néel** (☎ 04 92 31 32 38; 27 av Maréchal Juin), which also stages the annual Journées Tibétaines, a celebration of Tibetan culture, at the end of August. From October to June, free tours (with headphones for English speakers) start at 10.30am, 2pm and 4pm; and from April to September tours begin at 10.30am, 2pm, 3.30pm and 5pm. Drive out of town for 1km on the Nice road or take bus No 3 to the Stade Rolland stop.

MUSÉE GASSENDI
In the town centre, the eclectic **Musée Gassendi** (☎ 04 92 31 45 29; place des Récollets; adult/child €4/2; ⏰ 11am-7pm Apr-Sep, 1.30-5.30pm Wed-Mon Oct-Mar) displays five centuries of art, history and natural history on its four floors. There are displays of traditional Provençal and contemporary art, including the landscapes and still-lifes of the 19th-century painter Etienne and a large and striking clay wall by modern artist Andy Goldsworthy. One floor is dedicated to the 16th-century philosopher/scientist/painter Pierre Gassendi, who revived Epicureanism, a Greek school of philosophy.

RÉSERVE NATURELLE GÉOLOGIQUE
Digne is in the middle of the **Réserve Naturelle Géologique**, with spectacular fossil deposits, including the footprints of prehistoric birds as well as ammonites, and ram's horn spiral shells. Ask for the detailed regional map to the Digne and Sisteron areas at the tourist office. You'll need your own transport (or a patient thumb) to get to the 18 sites, although there's an impressive limestone slab right next to the road to Barles 3km north of Digne with around 500 giant ammonites.

The Réserve Naturelle's impressive headquarters, the **Centre de Géologie** (☎ 04 92 36 70 70; www.resgeol04.org; adult/child €4.60/2.75; ⏰ 9am-noon & 2-5.30pm Apr-Oct, Mon-Fri Nov-Mar) at St-Benoît, 2km north of town off the road to Barles, is well worth a visit. Artistically arranged outdoor

trails lead to a museum containing 10 aquariums, multimedia displays and plenty of fossils and plants. Take TUD bus No 2, get off at the Champourcin stop, then take the road to the left.

THERMAL SPA
Steep yourself in the healing warm waters, cover yourself in mud and seaweed treatments or luxuriate in herbal baths or massages at the **Établissement Thermal** (☎ 04 92 32 32 92; www.eurothermes.com in French; ⏰ Feb-early Dec), 2km east of Digne's centre. The cost of a good soak starts at €10 and goes up to €38 for a spa bath and massage. There's also a gym.

Sleeping
In July and August you may be required to take half-board at many of Digne's hotels. The tourist office has a full list of *gîtes d'étape* in the surrounding countryside.

Hôtel L'Origan (☎ /fax 04 92 31 62 13; 6 rue Pied de Ville; s with washbasin from €15, d with shower from €25) This is a little place in the old city, with an upmarket **restaurant** (menus €19) and affordable accommodation in old-fashioned but comfortable rooms.

Hôtel Central (☎ 04 92 31 31 91; www.lhotel-central.com in French; 26 blvd Gassendi; s/d with washbasin €25/28, r with shower/shower & toilet €33/42) A good, central, two-star hotel. Avoid the traffic-noise-plagued road-facing rooms.

Hôtel Le Coin Fleuri (☎ 04 92 31 04 51; 9 blvd Victor Hugo; s/d with shower & toilet from €38/48) Two-star rooms and a great garden to relax in.

Tonic Hotel (☎ 04 92 32 20 31; www.eurothermes.com in French; 36 route des Thermes; r from €60; P ⊗ ⊗ ⊗) A couple of kilometres from town on the way to the Établissement Thermal, the Tonic is pretty good value for what you get. That includes large, modern rooms with satellite TV and hairdryers plus an attractive location at the foot of steep, wooded hills. It also offers a range of health and beauty packages with half-board and treatments at the thermal spa starting at €268 for two days and nights.

Camping
Camping du Bourg (☎ 04 92 31 04 87; route de Barcelonnette; camping €10.50; ⏰ Apr-Oct) This park is 2km northeast of Digne (reduced to €10 if you're taking a cure). Take bus No 2 towards Barcelonnette and get off at Notre Dame du Bourg. From there it's a 600m walk.

Eating

Restaurant-Cafétéria Le Victor Hugo (☎ 04 92 31 57 23; 8-10 blvd Victor Hugo; plats du jour from €7; Ⓧ lunch Mon-Fri) One of the cheapest places for lunch.

Le Point Chaud (☎ 04 92 31 30 71; 95 blvd Gassendi; menu €12; Ⓧ Sat lunch & Sun) A local favourite for pizza, homemade pasta and a variety of fish and meat specialities.

La Braisière (☎ 04 92 31 59 63; 19 place de l'Évêché; lunch & dinner menus €10.80-24; Ⓧ closed Sat lunch) Away from the terraces on place du Général de Gaulle, La Braisière has good *menus* and a fine view over town. It does good *tartiflette* (€12) and *raclette* (€14).

SELF-CATERING

There's a **food market** (place du Général de Gaulle) on Wednesday and Saturday mornings.

There are a couple of good bread and pastry shops along blvd Gassendi plus the nearby **Boulangerie Pattisserie Andre Michel** (16 rue Pied de Ville), which sells tasty sweet and savoury treats.

Saveurs et Couleurs (7 blvd Gassendi) sells luxury local products.

There's also a **Casino Supermarket** (42 blvd Gassendi; Ⓧ 7.30am-12.30pm & 3.30-7.30pm).

Getting There & Away

BUS

The **bus station** (☎ 04 92 31 50 00; place du Tampinet; Ⓧ 9am-12.30pm & 3-6.30pm Mon-Sat) is behind the tourist office. Eleven regional companies operate buses to Nice (€14.60, 2¼ hours, two daily services Monday to Saturday) via Castellane (€10.50, 1¼ hours, one daily), Marseille (€14.10, 2½ hours, four daily) and Apt (€11.30, two hours, one daily).

There's also a shuttle bus linking Digne with the train station of Aix-en-Provence, timed to coincide with the TGV to and from Paris (€16.46, 1½ hours).

TRAIN

Digne's **train station** (☎ 04 92 31 00 67; av Pierre Sémard; Ⓧ ticket windows 8.15am-12.30pm & 1-8pm Mon-Fri, 8.15am-12.30pm & 1.45-4.45pm Sat) is a 10-minute walk westwards from the tourist office. There are four services daily to Marseille (€19.60, 2¼ hours) and three to Briançon (€21, 3½ hours) by bus to Chateau Arnoux and via St-Auban.

The two-car diesel trains operated by **Chemins de Fer de la Provence** (Digne ☎ 04 92 31 01 58, Nice ☎ 04 97 03 80 80) run along a scenic

and winding narrow-gauge line to Nice's Gare de Nice CP via St-Martin du Var, 26km northeast of Nice. The entire trip takes about 3¼ hours. There are four runs in each direction daily.

THE PERFUME OF PROVENCE

Perhaps the most typical Provençal summer sight and smell is of lavender *(lavande)*, the sweet purple flower harvested between 15 July and 15 August for its fine perfume.

Lavender farms, distilleries and ornamental gardens open to visitors are listed in the English-language brochure *Les Routes de la Lavande* (free from tourist offices or online at www.routes-lavande.com). You can find lavender fields at the Abbaye de Sénanque near Gordes, the **Musée de la Lavande** (Lavender Museum; ☎ 04 90 76 91 23) in Coustellet and many more carpeting the arid Sault region, east of Mont Ventoux on the Vaucluse plateau. The tourist office at Digne-les-Bains also provides information on several lavender tours and festivals.

GORGES DU VERDON

The gorgeous 25km Gorges du Verdon (also known as the Grand Canyon du Verdon), the largest canyon in Europe, slices through the limestone plateau midway between Avignon and Nice. They begin at Rougon (near the confluence of the Verdon and the Jabron) and continue westwards until the river flows into Lac de Ste-Croix. The village of Castellane (population 1349) is east of Rougon and is the main gateway for the gorges.

Carved by the greenish waters of the Verdon River, the gorges are 250m to 700m deep. The bottom is 8m to 90m wide, while the rims are 200m to 1500m apart.

Information

The best information source for the Gorges du Verdon is the **Castellane tourist office** (☎ 04 92 83 61 14; www.castellane.org; rue Nationale; Ⓧ 9am-12.30pm & 1.30-7pm Mon-Sat, 10am-12.30pm Sun Jul & Aug, 9am-noon & 2-6pm Mon-Fri, 10am-noon & 3-6pm Sat Sep-Jun), or try the **Moustiers Ste-Marie tourist office** (☎ 04 92 74 67 84; fax 04 92 74 60 65; Ⓧ 10am-noon & 2-7pm).

There's a small **tourist office** (☎ /fax 04 92 77 32 02, 04 92 77 38 02) in the centre of La Palud-sur-Verdon and a **Syndicat d'Initiative** (☎ /fax 04 94 85 68 40) in Trigance.

Sights & Activities

The bottom of the gorges can be visited only on foot or by raft, but motorists and cyclists can enjoy spectacular (if dizzying) views from two cliff-side roads.

The D952 follows the northern rim and passes the **Point Sublime** viewpoint, offering a spectacular, almost fisheye lens–like panorama of riotous rock formations, that deep, deep gorge and the rushing river way, way below. The GR4 trail leads to the bottom of the gorge from here. The best view from the northern side is from **Belvédère de l'Escalès** along route de Crêtes (D23). Drive to the third bend and hold your breath since the drop-off into the gorge is quite stunning. Retrace your route to the D952.

Another stunning view is offered by **La Corniche Sublime** (the D19 to the D71), which goes along the southern rim and takes you to such landmarks as the **Balcons de la Mescla** (Mescla Terraces) and **Pont de l'Artuby** (Artuby Bridge), the highest bridge in Europe.

A complete circuit of the Gorges du Verdon via Moustiers Ste-Marie involves about 140km of driving; the tourist office in Castellane has the good English-language brochure *Driving Tours* with 11 itineraries. The only real village en route is **La Palud-sur-Verdon** (930m), 2km northeast of the northern bank of the gorges. In summer, heavy traffic often slows travel to a crawl.

The bottom of the canyon, first explored in its entirety in 1905, presents walkers and white-water rafters with an overwhelming series of cliffs and narrows. You can walk most of it along the often-difficult GR4, which is covered by Didier-Richard's 1:50,000 map No 19, *Haute Provence-Verdon*. It is also included in the excellent English-language book *Canyon du Verdon – The Most Beautiful Hikes* (€4.12), available at Castellane or Moustiers tourist offices. The full GR4 takes two days, though short descents into the canyon are possible from a number of points. Bring along a torch (flashlight) and drinking water. Camping in the rough on gravel beaches along the way is illegal, however people do it.

Castellane's tourist office has a complete list of companies offering rafting, canyon-

ing, horse riding, mountaineering, biking and other outdoor pursuits.

Aboard Rafting (☎ /fax 04 92 83 76 11; www .aboard-rafting.com; ☒ Apr-Sep) runs white-water rafting trips (€30 to €75) as well as canyoning (€30 to €65), kayaking (€30) and hot-dogging (€45).

Sleeping & Eating

BUDGET

Gîte d'Étape de Fontaine Basse (☎ 04 94 85 68 36; fax 04 94 85 68 50; Trigance; dm incl breakfast €17) This place is 16km southeast of Castellane.

The tourist office has a full list of the area's many camping grounds. The river near Castellane is lined with seasonal camping areas that tend to be crowded and pricey in summer.

Domaine de Chasteuil Provence (☎ 04 92 83 61 21; www.chasteuil-provence.com; camping low/high season €14/20; ☒ May–mid-Sep; ☒) Just south of Castellane.

MID-RANGE

If you're looking for something inexpensive, Castellane is the place for you. Numerous hotels line the central square, place Marcel Sauvaire and place de l'Église.

Grand Hôtel du Levant (☎ 04 92 83 60 05; www .touring-levant.com; place Marcel Sauvaire; r €35-65; P) Offers good-value rooms with bathrooms.

Ma Petite Auberge (☎ 04 92 83 62 06; fax 04 92 83 68 49; rue de la République; d from €43) Also has a restaurant.

Studi Hôtel (☎ 04 92 83 76 47; fax 04 94 84 63 36; d €43; ☒) An excellent-value place, a 10-minute walk from town on the N85 out of Castellane (direction Digne-les-Bains). A week's stay in a two- to four-person studio costs €564.

La Bastide de Moustiers (☎ 04 92 70 47 47; www .bastide-moustiers.com; Moustiers-Ste Marie; d low/high season from €155/180; menus lunch/dinner €42/47; P ☒ ☒) This is the place for total indulgence, relaxation and especially for gourmet dining since this is part of the growing empire of French culinary legend Alain Ducasse. The rooms inside the thick stone-walled old farmhouse are elegant and, thank goodness, there's a place to park the helicopter. It's about 20km from Castellane.

Getting There & Away

Public transport to, from, and around the Gorges du Verdon is limited. **Autocars Sumian**

(☎ 04 42 67 60 34) runs buses from Marseille to Castellane via Aix-en-Provence (€19.90, 3½ hours), La Palud and Moustiers.

Getting Around

In July and August **Navettes Autocar** (☎ 04 92 83 40 27, 04 92 83 64 47) runs shuttle buses around the gorges daily except Sunday, linking Castellane with Point Sublime, La Palud and La Maline. Ask at the tourist office in Castellane for schedules and fares.

Aboard Rafting (see p813) rents mountain bikes for €10/20 per half/full day.

PRA-LOUP & LA FOUX D'ALLOS

The ski resort of Pra-Loup (elevation 1600m), 8.5km southwest of Barcelonnette and 70km southeast of Gap, is connected by a lift system across the Vallon des Agneliers with another ski resort called La Foux d'Allos. By road, Pra-Loup is 23.5km to the north, but there is no public transport available between the two resorts.

The majority of runs are for intermediate and advanced skiers and snowboarders. St-Paul-sur-Ubaye, in a valley below and to the northeast of Pra-Loup, has 25km of cross-country runs from 1400m to 1500m and Larche has 30km of runs from 1700m to 2000m.

Pra-Loup's 53 lifts are between 1600m and 2600m, with 160km of runs and a vertical drop of almost 1000m.

The Pra-Loup **tourist office** (☎ 04 92 84 10 04; www.praloup.com; ☯ 9am-noon & 2-6pm Jul & Aug, 9am-noon & 2-6pm Mon-Fri May, Jun & Sep-Nov, 9am-7pm Dec-Apr), **École de Ski Français** (ESF; ☎ 04 92 84 11 05) and post office, where you can also change money, are all inside the Maison de Pra-Loup. The La Foux d'Allos **tourist office** (☎ 04 92 83 80 70; www.valdallos.com in French) is in the Maison de la Foux on the main square.

Sleeping

Studios and apartments are usually the best option. The tourist offices have lists of all available establishments. Apartments are the main type of accommodation here and studios for two start at €165 per week during the low season and around €300 in the high season.

Getting There & Away

The nearest train station to Pra-Loup is Gap, from where there are a couple of buses daily travelling to Pra-Loup (€8.10, 1¾ hours) via Barcelonnette.

Buses link the village of La Foux d'Allos, which is 9km southeast of the resort, with Digne-les-Bains and Avignon.

It is possible to get to La Foux d'Allos from Nice by train departing Nice's Gare des Chemins de Fer de Provence to La Vœsubie-Plan-du-Var. The rest of the trip is by bus, with a change required at Thorame.

Côte d'Azur & Monaco

CONTENTS

Nice to Toulon	**818**
Nice	818
Antibes–Juan-les-Pins	831
Around Antibes	832
St-Paul de Vence	833
Vence	834
Cannes	834
Îles de Lérins	840
Grasse	840
Massif de l'Estérel	841
Fréjus & St-Raphaël	841
St-Tropez	844
The Var Hinterland	847
St-Tropez to Toulon	847
Toulon	848
Nice to Menton	**851**
The Corniches	851
Menton	852
Monaco (Principauté de Monaco)	**854**

Côte d'Azur
Monaco

A region of heart-palpitatingly dramatic ocean views, chic seaside towns, fine wine and great food, the beautiful Côte d'Azur (Azure Coast), also known as the French Riviera, stretches along the Mediterranean coast from Toulon to the Italian border.

Many towns on the coast – Nice, Monaco, Cannes, St-Tropez – are known as the playgrounds of the rich, famous and tanned. The reality is usually less glamorous and occasionally, at its worst, it can be a purgatory of traffic gridlock and overrun tourist attractions. Even so, the Côte d'Azur has much to entice visitors: sun, beach, warm sea water and all sorts of cultural activities.

The capital, Nice, is a good base for exploring the region. Following the coast west, you come to attractive Antibes, wealthy Cannes and, just west of the stunning red mountain range known as the Massif de l'Estérel, twin towns St-Raphaël and Fréjus. Inland, the hills over-looking the coast are dotted with villages such as Grasse, Vence and St-Paul de Vence.

Administratively part of Provence, Côte d'Azur also includes most of the *départements* of Alpes-Maritimes and Var. The forested Massif des Maures, and the tiny villages nestling inside it, stretches from St-Raphaël to Hyères. It's well worth a detour when you tire of the feel of sand between your toes.

West of fashionable St-Tropez you'll find the region's most unspoiled coastline, where capes and cliffs alternate with streams and beaches, many sheltered from the open sea by the Îles d'Hyères, three large islands (and a couple of tiny ones) some 10km offshore.

East of Nice, the foothills of the Alps plummet into the Mediterranean. Three coastal roads, known as corniches (and where you'll experience many of those dramatic views), pass villages overlooking the sea en route to Menton and the Italian border. The tiny principality of Monaco is roughly midway between Nice and Menton.

HIGHLIGHTS

- Savour the flavours of local **Niçois specialities** (p818) in old Nice
- Sample the liquid delights of **Maison des Vins Côtes de Provence** (p847)
- Admire the sculpture and artworks at **Fondation Maeght** (p833), St-Paul de Vence, or the **Musée d'Art Moderne et d'Art Contemporain** (p822)
- Make the most of the exuberance of **Nice's old-town nightlife** (p829)
- Be seen with the fashionable set in **St-Tropez** (p844)
- Spot the A-listers at the **Cannes Film Festival** (p836)
- Explore the wild and rocky coastline of the **corniches** (p851) east of Nice

 POPULATION: 1.100.000 | AREA: 4300 SQ KM

CÔTE D'AZUR

0 — 40 km
0 — 20 miles

MEDITERRANEAN SEA

ITALY
To Genoa (720km)

San Remo
Ventimiglia
Bordighera
Menton
Cap Martin
MONACO
Monte Carlo
Roquebrune-Cap-Martin
Beausoleil
Ste-Agnès
Gorbio
Castillon
Sospel
Saorge
Èze
La Turbie
St-Jean-Cap-Ferrat
Villefranche-sur-Mer
Nice
St-Martin-Vésubie
St-Jean-la-Rivière
Plan-du-Var
Comté de Nice
D2574
Èze-sur-Mer
Var
Antibes
Juan-les-Pins
Cap d'Antibes
Cagnes-sur-Mer
Biot
Vence
St-Paul-de-Vence
Cannes
Théoule-sur-Mer
Miramar
Le Trayas
Le Dramont
ALPES-MARITIMES
Plateau de Caussols
Réserve Géologique de Haute-Provence
Puget-Théniers
Entrevaux
Gourdon
Grasse
Mandelieu-La Napoule
Tourrettes
Massif de l'Esterel
Agay
St-Aygulf
Ste-Maxime
La Moutte
Plage de Tahiti
St-Tropez
Ramatuelle
Le Rayol
Le Lavandou
Cavalaire
La Croix-Valmer
Thorame-Haute
Annot
St-André-les-Alpes
Castellane
Barrême
Digne-les-Bains
Moustiers-Ste-Marie
La Palud-sur-Verdon
Rougon
Gorges du Verdon
Aiguines
Bauduen
Les Salles-sur-Verdon
Riez
Valensole
Ste-Croix
Comps-sur-Artuby
Bargème
Trigance
Bargemon
Callas
Figanières
Draguignan
Le Muy
Les Arcs-sur-Argens
Fréjus
Saint-Raphaël
La Garde-Freinet
Grimaud
Port Grimaud
Cogolin
Collobrières
Massif des Maures
Bormes-les-Mimosas
Hyères
Îles d'Hyères
Île de Porquerolles
Port-Cros
Île du Levant
Côte d'Azur
VAR
Lorgues
Salernes
Vaillauroze
Aups
Toutour
Entrecasteaux
Cotignac
Carcès
Abbaye du Thoronet
Le Thoronet
Cabasse
Le Luc
Le Cannet-des-Maures
La Sauvette
La Chartreuse de la Verne
Confaron
Pierrefeu-du-Var
Cuers
La Garde
Pignans
Sollies-Pont
Toulon
La Seyne-sur-Mer
Bandol
Sanary-sur-Mer
Six-Fours-les-Plages
Le Brusc
La Ciotat
Cassis
Sormiou
Aubagne
Roquevaire
Marseilles
L'Estaque
Marseilles-Provence Airport
BOUCHES-DU-RHÔNE
Cabriès
Aix-en-Provence
Gardanne
Meyrargues
Mont Ste-Victoire (1011m)
Montagne Ste-Victoire
St-Maximin-la-Ste-baume
Tretes
Rougiers
Brignoles
Le Beausset
Barjols
Tavernes
Montmeyan
Rians
Vinon
Ginasservis
St-Julien
Esparron
Gréoux-les-Bains
Manosque
Montagne du Lubéron
Parc Naturel Régional du Lubéron
Céreste
Forcalquier
Mane
Oraison
Les Mées
Volonne
Château-Arnoux
ALPES-DE-HAUTE-PROVENCE
To Sisteron (7.5km); Gap (55km); Grenoble (140km)
Ganagobie
Peyruis
Durance
VAUCLUSE
Sault
St-Christol
Plateau d'Albion
Lagarde d'Apt
Monts du Vaucluse
St-Saturnin-les-Apt
Roussillon
Apt
Gordes
Cadenet
Bonnieux
Lourmarin
Montagne du Lubéron
Parc Naturel Régional du Lubéron
Rognes
Gulf du Lion
To Corsica
To Tunisia & Algeria
Marseilles – Corsica
To Corsica & Sardinia

A8 · A50 · A51 · A57 · N7 · N85 · N96 · N98 · N202 · D2 · D3 · D4 · D14 · D25 · D26 · D28 · D30 · D71 · D559

CÔTE D'AZUR & MONACO

History

Occupied by the Ligurians from the 1st millennium BC, the eastern part of France's Mediterranean coast was colonised around 600 BC by Greeks from Asia Minor, who settled in Massalia (modern-day Marseille) and along the coast, including what are now Hyères, St-Tropez, Antibes and Nice. Called in to help Massalia against the threat of invasion by Celto-Ligurians from Entremont in 125 BC, the Romans defeated the Celts and Ligurians and created the Provincia Romana – the area between the Alps, the sea and the River Rhône – from which the name Provence is derived.

In 1388 Nice was incorporated into the lands of the House of Savoy. The rest of Provence became part of the French kingdom in 1482, and the centralist policies of the French kings saw the region's autonomy greatly reduced. In 1860, after an agreement between Napoleon III and the House of Savoy helped drive the Austrians from northern Italy, France took possession of Savoy and the area around Nice.

In the 19th century wealthy French, English, American and Russian tourists discovered the Côte d'Azur. Primarily a winter resort, the area attracted an increasing number of affluent visitors. The intensity and clarity of the region's colours and light appealed to many painters – particularly the impressionists – including Cézanne, Matisse and Picasso. Writers such as Collette and other celebrities were also attracted to the region and contributed to its fame. Little fishing ports became exclusive resorts, and in no time the most beautiful spots were occupied by private villas that looked more like castles. With improved rail and road access and the advent of paid holidays for all French workers in 1936, even more tourists flocked to the region.

Dangers & Annoyances

Theft, from backpacks, pockets, bags cars and even laundrettes, is a serious problem along the Côte d'Azur. Keep a very sharp eye on your bags, especially at train and bus stations, on overnight trains, in tourist offices, in fast-food restaurants and on the beaches. If you rent a car, drive with the doors locked and windows rolled up as thieves often lie in wait at red lights to pounce and snatch bags.

> **MUSEUM BUFF?**
>
> The excellent-value **Carte Musées Côte d'Azur** is a pass that gives free admission to some 60 Côte d'Azur museums. It costs €8/15/25 for one/five/seven days and is available at tourist offices and participating museums. If you'll only be staying in Nice, ask about the Carte Musées Ville de Nice, which allows entry into all of Nice's museums except the Chagall. It costs €6/18.30 for seven/15 days.

Getting There & Away

The efficient SNCF train network and regular bus connections link the Côte d'Azur with Provence and the rest of France. Roads into the region are good, but traffic in the cities can be a problem. There is an international airport at Nice and outside Toulon.

For information on ferry services from Nice and Toulon to Corsica, see p865.

Getting Around

SNCF trains shuttle back and forth along the coast between St-Raphaël and the Italian border. The area between St-Raphaël, where the train line veers inland, and Toulon can be reached by bus.

Except for the traffic-plagued high season, the Côte d'Azur is easily accessible by car. The fastest way to get around is by the boring A8 autoroute which, travelling west to east, starts near Aix-en-Provence, approaches the coast at Fréjus, skirts the Estérel range and runs more or less parallel to the coast from Cannes to the Italian border at Ventimiglia (Vintimille in French).

NICE TO TOULON

NICE

pop 342,738

Rich English folk – Queen Victoria for one – were the first to make Nice a fashionable destination for healthy, restorative holidays, strolling the seafront and lapping up the good weather. It's not so different today. The world still cools off in the sea that laps Nice's long, pebbly beaches or strolls the glorious long promenades, while gazing out at the uniquely beautiful marbling of the sea: here patches of deep blue, there chalky white.

It remains a fashionable city (considered the capital of the Riviera), but it's relaxed and fun too. Nice also makes a great base from which to explore the rest of the Côte d'Azur, as it is only a short train or bus ride from Monaco, Cannes and other Riviera hot spots. The city is also blessed with museums as fine as you'll find anywhere in the south of France.

There's a lively nightlife in the old city's narrow warren of streets, an old harbour and hilltop gardens to explore and great markets to nose around in too. Unsurprisingly Nice is enormously popular with young travellers, so there are lots of budget places to stay. However, there's a profusion of good hotels and entertainment options for all budgets. In short, Nice has plenty to offer everyone.

History

Nice was founded around 350 BC by the Greek seafarers who had settled Marseille. They named the colony Nikaia, apparently to commemorate a victory (*nike* in Greek) over a nearby town. In 154 BC the Greeks were followed by the Romans, who settled further uphill around what is now Cimiez, site of a number of Roman ruins.

By the 10th century, Nice was ruled by the counts of Provence but turned to Amadeus VII of the House of Savoy in 1388. In the 18th and 19th centuries it was temporarily occupied several times by the French, but did not definitively become part of France until 1860, when Napoleon III struck a deal (known as the treaty of Turin) with the House of Savoy.

During the Victorian period Nice became popular with the English aristocracy, who came to enjoy the city's mild winter climate. European royalty soon followed.

Orientation

Avenue Jean Médecin runs south from near the Gare Nice Ville (the main train station) to place Masséna. The modern city centre, the area north and west of place Masséna, includes the upmarket pedestrianised streets of rue de France and rue Masséna. Station Centrale and intercity bus stations are located three blocks east of place Masséna.

The famous promenade des Anglais follows the gently curved beachfront from the city centre to the airport, 6km west. Vieux Nice (old Nice) is delineated by blvd Jean Jaurès, quai des États-Unis and, east, the hill known as Le Château. Place Garibaldi is at the northeastern tip of Vieux Nice.

The wealthy residential neighbourhood of Cimiez, home to several outstanding museums, is just north of the city centre.

Information
BOOKSHOPS

Cat's Whiskers (☎ /fax 04 93 80 02 66; 26 rue Lamartine) New and second-hand guides and English-language novels.

Magellan Librairie de Voyages (☎ 04 93 82 31 81; 3 rue d'Italie) An excellent selection of maps and travel guides, including Lonely Planet in English.

Maison de la Presse (place Masséna) Also has a wide selection of maps and guides, plus books and magazines in English.

NICE IN...

Two days

Breakfast by the flower and produce markets on **cours Saleya** (p828), meander or rollerblade along the **promenade des Anglais** (p824), head up to the lovely gardens of the **château** (p822) before grabbing a tapas-style lunch of fried nibbles and peppered-*socca* in **Vieux Nice** (p827), then hit the pebbly beach. Head back into old Nice for dinner and a bar-crawl around some of the many lively **bars and pubs** (p828) here. The next day visit the excellent **Musée Matisse** (p823) and **Musée Marc Chagall** (p823). Lunch in pretty **Villefranche-sur-Mer** (p851) and then take off to **Èze** (p852) for unforgettable sea views.

Four days

Head west along the coast for a day wandering the narrow streets of laid-back **Antibes** (p831) and visiting the **Musée Picasso** (p832). The next day drive the spectacular corniches on the way to the exclusive principality of **Monaco** (p854) or head inland for a feast of art at **Matisse's chapel** (p834) in Vence and the **Fondation Maeght** (p833) in St-Paul de Vence.

CÔTE D'AZUR & MONACO

NICE

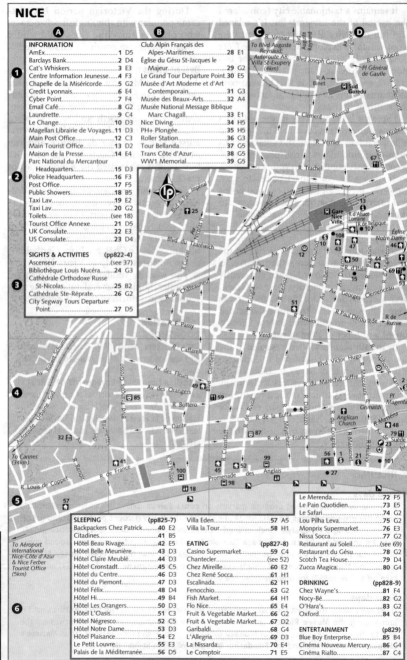

INFORMATION		
AmEx	1	D5
Barclays Bank	2	D4
Cat's Whiskers	3	E3
Centre Information Jeunesse	4	F3
Chapelle de la Miséricorde	5	G2
Credit Lyonnais	6	E4
Cyber Point	7	F4
Email Café	8	G2
Laundrette	9	C4
Le Change	10	D3
Magellan Librairie de Voyages	11	D3
Main Post Office	12	C3
Main Tourist Office	13	D3
Maison de la Presse	14	E4
Parc National du Mercantour Headquarters	15	D3
Police Headquarters	16	F3
Post Office	17	F5
Public Showers	18	B5
Taxi Lav	19	E2
Taxi Lav	20	G2
Toilets	(see 18)	
Tourist Office Annexe	21	D5
UK Consulate	22	E3
US Consulate	23	D4

SIGHTS & ACTIVITIES	(pp822-4)	
Ascenseur	(see 37)	
Bibliothèque Louis Nucéra	24	G3
Cathédrale Orthodoxe Russe St-Nicolas	25	B2
Cathédrale Ste-Réprate	26	G2
City Segway Tours Departure Point	27	D5

Club Alpin Français des Alpes-Maritimes	28	E1
Église du Gésu St-Jacques le Majeur	29	G2
Le Grand Tour Departure Point	30	E5
Musée d'Art Moderne et d'Art Contemporain	31	G3
Musée des Beaux-Arts	32	A4
Musée National Message Biblique Marc Chagall	33	E1
Nice Diving	34	H5
PH+ Plongée	35	H5
Roller Station	36	G3
Tour Bellanda	37	G5
Trans Côte d'Azur	38	G5
WW1 Memorial	39	G5

To Blvd Vernier
To Blvd Auguste Reynaud;
Autoroute A8;
Villa St-Exupery (4km)

SLEEPING	(pp825-7)	
Backpackers Chez Patrick	40	E2
Citadines	41	B5
Hôtel Beau Rivage	42	E5
Hôtel Belle Meunière	43	D3
Hôtel Claire Meublé	44	D3
Hôtel Cronstadt	45	C5
Hôtel du Centre	46	D3
Hôtel du Piemont	47	D3
Hôtel Félix	48	D4
Hôtel Hi	49	B4
Hôtel Les Orangers	50	D3
Hôtel L'Oasis	51	C3
Hôtel Négresco	52	C5
Hôtel Notre Dame	53	D3
Hôtel Plaisance	54	E2
Le Petit Louvre	55	D3
Palais de la Méditerranée	56	D5

Villa Eden	57	A5
Villa la Tour	58	H1

EATING	(pp827-8)	
Casino Supermarket	59	C4
Chantecler	(see 52)	
Chez Mireille	60	E2
Chez René Socca	61	H1
Escalinada	62	H1
Fenocchio	63	G2
Fish Market	64	H1
Flo Nice	65	E4
Fruit & Vegetable Market	66	G2
Fruit & Vegetable Market	67	D2
Garibaldi	68	G4
L'Allegria	69	D3
La Nissarda	70	E4
Le Comptoir	71	E5

Le Merenda	72	F5
Le Pain Quotidien	73	E5
Le Safari	74	G2
Lou Pilha Leva	75	G2
Monprix Supermarket	76	E3
Nissa Socca	77	G2
Restaurant au Soleil	(see 69)	
Restaurant du Gésu	78	G2
Scotch Tea House	79	D4
Zucca Magica	80	G4

DRINKING	(pp828-9)	
Chez Wayne's	81	F4
Nocy-Bé	82	G2
O'Hara's	83	G2
Oxford	84	G2

ENTERTAINMENT	(p829)	
Blue Boy Enterprise	85	B4
Cinéma Nouveau Mercury	86	G4
Cinéma Rialto	87	C4

To Cannes (34km)

To Aéroport International Nice-Côte d'Azur & Nice Ferber Tourist Office (5km)

CÔTE D'AZUR & MONACO

To Cimiez (1.2km); Musée Matisse (1.3km);
Musée et Site Archéologiques (1.4km);
Monastère Notre Dame de Cimiez (1.5km)

0 — 400 m
0 — 0.2 miles

0 — 100 m
0 — 0.1 miles

VIEUX NICE

Parc du Château

Colline du Château

See Enlargement

Pl Garibaldi

To Auberge de Jeunesse (2.5km)

Jardin Albert 1er

Espace Masséna

Palais de Justice

Pl Pierre Gautier

VIEUX NICE

Baie des Anges

Colline du Château

Parc du Château

Pl Rôbilante

Pl Ile de Beauté

Bassin Lympia

Bassin des Amiraux

Bassin du Commerce

To Monaco via Corniche Inférieure (N98) (18km)

MEDITERRANEAN SEA

Cinémathèque de Nice	**88**	G3
Ghost	**89**	G2
Happy Bar	(see 49)	
Jonathan's	**90**	G2
Le Bar des Oiseaux	**91**	G2
Opéra de Nice	**92**	E5
SHOPPING □	(p829)	
À l'Olivier	**93**	E5
Flower Market	**94**	F5
Les Grandes Caves Caprioglio	**95**	G2
Moulin à Huile d'Olive Alziari	**96**	E5
Nice Étoile Shopping Mall	**97**	E3
TRANSPORT	(pp829-31)	
ANT Airport Buses	**98**	C5
ANT Airport Buses	**99**	C5
ANT Airport Buses	**100**	B5
Budget	**101**	D5
Budget	(see 108)	
Corsica Ferries Terminal	**102**	G5
Corsica Ferries Terminal	**103**	H6
Corsica Ferries Ticket Office	**104**	H5
Ferry Terminal	**105**	H6
Fnac	(see 97)	
Intercity Bus Station	**106**	G1
JLM	(see 108)	
Nicea Location Rent	**107**	D2
Rent a Car Système	**108**	D3
SNCM Office	(see 105)	
Station Centrale	**109**	F4
Sunbus Information Office	**110**	F4

EMERGENCY
Police Headquarters (☎ 04 92 17 22 22, Foreign Tourist Department ☎ 04 92 17 20 63; 1 av Maréchal Foch)

INTERNET ACCESS
Cyber Point (☎ 04 93 92 70 63; 10 av Félix Faure; per 30/60min €3/5; ☯ 10.30am-1.30pm & 2.30-7pm Mon-Sat)
Email café (☎ 04 93 62 68 86; ☯ 7.30am-7pm Mon-Sat; per 10/30/60min €1/2.5/4.5) In the old town, here you can surf with a sandwich and a coffee.

LAUNDRY
Self-service laundrettes are plentiful around Gare Nice Ville. It will cost about €3 for a small load of around 5kg.
Laundrette (rue de Buffa; ☯ 7am-9pm)
Taxi Lav (22 rue Pertinax; ☯ 7am-9pm) Old Town (13 rue du Pont Vieux; ☯ 7am-9pm)

MONEY
AmEx (☎ 04 93 16 53 53; 11 promenade des Anglais; ☯ 9am-7pm Mon-Sat, 10am-1pm & 1.30-5.30pm Sun) Poste restante services are also available here.
Barclays Bank (2 rue Alphonse Karr) There's a change counter here.
Le Change (☎ 04 93 88 56 80; 17 av Thiers; ☯ 7.30am-8pm) Opposite the Gare Nice Ville, to the right as you exit the terminal building. It has decent rates.

POST
Main Post Office (23 av Thiers) In a fantastic red-brick building. It also exchanges foreign currency.
Post Office (2 rue Louis Gassin) In Vieux Nice.

TOURIST INFORMATION
Airport Tourist Information Desk (☎ 08 92 70 74 07; ☯ 8am-9pm daily high season, closed Sun low season) Inside Terminal 1.
Centre Information Jeunesse (☎ 04 93 80 93 93; 19 rue Gioffrédo; ☯ 10am-7pm Mon-Fri)
Main Tourist Office (☎ 0 892 353 535; www.nicetourism.com; av Thiers; ☯ 8am-8pm Mon-Sat, 9am-7pm Sun Jun-Sep, 8am-7pm Mon-Sat, 9am-6pm Sun Oct-May) The most convenient office next to the Gare Nice Ville.
Nice Ferber Tourist Office Branch (☎ 04 93 83 32 64; promenade des Anglais) Towards town from the airport terminal.
Parc National du Mercantour headquarters (☎ 04 93 16 78 88; www.parc-mercantour.fr; 23 rue d'Italie) Stocks numerous guides including the excellent and free Les Guides Randoxygène series, which details 25 canyoning routes, 40 mountain-biking (VTT) trails and hiking trails in the park.

Tourist Office Annexe (☎ 0892 70 74 07; fax 04 92 14 48 03; 5 promenade des Anglais; ☯ 8am-8pm Mon-Sat, 9am-7pm Sun Jun-Sep; 9am-6pm Mon-Sat Oct-May) Less crowded than the main office.

Sights
VIEUX NICE
This area of narrow, winding streets between quai des États-Unis and the Musée d'Art Moderne et d'Art Contemporain has looked the same since the 1700s. Arcadelined **place Garibaldi**, built during the latter half of the 18th century, is named after Giuseppe Garibaldi (1807–82). One of the great heroes of Italian unification, he was born in Nice and is buried in the cemetery in the Parc du Château.

Interesting churches in Vieux Nice include baroque **Cathédrale Ste-Réparate** (place Rossetti), built around 1650; the blue-grey and yellow **Église du Gésu St-Jacques Le Majeur** (place du Gésu), close to rue Rossetti, whose baroque ornamentation dates from the mid-17th century; and the mid-18th-century **Chapelle de la Miséricorde**, which is next to place Pierre Gautier.

Rue Benoît Bunico, which runs perpendicular to rue Rossetti, served as Nice's Jewish ghetto after a 1430 law restricted where Jews could live. Gates at each end were locked at sunset.

PARC DU CHÂTEAU
At the eastern end of quai des États-Unis, atop a 92m-high hill, is this shady public park where local families come to stroll, admire the panoramic views of Nice and the sparkling Baie des Anges, or visit the artificial waterfall. It's a great place to escape the heat on a summer afternoon.

The hill and the park are named after a 12th-century chateau, which was razed by Louis XIV in 1706. To get to the top of the hill, take the **ascenseur** (lift; adult single/return €0.60/0.90, child €0.30/0.45; ☯ 9am-7.50pm daily Jul & Aug, 9am-7pm Apr-Jun & Sep, 9am-5.50pm Oct-Mar) from under Tour Bellanda. Alternatively, walk up montée Lesage or climb the steps at the eastern end of rue Rossetti.

MUSÉE D'ART MODERNE ET D'ART CONTEMPORAIN
The **Musée d'Art Moderne et d'Art Contemporain** (Museum of Modern & Contemporary Art; ☎ 04 93 62 61 62; www.mamac-nice.org; av St-Jean Baptiste; adult/student

€4/2.50; ☺ 10am-6pm Wed-Mon), Nice's pride and joy in the architectural as well as the art stakes, specialises in French and American avant-garde works from the 1960s to the present. The exhibits explode with colour in the fabulously light, large display spaces. Glass walkways connect the four marble-coated towers, on top of which is a must-see rooftop garden and gallery featuring pieces by Nice-born Yves Klein (1928–62). Other highlights include Andy Warhol's *Campbell's Soup Can* (1965), a shopping trolley wrapped by Christo, Armen's creepy *Venus aux Ongles Rouge*, and a pea-green Model-T Ford compressed into a 1.6m-high block by Marseille-born sculptor, César. The pop art sculptor Niki de St-Phalle (1930–2002) donated an impressive collection of her works to the museum before she died.

Next door is Nice's library, **Bibliothèque Louis Nucéra**, marked by a cubical 'head' of administrative offices over the underground reading rooms.

MUSÉE NATIONAL MESSAGE BIBLIQUE MARC CHAGALL

The **Musée National Message Biblique Marc Chagall** (Marc Chagall Biblical Message Museum; ☎ 04 93 53 87 20; adult/student Jul-Sep €5.80/4.25, rest of year €5.50/4; ☺ 10am-6pm Wed-Mon Jul-Sep, to 5pm Oct-Jun), contains a series of large, impressive and colourful series of paintings of *Old Testament* scenes. Don't miss the mosaic of the rose window at Metz Cathedral, viewed through a plate-glass window across a small pond. Take bus No 15 from place Masséna to the front of the museum or walk.

MUSÉE MATISSE

Northeast of the Gare Nice Ville about 2.5km, in the bourgeois district of Cimiez, the **Musée Matisse** (Matisse Museum; ☎ 04 93 81 08 08; www.musee-matisse-nice.org; 164 av des Arènes de Cimiez; adult/student €4/2.50; ☺ 10am-6pm Wed-Mon) houses a fine collection of works by Henri Matisse. Its permanent collection is displayed in a red-ochre, 17th-century Genoese mansion and the **Parc des Arènes**. Temporary exhibitions are hosted in the basement building that leads through to the stucco-decorated villa. Well-known pieces in the permanent collection include Matisse's blue paper cut-outs of *Blue Nude IV* and *Woman with Amphora*. The collection is striking for its variety: Matisse worked in a wide range of media, well represented here,

including cloth, paper, bronze, oil paint and pen and ink.

Matisse is buried in the cemetery of the **Monastère Notre Dame de Cimiez** (Cimiez Notre Dame Monastery; ☎ 04 93 81 00 04; ☺ 8.30am-12.30pm & 2.30-6.30pm), which today houses a small **museum** (admission free; ☺ 10am-noon & 3-6pm Mon-Sat) illustrating the everyday lives and activities of the monastery's monks. The artist's grave is signposted *sépulture Henri Matisse* from the cemetery's main entrance (next to the monastery church on av Bellanda). A flight of stairs leads from the eastern end of the olive grove to av Bellanda.

Take bus No 15, 17, 20, 22 or 25 from Station Centrale to the Arènes stop.

MUSÉE ET SITE ARCHÉOLOGIQUES

Behind the Musée Matisse, on the eastern side of the Parc des Arènes, lie the ruins of the Roman city of Cemenelum – the focus of the **Musée et Site Archéologiques** (Archaeology Museum; ☎ 04 93 81 59 57; 160 av des Arènes de Cimiez; adult/student €4/2.50; ☺ 10am-noon & 2-6pm Wed-Mon Apr-Sep, 10am-1pm & 2-5pm Wed-Mon Oct-Mar). The public baths and amphitheatre – the venue for outdoor concerts during the Nice Jazz Festival (p825) – can both be visited.

To get here from Museé Matisse, turn left out of the main park entrance on av des Arènes de Cimiez, walk 100m, then turn left again onto av Monte Croce, where the main entrance to the archaeological site is located.

CATHÉDRALE ORTHODOXE RUSSE ST-NICOLAS

The multicoloured **Cathédrale Orthodoxe Russe St-Nicolas** (Russian Orthodox Cathedral of St-Nicolas; ☎ 04 93 96 88 02; av Nicolas II; ☺ 9am-noon & 2.30-6pm, closed Sun morning), crowned by six onion domes, was built between 1902 and 1912 in early-17th-century style. It is opposite 17 blvd du Tzaréwich, an easy 15-minute walk from Gare Nice Ville. Step inside and you're transported to imperial Russia. Shorts, mini-skirts and sleeveless shirts are forbidden.

MUSÉE DES BEAUX-ARTS

The **Musée des Beaux-Arts** (Fine Arts Museum; ☎ 04 92 15 28 28; 33 av des Baumettes; adult/student €4/2.50; ☺ 10am-noon & 2-6pm Tue-Sun) is housed in a fantastic late-19th-century villa and displays works by Boudin, Dufy, Fragonard, Sisley and Rodin.

Activities

For information on the region's **walking** and **mountain-biking** trails, go to the headquarters of **Parc National du Mercantour** (see p822) or **Club Alpin Français** (CAF; ☎ 04 93 62 59 99; 14 av Mirabeau).

CITY WALKING

The palm-lined **promenade des Anglais** (English promenade), established by Nice's English colony in 1822 as a seaside walking path, provides a fine stage for a stroll along the beach and the Baie des Anges (Bay of Angels). Don't miss the magnificent façade of the Art Deco **Palais de la Méditerranée** (13-17 promenade des Anglais), formerly a lavish casino and theatre that fell into ruin after its owners experienced financial difficulties in the 1970s. Keeping the arcaded façade, the Palais has been restored to its former glory. It reopened in 2004 as a plush four-star hotel and casino (see p827).

Enjoy a stroll along **Quai des États-Unis**, the promenade leading east to Vieux Nice that honours the 1917 decision by President Wilson for the USA to enter WWI; a colossal **memorial** commemorating the 4000 people from Nice who died during the war is carved in the rock at the eastern end of the quay.

Other pleasant walking spots are **Jardin Albert 1er**, laid out in the late 19th century; **Espace Masséna**, a public square enlivened by fountains; **place Masséna**, with early-19th-century, neoclassical arcaded buildings in shades of ochre and red; **av Jean Médecin**, Nice's main commercial street; and **Cimiez**, the most exclusive quarter in Nice, just north of the city.

INLINE SKATING

Promenade des Anglais is *the* place to skate. **Roller Station** (☎ 04 93 62 99 05; 49 quai des États-Unis)

rents skates and protective kneepads for €7 a day and bikes for €15 a day. A piece of identification is required as a deposit.

WATER SPORTS

If you don't like the feel of sand in your bathing suit, Nice's **beaches** are for you: they are covered with smooth, round pebbles. Free sections of beach alternate with 15 **plages concédées** (private beaches), for which you have to pay by renting a chair (around €11 a day) or mattress (around €9).

On the beach you can hire a catamaran, paddleboats, sailboards and jet skis, go parascending and water-skiing, or give paragliding a go.

There are outdoor showers on every beach, and indoor showers and toilets opposite 50 promenade des Anglais.

Dive companies **PH+ Plongée** (☎ 04 93 26 09 03; 3 quai des Deux Emmanuel) and **Nice Diving** (☎ 04 93 89 42 44; www.nicediving.com; 14 quai des Docks) offer courses, organise diving expeditions and rent equipment. An introductory dive costs around €33 with equipment.

Tours

The tourist office organises **guided walking tours** (€12; 9.30am Sat May-Oct) of Vieux Nice in English, starting at the tourist office annexe on promenade de Anglais.

See Nice aboard the buses of **Le Grand Tour** (☎ 04 92 29 17 00; adult/student/child €17/13/9; 1½hr) A headphone commentary in several languages is provided. Tours depart from the Jardin Albert 1er on the Promenade Anglais.

Trans Côte d'Azur (☎ 04 92 00 42 30; quai Lunel) organises glass-bottom boat trips around the Baie des Anges (adult/child €11/6) and runs cruises to the Îles de Lérins (€23; see p840), and transfers to St-Tropez (€42) and Monaco (€20).

EASY RIDERS

If walking the promenade des Anglais seems unthinkably hard work and skating its length seems a tad *passé* then climb aboard a Segway personal transporter (electronic, two-wheeled gyroscopic chariots) with **City Segway Tours** (☎ 01 56 58 10 54; www.citysegwaytours.com; 16 rue de la Buffa; €45). The three-hour tours, operating from March to November, take you effortlessly (but very conspicuously) along the seafront and into the old town. Day tours include shopping for a picnic on the cours Saleya, which you eat in the lovely gardens of the Château above town. Night tours include a whiz around Vieux Nice. It takes two minutes to master the controls (movement is controlled using your balance). It's a fun, if slightly silly, way to see the city.

Tours start in front of the Palais de la Méditerranée, but you have to book in advance online.

Festivals & Events

The colourful **Carnaval de Nice** (www.nicecarna val.com), held every spring around Mardi Gras (Shrove Tuesday), fills the streets with flower-bedecked floats and musicians.

The week-long **Nice Jazz Festival** (www.nice jazzfest.com) sets the town jiving in July, taking up the entire Arènes de Cimiez, Roman ruins and all. The music starts around 7pm and there can be up to 15 bands playing at three or four venues around the park throughout the evening. The programming is largely pop, rock and world with few jazz artists. Big-name performers in the past have included Peter Gabriel, Bryan Ferry, BB King, Dee Dee Bridgewater, Air, Cheb Mami and Dr John.

Sleeping

Nice has a surfeit of reasonably priced places to stay, particularly in the city centre and around the main railway station. Accommodation is scarcer in and around the old town but plentiful (and pricier) close to and on the seafront.

The tourist offices have information on Logis de France hotels, and Gîtes de France if you want a rural experience in the region.

BUDGET
Hostels

Hôtel Belle Meunière (☎ 04 93 88 66 15; fax 04 93 82 51 76; 21 av Durante; dm with shower & toilet under 26 yrs €15, d with shower/shower & toilet €47/51) A great and central option. The large four-bed dorm rooms are posh, panelled affairs and the place touts a great tree-studded garden to lounge in. Rates include breakfast.

Villa St Exupéry (☎ 04 93 84 42 83; www.villa saintexupery.com; 22 av Gravier; dm/s/d from €18/28/44; P ⌨) A fair trek out of town, this hostel in a lovely old former monastery with large grounds and gardens has been recommended by a number of readers. There's no curfew, a very friendly vibe and free Internet access, breakfast and station shuttle. It's also something of a party spot, so noise can be a problem. There are some new and wonderful private rooms, although some of the dorms, sharing too few bathrooms, are less appealing. From the town centre take bus No 1 or 2 along av Jean Médecin and get off at the Gravier stop.

Backpackers Chez Patrick (☎ 04 93 80 30 72; chezpatrick@voila.fr; 32 rue Pertinax; dm €18-21, r with 2 or 3 beds per person €20-25) A popular 24-bed spot. There's no curfew and Patrick, who runs the place, can direct party-mad backpackers to the hot spot of the moment.

Auberge de Jeunesse (☎ 04 93 89 23 64; fax 04 92 04 03 10; route Forestière de Mont Alban; dm incl breakfast €14; ☻ curfew midnight) This is 4km east of Gare Nice Ville. Rooms are locked from noon to 5pm. Take bus No 14 (last one at 8.20pm) from the Station Centrale bus terminal on square Général Leclerc, which is linked to Gare Nice Ville by bus Nos 15 and 17, and get off at the L'Auberge stop.

Hotels – Train Station Area

The quickest way to get to all these hotels is to walk straight down the steps opposite Gare Nice Ville onto av Durante.

Hôtel Les Orangers (☎ 04 93 87 51 41; fax 04 93 82 57 82; 10bis av Durante; dm in 6-bed r €16, s/d with shower €25/40) Occupying a turn-of-the-20th-century townhouse, Les Orangers is recommended for its large-windowed, sunlit rooms, although this scruffy old place could do with a refit. Rooms come with a fridge (and hotplate on request).

Rue d'Alsace-Lorraine is dotted with more upmarket two-star hotels: one of the cheapest is **Hôtel du Piemont** (☎ 04 93 88 25 15; hotel-du-piemont@wanadoo.fr; 19 rue d'Alsace-Lorraine; s/d with washbasin from €19/22, with shower from €22/27, with shower & toilet from €32/34).

Hotels – City Centre

Le Petit Louvre (☎ 04 93 80 15 54; petitlouvr@wanadoo .fr; 10 rue Emma Tiranty; s/d/tr with shower €37/43/57, s/d with shower & toilet €40/49; P) Midway between the sea and the station, this colourful place is run by friendly proprietors. A faceless *Mona Lisa* greets guests as they enter, and corridors are adorned with an eclectic bunch of paintings. There's no air-con but there are fans. Cheap parking is available locally for guests.

MID-RANGE

Near Gare Nice Ville there are several two- and three-star hotels on rue d'Angleterre, rue d'Alsace-Lorraine, rue de Suisse, rue de Russie and av Durante.

Villa Eden (☎ 04 93 86 53 70; hotelvilllaeden@caramail .com; 99bis promenade des Anglais; s/d/tr €50/75/90; P ☒) Across the street from the beach and a good option for those who want to devote their stay to sunbathing. Some of the comfortable, old-fashioned rooms have terraces facing the sea.

Hôtel Claire Meublé (☎ 04 93 87 87 61; hotel _clair_meuble@hotmail.com; 6 rue d'Italie; 2-/3-/4-/5-person studio €42/50/64/70) A spotless place with compact, fully equipped studios well suited for self-catering families and couples.

Hôtel L'Oasis (☎ 04 93 88 12 29; www.hoteloasis -nice.com; 23 rue Gounod; s/d from 43/84; P X 🐾) An attractive period house where the playwright Chekhov wrote *The Three Sisters*. In a quiet close not far from the sea, the Oasis has a verdant, shady garden, appealing rooms and parking (€8).

Hôtel Cronstadt (☎ 04 93 82 00 30; www.hotelcron stadt.com; 3 rue Cronstadt; s €60-70, d €65-75). Near the sea and a welcoming, homely place. Rooms are quiet and graceful. The rates include breakfast.

Hôtel Félix (☎ 04 93 88 67 73; www.hotel-felix.com; 41 rue Masséna; r high/low season €70/50; 🐾 💻) This has considerable appeal, with small brightly coloured rooms equipped with hairdryers, air-con and satellite TV. Some of the soundproofed rooms have balconies overlooking rue Masséna and the telephones have modem plugs.

Citadines (☎ 08 25 01 03 62; www.citadines.com; 3-5 blvd François Grosso; d studio/4-person apt €125/176; P 🐾) Near the seafront and well equipped with modern fittings and full self-catering facilities in smart studios and slightly larger one-bedroom apartments (which also come with a double sofa bed), this makes a good standby, although the somewhat bland décor is typical of this relentlessly uniform chain of 'aparthotels'.

The following places in the centre of town are also recommended for value, comfort and cleanliness:

Hôtel du Centre (☎ 04 93 88 83 85; hotel-centre@ webstore.fr; 2 rue de Suisse; d hall shower €28.50, s/d with shower & toilet €50/59) An attractively renovated place with very neat rooms.

Hôtel Notre Dame (☎ 04 93 88 70 44; fax 04 93 82 20 38; 22 rue de Russie; s/d/q with shower & toilet €39/42/60) A basic but popular place (so book ahead) offering spacious rooms.

Hôtel Plaisance (☎ 04 93 85 11 90; hotelplaisance@ wanadoo.fr; 20 rue de Paris; s/d from €46/56; P 🐾) With soundproofed rooms with TVs and modern bathrooms.

TOP END

Hôtel Beau Rivage (☎ 04 92 47 82 82; www.nicebeau rivage.com; 24 rue St-François de Paule; r €140-300; 🐾) Out went the *belle époque* chintz Matisse would have known when he stayed here in 1916 and in came cool minimalism in the 2004 refit: all cream marble and chocolate suede sofas. Rooms are smart and restful, although on the small side given the price.

Hôtel Négresco (☎ 04 93 16 64 00; www.hotel -negresco-nice.com; 37 promenade des Anglais; r €225-780) Still in the *belle époque* style, the Negresco is the four-star *grande dame* of the seafront who, dare we say it, is starting to show her age next to her brash young luxury rivals nearby. This pink-domed, green-shuttered monument is still strong on service though. And anyway, where else will you be able to relax on your own Louis Quatorze chair as you contemplate the original and valuable art hanging in your room or peruse the

AUTHOR'S CHOICE

Hôtel Hi (☎ 04 97 07 26 26; www.hotel-hi-nice.cote.azur.fr; 3 av des Fleurs; r €175-500; X 🐾 💻 🏊) Step inside this modern, hi-tech place and you could be forgiven for thinking you've somehow boarded an ultrastylish, candy-coloured, interstellar spaceship. Philippe Starck had a hand in designing the functional, modular panelling in ice-cream limes and purples, all built around a large, light atrium, forming the space-age canteen-cum-restaurant-cum-bar and dance floor. There's also a modish rooftop plunge pool overlooking town and the Alps. Rooms are similarly striking with bright panels of colour and modern entertainment systems. A rather glam clientele, such as fashion designer Jean Paul Gaultier or rock stars like the band REM, may teleport in to join you.

If your budget doesn't quite stretch to the Hi consider **Villa la Tour** (☎ 04 93 80 08 15; www .villa-la-tour.com; 4 rue de la Tour; r from €56; 🐾), a great new place in Vieux Nice set up by a former manager at the Negresco Hotel, so good service and charm are a given. The well-equipped rooms are individually decorated with contemporary flair, there's a cute roof patio, a good breakfast (continental/buffet €3.50/7) and, best of all, you're just a stumble from the bars and *socca* joints of the old town.

menu of the Négresco's Michelin-starred, fine-dining restaurant, Chantecler?

Palais de la Mediterranée (☎ 04 92 14 77 00; www .lepalaisdelamediterranee.com; r €280-680; P ✗ ✗ ✗) The Negresco's latest rival has been rebuilt from the ruins of the old casino. The utter luxury of the original 1920s house of art and gambling was revived with the 2004 reopening of a four-star hotel and casino. Rooms are huge and the sea views from the rooms, the café and the restaurant are spectacularly framed by the massive pillars of that Art Deco façade, which also serves to cut out the sight (and noise) of the traffic below. There is disabled access at the Palais.

Eating

You won't have any problems finding good, interesting food in all price ranges in the city. Many of the local specialities are served by inexpensive, bustling places in the Vieux Nice (such as Chez Rene, right) and seafood is always a good bet, but a there's a wide range of options including some highly regarded, fine-dining restaurants.

RESTAURANTS – VIEUX NICE

The cours Saleya and the narrow streets of Vieux Nice are lined with restaurants, cafés and pizzerias of varying quality. Local specialities to watch out for include *socca* (a thin layer of chickpea flour and olive oil batter fried on a griddle and served with pepper), *salade niçoise, ratatouille* and *farcis* (stuffed vegetables, especially stuffed zucchini flowers).

Nissa Socca (☎ 04 93 80 18 35; 5 rue Ste-Réparate; menu €13, dishes from €6; ☺ closed Sun & lunch Mon) This is a good place to try many of those local specialities. It's a perennial favourite with locals, and specialises in Niçois dishes.

Lou Pilha Leva (place Centrale; dishes from €3; ☺ 11am-10pm) It won't win any prizes for ambience (you eat on outdoor wooden tables under an awning) but the *pissaladiére* (thin crust topped with onions and anchovies or olives), *soupe au pistou* (soup of vegetables, noodles, beans, basil and garlic) and other Niçois specialities are prepared the way *maman* would. Order at the counter, grab your plate and a waiter will come around for your drink order.

Restaurant du Gésu (☎ 04 93 62 26 46; 1 place du Gésu; plat du jour & pizzas from €7; ☺ lunch & dinner Mon-Sat) An exuberant place decorated with foot-

ball pennants with a terrace in front of Église du Gésu St-Jacques le Majeur. The pizzas and pastas are exceptionally well prepared.

Escalinada (☎ 04 93 62 11 71; 22 rue Pairolière; menu €20; ☺ lunch & dinner) Enchanting (smiling staff, candlelit terrace), you can get a decent bottle of wine and good, unpretentious fare such as *daube* (stew) and rouget fillets. The house speciality is *testicules de mouton panés* (sheep's testicles in batter).

Le Merenda (4 rue de la Terrasse; starters from €9, mains around €16; ☺ lunch & dinner Mon-Fri) Tiny and annoying (no phone, no credit cards, no phone reservations, as the blackboard menu proudly announces) but if you can manage a reservation (in person), you won't be disappointed by the first-rate food, which is hearty regional comfort food served to a mostly mature clientele. House specialities include *pâtes au pistou* (pasta with pesto sauce), stockfish and a range of French/Provençal dishes.

Le Safari (☎ 04 93 80 18 44; 1 cours Saleya; mains from €14, menu €28; ☺ lunch & dinner) Far and away the best of the lot on buzzing, touristy cours Saleya. Avoiding the heaviness of cheaper Provençal food, this local favourite brings a lighter touch to specialities such as *farcis* and stockfish. Good seafood choices might include octopus salad and langoustine pasta.

RESTAURANTS – CITY CENTRE

The rue Masséna pedestrian mall and nearby streets and squares, including rue de France and place Magenta, are crammed with touristy outdoor cafés and restaurants. Unfortunately most of them don't offer particularly good value.

Zucca Magica (☎ 04 93 56 25 27; 4bis quai Papacino; lunch/dinner menus €18/22; lunch & dinner Tue-Sat) Near the old port and always packed with regulars, along with the riot of pumpkins, squashes and gourd memorabilia that crowd the diners. The décor may be bizarre but the food is down-to-earth, homely, vegetarian Italian. Course after course of cheesy, vegie delicacies make dining here a veritable cheese assault course for your tummy. Book ahead.

La Nissarda (☎ 04 93 85 26 29; 17 rue Gubernatis; lunch menus €12 & €17, dinner menu €24; Mon-Sat) Fresh, well-prepared Provençal specialities plus a hearty *bœuf bourguignon* in the small, welcoming dining room are what to expect.

Flo Nice (☎ 04 93 13 38 39; 4 rue Sacha Guitry; menus €30; noon-3pm & 7pm-midnight) Housed in a converted theatre in which the glassed-in kitchen occupies centre stage, this is part of the Parisian Brasserie Flo chain. Like its cousins to the north, the restaurant turns out flawlessly executed dishes with an emphasis on fish and plentiful seafood platters.

Le Comptoir (☎ 04 93 92 08 80; 20 rue St-François de Paule; menu €30; closed Sat & Sun lunch) A smart place close to the seashore. The restaurant is decked out in Art Deco style and has a terrace too. The food has Italian and French flavours, such as *gnocchi* with *daube*.

Chantecler (☎ 04 93 16 64 00; 37 promenade des Anglais) Last seen trying to win back one of its two prized Michelin stars in 2004, but still the place for a mind-blowing traditional French meal in a luxurious setting inside Hôtel Négresco (p826). Expect impeccable service, tantalising cuisine and a hefty €100 per-head (at least) bill.

RESTAURANTS – TRAIN STATION AREA

There's plenty of value-for-money fare in this area, but head south if you're after finer dining.

L'Allegria (☎ 04 93 87 42 00; rue d'Italie; menus from €11; Tue-Sat) Corsican chants and energetic guitar duets are on hand to help the food go down. If it's a chilly day, ask for a filling, large bowl of *soupe corse* (with vegetables and beans), one of Corsica's staple soups.

Restaurant au Soleil (☎ 04 93 88 77 74; 9 rue d'Italie; menu €12; lunch & dinner, closed Sat year-round, Nov & Dec) Next door to L'Allegria, unpretentious and very friendly. It offers good local cuisine at unbeatable prices, including an all-day omelette breakfast for €5.50.

Chez Mireille (☎ 04 93 85 27 23; cnr blvd Raimbaldi & rue Miron; paella €20; lunch & dinner Wed-Sun) Specialises in paella, paella and more paella.

CAFÉS

Le Pain Quotidien (cnr rue Louis Gassin & Cours Saleya; breakfast from €6, brunch €18; 7am-7pm) *The* place in town to have breakfast or to tackle the mother of all brunches. Choose your breakfast formula, enjoy the excellent hot chocolate and take in the colour and fragrance of the adjacent flower market from the terrace or from inside through the large windows.

Scotch Tea House (☎ 04 93 87 75 62; 4 av de Suède; dishes €7.50-15; 9am-8pm Mon-Sat) Home-made cakes and hearty tarts – just like grandma bakes – make this a good, old-fashioned afternoon tea kind of place.

Fenocchio (☎ 04 93 80 72 52; 2 place Rossetti; 9am-midnight Feb-Oct) The mecca of ice cream and sorbet in town, with 86 flavours made on the premises, including tomato-basil and prune for the truly adventurous.

SELF-CATERING

There's a fantastic **fruit & vegetable market** (cours Saleya; 7am-1pm Tue-Sun) in front of the Palais de Justice selling every type of fresh, dried and preserved produce and another, cheaper and less touristy one that begins on av Malaussena, north of Gare Nice Ville. It's open the same hours. There's also a fresh **fish market** (place St-François; 6am-1pm Tue-Sun).

There supermarkets across town.

Casino Supermarket (27 blvd Gambetta; 8.30am-8pm Mon-Sat) On the western side of the city.

Monoprix Supermarket (33 av Jean Médecin; 8.30am-8.30pm Mon-Sat); Garibaldi branch (place Garibaldi; 8.30am-8pm Mon-Sat)

Drinking

Terraced cafés and bars, perfect for quaffing beers and sipping pastis, abound in Nice. Almost all nightlife is in Vieux Nice, which throbs with activity on summer nights. The most popular pubs in Nice are run by Anglophones, with happy hours and live music.

Chez Wayne's (☎ 04 93 13 46 99; 15 rue de la Préfecture; 3pm-midnight) The best known place for liquor-fuelled carousing, hosts a quiz nightly except Tuesday, a ladies' night on Wednesday, karaoke on Sunday and live bands nightly. It opens later at weekends. Happy 'hour' is until 9pm.

Two fun British/Irish boozer-type places include **O'Haras** (☎ 04 93 80 43 22; 22 rue Droite; 11am-late), good for a pint of Guinness and **Oxford** (☎ 04 93 92 24 54; 4 rue Mascoïnat; until 4am), which offers a wide range of English and Irish draught beers.

Nocy-Bé (rue de la Préfecture; 10am-late) is a cool, dark Moroccan-style tea house where you can sit low on cushions and sip refreshing mint teas. **Le Pain Quotidien** (opposite) is a great place a coffee as well as breakfast.

Entertainment
The tourist office has detailed information on Nice's abundant cultural activities, many of which are listed in its free publications, *Nice Rendezvous* and *Côte d'Azur en Fêtes*. More useful is the weekly *Semaine des Spectacles* (€0.80), available from newsstands on Wednesday. Tickets to events of all sorts can be purchased at **Fnac** (☎ 04 92 17 77 77; 24 av Jean Médecin), inside the Nice Étoile shopping mall.

CINEMA
Nice has two cinemas offering nondubbed films, many of them in English: **Cinéma Nouveau Mercury** (recorded message in French ☎ 04 93 55 32 31; 16 place Garibaldi) and **Cinéma Rialto** (☎ 04 93 88 08 41; 4 rue de Rivoli). Art films (usually in the original version with French subtitles) are screened at **Cinémathèque de Nice** (☎ 04 92 04 06 66; 3 esplanade Kennedy), which is at the Acropolis conference centre and concert hall, Tuesday to Sunday.

LIVE MUSIC
Opéra de Nice (☎ 04 92 17 40 40; 4-6 rue St-François de Paule; box office 10am-5pm Mon-Sat) Built in 1885 and recently renovated this grand old place hosts operas and orchestral concerts. Tickets for operas, concerts and ballets cost €6 to €64, the opera house is closed between mid-June and September.

Le Bar des Oiseaux (☎ 04 93 80 27 33; 5 rue St-Vincent; 7am-midnight Mon-Sat) Attracts an assortment of artistic types and nonconformists for a programme of music, theatre and philosophical discussion sessions. Jazz is the strong point. You'll pay around €5 for admission when there's live music.

Jonathan's (☎ 04 93 62 57 62; 1 rue de la Loge; 8-11.30pm) Another live music venue where

(country, boogie-woogie, Irish folk etc) play every night in summer.

NIGHTCLUBS
Happy Bar (☎ 04 97 07 26 26; www.hi-hotel.com; 3 av des Fleurs; DJs Tue, Fri & Sat till late) A way from the centre or the old town, this is an ultracool bar in the space-age Hôtel Hi with a dance floor and DJs playing house and other bleep-bleep stuff three nights a week. It's a fairly quiet bar the rest of the week.

Ghost (☎ 04 93 92 93 37; 3 rue Barillerie; 8pm-2.30am Mon-Sat) A fun and relaxed club with comfortable *banquettes* (seating) and soft lighting. DJs lean towards world, trip-hop and house music.

Blue Boy Enterprise (☎ 04 93 44 68 24; 9 rue Spinetta; from 11pm) A trendy gay nightclub that also welcomes a straight crowd.

Shopping
Cours Saleya is divided between a wonderful flower market in the western half and a diverse food market on the eastern end, including stalls devoted to dried produce, mushrooms and *fruits glacés* (glazed or candied fruits), a regional speciality. The figs, ginger, tangerine slices and pears have to be tasted to be believed. Both markets open at 6am Tuesday to Sunday. The food market wraps up at 1pm and the flower market is open to 5.30pm (1pm Sunday).

The best-value place for wine-tasting and buying is a traditional wine cellar, and a good one is **Les Grandes Caves Caprioglio** (☎ 04 93 85 66 57; 16 rue de la Préfecture) sells wines from all over France, ranging from cheap, local tooth enamel stripper by the flagon to pricey Bandol and Burgundy by the bottle.

À l'Olivier (☎ 04 93 13 44 97; 7 rue St-François de Paule) and **Moulin à Huile d'Olive Alziari** (14 rue St-François de Paule), close to each other, both sell olive oil and its many and varied spin-offs.

Designer names abound above the beautiful fashion boutiques languishing along rue Paradis, av de Suède, rue Alphonse Karr and rue du Maréchal Joffre.

Nice Étoile shopping mall (av Jean Médecin) covers a large block of the city.

Getting There & Away
AIR
Nice's international airport, **Aéroport International Nice-Côte d'Azur** (☎ 08 20 42 33 33), is about 6km west of the city centre.

There are two terminals connected by a complementary **shuttle bus** (🕒 at least every 10min btwn 6am-11pm).

BMIBaby (www.bmibaby.com) and **easyJet** (www.easyjet.com) have services to Nice from various UK airports.

BOAT

The fastest and least expensive SNCM ferries from mainland France to Corsica depart from Nice (see p865).

The **SNCM office** (🕾 04 93 13 66 66; ferry terminal, quai du Commerce) issues tickets (otherwise try a travel agency in town). From av Jean Médecin take bus No 1 or 2 to the Port stop. You can also try **Corsica Ferries** (🕾 08 25 09 50 95; www.corsicaferries.com; quai Lunel).

BUS

Lines operated by some two dozen bus companies stop at the **intercity bus station** (🕾 04 93 85 61 81; 5 blvd Jean Jaurès). There's a busy information counter at the station.

There are slow but frequent services until about 7.30pm daily to Antibes (€4.20, 1¼ hours), Cannes (€5.90, 1½ hours), Grasse (€6.30, 1¼ hours), Menton (€5.10, 1¼ hours) and Monaco (€3.90 return, 45 minutes). Hourly buses run to Vence (€4.70, 50 minutes) and St-Paul de Vence (€4.30, one hour). To Castellane, the gateway to the Gorges du Verdon, there's one bus a day at 7.30am (€17.20, 1½ hours). Buses run to the ski resort of Isola 2000 to the north two times a day (€17.10, 2¼ hours).

For long-haul travel, **Intercars** (🕾 04 93 80 08 70), at the bus station, takes you to various European destinations; it sells Eurolines tickets for buses to London, Brussels and Amsterdam.

TRAIN

Nice's main train station, **Gare Nice Ville** (Gare Thiers; av Thiers) is 1.2km north of the beach.

There are fast and frequent services (up to 40 trains a day in each direction) to towns up and down the coast from St-Raphaël to Ventimiglia (across the Italian border): Antibes (€3.50, 25 minutes), Cannes (€5.20, 40 minutes), Menton (€3.90, 35 minutes), Monaco (€3, 20 minutes) and St-Raphaël (€9.20, 45 minutes).

There are two or three TGVs that link Nice with Paris' Gare de Lyon (€81, 5½ hours), via Lyon (€55.50, 4½ hours).

Lost luggage and other problems are handled by **SOS Voyageurs** (🕾 04 93 16 02 61; 🕒 9am-noon & 3-6pm Mon-Fri).

The ever-popular, two-car diesel trains operated by **Les Chemins de Fer de la Provence** (in Nice 🕾 04 97 0 3 80 80, in Digne-les-Bains 🕾 04 92 31 01 58) make the scenic trip four times daily from Nice's **Gare du Sud** (🕾 04 93 82 10 17; 4bis rue Alfred Binet) to Digne-les-Bains (€17.40, 3¼ hours).

An equally scenic train trip run by the SNCF goes from Nice to Tende (€10, 1¾ hours) and on to Cuneo in Italy, stopping at a number of mountain villages. During summer you can break your journey a few times and qualify for reductions at local attractions, although this needs careful planning as there are not many services each day.

Getting Around
TO/FROM THE AIRPORT

Sunbus route No 23 (€1.30), which runs to the airport every 20 or 30 minutes from about 6am to 8pm, can be picked up at Gare Nice Ville or on blvd Gambetta, rue de France or av de la Californie. ANT's route 99 shuttles every half hour direct between Gare Nice Ville and both airport terminals daily from 8am to 9pm.

From the intercity bus station, you can also take the **ANT airport bus** (🕾 04 92 29 88 88; €3.50), which bears the symbol of an aeroplane (every 20 minutes; 30 minutes on Sunday). Bus No 99 also makes the airport run from the Gare Nice Ville.

A taxi from the airport to the centre of Nice will cost €25 to €30, depending on the time of day and whether you're at Terminal 1 or 2.

BUS

Local buses, run by Sunbus, cost €1.30/16 for a single/14 rides. After you time-stamp your ticket, it's valid for one hour and can be used for one transfer or return. The Nice by Bus pass, valid for one/five/seven days, costs €4/12.95/16.75 and includes a return trip to the airport. You can buy single trips, 14-trip cards and a day card on the bus. The other passes are sold in *tabacs* and kiosks as well as at the **Sunbus information office** (🕾 04 93 13 53 13; 10 av Félix Faure).

Station Centrale, Sunbus' main hub, takes up three sides of square Général Leclerc and contains a kiosk where you can get further information.

Bus No 12 links Gare Nice Ville with promenade des Anglais and the beach. To get from Gare Nice Ville to Vieux Nice and the intercity bus station, take bus No 2, 5 or 17. At night, four Noctambuses run north, east and west from place Masséna every half-hour from 9.10pm.

CAR & MOTORCYCLE

If you just want to tool around in the countryside for a day, your best bet is **Easycar** (in London ☎ 44-0906 33 33 33 3; www.easycar.com), which rents out subcompacts from Nice for as little as €27 per day, including 100km. Cars must be reserved either on the website or through its London call centre.

In Nice, try the following places, which offer subcompacts for around €37 a day, including 100km.

Budget (☎ 04 97 03 35 03; 1bis av Gustave V) Aubert branch (38 av Aubert)

JML (☎ 04 93 16 07 00; fax 04 93 16 07 48; 34 av Aubert)

Rent a Car Système (☎ 04 93 88 69 69; fax 04 93 88 43 36; 38 av Aubert)

Nicea Location Rent (☎ 04 93 16 10 30; fax 04 93 87 76 36; 12 rue de Belgique) rents 50cc scooters for €49 a day, and 125cc motorcycles for €73 a day.

TAXI

Some taxi drivers in Nice can be dishonest. Make sure the driver is using the meter and applying the right rate, clearly outlined in a laminated card, which the driver is required to display. There are taxi stands right outside the Gare Nice Ville and on av Félix Faure close to place Masséna; otherwise you can order one on ☎ 04 93 13 78 78.

ANTIBES–JUAN-LES-PINS

pop 73,383

Directly across the Baie des Anges from Nice, Antibes, Cap d'Antibes and neighbouring Juan-les-Pins have a surprising range of attractions packed into a relatively small space at the base of a peninsula. Antibes is the quintessential Mediterranean town where narrow cobblestone streets, festooned with plants and flowers, branch out from a central, covered marketplace. It boasts a fine Picasso museum and an extensive yacht-packed port. Cap d'Antibes is a favourite hideaway for the migrating rich

who own luxurious walled mansions amid the dense pines. Juan-les-Pins is popular for its 2km-long stretch of sandy beach and its sizzling nightlife.

Antibes was first settled around the 4th century BC by Greeks from Marseille, who named it Antipolis. It was later taken over by the Romans and then by the Grimaldi family, who ruled it from 1384 to 1608. Because of its position on the border of France and Savoy, it was fortified in the 17th and 18th centuries, but these fortifications were torn down in 1894 to allow the town to expand. Antibes has appealed to many artists over the years, most notably Picasso, Max Ernst and Nicolas de Staël.

Orientation

The centre of Antibes is place du Général de Gaulle linked to Juan-les-Pins by blvd du Président Wilson and to Cap d'Antibes by blvd Albert 1er. Avenue Robert Soleau links Antibes train station with place du Général de Gaulle. The bus station is just a few steps away, linked by rue de la République.

Information

BOOKSHOPS

Antibes Books-Heidi's English Bookshop (☎ 04 93 34 74 11; 24 rue Aubernon; 🕙 10am-7pm) Near cours Masséna, this shop stocks new and used English-language books.

INTERNET ACCESS

The Office (☎ 04 93 34 09 96; 8 blvd d'Aguillon; per min €0.10; 🕙 9.30am-9pm)

MONEY

Eurochange (4 rue Georges Clemenceau, Antibes; 🕙 9am-7pm Mon-Sat, 10am-1pm Sat)
Exchange Office (17 blvd Albert 1er, Antibes; 🕙 9am-7pm Mon-Sat, 10am-1pm Sat)

POST

Main Post Office (place des Martyrs de la Résistance, Antibes)

TOURIST INFORMATION

Antibes Tourist Office (☎ 04 92 90 53 00; www.antibesjuanlespins.com; 11 place de Gaulle; 🕙 9am-7pm daily Jul & Aug, 9am-12.30pm & 1.30-6pm Mon-Fri, 9am-noon & 2-6pm Sat Sep-Jun) In the town centre.
Juan-les-Pins Tourist Office (☎ 04 92 90 53 05; fax 04 92 90 55 13; 55 blvd Charles Guillaumont) Has similar hours to the Antibes office.

Sights & Activities

Housed in the evocative, 12th-century Château Grimaldi overlooking a terrific stretch of coast, **Musée Picasso** (☎ 04 92 90 54 20; adult/student €4.60/2.30; 10am-6pm Tue-Sun Jun-Sep, 10am-noon & 2-6pm Tue-Sun Oct-May) is undoubtedly Antibes' star museum. Picasso used the chateau as a studio for six months in 1946, where he would paint late into the night in a kind of trance, his work lit by powerful arc-lights. Today it houses an excellent collection of his paintings, lithographs, drawings and ceramics. The museum also contains works by other artists, including Léger, Miró, Ernst and Calder.

Other worthwhile sights include **Musée Peynet** (☎ 04 92 90 54 30; admission €3; 10am-6pm Tue-Sun Jun-Sep, 10am-noon & 2-6pm Oct-May) interesting for its exhibits of pictures, cartoons, sculptures and costumes by Antibes-born cartoonist Peynet and some good temporary exhibitions from other illustrators and cartoonists.

Antibes has one small, sandy beach, **Plage de la Gravette**, but the best **beaches** are located in Juan-les-Pins, including some free ones on blvd Littoral and blvd Charles Guillaumont.

Festivals & Events

Antibes' premier occasion is **Jazz à Juan** or the Festival de Jazz d'Antibes Juan-les-Pins, which takes place for a week in mid-July in La Pinède, the park next to the casino. The line-up is always first-rate, the acoustics are superb and the outdoor setting under the stars can't be beaten. Tickets can be reserved through the tourist office but it's usually possible to find something at the gate an hour before show time.

Sleeping & Eating

Accommodation is generally costly in Antibes or Juan-les-Pins.

Relais International de la Jeunesse (☎ 04 93 61 34 40; 60 blvd de la Garoupe; dm incl breakfast €14, sheets €3) Beautifully located in Cap d'Antibes. It's possible to pitch a tent on site for €8, not including breakfast. Take bus No 2A from the bus station to L'Antiquité stop.

Le Relais du Postillon (☎ 04 93 34 20 77; www .relaisdupostillon.com; 8 rue Championnet; r €44-82; mains €11-27) A friendly establishment in a sprawling 17th-century coach house. Each different room is beautifully decorated. The hotel runs a smart, good-quality restaurant with an accent on fish, such as langoustine risotto or crab and scampi. Book ahead for accommodation.

Hotel Savoy (☎ 04 93 61 13 82; hotelsavoysarl@aol .com; 144 blvd du Président Wilson; s/d high season €65/90, low season €52/58) The cheapest you'll find in Juan-les-Pins and right at the centre of the action. Rooms are soundproofed, have TV and a telephone, but the décor is a bit drab.

L'Étoile (☎ 04 93 34 26 30; www.hoteletoile.com; 2 av Gambetta; s/d €52/58;   ) Less central but offering good value for soundproofed rooms with TV and minibar.

Le Brulot (☎ 04 93 34 11 76; rue Frederick Isnard; menus €13; closed Sun & lunch Mon) A good bet for pizzas, seafood, pasta and *socca*.

Rice Bar (☎ 04 93 34 12 84; 1 rue des Bains; menus €10, €13 & €15; lunch & dinner Tue-Sun) The place to go for vegetarians, as many of the rice-based dishes are vegetable-adorned.

Marché Provençal (cours Masséna; mornings daily Jun-Aug, Tue-Sun Sep-May) One of the region's most colourful markets and a delightful place to pick up supplies. If you've missed the market, rue Sade is another good hunting ground for picnic goodies.

Getting There & Away

Antibes is an easy day trip by bus from Nice (€4.20, 1¼ hours) or Cannes (€2.20, 30 minutes).

AROUND ANTIBES
Biot
pop 7489

This charming *village perché* (perched village) was once a vital pottery-manufacturing centre specialising in large earthenware oil and wine containers. Although metal containers brought an end to this industry, Biot is still active in the production of handicrafts. The village streets are a pleasant place for a stroll, but you will have to get there early to beat the hordes.

The attractive **place des Arcades** dates from the 13th and 14th centuries. At the foot of the village is a **glass factory** where you can watch glass-blowers at work.

You can pick up information at the **tourist office** (☎ 04 93 65 78 00; www.biot-cotezaur.com in French; 46 rue St-Sébastien; 10am-7pm Mon-Fri Jul & Aug, 2.30-7pm Sat & Sun, 9am-noon & 2-6pm Mon-Fri, 2-6pm Sat & Sun rest of year).

Musée National Fernand Léger (☎ 04 92 91 50 30; www.musee-fernandleger.fr in French; chemin du Val de Pôme; adult/child €4/2.60; 🕙 10.30am-6pm Wed-Mon Jul-Sep, 10am-12.30pm & 2-5pm Wed-Mon Oct-Jun) is dedicated to the artist Fernand Léger (1881–1955) and contains 360 of his works, including paintings, mosaics, ceramics and stained-glass windows. A huge, colourful mosaic decorates the museum's façade.

Bus 10a runs (€1, 20 minutes, hourly) from Antibes station to Biot. For detailed information contact **Antibes bus station** (🕙 04 93 34 37 60).

Cagnes-sur-Mer
pop 44,207
Cagnes-sur-Mer is made up of Le Haut de Cagnes, the old hill town; Le Cros de Cagnes, the former fishing village by the beach; and Cagnes Ville, a rapidly-growing modern quarter. The old city is dominated by the 14th-century **Château Grimaldi** (☎ 04 92 02 47 30; place Grimaldi; adult/child €3/1.50, combined ticket with Musée Renoir €4.50; 🕙 10am-noon & 2-6pm Wed-Mon), which houses a museum of contemporary Mediterranean art and stages an annual international art festival.

Near Cagnes Ville is **Musée Renoir** (☎ 04 93 20 61 07; chemin des Collettes; adult/child €3/1.50; 🕙 10am-noon & 2-6pm Wed-Mon), the home and studio of Renoir from 1907 to 1919. It has retained its original décor and has several of the artist's works on display. The villa is set within a magnificent olive grove. Guided tours in English are available.

The **tourist office** (☎ 04 93 20 61 64; www.cagnes-tourisme.com in French; 6 blvd Maréchal Juin, Cagnes Ville; 🕙 9am-7pm Mon-Sat, 9am-noon & 3-7pm Sun Jul & Aug, 9am-noon & 2-7pm Mon-Sat Jun & Sep, 9am-noon & 2-6pm rest of year) is just off the A8.

TAM (🕙 04 93 85 61 81; www.rca.tm.fr in French) runs regular buses between Cagnes and Nice.

ST-PAUL DE VENCE
pop 2900
Once upon a time, St-Paul de Vence was a modest village on a hill overlooking the coast, about 10km north of Cagnes-sur-Mer. Fortified in the 16th century, it remained beautifully intact and began to attract artists such as the Russian painter Marc Chagall, who moved to the village in 1966. St-Paul was also a favourite hang-out of singer/actor Yves Montand, who met and married his wife, actress Simone Signoret, here.

The cobblestones of the narrow streets, have been polished smooth by the cease-less flow of visitors and it can all get a bit wearing in summer. St-Paul may be looking weary from its annual onslaught but there is a hard nugget of fine art underneath it all. Braque, Chagall, Dufy and Picasso often dined at La Colombe d'Or and paid for their meals with their creations. The restaurant now houses one of France's most fascinating private art collections. The village is crammed with galleries of wildly varying quality,

Perhaps the most compelling reason for coming to town is to visit the nearby Fondation Maeght, the former home of a fabulously wealthy art dealer, which hosts an exceptional collection of 20th-century works featuring Braque, Bonnard, Chagall, Matisse, Miró and Léger.

Orientation & Information
The village is defined by one main street, rue Grande, which leads up to the cemetery containing the tomb of Marc Chagall. The **tourist office** (☎ 04 93 32 86 95; artdevivre@wanadoo.fr; 2 rue Grande; 🕙 10am-7pm Jun-Sep, 10am-6pm Oct-May) is on the right as you enter the walled village. The post office is outside the walled village across from the bus stop. There is a currency exchange and an ATM.

Fondation Maeght
Inaugurated in 1964, **Fondation Maeght** (Maeght Foundation; ☎ 04 93 32 81 63; adult/student €11/9.50; 🕙 10am-7pm Jul-Sep, 10am-12.30pm & 2.30-6pm Oct-Jun) is the finest museum in the region. Its extraordinary collection of painting and sculpture is exhibited on a rotating basis, and there are several temporary exhibitions a year. In the gardens behind the museum, visitors can stroll through **Miró Labyrinth**, an outdoor sculpture garden studded with reflecting pools and mosaics by the Spanish surrealist, Joan Miró.

The museum is about 1km uphill from the bus stop outside the old village. If you're arriving by bus, it's best to see the museum in the morning when the walk uphill will be cooler and visit the village after lunch when the tour buses leave.

Eating
La Colombe d'Or (The Golden Dove; ☎ 04 93 32 77 78; mains €17-40; 🕙 lunch & dinner) This is a top-end choice and tables must be reserved long in advance. The lovely outdoor terrace has a

view over the hills but the art collection is indoors. No, you may not take a peek at the art collection unless you book a table or stay in one of the upstairs rooms (€360).

Un Coeur en Provence (☎ 04 93 32 87 81; light meals from €9; ☾ 10am-9pm Thu-Tue) Dedicated to poetry and simple, light dishes this is a laid-back tea salon. There are books stacked in a corner, occasional poetry readings, soft music and an array of fresh soup, salads, pancakes and tarts and several vegetarian options.

There's a **grocery store** immediately to your right after entering the village and plenty of benches for picnicking along the ramparts.

Getting There & Away
St-Paul is served by the Nice–Vence bus service (€4.30, one hour from Nice).

VENCE
pop 17,184
This pleasant but unremarkable town, 4km north of St-Paul de Vence, is noted for the exceptional **Chapelle du Rosaire** (☎ 04 93 58 03 26; 468 av Henri Matisse; admission €2.50; ☾ 2-5.30pm Mon, Wed & Sat, 10-11.30am & 2-5.30pm Tue & Thu). In 1943 an ailing Matisse moved to Vence and fell under the care of his former nurse and model, Monique Bourgeois, who had since become a Dominican nun. She persuaded the artist to design the chapel for her community, and the result is this treasure. Matisse, who regarded this as both his masterpiece and a summation of his artistic career, designed the entire interior including the chapel's stone altar, candlesticks, cross and even the priests' vestments displayed in an adjoining hall. The real impact comes from the colour of those huge stained-glass windows. A bright morning is the best time to come for the full, light-flooded effect.

The chapel is 800m north of Vence on route de St-Jeannet (the D2210). From place du Grand Jardin, head east along av de la Résistance, then turn right along av Tuby. At the next junction, bear right along av de Provence, then left onto av Henri Matisse. Vence is served by frequent buses from Nice (€4.70, 50 minutes).

CANNES
pop 68,214
It's the money of the affluent, spent with the nonchalance of those for whom it is no object, that continues to keep Cannes' expen-

sive hotels, fancy restaurants and exorbitant boutiques in business, and its yachts as big as ocean liners afloat. But the harbour, the bay, the hill west of the port called Le Suquet, the beachside promenade, the beaches and the people sunning themselves provide more than enough natural beauty to make at least a day trip here worth the effort.

Cannes hosts many festivals, the most renowned being the 10-day International Film Festival in mid-May, which sees the city's population treble overnight.

The film festival excepted, culture is hardly Cannes' strong point. It has just one museum and, since its speciality is ethnography, the only art you are likely to come across is in the many galleries scattered around town.

Perhaps the best way to spend time here is to wander along blvd de la Croisette, then sit and watch Cannes' human circus pass by in all its expensively but strangely dressed, permatanned, face-lifted, small-yappy-type-dog-carrying glory.

Cannes comes to life on a sunny day at any time of year and the view of town from Corniche de l'Estérel, with its background of the snowcapped Alpes-Maritimes in late winter, is a magnificent sight.

One big disappointment is the public beaches, which are small, crowded and often with rather murky water. You'll have to head out of town to the west to find good ones like Plages du Midi and Pages de la Bocca.

Orientation
Don't expect to be struck down by glitz the minute you set foot in Cannes: sex shops and peep shows abound near the train station on rue Jean Jaurès. Things improve along rue d'Antibes, the main shopping street a couple of blocks south. Several blocks further south is the huge Palais des Festivals et des Congrès, east of the Vieux Port (old port).

Cannes' most famous promenade, the magnificent, hotel-lined blvd de la Croisette, begins at the Palais des Festivals and continues east along the Baie de Cannes to Pointe de la Croisette. Place Bernard Cornut Gentille, where the bus station to Nice is located, is on the northwestern corner of Vieux Port.

Information
BOOKSHOPS
Cannes English Bookshop (☎ 04 93 99 40 08; 11 rue Bivouac Napoléon) For English-language novels.

CANNES

INFORMATION

AmEx Bureau de Change............1	D2
Cannes English Bookshop..........2	C2
Cannes Info Jeunesse...............3	B3
Cannes Réservation..................4	D1
Crédit Lyonnais.......................5	C2
Cybercafe Webstation..............6	D2
Laverie du Cygne.....................7	A4
Main Post Office.....................8	D2
Office Provencal Change...........9	D1
Station Cyber.........................10	E1
Touris' Office Annexe..............11	D1
Touris' Office........................12	D3

SIGHTS & ACTIVITIES (p837)

Musée de la Castre.................13	A3
Palais des Festivals et des Congrès...14	D3
Trans Côte d'Azur Ticket Office...15	B4

SLEEPING (pp837-8)

Alan Robert's Hôtel................16	D1
Grand Hôtel..........................17	E3
Hôtel Alizé...........................18	D2
Hôtel Atlantis........................19	D2
Hôtel de Bourgogne................20	D1
Hôtel Florella........................21	F1
Hôtel Florian.........................22	B2
Hôtel National.......................23	C2
Le Chantecler........................24	A2
Noga Hilton...........................25	F3

EATING (pp838-9)

Astoux & Brun.......................26	B2
Au Bons Enfants....................27	B2
Barbarella............................28	B2
Boulangerie-Pâtisserie.............29	A2
Ceneri.................................30	D1
Champion Supermarket............31	B2
La Piazza.............................32	C2
La Tarterie...........................33	B2
Le Petit Lardon.....................34	D2
	35 E2
Lenotre...............................36	D2
Marché Forville......................37	B2
Monoprix Supermarket............38	D1
Morning Food Market..............39	E1
Sushikan.............................40	E2

DRINKING (p839)

Bar La Renaissance................41	E2
Cat Corner..........................42	E3
Le Loft...............................43	B2
Morrison's Irish Pub...............44	E2

ENTERTAINMENT
Jimmy'z...............................45	C3
Le Vogue............................46	A2
Les Coulisses........................47	E3
Zanzibar.............................48	C2

TRANSPORT (pp839-40)

Alliance Location...................49	E2
Bus Station (to Nice)..............50	B3
Bus Station..........................51	D1
Palais Underground Car Park.....(see 14)
Rapides Côte d'Azur & Bus Azur...(see 50)

OTHER

Hôtel de Ville.......................52	B2

Vieux Port

Baie de Cannes

Le Suquet

Plage du Festival

Plages de la Croisette (Private Beaches)

Public Beach

Esplanade George Pompidou

Jetée Albert Edouard

Public Beach

To Iles de Lérins

To JKL (50m); Carlton Inter-Continental; Le Bar des Célébrités (100m); Hôtel Martinez; Amiral Hôtel 400m; Pointe de la Croisette & Palm Beach Casino (2km)

To Hôtel Molière (75m)

To Le Chailit (200m)

To Plage du Midi; Plages de la Bocca; Cannes-La Bocca, Parc Bellevue Camp Site (5.5km)

0 200 m
0 0.1 miles

CÔTE D'AZUR & MONACO

INTERNET ACCESS

Both the following places are close to the town centre and handy for the train station.

Cybercafé Webstation (☎ /fax 04 93 68 72 37; 26 rue Hoche; per 30/60min €3/6; ⊙ 10am-11pm Mon-Sat)

Station Cyber (☎ 04 93 38 49 97; 32 rue Jean Jaurès; per hr €6; ⊙ 10am-7pm) Has disabled access.

LAUNDRY

Laverie du Cygne (☎ 04 93 39 96 79; 58 rue Georges Clemenceau) The most convenient to the town centre.

MONEY

There are several banks along rue d'Antibes and on rue Buttura.

AmEx Bureau de Change (☎ 04 93 99 05 45; ⊙ 9am-7pm daily May-Sep, 9.30am-noon & 1.30-5.30pm Mon-Fri Oct-Apr) For card-related matters and money changing.

Crédit Lyonnais (13 rue d'Antibes) In town.

Office Provençal Change (☎ 04 93 39 34 37; cnr rue Maréchal Foch & rue Jean Jaurès) Inside Maison de la Chance.

POST

Main Post Office (22 rue Bivouac Napoléon; ⊙ 8am-7pm Mon-Fri, 8am-noon Sat). Has currency exchange and ATM.

TOURIST INFORMATION

Cannes Info Jeunesse office (☎ 04 93 06 31 31; 5 quai St-Pierre—La Pantiéro; ⊙ 8.30am-12.30pm & 2-5pm Mon-Fri)

STARRING AT CANNES

For 12 days in May, Cannes becomes the centre of the cinematic universe. Over 30,000 producers, distributors, directors, publicists, stars and hangers-on descend on Cannes each year to buy, sell or promote more than 2000 films. As the premier film event of the year, it attracts some 4000 journalists from around the world, guaranteeing a global spotlight to anyone with enough looks or prestige to grab it.

When the festival is in town La Croisette bursts into life. Sleek men and women stride down the boulevard, barking into their mobile phones in dozens of languages. The tuxedos and evening gowns come out at night for lavish and highly exclusive parties at the Carlton, Majestic or Noga Hilton hotels. Meanwhile, the uninvited mass around the stars as they emerge from chauffeured limos to climb the red carpeted stairs into the Palais des Festivals.

At the centre of the whirlwind is the 60,000-sq-metres Palais des Festivals (Festival Palace; dubbed 'the bunker' by locals) where the official selections are screened. Its stark concrete base is adorned with the hand prints and autographs of celebrities – Brigitte Bardot, David Lynch, Johnny Halliday and the like.

The palace was built to accommodate the first Cannes Film Festival, scheduled for 1 September 1939 as a response to Mussolini's fascist propaganda film festival in Venice. Hitler's invasion of Poland forced an abrupt end to the festival but it restarted in 1946. And the rest is history.

Over the years the festival split into 'in competition' and 'out of competition' sections. The goal of 'in competition' films is the prestigious Palme d'Or, awarded by the jury and its president to the film that best 'serves the evolution of cinematic art'. Notable winners include Francis Ford Coppola's *Apocalypse Now* (1979), David Lynch's *Wild at Heart* (1990), Mike Leigh's *Secrets and Lies* (1996) and Lars van Trier's *Dancer in the Dark* (2000). The 2004 winner was documentary maker and political agitator Michael Moore with his anti-Bush administration polemic *Fahrenheit 9/11*.

The vast majority of films are 'out of competition'. Behind the scenes there's the Marché (marketplace), where an estimated US$200 million worth of business is negotiated over distribution deals for obscure movies that won't be coming to a theatre near you.

The combination of hard-core commerce and Tinseltown glitz gives the film festival its special magic. For a concentrated dose, put on your best clothes, straighten your shoulders and march confidently into the bar of the Majestic in the early evening.

Getting film tickets to the Cannes Film Festival is governed by a complex system of passes that clearly determine who gets entry to which film. Unless you are somehow connected to the film industry and apply well in advance, you will not get a pass. What you can get are free tickets to selected individual films, usually after their first screening. Look for the booth of the **Cannes Cinephiles** (☎ 04 93 99 04 04), outside the Palais des Festivals, which distributes film tickets daily from 9am to 5.30pm. For the film festival programme, consult the official website www.festival-cannes.org.

Tourist Office (☎ 04 92 99 84 22; www.cannes.com; ☽ 9am-8pm daily Jul & Aug, 9am-7pm Mon-Sat Sep-Jun) On the ground floor of the Palais des Festivals.
Tourist Office Annexe (☎ 04 93 99 19 77; ☽ 9am-7pm Mon-Sat) Next to the train station.

Musée de la Castre

Musée de la Castre (☎ 04 93 38 55 26; adult/concession €3/2; ☽ 10am-1pm & 3-7pm Tue-Sun Jun-Aug, 10am-1pm & 2-6pm Tue-Sun Apr, May & Sep, 10am-1pm & 2-5pm Wed-Mon Oct-Mar), housed in the chateau atop Le Suquet, has a diverse collection of Mediterranean and Middle Eastern antiquities, as well as objects of ethnographic interest from all over the world.

Beaches

Unlike Nice, Cannes is endowed with a beach of the sandy variety, most of which is sectioned off for guests of the fancy hotels lining blvd de la Croisette. Sun worshippers pay around €19 a day for the privilege of stretching out in a lounge chair and another €6 for a parasol. This arrangement leaves only a small strip of sand near the Palais des Festivals for the bathing pleasure of picnicking hoi polloi. Free public beaches, **Plages du Midi** and **Plages de la Bocca**, stretch for several kilometres westwards from the Vieux Port along blvd Jean Hibert and blvd du Midi.

Tours

Cannes makes a good base for boat trips up and down the coast. **Trans Côte d'Azur** (☎ 04 92 98 71 30; www.trans-cote-azur.com; quai St-Pierre) runs boats to St-Tropez or Monaco (adult/child €31/16 return), Île de Porquerolles (€46/21) and San Remo (Italy; €41/19.50).

Sleeping

Hotel prices in Cannes fluctuate wildly according to the season. Prices given are for the high season in July and August; rooms can be 50% cheaper in the low season. Don't even consider staying in Cannes during the May film festival unless you've booked months in advance. Most upmarket places only accept 12-day bookings during this time.

If you still want to try, get in touch with **Cannes Réservation** (☎ 08 26 00 06 06; www.cannes-reservation.com; 8 blvd d'Alsace; ☽ 7am-7pm Mon-Sat).

BUDGET

Le Chalit (☎ 04 93 99 22 11; www.le-chalit.com; 27 av du Maréchal Galliéni; dm Apr-Sep €20, Oct-Mar €18, film festival €25-30, sheets €3; reception ☽ 8.30am-1pm & 5-8.30pm) Around 300m northwest of the station, this is one very pleasant private hostel. There is one kitchen with a food and drinks machine. There is no curfew. From July to September reservations are only accepted if you book three or more nights.

Hôtel Florella (☎ 04 93 38 48 11; fax 04 93 99 22 15; 55 blvd de la République; s/d with washbasin €40/45, with shower & toilet €60/64) A bit tatty but friendly, homely and good value.

Le Chanteclair (☎ /fax 04 93 39 68 88; 12 rue Forville; s/d with washbasin €33/36, with shower & toilet €40/42) This is a well-run hotel with functional whitewashed rooms in the colourful Le Suquet area, so it is close to many of the restaurants and the harbour.

Hôtel de Bourgogne (☎ 04 93 38 36 73; www.hotel-de-bourgogne.com; 11 rue du 24 Août; s/d with washbasin €33/40, d with shower/shower & toilet €55/65) The Bourgogne is a calm, orderly establishment with large, old-fashioned but rather dimly lit rooms.

Hôtel National (☎ 04 93 39 91 92; fax 04 92 98 44 06; 8 rue Maréchal Joffre; s/d €45/60; ⌨) A friendly, well-kept establishment. The well-equipped, newly furnished rooms are soundproofed, have TVs and hairdryers. Reserve and try to get a room overlooking the courtyard.

Camping

Parc Bellevue (☎ 04 93 47 28 97; fax 04 93 48 66 25; 67 av Maurice Chevalier, Cannes-La Bocca; camping for 2 adults, tent & car €20; ☽ Apr-Sep) About 5.5km west of the centre. The No 9 bus from the bus station on place Bernard Cornut Gentille stops 400m away.

MID-RANGE

Hôtel Florian (☎ 04 93 39 24 82; fax 04 92 99 18 30; 31 rue Commandant André; s/d €62/72; ⌨) Central, neat and modern. All rooms have private baths, TVs, telephones and hairdryers.

Hôtel Atlantis (☎ 04 93 39 18 72; www.cannes-hotel-atlantis.com; 4 rue de 24 Août; s/d with TV & minibar Jul & Aug €58/80, low season €42/50; ⌨ 🖵) This hotel has cheerful rooms with hairdryers, TVs and telephones. There's a spa and sauna for guests, plus cheaper use of a private beach (€7).

Alan Robert's Hôtel (☎ 04 93 38 05 07; www.cannes-hotels.com; 16 rue Jean Jaurès; s/d €54/65; ⌨) Inside a handsome, classical building opposite the train station, you'll find large-ish, soundproofed rooms all with satellite TV and telephones.

Hôtel Alizé (☎ 04 93 39 62 17; www.alizecannes.com; 29 rue Bivouac Napoléon; s/d €49/56; ❄ ▢) The rooms are not huge, you may recoil at the fake satin bedcovers and the early '90s décor but this remains a very central bet and, style aside, the rooms are well equipped (all have hairdryers, phones, satellite TV and a personal safe).

Hôtel Molière (☎ 04 93 38 16 16; www.hotel-moliere.com; 5 rue Molière; s/d from €79/97; ❄) This is an immaculate, comfortable period place with a picture postcard garden and a pastel-pink, wedding-cake exterior. Some rooms have balconies.

TOP END

During the film festival, Cannes' stratospherically expensive hotels are abuzz with the frantic comings-and-goings of journalists, paparazzi and stars. All of the top-end hotels are along blvd de la Croisette.

Grand Hôtel (☎ 04 93 38 15 45; www.grand-hotel-cannes.com; 45 blvd de la Croisette; s/d high season €168/198, low season €100/122) The Grand has an appealing if perhaps somewhat 1960s ambience and, compared to its neighbours on La Croisette, offers affordable luxury.

Hôtel Martinez (☎ 04 92 98 73 00; www.hotel-martinez.com; 73 blvd de la Croisette; r high season from €490, low season €260) Arguably the loveliest luxury place in town is an ultrasmart Art Deco-styled place with huge, fabulous rooms and a posh Givenchy Spa (treatments €40 to €160).

Other luxury places along la Croisette:

Carlton Inter-Continental (☎ 04 93 06 40 06; www.intercontinental.com; 58 blvd de la Croisette)

Noga Hilton (☎ 04 92 99 70 00; www.cannes.hilton.com; 50 blvd de la Croisette)

Eating

Rue du Marché Forville is the area for the few less expensive restaurants. There are lots of little, though not necessarily cheap, restaurants along rue St-Antoine and rue du Suquet.

Barbarella (☎ 04 92 99 17 33; 14-16 rue St-Dizier; dishes €10-18; ☺ 7pm-1am) An eye-catching, gay-friendly establishment.

Le petit Lardon (☎ 04 93 39 06 28; 3 rue du Batéguier; menus €21; ☺ lunch & dinner Tue-Sat) This place is small, intimate, friendly and reliable for reasonably priced local fare, such as *soupe de poisson* (fish soup) and *anchoiade* (anchovies, garlic and olive oil paste).

Astoux & Brun (☎ 04 93 39 21 87; 21 rue Félix Faure; menu €28; ☺ 10am-1am) *The* place for seafood.

Every type and size of oyster is available by the dozen here, as well as elaborate fish platters, scallops and mussels stuffed with garlic and parsley. In summer chefs draw the crowds by preparing the shellfish out front.

Aux Bons Enfants (80 rue Meynadier; menu €17; ☺ closed Sun & dinner Sat low season) Another, popular choice, offers regional dishes like *aïoli garni* (garlic mayonnaise with a platter of fresh vegies) and *mesclun* (a rather bitter salad of dandelion greens and other greenery) in a convivial atmosphere. It's also strong on fish. Credit cards are not accepted.

There are several other small restaurants at this end of rue Meynadier.

La Piazza (☎ 04 92 98 60 80; 9 place Bernard Cornut Gentille; mains €12, menu €19; ☺ lunch & dinner) A sprawling, friendly establishment that offers the best home-made pasta, risotto and pizza in town.

Au Rich-Lieu (☎ 04 93 39 98 75; 66 rue Meynadier; meals €15/20/24; ☺ lunch & dinner) If you love mussels you get unlimited quantities here (with fries) for only €9.20. Fish dishes and pizza are also available.

Sushikan (☎ 04 93 39 86 13; 5 rue Florian; dishes €2.50-4.50; ☺ lunch & dinner) This place is a smart sushi-on-a-conveyor-belt place that also does takeaways.

CAFÉS

Coffeehouses, cafés and *salons de thé* abound in upmarket Cannes.

Lenotre (☎ 04 92 92 56 00; 63 rue d'Antibes; breakfast around €7, lunch around €12; ☺ 8am-4.30pm) With a serene, classy dining room above the patisserie counter, the Lenotre is a great place to sip espresso, take breakfast or enjoy a light lunch of tarts and pastries among well-to-do ladies who lunch.

La Tarterie (☎ 04 93 39 67 43; 33 rue Bivouac Napoléon; ☺ 8.30am-4.30pm) The range of salads from €6 to €8 is good, but it's the house specialities – tarts and *clafoutis* (a kind of tart with fruit baked in a sweet batter) for €3 to €5 a slice – that bring in the crowds.

SELF-CATERING

The daily **food market** (place Gambetta; ☺ closed Mon in winter) is one of Cannes' main markets. **Marché Forville** (rue du Marché Forville), a fruit and vegetable market two blocks north of place Bernard Cornut Gentille, is open every morning except Monday (when a flea market takes its place).

Square Lord Brougham, next to the Vieux Port, is a great place for a picnic – buy filled baguettes and other lunch-time snacks from **Boulangerie-Pâtisserie** (12 rue Maréchal Foch) or go upmarket at **Lenotre** (see opposite) nearby. Locals go to **Ceneri** (22 rue Meynadier) for its wondrous cheeses.

Large supermarkets:

Champion Supermarket (6 rue Meynadier).

Monoprix Supermarket (9 rue Maréchal Foch) Take the second entrance on the corner of rue Jean Jaurès and rue Buttura.

Drinking

Generally speaking the streets north of blvd de la Croisette between the Grand Hotel and the rue des États Unis offer the best night-time bar (and club) hopping potential. La Croisette is of course the best place for a posey coffee while you take in its strange parade.

Bar La Renaissance (☎ 04 93 38 38 20; cnr rue Teisseire & rue Marceau) Small and cosy Renaissance, overlooking the bustling place Gambetta market, is a very down-to-earth bar. Black-and-white photos of yesterday's stars line the walls – a pleasant contrast to the simple wooden tables and chairs.

Morrisson's Irish Pub (☎ 04 92 98 16 17; 10 rue Teisseire; ☺ 5pm-2am) is very Dublin, but French-style. Guinness flows freely weekend nights. There's live music on Wednesday, Thursday and Sunday and happy hour is between 5pm and 8pm.

Entertainment

Ask the tourist office for a copy of the free monthly *Le Mois à Cannes,* which lists what's on and where. Nondubbed films are screened from time to time at the cinemas along rue Félix Faure and rue d'Antibes.

NIGHTCLUBS & DISCOS

Cannes' nightlife becomes world class during the film festival. Autograph hunters and stalkers of the A-list can track down their stalkees at some classy places:

Amiral Bar (Hôtel Martinez; see opposite; ☺ 9am-2.30am) A swanky, upmarket place in the fabulous Hotel Martinez that enables you to rub shoulders with glamorous company, at a price.

Jimmy'z (☎ 04 92 98 78 00; Palais des Festivals, blvd de la Croisette; ☺ midnight-dawn daily Jun-Sep, Fri, Sat & Sun rest of year) The Cannes branch of the legendary Monaco club.

Le Bar des Célébrités (☎ 04 93 06 40 06; 58 blvd de la Croisette; ☺ 11am-at least 1am) At the Carlton Inter-Continental.

Le Loft (☎ 04 93 39 40 39; 13 rue du Dr Gérard; ☺ 10.30am-2.30am Mon-Sat) A more low-key place.

You may or may not see celebrities at the following places, but you'll certainly rub shoulders with local rich kids.

Cat Corner (☎ 04 93 39 31 31; 22 rue Macé; ☺ 11pm-5am) There's a sniffy door policy, so try to look fabulous. Inside you'll mingle with beautiful people from around the globe.

Les Coulisses (☎ 04 932 99 17 17; 29 rue Commandant André; ☺ 6pm-2.30am) A glam bar close to the seafront.

Le Vogue (☎ 04 93 39 99 18; 20 rue du Suquet; ☺ 7pm-2.30am Tue-Sat) Draws a young and trendy crowd up to Le Suquet.

Zanzibar (☎ 04 93 39 30 75; 85 rue Félix Faure; ☺ 6pm-4am) The oldest and most venerable gay bar on the coast. Pretty boys party to house music beneath erotically evocative ceiling frescoes.

Getting There & Away
BUS

The train is usually quicker and cheaper if you want to go up and down the coast, but for trips to the interior, you'll have to take a bus. Buses to Nice (€5.90, 1½ hours, every 20 minutes), Nice airport (€12.70 for the 40-minute trip via the autoroute, €2.20 for the 1½-hour trip via the regular road, hourly from 8am to 7pm) and other destinations leave from place Bernard Cornut Gentille, next to Hôtel de Ville in Cannes centre. Most are operated by **Rapides Côte d'Azur** (information office ☎ 04 93 39 11 39).

TRAIN

There's an **information desk** (rue Jean Jaurès) at the train station, but no left-luggage office.

Destinations within easy reach include St-Raphaël (€5.50, 20 minutes, two an hour), from where you can get buses to St-Tropez and Toulon. Other destinations include Nice (€5.20, 40 minutes, two per hour) and Marseille (€22.30, two hours).

Getting Around
BUS

Serving Cannes and destinations up to 7km away from town is **Bus Azur** (☎ 08 25 82 55 99, 04 93 45 20 08; place Bernard Cornut Gentille). Its office is in the same building as Rapides Côte d'Azur.

CÔTE D'AZUR & MONACO

Single/10 tickets cost €1.30/8.50. Bus No 8 runs along the coast from place Bernard Cornut Gentille to the port and Palm Beach Casino on Pointe de la Croisette.

CAR & MOTORCYCLE

Car-rental agency **JKL** (☎ 04 97 06 37 77; www.jkl -forrent.com; 59 Angle de la Croisette) offers cars fit for a star (if you absolutely, positively have to get noticed, how about a yellow Humvee for €1000 a day?). Even if you don't have a Hummer, street parking can be a nightmare in Cannes, but there are plenty of pay car parks, which charge at least €2 an hour. The easiest park to get to is the Palais underground car park right next to the tourist office. The easy-to-spot entry is off blvd de la Croisette.

Alliance Location (☎ 04 93 38 62 62; 19 rue des Frères Pradignac) rents motorcycles (from €53 a day) and scooters (€38), as well as mobile phones (€11 plus calls).

TAXI

Taxis (☎ 04 93 38 91 91, 04 93 49 59 20) can be ordered by phone.

ÎLES DE LÉRINS

Two islands make up the Lérins and they are just a 20-minute boat ride from Cannes. The tiny eucalyptus- and pine-covered **Île Ste-Marguerite** is 1km from the mainland. It's where the enigmatic Man in the Iron Mask – immortalised by Alexandre Dumas in his novel *Le Vicomte de Bragelonne* (The Viscount of Bragelonne) and in the more recent 1998 Hollywood release *The Man in the Iron Mask* – was held during the late 17th century.

The island, home to 20 families and measuring only 3.25km by 1km, is encircled and crisscrossed by trails and paths. **Musée de la Mer** (☎ 04 93 38 55 26; adult/child €3/2; museum & cells 🕑 10.30am-1.15pm & 2.15-5.45pm Wed-Mon Apr-Sep, to 4.45pm Wed-Mon Oct-Mar), in the Fort Royal, has interesting exhibits dealing with the fort's history and various ships that have been wrecked off the island's coast. The door to the left as you enter leads to the old state prisons, built under Louis XIV and the home in 1685 to Huguenots imprisoned for their refusal to renounce their Protestant faith. The inventor of the steam boat, Claude François Dorothée, is said to have come up with the idea while in prison here in 1773.

The smaller, forested **Île St-Honorat**, which is just 1.5km long and 400m wide, was once the site of a renowned and powerful monastery founded in the 5th century. Today it is home to Cistercian monks who own the island but welcome people to visit their monastery and seven small chapels dotted around the island.

Neither island has a fantastic beach; in some places, sunbathers lie on mounds of dried seaweed. Camping, cycling and smoking are forbidden on both islands. There are no hotels, *gîtes* or camping areas.

All boats leave from the same point on the quai des Îles (along from Quai Max Laubeuf) on the western side of the harbour. **Compagnie Maritime Cannoise** (CMC; ☎ 04 93 38 66 33) runs ferries to Île Ste-Marguerite (€9 return, 20 minutes), while **Compagnie Estérel Chanteclair** (☎ 04 93 39 11 82) operates boats to Île St-Honorat (€10 return, 20 minutes, almost hourly between 7.30am and 4pm).

Trans Côte d'Azur (see p837) charges €10 for trips to/from Ste-Marguerite. **Les Bateaux de St-Raphaël** (see p843) has daily excursions to the islands.

GRASSE

pop 44,790

For centuries Grasse, with its distinct red and orange tile roofs rising up the slopes of the pre-Alps, has been one of France's most important centres of perfume production, along with Paris and Montpellier. Perfume is a natural product of the highly prized flowers – lavender, jasmine, centifolia roses, mimosa, orange blossom and violets – you'll see growing profusely in the countryside.

Orientation & Information

While the town of Grasse and its suburbs sprawl over a wide area of hill and valley, the old city is a small area, densely packed into the hillside. The N85, better known as Route Napoléon, runs right through Grasse, where it becomes the town's main (and often very congested) thoroughfare, blvd du Jeu de Ballon.

The tourist office marked **Grasse Espace Accueil** (☎ 04 93 36 21 68; www.grasse-riviera.com; place de la Foux; 🕑 9am-7pm Mon-Sat, 9am-1pm & 2-6pm Sun Jul-Sep, 9am-12.30pm & 2-6pm Mon-Sat Oct-Jun) is close to the bus station.

In town, there's a tiny **tourist office** (☎ 04 93 36 66 66; 22 cours Honoré Cresp; 🕑 9am-7pm daily ul-Sep, 9am-12.30pm & 2-6pm Mon-Fri Oct-Jun) inside the Palais de Congrès.

Banks abound on blvd du Jeu de Ballon. You can also change money at the **Change du Casino** (☎ 04 93 36 48 48; Palais de Congrès).

Perfumeries

While more than 40 perfumeries exist in Grasse, only a few are open to the public, offering free visits to their showrooms and an introduction to the art of perfume making. During the tour you'll be taken through every stage of perfume production, from extraction and distillation to the work of the 'noses'. It's unlikely that you'll know any of the perfumeries by name, as the perfumes are sold only from their factories or by mail order. Naturally there is a boutique attached to each perfumery where you can buy the house scents in all their forms, from essences to talcum powder. The perfumes are bewitching and less expensive than store-bought fragrances, but the scent usually doesn't linger long.

Fragonard (☎ 04 93 36 44 65; 20 blvd Fragonard; 9am-6.30pm Jun-Sep, 9am-12.30pm & 2-6pm Oct-May) is the most convenient perfumery if you're on foot.

Galimard (☎ 04 93 09 20 00; 73 route de Cannes; 9am-6.30pm Jun-Sep, 9am-12.30pm & 2-6pm Oct-May) is not far from Fragonard's factory, about 3km out of town. Unless you have wheels, a visit is not a feasible option.

Close by is Galimard's **Studio des Fragrances** (☎ 04 93 09 20 00; 5 route de Pégomas), where you can create your own unique fragrance during a seminar under the guidance of a professional *nez* (€34, two hours).

Molinard (☎ 04 92 42 33 11, 04 93 36 01 62; 60 blvd Victor Hugo; 9am-6.30pm Mon-Sat Jul-Sep, 9am-12.30pm & 2-6pm Mon-Sat Oct-Jun) is a much ritzier affair, with 'create your own perfume' sessions (€40, 1¼ hours) that include a seminar about the history of perfume, after which participants walk away with a Molinard diploma.

Getting There & Away

There's a **ticket office** at the bus station (☎ 04 93 36 08 43; place de la Buanderie; to 5.15pm). Several companies operate from here. **Rapides Côte d'Azur** (☎ 04 93 36 49 61) has buses to Nice (€6.30, 1¼ hours) via Cannes (€3.80, 45 minutes) every 30 minutes (hourly on Sunday).

MASSIF DE L'ESTÉREL

The most stunning natural feature of the entire Côte d'Azur (apart from the azure-blue sea) is the lump of red porphyry rock known as the Massif de l'Estérel. Covered by pine, oak and eucalyptus trees, this range is situated between St-Raphaël and Mandelieu-La Napoule, which is inland from Cannes.

A drive or walk along the Corniche de l'Estérel (also known as the Corniche d'Or and the N98), the coastal road that runs along the base of the range, is not to be missed as the views are spectacular. Along the way you will find many small summer resorts and inlets where you can swim. Some of the places worth visiting include **Le Dramont**, where the 36th US Division landed on 15 August 1944; **Agay**, a sheltered bay with an excellent beach; the resorts of **Le Trayas** and **Théoule-sur-Mer**; and **Mandelieu-La Napoule**, a pleasant resort with a large pleasure-boat harbour near a fabulously restored 14th-century castle. In summer when the Corniche de l'Estérel gets very crowded, choose the inland N7, which runs through the hills and feels like a whole different world.

There are all sorts of walks you can take in the Massif de l'Estérel, but for the more difficult trails you will need to come equipped with a good map, such as IGN's *Série Bleue* (1:25,000) No 3544ET. Many of the walks, such as those up to Pic de l'Ours (496m) and Pic du Cap Roux (452m), are signposted.

FRÉJUS & ST-RAPHAËL
pop 47,897 & pop 31,196

Fréjus, first settled by Massiliots (the Greeks who founded Marseille) and colonised by Julius Caesar around 49 BC as Forum Julii, is known for its Roman ruins. Once an important port, the town was sacked by various invaders, including the Saracens in the 10th century. Much of the town's commercial activity ceased after its harbour silted up in the 16th century. The ruins are often busy, but the lively town centre, with its rows of low, pastel buildings and shady plazas, is usually unclogged with tourists, leaving an appealing Provençal ambience.

At the foot of the Massif de l'Estérel is St-Raphaël, a beachside resort town southeast of Fréjus. St-Raphaël was one of the main landing bases of US and French troops in August 1944.

PROVENÇAL WINE AT A GLANCE

Long known for its rosé but little else, the region offers a wealth of great wines of all types and colours. There are more and more terrific little producers out there making excellent reds and whites. A good way to start planning tastings is with the free *Wine Routes of Provence* booklet and the excellent, unpretentious *100 Top Vineyards in Provence* (€10.50) by British resident and wine buff Ian Parkin, both available at the Maison des Vins Côtes de Provence (p847) and, if you're lucky, other tourist offices in the area.

Côtes de Provence
A large, geographically diverse appellation, with a variety of soils, altitudes and microclimates stretching roughly in the triangle between Aix-en-Provence, Toulon and St-Raphaël, means there's no such thing as a typical Côtes de Provence. Rosé makes up 75% of production.

Coteaux Varois
An island of vineyards around Brignoles (surrounded by Côtes de Provence vineyards), this appellation, which produces mostly rosé, is shaking off a reputation for mass-produced blandness. Quality is improving all the time.

Coteaux d'Aix
Half the wine made in this geographically broad appellation (stretching from Les Baux de Provence across to Aix-en-Provence and down to the salty Étang de Berre) is an usually fruity rosé but there are some well-regarded Bordeaux-style reds too.

There are a few smaller appellations well worth sampling including **Bandol** (especially for beefy, heavy, sometimes tanniny reds) **Cassis** (for delicate whites), **Muscat de Beaumes de Venise** (for sweet white) and **Bellet** (a tiny, obscure and expensive appellation better known for its whites and a good to name drop if you need to get the better of a sniffy *sommelier*).

Orientation

Although St-Raphaël is 2km from Fréjus, the suburbs of both have become so intertwined they seem almost to form a single town. Fréjus comprises the hillside Fréjus Ville, about 3km from the seafront, and Fréjus Plage, on the Golfe de Fréjus. The Roman remains are mostly in Fréjus Ville.

Information

MONEY
Banque National de Paris (BNP; rue Jean Jaurès) Just west of the Fréjus tourist office and there's an ATM.

POST
Fréjus Post Office (264 av Aristide Briand)
Post Office Branch (blvd de la Libération) Opposite the tourist office kiosk in Fréjus.
St-Raphaël Post Office (av Frédéric Mistral) East of the tourist office.

TOURIST INFORMATION
Fréjus Tourist Office (☎ 04 94 51 83 83; www.ville -frejus.fr in French; 325 rue Jean Jaurès; ☼ 9am-noon &

2-6pm Mon-Sat year-round, plus 10am-noon & 2-6pm Sun Jul & Aug) Staff make hotel reservations and distribute an excellent map of Fréjus locating its archaeological treasures.
St-Raphaël Tourist Office (☎ 04 94 19 52 52; www .saint-raphael.com; rue Waldeck Rousseau; ☼ 9am-7pm daily Jul & Aug, 9am-12.30pm & 2-6.30pm Mon-Sat Sep-Jun) Across the street from the train station.
Tourist Office Kiosk (☎ 04 94 51 48 42; ☼ 10am-noon & 3-7pm daily Jun–mid-Sep) By the beach opposite 11 blvd de la Libération in Fréjus.

Roman Ruins

West of Fréjus' old city (past the Porte des Gaules) is the mostly rebuilt 1st- and 2nd-century **arènes** (amphitheatre; ☎ 04 94 51 34 31; rue Henri Vadon; ☼ 10am-1pm & 2.30-6.30pm Mon-Sat Apr-Oct, 10am-noon & 1.30-5.30pm Mon-Fri, 9.30am-12.30pm & 1.30-5.30pm Sat Nov-Mar). The amphitheatre once seated an audience of 10,000 and is today used for rock concerts and bullfights.

At the southeastern end of rue des Moulins is **Porte d'Orée**, the only arcade of the thermal baths still standing. North of the old town are the remains of a **Roman theatre** (rue du Théâtre Romain; ☺ as for amphitheatre).

Le Groupe Épiscopal

On place Formigé, on the site of a Roman temple, is an episcopal ensemble, comprising an 11th- and 12th-century **cathedral** (☎ 04 94 51 26 30). One of the first Gothic buildings in the area, it retains certain Roman features. The carved wooden doors at the entrance were added during the Renaissance.

To the left of the cathedral is the octagonal 5th-century **baptistry**, with a Roman column on each of its eight corners. Stairs from the entrance porch lead up to the stunning 12th- and 13th-century **cloister**, which features some of the columns of the Roman temple and painted wooden ceilings from the 14th and 15th centuries. It looks onto a courtyard with a well-tended garden.

In the cathedral's cloister is the **Musée Archéologique** (Archaeological Museum; adult/student €3.80/2.50; ☺ 10am-1pm & 2.30-6.30pm Mon & Wed-Sat Apr-Oct, 10am-noon & 1.30-5.30pm Mon & Wed-Sat Nov-Mar), which has a marble statue of Hermes, a head of Jupiter, and a stunning 3rd-century mosaic depicting a leopard. Admission includes entry to the baptistry and cloister.

Activities

Fréjus Plage, lined with buildings from the 1950s, and St-Raphaël both have excellent sandy **beaches**.

St-Raphaël is a leading **diving** centre, thanks in part to the **WWII shipwrecks** off the coast. Most diving clubs in town organise dives to the wrecks, which range from a 42m-long US minesweeper to a landing craft destroyed by a rocket in 1944 during the Allied landings.

Plongée 83 (☎ 04 94 95 27 18; 29 av de la Gare, St-Raphaël) and **CIP** (☎ 04 94 52 34 99; Fréjus east port) organise night and day dives and courses for beginners.

Tours

Les Bateaux de St-Raphaël (☎ 04 94 95 17 46; fax 04 94 83 84 55; Gare Maritime, St-Raphaël) organises daily boat excursions from St-Raphaël to the Îles de Lérins (€16 return), and daily boats to St-Tropez and Port Grimaud (€13 return).

Sleeping & Eating

BUDGET

Auberge de Jeunesse Fréjus-St-Raphaël (☎ 04 94 53 18 75; fax 04 94 53 25 86; chemin du Counillier; dm incl breakfast €14) Near Fréjus Ville, in a 7-hectare park. If you arrive by train, get off at St-Raphaël, take bus No 7 and walk up the hill. In July and August bus No 6 goes directly to the hostel. From Fréjus' train station or from place Paul Vernet, bus No 3 is the best option.

Hôtel Riviera (☎ 04 94 51 31 46; fax 04 94 17 18 34; 90 rue Grisolle, Fréjus; r with shower €32, with shower & toilet €34, with bath & toilet €36) A backpackers' hotel in the best sense of the word. The rambling old building and dark but neat rooms are kept in good shape by a friendly young couple who clearly enjoy their clientele. The hotel has a **restaurant** (main course & 0.25L wine €9).

Camping

Holiday Green (☎ 04 94 19 88 30; www.holiday-green .com; route de Bagnols, Fréjus; camping €30; ☺ Apr-end Sep) This is a four-star place and one of the best of the dozen or so camping grounds around Fréjus. It's 7km from the beach but has its own large pool.

MID-RANGE

L'Aréna (☎ 04 94 17 09 40; www.arena-hotel.com; 145 rue du Général de Gaulle, Fréjus; s €60-80, d €80-160; menus €35/45/55; P ☒ ▣ ☎) The Arena is a simply delightful hotel with a flower-lined garden terrace, where you can eat wonderful breakfasts or lounge by the pool. The rooms are bright and summery, there's a decent **restaurant** serving refined and imaginative food and it's about 1km from the beaches. Highly recommended; with disabled access.

Hôtel L'Oasis (☎ 04 94 51 50 44; fax 04 94 53 01 04; www.hotel-oasis.net; impasse Jean-Baptiste Charcot, Fréjus Plage; r €38-65; ☺ mid-Feb–Oct; P ☒) A 27-room place set amid pine trees, with comfortable rooms with TV. There is also disabled access.

Hôtel Le Flore (☎ 04 94 51 38 35; fax 04 94 55 59 89; 35 rue Grisolle; s/d €53/56) The Flore is a two-star hotel on a main street. A couple of the front rooms have balconies.

Getting There & Away

Bus No 5, run by **Forum Cars** (in Fréjus ☎ 04 94 95 16 71), links Fréjus train station and place Paul Vernet with St-Raphaël.

Fréjus and St-Raphaël are on the train line from Nice to Marseille. There's a frequent service (€9.20, 95 minutes) from Nice to **St-Raphaël-Valescure train station** (information office ☎ 08 92 35 35 35; ⏰ 9.15am-1pm & 2.30-6pm), southeast of the centre.

ST-TROPEZ

pop 5542

A destination for the jet-set, the Eurotrashy and, in summer, too many visitors for comfort, St-Tropez has long since ceased to be the quiet, charming, isolated fishing village that attracted artists, writers and the glitterati here in the 20th century. The year things really changed for good was 1956 when *Et Dieu Créa la Femme* (And God Created Woman) starring Brigitte Bardot was shot here. Its stunning success brought about St-Tropez's rise to stardom – or destruction, depending on your point of view.

Attempts to keep St-Tropez small and exclusive have created at least one tangible result in the busiest summer months: you'll probably crawl into town behind huge traffic queues. Yachts, so out of proportion to the size of the old harbour that they block the view, chased away simple fishing boats a long time ago. And while painters and their easels jostle each other for space along the quay, in summer there's little of the intimate village air that artists (such as the pointillist Paul Signac) found so alluring.

But for all that it's still a place of interest and even, still, charm. Sitting in a café on place des Lices in late May, watching the locals engage in a game of *pétanque* (bowls) in the shade of the age-old plane trees, you could be in any little Provençal village (if you squint to ignore the exclusive boutiques and the expensive threads on display, that is).

St-Tropez is a fascinating place to watch the rich and famous at play, and a surprising proportion of the film, music and sporting A-list holiday here each summer. To get up close to them (apart from ogling them aboard their boats from the quayside cafés) it helps to be famous too – or rich at least. The clubs, restaurants, private beaches and hotels they patronise are seriously pricey and/or selective.

Orientation

St-Tropez lies at the end of a narrow peninsula on the southern side of the narrow Bay of St-Tropez, opposite the Massif des Maures. The old city, with its narrow streets, is packed between quai Jean Jaurès

(the main quay of Vieux Port), place de Lices (a lovely shady rectangular 'square' few blocks inland) and a handsome 16th century citadel overlooking the town from the northeast.

Information

Crédit Lyonnais (21 quai Suffren) At the port and there's an ATM.

Kreatik Café (☎ 04 94 97 40 61; 19 av Gal Lerclerc; ⏰ 10am-1am) The best place to go online.

Laverie du Port (quai de l'Épi; ⏰ 7am-10pm) Close to the town-facing edge of the car park near the port. A load will cost about €4.

Post Office (place Celli) One block from the port. There's also an exchange service.

Tourist Office (☎ 04 94 97 45 21; www.saint-tropez.st quai Jean Jaurès; ⏰ 9.30am-8.30pm Jul & Aug, 9.30am-12.30pm & 2-7pm Apr-Jun, Sep & Oct, 9.30am-12.30pm & 2-6pm Nov-Mar) It organises guided city tours (€6) every Thursday at 10.30am and distributes a wealth of informative brochures.

Sights

Musée de l'Annonciade (☎ 04 94 97 04 01; place Grammont, Vieux Port; adult/student €4.50/2.50; ⏰ 10am-noon & 3-7pm Wed-Mon Jun-Sep, 10am-noon & 2-6pm Wed-Mon Oct-May, closed Nov), in a disused chapel, contains an impressive collection of modern art, including works by Matisse, Bonnard, Dufy, Derain and Rouault. Signac, who set up his home and studio in St-Tropez, is well represented.

If you're bored with watching the antics of the rich and (maybe not so) famous, **Citadelle de St Tropez** (☎ 04 94 97 59 43; adult/concession €4/2.50; ⏰ 10am-12.30pm & 1.30-6.30pm Apr-Sep, 10am-12.30pm & 1.30-5.30pm Oct-Mar) is worth strolling to just for the views across the bay, a view you may share with the resident peacocks. Inside the citadel, which is just east of the town centre, there are displays recounting the town's maritime history and the Allied landings that took place here in 1944. The best photographs of St-Tropez can be taken from the citadel grounds.

Activities

BEACHES

About 4km southeast of the town is the start of a magnificent sandy beach, **Plage de Tahiti** and its continuation, Plage de Pampelonne. It runs for about 9km between Cap du Pinet and the rocky Cap Camarat. To get there on foot, head out of town along av de la Résistance (south of place des Lices) to route de la Belle Isnarde and then route de Tahiti. Otherwise, the bus to Ramatuelle, a village south of St-Tropez, stops at various points along a road that runs about 1km inland from the beach.

The coastline east of Toulon, from Le Lavandou to the St-Tropez peninsula (including spots around the peninsula), is well endowed with *naturiste* (nudist) beaches. Naturism is also legal in some other places, mostly in secluded spots or along sheltered streams further inland.

On the southern side of Cap Camarat is a secluded nudist beach, **Plage de l'Escalet**. Several streams around here also attract bathers in the buff. To get there you can take the bus to Ramatuelle, but you'll have to walk or, if lucky, hitch the 4km southeast to the beach. Closer to St-Tropez is **La Moutte**, a *naturiste* beach 4.5km east of town – take route des Salins, which runs between two of the houses owned by BB (as Bardot is known in France).

WALKING

The **Sentier Littoral** (Coastal Path) goes all the way south from St-Tropez to the beach of Cavalaire along some 35km of splendid rocky outcrops and hidden bays. In parts, the setting is reminiscent of the tropics minus the coconut palms. If the distance is too great, you can walk as far as Ramatuelle and return on the bus.

If you can read French, invest in the pocket-sized *Promenez-vous à Pied – Le Golfe de St-Tropez*, which details 26 walks around St-Tropez; buy a copy from the **Librairie du Port** (11 rue des Commerçants).

Sleeping
BUDGET & MID-RANGE

Surprise, surprise! There's not a cheap hotel to be found in St-Tropez. However, to the southeast along Plage de Pampelonne there are plenty of multistar camping grounds.

Le Baron (☎ 04 94 97 06 57; fax 04 94 97 58 72; 23 rue de l'Aïoli; r €54-100; ☒) Well worth the cash, Le Baron is calm and quiet. Rooms – all with TV and bathrooms – overlook the citadel. Some have balconies. Book ahead.

Lou Cagnard (☎ 04 94 97 00 24; www.hotel-lou -cagnard.com; 18 av Paul Roussel; r €44-100; P ☒) A very pleasant option with attractive rooms containing TVs and telephones, and in a

traditional Provençal *mas* (farmhouse) surrounded by shrubs and plants.

Hôtel La Méditerranée (☎ 04 94 97 00 44; www .hotelmediterranee.org; 21 blvd Louis Blanc; r high/low season €150/50; ☒) The Méditerranée is an excellent place, as the DJs who play the local bars and clubs will confirm to since they stay here. This solid, period house has recently refurbished rooms, a cosy restaurant and courtyard garden and a proprietor who can tell you where to find all the St-Trop hot spots.

TOP END

St-Tropez' top-end hotels are mostly open from early April to mid-October.

Le Yaca (☎ 04 94 55 81 00; www.hotel-le-yaca.fr; 1 blvd d'Aumale; s/d high season from €300/380, low season from €250/300; P ☒ ☒) A former home of the writer Collette and a place where artists such as Signac and Hollywood legends including Clark Cable have stayed – and where bigwigs continue to stay. This is *the* hotel for unashamed, indulgent relaxation. Lounge by the pool or feed the peacocks *pain au chocolat* from your balcony window at dawn. All rooms are beautifully and individually decorated and the better rooms have splendid views over town and the bay. The concierge can get you into any club or restaurant in town, so be nice to him.

Eating
RESTAURANTS

Quai Jean Jaurès is lined with restaurants, most with mediocre *menus* from €17 to €26 and a strategic view of the silverware and crystal of those dining on the decks of their yachts.

La Table du Marché (☎ 04 94 97 85 20; 38 rue Georges Clemenceau; lunch or dinner formule €18, menu €25; ☒ lunch & dinner) A great and stylish place for savoury and sweet pastries in the café at the front (daytime only), for sushi upstairs (summer only) or excellent, simple and reasonably priced brasserie style food (like the house terrine with onion chutney, scallop raviolis in thyme butter or tomato and basil tart) at the back.

Le Petit Charron (☎ 04 94 97 73 78; 5 rue Charrons; dishes €16-23; ☒ dinner Tue-Sat) Off place des Lices, this restaurant serves a delicious Provençal menu.

Le Fregate (☎ 04 94 97 07 08; 52-54 rue Allard; menus €19-27; ☒ lunch & dinner Thu-Tue) The blue and white décor here heralds the excellent fish dishes. Try the *aïoli* at €15 if it's on the daily offerings.

Auberge des Maures (☎ 04 94 97 01 50; 8 rue du Docteur Boutin; menu €40; ☽ dinner only) Off rue Allard, this place is not far from the port. The food is good, rich and traditional (such as fresh barbequed fish, rice-stuffed squid and a tasty crème caramel). The portions are hearty. Book ahead.

Café Joseph (☎ 04 94 97 01 66; 1 place de l'Hôtel de Ville; dishes €22-42; ☽ lunch & dinner) The constant beat of house music accompanies reliably decent food (inventive pasta dishes, good beef tartare), served to a very wealthy, often fabulous, sometimes strange, crowd of loyal locals. It's a tad pricey for what you get and the service can be snooty but the people-watching here is strangely compelling.

CAFÉS
Several cafés with vast, open-air terraces line quai Jean Jaurès. You will spend *beaucoup* to nurse a drink and watch tourists watching you, but if you must, try **Sénéquier** or **Le Gorille**.

Le Café (☎ 04 94 97 44 69; place des Lices) St-Tropez' most historic café, Le Café was one of the former haunts of BB and her glam friends and foes. Formally called Le Café des Arts, it should not to be confused with the place of that name on the corner of place des Lices and av du Maréchal Foch.

SELF-CATERING
The **place des Lices market** is held on Tuesday and Saturday mornings. There's also a **market** on place aux Herbes behind quai Jean Jaurès, open until about noon daily.

La Tarte Tropézienne (36 rue Georges Clemenceau) is a good way to beat the high food prices of St-Tropez. Sandwiches are made from freshly baked bread and you can finish up with the local speciality, *tarte Tropézienne*, a sweet sandwich filled with custard.

There's also the **Prisunic Supermarket** (9 av du Général Leclerc; ☽ 8am-8pm Mon-Sat).

Entertainment
If you think the cafés in town are expensive, then arrange an overdraft for the clubs: €13 to €25 is standard for a drink and you'll be watched to make sure you drink. Even if money is not a problem, getting in may be, so try to look fabulous. It will also help if you can say your first name is Paris or Puff and

your second name is Hilton or Daddy. Your reward for convincing the door staff will likely be admittance to the strange world of massive affluence and celebrity. Most bars open from around 11pm to dawn.

Le Café de Paris (☎ 04 94 97 00 56; Quai Suffren) Smart, lively and good for late-night carousing if the clubs don't appeal to you (or you to them).

Cohiba Café (☎ 04 94 97 26 20; 23 rue du Portail Neuf) This is a cosy, low-key place away from the quayside brouhaha. Knock back a cocktail or chew on a cigar from the humidor.

There are four clubs in town to try, all of them *trés en vogue*. Broadly speaking **Papagayo** (☎ 04 94 54 82 89; Residence du Port) and the gay-friendly **L'Esquinade** (☎ 04 94 97 87 45; 2 rue du Four) are slightly less picky about who they let in (although during May Papagayo becomes the official nightclub of the Cannes Film Festival) than the ultraswanky **VIP Room** (☎ 04 94 97 14 70; Residence du Port) or **Les Caves du Roy** (☎ 04 94 97 16 02; av Foch), another A-list celeb haunt.

Getting There & Away
BOAT
In July and August **MMG** (in Ste-Maxime ☎ 04 94 96 51 00) operates a shuttle-boat service from St-Tropez to Ste-Maxime and Port Grimaud. Between April and October, **Transports Maritimes Raphaelois** (in St-Raphaël ☎ 04 94 95 17 46) runs two to six boats daily from St-Tropez to St-Raphaël (€10, 50 minutes).

A day trip by boat from Nice or Cannes can be a good way to avoid St-Tropez' notorious traffic jams and high hotel prices. Trans Côte d'Azur runs day trips from Nice (see p824) and Cannes (see p837) between Easter and September.

BUS
St-Tropez **bus station** (av Général de Gaulle) is on the southwestern edge of town on the main road. There's an **information office** (☎ 04 94 54 62 36; ☽ 8am-noon & 2-6pm Mon-Fri, 8am-noon Sat) at the station. Buses to Ramatuelle (€8.30, 1½ hours, five daily) leave from the here and run parallel to the coast about 1km inland. **Sodetrav** (in Hyères ☎ 04 94 12 55 12) has eight buses daily from St-Raphaël-Valescure train station to St-Tropez bus station, via Fréjus (€7.60, 1¼ hours). Eight daily buses from St-Tropez to Toulon go inland before joining the coast at Cavalaire; they also stop at Le Lavandou and Hyères.

CAR
If you go to St-Tropez by car be prepared for long delays, both getting in and out of town. Here is a tip to minimise the frustration of waiting: avoid the coastal roads. Instead approach from the Provençale Autoroute (the A8) and exit at Le Muy (exit 35). Take the D558 road across the Massif des Maures and via La Garde Freinet to Port Grimaud. Park your car (easily) here and take the regular shuttle boat that runs to St-Tropez from Easter to October. Exit the same way.

Getting Around
MAS (☎ /fax 04 94 97 00 60; 3-5 rue Joseph Quaranta) rents mountain bikes. There are several car-hire places lining av du Général Leclerc.

To order a taxi ring ☎ 04 94 97 05 27. To order a taxi boat call **Taxi de Mer** (☎ 06 09 53 15 47; 5 quartier Neuf).

THE VAR HINTERLAND
Inland from St-Tropez and Fréjus, the dark-green wooded hills, sleepy hilltop villages and vineyards of the Var hinterland (broadly speaking north of the A8 and south of the Gorges du Verdon) are well worth a day or two of exploration if you have your own car. It's a great area in which to sample Provençal wines and makes a welcome escape from the crowded summer coast.

Villages and attractions worth stopping for include **Cabasse**, a quiet, shady village near a large trout-filled lake; **Tourtour**, a pretty hilltop village with views over the area's forests; and **Cotignac** an enchanting, plane-tree shaded town sitting below a cliff face peppered with grottos. Pure, fountains gush clear around the attractive town square and there are a couple of decent restaurants including **Hôtel Restaurant du Cours** (☎ 04 94 04 78 50; 18 cours Gambetta; menus €21-28), which serves tasty Provençal food.

Well worth the visit also is **Abbaye du Thoronet** (☎ 04 94 60 43 90; adult/child €6.10/free; 10am-6pm Mon-Sat, 10am-noon & 2-6.30pm Sun Sep, 10am-1pm & 2-5pm Mon-Sat, 10am-noon & 2-5pm Sun Oct-Mar), a remote, partly restored Cistercian monastery near Le Thoronet. The guided tours are well worthwhile and your guide may sing beautiful plainsong. The acoustics are incredible.

The area is one of the best places in Provence to sample a good range of its wines and to get an overview of many different styles. At Les Arcs-sur-Argens, on the N7, the **Maison des Vins Côtes de Provence** (☎ 04 94 99 50 29; 10am-8pm daily Jul & Aug, 10am-1pm & 1.30-6pm Mon-Sat Oct-Apr) offers free wine tastings and explanations in English.

For free maps of the area and brochures offering other itinerary ideas ask at the Toulon (p850) and Fréjus (p842) tourist offices.

ST-TROPEZ TO TOULON
Massif des Maures
Stretching from Hyères to Fréjus, this arc-shaped massif is covered with pine, chestnut and cork oak trees. The vegetation makes it appear almost black and gives rise to its name, which comes from the Provençal word *mauro* (dark pine wood).

The Massif des Maures offers superb walking and cycling opportunities. There are four roads you can take through the hills, the northernmost being a ridge road, the 85km-long **route des Crêtes**, which runs close to La Sauvette (779m), the massif's highest peak. It continues east through the village of **La Garde Freinet**, a perfect getaway from the summer hordes. Within the massif are a number of places worth visiting.

If you like chestnuts, the place to go is **Collobrières**, a small town renowned for its chestnut purée and *marrons glacés* (candied chestnuts). If you like wine, the area is a good place to sniff out some excellent Provençal nectar.

There are some interesting cultural sites too, such as the partly restored Cistertian **Abbaye de Thoronet** and, east of Collobrières, the ruins of a 12th- to 13th-century monastery, called **La Chartreuse de la Verne**. Northeast of the monastery is the village of **Grimaud**, notable for its castle ruins, small Roman church, windmill and pretty streets.

The tourist office in St-Tropez distributes a map/guide called *Tours in the Gulf of St-Tropez – Pays des Maures*, which describes four driving, cycling or walking itineraries.

Le Lavandou
pop 5200
Once a fishing village, Le Lavandou, about 5km southeast of Bormes-les-Mimosas, has become a very popular destination, thanks mainly to its 12km-long sandy beach. Although the town itself may not have much to offer, it is a good base for exploring the

nearby Massif des Maures, especially if you are interested in cycling. The resort is also close to the three idyllic Îles d'Hyères, which you can reach easily by boat.

For local information, Le Lavandou has a **tourist office** (☎ 04 94 00 40 50; www.lelavandou .com; quai Gabriel Péri; ☒ 9am-noon & 3-6pm, closed Sun low season).

Corniche des Maures

This 26km-long coastal road (part of the D559) stretches from Le Lavandou northeast to La Croix-Valmer. All along here you can enjoy breathtaking views. There are also lots of great beaches for swimming, sunbathing or windsurfing. Among the towns that the road passes through are Cavalaire, Pramousquier and Le Rayol.

Îles d'Hyères

The oldest and largest *naturiste* colony in the region is on Île du Levant, the easternmost of the three Hyères islands. Indeed, half of this 8km-long island is for naturists. Port-Cros is the smallest island and Porquerolles the largest.

PARC NATIONAL DE PORT-CROS

Created in 1963 to protect at least one small part of the Côte d'Azur from overdevelopment, Port-Cros is France's smallest national park, encompassing just 700 hectares of land – essentially the island of Port-Cros – as well as an 18-sq-km zone of water around it. The middle island of the Îles d'Hyères, Port-Cros is a marine reserve, but is also known for its rich variety of insects and butterflies. Keeping the water around it clean (compared with the rest of the coast) is one of the reserve's big challenges.

The park's **head office** (☎ 04 94 12 82 30; www .portcrosparcnational.fr in French; 50 rue St Claire, Hyères) is on the mainland. The island can be visited year-round, but walkers must stick to the marked paths. Fishing, camping and fires are not allowed.

GETTING THERE & AWAY

Boats to the Îles d'Hyères leave from various towns along the coast, including Le Lavandou and Hyères. **Vedettes Îles d'Or** (☎ 04 94 71 01 02; www.vedettesilesdor.fr in French), which has an office at the ferry terminal in Le Lavandou, operates boats to Île du Levant and Port Cros (adult/child return €22/17.50, 35

to 55 minutes). There is a supplement of €6.50 for visiting both islands. There are at least four boats a day in the warmer months (hourly in summer) but only four a week in winter. To Porquerolles there is a boat three times a week (daily in July and August) and the return adult/child fare is €27.70/21.30. Boats also sail from Hyères (one hour) in the high season.

Boats from Toulon run only from Easter to September (see p851).

TOULON
pop 166,442

Toulon is France's most important naval port: it's the base for the French navy's Mediterranean fleet. Partly as a result of heavy bombing in WWII, and partly due to the presence of dodgy bars and sex shops near the naval base, Toulon's run-down centre looks and feels grim (especially by night) compared to Nice, Cannes or even Marseille. Toulon is not a tourist magnet when pulsating Marseille, fine beaches and the tranquil Îles d'Hyères are so close, however a day trip is worthwhile.

Initially a Roman colony, Toulon only became part of France in 1481 – the city grew in importance after Henri IV founded an arsenal here. In the 17th century the port was enlarged by Vauban. The young Napoleon Bonaparte first made a name for himself in 1793 during a siege in which the English, who had taken over Toulon, were expelled.

By day the large, excellent market runs the length of Cours Lafayette. Perhaps the best way to see Toulon is from a distance, atop the giddying Mont Faron, where you will get a classic Côte d'Azur vista of cobalt sky, dazzling sea and pine-clad, resin-scented hills in one heady hit.

Orientation

Toulon is built around the *rade*, a sheltered bay lined with quays. To the west is the naval base and to the east the ferry terminal, from where boats set sail for Corsica. The city is at its liveliest along quai de la Sinse and quai Stalingrad (from where ferries depart for the Îles d'Hyères) and in the old city. The train station is northwest of the old city.

Separating the old city from the northern section is a multilane, multinamed thoroughfare (known as av du Maréchal Leclerc

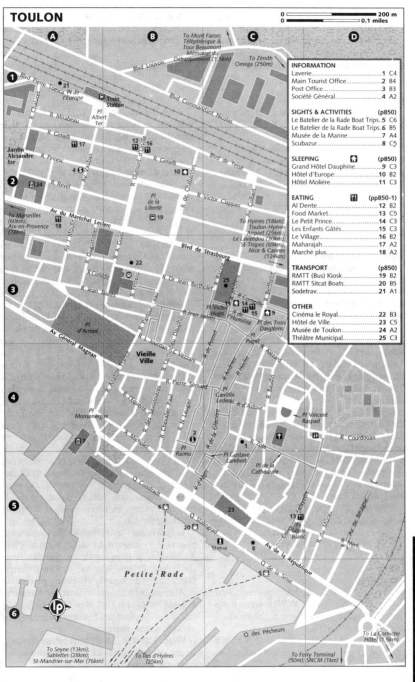

TOULON

0 —————— 200 m
0 —————— 0.1 miles

INFORMATION	
Laverie	**1** C4
Main Tourist Office	**2** B4
Post Office	**3** B3
Société Général	**4** A2

SIGHTS & ACTIVITIES	(p850)
Le Batelier de la Rade Boat Trips	**5** C6
Le Batelier de la Rade Boat Trips	**6** B5
Musée de la Marine	**7** A4
Scubazur	**8** C5

SLEEPING	(p850)
Grand Hôtel Dauphine	**9** C3
Hôtel d'Europe	**10** B2
Hôtel Molière	**11** C3

EATING	(pp850-1)
Al Dente	**12** B2
Food Market	**13** C5
Le Petit Prince	**14** C3
Les Enfants Gâtés	**15** C3
Le Village	**16** B2
Maharajah	**17** A2
Marché plus	**18** A2

TRANSPORT	(p850)
RMTT (Bus) Kiosk	**19** B2
RMTT Sitcat Boats	**20** B5
Sodetrav	**21** A1

OTHER	
Cinéma le Royal	**22** B3
Hôtel de Ville	**23** C5
Musée de Toulon	**24** A2
Théâtre Municipal	**25** C3

To Mont Faron; Téléphérique & Tour Beaumont Mémorial du Débarquement (1.5km)

To Zénith Omega (250m)

Blvd Louvois

Blvd Pierre Toesca

Pl de l'Europe

Blvd Commandant Nicolas

Train Station

R Chabaud

R Mirabeau

Pl Albert 1er

R Gimelli

R Drujon

R Gimelli

Blvd de Tessé

Jardin Alexandre 1er

R Peiresc

R Vauban

R Dumont d'Urville

R de Chabannes

R Revel

Av Vauban

Pl de la Liberté

R Victor Clappier

Av Colbert

Av du Maréchal Leclerc

To Marseilles (60km); Aix-en-Provence (78km)

R A Guiol

R Dromont

Blvd de Strasbourg

To Hyères (18km); Toulon-Hyères Airport (25km); Le Lavandou (30km); St-Tropez (69km); Nice & Cannes (124km)

R Comédie

R Dr Jean Berthelet

R Ferrero

R Pastoureau

R Jean Jaurès

Pl d'Armes

Av Général Magnan

Vieille Ville

R Racine

R Molière

R Corneille

Pl Victor Hugo

R Jean Jaurès

R de l'Humilité

R Berthelot

Pl des Trois Dauphins

R L'Jourdan du Dauphin

R C Vezzani

R Lamalgue

Pl Puget

R d'Alezard

R Anatole France

R l'Equerre

R des Savonnières

R Chevalier Paul

R N Laugier

R Andrieu

R Hoche

R Baudin

Pl Monsenergue

Pl Micholet

R Micholet

Pl Camille Ledeau

R d'Astour

Pl Vincent Raspail

R Courdouan

R Pierre Sémard

Pl Raimu

R Raimu

Pl Gustave Lambert

R de la Glacière

R Zola

Pl de la Cathédrale

Q Constadt

Petite Rade

To Seyne (13km); Sablettes (28km); St-Mandrier-sur-Mer (76km)

To Iles d'Hyères (25km)

Q de Stalingrad

Av de la République

Pl Louis Blanc

R du Mûrier

Av de Besagne

R Mart

Q de la Sinse

Q des Pêcheurs

To Ferry Terminal (50m); SNCM (1km)

To La Corniche Hôtel (1.5km)

and blvd de Strasbourg as it runs through the centre), which teems with traffic.

Women travelling on their own may wish to avoid some of the old city streets at night, particularly around rue Chevalier Paul and the western end of rue Pierre Sémard.

Information

Commercial banks line blvd de Strasbourg.

Société Generale (1bis av Vauban; ☼ 8.30am-noon & 1.30-4.45pm Mon-Fri) With an ATM.

Laverie (10 rue Zola; ☼ 7am-9pm) One of several laundrettes in the old city.

Main Tourist Office (☎ 04 94 18 53 00; www.toulon tourisme.com; place Raimu; ☼ 9am-6pm Mon-Sat, 10am-noon Sun high season, 9.30am-5.30pm Mon-Sat, 10am-noon Sun low season).

Post Office (rue Bertholet) Second entrance on rue Ferrero.

Sights & Activities

The **Musée de la Marine** (Naval Museum; ☎ 04 94 02 02 01; place Monsenergue; adult/student/child €4.60/2.30/ free; ☼ 9.30am-noon & 3-7pm daily Jul & Aug, 9.30am-noon & 2-6pm Wed-Mon Sep-Jun) is in the lovely old arsenal building and displays scale models of old ships and historic paintings of Toulon.

Overlooking the old city to the north is **Mont Faron** (580m), from where you can see Toulon's port in its true magnificence. Near the summit is the **Tour Beaumont Mémorial du Débarquement**, commemorating the Allied landings that took place along the coast here in August 1944. The steep road up to the summit is used for the Tour de Méditerranée (February) and Paris–Nice (March) professional cycling races. A **téléphérique** (cableway; ☎ 04 94 92 68 25; adult/child return €5.80/4; ☼ 9am-noon & 2-5.30pm Tue-Sun) climbs the mountain from av de Vence. Take bus No 40 from place de la Liberté.

Scubazur (☎ 04 94 92 19 29; 334 av de la République) is a 1st-class diving shop that has plenty of information on all the diving clubs and schools along the Côte d'Azur.

Tours

Excursions around the *rade*, with a commentary (in French only) on the events that took place here during WWII, leave from quai Stalingrad or quai de la Sinse. One-hour trips average €8.

Le Batelier de la Rade (☎ 04 94 46 24 65; quai de la Sinse) organises day trips out to the Îles d'Hyères (€20).

SNRTM (☎ 04 94 93 07 56) runs trips, some including a meal on board, to Cannes and St-Tropez between June and September.

Sleeping

Beware of the cheapest options in the old town and near the station; there are some pretty grim places.

Hôtel Molière (☎ 04 94 92 78 35; hotel.moliere@ tiscali.fr; 12 rue Molière; r with shower & toilet €35) Beside the opera house, this is the best of the budget options, offering homely rooms in a family-style establishment.

Hôtel d'Europe (☎ /fax 04 94 92 37 44; 7 rue de Chabannes; r with shower & toilet €47) East of the train station, the Europe has some decent rooms. Photos of each room category accompany the price list displayed in reception. Some of the rooms have little balconies.

La Corniche (☎ 04 94 41 35 12; www.hotel-corniche .com; 17 littoral Frédéric Mistral; s/d €70/75, with sea views €85/95; ❄) Along the coast, just out of the town centre, La Corniche has considerable charm and a good restaurant.

Grand Hôtel Dauphiné (☎ 04 94 92 20 28; fax 04 94 62 16 69; 10 rue Bertholet; s/d €44/50; **P**) With large rooms and near secure parking, this place will do.

Eating

Pricey restaurants, terraces and bars with occasional live music are abundant along the quays; *menus* start at around €20 and a tiny *bouillabaisse* or *aïoli garni* will set you back €15 to €20. Another lively area is place Victor Hugo and neighbouring place Puget.

Les Enfants Gâtés ('Spoiled Children'; ☎ 04 94 09 14 67; 7 rue Corneille; lunch menu €7.60; ☼ closed Sat & Sun high season, closed dinner Mon-Fri & lunch Sat low season) A very popular, modern place run by a young crowd. This is one of the most pleasant places in town to dine without breaking the bank.

Le Petit Prince (☎ 04 94 93 03 45; 10 rue de l'Humilité; mains €8-11; ☼ closed Sun & lunch Sat) Named after Antoine de St-Exupéry's book for children, the 'Little Prince' is close to Les Enfants Gâtés and is an equally charming place.

Also recommend on or near rue Gimelli:

Al Dente (☎ 04 94 93 02 50; 30 rue Gimelli; menu €10/18; ☼ closed lunch Sun) An elegant Italian place serving good home-made pasta.

Le Village (☎ 04 94 22 03 03; 10 rue Dumont d'Urville; dishes €9-15; ☼ closed Sun & lunch Sat) Unpretentious, modern food and jazz concerts.

Maharajah (☎ 04 94 91 93 46; 15 rue Gimelli; menus €10 & €20; ☺ lunch & dinner Tue-Sun) Known for its vegetarian *thalis* (trays with an assortment of dishes).

SELF-CATERING
The southern half of cours Lafayette is one long, excellent **open-air food market** (☺ 9am-early afternoon Tue-Sun) held, in typical Provençal style, under the plane trees. A few blocks south of the train station there is a small grocery shop, **Marché Plus** (av du Maréchal Leclerc).

Getting There & Away
BOAT
Ferries to Corsica and Sardinia are run by the **SNCM** (☎ 08 91 70 18 01), which has an **office** (49 av de l'Infanterie de Marine; ☺ 8.30am-noon & 2pm-5.45pm Mon-Fri, from 11.30am Sat) opposite the ferry terminal. For details, see the Getting There & Away section of the Corsica chapter.

Boats from Toulon to the Îles d'Hyères only run from Easter to September and are operated by several companies, such as **Trans Med 2000** (☎ 04 94 92 96 82). All depart from quai Stalingrad. The trip to Porquer-olles (€18 return) takes one hour. It's an-other 40 minutes to Port Cros, from where it's a 20-minute hop to Île du Levant (€30 return to tour all three islands).

BUS
From the Toulon bus terminal **Sodetrav** (☎ 04 94 12 55 00; 4 blvd Pierre Toesca) operates buses along the coast. Bus No 103 to Hyères runs east along the coast via Le Lavandou to St-Tropez (€17, two hours, eight daily).

TRAIN
There are frequent connections to coastal cities including Marseilles (€9.20, 50 min-utes, hourly), St-Raphaël, Cannes (€16.60, one hour 20 minutes, hourly), Monaco (€21.40, 2½ hours, frequent) and Menton.

Getting Around
Local buses are run by **RMTT** (☎ 04 94 03 87 03), which has an **information kiosk** (place de la liberté; ☺ 7.30am-7pm Mon-Fri, 8am-12.30pm & 1.30-6.30pm Sat) at the main local bus hub. Single/10 tickets cost €1.30/8.60. Buses generally run until around 7.30pm or 8.30pm. Sunday service is limited. Bus No 7 and 13 link the train station with quai Stalingrad. One-day bus tickets cost €3.30 and combined one-day bus, boat and cable-car tickets cost €5.

Sitcat boats (☎ 04 94 46 35 46; ticket office ☺ 8am-12.15pm & 2-5.15pm) run by **RMTT** (☎ 04 94 03 87 03), the local transport company, link quai Stalingrad with the towns on the peninsula across the harbour, including La Seyne (line 8M), St-Mandrier-sur-Mer (line 28M) and Sablettes (line 18M). The 20-minute ride costs the same as a bus ticket: €1.30 (€1.70 if you buy your ticket onboard, or €5 for an all-day bus, boat and cable-car ticket). Boats run from around 6am to 8pm.

NICE TO MENTON

THE CORNICHES
Nice and Menton (and the 30km of towns in between) are linked by three corniches (coastal roads), each one higher up the hill than the last. If you're in a hurry and don't mind missing the scenery, you can drive a bit further inland and take the A8.

Corniche Inférieure
The Corniche Inférieure (also known as the Basse Corniche, the Lower Corniche and the N98) sticks pretty close to the villa-lined waterfront and the nearby train line, passing (as it goes from Nice eastwards to Menton) through Villefranche-sur-Mer, St-Jean-Cap Ferrat, Beaulieu-sur-Mer, Èze-sur-Mer, Cap d'Ail, where there's a very pleasant **seaside hostel** (☎ 04 93 78 18 58; clajpaca@cote-dazur.com) right by the sea and Monaco.

VILLEFRANCHE-SUR-MER
Set in one of the Côte d'Azur's most charm-ing harbours, this little port (population 6877) overlooks the Cap Ferrat peninsula. It has a well-preserved 14th-century old city with a 16th-century citadel and a church dating from 100 years later. Steps break up the tiny streets that weave through the old city, the most interesting of which is rue Obscure. Keep a lookout for occasional glimpses of the sea as you wander through the streets that lead down to the fishing port. Villefranche was a particular favourite of Jean Cocteau, who painted the frescoes (1957) in the 17th-century **Chapelle St-Pierre**.

ST-JEAN-CAP FERRAT
Once a fishing village, the seaside resort of St-Jean-Cap Ferrat (population 1907) lies on the spectacular peninsula of Cap Ferrat,

which conceals a bounty of millionaires' villas. On the narrow isthmus of Cap Ferrat is the extravagant **Musée de Béatrice Ephrussi de Rothschild** (☎ 04 93 01 33 09; adult/student €8/6; ☿ 10am-7pm daily), housed in the Villa Île de France, which was built in the style of the great houses of Tuscany for the Baroness de Rothschild in 1912. It abounds with antique furniture, paintings, tapestries and porcelain and is surrounded by beautiful gardens. Admission includes entry to the gardens and the collections on the **rez-de-chaussée** (ground floor). It costs an extra €2 to view those on the 1st floor.

BEAULIEU-SUR-MER
This upmarket resort (population 3700) boasts the wonderful **Villa Grecque Kérylos** (☎ 04 93 76 44 09; av Gustave Eiffel; adult/student €7.50/5.50; ☿ 10am-7pm), a wonderful reproduction of an Athenian villa built by archaeologist Théodore Reinach in 1902. After visiting the luxurious marble interior, take a walk on the botanical trail through the gardens, planted with vegetation typical to Greece and the French coast.

Moyenne Corniche
The Moyenne Corniche, the middle coastal road (the N7), clings to the hillside, affording great views if you can find a place to pull over. It takes you from Nice past the Col de Villefranche, Èze and Beausoleil, the French town up the hill from Monte Carlo.

ÈZE
Perched on a rocky peak at an altitude of 427m is the picturesque village of Èze (population 2526), once occupied by Ligurians and Phoenicians. Below is its coastal counterpart, Èze-sur-Mer.

Make your way to the **exotic garden** for fabulous views up and down the coast. The German philosopher Friedrich Nietzsche (1844–1900) spent some time here, during which he started *Thus Spoke Zarathustra*. The spectacular walking path that links Èze-sur-Mer and Èze is named after him. Allow an hour to complete the walk The bus between Èze and Nice costs €3. There's also a train between Èze-sur-Mer and Nice.

Grande Corniche
The Grande Corniche, whose panoramas are by far the most spectacular, leaves Nice

as the D2564. It passes the **Col d'Èze**, where there's a great view; **La Turbie**, which is on a promontory directly above Monaco and offers a stunning night-time vista of the principality; and **Le Vistaëro**.

ROQUEBRUNE
Dominating this appealing hilltop village (population 11,966), which lies just between Monaco and Menton, is a medieval dungeon that is complete with a re-created manor house. Roquebrune's tortuous little streets, which lead up to the castle, are lined with shops selling handicrafts and souvenirs and are overrun with tourists in the high season. Carved out of the rock is the impressive rue Moncollet, with arcaded passages and stairways.

For more information, contact the **tourist office** (☎ 04 93 35 62 87; fax 04 93 28 57 00; 218 av Aristide Briand; ☿ 9am-12.30pm & 2-6.30pm Mon-Sat), in nearby **Cap Martin**, an exclusive suburb of Menton known for its sumptuous villas and famous past residents (Winston Churchill and the architect Le Corbusier among them).

MENTON
pop 29,266
Menton, a confection of elegant historic buildings in sugared-almond pastels, is only a few kilometres from the Italian border and reputed to be the warmest spot on the Côte d'Azur (especially during winter). In part because of the weather, Menton is popular with older holiday-makers, whose way of life and preferences have made the town's after-dark entertainment a tad tranquil compared to other spots along the coast. Guy de Maupassant, Robert Louis Stevenson, Gustave Flaubert and Katherine Mansfield all found solace in Menton. Jean Cocteau lived here from 1956 to 1958 and made a number of important contributions to the town. Today, Menton draws Italians from across the border, and retains a sedate charm free of the airs and pretensions found in other areas of the Côte d'Azur.

Menton is famed for its cultivation of lemons. Giant, larger-than-life sculptures made from lemons, lemons and yet more lemons take over the town for two weeks during the fabulous **Fête des Citrons** (Lemon Festival) in February. The festival kicks off on Mardi Gras.

Orientation

Promenade du Soleil runs southwest to northeast along the beach; the train line runs approximately parallel about 500m inland. Avenue Édouard VII links the train station with the beach. Avenue Boyer, home to the tourist office, is 350m to the east. From the station, turn left and walk along av de la Gare, then take the second right onto what appears to be a two-way divided promenade. The tourist office is about half-way down av Boyer.

The old town is on and around the hill at the northeastern end of promenade du Soleil. Vieux Port lies just beyond it.

Information

BOOKSHOPS

Librairie de la Presse (25 av Félix Faure) Stocks a fine range of guides, travel books and foreign-language newspapers.

INTERNET ACCESS

Café des Arts (☎ 04 93 35 78 67; 16 rue de la République; ☺ 8am-10pm Mon-Sat; per 15min €2). Log-on, *pastis* in hand, from an elegant green leather banquette.

MONEY

There are plenty of banks with exchange facilities along rue Partouneaux.

Barclays Bank (☎ 04 93 28 60 00; 39 av Félix Faure) Has an automatic exchange machine outside.

Crédit Lyonnais (av Boyer) Two doors down from the tourist office. There's another 24-hour currency machine outside.

POST

Post Office (cours George V) With a Cyberposte.

TOURIST INFORMATION

Information Office (☎ 04 92 10 97 10; fax 04 93 28 46 85; 24 rue St-Michel) More central than the tourist office. Runs thematic organised tours (Menton and the *belle époque*, artists, gardens etc) arranged by the Service du Patrimoine for €5 per person.

Tourist Office (☎ 04 92 41 76 76; www.menton.fr; 8 av Boyer; ☺ 9am-7pm Mon-Sat, 10am-noon Sun Jul & Aug; 8.30am-12.30pm & 2-6pm Mon-Fri, 9am-noon & 2-6pm Sat low season) Inside the Palais de l'Europe.

Sights & Activities

The early-17th-century **Église St-Michel** (Church of St Michael; usually ☺ 10am-noon & 3-5.15pm, closed Sat morning) is the grandest and possibly the prettiest baroque church in this part of France. It is perched in the centre of the old town, which has many narrow, winding passageways. The ornate interior is Italian in inspiration.

Musée Jean Cocteau (Jean Cocteau Museum; ☎ 04 93 57 72 30; quai Napoléon III; admission €3; ☺ 10am-noon & 2-6pm Wed-Mon), southwest of the Vieux Port, displays work by Jean Cocteau (1889–1963) – poet, dramatist, artist and film director – in a seafront bastion dating from 1636. Cocteau's work includes drawings, tapestries and mosaics. Do not miss Cocteau's frescoes in the **Salle des Mariages** (Marriage Hall; place Ardoïno; admission €1.50; ☺ 8.30am-noon & 1.30-5pm Mon-Fri) in the Hôtel de Ville.

The **beach** along promenade du Soleil is public but, like its counterpart in Nice, it's covered with smooth little rocks. There are more beaches directly north of the Vieux Port, including Plages des Sablettes with sand and clean water, and east of Port de Garavan, the main pleasure-boat harbour.

Base Nautique (☎ 04 93 35 49 70; promenade de la Mer) rents laser-class dinghies/catamarans/kayaks for €19/31/8 per hour. The **sailing school** also runs courses that cost €115 for five two-hour sessions.

Sleeping

BUDGET

Auberge de Jeunesse (☎ 04 93 35 93 14; fax 04 93 35 93 07; Plateau St-Michel; dm incl breakfast €14.40; ☺ reception closed noon-5pm, 10am to 5pm in winter; ℗) The hostel is in a lovely spot overlooking town and the bay. The walk from the train station is quite a hike uphill. Otherwise take a Line 6 bus and get off at Camping Saint Michel, 500m away. Curfew is midnight (10pm in winter).

Hôtel Le Terminus (☎ 04 92 10 49 80; fax 04 92 10 49 81; place de la Gare; s/d with washbasin €28/31, with shower & toilet €30/40; ℗) A no-star, but welcoming, clean place with a few rooms right next to the station. Hall showers are free. Reception is often closed but you can always find someone to help you in the bar-restaurant areas during opening times.

Camping

Camping Saint Michel (☎ 04 93 35 81 23; route des Ciappes de Castellar; camping €10.90; ☺ 1 Apr-15 Oct) One kilometre northeast of the train station up Plateau St-Michel, and close to the youth hostel.

MID-RANGE

Hôtel de Londres (☎ 04 93 35 74 62; www.hotel-de-londres.com; 15 av Carnot; s/d from €35/38, with bathroom from €53/58; P ❄) Close to the sea, central enough and exuding a certain charm, this appealing place with a leafy dining terrace and garden is our pick in town.

Saint Michel (☎ 04 93 57 46 33; fax 04 93 57 71 19; 1684 promenade du Soleil; s/d €60/70) This place has the best sea views in town.

Hôtel Claridges (☎ 04 93 35 72 53; www.claridges -menton.com; 39 av de Verdun; s/d from €43/62) A two-star place with comfortable rooms.

Hôtel des Arcades (☎ 04 93 35 70 62; fax 04 93 35 35 97; 41 av Félix Faure; s/d with washbasin €41/46, with shower & toilet €53/55) In town under the arches, this hotel is one of Menton's most picturesque, if no-frills, options.

Eating

There aren't any outstanding restaurants in town, so if you have wheels or a train timetable, consider breaking for the nearby Italian border. In town there are places to eat galore along av Félix Faure and its pedestrianised continuation, rue St-Michel. Place Clemenceau and place aux Herbes in the Vieille Ville are equally popular. The pricier restaurants with terraces fanned by cool breezes are along promenade du Soleil. Slightly cheaper places, including pizzerias, line quai de Monléon in the Vieille Ville.

Le Chaudron (☎ 04 93 35 90 25; 28 rue St-Michel; menu €20; ☽ closed Wed & dinner Tue) Offers filling salads (€8 to €12) and some fresh fish mains (€9 to €20).

Ulivo (☎ 04 93 35 45 65; place du Cap; menu €15; ☽ Fri-Wed) Run by an Italian family and serving home-made Mediterranean-style dishes.

SELF-CATERING

The **Marché Municipal** (Les Halles; quai de Monléon; ☽ 5am-1pm Tue-Sun), in the old town, sells all kinds of food.

The **8 à Huit** (7 rue Amiral Courbet) is the place for groceries and the **Comtesse du Barry** (36 rue Partouneaux) sells luxury foie gras products.

Getting There & Away

BUS

The **bus station** (☎ 04 93 28 43 27, information office ☎ 04 93 35 93 60) is next to 12 promenade Maréchal Leclerc, the northern continuation of av Boyer.

There are buses to Monaco (€2.10 return, 30 minutes), Nice (€5.10 return, 1¼ hours), Ste-Agnès (€7.20 return, 45 minutes) and Sospel (€4.90 return, 45 minutes). There are also buses to the Nice–Côte d'Azur airport (€16.10, 1½ hours) via Monaco run by **Bus RCA** (☎ 04 93 85 64 44).

TRAIN

Trains to Ventimiglia cost €2.10 and take 10 minutes. For more information on train services along the Côte d'Azur see p830.

Getting Around

TUM (Transports Urbains de Menton; ☎ 04 93 35 93 60) runs nine bus lines in the area. Lines 1 and 2 link the train station with the old town.

MONACO (PRINCIPAUTÉ DE MONACO)

pop 30,000

Tiny, glamorous Monaco (its territory only covers 1.95 sq km) is a fantasy land of perfectly groomed streets, lush gardens, chic boutiques and extravagantly opulent 19th-century pleasure palaces.

With a photogenic royal family whose heritage stretches back to the 13th century and a stream of high-rollers filling its famous casino or gathering for the annual Formula One Grand Prix race, Monaco never seems to go out of style.

The Principality of Monaco has been under the rule of the Grimaldi family for most of the period since 1297 and is a sovereign state with close ties to France. It has been ruled since 1949 by Prince Rainier III (b 1923). Rainier's rule has modernised Monaco and weaned it from its dependence on gambling revenue. His marriage to the much beloved Princess Grace (remembered from her Hollywood days as the actress Grace Kelly) restored Monaco's glamour.

Tourism in all its permutations, from day-trippers to conventioneers, is now the backbone of Monaco's economy. Prince Albert is the heir to the throne but the tabloids have always been more fascinated with the ever-changing personal lives of his two sisters, Caroline and Stephanie. The 2003 marriage of Stephanie to a circus acrobat was just another episode in the princess' unconventional life.

The citizens of Monaco (known as Monégasques), of whom there are only about

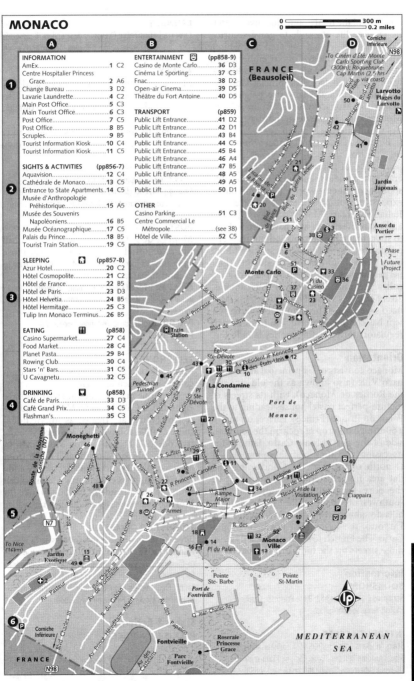

MONACO

0 —————— 300 m
0 —————— 0.2 miles

INFORMATION
AmEx...1	C2
Centre Hospitalier Princesse	
Grace..2	A6
Change Bureau 3	D2
Lavarie Laundrette.................4	C2
Main Post Office....................5	C3
Main Tourist Office................6	C3
Post Office.............................7	C5
Post Office.............................8	B5
Scruples..................................9	B5
Tourist Information Kiosk.....10	C4
Tourist Information Kiosk.....11	C5

SIGHTS & ACTIVITIES   (pp856-7)
Aquavision............................12	C4
Cathédrale de Monaco.........13	C5
Entrance to State Apartments..14	C5
Musée d'Anthropologie	
Préhistorique.......................15	A5
Musée des Souvenirs	
Napoléoniens........................16	B5
Musée Océanographique......17	C5
Palais du Prince....................18	B5
Tourist Train Station.............19	B5

SLEEPING   (pp857-8)
Azur Hotel............................20	C2
Hôtel Cosmopolite................21	C2
Hôtel de France....................22	B5
Hôtel de Paris.......................23	D3
Hôtel Helvetia......................24	B5
Hôtel Hermitage...................25	C3
Tulip Inn Monaco Terminus..26	B5

EATING   (p858)
Casino Supermarket..............27	C4
Food Market.........................28	C4
Planet Pasta.........................29	B4
Rowing Club.........................30	C4
Stars 'n' Bars........................31	C5
U Cavagnetu........................32	C5

DRINKING   (p858)
Café de Paris.........................33	D3
Café Grand Prix....................34	C5
Flashman's............................35	C3

ENTERTAINMENT   (pp858-9)
Casino de Monte Carlo..........36	D3
Cinéma Le Sporting...............37	C3
Fnac......................................38	D2
Open-air Cinema...................39	D5
Théâtre du Fort Antoine........40	D5

TRANSPORT   (p859)
Public Lift Entrance..............41	D2
Public Lift Entrance..............42	D1
Public Lift Entrance..............43	B4
Public Lift Entrance..............44	C5
Public Lift Entrance..............45	B4
Public Lift Entrance..............46	A4
Public Lift Entrance..............47	B5
Public Lift Entrance..............48	A5
Public Lift............................49	A5
Public Lift............................50	D1

OTHER
Casino Parking.....................51	C3
Centre Commercial Le	
Métropole........................(see 38)	
Hôtel de Ville.......................52	C5

FRANCE
(Beausoleil)

N98

Corniche
Inférieure

To Ciném d'Été; Monte
Carlo Sporting Club
(300m); Roquebrune;
Cap Martin (2.5 hrs
via coast)

Larvotto
Plages du
Larvotto

Jardin
Japonais

Anse du
Portier

Phase
2 –
Future
Project

Monte Carlo

Pl du
Casino

Train
Station

Église
Ste-Dévote

Pedestrian
Tunnel

Pl
Ste-
Dévote

La Condamine

Port de
Monaco

Monéghetti

Route de la Moyenne Corniche (N7)

N7

To Nice
(16km)

Rampe
Major

Pl
d'Armes

Jardin
Exotique

Pl du Palais

Monaco
Ville

Ciappaira

Pointe
Ste-Barbe

Pointe
St-Martin

Port de
Fontvieille

Corniche
Inférieure

FRANCE

N98

Fontvieille

Parc
Fontvieille

Roseraie
Princesse
Grace

MEDITERRANEAN
SEA

CÔTE D'AZUR & MONACO

5000 out of the total population, live an idyllic tax-free life of cradle-to-grave security. They have their own flag (red and white), own national holiday (19 November), own country telephone code and own traditional Monégasque dialect. The official language is French, although many street signs, particularly in Monaco Ville, are in French and Monégasque. There are no border formalities upon entering Monaco.

Because residents of Monaco don't pay income tax, the principality has become something of a tax haven for the jet set and entrepreneurs. Famous faces from the sporting or cinema worlds flit in and out of expensive boutiques or cruise the streets in Italian supercars. Money is safe in Monaco and so are the people who have it, so feel free to sport that emerald tiara without fear. The police presence in Monaco is striking (don't even think about running a red light), their perpetual vigilance aided by plain-clothed colleagues and hundreds of TV cameras. Street crime is virtually unknown, but Monaco's see-no-evil-hear-no-evil banking system has come under criticism from French regulators for tolerating money laundering.

Orientation

Monaco consists of six principal areas: Monaco Ville (also known as the old city and the Rocher de Monaco), with its streets of picture-perfect pastel houses leading to the Palais du Prince (Prince's Palace) on top of a 60m-high outcrop of rock on the southern side of the port; Monte Carlo, famous for its casino and high-end shopping, which is north of the port; La Condamine, the flat area immediately to the southwest of the port; Fontvieille, the industrial area southwest of Monaco Ville; Moneghetti, the hillside suburb west of La Condamine; and Larvotto, the beach area north of Monte Carlo. The French town of Beausoleil is just three streets up the hill from Monte Carlo.

Information

BOOKSHOPS

Scruples (☎ 93 50 43 52; 9 rue Princesse Caroline) An English-language bookshop.

INTERNET ACCESS

Stars 'n' Bars (☎ 93 50 95 95; info@starsnbars.com; 6 quai Antoine 1er; per 30min €5; 🕑 11am-midnight) There's a cybercorner inside this restaurant (p858).

LAUNDRY

Laverie Laundrette (1 Escalier de la Riviera, Beausoleil; 🕑 7am-7pm) On the border between Monaco and France.

MONEY

Monaco uses the euro along with the Monégasque franc coins, but the latter are difficult to find and not widely accepted outside the principality.

There are numerous banks in the vicinity of the casino. In La Condamine, try blvd Albert 1er.

AmEx (☎ 93 25 74 45; 35 blvd Princesse Charlotte; 🕑 9.30am-12.30pm & 2pm-5.30pm Mon-Fri)

Change Bureau (Jardins du Casino; 🕑 9am-7.30pm daily) At the entrance to the Monopole commercial centre.

POST

Monégasque stamps are valid only within Monaco. Postal rates are the same as those in France. There are post office branches in each of the areas of Monaco.

Main Post Office (1 av Henri Dunant) In Monte Carlo inside the Palais de la Scala. It does not exchange foreign currency.

Post Office (place de la Visitation, Monaco Ville)

Post Office (rue de la Côte)

TELEPHONE

Monaco's public telephones accept Monégasque or French *télécartes*.

Telephone numbers in Monaco only have eight digits. Calls between Monaco and the rest of France are treated as international calls. Dial 00 followed by Monaco's country code (377) when calling Monaco from France or abroad. To phone France from Monaco, dial 00 and France's country code (33). This applies even if only making a call from the eastern side of blvd de France (in Monaco) to its western side (in France)!

TOURIST INFORMATION

Direction du Tourisme et des Congrès de la Principauté de Monaco (☎ 92 16 61 16; www.monaco-tourisme.com; 2a blvd des Moulins; 🕑 9am-7pm Mon-Sat, 10am-noon Sun) Across the public gardens from the casino. From mid-June to late-September several tourist information kiosks open around the harbour.

Sights & Activities

PALAIS DU PRINCE

The changing of the guard takes place daily outside the **Palais du Prince** (Prince's Palace; ☎ 93 25 18 31), at the southern end of rue des Remparts in Monaco Ville, at precisely 11.55am. The guards, who carry out their duties of state in spiffy dress uniform (white in summer, black in winter), are apparently resigned to the comic-opera nature of their duties. You can also visit the **state apartments** (adult/child €6/3; 9.30am-6.30pm Jun-Sep, 10am-5pm Oct, closed Nov-May) with audioguide commentary.

A combined ticket including admission to the **Musée des Souvenirs Napoléoniens** – a display of Napoleon's personal effects in the southern wing of the palace – costs €8 (children €4).

MUSÉE OCÉANOGRAPHIQUE DE MONACO
If you're planning to see just one aquarium on your whole trip, the world-renowned **Musée Océanographique de Monaco** (93 15 36 00; av St-Martin, Monaco Ville; adult/student €11/6; 9.30am-7pm Jul & Aug, to 6.30pm Apr-Jun & Sep) should be it. It has 90 tanks, and upstairs there are all sorts of exhibits on ocean exploration. Bus Nos 1 and 2 are the alternatives to a relatively long walk up the hill.

CATHÉDRALE DE MONACO
Albeit unspectacular, the 1875 Romanesque-Byzantine **Cathédrale de Monaco** (4 rue Colonel) has one major draw: the grave of former Hollywood film star Grace Kelly (1929–82), which lies on the western side of the cathedral choir. Her modest tombstone, inscribed with the Latin words *Gratia Patricia Principis Rainerii III,* is heavily adorned with flowers. Tourists usually do a quick march around the cathedral to see her grave. Grace Patricia Kelly wed Prince Rainier III in 1956 and died in a car crash in 1982. The remains of other members of the royal family, buried in the church crypt since 1885, today rest behind Princess Grace's grave.

Between September and June, Sunday Mass at 10am is sung by Monaco's boys choir, Les Petits Chanteurs de Monaco.

JARDIN EXOTIQUE
The steep slopes of the wonderful **Jardin Exotique** (93 15 29 80; 62 blvd du Jardin Exotique; adult/student €6.40/3.20; 9am-7pm mid-May–mid-Sep, 9am-6pm mid-Sep–mid-May) are home to some 7000 varieties of cacti and succulents from all over the world. The spectacular view alone is worth at least half the admission fee, which also gets you into the **Musée d'Anthropologie Préhistorique** and includes a half-hour guided

visit to the **Observatory Caves**, a network of stalactite and stalagmite caves 279 steps down the hillside. From the tourist office, take bus No 2 to the Jardin Exotique terminus.

BEACHES
The nearest beaches, **Plages du Larvotto** and **Plage de Monte Carlo**, are a few kilometres east of Monte Carlo. In town sun worshippers lie their oiled bodies out to bake on giant concrete slabs on the eastern side of the jetty, at the northern end of quai des États-Unis.

Tours
You can explore the waters off Monaco in a glass-bottom boat (adult/student €11/8, 55 minutes) with **Aquavision** (92 16 15 15; www.aquavision-monaco.com; quai des États-Unis). Boats depart at 11am, 2.30pm and 4pm (2.30pm only May to October).

If the hills of Monaco are too much for you, the slightly tacky **Azur Express tourist train** (92 05 64 38) starts from opposite the Musée Océanographique. The 30-minute city tour costs €6 and it runs every day from 10.30am to 6pm (11am to 5pm in winter). Commentaries are in English, French, Italian and German.

Festivals & Events
GRAND PRIX AUTOMOBILE DE MONACO
In May of each year Monaco transforms itself into the giant racing circuit that is the Monaco Grand Prix, a unique arena in which the world's top Formula 1 drivers pit their skills against each other and against the city's narrow lanes, tortuous road layout and impossible hairpins. It's arguably the most thrilling and atmospheric of all the Formula 1 venues owing to the spectacular location and the fact that spectators can often get closer to the action than on more conventional circuits.

You can try to purchase tickets (from about €50) to get trackside from the **Automobile Club de Monaco** (www.amc.mc), but be warned it's a hugely popular event, so you'll need to get in early to stand a chance. Tickets for the better locations can be fiercely expensive.

Sleeping
BUDGET
Relais Internationale de la Jeunesse Thalassa (04 93 78 18 58; blvd de la Mer) Monaco has no

hostels. On Cap d'Ail, this is the closest to Monaco and is right by the sea.

MID-RANGE

Cheap hotels are nonexistent in Monaco. All is not lost though as the neighbouring town of Beausoleil is a better-value location for accommodation.

Azur Hotel (☎ 04 93 78 01 25; www.azurhotel.biz; 12 blvd de la Republique; s/d/tr from €42/52/62; ⓅⓍ) Probably the pick of places in the area for value, with appealing décor and location. It's also close to a couple of multistorey car parks.

Hôtel Cosmopolite (☎ 04 93 78 36 00; fax 04 93 41 84 22; 19 blvd du Général Leclerc; s/d €51/54) Comfortable rooms with TVs, telephones, minibars and hairdryers.

The above two hotels are three streets up from the casino and close to the Beausoleil market. When calling these hotels from Monaco (eg from the train station), dial 00 33, then the listed phone number (dropping the first 0). The following are in Monaco proper.

Hôtel de France (☎ 93 30 24 64; fax 92 16 13 34; 6 rue de la Turbie; s/d with shower & toilet €71/90) This two-star place has small rooms with showers, toilets and TVs; rates include breakfast.

Tulip Inn Monaco Terminus (☎ 92 05 63 00; www .terminus.monte-carlo.mc; 9 av Prince Pierre; s/d €130/170; Ⓧ) A three-star hotel in a 1960s brick of a building, the Tulip Inn offers rooms with soundproofing, hairdryers, TVs and telephones. Some have sea views.

Hôtel Helvetia (☎ 93 30 21 71; www.monte-carlo .mc/hotels/helvetia; 1bis rue Grimaldi; s/d €62/71) While this is a more expensive two-star hotel, it doesn't necessarily offer more comfort.

TOP END

World-famous places to spend a luxury holiday:

Hôtel de Paris (☎ 92 16 30 00; www.montecarlore sort.com; place du Casino; r from high season €570, low season €385) Spectacularly plush; where the writer Colette spent the last years of her life.

Hôtel Hermitage (☎ 92 16 40 00; www.montecarlo resort.com; square Beaumarchais; r 490 high season, low season from €355) The entrance is lined with Bentleys and Maseratis.

Eating

Finding a place to eat in Monaco won't be hard. The trick is to do it at a price you can

afford. For more choices grab the free *Monaco Shopping: Commerce and Restaurant Guide* booklet from the tourist office.

The lower end of the range restaurants tend to be in La Condamine along rue de la Turbie, and there are simple sandwich bars along quai Albert 1er. In Monte Carlo, there are a few sandwich and snack places inside the Centre Commercial Le Métropole.

Rowing Club (quai des États-Unis; mains €9-12; ☽ lunch Tue-Sat) The good food available in the quiet little bar and bolt hole above the where locals smoke and play cards is a closely kept local secret – until now.

Planet Pasta (☎ 93 50 80 14; 6 rue Imberty; pizza/ pasta €9-13, mains €17-22; ☽ lunch & dinner Tue-Sat) A reliable choice, serving filling portions of what its name advertises in a busy, often hot and stuffy dining room.

Stars 'n' Bars (☎ 93 50 95 95; 6 quai Antoine 1er; ☽ noon-3am Tue-Sun) On the south side of the port, this place has become a Monaco institution, despite being utterly American. It's a kind of huge country and western saloon where you can listen to live music and eat American-sized mains (€14 to €25) and huge salads (from €11) served by staff in starred-and-striped leather shorts and boots.

U Cavagnetu (☎ 93 30 35 80; 14 rue Comte Félix-Gastaldi; lunch menu €14.50, dinner menus €20 & €25) One of the few affordable restaurants specialising in Monégasque dishes.

SELF-CATERING

In La Condamine, there's a **food market** (place d'Armes; ☽ from 7am Mon-Sat) and a **Casino Supermarket** (blvd Albert 1er).

Drinking

Café de Paris (☎ 92 16 20 20; place du Casino). In Monte Carlo, this is the place to people-watch and spot the limo from the sprawling terrace. The action gets particularly intense after 10pm when the most exclusive rooms in the casino open.

Other drinking options:

Café Grand Prix (☎ 93 25 57 02; 1 quai Antoine 1er) Live music every night.

Flashman's (☎ 93 30 09 03; 7 av Princess Alice) An unreconstructed British boozer hosting a pot-bellied expat Brit crowd.

Entertainment

Monaco has a lively cultural scene of concerts, opera and ballet, held in the various

venues. Stop by the tourist office for a schedule of local events. Tickets for most cultural events are sold at **Fnac** (☎ 93 10 81 81;
Centre Commercial le Métropole, 17 av Spélugues).

CASINO
The drama of watching people risk their
money in Monte Carlo's spectacularly ornate
Casino de Monte Carlo (☎ 92 16 20 00; www.casino
-monte-carlo.com; European/Private Rooms ☺ from noon Sat
& Sun, from 2pm Mon-Fri), built between 1878 and
1910, makes visiting the gaming rooms almost worth the stiff entry fees: €10 for admission to the European Rooms, which have slot
machines, French roulette and *trente et quar-
ante;* and €20 for the Private Rooms, which
offer baccarat, blackjack, craps and American
roulette. You'll need to show your passport
or driving licence to enter the casino.

Gamblers can also head to the less glamorous gaming rooms adjoining the Café de
Paris (see opposite), which are more casual
and have lower minimum bets.

CINEMAS
Cinéma Le Sporting (☎ 0836 68 00 72; place du Casino; tickets €9) often has movies in their original language. An **open-air cinema** (parking des
Pêcheurs) has nightly shows at 9.30pm in July
and August, specialising in crowd-pleasing
blockbusters (€10 to €15).

THEATRE
A charming spot to while away a summer
evening is the 18th-century fortress, **Théâtre
du Fort Antoine** (☎ 93 50 80 00; av de la Quarantaine),
which is now used as an outside theatre.
Plays are staged here at 9pm or 9.30pm on
Monday in July and August.

Getting There & Away
BUS
There is no bus station in Monaco. Intercity buses leave from various stops around
the city.

CAR
Parking facilities are good in Monaco, with
some 25 official pay car parks scattered

around the principality. One of the most
convenient parks is the casino parking from
where you exit directly to the door of the
tourist office. It's cheaper to park in Beausoleil, if you can find a space.

Driving around Monaco is not recommended (or really necessary). If you are
thinking of driving, be aware that you cannot take your car up into Monaco Ville
unless you have either a Monaco or a 06
(Alpes-Maritimes) licence plate.

TRAIN
Trains to and from Monaco are run by the
French SNCF. For more information visit
the **information desk** (av Prince Pierre) at Monaco
train station.

Taking the train along the coast is highly
recommended – the Mediterranean Sea and
the mountains provide a truly magnificent
sight. There are frequent trains east to
Menton (€1.70, 10 minutes), Nice (€2.90,
20 minutes) and the first town across the
border in Italy, Ventimiglia (Vintimille in
French; €3, 25 minutes).

Getting Around
BUS
Monaco's urban bus system has six lines,
though in practice you are unlikely to ever
need to use the bus since Monaco is so
compact. The most useful bus is Line No
4, linking the train station with the tourist office and the casino. A ticket/*carnet* of
eight costs €1.30/5.25.

Full bus route details can be found in the
free Monaco map given out at the tourist
office.

LIFTS
Some 15 public lifts *(ascenseurs publics)* run
up and down the hillside, all marked on
the free town brochure distributed by the
tourist office. Most operate 24 hours, while
others run between 6am and midnight or
1am only.

TAXI
To order a taxi, call ☎ 93 15 01 01.

Corsica

CONTENTS

Bastia Area 867
Bastia 867
Cap Corse 871
The North Coast 872
Calvi 872
La Balagne 875
Île Rousse (Isula Rossa) 875
Porto to Ajaccio 876
Porto (Portu) 876
Évisa 878
Piana 878
Les Calanques 879
Cargèse (Carghjese) 879
Ajaccio (Ajacciu) 880
South of Ajaccio 885
Filitosa 885
Sartène (Sartè) 885
Bonifacio (Bunifaziu) 886
Corte Area 889
Corte (Corti) 889
Around Corte 892

Though Corsica (Corse) has been governed by mainland France for over 200 years, the island remains a nation apart, with its own distinctive language, customs and character – not to mention an entirely unique landscape. In many ways, Corsica resembles a miniature continent, with 1000km of sea-swept coastline, mountain ranges that stay snowcapped until July, a world-renowned marine reservation (Reserve Naturelle de Scandola), an uninhabited desert (Désert des Agriates) and a 'continental divide' running down the island's centre.

Much of the island is covered with *maquis* – a typically Corsican vegetation with fragrant shrubs that provide the herbs and spices used in Corsican cooking – but a single day's travel can carry you through a kaleidoscopic landscape of secret coves, booming waterfalls, plunging canyons, sweeping bays, megalithic menhirs and dense forests of chestnut and pine. Though the annual influx of tourists outnumbers the island's residents by six to one, Corsica has remained fiercely protective of its heritage, and away from the main holiday resorts, you'll discover the quiet fishing villages, remote mountain towns and deserted beaches that died out in the rest of the Mediterranean long ago.

From the ramshackle harbourfront of Bastia to the bustling streets of Ajaccio, and from the glittering bays of the west coast to the soaring central mountains, nowhere could be more deserving of the title of *l'ile de beâuté* – the island of beauty – than Corsica.

HIGHLIGHTS

- Sample the island's best at **Ajaccio's restaurants** (p883) and food markets
- Cruise the waters of the **Réserve Naturelle de Scandola** (p877)
- Explore Calvi's 15th-century **citadel** (p872)
- Meander along the clifftop road from **Calvi to Porto** (p866)
- Marvel at the **menhirs** (p885) of Filitosa
- Hike through the spectacular **Gorges de Spelunca** (p877)
- Explore isolated **Cap Corse** (p871), Corsica's unspoiled peninsula
- Ponder the permanence of the 'hanging buildings' of **Bonifacio** (p886)

★ Cap Corse
Calvi ★
Réserve Naturelle de Scandola ★
Gorges de Spelunca ★
Ajaccio ★
Filitosa ★
Bonifacio ★

- POPULATION: 260,150
- AREA: 8680 SQ KM

CORSICA

History

From the 11th to 13th centuries Corsica was ruled by the Italian city-state of Pisa, superseded in 1284 by its arch rival, Genoa. To prevent seaborne raids, mainly from North Africa, a massive defence system was constructed that included citadels and coastal watchtowers (many of which can still be seen around the coastline).

On several occasions, Corsican discontent with foreign rule led to open revolt. In 1755, after 25 years of sporadic warfare against the Genoese, Corsicans finally threw off the shackles and declared their independence, led by Pasquale Paoli (1725–1807), under whose rule they established a National Assembly and adopted the most democratic constitution in Europe.

The Corsicans made Corte their capital, outlawed blood vendettas, founded schools and established a university, but the island's independence was short-lived. In 1768 the Genoese ceded Corsica to the French king Louis XV, whose troops crushed Paoli's army in 1769.

The island has since been part of France, except for a period (1794–96) when it was under English domination, and during the German and Italian occupation of 1940–43. Corsica's most famous native son was Napoleon Bonaparte, emperor of France and, in the early 19th century, ruler of most of Europe.

Government & Politics

Despite having spent only 14 years as an autonomous country, the people of Corsica have retained a defiantly independent streak. Although Corsica is heavily subsidised by the French government, nationalists argue that the island should be an independent EU member. In fact, few Corsicans support the Front de Libération Nationale de la Corse (FLNC), whose slogans are spray-painted all over the island.

Since the assassination of Corsica's *préfet* (prefect), Claude Erignac, in Ajaccio in 1998, the French government has cracked down on the corruption that has dogged the island for decades. An undercover investigation into French bank Crédit Agricole in March 1998 uncovered US$150 million of unpaid agricultural loans. Shortly afterwards, a parliamentary report exposed organised gangs and continuing racketeering.

In 2001, the French parliament granted Corsica limited autonomy in exchange for an end to separatist violence, but the bill was overturned by France's high court because it breached the principle of national unity. The only victory for the autonomy movement was the right to have the Corsican language taught in schools.

Language

The Corsican language (Corsu) is more closely related to Italian than French. It's an important part of Corsican identity, and many people (especially at the university in Corte) are working to ensure its survival. Road signs are now bilingual or exclusively in Corsican. You'll see lots of French signs 'edited' with spray paint into their *nomi Corsi* (Corsican names).

THE MOOR'S HEAD

La Tête de Maure (Moor's Head) – a black head wearing a white bandanna and a hooped earring – is the emblem of Corsica. It has been a symbol of victory since the Crusades, but it first showed its face in Corsica in 1297.

Following the island's declaration of independence in 1755, Pasquale Paoli adopted the insignia as a national emblem. According to legend, the bandanna originally covered the Moor's eyes, and was raised to the forehead to symbolise the island's liberation.

When to Go

The best time to visit Corsica is in April and May, when the sun is shining, the olives are ripening, the wildflowers are blooming – and tourists are few. Many hotels, camping grounds and restaurants operate seasonally. Before Easter, there are practically no visitors, but in July and August, prices rocket and Corsica entertains an unending circus of holidaymakers.

Dangers & Annoyances

When Corsica makes the headlines, it's often because nationalist militants have turned nasty (previous acts include bombings, bank robberies and the murder of the prefect). But the violence is not targeted at tourists, and visitors have no need to worry about their safety.

CORSICA (CORSE)

0 — 40 km
0 — 20 miles

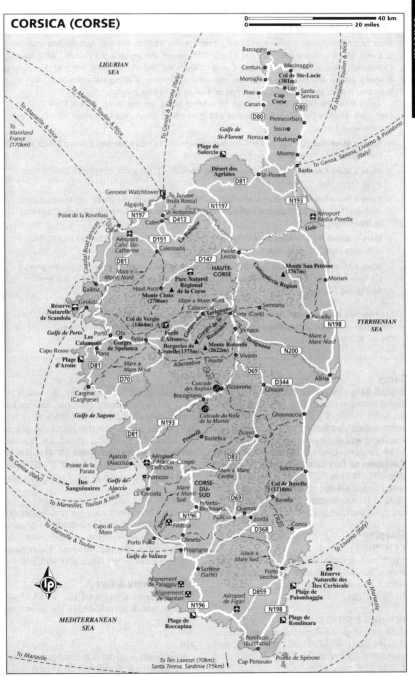

LIGURIAN SEA

To Marseille Toulon & Nice

To Marseille, Toulon & Nice

To Genoa & Savona (Italy)

To Marseille & Nice

To Mainland France (170km)

Barcaggio

Centuri

Macinaggio

Morsiglia

Col de Ste-Lucie (381m)

Pino

Luri

Santa Servara

Canari

Cap Corse

D80

Pietracorbara

D80

Sisco

Golfe de St-Florent

Nonza

Erbalunga

Plage de Saleccia

Miomo

To Genoa, Savona, Livorno & Piombino (Italy)

Désert des Agriates

St-Florent

Bastia

Genoese Watchtower

Île Rousse (Isula Rossa)

D81

N1197

N193

Algajola

St-Antonino

Aéroport Bastia-Poretta

Point de la Revellata

Cateri

D413

Calvi

D151

La Balagne

Golo

Aéroport Calvi-Ste-Catherine

Calenzana

D147

Ponte Leccia

Monte San Petrone (1767m)

D81

HAUTE-CORSE

Castagniccia Region

Moriani

Mare e Monti Nord

Parc Naturel Régional de la Corse

Galéria

Haut Asco

Monte Cinto (2706m)

Mare a Mare Nord

Girolata

Calacuccia

Réserve Naturelle de Scandola

Col de Vergio (1464m)

Tavignanu

Corte (Corti)

Sermanu

Pianellu

N198

TYRRHENIAN SEA

Golfe de Porto

Forêt d'Aitone

Gorges de la Restonica

Venaco

Mare a Mare Nord

Porto

Ota

Evisa

Les Calanques

Gorges de Spelunca

Bergeries de Grotelle(1375m)

Monte Rotondo (2622m)

Capo Rosso

Piana

Vivario

N200

Plage d'Arone

Mare a Mare Nord

Alternative Route

GR20

Aléria

D81

D70

Cascade des Anglais

Vizzavona

D69

D344

Cargèse (Carghjese)

Bocognano

Ghisoni

Golfe de Sagone

Cascade du Voile de la Mariée

Ghisonaccia

N193

Pruneli

Basteli ca

Zicavo

D81

D83

Ajaccio (Aiacciu)

Aéroport d'Ajaccio-Campo Dell'Oro

Mare a Mare Centre

Solenzara

Pointe de la Parata

Porticcio

CORSE-DU-SUD

Col de Bavella (1218m)

Îles Sanguinaires

Golfe d'Ajaccio

Mare e Monti Sud

D69

Bavella

La Crociata

Petreto-Bicchisano

Quenza

To Marseilles, Toulon & Nice

N196

Aullène

Zonza

Conca

Capo di Muro

Taravo

Filitosa

D368

GR20

Porto Pollo

Olmeto

To Marseille & Toulon

Golfe de Valinco

Propriano

Mare a Mare Sud

Sartène (Sarté)

Porto Vecchio

Réserve Naturelle des Îles Cerbicale

Alignement de Palaggiu

Plage de Palombaggia

Alignement de Stantari

Aéroport de Figari

D859

N198

To Marseille

To Genoa (Italy)

N196

Plage de Rondinara

MEDITERRANEAN SEA

Plage de Roccapina

Bonifacio (Bunifaziu)

To Marseille

To Îles Lavezzi (10km); Santa Teresa, Sardinia (15km)

Cap Pertusato

Pointe de Spérone

To Livorno (Italy)

Coastal Boat Services

CORSICA

CORSICA'S GREAT HIKES

Most of Corsica's superb hiking trails pass through the 3300-sq-km Parc Naturel Régional de la Corse. The legendary **GR20** (or Frá Li Monti, 'between the mountains') covers 160km from Calenzana (10km southeast of Calvi) to Conca (20km north of Porto Vecchio). Much of the route is above 2000m and passable only from mid-June to October. Walking the entire trail takes at least two weeks, so you'll need iron lungs as well as a head for heights.

Apart from the GR20, Corsica's most celebrated walks are the three Mare a Mare ('sea to sea') trails, and the two Mare e Monti (sea and mountains), linking the west coast with Corsica's mountainous interior.

- **Mare a Mare Sud** This five-day trail connects Propriano to Porto Vecchio, passing Zonza and the Aiguilles de Bavella en route. Open year-round.

- **Mare a Mare Centre** This seven-day trail links Porticcio (25km south of Ajaccio) with Ghison-accia. Open May to November.

- **Mare a Mare Nord** Connects Cargèse with Moriani (40km south of Bastia), one route passing through the forest of Vizzavona and the village of Vénaco. Allow seven to 12 days. Open May to November.

- **Mare e Monti Nord** Travels from Cargèse to Calenzana (via Évisa, Ota, Girolata and Galéria) and takes about 10 days. Open all year, but best in spring and autumn.

- **Mare e Monti Sud** This walk runs between the bays of the resorts of Porticcio and Propriano via Bisinao, Porto Pollo and Olmeto. It takes five days and is open year-round, but is best in spring and autumn.

Six hundred kilometres of trails are covered in *Walks in Corsica* (€18), published in the UK by Robertson McCarta. Lonely Planet's *Corsica* and *Walking in France* cover many hikes, including the GR20.

Tours

Objectif Nature (Map p868; ☎ /fax 04 95 32 54 34; objectif-nature@wanadoo.fr; 3 rue Notre Dame de Lourdes, Bastia) arranges guided cycling, walking, horse riding and fishing trips, as well as sea kayaking and diving excursions.

In Ajaccio, contact **Maison d'Information Randonées du Parc Naturel Régional de la Corse** (Map p881; ☎ 04 95 51 79 10; www.parc-naturel-corse .com; 2 rue Sgt Casolonga) or **Montagne Corse** (☎ 04 95 20 53 14; www.montagne-corse.com; 7 rue Méditerranée) for walking information.

Sleeping
CAMPING

Most of Corsica's camping grounds open from June to September. In remote areas, hikers can bivouac in *refuge* grounds for €3.50 a night.

REFUGES & GÎTES D'ÉTAPE

Refuges and *gîtes d'étape* (hikers' accommodation) line the GR20 and other trails, and cost from €9 per night. *Gîtes d'étapes* cost €10 to €15; most offer half-board too.

GÎTES

Depending on how far away the beach is, *gîtes ruraux* (country cottages, also called *meublés ruraux*) cost from €395 a week between June and September, but most places are booked up months ahead. In Ajaccio, contact **Relais des Gîtes Ruraux** (☎ 04 95 10 06 14; fax 04 95 10 54 39; 77 cours Napoléon, BP 1020181, Ajaccio Cedex 1) for information.

HOTELS

Corsica's hotel rooms are generally more expensive than mainland France; the minimum price is €30 in low season and €50 from June to September (the high season). Many rural hotels close between November and Easter.

Getting There & Away

Corsica levies a 'regional tax' of €4.57 on visitors, which is included in the following prices.

AIR

Corsica's main airports are at Ajaccio, Bastia, Figari (near Bonifacio) and Calvi.

Air France (☎ 0 820 820 820; www.airfrance.com) has year-round flights from Paris and Lyon to all airports except Figari. Seasonal flights operate from Bordeaux, Lille, Nantes, Mulhouse and Strasbourg to Bastia or Ajaccio. Air France also flies regularly from London to Corsica's main airports.

Compagnie Corse Méditeranée (☎ 0 820 820 820; www.ccm-airlines.com) flies from Bastia and Ajaccio to Marseille, Lyon and Nice year-round, and to Bordeaux, Lille, Lyon, Mulhouse Nantes and Strasbourg in summer.

Littoral Air (www.littoral-airlines.com in French) flies to Calvi, Bastia, Figari and Ajaccio.

BOAT
Mainland France
Most ferries between France (Nice, Marseille and Toulon) and Corsica (Ajaccio, Bastia, Calvi, Île Rousse, Porto Vecchio and Propriano) are handled by **Société Nationale Maritime Corse-Méditerranée** (SNCM; ☎ 0 891 701 801; online bookings www.sncm.fr).

Schedules and fares are listed in the SNCM timetable, available free from tourist and SNCM offices. In summer there are up to eight ferries daily; in winter there are as few as eight a week and fares are much cheaper. In high season, reservations are essential. Remember that ferries are dependent on weather conditions and boats can be cancelled at very short notice (often on the day of departure).

One-way tickets cost €30 (up to €42 for peak summer crossings) from Nice, €35 (€53 in peak periods) from Marseille or Toulon. Daytime crossings from Nice take around four hours. Most crossings from Marseille and Toulon are overnight: the cheapest couchette/most luxurious cabin costs €18/185 extra in summer.

For people under 25 and over 60, single fares are €27/15 in summer/winter from Nice, €40/20 from Marseille and Toulon. Children between four and 12 pay €17/13 in summer/winter from Nice, €19/7 from Marseille or Toulon. Under fours travel free.

Small cars cost €40 to €100 from Marseille or Toulon, or €40 to €108 from Nice, depending on the season. Motorcycles cost €21 to €59 and bicycles cost €10 to €14.

Corsica Ferries and SNCM also have 70km/h express NGV (Navire à Grande Vitesse) ferries from Nice to Calvi (three hours), Île Rousse (three hours), Ajaccio (four hours) and Bastia (four hours). Fares on these zippy NGVs are the same as on normal ferries, but there's a €5 to €8 supplement on peak-period crossings in summer.

In addition to basic fares, each port levies visitor taxes (€7.21 to €10.57 per passenger, €5.45 to €9.27 per vehicle), which vary according to the ports you use.

Italy
Between April and October, scheduled ferries link Corsica with the Italian mainland ports of Genoa, Livorno and Savona, and Porto Terres on neighbouring Sardinia. The season is shorter for smaller boats that cross between Bonifacio and Santa Teresa di Gallura on Sardinia.

Corsica Ferries and Moby Lines are the main operators on these routes. From Livorno (near Pisa and Florence) it's a two-hour voyage to Bastia. A Propriano–Porto Terres trip takes 3½ hours, Genoa–Bastia 6½ hours and Savona to Bastia/Calvi takes six/eight hours.

Fares from mainland Italy are lower than those from mainland France. Corsica Ferries charges €40 to €110 to transport a small car one way and upwards of €16/23 per person (up to €33/33 in high season) on a day/night crossing from Savona to Bastia, Calvi or Île Rousse. Passengers sailing with La Méridionale to Ajaccio or Propriano from Porto Terres pay €19, plus €35 for a car. For port taxes, add about €6 per passenger and €5 per car.

La Méridionale (CMN; France ☎ 08 10 20 13 20; www.cmn.fr), an SNCM subsidiary, has year-round sailings between Marseille and Ajaccio, Bastia and Propriano; and seasonal ferries (April to October) between Porto Terres (Sardinia) and Propriano and Ajaccio.

Corsica Ferries (France ☎ 08 25 09 50 95, Livorno ☎ 0586 88 13 80, Savona ☎ 019 215 62 47; www.corsicaferries.com) runs year-round from Nice to Ajaccio, Bastia, Calvi and Île Rousse, and from Toulon to Ajaccio and Bastia. It runs seasonal ferries from Livorno to Bastia (from April to early November) and from Savona to Bastia, Calvi and Île Rousse (from April to September).

Moby Lines (Corsica ☎ 04 95 34 84 94, Genoa ☎ 010 254 15 13, Livorno ☎ 0565 93 61; www.mobylines.it) has seasonal ferries (from May to September) from Genoa and Livorno to Bastia. Seasonal boats (from April to September) also

---

CORSICA'S TOP FIVE ROAD TRIPS

- **Cape Quest** (Cap Corse, four to six hours, D80) The roller-coaster road around Corsica's windswept peninsula snakes through the bays and fishing villages of the east coast, swings past Corsica's northernmost point, and shoots down the peninsula's windswept western clifftops.

- **West Coast Wonders** (Calvi to Porto, four to six hours, D81 and D81B) One of Corsica's most scenic drives, passing tiny inlets, vertical drops and thundering waves along the cliffs from Calvi to Porto. Take your time, savour the view – and look out for mountain goats.

- **Mountain Madness** (Porto to Vergio, three to four hours, D124 and D84) From Porto, this route climbs through Ota, Évisa and the Gorges de Spelunca to Col de Vergio (1464m), the highest road pass in Corsica. It's a spectacular journey through mountains, chestnut forests and canyons – bring plenty of spare film.

- **Peak Performance** (Zonza to Bavella, two to three hours, D268) The D268 connects Zonza with the Col de Bavella (1261m), a mountain landscape covered by flowers in spring and snow in winter. From the hilltop, you can drink in alpine views all the way to the hazy blue Mediterranean.

- **Hairpin High Jinks** (Vivario to Zicavo, two to four hours, D69) From Vivario, south of Corte, the D69 traverses peaks and valleys on its way through the Vizzavona Forest to Zicavo. Those without a head for heights should stay at home, but they'll be missing one of the island's classic drives.

---

operate between Santa Teresa di Gallura (Sardinia) and Bonifacio.

Getting Around

BUS
Corsica's buses are slow, infrequent and handled by several independent companies. On longer routes, mostly operated by **Eurocorse** (Ajaccio ☎ 04 95 21 06 30, Porto Vecchio ☎ 04 95 70 13 83), there are one, two or, at most, four runs daily. Except in high summer, buses rarely run on Sunday and holidays.

CAR & MOTORCYCLE
Travelling by road is the most convenient way to explore Corsica, but driving isn't easy. Most roads are spectacular but narrow, with hairpin curves and huge drops that demand nerves of steel. Count on averaging 50km/h (and look out for Corsican drivers). The speediest road is the east-coast N198 from Bastia to Bonifacio. A good road map (such as Michelin's yellow-jacketed 1:200,000 map No 90) is indispensable.

TRAIN
Corsica's single-track railway is at least a century behind the TGV, but it's a great (if bone-shattering) way to explore the island. In Corsica, trains are known as *U Trinighellu* ('the trembler'), and you only have to spend

five minutes on one to understand why. The tiny trains screech and judder their way through the mountains, stopping at tiny rural stations and, when necessary, for sheep, goats and cows.

The network's two lines meet at Ponte Leccia. Between September and July, the Ajaccio–Corte–Bastia line is served by four daily trains (two on Sunday and holidays). Two daily trains (coordinated with the Ajaccio–Corte–Bastia service) link Bastia with Ponte Leccia, Île Rousse and Calvi. Services are reduced in winter and increased in August.

Fares range from €9.70 (Bastia–Corte) to €24.50 (Ajaccio–Calvi). Children under 12 travel half-price; under fours travel free. Transporting a bicycle costs €18. For further details, contact **Chemins de Fer de Corse** (CFC; Bastia ☎ 04 95 32 80 61; www.ter-sncf.com/trains _touristiques/corse_anglais.htm).

Rail Passes
For return journeys of less than 200km within 48 hours, the *billet touristique* (tourist ticket) is 25% cheaper than a regular ticket, but is unavailable from July to September.

Holders of InterRail passes get 50% off normal fares. The CFC sells its own rail pass – the Carte Zoom – which costs €47 and buys unlimited train travel for seven days.

BASTIA AREA

BASTIA

pop 37,800
Bustling Bastia is Corsica's main centre of business and commerce. With its crumbling citadel, narrow streets, colourful tenement buildings and tree-lined squares, the city has a distinctly Italian atmosphere and was once the seat of the island's Genoese governors. Little effort has been made to smarten up the city for tourists, making it an authentic and atmospheric introduction to modern-day Corsica. You can easily spend a day exploring, the old port being Bastia's highlight – but most visitors move on pretty quickly.

Orientation

The focal point of the Bastia is place St-Nicolas. Bastia's main thoroughfares are the busy shopping street of boulevard Paoli and av Maréchal Sébastiani, which links the ferry port with the train station. The town's three older neighbourhoods are south of place St-Nicolas: Terra Vecchia (centred on place de l'Hôtel de Ville), the old port and the citadel.

Information

BOOKSHOPS
Librairie Album (☎ 04 95 31 08 59; 19 blvd Paoli; ☽ 8am-noon & 1.30-7.30pm Mon-Sat, 9am-12.30pm Sun) Big bookshop with an excellent travel section.
Librairie-Papeterie Papi (☎ 04 95 31 00 96; 5 rue César Campinchi; ☽ 7.30am-noon & 1.30-7pm Mon-Sat) Sells walking maps, topoguides and travel books.

EMERGENCY
Centre Hospitalier Général Paese Nuovo (☎ 04 95 59 11 11; Route Impériale)
Police National (☎ 04 95 54 50 22) Near the northern ferry terminal.

INTERNET ACCESS
Cyber Space (☎ 04 95 30 70 83; 3 blvd Paoli; per 15min/hr €1/3.80; ☽ 9am-midnight Mon-Sat, 4pm-midnight Sun) Mainly geared towards Internet gamers.
Oxy Cybercafé (☎ 04 95 58 27 96; rue Salvatore Viale; per hr €3.10; ☽ 9am-midnight Mon-Sat)

LAUNDRY
Le Lavoir du Port (☽ 7am-9pm) In the car park near the end of rue du Commandant Luce de Casabianca.

MONEY
Banks are dotted along place St-Nicolas, rue César Campinchi and rue du Conventionnel Salicetti. Most have ATMs. The exchange bureau in the southern ferry terminal is only open in summer.

POST
Post Office (av Maréchal Sébastiani; ☽ 8am-7pm Mon-Fri, 8am-noon Sat)

TOURIST OFFICES
Tourist Office (☎ 04 95 55 96 85; www.bastia-tourisme.com; place St-Nicolas; ☽ 8am-6pm Mon-Sat, 8am-1pm Sun)

Sights

Bastia can be covered in a half-day stroll starting with **place St-Nicolas**, a vast seafront esplanade laid out in the 19th century. The square is lined with trees and cafés, and at the southern end, a bizarre statue of **Napoleon Bonaparte** depicted as a muscle-bound Roman emperor stands guard, ringed by a phalanx of palm trees.

Between place St-Nicolas and the old port lies **Terra Vecchia**, a historic neighbourhood of old houses and tumbledown tenement blocks. Its centre is the shady **place de l'Hôtel de Ville**, now an open-air marketplace. On rue Napoléon, the baroque **Oratoire de l'Immaculée** once served as the seat of the Anglo-Corsican parliament.

The **old port** is an atmospheric jumble of boats, restaurants and crumbling buildings, dominated by the twin towers of the **Église St-Jean Baptiste**, which loom over the north side of the harbour. The best views are from **Jetée du Dragon** (Dragon Jetty) on the southern side of the harbour, where you can admire the luxury pleasure cruisers and watch the local blue and white fishing boats setting out to sea.

Bastia's most historic quarter juts out above the old port. The **citadel** in Terra Nova was built by the Genoese between the 15th and 17th centuries to protect Bastia's harbour. To reach it, climb the stairs through **Jardin Romieu**, the hillside park on the southern side of the harbour. Inside the citadel, winding streets lead to **Cathédrale Ste-Marie**, which contains one of the city's most precious relics, a mysterious black-oak crucifix hauled from the sea by fishermen in the 14th century.

CORSICA

BASTIA

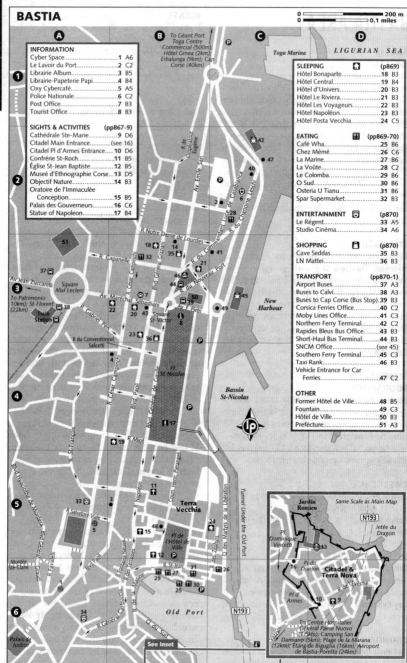

0 ————— 200 m
0 ————— 0.1 miles

INFORMATION
Cyber Space	1	A6
Le Lavoir du Port	2	C2
Librairie Album	3	B5
Librairie-Papeterie Papi	4	B4
Oxy Cybercafé	5	A5
Police Nationale	6	C2
Post Office	7	B3
Tourist Office	8	B3

SIGHTS & ACTIVITIES (pp867–9)
Cathédrale Ste-Marie	9	D6
Citadel Main Entrance	(see 16)	
Citadel Pl d'Armes Entrance	10	D6
Confrérie St-Roch	11	B5
Église St-Jean Baptiste	12	B5
Museé d'Ethnographie Corse	13	D5
Objectif Nature	14	B3
Oratoire de l'Immaculée Conception	15	B5
Palais des Gouverneurs	16	C6
Statue of Napoleon	17	B4

SLEEPING (p869)
Hôtel Bonaparte	18	B3
Hôtel Central	19	B4
Hôtel d'Univers	20	B3
Hôtel Le Riviera	21	B3
Hôtel Les Voyageurs	22	B3
Hôtel Napoléon	23	B3
Hôtel Posta Vecchia	24	C5

EATING (pp869–70)
Café Wha	25	B6
Chez Mémé	26	C6
La Marine	27	B6
La Voûte	28	C2
Le Colomba	29	B6
O Sud	30	B6
Osteria U Tianu	31	B6
Spar Supermarket	32	B3

ENTERTAINMENT (p870)
Le Régent	33	A5
Studio Cinéma	34	A6

SHOPPING (p870)
Cave Seddas	35	B3
LN Mattei	36	B3

TRANSPORT (pp870–1)
Airport Buses	37	A3
Buses to Calvi	38	A3
Buses to Cap Corse (Bus Stop)	39	B3
Corsica Ferries Office	40	C2
Moby Lines Office	41	C2
Northern Ferry Terminal	42	C2
Rapides Bleus Bus Office	43	B3
Short-Haul Bus Terminal	44	B3
SNCM Office	(see 45)	
Southern Ferry Terminal	45	C3
Taxi Rank	46	B3
Vehicle Entrance for Car Ferries	47	C2

OTHER
Former Hôtel de Ville	48	B5
Fountain	49	C3
Hôtel de Ville	50	B3
Préfecture	51	A3

To Géant Port
Toga Centre
Commercial (500m);
Hôtel Ginea (2km);
Erbalunga (9km); Cap
Corse (40km)

Toga Marina

LIGURIAN SEA

R de l'Impératrice Eugénie

Av Émile Sari

R du Commandant Luce de Casablanca

R du Chanoine Leschi

R Notre Dame de Lourdes

R Capanelle

Av Jean Zuccarelli

Square Mal Leclerc

To Patrimonio
10km); St-Florent
(22km)

R Gabriel Péri

R du Conventionnel Salicetti

Av Maréchal Sébastiani

R César Campinchi

Blvd Général Graziani

Blvd du Nouveau Port

Square St-Victor

Av F Pietri

New Harbour

Train Station

Bassin St-Nicolas

Pl St-Nicolas

R Miot

R St-François

Blvd Hyacinthe de Montera

Blvd Général Giraud

R Favalelli

R Salvatore Viale

Terra Vecchia

Cours Henri Pierangeli

Q des Martyrs de la Libération

Tunnel Under the Old Port

R Napoléon

Blvd Paoli

Blvd Général de Gaulle

Fontaine Neuve

R St-Jean

Pl de l'Hôtel de Ville

Montée Ste-Claire

R Général Carbuccia

R de la Marine

Q du Sud

Old Port

N193

Palais de Justice

See Inset

Inset:

Jardin Romieu

Same Scale as Main Map

N193

Jetée du Dragon

Pl Dominique Vincetti

Pl du Donjon

Citadel & Terra Nova

R de l'Évêché

Pl d'Armes

To Centre Hospitalier
Général Paese Nuovo
(1.5km); Camping San
Damiano (5km); Plage de la Marana
(12km); Étang de Biguglia (16km); Aéroport
de Bastia-Poretta (24km)

Close by, the fiery-orange **Palais des Gouverneurs** (Governors' Palace; place du Donjon) is home to Bastia's anthropology museum, **Musée d'Ethnographie Corse**. Both are currently closed as part of a €6 million restoration project. There's also an old Clarissian convent, which became a **prison** in the 19th century.

Activities

Objectif Nature (☎ /fax 04 95 32 54 34; objectif-nature@wanadoo.fr; 3 rue Notre Dame de Lourdes; ☺ 9am-6pm Mon-Sat) organises outdoor activities in the Bastia area, including kayaking, sea fishing, hiking, mountaineering and diving.

Sleeping

Like the rest of Corsica, Bastia's hotels hike up their prices in summer. Many have their reception desks on the 1st floor.

BUDGET

Hôtel Central (☎ 04 95 31 71 12; www.centralhotel.fr; 3 rue Miot; s €40-65, d €40-78 depending on season; ☒) As its name suggests, it's right in the city centre and the rooms have all been refurbished: the best have balconies and kitchenettes. You can also rent apartments (€50 to €65 per day, €305 to €420 per week).

Hôtel Le Riviera (☎ 04 95 31 07 16; www.corsehoteriviera.com in French; 1bis rue du Nouveau Port; s €40-60, d €60-80 depending on season; ☒) Rather like the rest of town – in dire need of some tender-loving care. The rooms are about as cheap as they get in Bastia, if you don't mind the odd spot of peeling plasterwork.

Camping

Camping San Damiano (☎ 04 95 33 68 02; www.campingsandamiano.com; camping low/high season €5.50/6.50; ☺ Apr-Oct) A shady seaside camping ground 5km south of Bastia, with furnished bungalows available. Served by the airport bus.

MID-RANGE

Hotel d'Univers (☎ 04 95 31 03 38; fax 04 95 31 19 91; 3 av Maréchal Sébastiani; s/d/tr low season €45/55/65, high season €60/70/80; ☒) The pick of Bastia's mid-range hotels, tucked between the old and new towns. The tasteful rooms have white walls, colourful bedspreads and wooden floors.

Hôtel Les Voyageurs (☎ 04 95 34 90 80; www.hotel-lesvoyageurs.com; 9 av Maréchal Sébastiani; d low season €52-80, high season €55-90; ☒) A smart three-star hotel with luxurious touches, up the street

from the Univers. Features include a lovely dining area behind a wrought-iron screen.

Hôtel Posta Vecchia (☎ 04 95 32 32 38; www.hotel-postavecchia.com; quai des Martyrs de la Libération; s/d with sea views €37/41, low season €54/60; ☒) One of the few hotels with sea views in Bastia. Don't be put off by the pebble-dash outside – inside the hotel is full of charm, and the old port is just around the corner.

Hôtel Napoléon (☎ 04 95 31 60 30; 43 blvd Paoli; d low season €49-75, high season €64-95) Another central option with small, comfortable doubles, though some of the décor is dated. Check out the colourful Corsican mural as you climb the stairs to reception.

Also recommended:

Hôtel Bonaparte (☎ 04 95 34 07 10; www.hotel-bonaparte-bastia.com; 45 blvd Général Graziani; s/d/tr low season €58/60/75, high season €68/87/100) Plain, modern hotel close to the port.

Hôtel Cyrnea (☎ 04 95 31 41 71; route de Cap; d low season €45-83; Ⓟ ☒) Purpose-built seafront hotel 2km north of Bastia.

Eating

For a quick *café créme* or ice cream, terraced cafés line place St-Nicolas. More restaurants are clustered around the old port, quai des Martyrs de la Libération and place de l'Hôtel de Ville.

La Voûte (☎ 04 95 32 47 11; 6 rue du Commandant Luce de Casabianca; lunch/dinner menu €12.95/20.70; ☺ Mon-Sat) Sophisticated French cuisine is served here under brick vaults or on a balcony with harbour view. The fish soup (€10) and *gambas à la provençale* (king prawns, €19) offer a true taste of the Mediterranean.

The old port is crammed with restaurants to suit all tastes: some are cosy and traditional, while others have packed terraces and lay on summer entertainment.

La Marine (☎ 06 12 21 38 09; 8 rue St-Jean; menus €12-21; ☺ Mon-Sat) An informal seafood restaurant that also offers pizzas and Corsican fare on its portside terrace; most of the fish literally comes straight off the boats.

Café Wha (☎ 04 95 34 25 79; Vieux Port; mains €7.80-14.90) A popular place on the old port, with a cheap Tex-Mex menu and regular theme nights. It serves generous *quesadillas* (€6 to €8) and fajitas (€8 to €10), and is nearly always chock-a-block with Bastiais and tourists alike.

Chez Mémé (☎ 04 95 31 44 12; quai des Martyrs de la Libération; menus €14-17) One of many seafront

COMIC BOOKS, CHECKMATE & CORSICAN BLUES

In April, Bastia hosts France's trendiest *bandes dessinées* (comics) festival, BD à Bastia. The graphic novel is a revered French art form, and the festival attracts big names from the pen-and-ink world – this is not the place to show off your second-rate Astérix collection.

In late summer, the tiny village of Patrimonio, about 10km west of Bastia, hosts **Nuits de la Guitare à Patrimonio** (☎ 04 95 37 12 15; www.festival-guitare-patrimonio.com), one of Europe's major guitar festivals. Jazz, blues, rock and classical guitar all find a home on the main outdoor stage.

Bastia's annual Italian Cinema Festival is held in February. There are British and Spanish film weeks later in the year. Other events include a Corsican music festival in October, and the island's hotly contested chess championships in November.

restaurants near the old port. It's a simple, unpretentious place that specialises in fish and shellfish: the €14 *menu corse* includes Corsican meats and cheeses.

Osteria U Tianu (☎ 04 95 31 36 67; 4 rue Rigo; menu €19; 7pm-1am Mon-Sat) This small, homely restaurant, hidden away down a backstreet behind the old port, is one of the best places in Bastia to sample authentic Corsican cuisine. The €19 five-course *menu* includes a range of traditional dishes and includes wine, so it's usually packed to the gunnels.

Also recommended:

Le Colomba (☎ 04 95 32 79 14; Vieux Port; pizzas €7-10) The best pizzas in the old port.

O Sud (☎ 04 95 31 00 90; Vieux Port; menus from €12) Upbeat restaurant next door to Café Wha.

SELF-CATERING

There's a lively morning **food market** (place de l'Hôtel de Ville; Tue-Sun). The large **Spar supermarket** (rue César Campinchi) is the most convenient place for supplies. Out of town, the huge Géant Port Toga Centre Commercial houses a Casino supermarket.

Entertainment

Le Régent (☎ 04 95 31 30 31; www.leregent.fr; rue César Campinchi) A large multi-screen cinema screening the latest releases (nearly always in French).

Studio Cinéma (☎ 04 95 31 12 94; www.studio-cinema.com; rue Miséricorde) A small arts cinema near the Palais de Justice that shows both French and international films, and also hosts several of Bastia's annual film weeks.

Shopping

Cave Seddas (3 av Emile Sari) is stocked with Corsican wines, while **LN Mattei** (15 blvd Général de Gaulle) is the place to buy the local liqueur, Cap Corse – Louis Napoléon Mattei invented

the liqueur in the late 19th century. Both of these shops sell Corsican jams, honeys and other delicacies.

Arrive at the Sunday **flea-market** (place St-Nicolas) before 9am for the best selection.

Getting There & Around

AIR

Aéroport Bastia-Poretta (☎ 04 95 54 54 54; www.bastia.aeroport.fr) is 24km south of the city. Buses (€8, seven to nine daily, fewer on Sunday) depart from outside the Préfecture building. The tourist office has schedules, and timetables are posted at the bus stop. A taxi to the airport costs €20 to €30.

BUS

The bus service in Bastia is bewildering – there is no central terminus and buses leave from several locations around town. The tourist office can provide timetables and show you where to catch your bus. Rue du Nouveau Port, north of the tourist office, is a makeshift terminus for buses serving villages south and west of Bastia.

Eurocorse (☎ 04 95 31 73 76) travels to Ajaccio (€18, three hours) via Corte (€10, two hours) twice daily except on Sundays.

Rapides Bleus (☎ 04 95 31 03 79; 1 av Maréchal Sébastiani) runs buses to Porto Vecchio (€18.50), with connections to Bonifacio and Sartène. It also sells tickets for the Eurocorse service to Corte and Ajaccio.

Les Beaux Voyages (☎ 04 95 65 11 35) travels to Calvi (€12.50, two hours) daily except Sunday. Buses leave at 4.30pm from outside the train station.

TRAIN

The **train station** (☎ 04 95 32 80 61; av Maréchal Sébastiani; 6am-8.40pm Mon-Sat, 8.40am-12.40pm & 4.15-8.40pm Sun) is beside the large roundabout on Square Mal Leclerc. Main destinations include Ajaccio (€20.70, four hours, four daily) via Corte, and Calvi (€15.70, three hours, three or four daily) via L'Île Rousse.

BOAT

The southern ferry terminal is at the eastern end of av François Pietri. The vehicle entrance is 600m north.

There's an **SNCM** (☎ 04 95 54 66 81; www.sncm .com; ☒ 8-11.45am & 2-5.45pm Mon-Fri, 8am-noon Sat) office in the southern terminal. Tickets are sold two hours before departure in the Corsica Marittima section of the terminal building.

Moby Lines (☎ 04 95 34 84 94; www.mobylines.it; 4 rue du Commandant Luce de Casabianca; ☒ 8am-noon & 2-6pm Mon-Fri, 8am-noon Sat) has a bureau in the ferry terminal, open two hours before each sailing.

The **Corsica Ferries** (☎ 04 95 32 95 95; corsicafér ries.com; 15bis rue Chanoine Leschi; ☒ 8.30am-noon & 2-6pm Mon-Fri, 9am-noon Sat) office is across the road from the ferry terminal.

CAP CORSE

The narrow peninsula at Corsica's upper tip stretches 40km north from Bastia. It's a wild, ruggedly beautiful area, sliced down the centre by mountains and ringed by spectacular coastline dotted with crumbling Genoese watchtowers, sandy coves and rocky cliffs.

Cap Corse can be visited by bus from Bastia, but the trip is more fun if you have your own transport. With legs of steel and time to spare, the area can also be explored by bike. Less energetic types can cover it in a day by car, but be prepared for some adventurous driving – Cap Corse's clifftop roads are not for the faint-hearted.

North of Bastia, the road winds through gentle bays and quiet fishing villages, including **Erbalunga**, **Sisco** and **Pietracorbara**, where you'll find one of the coast's best beaches.

At Santa Servara, the road splits in two. The western branch climbs though the village of Luri to the hilltop tower at **Col de Ste-Lucie**, where the Roman poet-philosopher Seneca was exiled in the 1st century. The second branch continues north to **Macinaggio**, a small fishing port and tourist town, and **Barcaggio**, near Corsica's northernmost point.

The west coast is wilder, with villages perched high on the steep cliffs and jagged inlets cut into the coastline. From Barcaggio, the road swings south to **Centuri**, with its traditional Corsican houses clustered around a pretty harbour. Further south, past the villages of **Pino** and **Canari**, you'll arrive at **Nonza**, where the houses tumble down the cliff in steep terraces to a vast grey-sand bay. The historic village is famous for the fortified tower perched above the beach and the 11th century chapel of St Julia (who was martyred in Nonza in the 5th century).

The final stretch passes sweeping bays on the way to **St-Florent**, a busy harbour at the end of the Cap Corse peninsula.

Sleeping & Eating

Macchia e Mare (☎ 04 95 35 21 36; www.macchia-e -mare.com in French; d Oct-Mar €44-53, Apr-Aug €45-63; P) In the east-coast village of Pietracorbara. The best rooms have sea views and terraces, and the white, sandy beach is moments away.

Le Vieux Moulin (☎ 04 95 35 60 15; www.le-vieux -moulin.net in French; d Apr-May & Oct €47-65, Jun-Sep €50-75; P) A traditional cottage hotel near Centuri harbour. The attached seafood restaurant is one of the most popular on the peninsula.

Les Tamaris (☎ 04 95 37 81 91; www.lestamaris .com; d May & Sep-Oct €51-58, Jun-Aug €60-75; P) This modern hotel in Canari is close to the beach and organises activities such as horse riding and local walks. Self-catering apartments cost €305 to €615 per week.

CAMPING

Camping La Pietra (☎ 04 95 35 27 49; ☒ May-Oct) A large, family-oriented camping ground near Sisco, which has all the creature comforts, but gets crowded in summer.

Camping L'Isulottu (☎ 04 95 35 62 81; www.paradisu .com; ☒ Feb-Nov; 🏊) A shady, secluded camping area near Morsiglia, south of Centuri, with swimming pool, restaurant and bar.

Getting There & Away

The main road around Cap Corse is the D80. **Société des Transports Interurbains Bastiais** (☎ 04 95 31 06 65) handles buses to Cap Corse. Destinations include Erbalunga (€2, six to eight daily), Pietracorbara (€2.60) and Macinaggio (€6.40, two daily except Sunday). Buses leave from av François Pietri, opposite the tourist office, in Bastia.

THE NORTH COAST

CALVI

pop 4800

The prosperous harbour town of Calvi sits at the edge of a sparkling crescent-shaped bay, backed by the snowy peaks of Monte Cinto (2706m) and its neighbours. Once a strategic military outpost, today Calvi is a thriving pleasure port that attracts sun seekers and weekend sailors from all over the Mediterranean, though the towers, bastions and clustered houses of its 15th-century citadel remain as relics of its martial past.

In 1794, a British expeditionary fleet assisting Pasquale Paoli's Corsican nationalist forces besieged and bombarded Calvi. In the course of the battle, a certain Captain Horatio Nelson was wounded by rock splinters and lost the use of his right eye.

Orientation

The citadel – also known as the Haute Ville (upper city) – is on a rocky promontory northeast of the Basse Ville (lower city). Blvd Wilson, the major thoroughfare through town, is uphill from the marina.

Information

BOOKSHOPS

Hall de la Presse (☎ 04 95 65 05 14; 13 blvd Wilson; 🕑 9am-noon & 2-6pm Mon-Sat) Sells topoguides and walking maps.

EMERGENCY

Antenne Médicale du SAMU (☎ 04 95 65 11 22; route du Stade)

INTERNET ACCESS

Café de l'Orient (☎ 04 95 65 00 16; quai Landry; connection/per min €1/0.10; 🕑 9am-late)

MONEY

Banks, including Crédit Lyonnais, can be found along blvd Wilson.

POST

Post Office (blvd Wilson)

TOURIST OFFICES

Tourist Office main office (☎ 04 95 65 16 67; omt .calvi@wanadoo.fr; 🕑 8.30am-1pm & 2.30-7pm Jun–mid-Sep, 9am-noon & 2-6pm Mon-Sat Oct-May); Citadel (🕑 9am-noon Mon-Sat, Jun-Sep) The main office is near the marina.

Sights & Activities

CITADEL

Set atop a granite promontory surrounded by massive Genoese fortifications, Calvi's 15th-century **citadel** dominates the harbour skyline. The town's loyalty to Genoa is recalled by the motto *Civitas Calvi Semper Fidelis* (the city of Calvi, forever faithful) carved over the citadel gateway. The majority of its buildings are closed to the public.

The **Palais des Gouverneurs** (Governors' Palace, place d'Armes) was once the seat of power for the Genoese administration and now serves (under the name Caserne Sampiero) as a base for the French Foreign Legion. Look out for soldiers wearing the regiment's distinctive white caps around town.

Up the hill from Caserne Sampiero is the 13th-century **Église St-Jean Baptiste**, rebuilt in 1570. The women of the local elite sat in the screened boxes, with grilles sheltering them from the rabble's inquisitive gaze. Near the altar is the *Christ des Miracles*, an ebony statue that was paraded around town in 1553 shortly before the besieging Turkish forces fell back. Credited with saving Calvi from the Saracens, the statue has become a much-revered relic.

CORSICAN POLYPHONY

Corsican band Les Nouvelles Polyphonies Corses won the heart of a nation with its magnetic polyphonic performance at the 1992 Winter Olympics in Albertville, France.

Corsican chants are traditionally sung a cappella (without musical accompaniment). *Paghjellas* feature three male voices – a tenor, baritone and bass – and mark the passage of life. Equally compelling are the church chants of the mountainous Castagniccia region, east of Corte. In Pigna, south of Île Rousse, summer polyphonic evenings are held in the **Casa Musicale** (☎ 04 95 61 77 31). Calvi hosts the five-day Rencontres Polyphoniques festival every September.

The recordings of the Sartène Male Voice Choir and contemporary bands I Muvrini, Canta U Populu Corsu and Les Nouvelles Polyphonies Corses are available on CD.

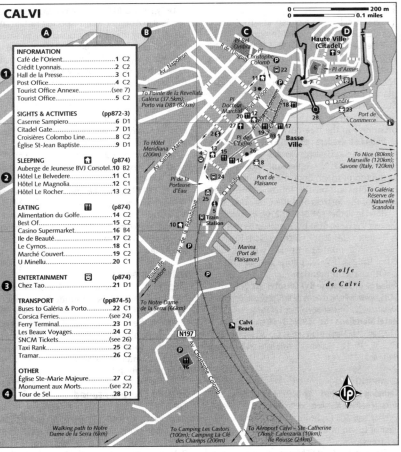

CALVI

0 ————— 200 m
0 ————— 0.1 miles

INFORMATION	
Café de l'Orient...........................1	C2
Crédit Lyonnais.........................2	C2
Hall de la Presse.......................3	C1
Post Office................................4	C2
Tourist Office Annexe.............(see 7)	
Tourist Office...........................5	C2

SIGHTS & ACTIVITIES	(pp872-3)
Caserne Sampiero.....................6	D1
Citadel Gate.............................7	D1
Croisières Colombo Line...........8	C2
Église St-Jean Baptiste..............9	D1

SLEEPING	(p874)
Auberge de Jeunesse BVJ Corsotel..10	B2
Hôtel Le Belvedere..................11	C1
Hôtel Le Magnolia...................12	C1
Hôtel Le Rocher......................13	C2

EATING	(p874)
Alimentation du Golfe..............14	C2
Best Of...................................15	C2
Casino Supermarket.................16	B4
Ile de Beauté..........................17	C2
Le Cyrnos...............................18	C1
Marché Couvert.......................19	C2
U Minellu................................20	C1

ENTERTAINMENT	(p874)
Chez Tao.................................21	D1

TRANSPORT	(pp874-5)
Buses to Galéria & Porto..........22	C1
Corsica Ferries.......................(see 24)	
Ferry Terminal.........................23	D1
Les Beaux Voyages..................24	C2
SNCM Tickets.........................(see 26)	
Taxi Rank...............................25	C2
Tramar...................................26	C2

OTHER	
Église Ste-Marie Majeure...........27	C2
Monument aux Morts............(see 22)	
Tour de Sel.............................28	D1

In the northern part of the citadel, a plaque marks the house where navigator Christopher Columbus was supposedly born – though the historical evidence is sketchy. The best views are from the citadel's ramparts, where you can gaze across the glittering Golfe du Calvi and the harbour.

BEACHES
Calvi's 4km of beach begins at the marina and runs east around the Golfe de Calvi.

Tours
Croisières Colombo Line (☎ 04 95 65 32 10; www .colombo-line.com in French; marina; ☼ Apr-Oct) offers glass-bottomed boat excursions (€45) to the seaside hamlets of Galéria and Girolata

(€50) via the Réserve Naturelle de Scandola nature reserve (see p877). Shorter trips just visit Scandola (€40).

Festivals & Events
Calvi's major events include **La Granitola** (an Easter penitential procession), a **fireworks festival** in May and Corsica's biggest **jazz festival** in June. More traditional tones can be heard at the **Rencontres Polyphoniques** music festival in September.

In autumn, **Le Festival du Vent** (☎ 04 95 65 16 67; www.le-festival-du-vent.com) celebrates wind in all its forms, with music, theatre and art exhibitions in town, sailing and windsurfing in the harbour and paragliding and air displays in the skies above Calvi.

Sleeping

Calvi's hotels aren't cheap at any time of year, and most are closed in winter.

Hôtel Le Magnolia (☎ 04 95 65 19 16; fax 04 95 65 08 02; cnr place du Marché & rue Alsace-Lorraine; s low/high season €65/85, d low season €77-97, high season €100-120; ☺ Apr-Jan; ☒) An elegant hotel ideally placed just behind the harbour, near Église Ste-Marie. The impeccable rooms have garden or sea views, and you can have breakfast or supper in the tree-covered courtyard.

Hôtel Le Belvedere (☎ 04 95 65 01 25; www.resa-hotels-calvi.com; place Christophe Colomb; d low season €45-54, high season €85-115; ☒) A pleasant, modern hotel at the top of town, opposite the citadel. The best rooms are on the top floor, with dual views of the fortress and the Golfe de Calvi.

Hôtel Le Rocher (☎ 04 95 65 20 04; www.hotel-le-rocher.com; blvd Wilson; d €90-190, 2-person apt per week €389-793, 4-person €645-1080; ☺ Apr-Sep; ☒) Provides rooms and mini-apartments with kitchenettes, fridges, TV, telephone and air-con.

Other recommendations:

Auberge de Jeunesse BVJ Corsotel (☎ 04 95 65 14 15; www.bvjhotel.com; av de la République; dm incl breakfast €22; ☺ Mar-Nov) Offers 120 budget beds.

Hotel Meridiana (☎ 04 95 65 31 38; fax 04 95 65 32 72; av Santa Maria; d low season €55-80, high season €90-158; ☒ ☒) Modern villa-style hotel set back from the town.

CAMPING

Camping Les Castors (☎ 04 95 65 13 30; www.castors.fr; route de Pietra Maggiore; adult/car/tent €8.20/2.90/3.20; ☺ May-Sep; ☒) Eight hundred metres southeast of town, in a sheltered spot under poplar trees.

Camping La Clé des Champs (☎ 04 95 65 00 86; camagni2@wanadoo.fr; route de Pietra Maggiore; per adult/car/tent €6/2/2.50; ☺ reception 9am-10.30pm Apr-Oct) South of Les Castors, but still only a short walk to the beach.

Eating

Calvi's restaurants are generally good, but you won't find many *menus* for under €12. From May to September, quai Landry and rue Clemenceau buzz with well-heeled visitors browsing for a place to eat.

Île de Beauté (☎ 04 95 65 00 46; quai Landry; menus €20) The best of the romantic cafés and restaurants along Calvi's waterfront. It specialises in fish and Corsican cuisine: delicacies include red mullet salad, sea bream in pesto sauce, and crab soup.

Le Cyrnos (☎ 04 95 65 06 10; quai Landry; menu €17; ☺ Mar-Nov) Another well-respected restaurant further along the quay, particularly renowned for the chef's *soupe de poissons* (fish soup).

U Minellu (☎ 04 95 65 05 52; Traverse à l'Église; menus €14-16; ☺ closed Sun in winter) A delightful family-run restaurant opposite Église Ste-Marie, serving Corsican dishes under a wooden awning lit by lanterns. The *menu Corse* (€16) includes regional specialities such as *brocciu* cannelloni, Corsican cooked pork, and chestnut and apple cake.

If you're looking for a snack on the move, head for **Best Of** (1 rue Clemenceau; ☺ 11.30am-10pm), which serves sandwiches and paninis (€4 to €6). The **marché couvert** (covered market; ☺ 8am-noon Mon-Sat) is near Église Ste-Marie Majeure. There's a large **Casino Supermarket** (av Christophe Colomb) south of the train station. Alternatively, try the well-stocked **Alimentation du Golfe** (rue Clemenceau).

Entertainment

Chez Tao (☎ 04 95 65 00 73; ☺ May-Oct) Calvi's best-known nightspot, founded by a member of the Russian White Cavalry escaping from the Crimean War. Celebrities and Corsicans alike head for this renowned piano bar for dancing and late-night drinking in summer – it's so hip it only has to open three months of the year.

Getting There & Around

AIR

Southeast of town (7km) is **Aéroport Calvi-Ste-Catherine** (☎ 04 95 65 88 88; www.calvi.aeroport.fr). Littoral Airlines and Air France link Calvi with Nice, Marseille, Lyon and other French cities. There is no bus service from Calvi to the airport. **Taxis** (☎ 04 95 65 03 10) can be picked up from place de la Porteuse d'Eau for around €15.

BOAT

The ferry terminal is below the southern side of the citadel. From Calvi there are express NGV ferries to Nice (2½ hours, five a week).

Ferry tickets can be bought at the port two hours before departure. At other times, SNCM tickets are handled by **Tramar** (☎ 04 95 65 01 38; quai Landry; ☺ 9am-noon & 2-6pm Mon-Fri, 9am-noon Sat). Tickets for Corsica Ferries are handled by **Les Beaux Voyages** (☎ 04 95 65 15 02; place de la Porteuse d'Eau).

BUS
The tourist office can provide bus information and can supply timetables. Buses to Bastia (€12.50, 2¼ hours) are run by **Les Beaux Voyages** (☎ 04 95 65 15 02; place de la Porteuse d'Eau).

From mid-May to mid-October, **Autocars SAIB** (☎ 04 95 22 41 99) runs buses from Calvi's Monument aux Morts (war memorial) to Galéria (1¼ hours) and Porto (three hours). There are no buses on Sunday.

TRAIN
Calvi's **train station** (☎ 04 95 65 00 61; ☺ until 7.30pm) is off av de la République. There are two departures daily to Ajaccio (€24.10), Bastia (€15.70) and the stations between.

From April to October, the single-car trains of CFC's Tramway de la Balagne (see p866) make 19 stops along the coast between Calvi and Île Rousse (45 minutes). The line is divided into three sectors – you need one ticket for each sector. *Carnets* (books) of six tickets (€8) are sold at stations.

LA BALAGNE
The Balagne is an area of low hills between the Monte Cinto massif and the sea. Its coastline stretches northeast from Galéria, all the way to **Désert des Agriates**, the maquis-covered desert east of Île Rousse. The coast between Calvi and Île Rousse is dotted with fine-sand beaches, including **Algajola**, **Aregno** and **Renalta**. Many are served by Le Tramway de la Balagne.

Inland, La Balagne is known as the 'Garden of Corsica', renowned for the fertility of its soil. The main town of **Calenzana** marks the northern terminus of the GR20 and Mare e Monti trails.

After the village of Cateri, bear right along the D413 for 2.5km to **St-Antonino**, dramatically perched on a hilltop and offering stunning views.

ÎLE ROUSSE (ISULA ROSSA)
pop 2300

The port of Île Rousse was founded by Pasquale Paoli in 1758 to compete with pro-Genoese Calvi, 24km northeast. During the 18th and 19th centuries, it became an important commercial harbour, but these days it's a busy beach resort and the main trade is in tourists. Its name comes from the red granite of Île de la Pietra, a rocky island (now connected to the mainland) with a Genoese watchtower that presides over the present-day port.

Orientation
From the main square of place Paoli, the old city stretches 400m northwest to the train station. The ferry port is on a peninsula north of town. The **tourist office** (☎ 04 95 60 04 35; www.ot-ile-rousse.fr in French; place Paoli; ☺ 9am-7pm Jul & Aug, 9am-12.30pm & 2-6.30pm May, Jun & Sep, 9am-noon & 2-6pm Mon-Fri Oct-Apr) is on the southern side of place Paoli.

Sights
Promenade a Marinella runs along the seafront. There is more sandy coastline east of town, near the **Musée Océanographique** (☎ 04 95 60 27 81), which houses eels, rays, fish and octopuses, but nothing much more impressive.

CORSICA'S TOP FIVE BEACHES

■ **Rondinara** (10km northeast of Bonifacio) A perfect ring of white sand enclosing a circular bay of crystal-clear water, with brilliant snorkelling and sheltered sunbathing.

■ **Algajola** (8km west of Île Rousse) Fantastic white-sand beach within easy reach of Île Rousse, served by the Tramway de la Balagne in summer. As with all Corsica's beaches, it's at its very best when there's no-one else around.

■ **Palombaggia** (3km southeast of Porto Vecchio) Like the other beaches near Porto Vecchio, this sandy cove ringed by pines and rocks is becoming well known – but arrive off-season and you might have the beach all to yourself.

■ **Rocapina** (12km south of Sartène) For those who like their beaches wild and windswept, Rocapina is just the ticket. Look out for the 'Lion of Rocapina' rock above the cove.

■ **Saleccia** (10km northwest of St-Florent) Corsica's most unspoiled beaches are hidden away in the Désert des Agriates. They can only be reached by sea or a long trek on foot or quad-bike, but you won't regret the effort – the island's beaches simply don't get any better.

Île de la Pietra, the island-turned-peninsula where the ferries dock, has a Genoese watchtower and a lighthouse.

The town's beaches are usually overflowing in summer, so if you're looking for empty sand, you might have better luck at nearby Lozari (7km east) or Guardiola (4km west).

Sleeping & Eating

Hôtel L'Isola Rossa (☎ 04 95 60 01 32; isolarossa@ absolucorse.com; promenade du Port; d €45-105 depending on season) One of a handful of pricey hotels lining the promenade. The seaside location is fantastic and the rooms have more character than other nearby hotels.

Splendid Hotel (☎ 04 95 60 00 24; www.le-splen did-hotel.com; s €45-62, d €50-92, tr €69-127 depending on season; P ⬚) Good value in a period building (which once served as a war hospital) near place Paoli. The rooms aren't grand but most have balconies and pleasant views.

Restaurant L'Île d'Or (☎ 04 95 60 12 05; place Paoli; menus €12-30) Salads, pizzas, pasta and fresh fish are the order of the day at this buzzy restaurant – and you can watch the nightly boules contests from the terrace.

Le Libecciu (☎ 04 95 60 13 82; rue Paoli; dishes €15-20; ⬚ noon-2am) This respected restaurant is particularly popular for its giant king prawns and delicious mussels.

Chez Paco (☎ 04 95 60 03 76; rue Paoli; menus €22 & €28; ⬚ Mon-Sat) An informal brasserie that does good simple seafood and light meals.

The daily covered market (place Paoli) sells fish, vegetables, fruit and Corsican goods.

Getting There & Away

On the Calvi–Bastia line, buses leave from av Paul Doumer. The train station (☎ 04 95 60 00 50) is between place Paoli and the ferry port. Île Rousse makes an easy day trip from Calvi.

Southeast of place Paoli, Tramar (☎ 04 95 60 09 56; av Joseph Calizi; ⬚ 8.30am-noon & 2-5.30pm Mon-Fri, 8.30am-noon Sat) handles ferry tickets.

PORTO TO AJACCIO

Corsica's wildest and most beautiful coastline runs from Calvi to Ajaccio.

PORTO (PORTU)

pop 460

The seaside village of Porto, which nestles among huge outcrops of red granite and fragrant groves of eucalyptus, is renowned for its fiery sunsets and proximity to the Réserve Naturelle de Scandola (Scandola Nature Reserve). Hotel prices are reasonable, making it a good base for exploring Les Calanques (p879), Girolata and the mountain villages of Ota and Évisa (p878).

Orientation

Porto is split into three sections: the marina area, the Vaita quarter further uphill and the main road from Calvi. There are shops, hotels and restaurants in all three districts. From the Calvi road to the marina is a walk of about 1km.

Information

The main tourist office (☎ 04 95 26 10 55; www .porto-tourisme.com in French; ⬚ 9am-noon & 2-6pm Mon-Sat Apr-Jun, Sep & Oct; ⬚ 9am-6pm Jul & Aug) is built into the wall below the marina's upper car park. It publishes a good English brochure, Hikes & Walks in the Area of Porto (€2.50).

Crédit Agricole has the only ATM in town. There's a currency exchange bureau next to the Spar supermarket, open only in summer.

Sights & Activities

Porto's seafront is surrounded by hotels and restaurants. A short trail leads up the rocks

---

UNDERWATER ADVENTURES

The Golfe de Porto offers fantastic diving. Top spots include Capo Rosso and the outskirts of the Réserve Naturelle de Scandola, where you'll glimpse multicoloured coral forests and all kinds of Mediterranean marine life.

Porto's accredited diving operators include École de Plongée Génération Bleue (☎ 04 95 26 24 88; www.generation-bleue.com; Porto Marina; ⬚ May-Oct) and Centre de Plongée du Golfe de Porto (☎ 04 95 26 10 29; www.plongeeporto.com in French; Porto Marina; ⬚ Apr-Nov). Both companies run diving courses and trips into the bay.

Other excellent locations in Corsica include the protected coastal areas around Finocchiarola (Cap Corse), Îles Lavezzi (Bonifacio) and Cerbicale (Porto Vecchio), and the bays of Galéria, Valinco (near Propriano) and Calvi.

to a **Genoese tower** (admission €2.50; 🕙 10am-noon & 2-7pm Apr-Jun, Sep & Oct; 9am-9pm Jul & Aug). Nearby, the marina overlooks the estuary of the Porto River. On the far side, across a footbridge, there's a modest pebbly **beach** and one of Corsica's best-known **eucalyptus groves**.

You can rent a boat from **Les Bateaux du Soleil** (☎ 06 08 69 75 20; half-day/full day €75/115) to visit the Réserve Naturelle de Scandola and Girolata independently. You'll be missing out on the educational experience of one of the excursions (see below), but you'll have more freedom to explore and for a group it would be cheaper.

Tours

From April to October **Nave Va Promenades en Mer** (☎ 04 95 26 15 16; www.naveva.com) and **Porto Linéa** (☎ 04 95 26 11 50, 06 08 16 89 71) offer excursions (€35 to €40 depending on season) to the Réserve Naturelle de Scandola, listed by Unesco for its unique marine environment. The boats afford incredible views of the fire-coloured coastline, and stop at Girolata, a remote fishing village only accessible by sea. There are shorter trips to Les Calanques (from €20).

Sleeping

Le Colombo (☎ 04 95 26 10 14; www.hotelcolombo.com; route de Calvi; d low/high season incl breakfast €59/120; 🕙 Apr-Oct; P 🞨) Charming little hotel on the Calvi road, with quirky décor and valley views. Get a balcony if you can.

Hôtel Calypso (☎ 04 95 26 11 54; www.hotel-la-calypso.com in French; marina; d low/high season €55/95; 🕙 Apr-Oct; P 🞨 🖳) One of the best hotels on the marina, in a pretty stone building decorated with awnings and window boxes. Small, smart and sophisticated.

Le Subrini (☎ 04 95 26 14 94; www.hotels-porto.com; marina; d low season €65-80, high season €90-110; 🕙 Apr-Oct; P 🞨) A luxurious hotel in a fabulous seafront position opposite Tour de Genoise. The rooms are spacious and comfortable and the views just don't get any better.

Le Golfe (☎ 04 95 26 13 33; marina; r low season €35-50, high season €55-70) This cheap hotel above a café offers basic rooms, some with little balconies overlooking the bay.

Other recommendations:

Cala di Sole (☎ 04 95 26 10 96; www.hotel-caladisole.com; Vaita quarter; d low season €50-60, high season €75-85; P 🞩) Modern motel with big rooms or apartments.

GORGES DE SPELUNCA

The partly paved trail linking Ota and Évisa was originally a mule track that carried supplies from Porto to the highland villages. These days, it's one of Corsica's great hikes. The trail winds along the plunging valley of the River Porto, past huge rock formations and soaring orange cliffs, some more than 1000m high. The trail passes the Genoese pont de Zaglia en route and takes about five hours return, but it's worth the effort (and the blisters). Aim to reach the gorge in late afternoon, when the fiery rocks are at their most vivid.

Other good walks near Évisa include the Sentier du Châtaigner (1½ hours), which travels through chestnut groves to a waterfall and mountain lake; and the 1½-hour hike uphill through the Forêt d'Aïtone to the Bocca a u Saltu (1391m) hilltop.

Le Riviera (☎ 04 95 26 10 15; www.hotel-restaurant-porto.com in French; marina; d low season €30-35, high season €38-48) Ultrabudget option with bay views.

CAMPING

Camping Les Oliviers (☎ 04 95 26 14 49; www.campinglesoliviers.com; per person/tent/car in summer €8.50/3.50/3.50, 4-person bungalow per week low/high season €367/640; 🕙 May-Nov; 🞨) Located on an olive-treed hillside near the supermarkets.

Le Funtana al' Ora (☎ 04 95 26 11 65; fax 04 95 26 15 48; per person/tent/car €5.50/2.20/2.20, 4-person bungalow per week low/high season €300/540; 🕙 Apr-Oct) Two kilometres east of Porto on the road to Évisa.

Eating

Le Sud (☎ 04 95 26 14 11; menu €25; 🕙 Apr-Oct) A sophisticated restaurant near the Tour Genoise, serving Mediterranean-style seafood and Corsican cooking on a veranda overlooking the rocks.

La Tour Genoise (☎ 04 95 26 17 11; menus €15.60-20.20; 🕙 Apr-Oct) Serves up Corsican cuisine and seafood in a cosy indoor restaurant or on a portside terrace.

Self-caterers can find two supermarkets near the pharmacy on the road from Calvi.

Getting There & Around

BUS

Autocars SAIB (☎ 04 95 22 41 99) has two buses daily, linking Porto and Ota with Ajaccio

CORSICA

CHESTNUT BREAD & BEER

The Corsicans have been planting *châtaigniers* (chestnut trees) since the 16th century. The tree became known as *l'arbre à pain* (the bread tree) because of the many uses the Corsicans found for chestnut flour (*farine de châtaigne*). These days the flour is mainly used to make pastries.

The meat of pigs raised on chestnuts is famous for its flavour. Other chestnut delights include *falculelli* (pressed, frittered *brocciu* cheese served on a chestnut leaf), *beignets au brocciu à la farine de châtaigne* (*brocciu* cheese frittered in chestnut flour), *délice à la châtaigne* (chestnut cake) and, last but certainly not least, *bière à la châtaigne* (chestnut beer).

(€11, two hours, none on Sunday). From May to October a bus runs from Porto to Calvi (€16, three hours).

Transports Mordiconi (☎ 04 95 48 00 44) connects Porto with Corte (€19, 2½ hours, one daily) via Évisa and Ota.

CAR & MOTORCYCLE
From May to late September, two and four wheels can be hired from **Porto Locations** (☎ /fax 04 95 26 10 13), across the street from the supermarkets. Daily rates for a scooter/car/mountain bike are €60/46/15.

TAXI
For a taxi contact **Mr Ceccaldi Félix** (☎ 04 95 26 12 92).

ÉVISA
pop 250 / elevation 830m
Surrounded by chestnut groves (*châtaigneraies*), the highland village of Évisa sits above a deep valley between the Gorges de Spelunca and the Forêt d'Aïtone. It makes an excellent base for hiking – several trails leave near the village, including the path through the Spelunca gorge itself, which ends near the tiny village of Ota.

Sights
The **Forêt d'Aïtone** (Aïtone Forest) contains Corsica's most impressive stands of laricio pines. These arrow-straight trees reach 60m in height and once provided beams and masts for Genoese ships. The forest begins

east of Évisa and stretches to the 1477m-high **Col de Vergio** (Vergio Hill). The **Cascades d'Aïtone** (Aïtone Falls) are 4km northeast of Évisa via the D84 and a short footpath.

Sleeping & Eating
Hôtel L'Aïtone (☎ 04 95 26 20 04; www.hotel-aitone.com; d low season €32-85, high season €56-100; 🕙 Feb-Nov; 🅿 🔲) Évisa's main hotel has rustic rooms, a homely restaurant and a welcoming country atmosphere. The more expensive rooms have balconies with panoramic valley views.

La Châtaigneraie (☎ 04 95 26 24 47; hotellachataigneraie@wanadoo.fr; d from €50) A traditional Corsican house offering simple, homely rooms on the western edge of the village, ideal after a long day's hike.

For cheap accommodation, dorm beds are available at **Gîte d'Étape Chez Marie** (☎ 04 95 26 11 37; dm €13) and **Gîte d'Étape Chez Félix** (☎ 04 95 26 12 92; dm €12, d €33.50-40) in Ota, further down the valley.

Village bars include Bar de la Poste and Modern Bar. Both are open daily and serve simple meals, cakes and good coffee.

Getting There & Away
There are two daily buses from Monday to Saturday from Évisa to Ajaccio (€10.70, two hours) via Ota and Porto.

PIANA
pop 500 / elevation 438m
The quiet hillside village of Piana affords breathtaking views of the Golfe de Porto and the soaring central mountains, and makes an excellent base for exploring Les Calanques. Good Friday is marked by La Granitola, a traditional festival during which

AUTHOR'S CHOICE

Hôtel des Roches Rouges (☎ 04 95 27 81 81; fax 04 95 27 81 76; d from €69; 🕙 Apr–mid-Nov) A grand old 30-room hotel dating from 1912, and without doubt one of Corsica's most romantic places to stay. The elegant double rooms have views of Les Calanques, Ficajola and the deep-blue Mediterranean, and the panoramic windows, antique dining room and period furnishings conjure the air of a bygone age. There are lots of luxury hotels in Corsica, but not many of them can match the 'Red Rocks' for atmosphere.

hooded penitents parade through the village to Piana's Église Ste-Marie.

The **syndicat d'initiative** (tourist office; ☎ 04 95 27 84 42; www.sipiana.com; ⊗ 8.30-11.30am, 1.30-4pm Mon-Fri, longer hours in summer) is next to the post office. It has lots of information on exploring Les Calanques, and distributes the free leaflet *Piana Randonnées*.

Nearby beaches include **Anse de Ficajola**, reached by a narrow 4km road from Piana, and **Plage d'Arone**, 11km southwest of town via the scenic D824. From the D824, a trail leads to the tower-topped **Capo Rosso**.

Hôtel Continental (☎ 04 95 27 83 12; www.continentalpiana.com; d low season €29-35, high season €32-38, ⊗ Apr-Sep) is an old, converted townhouse 100m uphill from the church, which has 17 old-fashioned rooms and antique décor to match.

Hôtel Le Scandola (☎ 04 95 27 80 07; fax 04 95 27 83 88; balcony d/tr incl breakfast €90/120; ⊗ Apr-Oct) is a modern hotel on the road towards Cargèse that offers comfort but not much character.

Buses between Porto and Ajaccio stop near the church and the post office.

LES CALANQUES

One of Corsica's most stunning natural sights is just outside Piana: Les Calanques de Piana (E Calanche in Corsican), a spectacular landscape of red granite cliffs and spiky outcrops, carved into bizarre shapes by the wind, water and weather. Less-rocky areas support pine and chestnut forests, the green foliage of which contrasts dramatically with the technicoloured granite.

Buses travelling from Ajaccio to Porto stop at the chalet.

CARGÈSE (CARGHJESE)
pop 900

Perched on cliffs between the Golfe de Sagone and Golfe de Pero, Cargèse feels more like a Greek village than a Corsican town – which is hardly surprising, as the town was founded by Greek settlers fleeing their Ottoman-controlled homeland in the 17th century. On Easter Monday and 15 August, a colourful religious procession, led by Cargèse's Greek-Catholic congregation, wends its way through the village.

Orientation & Information

The D81, Cargèse's main street, is called av de la République towards Ajaccio, and rue Colonel Fieschi towards Porto. The **tourist office** (☎ 04 95 26 41 31; www.cargese.net; rue du Docteur Dragacci; ⊗ 8.30am-7pm Jul & Aug, 9am-12.30pm & 2.30-6pm Mon-Fri Sep-Jun) is a few streets up from the Latin Church.

Sights & Activities

Cargèse is best known for its **twin churches** – one Eastern (Orthodox), the other Western (Catholic) – which face each other across hillside vegetable plots, like boxers squaring up for a fight. Both have fine views of the town and the glittering Golfe de Sagone. The interior of the Greek church – constructed from 1852 to 1870 by the faithful, who worked on Sunday after attending Divine Liturgy – is adorned with icons

---

HIKING IN LES CALANQUES

Though the Calanques are impressive from the main road, you have to take to one of the clifftop walking trails to fully appreciate the views. Eight kilometres southwest of Porto on the D81 is Le Chalet des Roches Bleues, a souvenir shop that makes a useful landmark. Four trails begin nearby:

■ **Chemin des Muletiers** The steep, one-hour 'Mule-Drivers' Trail' begins 400m towards Piana from the chalet; the trailhead is 15m downhill from the sanctuary dedicated to the Virgin Mary. Trail markings are blue.

■ **Chemin du Château Fort** A one-hour trail to a fortress-shaped rock with stunning views of the Golfe de Porto. It begins 700m towards Porto from the chalet; the trailhead is on the D81 right of the Tête de Chien (Dog's Head) rock. Trail markings are blue.

■ **La Châtaigneraie** A three-hour circuit through chestnut groves, beginning 25m uphill from the chalet.

■ **La Corniche** A steep, forested, 40-minute walk to a fantastic view of Les Calanques. Begins on the bridge 50m towards Porto from the chalet. Trail markings are yellow.

brought from Greece in the 1670s by the original settlers.

Cargèse's **port**, where fishing boats dock beside luxury leisure cruisers, is downhill from the churches.

The Genoese **towers** atop Pointe d'Omigna and Pointe de Cargèse overlook **Plage de Pero**, a long beach of white sand 1km north of Cargèse. Take the road downhill from the top of rue Colonel Fieschi.

Tours

Croisières Grand Bleu (☎ 04 95 26 40 24; http://croisiere.grandbleu.free.fr in French; rue Marbeuf) offers boat excursions in the Golfe de Porto, including visits to Girolata and tours of the Réserve Naturelle de Scandola. Prices vary depending on season.

Sleeping & Eating

M'hôtel Punta e Mare (☎ 04 95 26 44 33; www.hotel-puntaemare.com in French; chemin de Paomia; d with sea views low season €40-60, high season €65-85; P) A cosy, welcoming motel set back from the main town. The smart rooms offer great year-round value and there's a lovely breakfast terrace shaded by trees and climbing plants.

Le Cyrnos (☎ /fax 04 95 26 49 47; www.torraccia.com; rue de le République; d with sea view low/high season €40/60) In the centre of the village, with quaint, good-value rooms in a lemon-yellow townhouse. The rooms facing the road are cheaper.

Hôtel Le St-Jean (☎ 04 95 26 46 68; www.lesaintjean.com in French; place St-Jean; d with/without sea view €70/63; P ⚓) Near the old *lavoir* (laundry) on the main road from Porto, the St-Jean is a large café-restaurant that offers modern, villa-style rooms upstairs. Most have balconies overlooking the bay.

A Volta (☎ 04 95 26 41 96; rue du Docteur Petrolacci; menu €22; ⚓ May-Sep) A simple seafood restaurant offering a varied local *menu* and a fabulous ocean view.

There are a few summer-only restaurants on Pero beach, including **A Piaghja** (☎ 04 95 26 47 49; Plage de Pero; mains €10-15; ⚓ Jun-Sep), which does pizzas and seafood and has weekly music nights.

Getting There & Away

Two daily buses from Ota (1½ hours) via Porto (one hour) to Ajaccio (one hour) stop in front of the post office.

AJACCIO (AJACCIU)
pop 60,000

The pastel-shaded port of Ajaccio (pronounced Ajaxio) is the most cosmopolitan city in Corsica. With its designer shops, fashionable restaurants and hectic traffic, it's one of the few Corsican towns that seems to have its feet in the 21st century; but inland from the harbour, the modern shopping streets lead into the alleyways and narrow lanes of the old city, where 18th-century townhouses stand side-by-side with tiny restaurants and brightly coloured tenement blocks. For educational value, there are several museums dedicated to Ajaccio's most famous native son, Napoleon Bonaparte.

Orientation

Ajaccio's main street is cours Napoléon, which stretches from place de Gaulle northwards to the train station and beyond. The old city is south of place Foch. The port is on the eastern side of town, from where a tree-lined promenade leads west along plage St-Francois.

Information
BOOKSHOPS
Album (2 place Foch; ⚓ 8.30am-noon & 2.30-7pm Mon-Sat, 8.30am-noon Sun Oct-May)

EMERGENCY
Centre Hospitalier de la Miséricorde (☎ 04 95 29 90 90; 27 av Impératrice Eugénie; ⚓ 24hr)
Police Station (☎ 04 95 29 21 47; rue Général Firoella)

INTERNET ACCESS
Absolut Game (☎ 04 95 21 56 60; av de Paris; per hr €3; ⚓ 9-2am)
Game Net (☎ 04 95 50 72 79; 2 av de Paris; per 15min/hr €2/5; ⚓ 9am-noon & 2-9pm Mon-Fri, 2-9pm Sat & Sun)

LAUNDRY
Lavomatique (rue Maréchal Ornano; ⚓ 8am-10pm)

MONEY
Banks are found along place de Gaulle and cours Napoléon.
Banque Populaire (place Foch) ATM.
BNP (33 cours Napoléon) ATM.

POST
Main Post Office (13 cours Napoléon; ⚓ 8am-6.45pm Mon-Fri, 8am-noon Sat)

AJACCIO (AJACCIU)

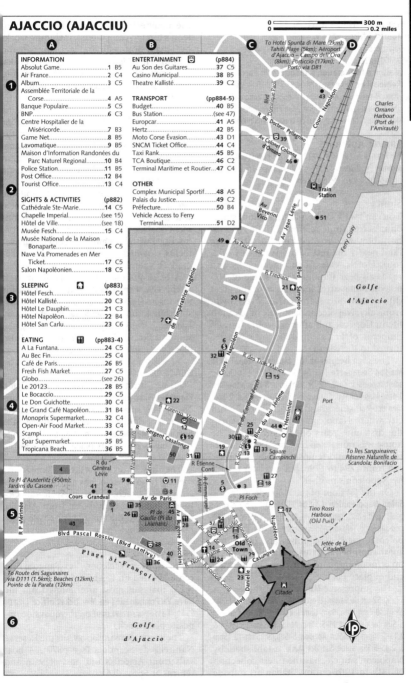

| 0 | 300 m |
| 0 | 0.2 miles |

INFORMATION
Absolut Game..........................1 B5
Air France..............................2 C4
Album...................................3 C5
Assemblée Territoriale de la
　Corse..................................4 A5
Banque Populaire......................5 C5
BNP.....................................6 C3
Centre Hospitalier de la
　Miséricorde...........................7 B3
Game Net...............................8 B5
Lavomatique............................9 B5
Maison d'Information Randonées du
　Parc Naturel Régional..............10 B4
Police Station.........................11 B5
Post Office............................12 B4
Tourist Office.........................13 C4

SIGHTS & ACTIVITIES (p882)
Cathédrale Ste-Marie.................14 C5
Chapelle Impérial...................(see 15)
Hôtel de Ville......................(see 18)
Musée Fesch..........................15 C4
Musée National de la Maison
　Bonaparte...........................16 C5
Nave Va Promenades en Mer
　Ticket...............................17 C5
Salon Napoléonien....................18 C5

SLEEPING (p883)
Hôtel Fesch...........................19 C4
Hôtel Kallisté........................20 C3
Hôtel Le Dauphin......................21 C3
Hôtel Napoléon........................22 B4
Hôtel San Carlu.......................23 C6

EATING (pp883-4)
A La Funtana..........................24 C5
Au Bec Fin............................25 C4
Café de Paris.........................26 B5
Fresh Fish Market.....................27 C5
Globo..............................(see 26)
Le 20123..............................28 B5
Le Bocaccio...........................29 C4
Le Don Guichotte......................30 C4
Le Grand Café Napoléon................31 B4
Monoprix Supermarket..................32 C4
Open-Air Food Market..................33 C4
Scampi................................34 C5
Spar Supermarket......................35 B5
Tropicana Beach.......................36 B5

ENTERTAINMENT (p884)
Au Son des Guitares...................37 C5
Casino Municipal......................38 B5
Theatre Kallisté......................39 C2

TRANSPORT (pp884-5)
Budget................................40 B5
Bus Station........................(see 47)
Europcar..............................41 A5
Hertz.................................42 B5
Moto Corse Évasion....................43 D1
SNCM Ticket Office....................44 C4
Taxi Rank.............................45 B5
TCA Boutique..........................46 C2
Terminal Maritime et Routier..........47 C4

OTHER
Complex Municipal Sportif.............48 A5
Palais du Justice.....................49 C2
Préfecture............................50 B4
Vehicle Access to Ferry
　Terminal.............................51 D2

To Hotel Spunta di Mare (2km);
Tahiti Plage (5km); Aéroport
d'Ajaccio – Campo dell'Oro
(8km); Porticcio (17km);
Porto via D81

Charles
Ornano
Harbour
(Port de
l'Amirauté)

R du Docteur Pellegrini

Av Colonel Colonna
d'Ornano

Cours Napoléon

Blvd Dominique Paoli

Train
Station

Av
Beverini
Vico

Av Jean Lévie

Ferry Quay

Golfe
d'Ajaccio

R Fredani

R des Trois Maries

Blvd Sampiero

Av Pascal Paoli

R de l'Impératrice Eugénie

Cours Napoléon

R Lorenzo Vero

R Cardinal Fesch

R du Roi Jérôme

L'Herminier

Blvd du Roi Jérôme

Port

Square
Campinchi

R Sergent Casalonga

R du Général Campi

R du Maréchal Ornano

R Bonaparte

Pl Foch

To Îles Sanguinaires;
Réserve Naturelle de
Scandola; Bonifacio

Tino Rossi
Harbour
(Old Port)

R Étienne
Conti

R Emmanuel
Arène

R du Général
Lévie

To Pl d'Austerlitz (450m);
Jardins du Casone

Cours Grandval

Av de Paris

Pl de
Gaulle (Pl du
Diamant)

Blvd Pascal Rossini (Blvd Lantivy)

Plage St-François

To Route des Saguinaires
via D111 (1.5km); Beaches (12km);
Pointe de la Parata (12km)

R P Mérimée

R Notre Dame
R Eugène Macchini
R du Roi de Rome
R St-Charles
R Cardinal Fesch
R Bonaparte
R Casanova
R Danielle

Old
Town

Citadel

Jetée de la
Citadelle

Golfe
d'Ajaccio

TOURIST INFORMATION

Tourist Office (☎ 04 95 51 53 03; www.tourisme.fr
/ajaccio; 3 blvd du Roi Jérôme; ☻ 8am-7pm Mon-Sat,
9am-1pm Sun)

**Maison d'Information Randonées du Parc Naturel
Régional de la Corse** (☎ 04 95 51 79 10; www.parc
-naturel-corse.com in French; 2 rue Sgt Casolonga;
☻ 8.30am-12.30pm & 2-6pm Mon-Fri) Provides information on Parc Naturel Régional de Corse and its hiking trails.

TRAVEL AGENCIES

Air France Ajaccio (☎ 04 95 51 53 03; 3 blvd du Roi
Jérôme; ☻ 8.30am-12.30pm & 2-6pm Mon-Fri, 8.30am-
noon Sat); Airport (☻ 6am-8pm)

Sights

You can't walk far in Ajaccio without stumbling across some reference to the Ajaccio-
born boy who became Emperor of France
(and nearly the rest of the Western world,
too). Hotels, cafés, boutiques, parks and
roads all bear the illustrious name of Napoléon Bonaparte, and statues of the great
(little) man are scattered all over town.
Ironically, Napoléon spent little of his adult
life in Corsica, and after crowning himself
Emperor of France in 1804, he never returned to the island.

The saga begins at the **Musée National de la
Maison Bonaparte** (☎ 04 95 21 43 89; rue St-Charles;
adult/concession €4/2.60; ☻ 9am-noon & 2-6pm Tue-Sun,
2-6pm Mon Apr-Sep, 10am-noon & 2-5pm Tue-Sat, 2-5pm
Mon Oct-Mar), the grand building in the old
city where Napoleon was born and spent
the first nine years of his childhood. The
house was ransacked by Corsican nationalists in 1793, and requisitioned by the English from 1794 to 1796, but was later rebuilt
by Napoléon's mother.

On the 1st floor of the Hôtel de Ville, the
Salon Napoléonien (☎ 04 95 21 90 15; place Foch;
adult/child €2.30/free; ☻ 9-11.45am & 2-5.45pm Mon-Fri
mid-Jun–mid-Sep, to 4.45pm rest of year) exhibits Napoleonic medals, paintings and busts in a
lavish chamber. A **statue** of Napoléon stands
on a fountain guarded by four lions at the
end of place Foch.

The impressive **Musée Fesch** (☎ 04 95 21 48
17; 50-52 rue du Cardinal Fesch; adult/student €5.35/3.80;
☻ 1.30-6pm Mon, 9am-6pm Tue-Fri, 10.30am-6pm Sat
& Sun Jul & Aug, 1.15-5.15pm Mon, 9.15am-12.15pm &
2.15-5.15pm Tue-Sun Apr-Jun & Sep, 9.15am-12.15pm
& 2.15-5.15pm Tue-Sat Oct-Mar), established by
Napoléon's uncle, has the finest collection
of 14th-to-19th-century Italian art outside

the Louvre (mostly looted during Napoléon's foreign campaigns), including works
by Titian, Botticelli, Raphael, Poussin and
Bellini. There is a separate fee for the **Chapelle Impériale** (adult/student €1.50/0.75), built in
the 1850s as a sepulchre for the Bonaparte
family.

The 16th-century **Cathédrale Ste-Marie** (rue
Forcioli Conti; ☻ 7-11.30am & 3-6.30pm Mon-Sat Apr-Sep,
to 6pm Oct-Mar, 7-11.30am Sun year-round) is in the
old city and contains Napoleon's baptismal
font and the *Vierge au Sacré-Cœur* (Virgin
of the Sacred Heart) by Eugène Delacroix
(1798–1863).

Last stop is place d'Austerlitz and the
Jardins du Casone, 800m west of place Foch,
where you'll find the city's grandest monument to Napoléon – a huge stone plinth,
inscribed with his battles and other achievements, crowned by a replica of the statue that
marks his tomb at Les Invalides in Paris.

A black-granite promontory 12km west
of the city, **Pointe de la Parata** is famed for
its sunsets. The group of islands visible offshore are known as **Îles Sanguinaires** (Bloody
Islands) because they turn a vivid red as the
sun sets. Bus No 5 travels to the point from
place de Gaulle several times daily.

BEACHES

Plage de Ricanto, popularly known as **Tahiti
Plage**, is 5km east of town, served by bus
No 1. The small beaches between Ajaccio
and Pointe de la Parata (**Ariane, Neptune, Palm
Beach** and **Marinella**) are served by bus No 5.
Both buses run from place du Général de
Gaulle.

The ritzy resort of **Porticcio**, 17km across
the bay from Ajaccio, has a great – if overcrowded – beach. Between April and October, there are daily boats from Ajaccio,
departing from the quayside opposite place
Foch (€5/8 single/return, 30 minutes).

Tours

From April to October, Îles Sanguinaires
can be visited on 2½-hour boat excursions
(€22) that sail most afternoons from the
Nave Va Promenades en Mer ticket office (☎ 04
95 51 31 31; www.naveva.com) on the quayside opposite place Foch.

The same company also visits the Réserve
Naturelle de Scandola (see p877). A boat
sails from Ajaccio's old port at 9am and
returns at 6pm (€46).

Sleeping

There are no budget options in Ajaccio, short of sleeping in your car – which you might have to do if you don't reserve ahead in summer.

Hôtel Napoléon (☎ 04 95 51 54 00; www.hotel -napoleon-ajaccio.com; 4 rue Lorenzo Vero; s/d low season €58/68, high season €85/100; P ⌘) With elegant, tasteful rooms set back from the hustle of cours Napoléon, this is one of Ajaccio's most stylish hotels – and in Boney's birthplace, how could you stay anywhere else?

Hôtel Kallisté (☎ 04 95 51 34 45; www.hotel-kalliste -ajaccio.com in French; 51 cours Napoléon; s/d low season €51/56, high season €58/68; ⌘ ✗ 💻) An excellent city hotel with clean lines and contemporary bedrooms. Stylish features such as the glass elevator, terracotta floors and exposed brickwork don't normally come this cheap.

Hôtel Fesch (☎ 04 95 51 62 62; www.hotel-fesch .com; 7 rue du Cardinal Fesch; s/d low season €54/63, high season €73/84; ⌘) A traditional hotel on one of Ajaccio's oldest streets. The period building, grand rooms and old-fashioned service make this a favourite with regular visitors, so book ahead.

Hôtel San Carlu (☎ 04 95 21 13 84; fax 04 95 21 09 99; 8 blvd Danielle Casanova; s low season €62-76, s high season €76-86, d low season €76-84, d high season €85-99; ⌘) One of the best hotels in the quiet old town, in a prime position overlooking the citadel. The top rooms have sea views with a price tag to match.

Also recommended:

Hôtel Le Dauphin (☎ 04 95 21 12 94; www.ledauphin hotel.com; 11 blvd Sampiero; s/d/tr low season €49/54/66, high season €54/60/69; P ⌘) Local café opposite the ferry port with standard rooms.

Hôtel Spunta di Mare (☎ 04 95 23 74 40; hotelspun tadimare@wanadoo.fr; Quartier St Joseph; s/d low season €48/57, high season €64/74; P) Modern seafront hotel 2km north of the city.

Eating

RESTAURANTS

In the old city, rue St-Charles and rue Conventionnel Chiappe are lined with tiny terraced restaurants that are always crammed in summer. It's a great place for a nighttime wander, even if you're not planning on eating.

Au Bec Fin (☎ 04 95 21 30 52; 3bis blvd du Roi-Jérôme; menu €13.90; ⌣ closed Sun & dinner Mon) A relaxed restaurant near the market, decked out as a 1930s brasserie. The excellent-value

menu includes grilled tuna, *carpaccio de boeuf* and salmon fillet.

Le 20123 (☎ 04 95 21 50 05; 2 rue du Roi de Rome; menu €26; ⌣ 7.30-11pm, closed Mon) This Corsican bistro started life in the village of Pila Canale (postcode 20123); when the owner upped sticks to Ajaccio, he decided to recreate his old restaurant – village square, water-pump, washing lines and all.

Le Scampi (☎ 04 95 21 38 09; 11 rue Conventionnel Chiappe; menus from €12.95; ⌣ closed dinner Fri & lunch Sat) Serves seafood and Corsican dishes (including sardines with *brocciu* cheese) on a flower-filled terrace.

Le Don Quichotte (☎ 04 95 21 27 30; rue des Halles; pizzas €7.60-10, menus from €12.50; ⌣ Mon-Sat) A down-to-earth Italian restaurant near the quay that's often packed with a local crowd who come for the delicious seafood and wood-fired pizzas.

A La Funtana (☎ 04 95 21 78 04; 7 rue Notre Dame; lunch/dinner menu €25/55, à la carte dishes €24-30; ⌣ lunch Tue-Sat, dinner in summer) One of Ajaccio's grandest *grandes tables*, regularly featured in the gourmet guides. The grilled lobster and *l'anima Corse* (a delicious pudding made with chestnut flour and *brocciu* cheese) are particularly renowned.

Other recommendations:

Le Boccaccio (☎ 04 95 21 16 77; 19 rue du Roi de Rome; dishes €18-30; ⌣ closed Wed Nov-Mar) High-quality Italian cuisine in the old town.

Tropicana Beach (☎ 04 95 51 12 98; blvd Pascal Rossini; menus from €12.50; ⌣ Mon-Sat) A seafront brasserie with a terrace above the waves.

CAFÉS

Ajaccio's thriving café culture centres on blvd du Roi Jérôme, quai Napoléon and place de Gaulle.

Le Grand Café Napoléon (☎ 04 95 21 42 54; 10 cours Napoléon; ⌣ Mon-Sat) The queen of cours Napoléon's terrace cafés, founded in 1821 and still going strong. Whether it's for afternoon coffee or supper in the grand dining room, this graceful establishment will fit the bill.

Café de Paris (☎ 04 95 51 03 90; dishes €8-15; place de Gaulle) A traditional café and brasserie with a fine terrace overlooking place de Gaulle.

Globo (☎ 04 95 21 01 54; dishes €8-15; ⌣ Mon-Sat) Next door to the Café de Paris, this hip café aims for a contemporary crowd, with modern fusion cooking and funky wooden furniture.

CORSICA

SELF-CATERING

Ajaccio's **open-air food market** (square Campinchi; 🕑 to noon, closed Mon) fills the area with Corsican atmosphere every morning. There's a daily **fish market** in the building behind the food market. Get there *very* early if you want to beat the restaurants to the day's catch.

Spar Supermarket (cours Grandval; 🕑 8.30am-12.30pm & 3-7.30pm Mon-Sat) is close to place de Gaulle, while **Monoprix Supermarket** (🕑 8.30am-7.15pm Mon-Sat; cours Napoléon) is not far away from the port.

Entertainment

Théâtre Kallisté (☎ 04 95 22 78 54; 6 av Colonel Colonna d'Ornano) Ajaccio's municipal theatre hosts music, dance and dramas.

Au Son des Guitares (☎ 04 95 51 15 47; 7 rue du Roi de Rome) A good bet for traditional music. It hosts local guitar bands most evenings from around 10pm.

Casino Municipal (☎ 04 95 50 40 60; blvd Pascal Rossini; 🕑 1pm-3am) The place to go if you have money to burn. There are poker machines, roulette and blackjack to soak up your cash, or you can simply relax in the piano bar.

PARTYING WITH NAPOLÉON

Fêtes Napoliennes, Ajaccio's annual celebration of its most beloved son, kicks off in mid-August. The varied programme of events includes displays, outdoor shows processions, and exhibitions, but the highlight is a huge street parade in which the participants dress up as Napoleonic soldiers. Usually the festival coincides with the fireworks display that lights up the night sky on 15 August to mark Napoléon's birthday.

Getting There & Away
AIR
Aéroport d'Ajaccio-Campo dell'Oro (☎ 04 95 23 56 56) is 8km east of the city centre.

BOAT
The ferry terminal is in the bus station. The **SNCM ticket office** (☎ 04 95 29 66 99; 3 quai l'Herminier; 🕑 8am-8pm Tue-Fri, to 6pm Mon, to 1pm Sat) is across the street. The SNCM bureau in the ferry terminal sells tickets a few hours before departure for evening ferries; tickets for vehicles are available at the port's vehicle entrance.

BUS
Bus companies operate from **Terminal Maritime et Routier** (quai l'Herminier). Most have ticket kiosks on the right as you enter the station. The **information counter** (☎ 04 95 51 55 45; 🕑 7am-7pm) provides schedules.

Eurocorse (☎ 04 95 21 06 30) travels to Bastia (€18, three hours, two daily), Bonifacio (€19.50, four hours, two or three daily), Calvi (€19.85, change at Ponte Leccia), Corte (€10.50, 2¾ hours, two daily) and Sartène (€11.50, two hours, two daily). Services run daily except Sundays; some routes operate reduced services out of season.

Autocars SAIB (☎ 04 95 22 41 99) travels to Porto (€11, two hours, two daily).

Autocars Ricci (☎ 04 95 51 08 19) also travels to Sartène (€10.70, two hours, two daily).

CAR
The main car-rental companies have airport bureaus as well as being in town.
Budget (☎ 04 95 21 17 18; 1 blvd Lantivy)
Europcar (☎ 04 95 21 05 49; 16 cours Grandval)
Hertz (☎ 04 95 21 70 94; 8 cours Grandval)

Hôtel Kallisté (p883) rents cars cheaply. A three-door car costs €49/227 per day/week, including unlimited mileage. Prices rise in July and August.

TRAIN
The **train station** (☎ 04 95 23 11 03; place de la Gare) is staffed until 6.30pm (to 8pm May to September). Services include Bastia (€20.70, four hours, three to four daily), Corte (€11, two hours, three to four daily) and Calvi (€24.10, five hours, two daily; change at Ponte-Leccia).

Getting Around
TO/FROM THE AIRPORT
Transports Corse d'Ajaccio (TCA) bus No 8 links the airport with Ajaccio's train and bus stations (€4.50). Hourly buses run from around 8am to 7pm from the bus station, 9am to 11pm from the airport. A taxi from the airport to Ajaccio costs €25 to €35.

BUS
TCA Boutique (☎ 04 95 23 29 41; 75 cours Napoléon) distributes bus maps and timetables. A single ticket/*carnet* of 10 costs €1.15/9. Most buses operate from place Général de Gaulle and cours Napoléon.

MOPED

Hôtel Kallisté (p883) rents mopeds for €31/157 per day/week in summer.

About 500m north of the train station, **Moto Corse Évasion** (☎ 04 95 20 52 05; fax 04 95 22 48 11; montée St-Jean) rents mountain bikes for €7/13 per half-day/full day.

TAXI

There's a **taxi rank** (☎ 04 95 21 00 87; place de Gaulle) or you can call **Radio Taxis Ajacciens** (☎ 04 95 25 09 13).

SOUTH OF AJACCIO

FILITOSA

Corsica's most important prehistoric site is 25km northwest of Propriano. Inhabited from 5850 BC until Roman times, the **megaliths** and **menhirs** of Filitosa have been intensely studied since their accidental discovery in 1946. The atmospheric hilltop site, shaded by 1000-year-old olive trees, has a small **museum** (☎ 04 95 74 00 91; admission €5; ☼ 8am-sunset) displaying major finds.

CORSICA BC (AND BEYOND)

For prehistory buffs, Corsica is a Mediterranean treasure trove. Other sites within driving distance of Filitosa include the figures and menhirs of the Alignement de Stantari and the Alignement de Palaggiu, and the eerie megaliths of Cauria, all southwest of Sartène near the D48. Theories abound regarding their purpose, ranging from magical armies to celestial communication centres, but the truth is no-one knows why they were made – which is half the fun.

SARTÈNE (SARTÈ)

pop 3500

The sombre hillside town of Sartène has long been suspicious of outsiders, and with good reason. In 1583 Barbary pirates raided the town and carried 400 people into slavery in North Africa; raids only ended in the 18th century. Sartène was notorious for its banditry and bloody vendettas. In the early 19th century a disagreement between rival landowners deteriorated into house-to-house fighting, forcing most of the population to flee.

Orientation & Information

From place de la Libération, Sartène's main square, cours Sœur Amélie leads south, while cours Général de Gaulle heads north. The old Santa Anna quarter is north of place de la Libération. The **tourist office** (☎ 04 95 77 15 40; 6 rue Borgo; ☼ 9am-noon Mon-Fri) is 30m uphill from place de la Libération. **Crédit Lyonnais** (14 cours Général de Gaulle) has an ATM.

Sights

Near the **WWI memorial** on place de la Libération is the granite **Église Ste-Marie**. Inside hangs the 32kg cross and 14kg chain used in the Procession du Catenacciu (p886). The arch through the **town hall** (formerly the Governors' Palace), on the northern side of the square, leads to the **Santa Anna quarter**, a residential neighbourhood of austere grey houses and solemn alleyways.

Musée de la Préhistoire Corse (Museum of Corsican Prehistory; ☎ 04 95 77 01 09; rue Croce; admission free; ☼ 10am-noon & 2-6pm Mon-Sat May-Sep), housed in a former 19th-century prison, displays exhibits on Corsica's prehistoric past.

Sleeping & Eating

Hôtel des Roches (☎ 04 95 77 07 61; hotel.des.roches@ wanadoo.fr; d €46-126 depending on season; ☼ Apr-Oct) Sartène's only central hotel is in a sober grey-granite building typical of the village. Inside, it's more welcoming, with snug rooms and a good restaurant. Rooms with a valley view cost more.

Hôtel La Villa Piana (☎ 04 95 77 07 04; www.lavilla piana.com; d €55-95 depending on season; ☼ Apr–mid-Oct; P ≋) Situated 1.5km outside Sartène on the N196, this modern hotel offers private terraces and fabulous valley views.

Aux Gourmets (☎ 04 95 77 16 08; 10 cours Sœur Amélie; menus €10-15; ☼ daily high season, closed Sun low season) Small, simple and Sartène's top eating spot, serving delicious Corsican specialities such as courgettes stuffed with *brocciu* (€9).

La Chaumière (☎ 04 95 77 07 13; 39 rue Médecin-Capitaine Louis Bénédetti; menu €15) This traditional restaurant serves Corsican food and Sartenaise specialities, including a delicious lamb-and-bean stew.

There's also a **Spar supermarket** (14 cours Général de Gaulle) for self-catering.

Getting There & Away

Sartène is on the **Eurocorse** (Ajaccio ☎ 04 95 21 06 30) bus line linking Ajaccio (€11.50, two

PROCESSION DU CATENACCIU

On Good Friday, the people of Sartène perform the Procession du Catenacciu, a colourful re-enactment of the Passion, in which the Catenacciu ('the chained one'), an anonymous, barefoot penitent covered in a red robe and cowl (to preserve his anonymity), carries a huge cross through the town while dragging a heavy chain shackled to the ankle. The Catenacciu is followed by a procession of penitents, clergy and local notables and, as the chain clatters by on the cobblestones, locals look on in great (if rather humourless) excitement. The penitent is chosen by the parish priest from applicants seeking to expiate a grave sin; hopefuls apply years in advance to fulfil the honoured role.

hours, two daily) with Bonifacio (€10, two hours, two daily). Buses stop at the **Ollandini travel agency** (☎ 04 95 77 18 41; cours Gabriel Péri), near the end of cours Sœur Amélie.

BONIFACIO (BUNIFAZIU)

pop 2700

The citadel of Bonifacio sits about 70m above the Mediterranean on a rock promontory sometimes called 'Corsica's Gibraltar'. On all sides, white limestone cliffs drop vertically into the sea, while the tall houses of the old city lean out precariously over the water. The northern side of the citadel overlooks Bonifacio Sound (Goulet de Bonifacio), while the southern ramparts afford views of Sardinia, 12km away across the Bouches de Bonifacio (Strait of Bonifacio).

With its dramatic clifftop location, fine architecture and lively marina, Bonifacio is one of Corsica's most appealing seaside towns – so it's hardly surprising that the town is overflowing with tourists in summer. From the geographical details in Homer's *Odyssey*, it's possible that Ulysses' encounter with the cannibalistic Laestrygonians was set in Bouches de Bonifacio.

Orientation

Bonifacio's marina lies at the southeastern corner of Bouches de Bonifacio. The citadel – also known as the Haute Ville (upper city) – occupies the promontory above the harbour, reached by car via av Charles de Gaulle, or on

foot by two sets of steps. The ferry terminal is further west along the marina.

Information

Boniboom (☎ 04 95 73 59 47; quai Jérôme Comparetti; per min/hr €0.15/8; ☼ 8-2am daily) Internet access.
Lavoir de la Marine (1 quai Jérôme Comparetti; €6.10; 7am-10pm) Laundrette.
Post Office (place Carrega; ☼ 8.30am-6pm Mon-Sat Jul–mid-Sep, 9am-noon & 2-5pm Mon-Fri, 9am-noon Sat mid-Sep–Jun).
Société Générale (38 rue St-Érasme; ☼ Mon-Fri) Exchanges currency and has the only ATM in town. In summer, there are exchange bureaus along the marina.
Tourist Office (☎ 04 95 73 11 88; www.bonifacio.com in French; 2 rue Fred Scamaroni; ☼ 9am-8pm daily Jul & Aug, 9am-noon & 2-6pm Mon-Fri, 9am-noon Sat Sep-Jun) In the citadel.

Sights & Activities
CITADEL

The steps linking rue St-Érasme with Porte de Gênes are known as Montée Rastello and Montée St-Roch further up. At the top of Montée St-Roch stands the **Porte de Gênes**, reached by a drawbridge dating from 1598. Just inside the gateway, you can visit the **Grand Bastion** (admission €2; ☼ 9am-6pm daily Jul & Aug, Mon-Sat Apr, May, Sep & Oct), above Porte de Gênes.

Close by, along the citadel's ramparts, there are great views from **place du Marché** and **place Manichella**. The two holes covered by glass pyramids in place Manichella were used to store grain, salted meats and other supplies to use during times of siege.

Crisscrossed by meandering alleyways lined with tall stone houses, the old city has a distinctly medieval feel. **Rue des Deux Empereurs** is so named because Charles V and Napoleon once slept in the houses at Nos 4 and 7. **Église Ste-Marie Majeure**, a 14th-century Romanesque church, is known for its loggia (roofed porch) and communal cistern, a vital asset in times of siege. The cistern is now used as a conference hall.

From the citadel, the **Escalier du Roi d'Aragon** (Staircase of the King of Aragon; admission €2; ☼ 9am-6pm daily Jul & Aug, Mon-Sat Apr, May, Sep & Oct) leads down the cliff. Its 187 steps were, according to legend, constructed by Aragonese troops in a single night during the siege of 1420. The staircase is closed if it's windy or stormy.

Outside the citadel, west along the limestone headland, stands **Église Ste-Dominique** – one of the only Gothic buildings in Corsica.

CORSICA

BONIFACIO (BUNIFAZIU)

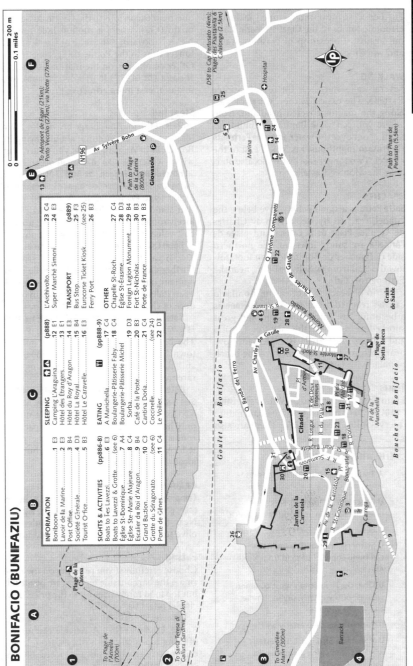

INFORMATION		SLEEPING	(p888)	L'Archivolto.............................23 C4
Boniboom...........................1 E3		Camping L'Araguina............12 E1		Super Marché Simoni.............24 E3
Lavoir de la Marine..............2 E3		Hôtel des Etrangers.............13 E1		
Post Office.........................3 B4		Hôtel du Roy d'Aragon........14 E3		**TRANSPORT** (p889)
Société Générale..................4 D3		Hôtel Le Royal....................15 B4		Bus Stop............................25 F3
Tourist Office.....................5 B3		Hôtel Le Caravelle...............16 E3		Eurocorse Ticket Kiosk.......(see 25)
				Ferry Port.........................26 B3
SIGHTS & ACTIVITIES (pp886-8)		**EATING** (pp888-9)		
Boats to I'es Lavezzi...............6 E3		A Manichella......................17 C4		**OTHER**
Boats to Lavezzi & Grotte.......(see 6)		Boulangerie-Pâtisserie Faby....18 C4		Chapelle St-Roch................27 C4
Église St-Dominique................7 A4		Boulangerie-Pâtisserie Michel		Église St-Erasme.................28 D3
Église Ste-Marie Majeure........8 C4		Sorba...............................19 D3		Foreign Legion Monument.....29 B4
Escalier du Roi d'Aragon.........9 B4		Café de la Poste..................20 B3		Fort St-Nicholas.................30 B3
Grand Bastion....................10 C3		Cantina Doria.....................21 C4		Porte de France.................31 B3
Grotte du Sdragonato........(see 6)		Coccinelle........................(see 24)		
Porte de Gênes.................11 C4		Le Voilier..........................22 D3		

Further west, near three ruined **mills**, the elaborate tombs of the **Cimetière Marin** stand out against a backdrop of crashing waves and wheeling gulls.

WALKING

Several walks start near the top of Montée Rastello. The easiest is the 2km stroll east along the maquis-covered headland, from where you can view Bonifacio's buildings arching out over the water. **Phare de Pertusato** (Pertusato Lighthouse) is 5.6km east of the citadel. Two longer marked walks also start near the Montée Rastello.

BEACHES

Sotta Rocca is a small pebbly cove below the citadel, reached by steps from av Charles de Gaulle. **Plage de la Catena** and **plage de l'Arinella** are sandy inlets on the northern side of Bouches de Bonifacio – on foot, follow the trail from av Sylvère Bohn, near the Esso petrol station.

A trio of beaches 3km east of Bonifacio can be reached from the D58. **Spérone** is a beautiful bay with white sand and great snorkelling opposite the islets of Cavallo and Lavezzi. **Piantarella** is a pleasant cove near Spérone, while **Calalonga** is a big beach popular with families.

Tours

From Easter to September, **Vedettes Christina** (☎ 04 95 73 09 77) runs trips to the island nature reserve of Îles Lavezzi (€25). There are also

---

THE WINDS OF CORSICA

- **A Tramuntana** A powerful, icy northerly wind.

- **U Grecale** Northeasterly wind that often heralds rain and storms in Corsica.

- **U Levante** A mild, balmy easterly wind.

- **U Sciroccu** Hot, southeasterly that can bring showers of sand from North Africa.

- **U Libecciu** The island's most common wind is southwesterly, dry in summer and wet in winter.

- **U Punente** Gentle westerly wind.

- **U Maestrale** Strong, northwesterly wind that can reach great speeds.

---

one-hour excursions to the Grotte du Sdragonato (€12), where a rooftop hole resembles a backwards silhouette of Corsica, and longer trips to the Pointe de Spérone (€15). Other companies on the marina, including **Thalassa** (☎ 04 95 73 10 17; thalassa@bonifacio.com), might offer a more attractive price.

Sleeping

Hotels at the marina charge heavily for their location. Don't even think about staying in Bonifacio in August, unless you're arriving with a wallet the size of a small ocean liner.

Hotel du Roy d'Aragon (☎ 04 95 73 03 99; www.roy aragon.com; 13 quai Jérôme Comparetti; d low season €45-79, high season €90-145; ✕ ✕) A refined hotel that stands out on the crowded quay. The lovely rooms with portside balconies are the best value in Bonifacio – book well ahead.

Hôtel La Caravelle (☎ 04 95 73 00 03; fax 04 95 73 00 41; 35 quai Jérôme Comparetti; d €114-144; ⌚ Apr-Oct) Further along the quay, the Caravelle is an opulent (and expensive) choice, decorated in an Italian Renaissance style with an overdose of cherubs and colourful frescoes.

Hôtel des Étrangers (☎ 04 95 73 01 09; fax 04 95 73 16 97; av Sylvère Bohn; d €43-71; ⌚ Apr-Oct; P ✕) The best deal in Bonifacio is just outside town. The large hotel offers 30 plain rooms and there's plenty of on-site parking – a rare treat in Bonifacio.

Hôtel Le Royal (☎ 04 95 73 00 51; fax 04 95 73 04 68; 6 rue Fred Scamaroni; r Jul & Aug €91.50-106, May, Jun, Sep & Oct €53.40-79.30, Oct-Apr €38.20-53.40) One of the only hotels in the citadel, it offers spacious rooms, some of which overlook the port. It looks shabby from the outside, but the location is hard to beat.

CAMPING

Camping L'Araguina (☎ 04 95 73 02 96; av Sylvère Bohn; per person/tent/car €5.50/1.70/1.85; ⌚ Mar-Oct) Near the Hôtel des Étrangers, shaded by olive trees and only a short walk into town.

Eating

Choose carefully if you're eating on the marina – the harbourside terraces are beautiful but the food rarely lives up to the price. The citadel offers better value.

Le Voilier (☎ 04 95 73 07 06; quai Jérôme Comparetti; 2 courses €19, menu €24.50) A reliable restaurant offering top-quality fish dishes, from langoustines roasted in butter to sea bream cooked with basil sauce.

BREAD OF THE DEAD & OTHER TREATS

Bonifacio's pastry speciality is *paides morts,* a nut and raisin bread, which delightfully translates as 'bread of the dead'. Other sweet Corsican delights include *fougazi* (flat, sugar-covered, aniseed-flavoured biscuits), *canistrelli* (sugar-crusted biscuits), *canistrone* (cheese tarts) and *moustachole* (bread with sugar crystals on top).

In the citadel, local specialities are baked at **Boulangerie-Pâtisserie Faby** (4 rue St-Jean Baptiste; ☑ 8am-8pm Jul & Aug, 8am-12.30pm & 4-7pm Sep-Jun). Try **Boulangerie-Pâtisserie Michel Sorba** (1-3 rue St-Érasme; ☑ 6am-8pm Jul & Aug, 8am-12.30pm & 4.30-7pm Tue-Sat, 8am-12.30pm Sun Sep-Jun) at the marina.

L'Archivolto (☎ 04 95 73 17 58; rue de l'Archivolto; plats du jour €7-14; ☑ Mon-Sat) A wonderfully quirky restaurant-cum-antique shop in the citadel, serving imaginative food in a dining room filled with bric-a-brac. Try the chicken in Pietra beer and the fresh herb tart with *brocciu.*

Cantina Doria (☎ 04 95 73 50 49; 27 rue Doria; menus €10-16.50; ☑ Apr-Oct) A classic Corsican eatery where diners sit on wooden benches, surrounded by farming tools, old photos and rusty signs. The *soupe Corse* (€6) is hearty enough for two, and the pork cooked in Pietra beer is a house speciality.

Café de la Poste (☎ 04 95 73 13 31; 5 rue Fred Scamaroni; menus €13.50-22) Housed in the town's former post office, this buzzy restaurant contains an informal café-bar, a good-value pizza-and-pasta joint, and a more sophisticated restaurant serving seafood and Corsican cuisine.

A Manichella (☎ 04 95 73 12 75; place du Marché; ☑ 9am-11pm Apr-Oct) A pleasant café offering light lunches, crepes and panoramic sea views near the city ramparts.

SELF CATERING
Super Marché Simoni (93 quai Jérôme Comparetti; ☑ 8am-12.30pm & 3.30-7.30pm Mon-Sat, 8am-12.30pm Sun) is on the marina. Next door, Coccinelle supermarket has a fresh bakery counter.

Getting There & Away
AIR
Bonifacio's airport, **Aéroport de Figari** (☎ 04 95 71 10 10), is 21km north of town. An airport bus runs from the town centre from the end of July to the beginning of September (€7 to €8).

BOAT
Ferries to Santa Teresa in Sardinia are offered by **Saremar** (☎ 04 95 73 00 96) and **Moby**

Lines (☎ 04 95 73 00 29) from Bonifacio's ferry port (50 minutes, two to seven daily).

Saremar charges €6.70/8.50 one way in low/high season, while Moby Lines charges €22/30 return. Cars cost between €21 and €43. Port taxes are €3.

BUS
Eurocorse (Porto Vecchio ☎ 04 95 70 13 83) runs two buses to Ajaccio (€19.50, four hours) via Sartène from Monday to Saturday. For Bastia, change at Porto Vecchio (€6.50, 45 minutes, two to four buses daily). Buses leave near the Eurocorse kiosk on the marina in summer only.

CORTE AREA

CORTE (CORTI)
pop 5700 / elevation 400m

When Pasquale Paoli led Corsica to independence in 1755, one of his first acts was to make this fortified town at the centre of the island the country's capital. To this day, Corte remains a potent symbol of Corsican independence and arguably the island's most authentic town. Paoli founded a national university here in 1765, but it was closed four years later when the short-lived Corsican republic foundered. Università di Corsica Pasquale Paoli was reopened in 1981 and now has about 3000 students.

Ringed with mountains and bordered in the east by the forest region of Castagniccia, it's also an excellent base for hiking. Some of the island's highest peaks are just west of town, and the city marks the midpoint on the Mare a Mare Nord trail.

Orientation
Corte's main street is cours Paoli, which is lined with shops and cafés. At its southern

CORSICA

CORTE (CORTI)

| 0 | 200 m |
| 0 | 0.1 miles |

	A		B		C		D	
INFORMATION			**SIGHTS & ACTIVITIES**	(p891)		**EATING**	(pp891-2)	
Caisse d'Epargne	1 B2	Belvédère	6 A4		A Merenda	16 B3	
Crédit Agricole	2 B2	Château (Nid d'Aigle)	7 A4		Bar L'Oriente	17 C3	
Hôpital Civile	3 C5	Citadelle Entrance	8 A4		Brasserie Le Bip's	18 B3	
Maison de la Presse	4 B3	Église de l'Annonciation	9 B4		Casanova Bakery	(see 23)	
Post Office	5 B2	Museu di a Corsica	10 A3		Casino Supermarket	19 C5	
Speed Laverie	(see 19)	Pallazu Nationale	11 A4		Chez Julien	20 B3	
Tourist Office	(see 8)				Eurospar Supermarket	21 B3	
		SLEEPING	(p891)		Grand Café	(see 14)	
		Hôtel de la Paix	12 B2		La Rivière des Vins	22 B3	
		Hôtel de la Poste	13 B2		La Trattoria	23 B3	
		Hôtel du Nord et de l'Europe	14 B3		Le Bip's	24 B3	
		Hôtel HR	15 D5		Le Gaffory	25 B4	
					U Museu	26 A4	
					OTHER		
					Chapelle Ste-Croix	27 B3	
					Fountain	28 B3	
					Fountain	29 B4	
					Statue of Pascale Paoli	30 B4	

To Ponte Leccia via N193 (18km); Calacuccia via D18 (40km); Bastia via D18 (77km)

To Gorges de Tavignanu Trailhead (300m)

Pl du Duc de Padoue

Av. du Général de Gaulle

Orta

To N193; Ponte Leccia (30km); Bastia (70km)

R. du Baron Mariani

R. St-Joseph

Cours Paoli

N193

R. Colonel Feracci

Rampe Ste-Croix

Citadel

R des Deux Villas

Av Xavier Luciani

Av Jean Nicoli

Universita di Corsica

Basse Ville

N200

Rampe Ribanelle

Pl Gaffory Haute Ville

Pl Paoli

To Police Station & N200 (500m); Aléria & West Coast (40km)

Chemin de Baliri

Av du Président Pierucci

Tavignanu

Quartier Porette

Sports Ground

Train Station

Pont Tavignanu

Pont Restonica

Restonica

Allée du 9 Septembre

N193

To D623 (250m); Gorges de la Restonica (16km)

To Camping Aliivetu (100m)

To Ajaccio via N193 (80km)

---

end is place Paoli, from where the narrow streets of the Haute Ville lead uphill to the citadel. The train station is downhill from cours Paoli.

Information

Banks with ATMs are found along cours Paoli. The post office also has an ATM.

Grand Café (22 cours Paoli; per 15min/hr €1/3.50; 7-2am) Internet access while you eat.

Hôpital Civile (☎ 04 95 45 05 00; allée du 9 Septembre)

Maison de la Presse (24 cours Paoli; 8am-6pm) Sells maps and walking guides and has a good Corsican section.

Police Station (☎ 04 95 46 04 81) On the road to Aléria.

Post Office (av du Baron Mariani)

Speed Laverie (☺ 8am-9pm) Laundrette in the same shopping complex as the Casino supermarket.

Tourist Office (☎ 04 95 46 26 70; corte.tourisme@ wanadoo.fr; La Citadelle; ☺ 9am-noon & 2-6pm Mon-Sat Apr & May, 9am-1pm & 2-7pm Mon-Sat Jun & Sep, 9am-8pm daily Jul & Aug, 9am-noon & 2-6pm Mon-Fri Oct-Mar)

Sights
CITADEL

Corte's citadel juts from a rocky outcrop above the Rivers Tavignanu and Restonica and the cobbled alleyways of the Haute Ville. The highest point of the citadel is the **château** (known as the Nid d'Aigle, or Eagle's Nest), built in 1419 by a Corsican nobleman allied with the Aragonese. It was expanded during the 18th and 19th centuries and served as a Foreign Legion base from 1962 until 1983.

The **Museu di a Corsica** (Museum of Corsica; ☎ 04 95 45 25 45; museu@sitec.fr; adult/student €3/2.30; ☺ 10am-6pm in summer, until 5pm Nov-Apr, closed Mon in low season) houses an outstanding exhibition on Corsican traditions, crafts, agriculture and anthropology. It has a small cinema and hosts art and music exhibitions on the ground floor. Captions are in French and Corsican.

Outside the ramparts, a path leads to **le belvédère** (viewing platform), which has views of the city and the Eagle's Nest. Close by, a precarious staircase leads down to the river.

OTHER SIGHTS

The Genoese-built **Palazzu Naziunale** (National Palace) was home to Corsica's government during the island's short-lived independence, but it is now occupied by a Corsican studies centre. The basement (once a prison) is used to display temporary exhibitions.

Further down the hill is the 15th-century **Église de l'Annonciation** (place Gaffory). The walls of nearby houses are pockmarked with bullet holes, reputedly from Corsica's war of independence.

Sleeping

Hôtel de la Paix (☎ 04 95 46 06 72; fax 04 95 46 23 84; av du Général de Gaulle; s/d/tr from €35/42/55; P) A big, comfortable hotel with 60 spic-and-span rooms on a quiet square off cours Paoli. The in-house **Corsican restaurant** (menu €13) is decent, too.

Hôtel de la Poste (☎ 04 95 46 01 37; 2 place du Duc de Padoue; r €33.50) On the same square as Hôtel de la Paix, but looking worse for wear, this is a typically Corsican no-frills hotel with mismatched décor and run-down charm.

Hôtel du Nord et de L'Europe (☎ 04 95 46 00 68; www.hoteldunord-corte.com in French; 22 cours Paoli; s/d/tr low season €45/50/70, high season €65/70/90) A family-run hotel offering 15 rooms with high ceilings and soundproofed windows; the best have mountain views.

Hôtel HR (☎ 04 95 45 11 11; 6 allée du 9 Septembre; s/d low season €21/35, high season €40/52; P) Clean and functional, this hotel is outside the town centre and has an on-site laundrette and sauna, but don't expect much charm.

CAMPING

Camping Alivetu (☎ 04 95 46 11 09; fax 04 95 46 12 34; faubourg de St-Antoine; per adult/car/tent €5/2/2; ☺ Apr-Oct) Attractive and shaded by olive trees, this camping area is south of town.

Eating
RESTAURANTS

U Museu (☎ 04 95 61 08 36; rampe Ribanelle; menus €13-15; ☺ closed Sun Oct-Jun) Corte's outstanding Corsican restaurant serves traditional cuisine on a gazebo-covered terrace. Its menus include *civet de sanglier aux myrtes sauvages* (wild boar with myrtle), *soissons Corses* (Corsican lima beans) and *truite au peveronata* (trout in red pepper sauce).

La Trattoria (☎ 04 95 46 00 76; 6 cours Paoli; menus €9-14; ☺ closed Sun) A family-run restaurant held in high esteem by locals, serving up classic Corsican meat dishes and enormous salads. The next-door patisserie is rather good, too.

Le Bip's (☎ 04 95 46 06 26; 14 cours Paoli; fish dishes €7.60-13; ☺ Sun-Fri) This cellar restaurant is always packed with a boisterous crowd who come for the atmosphere and homely food. The restaurant is down a flight of stairs beside Brasserie Le Bip's.

Le Gaffory (☎ 04 95 61 05 58; place Gaffory; menus €11.50-16.50) Nestling in the shadow of Église de l'Annonciation, this restaurant offers pizzas, cheap Corsican food and multilanguage menus. The €16.50 menu includes wine.

Also recommended:

Bar L'Oriente (☎ 04 95 61 11 17; av Jean Nicoli; ☺ 9am-midnight) Funky student hang-out opposite the university.

Chez Julien (☎ 04 95 46 02 90; 24 cours Paoli; menu €13; ☽ Mon-Sat) Rustic restaurant offering meals with a Corsican twist.

La Rivière des Vins (☎ 04 95 46 37 04; 5 rampe Ste-Croix; menus €9.90-11; ☽ closed Sun Oct-Mar) Cosy wine bar serving charcuterie and cheese.

CAFÉS

A Merenda (☎ 04 95 46 30 99; 3 cours Paoli; ☽ 9am-midnight Mon-Sat) A café-bar and *salon du thé* with delicious coffee, ice cream and light meals, including *croques-monsieurs*.

Grand Café (☎ 04 95 46 00 33; 22 cours Paoli; ☽ 7-2am) A cosy café in the Hotel du Nord where you can leave your backpacks for free.

SELF-CATERING

Corte's top *boulangerie* is Casanova, next door to La Trattoria (see p891) – practically the whole town comes here to buy its cakes. There's also a **Eurospar** (7 av Xavier Luciani) and a **Casino Supermarket** (allée du 9 Septembre).

Getting There & Away

BUS

Eurocorse travels through town twice daily from Ajaccio (€10.50, 2¾ hours) towards Bastia (€10, two hours) except Sunday.

TRAIN

The **train station** (☎ 04 95 46 00 97; ☽ 6.30am-8.30pm Mon-Sat, 9.45am-noon & 4.45-8.35pm Sun) is east of the city centre. Destinations include Bastia (€9.70, two hours, three to four daily) and Ajaccio (€11.00, two hours, three to four daily).

AROUND CORTE

Southwest of Corte are the grey-granite **Gorges de la Restonica**. Some of the area's best walking trails begin 16km southwest of Corte at **Bergeries de Grotelle** (1375m), which is accessible via the D623. The **Lac de Mello** (Melu; 1711m) is a one-hour walk from the Bergeries (sheepfolds), while **Lac de Capitello** (Capitellu; 1930m) is 40 minutes further. Both lakes are ice-covered for much of the year.

West of Corte, there are walking trails around the **River Tavignanu Valley**. **Lac Nino** (Ninu; 1743m) is a 9½-hour walk from Corte. Twenty kilometres south, the 15-sq-km **Forêt de Vizzavona** has 43km of forest trails. Two waterfalls, the **Cascade des Anglais**, accessible from Vizzavona, and the **Cascade du Voile de la Mariée**, near Bocognano, are both worth the hike.

Directory

CONTENTS

Accommodation 893
Activities 896
Business Hours 898
Children 898
Climate 899
Courses 899
Customs 900
Dangers & Annoyances 900
Disabled Travellers 901
Discount Cards 902
Embassies & Consulates 902
Festivals & Events 903
Food 904
Gay & Lesbian Travellers 904
Holidays 905
Insurance 905
Internet Access 905
Legal Matters 906
Local Government 906
Maps 906
Money 908
Photography & Video 909
Post 909
Shopping 909
Solo Travellers 910
Telephone 910
Time 911
Tourist Information 911
Visas 911
Women Travellers 913
Work 913

PRACTICALITIES

- Use the metric system for weights and measures.

- Plugs will have two round pins, so you will need an international adapter; the electric current is 220V at 50Hz AC (you may need a transformer for 110V electrical appliances).

- Videos in France work on the PAL system while TV is Secam.

- Read the French *informations* in *Le Monde*, the righter-wing *Figaro* or the left-leaning *Libération*.

- Tune in to Radio France Info (105.5 FM) or the multilanguage RFI (738AM) for round-the-clock news; BBC World Service/Europe (648AM); Nova (101.5FM) for an eclectic blend of modern beats; Paris Jazz (98.1 FM) for jazz in the capital; Nostalgie, Skyrock and Fun Radio for commercial hits (see http://windowsmedia.com/radiotuner/MyRadio.asp for local frequencies).

- Pick up *France USA Contacts* (Fusac) magazine (www.fusac.fr) in Anglophone haunts in Paris for classified ads about housing, babysitting, jobs and language exchanges.

- Switch on French TV: private stations TF1 and M6; and state-owned France 2, France 3 and Arte.

ACCOMMODATION

Be it a luxurious castle, a quaint hotel room or a mountain *refuge*, France has accommodation of every sort and for every budget.

In general, hotels listed under 'budget' have doubles that cost less than two hostel beds, that is up to €40 (€50 in Paris). Most are equipped with a washbasin but lack private bath or toilet. Hall showers usually cost €2 or €3.

Hotels listed under 'mid-range' are usually in the range of €40 to €100 for a double room (up to €150 in Paris) and always have en-suite shower and toilet facilities. These places are comfortable and good value. Top-end accommodation will cost more than €100 (€150 in the capital). Of course, when it comes to the cream of French hotel opulence the price will skyrocket.

During periods of heavy domestic or foreign tourism (eg Easter, Christmas–New Year, the February–March school holidays, as well as July and August and most long weekends) popular destinations are packed out (reservations are a must) and hotels will charge peak rates.

Tourist offices will often make room reservations for you (sometimes there will be a small fee), though not over the phone – you have to stop by the office. While staff sometimes have information on vacancies, they rarely give recommendations.

Hotels almost always ask for a credit card number and written (faxed) confirmation, and some may require a deposit. Most places will hold a room only until a set hour, rarely later than 6pm or 7pm (and sometimes earlier).

Camping & Caravan Parks

Camping is immensely popular in France, and many of the thousands of camping areas are near rivers, lakes or oceans. Most close from October or November to March or April. Hostels sometimes let travellers pitch tents in the back garden.

In this book 'camping' refers to fixed-price deals for two or three people including a tent and a car. Otherwise the price is broken down per person/tent/car, but does not include extras. Rates are generally the same for campervan, plus an extra fee for electricity. Camping-ground offices are often closed for most of the day. Getting to and from most camping grounds without your own car or bike can often be slow and costly.

Gîtes de France (see below) coordinates farm camping and publishes an annual guide: *Camping à la Ferme*.

Camping in nondesignated spots *(camping sauvage)* is generally illegal, though sometimes tolerated (ask permission on private land). Except in Corsica, you probably won't have problems if you're at least 1500m from a camping area (or, in national parks, at least an hour's walk from the road). Camping on the beach is not a good idea in areas with high tidal variations. Always ask permission before camping on private land.

Gîtes Ruraux & B&Bs

Several types of accommodation – often in charming, traditional-style houses with gardens – are available through Gîtes de France for people who would like to spend time in rural areas and who have a vehicle.

A *gîte rural* is a self-contained holiday cottage (or part of a house) in a village or on a farm, and makes a great base from which to explore the surrounding area.

A *chambre d'hôte*, basically a bed and breakfast (B&B), is a room in a private house rented to travellers by the night. The website www.bbfrance.com is useful for arranging B&Bs and vacation rentals.

Ask about Gîtes de France offices and brochures and guides at local tourist offices, or contact directly the **Fédération Nationale des Gîtes de France** (☎ 01 49 70 75 75; www.gites-de -france.fr; 59 rue St-Lazare, 9e, Paris; metro Trinité).

Homestays

Under an arrangement known as *hôtes payants* or *hébergement chez l'habitant*, students, young people and tourists can stay with French families. In general you rent a room and have access (sometimes limited) to the family's kitchen and bathroom. Ask local tourist offices for details. Language schools such as Alliance Française can organise homestays.

Accueil Familial des Jeunes Étrangers (☎ 01 45 49 15 57; www.afje-paris.org; 23 rue du Cherche Midi, 6e, Paris; metro Sèvres Babylone) arranges welcoming homestays in carefully selected French families in central and greater Paris, from €550 per month, including breakfast.

France Lodge (☎ 01 56 33 85 80; 2 rue Meissonier, 17e, Paris; metro Wagram) arranges accommodation in private homes and apartments in Paris, for €22 to €40 per night per person.

Hostels & Foyers

Official hostels are known as *auberges de jeunesse*. A hostel bed generally costs around €20 including breakfast in Paris, and €8 to €13 in the provinces, where a sometimes-optional breakfast costs around €3.

France's major hostel associations, **Ligue Française pour les Auberges de la Jeunesse** (LFAJ; ☎ 01 44 16 78 78; www.auberges-de-jeunesse.com; 7 rue Vergniaud, 13e, Paris; metro Glacière) and **Fédération Unie des Auberges de Jeunesse** (FUAJ; ☎ 01 48 04 70 30; www.fuaj.org; 9 rue de Brantome, 3e, Paris; metro Rambuteau) will require you to have or purchase an Hostelling International card or a nightly Welcome Stamp. You can bring your own sleeping sheet or rent one for a small fee.

The nonprofit organisation **Union des Centres de Rencontres Internationales de France** (UCRIF; ☎ 01 40 26 57 64; www.ucrif.asso.fr) has 'international holiday centres' with bedrooms, dorm rooms and restaurant facilities.

In the university towns, *foyers d'étudiant* (student dormitories) are sometimes converted for use by travellers during summer. *Foyers de jeunes travailleurs* or *travailleuses* (workers' dormitories, usually mixed sex) often take passing visitors when they have room. Relatively unknown to travellers, these places frequently have space when other hostels are full.

Hotels

French hotels are rated with one to four stars, but these ratings are based on objective criteria (eg the size of the entry hall), not the quality of the service, the décor or the cleanliness. Prices often reflect these intangibles far more than they do the number of stars.

A double has one double bed, so specify if you prefer two twin beds *(deux lits séparés)*; triples and quads usually have two or three beds.

Look out for great weekend deals to 33 cities and towns in France, offering two nights' accommodation for the price of one and other discounts. See www.bon-week-end -en-villes.com for details.

Consortiums **Logis de France** (☎ 01 45 84 83 84; www.logis-de-france.fr), which publishes an annual guide with maps, and **Citotel** (☎ 04 73 746 590; www.citotel.com) group together affiliated hotels that meet strict standards of service and amenities while retaining their own identity and charm. They are usually reliable and good value. The **Best Western** (☎ 0800 91 40 01; www.bestwestern.com) group is increasingly muscling in on the upper end of mid-range accommodation.

Then you have the identical hotel chains. A remarkably cheap option for those travelling by car are the Accor group 'clones' in convenient (though uninspiring) locations on the outskirts of towns and cities, usually on the main access route.

Etap (☎ 0 836 68 89 00; www.etaphotel.com) Slightly more comfortable rooms for a few euros more, usually closer to the town centre.

Formule 1 (☎ 0 836 68 56 85; www.hotelformule1 .com) €22 to €28 for an efficient three-person room with hall shower and toilet.

Refuges & Gîtes d'Étape

A *refuge* (mountain hut or shelter) is a very basic dorm-room cabin established along trails in uninhabited mountainous areas and operated by national park authorities, Club Alpin Français (see p897) or other private organisations. *Refuges* are generally marked on hiking and climbing maps.

A bunk bed in the dorm usually costs between €10 and €16 per night. Meals are sometimes available. It's a good idea to make a reservation: you don't want to hike all the way there to find there's no room.

Gîtes d'étape, generally better equipped and more comfortable than *refuges* (some even have showers), are situated in less remote areas, often in villages. Contact Gîtes de France (see opposite) for information and an annual guide.

For more information about *gîtes d'étape* and *refuges* look on the website at www.gites -refuges.com, which has a France-wide directory. Otherwise contact a tourist office near where you'll be hiking. Regional guides with *refuge* listings are available.

Rental Accommodation

Finding an apartment for a long-term rental in France can be a gruelling ordeal for natives and foreigners alike. Landlords usually require substantial proof of financial responsibility and sufficient funds in France; many ask for a *caution* (guarantee) and a hefty deposit.

Classified ads appear in *De Particulier à Particulier* (www.pap.fr) and *La Centrale des Particuliers* (www.lacentrale.fr in French), both issued each Thursday. *Fusac* magazine (see p893) also has short- and long-term apartment ads by people who'll rent to foreigners at a price.

For the best selection of apartments outside Paris it's best to be on-site. Check places like bars and *tabacs* for free local newspapers (named after the number of the *département*) with classifieds listings. The ads can also be accessed on the Internet at www.maville.com (in French).

Self-Catering Apartments

Renting a studio or apartment can be an economical alternative for stays longer than a week, plus it gives you the opportunity to live as a native. The apartments are usually furnished and fully equipped, with kitchens. Watch out for hidden extra charges that can add up: cleaning fees, linen fees, electricity fees etc. Expect to pay from €70 to €120 per night or (at least) €270 per week, depending on the location.

B & W Apartment Hotels (☎ 800-755 8266; www .apartmenthotels.com; 140 East 56th St, NY, NY 10022) A variety of apartments throughout France.

Citadines (☎ 0 825 010 362; www.citadines.com)
A favourite with business travellers for its convenient
apartments.
Maeva (☎ 0 825 070 060, 01 53 61 62 00; www.orion
-vacances.com) Apartment hotels primarily in mountain
and sea resorts.

A small hotel that rents rooms with kitchenettes, generally by the week, is known as
a *hôtel meublé*. They are common on the
Côte d'Azur.

ACTIVITIES

France's varied geography and climate make
it a superb place for a wide range of outdoor
pursuits. From the snowy peaks, rivers,
lakes and canyons of the Alps to the striking
mountains and volcanic peaks of the Massif
Central – not to mention 3000km of coastline from the Mediterranean to the Straits
of Dover – France's stunning scenery lends
itself to adventure sports and exhilarating
outdoor activities of all kinds.

See the individual destinations for details and check with both local and regional
tourist offices and websites for information
on local activities, clubs and companies (see
p911).

Some hostels, for example those run
by the Fédération Unie des Auberges de
Jeunesse (FUAJ; see p894), offer week-long
sports *stages* (training courses).

Adventure Sports

France is a fantastic place for adventurous
activities. In large cities and picturesque
places – particularly the Côte d'Azur and
the Alps – local companies offer all kinds of
high adrenaline pursuits such as canyoning
and bungy jumping.

If you are interested in *alpinisme* (mountaineering) or *escalade* (rock climbing), you
can arrange climbs with guides – and other
alpine activities – through the Club Alpin
Français (see opposite).

Deltaplane (hang-gliding) and *parapente*
(paragliding) are all the rage in many parts
of France. See the Pyrenees, Brittany, Massif
Central and Languedoc-Roussillon chapters
for more information or contact **Fédération
Française de Vol Libre** (☎ 04 97 03 82 82; www.ffvl.fr
in French) in Nice.

Vol à voile (gliding) is most popular in
France's south, where the temperatures are
warmer and the thermals better. Causse

Méjean (eg near Florac; p746) in Languedoc
is one of the most popular spots. For the addresses and details of gliding clubs around
France, contact the **Fédération Française de Vol
à Voile** (FFVV; ☎ 01 45 44 04 78; www.ffvv.org; 29 rue
de Sèvres, 6e, Paris).

For details on *montgolfière* flights in the
Loire Valley, see p401 and in Burgundy,
see p428).

Speleology, the scientific study of caves,
was pioneered in France; there are still some
great places for cave exploration. Club Alpin
Français (see opposite) has information.

Cycling

The French take their cycling very seriously,
and whole parts of the country almost grind
to a halt during the annual Tour de France
(see p).

A *vélo tout-terrain* (VTT, or mountain
bike) is a fantastic tool for exploring the
countryside. Some GR and GRP trails (see
opposite) are open to mountain bikers, but
take care not to startle walkers. A *piste cyclable* is a bicycle path.

Some of the best areas for cycling (with
varying grades of difficulty) are around the
Alpine resorts of Annecy (p508) and Chambéry (p512) and through the Pyrenees. In
southwestern France, the Dordogne and
Quercy offer a vast network of scenic,
tranquil roads for cycle tourists, while the
beautiful Mont Aigoual region has a huge
network of paths (see p741). The Loire Valley and coastal regions such as Brittany,
Normandy and the Atlantic coast offer a
wealth of easier options.

For maps, see p908. Lonely Planet's *Cycling France* includes essential maps, advice,
directions, and technical tips. For information on transporting your bicycle and bike
rental, see p922. Details on places that rent
bikes appear at the end of each city or town
listing under Getting Around.

Skiing

France has more than 400 ski resorts in the
Alps, the Jura, the Pyrenees, the Vosges,
the Massif Central and even the mountains of Corsica. The ski season generally
lasts from December to March or April.
January and February tend to have the best
overall conditions, but the slopes can be
very crowded during the February–March
school holidays.

SKIING SUPERLATIVES

France can claim a fair few superlatives in the world of skiing.

- The world's largest ski area is Les Portes du Soleil at Morzine-Avoriaz (p507), northwest of Chamonix. France's longest vertical drop (2500m) is at Les Arcs (p494), near Bourg St-Maurice.

- Europe's highest resort is Val Thorens (2300m), west of Méribel (p516) .

- Europe's largest skiable glacier, which measures almost 200 hectares, is at Les Deux Alpes (p530) in the spectacular Parc National des Écrins.

- One of France's longest unofficial trails (20km) is in the Vallée Blanche (p501) at Chamonix; the longest official (groomed) one – some 16km – is the black-marked Sarenne Trail (p531) at Alpe d'Huez.

The Alps have some of Europe's finest – and priciest – ski facilities. In a few places, you can even ski on glaciers during the summer (for details, see p493 and individual destinations).

Much cheaper and less glitzy, smaller, low-altitude stations in the Pyrenees and the Massif Central are more suited to beginners and intermediates. In the Alps, low-altitude skiing is popular on the Vercors massif (p528).

Ski de fond (cross-country skiing) is possible at high-altitude resorts but is usually much better in the valleys. Undoubtedly some of the best trails are in the Jura range (p535).

One of the cheapest ways to ski in France is to buy a package deal before leaving home. Ask your travel agency for details. Many hostels in the Alps offer reasonable week-long packages in winter. Websites for online bookings include www.discover-france.info, www.ski-europe.com and www.alpsweek.com.

Paris-based **Ski France** (Ski France; ☎ 01 47 42 23 32; www.skifrance.fr; 61 blvd Haussmann 8e, Paris; metro Opéra) has information and an annual brochure covering more than 50 ski resorts. The Club Alpin Français office (see right) may also be able to provide information on alpine activities.

Walking

The French countryside is crisscrossed by a staggering 120,000km of *sentiers balisés* (marked walking paths), which pass through every imaginable terrain in every region of the country. No permits are needed for hiking, but there are restrictions on where you can camp, especially in national parks.

Probably the best known trails are the *sentiers de grande randonnée*, long-distance footpaths marked by red-and-white-striped track indicators. Some trails are many hundreds of kilometres long, such as the GR5, which goes from the Netherlands through the French Alps to Nice.

The *grandes randonnées de pays* (GRP) trails, whose markings are yellow, are designed for intense exploration of one particular area. Other types of trails include *sentiers de promenade randonnée* (PR), walking paths marked in yellow; *drailles*, paths used by cattle to get to high-altitude summer pastures; and *chemins de halage*, canal towpaths. Shorter day-hike trails are often known as *sentiers de petites randonnées* or *sentiers de pays*.

Fédération Française de la Randonnée Pédestre (FFRP; French Ramblers' Association) has an **information centre and bookshop** (Map pp96-8; ☎ 01 44 89 93 93; www.ffrp.asso.fr in French; 14 rue Riquet 19e, Paris; metro Pernety) in Paris.

The **Club Alpin Français** (Map pp96-8; ☎ 01 53 72 87 00; www.clubalpin.com; 24 av de Laumière, 19e, Paris; metro Laumière) has a centre in Paris with useful information – joining is probably worthwhile if you're doing a great deal of hiking.

Lonely Planet's *Walking in France* is full of lively detail and essential practical information. For details on *refuges* (mountain huts) and other overnight accommodation for walkers, such as *gîtes d'étape*, (see p894). For maps, see p908.

Water Sports

France has lovely beaches along all of its coasts – the English Channel, the Atlantic and the Mediterranean – as well as on lakes such as Lac d'Annecy and Lake Geneva. The fine, sandy beaches stretching along the family-oriented Atlantic Coast (eg near La Rochelle; p620) are much less crowded than their rather pebbly counterparts on the Côte d'Azur. Corsica has some magnificent spots. Brittany and the north coast are also popular (though cooler) beach destinations.

The general public is free to use any beach not marked as private.

The best surfing in France is on the Atlantic coast around Biarritz (p654), where waves can reach heights of 4m. Windsurfing is popular wherever there's water and a breeze, and renting equipment is often possible on lakes.

White-water rafting, canoeing and kayaking are practised on many French rivers, especially in the Massif Central and the Alps. The **Fédération Française de Canoë-Kayak** (FFCK; ☎ 01 45 11 08 50; www.ffck.org in French) can supply information on canoeing and kayaking clubs around the country.

BUSINESS HOURS

French business hours are regulated by the controversial 35hr week work limit. Shop hours are usually 9am or 9.30am to 7pm or 8pm, often with a midday break from noon or 1pm to 2pm or 3pm. The midday break is uncommon in Paris. French law requires that most businesses close on Sunday; exceptions include grocery stores, *boulangeries*, patisseries, florists and businesses catering exclusively to the tourist trade. Many will also close on one other weekday, usually Monday.

Restaurants are usually open for lunch between noon or 12.30pm and 2pm and for dinner from 7.30pm; they are often closed on one or two days of the week. Cafés open early morning until around midnight. Bars usually open early evening and close at 1am or 2am.

National museums are closed on Tuesday and local museums are closed on Monday, though in summer some open daily. Local or less famous regional museums may close at lunchtime.

Banks usually open from 8am or 9am to 11.30am or 1pm and then 1.30pm or 2pm to 4.30pm or 5pm, Monday to Friday or Tuesday to Saturday. Exchange services may end half an hour before closing time.

Post offices generally open from 8.30am or 9am to 5pm or 6pm on weekdays (perhaps with a midday break) and Saturday morning from 8am to noon.

Supermarkets open Monday to Saturday usually from about 9am or 9.30am to 7pm or 8pm (plus a midday break in smaller towns); some open on Sunday morning. Small food shops may shut on Monday also, so Saturday morning may be your last chance to stock up on provisions until Tuesday. Open-air markets start at about 6am and finish at 1pm or 1.30pm. Many service stations have small groceries open 24 hours a day.

CHILDREN

Country France can be a great place for travel with children and, while big cities can be more difficult, lots of activities are on offer for *les enfants*, especially in Paris.

Practicalities

France is generally child-friendly but children are expected to behave themselves in public. French parents would not ordinarily take their children to a restaurant any more sophisticated than a corner café. Chain restaurants such as Hippopotamus and Bistro Romain are casual and serve the kind of food that most kids like. Take drinks with you on sightseeing days to avoid costly café stops. Picnics can be a great way to feed the troops and enjoy local produce.

The weekly entertainment magazine *L'Officiel des Spectacles* advertises babysitting services *(gardes d'enfants)* in Paris. It's out on Wednesday and is available at any newsstand.

Most car-rental firms in France have children's safety seats for hire at a nominal cost, but it is essential that you book them in advance. The same goes for high chairs and cots (cribs); they're standard in most restaurants and hotels but numbers are limited. The choice of baby food, infant formula, soy and cow's milk, disposable nappies (diapers) and the like is as great in French supermarkets as it is back home, but the opening hours may be quite different. Run out of nappies on Saturday afternoon and you could be facing a long and messy weekend.

As an alternative to hotels, you might prefer renting a self-contained apartment or *gîte* (cottage), which provides a comfortable base for exploring an area and makes you less reliant on eating out. The fancier camping grounds have pools and children's facilities.

Sights & Activities

Include the kids in the trip planning: if they've helped to work out the itinerary and activities they will be much more interested when they get there. Lonely Planet's *Travel with Children* is a good source of information.

Paris' narrow streets and metro stairways can be a trial, but the capital has wonderful parks with amusements and activities like pony rides and puppet shows, as well as attractions like La Villette (p130) and Disneyland Resort (p184).

Beaches are always a child-pleaser, and the Atlantic coast is especially popular with families. The French Alps also have lots of outdoor activities year-round, like horse riding or snow-shoe walking. You might also get them into some light hiking or bike riding (see p896).

Try to find things that will capture their imagination: discovering volcanoes at Vulcania (p553); marvelling at how Airbus planes are put together in Toulouse (p800); exploring the lavish castles of the Loire Valley (p395); riding the 'Magic Carpet' at Futuroscope cinematic theme park (p619); or simply cavorting in lavender fields in Provence.

CLIMATE
In general, France has a temperate climate with mild winters, except in mountainous areas and Alsace. For climatic considerations concerning your trip, see p13.

COURSES
Art, cuisine, language, cinema – the best of France is there for the learning. The website www.edufrance.fr/en has information about higher education, while www.studyabroad links.com can help you find specific courses and summer programmes.

Cooking
For information on cooking short courses and specialised sessions, like pastry making, see p79.

RAIN, HAIL, SNOW OR SHINE

Discover what France's weather-forecasters are saying at www.meteo.fr (in French) or call:

National forecast	☎ 0 836 701 234
Regional forecasts	☎ 0 836 680 000
Département forecasts	☎ 0 836 6802 +
	2-digit *département* number
Mountain areas & snow forecasts	☎ 0 836 680 404
Marine forecast	☎ 0 836 680 808

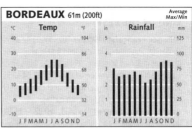

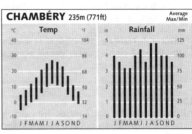

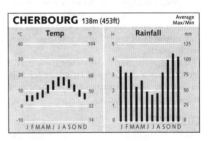

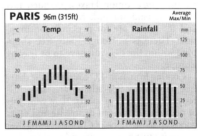

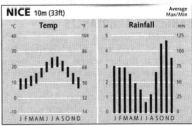

CINQ OF THE BEST

Alliance Française (Map p99-101; ☎ 01 42 84 90 00; www.alliancefr.org; 101 blvd Raspail, 6e Paris; metro St-Placide) This venerable institution for the worldwide promotion of French language and civilisation offers a variety of classes including literature, cooking or business French.

Université de Provence (Map p777; ☎ 04 42 95 32 17; www.up.univ-mrs.fr/wscefee in French; 29 av Robert Schumann, Aix-en-Provence) A popular choice in lovely Aix: academic language and methodology courses, as well as writing workshops and basic French classes.

Amboise Eurocentre (Map p413; ☎ 02 47 23 10 60; www.eurocentres.com; 9 Mail St-Thomas, Amboise) Dip into French language and culture at this small, well-organised school in the charming Loire Valley.

Besançon Centre de Linguistique Appliquée (Map p538; ☎ 03 81 66 52 00; http://cla.univ-fcomte.fr/; 6 rue Gabriel Plançon, Besançon) In this beautiful city, one of France's largest language schools with a variety of language and culture classes.

Institut de Français (☎ 04 93 01 88 44; www.institutdefrancais.com; 23 av Général Leclerc, Villefranche-sur-Mer) The only distraction from this intensive, total immersion course is the spectacular Mediterranean sea beckoning from beyond the classrooms.

Language

All manner of French courses are held in Paris and provincial cities and towns. Many can also arrange accommodation. Prices and courses vary greatly and can often be tailored to your needs (for a fee). Expect to pay upwards of €500 for an intensive four-week course.

The government site www.diplomatie .gouv.fr has a directory of language schools in France, as does *Europa Pages* (www.europa-pages.com/france).

CUSTOMS

Goods brought in and exported within the EU incur no additional taxes, provided duty has been paid somewhere within the EU and the goods are for personal consumption. There is no longer duty-free shopping within the EU; you have to be leaving Europe.

Coming from non-EU countries, the duty-free allowances (for adults) are: 200 cigarettes, 50 cigars, 1L of spirits, 2L of wine, 50g of perfume, 250ml eau de toilette and other goods up to the value of €183. Anything over the limit must be declared and paid for.

DANGERS & ANNOYANCES

In general, France is a safe place in which to live and travel, but crime has risen dramatically in the last several years. Property crime is a *major* problem but it is extremely unlikely that you will be physically assaulted while walking down the street. Always check your government's travel advisory warnings. Advice for women is on p913.

Hunters

The hunting season usually runs from the end of September to the end of February. If you see signs reading *'chasseurs'* or *'chasse gardée'* strung up or tacked to trees, you might want to think twice about wandering into the area. As well as millions of wild animals, fifty French hunters die each year after being shot by other hunters. Hunting is traditional and common place in all rural areas in France, especially Les Vosges, Sologne, the southwest and the Baie de Somme.

Natural Dangers

There are powerful tides and strong undertows along the Atlantic coast, Brittany and Normandy. Only swim in Zones de Baignade Surveillée (monitored beaches with life guards). Many people drown each year, especially on the Atlantic coast. Be aware of tide times, and if sleeping on a beach, always ensure you are above the high tidemark.

Thunderstorms in the mountains and hot southern plains can be extremely sudden and violent. So check the weather report before you set out on a long walk and be very well prepared if you're heading into the high country of the Alps or Pyrenees.

Smoking

By nature many French people dismiss laws they consider stupid or intrusive. Laws banning smoking in public places do exist, for example, but no-one pays much attention to them. In restaurants, diners will often smoke in the non-smoking sections – and the waiter will happily bring them an ashtray.

Strikes

France is the only European country in which public workers enjoy an unlimited right to strike and avail themselves of it with carefree abandon. An air traffic controllers strike in June 2002 disrupted air travel across Europe, and 2003 was the year of festival cancellations all over the country as arts workers protested. Aggrieved truck drivers have been known to block the autoroutes and farmers agitating for more government support occasionally dump tonnes of produce on major arteries.

Getting caught in one of the 'social dialogues' that characterise labour relations in France can put a serious crimp in your travel plans. It's best to leave some wriggle room in your schedule, particularly around the departure times.

Theft

The problems you're most likely to encounter are thefts (which can be aggressive), mainly pick-pocketing/bag snatching, especially in dense crowds and public places. A common ploy is for one person to distract you while another steals your wallet, camera or bag. Tired tourists on the train from the airport are a frequent target. Big cities – notably Paris, Marseille and Nice – have high crime levels. Particularly in Paris, museums are beset by organised gangs of seemingly innocuous children who are trained pickpockets.

Although there's no need whatsoever to travel in fear, a few simple precautions will minimise your chances of being ripped off.

- Photocopy your passport, credit cards, plane tickets, driver's licence, and other important documents – leave one copy at home and keep another one with you, separate from the originals.
- A hidden money belt remains the safest way to carry money and valuable documents.
- Take only what you need on busy sightseeing days: use the hotel/hostel safe.
- On trains, keep bags as close as possible: the luggage racks (if in use) at the ends of the carriage are an easy target for thieves; in sleeping compartments, lock the door carefully at night.
- Be especially vigilant at train stations, airports, fast-food outlets, cinemas, outdoor cafés, public transport and beaches.

TRAVELLING BY CAR

Car thefts and break-ins of parked cars are a frequent problem. Gangs cruise seemingly tranquil tourist areas for unattended vehicles. Foreign or out-of-town plates and rental stickers are a dead giveaway and will be targeted. *Never, ever* leave anything valuable (or otherwise) inside your car. Hiding your bags in the trunk is risky; in hatchbacks it is an open invitation to theft.

Aggressive theft from cars stopped at red lights is a problem, especially in the south at intersections and autoroute exits. Thieves are usually on motorcycle. Your car should have autolocking doors (and air-conditioning).

DISABLED TRAVELLERS

France is not well equipped for *handicapés* (disabled people): kerb ramps are few and far between; older public facilities and budget hotels often lack lifts; cobblestone streets are a nightmare to navigate in a wheelchair; and the Paris metro, most of it built decades ago, is hopeless. But disabled people who would like to visit France can overcome these difficulties.

The French government has increased efforts to improve conditions for disabled people, creating the national *Tourisme et Handicap* rating. This classification is given to sites, restaurants and hotels that meet strict requirements and standards: different symbols indicate whether establishments have access for people with physical, mental, hearing and/or seeing disabilities. Places marked *Accessible normes handicapés* subscribe to certain access standards, but the rating is not officially verified.

With the SNCF, a traveller in a wheelchair *(fauteuil roulant)* can travel in both TGV and regular trains (make a reservation at least a few hours before departure). Details are available in SNCF's booklet *Guide du Voyageur à Mobilité Réduite*. You can also contact **SNCF Accessibilité** (☎ 0 800 154 753) which has information (French only) for travellers with physical, sight and hearing disabilities.

Tourism for All (☎ 0845-124 9971; outside UK 44-208 760 0027; www.tourismforall.info) is a UK-based group that publishes an information guide to France which can be ordered online. **Access Project** (www.accessproject-phsp.org; 39 Bradley Gardens, West Ealing, London W13 8HE) publishes a fairly dated but useful guide, *Access in Paris*. The **Paris Tourist Office** (p111) also has information and brochures.

If you speak French, specialised guidebooks with comprehensive information for travellers with physical disabilities include Bernic's *Guide Rousseau* and the Petit Futé *Handiguide*. They are available at major bookshops. The portal www.jaccede.com (in French) has loads of information, reviews and links.

Michelin's *Guide Rouge* indicates those hotels with lifts and facilities for disabled people, while Gîtes de France (see p894) can provide a list of *gîtes ruraux* and *chambres d'hôtes* with disabled access.

Specialised travel agencies abroad include US-based **Wheels Up!** (☎ 1-888 38 4335; www.wheelsup.com) and UK-based **Access Travel** (☎ 01942 888 844; www.access-travel.co.uk).

Organisations
Association des Paralysées de France (AFP; ☎ 01 53 80 92 97; 13 Place de Rungis, 13e, Paris) This national organisation has branches throughout France with region-specific information.

Groupement pour l'Insertion des Personnes Handicapées Physiques (☎ 01 43 95 66 36; 10 rue Georges de Porto Riche, 14e, Paris; metro Porte d'Orléans) Provides vehicles outfitted for people in wheelchairs; the national office will put you in touch with local services.

DISCOUNT CARDS
Student, Youth & Teachers' Cards
These cards, available from student unions and travel agencies, can get fantastic discounts, but not all places will recognise them. An International Student Identity Card (ISIC; €12) can pay for itself through half-price admissions, discounted air and ferry tickets, and cheap meals in student cafeterias. Many places stipulate a maximum age, usually 24 or 25. For more details, check the International Student Travel Confederation (ISTC; www.istc.org) website.

If you're under 26 but not a student, you can apply for an International Youth Travel Card (ITYC or Go25, €12), also issued by ISTC, which entitles you to much the same discounts as an ISIC. The European Youth Card (Euro<26 card) offers similar discounts across 35 European countries for nonstudents under 26 (see www.euro26.org).

Teachers, professional artists, museum conservators and certain categories of students are admitted to some museums free. Bring along proof of affiliation, for example, an International Teacher Identity Card (ITIC).

Seniors Cards
Senior citizens are entitled to discounts in France on things like public transport, museum admission fees, public theatres and so on. The **Société Nationale des Chemins de Fer** (SNCF; www.sncf.fr) issues the Carte Senior (€45) to those aged over 60, which gives reductions of 25% to 50% on train tickets, valid for one year.

Camping Card International
The Camping Card International is a form of ID that can be used instead of a passport when checking into a camping ground and includes third-party insurance. As a result, many camping grounds offer a small discount if you sign in with one. CCIs are issued by automobile associations, camping federations and, sometimes, on the spot at camping grounds.

EMBASSIES & CONSULATES
French Embassies & Consulates
France's diplomatic and consular representatives abroad are listed on the website www.france.diplomatie.fr. For some of the following countries, additional consulates exist.

Australia Canberra (☎ 02-6216 0100; www.ambafrance
-au.org; 6 Perth Ave, Yarralumla, ACT 2600) Sydney Consulate
(☎ 02-9261 5779; www.consulfrance-sydney.org; 20th fl,
St Martin's Tower, 31 Market St, Sydney, NSW 2000)
Belgium Brussels (☎ 02-548 8711; www.ambafrance
-be.org; 65 rue Ducale, 1000) Brussels Consulate (☎ 02-
229 8500; www.consulfrance-bruxelles.org; 12a Place de
Louvain, 1000)
Canada Ottawa (☎ 613-789 1795; www.ambafrance
-ca.org; 42 Sussex Dr, Ottawa, Ont K1M 2C9) Toronto
Consulate (☎ 416-925 8041; www.consulfrance-toronto
.org; 130 Bloor West, Ste 400, Ont M5S 1N5)
Germany Berlin (☎ 030-590 039 000; www.botschaft
-frankreich.de; Parizer Platz 5, 10117) Munich Consulate
(☎ 089-419 4110; Möhlstrasse 5, 81675)
Ireland Dublin (☎ 01-217 5000; www.ambafrance
-ie.org; 36 Ailesbury Rd, Ballsbridge, 4)
Italy Rome (☎ 06-686 011; www.ambafrance-it.org;
Piazza Farnese 67, 00186)
Netherlands The Hague (☎ 070-312 5800; www
.ambafrance-nl.org; Smidsplein 1, 2514 BT) Amsterdam
Consulate (☎ 020-530 6969; www.consulfrance-amster
dam.org; Vijzelgracht 2, 1017 HR)
New Zealand Wellington (☎ 04-384 2555; www.am
bafrance-nz.org; Rural Bank Bldg, 34–42 Manners St)
South Africa Pretoria (☎ 012-42 51 6000; www.amba
france-rsa.org; 250 Melk St, New Muckleneuk, 0181)
Spain Madrid (☎ 91-423 8900; www.ambafrance-es.org;
Calle de Salustiano, Olozaga 9, 28001) Barcelona Consulate
(☎ 93-270 3000; www.consulfrance-barcelone.org;
Ronda Universitat 22, 08007)
Switzerland Berne (☎ 031-359 2111; www.amba
france-ch.org; Schosshaldenstrasse 46, 3006) Geneva
Consulate (☎ 022-319 0000; www.consulfrance-geneve
.org; 11 rue Imbert Galloix, 1205)
UK London (☎ 020-7073 1000; www.ambafrance-uk.org;
58 Knightsbridge, London SW1X 7JT) Consulate (☎ 020-
7073 1200; 21 Cromwell Rd, London SW7 2EN) Visa section
(☎ 020-7838 2051; 6A Cromwell Place SW7 2EW)
USA Washington (☎ 202-944 6000; www.ambafrance
-us.org; 4101 Reservoir Rd NW, DC 20007) New York Consulate (☎ 212-606 3600/89; www.consulfrance-newyork
.org; 934 Fifth Ave, NY 10021) San Francisco Consulate
(☎ 415-397 4330; www.consulfrance-sanfrancisco.org;
540 Bush St, CA 94108)

Embassies & Consulates in France
All foreign embassies are in Paris. Many
countries – including the UK, USA, Canada,
Japan and most European countries – also
have consulates in other major cities such as
Nice, Marseille and Lyon. To find an embassy
or consulate not listed here, look up 'Ambas-
sades et Consulats' in the *Yellow Pages* (Pages
Jaunes; www.pagesjaunes.fr) for Paris.

Australia Paris (Map pp99-101; ☎ 01 40 59 33 00; www
.austgov.fr; 4 rue Jean Rey, 15e; metro Bir Hakeim)
Belgium Paris (Map pp93-5; ☎ 01 44 09 39 39; 9 rue de
Tilsitt, 17e; metro Charles de Gaulle-Étoile)
Canada Paris (Map pp93-5; ☎ 01 44 43 29 00; www
.amb-canada.fr; 35 av Montaigne, 8e; metro Franklin
D Roosevelt) Nice Consulate (Map pp820-1; ☎ 04 93 92 93
22; 10 rue Lamartine)
Germany Paris (Map pp93-5; ☎ 01 53 83 45 00; www
.amb-allemagne.fr; 13-15 av Franklin D Roosevelt, 8e;
metro Franklin D Roosevelt)
Ireland Paris (Map pp93-5; ☎ 01 70 20 00 20; 33 rue
Miromesnil, 8e; metro Miromesnil)
Italy Paris (Map pp99-101; ☎ 01 49 54 03 00; www.amb
-italie.fr; 51 rue de Varenne, 7e; metro Rue du Bac)
Japan Paris (Map pp93-5; ☎ 01 48 88 62 00; www.amb
-japon.fr; 7 av Hoche, 8e; metro Courcelles)
Netherlands Paris (Map pp99-101; ☎ 01 40 62 33 00;
www.amb-pays-bas.fr; 7 rue Eblé, 7e; metro St-François
Xavier)
New Zealand Paris (Map pp93-5; ☎ 01 45 01 43 43;
www.nzembassy.com; 7ter rue Léonard de Vinci, 16e;
metro Victor Hugo)
South Africa Paris (Map pp99-101; ☎ 01 45 55 92 37;
59 quai d'Orsay, 7e; metro Invalides)
Spain Paris (Map pp93-5; ☎ 01 44 43 18 00; 22 av
Marceau, 8e; metro Alma Marceau)
Switzerland Paris (Map pp93-5; ☎ 01 49 55 67 00;
142 rue de Grenelle, 7e; metro Varenne)
UK Paris (Map pp93-5; ☎ 01 44 51 31 00; www.amb
-grandebretagne.fr; 35 rue du Faubourg St-Honoré, 8e;
metro Concorde) Consulate (Map pp93-5; ☎ 01 44 51 31
02; 16bis rue d'Anjou, 8e; metro Madeleine) Nice Consulate
(Map pp820-1; ☎ 04 93 62 13 56; 26 av Notre Dame)
Marseille Consulate (off Map pp764-5; ☎ 04 91 15 72 10;
24 av du Prado)
USA Paris (Map pp93-5; ☎ 01 43 12 22 22; www.amb
-usa.fr; 2 av Gabriel, 8e; metro Concorde) Consulate (Map
pp93-5; ☎ 01 43 12 47 08; 2 rue St-Florentin, 1er; metro
Concorde) Nice Consulate (Map pp820-1; ☎ 04 93 88 89
55; 7 av Gustav V, 06000) Marseille Consulate (Map pp764-5;
☎ 04 91 54 92 00; place Varian Fry)

FESTIVALS & EVENTS
Most French cities have at least one major
music, dance, theatre, cinema or art festival
each year. Villages hold *foires* (fairs) and
fêtes (festivals) to honour anything from
a local saint to the year's garlic crop. We
list these important annual events in city
and town sections; for precise details about
dates, contact the local tourist office. During big events towns get extremely busy and
accommodation is usually booked out in
advance.

MARCH & APRIL

Feria Pascale (p803; www.ville-ales.fr/feria in French)
In the ancient *arène* of Arles, this Feria kicks the bullfight
season with much cavorting and merriment (Easter).

MAY & JUNE

May Day Across France, the workers' day is celebrated
with trade union parades and diverse protests. People give
each other *muguet* (lilies of the valley) for good luck. No
one works – except waiters and *muguet* sellers (1 May).

International Film Festival (p836; www.festival-cannes
.com) The stars walk the red carpet at Cannes, the epitome
of see-and-be-seen cinema events in Europe (mid-May).

Fête de la Musique (www.fetedelamusique.culture.fr)
Bands, orchestras, crooners, buskers and spectators take to
the streets for this national celebration of music (21 June).

JULY

National Day Fireworks, parades and all-round hoo-ha to
commemorate the storming of the Bastille in 1789, symbol
of the French Revolution (14 July).

Gay Pride (www.gaypride.fr in French) Effervescent
street parades, performances and parties throughout Paris
(p136) and other major cities (July).

Festival International d'Art Lyrique (p780; www
.festival-aix.com) Attracting the world's best classical
music, opera, ballet and buskers, Aix-en-Provence is the
place to be for the discerning visitor (July).

Festival d'Avignon (p787; www.festival-avignon.com)
Actors, dancers and musicians flock to Avignon to perform
in the official and fringe art festivals (late July & early
August).

Fêtes de Bayonne (p651) Bullfighting, cow-chasing and
Basque music are the order of the day at Bayonne's biggest
event (July).

Nice Jazz Festival (p825; www.nicejazzfest.com) See
jazz cats and other pop, rock and world artists take over
public spaces and the Roman ruins of Nice (July).

AUGUST & SEPTEMBER

Festival Interceltique (p309; www.festival-intercelt
ique.com) This massive event pulls hundreds of thousands
of Celts to Lorient from all over Brittany and the UK for a
massive celebration of their shared Celtic culture (August).

American Film Festival (p255; www.festival-deauville
.com) The silver screen comes to the seaside at this celebration of Hollywood cinema in Deauville (September).

Braderie de Lille (p205) Three days of madness and
mussel-munching as this colossal flea market engulfs the city
with antiques, handicrafts and bric-a-brac (early September).

DECEMBER

Christmas Markets Alsace is the place to be for a
traditional-style festive season, with world-famous
Christmas markets, decorations and celebrations.

FOOD

Our special food and drinks chapter (p63) is
full of succulent information about French
gastronomy.

In this book, we usually indicate the price
of *menus* (two- or three-course set menus);
ordering à la carte (from the menu) is generally more expensive.

Budget eating options are usually more
casual places with simple meals under €10 or
set *menus* for around €8 to €13. Mid-range
restaurants will have more atmosphere and
offer seasonal specialities and fine local flavours, with *menus* from €15 to €25 (less at
lunchtime). In France, 'top-end' restaurants
are superb establishments with impeccable
quality and service and *menus* from €25.

GAY & LESBIAN TRAVELLERS

France is one of Europe's most liberal countries when it comes to homosexuality, in
part because of the long French tradition of
public tolerance towards people who choose
not to live by conventional social codes.
Paris has been a thriving gay and lesbian
centre since the late 1970s. Montpellier,
Lyon, Toulouse, Bordeaux and many other
towns also have significant active communities. Predictably, attitudes towards homosexuality tend to become more conservative
in the countryside and villages. France's lesbian scene is much less public than its gay
counterpart and is centred mainly around
women's cafés and bars, which are the best
place to find information.

Gay Pride marches are held in major
French cities each June.

There are a number of useful gay and
lesbian publications:
Action Act Up's free monthly publication with information
and issues.
Guide Gai Pied A French- and English-language travel
guide.
Lesbia A women's monthy with articles and useful listings.
Spartacus International Gay Guide An English-
language travel guide for men.

Têtu A glossy men's monthly with a France-wide directory of bars, clubs and hotels. There are also listings for lesbians.
Women's Traveller An English-language travel guide for lesbians, published by Damron.

Online, www.gayscape.com (in French) has hundreds of links, while www.france.qrd .org is a 'queer resources directory' for gay and lesbian travellers. Another good site for finding out about gay events is http://cite gay.fr (in French).

Organisations

Most of France's major gay and lesbian organisations are based in Paris:

Act Up-Paris (☎ 01 48 06 13 89; www.actupparis.org in French; 45 rue Sedaine, 11e; metro Voltaire) This organisation defends France's gay community and can provide advice and information. Advice by phone is available 2pm to 6pm on Wednesday.

AIDES (☎ 0 820 160 120; www.aides.org in French; 119 rue des Pyrénées, 20e; metro Jourdain) France-wide organisation fighting against HIV/AIDS and for the rights and wellbeing of those affected.

Association des Médecins Gais (☎ 01 48 05 81 71) The Association of Gay Doctors, based in the Centre Gai et Lesbien, deals with gay-related health issues.

Centre Gai et Lesbien (CGL; Map pp102-4; ☎ 01 43 57 21 47; www.cglparis.org in French; 3 rue Keller, 11e; metro Ledru Rollin) A welcome and support centre. Friday is women's (only) day, with meetings, debates, outings and workshops.

SIDA-info service (☎ 0 800 840 800; www.sida-info -service.org in French) HIV/AIDS information service that can help with anonymous testing and treatment. Advice is available in foreign languages between 2pm and 7pm.

HOLIDAYS

The following *jours fériés* (public holidays) are observed in France:

New Year's Day (Jour de l'An) 1 January – parties in larger cities; fireworks are subdued by international standards.
Easter Sunday and Monday (Pâques & lundi de Pâques) Late March/April.
May Day (Fête du Travail) 1 May – traditional parades
Victoire 1945 8 May – the Allied victory in Europe that ended WWII.
Ascension Thursday (L'Ascension) May – celebrated on the 40th day after Easter.
Pentecost/Whit Sunday & Whit Monday (Pentecôte & lundi de Pentecôte) Mid-May to mid-June – celebrated on the seventh Sunday after Easter.
Bastille Day/National Day (Fête Nationale) 14 July – *the* national holiday.
Assumption Day (L'Assomption) 15 August.

All Saints' Day (La Toussaint) 1 November.
Remembrance Day (L'onze novembre) 11 November – celebrates the WWI armistice.
Christmas *(Noël)* 25 December.

The following are *not* public holidays in France: Shrove Tuesday (Mardi Gras; the first day of Lent); Maundy (or Holy) Thursday and Good Friday just before Easter; and Boxing Day (26 December). Good Friday and Boxing Day, however, are holidays in Alsace.

INSURANCE
Travel Insurance

A travel-insurance policy to cover theft, loss and medical problems is a good idea. Some policies specifically exclude dangerous activities, which can include scuba diving, motorcycling, even trekking.

You may prefer a policy that pays doctors or hospitals directly rather than you having to pay on the spot and claim later. If you have to claim later ensure you keep all documentation. Check that the policy covers ambulances or an emergency flight home. Paying for your airline ticket with a credit card often provides limited travel accident insurance. Ask your credit card company what it's prepared to cover.

See p929 for health insurance and p924 for car insurance.

INTERNET ACCESS

After somewhat of a late start, Internet cafés have sprung up all over the country and are listed under Information in the regional chapters of this guide. You'll pay around €3 to €5 per hour. You may also come across Netanoo (http://www.netanoo.com in French) phonecard-operated Internet terminals. A 120-unit *télécarte* will get you two hours' surfing time.

Roughly 1000 post offices across France have been equipped with a Cyberposte, a card-operated Internet terminal for public use. Access cards cost €7.60 for the first hour and €4.60 for a recharge. There is a list of post offices with a Cyberposte at www .cyberposte.com (in French).

If you're using your laptop, check that it is compatible with the 220V current in France; if not you will need a converter. You'll also need a telephone plug adaptor. Having a reputable global modem will prevent access problems that can occur with PC-card modems brought from home.

If you do not go with a global Internet Service Provider (ISP; such as AOL) make sure your ISP has a dial-up number in France. Local ISPs Free (www.free.com), Tiscali (www.tiscali.fr) and Wanadoo (www.wanadoo.fr in French) have cheap or free short-term membership (look out for free trial membership CD-ROMs). For WiFi users things are improving rapidly: wireless access points are being installed in major airports, hotel chains and cafés. Check sites like www.wifinder.com for access points.

For useful travel websites, see p15.

LEGAL MATTERS
Drugs & Alcohol
Contrary to popular belief, French law does not officially distinguish between 'hard' and 'soft' drugs. The penalty for any personal use of *stupéfiants* (including cannabis, amphetamines, ecstasy, heroine etc) can be a one-year jail sentence and a €3750 fine, but depending on the circumstances it might be anything from a stern word to a compulsory rehab programme.

Importing, possessing, selling or buying drugs can get you up to 10 years' prison and massive fines. Police have been searching chartered coaches, cars and passengers getting off trains for drugs just because they are coming from Amsterdam.

Being drunk in public places is punishable with a €150 fine.

Police
French police have wide powers of search and seizure, and can ask you to prove your identity at any time – whether or not there is plausible cause. Foreigners must be able

---

LEGAL AGES

- Driving: 18
- Buying alcohol: 16
- Age of majority: 18
- Age of sexual consent for everyone: 15
- Age considered minor under anti-child-pornography and child-prostitution laws: 18
- Voting: 18

---

to prove their legal status in France (eg passport, visa, residency permit) without delay.

If the police stop you for any reason, be polite and remain calm. Verbally (and of course physically) abusing a police officer can carry a hefty fine, and even imprisonment. You may refuse to sign a police statement, and have the right to ask for a copy.

People who are arrested are considered innocent until proven guilty, but can be held in custody until trial. The website www.service-public.fr has information on legal rights.

French police are very strict about security. Do not leave baggage unattended at airports or train stations: suspicious objects will be summarily blown up.

LOCAL GOVERNMENT
Metropolitan France (the mainland and Corsica) is made up of 22 *régions* (regions) which are subdivided into 96 *départements* (departments), which are subdivided into 324 arrondissements, which are in turn subdivided into *cantons*, which are subdivided into 36,400 *communes* (communes).

Invariably named after a geographic feature, *départements* tout a two-digit code (see the map opposite) which make up the first two digits of the area's postcode.

MAPS
In Paris, the best place to find a full selection of maps is at the **Espace IGN** (Map pp93-5; ☎ 01 43 98 85 12; 107 rue La Boétie, 8e; metro Franklin D Roosevelt). The two major map producers are Michelin (www.michelin-travel.com) and Institut Géographique National (IGN; www.ign.fr in French): their websites list sales outlets. Road maps and city maps are available at Maisons de la Presse (large newsagencies found all over France), bookshops, tourist offices, and even some newspaper kiosks. IGN publishes themed maps about wine, museums and so on.

The book in your hand contains over 145 city and town maps. Lonely Planet publishes a laminated *Paris City Map*. Michelin has excellent road maps of cities and towns, which are coordinated with its travel guides. Plans-Guides Blay offers orange-jacketed street maps of 125 French cities and towns.

For road maps, *Environs de Paris* (Michelin) will help you with the very confusing drive out of Paris. Michelin's *Atlas Routier France*, which covers the whole country in

RÉGIONS & DÉPARTEMENTS

0 ⬛══ 200 km
0 ⬛══ 120 miles

ALSACE
67 Bas-Rhin
68 Haut-Rhin

AQUITAINE
24 Dordogne
33 Gironde
40 Landes
47 Lot-et-Garonne
64 Pyrénées-Atlantiques

AUVERGNE
03 Allier
15 Cantal
43 Haute-Loire
63 Puy-de-Dôme

BASSE-NORMANDIE
14 Calvados
50 Manche
61 Orne

BRETAGNE
22 Côtes d'Armor
29 Finistère
35 Ille-et-Vilaine
56 Morbihan

BOURGOGNE
21 Côte d'Or
58 Nièvre
71 Saône-et-Loire
89 Yonne

CENTRE
18 Cher
28 Eure-et-Loir
36 Indre
37 Indre-et-Loire
41 Loir-et-Cher
45 Loiret

CHAMPAGNE-ARDENNE
08 Ardennes
10 Aube
51 Marne
52 Haute-Marne

CORSE
2A Corse-du-Sud
2B Haute-Corse

FRANCHE-COMTÉ
25 Doubs
39 Jura
70 Haute-Saône
90 Territoire de Belfort

HAUTE-NORMANDIE
27 Eure
76 Seine-Maritime

LAUGUEDOC-ROUSSILLON
11 Aude
30 Gard
34 Hérault
48 Lozère
66 Pyrénées-Orientales

LIMOUSIN
19 Corrèze
23 Creuse
87 Haute-Vienne

LORRAINE
54 Meurthe-et-Moselle
55 Meuse
57 Moselle
88 Vosges

MIDI-PYRÉNÉES
09 Ariège
12 Aveyron
31 Haute-Garonne
32 Gers
46 Lot
65 Hautes-Pyrénées
81 Tarn
82 Tarn-et-Garonne

NORD-PAS-DE-CALAIS
59 Nord
62 Pas-de-Calais

PAS DE LA LOIRE
44 Loire-Atlantique
49 Maine-et-Loire
53 Mayenne
72 Sarthe
85 Vendée

PICARDIE
02 Aisne
60 Oise
80 Somme

POITOU-CHARENTES
16 Charente
17 Charente-Maritime
79 Deux-Sèvres
86 Vienne

PROVENCE-ALPES-CÔTE D'AZUR
04 Alpes-de-Haute-Provence
05 Hautes-Alpes
06 Alpes-Maritimes
13 Bouches-du-Rhône
83 Var
84 Vaucluse

RÉGION PARISIENNE
75 Ville de Paris
77 Yvelines
78 Seine-et-Marne
91 Essonne
92 Haut-de-Seine
93 Seine-St-Denis
94 Val-de-Marne
95 Val-d'Oise

RHÔNE-ALPES
01 Ain
07 Ardèche
26 Drôme
38 Isère
42 Loire
69 Rhône
73 Savoie
74 Haute-Savoie

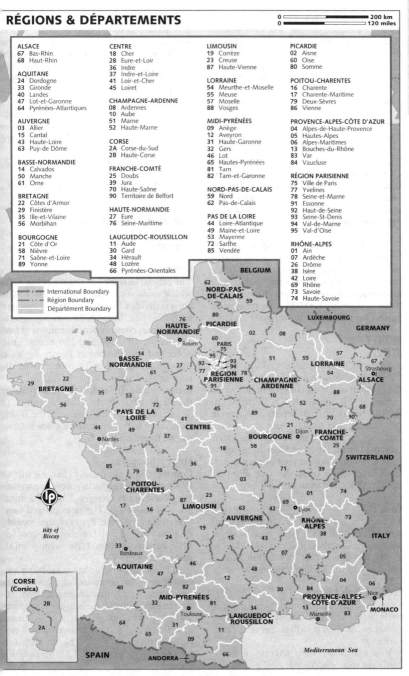

DIRECTORY

1:200,000 scale (1cm = 2km), is the best for long-distance driving. *France – Routes, Autoroutes* (IGN) is also good for plotting cross-country travel.

If you're concentrating on just a few regions, it is easier and more cose effective to buy Michelin's yellow-jacketed fold-out maps or IGN's fold-out regional maps.

Walking & Cycling

The FFRP (see p897) publishes some 120 topoguides in French, map-equipped booklets on major trails. Local organisations also produce topoguides with details on trail conditions, flora and fauna, mountain shelters and so on – ask local bookshops and tourist offices. English translations of some topoguides are available through UK publisher Robertson McCarta.

IGN has a variety of great maps and topoguides that are ideal for hiking, biking or walking. Its specialised *cyclocartes* (cycle maps) show dozens of suggested bicycle tours around France. Didier et Richard publishes a series of 1:50,000-scale trail maps, perfect for walking or for off-road cycling.

MONEY
ATMs

Automated Teller Machines (ATMs), or *distributeurs automatiques de billets* (DAB), are the cheapest and most convenient way to get money. ATMs are situated in all major cities and towns (though are more scarce in rural areas), and usually offer an excellent exchange rate. Many are linked to the international Cirrus, Plus and Maestro networks so that you can draw on your home account. Cash advances on credit cards are also possible at ATMs, but incur charges.

Cash

You always get a better exchange rate incountry, though it's a good idea to arrive with enough local currency to take a taxi to a hotel if you have to. Carry as little cash as possible while travelling around.

Credit & Debit Cards

Credit and debit cards are convenient, relatively secure and will usually offer a better exchange rate than travellers cheques or cash exchanges.

Visa and MasterCard (Access or Eurocard) are widely accepted; AmEx cards are useful at more upmarket establishments and allow you to get cash at AmEx office and certain ATMs. In general, all three cards can be used in shops, supermarkets for train travel, car rentals, autoroute toll and cash advances. Don't assume that you can pay for a meal or a budget hotel with a credit card – inquire first.

Getting a cash advance against a credit card is usually an expensive way to go a fees (and interest) are charged. Debit card fees are usually much less.

For lost cards, these numbers operate 24 hours:

AmEx (☎ 01 47 77 72 00) AmEx offices arrange on-the-spot replacements.
Diners Club (☎ 0 810 314 159)
MasterCard, Eurocard & Access (Eurocard France; ☎ 0 800 901 387)
Visa (Carte Bleue; ☎ 0 800 902 033)

Currency

The official currency of France is the euro which came into circulation in 2002. One euro is divided into 100 cents or centimes with one, two, five, 10, 20 and 50 centime coins. Notes come in denominations of five 10, 20, 50, 100, 200 and 500 euros. Euro notes and coins issued in France are valid throughout the other 11 countries in the euro zone: Austria, Belgium, Finland, Germany, Greece, Ireland, Italy, Luxembourg the Netherlands, Portugal and Spain.

Exchange rates are given on the inside front cover of this book and a guide to costs can be found on p13.

Moneychangers

Commercial banks usually charge a stiff €3 to €4.50 per foreign-currency transaction (eg BNP Paribas charges 3.3% or a minimum of about €4). The rates offered vary so it pays to compare. Banks charge roughly €3.40 to €5.30 to cash travellers cheques (eg BNP Paribas charges 1.5%, with a minimum charge of €4).

In Paris, bureaux de change are faster and easier, open longer hours and give better rates than most banks. In general, post offices in Paris can offer the best exchange rates and accept banknotes in various currencies as well as travellers cheques issued by American Express or Visa. The commission for travellers cheques is 1.5% (minimum about €4).

It's best to familiarise yourself with rates offered by the post office and compare them with those at bureaux de change, which are not generally allowed to charge commissions. On small transactions, even exchange places with less-than-optimal rates may leave you with more euros in your pocket.

Travellers Cheques

The most flexible travellers cheques are those issued by AmEx (in US dollars or euros) and Visa (in euros) because they can be changed at many post offices as well as commercial banks and exchange bureaux. Note that you will not be able to pay most merchants with travellers cheques directly. AmEx offices don't charge commission on their own travellers cheques.

For lost travellers cheques call **AmEx** (☎ 0 800 908 600) and **Thomas Cook** (☎ 0 800 908 330) for replacements. For **Visa** and **Mastercard**, see opposite.

PHOTOGRAPHY & VIDEO

Colour-print film is widely available, but it's fairly expensive in France compared to a lot of other countries, so it pays to stock up ahead of time. Developing a 24-exposure film costs from €8 to €14. For slides (dia-positives), avoid Kodachrome: it's difficult to process quickly in France and may not be handled correctly. You can easily obtain video cartridges in large towns, but it's good to come with a few from home.

A good companion when on the road is *Travel Photography: A Guide to Taking Better Pictures,* by travel photographer Richard I'Anson.

POST

Each of France's post offices is marked with a yellow or brown sign reading 'La Poste'. Since La Poste also has banking, finance and bill-paying functions, queues can be long, but there are automatic machines for postage.

Postal Rates

Domestic letters of up to 20g cost €0.50. For international post, there are three different zones: a letter/package under 20g/2kg costs €0.50/12.50 to Zone A (EU, Switzerland, Iceland, Norway); €0.75/14 to Zone B (the rest of Europe and Africa); and €0.90/20.50 to Zone C (North and South America, Asia & Middle East, Australasia).

Rates are automatically given for *prioritaire* (somewhat fast post); specify if you want the cheaper *économique* (rather slow post).

Worldwide express-mail delivery, called **Chronopost** (☎ 0 825 801 801), costs a fortune and is not as rapid as advertised.

All mail to France *must* include the five-digit postcode, which begins with the two-digit number of the *département* (postcodes are listed under the main city or town headings in this book). The notation 'CEDEX' after a town name simply means that mail sent to that address is collected at the post office, rather than delivered to the door.

Receiving Mail

Picking up poste-restante mail costs €0.50; you must show your passport or national ID card. Mail will be kept 15 days. Poste-restante mail not addressed to a particular branch goes to the city's main post office.

AmEx has a poste-restante service (mail is held for 30 days or returned to sender). There's a €0.76 if you don't have an AmEx card or travellers cheques. AmEx addresses are given in the relevant city listings.

SHOPPING

France is renowned for its luxury goods, particularly *haute couture,* high-quality clothing accessories (eg Hermès scarves), lingerie, perfume and cosmetics. Such goods may not be any cheaper here than at home.

Sale periods *(soldes)* – held for three weeks in January and July – can be a gold mine for fashion finds. The fashion- and budget-conscious should also look out for the words *dégriffés* (cut price; usually the labels have been cut out) or *dépôt-vente* (ex-showroom garments sold at steep mark-downs).

For local crafts and art it's best to go directly to the source. In Brittany, look for colourful Quimper faïence and in Normandy pick up unique Rouen faïence or some intricate lace from Alençon. Other good buys include crystal and glassware from Baccarat in southern Lorraine or enamel and porcelain from Limoges in Limousin.

Even though wines from Bordeaux, Burgundy, Alsace and Champagne are available everywhere, you'll get a better selection in a local wine shop. Local brandies make good souvenirs since they may not be available in your home country, such as cognacs (from Cognac!) and Calvados, Pommeau or

DIRECTORY

Fécamp Bénédictine (from Normandy). Corsicans sell unusual liqueurs in local markets and Charentes is the place to pick up Pineau de Charentes.

Goodies that travel well include macaroons from St-Émilion, *calissons* from Aix-en-Provence and candied fruit from Nice. For information on local shopping options, see the individual towns and cities.

Non-EU residents can get a rebate of some of the 19.6% value-added tax (VAT) for large purchases, including when several different purchases are made in the one department store. There are forms to fill out in-store which must be shown, with the purchases, upon departure.

SOLO TRAVELLERS

Travelling by yourself in France is easy and rewarding, and shouldn't pose any problems. Many hotels will charge the same price for single and double rooms, and if single prices are available, they tend not to be significantly cheaper. It is quite common to eat in restaurants alone in France, particularly at lunch, when *menus* are also considerably cheaper – you might want to make that the main meal of the day. Women shouldn't encounter any particular problems travelling alone in France, but may come across some minor hassles. See p913 for more information.

TELEPHONE

A quarter of a century ago, France had one of the worst telephone systems in Western Europe. But thanks to massive investment, the country now has one of the most modern and sophisticated telecommunications systems in the world.

Domestic Dialling

France has five telephone dialling areas. You dial the same 10-digit number no matter where you are, but it is cheaper to call locally.

For France Telecom's directory inquiries *(services des renseignements)*, dial ☎ 12 (around €0.45 per minute). Not all operators speak English.

Domestic rates are billed at about €0.15 for three minutes with a *télécarte*, but numbers starting with 08 are more expensive.

Emergency numbers (see inside the front cover) and 0 800 numbers can be dialled free from public and private telephones.

International Dialling

To call France from another country, dial your country's international access code, then dial ☎ 33 (France's country code), then omit the 0 at the beginning of the 10-digit local number.

To call someone outside France, dial the international access code (☎ 00), the country code, the area code (without the initial zero if there is one) and the local number. International Direct Dial (IDD) calls to almost anywhere in the world can be placed from public telephones.

To make a reverse-charges (collect) call *(en PCV)* or a person-to-person call *(avec préavis)*, dial ☎ 3123 or ☎ 0 800 990 011 (for the USA and Canada) and ☎ 0 800 990 061 for Australia. Expect to pay about €12 for a three-minute call.

For directory inquiries for numbers outside France, dial ☎ 3212. The cost is about €2.50.

Hotels, *gîtes,* hostels and pensions are free to meter their calls as they like. The surcharge is usually around €0.30 per minute but can be higher.

Phonecards (see below) offer much, much better international rates than Country Direct services (which allow you to be billed by the long-distance carrier you use at home).

Mobile Phones

France uses GSM 900/1800, which is compatible with the rest of Europe and Australia but not with the North American GSM 1900 or the totally different system in Japan (though some North Americans have GSM 1900/900 phones that do work here). If you have a GSM phone, check with your service provider about using it in France, and beware of calls being routed internationally (very expensive for a 'local' call).

The three major providers of mobile phone access are **SFR** (0 800 106 000; www.sfr.com), **Bouygues** (☎ 0 810 630 100; www.bouygtel.com) and France Telecom's **Orange** (☎ 0 800 830 800; www.orange.fr). If you already have a compatible phone, you can buy a 'prepay' phone kit which gives you a SIM-card with a mobile phone number and a set number of calls. When these run out you purchase a recharge card at most *tabacs.* You can also get similar 'prepay' deals that include the phone itself.

Mobile phone numbers in France always begin with 06. France has a 'caller pays' system which means that you do not pay to receive a call on your mobile phone unless it is an international call.

Public Phones & Telephone Cards
Almost all public telephones in France are card-operated – coin-operated phones are virtually nonexistent. Most public phones have a button displaying two flags which you push for explanations in English.

Cards can be purchased for €7.50 or €15 at post offices, *tabacs* (tobacconists) and anywhere that you see a blue sticker reading *'télécarte en vente ici'*. There are two kinds of phone cards, *cartes à puce* (cards with a magnetic chip, that are inserted chip-first into public phones) and *cartes à code* (that you can use from public or private phones by dialling the free access number and then punching in the card's scratch-off code).

Your choice of card will depend on your needs. France Telecom offers different cards suited to national and international dialling. For help in English on all France Telecom's services, dial ☎ 0 800 364 775.

A whole bevy of other cards are available for cheap international calls, especially in Paris, and most can be used elsewhere in Europe. Compare the rates on the posters, or ask which one is best for the place you're calling.

TIME
France uses the 24hr clock and is on Central European Time, which is one hour ahead of GMT/UTC. During daylight-saving time, which runs from the last Sunday in March to the last Sunday in October, France is two hours ahead of GMT/UTC.

Without taking daylight-saving time into account, when it's noon in Paris it's 3am in San Francisco, 6am in New York, 11am in London, 8pm in Tokyo, 9pm in Sydney and 11pm in Auckland. The Australian eastern coast is between eight and 10 hours ahead of France. Refer to the time-zone world map on p931 for additional data.

TOURIST INFORMATION
Local Tourist Offices
Every city, town, village and hamlet seems to have either an *office de tourisme* (a tourist office run by some unit of local government) or a *syndicat d'initiative* (a tourist office run by an organisation of local merchants). Both are

excellent resources for local maps, accommodation, restaurants and activities. Very few of their many, many brochures are on display. If you have a special interest, such as walking tours, cycling or wine sampling, ask about it. Some have limited currency-exchange services. Many tourist offices will make local hotel reservations, usually for a small fee.

Regional tourist offices *(Comité Régional de Tourisme)* and their websites are great for regionwide information, particularly concerning activities. The website www.fncrt.com (in French) links to the different CRTs.

Details on local tourist offices appear under Information at the beginning of each city, town or area listing.

Tourist Offices Abroad
French government tourist offices (usually called Maisons de la France) can provide every imaginable sort of tourist information on France, most of it in the form of brochures. The general website www.franceguide.com lets you access the site for your home country.

Australia (☎ 02-9231 5244; 25 Bligh St, 22nd floor, Sydney, NSW 2000)
Belgium (☎ 0902 88 025; 21 ave de la Toison d'Or, 1050 Brussels)
Canada (☎ 514-876 9881; 1981 McGill College Ave, Suite 490, Montreal, Que H3A 2W9)
Germany (☎ 0190 570 025; Westendstrasse 47, D-60325 Frankfurt)
Ireland (☎ 01560 235 235; 10 Suffolk St, Dublin 2)
Italy (☎ 166 116 216; Via Larga 7, 20122 Milan)
Netherlands (☎ 0900 112 2332; Prinsengracht 670, 1017 KX Amsterdam)
Spain Madrid (☎ 807 117 181; Plaza de España 18, 28008) Barcelona (☎ 807 117 181; Gran Via Corts Catalanes 656, 08010)
Switzerland Zurich (☎ 01-211 3085; Rennweg 42) Geneva (☎ 0900 900 699; 2 rue Thalberg, 1201)
UK (☎ 09068 244 123; 178 Piccadilly, London W1V 9AL)
USA New York (☎ 410-282 8310; 444 Madison Ave, 16th fl, NY 10022-6903) Los Angeles (☎ 310-271 6665; 9454 Wilshire Blvd, Ste 715, Beverly Hills, CA 90212-2967)

VISAS
For up-to-date information on visa requirements, see the Foreign Affairs Ministry site, www.diplomatie.gouv.fr under 'Entering France'.

EU nationals and citizens of Switzerland, Iceland and Norway need only a passport or national identity card to enter France and stay in the country. However, for nationals of the 10 new (in 2004) member countries, conditions for living and working in France vary from those for nationals of the original countries.

Citizens of Australia, the USA, Canada, New Zealand, Japan and Israel do not need visas to visit France as tourists for up to three months; the same goes for citizens of EU candidate countries (except Turkey).

As a practical matter, if you don't need a visa to visit France, no-one is likely to kick you out after three months. The unspoken policy seems to be that you can stay and spend your money in France as long as you don't try to work, apply for social services or commit a crime. Being in a *situation irrégulière* is nonetheless illegal, and without a *carte de séjour* you can face real problems renting an apartment, opening a bank account and so on.

Tourist (Schengen) Visa

Those not exempt will need a Schengen Visa, named after the Schengen agreement that abolished passport controls between Austria, Belgium, Denmark, Finland, France, Germany, Greece, Iceland, Italy, Luxembourg, the Netherlands, Norway, Portugal, Spain and Sweden. A Schengen visa allows unlimited travel throughout the entire zone within a 90-day period.

Applications are made with the consulate of the country you are entering first, or that will be your main destination. Among other things, you will need medical insurance and proof of sufficient funds to support yourself. See www.eurovisa.com for information.

If you enter France overland, it is unlikely that your visa will be checked at the border, but major problems can arise if you don't have one later on.

Tourist visas *cannot* be extended except in emergencies (such as medical problems); you'll need to leave and reapply from outside France when your visa expires.

Long-Stay & Student Visas

This is the first step if you'd like to work or study in France, or stay for over three months. Long-stay and student visas will allow you to enter France and apply for a *carte de séjour* (residency permit). Contact the French embassy or consulate nearest your residence, and begin your application

well in advance as it can take months. Tourist visas cannot be changed into student visas after arrival. However, short-term visas are available for students sitting university-entrance exams in France.

Working Holiday Visa

Citizens of Australia, Canada, Japan and New Zealand aged between 18 and 29 years (inclusive) are now eligible for a one-year, multiple-entry Working Holiday Visa, allowing combined tourism and employment in France. You have to apply to the embassy or consulate in your home country, and must prove you have a return ticket, insurance and sufficient funding to get through the start of your stay. Make sure you get in early with the application, as quotas apply.

Once you have arrived in France and have found a job, you must apply for a Temporary Work Permit *(autorisation provisoire de travail)*, which will only be valid for the duration of the employment position offered. The permit can be renewed under the same conditions up to the limit of the authorised length of stay.

The idea is to supplement your funds with unskilled work. You can also study or do training programmes, but the visa can not be extended, nor turned into a student visa. After one year you *must* go home.

Once in France, the Centre d'Information et Documentation Jeunesse (CIDJ; see opposite) can help with information.

Carte de Séjour

Once issued with a long-stay visa, you can apply for a *carte de séjour* (residence permit), and are usually required to do so within eight days of arrival in France. Make sure you have all the necessary documents *before* you arrive. EU passport-holders and citizens of Switzerland, Iceland and Norway no longer need a *carte de séjour* to reside or work in France. Other foreign nationals must contact the local *préfecture* (prefecture), or *commissariat* (police station) for their permit.

Students of all nationalities must apply for a *carte de séjour* at the **Centre des Étudiants** (Map pp99-101; 13 rue Miollis, 15e, Paris; metro Cambronne or Ségur) in Paris. For more information (in French) see the Paris Préfecture website (www.prefecture-police-paris.interieur .gouv.fr), or the national migrations office website (www.omi.social.fr).

WOMEN TRAVELLERS

For information about health issues while travelling, see p930.

Safety Precautions

Women tend to attract more unwanted attention than men, but female travellers need not walk around France in fear; people are rarely assaulted on the street. Be aware of your surroundings and of situations that could be potentially dangerous: empty streets, lonely beaches, dark corners of large train stations. Using the metros late at night is generally OK, as stations are rarely deserted, but there are a few to avoid. See p112 for details.

In some places women may have to deal with what might be called low-intensity sexual harassment: 'playful' comments and invitations that can become overbearing or aggressive, and which some women find threatening or offensive. Remain polite and keep your distance. Hearing a foreign accent may provoke further unwanted attention.

Be alert to vibes in cheap hotels, sometimes staffed by apparently unattached men who may pay far more attention to your comings and goings than you would like. Change hotels if you feel uncomfortable, or allude to the imminent arrival of your husband (whether you have one or not).

On overnight trains, you may prefer to ask (when reserving) if there's a women's compartment available. If your compartment companions are overly attentive, don't hesitate to ask the conductor for a change of compartment. Second-class sleeping cars offer greater security than a *couchette*.

You can reach France's national **rape crisis hotline** (☎ 0 800 059 595) toll-free from any telephone without using a phonecard. It's run by a Paris women's organisation, **Viols Femmes Informations** (9 villa d'Este, 13e; metro Porte d'Ivry).

The **police** (☎ 17) will take you to the hospital if you have been attacked or injured. In Paris, medical, psychological and legal services are available to people referred by the police at the 24hr **Service Médico-Judiciaire** (☎ 01 42 34 84 46) of the Hôtel Dieu hospital (Map pp93–5).

Organisations

The women-only **Maison des Femmes** (Map pp102-4; ☎ 01 43 43 41 13; 163 rue Charenton, 12e; metro Reuilly Diderot) is the main meeting place for women of all ages and nationalities.

WORK

EU nationals have an automatic right to work in France. Non-EU citizens will need to apply for a work permit, for which they first need a *carte de séjour* or a Working Holiday Visa (see opposite), as well as a written promise of employment. Permits can be refused on the grounds of high local unemployment.

Working 'in the black' (that is, without documents) is difficult and risky for non-EU travellers. The only instance in which the government turns a blind eye to undocumented workers is during fruit harvests (mid-May to November) and the *vendange* grape harvest (mid-September to mid- or late October).

Even with a permit, employers generally must pay 'foreigner fees' for non-EU employees, and must prove that the job cannot be done by an EU-citizen (there are some exceptions for artists and computing and translation specialists). So getting qualified work is extremely difficult.

Summer and casual work is more flexible, and can be found in restaurants and hotels (particularly in the Alps). Teaching English is another option, either for a company or through private lessons.

Au-pair work is also very popular and can be done legally even by non-EU citizens, but they must contact the placement agency from their home country at least three months in advance.

The administration for freelance workers *(travailleurs indépendants)* is **URSSAF** (☎ 01 49 20 10 10; www.urssaf.fr in French; 3 rue Franklin 93100, Montreuil). Organising freelance work status is complicated; it is highly advisable to consult a local attorney experienced in immigration matters.

France's national employment service, the **Agence National pour l'Emploi** (ANPE; www.anpe .fr in French) has offices throughout France; the website has job listings.

The **Centre d'Information et de Documentation Jeunesse** (CIDJ; Map pp99-101; ☎ 01 44 49 12 00; www.cidj.com; 101 quai Branly, 15e; metro Champ de Mars) provides all sorts of information for young people on jobs, housing, education and more: in 2004 they advertised 20,000 summer jobs on their website.

In Paris, the magazine *Fusac* (see p893) advertises jobs for English speakers, including au-pair work, babysitting and language teaching.

Transport

CONTENTS

Getting there & Away	**914**
Entering The Country	914
Air	914
Land	916
Sea	919
Getting Around	**921**
Air	921
Bicycle	922
Boat	922
Bus	923
Car & Motorcycle	923
Hitching	925
Local Transport	926
Tours	926
Train	927

GETTING THERE & AWAY

ENTERING THE COUNTRY

Thanks to European integration you can cross fluidly between France and neighbouring countries without passing through customs or border checkpoints. If you are arriving from a non-EU country, you will have to show your passport – and your visa permit if you need one (see p911) – or your identity card if you are an EU citizen, and clear customs.

AIR
Airports

Air France (www.airfrance.com), the national carrier, and scores of other airlines link Paris with every part of the globe. France has two major international airports: **Roissy-Charles de Gaulle** (CDG; ☎ 01 48 62 12 12) and **Orly** (ORY; ☎ 01 49 75 15 15), both run by **Aéroports de Paris** (☎ 01 43 35 70 00; www.adp.fr). For details on these airports see p170.

A number of other airports have significant international services (mainly within Europe):

Bordeaux (BOD; ☎ 05 56 34 50 50; www.bordeaux
.aeroport.fr)

Lille (LIL; ☎ 03 20 49 68 68; www.lille.aeroport.fr in French)

Lyon (LYS; ☎ 0 826 800 826; www.lyon.aeroport.fr)

Marseille (MRS; ☎ 04 42 14 14 14; www.marseille
-provence.aeroport.fr)

Nantes (NTE; ☎ 02 40 84 80 00; www.nantes.aeroport.fr)

Nice (NCE; ☎ 0 820 423 333; www.nice.aeroport.fr)

Strasbourg (SXB; ☎ 03 88 64 67 67 www.strasbourg
.aeroport.fr)

Toulouse (TLS; ☎ 0 825 380 000; www.toulouse
.aeroport.fr)

Some airlines and budget carriers use small provincial airports for flights to the UK, continental Europe and, sometimes, North Africa. Smaller airports with international flights include Biarritz, Caen, Deauville, Metz-Nancy-Lorraine, Montpellier, Morlaix, Mulhouse-Basel (EuroAirport), Nîmes, Rennes, St-Étienne, Tours and Quimper. Relevant local airports are listed relevant destination chapters.

Airlines
Most of the world's major carriers serve Paris at the very least.

Aer Lingus (☎ 01 70 20 00 72; www.aerlingus.com; airline code EI; hub Dublin)

Air Canada (☎ 0 825 880 881; www.aircanada.ca; airline code AC; hub Toronto)

Air France (☎ 0 820 820 820; www.airfrance.com; airline code AF; hub Paris)

Alitalia (☎ 0 820 315 315; www.alitalia.com; airline code AZ; hub Rome)

American Airlines (☎ 0 810 872 872; www.american airlines.com; airline code AA; hub Dallas)

Austrian Airlines (☎ 0 820 816 816; www.austrian airlines.com; airline code OS; hub Vienna)

Basiqair (☎ 0 821 231 214; www.basiqair.com; airline code HV; hub Amsterdam)
BMI BritishMidland (short haul ☎ 0870 6070 555, long haul ☎ 0870 6070 555; www.flybmi.com; airline code BD; hub London)
British Airways (☎ 0 825 825 400; www .british airways.com; airline code BA; hub London)
Cathay Pacific (☎ 01 41 43 75 75; www.cathaypacific .com; airline code CX; hub Hong Kong)
Continental Airlines (☎ 01 42 99 09 09; www .contin ental.com; airline code CO; hub Houstan)
easyJet (☎ 44-023-568 4880; www.easyjet.com; airline code EZY; hub London Luton)
Flybe (☎ 44-0871 700 0535; www.flybe.com; airline code BE; hub Southampton)
Iberia (☎ 0 820 075 075; www.iberia.com; airline code IB; hub Madrid)
KLM (☎ 0 890 710 710; www.klm.com; airline code KL; hub Amsterdam)
Lufthansa (☎ 0 820 020 030; www.lufthansa.com; airline code LH; hub Frankfurt)
Olympic Airlines (☎ 01 44 94 58 58; www .olympic airlines.com; airline code OA; hub Athens)
Qantas Airways (☎ 0 820 820 500; www.qantas.com; airline code QF; hub Sydney)
Ryanair (www.ryanair.com; airline code FR; hub London Stansted, Dublin)
Singapore Airlines (☎ 01 53 65 79 01; www .singa poreair.com; airline code SQ; hub Singapore)
South African Airways (☎ 01 55 61 94 55; www .flysaa.com; airline code SA; hub Johannesburg)
Thai Airways International (☎ 01 44 20 70 15; www.thaiair.com; airline code TG; hub Bangkok)

Tickets
A bit of research – calling around, checking Internet sites, comparing the airline and travel agent prices, scouring newspapers – can often result in real savings on your air ticket. Start early: some of the cheapest tickets have to be bought well in advance.

We mention well-known travel agents later in this chapter, under individual country headings. For cheap tickets from no-frill carriers, contact them directly or use online ticket searches. Good online agencies·
Anyway (www.anyway.com in French) French-based discount site.
Cheap Tickets (www.cheaptickets.com)
Expedia (www.expedia.com)
Last Minute (www.lastminute.com)
Priceline (www.priceline.com) With this US-based site you can bid for a ticket online.
Travel Cuts (www.travelcuts.com)
Travelocity (www.travelocity.co.uk)

Budget carriers such as Ryanair, BMI and easyJet have sprung up mushroom-like all over Europe. Usually tickets are bought directly from the airline, online or by phone. Bear in mind that budget-airlines are often changing their routes and going into liquidation, so check websites for up-to-date information.

INTERCONTINENTAL (RTW) TICKETS
Round-the-world (RTW) tickets can be a great way to combine destinations, and can be no more expensive than an ordinary return fare for residents of Australasia. The flight dates (but not the overall routing) are changeable en route. The departure date from your home country usually determines the fare (that is, whether you're charged high- or low-season rates). Validity usually lasts for a year.

Australia & New Zealand
From Melbourne or Sydney, many major airlines fly to Europe. Return tickets to Paris range from A$1900 to A$3000. Fares from Perth are about A$200 cheaper. A return flight from Auckland will cost from NZ$1900. A RTW ticket is worth considering, it might be better value than the return fare. Small agencies advertise in the *New Zealand Herald*, *Sydney Morning Herald* and the Melbourne *Age*. Other major dealers in cheap fares, with many branches:
Flight Centre (Australia-wide ☎ 131 131, in New Zealand ☎ 0800 24 35 44; www.flightcentre.com)
STA Travel (Australia-wide ☎ 1300 733 035, ☎ 0508 782 872; www.statravel.com)

Canada
From Toronto or Montreal, return flights on Air Canada to Paris are available from about C$820 in the low season; prices are C$200 or C$300 more from Vancouver. For lower fares, scan the travel-agency ads in the *Globe & Mail, Toronto Star* and *Vancouver Province*. **Travel CUTS** (☎ 1 888 359 2887; www .travelcuts.com) has branches across Canada.

Continental Europe
Most European airlines fly into Paris. Air France offers competitive fares on most of its routes as well as good discounts for young people, seniors and couples (married or legally cohabiting). Local travel agencies and online ticket sites follow.

TRANSPORT

DENMARK

Kilroy Travels (☎ 70 80 80 15; www.kilroytravels.com; Skindergade 28, Copenhagen)
STA Travel (☎ 33 14 15 01; www.statravel.dk; Fiolstraede 18, Copenhagen)

GERMANY

STA Travel (☎ 030-310 00 40; www.statravel.de; Hardenbergstrasse 9, Berlin)

ITALY

Viaggi Wasteels (☎ 091 34 96 86; Viale Piemonte, Palermo)
CTS Viaggi (☎ 06 462 043 116; www.cts.it; Via Genova, Rome) One of many branches throughout Italy.

THE NETHERLANDS

Kilroy Travels (☎ 020-524 51 00; wwww.kilroytravels .com; Singel 413, Amsterdam)
ISSTA (☎ 020-618 80 31; 226 Overtoom Straat, Amsterdam)

NORWAY

Kilroy Travels (☎ 81 55 96 33; wwww.kilroytravels .com; Nedre Slottsgate 23, Oslo)
STA Travel (☎ 81 55 99 05; www.statravel.no; Karl Johansgate 8, Oslo)

SWEDEN

Kilroy Travels (☎ 0771-545769; wwww.kilroytravels .com; Kungsgatan 4, Stockholm)
STA Travel (☎ 0771-611010; www.statravel.se; Kungsgatan 30, Stockholm)

SWITZERLAND

STA Travel (☎ 022-818 02 00; www.statravel.ch; rue de Rive 10, Geneva)

The UK & Ireland

Low-cost carriers now offer astounding rates from the UK and Ireland to destinations throughout France. Some of the best deals, especially to destinations other than Paris such as Lyon, Marseille Toulouse and La Rochelle, are offered by Ryanair, Flybe and easyJet. Prices vary wildly from a ridiculously low UK£17 between London and Paris. Aer Lingus flies from Dublin or Shannon to Paris' Charles de Gaulle for €115 return.

Air France and British Airways link cities throughout the UK and France, fares are often very reasonable. Other airlines that may have decent prices include British Midland and KLM (UK).

Look for special deals in the travel pages of the weekend broadsheet newspapers, as well as in *Time Out*, the *Evening Standard* and the free magazine *TNT*.

Recommended travel agencies and online ticket sites:
Cheap Flights (www.cheapflights.co.uk)
Cheapest Flights (www.cheapestflights.co.uk)
Online Travel (www.onlinetravel.com) Good deals on flights from more than a dozen British cities.
STA Travel (☎ 0870 1 600 599; www.statravel.co.uk) Caters especially to student and youth travel.
Usit Voyages (in Dublin ☎ 01-602 1600, in Paris ☎ 01 42 34 56 90; Irish Republic www.usitworld.com)

The USA

The flight options across the North Atlantic, the world's busiest long-haul air corridor, are bewildering. A return flight from New York to Paris costs around US$370 in the low season and US$800 in the high season; even lower promotional fares are sometimes on offer. Tickets from the west coast are US$150 to US$250 higher.

The *New York Times*, *LA Times*, *Chicago Tribune* and *San Francisco Chronicle* all have weekly travel sections in which you'll find any number of travel-agency ads. Independent periodicals such as the *San Francisco Guardian* and New York's *Village Voice* are other good places to check.

There are a number of local travel agencies and online ticket sites:
Expedia (www.expedia.com)
Flight Centre (www.flightcentre.com)
STA Travel (www.statravel.com)
Travelocity (www.travelocity.com)

STAND-BY & COURIER FLIGHTS

Other rock-bottom options for discounted – and even free – air travel include charter, stand-by and courier flights.
Airhitch (☎ 877-247-4482; www.airhitch.org) Specialises in stand-by flights.
Courier Travel (☎ 303 570 7586; www.couriertravel .org) A comprehensive search engine for courier and stand-by flights.
International Association of Air Travel Couriers (☎ 561-582 8320; www.courier.org)

LAND

If you are doing a lot of travel around Europe, look for discount bus and train passes, which can be conveniently combined with discount air fares.

Bus

Buses are slower and less comfortable than trains, but are cheaper, especially if you qualify for discount rates (people under 26, over 60, teachers and students) or get one of the reduced-price fares on offer at times.

BUSABOUT

From April to October, the UK-based **Busabout** (in London ☎ 207 950 1661; www.busabout.com), based in London, links 41 European cities in 11 countries, mostly in Western Europe, and offers a Europe-wide bus pass. Within France the buses stop at Bordeaux, Tours, Paris, Avignon and Nice. There are two types of pass available:

Flexipass Allows for a set number of travelling days within an certain number of days within the entire six-month operating season. Full/discount passes costs €419/379 for eight days and €729/649 for 16 days.
Unlimited Pass Allows for unlimited use of the bus system within a set period. Full/discount passes cost €359/329 for two weeks, €729/649 for six weeks or €1239/1109 for the six-month season.

You can hop on or off the buses as you like, and can pay extra for additional links to places like Croatia. On-board guides can take care of hostel reservations or you can book ahead online – in many places the pick-up/drop-off point is a central hostel. For information and bookings, check out its website.

EUROLINES

Eurolines (☎ 08 92 69 52 52, 01 43 54 11 99; www.euro lines .com) groups together more than 30 European coach operators and links points all across Europe as well as Morocco and Russia. Eurolines' all-Europe website has links to each national company's site and gives detailed information on fares, routes, bookings and special deals. You can usually book online. Return tickets cost about 20% less than two one-ways. In summer make reservations at least two working days in advance. The main hub is Paris. Sample one-way fares:

Route	Full Fare (€)	Duration (hr)
Paris–Prague	75	16
Paris–Amsterdam	46	8
Bordeaux–Barcelona	55	10¼
Nice–Rome	67	10
Lyon–Berlin	90	20

The Eurolines Travel Pass is a flexible ticket that allows for unlimited travel within a set period between 31 European cities, including several in France – but you are not able to visit other cities en route. A 15-/30-/60-day pass during high season (June to September) will cost €285/425/490 for adults and €240/345/380 for the discount (youth/senior) fares. The rest of the year the cost is €220/310/390 for adults and €185/250/310 for discount fares.

INTERCARS

French coach company **Intercars** (www.intercars .fr in French) links France with cities throughout in Europe, notably Eastern Europe and Russia. The office in **Paris** (☎ 01 42 19 99 35; 139bis rue de Vaugirard, 15e; metro Falguière) links with Berlin (€77, 13 hours), Moscow (€234, 50 hours) and many places in between. From **Lyon** (☎ 04 78 37 20 80; Perrache bus station) you can reach Venice, Naples, Porto, Minsk or Zagreb. From **Nice** (☎ 04 93 80 08 70; Nice bus station) you can reach San Sebastian, Casablanca and Warsaw.

You can reserve by emailing the agency closest to your place of departure.

Car & Motorcycle

Arriving in France by car is easy to do. At some border points you may be asked for passport or identity card (your driver's licence will not be sufficient ID). Police searches are not uncommon for vehicles entering France, particularly from Spain and Belgium (via which drugs from Morocco or the Netherlands can enter France). See p923 for details about driving in France.

EUROTUNNEL

The Channel Tunnel, inaugurated in 1994, is the first dry-land link between England and France since the Ice Age.

High-speed **Eurotunnel shuttle trains** (in the UK ☎ 0870 535 3535, in France ☎ 03 21 00 61 00; www .eurotunnel.com) whisk cars, motorcycles and coaches from Folkestone through the Channel Tunnel to Coquelles, 5km southwest of Calais, in air-conditioned and soundproofed comfort. Shuttles run 24 hours a day, every day of the year, with up to five departures an hour during peak periods (one an hour from 1am to 5am). LPG and CNG tanks are not permitted, which eliminates many campers and caravans.

TRANSPORT

Prices vary with market demand, but the regular one-way fare for a passenger car, including all its passengers, costs from UK£150 (in February or March) to UK£250 (in July or August); return passage costs twice as much. Return fares valid for less than five days are much cheaper. The fee for a bicycle, including its rider, is UK£32 re-turn; advance reservations are mandatory. To take advantage of promotional fares you must book at least one day ahead.

Train

Rail services link France with every country in Europe; schedules are available from major train stations in France and abroad.

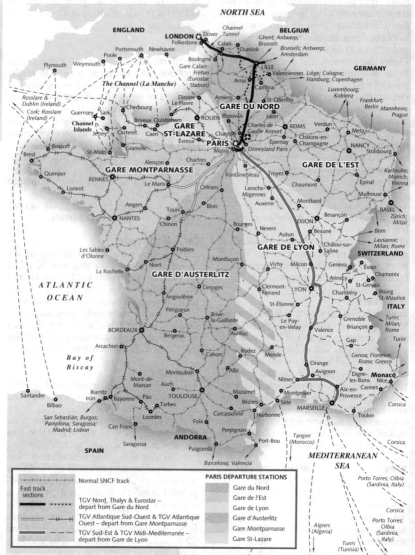

Because of different track gauges and electrification systems, you sometimes have to change trains at the border (eg when travelling to Spain). Many national rail companies are linked to Paris:

Austria (☎ 01-93 00 00; www.oebb.at)
Belgium (☎ 02-528 28.28; www.b-rail.be)
Germany (☎ 0800 1 50 70 90; www.bahn.de)
Italy (☎ 89 20 21; www.trenitalia.it)
The Netherlands (☎ 06 92 96; www.ns.nl)
Spain (☎ 902 24 02 02; www.renfe.es)
Switzerland (☎ 0900 300 300; www.sbb.ch)

The **Thalys** (www.thalys.com) service links Paris' Gare du Nord to Brussels-Midi (from €65, 1½ hours, 20 per day), Amsterdam CS (from €87, 4¼ hours, five per day) and Cologne's Hauptbahnhof (€78, four hours, seven per day).

You can book tickets and get information from **Rail Europe** (www.raileurope.com) up to two months ahead. In France ticketing is handled by the national train network **SNCF** (☎ 08 92 35 35 35; www.sncf.com). Telephone and Internet bookings are possible, but they won't post tickets outside France. See p928 for information about discounts.

EUROPEAN TRAIN PASSES
These discount passes are worthwhile only if you plan to travel extensively around France by train and other European countries.

Eurail Passes (www.eurail.com) A variety of passes are available to non-European residents for travel in 17 countries. For people over/under 26, 15 days' consecutive, unlimited travel costs €588/414; and five days' travel over a two-month period costs €356/249.

InterRail (www.raileurope.co.uk/inter-rail) and **Euro-Domino** passes are available to European residents. All are valid on the French national train network and allow unlimited travel for varying periods of time.

See p928 for discounts and passes from the SNCF and for travel within France. Eurail and some other train passes must be validated at a train station ticket window before you begin your first journey, in order to begin the period of validity.

EUROSTAR
On the highly civilised **Eurostar** (in France ☎ 08 92 35 35 39, in the UK ☎ 08705 186 186; www.eurostar .com), the trip from London to Paris takes just two hours and 35 minutes. There are direct daily services between London and Ashford (Kent) and Paris, Brussels, Lille, Parc Disneyland Paris and Calais-Fréthun. A direct seasonal service goes from London and Ashford to Avignon (May to October) and the French Alps (November to April).

A full-fare, 2nd-class ticket from London to Paris can be as low as UK£50 (and as high as £300). From Paris, the trip to London varies immensely from €60 to €525. You'll get the best deals if you stay over a Saturday night, if you book 14 or seven days ahead, if you're under 25 or if you're a student. Student travel agencies often have youth fares not available directly from Eurostar.

SEA
Tickets for ferry travel to/from the UK, the Channel Islands and Ireland are available from most travel agencies in France and the countries served. Except where noted, the prices given below are for standard one-way tickets; in some cases, return fares cost less than two one-way tickets. Prices vary greatly according to the season and the demand. There are discounts for children.

Note that if you're travelling with a vehicle you are usually denied access to it during the voyage.

The Channel Islands
Passenger-only catamarans operated by **Hugo Express** (in France ☎ 02 33 61 08 88) link the Channel Islands with two small ports on the western coast of Normandy: Granville (daily April to September, weekends only in March) and Carteret (daily April to September). The one-way pedestrian fare is UK£35.

Émeraude Lines (in the UK ☎ 01534 766 566, in France ☎ 0 825 165 180; www.emeraudelines.com) runs express car ferries between Jersey and St-Malo (foot passenger/car and two adults from UK£35/114, 1¼ hours).

Ireland
Eurail pass holders pay 50% of the adult pedestrian fare for crossings between Ireland and France on Irish Ferries (make sure you book ahead).

Irish Ferries (☎ 01-638 3333, in France ☎ 01 43 94 46 94; www.irishferries.ie) has overnight services from Rosslare to either Cherbourg (18½ hours) or Roscoff (16 hours) every other day (three times a week from mid-September to October, with a possible break in service from November to February). A pedestrian/car with two adults costs around €90/389. There are special prices for five- and nine-day returns.

From April to September, **Brittany Ferries** (☎ 0870 366 5333, in France ☎ 0 825 828 828; www .brittany-ferries.com) runs a car ferry every Saturday from Cork (Ringaskiddy) to Roscoff (14 hours), and every Friday in the other direction. Foot passengers pay around €198 for a three-person couchette.

Freight ferries run by **P&O Irish Sea** (☎ 0870 242 4777; www.poirishsea.com) link Rosslare with Cherbourg (18 hours, three per week); cars with two passengers cost from €154. From April to September there is also a weekly Dublin–Cherbourg route (18 hours); cars with two adults cost €174. Foot passengers are not accepted on either service.

Italy

From late April to mid-October, the **Société Nationale Maritime Corse Méditerranée** (SNCM; ☎ 0 891 701 801; www.sncm.fr) has five or six car ferries per week from Marseille or Toulon to Porto Torres on the island of Sardinia (Sardaigne in French). The one-way adult pedestrian fare is around €100 and takes about 11 hours.

A variety of ferry companies ply the waters between Corsica and Italy. For details, see p865.

North Africa

SNCM and **Compagnie Tunisienne de Navigation** (CTN; www.ctn.com.tn) link Marseille with the Tunisian capital, Tunis (about 24 hours, three or four a week). The standard adult fare is €300 one way, with discounts for seniors and those under 25. In France, ticketing is handled by SNCM, which also links Marseille with Algiers (Alger in French; Algeria).

Compagnie Marocaine de Navigation (CoMaNav; ☎ 04 99 57 21 21) links Sète, 29km (20 minutes by train) southwest of Montpellier, with the Moroccan port of Tangier (Tanger; 36 hours, five to seven a month). The cheapest berth costs €168 (€228 in August and for some other summer sailings) one way; return tickets cost 15% to 20% less than two one-ways. Discounts are available if you're aged under 26 or in a group of four or more. In France ticketing is handled by SNCM.

Spain

If you would like to start your trip in southwestern France (or return to England from there), a couple of ferry services from northern Spain are worth considering.

P&O Ferries (in the UK ☎ 0870 598 0555, in France ☎ 0825013013; www.poferries.com) links Portsmouth with Bilbao (Santurtzi port, 35 hours and two nights *to* Bilbao, 29 hours and one night *from* Bilbao), which is only about 150km west of Biarritz, twice a week (once a week from late October to late March; no services from early January to early February). A one-way pedestrian ticket including a mandatory sleeping berth costs around €180.

From mid-March to mid-November, **Brittany Ferries** (☎ 0870 366 5333, in France ☎ 0 825 828 828; www.brittany-ferries.com) runs twice-weekly car-ferry services from Plymouth to Santander (24 hours), which is around 240km west of Biarritz. Foot passengers pay around €104; a couchette costs around €10 extra.

The UK

Fares vary widely according to demand, which depends on the season (July and August are especially popular) and the time of day (a Friday night ferry can cost much more than a Sunday morning one); the most expensive tickets can cost almost three times as much as the cheapest ones. Three- or five-day excursion (return) fares generally cost about the same as regular one-way tickets; special promotional return fares, often requiring advance booking, are sometimes cheaper than a standard one-way fare. On some overnight sailings you have to pay extra for a mandatory reclining seat (UK£5) or sleeping berth (UK£16 to UK£38).

Check out **Ferry Savers** (☎ 0870 990 8492; www .ferrysavers.com), which guarantees the lowest prices on Channel crossings. Ferry companies may try to make it hard for people who use supercheap, one-day return tickets for one-way passage – a huge backpack is a dead giveaway.

Eurail passes are *not* valid for ferry travel between the UK and France. Transporting bicycles is often (but not always) free.

TO BRITTANY

From mid-March to mid-November, Plymouth is linked to Roscoff (six hours for day crossings, one to three per day) by Brittany

Ferries. The one-way fare for foot passengers is around UK£35.

Brittany Ferries also links Portsmouth and Plymouth with St-Malo (8¾ hours for day crossing, one per day). Pedestrians pay from UK£27 one way.

From April to September, **Condor Ferries** (☎ 0845 345 2000, in France ☎ 02 99 20 03 00; www .condorferries.com) has at least one daily ferry linking Weymouth with St-Malo (UK£35) that can take anywhere from seven to 10 hours, including a stopover in Guernsey.

TO FAR NORTHERN FRANCE

The fastest way to cross the English Channel is between Dover and Calais, served by Hoverspeed's SeaCats (catamarans), which take 50 minutes. For foot passengers, a one-way trip (or a return completed within five days) costs UK£39. From Calais, there are five daily trains to Le Tréport, the northernmost town in Normandy (€19, five hours).

The Dover–Calais crossing is also handled by car ferries, run by **SeaFrance** (☎ 0870 571 1711, in France ☎ 0 804 044 045; www.seafrance .com; 1½hr; 15 daily) and **P&O Ferries** (☎ 0870 520 20 20; www.poferries .com; 1–1½hr; 29 daily) for about the same price.

Ferries run by **Norfolk Line** (☎ 03 28 59 01 01; www.norfolkline.com) link Loon Plage, about 25km west of Dunkirk, with Dover, while **Speed Ferries** (in the UK ☎ 01304-20 3000, in France ☎ 03 21 10 50 00; www.speedferries.com) offers an ultramodern, ultrafast catamaran service between Boulogne and Dover (50 minutes, five daily).

TO NORMANDY

The Newhaven–Dieppe route is handled by **Hoverspeed** (☎ 0870 240 8070, in France ☎ 00 800 1211 1211; www.hoverspeed.co.uk) and **Transmanche Ferries** (☎ 0800 917 1201; www.transmancheferries.com). The hovercraft trip (one to three daily) takes 2¼ hours, while the ferry trip (two daily) takes four hours. Pedestrians pay from UK£30 one way, with special deals available.

There's a 4¼-hour crossing (two or three per day) from Poole to Cherbourg with **Brittany Ferries** (☎ 0870 366 5333, in France ☎ 0 825 828 828; www.brittany-ferries.com). Foot passengers pay from UK£33 one way.

On the Portsmouth–Cherbourg route, Brittany Ferries, Condor Ferries and **P&O Portsmouth** (in the UK ☎ 0870 598 0555, in France ☎ 0 825 013 013; www.poferries.com) have two or three car ferries a day (five hours by day, eight hours overnight) and, from April to September, two faster catamarans a day. Foot passengers pay from UK£29 one way.

The Portsmouth–Le Havre crossing is handled by P&O Portsmouth (5½ hours by day, 7¾ hours overnight, three car ferries a day, fewer in winter). Passage costs somewhat more than Portsmouth–Cherbourg.

Brittany Ferries also has car-ferry services from Portsmouth to Caen (Ouistreham; six hours, three per day). Tickets cost the same as for Poole–Cherbourg.

The USA, Canada & Elsewhere

The days when you could earn your passage to Europe on a freighter have well and truly passed, but it's still possible to travel as a passenger on a cargo ship from North America (and ports further afield) to France's Atlantic coast. Such vessels typically carry five to 12 passengers (more than 12 would require a doctor on board). Good websites:

The Cruise People (www.cruisepeople.co.uk) In the UK.
Freighter World Cruises (www.freighterworld.com) In the USA.
Traveltips (www.traveltips.com)

GETTING AROUND

France's domestic transport network, much of it owned or subsidised by the government, tends to be monopolistic: the state-owned Société Nationale des Chemins de Fer Français (SNCF) takes care of most land transport between *départements,* and short-haul bus companies are either run by the *département* or grouped so each local company handles different destinations. In recent years domestic air travel has been partly deregulated, but local smaller carriers have struggled.

While the efficient train system can get you to major cities and towns, travel within rural regions on sparse public bus services can be slow and difficult – if not impossible. If you wish to see rural areas and visit small towns off the major train routes, you really need your own wheels.

AIR

All of France's major cities – as well as many minor ones – have airports, which we mention in the destination chapters. National carrier **Air France** (☎ 0 820 820 820; www .airfrance. com) continues to control the lion's share of

France's long-protected domestic airline industry, particularly since the demise of local carriers Aeris and Air Lib. Other local carriers have been bought by Air France. British budget carrier easyJet has begun flights linking Paris with Marseille, Nice and Toulouse. Other European budget carriers may soon try to muscle in on France's domestic market.

Until then, the stiffest competition in the transport price war comes from the *Train à Grande Vitesse* (TGV), which has made travel between some cities (eg Paris and Lyon or Marseille) faster and easier by train than by air.

Any French travel agency or Air France office can make bookings for domestic flights and supply details on the complicated fare options. Outside France, Air France representatives sell tickets for many domestic flights.

Up to 84% reduction is available if you fly during the week and buy your ticket three weeks in advance. Significant discounts are available to children, young people, families, seniors, and couples who are married or have proof of cohabitation. Special last-minute offers are posted on the Air France website every Wednesday.

BICYCLE

France is an eminently cyclable country, thanks in part to its extensive network of secondary and tertiary roads, many of which carry relatively light traffic. One pitfall: the roads rarely have proper shoulders (verges). Many French cities have a growing network of urban and suburban *pistes cyclables* (bicycle paths), and in some areas (eg around Bordeaux) such paths link one town to the next. *Never* leave your bicycle locked up outside overnight if you want to see it or most of its parts again.

French law dictates that bicycles must have two functioning brakes, a bell, a red reflector on the back and yellow reflectors on the pedals. After sunset and when visibility is poor, cyclists must turn on a white light in front and a red one in the rear. When being overtaken by a car or lorry, cyclists are required to ride in single file.

Bicycles are not allowed on most local or intercity buses or on trams. On some regional trains you can take a bicycle free of charge. On train timetables, a bicycle symbol indicates that bicycles are allowed on particular trains. On some regional trains, bikes have to be covered and stored in the luggage van. The SNCF baggage service **Sernam** (☎ 0 825 84 58 45) will transport your bicycle (or any other luggage) door to door or station to station for €44.90.

European Bike Express (☎ 01642-251 440; www .bike-express.co.uk) transports cyclists and their bikes from the UK to places all over France.

More information of interest to cyclists can be found on p896. A useful source is the **Fédération Française de Cyclisme** (☎ 01 49 35 69 00; www.ffc.fr in French).

Hire & Purchase

Most towns have at least one shop that hires *vélos tout-terrains* (mountain bikes), popularly known as VTTs (€12 to €20 a day), or cheaper touring bikes. In general, they require a deposit of €150 or €300, which you forfeit if the bike is damaged or stolen. Some cities (eg Strasbourg, p356, and La Rochelle, p624) have remarkably inexpensive rental agencies run by the municipality. For details about rental shops, see the city and town listings throughout this book.

A VTT can be purchased for €250. Reselling your bike at the end of your trip (for around two-thirds of its purchase price) is possible at certain bike shops and pawnbrokers. French-language websites www .argusvtt.net and www.velo101.com have classified ads and advice.

BOAT

For information on ferry services linking towns along the coast of France see individual town and city sections. For information on ferry services from other countries, see p919.

Canal Boating

One of the most relaxing ways to see France is to rent a houseboat for a leisurely cruise along canals and navigable rivers, stopping at your whim along the way. Changes in altitude are taken care of by a system of *écluses* (locks).

Boats generally accommodate from four to 12 passengers and are fully outfitted with bedding and cooking facilities. Anyone over 18 can pilot a river boat without a special licence, but first-time skippers are given a short instruction session. The speed limit is 6km/h on canals and 10km/h on rivers.

Prices start at €1100 a week for a small boat. Reservations are a must if you're boating during a holiday period. Quercy (p598) and Burgundy (p428) chapters. For information on inland waterway rental:

Crown Travel (☎ 01603-630 513; 8 Ber St, Norwich NR1 3EJ, UK) For canal-boat rental in Brittany, Alsace, Languedoc and other areas.

French Nautical Industries Federation (☎ 01 44 37 04 00; www.france-nautic.com) Information about rental companies throughout France.

Syndicat National des Loueurs de Bateaux de Plaisance (☎ 01 44 37 04 00; Port de Javel, 75015 Paris; metro Javel) Publishes a booklet listing rental companies.

BUS

Within France, bus services are provided by numerous different companies, usually based within one *département*. For travel between regions, a train is your best bet since inter-regional bus services are limited. Buses are used quite extensively for short-distance travel within *départements*, especially in rural areas with relatively few train lines (eg Brittany and Normandy) – but services are often slow and few and far between.

Over the years, certain uneconomical train lines have been replaced by SNCF buses – unlike regional buses, these are free for people with train passes. City and town entries include bus connections with other destinations.

CAR & MOTORCYCLE

Having your own wheels gives you exceptional freedom and allows you to visit more remote parts of France. Unfortunately it can be expensive and, in cities parking and traffic are frequently a major headache. Motorcyclists will find France great for touring, with winding roads of good quality and lots of stunning scenery. Just make sure your wet-weather gear is up to scratch.

France (along with Belgium) has the densest highway network in Europe. There are four types of intercity roads, which have alphanumeric designations:

Autoroutes (eg A14) Multilane highways, usually with tolls *(péages)*.

Routes Nationales (N, RN) National highways.

Routes Départementales (D) Local roads.

Routes Communales (C, V) Minor rural roads.

Information on tolls, rest areas, petrol (gas) stations and itineraries is available on www .france-nautic.com. The websites www.via michelin.com and www.mappy.fr give suggested itineraries for getting from one place to another.

By autoroute, the drive from Paris to Nice (about 950km; eight hours of driving) costs at least €130 in petrol and autoroute tolls. By comparison, a regular, one-way, 2nd-class TGV ticket for the 5½-hour Paris–Nice run costs around €90 per person.

Roads throughout France block up during holiday periods and long weekends.

As insurance is compulsory for all cars in France, the number of the appropriate roadside assistance company is written on the insurance papers that will be in the car or stuck to the inside of the windscreen. Rental drivers should call their rental company for assistance.

Motorcycle and moped rental is popular in southern France, especially in the beach resorts, but accidents are all too common. Where relevant, details on rental options appear at the end of city and town listings. To rent a moped, scooter or motorcycle you usually have to leave a large *caution* (deposit), which you forfeit – up to the value of the damage – if you cause an accident or if the bike is in some way damaged or stolen.

Bring Your Own Vehicle

A right-hand drive vehicle brought to France from the UK or Ireland must have deflectors affixed to the headlights to avoid dazzling oncoming traffic. A motor vehicle entering a foreign country must display a sticker identifying its country of registration. In the UK information on driving in France is available from the **RAC** (☎ 0870 010 6382; www.rac.co.uk) and the **AA** (☎ 0870 600 0371; www.theaa.com).

Driving Licence & Documents

All drivers must carry at all times: a national ID card or passport; a valid driver's licence (*permis de conduire*; most foreign licences can be used in France for up to a year); car-ownership papers, known as a *carte grise* (grey card); and proof of third-party (liability) insurance. An International Driving Permit (IDP) is valid for a year and can be issued by your local automobile association before you leave home.

ROAD DISTANCES (KM)

	Bayonne	Bordeaux	Brest	Caen	Cahors	Calais	Chambéry	Cherbourg	Clermont-Ferrand	Dijon	Grenoble	Lille	Lyons	Marseille	Nantes	Nice	Paris	Perpignan	Strasbourg	Toulouse	Tours
Bayonne	---																				
Bordeaux	184	---																			
Brest	811	623	---																		
Caen	764	568	376	---																	
Cahors	307	218	788	661	---																
Calais	164	876	710	339	875	---															
Chambéry	860	651	120	800	523	834	---														
Cherbourg	835	647	399	124	743	461	923	---													
Clermont-Ferrand	564	358	805	566	269	717	295	689	---												
Dijon	807	619	867	548	378	572	273	671	279	---											
Grenoble	827	657	1126	806	501	863	56	929	300	302	---										
Lille	997	809	725	353	808	112	767	476	650	505	798	---									
Lyons	831	528	1018	698	439	755	103	820	171	194	110	687	---								
Marseille	700	651	1271	1010	521	1067	344	1132	477	506	273	999	314	---							
Nantes	513	326	298	292	491	593	780	317	462	656	787	609	618	975	---						
Nice	858	810	1429	1168	679	1225	410	1291	636	664	337	1157	473	190	1131	---					
Paris	771	583	596	232	582	289	565	355	424	313	571	222	462	775	384	932	---				
Perpignan	499	451	1070	998	320	1149	478	1094	441	640	445	1081	448	319	773	476	857	---			
Strasbourg	1254	1066	1079	730	847	621	496	853	584	335	551	522	488	803	867	804	490	935	---		
Toulouse	300	247	866	865	116	991	565	890	890	727	533	923	536	407	568	564	699	205	1022	---	
Tours	536	348	490	246	413	531	611	369	369	418	618	463	449	795	197	952	238	795	721	593	---

Fuel & Spare Parts

Essence (petrol or gasoline), also known as *carburant* (fuel), is considerably more expensive in France (€1.10/L for 95 unleaded) than Australia or North America. Filling up (*faire le plein*) is most expensive at the rest stops along the autoroutes and cheapest at small rural petrol stations and supermarkets.

Many small petrol stations close on Sunday afternoons. If you are out in the country you may have to drive to a self-service supermarket petrol station and pay by credit card.

If your car is *en panne* (breaks down), you'll have to find a garage that handles your *marque* (make of car). There are Peugeot, Renault and Citroën garages all over the place, but if you have a non-French car you may have trouble finding someone to service it in more remote areas.

Hire

To hire a car in France you'll generally need to be over 21 years old and in possession of a valid driver's licence and an international credit card. Arranging your car rental or fly/drive package before you leave home is often considerably cheaper. Major rental companies include:

ADA (☎ 0 825 169 169; www.ada.fr in French)
Avis (☎ 0 820 050 505; www.avis.com)
Budget (☎ 0 825 003 564; www.budget.com)
Easycar (☎ 0906 333 333 3; www.easycar.com) Cheap rates and offices in Paris and Nice.
Europcar (☎ 0 825 358 358; www.europcar.com)
Hertz (☎ 0 825 342 343; www.hertz.com)
National Citer (☎ 01 44 38 61 61, 0 800 202 121; www.citer.com)
OTU Voyages (☎ 01 40 29 12 12; www.otu.fr in French) For students.

Deals can be found on the Internet, with travel agencies and through companies like **Auto Europe** (☎ 1-888 223 5555; www.autoeurope.com) in the US, **Holiday Autos** (☎ 0870 5300 400; www.holidayautos.co.uk) in the UK. In this guide car-rental addresses are listed under large cities and towns.

Insurance

Unlimited third-party liability insurance is mandatory for all automobiles entering

France, whether the owner accompanies the vehicle or not. As proof of insurance, the owner must present an international motor insurance card showing that the vehicle is insured in France. A temporary insurance policy is available from the vehicle-insurance department of the **French Customs Office** (Direction Générale des Douanes et Droits Indirects; ☎ 01 40 04 04 04; 23bis rue de l'Université, 7e, Paris) with a validity of eight to 30 days. Third-party liability insurance is provided by car-rental companies, but things such as collision-damage waivers (CDW) vary greatly from company to company. When comparing rates, the most important thing to check is the *franchise* (excess/deductible), which is usually €350 for a small car. Your credit card may cover CDW *(assurance tout risqué)* if you use it to pay for the car rental.

Purchase-Repurchase Plans

If you'll be needing a car in Europe for 17 days to six months (one year if you're studying or teaching in France), by far your cheapest option is to 'purchase' a brand-new one from **Peugeot** (www.peugeot-openeurope.com) or **Renault** (www.eurodrive.renault.com) and then, at the end of your trip, 'sell' it back to them. In reality, you pay only for the number of days you use the vehicle. Eligibility is restricted to people who are not residents of the EU (citizens of EU countries are eligible if they live outside the EU).

Prices include unlimited kilometres, 24-hour towing and breakdown service, and comprehensive insurance with – incredibly – no excess (deductible), so returning a damaged car is totally hassle-free. Extending your contract is possible (using a credit card), but you'll end up paying about double the prepaid per-day rate.

Cars can be picked up in cities all over France and returned to any other purchase repurchase centre, including other European capitals.

Road Rules

Enforcement of road safety rules has been stepped up in France over the last few years. French law requires that all passengers, including those in the back seat, wear seat belts, and children who weigh less than 18kg must travel in backward-facing child seats. A passenger car is permitted to carry a maximum of five people. North American drivers should remember that turning right on a red light is illegal in France.

You will be fined for going 10km over the speed limit. Unless otherwise posted, a limit of 50km/h applies in *all* areas designated as built-up, no matter how rural they may appear. Speed limits outside built-up areas:

- 90km/h (80km/h if it's raining) on undivided N and D highways
- 110km/h (100km/h if it's raining) on dual carriageways (divided highways) or short sections of highway with a divider strip
- 130km/h (110km/h in the rain, 60km/h in icy conditions) on autoroutes

Under the *priorité à droite* rule, any car entering an intersection (including a T-junction) from a road on your right has the right-of-way, unless the intersection is marked 'vous n'avez pas la priorité' (you do not have right of way) or 'cédez le passage' (give way). *Priorité à droite* is also suspended on priority roads, which are marked by an up-ended yellow square with a black square in the middle.

It is illegal to drive with a blood-alcohol concentration over 0.05% (0.5g per litre of blood) – the equivalent of two glasses of wine for a 75kg adult. There are periodic random breathalyser tests. Mobile phones may only be used when accompanied by a hands-free kit or speakerphone.

Motoring in Europe, published in the UK by the RAC, gives an excellent summary of road regulations in each European country, including parking rules. British drivers committing driving offences in France can receive on-the-spot fines and get penalty points added to their driving licence at home.

Riders of any type of two-wheeled vehicle with a motor (except motor-assisted bicycles) must wear a helmet. No special licence is required to ride a motorbike whose engine is smaller than 50cc, which is why you often find places renting scooters rated at 49.9cc.

HITCHING

Hitching is never entirely safe in any country in the world, and we don't recommend it. Travellers who decide to hitch should understand that they are taking a small but potentially serious risk. Remember that it's safer to travel in pairs and be sure to inform someone of where you are planning to go. Hitching is not really part of French culture, and is not recommended for women in France, even in pairs.

Hitching from city centres is pretty much hopeless: take public transport to the outskirts. It is illegal to hitch on autoroutes, but you can stand near the entrance ramps as long as you don't block traffic. Thumbing around the Côte d'Azur is nearly impossible. Remote rural areas are often a good bet, but once you get off the *routes nationales* there are few vehicles. If your itinerary includes a ferry crossing, it's worth trying to score a ride before the ferry goes, since vehicle tickets sometimes include a number of passengers free of charge. At dusk, give up and think about finding somewhere to stay.

Ride Share Organisations

A number of organisations around France put people looking for rides in touch with drivers going to the same destination. Usually you pay a per-kilometre fee to the driver, as well as a flat administration fee.

Allostop (☎ 0 825 803 666; www.allostop.net in French) The best known; based in Paris.

Autostop Bretagne (☎ 02 99 67 34 67; http://allo stoprennes.com in French) Rennes.

La Clef de Contact (☎ 03 80 66 31 31) Dijon.

Stop Plus (☎ 04 76 43 14 14) Grenoble.

Voyage au Fil (☎ 02 51 72 94 60) Nantes.

LOCAL TRANSPORT

France's cities and larger towns generally have excellent public-transport systems. Remember that French cities are small and compact – most can be visited entirely on foot.

There are underground subway systems (metros) in Paris, Lyon, Marseille, Lille and Toulouse.

Ultramodern tramways exist in Paris, Grenoble, Nantes, Lille, Strasbourg, Lyon, Nancy and Bordeaux, and are being built in cities across the country. Bus systems tend to be less reliable.

Details on routes, fares, tourist passes etc, are available at tourist offices and from local bus companies. We list information in the individual destination sections.

See p896 and p922 for information on bicycles and bike hire.

Taxi

All large and medium-sized train stations – and many small ones – have a taxi stand out the front. For details on the tariffs and regulations applicable in major cities, see p176.

In small cities and towns, where taxi drivers are unlikely to find another fare anywhere near where they let you off, there are four kinds of per-kilometre tariffs, set locally by the *préfecture*. Rates are more expensive at night and on Sundays and holidays.

Travel under 20km/h (or thereabouts) is calculated by time (about €15 an hour) rather than distance. There may be a surcharge of €1 to get picked up at a train station or airport, a fee of €0.90 per bag and a charge of €2.45 for a fourth passenger.

TOURS

Local tourist offices, museums, wineries, chateaux and private minibus companies all over France offer a wide variety of guided tours that you arrange locally. Some tourist offices also offer tours to destinations outside of town. Details appear under Tours in city listings and at the beginning of regional chapters. Details on guided hikes, cycling tours and other organised outdoor activities appear under Activities. Some places are difficult to visit unless you have wheels, or are much more interesting with expert commentary.

An extensive list of UK-based companies offering trips to France is available from the website of the **Association of British Tour Operators to France** (www.holidayfrance.org.uk).

There is a surfeit of companies that run activities-based tours, usually including accommodation, meals and transport.

ATG Oxford (www.atg-oxford.co.uk) Cycling and rambling holidays for independent travellers.

Butterfield & Robinson (www.butterfield.com) Canada-based company with upmarket walking and biking holidays.

CBT Tours (www.biketrip.net) Cycling tours from the USA.

Cycling for Softies (www.cycling-for-softies.co.uk) Unescorted cycling trips through rural France.

French Wine Explorers (www.wine-tours-france.com) Small group wine tours of Beaujolais, Bordeaux, Burgundy and the Rhône Valley.

Old Ipswich Tours (www.ipswichtours.com) Specialising in wine tours (USA based).

Ramblers Holidays (www.ramblersholidays.co.uk) Tours based on outdoor activities like walking, trekking and cross-country skiing.

TRAIN

France's superb rail network reaches almost every part of the country. Many towns and villages not on the SNCF train and bus network are served by bus lines linking *départements*.

France's most important train lines radiate from Paris like the spokes of a wheel, making train travel between provincial towns situated on different spokes infrequent and rather slow. In some cases you have to transit through Paris. For details, see the map on p918.

The pride and joy of SNCF – and the French – generally is the world-renowned TGV (*Train à Grande Vitesse*, www.tgv .com. Pronounced 'teh-zheh-veh', it reaches speeds of over 300km/h (186mph) and was developed in the 1960s and 70s. The first service was in 1981. The French are really exceedingly proud of the TGV.

TGV Atlantique Sud-Ouest & TGV Atlantique Ouest These link Paris' Gare Montparnasse with western and southwestern France, including Brittany (Rennes, Quimper, Brest), Nantes, Tours, Poitiers, La Rochelle, Bordeaux, Biarritz and Toulouse.

TGV Nord, Thalys & Eurostar These link Paris' Gare du Nord with Arras, Lille, Calais, Brussels, Amsterdam, Cologne and, via the Channel Tunnel, Ashford and London Waterloo.

TGV Sud-Est & TGV Midi-Méditerranée These link Paris' Gare de Lyon with the southeast, including Dijon, Lyon, Geneva, the Alps, Avignon, Marseille, Nice and Montpellier.

A line leading northeast to Strasbourg and Germany (called TGV Est) is planned for 2007. TGV lines are now connected to each other, making it possible to go directly from, say, Lyon to Nantes or Bordeaux to Lille, without switching trains in Paris. Stops on the link-up, which runs east and south of Paris, include Roissy Charles de Gaulle airport, Massy and Disneyland Paris.

A train that is not a TGV is often referred to as a *corail*, a *classique* or a TER *(train express régional)*. For details on Thalys and the Eurostar, see p919.

Classes & Sleeping Cars

Most French trains have both 1st- and 2nd-class sections. On overnight trains the 2nd-class couchette compartments have six berths, while those in 1st class have four. In addition to bed linen, you are issued a bottle of water and a little 'welcome kit'. Some couchette compartments are reserved for

---

STOWING YOUR LUGGAGE

Security on French trains has been heightened considerably with growing incidents of terrorism on public transport. Security measures change regularly, but bags may not be allowed to be stored in racks between carriages, but kept with the passenger. Where such storage is permitted, clear labelling of items with name and address of the owner is required.

Left-luggage lockers located at the train stations countrywide are no longer in operation, but in larger cities like Paris, Lyon and Marseille staffed left-luggage facilities – where items are handed over in person and x-rayed before being stowed – are still available. See Left Luggage under Information in the destinations sections for details of opening hours, rates etc.

---

women travelling alone or with children. On some overnight trains a 2nd-class *siège inclinable* (reclining seat) costs €1.50.

Many overnight trains have *voitures-lits* (sleeping cars), which provide private facilities, a continental breakfast and greater security. Second class holds up to three people. First-class compartments are somewhat larger and accommodate one or two people.

Costs

Significant discounts are available (see p928) on regular train fares. Full-price fares can be very expensive (eg TGV Paris–Lyon €73 one-way). Full-fare return (round-trip) passage costs twice as much as one-way. Travel in 1st class is 50% more expensive than 2nd class. Train tickets (including the TGV) are more expensive during the peak periods (commuting hours, weekends, holiday periods).

Fantastic deals are available exclusively on the website www.sncf.com: last-minute offers at up to 50% off, published on the site every Tuesday; and *Prem's* early bird deals (eg Paris–Nice €25) available only through online bookings made at least three weeks in advance.

Tickets & Reservations

You can buy a ticket with a credit card via the SNCF's website and either have it sent to you by post or collect it from any SNCF

SNCF DISCOUNT FARES

Discounted fares and passes are available at all SNCF stations. See earlier for discount European bus (p917) and train (p919) passes.

Children aged under four travel free of charge; those aged four to 11 travel for half-price. Discounted fares (25% reduction) automatically apply to: travellers aged 12 to 25, seniors aged over 60, one to four adults travelling with a child aged four to 11, two people taking a return journey together or anyone taking a return journey of at least 200km and spending a Saturday night away. Purchasing tickets well in advance will also usually get you a discounted fare. The **Découverte J30**, which must be purchased 30 to 60 days before the date of travel, offers savings of 45% to 55%. The **Découverte J8**, which you must buy eight days ahead, gets you 20% to 30% off.

Purchasing a one-year travel pass can yield a 50% discount (25% if the cheapest seats are sold): a **Carte 12-25** (€48) aimed at travellers aged 12 to 25; the **Carte Enfant Plus** (€63) for one to four adults travelling with a child aged four to 11; and a **Carte Sénior** (€49) for those aged over 60.

The **France Railpass** entitles nonresidents of France to unlimited travel on SNCF trains for four days over a one-month period. In 2nd class it costs US$218; each additional day of travel costs US$28. The **France Youthpass** entitles holders to four days of travel over a one-month period. In 2nd class it costs US$164, plus US$21 for each extra day. These two passes can be purchased from travel agencies or on www.eurorail.com.

ticket office. Nearly every SNCF station in the country has at least one *billeterie automatique* (automatic ticket machine) that accepts credit cards. Large stations often have separate ticket windows for *international, grandes lignes* (long-haul) and *banlieue* (suburban) lines, and *achat à l'avance* (advance purchase) and *départ du jour* (same-day departure).

Before boarding the train you must validate your ticket by time-stamping it in a *composteur,* one of those orange posts located at the start of the platform. If you forget, find a conductor on the train so they can punch it for you (otherwise you're likely to be fined). Tickets *can* be purchased on board the train (straight away from the conductor) with cash but there a surcharge is incurred.

Reserving in advance (€1.50) is optional unless: you're travelling by TGV, Eurostar or Thalys; you want a couchette (sleeping berth; €14) or a bed; or you'll be travelling during peak holiday periods when trains may be full. Reservations can be made by telephone or via the SNCF's website. Reservations can usually be changed before departure time by telephone.

Long-distance trains sometimes split at a station, that is, each half of the train leaves for a different destination. Verify the destination as you board the car, or you could wind up very, very far from where you want to go.

Health

CONTENTS

Before You Go   929
In Transit   929
In France   929

Travel health depends on your predeparture preparations, your daily health care while travelling and how you handle medical problems that do develop. France is a healthy place. Your main risks are likely to be sunburn, foot blisters, insect bites and mild stomach problems from eating and drinking too much.

BEFORE YOU GO

Prevention is the key to staying healthy. Planning before departure, particularly for pre-existing illnesses, will save trouble later. See your dentist before a long trip, carry a spare pair of contact lenses and glasses, and take your optical prescription. Bring medications in their original, clearly labelled, containers. A signed and dated letter from your physician describing your medical conditions and medications, including generic names, is also helpful. If carrying syringes or needles, be sure to have a physician's letter documenting their medical necessity.

Insurance

Citizens of the EU, Switzerland, Iceland, Norway or Liechtenstein, are coverd by the European Health Insurance Card for emergency health care or accidents while in France. It does not cover nonemergencies or emergency repatriation. This card is being phased in from mid-2004 to the end of 2005. Old documentation (such as the E111) will be available in the interim. Each family member will need a separate card. In the UK, get application forms from post offices or download them from the Department of Health website (www.dh.gov.uk).

Citizens from other countries will need to check if there is a reciprocal arrangement for free medical care between their country and the country visited. If you need health insurance, strongly consider a policy covering the worst possible scenario, such as an accident requiring an emergency flight home. Find out in advance if your insurance plan will make payments directly to providers or reimburse you later for overseas health expenditures.

Recommended Vaccinations

No vaccinations are required to travel to France. However, the WHO recommends that all travellers should be covered for diphtheria, tetanus, measles, mumps, rubella and polio, regardless of their destination.

IN TRANSIT

Deep Vein Thrombosis (DVT)

Blood clots may form in the legs during plane flights, chiefly because of prolonged immobility. The chief symptom of DVT is swelling or pain of the foot, ankle or calf, usually but not always on just one side. When a blood clot travels to the lungs, it may cause chest pain and breathing difficulties. Travellers with any of these symptoms should immediately seek medical attention.

To prevent the development of DVT on long flights walk about the cabin, contract the leg muscles while sitting, drink plenty of fluids and avoid alcohol and tobacco.

Jet Lag

To avoid jet lag (common when crossing more than five time zones) drink plenty of nonalchoholic fluids and eat light meals. Upon arrival, get exposure to natural sunlight and readjust your schedule (for meals, sleep and so on) as soon as possible.

IN FRANCE

Availability & Cost of Health Care

Excellent health care is readily available and for minor illnesses pharmacists can give valuable advice and sell medications. They can also advise on more specialised help and point you in the right direction. Dental care is usually good, however, it is sensible to have a dental check-up before a long trip.

Diarrhoea

If you develop diarrhoea, drink plenty of fluids, preferably an oral rehydration solution (eg Dioralyte). If diarrhoea is bloody, persists for more than 72 hours or is accompanied by fever, shaking, chills or severe abdominal pain seek immediate medical attention.

Environmental Hazards
ALTITUDE SICKNESS
Lack of oxygen at high altitudes (over 2500m) affects most people to some extent. Symptoms of Acute Mountain Sickness (AMS) usually develop in the first 24 hours at altitude but may be delayed up to three weeks. Mild symptoms are headache, lethargy, dizziness, difficulty sleeping and loss of appetite. Severe symptoms are breathlessness, a dry, irritative cough (followed by the production of pink, frothy sputum), severe headache, lack of coordination and balance, confusion, vomiting, irrational behaviour, drowsiness and unconsciousness. There's no rule as to what is too high: AMS can be fatal at 3000m, but 3500m to 4500m is the usual range.

Treat mild symptoms by resting at the same altitude until recovered, usually a day or two. Paracetamol or aspirin can be taken for headaches. If symptoms persist or grow worse, however, *immediate descent is necessary;* even 500m can help. Drug treatments should never be used to avoid descent or to enable further ascent. Diamox (acetazolamide) reduces the headache of AMS and helps the body acclimatise to the lack of oxygen. It is only available on prescription.

To prevent acute mountain sickness:

- Ascend slowly – have frequent rest days, spending two to three nights at each rise of 1000m. Acclimatisation takes place gradually.
- Sleep at a lower altitude than the greatest height reached during the day if possible. Also, once above 3000m, care should be taken not to increase the sleeping altitude by more than 300m per day.
- Drink extra fluids. Monitor hydration by ensuring that urine is clear and plentiful.
- Eat light, high-carbohydrate meals for more energy.
- Avoid alcohol, sedatives and tobacco.

HEAT EXHAUSTION
Heat exhaustion follows excessive fluid loss with inadequate replacement of fluids and salt. Symptoms include headache, dizziness and tiredness. Dehydration is already happening by the time you feel thirsty – aim to drink enough water to produce pale, diluted

urine. To treat heat exhaustion, replace lost fluids by drinking water and/or fruit juice and cool the body with cold water and fans.

HYPOTHERMIA
Even on a hot day in the mountains weather can change rapidly; carry waterproof garments and warm layers, and inform others of your route. Acute hypothermia follows a sudden drop of temperature over a short time. Chronic hypothermia is caused by a gradual loss of temperature over hours. Hypothermia starts with shivering, loss of judgment and clumsiness. Unless rewarming occurs, the sufferer deteriorates into apathy, confusion and coma. Prevent further heat loss by seeking shelter, warm dry clothing, hot sweet drinks and shared bodily warmth.

Sexual Health
Emergency contraception is available with a doctor's prescription in France. Condoms are readily available; when buying, look for a European CE mark, which means they've been rigorously tested. Keep them in a cool dry place or they may crack and perish.

Travelling with Children
All travellers with children should know how to treat minor ailments and when to seek medical advice. Be sure children are up to date with routine vaccinations, and discuss possible travel vaccines well before departure as some vaccines are not suitable for children under a year.

If your child has vomiting or diarrhoea, lost fluids and salts must be replaced. It may be helpful to take rehydration powders for reconstituting with boiled water.

Women's Health
Emotional stress, exhaustion and travelling across time zones can all contribute to an upset in the menstrual pattern. Some antibiotics, diarrhoea and vomiting can interfere with the effectiveness of oral contraceptives and lead to the risk of pregnancy – remember to take condoms just in case. Time zones, gastrointestinal upsets and antibiotics do not affect injectable contraception.

Travelling during pregnancy is usually possible but always consult your doctor before planning your trip. The most risky times for travel are during the first 12 weeks of pregnancy and after 30 weeks.

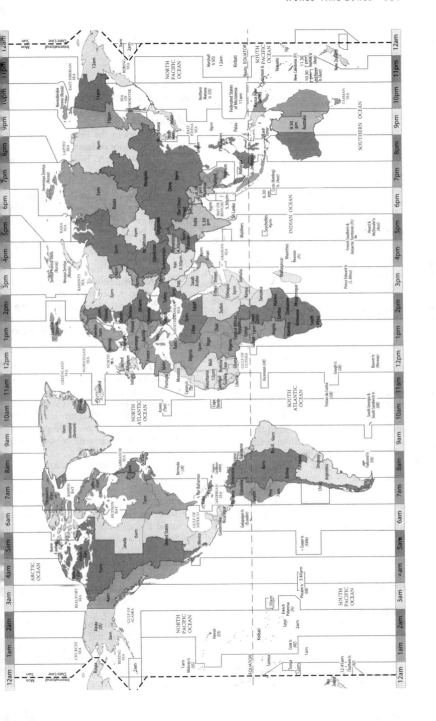

Language

CONTENTS

Pronunciation	932
Be Polite!	932
Gender	933
Accommodation	933
Conversation & Essentials	933
Directions	934
Emergencies	934
Health	934
Language Difficulties	935
Numbers	935
Paperwork	935
Question Words	935
Shopping & Services	935
Time & Dates	936
Transport	936
Travel With Children	937

Modern French developed from the *langue d'oïl*, a group of dialects spoken north of the Loire River that grew out of the vernacular Latin used during the late Gallo-Roman period. The *langue d'oïl* – particularly the Francien dialect spoken in the Île de France – eventually displaced the *langue d'oc*, the dialects spoken in the south of the country and from which the Mediterranean region of Languedoc got its name.

Standard French is taught and spoken in France, but its various accents and sub-dialects are an important source of identity in certain regions. In addition, some of the peoples subjected to French rule many centuries ago have preserved their traditional languages. These include Flemish in the far north; Alsatian in Alsace; Breton (a Celtic tongue similar to Cornish and Welsh) in Brittany; Basque (a language unrelated to any other) in the Basque Country; Catalan in Roussillon (Catalan is the official language of nearby Andorra and the first language of many in the Spanish province of Catalonia); Provençal in Provence; and Corsican on the island of Corsica.

For more information on food and dining in France, see p63. If you'd like a more comprehensive guide to the French language

Lonely Planet's compact *French Phrasebook* will cover most of your travel needs.

PRONUNCIATION

Most of letters in the French alphabet are pronounced more or less the same as their English counterparts. Here are a few that may cause confusion:

j	as the 's' in 'leisure', eg *jour* (day)
c	before **e** and **i**, as the 's' in 'sit'; before **a**, **o** and **u** it's pronounced as English 'k'. When undescored with a 'cedilla' (**ç**) it's always pronounced as the 's' in 'sit'.
r	pronounced from the back of the throat while constricting the muscles to restrict the flow of air
n, m	where a syllable ends in a single **n** or **m**, these letters are not pronounced, but the preceding vowel is given a nasal pronunciation

BE POLITE!

While the French rightly or wrongly have a reputation for assuming that all humans should speak French – until WWI it was the international language of culture and diplomacy – you'll find that any attempt to communicate in French will be very much appreciated.

What is often perceived as arrogance is often just a subtle objection to the assumption by many travellers that they should be able to speak English anywhere, and in any situation, and be understood. You can easily avoid the angst by approaching people politely, and addressing them in French. Even if the only sentence you can muster is *Pardon, madame/monsieur/mademoiselle, parlez-vous anglais?* (Excuse me, madam/sir/miss, do you speak English?), you're sure to be more warmly received than if you blindly address a stranger in English.

An important distinction is made in French between *tu* and *vous*, which both mean 'you'; *tu* is only used when addressing people you know well, children or animals. If you're addressing an adult who isn't a personal friend, *vous* should be used unless the person invites you to use *tu*. In general, younger people insist less on this distinction between polite and informal, and you will find that in many cases they use *tu* from the beginning of an acquaintance.

GENDER

All nouns in French are either masculine or feminine and adjectives reflect the gender of the noun they modify. The feminine form of many nouns and adjectives is indicated by a silent **e** added to the masculine form, as in *ami* and *amie* (the masculine and feminine for 'friend').

In the following phrases both masculine and feminine forms have been indicated where necessary. The masculine form comes first and is separated from the feminine by a slash. The gender of a noun is often indicated by a preceding article: 'the/a/some', *le/un/du* (m), *la/une/de la* (f); or one of the possessive adjectives, 'my/your/his/her', *mon/ton/son* (m), *ma/ta/sa* (f). With French, unlike English, the possessive adjective agrees in number and gender with the thing in question: 'his/her mother', *sa mère*.

ACCOMMODATION

I'm looking for a ...	*Je cherche ...*	zher shersh ...
campground	*un camping*	un kom·peeng
guesthouse	*une pension (de famille)*	ewn pon·syon (der fa·mee·ler)
hotel	*un hôtel*	un o·tel
youth hostel	*une auberge de jeunesse*	ewn o·berzh der zher·nes

Where is a cheap hotel?
Où est-ce qu'on peut trouver un hôtel pas cher?
oo es·kon per troo·vay un o·tel pa shair
What is the address?
Quelle est l'adresse?
kel e la·dres
Could you write the address, please?
Est-ce que vous pourriez écrire l'adresse, s'il vous plaît?
e·sker voo poo·ryay ay kreer la·dres seel voo play
Do you have any rooms available?
Est-ce que vous avez des chambres libres?
e·sker voo·za·vay day shom·brer lee·brer

I'd like (a) ...	*Je voudrais ...*	zher voo·dray ...
single room	*une chambre à un lit*	ewn shom·brer a un lee
double-bed	*une chambre*	ewn shom·brer

room	*avec un grand lit*	a·vek un gron lee
twin room with two beds	*une chambre avec des lits jumeaux*	ewn shom·brer a·vek day lee zhew·mo
room with a bathroom	*une chambre avec une salle de bains*	ewn shom·brer a·vek ewn sal der bun
to share a dorm	*coucher dans un dortoir*	koo·sher don zun dor·twa

MAKING A RESERVATION
(for phone or written requests)

To ...	*A l'attention de ...*
From ...	*De la part de ...*
Date	*Date*
I'd like to book ...	*Je voudrais réserver ...* (see the list under 'Accommodation' for bed and room options)
in the name of ...	*au nom de ...*
from ... (date) to ...	*du ... au ...*
credit card number expiry date	*carte de crédit numéro date d'expiration*
Please confirm availability and price.	*Veuillez confirmer la disponibilité et le prix.*

How much is it ...?	*Quel est le prix ...?*	kel e ler pree ...
per night	*par nuit*	par nwee
per person	*par personne*	par per·son

May I see it?
Est-ce que je peux voir la chambre?
es·ker zher per vwa la shom·brer
Where is the bathroom?
Où est la salle de bains? oo e la sal der bun
Where is the toilet?
Où sont les toilettes? oo·son lay twa·let
I'm leaving today.
Je pars aujourd'hui. zher par o·zhoor·dwee
We're leaving today.
Nous partons aujourd'hui. noo par·ton o·zhoor·dwee

CONVERSATION & ESSENTIALS

Hello.	*Bonjour.*	bon·zhoor
Goodbye.	*Au revoir.*	o·rer·vwa
Yes.	*Oui.*	wee

SIGNS

Entrée	Entrance
Sortie	Exit
Renseignements	Information
Ouvert	Open
Fermé	Closed
Interdit	Prohibited
Chambres Libres	Rooms Available
Complet	Full/No Vacancies
(Commissariat de) Police	Police Station
Toilettes/WC	Toilets
Hommes	Men
Femmes	Women

No.	Non.	no
Please.	S'il vous plaît.	seel voo play
Thank you.	Merci.	mair·see
You're welcome.	Je vous en prie.	zher voo·zon pree
	De rien. (inf)	der ree·en
Excuse me.	Excuse-moi.	ek·skew·zay·mwa
Sorry. (forgive me)	Pardon.	par·don

What's your name?
Comment vous appelez-vous? (pol) — ko·mon voo·za·pay·lay voo

Comment tu t'appelles? (inf) — ko·mon tew ta·pel

My name is ...
Je m'appelle ... — zher ma·pel ...

Where are you from?
De quel pays êtes-vous? — der kel pay·ee et·voo
De quel pays es-tu? (inf) — der kel pay·ee e·tew

I'm from ...
Je viens de ... — zher vyen der ...

I like ...
J'aime ... — zhem ...

I don't like ...
Je n'aime pas ... — zher nem pa ...

Just a minute.
Une minute. — ewn mee·newt

DIRECTIONS

Where is ...?
Où est ...? — oo e ...

Go straight ahead.
Continuez tout droit. — kon·teen·way too drwa

Turn left.
Tournez à gauche. — toor·nay a gosh

Turn right.
Tournez à droite. — toor·nay a drwat

at the corner
au coin — o kwun

at the traffic lights
aux feux — o fer

behind	derrière	dair·ryair
in front of	devant	der·von
far (from)	loin (de)	lwun (der)
near (to)	près (de)	pray (der)
opposite	en face de	on fas der

beach	la plage	la plazh
bridge	le pont	ler pon
castle	le château	ler sha·to
cathedral	la cathédrale	la ka·tay·dral
church	l'église	lay·gleez
island	l'île	leel
lake	le lac	ler lak
main square	la place centrale	la plas son·tral
museum	le musée	ler mew·zay
old city (town)	la vieille ville	la vyay veel
palace	le palais	ler pa·lay
quay	le quai	ler kay
riverbank	la rive	la reev
ruins	les ruines	lay rween
sea	la mer	la mair
square	la place	la plas
tourist office	l'office de tourisme	lo·fees der too·rees·mer
tower	la tour	la toor

EMERGENCIES

Help!
Au secours! — o skoor

There's been an accident!
Il y a eu un accident! — eel ya ew un ak·see·don

I'm lost.
Je me suis égaré/e. (m/f) — zhe me swee·zay·ga·ray

Leave me alone!
Fichez-moi la paix! — fee·shay·mwa la pay

Call ...!	Appelez ...!	a·play ...
a doctor	un médecin	un mayd·sun
the police	la police	la po·lees

HEALTH

I'm ill.
Je suis malade. — zher swee ma·lad

It hurts here.
J'ai une douleur ici. — zhay ewn doo·ler ee·see

I'm ...	Je suis ...	zher swee ...
asthmatic	asthmatique	(z)as·ma·teek
diabetic	diabétique	dee·a·bay·teek
epileptic	épileptique	(z)ay·pee·lep·teek

I'm allergic to ...	Je suis allergique ...	zher swee za·lair·zheek ...
antibiotics	aux antibiotiques	o zon·tee·byo·teek

bees	aux abeilles	o za·bay·yer
nuts	aux noix	o nwa
peanuts	aux cacahuètes	o ka·ka·wet
penicillin	à la pénicilline	a la pay·nee·see·leen

antiseptic	l'antiseptique	lon·tee·sep·teek
aspirin	l'aspirine	las·pee·reen
condoms	des préservatifs	day pray·zair·va·teef
contraceptive	le contraceptif	ler kon·tra·sep·teef
diarrhoea	la diarrhée	la dya·ray
medicine	le médicament	ler may·dee·ka·mon
nausea	la nausée	la no·zay
sunblock cream	la crème solaire	la krem so·lair
tampons	des tampons hygiéniques	day tom·pon ee·zhen·eek

15	quinze	kunz
16	seize	sez
17	dix-sept	dee·set
18	dix-huit	dee·zweet
19	dix-neuf	deez·nerf
20	vingt	vung
21	vingt et un	vung tay un
22	vingt-deux	vung·der
30	trente	tront
40	quarante	ka·ront
50	cinquante	sung·kont
60	soixante	swa·sont
70	soixante-dix	swa·son·dees
80	quatre-vingts	ka·trer·vung
90	quatre-vingt-dix	ka·trer·vung·dees
100	cent	son
1000	mille	meel

LANGUAGE DIFFICULTIES

Do you speak English?
Parlez-vous anglais? par·lay·voo ong·lay
Does anyone here speak English?
Y a-t-il quelqu'un qui ya·teel kel·kung kee
parle anglais? par long·glay
How do you say ... in French?
Comment est-ce qu'on ko·mon es·kon
dit ... en français? dee ... on fron·say
What does ... mean?
Que veut dire ...? ker ver deer ...
I understand.
Je comprends. zher kom·pron
I don't understand.
Je ne comprends pas. zher ner kom·pron pa
Could you write it down, please?
Est-ce que vous pourriez es·ker voo poo·ryay
l'écrire, s'il vous plaît? lay·kreer seel voo play
Can you show me (on the map)?
Pouvez-vous m'indiquer poo·vay·voo mun·dee·kay
(sur la carte)? (sewr la kart)

NUMBERS

0	zero	zay·ro
1	un	un
2	deux	der
3	trois	trwa
4	quatre	ka·trer
5	cinq	sungk
6	six	sees
7	sept	set
8	huit	weet
9	neuf	nerf
10	dix	dees
11	onze	onz
12	douze	dooz
13	treize	trez
14	quatorze	ka·torz

PAPERWORK

name	nom	nom
nationality	nationalité	na·syo·na·lee·tay
date/place	date/place	dat/plas
of birth	de naissance	der nay·sons
sex/gender	sexe	seks
passport	passeport	pas·por
visa	visa	vee·za

QUESTION WORDS

Who?	Qui?	kee
What?	Quoi?	kwa
What is it?	Qu'est-ce que c'est?	kes·ker say
When?	Quand?	kon
Where?	Où?	oo
Which?	Quel/Quelle?	kel
Why?	Pourquoi?	poor·kwa
How?	Comment?	ko·mon

SHOPPING & SERVICES

I'd like to buy ...
Je voudrais acheter ... zher voo·dray ash·tay ...
How much is it?
C'est combien? say kom·byun
I don't like it.
Cela ne me plaît pas. ser·la ner mer play pa
May I look at it?
Est-ce que je peux le voir? es·ker zher per ler vwar
I'm just looking.
Je regarde. zher rer·gard
It's cheap.
Ce n'est pas cher. ser nay pa shair
It's too expensive.
C'est trop cher. say tro shair
I'll take it.
Je le prends. zher ler pron

Can I pay by ...?	*Est-ce que je peux*	es·ker zher per
	payer avec ...?	pay-yay a·vek ...
credit card	*ma carte de*	ma kart der
	crédit	kray·dee
travellers	*des chèques*	day shek
cheques	*de voyage*	der vwa·yazh
more	*plus*	plew
less	*moins*	mwa
smaller	*plus petit*	plew per·tee
bigger	*plus grand*	plew gron
I'm looking	*Je cherche ...*	zhe shersh ...
for ...		
a bank	*une banque*	ewn bonk
the ... embassy	*l'ambassade*	lam·ba·sahd
	de ...	der ...
the hospital	*l'hôpital*	lo·pee·tal
the market	*le marché*	ler mar·shay
the police	*la police*	la po·lees
the post office	*le bureau de*	ler bew·ro der
	poste	post
a public phone	*une cabine*	ewn ka·been
	téléphonique	tay·lay·fo·neek
a public toilet	*les toilettes*	lay twa·let
the telephone	*la centrale*	la san·tral
centre	*téléphonique*	tay·lay·fo·neek

TIME & DATES

What time is it?	*Quelle heure est-il?*	kel er e til
It's (8) o'clock.	*Il est (huit) heures.*	il e (weet) er
It's half past ...	*Il est (...) heures et*	il e (...) er e
	demie.	day·mee
in the morning	*du matin*	dew ma·tun
in the afternoon	*de l'après-midi*	der la·pray·mee·dee
in the evening	*du soir*	dew swar
today	*aujourd'hui*	o·zhoor·dwee
tomorrow	*demain*	der·mun
yesterday	*hier*	yair
Monday	*lundi*	lun·dee
Tuesday	*mardi*	mar·dee
Wednesday	*mercredi*	mair·krer·dee
Thursday	*jeudi*	zher·dee
Friday	*vendredi*	von·drer·dee
Saturday	*samedi*	sam·dee
Sunday	*dimanche*	dee·monsh
January	*janvier*	zhon·vyay
February	*février*	fayv·ryay
March	*mars*	mars
April	*avril*	a·vreel
May	*mai*	may
June	*juin*	zhwun
July	*juillet*	zhwee·yay

August	*août*	oot
September	*septembre*	sep·tom·brer
October	*octobre*	ok·to·brer
November	*novembre*	no·vom·brer
December	*décembre*	day·som·brer

TRANSPORT
Public Transport

What time does	*À quelle heure*	a kel er
... leave/arrive?	*part/arrive ...?*	par/a·reev ...
boat	*le bateau*	ler ba·to
bus	*le bus*	ler bews
plane	*l'avion*	la·vyon
train	*le train*	ler trun
I'd like a ...	*Je voudrais*	zher voo·dray
ticket.	*un billet ...*	un bee·yay ...
one·way	*simple*	sum·pler
return	*aller et retour*	a·lay ay rer·toor
1st class	*de première classe*	der prem·yair klas
2nd class	*de deuxième classe*	der der·zyem klas

I want to go to ...	
Je voudrais aller à ...	zher voo·dray a·lay a ...
The train has been delayed.	
Le train est en retard.	ler trun et on rer·tar
The train has been cancelled.	
Le train a été annulé.	ler trun a ay·tay a·new·lay

the first	*le premier* (m)	ler prer·myay
	la première (f)	la prer·myair
the last	*le dernier* (m)	ler dair·nyay
	la dernière (f)	la dair·nyair
platform	*le numéro*	ler new·may·ro
number	*de quai*	der kay
ticket office	*le guichet*	ler gee·shay
timetable	*l'horaire*	lo·rair
train station	*la gare*	la gar

Private Transport

I'd like to hire	*Je voudrais*	zher voo·dray
a/an...	*louer ...*	loo·way ...
car	*une voiture*	ewn vwa·tewr
4WD	*un quatre-quatre*	un kat·kat
motorbike	*une moto*	ewn mo·to
bicycle	*un vélo*	un vay·lo

Is this the road to ...?	
C'est la route pour ...?	say la root poor ...
Where's a service station?	
Où est-ce qu'il y a	oo es·keel ya
une station-service?	ewn sta·syon·ser·vees
Please fill it up.	
Le plein, s'il vous plaît.	ler plun seel voo play
I'd like ... litres.	
Je voudrais ... litres.	zher voo·dray ... lee·trer

ROAD SIGNS

Cédez la Priorité	Give Way
Danger	Danger
Défense de Stationner	No Parking
Entrée	Entrance
Interdiction de Doubler	No Overtaking
Péage	Toll
Ralentissez	Slow Down
Sens Interdit	No Entry
Sens unique	One-way
Sortie	Exit

petrol/gas	*essence*	ay·sons
unleaded	*sans plomb*	son plom
leaded	*au plomb*	o plom
diesel	*diesel*	dyay·zel

(How long) Can I park here?
(Combien de temps) Est-ce que je peux stationner ici? (kom·byun der tom) es·ker zher per sta·syo·nay ee·see?

Where do I pay?
Où est-ce que je paie? oo es·ker zher pay?

I need a mechanic.
J'ai besoin d'un mécanicien. zhay ber·zwun dun may·ka·nee·syun

The car/motorbike has broken down (at ...)
La voiture/moto est tombée en panne (à ...) la vwa·tewr/mo·to ay tom·bay on pan (a ...)

The car/motorbike won't start.
La voiture/moto ne veut pas démarrer. la vwa·tewr/mo·to ner ver pa day·ma·ray

I have a flat tyre.
Mon pneu est à plat. mom pner ay ta pla

I've run out of petrol.
Je suis en panne d'essence. zher swee zon pan day·sons

I had an accident.
J'ai eu un accident. zhay ew un ak·see·don

TRAVEL WITH CHILDREN

Is there a/an ...?	*Y a-t-il ...?*	ya teel ...
I need a/an ...	*J'ai besoin ...*	zhay ber·zwun ...
baby change room	*d'un endroit pour changer le bébé*	dun on·drwa poor shon·zhay ler bay·bay
car baby seat	*d'un siège-enfant*	dun syezh·on·fon
child-minding service	*d'une garderie*	dewn gar·dree
children's menu	*d'un menu pour enfant*	dun mer·new poor on·fon
disposable nappies/diapers	*de couches-culottes*	der koosh·kew·lot
formula	*de lait maternisé*	de lay ma·ter·nee·zay
(English-speaking) babysitter	*d'une baby-sitter (qui parle anglais)*	dewn ba·bee·see·ter (kee parl ong·glay)
highchair	*d'une chaise haute*	dewn shay zot
potty	*d'un pot de bébé*	dun po der bay·bay
stroller	*d'une poussette*	dewn poo·set

Do you mind if I breastfeed here?
Cela vous dérange si j'allaite mon bébé ici? ser·la voo day·ron·zhe see zha·lay·ter mon bay·bay ee·see

Are children allowed?
Les enfants sont permis? lay zon·fon son pair·mee

LANGUAGE

Glossary

For a glossary of food and drink terms, see the Food & Drink chapter (p80).

(m) indicates masculine gender, (f) feminine gender and (pl) plural

accueil (m) – reception
alignements (m pl) – a series of standing stones, or menhirs, in straight lines
alimentation (f) – grocery store
AOC – appellation d'origine contrôlée; system of French wine classification
arrondissement (m) – administrative division of large city; abbreviated on signs as 1er (1st *arrondissement*), 2e or 2ème (2nd) etc
auberge de jeunesse (f) – (youth) hostel

baie (f) – bay
bassin (m) – bay or basin
bastide (f) – medieval settlement in southwestern France, usually built on a grid plan and surrounding an arcaded square
belle époque (f) – literally 'beautiful age'; era of elegance and gaiety characterising fashionable Parisian life in the period preceding WWI
billet (m) – ticket
billetterie (f) – ticket office or counter
billet jumelé (m) – combination ticket, good for more than one site, museum etc
boulangerie (f) – bakery or bread shop
boules (f pl) – a game not unlike lawn bowls played with heavy metal balls on a sandy pitch; also called *pétanque*
BP – *boîte postale*; post office box
brasserie (f) – restaurant usually serving food all day (original meaning: brewery)
bureau de poste (m) or **poste** (f) – post office
bureau de change (m) – exchange bureau

CAF – Club Alpin Français
carnet (m) – a book of five or 10 bus, tram or metro tickets sold at a reduced rate
carrefour (m) – crossroad
carte (f) – card; menu; map
caserne (f) – military barracks
cave (f) – wine cellar
chambre (f) – room
chambre d'hôte (f) – B&B
charcuterie (f) – pork butcher's shop and delicatessen; the prepared meats it sells
cimetière (m) – cemetery

col (m) – mountain pass
consigne (f) – left-luggage office
consigne automatique (f) – left-luggage locker
consigne manuelle (f) – left-luggage office
correspondance (f) – linking tunnel or walkway, eg in the metro; rail or bus connection
couchette (f) – sleeping berth on a train or ferry
cour (f) – courtyard
crémerie (f) – dairy or cheese shop
cyclisme (m) – cycling

dégustation (f) – tasting
demi (m) – 330mL glass of beer
demi-pension (f) – half-board (B&B with either lunch or dinner)
département (m) – administrative division of France
douane (f) – customs

église (f) – church
embarcadère (m) – pier or jetty
épicerie (f) – small grocery store
ESF – École de Ski Français; France's leading ski school

fauteuil (m) – seat on trains, ferries or at the theatre
fest-noz or **festou-noz** (pl) – night festival
fête (f) – festival
FN – Front National; National Front
forêt (f) – forest
formule or **formule rapide** (f) – similar to a *menu* but allows choice of whichever two of three courses you want (eg starter and main course or main course and dessert)
fouilles (f pl) – excavations at an archaeological site
foyer (m) – workers or students hostel
fromagerie (f) – cheese shop
FUAJ – Fédération Unie des Auberges de Jeunesse; France's major hostel association
funiculaire (m) – funicular railway

galerie (f) – covered shopping centre or arcade
gare or **gare SNCF** (f) – railway station
gare maritime (f) – ferry terminal
gare routière (f) – bus station
gendarmerie (f) – police station; police force
gîte d'étape (m) – hikers accommodation, usually in a village
gîte rural (m) – country cottage
golfe (m) – gulf
GR – *grande randonnée;* long-distance hiking trail
grand cru (m) – wine of exceptional quality

halles (f pl) – covered market; central food market
halte routière (f) – bus stop
horaire (m) – timetable or schedule
hôte payant (m) – paying guest
hôtel de ville (m) – city or town hall
hôtel particulier (m) – private mansion
hôtes payants (m pl) – paying guest
l'habitant or **hébergement chez** (m) – homestay

intra-muros – old city (literally 'within the walls')

jardin (m) – garden
jardin botanique (m) – botanic garden
jours fériés (m pl) – public holidays

laverie (f) or **lavomatique** (m) – laundrette

mairie (f) – city or town hall
maison de la presse (f) – newsagent
maison du parc (f) – a national park's headquarters and/or visitors centre
marché (m) – market
marché aux puces (m) – flea market
marché couvert (m) – covered market
mas (m) – farmhouse; tiny hamlet
menu (m) – fixed-price meal with two or more courses
mistral (m) – incessant north wind in southern France said to drive people crazy
musée (m) – museum

navette (f) – shuttle bus, train or boat

Occitan – a language also known as langue d'oc or sometimes Provençal, related to Catalan

palais de justice (m) – law courts
parapente – paragliding
pardon (m) – religious pilgrimage
parlement (m) – parliament
parvis (m) – square
pâtisserie (f) – cake and pastry shop
pensions de famille (f pl) – similar to B&Bs
pétanque (f) – a game not unlike lawn bowls played with heavy metal balls on a sandy pitch; also called *boules*
piste cyclable (f) – bicycle path
place (f) – square or plaza
plage (f) – beach
plan (m) – city map
plan du quartier (m) – map of nearby streets (hung on the wall near metro exits)
plat du jour (m) – daily special in a restaurant
pont (m) – bridge

port (m) – harbour or port
port de plaisance (m) – marina or pleasure-boat harbour
porte (f) – gate in a city wall
poste (f) or **bureau de poste** (m) – post office
préfecture (f) – prefecture (capital of a *département*)
presqu'île (f) – peninsula
pression (f) – draught beer
puy (m) – volcanic cone or peak

quai (m) – quay or railway platform
quartier (m) – quarter or district

refuge (m) – mountain hut, basic shelter for hikers
rez-de-chausée (m) – ground floor
rive (f) – bank of a river
rond point (m) – roundabout
routier (m) – trucker or truckers restaurant

sentier (m) – trail
service des urgences (f) – casualty ward
ski de fond – cross-country skiing
SNCF – Société Nationale des Chemins de Fer; state-owned railway company
SNCM – Société Nationale Maritime Corse-Méditerranée; state-owned ferry company linking Corsica and mainland France
sortie (f) – exit
spectacle (m) – performance, play or theatrical show
square (m) – public garden
supplément (m) – supplement or additional cost
syndicat d'initiative (m) – tourist office

tabac (m) – tobacconist (also selling bus tickets, phone-cards etc)
table d'orientation (f) – viewpoint indicator
taxe de séjour (f) – municipal tourist tax
télécarte (f) – phonecard
téléphérique (m) – cableway or cable car
télésiège (m) – chair lift
téléski (m) – ski lift or tow
TGV – *train à grande vitesse;* high-speed train or bullet train
tour (f) – tower
tour d'horloge (f) – clock tower

vallée (f) – valley
v.f. (f) – *version française;* a film dubbed in French
vieille ville (f) – old town or old city
ville neuve (f) – new town or new city
v.o. (f) – *version originale;* a nondubbed film with French subtitles
voie (f) – train platform
VTT – *vélo tout terrain;* mountain bike

Behind the Scenes

THIS BOOK

For this 6th edition of *France*, Nicola Williams co-ordinated a skilled team of authors comprising Oliver Berry, Steve Fallon, Annabel Hart, Jonathan Knight, Daniel Robinson, Miles Roddis and Andrew Stone. Nicola, Steve, Annabel, Daniel and Miles also made major contributions to previous editions, as did Teresa Fisher, Jeremy Gray, Leanne Logan, Paul Hellander, Oda O'Carroll and Jeanne Oliver. Dr Caroline Evans reviewed and contributed to the Health chapter.

THANKS from the Authors

Nicola Williams A big *grand merci* to my fellow authors for their good-humoured cooperation during what was, at times, a mind-boggling affair; to friends and acquaintances in Lyon for uncovering tasty places to eat, drink and enjoy over the years – and sharing them with me; and to my Frencher-than-German husband Matthias (not to mention Niko and Mischa) for being sweeter-than-Montélimar sweet.

Oliver Berry Lots of people helped during the writing of this book. Special thanks go to Susie Berry for love, support and lending me my wheels; to Laura Brammar for listening; to Carl and Si at o-region for keeping the show on the road; to the Hôtel L'Aïtone in Évisa for putting up with me; to Nicola Williams and Sam Trafford for patience, support and long-distance correspondence; and to all the staff of the many French tourist offices who helped along the way. I'd also like to thank the late Dorothy Carrington for writing the best book on Corsica anyone could hope to read.

Steve Fallon A number of people helped in the updating of the Paris chapter, but first and foremost stands resident Brenda Turnnidge, whose knowledge of all things Parisian – but especially fashion, transport and *les bonnes addresses* – never ceases to amaze and excite. Thanks, too, to Zahia Hafs, Olivier Cirendini, Caroline Guilleminot and Chew Terrière for assistance, ideas, hospitality and/or a few laughs during what was a very grey, very bleak winter in every way.

As always, I'd like to dedicate my efforts to my partner, Michael Rothschild, whose knowledge of menu French grows in direct proportion to… Well, *peu importe* (never mind).

Annabel Hart Special acknowledgment and thanks to Lonely Planet's Paris office and the wonderful people there, without whom none of this would have happened. Thanks especially to Didier, Olivier and, above all, *petite* Claire for her tactical and moral support. Thanks also to Georgia for being my 3am pen pal, Diana for cutting those last 200 words and Edouard for putting up with me. Thanks finally to editor Sam Trafford and co-ordinating author Nicola Williams for their hard work and understanding.

Jonathan Knight Thanks to hundreds of helpful tourist officials across southwestern France, particularly Séverine Michau, Samuel Buchwalder, Catherine Senand, Françoise Tetard, Séverine Pigeaud and David Morton. Thanks also to Sam and Nicola for assistance and deadline flexibility; to Grands Garages de Touraine for helping to get my trusty

THE LONELY PLANET STORY

The story begins with a classic travel adventure: Tony and Maureen Wheeler's 1972 journey across Europe and Asia to Australia. There was no useful information about the overland trail then, so Tony and Maureen published the first Lonely Planet guidebook to meet a growing need.

From a kitchen table, Lonely Planet has grown to become the largest independent travel publisher in the world, with offices in Melbourne (Australia), Oakland (USA) and London (UK). Today Lonely Planet guidebooks cover the globe. There is an ever-growing list of books and information in a variety of media. Some things haven't changed. The main aim is still to make it possible for adventurous travellers to get out there – to explore and better understand the world.

At Lonely Planet we believe travellers can make a positive contribution to the countries they visit – if they respect their host communities and spend their money wisely. Every year 5% of company profit is donated to charities around the world.

old four-wheeler back on the road; to Rose and Archie for company, wine, food and a bed in the tower; and most of all to Shellani for saying yes.

Daniel Robinson In Far Northern France, I am indebted to Jean-Christophe Le Goaër of Clairière de l'Armistice; Jocelyne Mitchell (PEI) and Laura Floyd (Ottowa) of the Vimy Canadian National Memorial; Alexandra Limousin of Boulogne's Nausicaä; and tourist office professionals Stéphanie Noël (Amiens), Stéphanie Seulin (Lille) and Madame Baudeuille (Boulogne). In Champagne, my research was nourished and lubricated by Jacqueline & Pascal Maillard and Jean-Paul Dzitko of Reim's Le Lion de Belfort and, in Troyes, Raquel & Elie Margen, Claude Margen, Olivier Galliot and my old friend Thierry Di Costanzo. In Lorraine, Jean-Pierre Collet of the Verdun municipality kindly provided up-to-the-minute mapping information. In Strasbourg, people who lent an enthusiastic hand include Claudine Lévy of the Agence de Développement Touristique du Bas-Rhin, Musica Schmidt of the Maison des Projets, Kiera Tchelistcheff of The Bookworm, Philippe Roth of Strasbourg's L'Assiette du Vin and the tourist office's Valérie Garnier. In Colmar, my special thanks go to Temple St-Mathieu organist Paul Florence, Cécile Lannoy of the tourist office and Aurélien, Adrien, Patricia & Jean-Michel Kempf. My travels around Alsace were considerably enlivened by the trans-Rhine visit of my Lonely Planet colleague Becca Blond.

Finally, I would like to thank Réka Kocsis of Sopron, Hungary and the 15e, for her warmth, enthusiasm and sense of adventure; and Kristy Marks of Sydney-based DriveAway Holidays, who arranged the purchase-repurchase Peugeot 206 that served me for 4250 problem-free kilometres.

Miles Roddis Thanks to so many cheerful tourist office staff. It was a pleasure to see once more Laurence Tapie and Myriam Blanchard (Bedous), Mathilde Lardat (Cauterets), Marie (Murat), Élodie Juillard (Le Mont-Dore) and Françoise Cros (Montpellier).

Thanks too to Myriam (Laruns), Stéphanie (Gavarnie), Fabrice Doucet (Lourdes), Mme Mourles (Millau), Xavier Brilhaut (Ste-Énimie), Benjamin Bonnet (Florac), Riccardo (Mende), Laurence Lescuyer and Virginie (St-Nectaire), Philippe (Clermont-Ferrand), Françoise Gioux (Vichy), Lise Gauthier (Orcival), Matthieu Aubignat-Fournet – good to meet another Durham graduate – (Thiers), Candice Taillandier (Ambert), Céline Charrat (Le Puy), Magani (Alès), Laurent Chateaux (Uzès), Armand Descombes (Nîmes), Francine (Agde), Véronique (Narbonne), Laure (Carcassonne), Sylvette (Foix), Dominique Fabre (Collioure), Marie-Pierre (Perpignan) and Agnès Chassin (Parc Naturel Régional Livradois-Forez). And a special thank you to ebullient Eddy Delobel (Service Relations Presse, Pau), also to reader Jennifer Barclay for a detailed and most helpful updating letter about Montpellier and its environs.

Andrew Stone For all the visits over the years and all the hospitality, my main thanks go to the Foucault and Peyre de Fabrègues families and in particular to Evelyn, Xavier, Michael and Sharmion. Special thanks to Ruth and Paulo at the Hub Lot for the Aix tips, to Michel Caraisco in Toulon for the Var tour and to Jean-Jacques Benetti at the Maison des Vins Côtes de Provence for the whistlestop wine tour. Thanks also to all the helpful tourism offices in the south and in particular thanks to Fabienne Fertilati in Nice and Nathalie Steinberg in Marseille. Finally, thanks to Fabienne Dupuis for all the tips, insights and, most importantly, the pints of Guinness.

CREDITS

France 6 was commissioned and developed in Lonely Planet's London office by Sam Trafford, and assessed by Sam Trafford and Susie Ashworth. The book was coordinated by Yvonne Byron (editorial) and Helen Rowley (cartography). Andrew Bain, Cinzia Cavallaro, Charlotte Harrison, Margedd Heliosz, John Hinman, Maryanne Netto, Nina Rousseau, Diana Saad and Helen Yeates assisted with editing and proofing. Paul Bazalicki, Christopher Crook, Csanad Csutoros, Piotr Czajkowski, Daniel Fennessy, Tadhagh Knaggs, Joelene Kowalski, Kusnandar, Mandy Sierp, Chris Thomas and Simon Tillema assisted with cartography. Chris Lee Ack and Lachlan Ross provided invaluable technical assistance. Jacqueline McLeod and Wibowo Rusli laid out the book, Pablo Gastar designed the colour content. Pepi Bluck designed the cover with artwork by Wendy Wright. Kate Evans, Sally Darmody, Adrianna Mammarella and Kate McDonald assisted with layout checking. Quentin Frayne prepared the Language chapter. Overseeing production were Glenn van der Knijff (Project Manager), Bruce Evans (Managing Editor) and Mark Griffiths (Managing Cartographer), who was assisted by Daniel Fennessy. Alison Lyall helped with map checking. The series was designed by James Hardy, with mapping development by Paul Piaia.

Our thoughts have been with our beloved late friend, Shelley Muir, during production of this 6th edition – an inspirational friend and colleague.

THANKS from Lonely Planet

Many thanks to the following travellers who used the last edition and wrote to us with helpful hints, useful advice and interesting anecdotes.

A Susan Alexander, J Anderson, Helene Andersson, **B** Sue Baker, Simon Ball, James Barisic, CM Beattie, Paola Benini, Cindy Bestland, Gail Bishko, Kate Black, Paul Bloomfield, Monica & Richard Booth, Truman Bradley, John Buckley, Chris Burin, M Burness, Maria Bursey, Alison Butcher, Robert Button, **C** Belinda Catterall, Kam Champaneri, Nikitas Chondroyannos, Greta Cleghorn, Colin Coffey, Marco Conte, Pat & John Cooper, Ali Coton, Florence Counil, Philip Crosby, **D** Lynn Dawson, Daniel De Groot, Audrey Dean, Joanna Delaney, Laura & Ami Diner, Terry Dolman, Fred Dugenet, Benjamin Dyson, **E** Robert Edmunds, **F** Rachel Faggetter, Craig Falls, Lea Feng, John Fletcher, Ian Fulcher, **G** Jason Galea, John Gibson, Amelia Greenberg, Martijn Grimmius, Pallav Gupta, **H** Jacob Halpin, Frank Harker, Jim Hendrickson, Lennart Henriksson, Katherine Hickey, Francis Higbie, Helen Hofsted, Tina Hough, Robert Hubbard, KA Humphries, Geoff Hutcheison, **J** Barry Johnston, Eve Jones, Philip Jones, Ronaele Jones, Michl Joos, **K** R Karlmarx, Mark Kemper, Pete Kitching, Madame Mary Ellen Kitler, Henry Koster, Ann Kramer, **L** Bart Langerwerf, Rebekah Lawrence, Tram Anh Le, Oliver Lewis, Nana Lim, Phil Linz, Ynyr Lloyd, **M** Peter MacLean, Suzy Mangion, Mark & Jaime Manson, Alison Matthews, Marco Mazzocchi, Dr JS McLintock, GJ Mensink, Peter Millett, Peter & June Millett, Peter Monk, **N** Travis Kane Nairn, Mikael Nojd, **O** Ruth O'Connell, Paul Ozorak, **P** Emma Payne, Murray Pearce, Inga Pfannebecker, Monique Pierre, Lizzy Pike, Alan & Maree Porter, **R** Susan Reilly, Stephane Reynolds, Lita Roberts, Terry Rolleri, **S** RR Sanderson, Eivind Stene, Kimberly Stewart, **T** Elizabeth Thorpe, Edward Tsui, Peter Tudor, Liz Turner, **U** Christina Unterwurzacher, **V** Esther Van Den Reek, Monique Van Erp, **W** Bill Wagman, Andy Ward, Joanna Wilding, Matthew Wilner-Reid, **Y** Barbara Yoshida, Andrew Young, **Z** Jabi Zabala

ACKNOWLEDGMENTS

Many thanks to the following for the use of their content:

Globe on back cover © Mountain High Maps 1993 Digital Wisdom, Inc.

RATP for the use of its transit map © RATP – CML Agence Cartographique.

SEND US YOUR FEEDBACK

We love to hear from travellers – your comments keep us on our toes and help make our books better. Our well-travelled team reads every word on what you loved or loathed about this book. Although we cannot reply individually to postal submissions, we always guarantee that your feedback goes straight to the appropriate authors, in time for the next edition. Each person who sends us information is thanked in the next edition – and the most useful submissions are rewarded with a free book.

To send us your updates – and find out about Lonely Planet events, newsletters and travel news – visit our award-winning website: **www.lonelyplanet.com/feedback**.

Note: We may edit, reproduce and incorporate your comments in Lonely Planet products such as guidebooks, websites and digital products, so let us know if you don't want your comments reproduced or your name acknowledged. For a copy of our privacy policy visit www.lonelyplanet.com/privacy.

Index

A
Abbatiale de la Ste-Trinité 248
Abbatiale de Pontigny 434-5
Abbatiale St-Pierre 582
Abbaye aux Dames 258
Abbaye aux Hommes 258
Abbaye de Cîteaux 458
Abbaye de Fontenay 459, 396-7
Abbaye de Fontevraud 424
Abbaye du Mont St-Michel 273-4
Abbaye du Thoronet 847
Abbaye St-Germain 431
Abbaye St-Guenolé 300
Abbaye St-Pierre 711
Abri du Cap Blanc 593
Abri Pataud 591
Académie Française 48, 123
accommodation 893-913
Accous 682-3
activities 896-8, *see also* individual
    entries
    Burgundy 428
    Massif Central 548
    safety 930
Agay 841
Agde 726-7
Agincourt 215
Aigues 809-10
Aigues Mortes 725, 807
Aiguille du Midi 499, 500
air travel
    Paris airports 170-2
    to/from France 915-16
    within France 921-2
Airbus factory 700-1
Aix-en-Provence 776-83, **777**
Ajaccio 880-5, **881**
Albert 227
Albi 705-9, **706**
Alençon 275-6
Alès 739-41
Alésia 459
Alignement de Palaggiu 885
Alignement de Stantari 885
Alpe d'Huez 528, 531
Alpine columbine 58
Alpine eryngo 58
Alps, the 489-545, **492**
    climate 491-2
    geography 491

history 491
skiing & snowboarding 493-6
travel to/from 496-7
Alsace 343-70, **343**
    customs 350
    food 67
    Judaism 351, 360
    language 345
    wine 70-1, 357-62
Ambert 564
Ambleteuse 215
Amboise 412-15, **413**
American Film Festival 904
American Military Cemetery,
    Colleville-sur-Mer 267
Amiens 227-30, **228**
Angers 418-22, **419**
Anglet 654
animals 57-8, *see also* individual entries
Anjou 418-24
Annecy 508-12, **509**, 7, 11
Annonay 487
Antibes 831-2
Apt 799-800
aquariums
    Aquarium du Laboratoire Arago 759
    Cité de la Mer, Dieppe 245
    Cité de la Mer, Cherbourg 269
    Grand Aquarium 284
    La Rochelle 622
    Marinarium 306
    Musée de la Mer, Biarritz 654
    Musée Océanographique de
        Monaco 857
    Nausicaä 217
    Océanopolis 297
Arbois 541
Arc de Triomphe
    Montpellier 721
    Nancy 372
    Orange 792
    Paris 53, 127
Arcachon 641-4, **642**
archaeology 27, 61
architecture 14, 52-4
Argelès-Gazost 680
Arles 800-6, **801**
Arromanches 266-7
art galleries, *see* museums & galleries

Artouste-Fabrèges 686
arts 47-55, *see also* individual entries
Asquins 442
Atelier Paul Cézanne 779
Atlantic Coast 609-45, **611**
ATMs 908
Aubazine 579-80
Aubenas 488
Aubusson 578-9
Aubusson tapestries, Mende 744
Auch 711-13, **712**
Australian National War Memorial,
    Villers-Bretonneux 226
Autun 459-62, **460**
Auxerre 429-33, **430**
Auxerrois 433
avalanches 492-3
Avallon 437-40, **438**
Aven Armand 746
Avignon 783-91, **784-5**
Avoriaz 507
Ax-les-Thermes 692
Azay-le-Rideau 411

B
Baccarat 376
Bagnères de Luchon 690-1
Balazuc 488
Balcons de la Mescla 813
Baldaccini, César 49
Ballon d'Alsace 369
ballooning, *see* hot-air ballooning
Bambouseraie de Prafrance 740
Banc d'Arguin 643
    bird reserve 644
Banyuls 759
Bar-sur-Aube 340
Barbie, Klaus 469
Barbizon School 54
Barcaggio 871
Barèges La Mongie 681
Barrage de la Rance 286
bars 74
Basilique de St-Denis 182-3
Basilique du Sacré Cœur 130
Basilique Notre Dame de Fourvière,
    Lyon 473
Basilique Notre Dame de la Garde 770
Basilique Notre Dame du Port 549
Basilique Notre Dame du Roncier 318

Basilique St-Sauveur 290
Basilique St-Sernin 697-8
Basilique St-Urbain 337
Basilique Ste-Madeleine 440-1
Basque Country 646-66, **648**
    food 69
    language 648
Bastia 867-71, **868**
bastides 583
Bastille 119
Bastille Day 136
Battle of Agincourt 215
Battle of Normandy 264-5, **265**
Battle of the Somme 223-7, **224**
    tours 223-4
Battle of Verdun 384-6
Baudelaire, Charles 48
Baume-les-Messieurs 542
Bayel 340
Bayeux 260-6, **261**
Bayeux Tapestry 28, 262
Bayeux War Cemetery 263
Bayonne 649-54, **650-1**
beaches 897-8
    Ajaccio 882
    Algajola 875
    Anglet 654
    Belle Île 314
    Biarritz 654
    Blériot Plage 211
    Bonifacio 888
    Canet-Plage 756
    Cannes 837
    Carcans Plage 637
    Cap Corse 871
    Concarneau 306
    Corsica 875
    Equihen Plage 217
    Fréjus 843
    Grande Plage, Quiberon 312
    Grande Plage, St-Malo 284
    Île de Ré 625-6
    Île d'Ouessant 299
    Le Portel 217
    Le Touquet 217
    Médoc, the 637
    Monaco 857
    Montpellier 725
    Morgat 301
    Nice 824
    Palombaggia 875

Perros-Guinec 293
Plage de Bon Secours 284, 140-1
Plage de l'Écluse 286
Plage de Rochebonne 284
Plage de Trestraou 293
Plage de Trestrignel 293
Plage des Bas Sablons 284
Plage du Château 293
Rocapina 875
Rondinara 875
Saleccia 875
Socoa 658
Soulac-sur-Mer 638
St-Jean de Luz 658
St-Malo 284
St-Tropez 844-5
Wimereux 217
Beaujeu 484
Beaujolais 484-5
Beaulieu-sur-Dordogne 581-2
Beaulieu-sur-Mer 852
Beaumont-Hamel Newfoundland
    Memorial, the Somme 226
Beaune 453-7, **455**
Beauvais 230-1
Beauvoir, Simone de 48
Bedous 682
beer 72-3, 351-2
Belfort 542
Belle-Île-en-Mer 313-14
Belleville 516
Belvédère de l'Escalès 813
Belvédère des Vautours 57
Bergerac 597-8
Bergeries de Grotelle 892
Bergheim 360
Berlioz, Hector 51
Bernadotte, Jean-Baptiste 672
Bertric Burée 587
Besançon 536-40, **538**
Besse-en-Chandesse 561
Beynac-et-Cazenac 596
Béziers 727
Biarritz 654-8, **655**
Bibliothèque Humaniste 359
Bibliothèque Nationale de France
    François Mitterrand 54, 129
bicycle travel, see cycling
Bidarray 666
Biot 832-3
bird-watching 57
    Baie de la Somme 217
    Bassin d'Arcachon 644
    Boulogne 217
    Camargue, the 806

Hunawihr 57, 361
Île de Ré 625
La Dombes 485
Le Teich Parc Ornithologique 645
Marais Audemarois 214
Munster 368
Parc Naturel Interrégional du
    Marais Poitevin 619-20
birds 57-8, see also bird-watching
    and individual entries
bison 57, 745
Bizet, Georges 51
blading, see in-line skating
Blésois 397-404
Blois 397-401, **398**
BMPT 54, 55
boat travel 918
    canal boating 281, 428, 922-3
    to/from France 919-1
boating
    Annecy 510
    Arcachon 643
    Avignon 787
    Bonifacio 888
    Camargue, the 808
    Cannes 837
    Condom 714
    Gorges du Tarn 745
    Nice 824
    Parc Naturel Interrégional du
        Marais Poitevin 619-20
    Quercy 598
    Toulon 850
    Toulouse 701
Bocuse, Paul 474, 479
Bonaparte, Napoleon 32, 191, 882, 884
Bonifacio 886-9, **887**, 684-5
Bonneval-sur-Arc 520
books 13-15
Borce 684
Bordeaux 628-37, **630**
    wine 71
bouchons 478-9
Boudin, Eugène 252
bouillabaisse 770
boules, see pétanque
Boulogne-sur-Mer 216-19, **218**
Bourges 396
Bout du Lac 510
Bouziès 603
Brancion 465
Braque, Georges 55
Brassens, Georges 52, 726
brasseries 74
bread 63, 359, 12

Brest 296-8
Briançon 532-5, **533**
Briare 396
Brittany 277-322, **280**
    activities 281
    customs 279, 319
    food 67
    language 279-81
Brive-La-Gaillarde 579
Brocéliande, see Forêt de Paimpont
brown bears 57, 683
bullfighting 648, 735, 804, 806
bungy jumping 896
Bunifaziu, see Bonifacio
Burgundy 425-65, **427**
    activities 428
    food 68
    wine 71, 453, 12
bus travel
    to/from France 917
    within France 923
business hours 898, see also inside
    front cover
Butte de Montfaucon 386
Butte de Montsec 386

C
cabaret 165
Cabasse 847
Caen 256-60, **257**
cafés 74
Cagnes-sur-Mer 833
Cahors 599-603, **600**
Calais 209-13, **210**
Calanques, the 771
Calvados 251-68
Calvi 872-5, **873**, 684-5
Camaret-sur-Mer 300
Camargue, the 800-10, **807**, 10
Camisard Revolt, the 739
Camus, Albert 627
canal boating 922-3
    Brittany 281
    Burgundy 428
    Paris 134-5
Canal de Bourgogne 428
Canal du Midi 600, 701, 726, 727
Canari 871
Cancale 289, 12
Candes-sur-Martin 424
Cannes 834-40, **835**
Cannes Film Festival 836
canoeing 898
    Alps 496
    Annecy 510

Conduché 603
Gorges de l'Ardèche 488
Gorges du Tarn 745-6
La Roque Gageac 596
Parc National des Écrins 529-30
Parc National des Pyrénées 681
Parc Naturel Interrégional du
    Marais Poitevin 619-20
River Gard 738
Superbagnères 691
Vézelay 441
canyoning 896
    Annecy 510
    Bedous 682
    Chambéry 514
    Chamonix 502
    Foix 692
    Gorges du Verdon 813
    Superbagnères 691
CAPC Musée d'Art Contemporain
    631
Cap Blanc-Nez 215
Cap Corse 871
Cap de la Chèvre 301
Cap Ferret 637, 644
Cap Gris-Nez 215
Cap Martin 852
Capo Rosso 876
car travel
    to/from France 917-19
    within France 923-5, **924**
Carcans Plage 637
Carcassonne 727-33, **728**
Carennac 608
Cargèse 879-80
Carghjese, see Cargèse
Carnac 310-12, 7
Carnon 725
Carpentras 796-7
Carré d'Art 734
Cascade des Anglais 892
Cascade du Voile de la Mariée
    892
Casino de Monte Carlo 859, 684-5
Cassel 214-15
Cassis 771, 684-5
Castelfranc 607
Castellane 812-13
Castres 709
Catacombes 123-4
Cathars, the 756-7
Cathédrale de Coutances 272
Cathédrale de Monaco 857
Cathédrale de Notre Dame de Paris
    119-20, 396-7

Cathédrale Notre Dame
    Amiens 227-9
    Bayeux 262
    Chantilly 195
    Clermont-Ferrand 549
    Laon 234
    Le Puy-en-Velay 565
    Reims 327, 8
    Rouen 240
    Strasbourg 349
    Verdun 383
Cathédrale Notre Dame de Chartres
    196-8
Cathédrale Orthodoxe Russe
    St-Nicolas 823
Cathédrale St-André 632
Cathédrale St-Bénigne 448
Cathédrale St-Corentin 303
Cathédrale St-Étienne
    Auxerre 431
    Bourges 396
    Cahors 599-601
    Limoges 575
    Metz 377
    Toulouse 698-700, 652-3
Cathédrale St-Front 585
Cathédrale St-Gatien 405
Cathédrale St-Jean
    Lyon 472, 428-9
    Perpignan 753
Cathédrale St-Just 727
Cathédrale St-Lazare 461
Cathédrale St-Maurice 420
Cathédrale St-Pierre
    Beauvais 231
    Compiègne 231
    Condom 714
    Poitiers 618
    Vannes 315
Cathédrale St-Pierre et St-Paul
    Nantes 613
    Troyes 336
Cathédrale St-Sacerdos 588
Cathédrale St-Sauveur 779
Cathédrale St-Vincent 283
Cathédrale Ste-Cécile 705-6
Cathédrale Ste-Croix 391
Cathédrale Ste-Marie
    Ajaccio 882
    Auch 711-12
    Bastia 867
    Bayonne 649-50
    St-Bertrand de Comminges 690
Cauria 885
Causse de Sauveterre 746

Causse du Larzac 747
Causse Méjean 746
Causse Noir 746-7
Cauterets 681, 686-90, **687**
Cave aux Sarcophages 424
cave paintings 27
    Lascaux 591, 595
caves, *see also individual entries under*
    grotte
    Abri du Cap Blanc 593
    Abri Pataud, Les Eyzies de Tayac
        591
    Arago Cave 756
    Aven Armand 746
    Dargilan 746
    Domme 596
    Gouffre de Padirac 608
    La Roque St-Christophe 594
    Saumur 423
    Troglodyte Valley 423-4
caving 514, 596, 603
cemeteries, *see individual entries*
    under Cimetière
Centre de Réintroduction des
    Cigognes, Hunawihr 360
Centre d'Histoire de la Résistance et
    de la Déportation, Lyon 475
Centre Mondial de la Paix, Verdun
    382-3
Centre Pompidou 116, 108-9
Centuri 871
Céret 756
Césars 49
Cézanne, Paul 55, 779
Chablis 433-4
Chagny 465
Chambéry 512-16, **513**
chamois 57, 519, 680
Chamonix 497-505, **498**
champagne 72
    Épernay 332-3
    houses 328, 332
    Nuits de Champagne, Troyes 338
    Reims 328
    Route Touristique du Champagne
        331, 340
Champagne Region 323-40, **325**
Champollion, Jean-François 604-5
Champs-Élysées 127
Chamrousse 528
chansons 52, 163-4

000 Map pages
000 Location of colour photographs

Chantier Médiéval de Guédelon 433
Chantilly 193-5, **193**
Chaos de Montpellier-le-Vieux 747
Chapelle de Notre Dame du Haut
    542, 8
Chapelle du Rosaire 834
Chapelle Notre-Dame-de-
    Rocamadour 300
Chapelle St-Pierre 851
charcuterie 65
Chardonnay 465
Chartres 196-9, **197**
Château Chinon 444
Château d'Amboise 412-14
Château d'Ancy-le-Franc 436-7
Château d'Angers 420
Château d'Annecy 509
Château d'Azay-le-Rideau 411
Château de Beauregard 404
Château de Beynac 596-7
Château de Biron 597
Château de Blois 53, 397-9, 396-7
Château de Bonaguil 607
Château de Brissac 395, 423
Château de Bussy-Rabutin 436
Château de Caen 256-7
Château de Cassaigne 716
Château de Castelnau-Bretenoux 608
Château de Castelnaud 596
Château de Chambord 53, 401-2, 6
Château de Chantilly 193-4
Château de Chenonceau 410, 396-7
Château de Cheverny 402-3
Château de Chinon 416
Château de Clérens 594
Château de Cognac 627
Château de Compiègne 232
Château de Cordès 558
Château de Cormatin 465
Château de Dinan 290
Château de Fontainebleau 53, 189-91
Château de Hautefort 585
Château de Josselin 318
Château de Jumilhac-le-Grand 585
Château de La Bussière 396
Château de La Rochepot 436
Château de la Verrerie 395, 462-3
Château de Langeais 411-12
Château de Losse 585
Château de Murol 561
Château de Pau 669
Château de Puyguilhem 585
Château de Puymartin 585
Château de Ratilly 436
Château de St-Brisson 396

Château de St-Fargeau 436
Château de Saumur 423
Château de Serrant 422
Château de Sully 436
Château de Sully-sur-Loire 395
Château de Tanlay 436
Château de Tournoël 554
Château de Vaux-le-Vicomte 192
Château de Verrieres 395
Château de Versailles 187-9, 140-1
Château de Villandry 410-11
Château des Comtes des Foix 692
Château des Ducs de Bretagne 613
Château des Ducs de Savoie 514
Château des Milandes 597
Château des Réaux 395
Château d'Eyrignac 585
Château d'If, Marseille 770
Château d'Ivoy 395
Château du Haut Kœnigsbourg 360
Château Gaillard 243
Châteauneuf-sur-Loire 395
chateaux, *see also* individual entries
    Burgundy 436-7
    Dordogne & Quercy 585
    Loire Valley 395-6, 401, 409-14
    tours 399, 410
Châtillon-sur-Seine 459
cheese 63-5, 78, 543, 562, 750
Chemilly 434
Chemin de la Croix 677
Chenonceaux 410
Cherbourg 269-71, **270**
chestnut trees 741
Chichée 434
children, travel with 22, 898-9, 937
    food 76
    health 930
    La Rochelle 622
    Lyon 473
    Musée du Jouet 364-5
    Muséum d'Histoire Naturelle,
        Tours 405
    Nausicaä 217
    Nigloland 339
    Paris 131, 134
    skiing 495
    Vulcania 553
Chinon 416-18, **417**
Chirac, Jacques 39-40
Chitry-le-Fort 434
chocolate 68, 78, 168, 486, 540, 651,
    653, 674
churches, *see individual entries under*
    Église

Ciboure 658-62
cider 73
Cimetière de Montmartre 130
Cimetière du Montparnasse 123
Cimetière du Père Lachaise 129
cimetière israélite, Sélestat 360
cinema 49-51, 475
    American Film Festival 255
    Cannes Film Festival 836
    Palme d'Or 51
Cingle de Montfort 596
Cirque de Gavarnie 690, 652-3
Cirque de Lescun 683
Cirque de Troumouse 690
Cirque du Lys 688
citadel, Calvi 872, 684-5
Citadelle Souterrraine 382
Cité de la Mer 245
Cité de la Musique 131
Cité de l'Espace 700
Cité des Sciences et de l'Industrie 131
Clairière de l'Armistice 233
Clermont-Ferrand 548-53, **550**
climate 13, 899
    Alps, the 491-2
    Brittany 279
    Burgundy 428
    Corsica 888
    Loire Region 390
    Provence 763
climbing
    Annecy 510
    Chambéry 514
    Méribel 517
Cluny 463-5, **464**
Cocteau, Jean 853
Cognac 627-8
Cointreau 420-1
Col de Guéry 558
Col de Ilseran 518
Col de la Faucille 545
Col de Montgenèvre 532
Col de St-Ignace 662
Col de Ste-Lucie 871
Col de Serre 562
Col de Vergio 878
Col d'Èze 857
Colette 48, 50, 433
Colleville-sur-Mer 267
Collias 738
Collioure 758-9
Collobrières 847
Collonges-la-Rouge 581
Colmar 362-7, **363**
Colombey-les-Deux-Églises 340

Compagnie des Guides 501
Compiègne 231-3, **232**
Concarneau 305-8, **307**
Conciergerie 120
Condom 713-15, **714**
Conduché 603
conservation organisations 60, 61-2
consulates 902-3
cooking courses 79-80
Corniche des Maures 848
Corniche Inférieure 851-2
Corrençon-en-Vercors 529
corrida, see bullfighting
Corse, see Corsica
Corsica 860-92, **863**
    accommodation 864
    food 69-70
    history 862
    language 862
    politics 862
    travel to/from 864-6
    travel within 866
Corte 889-92, **890**
Corti, see Corte
costs 13
    accommodation 893
    food 904
Côte Chalonnaise 465
Côte d'Albâtre 248-9
Côte d'Argent 637
Côte d'Azur 815-54, **817**
Côte de Beaune 453
Côte de Granit Rose 293
Côte de Nuits 452-3
Côte d'Émeraude 281-94
Côte des Bar 340
Côte d'Opale 215-19, **216**
Côte d'Or 444-59, **445**
C Sauvage 312-13
Côte de Granit Rose 293
Côte Vermeille 758-9
Cotentin Peninsula 268
Cotignac 847
Courbet, Gustave 54, 540
Courchevel 516
Courgis 434
courses
    cooking 79-80
    language 900
Coutances 271-2
Couvent Ste-Marie de la Tourette 485
credit cards 908
Croix Rousse, Lyon 474-5, **475**
Crozon 301
Crozon Peninsula 300-1

crystal manufacture 340, 376
cubism 55
culture 41-55
    Alsace 350
    Basque 648, 650, 660
    Brittany 279
    Catalan 753
customs regulations 900
Cyberposte 905
cycling 45, 136, 166, 922
    Alps, the 496
    Alsace 352
    Annecy 510
    Arcachon 643
    Bagnères de Luchon 690-1
    Beaujolais 484
    Bedous 682
    Chamonix 502
    Conduché 603
    Côte d'Or 453, 455
    Dinard 287
    Domaine National de
        Chambord 402
    Foix 692
    Gorges du Tarn 745
    Gorges du Verdon 813
    Île d'Ouessant 299
    La Roque Gageac 596
    Lyon 475-6
    maps 908
    Massif Central 548
    Massif des Maures 847
    Méribel 517
    Millau 749
    Nive Valley 665
    Parc Naturel Régional des Grands
        Causses 746
    Parc Naturel Regionel du
        Haut-Jura 544-5
    Parc Naturel Régional du
        Lubéron 799
    Paris 131-2
    Paris-Roubaix 233
    Prades 757
    Puy de Sancy 560
    Quercy 598
    St-Jean Pied de Port 665
    Sarlat-la-Canéda 588-9
    Tour de France 45, 136, 166
    Val d'Isère 518
    Vallée du Cousin 439
    Vézelay 441
    Voie Verte 465
    Voie Verte des Gaves 678
    Vosges, the 352

INDEX

INDEX

D

D-Day beaches 264-5, 266-8
    tours 268
    landings 35
da Vinci, Leonardo 413-14
Dadaism 55
Dali, Salvador 755
Dambach-la-Ville 359
d'Angers, David 420
Dargilan 746
Dauphiné 521-35
de Gaulle, Charles 30, 36-8, 205, 340
Deauville 254-6
Debussy, Claude 51
Deep Vein Thrombosis (DVT) 929
Défilé de Ruoms 488
Delacroix, Eugène 54
Delville Wood 226
denim 733
Dentelles de Montmirail 795
Depardieu, Gérard 50
départements 906-7, **907**
d'Estaing, Valéry Giscard 39
Dewulf and Marchand dunes 220
Dienne 562
Dieppe 245-8, **246**
Digne-les-Bains 810-12, 684-5
Dijon 444-52, **446-7**
Dinan 289-92, **291**, 140-1
Dinard 286-9, **287**
disabled travellers 901-2
Disneyland Resort Paris 184-5
diving
    Arcachon 643
    Corsica 876
    Nice 824
    St-Jean de Luz 660
    St-Raphaël 843
    Socoa 660
    Toulon 850
Dole 540-1
Domaine National de Chambord 402
Domme 595-6
donkey treks 684, 742
Dordogne, the 582-98, **572**, **592**
    food 68-9
Dordogne Périgourdine 595-7
Douarnenez 302
Doué-la-Fontaine 423
Dreyfus affair 34

000 Map pages
000 Location of colour photographs

drinks, *see also* wine
    alcoholic 70-3
    bars 74
    beer 73, 351-2
    cider 73
    cointreau 420
    nonalcoholic 73
drugs 906
Dune de Pyla 61, 644
Dunes de la Slack 215
dunes flamandes 220
Dunkirk 219-20

E

École Nationale d'Équitation 423
Écomusée d'Alsace 370
Écomusée de la Tradition Basque 660
economy 26, 42
Edict of Nantes 30
education 42
Église Abbatiale, Cluny 463
Église Abbatiale de St-Robert 564
Église des Dominicains 365
Église des Jacobins 698
Église Jeanne d'Arc 240
Église Monolithe 639
Église Notre Dame
    Alençon 275
    Dijon 448
Église Notre Dame de Pontorson 274
Église Notre Dame du Marthuret 553
Église Notre Dame la Grande 618
Église St-Eustache 116-17
Église St-Germain des Prés 122
Église St-Jean Baptiste
    Calvi 872
    St-Jean de Luz 660
Église St-Lazare 437
Église St-Michel 448
Église St-Michel des Lions 575
Église Ste-Catherine 252
Église Ste-Madeleine 336-7
Eiffel Tower 34, 125-6, **108-9**
electricity 893
email access 905-6
embassies 902-3
emergencies 109, 934, *see also inside front cover*
enamelware 573-5
Enclos Cigognes, Munster 57, 368
environmental issues 56-62
Épernay 331-4, **332**
Erbalunga 871
Espace Killy 517
Espelette 663

Esplanade des Invalides 125
Essoyes 340
Étang de Vaccarès 806
Étang du Fangassier 806
Étretat 249, **140-1**
Etsaut 684
European Court of Human Rights 350
European Parliament 350
Eurostar 919
Eurotunnel 917-19
Évian-les-Bains 508
Évisa 878
existentialism 48, 122
Èze 852, 11

F

Falaise aux Vautours 685
Falaise d'Amont 249
Falaise d'Aval 249
Far Northern France 200-34, **202**
Faubourg St-Germain 124-5
fauna, *see* animals *and* birds
fauvism 55, 758
faux de Verzy 331
Fécamp 248-9
Felletin 578
Ferney-Voltaire 545
ferry services 919-21
festivals 14, 903-4, *see also* special events
    American Film Festival 255
    Braderie de Lille 205
    Brest 2008 297
    Cannes Film Festival 836
    Christmas markets 352, 365
    Festival d'Avignon 787
    Festival de Cornouaille, Quimper 303
    Festival Interceltique, Lorient 309
    Fêtes de Bayonne 651
    Fêtes Napoliennes, Ajaccio 884
    Foire Régionale des Vins d'Alsace, Colmar 365
    food 73-4
    Gay Pride 94
    Grenoble Jazz Festival 525
    Hospices de Beaune wine auctions 456
    Nice Jazz Festival 825
    Nuits de Champagne, Troyes 338
    Paris 135-6
    snail festival, Beatric Burée 587
Festival Interceltique, Lorient 904
Fifth Republic 38-9
Figeac 604-5
Filitosa 885

INDEX

films, *see* cinema
Finistère 294-308
fires 59-60
fishing 518
Flame of Liberty 126
flamingos 58, 806
Flaubert, Gustave 48
Flavigny-sur-Ozerain 458-9
Fleury 385
flora, *see* plants
Florac 742-4
Foix 691-2
Fondation Maeght 833
Fontaine de Vaucluse 797-8
Fontainebleau 189-92, **190**
Fontaines Salées 442
food 21, 63-70, 904, **66**
   Alsace 67
   Auvergne 69
   Basque 69, 663
   brasseries 74
   Brittany 67
   Burgundy 68
   cafés 74
   chain restaurants 151
   cheese 63-5, 78, 543, 562, 750
   children 76
   cooking courses 79
   customs 76-7
   festivals 73-4
   Languedoc 69
   Loire Region 68
   Lyon 68
   Normandy 65-7
   Périgord 68-9
   Provence 69
   restaurants 75-6
   salons de thé 76
   vegetarian 76
   vocabulary 80-4
   winstubs 353
football 44, 165-6
forests 58
Forêt d'Aïtone 878
Forêt de Chantilly 194-5
Forêt de Fontainebleau 191
Forêt de la Chêne Rond 423
Forêt de Paimpont 318-19
Forêt de Vizzavona 892
Forêt Domaniale de Verdun 386
Forêt d'Orléans 394
Forêt du Crêt du Maure 510
Fort Boyard 626
Fort de Douaumont 385
Fort de Fermont 386

Fort de la Bastille, Grenoble 523-4
Fort de Souville 386
Fort de Vaux 386
Fort du Hackenberg 382
Forteresse de Polignac 568
Forum des Halles 116
Four-à-Chaux 344
Fourcès 716
Fourvière, Lyon 473
Foyer Ski de Fond Orcival Guéry 558
Fréjus 841-4
French Resistance, the 35
French Revolution, the 31, 32, 185
Fresque des Lyonnais 474
Front National (FN) 39, 46
Futuroscope, Poitiers 619

G
Gabas 686
galleries, *see* museums & galleries
Gauguin, Paul 55
Gavarnie 690
gay travellers 904-5
   Bordeaux 635
   Gay Pride 904
   Montpellier 724
   Paris 136, 161-2
   Strasbourg 355
Gèdre 690
Gennes 423
geography 56
geology 56
Germigny des Prés 395
giants 208
Gien 396
Giersberg 361
Gimel-les-Cascades 580-1
Gironde Estuary 637
Gitans 808
gîtes d'étape 895
gîtes ruraux 894
Giverny 243-4, **10**
Glacier des Sources d'Isère 518
Glacier du Mont de Lans 530
gliding 896
golden eagles 57
Golfe de Porto 876
Golfe du Morbihan 308-18, **317**
   islands 317-18
Gordes 798
Gorges de la Jonte 747
Gorges de la Ligne 488
Gorges de la Restonica 892
Gorges de l'Allier 568-9

Gorges de l'Ardèche 488
Gorges de Spelunca 877
Gorges du Tarn 745-6
Gorges du Verdon 812-14
Gouffre de Padirac 608
government 906-7, **907**
Grand' Place, Arras 221, **140-1**
Grand Balcon Nord 502
Grand Balcon Sud 502
Grand Ballon 369
Grand Pissaillas glacier 520
Grand Prix Automobile de Monaco 857
Grande Arche de La Défense 54, 180
Grande Corniche 852
Grandes Écuries, Château de Chantilly 194, **140-1**
Grande Île, Strasbourg 348-9
Grande Plage
   Quiberon 312
   St-Malo 284
Grande Pyramide 114
Grande Traversée du Jura 544
grandes randonnées (GR), *see* walks
Grasse 840-1
Grenoble 521-8, **522-3**
Grimaldi family 854
Grimaud 847
Grotte Chauvet-Pont d'Arc 27
Grotte de Font de Gaume 593
Grotte de la Mer de Glace 500
Grotte de l'Apothicairerie 313-14
Grotte de Lascaux I 595
Grotte de Lascaux II 595
Grotte de l'Ermitage 639
Grotte de Pech Merle 603
Grotte de Rouffignac 593
Grotte des Combarelles 593
Grotte du Grand Roc 593
Grottes de Bétharram 680
Grottes de Sare 663
Groupe Épiscopal 843
guillotine 31
Gujan Mestras 645

H
hang-gliding 896, *see also* paragliding
   Massif Central 548
   Ménez-Hom 300
   Millau 749
   Puy de Dôme 553
Haras National
   Cluny 463
   Compiègne 233
Hartmannswillerkopf 369

INDEX

Hau Kœnigsbourg 360
Haut Ribeaupierre 361
Haute Corniche 488
Hautvillers 331
health 929-30
heli-skiing 501-2, 518
Herrengarten lime tree 360
hiking, *see* walking
history 27-40
hitching 925-6
holidays 13, 905, *see also* festivals *and* special events
Honfleur 251-4
Horloge Astronomique, Besançon 537
horse racing 166
horse riding
    Accous 683
    Alps, the 496
    Camargue, the 808
    Gorges du Tarn 745
    Gorges du Verdon 813
    Haras National, Compiègne 233
hostels 894-5
hot-air ballooning 401, 428, 896
Hôtel des Invalides 125
Hôtel-Dieu des Hospices de Beaune 454, 396-7
hôtels particuliers
    Condom 714
    Dijon 448
    Paris 117
    Montpellier 721
    Toulouse 700
Houdini 399
Huelgoat 301-2
Hugo, Victor 47-8
Huguenots 30, 569
Hunawihr 361
Hundred Years' War 29
hunting 60, 396, 403, 900

I

ibex 57, 60, 519, 520
Île aux Moines 317-18
Île d'Aix 626
Île d'Arz 317-18
Île de Batz 296
Île de Groix 309
Île de la Cité 119-20
Île de la Pietra 876
Île de Ré 625

Île de St-Nicolas 308
Île des Landes 289
Île d'Oléron 626
Île d'Ouessant 298-300
Île du Grand Bé 283
Île Feydeau 613
Île Rousse 875-6
Île St-Honorat 840
Île St-Louis 120-1
Île Ste-Marguerite 840
Îles de Glénan 308
Îles de Lérins 840
Îles d'Hyères 848
Îles du Frioul 770-1
immigration 45-6, 52
impressionism 54-5
in-line skating
    Annecy 510
    Lyon 475
    Paris 132
    Voie Verte 465
Ingres, Jean Auguste Dominique 709-10
insects 57, 751
insurance
    car 924-5
    health 905, 929
    skiing 495-7
    travel 905
International Film Festival, Cannes 904
Internet
    access 905-6
    resources 15
Irsula Rosa, *see* Île Rousse
Issenheim Altarpiece 364
itineraries 16-22, 23
    Artsy Way, The 21, **21**
    Author's Favourite Trip 23, **23**
    Coast to Coast 17, **17**
    Kidding Around 22, **22**
    Mountain Adventure, A 19, **19**
    Quirky France 20, **20**
    Tastebuds on Tour 21, **21**
    Timeless Classics 16, **16**
    Tour de France 18, **18**
    World Heritage Sites 22, **22**
izards 59, 680

J

Jardin des Plantes 121-2
Jardin des Tuileries 115
Jardin du Luxembourg 123
Jargeau 394
jazz 51-2
    festivals, Paris 136
Jeu de Paume 115

Joan of Arc 29, 336, 390
    La Tour Jeanne d'Arc 240-1
    Les Fêtes Johanniques 329
    Maison de Jeanne d'Arc 391
Josselin 318
Joyeux 484
Juan-les-Pins 831-2
Judaism 118, 351
Juno Beach 264, 267
Juppé, Alain 39
Jura, the 535-45, **536**

K

kayaking 898, *see also* canoeing
    Arcachon 643
    Camargue, the 808
    Dinard 287
    Gorges du Tarn 745
    River Gard 738
Kaysersberg 362
Kerlescan megaliths 310-11
Kermario megaliths 311
King Arthur 279
Klein, Yves 55

L

La Balagne 875
La Bourboule 561
La Cazelle 745
La Chaise Dieu 564
La Cité, Carcassonne 730, 9
La Clusaz 512
La Corniche Sublime 813
La Coupole 214
La Couvertoirade 747
La Croix des Boutières 569
La Défense 179-82, **179**, 8
La Dombes 485
La Face de Bellevarde 517
La Falaise aux Vautours 57
La Foux d'Allos 814
La Garde Freinet 847
La Grande Motte 725
La Grande Pêche à la Morue 292
La Malène 745
La Marseillaise 349
La Meije 530-1
La Moutte 845
La Palud-sur-Verdon 813
La Piscine Musée d'Art et d'Industrie 205
La Puisaye 433
La Rhune 662-3
La Rochelle 620-5, **621**, 428-9
La Romieu 716

La Roque Gageac 596
La Roque St-Christophe 594
La Sauvette 847
La Sologne 396
La Turbie 852
La Villette 130-1
Labouiche 692
Lac Blanc 502
Lac Chambon 561
Lac d'Annecy 509-13, 11
Lac de Capitello 892
Lac de Gaube 688
Lac de Guéry 558
Lac de Mello 892
Lac du Chevril 519
Lac du Mont Cénis 520
Lac Nino 892
Lac Pavin 561
Lacanau-Océan 637
lace-making 211, 262, 275, 565
Lake Geneva 507
Lake Tueda 517
Landévennec 300
Langeais 411-12
Langres 340
language 41, 932-7, 938-9
    Alsatian 345
    Basque 648
    Breton 279-81
    Catalan 751
    Corsican 862
    courses 900
    food vocabulary 80-4
    Occitan 720
    Provençal 763
Languedoc 720-59, **719**, **740**
    food 69
    wine 71
Lans-en-Vercors 528, 529
Lanslebourg 520
Laon 233-4
Larche 814
Larressingle 716
Laruns 685-6
Lascaux 27, 591, 595
Latin Quarter 121-2
Lectoure 716
legal matters 906
Léger, Fernand 832-3
Le Brévent 499
Le Bugue 591
Le Chambon-sur-Lignon 569
Le Clos Lucé 413-4
Le Conquet 298
Le Corbusier 53, 542

Le Creusot 462-3
Le Dramont 841
Le Grand Bornand 512
Le Grand Serre Chevalier 535
Le Havre 249-51
Le Lavandou 847-8
Le Magasin 524
Le Ménec 310-11
Le Mont-Dore 558-61, **559**
Le Moustier 594
Le Pen, Jean-Marie 40, 46
Le Puy-en-Velay 564-8, **566**
Le Saut aux Loups 424
Le Semnoz 512
Le Teich Parc Ornithologique 645
Le Thot – Espace Cro-Magnon 594,
    428-9
Le Touquet 217
Le Trayas 841
Le Vaisseau 351
Le Vistaëro 852
leagal matters 906
Les Andelys 243
Les Arcs-sur-Argens 847
Les Arènes
    Arles 802
    Nîmes 733
Les Baux de Provence 791
Les Calanques de Piana 879
Les Deux Alpes 528, 530-1
Les Eyzies de Tayac 591-2
Les Get 507
Les Gorges du Gardon 738
Les Maisons Satie 252
Les Perrières 424
Les Portes du Solei 507
Les Riceys 340
Les Rousses 545
Les Stes-Maries de la Mer 807-9
lesbian travellers 904-5, see also gay
    travellers
Lescun 683-4
libraries, see individual entries under
    bibliothèque
Lille 202-9, **204**, 140-1
Lilleau des Niges 625
Limeuil 592
Limoges 573-7, **574**
Limousin 572-82, **572**
literature 47-9
    Paris 124
Loches 415-16
Locronan 302
L'Odyssée Blanche – Parc du Chien
    Polaire 544

Loire Region 387-424, **389**
    climate 390
    food 68
    history 390
    transport 390
    wine 71
Longues-sur-Mer 267
Lorient 308-10
Lorraine 370-86, **371**
Lorraine American Cemetery
    386
Louis XIV 30, 128
Louis XVI 31, 87, 185, 330
Lourdes 675-80, **676**
Louvre 54, 113-15, 7
Lubéron, the 799-800, 684-5
Luchon, see Bagnères de Luchon
Lumière brothers 49, 475
Luzech 607
Lyon 468-84, **470-2**, **475**
    accommodation 476-8
    activities 475-6
    entertainment 482-3
    food 68
    information 469-72
    sights 472-5
    travel to/from 483
    travel within 483-4

M
Macinaggio 871
Mâcon 465
magazines 160, 893
Maginot Line, the 35, 344, 386
Maison de la Magie 399
Maison des Mégalithes 310
Malaucène 795
Malraux, André 249-50
Manche 268-76
Mandelieu-La Napoule 841
Manet, Édouard 54
maps 906-8
maquis 58
Maquis Bernard Résistance
    Cemetery 444
Marais 117-19
Marais Audemarois 214
Marais Poitevin 619-20
Marie Antoinette 87, 120, 128, 188,
    330
markets
    Paris 168, 169
    Provence 776, 797
    truffles, Uzès 739
marmots 57, 519, 680

Marseille 763-76, **764-5**, **768**
  accommodation 772
  food 773-4
  information 767
  sights 769-71
  travel to/from 775
  travel within 776
Marshall Plan 36
Massif Central 546-69, **548**
Massif de l'Estérel 841
Massif des Maures 847
Massif des Vosges 367-9
Matisse, Henri 55, 823, 834
May Day celebrations 904
Médoc, the 637-8
megalithic sites 52
  Carnac 310-11
  Filitosa 885
Megève 506-7
Mémorial de Verdun 385
Mémorial Indien, Arras 225
Mémorial – Un Musée pour la Paix 256
Mende 744
Ménec megaliths 310-11
Ménerbes 800
Ménez-Hom 300
Menthon-St-Bernard 512
Menton 852-4
Mer de Glace 500
Méribel 516-17
Métabief Mont d'Or 543-4
Metz 377-82, **378-9**
Meuse-Argonne American Cemetery 386
Micropolis 751
Mijoux 545
military cemeteries, *see* WWI *and* WWII
Millau 747-50, **748**
Millet, Jean-François 54
Mittelbergheim 359
Mitterrand, François 39
mobile phones 910-11
Moët & Chandon 333
Moirans-en-Montagne 544
Moissac 711
Monaco 854-9, **855**
Monet, Claude 54, 243-4
money 13, 908-9, *see also inside front cover*
  discount cards 902

Monistrol d'Allier 568-9
Monpazier 597
Mont Aigoual 742
Mont Blanc 56, 497, 10
Mont Canigou 757, 758
Mont Faron 850
Mont Frugy 303
Mont Lozère 741-2
Mont Mézenc 569
Mont St-Cyr 601
Mont St-Michel 272-5
Mont St-Romain 465
Mont Ste-Odile 358-9
Mont Serein 795
Mont Sinaï 331
Mont Ventoux 795-6
Montauban 709-11
Montbenoît 544
Monte Carlo 856, 859
Montélimar 487
Montgolfier brothers 487
Monthou-sur-Cher 401
Montignac 594-5
Montlouis-sur-Loire 409
Monmartre 130, **108**, 6
Montparnasse 123-4
Montpellier 720-5, **722-3**
Montréal 716
Monts Dômes 554
Monts Dore 554
Monts du Cantal 61, 554
Montsoreau 424
Morbihan Coast 308-18
Morgat 301
Morzine 507
Mosquée de Paris 122
motorcycle travel, *see also* car travel
  to/from France 917-19
  within France 923-5
mouflons 57
Moulin Rouge 165
mountain biking, *see* cycling
mountaineering 896
Moyenne Corniche 852
Mulhouse 369-70
Munster 368
Mur Païen 359
murals
  Cité de la Création, Lyon 474
  metro, Paris 174-5
Murat 562-3
museums & galleries
  Galerie David d'Angers 420
  Galerie Municipale du Château
    d'Eau 700

Galerie Nationale du Jeu de
  Paume 115
Le Magasin 524
Les Maisons Satie 252
Musée Alsacien 350
Musée Animé du Vin 426-7
Musée Archéologique 448-9
Musée Bartholdi 364
Musée Basque et de l'Histoire de
  Bayonne 650
Musée Camarguais 807
Musée Carnavalet 118
Musée Claude Monet 243-4, 10
Musée d'Archéologique d'Arles 802
Musée d'Art Américain 244
Musée d'Art et d'Histoire, La
  Défense 183
Musée d'Art et d'Histoire du
  Judaïsme 118
Musée d'Art Moderne, Céret 756
Musée d'Art Moderne, Lille 203-4
Musée d'Art Moderne, Troyes 337
Musée d'Art Moderne et
  Contemporain, Strasbourg 350
Musée d'Art Moderne et
  Contemporain, Nice 822-3
Musée d'Art Roger Quilliot 551
Musée d'Automobiles 327
Musée de Béatrice Ephrussi de
  Rothschild 853
Musée de Grenoble 524
Musée de la Civilisation
  Gallo-Romaine 473
Musée de la Cohue 315-16
Musée de la Compagnie des
  Indes 309
Musée de la Guerre 211
Musée de la Mer, Biarritz 654
Musée de la Mer, Îles des Lérins
  840
Musée de la Mer, Paimpol 292
Musée de la Mode 769
Musée de la Résistance et de la
  Déportation, Limoges 575
Musée de la Résistance et de la
  Déportation de l'Isère 524
Musée de la Tapisserie de Bayeux
  262
Musée de la Vigne et du Vin
  d'Anjou 422
Musée de l'Annonciade 844
Musée de l'Armagnac 714
Musée de l'Art Troyen 337
Musée de l'École de Nancy 372
Musée de l'Hôtel Goüin 405

Musée de l'Imprimerie 474
Musée de l'Impression sur Étoffes 370
Musée de l'Œuvre Notre-Dame 349-50
Musée de Picardie 229
Musée de Préhistoire 310
Musée Départemental de la Tapisserie 578
Musée des Arts Décoratifs 474
Musée des Arts et Métiers 118-19
Musée des Augustins 698
Musée des Beaux-Arts, Arras 221
Musée des Beaux-Arts, Bordeaux 632
Musée des Beaux-Arts, Dijon 448
Musée des Beaux-Arts, Lyon 473
Musée des Beaux-Arts, Nancy 372-3
Musée des Beaux-Arts, Nice 823
Musée des Beaux-Arts, Orléans 391
Musée des Beaux-Arts, Rennes 319
Musée des Beaux-Arts, Tours 405
Musée des Beaux-Arts André-Malraux 249-50
Musée des Beaux-Arts et d'Archéologie 537
Musée des Beaux-Arts et de la Dentelle 275
Musée des Égouts de Paris 126
Musée des Jacobins 712-13
Musée des Phares et des Balises 299
Musée des Tissus 474
Musée d'Histoire de Marseille 769
Musée d'Histoire et d'Archéologie 316
Musée d'Histoire Naturelle, Dijon 449
Musée d'Histoire Naturelle, Nantes 612, **428-9**
Musée d'Orsay 54, 124-5, 9
Musée du Bateau 302
Musée du Champignon 423
Musée du Château de St-Malo 283
Musée du Châtillonnais 459
Musée du Jouet 364-5
Musée du Louvre 54, 113-14
Musée du Luxembourg 123
Musée du Papier Peint 370
Musée du Périgord 585
Musée du Quay Branly 53
Musée du Santon 769
Musée d'Unterlinden 364
Musée et Site Archéologiques 823
Musée Eugène Boudin 252

Musée Français du Chemin de Fer 370
Musée Franco-Australien 226
Musée Goya 709
Musée Granet 779
Musée Historique Lorrain 373
Musée Ingres 709-10
Musée Jean Cocteau 853
Musée Jean Lurçat et de la Tapisserie Contemporaine 420
Musée Lapidaire, Avignon 787
Musée Lapidaire, Lectoure 716
Musée Lumière 475
Musée Maritime Neptunea 622
Musée Matisse 823
Musée Mémorial 1944 Bataille de Normandie 262
Musée National de la Coopération Franco-Américaine 234
Musée National de l'Automobile 369-70
Musée National de Préhistoire 591
Musée National d'Histoire Naturelle 122
Musée National du Moyen Âge 121
Musée National Message Biblique Marc Chagall 823
Musée Océanographique de Monaco 857
Musée Picasso, Antibes 832
Musée Picasso, Paris 118
Musée Pierre de Luxembourg 791
Musée Reattu 803
Musée Rodin 125
Musée St-Remi 327
Musée Thomas Henry 269
Musée Toulouse-Lautrec 706-7
Museon Arlaten 802-3
Museu di a Corsica 891
Muséum d'Histoire Naturelle, Tours 405
Vesunna Musée Gallo-Romain de Périgueux 54, 586
music 51-2
Cité de la Musique, Paris 131
mustard 449

N
Najac 606-7, **428-9**
Nancy 370-6, **374-5**, **396-7**
Nantes 612-17, **614-5**
Napoleon Bonaparte 32, 191, 882, 884
Narbonne 727
National Day 904

national parks & reserves 58-9, *see also individual entries under* Parc *and* Réserve
Alps, the 492
naturism 626, 848, 845
Natzweiler-Struthof 357
Nausicaä, Boulogne-sur-Mer 217
newspapers 46, 893
Nice 818-31, **820-1**
accommodation 825-7
activities 824
food 827-8
information 819-22
sights 822-3
travel to/from 829-30
travel within 830-1
Nièvre 442-4
Nîmes 733-7, **734**
Nonza 871
Normandy 235-76, **237**
history 238
travel to/from 238
Notre Dame Cathedral, Paris 119-20, **396-7**
nougat 487
Noyers-sur-Serein 435
nuclear
power 60, 485
testing 39
waste 60-1

O
Obernai 358
Océanopolis 297
oil spills 60
Omaha Beach 264-5, 267, 6
Oradour-sur-Glane 577
Orange 791-3
Orangerie, Paris 115
orchids 58
Orcival 558
Orléanais 390-7
Orléans 390-4, **392**
Ornans 540
ospreys 58
Ossuaire de Douaumont 385
oysters 289, 645, 12
Ota 878

P
Pagode de Chanteloup 415
Paimpol 292-3
Paimpont 318
painting 21, 54-5
Palais Bénédictine 248

INDEX

Palais de l'Europe 350
Palais des Beaux-Arts 203
Palais des Droits de l'Homme 350
Palais des Ducs et des États de
    Bourgogne 445-8
Palais des Papes 52, 786, **684-5**
Palais des Rois de Majorque 753
Palais du Prince 856-7
Palais du Tau 327
Palais Rohan 350
Palais Royal 115-16
Palavas-les-Flots 725
Palme d'Or 51
Panthéon 121
paragliding 896, see also hang-gliding
    Accous 682-3
    Alps, the 496
    Chamonix 502
    Les Deux Alpes, 531
    Millau 749
    Nice 824
    Paray-le-Monial 463
    Parc National des Écrins 529-30
    Superbagnères 691
parapente, see paragliding
Parc de la Villette 130-1
Parc des Oiseaux 57
Parc du Gévaudan 57, 745
Parc National de la Vanoise 57-60,
    519-21, **428-9**
Parc National de Port-Cros 59, 848
Parc National des Cévennes 58, 59,
    741-2
Parc National des Écrins 59, 529-30
Parc National des Pyrénées 59, 680-1
Parc National du Mercantour 57, 59
Parc Naturel Interrégional du Marais
    Poitevin 619-20
Parc Naturel Régional d'Armorique 300
Parc Naturel Régional de Camargue
    806-7
Parc Naturel Régional de Chartreuse
    516
Parc Naturel Régional de la Montagne
    de Reims 61, 331
Parc Naturel Régional des Ballons des
    Vosges 367
Parc Naturel Régional des Grands
    Causses 57, 61, 746-7
Parc Naturel Régional des Volcans
    d'Auvergne 61, 554-63

000 Map pages
000 Location of colour photographs

Parc Naturel Régionel du Haut-Jura
    544-5
Parc Naturel Régional du Lubéron
    799, 800
Parc Naturel Régional du Massif des
    Bauges 516
Parc Naturel Régional du Morvan
    442-4
Parc Naturel Régional du Pilat 487
Parc Naturel Régional du Vercors 528-9
Parc Naturel Régional Livradois-Forez
    563-9
Parc Naturel Régional Nord-Pas-de-
    Calais 215
Parc Ornithologique, Le Tech 57
Parc Ornithologique du Marquenterre
    217
Paris 85-176, **90-108**, **108-9**
    accommodation 136-47
    activities 131-2
    arrondissements 88, **88**
    drinking 158-60
    entertainment 160-7
    festivals 135-6
    food 147-58
    information 89-112
    metro 173-6, **facing 108**
    shopping 167-70
    sights 113-31
    tourist information 111-12
    tours 134-5
    travel agencies 112
    travel to/from 170-1
    travel within 171-6
    walking tour 132-4, **133**
passports 911-12, 914 see also visas
Pasteur, Louis 540-1
Pas de Peyrol 562
Pau 669-75, **673**
pelota 648, 653
Péronne 225-6
Pérouges 485
Perpignan 751-6, **752**
Perrier 737-8
Perros-Guirec 293-4
pétanque 45, 749
    festival 749
Petit Train d'Artouste 686
Petit Train de la Rhune 662
Petite France 349
Peyrepertuse fortress 757
photography 909

Piaf, Edith 132
Piana 878-9
Pic du Jer 678
Pic du Midi de Bigorre 690
Picasso, Pablo 55, 118, 130, 832
Pierre-Perthuis 442
Pietracorbara 871
Pigalle 130
pilgrimage routes see Santiago de
    Compostela and walks
Pino 871
Place de la Concorde 127-8
Place Stanislas 372, **396-7**
Plage de Bon Secours 284, **140-1**
Plage de l'Écluse 286
Plage de l'Escalet 845
Plage de Rochebonne 284
Plage de Tahiti 844-5
Plage de Trestraou 293
Plage de Trestrignel 293
Plage des Bas Sablons 284
Plage des Grands Sables 314
Plage des Sables Blancs
Plage du Cabellou 306
Plage du Château 293
planning 13-15, see also itineraries
    discount cards 902
    health 929
    public holidays 905
plants 58
Plan Vigipirate 901
Plomb du Cantal 562
Point Sublime 813
point zéro des routes de France 119
Pointe de la Parata 882
Pointe de Pen-Hir 301
Pointe du Grouin 289
Pointe du Hoc Ranger Memorial 267-8
Pointe Helbronner 499
pointillism 55, 601
Poitiers 617-19
Poligny 541
politics 26, 39-40
    Corsica 862
Pomègues 770-1
Pompidou, Georges 39
Pompidou Centre 116, **108-9**
Pont-Aven school 319
Pont d'Arc 488, **428-9**
Pont d'Avignon 786
Pont de l'Artuby 813
Pont d'Espagne 688
Pont du Gard 738, **652-3**
Pont Neuf 120
Pont St-Bénézet 786

Pont Valentré 599
Pontigny 434-5
Pontorson 273-5
population 26, 43
porcelainware 573-5
Porquerolles 848
Port-Cros 59, 848
Port de Donnant 314
Port Kérel 314
Port-Vendres 759
Porto 876-8
Portu, see Porto
postal services 909
Poussin, Nicolas 54
power generation 60
Pra-Loup 814
Prades 568, 757
prehistoric sites 591-5, see also
    megalithic sites
Presqu'île de Crozon 300-1
Proust, Marcel 48
Provence 760-814, **762**
    culture 684-5
    food 69
    language 763
ptarmigans 57
public holidays 13, 905
public transport 926
Pupillin 541
Puy de Dôme 553
Puy de Sancy 559-60
Puy l'Évêque 607
Puy Mary 562
Pyrenees, the 667-92, **670-1**

Q
Quercy 598-608, **572**
Quéribus fortress 757
Quiberon 312-13
Quimper 302-5, **304**
quirky France 14, 20

R
Rabelais, François 47, 48
radio 893
rafting 898
    Alps 498
    Annecy 510
    Gorges du Verdon 813
    Parc National des Pyrénées 681
    Superbagnères 691
Rance Estuary 281
Rashi 337
Ratonneau 770-1
Ravel, Maurice 51

Ravin de la Mort 385-6
realism 54
refuges 895
regional parks, see individual entries
    under Parc Naturel Régional
régions 906-7, **907**
Reims 325-30, **326**
religion 46-7
Rémy Martin 628
Rennes 319-22, **320**
Renoir, Pierre-Auguste 55
Réserve de Bisons d'Europe 57, 745
Réserve Naturelle de Scandola 58, 876
Réserve Naturelle de Tueda 517
Réserve Naturelle Géologique 811
Réserve Naturelle Géologique de
    Haute-Provence 61
Réserve Naturelle Marine 759
restaurants 75-6
Rhône Valley 466-88, **468**
    wine 72
Ribeauvillé 360-2
Riom 553-4
Riquewihr 361-2
River Gard 738
River Garonne 701, 652-3
River Rance 290, 140-1
Roc de Chère 510
Rocamadour 607-8
Rochefort 626
Rochemenier 424
Rocher de la Vierge 655
rock climbing 896
    Conduché 603
    Forêt de Fontainebleau 191
    La Roque Gageac 596
    Millau 749
Rodin, Auguste 125
Rodolphe Potassium Mine 370
Roman architecture 52
Roman sites
    Alésia 459
    Arc de Triomphe, Orange 792
    Autun 461
    Bordeaux 631
    Cahors 599
    Fontaines Salées 442
    Fourvière, Lyon 473
    Fréjus 842-3
    Gennes 423
    Les Arènes, Arles 802
    Les Arènes, Nîmes 733
    Maison Carrée, Nîmes 733-4
    Nice 823
    Nîmes 733-5

Périgueux 585-6
Pont du Gard 738, 652-3
Reims 328
Séviac 716
Théâtre Antique, Arles 802
Théâtre Antique, Orange 792
Vaison-la-Romaine 793-4
Vienne 486
Ronchamp 542
Roquebrune 852
Roquefort 750-1
Roscoff 294-6
Rouen 238-43, **239**
Rousseau, Jean-Jacques 47, 514
Roussillon 799
Roussillon Region 751-9, **719**
Route des Crêtes 368-9
Route du Vin d'Alsace 357-62
Route Pasteur 540-1
Route Touristique du Champagne 331,
    340, 396-7
Royan 627
Rue Grande, St-Paul de Vence 833,
    684-5
rugby 44-5
Ruoms 488
Russan 738

S
Sacré Cœur 130
safe travel
    hitching 925-6
    Paris 112
    security 901
    skiing 492-3
    walking 900
sailing
    Cherbourg 269
    Menton 853
    Nice 824
    Socoa 660
St-Benoît-sur-Loire 395
St Bertrand de Comminges 690
St-Brisson 443
St-Cirq Lapopie 603-4
St-Denis 182-4, **182**
St-Émilion 639-41, **640**
St-Étienne 485-6
St-Étienne de Baïgorry 666
St-Florent 871
St-George des Sept Voies 423
St-Germain 122-3
St-Gervais 506-7
St-Hilaire-St-Florent 423
St-Jean-Cap Ferrat 851-2

INDEX

St-Jean de Luz 658-62, **659**
St-Jean Pied de Port 663-6, **664**, 652-3
St-Léon-sur-Vézère 594
St-Malo 281-6, **282**
St-Martin de l'Ardèche 488
St-Martin de Ré 625-6
St-Martin-le-Redon 607
St-Mihiel American Cemetery 386
St-Nectaire 561-3
St-Omer 214
St-Paul de Vence 833-4, **684-5**
St-Paul-sur-Ubaye 814
St-Péray 488
St-Père-sous-Vézelay 442
St-Raphaël 841-4
St-Rémy de Provence 791
St-Servan 283-4, **282**
St-Tropez 844-7
St-Ulrich 361
Ste-Chapelle 120, **108-9**
Ste-Claude 544
Ste-Énimie 746
Ste-Eulalie 747
Ste-Ménehould 330
Saline Royal 540
salons de thé 76
Sancerre 396
Sanctuaires Notre Dame de Lourdes
    677, **652-3**
Sangatte 215
Santiago de Compostela 440, 565,
    578, 604, 665, 684, 711, 716
Saône-et-Loire 459-65
Sare 663
Sarlat-la-Canéda 587-91, **588**, **589**
Sartène 885-6
Sartre, Jean-Paul 48
Satie, Erik 252
Saugeais Republic 544
Saulieu 443
Sault 795
Saumur 423-4
Savelot 444
Savoy, the 497-521
Schœnenbourg 344
sea caves 301
seaweed harvesters 295
Sélestat 359-60
Semur-en-Auxois 457-8
senior travellers
    discount cards 902

000 Map pages
000 Location of colour photographs

Senlis 195-6
Sète 725-6
Séviac 716
Sévrier 512
shopping 909-10
    Calais 213
    food 77-9
    Paris markets 168, 169
    Provençal markets 776
    Troyes 336
Sisco 871
skiing 896-7
    Alpe d'Huez 531
    Alps, the 493-6
    Ax-les-Thermes 692
    Bagnères de Luchon 690-1
    Cauterets 686-8
    Chambéry 514
    Chamonix 500-2
    Col de Guéry 558
    Grande Traversée du Jura 544
    Grenoble 525
    Internet resources 493
    Le Grand Serre Chevalier 535
    Les Deux Alpes 530-1
    Massif Central 548
    Méribel 516-17
    Métabief Mont d'Or 543-4
    Parc National de la Vanoise 520
    Parc National des Cévennes 742
    Parc National des Pyrénées 681
    Parc Naturel Régionel du Haut-Jura
        544-5
    Parc Naturel Régional du Vercors
        528-9
    Portes du Solei 507
    Provence 814
    Puy de Dôme 553
    Puy de Sancy 559-60
    safety 492-3
    schools 495
    Super Besse 559-60
    Super Lioran 562
    Val d'Isère 518
    Vosges, the 367
ski touring 501-2
skydiving 496
smoking 900
snorkelling 759
snow-shoeing
    Alsace 352
    Vosges, the 352
    Cauterets 688
snowboarding see skiing
soccer, see football

Socoa 658
Solignac 578
Sorbonne 121
Sotta Rocca 888
Soulac-sur-Mer 638-9
soupe des chiens 403
Souzay-Champigny 424
spas
    Aix-en-Provence 779
    Ax-les-Thermes 692
    Bagnères de Luchon 690-1
    Cauterets 686-8
    Digne-les-Bains 811
    Évian-les-Bains 508
    Le Mont-Dore 558-9
    St-Nectaire 561-3
    Thalasso Roscoff 295
    Vichy 556
special events 903-4, see also festivals
    Grand Prix Automobile de Monaco
        857
spectator sports 183
spelunking see caving
sports 43-5, see also individual sports
    adventure 896
    Paris 165-6
Stade de France 165, 183
Statue of Liberty, Colmar 364
Stevenson, Robert Louis 742-3
storks 57, 58, 331, 361, 368
Strasbourg 345-57, **346-8**
    accommodation 352-3
    activities 351-2
    drinking 354-5
    entertainment 355-6
    food 353
    information 345-8
    sights 348-51
    travel to/from 356
    travel within 356-7
Strauss, Levi 733
Super Besse 559-60, 561
Superbagnères 691
surfing 898, see also beaches
    Biarritz 654
    Soulac-sur-Mer 638
    St-Jean de Luz 660
swimming 897, see also beaches
    Annecy 509-10
    Dinard 286-7
    Paris 132

T
Tain l'Hermitage 486
Taittinger 328

Talloires 512
Tanlay 436
tapestries
    Aubusson 578-9, 744
    Bayeux Tapestry 262
    Galerie Nationale de la Tapisserie 231
    Gobelins tapestries, Pau 669
    L'Exposition Tapisseries d'Aubusson-Felletin 578
    Manufacture des Gobelins 129-30
    Manufacture Nationale de la Tapisserie 231
    Musée Jean Lurçat et de la Tapisserie Contemporaine 420
Tautavel 756-7
telephone services 910-11
Temple St-Mathieu, Colmar 365
tennis 45, 136, 166
Têt Valley 757-8
thalassotherapy, see spas
theft 112, 901
Théoule-sur-Mer 841
thermal baths, see spas
Thiepval Memorial 226
Thiers 563-4
Thonon-les-Bains 507
tides 900
Tignes 517, 518
time 911, 931
Tonnerre 435-6
Toulon 848-51, **849**
Toulouse 695-705, **696-7**, **699**, 652-3
Toulouse area 693-76, **695**
Toulouse-Lautrec, Henri de 706-7
Tour Beaumont Mémorial du Débarquement, Toulon 850
Tour de France 45, 136, 166
Touraine 404-18
tourist information 911
Tournus 465
Tours 404-9, **406-7**
tours 926
Tourtour 847
traboules 476
Train Bleu 34-5
Train Jaune, Têt Valley 757
train travel **918**
    discount fares 928
    rail passes 919, 928
    security 927
    to/from France 918-19
    within France 927
Tranchée des Baïonnettes, Verdun 385-6

trekking, see walking
Trésor de Vix 459
Troglodyte Valley 423-4
troglodytes 423-424, 593-4, 596, see also caves
Trompe-l'Œil murals 474
Trouville 254-6
Troyes 334-40, **335**, 396-7
Troyes School 337
Tulle 580
Turenne 581
TV 46, 51, 893

U
Ungersheim 370
Uzerche 579
Uzès 738-9

V
vaccinations 929
Vaison-la-Romaine 793-5
Val d'Azun 681
Val d'Isère 517-19
Valence 488
Valéry, Paul 726
Vallée Blanche descent 501
Vallée d'Aspe 681-4
Vallée de Baïgorry 666
Vallée de l'Ariège 691-2
Vallée de Marcadau 688
Vallée de Munster 368
Vallée des Gaves 678, 690
Vallée d'Ossau 684-6
Vallées Cévenoles 742
Vallon Pont d'Arc 488
van Gogh, Vincent 55, 803
Vannes 314-17, **315**
Var hinterland 847
Vauban, Sébastien le Prestre de 30, 283, 532, 537, 649
Vaucluse, the 783-800
Vaux-le-Vicomte 192
Veckring 382
vegetarian travellers 76
Vence 834
Vercingétorix 551
Verdun 382-6, **383**
    tours 384-5
Verne, Jules 229, 612-13
Vernet-les-Bains 758
Versailles 185-9, **186**
Verzy 331
Vesunna Musée Gallo-Romain de Périgueux 54, 586
Vézelay 440-2, **441**

Vézère Valley 591-5, **592**
Viaduc de Millau 747
Vichy 554-8, **555**
video systems 893, 909
Vieil Armand 369
Vienne 486-7
Village des Bories 799
Village Troglodytique de la Madeleine 593-4
Villandry 410-11
Villard de Lans 528, 529
Villars-les-Dombes 485
Villefranche-de-Conflent 757-8
Villefranche de Rouergue 605-6
Villefranche-sur-Mer 851
Villeneuve-lès-Avignon 791
Villers-Bretonneux 226
Vimy Canadian National Memorial & Park 224-5
visas 911-12, see also passports
Voie Verte 465
Voltaire 47
Volvic 554
Vosges, the 367-9
Vouvray 409
Vulcania 553
vultures 57, 685

W
walking 897, see also walks
    Alps, the 496
    Alsace 352
    Annecy 510
    Bagnères de Luchon 690-1
    Ballon d'Alsace 369
    Beaujolais 484
    Bedous 682
    Burgundy 428
    Camargue, the 807-8
    Cauterets 686-8
    Chamonix 502
    Cirque de Gavarnie 690
    Col de Guéry 558
    Conduché 603
    Corsica 864
    Corte 892
    Côte d'Opale 215
    Côte d'Or 453
    Dinard 287
    Domaine National de Chambord 402
    Foix 692
    Gorges de la Vallée de la Montane 580
    Gorges de Spelunca 877
    Gorges du Tarn 745

walking *continued*
Gorges du Verdon 813
Grenoble 525
Huelgoat 302
La Châtaigneraie 879
La Corniche 879
Les Calanques 879
Les Deux Alpes 531
Lescun 683-4
maps 908
Massif Central 548
Massif de l'Estérel 841
Massif des Maures 847
Méribel 517
Millau 749
Mont Ventoux 795
Parc National de la Vanoise 520
Parc National des Cévennes 742
Parc National des Écrins 529-30
Parc National des Pyrénées 681
Parc Naturel Régional des Grands Causses 746
Parc Naturel Régionel du Haut-Jura 544-5
Parc Naturel Régional du Lubéron 799
Parc Naturel Régional du Vercors 528-9
Prades 757
Puy de Dôme 553
Puy de Sancy 560
Quercy 598
Quimper 303
safety 493
St-Jean Pied de Port 665
Val d'Isère 518
Vallée d'Ossau 685
Vallée du Cousin 439
Voie Verte 465
Voie Verte des Gaves 678
Vosges, the 352, 367
walks
Chemin de la Mâture 684
Chemin des Cascades 688
Chemin des Muletiers 879
Chemin du Château 879
GR Littoral trail 215
GR2 428
GR3 396
GR4 548, 795, 813

GR5 369, 496, 520
GR6 598
GR7 428, 453, 569
GR9 795, 799
GR10 665, 683-4
GR20 864
GR21 245
GR34 289
GR36 598
GR46 598
GR55 520
GR60 745
GR62 749
GR65 598, 665
GR73 569
GR76 428, 453
GR92 799
GR97 799
GR652 598
GR653 684
Le Grand Tour de Haute Maurienne 520
Mare a Mare trails 864
Mare e Monti trails 864
pilgrimage routes 440, 565, 578, 604, 665, 684, 711, 716
Sentier de la Briance 578
Sentier de la Vallée du Tarn 745
sentier des douaniers 293
Sentier Littoral 845
war memorials, *see* WWI *and* WWII
Wars of Religion 30
water sports 897-8, *see also individual entries*
weights and measures 893, *see also inside front cover*
white-water rafting, *see also* rafting
Monistrol d'Allier 568-9
wildlife, *see* animals, birds *and* plants
William the Conqueror 259
windsurfing 898
Arcachon 643
Dinard 287
Socoa 660
wine 70-2
Alsace 70-1, 357-62
Bordeaux 71
Burgundy 71, 453, 12
champagne 72, 328, 332-3, 338
Cognac 627
Foire Régionale des Vins d'Alsace 365
Languedoc 71
Loire Region 71
Rhône Region 72

wine-growing
Alsace 357-62
Basque Region 666
Beaujolais 484, 428-9
Bergerac 597-8
Bordeaux 637
Cahors 607
Chablis 434
Côte d'Or 452-3
Côte des Blancs 331
Jura, the 540-1
Mâconnais 465
Médoc, the 637-8
Montagne de Reims 331
Provence 842
Tours area 409
Vallée de la Marne 331
wine-tasting
Amboise 414
Angers 421
Beaune 454-5
Bordeaux 632
Chinon 417
Côte d'Or 453
Médoc, the 638
Provence 847
Route du Vin d'Alsace 357-62
Route Touristique du Champagne 331, 340, 396-7
St-Émilion 640-1
Sentier des Clos 434
Sentier des Grands Crus 434
Sentier Viticole du Frankstein 359
Sentier Viticole du Schenkenberg 358
winstubs 353
Wissant 215
wolves 57, 745
women in france 47
women travellers 910, 913
health 930
work 912, 913
World Heritage Sites 22, 59
Abbaye de Fontevraud 424
Basilique Notre Dame du Port 549
Cathédrale Notre Dame, Amiens 227-9
Cathédrale Notre Dame, Reims 327
Cathédrale St-André 632
Cathédrale Ste-Marie, Auch 111-12
Grande Île, Strasbourg 348-9
Loire Region 388
Lyon 468
Mont St-Michel 272-5
public sqaures in Nancy 372

Pont du Gard 738, 652-3
St-Émilion 639-41
Saline Royal 540
WWI 34-5
    American Memorials, Verdun 386
    Australian National War
        Memorial 226
    Battle of the Somme 223-7, **224**
    Battle of Verdun 384-6
    Beaumont-Hamel Newfoundland
        Memorial 226
    Clairière de l'Armistice 233
    Hartmannswillerkopf 369
    Historial de la Grande Guerre 225
    La Chapellette Commonwealth
        Cemetery 225
    Lorraine American Cemetery 386
    Mémorial Indien 225
    Meuse-Argonne American
        Cemetery 386

Monument de l'Ulster 226
New Zealand National
    Memorial 227
St-Mihiel American Cemetery 386
South African National Memorial
    226-7
Thiepval Memorial 226
Verdun 382-6
Vimy Canadian National Memorial
    & Park 224-5
WWII 35
    American Military Cemetery 267
    Battle of Normandy 264-5, **265**
    Bayeux War Cemetery 263
    Canadian Military Cemetery,
        Bény-sur-Mer 267
    Canadian Military Cemetery,
        Dieppe 245
    D-Day beaches 266-8
    Dunkirk 219-20

German Military Cemetery,
    La Cambe 267
Maginot Line, the 35, 344, 386
Maquis Bernard Résistance
    Cemetery 444
Mémorial – Un Musée pour la
    Paix 256
Musée 39-45 216
Musée Mémorial 1944 Bataille de
    Normandie 262
Natzweiler-Struthof 357
Oradour-sur-Glane 577
Pointe du Hoc Ranger Memorial
    267-8
Tour Beaumont Mémorial du
    Débarquement 850

Y
Yitzhaki, Rabbi Shlomo, *see* Rashi
Yonne 429-42

MAP LEGEND

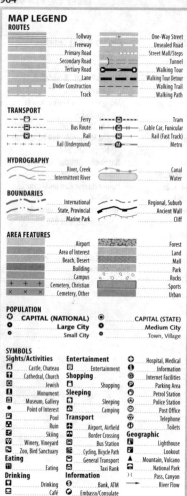

ROUTES

Tollway	One-Way Street
Freeway	Unsealed Road
Primary Road	Street Mall/Steps
Secondary Road	Tunnel
Tertiary Road	Walking Tour
Lane	Walking Tour Detour
Under Construction	Walking Trail
Track	Walking Path

TRANSPORT

Ferry	Tram
Bus Route	Cable Car, Funicular
Rail	Rail (Fast Track)
Rail (Underground)	Metro

HYDROGRAPHY

River, Creek	Canal
Intermittent River	Water

BOUNDARIES

International	Regional, Suburb
State, Provincial	Ancient Wall
Marine Park	Cliff

AREA FEATURES

Airport	Forest
Area of Interest	Land
Beach, Desert	Mall
Building	Park
Campus	Rocks
Cemetery, Christian	Sports
Cemetery, Other	Urban

POPULATION

CAPITAL (NATIONAL)	CAPITAL (STATE)
Large City	Medium City
Small City	Town, Village

SYMBOLS

Sights/Activities
- Castle, Chateau
- Cathedral, Church
- Jewish
- Monument
- Museum, Gallery
- Point of Interest
- Pool
- Ruin
- Skiing
- Winery, Vineyard
- Zoo, Bird Sanctuary

Eating
- Eating

Drinking
- Drinking
- Café

Entertainment
- Entertainment

Shopping
- Shopping

Sleeping
- Sleeping
- Camping

Transport
- Airport, Airfield
- Border Crossing
- Bus Station
- Cycling, Bicycle Path
- General Transport
- Taxi Rank

Information
- Bank, ATM
- Embassy/Consulate
- Hospital, Medical
- Information
- Internet Facilities
- Parking Area
- Petrol Station
- Police Station
- Post Office
- Telephone
- Toilets

Geographic
- Lighthouse
- Lookout
- Mountain, Volcano
- National Park
- Pass, Canyon
- River Flow

LONELY PLANET OFFICES

Australia
Head Office
Locked Bag 1, Footscray, Victoria 3011
☎ 03 8379 8000, fax 03 8379 8111
talk2us@lonelyplanet.com.au

USA
150 Linden St, Oakland, CA 94607
☎ 510 893 8555, toll free 800 275 8555
fax 510 893 8572, info@lonelyplanet.com

UK
72–82 Rosebery Ave,
Clerkenwell, London EC1R 4RW
☎ 020 7841 9000, fax 020 7841 9001
go@lonelyplanet.co.uk

Published by Lonely Planet Publications Pty Ltd
ABN 36 005 607 983

© Lonely Planet 2005

© photographers as indicated 2005

Cover photographs: Eiffel Tower, Robert Landau/APL Corbis (front); Vineyards along the Route du Vin (winery route), Greg Elms/Lonely Planet Images (back). Many of the images in this guide are available for licensing from Lonely Planet Images: www.lonelyplanetimages.com

Printed through The Bookmaker International Ltd
Printed in China